Published by Collins
An imprint of HarperCollins Publishers
Westerhill Road
Bishopbriggs
Glasgow G64 2QT

Fourth Edition 2017

10 9 8 7 6 5 4 3 2 1

© HarperCollins Publishers 2005, 2006,
2010, 2017

ISBN 978-0-00-818366-0

Collins® is a registered trademark of
HarperCollins Publishers Limited

www.collins.co.uk/languagesupport

Typeset by Davidson Publishing Solutions,
Glasgow

Printed in Great Britain by Clays Ltd, St Ives plc

The contents of this publication are
believed correct at the time of printing.
Nevertheless, the Publisher can accept no
responsibility for errors or omissions,
changes in the detail given or for any
expense or loss thereby caused.

HarperCollins does not warrant that any
website mentioned in this title will be
provided uninterrupted, that any website
will be error free, that defects will be
corrected, or that the website or the server
that makes it available are free of viruses or
bugs. For full terms and conditions please
refer to the site terms provided on the
website.

A catalogue record for this book is available
from the British Library.

If you would like to comment on any aspect
of this book, please contact us at the given
address or online.
E-mail: dictionaries@harpercollins.co.uk
 facebook.com/collinsdictionary
 @collinsdict

Acknowledgements
We would like to thank those authors and
publishers who kindly gave permission for
copyright material to be used in the Collins
Corpus. We would also like to thank Times
Newspapers Ltd for providing valuable data.

EDITOR
Susie Beattie

CONTRIBUTORS
Pierre-Henri Cousin, Lorna Sinclair Knight,
          son, Claude Nimmo,
        , Hélène Lewis,
        pbell, Renée Birks,
        Allain, Christine Penman,
        , Catherine E. Love,
        urent Jouet,
        nan

        ISHER
        lie
        s

        PPORT

Table des matières

Contents

Introduction

You may be starting French for the first time, or you may wish to extend your knowledge of the language. Perhaps you want to read and study French books, newspapers and magazines, or perhaps simply have a conversation with French speakers. Whatever the reason, whether you're a student, a tourist or want to use French for business, this is the ideal book to help you understand and communicate. This modern, user-friendly dictionary gives priority to everyday vocabulary and the language of current affairs, business, computing and tourism, and, as in all Collins dictionaries, the emphasis is firmly placed on contemporary language and expressions.

How to use the dictionary
Below you will find an outline of how information is presented in your dictionary. Our aim is to give you the maximum amount of detail in the clearest and most helpful way.

Entries
A typical entry in your dictionary will be made up of the following elements:

Phonetic transcription
Phonetics appear in square brackets immediately after the headword. They are shown using the International Phonetic Alphabet (IPA), and a complete list of the symbols used in this system can be found on pages x and xi.

Grammatical information
All words belong to one of the following parts of speech: noun, verb, adjective, adverb, pronoun, article, conjunction, preposition.

Nouns can be singular or plural and, in French, masculine or feminine. Verbs can be transitive, intransitive, reflexive or impersonal. Parts of speech appear in *italics* immediately after the phonetic spelling of the headword. The gender of the translation appears in *italics* immediately following the key element of the translation.

Often a word can have more than one part of speech. Just as the English word **chemical** can be an adjective or a noun, the French word **rose** can be an adjective ("pink") or a feminine noun ("rose"). In the same way the verb **to walk** is sometimes transitive, ie it takes an object ("to walk the dog") and sometimes intransitive, ie it doesn't take an object ("to walk to school"). To help you find the meaning you are looking for quickly and for clarity of presentation, the different part of speech categories are separated by a right facing triangle ▷.

Meaning divisions

Most words have more than one meaning. Take, for example, **punch** which can be, amongst other things, a blow with the fist or an object used for making holes. Other words are translated differently depending on the context in which they are used. The transitive verb **to roll up**, for example, can be translated by "rouler" or "retrousser" depending on what it is you are rolling up. To help you select the most appropriate translation in every context, entries are divided according to meaning. Different meanings are introduced by an "indicator" in *italics* and in brackets. Thus, the examples given above will be shown as follows:

> **punch** *n* (*blow*) coup *m* de poing; (*tool*) poinçon *m*
> **roll up** *vt* (*carpet, cloth, map*) rouler; (*sleeves*) retrousser

Likewise, some words can have a different meaning when used to talk about a specific subject area or field. For example, **bishop**, which we generally use to mean a high-ranking clergyman, is also the name of a chess piece. To show English speakers which translation to use, we have added "subject field labels" in *italics*, starting with a capital letter, and in brackets, in this case (*Chess*):

> **bishop** *n* évêque *m*; (*Chess*) fou *m*

Field labels are often shortened to save space. You will find a complete list of abbreviations used in the dictionary on pages viii and ix.

Translations

Most English words have a direct translation in French and vice versa, as shown in the examples given above. Sometimes, however, no exact equivalent exists in the target language. In such cases we have given an approximate equivalent, indicated by the sign ≈. An example is **National Insurance**, the French equivalent of which is "Sécurité Sociale". There is no exact equivalent since the systems of the two countries are quite different:

> **National Insurance** *n* (*Brit*) ≈ Sécurité Sociale

On occasion it is impossible to find even an approximate equivalent. This may be the case, for example, with the names of types of food:

> **mince pie** *n* *sorte de tarte aux fruits secs*

Here the translation (which doesn't exist) is replaced by an explanation. For increased clarity the explanation, or "gloss", is shown in *italics*.

It is often the case that a word, or a particular meaning of a word, cannot be translated in isolation. The translation of **Dutch**, for example, is "hollandais(e), neérlandais(e)". However, the phrase **to go Dutch** is rendered by "partager les frais".

Even an expression as simple as **washing powder** needs a separate translation since it translates as "lessive (en poudre)", not "poudre à laver". This is where your dictionary will prove to be particularly informative and useful since it contains an abundance of compounds, phrases and idiomatic expressions.

Levels of formality and familiarity

In English you instinctively know when to say "I don't have any money" and when to say "I'm broke" or "I'm a bit short of cash". When you are trying to understand someone who is speaking French, however, or when you yourself try to speak French, it is important to know what is polite and what is less so, and what you can say in a relaxed situation but not in a formal context. To help you with this, on the French–English side we have added the label (*fam*) to show that a French meaning or expression is colloquial, while those meanings or expressions which are vulgar are given an exclamation mark (*fam!*), warning you they can cause serious offence. Note also that on the English–French side, colloquial English words are labelled as (*inf*), vulgar or offensive English words as (*inf!*) and vulgar French translations as (*!*).

Keywords

Words labelled in the text as KEYWORDS, such as **be** and **do** or their French equivalents **être** and **faire**, have been given special treatment because they form the basic elements of the language. This extra help will ensure that you know how to use these complex words with confidence.

Highlighting

Words that appear with a shaded background, such as **ability** and **acheter** are words that are specified or commonly associated with GCSE exams and other exams of a similar level. The highlighting helps you spot your essential exam vocabulary quickly.

Cultural information

Entries which appear distinguished in the text by a column of dots explain aspects of culture in French and English-speaking countries. Subject areas covered include politics, education, media and national festivals, for example **Assemblée nationale**, **baccalauréat**, **BBC** and **Hallowe'en**.

Abréviations

Abbreviations

abréviation	*ab(b)r*	abbreviation
adjectif, locution adjectivale	*adj*	adjective, adjectival phrase
administration	*Admin*	administration
adverbe, locution adverbiale	*adv*	adverb, adverbial phrase
agriculture	*Agr*	agriculture
anatomie	*Anat*	anatomy
architecture	*Archit*	architecture
article défini	*art déf*	definite article
article indéfini	*art indéf*	indefinite article
automobile	*Aut(o)*	the motor car and motoring
aviation, voyages aériens	*Aviat*	flying, air travel
biologie	*Bio(l)*	biology
botanique	*Bot*	botany
anglais britannique	*Brit*	British English
chimie	*Chem*	chemistry
cinéma	*Ciné, Cine*	cinema
commerce, finance, banque	*Comm*	commerce, finance, banking
informatique	*Comput*	computing
conjonction	*conj*	conjunction
construction	*Constr*	building
nom utilisé comme adjectif	*cpd*	compound element
cuisine	*Culin*	cookery
article défini	*def art*	definite article
déterminant: article; adjectif démonstratif *ou* indéfini etc	*dét*	determiner: article, demonstrative etc
économie	*Écon, Econ*	economics
électricité, électronique	*Élec, Elec*	electricity, electronics
en particulier	*esp*	especially
exclamation, interjection	*excl*	exclamation, interjection
féminin	*f*	feminine
langue familière (! emploi vulgaire)	*fam(!)*	colloquial usage (! particularly offensive)
emploi figuré	*fig*	figurative use
(verbe anglais) dont la particule est inséparable	*fus*	(phrasal verb) where the particle is inseparable
généralement	*gén, gen*	generally
géographie, géologie	*Géo, Geo*	geography, geology
géométrie	*Géom, Geom*	geometry
langue familière (! emploi vulgaire)	*inf(!)*	colloquial usage (! particularly offensive)
infinitif	*infin*	infinitive
informatique	*Inform*	computing
invariable	*inv*	invariable
irrégulier	*irrég, irreg*	irregular
domaine juridique	*Jur*	law

Abréviations

Abbreviations

grammaire, linguistique	Ling	grammar, linguistics
masculin	m	masculine
mathématiques, algèbre	Math	mathematics, calculus
médecine	Méd, Med	medical term, medicine
masculin ou féminin	m/f	masculine or feminine
domaine militaire, armée	Mil	military matters
musique	Mus	music
nom	n	noun
navigation, nautisme	Navig, Naut	sailing, navigation
nom ou adjectif numéral	num	numeral noun or adjective
	o.s.	oneself
péjoratif	péj, pej	derogatory, pejorative
photographie	Phot(o)	photography
physiologie	Physiol	physiology
pluriel	pl	plural
politique	Pol	politics
participe passé	pp	past participle
préposition	prép, prep	preposition
pronom	pron	pronoun
psychologie, psychiatrie	Psych	psychology, psychiatry
temps du passé	pt	past tense
quelque chose	qch	
quelqu'un	qn	
religion, domaine ecclésiastique	Rel	religion
	sb	somebody
enseignement, système scolaire et universitaire	Scol	schooling, schools and universities
singulier	sg	singular
	sth	something
subjonctif	sub	subjunctive
sujet (grammatical)	su(b)j	(grammatical) subject
superlatif	superl	superlative
techniques, technologie	Tech	technical term, technology
télécommunications	Tél, Tel	telecommunications
télévision	TV	television
typographie	Typ(o)	typography, printing
anglais des USA	US	American English
verbe (auxiliare)	vb (aux)	(auxiliary) verb
verbe intransitif	vi	intransitive verb
verbe transitif	vt	transitive verb
zoologie	Zool	zoology
marque déposée	®	registered trademark
indique une équivalence culturelle	≈	introduces a cultural equivalent

Transcription phonétique

Consonnes

poupée	p	
bombe	b	
tente thermal	t	
dinde	d	
coq qui képi	k	
gag bague	g	
sale ce nation	s	
zéro rose	z	
tache chat	ʃ	
gilet juge	ʒ	
	tʃ	
	dʒ	
fer phare	f	
valve	v	
	θ	
	ð	
lent salle	l	
rare rentrer	ʀ	
	r	
maman femme	m	
non nonne	n	
agneau vigne	ɲ	
	ŋ	
hop	h	
yeux paille pied	j	
nouer oui	w	
huile lui	ɥ	
	x	

Consonants

p	*puppy*	
b	*baby*	
t	*tent*	
d	*daddy*	
k	*cork kiss chord*	
g	*gag guess*	
s	*so rice kiss*	
z	*cousin buzz*	
ʃ	*sheep sugar*	
ʒ	*pleasure beige*	
tʃ	*church*	
dʒ	*judge general*	
f	*farm raffle*	
v	*very rev*	
θ	*thin maths*	
ð	*that other*	
l	*little ball*	
ʀ		
r	*rat rare*	
m	*mummy comb*	
n	*no ran*	
ɲ		
ŋ	*singing bank*	
h	*hat reheat*	
j	*yet*	
w	*wall bewail*	
ɥ		
x	*loch*	

Divers

pour l'anglais: le "r" final se prononce en liaison devant une voyelle

ʳ

pour l'anglais: précède la syllabe accentuée

ˈ

Miscellaneous

in English transcription: final "r" can be pronounced before a vowel

in French wordlist: no liaison before aspirate "h"

NB: p, b, t, d, k, g sont suivis d'une aspiration en anglais.
p, b, t, d, k, g are not aspirated in French.

En règle générale, la prononciation est donnée entre crochets après chaque entrée. Toutefois, du côté anglais–français et dans le cas des expressions composées de deux ou plusieurs mots non réunis par un trait d'union et faisant l'objet d'une entrée séparée, la prononciation doit être cherchée sous chacun des mots constitutifs de l'expression en question.

Phonetic transcription

Voyelles

ici vie lyrique	i i:	
	ɪ	
jouer été	e	
lait jouet merci	ɛ	
plat amour	a æ	
bas pâte	ɑ ɑ:	
	ʌ	
le premier	ə	
beurre peur	œ	
peu deux	ø ə:	
or homme	ɔ	
mot eau gauche	o ɔ:	
genou roue	u	
	u:	
rue urne	y	

Vowels

i i:	heel bead
ɪ	hit pity
ɛ	set tent
æ	bat apple
ɑ:	after car calm
ʌ	fun cousin
ə	over above
ə:	urgent fern work
ɔ	wash pot
ɔ:	born cork
u	full hook
u:	boom shoe

Diphtongues

Diphthongs

ɪə	beer tier
ɛə	tear fair there
eɪ	date plaice day
aɪ	life buy cry
au	owl foul now
əu	low no
ɔɪ	boil boy oily
uə	poor tour

Nasales

matin plein	ɛ̃
brun	œ̃
sang an dans	ɑ̃
non pont	ɔ̃

Nasal vowels

NB: La mise en équivalence de certains sons n'indique qu'une ressemblance approximative.

The pairing of some vowel sounds only indicates approximate equivalence.

In general, we give the pronunciation of each entry in square brackets after the word in question. However, on the English–French side, where the entry is composed of two or more unhyphenated words, each of which is given elsewhere in this dictionary, you will find the pronunciation of each word in its alphabetical position.

French verb forms

1 Present participle **2** Past participle **3** Present **4** Imperfect **5** Future **6** Conditional
7 Present subjunctive **8** Impératif

acquérir 1 acquérant **2** acquis **3** acquiers,
acquérons, acquièrent **4** acquérais
5 acquerrai **7** acquière

ALLER 1 allant **2** allé **3** vais, vas, va, allons,
allez, vont **4** allais **5** irai **6** irais **7** aille

asseoir 1 asseyant **2** assis **3** assieds,
asseyons, asseyez, asseyent **4** asseyais
5 assiérai **7** asseye

atteindre 1 atteignant **2** atteint **3** atteins,
atteignons **4** atteignais **7** atteigne

AVOIR 1 ayant **2** eu **3** ai, as, a, avons, avez,
ont **4** avais **5** aurai **6** aurais **7** aie, aies, ait,
ayons, ayez, aient

battre 1 battant **2** battu **3** bats, bat, battons
4 battais **7** batte

boire 1 buvant **2** bu **3** bois, buvons, boivent
4 buvais **7** boive

bouillir 1 bouillant **2** bouilli **3** bous,
bouillons **4** bouillais **7** bouille

conclure 1 concluant **2** conclu **3** conclus,
concluons **4** concluais **7** conclue

conduire 1 conduisant **2** conduit **3** conduis,
conduisons **4** conduisais **7** conduise

connaître 1 connaissant **2** connu **3** connais,
connaît, connaissons **4** connaissais
7 connaisse

coudre 1 cousant **2** cousu **3** couds, cousons,
cousez, cousent **4** cousais **7** couse

courir 1 courant **2** couru **3** cours, courons
4 courais **5** courrai **7** coure

couvrir 1 couvrant **2** couvert **3** couvre,
couvrons **4** couvrais **7** couvre

craindre 1 craignant **2** craint **3** crains,
craignons **4** craignais **7** craigne

croire 1 croyant **2** cru **3** crois, croyons,
croient **4** croyais **7** croie

croître 1 croissant **2** crû, crue, crus, crues
3 croîs, croissons **4** croissais **7** croisse

cueillir 1 cueillant **2** cueilli **3** cueille,
cueillons **4** cueillais **5** cueillerai **7** cueille

devoir 1 devant **2** dû, due, dus, dues **3** dois,
devons, doivent **4** devais **5** devrai **7** doive

dire 1 disant **2** dit **3** dis, disons, dites,
disent **4** disais **7** dise

dormir 1 dormant **2** dormi **3** dors, dormons
4 dormais **7** dorme

écrire 1 écrivant **2** écrit **3** écris, écrivons
4 écrivais **7** écrive

ÊTRE 1 étant **2** été **3** suis, es, est, sommes,
êtes, sont **4** étais **5** serai **6** serais **7** sois,
sois, soit, soyons, soyez, soient

FAIRE 1 faisant **2** fait **3** fais, fais, fait,
faisons, faites, font **4** faisais **5** ferai
6 ferais **7** fasse

falloir 2 fallu **3** faut **4** fallait **5** faudra
7 faille

FINIR 1 finissant **2** fini **3** finis, finis, finit,
finissons, finissez, finissent **4** finissais
5 finirai **6** finirais **7** finisse

fuir 1 fuyant **2** fui **3** fuis, fuyons, fuient
4 fuyais **7** fuie

joindre 1 joignant **2** joint **3** joins, joignons
4 joignais **7** joigne

lire 1 lisant **2** lu **3** lis, lisons **4** lisais **7** lise

luire 1 luisant **2** lui **3** luis, luisons **4** luisais
7 luise

maudire 1 maudissant **2** maudit
3 maudis, maudissons **4** maudissait
7 maudisse

mentir 1 mentant **2** menti **3** mens,
mentons **4** mentais **7** mente

mettre 1 mettant **2** mis **3** mets, mettons
4 mettais **7** mette

mourir 1 mourant **2** mort **3** meurs,
mourons, meurent **4** mourais **5** mourrai
7 meure

naître 1 naissant **2** né **3** nais, naît,
naissons **4** naissais **7** naisse

offrir 1 offrant **2** offert **3** offre, offrons
4 offrais **7** offre

PARLER 1 parlant **2** parlé **3** parle, parles,
parle, parlons, parlez, parlent **4** parlais,
parlais, parlait, parlions, parliez, parlaient
5 parlerai, parleras, parlera, parlerons,

parlerez, parleront **6** parlerais, parlerais, parlerait, parlerions, parleriez, parleraient **7** parle, parles, parle, parlions, parliez, parlent **8** parle! parlons! parlez!

partir 1 partant **2** parti **3** pars, partons **4** partais **7** parte

plaire 1 plaisant **2** plu **3** plais, plaît, plaisons **4** plaisais **7** plaise

pleuvoir 1 pleuvant **2** plu **3** pleut, pleuvent **4** pleuvait **5** pleuvra **7** pleuve

pourvoir 1 pourvoyant **2** pourvu **3** pourvois, pourvoyons, pourvoient **4** pourvoyais **7** pourvoie

pouvoir 1 pouvant **2** pu **3** peux, peut, pouvons, peuvent **4** pouvais **5** pourrai **7** puisse

prendre 1 prenant **2** pris **3** prends, prenons, prennent **4** prenais **7** prenne

prévoir *like* **voir 5** prévoirai

RECEVOIR 1 recevant **2** reçu **3** reçois, reçois, reçoit, recevons, recevez, rerçoivent **4** recevais **5** recevrai **6** recevrais **7** reçoive

RENDRE 1 rendant **2** rendu **3** rends, rends, rend, rendons, rendez, rendent **4** rendais **5** rendrai **6** rendrais **7** rende

résoudre 1 résolvant **2** résolu **3** résous, résout, résolvons **4** résolvais **7** résolve

rire 1 riant **2** ri **3** ris, rions **4** riais **7** rie

savoir 1 sachant **2** su **3** sais, savons, savent **4** savais **5** saurai **7** sache **8** sache! sachons! sachez!

servir 1 servant **2** servi **3** sers, servons **4** servais **7** serve

sortir 1 sortant **2** sorti **3** sors, sortons **4** sortais **7** sorte

souffrir 1 souffrant **2** souffert **3** souffre, souffrons **4** souffrais **7** souffre

suffire 1 suffisant **2** suffi **3** suffis, suffisons **4** suffisais **7** suffise

suivre 1 suivant **2** suivi **3** suis, suivons **4** suivais **7** suive

taire 1 taisant **2** tu **3** tais, taisons **4** taisais **7** taise

tenir 1 tenant **2** tenu **3** tiens, tenons, tiennent **4** tenais **5** tiendrai **7** tienne

vaincre 1 vainquant **2** vaincu **3** vaincs, vainc, vainquons **4** vainquais **7** vainque

valoir 1 valant **2** valu **3** vaux, vaut, valons **4** valais **5** vaudrai **7** vaille

venir 1 venant **2** venu **3** viens, venons, viennent **4** venais **5** viendrai **7** vienne

vivre 1 vivant **2** vécu **3** vis, vivons **4** vivais **7** vive

voir 1 voyant **2** vu **3** vois, voyons, voient **4** voyais **5** verrai **7** voie

vouloir 1 voulant **2** voulu **3** veux, veut, voulons, veulent **4** voulais **5** voudrai **7** veuille **8** veuillez!

For additional information on French verb formation see pages 6–75 of the Grammar section.

Les nombres

		Numbers
un (une)	1	one
deux	2	two
trois	3	three
quatre	4	four
cinq	5	five
six	6	six
sept	7	seven
huit	8	eight
neuf	9	nine
dix	10	ten
onze	11	eleven
douze	12	twelve
treize	13	thirteen
quatorze	14	fourteen
quinze	15	fifteen
seize	16	sixteen
dix-sept	17	seventeen
dix-huit	18	eighteen
dix-neuf	19	nineteen
vingt	20	twenty
vingt et un (une)	21	twenty-one
vingt-deux	22	twenty-two
trente	30	thirty
quarante	40	forty
cinquante	50	fifty
soixante	60	sixty
soixante-dix	70	seventy
soixante-et-onze	71	seventy-one
soixante-douze	72	seventy-two
quatre-vingts	80	eighty
quatre-vingt-un (-une)	81	eighty-one
quatre-vingt-dix	90	ninety
cent	100	a hundred, one hundred
cent un (une)	101	a hundred and one
deux cents	200	two hundred
deux cent un (une)	201	two hundred and one
quatre cents	400	four hundred
mille	1000	a thousand
cinq mille	5 000	five thousand
un million	1 000 000	a million

Les nombres

premier (première), 1er (1ère)
deuxième, 2e ou 2ème
troisième, 3e ou 3ème
quatrième, 4e ou 4ème
cinquième, 5e ou 5ème
sixième, 6e ou 6ème
septième
huitième
neuvième
dixième
onzième
douzième
treizième
quartorzième
quinzième
seizième
dix-septième
dix-huitième
dix-neuvième
vingtième
vingt-et-unième
vingt-deuxième
trentième
centième
cent-unième
millième

Numbers

first, 1st
second, 2nd
third, 3rd
fourth, 4th
fifth, 5th
sixth, 6th
seventh
eighth
ninth
tenth
eleventh
twelfth
thirteenth
fourteenth
fifteenth
sixteenth
seventeenth
eighteenth
nineteenth
twentieth
twenty-first
twenty-second
thirtieth
hundredth
hundred-and-first
thousandth

L'heure

quelle heure est-il?
  il est ...

minuit
une heure (du matin)
une heure cinq
une heure dix
une heure et quart
une heure vingt-cinq
une heure et demie,
  une heure trente
deux heures moins vingt-cinq,
  une heure trente-cinq
deux heures moins vingt,
  une heure quarante
deux heures moins le quart,
  une heure quarante-cinq
deux heures moins dix,
  une heure cinquante
midi
deux heures (de l'après-midi),
  quatorze heures
sept heures (du soir),
  dix-sept heures

à quelle heure?
à minuit
à sept heures

dans vingt minutes
il y a un quart d'heure

The time

what time is it?
  it's ...

midnight, twelve p.m.
one o'clock (in the morning), one (a.m.)
five past one
ten past one
a quarter past one, one fifteen
twenty-five past one, one twenty-five
half-past one,
  one thirty
twenty-five to two,
  one thirty-five
twenty to two,
  one forty
a quarter to two,
  one forty-five
ten to two,
  one fifty
twelve o'clock, midday, noon
two o'clock (in the afternoon),
  two (p.m.)
seven o'clock (in the evening),
  seven (p.m.)

(at) what time?
at midnight
at seven o'clock

in twenty minutes
fifteen minutes ago

La date

The date

aujourd'hui	today
demain	tomorrow
après-demain	the day after tomorrow
hier	yesterday
avant-hier	the day before yesterday
la veille	the day before, the previous day
le lendemain	the next or following day
le matin	morning
le soir	evening
ce matin	this morning
ce soir	this evening
cet après-midi	this afternoon
hier matin	yesterday morning
hier soir	yesterday evening
demain matin	tomorrow morning
demain soir	tomorrow evening
dans la nuit du samedi au dimanche	during Saturday night, during the night of Saturday to Sunday
il viendra samedi	he's coming on Saturday
le samedi	on Saturdays
tous les samedis	every Saturday
samedi passé ou dernier	last Saturday
samedi prochain	next Saturday
samedi en huit	a week on Saturday
samedi en quinze	a fortnight or two weeks on Saturday
du lundi au samedi	from Monday to Saturday
tous les jours	every day
une fois par semaine	once a week
une fois par mois	once a month
deux fois par semaine	twice a week
il y a une semaine ou huit jours	a week ago
il y a quinze jours	a fortnight or two weeks ago
l'année passée ou dernière	last year
dans deux jours	in two days
dans huit jours ou une semaine	in a week
dans quinze jours	in a fortnight or two weeks
le mois prochain	next month
l'année prochaine	next year
quel jour sommes-nous?	*what day is it?*
le 1er/24 octobre 2017	the 1st/24th of October 2017, October 1st/24th 2017
en 2017	in 2017
mille neuf cent quatre-vingt seize	nineteen ninety-six
44 av. J.-C.	44 BC
14 apr. J.-C.	14 AD
au XIXe (siècle)	in the nineteenth century
dans les années trente	in the thirties
il était une fois ...	once upon a time ...

6 (*provenance*) from; **boire à la bouteille** to drink from the bottle

7 (*caractérisation, manière*): **l'homme aux yeux bleus** the man with the blue eyes; **à la russe** the Russian way; **glace à la framboise** raspberry ice cream

8 (*but, destination*): **tasse à café** coffee cup; **maison à vendre** house for sale; **je n'ai rien à lire** I don't have anything to read; **à bien réfléchir** ... thinking about it ..., on reflection ...; **problème à régler** problem to sort out

9 (*rapport, évaluation, distribution*): **100 km/ unités à l'heure** 100 km/units per *ou* an hour; **payé à l'heure** paid by the hour; **cinq à six** five to six

10 (*conséquence, résultat*): **à ce qu'il prétend** according to him; **à leur grande surprise** much to their surprise; **à nous trois nous n'avons pas su le faire** we couldn't do it even between the three of us; **ils sont arrivés à quatre** four of them arrived (together)

---

a [a] *vb voir* **avoir**

 MOT-CLÉ

à [a] (*à+le* = **au**, *à+les* = **aux**) *prép* **1** (*endroit, situation*) at, in; **être à Paris/au Portugal** to be in Paris/Portugal; **être à la maison/à l'école** to be at home/at school; **à la campagne** in the country; **c'est à 10 m/km/à 20 minutes (d'ici)** it's 10 m/km/20 minutes away

2 (*direction*) to; **aller à Paris/au Portugal** to go to Paris/Portugal; **aller à la maison/à l'école** to go home/to school; **à la campagne** to the country

3 (*temps*): **à 3 heures/minuit** at 3 o'clock/midnight; **au printemps** in the spring; **au mois de juin** in June; **à Noël/Pâques** at Christmas/Easter; **au départ** at the start, at the outset; **à demain/la semaine prochaine!** see you tomorrow/next week!; **visites de 5 heures à 6 heures** visiting from 5 *ou* till 6 o'clock

4 (*attribution, appartenance*) to; **le livre est à Paul/à lui/à nous** this book is Paul's/his/ours; **donner qch à qn** to give sth to sb; **un ami à moi** a friend of mine; **c'est à moi de le faire** it's up to me to do it

5 (*moyen*) with; **se chauffer au gaz** to have gas heating; **à bicyclette** on a *ou* by bicycle; **à pied** on foot; **à la main/machine** by hand/machine; **à la télévision/la radio** on television/the radio

---

abaisser [abese] *vt* to lower, bring down; (*manette*) to pull down; (*fig*) to debase; to humiliate; **s'abaisser** *vi* to go down; (*fig*) to demean o.s.; **s'~ à faire/à qch** to stoop *ou* descend to doing/to sth

abandon [abɑ̃dɔ̃] *nm* abandoning; deserting; giving up; withdrawal; surrender, relinquishing; (*fig*) lack of constraint; relaxed pose *ou* mood; **être à l'~** to be in a state of neglect; **laisser à l'~** to abandon

abandonner [abɑ̃dɔne] *vt* (*personne*) to leave, abandon, desert; (*projet, activité*) to abandon, give up; (*Sport*) to retire *ou* withdraw from; (*Inform*) to abort; (*céder*) to surrender, relinquish; **s'abandonner** *vi* to let o.s. go; **s'~ à** (*paresse, plaisirs*) to give o.s. up to; **~ qch à qn** to give sth up to sb

abasourdir [abazurdir] *vt* to stun, stagger

abat-jour [abaʒur] *nm inv* lampshade

abats [aba] *vb voir* **abattre** ▷ *nmpl* (*de bœuf, porc*) offal *sg* (*Brit*), entrails (*US*); (*de volaille*) giblets

abattement [abatmɑ̃] *nm* (*physique*) enfeeblement; (*moral*) dejection, despondency; (*déduction*) reduction; **~ fiscal** ≈ tax allowance

abattoir [abatwar] *nm* abattoir (*Brit*), slaughterhouse

abattre [abatr] *vt* (*arbre*) to cut down, fell; (*mur, maison*) to pull down; (*avion, personne*) to shoot down; (*animal*) to shoot, kill; (*fig: physiquement*) to wear out, tire out; (: *moralement*) to demoralize; **s'abattre** *vi* to crash down; **ne pas se laisser ~** to keep one's spirits up, not to let things get one down; **s'~ sur** (*pluie*) to beat down on; (: *coups, injures*) to rain down on; **~ ses cartes** (*aussi fig*) to lay one's cards on the table; **~ du travail** *ou* **de la besogne** to get through a lot of work

abbaye [abei] *nf* abbey

abbé [abe] *nm* priest; (*d'une abbaye*) abbot;
M l'~ Father

abcès [apsɛ] *nm* abscess

abdiquer [abdike] *vi* to abdicate ▷ *vt* to
renounce, give up

abdominal, e, -aux [abdɔminal, -o] *adj*
abdominal ▷ *nmpl* **faire des ~** to do sit-ups

abeille [abɛj] *nf* bee

aberrant, e [abɛrɑ̃, ɑ̃t] *adj* absurd

aberration [abɛrasjɔ̃] *nf* aberration

abêtir [abetir] *vt* to make idiots (*ou* an idiot) of

abîme [abim] *nm* abyss, gulf

abîmer [abime] *vt* to spoil, damage;
s'abîmer *vi* to get spoilt *ou* damaged; (*fruits*)
to spoil; (*tomber*) to sink, founder; **s'~ les
yeux** to ruin one's eyes *ou* eyesight

ablation [ablasjɔ̃] *nf* removal

aboiement [abwamɑ̃] *nm* bark,
barking *no pl*

abois [abwa] *nmpl*: **aux ~** at bay

abolir [abɔlir] *vt* to abolish

abominable [abɔminabl] *adj* abominable

abondance [abɔ̃dɑ̃s] *nf* abundance; (*richesse*)
affluence; **en ~** in abundance

abondant, e [abɔ̃dɑ̃, -ɑ̃t] *adj* plentiful,
abundant, copious

abonder [abɔ̃de] *vi* to abound, be plentiful; **~
en** to be full of, abound in; **~ dans le sens de
qn** to concur with sb

abonné, e [abɔne] *nm/f* subscriber; season
ticket holder ▷ *adj*: **être ~ à un journal** to
subscribe to *ou* have a subscription to a
periodical; **être ~ au téléphone** to be on the
(tele)phone

abonnement [abɔnmɑ̃] *nm* subscription;
(*pour transports en commun, concerts*) season
ticket

abonner [abɔne] *vt*: **s'abonner à** to subscribe
to, take out a subscription to; **s'~ aux tweets
de qn** to follow sb on Twitter

abord [abɔr] *nm*: **être d'un ~ facile** to be
approachable; **être d'un ~ difficile** (*personne*)
to be unapproachable; (*lieu*) to be hard to
reach *ou* difficult to get to; **de prime ~, au
premier ~** at first sight, initially; **abords**
nmpl (*environs*) surroundings; **d'~** *adv* first;
tout d'~ first of all

abordable [abɔrdabl] *adj* (*personne*)
approachable; (*marchandise*) reasonably
priced; (*prix*) affordable, reasonable

aborder [abɔrde] *vi* to land ▷ *vt* (*sujet,
difficulté*) to tackle; (*personne*) to approach;
(*rivage etc*) to reach; (*Navig: attaquer*) to board;
(: *heurter*) to collide with

aboutir [abutir] *vi* (*négociations etc*) to
succeed; (*abcès*) to come to a head; **~ à/dans/
sur** to end up at/in/on; **n'~ à rien** to come to
nothing

aboyer [abwaje] *vi* to bark

abréger [abreʒe] *vt* (*texte*) to shorten,
abridge; (*mot*) to abbreviate;
(*réunion, voyage*) to cut short, shorten

abreuver [abrœve] *vt* to water; (*fig*): **~ qn de**
to shower *ou* swamp sb with; (*injures etc*) to
shower sb with; **s'abreuver** *vi* to drink

abreuvoir [abrœvwar] *nm* watering place

abréviation [abrevjasjɔ̃] *nf* abbreviation

abri [abri] *nm* shelter; **être à l'~** to be under
cover; **se mettre à l'~** to shelter; **à l'~ de**
sheltered from; (*danger*) safe from

abricot [abriko] *nm* apricot

abriter [abrite] *vt* to shelter; (*loger*) to
accommodate; **s'abriter** *vi* to shelter, take
cover

abrupt, e [abrypt] *adj* sheer, steep; (*ton*)
abrupt

abruti, e [abryti] *adj* stunned, dazed ▷ *nm/f*
(*fam*) idiot; **~ de travail** overworked

absence [apsɑ̃s] *nf* absence; (*Méd*) blackout;
en l'~ de in the absence of; **avoir des ~s** to
have mental blanks

absent, e [apsɑ̃, -ɑ̃t] *adj* absent; (*chose*)
missing, lacking; (*distrait: air*) vacant,
faraway ▷ *nm/f* absentee

absenter [apsɑ̃te]: **s'absenter** *vi* to take time
off work; (*sortir*) to leave, go out

absolu, e [apsɔly] *adj* absolute; (*caractère*)
rigid, uncompromising ▷ *nm* (*Philosophie*): **l'~**
the Absolute; **dans l'~** in the absolute, in a
vacuum

absolument [apsɔlymɑ̃] *adv* absolutely

absorbant, e [apsɔrbɑ̃, -ɑ̃t] *adj* absorbent;
(*tâche*) absorbing, engrossing

absorber [apsɔrbe] *vt* to absorb; (*gén Méd:
manger, boire*) to take; (*Écon: firme*) to take over,
absorb

abstenir [apstənir]: **s'abstenir** *vi* (*Pol*) to
abstain; **s'~ de qch/de faire** to refrain from
sth/from doing

abstraction [apstraksjɔ̃] *nf* abstraction;
faire ~ de to set *ou* leave aside; **~ faite de …**
leaving aside …

abstrait, e [apstrɛ, -ɛt] *adj* abstract ▷ *nm*:
dans l'~ in the abstract

absurde [apsyrd] *adj* absurd ▷ *nm* absurdity;
(*Philosophie*): **l'~** absurd; **par l'~** ad exorbitant;

abus [aby] *nm* (*excès*) abuse, misuse; (*injustice*)
abuse; **~ de confiance** breach of trust;
(*détournement de fonds*) embezzlement; **il y a
de l'~!** (*fam*) that's a bit much!

abuser [abyze] *vi* to go too far, overstep the
mark ▷ *vt* to deceive, mislead; **s'abuser** *vi*
(*se méprendre*) to be mistaken; **~ de** *vt* (*force,
droit*) to misuse; (*alcool*) to take to excess;
(*violer, duper*) to take advantage of

abusif, -ive [abyzif, -iv] *adj* exorbitant;
(*punition*) excessive; (*pratique*) improper

acabit [akabi] *nm*: **du même ~** of the same
type

académie [akademi] *nf* (*société*) learned
society; (*école: d'art, de danse*) academy; (*Art:
nu*) nude; (*Scol: circonscription*) ≈ regional
education authority; **l'A~ (française)** the
French Academy; *see note*

acajou [akaʒu] *nm* mahogany

acariâtre [akaʀjɑtʀ] *adj* sour(-tempered)
(*Brit*), cantankerous

accablant, e [akablɑ̃, -ɑ̃t] *adj* (*chaleur*)
oppressive; (*témoignage, preuve*)
overwhelming

accablement [akabləmɑ̃] *nm* deep
despondency

accabler [akable] *vt* to overwhelm,
overcome; (*témoignage*) to condemn, damn;
~ **qn d'injures** to heap *ou* shower abuse on
sb; ~ **qn de travail** to overwork sb; **accablé
de dettes/soucis** weighed down with debts/
cares

accalmie [akalmi] *nf* lull

accaparer [akapaʀe] *vt* to monopolize;
(*travail etc*) to take up (all) the time *ou*
attention of

accéder [aksede]: ~ **à** *vt* (*lieu*) to reach; (*fig*:
pouvoir) to accede to; (: *poste*) to attain;
(*accorder*: *requête*) to grant, accede to

accélérateur [akseleʀatœʀ] *nm* accelerator

accélération [akseleʀasjɔ̃] *nf* speeding up;
acceleration

accélérer [akseleʀe] *vt* (*mouvement, travaux*) to
speed up ▷ *vi* (*Auto*) to accelerate

accent [aksɑ̃] *nm* accent; (*inflexions expressives*)
tone (of voice); (*Phonétique, fig*) stress; **aux ~s
de** (*musique*) to the strains of; **mettre l'~ sur**
(*fig*) to stress; ~ **aigu/grave/circonflexe**
acute/grave/circumflex accent

accentuer [aksɑ̃tɥe] *vt* (*Ling: orthographe*) to
accent; (: *phonétique*) to stress, accent; (*fig*) to
accentuate, emphasize; (: *effort, pression*) to
increase; **s'accentuer** *vi* to become more
marked *ou* pronounced

acceptation [akseptasjɔ̃] *nf* acceptance

accepter [aksepte] *vt* to accept; (*tolérer*):
~ **que qn fasse** to agree to sb doing; ~ **de
faire** to agree to do

accès [aksɛ] *nm* (*à un lieu, Inform*) access; (*Méd*)
attack; (: *de toux*) fit; (*de fièvre*) bout ▷ *nmpl*
(*routes etc*) means of access, approaches; **d'~
facile/malaisé** easily/not easily accessible;
facile d'~ easy to get to; **donner ~ à** (*lieu*) to
give access to; (*carrière*) to open the door to;

avoir ~ auprès de qn to have access to sb; **l'~
aux quais est interdit aux personnes non
munies d'un billet** ticket-holders only on
platforms, no access to platforms without a
ticket; ~ **de colère** fit of anger; ~ **de joie** burst
of joy

accessible [aksesibl] *adj* accessible;
(*personne*) approachable; (*livre, sujet*): ~ **à qn**
within the reach of sb; (*sensible*): ~ **à la pitié/
l'amour** open to pity/love

accessoire [akseswaʀ] *adj* secondary, of
secondary importance; (*frais*) incidental
▷ *nm* accessory; (*Théât*) prop

accident [aksidɑ̃] *nm* accident; **par ~** by
chance; ~ **de parcours** mishap; ~ **de la route**
road accident; ~ **du travail** accident at work;
industrial injury *ou* accident; ~**s de terrain**
unevenness of the ground

accidenté, e [aksidɑ̃te] *adj* damaged *ou*
injured (in an accident); (*relief, terrain*)
uneven; hilly

accidentel, le [aksidɑ̃tɛl] *adj* accidental

acclamation [aklamasjɔ̃] *nf*: **par ~** (*vote*) by
acclamation; **acclamations** *nfpl* cheers,
cheering *sg*

acclamer [aklame] *vt* to cheer, acclaim

acclimater [aklimate] *vt* to acclimatize;
s'acclimater *vi* to become acclimatized

accolade [akɔlad] *nf* (*amicale*) embrace;
(*signe*) brace; **donner l'~ à qn** to embrace sb

accommodant, e [akɔmɔdɑ̃, -ɑ̃t] *adj*
accommodating, easy-going

accommoder [akɔmɔde] *vt* (*Culin*) to
prepare; (*points de vue*) to reconcile; ~ **qch à**
(*adapter*) to adapt sth to; **s'accommoder de** to
put up with; (*se contenter de*) to make do with;
s'~ à (*s'adapter*) to adapt to

accompagnateur, -trice [akɔ̃paɲatœʀ,
-tʀis] *nm/f* (*Mus*) accompanist; (*de voyage*)
guide; (*de voyage organisé*) courier; (*d'enfants*)
accompanying adult

accompagner [akɔ̃paɲe] *vt* to accompany,
be *ou* go *ou* come with; (*Mus*) to accompany;
s'accompagner de to bring, be accompanied by

accompli, e [akɔ̃pli] *adj* accomplished

accomplir [akɔ̃pliʀ] *vt* (*tâche, projet*) to carry
out; (*souhait*) to fulfil; **s'accomplir** *vi* to be
fulfilled

accord [akɔʀ] *nm* (*entente, convention, Ling*)
agreement; (*entre des styles, tons etc*) harmony;
(*consentement*) agreement, consent; (*Mus*)
chord; **donner son ~** to give one's
agreement; **mettre deux personnes d'~** to
make two people come to an agreement,
reconcile two people; **se mettre d'~** to come
to an agreement (with each other); **être d'~**
to agree; **être d'~ avec qn** to agree with sb;
d'~! OK!, right!; **d'un commun ~** of one
accord; ~ **parfait** (*Mus*) tonic chord

accordéon [akɔʀdeɔ̃] *nm* accordion

accorder [akɔʀde] *vt* (*faveur, délai*) to grant;
(*attribuer*): ~ **de l'importance/de la valeur à**

accoster [akɔste] vt (*Navig*) to draw alongside; (*personne*) to accost ▷ vi (*Navig*) to berth

accotement [akɔtmɑ̃] nm (*de route*) verge (Brit), shoulder; ~ **stabilisé/non stabilisé** hard shoulder/soft verge *ou* shoulder

accouchement [akuʃmɑ̃] nm delivery, (child)birth; (*travail*) labour (Brit), labor (US); ~ **à terme** delivery at (full) term; ~ **sans douleur** natural childbirth

accoucher [akuʃe] vi to give birth, have a baby; (*être en travail*) to be in labour (Brit) *ou* labor (US) ▷ vt to deliver; ~ **d'un garçon** to give birth to a boy

accoucheur [akuʃœʀ] nm: (*médecin*) ~ obstetrician

accouder [akude]: **s'accouder** vi: **s'~ à/ contre/sur** to rest one's elbows on/against/ on; **accoudé à la fenêtre** leaning on the windowsill

accoudoir [akudwaʀ] nm armrest

accoupler [akuple] vt to couple; (*pour la reproduction*) to mate; **s'accoupler** vi to mate

accourir [akuʀiʀ] vi to rush *ou* run up

accoutrement [akutʀəmɑ̃] nm (*péj*) getup (Brit), outfit

accoutumance [akutymɑ̃s] nf (*gén*) adaptation; (*Méd*) addiction

accoutumé, e [akutyme] adj (*habituel*) customary, usual; **comme à l'~e** as is customary *ou* usual

accoutumer [akutyme] vt: ~ **qn à qch/faire** to accustom sb to sth/to doing; **s'accoutumer à** to get accustomed *ou* used to

accréditer [akʀedite] vt (*nouvelle*) to substantiate; ~ **qn (auprès de)** to accredit sb (to)

accroc [akʀo] nm (*déchirure*) tear; (*fig*) hitch, snag; **sans** ~ without a hitch; **faire un** ~ **à** (*vêtement*) to make a tear in, tear; (*fig: règle etc*) to infringe

accrochage [akʀɔʃaʒ] nm hanging (up); hitching (up); (*Auto*) (minor) collision; (*Mil*) encounter, engagement; (*dispute*) clash, brush

accrocher [akʀɔʃe] vt (*suspendre*): ~ **qch à** to hang sth (up) on; (*attacher: remorque*) to hitch sth (up) to; (*heurter*) to catch; to hit; (*déchirer*): ~ **qch à** to catch sth (on); (*Mil*) to engage; (*fig*) to catch, attract ▷ vi to stick, get stuck; (*fig: pourparlers etc*) to hit a snag; (*plaire: disque etc*) to catch on; **s'accrocher** vi (*se disputer*) to have a clash *ou* brush; (*ne pas céder*) to hold one's own, hang on in (*fam*); **il a accroché ma voiture** he bumped into my car; **s'~ à** (*rester pris à*) to catch on; (*agripper, fig*) to hang on *ou* cling to

accroissement [akʀwasmɑ̃] nm increase

accroître [akʀwatʀ] vt, **s'accroître** vi to increase

accroupir [akʀupiʀ]: **s'accroupir** vi to squat, crouch (down)

accru, e [akʀy] pp de **accroître**

accueil [akœj] nm welcome; (*endroit*) reception (desk); (: *dans une gare*) information kiosk; **comité/centre d'~** reception committee/centre

accueillant, e [akœjɑ̃, -ɑ̃t] adj welcoming, friendly

accueillir [akœjiʀ] vt to welcome; (*aller chercher*) to meet, collect; (*loger*) to accommodate

acculer [akyle] vt: ~ **qn à** *ou* **contre** to drive sb back against; ~ **qn dans** to corner sb in; ~ **qn à** (*faillite*) to drive sb to the brink of

accumuler [akymyle] vt to accumulate, amass; **s'accumuler** vi to accumulate; to pile up

accusation [akyzasjɔ̃] nf (*gén*) accusation; (*Jur*) charge; (*partie*): l'~ the prosecution; **mettre en** ~ to indict; **acte d'**~ bill of indictment

accusé, e [akyze] nm/f accused; (*prévenu(e)*) defendant ▷ nm: ~ **de réception** acknowledgement of receipt

accuser [akyze] vt to accuse; (*fig*) to emphasize, bring out; (: *montrer*) to show; **s'accuser** vi (*s'accentuer*) to become more marked; ~ **qn de** to accuse sb of; (*Jur*) to charge sb with; ~ **qn/qch de qch** (*rendre responsable*) to blame sb/sth for sth; **s'~ de qch/d'avoir fait qch** to admit sth/having done sth; to blame o.s. for sth/for having done sth; ~ **réception de** to acknowledge receipt of; ~ **le coup** (*aussi fig*) to be visibly affected

acerbe [asɛʀb] adj caustic, acid

acéré, e [aseʀe] adj sharp

acharné, e [aʃaʀne] adj (*lutte, adversaire*) fierce, bitter; (*travail*) relentless, unremitting

acharner [aʃaʀne]: **s'acharner** vi: **s'~ sur** to go at fiercely, hound; **s'~ contre** to set o.s. against; to dog, pursue; (*malchance*) to hound; **s'~ à faire** to try doggedly to do; to persist in doing

achat [aʃa] nm buying *no pl*; (*article acheté*) purchase; **faire l'~ de** to buy, purchase; **faire des ~s** to do some shopping, buy a few things

acheminer [aʃmine] vt (*courrier*) to forward, dispatch; (*troupes*) to convey, transport; (*train*) to route; **s'~ vers** to head for

acheter [aʃte] vt to buy, purchase; (*soudoyer*) to buy, bribe; ~ **qch à** (*marchand*) to buy *ou* purchase sth from; (*ami etc: offrir*) to buy sth for; ~ **à crédit** to buy on credit

acheteur, -euse [aʃtœʀ, -øz] nm/f buyer; shopper; (*Comm*) buyer; (*Jur*) vendee, purchaser

achever [aʃ(ə)ve] vt to complete, finish; (*blessé*) to finish off; **s'achever** vi to end

acide [asid] *adj* sour, sharp; (*ton*) acid, biting; (*Chimie*) acid(ic) ▷ *nm* acid

acidulé, e [asidyle] *adj* slightly acid; **bonbons ~s** acid drops (*Brit*), ≈ lemon drops (*US*)

acier [asje] *nm* steel; ~ **inoxydable** stainless steel

aciérie [asjeʀi] *nf* steelworks *sg*

acné [akne] *nf* acne

acolyte [akɔlit] *nm* (*péj*) associate

acompte [akɔ̃t] *nm* deposit; (*versement régulier*) instalment; (*sur somme due*) payment on account; (*sur salaire*) advance; **un ~ de 10 euros** 10 euros on account

à-côté [akote] *nm* side-issue; (*argent*) extra

à-coup [aku] *nm* (*du moteur*) hic(c)ough; (*fig*) jolt; **sans ~s** smoothly; **par ~s** by fits and starts

acoustique [akustik] *nf* (*d'une salle*) acoustics *pl*; (*science*) acoustics *sg* ▷ *adj* acoustic

acquéreur [akeʀœʀ] *nm* buyer, purchaser; **se porter/se rendre ~ de qch** to announce one's intention to purchase/to purchase sth

acquérir [akeʀiʀ] *vt* to acquire; (*par achat*) to purchase, acquire; (*valeur*) to gain; (*résultats*) to achieve; **ce que ses efforts lui ont acquis** what his efforts have won *ou* gained (for) him

acquis, e [aki, -iz] *pp de* **acquérir** ▷ *nm* (accumulated) experience; (*avantage*) gain ▷ *adj* (*achat*) acquired; (*valeur*) gained; (*résultats*) achieved; **être ~ à** (*plan, idée*) to be in full agreement with; **son aide nous est ~e** we can count on *ou* be sure of his help; **tenir qch pour ~** to take sth for granted

acquit [aki] *vb voir* **acquérir** ▷ *nm* (*quittance*) receipt; **pour ~** received; **par ~ de conscience** to set one's mind at rest

acquitter [akite] *vt* (*Jur*) to acquit; (*facture*) to pay, settle; **s'~ de** to discharge; (*promesse, tâche*) to fulfil (*Brit*), fulfill (*US*), carry out

âcre [akʀ] *adj* acrid, pungent

acrobate [akʀɔbat] *nm/f* acrobat

acrobatie [akʀɔbasi] *nf* (*art*) acrobatics *sg*; (*exercice*) acrobatic feat; **~ aérienne** aerobatics *sg*

acte [akt] *nm* act, action; (*Théât*) act; **actes** *nmpl* (*compte-rendu*) proceedings; **prendre ~ de** to note, take note of; **faire ~ de présence** to put in an appearance; **faire ~ de candidature** to submit an application; **~ d'accusation** charge (*Brit*), bill of indictment; **~ de baptême** baptismal certificate; **~ de mariage/naissance** marriage/birth certificate; **~ de vente** bill of sale

acteur [aktœʀ] *nm* actor

actif, -ive [aktif, -iv] *adj* active ▷ *nm* (*Comm*) assets *pl*; (*Ling*) active (voice); (*fig*): **avoir à son ~** to have to one's credit; **actifs** *nmpl* people in employment; **~ toxique** toxic asset; **mettre à son ~** to add to one's list of achievements; **l'~ et le passif** assets and liabilities; **prendre une part active à qch** to take an active part in sth; **population active** working population

action [aksjɔ̃] *nf* (*gén*) action; (*Comm*) share; **une bonne/mauvaise ~** a good/an unkind deed; **mettre en ~** to put into action; **passer à l'~** to take action; **sous l'~ de** under the effect of; **l'~ syndicale** (the) union action; **un film d'~** an action film *ou* movie; **~ en diffamation** libel action; **~ de grâce(s)** (*Rel*) thanksgiving

actionnaire [aksjɔnɛʀ] *nm/f* shareholder

actionner [aksjɔne] *vt* to work; (*mécanisme*) to activate; (*machine*) to operate

activer [aktive] *vt* to speed up; (*Chimie*) to activate; **s'activer** *vi* (*s'affairer*) to bustle about; (*se hâter*) to hurry up

activité [aktivite] *nf* activity; **en ~** (*volcan*) active; (*fonctionnaire*) in active life; (*militaire*) on active service

actrice [aktʀis] *nf* actress

actualiser [aktɥalize] *vt* to actualize; (*mettre à jour*) to bring up to date

actualité [aktɥalite] *nf* (*d'un problème*) topicality; (*événements*): **l'~** current events; **les ~s** (*Ciné, TV*) the news; **l'~ politique/sportive** the political/sports *ou* sporting news; **les ~s télévisées** the television news; **d'~** topical

actuel, le [aktɥɛl] *adj* (*présent*) present; (*d'actualité*) topical; (*non virtuel*) actual; **à l'heure ~le** at this moment in time, at the moment

actuellement [aktɥɛlmɑ̃] *adv* at present, at the present time

acuité [akɥite] *nf* acuteness

acuponcteur, acupuncteur [akypɔ̃ktœʀ] *nm* acupuncturist

acuponcture, acupuncture [akypɔ̃ktyʀ] *nf* acupuncture

adaptateur, -trice [adaptatœʀ, -tʀis] *nm/f* adapter

adapter [adapte] *vt* to adapt; **s'~ (à)** (*personne*) to adapt (to); (: *objet, prise etc*) to apply (to); **~ qch à** (*approprier*) to adapt sth to (fit); **~ qch sur/dans/à** (*fixer*) to fit sth on/into/to

additif [aditif] *nm* additional clause; (*substance*) additive; **~ alimentaire** food additive

addition [adisjɔ̃] *nf* addition; (*au café*) bill

additionner [adisjɔne] *vt* to add (up); **s'additionner** *vi* to add up; **~ un produit d'eau** to add water to a product

adepte [adɛpt] *nm/f* follower

adéquat, e [adekwa(t), at] *adj* appropriate, suitable

adhérent, e [adeʀɑ̃, -ɑ̃t] *nm/f* (*de club*) member

adhérer [adeʀe] *vi* (*coller*) to adhere, stick; **~ à** (*coller*) to adhere *ou* stick to; (*se rallier à: parti, club*) to join; to be a member of; (: *opinion, mouvement*) to support

adhésif, -ive [adezif, -iv] *adj* adhesive, sticky; **ruban ~** sticky *ou* adhesive tape ▷ *nm* adhesive

adhésion [adezjɔ̃] nf (à un club) joining; membership; (à une opinion) support

adieu, x [adjø] excl goodbye ▷ nm farewell; **dire ~ à qn** to say goodbye ou farewell to sb; **dire ~ à qch** (renoncer) to say ou wave goodbye to sth

adjectif [adʒɛktif] nm adjective; **~ attribut** adjectival complement; **~ épithète** attributive adjective

adjoindre [adʒwɛ̃dR] vt: **~ qch à** to attach sth to; (ajouter) to add sth to; **~ qn à** (personne) to appoint sb as an assistant to; (comité) to appoint sb to, attach sb to; **s'adjoindre** vt (collaborateur etc) to take on, appoint

adjoint, e [adʒwɛ̃, -wɛ̃t] pp de **adjoindre** ▷ nm/f assistant; **~ au maire** deputy mayor; **directeur ~** assistant manager

adjudant [adʒydɑ̃] nm (Mil) warrant officer; **~-chef** ≈ warrant officer 1st class (Brit), ≈ chief warrant officer (US)

adjuger [adʒyʒe] vt (prix, récompense) to award; (lors d'une vente) to auction (off); **s'adjuger** vt to take for o.s.; **adjugé!** (vendu) gone!, sold!

adjurer [adʒyRe] vt: **~ qn de faire** to implore ou beg sb to do

admettre [admɛtR] vt (visiteur, nouveau-venu) to admit, let in; (candidat: Scol) to pass; (Tech: gaz, eau, air) to admit; (tolérer) to allow, accept; (reconnaître) to admit, acknowledge; (supposer) to suppose; **j'admets que ...** I admit that ...; **je n'admets pas que tu fasses cela** I won't allow you to do that; **admettons que ...** let's suppose that ...; **admettons** let's suppose so

administrateur, -trice [administratœR, -tRis] nm/f (Comm) director; (Admin) administrator; **~ délégué** managing director; **~ judiciaire** receiver

administration [administrasjɔ̃] nf administration; **l'A~** ≈ the Civil Service

administrer [administRe] vt (firme) to manage, run; (biens, remède, sacrement etc) to administer

admirable [admiRabl] adj admirable, wonderful

admirateur, -trice [admiRatœR, -tRis] nm/f admirer

admiration [admiRasjɔ̃] nf admiration; **être en ~ devant** to be lost in admiration before

admirer [admiRe] vt to admire

admis, e [admi, -iz] pp de **admettre**

admissible [admisibl] adj (candidat) eligible; (comportement) admissible, acceptable; (Jur) receivable

admission [admisjɔ̃] nf admission; **tuyau d'~** intake pipe; **demande d'~** application for membership; **service des ~s** admissions

ADN sigle m (= acide désoxyribonucléique) DNA

adolescence [adɔlesɑ̃s] nf adolescence

adolescent, e [adɔlesɑ̃, -ɑ̃t] nm/f adolescent, teenager

adonner [adɔne]: **s'adonner à** vt (sport) to devote o.s. to; (boisson) to give o.s. over to

adopter [adɔpte] vt to adopt; (projet de loi etc) to pass

adoptif, -ive [adɔptif, -iv] adj (parents) adoptive; (fils, patrie) adopted

adorable [adɔRabl] adj adorable

adorer [adɔRe] vt to adore; (Rel) to worship

adosser [adose] vt: **~ qch à ou contre** to stand sth against; **s'~ à ou contre** to lean with one's back against; **être adossé à ou contre** to be leaning with one's back against

adoucir [adusiR] vt (goût, température) to make milder; (avec du sucre) to sweeten; (peau, voix, eau) to soften; (caractère, personne) to mellow; (peine) to soothe, allay; **s'adoucir** vi to become milder; to soften; (caractère) to mellow

adresse [adRes] nf (voir adroit) skill, dexterity; (domicile, Inform) address; **à l'~ de** (pour) for the benefit of; **~ électronique** email address; **~ Web** web address

adresser [adRese] vt (lettre: expédier) to send; (: écrire l'adresse sur) to address; (injure, compliments) to address; **~ qn à un docteur/ bureau** to refer ou send sb to a doctor/an office; **~ la parole à qn** to speak to ou address sb; **s'adresser à** (parler à) to speak to, address; (s'informer auprès de) to go and see, go and speak to; (: bureau) to enquire at; (livre, conseil) to be aimed at

adroit, e [adRwa, -wat] adj (joueur, mécanicien) skilful (Brit), skillful (US), dext(e)rous; (politicien etc) shrewd, skilled

ADSL sigle m (= asymmetrical digital subscriber line) ADSL, broadband; **avoir l'~** to have broadband

adulte [adylt] nm/f adult, grown-up ▷ adj (personne, attitude) adult, grown-up; (chien, arbre) fully-grown, mature; **l'âge ~** adulthood; **formation/film pour ~s** adult training/film

adultère [adyltɛR] adj adulterous ▷ nm/f adulterer/adulteress ▷ nm (acte) adultery

advenir [advəniR] vi to happen; **qu'est-il advenu de ...?** what has become of ...?; **quoi qu'il advienne** whatever befalls ou happens

adverbe [advɛRb] nm adverb; **~ de manière** adverb of manner

adversaire [advɛRsɛR] nm/f (Sport, gén) opponent, adversary; (Mil) adversary, enemy

adverse [advɛRs] adj opposing

aération [aeRasjɔ̃] nf airing; (circulation de l'air) ventilation; **conduit d'~** ventilation shaft; **bouche d'~** air vent

aérer [aeRe] vt to air; (fig) to lighten; **s'aérer** vi to get some (fresh) air

aérien, ne [aeRjɛ̃, -ɛn] adj (Aviat) air cpd, aerial; (câble, métro) overhead; (fig) light; **compagnie ~ne** airline (company); **ligne ~ne** airline

aérobic [aeRɔbik] nf aerobics sg

aérogare [aeRɔgaR] nf airport (buildings); (en ville) air terminal

aéroglisseur [aeRɔglisœR] nm hovercraft

Aéronavale [aeʀɔnaval] nf ≈ Fleet Air Arm (Brit), ≈ Naval Air Force (US)

aérophagie [aeʀɔfaʒi] nf (Méd) wind, aerophagia (Méd); **il fait de l'~** he suffers from abdominal wind

aéroport [aeʀɔpɔʀ] nm airport; **~ d'embarquement** departure airport

aéroporté, e [aeʀɔpɔʀte] adj airborne, airlifted

aérosol [aeʀɔsɔl] nm aerosol

affable [afabl] adj affable

affaiblir [afebliʀ] vt to weaken; **s'affaiblir** vi to weaken, grow weaker; (vue) to grow dim

affaire [afɛʀ] nf (problème, question) matter; (criminelle, judiciaire) case; (scandaleuse etc) affair; (entreprise) business; (marché, transaction) (business) deal, (piece of) business no pl; (occasion intéressante) good deal; **affaires** nfpl (activité commerciale) business sg; (effets personnels) things, belongings; **~s de sport** sports gear; **tirer qn/se tirer d'~** to get sb/o.s. out of trouble; **ceci fera l'~** this will do (nicely); **avoir ~ à** (comme adversaire) to be faced with; (en contact) to be dealing with; **tu auras ~ à moi!** (menace) you'll have me to contend with!; **c'est une ~ de goût/d'argent** it's a question ou matter of taste/money; **c'est l'~ d'une minute/heure** it'll only take a minute/an hour; **ce sont mes ~s** (cela me concerne) that's my business; **occupe-toi de tes ~s!** mind your own business!; **toutes ~s cessantes** forthwith; **les ~s étrangères** (Pol) foreign affairs

affairer [afeʀe]: **s'affairer** vi to busy o.s., bustle about

affaisser [afese]: **s'affaisser** vi (terrain, immeuble) to subside, sink; (personne) to collapse

affaler [afale]: **s'affaler** vi: **s'~ dans/sur** to collapse ou slump into/onto

affamé, e [afame] adj starving, famished

affectation [afɛktasjɔ̃] nf (voir affecter) allotment; appointment; posting; (voir affecté) affectedness

affecter [afɛkte] vt (émouvoir) to affect, move; (feindre) to affect, feign; (telle ou telle forme etc) to take on, assume; **~ qch à** to allocate ou allot sth to; **~ qn à** to appoint sb to; (diplomate) to post sb to; **~ qch de** (de coefficient) to modify sth by

affectif, -ive [afɛktif, -iv] adj emotional, affective

affection [afɛksjɔ̃] nf affection; (mal) ailment; **avoir de l'~ pour** to feel affection for; **prendre en ~** to become fond of

affectionner [afɛksjɔne] vt to be fond of

affectueusement [afɛktɥøzmɑ̃] adv affectionately

affectueux, -euse [afɛktɥø, -øz] adj affectionate

affermir [afɛʀmiʀ] vt to consolidate, strengthen

affichage [afiʃaʒ] nm billposting, billsticking; (électronique) display; **"~ interdit"** "stick no bills", "billsticking prohibited"; **à cristaux liquides** liquid crystal display, LCD; **~ numérique** ou **digital** digital display

affiche [afiʃ] nf poster; (officielle) (public) notice; (Théât) bill; **être à l'~** (Théât) to be on; **tenir l'~** to run

afficher [afiʃe] vt (affiche) to put up, post up; (réunion) to put up a notice about; (électroniquement) to display; (fig) to exhibit, display; **s'afficher** vi (péj) to flaunt o.s.; (électroniquement) to be displayed; **"défense d'~"** "no bill posters"

affilée [afile]: **d'~** adv at a stretch

affiler [afile] vt to sharpen

affilier [afilje] vt: **s'affilier à** to become affiliated to

affiner [afine] vt to refine; **s'affiner** vi to become (more) refined

affirmatif, -ive [afiʀmatif, -iv] adj affirmative ▷ nf: **répondre par l'affirmative** to reply in the affirmative; **dans l'affirmative** (si oui) if (the answer is) yes ..., if he does (ou you do etc) ...

affirmation [afiʀmasjɔ̃] nf assertion

affirmer [afiʀme] vt (prétendre) to maintain, assert; (autorité etc) to assert; **s'affirmer** vi to assert o.s.; to assert itself

affligé, e [afliʒe] adj distressed, grieved; **~ de** (maladie, tare) afflicted with

affliger [afliʒe] vt (peiner) to distress, grieve

affluence [aflyɑ̃s] nf crowds pl; **heures d'~** rush hour sg; **jours d'~** busiest days

affluent [aflyɑ̃] nm tributary

affluer [aflye] vi (secours, biens) to flood in, pour in; (sang) to rush, flow

affolant, e [afɔlɑ̃, -ɑ̃t] adj terrifying

affolement [afɔlmɑ̃] nm panic

affoler [afɔle] vt to throw into a panic; **s'affoler** vi to panic

affranchir [afʀɑ̃ʃiʀ] vt to put a stamp ou stamps on; (à la machine) to frank (Brit), meter (US); (esclave) to enfranchise, emancipate; (fig) to free, liberate; **s'affranchir de** to free o.s. from; **machine à ~** franking machine, postage meter

affranchissement [afʀɑ̃ʃismɑ̃] nm franking (Brit), metering (US); freeing; (Postes: prix payé) postage; **tarifs d'~** postage rates

affréter [afʀete] vt to charter

affreux, -euse [afʀø, -øz] adj dreadful, awful

affront [afʀɔ̃] nm affront

affrontement [afʀɔ̃tmɑ̃] nm (Mil, Pol) clash, confrontation

affronter [afʀɔ̃te] vt to confront, face; **s'affronter** to confront each other

affubler [afyble] vt (péj): **~ qn de** to rig ou deck sb out in; (surnom) to attach to sb

affût [afy] nm (de canon) gun carriage; **à l'~ (de)** (gibier) lying in wait (for); (fig) on the look-out (for)

affûter [afyte] vt to sharpen, grind
Afghanistan [afganistɑ̃] nm: l'~ Afghanistan
afin [afɛ̃]: **~ que** conj so that, in order that; **~ de faire** in order to do, so as to do
africain, e [afʀikɛ̃, -ɛn] adj African ▷ nm/f: A~, e African
Afrique [afʀik] nf: l'~ Africa; l'~ **australe/du Nord/du Sud** southern/North/South Africa
agacer [agase] vt to pester, tease; (involontairement) to irritate, aggravate; (aguicher) to excite, lead on
âge [ɑʒ] nm age; **quel ~ as-tu?** how old are you?; **une femme d'un certain ~** a middle-aged woman, a woman who is getting on (in years); **bien porter son ~** to wear well; **prendre de l'~** to be getting on (in years), grow older; **limite d'~** age limit; **dispense d'~** special exemption from age limit; **le troisième ~** (personnes âgées) senior citizens; (période) retirement; l'~ **ingrat** the awkward ou difficult age; **~ légal** legal age; **~ mental** mental age; l'~ **mûr** maturity, middle age; **~ de raison** age of reason
âgé, e [ɑʒe] adj old, elderly; **~ de 10 ans** 10 years old
agence [aʒɑ̃s] nf agency, office; (succursale) branch; **~ immobilière** estate agent's (office) (Brit), real estate office (US); **~ matrimoniale** marriage bureau; **~ de placement** employment agency; **~ de publicité** advertising agency; **~ de voyages** travel agency
agencer [aʒɑ̃se] vt to put together; (local) to arrange, lay out
agenda [aʒɛ̃da] nm diary; **~ électronique** PDA
agenouiller [aʒ(ə)nuje]: **s'agenouiller** vi to kneel (down)
agent, e [aʒɑ̃, ɑ̃t] nm/f (aussi: **~(e) de police**) policeman/policewoman; (Admin) official, officer; (fig: élément, facteur) agent; **~ d'assurances** insurance broker; **~ de change** stockbroker; **~ commercial** sales representative; **~ immobilier** estate agent (Brit), realtor (US); **~ (secret)** (secret) agent
agglomération [aglɔmeʀasjɔ̃] nf town; (Auto) built-up area; l'~ **parisienne** the urban area of Paris
aggloméré [aglɔmeʀe] nm (bois) chipboard; (pierre) conglomerate
aggraver [agʀave] vt to worsen, aggravate; (Jur: peine) to increase; **s'aggraver** vi to worsen; **~ son cas** to make one's case worse
agile [aʒil] adj agile, nimble
agir [aʒiʀ] vi (se comporter) to behave, act; (faire quelque chose) to act, take action; (avoir de l'effet) to act; **il s'agit de** it's a matter ou question of; (ça traite de) it is about; (il importe que): **il s'agit de faire** we (ou you etc) must do; **de quoi s'agit-il?** what is it about?
agitation [aʒitasjɔ̃] nf (hustle and) bustle; (trouble) agitation, excitement; (politique) unrest, agitation

agité, e [aʒite] adj (remuant) fidgety, restless; (troublé) agitated, perturbed; (journée) hectic; (mer) rough; (sommeil) disturbed, broken
agiter [aʒite] vt (bouteille, chiffon) to shake; (bras, mains) to wave; (préoccuper, exciter) to trouble, perturb; **s'agiter** vi to bustle about; (dormeur) to toss and turn; (enfant) to fidget; (Pol) to grow restless; **"~ avant l'emploi"** "shake before use"
agneau, x [aɲo] nm lamb; (toison) lambswool
agonie [agɔni] nf mortal agony, death pangs pl; (fig) death throes pl
agrafe [agʀaf] nf (de vêtement) hook, fastener; (de bureau) staple; (Méd) clip
agrafer [agʀafe] vt to fasten; to staple
agrafeuse [agʀaføz] nf stapler
agrandir [agʀɑ̃diʀ] vt (magasin, domaine) to extend, enlarge; (trou) to enlarge, make bigger; (Photo) to enlarge, blow up; **s'agrandir** vi (ville, famille) to grow, expand; (trou, écart) to get bigger
agrandissement [agʀɑ̃dismɑ̃] nm extension; enlargement; (photographie) enlargement
agréable [agʀeabl] adj pleasant, nice
agréé, e [agʀee] adj: **concessionnaire ~** registered dealer; **magasin ~** registered dealer('s)
agréer [agʀee] vt (requête) to accept; **~ à** vt to please, suit; **veuillez ~, Monsieur/ Madame, mes salutations distinguées** (personne nommée) yours sincerely; (personne non nommée) yours faithfully
agrégation [agʀegasjɔ̃] nf highest teaching diploma in France; see note

● **AGRÉGATION**
●
● The agrégation, informally known as the
● "agrég", is a prestigious competitive
● examination for the recruitment of
● secondary school teachers in France. The
● number of candidates always far exceeds
● the number of vacant posts. Most
● teachers of 'classes préparatoires' and
● most university lecturers have passed the
● agrégation.

agrégé, e [agʀeʒe] nm/f holder of the agrégation
agrément [agʀemɑ̃] nm (accord) consent, approval; (attraits) charm, attractiveness; (plaisir) pleasure; **voyage d'~** pleasure trip
agrémenter [agʀemɑ̃te] vt: **~ (de)** to embellish (with), adorn (with)
agresser [agʀese] vt to attack
agresseur [agʀesœʀ] nm aggressor, attacker; (Pol, Mil) aggressor
agressif, -ive [agʀesif, -iv] adj aggressive
agricole [agʀikɔl] adj agricultural, farm cpd
agriculteur, -trice [agʀikyltœʀ, -tʀis] nm/f farmer

agriculture [agrikyltyr] nf agriculture; farming

agripper [agripe] vt to grab, clutch; (pour arracher) to snatch, grab; **s'~ à** to cling (on) to, clutch, grip

agroalimentaire [agroalimɑ̃tɛr] adj farming cpd ▷ nm farm-produce industry; **l'~** agribusiness

agrumes [agrym] nmpl citrus fruit(s)

aguerrir [agerir] vt to harden; **s'~ (contre)** to become hardened (to)

aguets [agɛ]: **aux ~** adv: **être aux ~** to be on the look-out

aguicher [agiʃe] vt to entice

ahuri, e [ayri] adj (stupéfait) flabbergasted; (idiot) dim-witted

ai [ɛ] vb voir **avoir**

aide [ɛd] nm/f assistant ▷ nf assistance, help; (secours financier) aid; **à l'~ de** with the help ou aid of; **aller à l'~ de qn** to go to sb's aid, go to help sb; **venir en ~ à qn** to help sb, come to sb's assistance; **appeler (qn) à l'~** to call for help (from sb); **à l'~!** help!; **~ de camp** nm aide-de-camp; **~ comptable** nm accountant's assistant; **~ électricien** nm electrician's mate; **~ familiale** nf mother's help, ≈ home help; **~ judiciaire** nf legal aid; **~ de laboratoire** nm/f laboratory assistant; **~ ménagère** nf ≈ home help (Brit) ou helper (US); **~ sociale** nf (assistance) state aid; **~ soignant, e** nm/f auxiliary nurse; **~ technique** nf ≈ VSO (Brit), ≈ Peace Corps (US)

aide-éducateur, -trice [ɛdmedykatœr, tris] nm/f classroom assistant

aide-mémoire [ɛdmemwar] nm inv memoranda pages pl; (key facts) handbook

aider [ede] vt to help; **~ à qch** to help (towards) sth; **~ qn à faire qch** to help sb to do sth; **s'~ de** (se servir de) to use, make use of

aide-soignant, e [ɛdswaɲɑ̃, ɑ̃t] nm/f auxiliary nurse

aie etc [ɛ] vb voir **avoir**

aïe [aj] excl ouch!

aïeul, e [ajœl] nm/f grandparent, grandfather/grandmother; (ancêtre) forebear

aïeux [ajø] nmpl grandparents; forebears, forefathers

aigle [ɛgl] nm eagle

aigre [ɛgr] adj sour, sharp; (fig) sharp, cutting; **tourner à l'~** to turn sour

aigre-doux, -douce [ɛgrədu, -dus] adj (fruit) bitter-sweet; (sauce) sweet and sour

aigreur [ɛgrœr] nf sourness; sharpness; **~s d'estomac** heartburn sg

aigrir [egrir] vt (personne) to embitter; (caractère) to sour; **s'aigrir** vi to become embittered; to sour; (lait etc) to turn sour

aigu, ë [egy] adj (objet, arête) sharp, pointed; (son, voix) high-pitched, shrill; (note) high(-pitched); (douleur, intelligence) acute, sharp

aiguille [egɥij] nf needle; (de montre) hand; **à tricoter** knitting needle

aiguiller [egɥije] vt (orienter) to direct; (Rail) to shunt

aiguilleur [egɥijœr] nm: **~ du ciel** air traffic controller

aiguillon [egɥijɔ̃] nm (d'abeille) sting; (fig) spur, stimulus

aiguillonner [egɥijɔne] vt to spur ou goad on

aiguiser [egize] vt to sharpen, grind; (fig) to stimulate; (: esprit) to sharpen; (: sens) to excite

ail [aj] nm garlic

aile [ɛl] nf wing; (de voiture) wing (Brit), fender (US); **battre de l'~** (fig) to be in a sorry state; **voler de ses propres ~s** to stand on one's own two feet; **~ libre** hang-glider

aileron [ɛlrɔ̃] nm (de requin) fin; (d'avion) aileron

ailier [elje] nm (Sport) winger

aille etc [aj] vb voir **aller**

ailleurs [ajœr] adv elsewhere, somewhere else; **partout/nulle part ~** everywhere/nowhere else; **d'~** adv (du reste) moreover, besides; **par ~** adv (d'autre part) moreover, furthermore

aimable [ɛmabl] adj kind, nice; **vous êtes bien ~** that's very nice ou kind of you, how kind (of you)!

aimant¹ [ɛmɑ̃] nm magnet

aimant², e [ɛmɑ̃, -ɑ̃t] adj loving, affectionate

aimer [eme] vt to love; (d'amitié, affection, par goût) to like; (souhait): **j'aimerais ...** I would like ...; **s'aimer** to love each other; to like each other; **je n'aime pas beaucoup Paul** I don't like Paul much, I don't care much for Paul; **~ faire qch** to like doing sth, like to do sth; **j'aime faire du ski** I like skiing; **je t'aime** I love you; **aimeriez-vous que je vous accompagne?** would you like me to come with you?; **j'aimerais (bien) m'en aller** I should (really) like to go; **bien ~ qn/qch** to like sb/sth; **j'aime mieux Paul (que Pierre)** I prefer Paul (to Pierre); **j'aime mieux ou autant vous dire que** I may as well tell you that; **j'aimerais autant ou mieux y aller maintenant** I'd sooner ou rather go now; **j'aime assez aller au cinéma** I quite like going to the cinema

aine [ɛn] nf groin

aîné, e [ene] adj elder, older; (le plus âgé) eldest, oldest ▷ nm/f oldest child ou one, oldest boy ou son/girl ou daughter; **aînés** nmpl (fig: anciens) elders; **il est mon ~ (de 2 ans)** he's (2 years) older than me, he's (2 years) my senior

ainsi [ɛ̃si] adv (de cette façon) like this, in this way, thus; (ce faisant) thus ▷ conj thus, so; **~ que** (comme) (just) as; (et aussi) as well as; **pour ~ dire** so to speak, as it were; **~ donc** and so; **~ soit-il** (Rel) so be it; **et ~ de suite** and so on (and so forth)

air [ɛr] nm air; (mélodie) tune; (expression) look, air; (atmosphère, ambiance): **dans l'~** in the air (fig); **prendre de grands ~s (avec qn)** to give

o.s. airs (with sb); **en l'~** (up) into the air;
tirer en l'~ to fire shots in the air; **paroles/
menaces en l'~** empty words/threats;
prendre l'~ to get some (fresh) air; (*avion*) to
take off; **avoir l'~** (*sembler*) to look, appear;
avoir l'~ triste to look ou seem sad; **avoir l'~
de qch** to look like sth; **avoir l'~ de faire** to
look as though one is doing, appear to be
doing; **courant d'~** draught (Brit), draft (US);
le grand ~ the open air; **mal de l'~**
air-sickness; **tête en l'~** scatterbrain;
~ comprimé compressed air; **~ conditionné**
air-conditioning
airbag [ɛʀbag] nm airbag
aisance [ɛzɑ̃s] nf ease; (*Couture*) easing,
freedom of movement; (*richesse*) affluence;
être dans l'~ to be well-off ou affluent
aise [ɛz] nf comfort ▷ adj: **être bien ~ de/que**
to be delighted to/that; **aises** nfpl: **aimer ses
~s** to like one's (creature) comforts; **prendre
ses ~s** to make o.s. comfortable; **frémir d'~**
to shudder with pleasure; **être à l'~** ou **à son
~** to be comfortable; (*pas embarrassé*) to be at
ease; (*financièrement*) to be comfortably off; **se
mettre à l'~** to make o.s. comfortable; **être
mal à l'~** ou **à son ~** to be uncomfortable;
(*gêné*) to be ill at ease; **mettre qn à l'~** to put
sb at his (ou her) ease; **mettre qn mal à l'~** to
make sb feel ill at ease; **à votre ~** please
yourself, just as you like; **en faire à son ~** to
do as one likes; **en prendre à son ~ avec qch**
to be free and easy with sth, do as one likes
with sth
aisé, e [eze] adj easy; (*assez riche*) well-to-do,
well-off
aisselle [ɛsɛl] nf armpit
ait [ɛ] vb voir **avoir**
ajonc [aʒɔ̃] nm gorse no pl
ajourner [aʒuʀne] vt (*réunion*) to adjourn;
(*décision*) to defer, postpone; (*candidat*) to
refer; (*conscrit*) to defer
ajouter [aʒute] vt to add; **~ à** (*accroître*) to add
to; **s'~ à** to add to; **~ que** to add that; **~ foi à** to
lend ou give credence to
ajusté, e [aʒyste] adj: **bien ~** (*robe etc*) close-
fitting
ajuster [aʒyste] vt (*régler*) to adjust; (*vêtement*)
to alter; (*arranger*): **~ sa cravate** to adjust
one's tie; (*coup de fusil*) to aim; (*cible*) to aim at;
(*adapter*): **~ qch à** to fit sth to
alarme [alaʀm] nf alarm; **donner l'~** to give
ou raise the alarm; **jeter l'~** to cause alarm
alarmer [alaʀme] vt to alarm; **s'alarmer** vi
to become alarmed
alarmiste [alaʀmist] adj alarmist
Albanie [albani] nf: **l'~** Albania
album [albɔm] nm album; **~ à colorier**
colouring book; **~ de timbres** stamp album
albumine [albymin] nf albumin; **avoir** ou
faire de l'~ to suffer from albuminuria
alcool [alkɔl] nm: **l'~** alcohol; **un ~** a spirit, a
brandy; **bière sans ~** non-alcoholic ou

alcohol-free beer; **~ à brûler** methylated
spirits (Brit), wood alcohol (US); **~ à 90°**
surgical spirit; **~ camphré** camphorated
alcohol; **~ de prune** etc plum etc brandy
alcoolique [alkɔlik] adj, nm/f alcoholic
alcoolisé, e [alkɔlize] adj alcoholic; **une
boisson non ~e** a soft drink
alcoolisme [alkɔlism] nm alcoholism
alcootest®, alcotest® [alkɔtɛst] nm (*objet*)
Breathalyser®; (*test*) breath-test; **faire subir
l'alco(o)test à qn** to Breathalyse® sb
aléas [alea] nmpl hazards
aléatoire [aleatwaʀ] adj uncertain; (*Inform,
Statistique*) random
alentour [alɑ̃tuʀ] adv around (about);
alentours nmpl surroundings; **aux ~s de** in
the vicinity ou neighbourhood of, around
about; (*temps*) around about
alerte [alɛʀt] adj agile, nimble; (*style*) brisk,
lively ▷ nf alert; warning; **donner l'~** to give
the alert; **à la première ~** at the first sign of
trouble ou danger; **~ à la bombe** bomb scare
alerter [alɛʀte] vt to alert
algèbre [alʒɛbʀ] nf algebra
Alger [alʒe] n Algiers
Algérie [alʒeʀi] nf: **l'~** Algeria
algérien, ne [alʒeʀjɛ̃, -ɛn] adj Algerian
▷ nm/f: **A~, ne** Algerian
algue [alg] nf seaweed no pl; (*Bot*) alga
alibi [alibi] nm alibi
aliéné, e [aljene] nm/f insane person,
lunatic (*péj*)
aligner [aliɲe] vt to align, line up; (*idées,
chiffres*) to string together; (*adapter*): **~ qch sur**
to bring sth into alignment with; **s'aligner**
vi (*soldats etc*) to line up; **s'~ sur** (*Pol*) to align
o.s. with
aliment [alimɑ̃] nm food; **~ complet** whole
food
alimentaire [alimɑ̃tɛʀ] adj food cpd; (*péj*:
besogne) done merely to earn a living;
produits ~s foodstuffs, foods
alimentation [alimɑ̃tasjɔ̃] nf feeding; (*en
eau etc, de moteur*) supplying, supply;
(*commerce*) food trade; (*produits*) groceries pl;
(*régime*) diet; (*Inform*) feed; **~ (générale)**
(general) grocer's; **~ de base** staple diet; **~ en
feuilles/en continu/en papier** form/
stream/sheet feed
alimenter [alimɑ̃te] vt to feed; (*Tech*): **~ (en)**
to supply (with), feed (with); (*fig*) to sustain,
keep going
alinéa [alinea] nm paragraph; **"nouvel ~"**
"new line"
aliter [alite]: **s'aliter** vi to take to one's bed;
infirme alité bedridden person ou invalid
allaiter [alete] vt (*femme*) to (breast-)feed,
nurse; (*animal*) to suckle; **~ au biberon** to
bottle-feed
allant [alɑ̃] nm drive, go
alléchant, e [aleʃɑ̃, -ɑ̃t] adj tempting,
enticing

allécher [alefe] vt: ~ **qn** to make sb's mouth water; to tempt sb, entice sb

allée [ale] nf (de jardin) path; (en ville) avenue, drive; ~**s et venues** comings and goings

allégé, e [aleʒe] adj (yaourt etc) low-fat

alléger [aleʒe] vt (voiture) to make lighter; (chargement) to lighten; (souffrance) to alleviate, soothe

allègre [alɛɡʀ] adj lively, jaunty (Brit); (personne) gay, cheerful

alléguer [alege] vt to put forward (as proof ou an excuse)

Allemagne [almaɲ] nf: **l'**~ Germany; **l'**~ **de l'Est/Ouest** East/West Germany; **l'**~ **fédérale (RFA)** the Federal Republic of Germany (FRG)

allemand, e [almɑ̃, -ɑ̃d] adj German ▷ nm (Ling) German ▷ nm/f: **A**~, **e** German; **A**~ **de l'Est/l'Ouest** East/West German

aller [ale] nm (trajet) outward journey; (billet): ~ **(simple)** single (Brit) ou one-way ticket; ~ **(et) retour (AR)** (trajet) return ou journey (Brit), round trip (US); (billet) return (Brit) ou round-trip (US) ticket ▷ vi (gén) to go; ~ **à** (convenir) to suit; (forme, pointure etc) to fit; **cela me va** (couleur) that suits me; (vêtement) that suits me; that fits me; (projet, disposition) that suits me, that's fine ou OK by me; ~ **à la chasse/pêche** to go hunting/fishing; ~ **avec** (couleurs, style etc) to go (well) with; **je vais le faire/me fâcher** I'm going to do it/to get angry; ~ **voir/chercher qn** to go and see/look for sb; **comment allez-vous?** how are you?; **comment ça va?** how are you?; (affaires etc) how are things?; **ça va?** — **oui (ça va)!** how are things? — fine!; **pour ~ à** how do I get to; **ça va (comme ça)** that's fine (as it is); **il va bien/mal** he's well/ not well, he's fine/ill; **ça va bien/mal** (affaires etc) it's going well/not going well; **tout va bien** everything's fine; **ça ne va pas!** (mauvaise humeur etc) that's not on!, hey, come on!; **ça ne va pas sans difficultés** it's not without difficulties; ~ **mieux** to be better; **il y va de leur vie** their lives are at stake; **se laisser** ~ to let o.s. go; **s'en aller** vi (partir) to be off, go, leave; (disparaître) to go away; ~ **jusqu'à** to go as far as; **ça va de soi, ça va sans dire** that goes without saying; **tu y vas un peu fort** you're going a bit (too) far; **allez!** go on!; come on!; **allons!** come now!; **allons-y!** let's go!; **allez, au revoir!** right ou OK then, bye-bye!

allergie [alɛʀʒi] nf allergy

allergique [alɛʀʒik] adj allergic; ~ **à** allergic to

alliage [aljaʒ] nm alloy

alliance [aljɑ̃s] nf (Mil, Pol) alliance; (mariage) marriage; (bague) wedding ring; **neveu par** ~ nephew by marriage

allier [alje] vt (métaux) to alloy; (Pol, gén) to ally; (fig) to combine; **s'allier** vi to become allies; (éléments, caractéristiques) to combine; **s'**~ **à** to become allied to ou with

allô [alo] excl hullo, hallo

allocation [alɔkasjɔ̃] nf allowance; ~ **(de) chômage** unemployment benefit; ~ **(de) logement** rent allowance; ~**s familiales** ≈ child benefit no pl; ~**s de maternité** maternity allowance

allocution [alɔkysjɔ̃] nf short speech

allonger [alɔ̃ʒe] vt to lengthen, make longer; (étendre: bras, jambe) to stretch (out); (sauce) to spin out, make go further; **s'allonger** vi to get longer; (se coucher) to lie down, stretch out; ~ **le pas** to hasten one's step(s)

allouer [alwe] vt: ~ **qch à** to allocate sth to, allot sth to

allumage [alymaʒ] nm (Auto) ignition

allume-cigare [alymsigaʀ] nm inv cigar lighter

allumer [alyme] vt (lampe, phare, radio) to put ou switch on; (pièce) to put ou switch the light(s) on in; (feu, bougie, cigare, pipe, gaz) to light; (chauffage) to put on; **s'allumer** vi (lumière, lampe) to come ou go on; ~ **(la lumière ou l'électricité)** to put on the light

allumette [alymɛt] nf match; (morceau de bois) matchstick; (Culin): ~ **au fromage** cheese straw; ~ **de sûreté** safety match

allure [alyʀ] nf (vitesse) speed; (: à pied) pace; (démarche) walk; (maintien) bearing; (aspect, air) look; **avoir de l'**~ to have style; **à toute** ~ at full speed

allusion [a(l)lyzjɔ̃] nf allusion; (sous-entendu) hint; **faire** ~ **à** to allude ou refer to; to hint at

⭕ **MOT-CLÉ**

alors [alɔʀ] adv **1** (à ce moment-là) then, at that time; **il habitait alors à Paris** he lived in Paris at that time; **jusqu'alors** up till ou until then

2 (par conséquent) then; **tu as fini? alors je m'en vais** have you finished? I'm going then

3 (expressions): **alors? quoi de neuf?** well ou so? what's new?; **et alors?** so (what)?; **ça alors!** (well) really!

▷ conj: **alors que 1** (au moment où) when, as; **il est arrivé alors que je partais** he arrived as I was leaving

2 (tandis que) whereas, while; **alors que son frère travaillait dur, lui se reposait** while his brother was working hard, HE would rest

3 (bien que) even though; **il a été puni alors qu'il n'a rien fait** he was punished, even though he had done nothing

4 (pendant que) while, when; **alors qu'il était à Paris, il a visité ...** while ou when he was in Paris, he visited ...

alouette [alwɛt] nf (sky)lark

alourdir [aluʀdiʀ] vt to weigh down, make heavy; **s'alourdir** vi to grow heavy ou heavier

aloyau [alwajo] nm sirloin

Alpes [alp] nfpl: **les** ~ the Alps

alphabet [alfabɛ] nm alphabet; (livre) ABC (book), primer

alphabétique [alfabetik] adj alphabetic(al); **par ordre ~** in alphabetical order

alphabétiser [alfabetize] vt to teach to read and write; (pays) to eliminate illiteracy in

alpinisme [alpinism] nm mountaineering, climbing

alpiniste [alpinist] nm/f mountaineer, climber

Alsace [alzas] nf: **l'~** Alsace

alsacien, ne [alzasjɛ̃, -ɛn] adj Alsatian ▷ nm/f: **A~, ne** Alsatian

altérer [altere] vt (faits, vérité) to falsify, distort; (qualité) to debase, impair; (données) to corrupt; (donner soif à) to make thirsty; **s'altérer** vi to deteriorate; to spoil

altermondialisme [altɛrmɔ̃djalism] nm anti-globalism

altermondialiste [altɛrmɔ̃djalist] adj, nm/f anti-globalist

alternateur [altɛrnatœr] nm alternator

alternatif, -ive [altɛrnatif, -iv] adj alternating ▷ nf alternative

alternative nf (choix) alternative

alternativement [altɛrnativmɑ̃] adv alternately

alterner [altɛrne] vt to alternate ▷ vi: **~ (avec)** to alternate (with); **(faire) ~ qch avec qch** to alternate sth with sth

Altesse [altɛs] nf Highness

altitude [altityd] nf altitude, height; **à 1000 m d'~** at a height ou an altitude of 1000 m; **en ~** at high altitudes; **perdre/prendre de l'~** to lose/gain height; **voler à haute/basse ~** to fly at a high/low altitude

alto [alto] nm (instrument) viola ▷ nf (contr)alto

aluminium [alyminjɔm] nm aluminium (Brit), aluminum (US)

amabilité [amabilite] nf kindness; **il a eu l'~ de** he was kind ou good enough to

amadouer [amadwe] vt to coax, cajole; (adoucir) to mollify, soothe

amaigrir [amegrir] vt to make thin ou thinner

amaigrissant, e [amegrisɑ̃, -ɑ̃t] adj: **régime ~** slimming (Brit) ou weight-reduction (US) diet

amalgame [amalgam] nm amalgam; (fig: de gens, d'idées) hotch-potch, mixture

amande [amɑ̃d] nf (de l'amandier) almond; (de noyau de fruit) kernel; **en ~** (yeux) almond cpd, almond-shaped

amandier [amɑ̃dje] nm almond (tree)

amant [amɑ̃] nm lover

amarrer [amare] vt (Navig) to moor; (gén) to make fast

amas [amɑ] nm heap, pile

amasser [amase] vt to amass; **s'amasser** vi to pile up, accumulate; (foule) to gather

amateur [amatœr] nm amateur; **en ~** (péj) amateurishly; **musicien/sportif ~** amateur musician/sportsman; **~ de musique/sport** etc music/sport etc lover

amazone [amazɔn] nf horsewoman; **en ~** side-saddle

ambassade [ɑ̃basad] nf embassy; (mission): **en ~** on a mission; **l'~ de France** the French Embassy

ambassadeur, -drice [ɑ̃basadœr, -dris] nm/f ambassador/ambassadress

ambiance [ɑ̃bjɑ̃s] nf atmosphere; **il y a de l'~** everyone's having a good time

ambiant, e [ɑ̃bjɑ̃, -ɑ̃t] adj (air, milieu) surrounding; (température) ambient

ambigu, ë [ɑ̃bigy] adj ambiguous

ambitieux, -euse [ɑ̃bisjø, -øz] adj ambitious

ambition [ɑ̃bisjɔ̃] nf ambition

ambulance [ɑ̃bylɑ̃s] nf ambulance

ambulancier, -ière [ɑ̃bylɑ̃sje, -jɛr] nm/f ambulanceman/woman (Brit), paramedic (US)

ambulant, e [ɑ̃bylɑ̃, -ɑ̃t] adj travelling, itinerant

âme [am] nf soul; **rendre l'~** to give up the ghost; **bonne ~** (aussi ironique) kind soul; **un joueur/tricheur dans l'~** a gambler/cheat through and through; **~ sœur** kindred spirit

amélioration [ameljɔrasjɔ̃] nf improvement

améliorer [ameljɔre] vt to improve; **s'améliorer** vi to improve, get better

aménager [amenaʒe] vt (agencer: espace, local) to fit out; (: terrain) to lay out; (: quartier, territoire) to develop; (installer) to fix up, put in; **ferme aménagée** converted farmhouse

amende [amɑ̃d] nf fine; **mettre à l'~** to penalize; **faire ~ honorable** to make amends

amener [am(ə)ne] vt to bring; (causer) to bring about; (baisser: drapeau, voiles) to strike; **s'amener** vi (fam) to show up, turn up; **~ qn à qch/à faire** to lead sb to sth/to do

amenuiser [amənɥize]: **s'amenuiser** vi to dwindle; (chances) to grow slimmer, lessen

amer, amère [amɛr] adj bitter

américain, e [amerikɛ̃, -ɛn] adj American ▷ nm (Ling) American (English) ▷ nm/f: **A~, e** American; **en vedette ~e** as a special guest (star)

Amérique [amerik] nf America; **l'~ centrale** Central America; **l'~ latine** Latin America; **l'~ du Nord** North America; **l'~ du Sud** South America

amertume [amɛrtym] nf bitterness

ameublement [amœbləmɑ̃] nm furnishing; (meubles) furniture; **articles d'~** furnishings; **tissus d'~** soft furnishings, furnishing fabrics

ameuter [amøte] vt (badauds) to draw a crowd of; (peuple) to rouse, stir up

ami, e [ami] nm/f friend; (amant/maîtresse) boyfriend/girlfriend ▷ adj: **pays/groupe ~** friendly country/group; **être (très) ~ avec qn**

to be (very) friendly with sb; **être ~ de l'ordre** to be a lover of order; **un ~ des arts** a patron of the arts; **un ~ des chiens** a dog lover; **petit ~/petite ~e** (fam) boyfriend/girlfriend

amiable [amjabl] : **à l'~** adv (Jur) out of court; (gén) amicably

amiante [amjɑ̃t] nm asbestos

amical, e, -aux [amikal, -o] adj friendly ▷ nf (club) association

amicalement [amikalmɑ̃] adv in a friendly way; (formule épistolaire) regards

amidon [amidɔ̃] nm starch

amincir [amɛ̃siʀ] vt (objet) to thin (down); **s'amincir** vi to get thinner ou slimmer; **~ qn** to make a liking to; **faire** ou **présenter ses ~s à qn** to send sb one's best wishes; **~s** (formule épistolaire) (with) best wishes

amincissant, e [amɛ̃sisɑ̃, -ɑ̃t] adj slimming; **régime ~** diet; **crème ~e** slimming cream

amiral, -aux [amiʀal, -o] nm admiral

amitié [amitje] nf friendship; **prendre en ~** to take a liking to; **faire** ou **présenter ses ~s à qn** to send sb one's best wishes; **~s** (formule épistolaire) (with) best wishes

ammoniaque [amɔnjak] nf ammonia (water)

amnistie [amnisti] nf amnesty

amoindrir [amwɛ̃dʀiʀ] vt to reduce

amollir [amɔliʀ] vt to soften

amonceler [amɔ̃s(ə)le] vt to pile ou heap up; **s'amonceler** to pile ou heap up; (fig) to accumulate

amont [amɔ̃] : **en ~** adv upstream; (sur une pente) uphill; **en ~ de** prép upstream from; uphill from, above

amorce [amɔʀs] nf (sur un hameçon) bait; (explosif) cap; (tube) primer; (: contenu) priming; (fig: début) beginning(s), start

amorcer [amɔʀse] vt to bait; to prime; (commencer) to begin, start

amorphe [amɔʀf] adj passive, lifeless

amortir [amɔʀtiʀ] vt (atténuer: choc) to absorb, cushion; (bruit, douleur) to deaden; (Comm: dette) to pay off, amortize; (: mise de fonds, matériel) to write off; **~ un abonnement** to make a season ticket pay (for itself)

amortisseur [amɔʀtisœʀ] nm shock absorber

amour [amuʀ] nm love; (liaison) love affair, love; (statuette etc) cupid; **un ~ de** a lovely little; **l'~** de love

amouracher [amuʀaʃe] : **s'amouracher de** vt (péj) to become infatuated with

amoureux, -euse [amuʀø, -øz] adj (regard, tempérament) amorous; (vie, problèmes) love cpd; (personne) : **être ~ (de qn)** to be in love (with sb) ▷ nm/f lover ▷ nmpl courting couple(s); **tomber ~ de qn** to fall in love with sb; **être ~ de qch** to be passionately fond of sth; **un ~ de la nature** a nature lover

amour-propre (pl **amours-propres**) [amuʀpʀɔpʀ] nm self-esteem, pride

amovible [amɔvibl] adj removable, detachable

ampère [ɑ̃pɛʀ] nm amp(ere)

amphithéâtre [ɑ̃fiteatʀ] nm amphitheatre; (d'université) lecture hall ou theatre

ample [ɑ̃pl] adj (vêtement) roomy, ample; (gestes, mouvement) broad; (ressources) ample; **jusqu'à plus ~ informé** (Admin) until further details are available

amplement [ɑ̃pləmɑ̃] adv amply; **~ suffisant** ample, more than enough

ampleur [ɑ̃plœʀ] nf scale, size; (de dégâts, problème) extent, magnitude

amplificateur [ɑ̃plifikatœʀ] nm amplifier

amplifier [ɑ̃plifje] vt (son, oscillation) to amplify; (fig) to expand, increase

ampoule [ɑ̃pul] nf (électrique) bulb; (de médicament) phial; (aux mains, pieds) blister

ampoulé, e [ɑ̃pule] adj (péj) pompous, bombastic

amputer [ɑ̃pyte] vt (Méd) to amputate; (fig) to cut ou reduce drastically; **~ qn d'un bras/pied** to amputate sb's arm/foot

amusant, e [amyzɑ̃, -ɑ̃t] adj (divertissant, spirituel) entertaining, amusing; (comique) funny, amusing

amuse-gueule [amyzgœl] nm inv appetizer, snack

amusement [amyzmɑ̃] nm (voir amusé) amusement; (voir amuser) entertaining, amusing; (jeu etc) pastime, diversion

amuser [amyze] vt (divertir) to entertain, amuse; (égayer, faire rire) to amuse; (détourner l'attention de) to distract; **s'amuser** vi (jouer) to amuse o.s., play; (se divertir) to enjoy o.s., have fun; (fig) to mess around; **s'~ de qch** (trouver comique) to find sth amusing; **s'~ avec** ou **de qn** (duper) to make a fool of sb

amygdale [amidal] nf tonsil; **opérer qn des ~s** to take sb's tonsils out

an [ɑ̃] nm year; **être âgé de** ou **avoir 3 ans** to be 3 (years old); **en l'an 1980** in the year 1980; **le jour de l'an, le premier de l'an, le nouvel an** New Year's Day

analogique [analɔʒik] adj (Logique: raisonnement) analogical; (calculateur, montre etc) analogue; (Inform) analog

analogue [analɔg] adj: **~ (à)** analogous (to), similar (to)

analphabète [analfabɛt] nm/f illiterate

analyse [analiz] nf analysis; (Méd) test; **faire l'~ de** to analyse; **une ~ approfondie** an in-depth analysis; **en dernière ~** in the last analysis; **avoir l'esprit d'~** to have an analytical turn of mind; **~ grammaticale** grammatical analysis, parsing (Scol)

analyser [analize] vt to analyse; (Méd) to test

ananas [anana(s)] nm pineapple

anarchie [anaʀʃi] nf anarchy

anatomie [anatɔmi] nf anatomy

ancêtre [ɑ̃sɛtʀ] nm/f ancestor; (fig): **l'~ de** the forerunner of

anchois [ɑ̃ʃwa] nm anchovy

ancien, ne [ɑ̃sjɛ̃, -ɛn] adj old; (de jadis, de l'antiquité) ancient; (précédent, ex-) former, old; (par l'expérience) senior ▷ nm (mobilier ancien): **l'~ antiques** pl ▷ nm/f (dans une tribu etc) elder; **un ~ ministre** a former minister; **mon ~ne voiture** my previous car; **être plus ~ que qn dans une maison** to have been in a firm longer than sb; (dans la hiérarchie) to be senior to sb in a firm; **~ combattant** ex-serviceman; **~ (élève)** (Scol) ex-pupil (Brit), alumnus (US)
anciennement [ɑ̃sjɛnmɑ̃] adv formerly
ancienneté [ɑ̃sjɛnte] nf oldness; antiquity; (Admin) (length of) service; (privilèges obtenus) seniority
ancre [ɑ̃kʀ] nf anchor; **jeter/lever l'~** to cast/ weigh anchor; **à l'~** at anchor
ancrer [ɑ̃kʀe] vt (Constr: câble etc) to anchor; (fig) to fix firmly; **s'ancrer** vi (Navig) to (cast) anchor
Andorre [ɑ̃dɔʀ] nf Andorra
andouille [ɑ̃duj] nf (Culin) sausage made of chitterlings; (fam) clot, nit
âne [ɑn] nm donkey, ass; (péj) dunce, fool
anéantir [aneɑ̃tiʀ] vt to annihilate, wipe out; (fig) to obliterate, destroy; (déprimer) to overwhelm
anémie [anemi] nf anaemia
anémique [anemik] adj anaemic
ânerie [ɑnʀi] nf stupidity; (parole etc) stupid ou idiotic comment etc
anesthésie [anɛstezi] nf anaesthesia; **sous ~** under anaesthetic; **~ générale/locale** general/local anaesthetic; **faire une ~ locale à qn** to give sb a local anaesthetic
ange [ɑ̃ʒ] nm angel; **être aux ~s** to be over the moon; **~ gardien** guardian angel
angélus [ɑ̃ʒelys] nm angelus; (cloches) evening bells pl
angine [ɑ̃ʒin] nf sore throat, throat infection; **~ de poitrine** angina (pectoris)
anglais, e [ɑ̃glɛ, -ɛz] adj English ▷ nm (Ling) English ▷ nm/f: **A~, e** Englishman/woman; **les A~** the English; **filer à l'~e** to take French leave; **à l'~e** (Culin) boiled
angle [ɑ̃gl] nm angle; (coin) corner; **~ droit/ obtus/aigu/mort** right/obtuse/acute/dead angle
Angleterre [ɑ̃glətɛʀ] nf: **l'~** England
anglo... [ɑ̃glɔ] préfixe Anglo-, anglo(-)
anglophone [ɑ̃glɔfɔn] adj English-speaking
angoisse [ɑ̃gwas] nf: **l'~** anguish no pl
angoissé, e [ɑ̃gwase] adj anguished; (personne) distressed
angoisser [ɑ̃gwase] vt to harrow, cause anguish to ▷ vi to worry, fret
anguille [ɑ̃gij] nf eel; **~ de mer** conger (eel); **il y a ~ sous roche** (fig) there's something going on, there's something beneath all this
anicroche [anikʀɔʃ] nf hitch, snag
animal, e, -aux [animal, -o] adj, nm animal; **~ domestique/sauvage** domestic/wild animal

animateur, -trice [animatœʀ, -tʀis] nm/f (de télévision) host; (de music-hall) compère; (de groupe) leader, organizer; (Ciné: technicien) animator
animation [animasjɔ̃] nf (voir animé) busyness; liveliness; (Ciné: technique) animation; **animations** nfpl (activité) activities; **centre d'~** = community centre
animé, e [anime] adj (rue, lieu) busy, lively; (conversation, réunion) lively, animated; (opposé à inanimé, aussi Ling) animate
animer [anime] vt (ville, soirée) to liven up, enliven; (mettre en mouvement) to drive; (stimuler) to drive, impel; **s'animer** vi to liven up, come to life
anis [ani(s)] nm (Culin) aniseed; (Bot) anise
ankyloser [ɑ̃kiloze]: **s'ankyloser** vi to get stiff
anneau, x [ano] nm (de rideau, bague) ring; (de chaîne) link; (Sport): **exercices aux ~x** ring exercises
année [ane] nf year; **souhaiter la bonne ~ à qn** to wish sb a Happy New Year; **tout au long de l'~** all year long; **d'une ~ à l'autre** from one year to the next; **d'~ en ~** from year to year; **l'~ scolaire/fiscale** the school/tax year
annexe [anɛks] adj (problème) related; (document) appended; (salle) adjoining ▷ nf (bâtiment) annexe(e); (de document, ouvrage) annex, appendix; (jointe à une lettre, un dossier) enclosure
anniversaire [anivɛʀsɛʀ] nm birthday; (d'un événement, bâtiment) anniversary ▷ adj: **jour ~** anniversary
annonce [anɔ̃s] nf announcement; (signe, indice) sign; (aussi: **~ publicitaire**) advertisement; (Cartes) declaration; **~ personnelle** personal message; **les petites ~s** the small ou classified ads
annoncer [anɔ̃se] vt to announce; (être le signe de) to herald; (Cartes) to declare; **je vous annonce que ...** I wish to tell you that ...; **s'annoncer bien/difficile** vi to look promising/difficult; **~ la couleur** (fig) to lay one's cards on the table
annonceur, -euse [anɔ̃sœʀ, -øz] nm/f (TV, Radio: speaker) announcer; (publicitaire) advertiser
annuaire [anɥɛʀ] nm yearbook, annual; **~ téléphonique** (telephone) directory, phone book
annuel, le [anɥɛl] adj annual, yearly
annuité [anɥite] nf annual instalment
annulation [anylasjɔ̃] nf cancellation; annulment; quashing; repeal
annuler [anyle] vt (rendez-vous, voyage) to cancel, call off; (mariage) to annul; (jugement) to quash (Brit), repeal (US); (résultats) to declare void; (Math, Physique) to cancel out; **s'annuler** to cancel each other out
anodin, e [anɔdɛ̃, -in] adj harmless; (sans importance) insignificant, trivial

anonymat [anɔnima] *nm* anonymity; **garder l'~** to remain anonymous

anonyme [anɔnim] *adj* anonymous; *(fig)* impersonal

anorak [anɔrak] *nm* anorak

anorexie [anɔreksi] *nf* anorexia

anormal, e, -aux [anɔrmal, -o] *adj* abnormal; *(insolite)* unusual, abnormal

ANPE *sigle f* (= *Agence nationale pour l'emploi*) national employment agency (functions include job creation)

anse [ɑ̃s] *nf* handle; *(Géo)* cove

antan [ɑ̃tɑ̃] : **d'~** *adj* of yesteryear, of long ago

antarctique [ɑ̃tarktik] *adj* Antarctic ▷ *nm*: **l'A~** the Antarctic; **le cercle A~** the Antarctic Circle; **l'océan A~** the Antarctic Ocean

antécédent [ɑ̃tesedɑ̃] *nm* (*Ling*) antecedent; **antécédents** *nmpl* (*Méd etc*) past history *sg*; **~s professionnels** record, career to date

antenne [ɑ̃tɛn] *nf* (*de radio, télévision*) aerial; *(d'insecte)* antenna, feeler; *(poste avancé)* outpost; *(petite succursale)* sub-branch; **sur l'~** on the air; **passer à/avoir l'~** to go/be on the air; **deux heures d'~** two hours' broadcasting time; **hors ~** off the air; **~ chirurgicale** (*Mil*) advance surgical unit; **~ parabolique** satellite dish

antérieur, e [ɑ̃terjœr] *adj* (*d'avant*) previous, earlier; *(de devant)* front; **~ à** prior ou previous to; **passé/futur ~** (*Ling*) past/future anterior

anti... [ɑ̃ti] *préfixe* anti...

antialcoolique [ɑ̃tialkɔlik] *adj* anti-alcohol; **ligue ~** temperance league

antiatomique [ɑ̃tiatɔmik] *adj*: **abri ~** fallout shelter

antibiotique [ɑ̃tibjɔtik] *nm* antibiotic

antibrouillard [ɑ̃tibrujar] *adj*: **phare ~** fog lamp

anticipation [ɑ̃tisipasjɔ̃] *nf* anticipation; (*Comm*) payment in advance; **par ~** in anticipation, in advance; **livre/film d'~** science fiction book/film

anticipé, e [ɑ̃tisipe] *adj* (*règlement, paiement*) early, in advance; (*joie etc*) anticipated, early; **avec mes remerciements ~s** thanking you in advance ou anticipation

anticiper [ɑ̃tisipe] *vt* (*événement, coup*) to anticipate, foresee; (*paiement*) to pay ou make in advance ▷ *vi* to look ou think ahead; (*en racontant*) to jump ahead; (*prévoir*) to anticipate; **~ sur** to anticipate

anticonceptionnel, le [ɑ̃tikɔ̃sɛpsjɔnɛl] *adj* contraceptive

anticorps [ɑ̃tikɔr] *nm* antibody

antidote [ɑ̃tidɔt] *nm* antidote

antigel [ɑ̃tiʒɛl] *nm* antifreeze

antihistaminique [ɑ̃tiistaminik] *nm* antihistamine

antillais, e [ɑ̃tijɛ, -ɛz] *adj* West Indian, Caribbean ▷ *nm/f*: **A~, e** West Indian, Caribbean

Antilles [ɑ̃tij] *nfpl*: **les ~** the West Indies; **les Grandes/Petites ~** the Greater/Lesser Antilles

antilope [ɑ̃tilɔp] *nf* antelope

antimite, antimites [ɑ̃timit] *adj, nm*: **(produit) ~(s)** mothproofer, moth repellent

antimondialisation [ɑ̃timɔ̃djalizasjɔ̃] *nf* anti-globalization

antipathique [ɑ̃tipatik] *adj* unpleasant, disagreeable

antipelliculaire [ɑ̃tipelikylɛr] *adj* anti-dandruff

antipodes [ɑ̃tipɔd] *nmpl* (*Géo*): **les ~** the antipodes; *(fig)*: **être aux ~ de** to be the opposite extreme of

antiquaire [ɑ̃tikɛr] *nm/f* antique dealer

antique [ɑ̃tik] *adj* antique; (*très vieux*) ancient, antiquated

antiquité [ɑ̃tikite] *nf* (*objet*) antique; **l'A~** Antiquity; **magasin/marchand d'~s** antique shop/dealer

antirabique [ɑ̃tirabik] *adj* rabies *cpd*

antirouille [ɑ̃tiruj] *adj inv* anti-rust *cpd*; **peinture ~** antirust paint; **traitement ~** rustproofing

antisémite [ɑ̃tisemit] *adj* anti-Semitic

antiseptique [ɑ̃tisɛptik] *adj, nm* antiseptic

antiviral, e, -aux [ɑ̃tiviral, -o] *adj* (*Med*) antiviral

antivirus [ɑ̃tivirys] *nm* (*Inform*) antivirus (program)

antivol [ɑ̃tivɔl] *adj, nm*: **(dispositif) ~** antitheft device; (*pour vélo*) padlock

antre [ɑ̃tr] *nm* den, lair

anxiété [ɑ̃ksjete] *nf* anxiety

anxieux, -euse [ɑ̃ksjø, -øz] *adj* anxious, worried; **être ~ de faire** to be anxious to do

AOC *sigle f* (= *Appellation d'origine contrôlée*) guarantee of quality of wine; *see note*

> ● **AOC**
> ●
> ● *AOC* ("appellation d'origine contrôlée") is
> ● the highest French wine classification. It
> ● indicates that the wine meets strict
> ● requirements concerning vineyard of
> ● origin, type of grape, method of
> ● production and alcoholic strength.

août [u(t)] *nm* August; *voir aussi* **juillet**; **Assomption**

apaiser [apeze] *vt* (*colère*) to calm, quell, soothe; (*faim*) to appease, assuage; (*douleur*) to soothe; (*personne*) to calm (down), pacify; **s'apaiser** *vi* (*tempête, bruit*) to die down, subside; (*personne*) to calm down

apanage [apanaʒ] *nm*: **être l'~ de** to be the privilege ou prerogative of

aparté [aparte] *nm* (*Théât*) aside; (*entretien*) private conversation; **en ~** *adv* in an aside (*Brit*); (*entretien*) in private

apathique [apatik] *adj* apathetic

apatride [apatrid] *nm/f* stateless person

apercevoir [apɛrsəvwar] *vt* to see; **s'apercevoir de** *vt* to notice; **s'~ que** to notice that; **sans s'en ~** without realizing ou noticing

aperçu, e [apɛʀsy] pp de **apercevoir** ▷ nm (vue d'ensemble) general survey; (intuition) insight

apéritif, -ive [apeʀitif, -iv] adj which stimulates the appetite ▷ nm (boisson) aperitif; (réunion) (pre-lunch ou -dinner) drinks pl; **prendre l'~** to have drinks (before lunch ou dinner) ou an aperitif

à-peu-près [apøpʀɛ] nm inv (péj) vague approximation

apeuré, e [apœʀe] adj frightened, scared

aphte [aft] nm mouth ulcer

apiculture [apikyltyʀ] nf beekeeping, apiculture

apitoyer [apitwaje] vt to move to pity; **~ qn sur qn/qch** to move sb to pity for sb/over sth; **s'~ (sur qn/qch)** to feel pity ou compassion (for sb/over sth)

aplanir [aplaniʀ] vt to level; (fig) to smooth away, iron out

aplatir [aplatiʀ] vt to flatten; **s'aplatir** vi to become flatter; (écrasé) to be flattened; (fig) to lie flat on the ground; (: fam) to fall flat on one's face; (: péj) to grovel

aplomb [aplɔ̃] nm (équilibre) balance, equilibrium; (fig) self-assurance; (: péj) nerve; **d'~** adv steady; (Constr) plumb

APN sigle m (= appareil photo(graphique) numérique) digital camera

apogée [apɔʒe] nm (fig) peak, apogee

apologie [apɔlɔʒi] nf praise; (Jur) vindication

a posteriori [apɔsteʀjɔʀi] adv after the event, with hindsight, a posteriori

apostrophe [apɔstʀɔf] nf (signe) apostrophe; (appel) interpellation

apostropher [apɔstʀɔfe] vt (interpeller) to shout at, address sharply

apothéose [apɔteoz] nf pinnacle (of achievement); (Mus etc) grand finale

apôtre [apotʀ] nm apostle, disciple

apparaître [apaʀɛtʀ] vi to appear ▷ vb copule to appear, seem

apparat [apaʀa] nm: **tenue/dîner d'~** ceremonial dress/dinner

appareil [apaʀɛj] nm (outil, machine) piece of apparatus, device; (électrique etc) appliance; (politique, syndical) machinery; (avion) (aero) plane (Brit), (air)plane (US), aircraft inv; (téléphonique) telephone; (dentier) brace (Brit), braces (US); **~ digestif/reproducteur** digestive/reproductive system ou apparatus; **l'~ productif** the means of production; **qui est à l'~?** who's speaking?; **dans le plus simple ~** in one's birthday suit; **~ (photo)** camera; **~ numérique** digital camera

appareiller [apaʀeje] vi (Navig) to cast off, get under way ▷ vt (assortir) to match up

appareil photo (pl **appareils photos**) [apaʀɛjfɔto] nm camera

apparemment [apaʀamɑ̃] adv apparently

apparence [apaʀɑ̃s] nf appearance; **malgré**

les ~s despite appearances; **en ~** apparently, seemingly

apparent, e [apaʀɑ̃, -ɑ̃t] adj visible; (évident) obvious; (superficiel) apparent; **coutures ~es** topstitched seams; **poutres ~es** exposed beams

apparenté, e [apaʀɑ̃te] adj: **~ à** related to; (fig) similar to

apparition [apaʀisjɔ̃] nf appearance; (surnaturelle) apparition; **faire son ~** to appear

appartement [apaʀtəmɑ̃] nm flat (Brit), apartment (US)

appartenir [apaʀtəniʀ]: **~ à** vt to belong to; (faire partie de) to belong to, be a member of; **il lui appartient de** it is up to him to

apparu, e [apaʀy] pp de **apparaître**

appât [apa] nm (Pêche) bait; (fig) lure, bait

appâter [apate] vt (hameçon) to bait; (poisson, fig) to lure, entice

appauvrir [apovʀiʀ] vt to impoverish; **s'appauvrir** vi to grow poorer, become impoverished

appel [apɛl] nm call; (nominal) roll call; (: Scol) register; (Mil: recrutement) call-up; (Jur) appeal; **faire ~ à** (invoquer) to appeal to; (avoir recours à) to call on; (nécessiter) to call for, require; **faire** ou **interjeter ~** (Jur) to appeal, lodge an appeal; **faire l'~** to call the roll; (Scol) to call the register; **indicatif d'~** call sign; **numéro d'~** (Tél) number; **produit d'~** (Comm) loss leader; **sans ~** (fig) final, irrevocable; **~ d'air** in-draught; **~ d'offres** (Comm) invitation to tender; **faire un ~ de phares** to flash one's headlights; **~ (téléphonique)** (tele)phone call

appelé [ap(ə)le] nm (Mil) conscript

appeler [ap(ə)le] vt to call; (Tél) to call, ring; (faire venir: médecin etc) to call, send for; (fig: nécessiter) to call for, demand; **~ au secours** to call for help; **~ qn à l'aide** ou **au secours** to call to sb to help; **~ qn à un poste/des fonctions** to appoint sb to a post/assign duties to sb; **être appelé à** (fig) to be destined to; **~ qn à comparaître** (Jur) to summon sb to appear; **en ~ à** to appeal to; **s'appeler** vi: **elle s'appelle Gabrielle** her name is Gabrielle, she's called Gabrielle; **comment vous appelez-vous?** what's your name?; **comment ça s'appelle?** what is it ou that called?; **être appelé à** (fig) to be destined to

appendice [apɛ̃dis] nm appendix

appendicite [apɛ̃disit] nf appendicitis

appentis [apɑ̃ti] nm lean-to

appesantir [apəzɑ̃tiʀ]: **s'appesantir** vi to grow heavier; **s'~ sur** (fig) to dwell at length on

appétissant, e [apetisɑ̃, -ɑ̃t] adj appetizing, mouth-watering

appétit [apeti] nm appetite; **couper l'~ à qn** to take away sb's appetite; **bon ~!** enjoy your meal!

applaudir [aplodiʀ] vt to applaud ▷ vi to applaud, clap; **~ à** vt (décision) to applaud, commend

applaudissements [aplodismɑ̃] *nmpl* applause *sg*, clapping *sg*

appli [apli] *nf* app

application [aplikasjɔ̃] *nf* application; (*d'une loi*) enforcement; **mettre en ~** to implement

applique [aplik] *nf* wall lamp

appliquer [aplike] *vt* to apply; (*loi*) to enforce; (*donner: gifle, châtiment*) to give; **s'appliquer** *vi* (*élève etc*) to apply o.s.; **s'~ à** (*loi, remarque*) to apply to; **s'~ à faire qch** to apply o.s. to doing sth, take pains to do sth; **s'~ sur** (*coïncider avec*) to fit over

appoint [apwɛ̃] *nm* (*extra*) contribution *ou* help; **avoir/faire l'~** (*en payant*) to have/give the right change *ou* money; **chauffage d'~** extra heating

appointements [apwɛ̃tmɑ̃] *nmpl* salary *sg*, stipend

apport [apɔʀ] *nm* supply; (*argent, biens etc*) contribution

apporter [apɔʀte] *vt* to bring; (*preuve*) to give, provide; (*modification*) to make; (*remarque*) to contribute, add

apposer [apoze] *vt* to append; (*sceau etc*) to affix

appréciable [apʀesjabl] *adj* (*important*) appreciable, significant

apprécier [apʀesje] *vt* to appreciate; (*évaluer*) to estimate, assess; **j'~ais que tu ...** I should appreciate (it) if you ...

appréhender [apʀeɑ̃de] *vt* (*craindre*) to dread; (*arrêter*) to apprehend; **~ que** to fear that; **~ de faire** to dread doing

appréhension [apʀeɑ̃sjɔ̃] *nf* apprehension

apprendre [apʀɑ̃dʀ] *vt* to learn; (*événement, résultats*) to learn of, hear of; **~ qch à qn** (*informer*) to tell sb (of) sth; (*enseigner*) to teach sb sth; **tu me l'apprends!** that's news to me!; **~ à faire qch** to learn to do sth; **~ à qn à faire qch** to teach sb to do sth

apprenti, e [apʀɑ̃ti] *nm/f* apprentice; (*fig*) novice, beginner

apprentissage [apʀɑ̃tisaʒ] *nm* learning; (*Comm, Scol: période*) apprenticeship; **école** *ou* **centre d'~** training school *ou* centre; **faire l'~ de qch** (*fig*) to be initiated into sth

apprêté, e [apʀete] *adj* (*fig*) affected

apprêter [apʀete] *vt* to dress, finish; **s'apprêter** *vi*: **s'~ à qch/à faire qch** to prepare for sth/for doing sth

appris, e [apʀi, -iz] *pp de* **apprendre**

apprivoiser [apʀivwaze] *vt* to tame

approbation [apʀɔbasjɔ̃] *nf* approval; **digne d'~** (*conduite, travail*) praiseworthy, commendable

approchant, e [apʀɔʃɑ̃, -ɑ̃t] *adj* similar, close; **quelque chose d'~** something similar

approche [apʀɔʃ] *nf* approaching; (*arrivée, attitude*) approach; **approches** *nfpl* (*abords*) surroundings; **à l'~ du bateau/de l'ennemi** as the ship/enemy approached *ou* drew near; **l'~ d'un problème** the approach to a problem; **travaux d'~** (*fig*) manoeuvrings

approcher [apʀɔʃe] *vi* to approach, come near ▷ *vt* (*vedette, artiste*) to approach, come close to; (*rapprocher*): **~ qch (de qch)** to bring *ou* put *ou* move sth near (to sth); **~ de** *vt* (*lieu, but*) to draw near to; (*quantité, moment*) to approach; **s'approcher de** *vt* to approach, go *ou* come *ou* move near to; **approchez-vous** come *ou* go nearer

approfondir [apʀɔfɔ̃diʀ] *vt* to deepen; (*question*) to go further into; **sans ~** without going too deeply into it

approprié, e [apʀɔpʀije] *adj*: **~ (à)** appropriate (to), suited (to)

approprier [apʀɔpʀije] *vt* (*adapter*) adapt; **s'approprier** *vt* to appropriate, take over; **s'~ en** to stock up with

approuver [apʀuve] *vt* to agree with; (*autoriser: loi, projet*) to approve, pass; (*trouver louable*) to approve of; **je vous approuve entièrement/ne vous approuve pas** I agree with you entirely/don't agree with you; **lu et approuvé** (read and) approved

approvisionner [apʀɔvizjɔne] *vt* to supply; (*compte bancaire*) to pay funds into; **~ qn en** to supply sb with; **s'approvisionner** *vi*: **s'~ dans un certain magasin/au marché** to shop in a certain shop/at the market; **s'~ en** to stock up with

approximatif, -ive [apʀɔksimatif, -iv] *adj* approximate, rough; (*imprécis*) vague

appt *abr* = **appartement**

appui [apɥi] *nm* support; **prendre ~ sur** to lean on; (*objet*) to rest on; **point d'~** fulcrum; (*fig*) something to lean on; **à l'~ de** (*pour prouver*) in support of; **à l'~** *adv* to support one's argument; **l'~ de la fenêtre** the windowsill, the window ledge

appui-tête, appuie-tête [apɥitɛt] *nm inv* headrest

appuyer [apɥije] *vt* (*poser*): **~ qch sur/ contre/à** to lean *ou* rest sth on/against/on; (*soutenir: personne, demande*) to support, back (up) ▷ *vi*: **~ sur** (*bouton*) to press, push; (*mot, détail*) to stress, emphasize; **~ sur le frein** to brake, to apply the brakes; **s'appuyer sur** *vt* (*chose: peser sur*) to rest (heavily) on, press against; to lean on; (*compter sur*) to rely on; **s'~ sur qn** to lean on sb; **~ contre** (*toucher: mur, porte*) to lean *ou* rest against; **~ à droite** *ou* **sur sa droite** to bear (to the) right; **~ sur le champignon** to put one's foot down

âpre [ɑpʀ] *adj* acrid, pungent; (*fig*) harsh; (*lutte*) bitter; **~ au gain** grasping, greedy

après [apʀɛ] *prép* after ▷ *adv* afterwards; **deux heures ~** two hours later; **~ qu'il est parti/ avoir fait** after he left/having done; **courir ~ qn** to run after sb; **crier ~ qn** to shout at sb; **être toujours ~ qn** (*critiquer etc*) to be always on at sb; **~ quoi** after which; **d'~** *prép* (*selon*) according to; **~ lui** according to him; **d'~ moi** in my opinion; **~ coup** *adv* after the event, afterwards; ~ **tout** adv (au fond) after all; **et (puis)** ~? so what?

après-demain [apʀɛdmɛ̃] adv the day after tomorrow

après-guerre [apʀɛgɛʀ] nm post-war years pl; **d'~** adj post-war

après-midi [apʀɛmidi] nm ou f inv afternoon

après-rasage [apʀɛʀazaʒ] nm inv after-shave

après-shampooing [apʀɛʃɑ̃pwɛ̃] nm inv conditioner

après-ski [apʀɛski] nm inv (chaussure) snow boot; (moment) après-ski

après-soleil [apʀɛsɔlɛj] adj inv after-sun cpd ▷ nm after-sun cream ou lotion

à-propos [apʀɔpo] nm (d'une remarque) aptness; **faire preuve d'~** to show presence of mind, do the right thing; **avec ~** suitably, aptly

apte [apt] adj: ~ **à qch/faire qch** capable of sth/doing sth; ~ **(au service)** (Mil) fit (for service)

aquarelle [akwaʀɛl] nf (tableau) watercolour (Brit), watercolor (US); (genre) watercolo(u)rs pl, aquarelle

aquarium [akwaʀjɔm] nm aquarium

arabe [aʀab] adj Arabic; (désert, cheval) Arabian; (nation, peuple) Arab ▷ nm (Ling) Arabic ▷ nm/f: **A~** Arab

Arabie [aʀabi] nf: **l'~** Arabia; **l'~ Saoudite ou Séoudite** Saudi Arabia

arachide [aʀaʃid] nf groundnut (plant); (graine) peanut, groundnut

araignée [aʀeɲe] nf spider; ~ **de mer** spider crab

arbitraire [aʀbitʀɛʀ] adj arbitrary

arbitre [aʀbitʀ] nm (Sport) referee; (: Tennis, Cricket) umpire; (fig) arbiter, judge; (Jur) arbitrator

arbitrer [aʀbitʀe] vt to referee; to umpire; to arbitrate

arborer [aʀbɔʀe] vt to bear, display; (avec ostentation) to sport

arbre [aʀbʀ] nm tree; (Tech) shaft; ~ **à cames** (Auto) camshaft; ~ **fruitier** fruit tree; ~ **généalogique** family tree; ~ **de Noël** Christmas tree; ~ **de transmission** (Auto) driveshaft

arbuste [aʀbyst] nm small shrub, bush

arc [aʀk] nm (arme) bow; (Géom) arc; (Archit) arch; ~ **de cercle** arc of a circle; **en ~ de cercle** adj semi-circular

arcade [aʀkad] nf arch(way); ~**s** arcade sg, arches; ~ **sourcilière** arch of the eyebrows

arcanes [aʀkan] nmpl mysteries

arc-boutant (pl **arcs-boutants**) [aʀkbutɑ̃] nm flying buttress

arceau, x [aʀso] nm (métallique etc) hoop

arc-en-ciel (pl **arcs-en-ciel**) [aʀkɑ̃sjɛl] nm rainbow

arche [aʀʃ] nf arch; ~ **de Noé** Noah's Ark

archéologie [aʀkeɔlɔʒi] nf arch(a)eology

archéologue [aʀkeɔlɔg] nm/f arch(a)eologist

archet [aʀʃɛ] nm bow

archevêque [aʀʃəvɛk] nm archbishop

archi... [aʀʃi] préfixe (très) dead, extra

archipel [aʀʃipɛl] nm archipelago

architecte [aʀʃitɛkt] nm architect

architecture [aʀʃitɛktyʀ] nf architecture

archive [aʀʃiv] nf file

archives [aʀʃiv] nfpl (collection) archives

arctique [aʀktik] adj Arctic ▷ nm: **l'A~** the Arctic; **le cercle A~** the Arctic Circle; **l'océan A~** the Arctic Ocean

ardemment [aʀdamɑ̃] adv ardently, fervently

ardent, e [aʀdɑ̃, -ɑ̃t] adj (soleil) blazing; (fièvre) raging; (amour) ardent, passionate; (prière) fervent

ardeur [aʀdœʀ] nf blazing heat; (fig) fervour, ardour

ardoise [aʀdwaz] nf slate

ardu, e [aʀdy] adj (travail) arduous; (problème) difficult; (pente) steep, abrupt

arène [aʀɛn] nf arena; (fig): **l'~ politique** the political arena; **arènes** nfpl bull-ring sg

arête [aʀɛt] nf (de poisson) bone; (d'une montagne) ridge; (Géom etc) edge (where two faces meet)

argent [aʀʒɑ̃] nm (métal) silver; (monnaie) money; (couleur) silver; **en avoir pour son ~** to get value for money; **gagner beaucoup d'~** to earn a lot of money; ~ **comptant** (hard) cash; ~ **de poche** pocket money; ~ **liquide** ready money, (ready) cash

argenté, e [aʀʒɑ̃te] adj silver(y); (métal) silver-plated

argenterie [aʀʒɑ̃tʀi] nf silverware; (en métal argenté) silver plate

argentin, e [aʀʒɑ̃tɛ̃, -in] adj Argentinian, Argentine ▷ nm/f: **A~, e** Argentinian, Argentine

Argentine [aʀʒɑ̃tin] nf: **l'~** Argentina, the Argentine

argentique [aʀʒɑ̃tik] adj (appareil photo) film cpd

argile [aʀʒil] nf clay

argot [aʀgo] nm slang; see note

ARGOT

Argot was the term originally used to describe the jargon of the criminal underworld, characterized by colourful images and distinctive intonation and designed to confuse the outsider. Some French authors write in *argot* and so have helped it spread and grow. More generally, the special vocabulary used by any social or professional group is also known as *argot*.

argotique [aʀgɔtik] adj slang cpd; (très familier) slangy

argument [aʀgymɑ̃] nm argument

argumentaire [aʀgymɑ̃tɛʀ] nm list of sales points; (brochure) sales leaflet

argumenter [aʀgymɑ̃te] vi to argue

argus [aʀgys] nm guide to second-hand car etc prices

aride [aʀid] adj arid

aristocratie [aʀistɔkʀasi] nf aristocracy

aristocratique [aʀistɔkʀatik] adj aristocratic

arithmétique [aʀitmetik] adj arithmetic(al) ▷ nf arithmetic

armateur [aʀmatœʀ] nm shipowner

armature [aʀmatyʀ] nf framework; (de tente etc) frame; (de corset) bone; (de soutien-gorge) wiring

arme [aʀm] nf weapon; (section de l'armée) arm; **armes** nfpl weapons, arms; (blason) (coat of) arms; **les ~s** (profession) soldiering sg; **à ~s égales** on equal terms; **en ~s** up in arms; **passer par les ~s** to execute (by firing squad); **prendre/présenter les ~s** to take up/present arms; **se battre à l'~ blanche** to fight with blades; **~ à feu** firearm; **~s de destruction massive** weapons of mass destruction

armée [aʀme] nf army; **~ de l'air** Air Force; **l'~ du Salut** the Salvation Army; **~ de terre** Army

armement [aʀməmɑ̃] nm (matériel) arms pl, weapons pl; (: d'un pays) arms pl, armament; (action d'équiper: d'un navire) fitting out; **~s nucléaires** nuclear armaments; **course aux ~s** arms race

armer [aʀme] vt to arm; (arme à feu) to cock; (appareil photo) to wind on; **~ qch de** to fit sth with; (renforcer) to reinforce sth with; **~ qn de** to arm ou equip sb with; **s'armer de** to arm o.s. with

armistice [aʀmistis] nm armistice; **l'A~** ≈ Remembrance (Brit) ou Veterans (US) Day

armoire [aʀmwaʀ] nf (tall) cupboard; (penderie) wardrobe (Brit), closet (US); **~ à pharmacie** medicine chest

armoiries [aʀmwaʀi] nfpl coat of arms sg

armure [aʀmyʀ] nf armour no pl, suit of armour

armurier [aʀmyʀje] nm gunsmith; (Mil, d'armes blanches) armourer

arnaque [aʀnak] (fam) nf swindling; **c'est de l'~** it's daylight robbery

arnaquer [aʀnake] (fam) vt to do (fam), swindle; **se faire ~** to be had (fam) ou done

arobase [aʀɔbaz] nf (Inform) "at" symbol, @; **"paul ~ société point fr"** "paul at société dot fr"

aromates [aʀɔmat] nmpl seasoning sg, herbs (and spices)

aromathérapie [aʀɔmateʀapi] nf aromatherapy

aromatisé, e [aʀɔmatize] adj flavoured

arôme [aʀom] nm aroma; (d'une fleur etc) fragrance

arpenter [aʀpɑ̃te] vt to pace up and down

arpenteur [aʀpɑ̃tœʀ] nm land surveyor

arqué, e [aʀke] adj arched; (jambes) bow cpd, bandy

arrache-pied [aʀaʃpje]: **d'~** adv relentlessly

arracher [aʀaʃe] vt to pull out; (page etc) to tear off, tear out; (déplanter: légume, herbe, souche) to pull up; (bras etc: par explosion) to blow off; (: par accident) to tear off; **s'arracher** vt (article très recherché) to fight over; **~ qch à qn** to snatch sth from sb; (fig) to wring sth out of sb, wrest sth from sb; **~ qn à** (solitude, rêverie) to drag sb out of; (famille etc) to tear ou wrench sb away from; **se faire ~ une dent** to have a tooth ou pulled (US); **s'~ de** (lieu) to tear o.s. away from; (habitude) to force o.s. out of

arraisonner [aʀɛzɔne] vt to board and search

arrangeant, e [aʀɑ̃ʒɑ̃, -ɑ̃t] adj accommodating, obliging

arrangement [aʀɑ̃ʒmɑ̃] nm arrangement

arranger [aʀɑ̃ʒe] vt to arrange; (réparer) to fix, put right; (régler) to settle, sort out; (convenir à) to suit, be convenient for; **cela m'arrange** that suits me (fine); **s'arranger** vi (se mettre d'accord) to come to an agreement ou arrangement; (s'améliorer: querelle, situation) to be sorted out; (se débrouiller): **s'~ pour que ...** to arrange things so that ...; **je vais m'~** I'll manage; **ça va s'~** it'll sort itself out; **s'~ pour faire** to make sure that ou see to it that one can do

arrestation [aʀɛstasjɔ̃] nf arrest

arrêt [aʀɛ] nm stopping; (de bus etc) stop; (Jur) judgment, decision; (Football) save; **arrêts** nmpl (Mil) arrest sg; **être à l'~** to be stopped, have come to a halt; **rester ou tomber en ~ devant** to stop short in front of; **sans ~** without stopping, non-stop; (fréquemment) continually; **~ d'autobus** bus stop; **~ facultatif** request stop; **~ de mort** capital sentence; **~ de travail** stoppage (of work)

arrêté, e [aʀete] adj firm, fixed ▷ nm order, decree; **~ municipal** ≈ bylaw, byelaw

arrêter [aʀete] vt to stop; (chauffage etc) to turn off, switch off; (Comm: compte) to settle; (Couture: point) to fasten off; (fixer: date etc) to appoint, decide on; (criminel, suspect) to arrest; **s'arrêter** vi (s'interrompre) to stop o.s.; **~ de faire** to stop doing; **arrête de te plaindre** stop complaining; **ne pas ~ de faire** to keep on doing; **s'~ de faire** to stop doing; **s'~ sur** (choix, regard) to fall on

arrhes [aʀ] nfpl deposit sg

arrière [aʀjɛʀ] nm back; (Sport) fullback ▷ adj inv: **siège/roue ~** back ou rear seat/wheel; **arrières** nmpl (fig): **protéger ses ~s** to protect the rear; **à l'~** adv behind, at the back; **en ~** adv behind; (regarder) back, behind; (tomber, aller) backwards; **en ~ de** prép behind

arriéré, e [aʀjeʀe] adj (péj) backward ▷ nm (d'argent) arrears pl

arrière-goût [aʀjɛʀgu] nm aftertaste

arrière-grand-mère (pl **arrière-grand-mères**) [aʀjɛʀɡʀɑ̃mɛʀ] nf great-grandmother

arrière-grand-père (pl **arrière-grands-pères**) [aʀjɛʀɡʀɑ̃pɛʀ] nm great-grandfather

arrière-pays [aʀjɛʀpei] nm inv hinterland

arrière-pensée [aʀjɛʀpɑ̃se] nf ulterior motive; (doute) mental reservation

arrière-plan [aʀjɛʀplɑ̃] nm background; **à l'~** in the background; **d'~** adj (Inform) background cpd

arrière-saison [aʀjɛʀsezɔ̃] nf late autumn

arrière-train [aʀjɛʀtʀɛ̃] nm hindquarters pl

arrimer [aʀime] vt (cargaison) to stow; (fixer) to secure, fasten securely

arrivage [aʀivaʒ] nm consignment

arrivée [aʀive] nf arrival; (ligne d'arrivée) finish; **~ d'air/de gaz** air/gas inlet; **courrier à l'~** incoming mail; **à mon ~** when I arrived

arriver [aʀive] vi to arrive; (survenir) to happen, occur; **j'arrive!** (I'm) just coming!; **il arrive à Paris à 8 h** he gets to ou arrives in Paris at 8; **~ à destination** to arrive at one's destination; **~ à** (atteindre) to reach; **~ à (faire) qch** (réussir) to manage to (do) sth; **~ à échéance** to fall due; **en ~ à faire ...** to end up doing ..., get to the point of doing ...; **il arrive que ...** it happens that ...; **il lui arrive de faire ...** he sometimes does ...

arriviste [aʀivist] nm/f go-getter

arrobase [aʀɔbaz] nf (Inform) @, 'at' sign

arrogance [aʀɔɡɑ̃s] nf arrogance

arrogant, e [aʀɔɡɑ̃, -ɑ̃t] adj arrogant

arrondir [aʀɔ̃diʀ] vt (forme, objet) to round; (somme) to round off; **s'arrondir** vi to become round(ed); **~ ses fins de mois** to supplement one's pay

arrondissement [aʀɔ̃dismɑ̃] nm (Admin) ≈ district

arroser [aʀoze] vt to water; (victoire etc) to celebrate (over a drink); (Culin) to baste

arrosoir [aʀozwaʀ] nm watering can

arsenal, -aux [aʀsənal, -o] nm (Navig) naval dockyard; (Mil) arsenal; (fig) gear, paraphernalia

art [aʀ] nm art; **avoir l'~ de faire** (fig: personne) to have a talent for doing; **les ~s** the arts; **livre/critique d'~** art book/ critic; **objet d'~** object d'art; **~ dramatique** dramatic art; **~s martiaux** martial arts; **~s et métiers** applied arts and crafts; **~s ménagers** home economics sg; **~s plastiques** plastic arts

artère [aʀtɛʀ] nf (Anat) artery; (rue) main road

arthrite [aʀtʀit] nf arthritis

artichaut [aʀtiʃo] nm artichoke

article [aʀtikl] nm article; (Comm) item, article; **faire l'~** (Comm) to do one's sales spiel; **faire l'~ de** (fig) to sing the praises of; **à l'~ de la mort** at the point of death; **~ défini/ indéfini** definite/indefinite article; **~ de fond** (Presse) feature article; **~s de bureau** office equipment; **~s de voyage** travel goods ou items

articulation [aʀtikylasjɔ̃] nf articulation; (Anat) joint

articuler [aʀtikyle] vt to articulate; **s'articuler (sur)** vi (Anat, Tech) to articulate (with); **s'~ autour de** (fig) to centre around ou on, turn on

artifice [aʀtifis] nm device, trick

artificiel, le [aʀtifisjɛl] adj artificial

artisan [aʀtizɑ̃] nm artisan, (self-employed) craftsman; **l'~ de la victoire/du malheur** the architect of victory/of the disaster

artisanal, e, -aux [aʀtizanal, -o] adj of ou made by craftsmen; (péj) cottage industry cpd, unsophisticated; **de fabrication ~e** home-made

artisanat [aʀtizana] nm arts and crafts pl

artiste [aʀtist] nm/f artist; (Théât, Mus) artist, performer; (: de variétés) entertainer

artistique [aʀtistik] adj artistic

as vb [a] voir **avoir** ▷ nm [ɑs] ace

ascendance [asɑ̃dɑ̃s] nf (origine) ancestry; (Astrologie) ascendant

ascendant, e [asɑ̃dɑ̃, -ɑ̃t] adj upward ▷ nm influence; **ascendants** nmpl ascendants

ascenseur [asɑ̃sœʀ] nm lift (Brit), elevator (US)

ascension [asɑ̃sjɔ̃] nf ascent; (de montagne) climb; **l'A~** (Rel) the Ascension; (: jour férié) Ascension (Day); see note; **(île de) l'A~** Ascension Island

● L'ASCENSION

● The fête de l'Ascension is a public holiday in France. It always falls on a Thursday, usually in May. Many French people take the following Friday off work too and enjoy a long weekend.

aseptisé, e [aseptize] (péj) adj sanitized

asiatique [azjatik] adj Asian, Asiatic ▷ nm/f: **A~** Asian

Asie [azi] nf: **l'~** Asia

asile [azil] nm (refuge) refuge, sanctuary; (Pol): **droit d'~** (political) asylum; (pour malades, vieillards etc) home; **accorder l'~ politique à qn** to grant ou give sb political asylum; **chercher/trouver ~ quelque part** to seek/ find refuge somewhere

aspect [aspɛ] nm appearance, look; (fig) aspect, side; (Ling) aspect; **à l'~ de** at the sight of

asperge [aspɛʀʒ] nf asparagus no pl

asperger [aspɛʀʒe] vt to spray, sprinkle

aspérité [asperite] nf excrescence, protruding bit (of rock etc)

asphalte [asfalt] nm asphalt

asphyxier [asfiksje] vt to suffocate, asphyxiate; (fig) to stifle; **mourir asphyxié** to die of suffocation ou asphyxiation

aspirateur [aspiʀatœʀ] nm vacuum cleaner, hoover®; **passer l'~** to vacuum

aspirer [aspiʀe] vt (air) to inhale; (liquide) to suck (up); (appareil) to suck ou draw up; **~ à** vt to aspire to

aspirine [aspiʀin] nf aspirin

assagir [asaʒiʀ] vt, **s'assagir** vi to quieten down, settle down

assaillir [asajiʀ] vt to assail, attack; **~ qn de** (questions) to assail ou bombard sb with

assainir [aseniʀ] vt to clean up; (eau, air) to purify

assaisonnement [asɛzɔnmɑ̃] nm seasoning

assaisonner [asɛzɔne] vt to season; **bien assaisonné** highly seasoned

assassin [asasɛ̃] nm murderer; assassin

assassiner [asasine] vt to murder; (esp Pol) to assassinate

assaut [aso] nm assault, attack; **prendre d'~** to (take by) storm, assault; **donner l'~ (à)** to attack; **faire ~ de** (rivaliser) to vie with ou rival each other in

assécher [asefe] vt to drain

assemblage [asɑ̃blaʒ] nm (action) assembling; (Menuiserie) joint; **un ~ de** (fig) a collection of; **langage d'~** (Inform) assembly language

assemblée [asɑ̃ble] nf (réunion) meeting; (public, assistance) gathering; assembled people; (Pol) assembly; (Rel): **l'~ des fidèles** the congregation; **l'A~ nationale (AN)** the (French) National Assembly; see note

● **ASSEMBLÉE NATIONALE**
●
● The Assemblée nationale is the lower house
● of the French Parliament, the upper
● house being the "Sénat". It is housed in
● the Palais Bourbon in Paris. Its members,
● or "députés", are elected every five years.

assembler [asɑ̃ble] vt (joindre, monter) to assemble, put together; (amasser) to gather (together), collect (together); **s'assembler** vi to gather, collect

assener, asséner [asene] vt: **~ un coup à qn** to deal sb a blow

assentiment [asɑ̃timɑ̃] nm assent, consent; (approbation) approval

asseoir [aswaʀ] vt (malade, bébé) to sit up; (personne debout) to sit down; (autorité, réputation) to establish; **s'asseoir** vi to sit (o.s.) up; to sit (o.s.) down; **faire ~ qn** to ask sb to sit down; **asseyez-vous!, assieds-toi!** sit down!; **~ qch sur** to build sth on; (appuyer) to base sth on

assermenté, e [asɛʀmɑ̃te] adj sworn, on oath

asservir [asɛʀviʀ] vt to subjugate, enslave

assez [ase] adv (suffisamment) enough, sufficiently; (passablement) rather, quite, fairly; **~!** enough!, that'll do!; **~/pas ~ cuit** well enough done/underdone; **est-il ~ fort/rapide?** is he strong/fast enough?; **il est passé ~ vite** he went past rather ou quite ou

fairly fast; **~ de pain/livres** enough ou sufficient bread/books; **vous en avez ~?** have you got enough?; **en avoir ~ de qch** (en être fatigué) to have had enough of sth; **j'en ai ~!** I've had enough!; **travailler ~** to work (hard) enough

assidu, e [asidy] adj assiduous, painstaking; (régulier) regular; **~ auprès de qn** attentive towards sb

assied etc [asje] vb voir **asseoir**

assiéger [asjeʒe] vt to besiege, lay siege to; (foule, touristes) to mob, besiege

assiérai etc [asjeʀe] vb voir **asseoir**

assiette [asjɛt] nf plate; (contenu) plate(ful); (équilibre) seat; (de colonne) seating; (de navire) trim; **il n'est pas dans son ~** he's not feeling quite himself; **~ à dessert** dessert ou side plate; **~ anglaise** assorted cold meats; **~ creuse** (soup) dish, soup plate; **~ de l'impôt** basis of (tax) assessment; **~ plate** (dinner) plate

assigner [asine] vt: **~ qch à** to assign ou allot sth to; (valeur, importance) to attach sth to; (somme) to allocate sth to; (limites) to set ou fix sth to; (cause, effet) to ascribe ou attribute sth to; **~ qn à** (affecter) to assign sb to; **~ qn à résidence** (Jur) to give sb a compulsory order of residence

assimiler [asimile] vt to assimilate, absorb; (comparer): **~ qch/qn à** to liken ou compare sth/sb to; **s'assimiler** vi (s'intégrer) to be assimilated ou absorbed; **ils sont assimilés aux infirmières** (Admin) they are classed as nurses

assis, e [asi, -iz] pp de **asseoir** ⊳ adj sitting (down), seated ⊳ nf (Constr) course; (Géo) stratum (pl -a); (fig) basis (pl bases), foundation; **~ en tailleur** sitting cross-legged

assises [asiz] nfpl (Jur) assizes; (congrès) (annual) conference

assistance [asistɑ̃s] nf (public) audience; (aide) assistance; **porter ou prêter ~ à qn** to give sb assistance; **A~ publique (AP)** public health service; **enfant de l'A~ (publique)** child in care; **~ technique** technical aid

assistant, e [asistɑ̃, -ɑ̃t] nm/f assistant; (d'université) probationary lecturer; **les assistants** nmpl (auditeurs etc) those present; **~e sociale** social worker

assisté, e [asiste] adj (Auto) power assisted; **~ par ordinateur** computer-assisted; **direction ~e** power steering ⊳ nm/f person receiving aid from the State

assister [asiste] vt to assist; **~ à** vt (scène, événement) to witness; (conférence) to attend, be (present) at; (spectacle, match) to be at, see

association [asɔsjasjɔ̃] nf association; (Comm) partnership; **~ d'idées/images** association of ideas/images

associé, e [asɔsje] nm/f associate; (Comm) partner

associer [asɔsje] vt to associate; ~ **qn à** (profits) to give sb a share of; (affaire) to make sb a partner in; (joie, triomphe) to include sb in; ~ **qch à** (joindre, allier) to combine sth with; **s'associer** vi to join together; (Comm) to form a partnership ▷ vt (collaborateur) to take on (as a partner); **s'~ à** (couleurs, qualités) to be combined with; (opinions, joie de qn) to share in; **s'~ à** ou **avec qn pour faire** to join (forces) ou join together with sb to do

assoiffé, e [aswafe] adj thirsty; (fig): ~ **de** (sang) thirsting for; (gloire) thirsting after

assombrir [asɔ̃bʀiʀ] vt to darken; (fig) to fill with gloom; **s'assombrir** vi to darken; (devenir nuageux, fig: visage) to cloud over; (fig) to become gloomy

assommer [asɔme] vt (étourdir, abrutir) to knock out, stun; (fam: ennuyer) to bore stiff

Assomption [asɔ̃psjɔ̃] nf: **l'~** the Assumption; see note

● **L'ASSOMPTION**
●
● The fête de l'Assomption, more commonly
● known as "le 15 août" is a national
● holiday in France. Traditionally, large
● numbers of holidaymakers leave home
● on 15 August, frequently causing chaos
● on the roads.

assorti, e [asɔʀti] adj matched, matching; fromages/légumes ~**s** assorted cheeses/ vegetables; ~ **à** matching; ~ **de** accompanied with; (conditions, conseils) coupled with; **bien/ mal ~** well/ill-matched

assortiment [asɔʀtimɑ̃] nm (choix) assortment, selection; (harmonie de couleurs, formes) arrangement; (Comm: lot, stock) selection

assortir [asɔʀtiʀ] vt to match; **s'assortir** vi to go well together, match; ~ **qch à** to match sth with; ~ **qch de** to accompany sth with; **s'~ de** to be accompanied by

assoupi, e [asupi] adj dozing, sleeping; (fig) (be)numbed; (sens) dulled

assoupir [asupiʀ]: **s'assoupir** vi (personne) to doze off; (sens) to go numb

assouplir [asupliʀ] vt to make supple, soften; (membres, corps) to limber up, make supple; (fig) to relax; (: caractère) to soften, make more flexible; **s'assouplir** vi to soften; to limber up; to relax; to become more flexible

assouplissant [asuplisɑ̃] nm (fabric) softener

assourdir [asuʀdiʀ] vt (bruit) to deaden, muffle; (bruit) to deafen

assouvir [asuviʀ] vt to satisfy, appease

assujettir [asyʒetiʀ] vt to subject, subjugate; (fixer: planches, tableau) to fix securely; ~ **qn à** (règle, impôt) to subject sb to

assumer [asyme] vt (fonction, emploi) to assume, take on; (accepter: conséquence, situation) to accept

assurance [asyʀɑ̃s] nf (certitude) assurance; (confiance en soi) (self-)confidence; (contrat) insurance (policy); (secteur commercial) insurance; **prendre une ~ contre** to take out insurance ou an insurance policy against; ~ **contre l'incendie** fire insurance; ~ **contre le vol** insurance against theft; **société d'~, compagnie d'~s** insurance company; ~ **au tiers** third party insurance; ~ **maladie (AM)** health insurance; ~ **tous risques** (Auto) comprehensive insurance; ~**s sociales (AS)** ≈ National Insurance (Brit), ≈ Social Security (US)

assurance-vie (pl **assurances-vie**) [asyʀɑ̃svi] nf life assurance ou insurance

assuré, e [asyʀe] adj (réussite, échec, victoire etc) certain, sure; (démarche, voix) assured; (pas) steady, (self-)confident; (certain): ~ **de** confident of; (Assurances) insured ▷ nm/f insured (person); ~ **social** ≈ member of the National Insurance (Brit) ou Social Security (US) scheme

assurément [asyʀemɑ̃] adv assuredly, most certainly

assurer [asyʀe] vt (Comm) to insure; (stabiliser) to steady, stabilize; (victoire etc) to ensure, make certain; (frontières, pouvoir) to make secure; (service, garde) to provide, operate; ~ **qch à qn** (garantir) to secure ou guarantee sth for sb; (certifier) to assure sb of sth; ~ **à qn que** to assure sb that; **je vous assure que non/si** I assure you that that is not the case/ is the case; ~ **qn de** to assure sb of; ~ **ses arrières** (fig) to be sure one has something to fall back on; **s'assurer (contre)** vi (Comm) to insure o.s. (against); **s'~ de/que** (vérifier) to make sure of/that; **s'~ (de)** (aide de qn) to secure; **s'~ sur la vie** to take out life insurance; **s'~ le concours/la collaboration de qn** to secure sb's aid/collaboration

assureur [asyʀœʀ] nm insurance agent; (société) insurers pl

asthmatique [asmatik] adj, nm/f asthmatic

asthme [asm] nm asthma

asticot [astiko] nm maggot

astiquer [astike] vt to polish, shine

astre [astʀ] nm star

astreignant, e [astʀɛɲɑ̃, -ɑ̃t] adj demanding

astreindre [astʀɛ̃dʀ] vt: ~ **qn à qch** to force sth upon sb; ~ **qn à faire** to compel ou force sb to do; **s'~ à** to compel ou force o.s. to

astrologie [astʀɔlɔʒi] nf astrology

astronaute [astʀɔnot] nm/f astronaut

astronomie [astʀɔnɔmi] nf astronomy

astuce [astys] nf shrewdness, astuteness; (truc) trick, clever way; (plaisanterie) wisecrack

astucieux, -euse [astysjø, -øz] adj shrewd, clever, astute

atelier [atəlje] nm workshop; (de peintre) studio

athée [ate] adj atheistic ▷ nm/f atheist

Athènes [atɛn] n Athens

athlète [atlɛt] nm/f (Sport) athlete; (costaud) muscleman

athlétisme [atletism] nm athletics sg; **faire de l'~** to do athletics; **tournoi d'~** athletics meeting

atlantique [atlɑ̃tik] adj Atlantic ▷ nm: **l'(océan) A~** the Atlantic (Ocean)

atlas [atlas] nm atlas

atmosphère [atmɔsfɛʀ] nf atmosphere

atome [atom] nm atom

atomique [atɔmik] adj atomic, nuclear; (usine) nuclear; (nombre, masse) atomic

atomiseur [atɔmizœʀ] nm atomizer

atout [atu] nm trump; (fig) asset; (: plus fort) trump card; **"~ pique/trèfle"** "spades/clubs are trumps"

âtre [ɑtʀ] nm hearth

atroce [atʀɔs] adj atrocious, horrible

attabler [atable]: **s'attabler** vi to sit down at (the) table; **s'~ à la terrasse** to sit down (at a table) on the terrace

attachant, e [ataʃɑ̃, -ɑ̃t] adj engaging, likeable

attache [ataʃ] nf clip, fastener; (fig) tie; **attaches** nfpl (relations) connections; **à l'~** (chien) tied up

attacher [ataʃe] vt to tie up; (étiquette) to attach, tie on; (ceinture) to fasten; (souliers) to do up ▷ vi (poêle, riz) to stick; **s'attacher** vi (robe etc) to do up; **s'~ à** (par affection) to become attached to; **s'~ à faire qch** to endeavour to do sth; **~ qch à** to tie ou fasten ou attach sth to; **~ qn à** (fig: lier) to attach sb to; **~ du prix/de l'importance à** to attach great value/attach importance to

attaque [atak] nf attack; (cérébrale) stroke; (d'épilepsie) fit; **être/se sentir d'~** to be/feel on form; **~ à main armée** armed attack

attaquer [atake] vt to attack; (en justice) to sue, bring an action against; (travail) to tackle, set about ▷ vi to attack; **s'attaquer à** vt (personne) to attack; (épidémie, misère) to tackle, attack

attardé, e [atarde] adj (passants) late; (enfant) backward; (conceptions) old-fashioned

attarder [atarde]: **s'attarder** vi (sur qch, en chemin) to linger; (chez qn) to stay on

atteindre [atɛ̃dʀ] vt to reach; (blesser) to hit; (contacter) to reach, contact, get in touch with; (émouvoir) to affect

atteint, e [atɛ̃, -ɛ̃t] pp de **atteindre** ▷ adj (Méd): **être ~ de** to be suffering from ▷ nf attack; **hors d'~e** out of reach; **porter ~e à** to strike a blow at, undermine

atteler [atle] vt (cheval, bœufs) to hitch up; (wagons) to couple; **s'atteler à** (travail) to buckle down to

attelle [atɛl] nf splint

attenant, e [atnɑ̃, -ɑ̃t] adj: **~ (à)** adjoining

attendant [atɑ̃dɑ̃]: **en ~** adv (dans l'intervalle) meanwhile, in the meantime

attendre [atɑ̃dʀ] vt to wait for; (être destiné ou réservé à) to await, be in store for ▷ vi to wait; **je n'attends plus rien (de la vie)** I expect nothing more (from life); **attendez que je réfléchisse** wait while I think; **s'~ à (ce que)** (escompter) to expect (that); **je ne m'y attendais pas** I didn't expect that; **ce n'est pas ce à quoi je m'attendais** that's not what I expected; **attendez-moi, s'il vous plaît** wait for me, please; **~ un enfant** to be expecting a baby; **~ de pied ferme** to wait determinedly; **~ de faire/d'être** to wait until one does/is; **~ que** to wait until; **attendez qu'il vienne** wait until he comes; **~ qch de, ~ qch de** to expect sth of; **faire ~ qn** to keep sb waiting; **se faire ~** to keep people (ou us etc) waiting; **en attendant** adv voir **attendant**

attendrir [atɑ̃dʀiʀ] vt to move (to pity); (viande) to tenderize; **s'~ (sur)** to be moved ou touched (by)

attendrissant, e [atɑ̃dʀisɑ̃, -ɑ̃t] adj moving, touching

attendu, e [atɑ̃dy] pp de **attendre** ▷ adj (événement) long-awaited; (prévu) expected ▷ nm: **~s** reasons adduced for a judgment; **~ que** conj considering that, since

attentat [atɑ̃ta] nm (contre une personne) assassination attempt; (contre un bâtiment) attack; **~ à la bombe** bomb attack; **~ à la pudeur** (exhibitionnisme) indecent exposure no pl; (agression) indecent assault no pl; **~ suicide** suicide bombing

attente [atɑ̃t] nf wait; (espérance) expectation; **contre toute ~** contrary to (all) expectations

attenter [atɑ̃te]: **~ à** vt (liberté) to violate; **~ à la vie de qn** to make an attempt on sb's life; **~ à ses jours** to make an attempt on one's life

attentif, -ive [atɑ̃tif, -iv] adj (auditeur) attentive; (soin) scrupulous; (travail) careful; **~ à** paying attention to; (devoir) mindful of; **~ à faire** careful to do

attention [atɑ̃sjɔ̃] nf attention; (prévenance) attention, thoughtfulness no pl; **mériter ~** to be worthy of attention; **à l'~ de** for the attention of; **porter qch à l'~ de qn** to bring sth to sb's attention; **attirer l'~ de qn sur qch** to draw sb's attention to sth; **faire ~ (à)** to be careful (of); **faire ~ (à ce) que** to be ou make sure that; **~! careful!, watch!, watch out!; ~ à la voiture!** watch out for that car!; **~, si vous ouvrez cette lettre** (sanction) just watch out, if you open that letter; **~, respectez les consignes de sécurité** be sure to observe the safety instructions

attentionné, e [atɑ̃sjɔne] adj thoughtful, considerate

atténuer [atenɥe] vt (douleur) to alleviate, ease; (couleurs) to soften; (diminuer) to lessen; (amoindrir) to mitigate the effects of; **s'atténuer** vi to ease; (violence etc) to abate

atterrer [atere] vt to dismay, appal

atterrir [ateʀiʀ] vi to land

atterrissage [aterisaʒ] nm landing; **~ sur le ventre/sans visibilité/forcé** belly/blind/forced landing

attestation [atɛstasjɔ̃] nf certificate, testimonial; **~ médicale** doctor's certificate

attester [atɛste] vt to testify to, vouch for; (démontrer) to attest, testify to; **~ que** to testify that

attirail [atiʀaj] nm gear; (péj) paraphernalia

attirant, e [atiʀɑ̃, -ɑ̃t] adj attractive, appealing

attirer [atiʀe] vt to attract; (appâter) to lure, entice; **~ qn dans un coin/vers soi** to draw sb into a corner/towards one; **~ l'attention de qn** to attract sb's attention; **~ l'attention de qn sur qch** to draw sb's attention to sth; **~ des ennuis à qn** to make trouble for sb; **s'~ des ennuis** to bring trouble upon o.s., get into trouble

attiser [atize] vt (feu) to poke (up), stir up; (fig) to fan the flame of, stir up

attitré, e [atitʀe] adj qualified; (agréé) accredited, appointed

attitude [atityd] nf attitude; (position du corps) bearing

attouchements [atuʃmɑ̃] nmpl touching sg; (sexuels) fondling sg, stroking sg

attraction [atʀaksjɔ̃] nf attraction; (de cabaret, cirque) number

attrait [atʀɛ] nm appeal, attraction; (plus fort) lure; **attraits** nmpl attractions; **éprouver de l'~ pour** to be attracted to

attrape-nigaud [atʀapnigo] nm con

attraper [atʀape] vt to catch; (habitude, amende) to get, pick up; (fam: duper) to con, take in (Brit); **se faire ~** (fam) to be told off

attrayant, e [atʀɛjɑ̃, -ɑ̃t] adj attractive

attribuer [atʀibɥe] vt (prix) to award; (rôle, tâche) to allocate, assign; (imputer): **~ qch à** to attribute sth to, ascribe sth to, put sth down to; **s'attribuer** vt (s'approprier) to claim for o.s.

attribut [atʀiby] nm attribute; (Ling) complement

attrister [atʀiste] vt to sadden; **s'~ de qch** to be saddened by sth

attroupement [atʀupmɑ̃] nm crowd, mob

attrouper [atʀupe]: **s'attrouper** vi to gather

au [o] prép voir **à**

aubaine [obɛn] nf godsend; (financière) windfall; (Comm) bonanza

aube [ob] nf dawn, daybreak; (Rel) alb; **à l'~** at dawn ou daybreak; **à l'~ de** (fig) at the dawn of

aubépine [obepin] nf hawthorn

auberge [obɛʀʒ] nf inn; **~ de jeunesse** youth hostel

aubergine [obɛʀʒin] nf aubergine (Brit), eggplant (US)

aubergiste [obɛʀʒist] nm/f inn-keeper, hotel-keeper

aucun, e [okœ̃, -yn] adj, pron no; (positif) any ▷ pron none; (positif) any(one); **il n'y a ~ livre** there isn't any book, there is no book; **je n'en vois ~ qui ...** I can't see any which ..., I (can) see none which ...; **~ homme** no man; **sans ~ doute** without any doubt; **sans ~e hésitation** without hesitation; **plus qu'~ autre** more than any other; **il le fera mieux qu'~ de nous** he'll do it better than any of us; **plus qu'~ de ceux qui ...** more than any of those who ...; **en ~e façon** in no way at all; **~ des deux** neither of the two; **~ d'entre eux** none of them; **d'~s** (certains) some

aucunement [okynmɑ̃] adv in no way, not in the least

audace [odas] nf daring, boldness; (péj) audacity; **il a eu l'~ de ...** he had the audacity to ...; **vous ne manquez pas d'~!** you're not lacking in nerve ou cheek!

audacieux, -euse [odasjø, -øz] adj daring, bold

au-delà [od(ə)la] adv beyond ▷ nm: **l'~** the hereafter; **~ de** prép beyond

au-dessous [odsu] adv underneath; below; **~ de** prép under(neath), below; (limite, somme etc) below, under; (dignité, condition) below

au-dessus [odsy] adv above; **~ de** prép above

au-devant [od(ə)vɑ̃]: **~ de** prép: **aller ~ de** (personne, danger) to go (out) and meet; (souhaits de qn) to anticipate

audience [odjɑ̃s] nf audience; (Jur: séance) hearing; **trouver ~ auprès de** to arouse much interest among, get the (interested) attention of

audimat® [odimat] nm (taux d'écoute) ratings pl

audio-visuel, le [odjovizɥɛl] adj audio-visual ▷ nm (équipement) audio-visual aids pl; (méthodes) audio-visual methods pl; **l'~** radio and television

auditeur, -trice [oditœʀ, -tʀis] nm/f (à la radio) listener; (à une conférence) member of the audience, listener; **~ libre** unregistered student (attending lectures), auditor (US)

audition [odisjɔ̃] nf (ouïe, écoute) hearing; (Jur: de témoins) examination; (Mus, Théât: épreuve) audition

auditoire [oditwaʀ] nm audience

auge [oʒ] nf trough

augmentation [ɔgmɑ̃tasjɔ̃] nf (action) increasing; raising; (résultat) increase; **~ (de salaire)** rise (in salary) (Brit), (pay) raise (US)

augmenter [ɔgmɑ̃te] vt to increase, (salaire, prix) to increase, raise, put up; (employé) to increase the salary of, give a (salary) rise (Brit) ou (pay) raise (US) to ▷ vi to increase; **~ de poids/volume** to gain (in) weight/volume

augure [ogyʀ] nm soothsayer, oracle; **de bon/mauvais ~** of good/ill omen

augurer [ogyʀe] vt: **~ qch de** to foresee sth (coming) from ou out of; **~ bien de** to augur well for

aujourd'hui [oʒuʀdɥi] adv today; **~ en huit/quinze** a week/two weeks today, a week/two weeks from now; **à dater** ou **partir d'~** from today('s date)

aumône [omon] nf alms sg (pl inv); **faire l'~**

(à qn) to give alms (to sb); **faire l'~ de qch à qn** (fig) to favour sb with sth

aumônier [omonje] nm chaplain

auparavant [oparavã] adv before(hand)

auprès [oprɛ]: **~ de** prép next to, close to; (recourir, s'adresser) to; (en comparaison de) compared with, next to; (dans l'opinion de) in the opinion of

auquel [okel] pron voir **lequel**

aura etc [ɔra] vb voir **avoir**

aurai etc [ɔre] vb voir **avoir**

auréole [ɔreɔl] nf halo; (tache) ring

aurons etc [ɔrɔ̃] vb voir **avoir**

aurore [ɔrɔr] nf dawn, daybreak; **~ boréale** northern lights pl

ausculter [oskylte] vt to sound

aussi [osi] adv (également) also, too; (de comparaison) as ▷ conj therefore, consequently; **~ fort que** as strong as; **moi ~** me too; **lui ~** (sujet) he too; (objet) him too; **~ bien que** (de même que) as well as

aussitôt [osito] adv straight away, immediately; **~ que** as soon as; **~ envoyé** as soon as it is (ou was) sent; **~ fait** no sooner done

austère [ostɛr] adj austere; (sévère) stern

austral, e [ostral] adj southern; **l'océan A~** the Antarctic Ocean; **les Terres A~es** Antarctica

Australie [ostrali] nf: **l'~** Australia

australien, ne [ostraljɛ̃, -ɛn] adj Australian ▷ nm/f: **A~, ne** Australian

autant [otã] adv so much; **je ne savais pas que tu la détestais** – I didn't know you hated her so much; (comparatif): **~ (que)** as much (as); (nombre) as many (as); **~ (de)** so much (ou many); as much (ou many); **n'importe qui aurait pu en faire ~** anyone could have done the same ou as much; **~ partir** we (ou you etc) may as well leave; **~ ne rien dire** best not say anything; **~ dire que ...** one might as well say that ...; **fort ~ que courageux** as strong as he is brave; **pour ~** for all that; **il n'est pas découragé pour ~** he isn't discouraged for all that; **pour ~ que** conj assuming, as long as; **d'~** adv accordingly, in proportion; **d'~ plus/mieux (que)** all the more/the better (since)

autel [otel] nm altar

auteur [otœr] nm author; **l'~ de cette remarque** the person who said that; **droit d'~** copyright

authenticité [otãtisite] nf authenticity

authentique [otãtik] adj authentic, genuine

auto [oto] nf car; **~s tamponneuses** bumper cars, dodgems

autobiographie [otobjɔgrafi] nf autobiography

autobronzant [otobrɔ̃zã] nm self-tanning cream (or lotion etc)

autobus [otobys] nm bus

autocar [otokar] nm coach

autochtone [otoktɔn] nm/f native

autocollant, e [otokɔlã, -ãt] adj self-adhesive; (enveloppe) self-seal ▷ nm sticker

auto-couchettes [otokuʃet] adj inv: **train ~** car sleeper train, motorail® train (Brit)

autocuiseur [otokwizœr] nm (Culin) pressure cooker

autodéfense [otodefãs] nf self-defence; **groupe d'~** vigilante committee

autodidacte [otodidakt] nm/f self-taught person

auto-école [otoekɔl] nf driving school

autographe [otograf] nm autograph

automate [otomat] nm (robot) automaton; (machine) (automatic) machine

automatique [otomatik] adj automatic ▷ nm: **l'~** (Tél) ≈ direct dialling

automatiquement [otomatikmã] adv automatically

automatiser [otomatize] vt to automate

automne [otɔn] nm autumn (Brit), fall (US)

automobile [otomobil] adj motor cpd ▷ nf (motor) car; **l'~** motoring; (industrie) the car ou automobile (US) industry

automobiliste [otomobilist] nm/f motorist

automutiler [otomytile]: **s'automutiler** vpr to self-harm

autonome [otonom] adj autonomous

autonomie [otonomi] nf autonomy; (Pol) self-government, autonomy; **~ de vol** range

autopsie [otɔpsi] nf post-mortem (examination), autopsy

autoradio [otoradjo] nf car radio

autorisation [otorizasjɔ̃] nf permission, authorization; (papiers) permit; **donner à qn l'~ de** to give sb permission to, authorize sb to; **avoir l'~ de faire** to be allowed ou have permission to do, be authorized to do

autorisé, e [otorize] adj (opinion, sources) authoritative; (permis): **~ à faire** authorized ou permitted to do; **dans les milieux ~s** in official circles

autoriser [otorize] vt to give permission for, authorize; (fig) to allow (of), sanction; **~ qn à faire** to give permission to sb to do, authorize sb to do

autoritaire [otoritɛr] adj authoritarian

autorité [otorite] nf authority; **faire ~** to be authoritative; **~s constituées** constitutional authorities

autoroute [otorut] nf motorway (Brit), expressway (US); **~ de l'information** (Inform) information superhighway

● **AUTOROUTE**
●
● Motorways in France, indicated by blue
● road signs with the letter A followed by a
● number, are toll roads. The speed limit is
● 130 km/h (110 km/h when it is raining).
● At the tollgate, the lanes marked "réservé"
● and with an orange "t" are reserved for
● people who subscribe to "télépéage", an
● electronic payment system.

auto-stop [otostɔp] nm: l'~ hitch-hiking; **faire de l'~** to hitch-hike; **prendre qn en ~** to give sb a lift

auto-stoppeur, -euse [ɔtɔstɔpœʀ, -øz] nm/f hitch-hiker, hitcher (Brit)

autour [otuʀ] adv around; ~ **de** prép around; (environ) around, about; **tout ~** adv all around

 MOT-CLÉ

autre [otʀ] adj **1** (différent) other, different; **je préférerais un autre verre** I'd prefer another ou a different glass; **d'autres verres** different glasses; **se sentir autre** to feel different; **la difficulté est autre** the difficulty is ou lies elsewhere

2 (supplémentaire) other; **je voudrais un autre verre d'eau** I'd like another glass of water

3: autre chose something else; **autre part** somewhere else; **d'autre part** on the other hand

▷ pron **1: un autre** another (one); **nous/vous autres** us/you; **d'autres** others; **l'autre** the other (one); **les autres** the others; (autrui) others; **l'un et l'autre** both of them; **ni l'un ni l'autre** neither of them; **se détester l'un l'autre/les uns les autres** to hate each other ou one another; **d'une semaine/minute à l'autre** from one week/minute ou moment to the next; (incessamment) any week/minute ou moment now; **de temps à autre** from time to time; **entre autres** (personnes) among others; (choses) among other things

2 (expressions): **j'en ai vu d'autres** I've seen worse; **à d'autres!** pull the other one!

autrefois [otʀəfwa] adv in the past

autrement [otʀəmɑ̃] adv differently; (d'une manière différente) in another way; (sinon) otherwise; **je n'ai pas pu faire ~** I couldn't do anything else, I couldn't do otherwise; ~ **dit** in other words; (c'est-à-dire) that is to say

Autriche [otʀiʃ] nf: l'~ Austria

autrichien, ne [otʀiʃjɛ̃, -ɛn] adj Austrian ▷ nm/f: **A~, ne** Austrian

autruche [otʀyʃ] nf ostrich; **faire l'~** (fig) to bury one's head in the sand

autrui [otʀɥi] pron others

auvent [ovɑ̃] nm canopy

aux [o] prép voir **à**

auxiliaire [ɔksiljɛʀ] adj, nm/f auxiliary

auxquels, auxquelles [okɛl] pron voir **lequel**

avachi, e [avaʃi] adj limp, flabby; (chaussure, vêtement) out-of-shape; (personne): ~ **sur qch** slumped on ou across sth

aval [aval] nm (accord) endorsement, backing; (Géo): **en ~** downstream, downriver; (sur une pente) downhill; **en ~ de** downstream ou downriver from; downhill from

avalanche [avalɑ̃ʃ] nf avalanche; ~ **poudreuse** powder snow avalanche

avaler [avale] vt to swallow

avance [avɑ̃s] nf (de troupes etc) advance; (progrès) progress; (d'argent) advance; (opposé à retard) lead; being ahead of schedule; **avances** nfpl overtures; (amoureuses) advances; **une ~ de 300 m/4 h** (Sport) a 300 m/4 hour lead; (être) **en ~** (to be) early; (sur un programme) (to be) ahead of schedule; **on n'est pas en ~!** we're kind of late!; **être en ~ sur qn** to be ahead of sb; **d'~, à l'~, par ~** in advance; ~ (**du**) **papier** (Inform) paper advance

avancé, e [avɑ̃se] adj advanced; (travail etc) well on, well under way; (fruit, fromage) overripe ▷ nf projection; overhang; **il est ~ pour son âge** he is advanced for his age

avancement [avɑ̃smɑ̃] nm (professionnel) promotion; (de travaux) progress

avancer [avɑ̃se] vi to move forward, advance; (projet, travail) to make progress; (être en saillie) to overhang; to project; (montre, réveil) to be fast; (: d'habitude) to gain ▷ vt to move forward, advance; (argent) to advance; (montre, pendule) to put forward; (faire progresser: travail etc) to advance, move on; **s'avancer** vi to move forward, advance; (fig) to commit o.s.; (faire saillie) to project; **j'avance (d'une heure)** I'm (an hour) fast

avant [avɑ̃] prép before ▷ adv: **trop/plus ~** too far/further forward ▷ adj inv: **siège/roue ~** front seat/wheel ▷ nm (d'un véhicule, bâtiment) front; (Sport: joueur) forward; ~ **qu'il parte/de partir** before he leaves/leaving; ~ **qu'il (ne) pleuve** before it rains (ou rained); ~ **tout** (surtout) above all; **à l'~** (dans un véhicule) in (the) front; **en ~** adv (se pencher, tomber) forward(s); **partir en ~** to go on ahead; **en ~ de** prép in front of sb; **aller de l'~** to steam ahead (fig), make good progress

avantage [avɑ̃taʒ] nm advantage; (Tennis): ~ **service/dehors** advantage ou van (Brit) ou ad (US) in/out; **tirer ~ de** to take advantage of; **vous auriez ~ à faire** you would be well-advised to do, it would be to your advantage to do; **à l'~ de qn** to sb's advantage; **être à son ~** to be at one's best; **~s en nature** benefits in kind; **~s sociaux** fringe benefits

avantager [avɑ̃taʒe] vt (favoriser) to favour; (embellir) to flatter

avantageux, -euse [avɑ̃taʒø, -øz] adj (prix) attractive; (intéressant) attractively priced; (portrait, coiffure) flattering; **conditions avantageuses** favourable terms

avant-bras [avɑ̃bʀa] nm inv forearm

avant-coureur [avɑ̃kuʀœʀ] adj inv (bruit etc) precursory; **signe ~** advance indication ou sign

avant-dernier, -ière [avɑ̃dɛʀnje, -jɛʀ] adj, nm/f next to last, last but one

avant-goût [avɑ̃gu] nm foretaste

avant-hier [avɑ̃tjɛʀ] adv the day before yesterday

avant-première [avɑ̃pʀəmjɛʀ] *nf* (*de film*) preview; **en** ~ as a preview, in a preview showing

avant-projet [avɑ̃pʀɔʒɛ] *nm* preliminary draft

avant-propos [avɑ̃pʀɔpo] *nm* foreword

avant-veille [avɑ̃vɛj] *nf*: **l'** ~ two days before

avare [avaʀ] *adj* miserly, avaricious ▷ *nm/f* miser; ~ **de compliments** stingy *ou* sparing with one's compliments

avarié, e [avaʀje] *adj* (*viande, fruits*) rotting, going off (*Brit*); (*Navig: navire*) damaged

avaries [avaʀi] *nfpl* (*Navig*) damage *sg*

avec [avɛk] *prép* with; (*à l'égard de*) to(wards), with ▷ *adv* (*fam*) with it (*ou* him *etc*); ~ **habileté/lenteur** skilfully/slowly; ~ **eux/ces maladies** with them/these diseases; ~ **ça** (*malgré ça*) for all that; **et** ~ **ça?** (*dans un magasin*) anything ou something else?

avenant, e [avnɑ̃, -ɑ̃t] *adj* pleasant ▷ *nm* (*Assurances*) additional clause; **à l'** ~ *adv* in keeping

avènement [avɛnmɑ̃] *nm* (*d'un roi*) accession, succession; (*d'un changement*) advent; (*d'une politique, idée*) coming

avenir [avniʀ] *nm*: **l'** ~ the future; **à l'** ~ in future; **sans** ~ with no future, without a future; **carrière/politicien d'** ~ career/politician with prospects *ou* a future

aventure [avɑ̃tyʀ] *nf*: **l'** ~ adventure; **une** ~ an adventure; (*amoureuse*) an affair; **partir à l'** ~ to go off in search of adventure; (*au hasard*) to go where one's fancy takes one; **roman/film d'** ~ adventure story/film

aventurer [avɑ̃tyʀe] *vt* (*somme, réputation, vie*) to stake; (*remarque, opinion*) to venture; **s'aventurer** *vi* to venture; **s'** ~ **à faire qch** to venture into sth

aventureux, -euse [avɑ̃tyʀø, -øz] *adj* adventurous, venturesome; (*projet*) risky, chancy

avenue [avny] *nf* avenue

avérer [aveʀe]: **s'avérer** *vr*: **s'** ~ **faux/coûteux** to prove (to be) wrong/expensive

averse [avɛʀs] *nf* shower

averti, e [avɛʀti] *adj* (well-)informed

avertir [avɛʀtiʀ] *vt*: ~ **qn (de qch/que)** to warn sb (of sth/that); (*renseigner*) to inform sb (of sth/that); ~ **qn de ne pas faire qch** to warn sb not to do sth

avertissement [avɛʀtismɑ̃] *nm* warning

avertisseur [avɛʀtisœʀ] *nm* horn, siren; ~ **(d'incendie)** (fire) alarm

aveu, x [avø] *nm* confession; **passer aux** ~**x** to make a confession; **de l'** ~ **de** according to

aveugle [avœgl] *adj* blind ▷ *nm/f* blind person; **les** ~**s** the blind; **test en (double)** ~ (double) blind test

aveuglément [avœglemɑ̃] *adv* blindly

aveugler [avœgle] *vt* to blind

aviateur, -trice [avjatœʀ, -tʀis] *nm/f* aviator, pilot

aviation [avjasjɔ̃] *nf* (*secteur commercial*) aviation; (*sport, métier de pilote*) flying; (*Mil*) air force; **terrain d'** ~ airfield; ~ **de chasse** fighter force

avide [avid] *adj* eager; (*péj*) greedy, grasping; ~ **de** (*sang etc*) thirsting for; ~ **d'honneurs/ d'argent** greedy for honours/money; ~ **de connaître/d'apprendre** eager to know/ learn

avilir [aviliʀ] *vt* to debase

avion [avjɔ̃] *nm* (aero)plane (*Brit*), (air)plane (*US*); **aller (quelque part) en** ~ to go (somewhere) by plane, fly (somewhere); **par** ~ by airmail; ~ **de chasse** fighter; ~ **de ligne** airliner; ~ **à réaction** jet (plane)

aviron [aviʀɔ̃] *nm* oar; (*sport*): **l'** ~ rowing

avis [avi] *nm* opinion; (*notification*) notice; (*Comm*): ~ **de crédit/débit** credit/debit advice; **à mon** ~ in my opinion; **je suis de votre** ~ I share your opinion, I am of your opinion; **être d'** ~ **que** to be of the opinion that; **changer d'** ~ to change one's mind; **sauf** ~ **contraire** unless you hear to the contrary; **sans** ~ **préalable** without notice; **jusqu'à nouvel** ~ until further notice; ~ **de décès** death announcement

avisé, e [avize] *adj* sensible, wise; **être bien/ mal** ~ **de faire** to be well-/ill-advised to do

aviser [avize] *vt* (*voir*) to notice, catch sight of; (*informer*): ~ **qn de/que** to advise *ou* inform *ou* notify sb of/that ▷ *vi* to think about things, assess the situation; **nous** ~**ons sur place** we'll work something out once we're there; **s'** ~ **de qch/que** to become suddenly aware of sth/that; **s'** ~ **de faire** to take it into one's head to do

avocat, e [avɔka, -at] *nm/f* (*Jur*) ≈ barrister (*Brit*), lawyer; (*fig*) advocate, champion ▷ *nm* (*Culin*) avocado (pear); **se faire l'** ~ **du diable** to be the devil's advocate; **l'** ~ **de la défense/ partie civile** the counsel for the defence/ plaintiff; ~ **d'affaires** business lawyer; ~ **général** assistant public prosecutor

avoine [avwan] *nf* oats *pl*

○ **MOT-CLÉ**

avoir [avwaʀ] *nm* assets *pl*, resources *pl*; (*Comm*) credit; **avoir fiscal** tax credit
▷ *vt* **1** (*posséder*) to have; **elle a deux enfants/ une belle maison** she has (got) two children/a lovely house; **il a les yeux bleus** he has (got) blue eyes; **vous avez du sel?** do you have any salt?; **avoir du courage/de la patience** to be brave/patient

2 (*éprouver*): **qu'est-ce que tu as?, qu'as-tu?** what's wrong?, what's the matter?; **avoir de la peine** to be *ou* feel sad; *voir aussi* **faim, peur** *etc*

3 (*âge, dimensions*) to be; **il a 3 ans** he is 3 (years old); **le mur a 3 mètres de haut** the wall is 3 metres high

4 (*fam: duper*) to do, have; **on vous a eu!** you've been done *ou* had!; (*fait une plaisanterie*) we *ou* they had you there

5: en avoir contre qn to have a grudge against sb; **en avoir assez** to be fed up; **j'en ai pour une demi-heure** it'll take me half an hour; **n'avoir que faire de qch** to have no use for sth

6 (*obtenir, attraper*) to get; **j'ai réussi à avoir mon train** I managed to get *ou* catch my train; **j'ai réussi à avoir le renseignement qu'il me fallait** I managed to get (hold of) the information I needed

▷ *vb aux* **1** to have; **avoir mangé/dormi** to have eaten/slept; **hier je n'ai pas mangé** I didn't eat yesterday

2 (*avoir+à+infinitif*): **avoir à faire qch** to have to do sth; **vous n'avez qu'à lui demander** you only have to ask him; **tu n'as pas à me poser des questions** it's not for you to ask me questions

▷ *vb impers* **1**: **il y a** (+*singulier*) there is; (+*pluriel*) there are; **il y avait du café/des gâteaux** there was coffee/there were cakes; **qu'y-a-t-il?, qu'est-ce qu'il y a?** what's the matter?, what is it?; **il doit y avoir une explication** there must be an explanation; **il n'y a qu'à ...** we (*ou* you *etc*) will just have to ...; **il ne peut y en avoir qu'un** there can only be one

2 (*temporel*): **il y a 10 ans** 10 years ago; **il y a 10 ans/longtemps que je le connais** I've known him for 10 years/a long time; **il y a 10 ans qu'il est arrivé** it's 10 years since he arrived

avoisiner [avwazine] *vt* to be near *ou* close to; (*fig*) to border *ou* verge on
avortement [avɔʀtəmɑ̃] *nm* abortion
avorter [avɔʀte] *vi* (*Méd*) to have an abortion; (*fig*) to fail; **faire ~** to abort; **se faire ~** to have an abortion
avoué, e [avwe] *adj* avowed ▷ *nm* (*Jur*) ≈ solicitor (*Brit*), lawyer
avouer [avwe] *vt* (*crime, défaut*) to confess (to) ▷ *vi* (*se confesser*) to confess; (*admettre*) to admit; **~ avoir fait/que** to admit *ou* confess to having done/that; **~ que oui/non** to admit that that is so/not so
avril [avʀil] *nm* April; *voir aussi* **juillet**
axe [aks] *nm* axis (*pl* axes); (*de roue etc*) axle; **dans l'~ de** directly in line with; (*fig*) main line; **~ routier** trunk road (*Brit*), main road, highway (*US*)
axer [akse] *vt*: **~ qch sur** to centre sth on
ayons *etc* [ɛjɔ̃] *vb voir* **avoir**
azote [azɔt] *nm* nitrogen

baba [baba] *adj inv*: **en être ~** (*fam*) to be flabbergasted ▷ *nm*: **~ au rhum** rum baba
babines [babin] *nfpl* chops
babiole [babjɔl] *nf* (*bibelot*) trinket; (*vétille*) trifle
bâbord [babɔʀ] *nm*: **à ou par ~** to port, on the port side
baby-foot [babifut] *nm inv* table football
baby-sitting [babisitiŋ] *nm* baby-sitting; **faire du ~** to baby-sit
bac [bak] *nm* (*Scol*) = **baccalauréat**; (*bateau*) ferry; (*récipient*) tub; (: *Photo etc*) tray; (: *Industrie*) tank; **~ à glace** ice-tray; **~ à légumes** vegetable compartment *ou* rack
baccalauréat [bakalɔʀea] *nm* ≈ A-levels *pl* (*Brit*), ≈ high school diploma (*US*); *see note*

● **BACCALAURÉAT**
●
● The *baccalauréat* or "*bac*" is the school-
● leaving examination taken at a French
● "lycée" at the age of 18; it marks the end
● of seven years' secondary education.
● Several subject combinations are
● available, although in all cases a broad
● range is studied. Successful candidates
● can go on to university, if they so wish.

bâche [baʃ] *nf* tarpaulin, canvas sheet
bachelier, -ière [baʃəlje, -jɛʀ] *nm/f* holder of the *baccalauréat*
bâcler [bakle] *vt* to botch (up)

badaud, e [bado, -od] *nm/f* idle onlooker

badigeonner [badiʒɔne] *vt* to distemper; to colourwash; (*péj: barbouiller*) to daub; (*Méd*) to paint

badiner [badine] *vi*: ~ **avec qch** to treat sth lightly; **ne pas** ~ **avec qch** not to trifle with sth

baffe [baf] *nf* (*fam*) slap, clout

baffle [bafl] *nm* baffle (board)

bafouer [bafwe] *vt* to deride, ridicule

bafouiller [bafuje] *vi, vt* to stammer

bâfrer [bafʀe] *vi, vt* (*fam*) to guzzle, gobble

bagage [bagaʒ] *nm*: ~**s** luggage *sg*, baggage *sg*; (*connaissances*) background, knowledge; **faire ses** ~**s** to pack (one's bags); ~ **littéraire** (stock of) literary knowledge; ~**s à main** hand-luggage

bagarre [bagaʀ] *nf* fight, brawl; **il aime la** ~ he loves a fight, he likes fighting

bagarrer [bagaʀe]: **se bagarrer** *vi* to (have a) fight

bagatelle [bagatɛl] *nf* trifle, trifling sum (*ou* matter)

bagne [baɲ] *nm* penal colony; **c'est le** ~ (*fig*) it's forced labour

bagnole [baɲɔl] *nf* (*fam*) car, wheels *pl* (*Brit*)

bagout [bagu] *nm* glibness; **avoir du** ~ to have the gift of the gab

bague [bag] *nf* ring; ~ **de fiançailles** engagement ring; ~ **de serrage** clip

baguette [bagɛt] *nf* stick; (*cuisine chinoise*) chopstick; (*de chef d'orchestre*) baton; (*pain*) stick of (French) bread; (*Constr: moulure*) beading; **mener qn à la** ~ to rule sb with a rod of iron; ~ **magique** magic wand; ~ **de sourcier** divining rod; ~ **de tambour** drumstick

baie [bɛ] *nf* (*Géo*) bay; (*fruit*) berry; ~ (**vitrée**) picture window

baignade [bɛɲad] *nf* (*action*) bathing; (*bain*) bathe; (*endroit*) bathing place; "~ **interdite**" "no bathing"

baigner [beɲe] *vt* (*bébé*) to bath ▷ *vi*: ~ **dans son sang** to lie in a pool of blood; ~ **dans la brume** to be shrouded in mist; **se baigner** *vi* to go swimming *ou* bathing; (*dans une baignoire*) to have a bath; **ça baigne!** (*fam*) everything's great!

baignoire [beɲwaʀ] *nf* bath(tub); (*Théât*) ground-floor box

bail, baux [baj, bo] *nm* lease; **donner** *ou* **prendre qch à** ~ to lease sth

bâillement [bajmã] *nm* yawn

bâiller [baje] *vi* to yawn; (*être ouvert*) to gape

bâillonner [bajɔne] *vt* to gag

bain [bɛ̃] *nm* (*dans une baignoire, Photo, Tech*) bath; (*dans la mer, une piscine*) swim; **costume de** ~ bathing costume (*Brit*), swimsuit; **prendre un** ~ to have a bath; **se mettre dans le** ~ (*fig*) to get into (the way of) it *ou* things; ~ **de bouche** mouthwash; ~ **de foule** walkabout; ~ **moussant** bubble bath; ~ **de pieds** footbath; (*au bord de la mer*) paddle; ~ **de siège** hip bath; ~ **de soleil** sunbathing *no pl*;

prendre un ~ **de soleil** to sunbathe; ~**s de mer** sea bathing *sg*; ~**s(-douches) municipaux** public baths

bain-marie (*pl* **bains-marie**) [bɛ̃maʀi] *nm* double boiler; **faire chauffer au** ~ (*boîte etc*) to immerse in boiling water

baiser [beze] *nm* kiss ▷ *vt* (*main, front*) to kiss; (*fam!*) to screw (!)

baisse [bɛs] *nf* fall, drop; (*Comm*): "~ **sur la viande**" "meat prices down"; **en** ~ (*cours, action*) falling; **à la** ~ downwards

baisser [bese] *vt* to lower; (*radio, chauffage*) to turn down; (*Auto: phares*) to dip (*Brit*), lower (*US*) ▷ *vi* to fall, drop, go down; (*vue, santé*) to fail, dwindle; **se baisser** *vi* to bend down

bal [bal] *nm* dance; (*grande soirée*) ball; ~ **costumé/masqué** fancy-dress/masked ball; ~ **musette** dance (*with accordion accompaniment*)

balade [balad] (*fam*) *nf* (*à pied*) walk, stroll; (*en voiture*) drive; **faire une** ~ to go for a walk *ou* stroll; to go for a drive

balader [balade] (*fam*) *vt* (*traîner*) to trail around; **se balader** *vi* to go for a walk *ou* stroll; to go for a drive

baladeur [baladœʀ] *nm* personal stereo, Walkman®; ~ **numérique** MP3 player

balafre [balafʀ] *nf* gash, slash; (*cicatrice*) scar

balai [balɛ] *nm* broom, brush; (*Auto: d'essuie-glace*) blade; (*Mus: de batterie etc*) brush; **donner un coup de** ~ to give the floor a sweep; ~ **mécanique** carpet sweeper

balai-brosse (*pl* **balais-brosses**) [balɛbʀɔs] *nm* (long-handled) scrubbing brush

balance [balɑ̃s] *nf* (*à plateaux*) scales *pl*; (*de précision*) balance; (*Comm, Pol*): ~ **des comptes** *ou* **paiements** balance of payments; (*signe*): **la B**~ Libra, the Scales; **être de la B**~ to be Libra; ~ **commerciale** balance of trade; ~ **des forces** balance of power; ~ **romaine** steelyard

balancer [balɑ̃se] *vt* to swing; (*lancer*) to fling, chuck; (*renvoyer, jeter*) to chuck out ▷ *vi* to swing; **se balancer** *vi* to swing; (*bateau*) to rock; (*branche*) to sway; **se** ~ **de qch** (*fam*) not to give a toss about sth

balançoire [balɑ̃swaʀ] *nf* swing; (*sur pivot*) seesaw

balayer [baleje] *vt* (*feuilles etc*) to sweep up, brush up; (*pièce, cour*) to sweep; (*chasser*) to sweep away *ou* aside; (*radar*) to scan; (: *phares*) to sweep across

balayeur, -euse [balɛjœʀ, -øz] *nm/f* road sweeper ▷ *nf* (*engin*) road sweeper

balbutier [balbysje] *vi, vt* to stammer

balcon [balkɔ̃] *nm* balcony; (*Théât*) dress circle

Bâle [bal] *n* Basle *ou* Basel

Baléares [baleaʀ] *nfpl*: **les** ~ the Balearic Islands, the Balearics

baleine [balɛn] *nf* whale; (*de parapluie*) rib; (*de corset*) bone

balise [baliz] *nf* (*Navig*) beacon, (marker) buoy; (*Aviat*) runway light, beacon; (*Auto, Ski*) sign, marker

baliser [balize] *vt* to mark out (with beacons *ou* lights *etc*)

balivernes [balivɛʀn] *nfpl* twaddle *sg* (*Brit*), nonsense *sg*

ballant, e [balɑ̃, -ɑ̃t] *adj* dangling

balle [bal] *nf* (*de fusil*) bullet; (*de sport*) ball; (*du blé*) chaff; (*paquet*) bale; (*fam: franc*) franc; **~ perdue** stray bullet

ballerine [bal(ə)ʀin] *nf* (*danseuse*) ballet dancer; (*chaussure*) pump, ballet shoe

ballet [balɛ] *nm* ballet; (*fig*): **~ diplomatique** diplomatic to-ings and fro-ings

ballon [balɔ̃] *nm* (*de sport*) ball; (*jouet, Aviat, de bande dessinée*) balloon; (*de vin*) glass; **~ d'essai** (*météorologique*) pilot balloon; (*fig*) feeler(s); **~ de football** football; **~ d'oxygène** oxygen bottle

ballot [balo] *nm* bundle; (*péj*) nitwit

ballottage [balɔtaʒ] *nm* (*Pol*) second ballot

ballotter [balɔte] *vi* to roll around; (*bateau etc*) to toss ▷ *vt* to shake *ou* throw about; to toss; **être ballotté entre** (*fig*) to be shunted between; (: *indécis*) to be torn between

balnéaire [balneɛʀ] *adj* seaside *cpd*; **station ~** seaside resort

balourd, e [baluʀ, -uʀd] *adj* clumsy ▷ *nm/f* clodhopper

balustrade [balystʀad] *nf* railings *pl*, handrail

bambin [bɑ̃bɛ̃] *nm* little child

bambou [bɑ̃bu] *nm* bamboo

ban [bɑ̃] *nm* round of applause, cheer; **être/ mettre au ~ de** to be outlawed/to outlaw from; **le ~ et l'arrière-ban de sa famille** every last one of his relatives; **~s (de mariage)** banns, bans

banal, e [banal] *adj* banal, commonplace; (*péj*) trite; **four/moulin ~** village oven/mill

banalité [banalite] *nf* banality; (*remarque*) truism, trite remark

banane [banan] *nf* banana; (*sac*) waist-bag, bum-bag

banc [bɑ̃] *nm* seat, bench; (*de poissons*) shoal; **~ des accusés** dock; **~ d'essai** (*fig*) testing ground; **~ de sable** sandbank; **~ des témoins** witness box; **~ de touche** dugout

bancaire [bɑ̃kɛʀ] *adj* banking; (*chèque, carte*) bank *cpd*

bancal, e [bɑ̃kal] *adj* wobbly; (*personne*) bow-legged; (*fig: projet*) shaky

bandage [bɑ̃daʒ] *nm* bandaging; (*pansement*) bandage; **~ herniaire** truss

bande [bɑ̃d] *nf* (*de tissu etc*) strip; (*Méd*) bandage; (*motif, dessin*) stripe; (*Ciné*) film; (*Radio, groupe*) band; (*péj*): **une ~ de** a bunch *ou* crowd of; **par la ~** in a roundabout way; **donner de la ~** to list; **faire ~ à part** to keep to o.s.; **~ dessinée (BD)** strip cartoon (*Brit*), comic strip; **~ magnétique** magnetic tape;

~ passante (*Inform*) bandwidth; **~ perforée** punched tape; **~ de roulement** (*de pneu*) tread; **~ sonore** sound track; **~ de terre** strip of land; **~ Velpeau®** (*Méd*) crêpe bandage

bande-annonce (*pl* **bandes-annonces**) [bɑ̃danɔ̃s] *nf* (*Ciné*) trailer

bandeau, x [bɑ̃do] *nm* headband; (*sur les yeux*) blindfold; (*Méd*) head bandage

bander [bɑ̃de] *vt* (*blessure*) to bandage; (*muscle*) to tense; (*arc*) to bend ▷ *vi* (*fam!*) to have a hard on (!); **~ les yeux à qn** to blindfold sb

banderole [bɑ̃dʀɔl] *nf* banderole; (*dans un défilé etc*) streamer

bandit [bɑ̃di] *nm* bandit

banditisme [bɑ̃ditism] *nm* violent crime, armed robberies *pl*

bandoulière [bɑ̃duljɛʀ] *nf*: **en ~** (slung *ou* worn) across the shoulder

Bangladesh [bɑ̃gladɛʃ] *nm*: **le ~** Bangladesh

banlieue [bɑ̃ljø] *nf* suburbs *pl*; **quartiers de ~** suburban areas; **trains de ~** commuter trains

banlieusard, e [bɑ̃ljøzaʀ, -aʀd] *nm/f* suburbanite

bannière [banjɛʀ] *nf* banner

bannir [baniʀ] *vt* to banish

banque [bɑ̃k] *nf* bank; (*activités*) banking; **~ des yeux/du sang** eye/blood bank; **~ d'affaires** merchant bank; **~ de dépôt** deposit bank; **~ de données** (*Inform*) data bank; **~ d'émission** bank of issue

banqueroute [bɑ̃kʀut] *nf* bankruptcy

banquet [bɑ̃kɛ] *nm* (*de club*) dinner; (*de noces*) reception; (*d'apparat*) banquet

banquette [bɑ̃kɛt] *nf* seat

banquier [bɑ̃kje] *nm* banker

banquise [bɑ̃kiz] *nf* ice field

baptême [batɛm] *nm* (*sacrement*) baptism; (*cérémonie*) christening; baptism; (*d'un navire*) launching; (*d'une cloche*) consecration, dedication; **~ de l'air** first flight

baptiser [batize] *vt* to christen; to baptize; to launch; to consecrate, dedicate

baquet [bakɛ] *nm* tub, bucket

bar [baʀ] *nm* bar; (*poisson*) bass

baraque [baʀak] *nf* shed; (*fam*) house; **~ foraine** fairground stand

baraqué, e [baʀake] (*fam*) *adj* well-built, hefty

baraquements [baʀakmɑ̃] *nmpl* huts (*for refugees, workers etc*)

baratin [baʀatɛ̃] *nm* (*fam*) smooth talk, patter

baratiner [baʀatine] *vt* (*fam*) to chat up

barbant, e [baʀbɑ̃, -ɑ̃t] *adj* (*fam*) deadly (boring)

barbare [baʀbaʀ] *adj* barbaric ▷ *nm/f* barbarian

barbarie [baʀbaʀi] *nf* barbarism; (*cruauté*) barbarity

barbe [baʀb] *nf* beard; (**au nez et) à la ~ de qn** (*fig*) under sb's very nose; **la ~!** (*fam*) damn it!; **quelle ~!** (*fam*) what a drag *ou* bore!; **~ à papa** candy-floss (*Brit*), cotton candy (*US*)

barbelé [baʀbəle] *adj, nm*: **(fil de fer)** ~ barbed wire *no pl*

barber [baʀbe] *vt (fam)* to bore stiff

barbiturique [baʀbityʀik] *nm* barbiturate

barboter [baʀbɔte] *vi* to paddle, dabble ▷ *vt (fam)* to filch

barbouiller [baʀbuje] *vt* to daub; *(péj: écrire, dessiner)* to scribble; **avoir l'estomac barbouillé** to feel queasy *ou* sick

barbu, e [baʀby] *adj* bearded

barda [baʀda] *nm (fam)* kit, gear

barder [baʀde] *vt (Culin: rôti, volaille)* to bard ▷ *vi (fam)*: **ça va ~** sparks will fly

barème [baʀɛm] *nm (Scol)* scale; *(liste)* table; **~ des salaires** salary scale

baril [baʀi(l)] *nm (tonneau)* barrel; *(de poudre)* keg

bariolé, e [baʀjɔle] *adj* many-coloured, rainbow-coloured

baromètre [baʀɔmɛtʀ] *nm* barometer; **~ anéroïde** aneroid barometer

baron [baʀɔ̃] *nm* baron

baronne [baʀɔn] *nf* baroness

baroque [baʀɔk] *adj (Art)* baroque; *(fig)* weird

barque [baʀk] *nf* small boat

barquette [baʀkɛt] *nf* small boat-shaped tart; *(récipient: en aluminium)* tub; *(: en bois)* basket; *(pour repas)* tray; *(pour fruits)* punnet

barrage [baʀaʒ] *nm* dam; *(sur route)* roadblock, barricade; **~ de police** police roadblock

barre [baʀ] *nf (de fer etc)* rod; *(Navig)* helm; *(écrite)* line, stroke; *(Danse)* barre; *(niveau)*: **la livre a franchi la ~ des 1,70 euros** the pound has broken the 1.70 euros barrier; *(Jur)*: **comparaître à la ~** to appear as a witness; **être à** *ou* **tenir la ~** *(Navig)* to be at the helm; **coup de ~** *(fig)*: **c'est le coup de ~!** it's daylight robbery!; **j'ai le coup de ~!** I'm all in!; **~ fixe** *(Gym)* horizontal bar; **~ de mesure** *(Mus)* bar line; **~ à mine** crowbar; **~s parallèles/asymétriques** *(Gym)* parallel/asymmetric bars

barreau, x [baʀo] *nm* bar; *(Jur)*: **le ~** the Bar

barrer [baʀe] *vt (route etc)* to block; *(mot)* to cross out; *(chèque)* to cross *(Brit)*; *(Navig)* to steer; **se barrer** *vi (fam)* to clear off

barrette [baʀɛt] *nf (pour cheveux)* (hair) slide *(Brit)* ou clip *(US)*; *(broche)* brooch

barricader [baʀikade] *vt* to barricade; **se barricader** *vi*: **se ~ chez soi** *(fig)* to lock o.s. in

barrière [baʀjɛʀ] *nf* fence; *(obstacle)* barrier; *(porte)* gate; **la Grande B~** the Great Barrier Reef; **~ de dégel** *(Admin: on roadsigns)* no heavy vehicles — road liable to subsidence due to thaw; **~s douanières** trade barriers

barrique [baʀik] *nf* barrel, cask

bar-tabac [baʀtaba] *nm* bar *(which sells tobacco and stamps)*

bas, basse [bɑ, bɑs] *adj* low; *(action)* low, ignoble ▷ *nm (vêtement)* stocking; *(partie inférieure)*: **le ~ de** the lower part *ou* foot *ou* bottom of ▷ *nf (Mus)* bass ▷ *adv* low; *(parler)* softly; **plus ~** lower down; more softly; *(dans un texte)* further on, below; **la tête ~se** with lowered head; *(fig)* with head hung low; **avoir la vue ~se** to be short-sighted; **au ~ mot** at the lowest estimate; **enfant en ~ âge** infant, young child; **en ~** down below; *(d'une liste, d'un mur etc)* at *(ou* to) the bottom; *(dans une maison)* downstairs; **en ~ de** at the bottom of; **de ~ en haut** upwards; from the bottom to the top; **des hauts et des ~** ups and downs; **un ~ de laine** *(fam: économies)* money under the mattress *(fig)*; **mettre ~** *vi (animal)* to give birth; **à ~ la dictature!** down with dictatorship!; **~ morceaux** *(viande)* cheap cuts

basané, e [bazane] *adj (teint)* tanned, bronzed; *(foncé: péj)* swarthy

bas-côté [bɑkote] *nm (de route)* verge *(Brit)*, shoulder *(US)*; *(d'église)* (side) aisle

bascule [baskyl] *nf*: **(jeu de)** ~ seesaw; **(balance à)** ~ scales *pl*; **fauteuil à** ~ rocking chair; **système à** ~ tip-over device; rocker device

basculer [baskyle] *vi* to fall over, topple (over); *(benne)* to tip up ▷ *vt (aussi*: **faire ~)** to topple over; *(contenu)* to tip out; *(benne)* tip up

base [bɑz] *nf* base; *(Pol)*: **la ~** the rank and file, the grass roots; *(fondement, principe)* basis *(pl* bases); **jeter les ~s de** to lay the foundations of; **à la ~ de** *(fig)* at the root of; **sur la ~ de** *(fig)* on the basis of; **de ~** basic; **à ~ de café** *etc* coffee *etc* -based; **~ de données** *(Inform)* database; **~ de lancement** launching site

baser [bɑze] *vt*: **~ qch sur** to base sth on; **se ~ sur** *(données, preuves)* to base one's argument on; **être basé à/dans** *(Mil)* to be based at/in

bas-fond [bɑfɔ̃] *nm (Navig)* shallow; **bas-fonds** *nmpl (fig)* dregs

basilic [bazilik] *nm (Culin)* basil

basket [baskɛt], **basket-ball** [baskɛtbol] *nm* basketball

baskets [baskɛt] *nfpl (chaussures)* trainers *(Brit)*, sneakers *(US)*

basque [bask] *adj, nm (Ling)* Basque ▷ *nm/f*: **B~** Basque; **le Pays ~** the Basque country

basse [bɑs] *adj voir* **bas** ▷ *nf (Mus)* bass

basse-cour [bɑskuʀ] *(pl* basses-cours) *nf* farmyard; *(animaux)* farmyard animals

bassin [basɛ̃] *nm (cuvette)* bowl; *(pièce d'eau)* pond, pool; *(de fontaine, Géo)* basin; *(Anat)* pelvis; *(portuaire)* dock; **~ houiller** coalfield

bassine [basin] *nf* basin; *(contenu)* bowl, bowlful

basson [bɑsɔ̃] *nm* bassoon

bas-ventre [bɑvɑ̃tʀ] *nm* (lower part of the) stomach

bat [ba] *vb voir* **battre**

bataille [batɑj] *nf* battle; *(rixe)* fight; **en ~** *(en travers)* at an angle; *(en désordre)* awry; **elle avait les cheveux en ~** her hair was a mess; **~ rangée** pitched battle

bâtard, e [bɑtaʀ, -aʀd] *adj* (*enfant*) illegitimate; (*fig*) hybrid ▷ *nm/f* illegitimate child, bastard (*péj*) ▷ *nm* (*Boulangerie*) ≈ Vienna loaf; **chien ~** mongrel

bateau, x [bato] *nm* boat; (*grand*) ship ▷ *adj inv* (*banal, rebattu*) hackneyed; **~ de pêche/à moteur/à voiles** fishing/motor/sailing boat

bateau-mouche [batomuʃ] *nm* (*passenger*) pleasure boat (*on the Seine*)

bâti, e [bɑti] *adj* (*terrain*) developed ▷ *nm* (*armature*) frame; (*Couture*) tacking; **bien ~** (*personne*) well-built

batifoler [batifɔle] *vi* to frolic *ou* lark about

bâtiment [bɑtimɑ̃] *nm* building; (*Navig*) ship, vessel; (*industrie*): **le ~** the building trade

bâtir [bɑtiʀ] *vt* to build; (*Couture*): *jupe, ourlet*) to tack; **fil à ~** (*Couture*) tacking thread

bâtisse [bɑtis] *nf* building

bâton [bɑtɔ̃] *nm* stick; **mettre des ~s dans les roues à qn** to put a spoke in sb's wheel; **à ~s rompus** informally; **parler à ~s rompus** to chat about this and that; **~ de rouge (à lèvres)** lipstick; **~ de ski** ski stick

bats [ba] *vb voir* **battre**

battage [bataʒ] *nm* (*publicité*) (hard) plugging

battant, e [batɑ̃, -ɑ̃t] *vb voir* **battre** ▷ *adj*: **pluie ~e** lashing rain ▷ *nm* (*de cloche*) clapper; (*de volets*) shutter, flap; (*de porte*) side; (*fig: personne*) fighter; **porte à double ~** double door; **tambour ~** briskly

battement [batmɑ̃] *nm* (*de cœur*) beat; (*intervalle*) interval (*between classes, trains etc*); **~ de paupières** blinking *no pl* (*of eyelids*); **un ~ de 10 minutes**, **10 minutes de ~** 10 minutes to spare

batterie [batʀi] *nf* (*Mil, Élec*) battery; (*Mus*) drums *pl*, drum kit; **~ de cuisine** kitchen utensils *pl*; (*casseroles etc*) pots and pans *pl*; **une ~ de tests** a string of tests

batteur [batœʀ] *nm* (*Mus*) drummer; (*appareil*) whisk

battre [batʀ] *vt* to beat; (*pluie, vagues*) to beat *ou* lash against; (*œufs etc*) to beat up, whisk; (*blé*) to thresh; (*cartes*) to shuffle; (*passer au peigne fin*) to scour ▷ *vi* (*cœur*) to beat; (*volets etc*) to bang, rattle; **se battre** *vi* to fight; **~ la mesure** to beat time; **~ en brèche** (*Mil: mur*) to batter; (*fig: théorie*) to demolish; (: *institution etc*) to attack; **~ son plein** to be at its height, be going full swing; **~ pavillon britannique** to fly the British flag; **~ des mains** to clap one's hands; **~ des ailes** to flap its wings; **~ de l'aile** (*fig*) to be in a bad way *ou* in bad shape; **~ la semelle** to stamp one's feet; **~ en retraite** to beat a retreat

baume [bom] *nm* balm

bavard, e [bavaʀ, -aʀd] *adj* (*very*) talkative; gossipy

bavarder [bavaʀde] *vi* to chatter; (*indiscrètement*) to gossip; (: *révéler un secret*) to blab

bave [bav] *nf* dribble; (*de chien etc*) slobber, slaver (*Brit*), drool (*US*); (*d'escargot*) slime

baver [bave] *vi* to dribble; (*chien*) to slobber, slaver (*Brit*), drool (*US*); (*encre, couleur*) to run; **en ~** (*fam*) to have a hard time (of it)

baveux, -euse [bavø, -øz] *adj* dribbling; (*omelette*) runny

bavoir [bavwaʀ] *nm* (*de bébé*) bib

bavure [bavyʀ] *nf* smudge; (*fig*) hitch; (*policière etc*) blunder

bayer [baje] *vi*: **~ aux corneilles** to stand gaping

bazar [bazaʀ] *nm* general store; (*fam*) jumble

bazarder [bazaʀde] *vt* (*fam*) to chuck out

BCBG *sigle adj* (= *bon chic bon genre*) smart and trendy, ≈ preppy

BD *sigle f* = **bande dessinée**; (= *base de données*) DB

bd *abr* = **boulevard**

béant, e [beɑ̃, -ɑ̃t] *adj* gaping

béat, e [bea, -at] *adj* showing open-eyed wonder; (*sourire etc*) blissful

béatitude [beatityd] *nf* bliss

beau, bel, belle, beaux [bo, bɛl] *adj* beautiful, lovely; (*homme*) handsome ▷ *nf* (*Sport*) decider ▷ *adv*: **il fait ~** the weather's fine ▷ *nm*: **avoir le sens du ~** to have an aesthetic sense; **le temps est au ~** the weather is set fair; **un ~ geste** (*fig*) a fine gesture; **un ~ salaire** a good salary; **un ~ gâchis/rhume** a fine mess/nasty cold; **en faire/dire de belles** to do/say (some) stupid things; **le ~ monde** high society; **~ parleur** smooth talker; **un ~ jour** one (fine) day; **de plus belle** more than ever, even more; **bel et bien** well and truly; (*vraiment*) really (and truly); **le plus ~ c'est que ...** the best of it is that ...; **c'est du ~!** that's great, that is!; **on a ~ essayer** however hard *ou* no matter how hard we try; **il a ~ jeu de protester** *etc* it's easy for him to protest *etc*; **faire le ~** (*chien*) to sit up and beg

 MOT-CLÉ

beaucoup [boku] *adv* **1** a lot; **il boit beaucoup** he drinks a lot; **il ne boit pas beaucoup** he doesn't drink much *ou* a lot

2 (*suivi de plus, trop etc*) much, a lot, far; **il est beaucoup plus grand** he is much *ou* a lot *ou* far taller; **c'est beaucoup plus cher** it's a lot *ou* much more expensive; **il a beaucoup plus de temps que moi** he has much *ou* a lot more time than me; **il y a beaucoup plus de touristes ici** there are a lot *ou* many more tourists here; **beaucoup trop vite** much too fast; **il fume beaucoup trop** he smokes far too much

3: **beaucoup de** (*nombre*) many, a lot of; (*quantité*) a lot of; **pas beaucoup de** (*nombre*) not many, not a lot of; (*quantité*) not much, not a lot of; **beaucoup d'étudiants/de touristes** a lot of *ou* many students/tourists; **beaucoup de courage** a lot of courage; **il n'a**

pas beaucoup d'argent he hasn't got much *ou* a lot of money; **il n'y a pas beaucoup de touristes** there aren't many *ou* a lot of tourists

4: **de beaucoup** by far
▷ *pron*: **beaucoup le savent** lots of people know that

beau-fils (*pl* **beaux-fils**) [bofis] *nm* son-in-law; (*remariage*) stepson

beau-frère (*pl* **beaux-frères**) [bofʀɛʀ] *nm* brother-in-law

beau-père (*pl* **beaux-pères**) [bopɛʀ] *nm* father-in-law; (*remariage*) stepfather

beauté [bote] *nf* beauty; **de toute ~** beautiful; **en ~** *adv* with a flourish, brilliantly; **finir qch en ~** to complete sth brilliantly

beaux-arts [bozaʀ] *nmpl* fine arts

beaux-parents [bopaʀɑ̃] *nmpl* wife's/husband's family, in-laws

bébé [bebe] *nm* baby

bec [bɛk] *nm* beak, bill; (*de plume*) nib; (*de cafetière etc*) spout; (*de casserole etc*) lip; (*d'une clarinette etc*) mouthpiece; (*fam*) mouth; **clouer le ~ à qn** (*fam*) to shut sb up; **ouvrir le ~** (*fam*) to open one's mouth; **~ de gaz** (*street*) gaslamp; **~ verseur** pouring lip

bécane [bekan] *nf* (*fam*) bike

bec-de-lièvre (*pl* **becs-de-lièvre**) [bɛkdəljɛvʀ] *nm* harelip

bêche [bɛʃ] *nf* spade

bêcher [beʃe] *vt* (*terre*) to dig; (*personne: critiquer*) to slate; (: *snober*) to look down on

bécoter [bekɔte]: **se bécoter** *vi* to smooch

becqueter [bɛkte] *vt* (*fam*) to eat

bedaine [bədɛn] *nf* paunch

bedonnant, e [bədɔnɑ̃, -ɑ̃t] *adj* paunchy, potbellied

bée [be] *adj*: **bouche ~** gaping

beffroi [befʀwa] *nm* belfry

bégayer [begeje] *vt, vi* to stammer

bègue [bɛg] *nm/f*: **être ~** to have a stammer

beige [bɛʒ] *adj* beige

beignet [bɛɲɛ] *nm* fritter

bel [bɛl] *adj m voir* **beau**

bêler [bele] *vi* to bleat

belette [bəlɛt] *nf* weasel

belge [bɛlʒ] *adj* Belgian ▷ *nm/f*: **B~** Belgian; *see note*

Belgique [bɛlʒik] *nf*: **la ~** Belgium

bélier [belje] *nm* ram; (*engin*) (battering) ram; (*signe*): **le B~** Aries, the Ram; **être du B~** to be Aries

belle [bɛl] *adj voir* **beau** ▷ *nf* (*Sport*): **la ~** the decider

belle-fille (*pl* **belles-filles**) [bɛlfij] *nf* daughter-in-law; (*remariage*) stepdaughter

belle-mère (*pl* **belles-mères**) [bɛlmɛʀ] *nf* mother-in-law; (*remariage*) stepmother

belle-sœur (*pl* **belles-sœurs**) [bɛlsœʀ] *nf* sister-in-law

belliqueux, -euse [belikø, -øz] *adj* aggressive, warlike

belvédère [belvedɛʀ] *nm* panoramic viewpoint (*or small building there*)

bémol [bemɔl] *nm* (*Mus*) flat

bénédiction [benediksjɔ̃] *nf* blessing

bénéfice [benefis] *nm* (*Comm*) profit; (*avantage*) benefit; **au ~ de** in aid of

bénéficier [benefisje] *vi*: **~ de** to enjoy; (*profiter*) to benefit by *ou* from; (*obtenir*) to get, be given

bénéfique [benefik] *adj* beneficial

Benelux [benelyks] *nm*: **le ~** Benelux, the Benelux countries

bénévole [benevɔl] *adj* voluntary, unpaid

bénin, -igne [benɛ̃, -iɲ] *adj* minor, mild; (*tumeur*) benign

bénir [beniʀ] *vt* to bless

bénit, e [beni, -it] *adj* consecrated; **eau ~e** holy water

benjamin, e [bɛ̃ʒamɛ̃, -in] *nm/f* youngest child; (*Sport*) under-13

benne [bɛn] *nf* skip; (*de téléphérique*) (cable) car; **~ basculante** tipper (*Brit*), dump *ou* dumper truck (*Brit*); **~ à ordures** (*amovible*) skip

BEP *sigle m* (= *Brevet d'études professionnelles*) school-leaving diploma, taken at approx. 18 years

béquille [bekij] *nf* crutch; (*de bicyclette*) stand

berceau, x [bɛʀso] *nm* cradle, crib

bercer [bɛʀse] *vt* to rock, cradle; (*musique etc*) to lull; **~ qn de** (*promesses etc*) to delude sb with

berceur, -euse [bɛʀsœʀ, -øz] *adj* soothing ▷ *nf* (*chanson*) lullaby

berceuse *nf* lullaby

béret [beʀɛ], **béret basque** [beʀɛbask] *nm* beret

berge [bɛʀʒ] *nf* bank

berger, -ère [bɛʀʒe, -ɛʀ] *nm/f* shepherd/shepherdess; **~ allemand** (*chien*) alsatian (dog) (*Brit*), German shepherd (dog) (*US*)

Berlin [bɛʀlɛ̃] *n* Berlin; **~-Est/-Ouest** East/West Berlin

berlingot [bɛʀlɛ̃go] *nm* (*emballage*) carton (*pyramid shaped*); (*bonbon*) lozenge

berlue [bɛʀly] *nf*: **j'ai la ~** I must be seeing things

Bermudes [bɛʀmyd] *nfpl*: **les (îles) ~** Bermuda

Berne [bɛʀn] *n* Bern

berner [bɛʀne] *vt* to fool

besogne [bəzɔɲ] *nf* work *no pl*, job

besoin [bəzwɛ̃] *nm* need; (*pauvreté*): **le ~** need, want; **le ~ d'argent/de gloire** the need for money/glory; **~s (naturels)** nature's needs; **faire ses ~s** to relieve o.s.; **avoir ~ de qch/**

faire qch to need sth/to do sth; **il n'y a pas ~ de (faire)** there is no need to (do); **au ~, si ~ est** if need be; **pour les ~s de la cause** for the purpose in hand; **être dans le ~** to be in need *ou* want

bestial, e, -aux [bɛstjal, -o] *adj* bestial, brutish ▷ *nmpl* cattle

bestiole [bɛstjɔl] *nf* (tiny) creature

bétail [betaj] *nm* livestock, cattle *pl*

bête [bɛt] *nf* animal; *(bestiole)* insect, creature ▷ *adj* stupid, silly; **les ~s** (the) animals; **chercher la petite ~** to nit-pick; **~ noire** pet hate, bugbear (*Brit*); **~ sauvage** wild beast; **~ de somme** beast of burden

bêtement [bɛtmɑ̃] *adv* stupidly; **tout ~** quite simply

bêtise [betiz] *nf* stupidity; *(action, remarque)* stupid thing (to say *ou* do); *(bonbon)* type of mint sweet (*Brit*) *ou* candy (*US*); **faire/dire une ~** to do/say something stupid

béton [betɔ̃] *nm* concrete; **(en) ~** *(fig: alibi, argument)* cast iron; **~ armé** reinforced concrete; **~ précontraint** prestressed concrete

bétonnière [betɔnjɛʀ] *nf* cement mixer

betterave [bɛtʀav] *nf* *(rouge)* beetroot (*Brit*), beet (*US*); **~ fourragère** mangel-wurzel; **~ sucrière** sugar beet

beugler [bøgle] *vi* to low; *(péj: radio etc)* to blare ▷ *vt* *(péj: chanson etc)* to bawl out

Beur [bœʀ] *adj, nm/f see note*

beurre [bœʀ] *nm* butter; **mettre du ~ dans les épinards** *(fig)* to add a little to the kitty; **~ de cacao** cocoa butter; **~ noir** brown butter (sauce)

beurrer [bœʀe] *vt* to butter

beurrier [bœʀje] *nm* butter dish

beuverie [bœvʀi] *nf* drinking session

bévue [bevy] *nf* blunder

Beyrouth [beʀut] *n* Beirut

biais [bjɛ] *nm* *(moyen)* device, expedient; *(aspect)* angle; *(bande de tissu)* piece of cloth cut on the bias; **en ~, de ~** *(obliquement)* at an angle; *(fig)* indirectly; **par le ~ de** by means of

biaiser [bjeze] *vi* *(fig)* to sidestep the issue

bibelot [biblo] *nm* trinket, curio

biberon [bibʀɔ̃] *nm* *(feeding)* bottle; **nourrir au ~** to bottle-feed

bible [bibl] *nf* bible

bibliobus [biblijɔbys] *nm* mobile library van

bibliographie [biblijɔgʀafi] *nf* bibliography

bibliothécaire [biblijɔtekɛʀ] *nm/f* librarian

bibliothèque [biblijɔtɛk] *nf* library; *(meuble)* bookcase; **~ municipale** public library

bic® [bik] *nm* Biro®

bicarbonate [bikaʀbɔnat] *nm*: **~ (de soude)** bicarbonate of soda

biceps [bisɛps] *nm* biceps

biche [biʃ] *nf* doe

bichonner [biʃɔne] *vt* to groom

bicolore [bikɔlɔʀ] *adj* two-coloured (*Brit*), two-colored (*US*)

bicoque [bikɔk] *nf* *(péj)* shack, dump

bicyclette [bisiklɛt] *nf* bicycle

bide [bid] *nm* *(fam: ventre)* belly; *(Théât)* flop

bidet [bidɛ] *nm* bidet

bidon [bidɔ̃] *nm* can ▷ *adj inv* *(fam)* phoney

bidonville [bidɔ̃vil] *nm* shanty town

bidule [bidyl] *nm* *(fam)* thingamajig

 MOT-CLÉ

bien [bjɛ̃] *nm* **1** *(avantage, profit)*: **faire le bien** to do good; **faire du bien à qn** to do sb good; **ça fait du bien de faire** it does you good to do; **dire du bien de** to speak well of; **c'est pour son bien** it's for his own good; **changer en bien** to change for the better; **le bien public** the public good; **vouloir du bien à qn** *(vouloir aider)* to have sb's (best) interests at heart; **je te veux du bien** *(pour mettre en confiance)* I don't wish you any harm **2** *(possession, patrimoine)* possession, property; **son bien le plus précieux** his most treasured possession; **avoir du bien** to have property; **biens (de consommation** *etc)* (consumer *etc)* goods; **biens durables** (consumer) durables

3 *(moral)*: **le bien** good; **distinguer le bien du mal** to tell good from evil

▷ *adv* **1** *(de façon satisfaisante)* well; **elle travaille/mange bien** she works/eats well; **aller** *or* **se porter bien** to be well; **croyant bien faire, je/il ...** thinking I/he was doing the right thing, I/he ...; **tiens-toi bien!** *(assieds-toi correctement)* sit up straight!; *(debout)* stand up straight!; *(sois sage)* behave yourself!; *(prépare-toi)* wait for it!

2 *(valeur intensive)* quite; **bien jeune** quite young; **bien assez** quite enough; **bien mieux** (very) much better; **bien du temps/ des gens** quite a time/a number of people; **j'espère bien y aller** I do hope to go; **je veux bien le faire** *(concession)* I'm quite willing to do it; **il faut bien le faire** it has to be done; **il y a bien deux ans** at least two years ago; **cela fait bien deux ans que je ne l'ai pas vu** I haven't seen him for at least *ou* a good two years; **il semble bien que** it really seems that; **peut-être bien** it could well be; **aimer bien** to like; **Paul est bien venu, n'est-ce pas?** Paul HAS come, hasn't he?; **où peut-il**

bien être passé? where on earth can he have got to?

3 (*conséquence, résultat*): **si bien que** with the result that; **on verra bien** we'll see; **faire bien de ...** to be right to ...
▷ *excl* right!, OK!, fine!; **eh bien!** well!; **(c'est) bien fait!** it serves you (*ou* him *etc*) right!; **bien sûr!**, **bien entendu!** certainly!, of course!
▷ *adj inv* **1** (*en bonne forme, à l'aise*): **je me sens bien, je suis bien** I feel fine; **je ne me sens pas bien, je ne suis pas bien** I don't feel well; **on est bien dans ce fauteuil** this chair is very comfortable
2 (*joli, beau*) good-looking; **tu es bien dans cette robe** you look good in that dress
3 (*satisfaisant*) good; **elle est bien, cette maison/secrétaire** it's a good house/she's a good secretary; **c'est très bien (comme ça)** it's fine (like that); **ce n'est pas si bien que ça** it's not as good *ou* great as all that; **c'est bien?** is that all right?
4 (*moralement*) right; (: *personne*) good, nice; (*respectable*) respectable; **ce n'est pas bien de ...** it's not right to ...; **elle est bien, cette femme** she's a nice woman, she's a good sort; **des gens bien** respectable people
5 (*en bons termes*): **être bien avec qn** to be on good terms with sb

bien-aimé, e [bjɛ̃neme] *adj, nm/f* beloved
bien-être [bjɛ̃nɛtʀ] *nm* well-being
bienfaisance [bjɛ̃fəzɑ̃s] *nf* charity
bienfait [bjɛ̃fɛ] *nm* act of generosity, benefaction; (*de la science etc*) benefit
bienfaiteur, -trice [bjɛ̃fɛtœʀ, -tʀis] *nm/f* benefactor/benefactress
bien-fondé [bjɛ̃fɔ̃de] *nm* soundness
bien que [bjɛ̃k] *conj* although
bienséant, e [bjɛ̃seɑ̃, -ɑ̃t] *adj* proper, seemly
bientôt [bjɛ̃to] *adv* soon; **à ~** see you soon
bienveillant, e [bjɛ̃vejɑ̃, -ɑ̃t] *adj* kindly
bienvenu, e [bjɛ̃vny] *adj* welcome ▷ *nm/f*: **être le ~/la ~e** to be welcome ▷ *nf*: **souhaiter la ~e à** to welcome; **~e à** welcome to
bière [bjɛʀ] *nf* (*boisson*) beer; (*cercueil*) bier; **~ blonde** lager; **~ brune** brown ale (*Brit*), dark beer (*US*); **~ (à la) pression** draught beer
biffer [bife] *vt* to cross out
bifteck [biftɛk] *nm* steak
bifurquer [bifyʀke] *vi* (*route*) to fork; (*véhicule*) to turn off
bigarré, e [bigaʀe] *adj* multicoloured (*Brit*), multicolored (*US*); (*disparate*) motley
bigorneau, x [bigɔʀno] *nm* winkle
bigot, e [bigo, -ɔt] (*péj*) *adj* bigoted ▷ *nm/f* bigot
bigoudi [bigudi] *nm* curler
bijou, x [biʒu] *nm* jewel
bijouterie [biʒutʀi] *nf* (*magasin*) jeweller's (shop) (*Brit*), jewelry store (*US*); (*bijoux*) jewellery, jewelry

bijoutier, -ière [biʒutje, -jɛʀ] *nm/f* jeweller (*Brit*), jeweler (*US*)
bikini [bikini] *nm* bikini
bilan [bilɑ̃] *nm* (*Comm*) balance sheet(s); (*annuel*) end of year statement; (*fig*) (*net*) outcome; (: *de victimes*) toll; **faire le ~ de** to assess; to review; **déposer son ~** to file a bankruptcy statement; **~ de santé** (*Méd*) check-up; **~ social** *statement of a firm's policies towards its employees*
bile [bil] *nf* bile; **se faire de la ~** (*fam*) to worry o.s. sick
bilieux, -euse [biljø, -øz] *adj* bilious; (*fig: colérique*) testy
bilingue [bilɛ̃g] *adj* bilingual
billard [bijaʀ] *nm* billiards *sg*; (*table*) billiard table; **c'est du ~** (*fam*) it's a cinch; **passer sur le ~** (*fam*) to have an (*ou* one's) operation; **~ électrique** pinball
bille [bij] *nf* ball; (*du jeu de billes*) marble; (*de bois*) log; **jouer aux ~s** to play marbles
billet [bijɛ] *nm* (*aussi*: **~ de banque**) (bank) note; (*de cinéma, de bus etc*) ticket; (*courte lettre*) note; **~ à ordre** *ou* **de commerce** (*Comm*) promissory note, IOU; **~ d'avion/de train** plane/train ticket; **~ circulaire** round-trip ticket; **~ doux** love letter; **~ de faveur** complimentary ticket; **~ de loterie** lottery ticket; **~ de quai** platform ticket; **~ électronique** e-ticket
billetterie [bijetʀi] *nf* ticket office; (*distributeur*) ticket dispenser; (*Banque*) cash dispenser
billion [biljɔ̃] *nm* billion (*Brit*), trillion (*US*)
billot [bijo] *nm* block
bimensuel, le [bimɑ̃sɥɛl] *adj* bimonthly, twice-monthly
binette [binɛt] *nf* (*outil*) hoe
bio [bjo] *adj* (*fam*: = *biologique*) (*produits, aliments*) organic
bio... [bjo] *préfixe* bio...
biocarburant [bjokaʀbyʀɑ̃] *nm* biofuel
biochimie [bjoʃimi] *nf* biochemistry
biodiversité [bjodivɛʀsite] *nf* biodiversity
bioéthique [bjoetik] *nf* bioethics *sg*
biographie [bjɔgʀafi] *nf* biography
biologie [bjɔlɔʒi] *nf* biology
biologique [bjɔlɔʒik] *adj* biological; (*produits, aliments*) organic
biologiste [bjɔlɔʒist] *nm/f* biologist
biométrie *nf* biometrics
biotechnologie [bjotɛknɔlɔʒi] *nf* biotechnology
bioterrorisme [bjotɛʀɔʀism] *nm* bioterrorism
bioterroriste [bjotɛʀɔʀist] *nm/f* bioterrorist
bipolaire [bipɔlɛʀ] *adj* bipolar
Birmanie [biʀmani] *nf*: **la ~** Burma
bis, e [*adj* bi, *adj, nf* biz, *adv, excl, nm* bis] *adj* (*couleur*) greyish brown ▷ *adv*: **12 ~** 12a *ou* A ▷ *excl, nm* encore ▷ *nf* (*baiser*) kiss; (*vent*) North wind; **faire une** *ou* **la ~e à qn** to kiss

sb; **grosses ~es (de)** (*sur lettre*) love and kisses (from)

bisannuel, le [bizanɥɛl] *adj* biennial

biscornu, e [biskɔʀny] *adj* crooked; (*bizarre*) weird(-looking)

biscotte [biskɔt] *nf* toasted bread (*sold in packets*)

biscuit [biskɥi] *nm* biscuit (*Brit*), cookie (*US*); (*gâteau*) sponge cake; ~ **à la cuiller** sponge finger

bise [biz] *adj f, nf voir* **bis**

bisexuel, le [bisɛksɥɛl] *adj, nm/f* bisexual

bisou [bizu] *nm* (*fam*) kiss

bissextile [bisɛkstil] *adj*: **année ~** leap year

bistouri [bisturi] *nm* lancet

bistro, bistrot [bistro] *nm* bistro, café

bitume [bitym] *nm* asphalt

bizarre [bizaʀ] *adj* strange, odd

blafard, e [blafaʀ, -aʀd] *adj* wan

blague [blag] *nf* (*propos*) joke; (*farce*) trick; **sans ~!** no kidding!; ~ **à tabac** tobacco pouch

blaguer [blage] *vi* to joke ▷ *vt* to tease

blaireau, x [blɛʀo] *nm* (*Zool*) badger; (*brosse*) shaving brush

blairer [blɛʀe] *vt*: **je ne peux pas le ~** I can't bear ou stand him

blâme [blɑm] *nm* blame; (*sanction*) reprimand

blâmer [blɑme] *vt* (*réprouver*) to blame; (*réprimander*) to reprimand

blanc, blanche [blɑ̃, blɑ̃ʃ] *adj* white; (*non imprimé*) blank; (*innocent*) pure ▷ *nm/f* white, white man/woman ▷ *nm* (*couleur*) white; (*linge*): **le ~** whites *pl*; (*espace non écrit*) blank; (*aussi*: ~ **d'œuf**) (egg-)white; (*aussi*: ~ **de poulet**) breast, white meat; (*aussi*: **vin ~**) white wine ▷ *nf* (*Mus*) minim (*Brit*), half-note (*US*); (*fam*: *drogue*) smack; **d'une voix blanche** in a toneless voice; **aux cheveux ~s** white-haired; **le ~ de l'œil** the white of the eye; **laisser en ~** to leave blank; **chèque en ~** blank cheque; **à ~** *adv* (*chauffer*) white-hot; (*tirer, charger*) with blanks; **saigner à ~** to bleed white; ~ **cassé** off-white

blancheur [blɑ̃ʃœʀ] *nf* whiteness

blanchir [blɑ̃ʃiʀ] *vt* (*gén*) to whiten; (*linge, fig*: *argent*) to launder; (*Culin*) to blanch; (*fig*: *disculper*) to clear ▷ *vi* to grow white; (*cheveux*) to go white; **blanchi à la chaux** whitewashed

blanchisserie [blɑ̃ʃisʀi] *nf* laundry

blason [blazɔ̃] *nm* coat of arms

blasphème [blasfɛm] *nm* blasphemy

blazer [blazɛʀ] *nm* blazer

blé [ble] *nm* wheat; ~ **en herbe** wheat on the ear; ~ **noir** buckwheat

bled [blɛd] *nm* (*péj*) hole; (*en Afrique du Nord*): **le ~** the interior

blême [blɛm] *adj* pale

blessant, e [blɛsɑ̃, -ɑ̃t] *adj* hurtful

blessé, e [blese] *adj* injured ▷ *nm/f* injured person, casualty; **un ~ grave, un grand ~** a seriously injured ou wounded person

blesser [blese] *vt* to injure; (*délibérément: Mil etc*) to wound; (*souliers etc, offenser*) to hurt; **se blesser** to injure o.s.; **se ~ au pied** *etc* to injure one's foot *etc*

blessure [blesyʀ] *nf* (*accidentelle*) injury; (*intentionnelle*) wound

bleu, e [blø] *adj* blue; (*bifteck*) very rare ▷ *nm* (*couleur*) blue; (*novice*) greenhorn; (*contusion*) bruise; (*vêtement: aussi*: ~**s**) overalls *pl* (*Brit*), coveralls *pl* (*US*); **avoir une peur ~e** to be scared stiff; **zone ~e** ≈ restricted parking area; **fromage ~** blue cheese; **au ~** (*Culin*) au bleu; ~ (**de lessive**) ≈ blue bag; ~ **de méthylène** (*Méd*) methylene blue; ~ **marine/nuit/roi** navy/midnight/royal blue

bleuet [bløɛ] *nm* cornflower

bleuté, e [bløte] *adj* blue-shaded

blinder [blɛ̃de] *vt* to armour (*Brit*), armor (*US*); (*fig*) to harden

bloc [blɔk] *nm* (*de pierre etc, Inform*) block; (*de papier à lettres*) pad; (*ensemble*) group, block; **serré à ~** tightened right down; **en ~** as a whole; wholesale; **faire ~** to unite; ~ **opératoire** operating ou theatre block; ~ **sanitaire** toilet block; ~ **sténo** shorthand notebook

blocage [blɔkaʒ] *nm* (*voir bloquer*) blocking; jamming; (*des prix*) freezing; (*Psych*) hang-up

bloc-notes (*pl* **blocs-notes**) [blɔknɔt] *nm* note pad

blocus [blɔkys] *nm* blockade

blog, blogue [blɔg] *nm* blog

blogging [blɔgiŋ] *nm* blogging

bloguer [blɔge] *vi* to blog

blogueur, -euse [blɔgœʀ, -øz] *nm/f* blogger

blond, e [blɔ̃, -ɔ̃d] *adj* fair; (*plus clair*) blond; (*sable, blés*) golden ▷ *nm/f* fair-haired ou blond man/woman; ~ **cendré** ash blond

bloquer [blɔke] *vt* (*passage*) to block; (*pièce mobile*) to jam; (*crédits, compte*) to freeze; (*personne, négociations etc*) to hold up; (*regrouper*) to group; ~ **les freins** to jam on the brakes

blottir [blɔtiʀ]: **se blottir** *vi* to huddle up

blouse [bluz] *nf* overall

blouson [bluzɔ̃] *nm* blouson (jacket); ~ **noir** (*fig*) ≈ rocker

blue-jean [bludʒin], **blue-jeans** [bludʒins] *nm* jeans

bluff [blœf] *nm* bluff

bluffer [blœfe] *vi, vt* to bluff

bobard [bɔbaʀ] *nm* (*fam*) tall story

bobine [bɔbin] *nf* (*de fil*) reel; (*de machine à coudre*) spool; (*de machine à écrire*) ribbon; (*Élec*) coil; ~ **(d'allumage)** (*Auto*) coil; ~ **de pellicule** (*Photo*) roll of film

bobo [bɔbo] *abr m/f* (= *bourgeois bohème*) boho

bocal, -aux [bɔkal, -o] *nm* jar

bock [bɔk] *nm* (*beer*) glass; (*contenu*) glass of beer

body [bɔdi] *nm* body(suit); (*Sport*) leotard

bœuf (*pl* **bœufs**) [bœf, bø] *nm* ox; (*Culin*) beef; (*Mus: fam*) jam session

bof [bɔf] *excl* (*fam: indifférence*) don't care!,

meh; (*pas terrible*) nothing special

bogue [bɔg] *nf* (*Bot*) husk ▷ *nm* (*Inform*) bug

bohème [bɔɛm] *adj* happy-go-lucky, unconventional

bohémien, ne [bɔemjɛ̃, -ɛn] *adj* Bohemian ▷ *nm/f* gipsy

boire [bwaʀ] *vt* to drink; (*s'imprégner de*) to soak up; ~ **un coup** to have a drink

bois [bwa] *vb voir* **boire** ▷ *nm* wood; (*Zool*) antler; (*Mus*): **les** ~ the woodwind; **de** ~, **en** ~ wooden; ~ **vert** green wood; ~ **mort** deadwood; ~ **de lit** bedstead

boisé, e [bwaze] *adj* woody, wooded

boisson [bwasɔ̃] *nf* drink; **pris de** ~ drunk, intoxicated; ~**s alcoolisées** alcoholic beverages *ou* drinks; ~**s non alcoolisées** soft drinks

boîte [bwat] *nf* box; (*fam: entreprise*) firm, company; **aliments en** ~ canned *ou* tinned (*Brit*) foods; ~ **à gants** glove compartment; ~ **à musique** musical box; ~ **à ordures** dustbin (*Brit*), trash can (*US*); ~ **aux lettres** letter box, mailbox (*US*); (*Inform*) mailbox; ~ **crânienne** cranium; ~ **d'allumettes** box of matches; (*vide*) matchbox; ~ **de conserves** can *ou* tin (*Brit*) (of food); ~ **de nuit** night club; ~ **de sardines/petits pois** can *ou* tin (*Brit*) of sardines/peas; **mettre qn en** ~ (*fam*) to have a laugh at sb's expense; ~ **de vitesses** gear box; ~ **noire** (*Aviat*) black box; ~ **postale (BP)** PO box; ~ **vocale** voice mail

boiter [bwate] *vi* to limp; (*fig*) to wobble; (*raisonnement*) to be shaky

boîtier [bwatje] *nm* case; (*d'appareil photo*) body; ~ **de montre** watch case

boive *etc* [bwav] *vb voir* **boire**

bol [bɔl] *nm* bowl; (*contenu*): **un** ~ **de café** *etc* a bowl of coffee *etc*; **un** ~ **d'air** a breath of fresh air; **en avoir ras le** ~ (*fam*) to have had a bellyful; **avoir du** ~ (*fam*) to be lucky

bolide [bɔlid] *nm* racing car; **comme un** ~ like a rocket

bombardement [bɔ̃baʀdəmɑ̃] *nm* bombing

bombarder [bɔ̃baʀde] *vt* to bomb; ~ **qn de** (*cailloux, lettres*) to bombard sb with; ~ **qn directeur** to thrust sb into the director's seat

bombe [bɔ̃b] *nf* bomb; (*atomiseur*) (aerosol) spray; (*Équitation*) riding cap; **faire la** ~ (*fam*) to go on a binge; ~ **atomique** atomic bomb; ~ **à retardement** time bomb

bombé, e [bɔ̃be] *adj* rounded; (*mur*) bulging; (*front*) domed; (*route*) steeply cambered

bomber [bɔ̃be] *vi* to bulge; (*route*) to camber ▷ *vt*: ~ **le torse** to swell out one's chest

MOT-CLÉ

bon, bonne [bɔ̃, bɔn] *adj* **1** (*agréable, satisfaisant*) good; **un bon repas/restaurant** a good meal/restaurant; **être bon en maths** to be good at maths

2 (*charitable*): **être bon (envers)** to be good (to), to be kind (to); **vous êtes trop bon** you're too kind

3 (*correct*) right; **le bon numéro/moment** the right number/moment

4 (*souhaits*): **bon anniversaire!** happy birthday!; **bon courage!** good luck!; **bon séjour!** enjoy your stay!; **bon voyage!** have a good trip!; **bon week-end!** have a good weekend!; **bonne année!** happy New Year!; **bonne chance!** good luck!; **bonne fête!** happy holiday!; **bonne nuit!** good night!

5 (*approprié*): **bon à/pour** fit to/for; **bon à jeter** fit for the bin; **c'est bon à savoir** that's useful to know; **à quoi bon (...)?** what's the point *ou* use (of ...)?

6 (*intensif*): **ça m'a pris deux bonnes heures** it took me a good two hours; **un bon nombre de** a good number of

7: **bon enfant** *adj inv* accommodating, easy-going; **bonne femme** (*péj*) woman; **de bonne heure** early; **bon marché** *adj inv* cheap; **bon mot** witticism; **pour faire bon poids ...** to make up for it ...; **bon sens** common sense; **bon vivant** jovial chap; **bonnes œuvres** charitable works, charities; **bonne sœur** nun

▷ *nm* **1** (*billet*) voucher; (*aussi*: **bon cadeau**) gift voucher; **bon de caisse** cash voucher; **bon d'essence** petrol coupon; **bon à tirer** pass for press; **bon du Trésor** Treasury bond

2: **avoir du bon** to have its good points; **il y a du bon dans ce qu'il dit** there's some sense in what he says; **pour de bon** for good

▷ *nm/f*: **un bon à rien** a good-for-nothing

▷ *adv*: **il fait bon** it's *ou* the weather is fine; **sentir bon** to smell good; **tenir bon** to stand firm; **juger bon de faire ...** to think fit to do ...

▷ *excl* right!, good!; **ah bon?** really?; **bon, je reste** right, I'll stay; *voir aussi* **bonne**

bonbon [bɔ̃bɔ̃] *nm* (boiled) sweet

bonbonne [bɔ̃bɔn] *nf* demijohn; carboy

bond [bɔ̃] *nm* leap; (*d'une balle*) rebound, ricochet; **faire un** ~ to leap in the air; **d'un seul** ~ in one bound, with one leap; ~ **en avant** (*fig: progrès*) leap forward

bondé, e [bɔ̃de] *adj* packed (full)

bondir [bɔ̃diʀ] *vi* to leap; ~ **de joie** (*fig*) to jump for joy; ~ **de colère** (*fig*) to be hopping mad

bonheur [bɔnœʀ] *nm* happiness; **avoir le** ~ **de** to have the good fortune to; **porter** ~ (**à qn**) to bring (sb) luck; **au petit** ~ haphazardly; **par** ~ fortunately

bonhomie [bɔnɔmi] *nf* good-naturedness

bonhomme [bɔnɔm] (*pl* **bonshommes**) [bɔ̃zɔm] *nm* fellow ▷ *adj* good-natured; **un vieux** ~ an old chap; **aller son** ~ **de chemin** to carry on in one's own sweet way; ~ **de neige** snowman

bonifier [bɔnifje]: **se bonifier** vi to improve
boniment [bɔnimɑ̃] nm patter no pl
bonjour [bɔ̃ʒuʀ] excl, nm hello; (selon l'heure)
good morning (ou afternoon); **donner** ou
souhaiter le ~ à qn to bid sb good morning
ou afternoon; **c'est simple comme ~!** it's
easy as pie!
bonne [bɔn] adj f voir **bon** ▷ nf (domestique)
maid; **~ à toute faire** general help;
~ d'enfant nanny
bonnement [bɔnmɑ̃] adv: **tout ~** quite
simply
bonnet [bɔnɛ] nm bonnet, hat; (de soutien-
gorge, lac) cup; **~ d'âne** dunce's cap; **~ de bain**
bathing cap; **~ de nuit** nightcap
bonsoir [bɔ̃swaʀ] excl good evening
bonté [bɔ̃te] nf kindness no pl; **avoir la ~ de** to
be kind ou good enough to
bonus [bɔnys] nm (Assurances) no-claims
bonus; (de DVD) extras pl
bord [bɔʀ] nm (de table, verre, falaise) edge; (de
rivière, lac) bank; (de route) side; (de vêtement)
edge, border; (de chapeau) brim; **(monter) à ~**
(to go) on board; **jeter par-dessus ~** to throw
overboard; **le commandant de ~/les
hommes du ~** the ship's master/crew; **du
même ~** (fig) of the same opinion; **au ~ de la
mer/route** at the seaside/roadside; **être au ~
des larmes** to be on the verge of tears; **virer
de ~** (Navig) to tack; **sur les ~s** (fig) slightly; **de
tous ~s** on all sides; **~ du trottoir** kerb (Brit),
curb (US)
bordeaux [bɔʀdo] nm Bordeaux ▷ adj inv
maroon
bordel [bɔʀdɛl] nm brothel; (fam!) bloody
(Brit) ou goddamn (US) mess (!) ▷ excl hell!
bordelais, e [bɔʀdəlɛ, -ɛz] adj of ou from
Bordeaux
border [bɔʀde] vt (être le long de) to line,
border; (garnir): **~ qch de** to line sth with; to
trim sth with; (qn dans son lit) to tuck up
bordereau, x [bɔʀdəʀo] nm docket, slip
bordure [bɔʀdyʀ] nf border; (sur un vêtement)
trim(ming), border; **en ~ de** on the edge of
borgne [bɔʀɲ] adj one-eyed; **hôtel ~** shady
hotel; **fenêtre ~** obstructed window
borne [bɔʀn] nf boundary stone; (aussi:
~ kilométrique) kilometre-marker,
≈ milestone; **bornes** nfpl (fig) limits;
dépasser les ~s to go too far; **sans ~(s)**
boundless
borné, e [bɔʀne] adj narrow; (obtus: personne)
narrow-minded
borner [bɔʀne] vt (délimiter) to limit; (limiter)
to confine; **se ~ à faire** (se contenter de) to
content o.s. with doing; (se limiter à) to limit
o.s. to doing
bosniaque [bɔznjak] adj Bosnian ▷ nm/f: **B~**
Bosnian
Bosnie-Herzégovine [bɔsniɛʀzegɔvin] nf
Bosnia-Herzegovina
bosquet [bɔskɛ] nm copse (Brit), grove

bosse [bɔs] nf (de terrain etc) bump; (enflure)
lump; (du bossu, du chameau) hump; **avoir la ~
des maths** etc (fam) to have a gift for maths
etc; **il a roulé sa ~** (fam) he's been around
bosser [bɔse] vi (fam) to work; (: dur) to slave
(away), slog (hard) (Brit)
bossu, e [bɔsy] nm/f hunchback
botanique [bɔtanik] nf botany ▷ adj
botanic(al)
botte [bɔt] nf (soulier) (high) boot; (Escrime)
thrust; (gerbe): **~ de paille** bundle of straw;
~ de radis/d'asperges bunch of radishes/
asparagus; **~s de caoutchouc** wellington boots
botter [bɔte] vt to put boots on; (donner un coup
de pied à) to kick; (fam): **ça me botte** I fancy
that
bottin® [bɔtɛ̃] nm directory
bottine [bɔtin] nf ankle boot
bouc [buk] nm goat; (barbe) goatee;
~ émissaire scapegoat
boucan [bukɑ̃] nm din, racket
bouche [buʃ] nf mouth; **une ~ à nourrir** a
mouth to feed; **les ~s inutiles** the non-
productive members of the population; **faire
du ~ à ~ à qn** to give sb the kiss of life (Brit),
give sb mouth-to-mouth resuscitation; **de ~
à oreille** confidentially; **pour la bonne ~**
(pour la fin) till last; **faire venir l'eau à la ~** to
make one's mouth water; **~ cousue!** mum's
the word!; **rester ~ bée** to stand open-
mouthed; **~ d'aération** air vent; **~ de
chaleur** hot air vent; **~ d'égout** manhole;
~ d'incendie fire hydrant; **~ de métro** métro
entrance
bouché, e [buʃe] adj (flacon etc) stoppered;
(temps, ciel) overcast; (carrière) blocked; (péj:
personne) thick; (trompette) muted; **avoir le
nez ~** to have a blocked-(up) nose; **c'est un
secteur ~** there's no future in that area;
l'évier est ~ the sink's blocked
bouchée [buʃe] nf mouthful; **ne faire
qu'une ~ de** (fig) to make short work of; **pour
une ~ de pain** (fig) for next to nothing; **~s à la
reine** chicken vol-au-vents
boucher [buʃe] nm butcher ▷ vt (pour colmater)
to stop up; (trou) to fill up; (obstruer) to block
(up); **se boucher** vi (tuyau etc) to block up, get
blocked up; **j'ai le nez bouché** my nose is
blocked; **se ~ le nez** to hold one's nose
bouchère [buʃɛʀ] nf butcher
boucherie [buʃʀi] nf butcher's (shop);
(métier) butchery; (fig) slaughter, butchery
bouche-trou [buʃtʀu] nm (fig) stop-gap
bouchon [buʃɔ̃] nm (en liège) cork; (autre
matière) stopper; (de tube) top; (fig:
embouteillage) holdup; (Pêche) float; **~ doseur**
measuring cap
boucle [bukl] nf (forme, figure, aussi Inform) loop;
(objet) buckle; **~ (de cheveux)** curl; **~ d'oreille**
earring
bouclé, e [bukle] adj (cheveux) curly; (tapis)
uncut

boucler [bukle] vt (fermer: ceinture etc) to fasten; (: magasin) to shut; (terminer) to finish off; (: circuit) to complete; (budget) to balance; (enfermer) to shut away; (: condamné) to lock up; (: quartier) to seal off ▷ vi to curl; **faire ~** (cheveux) to curl; **~ la boucle** (Aviat) to loop the loop

bouclier [buklije] nm shield

bouddhiste [budist] nm/f Buddhist

bouder [bude] vi to sulk ▷ vt (chose) to turn one's nose up at; (personne) to refuse to have anything to do with

boudin [budɛ̃] nm (Culin): **~ (noir)** black pudding; (Tech) roll; **~ blanc** white pudding

boue [bu] nf mud

bouée [bwe] nf buoy; (de baigneur) rubber ring; **~ (de sauvetage)** lifebuoy; (fig) lifeline

boueux, -euse [bwø, -øz] adj muddy ▷ nm (fam) refuse (Brit) ou garbage (US) collector

bouffe [buf] nf (fam) grub, food

bouffée [bufe] nf (de cigarette) puff; **une ~ d'air pur** a breath of fresh air; **~ de chaleur** (gén) blast of hot air; (Méd) hot flush (Brit) ou flash (US); **~ de fièvre/de honte** flush of fever/shame; **~ d'orgueil** fit of pride

bouffer [bufe] vi (fam) to eat; (Couture) to puff out ▷ vt (fam) to eat

bouffi, e [bufi] adj swollen

bougeoir [buʒwar] nm candlestick

bougeotte [buʒɔt] nf: **avoir la ~** to have the fidgets

bouger [buʒe] vi to move; (dent etc) to be loose; (changer) to alter; (agir) to stir; (s'activer) to get moving ▷ vt to move; **les prix/les couleurs n'ont pas bougé** prices/colours haven't changed; **se bouger** (fam) to move (oneself)

bougie [buʒi] nf candle; (Auto) spark(ing) plug

bougon, ne [bugɔ̃, -ɔn] adj grumpy

bougonner [bugɔne] vi, vt to grumble

bouillabaisse [bujabɛs] nf type of fish soup

bouillant, e [bujɑ̃, -ɑ̃t] adj (qui bout) boiling; (très chaud) boiling (hot); (fig: ardent) hot-headed; **~ de colère** etc seething with anger etc

bouillie [buji] nf gruel; (de bébé) cereal; **en ~** (fig) crushed

bouillir [bujir] vi to boil ▷ vt (aussi: **faire ~**: Culin) to boil; **~ de colère** etc to seethe with anger etc

bouilloire [bujwar] nf kettle

bouillon [bujɔ̃] nm (Culin) stock no pl; (bulles, écume) bubble; **~ de culture** culture medium

bouillonner [bujɔne] vi to bubble; (fig: idées) to bubble up; (torrent) to foam

bouillotte [bujɔt] nf hot-water bottle

boulanger, -ère [bulɑ̃ʒe, -ɛr] nm/f baker ▷ nf (femme du boulanger) baker's wife

boulangerie [bulɑ̃ʒri] nf bakery, baker's (shop); (commerce) bakery; **~ industrielle** bakery

boulangerie-pâtisserie (pl **boulangeries-pâtisseries**) [bulɑ̃ʒripatisri] nf baker's and confectioner's (shop)

boule [bul] nf (gén) ball; (de pétanque) bowl; (de machine à écrire) golf ball; **roulé en ~** curled up in a ball; **se mettre en ~** (fig) to fly off the handle, blow one's top; **perdre la ~** (fig: fam) to go off one's rocker; **~ de gomme** (bonbon) gum(drop), pastille; **~ de neige** snowball; **faire ~ de neige** (fig) to snowball

bouleau, x [bulo] nm (silver) birch

bouledogue [buldɔg] nm bulldog

boulet [bulɛ] nm (aussi: **~ de canon**) cannonball; (de bagnard) ball and chain; (charbon) (coal) nut

boulette [bulɛt] nf (de viande) meatball

boulevard [bulvar] nm boulevard

bouleversant, e [bulvɛrsɑ̃, -ɑ̃t] adj (récit) deeply distressing; (nouvelle) shattering

bouleversement [bulvɛrsəmɑ̃] nm (politique, social) upheaval

bouleverser [bulvɛrse] vt (émouvoir) to overwhelm; (causer du chagrin à) to distress; (pays, vie) to disrupt; (papiers, objets) to turn upside down, upset

boulimie [bulimi] nf bulimia; compulsive eating

boulimique [bulimik] adj bulimic

boulon [bulɔ̃] nm bolt

boulot¹ [bulo] nm (fam: travail) work

boulot², te [bulo, -ɔt] adj plump, tubby

boum [bum] nm bang ▷ nf (fam) party

bouquet [bukɛ] nm (de fleurs) bunch (of flowers), bouquet; (de persil etc) bunch; (parfum) bouquet; (fig) crowning piece; **c'est le ~!** that's the last straw!; **~ garni** (Culin) bouquet garni

bouquin [bukɛ̃] nm (fam) book

bouquiner [bukine] vi (fam) to read

bouquiniste [bukinist] nm/f bookseller

bourbeux, -euse [burbø, -øz] adj muddy

bourbier [burbje] nm (quag)mire

bourde [burd] nf (erreur) howler; (gaffe) blunder

bourdon [burdɔ̃] nm bumblebee

bourdonner [burdɔne] vi to buzz; (moteur) to hum

bourg [bur] nm small market town (ou village)

bourgeois, e [burʒwa, -waz] adj (péj) ≈ (upper) middle class; bourgeois; (maison etc) very comfortable ▷ nm/f (autrefois) burgher

bourgeoisie [burʒwazi] nf ≈ upper middle classes pl; bourgeoisie; **petite ~** middle classes

bourgeon [burʒɔ̃] nm bud

Bourgogne [burgɔɲ] nf: **la ~** Burgundy ▷ nm: **bourgogne** Burgundy (wine)

bourguignon, ne [burgiɲɔ̃, -ɔn] adj of ou from Burgundy, Burgundian; **bœuf ~** bœuf bourguignon

bourlinguer [burlɛ̃ge] vi to knock about a lot, get around a lot

bourrade [buʀad] nf shove, thump

bourrage [buʀaʒ] nm (papier) jamming; ~ **de crâne** brainwashing; (Scol) cramming

bourrasque [buʀask] nf squall

bourratif, -ive [buʀatif, -iv] (fam) adj filling, stodgy

bourré, e [buʀe] adj (rempli): ~ **de** crammed full of; (fam: ivre) pickled, plastered

bourreau, x [buʀo] nm executioner; (fig) torturer; ~ **de travail** workaholic, glutton for work

bourrelet [buʀlɛ] nm draught (Brit) ou draft (US) excluder; (de peau) fold ou roll (of flesh)

bourrer [buʀe] vt (pipe) to fill; (poêle) to pack; (valise) to cram (full); ~ **de** to cram (full) with, stuff with; ~ **de coups** to hammer blows on, pummel; ~ **le crâne à qn** to pull the wool over sb's eyes; (endoctriner) to brainwash sb

bourrique [buʀik] nf (âne) ass

bourru, e [buʀy] adj surly, gruff

bourse [buʀs] nf (subvention) grant; (porte-monnaie) purse; **sans ~ délier** without spending a penny; **la B~** the Stock Exchange; ~ **du travail** ≈ trades union council (regional headquarters)

boursier, -ière [buʀsje, -jɛʀ] adj (Comm) Stock Market cpd ▷ nm/f (Scol) grant-holder

boursoufler [buʀsufle] vt to puff up, bloat; **se boursoufler** vi (visage) to swell ou puff up; (peinture) to blister

bous [bu] vb voir **bouillir**

bousculade [buskylad] nf (hâte) rush; (poussée) crush

bousculer [buskyle] vt to knock over; (heurter) to knock into; (fig) to push, rush

bouse [buz] nf: ~ **(de vache)** (cow) dung no pl (Brit), manure no pl

bousiller [buzije] vt (fam) to wreck

boussole [busɔl] nf compass

bout [bu] vb voir **bouillir** ▷ nm bit; (extrémité: d'un bâton etc) tip; (: d'une ficelle, table, rue, période) end; **au ~ de** at the end of, after; **au ~ du compte** at the end of the day; **pousser qn à ~** to push sb to the limit (of his patience); **venir à ~ de** to manage to finish (off) ou overcome; ~ **à ~** end to end; **à tout ~ de champ** at every turn; **d'un ~ à l'autre, de ~ en ~** from one end to the other; **à ~ portant** at point-blank range; **un ~ de chou** (enfant) a little tot; ~ **d'essai** (Ciné etc) screen test; ~ **filtre** filter tip

boutade [butad] nf quip, sally

boute-en-train [butãtʀɛ̃] nm inv live wire (fig)

bouteille [butɛj] nf bottle; (de gaz butane) cylinder

boutique [butik] nf shop (Brit), store (US); (de grand couturier, de mode) boutique

bouton [butɔ̃] nm (de vêtement, électrique etc) button; (Bot) bud; (sur la peau) spot; (de porte) knob; ~ **de manchette** cuff-link; ~ **d'or** buttercup

boutonner [butɔne] vt to button up, do up;

se boutonner to button one's clothes up

boutonnière [butɔnjɛʀ] nf buttonhole

bouton-pression (pl **boutons-pression**) [butɔ̃pʀesjɔ̃] nm press stud, snap fastener

bouture [butyʀ] nf cutting; **faire des ~s** to take cuttings

bovin, e [bɔvɛ̃, -in] adj bovine ▷ nm: ~**s** cattle pl

bowling [boliŋ] nm (tenpin) bowling; (salle) bowling alley

box [bɔks] nm lock-up (garage); (de salle, dortoir) cubicle; (d'écurie) loose-box; (aussi: ~-**calf**) box calf; **le ~ des accusés** the dock

boxe [bɔks] nf boxing

boxeur [bɔksœʀ] nm boxer

boyaux [bwajo] nmpl (viscères) entrails, guts

BP sigle f = **boîte postale**

bracelet [bʀaslɛ] nm bracelet

braconnier [bʀakɔnje] nm poacher

brader [bʀade] vt to sell off, sell cheaply

braderie [bʀadʀi] nf clearance sale; (par des particuliers) ≈ car boot sale (Brit), ≈ garage sale (US); (magasin) discount store; (sur marché) cut-price (Brit) ou cut-rate (US) stall

braguette [bʀagɛt] nf fly, flies pl (Brit), zipper (US)

brailler [bʀaje] vi to bawl, yell ▷ vt to bawl out, yell out

braire [bʀɛʀ] vi to bray

braise [bʀɛz] nf embers pl

brancard [bʀãkaʀ] nm (civière) stretcher; (bras, perche) shaft

brancardier [bʀãkaʀdje] nm stretcher-bearer

branchages [bʀãʃaʒ] nmpl branches, boughs

branche [bʀãʃ] nf branch; (de lunettes) side(-piece)

branché, e [bʀãʃe] adj (fam) switched-on, trendy ▷ nm/f (fam) trendy

brancher [bʀãʃe] vt to connect (up); (en mettant la prise) to plug in; ~ **qn/qch sur** (fig) to get sb/sth launched onto

brandir [bʀãdiʀ] vt (arme) to brandish, wield; (document) to flourish, wave

branle [bʀãl] nm: **mettre en ~** to set swinging; **donner le ~ à** to set in motion

branle-bas [bʀãlbɑ] nm inv commotion

braquer [bʀake] vi (Auto) to turn (the wheel) ▷ vt (revolver etc): ~ **qch sur** to aim sth at, point sth at; (mettre en colère): ~ **qn** to antagonize sb, put sb's back up; ~ **son regard sur** to fix one's gaze on; **se braquer** vi: **se ~ (contre)** to take a stand (against)

bras [bʀa] nm arm; (de fleuve) branch ▷ nmpl (fig: travailleurs) labour sg (Brit), labor sg (US), hands; ~ **dessus ~ dessous** arm in arm; **à ~ raccourcis** with fists flying; **à tour de ~** with all one's might; **baisser les ~** to give up; **se retrouver avec qch sur les ~** (fam) to be landed with sth; ~ **droit** (fig) right hand man; ~ **de fer** arm-wrestling; **une partie de ~ de fer** (fig) a trial of strength; ~ **de levier**

lever arm; **~ de mer** arm of the sea, sound
brasier [bʀɑzje] nm blaze, (blazing) inferno; (fig) inferno
bras-le-corps [bʀɑlkɔʀ]: **à ~** adv (a)round the waist
brassard [bʀɑsaʀ] nm armband
brasse [bʀɑs] nf (nage) breast-stroke; (mesure) fathom; **~ papillon** butterfly(-stroke)
brassée [bʀɑse] nf armful; **une ~ de** (fig) a number of
brasser [bʀɑse] vt (bière) to brew; (remuer: salade) to toss; (: cartes) to shuffle; (fig) to mix; **~ l'argent/les affaires** to handle a lot of money/business
brasserie [bʀɑsʀi] nf (restaurant) bar (selling food), brasserie; (usine) brewery
brave [bʀɑv] adj (courageux) brave; (bon, gentil) good, kind
braver [bʀɑve] vt to defy
bravo [bʀɑvo] excl bravo! ▷ nm cheer
bravoure [bʀɑvuʀ] nf bravery
break [bʀɛk] nm (Auto) estate car (Brit), station wagon (US)
brebis [bʀəbi] nf ewe; **~ galeuse** black sheep
brèche [bʀɛʃ] nf breach, gap; **être sur la ~** (fig) to be on the go
bredouille [bʀəduj] adj empty-handed
bredouiller [bʀəduje] vi, vt to mumble, stammer
bref, brève [bʀɛf, bʀɛv] adj short, brief ▷ adv in short ▷ nf (voyelle) short vowel; (information) brief news item; **d'un ton ~** sharply, curtly; **en ~** in short, in brief; **à ~ délai** shortly
Brésil [bʀezil] nm: **le ~** Brazil
brésilien, ne [bʀeziljɛ̃, -ɛn] adj Brazilian ▷ nm/f: **B~, ne** Brazilian
Bretagne [bʀətaɲ] nf: **la ~** Brittany
bretelle [bʀətɛl] nf (de fusil etc) sling; (de vêtement) strap; (d'autoroute) slip road (Brit), entrance ou exit ramp (US); **bretelles** nfpl (pour pantalon) braces (Brit), suspenders (US); **~ de contournement** (Auto) bypass; **~ de raccordement** (Auto) access road
breton, ne [bʀətɔ̃, -ɔn] adj Breton ▷ nm (Ling) Breton ▷ nm/f: **B~, ne** Breton
breuvage [bʀœvaʒ] nm beverage, drink
brève [bʀɛv] adj f, nf voir **bref**
brevet [bʀəvɛ] nm diploma, certificate; **~ d'apprentissage** certificate of apprenticeship; **~ (des collèges)** school certificate, taken at approx. 16 years; **~ (d'invention)** patent
breveté, e [bʀəvte] adj patented; (diplômé) qualified
bribes [bʀib] nfpl bits, scraps; (d'une conversation) snatches; **par ~** piecemeal
bricolage [bʀikɔlaʒ] nm: **le ~** do-it-yourself (jobs); (péj) patched-up job
bricole [bʀikɔl] nf (babiole, chose insignifiante) trifle; (petit travail) small job
bricoler [bʀikɔle] vi to do odd jobs; (en

amateur) to do DIY jobs; (passe-temps) to potter about ▷ vt (réparer) to fix up; (mal réparer) to tinker with; (trafiquer: voiture etc) to doctor, fix
bricoleur, -euse [bʀikɔlœʀ, -øz] nm/f handyman/woman, DIY enthusiast
bride [bʀid] nf bridle; (d'un bonnet) string, tie; **à ~ abattue** flat out, hell for leather; **tenir en ~** to keep in check; **lâcher la ~ à, laisser la ~ sur le cou à** to give free rein to
bridé, e [bʀide] adj: **yeux ~s** slit eyes
bridge [bʀidʒ] nm (Cartes) bridge
brièvement [bʀijɛvmɑ̃] adv briefly
brigade [bʀigad] nf (Police) squad; (Mil) brigade
brigadier [bʀigadje] nm (Police) ≈ sergeant; (Mil) bombardier; corporal
brigandage [bʀigɑ̃daʒ] nm robbery
briguer [bʀige] vt to aspire to; (suffrages) to canvass
brillamment [bʀijamɑ̃] adv brilliantly
brillant, e [bʀijɑ̃, -ɑ̃t] adj brilliant; (remarquable) bright; (luisant) shiny, shining ▷ nm (diamant) brilliant
briller [bʀije] vi to shine
brimer [bʀime] vt to harass; to bully
brin [bʀɛ̃] nm (de laine, ficelle etc) strand; (fig): **un ~ de** a bit of; **un ~ mystérieux** etc (fam) a weeny bit mysterious etc; **~ d'herbe** blade of grass; **~ de muguet** sprig of lily of the valley; **~ de paille** wisp of straw
brindille [bʀɛ̃dij] nf twig
brio [bʀijo] nm brilliance; (Mus) brio; **avec ~** brilliantly, with panache
brioche [bʀijɔʃ] nf brioche (bun); (fam: ventre) paunch
brique [bʀik] nf brick; (de lait) carton; (fam) 10 000 francs ▷ adj inv brick red
briquer [bʀike] vt (fam) to polish up
briquet [bʀikɛ] nm (cigarette) lighter
brise [bʀiz] nf breeze
briser [bʀize] vt to break; **se briser** vi to break
britannique [bʀitanik] adj British ▷ nm/f: **B~** Briton, British person; **les B~s** the British
brocante [bʀɔkɑ̃t] nf (objets) secondhand goods pl, junk; (commerce) secondhand trade; junk dealing
brocanteur, -euse [bʀɔkɑ̃tœʀ, -øz] nm/f junk shop owner; junk dealer
broche [bʀɔʃ] nf brooch; (Culin) spit; (fiche) spike, peg; (Méd) pin; **à la ~** spit-roasted, roasted on a spit
broché, e [bʀɔʃe] adj (livre) paper-backed; (tissu) brocaded
brochet [bʀɔʃɛ] nm pike inv
brochette [bʀɔʃɛt] nf (ustensile) skewer; (plat) kebab; **~ de décorations** row of medals
brochure [bʀɔʃyʀ] nf pamphlet, brochure, booklet
broder [bʀɔde] vt to embroider ▷ vi: **~ (sur des faits ou une histoire)** to embroider the facts

broderie [bʀɔdʀi] nf embroidery
broncher [bʀɔ̃ʃe] vi: **sans ~** without flinching, without turning a hair
bronches [bʀɔ̃ʃ] nfpl bronchial tubes
bronchite [bʀɔ̃ʃit] nf bronchitis
bronze [bʀɔ̃z] nm bronze
bronzer [bʀɔ̃ze] vt to tan ▷ vi to get a tan; **se bronzer** to sunbathe
brosse [bʀɔs] nf brush; **donner un coup de ~ à qch** to give sth a brush; **coiffé en ~** with a crewcut; **~ à cheveux** hairbrush; **~ à dents** toothbrush; **~ à habits** clothesbrush
brosser [bʀɔse] vt (nettoyer) to brush; (fig: tableau etc) to paint; to draw; **se brosser** vt, vi to brush one's clothes; **se ~ les dents** to brush one's teeth; **tu peux te ~!** (fam) you can sing for it!
brouette [bʀuɛt] nf wheelbarrow
brouhaha [bʀuaa] nm hubbub
brouillard [bʀujaʀ] nm fog; **être dans le ~** (fig) to be all at sea
brouille [bʀuj] nf quarrel
brouiller [bʀuje] vt (œufs, message) to scramble; (idées) to mix up; to confuse; (Radio) to cause interference to; (délibérément) to jam; (rendre trouble) to cloud; (désunir: amis) to set at odds; **se brouiller** vi (ciel, vue) to cloud over; (détails) to become confused; **se ~ (avec)** to fall out (with); **~ les pistes** to cover one's tracks; (fig) to confuse the issue
brouillon, ne [bʀujɔ̃, -ɔn] adj (sans soin) untidy; (qui manque d'organisation) disorganized, unmethodical ▷ nm (first) draft; **cahier de ~** rough (work) book; **(papier) ~** rough paper
broussailles [bʀusaj] nfpl undergrowth sg
broussailleux, -euse [bʀusajø, -øz] adj bushy
brousse [bʀus] nf: **la ~** the bush
brouter [bʀute] vt to graze on ▷ vi to graze; (Auto) to judder
broutille [bʀutij] nf trifle
broyer [bʀwaje] vt to crush; **~ du noir** to be down in the dumps
bru [bʀy] nf daughter-in-law
brugnon [bʀyɲɔ̃] nm nectarine
bruiner [bʀɥine] vb impers: **il bruine** it's drizzling, there's a drizzle
bruire [bʀɥiʀ] vi (eau) to murmur; (feuilles, étoffe) to rustle
bruit [bʀɥi] nm: **un ~** a noise, a sound; (fig: rumeur) a rumour (Brit), a rumor (US); **le ~** noise; **pas/trop de ~** no/too much noise; **sans ~** without a sound, noiselessly; **faire du ~** to make a noise; **~ de fond** background noise
bruitage [bʀɥitaʒ] nm sound effects pl
brûlant, e [bʀylɑ̃, -ɑ̃t] adj burning (hot); (liquide) boiling (hot); (regard) fiery; (sujet) red-hot
brûlé, e [bʀyle] adj (fig: démasqué) blown; (: homme politique etc) discredited ▷ nm: **odeur de ~** smell of burning

brûle-pourpoint [bʀylpuʀpwɛ̃]: **à ~** adv point-blank
brûler [bʀyle] vt to burn; (eau bouillante) to scald; (consommer: électricité, essence) to use; (feu rouge, signal) to go through (without stopping) ▷ vi to burn; (jeu): **tu brûles** you're getting warm ou hot; **se brûler** to burn o.s.; (s'ébouillanter) to scald o.s.; **se ~ la cervelle** to blow one's brains out; **~ les étapes** to make rapid progress; (aller trop vite) to cut corners; **~ (d'impatience) de faire qch** to burn with impatience to do sth, be dying to do sth
brûlure [bʀylyʀ] nf (lésion) burn; (sensation) burning no pl, burning sensation; **~s d'estomac** heartburn sg
brume [bʀym] nf mist
brumeux, -euse [bʀymø, -øz] adj misty; (fig) hazy
brumisateur [bʀymizatœʀ] nm atomizer
brun, e [bʀœ̃, -yn] adj (gén, bière) brown; (cheveux, personne, tabac) dark; **elle est ~e** she's got dark hair ▷ nm (couleur) brown ▷ nf (cigarette) cigarette made of dark tobacco; (bière) ≈ brown ale, ≈ stout
brunch [bʀœntʃ] nm brunch
brunir [bʀyniʀ] vi: **se brunir** to get a tan ▷ vt to tan
brushing [bʀœʃiŋ] nm blow-dry
brusque [bʀysk] adj (soudain) abrupt, sudden; (rude) abrupt, brusque
brusquer [bʀyske] vt to rush
brut, e [bʀyt] adj raw, crude, rough; (diamant) uncut; (soie, minéral, Inform: données) raw; (Comm) gross ▷ nf brute; **(champagne) ~** brut champagne; **(pétrole) ~** crude (oil)
brutal, e, -aux [bʀytal, -o] adj brutal
brutaliser [bʀytalize] vt to handle roughly, manhandle
Bruxelles [bʀysɛl] n Brussels
bruyamment [bʀɥijamɑ̃] adv noisily
bruyant, e [bʀɥijɑ̃, -ɑ̃t] adj noisy
bruyère [bʀyjɛʀ] nf heather
BTS sigle m (= Brevet de technicien supérieur) vocational training certificate taken at end of two-year higher education course
bu, e [by] pp de **boire**
buccal, e, -aux [bykal, -o] adj: **par voie ~e** orally
bûche [byʃ] nf log; **prendre une ~** (fig) to come a cropper (Brit), fall flat on one's face; **~ de Noël** Yule log
bûcher [byʃe] nm (funéraire) pyre; bonfire; (supplice) stake ▷ vi (fam: étudier) to swot (Brit), grind (US), slave (away) ▷ vt to swot up (Brit), cram, slave away at
bûcheron [byʃʀɔ̃] nm woodcutter
bûcheur, -euse [byʃœʀ, -øz] nm/f (fam: étudiant) swot (Brit), grind (US)
budget [bydʒɛ] nm budget
buée [bɥe] nf (sur une vitre) mist; (de l'haleine) steam

buffet [byfɛ] nm (meuble) sideboard; (de réception) buffet; ~ **(de gare)** (station) buffet, snack bar

buffle [byfl] nm buffalo

buis [bɥi] nm box tree; (bois) box(wood)

buisson [bɥisɔ̃] nm bush

buissonnière [bɥisɔnjɛʀ] adj f: **faire l'école ~** to play truant (Brit), skip school

bulbe [bylb] nm (Bot, Anat) bulb; (coupole) onion-shaped dome

Bulgarie [bylgaʀi] nf: **la ~** Bulgaria

bulle [byl] adj, nm: (papier) ~ manil(l)a paper ▷ nf bubble; (de bande dessinée) balloon; (papale) bull; ~ **de savon** soap bubble

bulletin [byltɛ̃] nm (communiqué, journal) bulletin; (papier) form; (: de bagages) ticket; (Scol) report; ~ **d'informations** news bulletin; ~ **de naissance** birth certificate; ~ **de salaire** pay slip; ~ **de santé** medical bulletin; ~ **(de vote)** ballot paper; ~ **météorologique** weather report

bureau, x [byʀo] nm (meuble) desk; (pièce, service) office; ~ **de change** (foreign) exchange office ou bureau; ~ **d'embauche** ≈ job centre; ~ **d'études** design office; ~ **de location** box office; ~ **des objets trouvés** lost property office (Brit), lost and found (US); ~ **de placement** employment agency; ~ **de poste** post office; ~ **de tabac** tobacconist's (shop), smoke shop (US); ~ **de vote** polling station

bureaucratie [byʀokʀasi] nf bureaucracy

burin [byʀɛ̃] nm cold chisel; (Art) burin

burlesque [byʀlɛsk] adj ridiculous; (Littérature) burlesque

bus vb [by] voir **boire** ▷ nm [bys] (véhicule, aussi Inform) bus

busqué, e [byske] adj: **nez ~** hook(ed) nose

buste [byst] nm (Anat) chest; (: de femme) bust; (sculpture) bust

but [by] vb voir **boire** ▷ nm (cible) target; (fig) goal, aim; (Football etc) goal; **de ~ en blanc** point-blank; **avoir pour ~ de faire** to aim to do; **dans le ~ de** with the intention of

butane [bytan] nm butane; (domestique) calor gas® (Brit), butane

buté, e [byte] adj stubborn, obstinate ▷ nf (Archit) abutment; (Tech) stop

buter [byte] vi: ~ **contre** ou **sur** to bump into; (trébucher) to stumble against ▷ vt to antagonize; **se buter** vi to get obstinate, dig in one's heels

butin [bytɛ̃] nm booty, spoils pl; (d'un vol) loot

butiner [bytine] vi (abeilles) to gather nectar

butte [byt] nf mound, hillock; **être en ~ à** to be exposed to

buvais etc [byvɛ] vb voir **boire**

buvard [byvaʀ] nm blotter

buvette [byvɛt] nf refreshment room ou stall; (comptoir) bar

buveur, -euse [byvœʀ, -øz] nm/f drinker

C

c' [s] pron voir **ce**

CA sigle m = **chiffre d'affaires; conseil d'administration; corps d'armée** ▷ sigle f = **chambre d'agriculture**

ça [sa] pron (pour désigner) this; (: plus loin) that; (comme sujet indéfini) it; **ça m'étonne que** it surprises me that; **ça va?** how are you?; how are things?; (d'accord?) OK?, all right?; **où ça?** where's that?; **pourquoi ça?** why's that?; **qui ça?** who's that?; **ça alors!** (désapprobation) well, really!; (étonnement) heavens!; **c'est ça** that's right; **ça y est** that's it

çà [sa] adv: **çà et là** here and there

cabane [kaban] nf hut, cabin

cabaret [kabaʀɛ] nm night club

cabas [kaba] nm shopping bag

cabillaud [kabijo] nm cod inv

cabine [kabin] nf (de bateau) cabin; (de plage) (beach) hut; (de piscine etc) cubicle; (de camion, train) cab; (d'avion) cockpit; ~ **(d'ascenseur)** lift cage; ~ **d'essayage** fitting room; ~ **de projection** projection room; ~ **spatiale** space capsule; ~ **(téléphonique)** call ou (tele)phone box, (tele)phone booth

cabinet [kabinɛ] nm (petite pièce) closet; (de médecin) surgery (Brit), office (US); (de notaire etc) office; (: clientèle) practice; (Pol) cabinet; (d'un ministre) advisers pl; **cabinets** nmpl (w.-c.) toilet sg; ~ **d'affaires** business consultants' (bureau), business partnership; ~ **de toilette** toilet; ~ **de travail** study

câble [kɑbl] nm cable; **le ~** (TV) cable television, cablevision (US)

cabosser [kabɔse] vt to dent

cabrer [kɑbʀe]: **se cabrer** vi (cheval) to rear up; (avion) to nose up; (fig) to revolt, rebel; to jib

cabriole [kabʀijɔl] nf caper; (gymnastique etc) somersault

cacahuète [kakaɥɛt] nf peanut

cacao [kakao] nm cocoa (powder); (boisson) cocoa

cache [kaʃ] nm mask, card (for masking) ▷ nf hiding place

cache-cache [kaʃkaʃ] nm: **jouer à ~** to play hide-and-seek

cachemire [kaʃmiʀ] nm cashmere ▷ adj: **dessin ~** paisley pattern; **le C~** Kashmir

cache-nez [kaʃne] nm inv scarf, muffler

cacher [kaʃe] vt to hide, conceal; **~ qch à qn** to hide ou conceal sth from sb; **se cacher** vi (volontairement) to hide; (être caché) to be hidden ou concealed; **il ne s'en cache pas** he makes no secret of it

cachet [kaʃe] nm (comprimé) tablet; (sceau: du roi) seal; (: de la poste) postmark; (rétribution) fee; (fig) style, character

cacheter [kaʃte] vt to seal; **vin cacheté** vintage wine

cachette [kaʃɛt] nf hiding place; **en ~** on the sly, secretly

cachot [kaʃo] nm dungeon

cachotterie [kaʃɔtʀi] nf mystery; **faire des ~s** to be secretive

cactus [kaktys] nm cactus

cadavre [kadavʀ] nm corpse, (dead) body

Caddie® [kadi] nm (supermarket) trolley (Brit), (grocery) cart (US)

cadeau, x [kado] nm present, gift; **faire un ~ à qn** to give sb a present ou gift; **faire ~ de qch à qn** to make a present of sth to sb, give sb sth as a present

cadenas [kadnɑ] nm padlock

cadence [kadɑ̃s] nf (Mus) cadence; (: rythme) rhythm; (de travail etc) rate; **cadences** nfpl (en usine) production rate sg; **en ~** rhythmically; in time

cadet, te [kadɛ, -ɛt] adj younger; (le plus jeune) youngest ▷ nm/f youngest child ou one, youngest boy ou son/girl ou daughter; **il est mon ~ de deux ans** he's two years younger than me, he's two years my junior; **les ~s** (Sport) the minors (15–17 years); **le ~ de mes soucis** the least of my worries

cadran [kadʀɑ̃] nm dial; **~ solaire** sundial

cadre [kadʀ] nm frame; (environnement) surroundings pl; (limites) scope ▷ nm/f (Admin) managerial employee, executive ▷ adj: **loi ~** outline ou blueprint law; **~ moyen/supérieur** (Admin) middle/senior management employee, junior/senior executive; **rayer qn des ~s** to discharge sb; to dismiss sb; **dans le ~ de** (fig) within the framework ou context of

cadrer [kadʀe] vi: **~ avec** to tally ou correspond with ▷ vt (Ciné, Photo) to frame

cafard [kafaʀ] nm cockroach; **avoir le ~** to be down in the dumps, be feeling low

café [kafe] nm coffee; (bistro) café ▷ adj inv coffee cpd; **~ crème** coffee with cream; **~ au lait** white coffee; **~ noir** black coffee; **~ en grains** coffee beans; **~ en poudre** instant coffee; **~ liégeois** coffee ice cream with whipped cream

cafétéria [kafeteʀja] nf cafeteria

café-tabac [kafetaba] nm tobacconist's or newsagent's also serving coffee and spirits

cafetière [kaftjɛʀ] nf (pot) coffee-pot

cafouiller [kafuje] vi to get in a shambles; (machine etc) to work in fits and starts

cage [kaʒ] nf cage; **~ (des buts)** goal; **en ~** in a cage, caged up ou in; **~ d'ascenseur** lift shaft; **~ d'escalier** (stair)well; **~ thoracique** rib cage

cageot [kaʒo] nm crate

cagibi [kaʒibi] nm shed

cagnotte [kaɲɔt] nf kitty

cagoule [kagul] nf cowl; hood; (Ski etc) cagoule; (passe-montagne) balaclava

cahier [kaje] nm notebook; (Typo) signature; (revue): **~s** journal; **~ de revendications/doléances** list of claims/grievances; **~ de brouillons** rough book, jotter; **~ des charges** specification; **~ d'exercices** exercise book

cahot [kao] nm jolt, bump

caïd [kaid] nm big chief, boss

caille [kaj] nf quail

cailler [kaje] vi (lait) to curdle; (sang) to clot; (fam) to be cold

caillot [kajo] nm (blood) clot

caillou, x [kaju] nm (little) stone

caillouteux, -euse [kajutø, -øz] adj stony; pebbly

Caire [kɛʀ] nm: **le ~** Cairo

caisse [kɛs] nf box; (où l'on met la recette) cashbox; (: machine) till; (où l'on paye) cash desk (Brit), checkout counter; (: au supermarché) cashier's desk; (Tech) case, casing; **faire sa ~** (Comm) to count the takings; **~ claire** (Mus) side ou snare drum; **~ éclair** express checkout; **~ enregistreuse** cash register; **~ d'épargne** (CE) savings bank; **~ noire** slush fund; **~ de retraite** pension fund; **~ de sortie** checkout; voir **grosse**

caissier, -ière [kesje, -jɛʀ] nm/f cashier

cajoler [kaʒɔle] vt to wheedle, coax; to surround with love and care, make a fuss of

cake [kɛk] nm fruit cake

calandre [kalɑ̃dʀ] nf radiator grill; (machine) calender, mangle

calanque [kalɑ̃k] nf rocky inlet

calcaire [kalkɛʀ] nm limestone ▷ adj (eau) hard; (Géo) limestone cpd

calciné, e [kalsine] adj burnt to ashes

calcul [kalkyl] nm calculation; **le ~** (Scol) arithmetic; **~ différentiel/intégral** differential/integral calculus; **~ mental** mental arithmetic; **~ (biliaire)** (gall)stone; **~ (rénal)** (kidney) stone; **d'après mes ~s** by my reckoning

calculateur [kalkylatœr] nm, **calculatrice** [kalkylatris] nf calculator

calculer [kalkyle] vt to calculate, work out, reckon; (combiner) to calculate; **~ qch de tête** to work sth out in one's head

calculette [kalkylɛt] nf (pocket) calculator

cale [kal] nf (de bateau) hold; (en bois) wedge, chock; **~ sèche** ou **de radoub** dry dock

calé, e [kale] adj (fam) clever, bright

caleçon [kalsɔ̃] nm (d'homme) boxer shorts; (de femme) leggings; **~ de bain** bathing trunks pl

calembour [kalābur] nm pun

calendrier [kalādrije] nm calendar; (fig) timetable

calepin [kalpɛ̃] nm notebook

caler [kale] vt to wedge, chock up; **~ (son moteur/véhicule)** to stall (one's engine/ vehicle); **se ~ dans un fauteuil** to make o.s. comfortable in an armchair ▷ vi (moteur, véhicule) to stall

calfeutrer [kalføtre] vt to (make) draughtproof (Brit) ou draftproof (US); **se calfeutrer** vi to make o.s. snug and comfortable

calibre [kalibr] nm (d'un fruit) grade; (d'une arme) bore, calibre (Brit), caliber (US); (fig) calibre, calibre

califourchon [kalifurʃɔ̃]: **à ~** adv astride; **à ~ sur** astride, straddling

câlin, e [kalɛ̃, -in] adj cuddly, cuddlesome; (regard, voix) tender

câliner [kaline] vt to fondle, cuddle

calmant [kalmā] nm tranquillizer, sedative; (contre la douleur) painkiller

calme [kalm] adj calm, quiet ▷ nm calm(ness), quietness; **sans perdre son ~** without losing one's cool ou calmness; **~ plat** (Navig) dead calm

calmer [kalme] vt to calm (down); (douleur, inquiétude) to ease, soothe; **se calmer** vi to calm down

calomnie [kalɔmni] nf slander; (écrite) libel

calomnier [kalɔmnje] vt to slander; to libel

calorie [kalɔri] nf calorie

calotte [kalɔt] nf (coiffure) skullcap; (gifle) slap; **la ~** (péj: clergé) the cloth, the clergy; **~ glaciaire** icecap

calquer [kalke] vt to trace; (fig) to copy exactly

calvaire [kalvɛr] nm (croix) wayside cross, calvary; (souffrances) suffering, martyrdom

calvitie [kalvisi] nf baldness

camarade [kamarad] nm/f friend, pal; (Pol) comrade

camaraderie [kamaradri] nf friendship

Cambodge [kābɔdʒ] nm: **le ~** Cambodia

cambouis [kābwi] nm dirty oil ou grease

cambrer [kābre] vt to arch; **se cambrer** vi to arch one's back; **~ la taille** ou **les reins** to arch one's back

cambriolage [kābrijolaʒ] nm burglary

cambrioler [kābrijole] vt to burgle (Brit), burglarize (US)

cambrioleur, -euse [kābrijolœr, -øz] nm/f burglar

camelote [kamlɔt] (fam) nf rubbish, trash, junk

caméra [kamera] nf (Ciné, TV) camera; (d'amateur) cine-camera

Cameroun [kamrun] nm: **le ~** Cameroon

caméscope® [kameskɔp] nm camcorder

camion [kamjɔ̃] nm lorry (Brit), truck; (plus petit, fermé) van; (charge): **~ de sable/cailloux** lorry-load (Brit) ou truck-load of sand/stones; **~ de dépannage** breakdown (Brit) ou tow (US) truck

camion-citerne (pl **camions-citernes**) [kamjɔ̃sitɛrn] nm tanker

camionnette [kamjonɛt] nf (small) van

camionneur [kamjonœr] nm (entrepreneur) haulage contractor (Brit), trucker (US); (chauffeur) lorry (Brit) ou truck driver; van driver

camisole [kamizɔl] nf: **~ (de force)** straitjacket

camomille [kamɔmij] nf camomile; (boisson) camomile tea

camoufler [kamufle] vt to camouflage; (fig) to conceal, cover up

camp [kā] nm camp; (fig) side; **~ de nudistes/ vacances** nudist/holiday camp; **~ de concentration** concentration camp

campagnard, e [kāpaɲar, -ard] adj country cpd ▷ nm/f countryman/woman

campagne [kāpaɲ] nf country, countryside; (Mil, Pol, Comm) campaign; **en ~** (Mil) in the field; **à la ~** in/to the country; **faire ~ pour** to campaign for; **~ électorale** election campaign; **~ de publicité** advertising campaign

camper [kāpe] vi to camp ▷ vt (chapeau etc) to pull ou put on firmly; (dessin) to sketch; **se ~ devant** to plant o.s. in front of

campeur, -euse [kāpœr, -øz] nm/f camper

camping [kāpiŋ] nm camping; (terrain de) **~** campsite, camping site; **faire du ~** to go camping; **faire du ~ sauvage** to camp rough

camping-car [kāpiŋkar] nm camper, motorhome (US)

camping-gaz® [kāpiŋgaz] nm inv camp(ing) stove

Canada [kanada] nm: **le ~** Canada

canadien, ne [kanadjɛ̃, -ɛn] adj Canadian ▷ nm/f: **C~, ne** Canadian ▷ nf (veste) fur-lined jacket

canaille [kanaj] nf (péj) scoundrel; (populace) riff-raff ▷ adj raffish, rakish

canal, -aux [kanal, -o] nm canal; (naturel, TV) channel; (Admin): **par le ~ de** through (the medium of), via; **~ de distribution/télévision** distribution/television channel; **~ de Panama/Suez** Panama/Suez Canal

canalisation [kanalizasjɔ̃] nf (tuyau) pipe

canaliser [kanalize] vt to canalize; (fig) to channel

canapé [kanape] nm settee, sofa; (Culin) canapé, open sandwich

canard [kanaʀ] nm duck; (fam: journal) rag

canari [kanaʀi] nm canary

cancans [kɑ̃kɑ̃] nmpl (malicious) gossip sg

cancer [kɑ̃sɛʀ] nm cancer; (signe): **le C~** Cancer, the Crab; **être du C~** to be Cancer; **il a un ~** he has cancer

cancre [kɑ̃kʀ] nm dunce

candeur [kɑ̃dœʀ] nf ingenuousness

candidat, e [kɑ̃dida, -at] nm/f candidate; (à un poste) applicant, candidate

candidature [kɑ̃didatyʀ] nf (Pol) candidature; (à poste) application; **poser sa ~** to submit an application, apply; **poser sa ~ à un poste** to apply for a job; **~ spontanée** unsolicited job application

candide [kɑ̃did] adj ingenuous, guileless, naïve

cane [kan] nf (female) duck

caneton [kantɔ̃] nm duckling

canette [kanɛt] nf (de bière) (flip-top) bottle; (de machine à coudre) spool

canevas [kanva] nm (Couture) canvas (for tapestry work); (fig) framework, structure

caniche [kaniʃ] nm poodle

canicule [kanikyl] nf scorching heat; midsummer heat, dog days pl

canif [kanif] nm penknife, pocket knife

canin, e [kanɛ̃, -in] adj canine ▷ nf canine (tooth), eye tooth

caniveau, x [kanivo] nm gutter

canne [kan] nf (walking) stick; **~ à pêche** fishing rod; **~ à sucre** sugar cane; **les ~s blanches** (les aveugles) the blind

cannelle [kanɛl] nf cinnamon

canoë [kanɔe] nm canoe; (sport) canoeing; **~ (kayak)** kayak

canon [kanɔ̃] nm (arme) gun; (Hist) cannon; (d'une arme: tube) barrel; (fig) model; (Mus) canon ▷ adj: **droit ~** canon law; **~ rayé** rifled barrel

canot [kano] nm boat, ding(h)y; **~ pneumatique** rubber ou inflatable ding(h)y; **~ de sauvetage** lifeboat

canotier [kanɔtje] nm boater

cantatrice [kɑ̃tatʀis] nf (opera) singer

cantine [kɑ̃tin] nf canteen; (réfectoire d'école) dining hall

cantique [kɑ̃tik] nm hymn

canton [kɑ̃tɔ̃] nm district (consisting of several communes); see note; (en Suisse) canton

● **CANTON**
●
● A French canton is the administrative
● division represented by a councillor in
● the "Conseil général". It comprises a
● number of "communes" and is, in turn,
● a subdivision of an "arrondissement".
● In Switzerland the cantons are the 23
● autonomous political divisions which
● make up the Swiss confederation.

cantonade [kɑ̃tɔnad]: **à la ~** adv to everyone in general; (crier) from the rooftops

cantonner [kɑ̃tɔne] vt (Mil) to billet (Brit), quarter; to station; **se ~ dans** to confine o.s. to

cantonnier [kɑ̃tɔnje] nm roadmender

canular [kanylaʀ] nm hoax

caoutchouc [kautʃu] nm rubber; **~ mousse** foam rubber; **en ~** rubber cpd

CAP sigle m (= Certificat d'aptitude professionnelle) vocational training certificate taken at secondary school

cap [kap] nm (Géo) cape; (promontoire) headland; (fig) hurdle; (tournant) watershed; (Navig): **changer de ~** to change course; **mettre le ~ sur** to head ou steer for; **doubler** ou **passer le ~** (fig) to get over the worst; **Le C~** Cape Town; **le ~ de Bonne Espérance** the Cape of Good Hope; **le ~ Horn** Cape Horn; **les îles du C~ Vert** (aussi: **le C~-Vert**) the Cape Verde Islands

capable [kapabl] adj able, capable; **~ de qch/faire** capable of sth/doing; **il est ~ d'oublier** he could easily forget; **spectacle ~ d'intéresser** show likely to be of interest

capacité [kapasite] nf (compétence) ability; (Jur, Inform, d'un récipient) capacity; **~ (en droit)** basic legal qualification

cape [kap] nf cape, cloak; **rire sous ~** to laugh up one's sleeve

CAPES [kapɛs] sigle m (= Certificat d'aptitude au professorat de l'enseignement du second degré) secondary teaching diploma; see note

● **CAPES**
●
● The French CAPES ("certificat d'aptitude
● au professorat de l'enseignement du
● second degré") is a competitive
● examination sat by prospective
● secondary school teachers after the
● "licence". Successful candidates become
● fully qualified teachers ("professeurs
● certifiés").

capillaire [kapilɛʀ] adj (soins, lotion) hair cpd; (vaisseau etc) capillary; **artiste ~** hair artist ou designer

capitaine [kapitɛn] nm captain; **~ des pompiers** fire chief (Brit), fire marshal (US); **~ au long cours** master mariner

capital, e, -aux [kapital, -o] *adj* (*œuvre*) major; (*question, rôle*) fundamental; (*Jur*) capital ▷ *nm* capital; (*fig*) stock; asset ▷ *nf* (*ville*) capital; (*lettre*) capital (letter); **d'une importance ~e** of capital importance; **capitaux** *nmpl* (*fonds*) capital *sg*, money *sg*; **les sept péchés capitaux** the seven deadly sins; **peine ~e** capital punishment; **~ (social)** authorized capital; **~ d'exploitation** working capital
capitalisme [kapitalism] *nm* capitalism
capitaliste [kapitalist] *adj, nm/f* capitalist
capitonné, e [kapitɔne] *adj* padded
caporal, -aux [kapɔral, -o] *nm* lance corporal
capot [kapo] *nm* (*Auto*) bonnet (*Brit*), hood (*US*)
capote [kapɔt] *nf* (*de voiture*) hood (*Brit*), top (*US*); (*de soldat*) greatcoat; **~ (anglaise)** (*fam*) rubber, condom
capoter [kapɔte] *vi* to overturn; (*négociations*) to founder
câpre [kɑpr] *nf* caper
caprice [kapris] *nm* whim, caprice; passing fancy; **caprices** *nmpl* (*de la mode etc*) vagaries; **faire un ~** to throw a tantrum; **faire des ~s** to be temperamental
capricieux, -euse [kaprisjø, -øz] *adj* (*fantasque*) capricious; whimsical; (*enfant*) temperamental
Capricorne [kaprikɔrn] *nm*: **le ~** Capricorn, the Goat; **être du ~** to be Capricorn
capsule [kapsyl] *nf* (*de bouteille*) cap; (*amorce*) primer; cap; (*Bot etc, spatiale*) capsule
capter [kapte] *vt* (*ondes radio*) to pick up; (*eau*) to harness; (*fig*) to win, capture
captivant, e [kaptivã, -ãt] *adj* captivating
captivité [kaptivite] *nf* captivity; **en ~** in captivity
capture [kaptyr] *nf* (*action*) capture, catching; **~ d'écran** (*Inform*) screenshot
capturer [kaptyre] *vt* to capture, catch
capuche [kapyʃ] *nf* hood
capuchon [kapyʃɔ̃] *nm* hood; (*de stylo*) cap, top
capucine [kapysin] *nf* (*Bot*) nasturtium
caquet [kakɛ] *nm*: **rabattre le ~ à qn** to bring sb down a peg or two
caqueter [kakte] *vi* (*poule*) to cackle; (*fig*) to prattle
car [kar] *nm* coach (*Brit*), bus ▷ *conj* because, for; **~ de police** police van; **~ de reportage** broadcasting *ou* radio van
carabine [karabin] *nf* carbine, rifle; **~ à air comprimé** airgun
caractère [karaktɛr] *nm* (*gén*) character; **en ~s gras** in bold type; **en petits ~s** in small print; **en ~s d'imprimerie** in block capitals; **avoir du ~** to have character; **avoir bon/mauvais ~** to be good-/ill-natured *ou* tempered; **~ de remplacement** wild card (*Inform*); **~s/seconde (cps)** characters per second (cps)
caractériel, le [karakterjɛl] *adj* (*enfant*) (emotionally) disturbed ▷ *nm/f* problem child; **troubles ~s** emotional problems

caractérisé, e [karakterize] *adj*: **c'est une grippe/de l'insubordination ~e** it is a clear-cut) case of flu/insubordination
caractériser [karakterize] *vt* to characterize; **se ~ par** to be characterized *ou* distinguished by
caractéristique [karakteristik] *adj, nf* characteristic
carafe [karaf] *nf* decanter; (*pour eau, vin ordinaire*) carafe
caraïbe [karaib] *adj* Caribbean; **les Caraïbes** *nfpl* the Caribbean (Islands); **la mer des C~s** the Caribbean Sea
carambolage [karɑ̃bɔlaʒ] *nm* multiple crash, pileup
caramel [karamɛl] *nm* (*bonbon*) caramel, toffee; (*substance*) caramel
carapace [karapas] *nf* shell
caravane [karavan] *nf* caravan
caravaning [karavaniŋ] *nm* caravanning; (*emplacement*) caravan site
carbone [karbɔn] *nm* carbon; (*feuille*) carbon, sheet of carbon paper; (*double*) carbon (copy)
carbonique [karbɔnik] *adj*: **gaz ~** carbon dioxide; **neige ~** dry ice
carbonisé, e [karbɔnize] *adj* charred; **mourir ~** to be burned to death
carburant [karbyrã] *nm* (*motor*) fuel
carburateur [karbyratœr] *nm* carburettor
carcan [karkɑ̃] *nm* (*fig*) yoke, shackles *pl*
carcasse [karkas] *nf* carcass; (*de véhicule etc*) shell
cardiaque [kardjak] *adj* cardiac, heart *cpd* ▷ *nm/f* heart patient; **être ~** to have a heart condition
cardigan [kardigã] *nm* cardigan
cardiologue [kardjɔlɔg] *nm/f* cardiologist, heart specialist
carême [karɛm] *nm*: **le C~** Lent
carence [karɑ̃s] *nf* incompetence, inadequacy; (*manque*) deficiency; **~ vitaminique** vitamin deficiency
caresse [karɛs] *nf* caress
caresser [karese] *vt* to caress; (*animal*) to stroke, fondle; (*fig: projet, espoir*) to toy with
cargaison [kargɛzɔ̃] *nf* cargo, freight
cargo [kargo] *nm* cargo boat, freighter; **~ mixte** cargo and passenger ship
caricature [karikatyr] *nf* caricature; (*politique etc*) (satirical) cartoon
carie [kari] *nf*: **la ~ (dentaire)** tooth decay; **une ~** a bad tooth
carillon [karijɔ̃] *nm* (*d'église*) bells *pl*; (*de pendule*) chimes *pl*; (*de porte*): **~ (électrique)** (electric) door chime *ou* bell
caritatif, -ive [karitatif, -iv] *adj* charitable
carnassier, -ière [karnasje, -jɛr] *adj* carnivorous ▷ *nm* carnivore
carnaval [karnaval] *nm* carnival
carnet [karnɛ] *nm* (*calepin*) notebook; (*de tickets, timbres etc*) book; (*d'école*) school report; (*journal intime*) diary; **~ d'adresses** address

book; **~ de chèques** cheque book (Brit), checkbook (US); **~ de commandes** order book; **~ de notes** (Scol) (school) report; **~ à souches** counterfoil book

carotte [kaʀɔt] nf (aussi fig) carrot

carpette [kaʀpɛt] nf rug

carré, e [kaʀe] adj square; (fig: franc) straightforward ▷ nm (de terrain, jardin) patch, plot; (Navig: salle) wardroom; (Math) square; **~ blanc** (TV) "adults only" symbol; (Cartes): **~ d'as/de rois** four aces/kings; **élever un nombre au ~** to square a number; **mètre/ kilomètre ~** square metre/kilometre; **~ de soie** silk headsquare ou headscarf; **~ d'agneau** loin of lamb

carreau, x [kaʀo] nm (en faïence etc) (floor) tile; (au mur) (wall) tile; (window) pane; (motif) check, square; (Cartes: couleur) diamonds pl; (: carte) diamond; **tissu à ~x** checked fabric; **papier à ~x** squared paper

carrefour [kaʀfuʀ] nm crossroads sg

carrelage [kaʀlaʒ] nm tiling; (sol) (tiled) floor

carrelet [kaʀlɛ] nm (poisson) plaice

carrément [kaʀemɑ̃] adv (franchement) straight out, bluntly; (sans détours, sans hésiter) straight; (nettement) definitely; (intensif) completely; **c'est ~ impossible** it's completely impossible; **il l'a ~ mis à la porte** he threw him straight out

carrière [kaʀjɛʀ] nf (de roches) quarry; (métier) career; **militaire de ~** professional soldier; **faire ~ dans** to make one's career in

carrossable [kaʀɔsabl] adj suitable for (motor) vehicles

carrosse [kaʀɔs] nm (horse-drawn) coach

carrosserie [kaʀɔsʀi] nf body, bodywork no pl (Brit); (activité, commerce) coachwork (Brit), (car) body manufacturing; **atelier de ~** (pour réparations) body shop, panel beaters' (yard) (Brit)

carrure [kaʀyʀ] nf build; (fig) stature, calibre

cartable [kaʀtabl] nm (d'écolier) satchel, (school)bag

carte [kaʀt] nf (de géographie) map; (marine, du ciel) chart; (de fichier, d'abonnement etc, à jouer) card; (au restaurant) menu; (aussi: **~ postale**) (post)card; (aussi: **~ de visite**) (visiting) card; **avoir/donner ~ blanche** to have/give carte blanche ou a free hand; **tirer les ~s à qn** to read sb's cards; **jouer aux ~s** to play cards; **jouer ~ sur table** (fig) to put one's cards on the table; **à la ~** (au restaurant) à la carte; **~ à circuit imprimé** printed circuit; **~ à puce** smartcard, chip and PIN card; **~ bancaire** cash card; **C~ Bleue®** debit card; **~ de crédit** credit card; **~ de fidélité** loyalty card; **la ~ des vins** the wine list; **~ d'état-major** ≈ Ordnance (Brit) ou Geological (US) Survey map; **~ d'identité** identity card; **la ~ grise** (Auto) ≈ (the) car registration document; **~ jeune** young person's railcard; **~ mémoire** (d'appareil photo numérique) memory card; **~**

perforée punch(ed) card; **~ routière** road map; **~ de séjour** residence permit; **~ SIM** SIM card; (: de la boîte de vitesses) casing; **la ~ verte** (Auto) the green card

carter [kaʀtɛʀ] nm (Auto: d'huile) sump (Brit), oil pan (US); (: de la boîte de vitesses) casing; (de bicyclette) chain guard

carton [kaʀtɔ̃] nm (matériau) cardboard; (boîte) (cardboard) box; (d'invitation) invitation card; (Art) sketch; cartoon; **en ~** cardboard cpd; **faire un ~** (au tir) to have a go at the rifle range; to score a hit; **~ (à dessin)** portfolio

carton-pâte [kaʀtɔ̃pat] nm pasteboard; **de ~** (fig) cardboard cpd

cartouche [kaʀtuʃ] nf cartridge; (de cigarettes) carton

cas [kɑ] nm case; **faire peu de ~/grand ~ de** to attach little/great importance to; **ne faire aucun ~ de** to take no notice of; **le ~ échéant** if need be; **en aucun ~** on no account, under no circumstances (whatsoever); **au ~ où** in case; **dans ce ~** in that case; **en ~ de** in case of, in the event of; **en ~ de besoin** if need be; **en ~ d'urgence** in an emergency; **en ce ~** in that case; **en tout ~** in any case, at any rate; **~ de conscience** matter of conscience; **~ de force majeure** case of absolute necessity; (Assurances) act of God; **~ limite** borderline case; **~ social** social problem

casanier, -ière [kazanje, -jɛʀ] adj stay-at-home

cascade [kaskad] nf waterfall, cascade; (fig) stream, torrent

cascadeur, -euse [kaskadœʀ, -øz] nm/f stuntman/girl

case [kɑz] nf (hutte) hut; (compartiment) compartment; (pour le courrier) pigeonhole; (d'échiquier) square; (sur un formulaire, de mots croisés) box

caser [kɑze] (fam) vt (mettre) to put; (loger) to put up; (péj) to find a job for; to marry off; **se caser** vi (se marier) to settle down; (trouver un emploi) to find a (steady) job

caserne [kazɛʀn] nf barracks

cash [kaʃ] adv: **payer ~** to pay cash down

casier [kazje] nm (à journaux etc) rack; (de bureau) filing cabinet; (: à cases) set of pigeonholes; (case) compartment; (pour courrier) pigeonhole; (: à clef) locker; (Pêche) lobster pot; **~ à bouteilles** bottle rack; **~ judiciaire** police record

casino [kazino] nm casino

casque [kask] nm helmet; (chez le coiffeur) (hair-)dryer; (pour audition) (head-)phones pl, headset; **les C~s bleus** the UN peacekeeping force

casquette [kaskɛt] nf cap

cassant, e [kasɑ̃, -ɑ̃t] adj brittle; (fig) brusque, abrupt

cassation [kasasjɔ̃] nf: **se pourvoir en ~** to lodge an appeal; **recours en ~** appeal to the Supreme Court

casse [kas] nf (pour voitures): **mettre à la ~** to scrap, send to the breakers (Brit); (dégâts): **il y a eu de la ~** there were a lot of breakages; (Typo): **haut/bas de ~** upper/lower case

casse-cou [kasku] adj inv daredevil, reckless; **crier ~ à qn** to warn sb (against a risky undertaking)

casse-croûte [kaskrut] nm inv snack

casse-noisettes [kasnwazet], **casse-noix** [kasnwa] nm inv nutcrackers pl

casse-pieds [kaspje] adj, nm/f inv (fam): **il est ~, c'est un ~** he's a pain (in the neck)

casser [kase] vt to break; (Admin: gradé) to demote; (Jur) to quash; (Comm): **~ les prix** to slash prices; **se casser** vi to break; (fam) to go, leave ▷ vt: **~ les pieds à qn** (fam: irriter) to get on sb's nerves; **se ~ la jambe/une jambe** to break one's leg/a leg; **se ~ la tête** (fam) to go to a lot of trouble; **à tout ~** fantastic, brilliant; **se ~ net** to break clean off

casserole [kasrɔl] nf saucepan; **à la ~** (Culin) braised

casse-tête [kastɛt] nm inv (fig) brain teaser; (difficultés) headache (fig)

cassette [kaset] nf (bande magnétique) cassette; (coffret) casket; **~ numérique** digital compact cassette; **~ vidéo** video

casseur [kasœr] nm hooligan; rioter

cassis [kasis] nm blackcurrant; (de la route) dip, bump

cassoulet [kasule] nm sausage and bean hotpot

cassure [kasyr] nf break, crack

castor [kastɔr] nm beaver

castrer [kastre] vt (mâle) to castrate; (femelle) to spay; (cheval) to geld; (chat, chien) to doctor (Brit), fix (US)

catalogue [katalɔg] nm catalogue

cataloguer [kataloge] vt to catalogue, list; (péj) to put a label on

catalyseur [katalizœr] nm catalyst

catalytique [katalitik] adj catalytic; **pot ~** catalytic converter

catastrophe [katastrɔf] nf catastrophe, disaster; **atterrir en ~** to make an emergency landing; **partir en ~** to rush away

catch [katʃ] nm (all-in) wrestling

catéchisme [kateʃism] nm catechism

catégorie [kategɔri] nf category; (Boucherie): **morceaux de première/deuxième ~** prime/ second cuts

catégorique [kategɔrik] adj categorical

cathédrale [katedral] nf cathedral

catholique [katɔlik] adj, nm/f (Roman) Catholic; **pas très ~** a bit shady ou fishy

catimini [katimini]: **en ~** adv on the sly, on the quiet

cauchemar [koʃmar] nm nightmare

cause [koz] nf cause; (Jur) lawsuit, case; brief; **faire ~ commune avec qn** to take sides with sb; **être ~ de** to be the cause of; **à ~ de** because of, owing to; **pour ~ de** on account of; owing to; **(et) pour ~** and for (a very) good reason; **être en ~** (intérêts) to be at stake; (personne) to

be involved; (qualité) to be in question; **mettre en ~** to implicate; to call into question; **remettre en ~** to challenge, call into question; **c'est hors de ~** it's out of the question; **en tout état de ~** in any case

causer [koze] vt to cause ▷ vi to chat, talk

causerie [kozri] nf talk

causette [kozet] nf: **faire ou un brin de ~** to have a chat

caution [kosjɔ̃] nf guarantee, security; deposit; (Jur) bail (bond); (fig) backing, support; **payer la ~ de qn** to stand bail for sb; **se porter ~ pour qn** to stand security for sb; **libéré sous ~** released on bail; **sujet à ~** unconfirmed

cautionner [kosjone] vt to guarantee; (soutenir) to support

cavalcade [kavalkad] nf (fig) stampede

cavalier, -ière [kavalje, -jɛr] adj (désinvolte) offhand ▷ nm/f rider; (au bal) partner ▷ nm (Échecs) knight; **faire ~ seul** to go it alone; **allée ou piste cavalière** riding path

cave [kav] nf cellar; (cabaret) (cellar) nightclub ▷ adj: **yeux ~s** sunken eyes; **joues ~s** hollow cheeks

caveau, x [kavo] nm vault

caverne [kavɛrn] nf cave

CCP sigle m = **compte chèque postal**

CD sigle m (= chemin départemental) secondary road, ≈ B road (Brit); (= compact disc) CD; (= comité directeur) steering committee

CDI sigle m (= Centre de documentation et d'information) school library; (= contrat à durée indéterminée) permanent ou open-ended contract

CD-ROM sigle m inv (= Compact Disc Read Only Memory) CD-Rom

CE sigle f (= Communauté européenne) EC; (Comm) = **caisse d'épargne** ▷ sigle m (Industrie) = **comité d'entreprise**; (Scol) = **cours élémentaire**

 MOT-CLÉ

ce, cette [sə, sɛt] (devant nm **cet** + voyelle ou h aspiré) (pl **ces**) adj dém (proximité) this; these pl; (non-proximité) that; those pl; **cette maison(-ci/là)** this/that house; **cette nuit** (qui vient) tonight; (passée) last night
▷ pron 1: **c'est** it's ou it is; **c'est petit/grand/un livre** it's ou it is small/big/a book; **c'est un peintre** he's ou he is a painter; **ce sont des peintres** they're ou they are painters; **c'est le facteur** etc (à la porte) it's the postman etc; **qui est-ce?** who is it?; (en désignant) who is he/she?; **qu'est-ce?** what is it?; **c'est toi qui lui as parlé** it was you who spoke to him
2: **c'est que: c'est qu'il est lent/qu'il n'a pas faim** the fact is, he's slow/he's not hungry
3 (expressions): **c'est ça** (correct) that's it, that's right; **c'est toi qui le dis!** that's what YOU say!; voir aussi **c'est-à-dire** voir **-ci**; **est-ce que**; **n'est-ce pas**

4: ce qui, ce que what; **ce qui me plaît, c'est sa franchise** what I like about him *ou* her is his *ou* her frankness; *(chose qui)*: **il est bête, ce qui me chagrine** he's stupid, which saddens me; **tout ce qui bouge** everything that *ou* which moves; **tout ce que je sais** all I know; **ce dont j'ai parlé** what I talked about; **ce que c'est grand!** it's so big!

ceci [səsi] *pron* this

cécité [sesite] *nf* blindness

céder [sede] *vt* to give up ▷ *vi (pont, barrage)* to give way; *(personne)* to give in; **~ à** to yield to, give in to

cédérom [sederɔm] *nm* CD-ROM

CEDEX [sedɛks] *sigle m (= courrier d'entreprise à distribution exceptionnelle)* accelerated postal service for bulk users

cédille [sedij] *nf* cedilla

cèdre [sɛdʀ] *nm* cedar

CEI *sigle f (= Communauté des États indépendants)* CIS

ceinture [sɛtyʀ] *nf* belt; *(taille)* waist; *(fig)* ring; belt; circle; **~ de sauvetage** lifebelt *(Brit)*, life preserver *(US)*; **~ de sécurité** safety *ou* seat belt; **~ (de sécurité) à enrouleur** inertia reel seat belt; **~ verte** green belt

cela [s(ə)la] *pron* that; *(comme sujet indéfini)* it; **~ m'étonne que** it surprises me that; **quand/où ~?** when/where (was that)?

célèbre [selɛbʀ] *adj* famous

célébrer [selebʀe] *vt* to celebrate; *(louer)* to extol

céleri [sɛlʀi] *nm*: **~(-rave)** celeriac; **~ (en branche)** celery

célibat [seliba] *nm* celibacy, bachelor/spinsterhood

célibataire [selibatɛʀ] *adj* single, unmarried ▷ *nm/f* bachelor/unmarried *ou* single woman; **mère ~** single *ou* unmarried mother

celle, celles [sɛl] *pron voir* **celui**

cellier [selje] *nm* storeroom

cellule [selyl] *nf (gén)* cell; **~ (photo-électrique)** electronic eye; **~ souche** stem cell

cellulite [selylit] *nf* cellulite

🔑 MOT-CLÉ

celui, celle [səlɥi, sɛl] *(mpl* **ceux**, *fpl* **celles**) *pron* **1**: **celui-ci/là, celle-ci/là** this one/that one; **ceux-ci, celles-ci** these (ones); **ceux-là, celles-là** those (ones); **celui de mon frère** my brother's; **celui du salon/du dessous** the one in *(ou* from) the lounge/below
2: **celui qui bouge** the one which *ou* that moves; *(personne)* the one who moves; **celui que je vois** the one (which *ou* that) I see; *(personne)* the one (whom) I see; **celui dont je parle** the one I'm talking about
3 *(valeur indéfinie)*: **celui qui veut** whoever wants

cendre [sãdʀ] *nf* ash; **~s** *(d'un foyer)* ash(es), cinders; *(volcaniques)* ash *sg*; *(d'un défunt)* ashes; **sous la ~** *(Culin)* in (the) embers

cendrier [sãdʀije] *nm* ashtray

cène [sɛn] *nf*: **la ~** (Holy) Communion; *(Art)* the Last Supper

censé, e [sãse] *adj*: **être ~ faire** to be supposed to do

censeur [sãsœʀ] *nm (Scol)* deputy head *(Brit)*, vice-principal *(US)*; *(Ciné, Pol)* censor

censure [sãsyʀ] *nf* censorship

censurer [sãsyʀe] *vt (Ciné, Presse)* to censor; *(Pol)* to censure

cent [sã] *num* a hundred, one hundred; **pour ~ (%)** per cent (%); **faire les ~ pas** to pace up and down ▷ *nm (US, Canada, partie de l'euro etc)* cent

centaine [sãtɛn] *nf*: **une ~ (de)** about a hundred, a hundred or so; *(Comm)* a hundred; **plusieurs ~s (de)** several hundred; **des ~s (de)** hundreds (of)

centenaire [sãtnɛʀ] *adj* hundred-year-old ▷ *nm/f* centenarian ▷ *nm (anniversaire)* centenary; *(monnaie)* cent

centième [sãtjɛm] *num* hundredth

centigrade [sãtigʀad] *nm* centigrade

centilitre [sãtilitʀ] *nm* centilitre *(Brit)*, centiliter *(US)*

centime [sãtim] *nm* centime; **~ d'euro** euro cent

centimètre [sãtimɛtʀ] *nm* centimetre *(Brit)*, centimeter *(US)*; *(ruban)* tape measure, measuring tape

central, e, -aux [sãtʀal, -o] *adj* central ▷ *nm*: **~ (téléphonique)** (telephone) exchange ▷ *nf* power station; **~e d'achat** *(Comm)* central buying service; **~e électrique/nucléaire** electric/nuclear power station; **~e syndicale** group of affiliated trade unions

centre [sãtʀ] *nm* centre *(Brit)*, center *(US)*; **~ commercial/sportif/culturel** shopping/sports/arts centre; **~ aéré** outdoor centre; **~ d'appels** call centre; **~ d'apprentissage** training college; **~ d'attraction** centre of attraction; **~ de gravité** centre of gravity; **~ de loisirs** leisure centre; **~ d'enfouissement des déchets** landfill site; **~ hospitalier** hospital complex; **~ de tri** *(Postes)* sorting office; **~s nerveux** *(Anat)* nerve centres

centre-ville *(pl* **centres-villes)** [sãtʀəvil] *nm* town centre *(Brit)* ou center *(US)*, downtown (area) *(US)*

centuple [sãtypl] *nm*: **le ~ de qch** a hundred times sth; **au ~** a hundredfold

cep [sɛp] *nm (vine)* stock

cèpe [sɛp] *nm (edible)* boletus

cependant [s(ə)pãdã] *adv* however, nevertheless

céramique [seʀamik] *adj* ceramic ▷ *nf* ceramic; *(art)* ceramics *sg*

cercle [sɛʀkl] *nm* circle; *(objet)* band, hoop; **décrire un ~** *(avion)* to circle; *(projectile)* to describe a circle; **~ d'amis** circle of friends; **~ de famille** family circle; **~ vicieux** vicious circle

cercueil [sɛʀkœj] nm coffin

céréale [seʀeal] nf cereal

cérémonie [seʀemɔni] nf ceremony; **sans ~** (inviter, manger) informally; **cérémonies** nfpl (péj) fuss sg, to-do sg

cerf [sɛʀ] nm stag

cerfeuil [sɛʀfœj] nm chervil

cerf-volant [sɛʀvɔlɑ̃] nm kite; **jouer au ~** to fly a kite

cerise [s(ə)ʀiz] nf cherry

cerisier [s(ə)ʀizje] nm cherry (tree)

cerner [sɛʀne] vt (Mil etc) to surround; (fig: problème) to delimit, define

cernes [sɛʀn] nfpl (dark) rings, shadows (under the eyes)

certain, e [sɛʀtɛ̃, -ɛn] adj certain; (sûr): **~ (de/ que)** certain ou sure (of/ that); **d'un ~ âge** past one's prime, not so young; **un ~ temps** (quite) some time; **sûr et ~** absolutely certain; **un ~ Georges** someone called Georges; **~s** pron some

certainement [sɛʀtɛnmɑ̃] adv (probablement) most probably ou likely; (bien sûr) certainly, of course

certes [sɛʀt] adv (sans doute) admittedly; (bien sûr) of course; indeed (yes)

certificat [sɛʀtifika] nm certificate; **C~ d'études (primaires)** former school leaving certificate (taken at the end of primary education); **C~ de fin d'études secondaires** school leaving certificate

certifier [sɛʀtifje] vt to certify, guarantee; **~ à qn que** to assure sb that, guarantee to sb that; **~ qch à qn** to guarantee sth to sb

certitude [sɛʀtityd] nf certainty

cerveau, x [sɛʀvo] nm brain; **~ électronique** electronic brain

cervelas [sɛʀvəla] nm saveloy

cervelle [sɛʀvɛl] nf (Anat) brain; (Culin) brain(s); **se creuser la ~** to rack one's brains

CES sigle m (= Collège d'enseignement secondaire) ≈ (junior) secondary school (Brit), ≈ junior high school (US)

ces [se] adj dém voir **ce**

cesse [sɛs]: **sans ~** adv (tout le temps) continually, constantly; (sans interruption) continuously; **il n'avait de ~ que** he would not rest until

cesser [sese] vt to stop ▷ vi to stop, cease; **~ de faire** to stop doing; **faire ~** (bruit, scandale) to put a stop to

cessez-le-feu [seselføf] nm inv ceasefire

c'est-à-dire [sɛtadiʀ] adv that is (to say); (demander de préciser): **~?** what does that mean?; **~ que ...** (en conséquence) which means that ...; (manière d'excuse) well, in fact ...

cet [sɛt] adj dém voir **ce**

ceux [sø] pron voir **celui**

CFC sigle mpl (= chlorofluorocarbures) CFC

CFDT sigle f (= Confédération française démocratique du travail) trade union

CGT sigle f (= Confédération générale du travail) trade union

chacun, e [ʃakœ̃, -yn] pron each; (indéfini) everyone, everybody

chagrin, e [ʃagʀɛ̃, -in] adj morose ▷ nm grief, sorrow; **avoir du ~** to be grieved ou sorrowful

chagriner [ʃagʀine] vt to grieve, distress; (contrarier) to bother, worry

chahut [ʃay] nm uproar

chahuter [ʃayte] vt to rag, bait ▷ vi to make an uproar

chaîne [ʃɛn] nf chain; (Radio, TV: stations) channel; (Inform) string; **chaînes** nfpl (liens, asservissement) fetters, bonds; **travail à la ~** production line work; **réactions en ~** chain reactions; **faire la ~** to form a (human) chain; **~ alimentaire** food chain; **~ compacte** music centre; **~ d'entraide** mutual aid association; **~ (haute-fidélité ou hi-fi)** hi-fi system; **~ (de montage ou de fabrication)** production ou assembly line; **~ (de montagnes)** (mountain) range; **~ de solidarité** solidarity network; **~ (stéréo ou audio)** stereo (system)

chaînette [ʃenɛt] nf (small) chain

chair [ʃɛʀ] nf flesh ▷ adj: (couleur) **~** flesh-coloured; **avoir la ~ de poule** to have goose pimples ou goose flesh; **bien en ~** plump, well-padded; **~ et en os** in the flesh; **~ à saucisse** sausage meat

chaire [ʃɛʀ] nf (d'église) pulpit; (d'université) chair

chaise [ʃɛz] nf chair; **~ de bébé** high chair; **~ électrique** electric chair; **~ longue** deckchair

châle [ʃal] nm shawl

chaleur [ʃalœʀ] nf heat; (fig: d'accueil) warmth; fire, fervour (Brit), fervor (US); heat; **en ~** (Zool) on heat

chaleureux, -euse [ʃalœʀø, -øz] adj warm

chaloupe [ʃalup] nf launch; (de sauvetage) lifeboat

chalumeau, x [ʃalymo] nm blowlamp (Brit), blowtorch

chalutier [ʃalytje] nm trawler; (pêcheur) trawlerman

chamailler [ʃamaje]: **se chamailler** vi to squabble, bicker

chambouler [ʃɑ̃bule] vt to disrupt, turn upside down

chambre [ʃɑ̃bʀ] nf bedroom; (Tech) chamber; (Pol) chamber, house; (Jur) court; (Comm) chamber; federation; **faire ~ à part** to sleep in separate rooms; **stratège/alpiniste en ~** armchair strategist/mountaineer; **~ à un lit/ deux lits** single/twin-bedded room; **~ pour une/deux personne(s)** single/double room; **~ d'accusation** court of criminal appeal; **~ d'agriculture** (CA) body responsible for the agricultural interests of a département; **~ à air**

(de pneu) (inner) tube; **~ d'amis** spare *ou* guest room; **~ de combustion** combustion chamber; **~ de commerce et d'industrie (CCI)** chamber of commerce and industry; **~ à coucher** bedroom; **la C~ des députés** the Chamber of Deputies, ≈ the House (of Commons) *(Brit)*, ≈ the House of Representatives *(US)*; **~ forte** strongroom; **~ froide** *ou* **frigorifique** cold room; **~ à gaz** gas chamber; **~ d'hôte** ≈ bed and breakfast *(in private home)*; **~ des machines** engine-room; **~ des métiers (CM)** *chamber of commerce for trades*; **~ meublée** bedsit(ter) *(Brit)*, furnished room; **~ noire** *(Photo)* dark room

chambrer [ʃɑ̃bʀe] *vt (vin)* to bring to room temperature

chameau, x [ʃamo] *nm* camel

chamois [ʃamwa] *nm* chamois ▷ *adj:* **(couleur) ~** fawn, buff

champ [ʃɑ̃] *nm (aussi Inform)* field; *(Photo: aussi:* **dans le ~)** in the picture; **prendre du ~** to draw back; **laisser le ~ libre à qn** to leave sb a clear field; **~ d'action** sphere of operation(s); **~ de bataille** battlefield; **~ de courses** racecourse; **~ d'honneur** field of honour; **~ de manœuvre** *(Mil)* parade ground; **~ de mines** minefield; **~ de tir** shooting *ou* rifle range; **~ visuel** field of vision

champagne [ʃɑ̃paɲ] *nm* champagne

champêtre [ʃɑ̃pɛtʀ] *adj* country *cpd*, rural

champignon [ʃɑ̃piɲɔ̃] *nm* mushroom; *(terme générique)* fungus; *(fam: accélérateur)* accelerator, gas pedal *(US)*; **~ de couche** *ou* **de Paris** button mushroom; **~ vénéneux** toadstool, poisonous mushroom

champion, ne [ʃɑ̃pjɔ̃, -ɔn] *adj, nm/f* champion

championnat [ʃɑ̃pjɔna] *nm* championship

chance [ʃɑ̃s] *nf:* **la ~** luck; **une ~** a stroke *ou* piece of luck *ou* good fortune; *(occasion)* a lucky break; **chances** *nfpl (probabilités)* chances; **avoir de la ~** to be lucky; **il a des ~s de gagner** he has a chance of winning; **il y a de fortes ~s pour que Paul soit malade** it's highly probable that Paul is ill; **bonne ~!** good luck!; **encore une ~ que tu viennes!** it's lucky you're coming!; **je n'ai pas de ~** I'm out of luck; *(toujours)* I never have any luck; **donner sa ~ à qn** to give sb a chance

chanceler [ʃɑ̃sle] *vi* to totter

chancelier [ʃɑ̃səlje] *nm (allemand)* chancellor; *(d'ambassade)* secretary

chanceux, -euse [ʃɑ̃sø, -øz] *adj* lucky, fortunate

chandail [ʃɑ̃daj] *nm (thick)* jumper *ou* sweater

Chandeleur [ʃɑ̃dlœʀ] *nf:* **la ~** Candlemas

chandelier [ʃɑ̃dəlje] *nm* candlestick; *(à plusieurs branches)* candelabra

chandelle [ʃɑ̃dɛl] *nf (tallow)* candle; *(Tennis):* **faire une ~** to lob; *(Aviat):* **monter en ~** to climb vertically; **tenir la ~** to play gooseberry; **dîner aux ~s** candlelight dinner

change [ʃɑ̃ʒ] *nm (Comm)* exchange; **opérations de ~** (foreign) exchange transactions; **contrôle des ~s** exchange control; **gagner/perdre au ~** to be better/worse off (for it); **donner le ~ à qn** *(fig)* to lead sb up the garden path

changement [ʃɑ̃ʒmɑ̃] *nm* change; **~ de vitesse** *(dispositif)* gears *pl; (action)* gear change

changer [ʃɑ̃ʒe] *vt (modifier)* to change, alter; *(remplacer, Comm, rhabiller)* to change ▷ *vi* to change, alter; **se changer** *vi* to change (o.s.); **~ de** *(remplacer: adresse, nom, voiture etc)* to change one's; **~ de train** to change trains; **~ d'air** to get a change of air; **~ de couleur/direction** to change colour/direction; **~ d'avis, ~ d'idée** to change one's mind; **~ de place avec qn** to change places with sb; **~ de vitesse** *(Auto)* to change gear; **si cela lui chante** *(fam)* if he feels like it *ou* fancies it

chanson [ʃɑ̃sɔ̃] *nf* song

chant [ʃɑ̃] *nm* song; *(art vocal)* singing; *(d'église)* hymn; *(de poème)* canto; *(Tech):* **posé de** *ou* **sur ~** placed edgeways; **~ de Noël** Christmas carol

chantage [ʃɑ̃taʒ] *nm* blackmail; **faire du ~** to use blackmail; **soumettre qn à un ~** to blackmail sb

chanter [ʃɑ̃te] *vt, vi* to sing; **~ juste/faux** to sing in tune/out of tune; **si cela lui chante** *(fam)* if he feels like it *ou* fancies it

chanteur, -euse [ʃɑ̃tœʀ, -øz] *nm/f* singer; **~ de charme** crooner

chantier [ʃɑ̃tje] *nm (building)* site; *(sur une route)* roadworks *pl;* **mettre en ~** to start work on; **~ naval** shipyard

chantilly [ʃɑ̃tiji] *nf voir* **crème**

chantonner [ʃɑ̃tone] *vi, vt* to sing to oneself, hum

chanvre [ʃɑ̃vʀ] *nm* hemp

chaparder [ʃapaʀde] *vt* to pinch

chapeau, x [ʃapo] *nm* hat; *(Presse)* introductory paragraph; **~!** well done!; **~ melon** bowler hat; **~ mou** trilby; **~x de roues** hub caps

chapelet [ʃaplɛ] *nm (Rel)* rosary; *(fig):* **un ~ de** a string of; **dire son ~** to tell one's beads

chapelle [ʃapɛl] *nf* chapel; **~ ardente** chapel of rest

chapelure [ʃaplyʀ] *nf* (dried) breadcrumbs *pl*

chapiteau, x [ʃapito] *nm (Archit)* capital; *(de cirque)* marquee, big top

chapitre [ʃapitʀ] *nm* chapter; *(fig)* subject, matter; **avoir voix au ~** to have a say in the matter

chaque [ʃak] *adj* each, every; *(indéfini)* every

char [ʃaʀ] *nm (à foin etc)* cart, waggon;

(de carnaval) float; ~ (**d'assaut**) tank; ~ **à voile** sand yacht

charabia [ʃaʀabja] nm (péj) gibberish, gobbledygook (Brit)

charade [ʃaʀad] nf riddle; (mimée) charade

charbon [ʃaʀbɔ̃] nm coal; ~ **de bois** charcoal

charcuterie [ʃaʀkytʀi] nf (magasin) pork butcher's shop and delicatessen; (produits) cooked pork meats pl

charcutier, -ière [ʃaʀkytje, -jɛʀ] nm/f pork butcher

chardon [ʃaʀdɔ̃] nm thistle

charge [ʃaʀʒ] nf (fardeau) load; (explosif, Élec, Mil, Jur) charge; (rôle, mission) responsibility; **charges** nfpl (du loyer) service charges; **à la ~ de** (dépendant de) dependant upon, supported by; (aux frais de) chargeable to, payable by; **j'accepte, à ~ de revanche** I accept, provided I can do the same for you (in return) one day; **prendre en ~** to take charge of; (véhicule) to take on; (dépenses) to take care of; **~ utile** (Auto) live load; (Comm) payload; **~s sociales** social security contributions

chargé [ʃaʀʒe] adj (voiture, animal, personne) laden; (fusil, batterie, caméra) loaded; (occupé: emploi du temps, journée) busy, full; (estomac) heavy, full; (langue) furred; (décoration, style) heavy, ornate ▷ nm: ~ **d'affaires** chargé d'affaires; ~ **de cours** lecturer; ~ **de** (responsable de) responsible for

chargement [ʃaʀʒəmɑ̃] nm (action) loading, charging; (objets) load

charger [ʃaʀʒe] vt (voiture, fusil, caméra) to load; (batterie) to charge ▷ vi (Mil etc) to charge; **se ~ de** vt to see to, take care of; ~ **qn de qch/faire qch** to give sb the responsibility for sth/of doing sth; to put sb in charge of sth/doing sth; **se ~ de faire qch** to take it upon o.s. to do sth

chariot [ʃaʀjo] nm trolley; (charrette) waggon; ~ **élévateur** fork-lift truck

charité [ʃaʀite] nf charity; **faire la ~** to give to charity; to do charitable works; **faire la ~ à** to give (something) to; **fête/vente de ~** fête/sale in aid of charity

charmant, e [ʃaʀmɑ̃, -ɑ̃t] adj charming

charme [ʃaʀm] nm charm; **charmes** nmpl (appas) charms; **c'est ce qui en fait le ~** that is its attraction; **faire du ~** to be charming, turn on the charm; **aller ou se porter comme un ~** to be in the pink

charmer [ʃaʀme] vt to charm; **je suis charmé de ...** I'm delighted to ...

charnel, le [ʃaʀnɛl] adj carnal

charnière [ʃaʀnjɛʀ] nf hinge; (fig) turning-point

charnu, e [ʃaʀny] adj fleshy

charpente [ʃaʀpɑ̃t] nf frame(work); (fig) structure, framework; (carrure) build, frame

charpentier [ʃaʀpɑ̃tje] nm carpenter

charpie [ʃaʀpi] nf: **en ~** (fig) in shreds ou ribbons

charrette [ʃaʀɛt] nf cart

charrier [ʃaʀje] vt to carry (along); to cart, carry ▷ vi (fam) to exaggerate

charrue [ʃaʀy] nf plough (Brit), plow (US)

charter [tʃaʀtœʀ] nm (vol) charter flight; (avion) charter plane

chasse [ʃas] nf hunting; (au fusil) shooting; (poursuite) chase; (aussi: ~ **d'eau**) flush; **la ~ est ouverte** the hunting season is open; **la ~ est fermée** it is the close (Brit) ou closed (US) season; **aller à la ~** to go hunting; **prendre en ~, donner la ~ à** to give chase to; **tirer la ~ (d'eau)** to flush the toilet, pull the chain; ~ **aérienne** aerial pursuit; ~ **à courre** hunting; ~ **à l'homme** manhunt; ~ **gardée** private hunting grounds pl; ~ **sous-marine** underwater fishing

chasse-neige [ʃasnɛʒ] nm inv snowplough (Brit), snowplow (US)

chasser [ʃase] vt to hunt; (expulser) to chase away ou out, drive away ou out; (dissiper) to chase ou sweep away; to dispel, drive away

chasseur, -euse [ʃasœʀ, -øz] nm/f hunter ▷ nm (avion) fighter; (domestique) page (boy), messenger (boy); ~ **d'images** roving photographer; ~ **de têtes** (fig) headhunter; ~s **alpins** mountain infantry

châssis [ʃasi] nm (Auto) chassis; (cadre) frame; (de jardin) cold frame

chat¹ [ʃa] nm cat; ~ **sauvage** wildcat

chat² [tʃat] nm (Internet: salon) chat room; (conversation) chat

châtaigne [ʃatɛɲ] nf chestnut

châtaignier [ʃatɛɲe] nm chestnut (tree)

châtain [ʃatɛ̃] adj inv chestnut (brown); (personne) chestnut-haired

château, x [ʃato] nm (forteresse) castle; (résidence royale) palace; (manoir) mansion; ~ **d'eau** water tower; ~ **fort** stronghold, fortified castle; ~ **de sable** sand castle

châtier [ʃatje] vt to punish, castigate; (fig: style) to polish, refine

châtiment [ʃatimɑ̃] nm punishment, castigation; ~ **corporel** corporal punishment

chaton [ʃatɔ̃] nm (Zool) kitten; (Bot) catkin; (de bague) bezel; stone

chatouiller [ʃatuje] vt to tickle; (l'odorat, le palais) to titillate

chatouilleux, -euse [ʃatujø, -øz] adj ticklish; (fig) touchy, over-sensitive

chatoyer [ʃatwaje] vi to shimmer

châtrer [ʃatʀe] vt (mâle) to castrate; (femelle) to spay; (cheval) to geld; (chat, chien) to doctor (Brit), fix (US); (fig) to mutilate

chatte [ʃat] nf (she-)cat

chatter [tʃate] vi (Internet) to chat

chaud, e [ʃo, -od] adj (gén) warm; (très chaud) hot; (fig: félicitations) hearty; (discussion) heated; **il fait ~** it's warm; it's hot; **manger ~** to have something hot to eat; **avoir ~** to be warm; to be hot; **tenir ~** to keep hot; **ça me**

tient – it keeps me warm; **tenir au ~** to keep in a warm place; **rester au ~** to stay in the warm

chaudière [ʃodjɛʀ] *nf* boiler

chaudron [ʃodʀɔ̃] *nm* cauldron

chauffage [ʃofaʒ] *nm* heating; **~ au gaz/à l'électricité/au charbon** gas/electric/solid fuel heating; **~ central** central heating; **~ par le sol** underfloor heating

chauffard [ʃofaʀ] *nm* (*péj*) reckless driver; road hog; (*après un accident*) hit-and-run driver

chauffe-eau [ʃofo] *nm inv* water heater

chauffer [ʃofe] *vt* to heat up, warm up; (*trop chauffer: moteur*) to overheat; **se chauffer** *vi* (*se mettre en train*) to warm up; (*au soleil*) to warm o.s.

chauffeur [ʃofœʀ] *nm* driver; (*privé*) chauffeur; **voiture avec/sans ~** chauffeur-driven/self-drive car; **~ de taxi** taxi driver

chaume [ʃom] *nm* (*du toit*) thatch; (*tiges*) stubble

chaumière [ʃomjɛʀ] *nf* (thatched) cottage

chaussée [ʃose] *nf* road(way); (*digue*) causeway

chausse-pied [ʃospje] *nm* shoe-horn

chausser [ʃose] *vt* (*bottes, skis*) to put on; (*enfant*) to put shoes on; (*soulier*) to fit; **~ du 38/42** to take size 38/42; **~ grand/bien** to be big-/well-fitting; **se chausser** to put one's shoes on

chaussette [ʃosɛt] *nf* sock

chausson [ʃosɔ̃] *nm* slipper; (*de bébé*) bootee; **~ (aux pommes)** (apple) turnover

chaussure [ʃosyʀ] *nf* shoe; (*commerce*): **la ~** the shoe industry *ou* trade; **~s basses** flat shoes; **~s montantes** ankle boots; **~ de ski** ski boots

chauve [ʃov] *adj* bald

chauve-souris (*pl* **chauves-souris**) [ʃovsuʀi] *nf* bat

chauvin, e [ʃovɛ̃, -in] *adj* chauvinistic; jingoistic

chaux [ʃo] *nf* lime; **blanchi à la ~** whitewashed

chavirer [ʃaviʀe] *vi* to capsize, overturn

chef [ʃɛf] *nm* head, leader; (*patron*) boss; (*de cuisine*) chef; **au premier ~** extremely, to the nth degree; **de son propre ~** on his *ou* her own initiative; **général/commandant en ~** general-/commander-in-chief; **~ d'accusation** (*Jur*) charge, count (of indictment); **~ d'atelier** (shop) foreman; **~ de bureau** head clerk; **~ de clinique** senior hospital lecturer; **~ d'entreprise** company head; **~ d'équipe** team leader; **~ d'état** head of state; **~ de famille** head of the family; **~ de file** (*de parti etc*) leader; **~ de gare** station master; **~ d'orchestre** conductor (*Brit*), leader (*US*); **~ de rayon** department(al) supervisor; **~ de service** departmental head

chef-d'œuvre (*pl* **chefs-d'œuvre**) [ʃɛdœvʀ] *nm* masterpiece

chef-lieu (*pl* **chefs-lieux**) [ʃɛfljø] *nm* county town

chemin [ʃəmɛ̃] *nm* path; (*itinéraire, direction, trajet*) way; **en ~, ~ faisant** on the way; **~ de fer** railway (*Brit*), railroad (*US*); **par ~ de fer** by rail; **les ~s de fer** the railways (*Brit*), the railroad (*US*); **~ de terre** dirt track

cheminée [ʃəmine] *nf* chimney; (*à l'intérieur*) chimney piece, fireplace; (*de bateau*) funnel

cheminement [ʃəminmɑ̃] *nm* progress; course

cheminot [ʃəmino] *nm* railwayman (*Brit*), railroad worker (*US*)

chemise [ʃəmiz] *nf* shirt; (*dossier*) folder; **~ de nuit** nightdress

chemisier [ʃəmizje] *nm* blouse

chenal, -aux [ʃənal, -o] *nm* channel

chêne [ʃɛn] *nm* oak (tree); (*bois*) oak

chenil [ʃənil] *nm* kennels *pl*

chenille [ʃənij] *nf* (*Zool*) caterpillar; (*Auto*) caterpillar track; **véhicule à ~s** tracked vehicle, caterpillar

chèque [ʃɛk] *nm* cheque (*Brit*), check (*US*); **faire/toucher un ~** to write/cash a cheque; **par ~** by cheque; **~ barré/sans provision** crossed (*Brit*)/bad cheque; **~ en blanc** blank cheque; **~ au porteur** cheque to bearer; **~ postal** post office cheque; ≈ giro cheque (*Brit*); **~ de voyage** traveller's cheque

chéquier [ʃekje] *nm* cheque book (*Brit*), checkbook (*US*)

cher, -ère [ʃɛʀ] *adj* (*aimé*) dear; (*coûteux*) expensive, dear ▷ *adv*: **coûter/payer ~** to cost/pay a lot ▷ *nf*: **la bonne chère** good food; **cela coûte ~** it's expensive, it costs a lot of money; **mon ~, ma chère** my dear

chercher [ʃɛʀʃe] *vt* to look for; (*gloire etc*) to seek; **~ des ennuis/la bagarre** to be looking for trouble/a fight; **aller ~** to go for, go and fetch; **~ à faire** to try to do

chercheur, -euse [ʃɛʀʃœʀ, -øz] *nm/f* researcher, research worker; **~ de** seeker of; hunter of; **~ d'or** gold digger

chère [ʃɛʀ] *adj f, nf voir* **cher**

chéri, e [ʃeʀi] *adj* beloved, dear; **(mon) ~** darling

chérir [ʃeʀiʀ] *vt* to cherish

cherté [ʃɛʀte] *nf*: **la ~ de la vie** the high cost of living

chétif, -ive [ʃetif, -iv] *adj* puny, stunted

cheval, -aux [ʃəval, -o] *nm* horse; (*Auto*): **~ (vapeur) (CV)** horsepower *no pl*; **50 chevaux (au frein)** 50 brake horsepower, 50 b.h.p.; **10 chevaux (fiscaux)** 10 horsepower (*for tax purposes*); **faire du ~** to ride; **à ~** on horseback; **à ~ sur** astride, straddling; (*fig*) overlapping; **~ d'arçons** vaulting horse; **~ à bascule** rocking horse; **~ de bataille** charger; (*fig*) hobby-horse; **~ de course** race horse; **chevaux de bois** (*des manèges*) wooden (fairground) horses; (*manège*) merry-go-round

chevalet [ʃəvalɛ] nm easel

chevalier [ʃəvalje] nm knight; **~ servant** escort

chevalière [ʃəvaljɛʀ] nf signet ring

chevalin, e [ʃəvalɛ̃, -in] adj of horses, equine; (péj) horsy; **boucherie ~e** horse-meat butcher's

chevaucher [ʃəvoʃe] vi (aussi: **se ~**) to overlap (each other) ▷ vt to be astride, straddle

chevaux [ʃəvo] nmpl voir **cheval**

chevelu, e [ʃəvly] adj with a good head of hair, hairy (péj)

chevelure [ʃəvlyʀ] nf hair no pl

chevet [ʃəvɛ] nm: **au ~ de qn** at sb's bedside; **lampe de ~** bedside lamp

cheveu, x [ʃəvø] nm hair ▷ nmpl (chevelure) hair sg; **avoir les ~x courts/en brosse** to have short hair/a crew cut; **se faire couper les ~x** to get ou have one's hair cut; **tiré par les ~x** (histoire) far-fetched

cheville [ʃəvij] nf (Anat) ankle; (de bois) peg; (pour enfoncer une vis) plug; **être en ~ avec qn** to be in cahoots with sb; **~ ouvrière** (fig) kingpin

chèvre [ʃɛvʀ] nf (she-)goat; **ménager la ~ et le chou** to try to please everyone

chevreau, x [ʃəvʀo] nm kid

chèvrefeuille [ʃɛvʀəfœj] nm honeysuckle

chevreuil [ʃəvʀœj] nm roe deer inv; (Culin) venison

chevronné, e [ʃəvʀɔne] adj seasoned, experienced

⭕ MOT-CLÉ

chez [ʃe] prép **1** (à la demeure de) at; (: direction) to; **chez qn** at/to sb's house ou place; **je suis chez moi** I'm at home; **je rentre chez moi** I'm going home; **allons chez Nathalie** let's go to Nathalie's

2 (+profession) at; (: direction) to; **chez le boulanger/dentiste** at ou to the baker's/dentist's

3 (dans le caractère, l'œuvre de) in; **chez les renards/Racine** in foxes/Racine; **chez ce poète** in this poet's work; **chez les Français** among the French; **chez lui, c'est un devoir** for him, it's a duty

▷ nm inv: **mon chez moi/ton chez toi** etc my/your etc home ou place; **c'est ce que je préfère chez lui** that's what I like best about him

4 (à l'entreprise de): **il travaille chez Renault** he works for Renault, he works at Renault('s)

chez-soi [ʃeswa] nm inv home

chic [ʃik] adj inv chic, smart; (généreux) nice, decent ▷ nm stylishness; **avoir le ~ de** ou **pour** to have the knack of ou for; **de ~** adv off the cuff; **~!** great!, terrific!

chicane [ʃikan] nf (obstacle) zigzag; (querelle) squabble

chicaner [ʃikane] vi (ergoter): **~ sur** to quibble about

chiche [ʃiʃ] adj (mesquin) niggardly, mean; (pauvre) meagre (Brit), meager (US) ▷ excl (en réponse à un défi) you're on!; **tu n'es pas ~ de lui parler!** you wouldn't (dare) speak to her!

chichis [ʃiʃi] (fam) nmpl fuss sg

chicorée [ʃikɔʀe] nf (café) chicory; (salade) endive; **~ frisée** curly endive

chien [ʃjɛ̃] nm dog; (de pistolet) hammer; **temps de ~** rotten weather; **vie de ~** dog's life; **couché en ~ de fusil** curled up; **~ d'aveugle** guide dog; **~ de chasse** gun dog; **~ de garde** guard dog; **~ policier** police dog; **~ de race** pedigree dog; **~ de traîneau** husky

chiendent [ʃjɛ̃dɑ̃] nm couch grass

chien-loup (pl **chiens-loups**) [ʃjɛ̃lu] nm wolfhound

chienne [ʃjɛn] nf (she-)dog, bitch

chier [ʃje] vi (fam!) to crap (!), shit (!); **faire ~ qn** (importuner) to bug sb; (causer des ennuis à) to piss sb around (!); **se faire ~** (s'ennuyer) to be bored rigid

chiffon [ʃifɔ̃] nm (piece of) rag

chiffonner [ʃifɔne] vt to crumple, crease; (tracasser) to concern

chiffre [ʃifʀ] nm (représentant un nombre) figure; numeral; (montant, total) total, sum; (d'un code) code, cipher; **~s romains/arabes** roman/arabic figures ou numerals; **en ~s ronds** in round figures; **écrire un nombre en ~s** to write a number in figures; **~ d'affaires (CA)** turnover; **~ de ventes** sales figures

chiffrer [ʃifʀe] vt (dépense) to put a figure to, assess; (message) to (en)code, cipher ▷ vi: **~ à, se ~ à** to add up to

chignon [ʃiɲɔ̃] nm chignon, bun

Chili [ʃili] nm: **le ~** Chile

chilien, ne [ʃiljɛ̃, -ɛn] adj Chilean ▷ nm/f: **C~, ne** Chilean

chimie [ʃimi] nf chemistry

chimiothérapie [ʃimjɔteʀapi] nf chemotherapy

chimique [ʃimik] adj chemical; **produits ~s** chemicals

chimpanzé [ʃɛ̃pɑ̃ze] nm chimpanzee

Chine [ʃin] nf: **la ~** China; **la ~ libre, la république de ~** the Republic of China, Nationalist China (Taiwan)

chine [ʃin] nm rice paper; (porcelaine) china (vase)

chinois, e [ʃinwa, -waz] adj Chinese; (fig: péj) pernickety, fussy ▷ nm (Ling) Chinese ▷ nm/f: **C~, e** Chinese

chiot [ʃjo] nm pup(py)

chiper [ʃipe] vt (fam) to pinch

chipoter [ʃipɔte] vi (manger) to nibble; (ergoter) to quibble, haggle

chips [ʃips] nfpl (aussi: **pommes ~**) crisps (Brit), (potato) chips (US)

chiquenaude [ʃiknod] nf flick, flip

chirurgical, e, -aux [ʃiʁyʁʒikal, -o] *adj* surgical

chirurgie [ʃiʁyʁʒi] *nf* surgery; **~ esthétique** cosmetic *ou* plastic surgery

chirurgien, ne [ʃiʁyʁʒjɛ̃] *nm/f* surgeon; **~ dentiste** dental surgeon

chlore [klɔʁ] *nm* chlorine

choc [ʃɔk] *nm* (*heurt*) impact; shock; (*collision*) crash; (*moral*) shock; (*affrontement*) clash ▷ *adj*: **prix ~** amazing *ou* incredible price/ prices; **de ~** (*troupe, traitement*) shock *cpd*; (*patron etc*) high-powered; **~ opératoire/ nerveux** post-operative/nervous shock; **~ en retour** return shock; (*fig*) backlash

chocolat [ʃɔkɔla] *nm* chocolate; (*boisson*) (hot) chocolate; **~ chaud** hot chocolate; **~ à cuire** cooking chocolate; **~ au lait** milk chocolate; **~ en poudre** drinking chocolate

chœur [kœʁ] *nm* (*chorale*) choir; (*Opéra, Théât*) chorus; (*Archit*) choir, chancel; **en ~** in chorus

choisir [ʃwaziʁ] *vt* to choose; (*entre plusieurs*) to choose, select; **~ de faire qch** to choose *ou* opt to do sth

choix [ʃwa] *nm* choice; selection; **avoir le ~** to have the choice; **je n'avais pas le ~** I had no choice; **de premier ~** (*Comm*) class *ou* grade one; **de ~** choice *cpd*, selected; **au ~** as you wish *ou* prefer; **de mon/son ~** of my/his *ou* her choosing

chômage [ʃomaʒ] *nm* unemployment; **mettre au ~** to make redundant, put out of work; **être au ~** to be unemployed *ou* out of work; **~ partiel** short-time working; **~ structurel** structural unemployment; **~ technique** lay-offs *pl*

chômeur, -euse [ʃomœʁ, -øz] *nm/f* unemployed person, person out of work

chope [ʃɔp] *nf* tankard

choper [ʃɔpe] (*fam*) *vt* (*objet, maladie*) to catch

choquer [ʃɔke] *vt* (*offenser*) to shock; (*commotionner*) to shake (up)

choral, e [kɔʁal] *adj* choral ▷ *nf* choral society, choir

choriste [kɔʁist] *nm/f* choir member; (*Opéra*) chorus member

chose [ʃoz] *nf* thing ▷ *nm* (*fam: machin*) thingamajig ▷ *adj inv*: **être/se sentir tout ~** (*bizarre*) to be/feel a bit odd; (*malade*) to be/feel out of sorts; **dire bien des ~s à qn** to give sb's regards to sb; **parler de ~(s) et d'autre(s)** to talk about one thing and another; **c'est peu de ~** it's nothing much

chou, x [ʃu] *nm* cabbage ▷ *adj inv* cute; **mon petit ~** (my) sweetheart; **faire ~ blanc** to draw a blank; **feuille de ~** (*fig: journal*) rag; **~ à la crème** cream bun (*made of choux pastry*); **~ de Bruxelles** Brussels sprout

chouchou, te [ʃuʃu, -ut] *nm/f* (*Scol*) teacher's pet

choucroute [ʃukʁut] *nf* sauerkraut; **~ garnie** sauerkraut with cooked meats and potatoes

chouette [ʃwɛt] *nf* owl ▷ *adj* (*fam*) great, smashing

chou-fleur (*pl* **choux-fleurs**) [ʃuflœʁ] *nm* cauliflower

choyer [ʃwaje] *vt* to cherish; to pamper

chrétien, ne [kʁetjɛ̃, -ɛn] *adj, nm/f* Christian

Christ [kʁist] *nm*: **le ~** Christ; **christ** (*crucifix etc*) figure of Christ; **Jésus ~** Jesus Christ

christianisme [kʁistjanism] *nm* Christianity

chrome [kʁom] *nm* chromium; (*revêtement*) chrome, chromium

chromé, e [kʁome] *adj* chrome-plated, chromium-plated

chronique [kʁɔnik] *adj* chronic ▷ *nf* (*de journal*) column, page; (*historique*) chronicle; (*Radio, TV*): **la ~ sportive/théâtrale** the sports/theatre review; **la ~ locale** local news and gossip

chronologique [kʁɔnɔlɔʒik] *adj* chronological

chronomètre [kʁɔnɔmɛtʁ] *nm* stopwatch

chronométrer [kʁɔnɔmetʁe] *vt* to time

chrysanthème [kʁizɑ̃tɛm] *nm* chrysanthemum

> ● **CHRYSANTHÈME**
> ●
> ● Chrysanthemums are strongly
> ● associated with funerals in France, and
> ● therefore should not be given as gifts.

chuchotement [ʃyʃɔtmɑ̃] *nm* whisper

chuchoter [ʃyʃɔte] *vt, vi* to whisper

chut *excl* [ʃyt] sh!

chute [ʃyt] *nf* fall; (*de bois, papier: déchet*) scrap; **la ~ des cheveux** hair loss; **faire une ~ (de 10 m)** to fall (10 m); **~s de pluie/neige** rain/ snowfalls; **~ (d'eau)** waterfall; **~ du jour** nightfall; **~ libre** free fall; **~ des reins** small of the back

Chypre [ʃipʁ] *nm/f* Cyprus

-ci, ci- [si] *adv ou* **par**; **ci-contre**; **ci-joint** *etc* ▷ *adj dém*: **ce garçon-/-là** this/that boy; **ces femmes-/-là** these/those women

cible [sibl] *nf* target

ciboulette [sibulɛt] *nf* (small) chive

cicatrice [sikatʁis] *nf* scar

cicatriser [sikatʁize] *vt* to heal; **se cicatriser** to heal (up), form a scar

ci-contre [sikɔ̃tʁ] *adv* opposite

ci-dessous [sidəsu] *adv* below

ci-dessus [sidəsy] *adv* above

cidre [sidʁ] *nm* cider

Cie *abr* (= **compagnie**) Co

ciel [sjɛl] *nm* sky; (*Rel*) heaven; **ciels** *nmpl* (*Peinture etc*) skies; **cieux** *nmpl* sky *sg*, skies; (*Rel*) heaven *sg*; **à ~ ouvert** open-air; (*mine*) opencast; **tomber du ~** (*arriver à l'improviste*) to appear out of the blue; (*être stupéfait*) to be unable to believe one's eyes; **C-!** good heavens!; **~ de lit** canopy

cierge [sjɛrʒ] nm candle; **~ pascal** Easter candle
cieux [sjø] nmpl voir **ciel**
cigale [sigal] nf cicada
cigare [sigar] nm cigar
cigarette [sigarɛt] nf cigarette; **~ (à) bout filtre** filter cigarette
ci-gît [siʒi] adv here lies
cigogne [sigɔɲ] nf stork
ci-inclus, e [siɛ̃kly, -yz] adj, adv enclosed
ci-joint, e [siʒwɛ̃, -ɛt] adj, adv enclosed; (to email) attached; **veuillez trouver ~** please find enclosed or attached
cil [sil] nm (eye)lash
cime [sim] nf top; (montagne) peak
ciment [simɑ̃] nm cement; **~ armé** reinforced concrete
cimetière [simtjɛr] nm cemetery; (d'église) churchyard; **~ de voitures** scrapyard
cinéaste [sineast] nm/f film-maker
cinéma [sinema] nm cinema; **aller au ~** to go to the cinema ou pictures ou movies; **~ d'animation** cartoon (film)
cinématographique [sinematografik] adj film cpd, cinema cpd
cinglant, e [sɛ̃glɑ̃, -ɑ̃t] adj (propos, ironie) scathing, biting; (échec) crushing
cinglé, e [sɛ̃gle] adj (fam) crazy
cinq [sɛ̃k] num five
cinquantaine [sɛ̃kɑ̃tɛn] nf: **une ~ (de)** about fifty; **avoir la ~** (âge) to be around fifty
cinquante [sɛ̃kɑ̃t] num fifty
cinquantenaire [sɛ̃kɑ̃tnɛr] adj, nm/f fifty-year-old
cinquième [sɛ̃kjɛm] num fifth ▷ nf (Scol) year 8 (Brit), seventh grade (US)
cintre [sɛ̃tr] nm coat-hanger; (Archit) arch; **plein ~** semicircular arch
cintré, e [sɛ̃tre] adj curved; (chemise) fitted, slim-fitting
cirage [siraʒ] nm (shoe) polish
circonflexe [sirkɔ̃flɛks] adj: **accent ~** circumflex accent
circonscription [sirkɔ̃skripsjɔ̃] nf district; **~ électorale** (d'un député) constituency; **~ militaire** military area
circonscrire [sirkɔ̃skrir] vt to define, delimit; (incendie) to contain; (propriété) to mark out; (sujet) to define
circonstance [sirkɔ̃stɑ̃s] nf circumstance; (occasion) occasion; **œuvre de ~** occasional work; **air de ~** fitting air; **tête de ~** appropriate demeanour (Brit) ou demeanor (US); **~s atténuantes** mitigating circumstances
circuit [sirkɥi] nm (trajet) tour, (round) trip; (Élec, Tech) circuit; **~ automobile** motor circuit; **~ de distribution** distribution network; **~ fermé** closed circuit; **~ intégré** integrated circuit
circulaire [sirkylɛr] adj, nf circular
circulation [sirkylasjɔ̃] nf circulation; (Auto): **la ~** (the) traffic; **bonne/mauvaise ~** good/bad circulation; **mettre en ~** to put into circulation

circuler [sirkyle] vi (véhicules) to drive (along); (passants) to walk along; (train etc) to run; (sang, devises) to circulate; **faire ~** (nouvelle) to spread (about), circulate; (badauds) to move on
cire [sir] nf wax; **~ à cacheter** sealing wax
ciré [sire] nm oilskin
cirer [sire] vt to wax, polish
cirque [sirk] nm circus; (arène) amphitheatre (Brit), amphitheater (US); (Géo) cirque; (fig: désordre) chaos, bedlam; (: chichis) carry-on; **quel ~!** what a carry-on!
cisaille [sizaj], **cisailles** nf(pl) (gardening) shears pl
ciseau, x [sizo] nm: **~ (à bois)** chisel ▷ nmpl (paire de ciseaux) (pair of) scissors; **sauter en ~x** to do a scissors jump; **à froid** cold chisel
ciseler [sizle] vt to chisel, carve
citadin, e [sitadɛ̃, -in] nm/f city dweller ▷ adj town cpd, city cpd, urban
citation [sitasjɔ̃] nf (d'auteur) quotation; (Jur) summons sg; (Mil: récompense) mention
cité [site] nf town; (plus grande) city; **~ ouvrière** (workers') housing estate; **~ universitaire** students' residences pl
citer [site] vt (un auteur) to quote (from); (nommer) to name; (Jur) to summon; **~ (en exemple)** (personne) to hold up (as an example); **je ne veux ~ personne** I don't want to name names
citerne [sitɛrn] nf tank
citoyen, ne [sitwajɛ̃, -ɛn] nm/f citizen
citron [sitrɔ̃] nm lemon; **~ pressé** (fresh) lemon juice; **~ vert** lime
citronnade [sitrɔnad] nf still lemonade
citrouille [sitruj] nf pumpkin
civet [sive] nm stew; **~ de lièvre** jugged hare; **~ de lapin** rabbit stew
civière [sivjɛr] nf stretcher
civil, e [sivil] adj (Jur, Admin, poli) civil; (non militaire) civilian ▷ nm civilian; **en ~** in civilian clothes; **dans le ~** in civilian life
civilisation [sivilizasjɔ̃] nf civilization
clair, e [klɛr] adj light; (chambre) light, bright; (eau, son, fig) clear ▷ adv: **voir ~** to see clearly ▷ nm: **mettre au ~** (notes etc) to tidy up; **tirer qch au ~** to clear sth up, clarify sth; **bleu ~** light blue; **pour être ~** so as to make it plain; **y voir ~** (comprendre) to understand, see; **le plus ~ de son temps/argent** the better part of his time/money; **en ~** (non codé) in clear; **~ de lune** moonlight
clairement [klɛrmɑ̃] adv clearly
clairière [klɛrjɛr] nf clearing
clairon [klɛrɔ̃] nm bugle
claironner [klɛrɔne] vt (fig) to trumpet, shout from the rooftops
clairsemé, e [klɛrsəme] adj sparse
clairvoyant, e [klɛrvwajɑ̃, -ɑ̃t] adj perceptive, clear-sighted

clandestin, e [klɑ̃dɛstɛ̃, -in] adj clandestine, covert; (Pol) underground, clandestine; (travailleur, immigration) illegal; **passager ~** stowaway

clapier [klapje] nm (rabbit) hutch

clapoter [klapɔte] vi to lap

claque [klak] nf (gifle) slap; (Théât) claque ▷ nm (chapeau) opera hat

claquer [klake] vi (drapeau) to flap; (porte) to bang, slam; (fam: mourir) to snuff it; (coup de feu) to ring out ▷ vt (porte) to slam, bang; (doigts) to snap; (fam: dépenser) to blow; **elle claquait des dents** her teeth were chattering; **être claqué** (fam) to be dead tired; **se ~ un muscle** to pull ou strain a muscle

claquettes [klakɛt] nfpl tap-dancing sg; (chaussures) flip-flops

clarinette [klarinɛt] nf clarinet

clarté [klarte] nf lightness; brightness; (d'un son, de l'eau) clearness; (d'une explication) clarity

classe [klɑs] nf class; (Scol: local) class(room); (: leçon) class; (: élèves) class, form; **1ère/2ème ~** 1st/2nd class; **un (soldat de) deuxième ~** (Mil: armée de terre) ≈ private (soldier); (: armée de l'air) ≈ aircraftman (Brit), ≈ airman basic (US); **de ~** luxury cpd; **faire ses ~s** (Mil) to do one's (recruit's) training; **faire la ~** (Scol) to be a ou the teacher; to teach; **aller en ~** to go to school; **aller en ~ verte/de neige/de mer** to go to the countryside/skiing/to the seaside with the school; **~ préparatoire** class which prepares students for the Grandes Écoles entry exams; see note; **~ sociale** social class; **~ touriste** economy class

○ **CLASSES PRÉPARATOIRES**
○
○ Classes préparatoires are the two years of
○ intensive study which coach students for
○ the competitive entry examinations to
○ the "grandes écoles". These extremely
○ demanding courses follow the
○ "baccalauréat" and are usually done at a
○ "lycée". Schools which provide such
○ classes are more highly regarded than
○ those which do not.

classement [klɑsmɑ̃] nm classifying; filing; grading; closing; (rang: Scol) place; (: Sport) placing; (liste: Scol) class list (in order of merit); (: Sport) placings pl; **premier au ~ général** (Sport) first overall

classer [klɑse] vt (idées, livres) to classify; (papiers) to file; (candidat, concurrent) to grade; (personne: juger: péj) to rate; (Jur: affaire) to close; **se ~ premier/dernier** to come first/last; (Sport) to finish first/last

classeur [klɑsœr] nm (cahier) file; (meuble) filing cabinet; **~ à feuillets mobiles** ring binder

classique [klasik] adj (sobre: coupe etc)

classic(al), classical; (habituel) standard, classic ▷ nm classic; classical author; **études ~s** classical studies, classics

clause [kloz] nf clause

clavecin [klav(ə)sɛ̃] nm harpsichord

clavicule [klavikyl] nf clavicle, collarbone

clavier [klavje] nm keyboard

clé, clef [kle] nf key; (Mus) clef; (de mécanicien) spanner (Brit), wrench (US) ▷ adj: **problème/ position ~** key problem/position; **mettre sous ~** to place under lock and key; **prendre la ~ des champs** to run away, make off; **prix ~s en main** (d'une voiture) on-the-road price; (d'un appartement) price with immediate entry; **~ de sol/de fa/d'ut** treble/bass/alto clef; **livre/film etc à ~** book/film etc in which real people are depicted under fictitious names; **à la ~** (à la fin) at the end of it all; **~ anglaise = clé à molette**; **~ de contact** ignition key; **~ à molette** adjustable spanner (Brit) ou wrench, monkey wrench; **~ USB** USB key; **~ de voûte** keystone

clément, e [klemɑ̃, -ɑ̃t] adj (temps) mild; (indulgent) lenient

clerc [klɛr] nm: **~ de notaire** ou **d'avoué** lawyer's clerk

clergé [klɛrʒe] nm clergy

cliché [kliʃe] nm (fig) cliché; (Photo) negative; print; (Typo) (printing) plate; (Ling) cliché

client, e [klijɑ̃, -ɑ̃t] nm/f (acheteur) customer, client; (d'hôtel) guest, patron; (du docteur) patient; (de l'avocat) client

clientèle [klijɑ̃tɛl] nf (du magasin) customers pl, clientèle; (du docteur, de l'avocat) practice; **accorder sa ~ à** to give one's custom to; **retirer sa ~ à** to take one's business away from

cligner [kliɲe] vi: **~ des yeux** to blink (one's eyes); **~ de l'œil** to wink

clignotant [kliɲɔtɑ̃] nm (Auto) indicator

clignoter [kliɲɔte] vi (étoiles etc) to twinkle; (lumière: à intervalles réguliers) to flash; (: vaciller) to flicker; (yeux) to blink

climat [klima] nm climate

climatisation [klimatizasjɔ̃] nf air conditioning

climatisé, e [klimatize] adj air-conditioned

clin d'œil [klɛ̃dœj] nm wink; **en un ~** in a flash

clinique [klinik] adj clinical ▷ nf nursing home, (private) clinic

clinquant, e [klɛ̃kɑ̃, -ɑ̃t] adj flashy

clip [klip] nm (pince) clip; (boucle d'oreille) clip-on; (vidéo) pop (ou promotional) video

cliquer [klike] vi (Inform) to click; **~ deux fois** to double-click ▷ vt to click; **~ sur** to click on

cliqueter [klikte] vi to clash; (ferraille, clefs, monnaie) to jangle, jingle; (verres) to chink

clochard, e [klɔʃar, -ard] nm/f tramp

cloche [klɔʃ] nf (d'église) bell; (fam) clot; (chapeau) cloche (hat); **~ à fromage** cheese-cover

cloche-pied [klɔʃpje]: **à ~** *adv* on one leg, hopping (along)

clocher [klɔʃe] *nm* church tower; (*en pointe*) steeple ▷ *vi* (*fam*) to be *ou* go wrong; **de ~** (*péj*) parochial

cloison [klwazõ] *nf* partition (wall); **~ étanche** (*fig*) impenetrable barrier, brick wall (*fig*)

cloître [klwatʀ] *nm* cloister

cloîtrer [klwatʀe] *vt*: **se cloîtrer** to shut o.s. away; (*Rel*) to enter a convent *ou* monastery

clonage [klɔnaʒ] *nm* cloning

clone [klon] *nm* clone

cloner [klone] *vt* to clone

cloque [klɔk] *nf* blister

clore [klɔʀ] *vt* to close; **~ une session** (*Inform*) to log out

clos, e [klo, -oz] *pp de* **clore** ▷ *adj voir* **maison**; **huis**; **vase** ▷ *nm* (enclosed) field

clôture [klotyʀ] *nf* closure, closing; (*barrière*) enclosure, fence

clôturer [klotyʀe] *vt* (*terrain*) to enclose, close off; (*festival, débats*) to close

clou [klu] *nm* nail; (*Méd*) boil; **clous** *nmpl* = **passage clouté**; **pneus à ~s** studded tyres; **le ~ du spectacle** the highlight of the show; **~ de girofle** clove

clouer [klue] *vt* to nail down (*ou* up); (*fig*): **~ sur/contre** to pin to/against

clown [klun] *nm* clown; **faire le ~** (*fig*) to clown (about), play the fool

club [klœb] *nm* club

CMU *sigle f* (= *couverture maladie universelle*) *system of free health care for those on low incomes*

CNRS *sigle m* (= *Centre national de la recherche scientifique*) ≈ SERC (Brit), ≈ NSF (US)

coaguler [kɔagyle] *vi, vt,* **se coaguler** *vi* (*sang*) to coagulate

coasser [kɔase] *vi* to croak

cobaye [kɔbaj] *nm* guinea-pig

coca® [kɔka] *nm* Coke®

cocaïne [kɔkain] *nf* cocaine

cocasse [kɔkas] *adj* comical, funny

coccinelle [kɔksinɛl] *nf* ladybird (Brit), ladybug (US)

cocher [kɔʃe] *nm* coachman ▷ *vt* to tick off; (*entailler*) to notch

cochère [kɔʃɛʀ] *adj f voir* **porte**

cochon, ne [kɔʃõ, -ɔn] *nm* pig ▷ *nm/f* (*péj*: *sale*) (filthy) pig; (*: méchant*) swine ▷ *adj* (*fam*) dirty, smutty; **~ d'Inde** guinea-pig; **~ de lait** (*Culin*) sucking pig

cochonnerie [kɔʃɔnʀi] *nf* (*fam: saleté*) filth; (*: marchandises*) rubbish, trash

cocktail [kɔktɛl] *nm* cocktail; (*réception*) cocktail party

coco [kɔko] *nm voir* **noix**; (*fam*) bloke (Brit), dude (US)

cocorico [kɔkɔʀiko] *excl, nm* cock-a-doodle-do

cocotier [kɔkɔtje] *nm* coconut palm

cocotte [kɔkɔt] *nf* (*en fonte*) casserole; **ma ~** (*fam*) sweetie (pie); **~ (minute)**® pressure

cooker; **~ en papier** paper shape

cocu [kɔky] *nm* cuckold

code [kɔd] *nm* code ▷ *adj*: **phares ~s** dipped lights; **se mettre en ~(s)** to dip (Brit) *ou* dim (US) one's (head)lights; **~ à barres** bar code; **~ de caractère** (*Inform*) character code; **~ civil** Common Law; **~ machine** machine code; **~ pénal** penal code; **~ postal** (*numéro*) postcode (Brit), zip code (US); **~ de la route** highway code; **~ secret** cipher

cœur [kœʀ] *nm* heart; (*Cartes: couleur*) hearts *pl*; (*: carte*) heart; (*Culin*): **~ de laitue/d'artichaut** lettuce/artichoke heart; (*fig*): **~ du débat** heart of the debate; **~ de l'été** height of summer; **~ de la forêt** depths *pl* of the forest; **affaire de ~** love affair; **avoir bon ~** to be kind-hearted; **avoir mal au ~** to feel sick; **contre** *ou* **sur son ~** to one's breast; **opérer qn à ~ ouvert** to perform open-heart surgery on sb; **recevoir qn à ~ ouvert** to welcome sb with open arms; **parler à ~ ouvert** to open one's heart; **de tout son ~** with all one's heart; **avoir le ~ gros** *ou* **serré** to have a heavy heart; **en avoir le ~ net** to be clear in one's own mind (about it); **par ~** by heart; **de bon ~** willingly; **avoir à ~ de faire** to be very keen to do; **cela lui tient à ~** that's (very) close to his heart; **prendre les choses à ~** to take things to heart; **à ~ joie** to one's heart's content; **être de tout ~ avec qn** to be (completely) in accord with sb

coffre [kɔfʀ] *nm* (*meuble*) chest; (*coffre-fort*) safe; (*d'auto*) boot (Brit), trunk (US); **avoir du ~** (*fam*) to have a lot of puff

coffre-fort (*pl* **coffres-forts**) [kɔfʀəfɔʀ] *nm* safe

coffret [kɔfʀɛ] *nm* casket; **~ à bijoux** jewel box

cognac [kɔnak] *nm* brandy, cognac

cogner [kɔne] *vi* to knock, bang; **se cogner** *vi* to bump o.s.; **se ~ contre** to knock *ou* bump into; **se ~ la tête** to bang one's head

cohérent, e [kɔeʀã, -ãt] *adj* coherent, consistent

cohorte [kɔɔʀt] *nf* troop

cohue [kɔy] *nf* crowd

coi, coite [kwa, kwat] *adj*: **rester ~** to remain silent

coiffe [kwaf] *nf* headdress

coiffé, e [kwafe] *adj*: **bien/mal ~** with tidy/untidy hair; **~ d'un béret** wearing a beret; **~ en arrière** with one's hair brushed *ou* combed back; **~ en brosse** with a crew cut

coiffer [kwafe] *vt* (*fig: surmonter*) to cover, top; **~ qn** to do sb's hair; **~ qn d'un béret** to put a beret on sb; **se coiffer** *vi* to do one's hair; to put on a *ou* one's hat

coiffeur, -euse [kwafœʀ, -øz] *nm/f* hairdresser ▷ *nf* (*table*) dressing table

coiffure [kwafyʀ] *nf* (*cheveux*) hairstyle, hairdo; (*chapeau*) hat, headgear *no pl*; (*art*): **la ~** hairdressing

coin [kwɛ̃] nm corner; (pour graver) die; (pour coincer) wedge; (poinçon) hallmark; **l'épicerie du ~** the local grocer; **dans le ~** (aux alentours) in the area, around about; (habiter) locally; **je ne suis pas du ~** I'm not from here; **au ~ du feu** by the fireside; **du ~ de l'œil** out of the corner of one's eye; **regard en ~** side(ways) glance; **sourire en ~** half-smile

coincé, e [kwɛ̃se] adj stuck, jammed; (fig: inhibé) inhibited, with hang-ups

coincer [kwɛ̃se] vt to jam; (fam) to catch (out); to nab; **se coincer** vi to get stuck ou jammed

coïncidence [kɔɛ̃sidɑ̃s] nf coincidence

coïncider [kɔɛ̃side] vi: **~ (avec)** to coincide (with); (correspondre: témoignage etc) to correspond ou tally (with)

coing [kwɛ̃] nm quince

col [kɔl] nm (de chemise) collar; (encolure, cou) neck; (de montagne) pass; **~ roulé** polo-neck; **~ de l'utérus** cervix

colère [kɔlɛʀ] nf anger; **une ~** a fit of anger; **être en ~ (contre qn)** to be angry (with sb); **mettre qn en ~** to make sb angry; **se mettre en ~ contre qn** to get angry with sb; **se mettre en ~** to get angry

coléreux, -euse [kɔleʀø, -øz], **colérique** [kɔleʀik] adj quick-tempered, irascible

colifichet [kɔlifiʃɛ] nm trinket

colimaçon [kɔlimasɔ̃] nm: **escalier en ~** spiral staircase

colin [kɔlɛ̃] nm hake

colique [kɔlik] nf diarrhoea (Brit), diarrhea (US); (douleurs) colic (pains pl); (fam: personne ou chose ennuyeuse) pain

colis [kɔli] nm parcel; **par ~ postal** by parcel post

collaborateur, -trice [kɔlabɔʀatœʀ, -tʀis] nm/f (aussi Pol) collaborator; (d'une revue) contributor

collaborer [kɔ(l)labɔʀe] vi to collaborate; (aussi: **~ à**) to collaborate on; (revue) to contribute to

collant, e [kɔlɑ̃, -ɑ̃t] adj sticky; (robe etc) clinging, skintight; (péj) clinging ▷ nm (bas) tights pl; (de danseur) leotard

collation [kɔlasjɔ̃] nf light meal

colle [kɔl] nf glue; (à papiers peints) (wallpaper) paste; (devinette) teaser, riddle; (Scol fam) detention; **~ forte** superglue®

collecte [kɔlɛkt] nf collection; **faire une ~** to take up a collection

collectif, -ive [kɔlɛktif, -iv] adj collective; (visite, billet etc) group cpd ▷ nm: **~ budgétaire** mini-budget (Brit), mid-term budget; **immeuble ~** block of flats

collection [kɔlɛksjɔ̃] nf collection; (Édition) series; **pièce de ~** collector's item; **faire (la) ~ de** to collect; (toute) **une ~ de ...** (fig) a (complete) set of ...

collectionner [kɔlɛksjɔne] vt (tableaux, timbres) to collect

collectionneur, -euse [kɔlɛksjɔnœʀ, -øz] nm/f collector

collectivité [kɔlɛktivite] nf group; **la ~** the community, the collectivity; **les ~s locales** local authorities

collège [kɔlɛʒ] nm (école) (secondary) school; see note; (assemblée) body; **~ électoral** electoral college

> ● **COLLÈGE**
> ●
> ● A collège is a state secondary school for
> ● children between 11 and 15 years of age.
> ● Pupils follow a national curriculum
> ● which prescribes a common core along
> ● with several options. Schools are free to
> ● arrange their own timetable and choose
> ● their own teaching methods. Before
> ● leaving this phase of their education,
> ● students are assessed by examination
> ● and course work for their "brevet des
> ● collèges".

collégien, ne [kɔleʒjɛ̃, -ɛn] nm/f secondary school pupil (Brit), high school student (US)

collègue [kɔ(l)lɛg] nm/f colleague

coller [kɔle] vt (papier, timbre) to stick (on); (affiche) to stick up; (appuyer, placer contre): **~ son front à la vitre** to press one's face to the window; (enveloppe) to stick down; (morceaux) to stick ou glue together; (Inform) to paste; (fam: mettre, fourrer) to stick, shove; (Scol fam) to keep in, give detention to ▷ vi (être collant) to be sticky; (adhérer) to stick; **~ qch sur** to stick (ou paste ou glue) sth on(to); **~ à** to stick to; (fig) to cling to; **être collé à un examen** (fam) to fail an exam

collet [kɔlɛ] nm (piège) snare, noose; (cou): **prendre qn au ~** to grab sb by the throat; **~ monté** adj inv straight-laced

collier [kɔlje] nm (bijou) necklace; (de chien, Tech) collar; **~ (de barbe), barbe en ~** narrow beard along the line of the jaw; **~ de serrage** choke collar

collimateur [kɔlimatœʀ] nm: **être dans le ~** (fig) to be in the firing line; **avoir qn/qch dans le ~** (fig) to have sb/sth in one's sights

colline [kɔlin] nf hill

collision [kɔlizjɔ̃] nf collision, crash; **entrer en ~ (avec)** to collide (with)

colloque [kɔlɔk] nm colloquium, symposium

collyre [kɔliʀ] nm (Méd) eye lotion

colmater [kɔlmate] vt (fuite) to seal off; (brèche) to plug, fill in

colombe [kɔlɔ̃b] nf dove

Colombie [kɔlɔ̃bi] nf: **la ~** Colombia

colon [kɔlɔ̃] nm settler; (enfant) boarder (in children's holiday camp)

colonel [kɔlɔnɛl] nm colonel; (de l'armée de l'air) group captain

colonie [kɔlɔni] nf colony; **~ (de vacances)** holiday camp (for children)

colonne [kɔlɔn] nf column; **se mettre
en ~ par deux/quatre** to get into twos/fours;
en ~ par deux in double file; **~ de secours**
rescue party; **~ (vertébrale)** spine, spinal
column

colorant [kɔlɔrɑ̃] nm colo(u)ring

colorer [kɔlɔre] vt to colour (Brit), color (US);
se colorer vi to turn red; to blush

colorier [kɔlɔrje] vt to colo(u)r (in); **album
à ~** colouring book

coloris [kɔlɔri] nm colo(u)r, shade

colporter [kɔlpɔrte] vt to peddle

colza [kɔlza] nm rape(seed)

coma [kɔma] nm coma; **être dans le ~** to be
in a coma

combat [kɔ̃ba] vb voir **combattre** ▷ nm fight;
fighting no pl; **~ de boxe** boxing match; **~ de
rues** street fighting no pl; **~ singulier** single
combat

combattant [kɔ̃batɑ̃] vb voir **combattre** ▷ nm
combatant; (d'une rixe) brawler; **ancien ~** war
veteran

combattre [kɔ̃batr] vi to fight ▷ vt to fight;
(épidémie, ignorance) to combat, fight against

combien [kɔ̃bjɛ̃] adv (quantité) how much;
(nombre) how many; (exclamatif) how; **~ de**
how much; (nombre) how many; **~ de temps**
how long, how much time; **c'est ~?, ça fait
~?** how much is it?; **~ coûte/pèse ceci?** how
much does this cost/weigh?; **vous mesurez
~?** what size are you?; **ça fait ~ en largeur?**
how wide is that?; **on est le ~ aujourd'hui?**
(fam) what's the date today?

combinaison [kɔ̃binɛzɔ̃] nf combination;
(astuce) device, scheme; (de femme) slip;
(d'aviateur) flying suit; (de plongée) wetsuit;
(bleu de travail) boilersuit (Brit), coveralls pl (US)

combine [kɔ̃bin] nf trick; (péj) scheme, fiddle
(Brit)

combiné [kɔ̃bine] nm (aussi: **~ téléphonique**)
receiver; (Ski) combination (event); (vêtement
de femme) corselet

combiner [kɔ̃bine] vt to combine; (plan,
horaire) to work out, devise

comble [kɔ̃bl] adj (salle) packed (full) ▷ nm
(du bonheur, plaisir) height; **combles** nmpl
(Constr) attic sg, loft sg; **de fond en ~** from
top to bottom; **pour ~ de malchance** to cap
it all; **c'est le ~!** that beats everything!,
that takes the biscuit! (Brit); **sous les ~s** in
the attic

combler [kɔ̃ble] vt (trou) to fill in; (besoin,
lacune) to fill; (déficit) to make good; (satisfaire)
to gratify, fulfil (Brit), fulfill (US); **~ qn de joie**
to fill sb with joy; **~ qn d'honneurs** to
shower sb with honours

combustible [kɔ̃bystibl] adj combustible
▷ nm fuel

comédie [kɔmedi] nf comedy; (fig)
playacting no pl; **jouer la ~** (fig) to put on an
act; **faire une ~** (fig) to make a fuss; **la C~
française** see note; **~ musicale** musical

 COMÉDIE FRANÇAISE

Founded in 1680 by Louis XIV, the Comédie
française is the French national theatre.
The company is subsidized by the state
and mainly performs in the Palais Royal
in Paris, tending to concentrate on
classical French drama.

comédien, ne [kɔmedjɛ̃, -ɛn] nm/f actor/
actress; (comique) comedy actor/actress,
comedian/comedienne; (fig) sham

comestible [kɔmɛstibl] adj edible;
comestibles nmpl foods

comique [kɔmik] adj (drôle) comical; (Théât)
comic ▷ nm (artiste) comic, comedian; **le ~ de
qch** the funny ou comical side of sth

comité [kɔmite] nm committee; **petit ~**
select group; **~ directeur** management
committee; **~ d'entreprise (CE)** works
council; **~ des fêtes** festival committee

commandant [kɔmɑ̃dɑ̃] nm (gén)
commander, commandant; (Mil: grade)
major; (: armée de l'air) squadron leader;
(Navig) captain; **~ (de bord)** (Aviat) captain

commande [kɔmɑ̃d] nf (Comm) order;
(Inform) command; **commandes** nfpl (Aviat
etc) controls; **passer une ~ (de)** to put in an
order (for); **sur ~** to order; **~ à distance**
remote control; **véhicule à double ~** vehicle
with dual controls

commandement [kɔmɑ̃dmɑ̃] nm
command; (ordre) command, order; (Rel)
commandment

commander [kɔmɑ̃de] vt (Comm) to order;
(diriger, ordonner) to command; **~ à** (Mil) to
command; (contrôler, maîtriser) to have control
over; **~ à qn de faire** to command ou order sb
to do

commando [kɔmɑ̃do] nm commando
(squad)

MOT-CLÉ

comme [kɔm] prép 1 (comparaison) like; **tout
comme son père** just like his father; **fort
comme un bœuf** as strong as an ox; **joli
comme tout** ever so pretty

2 (manière) like; **faites-le comme ça** do it like
this, do it this way; **comme ça ou cela on
n'aura pas d'ennuis** that way we won't
have any problems; **comme ci, comme ça**
so-so, middling; **comment ça va? — comme
ça** how are things? — OK; **comme on dit** as
they say

3 (en tant que) as a; **donner comme prix** to
give as a prize; **travailler comme secrétaire**
to work as a secretary

4: **comme quoi** (d'où il s'ensuit que) which
shows that; **il a écrit une lettre comme
quoi il ...** he's written a letter saying that ...

5: **comme il faut** adv properly

▷ adj (correct) proper, correct
▷ conj **1** (ainsi que) as; **elle écrit comme elle parle** she writes as she talks; **comme si** as if **2** (au moment où, alors que) as; **il est parti comme j'arrivais** he left as I arrived **3** (parce que, puisque) as, since; **comme il était en retard**, il ... as he was late, he ...
▷ adv: **comme il est fort/c'est bon!** he's so strong/it's so good!; **il est malin comme c'est pas permis** he's as smart as anything

commémorer [kɔmemɔre] vt to commemorate
commencement [kɔmɑ̃smɑ̃] nm beginning, start, commencement; **commencements** nmpl (débuts) beginnings
commencer [kɔmɑ̃se] vt to begin, start, commence ▷ vi to begin, start, commence; **~ à** ou **de faire** to begin ou start doing; **~ par qch** to begin with sth; **~ par faire qch** to begin by doing sth
comment [kɔmɑ̃] adv how; **~?** (que dites-vous) (I beg your) pardon?; **~!** what! ▷ nm: **le ~ et le pourquoi** the whys and wherefores; **et ~!** and how!; **~ donc!** of course!; **~ faire?** how will we do it?; **~ se fait-il que ...?** how is it that ...?
commentaire [kɔmɑ̃tɛr] nm comment; remark; **~ (de texte)** (Scol) commentary; **~ sur image** voice-over
commenter [kɔmɑ̃te] vt (jugement, événement) to comment (up)on; (Radio, TV: match, manifestation) to cover, give a commentary on
commérages [kɔmeraʒ] nmpl gossip sg
commerçant, e [kɔmɛrsɑ̃, -ɑ̃t] adj commercial; trading; (rue) shopping cpd; (personne) commercially shrewd ▷ nm/f shopkeeper, trader
commerce [kɔmɛrs] nm (activité) trade, commerce; (boutique) business; **le petit ~** small shop owners pl, small traders pl; **faire ~ de** to trade in; (fig: péj) to trade on; **chambre de ~** Chamber of Commerce; **livres de ~** (account) books; **vendu dans le ~** sold in the shops; **vendu hors-~** sold directly to the public; **~ en** ou **de gros/détail** wholesale/retail trade; **~ électronique** e-commerce; **~ équitable** fair trade; **~ intérieur/extérieur** home/foreign trade
commercial, e, -aux [kɔmɛrsjal, -o] adj commercial, trading; (péj) commercial ▷ nm: **les commerciaux** the commercial people
commercialiser [kɔmɛrsjalize] vt to market
commère [kɔmɛr] nf gossip
commettre [kɔmɛtr] vt to commit; **se commettre** vi to compromise one's good name
commis[1] [kɔmi] nm (de magasin) (shop) assistant (Brit), sales clerk (US); (de banque) clerk; **~ voyageur** commercial traveller (Brit) ou traveler (US)
commis[2], **e** [kɔmi, -iz] pp de **commettre**

commissaire [kɔmisɛr] nm (de police) ≈ (police) superintendent (Brit), ≈ (police) captain (US); (de rencontre sportive etc) steward; **~ du bord** (Navig) purser; **~ aux comptes** (Admin) auditor
commissaire-priseur (pl **commissaires-priseurs**) [kɔmisɛrprizœr] nm (official) auctioneer
commissariat [kɔmisarja] nm: **~ (de police)** police station; (Admin) commissionership
commission [kɔmisjɔ̃] nf (comité, pourcentage) commission; (message) message; (course) errand; **commissions** nfpl (achats) shopping sg; **~ d'examen** examining board
commode [kɔmɔd] adj (pratique) convenient, handy; (facile) easy; (air, personne) easy-going; (personne): **pas ~** awkward (to deal with) ▷ nf chest of drawers
commodité [kɔmɔdite] nf convenience
commotion [kɔmosjɔ̃] nf: **~ (cérébrale)** concussion
commotionné, e [kɔmosjɔne] adj shocked, shaken
commun, e [kɔmœ̃, -yn] adj common; (pièce) communal, shared; (réunion, effort) joint ▷ nf (Admin) commune; ≈ district; (: urbaine) ≈ borough; **communs** nmpl (bâtiments) outbuildings; **cela sort du ~** it's out of the ordinary; **le ~ des mortels** the common run of people; **sans ~e mesure** incomparable; **être ~ à** (chose) to be shared by; **en ~ (faire)** jointly; **mettre en ~** to pool, share; **peu ~** unusual; **d'un ~ accord** of one accord; with one accord
communauté [kɔmynote] nf community; (Jur): **régime de la ~** communal estate settlement
commune [kɔmyn] adj f, nf voir **commun**
communicatif, -ive [kɔmynikatif, -iv] adj (personne) communicative; (rire) infectious
communication [kɔmynikasjɔ̃] nf communication; **~ (téléphonique)** (telephone) call; **avoir la ~ (avec)** to get ou be through (to); **vous avez la ~** you're through; **donnez-moi la ~ avec** put me through to; **mettre qn en ~ avec qn** (en contact) to put sb in touch with sb; (au téléphone) to connect sb with sb; **~ interurbaine** long-distance call; **~ en PCV** reverse charge (Brit) ou collect (US) call; **~ avec préavis** personal call
communier [kɔmynje] vi (Rel) to receive communion; (fig) to be united
communion [kɔmynjɔ̃] nf communion
communiquer [kɔmynike] vt (nouvelle, dossier) to pass on, convey; (maladie) to pass on; (peur etc) to communicate; (chaleur, mouvement) to transmit ▷ vi to communicate; **~ avec** (salle) to communicate with; **se ~ à** (se propager) to spread to
communisme [kɔmynism] nm communism
communiste [kɔmynist] adj, nm/f communist

commutateur [kɔmytatœʀ] nm (Élec)
(change-over) switch, commutator

compact, e [kɔ̃pakt] adj (dense) dense;
(appareil) compact

compagne [kɔ̃paɲ] nf companion

compagnie [kɔ̃paɲi] nf (firme, Mil) company;
(groupe) gathering; (présence): **la ~ de qn** sb's
company; **homme/femme de ~** escort; **tenir
~ à qn** to keep sb company; **fausser ~ à qn** to
give sb the slip, slip ou sneak away from sb;
en ~ de in the company of; **Dupont et ~,
Dupont et Cie** Dupont and Company,
Dupont and Co; **~ aérienne** airline
(company)

compagnon [kɔ̃paɲɔ̃] nm companion;
(autrefois: ouvrier) craftsman; journeyman

comparable [kɔ̃paʀabl] adj: **~ (à)** comparable
(to)

comparaison [kɔ̃paʀɛzɔ̃] nf comparison;
(métaphore) simile; **en ~ (de)** in comparison
(with); **par ~ (à)** by comparison (with)

comparaître [kɔ̃paʀɛtʀ] vi: **~ (devant)** to
appear (before)

comparer [kɔ̃paʀe] vt to compare; **~ qch/qn
à ou et** (pour choisir) to compare sth/sb with ou
and; (pour établir une similitude) to compare sth/
sb to ou and

compartiment [kɔ̃paʀtimɑ̃] nm
compartment

comparution [kɔ̃paʀysjɔ̃] nf appearance

compas [kɔ̃pa] nm (Géom) (pair of)
compasses pl; (Navig) compass

compatible [kɔ̃patibl] adj compatible;
~ (avec) compatible (with)

compatir [kɔ̃patiʀ] vi: **~ (à)** to sympathize
(with)

compatriote [kɔ̃patʀijɔt] nm/f compatriot,
fellow countryman/woman

compensation [kɔ̃pɑ̃sasjɔ̃] nf
compensation; (Banque) clearing; **en ~** ou
as compensation

compenser [kɔ̃pɑ̃se] vt to compensate for,
make up for

compère [kɔ̃pɛʀ] nm accomplice; fellow
musician ou comedian etc

compétence [kɔ̃petɑ̃s] nf competence

compétent, e [kɔ̃petɑ̃, -ɑ̃t] adj (apte)
competent, capable; (Jur) competent

compétition [kɔ̃petisjɔ̃] nf (gén)
competition; (Sport: épreuve) event; **la ~**
competitive sport; **être en ~ avec** to be
competing with; **la ~ automobile** motor
racing

complainte [kɔ̃plɛ̃t] nf lament

complaire [kɔ̃plɛʀ]: **se complaire** vi: **se ~
dans/parmi** to take pleasure in/in being
among

complaisance [kɔ̃plɛzɑ̃s] nf kindness; (péj)
indulgence; (: fatuité) complacency;
attestation de ~ certificate produced to oblige
a patient etc; **pavillon de ~** flag of
convenience

complaisant, e [kɔ̃plɛzɑ̃, -ɑ̃t] vb voir
complaire ▷ adj (aimable) kind; obliging; (péj)
accommodating; (: fat) complacent

complément [kɔ̃plemɑ̃] nm complement;
(reste) remainder; (Ling) complement;
~ d'information (Admin) supplementary ou
further information; **~ d'agent** agent;
~ (d'objet) direct/indirect direct/indirect
object; **~ (circonstanciel) de lieu/temps**
adverbial phrase of place/time; **~ de nom**
possessive phrase

complémentaire [kɔ̃plemɑ̃tɛʀ] adj
complementary; (additionnel) supplementary

complet, -ète [kɔ̃plɛ, -ɛt] adj complete;
(plein: hôtel etc) full ▷ nm (aussi: **~-veston**) suit;
pain ~ wholemeal bread; **au (grand) ~** all
together

complètement [kɔ̃plɛtmɑ̃] adv (en entier)
completely; (absolument: fou, faux etc)
absolutely; (à fond: étudier etc) fully,
in depth

compléter [kɔ̃plete] vt (porter à la quantité
voulue) to complete; (augmenter: connaissances,
études) to complement, supplement;
(: garde-robe) to add to; **se compléter** vi
(personnes) to complement one another;
(collection etc) to become complete

complexe [kɔ̃plɛks] adj complex ▷ nm (Psych)
complex, hang-up; (bâtiments):
~ hospitalier/industriel hospital/
industrial complex

complexé, e [kɔ̃plɛkse] adj mixed-up,
hung-up

complication [kɔ̃plikasjɔ̃] nf complexity,
intricacy; (difficulté, ennui) complication;
complications nfpl (Méd) complications

complice [kɔ̃plis] nm accomplice

complicité [kɔ̃plisite] nf complicity

compliment [kɔ̃plimɑ̃] nm (louange)
compliment; **compliments** nmpl (félicitations)
congratulations

compliqué, e [kɔ̃plike] adj complicated,
complex, intricate; (personne) complicated

compliquer [kɔ̃plike] vt to complicate; **se
compliquer** vi (situation) to become
complicated; **se ~ la vie** to make life difficult
ou complicated for o.s

complot [kɔ̃plo] nm plot

comportement [kɔ̃pɔʀtəmɑ̃] nm
behaviour (Brit), behavior (US); (Tech:
d'une pièce, d'un véhicule) behavio(u)r,
performance

comporter [kɔ̃pɔʀte] vt (consister en) to
consist of, be composed of, comprise; (être
équipé de) to have; (impliquer) to entail, involve;
se comporter vi to behave; (Tech) to behave,
perform

composant [kɔ̃pozɑ̃] nm component,
constituent

composé, e [kɔ̃poze] adj (visage, air) studied;
(Bio, Chimie, Ling) compound ▷ nm (Chimie,
Ling) compound; **~ de** made up of

composer [kɔ̃poze] vt (musique, texte) to compose; (mélange, équipe) to make up; (faire partie de) to make up, form; (Typo) to (type)set ▷ vi (Scol) to sit ou do a test; (transiger) to come to terms; **se ~ de** to be composed of, be made up of; **~ un numéro** (au téléphone) to dial a number

compositeur, -trice [kɔ̃pozitœʀ, -tʀis] nm/f (Mus) composer; (Typo) compositor, typesetter

composition [kɔ̃pozisjɔ̃] nf composition; (Scol) test; (Typo) (type)setting, composition; **de bonne ~** (accommodant) easy to deal with; **amener qn à ~** to get sb to come to terms; **~ française** (Scol) French essay

composter [kɔ̃poste] vt to date-stamp; (billet) to punch

● **COMPOSTER**
●
● In France you have to punch your ticket
● on the platform to validate it before
● getting onto the train.

compote [kɔ̃pɔt] nf stewed fruit no pl; **~ de pommes** stewed apples

compréhensible [kɔ̃pʀeɑ̃sibl] adj comprehensible; (attitude) understandable

compréhensif, -ive [kɔ̃pʀeɑ̃sif, -iv] adj understanding

comprendre [kɔ̃pʀɑ̃dʀ] vt to understand; (se composer de) to comprise, consist of; (inclure) to include; **se faire ~** to make o.s. understood; to get one's ideas across; **mal ~** to misunderstand

compresse [kɔ̃pʀɛs] nf compress

compression [kɔ̃pʀesjɔ̃] nf compression; (d'un crédit etc) reduction

comprimé, e [kɔ̃pʀime] adj: **air ~** compressed air ▷ nm tablet

comprimer [kɔ̃pʀime] vt to compress; (fig: crédit etc) to reduce, cut down

compris, e [kɔ̃pʀi, -iz] pp de **comprendre** ▷ adj (inclus) included; **~? understood?**, is that clear?; **~ entre** (situé) contained between; **la maison ~e/non ~e, y/non ~ la maison** including/excluding the house; **service ~** service (charge) included; **100 euros tout ~** 100 euros all inclusive ou all-in

compromettre [kɔ̃pʀɔmɛtʀ] vt to compromise

compromis [kɔ̃pʀɔmi] vb voir **compromettre** ▷ nm compromise

comptabilité [kɔ̃tabilite] nf (activité, technique) accounting, accountancy; (d'une société: comptes) accounts pl, books pl; (: service) accounts office ou department; **~ à partie double** double-entry book-keeping

comptable [kɔ̃tabl] nm/f accountant ▷ adj accounts cpd, accounting

comptant [kɔ̃tɑ̃] adv: **payer ~** to pay cash; **acheter ~** to buy for cash

compte [kɔ̃t] nm count, counting; (total, montant) count, (right) number; (bancaire, facture) account; **comptes** nmpl accounts, books; (fig) explanation sg; **ouvrir un ~** to open an account; **rendre des ~s à qn** (fig) to be answerable to sb; **faire le ~ de** to count up, make a count of; **tout ~ fait** on the whole; **à ce ~-là** (dans ce cas) in that case; (à ce train-là) at that rate; **en fin de ~** (fig) all things considered, weighing it all up; **au bout du ~** in the final analysis; **à bon ~** at a favourable price; (fig) lightly; **avoir son ~** (fig: fam) to have had it; **s'en tirer à bon ~** to get off lightly; **pour le ~ de** on behalf of; **pour son propre ~** for one's own benefit; **sur le ~ de qn** (à son sujet) about sb; **travailler à son ~** to work for oneself; **mettre qch sur le ~ de qn** (le rendre responsable) to attribute sth to sb; **prendre qch à son ~** to take responsibility for sth; **trouver son ~ à qch** to do well out of sth; **régler un ~** (s'acquitter de qch) to settle an account; (se venger) to get one's own back; **rendre ~** (à qn) **de qch** to give an account of sth; **rendre des ~s à qn** (fig) to be answerable to sb; **tenir ~ de qch** to take sth into account; **~ tenu de** taking into account; **~ en banque** bank account; **~ chèque(s)** current account; **~ chèque postal (CCP)** Post Office account; **~ client** (sur bilan) accounts receivable; **~ courant (CC)** current account; **~ de dépôt** deposit account; **~ d'exploitation** operating account; **~ fournisseur** (sur bilan) accounts payable; **~ à rebours** countdown; **~ rendu** account, report; (de film, livre) review; voir aussi **rendre**

compte-gouttes [kɔ̃tɡut] nm inv dropper

compter [kɔ̃te] vt to count; (facturer) to charge for; (avoir à son actif, comporter) to have; (prévoir) to allow, reckon; (tenir compte de, inclure) to include; (penser, espérer): **~ réussir/revenir** to expect to succeed/return ▷ vi to count; (être économe) to economize; (être non négligeable) to count, matter; (valoir): **~ pour** to count for; (figurer): **~ parmi** to be ou rank among; **~ sur** to count (up)on; **~ avec qch/qn** to reckon with ou take account of sth/sb; **~ sans qch/qn** to reckon without sth/sb; **sans ~ que** besides which; **à ~ du 10 janvier** (Comm) (as) from 10th January

compteur [kɔ̃tœʀ] nm meter; **~ de vitesse** speedometer

comptine [kɔ̃tin] nf nursery rhyme

comptoir [kɔ̃twaʀ] nm (de magasin) counter; (de café) counter, bar; (colonial) trading post

compulser [kɔ̃pylse] vt to consult

comte, comtesse [kɔ̃t, kɔ̃tɛs] nm/f count/countess

con, ne [kɔ̃, kɔn] adj (fam!) bloody (Brit) ou damned stupid (!)

concéder [kɔ̃sede] vt to grant; (défaite, point) to concede; **~ que** to concede that

concentré [kɔ̃sɑ̃tʀe] nm concentrate; **~ de tomates** tomato purée

concentrer [kɔ̃sɑ̃tʀe] vt to concentrate; **se concentrer** vi to concentrate

concept [kɔ̃sɛpt] nm concept

conception [kɔ̃sɛpsjɔ̃] nf conception; (d'une machine etc) design

concerner [kɔ̃sɛʀne] vt to concern; **en ce qui me concerne** as far as I am concerned; **en ce qui concerne ceci** as far as this is concerned, with regard to this

concert [kɔ̃sɛʀ] nm concert; **de ~** adv in unison; together; (décider) unanimously

concerter [kɔ̃sɛʀte] vt to devise; **se concerter** vi (collaborateurs etc) to put our (ou their etc) heads together, consult (each other)

concession [kɔ̃sesjɔ̃] nf concession

concessionnaire [kɔ̃sesjɔnɛʀ] nm/f agent, dealer

concevoir [kɔ̃s(ə)vwaʀ] vt (idée, projet) to conceive (of); (méthode, plan d'appartement, décoration etc) to plan, design; (comprendre) to understand; (enfant) to conceive; **maison bien/mal conçue** well-/badly-designed ou -planned house

concierge [kɔ̃sjɛʀʒ] nm/f caretaker; (d'hôtel) head porter

conciliabules [kɔ̃siljabyl] nmpl (private) discussions, confabulations (Brit)

concilier [kɔ̃silje] vt to reconcile; **se ~ qn/l'appui de qn** to win sb over/sb's support

concis, e [kɔ̃si, -iz] adj concise

concitoyen, ne [kɔ̃sitwajɛ̃, -ɛn] nm/f fellow citizen

concluant, e [kɔ̃klyɑ̃, -ɑ̃t] vb voir **conclure** ▷ adj conclusive

conclure [kɔ̃klyʀ] vt to conclude; (signer: accord, pacte) to enter into; (déduire): **~ qch de qch** to deduce sth from sth; **~ à l'acquittement** to decide in favour of an acquittal; **~ au suicide** to come to the conclusion (ou Jur) to pronounce) that it is a case of suicide; **~ un marché** to clinch a deal; **j'en conclus que** from that I conclude that

conclusion [kɔ̃klyzjɔ̃] nf conclusion; **conclusions** nfpl (Jur) submissions; findings; **en ~** in conclusion

conçois [kɔ̃swa], **conçoive** etc [kɔ̃swav] vb voir **concevoir**

concombre [kɔ̃kɔ̃bʀ] nm cucumber

concorder [kɔ̃kɔʀde] vi to tally, agree

concourir [kɔ̃kuʀiʀ] vi (Sport) to compete; **~ à** vt (effet etc) to work towards

concours [kɔ̃kuʀ] vb voir **concourir** ▷ nm competition; (Scol) competitive examination; (assistance) aid, help; **recrutement par voie de ~** recruitment by (competitive) examination; **apporter son ~ à** to give one's support to; **~ de circonstances** combination of circumstances; **~ hippique** horse show; voir **hors-concours**

concret, -ète [kɔ̃kʀɛ, -ɛt] adj concrete

concrétiser [kɔ̃kʀetize] vt to realize; **se concrétiser** vi to materialize

conçu, e [kɔ̃sy] pp de **concevoir**

concubinage [kɔ̃kybinaʒ] nm (Jur) cohabitation

concurrence [kɔ̃kyʀɑ̃s] nf competition; **jusqu'à ~ de** up to; **faire ~ à** to be in competition with; **~ déloyale** unfair competition

concurrent, e [kɔ̃kyʀɑ̃, -ɑ̃t] adj competing ▷ nm/f (Sport, Écon etc) competitor; (Scol) candidate

condamner [kɔ̃dane] vt (blâmer) to condemn; (Jur) to sentence; (porte, ouverture) to fill in, block up; (malade) to give up (hope for); (obliger): **~ qn à qch/à faire** to condemn sb to sth/to do; **~ qn à deux ans de prison** to sentence sb to two years' imprisonment; **~ qn à une amende** to impose a fine on sb

condensation [kɔ̃dɑ̃sasjɔ̃] nf condensation

condenser [kɔ̃dɑ̃se]: **se condenser** vi to condense

condisciple [kɔ̃disipl] nm/f school fellow, fellow student

condition [kɔ̃disjɔ̃] nf condition; **conditions** nfpl (tarif, prix) terms; (circonstances) conditions; **sans ~** adj unconditional ▷ adv unconditionally; **sous ~ que** on condition that; **à ~ de ou que** provided that; **en bonne ~** in good condition; **mettre en ~** (Sport etc) to get fit; (Psych) to condition (mentally); **~s de vie** living conditions

conditionnel, le [kɔ̃disjɔnɛl] adj conditional ▷ nm conditional (tense)

conditionnement [kɔ̃disjɔnmɑ̃] nm (emballage) packaging; (fig) conditioning

conditionner [kɔ̃disjɔne] vt (déterminer) to determine; (Comm: produit) to package; (fig: personne) to condition; **air conditionné** air conditioning; **réflexe conditionné** conditioned reflex

condoléances [kɔ̃dɔleɑ̃s] nfpl condolences

conducteur, -trice [kɔ̃dyktœʀ, -tʀis] adj (Élec) conducting ▷ nm/f (Auto etc) driver; (d'une machine) operator ▷ nm (Élec etc) conductor

conduire [kɔ̃dɥiʀ] vt (véhicule, passager) to drive; (délégation, troupeau) to lead; **se conduire** vi to behave; **~ vers/à** to lead towards/to; **~ qn quelque part** to take sb somewhere; to drive sb somewhere

conduite [kɔ̃dɥit] nf (en auto) driving; (comportement) behaviour (Brit), behavior (US); (d'eau, de gaz) pipe; **sous la ~ de** led by; **~ forcée** pressure pipe; **~ à gauche** left-hand drive; **~ intérieure** saloon (car)

cône [kon] nm cone; **en forme de ~** cone-shaped

confection [kɔ̃fɛksjɔ̃] nf (fabrication) making; (Couture): **la ~** the clothing industry, the rag trade (fam); **vêtement de ~** ready-to-wear ou off-the-peg garment

confectionner [kɔ̃fɛksjɔne] vt to make

conférence [kɔ̃feʀɑ̃s] nf (exposé) lecture; (pourparlers) conference; **~ de presse** press conference; **~ au sommet** summit (conference)

conférencier, -ière [kɔ̃ferɑ̃sje, -jɛʀ] nm/f lecturer

confesser [kɔ̃fese] vt to confess; **se confesser** vi (Rel) to go to confession

confession [kɔ̃fɛsjɔ̃] nf confession; (culte: catholique etc) denomination

confetti [kɔ̃feti] nm confetti no pl

confiance [kɔ̃fjɑ̃s] nf (en l'honnêteté de qn) confidence, trust; (en la valeur de qch) faith; **avoir ~ en** to have confidence ou faith in, trust; **faire ~ à** to trust; **en toute ~** with complete confidence; **de ~** trustworthy, reliable; **mettre qn en ~** to win sb's trust; **vote de ~** (Pol) vote of confidence; **inspirer ~ à** to inspire confidence in; **~ en soi** self-confidence; voir **question**

confiant, e [kɔ̃fjɑ̃, -ɑ̃t] adj confident; trusting

confidence [kɔ̃fidɑ̃s] nf confidence

confidentiel, le [kɔ̃fidɑ̃sjɛl] adj confidential

confier [kɔ̃fje] vt: **~ à qn** (objet en dépôt, travail etc) to entrust to sb; (secret, pensée) to confide to sb; **se ~ à qn** to confide in sb

confins [kɔ̃fɛ̃] nmpl: **aux ~ de** on the borders of

confirmation [kɔ̃firmasjɔ̃] nf confirmation

confirmer [kɔ̃firme] vt to confirm; **~ qn dans une croyance/ses fonctions** to strengthen sb in a belief/his duties

confiserie [kɔ̃fizri] nf (magasin) confectioner's ou sweet shop (Brit), candy store (US); **confiseries** nfpl (bonbons) confectionery sg, sweets, candy no pl

confisquer [kɔ̃fiske] vt to confiscate

confit, e [kɔ̃fi, -it] adj: **fruits ~s** crystallized fruits ▷ nm: **~ d'oie** potted goose

confiture [kɔ̃fityr] nf jam; **~ d'oranges** (orange) marmalade

conflit [kɔ̃fli] nm conflict

confondre [kɔ̃fɔ̃dr] vt (jumeaux, faits) to confuse, mix up; (témoin, menteur) to confound; **se confondre** vi to merge; **se ~ en excuses** to offer profuse apologies, apologize profusely; **~ qch/qn avec qch/qn d'autre** to mistake sth/sb for sth/sb else

confondu, e [kɔ̃fɔ̃dy] pp de **confondre** ▷ adj (stupéfait) speechless, overcome; **toutes catégories ~es** taking all categories together

conforme [kɔ̃fɔrm] adj: **~ à** (en accord avec: loi, règle) in accordance with, in keeping with; (identique à) true to; **copie certifiée ~** (Admin) certified copy; **~ à la commande** as per order

conformément [kɔ̃fɔrmemɑ̃] adv: **~ à** in accordance with

conformer [kɔ̃fɔrme] vt: **~ qch à** to model sth on; **se ~ à** to conform to

confort [kɔ̃fɔr] nm comfort; **tout ~** (Comm) with all mod cons (Brit) ou modern conveniences

confortable [kɔ̃fɔrtabl] adj comfortable

confrère [kɔ̃frɛr] nm colleague; fellow member

confronter [kɔ̃frɔ̃te] vt to confront; (textes) to compare, collate

confus, e [kɔ̃fy, -yz] adj (vague) confused; (embarrassé) embarrassed

confusion [kɔ̃fyzjɔ̃] nf (voir confus) confusion; embarrassment; (voir confondre) confusion; mixing up; (erreur) confusion; **des peines** (Jur) concurrency of sentences

congé [kɔ̃ʒe] nm (vacances) holiday; (arrêt de travail) time off no pl, leave no pl; (Mil) leave no pl; (avis de départ) notice; **en ~** on holiday; off (work); on leave; **semaine/jour de ~** week/day off; **prendre ~ de qn** to take one's leave of sb; **donner son ~ à** to hand ou give in one's notice to; **~ de maladie** sick leave; **~ de maternité** maternity leave; **~s payés** paid holiday ou leave

congédier [kɔ̃ʒedje] vt to dismiss

congélateur [kɔ̃ʒelatœr] nm freezer, deep freeze

congeler [kɔ̃ʒ(ə)le] vt to freeze; **les produits congelés** frozen foods; **se congeler** vi to freeze

congestion [kɔ̃ʒɛstjɔ̃] nf congestion; **~ cérébrale** stroke; **~ pulmonaire** congestion of the lungs

congestionner [kɔ̃ʒɛstjɔne] vt to congest; (Méd) to flush

Congo [kɔ̃go] nm: **le ~** (pays, fleuve) the Congo

congrès [kɔ̃grɛ] nm congress

conifère [kɔnifɛr] nm conifer

conjecture [kɔ̃ʒɛktyr] nf conjecture, speculation no pl

conjoint, e [kɔ̃ʒwɛ̃, -wɛ̃t] adj joint ▷ nm/f spouse

conjonction [kɔ̃ʒɔ̃ksjɔ̃] nf (Ling) conjunction

conjonctivite [kɔ̃ʒɔ̃ktivit] nf conjunctivitis

conjoncture [kɔ̃ʒɔ̃ktyr] nf circumstances pl; **la ~ (économique)** the economic climate ou situation

conjugaison [kɔ̃ʒygɛzɔ̃] nf (Ling) conjugation

conjuguer [kɔ̃ʒyge] vt (Ling) to conjugate; (efforts etc) to combine

conjuration [kɔ̃ʒyrasjɔ̃] nf conspiracy

conjurer [kɔ̃ʒyre] vt (sort, maladie) to avert; (implorer): **~ qn de faire qch** to beseech ou entreat sb to do sth

connaissance [kɔnɛsɑ̃s] nf (savoir) knowledge no pl; (personne connue) acquaintance; (conscience) consciousness; **connaissances** nfpl knowledge no pl; **être sans ~** to be unconscious; **perdre/reprendre ~** to lose/regain consciousness; **à ma/sa ~** to (the best of) my/his knowledge; **faire ~ avec qn ou la ~ de qn** (rencontrer) to meet sb; (apprendre à connaître) to get to know sb; **avoir ~ de** to be aware of; **prendre ~ de** (document etc) to peruse; **en ~ de cause** with full knowledge of the facts; **de ~** (personne, visage) familiar

connaisseur, -euse [kɔnɛsœr, -øz] nm/f connoisseur ▷ adj expert

connaître [kɔnɛtr] vt to know; (éprouver) to experience; (avoir: succès) to have; to enjoy;

~ de nom/vue to know by name/sight; **se connaître** vi to know each other; (soi-même) to know o.s.; **ils se sont connus à Genève** they (first) met in Geneva; **s'y ~ en qch** to know about sth

connecter [kɔnɛkte] vt to connect; **se ~ à Internet** to log onto the Internet

connerie [kɔnʀi] nf (fam) (bloody) stupid (Brit) ou damn-fool (US) thing to do ou say

connexion [kɔnɛksjɔ̃] nf connection

connu, e [kɔny] pp de **connaître** ▷ adj (célèbre) well-known

conquérir [kɔ̃keʀiʀ] vt to conquer, win

conquête [kɔ̃kɛt] nf conquest

consacrer [kɔ̃sakʀe] vt (Rel) to consecrate; **~ qch (à)** to consecrate sth (to); (fig: usage etc) to sanction, establish; (employer): **~ qch à** to devote ou dedicate sth to; **se ~ à qch/faire** to dedicate ou devote o.s. to sth/to doing

conscience [kɔ̃sjɑ̃s] nf conscience; (perception) consciousness; **avoir/prendre ~ de** to be/become aware of; **perdre/reprendre ~** to lose/regain consciousness; **avoir bonne/mauvaise ~** to have a clear/guilty conscience; **en (toute) ~** in all conscience

consciencieux, -euse [kɔ̃sjɑ̃sjø, -øz] adj conscientious

conscient, e [kɔ̃sjɑ̃, -ɑ̃t] adj conscious; **~ de** aware ou conscious of

conscrit [kɔ̃skʀi] nm conscript

consécutif, -ive [kɔ̃sekytif, -iv] adj consecutive; **~ à** following upon

conseil [kɔ̃sɛj] nm (avis) piece of advice, advice no pl; (assemblée) council; (expert): **~ en recrutement** recruitment consultant ▷ adj: **ingénieur-~** engineering consultant; **tenir ~** to hold a meeting; to deliberate; **donner un ~ ou des ~s à** to give sb (a piece of) advice; **demander ~ à qn** to ask sb's advice; **prendre ~ (auprès de qn)** to take advice (from sb); **~ d'administration (CA)** board (of directors); **~ de classe** (Scol) meeting of teachers, parents and class representatives to discuss pupils' progress; **~ de discipline** disciplinary committee; **~ général** regional council; see note; **~ de guerre** court-martial; **le ~ des ministres** ≈ the Cabinet; **~ municipal (CM)** town council; **~ régional** regional board of elected representatives; **~ de révision** recruitment ou draft (US) board

○ **CONSEIL GÉNÉRAL**
○
○ Each "département" of France is run by
○ a Conseil général, whose remit covers
○ personnel, transport infrastructure,
○ housing, school grants and economic
○ development. The council is made up of
○ "conseillers généraux", each of whom
○ represents a "canton" and is elected for
○ a six-year term. Half of the council's
○ membership are elected every three years.

conseiller¹ [kɔ̃seje] vt (personne) to advise; (méthode, action) to recommend, advise; **~ qch à qn** to recommend sth to sb; **~ à qn de faire qch** to advise sb to do sth

conseiller², -ière [kɔ̃seje, -ɛʀ] nm/f adviser; **~ général** regional councillor; **~ matrimonial** marriage guidance counsellor; **~ municipal** town councillor; **~ d'orientation** (Scol) careers adviser (Brit), (school) counselor (US)

consentement [kɔ̃sɑ̃tmɑ̃] nm consent

consentir [kɔ̃sɑ̃tiʀ] vt: **~ (à qch/faire)** to agree ou consent (to sth/to doing); **~ qch à qn** to grant sb sth

conséquence [kɔ̃sekɑ̃s] nf consequence, outcome; **conséquences** nfpl consequences, repercussions; **en ~** (donc) consequently; (de façon appropriée) accordingly; **ne pas tirer à ~** to be unlikely to have any repercussions; **sans ~** unimportant; **de ~** important

conséquent, e [kɔ̃sekɑ̃, -ɑ̃t] adj logical, rational; (fam: important) substantial; **par ~** consequently

conservateur, -trice [kɔ̃sɛʀvatœʀ, -tʀis] adj conservative ▷ nm/f (Pol) conservative; (de musée) curator ▷ nm (pour aliments) preservative

conservatoire [kɔ̃sɛʀvatwaʀ] nm academy; (Écologie) conservation area

conserve [kɔ̃sɛʀv] nf (gén pl) canned ou tinned (Brit) food; **~s de poisson** canned ou tinned (Brit) fish; **en ~** canned, tinned (Brit); **de ~** (ensemble) in concert; (naviguer) in convoy

conserver [kɔ̃sɛʀve] vt (faculté) to retain, keep; (habitude) to keep up; (amis, livres) to keep; (préserver, Culin) to preserve; **se conserver** vi (aliments) to keep; **"~ au frais"** "store in a cool place"

considérable [kɔ̃sideʀabl] adj considerable, significant, extensive

considération [kɔ̃sideʀasjɔ̃] nf consideration; (estime) esteem, respect; **considérations** nfpl (remarques) reflections; **prendre en ~** to take into consideration ou account; **ceci mérite ~** this is worth considering; **en ~ de** given, because of

considérer [kɔ̃sideʀe] vt to consider; (regarder) to consider, study; **~ qch comme** to regard sth as

consigne [kɔ̃siɲ] nf (Comm) deposit; (de gare) left luggage (office) (Brit), checkroom (US); (punition: Scol) detention; (: Mil) confinement to barracks; (ordre, instruction) instructions pl; **~ automatique** left-luggage locker; **~s de sécurité** safety instructions

consigner [kɔ̃siɲe] vt (note, pensée) to record; (marchandises) to deposit; (punir: Mil) to confine to barracks; (: élève) to put in detention; (Comm) to put a deposit on

consistant, e [kɔ̃sistɑ̃, -ɑ̃t] adj thick; solid

consister [kɔ̃siste] vi: **~ en/dans/à faire** to consist of/in/in doing

consœur [kɔ̃sœʀ] nf (lady) colleague; fellow member

console [kɔ̃sɔl] nf console; ~ **graphique** ou **de visualisation** (Inform) visual display unit, VDU; ~ **de jeux** games console

consoler [kɔ̃sɔle] vt to console; **se ~ (de qch)** to console o.s. (for sth)

consolider [kɔ̃sɔlide] vt to strengthen, reinforce; (fig) to consolidate; **bilan consolidé** consolidated balance sheet

consommateur, -trice [kɔ̃sɔmatœʀ, -tʀis] nm/f (Écon) consumer; (dans un café) customer

consommation [kɔ̃sɔmasjɔ̃] nf (Écon) consumption; (Jur) consummation; (boisson) drink; ~ **aux 100 km** (Auto) (fuel) consumption p. 100 km, ≈ miles per gallon (mpg), ≈ gas mileage (US); **de** ~ (biens, société) consumer cpd

consommer [kɔ̃sɔme] vt (personne) to eat ou drink, consume; (voiture, usine, poêle) to use, consume; (Jur: mariage) to consummate ▷ vi (dans un café) to (have a) drink

consonne [kɔ̃sɔn] nf consonant

conspirer [kɔ̃spiʀe] vi to conspire, plot; ~ **à** (tendre à) to conspire to

constamment [kɔ̃stamɑ̃] adv constantly

constant, e [kɔ̃stɑ̃, -ɑ̃t] adj constant; (personne) steadfast ▷ nf constant

constat [kɔ̃sta] nm (d'huissier) certified report (by bailiff); (de police) report; (observation) (observed) fact, observation; (affirmation) statement; ~ **(à l'amiable)** (jointly agreed) statement for insurance purposes; ~ **d'échec** acknowledgement of failure

constatation [kɔ̃statasjɔ̃] nf noticing; certifying; (remarque) observation

constater [kɔ̃state] vt (remarquer) to note, notice; (Admin, Jur: attester) to certify; (dégâts) to note; ~ **que** (dire) to state that

consterner [kɔ̃stɛʀne] vt to dismay

constipé, e [kɔ̃stipe] adj constipated; (fig) stiff

constitué, e [kɔ̃stitɥe] adj: ~ **de** made up ou composed of; **bien ~** of sound constitution; well-formed

constituer [kɔ̃stitɥe] vt (comité, équipe) to set up, form; (dossier, collection) to put together, build up; (éléments, parties: composer) to make up, constitute; (représenter, être) to constitute; **se ~ prisonnier** to give o.s. up; **se ~ partie civile** to bring an independent action for damages

constitution [kɔ̃stitysjɔ̃] nf setting up; building up; (composition) composition, make-up; (santé, Pol) constitution

constructeur [kɔ̃stʀyktœʀ] nm/f manufacturer, builder

constructif, -ive [kɔ̃stʀyktif, -iv] adj (positif) constructive

construction [kɔ̃stʀyksjɔ̃] nf construction, building

construire [kɔ̃stʀɥiʀ] vt to build, construct; **se construire** vi: **l'immeuble s'est**

construit très vite the building went up ou was built very quickly

consul [kɔ̃syl] nm consul

consulat [kɔ̃syla] nm consulate

consultant, e [kɔ̃syltɑ̃, -ɑ̃t] adj, nm consultant

consultation [kɔ̃syltasjɔ̃] nf consultation; **consultations** nfpl (Pol) talks; **être en** ~ (délibération) to be in consultation; (médecin) to be consulting; **aller à la** ~ (Méd) to go to the surgery (Brit) ou doctor's office (US); **heures de** ~ (Méd) surgery (Brit) ou office (US) hours

consulter [kɔ̃sylte] vt to consult; **se** ~ (médecin) to hold surgery (Brit), be in (the office) (US); **se consulter** vi to confer

consumer [kɔ̃syme] vt to consume; **se consumer** vi to burn; **se ~ de chagrin/ douleur** to be consumed with sorrow/grief

contact [kɔ̃takt] nm contact; **au** ~ **de** (air, peau) on contact with; (gens) through contact with; **mettre/couper le** ~ (Auto) to switch on/off the ignition; **entrer en** ~ (fils, objets) to come into contact, make contact; **se mettre en ~ avec** (Radio) to make contact with; **prendre** ~ **avec** (relation d'affaires, connaissance) to get in touch ou contact with

contacter [kɔ̃takte] vt to contact, get in touch with

contagieux, -euse [kɔ̃taʒjø, -øz] adj infectious; (par le contact) contagious

contaminer [kɔ̃tamine] vt (par un virus) to infect; (par des radiations) to contaminate

conte [kɔ̃t] nm tale; ~ **de fées** fairy tale

contempler [kɔ̃tɑ̃ple] vt to contemplate, gaze at

contemporain, e [kɔ̃tɑ̃pɔʀɛ̃, -ɛn] adj, nm/f contemporary

contenance [kɔ̃tnɑ̃s] nf (d'un récipient) capacity; (attitude) bearing, attitude; **perdre** ~ to lose one's composure; **se donner une** ~ to give the impression of composure; **faire bonne** ~ **(devant)** to put on a bold front (in the face of)

conteneur [kɔ̃tnœʀ] nm container; ~ **(de bouteilles)** bottle bank

contenir [kɔ̃t(ə)niʀ] vt to contain; (avoir une capacité de) to hold; **se contenir** vi (se retenir) to control o.s. ou one's emotions, contain o.s.

content, e [kɔ̃tɑ̃, -ɑ̃t] adj pleased, glad; ~ **de** pleased with; **je serais ~ que tu ...** I would be pleased if you ...

contenter [kɔ̃tɑ̃te] vt to satisfy, please; (envie) to satisfy; **se ~ de** to content o.s. with

contentieux [kɔ̃tɑ̃sjø] nm (Comm) litigation; (: service) litigation department; (Pol etc) contentious issues pl

contenu, e [kɔ̃t(ə)ny] pp de **contenir** ▷ nm (d'un bol) contents pl; (d'un texte) content

conter [kɔ̃te] vt to recount, relate; **en ~ de belles à qn** to tell tall stories to sb

contestable [kɔ̃tɛstabl] adj questionable

contestation [kɔ̃tɛstasjɔ̃] nf questioning,

contesting; (Pol): **la** ~ anti-establishment activity, protest

conteste [kɔ̃tɛst]: **sans** ~ adv unquestionably, indisputably

contester [kɔ̃teste] vt to question, contest ▷ vi (Pol: gén) to rebel (against established authority), protest

contexte [kɔ̃tɛkst] nm context

contigu, ë [kɔ̃tigy] adj: ~ **(à)** adjacent (to)

continent [kɔ̃tinɑ̃] nm continent

continu, e [kɔ̃tiny] adj continuous; **faire la journée** ~**e** to work without taking a full lunch break; **(courant)** ~ direct current, DC

continuel, le [kɔ̃tinɥɛl] adj (qui se répète) constant, continual; (continu) continuous

continuer [kɔ̃tinɥe] vt (travail, voyage etc) to continue (with), carry on (with), go on with; (prolonger: alignement, rue) to continue ▷ vi (pluie, vie, bruit) to continue, go on; (voyageur) to go on; **se continuer** vi to carry on; ~ **à** ou **de faire** to go on ou continue doing

contorsionner [kɔ̃tɔʀsjɔne]: **se contorsionner** vi to contort o.s., writhe about

contour [kɔ̃tuʀ] nm outline, contour; **contours** nmpl (d'une rivière etc) windings

contourner [kɔ̃tuʀne] vt to bypass, walk ou drive) round; (difficulté) to get round

contraceptif, -ive [kɔ̃tʀasɛptif, -iv] adj, nm contraceptive

contraception [kɔ̃tʀasɛpsjɔ̃] nf contraception

contracté, e [kɔ̃tʀakte] adj (muscle) tense, contracted; (personne: tendu) tense, tensed up; **article** ~ (Ling) contracted article

contracter [kɔ̃tʀakte] vt (muscle etc) to tense, contract; (maladie, dette, obligation) to contract; (assurance) to take out; **se contracter** vi (métal, muscles) to contract

contractuel, le [kɔ̃tʀaktɥɛl] adj contractual ▷ nm/f (agent) traffic warden; (employé) contract employee

contradiction [kɔ̃tʀadiksjɔ̃] nf contradiction

contradictoire [kɔ̃tʀadiktwaʀ] adj contradictory, conflicting; **débat** ~ (open) debate

contraignant, e [kɔ̃tʀɛɲɑ̃, -ɑ̃t] vb voir **contraindre** ▷ adj restricting

contraindre [kɔ̃tʀɛ̃dʀ] vt: ~ **qn à faire** to force ou compel sb to do

contraint, e [kɔ̃tʀɛ̃, -ɛ̃t] pp de **contraindre** ▷ nf constraint

contraire [kɔ̃tʀɛʀ] adj, nm opposite; ~ **à** contrary to; **au** ~ adv on the contrary

contrarier [kɔ̃tʀaʀje] vt (personne) to annoy, bother; (fig) to impede; (projets) to thwart, frustrate

contrariété [kɔ̃tʀaʀjete] nf annoyance

contraste [kɔ̃tʀast] nm contrast

contrat [kɔ̃tʀa] nm contract; (fig: accord, pacte) agreement; ~ **de travail** employment contract

contravention [kɔ̃tʀavɑ̃sjɔ̃] nf (infraction): ~ **à** contravention of; (amende) fine; (PV pour stationnement interdit) parking ticket; **dresser** ~ **à** (automobiliste) to book; to write out a parking ticket for

contre [kɔ̃tʀ] prép against; (en échange) (in exchange) for; **par** ~ on the other hand

contrebande [kɔ̃tʀəbɑ̃d] nf (trafic) contraband, smuggling; (marchandise) contraband, smuggled goods pl; **faire la** ~ **de** to smuggle

contrebandier, -ière [kɔ̃tʀəbɑ̃dje, -jɛʀ] nm/f smuggler

contrebas [kɔ̃tʀəba]: **en** ~ adv (down) below

contrebasse [kɔ̃tʀəbas] nf (double) bass

contrecarrer [kɔ̃tʀəkaʀe] vt to thwart

contrecœur [kɔ̃tʀəkœʀ]: **à** ~ adv (be) grudgingly, reluctantly

contrecoup [kɔ̃tʀəku] nm repercussions pl; **par** ~ as an indirect consequence

contredire [kɔ̃tʀədiʀ] vt (personne) to contradict; (témoignage, assertion, faits) to refute; **se contredire** vi to contradict o.s.

contrée [kɔ̃tʀe] nf region; land

contrefaçon [kɔ̃tʀəfasɔ̃] nf forgery; ~ **de brevet** patent infringement

contrefaire [kɔ̃tʀəfɛʀ] vt (document, signature) to forge, counterfeit; (personne, démarche) to mimic; (dénaturer: sa voix etc) to disguise

contre-indication [kɔ̃tʀɛ̃dikasjɔ̃] (pl **contre-indications**) nf (Méd) contra-indication; **"~ en cas d'eczéma"** "should not be used by people with eczema"

contre-indiqué, e [kɔ̃tʀɛ̃dike] adj (Méd) contraindicated; (déconseillé) unadvisable, ill-advised

contre-jour [kɔ̃tʀəʒuʀ]: **à** ~ adv against the light

contremaître [kɔ̃tʀəmɛtʀ] nm foreman

contrepartie [kɔ̃tʀəpaʀti] nf compensation; **en** ~ in compensation; in return

contre-pied [kɔ̃tʀəpje] nm (inverse, opposé): **le** ~ **de ...** the exact opposite of ...; **prendre le** ~ **de** to take the opposing view of; to take the opposite course to; **prendre qn à** ~ (Sport) to wrong-foot sb

contre-plaqué [kɔ̃tʀəplake] nm plywood

contrepoids [kɔ̃tʀəpwa] nm counterweight, counterbalance; **faire** ~ to act as a counterbalance

contrepoison [kɔ̃tʀəpwazɔ̃] nm antidote

contrer [kɔ̃tʀe] vt to counter

contresens [kɔ̃tʀəsɑ̃s] nm (erreur) misinterpretation; (mauvaise traduction) mistranslation; (absurdité) nonsense no pl; **à** ~ adv the wrong way

contretemps [kɔ̃tʀətɑ̃] nm hitch, contretemps; **à** ~ adv (Mus) out of time; (fig) at an inopportune moment

contrevenir [kɔ̃tʀəvniʀ]: ~ **à** vt to contravene

contribuable [kɔ̃tʀibɥabl] nm/f taxpayer

contribuer [kɔ̃tʀibɥe]: ~ **à** vt to contribute towards

contribution [kɔ̃tʀibysjɔ̃] nf contribution; **les –s** (bureaux) the tax office; **mettre à –** to call upon; **~s directes/indirectes** direct/ indirect taxation

contrôle [kɔ̃tʀol] nm checking no pl, check; supervision; monitoring; (test) test, examination; **perdre le – de son véhicule** to lose control of one's vehicle; **~ des changes** (Comm) exchange controls; **~ continu** (Scol) continuous assessment; **~ d'identité** identity check; **~ des naissances** birth control; **~ des prix** price control

contrôler [kɔ̃tʀole] vt (vérifier) to check; (surveiller: opérations) to supervise; (: prix) to monitor, control; (maîtriser, Comm: firme) to control; **se contrôler** vi to control o.s.

contrôleur, -euse [kɔ̃tʀolœʀ, -øz] nm/f (de train) (ticket) inspector; (de bus) (bus) conductor/tress; **~ de la navigation aérienne, ~ aérien** air traffic controller; **~ financier** financial controller

contrordre [kɔ̃tʀɔʀdʀ] nm counter-order, countermand; **sauf ~** unless otherwise directed

controversé, e [kɔ̃tʀovɛʀse] adj (personnage, question) controversial

contusion [kɔ̃tyzjɔ̃] nf bruise, contusion

convaincre [kɔ̃vɛ̃kʀ] vt: **~ qn (de qch)** to convince sb (of sth); **~ qn (de faire)** to persuade sb (to do); **~ qn de** (Jur: délit) to convict sb of

convalescence [kɔ̃valesɑ̃s] nf convalescence; **maison de ~** convalescent home

convenable [kɔ̃vnabl] adj suitable; (décent) acceptable, proper; (assez bon) decent, acceptable; adequate, passable

convenance [kɔ̃vnɑ̃s] nf: **à ma/votre ~** to my/your liking; **convenances** nfpl proprieties

convenir [kɔ̃vniʀ] vi to be suitable; **~ à** to suit; **il convient de** it is advisable to; (bienséant) it is right ou proper to; **~ de** (bien-fondé de qch) to admit (to), acknowledge; (date, somme etc) to agree upon; **~ que** (admettre) to admit that, acknowledge the fact that; **~ de faire qch** to agree to do sth; **il a été convenu que** it has been agreed that; **comme convenu** as agreed

convention [kɔ̃vɑ̃sjɔ̃] nf convention; **conventions** nfpl (convenances) convention sg, social conventions; **de ~** conventional; **~ collective** (Écon) collective agreement

conventionné, e [kɔ̃vɑ̃sjɔne] adj (Admin) applying charges laid down by the state

convenu, e [kɔ̃vny] pp de **convenir** ▷ adj agreed

conversation [kɔ̃vɛʀsasjɔ̃] nf conversation; **avoir de la ~** to be a good conversationalist

convertir [kɔ̃vɛʀtiʀ] vt: **~ qn (à)** to convert sb (to); **~ qch en** to convert sth into; **se ~ (à)** to be converted (to)

conviction [kɔ̃viksjɔ̃] nf conviction

convienne etc [kɔ̃vjɛn] vb voir **convenir**

convier [kɔ̃vje] vt: **~ qn à** (dîner etc) to (cordially) invite sb to; **~ qn à faire** to urge sb to do

convive [kɔ̃viv] nm/f guest (at table)

convivial, e [kɔ̃vivjal] adj (Inform) user-friendly

convocation [kɔ̃vokasjɔ̃] nf (voir convoquer) convening, convoking; summoning; invitation; (document) notification to attend; summons sg

convoi [kɔ̃vwa] nm (de voitures, prisonniers) convoy; (train) train; **~ (funèbre)** funeral procession

convoiter [kɔ̃vwate] vt to covet

convoquer [kɔ̃voke] vt (assemblée) to convene, convoke; (subordonné, témoin) to summon; (candidat) to ask to attend; **~ qn (à)** (réunion) to invite sb (to attend)

convoyeur [kɔ̃vwajœʀ] nm (Navig) escort ship; **~ de fonds** security guard

cookie [kuki] nm (Inform) cookie

coopération [kooperasjɔ̃] nf co-operation; (Admin): **la C~** ≈ Voluntary Service Overseas (Brit) ou the Peace Corps (US) (done as alternative to military service)

coopérer [koopere] vi: **~ (à)** to co-operate (in)

coordonné, e [kɔɔʀdɔne] adj coordinated ▷ nf (Ling) coordinate clause; **coordonnés** nmpl (vêtements) coordinates; **coordonnées** nfpl (Math) coordinates; (détails personnels) address, phone number, schedule etc; whereabouts

coordonner [kɔɔʀdɔne] vt to coordinate

copain, copine [kɔpɛ̃, kɔpin] nm/f mate (Brit), pal; (petit ami) boyfriend; (petite amie) girlfriend ▷ adj: **être ~ avec** to be pally with

copeau, x [kɔpo] nm shaving; (de métal) turning

copie [kɔpi] nf copy; (Scol) script, paper; exercise; **~ certifiée conforme** certified copy; **~ papier** (Inform) hard copy

copier [kɔpje] vt, vi to copy; **~ coller** (Inform) copy and paste; **~ sur** to copy from

copieur [kɔpjœʀ] nm (photo)copier

copieux, -euse [kɔpjø, -øz] adj copious, hearty

copine [kɔpin] nf voir **copain**

copropriété [kɔpʀopʀijete] nf co-ownership, joint ownership; **acheter en ~** to buy on a co-ownership basis

coq [kɔk] nm cockerel, rooster ▷ adj inv (Boxe): **poids ~** bantamweight; **~ de bruyère** grouse; **~ du village** (fig: péj) ladykiller; **~ au vin** coq au vin

coq-à-l'âne [kɔkalɑn] nm inv abrupt change of subject

coque [kɔk] nf (de noix, mollusque) shell; (de bateau) hull; **à la ~** (Culin) (soft-)boiled

coquelicot [kɔkliko] nm poppy

coqueluche [kɔklyʃ] nf whooping-cough;

(*fig*): **être la ~ de qn** to be sb's flavour of the month

coquet, te [kɔkɛ, -ɛt] *adj* appearance-conscious; (*joli*) pretty; (*logement*) smart, charming

coquetier [kɔk(ə)tje] *nm* egg-cup

coquillage [kɔkijaʒ] *nm* (*mollusque*) shellfish *inv*; (*coquille*) shell

coquille [kɔkij] *nf* shell; (*Typo*) misprint; **~ de beurre** shell of butter; **~ d'œuf** *adj* (*couleur*) eggshell; **~ de noix** nutshell; **~ St Jacques** scallop

coquin, e [kɔkɛ̃, -in] *adj* mischievous, roguish; (*polisson*) naughty ▷ *nm/f* (*péj*) rascal

cor [kɔʀ] *nm* (*Mus*) horn; (*Méd*): **~ (au pied)** corn; **réclamer à ~ et à cri** to clamour for; **~ anglais** cor anglais; **~ de chasse** hunting horn

corail, -aux [kɔʀaj, -o] *nm* coral *no pl*

Coran [kɔʀɑ̃] *nm*: **le ~** the Koran

corbeau, x [kɔʀbo] *nm* crow

corbeille [kɔʀbɛj] *nf* basket; (*Inform*) recycle bin; (*Bourse*): **la ~ ≈** the floor (of the Stock Exchange); **~ de mariage** (*fig*) wedding presents *pl*; **~ à ouvrage** work-basket; **~ à pain** breadbasket; **~ à papier** waste paper basket *ou* bin

corbillard [kɔʀbijaʀ] *nm* hearse

corde [kɔʀd] *nf* rope; (*de violon, raquette, d'arc*) string; (*trame*): **la ~** the thread; (*Athlétisme, Auto*): **la ~** the rails *pl*; **les ~s** (*Boxe*) the ropes; **les (instruments à) ~s** (*Mus*) the strings, the stringed instruments; **semelles de ~** rope soles; **tenir la ~** (*Athlétisme, Auto*) to be in the inside lane; **tomber des ~s** to rain cats and dogs; **tirer sur la ~** to go too far; **la ~ sensible** the right chord; **usé jusqu'à la ~** threadbare; **~ à linge** washing *ou* clothes line; **~ lisse** (climbing) rope; **~ à nœuds** knotted climbing rope; **~ raide** tightrope; **~ à sauter** skipping rope; **~s vocales** vocal cords

cordée [kɔʀde] *nf* (*d'alpinistes*) rope, roped party

cordialement [kɔʀdjalmɑ̃] *adv* cordially, heartily; (*formule épistolaire*) (kind) regards

cordon [kɔʀdɔ̃] *nm* cord, string; **~ sanitaire/ de police** sanitary/police cordon; **~ littoral** sandbank, sandbar; **~ ombilical** umbilical cord

cordonnerie [kɔʀdɔnʀi] *nf* shoe repairer's *ou* mender's (shop)

cordonnier [kɔʀdɔnje] *nm* shoe repairer *ou* mender, cobbler

Corée [kɔʀe] *nf*: **la ~** Korea; **la ~ du Sud/du Nord** South/North Korea; **la République (démocratique populaire) de ~** the (Democratic People's) Republic of Korea

coriace [kɔʀjas] *adj* tough

corne [kɔʀn] *nf* horn; (*de cerf*) antler; (*de la peau*) callus; **~ d'abondance** horn of plenty; **~ de brume** (*Navig*) foghorn

cornée [kɔʀne] *nf* cornea

corneille [kɔʀnɛj] *nf* crow

cornemuse [kɔʀnəmyz] *nf* bagpipes *pl*; **joueur de ~** piper

cornet [kɔʀnɛ] *nm* (paper) cone; (*de glace*) cornet, cone; **~ à pistons** cornet

corniche [kɔʀniʃ] *nf* (*de meuble, neigeuse*) cornice; (*route*) coast road

cornichon [kɔʀniʃɔ̃] *nm* gherkin

Cornouailles [kɔʀnwaj] *nf(pl)* Cornwall

corporation [kɔʀpɔʀasjɔ̃] *nf* corporate body; (*au Moyen-Âge*) guild

corporel, le [kɔʀpɔʀɛl] *adj* bodily; (*punition*) corporal; **soins ~s** care *sg* of the body

corps [kɔʀ] *nm* (*gén*) body; (*cadavre*) (dead) body; **à son ~ défendant** against one's will; **à ~ perdu** headlong; **perdu ~ et biens** lost with all hands; **prendre ~** to take shape; **faire ~ avec** to be joined to; to form one body with; **~ d'armée (CA)** army corps; **~ de ballet** corps de ballet; **~ constitués** (*Pol*) constitutional bodies; **le ~ consulaire (CC)** the consular corps; **~ à ~** *adv* hand-to-hand ▷ *nm* clinch; **le ~ du délit** (*Jur*) corpus delicti; **le ~ diplomatique (CD)** the diplomatic corps; **le ~ électoral** the electorate; **le ~ enseignant** the teaching profession; **~ étranger** (*Méd*) foreign body; **~ expéditionnaire** task force; **~ de garde** guardroom; **~ législatif** legislative body; **le ~ médical** the medical profession

corpulent, e [kɔʀpylɑ̃, -ɑ̃t] *adj* stout (*Brit*), corpulent

correct, e [kɔʀɛkt] *adj* (*exact*) accurate, correct; (*bienséant, honnête*) correct; (*passable*) adequate

correcteur, -trice [kɔʀɛktœʀ, -tʀis] *nm/f* (*Scol*) examiner, marker; (*Typo*) proofreader

correction [kɔʀɛksjɔ̃] *nf* (*voir corriger*) correction; marking; (*voir correct*) correctness; (*rature, surcharge*) correction, emendation; (*coups*) thrashing; **~ sur écran** (*Inform*) screen editing; **~ (des épreuves)** proofreading

correctionnel, le [kɔʀɛksjɔnɛl] *adj* (*Jur*): **tribunal ~ ≈** criminal court

correspondance [kɔʀɛspɔ̃dɑ̃s] *nf* correspondence; (*de train, d'avion*) connection; **ce train assure la ~ avec l'avion de 10 heures** this train connects with the 10 o'clock plane; **cours par ~** correspondence course; **vente par ~** mail-order business

correspondant, e [kɔʀɛspɔ̃dɑ̃, -ɑ̃t] *nm/f* correspondent; (*Tél*) person phoning (*ou* being phoned)

correspondre [kɔʀɛspɔ̃dʀ] *vi* (*données, témoignages*) to correspond, tally; (*chambres*) to communicate; **~ à** to correspond to; **~ avec qn** to correspond with sb

corrida [kɔʀida] *nf* bullfight

corridor [kɔʀidɔʀ] *nm* corridor, passage

corrigé [kɔʀiʒe] *nm* (*Scol: d'exercice*) correct version; fair copy

corriger [kɔriʒe] vt (devoir) to correct, mark; (texte) to correct, emend; (erreur, défaut) to correct, put right; (punir) to thrash; **~ qn de** (défaut) to cure sb of; **se ~ de** to cure o.s. of

corroborer [kɔrɔbɔre] vt to corroborate

corrompre [kɔrɔ̃pr] vt (dépraver) to corrupt; (acheter: témoin etc) to bribe

corruption [kɔrypsjɔ̃] nf corruption; (de témoins) bribery

corsage [kɔrsaʒ] nm (d'une robe) bodice; (chemisier) blouse

corsaire [kɔrsɛr] nm pirate, corsair; privateer

corse [kɔrs] adj Corsican ▷ nm/f: **C~** Corsican ▷ nf: **la C~** Corsica

corsé, e [kɔrse] adj vigorous; (café etc) full-flavoured (Brit) ou -flavored (US); (goût) full; (sauce) spicy; (problème) tough, tricky

corset [kɔrsɛ] nm corset; (d'une robe) bodice; **~ orthopédique** surgical corset

cortège [kɔrtɛʒ] nm procession

cortisone [kɔrtizɔn] nf (Méd) cortisone

corvée [kɔrve] nf chore, drudgery no pl; (Mil) fatigue (duty)

cosmétique [kɔsmetik] nm (pour les cheveux) hair-oil; (produit de beauté) beauty care product

cosmopolite [kɔsmɔpɔlit] adj cosmopolitan

cossu, e [kɔsy] adj opulent-looking, well-to-do

costaud, e [kɔsto, -od] adj strong, sturdy

costume [kɔstym] nm (d'homme) suit; (de théâtre) costume

costumé, e [kɔstyme] adj dressed up

cote [kɔt] nf (en Bourse etc) quotation; quoted value; (d'un cheval): **la ~ de** the odds pl on; (d'un candidat etc) rating; (mesure: sur une carte) spot height; (: sur un croquis) dimension; (de classement) (classification) mark; reference number; **avoir la ~** to be very popular; **inscrit à la ~** quoted on the Stock Exchange; **~ d'alerte** danger ou flood level; **~ mal taillée** (fig) compromise; **~ de popularité** popularity rating

coté, e [kɔte] adj: **être ~** to be listed ou quoted; **être ~ en Bourse** to be quoted on the Stock Exchange; **être bien/mal ~** to be highly/poorly rated

côte [kot] nf (rivage) coast(line); (pente) slope; (: sur une route) hill; (Anat) rib; (d'un tricot, tissu) rib, ribbing no pl; **~ à ~** adv side by side; **la C~ (d'Azur)** the (French) Riviera; **la C~ d'Ivoire** the Ivory Coast; **~ de porc** pork chop

côté [kote] nm (gén) side; (direction) way, direction; **de chaque ~ (de)** on each side of; **de tous les ~s** from all directions; **de quel ~ est-il parti?** which way ou in which direction did he go?; **de ce/de l'autre ~** this/the other way; **d'un ~ ... de l'autre ~ ...** (alternative) on the one hand ... on the other (hand) ...; **du ~ de** (provenance) from; (direction) towards; **du ~ de Lyon** (proximité) near Lyons;

du ~ gauche on the left-hand side; **de ~** adv (regarder) sideways; on one side; to one side; aside; **laisser de ~** to leave on one side; **mettre de ~** to put aside, put on one side; **mettre de l'argent de ~** to save some money; **de mon ~** (quant à moi) for my part; **à ~** adv (right) nearby; (voisins) next door; (d'autre part) besides; **à ~ de** beside; next to; (fig) in comparison to; **à ~ (de la cible)** off target, wide (of the mark); **être aux ~s de** to be by the side of

coteau, x [kɔto] nm hill

Côte d'Ivoire [kotdivwar] nf: **la ~** Côte d'Ivoire, the Ivory Coast

côtelette [kotlɛt] nf chop

côtier, -ière [kotje, -jɛr] adj coastal

cotisation [kɔtizasjɔ̃] nf subscription, dues pl; (pour une pension) contributions pl

cotiser [kɔtize] vi: **~ (à)** to pay contributions (to); (à une association) to subscribe (to); **se cotiser** vi to club together

coton [kɔtɔ̃] nm cotton; **~ hydrophile** cotton wool (Brit), absorbent cotton (US)

Coton-Tige® [kɔtɔ̃tiʒ] nm cotton bud

côtoyer [kotwaje] vt to be close to; (rencontrer) to rub shoulders with; (longer) to run alongside; (fig: friser) to be bordering ou verging on

cou [ku] nm neck

couchant [kuʃɑ̃] adj: **soleil ~** setting sun

couche [kuʃ] nf (strate: gén, Géo) layer, stratum (pl -a); (de peinture, vernis) coat; (de poussière, crème) layer; (de bébé) nappy (Brit), diaper (US); **~ d'ozone** ozone layer; **couches** nfpl (Méd) confinement sg; **~s sociales** social levels ou strata

couché, e [kuʃe] adj (étendu) lying down; (au lit) in bed

coucher [kuʃe] nm (du soleil) setting ▷ vt (personne) to put to bed; (: loger) to put up; (objet) to lay on its side; (écrire) to inscribe, couch ▷ vi (dormir) to sleep, spend the night; **~ avec qn** to sleep with sb, to go to bed with sb; **se coucher** vi (pour dormir) to go to bed; (pour se reposer) to lie down; (soleil) to set, go down; **à prendre avant le ~** (Méd) take at night ou before going to bed; **~ de soleil** sunset

couchette [kuʃɛt] nf couchette; (de marin) bunk; (pour voyageur, sur bateau) berth

coucou [kuku] nm cuckoo ▷ excl peek-a-boo

coude [kud] nm (Anat) elbow; (de tuyau, de la route) bend; **~ à ~** adv shoulder to shoulder, side by side

coudre [kudr] vt (bouton) to sew on; (robe) to sew (up) ▷ vi to sew

couenne [kwan] nf (de lard) rind

couette [kwɛt] nf duvet; **couettes** nfpl (cheveux) bunches

couffin [kufɛ̃] nm Moses basket; (straw) basket

couler [kule] vi to flow, run; (fuir: stylo, récipient) to leak; (nez) to run; (sombrer: bateau) to sink ▷ vt *(cloche, sculpture)* to cast; *(bateau)* to sink; *(faire échouer: personne)* to bring down, ruin; (: *passer*): **une vie heureuse** to enjoy a happy life; **se ~ dans** *(interstice etc)* to slip into; **faire ~** *(eau)* to run; **faire ~ un bain** to run a bath; **il a coulé une bielle** *(Auto)* his big end went; **~ de source** to follow on naturally; **~ à pic** to sink *ou* go straight to the bottom

couleur [kulœʀ] *nf* colour *(Brit)*, color *(US)*; *(Cartes)* suit; **couleurs** *nfpl (du teint)* colo(u)r *sg*; **les ~s** *(Mil)* the colo(u)rs; **en ~s** *(film)* in colo(u)r; **télévision en ~s** colo(u)r television; **de ~** *(homme, femme: vieilli)* colo(u)red; **sous ~ de** on the pretext of; **de quelle ~ what** colo(u)r

couleuvre [kulœvʀ] *nf* grass snake

coulisse [kulis] *nf (Tech)* runner; **coulisses** *nfpl (Théât)* wings; *(fig)*: **dans les ~s** behind the scenes; **porte à ~** sliding door

coulisser [kulise] *vi* to slide, run

couloir [kulwaʀ] *nm* corridor, passage; *(d'avion)* aisle; *(de bus)* gangway; (: *sur la route)* bus lane; *(Sport: de piste)* lane; *(Géo)* gully; **~ aérien** air corridor *ou* lane; **~ de navigation** shipping lane

coup [ku] *nm (heurt, choc)* knock; *(affectif)* blow, shock; *(agressif)* blow; *(avec arme à feu)* shot; *(de l'horloge)* chime; *(Sport: golf)* stroke; *(tennis)* shot; blow; *(fam: fois)* time; *(Échecs)* move; **~ de coude/genou** nudge (with the elbow)/with the knee; **à ~s de hache/marteau** (hitting) with an axe/a hammer; **~ de tonnerre** clap of thunder; **~ de sonnette** ring of the bell; **~ de crayon/pinceau** stroke of the pencil/brush; **donner un ~ de balai** to give the floor a sweep, sweep up; **donner un ~ de chiffon** to go round with the duster; **avoir le ~** *(fig)* to have the knack; **être dans le/hors du ~** to be/not to be in on it; *(à la page)* to be hip *ou* trendy; **du ~** as a result; **boire un ~** to have a drink; **d'un seul ~** *(subitement)* suddenly; *(à la fois)* at one go; in one blow; **du ~** so (you see); **du premier ~** first time *ou* go, at the first attempt; **du même ~** at the same time; **à ~ sûr** definitely, without fail; **après ~** afterwards; **~ sur ~** in quick succession; **être sur un ~** to be on to something; **sur le ~** outright; **sous le ~ de** *(surprise etc)* under the influence of; **tomber sous le ~ de la loi** to constitute a statutory offence; **à tous les ~s** every time; **tenir le ~** to hold out; **il a raté son ~** he missed his turn; **pour le ~** for once; **bas: donner un ~ bas à qn** to hit sb below the belt; **~ de chance** stroke of luck; **~ de chapeau** *(fig)* pat on the back; **~ de couteau** stab (of a knife); **~ dur** hard blow; **~ d'éclat** (great) feat; **~ d'envoi** kick-off; **~ d'essai** first attempt; **~ d'état** coup d'état; **~ de feu** shot; **~ de filet** *(Police)* haul; **~ de foudre** *(fig)* love at first sight; **~ fourré** stab in the back; **~ franc** free kick; **~ de frein** (sharp) braking *no pl*; **~ de**

fusil rifle shot; **~ de grâce** coup de grâce; **~ du lapin** *(Auto)* whiplash; **~ de main**: **donner un coup de main à qn** to give sb a (helping) hand; **~ de maître** master stroke; **~ d'œil** glance; **~ de pied** kick; **~ de poing** punch; **~ de soleil** sunburn *no pl*; **~ de sonnette** ring of the bell; **~ de téléphone** phone call; **~ de tête** *(fig)* (sudden) impulse; **~ de théâtre** *(fig)* dramatic turn of events; **~ de tonnerre** clap of thunder; **~ de vent** gust of wind; **en ~ de vent** *(rapidement)* in a tearing hurry

coupable [kupabl] *adj* guilty; *(pensée)* guilty, culpable ▷ *nm/f (gén)* culprit; *(Jur)* guilty party; **~ de** guilty of

coupe [kup] *nf (verre)* goblet; *(à fruits)* dish; *(Sport)* cup; *(de cheveux, de vêtement)* cut; *(graphique, plan)* (cross) section; **être sous la ~ de** to be under the control of sb; **faire des ~s sombres dans** to make drastic cuts in

coupe-papier [kuppapje] *nm inv* paper knife

couper [kupe] *vt* to cut; *(retrancher)* to cut (out), take out; *(route, courant)* to cut off; *(appétit)* to take away; *(fièvre)* to take down, reduce; *(vin, cidre)* to blend; (: *à table)* to dilute (with water) ▷ *vi* to cut; *(prendre un raccourci)* to take a short-cut; *(Cartes: diviser le paquet)* to cut; (: *avec l'atout)* to trump; **se couper** *(se blesser)* to cut o.s.; *(en témoignant etc)* to give o.s. away; **~ l'appétit à qn** to spoil sb's appetite; **~ la parole à qn** to cut sb short; **~ les vivres à qn** to cut off sb's vital supplies; **~ le contact** *ou* **l'allumage** *(Auto)* to turn off the ignition; **~ les ponts avec qn** to break with sb; **se faire ~ les cheveux** to have *ou* get one's hair cut; **nous avons été coupés** we've been cut off

couple [kupl] *nm* couple; **~ de torsion** torque

couplet [kuplɛ] *nm* verse

coupole [kupɔl] *nf* dome; cupola

coupon [kupɔ̃] *nm (ticket)* coupon; *(de tissu)* remnant; roll

coupon-réponse *(pl* **coupons-réponses**) [kupɔ̃repɔ̃s] *nm* reply coupon

coupure [kupyʀ] *nf* cut; *(billet de banque)* note; *(de journal)* cutting; **~ de courant** power cut

cour [kuʀ] *nf (de ferme, jardin)* (court)yard; *(d'immeuble)* back yard; *(Jur, royale)* court; **faire la ~ à qn** to court sb; **~ d'appel** appeal court *(Brit)*, appellate court *(US)*; **~ d'assises** court of assizes, ≈ Crown Court *(Brit)*; **~ de cassation** final court of appeal; **~ des comptes** *(Admin)* revenue court; **~ martiale** court-martial; **~ de récréation** *(Scol)* playground, schoolyard

courage [kuʀaʒ] *nm* courage, bravery

courageux, -euse [kuʀaʒø, -øz] *adj* brave, courageous

couramment [kuʀamɑ̃] *adv* commonly; *(parler)* fluently

courant, e [kuʀɑ̃, -ɑ̃t] *adj (fréquent)* common; *(Comm, gén: normal)* standard; *(en cours)* current ▷ *nm* current; *(fig)* movement;

(: *d'opinion*) trend; **être au ~ (de)** (*fait, nouvelle*) to know (about); **mettre qn au ~ (de)** (*fait, nouvelle*) to teach sb (about); (*nouveau travail etc*) to teach sb the basics (of), brief sb (about); **se tenir au ~ (de)** (*techniques etc*) to keep o.s. up-to-date (on); **dans le ~ de** (*pendant*) in the course of; **~ octobre** *etc* in the course of October *etc*; **le 10 ~** (*Comm*) the 10th inst.; **~ d'air** draught (Brit), draft (US); **~ électrique** (electric) current, power

courbature [kurbatyr] *nf* ache

courbe [kurb] *adj* curved ▷ *nf* curve; **~ de niveau** contour line

courber [kurbe] *vt* to bend; **~ la tête** to bow one's head; **se courber** *vi* (*branche etc*) to bend, curve; (*personne*) to bend (down)

coureur, -euse [kurœr, -øz] *nm/f* (*Sport*) runner (*ou* driver); (*péj*) womanizer/ manhunter; **~ cycliste/automobile** racing cyclist/driver

courge [kurʒ] *nf* (*Bot*) gourd; (*Culin*) marrow

courgette [kurʒɛt] *nf* courgette (Brit), zucchini (US)

courir [kurir] *vi* (*gén*) to run; (*se dépêcher*) to rush; (*fig: rumeurs*) to go round; (*Comm: intérêt*) to accrue ▷ *vt* (*Sport: épreuve*) to compete in; (*risque*) to run; (*danger*) to face; **~ les cafés/bals** to do the rounds of the cafés/ dances; **le bruit court que** the rumour is going round that; **par les temps qui courent** at the present time; **~ après qn** to run after sb, chase (after) sb; **laisser ~** to let things alone; **faire ~ qn** to make sb run around (all over the place); **tu peux (toujours) ~!** you've got a hope!

couronne [kurɔn] *nf* crown; (*de fleurs*) wreath, circlet; **~ (funéraire** *ou* **mortuaire)** (funeral) wreath

courons [kurɔ̃], **courrai** *etc* [kure] *vb voir* **courir**

courriel [kurjɛl] *nm* email

courrier [kurje] *nm* mail, post; (*lettres à écrire*) letters *pl*; (*rubrique*) column; **qualité ~** letter quality; **long/moyen ~** *adj* (*Aviat*) long-/ medium-haul; **~ du cœur** problem page; **~ électronique** electronic mail, email; **est-ce que j'ai du ~?** are there any letters for me?

courroie [kurwa] *nf* strap; (*Tech*) belt; **~ de transmission/de ventilateur** driving/ fan belt

courrons *etc* [kurɔ̃] *vb voir* **courir**

cours [kur] *vb voir* **courir** ▷ *nm* (*leçon*) class; (: *particulier*) lesson; (*série de leçons*) course; (*cheminement*) course; (*écoulement*) flow; (*avenue*) walk; (*Comm: de devises*) rate; (: *de denrées*) price; (*Bourse*) quotation; **donner libre ~ à** to give free expression to; **avoir ~** (*monnaie*) to be legal tender; (*fig*) to be current; (*Scol*) to have a class *ou* lecture; **en ~** (*année*) current; (*travaux*) in progress; **en ~ de route** on the way; **au ~ de** in the course of,

during; **le ~ du change** the exchange rate; **~ d'eau** waterway; **~ élémentaire (CE)** 2nd and 3rd years of primary school; **~ moyen (CM)** 4th and 5th years of primary school; **~ préparatoire** ≈ infants' class (Brit), ≈ 1st grade (US); **~ du soir** night school

course [kurs] *nf* running; (*Sport: épreuve*) race; (*trajet: du soleil*) course; (: *d'un projectile*) flight; (: *d'une pièce mécanique*) travel; (*excursion*) outing; climb; (*d'un taxi, autocar*) journey, trip; (*petite mission*) errand; **courses** *nfpl* (*achats*) shopping *sg*; (*Hippisme*) races; **faire les** *ou* **ses ~s** to go shopping; **jouer aux ~s** to bet on the races; **à bout de ~** (*épuisé*) exhausted; **~ automobile** car race; **~ de côte** (*Auto*) hill climb; **~ par étapes** *ou* **d'étapes** race in stages; **~ d'obstacles** obstacle race; **~ à pied** walking race; **~ de vitesse** sprint; **~s de chevaux** horse racing

court, e [kur, kurt] *adj* short ▷ *adv* short ▷ *nm*: **~ (de tennis)** (tennis) court; **tourner ~** to come to a sudden end; **couper ~ à** to cut short; **à ~ de** short of; **prendre qn de ~** to catch sb unawares; **pour faire ~** briefly, to cut a long story short; **ça fait ~** that's not very long; **tirer à la ~e paille** to draw lots; **faire la ~e échelle à qn** to give sb a leg up; **~ métrage** (*Ciné*) short (film)

court-circuit (*pl* **courts-circuits**) [kursirkɥi] *nm* short-circuit

courtier, -ière [kurtje, -jɛr] *nm/f* broker

courtiser [kurtize] *vt* to court, woo

courtois, e [kurtwa, -waz] *adj* courteous

courtoisie [kurtwazi] *nf* courtesy

couru, e [kury] *pp de* **courir** ▷ *adj* (*spectacle etc*) popular; **c'est ~ (d'avance)!** (*fam*) it's a safe bet!

cousais *etc* [kuze] *vb voir* **coudre**

couscous [kuskus] *nm* couscous

cousin, e [kuzɛ̃, -in] *nm/f* cousin ▷ *nm* (*Zool*) mosquito; **~ germain** first cousin

coussin [kusɛ̃] *nm* cushion; **~ d'air** (*Tech*) air cushion

cousu, e [kuzy] *pp de* **coudre** ▷ *adj*: **~ d'or** rolling in riches

coût [ku] *nm* cost; **le ~ de la vie** the cost of living

coûtant [kutɑ̃] *adj m*: **au prix ~** at cost price

couteau, x [kuto] *nm* knife; **~ à cran d'arrêt** flick-knife; **~ de cuisine** kitchen knife; **~ à pain** bread knife; **~ de poche** pocket knife

coûter [kute] *vt* to cost ▷ *vi* to cost; **~ à qn** to cost sb a lot; **~ cher** to be expensive; **~ cher à qn** (*fig*) to cost sb dear *ou* dearly; **combien ça coûte?** how much is it?, what does it cost?; **coûte que coûte** at all costs

coûteux, -euse [kutø, -øz] *adj* costly, expensive

coutume [kutym] *nf* custom; **de ~** usual, customary

couture [kutyr] *nf* sewing; (*profession*) dress-making; (*points*) seam

couturier [kutyʀje] nm fashion designer, couturier

couturière [kutyʀjɛʀ] nf dressmaker

couvée [kuve] nf brood, clutch

couvent [kuvɑ̃] nm (de sœurs) convent; (de frères) monastery; (établissement scolaire) convent (school)

couver [kuve] vt to hatch; (maladie) to be sickening for ▷ vi (feu) to smoulder (Brit), smolder (US); (révolte) to be brewing; **~ qn/qch des yeux** to look lovingly at sb/sth; (convoiter) to belch longingly at sb/sth

couvercle [kuvɛʀkl] nm lid; (de bombe aérosol etc, qui se visse) cap, top

couvert, e [kuvɛʀ, -ɛʀt] pp de **couvrir** ▷ adj (ciel) overcast; (coiffé d'un chapeau) wearing a hat ▷ nm place setting; (place à table) place; (au restaurant) cover charge; **couverts** nmpl place settings; (ustensiles) cutlery sg; **~ de** covered with ou in; **bien ~** (habillé) well wrapped up; **mettre le ~** to lay the table; **à ~** under cover; **sous le ~ de** under the shelter of; (fig) under cover of

couverture [kuvɛʀtyʀ] nf (de lit) blanket; (de bâtiment) roofing; (de livre, fig: d'un espion etc, Assurances) cover; (Presse) coverage; **de ~** (lettre etc) covering; **~ chauffante** electric blanket

couveuse [kuvøz] nf (à poules) sitter, brooder; (de maternité) incubator

couvre-feu, x [kuvʀəfø] nm curfew

couvre-lit [kuvʀəli] nm bedspread

couvreur [kuvʀœʀ] nm roofer

couvrir [kuvʀiʀ] vt to cover; (dominer, étouffer: voix, pas) to drown out; (erreur) to cover up; (Zool: s'accoupler à) to cover; **se couvrir** vi (ciel) to cloud over; (s'habiller) to cover up, wrap up; (se coiffer) to put on one's hat; (par une assurance) to cover o.s.; **se ~ de** (fleurs, boutons) to become covered in

cow-boy [koboj] nm cowboy

crabe [kʀab] nm crab

cracher [kʀaʃe] vi to spit ▷ vt to spit out; (fig: lave etc) to belch (out); **~ du sang** to spit blood

crachin [kʀaʃɛ̃] nm drizzle

crack [kʀak] nm (intellectuel) whiz kid; (sportif) ace; (poulain) hot favourite (Brit) ou favorite (US)

craie [kʀɛ] nf chalk

craindre [kʀɛ̃dʀ] vt to fear, be afraid of; (être sensible à: chaleur, froid) to be easily damaged by; **~ de/que** to be afraid of/that; **je crains qu'il (ne) vienne** I am afraid he may come

crainte [kʀɛ̃t] nf fear; **de ~ de/que** for fear of/that

craintif, -ive [kʀɛ̃tif, -iv] adj timid

cramoisi, e [kʀamwazi] adj crimson

crampe [kʀɑ̃p] nf cramp; **~ d'estomac** stomach cramp; **j'ai une ~ à la jambe** I've got cramp in my leg

crampon [kʀɑ̃pɔ̃] nm (de semelle) stud; (Alpinisme) crampon

cramponner [kʀɑ̃pɔne]: **se cramponner** vi: **se ~ (à)** to hang ou cling on (to)

cran [kʀɑ̃] nm (entaille) notch; (de courroie) hole; (courage) guts pl; **~ d'arrêt/de sûreté** safety catch; **~ de mire** bead

crâne [kʀɑn] nm skull

crâner [kʀɑne] vi (fam) to swank, show off

crapaud [kʀapo] nm toad

crapule [kʀapyl] nf villain

craquement [kʀakmɑ̃] nm crack, snap; (du plancher) creak, creaking no pl

craquer [kʀake] vi (bois, plancher) to creak; (fil, branche) to snap; (couture) to come apart, burst; (fig: accusé) to break down, fall apart; (: être enthousiasmé) to go wild ▷ vt: **~ une allumette** to strike a match; **j'ai craqué** (fam) I couldn't resist it

crasse [kʀas] nf grime, filth ▷ adj (fig: ignorance) crass

crasseux, -euse [kʀasø, øz] adj filthy

cravache [kʀavaʃ] nf (riding) crop

cravate [kʀavat] nf tie

crawl [kʀol] nm crawl; **dos ~é** backstroke

crayon [kʀɛjɔ̃] nm pencil; (de rouge à lèvres etc) stick, pencil; **écrire au ~** to write in pencil; **~ à bille** ball-point pen; **~ de couleur** crayon; **~ optique** light pen

crayon-feutre (pl **crayons-feutres**) [kʀɛjɔ̃føtʀ] nm felt(-tip) pen

créancier, -ière [kʀeɑ̃sje, -jɛʀ] nm/f creditor

création [kʀeasjɔ̃] nf creation

créature [kʀeatyʀ] nf creature

crèche [kʀɛʃ] nf (de Noël) crib; see note; (garderie) crèche, day nursery

---

CRÈCHE

In France the Christmas crib (crèche) usually contains figurines representing a miller, a wood-cutter and other villagers as well as the Holy Family and the traditional cow, donkey and shepherds. The Three Wise Men are added to the nativity scene at Epiphany (6 January, Twelfth Night).

---

crédit [kʀedi] nm (gén) credit; **crédits** nmpl funds; **acheter à ~** to buy on credit ou on easy terms; **faire ~ à qn** to give sb credit; **~ municipal** pawnshop; **~ relais** bridging loan

créditer [kʀedite] vt: **~ un compte (de)** to credit an account (with)

crédule [kʀedyl] adj credulous, gullible

créer [kʀee] vt to create; (Théât: pièce) to produce (for the first time); (: rôle) to create

crémaillère [kʀemajɛʀ] nf (Rail) rack; (tige crantée) trammel; **direction à ~** (Auto) rack and pinion steering; **pendre la ~** to have a house-warming party

crématoire [kʀematwaʀ] adj: **four ~** crematorium

crème [kʀɛm] nf cream; (entremets) cream dessert ▷ adj inv cream; **un (café)** ~ ≈ a white coffee; ~ **anglaise** (egg) custard; ~ **chantilly** whipped cream, crème Chantilly; ~ **fouettée** whipped cream; ~ **glacée** ice cream; ~ **à raser** shaving cream; ~ **solaire** sun cream

crémerie [kʀɛmʀi] nf dairy; (tearoom) teashop

crémeux, -euse [kʀemø, -øz] adj creamy

créneau, x [kʀeno] nm (de fortification) crenel(le); (fig, aussi Comm) gap, slot; (Auto): **faire un** ~ to reverse into a parking space (between cars alongside the kerb)

crêpe [kʀɛp] nf (galette) pancake ▷ nm (tissu) crêpe; (de deuil) black mourning crêpe; (ruban) black armband (ou hatband ou ribbon); **semelle (de)** ~ crêpe sole; ~ **de Chine** crêpe de Chine

crêpé, e [kʀepe] adj (cheveux) backcombed

crêperie [kʀepʀi] nf pancake shop ou restaurant

crépiter [kʀepite] vi to sputter, splutter, crackle

crépu, e [kʀepy] adj frizzy, fuzzy

crépuscule [kʀepyskyl] nm twilight, dusk

cresson [kʀesɔ̃] nm watercress

crête [kʀɛt] nf (de coq) comb; (de vague, montagne) crest

creuser [kʀøze] vt (trou, tunnel) to dig; (sol) to dig a hole in; (bois) to hollow out; (fig) to go (deeply) into; **ça creuse** that gives you a real appetite; **se** ~ **(la cervelle)** to rack one's brains

creux, -euse [kʀø, -øz] adj hollow ▷ nm hollow; (fig: sur graphique etc) trough; **heures creuses** slack periods; (électricité, téléphone) off-peak periods; **le** ~ **de l'estomac** the pit of the stomach; **avoir un** ~ (fam) to be hungry

crevaison [kʀəvɛzɔ̃] nf puncture, flat

crevasse [kʀəvas] nf (dans le sol) crack, fissure; (de glacier) crevasse; (de la peau) crack

crevé, e [kʀəve] adj (fam: fatigué) shattered (Brit), exhausted

crever [kʀəve] vt (papier) to tear, break; (tambour, ballon) to burst ▷ vi (pneu) to burst; (automobiliste) to have a puncture (Brit) ou a flat (tire) (US); (abcès, outre, nuage) to burst (open); (fam) to die; **cela lui a crevé un œil** it blinded him in one eye; ~ **l'écran** to have real screen presence

crevette [kʀəvɛt] nf: ~ **(rose)** prawn; ~ **grise** shrimp

cri [kʀi] nm cry, shout; (d'animal: spécifique) cry, call; **à grands** ~s at the top of one's voice; **c'est le dernier** ~ (fig) it's the latest fashion

criant, e [kʀijɑ̃, -ɑ̃t] adj (injustice) glaring

criard, e [kʀijaʀ, -aʀd] adj (couleur) garish, loud; (voix) yelling

crible [kʀibl] nm riddle; (mécanique) screen, jig; **passer qch au** ~ to put sth through a riddle; (fig) to go over sth with a fine-tooth comb

criblé, e [kʀible] adj: ~ **de** riddled with

cric [kʀik] nm (Auto) jack

crier [kʀije] vi (pour appeler) to shout, cry (out); (de peur, de douleur etc) to scream, yell; (fig: grincer) to squeal, screech ▷ vt (ordre, injure) to shout (out), yell (out); **sans** ~ **gare** without warning; ~ **grâce** to cry for mercy; ~ **au secours** to shout for help

crime [kʀim] nm crime; (meurtre) murder

criminel, le [kʀiminɛl] adj criminal ▷ nm/f criminal; murderer; ~ **de guerre** war criminal

crin [kʀɛ̃] nm (de cheval) hair no pl; (fibre) horsehair; **à tous** ~**s, à tout** ~ diehard, out-and-out

crinière [kʀinjɛʀ] nf mane

crique [kʀik] nf creek, inlet

criquet [kʀikɛ] nm grasshopper

crise [kʀiz] nf crisis (pl crises); (Méd) attack; (: d'épilepsie) fit; ~ **cardiaque** heart attack; ~ **de foi** crisis of belief; **avoir une** ~ **de foie** to have really bad indigestion; ~ **de nerfs** attack of nerves; **piquer une** ~ **de nerfs** to go hysterical

crisper [kʀispe] vt to tense; (poings) to clench; **se crisper** to tense; to clench; (personne) to get tense

crisser [kʀise] vi (neige) to crunch; (tissu) to rustle; (pneu) to screech

cristal, -aux [kʀistal, -o] nm crystal; **crystaux** nmpl (objets) crystal(ware) sg; ~ **de plomb** (lead) crystal; ~ **de roche** rock-crystal; **cristaux de soude** washing soda sg

cristallin, e [kʀistalɛ̃, -in] adj crystal-clear ▷ nm (Anat) crystalline lens

critère [kʀitɛʀ] nm criterion (pl -ia)

critiquable [kʀitikabl] adj open to criticism

critique [kʀitik] adj critical ▷ nm/f (de théâtre, musique) critic ▷ nf criticism; (Théât etc: article) review; **la** ~ (activité) criticism; (personnes) the critics pl

critiquer [kʀitike] vt (dénigrer) to criticize; (évaluer, juger) to assess, examine (critically)

croasser [kʀɔase] vi to caw

croate [kʀɔat] adj Croatian ▷ nm (Ling) Croat, Croatian ▷ nm/f: **C-** Croat, Croatian

Croatie [kʀɔasi] nf: **la** ~ Croatia

croc [kʀo] nm (dent) fang; (de boucher) hook

croc-en-jambe (pl crocs-en-jambe) [kʀɔkɑ̃ʒɑ̃b] nm: **faire un** ~ **à qn** to trip sb up

croche [kʀɔʃ] nf (Mus) quaver (Brit), eighth note (US); **double** ~ semiquaver (Brit), sixteenth note (US)

croche-pied [kʀɔʃpje] nm = croc-en-jambe

crochet [kʀɔʃɛ] nm hook; (clef) picklock; (détour) detour; (Boxe): ~ **du gauche** left hook; (Tricot: aiguille) crochet hook; (: technique) crochet; **crochets** nmpl (Typo) square brackets; **vivre aux** ~**s de qn** to live ou sponge off sb

crochu, e [kʀɔʃy] adj hooked; claw-like

crocodile [kʀɔkɔdil] nm crocodile

croire [kʀwaʀ] vt to believe; ~ **qn honnête** to

believe sb (to be) honest; **se ~ fort** to think one is strong; **~ que** to believe ou think that; **vous croyez?** do you think so?; **~e être/faire** to think one is/does; **~ à**, **~ en** to believe in

croîs etc [kʀwa] vb voir **croître**

croisade [kʀwazad] nf crusade

croisé, e [kʀwaze] adj (veston) double-breasted ▷ nm (guerrier) crusader ▷ nf (fenêtre) window, casement; **~ d'ogives** intersecting ribs; **à la ~e des chemins** at the crossroads

croisement [kʀwazmã] nm (carrefour) crossroads sg; (Bio) crossing; (: résultat) crossbreed

croiser [kʀwaze] vt (personne, voiture) to pass; (route) to cross, cut across; (Bio) to cross ▷ vi (Navig) to cruise; **~ les jambes/bras** to cross one's legs/ fold one's arms; **se croiser** vi (personnes, véhicules) to pass each other; (routes) to cross, intersect; (lettres) to cross (in the post); (regards) to meet; **se ~ les bras** (fig) to fold one's arms, to twiddle one's thumbs

croisière [kʀwazjɛʀ] nf cruise; **vitesse de ~** (Auto etc) cruising speed

croissance [kʀwasãs] nf growing, growth; **troubles de la ~** growing pains; **maladie de ~** growth disease; **~ économique** economic growth

croissant, e [kʀwasã, -ãt] vb voir **croître** ▷ adj growing; rising ▷ nm (à manger) croissant; (motif) crescent; **~ de lune** crescent moon

croître [kʀwatʀ] vi to grow; (lune) to wax

croix [kʀwa] nf cross; **en ~** adj, adv in the form of a cross; **la C~ Rouge** the Red Cross

croque-madame [kʀɔkmadam] nm inv toasted cheese sandwich with a fried egg on top

croque-monsieur [kʀɔkməsjø] nm inv toasted ham and cheese sandwich

croquer [kʀɔke] vt (manger) to crunch; (: fruit) to munch; (dessiner) to sketch ▷ vi to be crisp ou crunchy; **chocolat à ~** plain dessert chocolate

croquis [kʀɔki] nm sketch

cross [kʀɔs], **cross-country** [kʀɔskuntʀi] (pl **cross-(countries)**) nm cross-country race ou run; cross-country racing ou running

crosse [kʀɔs] nf (de fusil) butt; (de revolver) grip; (d'évêque) crook, crosier; (de hockey) hockey stick

crotte [kʀɔt] nf droppings pl; **~!** (fam) damn!

crotté, e [kʀɔte] adj muddy, mucky

crottin [kʀɔtɛ̃] nm dung, manure; (fromage) (small round) cheese (made of goat's milk)

crouler [kʀule] vi (s'effondrer) to collapse; (être délabré) to be crumbling

croupe [kʀup] nf croup, rump; **en ~** pillion

croupir [kʀupiʀ] vi to stagnate

croustillant, e [kʀustijã, -ãt] adj crisp; (fig) spicy

croûte [kʀut] nf crust; (du fromage) rind; (de vol-au-vent) case; (Méd) scab; **en ~** (Culin) in pastry, in a pie; **~ aux champignons** mushrooms on toast; **~ au fromage** cheese

on toast no pl; **~ de pain** (morceau) crust (of bread); **~ terrestre** earth's crust

croûton [kʀutõ] nm (Culin) crouton; (bout du pain) crust, heel

croyable [kʀwajabl] adj believable, credible

croyant, e [kʀwajã, -ãt] vb voir **croire** ▷ adj: **être/ne pas être ~** to be/not to be a believer ▷ nm/f believer

CRS sigle fpl (= Compagnies républicaines de sécurité) state security police force ▷ sigle m member of the CRS

cru, e [kʀy] pp de **croire** ▷ adj (non cuit) raw; (lumière, couleur) harsh; (description) crude; (paroles, langage: franc) blunt; (: grossier) crude ▷ nm (vignoble) vineyard; (vin) wine ▷ nf (d'un cours d'eau) swelling, rising; **de son (propre) ~** (fig) of his own devising; **monter à ~** to ride bareback; **du ~** local; **en ~e** in spate; **un grand ~** a great vintage; **jambon ~** Parma ham

crû [kʀy] pp de **croître**

cruauté [kʀyote] nf cruelty

cruche [kʀyʃ] nf pitcher, (earthenware) jug

crucifix [kʀysifi] nm crucifix

crucifixion [kʀysifiksjõ] nf crucifixion

crudité [kʀydite] nf crudeness no pl; harshness no pl; **crudités** nfpl (Culin) selection of raw vegetables

crue [kʀy] nf (inondation) flood; voir aussi **cru**

cruel, le [kʀyɛl] adj cruel

crus, crûs etc [kʀy] vb voir **croire**; **croître**

crustacés [kʀystase] nmpl shellfish

Cuba [kyba] nm: **le ~** Cuba

cubain, e [kybɛ̃, -ɛn] adj Cuban ▷ nm/f: **C~, e** Cuban

cube [kyb] nm cube; (jouet) brick, building block; **gros ~** powerful motorbike; **mètre ~** cubic metre; **2 au ~ = 8** 2 cubed is 8; **élever au ~** to cube

cueillette [kœjɛt] nf picking; (quantité) crop, harvest

cueillir [kœjiʀ] vt (fruits, fleurs) to pick, gather; (fig) to catch

cuiller [kɥijɛʀ], **cuillère** [kɥijɛʀ] nf spoon; **~ à café** coffee spoon; (Culin) ≈ teaspoonful; **~ à soupe** soup spoon; (Culin) ≈ tablespoonful

cuillerée [kɥijʀe] nf spoonful; (Culin): **~ à soupe/café** tablespoonful/teaspoonful

cuir [kɥiʀ] nm leather; (avant tannage) hide; **~ chevelu** scalp

cuire [kɥiʀ] vt: **(faire) ~** (aliments) to cook; (au four) to bake; (poterie) to fire ▷ vi to cook; (picoter) to smart, sting, burn; **bien cuit** (viande) well done; **trop cuit** overdone; **pas assez cuit** underdone; **cuit à point** medium done; done to a turn

cuisant, e [kɥizã, -ãt] vb voir **cuire** ▷ adj (douleur) smarting, burning; (fig: souvenir, échec) bitter

cuisine [kɥizin] nf (pièce) kitchen; (art culinaire) cookery, cooking; (nourriture) cooking, food; **faire la ~** to cook

cuisiné, e [kɥizine] adj: **plat ~** ready-made meal ou dish

cuisiner [kɥizine] vt to cook; (fam) to grill ▷ vi to cook

cuisinier, -ière [kɥizinje, -jɛʀ] nm/f cook ▷ nf (poêle) cooker; **cuisinière électrique/à gaz** electric/gas cooker

cuisse [kɥis] nf (Anat) thigh; (Culin) leg

cuisson [kɥisɔ̃] nf cooking; (de poterie) firing

cuit, e [kɥi, -it] pp de **cuire** ▷ nf (fam): **prendre une ~** to get plastered ou smashed

cuivre [kɥivʀ] nm copper; **les ~s** (Mus) the brass; **~ rouge** copper; **~ jaune** brass

cul [ky] nm (fam!) arse (Brit) (!), ass (US) (!), bum (Brit); **~ de bouteille** bottom of a bottle

culbute [kylbyt] nf somersault; (accidentelle) tumble, fall

culminant, e [kylminɑ̃, -ɑ̃t] adj: **point ~** highest point; (fig) height, climax

culminer [kylmine] vi to reach its highest point; to tower

culot [kylo] (fam) nm (d'ampoule) cap; (effronterie) cheek, nerve

culotte [kylɔt] nf (de femme) panties pl, knickers pl (Brit); (d'homme) underpants pl; (pantalon) trousers pl (Brit), pants pl (US); **~ de cheval** riding breeches pl

culpabilité [kylpabilite] nf guilt

culte [kylt] adj: **livre/film ~** cult film/book ▷ nm (religion) religion; (hommage, vénération) worship; (protestant) service

cultivateur, -trice [kyltivatœʀ, -tʀis] nm/f farmer

cultivé, e [kyltive] adj (personne) cultured, cultivated

cultiver [kyltive] vt to cultivate; (légumes) to grow, cultivate

culture [kyltyʀ] nf cultivation; growing; (connaissances etc) culture; **(champs de) ~s** land(s) under cultivation; **les ~s intensives** intensive farming; **~ physique** physical training

culturel, le [kyltyʀɛl] adj cultural

culturisme [kyltyʀism] nm body-building

cumin [kymɛ̃] nm (Culin) cumin

cumuler [kymyle] vt (emplois, honneurs) to hold concurrently; (salaires) to draw concurrently; (Jur: droits) to accumulate

cupide [kypid] adj greedy, grasping

cure [kyʀ] nf (Méd) course of treatment; (Rel) cure, ≈ living; presbytery, ≈ vicarage; **faire une ~ de fruits** to go on a fruit cure ou diet; **faire une ~ thermale** to take the waters; **n'avoir ~ de** to pay no attention to; **~ d'amaigrissement** slimming course; **~ de repos** rest cure; **~ de sommeil** sleep therapy no pl

curé [kyʀe] nm parish priest; **M le ~** ≈ Vicar

cure-dent [kyʀdɑ̃] nm toothpick

cure-pipe [kyʀpip] nm pipe cleaner

curer [kyʀe] vt to clean out; **se ~ les dents** to pick one's teeth

curieusement [kyʀjøzmɑ̃] adv oddly

curieux, -euse [kyʀjø, -øz] adj (étrange) strange, curious; (indiscret) curious, inquisitive; (intéressé) inquiring, curious ▷ nmpl (badauds) onlookers, bystanders

curiosité [kyʀjozite] nf curiosity, inquisitiveness; (objet) curio(sity); (site) unusual feature ou sight

curriculum vitae [kyʀikylɔmvite] nm inv curriculum vitae

curseur [kyʀsœʀ] nm (Inform) cursor; (de règle) slide; (de fermeture-éclair) slider

cutané, e [kytane] adj cutaneous, skin cpd

cuti-réaction [kytiʀeaksjɔ̃] nf (Méd) skin-test

cuve [kyv] nf vat; (à mazout etc) tank

cuvée [kyve] nf vintage

cuvette [kyvɛt] nf (récipient) bowl, basin; (du lavabo) (wash)basin; (des w.-c.) pan; (Géo) basin

CV sigle m (Auto) = **cheval vapeur**; (Admin) = **curriculum vitae**

cyanure [sjanyʀ] nm cyanide

cybercafé [sibɛʀkafe] nm Internet café

cyberespace [sibɛʀɛspas] nm cyberspace

cybernaute [sibɛʀnot] nm/f Internet user

cyclable [siklabl] adj: **piste ~** cycle track

cycle [sikl] nm cycle; (Scol): **premier/second ~** ≈ middle/upper school (Brit), ≈ junior/senior high school (US)

cyclisme [siklism] nm cycling

cycliste [siklist] nm/f cyclist ▷ adj cycle cpd; **coureur ~** racing cyclist

cyclomoteur [siklomotœʀ] nm moped

cyclone [siklon] nm hurricane

cygne [siɲ] nm swan

cylindre [silɛ̃dʀ] nm cylinder; **moteur à 4 ~s en ligne** straight-4 engine

cylindrée [silɛ̃dʀe] nf (Auto) (cubic) capacity; **une (voiture de) grosse ~** a big-engined car

cymbale [sɛ̃bal] nf cymbal

cynique [sinik] adj cynical

cystite [sistit] nf cystitis

d

d' prép, art voir de

dactylo [daktilo] nf (aussi: **~graphe**) typist; (aussi: **~graphie**) typing, typewriting

dactylographier [daktilɔgʀafje] vt to type (out)

dada [dada] nm hobby-horse

daigner [deɲe] vt to deign

daim [dɛ̃] nm (fallow) deer inv; (peau) buckskin; (cuir suédé) suede

dalle [dal] nf slab; (au sol) paving stone, flag(stone); **que ~** nothing at all, damn all (Brit)

daltonien, ne [daltɔnjɛ̃, -ɛn] adj colour-blind (Brit), color-blind (US)

dam [dam] nm: **au grand ~ de** much to the detriment (ou annoyance) of

dame [dam] nf lady; (Cartes, Échecs) queen; **dames** nfpl (jeu) draughts sg (Brit), checkers sg (US); **les (toilettes des) ~s** the ladies' (toilets); **~ de charité** benefactress; **~ de compagnie** lady's companion

damner [dɑne] vt to damn

dancing [dɑ̃siŋ] nm dance hall

Danemark [danmaʀk] nm: **le ~** Denmark

danger [dɑ̃ʒe] nm danger; **mettre en ~** (personne) to put in danger; (projet, carrière) to jeopardize; **être en ~** (personne) to be in danger; **être en ~ de mort** to be in peril of one's life; **être hors de ~** to be out of danger

dangereux, -euse [dɑ̃ʒʀø, -øz] adj dangerous

danois, e [danwa, -waz] adj Danish ▷ nm (Ling) Danish ▷ nm/f: **D~, e** Dane

---

dans [dɑ̃] prép **1** (position) in; (à l'intérieur de) inside; **c'est dans le tiroir/le salon** it's in the drawer/lounge; **dans la boîte** in ou inside the box; **marcher dans la ville/la rue** to walk about the town/along the street; **je l'ai lu dans le journal** I read it in the newspaper; **être dans les meilleurs** to be among ou one of the best

2 (direction) into; **elle a couru dans le salon** she ran into the lounge; **monter dans une voiture/le bus** to get into a car/on to the bus

3 (provenance) out of, from; **je l'ai pris dans le tiroir/salon** I took it out ou from the drawer/lounge; **boire dans un verre** to drink out of ou from a glass

4 (temps) in; **dans deux mois** in two months, in two months' time

5 (approximation) about; **dans les 20 euros** about 20 euros

---

danse [dɑ̃s] nf: **la ~** dancing; (classique) (ballet) dancing; **une ~** a dance; **~ du ventre** belly dancing

danser [dɑ̃se] vi, vt to dance

danseur, -euse [dɑ̃sœʀ, -øz] nm/f ballet dancer; (au bal etc) dancer; (: cavalier) partner; **~ de claquettes** tap-dancer; **en danseuse** (à vélo) standing on the pedals

dard [daʀ] nm sting (organ)

date [dat] nf date; **faire ~** to mark a milestone; **de longue ~** adj longstanding; **~ de naissance** date of birth; **~ limite** deadline; (d'un aliment: aussi: **~ limite de vente**) sell-by date

dater [date] vt, vi to date; **~ de** to date from, go back to; **à ~ de** (as) from

datte [dat] nf date

dauphin [dofɛ̃] nm (Zool) dolphin; (du roi) dauphin; (fig) heir apparent

davantage [davɑ̃taʒ] adv more; (plus longtemps) longer; **~ de** more; **~ que** more than

---

de, d' [de, d] (de + le = **du**, de + les = **des**) prép **1** (appartenance) of; **le toit de la maison** the roof of the house; **la voiture d'Elisabeth/de mes parents** Elizabeth's/my parents' car

2 (provenance) from; **il vient de Londres** he comes from London; **de Londres à Paris** from London to Paris; **elle est sortie du cinéma** she came out of the cinema

3 (moyen) with; **je l'ai fait de mes propres mains** I did it with my own two hands

4 (caractérisation, mesure): **un mur de brique/ bureau d'acajou** a brick wall/mahogany desk; **un billet de 10 euros** a 10 euro note; **une pièce de 2 m de large** ou **large de 2 m** a room 2 m wide, a 2m-wide room; **un bébé de 10 mois** a 10-month-old baby; **12 mois de**

crédit/travail 12 months' credit/work; **elle est payée 20 euros de l'heure** she's paid 20 euros an hour *ou* per hour; **augmenter de 10 euros** to increase by 10 euros; **trois jours de libres** three free days, three days free; **un verre d'eau** a glass of water; **il mange de tout** he'll eat anything

5 (*rapport*) from; **de quatre à six** from four to six

6 (*cause*): **mourir de faim** to die of hunger; **rouge de colère** red with fury

7 (*vb+de+infin*) to; **il m'a dit de rester** he told me to stay

8 (*de la part de*): **estimé de ses collègues** respected by his colleagues

9 (*en apposition*): **cet imbécile de Paul** that idiot Paul; **le terme de franglais** the term "franglais"

▷ *art* **1** (*phrases affirmatives*): some (*souvent omis*); **du vin, de l'eau, des pommes** (some) wine, (some) water, (some) apples; **des enfants sont venus** some children came; **pendant des mois** for months

2 (*phrases interrogatives et négatives*): any; **a-t-il du vin?** has he got any wine?; **il n'a pas de pommes/d'enfants** he hasn't (got) any apples/children, he has no apples/children

dé [de] *nm* (*à jouer*) die *ou* dice; (*aussi*: **dé à coudre**) thimble; **dés** *nmpl* (*jeu*) (game of) dice; **un coup de dés** a throw of the dice; **couper en dés** (*Culin*) to dice

dealer [dilœʀ] *nm* (*fam*) (drug) pusher

déambuler [deãbyle] *vi* to stroll about

débâcle [debɑkl] *nf* rout

déballer [debale] *vt* to unpack

débandade [debɑ̃dad] *nf* scattering; (*déroute*) rout

débarbouiller [debaʀbuje] *vt* to wash; **se débarbouiller** *vi* to wash (one's face)

débarcadère [debaʀkadɛʀ] *nm* landing stage (Brit), wharf

débardeur [debaʀdœʀ] *nm* docker, stevedore; (*maillot*) slipover; (*pour femme*) vest top; (*pour homme*) sleeveless top

débarquer [debaʀke] *vt* to unload, land ▷ *vi* to disembark; (*fig*) to turn up

débarras [debaʀɑ] *nm* (*pièce*) lumber room; (*placard*) junk cupboard; (*remise*) outhouse; **bon ~!** good riddance!

débarrasser [debaʀase] *vt* to clear ▷ *vi* (*enlever le couvert*) to clear away; **~ qn de** (*vêtements, paquets*) to relieve sb of; (*habitude, ennemi*) to rid sb of; **~ qch de** (*fouillis etc*) to clear sth of; **se débarrasser de** *vt* to get rid of; to rid o.s. of

débat [deba] *vb voir* **débattre** ▷ *nm* discussion, debate; **débats** *nmpl* (*Pol*) proceedings, debates

débattre [debatʀ] *vt* to discuss, debate; **se débattre** *vi* to struggle

débaucher [deboʃe] *vt* (*licencier*) to lay off, dismiss; (*salarié d'une autre entreprise*) to poach; (*entraîner*) to lead astray, debauch; (*inciter à la grève*) to incite

débile [debil] *adj* weak, feeble; (*fam: idiot*) dim-witted

débit [debi] *nm* (*d'un liquide, fleuve*) (rate of) flow; (*d'un magasin*) turnover (of goods); (*élocution*) delivery; (*bancaire*) debit; **avoir un ~ de 10 euros** to be 10 euros in debit; **~ de boissons** drinking establishment; **~ de tabac** tobacconist's (shop) (Brit), tobacco *ou* smoke shop (US)

débiter [debite] *vt* (*compte*) to debit; (*liquide, gaz*) to yield, produce, give out; (*couper: bois, viande*) to cut up; (*vendre*) to retail; (*péj: paroles etc*) to come out with, churn out

débiteur, -trice [debitœʀ, -tʀis] *nm/f* debtor ▷ *adj* in debit; (*compte*) debit *cpd*

déblayer [debleje] *vt* to clear; **~ le terrain** (*fig*) to clear the ground

débloquer [deblɔke] *vt* (*frein, fonds*) to release; (*prix, crédits*) to free ▷ *vi* (*fam*) to talk rubbish

déboires [debwaʀ] *nmpl* setbacks

déboiser [debwaze] *vt* to clear of trees; (*région*) to deforest; **se déboiser** *vi* (*colline, montagne*) to become bare of trees

déboîter [debwate] *vt* (*Auto*) to pull out; **se ~ le genou** *etc* to dislocate one's knee *etc*

débonnaire [debɔnɛʀ] *adj* easy-going, good-natured

débordé, e [debɔʀde] *adj*: **être ~ de** (*travail, demandes*) to be snowed under with

déborder [debɔʀde] *vi* to overflow; (*lait etc*) to boil over ▷ *vt* (*Mil, Sport*) to outflank; **~ (de) qch** (*dépasser*) to extend beyond sth; **~ de** (*joie, zèle*) to be brimming over with *ou* bursting with

débouché [debuʃe] *nm* (*pour vendre*) outlet; (*perspective d'emploi*) opening; (*sortie*): **au ~ de la vallée** where the valley opens out (onto the plain)

déboucher [debuʃe] *vt* (*évier, tuyau etc*) to unblock; (*bouteille*) to uncork, open ▷ *vi*: **~ de** to emerge from, come out of; **~ sur** to come out onto; to open out onto; (*fig*) to arrive at, lead up to; (*études*) to lead on to

débourser [debuʀse] *vt* to pay out, lay out

déboussoler [debusɔle] *vt* to disorientate, disorient

debout [dəbu] *adv*: **être ~** (*personne*) to be standing, stand; (*: levé, éveillé*) to be up (and about); (*chose*) to be upright; **être encore ~** (*fig: en état*) to be still going; to be still standing; to be still up; **mettre qn ~** to get sb to his feet; **mettre qch ~** to stand sth up; **se mettre ~** to get up (on one's feet); **se tenir ~** to stand; **~! stand up!**; (*du lit*) get up!; **cette histoire ne tient pas ~** this story doesn't hold water

déboutonner [debutɔne] *vt* to undo, unbutton; **se déboutonner** *vi* to come undone *ou* unbuttoned

débraillé, e [debraje] adj slovenly, untidy

débrancher [debrɑ̃ʃe] vt (appareil électrique) to unplug; (téléphone, courant électrique) to disconnect, cut off

débrayage [debrɛjaʒ] nm (Auto) clutch; (: action) disengaging the clutch; (grève) stoppage; **faire un double ~** to double-declutch

débrayer [debrɛje] vi (Auto) to declutch, disengage the clutch; (cesser le travail) to stop work

débris [debri] nm (fragment) fragment ▷ nmpl (déchets) pieces, debris sg; rubbish sg (Brit), garbage sg (US); **des ~ de verre** bits of glass

débrouillard, e [debrujar, -ard] adj smart, resourceful

débrouiller [debruje] vt to disentangle, untangle; (fig) to sort out, unravel; **se débrouiller** vi to manage; **débrouillez-vous** you'll have to sort things out yourself

début [deby] nm beginning, start; **débuts** nmpl (de carrière) début sg; **faire ses ~s** to start out; **au ~** in ou at the beginning, at first; **au ~ de** at the beginning ou start of; **dès le ~** from the start; **~ juin** in early June

débutant, e [debytɑ̃, -ɑ̃t] nm/f beginner, novice

débuter [debyte] vi to begin, start; (faire ses débuts) to start out

deçà [dəsa]: **en ~ de** prép this side of; **en ~** adv on this side

décadence [dekadɑ̃s] nf decadence; decline

décaféiné, e [dekafeine] adj decaffeinated, caffeine-free

décalage [dekalaʒ] nm move forward ou back; shift forward ou back; (écart) gap; (désaccord) discrepancy; **~ horaire** time difference (between time zones), time-lag

décaler [dekale] vt (dans le temps: avancer) to bring forward; (: retarder) to put back; (changer de position) to shift forward ou back; **~ de 10 cm** to move forward ou back by 10 cm; **~ de deux heures** to bring ou move forward two hours; to put back two hours

décalquer [dekalke] vt to trace; (par pression) to transfer

décamper [dekɑ̃pe] vi to clear out ou off

décaper [dekape] vt to strip; (avec abrasif) to scour; (avec papier de verre) to sand

décapiter [dekapite] vt to behead; (par accident) to decapitate; (fig) to cut the top off; (: organisation) to remove the top people from

décapotable [dekapɔtabl] adj convertible

décapsuleur [dekapsylœr] nm bottle-opener

décarcasser [dekarkase] vt: **se ~ pour qn/ pour faire qch** (fam) to slog one's guts out for sb/to do sth

décédé, e [desede] adj deceased

décéder [desede] vi to die

déceler [desle] vt to discover, detect; (révéler)

to indicate, reveal

décembre [desɑ̃br] nm December; voir aussi **juillet**

décemment [desamɑ̃] adv decently

décennie [deseni] nf decade

décent, e [desɑ̃, -ɑ̃t] adj decent

déception [desɛpsjɔ̃] nf disappointment

décerner [desɛrne] vt to award

décès [desɛ] nm death, decease; **acte de ~** death certificate

décevant, e [desvɑ̃, -ɑ̃t] adj disappointing

décevoir [des(ə)vwar] vt to disappoint

déchaîner [deʃene] vt (passions, colère) to unleash; (rires etc) to give rise to, arouse; **se déchaîner** vi to be unleashed; (rires) to burst out; (se mettre en colère) to fly into a rage; **se ~ contre qn** to unleash one's fury on sb

déchanter [deʃɑ̃te] vi to become disillusioned

décharge [deʃarʒ] nf (dépôt d'ordures) rubbish tip ou dump; (électrique) electrical discharge; (salve) volley of shots; **à la ~ de** in defence of

décharger [deʃarʒe] vt (marchandise, véhicule) to unload; (Élec) to discharge; (arme: neutraliser) to unload; (: faire feu) to discharge, fire; **~ qn de** (responsabilité) to relieve sb of, release sb from; **~ sa colère (sur)** to vent one's anger (on); **~ sa conscience** to unburden one's conscience; **se ~ dans** (se déverser) to flow into; **se ~ d'une affaire sur qn** to hand a matter over to sb

décharné, e [deʃarne] adj bony, emaciated, fleshless

déchausser [deʃose] vt (personne) to take the shoes off; (skis) to take off; **se déchausser** vi to take off one's shoes; (dent) to come ou work loose

déchéance [deʃeɑ̃s] nf (déclin) degeneration, decay, decline; (chute) fall

déchet [deʃɛ] nm (de bois, tissu etc) scrap; (perte: gén Comm) wastage, waste; **déchets** nmpl (ordures) refuse sg, rubbish sg (Brit), garbage sg (US); **~s nucléaires** nuclear waste; **~s radioactifs** radioactive waste

déchiffrer [deʃifre] vt to decipher

déchiqueter [deʃikte] vt to tear ou pull to pieces

déchirant, e [deʃirɑ̃, -ɑ̃t] adj heart-breaking, heart-rending

déchirement [deʃirmɑ̃] nm (chagrin) wrench, heartbreak; (gén pl: conflit) rift, split

déchirer [deʃire] vt to tear, rip; (mettre en morceaux) to tear up; (pour ouvrir) to tear off; (arracher) to tear out; (fig) to tear apart; **se déchirer** vi to tear, rip; **se ~ un muscle/ tendon** to tear a muscle/tendon

déchirure [deʃiryr] nf (accroc) tear, rip; **~ musculaire** torn muscle

déchoir [deʃwar] vi (personne) to lower o.s., demean o.s.; **~ de** to fall from

déchu, e [deʃy] pp de **déchoir** ▷ adj fallen; (roi) deposed

décidé, e [deside] adj (personne, air)
determined; **c'est ~** it's decided; **être ~ à
faire** to be determined to do

décidément [desidemã] adv undoubtedly;
really

décider [deside] vt: **~ qch** to decide on sth;
~ de faire/que to decide to do/that; **~ qn (à
faire qch)** to persuade ou induce sb (to do
sth); **~ de qch** to decide upon sth; (chose) to
determine sth; **se décider** vi (personne) to
decide, make up one's mind; (problème, affaire)
to be resolved; **se ~ à qch** to decide on sth;
se ~ à faire to decide ou make up one's mind
to do; **se ~ pour qch** to decide on ou in favour
of sth

décimal, e, -aux [desimal, -o] adj, nf
decimal

décimètre [desimɛtʀ] nm decimetre (Brit),
decimeter (US); **double ~** (20 cm) ruler

décisif, -ive [desizif, -iv] adj decisive; (qui
l'emporte): **le facteur/l'argument ~** the
deciding factor/argument

décision [desizjɔ̃] nf decision; (fermeté)
decisiveness, decision; **prendre une ~** to
make a decision; **prendre la ~ de faire** to
take the decision to do; **emporter** ou **faire
la ~** to be decisive

déclaration [deklaʀasjɔ̃] nf declaration;
registration; (discours: Pol etc) statement;
(compte rendu) report; **fausse ~**
misrepresentation; **~ (d'amour)** declaration;
~ de décès registration of death; **~ de guerre**
declaration of war; **~ (d'impôts)** statement
of income, tax declaration, ≈ tax return; **~ (de
sinistre)** (insurance) claim; **~ de revenus**
statement of income; **faire une ~ de vol** to
report a theft

déclarer [deklaʀe] vt to declare, announce;
(revenus, employés, marchandises) to declare;
(décès, naissance) to register; (vol etc: à la police)
to report; **rien à ~** nothing to declare; **se
déclarer** vi (feu, maladie) to break out; **~ la
guerre** to declare war

déclencher [deklɑ̃ʃe] vt (mécanisme etc) to
release; (sonnerie) to set off, activate; (attaque,
grève) to launch; (provoquer) to trigger off; **se
déclencher** vi to release itself; (sonnerie) to
go off

déclic [deklik] nm trigger mechanism; (bruit)
click

décliner [dekline] vi to decline ▷ vt
(invitation) to decline, refuse; (responsabilité) to
refuse to accept; (nom, adresse) to state; (Ling)
to decline; **se décliner** (Ling) to decline

décocher [dekɔʃe] vt to hurl; (flèche, regard) to
shoot

décoiffer [dekwafe] vt: **~ qn** to mess up sb's
hair; to take sb's hat off; **je suis toute
décoiffée** my hair is in a real mess; **se
décoiffer** vi to take off one's hat

déçois etc [deswa], **déçoive** etc [deswav] vb
voir **décevoir**

décollage [dekɔlaʒ] nm (Aviat, Écon) takeoff

décoller [dekɔle] vt to unstick ▷ vi (avion) to
take off; (projet, entreprise) to take off, get off
the ground; **se décoller** vi to come unstuck

décolleté, e [dekɔlte] adj low-necked, low-
cut; (femme) wearing a low-cut dress ▷ nm
low neck(line); (épaules) (bare) neck and
shoulders; (plongeant) cleavage

décolorer [dekɔlɔʀe] vt (tissu) to fade;
(cheveux) to bleach, lighten; **se décolorer** vi
to fade; **se faire ~ les cheveux** to have one's
hair bleached

décombres [dekɔ̃bʀ] nmpl rubble sg, debris sg

décommander [dekɔmɑ̃de] vt to cancel;
(invités) to put off; **se décommander** vi to
cancel, cry off

décomposé, e [dekɔ̃poze] adj (pourri)
decomposed; (visage) haggard, distorted

décompte [dekɔ̃t] nm deduction; (facture)
breakdown (of an account), detailed account

déconcerter [dekɔ̃sɛʀte] vt to disconcert,
confound

déconfit, e [dekɔ̃fi, -it] adj crestfallen,
downcast

décongeler [dekɔ̃ʒ(ə)le] vt to thaw (out)

déconner [dekɔne] vi (faml: en parlant) to talk
(a load of) rubbish (Brit) ou garbage (US);
(: faire des bêtises) to muck about; **sans ~** no
kidding

déconseiller [dekɔ̃seje] vt: **~ qch (à qn)** to
advise (sb) against sth; **~ à qn de faire** to
advise sb against doing; **c'est déconseillé**
it's not advised ou advisable

décontracté, e [dekɔ̃tʀakte] adj relaxed,
laid-back (fam)

décontracter [dekɔ̃tʀakte] vt, **se
décontracter** vi to relax

déconvenue [dekɔ̃vny] nf disappointment

décor [dekɔʀ] nm décor; (paysage) scenery;
décors nmpl (Théât) scenery sg, decor sg; (Ciné)
set sg; **changement de ~** (fig) change of
scene; **entrer dans le ~** (fig) to run off the
road; **en ~ naturel** (Ciné) on location

décorateur, -trice [dekɔʀatœʀ, -tʀis] nm/f
(interior) decorator; (Ciné) set designer

décoration [dekɔʀasjɔ̃] nf decoration

décorer [dekɔʀe] vt to decorate

décortiquer [dekɔʀtike] vt to shell; (riz) to
hull; (fig: texte) to dissect

découcher [dekuʃe] vi to spend the night
away

découdre [dekudʀ] vt (vêtement, couture) to
unpick, take the stitching out of; (bouton) to
take off; **se découdre** vi to come unstitched;
(bouton) to come off; **en ~** (fig) to fight, do
battle

découler [dekule] vi: **~ de** to ensue ou follow
from

découper [dekupe] vt (papier, tissu etc) to cut
up; (volaille, viande) to carve; (détacher: manche,
article) to cut out; **se ~ sur** (ciel, fond) to stand
out against

décourager [dekuʀaʒe] vt to discourage, dishearten; (*dissuader*) to discourage, put off; **se décourager** vi to lose heart, become discouraged; **~ qn de faire/de qch** to discourage sb from doing/from sth, put sb off doing/sth

décousu, e [dekuzy] pp de **découdre** ▷ adj unstitched; (*fig*) disjointed, disconnected

découvert, e [dekuvɛʀ, -ɛʀt] pp de **découvrir** ▷ adj (*tête*) bare, uncovered; (*lieu*) open, exposed ▷ nm (*bancaire*) overdraft ▷ nf discovery; **à ~** adv (Mil) exposed, without cover; (*fig*) openly ▷ adj (Comm) overdrawn; **à visage ~** openly; **aller à la ~e de** to go in search of; **faire la ~e de** to discover

découvrir [dekuvʀiʀ] vt to discover; (*apercevoir*) to see; (*enlever ce qui couvre ou protège*) to uncover; (*montrer, dévoiler*) to reveal; **se découvrir** vi (*chapeau*) to take off one's hat; (*se déshabiller*) to take something off; (*au lit*) to uncover o.s.; (*ciel*) to clear; **se ~ des talents** to find hidden talents in o.s.

décret [dekʀɛ] nm decree

décréter [dekʀete] vt to decree; (*ordonner*) to order

décrié, e [dekʀije] adj disparaged

décrire [dekʀiʀ] vt to describe; (*courbe, cercle*) to follow, describe

décrocher [dekʀɔʃe] vt (*dépendre*) to take down; (*téléphone*) to take off the hook; (: *pour répondre*): **~ (le téléphone)** to pick up ou lift the receiver; (*fig: contrat etc*) to get, land ▷ vi (*fam: abandonner*) to drop out; (*cesser d'écouter*) to switch off; **se décrocher** vi (*tableau, rideau*) to fall down

décroître [dekʀwatʀ] vi to decrease, decline diminish

décrypter [dekʀipte] vt to decipher

déçu, e [desy] pp de **décevoir** ▷ adj disappointed

décupler [dekyple] vt, vi to increase tenfold

dédaigner [dedeɲe] vt to despise, scorn; (*négliger*) to disregard, spurn; **~ de faire** to consider it beneath one to do, not deign to do

dédaigneux, -euse [dedɛɲø, -øz] adj scornful, disdainful

dédain [dedɛ̃] nm scorn, disdain

dédale [dedal] nm maze

dedans [dədɑ̃] adv inside; (*pas en plein air*) indoors, inside ▷ nm inside; **au ~** on the inside; inside; **en ~** (*vers l'intérieur*) inwards; *voir aussi* **là**

dédicacer [dedikase] vt: **~ (à qn)** to sign (for sb), autograph (for sb), inscribe (to sb)

dédier [dedje] vt to dedicate; **~ à** to dedicate to

dédire [dediʀ]: **se dédire** vi to go back on one's word; (*se rétracter*) to retract, recant

dédommagement [dedɔmaʒmɑ̃] nm compensation

dédommager [dedɔmaʒe] vt: **~ qn (de)** to compensate sb (for); (*fig*) to repay sb (for)

dédouaner [dedwane] vt to clear through customs

dédoubler [deduble] vt (*classe, effectifs*) to split (into two); (*couverture etc*) to unfold; (*manteau*) to remove the lining of; **~ un train/les trains** to run a relief train/additional trains; **se dédoubler** vi (Psych) to have a split personality

déduire [dedɥiʀ] vt: **~ qch (de)** (*ôter*) to deduct sth (from); (*conclure*) to deduce ou infer sth (from)

déesse [dees] nf goddess

défaillance [defajɑ̃s] nf (*syncope*) blackout; (*fatigue*) (sudden) weakness no pl; (*technique*) fault, failure; (*morale etc*) weakness; **~ cardiaque** heart failure

défaillir [defajiʀ] vi to faint; to feel faint; (*mémoire etc*) to fail

défaire [defɛʀ] vt (*installation, échafaudage*) to take down, dismantle; (*paquet etc, nœud, vêtement*) to undo; (*bagages*) to unpack; (*ouvrage*) to undo, unpick; (*cheveux*) to take out; **se défaire** vi to come undone; **se ~ de** vt (*se débarrasser de*) to get rid of; (*se séparer de*) to part with; **~ le lit** (*pour changer les draps*) to strip the bed; (*pour se coucher*) to turn back the bedclothes

défait, e [defɛ, -ɛt] pp de **défaire** ▷ adj (*visage*) haggard, ravaged ▷ nf defeat

défalquer [defalke] vt to deduct

défaut [defo] nm (*moral*) fault, failing, defect; (*d'étoffe, métal*) fault, flaw, defect; (*manque, carence*): **~ de** lack of; shortage of; (Inform) bug; **~ de la cuirasse** (*fig*) chink in the armour (Brit) ou armor (US); **en ~** at fault; in the wrong; **prendre qn en ~** to catch sb out; **faire ~** (*manquer*) to be lacking; **à ~** adv failing that; **à ~ de** for lack ou want of; **par ~** (Jur) in his (ou her etc) absence

défavorable [defavɔʀabl] adj unfavourable (Brit), unfavorable (US)

défavoriser [defavɔʀize] vt to put at a disadvantage

défection [defɛksjɔ̃] nf defection, failure to give support ou assistance; failure to appear; **faire ~** (*d'un parti etc*) to withdraw one's support, leave

défectueux, -euse [defɛktɥø, -øz] adj faulty, defective

défendre [defɑ̃dʀ] vt to defend; (*interdire*) to forbid; **~ à qn qch/de faire** to forbid sb sth/to do; **il est défendu de cracher** spitting (is) prohibited ou is not allowed; **c'est défendu** it is forbidden; **se défendre** vi to defend o.s.; **il se défend** (*fig*) he can hold his own; **ça se défend** (*fig*) it holds together; **se ~ de/contre** (*se protéger*) to protect o.s. from/against; **se ~ de** (*se garder de*) to refrain from; (*nier*): **se ~ de vouloir** to deny wanting

défense [defɑ̃s] nf defence (Brit), defense (US); (*d'éléphant etc*) tusk; **ministre de la ~** Minister of Defence (Brit), Defence Secretary;

la ~ **nationale** defence, the defence of the realm (Brit); **la ~ contre avions** anti-aircraft defence; **"~ de fumer/cracher"** "no smoking/spitting", "smoking/spitting prohibited"; **prendre la ~ de qn** to stand up for sb; **~ des consommateurs** consumerism

déférer [defere] vt (Jur) to refer; **~ à** (requête, décision) to defer to; **~ qn à la justice** to hand sb over to justice

déferler [defɛʀle] vi (vagues) to break; (fig) to surge

défi [defi] nm (provocation) challenge; (bravade) defiance; **mettre qn au ~ de faire qch** to challenge sb to do sth; **relever un ~** to take up ou accept a challenge; **lancer un ~ à qn** to challenge sb to; **sur un ton de ~** defiantly

déficit [defisit] nm (Comm) deficit; (Psych etc: manque) defect; **~ budgétaire** budget deficit; **être en ~** to be in deficit

déficitaire [defisitɛʀ] adj (année, récolte) bad; **entreprise/budget ~** business/budget in deficit

défier [defje] vt (provoquer) to challenge; (fig) to defy, brave; **se ~ de** (se méfier de) to distrust, mistrust; **~ qn de faire** to challenge ou defy sb to do; **~ qn à** to challenge sb to; **~ toute comparaison/concurrence** to be incomparable/unbeatable

défigurer [defigyʀe] vt to disfigure; (boutons etc) to mar ou spoil (the looks of); (fig: œuvre) to mutilate, deface

défilé [defile] nm (Géo) (narrow) gorge ou pass; (soldats) parade; (manifestants) procession, march; **un ~ de** (voitures, visiteurs etc) a stream of

défiler [defile] vi (troupes) to march past; (sportifs) to parade; (manifestants) to march; (visiteurs) to pour, stream; **faire ~ un document** (Inform) to scroll a document; **se défiler** vi (se dérober) to slip away, sneak off; **faire ~** (bande, film) to put on; (Inform) to scroll; **il s'est défilé** (fam) he wriggled out of it

définir [definiʀ] vt to define

définitif, -ive [definitif, -iv] adj (final) final, definitive; (pour longtemps) permanent, definitive; (sans appel) final, definite ▷ nf: **en définitive** eventually; (somme toute) when all is said and done

définitivement [definitivmɑ̃] adv definitively; permanently; definitely

défoncer [defɔ̃se] vt (caisse) to stave in; (porte) to smash in ou down; (lit, fauteuil) to burst (the springs of); (terrain, route) to rip ou plough up; **se défoncer** vi (se donner à fond) to give it all one's got

déformer [defɔʀme] vt to put out of shape; (corps) to deform; (pensée, fait) to distort; **se déformer** vi to lose its shape

défouler [defule]: **se défouler** vi (Psych) to work off one's tensions, release one's pent-up feelings; (gén) to unwind, let off steam

défraîchir [defʀeʃiʀ]: **se défraîchir** vi to fade; to become shop-soiled

défricher [defʀiʃe] vt to clear (for cultivation)

défunt, e [defœ̃, -œ̃t] adj: **son ~ père** his late father ▷ nm/f deceased

dégagé, e [degaʒe] adj (route, ciel) clear; (ton, air) casual, jaunty; **sur un ton ~** casually

dégagement [degaʒmɑ̃] nm emission; freeing; clearing; (espace libre) clearing; passage; clearance; (Football) clearance; **voie de ~** slip road; **itinéraire de ~** alternative route (to relieve traffic congestion)

dégager [degaʒe] vt (exhaler) to give off, emit; (délivrer) to free, extricate; (Mil: troupes) to relieve; (désencombrer) to clear; (isoler, mettre en valeur) to bring out; (crédits) to release; **se dégager** vi (odeur) to emanate, be given off; (passage, ciel) to clear; **~ qn de** (engagement, parole etc) to release ou free sb from; **se ~ de** (fig: engagement etc) to get out of; (: promesse) to go back on

dégarnir [degaʀniʀ] vt (vider) to empty, clear; **se dégarnir** vi to empty; to be cleaned out ou cleared; (tempes, crâne) to go bald

dégâts [dega] nmpl damage sg; **faire des ~** to damage

dégel [deʒɛl] nm thaw; (fig: des prix etc) unfreezing

dégeler [deʒle] vt to thaw (out); (fig) to unfreeze ▷ vi to thaw (out); **se dégeler** vi (fig) to thaw out

dégénérer [deʒeneʀe] vi to degenerate; (empirer) to go from bad to worse; (devenir): **~ en** to degenerate into

dégingandé, e [deʒɛ̃gɑ̃de] adj gangling, lanky

dégivrer [deʒivʀe] vt (frigo) to defrost; (vitres) to de-ice

dégonflé, e [degɔ̃fle] adj (pneu) flat; (fam) chicken ▷ nm/f (fam) chicken

dégonfler [degɔ̃fle] vt (pneu, ballon) to let down, deflate ▷ vi (désenfler) to go down; **se dégonfler** vi (fam) to chicken out

dégouliner [deguline] vi to trickle, drip; **~ de** to be dripping with

dégourdi, e [deguʀdi] adj smart, resourceful

dégourdir [deguʀdiʀ] vt to warm (up); **se ~ (les jambes)** to stretch one's legs

dégoût [degu] nm disgust, distaste

dégoûtant, e [degutɑ̃, -ɑ̃t] adj disgusting

dégoûté, e [degute] adj disgusted; **~ de** sick of

dégoûter [degute] vt to disgust; **cela me dégoûte** I find this disgusting ou revolting; **~ qn de qch** to put sb off sth; **se ~ de** to get ou become sick of

dégrader [degʀade] vt (Mil: officier) to degrade; (abîmer) to damage, deface; (avilir) to degrade, debase; **se dégrader** vi (relations, situation) to deteriorate

dégrafer [degʀafe] vt to unclip, unhook, unfasten

degré [dəgʀe] nm degree; (d'escalier) step; **brûlure au 1er/2ème ~** 1st/2nd degree burn; **équation du 1er/2ème ~** linear/quadratic equation; **le premier ~** (*Scol*) primary level; **alcool à 90 ~s** surgical spirit; **vin de 10 ~s** 10° wine (*on Gay-Lussac scale*); **par ~(s)** adv by degrees, gradually

dégressif, -ive [degʀesif, -iv] adj on a decreasing scale, degressive; **tarif ~** decreasing rate of charge

dégringoler [degʀɛ̃gɔle] vi to tumble (down); (*fig: prix, monnaie etc*) to collapse

dégrossir [degʀosiʀ] vt (*bois*) to trim; (*fig*) to work out roughly; (: *personne*) to knock the rough edges off

déguenillé, e [degnije] adj ragged, tattered

déguerpir [degɛʀpiʀ] vi to clear off

dégueulasse [degœlas] adj (*fam*) disgusting

dégueuler [degœle] vi (*fam*) to puke, throw up

déguisement [degizmɑ̃] nm disguise; (*habits: pour s'amuser*) fancy dress; (: *pour tromper*) disguise

déguiser [degize] vt to disguise; **se déguiser (en)** vi (*se costumer*) to dress up (as); (*pour tromper*) to disguise o.s. (as)

dégustation [degystasjɔ̃] nf tasting; (*de fromages etc*) sampling; savouring (*Brit*), savoring (*US*); (*séance*): **~ de vin(s)** wine-tasting

déguster [degyste] vt (*vins*) to taste; (*fromages etc*) to sample; (*savourer*) to enjoy, savour (*Brit*), savor (*US*)

dehors [dəɔʀ] adv outside; (*en plein air*) outdoors, outside ▷ nm outside ▷ nmpl (*apparences*) appearances, exterior sg; **mettre ou jeter ~** to throw out; **au ~** outside; (*en apparence*) outwardly; **au ~ de** outside; **de ~** from outside; **en ~** outside; outwards; **en ~ de** apart from

déjà [deʒa] adv already; (*auparavant*) before, already; **as-tu ~ été en France?** have you been to France before?; **c'est ~ pas mal** that's not too bad (at all); **c'est ~ quelque chose** (at least) it's better than nothing; **quel nom, ~?** what was the name again?

déjeuner [deʒœne] vi to (have) lunch; (*le matin*) to have breakfast ▷ nm lunch; (*petit déjeuner*) breakfast; **~ d'affaires** business lunch

déjouer [deʒwe] vt to elude, to foil, thwart

delà [dəla] adv: **par ~, en ~ (de), au ~ (de)** beyond

délabrer [delabʀe]: **se délabrer** vi to fall into decay, become dilapidated

délacer [delase] vt (*chaussures*) to undo, unlace

délai [dele] nm (*attente*) waiting period; (*sursis*) extension (of time); (*temps accordé*; aussi: **~s**) time limit; **sans ~** without delay; **à bref ~** shortly, very soon; at short notice; **dans les ~s** within the time limit; **un ~ de 30 jours** a period of 30 days; **comptez un ~ de livraison de 10 jours** allow 10 days for delivery

délaisser [delese] vt (*abandonner*) to abandon, desert; (*négliger*) to neglect

délasser [delase] vt (*reposer*) to relax; (*divertir*) to divert, entertain; **se délasser** vi to relax

délavé, e [delave] adj faded

délayer [deleje] vt (*Culin*) to mix (with water etc); (*peinture*) to thin down; (*fig*) to pad out, spin out

delco® [dɛlko] nm (*Auto*) distributor; **tête de ~** distributor cap

délecter [delɛkte]: **se délecter** vi: **se ~ de** to revel ou delight in

délégué, e [delege] adj delegated ▷ nm/f delegate; representative; **ministre ~ à** minister with special responsibility for

déléguer [delege] vt to delegate

délibéré, e [delibeʀe] adj (*conscient*) deliberate; (*déterminé*) determined, resolute; **de propos ~** (*à dessein, exprès*) intentionally

délibérer [delibeʀe] vi to deliberate

délicat, e [delika, -at] adj delicate; (*plein de tact*) tactful; (*attentionné*) thoughtful; (*exigeant*) fussy, particular; **procédés peu ~s** unscrupulous methods

délicatement [delikatmɑ̃] adv delicately; (*avec douceur*) gently

délice [delis] nm delight

délicieux, -euse [delisjø, -øz] adj (*au goût*) delicious; (*sensation, impression*) delightful

délimiter [delimite] vt (*terrain*) to delimit, demarcate

délinquance [delɛ̃kɑ̃s] nf criminality; **~ juvénile** juvenile delinquency

délinquant, e [delɛ̃kɑ̃, -ɑ̃t] adj, nm/f delinquent

délirant, e [deliʀɑ̃, -ɑ̃t] adj (*Méd: fièvre*) delirious; (*imagination*) frenzied; (*fam: déraisonnable*) crazy

délirer [deliʀe] vi to be delirious; **tu délires!** (*fam*) you're crazy!

délit [deli] nm (criminal) offence; **~ de droit commun** violation of common law; **~ de fuite** failure to stop after an accident; **~ d'initiés** insider dealing ou trading; **~ de presse** violation of the press laws

délivrer [delivʀe] vt (*prisonnier*) to (set) free, release; (*passeport, certificat*) to issue; **~ qn de** (*ennemis*) to set sb free from, deliver ou free sb from; (*fig*) to rid sb of

déloger [delɔʒe] vt (*locataire*) to turn out; (*objet coincé, ennemi*) to dislodge

déloyal, e, -aux [delwajal, -o] adj (*personne, conduite*) disloyal; (*procédé*) unfair

deltaplane® [dɛltaplan] nm hang-glider

déluge [delyʒ] nm (*biblique*) Flood, Deluge; (*grosse pluie*) downpour, deluge; (*grand nombre*): **~ de** flood of

déluré, e [delyʀe] adj smart, resourceful; (*péj*) forward, pert

demain [d(ə)mɛ̃] adv tomorrow; **~ matin/soir** tomorrow morning/evening; **~ midi** tomorrow at midday; **à ~!** see you tomorrow!

demande [d(ə)mãd] nf (requête) request; (revendication) demand; (Admin, formulaire) application; (Écon): **la ~** demand; **"~s d'emploi"** "situations wanted"; **à la ~ générale** by popular request; **~ en mariage** (marriage) proposal; **faire sa ~ (en mariage)** to propose (marriage); **~ de naturalisation** application for naturalization; **~ de poste** job application

demandé, e [d(ə)mãde] adj (article etc): **très ~** (very) much in demand

demander [d(ə)mãde] vt (question: date, heure, chemin) to ask; (requérir, nécessiter) to require, demand; **~ qch à qn** to ask sb for sth, ask sb sth; **ils demandent deux secrétaires et un ingénieur** they're looking for two secretaries and an engineer; **~ la main de qn** to ask for sb's hand (in marriage); **~ pardon à qn** to apologize to sb; **à ou de voir/faire** to ask to see/ask if one can do; **~ à qn de faire** to ask sb to do; **~ que/pourquoi** to ask that/why; **se ~ si/pourquoi** etc to wonder if/why etc; (sens purement réfléchi) to ask o.s. if/why etc; **on vous demande au téléphone** you're wanted on the phone, there's someone for you on the phone; **il ne demande que ça** that's all he wants; **je ne demande pas mieux** I'm asking nothing more; **il ne demande qu'à faire** all he wants is to do

demandeur, -euse [damãdœr, -øz] nm/f: **~ d'asile** asylum-seeker; **~ d'emploi** jobseeker

démangeaison [demãʒɛzɔ̃] nf itching; **avoir des ~s** to be itching

démanger [demãʒe] vi to itch; **la main me démange** my hand is itching; **l'envie ou ça me démange de faire** I'm itching to do

démanteler [demãtle] vt to break up; to demolish

démaquillant [demakijã] nm make-up remover

démaquiller [demakije] vt: **se démaquiller** to remove one's make-up

démarche [demarʃ] nf (allure) gait, walk; (intervention) step; approach; (fig: intellectuelle) thought processes pl; approach; **faire ou entreprendre des ~s** to take action; **faire des ~s auprès de qn** to approach sb; **faire les ~s nécessaires (pour obtenir qch)** to take the necessary steps (to obtain sth)

démarcheur, -euse [demarʃœr, -øz] nm/f (Comm) door-to-door salesman/woman; (Pol etc) canvasser

démarque [demark] nf (Comm: d'un article) mark-down

démarrage [demaraʒ] nm starting no pl, start; **~ en côte** hill start

démarrer [demare] vt to start up ▷ vi (conducteur) to start (up); (véhicule) to move off; (travaux, affaire) to get moving; (coureur: accélérer) to pull away

démarreur [demarœr] nm (Auto) starter

démêlant, e [demelã, -ãt] adj: **baume ~, crème ~e** (hair) conditioner ▷ nm conditioner

démêler [demele] vt to untangle, disentangle

démêlés [demele] nmpl problems

déménagement [demenaʒmã] nm (du point de vue du locataire etc) move; (: du déménageur) removal (Brit), moving (US); **entreprise/ camion de ~** removal (Brit) ou moving (US) firm/van

déménager [demenaʒe] vt (meubles) to (re)move ▷ vi to move (house)

déménageur [demenaʒœr] nm removal man (Brit), (furniture) mover (US); (entrepreneur) furniture remover

démener [demne]: **se démener** vi to thrash about; (fig) to exert o.s.

dément, e [demã, -ãt] vb voir **démentir** ▷ adj (fou) mad (Brit), crazy; (fam) brilliant, fantastic

démentiel, le [demãsjɛl] adj insane

démentir [demãtir] vt (nouvelle, témoin) to refute; (faits etc) to belie, refute; **~ que** to deny that; **ne pas se ~** not to fail, keep up

démerder [demerde]: **se démerder** vi (fam!) to bloody well manage for o.s.

démesuré, e [deməzyre] adj immoderate, disproportionate

démettre [demɛtr] vt: **~ qn de** (fonction, poste) to dismiss sb from; **se ~ (de ses fonctions)** to resign (from) one's duties; **se ~ l'épaule** etc to dislocate one's shoulder etc

demeurant [dəmœrã]: **au ~** adv for all that

demeure [dəmœr] nf residence; **dernière ~** (fig) last resting place; **mettre qn en ~ de faire** to enjoin ou order sb to do; **à ~** adv permanently

demeurer [d(ə)mœre] vi (habiter) to live; (séjourner) to stay; (rester) to remain; **en ~ là** (personne) to leave it at that; (: choses) to be left at that

demi, e [dəmi] adj half; **et ~, trois heures/ bouteilles et ~es** three and a half hours/ bottles, three hours/bottles and a half ▷ nm (bière: = 0.25 litre) ≈ half-pint; (Football) half-back; **il est 2 heures et ~** it's half past 2; **il est midi et ~** it's half past 12; **~ de mêlée/ d'ouverture** (Rugby) scrum/fly half; **à ~** adv half-; **ouvrir à ~** to half-open; **faire les choses à ~** to do things by halves; **à la ~e** (heure) on the half-hour

demi-cercle [dəmisɛrkl] nm semicircle; **en ~** adj semicircular ▷ adv in a semicircle

demi-douzaine [dəmiduzɛn] nf half-dozen, half a dozen

demi-finale [dəmifinal] nf semifinal

demi-frère [dəmifrɛr] nm half-brother

demi-heure [dəmijœr] nf: **une ~** a half-hour, half an hour

demi-journée [dəmiʒurne] nf half-day, half a day

demi-litre [dəmilitʀ] *nm* half-litre (Brit), half-liter (US), half a litre *ou* liter

demi-livre [dəmilivʀ] *nf* half-pound, half a pound

demi-mot [dəmimo]: **à ~** *adv* without having to spell things out

demi-pension [dəmipɑ̃sjɔ̃] *nf* half-board; **être en ~** (*Scol*) to take school meals

demi-pensionnaire [dəmipɑ̃sjɔnɛʀ] *nm/f*: **être ~** to take school lunches

demi-place [dəmiplas] *nf* half-price; (*Transports*) half-fare

démis, e [demi, -iz] *pp de* **démettre** ▷ *adj* (*épaule etc*) dislocated

demi-sel [dəmisɛl] *adj inv* slightly salted

demi-sœur [dəmisœʀ] *nf* half-sister

démission [demisjɔ̃] *nf* resignation; **donner sa ~** to give *ou* hand in one's notice, hand in one's resignation

démissionner [demisjɔne] *vi* (*de son poste*) to resign, give *ou* hand in one's notice

demi-tarif [dəmitaʀif] *nm* half-price; (*Transports*) half-fare; **voyager à ~** to travel half-fare

demi-tour [dəmituʀ] *nm* about-turn; **faire un ~** (*Mil etc*) to make an about-turn; **faire ~** to turn (and go) back; (*Auto*) to do a U-turn

démocratie [demɔkʀasi] *nf* democracy; **~ populaire/libérale** people's/liberal democracy

démocratique [demɔkʀatik] *adj* democratic

démodé, e [demɔde] *adj* old-fashioned

demoiselle [d(ə)mwazɛl] *nf* (*jeune fille*) young lady; (*célibataire*) single lady, maiden lady; **~ d'honneur** bridesmaid

démolir [demɔliʀ] *vt* to demolish; (*fig: personne*) to do for

démon [demɔ̃] *nm* demon, fiend; evil spirit; (*enfant turbulent*) devil, demon; **le ~ du jeu/des femmes** a mania for gambling/women; **le D~** the Devil

démonstration [demɔ̃stʀasjɔ̃] *nf* demonstration; (*aérienne, navale*) display

démonté, e [demɔ̃te] *adj* (*mer*) raging, wild

démonter [demɔ̃te] *vt* (*machine etc*) to take down, dismantle; (*pneu, porte*) to take off; (*cavalier*) to throw, unseat; (*fig: personne*) to disconcert; **se démonter** *vi* (*meuble*) to be dismantled, be taken to pieces; (*personne*) to lose countenance

démontrer [demɔ̃tʀe] *vt* to demonstrate, show

démordre [demɔʀdʀ] *vi* (*aussi*: **ne pas ~ de**) to refuse to give up, stick to

démouler [demule] *vt* (*gâteau*) to turn out

démuni, e [demyni] *adj* (*sans argent*) impoverished; **~ de** without, lacking in

démunir [demyniʀ] *vt*: **~ qn de** to deprive sb of; **se ~ de** to part with, give up

dénaturer [denatyʀe] *vt* (*goût*) to alter (completely); (*pensée, fait*) to distort, misrepresent

dénicher [deniʃe] *vt* (*fam*) ▷ *vt* (*objet*) to unearth; (*restaurant etc*) to discover

dénier [denje] *vt* to deny; **~ qch à qn** to deny sb sth

dénigrer [denigʀe] *vt* to denigrate, run down

dénivellation [denivelasjɔ̃] *nf*, **dénivellement** [denivɛlmɑ̃] *nm* difference in level; (*pente*) ramp; (*creux*) dip

dénombrer [denɔ̃bʀe] *vt* (*compter*) to count; (*énumérer*) to enumerate, list

dénomination [denɔminasjɔ̃] *nf* designation, appellation

dénommé, e [denɔme] *adj*: **le ~ Dupont** the man by the name of Dupont

dénoncer [denɔ̃se] *vt* to denounce; **se dénoncer** *vi* to give o.s. up, come forward

dénouement [denumɑ̃] *nm* outcome, conclusion; (*Théât*) dénouement

dénouer [denwe] *vt* to unknot, undo

dénoyauter [denwajote] *vt* to stone; **appareil à ~** stoner

denrée [dɑ̃ʀe] *nf* commodity; (*aussi*: **~ alimentaire**) food(stuff)

dense [dɑ̃s] *adj* dense

densité [dɑ̃site] *nf* denseness; (*Physique*) density

dent [dɑ̃] *nf* tooth; **avoir/garder une ~ contre qn** to have/hold a grudge against sb; **se mettre qch sous la ~** to eat sth; **être sur les ~s** to be on one's last legs; **faire ses ~s** to teethe, cut (one's) teeth; **en ~s de scie** serrated; (*irrégulier*) jagged; **avoir les ~s longues** (*fig*) to be ruthlessly ambitious; **~ de lait/sagesse** milk/wisdom tooth

dentaire [dɑ̃tɛʀ] *adj* dental; **cabinet ~** dental surgery; **école ~** dental school

dentelé, e [dɑ̃tle] *adj* jagged, indented

dentelle [dɑ̃tɛl] *nf* lace *no pl*

dentier [dɑ̃tje] *nm* denture

dentifrice [dɑ̃tifʀis] *adj, nm*: **(pâte) ~** toothpaste; **eau ~** mouthwash

dentiste [dɑ̃tist] *nm/f* dentist

dentition [dɑ̃tisjɔ̃] *nf* teeth *pl*, dentition

dénuder [denyde] *vt* to bare; **se dénuder** (*personne*) to strip

dénué, e [denɥe] *adj*: **~ de** lacking in; (*intérêt*) devoid of

dénuement [denɥmɑ̃] *nm* destitution

déodorant [deɔdɔʀɑ̃] *nm* deodorant

déontologie [deɔ̃tɔlɔʒi] *nf* code of ethics; (*professionnelle*) (professional) code of practice

dépannage [depanaʒ] *nm*: **service/camion de ~** (*Auto*) breakdown service/truck

dépanner [depane] *vt* (*voiture, télévision*) to fix, repair; (*fig*) to bail out, help out

dépanneuse [depanøz] *nf* breakdown lorry (Brit), tow truck (US)

dépareillé, e [depaʀeje] *adj* (*collection, service*) incomplete; (*gant, volume, objet*) odd

départ [depaʀ] *nm* leaving *no pl*, departure; (*Sport*) start; (*sur un horaire*) departure; **à son ~** when he left; **au ~** (*au début*) initially, at the start; **courrier au ~** outgoing mail; **la veille de son ~** the day before he leaves/left

départager [depaʀtaʒe] *vt* to decide between

département [depaʀtəmɑ̃] *nm* department; *see note*

○ **DÉPARTEMENTS**

France is divided into administrative units called *départements*. There are 96 of these in metropolitan France and a further five overseas. These local government divisions are headed by a state-appointed "préfet", and administered by an elected "Conseil général". *Départements* are usually named after prominent geographical features such as rivers or mountain ranges.

dépassé, e [depase] *adj* superseded, outmoded; (*fig*) out of one's depth

dépasser [depase] *vt* (*véhicule, concurrent*) to overtake; (*endroit*) to pass, go past; (*somme, limite*) to exceed; (*fig: en beauté etc*) to surpass, outshine; (*être en saillie sur*) to jut out above (*ou* in front of); (*dérouter*): **cela me dépasse** it's beyond me ▷ *vi* (*Auto*) to overtake; (*jupon*) to show; **se dépasser** *vi* to excel o.s.

dépaysé, e [depeize] *adj* disoriented

dépaysement [depeizmɑ̃] *nm* disorientation; change of scenery

dépecer [depase] *vt* (*boucher*) to joint, cut up; (*animal*) to dismember

dépêche [depɛʃ] *nf* dispatch; **~ (télégraphique)** telegram, wire

dépêcher [depeʃe] *vt* to dispatch; **se dépêcher** *vi* to hurry; **se ~ de faire qch** to hasten to *ou* be quick to do sth

dépeindre [depɛ̃dʀ] *vt* to depict

dépendance [depɑ̃dɑ̃s] *nf* (*interdépendance*) dependence *no pl*, dependency; (*bâtiment*) outbuilding

dépendre [depɑ̃dʀ] *vt* (*tableau*) to take down; **~ de** to depend on, to be dependent on; (*appartenir*) to belong to; **ça dépend** it depends

dépens [depɑ̃] *nmpl*: **aux ~ de** at the expense of

dépense [depɑ̃s] *nf* spending *no pl*, expense, expenditure *no pl*, (*fig*) consumption; (*: de temps, de forces*) expenditure; **pousser qn à la ~** to make sb incur an expense; **~ physique** (physical) exertion; **~s de fonctionnement** revenue expenditure; **~s d'investissement** capital expenditure; **~s publiques** public expenditure

dépenser [depɑ̃se] *vt* to spend; (*gaz, eau*) to use; (*fig*) to expend, use up; **se dépenser** *vi* (*se fatiguer*) to exert o.s.

dépensier, -ière [depɑ̃sje, -jɛʀ] *adj*: **il est ~** he's a spendthrift

dépérir [depeʀiʀ] *vi* (*personne*) to waste away; (*plante*) to wither

dépêtrer [depetʀe] *vt*: **se ~ de** (*situation*) to extricate o.s. from

dépeupler [depœple] *vt* to depopulate; **se dépeupler** *vi* to become depopulated

dépilatoire [depilatwaʀ] *adj* depilatory, hair-removing; **crème ~** hair-removing *ou* depilatory cream

dépister [depiste] *vt* to detect; (*Méd*) to screen; (*voleur*) to track down; (*poursuivants*) to throw off the scent

dépit [depi] *nm* vexation, frustration; **en ~ de** *prép* in spite of; **en ~ du bon sens** contrary to all good sense

dépité, e [depite] *adj* vexed, frustrated

déplacé, e [deplase] *adj* (*propos*) out of place, uncalled-for; **personne ~e** displaced person

déplacement [deplasmɑ̃] *nm* moving; shifting; transfer; (*voyage*) trip, travelling *no pl* (*Brit*), traveling *no pl* (*US*); **en ~** away (on a trip); **~ d'air** displacement of air; **~ de vertèbre** slipped disc

déplacer [deplase] *vt* (*table, voiture*) to move, shift; (*employé*) to transfer, move; **se déplacer** *vi* (*objet*) to move; (*organe*) to become displaced; (*personne: bouger*) to move, walk; (*: voyager*) to travel ▷ *vt*: **se ~ une vertèbre** to slip a disc

déplaire [deplɛʀ] *vi*: **ceci me déplaît** I don't like this, I dislike this; **il cherche à nous ~** he's trying to displease us *ou* be disagreeable to us; **se ~ quelque part** to dislike it *ou* be unhappy somewhere

déplaisant, e [deplɛzɑ̃, -ɑ̃t] *vb voir* **déplaire** ▷ *adj* disagreeable, unpleasant

dépliant [deplijɑ̃] *nm* leaflet

déplier [deplije] *vt* to unfold; **se déplier** *vi* (*parachute*) to open

déplorer [deplɔʀe] *vt* (*regretter*) to deplore; (*pleurer sur*) to lament

déployer [deplwaje] *vt* to open out, spread; (*Mil*) to deploy; (*montrer*) to display, exhibit

déporter [depɔʀte] *vt* (*Pol*) to deport; (*dévier*) to carry off course; **se déporter** *vi* (*voiture*) to swerve

déposer [depoze] *vt* (*gén: mettre, poser*) to lay down, put down, set down; (*à la banque, à la consigne*) to deposit; (*caution*) to put down; (*passager*) to drop (off), set down; (*démonter: serrure, moteur*) to take out; (*: rideau*) to take down; (*roi*) to depose; (*Admin: faire enregistrer*) to file; (*marque*) to register; (*plainte*) to lodge ▷ *vi* to form a sediment *ou* deposit; (*Jur*): **~ (contre)** to testify *ou* give evidence (against); **se déposer** *vi* to settle; **~ son bilan** (*Comm*) to go into (voluntary) liquidation

dépositaire [depozitɛʀ] *nm/f* (*Jur*) depository; (*Comm*) agent; **~ agréé** authorized agent

déposition [depozisjɔ̃] *nf* (*Jur*) deposition, statement

dépôt [depo] *nm* (*à la banque, sédiment*) deposit; (*entrepôt, réserve*) warehouse, store; (*gare*) depot; (*prison*) cells *pl*; **~ d'ordures** rubbish

(Brit) ou garbage (US) dump, tip (Brit); **~ de bilan** (voluntary) liquidation; **~ légal** registration of copyright

dépotoir [depɔtwaʀ] nm dumping ground, rubbish (Brit) ou garbage (US) dump; **~ nucléaire** nuclear (waste) dump

dépouiller [depuje] vt (animal) to skin; (spolier) to deprive of one's possessions; (documents) to go through, peruse; **~ qn/qch de** to strip sb/sth of; **~ le scrutin** to count the votes

dépourvu, e [depuʀvy] adj: **~ de** lacking in, without; **au ~** adv: **prendre qn au ~** to catch sb unawares

déprécier [depʀesje] vt to reduce the value of; **se déprécier** vi to depreciate

dépression [depʀesjɔ̃] nf depression; **~ (nerveuse)** (nervous) breakdown

déprimant, e [depʀimɑ̃, -ɑ̃t] adj depressing

déprimer [depʀime] vt to depress

⊙ **MOT-CLÉ**

depuis [dəpɥi] prép **1** (point de départ dans le temps) since; **il habite Paris depuis 1983/l'an dernier** he has been living in Paris since 1983/last year; **depuis quand?** since when?; **depuis quand le connaissez-vous?** how long have you known him?; **depuis lors** since then

2 (temps écoulé) for; **il habite Paris depuis cinq ans** he has been living in Paris for five years; **je le connais depuis trois ans** I've known him for three years; **depuis combien de temps êtes-vous ici?** how long have you been here?

3 (lieu): **il a plu depuis Metz** it's been raining since Metz; **elle a téléphoné depuis Valence** she rang from Valence

4 (quantité, rang) from; **depuis les plus petits jusqu'aux plus grands** from the youngest to the oldest

▷ adv (temps) since (then); **je ne lui ai pas parlé depuis** I haven't spoken to him since (then); **depuis que** conj (ever) since; **depuis qu'il m'a dit ça** (ever) since he said that to me

député, e [depyte] nm/f (Pol) deputy, ≈ Member of Parliament (Brit), ≈ Congressman/woman (US)

députer [depyte] vt to delegate; **~ qn auprès de** to send sb (as a representative) to

déraciner [deʀasine] vt to uproot

dérailler [deʀaje] vi (train) to be derailed, go off ou jump the rails; (fam) to be completely off the track; **faire ~** to derail

déraisonner [deʀɛzɔne] vi to talk nonsense, rave

dérangement [deʀɑ̃ʒmɑ̃] nm (gêne, déplacement) trouble; (gastrique etc) disorder; (mécanique) breakdown; **en ~** (téléphone) out of order

déranger [deʀɑ̃ʒe] vt (personne) to trouble, bother, disturb; (projets) to disrupt, upset; (objets, vêtements) to disarrange; **se déranger** to put o.s. out; (se déplacer) to (take the trouble to) come (ou go) out; **surtout ne vous dérangez pas pour moi** please don't put yourself out on my account; **est-ce que cela vous dérange si ...?** do you mind if ...?; **ça te dérangerait de faire ...?** would you mind doing ...?; **ne vous dérangez pas** don't go to any trouble; don't disturb yourself

déraper [deʀape] vi (voiture) to skid; (personne, semelles, couteau) to slip; (fig: économie etc) to go out of control

dérégler [deʀegle] vt (mécanisme) to put out of order, cause to break down; (estomac) to upset; **se dérégler** vi to break down, go wrong

dérider [deʀide] vt: **se dérider** vi to cheer up

dérision [deʀizjɔ̃] nf derision; **tourner en ~** to deride; **par ~** in mockery

dérisoire [deʀizwaʀ] adj derisory

dérive [deʀiv] nf (de dériveur) centre-board; **aller à la ~** (Navig, fig) to drift; **~ des continents** (Géo) continental drift

dérivé, e [deʀive] adj derived ▷ nm (Ling) derivative; (Tech) by-product ▷ nf (Math) derivative

dériver [deʀive] vt (Math) to derive; (cours d'eau etc) to divert ▷ vi (bateau) to drift; **~ de** to derive from

dermatologue [dɛʀmatɔlɔg] nm/f dermatologist

dernier, -ière [dɛʀnje, -jɛʀ] adj (dans le temps, l'espace) last; (le plus récent: gén avant n) latest, last; (final, ultime: effort) final; (échelon, grade) top, highest ▷ nm (étage) top floor; **lundi/le mois ~** last Monday/month; **du ~ chic** extremely smart; **le ~ cri** the last word (in fashion); **les ~s honneurs** the last tribute; **le ~ soupir, rendre le ~ soupir** to breathe one's last; **en ~** adv last; **ce ~, cette dernière** the latter

dernièrement [dɛʀnjɛʀmɑ̃] adv recently

dérobé, e [deʀɔbe] adj (porte) secret, hidden; **à la ~e** surreptitiously

dérober [deʀɔbe] vt to steal; (cacher): **~ qch à (la vue de) qn** to conceal ou hide sth from sb('s view); **se dérober** vi (s'esquiver) to slip away; (fig) to shy away; **se ~ sous** (s'effondrer) to give way beneath; **se ~ à** (justice, regards) to hide from; (obligation) to shirk

dérogation [deʀɔgasjɔ̃] nf (special) dispensation

déroger [deʀɔʒe]: **~ à** vt to go against, depart from

dérouiller [deʀuje] vt: **se ~ les jambes** to stretch one's legs (fig)

déroulement [deʀulmɑ̃] nm (d'une opération etc) progress

dérouler [deʀule] vt (ficelle) to unwind; (papier) to unroll; **se dérouler** vi to unwind;

to unroll, come unrolled; (avoir lieu) to take place; (se passer) to go; **tout s'est déroulé comme prévu** everything went as planned

dérouter [deRute] vt (avion, train) to reroute, divert; (étonner) to disconcert, throw (out)

derrière [dɛRjɛR] adv, prép behind ▷ nm (d'une maison) back; (postérieur) behind, bottom; **les pattes de** ~ the back legs, the hind legs; **par** ~ from behind; (fig) in an underhand way, behind one's back

des [de] art voir **de**

dès [dɛ] prép from; ~ **que** conj as soon as; ~ **à présent** here and now; ~ **son retour** as soon as he was (ou is) back; ~ **réception** upon receipt; ~ **lors** adv from then on; ~ **lors que** conj from the moment (that)

désabusé, e [dezabyze] adj disillusioned

désaccord [dezakɔR] nm disagreement

désaccordé, e [dezakɔRde] adj (Mus) out of tune

désaffecté, e [dezafɛkte] adj disused

désagréable [dezagReabl] adj unpleasant, disagreeable

désagréger [dezagReʒe]: **se désagréger** vi to disintegrate, break up

désagrément [dezagRemã] nm annoyance, trouble no pl

désaltérer [dezaltere] vt: **se désaltérer** to quench one's thirst; **ça désaltère** it's thirst-quenching, it quenches your thirst

désapprobateur, -trice [dezapRɔbatœR, -tRis] adj disapproving

désapprouver [dezapRuve] vt to disapprove of

désarmant, e [dezaRmã, -ãt] adj disarming

désarroi [dezaRwa] nm helplessness, disarray

désastre [dezastR] nm disaster

désastreux, -euse [dezastRø, -øz] adj disastrous

désavantage [dezavãtaʒ] nm disadvantage; (inconvénient) drawback, disadvantage

désavantager [dezavãtaʒe] vt to put at a disadvantage

descendre [desãdR] vt (escalier, montagne) to go (ou come) down; (valise, paquet) to take ou get down; (étagère etc) to lower; (fam: abattre) to shoot down; (: boire) to knock back ▷ vi to go (ou come) down; (passager: s'arrêter) to get out, alight; (niveau, température) to go down, fall, drop; (marée) to go out; ~ **à pied/ en voiture** to walk/drive down, go down on foot/by car; ~ **de** (famille) to be descended from; ~ **du train** to get out ou off the train; ~ **d'un arbre** to climb down from a tree; ~ **de cheval** to dismount, get off one's horse; ~ **à l'hôtel** to stay at a hotel; ~ **dans la rue** (manifester) to take to the streets; ~ **en ville** to go into town, go down town

descente [desãt] nf descent, going down; (chemin) way down; (Ski) downhill (race); **au milieu de la** ~ halfway down; **freinez dans**

les ~**s** use the brakes going downhill; ~ **de lit** bedside rug; ~ **(de police)** (police) raid

description [dɛskRipsjõ] nf description

désemparé, e [dezãpaRe] adj bewildered, distraught; (bateau, avion) crippled

désemplir [dezãpliR] vi: **ne pas** ~ to be always full

déséquilibre [dezekilibR] nm (position): **être en** ~ to be unsteady; (fig: des forces, du budget) imbalance; (Psych) unbalance

déséquilibré, e [dezekilibRe] nm/f (Psych) unbalanced person

déséquilibrer [dezekilibRe] vt to throw off balance

désert, e [dezɛR, -ɛRt] adj deserted ▷ nm desert

déserter [dezɛRte] vi, vt to desert

désertique [dezɛRtik] adj desert cpd; (inculte) barren, empty

désespéré, e [dezɛspeRe] adj desperate; (regard) despairing; **état** ~ (Méd) hopeless condition

désespérer [dezɛspeRe] vt to drive to despair; **se désespérer** vi to despair; ~ **de** to despair of

désespoir [dezɛspwaR] nm despair; **être** ou **faire le** ~ **de qn** to be the despair of sb; **en** ~ **de cause** in desperation

déshabiller [dezabije] vt to undress; **se déshabiller** vi to undress (o.s.)

déshérité, e [dezeRite] adj disinherited ▷ nm/f: **les** ~**s** (pauvres) the underprivileged, the deprived

déshériter [dezeRite] vt to disinherit

déshonneur [dezɔnœR] nm dishonour (Brit), dishonor (US), disgrace

déshydraté, e [dezidRate] adj dehydrated

desiderata [dezideRata] nmpl requirements

désigner [dezine] vt (montrer) to point out, indicate; (dénommer) to denote, refer to; (nommer: candidat etc) to name, appoint

désinfectant, e [dezɛ̃fɛktã, -ãt] adj, nm disinfectant

désinfecter [dezɛ̃fɛkte] vt to disinfect

désintégrer [dezɛ̃tegRe] vt to break up; **se désintégrer** vi to disintegrate

désintéressé, e [dezɛ̃teRese] adj (généreux, bénévole) disinterested, unselfish

désintéresser [dezɛ̃teRese] vt: **se désintéresser (de)** to lose interest (in)

désintoxication [dezɛ̃tɔksikasjõ] nf treatment for alcoholism (ou drug addiction); **faire une cure de** ~ to have ou undergo treatment for alcoholism (ou drug addiction)

désinvolte [dezɛ̃vɔlt] adj casual, off-hand

désinvolture [dezɛ̃vɔltyR] nf casualness

désir [deziR] nm wish; (fort, sensuel) desire

désirer [deziRe] vt to want, wish for; (sexuellement) to desire; **je désire ...** (formule de politesse) I would like ...; **il désire que tu l'aides** he would like ou he wants you to help

him; ~ **faire** to want ou wish to do; **ça laisse
à** ~ it leaves something to be desired
désister [deziste]: **se désister** vi to stand
down, withdraw
désobéir [dezɔbeiʀ] vi: ~ **(à qn/qch)** to
disobey (sb/sth)
désobéissant, e [dezɔbeisɑ̃, -ɑ̃t] adj
disobedient
désobligeant, e [dezɔbliʒɑ̃, -ɑ̃t] adj
disagreeable, unpleasant
désodorisant [dezɔdɔʀizɑ̃] nm air freshener,
deodorizer
désœuvré, e [dezœvʀe] adj idle
désolé, e [dezɔle] adj (paysage) desolate; **je
suis** ~ I'm sorry
désoler [dezɔle] vt to distress, grieve; **se
désoler** vi to be upset
désopilant, e [dezɔpilɑ̃, -ɑ̃t] adj screamingly
funny, hilarious
désordonné, e [dezɔʀdɔne] adj untidy,
disorderly
désordre [dezɔʀdʀ] nm disorder(liness),
untidiness; (anarchie) disorder; **désordres**
nmpl (Pol) disturbances, disorder sg; **en** ~ in a
mess, untidy
désorienté, e [dezɔʀjɑ̃te] adj disorientated;
(fig) bewildered
désormais [dezɔʀmɛ] adv in future, from
now on
désosser [dezɔse] vt to bone
desquels, desquelles [dekɛl] prép + pron voir
lequel
desséché, e [deseʃe] adj dried up
dessécher [deseʃe] vt (terre, plante) to dry out,
parch; (peau) to dry out; (volontairement:
aliments etc) to dry, dehydrate; (fig: cœur) to
harden; **se dessécher** vi to dry out; (peau,
lèvres) to go dry
dessein [desɛ̃] nm design; **dans le** ~ **de** with
the intention of; **à** ~ intentionally,
deliberately
desserrer [desere] vt to loosen; (frein) to
release; (poing, dents) to unclench; (objets
alignés) to space out; **ne pas** ~ **les dents** not to
open one's mouth
dessert [desɛʀ] vb voir **desservir** ▷ nm
dessert, pudding
desserte [desɛʀt] nf (table) side table;
(transport): **la** ~ **du village est assurée par
autocar** there is a coach service to the
village; **chemin** ou **voie de** ~ service road
desservir [desɛʀviʀ] vt (ville, quartier) to serve;
(: voie de communication) to lead into; (vicaire:
paroisse) to serve; (nuire à: personne) to do a
disservice to; (débarrasser): ~ **(la table)** to clear
the table
dessin [desɛ̃] nm (œuvre, art) drawing; (motif)
pattern, design; (contour) (out)line; **le** ~
industriel draughtsmanship (Brit),
draftsmanship (US); ~ **animé** cartoon (film);
~ **humoristique** cartoon
dessinateur, -trice [desinatœʀ, -tʀis] nm/f

drawer; (de bandes dessinées) cartoonist;
(industriel) draughtsman (Brit), draftsman
(US); **dessinatrice de mode** fashion
designer
dessiner [desine] vt to draw; (concevoir:
carrosserie, maison) to design; (robe: taille) to
show off; **se dessiner** vi (forme) to be
outlined; (fig: solution) to emerge
dessous [d(ə)su] adv underneath, beneath
▷ nm underside; (étage inférieur): **les voisins
du** ~ the downstairs neighbours ▷ nmpl (sous-
vêtements) underwear sg; (fig) hidden aspects;
en ~ underneath; below; (fig: en catimini) slyly,
on the sly; **par** ~ underneath; below; **de** ~ **le
lit** from under the bed; **au** ~ below; **au-~
de** prép below; (peu digne de) beneath; **au-~ de
tout** the (absolute) limit; **avoir le** ~ to get the
worst of it
dessous-de-plat [dəsudpla] nm inv tablemat
dessus [d(ə)sy] adv on top; (collé, écrit) on it
▷ nm top; (étage supérieur): **les
voisins/l'appartement du** ~ the upstairs
neighbours/flat; **en** ~ above; **par** ~ adv over it
▷ prép over; **au-~** above; **au-~ de** above; **avoir/
prendre le** ~ to have/get the upper hand;
reprendre le ~ to get over it; **bras** ~ **bras
dessous** arm in arm; **sens** ~ **dessous** upside
down; voir **ci-là-**
dessus-de-lit [dəsydli] nm inv bedspread
destin [dɛstɛ̃] nm fate; (avenir) destiny
destinataire [dɛstinatɛʀ] nm/f (Postes)
addressee; (d'un colis) consignee; (d'un mandat)
payee; **aux risques et périls du** ~ at owner's
risk
destination [dɛstinasjɔ̃] nf (lieu) destination;
(usage) purpose; **à** ~ **de** (avion etc) bound for;
(voyageur) bound for, travelling to
destinée [dɛstine] nf fate; (existence, avenir)
destiny
destiner [dɛstine] vt: ~ **qn à** (poste, sort) to
destine sb for; ~ **qn/qch à** (prédestiner) to mark
sb/sth out for; ~ **qch à** (envisager d'affecter) to
intend to use sth for; ~ **qch à qn** (envisager de
donner) to intend sb to have sth, intend to
give sth to sb; (adresser) to intend sth for sb;
se ~ **à l'enseignement** to intend to become
a teacher; **être destiné à** (sort) to be destined
to + verbe; (usage) to be intended ou meant for;
(sort) to be in store for
destruction [dɛstʀyksjɔ̃] nf destruction
désuet, -ète [desɥɛ, -ɛt] adj outdated,
outmoded
détachant [detaʃɑ̃] nm stain remover
détachement [detaʃmɑ̃] nm detachment;
(fonctionnaire, employé): **être en** ~ to be on
secondment (Brit) ou a posting
détacher [detaʃe] vt (enlever) to detach,
remove; (délier) to untie; (Admin): ~ **qn
(auprès de ou à)** to post sb (to), send sb on
secondment (to) (Brit); (Mil) to detail;
(vêtement: nettoyer) to remove the stains from;
se détacher vi (se séparer) to come off; (page)

to come out; (se défaire) to come undone;
(Sport) to pull ou break away; (se délier: chien,
prisonnier) to break loose; **se ~ sur** to stand
out against; **se ~ de** (se désintéresser) to grow away
from

détail [detaj] nm detail; (Comm): **le ~** retail;
prix de ~ retail price; **au ~** adv (Comm) retail;
(: individuellement) separately; **donner le ~ de**
to give a detailed account of; (compte) to give
a breakdown of; **en ~** in detail

détaillant, e [detajɑ̃, -ɑ̃t] nm/f retailer

détaillé, e [detaje] adj (récit, plan, explications)
detailed; (facture) itemized

détailler [detaje] vt (Comm) to sell retail; to
sell separately; (expliquer) to explain in detail;
to detail; (examiner) to look over, examine

détaler [detale] vi (lapin) to scamper off; (fam:
personne) to make off, scarper (fam)

détartrant [detaʀtʀɑ̃] nm descaling agent
(Brit), scale remover

détaxer [detakse] vt (réduire) to reduce the tax
on; (ôter) to remove the tax on

détecter [detɛkte] vt to detect

détective [detɛktiv] nm detective; **~ (privé)**
private detective ou investigator

déteindre [detɛ̃dʀ] vi to fade; (au lavage) to
run; **~ sur** (vêtement) to run into; (fig) to rub
off on

détendre [detɑ̃dʀ] vt (fil) to slacken, loosen;
(personne, atmosphère, corps, esprit) to relax;
(: situation) to relieve; **se détendre** vi (ressort)
to lose its tension; (personne) to relax

détenir [det(ə)niʀ] vt (fortune, objet, secret) to
be in possession of; (prisonnier) to detain;
(record) to hold; **~ le pouvoir** to be in power

détente [detɑ̃t] nf relaxation; (Pol) détente;
(d'une arme) trigger; (d'un athlète qui saute)
spring

détention [detɑ̃sjɔ̃] nf (de fortune, objet, secret)
possession; (captivité) detention; (de record)
holding; **~ préventive** (pre-trial) custody

détenu, e [det(ə)ny] pp de **détenir** ▷ nm/f
prisoner

détergent [detɛʀʒɑ̃] nm detergent

détériorer [deteʀjɔʀe] vt to damage; **se
détériorer** vi to deteriorate

déterminé, e [detɛʀmine] adj (résolu)
determined; (précis) specific, definite

déterminer [detɛʀmine] vt (fixer) to
determine; (décider): **~ qn à faire** to decide sb
to do; **se ~ à faire** to make up one's mind to
do

déterrer [detere] vt to dig up

détestable [detɛstabl] adj foul, detestable

détester [detɛste] vt to hate, detest

détonner [detɔne] vi (Mus) to go out of tune;
(fig) to clash

détour [detuʀ] nm detour; (tournant) bend,
curve; (fig: subterfuge) roundabout means; **ça
vaut le ~** it's worth the trip; **sans ~** (fig) plainly

détourné, e [deturne] adj (sentier, chemin,
moyen) roundabout

détournement [deturnəmɑ̃] nm diversion,
rerouting; **~ d'avion** hijacking; **~ (de fonds)**
embezzlement ou misappropriation (of
funds); **~ de mineur** corruption of a minor

détourner [deturne] vt to divert; (avion) to
divert, reroute; (: par la force) to hijack; (yeux,
tête) to turn away; (de l'argent) to embezzle,
misappropriate; **se détourner** vi to turn
away; **~ la conversation** to change the
subject; **~ qn de son devoir** to divert sb from
his duty; **~ l'attention (de qn)** to distract ou
divert (sb's) attention

détoxifier [detɔksifje] vt (organisme, corps) to
detox

détracteur, -trice [detʀaktœʀ, -tʀis] nm/f
disparager, critic

détraquer [detʀake] vt to put out of order;
(estomac) to upset; **se détraquer** vi to go
wrong

détrempé, e [detʀɑ̃pe] adj (sol) sodden,
waterlogged

détresse [detʀɛs] nf distress; **en ~** (avion etc)
in distress; **appel/signal de ~** distress call/
signal

détriment [detʀimɑ̃] nm: **au ~ de** to the
detriment of

détritus [detʀitys] nmpl rubbish sg, refuse sg,
garbage sg (US)

détroit [detʀwa] nm strait; **le ~ de Bering** ou
Behring the Bering Strait; **le ~ de Gibraltar**
the Straits of Gibraltar; **le ~ du Bosphore** the
Bosphorus; **le ~ de Magellan** the Strait of
Magellan, the Magellan Strait

détromper [detʀɔ̃pe] vt to disabuse; **se
détromper** vi: **détrompez-vous** don't
believe it

détruire [detʀɥiʀ] vt to destroy; (fig: santé,
réputation) to ruin; (documents) to shred

dette [dɛt] nf debt; **~ publique** ou **de l'État**
national debt

DEUG [dœg] sigle m (formerly) = **Diplôme
d'études universitaires générales** see note

● **DEUG**

● The DEUG was a two-year university
● diploma, which, following educational
● reform, was replaced by the first two
● years of the "licence générale".

deuil [dœj] nm (perte) bereavement; (période)
mourning; (chagrin) grief; **porter le ~** to wear
mourning; **prendre le/être en ~** to go into/
be in mourning

deux [dø] num two; **les ~** both; **ses ~ mains**
both his hands, his two hands; **à ~ pas** a
short distance away; **tous les ~ mois** every
two months, every other month; **~ fois**
twice

deuxième [døzjɛm] num second

deuxièmement [døzjɛmmɑ̃] adv secondly,
in the second place

deux-pièces [døpjɛs] *nm inv* (*tailleur*) two-piece (suit); (*de bain*) two-piece (swimsuit); (*appartement*) two-roomed flat (Brit) ou apartment (US)

deux-points *nm inv* colon *sg*

deux-roues [døʀu] *nm inv* two-wheeled vehicle

devais *etc* [dəvɛ] *vb voir* **devoir**

dévaler [devale] *vt* to hurtle down

dévaliser [devalize] *vt* to rob, burgle

dévaloriser [devalɔʀize] *vt* to reduce the value of; **se dévaloriser** *vi* to depreciate

dévaluation [devalɥasjɔ̃] *nf* depreciation; (*Écon: mesure*) devaluation

devancer [d(ə)vɑ̃se] *vt* to be ahead of; (*distancer*) to get ahead of; (*arriver avant*) to arrive before; (*prévenir*) to anticipate; **~ l'appel** (Mil) to enlist before call-up

devant [d(ə)vɑ̃] *vb voir* **devoir** ▷ *adv* in front; (*à distance: en avant*) ahead ▷ *prép* in front of; (*en avant*) ahead of; (*avec mouvement: passer*) past; (*fig*) before, in front of; (*: face à*) faced with, in the face of; (*: vu*) in view of ▷ *nm* front; **prendre les ~s** to make the first move; **de ~** (*roue, porte*) front; **les pattes de ~** the front legs, the forelegs; **par ~** (*boutonner*) at the front; (*entrer*) the front way; **par-~ notaire** in the presence of a notary; **aller au-~ de qn** to go out to meet sb; **aller au-~ de** (*désirs de qn*) to anticipate; **aller au-~ des ennuis** ou **difficultés** to be asking for trouble

devanture [d(ə)vɑ̃tyʀ] *nf* (*façade*) (shop) front; (*étalage*) display; (*vitrine*) (shop) window

déveine [devɛn] *nf* rotten luck *no pl*

développement [dev(ə)lɔpmɑ̃] *nm* development; **pays en voie de ~** developing countries

développer [dev(ə)lɔpe] *vt* to develop; **se développer** *vi* to develop

devenir [dəv(ə)niʀ] *vi* to become; **~ instituteur** to become a teacher; **que sont-ils devenus?** what has become of them?

dévergondé, e [devɛʀgɔ̃de] *adj* wild, shameless

déverser [devɛʀse] *vt* (*liquide*) to pour (out); (*ordures*) to tip (out); **se ~ dans** (*fleuve, mer*) to flow into

dévêtir [devetiʀ] *vt*, **se dévêtir** *vi* to undress

devez [dəve] *vb voir* **devoir**

déviation [devjasjɔ̃] *nf* deviation; (*Auto*) diversion (Brit), detour (US); **~ de la colonne (vertébrale)** curvature of the spine

devienne *etc* [dəvjɛn] *vb voir* **devenir**

dévier [devje] *vt* (*fleuve, circulation*) to divert; (*coup*) to deflect ▷ *vi* to veer (off course); **(faire) ~** (*projectile*) to deflect; (*véhicule*) to push off course

devin [dəvɛ̃] *nm* soothsayer, seer

deviner [d(ə)vine] *vt* to guess; (*prévoir*) to foretell, foresee; (*apercevoir*) to distinguish

devinette [d(ə)vinɛt] *nf* riddle

devis [d(ə)vi] *nm* estimate, quotation; **~ descriptif/estimatif** detailed/preliminary estimate

dévisager [devizaʒe] *vt* to stare at

devise [dəviz] *nf* (*formule*) motto, watchword; (*Écon: monnaie*) currency; **devises** *nfpl* (*argent*) currency *sg*

deviser [dəvize] *vi* to converse

dévisser [devise] *vt* to unscrew, undo; **se dévisser** *vi* to come unscrewed

dévoiler [devwale] *vt* to unveil

devoir [d(ə)vwaʀ] *nm* duty; (*Scol*) piece of homework, homework *no pl*; (*: en classe*) exercise ▷ *vt* (*argent, respect*): **~ qch (à qn)** to owe (sb) sth; **combien est-ce que je vous dois?** how much do I owe you?; (*suivi de l'infinitif: obligation*): **il doit le faire** he has to do it, he must do it; (*: fatalité*): **cela devait arriver un jour** it was bound to happen; (*: intention*): **il doit partir demain** he is due to leave tomorrow; (*: probabilité*): **il doit être tard** it must be late; **se faire un ~ de faire qch** to make it one's duty to do sth; **~s de vacances** homework set for the holidays; **se ~ de faire qch** to be duty bound to do sth; **je devrais faire** I ought to ou should do; **tu n'aurais pas dû** you ought not to have ou shouldn't have; **comme il se doit** (*comme il faut*) as is right and proper

dévolu, e [devɔly] *adj*: **~ à** allotted to ▷ *nm*: **jeter son ~ sur** to fix one's choice on

dévorer [devɔʀe] *vt* to devour; (*feu, soucis*) to consume; **~ qn/qch des yeux** ou **du regard** (*fig*) to eye sb/sth intently; (*: convoitise*) to eye sb/sth greedily

dévot, e [devo, -ɔt] *adj* devout, pious ▷ *nm/f* devout person; **un faux ~** a falsely pious person

dévotion [devosjɔ̃] *nf* devoutness; **être à la ~ de qn** to be totally devoted to sb; **avoir une ~ pour qn** to worship sb

dévoué, e [devwe] *adj* devoted

dévouement [devumɑ̃] *nm* devotion, dedication

dévouer [devwe]: **se dévouer** *vi* (*se sacrifier*): **se ~ (pour)** to sacrifice o.s. (for); (*se consacrer*): **se ~ à** to devote ou dedicate o.s. to

dévoyé, e [devwaje] *adj* delinquent

devrai *etc* [dəvʀe] *vb voir* **devoir**

dézipper [dezipe] *vt* (*Inform*) to unzip

diabète [djabɛt] *nm* diabetes *sg*

diabétique [djabetik] *nm/f* diabetic

diable [djabl] *nm* devil; **une musique du ~** an unholy racket; **il fait une chaleur du ~** it's fiendishly hot; **avoir le ~ au corps** to be the very devil

diabolo [djabɔlo] *nm* (*jeu*) diabolo; (*boisson*) lemonade and fruit cordial; **~(-menthe)** lemonade and mint cordial

diagnostic [djagnɔstik] *nm* diagnosis *sg*

diagnostiquer [djagnɔstike] *vt* to diagnose

diagonal, e, -aux [djagɔnal, -o] *adj, nf*
diagonal; **en ~e** diagonally; **lire en ~e** *(fig)* to
skim through

diagramme [djagʀam] *nm* chart, graph

dialecte [djalɛkt] *nm* dialect

dialogue [djalɔg] *nm* dialogue; **~ de sourds**
dialogue of the deaf

diamant [djamɑ̃] *nm* diamond

diamètre [djamɛtʀ] *nm* diameter

diapason [djapazɔ̃] *nm* tuning fork; *(fig)*:
être/se mettre au ~ (de) to be/get in tune
(with)

diaphragme [djafʀagm] *nm* *(Anat, Photo)*
diaphragm; *(contraceptif)* diaphragm, cap;
ouverture du ~ *(Photo)* aperture

diapo [djapo], **diapositive** [djapozitiv] *nf*
transparency, slide

diarrhée [djaʀe] *nf* diarrhoea *(Brit)*, diarrhea
(US)

dictateur [diktatœʀ] *nm* dictator

dictature [diktatyʀ] *nf* dictatorship

dictée [dikte] *nf* dictation; **prendre sous ~** to
take down *(sth dictated)*

dicter [dikte] *vt* to dictate

dictionnaire [diksjɔnɛʀ] *nm* dictionary;
~ géographique gazetteer

dicton [diktɔ̃] *nm* saying, dictum

dièse [djɛz] *nm* *(Mus)* sharp

diesel [djezɛl] *nm, adj inv* diesel

diète [djɛt] *nf* *(jeûne)* starvation diet; *(régime)*
diet; **être à la ~** to be on a diet

diététique [djetetik] *nf* dietetics *sg* ▷ *adj*:
magasin ~ health food shop *(Brit)* ou store
(US)

dieu, x [djø] *nm* god; **D~** God; **le bon D~** the
good Lord; **mon D~!** good heavens!

diffamation [difamasjɔ̃] *nf* slander; *(écrite)*
libel; **attaquer qn en ~** to sue sb for slander
(ou libel)

différé [difeʀe] *adj* *(Inform)*: **traitement ~**
batch processing; **crédit ~** deferred credit
▷ *nm* *(TV)*: **en ~** (pre-)recorded

différemment [difeʀamɑ̃] *adv* differently

différence [difeʀɑ̃s] *nf* difference; **à la ~ de**
unlike

différencier [difeʀɑ̃sje] *vt* to differentiate;
se différencier *vi* *(organisme)* to become
differentiated; **se ~ de** to differentiate o.s.
from; *(être différent)* to differ from

différend [difeʀɑ̃] *nm* difference (of
opinion), disagreement

différent, e [difeʀɑ̃, -ɑ̃t] *adj* *(dissemblable)*
different; **~ de** different from; **~s objets**
different ou various objects; **à ~es reprises**
on various occasions

différer [difeʀe] *vt* to postpone, put off ▷ *vi*:
~ (de) to differ (from); **~ de faire** *(tarder)* to
delay doing

difficile [difisil] *adj* difficult; *(exigeant)* hard
to please, difficult (to please); **faire le** ou **la ~**
to be hard to please, be difficult

difficilement [difisilmɑ̃] *adv* *(marcher,*

s'expliquer etc) with difficulty; **~ lisible/
compréhensible** difficult ou hard to read/
understand

difficulté [difikylte] *nf* difficulty; **en ~**
(bateau, alpiniste) in trouble ou difficulties;
avoir de la ~ à faire to have difficulty (in)
doing

difforme [difɔʀm] *adj* deformed, misshapen

diffuser [difyze] *vt* *(chaleur, bruit, lumière)* to
diffuse; *(émission, musique)* to broadcast;
(nouvelle, idée) to circulate; *(Comm: livres,
journaux)* to distribute

digérer [diʒeʀe] *vt* *(personne)* to digest;
(: machine) to process; *(fig: accepter)* to
stomach, put up with

digestif, -ive [diʒɛstif, -iv] *adj* digestive
▷ *nm* (after-dinner) liqueur

digestion [diʒɛstjɔ̃] *nf* digestion

digne [diɲ] *adj* dignified; **~ de** worthy of; **~ de
foi** trustworthy

dignité [diɲite] *nf* dignity

digue [dig] *nf* dike, dyke; *(pour protéger la côte)*
sea wall

dilapider [dilapide] *vt* to squander, waste;
(détourner: biens, fonds publics) to embezzle,
misappropriate

dilemme [dilɛm] *nm* dilemma

dilettante [diletɑ̃t] *nm/f* dilettante; **en ~** in a
dilettantish way

diligence [diliʒɑ̃s] *nf* stagecoach, diligence;
(empressement) despatch; **faire ~** to make haste

diluer [dilɥe] *vt* to dilute

diluvien, ne [dilyvjɛ̃, -ɛn] *adj*: **pluie ~ne**
torrential rain

dimanche [dimɑ̃ʃ] *nm* Sunday; **le ~ des
Rameaux/de Pâques** Palm/Easter Sunday;
voir aussi **lundi**

dimension [dimɑ̃sjɔ̃] *nf* *(grandeur)* size; *(gén
pl: cotes, Math: de l'espace)* dimension;
(dimensions) dimensions

diminué, e [diminɥe] *adj* *(personne:
physiquement)* run-down; *(: mentalement)* less
alert

diminuer [diminɥe] *vt* to reduce, decrease;
(ardeur etc) to lessen; *(personne: physiquement)* to
undermine; *(dénigrer)* to belittle ▷ *vi* to
decrease, diminish

diminutif [diminytif] *nm* *(Ling)* diminutive;
(surnom) pet name

diminution [diminysjɔ̃] *nf* decreasing,
diminishing

dinde [dɛ̃d] *nf* turkey; *(femme stupide)* goose

dindon [dɛ̃dɔ̃] *nm* turkey

dîner [dine] *nm* dinner ▷ *vi* to have dinner;
~ d'affaires/de famille business/family
dinner

dingue [dɛ̃g] *adj* *(fam)* crazy

dinosaure [dinozɔʀ] *nm* dinosaur

diplomate [diplɔmat] *adj* diplomatic ▷ *nm*
diplomat; *(fig: personne habile)* diplomatist;
(Culin: gâteau) dessert made of sponge cake, candied
fruit and custard, ≈ trifle *(Brit)*

diplomatie [diplɔmasi] nf diplomacy

diplôme [diplom] nm diploma certificate; (examen) (diploma) examination; **avoir des ~s** to have qualifications

diplômé, e [diplome] adj qualified

dire [diʀ] nm: **au ~ de** according to; **leurs ~s** what they say ▷ vt to say; (secret, mensonge) to tell; **~ l'heure/la vérité** to tell the time/the truth; **dis pardon/merci** say sorry/thank you; **~ qch à qn** to tell sb sth; **~ à qn qu'il fasse** ou **de faire** to tell sb to do; **~ que** to say that; **on dit que** they say that; **comme on dit** as they say; **on dirait que** it looks (ou sounds etc) as though; **on dirait du vin** you'd ou one would think it was wine; **que dites-vous de** (penser) what do you think of; **si cela lui dit** if he feels like it, if he fancies it; **cela ne me dit rien** that doesn't appeal to me; **à vrai ~** truth to tell; **pour ainsi ~** so to speak; **cela va sans ~** that goes without saying; **dis donc!, dites donc!** (pour attirer l'attention) hey!; (au fait) by the way; **et ~ que ...** and to think that ...; **ceci** ou **cela dit** that being said; (à ces mots) whereupon; **c'est dit, voilà qui est dit** so that's settled; **il n'y a pas à ~** there's no getting away from it; **c'est ~ si ...** that just shows that ...; **c'est beaucoup/peu ~** that's saying a lot/not saying much; **se dire** vi (à soi-même) to say to oneself; (se prétendre): **se ~ malade** etc to say (that) one is ill etc; **ça se dit ... en anglais** that is ... in English; **ça ne se dit pas** (impoli) you shouldn't say that; (pas en usage) you don't say that; **cela ne se dit pas comme ça** you don't say it like that; **se ~ au revoir** to say goodbye (to each other)

direct, e [diʀɛkt] adj direct ▷ nm (train) through train; **en ~** (émission) live; **train/bus ~** express train/bus

directement [diʀɛktəmɑ̃] adv directly

directeur, -trice [diʀɛktœʀ, -tʀis] nm/f (d'entreprise) director; (de service) manager/eress; (d'école) head(teacher) (Brit), principal (US); **comité ~** management ou steering committee; **~ général** general manager; **~ de thèse** ≈ PhD supervisor

direction [diʀɛksjɔ̃] nf (d'entreprise) management; conducting; supervision; (Auto) steering; (sens) direction; **sous la ~ de** (Mus) conducted by; **en ~ de** (avion, train, bateau) for; **"toutes ~s"** (Auto) "all routes"

dirent [diʀ] vb voir **dire**

dirigeant, e [diʀiʒɑ̃, -ɑ̃t] adj managerial; (classes) ruling ▷ nm/f (d'un parti etc) leader; (d'entreprise) manager, member of the management

diriger [diʀiʒe] vt (entreprise) to manage, run; (véhicule) to steer; (orchestre) to conduct; (recherches, travaux) to supervise, be in charge of; (braquer: regard, arme): **~ sur** (arme) to point ou level ou aim at; (fig: critiques): **~ contre** aim at; **~ son regard sur** to look in the direction of; **se diriger** vi (s'orienter) to find one's way; **se ~ vers** ou **sur** to make ou head for

dis [di], **disais** etc [dizɛ] vb voir **dire**

discernement [disɛʀnəmɑ̃] nm discernment, judgment

discerner [disɛʀne] vt to discern, make out

discipline [disiplin] nf discipline

discipliner [disipline] vt to discipline; (cheveux) to control

discontinu, e [diskɔ̃tiny] adj intermittent; (bande: sur la route) broken

discontinuer [diskɔ̃tinɥe] vi: **sans ~** without stopping, without a break

discordant, e [diskɔʀdɑ̃, -ɑ̃t] adj discordant; conflicting

discothèque [diskɔtɛk] nf (disques) record collection; (: dans une bibliothèque): **~ (de prêt)** record library; (boîte de nuit) disco(thèque)

discours [diskuʀ] nm speech; **~ direct/indirect** (Ling) direct/indirect ou reported speech

discret, -ète [diskʀɛ, -ɛt] adj discreet; (fig: musique, style, maquillage) unobtrusive; (: endroit) quiet

discrétion [diskʀesjɔ̃] nf discretion; **à la ~ de qn** at sb's discretion; in sb's hands; **à ~** (boisson etc) unlimited, as much as one wants

discrimination [diskʀiminasjɔ̃] nf discrimination; **sans ~** indiscriminately

disculper [diskylpe] vt to exonerate

discussion [diskysjɔ̃] nf discussion

discutable [diskytabl] adj (contestable) doubtful; (à débattre) debatable

discuté, e [diskyte] adj controversial

discuter [diskyte] vt (contester) to question, dispute; (débattre: prix) to discuss ▷ vi to talk; (protester) to argue; **~ de** to discuss

dise etc [diz] vb voir **dire**

diseuse [dizøz] nf: **~ de bonne aventure** fortune-teller

disgracieux, -euse [disgʀasjø, -øz] adj ungainly, awkward

disjoindre [disʒwɛ̃dʀ] vt to take apart; **se disjoindre** vi to come apart

disjoncteur [disʒɔ̃ktœʀ] nm (Élec) circuit breaker

disloquer [dislɔke] vt (membre) to dislocate; (chaise) to dismantle; (troupe) to disperse; **se disloquer** vi (parti, empire) to break up; (meuble) to come apart; **se ~ l'épaule** to dislocate one's shoulder

disons etc [dizɔ̃] vb voir **dire**

disparaître [dispaʀɛtʀ] vi to disappear; (à la vue) to vanish, disappear; to be hidden ou concealed; (être manquant) to go missing, disappear; (se perdre: traditions etc) to die out; (personne: mourir) to die; **faire ~** (objet, tache, trace) to remove; (personne, douleur) to get rid of

disparition [dispaʀisjɔ̃] nf disappearance; **espèce en voie de ~** endangered species

disparu, e [dispaʀy] pp de **disparaître** ▷ nm/f missing person; (défunt) departed; **être porté ~** to be reported missing

dispensaire [dispɑ̃sɛʀ] nm community clinic

dispenser [dispɑ̃se] vt (donner) to lavish, bestow; (exempter): ~ **qn de** to exempt sb from; **se ~ de** vt to avoid, to get out of

disperser [dispɛʀse] vt to scatter; (fig: son attention) to dissipate; **se disperser** vi to scatter; (fig) to dissipate one's efforts

disponibilité [disponibilite] nf availability; (Admin): **être en ~** to be on leave of absence; **disponibilités** nfpl (Comm) liquid assets

disponible [disponibl] adj available

dispos [dispo] adj m: (**frais et**) **~** fresh (as a daisy)

disposé, e [dispoze] adj (d'une certaine manière) arranged, laid-out; **bien/mal ~** (humeur) in a good/bad mood; **bien/mal ~ pour** ou **envers qn** well/badly disposed towards sb; **~ à** (prêt à) willing ou prepared to

disposer [dispoze] vt (arranger, placer) to arrange; (inciter): **~ qn à qch/faire qch** to dispose ou incline sb towards sth/to do sth ▷ vi: **vous pouvez ~** you may leave; **~ de** vt to have (at one's disposal); **se ~ à faire** to prepare to do, be about to do

dispositif [dispozitif] nm device; (fig) system, plan of action; set-up; (d'un texte de loi) operative part; **~ de sûreté** safety device

disposition [dispozisjɔ̃] nf (arrangement) arrangement, layout; (humeur) mood; (tendance) tendency; **dispositions** nfpl (mesures) steps, measures; (préparatifs) arrangements; (de loi, testament) provisions; (aptitudes) bent sg, aptitude sg; **prendre ses ~s** to make arrangements; **avoir des ~s pour la musique** etc to have a special aptitude for music etc; **à la ~ de qn** at sb's disposal; **je suis à votre ~** I am at your service

disproportionné, e [dispʀopɔʀsjone] adj disproportionate, out of all proportion

dispute [dispyt] nf quarrel, argument

disputer [dispyte] vt (match) to play; (combat) to fight; (course) to run; **se disputer** vi to quarrel, have a quarrel; (match, combat, course) to take place; **~ qch à qn** to fight with sb for ou over sth

disquaire [diskɛʀ] nm/f record dealer

disqualifier [diskalifje] vt to disqualify; **se disqualifier** vi to bring discredit on o.s.

disque [disk] nm (Mus) record; (Inform) disk, disc; (forme, pièce) disc; (Sport) discus; **~ compact** compact disc; **~ compact interactif** CD-I®; **~ dur** hard disk; **~ d'embrayage** (Auto) clutch plate; **~ laser** compact disc; **~ de stationnement** parking disc; **~ système** system disk

disquette [diskɛt] nf floppy (disk), diskette

disséminer [disemine] vt to scatter; (troupes: sur un territoire) to disperse

disséquer [diseke] vt to dissect

dissertation [disɛʀtasjɔ̃] nf (Scol) essay

dissimuler [disimyle] vt to conceal; **se dissimuler** vi to conceal o.s.; to be concealed

dissipé, e [disipe] adj (indiscipliné) unruly

dissiper [disipe] vt to dissipate; (fortune) to squander, fritter away; **se dissiper** vi (brouillard) to clear, disperse; (doutes) to disappear, melt away; (élève) to become undisciplined ou unruly

dissolvant, e [disɔlvɑ̃, -ɑ̃t] vb voir **dissoudre** ▷ nm (Chimie) solvent; **~ (gras)** nail polish remover

dissonant, e [disɔnɑ̃, -ɑ̃t] adj discordant

dissoudre [disudʀ] vt, **se dissoudre** vi to dissolve

dissuader [disɥade] vt, **~ qn de faire/de qch** to dissuade sb from doing/from sth

dissuasion [disɥazjɔ̃] nf dissuasion; **force de ~** deterrent power

distance [distɑ̃s] nf distance; (fig: écart) gap; **à ~** at ou from a distance; (mettre en marche, commander) by remote control; (**situé**) **à ~** (Inform) remote; **tenir qn à ~** to keep sb at a distance; **se tenir à ~** to keep one's distance; **à une ~ de 10 km, à 10 km de ~** 10 km away, at a distance of 10 km; **à deux ans de ~** with a gap of two years; **prendre ses ~s** to space out; **garder ses ~s** to keep one's distance; **tenir la ~** (Sport) to cover the distance, last the course; **~ focale** (Photo) focal length

distancer [distɑ̃se] vt to outdistance, leave behind

distant, e [distɑ̃, -ɑ̃t] adj (réservé) distant, aloof; (éloigné) distant, far away; **~ de** (lieu) far away ou a long way from; **~ de 5 km (d'un lieu)** 5 km away (from a place)

distendre [distɑ̃dʀ] vt, **se distendre** vi to distend

distillerie [distilʀi] nf distillery

distinct, e [distɛ̃(kt), distɛ̃kt] adj distinct

distinctement [distɛ̃ktəmɑ̃] adv distinctly

distinctif, -ive [distɛ̃ktif, -iv] adj distinctive

distingué, e [distɛ̃ge] adj distinguished

distinguer [distɛ̃ge] vt to distinguish; **se distinguer** vi (s'illustrer) to distinguish o.s.; (différer): **se ~ (de)** to distinguish o.s. ou be distinguished (from)

distraction [distʀaksjɔ̃] nf (manque d'attention) absent-mindedness; (oubli) lapse (in concentration ou attention); (détente) diversion, recreation; (passe-temps) distraction, entertainment

distraire [distʀɛʀ] vt (déranger) to distract; (divertir) to entertain, divert; (détourner: somme d'argent) to divert, misappropriate; **se distraire** vi to amuse ou enjoy o.s.

distrait, e [distʀɛ, -ɛt] pp de **distraire** ▷ adj absent-minded

distrayant, e [distʀɛjɑ̃, -ɑ̃t] vb voir **distraire** ▷ adj entertaining

distribuer [distʀibɥe] vt to distribute; to hand out; (Cartes) to deal (out); (courrier) to deliver

distributeur [distʀibytœʀ] nm (Auto, Comm) distributor; (automatique) (vending) machine; **~ de billets** (Rail) ticket machine; (Banque) cash dispenser

distribution [distribysjɔ̃] nf distribution; (postale) delivery; (choix d'acteurs) casting; **circuits de ~** (Comm) distribution network; **~ des prix** (Scol) prize giving

dit, e [di, dit] pp de **dire** ▷ adj (fixé): **le jour ~** the arranged day; (surnommé): **X, ~ Pierrot** X, known as ou called Pierrot

dites [dit] vb voir **dire**

divaguer [divage] vi to ramble; (malade) to rave

divan [divɑ̃] nm divan

diverger [divɛrʒe] vi to diverge

divers, e [divɛr, -ɛrs] adj (varié) diverse, varied; (différent) different, various; **(frais) ~** (Comm) sundries, miscellaneous (expenses); **"~"** (rubrique) "miscellaneous"; **~es personnes** various ou several people

diversifier [divɛrsifje] vt, **se diversifier** vi to diversify

diversité [divɛrsite] nf diversity, variety

divertir [divɛrtir] vt to amuse, entertain; **se divertir** vi to amuse ou enjoy o.s.

divertissement [divɛrtismɑ̃] nm entertainment; (Mus) divertimento, divertissement

divin, e [divɛ̃, -in] adj divine; (fig: excellent) heavenly, divine

diviser [divize] vt (gén, Math) to divide; (morceler, subdiviser) to divide (up), split (up); **se ~ en** to divide into; **~ par** to divide by

division [divizjɔ̃] nf (gén) division; **~ du travail** (Écon) division of labour

divorce [divɔrs] nm divorce

divorcé, e [divɔrse] nm/f divorcee

divorcer [divɔrse] vi to get a divorce, get divorced; **~ de** ou **d'avec qn** to divorce sb

divulguer [divylge] vt to disclose, divulge

dix [di, dis, diz] num ten

dix-huit [dizɥit] num eighteen

dix-huitième [dizɥitjɛm] num eighteenth

dixième [dizjɛm] num tenth

dix-neuf [diznœf] num nineteen

dix-neuvième [diznœvjɛm] num nineteenth

dix-sept [disɛt] num seventeen

dix-septième [disɛtjɛm] num seventeenth

dizaine [dizɛn] nf (10) ten; (environ 10): **une ~ (de)** about ten, ten or so

do [do] nm (note) C; (en chantant la gamme) do(h)

docile [dɔsil] adj docile

dock [dɔk] nm dock; (hangar, bâtiment) warehouse

docker [dɔkɛr] nm docker

docteur, e [dɔktœr] nm/f doctor; **~ en médecine** doctor of medicine

doctorat [dɔktɔra] nm: **~ (d'Université)** ≈ doctorate; **~ d'État** ≈ PhD; **~ de troisième cycle** ≈ doctorate

doctoresse [dɔktɔrɛs] nf lady doctor

doctrine [dɔktrin] nf doctrine

document [dɔkymɑ̃] nm document

documentaire [dɔkymɑ̃tɛr] adj, nm documentary

documentaliste [dɔkymɑ̃talist] nm/f archivist; (Presse, TV) researcher

documentation [dɔkymɑ̃tasjɔ̃] nf documentation, literature; (Presse, TV: service) research

documenter [dɔkymɑ̃te] vt: **se ~ (sur)** to gather information ou material (on ou about)

dodo [dodo] nm: **aller faire ~** to go to beddy-byes

dodu, e [dody] adj plump

dogue [dɔg] nm mastiff

doigt [dwa] nm finger; **à deux ~s de** within an ace (Brit) ou an inch of; **un ~ de lait/whisky** a drop of milk/whisky; **désigner** ou **montrer du ~** to point at; **au ~ et à l'œil** to the letter; **connaître qch sur le bout du ~** to know sth backwards; **mettre le ~ sur la plaie** (fig) to find the sensitive spot; **~ de pied** toe

doigté [dwate] nm (Mus) fingering; (fig: habileté) diplomacy, tact

doit etc [dwa] vb voir **devoir**

doléances [dɔleɑ̃s] nfpl complaints; (réclamations) grievances

dollar [dɔlar] nm dollar

domaine [dɔmɛn] nm estate, property; (fig) domain, field; **tomber dans le ~ public** (livre etc) to be out of copyright; **dans tous les ~s** in all areas

domestique [dɔmɛstik] adj domestic ▷ nm/f servant, domestic

domestiquer [dɔmɛstike] vt to domesticate; (vent, marées) to harness

domicile [dɔmisil] nm home, place of residence; **à ~** at home; **élire ~ à** to take up residence in; **sans ~ fixe** of no fixed abode; **~ conjugal** marital home; **~ légal** domicile; **livrer à ~** to deliver

domicilié, e [dɔmisilje] adj: **être ~ à** to have one's home in ou at

dominant, e [dɔminɑ̃, -ɑ̃t] adj dominant; (plus important: opinion) predominant ▷ nf (caractéristique) dominant characteristic; (couleur) dominant colour

dominer [dɔmine] vt to dominate; (passions etc) to control, master; (sujet) to master; (surpasser) to outclass, surpass; (surplomber) to tower above, dominate ▷ vi to be in the dominant position; **se dominer** vi to control o.s.

domino [dɔmino] nm domino; **dominos** nmpl (jeu) dominoes sg

dommage [dɔmaʒ] nm (préjudice) harm, injury; **~s** (dégâts, pertes) damage no pl; **c'est ~ de faire/que** it's a shame ou pity to do/that; **quel ~!, c'est ~!** what a pity ou shame!; **~s corporels** physical injury

dommages-intérêts [dɔmaʒ(əz)ɛ̃terɛ] nmpl damages

dompter [dɔ̃(p)te] vt to tame

dompteur, -euse [dɔ̃tœʀ, -øz] *nm/f* trainer; *(de lion)* lion tamer

DOM-ROM [dɔmʀɔm], **DOM-TOM** [dɔmtɔm] *sigle m ou mpl* (= *Département(s) et Régions/Territoire(s) d'outre-mer)* French overseas departments and regions; *see note*

 MOT-CLÉ

DOM-TOM, ROM ET COM

There are five "Départements d'outre-mer" or DOMs: Guadeloupe, Martinique, La Réunion, French Guyana and Mayotte. They are run in the same way as metropolitan "départements" and their inhabitants are French citizens. In administrative terms they are also "Régions", and in this regard are also referred to as "ROM" (Régions d'outre-mer").

The term "DOM-TOM" is still commonly used, but the term "Territoire d'outre-mer" has been superseded by that of "Collectivité d'outre-mer" (COM). The COMs include French Polynesia, Wallis-and-Futuna, New Caledonia and polar territories. They are independent, but each is supervised by a representative of the French government.

don [dɔ̃] *nm (cadeau)* gift; *(charité)* donation; *(aptitude)* gift, talent; **avoir des ~s pour** to have a gift *ou* talent for; **faire ~ de** to make a gift of; **~ en argent** cash donation; **elle a le ~ de m'énerver** she's got a knack of getting on my nerves

donc [dɔ̃k] *conj* therefore, so; *(après une digression)* so, then; *(intensif)*: **voilà ~ la solution** so there's the solution; **je disais ~ que ...** as I was saying, ...; **venez ~ dîner à la maison** do come for dinner; **allons ~!** come now!; **faites ~** go ahead

donjon [dɔ̃ʒɔ̃] *nm* keep

donné, e [dɔne] *adj (convenu: lieu, heure)* given; *(pas cher)* very cheap; **données** *nfpl (Math, Inform, gén)* data; **c'est ~** it's a gift; **étant ~ que ...** given that ...

données [dɔne] *nfpl* data

donner [dɔne] *vt* to give; *(vieux habits etc)* to give away; *(spectacle)* to put on; *(film)* to show; **~ qch à qn** to give sb sth, give sth to sb; **~ sur** *(fenêtre, chambre)* to look (out) onto; **~ dans** *(piège etc)* to fall into; **faire ~ l'infanterie** *(Mil)* to send in the infantry; **~ l'heure à qn** to tell sb the time; **~ le ton** *(fig)* to set the tone; **~ à penser/entendre que ...** to make one think/give one to understand that ...; **ça donne soif/faim** it makes you (feel) thirsty/hungry; **se ~ à fond (à son travail)** to give one's all (to one's work); **se ~ du mal** *ou* **de la peine (pour faire qch)** to go to a lot of trouble (to do sth); **s'en ~ à cœur joie** *(fam)* to have a great time (of it)

dont [dɔ̃] *pron relatif* **1** *(appartenance: objets)* whose, of which; *(appartenance: êtres animés)* whose; **la maison dont le toit est rouge** the house the roof of which is red, the house whose roof is red; **l'homme dont je connais la sœur** the man whose sister I know **2** *(parmi lesquel(le)s)*: **deux livres, dont l'un est ...** two books, one of which is ...; **il y avait plusieurs personnes, dont Gabrielle** there were several people, among them Gabrielle; **10 blessés, dont 2 grièvement** 10 injured, 2 of them seriously **3** *(complément d'adjectif, de verbe)*: **le fils dont il est si fier** the son he's so proud of; **le pays dont il est originaire** the country he's from; **ce dont je parle** what I'm talking about; **la façon dont il l'a fait** the way (in which) he did it

dopage [dɔpaʒ] *nm (Sport)* drug use; *(de cheval)* doping

doré, e [dɔʀe] *adj* golden; *(avec dorure)* gilt, gilded

dorénavant [dɔʀenavɑ̃] *adv* from now on, henceforth

dorer [dɔʀe] *vt (cadre)* to gild; **(faire) ~** *(Culin)* to brown; *(: gâteau)* to glaze; **se ~ au soleil** to sunbathe; **~ la pilule à qn** to sugar the pill for sb

dorloter [dɔʀlɔte] *vt* to pamper, cosset (Brit); **se faire ~** to be pampered *ou* cosseted

dormir [dɔʀmiʀ] *vi* to sleep; *(être endormi)* to be asleep; **~ à poings fermés** to sleep very soundly

dortoir [dɔʀtwaʀ] *nm* dormitory

dorure [dɔʀyʀ] *nf* gilding

dos [do] *nm* back; *(de livre)* spine; **"voir au ~"** "see over"; **robe décolletée dans le ~** low-backed dress; **de ~** from the back, from behind; **~ à ~** back to back; **sur le ~** on one's back; **à ~ de chameau** riding on a camel; **avoir bon ~** to be a good excuse; **se mettre qn à ~** to turn sb against one

dosage [dozaʒ] *nm* mixture

dose [doz] *nf (Méd)* dose; **forcer la ~** *(fig)* to overstep the mark

doser [doze] *vt* to measure out; *(mélanger)* to mix in the correct proportions; *(fig)* to expend in the right amounts *ou* proportions; to strike a balance between; **il faut savoir ~ ses efforts** you have to be able to pace yourself

dossard [dosaʀ] *nm* number *(worn by competitor)*

dossier [dosje] *nm (renseignements, fichier)* file; *(enveloppe)* folder, file; *(de chaise)* back; *(Presse)* feature; *(Inform)* folder; **un ~ scolaire** a school report; **le ~ social/monétaire** *(fig)* the social/financial question; **~ suspendu** suspension file

dot [dɔt] nf dowry

doter [dɔte] vt: ~ **qn/qch de** to equip sb/sth with

douane [dwan] nf (*poste, bureau*) customs pl; (*taxes*) (customs) duty; **passer la ~** to go through customs; **en ~** (*marchandises, entrepôt*) bonded

douanier, -ière [dwanje, -jɛʀ] adj customs cpd ▷ nm customs officer

double [dubl] adj, adv double ▷ nm (*2 fois plus*): **le ~ (de)** twice as much (*ou* many) (as), double the amount (*ou* number) (of); (*autre exemplaire*) duplicate, copy; (*sosie*) double; (*Tennis*) doubles sg; **voir ~** to see double; **en ~ (exemplaire)** in duplicate; **faire ~ emploi** to be redundant; **à ~ sens** with a double meaning; **à ~ tranchant** two-edged; **~ carburateur** twin carburettor; **à ~s commandes** dual-control; **~ messieurs/ mixte** men's/mixed doubles sg; **~ toit** (*de tente*) fly sheet; **~ vue** second sight

double-cliquer [dubl(ə)klike] vi (*Inform*) to double-click

doubler [duble] vt (*multiplier par 2*) to double; (*vêtement*) to line; (*dépasser*) to overtake, pass; (*film*) to dub; (*acteur*) to stand in for ▷ vi to double, increase twofold; **se ~ de** to be coupled with; **~ (la classe)** (*Scol*) to repeat a year; **~ un cap** (*Navig*) to round a cape; (*fig*) to get over a hurdle

doublure [dublyʀ] nf lining; (*Ciné*) stand-in

douce [dus] adj f voir **doux**

douceâtre [dusɑtʀ] adj sickly sweet

doucement [dusmɑ̃] adv gently; (*à voix basse*) softly; (*lentement*) slowly

doucereux, -euse [dusʀø, -øz] adj (*péj*) sugary

douceur [dusœʀ] nf softness; sweetness; (*de climat*) mildness; (*de quelqu'un*) gentleness; **douceurs** nfpl (*friandises*) sweets (*Brit*), candy sg (*US*); **en ~** gently

douche [duʃ] nf shower; **douches** nfpl shower room sg; **prendre une ~** to have *ou* take a shower; **~ écossaise** (*fig*): **~ froide** (*fig*) let-down

doucher [duʃe] vt: **~ qn** to give sb a shower; (*mouiller*) to drench sb; (*fig*) to give sb a telling-off; **se doucher** vi to have *ou* take a shower

doudoune [dudun] nf padded jacket; (*fam*) boob

doué, e [dwe] adj gifted, talented; **~ de** endowed with; **être ~ pour** to have a gift for

douille [duj] nf (*Élec*) socket; (*de projectile*) case

douillet, te [dujɛ, -ɛt] adj cosy; (*péj: à la douleur*) soft

douleur [dulœʀ] nf pain; (*chagrin*) grief, distress; **ressentir des ~s** to feel pain; **il a eu la ~ de perdre son père** he suffered the grief of losing his father

douloureux, -euse [duluʀø, -øz] adj painful

doute [dut] nm doubt; **sans ~** adv no doubt;

(*probablement*) probably; **sans nul** *ou* **aucun ~** without (a) doubt; **hors de ~** beyond doubt; **nul ~ que** there's no doubt that; **mettre en ~** to call into question; **mettre en ~ que** to question whether

douter [dute] vt to doubt; **~ de** vt (*allié, sincérité de qn*) to have (one's) doubts about, doubt; (*résultat, réussite*) to be doubtful of; **~ que** to doubt whether *ou* if; **j'en doute** I have my doubts; **se ~ de qch/que** to suspect sth/that; **je m'en doutais** I suspected as much; **il ne se doutait de rien** he didn't suspect a thing

douteux, -euse [dutø, -øz] adj (*incertain*) doubtful; (*discutable*) dubious, questionable; (*péj*) dubious-looking

Douvres [duvʀ] n Dover

doux, douce [du, dus] adj (*lisse, moelleux, pas vif: couleur, non calcaire: eau*) soft; (*sucré, agréable*) sweet; (*peu fort: moutarde etc, clément: climat*) mild; (*pas brusque*) gentle; **en douce** (*partir etc*) on the quiet

douzaine [duzɛn] nf (*12*) dozen; (*environ 12*): **une ~ (de)** a dozen or so, twelve or so

douze [duz] num twelve

douzième [duzjɛm] num twelfth

doyen, ne [dwajɛ̃, -ɛn] nm/f (*en âge, ancienneté*) most senior member; (*de faculté*) dean

dragée [dʀaʒe] nf sugared almond; (*Méd*) (sugar-coated) pill

dragon [dʀagɔ̃] nm dragon

draguer [dʀage] vt (*rivière: pour nettoyer*) to dredge; (*: pour trouver qch*) to drag; (*fam*) to try and pick up, chat up (*Brit*) ▷ vi to try and pick sb up, chat sb up (*Brit*)

dramatique [dʀamatik] adj dramatic; (*tragique*) tragic ▷ nf (*TV*) (television) drama

dramaturge [dʀamatyʀʒ] nm dramatist, playwright

drame [dʀam] nm (*Théât*) drama; (*catastrophe*) drama, tragedy; **~ familial** family drama

drap [dʀa] nm (*de lit*) sheet; (*tissu*) woollen fabric; **~ de plage** beach towel

drapeau, x [dʀapo] nm flag; **sous les ~x** with the colours (*Brit*) *ou* colors (*US*), in the army

drap-housse (*pl* **draps-housses**) [dʀaus] nm fitted sheet

dresser [dʀese] vt (*mettre vertical, monter: tente*) to put up, erect; (*fig: liste, bilan, contrat*) to draw up; (*animal*) to train; **se dresser** vi (*falaise, obstacle*) to stand; (*avec grandeur, menace*) to tower (up); (*personne*) to draw o.s. up; **~ l'oreille** to prick up one's ears; **~ la table** to set *ou* lay the table; **~ qn contre qn d'autre** to set sb against sb else; **~ un procès-verbal** *ou* **une contravention à qn** to book sb

drogue [dʀɔg] nf drug; **la ~** drugs pl; **~ dure/ douce** hard/soft drugs pl

drogué, e [dʀɔge] nm/f drug addict

droguer [dʀɔge] vt (victime) to drug; (malade) to give drugs to; **se droguer** vi (aux stupéfiants) to take drugs; (péj: de médicaments) to dose o.s. up

droguerie [dʀɔgʀi] nf ≈ hardware shop (Brit) ou store (US)

droguiste [dʀɔgist] nm ≈ keeper (ou owner) of a hardware shop ou store

droit, e [dʀwa, dʀwat] adj (non courbe) straight; (vertical) upright, straight; (fig: loyal, franc) upright, straight(forward); (opposé à gauche) right, right-hand ▷ adv straight ▷ nm (prérogative, Boxe) right; (taxe) duty, tax; (: d'inscription) fee; (lois, branche): **le ~** law ▷ nf (Pol) right (wing); (ligne) straight line; **~ au but** ou **au fait/cœur** straight to the point/heart; **avoir le ~ de** to be allowed to; **avoir ~ à** to be entitled to; **être en ~ de** to have a ou the right to; **faire ~ à** to grant, accede to; **être dans son ~** to be within one's rights; **à bon ~** (justement) with good reason; **de quel ~?** by what right?; **à qui de ~** to whom it may concern; **à ~e** on the right; (direction) (to the) right; **à ~ e de** to the right of; **de ~e, sur votre ~e** on your right; (Pol) right-wing; **~ d'auteur** copyright; **~s d'auteur** royalties; **avoir ~ de cité (dans)** (fig) to belong (to); **~ coutumier** common law; **~ de regard** right of access ou inspection; **~ de réponse** right to reply; **~ de visite** (right of) access; **~ de vote** (right to) vote; **~s d'auteur** royalties; **~s de douane** customs duties; **~s de l'homme** human rights; **~s d'inscription** enrolment ou registration fees

droitier, -ière [dʀwatje, -jɛʀ] nm/f right-handed person ▷ adj right-handed

droiture [dʀwatyʀ] nf uprightness, straightness

drôle [dʀol] adj (amusant) funny, amusing; (bizarre) funny, peculiar; **un ~ de ...** (bizarre) a strange ou funny ...; (intensif) an incredible ..., a terrific ...

drôlement [dʀolmɑ̃] adv funnily; peculiarly; (très) terribly, awfully; **il fait ~ froid** it's awfully cold

dromadaire [dʀɔmadɛʀ] nm dromedary

dru, e [dʀy] adj (cheveux) thick, bushy; (pluie) heavy ▷ adv (pousser) thickly; (tomber) heavily

du [dy] art voir **de** ▷ prép +dét = **de + le**

dû, due [dy] pp de **devoir** ▷ adj (somme) owing, owed; (: venant à échéance) due; (causé par): **dû à** due to ▷ nm due; (somme) dues pl

duc [dyk] nm duke

duchesse [dyʃɛs] nf duchess

dûment [dymɑ̃] adv duly

dune [dyn] nf dune

Dunkerque [dœ̃kɛʀk] n Dunkirk

duo [dɥo] nm (Mus) duet; (fig: couple) duo, pair

dupe [dyp] nf dupe ▷ adj: **(ne pas) être ~ de** (not) to be taken in by

duplex [dyplɛks] nm (appartement) split-level apartment, duplex; (TV): **émission en ~** link-up

duplicata [dyplikata] nm duplicate

duquel [dykɛl] prép + pron voir **lequel**

dur, e [dyʀ] adj (pierre, siège, travail, problème) hard; (lumière, voix, climat) harsh; (sévère) hard, harsh; (cruel) hard(-hearted); (porte, col) stiff; (viande) tough ▷ adv hard ▷ nf: **à la ~e** rough; **mener la vie ~e à qn** to give sb a hard time ▷ nm (fam: meneur) tough nut; **~ d'oreille** hard of hearing

durant [dyʀɑ̃] prép (au cours de) during; (pendant) for; **~ des mois, des mois ~** for months

durcir [dyʀsiʀ] vt, vi to harden; **se durcir** vi to harden

durée [dyʀe] nf length; (d'une pile etc) life; (déroulement: des opérations etc) duration; **pour une ~ illimitée** for an unlimited length of time; **de courte ~** (séjour, répit) brief, short-term; **de longue ~** (effet) long-term; **pile de longue ~** long-life battery

durement [dyʀmɑ̃] adv harshly

durer [dyʀe] vi to last

dureté [dyʀte] nf (voir dur) hardness; harshness; stiffness; toughness

durit® [dyʀit] nf (car radiator) hose

duvet [dyvɛ] nm down; (sac de couchage en) **~** down-filled sleeping bag

DVD sigle m (= digital versatile disc) DVD

dynamique [dinamik] adj dynamic

dynamisme [dinamism] nm dynamism

dynamite [dinamit] nf dynamite

dynamo [dinamo] nf dynamo

dyslexie [dislɛksi] nf dyslexia, word blindness

e

eau, x [o] *nf* water ▷ *nfpl* (*Méd*) waters;
prendre l'~ (*chaussure etc*) to leak, let in water;
prendre les ~x to take the waters; **faire ~** to
leak; **tomber à l'~** (*fig*) to fall through; **à l'~**
de rose slushy, sentimental; **~ bénite** holy
water; **~ de Cologne** eau de Cologne;
~ courante running water; **~ distillée**
distilled water; **~ douce** fresh water;
~ gazeuse sparkling (mineral) water;
~ de Javel bleach; **~ lourde** heavy water;
~ salée salt water; **~ de**
pluie rainwater; **~ salée** salt water; **~ de**
toilette toilet water; **~x ménagères** dirty
water (*from washing up etc*); **~x territoriales**
territorial waters; **~x usées** liquid waste
eau-de-vie [odvi] (*pl* **eaux-de-vie**) *nf* brandy
eau-forte [ofɔʀt] (*pl* **eaux-fortes**) *nf* etching
ébahi, e [ebai] *adj* dumbfounded,
flabbergasted
ébattre [ebatʀ]: **s'ébattre** *vi* to frolic
ébaucher [eboʃe] *vt* to sketch out, outline;
(*fig*): **~ un sourire/geste** to give a hint of a
smile/make a slight gesture; **s'ébaucher** *vi*
to take shape
ébène [ebɛn] *nf* ebony
ébéniste [ebenist] *nm* cabinetmaker
éberlué, e [ebɛʀlɥe] *adj* astounded,
flabbergasted
éblouir [ebluiʀ] *vt* to dazzle
éborgner [ebɔʀɲe] *vt*: **~ qn** to blind sb in
one eye

éboueur [ebwœʀ] *nm* dustman (*Brit*),
garbage man (*US*)
ébouillanter [ebujɑ̃te] *vt* to scald; (*Culin*) to
blanch; **s'ébouillanter** *vi* to scald o.s.
éboulement [ebulmɑ̃] *nm* falling rocks *pl*,
rock fall; (*amas*) heap of boulders *etc*
ébouler [ebule]: **s'ébouler** *vi* to crumble,
collapse
éboulis [ebuli] *nmpl* fallen rocks
ébouriffé, e [ebuʀife] *adj* tousled, ruffled
ébranler [ebʀɑ̃le] *vt* to shake; (*rendre instable:*
mur, santé) to weaken; **s'ébranler** *vi* (*partir*) to
move off
ébrécher [ebʀeʃe] *vt* to chip
ébriété [ebʀijete] *nf*: **en état d'~** in a state of
intoxication
ébrouer [ebʀue]: **s'ébrouer** *vi* (*souffler*) to
snort; (*s'agiter*) to shake o.s.
ébruiter [ebʀɥite] *vt*, **s'ébruiter** *vi* to spread
ébullition [ebylisjɔ̃] *nf* boiling point; **en ~**
boiling; (*fig*) in an uproar
écaille [ekaj] *nf* (*de poisson*) scale; (*de coquillage*)
shell; (*matière*) tortoiseshell; (*de roc etc*) flake
écailler [ekaje] *vt* (*poisson*) to scale; (*huître*) to
open; **s'écailler** *vi* to flake ou peel (off)
écarlate [ekaʀlat] *adj* scarlet
écarquiller [ekaʀkije] *vt*: **~ les yeux** to stare
wide-eyed
écart [ekaʀ] *nm* gap; (*embardée*) swerve; (*saut*)
sideways leap; (*fig*) departure, deviation;
à l'~ *adv* out of the way; **à l'~ de** *prép* away
from; (*fig*) out of; **faire un ~** (*voiture*) to
swerve; **faire le grand ~** (*Danse, Gymnastique*)
to do the splits; **~ de conduite**
misdemeanour
écarté, e [ekaʀte] *adj* (*lieu*) out-of-the-way,
remote; (*ouvert*) open: **les jambes ~es** legs apart;
les bras ~s arms outstretched
écarter [ekaʀte] *vt* (*séparer*) to move apart,
separate; (*éloigner*) to push back, move away;
(*ouvrir: bras, jambes*) to spread, open; (*: rideau*)
to draw (back); (*éliminer: candidat, possibilité*) to
dismiss; (*Cartes*) to discard; **s'écarter** *vi* to
part; (*personne*) to move away; **s'~ de** to
wander from
écervelé, e [esɛʀvəle] *adj* scatterbrained,
featherbrained
échafaud [eʃafo] *nm* scaffold
échafaudage [eʃafodaʒ] *nm* scaffolding; (*fig*)
heap, pile
échafauder [eʃafode] *vt* (*plan*) to construct
échalote [eʃalɔt] *nf* shallot
échancrure [eʃɑ̃kʀyʀ] *nf* (*de robe*) scoop
neckline; (*de côte, arête rocheuse*) indentation
échange [eʃɑ̃ʒ] *nm* exchange; **en ~** in
exchange; **en ~ de** in exchange ou return for;
libre ~ free trade; **~ de lettres/politesses/**
vues exchange of letters/civilities/views; **~s**
commerciaux trade; **~s culturels** cultural
exchanges
échanger [eʃɑ̃ʒe] *vt*: **~ qch (contre)** to
exchange sth (for)

échangeur [eʃɑ̃ʒœʀ] nm (Auto) interchange

échantillon [eʃɑ̃tijɔ̃] nm sample

échappement [eʃapmɑ̃] nm (Auto) exhaust; ~ **libre** cutout

échapper [eʃape]: ~ **à** vt (gardien) to escape (from); (punition, péril) to escape; ~ **à qn** (détail, sens) to escape sb; (objet qu'on tient: aussi: ~ **des mains de qn**) to slip out of sb's hands; **laisser ~** to let fall; (cri etc) to let out; **s'échapper** vi to escape; **l'~ belle** to have a narrow escape

écharde [eʃaʀd] nf splinter (of wood)

écharpe [eʃaʀp] nf scarf; (de maire) sash; (Méd) sling; **avoir le bras en ~** to have one's arm in a sling; **prendre en ~** (dans une collision) to hit sideways on

échasse [eʃas] nf stilt

échassier [eʃasje] nm wader

échauffer [eʃofe] vt (métal, moteur) to overheat; (fig: exciter) to fire, excite; **s'échauffer** vi (Sport) to warm up; (discussion) to become heated

échéance [eʃeɑ̃s] nf (d'un paiement: date) settlement date; (: somme due) financial commitment(s); (fig) deadline; **à brève/ longue ~** adj short-/long-term ▷ adv in the short/long term

échéant [eʃeɑ̃]: **le cas ~** adv if the case arises

échec [eʃɛk] nm failure; (Échecs): ~ **et mat/au roi** checkmate/check; **échecs** nmpl (jeu) chess sg; **mettre en ~** to put in check; **tenir en ~** to hold in check; **faire ~ à** to foil, thwart

échelle [eʃɛl] nf ladder; (fig, d'une carte) scale; **à l'~ de** on the scale of; **sur une grande/ petite ~** on a large/small scale; **faire la courte ~ à qn** to give sb a leg up; ~ **de corde** rope ladder

échelon [eʃ(ə)lɔ̃] nm (d'échelle) rung; (Admin) grade

échelonner [eʃ(ə)lɔne] vt to space out, spread out; (versement) **échelonné** (payment) by instalments

échevelé, e [eʃəvle] adj tousled, dishevelled; (fig) wild, frenzied

échine [eʃin] nf backbone, spine

échiquier [eʃikje] nm chessboard

écho [eko] nm echo; **échos** nmpl (potins) gossip sg, rumours; (Presse: rubrique) "news in brief"; **rester sans ~** (suggestion etc) to come to nothing; **se faire l'~ de** to repeat, spread about

échographie [ekografi] nf ultrasound (scan); **passer une ~** to have a scan

échoir [eʃwaʀ] vi (dette) to fall due; (délais) to expire; ~ **à** vt to fall to

échouer [eʃwe] vi to fail; (débris etc: sur la plage) to be washed up; (aboutir: personne dans un café etc) to arrive ▷ vt (bateau) to ground; **s'échouer** vi to run aground

échu, e [eʃy] pp de **échoir** ▷ adj due, mature

éclabousser [eklabuse] vt to splash; (fig) to tarnish

éclair [eklɛʀ] nm (d'orage) flash of lightning,

lightning no pl; (Photo: de flash) flash; (fig) flash, spark; (gâteau) éclair

éclairage [eklɛʀaʒ] nm lighting

éclaircie [eklɛʀsi] nf bright ou sunny interval

éclaircir [eklɛʀsiʀ] vt to lighten; (fig: mystère) to clear up; (point) to clarify; (Culin) to thin (down); **s'éclaircir** vi (ciel) to brighten up, clear; (cheveux) to go thin; (situation etc) to become clearer; **s'~ la voix** to clear one's throat

éclaircissement [eklɛʀsismɑ̃] nm clearing up, clarification

éclairer [eklɛʀe] vt (lieu) to light (up); (personne: avec une lampe de poche etc) to light the way for; (fig: instruire) to enlighten; (: rendre compréhensible) to shed light on ▷ vi: ~ **mal/ bien** to give a poor/good light; **s'éclairer** vi (phare, rue) to light up; (situation etc) to become clearer; **s'~ à la bougie/l'électricité** to use candlelight/have electric lighting

éclaireur, -euse [eklɛʀœʀ, -øz] nm/f (scout) (boy) scout/(girl) guide ▷ nm (Mil) scout; **partir en ~** to go off to reconnoitre

éclat [ekla] nm (de bombe, de verre) fragment; (du soleil, d'une couleur etc) brightness, brilliance; (d'une cérémonie) splendour; (scandale): **faire un ~** to cause a commotion; **action d'~** outstanding action; **voler en ~s** to shatter; **des ~s de verre** broken glass; flying glass; ~ **de rire** burst ou roar of laughter; ~ **de voix** shout

éclatant, e [eklatɑ̃, -ɑ̃t] adj brilliant, bright; (succès) resounding; (revanche) devastating

éclater [eklate] vi (pneu) to burst; (bombe) to explode; (guerre, épidémie) to break out; (groupe, parti) to break up; ~ **de rire/en sanglots** to burst out laughing/sobbing

éclipser [eklipse] vt to eclipse; **s'éclipser** vi to slip away

éclore [eklɔʀ] vi (œuf) to hatch; (fleur) to open (out)

écluse [eklyz] nf lock

écœurant, e [ekœʀɑ̃, -ɑ̃t] adj sickening; (gâteau etc) sickly

écœurer [ekœʀe] vt: ~ **qn** (nourriture) to make sb feel sick; (fig: conduite, personne) to disgust sb

école [ekɔl] nf school; **aller à l'~** to go to school; **faire ~** to collect a following; **les grandes ~s** prestige university-level colleges with competitive entrance examinations; ~ **maternelle** nursery school; see note; ~ **primaire** primary (Brit) ou grade (US) school; ~ **secondaire** secondary (Brit) ou high (US) school; ~ **privée/ publique/élémentaire** private/state/ elementary school; ~ **de dessin/danse/ musique** art/dancing/music school; ~ **hôtelière** catering college; ~ **normale (d'instituteurs) (ENI)** primary school teachers' training college; ~ **normale supérieure (ENS)** grande école for training secondary school teachers; ~ **de secrétariat** secretarial college

● **ÉCOLE MATERNELLE**
●
● Nursery school (kindergarten) (*l'école*
● *maternelle*) is publicly funded in France
● and, though not compulsory, is attended
● by most children between the ages of
● three and six. Statutory education begins
● with primary (grade) school (*l'école*
● *primaire*) and is attended by children
● between the ages of six and 10 or 11.

écolier, -ière [ekɔlje, -jɛʀ] *nm/f* schoolboy/girl
écologie [ekɔlɔʒi] *nf* ecology; (*sujet scolaire*) environmental studies *pl*
écologique [ekɔlɔʒik] *adj* ecological; environment-friendly
écologiste [ekɔlɔʒist] *nm/f* ecologist; environmentalist
éconduire [ekɔ̃dɥiʀ] *vt* to dismiss
économe [ekɔnɔm] *adj* thrifty ▷ *nm/f* (*de lycée etc*) bursar (Brit), treasurer (US)
économie [ekɔnɔmi] *nf* (*vertu*) economy, thrift; (*gain: d'argent, de temps etc*) saving; (*science*) economics *sg*; (*situation économique*) economy; **économies** *nfpl* (*pécule*) savings; **faire des ~s** to save up; **une ~ de temps/ d'argent** a saving in time/of money; **~ dirigée** planned economy; **~ de marché** market economy
économique [ekɔnɔmik] *adj* (*avantageux*) economical; (*Écon*) economic
économiser [ekɔnɔmize] *vt, vi* to save
économiseur [ekɔnɔmizœʀ] *nm*: **~ d'écran** (Inform) screen saver
écoper [ekɔpe] *vi* to bale out; (*fig*) to cop it; **~ (de)** *vt* to get
écorce [ekɔʀs] *nf* bark; (*de fruit*) peel
écorcher [ekɔʀʃe] *vt* (*animal*) to skin; (*égratigner*) to graze; **~ une langue** to speak a language brokenly; **s'~ le genou** *etc* to scrape ou graze one's knee *etc*
écorchure [ekɔʀʃyʀ] *nf* graze
écossais, e [ekɔsɛ, -ɛz] *adj* Scottish, Scots; (*whisky, confiture*) Scotch; (*écharpe, tissu*) tartan ▷ *nm* (Ling) Scots; (*: gaélique*) Gaelic; (*tissu*) tartan (cloth) ▷ *nm/f*: **É~, e** Scot, Scotsman/ woman; **les É~** the Scots
Écosse [ekɔs] *nf*: **l'~** Scotland
écosser [ekɔse] *vt* to shell
écotaxe [ekotaks] *nf* green tax
écoulement [ekulmã] *nm* (*de faux billets*) circulation; (*de stock*) selling
écouler [ekule] *vt* to dispose of; **s'écouler** vi (*eau*) to flow (out); (*foule*) to drift away; (*jours, temps*) to pass (by)
écourter [ekuʀte] *vt* to curtail, cut short
écoute [ekut] *nf* (Navig: *cordage*) sheet; (Radio, TV): **temps d'~** (listening *ou* viewing) time; **heure de grande ~** peak listening *ou* viewing time; **prendre l'~** to tune in; **rester à l'~ (de)** to stay tuned in (to); **~s téléphoniques** phone tapping *sg*

écouter [ekute] *vt* to listen to; **s'écouter** (*malade*) to be a bit of a hypochondriac; **si je m'écoutais** if I followed my instincts
écouteur [ekutœʀ] *nm* (Tél) receiver; **écouteurs** *nmpl* (*casque*) headphones, headset *sg*
écoutille [ekutij] *nf* hatch
écran [ekʀã] *nm* screen; (Inform) screen, VDU; **~ de fumée/d'eau** curtain of smoke/water; **porter à l'~** (Ciné) to adapt for the screen; **le petit ~** television, the small screen; **~ tactile** touchscreen; **~ total** sunblock
écrasant, e [ekʀazã, -ãt] *adj* overwhelming
écraser [ekʀaze] *vt* to crush; (*piéton*) to run over; (Inform) to overwrite; **se faire ~** to be run over; **écrase(-toi)!** shut up!; **s'~ (au sol)** *vi* to crash; **s'~ contre** to crash into
écrémé, e [ekʀeme] *adj* (*lait*) skimmed
écrevisse [ekʀəvis] *nf* crayfish *inv*
écrier [ekʀije]: **s'écrier** vi to exclaim
écrin [ekʀɛ̃] *nm* case, box
écrire [ekʀiʀ] *vt, vi* to write ▷ vi: **ça s'écrit comment?** how is it spelt?; **~ à qn que** to write and tell sb that; **s'écrire** vi to write to one another
écrit, e [ekʀi, -it] *pp de* **écrire** ▷ *adj*: **bien/ mal ~** well/badly written ▷ *nm* document; (*examen*) written paper; **par ~** in writing
écriteau, x [ekʀito] *nm* notice, sign
écriture [ekʀityʀ] *nf* writing; (Comm) entry; **écritures** *nfpl* (Comm) accounts, books; **l'É~ (sainte)**, **les É~s** the Scriptures
écrivain [ekʀivɛ̃] *nm* writer
écrou [ekʀu] *nm* nut
écrouer [ekʀue] *vt* to imprison; (*provisoirement*) to remand in custody
écrouler [ekʀule]: **s'écrouler** vi to collapse
écru, e [ekʀy] *adj* (*toile*) raw, unbleached; (*couleur*) off-white, écru
écueil [ekœj] *nm* reef; (*fig*) pitfall; stumbling block
éculé, e [ekyle] *adj* (*chaussure*) down-at-heel; (*fig: péj*) hackneyed
écume [ekym] *nf* foam; (Culin) scum; **~ de mer** meerschaum
écumer [ekyme] *vt* (Culin) to skim; (*fig*) to plunder ▷ vi (*mer*) to foam; (*fig*) to boil with rage
écumoire [ekymwaʀ] *nf* skimmer
écureuil [ekyʀœj] *nm* squirrel
écurie [ekyʀi] *nf* stable
écusson [ekysɔ̃] *nm* badge
écuyer, -ère [ekɥije, -ɛʀ] *nm/f* rider
eczéma [ɛgzema] *nm* eczema
édenté, e [edãte] *adj* toothless
EDF *sigle f* (= Électricité de France) national electricity company
édifice [edifis] *nm* building, edifice
édifier [edifje] *vt* to build, erect; (*fig*) to edify
Édimbourg [edɛ̃buʀ] *n* Edinburgh
éditer [edite] *vt* (*publier*) to publish; (*: disque*) to produce; (*préparer: texte, Inform: annoter*) to edit

éditeur, -trice [editœʀ, -tʀis] *nm/f* publisher; editor; **~ de textes** (*Inform*) text editor

édition [edisjɔ̃] *nf* editing *no pl*; (*série d'exemplaires*) edition; (*industrie du livre*): **l'~** publishing; **~ sur écran** (*Inform*) screen editing

édredon [edʀədɔ̃] *nm* eiderdown, comforter (*US*)

éducateur, -trice [edykatœʀ, -tʀis] *nm/f* teacher; (*en école spécialisée*) instructor; **~ spécialisé** specialist teacher

éducatif, -ive [edykatif, -iv] *adj* educational

éducation [edykasjɔ̃] *nf* education; (*familiale*) upbringing; (*manières*) (good) manners *pl*; **bonne/mauvaise ~** good/bad upbringing; **sans ~** bad-mannered, ill-bred; **l'É-(nationale)** = the Department for Education; **~ permanente** continuing education; **~ physique** physical education

édulcorant [edylkɔʀɑ̃] *nm* sweetener

éduquer [edyke] *vt* to educate; (*élever*) to bring up; (*faculté*) to train; **bien/mal éduqué** well/badly brought up

effacé, e [efase] *adj* (*fig*) retiring, unassuming

effacer [efase] *vt* to erase, rub out; (*bande magnétique*) to erase; (*Inform: fichier, fiche*) to delete; **s'effacer** *vi* (*inscription etc*) to wear off; (*pour laisser passer*) to step aside; **~ le ventre** to pull one's stomach in

effarant, e [efaʀɑ̃, -ɑ̃t] *adj* alarming

effarer [efaʀe] *vt* to alarm

effaroucher [efaʀuʃe] *vt* to frighten *ou* scare away; (*personne*) to alarm

effectif, -ive [efɛktif, -iv] *adj* real; effective ▷ *nm* (*Mil*) strength; (*Scol*) total number of pupils, size; **~s** numbers, strength *sg*; (*Comm*) manpower *sg*; **réduire l'~ de** to downsize

effectivement [efɛktivmɑ̃] *adv* effectively; (*réellement*) actually, really; (*en effet*) indeed

effectuer [efɛktɥe] *vt* (*opération, mission*) to carry out; (*déplacement, trajet*) to make, complete; (*mouvement*) to execute, make; **s'effectuer** *vi* to be carried out

efféminé, e [efemine] *adj* effeminate

effervescent, e [efɛʀvesɑ̃, -ɑ̃t] *adj* (*cachet, boisson*) effervescent; (*fig*) agitated, in a turmoil

effet [efɛ] *nm* (*résultat, artifice*) effect; (*impression*) impression; (*Comm*) bill; (*Jur: d'une loi, d'un jugement*): **avec ~ rétroactif** applied retrospectively; **effets** *nmpl* (*vêtements etc*) things; **~ de style/couleur/lumière** stylistic/colour/lighting effect; **~s de voix** dramatic effects with one's voice; **faire ~** (*médicament*) to take effect; **faire de l'~** (*médicament, menace*) to have an effect, be effective; (*impressionner*) to make an impression; **faire bon/mauvais ~ sur qn** to make a good/bad impression on sb; **sous l'~ de** under the effect of; **donner de l'~ à une** balle (*Tennis*) to put some spin on a ball; **à cet ~** to that end; **en ~** *adv* indeed; **~ (de commerce)** bill of exchange; **~ de serre** greenhouse effect; **~s spéciaux** (*Ciné*) special effects

efficace [efikas] *adj* (*personne*) efficient; (*action, médicament*) effective

efficacité [efikasite] *nf* efficiency; effectiveness

effilocher [efilɔʃe]: **s'effilocher** *vi* to fray

efflanqué, e [eflɑ̃ke] *adj* emaciated

effleurer [eflœʀe] *vt* to brush (against); (*sujet*) to touch upon; (*idée, pensée*): **~ qn** to cross sb's mind

effluves [eflyv] *nmpl* exhalation(s)

effondrer [efɔ̃dʀe]: **s'effondrer** *vi* to collapse

efforcer [efɔʀse]: **s'efforcer de** *vt*: **s'~ de faire** to try hard to do

effort [efɔʀ] *nm* effort; **faire un ~** to make an effort; **faire tous ses ~s** to try one's hardest; **faire l'~ de ...** to make the effort to ...; **sans ~** *adj* effortless ▷ *adv* effortlessly; **~ de mémoire** attempt to remember; **~ de volonté** effort of will

effraction [efʀaksjɔ̃] *nf* breaking-in; **s'introduire par ~ dans** to break into

effrayant, e [efʀejɑ̃, -ɑ̃t] *adj* frightening, fearsome; (*sens affaibli*) dreadful

effrayer [efʀeje] *vt* to frighten, scare; (*rebuter*) to put off; **s'effrayer (de)** *vi* to be frightened *ou* scared (by)

effréné, e [efʀene] *adj* wild

effriter [efʀite]: **s'effriter** *vi* to crumble; (*monnaie*) to be eroded; (*valeurs*) to slacken off

effroi [efʀwa] *nm* terror, dread *no pl*

effronté, e [efʀɔ̃te] *adj* insolent

effroyable [efʀwajabl] *adj* horrifying, appalling

effusion [efyzjɔ̃] *nf* effusion; **sans ~ de sang** without bloodshed

égal, e, -aux [egal, -o] *adj* (*identique, ayant les mêmes droits*) equal; (*plan: surface*) even, level; (*constant: vitesse*) steady; (*équitable*) even ▷ *nm/f* equal; **être ~ à** (*prix, nombre*) to be equal to; **ça m'est ~** it's all the same to me, it doesn't matter to me, I don't mind; **c'est ~, ...** all the same, ...; **sans ~** matchless, unequalled; **à l'~ de** (*comme*) just like; **d'~ à ~** as equals

également [egalmɑ̃] *adv* equally; evenly; steadily; (*aussi*) too, as well

égaler [egale] *vt* to equal

égaliser [egalize] *vt* (*sol, salaires*) to level (out); (*chances*) to equalize ▷ *vi* (*Sport*) to equalize

égalité [egalite] *nf* equality; evenness; steadiness; (*Math*) identity; **être à ~ (de points)** to be level; **~ de droits** equality of rights; **~ d'humeur** evenness of temper

égard [egaʀ] *nm*: **~s** *nmpl* consideration *sg*; **à cet ~** in this respect; **à certains ~s/tous ~s** in certain respects/all respects; **eu ~ à** in view of; **par ~ pour** out of consideration for; **sans**

~ pour without regard for; **à l'~ de** prép towards; (en ce qui concerne) concerning, as regards

égarement [egarmã] nm distraction; aberration

égarer [egare] vt (objet) to mislay; (moralement) to lead astray; **s'égarer** vi to get lost, lose one's way; (objet) to go astray; (fig: dans une discussion) to wander

égayer [egeje] vt (personne) to amuse; (: remonter) to cheer up; (récit, endroit) to brighten up, liven up

églantine [eglãtin] nf wild ou dog rose

églefin [egləfɛ̃] nm haddock

église [egliz] nf church; **aller à l'~** to go to church

égoïsme [egɔism] nm selfishness, egoism

égoïste [egɔist] adj selfish, egoistic ▷ nm/f egoist

égorger [egɔrʒe] vt to cut the throat of

égosiller [egozije]: **s'égosiller** vi to shout o.s. hoarse

égout [egu] nm sewer; **eaux d'~** sewage

égoutter [egute] vt (linge) to wring out; (vaisselle, fromage) to drain ▷ vi to drip; **s'égoutter** vi to drip

égouttoir [egutwar] nm draining board; (mobile) draining rack

égratigner [egratiɲe] vt to scratch; **s'égratigner** vi to scratch o.s.

égratignure [egratiɲyr] nf scratch

Égypte [eʒipt] nf: **l'~** Egypt

égyptien, ne [eʒipsjɛ̃, -ɛn] adj Egyptian ▷ nm/f: **É-, ne** Egyptian

eh [e] excl hey!; **eh bien** well

éhonté, e [eɔ̃te] adj shameless, brazen (Brit)

éjecter [eʒɛkte] vt (Tech) to eject; (fam) to kick ou chuck out

élaborer [elabɔre] vt to elaborate; (projet, stratégie) to work out; (rapport) to draft

élan [elã] nm (Zool) elk, moose; (Sport: avant le saut) run up; (de véhicule) momentum; (fig: de tendresse etc) surge; **prendre son ~/de l'~** to take a run up/gather speed; **perdre son ~** to lose one's momentum

élancé, e [elãse] adj slender

élancement [elãsmã] nm shooting pain

élancer [elãse]: **s'élancer** vi to dash, hurl o.s.; (fig: arbre, clocher) to soar (upwards)

élargir [elarʒir] vt to widen; (vêtement) to let out; (Jur) to release; **s'élargir** vi to widen; (vêtement) to stretch

élastique [elastik] adj elastic ▷ nm (de bureau) rubber band; (pour la couture) elastic no pl

électeur, -trice [elɛktœr, -tris] nm/f elector, voter

élection [elɛksjɔ̃] nf election; **élections** nfpl (Pol) election(s); **sa terre/patrie d'~** the land/country of one's choice; **~ partielle** ≈ by-election; **~s législatives/présidentielles** general/presidential election sg; see note

électorat [elɛktɔra] nm electorate

électricien, ne [elɛktrisjɛ̃, -ɛn] nm/f electrician

électricité [elɛktrisite] nf electricity; **allumer/éteindre l'~** to put on/off the light; **~ statique** static electricity

électrique [elɛktrik] adj electric(al)

électrocuter [elɛktrɔkyte] vt to electrocute

électroménager [elɛktromenaʒe] adj: **appareils ~s** domestic (electrical) appliances ▷ nm: **l'~** household appliances

électronique [elɛktrɔnik] adj electronic ▷ nf (science) electronics sg

électrophone [elɛktrɔfɔn] nm record player

élégance [elegãs] nf elegance

élégant, e [elegã, -ãt] adj elegant; (solution) neat, elegant; (attitude, procédé) courteous, civilized

élément [elemã] nm element; (pièce) component, part; **éléments** nmpl elements

élémentaire [elemãter] adj elementary; (Chimie) elemental

éléphant [elefã] nm elephant; **~ de mer** elephant seal

élevage [el(ə)vaʒ] nm breeding; (de bovins) cattle breeding ou rearing; (ferme) cattle farm; **truite d'~** farmed trout

élévation [elevasjɔ̃] nf (gén) elevation; (voir élever) raising; (voir s'élever) rise

élevé, e [el(ə)ve] adj (prix, sommet) high; (fig: noble) elevated; **bien/mal ~** well-/ill-mannered

élève [elɛv] nm/f pupil; **~ infirmière** student nurse

élever [el(ə)ve] vt (enfant) to bring up, raise; (bétail, volaille) to breed; (abeilles) to keep; (hausser: taux, niveau) to raise; (fig: âme, esprit) to elevate; (édifier: monument) to put up, erect; **s'élever** vi (avion, alpiniste) to go up; (niveau, température, aussi: cri etc) to rise; (survenir: difficultés) to arise; **s'~ à** (frais, dégâts) to amount to, add up to; **s'~ contre** to rise up against; **~ la voix** to raise one's voice; **~ une protestation/critique** to raise a protest/ make a criticism; **~ qn au rang de** to raise ou elevate sb to the rank of; **~ un nombre au carré/au cube** to square/cube a number

éleveur, -euse [el(ə)vœr, -øz] nm/f stock breeder

élimé, e [elime] adj worn (thin), threadbare

éliminatoire [eliminatwar] adj eliminatory; (Sport) disqualifying ▷ nf (Sport) heat

éliminer [elimine] vt to eliminate

élire [eliʀ] vt to elect; **~ domicile à** to take up residence in ou at

elle [ɛl] pron (sujet) she; (: chose) it; (complément) her; it; **~s** (sujet) they; (complément) them; **~-même** herself; itself; **~s-mêmes** themselves; voir **il**

élocution [elɔkysjɔ̃] nf delivery; **défaut d'~** speech impediment

éloge [elɔʒ] nm praise gen no pl; **faire l'~ de** to praise

élogieux, -euse [elɔʒjø, -øz] adj laudatory, full of praise

éloigné, e [elwaɲe] adj distant, far-off; (parent) distant

éloignement [elwaɲmɑ̃] nm removal; putting off; estrangement; (fig: distance) distance

éloigner [elwaɲe] vt (objet): **~ qch (de)** to move ou take sth away (from); (personne): **~ qn (de)** to take sb away ou remove sb (from); (échéance) to put off, postpone; (soupçons, danger) to ward off; **s'éloigner (de)** vi (personne) to go away (from); (véhicule) to move away (from); (affectivement) to become estranged (from)

élu, e [ely] pp de **élire** ▷ nm/f (Pol) elected representative

éluder [elyde] vt to evade

Élysée [elize] nm: (**le palais de) l'~** the Élysée palace; see note; **les Champs ~s** the Champs Élysées

○ **L'ÉLYSÉE**
○
○ The palais de l'Élysée, situated in the heart
○ of Paris just off the Champs Élysées, is
○ the official residence of the French
○ President. Built in the eighteenth
○ century, it has performed its present
○ function since 1876. A shorter form of its
○ name, "l'Élysée" is frequently used to
○ refer to the presidency itself.

émacié, e [emasje] adj emaciated

émail, -aux [emaj, -o] nm enamel

e-mail [imel] nm email; **envoyer qch par ~** to email sth

émaillé, e [emaje] adj enamelled; (fig): **~ de** dotted with

émanciper [emɑ̃sipe] vt to emancipate; **s'émanciper** vi (fig) to become emancipated ou liberated

émaner [emane]: **~ de** vt to emanate from; (Admin) to proceed from

emballage [ɑ̃balaʒ] nm wrapping; packing; (papier) wrapping; (carton) packaging

emballer [ɑ̃bale] vt to wrap (up); (dans un carton) to pack (up); (fig: fam) to thrill (to bits); **s'emballer** vi (moteur) to race; (cheval) to bolt; (fig: personne) to get carried away

embarcadère [ɑ̃baʀkadɛʀ] nm landing stage (Brit), pier

embarcation [ɑ̃baʀkasjɔ̃] nf (small) boat, (small) craft inv

embardée [ɑ̃baʀde] nf swerve; **faire une ~** to swerve

embarquement [ɑ̃baʀkəmɑ̃] nm embarkation; (de marchandises) loading; (de passagers) boarding

embarquer [ɑ̃baʀke] vt (personne) to embark; (marchandise) to load; (fam) to cart off; (: arrêter) to nick ▷ vi (passager) to board; (Navig) to ship water; **s'embarquer** vi to board; **s'~ dans** (affaire, aventure) to embark upon

embarras [ɑ̃baʀa] nm (obstacle) hindrance; (confusion) embarrassment; (ennuis): **être dans l'~** to be in a predicament ou an awkward position; (gêne financière) to be in difficulties; **~ gastrique** stomach upset; **vous n'avez que l'~ du choix** the only problem is choosing

embarrassant, e [ɑ̃baʀasɑ̃, -ɑ̃t] adj cumbersome; embarrassing; awkward

embarrasser [ɑ̃baʀase] vt (encombrer) to clutter (up); (gêner) to hinder, hamper; (fig) to cause embarrassment to; to put in an awkward position; **s'embarrasser de** vi to burden o.s. with

embauche [ɑ̃boʃ] nf hiring; **bureau d'~** labour office

embaucher [ɑ̃boʃe] vt to take on, hire; **s'embaucher comme** vi to get (o.s.) a job as

embaumer [ɑ̃bome] vt to embalm; (parfumer) to fill with its fragrance; **~ la lavande** to be fragrant with (the scent of) lavender

embellie [ɑ̃beli] nf bright spell, brighter period

embellir [ɑ̃beliʀ] vt to make more attractive; (une histoire) to embellish ▷ vi to grow lovelier ou more attractive

embêtant, e [ɑ̃bɛtɑ̃, -ɑ̃t] adj annoying

embêtement [ɑ̃bɛtmɑ̃] nm problem, difficulty; **embêtements** nmpl trouble sg

embêter [ɑ̃bɛte] vt to bother; **s'embêter** vi (s'ennuyer) to be bored; **ça m'embête** it bothers me; **il ne s'embête pas!** (ironique) he does all right for himself!

emblée [ɑ̃ble]: **d'~** adv straightaway

embobiner [ɑ̃bɔbine] vt (enjôler): **~ qn** to get round sb

emboîter [ɑ̃bwate] vt to fit together; **s'emboîter dans** to fit into; **s'~ (l'un dans l'autre)** to fit together; **~ le pas à qn** to follow in sb's footsteps

embonpoint [ɑ̃bɔ̃pwɛ̃] nm stoutness (Brit), corpulence; **prendre de l'~** to grow stout (Brit) ou corpulent

embouchure [ɑ̃buʃyʀ] nf (Géo) mouth; (Mus) mouthpiece

embourber [ɑ̃buʀbe]: **s'embourber** vi to get stuck in the mud; (fig): **s'~ dans** to sink into

embourgeoiser [ɑ̃buʀʒwaze]: **s'embourgeoiser** vi to adopt a middle-class outlook

embouteillage [ãbutɛjaʒ] nm traffic jam, (traffic) holdup (*Brit*)

emboutir [ãbutiʀ] vt (*Tech*) to stamp; (*heurter*) to crash into, ram

embranchement [ãbʀãʃmã] nm (*routier*) junction; (*classification*) branch

embraser [ãbʀaze]: **s'embraser** vi to flare up

embrasser [ãbʀase] vt to kiss; (*sujet, période*) to embrace, encompass; (*carrière*) to embark on; (*métier*) to go in for, take up; ~ **du regard** to take in (*with eyes*); **s'embrasser** vi to kiss (each other)

embrasure [ãbʀazyʀ] nf: **dans l'~ de la porte** in the door(way)

embrayage [ãbʀɛjaʒ] nm clutch

embrayer [ãbʀeje] vi (*Auto*) to let in the clutch ▷ vt (*fig: affaire*) to set in motion; ~ **qch** to begin on sth

embrocher [ãbʀɔʃe] vt to (put on a) spit (*ou* skewer)

embrouiller [ãbʀuje] vt (*fils*) to tangle (up); (*fiches, idées, personne*) to muddle up; **s'embrouiller** vi to get in a muddle

embruns [ãbʀœ̃] nmpl sea spray *sg*

embryon [ãbʀijõ] nm embryo

embûches [ãbyʃ] nfpl pitfalls, traps

embué, e [ãbɥe] adj misted up; **yeux ~s de larmes** eyes misty with tears

embuscade [ãbyskad] nf ambush; **tendre une ~ à** to lay an ambush for

éméché, e [emeʃe] adj tipsy, merry

émeraude [em(ə)ʀod] nf emerald ▷ adj inv emerald-green

émerger [emɛʀʒe] vi to emerge; (*faire saillie, aussi fig*) to stand out

émeri [em(ə)ʀi] nm: **toile** *ou* **papier ~** emery paper

émerveillement [emɛʀvɛjmã] nm wonderment

émerveiller [emɛʀveje] vt to fill with wonder; **s'émerveiller de** vi to marvel at

émettre [emɛtʀ] vt (*son, lumière*) to give out, emit; (*message etc: Radio*) to transmit; (*billet, timbre, emprunt, chèque*) to issue; (*hypothèse, avis*) to voice, put forward; (*vœu*) to express ▷ vi to broadcast; ~ **sur ondes courtes** to broadcast on short wave

émeus *etc* [emø] *vb voir* **émouvoir**

émeute [emøt] nf riot

émietter [emjete] vt (*pain, terre*) to crumble; (*fig*) to split up, disperse; **s'émietter** vi (*pain, terre*) to crumble

émigrer [emigʀe] vi to emigrate

émincer [emɛ̃se] vt (*Culin*) to slice thinly

éminent, e [eminã, -ãt] adj distinguished

émission [emisjõ] nf (*voir émettre*) emission; (*d'un message*) transmission; (*de billet, timbre, emprunt, chèque*) issue; (*Radio, TV*) programme, broadcast

emmagasiner [ãmagazine] vt (*to put into*) store; (*fig*) to store up

emmanchure [ãmãʃyʀ] nf armhole

emmêler [ãmele] vt to tangle (up); (*fig*) to muddle up; **s'emmêler** vi to get into a tangle

emménager [ãmenaʒe] vi to move in; ~ **dans** to move into

emmener [ãm(ə)ne] vt to take (with one); (*comme otage, capture*) to take away; ~ **qn au cinéma** to take sb to the cinema

emmerder [ãmɛʀde] (*fam!*) vt to bug, bother; **s'emmerder** vi (*s'ennuyer*) to be bored stiff; **je t'emmerde!** to hell with you!

emmitoufler [ãmitufle] vt to wrap up (warmly); **s'emmitoufler** vi to wrap (o.s.) up (warmly)

émoi [emwa] nm (*agitation, effervescence*) commotion; (*trouble*) agitation; **en ~** (*sens*) excited, stirred

émoticone [emotikɔn] nm (*Inform*) smiley

émotif, -ive [emotif, -iv] adj emotional

émotion [emosjõ] nf emotion; **avoir des ~s** (*fig*) to get a fright; **donner des ~s à** to give a fright to; **sans ~** without emotion, coldly

émousser [emuse] vt to blunt; (*fig*) to dull

émouvoir [emuvwaʀ] vt (*troubler*) to stir, affect; (*toucher, attendrir*) to move; (*indigner*) to rouse; (*effrayer*) to disturb, worry; **s'émouvoir** vi to be affected; to be moved; to be roused; to be disturbed *ou* worried

empailler [ãpaje] vt to stuff

empaqueter [ãpakte] vt to pack up

emparer [ãpaʀe]: **s'emparer de** vt (*objet*) to seize, grab; (*comme otage, Mil*) to seize; (*peur etc*) to take hold of

empâter [ãpate]: **s'empâter** vi to thicken out

empêchement [ãpɛʃmã] nm (unexpected) obstacle, hitch

empêcher [ãpeʃe] vt to prevent; ~ **qn de faire** to prevent *ou* stop sb (from) doing; ~ **que qch (n')arrive/qn (ne) fasse** to prevent sth from happening/sb from doing; **il n'empêche que** nevertheless, be that as it may; **il n'a pas pu s'~ de rire** he couldn't help laughing

empereur [ãpʀœʀ] nm emperor

empester [ãpɛste] vt (*lieu*) to stink out ▷ vi to stink, reek; ~ **le tabac/le vin** to stink *ou* reek of tobacco/wine

empêtrer [ãpetʀe] vt: **s'empêtrer dans** (*fils etc, aussi fig*) to get tangled up in

emphase [ãfaz] nf pomposity, bombast; **avec ~** pompously

empiéter [ãpjete]: ~ **sur** vt to encroach upon

empiffrer [ãpifʀe]: **s'empiffrer** vi (*péj*) to stuff o.s.

empiler [ãpile] vt to pile (up), stack (up); **s'empiler** vi to pile up

empire [ãpiʀ] nm empire; (*fig*) influence; **style E~** Empire style; **sous l'~ de** in the grip of

empirer [ãpiʀe] vi to worsen, deteriorate

emplacement [ãplasmã] nm site; **sur l'~ de** on the site of

emplette [ãplɛt] nf: **faire l'~ de** to purchase; **emplettes** shopping *sg*; **faire des ~s** to go shopping

emplir [ãpliʀ] vt to fill; **s'emplir (de)** vi to fill (with)

emploi [ãplwa] nm use; (Comm, Écon): **l'~** employment; (poste) job, situation; **d'~ facile** easy to use; **le plein ~** full employment; **mode d'~** directions for use; **~ du temps** timetable, schedule

employé, e [ãplwaje] nm/f employee; **~ de bureau/banque** office/bank employee ou clerk; **~ de maison** domestic (servant)

employer [ãplwaje] vt (outil, moyen, méthode, mot) to use; (ouvrier, main-d'œuvre) to employ; **s'~ à qch/à faire** to apply ou devote o.s. to sth/to doing

employeur, -euse [ãplwajœʀ, -øz] nm/f employer

empocher [ãpɔʃe] vt to pocket

empoigner [ãpwaɲe] vt to grab; **s'empoigner** (fig) to have a row ou set-to

empoisonner [ãpwazɔne] vt to poison; (empester: air, pièce) to stink out; (fam): **~ qn** to drive sb mad; **s'empoisonner** to poison o.s.; **~ l'atmosphère** (aussi fig) to poison the atmosphere; (aussi: **il nous empoisonne l'existence**) he's the bane of our life

emporté, e [ãpɔʀte] adj (personne, caractère) fiery

emporter [ãpɔʀte] vt to take (with one); (en dérobant ou enlevant, emmener: blessés, voyageurs) to take away; (entraîner) to carry away ou along; (arracher) to tear off; (rivière, vent) to carry away; (Mil: position) to take; (avantage, approbation) to win; **s'emporter** vi (de colère) to fly into a rage, lose one's temper; **la maladie qui l'a emporté** the illness which caused his death; **l'~** to gain victory; **l'~ (sur)** to get the upper hand (of); (méthode etc) to prevail (over); **boissons à ~** take-away drinks; **plats à ~** take-away meals

empreint, e [ãpʀɛ̃, -ɛ̃t] adj: **~ de** marked with; tinged with ▷ nf (de pied, main) print; (fig) stamp, mark; **~e (digitale)** fingerprint; **~e écologique** carbon footprint

empressé, e [ãpʀese] adj attentive; (péj) overanxious to please, overattentive

empressement [ãpʀesmã] nm eagerness

empresser [ãpʀese]: **s'empresser** vi: **s'~ auprès de qn** to surround sb with attentions; **s'~ de faire** to hasten to do

emprise [ãpʀiz] nf hold, ascendancy; **sous l'~ de** under the influence of

emprisonnement [ãpʀizɔnmã] nm imprisonment

emprisonner [ãpʀizɔne] vt to imprison, jail

emprunt [ãpʀœ̃] nm borrowing no pl, loan (from debtor's point of view); (Ling etc) borrowing; **nom d'~** assumed name; **~ d'État** government ou state loan; **~ public à 5%** 5% public loan

emprunté, e [ãpʀœ̃te] adj (fig) ill-at-ease, awkward

emprunter [ãpʀœ̃te] vt to borrow; (itinéraire) to take, follow; (style, manière) to adopt, assume

ému, e [emy] pp de **émouvoir** ▷ adj excited; (gratitude) touched; (compassion) moved

 MOT-CLÉ

en [ã] prép **1** (endroit, pays) in; (direction) to; **habiter en France/ville** to live in France/ town; **aller en France/ville** to go to France/ town

2 (moment, temps) in; **en été/juin** in summer/ June; **en 3 jours/20 ans** in 3 days/20 years

3 (moyen) by; **en avion/taxi** by plane/taxi

4 (composition) made of; **c'est en verre/coton/ laine** it's (made of) glass/cotton/wool; **en métal/plastique** made of metal/plastic; **un collier en argent** a silver necklace; **en deux volumes/une pièce** in two volumes/one piece

5 (description, état): **une femme (habillée) en rouge** a woman (dressed) in red; **peindre qch en rouge** to paint sth red; **en T/étoile** T-/star-shaped; **en chemise/chaussettes** in one's shirt sleeves/socks; **en soldat** as a soldier; **en civil** in civilian clothes; **cassé en plusieurs morceaux** broken into several pieces; **en réparation** being repaired, under repair; **en vacances** on holiday; **en bonne santé** healthy, in good health; **en deuil** in mourning; **le même en plus grand** the same but ou bigger

6 (avec gérondif) while; on; **en dormant** while sleeping, as one sleeps; **en sortant** on going out, as he etc went out; **sortir en courant** to run out; **en apprenant la nouvelle, il s'est évanoui** he fainted at the news ou when he heard the news

7 (matière): **fort en math** good at maths; **expert en** expert in

8 (conformité): **en tant que** as; **en bon politicien, il …** good politician that he is, he …, like a good ou true politician, he …; **je te parle en ami** I'm talking to you as a friend ▷ pron **1** (indéfini): **j'en ai/veux** I have/want some; **en as-tu?** have you got any?; **il n'y en a pas** there isn't ou aren't any; **je n'en veux pas** I don't want any; **j'en ai deux** I've got two; **combien y en a-t-il?** how many (of them) are there?; **j'en ai assez** I've got enough (of it ou them); (j'en ai marre) I've had enough; **où en étais-je?** where was I?

2 (provenance) from there; **j'en viens** I've come from there

3 (cause): **il en est malade/perd le sommeil** he is ill/can't sleep because of it

4 (de la part de): **elle en est aimée** she is loved by him (ou them etc)

5 (complément de nom, d'adjectif, de verbe): **j'en connais les dangers** I know its ou the dangers; **j'en suis fier/ai besoin** I am proud of it/need it; **il en est ainsi** ou **de même pour moi** it's the same for me, same here

ENA [ena] *sigle f* (= *École nationale d'administration*) grande école for training civil servants

encadrement [ākadʀəmā] *nm* framing; training; (*de porte*) frame; **~ du crédit** credit restrictions

encadrer [ākadʀe] *vt* (*tableau, image*) to frame; (*fig: entourer*) to surround; (*personnel, soldats etc*) to train; (*Comm: crédit*) to restrict

encaissé, e [ākese] *adj* (*vallée*) steep-sided; (*rivière*) with steep banks

encaisser [ākese] *vt* (*chèque*) to cash; (*argent*) to collect; (*fig: coup, défaite*) to take

encart [ākaʀ] *nm* insert; **~ publicitaire** publicity insert

en-cas [āka] *nm inv* snack

encastré, e [ākastʀe] *adj* (*four, baignoire*) built-in

enceinte [āsɛ̃t] *adj f:* **~ (de six mois)** (six months) pregnant ▷ *nf* (*mur*) wall; (*espace*) enclosure; **~ (acoustique)** speaker

encens [āsā] *nm* incense

encercler [āsɛʀkle] *vt* to surround

enchaîner [āʃene] *vt* to chain up; (*mouvements, séquences*) to link (together) ▷ *vi* to carry on

enchanté, e [āʃāte] *adj* (*ravi*) delighted; (*ensorcelé*) enchanted; **~ (de faire votre connaissance)** pleased to meet you, how do you do?

enchantement [āʃātmā] *nm* delight; (*magie*) enchantment; **comme par ~** as if by magic

enchère [āʃɛʀ] *nf* bid; **faire une ~** to (make a) bid; **mettre/vendre aux ~s** to put up for (sale by)/sell by auction; **les ~s montent** the bids are rising; **faire monter les ~s** (*fig*) to raise the bidding

enchevêtrer [āʃvetʀe] *vt* to tangle (up)

enclencher [āklāʃe] *vt* (*mécanisme*) to engage; (*fig: affaire*) to set in motion; **s'enclencher** *vi* to engage

enclin, e [āklɛ̃, -in] *adj:* **~ à qch/à faire** inclined *ou* prone to sth/to do

enclos [āklo] *nm* enclosure; (*clôture*) fence

enclume [āklym] *nf* anvil

encoche [ākɔʃ] *nf* notch

encoignure [ākɔɲyʀ] *nf* corner

encolure [ākɔlyʀ] *nf* (*tour de cou*) collar size; (*col, cou*) neck

encombrant, e [ākɔ̃bʀā, -āt] *adj* cumbersome, bulky

encombre [ākɔ̃bʀ]: **sans ~** *adv* without mishap *ou* incident

encombrement [ākɔ̃bʀəmā] *nm* (*d'un lieu*) cluttering (up); (*d'un objet: dimensions*) bulk; **être pris dans un ~** to be stuck in a traffic jam

encombrer [ākɔ̃bʀe] *vt* to clutter (up); (*gêner*) to hamper; **s'encombrer de** *vi* (*bagages etc*) to load *ou* burden o.s. with; **~ le passage** to block *ou* obstruct the way

encontre [ākɔ̃tʀ]: **à l'~ de** *prép* against, counter to

 MOT-CLÉ

encore [ākɔʀ] *adv* **1** (*continuation*) still; **il y travaille encore** he's still working on it; **pas encore** not yet

2 (*de nouveau*) again; **j'irai encore demain** I'll go again tomorrow; **encore une fois** (once) again

3 (*en plus*) more; **encore un peu de viande?** a little more meat?; **encore un effort** one last effort; **encore deux jours** two more days

4 (*intensif*) even, still; **encore plus fort/mieux** even louder/better, louder/better still; **hier encore** even yesterday; **non seulement ..., mais encore ...** not only ..., but also ...; **encore!** (*insatisfaction*) not again!; **quoi encore?** what now?

5 (*restriction*) even so *ou* then, only; **encore pourrais-je le faire si ...** even so, I might be able to do it if ...; **si encore** if only; **encore que** *conj* although

encouragement [ākuʀaʒmā] *nm* encouragement; (*récompense*) incentive

encourager [ākuʀaʒe] *vt* to encourage; **~ qn à faire qch** to encourage sb to do sth

encourir [ākuʀiʀ] *vt* to incur

encrasser [ākʀase] *vt* to foul up; (*Auto etc*) to soot up

encre [ākʀ] *nf* ink; **~ de Chine** Indian ink; **~ indélébile** indelible ink; **~ sympathique** invisible ink

encrier [ākʀije] *nm* inkwell

encroûter [ākʀute]: **s'encroûter** *vi* (*fig*) to get into a rut, get set in one's ways

encyclopédie [āsiklɔpedi] *nf* encyclopaedia (Brit), encyclopedia (US)

endetter [ādete] *vt*, **s'endetter** *vi* to get into debt

endiablé, e [ādjable] *adj* furious; (*enfant*) boisterous

endimanché, e [ādimāʃe] *adj* in one's Sunday best

endive [ādiv] *nf* chicory *no pl*

endoctriner [ādɔktʀine] *vt* to indoctrinate

endommager [ādɔmaʒe] *vt* to damage

endormi, e [ādɔʀmi] *pp de* **endormir** ▷ *adj* (*personne*) asleep; (*fig: indolent, lent*) sluggish; (*engourdi: main, pied*) numb

endormir [ādɔʀmiʀ] *vt* to put to sleep; (*chaleur etc*) to send to sleep; (*Méd: dent, nerf*) to anaesthetize; (*fig: soupçons*) to allay; **s'endormir** *vi* to fall asleep, go to sleep

endosser [ādose] *vt* (*responsabilité*) to take, shoulder; (*chèque*) to endorse; (*uniforme, tenue*) to put on, don

endroit [ādʀwa] *nm* place; (*localité*): **les gens de l'~** the local people; (*opposé à l'envers*) right side; **à cet ~** in this place; **à l'~** right side out; the right way up; (*vêtement*) the right way out; **à l'~ de** *prép* regarding, with regard to; **par ~s** in places; (*objet posé*) the right way round

enduire [ɑ̃dɥiʀ] vt to coat; ~ **qch de** to coat sth with

enduit, e [ɑ̃dɥi, -it] pp de **enduire** ▷ nm coating

endurance [ɑ̃dyʀɑ̃s] nf endurance

endurant, e [ɑ̃dyʀɑ̃, -ɑ̃t] adj tough, hardy

endurcir [ɑ̃dyʀsiʀ] vt (physiquement) to toughen; (moralement) to harden; **s'endurcir** vi (physiquement) to become tougher; (moralement) to become hardened

endurer [ɑ̃dyʀe] vt to endure, bear

énergétique [enɛʀʒetik] adj (ressources etc) energy cpd; (aliment) energizing

énergie [enɛʀʒi] nf (Physique) energy; (Tech) power; (fig: physique) energy; (: morale) vigour, spirit; ~ **éolienne/solaire** wind/solar power

énergique [enɛʀʒik] adj energetic; vigorous; (mesures) drastic, stringent

énervant, e [enɛʀvɑ̃, -ɑ̃t] adj irritating, annoying

énervé, e [enɛʀve] adj nervy, on edge; (agacé) irritated

énerver [enɛʀve] vt to irritate, annoy; **s'énerver** vi to get excited, get worked up

enfance [ɑ̃fɑ̃s] nf (âge) childhood; (fig) infancy; (enfants) children pl; **c'est l'~ de l'art** it's child's play; **petite ~** infancy; **souvenir/ami d'~** childhood memory/ friend; **retomber en ~** to lapse into one's second childhood

enfant [ɑ̃fɑ̃] nm/f child; ~ **adoptif/naturel** adopted/natural child; **bon ~** adj good-natured, easy-going; ~ **de chœur** nm (Rel) altar boy; ~ **prodige** child prodigy; ~ **unique** only child

enfantillage [ɑ̃fɑ̃tijaʒ] nm (péj) childish behaviour no pl

enfantin, e [ɑ̃fɑ̃tɛ̃, -in] adj childlike; (péj) childish; (langage) children's cpd

enfer [ɑ̃fɛʀ] nm hell; **allure/bruit d'~** horrendous speed/noise

enfermer [ɑ̃fɛʀme] vt to shut up; (à clef, interner) to lock up; **s'enfermer** to shut o.s. away; **s'~ à clé** to lock o.s. in; **s'~ dans la solitude/le mutisme** to retreat into solitude/silence

enfiévré, e [ɑ̃fjevʀe] adj (fig) feverish

enfiler [ɑ̃file] vt (vêtement): ~ **qch** to slip sth on, slip into sth; (insérer): ~ **qch dans** to stick sth into; (rue, couloir) to take; (perles) to string; (aiguille) to thread; **s'enfiler dans** vi to disappear into

enfin [ɑ̃fɛ̃] adv at last; (en énumérant) lastly; (de restriction, résignation) still; (eh bien) well; (pour conclure) in a word; (somme toute) after all

enflammer [ɑ̃flame] vt to set fire to; (Méd) to inflame; **s'enflammer** vi to catch fire; (Méd) to become inflamed

enflé, e [ɑ̃fle] adj swollen; (péj: style) bombastic, turgid

enfler [ɑ̃fle] vi to swell (up); **s'enfler** vi to swell

enfoncer [ɑ̃fɔ̃se] vt (clou) to drive in; (faire pénétrer): ~ **qch dans** to push (ou drive) sth into; (forcer: porte) to break open; (: plancher) to cause to cave in; (défoncer: côtes etc) to smash; (fam: surpasser) to lick, beat (hollow) ▷ vi (dans la vase etc) to sink in; (sol, surface porteuse) to give way; **s'enfoncer** vi to sink; **s'~ dans** to sink into; (forêt, ville) to disappear into; ~ **un chapeau sur la tête** to cram ou jam a hat on one's head; ~ **qn dans la dette** to drag sb into debt

enfouir [ɑ̃fwiʀ] vt (dans le sol) to bury; (dans un tiroir etc) to tuck away; **s'enfouir dans/sous** to bury o.s. in/under

enfourcher [ɑ̃fuʀʃe] vt to mount; ~ **son dada** (fig) to get on one's hobby-horse

enfreindre [ɑ̃fʀɛ̃dʀ] vt to infringe, break

enfuir [ɑ̃fɥiʀ]: **s'enfuir** vi to run away ou off

enfumer [ɑ̃fyme] vt to smoke out

engageant, e [ɑ̃gaʒɑ̃, -ɑ̃t] adj attractive, appealing

engagement [ɑ̃gaʒmɑ̃] nm taking on, engaging; starting; investing; (promesse) commitment; (Mil: combat) engagement; (: recrutement) enlistment; (Sport) entry; **prendre l'~ de faire** to undertake to do; **sans ~** (Comm) without obligation

engager [ɑ̃gaʒe] vt (embaucher) to take on; (: artiste) to engage; (commencer) to start; (lier) to bind, commit; (impliquer, entraîner) to involve; (investir) to invest, lay out; (faire intervenir) to engage; (Sport: concurrents, chevaux) to enter; (introduire: clé) to insert; (inciter): ~ **qn à faire** to urge sb to do; (faire pénétrer): ~ **qch dans** to insert sth into; ~ **qn à qch** to urge sth on sb; **s'engager** vi to get taken on; (Mil) to enlist; (promettre, politiquement) to commit o.s.; (débuter: conversation etc) to start (up); **s'~ à faire** to undertake to do; **s'~ dans** (rue, passage) to turn into, enter; (s'emboîter) to engage ou fit into; (fig: affaire, discussion) to enter into, embark on

engelures [ɑ̃ʒlyʀ] nfpl chilblains

engendrer [ɑ̃ʒɑ̃dʀe] vt to father; (fig) to create, breed

engin [ɑ̃ʒɛ̃] nm machine; (outil) instrument; (Auto) vehicle; (péj) gadget; (Aviat: avion) aircraft inv; (: missile) missile; ~ **blindé** armoured vehicle; ~ **(explosif)** (explosive) device; ~**s (spéciaux)** missiles

englober [ɑ̃glɔbe] vt to include

engloutir [ɑ̃glutiʀ] vt to swallow up; (fig: dépenses) to devour; **s'engloutir** vi to be engulfed

engoncé, e [ɑ̃gɔ̃se] adj: ~ **dans** cramped in

engorger [ɑ̃gɔʀʒe] vt to obstruct, block; **s'engorger** vi to become blocked

engouement [ɑ̃gumɑ̃] nm (sudden) passion

engouffrer [ɑ̃gufʀe] vt to swallow up, devour; **s'engouffrer dans** to rush into

engourdir [ɑ̃guʀdiʀ] vt to numb; (fig) to dull, blunt; **s'engourdir** vi to go numb

engrais [ãgʀɛ] nm manure; **~ (chimique)** (chemical) fertilizer; **~ organique/ inorganique** organic/inorganic fertilizer

engraisser [ãgʀese] vt to fatten (up); (terre: fertiliser) to fertilize ▷ vi (péj) to get fat(ter)

engrenage [ãgʀənaʒ] nm gears pl, gearing; (fig) chain

engueuler [ãgœle] vt (fam) to bawl at ou out

enhardir [ãaʀdiʀ]: **s'enhardir** vi to grow bolder

énigme [enigm] nf riddle

enivrer [ãnivʀe] vt: **s'enivrer** to get drunk; **s'~ de** (fig) to become intoxicated with

enjambée [ãʒãbe] nf stride; **d'une ~** with one stride

enjamber [ãʒãbe] vt to stride over; (pont etc) to span, straddle

enjeu, x [ãʒø] nm stakes pl

enjôler [ãʒole] vt to coax, wheedle

enjoliver [ãʒolive] vt to embellish

enjoliveur [ãʒolivœʀ] nm (Auto) hub cap

enjoué, e [ãʒwe] adj playful

enlacer [ãlase] vt (étreindre) to embrace, hug; (lianes) to wind round, entwine

enlaidir [ãlediʀ] vt to make ugly ▷ vi to become ugly

enlèvement [ãlɛvmã] nm removal; (rapt) abduction, kidnapping; **l'~ des ordures ménagères** refuse collection

enlever [ãl(ə)ve] vt (ôter: gén) to remove; (: vêtement, lunettes) to take off; (: Méd: organe) to remove; (emporter: ordures etc) to collect, take away; (kidnapper) to abduct, kidnap; (obtenir: prix, contrat) to win; (Mil: position) to take; (morceau de piano etc) to execute with spirit ou brio; (prendre): **~ qch à qn** to take sth (away) from sb; **s'enlever** vi (tache) to come out ou off; **la maladie qui nous l'a enlevé** (euphémisme) the illness which took him from us

enliser [ãlize]: **s'enliser** vi to sink, get stuck; (dialogue etc) to get bogged down

enneigé, e [ãneʒe] adj snowy; (col) snowed-up; (maison) snowed-in

ennemi, e [ɛnmi] adj hostile; (Mil) enemy cpd ▷ nm/f enemy; **être ~ de** to be strongly averse ou opposed to

ennui [ãnɥi] nm (lassitude) boredom; (difficulté) trouble no pl; **avoir des ~s** to have problems; **s'attirer des ~s** to cause problems for o.s.

ennuyer [ãnɥije] vt to bother; (lasser) to bore; **s'ennuyer** vi to be bored; (s'ennuyer de: regretter) to miss; **si cela ne vous ennuie pas** if it's no trouble to you

ennuyeux, -euse [ãnɥijø, -øz] adj boring, tedious; (agaçant) annoying

énoncé [enõse] nm terms pl; wording; (Ling) utterance

énoncer [enõse] vt to say, express; (conditions) to set out, lay down, state

enorgueillir [ãnɔʀɡœjiʀ]: **s'enorgueillir de** vt to pride o.s. on; to boast

énorme [enɔʀm] adj enormous, huge

énormément [enɔʀmemã] adv enormously, tremendously; **~ de neige/gens** an enormous amount of snow/number of people

énormité [enɔʀmite] nf enormity, hugeness; (propos) outrageous remark

enquérir [ãkeʀiʀ]: **s'enquérir de** vt to inquire about

enquête [ãkɛt] nf (de journaliste, de police) investigation; (judiciaire, administrative) inquiry; (sondage d'opinion) survey

enquêter [ãkete] vi to investigate; to hold an inquiry; (faire un sondage): **~ (sur)** to do a survey (on), carry out an opinion poll (on)

enquiers, enquière etc [ãkjɛʀ] vb voir **enquérir**

enquiquiner [ãkikine] vt to rile, irritate

enraciné, e [ãʀasine] adj deep-rooted

enragé, e [ãʀaʒe] adj (Méd) rabid, with rabies; (furieux) furiously angry; (fig) fanatical; **~ de** wild about

enrageant, e [ãʀaʒã, -ãt] adj infuriating

enrager [ãʀaʒe] vi to be furious, be in a rage; **faire ~ qn** to make sb wild with anger

enrayer [ãʀeje] vt to check, stop; **s'enrayer** vi (arme à feu) to jam

enregistrement [ãʀ(ə)ʒistʀəmã] nm recording; (Admin) registration; **~ des bagages** (à l'aéroport) baggage check-in; **~ magnétique** tape-recording

enregistrer [ãʀ(ə)ʒistʀe] vt (Mus) to record; (Inform) to save; (remarquer, noter) to note, record; (Comm: commande) to note, enter; (fig: mémoriser) to make a mental note of; (Admin) to register; (aussi: **faire ~**: bagages: par train) to register; (: à l'aéroport) to check in

enrhumé, e [ãʀyme] adj: **il est ~** he has a cold

enrhumer [ãʀyme]: **s'enrhumer** vi to catch a cold

enrichir [ãʀiʃiʀ] vt to make rich(er); (fig) to enrich; **s'enrichir** vi to get rich(er)

enrober [ãʀobe] vt: **~ qch de** to coat sth with; (fig) to wrap sth up in

enrôler [ãʀole] vt to enlist; **s'enrôler (dans)** vi to enlist (in)

enrouer [ãʀwe]: **s'enrouer** vi to go hoarse

enrouler [ãʀule] vt (fil, corde) to wind (up); **s'enrouler** to coil up; **~ qch autour de** to wind sth (a)round

ensanglanté, e [ãsãglãte] adj covered with blood

enseignant, e [ãsɛɲã, -ãt] adj teaching ▷ nm/f teacher

enseigne [ãsɛɲ] nf sign ▷ nm: **~ de vaisseau** lieutenant; **à telle ~ que** so much so that; **être logés à la même ~** (fig) to be in the same boat; **~ lumineuse** neon sign

enseignement [ãsɛɲ(ə)mã] nm teaching; (Admin) education; **~ ménager** home economics; **~ primaire** primary (Brit) ou

grade school (US) education; **~ secondaire**
secondary (Brit) ou high school (US) education
enseigner [ãseɲe] vt, vi to teach; **~ qch à qn/à
qn que** to teach sb sth/sb that
ensemble [ãsãbl] adv together ▷ nm
(assemblage, Math) set; (totalité): **l'~ du/de la**
the whole ou entire; (vêtements): **outfit**;
(vêtement féminin) ensemble, suit; (unité,
harmonie) unity; (résidentiel) housing
development; **aller ~** to go together;
impression/idée d'~ overall ou general
impression/idea; **dans l'~** (en gros) on the
whole; **dans son ~** overall, in general;
~ vocal/musical vocal/musical ensemble
ensemencer [ãsmãse] vt to sow
ensevelir [ãsəvliʁ] vt to bury
ensoleillé, e [ãsɔleje] adj sunny
ensommeillé, e [ãsɔmeje] adj sleepy, drowsy
ensorceler [ãsɔʁsəle] vt to enchant, bewitch
ensuite [ãsɥit] adv then, next; (plus tard)
afterwards, later; **~ de quoi** after which
ensuivre [ãsɥivʁ]: **s'ensuivre** vi to follow,
ensue; **il s'ensuit que ...** it follows that ...; **et
tout ce qui s'ensuit** and all that goes with it
entaille [ãtaj] nf (encoche) notch; (blessure) cut;
se faire une ~ to cut o.s.
entamer [ãtame] vt (pain, bouteille) to start;
(hostilités, pourparlers) to open; (fig: altérer) to
make a dent in; to damage
entasser [ãtase] vt (empiler) to pile up, heap
up; (tenir à l'étroit) to cram together;
s'entasser vi (s'amonceler) to pile up; to cram;
s'~ dans to cram into
entendre [ãtãdʁ] vt to hear; (comprendre) to
understand; (vouloir dire) to mean; (vouloir):
~ être obéi/que to intend ou mean to be
obeyed/that; **j'ai entendu dire que** I've
heard (it said) that; **je suis heureux de vous
l'~ dire** I'm pleased to hear you say it;
~ parler de to hear of; **laisser ~ que, donner
à ~ que** to let it be understood that; **~ raison**
to see sense, listen to reason; **qu'est-ce qu'il
ne faut pas ~!** whatever next!; **j'ai mal
entendu** I didn't catch what was said; **je
vous entends très mal** I can hardly hear
you; **s'entendre** vi (sympathiser) to get on; (se
mettre d'accord) to agree; **s'~ à qch/à faire** (être
compétent) to be good at sth/doing; **ça
s'entend** (est audible) it's audible; **je
m'entends** I mean; **entendons-nous!** let's
be clear about what we mean
entendu, e [ãtãdy] pp de **entendre** ▷ adj
(réglé) agreed; (au courant: air) knowing; **étant
~ que** since (it's understood ou agreed that);
(c'est) **~** all right, agreed; **c'est ~** (concession)
all right, granted; **bien ~** of course
entente [ãtãt] nf (entre amis, pays)
understanding, harmony; (accord, traité)
agreement, understanding; **à double ~** (sens)
with a double meaning
entériner [ãteʁine] vt to ratify, confirm
enterrement [ãtɛʁmã] nm burying;

(cérémonie) funeral, burial; (cortège funèbre)
funeral procession
enterrer [ãteʁe] vt to bury
entêtant, e [ãtɛtã, -ãt] adj heady
en-tête [ãtɛt] nm heading; (de papier à lettres)
letterhead; **papier à ~** headed notepaper
entêté, e [ãtete] adj stubborn
entêter [ãtete]: **s'entêter** vi: **s'~ (à faire)** to
persist in doing
enthousiasme [ãtuzjasm] nm enthusiasm;
avec ~ enthusiastically
enthousiasmer [ãtuzjasme] vt to fill with
enthusiasm; **s'~ (pour qch)** to get
enthusiastic (about sth)
enthousiaste [ãtuzjast] adj enthusiastic
enticher [ãtiʃe]: **s'enticher de** vt to become
infatuated with
entier, -ière [ãtje, -jɛʁ] adj (non entamé, en
totalité) whole; (total, complet: satisfaction etc)
complete; (fig: caractère) unbending, averse to
compromise ▷ nm (Math) whole; **en ~** totally;
in its entirety; **se donner tout ~ à qch** to
devote o.s. completely to sth; **lait ~** full-
cream milk; **pain ~** wholemeal bread;
nombre ~ whole number
entièrement [ãtjɛʁmã] adv entirely,
completely, wholly
entonner [ãtɔne] vt (chanson) to strike up
entonnoir [ãtɔnwaʁ] nm (ustensile) funnel;
(trou) shell-hole, crater
entorse [ãtɔʁs] nf (Méd) sprain; (fig): **~ à la
loi/au règlement** infringement of the law/
rule; **se faire une ~ à la cheville/au poignet**
to sprain one's ankle/wrist
entortiller [ãtɔʁtije] vt (envelopper): **~ qch
dans/avec** to wrap sth in/with; (enrouler): **~
qch autour de** to twist ou wind sth (a)round;
(fam): **~ qn** to get (a)round sb; (: duper) to
hoodwink sb (Brit), trick sb; **s'entortiller
dans** vi (draps) to roll o.s. up in; (fig: réponses)
to get tangled up in
entourage [ãtuʁaʒ] nm circle; (famille)
family (circle); (d'une vedette etc) entourage;
(ce qui enclôt) surround
entouré, e [ãtuʁe] adj (recherché, admiré)
popular; **~ de** surrounded by
entourer [ãtuʁe] vt to surround; (apporter son
soutien à) to rally round; **~ de** to surround
with; (trait) to encircle with; **s'entourer de** vi
to surround o.s. with; **s'~ de précautions** to
take all possible precautions
entracte [ãtʁakt] nm interval
entraide [ãtʁɛd] nf mutual aid ou assistance
entrain [ãtʁɛ̃] nm spirit; **avec ~** (répondre,
travailler) energetically; **faire qch sans ~** to do
sth half-heartedly ou without enthusiasm
entraînement [ãtʁɛnmã] nm training;
(Tech): **~ à chaîne/galet** chain/wheel drive;
manquer d'~ to be unfit; **~ par ergots/**
friction (Inform) tractor/friction feed
entraîner [ãtʁene] vt (tirer: wagons) to pull;
(charrier) to carry ou drag along; (Tech) to drive

(*emmener: personne*) to take (off); (*mener à l'assaut, influencer*) to lead; (*Sport*) to train; (*impliquer*) to entail; (*causer*) to lead to, bring about; **~ qn à faire** (*inciter*) to lead sb to do; **s'entraîner** *vi* (*Sport*) to train; **s'~ à qch/à faire** to train o.s. for sth/to do

entraîneur [ɑ̃tʀɛnœʀ] *nm/f* (*Sport*) coach, trainer ▷ *nm* (*Hippisme*) trainer

entraver [ɑ̃tʀave] *vt* (*circulation*) to hold up; (*action, progrès*) to hinder, hamper

entre [ɑ̃tʀ] *prép* between; (*parmi*) among(st); **l'un d'~ eux/nous** one of them/us; **le meilleur d'~ eux/nous** the best of them/us; **ils préfèrent rester ~ eux** they prefer to keep to themselves; **~ autres (choses)** among other things; **~ nous, ...** between ourselves ..., between you and me ...; **ils se battent ~ eux** they are fighting among(st) themselves

entrebâillé, e [ɑ̃tʀəbaje] *adj* half-open, ajar

entrechoquer [ɑ̃tʀəʃɔke]: **s'entrechoquer** *vi* to knock ou bang together

entrecôte [ɑ̃tʀəkot] *nf* entrecôte ou rib steak

entrecouper [ɑ̃tʀəkupe] *vt*, **~ qch de** to intersperse sth with; **~ un récit/voyage de** to interrupt a story/journey with; **s'entrecouper** *vi* (*traits, lignes*) to cut across each other

entrecroiser [ɑ̃tʀəkʀwaze] *vt*, **s'entrecroiser** *vi* to intertwine

entrée [ɑ̃tʀe] *nf* entrance; (*accès: au cinéma etc*) admission; (*billet*) (admission) ticket; (*Culin*) first course; (*Comm: de marchandises*) entry; (*Inform*) entry, input; **entrées** *nfpl*: **avoir ses ~s chez** ou **auprès de** to be a welcome visitor to; **d'~** *adv* from the outset; **erreur d'~** input error; **"~ interdite"** "no admittance ou entry"; **~ des artistes** stage door; **~ en matière** introduction; **~ principale** main entrance; **~ en scène** entrance; **~ de service** service entrance

entrefaites [ɑ̃tʀəfɛt]: **sur ces ~** *adv* at this juncture

entrefilet [ɑ̃tʀəfilɛ] *nm* (*article*) paragraph, short report

entrejambes [ɑ̃tʀəʒɑ̃b] *nm inv* crotch

entrelacer [ɑ̃tʀəlase] *vt*, **s'entrelacer** *vi* to intertwine

entremêler [ɑ̃tʀəmele] *vt*: **~ qch de** to (inter) mingle sth with

entremets [ɑ̃tʀəmɛ] *nm* (cream) dessert

entremise [ɑ̃tʀəmiz] *nf* intervention; **par l'~ de** through

entreposer [ɑ̃tʀəpoze] *vt* to store, put into storage

entrepôt [ɑ̃tʀəpo] *nm* warehouse

entreprenant, e [ɑ̃tʀəpʀənɑ̃, -ɑ̃t] *vb voir* **entreprendre** ▷ *adj* (*actif*) enterprising; (*trop galant*) forward

entreprendre [ɑ̃tʀəpʀɑ̃dʀ] *vt* (*se lancer dans*) to undertake; (*commencer*) to begin ou start (upon); (*personne*) to buttonhole; **~ qn sur un**

sujet to tackle sb on a subject; **~ de faire** to undertake to do

entrepreneur, -euse [ɑ̃tʀəpʀənœʀ] *nm/f*: **~ (en bâtiment)** (building) contractor; **~ de pompes funèbres** funeral director, undertaker

entrepris, e [ɑ̃tʀəpʀi, -iz] *pp de* **entreprendre** ▷ *nf* (*société*) firm, business; (*action*) undertaking, venture

entrer [ɑ̃tʀe] *vi* to go (ou come) in, enter ▷ *vt* (*Inform*) to input, enter; (*faire*) **~ qch dans** to get sth into; **~ dans** (*gén*) to enter; (*pièce*) to go (ou come) into, enter; (*club*) to join; (*heurter*) to run into; (*partager: vues, craintes de qn*) to share; (*être une composante de*) to go into; (*faire partie de*) to form part of; **~ au couvent** to enter a convent; **~ à l'hôpital** to go into hospital; **~ dans le système** (*Inform*) to log in; **~ en fureur** to become angry; **~ en ébullition** to start to boil; **~ en scène** to come on stage; **laisser ~ qn/qch** to let sb/sth in; **faire ~** (*visiteur*) to show in

entresol [ɑ̃tʀəsɔl] *nm* entresol, mezzanine

entre-temps [ɑ̃tʀətɑ̃] *adv* meanwhile, (in the) meantime

entretenir [ɑ̃tʀət(ə)niʀ] *vt* to maintain; (*amitié*) to keep alive; (*famille, maîtresse*) to support, keep; **~ qn (de)** to speak to sb (about); **s'entretenir (de)** to converse (about); **~ qn dans l'erreur** to let sb remain in ignorance

entretien [ɑ̃tʀətjɛ̃] *nm* maintenance; (*discussion*) discussion, talk; (*pour un emploi*) interview; **frais d'~** maintenance charges

entrevoir [ɑ̃tʀəvwaʀ] *vt* (*à peine*) to make out; (*brièvement*) to catch a glimpse of

entrevu, e [ɑ̃tʀəvy] *pp de* **entrevoir** ▷ *nf* meeting; (*audience*) interview

entrouvert, e [ɑ̃tʀuvɛʀ, -ɛʀt] *adj* half-open

énumérer [enymeʀe] *vt* to list, enumerate

envahir [ɑ̃vaiʀ] *vt* to invade; (*inquiétude, peur*) to come over

envahissant, e [ɑ̃vaisɑ̃, -ɑ̃t] *adj* (*péj: personne*) interfering, intrusive

enveloppe [ɑ̃v(ə)lɔp] *nf* (*de lettre*) envelope; (*Tech*) casing; outer layer; (*crédits*) budget; **mettre sous ~** to put in an envelope; **~ autocollante** self-seal envelope; **~ budgétaire** budget; **~ à fenêtre** window envelope

envelopper [ɑ̃v(ə)lɔpe] *vt* to wrap; (*fig*) to envelop, shroud; **s'~ dans un châle/une couverture** to wrap o.s. in a shawl/blanket

envenimer [ɑ̃vnime] *vt* to aggravate; **s'envenimer** *vi* (*plaie*) to fester; (*situation, relations*) to worsen

envergure [ɑ̃vɛʀgyʀ] *nf* (*d'un oiseau, avion*) wingspan; (*fig: étendue*) scope; (: *valeur*) calibre

enverrai *etc* [ɑ̃veʀe] *vb voir* **envoyer**

envers [ɑ̃vɛʀ] *prép* towards, to ▷ *nm* other side; (*d'une étoffe*) wrong side; **à l'~**

(verticalement) upside down; (pull) back to front; (vêtement) inside out; **~ et contre tous** ou **tout** against all opposition

envie [ãvi] nf (sentiment) envy; (souhait) desire, wish; (tache sur la peau) birthmark; (filet de peau) hangnail; **avoir ~ de** to feel like; (désir plus fort) to want; **avoir ~ de faire** to feel like doing; to want to do; **avoir ~ que** to wish that; **donner à qn l'~ de faire** to make sb want to do; **cette glace me fait ~** I fancy some of that ice cream

envier [ãvje] vt to envy; **~ qch à qn** to envy sb sth; **n'avoir rien à ~ à** to have no cause to be envious of

envieux, -euse [ãvjø, -øz] adj envious

environ [ãvirõ] adv: **~ 3 h/2 km, 3 h/2km ~** (around) about 3 o'clock/2 km, 3 o'clock/2 km or so; voir aussi **environs**

environnant, e [ãvirõnã, -ãt] adj surrounding

environnement [ãvirõnmã] nm environment

environs [ãvirõ] nmpl surroundings; **aux ~ de** around

envisager [ãvizaʒe] vt (examiner, considérer) to contemplate, view; (avoir en vue) to envisage; **~ de faire** to consider doing

envoi [ãvwa] nm sending; (paquet) parcel, consignment; **~ contre remboursement** (Comm) cash on delivery

envoler [ãvɔle]: **s'envoler** vi (oiseau) to fly away ou off; (avion) to take off; (papier, feuille) to blow away; (fig) to vanish (into thin air)

envoûter [ãvute] vt to bewitch

envoyé, e [ãvwaje] nm/f (Pol) envoy; (Presse) correspondent; **~ spécial** special correspondent ▷ adj: **bien ~** (remarque, réponse) well-aimed

envoyer [ãvwaje] vt to send; (lancer) to hurl, throw; **~ une gifle/un sourire à qn** to aim a blow/flash a smile at sb; **~ les couleurs** to run up the colours; **~ chercher** to send for; **~ par le fond** (bateau) to send to the bottom; **~ promener qn** (fam) to send sb packing; **~ un SMS à qn** to text sb

épagneul, e [epaɲœl] nm/f spaniel

épais, se [epɛ, -ɛs] adj thick

épaisseur [epesœr] nf thickness

épancher [epãʃe] vt to give vent to; **s'épancher** vi to open one's heart; (liquide) to pour out

épanouir [epanwir]: **s'épanouir** vi (fleur) to bloom, open out; (visage) to light up; (fig: se développer) to blossom (out); (: mentalement) to open up

épargne [eparɲ] nf saving; **l'~-logement** property investment

épargner [eparɲe] vt to save; (ne pas tuer ou endommager) to spare ▷ vi to save; **~ qch à qn** to spare sb sth

éparpiller [eparpije] vt to scatter; (pour répartir) to disperse; (fig: efforts) to dissipate; **s'éparpiller** vi to scatter; (fig) to dissipate one's efforts

épars, e [epar, -ars] adj (maisons) scattered; (cheveux) sparse

épatant, e [epatã, -ãt] adj (fam) super, splendid

épater [epate] vt (fam) to amaze; (impressionner) to impress

épaule [epol] nf shoulder

épauler [epole] vt (aider) to back up, support; (arme) to raise (to one's shoulder) ▷ vi to (take) aim

épaulette [epolet] nf (Mil, d'un veston) epaulette; (de combinaison) shoulder strap

épave [epav] nf wreck

épée [epe] nf sword

épeler [ep(ə)le] vt to spell

éperdu, e [eperdy] adj (personne) overcome; (sentiment) passionate; (fuite) frantic

éperon [eprõ] nm spur

épervier [epervje] nm (Zool) sparrowhawk; (Pêche) casting net

épi [epi] nm (de blé, d'orge) ear; (de maïs) cob; **~ de cheveux** tuft of hair; **stationnement/ se garer en ~** parking/to park at an angle to the kerb

épice [epis] nf spice

épicé, e [epise] adj highly spiced, spicy; (fig) spicy

épicer [epise] vt to spice; (fig) to add spice to

épicerie [episri] nf (magasin) grocer's shop; (denrées) groceries pl; **~ fine** delicatessen (shop)

épicier, -ière [episje, -jɛr] nm/f grocer

épidémie [epidemi] nf epidemic

épiderme [epiderm] nm skin, epidermis

épier [epje] vt to spy on, watch closely; (occasion) to look out for

épilepsie [epilɛpsi] nf epilepsy

épiler [epile] vt (jambes) to remove the hair from; (sourcils) to pluck; **s'~ les jambes** to remove the hair from one's legs; **s'~ les sourcils** to pluck one's eyebrows; **se faire ~** to get unwanted hair removed; **crème à ~** hair-removing ou depilatory cream; **pince à ~** eyebrow tweezers

épilogue [epilɔg] nm (fig) conclusion, dénouement

épiloguer [epilɔge] vi: **~ sur** to hold forth on

épinards [epinar] nmpl spinach sg

épine [epin] nf thorn, prickle; (d'oursin etc) spine, prickle; **~ dorsale** backbone

épineux, -euse [epinø, -øz] adj thorny, prickly

épingle [epɛ̃gl] nf pin; **tirer son ~ du jeu** to play one's game well; **tiré à quatre ~s** well turned-out; **monter qch en ~** to build sth up, make a thing of sth (fam); **~ à chapeau** hatpin; **~ à cheveux** hairpin; **virage en ~ à cheveux** hairpin bend; **~ de cravate** tie pin; **~ de nourrice** ou **de sûreté** ou **double** safety pin, nappy (Brit) ou diaper (US) pin

épingler [epɛ̃gle] vt (badge, décoration): **~ qch sur** to pin sth on(to); (Couture: tissu, robe) to pin together; (*fam*) to catch, nick

épique [epik] *adj* epic

épisode [epizɔd] *nm* episode; **film/roman à ~s** serialized film/novel, serial

épisodique [epizɔdik] *adj* occasional

éploré, e [eplɔʀe] *adj* in tears, tearful

épluche-légumes [eplyʃlegym] *nm inv* potato peeler

éplucher [eplyʃe] *vt* (*fruit, légumes*) to peel; (*comptes, dossier*) to go over with a fine-tooth comb

épluchures [eplyʃyʀ] *nfpl* peelings

éponge [epɔ̃ʒ] *nf* sponge; **passer l'~ (sur)** (*fig*) to let bygones be bygones (with regard to); **jeter l'~** (*fig*) to throw in the towel; **~ métallique** scourer

éponger [epɔ̃ʒe] *vt* (*liquide*) to mop *ou* sponge up; (*surface*) to sponge; (*fig: déficit*) to soak up, absorb; **s'~ le front** to mop one's brow

épopée [epɔpe] *nf* epic

époque [epɔk] *nf* (*de l'histoire*) age, era; (*de l'année, la vie*) time; **d'~** *adj* (*meuble*) period *cpd*; **à cette ~** at this (*ou* that) time *ou* period; **faire ~** to make history

époumoner [epumɔne]: **s'époumoner** *vi* to shout (*ou* sing) o.s. hoarse

épouse [epuz] *nf* wife

épouser [epuze] *vt* to marry; (*fig: idées*) to espouse; (: *forme*) to fit

épousseter [epuste] *vt* to dust

époustouflant, e [epustuflɑ̃, -ɑ̃t] *adj* staggering, mind-boggling

épouvantable [epuvɑ̃tabl] *adj* appalling, dreadful

épouvantail [epuvɑ̃taj] *nm* (*à moineaux*) scarecrow; (*fig*) bog(e)y; bugbear

épouvante [epuvɑ̃t] *nf* terror; **film d'~** horror film

épouvanter [epuvɑ̃te] *vt* to terrify

époux [epu] *nm* husband ▷ *nmpl*: **les ~** the (married) couple, the husband and wife

éprendre [epʀɑ̃dʀ]: **s'éprendre de** *vt* to fall in love with

épreuve [epʀœv] *nf* (*d'examen*) test; (*malheur, difficulté*) trial, ordeal; (*Photo*) print; (*Typo*) proof; (*Sport*) event; **à l'~ des balles/du feu** (*vêtement*) bulletproof/fireproof; **à toute ~** unfailing; **mettre à l'~** to put to the test; **~ de force** trial of strength; (*fig*) showdown; **~ de résistance** test of resistance; **~ de sélection** (*Sport*) heat

épris, e [epʀi, -iz] *pp voir* **éprendre** ▷ *adj*: **~ de** in love with

éprouvant, e [epʀuvɑ̃, -ɑ̃t] *adj* trying

éprouver [epʀuve] *vt* (*tester*) to test; (*mettre à l'épreuve*) to put to the test; (*marquer, faire souffrir*) to afflict, distress; (*ressentir*) to experience

éprouvette [epʀuvɛt] *nf* test tube

EPS *sigle f* (= *Éducation physique et sportive*) ≈ PE

épuisé, e [epɥize] *adj* exhausted; (*livre*) out of print

épuisement [epɥizmɑ̃] *nm* exhaustion; **jusqu'à ~ des stocks** while stocks last

épuiser [epɥize] *vt* (*fatiguer*) to exhaust, wear *ou* tire out; (*stock, sujet*) to exhaust; **s'épuiser** *vi* to wear *ou* tire o.s. out, exhaust o.s.; (*stock*) to run out

épuisette [epɥizɛt] *nf* landing net; shrimping net

épurer [epyʀe] *vt* (*liquide*) to purify; (*parti, administration*) to purge; (*langue, texte*) to refine

équateur [ekwatœʀ] *nm* equator; **(la république de) l'É~** Ecuador

équation [ekwasjɔ̃] *nf* equation; **mettre en ~** to equate; **~ du premier/second degré** simple/quadratic equation

équerre [ekɛʀ] *nf* (*à dessin*) (set) square; (*pour fixer*) brace; **en ~** at right angles; **à l'~, d'~** straight; **double ~** T-square

équilibre [ekilibʀ] *nm* balance; (*d'une balance*) equilibrium; **~ budgétaire** balanced budget; **garder/perdre l'~** to keep/lose one's balance; **être en ~** to be balanced; **mettre en ~** to make steady; **avoir le sens de l'~** to be well-balanced

équilibré, e [ekilibʀe] *adj* (*fig*) well-balanced, stable

équilibrer [ekilibʀe] *vt* to balance; **s'équilibrer** *vi* (*poids*) to balance; (*fig: défauts etc*) to balance each other out

équipage [ekipaʒ] *nm* crew; **en grand ~** in great array

équipe [ekip] *nf* team; (*bande: parfois péj*) bunch; **travailler par ~s** to work in shifts; **travailler en ~** to work as a team; **faire ~ avec** to team up with; **~ de chercheurs** research team; **~ de secours** *ou* **de sauvetage** rescue team

équipé, e [ekipe] *adj* (*cuisine etc*) equipped, fitted(-out) ▷ *nf* escapade; **bien/mal ~** well-/poorly-equipped

équipement [ekipmɑ̃] *nm* equipment; **équipements** *nmpl* amenities, facilities; installations; **biens/dépenses d'~** capital goods/expenditure; **ministère de l'É~** department of public works; **~s sportifs/collectifs** sports/community facilities *ou* resources

équiper [ekipe] *vt* to equip; (*voiture, cuisine*) to equip, fit out; **~ qn/qch de** to equip sb/sth with; **s'équiper** *vi* (*sportif*) to equip o.s., kit o.s. out

équipier, -ière [ekipje, -jɛʀ] *nm/f* team member

équitable [ekitabl] *adj* fair

équitation [ekitasjɔ̃] *nf* (horse-)riding; **faire de l'~** to go (horse-)riding

équivalent, e [ekivalɑ̃, -ɑ̃t] *adj, nm* equivalent

équivaloir [ekivalwaʀ]: **~ à** *vt* to be equivalent to; (*représenter*) to amount to

équivoque [ekivɔk] *adj* equivocal, ambiguous; (*louche*) dubious ▷ *nf* ambiguity

érable [eʀabl] nm maple

érafler [eʀafle] vt to scratch; **s'~ la main/les jambes** to scrape ou scratch one's hand/legs

éraflure [eʀaflyʀ] nf scratch

éraillé, e [eʀaje] adj (voix) rasping, hoarse

ère [eʀ] nf era; **en l'an 1050 de notre ~** in the year 1050 A.D.

érection [eʀɛksjɔ̃] nf erection

éreinter [eʀɛ̃te] vt to exhaust, wear out; (fig: critiquer) to slate; **s'~ (à faire qch/à qch)** to wear o.s. out (doing sth/with sth)

ériger [eʀiʒe] vt (monument) to erect; **~ qch en principe/loi** to make sth a principle/law; **s'~ en critique (de)** to set o.s. up as a critic (of)

ermite [eʀmit] nm hermit

éroder [eʀɔde] vt to erode

érotique [eʀɔtik] adj erotic

errer [eʀe] vi to wander

erreur [eʀœʀ] nf mistake, error; (Inform) error; (morale): **~s** nfpl errors; **être dans l'~** to be wrong; **induire qn en ~** to mislead sb; **par ~** by mistake; **sauf ~** unless I'm mistaken; **faire ~** to be mistaken; **~ de date** mistake in the date; **~ de fait** error of fact; **~ d'impression** (Typo) misprint; **~ judiciaire** miscarriage of justice; **~ de jugement** error of judgment; **~ matérielle ou d'écriture** clerical error; **~ tactique** tactical error

érudit, e [eʀydi, -it] adj erudite, learned ▷ nm/f scholar

éruption [eʀypsjɔ̃] nf eruption; (cutanée) outbreak; (: boutons) rash; (fig: de joie, colère, folie) outburst

es [ɛ] vb voir **être**

ès [ɛs] prép: **licencié ès lettres/sciences** ≈ Bachelor of Arts/Science; **docteur ès lettres** ≈ doctor of philosophy, ≈ PhD

ESB sigle f (= encéphalopathie spongiforme bovine) BSE

escabeau, x [ɛskabo] nm (tabouret) stool; (échelle) stepladder

escadron [ɛskadʀɔ̃] nm squadron

escalade [ɛskalad] nf climbing no pl; (Pol etc) escalation

escalader [ɛskalade] vt to climb, scale

escale [ɛskal] nf (Navig: durée) call; (: port) port of call; (Aviat) stop(over); **faire ~ à** to put in at, call in at; (Aviat) to stop over at; **~ technique** refuelling stop; **vol sans ~** nonstop flight

escalier [ɛskalje] nm stairs pl; **dans l'~** ou **les ~s** on the stairs; **descendre l'~** ou **les ~s** to go downstairs; **~ mécanique** ou **roulant** escalator; **~ de secours** fire escape; **~ de service** backstairs; **~ à vis** ou **en colimaçon** spiral staircase

escamoter [ɛskamɔte] vt (esquiver) to get round, evade; (faire disparaître) to conjure away; (dérober: portefeuille etc) to snatch; (train d'atterrissage) to retract; (mots) to miss out

escapade [ɛskapad] nf: **faire une ~** to go on a jaunt; (s'enfuir) to run away ou off

escargot [ɛskaʀgo] nm snail

escarpé, e [ɛskaʀpe] adj steep

escarpin [ɛskaʀpɛ̃] nm flat(-heeled) shoe

escient [ɛsjɑ̃] nm: **à bon ~** advisedly

esclaffer [ɛsklafe]: **s'esclaffer** vi to guffaw

esclandre [ɛsklɑ̃dʀ] nm scene, fracas

esclavage [ɛsklavaʒ] nm slavery

esclave [ɛsklav] nm/f slave; **être ~ de** (fig) to be a slave of

escompte [ɛskɔ̃t] nm discount

escompter [ɛskɔ̃te] vt (Comm) to discount; (espérer) to expect, reckon upon; **~ que** to reckon ou expect that

escorte [ɛskɔʀt] nf escort; **faire ~ à** to escort

escorter [ɛskɔʀte] vt to escort

escouade [ɛskwad] nf squad; (fig: groupe de personnes) group

escrime [ɛskʀim] nf fencing; **faire de l'~** to fence

escrimer [ɛskʀime]: **s'escrimer** vi: **s'~ à faire** to wear o.s. out doing

escroc [ɛskʀo] nm swindler, con-man

escroquer [ɛskʀɔke] vt: **~ qn (de qch)/qch à qn** to swindle sb (out of sth)/sth out of sb

escroquerie [ɛskʀɔkʀi] nf swindle

espace [ɛspas] nm space; **~ publicitaire** advertising space; **~ vital** living space

espacer [ɛspase] vt to space out; **s'espacer** vi (visites etc) to become less frequent

espadon [ɛspadɔ̃] nm swordfish inv

espadrille [ɛspadʀij] nf rope-soled sandal

Espagne [ɛspaɲ] nf: **l'~** Spain

espagnol, e [ɛspaɲɔl] adj Spanish ▷ nm (Ling) Spanish ▷ nm/f: **E~, e** Spaniard

espèce [ɛspɛs] nf (Bio, Bot, Zool) species inv; (gén: sorte) sort, kind, type; (péj): **~ de maladroit/de brute!** you clumsy oaf/you brute!; **espèces** nfpl (Comm) cash sg; (Rel) species; **de toute ~** of all kinds ou sorts; **en l'~** adv in the case in point; **payer en ~s** to pay (in) cash; **cas d'~** individual case; **l'~ humaine** humankind

espérance [ɛspeʀɑ̃s] nf hope; **~ de vie** life expectancy

espérer [ɛspeʀe] vt to hope for; **j'espère (bien)** I hope so; **~ que/faire** to hope that/to do; **~ en** to trust in

espiègle [ɛspjɛgl] adj mischievous

espion, ne [ɛspjɔ̃, -ɔn] nm/f spy; **avion ~** spy plane

espionnage [ɛspjɔnaʒ] nm espionage, spying; **film/roman d'~** spy film/novel

espionner [ɛspjɔne] vt to spy (up)on

esplanade [ɛsplanad] nf esplanade

espoir [ɛspwaʀ] nm hope; **l'~ de qch/de faire qch** the hope of sth/of doing sth; **avoir bon ~ que ...** to have high hopes that ...; **garder l'~ que ...** to remain hopeful that ...; **dans l'~ de/que** in the hope of/that; **reprendre ~** not to lose hope; **un ~ de la boxe/du ski** one of boxing's/skiing's hopefuls, one of the hopes of boxing/skiing; **sans ~** adj hopeless

esprit [ɛspri] nm (pensée, intellect) mind; (humour, ironie) wit; (mentalité, d'une loi etc, fantôme etc) spirit; l'~ **d'équipe/de compétition** team/competitive spirit; **faire de l'~** to try to be witty; **reprendre ses ~s** to come to; **perdre l'~** to lose one's mind; **avoir bon/mauvais ~** to be of a good/bad disposition; **avoir l'~ à faire qch** to have a mind to do sth; **avoir l'~ critique** to be critical; ~ **de contradiction** contrariness; ~ **de corps** esprit de corps; ~ **de famille** family loyalty; l'E~ **malin** (le diable) the Evil One; ~s **chagrins** fault-finders

esquimau, de, x [ɛskimo, -od] adj Eskimo ▷ nm (Ling) Eskimo; (glace): **E-®** ice lolly (Brit), popsicle (US) ▷ nm/f: **E-, de** Eskimo; **chien ~** husky

esquinter [ɛskɛ̃te] vt (fam) to mess up; **s'esquinter** vi: **s'~ à faire qch** to knock o.s. out doing sth

esquisse [ɛskis] nf sketch; l'~ **d'un sourire/ changement** a hint of a smile/of change

esquisser [ɛskise] vt to sketch; **s'esquisser** vi (amélioration) to begin to be detectable; ~ **un sourire** to give a hint of a smile

esquiver [ɛskive] vt to dodge; **s'esquiver** vi to slip away

essai [esɛ] nm trying; (tentative) attempt, try; (de produit) testing; (Rugby) try; (Littérature) essay; **essais** nmpl (Auto) trials; **à l'~** on a trial basis; **mettre à l'~** to put to the test; ~ **gratuit** (Comm) free trial

essaim [esɛ̃] nm swarm

essayer [eseje] vt (gén) to try; (vêtement, chaussures) to try (on); (restaurant, méthode, voiture) to try (out) ▷ vi to try; ~ **de faire** to try ou attempt to do; **s'~ à faire** to try one's hand at doing; **essayez un peu!** (menace) just you try!

essence [esɑ̃s] nf (de voiture) petrol (Brit), gas(oline) (US); (extrait de plante, Philosophie) essence; (espèce: d'arbre) species inv; **prendre de l'~** to get (some) petrol ou gas; **par ~** (essentiellement) essentially; ~ **de citron/rose** lemon/rose oil; ~ **sans plomb** unleaded petrol; ~ **de térébenthine** turpentine

essentiel, le [esɑ̃sjɛl] adj essential ▷ nm: l'~ **d'un discours/d'une œuvre** the essence of a speech/work of art; **emporter l'~** to take the essentials; **c'est l'~** (ce qui importe) that's the main thing; l'~ **de** (la majeure partie) the main part of

essieu, x [esjø] nm axle

essor [esɔr] nm (de l'économie etc) rapid expansion; **prendre son ~** (oiseau) to fly off

essorer [esɔre] vt (en tordant) to wring (out); (par la force centrifuge) to spin-dry; (salade) to spin; (: en secouant) to shake dry

essoreuse [esɔrøz] nf mangle, wringer; (à tambour) spin-dryer

essoufflé, e [esufle] adj out of breath, breathless

essouffler [esufle] vt to make breathless; **s'essouffler** vi to get out of breath; (fig: économie) to run out of steam

essuie-glace [esɥiɡlas] nm windscreen (Brit) ou windshield (US) wiper

essuyer [esɥije] vt to wipe; (fig: subir) to suffer; **s'essuyer** (après le bain) to dry o.s.; ~ **la vaisselle** to dry up, dry the dishes

est [ɛ] vb voir **être** ▷ nm [ɛst]: l'~ the east ▷ adj inv east; (région) east(ern); **à l'~** in the east; (direction) to the east, east(wards); **à l'~ de** (to the) east of; **les pays de l'E~** the eastern countries

estampe [ɛstɑ̃p] nf print, engraving

est-ce que [ɛskə] adv: ~ **c'est cher/c'était bon?** is it expensive/was it good?; **quand est-ce qu'il part?** when does he leave?, when is he leaving?; **où est-ce qu'il va?** where's he going?; voir aussi **que**

esthéticienne [ɛstetisjɛn] nf beautician

esthétique [ɛstetik] adj (sens, jugement) aesthetic; (beau) attractive, aesthetically pleasing ▷ nf aesthetics sg; l'~ **industrielle** industrial design

estimation [ɛstimasjɔ̃] nf valuation; assessment; (chiffre) estimate; **d'après mes ~s** according to my calculations

estime [ɛstim] nf esteem, regard; **avoir de l'~ pour qn** to think highly of sb

estimer [ɛstime] vt (respecter) to esteem, hold in high regard; (expertiser: bijou) to value; (évaluer: coût etc) to assess, estimate; (penser): ~ **que/être** to consider that/o.s. to be; **s'estimer** vi: **s'~ satisfait/heureux** to feel satisfied/happy; **j'estime la distance à 10 km** I reckon the distance to be 10 km

estival, e, -aux [ɛstival, -o] adj summer cpd; **station ~e** (summer) holiday resort

estivant, e [ɛstivɑ̃, -ɑ̃t] nm/f (summer) holiday-maker

estomac [ɛstɔma] nm stomach; **avoir mal à l'~** to have stomach ache; **avoir l'~ creux** to have an empty stomach

estomaqué, e [ɛstɔmake] adj flabbergasted

estomper [ɛstɔ̃pe] vt (Art) to shade off; (fig) to blur, dim; **s'estomper** vi (sentiments) to soften; (contour) to become blurred

estrade [ɛstrad] nf platform, rostrum

estragon [ɛstragɔ̃] nm tarragon

estuaire [ɛstɥɛr] nm estuary

et [e] conj and; **et lui?** what about him?; **et alors?, et (puis) après?** so what?; (ensuite) and then?

étable [etabl] nf cowshed

établi, e [etabli] adj established ▷ nm (work) bench

établir [etablir] vt (papiers d'identité, facture) to make out; (liste, programme) to draw up; (gouvernement, artisan etc: aider à s'installer) to set up, establish; (entreprise, atelier, camp) to set up; (réputation, usage, fait, culpabilité, relations) to establish; (Sport: record) to set; **s'établir** vi (se *faire: entente etc*) to be established; **s'~ (à son compte)** to set up in business; **s'~ à/près de** to settle in/near

établissement [etablismɑ̃] *nm* making out; drawing up; setting up, establishing; (*entreprise, institution*) establishment; **~ de crédit** credit institution; **~ hospitalier** hospital complex; **~ industriel** industrial plant, factory; **~ scolaire** school, educational establishment

étage [etaʒ] *nm* (*d'immeuble*) storey (*Brit*), story (*US*), floor; (*de fusée*) stage; (*Géo: de culture, végétation*) level; **au 2ème** ~ on the 2nd (*Brit*) *ou* 3rd (*US*) floor; **à l'~** upstairs; **maison à deux ~s** two-storey *ou* -story house; **c'est à quel ~?** what floor is it on?; **de bas ~** *adj* low-born; (*médiocre*) inferior

étagère [etaʒɛʀ] *nf* (*rayon*) shelf; (*meuble*) shelves *pl*, set of shelves

étai [etɛ] *nm* stay, prop

étain [etɛ̃] *nm* tin; (*Orfèvrerie*) pewter *no pl*

étais *etc* [etɛ] *vb voir* **être**

étal [etal] *nm* stall

étalage [etalaʒ] *nm* display; (*vitrine*) display window; **faire ~ de** to show off, parade

étaler [etale] *vt* (*carte, nappe*) to spread (out); (*peinture, liquide*) to spread; (*échelonner: paiements, dates, vacances*) to spread, stagger; (*exposer: marchandises*) to display; (*richesses, connaissances*) to parade; **s'étaler** *vi* (*liquide*) to spread out; (*fam*) to fall flat on one's face, come a cropper (*Brit*); **s'~ sur** (*paiements etc*) to be spread over

étalon [etalɔ̃] *nm* (*mesure*) standard; (*cheval*) stallion; **l'~-or** the gold standard

étanche [etɑ̃ʃ] *adj* (*récipient, aussi fig*) watertight; (*montre, vêtement*) waterproof; **~ à l'air** airtight

étancher [etɑ̃ʃe] *vt* (*liquide*) to stop (flowing); **~ sa soif** to quench *ou* slake one's thirst

étang [etɑ̃] *nm* pond

étant [etɑ̃] *vb voir* **être; donné**

étape [etap] *nf* stage; (*lieu d'arrivée*) stopping place; (: *Cyclisme*) staging point; **faire ~ à** to stop off at; **brûler les ~s** (*fig*) to cut corners

état [eta] *nm* (*Pol, condition*) state; (*d'un article d'occasion etc*) condition, state; (*liste*) inventory, statement; (*condition: professionnelle*) profession, trade; (: *sociale*) status; **en bon/mauvais ~** in good/poor condition; **en ~ (de marche)** in (working) order; **remettre en ~** to repair; **hors d'~** out of order; **être en ~/hors d'~ de faire** to be in a state/in no fit state to do; **en tout ~ de cause** in any event; **être dans tous ses ~s** to be in a state; **faire ~ de** (*alléguer*) to put forward; **en ~ d'arrestation** under arrest; **~ de grâce** (*Rel*) state of grace; (*fig*) honeymoon period; **en ~ de grâce** (*fig*) inspired; **en ~ d'ivresse** under the influence of drink; **~ de choses** (*situation*) state of affairs; **l'É~** the State; **~ civil** civil status; (*bureau*) registry office (*Brit*); **~ d'esprit** frame

of mind; **~ des lieux** inventory of fixtures; **~ de santé** state of health; **~ de siège/d'urgence** state of siege/emergency; **~ de veille** (*Psych*) waking state; **~s d'âme** moods; **les É~s barbaresques** the Barbary States; **les É~s du Golfe** the Gulf States; **~s de service** service record *sg*

étatiser [etatize] *vt* to bring under state control

état-major (*pl* **états-majors**) [etamaʒɔʀ] *nm* (*Mil*) staff; (*d'un parti etc*) top advisers *pl*; (*d'une entreprise*) top management

États-Unis [etazyni] *nmpl*: **les ~ (d'Amérique)** the United States (of America)

étau, x [eto] *nm* vice (*Brit*), vise (*US*)

étayer [eteje] *vt* to prop *ou* shore up; (*fig*) to back up

etc. [ɛtsetera] *adv* etc

et cætera, et cetera [ɛtsetera], **etc.** *adv* et cetera, and so on, etc

été [ete] *pp de* **être** ▷ *nm* summer; **en ~** in summer

éteindre [etɛ̃dʀ] *vt* (*lampe, lumière, radio, chauffage*) to turn *ou* switch off; (*cigarette, incendie, bougie*) to put out, extinguish; (*Jur: dette*) to extinguish; **s'éteindre** *vi* to go off; (*feu, lumière*) to go out; (*mourir*) to pass away

éteint, e [etɛ̃, -ɛ̃t] *pp de* **éteindre** ▷ *adj* (*fig*) lacklustre, dull; (*volcan*) extinct; **tous feux ~s** (*Auto: rouler*) without lights

étendard [etɑ̃daʀ] *nm* standard

étendre [etɑ̃dʀ] *vt* (*appliquer: pâte, liquide*) to spread; (*déployer: carte etc*) to spread out; (*sur un fil: lessive, linge*) to hang up *ou* out; (*bras, jambes, par terre: blessé*) to stretch out; (*diluer*) to dilute, thin; (*fig: agrandir*) to extend; (*fam: adversaire*) to floor; **s'étendre** *vi* (*augmenter, se propager*) to spread; (*terrain, forêt etc*): **s'~ jusqu'à/de ... à** to stretch as far as/from ... to; **s'~ (sur)** (*s'allonger*) to stretch out (upon); (*se coucher*) to lie down (on); (*fig: expliquer*): **s'~ (sur)** to elaborate *ou* enlarge (upon)

étendu, e [etɑ̃dy] *adj* extensive ▷ *nf* (*d'eau, de sable*) stretch, expanse; (*importance*) extent

éternel, le [etɛʀnɛl] *adj* eternal; **les neiges ~les** perpetual snow

éterniser [etɛʀnize]: **s'éterniser** *vi* to last for ages; (*personne*) to stay for ages

éternité [etɛʀnite] *nf* eternity; **il y a** *ou* **ça fait une ~ que** it's ages since; **de toute ~** from time immemorial; **ça a duré une ~** it lasted for ages

éternuement [etɛʀnymɑ̃] *nm* sneeze

éternuer [etɛʀnɥe] *vi* to sneeze

êtes [ɛt(z)] *vb voir* **être**

Éthiopie [etjɔpi] *nf*: **l'~** Ethiopia

éthique [etik] *adj* ethical ▷ *nf* ethics *sg*

ethnie [ɛtni] *nf* ethnic group

éthylisme [etilism] *nm* alcoholism

étiez [etje] *vb voir* **être**

étinceler [etɛ̃s(ə)le] *vi* to sparkle

étincelle [etɛ̃sɛl] *nf* spark

étiqueter [etikte] vt to label
étiquette [etiket] vb voir **étiqueter** ▷ nf label; (protocole): **l'~** etiquette
étirer [etire] vt to stretch; (ressort) to stretch out; **s'étirer** vi (personne) to stretch; (convoi, route): **s'~ sur** to stretch out over
étoffe [etɔf] nf material, fabric; **avoir l'~ d'un chef** etc to be cut out to be a leader etc; **avoir de l'~** to be a forceful personality
étoffer [etɔfe] vt to flesh out; **s'étoffer** vi to fill out
étoile [etwal] nf star ▷ adj: **danseuse** ou **danseur ~** leading dancer; **la bonne/mauvaise ~ de qn** sb's lucky/unlucky star; **à la belle ~** (out) in the open; **~ filante** shooting star; **~ de mer** starfish; **~ polaire** pole star
étoilé, e [etwale] adj starry
étonnant, e [etɔnɑ̃, -ɑ̃t] adj surprising
étonnement [etɔnmɑ̃] nm surprise, amazing; **à mon grand ~** ... to my great surprise ou amazement ...
étonner [etɔne] vt to surprise, amaze; **s'étonner que/de** to be surprised that/at; **cela m'~ait (que)** (j'en doute) I'd be (very) surprised (if)
étouffant, e [etufɑ̃, -ɑ̃t] adj stifling
étouffé, e [etufe] adj (asphyxié) suffocated; (assourdi: cris, rires) smothered ▷ nf: **à l'~e** (Culin: poisson, légumes) steamed; (: viande) braised
étouffer [etufe] vt to suffocate; (bruit) to muffle; (scandale) to hush up ▷ vi to suffocate; (avoir trop chaud; aussi fig) to feel stifled; **s'étouffer** vi (en mangeant etc) to choke; **on étouffe** it's stifling
étourderie [eturdəri] nf (caractère) absent-mindedness no pl; (faute) thoughtless blunder; **faute d'~** careless mistake
étourdi, e [eturdi] adj (distrait) scatterbrained, heedless
étourdir [eturdir] vt (assommer) to stun, daze; (griser) to make dizzy ou giddy
étourdissement [eturdismɑ̃] nm dizzy spell
étourneau, x [eturno] nm starling
étrange [etrɑ̃ʒ] adj strange
étranger, -ère [etrɑ̃ʒe, -ɛr] adj foreign; (pas de la famille, non familier) strange ▷ nm/f foreigner; stranger ▷ nm: **l'~** foreign countries; **à l'~** abroad; **de l'~** from abroad; **~ à** (mal connu) unfamiliar to; (sans rapport) irrelevant to
étrangler [etrɑ̃gle] vt to strangle; (fig: presse, libertés) to stifle; **s'étrangler** vi (en mangeant etc) to choke; (se resserrer) to make a bottleneck

○ **MOT-CLÉ**

être [ɛtr] nm being; **être humain** human being
▷ vb copule **1** (état, description) to be; **il est**

instituteur he is ou he's a teacher; **vous êtes grand/intelligent/fatigué** you are ou you're tall/clever/tired
2 (+à: appartenir) to be; **le livre est à Paul** the book is Paul's ou belongs to Paul; **c'est à moi/eux** it is ou it's mine/theirs
3 (+de: provenance): **il est de Paris** he is from Paris; (appartenance: 000): **il est des nôtres** he is one of us
4 (date): **nous sommes le 10 janvier** it's the 10th of January (today)
▷ vi to be; **je ne serai pas ici demain** I won't be here tomorrow
▷ vb aux **1** to have; to be; **être arrivé/allé** to have arrived/gone; **il est parti** he has left, he has gone
2 (forme passive) to be; **être fait par** to be made by; **il a été promu** he has been promoted
3 (+à +inf: obligation, but): **c'est à réparer** it needs repairing; **c'est à essayer** it should be tried; **il est à espérer que** ... it is ou it's to be hoped that ...
▷ vb impers **1**: **il est** avec adjectif it is; **il est impossible de le faire** it's impossible to do it
2 (heure, date): **il est 10 heures** it is ou it's 10 o'clock
3 (emphatique): **c'est moi** it's me; **c'est à lui de le faire** it's up to him to do it; voir aussi **est-ce que; n'est-ce pas; c'est-à-dire; ce**

étreindre [etrɛ̃dr] vt to clutch, grip; (amoureusement, amicalement) to embrace; **s'étreindre** vi to embrace
étrenner [etrene] vt to use (ou wear) for the first time
étrennes [etren] nfpl (cadeaux) New Year's present; (gratifications) ≈ Christmas box sg, ≈ Christmas bonus
étrier [etrije] nm stirrup
étriqué, e [etrike] adj skimpy
étroit, e [etrwa, -wat] adj narrow; (vêtement) tight; (fig: serré: liens, collaboration) close, tight; **à l'~** cramped; **~ d'esprit** narrow-minded
étude [etyd] nf studying; (ouvrage, rapport, Mus) study; (de notaire: bureau) office; (: charge) practice; (Scol: salle de travail) study room; **études** nfpl (Scol) studies; **être à l'~** (projet etc) to be under consideration; **faire des ~s (de droit/médecine)** to study (law/medicine); **~s secondaires/supérieures** secondary/higher education; **~ de cas** case study; **~ de faisabilité** feasibility study; **~ de marché** (Écon) market research
étudiant, e [etydjɑ̃, -ɑ̃t] adj, nm/f student
étudier [etydje] vt, vi to study
étui [etɥi] nm case
étuve [etyv] nf steamroom; (appareil) sterilizer
étuvée [etyve] : **à l'~** adv braised
eu, eue [y] pp de **avoir**
euh [ø] excl er

euro [øʁo] *nm* euro
Euroland [øʁɔlɑ̃d] *nm* Euroland
Europe [øʁɔp] *nf*: **l'~** Europe; **l'~ centrale** Central Europe; **l'~ verte** European agriculture
européen, ne [øʁɔpeɛ̃, -ɛn] *adj* European ▷ *nm/f*: **E-, ne** European
eus *etc* [y] *vb voir* **avoir**
eux [ø] *pron (sujet)* they; *(objet)* them; **~, ils ont fait ...** THEY did ...
évacuer [evakɥe] *vt (salle, région)* to evacuate, clear; *(occupants, population)* to evacuate; *(toxine etc)* to evacuate, discharge
évader [evade]: **s'évader** *vi* to escape
évaluer [evalɥe] *vt (expertiser)* to assess, evaluate; *(juger approximativement)* to estimate
évangile [evɑ̃ʒil] *nm* gospel; *(texte de la Bible)*: **É-** Gospel; **ce n'est pas l'É-** *(fig)* it's not gospel
évanouir [evanwiʁ]: **s'évanouir** *vi* to faint, pass out; *(disparaître)* to vanish, disappear
évanouissement [evanwismɑ̃] *nm (syncope)* fainting fit; *(Méd)* loss of consciousness
évaporer [evapɔʁe]: **s'évaporer** *vi* to evaporate
évasé, e [evaze] *adj (jupe etc)* flared
évasif, -ive [evazif, -iv] *adj* evasive
évasion [evazjɔ̃] *nf* escape; **littérature d'~** escapist literature; **~ des capitaux** *(Écon)* flight of capital; **~ fiscale** tax avoidance
évêché [eveʃe] *nm (fonction)* bishopric; *(palais)* bishop's palace
éveil [evɛj] *nm* awakening; **être en ~** to be alert; **mettre qn en ~, donner l'~ à qn** to arouse sb's suspicions; **activités d'~** early-learning activities
éveillé, e [eveje] *adj* awake; *(vif)* alert, sharp
éveiller [eveje] *vt* to (a)waken; *(soupçons etc)* to arouse; **s'éveiller** *vi* to (a)waken; *(fig)* to be aroused
événement [evɛnmɑ̃] *nm* event
éventail [evɑ̃taj] *nm* fan; *(choix)* range; **en ~** fanned out; fan-shaped
éventaire [evɑ̃tɛʁ] *nm* stall, stand
éventer [evɑ̃te] *vt (secret, complot)* to uncover; *(avec un éventail)* to fan; **s'éventer** *vi (parfum, vin)* to go stale
éventualité [evɑ̃tɥalite] *nf* eventuality; possibility; **dans l'~ de** in the event of; **parer à toute ~** to guard against all eventualities
éventuel, le [evɑ̃tɥɛl] *adj* possible
éventuellement [evɑ̃tɥɛlmɑ̃] *adv* possibly
évêque [evɛk] *nm* bishop
évertuer [evɛʁtɥe]: **s'évertuer** *vi*: **s'~ à faire** to try very hard to do
éviction [eviksjɔ̃] *nf* ousting, supplanting; *(de locataire)* eviction
évidemment [evidamɑ̃] *adv (bien sûr)* of course; *(certainement)* obviously
évidence [evidɑ̃s] *nf* obviousness; *(fait)* obvious fact; **se rendre à l'~** to bow before the evidence; **nier l'~** to deny the evidence;

à l'~ evidently; **de toute ~** quite obviously *ou* evidently; **en ~** conspicuous; **être en ~** to be clearly visible; **mettre en ~** *(fait)* to highlight
évident, e [evidɑ̃, -ɑ̃t] *adj* obvious, evident; **ce n'est pas ~** *(cela pose des problèmes)* it's not (all that) straightforward, it's not as simple as all that
évider [evide] *vt* to scoop out
évier [evje] *nm* (kitchen) sink
évincer [evɛ̃se] *vt* to oust, supplant
éviter [evite] *vt* to avoid; **~ de faire/que qch ne se passe** to avoid doing/sth happening; **~ qch à qn** to spare sb sth
évolué, e [evolɥe] *adj* advanced; *(personne)* broad-minded
évoluer [evolɥe] *vi (enfant, maladie)* to develop; *(situation, moralement)* to evolve, develop; *(aller et venir: danseur etc)* to move about, circle
évolution [evolysjɔ̃] *nf* development; evolution; **évolutions** *nfpl* movements
évoquer [evoke] *vt* to call to mind, evoke; *(mentionner)* to mention
ex- [ɛks] *préfixe* ex-; **son ~mari** her ex-husband; **son ~femme** his ex-wife
exact, e [ɛgza(kt), ɛgzakt] *adj (précis)* exact, accurate, precise; *(correct)* correct; *(ponctuel)* punctual; **l'heure ~e** the right *ou* exact time
exactement [ɛgzaktəmɑ̃] *adv* exactly, accurately, precisely; correctly; *(c'est cela même)* exactly
ex aequo [ɛgzeko] *adj* equally placed; **classé 1er ~** placed equal first; **arriver ~** to finish neck and neck
exagéré, e [ɛgzaʒeʁe] *adj (prix etc)* excessive
exagérer [ɛgzaʒeʁe] *vt* to exaggerate ▷ *vi (abuser)* to go too far; *(dépasser les bornes)* to overstep the mark; *(déformer les faits)* to exaggerate; **s'exagérer qch** to exaggerate sth
exalter [ɛgzalte] *vt (enthousiasmer)* to excite, elate; *(glorifier)* to exalt
examen [ɛgzamɛ̃] *nm* examination; *(Scol)* exam, examination; **à l'~** *(dossier, projet)* under consideration; *(Comm)* on approval; **~ blanc** mock exam(ination); **~ de la vue** sight test; **~ médical** (medical) examination; *(analyse)* test
examinateur, -trice [ɛgzaminatœʁ, -tʁis] *nm/f* examiner
examiner [ɛgzamine] *vt* to examine
exaspérant, e [ɛgzaspeʁɑ̃, -ɑ̃t] *adj* exasperating
exaspérer [ɛgzaspeʁe] *vt* to exasperate; *(aggraver)* to exacerbate
exaucer [ɛgzose] *vt (vœu)* to grant, fulfil; **~ qn** to grant sb's wishes
excédent [ɛksedɑ̃] *nm* surplus; **en ~** surplus; **payer 60 euros d'~** *(de bagages)* to pay 60 euros excess baggage; **~ de bagages** excess baggage; **~ commercial** trade surplus
excéder [ɛksede] *vt (dépasser)* to exceed; *(agacer)* to exasperate; **excédé de fatigue** exhausted; **excédé de travail** worn out with work

excellent, e [ɛksɛlɑ̃, -ɑ̃t] *adj* excellent
excentrique [ɛksɑ̃trik] *adj* eccentric; (*quartier*) outlying ▷ *nm/f* eccentric
excepté, e [ɛksɛpte] *adj*, *prép*: **les élèves ~s, ~ les élèves** except for *ou* apart from the pupils; **si/quand** except if/when; **~ que** except that
exception [ɛksɛpsjɔ̃] *nf* exception; **faire ~** to be an exception; **faire une ~** to make an exception; **sans ~** without exception; **à l'~ de** except for, with the exception of; **d'~** (*mesure, loi*) special, exceptional
exceptionnel, le [ɛksɛpsjɔnɛl] *adj* exceptional; (*prix*) special
exceptionnellement [ɛksɛpsjɔnɛlmɑ̃] *adv* exceptionally; (*par exception*) by way of an exception, on this occasion
excès [ɛksɛ] *nm* surplus ▷ *nmpl* excesses; **à l'~** (*méticuleux, généreux*) to excess; **avec ~** to excess; **sans ~** in moderation; **tomber dans l'~ inverse** to go to the opposite extreme; **~ de langage** immoderate language; **~ de pouvoir** abuse of power; **faire des ~** to overindulge; **~ de vitesse** speeding *no pl*, exceeding the speed limit; **~ de zèle** overzealousness *no pl*
excessif, -ive [ɛksesif, -iv] *adj* excessive
excitant, e [ɛksitɑ̃, -ɑ̃t] *adj* exciting ▷ *nm* stimulant
excitation [ɛksitasjɔ̃] *nf* (*état*) excitement
exciter [ɛksite] *vt* to excite; (*café etc*) to stimulate; **s'exciter** *vi* to get excited; **~ qn à** (*révolte etc*) to incite sb to
exclamation [ɛksklamasjɔ̃] *nf* exclamation
exclamer [ɛksklame]: **s'exclamer** *vi* to exclaim
exclu, e [ɛkskly] *adj*: **il est/n'est pas ~ que ~** it's out of the question/not impossible that ...
exclure [ɛksklyr] *vt* (*faire sortir*) to expel; (*ne pas compter*) to exclude, leave out; (*rendre impossible*) to exclude, rule out
exclusif, -ive [ɛksklyzif, -iv] *adj* exclusive; **avec la mission exclusive/dans le but ~ de ...** with the sole mission/aim of ...; **agent ~** sole agent
exclusion [ɛksklyzjɔ̃] *nf* expulsion; **à l'~ de** with the exclusion *ou* exception of
exclusivité [ɛksklyzivite] *nf* exclusiveness; (*Comm*) exclusive rights *pl*; **film passant en ~ à** film showing only at
excursion [ɛkskyrsjɔ̃] *nf* (*en autocar*) excursion, trip; (*à pied*) walk, hike; **faire une ~** to go on an excursion *ou* a trip; to go on a walk *ou* hike
excuse [ɛkskyz] *nf* excuse; **excuses** *nfpl* (*regret*) apology *sg*, apologies; **faire des ~s** to apologize; **faire ses ~s** to offer one's apologies; **mot d'~** (*Scol*) note from one's parent(s) (*to explain absence etc*); **lettre d'~s** letter of apology
excuser [ɛkskyze] *vt* to excuse; **~ qn de qch** (*dispenser*) to excuse sb from sth; **s'excuser**

(de) to apologize (for); **"excusez-moi"** "I'm sorry"; (*pour attirer l'attention*) "excuse me"; **se faire ~** to ask to be excused
exécrable [ɛgzekrabl] *adj* atrocious
exécuter [ɛgzekyte] *vt* (*prisonnier*) to execute; (*tâche etc*) to execute, carry out; (*Mus: jouer*) to perform, execute; (*Inform*) to run; **s'exécuter** *vi* to comply
exécutif, -ive [ɛgzekytif, -iv] *adj*, *nm* (*Pol*) executive
exécution [ɛgzekysjɔ̃] *nf* execution; carrying out; **mettre à ~** to carry out
exemplaire [ɛgzɑ̃plɛr] *adj* exemplary ▷ *nm* copy
exemple [ɛgzɑ̃pl] *nm* example; **par ~** for instance, for example; (*valeur intensive*) really!; **sans ~** (*bêtise, gourmandise etc*) unparalleled; **donner l'~** to set an example; **prendre ~ sur** to take as a model; **à l'~ de** just like; **pour l'~** (*punir*) as an example
exempt, e [ɛgzɑ̃, -ɑ̃t] *adj*: **~ de** (*dispensé de*) exempt from; (*sans*) free from; **~ de taxes** tax-free
exercer [ɛgzɛrse] *vt* (*pratiquer*) to exercise, practise; (*faire usage de: prérogative*) to exercise; (*effectuer: influence, contrôle, pression*) to exert; (*former*) to exercise, train; **s'exercer** *vi* (*médecin*) to be in practice; (*musicien*) to practise; (*se faire sentir: pression etc*): **s'~ (sur ou contre)** to be exerted (on); **s'~ à faire qch** to train o.s. to do sth
exercice [ɛgzɛrsis] *nm* practice; exercising; (*tâche, travail*) exercise; (*Comm, Admin: période*) accounting period; **l'~** (*sportive etc*) exercise; (*Mil*) drill; **en ~** (*juge*) in office; (*médecin*) practising; **dans l'~ de ses fonctions** in the discharge of his duties; **~s d'assouplissement** limbering-up (exercises)
exhaustif, -ive [ɛgzostif, -iv] *adj* exhaustive
exhiber [ɛgzibe] *vt* (*montrer: papiers, certificat*) to present, produce; (*péj*) to display, flaunt; **s'exhiber** *vi* (*personne*) to parade; (*exhibitionniste*) to expose o.s.
exhibitionniste [ɛgzibisjɔnist] *nm/f* exhibitionist
exhorter [ɛgzɔrte] *vt*: **~ qn à faire** to urge sb to do
exigeant, e [ɛgziʒɑ̃, -ɑ̃t] *adj* demanding; (*péj*) hard to please
exigence [ɛgziʒɑ̃s] *nf* demand, requirement
exiger [ɛgziʒe] *vt* to demand, require
exigu, ë [ɛgzigy] *adj* cramped, tiny
exil [ɛgzil] *nm* exile; **en ~** in exile
exiler [ɛgzile] *vt* to exile; **s'exiler** *vi* to go into exile
existence [ɛgzistɑ̃s] *nf* existence; **dans l'~** in life
exister [ɛgziste] *vi* to exist; **il existe un/des** there is a/are (some)
exonérer [ɛgzɔnere] *vt*: **~ de** to exempt from
exorbitant, e [ɛgzɔrbitɑ̃, -ɑ̃t] *adj* exorbitant

e

exorbité, e [ɛgzɔrbite] *adj:* **yeux ~s** bulging eyes

exotique [ɛgzɔtik] *adj* exotic; **yaourt aux fruits ~s** tropical fruit yoghurt

expatrier [ɛkspatrije] *vt (argent)* to take *ou* send out of the country; **s'expatrier** to leave one's country

expectative [ɛkspɛktativ] *nf:* **être dans l'~** to be waiting to see

expédient [ɛkspedjɑ̃] *nm (parfois péj)* expedient; **vivre d'~s** to live by one's wits

expédier [ɛkspedje] *vt (lettre, paquet)* to send; *(troupes, renfort)* to dispatch; *(péj: travail etc)* to dispose of, dispatch

expéditeur, -trice [ɛkspeditœr, -tris] *nm/f (Postes)* sender

expédition [ɛkspedisjɔ̃] *nf* sending; *(scientifique, sportive, Mil)* expedition; **~ punitive** punitive raid

expérience [ɛksperjɑ̃s] *nf (de la vie, des choses)* experience; *(scientifique)* experiment; **avoir de l'~** to have experience, be experienced; **avoir l'~ de** to have experience of sth; **faire l'~ de qch** to experience sth; **~ de chimie/d'électricité** chemical/electrical experiment

expérimenté, e [ɛksperimɑ̃te] *adj* experienced

expérimenter [ɛksperimɑ̃te] *vt (machine, technique)* to test out, experiment with

expert, e [ɛkspɛr, -ɛrt] *adj:* **~ en** expert in ▷ *nm (spécialiste)* expert; **~ en assurances** insurance valuer

expert-comptable *(pl* **experts-comptables)** [ɛkspɛrkɔ̃tabl] *nm* ≈ chartered *(Brit) ou* certified public *(US)* accountant

expertise [ɛkspɛrtiz] *nf* valuation; assessment; valuer's *(ou* assessor's) report; *(Jur)* (forensic) examination

expertiser [ɛkspɛrtize] *vt (objet de valeur)* to value; *(voiture accidentée etc)* to assess damage to

expier [ɛkspje] *vt* to expiate, atone for

expirer [ɛkspire] *vi (prendre fin, littéraire: mourir)* to expire; *(respirer)* to breathe out

explicatif, -ive [ɛksplikatif, -iv] *adj (mot, texte, note)* explanatory

explication [ɛksplikasjɔ̃] *nf* explanation; *(discussion)* discussion; *(dispute)* argument; **~ de texte** *(Scol)* critical analysis (of a text)

explicite [ɛksplisit] *adj* explicit

expliquer [ɛksplike] *vt* to explain; **~ (à qn) comment/que** to point out *ou* explain (to sb) how/that; **s'expliquer** *(se faire comprendre: personne)* to explain o.s.; *(se disputer)* to have it out; *(comprendre)*: **je m'explique son retard/absence** I understand his lateness/absence; **son erreur s'explique** one can understand his mistake; **s'~ avec qn** *(discuter)* to explain o.s. to sb

exploit [ɛksplwa] *nm* exploit, feat

exploitant [ɛksplwatɑ̃] *nm/f:* **~ (agricole)** farmer

exploitation [ɛksplwatasjɔ̃] *nf* exploitation; *(d'une entreprise)* running; *(entreprise)*: **~ agricole** farming concern

exploiter [ɛksplwate] *vt (personne, don)* to exploit; *(entreprise, ferme)* to run, operate; *(mine)* to exploit, work

explorer [ɛksplɔre] *vt* to explore

exploser [ɛksploze] *vi* to explode, blow up; *(engin explosif)* to go off; *(fig: joie, colère)* to burst out, explode; *(: personne: de colère)* to explode, flare up; **faire ~** *(bombe)* to explode, detonate; *(bâtiment, véhicule)* to blow up

explosif, -ive [ɛksplozif, -iv] *adj, nm* explosive

explosion [ɛksplozjɔ̃] *nf* explosion; **~ de joie/ colère** outburst of joy/rage; **~ démographique** population explosion

exportateur, -trice [ɛkspɔrtatœr, -tris] *adj* export *cpd*, exporting ▷ *nm* exporter

exportation [ɛkspɔrtasjɔ̃] *nf (action)* exportation; *(produit)* export

exporter [ɛkspɔrte] *vt* to export

exposant [ɛkspozɑ̃] *nm* exhibitor; *(Math)* exponent

exposé, e [ɛkspoze] *nm (écrit)* exposé; *(oral)* talk ▷ *adj:* **~ au sud** facing south, with a southern aspect; **bien ~** well situated; **très ~** very exposed

exposer [ɛkspoze] *vt (montrer: marchandise)* to display; *(: peinture)* to exhibit, show; *(parler de: problème, situation)* to explain, expose, set out; *(mettre en danger, orienter, Photo: maison etc)* to expose; **~ qn/qch à** to expose sb/sth to; **~ sa vie** to risk one's life; **s'exposer à** *(soleil, danger)* to expose o.s. to; *(critiques, punition)* to lay o.s. open to

exposition [ɛkspozisjɔ̃] *nf (voir exposer)* displaying; exhibiting; explanation, exposition; exposure; *(voir exposé)* aspect, situation; *(manifestation)* exhibition; *(Photo)* exposure; *(introduction)* exposition

exprès¹ [ɛksprɛ] *adv (délibérément)* on purpose; *(spécialement)* specially; **faire ~ de faire qch** to do sth on purpose

exprès², -esse [ɛksprɛs] *adj (ordre, défense)* express, formal ▷ *adj inv, adv (Postes: lettre, colis)* express; **envoyer qch en ~** to send sth express

express [ɛksprɛs] *adj, nm:* **(café) ~** espresso; **(train) ~** fast train

expressément [ɛkspresemɑ̃] *adv* expressly, specifically

expressif, -ive [ɛkspresif, -iv] *adj* expressive

expression [ɛkspresjɔ̃] *nf* expression; **réduit à sa plus simple ~** reduced to its simplest terms; **liberté/moyens d'~** freedom/means of expression; **~ toute faite** set phrase

exprimer [ɛksprime] *vt (sentiment, idée)* to express; *(faire sortir: jus, liquide)* to press out; **s'exprimer** *vi (personne)* to express o.s.

exproprier [ɛksprɔprije] *vt* to buy up *(ou* buy

the property of) by compulsory purchase, expropriate

expulser [ɛkspylse] vt (d'une salle, d'un groupe) to expel; (locataire) to evict; (Football) to send off

exquis, e [ɛkski, -iz] adj (gâteau, parfum, élégance) exquisite; (personne, temps) delightful

extase [ɛkstaz] nf ecstasy; **être en ~** to be in raptures

extasier [ɛkstazje]: **s'extasier** vi: **s'~ sur** to go into raptures over

extension [ɛkstɑ̃sjɔ̃] nf (d'un muscle, ressort) stretching; (Méd): **à l'~** in traction; (fig) extension; expansion

exténuer [ɛkstenɥe] vt to exhaust

extérieur, e [ɛksterjœr] adj (de dehors: porte, mur etc) outer, outside; (: commerce, politique) foreign; (: influences, pressions) external; (au dehors: escalier, w.-c.) outside; (apparent: calme, gaieté etc) outer ▷ nm (d'une maison, d'un récipient etc) outside, exterior; (d'une personne: apparence) exterior; (d'un pays, d'un groupe social): **l'~** the outside world; **à l'~** (dehors) outside; (fig: à l'étranger) abroad

extérieurement [ɛksterjœrmɑ̃] adv (de dehors) on the outside; (en apparence) on the surface

exterminer [ɛkstɛrmine] vt to exterminate, wipe out

externat [ɛkstɛrna] nm day school

externe [ɛkstɛrn] adj external, outer ▷ nm/f (Méd) non-resident medical student, extern (US); (Scol) day pupil

extincteur [ɛkstɛ̃ktœr] nm (fire) extinguisher

extinction [ɛkstɛ̃ksjɔ̃] nf extinction; (Jur: d'une dette) extinguishment; **~ de voix** (Méd) loss of voice

extorquer [ɛkstɔrke] vt (de l'argent, un renseignement): **~ qch à qn** to extort sth from sb

extra [ɛkstra] adj inv first-rate; (fam) fantastic; (marchandises) top-quality ▷ nm inv extra help ▷ préfixe extra(-)

extrader [ɛkstrade] vt to extradite

extraire [ɛkstrɛr] vt to extract; **~ qch de** to extract sth from

extrait, e [ɛkstrɛ, -ɛt] pp de **extraire** ▷ nm (de plante) extract; (de film, livre) extract, excerpt; **~ de naissance** birth certificate

extraordinaire [ɛkstraɔrdinɛr] adj extraordinary; (Pol, Admin: mesures etc) special; **ambassadeur ~** ambassador extraordinary; **assemblée ~** extraordinary meeting; **par ~** by some unlikely chance

extravagant, e [ɛkstravagɑ̃, -ɑ̃t] adj (personne, attitude) extravagant; (idée) wild

extraverti, e [ɛkstraverti] adj extrovert

extrême [ɛkstrɛm] adj, nm extreme; (intensif): **d'une ~ simplicité/brutalité** extremely simple/brutal; **d'un ~ à l'autre** from one extreme to another; **à l'~** in the extreme; **à l'~ rigueur** in the absolute extreme

extrêmement [ɛkstrɛmmɑ̃] adv extremely

extrême-onction (pl **extrêmes-onctions**) [ɛkstrɛmɔ̃ksjɔ̃] nf (Rel) last rites pl, Extreme Unction

Extrême-Orient [ɛkstrɛmɔrjɑ̃] nm: **l'~** the Far East

extrémité [ɛkstremite] nf (bout) end; (situation) straits pl, plight; (geste désespéré) extreme action; **extrémités** nfpl (pieds et mains) extremities; **à la dernière ~** (à l'agonie) on the point of death

exubérant, e [ɛgzyberɑ̃, -ɑ̃t] adj exuberant

exutoire [ɛgzytwar] nm outlet, release

f

F, f [ɛf] *nm inv* F, f ▷ *abr* = **féminin**; (= *franc*) fr.;
(= *Fahrenheit*) F; (= *frère*) Br(o).; (= *femme*) W;
(*appartement*): **un F2/F3** a 2-/3-roomed flat
(Brit) *ou* apartment (US); **F comme François**
F for Frederick (Brit) *ou* Fox (US)

fa [fa] *nm inv* (*Mus*) F; (*en chantant la gamme*) fa

fable [fabl] *nf* fable; (*mensonge*) story, tale

fabricant, e [fabʀikɑ̃, ɑ̃t] *nm/f*
manufacturer, maker

fabrication [fabʀikasjɔ̃] *nf* manufacture,
making

fabrique [fabʀik] *nf* factory

fabriquer [fabʀike] *vt* to make;
(*industriellement*) to manufacture, make;
(*construire: voiture*) to manufacture, build;
(: *maison*) to build; (*fig: inventer: histoire, alibi*) to
make up; (*fam*): **qu'est-ce qu'il fabrique?**
what is he up to?; **~ en série** to mass-produce

fabulation [fabylasjɔ̃] *nf* (*Psych*) fantasizing

fac [fak] *abr f* (*fam: Scol: = faculté*) Uni (Brit: *fam*)
≈ college (US)

façade [fasad] *nf* front, façade; (*fig*) façade

face [fas] *nf* face; (*fig: aspect*) side ▷ *adj*: **le
côté ~** heads; **perdre/sauver la ~** to lose/save
face; **regarder qn en ~** to look sb in the face;
la maison/le trottoir d'en ~ the house/
pavement opposite; **en ~ de** *prép* opposite;
(*fig*) in front of; **de ~** *adv* from the front; face
on; **~ à** *prép* facing; (*fig*) faced with, in the
face of; **faire ~ à** to face; **faire ~ à la
demande** (*Comm*) to meet the demand; **~ à ~**
adv facing each other ▷ *nm inv* encounter

fâché, e [faʃe] *adj* angry; (*désolé*) sorry

fâcher [faʃe] *vt* to anger; **se fâcher** *vi* to get
angry; **se ~ avec** (*se brouiller*) to fall out with

fâcheux, -euse [faʃø, -øz] *adj* unfortunate,
regrettable

facile [fasil] *adj* easy; (*accommodant: caractère*)
easy-going

facilement [fasilmɑ̃] *adv* easily

facilité [fasilite] *nf* easiness; (*disposition, don*)
aptitude; (*moyen, occasion, possibilité*): **il a la ~
de rencontrer les gens** he has every
opportunity to meet people; **facilités** *nfpl*
(*possibilités*) facilities; (*Comm*) terms; **~s de
crédit** credit terms; **~s de paiement** easy
terms

faciliter [fasilite] *vt* to make easier

façon [fasɔ̃] *nf* (*manière*) way; (*d'une robe etc*)
making-up; cut; (: *main-d'œuvre*) labour (Brit),
labor (US); (*imitation*): **châle ~ cachemire**
cashmere-style shawl; **façons** *nfpl* (*péj*) fuss
sg; **faire des ~s** (*péj: être affecté*) to be affected;
(: *faire des histoires*) to make a fuss; **de quelle ~?**
(in) what way?; **sans ~** *adv* without fuss ▷ *adj*
unaffected; **non merci, sans ~** no thanks,
honestly; **d'une autre ~** in another way; **en
aucune ~** in no way; **de ~ à so as to; de ~ à ce
que, de (telle) ~ que** so that; **de toute ~**
anyway, in any case; **(c'est une) ~ de parler**
it's a way of putting it; **travail à ~** tailoring

façonner [fasɔne] *vt* (*fabriquer*) to
manufacture; (*travailler: matière*) to shape,
fashion; (*fig*) to mould, shape

facteur, -trice [faktœʀ, -tʀis] *nm/f*
postman/woman (Brit), mailman/woman
(US) ▷ *nm* (*Math, gén: élément*) factor;
~ d'orgues organ builder; **~ de pianos** piano
maker; **~ rhésus** rhesus factor

factice [faktis] *adj* artificial

faction [faksjɔ̃] *nf* (*groupe*) faction; (*Mil*)
guard *ou* sentry (duty); watch; **en ~** on guard;
standing watch

facture [faktyʀ] *nf* (*à payer: gén*) bill; (: *Comm*)
invoice; (*d'un artisan, artiste*) technique,
workmanship

facturer [faktyʀe] *vt* to invoice

facultatif, -ive [fakyltatif, -iv] *adj* optional;
(*arrêt de bus*) request *cpd*

faculté [fakylte] *nf* (*intellectuelle, d'université*)
faculty; (*pouvoir, possibilité*) power

fade [fad] *adj* insipid

fagot [fago] *nm* (*de bois*) bundle of sticks

faible [fɛbl] *adj* weak; (*voix, lumière, vent*) faint;
(*élève, copie*) poor; (*rendement, intensité, revenu
etc*) low ▷ *nm* weak point; (*pour quelqu'un*)
weakness, soft spot; **~ d'esprit**
feeble-minded

faiblesse [fɛbles] *nf* weakness

faiblir [feblir] *vi* to weaken; (*lumière*) to dim;
(*vent*) to drop

faïence [fajɑ̃s] *nf* earthenware *no pl*; (*objet*)
piece of earthenware

faignant, e [fɛɲɑ̃, -ɑ̃t] *nm/f* = **fainéant, e**

faille [faj] *vb voir* **falloir** ▷ *nf* (*Géo*) fault; (*fig*) flaw, weakness

faillir [fajiʀ] *vi*: **j'ai failli tomber/lui dire** I almost *ou* nearly fell/told him; **~ à une promesse/un engagement** to break a promise/an agreement

faillite [fajit] *nf* bankruptcy; (*échec: d'une politique etc*) collapse; **être en ~** to be bankrupt; **faire ~** to go bankrupt

faim [fɛ̃] *nf* hunger; (*fig*): **~ d'amour/de richesse** hunger *ou* yearning for love/wealth; **avoir ~** to be hungry; **rester sur sa ~** (*aussi fig*) to be left wanting more

fainéant, e [fɛneɑ̃, -ɑ̃t] *nm/f* idler, loafer

◯ **MOT-CLÉ**

faire [fɛʀ] *vt* **1** (*fabriquer, être l'auteur de*) to make; (*produire*) to produce; (*construire: maison, bateau*) to build; **faire du vin/une offre/un film** to make wine/an offer/a film; **faire du bruit** to make a noise

2 (*effectuer: travail, opération*) to do; **que faites-vous?** (*quel métier etc*) what do you do?; (*quelle activité: au moment de la question*) what are you doing?; **que faire?** what are we going to do?, what can be done (about it)?; **faire la lessive/le ménage** to do the washing/the housework

3 (*études*) to do; (*sport, musique*) to play; **faire du droit/du français** to do law/French; **faire du rugby/piano** to play rugby/the piano; **faire du cheval/du ski** to go riding/skiing

4 (*visiter*): **faire les magasins** to go shopping; **faire l'Europe** to tour *ou* do Europe

5 (*distance*): **faire du 50 (à l'heure)** to do 50 (km an hour); **nous avons fait 1000 km en 2 jours** we did *ou* covered 1000 km in 2 days

6 (*simuler*): **faire le malade/l'ignorant** to act the invalid/the fool

7 (*transformer, avoir un effet sur*): **faire de qn un frustré/avocat** to make sb frustrated/a lawyer; **ça ne me fait rien** (*m'est égal*) I don't care *ou* mind; (*me laisse froid*) it has no effect on me; **ça ne fait rien** it doesn't matter; **faire que** (*impliquer*) to mean that

8 (*calculs, prix, mesures*): **deux et deux font quatre** two and two are *ou* make four; **ça fait 10 m/15 euros** it's 10 m/15 euros; **je vous le fais 10 euros** I'll let you have it for 10 euros; **je fais du 40** I take a size 40

9 (*vb+de*): **qu'a-t-il fait de sa valise/de sa sœur?** what has he done with his case/his sister?

10: **ne faire que**: **il ne fait que critiquer** (*sans cesse*) all he (ever) does is criticize; (*seulement*) he's only criticizing

11 (*dire*) to say; **vraiment?** **fit-il** really? he said

12 (*maladie*) to have; **faire du diabète/de la tension** to have diabetes *sg*/high blood pressure

▷ *vi* **1** (*agir, s'y prendre*) to act, do; **il faut faire vite** we (*ou* you *etc*) must act quickly; **comment a-t-il fait pour?** how did he manage to?; **faites comme chez vous** make yourself at home; **je n'ai pas pu faire autrement** there was nothing else I could do

2 (*paraître*) to look; **faire vieux/démodé** to look old/old-fashioned; **ça fait bien** it looks good; **tu fais jeune dans cette robe** that dress makes you look young(er)

3 (*remplaçant un autre verbe*) to do; **ne le casse pas comme je l'ai fait** don't break it as I did; **je peux le voir? — faites!** can I see it? — please do!; **remets-le en place — je viens de le faire** put it back in its place — I just have (done)

▷ *vb impers* **1**: **il fait beau** *etc* the weather is fine *etc*; *voir aussi* **jour**; **froid** *etc*

2 (*temps écoulé, durée*): **ça fait deux ans qu'il est parti** it's two years since he left; **ça fait deux ans qu'il y est** he's been there for two years

▷ *vb aux* **1**: **faire** (+*infinitif: action directe*) to make; **faire tomber/bouger qch** to make sth fall/move; **faire démarrer un moteur/chauffer de l'eau** to start up an engine/heat some water; **cela fait dormir** it makes you sleep; **faire travailler les enfants** to make the children work *ou* get the children to work; **il m'a fait traverser la rue** he helped me to cross the road

2 (*indirectement, par un intermédiaire*): **faire réparer qch** to get *ou* have sth repaired; **faire punir les enfants** to have the children punished; **il m'a fait ouvrir la porte** he got me to open the door

se faire *vi* **1** (*vin, fromage*) to mature

2 (*être convenable*): **cela se fait beaucoup/ne se fait pas** it's done a lot/not done

3 (+*nom ou pron*): **se faire une jupe** to make o.s. a skirt; **se faire des amis** to make friends; **se faire du souci** to worry; **se faire des illusions** to delude o.s.; **se faire beaucoup d'argent** to make a lot of money; **il ne s'en fait pas** he doesn't worry

4 (+*adj: devenir*): **se faire vieux** to be getting old; (*délibérément*): **se faire beau** to do o.s. up

5: **se faire à** (*s'habituer*) to get used to; **je n'arrive pas à me faire à la nourriture/au climat** I can't get used to the food/climate

6 (+*infinitif*): **se faire examiner la vue/opérer** to have one's eyes tested/have an operation; **se faire couper les cheveux** to get one's hair cut; **il va se faire tuer/punir** he's going to get himself killed/punished (himself); **il s'est fait aider** he got somebody to help him; **il s'est fait aider par Simon** he got Simon to help him; **se faire faire un vêtement** to get a garment made for o.s.

7 (*impersonnel*): **comment se fait-il/faisait-il que?** how is it/was it that?; **il peut se faire que nous utilisions ...** it's possible that we could use ...

faire-part [fɛʀpaʀ] nm inv announcement (of birth, marriage etc)

faisable [fəzabl] adj feasible

faisan, e [fəzɑ̃, -an] nm/f pheasant

faisandé, e [fəzɑ̃de] adj high (bad); (fig péj) corrupt, decadent

faisceau [fɛso] nm (de lumière etc) beam; (de branches etc) bundle

faisons etc [fəzɔ̃] vb voir **faire**

fait[1] [fɛ] vb voir **faire** ▷ nm (événement) event, occurrence; (réalité, donnée) fact; **le ~ que/de manger** the fact that/of eating; **être le ~ de** (causé par) to be the work of; **être au ~ (de)** to be informed (of); **mettre qn au ~** to inform sb, put sb in the picture; **au ~** (à propos) by the way; **en venir au ~** to get to the point; **de ~** adj (opposé à: de droit) de facto ▷ adv in fact; **du ~ de ceci/qu'il a menti** because of ou on account of this/his having lied; **de ce ~** therefore, for this reason; **en ~** in fact; **en ~ de repas** by way of a meal; **prendre ~ et cause pour qn** to support sb, side with sb; **prendre qn sur le ~** to catch sb in the act; **dire à qn son ~** to give sb a piece of one's mind; **hauts ~s** (exploits) exploits; **~ d'armes** feat of arms; **~ divers** (short) news item; **les ~s et gestes de qn** sb's actions ou doings

fait[2]**, e** [fɛ, fɛt] pp de **faire** ▷ adj (mûr: fromage, melon) ripe; (maquillé: yeux) made-up; (vernis: ongles) painted, polished; **un homme ~** a grown man; **tout(e) ~(e)** (préparé à l'avance) ready-made; **c'en est ~ de notre tranquillité** that's the end of our peace; **c'est bien ~ (pour lui ou eux** etc) it serves him (ou them etc) right

faîte [fɛt] nm top; (fig) pinnacle, height

faites [fɛt] vb voir **faire**

faitout [fɛtu] nm stewpot

falaise [falɛz] nf cliff

falloir [falwaʀ] vb impers: **il faut faire les lits** we (ou you etc) have to ou must make the beds; **il faut que je fasse les lits** I have to ou must make the beds; **il a fallu qu'il parte** he had to leave; **il faudrait qu'elle rentre** she should come ou go back, she ought to come ou go back; **il faut faire attention** you have to be careful; **il me faudrait 100 euros** I would need 100 euros; **il doit ~ du temps** that must take time; **il vous faut tourner à gauche après l'église** you have to turn left past the church; **nous avons ce qu'il (nous) faut** we have what we need; **il faut qu'il ait oublié** he must have forgotten; **il a fallu qu'il l'apprenne** he would have to hear about it; **il ne fallait pas** (pour remercier) you shouldn't have (done); **faut le faire!** (it) takes some doing! ▷ vi: **s'en falloir; il s'en est fallu de 10 euros/5 minutes** we (ou they etc) were 10 euros short/5 minutes late (ou early); **il s'en faut de beaucoup qu'il soit** ... he is far from being ...; **il s'en est fallu de peu que cela n'arrive** it very nearly happened; **ou peu**

s'en faut or just about, or as good as; **comme il faut** adj proper ▷ adv properly

falsifier [falsifje] vt to falsify

famé, e [fame] adj: **mal ~** disreputable, of ill repute

famélique [famelik] adj half-starved

fameux, -euse [famø, -øz] adj (illustre: parfois péj) famous; (bon: repas, plat etc) first-rate, first-class; (intensif): **un ~ problème** etc a real problem etc; **pas ~** not great, not much good

familial, e, -aux [familjal, -o] adj family cpd ▷ nf (Auto) family estate car (Brit), station wagon (US)

familiarité [familjaʀite] nf familiarity; informality; **familiarités** nfpl familiarities; **~ avec** (sujet, science) familiarity with

familier, -ière [familje, -jɛʀ] adj (connu, impertinent) familiar; (atmosphère) informal, friendly; (Ling) informal, colloquial ▷ nm regular (visitor)

famille [famij] nf family; **il a de la ~ à Paris** he has relatives in Paris

famine [famin] nf famine

fana [fana] adj, nm/f (fam) = **fanatique**

fanatique [fanatik] adj: **~ (de)** fanatical (about) ▷ nm/f fanatic

fanatisme [fanatism] nm fanaticism

faner [fane]: **se faner** vi to fade

fanfare [fɑ̃faʀ] nf (orchestre) brass band; (musique) fanfare; **en ~** (avec bruit) noisily

fanfaron, ne [fɑ̃faʀɔ̃, -ɔn] nm/f braggart

fantaisie [fɑ̃tezi] nf (spontanéité) fancy, imagination; (caprice) whim; extravagance; (Mus) fantasia ▷ adj: **bijou (de) ~** (piece of) costume jewellery (Brit) ou jewelry (US); **pain (de) ~** fancy bread

fantaisiste [fɑ̃tezist] adj (péj) unorthodox, eccentric ▷ nm/f (de music-hall) variety artist ou entertainer

fantasme [fɑ̃tasm] nm fantasy

fantasque [fɑ̃task] adj whimsical, capricious; fantastic

fantastique [fɑ̃tastik] adj fantastic

fantôme [fɑ̃tom] nm ghost, phantom

faon [fɑ̃] nm fawn (deer)

FAQ abr f (= foire aux questions) FAQ pl (= frequently asked questions)

farce [faʀs] nf (viande) stuffing; (blague) (practical) joke; (Théât) farce; **faire une ~ à qn** to play a (practical) joke on sb; **~s et attrapes** jokes and novelties

farcir [faʀsiʀ] vt (viande) to stuff; (fig): **~ qch de** to stuff sth with; **se farcir** (fam): **je me suis farci la vaisselle** I've got stuck ou landed with the washing-up

fardeau, x [faʀdo] nm burden

farder [faʀde] vt to make up; (vérité) to disguise; **se farder** to make o.s. up

farfelu, e [faʀfəly] adj wacky (fam), hare-brained

farine [faʀin] nf flour; **~ de blé** wheatflour; **~ de maïs** cornflour (Brit), cornstarch (US);

~ **lactée** (*pour bouillie*) baby cereal

farineux, -euse [faʀinø, -øz] *adj* (*sauce, pomme*) floury ▷ *nmpl* (*aliments*) starchy foods

farouche [faʀuʃ] *adj* shy, timid; (*sauvage*) savage, wild; (*violent*) fierce

fart [faʀt] *nm* (ski) wax

fascicule [fasikyl] *nm* volume

fascination [fasinasjɔ̃] *nf* fascination

fasciner [fasine] *vt* to fascinate

fascisme [faʃism] *nm* fascism

fasse *etc* [fas] *vb voir* **faire**

faste [fast] *nm* splendour (*Brit*), splendor (*US*) ▷ *adj*: **c'est un jour ~** it's his (*ou our etc*) lucky day

fastidieux, -euse [fastidjø, -øz] *adj* tedious, tiresome

fastueux, -euse [fastɥø, -øz] *adj* sumptuous, luxurious

fatal, e [fatal] *adj* fatal; (*inévitable*) inevitable

fatalité [fatalite] *nf* (*destin*) fate; (*coïncidence*) fateful coincidence; (*caractère inévitable*) inevitability

fatidique [fatidik] *adj* fateful

fatigant, e [fatigɑ̃, -ɑ̃t] *adj* tiring; (*agaçant*) tiresome

fatigue [fatig] *nf* tiredness, fatigue; (*détérioration*) fatigue; **les ~s du voyage** the wear and tear of the journey

fatigué, e [fatige] *adj* tired

fatiguer [fatige] *vt* to tire, make tired; (*Tech*) to put a strain on, strain; (*fig: agacer*) to annoy ▷ *vi* (*moteur*) to labour (*Brit*), labor (*US*), strain; **se fatiguer** *vi* to get tired; to tire o.s. (out); **se ~ à faire qch** to tire o.s. out doing sth

fatras [fatʀa] *nm* jumble, hotchpotch

faubourg [fobuʀ] *nm* suburb

fauché, e [foʃe] *adj* (*fam*) broke

faucher [foʃe] *vt* (*herbe*) to cut; (*champs, blés*) to reap; (*fig*) to cut down; (*véhicule*) to mow down; (*fam: voler*) to pinch, nick

faucille [fosij] *nf* sickle

faucon [fokɔ̃] *nm* falcon, hawk

faudra *etc* [fodʀa] *vb voir* **falloir**

faufiler [fofile] *vt* to tack, baste; **se faufiler** *vi*: **se ~ dans** to edge one's way into; **se ~ parmi/entre** to thread one's way among/ between

faune [fon] *nf* (*Zool*) wildlife, fauna; (*fig péj*) set, crowd ▷ *nm* faun; ~ **marine** marine (animal) life

faussaire [fosεʀ] *nm/f* forger

fausse [fos] *adj f voir* **faux**

faussement [fosmɑ̃] *adv* (*accuser*) wrongly, wrongfully; (*croire*) falsely, erroneously

fausser [fose] *vt* (*objet*) to bend, buckle; (*fig*) to distort; ~ **compagnie à qn** to give sb the slip

faut [fo] *vb voir* **falloir**

faute [fot] *nf* (*erreur*) mistake, error; (*péché, manquement*) misdemeanour; (*Football etc*) offence; (*Tennis*) fault; (*responsabilité*): **par la ~ de** through the fault of, because of; **c'est de sa/ma ~** it's his/my fault; **être en ~** to be in

the wrong; **prendre qn en ~** to catch sb out; ~ **de** (*temps, argent*) for ou through lack of; ~ **de mieux** for want of anything ou something better; **sans ~** *adv* without fail; ~ **de frappe** typing error; ~ **d'inattention** careless mistake; ~ **d'orthographe** spelling mistake; ~ **professionnelle** professional misconduct *no pl*

fauteuil [fotœj] *nm* armchair; ~ **à bascule** rocking chair; ~ **club** (big) easy chair; ~ **d'orchestre** seat in the front stalls (*Brit*) ou the orchestra (*US*); ~ **roulant** wheelchair

fauteur [fotœʀ] *nm*: ~ **de troubles** trouble-maker

fautif, -ive [fotif, -iv] *adj* (*incorrect*) incorrect, inaccurate; (*responsable*) at fault, in the wrong; (*coupable*) guilty ▷ *nm/f* culprit; **il se sentait ~** he felt guilty

fauve [fov] *nm* wildcat; (*peintre*) Fauve ▷ *adj* (*couleur*) fawn

faux¹ [fo] *nf* scythe

faux², fausse [fo, fos] *adj* (*inexact*) wrong; (*piano, voix*) out of tune; (*falsifié: billet*) fake, forged; (*sournois, postiche*) false ▷ *adv* (*Mus*) out of tune ▷ *nm* (*copie*) fake, forgery; (*opposé au vrai*): **le ~** falsehood; **le ~ numéro/la fausse clé** the wrong number/key; **faire fausse route** to go the wrong way; **faire ~ bond à qn** to let sb down; ~ **ami** (*Ling*) faux ami; ~ **col** detachable collar; ~ **départ** (*Sport, fig*) false start; ~ **frais** *nmpl* extras, incidental expenses; ~ **frère** (*fig péj*) false friend; ~ **mouvement** awkward movement; ~ **nez** false nose; ~ **nom** assumed name; ~ **pas** tripping *no pl*; (*fig*) faux pas; **faire un ~ pas** to trip; (*fig*) to make a faux pas; ~ **témoignage** (*délit*) perjury; **fausse alerte** false alarm; **fausse clé** skeleton key; **fausse couche** (*Méd*) miscarriage; **fausse joie** vain joy; **fausse note** wrong note

faux-filet [fofile] *nm* sirloin

faux-monnayeur [fomɔnεjœʀ] *nm* counterfeiter, forger

faveur [favœʀ] *nf* favour (*Brit*), favor (*US*); **traitement de ~** preferential treatment; **à la ~ de** under cover of; (*grâce à*) thanks to; **en ~ de** in favo(u)r of

favorable [favɔʀabl] *adj* favo(u)rable

favori, te [favɔʀi, -it] *adj, nm/f* favo(u)rite

favoriser [favɔʀize] *vt* to favour (*Brit*), favor (*US*)

fax [faks] *nm* fax

faxer [fakse] *vt* to fax

FB *abr* (= *franc belge*) BF, FB

fébrile [febʀil] *adj* feverish, febrile; **capitaux ~s** (*Écon*) hot money

fécond, e [fekɔ̃, -ɔ̃d] *adj* fertile

féconder [fekɔ̃de] *vt* to fertilize

fécondité [fekɔ̃dite] *nf* fertility

fécule [fekyl] *nf* potato flour

féculent [fekylɑ̃] *nm* starchy food

fédéral, e, -aux [federal, -o] *adj* federal

fée [fe] *nf* fairy

féerique [feʀik] adj magical, fairytale cpd
feignant, e [fɛɲɑ̃, -ɑ̃t] nm/f = **fainéant, e**
feindre [fɛ̃dʀ] vt to feign ▷ vi to dissemble;
~ **de faire** to pretend to do
feint, e [fɛ̃, fɛ̃t] pp de **feindre** ▷ adj feigned
▷ nf (Sport: escrime) feint; (: Football, Rugby)
dummy (Brit), fake (US); (fam: ruse) sham
fêler [fele] vt to crack
félicitations [felisitasjɔ̃] nfpl
congratulations
féliciter [felisite] vt: ~ **qn (de)** to
congratulate sb (on)
félin, e [felɛ̃, -in] adj feline ▷ nm (big) cat
fêlure [felyʀ] nf crack
femelle [fəmɛl] adj (aussi Élec, Tech) female
▷ nf female
féminin, e [feminɛ̃, -in] adj feminine; (sexe)
female; (équipe, vêtements etc) women's;
(parfois péj: homme) effeminate ▷ nm (Ling)
feminine
féministe [feminist] adj, nf feminist
femme [fam] nf woman; (épouse) wife; **être
très** ~ to be very much a woman; **devenir** ~
to attain womanhood; ~ **d'affaires**
businesswoman; ~ **de chambre**
chambermaid; ~ **fatale** femme fatale; ~ **au
foyer** housewife; ~ **d'intérieur** (real)
homemaker; ~ **de ménage** domestic help,
cleaning lady; ~ **du monde** society woman;
~-**objet** sex object; ~ **de tête** determined,
intellectual woman
fémur [femyʀ] nm femur, thighbone
fendre [fɑ̃dʀ] vt (couper en deux) to split;
(fissurer) to crack; (fig: traverser) to cut through;
to push one's way through; **se fendre** vi to
crack
fenêtre [f(ə)nɛtʀ] nf window; ~ **à guillotine**
sash window
fenouil [fənuj] nm fennel
fente [fɑ̃t] nf (fissure) crack; (de boîte à lettres etc)
slit
féodal, e, -aux [feɔdal, -o] adj feudal
fer [fɛʀ] nm iron; (de cheval) shoe; **fers** nmpl
(Méd) forceps; **mettre aux** ~**s** (enchaîner) to
put in chains; **au** ~ **rouge** with a red-hot
iron; **santé/main de** ~ iron constitution/
hand; ~ **à cheval** horseshoe; **en** ~ **à cheval**
(fig) horseshoe-shaped; ~ **forgé** wrought
iron; ~ **à friser** curling tongs; ~ **de lance**
spearhead; ~ **(à repasser)** iron; ~ **à souder**
soldering iron
ferai etc [fəʀe] vb voir **faire**
fer-blanc [fɛʀblɑ̃] nm tin(plate)
férié, e [feʀje] adj: **jour** ~ public holiday
ferions etc [fəʀjɔ̃] vb voir **faire**
ferme [fɛʀm] adj firm ▷ adv (travailler etc) hard;
(discuter) ardently ▷ nf (exploitation) farm;
(maison) farmhouse; **tenir** ~ to stand firm
fermé, e [fɛʀme] adj closed, shut; (gaz, eau etc)
off; (fig: personne) uncommunicative; (: milieu)
exclusive
fermenter [fɛʀmɑ̃te] vi to ferment

fermer [fɛʀme] vt to close; shut; (cesser
l'exploitation de) to close down, shut down;
(eau, lumière, électricité, robinet) to turn off;
(aéroport, route) to close ▷ vi to close, shut;
(magasin: définitivement) to close down, shut
down; **se fermer** vi (yeux) to close, shut; (fleur,
blessure) to close up; ~ **à clef** to lock; ~ **au
verrou** to bolt; ~ **les yeux (sur qch)** (fig) to
close one's eyes (on to sth); **se** ~ **à** (pitié, amour) to
close one's heart ou mind to
fermeté [fɛʀməte] nf firmness
fermeture [fɛʀmətyʀ] nf closing; shutting;
closing ou shutting down; putting ou turning
off; (dispositif) catch; fastening; fastener;
heure de ~ (Comm) closing time; **jour de** ~
(Comm) day on which the shop (etc) is closed;
~ **annuelle** (Comm) annual closure; ~ **éclair**®
ou **à glissière** zip (fastener) (Brit), zipper; voir
fermer
fermier, -ière [fɛʀmje, -jɛʀ] nm/f farmer ▷ nf
(femme de fermier) farmer's wife ▷ adj: **beurre/
cidre** ~ farm butter/cider
fermoir [fɛʀmwaʀ] nm clasp
féroce [feʀɔs] adj ferocious, fierce
ferons etc [fəʀɔ̃] vb voir **faire**
ferraille [feʀaj] nf scrap iron; **mettre à la** ~
to scrap; **bruit de** ~ clanking
ferrer [feʀe] vt (cheval) to shoe; (chaussure) to
nail; (canne) to tip; (poisson) to strike
ferronnerie [feʀɔnʀi] nf ironwork; ~ **d'art**
wrought iron work
ferroviaire [feʀɔvjɛʀ] adj rail cpd, railway cpd
(Brit), railroad cpd (US)
ferry [feʀe], **ferry-boat** [feʀebot] nm ferry
fertile [fɛʀtil] adj fertile; ~ **en incidents**
eventful, packed with incidents
féru, e [feʀy] adj: ~ **de** with a keen interest in
fervent, e [fɛʀvɑ̃, -ɑ̃t] adj fervent
fesse [fɛs] nf buttock; **les** ~**s** the bottom sg,
the buttocks
fessée [fese] nf spanking
festin [fɛstɛ̃] nm feast
festival [festival] nm festival
festivités [festivite] nfpl festivities,
merrymaking sg
festoyer [fɛstwaje] vi to feast
fêtard [fɛtaʀ, e] [fɛtaʀ, aʀd] (fam) nm/f (péj)
high liver, merrymaker
fête [fɛt] nf (religieuse) feast; (publique) holiday;
(en famille etc) celebration; (réception) party;
(kermesse) fête, fair, festival; (du nom) feast day,
name day; **faire la** ~ to live it up; **faire** ~ **à qn**
to give sb a warm welcome; **se faire une** ~ **de**
to look forward to; to enjoy; **ça va être sa** ~!
(fam) he's going to get it!; **jour de** ~ holiday;
les ~**s (de fin d'année)** the festive season; **la
salle/le comité des** ~**s** the village hall/
festival committee; **la** ~ **des Mères/Pères**
Mother's/Father's Day; ~ **de charité** charity
fair ou fête; ~ **foraine** (fun)fair; **la** ~ **de la
musique** see note; ~ **mobile** movable feast
(day); **la F~ Nationale** the national holiday

● **FÊTE DE LA MUSIQUE**
●
● The *Fête de la Musique* is a music festival
● which has taken place every year since
● 1981. On 21 June throughout France local
● musicians perform free of charge in
● parks, streets and squares.

fêter [fete] vt to celebrate; (*personne*) to have a celebration for

feu¹ [fø] adj inv: **~ son père** his late father

feu², x [fø] nm (*gén*) fire; (*signal lumineux*) light; (*de cuisinière*) ring; (*sensation de brûlure*) burning (sensation); **feux** nmpl fire sg; (*Auto*) (traffic) lights; **tous ~x éteints** (*Navig, Auto*) without lights; **au ~!** (*incendie*) fire!; **à ~ doux/vif** over a slow/brisk heat; **à petit ~** (*Culin*) over a gentle heat; (*fig*) slowly; **faire ~** to fire; **ne pas faire long ~** (*fig*) not to last long; **commander le ~** (*Mil*) to give the order to (open) fire; **tué au ~** (*Mil*) killed in action; **mettre à ~** (*fusée*) to fire off; **pris entre deux ~x** caught in the crossfire; **en ~** on fire; **être tout ~ tout flamme (pour)** (*passion*) to be aflame with passion (for); (*enthousiasme*) to be fired with enthusiasm (for); **prendre ~** to catch fire; **mettre le ~ à** to set fire to, set on fire; **faire du ~** to make a fire; **avez-vous du ~?** (*pour cigarette*) have you (got) a light?; **~ rouge/vert/orange** (*Auto*) red/green/amber (*Brit*) ou yellow (*US*) light; **donner le ~ vert à qch/qn** (*fig*) to give sth/sb the go-ahead ou green light; **~ arrière** (*Auto*) rear light; **~ d'artifice** firework; (*spectacle*) fireworks pl; **~ de camp** campfire; **~ de cheminée** chimney fire; **~ de joie** bonfire; **~ de paille** (*fig*) flash in the pan; **~x de brouillard** (*Auto*) fog lights ou lamps; **~x de croisement** (*Auto*) dipped (*Brit*) ou dimmed (*US*) headlights; **~x de position** (*Auto*) sidelights; **~x de route** (*Auto*) headlights (on full (*Brit*) ou high (*US*) beam); **~x de stationnement** parking lights

feuillage [fœjaʒ] nm foliage, leaves pl

feuille [fœj] nf (*d'arbre*) leaf; **~ (de papier)** sheet (of paper); **rendre ~ blanche** (*Scol*) to give in a blank paper; **~ de calcul** spreadsheet; **~ d'or/de métal** gold/metal leaf; **~ de chou** (*péj: journal*) rag; **~ d'impôts** tax form; **~ de maladie** medical expenses claim form; **~ morte** dead leaf; **~ de paye**, **~ de paie** pay slip; **~ de présence** attendance sheet; **~ de température** temperature chart; **~ de vigne** (*Bot*) vine leaf; (*sur statue*) fig leaf; **~ volante** loose sheet

feuillet [fœje] nm leaf, page

feuilleté, e [fœjte] adj (*Culin*) flaky; (*verre*) laminated; **pâte ~e** flaky pastry

feuilleter [fœjte] vt (*livre*) to leaf through

feuilleton [fœjtɔ̃] nm serial

feutre [føtʀ] nm felt; (*chapeau*) felt hat; (*stylo*) felt-tip(ped pen)

feutré, e [føtʀe] adj feltlike; (*pas, voix,*

atmosphère) muffled

fève [fɛv] nf broad bean; (*dans la galette des Rois*) charm (*hidden in cake eaten on Twelfth Night*)

février [fevʀije] nm February; *voir aussi* **juillet**

FF abr (= franc français) FF

FFF abr = Fédération française de football

fiable [fjabl] adj reliable

fiançailles [fjɑ̃saj] nfpl engagement sg

fiancé, e [fjɑ̃se] nm/f fiancé/fiancée ▷ adj: **être ~ (à)** to be engaged (to)

fiancer [fjɑ̃se]: **se fiancer** vi: **se ~ (avec)** to become engaged (to)

fibre [fibʀ] nf fibre, fiber (*US*); **avoir la ~ paternelle/militaire** to be a born father/soldier; **~ optique** optical fibre ou fiber; **~ de verre** fibreglass (*Brit*), fiberglass (*US*), glass fibre ou fiber

ficeler [fis(ə)le] vt to tie up

ficelle [fisɛl] nf string no pl; (*morceau*) piece ou length of string; (*pain*) stick of French bread; **ficelles** nfpl (*fig*) strings; **tirer sur la ~** (*fig*) to go too far

fiche [fiʃ] nf (*carte*) (index) card; (*formulaire*) form; (*Élec*) plug; **~ de paye** pay slip; **~ signalétique** (*Police*) identification card; **~ technique** data sheet, specification ou spec sheet

ficher [fiʃe] vt (*dans un fichier*) to file; (: *Police*) to put on file; (*fam: faire*) to do; (: *donner*) to give; (: *mettre*) to stick ou shove; (*planter*): **~ qch dans** to stick ou drive sth into; **~ qn à la porte** (*fam*) to chuck sb out; **fiche(-moi) le camp** (*fam*) clear off; **fiche-moi la paix** (*fam*) leave me alone; **se ~ dans** (*s'enfoncer*) to get stuck in, embed itself in; **se ~ de** (*fam: rire de*) to make fun of; (*être indifférent à*) to not care about

fichier [fiʃje] nm (*gén, Inform*) file; (*à cartes*) card index; **~ actif** ou **en cours d'utilisation** (*Inform*) active file; **~ d'adresses** mailing list; **~ d'archives** (*Inform*) archive file; **~ joint** (*Inform*) attachment

fichu, e [fiʃy] pp de **ficher** ▷ adj (*fam: fini, inutilisable*) bust, done for; (: *intensif*) wretched, darned ▷ nm (*foulard*) (head)scarf; **être ~ de** to be capable of; **mal ~** feeling lousy; useless; **bien ~** great

fictif, -ive [fiktif, -iv] adj fictitious

fiction [fiksjɔ̃] nf fiction; (*fait imaginé*) invention

fidèle [fidɛl] adj: **~ (à)** faithful (to) ▷ nm/f (*Rel*): **les ~s** the faithful; (*à l'église*) the congregation

fidélité [fidelite] nf (*d'un conjoint*) fidelity, faithfulness; (*d'un ami, client*) loyalty

fier¹ [fje]: **se ~ à** vt to trust

fier², fière [fjɛʀ] adj proud; **~ de** proud of; **avoir fière allure** to cut a fine figure

fierté [fjɛʀte] nf pride

fièvre [fjɛvʀ] nf fever; **avoir de la ~/39 de ~** to have a high temperature/a temperature of 39°C; **~ typhoïde** typhoid fever

fiévreux, -euse [fjevʀø, -øz] adj feverish

figé, e [fiʒe] *adj (manières)* stiff; *(société)* rigid; *(sourire)* set

figer [fiʒe] *vt* to congeal; *(fig: personne)* to freeze, root to the spot; **se figer** *vi* to congeal; *(personne)* to freeze; *(institutions etc)* to become set, stop moving

fignoler [fiɲɔle] *vt* to put the finishing touches to

figue [fig] *nf* fig

figuier [figje] *nm* fig tree

figurant, e [figyʀã, -ãt] *nm/f (Théât)* walk-on; *(Ciné)* extra

figure [figyʀ] *nf (visage)* face; *(image, tracé, forme, personnage)* figure; *(illustration)* picture, diagram; **faire ~ de** to look like; **faire bonne ~** to put up a good show; **faire triste ~** to be a sorry sight; **~ de rhétorique** figure of speech

figuré, e [figyʀe] *adj (sens)* figurative

figurer [figyʀe] *vi* to appear ▷ *vt* to represent; **se ~ que** to imagine that; **figurez-vous que ...** would you believe that ...?

fil [fil] *nm (brin, fig: d'une histoire)* thread; *(du téléphone)* cable, wire; *(textile de lin)* linen; *(d'un couteau: tranchant)* edge; **au ~ des années** with the passing of the years; **au ~ de l'eau** with the stream *ou* current; **de ~ en aiguille** one thing leading to another; **ne tenir qu'à un ~** *(vie, réussite etc)* to hang by a thread; **donner du ~ à retordre à qn** to make life difficult for sb; **coup de ~** *(fam)* phone call; **donner/recevoir un coup de ~** to make/get a phone call; **~ à coudre** (sewing) thread *ou* yarn; **~ dentaire** dental floss; **~ électrique** electric wire; **~ de fer** wire; **~ de fer barbelé** barbed wire; **~ à pêche** fishing line; **~ à plomb** plumb line; **~ à souder** soldering wire

filament [filamã] *nm (Élec)* filament; *(de liquide)* trickle, thread

filandreux, -euse [filãdʀø, -øz] *adj* stringy

filature [filatyʀ] *nf (fabrique)* mill; *(policière)* shadowing *no pl*, tailing *no pl*; **prendre qn en ~** to shadow *ou* tail sb

file [fil] *nf* line; *(Auto)* lane; **~ (d'attente)** queue *(Brit)*, line *(US)*; **prendre la ~** to join the (end of the) queue *ou* line; **prendre la ~ de droite** *(Auto)* to move into the right-hand lane; **se mettre en ~** to form a line; *(Auto)* to get into lane; **stationner en double ~** *(Auto)* to double-park; **à la ~** *adv (d'affilée)* in succession; *(à la suite)* one after another; **à la** *ou* **en ~ indienne** in single file

filer [file] *vt (tissu, toile, verre)* to spin; *(dérouler: câble etc)* to pay ou let out; *(prendre en filature)* to shadow, tail; *(fam: donner)*: **~ qch à qn** to slip sb sth ▷ *vi (bas, maille, liquide, pâte)* to run; *(aller vite)* to fly past *ou* by; *(fam: partir)* to make off; **~ à l'anglaise** to take French leave; **~ doux** to behave o.s., toe the line; **~ un mauvais coton** to be in a bad way

filet [file] *nm* net; *(Culin)* fillet; *(d'eau, de sang)* trickle; **tendre un ~** *(police)* to set a trap; **~ (à**

bagages) *(Rail)* luggage rack; **~ (à provisions)** string bag

filial, e, -aux [filjal, -o] *adj* filial ▷ *nf (Comm)* subsidiary; affiliate

filière [filjɛʀ] *nf (carrière)* path; **passer par la ~** to go through the (administrative) channels; **suivre la ~** to work one's way up (through the hierarchy)

filiforme [filifɔʀm] *adj* spindly; threadlike

filigrane [filigʀan] *nm (d'un billet, timbre)* watermark; **en ~** *(fig)* showing just beneath the surface

fille [fij] *nf* girl; *(opposé à fils)* daughter; **vieille ~** old maid; **~ de joie** prostitute; **~ de salle** waitress

fillette [fijɛt] *nf* (little) girl

filleul, e [fijœl] *nm/f* godchild, godson; goddaughter

film [film] *nm (pour photo)* (roll of) film; *(œuvre)* film, picture, movie; *(couche)* film; **~ muet/parlant** silent/talking picture *ou* movie; **~ alimentaire** clingfilm; **~ d'amour/d'animation/d'horreur** romantic/animated/horror film; **~ comique** comedy; **~ policier** thriller

filon [filɔ̃] *nm* vein, lode; *(fig)* lucrative line, money-spinner

fils [fis] *nm* son; **~ de famille** moneyed young man; **~ à papa** *(péj)* daddy's boy

filtre [filtʀ] *nm* filter; **"~ ou sans ~?"** *(cigarettes)* "tipped or plain?"; **~ à air** air filter

filtrer [filtʀe] *vt* to filter; *(fig: candidats, visiteurs)* to screen ▷ *vi* to filter (through)

fin¹ [fɛ̃] *nf* end; **fins** *nfpl (but)* ends; **à (la) ~ mai, ~ mai** at the end of May; **en ~ de semaine** at the end of the week; **prendre ~** to come to an end; **toucher à sa ~** to be drawing to a close; **mettre ~ à** to put an end to; **mener à bonne ~** to bring to a successful conclusion; **à cette ~** to this end; **à toutes ~s utiles** for your information; **à la ~** in the end, eventually; **en ~ de compte** in the end; **sans ~** *adj* endless ▷ *adv* endlessly; **~ de non-recevoir** *(Jur, Admin)* objection; **~ de section** *(de ligne d'autobus)* (fare) stage

fin², e [fɛ̃, fin] *adj (papier, couche, fil)* thin; *(cheveux, poudre, pointe, visage)* fine; *(taille)* neat, slim; *(esprit, remarque)* subtle; shrewd ▷ *adv (moudre, couper)* finely ▷ *nm*: **vouloir jouer au plus ~ (avec qn)** to try to outsmart sb ▷ *nf (alcool)* liqueur brandy; **c'est ~!** *(ironique)* how clever!; **~ prêt/soûl** quite ready/drunk; **un ~ gourmet** a gourmet; **un ~ tireur** a crack shot; **avoir la vue/l'ouïe ~e** to have keen eyesight/hearing, have sharp eyes/ears; **or/linge/vin ~** fine gold/linen/wine; **le ~ fond de** the very depths of; **le ~ mot de** the real story behind; **la ~e fleur de** the flower of; **une ~e mouche** *(fig)* a sly customer; **~es herbes** mixed herbs

final, e [final] *adj, nf* finale ▷ *nm (Mus)* finale; **quarts de ~e** quarter finals; **8èmes/16èmes**

de ~e 2nd/1st round (*in 5 round knock-out competition*)

finalement [finalmã] *adv* finally, in the end; (*après tout*) after all

finance [finãs] *nf* finance; **finances** *nfpl* (*situation financière*) finances; (*activités financières*) finance *sg*; **moyennant ~** for a fee *ou* consideration

financer [finãse] *vt* to finance

financier, -ière [finãsje, -jɛR] *adj* financial ▷ *nm* financier

finaud, e [fino, -od] *adj* wily

finesse [finɛs] *nf* thinness; (*raffinement*) fineness; neatness; slimness; (*subtilité*) subtlety; shrewdness; **finesses** *nfpl* (*subtilités*) niceties; finer points

fini, e [fini] *adj* finished; (*Math*) finite; (*intensif*): **un menteur ~** a liar through and through ▷ *nm* (*d'un objet manufacturé*) finish

finir [finiR] *vt* to finish ▷ *vi* to finish, end; **~ quelque part** to end *ou* finish up somewhere; **~ de faire** to finish doing; (*cesser*) to stop doing; **~ par faire** to end *ou* finish up doing; **il finit par m'agacer** he's beginning to get on my nerves; **~ en pointe/tragédie** to end in a point/in tragedy; **en ~ avec** to be *ou* have done with; **à n'en plus ~** (*route, discussions*) never-ending; **il va mal ~** he will come to a bad end; **c'est bientôt fini?** (*reproche*) have you quite finished?

finition [finisjɔ̃] *nf* finishing; (*résultat*) finish

finlandais, e [fɛ̃lãdɛ, -ɛz] *adj* Finnish ▷ *nm/f*: **F~, e** Finn

Finlande [fɛ̃lãd] *nf*: **la ~** Finland

finnois, e [finwa, -waz] *adj* Finnish ▷ *nm* (*Ling*) Finnish

fiole [fjɔl] *nf* phial

fioul [fjul] *nm* fuel oil

firme [fiRm] *nf* firm

fis [fi] *vb voir* **faire**

fisc [fisk] *nm* tax authorities *pl*, ≈ Inland Revenue (*Brit*), ≈ Internal Revenue Service (*US*)

fiscal, e, -aux [fiskal, -o] *adj* tax *cpd*, fiscal

fiscalité [fiskalite] *nf* tax system; (*charges*) taxation

fissure [fisyR] *nf* crack

fissurer [fisyRe] *vt* to crack; **se fissurer** *vi* to crack

fiston [fistɔ̃] *nm* (*fam*) son, lad

fit [fi] *vb voir* **faire**

fixation [fiksasjɔ̃] *nf* fixing; (*attache*) fastening; setting; (*de ski*) binding; (*Psych*) fixation

fixe [fiks] *adj* fixed; (*emploi*) steady, regular ▷ *nm* (*salaire*) basic salary; (*téléphone*) landline; **à heure ~** at a set time; **menu à prix ~** set menu

fixé, e [fikse] *adj* (*heure, jour*) appointed; **être ~ (sur)** (*savoir à quoi s'en tenir*) to have made up one's mind (about); to know for certain (about)

fixer [fikse] *vt* (*attacher*): **~ qch (à/sur)** to fix *ou* fasten sth (to/onto); (*déterminer*) to fix, set; (*Chimie, Photo*) to fix; (*poser son regard sur*) to stare at, look hard at; **se fixer** (*s'établir*) to settle down; **~ son choix sur qch** to decide on sth; **se ~ sur** (*attention*) to focus on

flacon [flakɔ̃] *nm* bottle

flageoler [flaʒɔle] *vi* to have knees like jelly

flageolet [flaʒɔlɛ] *nm* (*Mus*) flageolet; (*Culin*) dwarf kidney bean

flagrant, e [flagRã, -ãt] *adj* flagrant, blatant; **en ~ délit** in the act, in flagrante delicto

flair [flɛR] *nm* sense of smell; (*fig*) intuition

flairer [fleRe] *vt* (*humer*) to sniff (at); (*détecter*) to scent

flamand, e [flamã, -ãd] *adj* Flemish ▷ *nm* (*Ling*) Flemish ▷ *nm/f*: **F~, e** Fleming; **les F~s** the Flemish

flamant [flamã] *nm* flamingo

flambant [flãbã] *adv*: **~ neuf** brand new

flambé, e [flãbe] *adj* (*Culin*) flambé ▷ *nf* blaze; (*fig*) flaring-up, explosion

flambeau, x [flãbo] *nm* (flaming) torch; **se passer le ~** (*fig*) to hand down the (*ou* a) tradition

flambée [flãbe] *nf* (*feu*) blaze; (*Comm*): **~ des prix** (sudden) shooting up of prices

flamber [flãbe] *vi* to blaze (up) ▷ *vt* (*poulet*) to singe; (*aiguille*) to sterilize

flamboyer [flãbwaje] *vi* to blaze (up); (*fig*) to flame

flamme [flam] *nf* flame; (*fig*) fire, fervour; **en ~s** on fire, ablaze

flan [flã] *nm* (*Culin*) custard tart *ou* pie

flanc [flã] *nm* side; (*Mil*) flank; **à ~ de colline** on the hillside; **prêter le ~ à** (*fig*) to lay o.s. open to

flancher [flãʃe] *vi* (*cesser de fonctionner*) to fail, pack up; (*armée*) to quit

flanelle [flanɛl] *nf* flannel

flâner [flane] *vi* to stroll

flânerie [flanRi] *nf* stroll

flanquer [flãke] *vt* to flank; (*fam: mettre*) to chuck, shove; (: *jeter*): **~ par terre/à la porte** to fling to the ground/chuck out; (: *donner*): **~ la frousse à qn** to put the wind up sb, give sb an awful fright

flaque [flak] *nf* (*d'eau*) puddle; (*d'huile, de sang etc*) pool

flash (*pl* **flashes**) [flaʃ] *nm* (*Photo*) flash; **~ (d'information)** newsflash

flasque [flask] *adj* flabby ▷ *nf* (*flacon*) flask

flatter [flate] *vt* to flatter; (*caresser*) to stroke; **se ~ de qch** to pride o.s. on sth

flatterie [flatRi] *nf* flattery

flatteur, -euse [flatœR, -øz] *adj* flattering ▷ *nm/f* flatterer

fléau, x [fleo] *nm* scourge, curse; (*de balance*) beam; (*pour le blé*) flail

flèche [flɛʃ] *nf* arrow; (*de clocher*) spire; (*de grue*) jib; (*trait d'esprit, critique*) shaft; **monter en ~** (*fig*) to soar, rocket; **partir en ~** (*fig*) to be off like a shot; **à ~ variable** (*avion*) swing-wing *cpd*

fléchette [fleʃɛt] *nf* dart; **fléchettes** *nfpl* (*jeu*) darts *sg*

fléchir [fleʃiʀ] *vt* (*corps, genou*) to bend; (*fig*) to sway, weaken ▷ *vi* (*poutre*) to sag, bend; (*fig*) to weaken, flag; (: *baisser: prix*) to fall off

flemmard, e [flemaʀ, -aʀd] *nm/f* lazybones *sg*, loafer

flemme [flɛm] *nf* (*fam*): **j'ai la ~ de le faire** I can't be bothered

flétrir [fletʀiʀ] *vt* to wither; (*stigmatiser*) to condemn (in the most severe terms); **se flétrir** *vi* to wither

fleur [flœʀ] *nf* flower; (*d'un arbre*) blossom; **être en ~** (*arbre*) to be in blossom; **tissu à ~s** flowered *ou* flowery fabric; **la (fine) ~ de** (*fig*) the flower of; **être ~ bleue** to be soppy *ou* sentimental; **à ~ de terre** just above the ground; **faire une ~ à qn** to do sb a favour (*Brit*) *ou* favor (*US*); **~ de lis** fleur-de-lis

fleuri, e [flœʀi] *adj* (*jardin*) in flower *ou* bloom; surrounded by flowers; (*fig: style, tissu, papier*) flowery; (: *teint*) glowing

fleurir [flœʀiʀ] *vi* (*rose*) to flower; (*arbre*) to blossom; (*fig*) to flourish ▷ *vt* (*tombe*) to put flowers on; (*chambre*) to decorate with flowers

fleuriste [flœʀist] *nmf* florist

fleuve [flœv] *nm* river; **roman-~** saga; **discours-~** interminable speech

flexible [fleksibl] *adj* flexible

flic [flik] *nm* (*fam: péj*) cop

flipper *nm* [flipœʀ] pinball (machine) ▷ *vi* [flipe] (*fam: être déprimé*) to feel down, be on a downer; (: *être exalté*) to freak out

flirter [flœʀte] *vi* to flirt

flocon [flɔkɔ̃] *nm* flake; (*de laine etc: boulette*) flock; **~s d'avoine** oat flakes, porridge oats

flopée [flɔpe] *nf*: **une ~ de** loads of

floraison [flɔʀezɔ̃] *nf* flowering; blossoming; flourishing; *voir* **fleurir**

flore [flɔʀ] *nf* flora

florissant, e [flɔʀisɑ̃, -ɑ̃t] *vb voir* **fleurir** ▷ *adj* (*économie*) flourishing; (*santé, teint, mine*) blooming

flot [flo] *nm* flood, stream; (*marée*) flood tide; **flots** *nmpl* (*de la mer*) waves; **être à ~** (*Navig*) to be afloat; (*fig*) to be on an even keel; **à ~s** (*couler*) in torrents; **entrer à ~s** to stream *ou* pour in

flottant, e [flɔtɑ̃, -ɑ̃t] *adj* (*vêtement*) loose(-fitting); (*cours, barème*) floating

flotte [flɔt] *nf* (*Navig*) fleet; (*fam: eau*) water; (: *pluie*) rain

flottement [flɔtmɑ̃] *nm* (*fig*) wavering, hesitation; (*Écon*) floating

flotter [flɔte] *vi* to float; (*nuage, odeur*) to drift; (*drapeau*) to fly; (*vêtements*) to hang loose ▷ *vb impers* (*fam: pleuvoir*): **il flotte** it's raining ▷ *vt* to float; **faire ~** to float

flotteur [flɔtœʀ] *nm* float

flou, e [flu] *adj* fuzzy, blurred; (*fig*) woolly (*Brit*), vague; (*non ajusté: robe*) loose(-fitting)

fluctuation [flyktɥasjɔ̃] *nf* fluctuation

fluet, te [flyɛ, -ɛt] *adj* thin, slight; (*voix*) thin

fluide [flɥid] *adj* fluid; (*circulation etc*) flowing freely ▷ *nm* fluid; (*force*) (mysterious) power

fluor [flyɔʀ] *nm* fluorine; **dentifrice au ~** fluoride toothpaste

fluorescent, e [flyɔʀesɑ̃, -ɑ̃t] *adj* fluorescent

flûte [flyt] *nf* (*aussi*: **~ traversière**) flute; (*verre*) flute glass; (*pain*) (thin) baguette; **petite ~** piccolo; **~!** drat it!; **~ (à bec)** recorder; **~ de Pan** panpipes *pl*

flux [fly] *nm* incoming tide; (*écoulement*) flow; **le ~ et le reflux** the ebb and flow

FM *sigle f* (= *frequency modulation*) FM

foc [fɔk] *nm* jib

foi [fwa] *nf* faith; **sous la ~ du serment** under *ou* on oath; **ajouter ~ à** to lend credence to; **faire ~** (*prouver*) to be evidence; **digne de ~** reliable; **sur la ~ de** on the word *ou* strength of; **être de bonne/mauvaise ~** to be in good faith/not to be in good faith; **ma ~!** well!

foie [fwa] *nm* liver; **~ gras** foie gras; **crise de ~** stomach upset

foin [fwɛ̃] *nm* hay; **faire les ~s** to make hay; **faire du ~** (*fam*) to kick up a row

foire [fwaʀ] *nf* fair; (*fête foraine*) (fun) fair; (*fig: désordre, confusion*) bear garden; **~ aux questions** (*Internet*) frequently asked questions; **faire la ~** to whoop it up; **~ d'exposition** trade fair

fois [fwa] *nf* time; **une/deux ~** once/twice; **trois/vingt ~** three/twenty times; **deux ~ deux** twice two; **deux/quatre ~ plus grand (que)** twice/four times as big (as); **une ~** (*passé*) once; (*futur*) sometime; **une (bonne) ~ pour toutes** once and for all; **encore une ~** again, once more; **il était une ~** once upon a time; **une ~ que c'est fait** once it's done; **une ~ parti** once he (*ou* I *etc*) had left; **des ~** (*parfois*) sometimes; **si des ~ ...** (*fam*) if ever ...; **non mais des ~!** (*fam*) (now) look here!; **à la ~** (*ensemble*) (all) at once; **à la ~ grand et beau** both tall and handsome

foison [fwazɔ̃] *nf*: **une ~ de** an abundance of; **à ~** *adv* in plenty

foisonner [fwazɔne] *vi* to abound; **~ en** *ou* **de** to abound in

fol [fɔl] *adj m voir* **fou**

folie [fɔli] *nf* (*d'une décision, d'un acte*) madness, folly; (*état*) madness, insanity; (*acte*) folly; **la ~ des grandeurs** delusions of grandeur; **faire des ~s** (*en dépenses*) to be extravagant

folklorique [fɔlklɔʀik] *adj* folk *cpd*; (*fam*) weird

folle [fɔl] *adj f, nf voir* **fou**

follement [fɔlmɑ̃] *adv* (*très*) madly, wildly

foncé, e [fɔ̃se] *adj* dark; **bleu ~** dark blue

foncer [fɔ̃se] *vt* to make darker; (*Culin: moule etc*) to line ▷ *vi* to go darker; (*fam: aller vite*) to tear *ou* belt along; **~ sur** to charge at

foncier, -ière [fɔ̃sje, -jɛʀ] *adj* (*honnêteté etc*)

basic, fundamental; (*malhonnêteté*) deep-rooted; (*Comm*) real estate *cpd*

fonction [fɔ̃ksjɔ̃] *nf* (*rôle, Math, Ling*) function; (*emploi, poste*) post, position; **fonctions** *nfpl* (*professionnelles*) duties; **entrer en ~s** to take up one's post ou duties; to take up office; **voiture de ~** company car; **être ~ de** (*dépendre de*) to depend on; **en ~ de** (*par rapport à*) according to; **faire ~ de** to serve as; **la ~ publique** the state ou civil (*Brit*) service

fonctionnaire [fɔ̃ksjɔnɛR] *nm/f* state employee ou official; (*dans l'administration*) ≈ civil servant (*Brit*)

fonctionner [fɔ̃ksjɔne] *vi* to work, function; (*entreprise*) to operate, function; **faire ~** to work, operate

fond [fɔ̃] *nm voir aussi* **fonds**; (*d'un récipient, trou*) bottom; (*d'une salle, scène*) back; (*d'un tableau, décor*) background; (*opposé à la forme*) content; (*petite quantité*): **un ~ de verre** a drop; (*Sport*): **le ~** long distance (running); **course/épreuve de ~** long-distance race/trial; **au ~ de** at the bottom of; at the back of; **aller au ~ des choses** to get to the root of things; **le ~ de sa pensée** his (ou her) true thoughts ou feelings; **sans ~** *adj* bottomless; **envoyer par le ~** (*Navig: couler*) to sink, scuttle; **à ~** *adv* (*connaître, soutenir*) thoroughly; (*appuyer, visser*) right down ou home; **à ~ (de train)** *adv* (*fam*) full tilt; **dans le ~, au ~** *adv* (*en somme*) basically, really; **de ~ en comble** *adv* from top to bottom; **~ sonore** background noise; background music; **~ de teint** foundation

fondamental, e, -aux [fɔ̃damɑ̃tal, -o] *adj* fundamental

fondant, e [fɔ̃dɑ̃, -ɑ̃t] *adj* (*neige*) melting; (*poire*) that melts in the mouth; (*chocolat*) fondant

fondateur, -trice [fɔ̃datœR, -tRis] *nm/f* founder; **membre ~** founder (*Brit*) ou founding (*US*) member

fondation [fɔ̃dasjɔ̃] *nf* founding; (*établissement*) foundation; **fondations** *nfpl* (*d'une maison*) foundations; **travail de ~** foundation works *pl*

fondé, e [fɔ̃de] *adj* (*accusation etc*) well-founded ▷ *nm*: **~ de pouvoir** authorized representative; **mal ~** unfounded; **être à croire** to have grounds for believing ou good reason to believe

fondement [fɔ̃dmɑ̃] *nm* (*derrière*) behind; **fondements** *nmpl* foundations; **sans ~** *adj* (*rumeur etc*) groundless, unfounded

fonder [fɔ̃de] *vt* to found; (*fig*): **~ qch sur** to base sth on; **se ~ sur** (*personne*) to base o.s. on; **~ un foyer** (*se marier*) to set up home

fonderie [fɔ̃dRi] *nf* smelting works *sg*

fondre [fɔ̃dR] *vt* (*aussi*: **faire ~**) to melt; (*dans l'eau: sucre, sel*) to dissolve; (*fig: mélanger*) to merge, blend ▷ *vi* (*à la chaleur*) to melt; to dissolve; (*fig*) to melt away; (*se précipiter*): **~ sur** to swoop down on; **se fondre** *vi* (*se combiner, se confondre*) to merge into each other; to dissolve; **~ en larmes** to dissolve into tears

fonds [fɔ̃] *nm* (*de bibliothèque*) collection; (*Comm*): **~ (de commerce)** business; (*fig*): **~ de probité etc** fund of integrity *etc* ▷ *nmpl* (*argent*) funds; **à ~ perdus** *adv* with little or no hope of getting the money back; **être en ~** to be in funds; **mise de ~** investment, (capital) outlay; **F~ monétaire international (FMI)** International Monetary Fund (IMF); **~ de roulement** *nm* float

fondu, e [fɔ̃dy] *adj* (*beurre, neige*) melted; (*métal*) molten ▷ *nm* (*Ciné*): **~ (enchaîné)** dissolve ▷ *nf* (*Culin*) fondue

font [fɔ̃] *vb voir* **faire**

fontaine [fɔ̃tɛn] *nf* fountain; (*source*) spring

fonte [fɔ̃t] *nf* melting; (*métal*) cast iron; **la ~ des neiges** the (spring) thaw

foot [fut], **football** [futbol] *nm* football, soccer

footballeur, -euse [futbolœR, -øz] *nm/f* footballer (*Brit*), football ou soccer player

footing [futiŋ] *nm* jogging; **faire du ~** to go jogging

for [fɔR] *nm*: **dans ou en son ~ intérieur** in one's heart of hearts

forain, e [fɔRɛ̃, -ɛn] *adj* fairground *cpd* ▷ *nm* (*marchand*) stallholder; (*acteur etc*) fairground entertainer

forçat [fɔRsa] *nm* convict

force [fɔRs] *nf* strength; (*puissance: surnaturelle etc*) power; (*Physique, Mécanique*) force; **forces** *nfpl* (*physiques*) strength *sg*; (*Mil*) forces; (*effectifs*): **d'importantes ~s de police** large contingents of police; **avoir de la ~** to be strong; **être à bout de ~** to have no strength left; **à la ~ du poignet** (*fig*) by the sweat of one's brow; **à ~ de faire** by dint of doing; **arriver en ~** (*nombreux*) to arrive in force; **cas de ~ majeure** case of absolute necessity; (*Assurances*) act of God; **~ de la nature** natural force; **de ~** *adv* forcibly, by force; **de toutes mes/ses ~s** with all my/his strength; **par la ~** using force; **par la ~ des choses/d'habitude** by force of circumstances/habit; **à toute ~** (*absolument*) at all costs; **faire ~ de rames/voiles** to ply the oars/cram on sail; **être de ~ à faire** to be up to doing; **de première ~** first class; **la ~ armée** (*les troupes*) the army; **~ d'âme** fortitude; **~ de frappe** strike force; **~ d'inertie** force of inertia; **la ~ publique** the authorities responsible for public order; **~s d'intervention** (*Mil, Police*) peace-keeping force *sg*; **dans la ~ de l'âge** in the prime of life; **les ~s de l'ordre** the police

forcé, e [fɔRse] *adj* forced; (*bain*) unintended; (*inévitable*): **c'est ~!** it's inevitable!, it HAS to be!

forcément [fɔRsemɑ̃] *adv* necessarily; inevitably; (*bien sûr*) of course; **pas ~** not necessarily

f

forcené, e [fɔʀsəne] adj frenzied ▷ nm/f maniac

forcer [fɔʀse] vt (contraindre): ~ **qn à faire** to force sb to do; (porte, serrure, plante) to force; (moteur, voix) to strain ▷ vi (Sport) to overtax o.s.; **se ~ à faire qch** to force o.s. to do sth; ~ **la dose/ l'allure** to overdo it/increase the pace; ~ **l'attention/le respect** to command attention/ respect; ~ **la consigne** to bypass orders

forcir [fɔʀsiʀ] vi (grossir) to broaden out; (vent) to freshen

forer [fɔʀe] vt to drill, bore

forestier, -ière [fɔʀɛstje, -jɛʀ] adj forest cpd

forêt [fɔʀɛ] nf forest; **Office National des F~s** (Admin) ≈ Forestry Commission (Brit), ≈ National Forest Service (US); **la F~ Noire** the Black Forest

forfait [fɔʀfɛ] nm (Comm) fixed ou set price; all-in deal ou price; (crime) infamy; **déclarer ~** to withdraw; **gagner par ~** to win by a walkover; **travailler à ~** to work for a lump sum

forfaitaire [fɔʀfɛtɛʀ] adj set; inclusive

forge [fɔʀʒ] nf forge, smithy

forger [fɔʀʒe] vt to forge; (fig: personnalité) to form; (: prétexte) to contrive, make up

forgeron [fɔʀʒəʀɔ̃] nm (black)smith

formaliser [fɔʀmalize]: **se formaliser** vi: **se ~ (de)** to take offence (at)

formalité [fɔʀmalite] nf formality; **simple ~** mere formality

format [fɔʀma] nm size; **petit ~** small size; (Photo) 35 mm (film)

formater [fɔʀmate] vt (disque) to format; **non formaté** unformatted

formation [fɔʀmasjɔ̃] nf forming; (éducation) training; (Mus) group; (Mil, Aviat, Géo) formation; **la ~ permanente** ou **continue** continuing education; **la ~ professionnelle** vocational training

forme [fɔʀm] nf (gén) form; (d'un objet) shape, form; **formes** nfpl (bonnes manières) proprieties; (d'une femme) figure sg; **en ~ de poire** pear-shaped, in the shape of a pear; **sous ~ de** in the form of; in the guise of; **sous ~ de cachets** in the form of tablets; **être en (bonne** ou **pleine) ~, avoir la ~** (Sport etc) to be on form; **en bonne et due ~** in due form; **pour la ~** for the sake of form; **sans autre ~ de procès** (fig) without further ado; **prendre ~** to take shape

formel, le [fɔʀmɛl] adj (preuve, décision) definite, positive; (logique) formal

formellement [fɔʀmɛlmɑ̃] adv (interdit) strictly; (absolument) positively

former [fɔʀme] vt (gén) to form; (éduquer: soldat, ingénieur etc) to train; **se former** vi to form; to train

formidable [fɔʀmidabl] adj tremendous

formulaire [fɔʀmylɛʀ] nm form

formule [fɔʀmyl] nf (gén) formula; (formulaire) form; (expression) phrase; **selon la ~**

consacrée as one says; ~ **de politesse** polite phrase; (en fin de lettre) letter ending

formuler [fɔʀmyle] vt (émettre: réponse, vœux) to formulate; (expliciter: sa pensée) to express

fort, e [fɔʀ, fɔʀt] adj strong; (intensité, rendement) high, great; (corpulent) large; (doué): **être ~ (en)** to be good (at) ▷ adv (serrer, frapper) hard; (sonner) loud(ly); (beaucoup) greatly, very much; (très) very ▷ nm (édifice) fort; (point fort) strong point, forte; **le ~, les ~s** the strong; **c'est un peu ~!** it's a bit much!; **à plus ~e raison** even more so, all the more reason; **avoir ~ à faire avec qn** to have a hard job with sb; **se faire ~ de faire** to claim one can do; ~ **bien/peu** very well/few; **au plus ~ de** (au milieu de) in the thick of, at the height of; ~**e tête** rebel

forteresse [fɔʀtəʀɛs] nf fortress

fortifiant [fɔʀtifjɑ̃] nm tonic

fortifier [fɔʀtifje] vt to strengthen, fortify; (Mil) to fortify; **se fortifier** vi (personne, santé) to grow stronger

fortiori [fɔʀtjɔʀi]: **à ~** adv all the more so

fortuit, e [fɔʀtɥi, -it] adj fortuitous, chance cpd

fortune [fɔʀtyn] nf fortune; **faire ~** to make one's fortune; **de ~** adj makeshift; (compagnon) chance cpd

fortuné, e [fɔʀtyne] adj wealthy, well-off; **forum de discussion** (Internet) message board

forum [fɔʀɔm] nm forum

fosse [fos] nf (grand trou) pit; (tombe) grave; **la ~ aux lions/ours** the lions' den/bear pit; ~ **commune** common ou communal grave; ~ **(d'orchestre)** (orchestra) pit; ~ **à purin** cesspit; ~ **septique** septic tank; ~**s nasales** nasal fossae

fossé [fose] nm ditch; (fig) gulf, gap

fossette [fosɛt] nf dimple

fossile [fosil] nm fossil ▷ adj fossilized, fossil cpd

fossoyeur [foswajœʀ] nm gravedigger

fou, fol, folle [fu, fɔl] adj mad, crazy; (déréglé etc) wild, erratic; (mèche) stray; (herbe) wild; (fam: extrême, très grand) terrific, tremendous ▷ nm/f madman/woman ▷ nm (du roi) jester, fool; (Échecs) bishop; ~ **à lier, ~ furieux (folle furieuse)** raving mad; **être ~ de** to be mad ou crazy about; (chagrin, joie, colère) to be wild with; **faire le ~** to play ou act the fool; **avoir le ~ rire** to have the giggles

foudre [fudʀ] nf: **la ~** lightning; **foudres** nfpl (fig: colère) wrath sg

foudroyant, e [fudʀwajɑ̃, -ɑ̃t] adj devastating; (progrès) lightning cpd; (succès) stunning; (maladie, poison) violent

foudroyer [fudʀwaje] vt to strike down; ~ **qn du regard** to look daggers at sb; **il a été foudroyé** he was struck by lightning

fouet [fwɛ] nm whip; (Culin) whisk; **de plein ~** adv (se heurter) head on

fouetter [fwete] vt to whip; (crème) to whisk

fougère [fuʒɛʀ] nf fern

fougue [fug] nf ardour (Brit), ardor (US), spirit

fougueux, -euse [fugø, -øz] adj fiery, ardent

fouille [fuj] nf search; **fouilles** nfpl (archéologiques) excavations; **passer à la ~** to be searched

fouiller [fuje] vt to search; (creuser) to dig; (: archéologue) to excavate; (approfondir: étude etc) to go into ▷ vi (archéologue) to excavate; **~ dans/parmi** to rummage in/among

fouillis [fuji] nm jumble, muddle

fouiner [fwine] vi (péj): **~ dans** to nose around ou about in

foulard [fular] nm scarf

foule [ful] nf crowd; **la ~** crowds pl; **une ~ de** masses of; **venir en ~** to come in droves

foulée [fule] nf stride; **dans la ~ de** on the heels of

fouler [fule] vt to press; (sol) to tread upon; **se fouler** vi (fam) to overexert o.s.; **se ~ la cheville** to sprain one's ankle; **ne pas se ~** not to overexert o.s.; **il ne se foule pas** he doesn't put himself out; **~ aux pieds** to trample underfoot

foulure [fulyr] nf sprain

four [fur] nm oven; (de potier) kiln; (Théât: échec) flop; **allant au ~** ovenproof

fourbe [furb] adj deceitful

fourbu, e [furby] adj exhausted

fourche [furʃ] nf pitchfork; (de bicyclette) fork

fourchette [furʃet] nf fork; (Statistique) bracket, margin

fourgon [furgɔ̃] nm van; (Rail) wag(g)on; **~ mortuaire** hearse

fourgonnette [furgɔnet] nf (delivery) van

fourmi [furmi] nf ant; **avoir des ~s dans les jambes/mains** to have pins and needles in one's legs/hands

fourmilière [furmiljer] nf ant-hill; (fig) hive of activity

fourmiller [furmije] vi to swarm; **~ de** to be teeming with, be swarming with

fournaise [furnez] nf blaze; (fig) furnace, oven

fourneau, x [furno] nm stove

fournée [furne] nf batch

fourni, e [furni] adj (barbe, cheveux) thick; (magasin): **bien ~ (en)** well stocked (with)

fournir [furnir] vt to supply; (preuve, exemple) to provide, supply; (effort) to put in; **~ qch à qn** to supply sth to sb, supply ou provide sb with sth; **~ qn en** (Comm) to supply sb with; **se ~ chez** to shop at

fournisseur, -euse [furnisœr, -øz] nm/f supplier; (Internet): **~ d'accès à Internet** (Internet) service provider, ISP

fourniture [furnityr] nf supply(ing); **fournitures** nfpl supplies; **~s de bureau** office supplies, stationery; **~s scolaires** school stationery

fourrage [furaʒ] nm fodder

fourré, e [fure] adj (bonbon, chocolat) filled; (manteau, botte) fur-lined ▷ nm thicket

fourrer [fure] vt (fam) to stick, shove; **~ qch dans** to stick ou shove sth into; **se ~ dans/sous** to get into/under; **se ~ dans** (une mauvaise situation) to land o.s. in

fourre-tout [furtu] nm inv (sac) holdall; (péj) junk room (ou cupboard); (fig) rag-bag

fourrière [furjer] nf pound

fourrure [furyr] nf fur; (sur l'animal) coat; **manteau/col de ~** fur coat/collar

fourvoyer [furvwaje]: **se fourvoyer** vi to go astray, stray; **se ~ dans** to stray into

foutre [futr] vt (fam!) = **ficher**

foutu, e [futy] adj (fam!) = **fichu**

foyer [fwaje] nm (de cheminée) hearth; (fig) seat, centre; (famille) family; (domicile) home; (local de réunion) (social) club; (résidence) hostel; (salon) foyer; (Optique, Photo) focus; **lunettes à double ~** bi-focal glasses

fracas [fraka] nm din; crash

fracassant, e [frakasɑ̃, -ɑ̃t] adj (succès) sensational, staggering

fracasser [frakase] vt to smash; **se fracasser contre** ou **sur** to crash against

fraction [fraksjɔ̃] nf fraction

fractionner [fraksjone] vt to divide (up), split (up)

fracturation [fraktyrasjɔ̃] nf: **~ hydraulique** fracking

fracture [fraktyr] nf fracture; **~ du crâne** fractured skull; **~ de la jambe** broken leg

fracturer [fraktyre] vt (coffre, serrure) to break open; (os, membre) to fracture; **se ~ le crâne** to fracture one's skull

fragile [fraʒil] adj fragile, delicate; (fig) frail

fragilité [fraʒilite] nf fragility

fragment [fragmɑ̃] nm (d'un objet) fragment, piece; (d'un texte) passage, extract

fraîche [freʃ] adj f voir **frais**

fraîcheur [freʃœr] nf coolness; (d'un aliment) freshness; voir **frais**

fraîchir [freʃir] vi to get cooler; (vent) to freshen

frais, fraîche [fre, freʃ] adj (air, eau, accueil) cool; (petit pois, œufs, nouvelles, couleur, troupes) fresh; **le voilà ~!** he's in a (right) mess! ▷ adv (récemment) newly, fresh(ly); **il fait ~** it's cool; **servir ~** chill before serving, serve chilled ▷ nm: **mettre au ~** to put in a cool place; **prendre le ~** to take a breath of cool air ▷ nmpl (débours) expenses; (Comm) costs; charges; **faire des ~** to spend; to go to a lot of expense; **faire les ~ de** to bear the brunt of; **faire les ~ de la conversation** (parler) to do most of the talking; (en être le sujet) to be the topic of conversation; **il en a été pour ses ~** he could have spared himself the trouble; **rentrer dans ses ~** to recover one's expenses; **~ de déplacement** travel(ling) expenses; **~ d'entretien** upkeep; **~ généraux** overheads; **~ de scolarité** school fees, tuition (US)

fraise [frez] nf strawberry; (Tech) countersink (bit); (de dentiste) drill; **~ des bois** wild strawberry

framboise [fʀɑ̃bwaz] nf raspberry

franc, franche [fʀɑ̃, fʀɑ̃ʃ] adj (personne) frank, straightforward; (visage) open; (net: refus, couleur) clear; (: coupure) clean; (intensif) downright; (exempt): **~ de port** post free, postage paid; (zone, port) free; (boutique) duty-free ▷ adv: **parler ~** to be frank ou candid ▷ nm franc

français, e [fʀɑ̃sɛ, -ɛz] adj French ▷ nm (Ling) French ▷ nm/f: **F~, e** Frenchman/woman; **les F~** the French

France [fʀɑ̃s] nf: **la ~** France; **en ~** in France; **~ 2, ~ 3** state-owned television channels; see note

● **FRANCE TÉLÉVISION**
●
● France 2 and France 3 are state-owned
● television channels. France 2 is a national
● general interest and entertainment
● channel; France 3 provides regional news
● and information as well as programmes
● for the national network.

franche [fʀɑ̃ʃ] adj f voir **franc**

franchement [fʀɑ̃ʃmɑ̃] adv frankly; clearly; (nettement) definitely; (tout à fait) downright ▷ excl well, really!; voir **franc**

franchir [fʀɑ̃ʃiʀ] vt (obstacle) to clear, get over; (seuil, ligne, rivière) to cross; (distance) to cover

franchise [fʀɑ̃ʃiz] nf frankness; (douanière, d'impôt) exemption; (Assurances) excess; (Comm) franchise; **~ de bagages** baggage allowance

franc-maçon (pl francs-maçons) [fʀɑ̃masɔ̃] nm Freemason

franco [fʀɑ̃ko] adv (Comm): **~ (de port)** postage paid

francophone [fʀɑ̃kɔfɔn] adj French-speaking ▷ nm/f French speaker

franc-parler [fʀɑ̃paʀle] nm inv outspokenness; **avoir son ~** to speak one's mind

frange [fʀɑ̃ʒ] nf fringe; (cheveux) fringe (Brit), bangs (US)

frangipane [fʀɑ̃ʒipan] nf almond paste

franquette [fʀɑ̃kɛt]: **à la bonne ~** adv without any fuss

frappant, e [fʀapɑ̃, -ɑ̃t] adj striking

frappé, e [fʀape] adj (Culin) iced; **~ de panique** panic-stricken; **~ de stupeur** thunderstruck, dumbfounded

frapper [fʀape] vt to hit, strike; (étonner) to strike; (monnaie) to strike, stamp; **se frapper** vi (s'inquiéter) to get worked up; **~ à la porte** to knock at the door; **~ dans ses mains** to clap one's hands; **~ du poing sur** to bang one's fist on; **~ un grand coup** (fig) to strike a blow; **frappé de stupeur** dumbfounded

frasques [fʀask] nfpl escapades; **faire des ~** to get up to mischief

fraternel, le [fʀatɛʀnɛl] adj brotherly, fraternal

fraternité [fʀatɛʀnite] nf brotherhood

fraude [fʀod] nf fraud; (Scol) cheating; **passer qch en ~** to smuggle sth in (ou out); **~ fiscale** tax evasion

frauder [fʀode] vi, vt to cheat; **~ le fisc** to evade paying tax(es)

frauduleux, -euse [fʀodylø, -øz] adj fraudulent

frayer [fʀeje] vt to open up, clear ▷ vi to spawn; (fréquenter): **~ avec** to mix ou associate with; **se ~ un passage dans** to clear o.s. a path through, force one's way through

frayeur [fʀejœʀ] nf fright

fredonner [fʀədɔne] vt to hum

freezer [fʀizœʀ] nm freezing compartment

frein [fʀɛ̃] nm brake; **mettre un ~ à** (fig) to put a brake on, check; **sans ~** (sans limites) unchecked; **~ à main** handbrake; **~ moteur** engine braking; **~s à disques** disc brakes; **~s à tambour** drum brakes

freiner [fʀene] vi to brake ▷ vt (progrès etc) to check

frêle [fʀɛl] adj frail, fragile

frelon [fʀəlɔ̃] nm hornet

frémir [fʀemiʀ] vi (de froid, de peur) to shudder, shiver; (de colère) to shake; (de joie, feuillage) to quiver; (eau) to (begin to) bubble

frêne [fʀɛn] nm ash (tree)

frénétique [fʀenetik] adj frenzied, frenetic

fréquemment [fʀekamɑ̃] adv frequently

fréquent, e [fʀekɑ̃, -ɑ̃t] adj frequent

fréquentation [fʀekɑ̃tasjɔ̃] nf frequenting; seeing; **fréquentations** nfpl (relations) company sg; **avoir de mauvaises ~s** to be in with the wrong crowd, keep bad company

fréquenté, e [fʀekɑ̃te] adj: **très ~** (very) busy; **mal ~** patronized by disreputable elements

fréquenter [fʀekɑ̃te] vt (lieu) to frequent; (personne) to see; **se fréquenter** to see a lot of each other

frère [fʀɛʀ] nm brother ▷ adj: **partis/pays ~s** sister parties/countries

fresque [fʀɛsk] nf (Art) fresco

fret [fʀɛ(t)] nm freight

frétiller [fʀetije] vi to wriggle; to quiver; **~ de la queue** to wag its tail

fretin [fʀətɛ̃] nm: **le menu ~** the small fry

friable [fʀijabl] adj crumbly

friand, e [fʀijɑ̃, -ɑ̃d] adj: **~ de** very fond of ▷ nm (Culin) small minced-meat (Brit) ou ground-meat (US) pie; (: sucré) small almond cake; **~ au fromage** cheese puff

friandise [fʀijɑ̃diz] nf sweet

fric [fʀik] nm (fam) cash, bread

friche [fʀiʃ]: **en ~** adj, adv (lying) fallow

friction [fʀiksjɔ̃] nf (massage) rub, rub-down; (chez le coiffeur) scalp massage; (Tech, fig) friction

frictionner [fʀiksjɔne] vt to rub (down); to massage

frigidaire® [fʀiʒidɛʀ] nm refrigerator

frigide [fʀiʒid] adj frigid

frigo [fʀigo] nm (= frigidaire) fridge

frigorifique [fʀigoʀifik] adj refrigerating

frileux, -euse [fʀilø, -øz] adj sensitive to (the) cold; (fig) overcautious

frime [fʀim] nf (fam): **c'est de la ~** it's all put on; **pour la ~** just for show

frimer [fʀime] vi (fam) ▷ vi to show off

frimousse [fʀimus] nf (sweet) little face

fringale [fʀɛ̃gal] nf (fam): **avoir la ~** to be ravenous

fringant, e [fʀɛ̃gɑ̃, -ɑ̃t] adj dashing

fringues [fʀɛ̃g] nfpl (fam) clothes, gear no pl

fripé, e [fʀipe] adj crumpled

fripon, ne [fʀipɔ̃, -ɔn] adj roguish, mischievous ▷ nm/f rascal, rogue

fripouille [fʀipuj] nf scoundrel

frire [fʀiʀ] vt (aussi: **faire ~**) ▷ vi to fry

frisé, e [fʀize] adj (cheveux) curly; (personne) curly-haired ▷ nf: **(chicorée) ~e** curly endive

frisson [fʀisɔ̃], **frissonnement** [fʀisɔnmɑ̃] nm (de froid) shiver; (de peur) shudder; quiver

frissonner [fʀisɔne] vi (de fièvre, froid) to shiver; (d'horreur) to shudder; (feuilles) to quiver

frit, e [fʀi, fʀit] pp de **frire** ▷ adj fried ▷ nf: **(pommes) ~es** chips (Brit), French fries

friteuse [fʀitøz] nf chip pan (Brit); **~ électrique** deep (fat) fryer

friture [fʀityʀ] nf (huile) (deep) fat; (plat): **~ (de poissons)** fried fish; (Radio) crackle, crackling no pl; **fritures** nfpl (aliments frits) fried food sg

frivole [fʀivɔl] adj frivolous

froid, e [fʀwa, fʀwad] adj cold ▷ nm cold; (absence de sympathie) coolness no pl; **il fait ~** it's cold; **avoir ~** to be cold; **prendre ~** to catch a chill ou cold; **à ~** adv (démarrer) (from) cold; **(pendant) les grands ~s** (in) the depths of winter, (during) the cold season; **jeter un ~** (fig) to cast a chill; **être en ~ avec** to be on bad terms with; **battre ~ à qn** to give sb the cold shoulder

froidement [fʀwadmɑ̃] adv (accueillir) coldly; (décider) coolly

froideur [fʀwadœʀ] nf coolness no pl

froisser [fʀwase] vt to crumple (up), crease; (fig) to hurt, offend; **se froisser** vi to crumple, crease; (personne) to take offence (Brit) ou offense (US); **se ~ un muscle** to strain a muscle

frôler [fʀole] vt to brush against; (projectile) to skim past; (fig) to come very close to, come within a hair's breadth of

fromage [fʀɔmaʒ] nm cheese; **~ blanc** soft white cheese; **~ de tête** pork brawn

froment [fʀɔmɑ̃] nm wheat

froncer [fʀɔ̃se] vt to gather; **~ les sourcils** to frown

frondaisons [fʀɔ̃dɛzɔ̃] nfpl foliage sg

front [fʀɔ̃] nm forehead, brow; (Mil, Météorologie, Pol) front; **avoir le ~ de faire** to have the effrontery to do; **de ~** adv (se heurter) head-on; (rouler) together (2 or 3 abreast);

(simultanément) at once; **faire ~ à** to face up to; **~ de mer** (sea) front

frontalier, -ière [fʀɔ̃talje, -jɛʀ] adj border cpd, frontier cpd ▷ nm/f: **(travailleurs) ~s** workers who cross the border to go to work, commuters from across the border

frontière [fʀɔ̃tjɛʀ] nf (Géo, Pol) frontier, border; (fig) frontier, boundary

frotter [fʀote] vi to rub, scrape ▷ vt to rub; (pour nettoyer) to rub (up); (: avec une brosse: pommes de terre, plancher) to scrub; **~ une allumette** to strike a match; **se ~ à qn** to cross swords with sb; **se ~ à qch** to come up against sth; **se ~ les mains** (fig) to rub one's hands (gleefully)

fructifier [fʀyktifje] vi to yield a profit; **faire ~** to turn to good account

fructueux, -euse [fʀyktɥø, -øz] adj fruitful; profitable

frugal, e, -aux [fʀygal, -o] adj frugal

fruit [fʀɥi] nm fruit gen no pl; **~s de mer** (Culin) seafood(s); **~s secs** dried fruit sg

fruité, e [fʀɥite] adj (vin) fruity

fruitier, -ière [fʀɥitje, -jɛʀ] adj: **arbre ~** fruit tree ▷ nm/f fruiterer (Brit), fruit merchant (US)

fruste [fʀyst] adj unpolished, uncultivated

frustrer [fʀystʀe] vt to frustrate; (priver): **~ qn de qch** to deprive sb of sth

FS abr (= franc suisse) FS, SF

fuel [fjul], **fuel-oil** [fjulojl] nm fuel oil; (pour chauffer) heating oil

fugace [fygas] adj fleeting

fugitif, -ive [fyʒitif, -iv] adj (lueur, amour) fleeting; (prisonnier etc) runaway ▷ nm/f fugitive, runaway

fugue [fyg] nf (d'un enfant) running away no pl; (Mus) fugue; **faire une ~** to run away, abscond

fuir [fɥiʀ] vt to flee from; (éviter) to shun ▷ vi to run away; (gaz, robinet) to leak

fuite [fɥit] nf flight; (écoulement) leak, leakage; (divulgation) leak; **être en ~** to be on the run; **mettre en ~** to put to flight; **prendre la ~** to take flight

fulgurant, e [fylgyʀɑ̃, -ɑ̃t] adj lightning cpd, dazzling

fulminer [fylmine] vi: **~ (contre)** to thunder forth (against)

fumé, e [fyme] adj (Culin) smoked; (verre) tinted ▷ nf smoke; **partir en ~e** to go up in smoke

fumer [fyme] vi to smoke; (liquide) to steam ▷ vt to smoke; (terre, champ) to manure

fûmes [fym] vb voir **être**

fumet [fyme] nm aroma

fumeur, -euse [fymœʀ, -øz] nm/f smoker; (compartiment) **~s** smoking compartment

fumeux, -euse [fymø, -øz] adj (péj) woolly (Brit), hazy

fumier [fymje] nm manure

fumiste [fymist] nm (ramoneur) chimney sweep ▷ nm/f (péj: paresseux) shirker; (charlatan) phoney

funèbre [fynɛbʀ] *adj* funeral *cpd*; (*fig*) doleful; funereal

funérailles [fyneʀɑj] *nfpl* funeral *sg*

funeste [fynɛst] *adj* disastrous; deathly

fur [fyʀ]: **au ~ et à mesure** *adv* as one goes along; **au ~ et à mesure que** as; **au ~ et à mesure de leur progression** as they advance (*ou* advanced)

furet [fyʀɛ] *nm* ferret

fureter [fyʀ(ə)te] *vi* (*péj*) to nose about

fureur [fyʀœʀ] *nf* fury; (*passion*): **~ de** passion for; **être en ~** to be infuriated; **faire ~** to be all the rage

furibond, e [fyʀibɔ̃, -ɔ̃d] *adj* livid, absolutely furious

furie [fyʀi] *nf* fury; (*femme*) shrew, vixen; **en ~** (*mer*) raging

furieux, -euse [fyʀjø, -øz] *adj* furious

furoncle [fyʀɔ̃kl] *nm* boil

furtif, -ive [fyʀtif, -iv] *adj* furtive

fus [fy] *vb voir* **être**

fusain [fyzɛ̃] *nm* (*Bot*) spindle-tree; (*Art*) charcoal

fuseau, x [fyzo] *nm* (*pantalon*) (ski-)pants *pl*; (*pour filer*) spindle; **en ~** (*jambes*) tapering; (*colonne*) bulging; **~ horaire** time zone

fusée [fyze] *nf* rocket; **~ éclairante** flare

fuser [fyze] *vi* (*rires etc*) to burst forth

fusible [fyzibl] *nm* (*Élec: fil*) fuse wire; (: *fiche*) fuse

fusil [fyzi] *nm* (*de guerre, à canon rayé*) rifle, gun; (*de chasse, à canon lisse*) shotgun, gun; **~ à deux coups** double-barrelled rifle *ou* shotgun; **~ sous-marin** spear-gun

fusillade [fyzijad] *nf* gunfire *no pl*, shooting *no pl*; (*combat*) gun battle

fusiller [fyzije] *vt* to shoot; **~ qn du regard** to look daggers at sb

fusil-mitrailleur (*pl* **fusils-mitrailleurs**) [fyzimitʀɑjœʀ] *nm* machine gun

fusionner [fyzjɔne] *vi* to merge

fut [fy] *vb voir* **être**

fût [fy] *vb voir* **être** ▷ *nm* (*tonneau*) barrel, cask; (*de canon*) stock; (*d'arbre*) bole, trunk; (*de colonne*) shaft

futé, e [fyte] *adj* crafty; **Bison ~®** TV and radio traffic monitoring service

futile [fytil] *adj* (*inutile*) futile; (*frivole*) frivolous

futur, e [fytyʀ] *adj, nm* future; **son ~ époux** her husband-to-be; **au ~** (*Ling*) in the future

fuyant, e [fɥijɑ̃, -ɑ̃t] *vb voir* **fuir** ▷ *adj* (*regard etc*) evasive; (*lignes etc*) receding; (*perspective*) vanishing

fuyard, e [fɥijaʀ, -aʀd] *nm/f* runaway

Gabon [gabɔ̃] *nm*: **le ~** Gabon

gâcher [gɑʃe] *vt* (*gâter*) to spoil, ruin; (*gaspiller*) to waste; (*plâtre*) to temper; (*mortier*) to mix

gâchis [gɑʃi] *nm* (*désordre*) mess; (*gaspillage*) waste *no pl*

gadoue [gadu] *nf* sludge

gaffe [gaf] *nf* (*instrument*) boat hook; (*fam: erreur*) blunder; **faire ~** (*fam*) to watch out

gage [gaʒ] *nm* (*dans un jeu*) forfeit; (*fig: de fidélité*) token; **gages** *nmpl* (*salaire*) wages; (*garantie*) guarantee *sg*; **mettre en ~** to pawn; **laisser en ~** to leave as security

gageure [gaʒyʀ] *nf*: **c'est une ~** it's attempting the impossible

gagnant, e [gaɲɑ̃, -ɑ̃t] *adj*: **billet/numéro ~** winning ticket/number ▷ *adv*: **jouer ~** (*aux courses*) to be bound to win ▷ *nm/f* winner

gagne-pain [gaɲpɛ̃] *nm inv* job

gagner [gaɲe] *vt* (*concours, procès, pari*) to win; (*somme d'argent, revenu*) to earn; (*aller vers, atteindre*) to reach; (*s'emparer de*) to overcome; (*envahir*) to spread to; (*se concilier*): **~ qn** to win sb over ▷ *vi* to win; (*fig*) to gain; **~ du temps/de la place** to gain time/save space; **~ sa vie** to earn one's living; **~ du terrain** (*aussi fig*) to gain ground; **~ qn de vitesse** to outstrip sb; (*aussi fig*): **~ à faire** (*s'en trouver bien*) to be better off doing; **il y gagne** it's in his interest, it's to his advantage

gai, e [ge] *adj* cheerful; (*livre, pièce de théâtre*) light-hearted; (*un peu ivre*) merry

gaiement [gemɑ̃] *adv* cheerfully

gaieté [gete] nf cheerfulness; **gaietés** nfpl (souvent ironique) delights; **de ~ de cœur** with a light heart

gaillard, e [gajar, -ard] adj (robuste) sprightly; (grivois) bawdy, ribald ▷ nm/f (strapping) fellow/wench

gain [gɛ̃] nm (revenu) earnings pl; (bénéfice: gén pl) profits pl; (au jeu: gén pl) winnings pl; (fig: de temps, place) saving; (: avantage) benefit; (: lucre) gain; **avoir ~ de cause** to win the case; (fig) to be proved right; **obtenir ~ de cause** (fig) to win out

gaine [gɛn] nf (corset) girdle; (fourreau) sheath; (de fil électrique etc) outer covering

gala [gala] nm official reception; **soirée de ~** gala evening

galant, e [galɑ̃, -ɑ̃t] adj (courtois) courteous, gentlemanly; (entreprenant) flirtatious, gallant; (aventure, poésie) amorous; (scène, rendez-vous) romantic; **en ~e compagnie** (homme) with a lady friend; (femme) with a gentleman friend

galère [galɛr] nf galley

galérer [galere] vi (fam) to work hard, slave (away)

galerie [galri] nf gallery; (Théât) circle; (de voiture) roof rack; (fig: spectateurs) audience; **~ marchande** shopping mall; **~ de peinture** (private) art gallery

galet [galɛ] nm pebble; (Tech) wheel; **galets** nmpl pebbles, shingle sg

galette [galɛt] nf (gâteau) flat pastry cake; (crêpe) savoury pancake; **la ~ des Rois** cake traditionally eaten on Twelfth Night

○ **GALETTE DES ROIS**
○
○ A galette des Rois is a cake eaten on
○ Twelfth Night containing a figurine.
○ The person who finds it is the king
○ (or queen) and gets a paper crown. They
○ then choose someone else to be their
○ queen (or king).

galipette [galipɛt] nf somersault; **faire des ~s** to turn somersaults

Galles [gal] nfpl: **le pays de ~** Wales

gallois, e [galwa, -waz] adj Welsh ▷ nm (Ling) Welsh ▷ nm/f: **G~, e** Welshman(-woman)

galon [galɔ̃] nm (Mil) stripe; (décoratif) piece of braid; **prendre du ~** to be promoted

galop [galo] nm gallop; **au ~** at a gallop; **~ d'essai** (fig) trial run

galoper [galɔpe] vi to gallop

galopin [galɔpɛ̃] nm urchin, ragamuffin

gambader [gɑ̃bade] vi (animal, enfant) to leap about

gamin, e [gamɛ̃, -in] nm/f kid ▷ adj mischievous, playful

gamme [gam] nf (Mus) scale; (fig) range

gammé, e [game] adj: **croix ~e** swastika

gang [gɑ̃g] nm (de criminels) gang

gant [gɑ̃] nm glove; **prendre des ~s** (fig) to handle the situation with kid gloves; **relever le ~** (fig) to take up the gauntlet; **~ de crin** massage glove; **~ de toilette** (face) flannel (Brit), face cloth; **~s de boxe** boxing gloves; **~s de caoutchouc** rubber gloves

garage [garaʒ] nm garage; **~ à vélos** bicycle shed

garagiste [garaʒist] nm/f (propriétaire) garage owner; (mécanicien) garage mechanic

garantie [garɑ̃ti] nf guarantee, warranty; (gage) security, surety; **(bon de) ~** guarantee ou warranty slip; **~ de bonne exécution** performance bond

garantir [garɑ̃tir] vt to guarantee; (protéger): **~ de** to protect from; **je vous garantis que** I can assure you that; **garanti pure laine/2 ans** guaranteed pure wool/for 2 years

garce [gars] nf (péj) bitch (!)

garçon [garsɔ̃] nm boy; (célibataire): **vieux ~** bachelor; (jeune homme) boy, lad; (aussi: **~ de café**) waiter; **~ boucher/coiffeur** butcher's/hairdresser's assistant; **~ de courses** messenger; **~ d'écurie** stable lad; **~ manqué** tomboy

garçonnière [garsɔnjɛr] nf bachelor flat

garde [gard] nm (de prisonnier) guard; (de domaine etc) warden; (soldat, sentinelle) guardsman ▷ nf guarding; looking after; (soldats, Boxe, Escrime) guard; (faction) watch; (d'une arme) hilt; (Typo: aussi: **page** ou **feuille de ~**) flyleaf; (: collée) endpaper; **de ~** adj, adv on duty; **monter la ~** to stand guard; **être de ~** to be on one's guard; **mettre en ~** to warn; **mise en ~** warning; **prendre ~ (à)** to be careful (of); **avoir la ~ des enfants** (après divorce) to have custody of the children; **~ champêtre** nm rural policeman; **~ du corps** nm bodyguard; **~ d'enfants** nf child minder; **~ forestier** nm forest warden; **~ mobile** nm, nf mobile guard; **des Sceaux** nm ≈ Lord Chancellor (Brit), ≈ Attorney General (US); **~ à vue** nf (Jur) ≈ police custody

garde-à-vous [gardavu] nm inv: **être/se mettre au ~** to be at/stand to attention; **~ (fixe)!** (Mil) attention!

garde-barrière (pl **gardes-barrière(s)**) [gardəbarjɛr] nm/f level-crossing keeper

garde-boue [gardəbu] nm inv mudguard

garde-chasse (pl **gardes-chasse(s)**) [gardəʃas] nm gamekeeper

garde-malade (pl **gardes-malade(s)**) [gardəmalad] nf home nurse

garde-manger [gardmɑ̃ʒe] nm inv (boîte) meat safe; (placard) pantry, larder

garder [garde] vt (conserver) to keep; (: sur soi: vêtement, chapeau) to keep on; (surveiller: enfants) to look after; (: immeuble, lieu, prisonnier) to guard; **se garder** vi (aliment: se conserver) to keep; **se ~ de faire** to be careful not to do; **~ le lit/la chambre** to stay in bed/indoors; **~ le silence** to keep silent ou quiet; **~ la ligne** to

keep one's figure; **~ à vue** to keep in custody;
pêche/chasse gardée private fishing/
hunting (ground)
garderie [gardəri] nf day nursery, crèche
garde-robe [gardərɔb] nf wardrobe
gardien, ne [gardjɛ̃, -ɛn] nm/f (garde) guard;
(de prison) warder; (de domaine, réserve) warden;
(de musée etc) attendant; (de phare, cimetière)
keeper; (d'immeuble) caretaker; (fig) guardian;
~ de but goalkeeper; **~ de nuit** night
watchman; **~ de la paix** policeman
gare [gar] nf (railway) station, train station
(US) ▷ excl: **~ à ... mind ...!, watch out for ...!;
~ à ne pas ... mind you don't ...; **~ à toi!**
watch out!; **sans crier ~** without warning;
~ maritime harbour station; **~ routière** bus
station; (de camions) haulage (Brit) ou trucking
(US) depot; **~ de triage** marshalling yard
garer [gare] vt to park; **se garer** vi to park;
(pour laisser passer) to draw into the side
gargariser [gargarize]: **se gargariser** vi to
gargle; **se ~ de** (fig) to revel in
gargote [gargɔt] nf cheap restaurant, greasy
spoon (fam)
gargouille [garguj] nf gargoyle
gargouiller [garguje] vi (estomac) to rumble;
(eau) to gurgle
garnement [garnəmɑ̃] nm rascal, scallywag
garni, e [garni] adj (plat) served with
vegetables (and chips, pasta or rice) ▷ nm
(appartement) furnished accommodation no pl
(Brit) ou accommodations pl (US)
garnison [garnizɔ̃] nf garrison
garniture [garnityr] nf (Culin: légumes)
vegetables pl; (: persil etc) garnish; (: farce)
filling; (décoration) trimming; (protection)
fittings pl; **~ de cheminée** mantelpiece
ornaments pl; **~ de frein** (Auto) brake lining;
~ intérieure (Auto) interior trim;
~ périodique sanitary towel (Brit) ou
napkin (US)
gars [ga] nm lad; (type) guy
Gascogne [gaskɔɲ] nf: **la ~** Gascony; **le golfe
de ~** the Bay of Biscay
gas-oil [gazɔjl] nm diesel oil
gaspiller [gaspije] vt to waste
gastronome [gastrɔnɔm] nm/f gourmet
gastronomie [gastrɔnɔmi] nf gastronomy
gastronomique [gastrɔnɔmik] adj
gastronomic; **menu ~** gourmet menu
gâteau, x [gato] nm cake ▷ adj inv (fam: trop
indulgent): **papa-/maman-~** doting father/
mother; **~ d'anniversaire** birthday cake;
~ de riz ≈ rice pudding; **~ sec** biscuit
gâter [gate] vt to spoil; **se gâter** vi (dent, fruit)
to go bad; (temps, situation) to change for the
worse
gâterie [gatri] nf little treat
gâteux, -euse [gatø, -øz] adj senile
gauche [goʃ] adj left, left-hand; (maladroit)
awkward, clumsy ▷ nf (Pol) left (wing); **le
bras ~** the left arm; **le côté ~** the left-hand

side; (Boxe) left; **à ~** on the left; (direction) (to
the) left; **à ~ de** (on ou to the) left of; **à la ~ de**
to the left of; **sur votre ~** on your left; **de ~**
(Pol) left-wing
gaucher, -ère [goʃe, -ɛr] adj left-handed
gauchiste [goʃist] adj, nm/f leftist
gaufre [gofr] nf (pâtisserie) waffle; (de cire)
honeycomb
gaufrette [gofrɛt] nf wafer
gaulois, e [golwa, -waz] adj Gallic; (grivois)
bawdy ▷ nm/f: **G~,** e Gaul
gaver [gave] vt to force-feed; (fig): **~ de** to
cram with, fill up with; (personne): **se ~ de** to
stuff o.s. with
gaz [gaz] nm inv gas; **mettre les ~** (Auto) to put
one's foot down; **chambre/masque à ~** gas
chamber/mask; **~ en bouteille** bottled gas;
~ butane Calor gas® (Brit), butane gas;
~ carbonique carbon dioxide; **~ hilarant**
laughing gas; **~ lacrymogène** tear gas;
~ naturel natural gas; **~ de ville** town gas
(Brit), manufactured domestic gas; **ça sent
le ~** I can smell gas, there's a smell of gas
gaze [gaz] nf gauze
gazer [gaze] vt to gas ▷ vi (fam) to be going ou
working well
gazette [gazɛt] nf news sheet
gazeux, -euse [gazø, -øz] adj gaseous; (eau)
sparkling; (boisson) fizzy
gazoduc [gazodyk] nm gas pipeline
gazon [gazɔ̃] nm (herbe) turf, grass; (pelouse)
lawn
gazouiller [gazuje] vi (oiseau) to chirp;
(enfant) to babble
GDF sigle m (= Gaz de France) national gas company
geai [ʒɛ] nm jay
géant, e [ʒeɑ̃, -ɑ̃t] adj gigantic, giant; (Comm)
giant-size ▷ nm/f giant
geindre [ʒɛ̃dr] vi to groan, moan
gel [ʒɛl] nm frost; (de l'eau) freezing; (fig: des
salaires, prix) freeze; freezing; (produit de beauté)
gel; **~ douche** shower gel
gélatine [ʒelatin] nf gelatine
gelé, e [ʒəle] adj frozen ▷ nf jelly; (gel) frost;
~ blanche hoarfrost, white frost
geler [ʒ(ə)le] vt, vi to freeze; **il gèle** it's
freezing
gélule [ʒelyl] nf (Méd) capsule
gelures [ʒəlyr] nfpl frostbite sg
Gémeaux [ʒemo] nmpl: **les ~** Gemini, the
Twins; **être des ~** to be Gemini
gémir [ʒemir] vi to groan, moan
gênant, e [ʒenɑ̃, -ɑ̃t] adj (objet) awkward, in
the way; (histoire, personne) embarrassing
gencive [ʒɑ̃siv] nf gum
gendarme [ʒɑ̃darm] nm gendarme
gendarmerie [ʒɑ̃darməri] nf military police
force in countryside and small towns; their police
station or barracks
gendre [ʒɑ̃dr] nm son-in-law
gêné, e [ʒene] adj embarrassed; (dépourvu
d'argent) short (of money)

gêner [ʒene] vt (incommoder) to bother; (encombrer) to hamper; (bloquer le passage) to be in the way of; (déranger) to bother; (embarrasser): ~ **qn** to make sb feel ill-at-ease; **se gêner** to put o.s. out; **ne vous gênez pas!** (ironique) go right ahead!, don't mind me!; **je vais me ~!** (ironique) why should I care?

général, e, -aux [ʒeneral, -o] adj, nm general ⊳ nf: (**répétition**) **-e** final dress rehearsal; **en ~** usually, in general; **à la satisfaction ~e** to everyone's satisfaction

généralement [ʒeneralmɑ̃] adv generally

généraliser [ʒeneralize] vt, vi to generalize; **se généraliser** vi to become widespread

généraliste [ʒeneralist] nm/f (Méd) general practitioner, GP

génération [ʒenerasjɔ̃] nf generation

généreux, -euse [ʒenerø, -øz] adj generous

générique [ʒenerik] adj generic ⊳ nm (Ciné, TV) credits pl, credit titles pl

générosité [ʒenerozite] nf generosity

genêt [ʒ(ə)nɛ] nm (Bot) broom no pl

génétique [ʒenetik] adj genetic ⊳ nf genetics sg

Genève [ʒ(ə)nɛv] n Geneva

génial, e, -aux [ʒenjal, -o] adj of genius; (fam: formidable) fantastic, brilliant

génie [ʒeni] nm genius; (Mil): **le ~** ≈ the Engineers pl; **avoir du ~** to have genius; **~ civil** civil engineering; **~ génétique** genetic engineering

genièvre [ʒənjɛvʀ] nm (Bot) juniper (tree); (boisson) Dutch gin; **grain de ~** juniper berry

génisse [ʒenis] nf heifer; **foie de ~** ox liver

génital, e, -aux [ʒenital, -o] adj genital; **les parties ~es** the genitals

génois, e [ʒenwa, -waz] adj Genoese ⊳ nf (gâteau) ≈ sponge cake

génome [ʒenom] nm genome

genou, x [ʒ(ə)nu] nm knee; **à ~x** on one's knees; **se mettre à ~x** to kneel down

genre [ʒɑ̃ʀ] nm (espèce, sorte) kind, type, sort; (allure) manner; (Ling) gender; (Art) genre; (Zool etc) genus; **se donner du ~** to give o.s. airs; **avoir bon ~** to look a nice sort; **avoir mauvais ~** to be coarse-looking; **ce n'est pas son ~** it's not like him

gens [ʒɑ̃] nmpl (f in some phrases) people pl; **les ~ d'Église** the clergy; **les ~ du monde** society people; **~ de maison** domestics

gentil, le [ʒɑ̃ti, -ij] adj kind; (enfant: sage) good; (sympa: endroit etc) nice; **c'est très ~ à vous** it's very kind ou good ou nice of you

gentillesse [ʒɑ̃tijɛs] nf kindness

gentiment [ʒɑ̃timɑ̃] adv kindly

géo abr (= géographie) geography

géographie [ʒeɔgrafi] nf geography

geôlier [ʒolje] nm jailer

géologie [ʒeɔlɔʒi] nf geology

géomètre [ʒeɔmɛtʀ] nm: (**arpenteur-**)~ (land) surveyor

géométrie [ʒeɔmetri] nf geometry; **à ~ variable** (Aviat) swing-wing

géométrique [ʒeɔmetrik] adj geometric

géranium [ʒeranjɔm] nm geranium

gérant, e [ʒerɑ̃, -ɑ̃t] nm/f manager/manageress; **~ d'immeuble** managing agent

gerbe [ʒɛrb] nf (de fleurs, d'eau) spray; (de blé) sheaf; (fig) shower, burst

gercé, e [ʒɛrse] adj chapped

gerçure [ʒɛrsyr] nf crack

gérer [ʒere] vt to manage

germain, e [ʒɛrmɛ̃, -ɛn] adj: **cousin ~** first cousin

germe [ʒɛrm] nm germ

germer [ʒɛrme] vi to sprout; (semence, aussi fig) to germinate

Ghana [gana] nm: **le ~** Ghana

ghetto [geto] nm ghetto

gibet [ʒibɛ] nm gallows pl

gibier [ʒibje] nm (animaux) game; (fig) prey

giboulée [ʒibule] nf sudden shower

gicler [ʒikle] vi to spurt, squirt

gifle [ʒifl] nf slap (in the face)

gifler [ʒifle] vt to slap (in the face)

gigantesque [ʒigɑ̃tɛsk] adj gigantic

gigogne [ʒigɔɲ] adj: **lits ~s** truckle (Brit) ou trundle (US) beds; **tables/poupées ~s** nest of tables/dolls

gigot [ʒigo] nm leg (of mutton ou lamb)

gigoter [ʒigote] vi to wriggle (about)

gilet [ʒile] nm waistcoat; (pull) cardigan; (de corps) vest; **~ pare-balles** bulletproof jacket; **~ de sauvetage** life jacket

gin [dʒin] nm gin; **~-tonic** gin and tonic

gingembre [ʒɛ̃ʒɑ̃br] nm ginger

girafe [ʒiraf] nf giraffe

giratoire [ʒiratwar] adj: **sens ~** roundabout

girofle [ʒirɔfl] nm: **clou de ~** clove

girouette [ʒirwɛt] nf weather vane ou cock

gitan, e [ʒitɑ̃, -an] nm/f gipsy

gîte [ʒit] nm (maison) home; (abri) shelter; (du lièvre) form; **~ (rural)** (country) holiday cottage ou apartment, gîte (self-catering accommodation in the country)

givre [ʒivʀ] nm (hoar) frost

givré, e [ʒivʀe] adj covered in frost; (fam: fou) nuts; **citron ~/orange ~e** lemon/orange sorbet (served in fruit skin)

glace [glas] nf ice; (crème glacée) ice cream; (verre) sheet of glass; (miroir) mirror; (de voiture) window; **glaces** nfpl (Géo) ice sheets, ice sg; **de ~** (fig: accueil, visage) frosty, icy; **rester de ~** to remain unmoved

glacé, e [glase] adj (mains, vent, pluie) freezing; (lac) frozen; (boisson) iced

glacer [glase] vt to freeze; (boisson) to chill, ice; (gâteau) to ice (Brit), frost (US); (papier, *tissu)* to glaze; *(fig):* ~ **qn** *(intimider)* to chill sb; *(fig)* to make sb's blood run cold

glacial, e [glasjal] *adj* icy

glacier [glasje] *nm (Géo)* glacier; *(marchand)* ice-cream maker

glacière [glasjɛʀ] *nf* icebox

glaçon [glasɔ̃] *nm* icicle; *(pour boisson)* ice cube

glaïeul [glajœl] *nm* gladiola

glaise [glɛz] *nf* clay

gland [glɑ̃] *nm (de chêne)* acorn; *(décoration)* tassel; *(Anat)* glans

glande [glɑ̃d] *nf* gland

glander [glɑ̃de] *vi (fam)* to fart around *(Brit)* (!), screw around (US) (!)

glauque [glok] *adj* dull blue-green

glissade [glisad] *nf (par jeu)* slide; *(chute)* slip; *(dérapage)* skid; **faire des ~s** to slide

glissant, e [glisɑ̃, -ɑ̃t] *adj* slippery

glissement [glismɑ̃] *nm* sliding; *(fig)* shift; ~ **de terrain** landslide

glisser [glise] *vi (avancer)* to glide *ou* slide along; *(coulisser, tomber)* to slide; *(déraper)* to slip; *(être glissant)* to be slippery ▷ *vt* to slip; ~ **qch sous/dans/à** to slip sth under/into/to; ~ **sur** *(fig: détail etc)* to skate over; **se ~ dans/entre** to slip into/between

global, e, -aux [glɔbal, -o] *adj* overall

globe [glɔb] *nm* globe; **sous ~** under glass; ~ **oculaire** eyeball; **le ~ terrestre** the globe

globule [glɔbyl] *nm (du sang):* ~ **blanc/rouge** white/red corpuscle

globuleux, -euse [glɔbylø, -øz] *adj:* **yeux ~** protruding eyes

gloire [glwaʀ] *nf* glory; *(mérite)* distinction, credit; *(personne)* celebrity

glorieux, -euse [glɔʀjø, -øz] *adj* glorious

gloussement [glusmɑ̃] *nm (de poule)* cluck; *(rire)* chuckle

glousser [gluse] *vi* to cluck; *(rire)* to chuckle

glouton, ne [glutɔ̃, -ɔn] *adj* gluttonous, greedy

gluant, e [glyɑ̃, -ɑ̃t] *adj* sticky, gummy

glucose [glykoz] *nm* glucose

glycine [glisin] *nf* wisteria

GO *sigle fpl* (= **grandes ondes**) LW ▷ *sigle m* (= **gentil organisateur**) *title given to leaders on Club Méditerranée holidays; extended to refer to easy-going leader of any group*

go [go]: **tout de go** *adv* straight out

goal [gol] *nm* goalkeeper

gobelet [gɔblɛ] *nm (en métal)* tumbler; *(en plastique)* beaker; *(à dés)* cup

gober [gɔbe] *vt* to swallow

godasse [gɔdas] *nf (fam)* shoe

godet [gɔdɛ] *nm* pot; *(Couture)* unpressed pleat

goéland [gɔelɑ̃] *nm* (sea)gull

goélette [gɔelɛt] *nf* schooner

gogo [gogo] *nm (péj)* mug, sucker; **à ~** *adv* galore

goguenard, e [gɔgnaʀ, -aʀd] *adj* mocking

goinfre [gwɛ̃fʀ] *nm* glutton

golf [gɔlf] *nm (jeu)* golf; *(terrain)* golf course; ~ **miniature** crazy *ou* miniature golf

golfe [gɔlf] *nm* gulf; *(petit)* bay; **le ~ d'Aden** the Gulf of Aden; **le ~ de Gascogne** the Bay of Biscay; **le ~ du Lion** the Gulf of Lions; **le ~ Persique** the Persian Gulf

gomme [gɔm] *nf (à effacer)* rubber *(Brit)*, eraser; *(résine)* gum; **boule** *ou* **pastille de ~** throat pastille

gommer [gɔme] *vt (effacer)* to rub out *(Brit)*, erase; *(enduire de gomme)* to gum

gond [gɔ̃] *nm* hinge; **sortir de ses ~s** *(fig)* to fly off the handle

gondoler [gɔ̃dɔle]: **se gondoler** *vi* to warp, buckle; *(fam: rire)* to hoot with laughter; to be in stitches

gonflé, e [gɔ̃fle] *adj* swollen; *(ventre)* bloated; **il est ~** *(fam: courageux)* he's got some nerve; *(impertinent)* he's got a nerve

gonfler [gɔ̃fle] *vt (pneu, ballon)* to inflate, blow up; *(nombre, importance)* to inflate ▷ *vi (pied etc)* to swell (up); *(Culin: pâte)* to rise

gonfleur [gɔ̃flœʀ] *nm* air pump

gonzesse [gɔ̃zɛs] *nf (fam)* chick, bird *(Brit)*

goret [gɔʀɛ] *nm* piglet

gorge [gɔʀʒ] *nf (Anat)* throat; *(poitrine)* breast; *(Géo)* gorge; *(rainure)* groove; **avoir mal à la ~** to have a sore throat; **avoir la ~ serrée** to have a lump in one's throat

gorgé, e [gɔʀʒe] *adj:* ~ **de** filled with; *(eau)* saturated with ▷ *nf* mouthful; *(petite)* sip; *(grande)* gulp; **boire à petites/grandes ~es** to take little sips/big gulps

gorille [gɔʀij] *nm* gorilla; *(fam)* bodyguard

gosier [gozje] *nm* throat

gosse [gɔs] *nm/f* kid

goudron [gudrɔ̃] *nm (asphalte)* tar(mac) *(Brit)*, asphalt; *(du tabac)* tar

goudronner [gudrɔne] *vt* to tar(mac) *(Brit)*, asphalt

gouffre [gufʀ] *nm* abyss, gulf

goujat [guʒa] *nm* boor

goulot [gulo] *nm* neck; **boire au ~** to drink from the bottle

goulu, e [guly] *adj* greedy

gourd, e [guʀ, guʀd] *adj* numb (with cold); *(fam)* oafish

gourde [guʀd] *nf (récipient)* flask; *(fam)* (clumsy) clot *ou* oaf ▷ *adj* oafish

gourdin [guʀdɛ̃] *nm* club, bludgeon

gourer [guʀe] *(fam):* **se gourer** *vi* to boob

gourmand, e [guʀmɑ̃, -ɑ̃d] *adj* greedy

gourmandise [guʀmɑ̃diz] *nf* greed; *(bonbon)* sweet *(Brit)*, piece of candy (US)

gourmet [guʀmɛ] *nm* epicure

gourmette [guʀmɛt] *nf* chain bracelet

gousse [gus] *nf (de vanille etc)* pod; ~ **d'ail** clove of garlic

goût [gu] *nm* taste; *(fig: appréciation)* taste, liking; **le (bon) ~** good taste; **de bon ~** in good taste, tasteful; **de mauvais ~** in bad taste, tasteless; **avoir bon/mauvais ~** *(aliment)* to taste nice/ nasty; *(personne)* to have good/bad taste; **avoir du/manquer de ~** to have/lack taste; **avoir du ~ pour** to have a liking for; **prendre ~ à** to develop a taste *ou* a liking for

goûter [gute] *vt (essayer)* to taste; *(apprécier)* to enjoy ▷ *vi* to have (afternoon) tea ▷ *nm* (afternoon) tea; **~ à** to taste, sample; **~ de** to have a taste of; **~ d'enfants/d'anniversaire** children's tea/birthday party; **je peux ~?** can I have a taste?

goutte [gut] *nf* drop; *(Méd)* gout; *(alcool)* nip *(Brit)*, tot *(Brit)*, drop *(US)*; **gouttes** *nfpl (Méd)* drops; **~ à ~** *adv* a drop at a time; **tomber ~ à ~** to drip

goutte-à-goutte [gutagut] *nm inv (Méd)* drip; **alimenter au ~** to drip-feed

gouttelette [gutlɛt] *nf* droplet

gouttière [gutjɛʀ] *nf* gutter

gouvernail [guvɛʀnaj] *nm* rudder; *(barre)* helm, tiller

gouvernant, e [guvɛʀnɑ̃, -ɑ̃t] *adj* ruling *cpd* ▷ *nf* housekeeper; *(d'un enfant)* governess

gouvernement [guvɛʀnəmɑ̃] *nm* government

gouverner [guvɛʀne] *vt* to govern; *(diriger)* to steer; *(fig)* to control

grâce [gʀɑs] *nf (charme, Rel)* grace; *(faveur)* favour; *(Jur)* pardon; **grâces** *nfpl (Rel)* grace *sg*; **de bonne/mauvaise ~** with (a) good/bad grace; **dans les bonnes ~s de qn** in favour with sb; **faire ~ à qn de qch** to spare sb sth; **rendre ~(s) à** to give thanks to; **demander ~** to beg for mercy; **droit de ~** right of reprieve; **recours en ~** plea for pardon; **~ à** *prép* thanks to

gracier [gʀasje] *vt* to pardon

gracieux, -euse [gʀasjø, -øz] *adj (charmant, élégant)* graceful; *(aimable)* gracious, kind; **à titre ~** free of charge

grade [gʀad] *nm (Mil)* rank; *(Scol)* degree; **monter en ~** to be promoted

gradin [gʀadɛ̃] *nm (dans un théâtre)* tier; *(de stade)* step; **gradins** *nmpl (de stade)* terracing *no pl (Brit)*, standing area; **en ~s** terraced

gradué, e [gʀadɥe] *adj (exercices)* graded (for difficulty); *(thermomètre)* graduated; **verre ~** measuring jug

graduel, le [gʀadɥɛl] *adj* gradual; progressive

graduer [gʀadɥe] *vt (effort etc)* to increase gradually; *(règle, verre)* to graduate

graffiti [gʀafiti] *nmpl* graffiti

grain [gʀɛ̃] *nm (gén)* grain; *(de chapelet)* bead; *(Navig)* squall; *(averse)* heavy shower; *(fig: petite quantité)*: **un ~ de** a touch of; **~ de beauté** beauty spot; **~ de café** coffee bean; **~ de poivre** peppercorn; **~ de poussière** speck of dust; **~ de raisin** grape

graine [gʀɛn] *nf* seed; **mauvaise ~** *(mauvais sujet)* bad lot; **une ~ de voyou** a hooligan in the making

graissage [gʀesaʒ] *nm* lubrication, greasing

graisse [gʀɛs] *nf* fat; *(lubrifiant)* grease; **~ saturée** saturated fat

graisser [gʀese] *vt* to lubricate, grease; *(tacher)* to make greasy

graisseux, -euse [gʀesø, -øz] *adj* greasy; *(Anat)* fatty

grammaire [gʀamɛʀ] *nf* grammar

grammatical, e, -aux [gʀamatikal, -o] *adj* grammatical

gramme [gʀam] *nm* gramme

grand, e [gʀɑ̃, gʀɑ̃d] *adj (haut)* tall; *(gros, vaste, large)* big, large; *(long)* long; *(plus âgé)* big; *(adulte)* grown-up; *(important, brillant)* great ▷ *adv*: **~ ouvert** wide open; **un ~ buveur** a heavy drinker; **un ~ homme** a great man; **son ~ frère** his big *ou* older brother; **avoir ~ besoin de** to be in dire *ou* desperate need of; **il est ~ temps de** it's high time to; **il est assez ~ pour** he's big *ou* old enough to; **voir ~** to think big; **en ~** on a large scale; **au ~ air** in the open (air); **les ~s blessés/brûlés** the severely injured/burned; **de ~ matin** at the crack of dawn; **~ écart** splits *pl*; **~ ensemble** housing scheme; **~ jour** broad daylight; **~ livre** *(Comm)* ledger; **~ magasin** department store; **~ malade** very sick person; **~ public** general public; **~e personne** grown-up; **~e surface** hypermarket, superstore; **~es écoles** *prestige university-level colleges with competitive entrance examinations; see note*; **~es lignes** *(Rail)* main lines; **~es vacances** summer holidays *(Brit)* ou vacation *(US)*

GRANDES ÉCOLES

The *grandes écoles* are highly-respected institutes of higher education which train students for specific careers. Students who have spent two years after the "baccalauréat" in the "classes préparatoires" are recruited by competitive entry examination. The prestigious *grandes écoles* have a strong corporate identity and tend to furnish France with its intellectual, administrative and political élite.

grand-chose [gʀɑ̃ʃoz] *nm/f inv*: **pas ~** not much

Grande-Bretagne [gʀɑ̃dbʀətaɲ] *nf*: **la ~** (Great) Britain; **en ~** in (Great) Britain

grandeur [gʀɑ̃dœʀ] *nf (dimension)* size; *(fig: ampleur, importance)* magnitude; *(: gloire, puissance)* greatness; **~ nature** *adj* life-size

grandiose [gʀɑ̃djoz] *adj (paysage, spectacle)* imposing

grandir [gʀɑ̃diʀ] *vi (enfant, arbre)* to grow; *(bruit, hostilité)* to increase, grow ▷ *vt*: **~ qn** *(vêtement, chaussure)* to make sb look taller; *(fig)* to make sb grow in stature

grand-mère *(pl grand(s)-mères)* [gʀɑ̃mɛʀ] *nf* grandmother

grand-messe [gʀɑ̃mɛs] nf high mass
grand-peine [gʀɑ̃pɛn]: **à ~** adv with (great) difficulty
grand-père (pl **grands-pères**) [gʀɑ̃pɛʀ] nm grandfather
grand-route [gʀɑ̃ʀut] nf main road
grands-parents [gʀɑ̃paʀɑ̃] nmpl grandparents
grange [gʀɑ̃ʒ] nf barn
granit, granite [gʀanit] nm granite
graphique [gʀafik] adj graphic ▷ nm graph
grappe [gʀap] nf cluster; **~ de raisin** bunch of grapes
gras, se [gʀɑ, gʀɑs] adj (viande, soupe) fatty; (personne) fat; (surface, main, cheveux) greasy; (terre) sticky; (toux) loose, phlegmy; (rire) throaty; (plaisanterie) coarse; (crayon) soft-lead; (Typo) bold ▷ nm (Culin) fat; **faire la ~se matinée** to have a lie-in (Brit), sleep late; **matière ~se** fat (content)
grassement [gʀasmɑ̃] adv (généreusement): **~ payé** handsomely paid; (grossièrement: rire) coarsely
grassouillet, te [gʀasujɛ, -ɛt] adj podgy, plump
gratifiant, e [gʀatifjɑ̃, -ɑ̃t] adj gratifying, rewarding
gratin [gʀatɛ̃] nm (Culin) cheese- (où crumb-) topped dish; (: croûte) topping; **au ~** au gratin; **tout le ~ parisien** all the best people of Paris
gratiné [gʀatine] adj (Culin) au gratin; (fam) hellish ▷ nf (soupe) onion soup au gratin
gratis [gʀatis] adv, adj free
gratitude [gʀatityd] nf gratitude
gratte-ciel [gʀatsjɛl] nm inv skyscraper
gratte-papier [gʀatpapje] nm inv (péj) penpusher
gratter [gʀate] vt (frotter) to scrape; (enlever: avec un outil) to scrape off; (avec un ongle: bras, bouton) to scratch; (enlever avec un ongle) to scratch off ▷ vi (irriter) to be scratchy; (démanger) to itch; **se gratter** to scratch o.s.
gratuit, e [gʀatɥi, -ɥit] adj (entrée) free; (billet) free, complimentary; (fig) gratuitous
gravats [gʀava] nmpl rubble sg
grave [gʀav] adj (dangereux: maladie, accident) serious, bad; (sérieux: sujet, problème) serious, grave; (personne, air) grave, solemn; (voix, son) deep, low-pitched ▷ nm (Mus) low register; **ce n'est pas ~!** it's all right, don't worry; **blessé ~** seriously injured person
gravement [gʀavmɑ̃] adv seriously; badly; (parler, regarder) gravely
graver [gʀave] vt (plaque, nom) to engrave; (CD, DVD) to burn; (fig): **~ qch dans son esprit/sa mémoire** to etch sth in one's mind/memory
graveur [gʀavœʀ] nm engraver; **~ de CD/DVD** CD/DVD burner or writer
gravier [gʀavje] nm (loose) gravel no pl
gravillons [gʀavijɔ̃] nmpl gravel sg, loose chippings ou gravel

gravir [gʀaviʀ] vt to climb (up)
gravité [gʀavite] nf (de maladie, d'accident) seriousness; (de sujet, problème) gravity; (Physique) gravity
graviter [gʀavite] vi to revolve; **~ autour de** to revolve around
gravure [gʀavyʀ] nf engraving; (reproduction) print; plate
gré [gʀe] nm: **à son ~** adj to his liking ▷ adv as he pleases; **au ~ de** according to, following; **contre le ~ de qn** against sb's will; **de son (plein) ~** of one's own free will; **de ~ ou de force** whether one likes it or not; **de bon ~** willingly; **bon ~ mal ~** like it or not; willy-nilly; **de ~ à ~** (Comm) by mutual agreement; **savoir (bien) ~ à qn de qch** to be (most) grateful to sb for sth
grec, grecque [gʀɛk] adj Greek; (classique: vase etc) Grecian ▷ nm (Ling) Greek ▷ nm/f: **G~, G~que** Greek
Grèce [gʀɛs] nf: **la ~** Greece
greffe [gʀɛf] nf (Bot, Méd: de tissu) graft; (Méd: d'organe) transplant ▷ nm (Jur) office
greffer [gʀefe] vt (Bot, Méd: tissu) to graft; (Méd: organe) to transplant
greffier [gʀefje] nm clerk of the court
grêle [gʀɛl] adj (very) thin ▷ nf hail
grêler [gʀele] vb impers: **il grêle** it's hailing ▷ vt: **la région a été grêlée** the region was damaged by hail
grêlon [gʀɛlɔ̃] nm hailstone
grelot [gʀəlo] nm little bell
grelotter [gʀəlɔte] vi (trembler) to shiver
grenade [gʀənad] nf (explosive) grenade; (Bot) pomegranate; **~ lacrymogène** teargas grenade
grenadine [gʀənadin] nf grenadine
grenat [gʀəna] adj inv dark red
grenier [gʀənje] nm (de maison) attic; (de ferme) loft
grenouille [gʀənuj] nf frog
grès [gʀɛ] nm (roche) sandstone; (poterie) stoneware
grésiller [gʀezije] vi to sizzle; (Radio) to crackle
grève [gʀɛv] nf (d'ouvriers) strike; (plage) shore; **se mettre en/faire ~** to go on/be on strike; **~ bouchon** partial strike (in key areas of a company); **~ de la faim** hunger strike; **~ perlée** go-slow (Brit), slowdown (US); **~ sauvage** wildcat strike; **~ de solidarité** sympathy strike; **~ surprise** lightning strike; **~ sur le tas** sit down strike; **~ tournante** strike by rota; **~ du zèle** work-to-rule (Brit), slowdown (US)
gréviste [gʀevist] nm/f striker
gribouiller [gʀibuje] vt to scribble, scrawl ▷ vi to doodle
grièvement [gʀijɛvmɑ̃] adv seriously
griffe [gʀif] nf claw; (fig) signature; (: d'un couturier, parfumeur) label, signature
griffer [gʀife] vt to scratch

griffonner [gʀifɔne] vt to scribble

grignoter [gʀiɲɔte] vt (personne) to nibble at; (souris) to gnaw at ⊳ vi to nibble

gril [gʀil] nm steak ou grill pan

grillade [gʀijad] nf grill

grillage [gʀijaʒ] nm (treillis) wire netting; (clôture) wire fencing

grille [gʀij] nf (portail) (metal) gate; (clôture) railings pl; (d'égout) (metal) grate; (fig) grid

grille-pain [gʀijpɛ̃] nm inv toaster

griller [gʀije] vt (aussi: **faire ~**: pain) to toast; (: viande) to grill (Brit), broil (US); (: café) to roast; (châtaignes) to roast; (fig: ampoule etc) to burn out, blow; **~ un feu rouge** to jump the lights (Brit), run a stoplight (US) ⊳ vi (brûler) to be roasting

grillon [gʀijɔ̃] nm (Zool) cricket

grimace [gʀimas] nf grimace; (pour faire rire): **faire des ~s** to pull ou make faces

grimper [gʀɛ̃pe] vi, vt to climb ⊳ nm: **le ~** (Sport) rope-climbing; **~ à/sur** to climb (up)/ climb onto

grincer [gʀɛ̃se] vi (porte, roue) to grate; (plancher) to creak; **~ des dents** to grind one's teeth

grincheux, -euse [gʀɛ̃ʃø, -øz] adj grumpy

grippe [gʀip] nf flu, influenza; **avoir la ~** to have (the) flu; **prendre qn/qch en ~** (fig) to take a sudden dislike to sb/sth; **~ aviaire** bird flu; **~ porcine** swine flu

grippé, e [gʀipe] adj: **être ~** to have (the) flu; (moteur) to have seized up (Brit) ou jammed

gris, e [gʀi, gʀiz] adj grey (Brit), gray (US); (ivre) tipsy ⊳ nm (couleur) grey (Brit), gray (US); **il fait ~** it's a dull ou grey day; **faire ~e mine** to look miserable ou morose; **faire ~e mine à qn** to give sb a cool reception

grisaille [gʀizaj] nf greyness (Brit), grayness (US), dullness

griser [gʀize] vt to intoxicate; **se ~ de** (fig) to become intoxicated with

grisonner [gʀizɔne] vi to be going grey (Brit) ou gray (US)

grisou [gʀizu] nm firedamp

grive [gʀiv] nf (Zool) thrush

grivois, e [gʀivwa, -waz] adj saucy

Groenland [gʀɔenlɑ̃d] nm: **le ~** Greenland

grogner [gʀɔɲe] vi to growl; (fig) to grumble

grognon, ne [gʀɔɲɔ̃, -ɔn] adj grumpy, grouchy

groin [gʀwɛ̃] nm snout

grommeler [gʀɔmle] vi to mutter to o.s.

gronder [gʀɔ̃de] vi (canon, moteur, tonnerre) to rumble; (animal) to growl; (fig: révolte) to be brewing ⊳ vt to scold; **se faire ~** to get a telling-off

groom [gʀum] nm page, bellhop (US)

gros, se [gʀo, gʀos] adj big, large; (obèse) fat; (problème, quantité) great; (travaux, dégâts) extensive; (large: trait, fil) thick; (rhume, averse) heavy ⊳ adv: **risquer/gagner ~** to risk/win a lot ⊳ nm/f fat man/woman ⊳ nm (Comm): **le ~**

the wholesale business; **écrire ~** to write in big letters; **prix de ~** wholesale price; **par ~ temps/~se mer** in rough weather/heavy seas; **le ~ de** the main body of; (du travail etc) the bulk of; **en avoir ~ sur le cœur** to be upset; **en ~** roughly; (Comm) wholesale; **~ intestin** large intestine; **~ lot** jackpot; **~ mot** swearword, vulgarity; **~ œuvre** shell (of building); **~ plan** (Photo) close-up; **~ porteur** wide-bodied aircraft, jumbo (jet); **~ sel** cooking salt; **~ titre** headline; **~se caisse** big drum

groseille [gʀozɛj] nf: **~ (rouge)/(blanche)** red/white currant; **~ à maquereau** gooseberry

grosse [gʀos] adj f voir **gros** ⊳ nf (Comm) gross

grossesse [gʀosɛs] nf pregnancy; **~ nerveuse** phantom pregnancy

grosseur [gʀosœʀ] nf size; fatness; (tumeur) lump

grossier, -ière [gʀosje, -jɛʀ] adj coarse; (insolent) rude; (dessin) rough; (travail) roughly done; (imitation, instrument) crude; (évident: erreur) gross

grossièrement [gʀosjɛʀmɑ̃] adv (vulgairement) coarsely; (sommairement) roughly; crudely; (en gros) roughly

grossièreté [gʀosjɛʀte] nf coarseness, rudeness; (mot): **dire des ~s** to use coarse language

grossir [gʀosiʀ] vi (personne) to put on weight; (fig) to grow, get bigger; (rivière) to swell ⊳ vt to increase; (exagérer) to exaggerate; (au microscope) to magnify, enlarge; (vêtement): **~ qn** to make sb look fatter

grossiste [gʀosist] nm/f wholesaler

grosso modo [gʀosomɔdo] adv roughly

grotesque [gʀɔtɛsk] adj (extravagant) grotesque; (ridicule) ludicrous

grotte [gʀɔt] nf cave

grouiller [gʀuje] vi (foule) to mill about; (fourmis) to swarm about; **~ de** to be swarming with

groupe [gʀup] nm group; **cabinet de ~** group practice; **médecine de ~** group practice; **~ électrogène** generator; **~ de parole** support group; **~ de pression** pressure group; **~ sanguin** blood group; **~ scolaire** school complex

groupement [gʀupmɑ̃] nm grouping; (groupe) group; **~ d'intérêt économique (GIE)** ≈ trade association

grouper [gʀupe] vt to group; (ressources, moyens) to pool; **se grouper** vi to get together

grue [gʀy] nf crane; **faire le pied de ~** (fam) to hang around (waiting), kick one's heels (Brit)

grumeaux [gʀymo] nmpl (Culin) lumps

GSM [ʒeɛsɛm] nm, adj GSM

guenilles [gənij] nfpl rags

guenon [gənɔ̃] nf female monkey

guépard [gepaʀ] nm cheetah

guêpe [gɛp] nf wasp

guêpier [gepje] nm (fig) trap

guère [gɛʀ] adv (avec adjectif, adverbe): **ne ... ~** hardly; (avec verbe: pas beaucoup): **ne ... ~** (tournure négative) much; (pas souvent) hardly ever; (very) long; **il n'y a ~ que/de** there's hardly anybody (ou anything) but/hardly any; **ce n'est ~ difficile** it's hardly difficult; **nous n'avons ~ de temps** we have hardly any time

guéridon [geʀidɔ̃] nm pedestal table

guérilla [geʀija] nf guerrilla warfare

guérillero [geʀijeʀo] nm guerrilla

guérir [geʀiʀ] vt (personne, maladie) to cure; (membre, plaie) to heal ▷ vi (personne, malade) to recover, be cured; (maladie) to be cured; (plaie, chagrin, blessure) to heal; **~ de** to be cured of, recover from; **~ qn de** to cure sb of

guérison [geʀizɔ̃] nf (de maladie) curing; (de membre, plaie) healing; (de malade) recovery

guérisseur, -euse [geʀisœʀ, -øz] nm/f healer

guerre [gɛʀ] nf war; (méthode): **~ atomique/ de tranchées** atomic/trench warfare no pl; **en ~** at war; **faire la ~ à** to wage war against; **de ~ lasse** (fig) tired of fighting ou resisting; **de bonne ~** fair and square; **~ civile/ mondiale** civil/world war; **~ froide/sainte** cold/holy war; **~ d'usure** war of attrition

guerrier, -ière [gɛʀje, -jɛʀ] adj warlike ▷ nm/f warrior

guet [gɛ] nm: **faire le ~** to be on the watch ou look-out

guet-apens (pl **guets-apens**) [gɛtapɑ̃] nm ambush

guetter [gete] vt (épier) to watch (intently); (attendre) to watch (out) for; (: pour surprendre) to be lying in wait for

gueule [gœl] nf (d'animal) mouth; (fam: visage) mug; (: bouche) gob (!), mouth; **ta ~!** (fam) shut up!; **avoir la ~ de bois** (fam) to have a hangover, be hung over

gueuler [gœle] vi (fam) to bawl

gueuleton [gœltɔ̃] nm (fam) blowout (Brit), big meal

gui [gi] nm mistletoe

guichet [giʃɛ] nm (de bureau, banque) counter, window; (d'une porte) wicket, hatch; **les ~s** (à la gare, au théâtre) the ticket office; **jouer à ~s fermés** to play to a full house

guide [gid] nm (personne) guide; (livre) guide(book) ▷ nf (fille scout) (girl) guide (Brit), girl scout (US); **guides** nfpl (d'un cheval) reins

guider [gide] vt to guide

guidon [gidɔ̃] nm handlebars pl

guignol [giɲɔl] nm ≈ Punch and Judy show; (fig) clown

guillemets [gijmɛ] nmpl: **entre ~** in inverted commas ou quotation marks; **~ de répétition** ditto marks

guillotiner [gijɔtine] vt to guillotine

guindé, e [gɛ̃de] adj (personne, air) stiff, starchy; (style) stilted

Guinée [gine] nf: **la (République de) ~** (the Republic of) Guinea

guirlande [giʀlɑ̃d] nf (fleurs) garland; (de papier) paper chain; **~ lumineuse** lights pl, fairy lights pl (Brit); **~ de Noël** tinsel no pl

guise [giz] nf: **à votre ~** as you wish ou please; **en ~ de** by way of

guitare [gitaʀ] nf guitar

Guyane [gɥijan] nf: **la ~** Guyana; **la ~ (française)** (French) Guiana

gym [ʒim] nf (exercices) gym

gymnase [ʒimnaz] nm gym(nasium)

gymnaste [ʒimnast] nm/f gymnast

gymnastique [ʒimnastik] nf gymnastics sg; (au réveil etc) keep-fit exercises pl; **~ corrective** remedial gymnastics

gynécologie [ʒinekɔlɔʒi] nf gynaecology (Brit), gynecology (US)

gynécologique [ʒinekɔlɔʒik] adj gynaecological (Brit), gynecological (US)

gynécologue [ʒinekɔlɔg] nm/f gynaecologist (Brit), gynecologist (US)

h

habile [abil] *adj* skilful; *(malin)* clever

habileté [abilte] *nf* skill, skilfulness; cleverness

habillé, e [abije] *adj* dressed; *(chic)* dressy; *(Tech)*: **~ de** covered with; encased in

habillement [abijmɑ̃] *nm* clothes *pl*; *(profession)* clothing industry

habiller [abije] *vt* to dress; *(fournir en vêtements)* to clothe; *(couvrir)* to cover; **s'habiller** *vi* to dress (o.s.); *(se déguiser, mettre des vêtements chic)* to dress up; **s'~ de/en** to dress in/dress up as; **s'~ chez/à** to buy one's clothes from/at

habit [abi] *nm* outfit; **habits** *nmpl* *(vêtements)* clothes; **~ (de soirée)** evening dress; *(pour homme)* tails *pl*; **prendre l'~** *(Rel: entrer en religion)* to enter (holy) orders

habitant, e [abitɑ̃, -ɑ̃t] *nm/f* inhabitant; *(d'une maison)* occupant, occupier; **loger chez l'~** to stay with the locals

habitation [abitasjɔ̃] *nf* living; *(demeure)* residence, home; *(maison)* house; **~s à loyer modéré (HLM)** low-rent, state-owned housing, ≈ council flats *(Brit)*, ≈ public housing units *(US)*

habiter [abite] *vt* to live in; *(sentiment)* to dwell in ▷ *vi*: **~ à/dans** to live in *ou* at/in; **~ chez** *ou* **avec qn** to live with sb; **~ 16 rue Montmartre** to live at number 16 rue Montmartre; **~ rue Montmartre** to live in rue Montmartre

habitude [abityd] *nf* habit; **avoir l'~ de faire** to be in the habit of doing; *(expérience)* to be used to doing; **avoir l'~ des enfants** to be used to children; **prendre l'~ de faire qch** to get into the habit of doing sth; **perdre une ~** to get out of a habit; **d'~** usually; **comme d'~** as usual; **par ~** out of habit

habitué, e [abitye] *adj*: **être ~ à** to be used *ou* accustomed to ▷ *nm/f* *(de maison)* regular visitor; *(client)* regular (customer)

habituel, le [abityɛl] *adj* usual

habituer [abitye] *vt*: **~ qn à** to get sb used to; **s'habituer à** to get used to

'hache [ˈaʃ] *nf* axe

'hacher [ˈaʃe] *vt* *(viande)* to mince *(Brit)*, grind *(US)*; *(persil)* to chop; **~ menu** to mince *ou* grind finely; to chop finely

'hachis [ˈaʃi] *nm* mince *no pl* *(Brit)*, hamburger meat *(US)*; **~ de viande** minced *(Brit)* ou ground *(US)* meat; **hachis Parmentier** ≈ shepherd's pie

'hachisch [ˈaʃiʃ] *nm* hashish

'hachoir [ˈaʃwaʀ] *nm* chopper; *(meat)* mincer *(Brit)* ou grinder *(US)*; *(planche)* chopping board

'hagard, e [ˈagaʀ, -aʀd] *adj* wild, distraught

'haie [ˈɛ] *nf* hedge; *(Sport)* hurdle; *(fig: rang)* line, row; **200 m ~s** 200 m hurdles; **~ d'honneur** guard of honour

'haillons [ˈajɔ̃] *nmpl* rags

'haine [ˈɛn] *nf* hatred

'haïr [ˈaiʀ] *vt* to detest, hate; **se 'haïr** to hate each other

'hâlé, e [ˈɑle] *adj* *(sun)*tanned, sunburnt

haleine [alɛn] *nf* breath; **perdre ~** to get out of breath; **à perdre ~** until one is gasping for breath; **avoir mauvaise ~** to have bad breath; **reprendre ~** to get one's breath back; **hors d'~** out of breath; **tenir en ~** *(attention)* to hold spellbound; *(en attente)* to keep in suspense; **de longue ~** *adj* long-term

'haleter [ˈalte] *vi* to pant

'hall [ˈol] *nm* hall

'halle [ˈal] *nf* (covered) market; **halles** *nfpl* *(d'une grande ville)* central food market *sg*

hallucinant, e [alysinɑ̃, -ɑ̃t] *adj* staggering

hallucination [alysinasjɔ̃] *nf* hallucination

'halte [ˈalt] *nf* stop, break; *(escale)* stopping place; *(Rail)* halt ▷ *excl* stop!; **faire halte** to stop

haltère [altɛʀ] *nm* *(à boules, disques)* dumbbell, barbell; **(poids et) ~s** *(activité)* weightlifting *sg*

haltérophilie [alteʀɔfili] *nf* weightlifting

'hamac [ˈamak] *nm* hammock

'hamburger [ˈɑ̃buʀɡœʀ] *nm* hamburger

'hameau, x [ˈamo] *nm* hamlet

hameçon [amsɔ̃] *nm* *(fish)* hook

'hamster [ˈamstɛʀ] *nm* hamster

'hanche [ˈɑ̃ʃ] *nf* hip

'hand-ball [ˈɑ̃dbal] *nm* handball

'handicapé, e [ˈɑ̃dikape] *adj* disabled ▷ *nm/f* person with a disability; **handicapé mental** person with learning difficulties; **~ physique** person with a disability

'hangar [ˈɑ̃ɡaʀ] *nm* shed; *(Aviat)* hangar

'hanneton [ˈantɔ̃] *nm* cockchafer

'hanter [ˈɑ̃te] *vt* to haunt

'hantise ['ɑ̃tiz] nf obsessive fear

'happer ['ape] vt to snatch; (train etc) to hit

'haras ['aʀa] nm stud farm

'harassant, e ['aʀasɑ̃, -ɑ̃t] adj exhausting

'harcèlement ['aʀsɛlmɑ̃] nm harassment; **~ sexuel** sexual harassment

'harceler ['aʀsəle] vt (Mil, Chasse) to harass, harry; (importuner) to plague; **harceler qn de questions** to plague sb with questions

'hardi, e ['aʀdi] adj bold, daring

'hareng ['aʀɑ̃] nm herring; **hareng saur** kipper, smoked herring

'hargne ['aʀɲ] nf aggressivity, aggressiveness

'hargneux, -euse ['aʀɲø, -øz] adj (propos, personne) belligerent, aggressive; (chien) fierce

'haricot ['aʀiko] nm bean; **blanc/rouge** haricot/kidney bean; **~ vert** French (Brit) ou green bean

harmonica [aʀmɔnika] nm mouth organ

harmonie [aʀmɔni] nf harmony

harmonieux, -euse [aʀmɔnjø, -øz] adj harmonious; (couleurs, couple) well-matched

'harnacher ['aʀnaʃe] vt to harness

'harnais ['aʀnɛ] nm harness

'harpe ['aʀp] nf harp

'harponner ['aʀpɔne] vt to harpoon; (fam) to collar

'hasard ['azaʀ] nm: **le ~** chance, fate; **un ~** a coincidence; (aubaine, chance) a stroke of luck; **au ~** (sans but) aimlessly; (à l'aveuglette) at random, haphazardly; **par ~** by chance; **comme par ~** as if by chance; **à tout ~** (en espérant trouver ce qu'on cherche) on the off chance; (en cas de besoin) just in case

'hasarder ['azaʀde] vt (mot) to venture; (fortune) to risk; **se ~ à faire** to risk doing, venture to do

'hâte ['ɑt] nf haste; **à la ~** hurriedly, hastily; **en ~** posthaste, with all possible speed; **avoir ~ de** to be eager ou anxious to

'hâter ['ɑte] vt to hasten; **se 'hâter** to hurry; **se ~ de** to hurry ou hasten to

'hâtif, -ive ['ɑtif, -iv] adj (travail) hurried; (décision) hasty; (légume) early

'hausse ['os] nf rise, increase; (de fusil) backsight adjuster; **à la ~** upwards; **en ~** rising; **être en ~** to be going up

'hausser ['ose] vt to raise; **~ les épaules** to shrug (one's shoulders); **se ~ sur la pointe des pieds** to stand (up) on tiptoe ou tippy-toe (US)

'haut, e ['o, 'ot] adj high; (grand) tall; (son, voix) high(-pitched) ▷ adv high ▷ nm top (part); **de 3 m de ~, de 3 m** 3 m high, 3 m in height; **en ~e montagne** high up in the mountains; **en ~ lieu** in high places; **à ~e voix, (tout) ~** aloud, out loud; **des ~s et des bas** ups and downs; **du ~ de** from the top of; **tomber de ~** to fall from a height; (fig) to have one's hopes dashed; **dire qch bien ~** to say sth plainly; **prendre qch de (très) ~** to react haughtily to sth; **traiter qn de ~** to treat sb with disdain; **de ~ en bas** from top to bottom; downwards; **~ en couleur** (chose) highly coloured;

(personne): **un personnage ~ en couleur** a colourful character; **plus ~** higher up, further up; (dans un texte) above; (parler) louder; **en ~** up above; (être/aller) at (ou to) the top; (dans une maison) upstairs; **en ~ de** at the top of; **les mains!** hands up!, stick 'em up!; **la ~e couture/coiffure** haute couture/coiffure; **~ débit** (Inform) broadband; **~e fidélité** hi-fi, high fidelity; **la ~e finance** high finance; **~e trahison** high treason

'hautain, e ['otɛ̃, -ɛn] adj (personne, regard) haughty

'hautbois ['obwa] nm oboe

'haut-de-forme (pl **'hauts-de-forme**) ['odfɔʀm] nm top hat

'hauteur ['otœʀ] nf height; (Géo) height, hill; (fig) loftiness; haughtiness; **à ~ de** up to (the level of); **à ~ des yeux** at eye level; **à la ~ de** (sur la même ligne) level with; by; (fig: tâche, situation) equal to; **à la ~** (fig) up to it, equal to the task

'haut-fourneau (pl **'hauts-fourneaux**) ['ofuʀno] nm blast ou smelting furnace

'haut-le-cœur ['olkœʀ] nm inv retch, heave

'haut-parleur (pl **'haut-parleurs**) ['opaʀlœʀ] nm (loud)speaker

'havre ['avʀ] nm haven

Hawaii [awaj] n Hawaii; **les îles ~** the Hawaiian Islands

'Haye ['ɛ] n: **la ~** the Hague

'hayon ['ejɔ̃] nm tailgate

hebdo [ɛbdo] nm (fam) weekly

hebdomadaire [ɛbdɔmadɛʀ] adj, nm weekly

hébergement [ebɛʀʒemɑ̃] nm accommodation, lodging; taking in

héberger [ebɛʀʒe] vt (touristes) to accommodate, lodge; (amis) to put up; (réfugiés) to take in

hébergeur [ebɛʀʒœʀ] nm (Internet) host

hébété, e [ebete] adj dazed

hébreu, x [ebʀø] adj m, nm Hebrew

Hébrides [ebʀid] nf: **les ~** the Hebrides

hécatombe [ekatɔ̃b] nf slaughter

hectare [ɛktaʀ] nm hectare, 10,000 square metres

'hein ['ɛ̃] excl eh?; (sollicitant l'approbation): **tu m'approuves, ~?** so I did the right thing then?; **Paul est venu, ~?** Paul came, did he?; **que fais-tu, ~?** hey! what are you doing?

'hélas ['elɑs] excl alas! ▷ adv unfortunately

'héler ['ele] vt to hail

hélice [elis] nf propeller

hélicoptère [elikɔptɛʀ] nm helicopter

helvétique [ɛlvetik] adj Swiss

hématome [ematom] nm haematoma

hémicycle [emisikl] nm semicircle; (Pol): **l'~** the benches (in French parliament)

hémisphère [emisfɛʀ] nm: **~ nord/sud** northern/southern hemisphere

hémorragie [emɔʀaʒi] nf bleeding no pl, haemorrhage (Brit), hemorrhage (US); **~ cérébrale** cerebral haemorrhage; **~ interne** internal bleeding ou haemorrhage

hémorroïdes [emɔʀɔid] *nfpl* piles, haemorrhoids (*Brit*), hemorrhoids (*US*)

hennir ['eniʀ] *vi* to neigh, whinny

hennissement ['enismɑ̃] *nm* neighing, whinnying

hépatite [epatit] *nf* hepatitis, liver infection

herbe [ɛʀb] *nf* grass; (*Culin, Méd*) herb; **~s de Provence** mixed herbs; **en ~** unripe; (*fig*) budding; **touffe/brin d'~** clump/blade of grass

herbicide [ɛʀbisid] *nm* weed-killer

herboriste [ɛʀbɔʀist] *nm/f* herbalist

hère ['ɛʀ] *nm*: **pauvre ~** poor wretch

héréditaire [eʀeditɛʀ] *adj* hereditary

hérédité [eʀedite] *nf* heredity

hérisser ['eʀise] *vt*: **~ qn** (*fig*) to ruffle sb; **se hérisser** *vi* to bristle, bristle up

hérisson ['eʀisɔ̃] *nm* hedgehog

héritage [eʀitaʒ] *nm* inheritance; (*fig: coutumes, système*) heritage; (*: legs*) legacy; **faire un (petit) ~** to come into a (little) money

hériter [eʀite] *vi*: **~ de qch (de qn)** to inherit sth (from sb); **~ de qn** to inherit sb's property

héritier, -ière [eʀitje, -jɛʀ] *nm/f* heir/heiress

hermétique [ɛʀmetik] *adj* (*à l'air*) airtight; (*à l'eau*) watertight; (*fig: écrivain, style*) abstruse; (*: visage*) impenetrable

hermine [ɛʀmin] *nf* ermine

hernie ['ɛʀni] *nf* hernia

héroïne [eʀɔin] *nf* heroine; (*drogue*) heroin

héroïque [eʀɔik] *adj* heroic

héron ['eʀɔ̃] *nm* heron

héros ['eʀo] *nm* hero

hésitant, e [ezitɑ̃, -ɑ̃t] *adj* hesitant

hésitation [ezitasjɔ̃] *nf* hesitation

hésiter [ezite] *vi*: **~ (à faire)** to hesitate (to do); **~ sur qch** to hesitate over sth

hétéroclite [eteʀɔklit] *adj* heterogeneous; (*objets*) sundry

hétérogène [eteʀɔʒɛn] *adj* heterogeneous

hétérosexuel, le [eteʀɔsɛkɥɛl] *adj* heterosexual

hêtre ['ɛtʀ] *nm* beech

heure [œʀ] *nf* hour; (*Scol*) period; (*moment, moment fixé*) time; **c'est l'~** it's time; **pourriez-vous me donner l'~, s'il vous plaît?** could you tell me the time, please?; **quelle ~ est-il?** what time is it?; **2 ~s (du matin)** 2 o'clock (in the morning); **à la bonne ~!** (*parfois ironique*) splendid!; **être à l'~** to be on time; (*montre*) to be right; **le bus passe à l'~** the bus runs on the hour; **mettre à l'~** to set right; **100 km à l'~** ≈ 60 miles an *ou* per hour; **à toute ~** at any time; **24 ~s sur 24** round the clock, 24 hours a day; **à l'~ qu'il est** at this time (of day); (*fig*) now; **à l'~ actuelle** at the present time; **sur l'~** at once; **pour l'~** for the time being; **d'~ en ~** from one hour to the next; (*régulièrement*) hourly; **d'une ~ à l'autre** from hour to hour; **à une ~ avancée (de la nuit)** at a late hour (of the night); **de bonne ~** early; **deux ~s de marche/travail** two hours' walking/work; **une ~ d'arrêt** an hour's break *ou* stop; **~ d'été** summer time

(*Brit*), daylight saving time (*US*); **~ de pointe** rush hour; (*téléphone*) peak period; **~s de bureau** office hours; **~s supplémentaires** overtime *sg*

heureusement [œʀøzmɑ̃] *adv* (*par bonheur*) fortunately, luckily; **~ que ...** it's a good job that ..., fortunately ...

heureux, -euse [œʀø, -øz] *adj* happy; (*chanceux*) lucky, fortunate; (*judicieux*) felicitous, fortunate; **être ~ de qch** to be pleased *ou* happy about sth; **être ~ de faire/que** to be pleased *ou* happy to do/that; **s'estimer ~ de qch/que** to consider o.s. fortunate with sth/that; **encore ~ que ...** just as well that ...

heurt ['œʀ] *nm* (*choc*) collision; **heurts** *nmpl* (*fig*) clashes

heurter ['œʀte] *vt* (*mur*) to strike, hit; (*personne*) to collide with; (*fig*) to go against, upset; **se heurter** (*couleurs, tons*) to clash; **se ~ à** to collide with; (*fig*) to come up against; **~ qn de front** to clash head-on with sb

hexagone [ɛgzagɔn] *nm* hexagon; **l'H~** (*la France*) France (*because of its roughly hexagonal shape*)

hiberner [ibɛʀne] *vi* to hibernate

hibou, x ['ibu] *nm* owl

hideux, -euse ['idø, -øz] *adj* hideous

hier [jɛʀ] *adv* yesterday; **~ matin/soir/midi** yesterday morning/evening/lunchtime; **toute la journée d'~** all day yesterday; **toute la matinée d'~** all yesterday morning

hiérarchie ['jeʀaʀʃi] *nf* hierarchy

hi-fi ['ifi] *nf inv* hi-fi

hilare [ilaʀ] *adj* mirthful

hindou, e [ɛ̃du] *adj* Hindu ▷ *nm/f*: **H~, e** Hindu; (*Indien*) Indian

hippique [ipik] *adj* equestrian, horse *cpd*; **un club ~** a riding centre; **un concours ~** a horse show

hippisme [ipism] *nm* (horse-)riding

hippodrome [ipɔdʀom] *nm* racecourse

hippopotame [ipɔpɔtam] *nm* hippopotamus

hirondelle [iʀɔ̃dɛl] *nf* swallow

hirsute [iʀsyt] *adj* (*personne*) hairy; (*barbe*) shaggy; (*tête*) tousled

hisser ['ise] *vt* to hoist, haul up; **se hisser sur** to haul o.s. up onto

histoire [istwaʀ] *nf* (*science, événements*) history; (*anecdote, récit, mensonge*) story; (*affaire*) business *no pl*; (*chichis: gén pl*) fuss *no pl*; **histoires** *nfpl* (*ennuis*) trouble *sg*; **l'~ de France** French history, the history of France; **l'~ sainte** biblical history; **~ géo** humanities *pl*; **une ~ de** (*fig*) a question of

historique [istɔʀik] *adj* historical; (*important*) historic ▷ *nm* (*exposé, récit*): **faire l'~ de** to give the background to

hit-parade ['itpaʀad] *nm*: **le ~** the charts

hiver [ivɛʀ] *nm* winter; **en ~** in winter

hivernal, e, -aux [ivɛʀnal, -o] *adj* (*de l'hiver*) winter *cpd*; (*comme en hiver*) wintry

hiverner [ivɛʀne] *vi* to winter

HLM sigle m ou f (= habitations à loyer modéré) low-rent, state-owned housing; **un(e) ~** ≈ a council flat (ou house) (Brit), ≈ a public housing unit (US)

'**hobby** ['ɔbi] nm hobby

'**hocher** ['ɔʃe] vt: **~ la tête** to nod; (signe négatif ou dubitatif) to shake one's head

'**hochet** ['ɔʃe] nm rattle

'**hockey** ['ɔke] nm: **~ (sur glace/gazon)** (ice/field) hockey

'**hold-up** ['ɔldœp] nm inv hold-up

'**hollandais, e** ['ɔlɑ̃dɛ, -ɛz] adj Dutch ▷ nm (Ling) Dutch ▷ nm/f: '**Hollandais, e** Dutchman/woman; **les 'Hollandais** the Dutch

'**Hollande** ['ɔlɑ̃d] nf: **la ~** Holland ▷ nm: '**hollande** (fromage) Dutch cheese

'**homard** ['ɔmaʀ] nm lobster

homéopathique [ɔmeopatik] adj homoeopathic

homicide [ɔmisid] nm murder ▷ nm/f murderer/eress; **~ involontaire** manslaughter

hommage [ɔmaʒ] nm tribute; **hommages** nmpl: **présenter ses ~s** to pay one's respects; **rendre ~ à** to pay tribute ou homage to; **en ~ de** as a token of; **faire ~ de qch à qn** to present sb with sth

homme [ɔm] nm man; (espèce humaine): **l'~** man, mankind; **~ d'affaires** businessman; **~ des cavernes** caveman; **~ d'Église** churchman, clergyman; **~ d'État** statesman; **~ de loi** lawyer; **~ de main** hired man; **~ de paille** stooge; **~ politique** politician; **l'~ de la rue** the man in the street; **~ à tout faire** odd-job man

homme-grenouille (pl hommes-grenouilles) [ɔmgʀənuj] nm frogman

homogène [ɔmɔʒɛn] adj homogeneous

homologue [ɔmɔlɔg] nm/f counterpart, opposite number

homologué, e [ɔmɔlɔge] adj (Sport) officially recognized, ratified; (tarif) authorized

homonyme [ɔmɔnim] nm (Ling) homonym; (d'une personne) namesake

homosexuel, le [ɔmɔsɛksɥɛl] adj homosexual

'**Hong-Kong** ['ɔ̃gkɔ̃g] n Hong Kong

'**Hongrie** ['ɔ̃gʀi] nf: **la ~** Hungary

'**hongrois, e** ['ɔ̃gʀwa, -waz] adj Hungarian ▷ nm (Ling) Hungarian ▷ nm/f: '**Hongrois, e** Hungarian

honnête [ɔnɛt] adj (intègre) honest; (juste, satisfaisant) fair

honnêtement [ɔnɛtmɑ̃] adv honestly

honnêteté [ɔnɛtte] nf honesty

honneur [ɔnœʀ] nm honour; (mérite): **l'~ lui revient** the credit is his; **à qui ai-je l'~?** to whom have I the pleasure of speaking?; "**j'ai l'~ de ...**" "I have the honour of ..."; **en l'~ de** (personne) in honour of; (événement) on the occasion of; **faire ~ à** (engagements) to honour; (famille, professeur) to be a credit to; (fig: repas etc) to do justice to; **être à l'~** to be in the place of honour; **être en ~** to be in favour; **membre d'~** honorary member; **table d'~** top table

honorable [ɔnɔʀabl] adj worthy, honourable; (suffisant) decent

honoraire [ɔnɔʀɛʀ] adj honorary; **honoraires** nmpl fees; **professeur ~** professor emeritus

honorer [ɔnɔʀe] vt to honour; (estimer) to hold in high regard; (faire honneur à) to do credit to; **~ qn de** to honour sb with; **s'honorer de** to pride o.s. upon

honorifique [ɔnɔʀifik] adj honorary

'**honte** ['ɔ̃t] nf shame; **avoir ~ de** to be ashamed of; **faire ~ à qn** to make sb (feel) ashamed

'**honteux, -euse** ['ɔ̃tø, -øz] adj ashamed; (conduite, acte) shameful, disgraceful

hôpital, -aux [ɔpital, -o] nm hospital; **où est l'~ le plus proche?** where is the nearest hospital?

'**hoquet** ['ɔke] nm hiccough; **avoir le ~** to have (the) hiccoughs

'**hoqueter** ['ɔkte] vi to hiccough

horaire [ɔʀɛʀ] adj hourly ▷ nm timetable, schedule; **horaires** nmpl (heures de travail) hours; **~ flexible** ou **mobile** ou **à la carte** ou **souple** flex(i)time

horizon [ɔʀizɔ̃] nm horizon; (paysage) landscape, view; **sur l'~** on the skyline ou horizon

horizontal, e, -aux [ɔʀizɔ̃tal, -o] adj horizontal ▷ nf: **à l'~e** on the horizontal

horloge [ɔʀlɔʒ] nf clock; **l'~ parlante** the speaking clock; **~ normande** grandfather clock; **~ physiologique** biological clock

horloger, -ère [ɔʀlɔʒe, -ɛʀ] nm/f watchmaker; clockmaker

'**hormis** ['ɔʀmi] prép save

horoscope [ɔʀɔskɔp] nm horoscope

horreur [ɔʀœʀ] nf horror; **avoir ~ de** to loathe, detest; **quelle ~!** how awful!; **avoir ~ de** to loathe ou detest

horrible [ɔʀibl] adj horrible

horrifier [ɔʀifje] vt to horrify

horripiler [ɔʀipile] vt to exasperate

'**hors** ['ɔʀ] prép except (for); **~ de** out of; **~ ligne** (Inform) off line; **~ pair** outstanding; **~ de propos** inopportune; **~ série** (sur mesure) made-to-order; (exceptionnel) exceptional; **~ service (HS)**, **~ d'usage** out of service; **être ~ de soi** to be beside o.s.

'**hors-bord** ['ɔʀbɔʀ] nm inv outboard motor; (canot) speedboat (with outboard motor)

'**hors-d'œuvre** ['ɔʀdœvʀ] nm inv hors d'œuvre

'**hors-jeu** ['ɔʀʒø] nm inv being offside no pl

'**hors-la-loi** ['ɔʀlalwa] nm inv outlaw

hors-taxe [ɔʀtaks] adj (sur une facture, prix) excluding VAT; (boutique, marchandises) duty-free

hortensia [ɔʀtɑ̃sja] nm hydrangea

hospice [ɔspis] nm (de vieillards) home; (asile) hospice

hospitalier, -ière [ɔspitalje, -jɛʀ] adj (accueillant) hospitable; (Méd: service, centre) hospital cpd

hospitaliser [ɔspitalize] vt to take (ou send) to hospital, hospitalize

hospitalité [ɔspitalite] *nf* hospitality
hostie [ɔsti] *nf* host; (*Rel*)
hostile [ɔstil] *adj* hostile
hostilité [ɔstilite] *nf* hostility; **hostilités** *nfpl* hostilities
hôte [ot] *nm* (*maître de maison*) host; (*client*) patron; (*fig*) inhabitant, occupant ▷ *nm/f* (*invité*) guest; **~ payant** paying guest
hôtel [otɛl] *nm* hotel; **aller à l'~** to stay in a hotel; **~ (particulier)** (private) mansion; **~ de ville** town hall

⬤ HÔTELS
⬤
⬤
⬤ There are five categories of hotel in
⬤ France, from 1 star to 5 stars. Prices
⬤ include VAT but not breakfast. In some
⬤ towns, guests pay a small additional
⬤ tourist tax, the 'taxe de séjour', used to
⬤ offset tourism-related costs incurred by
⬤ the town.

hôtelier, -ière [otəlje, -jɛʀ] *adj* hotel *cpd* ▷ *nm/f* hotelier, hotel-keeper
hôtellerie [otɛlʀi] *nf* (*profession*) hotel business; (*auberge*) inn
hôtesse [otɛs] *nf* hostess; **~ de l'air** flight attendant; **~ (d'accueil)** receptionist
'hotte [ɔt] *nf* (*panier*) basket (*carried on the back*); (*de cheminée*) hood; **~ aspirante** cooker hood
'houblon [ublɔ̃] *nm* (*Bot*) hop; (*pour la bière*) hops *pl*
'houille [uj] *nf* coal; **~ blanche** hydroelectric power
'houle [ul] *nf* swell
'houleux, -euse [ulø, -øz] *adj* heavy, swelling; (*fig*) stormy, turbulent
'hourra [uʀa] *nm* cheer ▷ *excl* hurrah!
'houspiller [uspije] *vt* to scold
'housse [us] *nf* cover; (*pour protéger provisoirement*) dust cover; (*pour recouvrir à neuf*) loose ou stretch cover; **~ (penderie)** hanging wardrobe
'houx [u] *nm* holly
hovercraft [ovœʀkʀaft] *nm* hovercraft
'hublot [yblo] *nm* porthole
'huche [yʃ] *nf*: **~ à pain** bread bin
'huer [ɥe] *vt* to boo; (*hibou, chouette*) to hoot
huile [ɥil] *nf* oil; (*Art*) oil painting; (*fam*) bigwig; **mer d'~** (*très calme*) glassy sea, sea of glass; **faire tache d'~** (*fig*) to spread; **~ d'arachide** groundnut oil; **~ essentielle** essential oil; **~ de foie de morue** cod-liver oil; **~ de ricin** castor oil; **~ solaire** suntan oil; **~ de table** salad oil
huiler [ɥile] *vt* to oil
huileux, -euse [ɥilø, -øz] *adj* oily
huis [ɥi] *nm*: **à ~ clos** in camera
huissier [ɥisje] *nm* usher; (*Jur*) ≈ bailiff
'huit [ɥi(t)] *num* eight; **samedi en ~** a week on Saturday; **dans ~ jours** in a week('s time)
'huitaine [ɥiten] *nf*: **une ~ de** about eight, eight or so; **une ~ de jours** a week or so

'huitième [ɥitjem] *num* eighth
'huître [ɥitʀ] *nf* oyster
humain, e [ymɛ̃, -ɛn] *adj* human; (*compatissant*) humane ▷ *nm* human (being)
humanitaire [ymanitɛʀ] *adj* humanitarian
humanité [ymanite] *nf* humanity
humble [œ̃bl] *adj* humble
humecter [ymɛkte] *vt* to dampen; **s'~ les lèvres** to moisten one's lips
'humer [yme] *vt* (*parfum*) to inhale; (*pour sentir*) to smell
humeur [ymœʀ] *nf* mood; (*tempérament*) temper; (*irritation*) bad temper; **de bonne/mauvaise ~** in a good/bad mood; **être d'~ à faire qch** to be in the mood for doing sth
humide [ymid] *adj* (*linge*) damp; (*main, yeux*) moist; (*climat, chaleur*) humid; (*saison, route*) wet
humilier [ymilje] *vt* to humiliate; **s'~ devant qn** to humble o.s. before sb
humilité [ymilite] *nf* humility, humbleness
humoristique [ymɔʀistik] *adj* humorous; humoristic
humour [ymuʀ] *nm* humour; **avoir de l'~** to have a sense of humour; **~ noir** sick humour
'huppé, e [ype] *adj* crested; (*fam*) posh
'hurlement [yʀləmɑ̃] *nm* howling *no pl*, howl; yelling *no pl*, yell
'hurler [yʀle] *vi* to howl, yell; (*fig: vent*) to howl; (: *couleurs etc*) to clash; **~ à la mort** (*chien*) to bay at the moon
hurluberlu [yʀlybɛʀly] *nm* (*péj*) crank ▷ *adj* cranky
'hutte [yt] *nf* hut
hybride [ibʀid] *adj* hybrid
hydratant, e [idʀatɑ̃, -ɑ̃t] *adj* (*crème*) moisturizing
hydraulique [idʀolik] *adj* hydraulic
hydravion [idʀavjɔ̃] *nm* seaplane, hydroplane
hydrogène [idʀɔʒɛn] *nm* hydrogen
hydroglisseur [idʀɔɡlisœʀ] *nm* hydroplane
hyène [jɛn] *nf* hyena
hygiène [iʒjɛn] *nf* hygiene; **~ intime** personal hygiene
hygiénique [iʒenik] *adj* hygienic
hymne [imn] *nm* hymn; **~ national** national anthem
hyperlien [ipɛʀljɛ̃] *nm* (*Inform*) hyperlink
hypermarché [ipɛʀmaʀʃe] *nm* hypermarket
hypermétrope [ipɛʀmetʀɔp] *adj* long-sighted
hypertension [ipɛʀtɑ̃sjɔ̃] *nf* high blood pressure, hypertension
hypertexte [ipɛʀtekst] *nm* (*Inform*) hypertext
hypnose [ipnoz] *nf* hypnosis
hypnotiser [ipnotize] *vt* to hypnotize
hypnotiseur [ipnotizœʀ] *nm* hypnotist
hypocrisie [ipɔkʀizi] *nf* hypocrisy
hypocrite [ipɔkʀit] *adj* hypocritical ▷ *nm/f* hypocrite
hypothèque [ipotek] *nf* mortgage
hypothèse [ipotez] *nf* hypothesis; **dans l'~ où** assuming that
hystérique [isteʀik] *adj* hysterical

iceberg [isbɛʀg] *nm* iceberg
ici [isi] *adv* here; **jusqu'~** as far as this; (*temporel*) until now; **d'~ là** by then; **d'~ demain** by tomorrow; (*en attendant*) in the meantime; **d'~ peu** before long
icône [ikon] *nf* (*aussi Inform*) icon
idéal, e, -aux [ideal, -o] *adj* ideal ▷ *nm* ideal; (*système de valeurs*) ideals *pl*
idéaliste [idealist] *adj* idealistic ▷ *nm/f* idealist
idée [ide] *nf* idea; (*illusion*): **se faire des ~s** to imagine things, get ideas into one's head; **avoir dans l'~ que** to have an idea that; **mon ~, c'est que ...** I suggest that ..., I think that ...; **à l'~ de/que** at the idea of/that, at the thought of/that; **je n'ai pas la moindre ~** I haven't the faintest idea; **avoir ~ que** to have an idea that; **avoir des ~s larges/étroites** to be broad-/narrow-minded; **venir à l'~ de qn** to occur to sb; **en voilà des ~s!** the very idea!; **~ fixe** idée fixe, obsession; **~s noires** black ou dark thoughts; **~s reçues** accepted ideas ou wisdom
identifiant [idɑ̃tifjɑ̃] *nm* (*Inform*) login
identifier [idɑ̃tifje] *vt* to identify; **~ qch/qn à** to identify sth/sb with; **s'identifier** *vi*: **s'~ avec** ou **à qn/qch** (*héros etc*) to identify with sb/sth
identique [idɑ̃tik] *adj*: **~ (à)** identical (to)
identité [idɑ̃tite] *nf* identity; **~ judiciaire** (*Police*) ≈ Criminal Records Office
idiot, e [idjo, idjɔt] *adj* idiotic ▷ *nm/f* idiot

idiotie [idjɔsi] *nf* idiocy; (*propos*) idiotic remark
idole [idɔl] *nf* idol
if [if] *nm* yew
igloo [iglu] *nm* igloo
ignare [iɲaʀ] *adj* ignorant
ignoble [iɲɔbl] *adj* vile
ignorant, e [iɲɔʀɑ̃, -ɑ̃t] *adj* ignorant ▷ *nm/f*: **faire l'~** to pretend one doesn't know; **~ de** ignorant of, not aware of; **~ en** ignorant of, knowing nothing of
ignorer [iɲɔʀe] *vt* (*ne pas connaître*) not to know, be unaware ou ignorant of; (*être sans expérience de: plaisir, guerre etc*) not to know about, have no experience of; (*bouder: personne*) to ignore; **j'ignore comment/si** I do not know how/if; **~ que** to be unaware that, not to know that; **je n'ignore pas que ...** I'm not forgetting that ..., I'm not unaware that ...; **je l'ignore** I don't know
il [il] *pron* he; (*animal, chose, en tournure impersonnelle*) it, NB: *en anglais les navires et les pays sont en général assimilés aux femelles, et les bébés aux choses, si le sexe n'est pas spécifié;* **ils** they; **il neige** it's snowing; **Pierre est-il arrivé?** has Pierre arrived?; **il a gagné** he won; *voir aussi* **avoir**
île [il] *nf* island; **les Î~s** the West Indies; **l'~ de Beauté** Corsica; **l'~ Maurice** Mauritius; **les ~s anglo-normandes** the Channel Islands; **les ~s Britanniques** the British Isles; **les ~s Cocos** ou **Keeling** the Cocos ou Keeling Islands; **les ~s Cook** the Cook Islands; **les ~s Scilly** the Scilly Isles, the Scillies; **les ~s Shetland** the Shetland Islands, Shetland; **les ~s Sorlingues = les îles Scilly; les ~s Vierges** the Virgin Islands
illégal, e, -aux [ilegal, -o] *adj* illegal, unlawful (*Admin*)
illégitime [ileʒitim] *adj* illegitimate; (*optimisme, sévérité*) unjustified, unwarranted
illettré, e [iletʀe] *adj, nm/f* illiterate
illimité, e [ilimite] *adj* (*immense*) boundless, unlimited; (*congé, durée*) indefinite, unlimited
illisible [ilizibl] *adj* illegible; (*roman*) unreadable
illogique [ilɔʒik] *adj* illogical
illumination [ilyminasjɔ̃] *nf* illumination, floodlighting; (*inspiration*) flash of inspiration; **illuminations** *nfpl* illuminations, lights
illuminer [ilymine] *vt* to light up; (*monument, rue: pour une fête*) to illuminate; (*au moyen de projecteurs*) floodlight; **s'illuminer** *vi* to light up
illusion [ilyzjɔ̃] *nf* illusion; **se faire des ~s** to delude o.s.; **faire ~** to delude ou fool people; **~ d'optique** optical illusion
illusionniste [ilyzjɔnist] *nm/f* conjuror
illustration [ilystʀasjɔ̃] *nf* illustration; (*d'un ouvrage: photos*) illustrations *pl*
illustre [ilystʀ] *adj* illustrious, renowned
illustré, e [ilystʀe] *adj* illustrated ▷ *nm*

illustrated magazine; (*pour enfants*) comic
illustrer [ilystʀe] *vt* to illustrate; **s'illustrer**
to become famous, win fame
îlot [ilo] *nm* small island, islet; (*de maisons*)
block; (*petite zone*): **un ~ de verdure** an island
of greenery, a patch of green
ils [il] *pron* they
image [imaʒ] *nf* (*gén*) picture; (*comparaison,
ressemblance, Optique*) image; **~ de** picture ou
image of; **~ d'Épinal** (social) stereotype; **~ de
marque** brand image; (*d'une personne*)
(public) image; (*d'une entreprise*) corporate
image; **~ pieuse** holy picture
imagé, e [imaʒe] *adj* (*texte*) full of imagery;
(*langage*) colourful
imaginaire [imaʒineʀ] *adj* imaginary
imagination [imaʒinasjɔ̃] *nf* imagination;
(*chimère*) fancy, imagining; **avoir de l'~** to be
imaginative, have a good imagination
imaginer [imaʒine] *vt* to imagine; (*croire*):
qu'allez-vous ~ là? what on earth are you
thinking of?; (*inventer: expédient, mesure*) to
devise, think up; **s'imaginer** *vt* (*se figurer: scène
etc*) to imagine, picture; **s'~ à 60 ans** to picture
ou imagine o.s. at 60; **s'~ que** to imagine that;
s'~ pouvoir faire qch to think one can do sth;
j'imagine qu'il a voulu plaisanter I suppose
he was joking; **~ de faire** (*se mettre dans l'idée
de*) to dream up the idea of doing
imam [imam] *nm* imam
imbattable [ɛ̃batabl] *adj* unbeatable
imbécile [ɛ̃besil] *adj* idiotic ▷ *nm/f* idiot;
(*Méd*) imbecile
imbécillité [ɛ̃besilite] *nf* idiocy; imbecility;
idiotic action (*ou* remark *etc*)
imbiber [ɛ̃bibe] *vt*: **~ qch de** to moisten *ou*
wet sth with; **s'imbiber de** to become
saturated with; **imbibé(e) d'eau** (*chaussures,
étoffe*) saturated; (*terre*) waterlogged
imbu, e [ɛ̃by] *adj*: **~ de** full of; **~ de soi-même/
sa supériorité** full of oneself/one's
superiority
imbuvable [ɛ̃byvabl] *adj* undrinkable
imitateur, -trice [imitatœʀ, -tʀis] *nm/f* (*gén*)
imitator; (*Music-Hall: d'une personnalité*)
impersonator
imitation [imitasjɔ̃] *nf* imitation; (*de
personalité*) impersonation; **sac ~ cuir** bag in
imitation *ou* simulated leather; **à l'~ de** in
imitation of
imiter [imite] *vt* to imitate; (*personne*) to
imitate, impersonate; (*contrefaire: signature,
document*) to forge, copy; (*ressembler à*) to look
like; **il se leva et je l'imitai** he got up and I
did likewise
immaculé, e [imakyle] *adj* spotless,
immaculate; **l'I~e Conception** (*Rel*) the
Immaculate Conception
immangeable [ɛ̃mɑ̃ʒabl] *adj* inedible,
uneatable
immatriculation [imatʀikylasjɔ̃] *nf*
registration

immatriculer [imatʀikyle] *vt* to register;
faire/se faire ~ to register; **voiture
immatriculée dans la Seine** car with a
Seine registration (number)
immédiat, e [imedja, -at] *adj* immediate
▷ *nm*: **dans l'~** for the time being; **dans le
voisinage ~ de** in the immediate vicinity of
immédiatement [imedjatmɑ̃] *adv*
immediately
immense [imɑ̃s] *adj* immense
immerger [imɛʀʒe] *vt* to immerse,
submerge; (*câble etc*) to lay under water;
(*déchets*) to dump at sea; **s'immerger** *vi* (*sous-
marin*) to dive, submerge
immeuble [imœbl] *nm* building ▷ *adj* (*Jur*)
immovable, real; **~ locatif** block of rented
flats (*Brit*), rental building (*US*); **~ de rapport**
investment property
immigration [imigʀasjɔ̃] *nf* immigration
immigré, e [imigʀe] *nm/f* immigrant
imminent, e [iminɑ̃, -ɑ̃t] *adj* imminent,
impending
immiscer [imise]: **s'immiscer** *vi*: **s'~ dans** to
interfere in *ou* with
immobile [imɔbil] *adj* still, motionless; (*pièce
de machine*) fixed; (*fig*) unchanging; **rester/se
tenir ~** to stay/keep still
immobilier, -ière [imɔbilje, -jɛʀ] *adj*
property *cpd*, in real property ▷ *nm*: **l'~** the
property *ou* the real estate business
immobiliser [imɔbilize] *vt* (*gén*) to
immobilize; (*circulation, véhicule, affaires*) to
bring to a standstill; **s'immobiliser** (*personne*)
to stand still; (*machine, véhicule*) to come to a
halt *ou* a standstill
immonde [imɔ̃d] *adj* foul; (*sale: ruelle, taudis*)
squalid
immoral, e, -aux [imɔʀal, -o] *adj* immoral
immortel, le [imɔʀtɛl] *adj* immortal ▷ *nf*
(*Bot*) everlasting (flower)
immuable [imɥabl] *adj* (*inébranlable*)
immutable; (*qui ne change pas*) unchanging;
(*personne*): **~ dans ses convictions**
immoveable (in one's convictions)
immunisé, e [im(m)ynize] *adj*: **~ contre**
immune to
immunité [imynite] *nf* immunity;
~ diplomatique diplomatic immunity;
~ parlementaire parliamentary privilege
impact [ɛ̃pakt] *nm* impact; **point d'~** point of
impact
impair, e [ɛ̃pɛʀ] *adj* odd ▷ *nm* faux pas,
blunder; **numéros ~s** odd numbers

impardonnable [ɛ̃paʀdɔnabl] *adj*
unpardonable, unforgivable; **vous êtes ~
d'avoir fait cela** it's unforgivable of you to
have done that

imparfait, e [ɛ̃paʀfɛ, -ɛt] *adj* imperfect ▷ *nm*
(*Ling*) imperfect (tense)

impartial, e, -aux [ɛ̃paʀsjal, -o] *adj*
impartial, unbiased

impasse [ɛ̃pas] *nf* dead-end, cul-de-sac; (*fig*)
deadlock; **être dans l'~** (*négociations*) to have
reached deadlock; **~ budgétaire** budget deficit

impassible [ɛ̃pasibl] *adj* impassive

impatience [ɛ̃pasjɑ̃s] *nf* impatience

impatient, e [ɛ̃pasjɑ̃, -ɑ̃t] *adj* impatient;
~ de faire qch keen *ou* impatient to do sth

impatienter [ɛ̃pasjɑ̃te] *vt* to irritate, annoy;
s'impatienter *vi* to get impatient; **s'~ de/
contre** to lose patience at/with, grow
impatient at/with

impeccable [ɛ̃pekabl] *adj* faultless,
impeccable; (*propre*) spotlessly clean; (*chic*)
impeccably dressed; (*fam*) smashing

impensable [ɛ̃pɑ̃sabl] *adj* (*événement
hypothétique*) unthinkable; (*événement qui a eu
lieu*) unbelievable

imper [ɛ̃pɛʀ] *nm* (*imperméable*) mac

impératif, -ive [ɛ̃peʀatif, -iv] *adj*
imperative; (*Jur*) mandatory ▷ *nm* (*Ling*)
imperative; **impératifs** *nmpl* (*exigences: d'une
fonction, d'une charge*) requirements; (*de la mode*)
demands

impératrice [ɛ̃peʀatʀis] *nf* empress

imperceptible [ɛ̃pɛʀsɛptibl] *adj*
imperceptible

impérial, e, -aux [ɛ̃peʀjal, -o] *adj* imperial
▷ *nf* upper deck; **autobus à ~e** double-decker
bus

impérieux, -euse [ɛ̃peʀjø, -øz] *adj* (*caractère,
ton*) imperious; (*obligation, besoin*) pressing,
urgent

impérissable [ɛ̃peʀisabl] *adj* undying,
imperishable

imperméable [ɛ̃pɛʀmeabl] *adj* waterproof;
(*Géo*) impermeable; (*fig*): **~ à** impervious to
▷ *nm* raincoat; **~ à l'air** airtight

impertinent, e [ɛ̃pɛʀtinɑ̃, -ɑ̃t] *adj*
impertinent

imperturbable [ɛ̃pɛʀtyʀbabl] *adj* (*personne*)
imperturbable; (*sang-froid*) unshakeable;
rester ~ to remain unruffled

impétueux, -euse [ɛ̃petɥø, -øz] *adj* fiery

impitoyable [ɛ̃pitwajabl] *adj* pitiless,
merciless

implanter [ɛ̃plɑ̃te] *vt* (*usine, industrie, usage*) to
establish; (*colons etc*) to settle; (*idée, préjugé*) to
implant; **s'implanter dans** *vi* to be
established in; to settle in; to become
implanted in

impliquer [ɛ̃plike] *vt* to imply; **~ qn (dans)** to
implicate sb (in)

impoli, e [ɛ̃pɔli] *adj* impolite, rude

impopulaire [ɛ̃pɔpylɛʀ] *adj* unpopular

importance [ɛ̃pɔʀtɑ̃s] *nf* importance;
(*de somme*) size; (*de retard*): **avoir de l'~** to be
important; **sans ~** unimportant; **d'~**
important, considerable; **quelle ~?** what
does it matter?

important, e [ɛ̃pɔʀtɑ̃, -ɑ̃t] *adj* important;
(*en quantité: somme, retard*) considerable,
sizeable; (: *gamme, dégâts*) extensive; (*péj: airs,
ton*) self-important ▷ *nm*: **l'~** the important
thing

importateur, -trice [ɛ̃pɔʀtatœʀ, -tʀis] *adj*
importing ▷ *nm/f* importer; **pays ~ de blé**
wheat-importing country

importation [ɛ̃pɔʀtasjɔ̃] *nf* import;
introduction; (*produit*) import

importer [ɛ̃pɔʀte] *vt* (*Comm*) to import;
(*maladies, plantes*) to introduce ▷ *vi* (*être
important*) to matter; **~ à qn** to matter to sb; **il
importe de** it is important to; **il importe
qu'il fasse** he must do, it is important that
he should do; **peu m'importe** (*je n'ai pas de
préférence*) I don't mind; (*je m'en moque*) I don't
care; **peu importe** it doesn't matter; **peu
importe (que)** it doesn't matter (if); **peu
importe le prix** never mind the price; *voir
aussi* **n'importe**

importun, e [ɛ̃pɔʀtœ̃, -yn] *adj* irksome,
importunate; (*arrivée, visite*) inopportune,
ill-timed ▷ *nm* intruder

importuner [ɛ̃pɔʀtyne] *vt* to bother

imposable [ɛ̃pozabl] *adj* taxable

imposant, e [ɛ̃pozɑ̃, -ɑ̃t] *adj* imposing

imposer [ɛ̃poze] *vt* (*taxer*) to tax; (*Rel*): **~ les
mains** to lay on hands; **~ qch à qn** to impose
sth on sb; **s'imposer** *vi* (*être nécessaire*) to be
imperative; (*montrer sa proéminence*) to stand
out, emerge; (*artiste: se faire connaître*) to win
recognition, come to the fore; **en ~ to be
imposing; **en ~ à** to impress; **s'~ comme** to
emerge as; **s'~ par** to win recognition
through; **ça s'impose** it's essential, it's vital

impossibilité [ɛ̃posibilite] *nf* impossibility;
être dans l'~ de faire to be unable to do, find
it impossible to do

impossible [ɛ̃posibl] *adj* impossible ▷ *nm*: **l'~**
the impossible; **~ à faire** impossible to do; **il
m'est ~ de le faire** it is impossible for me to
do it, I can't possibly do it; **faire l'~ (pour
que)** to do one's utmost (so that); **si, par ~ ...**
if, by some miracle ...

imposteur [ɛ̃pɔstœʀ] *nm* impostor

impôt [ɛ̃po] *nm* tax; (*taxes*) taxation, taxes *pl*;
impôts *nmpl* (*contributions*) tax *sg*;
payer 1000 euros d'~s to pay 1,000 euros in
tax; **~ direct/indirect** direct/indirect tax; **~ sur
le chiffre d'affaires** corporation (*Brit*) *ou*
corporate (*US*) tax; **~ foncier** land tax; **~ sur
la fortune** wealth tax; **~ sur les plus-values**
capital gains tax; **~ sur le revenu** income
tax; **~ sur le RPP** personal income tax; **~ sur
les sociétés** tax on companies; **~s locaux**
rates, local taxes (*US*), ≈ council tax (*Brit*)

impotent, e [ɛ̃pɔtɑ̃, -ɑ̃t] *adj* disabled
impraticable [ɛ̃pratikabl] *adj* (*projet*)
impracticable, unworkable; (*piste*) impassable
imprécis, e [ɛ̃presi, -iz] *adj* (*contours, souvenir*)
imprecise, vague; (*tir*) inaccurate, imprecise
imprégner [ɛ̃preɲe] *vt* (*tissu, tampon*): ~ **(de)**
to soak *ou* impregnate (with); (*lieu, air*): ~ **(de)**
to fill (with); (*amertume, ironie*) to pervade;
s'imprégner de *vi* to become impregnated
with; to be filled with; (*fig*) to absorb
imprenable [ɛ̃prənabl] *adj* (*forteresse*)
impregnable; **vue ~** unimpeded outlook
impresario [ɛ̃presarjo] *nm* manager,
impresario
impression [ɛ̃presjɔ̃] *nf* impression; (*d'un
ouvrage, tissu*) printing; (*Photo*) exposure; **faire
bonne/mauvaise ~** to make a good/bad
impression; **donner une ~ de/l'~ que** to give
the impression of/that; **avoir l'~ de/que** to
have the impression of/that; **faire ~** to make
an impression; **~s de voyage** impressions of
one's journey
impressionnant, e [ɛ̃presjɔnɑ̃, -ɑ̃t] *adj*
(*imposant*) impressive; (*bouleversant*) upsetting
impressionner [ɛ̃presjɔne] *vt* (*frapper*) to
impress; (*troubler*) to upset; (*Photo*) to expose
imprévisible [ɛ̃previzibl] *adj* unforeseeable;
(*réaction, personne*) unpredictable
imprévoyant, e [ɛ̃prevwajɑ̃, -ɑ̃t] *adj* lacking
in foresight; (*en matière d'argent*) improvident
imprévu, e [ɛ̃prevy] *adj* unforeseen,
unexpected ▷ *nm* (*incident*) unexpected
incident; **l'~** the unexpected; **des vacances
pleines d'~** holidays full of surprises; **en cas
d'~** if anything unexpected happens; **sauf ~**
unless anything unexpected crops up
imprimante [ɛ̃primɑ̃t] *nf* (*Inform*) printer; **~ à
bulle d'encre** bubblejet printer; **~ à jet
d'encre** ink-jet printer; **~ à laser** laser
printer; **~ (ligne par) ligne** line printer; **~ à
marguerite** daisy-wheel printer
imprimé [ɛ̃prime] *nm* (*formulaire*) printed
form; (*Postes*) printed matter *no pl*; (*tissu*)
printed fabric; **~ à fleurs/pois** (*tissu*) a
floral/polka-dot print
imprimer [ɛ̃prime] *vt* to print; (*Inform*) to
print (out); (*apposer: visa, cachet*) to stamp;
(*empreinte etc*) to imprint; (*publier*) to publish;
(*communiquer: mouvement, impulsion*) to impart,
transmit
imprimerie [ɛ̃primri] *nf* printing;
(*établissement*) printing works *sg*; (*atelier*)
printing house, printery
imprimeur [ɛ̃primœr] *nm* printer;
~-éditeur/-libraire printer and publisher/
bookseller
impromptu, e [ɛ̃prɔ̃pty] *adj* impromptu;
(*départ*) sudden
impropre [ɛ̃prɔpr] *adj* inappropriate; **~ à**
unsuitable for
improviser [ɛ̃prɔvize] *vt, vi* to improvize;
s'improviser (*secours, réunion*) to be

improvized; **s'~ cuisinier** to (decide to) act as
cook; **~ qn cuisinier** to get sb to act as cook
improviste [ɛ̃prɔvist]: **à l'~** *adv*
unexpectedly, without warning
imprudence [ɛ̃prydɑ̃s] *nf* (*d'une personne, d'une
action*) carelessness *no pl*; (*d'une remarque*)
imprudence *no pl*; act of carelessness; (*000*)
foolish *ou* unwise action; **commettre une ~**
to do something foolish
imprudent, e [ɛ̃prydɑ̃, -ɑ̃t] *adj* (*conducteur,
geste, action*) careless; (*remarque*) unwise,
imprudent; (*projet*) foolhardy
impudent, e [ɛ̃pydɑ̃, -ɑ̃t] *adj* impudent
impudique [ɛ̃pydik] *adj* shameless
impuissant, e [ɛ̃pɥisɑ̃, -ɑ̃t] *adj* helpless;
(*sans effet*) ineffectual; (*sexuellement*) impotent
▷ *nm* impotent man; **à faire qch** powerless
to do sth
impulsif, -ive [ɛ̃pylsif, -iv] *adj* impulsive
impulsion [ɛ̃pylsjɔ̃] *nf* (*Élec, instinct*) impulse;
(*élan, influence*) impetus
impunément [ɛ̃pynemɑ̃] *adv* with impunity
inabordable [inabɔrdabl] *adj* (*lieu*)
inaccessible; (*cher*) prohibitive
inacceptable [inakseptabl] *adj*
unacceptable
inaccessible [inaksesibl] *adj* inaccessible;
(*objectif*) unattainable; (*insensible*): **~ à**
impervious to
inachevé, e [inaʃve] *adj* unfinished
inactif, -ive [inaktif, -iv] *adj* inactive, idle;
(*remède*) ineffective; (*Bourse: marché*) slack
inadapté, e [inadapte] *adj* (*Psych: adulte,
enfant*) maladjusted ▷ *nm/f* (*péj: adulte: asocial*)
misfit; **~ à** not adapted to, unsuited to
inadéquat, e [inadekwa, wat] *adj* inadequate
inadmissible [inadmisibl] *adj* inadmissible
inadvertance [inadvɛrtɑ̃s]: **par ~** *adv*
inadvertently
inaltérable [inalterabl] *adj* (*matière*) stable;
(*fig*) unchanging; **~ à** unaffected by; **couleur
~ (au lavage/à la lumière)** fast colour/fade-
resistant colour
inanimé, e [inanime] *adj* (*matière*)
inanimate; (*évanoui*) unconscious; (*sans vie*)
lifeless
inanition [inanisjɔ̃] *nf*: **tomber d'~** to faint
with hunger and exhaustion
inaperçu, e [inapɛrsy] *adj*: **passer ~** to go
unnoticed
inapte [inapt] *adj*: **~ à** incapable of; (*Mil*)
unfit for
inattaquable [inatakabl] *adj* (*Mil*)
unassailable; (*texte, preuve*) irrefutable
inattendu, e [inatɑ̃dy] *adj* unexpected ▷ *nm*:
l'~ the unexpected
inattentif, -ive [inatɑ̃tif, -iv] *adj*
inattentive; **~ à** (*dangers, détails*) heedless of
inattention [inatɑ̃sjɔ̃] *nf* inattention;
(*inadvertance*) **une minute d'~** a minute of
inattention, a minute's carelessness; **par ~**
inadvertently; **faute d'~** careless mistake

inauguration [inɔgyRasjɔ̃] nf unveiling; opening; **discours/cérémonie d'~** inaugural speech/ceremony

inaugurer [inɔgyRe] vt (*monument*) to unveil; (*exposition, usine*) to open; (*fig*) to inaugurate

inavouable [inavwabl] adj (*bénéfices*) undisclosable; (*honteux*) shameful

incalculable [ɛ̃kalkylabl] adj incalculable; **un nombre ~ de** countless numbers of

incandescence [ɛ̃kɑ̃desɑ̃s] nf incandescence; **en ~** incandescent, white-hot; **porter à ~** to heat white-hot; **lampe/manchon à ~** incandescent lamp/(gas) mantle

incapable [ɛ̃kapabl] adj incapable; **~ de faire** incapable of doing; (*empêché*) unable to do

incapacité [ɛ̃kapasite] nf (*incompétence*) incapability; (*Jur: impossibilité*) incapacity; **être dans l'~ de faire** to be unable to do; **~ permanente/de travail** permanent/industrial disablement; **~ électorale** ineligibility to vote

incarcérer [ɛ̃kaRseRe] vt to incarcerate, imprison

incarné, e [ɛ̃kaRne] adj incarnate; (*ongle*) ingrown

incarner [ɛ̃kaRne] vt to embody, personify; (*Théât*) to play; (*Rel*) to incarnate; **s'incarner dans** vi (*Rel*) to be incarnate in

incassable [ɛ̃kasabl] adj unbreakable

incendiaire [ɛ̃sɑ̃djɛR] adj incendiary; (*fig: discours*) inflammatory ▷ nm/f fire-raiser, arsonist

incendie [ɛ̃sɑ̃di] nm fire; **~ criminel** arson no pl; **~ de forêt** forest fire

incendier [ɛ̃sɑ̃dje] vt (*mettre le feu à*) to set fire to, set alight; (*brûler complètement*) to burn down

incertain, e [ɛ̃sɛRtɛ̃, -ɛn] adj uncertain; (*temps*) uncertain, unsettled; (*imprécis: contours*) indistinct, blurred

incertitude [ɛ̃sɛRtityd] nf uncertainty

incessamment [ɛ̃sesamɑ̃] adv very shortly

incident [ɛ̃sidɑ̃] nm incident; **~ de frontière** border incident; **~ de parcours** minor hitch *ou* setback; **~ technique** technical difficulties *pl*, technical hitch

incinérer [ɛ̃sineRe] vt (*ordures*) to incinerate; (*mort*) to cremate

incisif, -ive [ɛ̃sizif, -iv] adj incisive, cutting ▷ nf incisor

inciter [ɛ̃site] vt: **~ qn à (faire) qch** to prompt *ou* encourage sb to do sth; (*à la révolte etc*) to incite sb to do sth

incivilité [ɛ̃sivilite] nf (*grossièreté*) incivility; **incivilités** nfpl antisocial behaviour *sg*

inclinable [ɛ̃klinabl] adj (*dossier etc*) tilting; **siège à dossier ~** reclining seat

inclinaison [ɛ̃klinɛzɔ̃] nf (*déclivité: d'une route etc*) incline; (: *d'un toit*) slope; (*état penché: d'un mur*) lean; (: *de la tête*) tilt; (: *d'un navire*) list

inclination [ɛ̃klinasjɔ̃] nf (*penchant*) inclination, tendency; **montrer de l'~ pour les sciences** etc to show an inclination for the sciences etc; **~s égoïstes/altruistes** egoistic/altruistic tendencies; **~ de (la) tête** nod (of the head); **~ (de buste)** bow

incliner [ɛ̃kline] vt (*bouteille*) to tilt; (*tête*) to incline; (*inciter*): **~ qn à qch/à faire** to encourage sb towards sth/to do ▷ vi: **~ à qch/à faire** (*tendre à, pencher pour*) to incline towards sth/doing, tend towards sth/to do; **s'incliner** vi (*route*) to slope; (*toit*) to be sloping; **s'~ (devant)** to bow (before)

inclure [ɛ̃klyR] vt to include; (*joindre à un envoi*) to enclose; **jusqu'au 10 mars inclus** until 10th March inclusive

inclus, e [ɛ̃kly, -yz] pp de **inclure** ▷ adj included; (*joint à un envoi*) enclosed; (*compris: frais, dépense*) included; (*Math: ensemble*): **~ dans** included in; **jusqu'au troisième chapitre ~** up to and including the third chapter; **jusqu'au 10 mars ~** until 10th March inclusive

incognito [ɛ̃kɔɲito] adv incognito ▷ nm: **garder l'~** to remain incognito

incohérent, e [ɛ̃kɔeRɑ̃, -ɑ̃t] adj (*comportement*) inconsistent; (*geste, langage, texte*) incoherent

incollable [ɛ̃kɔlabl] adj (*riz*) that does not stick; (*fam: personne*): **il est ~** he's got all the answers

incolore [ɛ̃kɔlɔR] adj colourless

incommoder [ɛ̃kɔmɔde] vt (*chaleur, odeur*): **~ qn** to bother *ou* inconvenience sb; (*embarrasser*) to make sb feel uncomfortable *ou* ill at ease

incomparable [ɛ̃kɔ̃paRabl] adj not comparable; (*inégalable*) incomparable, matchless

incompatible [ɛ̃kɔ̃patibl] adj incompatible

incompétent, e [ɛ̃kɔ̃petɑ̃, -ɑ̃t] adj (*ignorant*) inexpert; (*incapable*) incompetent, not competent

incomplet, -ète [ɛ̃kɔ̃plɛ, -ɛt] adj incomplete

incompréhensible [ɛ̃kɔ̃pReɑ̃sibl] adj incomprehensible

incompris, e [ɛ̃kɔ̃pRi, -iz] adj misunderstood

inconcevable [ɛ̃kɔ̃svabl] adj (*conduite etc*) inconceivable; (*mystère*) incredible

inconciliable [ɛ̃kɔ̃siljabl] adj irreconcilable

inconditionnel, le [ɛ̃kɔ̃disjɔnɛl] adj unconditional; (*partisan*) unquestioning ▷ nm/f (*partisan*) unquestioning supporter

inconfort [ɛ̃kɔ̃fɔR] nm lack of comfort, discomfort

inconfortable [ɛ̃kɔ̃fɔRtabl] adj uncomfortable

incongru, e [ɛ̃kɔ̃gRy] adj unseemly; (*remarque*) ill-chosen, incongruous

inconnu, e [ɛ̃kɔny] adj unknown; (*sentiment, plaisir*) new, strange ▷ nm/f stranger; unknown person (*ou* artist etc) ▷ nm: **l'~** the unknown ▷ nf (*Math*) unknown; (*fig*) unknown factor

inconsciemment [ɛ̃kɔ̃sjamɑ̃] *adv*
unconsciously

inconscient, e [ɛ̃kɔ̃sjɑ̃, -ɑ̃t] *adj* unconscious;
(*irréfléchi*) thoughtless, reckless; (*sentiment*)
subconscious ▷ *nm* (*Psych*): **l'~** the
subconscious, the unconscious; **~ de**
unaware of

inconsidéré, e [ɛ̃kɔ̃sidere] *adj* ill-considered

inconsistant, e [ɛ̃kɔ̃sistɑ̃, -ɑ̃t] *adj* flimsy,
weak; (*crème etc*) runny

inconsolable [ɛ̃kɔ̃sɔlabl] *adj* inconsolable

incontestable [ɛ̃kɔ̃tɛstabl] *adj*
unquestionable, indisputable

incontinent, e [ɛ̃kɔ̃tinɑ̃, -ɑ̃t] *adj* (*Méd*)
incontinent ▷ *adv* (*tout de suite*) forthwith

incontournable [ɛ̃kɔ̃turnabl] *adj*
unavoidable

incontrôlable [ɛ̃kɔ̃trolabl] *adj* unverifiable;
(*irrépressible*) uncontrollable

inconvenant, e [ɛ̃kɔ̃vnɑ̃, -ɑ̃t] *adj* unseemly,
improper

inconvénient [ɛ̃kɔ̃venjɑ̃] *nm* (*d'une situation,
d'un projet*) disadvantage, drawback; (*d'un
remède, changement etc*) risk, inconvenience; **si
vous n'y voyez pas d'~** if you have no
objections; **y a-t-il un ~ à ...?** (*risque*) isn't
there a risk in ...?; (*objection*) is there any
objection to ...?

incorporer [ɛ̃kɔrpɔre] *vt*: **~ (à)** to mix in
(with); (*paragraphe etc*): **~ (dans)** to
incorporate (in); (*territoire, immigrants*): **~
(dans)** to incorporate (into); (*Mil*: *appeler*) to
recruit, call up; (: *affecter*): **~ qn dans** to enlist
sb into; **il a très bien su s'~ à notre groupe**
he was very easily incorporated into our
group

incorrect, e [ɛ̃kɔrɛkt] *adj* (*impropre,
inconvenant*) improper; (*défectueux*) faulty;
(*inexact*) incorrect; (*impoli*) impolite; (*déloyal*)
underhand

incorrigible [ɛ̃kɔriʒibl] *adj* incorrigible

incrédule [ɛ̃kredyl] *adj* incredulous; (*Rel*)
unbelieving

increvable [ɛ̃krəvabl] *adj* (*pneu*) puncture-
proof; (*fam*) tireless

incriminer [ɛ̃krimine] *vt* (*personne*) to
incriminate; (*action, conduite*) to bring under
attack; (*bonne foi, honnêteté*) to call into
question; **livre/article incriminé** offending
book/article

incroyable [ɛ̃krwajabl] *adj* incredible,
unbelievable

incruster [ɛ̃kryste] *vt* (*Art*): **~ qch dans/qch
de** to inlay sth into/sth with; (*radiateur etc*) to
coat with scale *ou* fur; **s'incruster** *vi* (*invité*) to
take root; (*radiateur etc*) to become coated
with scale *ou* fur; **s'~ dans** (*corps étranger,
caillou*) to become embedded in

inculpé, e [ɛ̃kylpe] *nm/f* accused

inculper [ɛ̃kylpe] *vt*: **~ (de)** to charge (with)

inculquer [ɛ̃kylke] *vt*: **~ qch à** to inculcate
sth in, instil sth into

inculte [ɛ̃kylt] *adj* uncultivated; (*esprit, peuple*)
uncultured; (*barbe*) unkempt

Inde [ɛ̃d] *nf*: **l'~** India

indécent, e [ɛ̃desɑ̃, -ɑ̃t] *adj* indecent

indéchiffrable [ɛ̃deʃifrabl] *adj* indecipherable

indécis, e [ɛ̃desi, -iz] *adj* (*par nature*)
indecisive; (*perplexe*) undecided

indéfendable [ɛ̃defɑ̃dabl] *adj* indefensible

indéfini, e [ɛ̃defini] *adj* (*imprécis, incertain*)
undefined; (*illimité, Ling*) indefinite

indéfiniment [ɛ̃definimɑ̃] *adv* indefinitely

indéfinissable [ɛ̃definisabl] *adj* indefinable

indélébile [ɛ̃delebil] *adj* indelible

indélicat, e [ɛ̃delika, -at] *adj* tactless;
(*malhonnête*) dishonest

indemne [ɛ̃dɛmn] *adj* unharmed

indemniser [ɛ̃dɛmnize] *vt*: **~ qn (de)** to
compensate sb (for); **se faire ~** to get
compensation

indemnité [ɛ̃dɛmnite] *nf* (*dédommagement*)
compensation *no pl*; (*allocation*) allowance;
~ de licenciement redundancy payment;
~ de logement housing allowance;
~ parlementaire ≈ MP's (*Brit*) *ou*
Congressman's (*US*) salary

indépendamment [ɛ̃depɑ̃damɑ̃] *adv*
independently; **~ de** independently of;
(*abstraction faite de*) irrespective of; (*en plus de*)
over and above

indépendance [ɛ̃depɑ̃dɑ̃s] *nf* independence;
~ matérielle financial independence

indépendant, e [ɛ̃depɑ̃dɑ̃, -ɑ̃t] *adj*
independent; **~ de** independent of; **chambre
~e** room with private entrance; **travailleur ~**
self-employed worker

indescriptible [ɛ̃deskriptibl] *adj*
indescribable

indésirable [ɛ̃dezirabl] *adj* undesirable

indestructible [ɛ̃dɛstryktibl] *adj*
indestructible; (*marque, impression*) indelible

indétermination [ɛ̃detɛrminasjɔ̃] *nf*
indecision, indecisiveness

indéterminé, e [ɛ̃detɛrmine] *adj* (*date, cause,
nature*) unspecified; (*forme, longueur, quantité*)
indeterminate; indeterminable

index [ɛ̃dɛks] *nm* (*doigt*) index finger; (*d'un
livre etc*) index; **mettre à l'~** to blacklist

indexé, e [ɛ̃dɛkse] *adj* (*Écon*): **~ (sur)** index-
linked (to)

indicateur [ɛ̃dikatœr] *nm* (*Police*) informer;
(*livre*) guide; (: *liste*) directory; (*Tech*) gauge;
indicator; (*Écon*) indicator ▷ *adj*: **poteau ~**
signpost; **tableau ~** indicator (board); **~ des
chemins de fer** railway timetable; **~ de
direction** (*Auto*) indicator; **~ immobilier**
property gazette; **~ de niveau** level, gauge;
~ de pression pressure gauge; **~ de rues**
street directory; **~ de vitesse** speedometer

indicatif, -ive [ɛ̃dikatif, -iv] *adj*: **à titre ~** for
(your) information ▷ *nm* (*Ling*) indicative;
(*d'une émission*) theme *ou* signature tune; (*Tél*)
dialling code (*Brit*), area code (*US*); **~ d'appel**

(Radio) call sign; **quel est l'~ de ...** what's the code for ...?

indication [ɛ̃dikasjɔ̃] nf indication; (renseignement) information no pl; **indications** nfpl (directives) instructions; **~ d'origine** (Comm) place of origin

indice [ɛ̃dis] nm (marque, signe) indication, sign; (Police: lors d'une enquête) clue; (Jur: présomption) piece of evidence; (Science, Écon, Tech) index; (Admin) grading; rating; **~ du coût de la vie** cost-of-living index; **~ inférieur** subscript; **~ d'octane** octane rating; **~ des prix** price index; **~ de traitement** salary grading; **~ de protection** (sun protection) factor

indicible [ɛ̃disibl] adj inexpressible

indien, ne [ɛ̃djɛ̃, -ɛn] adj Indian ▷ nm/f: **I~, ne** (d'Amérique) Native American; (d'Inde) Indian

indifféremment [ɛ̃diferamɑ̃] adv (sans distinction) equally; indiscriminately

indifférence [ɛ̃diferɑ̃s] nf indifference

indifférent, e [ɛ̃diferɑ̃, -ɑ̃t] adj (peu intéressé) indifferent; **~ à** (insensible à) indifferent to, unconcerned about; (peu intéressant pour) indifferent to; immaterial to; **ça m'est ~ (que ...)** it doesn't matter to me (whether ...); **elle m'est ~e** I am indifferent to her

indigence [ɛ̃diʒɑ̃s] nf poverty; **être dans l'~** to be destitute

indigène [ɛ̃diʒɛn] adj native, indigenous; (de la région) local ▷ nm/f native

indigeste [ɛ̃diʒɛst] adj indigestible

indigestion [ɛ̃diʒɛstjɔ̃] nf indigestion no pl; **avoir une ~** to have indigestion

indigne [ɛ̃diɲ] adj: **~ (de)** unworthy (of)

indigner [ɛ̃diɲe] vt to make indignant; **s'indigner (de/contre)** vi to be (ou become) indignant (at)

indiqué, e [ɛ̃dike] adj (date, lieu) given, appointed; (adéquat) appropriate, suitable; (conseillé) advisable; (remède, traitement) appropriate

indiquer [ɛ̃dike] vt (désigner): **~ qch/qn à qn** to point sth/sb out to sb; (faire connaître: médecin, restaurant) to tell sb of sth/sb; (pendule, aiguille) to show; (étiquette, plan) to show, indicate; (faire connaître: médecin, lieu): **~ qch/qn à qn** to tell sb of sth/sb; (renseigner sur) to point out, tell; (déterminer: date, lieu) to give, state; (dénoter) to indicate, point to; **~ du doigt** to point out; **~ de la main** to indicate with one's hand; **~ du regard** to glance towards ou in the direction of; **pourriez-vous m'~ les toilettes/l'heure?** could you direct me to the toilets/tell me the time?

indirect, e [ɛ̃dirɛkt] adj indirect

indiscipliné, e [ɛ̃disipline] adj undisciplined; (fig) unmanageable

indiscret, -ète [ɛ̃diskrɛ, -ɛt] adj indiscreet

indiscutable [ɛ̃diskytabl] adj indisputable

indispensable [ɛ̃dispɑ̃sabl] adj indispensable, essential; **~ à qn/pour faire qch** essential for sb/to do sth

indisposé, e [ɛ̃dispoze] adj indisposed, unwell

indisposer [ɛ̃dispoze] vt (incommoder) to upset; (déplaire à) to antagonize

indistinct, e [ɛ̃distɛ̃, -ɛ̃kt] adj indistinct

indistinctement [ɛ̃distɛ̃ktəmɑ̃] adv (voir, prononcer) indistinctly; (sans distinction) without distinction, indiscriminately

individu [ɛ̃dividy] nm individual

individuel, le [ɛ̃dividɥɛl] adj (gén) individual; (opinion, livret, contrôle, avantages) personal; **chambre ~le** single room; **maison ~le** detached house; **propriété ~le** personal ou private property

indolore [ɛ̃dɔlɔr] adj painless

indomptable [ɛ̃dɔ̃tabl] adj untameable; (fig) invincible, indomitable

Indonésie [ɛ̃dɔnezi] nf: **l'~** Indonesia

indu, e [ɛ̃dy] adj: **à une heure ~e** at some ungodly hour

induire [ɛ̃dɥir] vt: **~ qch de** to induce sth from; **~ qn en erreur** to lead sb astray, mislead sb

indulgent, e [ɛ̃dylʒɑ̃, -ɑ̃t] adj (parent, regard) indulgent; (juge, examinateur) lenient

industrialisé, e [ɛ̃dystrijalize] adj industrialized

industrie [ɛ̃dystri] nf industry; **~ automobile/textile** car/textile industry; **~ du spectacle** entertainment business

industriel, le [ɛ̃dystrijɛl] adj industrial; (produit industriellement: pain etc) mass-produced, factory-produced ▷ nm industrialist; (fabricant) manufacturer

inébranlable [inebrɑ̃labl] adj (masse, colonne) solid; (personne, certitude, foi) steadfast, unwavering

inédit, e [inedi, -it] adj (correspondance etc) (hitherto) unpublished; (spectacle, moyen) novel, original; (film) unreleased

ineffaçable [inefasabl] adj indelible

inefficace [inefikas] adj (remède, moyen) ineffective; (machine, employé) inefficient

inégal, e, -aux [inegal, -o] adj unequal; (irrégulier) uneven

inégalable [inegalabl(ə)] adj matchless

inégalé, e [inegale] adj (record) unmatched, unequalled; (beauté) unrivalled

inégalité [inegalite] nf inequality; unevenness no pl; **~ de deux hauteurs** difference ou disparity between two heights; **~s de terrain** uneven ground

inépuisable [inepɥizabl] adj inexhaustible

inerte [inɛrt] adj (immobile) lifeless; (apathique) passive, inert; (Physique, Chimie) inert

inespéré, e [inɛspere] adj unhoped-for, unexpected

inestimable [inɛstimabl] adj priceless; (fig: bienfait) invaluable

inévitable [inevitabl] adj unavoidable; (fatal, habituel) inevitable

inexact, e [inɛgzakt] adj inaccurate, inexact; (non ponctuel) unpunctual

inexcusable [inɛkskyzabl] *adj* inexcusable, unforgivable

inexplicable [inɛksplikabl] *adj* inexplicable

in extremis [inɛkstremis] *adv* at the last minute ▷ *adj* last-minute; (*testament*) death bed *cpd*

infaillible [ɛ̃fajibl] *adj* infallible; (*instinct*) infallible, unerring

infâme [ɛ̃fam] *adj* vile

infarctus [ɛ̃farktys] *nm*: ~ **(du myocarde)** coronary (thrombosis)

infatigable [ɛ̃fatigabl] *adj* tireless, indefatigable

infect, e [ɛ̃fɛkt] *adj* revolting; (*repas, vin*) revolting, foul; (*personne*) obnoxious; (*temps*) foul

infecter [ɛ̃fɛkte] *vt* (*atmosphère, eau*) to contaminate; (*Méd*) to infect; **s'infecter** *vi* to become infected ou septic

infection [ɛ̃fɛksjɔ̃] *nf* infection; (*puanteur*) stench

inférieur, e [ɛ̃ferjœr] *adj* lower; (*en qualité, intelligence*) inferior ▷ *nm/f* inferior; ~ **à** (*somme, quantité*) less ou smaller than; (*moins bon que*) inferior to; (*tâche: pas à la hauteur de*) unequal to

infernal, e, -aux [ɛ̃fɛrnal, -o] *adj* (*insupportable: chaleur, rythme*) infernal; (*enfant*) horrid; (*méchanceté, complot*) diabolical

infidèle [ɛ̃fidɛl] *adj* unfaithful; (*Rel*) infidel

infiltrer [ɛ̃filtre]: **s'infiltrer** *vi*: **s'~ dans** to penetrate into; (*liquide*) to seep into; (*fig: noyauter*) to infiltrate

infime [ɛ̃fim] *adj* minute, tiny; (*inférieur*) lowly

infini, e [ɛ̃fini] *adj* infinite ▷ *nm* infinity; **à l'~** (*Math*) to infinity; (*discourir*) ad infinitum, endlessly; (*agrandir, varier*) infinitely; (*à perte de vue*) endlessly (into the distance)

infiniment [ɛ̃finimã] *adv* infinitely; ~ **grand/petit** (*Math*) infinitely great/infinitesimal

infinité [ɛ̃finite] *nf*: **une ~ de** an infinite number of

infinitif, -ive [ɛ̃finitif, -iv] *adj, nm* infinitive

infirme [ɛ̃firm] *adj* disabled ▷ *nm/f* person with a disability; ~ **de guerre** person disabled during the war; ~ **du travail** industrially disabled person

infirmerie [ɛ̃firməri] *nf* sick bay

infirmier, -ière [ɛ̃firmje, -jɛr] *nm/f* nurse ▷ *adj*: **élève ~** student nurse; **infirmière chef** sister; **infirmière diplômée** registered nurse; **infirmière visiteuse** visiting nurse, ≈ district nurse (*Brit*)

infirmité [ɛ̃firmite] *nf* disability

inflammable [ɛ̃flamabl] *adj* (in)flammable

inflation [ɛ̃flasjɔ̃] *nf* inflation; ~ **rampante/galopante** creeping/galloping inflation

infliger [ɛ̃fliʒe] *vt*: ~ **qch (à qn)** to inflict sth (on sb); (*amende, sanction*) to impose sth (on sb)

influençable [ɛ̃flyãsabl] *adj* easily influenced

influence [ɛ̃flyãs] *nf* influence; (*d'un médicament*) effect

influencer [ɛ̃flyãse] *vt* to influence

influent, e [ɛ̃flyã, -ãt] *adj* influential

informateur, -trice [ɛ̃fɔrmatœr, -tris] *nm/f* informant

informaticien, ne [ɛ̃fɔrmatisjɛ̃, -ɛn] *nm/f* computer scientist

information [ɛ̃fɔrmasjɔ̃] *nf* (*renseignement*) piece of information; (*Presse, TV: nouvelle*) item of news; (*diffusion de renseignements, Inform*) information; (*Jur*) inquiry, investigation; **informations** *nfpl* (*TV*) news *sg*; **voyage d'~** fact-finding trip; **agence d'~** news agency; **journal d'~** quality (*Brit*) ou serious newspaper

informatique [ɛ̃fɔrmatik] *nf* (*technique*) data processing; (*science*) computer science ▷ *adj* computer *cpd*

informatiser [ɛ̃fɔrmatize] *vt* to computerize

informe [ɛ̃fɔrm] *adj* shapeless

informer [ɛ̃fɔrme] *vt*: ~ **qn (de)** to inform sb (of) ▷ *vi* (*Jur*): ~ **contre qn/sur qch** to initiate inquiries about sb/sth; **s'informer (sur)** to inform o.s. (about); **s'~ (de qch/si)** to inquire ou find out (about sth/whether ou if)

infos [ɛ̃fo] *nfpl* (= *informations*) news

infraction [ɛ̃fraksjɔ̃] *nf* offence; ~ **à** violation ou breach of; **être en ~** to be in breach of the law

infranchissable [ɛ̃frɑ̃ʃisabl] *adj* impassable; (*fig*) insuperable

infrarouge [ɛ̃fraruʒ] *adj, nm* infrared

infrastructure [ɛ̃frastryktyr] *nf* (*d'une route etc*) substructure; (*Aviat, Mil*) ground installations *pl*; (*Écon: touristique etc*) facilities *pl*

infuser [ɛ̃fyze] *vt* (*aussi*: **faire ~**: *thé*) to brew; (: *tisane*) to infuse ▷ *vi* to brew; to infuse; **laisser ~** (to leave) to brew

infusion [ɛ̃fyzjɔ̃] *nf* (*tisane*) infusion, herb tea

ingénier [ɛ̃ʒenje]: **s'ingénier** *vi*: **s'~ à faire** to strive to do

ingénierie [ɛ̃ʒeniri] *nf* engineering

ingénieur [ɛ̃ʒenjœr] *nm* engineer; ~ **agronome/chimiste** agricultural/chemical engineer; ~ **conseil** consulting engineer; ~ **du son** sound engineer

ingénieux, -euse [ɛ̃ʒenjø, -øz] *adj* ingenious, clever

ingénu, e [ɛ̃ʒeny] *adj* ingenuous, artless ▷ *nf* (*Théât*) ingénue

ingérer [ɛ̃ʒere]: **s'ingérer** *vi*: **s'~ dans** to interfere in

ingrat, e [ɛ̃gra, -at] *adj* (*personne*) ungrateful; (*sol*) poor; (*travail, sujet*) arid, thankless; (*visage*) unprepossessing

ingrédient [ɛ̃gredjã] *nm* ingredient

ingurgiter [ɛ̃gyrʒite] *vt* to swallow; **faire ~ qch à qn** to make sb swallow sth; (*fig: connaissances*) to force sth into sb

inhabitable [inabitabl] *adj* uninhabitable

inhabité, e [inabite] *adj* (*régions*) uninhabited; (*maison*) unoccupied

inhabituel, le [inabituɛl] *adj* unusual

inhibition [inibisjɔ̃] *nf* inhibition

inhumain, e [inymɛ̃, -ɛn] *adj* inhuman

inhumation [inymasjɔ̃] *nf* interment, burial

inhumer [inyme] *vt* to inter, bury

inimaginable [inimaʒinabl] *adj* unimaginable

ininterrompu, e [inɛ̃tɛrɔ̃py] *adj* (*file, série*) unbroken; (*flot, vacarme*) uninterrupted, non-stop; (*effort*) unremitting, continuous; (*suite, ligne*) unbroken

initial, e, -aux [inisjal, -o] *adj, nf* initial; **initiales** *nfpl* initials

initialiser [inisjalize] *vt* to initialize

initiation [inisjasjɔ̃] *nf* initiation; ~ **à** introduction to

initiative [inisjativ] *nf* initiative; **prendre l'~ de qch/de faire** to take the initiative for sth/of doing; **avoir de l'~** to have initiative, show enterprise; **esprit/qualités d'~** spirit/ qualities of initiative; **à** *ou* **sur l'~ de qn** on sb's initiative; **de sa propre ~** on one's own initiative

initier [inisje] *vt* to initiate; ~ **qn à** to initiate sb into; (*faire découvrir: art, jeu*) to introduce sb to; **s'initier à** *vi* (*métier, profession, technique*) to become initiated into

injecté, e [ɛ̃ʒekte] *adj*: **yeux ~s de sang** bloodshot eyes

injecter [ɛ̃ʒekte] *vt* to inject

injection [ɛ̃ʒeksjɔ̃] *nf* injection; **à ~** (*Auto*) fuel injection *cpd*

injure [ɛ̃ʒyʀ] *nf* insult, abuse *no pl*

injurier [ɛ̃ʒyʀje] *vt* to insult, abuse

injurieux, -euse [ɛ̃ʒyʀjø, -øz] *adj* abusive, insulting

injuste [ɛ̃ʒyst] *adj* unjust, unfair

injustice [ɛ̃ʒystis] *nf* injustice

inlassable [ɛ̃lasabl] *adj* tireless, indefatigable

inné, e [ine] *adj* innate, inborn

innocent, e [inɔsɑ̃, -ɑ̃t] *adj* innocent ▷ *nm/f* innocent person; **faire l'~** to play *ou* come the innocent

innocenter [inɔsɑ̃te] *vt* to clear, prove innocent

innombrable [inɔ̃bʀabl] *adj* innumerable

innommable [inɔmabl] *adj* unspeakable

innover [inɔve] *vi*: ~ **en matière d'art** to break new ground in the field of art

inoccupé, e [inɔkype] *adj* unoccupied

inodore [inɔdɔʀ] *adj* (*gaz*) odourless; (*fleur*) scentless

inoffensif, -ive [inɔfɑ̃sif, -iv] *adj* harmless, innocuous

inondation [inɔ̃dasjɔ̃] *nf* flooding *no pl*; (*torrent, eau*) flood

inonder [inɔ̃de] *vt* to flood; (*fig*) to inundate, overrun; ~ **de** (*fig*) to flood *ou* swamp with

inopiné, e [inɔpine] *adj* unexpected, sudden

inopportun, e [inɔpɔʀtœ̃, -yn] *adj* ill-timed, untimely; inappropriate; (*moment*) inopportune

inoubliable [inublijabl] *adj* unforgettable

inouï, e [inwi] *adj* unheard-of, extraordinary

inox [inɔks] *adj, nm* (= *inoxydable*) stainless (steel)

inqualifiable [ɛ̃kalifjabl] *adj* unspeakable

inquiet, -ète [ɛ̃kjɛ, -ɛt] *adj* (*par nature*) anxious; (*momentanément*) worried; ~ **de qch/ au sujet de qn** worried about sth/sb

inquiétant, e [ɛ̃kjetɑ̃, -ɑ̃t] *adj* worrying, disturbing

inquiéter [ɛ̃kjete] *vt* to worry, disturb; (*harceler*) to harass; **s'inquiéter** to worry, become anxious; **s'~ de** to worry about; (*s'enquérir de*) to inquire about

inquiétude [ɛ̃kjetyd] *nf* anxiety; **donner de l'~** *ou* **des ~s à** to worry; **avoir de l'~** *ou* **des ~s au sujet de** to feel anxious *ou* worried about

insaisissable [ɛ̃sezisabl] *adj* (*fugitif, ennemi*) elusive; (*différence, nuance*) imperceptible

insalubre [ɛ̃salybʀ] *adj* unhealthy, insalubrious

insatisfait, e [ɛ̃satisfɛ, -ɛt] *adj* (*non comblé*) unsatisfied; (: *passion, envie*) unfulfilled; (*mécontent*) dissatisfied

inscription [ɛ̃skʀipsjɔ̃] *nf* (*sur un mur, écriteau etc*) inscription; (*à une institution: voir s'inscrire*) enrolment; registration

inscrire [ɛ̃skʀiʀ] *vt* (*marquer: sur son calepin etc*) to note *ou* write down; (: *sur un mur, une affiche etc*) to write; (: *dans la pierre, le métal*) to inscribe; (*mettre: sur une liste, un budget etc*) to put down; (*enrôler: soldat*) to enlist; ~ **qn à** (*club, école etc*) to enrol sb at; **s'inscrire** *vi* (*pour une excursion etc*) to put one's name down; **s'~ (à)** (*club, parti*) to join; (*université*) to register *ou* enrol (at); (*examen, concours*) to register *ou* enter (for); **s'~ dans** (*se situer: négociations etc*) to come within the scope of; **s'~ en faux contre** to deny (strongly); (*Jur*) to challenge

insecte [ɛ̃sɛkt] *nm* insect

insecticide [ɛ̃sɛktisid] *nm* insecticide

insensé, e [ɛ̃sɑ̃se] *adj* insane, mad

insensibiliser [ɛ̃sɑ̃sibilize] *vt* to anaesthetize; (*à une allergie*) to desensitize; ~ **à qch** (*fig*) to cause to become insensitive to sth

insensible [ɛ̃sɑ̃sibl] *adj* (*nerf, membre*) numb; (*dur, indifférent*) insensitive; (*imperceptible*) imperceptible

inséparable [ɛ̃separabl] *adj*: ~ **(de)** inseparable (from) ▷ *nmpl*: ~**s** (*oiseaux*) lovebirds

insigne [ɛ̃siɲ] *nm* (*d'un parti, club*) badge ▷ *adj* distinguished; **insignes** *nmpl* (*d'une fonction*) insignia *pl*

insignifiant, e [ɛ̃siɲifjɑ̃, -ɑ̃t] *adj* insignificant; (*somme, affaire, détail*) trivial, insignificant

insinuer [ɛ̃sinɥe] *vt* to insinuate, imply; **s'insinuer dans** *vi* to seep into; (*fig*) to worm one's way into, creep into

insipide [ɛ̃sipid] *adj* insipid

insister [ɛ̃siste] vi to insist; (s'obstiner) to keep on; ~ **sur** (détail, note) to stress; ~ **pour qch/pour faire qch** to be insistent about sth/about doing sth

insolation [ɛ̃sɔlasjɔ̃] nf (Méd) sunstroke no pl; (ensoleillement) period of sunshine

insolent, e [ɛ̃sɔlɑ̃, -ɑ̃t] adj insolent

insolite [ɛ̃sɔlit] adj strange, unusual

insomnie [ɛ̃sɔmni] nf insomnia no pl, sleeplessness no pl; **avoir des ~s** to sleep badly, suffer from insomnia

insonoriser [ɛ̃sɔnɔrize] vt to soundproof

insouciant, e [ɛ̃susjɑ̃, -ɑ̃t] adj carefree; (imprévoyant) heedless; ~ **du danger** heedless of (the) danger

insoumis, e [ɛ̃sumi, -iz] adj (caractère, enfant) rebellious, refractory; (contrée, tribu) unsubdued; (Mil: soldat) absent without leave ▷ nm (Mil: soldat) absentee

insoupçonnable [ɛ̃supsɔnabl] adj unsuspected; (personne) above suspicion

insoupçonné, e [ɛ̃supsɔne] adj unsuspected

insoutenable [ɛ̃sutnabl] adj (argument) untenable; (chaleur) unbearable

inspecter [ɛ̃spɛkte] vt to inspect

inspecteur, -trice [ɛ̃spɛktœr, -tris] nm/f inspector; (des assurances) assessor; ~ **d'Académie** (regional) director of education; ~ **(de l'enseignement) primaire** primary school inspector; ~ **des finances** ≈ tax inspector (Brit), ≈ Internal Revenue Service agent (US); ~ **(de police)** (police) inspector

inspection [ɛ̃spɛksjɔ̃] nf inspection

inspirer [ɛ̃spire] vt (gén) to inspire ▷ vi (aspirer) to breathe in; **s'inspirer de** (artiste) to draw one's inspiration from; (tableau) to be inspired by; ~ **qch à qn** (œuvre, projet, action) to inspire sb with sth; (dégoût, crainte, horreur) to fill sb with sth; **ça ne m'inspire pas** I'm not keen on the idea

instable [ɛ̃stabl] adj (meuble, équilibre) unsteady; (population, temps) unsettled; (paix, régime, caractère) unstable

installation [ɛ̃stalasjɔ̃] nf (mise en place) installation; putting in ou up; fitting out; settling in; (appareils etc) fittings pl, installations pl; **installations** nfpl (industrielles) plant sg; (de sport, dans un camping) facilities; **l'~ électrique** wiring

installer [ɛ̃stale] vt (loger): ~ **qn** to get sb settled, install sb; (asseoir, coucher) to settle (down); (placer) to put, place; (meuble) to put in; (rideau, étagère, tente) to put up; (gaz, électricité etc) to put in, install; (appartement) to fit out; (aménager): ~ **une salle de bains dans une pièce** to fit out a room with a bathroom suite; **s'installer** vi (s'établir: artisan, dentiste etc) to set o.s. up; (se loger): **s'~ à l'hôtel/chez qn** to move into a hotel/in with sb; (emménager) to settle in; (sur un siège, à un emplacement) to settle (down); (fig: maladie, grève) to take a firm hold ou grip

instance [ɛ̃stɑ̃s] nf (Jur: procédure) (legal) proceedings pl; (Admin: autorité) authority; **instances** nfpl (prières) entreaties; **affaire en ~** matter pending; **courrier en ~** mail ready for posting; **être en ~ de divorce** to be awaiting a divorce; **train en ~ de départ** train on the point of departure; **tribunal de première ~** court of first instance; **en seconde ~** on appeal

instant [ɛ̃stɑ̃] nm moment, instant; **dans un ~** in a moment; **à l'~** this instant; **je l'ai vu à l'~** I've just this minute seen him, I saw him a moment ago; **à l'~ (même) où** at the (very) moment that ou when, (just) as; **à chaque ~, à tout ~** at any moment; constantly; **pour l'~** for the moment, for the time being; **par ~s** at times; **de tous les ~s** perpetual; **dès l'~ où ou que ...** from the moment when ..., since that moment when ...

instantané, e [ɛ̃stɑ̃tane] adj (lait, café) instant; (explosion, mort) instantaneous ▷ nm snapshot

instar [ɛ̃star]: **à l'~ de** prép following the example of, like

instaurer [ɛ̃stɔre] vt to institute; (couvre-feu) to impose; **s'instaurer** vi to set o.s. up; (collaboration, paix etc) to be established; (doute) to set in

instinct [ɛ̃stɛ̃] nm instinct; **d'~** (spontanément) instinctively; ~ **grégaire** herd instinct; ~ **de conservation** instinct of self-preservation

instinctivement [ɛ̃stɛ̃ktivmɑ̃] adv instinctively

instit [ɛ̃stit] (fam) nm/f (primary school) teacher

instituer [ɛ̃stitɥe] vt to establish, institute; **s'~ défenseur d'une cause** to set o.s up as defender of a cause

institut [ɛ̃stity] nm institute; ~ **de beauté** beauty salon; ~ **médico-légal** mortuary; **I~ universitaire de technologie (IUT)** ≈ Institute of technology

instituteur, -trice [ɛ̃stitytœr, -tris] nm/f (primary (Brit) ou grade (US) school) teacher

institution [ɛ̃stitysjɔ̃] nf institution; (collège) private school; **institutions** nfpl (structures politiques et sociales) institutions

instructif, -ive [ɛ̃stryktif, -iv] adj instructive

instruction [ɛ̃stryksjɔ̃] nf (enseignement, savoir) education; (Jur) (preliminary) investigation and hearing; (directive) instruction; (Admin: document) directive; **instructions** nfpl instructions; (mode d'emploi) directions, instructions; ~ **civique** civics sg; ~ **primaire/publique** primary/public education; ~ **religieuse** religious instruction; ~ **professionnelle** vocational training

instruire [ɛ̃strɥir] vt (élèves) to teach; (recrues) to train; (Jur: affaire) to conduct the investigation for; **s'instruire** to educate o.s.; **s'~ auprès de qn de qch** (s'informer) to find sth out from sb; **~ qn de qch** (*informer*) to inform *ou* advise sb of sth; **~ contre qn** (*Jur*) to investigate sb

instruit, e [ɛ̃stʁɥi, -it] *pp de* **instruire** ▷ *adj* educated

instrument [ɛ̃stʁymɑ̃] *nm* instrument; **~ à cordes/vent** stringed/wind instrument; **~ de mesure** measuring instrument; **~ de musique** musical instrument; **~ de travail** (working) tool

insu [ɛ̃sy] *nm*: **à l'~ de qn** without sb knowing

insubmersible [ɛ̃sybmɛʁsibl] *adj* unsinkable

insuffisant, e [ɛ̃syfizɑ̃, -ɑ̃t] *adj* (*en quantité*) insufficient; (*en qualité: élève, travail*) inadequate; (*sur une copie*) poor

insulaire [ɛ̃sylɛʁ] *adj* island *cpd*; (*attitude*) insular

insuline [ɛ̃sylin] *nf* insulin

insulte [ɛ̃sylt] *nf* insult

insulter [ɛ̃sylte] *vt* to insult

insupportable [ɛ̃sypɔʁtabl] *adj* unbearable

insurger [ɛ̃syʁʒe]: **s'insurger** *vi*: **s'~ (contre)** to rise up *ou* rebel (against)

insurmontable [ɛ̃syʁmɔ̃tabl] *adj* (*difficulté*) insuperable; (*aversion*) unconquerable

insurrection [ɛ̃syʁɛksjɔ̃] *nf* insurrection, revolt

intact [ɛ̃takt] *adj* intact

intangible [ɛ̃tɑ̃ʒibl] *adj* intangible; (*principe*) inviolable

intarissable [ɛ̃taʁisabl] *adj* inexhaustible

intégral, e, -aux [ɛ̃tegʁal, -o] *adj* complete ▷ *nf* (*Math*) integral; (*œuvres complètes*) complete works; **texte ~** unabridged version; **bronzage ~** all-over suntan

intégralement [ɛ̃tegʁalmɑ̃] *adv* in full, fully

intégralité [ɛ̃tegʁalite] *nf* (*d'une somme, d'un revenu*) whole (*ou* full) amount; **dans son ~** in its entirety

intégrant, e [ɛ̃tegʁɑ̃, -ɑ̃t] *adj*: **faire partie ~ de** to be an integral part of, be part and parcel of

intègre [ɛ̃tegʁ] *adj* perfectly honest, upright

intégrer [ɛ̃tegʁe] *vt*: **~ qch à** *ou* **dans** to integrate sth into; **s'intégrer** *vr*: **s'~ à** *ou* **dans** to become integrated into; **bien s'~** to fit in

intégrisme [ɛ̃tegʁism] *nm* fundamentalism

intellectuel, le [ɛ̃telɛktɥɛl] *adj, nm/f* intellectual; (*péj*) highbrow

intelligence [ɛ̃teliʒɑ̃s] *nf* intelligence; (*compréhension*): **l'~ de** the understanding of; (*complicité*): **regard d'~** glance of complicity, meaningful *ou* knowing look; (*accord*): **vivre en bonne ~ avec qn** to be on good terms with sb; **intelligences** *nfpl* (*Mil, fig*) secret contacts; **être d'~** to have an understanding, ~ **artificielle** artificial intelligence (A.I.)

intelligent, e [ɛ̃teliʒɑ̃, -ɑ̃t] *adj* intelligent; (*capable*): **~ en affaires** competent in business

intelligible [ɛ̃teliʒibl] *adj* intelligible

intempéries [ɛ̃tɑ̃peʁi] *nfpl* bad weather *sg*

intempestif, -ive [ɛ̃tɑ̃pɛstif, -iv] *adj* untimely

intenable [ɛ̃tnabl] *adj* unbearable

intendant, e [ɛ̃tɑ̃dɑ̃, -ɑ̃t] *nm/f* (*Mil*) quartermaster; (*Scol*) bursar; (*d'une propriété*) steward

intense [ɛ̃tɑ̃s] *adj* intense

intensif, -ive [ɛ̃tɑ̃sif, -iv] *adj* intensive; **cours ~** crash course; **~ en main-d'œuvre** labour-intensive; **~ en capital** capital-intensive

intenter [ɛ̃tɑ̃te] *vt*: **~ un procès contre** *ou* **à qn** to start proceedings against sb

intention [ɛ̃tɑ̃sjɔ̃] *nf* intention; (*Jur*) intent; **avoir l'~ de faire** to intend to do, have the intention of doing; **dans l'~ de faire qch** with a view to doing sth; **à l'~ de** *prép* for; (*renseignement*) for the benefit *ou* information of; (*film, ouvrage*) aimed at; **à cette ~** with this aim in view; **sans ~** unintentionally; **faire qch sans mauvaise ~** to do sth without ill intent; **agir dans une bonne ~** to act with good intentions

intentionné, e [ɛ̃tɑ̃sjɔne] *adj*: **bien ~** well-meaning *ou* -intentioned; **mal ~** ill-intentioned

interactif, -ive [ɛ̃teʁaktif, -iv] *adj* (*aussi Inform*) interactive

intercalaire [ɛ̃teʁkalɛʁ] *adj, nm*: (**feuillet**) **~** insert; (**fiche**) **~** divider

intercaler [ɛ̃teʁkale] *vt* to insert; **s'intercaler entre** *vi* to come in between; to slip in between

intercepter [ɛ̃teʁsɛpte] *vt* to intercept; (*lumière, chaleur*) to cut off

interchangeable [ɛ̃teʁʃɑ̃ʒabl] *adj* interchangeable

interclasse [ɛ̃teʁklas] *nm* (*Scol*) break (between classes)

interdiction [ɛ̃teʁdiksjɔ̃] *nf* ban; **~ de faire qch** ban on doing sth; **~ de séjour** (*Jur*) order banning ex-prisoner from frequenting specified places; **~ de fumer** no smoking

interdire [ɛ̃teʁdiʁ] *vt* to forbid; (*Admin: stationnement, meeting, passage*) to ban, prohibit; (:*journal, livre*) to ban; **~ qch à qn** to forbid sb sth; **~ à qn de faire** to forbid sb to do, prohibit sb from doing; (*empêchement*) to prevent *ou* preclude sb from doing; **s'interdire qch** *vi* (*éviter*) to refrain *ou* abstain from sth; (*se refuser*) **il s'interdit d'y penser** he doesn't allow himself to think about it

interdit, e [ɛ̃teʁdi, -it] *pp de* **interdire** ▷ *adj* (*stupéfait*) taken aback; (*défendu*) forbidden, prohibited ▷ *nm* interdict, prohibition; **film ~ aux moins de 18/12 ans** ≈ 18-/12A-rated film; **sens ~** one way; **stationnement ~** no parking; **~ de chéquier** having cheque book facilities suspended; **~ de séjour** subject to an "interdiction de séjour"

intéressant, e [ɛ̃teʁesɑ̃, -ɑ̃t] *adj* interesting; (*avantageux*) attractive; **faire l'~** to draw attention to o.s.

intéressé, e [ēterese] *adj* (*parties*) involved, concerned; (*amitié, motifs*) self-interested ▷ *nm*: **l'~** the interested party; **les ~s** those concerned *ou* involved

intéresser [ēterese] *vt* (*captiver*) to interest; (*toucher*) to be of interest *ou* concern to; (*concerner*) to affect, concern; (*Comm: travailleur*) to give a share in the profits to; (: *partenaire*) to interest (in the business); **s'intéresser à** *vi* to take an interest in, be interested in; **~ qn à qch** to get sb interested in sth

intérêt [ētere] *nm* (*aussi* Comm) interest; (*égoïsme*) self-interest; **porter de l'~ à qn** to take an interest in sb; **agir par ~** to act out of self-interest; **avoir des ~s dans** (*Comm*) to have a financial interest *ou* a stake in; **avoir ~ à faire** to do well to do; **tu as ~ à accepter** it's in your interest to accept; **tu as ~ te dépêcher** you'd better hurry; **il y a ~ à ...** it would be a good thing to ...; **~ composé** compound interest

intérieur, e [ēterjœr] *adj* (*mur, escalier, poche*) inside; (*commerce, politique*) domestic; (*cour, calme, vie*) inner; (*navigation*) inland ▷ *nm* (*d'une maison, d'un récipient etc*) inside; (*d'un pays, aussi: décor, mobilier*) interior; (*Pol*): **l'I~** (the Department of) the Interior, ≈ the Home Office (*Brit*); **à l'~ (de)** inside; (*fig*) within; **de l'~** (*fig*) from the inside; **en ~** (*Ciné*) in the studio; **vêtement d'~** indoor garment

intérieurement [ēterjœrmā] *adv* inwardly

intérim [ēterim] *nm* (*période*) interim period; (*travail*) temping; **agence d'~** temping agency; **assurer l'~ (de)** to deputize (for); **président par ~** interim president; **travailler en ~, faire de l'~** to temp

intérimaire [ēterimer] *adj* (*directeur, ministre*) acting; (*secrétaire, personnel*) temporary, interim ▷ *nm/f* (*secrétaire etc*) temporary, temp (*Brit*); (*suppléant*) deputy

interlocuteur, -trice [ēterlɔkytœr, -tris] *nm/f* speaker; (*Pol*): **~ valable** valid representative; **son ~** the person he *ou* she was speaking to

interloquer [ēterlɔke] *vt* to take aback

intermède [ētermɛd] *nm* interlude

intermédiaire [ētermedjɛr] *adj* intermediate; middle; half-way; (*solution*) temporary ▷ *nm/f* intermediary; (*Comm*) middleman; **sans ~** directly; **par l'~ de** through

interminable [ēterminabl] *adj* never-ending

intermittence [ētermitās] *nf*: **par ~** intermittently, sporadically

internat [ēterna] *nm* (*Scol*) boarding school

international, e, -aux [ēternasjɔnal, -o] *adj, nm/f* international

internaute [ēternot] *nm/f* Internet user

interne [ētern] *adj* internal ▷ *nm/f* (*Scol*) boarder; (*Méd*) houseman (*Brit*), intern (*US*)

interner [ēterne] *vt* (*Pol*) to intern; (*Méd*) to confine to a mental institution

Internet [ēternet] *nm*: **l'~** the Internet

interpeller [ēterpele] *vt* (*appeler*) to call out to; (*apostropher*) to shout at; (*Police*) to take in for questioning; (*Pol*) to question; (*concerner*) to concern; **s'interpeller** *vi* to exchange insults

interphone [ēterfɔn] *nm* intercom; (*d'immeuble*) entry phone

interposer [ēterpoze] *vt* to interpose; **s'interposer** *vi* to intervene; **par personnes interposées** through a third party

interprétation [ēterpretasjɔ̃] *nf* interpretation

interprète [ēterpret] *nm/f* interpreter; (*porte-parole*) spokesman

interpréter [ēterprete] *vt* to interpret; (*jouer*) to play; (*chanter*) to sing

interrogateur, -trice [ēterɔgatœr, -tris] *adj* questioning, inquiring ▷ *nm/f* (*Scol*) (oral) examiner

interrogatif, -ive [ēterɔgatif, -iv] *adj* (*Ling*) interrogative

interrogation [ēterɔgasjɔ̃] *nf* question; (*Scol*) (written *ou* oral) test

interrogatoire [ēterɔgatwar] *nm* (*Police*) questioning *no pl*; (*Jur, aussi fig*) cross-examination, interrogation

interroger [ēterɔʒe] *vt* to question; (*Inform*) to search; (*Scol: candidat*) to test; **~ qn (sur qch)** to question sb (about sth); **~ qn du regard** to look questioningly at sb, give sb a questioning look; **s'~ sur qch** to ask o.s. about sth, ponder (about) sth

interrompre [ēterɔ̃pr] *vt* (*gén*) to interrupt; (*travail, voyage*) to break off, interrupt; (*négociations*) to break off; (*match*) to stop; **s'interrompre** *vi* to break off

interrupteur [ēteryptœr] *nm* switch

interruption [ēterypsjɔ̃] *nf* interruption; (*pause*) break; **sans ~** without a break; **~ de grossesse** termination of pregnancy; **~ volontaire de grossesse** voluntary termination of pregnancy, abortion

intersection [ēterseksjɔ̃] *nf* intersection

interstice [ēterstis] *nm* crack, slit

interurbain [ēteryrbē] (*Tél*) *nm* long-distance call service ▷ *adj* long-distance

intervalle [ēterval] *nm* (*espace*) space; (*de temps*) interval; **dans l'~** in the meantime; **à deux jours d'~** two days apart; **à ~s rapprochés** at close intervals; **par ~s** at intervals

intervenir [ētervǝnir] *vi* (*gén*) to intervene; (*survenir*) to take place; (*faire une conférence*) to give a talk *ou* lecture; **~ auprès de/en faveur de qn** to intervene with/on behalf of sb; **la police a dû ~** police had to step in *ou* intervene; **les médecins ont dû ~** the doctors had to operate

intervention [ētervāsjɔ̃] *nf* intervention; (*conférence*) talk, paper; (*discours*) speech; **~ chirurgicale** operation

intervertir [ɛ̃tɛʀvɛʀtiʀ] *vt* to invert (the order of), reverse

interview [ɛ̃tɛʀvju] *nf* interview

interviewer [ɛ̃tɛʀvjuve] *vt* to interview ▷ *nm* [ɛ̃tɛʀvjuvœʀ] (*journaliste*) interviewer

intestin, e [ɛ̃tɛstɛ̃, -in] *adj* internal ▷ *nm* intestine; **~ grêle** small intestine

intime [ɛ̃tim] *adj* intimate; (*vie, journal*) private; (*convictions*) inmost; (*dîner, cérémonie*) held among friends, quiet ▷ *nm/f* close friend; **un journal ~** a diary

intimider [ɛ̃timide] *vt* to intimidate

intimité [ɛ̃timite] *nf* intimacy; (*vie privée*) privacy; private life; **dans l'~** in private; (*sans formalités*) with only a few friends, quietly

intitulé [ɛ̃tityle] *nm* title

intolérable [ɛ̃tɔleʀabl] *adj* intolerable

intox [ɛ̃tɔks] (*fam*) *nf* brainwashing

intoxication [ɛ̃tɔksikasjɔ̃] *nf* poisoning *no pl*; (*toxicomanie*) drug addiction; (*fig*) brainwashing; **~ alimentaire** food poisoning

intoxiquer [ɛ̃tɔksike] *vt* to poison; (*fig*) to brainwash; **s'intoxiquer** to poison o.s.

intraduisible [ɛ̃tʀadɥizibl] *adj* untranslatable; (*fig*) inexpressible

intraitable [ɛ̃tʀɛtabl] *adj* inflexible, uncompromising

intranet [ɛ̃tʀanɛt] *nm* intranet

intransigeant, e [ɛ̃tʀɑ̃ziʒɑ̃, -ɑ̃t] *adj* intransigent; (*morale, passion*) uncompromising

intransitif, -ive [ɛ̃tʀɑ̃zitif, -iv] *adj* (*Ling*) intransitive

intrépide [ɛ̃tʀepid] *adj* dauntless, intrepid

intrigue [ɛ̃tʀig] *nf* intrigue; (*scénario*) plot

intriguer [ɛ̃tʀige] *vi* to scheme ▷ *vt* to puzzle, intrigue

intrinsèque [ɛ̃tʀɛ̃sek] *adj* intrinsic

introduction [ɛ̃tʀɔdyksjɔ̃] *nf* introduction; **paroles/chapitre d'~** introductory words/chapter; **lettre/mot d'~** letter/note of introduction

introduire [ɛ̃tʀɔdɥiʀ] *vt* to introduce; (*visiteur*) to show in; (*aiguille, clef*): **~ qch dans** to insert *ou* introduce sth into; (*personne*): **~ à qch** to introduce to sth; (: *présenter*): **~ qn à qn/dans un club** to introduce sb to sb/to a club; **s'introduire** *vi* (*techniques, usages*) to be introduced; **s'~ dans** to gain entry into; (*dans un groupe*) to get o.s. accepted into; (*eau, fumée*) to get into; **~ au clavier** to key in

introuvable [ɛ̃tʀuvabl] *adj* which cannot be found; (*Comm*) unobtainable

introverti, e [ɛ̃tʀɔvɛʀti] *nm/f* introvert

intrus, e [ɛ̃tʀy, -yz] *nm/f* intruder

intrusion [ɛ̃tʀyzjɔ̃] *nf* intrusion; (*ingérence*) interference

intuition [ɛ̃tɥisjɔ̃] *nf* intuition; **avoir une ~** to have a feeling; **avoir l'~ de qch** to have an intuition of sth; **avoir de l'~** to have intuition

inusable [inyzabl] *adj* hard-wearing

inusité, e [inyzite] *adj* rarely used

inutile [inytil] *adj* useless; (*superflu*)

unnecessary

inutilement [inytilmɑ̃] *adv* needlessly

inutilisable [inytilizabl] *adj* unusable

invalide [ɛ̃valid] *adj* disabled ▷ *nm/f*: **~ de guerre** disabled ex-serviceman; **~ du travail** industrially disabled person

invariable [ɛ̃vaʀjabl] *adj* invariable

invasion [ɛ̃vazjɔ̃] *nf* invasion

invectiver [ɛ̃vɛktive] *vt* to hurl abuse at ▷ *vi*: **~ contre** to rail against

invendable [ɛ̃vɑ̃dabl] *adj* unsaleable, unmarketable

invendu, e [ɛ̃vɑ̃dy] *adj* unsold ▷ *nm* return; **invendus** *nmpl* unsold goods

inventaire [ɛ̃vɑ̃tɛʀ] *nm* inventory; (*Comm: liste*) stocklist; (: *opération*) stocktaking *no pl*; (*fig*) survey; **faire un ~** to make an inventory; (*Comm*) to take stock; **faire ou procéder à l'~** to take stock

inventer [ɛ̃vɑ̃te] *vt* to invent; (*subterfuge*) to devise, invent; (*histoire, excuse*) to make up, invent; **~ de faire** to hit on the idea of doing

inventeur, -trice [ɛ̃vɑ̃tœʀ, -tʀis] *nm/f* inventor

inventif, -ive [ɛ̃vɑ̃tif, -iv] *adj* inventive

invention [ɛ̃vɑ̃sjɔ̃] *nf* invention; (*imagination, inspiration*) inventiveness

inverse [ɛ̃vɛʀs] *adj* (*ordre*) reverse; (*sens*) opposite; (*rapport*) inverse ▷ *nm* reverse; inverse; **l'~** the opposite; **dans l'ordre ~** in the reverse order; **en proportion ~** in inverse proportion; **dans le sens ~ des aiguilles d'une montre** anti-clockwise; **en sens ~** in (*ou* from) the opposite direction; **à l'~** conversely

inversement [ɛ̃vɛʀsəmɑ̃] *adv* conversely

inverser [ɛ̃vɛʀse] *vt* to reverse, invert; (*Élec*) to reverse

investigation [ɛ̃vɛstigasjɔ̃] *nf* investigation, inquiry

investir [ɛ̃vɛstiʀ] *vt* to invest; **~ qn de** (*d'une fonction, d'un pouvoir*) to vest *ou* invest sb with; **s'investir** *vi* (*Psych*) to involve o.s.; **~ qn de** to vest *ou* invest sb with; **s'~ dans** to put a lot into

investissement [ɛ̃vɛstismɑ̃] *nm* investment; (*Psych*) involvement

investiture [ɛ̃vɛstityʀ] *nf* investiture; (*à une élection*) nomination

invétéré, e [ɛ̃vetere] *adj* (*habitude*) ingrained; (*bavard, buveur*) inveterate

invisible [ɛ̃vizibl] *adj* invisible; (*fig: personne*) not available

invitation [ɛ̃vitasjɔ̃] *nf* invitation; **à/sur l'~ de qn** at/on sb's invitation; **carte/lettre d'~** invitation card/letter

invité, e [ɛ̃vite] *nm/f* guest

inviter [ɛ̃vite] *vt* to invite; **~ qn à faire qch** to invite sb to do sth; (*chose*) to induce *ou* tempt sb to do sth

invivable [ɛ̃vivabl] *adj* unbearable, impossible

involontaire [ɛ̃vɔlɔ̃tɛʀ] *adj* (*mouvement*)

involuntary; (*insulte*) unintentional; (*complice*) unwitting

invoquer [ɛ̃vɔke] *vt* (*Dieu, muse*) to call upon, invoke; (*prétexte*) to put forward (as an excuse); (*témoignage*) to call upon; (*loi, texte*) to refer to; **~ la clémence de qn** to beg sb *ou* appeal to sb for clemency

invraisemblable [ɛ̃vʀɛsɑ̃blabl] *adj* (*fait, nouvelle*) unlikely, improbable; (*bizarre*) incredible

iode [jɔd] *nm* iodine

irai *etc* [iʀe] *vb voir* **aller**

Irak [iʀak] *nm*: **l'~** Iraq *ou* Irak

irakien, ne [iʀakjɛ̃, -ɛn] *adj* Iraqi ⊳ *nm/f*: **I~, ne** Iraqi

Iran [iʀɑ̃] *nm*: **l'~** Iran

iranien, ne [iʀanjɛ̃, -ɛn] *adj* Iranian ⊳ *nm* (*Ling*) Iranian ⊳ *nm/f*: **I~, ne** Iranian

irascible [iʀasibl] *adj* short-tempered, irascible

irions *etc* [iʀjɔ̃] *vb voir* **aller**

iris [iʀis] *nm* iris

irlandais, e [iʀlɑ̃dɛ, -ɛz] *adj, nm* (*Ling*) Irish ⊳ *nm/f*: **I~, e** Irishman/woman; **les I~** the Irish

Irlande [iʀlɑ̃d] *nf*: **l'~** (*pays*) Ireland; **la République d'~** the Irish Republic, the Republic of Ireland, Eire; **~ du Nord** Northern Ireland, Ulster; **~ du Sud** Southern Ireland, Irish Republic, Eire; **la mer d'~** the Irish Sea

ironie [iʀɔni] *nf* irony

ironique [iʀɔnik] *adj* ironical

ironiser [iʀɔnize] *vi* to be ironical

irons *etc* [iʀɔ̃] *vb voir* **aller**

irradier [iʀadje] *vi* to radiate ⊳ *vt* to irradiate

irraisonné, e [iʀɛzɔne] *adj* irrational, unreasoned

irrationnel, le [iʀasjɔnɛl] *adj* irrational

irréalisable [iʀealizabl] *adj* unrealizable; (*projet*) impracticable

irrécupérable [iʀekypeʀabl] *adj* unreclaimable, beyond repair; (*personne*) beyond redemption *ou* recall

irréductible [iʀedyktibl] *adj* indomitable, implacable; (*Math: fraction, équation*) irreducible

irréel, le [iʀeɛl] *adj* unreal

irréfléchi, e [iʀefleʃi] *adj* thoughtless

irrégularité [iʀegylaʀite] *nf* irregularity; (*de travail, d'effort, de qualité*) unevenness *no pl*

irrégulier, -ière [iʀegylje, -jɛʀ] *adj* irregular; (*surface, rythme, écriture*) uneven, irregular; (*travail, effort, qualité*) uneven; (*élève, athlète*) erratic

irrémédiable [iʀemedjabl] *adj* irreparable

irremplaçable [iʀɑ̃plasabl] *adj* irreplaceable

irréparable [iʀepaʀabl] *adj* beyond repair, irreparable; (*fig*) irreparable

irréprochable [iʀepʀoʃabl] *adj* irreproachable, beyond reproach; (*tenue, toilette*) impeccable

irrésistible [iʀezistibl] *adj* irresistible; (*preuve, logique*) compelling; (*amusant*) hilarious

irrésolu, e [iʀezɔly] *adj* irresolute

irrespectueux, -euse [iʀɛspɛktɥø, -øz] *adj* disrespectful

irrespirable [iʀɛspiʀabl] *adj* unbreathable; (*fig*) oppressive, stifling

irresponsable [iʀɛspɔ̃sabl] *adj* irresponsible

irriguer [iʀige] *vt* to irrigate

irritable [iʀitabl] *adj* irritable

irriter [iʀite] *vt* (*agacer*) to irritate, annoy; (*Méd: enflammer*) to irritate; **s'~ contre qn/de qch** to get annoyed *ou* irritated with sb/at sth

irruption [iʀypsjɔ̃] *nf* irruption *no pl*; **faire ~ dans** to burst into; **faire ~ chez qn** to burst in on sb

Islam [islam] *nm*: **l'~** Islam

islamique [islamik] *adj* Islamic

islamiste [islamist] *adj, nm/f* Islamic

islamophobie *nf* Islamophobia

Islande [islɑ̃d] *nf*: **l'~** Iceland

isolant, e [izɔlɑ̃, -ɑ̃t] *adj* insulating; (*insonorisant*) soundproofing ⊳ *nm* insulator

isolation [izɔlasjɔ̃] *nf* insulation; **~ thermique** thermal insulation; **~ acoustique** soundproofing

isolé, e [izɔle] *adj* isolated; (*Élec*) insulated; (*contre le froid*) insulated

isoler [izɔle] *vt* to isolate; (*prisonnier*) to put in solitary confinement; (*ville*) to cut off, isolate; (*Élec*) to insulate; (*contre le froid*) to insulate; **s'isoler** *vi* to isolate o.s.

isoloir [izɔlwaʀ] *nm* polling booth

Israël [isʀaɛl] *nm*: **l'~** Israel

israélien, ne [isʀaeljɛ̃, -ɛn] *adj* Israeli ⊳ *nm/f*: **I~, ne** Israeli

israélite [isʀaelit] *adj* Jewish; (*dans l'Ancien Testament*) Israelite ⊳ *nm/f*: **I~** Jew; Israelite

issu, e [isy] *adj*: **~ de** (*né de*) descended from; (*fig: résultant de*) stemming from ⊳ *nf* (*ouverture, sortie*) exit; (*solution*) way out, solution; (*dénouement*) outcome; **à l'~e de** at the conclusion *ou* close of; **rue sans ~e, voie sans ~e** dead end, no through road (*Brit*), no outlet (*US*); **~e de secours** emergency exit

Italie [itali] *nf*: **l'~** Italy

italien, ne [italjɛ̃, -ɛn] *adj* Italian ⊳ *nm* (*Ling*) Italian ⊳ *nm/f*: **I~, ne** Italian

italique [italik] *nm*: **en ~(s)** in italics

itinéraire [itineʀɛʀ] *nm* itinerary, route; **~ bis** alternative route

IUT *sigle m* = **Institut universitaire de technologie**

IVG *sigle f* (= *interruption volontaire de grossesse*) abortion

ivoire [ivwaʀ] *nm* ivory

ivre [ivʀ] *adj* drunk; **~ de** (*colère*) wild with; (*bonheur*) drunk *ou* intoxicated with; **~ mort** dead drunk

ivresse [ivʀɛs] *nf* drunkenness; (*euphorie*) intoxication

ivrogne [ivʀɔɲ] *nm/f* drunkard

j' [ʒ] *pron voir* **je**

jacasser [ʒakase] *vi* to chatter

jacinthe [ʒasɛ̃t] *nf* hyacinth; **~ des bois** bluebell

jadis [ʒadis] *adv* in times past, formerly

jaillir [ʒajiʀ] *vi (liquide)* to spurt out, gush out; *(lumière)* to flood out; *(fig)* to rear up; *(cris, réponses)* to burst out

jais [ʒɛ] *nm* jet; **(d'un noir) de ~** jet-black

jalousie [ʒaluzi] *nf* jealousy; *(store)* (venetian) blind

jaloux, -ouse [ʒalu, -uz] *adj* jealous; **être ~ de qn/qch** to be jealous of sb/sth

jamaïquain, e [ʒamaikɛ̃, -ɛn] *adj* Jamaican ▷ *nm/f:* **J~, e** Jamaican

Jamaïque [ʒamaik] *nf:* **la ~** Jamaica

jamais [ʒamɛ] *adv* never; *(sans négation)* ever; **ne ... ~** never; **~ de la vie!** never!; **si ... ~** if ever ...; **à (tout) ~, pour ~** for ever, for ever and ever; **je ne suis ~ allé en Espagne** I've never been to Spain

jambe [ʒɑ̃b] *nf* leg; **à toutes ~s** as fast as one's legs can carry one

jambon [ʒɑ̃bɔ̃] *nm* ham

jambonneau, x [ʒɑ̃bɔno] *nm* knuckle of ham

jante [ʒɑ̃t] *nf* (wheel) rim

janvier [ʒɑ̃vje] *nm* January; *voir aussi* **juillet**

Japon [ʒapɔ̃] *nm:* **le ~** Japan

japonais, e [ʒapɔnɛ, -ɛz] *adj* Japanese ▷ *nm (Ling)* Japanese ▷ *nm/f:* **J~, e** Japanese

japper [ʒape] *vi* to yap, yelp

jaquette [ʒakɛt] *nf (de cérémonie)* morning coat; *(de femme)* jacket; *(de livre)* dust cover, (dust) jacket

jardin [ʒaʀdɛ̃] *nm* garden; **~ d'acclimatation** zoological gardens *pl;* **~ botanique** botanical gardens *pl;* **~ d'enfants** nursery school; **~ potager** vegetable garden; **~ public** (public) park, public gardens *pl;* **~s suspendus** hanging gardens; **~ zoologique** zoological gardens

jardinage [ʒaʀdinaʒ] *nm* gardening

jardiner [ʒaʀdine] *vi* to garden, do some gardening

jardinier, -ière [ʒaʀdinje, -jɛʀ] *nm/f* gardener ▷ *nf (de fenêtre)* window box; **jardinière d'enfants** nursery school teacher; **jardinière (de légumes)** *(Culin)* mixed vegetables

jargon [ʒaʀgɔ̃] *nm (charabia)* gibberish; *(publicitaire, scientifique etc)* jargon

jarret [ʒaʀɛ] *nm* back of knee; *(Culin)* knuckle, shin

jarretelle [ʒaʀtɛl] *nf* suspender (Brit), garter (US)

jarretière [ʒaʀtjɛʀ] *nf* garter

jaser [ʒaze] *vi* to chatter, prattle; *(indiscrètement)* to gossip

jatte [ʒat] *nf* basin, bowl

jauge [ʒoʒ] *nf (capacité)* capacity, tonnage; *(instrument)* gauge; **~ (de niveau) d'huile** *(Auto)* dipstick

jaune [ʒon] *adj, nm* yellow ▷ *nm/f* Asiatic; *(briseur de grève)* blackleg ▷ *adv (fam):* **rire ~** to laugh on the other side of one's face; **~ d'œuf** (egg) yolk

jaunir [ʒoniʀ] *vi, vt* to turn yellow

jaunisse [ʒonis] *nf* jaundice

Javel [ʒavɛl] *nf voir* **eau**

javelot [ʒavlo] *nm* javelin; *(Sport):* **faire du ~** to throw the javelin

J.-C. *abr* = **Jésus-Christ**

je, j' [ʒə, ʒ] *pron* I

jean [dʒin] *nm* jeans *pl*

Jésus-Christ [ʒezykʀi(st)] *n* Jesus Christ; **600 avant/après ~** *ou* **J.-C.** 600 B.C./A.D.

jet¹ [ʒɛ] *nm (lancer: action)* throwing *no pl;* *(résultat)* throw; *(jaillissement: d'eaux)* jet; *(de sang)* spurt; *(de tuyau)* nozzle; *(fig):* **premier ~** *(ébauche)* rough outline; **arroser au ~** to hose; **d'un (seul) ~** *(d'un seul coup)* at *(ou* in) one go; **du premier ~** at the first attempt *ou* shot; **~ d'eau** spray; *(fontaine)* fountain

jet² [dʒɛt] *nm (avion)* jet

jetable [ʒətabl] *adj* disposable

jetée [ʒəte] *nf* jetty; *(grande)* pier

jeter [ʒəte] *vt (gén)* to throw; *(se défaire de)* to throw away *ou* out; *(son, lueur etc)* to give out; **~ qch à qn** to throw sth to sb; *(de façon agressive)* to throw sth at sb; *(Navig):* **~ l'ancre** to cast anchor; **~ un coup d'œil (à)** to take a look (at); **~ les bras en avant/la tête en arrière** to throw one's arms forward/one's head back(ward); **~ l'effroi parmi** to spread fear among; **~ un sort à qn** to cast a spell on sb; **~ qn dans la misère** to reduce sb to poverty; **~ qn dehors/en prison** to throw sb out/into prison; **~ l'éponge** (fig) to throw in the towel; **~ des fleurs à qn** (fig) to say lovely things to sb; **~ la pierre à qn** (accuser, blâmer) to accuse sb; **se ~ sur** to throw o.s. onto; **se ~ dans** (fleuve) to flow into; **se ~ par la fenêtre** to throw o.s. out of the window; **se ~ à l'eau** (fig) to take the plunge

jeton [ʒətɔ̃] nm (au jeu) counter; (de téléphone) token; **~s de présence** (director's) fees

jette etc [ʒɛt] vb voir **jeter**

jeu, x [ʒø] nm (divertissement, Tech: d'une pièce) play; (défini par des règles, Tennis: partie, Football etc: façon de jouer) game; (Théât etc) acting; (fonctionnement) working, interplay; (série d'objets, jouet) set; (Cartes) hand; (au casino): **le ~** gambling; **cacher son ~** (fig) to keep one's cards hidden, conceal one's hand; **c'est un ~ d'enfant!** (fig) it's child's play!; **en ~** at stake; at work; (Football) in play; **remettre en ~** to throw in; **entrer/mettre en ~** to come/bring into play; **par ~** (pour s'amuser) for fun; **d'entrée de ~** (tout de suite, dès le début) from the outset; **entrer dans le ~/le ~ de qn** (fig) to play the game/sb's game; **jouer gros ~** to play for high stakes; **se piquer/se prendre au ~** to get excited over/get caught up in the game; **~ d'arcade** video game; **~ de boules** game of bowls; (endroit) bowling pitch; (boules) set of bowls; **~ de cartes** card game; (paquet) pack of cards; **~ de construction** building set; **~ d'échecs** chess set; **~ d'écritures** (Comm) paper transaction; **~ électronique** electronic game; **~ de hasard** game of chance; **~ de mots** pun; **le ~ de l'oie** snakes and ladders sg; **~ d'orgue(s)** organ stop; **~ de patience** puzzle; **~ de physionomie** facial expressions pl; **~ de société** board game; **~ télévisé** television quiz; **~ vidéo** video game; **~x de lumière** lighting effects; **J-x olympiques (JO)** Olympic Games

jeudi [ʒødi] nm Thursday; **~ saint** Maundy Thursday; voir aussi **lundi**

jeun [ʒœ̃]: **à ~** adv on an empty stomach; **être à ~** to have eaten nothing; **rester à ~** not to eat anything

jeune [ʒɛn] adj young ▷ adv: **faire/s'habiller ~** to look/dress young; **les ~s** young people, the young; **~ fille** nf girl; **~ homme** nm young man; **~ loup** nm (Pol, Écon) young go-getter; **~ premier** leading man; **~s gens** nmpl young people; **~s mariés** nmpl newly weds

jeûne [ʒøn] nm fast

jeunesse [ʒœnɛs] nf youth; (aspect) youthfulness; (jeunes) young people pl, youth

joaillerie [ʒɔajʀi] nf jewel trade; jewellery (Brit), jewelry (US)

joaillier, -ière [ʒɔaje, -jɛʀ] nm/f jeweller

(Brit), jeweler (US)

jogging [dʒɔgin] nm jogging; (survêtement) tracksuit (Brit), sweatsuit (US); **faire du ~** to go jogging, jog

joie [ʒwa] nf joy

joindre [ʒwɛ̃dʀ] vt to join; **~ qch à** (à une lettre) to enclose sth with; (contacter) to contact, get in touch with; **~ un fichier à un mail** (Inform) to attach a file to an email; **~ les mains/talons** to put one's hands/heels together; **~ les deux bouts** (fig: du mois) to make ends meet; **se joindre** (mains etc) to come together; **se ~ à qn** to join sb; **se ~ à qch** to join in sth

joint, e [ʒwɛ̃, -ɛ̃t] pp de **joindre** ▷ adj: **~ (à)** (lettre, paquet) attached (to), enclosed (with); **pièce ~e** (de lettre) enclosure; (de mail) attachment ▷ nm joint; (ligne) join; (de ciment etc) pointing no pl; **chercher/trouver le ~** (fig) to look for/come up with the answer; **~ de cardan** cardan joint; **~ de culasse** cylinder head gasket; **~ de robinet** washer; **~ universel** universal joint

joker [ʒɔkɛʀ] nm (Cartes) joker; (Inform): **(caractère) ~** wild card

joli, e [ʒɔli] adj pretty, attractive; **une ~ somme/situation** a nice little sum/ situation; **un ~ gâchis** etc a nice mess etc; **c'est du ~!** (ironique) that's very nice!; **tout ça, c'est bien ~ mais ...** that's all very well but ...

jonc [ʒɔ̃] nm (bul) rush; (bague, bracelet) band

jonction [ʒɔ̃ksjɔ̃] nf joining; **(point de) ~** (de routes) junction; (de fleuves) confluence; **opérer une ~** (Mil etc) to rendez-vous

jongleur, -euse [ʒɔ̃glœʀ, -øz] nm/f juggler

jonquille [ʒɔ̃kij] nf daffodil

Jordanie [ʒɔʀdani] nf: **la ~** Jordan

joue [ʒu] nf cheek; **mettre en ~** to take aim at

jouer [ʒwe] vt (partie, carte, coup, Mus: morceau) to play; (somme d'argent, réputation) to stake, wager; (pièce, rôle) to perform; (film) to show; (simuler: sentiment) to affect, feign ▷ vi to play; (Théât, Ciné) to act, perform; (au casino) to gamble; (bois, porte: se voiler) to warp; (clef, pièce: avoir du jeu) to be loose; (entrer ou être en jeu) to come into play, come into it; **~ sur** (miser) to gamble on; **~ de** (Mus) to play; **~ du couteau/des coudes** to use knives/one's elbows; **~ à** (jeu, sport, roulette) to play; **~ au héros** to act ou play the hero; **~ avec** (risquer) to gamble with; **se ~ de** (difficultés) to make light of; **se ~ de qn** to deceive ou dupe sb; **~ un tour à qn** to play a trick on sb; **~ la comédie** (fig) to put on an act, put it on; **~ aux courses** to back horses, bet on horses; **~ à la baisse/ hausse** (Bourse) to play for a fall/rise; **~ serré** to play a close game; **~ de malchance** to be dogged with ill-luck; **~ sur les mots** to play with words; **à toi/nous de ~** it's your/our go ou turn; **bien joué!** well done!; **on joue Hamlet au théâtre X** Hamlet is on at the X theatre

jouet [ʒwɛ] nm toy; **être le ~ de** (illusion etc) to be the victim of

joueur, -euse [ʒwœr, -øz] nm/f player ▷ adj (enfant, chat) playful; **être beau/mauvais ~** to be a good/bad loser

joufflu, e [ʒufly] adj chubby(-cheeked)

joug [ʒu] nm yoke

jouir [ʒwir] vi (sexe: fam) to come ▷ vt: **~ de** to enjoy

jouissance [ʒwisɑ̃s] nf pleasure; (Jur) use

joujou [ʒuʒu] nm (fam) toy

jour [ʒur] nm day; (opposé à la nuit) day, daytime; (clarté) daylight; (fig: aspect): **sous un ~ favorable/nouveau** in a favourable/ new light; (ouverture) opening; (Couture) openwork no pl; **de ~** (crème, service) day cpd; **travailler de ~** to work during the day; **voyager de ~** to travel by day; **au ~ le ~** from day to day; **de nos ~s** these days, nowadays; **tous les ~s** every day; **de ~ en ~** day by day; **d'un ~ à l'autre** from one day to the next; **du ~ au lendemain** overnight; **il fait ~** it's daylight; **en plein ~** in broad daylight; **au ~** in daylight; **au petit ~** at daybreak; **au grand ~** (fig) in the open; **mettre au ~** to disclose, uncover; **être à ~** to be up to date; **mettre à ~** to bring up to date, update; **mise à ~** updating; **donner le ~ à** to give birth to; **voir le ~** to be born; **se faire ~** (fig) to become clear; **~ férié** public holiday; **le J** D-day; **~ ouvrable** working day

journal, -aux [ʒurnal, -o] nm (news)paper; (personnel) journal; (intime) diary; **~ de bord** log; **~ de mode** fashion magazine; **le J~ officiel (de la République française) (JO)** bulletin giving details of laws and official announcements; **~ parlé/télévisé** radio/ television news sg

journalier, -ière [ʒurnalje, -jɛr] adj daily; (banal) everyday ▷ nm day labourer

journalisme [ʒurnalism] nm journalism

journaliste [ʒurnalist] nm/f journalist

journée [ʒurne] nf day; **la ~ continue** the 9 to 5 working day (with short lunch break)

journellement [ʒurnɛlmɑ̃] adv (tous les jours) daily; (souvent) every day

joyau, x [ʒwajo] nm gem, jewel

joyeux, -euse [ʒwajø, -øz] adj joyful, merry; **~ Noël!** Merry ou Happy Christmas!; **joyeuses Pâques!** Happy Easter!; **~ anniversaire!** many happy returns!

jubiler [ʒybile] vi to be jubilant, exult

jucher [ʒyʃe] vt: **~ qch sur** to perch sth (up)on ▷ vi (oiseau): **~ sur** to perch (up)on; **se ~ sur** to perch o.s. (up)on

judas [ʒyda] nm (trou) spy-hole

judiciaire [ʒydisjɛr] adj judicial

judicieux, -euse [ʒydisjø, -øz] adj judicious

judo [ʒydo] nm judo

juge [ʒyʒ] nm judge; **~ d'instruction** examining (Brit) ou committing (US) magistrate; **~ de paix** justice of the peace;

~ de touche linesman

jugé [ʒyʒe] **au ~** adv by guesswork

jugement [ʒyʒmɑ̃] nm judgment; (Jur: au pénal) sentence; (: au civil) decision; **~ de valeur** value judgment

jugeote [ʒyʒɔt] nf (fam) gumption

juger [ʒyʒe] vt to judge; (estimer) to consider ▷ nm: **au ~** by guesswork; **~ qn/qch satisfaisant** to consider sb/sth (to be) satisfactory; **~ que** to think ou consider that; **~ bon de faire** to consider it a good idea to do, see fit to do; **~ de** vt to judge; **jugez de ma surprise** imagine my surprise

juif, -ive [ʒɥif, -iv] adj Jewish ▷ nm/f: **J~, ive** Jewish man/woman ou Jew

juillet [ʒɥijɛ] nm July; **le premier ~** the first of July (Brit), July first (US); **le deux/onze ~** the second/eleventh of July, July second/ eleventh; **il est venu le 5** ~ he came on 5th July ou July 5th; **en ~** in July; **début/fin ~** at the beginning/end of July; see note

juin [ʒɥɛ̃] nm June; voir aussi **juillet**

jumeau, -elle, x [ʒymo, -ɛl] adj, nm/f twin; **maisons jumelles** semidetached houses

jumelage [ʒymlaʒ] nm twinning

jumeler [ʒymle] vt to twin; **roues jumelées** double wheels; **billets de loterie jumelés** double series lottery tickets; **pari jumelé** double bet

jumelle [ʒymɛl] adj f, nf voir **jumeau** ▷ vb voir **jumeler**

jument [ʒymɑ̃] nf mare

jungle [ʒɔ̃gl] nf jungle

jupe [ʒyp] nf skirt

jupon [ʒypɔ̃] nm waist slip ou petticoat

juré, e [ʒyre] nm/f juror ▷ adj: **ennemi ~** sworn ou avowed enemy

jurer [ʒyre] vt (obéissance etc) to swear, vow ▷ vi (dire des jurons) to swear, curse; (dissoner): **~ (avec)** to clash (with); (s'engager): **~ de faire/ que** to swear ou vow to do/that; (affirmer): **~ que** to swear ou vouch that; **~ de qch** (s'en porter garant) to swear to sth; **ils ne jurent que par lui** they swear by him; **je vous jure!** honestly!

juridique [ʒyridik] adj legal

juron [ʒyrɔ̃] nm curse, swearword

jury [ʒyri] nm (Jur) jury; (Art, Sport) panel of judges; (Scol) board (of examiners), jury

jus [ʒy] *nm* juice; *(de viande)* gravy, (meat) juice; ~ **de fruits** fruit juice; ~ **de raisin/tomates** grape/tomato juice

jusque [ʒysk]: **jusqu'à** *prép (endroit)* as far as, (up) to; *(moment)* until, till; *(limite)* up to; ~ **sur/dans** up to, as far as; *(y compris)* even on/in; ~ **vers** until about; **jusqu'à ce que** *conj* until; **~-là** *(temps)* until then; *(espace)* up to there; **jusqu'ici** *(temps)* until now; *(espace)* up to here; **jusqu'à présent** *ou* **maintenant** until now, so far; **jusqu'où?** how far?

justaucorps [ʒystokɔʀ] *nm inv (Danse, Sport)* leotard

juste [ʒyst] *adj (équitable)* just, fair; *(légitime)* just, justified; *(exact, vrai)* right; *(pertinent)* apt; *(étroit, insuffisant)* tight; *(insuffisant)* on the short side ▷ *adv* right; tight; *(chanter)* in tune; *(seulement)* just; ~ **assez/au-dessus** just enough/above; **pouvoir tout** ~ **faire** to be only just able to do; **au** ~ exactly, actually; **comme de** ~ of course, naturally; **le** ~ **milieu** the happy medium; **c'était** ~ it was a close thing; **à** ~ **titre** rightfully

justement [ʒystəmɑ̃] *adv* rightly; justly; *(précisément)* just, precisely; **c'est** ~ **ce qu'il fallait faire** that's just *ou* precisely what needed doing

justesse [ʒystɛs] *nf (précision)* accuracy; *(d'une remarque)* aptness; *(d'une opinion)* soundness; **de** ~ only just, by a narrow margin

justice [ʒystis] *nf (équité)* fairness, justice; *(Admin)* justice; **rendre la** ~ to dispense justice; **traduire en** ~ to bring before the courts; **obtenir** ~ to obtain justice; **rendre** ~ **à qn** to do sb justice; **se faire** ~ to take the law into one's own hands; *(se suicider)* to take one's life

justicier, -ière [ʒystisje, -jɛʀ] *nm/f* judge, righter of wrongs

justificatif, -ive [ʒystifikatif, -iv] *adj (document etc)* supporting ▷ *nm* supporting proof; **pièce justificative** written proof

justifier [ʒystifje] *vt* to justify; ~ **de** *vt* to prove; **non justifié** unjustified; **justifié à droite/gauche** ranged right/left

juteux, -euse [ʒytø, -øz] *adj* juicy

juvénile [ʒyvenil] *adj* young, youthful

K, k [kɑ] *nm inv* K, k ▷ *abr (= kilo)* kg; **K comme Kléber** K for King

K 7 [kaset] *nf* cassette

kaki [kaki] *adj inv* khaki

kangourou [kɑ̃guʀu] *nm* kangaroo

karaté [kaʀate] *nm* karate

karting [kaʀtiŋ] *nm* go-carting, karting

kascher [kaʃɛʀ] *adj inv* kosher

kayak [kajak] *nm* kayak; **faire du** ~ to go kayaking

képi [kepi] *nm* kepi

kermesse [kɛʀmɛs] *nf* bazaar, (charity) fête; village fair

kidnapper [kidnape] *vt* to kidnap

kilo [kilo] *nm* kilo

kilogramme [kilɔgʀam] *nm* kilogramme (Brit), kilogram (US)

kilométrage [kilɔmetʀaʒ] *nm* number of kilometres travelled, ≈ mileage

kilomètre [kilɔmetʀ] *nm* kilometre (Brit), kilometer (US); **~s-heure** kilometres per hour

kilométrique [kilɔmetʀik] *adj (distance)* in kilometres; **compteur** ~ ≈ mileage indicator

kinésithérapeute [kineziteʀapøt] *nm/f* physiotherapist

kiosque [kjɔsk] *nm* kiosk, stall; *(Tél etc)* telephone and/or videotext information service; ~ **à journaux** newspaper kiosk

kir [kiʀ] *nm* kir *(white wine with blackcurrant liqueur)*

kit [kit] *nm* kit; ~ **piéton** *ou* **mains libres** hands-free kit; **en** ~ in kit form

k

kiwi [kiwi] *nm* (*Zool*) kiwi; (*Bot*) kiwi (fruit)
klaxon [klaksɔn] *nm* horn
klaxonner [klaksɔne] *vi, vt* to hoot (*Brit*),
honk (one's horn) (*US*)
km *abr* (= *kilomètre*) km
km/h *abr* (= *kilomètres/heure*) km/h, kph
K.-O. [kao] *adj inv* shattered, knackered
Kosovo [kɔsɔvo] *nm*: **le ~** Kosovo
Koweit, Kuweit [kɔwɛt] *nm*: **le ~** Kuwait,
Koweit
k-way® [kawɛ] *nm* (lightweight nylon)
cagoule
kyste [kist] *nm* cyst

l' [l] *art déf* voir **le**
la [la] *art déf, pron. voir* **le** ▷ *nm* (*Mus*) A; (*en
chantant la gamme*) la
là [la] *adv voir aussi* **-ci; celui** there; (*ici*) here;
(*dans le temps*) then; **est-ce que Catherine est
là?** is Catherine there (*ou* here)?; **elle n'est
pas là** she isn't here; **c'est là que** this is
where; **là où** where; **de là** (*fig*) hence; **par là**
(*fig*) by that; **tout est là** (*fig*) that's what it's
all about
là-bas [labɑ] *adv* there
label [labɛl] *nm* stamp, seal
labeur [labœʀ] *nm* toil *no pl*, toiling *no pl*
labo [labo] *nm* (= *laboratoire*) lab
laboratoire [labɔʀatwaʀ] *nm* laboratory;
~ de langues/d'analyses language/
(medical) analysis laboratory
laborieux, -euse [labɔʀjø, -øz] *adj* (*tâche*)
laborious; **classes laborieuses** working
classes
labour [labuʀ] *nm* ploughing *no pl* (*Brit*),
plowing *no pl* (*US*); **labours** *nmpl* (*champs*)
ploughed fields; **cheval de ~** plough- *ou* cart-
horse; **bœuf de ~** ox
labourer [labuʀe] *vt* to plough (*Brit*), plow
(*US*); (*fig*) to make deep gashes *ou* furrows in
labyrinthe [labiʀɛ̃t] *nm* labyrinth, maze
lac [lak] *nm* lake; **le ~ Léman** Lake Geneva;
les Grands L~s the Great Lakes; *voir aussi*
lacs
lacer [lase] *vt* to lace *ou* do up
lacérer [laseʀe] *vt* to tear to shreds

lacet [lasɛ] nm (de chaussure) lace; (de route) sharp bend; (piège) snare; **chaussures à ~s** lace-up ou lacing shoes

lâche [laʃ] adj (poltron) cowardly; (desserré) loose, slack; (morale, mœurs) lax ▷ nm/f coward

lâcher [laʃe] nm (de ballons, oiseaux) release ▷ vt to let go of; (ce qui tombe, abandonner) to drop; (oiseau, animal: libérer) to release, set free; (fig: mot, remarque) to let slip, come out with; (Sport: distancer) to leave behind ▷ vi (fil, amarres) to break, give way; (freins) to fail; **~ les amarres** (Navig) to cast off (the moorings); **~ prise** to let go

lâcheté [laʃte] nf cowardice; (bassesse) lowness

lacrymogène [lakʀimɔʒɛn] adj: **grenade/ gaz ~** tear gas grenade/tear gas

lacté, e [lakte] adj milk cpd

lacune [lakyn] nf gap

là-dedans [ladədɑ̃] adv inside (there), in it; (fig) in that

là-dessous [ladsu] adv underneath, under there; (fig) behind that

là-dessus [ladsy] adv on there; (fig: sur ces mots) at that point; (: à ce sujet) about that

ladite [ladit] adj voir **ledit**

lagune [lagyn] nf lagoon

là-haut [lao] adv up there

laïc [laik] adj, nm/f = **laïque**

laid, e [lɛ, lɛd] adj ugly; (fig: acte) mean, cheap

laideur [lɛdœʀ] nf ugliness no pl; meanness no pl

lainage [lɛnaʒ] nm (vêtement) woollen garment; (étoffe) woollen material

laine [lɛn] nf wool; **~ peignée** worsted (wool); **~ à tricoter** knitting wool; **~ de verre** glass wool; **~ vierge** new wool

laïque [laik] adj lay, civil; (Scol) state cpd (as opposed to private and Roman Catholic) ▷ nm/f layman(-woman)

laisse [lɛs] nf (de chien) lead, leash; **tenir en ~** to keep on a lead ou leash

laisser [lese] vt to leave ▷ vb aux: **~ qn faire** to let sb do; **se ~ exploiter** to let o.s. be exploited; **se ~ aller** to let o.s. go; **~ qn tranquille** to leave sb alone; **laisse-toi faire** let me (ou him) do it; **rien ne laisse penser que …** there is no reason to think that …; **cela ne laisse pas de surprendre** nonetheless it is surprising

laisser-aller [leseale] nm carelessness, slovenliness

laissez-passer [lesepase] nm inv pass

lait [lɛ] nm milk; **frère/sœur de ~** foster brother/sister; **~ écrémé/entier/concentré/ condensé** skimmed/full-fat/condensed/ evaporated milk; **~ en poudre** powdered milk, milk powder; **~ de chèvre/vache** goat's/cow's milk; **~ maternel** mother's milk; **~ démaquillant/de beauté** cleansing/ beauty lotion

laitage [lɛtaʒ] nm dairy product

laiterie [lɛtʀi] nf dairy

laitier, -ière [letje, -jɛʀ] adj dairy cpd ▷ nm/f milkman/dairywoman

laiton [lɛtɔ̃] nm brass

laitue [lety] nf lettuce

laïus [lajys] nm (péj) spiel

lambeau, x [lɑ̃bo] nm scrap; **en ~x** in tatters, tattered

lambris [lɑ̃bʀi] nm panelling no pl

lame [lam] nf blade; (vague) wave; (lamelle) strip; **~ de fond** ground swell no pl; **~ de rasoir** razor blade

lamelle [lamɛl] nf (lame) small blade; (morceau) sliver; (de champignon) gill; **couper en ~s** to slice thinly

lamentable [lamɑ̃tabl] adj (déplorable) appalling; (pitoyable) pitiful

lamenter [lamɑ̃te]: **se lamenter** vi: **se ~ (sur)** to moan (over)

lampadaire [lɑ̃padɛʀ] nm (de salon) standard lamp; (dans la rue) street lamp

lampe [lɑ̃p] nf lamp; (Tech) valve; **~ à alcool** spirit lamp; **~ à pétrole** oil lamp; **~ à bronzer** sunlamp; **~ de poche** torch (Brit), flashlight (US); **~ à souder** blowlamp; **~ témoin** warning light; **~ halogène** halogen lamp

lampion [lɑ̃pjɔ̃] nm Chinese lantern

lance [lɑ̃s] nf spear; **~ d'arrosage** garden hose; **~ à eau** water hose; **~ d'incendie** fire hose

lancée [lɑ̃se] nf: **être/continuer sur sa ~** to be under way/keep going

lancement [lɑ̃smɑ̃] nm launching no pl, launch; **offre de ~** introductory offer

lance-pierres [lɑ̃spjɛʀ] nm inv catapult

lancer [lɑ̃se] nm (Sport) throwing no pl, throw; (Pêche) rod and reel fishing ▷ vt to throw; (émettre, projeter) to throw out, send out; (produit, fusée, bateau, artiste) to launch; (injure) to hurl, fling; (proclamation, mandat d'arrêt) to issue; (emprunt) to float; (moteur) to send roaring away; **~ qch à qn** to throw sth to sb; (de façon agressive) to throw sth at sb; **~ un cri** ou **un appel** to shout ou call out; **se lancer** vi (prendre de l'élan) to build up speed; (se précipiter): **se ~ sur** ou **contre** to rush at; **se ~ dans** (discussion) to launch into; (aventure) to embark on; (les affaires, la politique) to go into; **~ du poids** nm putting the shot

lancinant, e [lɑ̃sinɑ̃, -ɑ̃t] adj (regrets etc) haunting; (douleur) shooting

landau [lɑ̃do] nm pram (Brit), baby carriage (US)

lande [lɑ̃d] nf moor

langage [lɑ̃gaʒ] nm language; **~ d'assemblage** (Inform) assembly language; **~ du corps** body language; **~ évolué/ machine** (Inform) high-level/machine language; **~ de programmation** (Inform) programming language

langouste [lɑ̃gust] nf crayfish inv

langoustine [lɑ̃gustin] nf Dublin Bay prawn

langue [lɑ̃g] nf (Anat, Culin) tongue; (Ling) language; (bande): **~ de terre** spit of land; **tirer la ~ (à)** to stick out one's tongue (at);

donner sa ~ au chat to give up, give in; **de ~ française** French-speaking; **~ de bois** officialese; **~ maternelle** native language, mother tongue; **(de voiture)** (side)light; **~ rouge** *(fig)* tail-ender; **~ vénitienne** Chinese lantern

langueur [lɑ̃gœr] *nf* languidness

languir [lɑ̃gir] *vi* to languish; *(conversation)* to flag; **se languir** *vi* to be languishing; **faire ~ qn** to keep sb waiting

lanière [lanjɛr] *nf (de fouet)* lash; *(de valise, bretelle)* strap

lanterne [lɑ̃tɛrn] *nf (portable)* lantern; *(électrique)* light, lamp; *(de voiture)* (side)light; **~ rouge** *(fig)* tail-ender; **~ vénitienne** Chinese lantern

laper [lape] *vt* to lap up

lapidaire [lapidɛr] *adj* stone *cpd*; *(fig)* terse

lapin [lapɛ̃] *nm* rabbit; *(peau)* rabbitskin; *(fourrure)* cony; **coup du ~** rabbit punch; **poser un ~ à qn** to stand sb up; **~ de garenne** wild rabbit

Laponie [laponi] *nf:* **la ~** Lapland

laps [laps] *nm:* **~ de temps** space of time, time *no pl*

laque [lak] *nf (vernis)* lacquer; *(brute)* shellac; *(pour cheveux)* hair spray ▷ *nm* lacquer; piece of lacquer ware

laquelle [lakɛl] *pron voir* **lequel**

larcin [larsɛ̃] *nm* theft

lard [lar] *nm (graisse)* fat; *(bacon)* (streaky) bacon

lardon [lardɔ̃] *nm (Culin)* piece of chopped bacon; *(fam: enfant)* kid

large [larʒ] *adj* wide; broad; *(fig)* generous ▷ *adv* **calculer/voir ~** to allow extra/think big ▷ *nm (largeur):* **5 m de ~** 5 m wide *ou* in width; *(mer):* **le ~** the open sea; **en ~** *adv* sideways; **au ~ de** off; **~ d'esprit** broadminded; **ne pas en mener ~** to have one's heart in one's boots

largement [larʒəmɑ̃] *adv* widely; *(de loin)* greatly; *(amplement, au minimum)* easily; *(sans compter: donner etc)* generously; **c'est ~ suffisant** that's ample

largesse [larʒɛs] *nf* generosity; **largesses** *nfpl (dons)* liberalities

largeur [larʒœr] *nf (qu'on mesure)* width; *(impression visuelle)* wideness, width; breadth; *(d'esprit)* broadness

larguer [large] *vt* to drop; *(fam: se débarrasser de)* to get rid of; **~ les amarres** to cast off (the moorings)

larme [larm] *nf* tear; *(fig):* **une ~ de** a drop of; **en ~s** in tears; **pleurer à chaudes ~s** to cry one's eyes out, cry bitterly

larmoyer [larmwaje] *vi (yeux)* to water; *(se plaindre)* to whimper

larvé, e [larve] *adj (fig)* latent

laryngite [larɛ̃ʒit] *nf* laryngitis

las, lasse [lɑ, lɑs] *adj* weary

laser [lazɛr] *nm:* **(rayon) ~** laser (beam); **chaîne** *ou* **platine ~** compact disc (player);

disque ~ compact disc

lasse [lɑs] *adj f voir* **las**

lasser [lɑse] *vt* to weary, tire; **se ~ de** to grow weary *ou* tired of

latéral, e, -aux [lateral, -o] *adj* side *cpd*, lateral

latin, e [latɛ̃, -in] *adj* Latin ▷ *nm (Ling)* Latin ▷ *nm/f:* **L-, e** Latin; **j'y perds mon ~** it's all Greek to me

latitude [latityd] *nf* latitude; *(fig):* **avoir la ~ de faire** to be left free *ou* at liberty to do; **à 48° de ~ Nord** at latitude 48° North; **sous toutes les ~s** *(fig)* world-wide, throughout the world

latte [lat] *nf* lath, slat; *(de plancher)* board

lauréat, e [lɔrea, -at] *nm/f* winner

laurier [lɔrje] *nm (Bot)* laurel; *(Culin)* bay leaves *pl*; **lauriers** *nmpl (fig)* laurels

lavable [lavabl] *adj* washable

lavabo [lavabo] *nm* washbasin; **lavabos** *nmpl* toilet *sg*

lavage [lavaʒ] *nm* washing *no pl*, wash; **~ d'estomac/d'intestin** stomach/intestinal wash; **~ de cerveau** brainwashing *no pl*

lavande [lavɑ̃d] *nf* lavender

lave [lav] *nf* lava *no pl*

lave-linge [lavlɛ̃ʒ] *nm inv* washing machine

laver [lave] *vt* to wash; *(tache)* to wash off; *(fig: affront)* to avenge; **se laver** *vi* to have a wash, wash; **se ~ les mains/dents** to wash one's hands/clean one's teeth; **~ la vaisselle/le linge** to wash the dishes/clothes; **~ qn de** *(accusation)* to clear sb of

laverie [lavri] *nf:* **~ (automatique)** launderette

lavette [lavɛt] *nf (chiffon)* dish cloth; *(brosse)* dish mop; *(fam: homme)* wimp, drip

laveur, -euse [lavœr, -øz] *nm/f* cleaner

lave-vaisselle [lavvesɛl] *nm inv* dishwasher

lavoir [lavwar] *nm* wash house; *(bac)* washtub; *(évier)* sink

laxatif, -ive [laksatif, -iv] *adj, nm* laxative

layette [lɛjɛt] *nf* layette

 MOT-CLÉ

le, l', la [lə, l, la] *(pl* **les**) *art déf* **1** le; **le livre/ la pomme/l'arbre** the book/the apple/the tree; **les étudiants** the students
2 *(noms abstraits):* **le courage/l'amour/la jeunesse** courage/love/youth
3 *(indiquant la possession):* **se casser la jambe** *etc* to break one's leg *etc*; **levez la main** put your hand up; **avoir les yeux gris/le nez rouge** to have grey eyes/a red nose
4 *(temps):* **le matin/soir** in the morning/ evening; mornings/evenings; **le jeudi** *etc (d'habitude)* on Thursdays *etc*; *(ce jeudi-là etc)* on (the) Thursday; **nous venons le 3 décembre** *(parlé)* we're coming on the 3rd of December *ou* on December the 3rd; *(écrit)* we're coming (on) 3rd *ou* 3 December

5 (*distribution, évaluation*) a, an; **trois euros le mètre/kilo** three euros a *ou* per metre/kilo; **le tiers/quart de** a third/quarter of
▷ *pron* **1** (*personne: mâle*) him; (: *femelle*) her; (: *pluriel*) them; **je le/la/les vois** I can see him/her/them
2 (*animal, chose: singulier*) it; (: *pluriel*) them; **je le** (*ou* **la**) **vois** I can see it; **je les vois** I can see them
3 (*remplaçant une phrase*): **je ne le savais pas** I didn't know (about it); **il était riche et ne l'est plus** he was once rich but no longer is

lécher [leʃe] *vt* to lick; (*laper: lait, eau*) to lick *ou* lap up; (*finir, polir*) to over-refine; **~ les vitrines** to go window-shopping; **se ~ les doigts/lèvres** to lick one's fingers/lips

lèche-vitrines [lɛʃvitrin] *nm inv*: **faire du ~** to go window-shopping

leçon [l(ə)sɔ̃] *nf* lesson; **faire la ~** to teach; **faire la ~ à** (*fig*) to give a lecture to; **~s de conduite** driving lessons; **~s particulières** private lessons *ou* tuition *sg* (*Brit*)

lecteur, -trice [lɛktœʀ, -tʀis] *nm/f* reader; (*d'université*) (foreign language) assistant (*Brit*), (foreign) teaching assistant (*US*) ▷ *nm* (*Tech*): **~ de cassettes** cassette player; **~ de disquette(s)** disk drive; **~ de CD/DVD** (*Inform: d'ordinateur*) CD/DVD drive; (*de salon*) CD/DVD player; **~ MP3** MP3 player

lecture [lɛktyʀ] *nf* reading

ledit [lədi], **ladite** [ladit] (*mpl* **lesdits**) [ledi] (*fpl* **lesdites**) [ledit] *adj* the aforesaid

légal, e, -aux [legal, -o] *adj* legal

légaliser [legalize] *vt* to legalize

légalité [legalite] *nf* legality, lawfulness; **être dans/sortir de la ~** to be within/step outside the law

légendaire [leʒɑ̃dɛʀ] *adj* legendary

légende [leʒɑ̃d] *nf* (*mythe*) legend; (*de carte, plan*) key, legend; (*de dessin*) caption

léger, -ère [leʒe, -ɛʀ] *adj* light; (*bruit, retard*) slight; (*boisson, parfum*) weak; (*couche, étoffe*) thin; (*superficiel*) thoughtless; (*volage*) free and easy; flighty; (*peu sérieux*) lightweight; **blessé ~** slightly injured person; **à la légère** *adv* (*parler, agir*) rashly, thoughtlessly

légèrement [leʒɛʀmɑ̃] *adv* (*s'habiller, bouger*) lightly; thoughtlessly, rashly; **~ plus grand** slightly bigger; **manger ~** to eat a light meal

légèreté [leʒɛʀte] *nf* lightness; thoughtlessness; (*d'une remarque*) flippancy

législatif, -ive [leʒislatif, -iv] *adj* legislative; **législatives** *nfpl* general election *sg*

légitime [leʒitim] *adj* (*Jur*) lawful, legitimate; (*enfant*) legitimate; (*fig*) rightful, legitimate; **en état de ~ défense** in self-defence

legs [lɛg] *nm* legacy

léguer [lege] *vt*: **~ qch à qn** (*Jur*) to bequeath sth to sb; (*fig*) to hand sth down *ou* pass sth on to sb

légume [legym] *nm* vegetable; **~s verts** green vegetables; **~s secs** pulses

lendemain [lɑ̃dmɛ̃] *nm*: **le ~** the next *ou* following day; **le ~ matin/soir** the next *ou* following morning/evening; **le ~ de** the day after; **au ~ de** in the days following; in the wake of; **penser au ~** to think of the future; **sans ~** short-lived; **de beaux ~s** bright prospects; **des ~s qui chantent** a rosy future

lent, e [lɑ̃, lɑ̃t] *adj* slow

lentement [lɑ̃tmɑ̃] *adv* slowly

lenteur [lɑ̃tœʀ] *nf* slowness *no pl*; **lenteurs** *nfpl* (*actions, décisions lentes*) slowness *sg*

lentille [lɑ̃tij] *nf* (*Optique*) lens *sg*; (*Bot*) lentil; **~ d'eau** duckweed; **~s de contact** contact lenses

léopard [leɔpaʀ] *nm* leopard

lèpre [lɛpʀ] *nf* leprosy

○ **MOT-CLÉ**

lequel, laquelle [ləkɛl, lakɛl] (*mpl* **lesquels**, *fpl* **lesquelles**) (*à* + *lequel* = **auquel**, *de* + *lequel* = **duquel**) *pron* **1** (*interrogatif*) which, which one; **lequel des deux?** which one?
2 (*relatif: personne: sujet*) who; (: *objet, après préposition*) whom; (: *sujet: possessif*) whose; (: *chose*) which; **je l'ai proposé au directeur, lequel est d'accord** I suggested it to the director, who agrees; **la femme à laquelle j'ai acheté mon chien** the woman from whom I bought my dog; **le pont sur lequel nous sommes passés** the bridge (over) which we crossed; **un homme sur la compétence duquel on peut compter** a man whose competence one can count on
▷ *adj*: **auquel cas** in which case

les [le] *art déf*, *pron voir* **le**

lesbienne [lɛsbjɛn] *nf* lesbian

lesdits [ledi], **lesdites** [ledit] *adj voir* **ledit**

léser [leze] *vt* to wrong; (*Méd*) to injure

lésiner [lezine] *vi*: **ne pas ~ sur les moyens** (*pour mariage etc*) to push the boat out

lésion [lezjɔ̃] *nf* lesion, damage *no pl*; **~s cérébrales** brain damage

lesquels, lesquelles [lekɛl] *pron voir* **lequel**

lessive [lesiv] *nf* (*poudre*) washing powder; (*linge*) washing *no pl*, wash; (*opération*) washing *no pl*; **faire la ~** to do the washing

lessiver [lesive] *vt* to wash; (*fam: fatiguer*) to tire out, exhaust

lest [lɛst] *nm* ballast; **jeter** *ou* **lâcher du ~** (*fig*) to make concessions

leste [lɛst] *adj* (*personne, mouvement*) sprightly, nimble; (*désinvolte: manières*) offhand; (*osé: plaisanterie*) risqué

lettre [lɛtR] *nf* letter; **lettres** *nfpl* (*étude, culture*) literature *sg*; (*Scol*) arts (subjects); **à la ~** (*au sens propre*) literally; (*ponctuellement*) to the letter; **en ~s majuscules** *ou* **capitales** in capital letters, in capitals; **en toutes ~s** in words, in full; **~ de change** bill of exchange; **~ piégée** letter bomb; **~ de voiture (aérienne)** (*air*) waybill, (*air*) bill of lading; **~s de noblesse** pedigree

leucémie [løsemi] *nf* leukaemia

 MOT-CLÉ

leur [lœR] *adj poss* their; **leur maison** their house; **leurs amis** their friends; **à leur approche** as they came near; **à leur vue** at the sight of them
▷ *pron* **1** (*objet indirect*) (to) them; **je leur ai dit la vérité** I told them the truth; **je le leur ai donné** I gave it to them, I gave them it
2 (*possessif*): **le(la) leur, les leurs** theirs

leurre [lœR] *nm* (*appât*) lure; (*fig*) delusion; (*: piège*) snare

leurrer [lœRe] *vt* to delude, deceive

leurs [lœR] *adj voir* **leur**

levain [ləvɛ̃] *nm* leaven; **sans ~** unleavened

levé, e [ləve] *adj*: **être ~** to be up ▷ *nm*: **~ de terrain** land survey; **à mains ~es** (*vote*) by a show of hands; **au pied ~** at a moment's notice

levée [ləve] *nf* (*Postes*) collection; (*Cartes*) trick; **~ de boucliers** general outcry; **~ du corps** *collection of the body from the house of the deceased, before funeral*; **~ d'écrou** release from custody; **~ de terre** levee; **~ de troupes** levy

lever [ləve] *vt* (*vitre, bras etc*) to raise; (*soulever de terre, supprimer: interdiction, siège*) to lift; (*: difficulté*) to remove; (*séance*) to close; (*impôts, armée*) to levy; (*Chasse: lièvre*) to start; (*: perdrix*) to flush; (*fam: fille*) to pick up ▷ *vi* (*Culin*) to rise ▷ *nm*: **au ~** on getting up; **se lever** *vi* to get up; (*soleil*) to rise; (*jour*) to break; (*brouillard*) to lift; **levez-vous!, lève-toi!** stand up!, get up!; **ça va se ~** (*temps*) it's going to clear up; **~ du jour** daybreak; **~ du rideau** (*Théât*) curtain; **~ de rideau** (*pièce*) curtain raiser; **~ de soleil** sunrise

levier [ləvje] *nm* lever; **faire ~ sur** to lever up (*ou* off); **~ de changement de vitesse** gear lever

lèvre [lɛvR] *nf* lip; **lèvres** *nfpl* (*d'une plaie*) edges; **petites/grandes ~s** labia minora/majora; **du bout des ~s** half-heartedly

lévrier [levRije] *nm* greyhound

levure [ləvyR] *nf* yeast; **~ chimique** baking powder

lexique [lɛksik] *nm* vocabulary, lexicon; (*glossaire*) vocabulary

lézard [lezaR] *nm* lizard; (*peau*) lizard skin

lézarde [lezaRd] *nf* crack

liaison [ljɛzɔ̃] *nf* (*rapport*) connection, link; (*Rail, Aviat etc*) link; (*relation: d'amitié*) friendship; (*: d'affaires*) relationship; (*: amoureuse*) affair; (*Culin, Phonétique*) liaison; **entrer/être en ~ avec** to get/be in contact with; **~ radio** radio contact; **~ (de transmission de données)** (*Inform*) data link

liane [ljan] *nf* creeper

liant, e [ljã, -ãt] *adj* sociable

liasse [ljas] *nf* wad, bundle

Liban [libã] *nm*: **le ~** (the) Lebanon

libanais (libane, -ɛz] *adj* Lebanese ▷ *nm/f*: **L~, e** Lebanese

libeller [libele] *vt* (*chèque, mandat*): **~ (au nom de)** to make out (to); (*lettre*) to word

libellule [libelyl] *nf* dragonfly

libéral, e, -aux [libeRal, -o] *adj, nm/f* liberal; **les professions ~es** liberal professions

libérer [libeRe] *vt* (*délivrer*) to free, liberate; (*: moralement, Psych*) to liberate; (*relâcher: prisonnier*) to release; (*: soldat*) to discharge; (*dégager: gaz, cran d'arrêt*) to release; (*Écon: échanges commerciaux*) to ease restrictions on; **se libérer** *vi* (*de rendez-vous*) to get out of previous engagements, try and be free; **~ qn de** (*liens, dette*) to free sb from; (*promesse*) to release sb from

liberté [libɛRte] *nf* freedom; (*loisir*) free time; **libertés** *nfpl* (*privautés*) liberties; **mettre/être en ~** to set/be free; **en ~ provisoire/surveillée/conditionnelle** on bail/probation/parole; **~ d'association** right of association; **~ de conscience** freedom of conscience; **~ du culte** freedom of worship; **~ d'esprit** independence of mind; **~ d'opinion** freedom of thought; **~ de la presse** freedom of the press; **~ de réunion** right to hold meetings; **~ syndicale** union rights *pl*; **~s individuelles** personal freedom *sg*; **~s publiques** civil rights

libraire [libRɛR] *nm/f* bookseller

librairie [libRɛRi] *nf* bookshop

libre [libR] *adj* free; (*route*) clear; (*place etc*) vacant, free; (*fig: propos, manières*) open; (*ligne*) not engaged; (*Scol*) non-state, private and Roman Catholic (*as opposed to "laïque"*); **~ (place)** free; **~ de qch/de faire** free from sth/to do; **vente ~** (*Comm*) unrestricted sale; **~ arbitre** free will; **~ concurrence** free-market economy; **~ entreprise** free enterprise

libre-échange [libReʃɑ̃ʒ] *nm* free trade

libre-service [libRəsɛRvis] *nm inv* (*magasin*) self-service store; (*restaurant*) self-service restaurant

Libye [libi] *nf*: **la ~** Libya

licence [lisɑ̃s] *nf* (*permis*) permit; (*diplôme*) (first) degree; *see note*; (*liberté*) liberty; (*poétique, orthographique*) licence (*Brit*), license (*US*); (*des mœurs*) licentiousness; **~ ès lettres/en droit** arts/law degree

LICENCE

The *licence générale* is a three-year university course undertaken after completing secondary education. The *licence professionnelle* is a one-year course open to students already in possession of a university-level qualification or having completed the first two years of a *licence générale*.

licencié, e [lisɑ̃sje] *nm/f (Scol):* **~ ès lettres/ en droit** ≈ Bachelor of Arts/Law, arts/law graduate; *(Sport)* permit-holder

licenciement [lisɑ̃simɑ̃] *nm* dismissal; redundancy; laying off *no pl*

licencier [lisɑ̃sje] *vt (renvoyer)* to dismiss; *(débaucher)* to make redundant; to lay off

licite [lisit] *adj* lawful

lie [li] *nf* dregs *pl*, sediment

lié, e [lje] *adj:* **très ~ avec** *(fig)* very friendly with *ou* close to; **~ par** *(serment, promesse)* bound by; **avoir partie ~e (avec qn)** to be involved (with sb)

Liechtenstein [liʃtɛnʃtajn] *nm:* **le ~** Liechtenstein

liège [ljɛʒ] *nm* cork

lien [ljɛ̃] *nm (corde, fig: affectif, culturel)* bond; *(rapport)* link, connection; *(analogie)* link; **~ de parenté** family tie; **~ hypertexte** hyperlink

lier [lje] *vt (attacher)* to tie up; *(joindre)* to link up; *(fig: unir, engager)* to bind; *(Culin)* to thicken; **~ qch à** *(attacher)* to tie sth to; *(associer)* to link sth to; **~ conversation (avec)** to strike up a conversation (with); **se ~ avec** to make friends with; **~ connaissance avec** to get to know

lierre [ljɛʀ] *nm* ivy

liesse [ljɛs] *nf:* **être en ~** to be jubilant

lieu, x [ljø] *nm* place; **lieux** *nmpl (locaux)* premises; *(endroit: d'un accident etc)* scene *sg*; **en ~ sûr** in a safe place; **en haut ~** in high places; **vider** *ou* **quitter les ~x** to leave the premises; **arriver/être sur les ~x** to arrive/ be on the scene; **en premier ~** in the first place; **en dernier ~** lastly; **avoir ~** to take place; **avoir ~ de faire** to have grounds *ou* good reason for doing; **tenir ~ de** to take the place of; *(servir de)* to serve as; **donner ~ à** to give rise to, give cause for; **au ~ de** instead of; **au ~ qu'il y aille** instead of him going; **~ commun** commonplace; **~ géométrique** locus; **~ de naissance** place of birth

lieu-dit *(pl* **lieux-dits)** [ljødi] *nm* locality

lieutenant [ljøtnɑ̃] *nm* lieutenant; **~ de vaisseau** *(Navig)* lieutenant

lièvre [ljɛvʀ] *nm* hare; *(coureur)* pacemaker; **lever un ~** *(fig)* to bring up a prickly subject

ligament [ligamɑ̃] *nm* ligament

ligne [liɲ] *nf (gén)* line; *(Transports: liaison)* service; *(: trajet)* route; *(silhouette)* figure; **garder la ~** to keep one's figure; **en ~** *(Inform)* online;

en ~ droite as the crow flies; **"à la ~"** "new paragraph"; **entrer en ~ de compte** to be taken into account; to come into it; **~ de but/ médiane** goal/halfway line; **~ d'arrivée/de départ** finishing/starting line; **~ de conduite** course of action; **~ directrice** guiding line; **~ fixe** *(Tél)* landline; **~ d'horizon** skyline; **~ de mire** line of sight; **~ de touche** touchline

ligné, e [liɲe] *adj:* **papier ~** ruled paper ▷ *nf (race, famille)* line, lineage; *(postérité)* descendants *pl*

ligoter [ligɔte] *vt* to tie up

ligue [lig] *nf* league

liguer [lige]: **se liguer** *vi* to form a league; **se ~ contre** *(fig)* to combine against

lilas [lila] *nm* lilac

limace [limas] *nf* slug

limande [limɑ̃d] *nf* dab

lime [lim] *nf (Tech)* file; *(Bot)* lime; **~ à ongles** nail file

limer [lime] *vt (bois, métal)* to file (down); *(ongles)* to file; *(fig: prix)* to pare down

limier [limje] *nm (Zool)* bloodhound; *(détective)* sleuth

limitation [limitasjɔ̃] *nf* limitation, restriction; **sans ~ de temps** with no time limit; **~ des naissances** birth control; **~ de vitesse** speed limit

limite [limit] *nf (de terrain)* boundary; *(partie ou point extrême)* limit; **dans la ~ de** within the limits of; **à la ~** *(au pire)* if the worst comes (*ou* came) to the worst; **sans ~s** *(bêtise, richesse, pouvoir)* limitless, boundless; **vitesse/charge ~** maximum speed/load; **cas ~** borderline case; **date ~** deadline; **date ~ de vente/ consommation** sell-by/best-before date; **prix ~** upper price limit; **d'âge** maximum age, age limit

limiter [limite] *vt (restreindre)* to limit, restrict; *(délimiter)* to border, form the boundary of; **se ~ (à qch/à faire)** *(personne)* to limit *ou* confine o.s. (to sth/to doing sth); **se ~ à** *(chose)* to be limited to

limitrophe [limitʀɔf] *adj* border *cpd;* **~ de** bordering on

limoger [limɔʒe] *vt* to dismiss

limon [limɔ̃] *nm* silt

limonade [limɔnad] *nf* lemonade *(Brit)*, (lemon) soda *(US)*

lin [lɛ̃] *nm (Bot)* flax; *(tissu, toile)* linen

linceul [lɛ̃sœl] *nm* shroud

linge [lɛ̃ʒ] *nm (serviettes etc)* linen; *(pièce de tissu)* cloth; *(aussi:* **~ de corps)** underwear; *(aussi:* **~ de toilette)** towel; *(lessive)* washing; **~ sale** dirty linen

lingerie [lɛ̃ʒʀi] *nf* lingerie, underwear

lingot [lɛ̃go] *nm* ingot

linguistique [lɛ̃gɥistik] *adj* linguistic ▷ *nf* linguistics *sg*

lion, ne [ljɔ̃, ljɔn] *nm/f* lion/lioness; *(signe):* **le L~** Leo, the Lion; **être du L~** to be Leo; **~ de mer** sea lion

lionceau, x [ljɔ̃so] nm lion cub
liqueur [likœʀ] nf liqueur
liquidation [likidasjɔ̃] nf (vente) sale, liquidation; (Comm) clearance (sale); **~ judiciaire** compulsory liquidation
liquide [likid] adj liquid ▷ nm liquid; (Comm): **en ~** in ready money ou cash; **je n'ai pas de ~** I haven't got any cash
liquider [likide] vt (société, biens, témoin gênant) to liquidate; (compte, problème) to settle; (Comm: articles) to clear, sell off
liquidités [likidite] nfpl (Comm) liquid assets
lire [liʀ] nf (monnaie) lira ▷ vt, vi to read; **~ qch à qn** to read sth (out) to sb
lis vb [li] voir **lire** ▷ nm [lis] = **lys**
Lisbonne [lizbɔn] n Lisbon
liseuse [lizøz] nf (Inform) e-reader
lisible [lizibl] adj legible; (digne d'être lu) readable
lisière [lizjɛʀ] nf (de forêt) edge; (de tissu) selvage
lisons [lizɔ̃] vb voir **lire**
lisse [lis] adj smooth
lisseur [li:sœʀ] nm straighteners pl
liste [list] nf list; (Inform) listing; **faire la ~ de** to list, make out a list of; **~ d'attente** waiting list; **~ civile** civil list; **~ électorale** electoral roll; **~ de mariage** wedding (present) list; **~ noire** hit list
listing [listiŋ] nm (Inform) printout; **qualité ~** draft quality
lit [li] nm (gén) bed; **petit ~, ~ à une place** single bed; **grand ~, ~ à deux places** double bed; **faire son ~** to make one's bed; **aller/se mettre au ~** to go to/get into bed; **chambre avec un grand ~** room with a double bed; **prendre le ~** to take to one's bed; **d'un premier ~** (Jur) of a first marriage; **~ de camp** camp bed (Brit), cot (US); **~ d'enfant** cot (Brit), crib (US)
literie [litʀi] nf bedding; (linge) bedding, bedclothes pl
litière [litjɛʀ] nf litter
litige [litiʒ] nm dispute; **en ~** in contention
litre [litʀ] nm litre; (récipient) litre measure
littéraire [liteʀɛʀ] adj literary ▷ nm/f arts student; **elle est très ~** she's very literary
littéral, e, -aux [liteʀal, -o] adj literal
littérature [liteʀatyʀ] nf literature
littoral, e, -aux [litɔʀal, -o] adj coastal ▷ nm coast
liturgie [lityʀʒi] nf liturgy
livide [livid] adj livid, pallid
livraison [livʀɛzɔ̃] nf delivery; **~ à domicile** home delivery (service)
livre [livʀ] nm book; (imprimerie etc): **le ~** the book industry ▷ nf (poids, monnaie) pound; **traduire qch à ~ ouvert** to translate sth off the cuff ou at sight; **~ blanc** official report (on war, natural disaster etc, prepared by independent body); **~ de bord** (Navig) logbook; **~ de comptes** account(s) book; **~ de cuisine** cookery book (Brit), cookbook; **~ de messe** mass ou prayer book; **~ d'or** visitors' book;

~ de poche paperback (small and cheap); **~ sterling** pound sterling; **~ verte** green pound
livré, e [livʀe] nf livery ▷ adj: **~ à** (l'anarchie etc) given over to; **~ à soi-même** left to oneself ou one's own devices
livrer [livʀe] vt (Comm) to deliver; (otage, coupable) to hand over; (secret, information) to give away; **se ~** (se confier) to confide in; (se rendre) to give o.s. up to; (s'abandonner à: débauche etc) to give o.s. up ou over to; (faire: pratiques, actes) to indulge in; (travail) to be engaged in, engage in; (: sport) to practise; (: enquête) to carry out; **~ bataille** to give battle
livret [livʀɛ] nm booklet; (d'opéra) libretto; **~ de caisse d'épargne** (savings) bank-book; **~ de famille** (official) family record book; **~ scolaire** (school) report book
livreur, -euse [livʀœʀ, -øz] nm/f delivery boy ou man/girl ou woman
local, e, -aux [lɔkal, -o] adj local ▷ nm (salle) premises ▷ nmpl premises
localiser [lɔkalize] vt (repérer) to locate, place; (limiter) to localize, confine
localité [lɔkalite] nf locality
locataire [lɔkatɛʀ] nm/f tenant; (de chambre) lodger
location [lɔkasjɔ̃] nf (par le locataire) renting; (par l'usager: de voiture etc) hiring (Brit), renting (US); (par le propriétaire) renting out, letting; hiring out (Brit); (de billets, places) booking; (bureau) booking office; **"~ de voitures"** "car hire (Brit) ou rental (US)"; **habiter en ~** to live in rented accommodation; **prendre une ~ (pour les vacances)** to rent a house etc (for the holidays)
locomotive [lɔkɔmɔtiv] nf locomotive, engine; (fig) pacesetter, pacemaker
locution [lɔkysjɔ̃] nf phrase
loge [lɔʒ] nf (Théât: d'artiste) dressing room; (: de spectateurs) box; (de concierge, franc-maçon) lodge
logement [lɔʒmɑ̃] nm flat (Brit), apartment (US); accommodation no pl (Brit), accommodations pl (US); (Pol, Admin): **le ~** housing; **chercher un ~** to look for a flat ou apartment, look for accommodation(s); **construire des ~s bon marché** to build cheap housing sg; **crise du ~** housing shortage; **~ de fonction** (Admin) company flat ou apartment, accommodation(s) provided with one's job
loger [lɔʒe] vt to accommodate ▷ vi to live; **être logé, nourri** to have board and lodging; **se loger: trouver à se ~** to find accommodation; **se ~ dans** (balle, flèche) to lodge itself in
logeur, -euse [lɔʒœʀ, -øz] nm/f landlord/landlady
logiciel [lɔʒisjɛl] nm (Inform) piece of software
logique [lɔʒik] adj logical ▷ nf logic; **c'est ~** it stands to reason

logis [lɔʒi] nm home; abode, dwelling

logo [logo], **logotype** [lɔgɔtip] nm logo

loi [lwa] nf law; **faire la ~** to lay down the law; **les ~s de la mode** (fig) to the dictates of fashion; **proposition de ~** (private member's) bill; **projet de ~** (government) bill

loin [lwɛ̃] adv far; (dans le temps: futur) a long way off; (: passé) a long time ago; **plus ~** further; **moins ~ (que)** not as far (as); **~ de** far from; **~ d'ici** a long way from here; **pas ~ de 100 euros** not far off 100 euros; **au ~** far off; **de ~** adv from a distance; (fig: de beaucoup) by far; **il vient de ~** he's come a long way; he comes from a long way away; **de ~ en ~** here and there; (de temps en temps) (every) now and then; **~ de là** (au contraire) far from it

lointain, e [lwɛ̃tɛ̃, -ɛn] adj faraway, distant; (dans le temps: passé) distant, far-off; (cause, parent) remote, distant ▷ nm: **dans le ~** in the distance

loir [lwaʀ] nm dormouse

Loire [lwaʀ] nf: **la ~** the Loire

loisir [lwazir] nm: **heures de ~** spare time; **loisirs** nmpl (temps libre) leisure sg; (activités) leisure activities; **avoir le ~ de faire** to have the time ou opportunity to do; **(tout) à ~** (en prenant son temps) at leisure; (autant qu'on le désire) at one's pleasure

londonien, ne [lɔ̃dɔnjɛ̃, -ɛn] adj London cpd, of London ▷ nm/f: **L~, ne** Londoner

Londres [lɔ̃dʀ] n London

long, longue [lɔ̃, lɔ̃g] adj long ▷ adv: **en savoir ~** to know a great deal ▷ nm: **de 3 m de ~** 3 m long, 3 m in length ▷ **à la longue** in the end; **faire ~ ~ feu** to fizzle out; **ne pas faire ~ feu** not to last long; **au ~ cours** (Navig) ocean cpd, ocean-going; **de longue date** adj long-standing; **longue durée** adj long-term; **de longue haleine** adj long-term; **être ~ à faire** to take a long time to do; **en ~** adv lengthwise, lengthways; **(tout) le ~ de** (all) along; **tout au ~ de** (année, vie) throughout; **de ~ en large** (marcher) to and fro, up and down; **en ~ et en large** (fig) in every detail

longer [lɔ̃ʒe] vt to go (ou walk ou drive) along(side); (mur, route) to border

longiligne [lɔ̃ʒiliɲ] adj long-limbed

longitude [lɔ̃ʒityd] nf longitude; **à 45° de ~ ouest** at 45° longitude west

longtemps [lɔ̃tɑ̃] adv (for) a long time, (for) long; **ça ne va pas durer ~** it won't last long; **avant ~** before long; **pour/pendant ~** for a long time; **je n'en ai pas pour ~** I shan't be long; **mettre ~ à faire** to take a long time to do; **il en a pour ~** he'll be a long time; **il y a ~ que je travaille** I have been working (for) a long time; **il n'y a pas ~ que je l'ai rencontré** it's not long since I met him

longue [lɔ̃g] adj f voir **long** ▷ nf: **à la ~** in the end

longuement [lɔ̃gmɑ̃] adv (longtemps: parler, regarder) for a long time; (en détail: expliquer, raconter) at length

longueur [lɔ̃gœʀ] nf length; **longueurs** nfpl (fig: d'un film etc) tedious parts; **sur une ~ de 10 km** for ou over 10 km; **en ~** adv lengthwise, lengthways; **tirer en ~** to drag on; **à ~ de journée** all day long; **d'une ~** (gagner) by a length; **~ d'onde** wavelength

longue-vue [lɔ̃gvy] nf telescope

look [luk] (fam) nm look, image

lopin [lɔpɛ̃] nm: **~ de terre** patch of land

loque [lɔk] nf (personne) wreck; **loques** nfpl (habits) rags; **être ou tomber en ~s** to be in rags

loquet [lɔkɛ] nm latch

lorgner [lɔʀɲe] vt to eye; (fig: convoiter) to have one's eye on

lors [lɔʀ]: **~ de** prép (au moment de) at the time of; (pendant) during; **~ même que** even though

lorsque [lɔʀsk] conj when, as

losange [lɔzɑ̃ʒ] nm diamond; (Géom) lozenge; **en ~** diamond-shaped

lot [lo] nm (part) share; (de loterie) prize; (fig: destin) fate, lot; (Comm, Inform) batch; **le gros ~** the jackpot; **~ de consolation** consolation prize

loterie [lɔtʀi] nf lottery; (tombola) raffle; **L~ nationale** French national lottery

loti, e [lɔti] adj: **bien/mal ~** well-/badly off, lucky/unlucky

lotion [losjɔ̃] nf lotion; **~ après rasage** after-shave (lotion); **~ capillaire** hair lotion

lotissement [lɔtismɑ̃] nm (groupe de maisons, d'immeubles) housing development; (parcelle) (building) plot, lot

loto [lɔto] nm lotto

lotte [lɔt] nf (Zool: de rivière) burbot; (: de mer) monkfish

louable [lwabl] adj (appartement, garage) rentable; (action, personne) praiseworthy, commendable

louange [lwɑ̃ʒ] nf: **à la ~ de** in praise of; **louanges** nfpl praise sg

loubar, loubard [lubaʀ] nm (fam) lout

louche [luʃ] adj shady, fishy, dubious ▷ nf ladle

loucher [luʃe] vi to squint; (fig): **~ sur** to have one's (beady) eye on

louer [lwe] vt (maison: propriétaire) to let, rent (out); (: locataire) to rent; (voiture etc: entreprise) to hire out (Brit), rent (out); (locataire) to hire (Brit), rent; (réserver) to book; (faire l'éloge de) to praise; **"à ~"** "to let" (Brit), "for rent" (US); **~ qn de** to praise sb for; **se ~ de** to congratulate o.s. on

loup [lu] nm wolf; (poisson) bass; (masque) (eye) mask; **jeune ~** young go-getter; **~ de mer** (marin) old seadog

loupe [lup] nf magnifying glass; **~ de noyer** burr walnut; **à la ~** (fig) in minute detail

louper [lupe] vt (fam: manquer) to miss; (: gâcher) to mess up, bungle; (examen) to flunk

lourd, e [luʀ, luʀd] adj heavy; (chaleur, temps) sultry; (fig: personne, style) heavy-handed
▷ adv: **peser ~** to be heavy; **~ de** (menaces) charged with; (conséquences) fraught with; **artillerie/industrie ~e** heavy artillery/industry

lourdaud, e [luʀdo, -od] adj clumsy

lourdement [luʀdəmɑ̃] adv heavily; **se tromper ~** to make a big mistake

lourdeur [luʀdœʀ] nf heaviness; **~ d'estomac** indigestion no pl

loutre [lutʀ] nf otter; (fourrure) otter skin

louveteau, X [luvto] nm (Zool) wolf-cub; (scout) cub (scout)

louvoyer [luvwaje] vi (Navig) to tack; (fig) to hedge, evade the issue

loyal, e, -aux [lwajal, -o] adj (fidèle) loyal, faithful; (fair-play) fair

loyauté [lwajote] nf loyalty, faithfulness; fairness

loyer [lwaje] nm rent; **~ de l'argent** interest rate

lu, e [ly] pp de **lire**

lubie [lybi] nf whim, craze

lubrifiant [lybʀifjɑ̃] nm lubricant

lubrifier [lybʀifje] vt to lubricate

lubrique [lybʀik] adj lecherous

lucarne [lykaʀn] nf skylight

lucide [lysid] adj (conscient) lucid; (accidenté) conscious; (perspicace) clear-headed

lucratif, -ive [lykʀatif, -iv] adj lucrative, profitable; **à but non ~** non profit-making

lueur [lɥœʀ] nf (chatoyante) glimmer no pl; (métallique, mouillée) gleam no pl; (rougeoyante) glow no pl; (pâle) (faint) light; (fig) spark; (: d'espérance) glimmer, gleam

luge [lyʒ] nf sledge (Brit), sled (US); **faire de la ~** to sledge (Brit), sled (US), toboggan

lugubre [lygybʀ] adj gloomy; dismal

 MOT-CLÉ

lui [lɥi] pp de **luire**
▷ pron **1** (objet indirect: mâle) (to) him; (: femelle) (to) her; (: chose, animal) (to) it; **je lui ai parlé** I have spoken to him (ou to her); **il lui a offert un cadeau** he gave him (ou her) a present; **je le lui ai donné** I gave it to him (ou her)
2 (après préposition, comparatif: personne) him; (: chose, animal) it; **elle est contente de lui** she is pleased with him; **je la connais mieux que lui** I know her better than he does; I know her better than him; **cette voiture est à lui** this car belongs to him, this is HIS car; **c'est à lui de jouer** it's his turn ou go
3 (sujet, forme emphatique) he; **lui, il est à Paris** HE is in Paris; **c'est lui qui l'a fait** HE did it

4 (objet, forme emphatique) him; **c'est lui que j'attends** I'm waiting for HIM
5: **lui-même** himself; itself

luire [lɥiʀ] vi (gén) to shine, gleam; (surface mouillée) to glisten; (reflets chauds, cuivrés) to glow

lumière [lymjɛʀ] nf light; **lumières** nfpl (d'une personne) knowledge sg, wisdom sg; **à la ~ de** by the light of; (fig: événements) in the light of; **fais de la ~** let's have some light, give us some light; **faire (toute) la ~ sur** (fig) to clarify (completely); **mettre en ~** (fig) to highlight; **~ du jour/soleil** day/sunlight

luminaire [lyminɛʀ] nm lamp, light

lumineux, -euse [lyminø, -øz] adj (émettant de la lumière) luminous; (éclairé) illuminated; (ciel, journée, couleur) bright; (relatif à la lumière: rayon etc) of light, light cpd; (fig: regard) radiant

lunatique [lynatik] adj whimsical, temperamental

lundi [lœ̃di] nm Monday; **on est ~** it's Monday; **le ~ 20 août** Monday 20th August; **il est venu ~** he came on Monday; **le(s) ~(s)** on Mondays; **à ~!** see you (on) Monday!; **~ de Pâques** Easter Monday; **~ de Pentecôte** Whit Monday (Brit)

lune [lyn] nf moon; **pleine/nouvelle ~** full/new moon; **être dans la ~** (distrait) to have one's head in the clouds; **~ de miel** honeymoon

lunette [lynɛt] nf: **~s** nfpl glasses, spectacles; (protectrices) goggles; **~ d'approche** telescope; **~ arrière** (Auto) rear window; **~s noires** dark glasses; **~s de soleil** sunglasses

lus etc [ly] vb voir **lire**

lustre [lystʀ] nm (de plafond) chandelier; (fig: éclat) lustre

lustrer [lystʀe] vt: **~ qch** (faire briller) to make sth shine; (user) to make sth shiny

lut [ly] vb voir **lire**

luth [lyt] nm lute

lutin [lytɛ̃] nm imp, goblin

lutte [lyt] nf (conflit) struggle; (Sport): **la ~** wrestling; **de haute ~** after a hard-fought struggle; **~ des classes** class struggle; **~ libre** (Sport) all-in wrestling

lutter [lyte] vi to fight, struggle; (Sport) to wrestle

luxe [lyks] nm luxury; **un ~ de** (détails, précautions) a wealth of; **de ~** adj luxury cpd

Luxembourg [lyksɑ̃buʀ] nm: **le ~** Luxembourg

luxembourgeois, e [lyksɑ̃buʀʒwa, -waz] adj of ou from Luxembourg ▷ nm/f: **L~, e** inhabitant ou native of Luxembourg

luxer [lykse] vt: **se ~ l'épaule** to dislocate one's shoulder

luxueux, -euse [lyksɥø, -øz] adj luxurious

luxure [lyksyʀ] nf lust

luxuriant, e [lyksyʀjɑ̃, -ɑ̃t] adj luxuriant, lush

lycée [lise] *nm* (state) secondary (*Brit*) *ou* high (*US*) school; **~ technique** technical secondary *ou* high school; *see note*

lycéen, ne [liseɛ̃, -ɛn] *nm/f* secondary school pupil
Lyon [ljɔ̃] *n* Lyons
lyophilisé, e [ljofilize] *adj* (*café*) freeze-dried
lyrique [liʀik] *adj* lyrical; (*Opéra*) lyric; **artiste ~** opera singer; **comédie ~** comic opera; **théâtre ~** opera house (*for light opera*)
lys [lis] *nm* lily

M, m [ɛm] *nm inv* M, m ▷ *abr* = **majeur; masculin; mètre; Monsieur;** (= *million*) M; **M comme Marcel** M for Mike
m' [m] *pron voir* **me**
ma [ma] *adj poss voir* **mon**
macaron [makaʀɔ̃] *nm* (*gâteau*) macaroon; (*insigne*) (round) badge
macaroni [makaʀɔni] *nm*, **macaronis** *nmpl* macaroni *sg*; **~(s) au gratin** macaroni cheese (*Brit*), macaroni and cheese (*US*)
Macédoine [masedwan] *nf* Macedonia
macédoine [masedwan] *nf*: **~ de fruits** fruit salad; **~ de légumes** mixed vegetables *pl*
macérer [maseʀe] *vi, vt* to macerate; (*dans du vinaigre*) to pickle
mâcher [mɑʃe] *vt* to chew; **ne pas ~ ses mots** not to mince one's words; **~ le travail à qn** (*fig*) to spoon-feed sb, do half sb's work for him
machin [maʃɛ̃] *nm* (*fam*) thingamajig, thing; (*personne*): **M~(e)** *nm(f)* what's-his-(*ou* her)-name
machinal, e, -aux [maʃinal, -o] *adj* mechanical, automatic
machinalement [maʃinalmɑ̃] *adv* mechanically, automatically
machination [maʃinasjɔ̃] *nf* scheming, frame-up
machine [maʃin] *nf* machine; (*locomotive; de navire etc*) engine; (*fig: rouages*) machinery; (*fam: personne*): **M~** what's-her-name; **faire ~ arrière** (*Navig*) to go astern; (*fig*) to back-

pedal; ~ **à laver/coudre/tricoter** washing/
sewing/knitting machine; ~ **à écrire**
typewriter; ~ **à sous** fruit machine; ~ **à
vapeur** steam engine

macho [matʃo] (*fam*) *nm* male chauvinist

mâchoire [maʃwaR] *nf* jaw; ~ **de frein** brake
shoe

mâchonner [maʃɔne] *vt* to chew (at)

maçon [masɔ̃] *nm* bricklayer; (*constructeur*)
builder

maçonnerie [masɔnRi] *nf* (*murs: de brique*)
brickwork; (: *de pierre*) masonry, stonework;
(*activité*) bricklaying; building; ~ **de béton**
concrete

maculer [makyle] *vt* to stain; (*Typo*) to
mackle

Madagascar [madagaskaR] *nf* Madagascar

Madame [madam] (*pl* **Mesdames**) [medam]
nf: ~ **X** Mrs X; **occupez-vous de** ~/**Monsieur/
Mademoiselle** please serve this lady/
gentleman/(young) lady; **bonjour** ~/
Monsieur/Mademoiselle good morning;
(*ton déférent*) good morning Madam/Sir/
Madam; (*le nom est connu*) good morning Mrs
X/Mr X/Miss X; ~/**Monsieur/Mademoiselle!**
(*pour appeler*) excuse me!; (*ton déférent*) Madam/
Sir/Miss!; ~/**Monsieur/Mademoiselle** (*sur
lettre*) Dear Madam/Sir/Madam; **chère** ~/**cher
Monsieur/chère Mademoiselle** Dear Mrs X/
Mr X/Miss X; ~ **la Directrice** the director; the
manageress; the head teacher; **Mesdames**
Ladies; **mesdames; mesdemoiselles,
messieurs** ladies and gentlemen

madeleine [madlɛn] *nf* madeleine, ≈ sponge
finger cake

Mademoiselle [madmwazɛl] (*pl
Mesdemoiselles*) [medmwazɛl] *nf* Miss; *voir
aussi* **Madame**

Madère [madɛR] *nf* Madeira ▷ *nm*: **madère**
Madeira (wine)

Madrid [madRid] *n* Madrid

magasin [magazɛ̃] *nm* (*boutique*) shop; (*entrepôt*)
warehouse; (*d'arme, appareil photo*) magazine;
en ~ (*Comm*) in stock; **faire les** ~**s** to go (a)round
the shops, do the shops; ~ **d'alimentation**
grocer's (shop) (*Brit*), grocery store (*US*)

⬤ **MAGASINS**
⬤
⬤ French shops are usually open from 9am
⬤ to noon and from 2pm to 7pm. Most
⬤ shops are closed on Sunday and some do
⬤ not open on Monday. In bigger towns and
⬤ shopping centres, most shops are open
⬤ throughout the day.

magazine [magazin] *nm* magazine

Maghreb [magRɛb] *nm*: **le** ~ the Maghreb,
North(-West) Africa

maghrébin, e [magRebɛ̃, -in] *adj* of ou from
the Maghreb, North African ▷ *nm/f*: **M**~, **e**
North African, Maghrebi

magicien, ne [maʒisjɛ̃, -ɛn] *nm/f* magician

magie [maʒi] *nf* magic; ~ **noire** black magic

magique [maʒik] *adj* (*occulte*) magic; (*fig*)
magical

magistral, e, -aux [maʒistRal, -o] *adj* (*œuvre,
adresse*) masterly; (*ton*) authoritative; (*gifle
etc*) sound, resounding; (*ex cathedra*):
enseignement ~ lecturing, lectures *pl*;
cours ~ lecture

magistrat [maʒistRa] *nm* magistrate

magnat [magna] *nm* tycoon, magnate

magnétique [maɲetik] *adj* magnetic

magnétiser [maɲetize] *vt* to magnetize;
(*fig*) to mesmerize, hypnotize

magnétophone [maɲetɔfɔn] *nm* tape
recorder; ~ **à cassettes** cassette recorder

magnétoscope [maɲetɔskɔp] *nm*: ~ (**à
cassette**) video (recorder)

magnifique [maɲifik] *adj* magnificent

magot [mago] *nm* (*argent*) pile (of money);
(*économies*) nest egg

magouille [maguj] *nf* (*fam*) scheming

magret [magRɛ] *nm*: ~ **de canard** duck breast

mai [mɛ] *nm* May; *see note*; *voir aussi* **juillet**

⬤ **LE PREMIER MAI**
⬤
⬤ *Le premier mai* is a public holiday in France
⬤ and commemorates the trades union
⬤ demonstrations in the United States in
⬤ 1886 when workers demanded the right
⬤ to an eight-hour working day. Sprigs of
⬤ lily of the valley are traditionally
⬤ exchanged. *Le 8 mai* is also a public
⬤ holiday and commemorates the
⬤ surrender of the German army to
⬤ Eisenhower on 7 May, 1945. It is marked
⬤ by parades of ex-servicemen and
⬤ ex-servicewomen in most towns. The
⬤ social upheavals of May and June 1968,
⬤ with their student demonstrations,
⬤ workers' strikes and general rioting, are
⬤ usually referred to as "les événements de
⬤ mai 68". De Gaulle's Government
⬤ survived, but reforms in education and a
⬤ move towards decentralization ensued.

maigre [mɛgR] *adj* (very) thin, skinny;
(*viande*) lean; (*fromage*) low-fat; (*végétation*)
thin, sparse; (*fig*) poor, meagre, skimpy
▷ *adv*: **faire** ~ not to eat meat; **jours** ~**s** days of
abstinence, fish days

maigreur [mɛgRœR] *nf* thinness

maigrir [megRiR] *vi* to get thinner, lose
weight ▷ *vt*: ~ **qn** (*vêtement*) to make sb look
slim(mer); ~ **de 2 kilos** to lose 2 kilos

mail [mɛl] *nm* email

maille [maj] *nf* (*boucle*) stitch; (*ouverture*) hole
(in the mesh); **avoir** ~ **à partir avec qn** to
have a brush with sb; ~ **à l'endroit/à
l'envers** knit one/purl one; (*boucle*) plain/
purl stitch

maillet [majɛ] nm mallet

maillon [majɔ̃] nm link

maillot [majo] nm (aussi: ~ **de corps**) vest; (de danseur) leotard; (de sportif) jersey; ~ **de bain** swimming ou bathing (Brit) costume, swimsuit; (d'homme) (swimming ou bathing (Brit)) trunks pl; ~ **deux pièces** two-piece swimsuit, bikini; ~ **jaune** yellow jersey

main [mɛ̃] nf hand; **la ~ dans la ~** hand in hand; **à deux ~s** with both hands; **à une ~** with one hand; **à la ~** (tenir, avoir) in one's hand; (faire, tricoter etc) by hand; **se donner la ~** to hold hands; **donner** ou **tendre la ~ à qn** to hold out one's hand to sb; **se serrer la ~** to shake hands; **serrer la ~ à qn** to shake hands with sb; **sous la ~** to ou at hand; **haut les ~s!** hands up!; **à ~ levée** (Art) freehand; **à ~s levées** (voter) with a show of hands; **attaque à ~ armée** armed attack; **à droite/gauche** to the right/left; **à remettre en ~s propres** to be delivered personally; **de première ~** (renseignement) first-hand; (Comm: voiture etc) with only one previous owner; **faire ~ basse sur** to help o.s. to; **mettre la dernière ~ à** to put the finishing touches to; **mettre la ~ à la pâte** (fig) to lend a hand; **avoir/passer la ~** (Cartes) to lead/hand over the lead; **s'en laver les ~s** (fig) to wash one's hands of it; **se faire/perdre la ~** to get one's hand in/lose one's touch; **avoir qch bien en ~** to have got the hang of sth; **en un tour de ~** (fig) in the twinkling of an eye; **~ courante** handrail

main-d'œuvre [mɛ̃dœvʀ] nf manpower, labour (Brit), labor (US)

main-forte [mɛ̃fɔʀt] nf: **prêter ~ à qn** to come to sb's assistance

mainmise [mɛ̃miz] nf seizure; (fig): **avoir la ~ sur** to have a grip on stranglehold on

mains-libres [mɛ̃libʀ] adj inv (téléphone, kit) hands-free

maint, e [mɛ̃, mɛ̃t] adj many a; **~s** many; **à ~es reprises** time and (time) again

maintenant [mɛ̃tnɑ̃] adv now; (actuellement) nowadays

maintenir [mɛ̃tniʀ] vt (retenir, soutenir) to support; (contenir: foule etc) to keep in check, hold back; (conserver) to maintain, uphold; (affirmer) to maintain; **se maintenir** vi (paix, temps) to hold; (prix) to keep steady; (préjugé) to persist; (malade) to remain stable

maintien [mɛ̃tjɛ̃] nm maintaining, upholding; (attitude) bearing; **~ de l'ordre** maintenance of law and order

maire [mɛʀ] nm mayor

mairie [meʀi] nf (bâtiment) town hall; (administration) town council

mais [mɛ] conj but; **~ non!** of course not!; **~ enfin** but after all; (indignation) look here!; **~ encore?** is that all?

maïs [mais] nm maize (Brit), corn (US)

maison [mɛzɔ̃] nf (bâtiment) house; (chez-soi) home; (Comm) firm; (famille): **ami de la ~** friend of the family ▷ adj inv (Culin) home-made; (: au restaurant) made by the chef; (Comm) in-house, own; (fam) first-rate; **à la ~** at home; (direction) home; **~ d'arrêt** (short-stay) prison; **~ centrale** prison; **~ close** brothel; **~ de correction** ≈ remand home (Brit), ≈ reformatory (US); **~ de la culture** ≈ arts centre; **~ des jeunes** ≈ youth club; **~ mère** parent company; **~ de passe** = maison close; **~ de repos** convalescent home; **~ de retraite** old people's home; **~ de santé** home for mentally ill people

maisonnée [mɛzɔne] nf household, family

maisonnette [mɛzɔnɛt] nf small house

maître, -esse [mɛtʀ, mɛtʀɛs] nm/f master/ mistress; (Scol) teacher, schoolmaster(-mistress) ▷ nm (peintre etc) master; (titre): **M~ (M^e)** Maître, term of address for lawyers etc ▷ nf (amante) mistress ▷ adj (principal, essentiel) main; **maison de ~** family seat; **être ~ de** (soi-même, situation) to be in control of; **se rendre ~ de** (pays, ville) to gain control of; (situation, incendie) to bring under control; **être passé ~ dans l'art de** to be a (past) master in the art of; **une maîtresse femme** a forceful woman; **~ d'armes** fencing master; **~ auxiliaire (MA)** (Scol) temporary teacher; **~ chanteur** blackmailer; **~ de chapelle** choirmaster; **~ de conférences** ≈ senior lecturer (Brit), ≈ assistant professor (US); **~/maîtresse d'école** teacher, schoolmaster/-mistress; **~ d'hôtel** (domestique) butler; (d'hôtel) head waiter; **~ de maison** host; **~ nageur** lifeguard; **~ d'œuvre** (Constr) project manager; **~ d'ouvrage** (Constr) client; **~ queux** chef; **maîtresse de maison** hostess; (ménagère) housewife

maîtrise [mɛtʀiz] nf (aussi: ~ **de soi**) self-control, self-possession; (habileté) skill, mastery; (suprématie) mastery, command; (diplôme) ≈ master's degree; see note; (chefs d'équipe) supervisory staff

● **MAÎTRISE**
●
● The maîtrise was formerly a French
● degree which was awarded to
● university students if they successfully
● completed two more years' study after
● the "DEUG".

maîtriser [mɛtʀize] vt (cheval, incendie) to (bring under) control; (sujet) to master; (émotion) to control, master; **se maîtriser** to control o.s.

majestueux, -euse [maʒɛstɥø, -øz] adj majestic

majeur, e [maʒœʀ] adj (important) major; (Jur) of age; (fig) adult ▷ nm/f (Jur) person who has come of age ou attained his (ou her) majority

▷ *nm* (*doigt*) middle finger; **en ~e partie** for the most part; **la ~e partie de** most of

majoration [maʒɔrasjɔ̃] *nf* increase

majorer [maʒɔre] *vt* to increase

majoritaire [maʒɔritɛr] *adj* majority *cpd*; **système/scrutin ~** majority system/ballot

majorité [maʒɔrite] *nf* (*gén*) majority; (*parti*) party in power; **en ~** (*composé etc*) mainly; **avoir la ~** to have the majority

majuscule [maʒyskyl] *adj*, *nf*: **(lettre) ~** capital (letter)

mal, maux [mal, mo] *nm* (*opposé au bien*) evil; (*tort, dommage*) harm; (*douleur physique*) pain, ache; (*maladie*) illness, sickness *no pl*; (*difficulté, peine*) trouble; (*souffrance morale*) pain ▷ *adv* badly: **c'est ~ (de faire)** it's bad *ou* wrong (to do); **être ~ (à l'aise)** to be uncomfortable; **être ~ avec qn** to be on bad terms with sb; **être au plus ~** (*malade*) to be very bad; (*brouillé*) to be at daggers drawn; **il comprend ~** he has difficulty in understanding; **il a ~ compris** he misunderstood; **se sentir** *ou* **se trouver ~** to feel ill *ou* unwell; **~ tourner** to go wrong; **dire/penser du ~ de** to speak/think ill of; **ne vouloir du ~ à personne** to wish nobody any ill; **il n'a rien fait de ~** he has done nothing wrong; **avoir du ~ à faire qch** to have trouble doing sth; **se donner du ~ pour faire qch** to go to a lot of trouble to do sth; **ne voir aucun ~ à** to see no harm in, see nothing wrong in; **craignant ~ faire** fearing he *etc* was doing the wrong thing; **sans penser** *ou* **songer à ~** without meaning any harm; **faire du ~ à qn** to hurt sb; to harm sb; **se faire ~** to hurt o.s.; **se faire ~ au pied** to hurt one's foot; **ça fait ~** it hurts; **j'ai ~ (ici)** it hurts (here); **j'ai ~ au dos** my back aches, I've got a pain in my back; **avoir ~ à la tête/à la gorge** to have a headache/a sore throat; **avoir ~ aux dents/à l'oreille** to have toothache/earache; **avoir le ~ de l'air** to be airsick; **avoir le ~ du pays** to be homesick; **~ de mer** seasickness; **~ de la route** carsickness; **~ en point** *adj inv* in a bad state; **maux de ventre** stomach ache *sg*; *voir aussi* **cœur**

malade [malad] *adj* ill, sick; (*poitrine, jambe*) bad; (*plante*) diseased; (*fig: entreprise, monde*) ailing ▷ *nm/f* invalid, sick person; (*à l'hôpital etc*) patient; **tomber ~** to fall ill; **être ~ du cœur** to have heart trouble *ou* a bad heart; **grand ~** seriously ill person; **~ mental** mentally ill person

maladie [maladi] *nf* (*spécifique*) disease, illness; (*mauvaise santé*) illness, sickness; (*fig: manie*) mania; **être rongé par la ~** to be wasting away (through illness); **~ d'Alzheimer** Alzheimer's disease; **~ de peau** skin disease

maladif, -ive [maladif, -iv] *adj* sickly; (*curiosité, besoin*) pathological

maladresse [maladrɛs] *nf* clumsiness *no pl*; (*gaffe*) blunder

maladroit, e [maladrwa, -wat] *adj* clumsy

malaise [malɛz] *nm* (*Méd*) feeling of faintness; feeling of discomfort; (*fig*) uneasiness, malaise; **avoir un ~** to feel faint *ou* dizzy

malaisé, e [maleze] *adj* difficult

Malaisie [malɛzi] *nf*: **la ~** Malaysia; **la péninsule de ~** the Malay Peninsula

malaria [malarja] *nf* malaria

malaxer [malakse] *vt* (*pétrir*) to knead; (*mêler*) to mix

malbouffe [malbuf] *nf* (*fam*): **la ~** junk food

malchance [malʃɑ̃s] *nf* misfortune, ill luck *no pl*; **par ~** unfortunately; **quelle ~!** what bad luck!

malchanceux, -euse [malʃɑ̃sø, -øz] *adj* unlucky

mâle [mɑl] *adj* (*Élec, Tech*) male; (*viril: voix, traits*) manly ▷ *nm* male

malédiction [malediksjɔ̃] *nf* curse

malencontreux, -euse [malɑ̃kɔ̃trø, -øz] *adj* unfortunate, untoward

malentendant, e [malɑ̃tɑ̃dɑ̃, -ɑ̃t] *nm/f*: **les ~s** the hard of hearing

malentendu [malɑ̃tɑ̃dy] *nm* misunderstanding; **il y a eu un ~** there's been a misunderstanding

malfaçon [malfasɔ̃] *nf* fault

malfaisant, e [malfəzɑ̃, -ɑ̃t] *adj* evil, harmful

malfaiteur [malfɛtœr] *nm* lawbreaker, criminal; (*voleur*) burglar, thief

malfamé, e [malfame] *adj* disreputable, of ill repute

malgache [malgaʃ] *adj* Malagasy, Madagascan ▷ *nm* (*Ling*) Malagasy ▷ *nm/f*: **M~** Malagasy, Madagascan

malgré [malgre] *prép* in spite of, despite; **~ tout** *adv* in spite of everything

malhabile [malabil] *adj* clumsy

malheur [malœr] *nm* (*situation*) adversity, misfortune; (*événement*) misfortune; (: *plus fort*) disaster, tragedy; **par ~** unfortunately; **quel ~!** what a shame *ou* pity!; **faire un ~** (*fam: un éclat*) to do something desperate; (: *avoir du succès*) to be a smash hit

malheureusement [malœrøzmɑ̃] *adv* unfortunately

malheureux, -euse [malœrø, -øz] *adj* (*triste*) unhappy, miserable; (*infortuné, regrettable*) unfortunate; (*malchanceux*) unlucky; (*insignifiant*) wretched ▷ *nm/f* (*infortuné, misérable*) poor soul; (*indigent, miséreux*) unfortunate creature; **les ~** the destitute; **avoir la main malheureuse** (*au jeu*) to be unlucky; (*tout casser*) to be ham-fisted

malhonnête [malɔnɛt] *adj* dishonest

malhonnêteté [malɔnɛtte] *nf* dishonesty; rudeness *no pl*

malice [malis] *nf* mischievousness; (*méchanceté*): **par ~** out of malice *ou* spite; **sans ~** guileless

malicieux, -euse [malisjø, -øz] *adj*
mischievous

malin, -igne [malɛ̃, -iɲ] (*f gén* **maline**) *adj*
(*futé*) smart, shrewd; (*: sourire*) knowing;
(*Méd, influence*) malignant; **faire le ~** to show
off; **éprouver un ~ plaisir à** to take
malicious pleasure in

malingre [malɛ̃gʀ] *adj* puny

malle [mal] *nf* trunk; (*Auto*): **~ (arrière)** boot
(*Brit*), trunk (*US*)

mallette [malɛt] *nf* (*valise*) (small) suitcase;
(*aussi*: **~ de voyage**) overnight case; (*pour
documents*) attaché case

malmener [malməne] *vt* to manhandle; (*fig*)
to give a rough ride to

malodorant, e [malɔdɔʀɑ̃, -ɑ̃t] *adj* foul-
smelling

malotru [malɔtʀy] *nm* lout, boor

malpoli, e [malpɔli] *nm/f* rude individual
▷ *adj* impolite

malpropre [malpʀɔpʀ] *adj* (*personne, vêtement*)
dirty; (*travail, casserole*) slovenly; (*histoire, plaisanterie*)
unsavoury (*Brit*), unsavory (*US*), smutty;
(*malhonnête*) dishonest

malsain, e [malsɛ̃, -ɛn] *adj* unhealthy

malt [malt] *nm* malt; **pur ~** (*whisky*) malt
(whisky)

Malte [malt] *nf* Malta

maltraiter [maltʀete] *vt* (*brutaliser*) to
manhandle, ill-treat; (*critiquer, éreinter*) to
slate (*Brit*), roast

malveillance [malvɛjɑ̃s] *nf* (*animosité*) ill
will; (*intention de nuire*) malevolence; (*Jur*)
malicious intent *no pl*

malversation [malvɛʀsasjɔ̃] *nf*
embezzlement, misappropriation (of funds)

mal-vivre [malvivʀ] *nm inv* malaise

maman [mamɑ̃] *nf* mum(my) (*Brit*), mom (*US*)

mamelle [mamɛl] *nf* teat

mamelon [mamlɔ̃] *nm* (*Anat*) nipple; (*colline*)
knoll, hillock

mamie [mami] *nf* (*fam*) granny

mammifère [mamifɛʀ] *nm* mammal

mammouth [mamut] *nm* mammoth

manche [mɑ̃ʃ] *nf* (*de vêtement*) sleeve; (*d'un jeu,
tournoi*) round; (*Géo*): **la M~** the (English)
Channel ▷ *nm* (*d'outil, casserole*) handle; (*de
pelle, pioche etc*) shaft; (*de violon, guitare*) neck;
(*fam*) clumsy oaf; **faire la ~** to pass the hat;
~ à air (*Aviat*) wind-sock; **à ~s courtes/
longues** short-/long-sleeved; **~ à balai** *nm*
broomstick; (*Aviat, Inform*) joystick *m inv*

manchette [mɑ̃ʃɛt] *nf* (*de chemise*) cuff; (*coup*)
forearm blow; (*titre*) headline

manchot [mɑ̃ʃo] *nm* one-armed man;
armless man; (*Zool*) penguin

mandarine [mɑ̃daʀin] *nf* mandarin
(orange), tangerine

mandat [mɑ̃da] *nm* (*postal*) postal *ou* money
order; (*d'un député etc*) mandate; (*procuration*)
power of attorney, proxy; (*Police*) warrant;
~ d'amener summons *sg*; **~ d'arrêt** warrant

for arrest; **~ de dépôt** committal order; **~ de
perquisition** (*Police*) search warrant

mandataire [mɑ̃datɛʀ] *nm/f* (*représentant,
délégué*) representative; (*Jur*) proxy

manège [manɛʒ] *nm* riding school; (*à la foire*)
roundabout (*Brit*), merry-go-round; (*fig*)
game, ploy; **faire un tour de ~** to go for a ride
on a *ou* the roundabout *etc*; **~ (de chevaux de
bois*) roundabout (*Brit*), merry-go-round

manette [manɛt] *nf* lever, tap; **~ de jeu**
(*Inform*) joystick

mangeable [mɑ̃ʒabl] *adj* edible, eatable

mangeoire [mɑ̃ʒwaʀ] *nf* trough, manger

manger [mɑ̃ʒe] *vt* to eat; (*ronger: rouille etc*) to
eat into *ou* away; (*utiliser, consommer*) to eat up
▷ *vi* to eat; **donner à ~ à** (*enfant*) to feed

mangeur, -euse [mɑ̃ʒœʀ, -øz] *nm/f* eater

mangue [mɑ̃g] *nf* mango

maniable [manjabl] *adj* (*outil*) handy; (*voiture,
voilier*) easy to handle; manoeuvrable (*Brit*),
maneuverable (*US*); (*fig: personne*) easily
influenced, manipulable

maniaque [manjak] *adj* (*pointilleux,
méticuleux*) finicky, fussy; (*atteint de manie*)
suffering from a mania ▷ *nm/f* (*méticuleux*)
fusspot; (*fou*) maniac

manie [mani] *nf* mania; (*tic*) odd habit; **avoir
la ~ de** to be obsessive about

manier [manje] *vt* to handle; **se manier** *vi*
(*fam*) to get a move on

maniéré, e [manjeʀe] *adj* affected

manière [manjɛʀ] *nf* (*façon*) way, manner;
(*genre, style*) style; **manières** *nfpl* (*attitude*)
manners; (*chichis*) fuss *sg*; **de ~ à** so as to; **de
telle ~ que** in such a way that; **de cette ~** in
this way *ou* manner; **d'une ~ générale**
generally speaking, as a general rule; **de
toute ~** in any case; **d'une ~ certaine** in a
(certain) way; **faire des ~s** to put on airs;
employer la ~ forte to use strong-arm
tactics

manif [manif] *nf* (*manifestation*) demo

manifestant, e [manifɛstɑ̃, -ɑ̃t] *nm/f*
demonstrator

manifestation [manifɛstasjɔ̃] *nf* (*de joie,
mécontentement*) expression, demonstration;
(*symptôme*) outward sign; (*fête etc*) event; (*Pol*)
demonstration

manifeste [manifɛst] *adj* obvious, evident
▷ *nm* manifesto

manifester [manifɛste] *vt* (*volonté, intentions*)
to show, indicate; (*joie, peur*) to express, show
▷ *vi* (*Pol*) to demonstrate; **se manifester** *vi*
(*émotion*) to show *ou* express itself; (*difficultés*)
to arise; (*symptômes*) to appear; (*témoin etc*) to
come forward

manigance [manigɑ̃s] *nf* scheme

manigancer [manigɑ̃se] *vt* to plot, devise

manipulation [manipylasjɔ̃] *nf* handling;
(*Pol, génétique*) manipulation

manipuler [manipyle] *vt* to handle; (*fig*) to
manipulate

m

manivelle [manivɛl] nf crank

mannequin [mankɛ̃] nm (*Couture*) dummy; (*Mode*) model

manœuvre [manœvR] nf (*gén*) manoeuvre (*Brit*), maneuver (*US*) ▷ nm (*ouvrier*) labourer (*Brit*), laborer (*US*)

manœuvrer [manœvRe] vt to manoeuvre (*Brit*), maneuver (*US*); (*levier, machine*) to operate; (*personne*) to manipulate ▷ vi to manoeuvre ou maneuver

manoir [manwaR] nm manor ou country house

manque [mɑ̃k] nm (*insuffisance*): ~ **de** lack of; (*vide*) emptiness, gap; (*Méd*) withdrawal; **manques** nmpl (*lacunes*) faults, defects; **par ~ de** for want of; **~ à gagner** loss of profit ou earnings; **être en état de ~** to suffer withdrawal symptoms

manqué [mɑ̃ke] adj failed; **garçon ~** tomboy

manquer [mɑ̃ke] vi (*faire défaut*) to be lacking; (*être absent*) to be missing; (*échouer*) to fail ▷ vt to miss ▷ vb impers: **il (nous) manque encore 10 euros** we are still 10 euros short; **il manque des pages (au livre)** there are some pages missing ou some pages are missing (from the book); **l'argent qui leur manque** the money they need ou are short of; **le pied/la voix lui manqua** he missed his footing/his voice failed him; **~ à qn** (*absent etc*): **il/cela me manque** I miss him/that; **~ à** vt (*règles etc*) to be in breach of, fail to observe; **~ de** vt to lack; (*Comm*) to be out of (stock of); **ne pas ~ de faire, je ne ~ai pas de le lui dire** I'll be sure to tell him; **~ (de) faire**, **il a manqué (de) se tuer** he very nearly got killed; **il ne manquerait plus qu'il fasse** all we need now is for him to do; **je n'y manquerai pas** leave it to me, I'll definitely do it

mansarde [mɑ̃saRd] nf attic

mansardé, e [mɑ̃saRde] adj: **chambre ~e** attic room

manteau, x [mɑ̃to] nm coat; **~ de cheminée** mantelpiece; **sous le ~** (*fig*) under cover

manucure [manykyR] nf manicurist

manuel, le [manɥɛl] adj manual ▷ nm/f manually gifted pupil (*as opposed to intellectually gifted*) ▷ nm (*ouvrage*) manual, handbook

manufacture [manyfaktyR] nf (*établissement*) factory; (*fabrication*) manufacture

manufacturé, e [manyfaktyRe] adj manufactured

manuscrit, e [manyskRi, -it] adj handwritten ▷ nm manuscript

manutention [manytɑ̃sjɔ̃] nf (*Comm*) handling; (*local*) storehouse

mappemonde [mapmɔ̃d] nf (*plane*) map of the world; (*sphère*) globe

maquereau, x [makRo] nm (*Zool*) mackerel inv; (*fam: proxénète*) pimp

maquette [makɛt] nf (*d'un décor, bâtiment, véhicule*) (scale) model; (*Typo*) mockup; (: *d'une page illustrée, affiche*) paste-up; (: *prêt à la reproduction*) artwork

maquillage [makijaʒ] nm making up; faking; (*produits*) make-up

maquiller [makije] vt (*personne, visage*) to make up; (*truquer: passeport, statistique*) to fake; (: *voiture volée*) to do over (respray etc); **se maquiller** vi to make o.s. up

maquis [maki] nm (*Géo*) scrub; (*fig*) tangle; (*Mil*) maquis, underground fighting no pl

maraîcher, -ère [maReʃe, maReʃɛR] adj: **cultures maraîchères** market gardening sg ▷ nm/f market gardener

marais [maRɛ] nm marsh, swamp; **~ salant** saltworks

marasme [maRasm] nm (*Pol, Écon*) stagnation, sluggishness; (*accablement*) dejection, depression

marathon [maRatɔ̃] nm marathon

maraudeur, -euse [maRodœR, -øz] nm/f marauder; prowler

marbre [maRbR] nm (*pierre, statue*) marble; (*d'une table, commode*) marble top; (*Typo*) stone, bed; **rester de ~** to remain stonily indifferent

marc [maR] nm (*de raisin, pommes*) marc; **~ de café** coffee grounds pl ou dregs pl

marchand, e [maRʃɑ̃, -ɑ̃d] nm/f shopkeeper, tradesman(-woman); (*au marché*) stallholder; (*spécifique*): **~ de cycles/tapis** bicycle/carpet dealer; **~ de charbon/vins** coal/wine merchant ▷ adj: **prix/valeur ~(e)** market price/value; **qualité ~e** standard quality; **~ en gros/au détail** wholesaler/retailer; **~ de biens** real estate agent; **~ de canons** (*péj*) arms dealer; **~ de couleurs** ironmonger (*Brit*), hardware dealer (*US*); **~/e de fruits** fruiterer (*Brit*), fruit seller (*US*); **~/e de journaux** newsagent; **~/e de légumes** greengrocer (*Brit*), produce dealer (*US*); **~/e de poisson** fishmonger (*Brit*), fish seller (*US*); **~/e de(s) quatre-saisons** costermonger (*Brit*), street vendor (selling fresh fruit and vegetables); **~ de sable** (*fig*) sandman; **~ de tableaux** art dealer

marchander [maRʃɑ̃de] vt (*article*) to bargain ou haggle over; (*éloges*) to be sparing with ▷ vi to bargain, haggle

marchandise [maRʃɑ̃diz] nf goods pl, merchandise no pl

marche [maRʃ] nf (*d'escalier*) step; (*activité*) walking; (*promenade, trajet, allure*) walk; (*démarche*) walk, gait; (*Mil etc, Mus*) march; (*fonctionnement*) running; (*progression*) progress; (*des événements*) course; **à une heure de ~** an hour's walk (away); **ouvrir/fermer la ~** to lead the way/bring up the rear; **dans le sens de la ~** (*Rail*) facing the engine; **en ~** (*monter etc*) while the vehicle is moving ou in motion; **mettre en ~** to start; **remettre qch en ~** to set ou start sth going again; **se mettre en ~** (*personne*) to get moving; (*machine*) to start; **être en état de ~** to be in working order; **~ arrière** (*Auto*) reverse (gear);

faire ~ arrière (*Auto*) to reverse; (*fig*) to backtrack, back-pedal; **~ à suivre** (correct) procedure; (*sur notice*) (step by step) instructions *pl*

marché [maʀʃe] *nm* (*lieu, Comm, Écon*) market; (*ville*) trading centre; (*transaction*) bargain, deal; **par-dessus le ~** into the bargain; **faire son ~** to do one's shopping; **mettre le ~ en main à qn** to tell sb to take it or leave it; **~ au comptant** (*Bourse*) spot market; **~ aux fleurs** flower market; **~ noir** black market; **faire du ~ noir** to buy and sell on the black market; **~ aux puces** flea market; **~ à terme** (*Bourse*) forward market; **~ du travail** labour market

marchepied [maʀʃəpje] *nm* (*Rail*) step; (*Auto*) running board; (*fig*) stepping stone

marcher [maʀʃe] *vi* to walk; (*Mil*) to march; (*aller: voiture, train, affaires*) to go; (*prospérer*) to go well; (*fonctionner*) to work, run; (*fam: consentir*) to go along, agree; (: *croire naïvement*) to be taken in; **~ sur** to walk on; (*mettre le pied sur*) to step on ou in; (*Mil*) to march upon; **~ dans** (*herbe etc*) to walk in ou on; (*flaque*) to step in; **faire ~ qn** (*pour rire*) to pull sb's leg; (*pour tromper*) to lead sb up the garden path

marcheur, -euse [maʀʃœʀ, -øz] *nm/f* walker

mardi [maʀdi] *nm* Tuesday; **M~ gras** Shrove Tuesday; *voir aussi* **lundi**

mare [maʀ] *nf* pond; (*flaque*) pool; **~ de sang** pool of blood

marécage [maʀekaʒ] *nm* marsh, swamp

marécageux, -euse [maʀekaʒø, -øz] *adj* marshy, swampy

maréchal, -aux [maʀeʃal, -o] *nm* marshal; **~ des logis** (*Mil*) sergeant

maréchal-ferrant (*pl* **maréchaux-ferrants**) [maʀeʃalferɑ̃, maʀeʃo-] *nm* blacksmith

marée [maʀe] *nf* tide; (*poissons*) fresh (sea) fish; **~ haute/basse** high/low tide; **~ montante/descendante** rising/ebb tide; **~ noire** oil slick

marelle [maʀɛl] *nf*: **(jouer à) la ~** (to play) hopscotch

margarine [maʀgaʀin] *nf* margarine

marge [maʀʒ] *nf* margin; **en ~** in the margin; **en ~ de** (*fig*) on the fringe of; (*en dehors de*) cut off from; (*qui se rapporte à*) connected with; **~ bénéficiaire** profit margin, mark-up; **~ de sécurité** safety margin

marginal, e, -aux [maʀʒinal, -o] *adj* marginal ▷ *nm/f* (*original*) eccentric; (*déshérité*) dropout

marguerite [maʀgøʀit] *nf* marguerite, (*oxeye*) daisy; (*d'imprimante*) daisy-wheel

mari [maʀi] *nm* husband

mariage [maʀjaʒ] *nm* (*union, état, fig*) marriage; (*noce*) wedding; **~ civil/religieux** registry office (*Brit*) ou civil/church wedding; **un ~ de raison/d'amour** a marriage of convenience/a love match; **~ blanc** unconsummated marriage; **~ en blanc** white wedding

marié, e [maʀje] *adj* married ▷ *nm/f* (*bride*) groom/bride; **les ~s** the bride and groom; **les (jeunes) ~s** the newly-weds

marier [maʀje] *vt* to marry; (*fig*) to blend; **se ~ (avec)** to marry, get married (to); (*fig*) to blend (with)

marin, e [maʀɛ̃, -in] *adj* sea *cpd*, marine ▷ *nm* sailor ▷ *nf* navy; (*Art*) seascape; (*couleur*) navy (blue); **avoir le pied ~** to be a good sailor; (*garder son équilibre*) to have one's sea legs; **~e de guerre** navy; **~e marchande** merchant navy; **~e à voiles** sailing ships *pl*

marine [maʀin] *adj f, nf voir* **marin** ▷ *adj inv* navy (blue) ▷ *nm* (*Mil*) marine

mariner [maʀine] *vi, vt* to marinate, marinade

marionnette [maʀjɔnɛt] *nf* puppet

maritalement [maʀitalmɑ̃] *adv*: **vivre ~** to live together (as husband and wife)

maritime [maʀitim] *adj* sea *cpd*, maritime; (*ville*) coastal, seaside; (*droit*) shipping, maritime

mark [maʀk] *nm* mark

marmelade [maʀməlad] *nf* (*compote*) stewed fruit, compote; **~ d'oranges** (*orange*) marmalade; **en ~** (*fig*) crushed (to a pulp)

marmite [maʀmit] *nf* (cooking-)pot

marmonner [maʀmɔne] *vt, vi* to mumble, mutter

marmot [maʀmo] *nm* (*fam*) brat

marmotter [maʀmɔte] *vt* (*prière*) to mumble, mutter

Maroc [maʀɔk] *nm*: **le ~** Morocco

marocain, e [maʀɔkɛ̃, -ɛn] *adj* Moroccan ▷ *nm/f*: **M~, e** Moroccan

maroquinerie [maʀɔkinʀi] *nf* (*industrie*) leather craft; (*commerce*) leather shop; (*articles*) fine leather goods *pl*

marquant, e [maʀkɑ̃, -ɑ̃t] *adj* outstanding

marque [maʀk] *nf* mark; (*Sport, Jeu*) score; (*Comm: de nourriture*) brand; (: *de voiture, produits manufacturés*) make; (: *de disques*) label; (*insigne: d'une fonction*) badge; (*fig*): **~ d'affection** token of affection; **~ de joie** sign of joy; **à vos ~s!** (*Sport*) on your marks!; **de ~** *adj* (*Comm*) brand-name *cpd*; proprietary; (*fig*) high-class; (: *personnage, hôte*) distinguished; **produit de ~** quality product; **~ déposée** registered trademark; **~ de fabrique** trademark; **une grande ~ de vin** a well-known brand of wine

marquer [maʀke] *vt* to mark; (*inscrire*) to write down; (*bétail*) to brand; (*Sport: but etc*) to score; (: *joueur*) to mark; (*accentuer: taille etc*) to emphasize; (*manifester: refus, intérêt*) to show ▷ *vi* (*événement, personnalité*) to stand out, be outstanding; (*Sport*) to score; **~ qn de son influence/empreinte** to have an influence/leave its impression on sb; **~ un temps d'arrêt** to pause momentarily; **~ le pas** (*fig*) to mark time; **il a marqué ce jour-là d'une pierre blanche** that was a red-letter day for him; **~ les points** (*tenir la marque*) to keep the score

marqueterie [maʀkɛtʀi] nf inlaid work, marquetry

marquis, e [maʀki, -iz] nm/f marquis ou marquess/marchioness ▷ nf (auvent) glass canopy ou awning

marraine [maʀɛn] nf godmother; (d'un navire, d'une rose etc) namer

marrant, e [maʀɑ̃, -ɑ̃t] adj (fam) funny

marre [maʀ] adv (fam): **en avoir ~ de** to be fed up with

marrer [maʀe]: **se marrer** vi (fam) to have a (good) laugh

marron, ne [maʀɔ̃, -ɔn] nm (fruit) chestnut ▷ adj inv brown ▷ adj (péj) crooked; (: faux) bogus; **~s glacés** marrons glacés

marronnier [maʀɔnje] nm chestnut (tree)

mars [maʀs] nm March; voir aussi **juillet**

● **LA MARSEILLAISE**
●
● The Marseillaise has been France's
● national anthem since 1879. The words of
● the "Chant de guerre de l'armée du
● Rhin", as the song was originally called,
● were written to an anonymous tune by
● an army captain called Rouget de Lisle in
● 1792. Adopted as a marching song by the
● Marseille battalion, it was finally
● popularized as the Marseillaise.

Marseille [maʀsɛj] n Marseilles

marsouin [maʀswɛ̃] nm porpoise

marteau, x [maʀto] nm hammer; (de porte) knocker; **~ pneumatique** pneumatic drill; **être ~** (fam) to be nuts

marteau-piqueur (pl marteaux-piqueurs) [maʀtopikœʀ] nm pneumatic drill

marteler [maʀtəle] vt to hammer; (mots, phrases) to rap out

martien, ne [maʀsjɛ̃, -ɛn] adj Martian, of ou from Mars

martyr, e [maʀtiʀ] nm/f martyr ▷ adj martyred; **enfants ~s** battered children

martyre [maʀtiʀ] nm martyrdom; (fig: sens affaibli) agony, torture; **souffrir le ~** to suffer agonies

martyriser [maʀtiʀize] vt (Rel) to martyr; (fig) to bully; (: enfant) to batter

marxiste [maʀksist] adj, nm/f Marxist

mascara [maskaʀa] nm mascara

masculin, e [maskylɛ̃, -in] adj masculine; (sexe, population) male; (équipe, vêtements) men's; (viril) manly ▷ nm masculine

masochiste [mazɔʃist] adj masochistic ▷ nm/f masochist

masque [mask] nm mask; **~ de beauté** face pack; **~ à gaz** gas mask; **~ de plongée** diving mask

masquer [maske] vt (cacher: porte, goût) to hide, conceal; (dissimuler: vérité, projet) to mask, obscure

massacre [masakʀ] nm massacre, slaughter; **jeu de ~** (fig) wholesale slaughter

massacrer [masakʀe] vt to massacre, slaughter; (fig: adversaire) to slaughter; (: texte etc) to murder

massage [masaʒ] nm massage

masse [mas] nf mass; (péj): **la ~** the masses pl; (Élec) earth; (maillet) sledgehammer; **masses** nfpl masses; **une ~ de, des ~s de** (fam) masses ou loads of; **en ~** adv (en bloc) in bulk; (en foule) en masse ▷ adj (exécutions, production) mass cpd; **~ monétaire** (Écon) money supply; **~ salariale** (Comm) wage(s) bill

masser [mase] vt (assembler: gens) to gather; (pétrir) to massage; **se masser** vi (foule) to gather

masseur, -euse [masœʀ, -øz] nm/f (personne) masseur(-euse) ▷ nm (appareil) massager

massif, -ive [masif, -iv] adj (porte) solid, massive; (visage) heavy, large; (bois, or) solid; (dose) massive; (déportations etc) mass cpd ▷ nm (montagneux) massif; (de fleurs) clump, bank; **le M~ Central** the Massif Central

massue [masy] nf club, bludgeon ▷ adj inv: **argument ~** sledgehammer argument

mastic [mastik] nm (pour vitres) putty; (pour fentes) filler

mastiquer [mastike] vt (aliment) to chew, masticate; (fente) to fill; (vitre) to putty

mat, e [mat] adj (couleur, métal) mat(t); (bruit, son) dull ▷ adj inv (Échecs): **être ~** to be checkmate

mât [mɑ] nm (Navig) mast; (poteau) pole, post

match [matʃ] nm match; **~ nul** draw, tie (US); **faire ~ nul** to draw (Brit), tie (US); **~ aller** first leg; **~ retour** second leg, return match

matelas [matla] nm mattress; **~ pneumatique** air bed ou mattress; **~ à ressorts** spring ou interior-sprung mattress

matelassé, e adj padded; (tissu) quilted

matelot [matlo] nm sailor, seaman

mater [mate] vt (personne) to bring to heel, subdue; (révolte) to put down; (fam) to watch, look at

matérialiser [mateʀjalize]: **se matérialiser** vi to materialize

matérialiste [mateʀjalist] adj materialistic ▷ nm/f materialist

matériau, x [mateʀjo] nm material; **matériaux** nmpl material(s); **~x de construction** building materials

matériel, le [mateʀjɛl] adj material; (organisation, aide, obstacle) practical; (fig: péj: personne) materialistic ▷ nm equipment no pl; (de camping etc) gear no pl; (Inform) hardware; **il n'a pas le temps ~ de le faire** he doesn't have the time (needed) to do it; **~ d'exploitation** (Comm) plant; **~ roulant** rolling stock

maternel, le [mateʀnɛl] adj (amour, geste) motherly, maternal; (grand-père, oncle) maternal ▷ nf (aussi: **école ~le**) (state) nursery school

maternité [maternite] nf (établissement) maternity hospital; (état de mère) motherhood, maternity; (grossesse) pregnancy; **congé de ~** maternity leave

mathématique [matematik] adj mathematical

mathématiques [matematik] nfpl mathematics sg

maths [mat] nfpl maths (Brit), math (US)

matière [matjer] nf (Physique) matter; (Comm, Tech) material; matter no pl; (fig: d'un livre etc) subject matter, material; (Scol) subject; **en ~ de** as regards; **donner ~ à** to give cause to; **~ plastique** plastic; **~s fécales** faeces; **~s grasses** fat (content) sg; **~s premières** raw materials

Matignon [matiɲɔ̃] nm: **(l'hôtel) ~** the French Prime Minister's residence; see note

● **HÔTEL MATIGNON**
●
● The hôtel Matignon is the Paris office and
● residence of the French Prime Minister.
● By extension, the term "Matignon" is
● often used to refer to the Prime Minister
● and his or her staff.

matin [matɛ̃] nm, adv morning; **le ~** (pendant le matin) in the morning; **demain/hier/dimanche ~** tomorrow/yesterday/Sunday morning; **tous les ~s** every morning; **le lendemain ~** (the) next morning; **du ~ au soir** from morning till night; **une heure du ~** one o'clock in the morning; **de grand** ou **bon ~** early in the morning

matinal, e, -aux [matinal, -o] adj (toilette, gymnastique) morning cpd; (de bonne heure) early; **être ~** (personne) to be up early; (: habituellement) to be an early riser

matinée [matine] nf morning; (spectacle) matinée, afternoon performance

matou [matu] nm tom(cat)

matraque [matrak] nf (de malfaiteur) cosh (Brit), club; (de policier) truncheon (Brit), billy (US)

matricule [matrikyl] nf (aussi: **registre ~**) roll, register ▷ nm (aussi: **numéro ~**: Mil) regimental number; (: Admin) reference number

matrimonial, e, -aux [matrimɔnjal, -o] adj marital, marriage cpd

maudire [modir] vt to curse

maudit, e [modi, -it] adj (fam: satané) blasted, confounded

maugréer [mogree] vi to grumble

maussade [mosad] adj (air, personne) sullen; (ciel, temps) gloomy

mauvais, e [mɔvɛ, -ɛz] adj bad; (méchant, malveillant) malicious, spiteful; (faux): **le ~ numéro** the wrong number ▷ nm: **le ~** the bad side ▷ adv: **il fait ~** the weather is bad; **sentir ~** to have a nasty smell, smell bad ou nasty; **la mer est ~e** the sea is rough; **~ coucheur** awkward customer; **~ coup** (fig) criminal venture; **~ garçon** tough; **~ pas** tight spot; **~ plaisant** hoaxer; **~e plaisanterie** nasty trick; **~ traitements** ill treatment sg; **~ joueur** bad loser; **~e herbe** weed; **~e langue** gossip, scandalmonger (Brit); **~e passe** difficult situation; (période) bad patch; **~e tête** rebellious ou headstrong customer

mauve [mov] adj (couleur) mauve ▷ nf (Bot) mallow

maux [mo] nmpl voir **mal**

maximal, e, -aux [maksimal, -o] adj maximal

maximum [maksimɔm] adj, nm maximum; **atteindre un/son ~** to reach a/his peak; **au ~** adv (le plus possible) to the full; as much as one can; (tout au plus) at the (very) most ou maximum; **faire le ~** to do one's level best

mayonnaise [majɔnɛz] nf mayonnaise

mazout [mazut] nm (fuel) oil; **chaudière/poêle à ~** oil-fired boiler/stove

me, m' [mə, m] pron (direct: téléphoner, attendre etc) me; (indirect: parler, donner etc) (to) me; (réfléchi) myself

mec [mɛk] nm (fam) guy, bloke (Brit)

mécanicien, ne [mekanisjɛ̃, -ɛn] nm/f mechanic; (Rail) (train ou engine) driver; **~ navigant** ou **de bord** (Aviat) flight engineer

mécanique [mekanik] adj mechanical ▷ nf (science) mechanics sg; (technologie) mechanical engineering; (mécanisme) mechanism; engineering; works pl; **ennui ~** engine trouble no pl; **s'y connaître en ~** to be mechanically minded; **~ hydraulique** hydraulics sg; **~ ondulatoire** wave mechanics sg

mécanisme [mekanism] nm mechanism; **~ des taux de change** exchange rate mechanism

méchamment [meʃamɑ̃] adv nastily, maliciously; spitefully; viciously

méchanceté [meʃɑ̃ste] nf (d'une personne, d'une parole) nastiness, maliciousness, spitefulness; (parole, action) nasty ou spiteful ou malicious remark (ou action); **dire des ~s à qn** to say spiteful things to sb

méchant, e [meʃɑ̃, -ɑ̃t] adj nasty, malicious, spiteful; (enfant: pas sage) naughty; (animal) vicious; (avant le nom: péjoratif) nasty

mèche [meʃ] nf (de lampe, bougie) wick; (d'un explosif) fuse; (Méd) pack, dressing; (de vilebrequin, perceuse) bit; (de dentiste) drill; (de fouet) lash; (de cheveux) lock; **se faire faire des ~s** (chez le coiffeur) to have highlights put in one's hair, have one's hair streaked; **vendre la ~** to give the game away; **de ~ avec** in league with

méchoui [meʃwi] nm whole sheep barbecue

méconnaissable [mekɔnɛsabl] adj unrecognizable

méconnaître [mekɔnɛtʀ] vt (ignorer) to be unaware of; (mésestimer) to misjudge

mécontent, e [mekɔ̃tɑ̃, -ɑ̃t] adj: ~ (de) (insatisfait) discontented ou dissatisfied ou displeased (with); (contrarié) annoyed (at) ▷ nm/f malcontent, dissatisfied person

mécontentement [mekɔ̃tɑ̃tmɑ̃] nm dissatisfaction, discontent, displeasure; (irritation) annoyance

Mecque [mɛk] nf: **la ~** Mecca

médaille [medaj] nf medal

médaillon [medajɔ̃] nm (portrait) medallion; (bijou) locket; (Culin) médaillon; **en ~** (carte etc) inset

médecin [medsɛ̃] nm doctor; **~ du bord** (Navig) ship's doctor; **~ généraliste** general practitioner, GP; **~ légiste** forensic scientist (Brit), medical examiner (US); **~ traitant** family doctor, GP

médecine [medsin] nf medicine; **~ générale** general medicine; **~ infantile** paediatrics sg (Brit), pediatrics sg (US); **~ légale** forensic medicine; **~ préventive** preventive medicine; **~ du travail** occupational ou industrial medicine; **~s parallèles** ou **douces** alternative medicine

média [medja] nmpl: **les ~** the media

médiatique [medjatik] adj media cpd

médiatisé, e [medjatize] adj reported in the media; **ce procès a été très ~** (péj) this trial was turned into a media event

médical, e, -aux [medikal, -o] adj medical; **visiteur** ou **délégué ~** medical rep ou representative; **passer une visite ~e** to have a medical

médicament [medikamɑ̃] nm medicine, drug

médiéval, e, -aux [medjeval, -o] adj medieval

médiocre [medjɔkʀ] adj mediocre, poor

médire [mediʀ] vi: **~ de** to speak ill of

médisance [medizɑ̃s] nf scandalmongering no pl (Brit), mud-slinging no pl; (propos) piece of scandal ou malicious gossip

méditer [medite] vt (approfondir) to meditate on, ponder (over); (combiner) to meditate ▷ vi to meditate; **~ de faire** to contemplate doing, plan to do

Méditerranée [mediteʀane] nf: **la (mer) ~** the Mediterranean (Sea)

méditerranéen, ne [mediteʀaneɛ̃, -ɛn] adj Mediterranean ▷ nm/f: **M~, ne** Mediterranean

méduse [medyz] nf jellyfish

meeting [mitiŋ] nm (Pol, Sport) rally, meeting; **~ d'aviation** air show

méfait [mefɛ] nm (faute) misdemeanour, wrongdoing; **méfaits** nmpl (ravages) ravages, damage sg

méfiance [mefjɑ̃s] nf mistrust, distrust

méfiant, e [mefjɑ̃, -ɑ̃t] adj mistrustful, distrustful

méfier [mefje]: **se méfier** vi to be wary; (faire attention) to be careful; **se ~ de** vt to mistrust, distrust, be wary of; to be careful about

méga-octet [megaɔktɛ] nm megabyte

mégarde [megaʀd] nf: **par ~** (accidentellement) accidentally; (par erreur) by mistake

mégère [meʒɛʀ] nf (péj: femme) shrew

mégot [mego] nm cigarette end ou butt

meilleur, e [mɛjœʀ] adj, adv better; (valeur superlative) best ▷ nm: **le ~** (celui qui ...) the best (one); (ce qui ...) the best ▷ nf: **la ~e** the best (one); **le ~ des deux** the better of the two; **il fait ~ qu'hier** it's better weather than yesterday; **de ~e heure** earlier; **~ marché** cheaper

mél [mɛl] nm email

mélancolie [melɑ̃kɔli] nf melancholy, gloom

mélancolique [melɑ̃kɔlik] adj melancholy, gloomy

mélange [melɑ̃ʒ] nm (opération) mixing; blending; (résultat) mixture; blend; **sans ~** unadulterated

mélanger [melɑ̃ʒe] vt (substances) to mix; (vins, couleurs) to blend; (mettre en désordre, confondre) to mix up, muddle (up); **se mélanger** (liquides, couleurs) to blend, mix

mélasse [melas] nf treacle, molasses sg

mêlée [mele] nf (bataille, cohue) mêlée, scramble; (lutte, conflit) tussle, scuffle; (Rugby) scrum(mage)

mêler [mele] vt (substances, odeurs, races) to mix; (embrouiller) to muddle (up), mix up; **se mêler** vi to mix; (se joindre, s'allier) to mingle; **se ~ à** (personne) to join; (s'associer à) to mix with; (: odeurs etc) to mingle with; **se ~ de** (personne) to meddle with, interfere in; **mêle-toi de tes affaires!** mind your own business!; **~ à** ou **avec** ou **de** to mix with; to mingle with; **~ qn à** (affaire) to get sb mixed up ou involved in

mélodie [melɔdi] nf melody

mélodieux, -euse [melɔdjø, -øz] adj melodious, tuneful

melon [məlɔ̃] nm (Bot) (honeydew) melon; (aussi: **chapeau ~**) bowler (hat); **~ d'eau** watermelon

membre [mɑ̃bʀ] nm (Anat) limb; (personne, pays, élément) member ▷ adj member cpd; **être ~ de** to be a member of; **~ (viril)** (male) organ

mémé [meme] nf (fam) granny; (: vieille femme) old dear

O **MOT-CLÉ**

même [mɛm] adj **1** (avant le nom) same; **en même temps** at the same time; **ils ont les mêmes goûts** they have the same ou similar tastes

2 (après le nom: renforcement): **il est la loyauté même** he is loyalty itself; **ce sont ses paroles/celles-là même** they are his very words/the very ones

▷ pron: **le (la) même** the same one

▷ *adv* **1** (*renforcement*): **il n'a même pas pleuré** he didn't even cry; **même lui l'a dit** even HE said it; **ici même** in this very place; **même si** even if

2: **à même** (*ooo*): **à même la bouteille** straight from the bottle; **à même la peau** next to the skin; **être à même de faire** to be in a position to do, be able to do; **mettre qn à même de faire** to enable sb to do

3: **de même** likewise; **faire de même** to do likewise *ou* the same; **lui de même** so does (*ou* did *ou* is) he; **de même que** just as; **il en va de même pour** the same goes for

mémo [memo] (*fam*) *nm* memo

mémoire [memwaʀ] *nf* memory ▷ *nm* (*Admin, Jur*) memorandum; (*Scol*) dissertation, paper; **avoir la ~ des visages/chiffres** to have a (good) memory for faces/figures; **n'avoir aucune ~** to have a terrible memory; **avoir de la ~** to have a good memory; **à la ~ de** to the *ou* in memory of; **pour ~** *adv* for the record; **de ~** *adv* from memory; **de ~ d'homme** in living memory; **mettre en ~** (*Inform*) to store; **~ morte** read-only memory, ROM; **~ vive** random access memory, RAM

mémoires [memwaʀ] *nmpl* memoirs

mémorable [memɔʀabl] *adj* memorable

menace [mənas] *nf* threat; **~ en l'air** empty threat

menacer [mənase] *vt* to threaten; **~ qn de qch/de faire qch** to threaten sb with sth/to do sth

ménage [menaʒ] *nm* (*travail*) housekeeping, housework; (*couple*) (married) couple; (*famille, Admin*) household; **faire le ~** to do the housework; **faire des ~s** to work as a cleaner (*in private homes*); **monter son ~** to set up house; **se mettre en ~ (avec)** to set up house (with); **heureux en ~** happily married; **faire bon ~ avec** to get on well with; **~ de poupée** doll's kitchen set; **~ à trois** love triangle

ménagement [menaʒmã] *nm* care and attention; **ménagements** *nmpl* (*égards*) consideration *sg*, attention *sg*

ménager¹ [menaʒe] *vt* (*traiter avec mesure*) to handle with tact; to treat considerately; (*utiliser*) to use with care; (: *avec économie*) to use sparingly; (*prendre soin de*) to take (great) care of, look after; (*organiser*) to arrange; (*installer*) to put in; to make; **se ménager** to look after o.s.; **~ qch à qn** (*réserver*) to have sth in store for sb

ménager², -ère [menaʒe, -ɛʀ] *adj* household *cpd*, domestic ▷ *nf* (*femme*) housewife; (*couverts*) canteen (of cutlery)

mendiant, e [mãdjã, -ãt] *nm/f* beggar

mendier [mãdje] *vi* to beg ▷ *vt* to beg (for); (*fig: éloges, compliments*) to fish for

mener [məne] *vt* to lead; (*enquête*) to conduct; (*affaires*) to manage, conduct, run ▷ *vi*: **~ (à la marque)** to lead, be in the lead; **~ à/dans**

(*emmener*) to take to/into; **~ qch à bonne fin** *ou* **à terme** *ou* **à bien** to see sth through (to a successful conclusion), complete sth successfully

meneur, -euse [mənœʀ, -øz] *nm/f* leader; (*péj: agitateur*) ringleader; **~ d'hommes** born leader; **~ de jeu** host, quizmaster (*Brit*)

méningite [menɛ̃ʒit] *nf* meningitis *no pl*

ménopause [menopoz] *nf* menopause

menotte [mənɔt] *nf* (*langage enfantin*) handie; **menottes** *nfpl* handcuffs; **passer les ~s à** to handcuff

mensonge [mãsɔ̃ʒ] *nm*: **le ~** lying *no pl*; **un ~** a lie

mensonger, -ère [mãsɔ̃ʒe, -ɛʀ] *adj* false

mensualité [mãsɥalite] *nf* (*somme payée*) monthly payment; (*somme perçue*) monthly salary

mensuel, le [mãsɥɛl] *adj* monthly ▷ *nm/f* (*employé*) employee paid monthly ▷ *nm* (*Presse*) monthly

mensurations [mãsyʀasjɔ̃] *nfpl* measurements

mental, e, -aux [mãtal, -o] *adj* mental

mentalité [mãtalite] *nf* mentality

menteur, -euse [mãtœʀ, -øz] *nm/f* liar

menthe [mãt] *nf* mint; **~ (à l'eau)** peppermint cordial

mention [mãsjɔ̃] *nf* (*note*) note, comment; (*Scol*): **~ (très) bien/passable** (*very*) good/satisfactory pass; **faire ~ de** to mention; **"rayer la ~ inutile"** "delete as appropriate"

mentionner [mãsjɔne] *vt* to mention

mentir [mãtiʀ] *vi* to lie

menton [mãtɔ̃] *nm* chin

menu, e [məny] *adj* (*mince*) slim, slight; (*petit*) tiny; (*frais, difficulté*) minor ▷ *adv* (*couper, hacher*) very fine ▷ *nm* menu; **par le ~** (*raconter*) in minute detail; **~ touristique** popular *ou* tourist menu; **~e monnaie** small change

menuiserie [mənɥizʀi] *nf* (*travail*) joinery, carpentry; (*d'amateur*) woodwork; (*local*) joiner's workshop; (*ouvrages*) woodwork *no pl*

menuisier [mənɥizje] *nm* joiner, carpenter

méprendre [mepʀãdʀ]: **se méprendre** *vi*: **se ~ sur** to be mistaken about

mépris, e [mepʀi, -iz] *pp de* **méprendre** ▷ *nm* (*dédain*) contempt, scorn; (*indifférence*): **le ~ de** contempt *ou* disregard for; **au ~ de** regardless of, in defiance of

méprisable [mepʀizabl] *adj* contemptible, despicable

méprisant, e [mepʀizã, -ãt] *adj* contemptuous, scornful

méprise [mepʀiz] *nf* mistake, error; (*malentendu*) misunderstanding

mépriser [mepʀize] *vt* to scorn, despise; (*gloire, danger*) to scorn, spurn

mer [mɛʀ] *nf* sea; (*marée*) tide; **~ fermée** inland sea; **en ~** at sea; **prendre la ~** to put out to sea; **en haute** *ou* **pleine ~** off shore, on the open sea; **la ~ Adriatique** the Adriatic

(Sea); **la ~ des Antilles** ou **des Caraïbes** the Caribbean (Sea); **la ~ Baltique** the Baltic (Sea); **la ~ Caspienne** the Caspian Sea; **la ~ de Corail** the Coral Sea; **la ~ Égée** the Aegean (Sea); **la ~ Ionienne** the Ionian Sea; **la ~ Morte** the Dead Sea; **la ~ Noire** the Black Sea; **la ~ du Nord** the North Sea; **la ~ Rouge** the Red Sea; **la ~ des Sargasses** the Sargasso Sea; **les ~s du Sud** the South Seas; **la ~ Tyrrhénienne** the Tyrrhenian Sea

mercenaire [mɛʀsənɛʀ] *nm* mercenary, hired soldier

mercerie [mɛʀsəʀi] *nf* (*Couture*) haberdashery (*Brit*), notions *pl* (*US*); (*boutique*) haberdasher's (shop) (*Brit*), notions store (*US*)

merci [mɛʀsi] *excl* thank you ▷ *nf*: **à la ~ de qn/qch** at sb's mercy/the mercy of sth; **~ beaucoup** thank you very much; **~ de** ou **pour** thank you for; **sans ~** *adj* merciless ▷ *adv* mercilessly

mercredi [mɛʀkʀədi] *nm* Wednesday; **~ des Cendres** Ash Wednesday; *voir aussi* **lundi**

mercure [mɛʀkyʀ] *nm* mercury

merde [mɛʀd] (*fam!*) *nf* shit (!) ▷ *excl* (bloody) hell (!)

mère [mɛʀ] *nf* mother ▷ *adj inv* mother *cpd*; **~ célibataire** single parent, unmarried mother; **~ de famille** housewife, mother

merguez [mɛʀgɛz] *nf* spicy North African sausage

méridional, e, -aux [meʀidjɔnal, -o] *adj* southern; (*du midi de la France*) Southern (French) ▷ *nm/f* Southerner

meringue [məʀɛ̃g] *nf* meringue

mérite [meʀit] *nm* merit; **avoir du ~** (**à faire qch**) to deserve credit (for doing sth); **le ~** (**de ceci**) **lui revient** the credit (for this) is his

mériter [meʀite] *vt* to deserve; **~ de réussir** to deserve to succeed; **il mérite qu'on fasse ...** he deserves people to do ...

merlan [mɛʀlɑ̃] *nm* whiting

merle [mɛʀl] *nm* blackbird

merveille [mɛʀvɛj] *nf* marvel, wonder; **faire ~** ou **des ~s** to work wonders; **à ~** perfectly, wonderfully

merveilleux, -euse [mɛʀvɛjø, -øz] *adj* marvellous, wonderful

mes [me] *adj poss voir* **mon**

mésange [mezɑ̃ʒ] *nf* tit(mouse); **~ bleue** bluetit

mésaventure [mezavɑ̃tyʀ] *nf* misadventure, misfortune

Mesdames [medam] *nfpl voir* **Madame**

Mesdemoiselles [medmwazɛl] *nfpl voir* **Mademoiselle**

mesquin, e [mɛskɛ̃, -in] *adj* mean, petty

mesquinerie [mɛskinʀi] *nf* meanness *no pl*, pettiness *no pl*; (*procédé*) mean trick

message [mesaʒ] *nm* message; **~ d'erreur** (*Inform*) error message; **~ électronique** (*Inform*) email; **~ publicitaire** advertisement; **~ téléphoné** telegram dictated by telephone; **~ SMS** text message

messager, -ère [mesaʒe, -ɛʀ] *nm/f* messenger

messagerie [mesaʒʀi] *nf*: **~s aériennes/maritimes** air freight/shipping service *sg*; (*Internet*): **~ électronique** electronic mail, email; **~s de presse** press distribution service; **~ instantanée** instant messenger, IM; **~ rose** lonely hearts and contact service on videotext; **~ vocale** voice mail

messe [mɛs] *nf* mass; **aller à la ~** to go to mass; **~ de minuit** midnight mass; **faire des ~s basses** (*fig, péj*) to mutter

Messieurs [mesjø] *nmpl voir* **Monsieur**

mesure [məzyʀ] *nf* (*évaluation, dimension*) measurement; (*étalon, récipient, contenu*) measure; (*Mus: cadence*) time, tempo; (: *division*) bar; (*retenue*) moderation; (*disposition*) measure, step; **unité/système de ~** unit/system of measurement; **sur ~** (*costume*) made-to-measure; (*fig*) personally adapted; **à la ~ de** (*fig: personne*) worthy of; (*chambre etc*) on the same scale as; **dans la ~ où** insofar as, inasmuch as; **dans une certaine ~** to some ou a certain extent; **à ~ que** as; **en ~** (*Mus*) in time ou tempo; **être en ~ de** to be in a position to; **dépasser la ~** (*fig*) to overstep the mark

mesurer [məzyʀe] *vt* to measure; (*juger*) to weigh up, assess; (*limiter*) to limit, ration; (*modérer: ses paroles etc*) to moderate; (*proportionner*): **~ qch à** to match sth to, gear sth to; **se ~ avec** to have a confrontation with; to tackle; **il mesure 1 m 80** he's 1 m 80 tall

met [mɛ] *vb voir* **mettre**

métal, -aux [metal, -o] *nm* metal

métallique [metalik] *adj* metallic

météo [meteo] *nf* (*bulletin*) (weather) forecast; (*service*) ≈ Met Office (*Brit*), ≈ National Weather Service (*US*)

météorologie [meteɔʀɔlɔʒi] *nf* (*étude*) meteorology; (*service*) ≈ Meteorological Office (*Brit*), ≈ National Weather Service (*US*)

méthode [metɔd] *nf* method; (*livre, ouvrage*) manual, tutor

méticuleux, -euse [metikylø, -øz] *adj* meticulous

métier [metje] *nm* (*profession: gén*) job; (: *manuel*) trade; (: *artisanal*) craft; (*technique, expérience*) (acquired) skill ou technique; (*aussi*: **~ à tisser**) (weaving) loom; **être du ~** to be in the trade ou profession

métrage [metʀaʒ] *nm* (*de tissu*) length; (*Ciné*) footage, length; **long/moyen/court ~** feature ou full-length/medium-length/short film

mètre [mɛtʀ] *nm* metre (*Brit*), meter (*US*); (*règle*) (metre ou meter) rule; (*ruban*) tape measure; **~ carré/cube** square/cubic metre ou meter

métrique [metʀik] *adj* metric ▷ *nf* metrics *sg*

métro [metʀo] nm underground (Brit), subway (US)

métropole [metʀopɔl] nf (capitale) metropolis; (pays) home country

mets [mɛ] nm dish ▷ vb voir **mettre**

metteur [metœʀ] nm: **~ en scène** (Théât) producer; (Ciné) director; **~ en ondes** (Radio) producer

 MOT-CLÉ

mettre [metʀ] vt **1** (placer) to put; **mettre en bouteille/en sac** put your bottle/put in bags ou sacks; **mettre qch à la poste** to post sth (Brit), mail sth (US); **mettre en examen (pour)** to charge (with) (Brit), indict (for) (US); **mettre une note gaie/amusante** to inject a cheerful/an amusing note; **mettre qn debout/assis** to help sb up ou to their feet/help sb to sit down

2 (vêtements: revêtir) to put on; (: porter) to wear; **mets ton gilet** put your cardigan on; **je ne mets plus mon manteau** I no longer wear my coat

3 (faire fonctionner: chauffage, électricité) to put on; (: réveil, minuteur) to set; (installer: gaz, eau) to put in, lay on; **mettre en marche** to start up

4 (consacrer): **mettre du temps/deux heures à faire qch** to take time/two hours to do sth; **y mettre du sien** to pull one's weight

5 (noter, écrire) to say, put (down); **qu'est-ce qu'il a mis sur la carte?** what did he say ou write on the card?; **mettez au pluriel ...** put ... into the plural

6 (supposer): **mettons que ...** let's suppose ou say that ...

7 (faire + vb): **faire mettre le gaz/l'électricité** to have gas/electricity put in ou installed

se mettre vi **1** (se placer): **vous pouvez vous mettre là** you can sit (ou stand) there; **où ça se met?** where does it go?; **se mettre au lit** to get into bed; **se mettre au piano** to sit down at the piano; **se mettre à l'eau** to get into the water; **se mettre de l'encre sur les doigts** to get ink on one's fingers

2 (s'habiller): **se mettre en maillot de bain** to get into ou put on a swimsuit; **n'avoir rien à se mettre** to have nothing to wear

3 (dans rapports): **se mettre bien/mal avec qn** to get on the right/wrong side of sb; **se mettre qn à dos** to get on sb's bad side; **se mettre avec qn** (prendre parti) to side with sb; (faire équipe) to team up with sb; (en ménage) to move in with sb

4: **se mettre à** to begin, start; **se mettre à faire** to begin ou start doing ou to do; **se mettre au piano** to start learning the piano; **se mettre au régime** to go on a diet; **se mettre au travail/à l'étude** to get down to work/one's studies; **il est temps de s'y mettre** it's time we got down to it ou got on with it

meuble [mœbl] nm (objet) piece of furniture; (ameublement) furniture no pl ▷ adj (terre) loose, friable; (Jur): **biens ~s** movables

meublé [mœble] nm (pièce) furnished room; (appartement) furnished flat (Brit) ou apartment (US)

meubler [mœble] vt to furnish; (fig): **~ qch (de)** to fill sth (with); **se meubler** to furnish one's house

meuf [mœf] nf (fam) woman

meugler [møgle] vi to low, moo

meule [møl] nf (à broyer) millstone; (à aiguiser) grindstone; (à polir) buff wheel; (de foin, blé) stack; (de fromage) round

meunier, -ière [mønje, -jɛʀ] nm miller ▷ nf miller's wife ▷ adj f (Culin) meunière

meurs etc [mœʀ] vb voir **mourir**

meurtre [mœʀtʀ] nm murder

meurtrier, -ière [mœʀtʀije, -jɛʀ] adj (arme, épidémie, combat) deadly; (accident) fatal; (carrefour, route) lethal; (fureur, instincts) murderous ▷ nm/f murderer(-ess) ▷ nf (ouverture) loophole

meurtrir [mœʀtʀiʀ] vt to bruise; (fig) to wound

meurtrissure [mœʀtʀisyʀ] nf bruise; (fig) scar

meus etc [mœ] vb voir **mouvoir**

meute [møt] nf pack

mexicain, e [mɛksikɛ̃, -ɛn] adj Mexican ▷ nm/f: **M-, e** Mexican

Mexico [mɛksiko] n Mexico City

Mexique [mɛksik] nm: **le ~** Mexico

mi [mi] nm (Mus) E; (en chantant la gamme) mi

mi... [mi] préfixe half(-), mid-; **à la ~nvier** in mid-January; **à ~mbes/-corps** (up ou down) to the knees/waist; **à ~uteur/-pente** halfway up (ou down)/up (ou down) the hill

miauler [mjole] vi to miaow

mi-bas [miba] nm inv knee-length sock

miche [miʃ] nf round ou cob loaf

mi-chemin [miʃmɛ̃]: **à ~** adv halfway, midway

mi-clos, e [miklo, -kloz] adj half-closed

micro [mikʀo] nm mike, microphone; (Inform) micro; **~ cravate** lapel mike

microbe [mikʀɔb] nm germ, microbe

micro-onde [mikʀɔ̃d] nf: **four à ~s** microwave oven

micro-ordinateur [mikʀɔɔʀdinatœʀ] nm microcomputer

microscope [mikʀɔskɔp] nm microscope; **au ~** under ou through the microscope

microscopique [mikʀɔskɔpik] adj microscopic

midi [midi] nm (milieu du jour) midday, noon; (moment du déjeuner) lunchtime; (sud) south; (: de la France): **le M~** the South (of France), the Midi; **à ~** at 12 (o'clock) ou midday ou noon; **tous les ~s** every lunchtime; **le repas de ~** lunch; **en plein ~** (right) in the middle of the day; (sud) facing south

mie [mi] nf inside (of the loaf)

m

miel [mjɛl] nm honey; **être tout ~** (fig) to be all sweetness and light

mielleux, -euse [mjɛlø, -øz] adj (péj: personne) sugary, syrupy

mien, ne [mjɛ̃, mjɛn] adj, pron: **le (la) ~(ne), les ~s** mine; **les ~s** (ma famille) my family

miette [mjɛt] nf (de pain, gâteau) crumb; (fig: de la conversation etc) scrap; **en ~s** (fig) in pieces ou bits

⬤ **MOT-CLÉ**

mieux [mjø] adv **1** (d'une meilleure façon): **mieux (que)** better (than); **elle travaille/mange mieux** she works/eats better; **aimer mieux** to prefer; **j'attendais mieux de vous** I expected better of you; **elle va mieux** she is better; **de mieux en mieux** better and better **2** (de la meilleure façon) best; **ce que je sais le mieux** what I know best; **les livres les mieux faits** the best made books **3** (intensif): **vous feriez mieux de faire ...** you would be better to do ...; **crier à qui mieux mieux** to try to shout each other down ▷ adj inv **1** (plus à l'aise, en meilleure forme) better; **se sentir mieux** to feel better **2** (plus satisfaisant) better; **c'est mieux ainsi** it's better like this; **c'est le mieux des deux** it's the better of the two; **le/la mieux, les mieux** the best; **demandez-lui, c'est le mieux** ask him, it's the best thing **3** (plus joli) better-looking; (plus gentil) nicer; **il est mieux que son frère** (plus beau) he's better-looking than his brother; (plus gentil) he's nicer than his brother; **il est mieux sans moustache** he looks better without a moustache **4**: **au mieux** at best; **au mieux avec** on the best of terms with; **pour le mieux** for the best; **qui mieux est** even better, better still ▷ nm **1** (progrès) improvement **2**: **de mon/ton mieux** as best I/you can (ou could); **faire de son mieux** to do one's best; **du mieux qu'il peut** the best he can; **faute de mieux** for lack ou want of anything better, failing anything better

mièvre [mjɛvʀ] adj sickly sentimental

mignon, ne [miɲɔ̃, -ɔn] adj sweet, cute

migraine [migʀɛn] nf headache; (Méd) migraine

mijoter [miʒɔte] vt to simmer; (préparer avec soin) to cook lovingly; (affaire, projet) to plot, cook up ▷ vi to simmer

mil [mil] num = **mille**

milieu, x [miljø] nm (centre) middle; (fig) middle course ou way; (aussi: **juste ~**) happy medium; (Bio, Géo) environment; (entourage social) milieu; (familial) background; circle; (pègre): **le ~** the underworld; **au ~ de** in the middle of; **au beau ou en plein ~ (de)** right in the middle (of); **~ de terrain** (Football: joueur) midfield player; (: joueurs) midfield

militaire [militɛʀ] adj military, army cpd ▷ nm serviceman; **service ~** military service

militant, e [militɑ̃, -ɑ̃t] adj, nm/f militant

militer [milite] vi to be a militant; **~ pour/contre** to militate in favour of/against

mille [mil] num a ou one thousand ▷ nm (mesure): **~ (marin)** nautical mile; **mettre dans le ~** to hit the bull's-eye; (fig) to be bang on (target)

millefeuille [milfœj] nm cream ou vanilla slice

millénaire [milenɛʀ] nm millennium ▷ adj thousand-year-old; (fig) ancient

mille-pattes [milpat] nm inv centipede

millésimé, e [milezime] adj vintage cpd

millet [mijɛ] nm millet

milliard [miljaʀ] nm milliard, thousand million (Brit), billion (US)

milliardaire [miljaʀdɛʀ] nm/f multimillionaire (Brit), billionaire (US)

millier [milje] nm thousand; **un ~ (de)** a thousand or so, about a thousand; **par ~s** in (their) thousands, by the thousand

milligramme [miligʀam] nm milligramme (Brit), milligram (US)

millimètre [milimɛtʀ] nm millimetre (Brit), millimeter (US)

million [miljɔ̃] nm million; **deux ~s de** two million; **riche à ~s** worth millions

millionnaire [miljɔnɛʀ] nm/f millionaire

mime [mim] nm/f (acteur) mime(r); (imitateur) mimic ▷ nm (art) mime, miming

mimer [mime] vt to mime; (singer) to mimic, take off

mimique [mimik] nf (funny) face; (signes) gesticulations pl, sign language no pl

minable [minabl] adj (personne) shabby(-looking); (travail) pathetic

mince [mɛ̃s] adj thin; (personne, taille) slim, slender; (fig: profit, connaissances) slight, small; (: prétexte) weak ▷ excl: **~ (alors)!** darn it!

minceur [mɛ̃sœʀ] nf thinness; (d'une personne) slimness, slenderness

mincir [mɛ̃siʀ] vi to get slimmer ou thinner

mine [min] nf (physionomie) expression, look; (extérieur) exterior, appearance; (de crayon) lead; (gisement, exploitation, explosif) mine; **mines** nfpl (péj) simpering airs; **les M~s** (Admin) the national mining and geological service, the government vehicle testing department; **avoir bonne ~** (personne) to look well; (ironique) to look an utter idiot; **avoir mauvaise ~** to look unwell; **faire ~ de faire** to make a pretence of doing; **ne pas payer de ~** to be not much to look at; **~ de rien** adv with a casual air; although you wouldn't think so; **~ de charbon** coal mine; **à ciel ouvert** opencast (Brit) ou open-air (US) mine

miner [mine] vt (saper) to undermine, erode; (Mil) to mine

minerai [minʀɛ] nm ore

minéral, e, -aux [mineʀal, -o] *adj* mineral; (*Chimie*) inorganic ▷ *nm* mineral

minéralogique [mineʀalɔʒik] *adj* mineralogical; **plaque ~** number (*Brit*) *ou* license (*US*) plate; **numéro ~** registration (*Brit*) *ou* license (*US*) number

minet, te [minɛ, -ɛt] *nm/f* (*chat*) pussy-cat; (*péj*) young trendy

mineur, e [minœʀ] *adj* minor ▷ *nm/f* (*Jur*) minor ▷ *nm* (*travailleur*) miner; (*Mil*) sapper; **~ de fond** face worker

miniature [minjatyʀ] *adj, nf* miniature

minibus [minibys] *nm* minibus

mini-cassette [minikasɛt] *nf* cassette (recorder)

minier, -ière [minje, -jɛʀ] *adj* mining

mini-jupe [miniʒyp] *nf* mini-skirt

minimal, e, -aux [minimal, -o] *adj* minimum

minime [minim] *adj* minor, minimal ▷ *nm/f* (*Sport*) junior

minimiser [minimize] *vt* to minimize; (*fig*) to play down

minimum [minimɔm] *adj, nm* minimum; **au ~** at the very least; **~ vital** (*salaire*) living wage; (*niveau de vie*) subsistence level

ministère [ministɛʀ] *nm* (*cabinet*) government; (*département*) ministry (*Brit*), department; (*Rel*) ministry; **~ public** (*Jur*) Prosecution, State Prosecutor

ministre [ministʀ] *nm* minister (*Brit*), secretary; (*Rel*) minister; **~ d'État** senior minister *ou* secretary

Minitel® [minitɛl] *nm* (*formerly*) videotext terminal and service

● **MINITEL**
●
● **Minitel**® was a public information
● system provided by France-Télécom to
● telephone subscribers from the early 80s
● until 2012. Among the services available
● were a computerized telephone directory
● and information on travel timetables,
● stock-market news and situations
● vacant. Subscribers paid for their time
● on screen as part of their phone bill.
● Although this information also became
● available on the Internet, the special
● Minitel® screens, terminals and
● keyboards were still very much a part
● of French daily life.

minoritaire [minɔʀitɛʀ] *adj* minority *cpd*

minorité [minɔʀite] *nf* minority; **être en ~** to be in the *ou* a minority; **mettre en ~** (*Pol*) to defeat

minuit [minɥi] *nm* midnight

minuscule [minyskyl] *adj* minute, tiny ▷ *nf*: (*lettre*) **~** small letter

minute [minyt] *nf* minute; (*Jur: original*) minute, draft ▷ *excl* just a minute!, hang on!; **à la ~** (*présent*) (just) this instant; (*passé*) there and then; **entrecôte** *ou* **steak ~** minute steak

minuter [minyte] *vt* to time

minuterie [minytʀi] *nf* time switch

minutieux, -euse [minysjø, -øz] *adj* (*personne*) meticulous; (*inspection*) minutely detailed; (*travail*) requiring painstaking attention to detail

mirabelle [miʀabɛl] *nf* (*fruit*) (cherry) plum; (*eau-de-vie*) plum brandy

miracle [miʀakl] *nm* miracle

mirage [miʀaʒ] *nm* mirage

mire [miʀ] *nf* (*d'un fusil*) sight; (*TV*) test card; **point de ~** target; (*fig*) focal point; **ligne de ~** line of sight

miroir [miʀwaʀ] *nm* mirror

miroiter [miʀwate] *vi* to sparkle, shimmer; **faire ~ qch à qn** to paint sth in glowing colours for sb, dangle sth in front of sb's eyes

mis, e [mi, miz] *pp de* **mettre** ▷ *adj* (*couvert, table*) set, laid; (*personne*): **bien ~** well dressed ▷ *nf* (*argent: au jeu*) stake; (*tenue*) clothing; attire; **être de ~e** to be acceptable *ou* in season; **~e en bouteilles** bottling; **~e en examen** charging, indictment; **~e à feu** blast-off; **~e de fonds** capital outlay; **~e à jour** (*Inform*) update; **~e à mort** kill; **~e à pied** (*d'un employé*) suspension; lay-off; **~e au pied** (*d'une affaire, entreprise*) setting up; **~e en plis** set; **~e au point** (*Photo*) focusing; (*fig*) clarification; **~e à prix** reserve (*Brit*) *ou* upset price; **~e en scène** production

mise [miz] *adj f, nf voir* **mis**

miser [mize] *vt* (*enjeu*) to stake, bet; **~ sur** *vt* (*cheval, numéro*) to bet on; (*fig*) to bank *ou* count on

misérable [mizeʀabl] *adj* (*lamentable, malheureux*) pitiful, wretched; (*pauvre*) poverty-stricken; (*insignifiant, mesquin*) miserable ▷ *nm/f* wretch; (*miséreux*) poor wretch

misère [mizɛʀ] *nf* (*pauvreté*) (extreme) poverty, destitution; **misères** *nfpl* (*malheurs*) woes, miseries; (*ennuis*) little troubles; **être dans la ~** to be destitute *ou* poverty-stricken; **salaire de ~** starvation wage; **faire des ~s à qn** to torment sb; **~ noire** utter destitution, abject poverty

missile [misil] *nm* missile

mission [misjɔ̃] *nf* mission; **partir en ~** (*Admin, Pol*) to go on an assignment

missionnaire [misjɔnɛʀ] *nm/f* missionary

mit [mi] *vb voir* **mettre**

mité, e [mite] *adj* moth-eaten

mi-temps [mitɑ̃] *nf inv* (*Sport: période*) half; (*: pause*) half-time; **à ~** *adj, adv* part-time

miteux, -euse [mitø, -øz] *adj* seedy, shabby

mitigé, e [mitiʒe] *adj* (*conviction, ardeur*) lukewarm; (*sentiments*) mixed

mitonner [mitɔne] *vt* (*préparer*) to cook with loving care; (*fig*) to cook up quietly

mitoyen, ne [mitwajɛ̃, -ɛn] *adj* (*mur*)

m

common, party *cpd*; **maisons ~nes** semi-detached houses; (*plus de deux*) terraced (Brit) *ou* row (US) houses

mitrailler [mitʀaje] *vt* to machine-gun; (*fig: photographier*) to snap away at; **~ qn de** to pelt *ou* bombard sb with

mitraillette [mitʀajɛt] *nf* submachine gun

mitrailleuse [mitʀajøz] *nf* machine gun

mi-voix [mivwa]: **à ~** *adv* in a low *ou* hushed voice

mixage [miksaʒ] *nm* (*Ciné*) (sound) mixing

mixer, mixeur [miksœʀ] *nm* (*Culin*) (food) mixer

mixte [mikst] *adj* (*gén*) mixed; (*Scol*) mixed, coeducational; **à usage ~** dual-purpose; **cuisinière ~** combined gas and electric cooker; **équipe ~** combined team

mixture [mikstyʀ] *nf* mixture; (*fig*) concoction

MJC *sigle f* (= *maison des jeunes et de la culture*) community arts centre and youth club

Mlle (*pl* **Mlles**) *abr* = **Mademoiselle**

MM *abr* = **Messieurs** *voir* **Monsieur**

Mme (*pl* **Mmes**) *abr* = **Madame**

mobile [mɔbil] *adj* mobile; (*amovible*) loose, removable; (*pièce de machine*) moving; (*élément de meuble etc*) movable ▷ *nm* (*motif*) motive; (*œuvre d'art*) mobile; (*Physique*) moving object *ou* body; (**téléphone**) **~** mobile (phone) (Brit), cell (phone) (US)

mobilier, -ière [mɔbilje, -jɛʀ] *adj* (*Jur*) personal ▷ *nm* (*meubles*) furniture; **valeurs mobilières** transferable securities; **vente mobilière** sale of personal property *ou* chattels

mobiliser [mɔbilize] *vt* (*Mil*, *gén*) to mobilize

mobylette® [mɔbilɛt] *nf* moped

mocassin [mɔkasɛ̃] *nm* moccasin

moche [mɔʃ] *adj* (*fam*: laid) ugly; (: *mauvais*, *méprisable*) rotten

modalité [mɔdalite] *nf* form, mode; **modalités** *nfpl* (*d'un accord etc*) clauses, terms; **~s de paiement** methods of payment

mode [mɔd] *nf* fashion; (*commerce*) fashion trade *ou* industry ▷ *nm* (*manière*) form, mode, method; (*Ling*) mood; (*Inform*, *Mus*) mode; **travailler dans la ~** to be in the fashion business; **à la ~** fashionable, in fashion; **~ dialogué** (*Inform*) interactive *ou* conversational mode; **~ d'emploi** directions *pl* (for use); **~ de paiement** method of payment; **~ de vie** way of life

modèle [mɔdɛl] *adj* model ▷ *nm* model; (*qui pose: de peintre*) sitter; (*type*) type; (*gabarit*, *patron*) pattern; **~ courant** *ou* **de série** (*Comm*) production model; **~ déposé** registered design; **~ réduit** small-scale model

modeler [mɔdle] *vt* (*Art*) to model, mould; (*vêtement*, *érosion*) to mould, shape; **~ qch sur/ d'après** to model sth on

modem [mɔdɛm] *nm* (*Inform*) modem

modéré, e [mɔdeʀe] *adj*, *nm/f* moderate

modérer [mɔdeʀe] *vt* to moderate; **se modérer** *vi* to restrain o.s

moderne [mɔdɛʀn] *adj* modern ▷ *nm* (*Art*) modern style; (*ameublement*) modern furniture

moderniser [mɔdɛʀnize] *vt* to modernize

modeste [mɔdɛst] *adj* modest; (*origine*) humble, lowly

modestie [mɔdɛsti] *nf* modesty; **fausse ~** false modesty

modifier [mɔdifje] *vt* to modify, alter; (*Ling*) to modify; **se modifier** *vi* to alter

modique [mɔdik] *adj* (*salaire*, *somme*) modest

modiste [mɔdist] *nf* milliner

module [mɔdyl] *nm* module

moelle [mwal] *nf* marrow; (*fig*) pith, core; **~ épinière** spinal chord

moelleux, -euse [mwalø, -øz] *adj* soft; (*au goût*, *à l'ouïe*) mellow; (*gracieux*, *souple*) smooth; (*gâteau*) light and moist

mœurs [mœʀ] *nfpl* (*conduite*) morals; (*manières*) manners; (*pratiques sociales*) habits; (*mode de vie*) life style *sg*; (*d'une espèce animale*) behaviour *sg* (Brit), behavior *sg* (US); **femme de mauvaises ~** loose woman; **passer dans les ~** to become the custom; **contraire aux bonnes ~** contrary to proprieties

mohair [mɔɛʀ] *nm* mohair

moi [mwa] *pron me; (emphatique)*: **~, je ...** for my part, I ..., I myself ...; **c'est ~ qui l'ai fait** I did it, it was me who did it; **apporte-le-~** bring it to me; **à ~ ~** mine; (*dans un jeu*) my turn ▷ *nm inv* (*Psych*) ego, self; **à ~!** (*à l'aide*) help (me)!

moi-même [mwamɛm] *pron* myself; (*emphatique*) I myself

moindre [mwɛ̃dʀ] *adj* lesser; lower; **le (la) ~**, **les ~s** the least; the slightest; **le (la) ~ de** the least of; **c'est la ~ des choses** it's nothing at all

moine [mwan] *nm* monk, friar

moineau, x [mwano] *nm* sparrow

 MOT-CLÉ

moins [mwɛ̃] *adv* **1** *comparatif*; **moins (que)** less (than); **moins grand que** less tall than, not as tall as; **il a trois ans de moins que moi** he's three years younger than me; **il est moins intelligent que moi** he's not as clever as me, he's less clever than me; **moins je travaille, mieux je me porte** the less I work, the better I feel

2 *superlatif*; **le moins** (the) least; **c'est ce que j'aime le moins** it's what I like (the) least; **le(la) moins doué(e)** the least gifted; **au moins, du moins** at least; **pour le moins** at the very least

3: **moins de** (*quantité*) less (than); (*nombre*) fewer (than); **moins de sable/d'eau** less sand/water; **moins de livres/gens** fewer books/people; **moins de deux ans** less than

two years; **moins de midi** not yet midday 4: **de moins, en moins** (000): **100 euros/3 jours de moins** 100 euros/3 days less; **trois livres en moins** three books fewer; three books too few; **de l'argent en moins** less money; **le soleil en moins** but for the sun, minus the sun; **de moins en moins** less and less; **en moins de deux** in a flash *ou* a trice 5: **à moins de, à moins que** unless; **à moins de faire** unless we do (*ou* he does *etc*); **à moins que tu ne fasses** unless you do; **à moins d'un accident** barring any accident ▷ *prép*: **quatre moins deux** four minus two; **dix heures moins cinq** five to ten; **il fait moins cinq** it's five (degrees) below (freezing), it's minus five; **il est moins cinq** it's five to
▷ *nm* (*signe*) minus sign

mois [mwa] *nm* month; (*salaire, somme dû*) (monthly) pay *ou* salary; **treizième ~, double ~** extra month's salary

moisi, e [mwazi] *adj* mouldy (Brit), moldy (US), mildewed ▷ *nm* mould, mold, mildew; **odeur de ~** musty smell

moisir [mwaziʀ] *vi* to go mouldy (Brit) *ou* moldy (US); (*fig*) to rot; (*personne*) to hang about ▷ *vt* to make mouldy *ou* moldy

moisissure [mwazisyʀ] *nf* mould *no pl* (Brit), mold *no pl* (US)

moisson [mwasɔ̃] *nf* harvest; (*époque*) harvest (time); (*fig*): **faire une ~ de** to gather a wealth of

moissonner [mwasɔne] *vt* to harvest, reap; (*fig*) to collect

moissonneur, -euse [mwasɔnœʀ, -øz] *nm/f* harvester, reaper ▷ *nf* (*machine*) harvester

moissonneuse *nf* (*machine*) harvester

moite [mwat] *adj* (*peau, mains*) sweaty, sticky; (*atmosphère*) muggy

moitié [mwatje] *nf* half; (*épouse*): **sa ~** his better half; **la ~** half; **la ~ de** half (of), half the amount (*ou* number) of; **la ~ du temps/des gens** half the time/the people; **à la ~ de** halfway through; **~ moins grand** half as tall; **~ plus long** half as long again, longer by half; **à ~** half (*avant le verbe*), half- (*avant l'adjectif*); **à ~ prix** (at) half price, half-price; **de ~ by half; ~ ~** half-and-half

moka [mɔka] *nm* (*café*) mocha coffee; (*gâteau*) mocha cake

mol [mɔl] *adj m voir* **mou**

molaire [mɔlɛʀ] *nf* molar

molester [mɔlɛste] *vt* to manhandle, maul (about)

molle [mɔl] *adj f voir* **mou**

mollement [mɔlmɑ̃] *adv* softly; (*péj: travailler*) sluggishly; (*protester*) feebly

mollet [mɔlɛ] *nm* calf ▷ *adj m*: **œuf ~** soft-boiled egg

molletonné, e [mɔltɔne] *adj* (*gants etc*) fleece-lined

mollir [mɔliʀ] *vi* (*jambes*) to give way; (*Navig: vent*) to drop, die down; (*fig: personne*) to relent; (: *courage*) to fail, flag; (*substance*) to go soft

mollusque [mɔlysk] *nm* (Zool) mollusc; (*fig: personne*) lazy lump

môme [mom] *nm/f* (*fam: enfant*) brat; (: *fille*) bird (Brit), chick

moment [mɔmɑ̃] *nm* moment; (*occasion*): **profiter du ~** to take (advantage of) the opportunity; **ce n'est pas le ~** this is not the right time; **à un certain ~** at some point; **à un ~ donné** at a certain point; **à quel ~?** when exactly?; **au même ~** at the same time; (*instant*) at the same moment; **pour un bon ~** for a good while; **pour le ~** for the moment, for the time being; **au ~ de** at the time of; **au ~ où** as; at a time when; **à tout ~** at any time *ou* moment; (*continuellement*) constantly, continually; **en ce ~** at the moment; (*aujourd'hui*) at present; **sur le ~** at the time; **par ~s** now and then, at times; **d'un ~ à l'autre** any time (now); **du ~ où** *ou* **que** seeing that, since; **n'avoir pas un ~ à soi** not to have a minute to oneself

momentané, e [mɔmɑ̃tane] *adj* temporary, momentary

momentanément [mɔmɑ̃tanemɑ̃] *adv* for a moment, for a while

momie [mɔmi] *nf* mummy

mon [mɔ̃], **ma** [ma] (*pl* **mes**) [me] *adj poss* my

Monaco [mɔnako] *nm*: **le ~** Monaco

monarchie [mɔnaʀʃi] *nf* monarchy

monastère [mɔnastɛʀ] *nm* monastery

monceau, x [mɔ̃so] *nm* heap

mondain, e [mɔ̃dɛ̃, -ɛn] *adj* (*soirée, vie*) society *cpd*; (*obligations*) social; (*peintre, écrivain*) fashionable; (*personne*) society *cpd* ▷ *nm/f* society man/woman, socialite ▷ *nf*: **la M~e, la police ~e** ≈ the vice squad

monde [mɔ̃d] *nm* world; (*personnes mondaines*): **le ~** (high) society; (*milieu*): **être du même ~** to move in the same circles; (*gens*): **il y a du ~** (*beaucoup de gens*) there are a lot of people; (*quelques personnes*) there are some people; **y a-t-il du ~ dans le salon?** is there anybody in the lounge?; **beaucoup/peu de ~** many/few people; **le meilleur** *etc* **du ~** the best *etc* in the world; **mettre au ~** to bring into the world; **pas le moins du ~** not in the least; **se faire un ~ de qch** to make a great deal of fuss about sth; **tour du ~** round-the-world trip; **homme/femme du ~** society man/woman

mondial, e, -aux [mɔ̃djal, -o] *adj* (*population*) world *cpd*; (*influence*) world-wide

mondialement [mɔ̃djalmɑ̃] *adv* throughout the world

mondialisation [mɔ̃djalizasjɔ̃] *nf* globalization; (*d'une technique*) global application; (*d'un conflit*) global spread

monégasque [mɔnegask] *adj* Monegasque, of *ou* from Monaco ▷ *nm/f*: **M~** Monegasque

monétaire [mɔnetɛʀ] *adj* monetary

moniteur, -trice [mɔnitœʀ, -tʀis] *nm/f*
(*Sport*) instructor/instructress; (*de colonie de vacances*) supervisor ▷ *nm* (*écran*) monitor; ~ **cardiaque** cardiac monitor; ~ **d'auto-école** driving instructor

monnaie [mɔnɛ] *nf* (*pièce*) coin; (*Écon: gén: moyen d'échange*) currency; (*petites pièces*): **avoir de la ~** to have (some) change; **faire de la ~** to get (some) change; **avoir/faire la ~ de 20 euros** to have/get change for 20 euros; **faire *ou* donner à qn la ~ de 20 euros** to give sb change for 20 euros, change 20 euros for sb; **rendre à qn la ~ (sur 20 euros)** to give sb the change (from *ou* out of 20 euros); **servir de ~ d'échange** (*fig*) to be used as a bargaining counter ou as bargaining counters; **payer en ~ de singe** to fob (sb) off with empty promises; **c'est ~ courante** it's a common occurrence; **~ légale** legal tender

monnayer [mɔneje] *vt* to convert into cash; (*talent*) to capitalize on

monologue [mɔnɔlɔg] *nm* monologue, soliloquy; **~ intérieur** stream of consciousness

monologuer [mɔnɔlɔge] *vi* to soliloquize

monoparental, e, -aux [mɔnɔpaʀɑ̃tal, -o] *adj*: **famille monoparentale** single-parent *ou* one-parent family

monopole [mɔnɔpɔl] *nm* monopoly

monotone [mɔnɔtɔn] *adj* monotonous

Monsieur [məsjø] (*pl* **Messieurs**) [mesjø] *nm* (*titre*) Mr; (*homme quelconque*): **un/le monsieur** a/the gentleman; **~, ...** (*en tête de lettre*) Dear Sir, ...; *voir aussi* **Madame**

monstre [mɔ̃stʀ] *nm* monster ▷ *adj* (*fam: effet, publicité*) massive; **un travail ~** a fantastic amount of work; an enormous job; **~ sacré** superstar

monstrueux, -euse [mɔ̃stʀyø, -øz] *adj* monstrous

mont [mɔ̃] *nm*: **par ~s et par vaux** up hill and down dale; **le M~ Blanc** Mont Blanc; **~ de Vénus** mons veneris

montage [mɔ̃taʒ] *nm* putting up; (*d'un bijou*) mounting, setting; (*d'une machine etc*) assembly; (*Photo*) photomontage; (*Ciné*) editing; **~ sonore** sound editing

montagnard, e [mɔ̃taɲaʀ, -aʀd] *adj* mountain *cpd* ▷ *nm/f* mountain-dweller

montagne [mɔ̃taɲ] *nf* (*cime*) mountain; (*région*): **la ~** the mountains *pl*; **la haute ~** the high mountains; **les ~s Rocheuses** the Rocky Mountains, the Rockies; **~s russes** big dipper *sg*, switchback *sg*

montagneux, -euse [mɔ̃taɲø, -øz] *adj* mountainous; (*basse montagne*) hilly

montant, e [mɔ̃tɑ̃, -ɑ̃t] *adj* (*mouvement, marée*) rising; (*chemin*) uphill; (*robe, corsage*) high-necked ▷ *nm* (*somme, total*) (sum) total, (total) amount; (*de fenêtre*) upright; (*de lit*) post

monte-charge [mɔ̃tʃaʀʒ] *nm inv* goods lift, hoist

montée [mɔ̃te] *nf* rising, rise; (*escalade*) ascent,

climb; (*chemin*) way up; (*côte*) hill; **au milieu de la ~** halfway up; **le moteur chauffe dans les ~s** the engine overheats going uphill

Monténégro [mɔ̃tenegro] *nm*: **le ~** Montenegro

monter [mɔ̃te] *vt* (*escalier, côte*) to go (*ou* come) up; (*valise, paquet*) to take (*ou* bring) up; (*cheval*) to mount; (*femelle*) to cover, serve; (*étagère*) to raise; (*tente, échafaudage*) to put up; (*machine*) to assemble; (*bijou*) to mount, set; (*Couture*) to sew on; (: *manche*) to set in; (*Ciné*) to edit; (*Théât*) to put on, stage; (*société, coup etc*) to set up; (*fournir, équiper*) to equip ▷ *vi* to go (*ou* come) up; (*avion, voiture*) to climb, go up; (*chemin, niveau, température, voix, prix*) to go up, rise; (*brouillard, bruit*) to rise, come up; (*passager*) to get on; (*à cheval*): **~ bien/mal** to ride well/badly; **~ à cheval** to get on *ou* mount a horse; (*faire du cheval*) to ride (a horse); **~ à bicyclette** to get on *ou* mount a bicycle, to (ride a) bicycle; **~ à pied/en voiture** to walk/ drive up, go up on foot/by car; **~ dans le train/l'avion** to get into the train/plane, board the train/plane; **~ sur** to climb up onto; **~ sur *ou* à un arbre/une échelle** to climb (up) a tree/ladder; **~ à bord** to (get on) board; **~ à la tête de qn** to go to sb's head; **~ sur les planches** to go on the stage; **~ en grade** to be promoted; **se monter** (*s'équiper*) to equip o.s., get kitted out (*Brit*); **se ~ à** (*frais etc*) to add up to, come to; **~ qn contre qn** to set sb against sb; **~ la tête à qn** to give sb ideas

montgolfière [mɔ̃gɔlfjɛʀ] *nf* hot-air balloon

montre [mɔ̃tʀ] *nf* watch; (*ostentation*): **pour la ~** for show; **~ en main** exactly, to the minute; **faire ~ de** to display, show; **contre la ~** (*Sport*) against the clock; **~ de plongée** diver's watch

Montréal [mɔ̃real] *n* Montreal

montre-bracelet (*pl* **montres-bracelets**) [mɔ̃tʀabʀaslɛ] *nf* wrist watch

montrer [mɔ̃tʀe] *vt* to show; **se montrer** to appear; **~ qch à qn** to show sb sth; **~ qch du doigt** to point to sth, point one's finger at sth; **se ~ intelligent** to prove to (be) intelligent

monture [mɔ̃tyʀ] *nf* (*bête*) mount; (*d'une bague*) setting; (*de lunettes*) frame

monument [mɔnymɑ̃] *nm* monument; **~ aux morts** war memorial

moquer [mɔke]: **se ~ de** *vt* to make fun of, laugh at; (*fam: se désintéresser de*) to not care about; (*tromper*): **se ~ de qn** to take sb for a ride

moquerie [mɔkʀi] *nf* mockery *no pl*

moquette [mɔkɛt] *nf* fitted carpet, wall-to-wall carpeting *no pl*

moqueur, -euse [mɔkœʀ, -øz] *adj* mocking

moral, e, -aux [mɔʀal, -o] *adj* moral ▷ *nm* morale ▷ *nf* (*conduite*) morals *pl* (*règles*), moral code, ethic; (*valeurs*) moral standards *pl*, morality; (*science*) ethics *sg*, moral philosophy; (*conclusion: d'une fable etc*) moral;

au ~, **sur le plan** ~ morally; **avoir le** ~ (fam) to be in good spirits; **avoir le** ~ **à zéro** to be really down; **faire la** ~**e à** to lecture, preach at

moralité [mɔralite] nf (d'une action, attitude) morality; (conduite) morals pl; (conclusion, enseignement) moral

morceau, x [mɔrso] nm piece, bit; (d'une œuvre) passage, extract; (Mus) piece; (Culin: de viande) cut; (de sucre) lump; **mettre en ~x** to pull to pieces ou bits; **manger un ~** to have a bite (to eat)

morceler [mɔrsəle] vt to break up, divide up

mordant, e [mɔrdɑ̃, -ɑ̃t] adj (ton, remarque) scathing, cutting; (froid) biting ▷ nm (dynamisme, énergie) spirit; (fougue) bite, punch

mordiller [mɔrdije] vt to nibble at, chew at

mordre [mɔrdr] vt to bite; (lime, vis) to bite into ▷ vi (poisson) to bite; ~ **dans** to bite into; ~ **sur** (fig) to go over into, overlap into; ~ **à qch** (comprendre, aimer) to take to; ~ **à l'hameçon** to bite, rise to the bait

mordu, e [mɔrdy] pp de **mordre** ▷ adj (amoureux) smitten ▷ nm/f enthusiast; **un ~ du jazz/de la voile** a jazz/sailing fanatic ou buff

morfondre [mɔrfɔ̃dr]: **se morfondre** vi to mope

morgue [mɔrg] nf (arrogance) haughtiness; (lieu: de la police) morgue; (: à l'hôpital) mortuary

morne [mɔrn] adj (personne, visage) glum, gloomy; (temps, vie) dismal, dreary

morose [mɔroz] adj sullen, morose; (marché) sluggish

mors [mɔr] nm bit

morse [mɔrs] nm (Zool) walrus; (Tél) Morse (code)

morsure [mɔrsyr] nf bite

mort¹ [mɔr] nf death; **se donner la ~** to take one's own life; **de ~** (silence, pâleur) deathly; **blessé à ~** fatally wounded ou injured; **la vie, à la ~** for better, for worse; ~ **clinique** brain death; ~ **subite du nourrisson**, ~ **au berceau** cot death

mort² [mɔr, mɔrt] pp de **mourir** ▷ adj dead ▷ nm/f (défunt) dead man/woman; (victime): **il y a eu plusieurs ~s** several people were killed, there were several killed ▷ nm (Cartes) dummy; ~ **ou vif** dead or alive; ~ **de peur/fatigue** frightened to death/dead tired; ~**s et blessés** casualties; **faire le ~** to play dead; (fig) to lie low

mortalité [mɔrtalite] nf mortality, death rate

mortel, le [mɔrtɛl] adj (poison etc) deadly, lethal; (accident, blessure) fatal; (silence, ennemi) deadly; (Rel: danger, frayeur, péché) mortal; (fig: froid) deathly; (: ennui, soirée) deadly (boring) ▷ nm/f mortal

mortier [mɔrtje] nm (gén) mortar

mort-né, e [mɔrne] adj (enfant) stillborn; (fig) abortive

mortuaire [mɔrtɥɛr] adj funeral cpd; **avis ~s** death announcements, intimations; **chapelle ~** mortuary chapel; **couronne ~** (funeral) wreath; **domicile ~** house of the deceased; **drap ~** pall

morue [mɔry] nf (Zool) cod inv; (Culin: salée) salt-cod

mosaïque [mɔzaik] nf (Art) mosaic; (fig) patchwork

Moscou [mɔsku] n Moscow

mosquée [mɔske] nf mosque

mot [mo] nm word; (message) line, note; (bon mot etc) saying; **le ~ de la fin** the last word; ~ **à** ~ adj, adv word for word; ~ **pour** ~ word for word, verbatim; **sur** ou **à ces ~s** with these words; **en un ~** in a word; **à ~s couverts** in veiled terms; **prendre qn au ~** to take sb at his word; **se donner le ~** to send the word round; **avoir son ~ à dire** to have a say; ~ **d'ordre** watchword; ~ **de passe** password; ~**s croisés** crossword (puzzle) sg

motard [mɔtar] nm biker; (policier) motorcycle cop

mot-dièse [modjɛz] nm (Inform: Twitter) hashtag

motel [mɔtɛl] nm motel

moteur, -trice [mɔtœr, -tris] adj (Anat, Physiol) motor; (Tech) driving; (Auto): **à 4 roues motrices** 4-wheel drive ▷ nm engine, motor; (fig) mover, mainspring; **à ~** power-driven, motor cpd; ~ **à deux temps** two-stroke engine; ~ **à explosion** internal combustion engine; ~ **à réaction** jet engine; ~ **de recherche** search engine; ~ **thermique** heat engine

motif [mɔtif] nm (cause) motive; (décoratif) design, pattern, motif; (d'un tableau) subject, motif; (Mus) figure, motif; **motifs** nmpl (Jur) grounds pl; **sans ~** adj groundless

motivation [mɔtivasjɔ̃] nf motivation

motiver [mɔtive] vt (justifier) to justify, account for; (Admin, Jur, Psych) to motivate

moto [mɔto] nf (motor)bike; ~ **verte** ou **de trial** trail (Brit) ou dirt (US) bike

motocyclette [mɔtosiklɛt] nf motorbike, motorcycle

motocycliste [mɔtosiklist] nm/f motorcyclist

motorisé, e [mɔtorize] adj (troupe) motorized; (personne) having one's own transport

motrice [mɔtris] adj f voir **moteur**

motte [mɔt] nf: ~ **de terre** lump of earth, clod (of earth); ~ **de gazon** turf, sod; ~ **de beurre** lump of butter

mou, mol, molle [mu, mɔl] adj soft; (péj: visage, traits) flabby; (: geste) limp; (: empoté) sluggish; (: résistance, protestations) feeble ▷ nm (homme mou) wimp; (abats) lights pl, lungs pl; (de la corde): **avoir du ~** to be slack; **donner du ~** to slacken, loosen; **avoir les jambes molles** to be weak at the knees

mouche [muʃ] nf fly; (Escrime) button; (de taffetas) patch; **prendre la ~** to go into a huff; **faire ~** to score a bull's-eye

moucher [muʃe] vt (enfant) to blow the nose of; (chandelle) to snuff (out); **se moucher** vi to blow one's nose

moucheron [muʃʀɔ̃] nm midge

mouchoir [muʃwaʀ] nm handkerchief, hanky; **~ en papier** tissue, paper hanky

moudre [mudʀ] vt to grind

moue [mu] nf pout; **faire la ~** to pout; (fig) to pull a face

mouette [mwɛt] nf (sea)gull

moufle [mufl] nf (gant) mitt(en); (Tech) pulley block

mouillé, e [muje] adj wet

mouiller [muje] vt (humecter) to wet, moisten; (tremper): **~ qn/qch** to make sb/sth wet; (Culin: ragoût) to add stock ou wine to; (couper, diluer) to water down; (mine etc) to lay ▷ vi (Navig) to lie ou be at anchor; **se mouiller** to get wet; (fam: prendre des risques) to commit o.s. to; to get (o.s.) involved; **~ l'ancre** to drop ou cast anchor

moulant, e [mulɑ̃, -ɑ̃t] adj figure-hugging

moule [mul] vb voir **moudre** ▷ nf (mollusque) mussel ▷ nm (creux, Culin) mould (Brit), mold (US); (modèle plein) cast; **~ à gâteau** nm cake tin (Brit) ou pan (US); **~ à gaufre** nm waffle iron; **~ à tarte** nm pie ou flan dish

moulent [mul] vb voir **moudre**; **mouler**

mouler [mule] vt (brique) to mould (Brit), mold (US); (statue) to cast; (visage, bas-relief) to make a cast of; (lettre) to shape with care; (vêtement) to hug, fit closely round; **~ qch sur** (fig) to model sth on

moulin [mulɛ̃] nm mill; (fam) engine; **~ à café** coffee mill; **~ à eau** watermill; **~ à légumes** (vegetable) shredder; **~ à paroles** chatterbox; **~ à poivre** pepper mill; **~ à prières** prayer wheel; **~ à vent** windmill

moulinet [mulinɛ] nm (de treuil) winch; (de canne à pêche) reel; (mouvement): **faire des ~s avec qch** to whirl sth around

moulinette® [mulinɛt] nf (vegetable) shredder

moulu, e [muly] pp de **moudre** ▷ adj (café) ground

mourant, e [muʀɑ̃, -ɑ̃t] vb voir **mourir** ▷ adj dying ▷ nm/f dying man/woman

mourir [muʀiʀ] vi to die; (civilisation) to die out; **~ assassiné** to be murdered; **~ de froid/faim/vieillesse** to die of exposure/hunger/old age; **~ de faim/d'ennui** (fig) to be starving/be bored to death; **~ d'envie de faire** to be dying to do; **s'ennuyer à ~** to be bored to death

mousse [mus] nf (Bot) moss; (de savon) lather; (écume: sur eau, bière) froth, foam; (: shampooing) lather; (de champagne) bubbles pl; (Culin) mousse; (en caoutchouc etc) foam ▷ nm (Navig) ship's boy; **bain de ~** bubble bath; **bas ~** stretch stockings; **balle ~** rubber ball; **~ carbonique** (fire-fighting) foam; **~ de nylon** nylon foam; (tissu) stretch nylon; **~ à raser** shaving foam

mousseline [muslin] nf (Textiles) muslin;

chiffon; **pommes ~** (Culin) creamed potatoes

mousser [muse] vi (bière, détergent) to foam; (savon) to lather

mousseux, -euse [musø, -øz] adj (chocolat) frothy; (eau) foamy, frothy; (vin) sparkling ▷ nm: (vin) **~** sparkling wine

mousson [musɔ̃] nf monsoon

moustache [mustaʃ] nf moustache; **moustaches** nfpl (d'animal) whiskers pl

moustachu, e [mustaʃy] adj with a moustache

moustiquaire [mustikɛʀ] nf (rideau) mosquito net; (chassis) mosquito screen

moustique [mustik] nm mosquito

moutarde [mutaʀd] nf mustard ▷ adj inv mustard(-coloured)

mouton [mutɔ̃] nm (Zool, péj) sheep inv; (peau) sheepskin; (Culin) mutton

mouvement [muvmɑ̃] nm (gen, aussi: mécanisme) movement; (ligne courbe) contours pl; (fig: tumulte, agitation) activity, bustle; (: impulsion) impulse; reaction; (geste) gesture; (Mus: rythme) tempo; **avoir un bon ~** to make a nice gesture; **en ~** in motion; on the move; **mettre qch en ~** to set sth in motion, set sth going; **~ d'humeur** fit ou burst of temper; **~ d'opinion** trend of (public) opinion; **le ~ perpétuel** perpetual motion

mouvementé, e [muvmɑ̃te] adj (vie, poursuite) eventful; (réunion) turbulent

mouvoir [muvwaʀ] vt (levier, membre) to move; (machine) to drive; **se mouvoir** vi to move

moyen, ne [mwajɛ̃, -ɛn] adj average; (tailles, prix) medium; (de grandeur moyenne) medium-sized ▷ nm (façon) means sg, way ▷ nf average; (Statistique) mean; (Scol: à l'examen) pass mark; (Auto) average speed; **moyens** nmpl (capacités) means; **très ~** (résultats) pretty poor; **je n'en ai pas les ~s** I can't afford it; **au ~ de** by means of; **y a-t-il ~ de ...?** is it possible to ...?, can one ...?; **par quel ~?** how?, which way?, by which means?; **par tous les ~s** by every possible means, every possible way; **avec les ~s du bord** (fig) with what's available ou what comes to hand; **employer les grands ~s** to resort to drastic measures; **par ses propres ~s** all by oneself; **en ~ne** on (an) average; **faire la ~ne** to work out the average; **~ de locomotion/d'expression** means of transport/expression; **~ âge** Middle Ages; **~ de transport** means of transport; **~ne d'âge** average age; **~ne entreprise** (Comm) medium-sized firm

moyennant [mwajɛnɑ̃] prép (somme) for; (service, conditions) in return for; (travail, effort) with

Moyen-Orient [mwajɛnɔʀjɑ̃] nm: **le ~** the Middle East

moyeu, x [mwajø] nm hub

MSF sigle mpl = **Médecins sans frontières**

MST sigle f (= maladie sexuellement transmissible) STD (= sexually transmitted disease)

mû, mue [my] *pp de* **mouvoir**

muer [mɥe] *vi (oiseau, mammifère)* to moult (Brit), molt (US); *(serpent)* to slough (its skin); *(jeune garçon)*: **il mue** his voice is breaking; **se ~ en** to transform into

muet, te [mɥɛ, -ɛt] *adj* with a speech impairment; *(fig)*: **~ d'admiration** *etc* speechless with admiration *etc*; *(joie, douleur, Ciné)* silent; *(Ling: lettre)* silent, mute; *(carte)* blank ▷ *nm/f* person with a speech impairment ▷ *nm*: **le ~** *(Ciné)* the silent cinema *ou (esp US)* movies

mufle [myfl] *nm* muzzle; *(goujat)* boor ▷ *adj* boorish

mugir [myʒiʀ] *vi (bœuf)* to bellow; *(vache)* to low, moo; *(fig)* to howl

muguet [mygɛ] *nm (Bot)* lily of the valley; *(Méd)* thrush

mule [myl] *nf (Zool)* (she-)mule

mulet [mylɛ] *nm (Zool)* (he-)mule; *(poisson)* mullet

multinational, e, -aux [myltinasjɔnal, -o] *adj, nf* multinational

multiple [myltipl] *adj* multiple, numerous; *(varié)* many, manifold ▷ *nm (Math)* multiple

multiplication [myltiplikasjɔ̃] *nf* multiplication

multiplier [myltiplije] *vt* to multiply; **se multiplier** *vi* to multiply; *(fig: personne)* to be everywhere at once

municipal, e, -aux [mynisipal, -o] *adj (élections, stade)* municipal; *(conseil)* town *cpd*; **piscine/bibliothèque ~e** public swimming pool/library

municipalité [mynisipalite] *nf (corps municipal)* town council, corporation; *(commune)* town, municipality

munir [myniʀ] *vt*: **~ qn/qch de** to equip sb/ sth with; **se ~ de** to provide o.s. with

munitions [mynisjɔ̃] *nfpl* ammunition *sg*

mur [myʀ] *nm* wall; *(fig)* stone *ou* brick wall; **faire le ~** *(interne, soldat)* to jump the wall; **~ du son** sound barrier

mûr, e [myʀ] *adj* ripe; *(personne)* mature ▷ *nf (de la ronce)* blackberry; *(du mûrier)* mulberry

muraille [myʀaj] *nf* (high) wall

mural, e, -aux [myʀal, -o] *adj* wall *cpd* ▷ *nm (Art)* mural

mûre [myʀ] *nf* blackberry

muret [myʀɛ] *nm* low wall

mûrir [myʀiʀ] *vi (fruit, blé)* to ripen; *(abcès, furoncle)* to come to a head; *(fig: idée, personne)* to mature; *(projet)* to develop ▷ *vt (fruit, blé)* to ripen; *(personne)* to (make) mature; *(pensée, projet)* to nurture

murmure [myʀmyʀ] *nm* murmur; **murmures** *nmpl (plaintes)* murmurings, mutterings

murmurer [myʀmyʀe] *vi* to murmur; *(se plaindre)* to mutter, grumble

muscade [myskad] *nf (aussi:* **noix (de) ~)** nutmeg

muscat [myska] *nm (raisin)* muscat grape; *(vin)* muscatel (wine)

muscle [myskl] *nm* muscle

musclé, e [myskle] *adj (personne, corps)* muscular; *(fig: politique, régime etc)* strong-arm *cpd*

museau, x [myzo] *nm* muzzle; *(Culin)* brawn

musée [myze] *nm* museum; *(de peinture)* art gallery

museler [myzle] *vt* to muzzle

muselière [myzəljɛʀ] *nf* muzzle

musette [myzɛt] *nf (sac)* lunch bag ▷ *adj inv (orchestre etc)* accordion *cpd*

musical, e, -aux [myzikal, -o] *adj* musical

music-hall [myzikol] *nm (salle)* variety theatre; *(genre)* variety

musicien, ne [myzisjɛ̃, -ɛn] *adj* musical ▷ *nm/f* musician

musique [myzik] *nf* music; *(fanfare)* band; **faire de la ~** to make music; *(jouer d'un instrument)* to play an instrument; **~ de chambre** chamber music; **~ de fond** background music

---

● FÊTE DE LA MUSIQUE

● The *Fête de la Musique* is a music festival
● which takes place every year on 21 June.
● Throughout France, local musicians
● perform free of charge in parks, streets
● and squares.

---

musulman, e [myzylmɑ̃, -an] *adj, nm/f* Moslem, Muslim

mutation [mytasjɔ̃] *nf (Admin)* transfer; *(Bio)* mutation

muter [myte] *vt (Admin)* to transfer, move

mutilé, e [mytile] *nm/f* person with a disability *(through loss of limbs)*; **~ de guerre** disabled ex-serviceman; **grand ~** severely disabled person

mutiler [mytile] *vt* to mutilate, maim; *(fig)* to mutilate, deface

mutin, e [mytɛ̃, -in] *adj (enfant, air, ton)* mischievous, impish ▷ *nm/f (Mil, Navig)* mutineer

mutinerie [mytinʀi] *nf* mutiny

mutisme [mytism] *nm* silence

mutuel, le [mytɥɛl] *adj* mutual ▷ *nf* mutual benefit society

myope [mjɔp] *adj* short-sighted

myosotis [mjɔzɔtis] *nm* forget-me-not

myrtille [miʀtij] *nf* blueberry, bilberry (Brit)

mystère [mistɛʀ] *nm* mystery

mystérieux, -euse [misteʀjø, -øz] *adj* mysterious

mystifier [mistifje] *vt* to fool, take in; *(tromper)* to mystify

mythe [mit] *nm* myth

mythologie [mitɔlɔʒi] *nf* mythology

m

n' [n] adv voir **ne**

nacre [nakʀ] nf mother-of-pearl

nage [naʒ] nf swimming; (*manière*) style of swimming, stroke; **traverser/s'éloigner à la ~** to swim across/away; **en ~** bathed in sweat; **~ indienne** sidestroke; **~ libre** freestyle; **~ papillon** butterfly

nageoire [naʒwaʀ] nf fin

nager [naʒe] vi to swim; (*fig: ne rien comprendre*) to be all at sea; **~ dans** to be swimming in; (*vêtements*) to be lost in; **~ dans le bonheur** to be overjoyed

nageur, -euse [naʒœʀ, -øz] nm/f swimmer

naguère [nagɛʀ] adv (*il y a peu de temps*) not long ago; (*autrefois*) formerly

naïf, -ïve [naif, naiv] adj naïve

nain, e [nɛ̃, nɛn] nm/f person of small stature

naissance [nɛsɑ̃s] nf birth; **donner ~ à** to give birth to; (*fig*) to give rise to; **prendre ~** to originate; **aveugle de ~** born blind; **Français de ~** French by birth; **à la ~ des cheveux** at the roots of the hair; **lieu de ~** place of birth

naître [nɛtʀ] vi to be born; (*conflit, complications*): **~ de** to arise from, be born out of; **~ à** (*amour, poésie*) to awaken to; **je suis né en 1960** I was born in 1960; **il naît plus de filles que de garçons** there are more babies born than boys; **faire ~** (*fig*) to give rise to, arouse

naïveté [naivte] nf naivety

nana [nana] nf (*fam: fille*) bird (Brit), chick

nantir [nɑ̃tiʀ] vt: **~ qn de** to provide sb with; **les nantis** (*péj*) the well-to-do

nappe [nap] nf tablecloth; (*fig*) sheet; (*de pétrole, gaz*) layer; **~ de mazout** oil slick; **~ (phréatique)** water table

napperon [napʀɔ̃] nm table-mat; **~ individuel** place mat

narcodollars [naʀkodɔlaʀ] nmpl drug money *no pl*

narguer [naʀge] vt to taunt

narine [naʀin] nf nostril

narquois, e [naʀkwa, -waz] adj derisive, mocking

natal, e [natal] adj native

natalité [natalite] nf birth rate

natation [natasjɔ̃] nf swimming; **faire de la ~** to go swimming (*regularly*)

natif, -ive [natif, -iv] adj native

nation [nasjɔ̃] nf nation; **les N~s unies (NU)** the United Nations (UN)

national, e, -aux [nasjonal, -o] adj national ▷ nf: (*route*) **~e** ≈ A road (Brit), ≈ state highway (US); **obsèques ~es** state funeral

nationaliser [nasjonalize] vt to nationalize

nationalisme [nasjonalism] nm nationalism

nationalité [nasjonalite] nf nationality; **de ~ française** of French nationality

natte [nat] nf (*tapis*) mat; (*cheveux*) plait

naturaliser [natyralize] vt to naturalize; (*empailler*) to stuff

nature [natyʀ] nf nature ▷ adj, adv (Culin) plain, without seasoning or sweetening; (*café, thé: sans lait*) black; (: *sans sucre*) without sugar; (*yaourt*) natural; **payer en ~** to pay in kind; **peint d'après ~** painted from life; **être de ~ à faire qch** (*propre à*) to be the sort of thing (*ou* person) to do sth; **~ morte** still-life

naturel, le [natyʀɛl] adj natural ▷ nm naturalness; (*caractère*) disposition, nature; (*autochtone*) native; (*aussi*: **au ~**: Culin) in water; in its own juices

naturellement [natyʀɛlmɑ̃] adv naturally; (*bien sûr*) of course

naufrage [nofʀaʒ] nm (ship)wreck; (*fig*) wreck; **faire ~** to be shipwrecked

nauséabond, e [nozeabɔ̃, -ɔ̃d] adj foul, nauseous

nausée [noze] nf nausea; **avoir la ~** to feel sick; **avoir des ~s** to have waves of nausea, feel nauseous *ou* sick

nautique [notik] adj nautical, water *cpd*; **sports ~s** water sports

naval, e [naval] adj naval; (*industrie*) shipbuilding

navet [navɛ] nm turnip; (*péj: film*) third-rate film

navette [navɛt] nf shuttle; (*en car etc*) shuttle (service); **faire la ~ (entre)** to go to and fro (between), shuttle (between); **~ spatiale** space shuttle

navigateur [navigatœʀ] nm (Navig) seafarer, sailor; (Aviat) navigator; (Inform) browser

navigation [navigasjɔ̃] nf navigation, sailing; (Comm) shipping; **compagnie de ~**

shipping company; **~ spatiale** space navigation

naviguer [navige] vi to navigate, sail; **~ sur Internet** to browse the Internet

navire [naviʀ] nm ship; **~ de guerre** warship; **~ marchand** merchantman

navrer [navʀe] vt to upset, distress; **je suis navré (de/de faire/que)** I'm so sorry (for/for doing/that)

ne, n' [nə, n] adv voir **pas**; **plus**; **jamais** etc; (sans valeur négative: non traduit): **c'est plus loin que je ne le croyais** it's further than I thought

né, e [ne] pp de **naître**; **né en 1960** born in 1960; **née Scott** née Scott; **né(e) de ... et de ... son/daughter of ... and of ...**; **né d'une mère française** having a French mother; **né pour commander** born to lead ▷ adj: **un comédien né** a born comedian

néanmoins [neɑ̃mwɛ̃] adv nevertheless, yet

néant [neɑ̃] nm nothingness; **réduire à ~** to bring to nought; (espoir) to dash

nécessaire [neseseʀ] adj necessary ▷ nm necessary; (sac) kit; **faire le ~** to do the necessary; **n'emporter que le strict ~** to take only what is strictly necessary; **~ de couture** sewing kit; **~ de toilette** toilet bag; **~ de voyage** overnight bag

nécessité [nesesite] nf necessity; **se trouver dans la ~ de faire qch** to find it necessary to do sth; **par ~** out of necessity

nécessiter [nesesite] vt to require

nécrologique [nekʀɔlɔʒik] adj: **article ~** obituary; **rubrique ~** obituary column

nectar [nektaʀ] nm nectar

néerlandais, e [neɛʀlɑ̃dɛ, -ɛz] adj Dutch, of the Netherlands ▷ nm (Ling) Dutch ▷ nm/f: **N~, e** Dutchman/woman; **les N~** the Dutch

nef [nɛf] nf (d'église) nave

néfaste [nefast] adj (nuisible) harmful; (funeste) ill-fated

négatif, -ive [negatif, iv] adj negative ▷ nm (Photo) negative

négligé, e [negliʒe] adj (en désordre) slovenly ▷ nm (tenue) negligee

négligeable [negliʒabl] adj insignificant, negligible

négligent, e [negliʒɑ̃, -ɑ̃t] adj careless; (Jur etc) negligent

négliger [negliʒe] vt (épouse, jardin) to neglect; (tenue) to be careless about; (avis, précautions) to disregard, overlook; **~ de faire** to fail to do, not bother to do; **se négliger** to neglect o.s

négoce [negɔs] nm trade

négociant, e [negɔsjɑ̃, jɑ̃t] nm/f merchant

négociation [negɔsjasjɔ̃] nf negotiation; **~s collectives** collective bargaining sg

négocier [negɔsje] vi, vt to negotiate

nègre [negʀ] nm (péj) Negro (!); (péj: écrivain) ghost writer ▷ adj (péj) Negro (!)

neige [nɛʒ] nf snow; **battre les œufs en ~** (Culin) to whip ou beat the egg whites until stiff; **~ carbonique** dry ice; **~ fondue** (par terre) slush; (qui tombe) sleet; **~ poudreuse** powdery snow

neiger [neʒe] vi to snow

nénuphar [nenyfaʀ] nm water-lily

néon [neɔ̃] nm neon

néo-zélandais, e [neɔzelɑ̃dɛ, -ɛz] adj New Zealand cpd ▷ nm/f: **N~, e** New Zealander

Népal [nepal] nm: **le ~** Nepal

nerf [nɛʀ] nm nerve; (fig) spirit; (: forces) stamina; **nerfs** nmpl nerves; **être ou vivre sur les ~s** to live on one's nerves; **être à bout de ~s** to be at the end of one's tether; **passer ses ~s sur qn** to take it out on sb

nerveux, -euse [nɛʀvø, -øz] adj nervous; (cheval) highly-strung; (irritable) touchy, nervy; (voiture) nippy, responsive; (tendineux) sinewy

nervosité [nɛʀvozite] nf nervousness; (émotivité) excitability, tenseness

nervure [nɛʀvyʀ] nf (de feuille) vein; (Archit, Tech) rib

n'est-ce pas [nɛspa] adv isn't it?, won't you? etc (selon le verbe qui précède); **c'est bon, ~?** it's good, isn't it?; **il a peur, ~?** he's afraid, isn't he?; **~ que c'est bon?** don't you think it's good?; **lui, ~, il peut se le permettre** he, of course, can afford to do that, can't he?

net, nette [nɛt] adj (sans équivoque, distinct) clear; (photo) sharp; (évident) definite; (amélioration, différence) marked, distinct; (propre) neat, clean; (Comm: prix, salaire, poids) net ▷ adv (refuser) flatly ▷ nm: **mettre au ~** to copy out; **s'arrêter ~** to stop dead; **la lame a cassé ~** the blade snapped clean through; **faire place nette** to make a clean sweep; **~ d'impôt** tax free

Net [nɛt] nm (Internet): **le ~** the Net

netiquette [netiket] nf netiquette

nettement [nɛtmɑ̃] adv (distinctement) clearly; (évidemment) definitely; (incontestablement) decidedly; (avec comparatif, superlatif): **~ mieux** definitely ou clearly better

netteté [nɛtte] nf clearness

nettoyage [netwajaʒ] nm cleaning; **~ à sec** dry cleaning

nettoyer [netwaje] vt to clean; (fig) to clean out

neuf¹ [nœf] num nine

neuf², neuve [nœf, nœv] adj new ▷ nm: **repeindre à ~** to redecorate; **remettre à ~** to do up (as good as new), refurbish; **n'acheter que du ~** to buy everything new; **quoi de ~?** what's new?

neutre [nøtʀ] adj neutral; **~ en carbone** carbon-neutral ▷ nm (Ling) neuter

neuve [nœv] adj f voir **neuf**

neuvième [nœvjɛm] num ninth

neveu, x [nəvø] nm nephew

névrosé, e [nevroze] adj, nm/f neurotic

New York [njujɔʀk] n New York

nez [ne] nm nose; **rire au ~ de qn** to laugh in sb's face; **avoir du ~** to have flair; **avoir le ~**

fin to have foresight; **~ à ~ avec** face to face with; **à vue de ~** roughly

ni [ni] *conj*: **ni ... ni** neither ... nor; **je n'aime ni les lentilles ni les épinards** I like neither lentils nor spinach; **il n'a dit ni oui ni non** he didn't say either yes or no; **elles ne sont venues ni l'une ni l'autre** neither of them came; **il n'a rien vu ni entendu** he didn't see or hear anything

niais, e [njɛ, -ɛz] *adj* silly, thick

niche [niʃ] *nf* (*du chien*) kennel; (*de mur*) recess, niche; (*farce*) trick

nicher [niʃe] *vi* to nest; **se ~ dans** (*personne: se blottir*) to snuggle into; (: *se cacher*) to hide in; (*objet*) to lodge itself in

nid [ni] *nm* nest; (*fig: repaire etc*) den, lair; **~ d'abeilles** (*Couture, Textile*) honeycomb stitch; **~ de poule** pothole

nièce [njɛs] *nf* niece

nier [nje] *vt* to deny

nigaud, e [nigo, -od] *nm/f* booby, fool

Nil [nil] *nm*: **le ~** the Nile

n'importe [nɛ̃pɔʀt] *adv*: **~!** no matter!; **~ qui/quoi/où** anybody/anything/anywhere; **~ quoi!** (*fam: désapprobation*) what rubbish!; **~ quand** any time; **~ quel/quelle** any; **~ lequel/laquelle** any (one); **~ comment** (*sans soin*) carelessly; **~ comment, il part ce soir** he's leaving tonight in any case

niveau, x [nivo] *nm* level; (*des élèves, études*) standard; **au ~ de** at the level of; (*personne*) on a level with; **de ~ (avec)** level (with); **le ~ de la mer** sea level; **~ (à bulle)** spirit level; **~ (d'eau)** water level; **~ de vie** standard of living

niveler [nivle] *vt* to level

NN *abr* (= *nouvelle norme*) revised standard of hotel classification

noble [nɔbl] *adj* noble; (*de qualité: métal etc*) precious ▷ *nm/f* noble(man/-woman)

noblesse [nɔblɛs] *nf* (*classe sociale*) nobility; (*d'une action etc*) nobleness

noce [nɔs] *nf* wedding; (*gens*) wedding party (*ou* guests *pl*); **il a épousée en secondes ~s** she was his second wife; **faire la ~** (*fam*) to go on a binge; **~s d'or/d'argent/de diamant** golden/silver/diamond wedding

nocif, -ive [nɔsif, -iv] *adj* harmful, noxious

nocturne [nɔktyʀn] *adj* nocturnal ▷ *nf* (*Sport*) floodlit fixture; (*d'un magasin*) late opening

Noël [nɔɛl] *nm* Christmas; **la (fête de) ~** Christmas time

nœud [nø] *nm* (*de corde, du bois, Navig*) knot; (*ruban*) bow; (*fig: liens*) bond, tie; (: *d'une question*) crux; (*Théât etc*): **le ~ de l'action** the web of events; **~ coulant** noose; **~ gordien** Gordian knot; **~ papillon** bow tie

noir, e [nwaʀ] *adj* black; (*obscur, sombre*) dark ▷ *nm/f* black man/woman ▷ *nm*: **dans le ~** in the dark ▷ *nf* (*Mus*) crotchet (*Brit*), quarter note (*US*); **il fait ~** it is dark; **au ~** *adv* (*acheter,*

vendre) on the black market; **travail au ~** moonlighting; **travailler au ~** to work on the side

noircir [nwaʀsiʀ] *vt, vi* to blacken

noisette [nwazɛt] *nf* hazelnut; (*morceau: beurre etc*) small knob ▷ *adj* (*yeux*) hazel

noix [nwa] *nf* walnut; (*fam*) twit; (*Culin*): **une ~ de beurre** a knob of butter; **à la ~** (*fam*) worthless; **~ de cajou** cashew nut; **~ de coco** coconut; **~ muscade** nutmeg; **~ de veau** (*Culin*) round fillet of veal

nom [nɔ̃] *nm* name; (*Ling*) noun; **connaître qn de ~** to know sb by name; **au ~ de** in the name of; **~ d'une pipe** *ou* **d'un chien!** (*fam*) for goodness' sake!; **~ de Dieu!** (*fam!*) bloody hell! (*Brit*); **~ commun/propre** common/proper noun; **~ composé** (*Ling*) compound noun; **~ déposé** trade name; **~ d'emprunt** assumed name; **~ de famille** surname; **~ de fichier** file name; **~ de jeune fille** maiden name; **~ d'utilisateur** (*Inform*) username

nomade [nɔmad] *adj* nomadic ▷ *nm/f* nomad

nombre [nɔ̃bʀ] *nm* number; **venir en ~** to come in large numbers; **depuis ~ d'années** for many years; **ils sont au ~ de trois** there are three of them; **au ~ de mes amis** among my friends; **sans ~** countless; **(bon) ~ de** (*beaucoup, plusieurs*) a (large) number of; **~ premier/entier** prime/whole number

nombreux, -euse [nɔ̃bʀø, -øz] *adj* many, numerous; (*avec nom sg*) large (etc); **peu ~** few; small; **de ~ cas** many cases

nombril [nɔ̃bʀi(l)] *nm* navel

nommer [nɔme] *vt* (*baptiser*) to name, give a name to; (*qualifier*) to call; (*mentionner*) to name, give the name of; (*élire*) to appoint, nominate; **se nommer**: **il se nomme Pascal** his name's Pascal, he's called Pascal

non [nɔ̃] *adv* (*réponse*) no; (*suivi d'un adjectif, adverbe*) not; **Paul est venu, ~?** Paul came, didn't he?; **répondre** *ou* **dire que ~** to say no; **~ pas que** not that; **~ plus**: **moi non plus** neither do I, I don't either; **je préférerais que ~** I would prefer not; **il se trouve que ~** perhaps not; **je pense que ~** I don't think so; **~ mais!** well really!; **~ mais des fois!** you must be joking!; **~ alcoolisé** non-alcoholic; **~ loin/seulement** not far/only

nonante [nɔnɑ̃t] *num* (*Belgique, Suisse*) ninety

nonchalant, e [nɔ̃ʃalɑ̃, -ɑ̃t] *adj* nonchalant, casual

non-fumeur, -euse [nɔ̃fymœʀ, øz] *nm/f* non-smoker

non-sens [nɔ̃sɑ̃s] *nm* absurdity

nord [nɔʀ] *nm* North ▷ *adj* northern; north; **au ~** (*situation*) in the north; (*direction*) to the north; **au ~ de** north of, to the north of; **perdre le ~** to lose one's way (*fig*)

nord-africain, e [nɔʀafʀikɛ̃, -ɛn] *adj* North-African ▷ *nm/f*: **Nord-Africain, e** North African

nord-est [nɔʀɛst] *nm* North-East

nord-ouest [nɔRwɛst] nm North-West

normal, e, -aux [nɔRmal, -o] adj normal
▷ nf: **la ~e** the norm, the average; **c'est tout à fait ~** it's perfectly natural; **vous trouvez ça ~?** does it seem right to you?

normalement [nɔRmalmɑ̃] adv (en général) normally; (comme prévu): **~, il le fera demain** he should be doing it tomorrow, he's supposed to do it tomorrow

normand, e [nɔRmɑ̃, -ɑ̃d] adj (de Normandie) Norman ▷ nm/f: **N~, e** (de Normandie) Norman

Normandie [nɔRmɑ̃di] nf: **la ~** Normandy

norme [nɔRm] nf norm; (Tech) standard

Norvège [nɔRvɛʒ] nf: **la ~** Norway

norvégien, ne [nɔRveʒjɛ̃, -ɛn] adj Norwegian ▷ nm (Ling) Norwegian ▷ nm/f: **N~, ne** Norwegian

nos [no] adj poss voir **notre**

nostalgie [nɔstalʒi] nf nostalgia

nostalgique [nɔstalʒik] adj nostalgic

notable [nɔtabl] adj notable, noteworthy; (marqué) noticeable, marked ▷ nm prominent citizen

notaire [nɔtɛR] nm notary; solicitor

notamment [nɔtamɑ̃] adv in particular, among others

note [nɔt] nf (écrite, Mus) note; (Scol) mark (Brit), grade; (facture) bill; **prendre des ~s** to take notes; **prendre ~ de** to note; (par écrit) to note, write down; **dans la ~** exactly right; **forcer la ~** to exaggerate; **une ~ de tristesse/ de gaieté** a sad/happy note; **~ de service** memorandum

noté, e [nɔte] adj: **être bien/mal ~** (employé etc) to have a good/bad record

noter [nɔte] vt (écrire) to write down, note; (remarquer) to note, notice; (Scol, Admin: donner une appréciation: devoir) to mark, give a mark to; **notez bien que ...** (please) note that ...

notice [nɔtis] nf summary, short article; (brochure): **~ explicative** explanatory leaflet, instruction booklet

notifier [nɔtifje] vt: **~ qch à qn** to notify sb of sth, notify sth to sb

notion [nɔsjɔ̃] nf notion, idea; **notions** nfpl (rudiments) rudiments

notoire [nɔtwaR] adj widely known; (en mal) notorious; **le fait est ~** the fact is common knowledge

notre [nɔtR(ə)] (pl **nos** [no]) adj poss our

nôtre [notR] adj ours ▷ pron: **le/la ~** ours; **les ~s** ours; (alliés etc) our own people; **soyez des ~s** join us

nouer [nwe] vt to tie, knot; (fig: alliance etc) to strike up; **~ la conversation** to start a conversation; **se nouer** vi: **c'est là où l'intrigue se noue** it's at that point that the strands of the plot come together; **ma gorge se noua** a lump came to my throat

noueux, -euse [nwø, -øz] adj gnarled

nouille [nuj] nf (fam) noodle (Brit), fathead; **nouilles** nfpl (pâtes) noodles; pasta sg

nourrice [nuRis] nf ≈ child-minder; (autrefois) wet-nurse

nourrir [nuRiR] vt to feed; (fig: espoir) to harbour, nurse; **logé nourri** with board and lodging; **~ au sein** to breast-feed; **se ~ de légumes** to live on vegetables

nourrissant, e [nuRisɑ̃, -ɑ̃t] adj nourishing, nutritious

nourrisson [nuRisɔ̃] nm (unweaned) infant

nourriture [nuRityR] nf food

nous [nu] pron (sujet) we; (objet) us

nous-mêmes [numɛm] pron ourselves

nouveau, nouvel, -elle, x [nuvo, -ɛl] adj new; (original) novel ▷ nm/f new pupil (ou employee) ▷ nm: **il y a du ~** there's something new ▷ nf (piece of) news sg; (Littérature) short story; **nouvelles** nfpl (Presse, TV) news; **de ~ à ~** again; **je suis sans nouvelles de lui** I haven't heard from him; **Nouvel An** New Year; **~ venu, nouvelle venue** newcomer; **~x mariés** newly-weds; **nouvelle vague** new wave

nouveau-né, e [nuvone] nm/f newborn (baby)

nouveauté [nuvote] nf novelty; (chose nouvelle) innovation, something new; (Comm) new film (ou book ou creation etc)

nouvel adj m, **nouvelle** adj f, nf [nuvɛl] voir **nouveau**

Nouvelle-Calédonie [nuvɛlkaledɔni] nf: **la ~** New Caledonia

nouvellement [nuvɛlmɑ̃] adv (arrivé etc) recently, newly

Nouvelle-Zélande [nuvɛlzelɑ̃d] nf: **la ~** New Zealand

novembre [nɔvɑ̃bR] nm November; see note; voir aussi **juillet**

LE 11 NOVEMBRE

Le 11 novembre is a public holiday in France and commemorates the signing of the armistice, near Compiègne, at the end of the First World War.

---

novice [nɔvis] adj inexperienced ▷ nm/f novice

noyade [nwajad] nf drowning no pl

noyau, x [nwajo] nm (de fruit) stone; (Bio, Physique) nucleus; (Élec, Géo, fig: centre) core; (fig: d'artistes etc) group; (: de résistants etc) cell

noyauter [nwajote] vt (Pol) to infiltrate

noyer [nwaje] nm walnut (tree); (bois) walnut ▷ vt to drown; (fig) to flood; to submerge; (Auto: moteur) to flood; **se noyer** to be drowned, drown; (suicide) to drown o.s.; **~ son chagrin** to drown one's sorrows; **~ le poisson** to duck the issue

nu, e [ny] adj naked; (membres) naked, bare; (chambre, fil, plaine) bare ▷ nm (Art) nude; **le nu intégral** total nudity; **tout nu** stark naked; **se mettre nu** to strip; **mettre à nu** to bare

nuage [nɥaʒ] *nm* cloud; **être dans les ~s** (*distrait*) to have one's head in the clouds; **~ de lait** drop of milk

nuageux, -euse [nɥaʒø, -øz] *adj* cloudy

nuance [nɥɑ̃s] *nf* (*de couleur, sens*) shade; **il y a une ~ (entre)** there's a slight difference (between); **une ~ de tristesse** a tinge of sadness

nuancer [nɥɑ̃se] *vt* (*pensée, opinion*) to qualify

nucléaire [nykleɛʀ] *adj* nuclear ▷ *nm*: **le ~** nuclear power

nudiste [nydist] *adj, nm/f* nudist

nuée [nɥe] *nf*: **une ~ de** a cloud *ou* host *ou* swarm of

nues [ny] *nfpl*: **tomber des ~** to be taken aback; **porter qn aux ~** to praise sb to the skies

nuire [nɥiʀ] *vi* to be harmful; **~ à** to harm, do damage to

nuisible [nɥizibl] *adj* harmful; (**animal**) **~** pest

nuit [nɥi] *nf* night; **payer sa ~** to pay for one's overnight accommodation; **il fait ~** it's dark; **cette ~ (hier)** last night; (*aujourd'hui*) tonight; **de ~ (vol, service)** night *cpd*; **~ blanche** sleepless night; **~ de noces** wedding night; **~ de Noël** Christmas Eve

nul, nulle [nyl] *adj* (*aucun*) no; (*minime*) nil, non-existent; (*non valable*) null; (*péj*) useless, hopeless ▷ *pron* none, no one; **résultat ~, match ~** draw; **nulle part** *adv* nowhere

nullement [nylmɑ̃] *adv* by no means

nullité [nylite] *nf* nullity; (*péj*) hopelessness; (: *personne*) hopeless individual, nonentity

numérique [nymerik] *adj* numerical; (*Inform, TV*: *affichage, son, télévision*) digital

numéro [nymero] *nm* number; (*spectacle*) act, turn; (*Presse*) issue, number; **faire** *ou* **composer un ~** to dial a number; **~ d'identification personnel** personal identification number (PIN); **~ d'immatriculation** *ou* **minéralogique** *ou* **de police** registration (Brit) *ou* license (US) number; **~ de téléphone** (tele)phone number; **~ vert** ≈ Freefone® number (Brit), ≈ toll-free number (US)

numéroter [nymerote] *vt* to number

nu-pieds [nypje] *nm inv* sandal ▷ *adj inv* barefoot

nuque [nyk] *nf* nape of the neck

nu-tête [nytɛt] *adj inv* bareheaded

nutritif, -ive [nytritif, -iv] *adj* (*besoins, valeur*) nutritional; (*aliment*) nutritious, nourishing

nylon [nilɔ̃] *nm* nylon

oasis [ɔazis] *nf ou m* oasis

obéir [ɔbeiʀ] *vi* to obey; **~ à** to obey; (*moteur, véhicule*) to respond to

obéissance [ɔbeisɑ̃s] *nf* obedience

obéissant, e [ɔbeisɑ̃, -ɑ̃t] *adj* obedient

obèse [ɔbɛz] *adj* obese

obésité [ɔbezite] *nf* obesity

objecter [ɔbʒɛkte] *vt* (*prétexter*) to plead, put forward as an excuse; **~ qch à** (*argument*) to put forward sth against; **~ (à qn) que** to object (to sb) that

objecteur [ɔbʒɛktœʀ] *nm*: **~ de conscience** conscientious objector

objectif, -ive [ɔbʒɛktif, -iv] *adj* objective ▷ *nm* (*Optique, Photo*) lens *sg*; (*Mil: fig*) objective; **~ grand angulaire/à focale variable** wide-angle/zoom lens

objection [ɔbʒɛksjɔ̃] *nf* objection; **~ de conscience** conscientious objection

objectivité [ɔbʒɛktivite] *nf* objectivity

objet [ɔbʒɛ] *nm* (*chose*) object; (*d'une discussion, recherche*) subject; **être** *ou* **faire l'~ de** (*discussion*) to be the subject of; (*soins*) to be given *ou* shown; **sans ~** purposeless; (*sans fondement*) groundless; **~ d'art** objet d'art; **~s personnels** personal items; **~s de toilette** toiletries; **~s trouvés** lost property *sg* (Brit), lost-and-found *sg* (US); **~s de valeur** valuables

obligation [ɔbligasjɔ̃] *nf* obligation; (*gén pl*: *devoir*) duty; (*Comm*) bond, debenture; **sans ~ d'achat** with no obligation (to buy); **être**

dans l'~ de faire to be obliged to do; **avoir l'~ de faire** to be under an obligation to do; **~s familiales** family obligations *ou* responsibilities; **~s militaires** military obligations *ou* duties

obligatoire [ɔbligatwaʀ] *adj* compulsory, obligatory

obligatoirement [ɔbligatwaʀmɑ̃] *adv* compulsorily; (*fatalement*) necessarily; (*fam: sans aucun doute*) inevitably

obligé, e [ɔbliʒe] *adj* (*redevable*): **être très ~ à qn** to be most obliged to sb; (*contraint*): **je suis (bien) ~ (de le faire)** I have to (do it); (*nécessaire: conséquence*) necessary; **c'est ~!** it's inevitable!

obligeance [ɔbliʒɑ̃s] *nf*: **avoir l'~ de** to be kind *ou* good enough to

obligeant, e [ɔbliʒɑ̃, -ɑ̃t] *adj* obliging; kind

obliger [ɔbliʒe] *vt* (*contraindre*): **~ qn à faire** to force *ou* oblige sb to do; (*Jur: engager*) to bind; (*rendre service à*) to oblige; **je suis bien obligé (de le faire)** I have to (do it)

oblique [ɔblik] *adj* oblique; **regard ~** sidelong glance; **en ~** *adv* diagonally

obliquer [ɔblike] *vi*: **~ vers** to turn off towards

oblitérer [ɔblitere] *vt* (*timbre-poste*) to cancel; (*Méd: canal, vaisseau*) to obstruct

obnubiler [ɔbnybile] *vt* to obsess

obscène [ɔpsɛn] *adj* obscene

obscur, e [ɔpskyʀ] *adj* (*sombre*) dark; (*fig: raisons*) obscure; (*: sentiment, malaise*) vague; (*: personne, vie*) humble, lowly

obscurcir [ɔpskyʀsiʀ] *vt* to darken; (*fig*) to obscure; **s'obscurcir** *vi* to grow dark

obscurité [ɔpskyʀite] *nf* darkness; **dans l'~** in the dark, in darkness; (*anonymat, médiocrité*) in obscurity

obsédé, e [ɔpsede] *nm/f* fanatic; **~(e) sexuel(le)** sex maniac

obséder [ɔpsede] *vt* to obsess, haunt

obsèques [ɔpsɛk] *nfpl* funeral *sg*

observateur, -trice [ɔpsɛʀvatœʀ, -tʀis] *adj* observant, perceptive ▷ *nm/f* observer

observation [ɔpsɛʀvasjɔ̃] *nf* observation; (*d'un règlement etc*) observance; (*commentaire*) observation, remark; (*reproche*) reproof; **en ~** (*Méd*) under observation

observatoire [ɔpsɛʀvatwaʀ] *nm* observatory; (*lieu élevé*) observation post, vantage point

observer [ɔpsɛʀve] *vt* (*regarder*) to observe, watch; (*examiner*) to examine; (*scientifiquement, aussi: règlement, jeûne etc*) to observe; (*surveiller*) to watch; (*remarquer*) to observe, notice; **faire ~ qch à qn** (*dire*) to point out sth to sb; **s'observer** *vi* (*se surveiller*) to keep a check on o.s.

obsession [ɔpsesjɔ̃] *nf* obsession; **avoir l'~ de** to have an obsession with

obstacle [ɔpstakl] *nm* obstacle; (*Équitation*) jump, hurdle; **faire ~ à** (*lumière*) to block out; (*projet*) to hinder, put obstacles in the path of; **~s antichars** tank defences

obstiné, e [ɔpstine] *adj* obstinate

obstiner [ɔpstine]: **s'obstiner** *vi* to insist, dig one's heels in; **s'~ à faire** to persist (obstinately) in doing; **s'~ sur qch** to keep working at sth, labour away at sth

obstruer [ɔpstʀye] *vt* to block, obstruct; **s'obstruer** *vi* to become blocked

obtenir [ɔptəniʀ] *vt* to obtain, get; (*total*) to arrive at, reach; (*résultat*) to achieve, obtain; **~ de pouvoir faire** to obtain permission to do; **~ qch à qn** to obtain sth for sb; **~ de qn qu'il fasse** to get sb to agree to do(ing)

obturateur [ɔptyʀatœʀ] *nm* (*Photo*) shutter; **~ à rideau** focal plane shutter

obus [ɔby] *nm* shell; **~ explosif** high-explosive shell; **~ incendiaire** incendiary device, fire bomb

occasion [ɔkazjɔ̃] *nf* (*aubaine, possibilité*) opportunity; (*circonstance*) occasion; (*Comm: article non neuf*) secondhand buy; (*: acquisition avantageuse*) bargain; **à plusieurs ~s** on several occasions; **à la première ~** at the first *ou* earliest opportunity; **avoir l'~ de faire** to have the opportunity to do; **être l'~ de** to occasion, give rise to; **à l'~** *adv* sometimes, on occasions; (*un jour*) some time; **à l'~ de** on the occasion of; **d'~** *adj, adv* secondhand

occasionnel, le [ɔkazjɔnɛl] *adj* (*fortuit*) chance *cpd*; (*non régulier*) occasional; (*: travail*) casual

occasionnellement [ɔkazjɔnɛlmɑ̃] *adv* occasionally, from time to time

occasionner [ɔkazjɔne] *vt* to cause, bring about; **~ qch à qn** to cause sb sth

occident [ɔksidɑ̃] *nm*: **l'O~** the West

occidental, e, -aux [ɔksidɑ̃tal, -o] *adj* western; (*Pol*) Western ▷ *nm/f* Westerner

occupation [ɔkypasjɔ̃] *nf* occupation; **l'O~** the Occupation (of France)

occupé, e [ɔkype] *adj* (*Mil, Pol*) occupied; (*personne: affairé, pris*) busy; (*esprit: absorbé*) occupied; (*place, sièges*) taken; (*toilettes*) engaged; **la ligne est ~e** the line's engaged (*Brit*) *ou* busy (*US*)

occuper [ɔkype] *vt* to occupy; (*poste, fonction*) to hold; (*main-d'œuvre*) to employ; **s'~ qch** to occupy o.s *ou* keep o.s. busy (with sth); **s'~ de** (*être responsable de*) to be in charge of; (*se charger de: affaire*) to take charge of, deal with; (*: clients etc*) to attend to; (*s'intéresser à, pratiquer: politique etc*) to be involved in; **ça occupe trop de place** it takes up too much room

occurrence [ɔkyʀɑ̃s] *nf*: **en l'~** in this case

océan [ɔseɑ̃] *nm* ocean; **l'~ Indien** the Indian Ocean

octante [ɔktɑ̃t] *num* (*Belgique, Suisse*) eighty

octet [ɔktɛ] *nm* byte

octobre [ɔktɔbʀ] *nm* October; *voir aussi* **juillet**

octroyer [ɔktʀwaje] *vt*: **~ qch à qn** to grant sth to sb, grant sb sth

oculiste [ɔkylist] *nm/f* eye specialist, oculist
odeur [ɔdœʀ] *nf* smell
odieux, -euse [ɔdjø, -øz] *adj* odious, hateful
odorant, e [ɔdɔʀɑ̃, -ɑ̃t] *adj* sweet-smelling, fragrant
odorat [ɔdɔʀa] *nm* (sense of) smell; **avoir l'~ fin** to have a keen sense of smell
œil [œj] (*pl* **yeux**) [jø] *nm* eye; **avoir un ~ poché** *ou* **au beurre noir** to have a black eye; **à l'~** (*fam*) for free; **à l'~ nu** with the naked eye; **tenir qn à l'~** to keep an eye *ou* a watch on sb; **avoir l'~ à** to keep an eye on; **faire de l'~ à qn** to make eyes at sb; **voir qch d'un bon/mauvais ~** to view sth in a favourable/an unfavourable light; **à l'~ vif** with a lively expression; **à mes/ses yeux** in my/his eyes; **de ses propres yeux** with his own eyes; **fermer les yeux (sur)** (*fig*) to turn a blind eye (to); **les yeux fermés** (*aussi fig*) with one's eyes shut; **ouvrir l'~** (*fig*) to keep one's eyes open *ou* an eye out; **fermer l'~** to get a moment's sleep; **~ pour ~, dent pour dent** an eye for an eye, a tooth for a tooth; **pour les beaux yeux de qn** (*fig*) for love of sb; **~ de verre** glass eye
œillères [œjɛʀ] *nfpl* blinkers (*Brit*), blinders (*US*); **avoir des ~** (*fig*) to be blinkered, wear blinders
œillet [œjɛ] *nm* (*Bot*) carnation; (*trou*) eyelet
œuf [œf] *nm* egg; **étouffer dans l'~** to nip in the bud; **~ à la coque/dur/mollet** boiled/hard-boiled/soft-boiled egg; **~ au plat/poché** fried/poached egg; **~s brouillés** scrambled eggs; **~ de Pâques** Easter egg; **~ à repriser** darning egg
œuvre [œvʀ] *nf* (*tâche*) task, undertaking; (*ouvrage achevé, livre, tableau etc*) work; (*ensemble de la production artistique*) works *pl*; (*organisation charitable*) charity ▷ *nm* (*d'un artiste*) works *pl*; (*Constr*): **le gros ~** the shell; **œuvres** *nfpl* (*actes*) deeds, works; **être/se mettre à l'~** to be at/get (down) to work; **mettre en ~** (*moyens*) to make use of; (*plan, loi, projet etc*) to implement; **~ d'art** work of art; **bonnes ~s** good works *ou* deeds; **~s de bienfaisance** charitable works
offense [ɔfɑ̃s] *nf* (*affront*) insult; (*Rel: péché*) transgression, trespass
offenser [ɔfɑ̃se] *vt* to offend, hurt; (*principes, Dieu*) to offend against; **s'offenser de** *vi* to take offence (*Brit*) *ou* offense (*US*) at
offert, e [ɔfɛʀ, -ɛʀt] *pp de* **offrir**
office [ɔfis] *nm* (*charge*) office; (*agence*) bureau, agency; (*Rel*) service ▷ *nm ou f* (*pièce*) pantry; **faire ~ de** to act as; to do duty as; **d'~** *adv* automatically; **bons ~s** (*Pol*) good offices; **~ du tourisme** tourist office
officiel, le [ɔfisjɛl] *adj, nm/f* official
officier [ɔfisje] *nm* officer ▷ *vi* (*Rel*) to officiate; **~ de l'état-civil** registrar; **~ ministériel** member of the legal profession; **~ de police** ≈ police officer

officieux, -euse [ɔfisjø, -øz] *adj* unofficial
offrande [ɔfʀɑ̃d] *nf* offering
offre [ɔfʀ] *vb voir* **offrir** ▷ *nf* offer; (*aux enchères*) bid; (*Admin: soumission*) tender; (*Écon*): **l'~ et la demande** supply and demand; **~ d'emploi** job advertised; **"~s d'emploi"** "situations vacant"; **~ publique d'achat (OPA)** takeover bid; **~s de service** offer of service
offrir [ɔfʀiʀ] *vt*: **~ (à qn)** to offer (to sb); (*faire cadeau*) to give to (sb); **s'offrir** *vi* (*se présenter: occasion, paysage*) to present itself ▷ *vt* (*se payer: vacances, voiture*) to treat o.s. to; **~ (à qn) de faire qch** to offer to do sth (for sb); **~ à boire à qn** (*chez soi*) to offer sb a drink; **je vous offre un verre** I'll buy you a drink; **s'~ à faire qch** to offer *ou* volunteer to do sth; **s'~ comme guide/en otage** to offer one's services as (a) guide/offer o.s. as (a) hostage; **s'~ aux regards** (*personne*) to expose o.s. to the public gaze
offusquer [ɔfyske] *vt* to offend; **s'offusquer de** to take offence (*Brit*) *ou* offense (*US*) at, be offended by
OGM *sigle m* (= *organisme génétiquement modifié*) GMO (= *genetically modified organism*); **culture ~** GM crop
oie [wa] *nf* (*Zool*) goose; **~ blanche** (*fig*) young innocent
oignon [ɔɲɔ̃] *nm* (*Culin*) onion; (*de tulipe etc: bulbe*) bulb; (*Méd*) bunion; **ce ne sont pas tes ~s** (*fam*) that's none of your business
oiseau, x [wazo] *nm* bird; **~ de proie** bird of prey
oisif, -ive [wazif, -iv] *adj* idle ▷ *nm/f* (*péj*) man/lady of leisure
oléoduc [ɔleɔdyk] *nm* (oil) pipeline
olive [ɔliv] *nf* (*Bot*) olive ▷ *adj inv* olive-green
olivier [ɔlivje] *nm* olive (tree); (*bois*) olive (wood)
OLP *sigle f* (= *Organisation de libération de la Palestine*) PLO
olympique [ɔlɛ̃pik] *adj* Olympic
ombragé, e [ɔ̃bʀaʒe] *adj* shaded, shady
ombrageux, -euse [ɔ̃bʀaʒø, -øz] *adj* (*cheval*) skittish, nervous; (*personne*) touchy, easily offended
ombre [ɔ̃bʀ] *nf* (*espace non ensoleillé*) shade; (*ombre portée, tache*) shadow; **à l'~** in the shade; (*fam: en prison*) behind bars; **à l'~ de** in the shade of; (*tout près de, fig*) in the shadow of; **tu me fais de l'~** you're in my light; **ça nous donne de l'~** it gives us (some) shade; **il n'y a pas l'~ d'un doute** there's not the shadow of a doubt; **dans l'~** in the shade; (*fig*) in the dark; **vivre dans l'~** (*fig*) to live in obscurity; **laisser dans l'~** (*fig*) to leave in the dark; **~ à paupières** eye shadow; **~ portée** shadow; **~s chinoises** (*spectacle*) shadow show *sg*
ombrelle [ɔ̃bʀɛl] *nf* parasol, sunshade
omelette [ɔmlɛt] *nf* omelette; **~ baveuse** runny omelette; **~ au fromage/au jambon** cheese/ham omelette; **~ aux herbes** omelette with herbs; **~ norvégienne** baked Alaska

omettre [ɔmɛtʀ] *vt* to omit, leave out; **~ de faire** to fail *ou* omit to do

omnibus [ɔmnibys] *nm* slow *ou* stopping train

omoplate [ɔmɔplat] *nf* shoulder blade

 MOT-CLÉ

on [ɔ̃] *pron* **1** (*indéterminé*) you, one; **on peut le faire ainsi** you *ou* one can do it like this, it can be done like this; **on dit que ...** they say that ..., it is said that ..

2 (*quelqu'un*): **on les a attaqués** they were attacked; **on vous demande au téléphone** there's a phone call for you, you're wanted on the phone; **on frappe à la porte** someone's knocking at the door

3 (*nous*) we; **on va y aller demain** we're going tomorrow

4 (*les gens*) they; **autrefois, on croyait ...** they used to believe ..

5: **on ne peut plus** *adv*: **on ne peut plus stupide** as stupid as can be

oncle [ɔ̃kl] *nm* uncle

onctueux, -euse [ɔ̃ktɥø, -øz] *adj* creamy, smooth; (*fig*) smooth, unctuous

onde [ɔ̃d] *nf* (*Physique*) wave; **sur l'~** on the waters; **sur les ~s** on the radio; **mettre en ~s** to produce for the radio; **~ de choc** shock wave; **~s courtes (OC)** short wave *sg*; **petites ~s (PO)**, **~s moyennes (OM)** medium wave *sg*; **grandes ~s (GO)**, **~s longues (OL)** long wave *sg*; **~s sonores** sound waves

ondée [ɔ̃de] *nf* shower

on-dit [ɔ̃di] *nm inv* rumour

onduler [ɔ̃dyle] *vi* to undulate; (*cheveux*) to wave

onéreux, -euse [ɔneʀø, -øz] *adj* costly; **à titre ~** in return for payment

ongle [ɔ̃gl] *nm* (*Anat*) nail; **manger** *ou* **ronger ses ~s** to bite one's nails; **se faire les ~s** to do one's nails

ont [ɔ̃] *vb voir* **avoir**

ONU [ɔny] *sigle f* (= *Organisation des Nations unies*) UN(O)

onze ['ɔ̃z] *num* eleven

onzième [ɔ̃zjɛm] *num* eleventh

OPA *sigle f* = **offre publique d'achat**

opaque [ɔpak] *adj* (*vitre, verre*) opaque; (*brouillard, nuit*) impenetrable

opéra [ɔpeʀa] *nm* opera; (*édifice*) opera house

opérateur, -trice [ɔpeʀatœʀ, -tʀis] *nm/f* operator; **~ (de prise de vues)** cameraman

opération [ɔpeʀasjɔ̃] *nf* operation; (*Comm*) dealing; **salle/table d'~** operating theatre/table; **~ de sauvetage** rescue operation; **~ à cœur ouvert** open-heart surgery *no pl*

opératoire [ɔpeʀatwaʀ] *adj* (*manœuvre, méthode*) operating; (*choc etc*) post-operative

opérer [ɔpeʀe] *vt* (*Méd*) to operate on; (*faire, exécuter*) to carry out, make ▷ *vi* (*remède: faire*

effet) to act, work; (*procéder*) to proceed; (*Méd*) to operate; **s'opérer** *vi* (*avoir lieu*) to occur, take place; **se faire ~** to have an operation; **se faire ~ des amygdales/du cœur** to have one's tonsils out/have a heart operation

opérette [ɔpeʀɛt] *nf* operetta, light opera

ophtalmologie [ɔftalmɔlɔʒi] *nf* ophthalmology

opiner [ɔpine] *vi*: **~ de la tête** to nod assent ▷ *vt*: **~ à** to consent to

opinion [ɔpinjɔ̃] *nf* opinion; **l'~ (publique)** public opinion; **avoir bonne/mauvaise ~ de** to have a high/low opinion of

opportun, e [ɔpɔʀtœ̃, -yn] *adj* timely, opportune; **en temps ~** at the appropriate time

opportuniste [ɔpɔʀtynist] *adj, nm/f* opportunist

opposant, e [ɔpozɑ̃, -ɑ̃t] *adj* opposing ▷ *nm/f* opponent

opposé, e [ɔpoze] *adj* (*direction, rive*) opposite; (*faction*) opposing; (*couleurs*) contrasting; (*opinions, intérêts*) conflicting; (*contre*): **~ à** opposed to, against ▷ *nm*: **l'~** the other *ou* opposite side (*ou* direction); (*contraire*) the opposite; **être ~ à** to be opposed to; **à l'~** (*fig*) on the other hand; **à l'~ de** on the other *ou* opposite side from; (*fig*) contrary to, unlike

opposer [ɔpoze] *vt* (*meubles, objets*) to place opposite each other; (*personnes, armées, équipes*) to oppose; (*couleurs, termes, tons*) to contrast; (*comparer: livres, avantages*) to contrast; **~ qch à** (*comme obstacle, défense*) to set sth against; (*comme objection*) to put sth forward against; (*en contraste*) to set sth opposite; to match sth with; **s'opposer** *vi* (*équipes*) to confront each other; (*opinions*) to conflict; (*couleurs, styles*) to contrast; **s'~ à** (*interdire, empêcher*) to oppose; (*tenir tête à*) to rebel against; **sa religion s'y oppose** it's against his religion; **s'~ à ce que qn fasse** to be opposed to sb's doing

opposition [ɔpozisjɔ̃] *nf* opposition; **par ~** in contrast; **par ~ à** as opposed to, in contrast with; **entrer en ~ avec** to come into conflict with; **être en ~ avec** (*idées, conduite*) to be at variance with; **faire ~ à un chèque** to stop a cheque

oppressant, e [ɔpʀesɑ̃, -ɑ̃t] *adj* oppressive

oppresser [ɔpʀese] *vt* to oppress; **se sentir oppressé** to feel breathless

oppression [ɔpʀesjɔ̃] *nf* oppression; (*malaise*) feeling of suffocation

opprimer [ɔpʀime] *vt* (*asservir: peuple, faibles*) to oppress; (*étouffer: liberté, opinion*) to suppress, stifle; (*chaleur etc*) to suffocate, oppress

opter [ɔpte] *vi*: **~ pour** to opt for; **~ entre** to choose between

opticien, ne [ɔptisjɛ̃, -ɛn] *nm/f* optician

optimisme [ɔptimism] *nm* optimism

optimiste [ɔptimist] *adj* optimistic ▷ *nm/f* optimist

option [ɔpsjɔ̃] nf option; (Auto: supplément) optional extra; **matière à ~** (Scol) optional subject (Brit), elective (US); **prendre une ~ sur** to take (out) an option on; **~ par défaut** (Inform) default (option)

optique [ɔptik] adj (nerf) optic; (verres) optical ▷ nf (Photo: lentilles etc) optics pl; (science, industrie) optics sg; (fig: manière de voir) perspective

opulent, e [ɔpylɑ̃, -ɑ̃t] adj wealthy, opulent; (formes, poitrine) ample, generous

or [ɔʀ] nm gold ▷ conj now, but; **d'or** (fig) golden; **en or** gold cpd; (occasion) golden; **un mari/enfant en or** a treasure; **une affaire en or** (achat) a real bargain; (commerce) a gold mine; **plaqué or** gold-plated; **or noir** black gold; **il croyait gagner et il a perdu** he was sure he would win and yet he lost

orage [ɔʀaʒ] nm (thunder)storm

orageux, -euse [ɔʀaʒø, -øz] adj stormy

oral, e, -aux [ɔʀal, -o] adj (déposition, promesse) oral, verbal; (Méd): **par voie ~e** by mouth, orally ▷ nm (Scol) oral

orange [ɔʀɑ̃ʒ] adj inv, nf orange; **~ sanguine** blood orange; **~ pressée** freshly-squeezed orange juice

orangé, e [ɔʀɑ̃ʒe] adj orangey, orange-coloured

orangeade [ɔʀɑ̃ʒad] nf orangeade

oranger [ɔʀɑ̃ʒe] nm orange tree

orateur [ɔʀatœʀ] nm speaker; orator

orbite [ɔʀbit] nf (Anat) (eye-)socket; (Physique) orbit; **mettre sur ~** to put into orbit; (fig) to launch; **dans l'~ de** (fig) within the sphere of influence of

Orcades [ɔʀkad] nfpl: **les ~** the Orkneys, the Orkney Islands

orchestre [ɔʀkɛstʀ] nm orchestra; (de jazz, danse) band; (places) stalls pl (Brit), orchestra (US)

orchestrer [ɔʀkɛstʀe] vt (Mus) to orchestrate; (fig) to mount, stage-manage

orchidée [ɔʀkide] nf orchid

ordinaire [ɔʀdinɛʀ] adj ordinary; (coutumier: maladresse etc) usual; (de tous les jours) everyday; (modèle, qualité) standard; (péj: commun) common ▷ nm ordinary; (menus) everyday fare ▷ nf (essence) ≈ two-star (petrol) (Brit), ≈ regular (gas) (US); **d'~** usually, normally; **à l'~** usually, ordinarily; **comme à l'~** as usual

ordinateur [ɔʀdinatœʀ] nm computer; **mettre sur ~** to computerize, put on computer; **~ de bureau** desktop computer; **~ individuel** ou **personnel** personal computer; **~ portable** laptop (computer)

ordonnance [ɔʀdɔnɑ̃s] nf organization; (groupement, disposition) layout; (Méd) prescription; (Jur) order; (Mil) orderly, batman (Brit); **d'~** (Mil) regulation cpd; **officier d'~** aide-de-camp

ordonné, e [ɔʀdɔne] adj tidy, orderly; (Math) ordered ▷ nf (Math) Y-axis, ordinate

ordonner [ɔʀdɔne] vt (agencer) to organize, arrange; (: meubles, appartement) to lay out, arrange; (donner un ordre): **~ à qn de faire** to order sb to do; (Math) to (arrange in) order; (Rel) to ordain; (Méd) to prescribe; (Jur) to order; **s'ordonner** vi (faits) to organize themselves

ordre [ɔʀdʀ] nm (gén) order; (propreté et soin) orderliness, tidiness; (association professionnelle, honorifique) association; (Comm): **à l'~ de** payable to; (nature): **d'~ pratique** of a practical nature; **ordres** nmpl (Rel) holy orders; **avoir de l'~** to be tidy ou orderly; **mettre en ~** to tidy (up), put in order; **mettre bon ~ à** to put to rights, sort out; **procéder par ~** to take things one at a time; **par ~ alphabétique/d'importance** in alphabetical order/in order of importance; **être aux ~s de qn/sous les ~s de qn** to be at sb's disposal/under sb's command; **rappeler qn à l'~** to call sb to order; **jusqu'à nouvel ~** until further notice; **dans le même ~ d'idées** in this connection; **par ~ d'entrée en scène** in order of appearance; **un ~ de grandeur** some idea of the size (ou amount); **de premier ~** first-rate; **~ de grève** strike call; **~ du jour** (d'une réunion) agenda; (Mil) order of the day; **à l'~ du jour** on the agenda; (fig) topical; (Mil: citer) in dispatches; **~ de mission** (Mil) orders pl; **~ public** law and order; **~ de route** marching orders pl

ordure [ɔʀdyʀ] nf filth no pl; (propos, écrit) obscenity, (piece of) filth; **ordures** nfpl (balayures, déchets) rubbish sg, refuse sg; **~s ménagères** household refuse

oreille [ɔʀɛj] nf (Anat) ear; (de marmite, tasse) handle; (Tech: d'un écrou) wing; **avoir l'~ fine** to have a good ear (for music); **avoir l'~ basse** crestfallen, dejected; **se faire tirer l'~** to take a lot of persuading; **dire qch à l'~ de qn** to have a word in sb's ear (about sth)

oreiller [ɔʀeje] nm pillow

oreillons [ɔʀejɔ̃] nmpl mumps sg

ores [ɔʀ]: **d'~ et déjà** adv already

orfèvrerie [ɔʀfɛvʀəʀi] nf (art, métier) goldsmith's (ou silversmith's) trade; (ouvrage) (silver ou gold) plate

organe [ɔʀgan] nm organ; (véhicule, instrument) instrument; (voix) voice; (porte-parole) representative, mouthpiece; **~s de commande** (Tech) controls; **~s de transmission** (Tech) transmission system sg

organigramme [ɔʀganigʀam] nm (hiérarchique, structure) organization chart; (des opérations) flow chart

organique [ɔʀganik] adj organic

organisateur, -trice [ɔʀganizatœʀ, -tʀis] nm/f organizer

organisation [ɔʀganizasjɔ̃] nf organization; **O~ des Nations unies (ONU)** United Nations (Organization) (UN, UNO); **O~**

mondiale de la santé (OMS) World Health Organization (WHO); **O~ du traité de l'Atlantique Nord (OTAN)** North Atlantic Treaty Organization (NATO)

organiser [ɔʀɡanize] vt to organize; (mettre sur pied: service etc) to set up; **s'organiser** vi to get organized

organisme [ɔʀɡanism] nm (Bio) organism; (corps humain) body; (Admin, Pol etc) body, organism

organiste [ɔʀɡanist] nm/f organist

orgasme [ɔʀɡasm] nm orgasm, climax

orge [ɔʀʒ] nf barley

orgue [ɔʀɡ] nm organ; **orgues** nfpl organ sg; **~ de Barbarie** barrel ou street organ

orgueil [ɔʀɡœj] nm pride

orgueilleux, -euse [ɔʀɡœjø, -øz] adj proud

Orient [ɔʀjɑ̃] nm: **l'~** the East, the Orient

oriental, e, -aux [ɔʀjɑ̃tal, -o] adj (langue, produit) oriental, eastern; (frontière) eastern ▷ nm/f: **O~, e** Oriental

orientation [ɔʀjɑ̃tasjɔ̃] nf positioning; adjustment; (de recherches) orientation; direction; (d'une maison etc) aspect; (d'un journal) leanings pl; **avoir le sens de l'~** to have a (good) sense of direction; **course d'~** orienteering exercise; **~ professionnelle** careers advice ou guidance; (service) careers advisory service

orienté, e [ɔʀjɑ̃te] adj (fig: article, journal) slanted; **bien/mal ~** (appartement) well/badly positioned; **~ au sud** facing south, with a southern aspect

orienter [ɔʀjɑ̃te] vt (situer) to position; (placer, disposer: pièce mobile) to adjust, position; (tourner: antenne) to direct, turn; (voyageur, touriste, recherches) to direct; (fig: élève) to orientate; **s'orienter** vi (se repérer) to find one's bearings; **s'~ vers** (fig) to turn towards

origan [ɔʀiɡɑ̃] nm oregano

originaire [ɔʀiʒinɛʀ] adj original; **être ~ de** (pays, lieu) to be a native of; (provenir de) to originate from; to be native to

original, e, -aux [ɔʀiʒinal, -o] adj original; (bizarre) eccentric ▷ nm/f (fam: excentrique) eccentric; (: fantaisiste) joker ▷ nm (document etc, Art) original; (dactylographie) top copy

origine [ɔʀiʒin] nf origin; (d'un message, appel téléphonique) source; (d'une révolution, réussite) root; **origines** nfpl (d'une personne) origins; (d'un pays) of origin; (pneus etc) original; (bureau postal) dispatching; **d'~ française** of French origin; **dès l'~** at ou from the outset; **à l'~** originally; **avoir son ~ dans** to have its origins in, originate in

originel, le [ɔʀiʒinɛl] adj original

orme [ɔʀm] nm elm

ornement [ɔʀnəmɑ̃] nm ornament; (fig) embellishment, adornment; **~s sacerdotaux** vestments

orner [ɔʀne] vt to decorate, adorn; **~ qch de** to decorate sth with

ornière [ɔʀnjɛʀ] nf rut; (fig): **sortir de l'~** (routine) to get out of the rut; (impasse) to get out of a spot

orphelin, e [ɔʀfəlɛ̃, -in] adj orphan(ed) ▷ nm/f orphan; **~ de père/mère** fatherless/motherless

orphelinat [ɔʀfəlina] nm orphanage

orteil [ɔʀtɛj] nm toe; **gros ~** big toe

orthographe [ɔʀtɔɡʀaf] nf spelling

ortie [ɔʀti] nf (stinging) nettle; **~ blanche** white dead-nettle

os [ɔs] nm bone; **sans os** (Boucherie) off the bone, boned; **os à moelle** marrowbone

osciller [ɔsile] vi (pendule) to swing; (au vent etc) to rock; (Tech) to oscillate; (fig): **~ entre** to waver ou fluctuate between

osé, e [oze] adj daring, bold

oseille [ozɛj] nf sorrel

oser [oze] vi, vt to dare; **~ faire** to dare (to) do

osier [ozje] nm (Bot) willow; **d'~, en ~** wicker(work) cpd

ossature [ɔsatyʀ] nf (Anat: squelette) frame, skeletal structure; (: du visage) bone structure; (fig) framework

osseux, -euse [ɔsø, -øz] adj bony; (tissu, maladie, greffe) bone cpd

ostensible [ɔstɑ̃sibl] adj conspicuous

otage [ɔtaʒ] nm hostage; **prendre qn comme ~** to take sb hostage

OTAN [ɔtɑ̃] sigle f (= Organisation du traité de l'Atlantique Nord) NATO

otarie [ɔtaʀi] nf sea-lion

ôter [ote] vt to remove; (soustraire) to take away; **~ qch à qn** to take sth (away) from sb; **~ qch de** to remove sth from; **six ôté de dix égale quatre** six from ten equals ou is four

otite [ɔtit] nf ear infection

ou [u] conj or; **ou ... ou** either ... or; **ou bien** or (else)

MOT-CLÉ

où [u] pron relatif **1** (position, situation) where, that (souvent omis); **la chambre où il était** the room (that) he was in, the room where he was; **la ville où je l'ai rencontré** the town where I met him; **la pièce d'où il est sorti** the room he came out of; **le village d'où je viens** the village I come from; **les villes par où il est passé** the towns he went through **2** (temps, état) that (souvent omis); **le jour où il est parti** the day (that) he left; **au prix où c'est** at the price it is
▷ adv **1** (interrogation) where; **où est-il/va-t-il?** where is he/is he going?; **par où?** which way?; **d'où vient que ...?** how come ...?
2 (position) where; **je sais où il est** I know where he is; **où que l'on aille** wherever you go

ouate [wat] nf cotton wool (Brit), cotton (US); (bourre) padding, wadding; **~ hydrophile** cotton wool (Brit), (absorbent) cotton (US)

oubli [ubli] nm (*acte*): **l'~ de** forgetting; (*trou de mémoire*) lapse of memory; (*étourderie*) forgetfulness *no pl*; (*négligence*) omission, oversight; (*absence de souvenirs*) oblivion; **~ de soi** self-effacement, self-negation; **tomber dans l'~** to sink into oblivion

oublier [ublije] vt (*gén*) to forget; (*ne pas voir: erreurs etc*) to miss; (*ne pas mettre: virgule, nom*) to leave out, forget; (*laisser quelque part: chapeau etc*) to leave behind; **s'oublier** vi to forget o.s.; (*enfant, animal*) to have an accident (*euphemism*); **~ l'heure** to forget (about) the time

oubliettes [ublijɛt] nfpl dungeon *sg*; (**jeter**) **aux ~** (*fig*) (to put) completely out of mind

ouest [wɛst] nm west ▷ adj inv west; (*région*) western; **à l'~** in the west; (*direction*) (to the) west, westwards; **à l'~ de** (to the) west of; **vent d'~** westerly wind

ouf [uf] excl phew!

oui [wi] adv yes; **répondre (par) ~** to answer yes; **mais ~, bien sûr** yes, of course; **je pense que ~** I think so; **pour un ~ ou pour un non** for no apparent reason

ouï-dire ['widiʀ]: **par ~** adv by hearsay

ouïe [wi] nf hearing; **ouïes** nfpl (*de poisson*) gills; (*de violon*) sound-hole *sg*

ouragan [uʀagɑ̃] nm hurricane; (*fig*) storm

ourlet [uʀlɛ] nm hem; (*de l'oreille*) rim; **faire un ~ à** to hem

ours [uʀs] nm bear; **~ brun/blanc** brown/polar bear; **~ marin** fur seal; **~ mal léché** uncouth fellow; **~ (en peluche)** teddy (bear)

oursin [uʀsɛ̃] nm sea urchin

ourson [uʀsɔ̃] nm (bear-)cub

ouste [ust] excl hop it!

outil [uti] nm tool

outiller [utije] vt (*ouvrier, usine*) to equip

outrage [utʀaʒ] nm insult; **faire subir les derniers ~s à** (*femme*) to ravish; **~ aux bonnes mœurs** (*Jur*) outrage to public decency; **~ à magistrat** (*Jur*) contempt of court; **~ à la pudeur** (*Jur*) indecent behaviour *no pl*

outrager [utʀaʒe] vt to offend gravely; (*fig: contrevenir à*) to outrage, insult

outrance [utʀɑ̃s] nf excessiveness *no pl*, excess; **à ~** adv excessively, to excess

outre [utʀ] nf goatskin, water skin ▷ prép besides ▷ adv: **passer ~** to carry on regardless; **passer ~ à** to disregard, take no notice of; **en ~** besides, moreover; **~ que** apart from the fact that; **~ mesure** to excess; (*manger, boire*) immoderately

outre-Atlantique [utʀatlɑ̃tik] adv across the Atlantic

outre-Manche [utʀəmɑ̃ʃ] adv across the Channel

outre-mer [utʀəmɛʀ] adv overseas; **d'~** overseas

outrepasser [utʀəpɑse] vt to go beyond, exceed

ouvert, e [uvɛʀ, -ɛʀt] pp de **ouvrir** ▷ adj open; (*robinet, gaz etc*) on; **à bras ~s** with open arms

ouvertement [uvɛʀtəmɑ̃] adv openly

ouverture [uvɛʀtyʀ] nf opening; (*Mus*) overture; (*Pol*): **l'~** the widening of the political spectrum; (*Photo*): **~ (du diaphragme)** aperture; **ouvertures** nfpl (*propositions*) overtures; **~ d'esprit** open-mindedness; **heures d'~** (*Comm*) opening hours; **jours d'~** (*Comm*) days of opening

ouvrable [uvʀabl] adj: **jour ~** working day, weekday; **heures ~s** business hours

ouvrage [uvʀaʒ] nm (*tâche, de tricot etc, Mil*) work *no pl*; (*objet: Couture, Art*) (piece of) work; (*texte, livre*) work; **panier ou corbeille à ~** work basket; **~ d'art** (*Génie Civil*) bridge or tunnel etc

ouvragé, e [uvʀaʒe] adj finely embroidered (*ou* worked *ou* carved)

ouvre-boîte, ouvre-boîtes [uvʀəbwat] nm inv tin (*Brit*) *ou* can opener

ouvre-bouteille, ouvre-bouteilles [uvʀə butɛj] nm inv bottle-opener

ouvreuse [uvʀøz] nf usherette

ouvrier, -ière [uvʀije, -jɛʀ] nm/f worker ▷ nf (*Zool*) worker (bee) ▷ adj working-class; (*problèmes, conflit*) industrial; (*mouvement*) labour cpd (*Brit*), labor cpd (*US*); (*revendications*) workers'; **classe ouvrière** working class; **~ agricole** farmworker; **~ qualifié** skilled worker; **~ spécialisé (OS)** semiskilled worker; **~ d'usine** factory worker

ouvrir [uvʀiʀ] vt (*gén*) to open; (*brèche, passage*) to open up; (*commencer l'exploitation de, créer*) to open (up); (*eau, électricité, chauffage, robinet*) to turn on; (*Méd: abcès*) to open up, cut open ▷ vi to open; to open up; (*Cartes*): **~ à trèfle** to open in clubs; **s'ouvrir** vi to open; **s'~ à** (*art etc*) to open one's mind to; **s'~ à qn (de qch)** to open one's heart to sb (about sth); **s'~ les veines** to slash *ou* cut one's wrists; **~ sur** to open onto; **~ l'appétit à qn** to whet sb's appetite; **~ des horizons** to open up new horizons; **~ l'esprit** to broaden one's horizons; **~ une session** (*Inform*) to log in

ovaire [ovɛʀ] nm ovary

ovale [oval] adj oval

OVNI [ovni] sigle m (= *objet volant non identifié*) UFO

oxyder [okside]: **s'oxyder** vi to become oxidized

oxygéné, e [oksiʒene] adj: **eau ~e** hydrogen peroxide; **cheveux ~s** bleached hair

oxygène [oksiʒɛn] nm oxygen; (*fig*): **cure d'~** fresh air cure

ozone [ozon] nm ozone; **trou dans la couche d'~** hole in the ozone layer

p

pacifique [pasifik] adj (personne) peaceable; (intentions, coexistence) peaceful ▷ nm: **le P~**, **l'océan P~** the Pacific (Ocean)

pack [pak] nm pack

pacotille [pakɔtij] nf (péj) cheap junk pl; **de ~** cheap

PACS [paks] sigle m (= pacte civil de solidarité) ≈ civil partnership

pacser [pakse]: **se pacser** vi ≈ to form a civil partnership

pacte [pakt] nm pact, treaty

pagaie [pagɛ] nf paddle

pagaille [pagaj] nf mess, shambles sg; **il y en a en ~** there are loads ou heaps of them

pagayer [pageje] vi to paddle

page [paʒ] nf page; (passage: d'un roman) passage ▷ nm page (boy); **mettre en ~s** to make up (into pages); **mise en ~** layout; **à la ~** (fig) up-to-date; **~ d'accueil** (Inform) home page; **~ blanche** blank page; **~ de garde** endpaper; **~ Web** (Inform) web page

païen, ne [pajɛ̃, -ɛn] adj, nm/f pagan, heathen

paillasson [pajasɔ̃] nm doormat

paille [paj] nf straw; (défaut) flaw; **être sur la ~** to be ruined; **~ de fer** steel wool

paillette [pajɛt] nf speck, flake; **paillettes** nfpl (décoratives) sequins, spangles; **lessive en ~s** soapflakes pl

pain [pɛ̃] nm (substance) bread; (unité) loaf (of bread); (morceau): **~ de cire** etc bar of wax etc; (Culin): **~ de poisson/légumes** fish/vegetable

loaf; **petit ~** (bread) roll; **~ bis/complet** brown/wholemeal (Brit) ou wholewheat (US) bread; **~ de campagne** farmhouse bread; **~ d'épice** ≈ gingerbread; **~ grillé** toast; **~ de mie** sandwich loaf; **~ perdu** French toast; **~ de seigle** rye bread; **~ de sucre** sugar loaf; **~ au chocolat** pain au chocolat; **~ aux raisins** currant pastry

pair, e [pɛR] adj (nombre) even ▷ nm peer; **aller de ~ (avec)** to go hand in hand ou together (with); **au ~** (Finance) at par; **valeur au ~** par value; **jeune fille au ~** au pair

paire [pɛR] nf pair; **une ~ de lunettes/tenailles** a pair of glasses/pincers; **faire la ~**: **les deux font la paire** they are two of a kind

paisible [pezibl] adj peaceful, quiet

paître [pɛtR] vi to graze

paix [pɛ] nf peace; (fig) peacefulness, peace; **faire la ~ avec** to make peace with; **avoir la ~** to have peace (and quiet); **fiche-lui la ~!** (fam) leave him alone!

Pakistan [pakistɑ̃] nm: **le ~** Pakistan

palace [palas] nm luxury hotel

palais [palɛ] nm palace; (Anat) palate; **le P~Bourbon** the seat of the French National Assembly; **le P~ de l'Élysée** the Élysée Palace; **~ des expositions** exhibition centre; **le P~ de Justice** the Law Courts pl

pâle [pɑl] adj pale; (fig): **une ~ imitation** a pale imitation; **bleu ~** pale blue; **~ de colère** white ou pale with anger

Palestine [palɛstin] nf: **la ~** Palestine

palet [palɛ] nm disc; (Hockey) puck

paletot [palto] nm (short) coat

palette [palɛt] nf (de peintre) palette; (de produits) range

pâleur [pɑlœR] nf paleness

palier [palje] nm (d'escalier) landing; (fig) level, plateau; (: phase stable) levelling (Brit) ou leveling (US) off, new level; (Tech) bearing; **nos voisins de ~** our neighbo(u)rs across the landing (Brit) ou the hall (US); **en ~** adv level; **par ~s** in stages

pâlir [pɑliR] vi to turn ou go pale; (couleur) to fade; **faire ~ qn** (de jalousie) to make sb green (with envy)

palissade [palisad] nf fence

pallier [palje] vt: **~ à** vt to offset, make up for

palmarès [palmaRɛs] nm record (of achievements); (Scol) prize list; (Sport) list of winners

palme [palm] nf (Bot) palm leaf; (symbole) palm; (de plongeur) flipper; **~s (académiques)** decoration for services to education

palmé, e [palme] adj (pattes) webbed

palmier [palmje] nm palm tree; (gâteau) heart-shaped biscuit made of flaky pastry

pâlot, te [palo, -ɔt] adj pale, peaky

palourde [paluRd] nf clam

palper [palpe] vt to feel, finger

palpitant, e [palpitɑ̃, -ɑ̃t] adj thrilling, gripping

palpiter [palpite] vi (cœur, pouls) to beat; (: plus fort) to pound, throb; (narines, chair) to quiver

paludisme [palydism] nm malaria

pamphlet [pɑ̃flɛ] nm lampoon, satirical tract

pamplemousse [pɑ̃pləmus] nm grapefruit

pan [pɑ̃] nm section, piece; (côté: d'un prisme, d'une tour) side, face ▷ excl bang!; ~ **de chemise** shirt tail; ~ **de mur** section of wall

panache [panaʃ] nm plume; (fig) spirit, panache

panaché, e [panaʃe] adj: œillet ~ variegated carnation; **glace ~e** mixed ice cream; **salade ~e** mixed salad ▷ nm (bière) shandy

pancarte [pɑ̃kaʀt] nf sign, notice; (dans un défilé) placard

pancréas [pɑ̃kʀeɑs] nm pancreas

pandémie [pɑ̃demi] nf pandemic

pané, e [pane] adj fried in breadcrumbs

panier [panje] nm basket; (à diapositives) magazine; **mettre au ~** to chuck away; ~ **de crabes: c'est un panier de crabes** (fig) they're constantly at one another's throats; ~ **percé** (fig) spendthrift; ~ **à provisions** shopping basket; ~ **à salade** (Culin) salad shaker; (Police) paddy wagon, police van

panier-repas (pl **paniers-repas**) [panjeʀ(ə)pa] nm packed lunch

panique [panik] adj panicky ▷ nf panic

paniquer [panike] vi to panic

panne [pan] nf (d'un mécanisme, moteur) breakdown; **être/tomber en ~** to have broken down/break down; **être en ~ d'essence** ou **en ~ sèche** to have run out of petrol (Brit) ou gas (US); **mettre en ~** (Navig) to bring to; ~ **d'électricité** ou **de courant** power ou electrical failure

panneau, x [pano] nm (écriteau) sign, notice; (de boiserie, de tapisserie etc) panel; **tomber dans le ~** (fig) to walk into the trap; ~ **d'affichage** notice (Brit) ou bulletin (US) board; ~ **électoral** board for election poster; ~ **indicateur** signpost; ~ **publicitaire** hoarding (Brit), billboard (US); ~ **de signalisation** roadsign; ~ **solaire** solar panel

panoplie [panɔpli] nf (jouet) outfit; (d'armes) display; (fig) array

panorama [panɔʀama] nm (vue) all-round view, panorama; (peinture) panorama; (fig: étude complète) complete overview

panse [pɑ̃s] nf paunch

pansement [pɑ̃smɑ̃] nm dressing, bandage; ~ **adhésif** sticking plaster (Brit), bandaid® (US)

panser [pɑ̃se] vt (plaie) to dress, bandage; (bras) to put a dressing on, bandage; (cheval) to groom

pantacourt [pɑ̃takuʀ] nm cropped trousers pl

pantalon [pɑ̃talɔ̃] nm trousers pl (Brit), pants pl (US), pair of trousers ou pants; ~ **de ski** ski pants pl

panthère [pɑ̃tɛʀ] nf panther

pantin [pɑ̃tɛ̃] nm (jouet) jumping jack; (péj: personne) puppet

pantois [pɑ̃twa] adj m: **rester ~** to be flabbergasted

pantoufle [pɑ̃tufl] nf slipper

paon [pɑ̃] nm peacock

papa [papa] nm dad(dy)

pape [pap] nm pope

paperasse [papʀas] nf (péj) bumf no pl, papers pl; forms pl

paperasserie [papʀasʀi] nf (péj) red tape no pl; paperwork no pl

papeterie [papɛtʀi] nf (fabrication du papier) paper-making (industry); (usine) paper mill; (magasin) stationer's (shop (Brit)); (articles) stationery

papetier, -ière [paptje, -jɛʀ] nm/f paper-maker; stationer

papi [papi] nm (fam) granddad

papier [papje] nm paper; (feuille) sheet ou piece of paper; (article) article; (écrit officiel) document; **papiers** nmpl (aussi: **~s d'identité**) (identity) papers; **sur le ~** (théoriquement) on paper; **noircir du ~** to write page after page; ~ **couché/glacé** art/glazed paper; ~ **(d') aluminium** aluminium (Brit) ou aluminum (US) foil, tinfoil; ~ **d'Arménie** incense paper; ~ **bible** India ou bible paper; ~ **de brouillon** rough ou scrap paper; ~ **bulle** manil(l)a paper; ~ **buvard** blotting paper; ~ **calque** tracing paper; ~ **carbone** carbon paper; ~ **collant** Sellotape® (Brit), Scotch tape® (US), sticky tape; ~ **en continu** continuous stationery; ~ **à dessin** drawing paper; ~ **d'emballage** wrapping paper; ~ **gommé** gummed paper; ~ **hygiénique** ou **(de) toilette** toilet paper; ~ **journal** newsprint; (pour emballer) newspaper; ~ **à lettres** writing paper, notepaper; ~ **mâché** papier-mâché; ~ **machine** typing paper; ~ **peint** wallpaper; ~ **pelure** India paper; ~ **à pliage accordéon** fanfold paper; ~ **de soie** tissue paper; ~ **thermique** thermal paper; ~ **de tournesol** litmus paper; ~ **de verre** sandpaper

papillon [papijɔ̃] nm butterfly; (fam: contravention) (parking) ticket; (Tech: écrou) wing ou butterfly nut; ~ **de nuit** moth

papillote [papijɔt] nf (pour cheveux) curlpaper; (de gigot) (paper) frill; **en ~** cooked in tinfoil

papoter [papɔte] vi to chatter

paquebot [pakbo] nm liner

pâquerette [pakʀɛt] nf daisy

Pâques [pak] nm, nfpl Easter; **faire ses ~** to do one's Easter duties; **l'île de ~** Easter Island

● **PÂQUES**
●
●
● In France, Easter eggs are said to be
● brought by the Easter bells or cloches de
● Pâques which fly from Rome and drop
● them in people's gardens.

paquet [pakɛ] nm packet; (colis) parcel; (ballot) bundle; (dans négociations) package (deal); (*fig*: *tas*): **~ de pile** ou heap of; **paquets** *nmpl* (*bagages*) bags; **mettre le ~** (*fam*) to give one's all; **~ de mer** big wave

paquet-cadeau (*pl* **paquets-cadeaux**) [pakɛkado] *nm* gift-wrapped parcel

par [paʀ] *prép* by; **finir** *etc* **~** to end *etc* with; **~ amour** out of love; **passer ~ Lyon/la côte** to go via ou through Lyons/along the coast; **~ la fenêtre** (*jeter, regarder*) out of the window; **trois ~ jour/personne** three a ou per day/head; **deux ~ deux** two at a time; (*marcher etc*) in twos; **où?** which way?; **~ ici** this way; (*dans le coin*) round here; **~-ci, ~-là** here and there; **~ temps de pluie** in wet weather

parabolique [paʀabɔlik] *adj* parabolic; **antenne ~** satellite dish

parachever [paʀaʃve] *vt* to perfect

parachute [paʀaʃyt] *nm* parachute

parachutiste [paʀaʃytist] *nm/f* parachutist; (*Mil*) paratrooper

parade [paʀad] *nf* (*spectacle, défilé*) parade; (*Escrime, Boxe*) parry; (*ostentation*): **faire ~ de** to display, show off; (*défense, riposte*): **trouver la ~ à une attaque** to find the answer to an attack; **de ~** *adj* ceremonial; (*superficiel*) superficial; outward

paradis [paʀadi] *nm* heaven, paradise; **P~ terrestre** (*Rel*) Garden of Eden; (*fig*) heaven on earth

paradoxe [paʀadɔks] *nm* paradox

paraffine [paʀafin] *nf* paraffin; paraffin wax

parages [paʀaʒ] *nmpl* (*Navig*) waters; **dans les ~ (de)** in the area ou vicinity (of)

paragraphe [paʀagʀaf] *nm* paragraph

paraître [paʀɛtʀ] *vb copule* to seem, look, appear ▷ *vi* to appear; (*être visible*) to show; (*Presse, Édition*) to be published, come out, appear; (*briller*) to show off; **laisser ~ qch** to let (sth) show ▷ *vb impers*: **il paraît que** it seems ou appears that; **il me paraît que** it seems to me that; **il paraît absurde de** it seems absurd to; **il ne paraît pas son âge** he doesn't look his age; **~ en justice** to appear before the court(s); **~ en scène/en public/à l'écran** to appear on stage/in public/on the screen

parallèle [paʀalɛl] *adj* parallel; (*police, marché*) unofficial; (*société, énergie*) alternative ▷ *nm* (*comparaison*): **faire un ~ entre** to draw a parallel between; (*Géo*) parallel ▷ *nf* parallel (line); **en ~** in parallel; **mettre en ~** (*choses opposées*) to compare; (*choses semblables*) to parallel

paralyser [paʀalize] *vt* to paralyze

paramédical, e, -aux [paʀamedikal, -o] *adj* paramedical; **personnel ~** paramedics *pl*, paramedical workers *pl*

paraphrase [paʀafʀaz] *nf* paraphrase

parapluie [paʀaplɥi] *nm* umbrella; **~ atomique** ou **nucléaire** nuclear umbrella; **~ pliant** telescopic umbrella

parasite [paʀazit] *nm* parasite ▷ *adj* (*Bot, Bio*)

parasitic(al); **parasites** *nmpl* (*Tél*) interference *sg*

parasol [paʀasɔl] *nm* parasol, sunshade

paratonnerre [paʀatɔnɛʀ] *nm* lightning conductor

paravent [paʀavã] *nm* folding screen; (*fig*) screen

parc [paʀk] *nm* (*public*) park, gardens *pl*; (*de château etc*) grounds *pl*; (*pour le bétail*) pen, enclosure; (*d'enfant*) playpen; (*Mil*: *entrepôt*) depot; (*ensemble d'unités*) stock; (*de voitures etc*) fleet; **~ d'attractions** amusement park; **~ automobile** (*d'un pays*) number of cars on the roads; **~ à huîtres** oyster bed; **~ à thème** theme park; **~ national** national park; **~ naturel** nature reserve; **~ de stationnement** car park; **~ zoologique** zoological gardens *pl*

parcelle [paʀsɛl] *nf* fragment, scrap; (*de terrain*) plot, parcel

parce que [paʀskə] *conj* because

parchemin [paʀʃəmɛ̃] *nm* parchment

parcmètre [paʀkmɛtʀ], **parcomètre** [paʀkɔmɛtʀ] *nm* parking meter

parcourir [paʀkuʀiʀ] *vt* (*trajet, distance*) to cover; (*article, livre*) to skim ou glance through; (*lieu*) to go all over, travel up and down; (*frisson, vibration*) to run through; **~ des yeux** to run one's eye over

parcours [paʀkuʀ] *vb voir* **parcourir** ▷ *nm* (*trajet*) journey; (*itinéraire*) route; (*Sport*: *terrain*) course; (: *tour*) round; run; lap; **~ du combattant** assault course

par-dessous [paʀdəsu] *prép, adv* under(neath)

pardessus [paʀdəsy] *nm* overcoat

par-dessus [paʀdəsy] *prép* over (the top of) ▷ *adv* over (the top); **~ le marché** on top of it all; **~ tout** above all; **en avoir ~ la tête** to have had enough

par-devant [paʀdəvã] *prép* in the presence of, before ▷ *adv* at the front; (*passer*) round the front

pardon [paʀdɔ̃] *nm* forgiveness *no pl* ▷ *excl* (*excuses*) (I'm) sorry; (*pour interpeller etc*) excuse me; **demander ~ à qn (de)** to apologize to sb (for); **je vous demande ~** I'm sorry; (*pour interpeller*) excuse me; (*demander de répéter*) (I beg your) pardon? (*Brit*), pardon me? (*US*)

pardonner [paʀdɔne] *vt* to forgive; **~ qch à qn** to forgive sb for sth; **qui ne pardonne pas** (*maladie, erreur*) fatal

paré, e [paʀe] *adj* ready, prepared

pare-balles [paʀbal] *adj inv* bulletproof

pare-brise [paʀbʀiz] *nm inv* windscreen (*Brit*), windshield (*US*)

pare-chocs [paʀʃɔk] *nm inv* bumper (*Brit*), fender (*US*)

pare-feu [paʀfø] *nm inv* (*de foyer*) fireguard; (*Inform*) firewall ▷ *adj inv*

pareil, le [paʀɛj] *adj* (*identique*) the same, alike; (*similaire*) similar; (*tel*): **un courage/livre ~** such courage/a book, courage/a book like this; **de ~s livres** such books ▷ *adv*:

p

habillés ~ dressed the same (way), dressed alike; **faire ~** to do the same (thing); **j'en veux un ~** I'd like one just like it; **rien de ~** no (ou any) such thing, nothing (ou anything) like it; **ses ~s** one's fellow men; one's peers; **ne pas avoir son (sa) ~(le)** to be second to none; **~ à** the same as; similar to; **sans ~** unparalleled, unequalled; **c'est du ~ au même** it comes to the same thing, it's six (of one) and half-a-dozen (of the other); **en ~ cas** in such a case; **rendre à qn la ~le à qn** to pay sb back in his own coin

parent, e [paʀɑ̃, -ɑ̃t] nm/f: **un/une ~/e** a relative ou relation ▷ adj: **être ~ de** to be related to; **parents** nmpl (père et mère) parents; (famille, proches) relatives, relations; **~ unique** lone parent; **~s par alliance** relatives ou relations by marriage; **~s en ligne directe** blood relations

parenté [paʀɑ̃te] nf (lien) relationship; (personnes) relatives pl, relations pl

parenthèse [paʀɑ̃tɛz] nf (ponctuation) bracket, parenthesis; (Math) bracket; (digression) parenthesis, digression; **ouvrir/ fermer la ~** to open/close brackets; **entre ~s** in brackets; (fig) incidentally

parer [paʀe] vt to adorn; (Culin) to dress, trim; (éviter) to ward off; **~ à** (danger) to ward off; (inconvénient) to deal with; **se ~ de** (fig: qualité, titre) to assume; **~ à toute éventualité** to be ready for every eventuality; **~ au plus pressé** to attend to what's most urgent

paresse [paʀɛs] nf laziness

paresseux, -euse [paʀɛsø, -øz] adj lazy; (fig) slow, sluggish ▷ nm (Zool) sloth

parfaire [paʀfɛʀ] vt to perfect, complete

parfait, e [paʀfɛ, -ɛt] pp de **parfaire** ▷ adj perfect ▷ nm (Ling) perfect (tense); (Culin) parfait ▷ excl fine, excellent

parfaitement [paʀfɛtmɑ̃] adv perfectly ▷ excl (most) certainly

parfois [paʀfwa] adv sometimes

parfum [paʀfœ̃] nm (produit) perfume, scent; (odeur: de fleur) scent, fragrance; (: de tabac, vin) aroma; (goût: de glace, milk-shake) flavour (Brit), flavor (US)

parfumé, e [paʀfyme] adj (fleur, fruit) fragrant; (papier à lettres etc) scented; (femme) wearing perfume ou scent, perfumed; (aromatisé): **~ au café** coffee-flavoured (Brit) ou -flavored (US)

parfumer [paʀfyme] vt (odeur, bouquet) to perfume; (mouchoir) to put scent ou perfume on; (crème, gâteau) to flavour (Brit), flavor (US); **se parfumer** to put on (some) perfume ou scent; (d'habitude) to use perfume ou scent

parfumerie [paʀfymʀi] nf (commerce) perfumery; (produits) perfumes pl; (boutique) perfume shop (Brit) ou store (US)

pari [paʀi] nm bet, wager; (Sport) bet; **~ mutuel urbain (PMU)** system of betting on horses

parier [paʀje] vt to bet; **j'aurais parié que si/ non** I'd have said he (ou you etc) would/ wouldn't

Paris [paʀi] n Paris

parisien, ne [paʀizjɛ̃, -ɛn] adj Parisian; (Géo, Admin) Paris cpd ▷ nm/f: **P~, ne** Parisian

parité [paʀite] nf parity; **~ de change** (Écon) exchange parity; (Pol): **~ hommes-femmes** balanced representation of men and women

parjure [paʀʒyʀ] nm (faux serment) false oath, perjury; (violation de serment) breach of oath, perjury ▷ nm/f perjurer

parking [paʀkiŋ] nm (lieu) car park (Brit), parking lot (US)

parlant, e [paʀlɑ̃, -ɑ̃t] adj (fig) graphic, vivid; (: comparaison, preuve) eloquent; (Ciné) talking ▷ adv: **généralement ~** generally speaking

parlement [paʀləmɑ̃] nm parliament; **le P~ européen** the European Parliament

parlementaire [paʀləmɑ̃tɛʀ] adj parliamentary ▷ nm/f (député) ≈ Member of Parliament (Brit) ou Congress (US); parliamentarian; (négociateur) negotiator, mediator

parlementer [paʀləmɑ̃te] vi (ennemis) to negotiate, parley; (s'entretenir, discuter) to argue at length, have lengthy talks

parler [paʀle] nm speech; dialect ▷ vi to speak, talk; (avouer) to talk; **~ (à qn) de** to talk ou speak (to sb) about; **~ pour qn** (intercéder) to speak for sb; **~ en l'air** to say the first thing that comes into one's head; **~ le/en français** to speak French/in French; **~ affaires** to talk business; **~ en dormant/du nez** to talk in one's sleep/through one's nose; **sans ~ de** (fig) not to mention, to say nothing of; **tu parles!** you must be joking!; (bien sûr) you bet!; **n'en parlons plus!** let's forget it!

parloir [paʀlwaʀ] nm (d'une prison, d'un hôpital) visiting room; (Rel) parlour (Brit), parlor (US)

parmi [paʀmi] prép among(st)

paroi [paʀwa] nf wall; (cloison) partition; **~ rocheuse** rock face

paroisse [paʀwas] nf parish

parole [paʀɔl] nf (faculté): **la ~** speech; (mot, promesse) word; (Rel): **la bonne ~** the word of God; **paroles** nfpl (Mus) words, lyrics; **tenir ~** to keep one's word; **avoir la ~** to have the floor; **n'avoir qu'une ~** to be true to one's word; **donner la ~ à qn** to hand over to sb; **prendre la ~** to speak; **demander la ~** to ask for permission to speak; **perdre la ~** to lose the power of speech; (fig) to lose one's tongue; **je le crois sur ~** I'll take his word for it, I'll take him at his word; **temps de ~** (TV, Radio etc) discussion time; **ma ~!** my word!, good heavens!; **~ d'honneur** word of honour (Brit) ou honor (US)

parquer [paʀke] vt (voiture, matériel) to park; (bestiaux) to pen (in ou up); (prisonniers) to pack in

parquet [paʀkɛ] nm (parquet) floor; (Jur: bureau) public prosecutor's office; **le ~ (général)** (magistrats) ≈ the Bench

parrain [paʀɛ̃] nm godfather; (d'un navire) namer; (d'un nouvel adhérent) sponsor, proposer

parrainer [paʀene] vt (nouvel adhérent) to sponsor, propose; (entreprise) to promote, sponsor

pars [paʀ] vb voir **partir**

parsemer [paʀsəme] vt (feuilles, papiers) to be scattered over; **~ qch de** to scatter sth with

part [paʀ] vb voir **partir** ▷ nf (qui revient à qn) share; (fraction, partie) part; (de gâteau, fromage) portion; (Finance) (non-voting) share; **prendre ~ à** (débat etc) to take part in; (soucis, douleur de qn) to share in; **faire ~ de qch à qn** to announce sth to sb, inform sb of sth; **pour ma ~** as for me, as far as I'm concerned; **à ~ entière** adj full; **de la ~ de** (au nom de) on behalf of; (donné par) from; **c'est de la ~ de qui?** (au téléphone) who's calling ou speaking (please)?; **de toute(s) ~(s)** from all sides ou quarters; **de ~ et d'autre** on both sides, on either side; **de ~ en ~** right through; **d'une ~ ... d'autre ~** on the one hand ... on the other hand; **d'autre ~** (de plus) moreover; **nulle autre/quelque ~** nowhere/elsewhere/ somewhere; **à ~** adv separately; (de côté) aside ▷ prép apart from, except for ▷ adj exceptional, special; **pour une large** ou **bonne ~** to a great extent; **prendre qch en bonne/mauvaise ~** to take sth well/badly; **faire la ~ des choses** to make allowances; **faire la ~ du feu** (fig) to cut one's losses; **faire la ~ (trop) belle à qn** to give sb more than his (ou her) share

partage [paʀtaʒ] nm voir **partager** sharing (out) no pl, share-out; sharing; dividing up; (Pol: de suffrages) share; **recevoir qch en ~** to receive sth as one's share (ou lot); **sans ~** undivided

partager [paʀtaʒe] vt to share; (distribuer, répartir) to share (out); (morceler, diviser) to divide (up); **se partager** vt (héritage etc) to share between themselves (ou ourselves etc)

partance [paʀtɑ̃s]: **en ~** adv outbound, due to leave; **en ~ pour** (bound) for

partenaire [paʀtənɛʀ] nm/f partner; **~s sociaux** management and workforce

parterre [paʀtɛʀ] nm (de fleurs) (flower) bed, border; (Théât) stalls pl

parti [paʀti] nm (Pol) party; (décision) course of action; (personne à marier) match; **tirer ~ de** to take advantage of, turn to good account; **prendre le ~ de faire** to make up one's mind to do, resolve to do; **prendre le ~ de qn** to stand up for sb, side with sb; **prendre ~ (pour/contre)** to take sides ou a stand (for/ against); **prendre son ~ de** to come to terms with; **~ pris** bias

partial, e, -aux [paʀsjal, -o] adj biased, partial

participant, e [paʀtisipɑ̃, -ɑ̃t] nm/f participant; (à un concours) entrant; (d'une société) member

participation [paʀtisipasjɔ̃] nf participation; (financière) contribution; sharing; (Comm) interest; **la ~ aux bénéfices** profit-sharing; **la ~ ouvrière** worker participation; **"avec la ~ de ..."** "featuring ..."

participer [paʀtisipe]: **~ à** vt (course, réunion) to take part in; (profits etc) to share in; (frais etc) to contribute to; (entreprise: financièrement) to cooperate in; (chagrin, succès de qn) to share (in); **~ de** vt to partake of

particularité [paʀtikylaʀite] nf particularity; (distinctive) characteristic, feature

particulier, -ière [paʀtikylje, -jɛʀ] adj (personnel, privé) private; (étrange) peculiar, odd; (spécial) special, particular; (caractéristique) characteristic, distinctive; (spécifique) particular ▷ nm (individu: Admin) private individual; **"~ vend ..."** (Comm) "for sale privately ...", "for sale by owner ..." (US); **~ à** peculiar to; **en ~** adv (surtout) in particular, particularly; (à part) separately; (en privé) in private

particulièrement [paʀtikyljɛʀmɑ̃] adv particularly

partie [paʀti] nf (gén) part; (profession, spécialité) field, subject; (Jur etc: protagonistes) party; (de cartes, tennis etc) game; (fig: lutte, combat) struggle, fight; **une ~ de campagne/ de pêche** an outing in the country/a fishing party ou trip; **en ~** partly, in part; **faire ~ de** to belong to; (chose) to be part of; **prendre qn à ~** to take sb to task; (malmener) to set on sb; **en grande ~** largely, in the main; **ce n'est que ~ remise** it will be for another time ou the next time; **avoir ~ liée avec qn** to be in league with sb; **~ civile** (Jur) party claiming damages in a criminal case

partiel, le [paʀsjɛl] adj partial ▷ nm (Scol) class exam

partir [paʀtiʀ] vi (gén) to go; (quitter) to go, leave; (s'éloigner) to go (ou drive etc) away ou off; (moteur) to start; (pétard) to go off; (bouchon) to come out; (bouton) to come off; (tache) to go, come out; **~ de** (lieu: quitter) to leave; (: commencer à) to start from; (date) to run ou start from; **pour/à** (lieu, pays etc) to leave for/go off to; **à ~ de** from

partisan, e [paʀtizɑ̃, -an] nm/f partisan; (d'un parti, régime etc) supporter ▷ adj (lutte, querelle) partisan, one-sided; **être ~ de qch/ faire** to be in favour (Brit) ou favor (US) of sth/ doing

partition [paʀtisjɔ̃] nf (Mus) score

partout [paʀtu] adv everywhere; **~ où il allait** everywhere ou wherever he went; **trente ~** (Tennis) thirty all

paru [paʀy] pp de **paraître**

parure [paʀyʀ] nf (bijoux etc) finery no pl; jewellery no pl (Brit), jewelry no pl (US); (assortiment) set

P

parution [paʁysjɔ̃] *nf* publication, appearance

parvenir [paʁvəniʁ]: **~ à** *vt* (*atteindre*) to reach; (*obtenir, arriver à*) to attain; (*réussir*): **à faire** to manage to do, succeed in doing; **faire ~ qch à qn** to have sth sent to sb

 MOT-CLÉ

pas[1] [pɑ] *adv* **1** (*en corrélation avec ne, non etc*) not; **il ne pleure pas** (*habituellement*) he does not *ou* doesn't cry; (*maintenant*) he's not *ou* isn't crying; **je ne mange pas de viande** I don't *ou* do not eat meat; **il n'a pas pleuré/ne pleurera pas** he did not *ou* didn't/will not *ou* won't cry; **ils n'ont pas de voiture/d'enfants** they haven't got a car/ any children, they have no car/children; **il m'a dit de ne pas le faire** he told me not to do it; **non pas que ...** not that ..
2 (*employé sans ne etc*): **pas moi** not me, not I, I don't (*ou* can't *etc*); **elle travaille, (mais) lui pas** *ou* **pas lui** she works but he doesn't *ou* does not; **une pomme pas mûre** an apple which isn't ripe; **pas plus tard qu'hier** only yesterday; **pas du tout** not at all; **pas de sucre, merci** no sugar, thanks; **ceci est à vous ou pas?** is this yours or not?, is this yours or isn't it?
3: **pas mal** (*joli: personne, maison*) not bad; **pas mal fait** not badly done *ou* made; **comment ça va? — pas mal** how are things? — not bad; **pas mal de** quite a lot of

pas[2] [pɑ] *nm* (*démarche*) tread; (*enjambée, Danse, fig: étape*) step; (*bruit*) (foot)step; (*trace*) footprint; (*allure, mesure*) pace; (*d'un cheval*) walk; (*Tech: de vis, d'écrou*) thread; **à ~** step by step; **au ~** at a walking pace; **de ce ~** (*à l'instant même*) straightaway, at once; **marcher à grands ~** to stride along; **mettre qn au ~** to bring sb to heel; **au ~ de gymnastique/de course** at a jog trot/at a run; **à ~ de loup** stealthily; **faire les cent ~** to pace up and down; **faire les premiers ~** to make the first move; **retourner** *ou* **revenir sur ses ~** to retrace one's steps; **se tirer d'un mauvais ~** to get o.s. out of a tight spot; **sur le ~ de la porte** on the doorstep; **le ~ de Calais** (*détroit*) the Straits *pl* of Dover; **~ de porte** (*fig*) key money

passage [pɑsaʒ] *nm* (*fait de passer*) *voir* **passer**; (*lieu, prix de la traversée, extrait de livre etc*) passage; (*chemin*) way; (*itinéraire*): **sur le ~ du cortège** along the route of the procession; **"laissez/ n'obstruez pas le ~"** "keep clear/do not obstruct"; **au ~** (*en passant*) as I (*ou* he *etc*) went by; **de ~** (*touristes*) passing through; (*amants etc*) casual; **~ clouté** pedestrian crossing; **"~ interdit"** "no entry"; **~ à niveau** level (*Brit*) *ou* grade (*US*) crossing; **"~ protégé"** right of way over secondary road(s) on your right;

~ souterrain subway (*Brit*), underpass; **~ à tabac** beating-up; **~ à vide** (*fig*) bad patch

passager, -ère [pɑsaʒe, -ɛʀ] *adj* passing; (*hôte*) short-stay *cpd*; (*oiseau*) migratory ▷ *nm/f* passenger; **~ clandestin** stowaway

passant, e [pɑsɑ̃, -ɑ̃t] *adj* (*rue, endroit*) busy ▷ *nm/f* passer-by ▷ *nm* (*pour ceinture etc*) loop; **en ~: remarquer qch en passant** to notice sth in passing

passe [pɑs] *nf* (*Sport, magnétique*) pass; (*Navig*) channel ▷ *nm* (*passe-partout*) master *ou* skeleton key; **être en ~ de faire** to be on the way to doing; **être dans une mauvaise ~** (*fig*) to be going through a bad patch; **être dans une bonne ~** (*fig*) to be in a healthy situation; **~ d'armes** (*fig*) heated exchange

passé, e [pɑse] *adj* (*événement, temps*) past; (*dernier: semaine etc*) last; (*couleur, tapisserie*) faded; (*précédent*): **dimanche ~** last Sunday ▷ *prép* after ▷ *nm* past; (*Ling*) past (tense); **il est ~ midi** *ou* **midi ~** it's gone (*Brit*) *ou* past twelve; **~ de mode** out of fashion; **~ composé** perfect (tense); **~ simple** past historic

passe-partout [pɑspaʀtu] *nm inv* master *ou* skeleton key ▷ *adj inv* all-purpose

passeport [pɑspɔʀ] *nm* passport

passer [pɑse] *vi* (*se rendre, aller*) to go; (*voiture, piétons: défiler*) to pass (by), go by; (*faire une halte rapide: facteur, laitier etc*) to come, call; (: *pour rendre visite*) to call ou drop in; (*courant, air, lumière, franchir un obstacle etc*) to get through; (*accusé, projet de loi*): **~ devant** to come before; (*film, émission*) to be on; (*temps, jours*) to pass, go by; (*liquide, café*) to go through; (*être digéré, avalé*) to go down; (*couleur, papier*) to fade; (*mode*) to die out; (*douleur*) to pass, go away; (*Cartes*) to pass; (*Scol*): **~ dans la classe supérieure** to go up (to the next class); (*devenir*): **~ président** to be appointed *ou* become president ▷ *vt* (*frontière, rivière etc*) to cross; (*douane*) to go through; (*examen*) to sit, take; (*visite médicale etc*) to have; (*journée, temps*) to spend; (*donner*): **~ qch à qn** (*sel etc*) to pass sth to sb; (*prêter*) to lend sb sth; (*lettre, message*) to pass sth on to sb; (*tolérer*) to let sb get away with sth; (*transmettre*): **~ qch à qn** to pass sth on to sb; (*enfiler: vêtement*) to slip on; (*faire entrer, mettre*): **(faire) ~ qch dans/ par** to get sth into/through; (*café*) to pour the water on; (*thé, soupe*) to strain; (*film, pièce*) to show, put on; (*disque*) to play, put on; (*commande*) to place; (*marché, accord*) to agree on; (*tolérer*): **~ qch à qn** to let sb get away with sth; **se passer** *vi* (*avoir lieu: scène, action*) to take place; (*se dérouler: entretien etc*) to go; (*arriver*): **que s'est-il passé?** what happened?; (*s'écouler: semaine etc*) to pass, go by; **se ~ de** *vt* to go *ou* do without; **se ~ les mains sous l'eau/de l'eau sur le visage** to put one's hands under the tap/run water over one's face; **en passant** in passing; **~ par** to go through; **passez devant/par ici** go in front/

this way; **~ sur** vt (faute, détail inutile) to pass over; **~ dans les mœurs/l'usage** to become the custom/normal usage; **~ avant qch/qn** (fig) to come before sth/sb; **~ un coup de fil à qn** (fam) to give sb a ring; **laisser ~** (air, lumière, personne) to let through; (occasion) to let slip, miss; (erreur) to overlook; **faire ~** (message) to get over ou across; **faire ~ à qn le goût de qch** to cure sb of his (ou her) taste for sth; **~ à la radio/fouille** to be X-rayed/searched; **~ à la radio/télévision** to be on the radio/on television; **~ à table** to sit down to eat; **~ au salon** to go through to ou into the sitting room; **~ son tour** to miss one's turn; **~ à l'opposition** to go over to the opposition; **~ aux aveux** to confess, make a confession; **~ à l'action** to go into action; **~ pour riche** to be taken for a rich man; **il passait pour avoir** he was said to have; **faire ~ qn/qch pour** to make sb/sth out to be; **passe encore de le penser, mais de le dire!** it's one thing to think it, but to say it!; **passons!** let's say no more (about it); **et j'en passe!** and that's not all!; **~ en seconde, ~ la seconde** (Auto) to change into second; **~ qch en fraude** to smuggle sth in (ou out); **~ la main par la portière** to stick one's hand out of the door; **~ le balai/l'aspirateur** to sweep up/hoover; **~ commande/la parole à qn** to hand over to sb; **je vous passe M. X** (je vous mets en communication avec lui) I'm putting you through to Mr X; (je lui passe l'appareil) here is Mr X, I'll hand you over to Mr X; **je vous passe M. Dupont** (je vous mets en communication avec lui) I'm putting you through to Mr Dupont; (je lui passe l'appareil) here is Mr Dupont, I'll hand you over to Mr Dupont; **~ prendre** to (come and) collect

passerelle [pɑsʀɛl] nf footbridge; (de navire, avion) gangway; (Navig): **~ (de commandement)** bridge

passe-temps [pɑstɑ̃] nm inv pastime

passible [pɑsibl] adj: **~ de** liable to

passif, -ive [pɑsif, -iv] adj passive ▷ nm (Ling) passive; (Comm) liabilities pl

passion [pɑsjɔ̃] nf passion; **avoir la ~ de** to have a passion for; **fruit de la ~** passion fruit

passionnant, e [pɑsjɔnɑ̃, -ɑ̃t] adj fascinating

passionné, e [pɑsjɔne] adj (personne, tempérament) passionate; (description, récit) impassioned ▷ nm/f: **c'est un ~ d'échecs** he's a chess fanatic; **être ~ de** ou **pour qch** to have a passion for sth

passionner [pɑsjɔne] vt (personne) to fascinate, grip; (débat, discussion) to inflame; **se ~ pour** to take an avid interest in; to have a passion for

passoire [pɑswaʀ] nf sieve; (à légumes) colander; (à thé) strainer

pastèque [pɑstɛk] nf watermelon

pasteur [pɑstœʀ] nm (protestant) minister, pastor

pasteurisé, e [pɑstœʀize] adj pasteurized

pastille [pɑstij] nf (à sucer) lozenge, pastille; (de papier etc) (small) disc; **~s pour la toux** cough drops ou lozenges

patate [patat] nf spud; **~ douce** sweet potato

patauger [patoʒe] vi (pour s'amuser) to splash about; (avec effort) to wade about; (fig) to flounder; **~ dans** (en marchant) to wade through

pâte [pɑt] nf (à tarte) pastry; (à pain) dough; (à frire) batter; (substance molle) paste; cream; **pâtes** nfpl (macaroni etc) pasta sg; **fromage à ~ dure/molle** hard/soft cheese; **~ d'amandes** almond paste, marzipan; **~ brisée** shortcrust (Brit) ou pie crust (US) pastry; **~ à choux/feuilletée** choux/puff ou flaky (Brit) pastry; **~ de fruits** crystallized fruit no pl; **~ à modeler** modelling clay, Plasticine® (Brit); **~ à papier** paper pulp

pâté [pɑte] nm (charcuterie: terrine) pâté; (tache) ink blot; (de sable) sandpie; **~ (en croûte)** ≈ meat pie; **~ de foie** liver pâté; **~ de maisons** block (of houses)

pâtée [pɑte] nf mash, feed

patente [patɑ̃t] nf (Comm) trading licence (Brit) ou license (US)

paternel, le [patɛʀnɛl] adj (amour, soins) fatherly; (ligne, autorité) paternal

pâteux, -euse [pɑtø, -øz] adj thick; pasty; **avoir la bouche** ou **langue pâteuse** to have a furred (Brit) ou coated tongue

pathétique [patetik] adj pathetic, moving

patience [pasjɑ̃s] nf patience; **être à bout de ~** to have run out of patience; **perdre/prendre ~** to lose (one's)/have patience

patient, e [pasjɑ̃, -ɑ̃t] adj, nm/f patient

patienter [pasjɑ̃te] vi to wait

patin [patɛ̃] nm skate; (sport) skating; (de traîneau, luge) runner; (pièce de tissu) cloth pad (used as slippers to protect polished floor); **~ (de frein)** brake block; **~s (à glace)** (ice) skates; **~s à roulettes** roller skates

patinage [patinaʒ] nm skating; **~ artistique/de vitesse** figure/speed skating

patiner [patine] vi to skate; (embrayage) to slip; (roue, voiture) to spin; **se patiner** vi (meuble, cuir) to acquire a sheen, become polished

patineur, -euse [patinœʀ, -øz] nm/f skater

patinoire [patinwaʀ] nf skating rink, (ice) rink

pâtir [pɑtiʀ]: **~ de** vt to suffer because of

pâtisserie [pɑtisʀi] nf (boutique) cake shop; (métier) confectionery; (à la maison) pastry- ou cake-making, baking; **pâtisseries** nfpl (gâteaux) pastries, cakes

pâtissier, -ière [pɑtisje, -jɛʀ] nm/f pastrycook; confectioner

patois [patwa] nm dialect, patois

patraque [patʀak] (fam) adj peaky, off-colour

patrie [patʀi] nf homeland

patrimoine [patʀimwan] nm inheritance, patrimony; (culture) heritage; **~ génétique** ou **héréditaire** genetic inheritance

P

● Once a year, important public buildings
● are open to the public for a weekend.
● During these **Journées du Patrimoine**,
● there are guided visits and talks based on
● a particular theme.

patriotique [patʀijɔtik] *adj* patriotic

patron, ne [patʀɔ̃, -ɔn] *nm/f* (*chef*) boss, manager(-ess); (*propriétaire*) owner, proprietor(-tress); (*employeur*) employer; (*Méd*) ≈ senior consultant; (*Rel*) patron saint ▷ *nm* (*Couture*) pattern; **~ de thèse** supervisor (of postgraduate thesis)

patronat [patʀɔna] *nm* employers *pl*

patronner [patʀɔne] *vt* to sponsor, support

patrouille [patʀuj] *nf* patrol

patte [pat] *nf* (*jambe*) leg; (*pied: de chien, chat*) paw; (: *d'oiseau*) foot; (*languette*) strap; (: *de poche*) flap; (*favoris*): **~s (de lapin)** (short) sideburns; **à ~s d'éléphant** *adj* (*pantalon*) flared; **~s de mouche** (*fig*) spidery scrawl *sg*; **~s d'oie** (*fig*) crow's feet

pâturage [pɑtyʀaʒ] *nm* pasture

paume [pom] *nf* palm

paumé, e [pome] *nm/f* (*fam*) drop-out

paumer [pome] *vt* (*fam*) to lose

paupière [popjɛʀ] *nf* eyelid

pause [poz] *nf* (*arrêt*) break; (*en parlant, Mus*) pause; **~ de midi** lunch break

pauvre [povʀ] *adj* poor ▷ *nm/f* poor man/woman; **les ~s** the poor; **~ en calcium** low in calcium

pauvreté [povʀəte] *nf* (*état*) poverty; **pauvreté énergétique** fuel poverty

pavaner [pavane]: **se pavaner** *vi* to strut about

pavé, e [pave] *adj* (*cour*) paved; (*rue*) cobbled ▷ *nm* (*bloc*) paving stone; cobblestone; (*pavage*) paving; (*bifteck*) slab of steak; (*fam: livre*) hefty tome; **être sur le ~** (*sans domicile*) to be on the streets; (*sans emploi*) to be out of a job; **~ numérique** (*Inform*) keypad

pavillon [pavijɔ̃] *nm* (*de banlieue*) small (detached) house; (*kiosque*) lodge; pavilion; (*d'hôpital*) ward; (*Mus: de cor etc*) bell; (*Anat: de l'oreille*) pavilion, pinna; (*Navig*) flag; **~ de complaisance** flag of convenience

pavoiser [pavwaze] *vt* to deck with flags ▷ *vi* to put out flags; (*fig*) to rejoice, exult

pavot [pavo] *nm* poppy

payant, e [pejɑ̃, -ɑ̃t] *adj* (*spectateurs etc*) paying; (*billet*) that you pay for, to be paid for; (*fig: entreprise*) profitable; (*effort*) which pays off; **c'est ~** you have to pay, there is a charge

paye [pɛj] *nf* pay, wages *pl*

payer [peje] *vt* (*créancier, employé, loyer*) to pay; (*achat, réparations, fig: faute*) to pay for ▷ *vi* to pay; (*métier*) to be well-paid, pay; (*effort, tactique etc*) to pay off; **être bien/mal payé** to be well/badly paid; **il me l'a fait ~ 10 euros**

he charged me 10 euros for it; **~ qn de** (*ses efforts, peines*) to reward sb for; **~ qch à qn** to buy sth for sb, buy sb sth; **ils nous ont payé le voyage** they paid for our trip; **~ de sa personne** to give of oneself; **~ d'audace** to act with great daring; **~ cher qch** to pay dear(ly) for sth; **cela ne paie pas de mine** it doesn't look much; **se ~ qch** to buy o.s. sth; **se ~ de mots** to shoot one's mouth off; **se ~ la tête de qn** to take the mickey out of sb (*Brit*), make a fool of sb; (*duper*) to take sb for a ride

pays [pei] *nm* (*territoire, habitants*) country, land; (*région*) region; (*village*) village; **du ~** *adj* local; **le ~ de Galles** Wales

paysage [peizaʒ] *nm* landscape

paysan, ne [peizɑ̃, -an] *nm/f* countryman/-woman; farmer; (*péj*) peasant ▷ *adj* (*rural*) country *cpd*; (*agricole*) farming, farmers'

Pays-Bas [peiba] *nmpl*: **les ~** the Netherlands

PC *sigle m* (*Pol*) = **parti communiste**; (*Inform*: = *personal computer*) PC; (= *prêt conventionné*) type of loan for house purchase; (*Constr*) = **permis de construire**; (*Mil*) = **poste de commandement**

PDA *sigle m* (= *personal digital assistant*) PDA

PDG *sigle m* = **président directeur général**

péage [peaʒ] *nm* toll; (*endroit*) tollgate; **pont à ~** toll bridge

peau, x [po] *nf* skin; (*cuir*): **gants de ~** leather gloves; **être bien/mal dans sa ~** to be at ease/ill-at-ease; **se mettre dans la ~ de qn** to put o.s. in sb's place ou shoes; **faire ~ neuve** (*se renouveler*) to change one's image; **~ de chamois** (*chiffon*) chamois leather, shammy; **~ d'orange** orange peel

Peau-Rouge [poʀuʒ] *nm/f* American Indian

péché [peʃe] *nm* sin; **~ mignon** weakness

pêche [pɛʃ] *nf* (*sport, activité*) fishing; (*poissons pêchés*) catch; (*fruit*) peach; **aller à la ~** to go fishing; **avoir la ~** (*fam*) to be on (top) form; **~ à la ligne** (*en rivière*) angling; **~ sous-marine** deep-sea fishing

pécher [peʃe] *vi* (*Rel*) to sin; (*fig: personne*) to err; (: *chose*) to be flawed; **~ contre la bienséance** to break the rules of good behaviour

pêcher [peʃe] *nm* peach tree ▷ *vi* to go fishing; (*en rivière*) to go angling ▷ *vt* (*attraper*) to catch, land; (*chercher*) to fish for; **~ au chalut** to trawl

pécheur, -eresse [peʃœʀ, peʃʀɛs] *nm/f* sinner

pêcheur [peʃœʀ] *nm voir* **pêcher** fisherman; (*à la ligne*) angler; **~ de perles** pearl diver

pécule [pekyl] *nm* savings *pl*, nest egg; (*d'un détenu*) earnings *pl* (*paid on release*)

pédagogie [pedagɔʒi] *nf* educational methods *pl*, pedagogy

pédagogique [pedagɔʒik] *adj* educational; **formation ~** teacher training

pédale [pedal] *nf* pedal; **mettre la ~ douce** to soft-pedal

pédalo [pedalo] nm pedalo, pedal-boat
pédant, e [pedɑ̃, -ɑ̃t] adj (péj) pedantic ▷ nm/f pedant
pédestre [pedɛstʀ] adj: **tourisme ~** hiking; **randonnée ~** (activité) rambling; (excursion) ramble; **sentier ~** pedestrian footpath
pédiatre [pedjatʀ] nm/f paediatrician (Brit), pediatrician ou pediatrist (US), child specialist
pédicure [pedikyʀ] nm/f chiropodist
pègre [pɛgʀ] nf underworld
peignais etc [pɛɲɛ] vb voir **peindre**
peigne [pɛɲ] vb voir **peindre; peigner** ▷ nm comb
peigner [pɛɲe] vt to comb (the hair of); **se peigner** vi to comb one's hair
peignoir [pɛɲwaʀ] nm dressing gown; **~ de bain** bathrobe; **~ de plage** beach robe
peindre [pɛ̃dʀ] vt to paint; (fig) to portray, depict
peine [pɛn] nf (affliction) sorrow, sadness no pl; (mal, effort) trouble no pl, effort; (difficulté) difficulty; (punition, châtiment) punishment; (Jur) sentence; **faire de la ~ à qn** to distress ou upset sb; **prendre la ~ de faire** to go to the trouble of doing; **se donner de la ~** to make an effort; **ce n'est pas la ~ de faire** there's no point in doing, it's not worth doing; **ce n'est pas la ~ que vous fassiez** there's no point (in) you doing; **avoir de la ~** to be sad; **avoir de la ~ à faire** to have difficulty doing; **donnez-vous** ou **veuillez-vous donner la ~ d'entrer** please do come in; **c'est ~ perdue** it's a waste of time (and effort); **à ~** adv scarcely, hardly, barely; **à ~ ... que** hardly ... than, no sooner ... than; **c'est à ~ si ...** it's (ou it was) a job to ...; **sous ~:** **sous peine d'être puni** for fear of being punished; **défense d'afficher sous ~ d'amende** billposters will be fined; **~ capitale** capital punishment; **~ de mort** death sentence ou penalty
peiner [pene] vi to work hard; to struggle; (moteur, voiture) to labour (Brit), labor (US) ▷ vt to grieve, sadden
peintre [pɛ̃tʀ] nm painter; **~ en bâtiment** house painter, painter and decorator; **~ d'enseignes** signwriter
peinture [pɛ̃tyʀ] nf painting; (couche de couleur, couleur) paint; (surfaces peintes: aussi: **~s**) paintwork; **je ne peux pas le voir en ~** I can't stand the sight of him; **~ mate/brillante** matt/gloss paint; **"~ fraîche"** "wet paint"
péjoratif, -ive [peʒɔʀatif, -iv] adj pejorative, derogatory
Pékin [pekɛ̃] n Beijing
pelage [pəlaʒ] nm coat, fur
pêle-mêle [pɛlmɛl] adv higgledy-piggledy
peler [pəle] vt, vi to peel
pèlerin [pɛlʀɛ̃] nm pilgrim
pèlerinage [pɛlʀinaʒ] nm (voyage) pilgrimage; (lieu) place of pilgrimage, shrine

pelle [pɛl] nf shovel; (d'enfant, de terrassier) spade; **~ à gâteau** cake slice; **~ mécanique** mechanical digger
pellicule [pelikyl] nf film; **pellicules** nfpl (Méd) dandruff sg
pelote [pəlɔt] nf (de fil, laine) ball; (d'épingles) pin cushion; **~ basque** pelota
peloton [pəlɔtɔ̃] nm (groupe: de personnes) group; (: de pompiers, gendarmes) squad; (: Sport) pack; (de laine) ball; **~ d'exécution** firing squad
pelotonner [pəlɔtɔne]: **se pelotonner** vi to curl (o.s.) up
pelouse [pəluz] nf lawn; (Hippisme) spectating area inside racetrack
peluche [pəlyʃ] nf (bit of) fluff; **animal en ~** soft toy, fluffy animal; **chien/lapin en ~** fluffy dog/rabbit
pelure [pəlyʀ] nf peeling, peel no pl; **~ d'oignon** onion skin
pénal, e, -aux [penal, -o] adj penal
pénalité [penalite] nf penalty
penaud, e [pəno, -od] adj sheepish, contrite
penchant [pɑ̃ʃɑ̃] nm: **un ~ à faire/à qch** a tendency to do/to sth; **un ~ pour qch** a liking ou fondness for sth
pencher [pɑ̃ʃe] vi to tilt, lean over ▷ vt to tilt; **se pencher** vi to lean over; (se baisser) to bend down; **se ~ sur** to bend over; (fig: problème) to look into; **se ~ au dehors** to lean out; **~ pour** to be inclined to favour (Brit) ou favor (US)
pendaison [pɑ̃dɛzɔ̃] nf hanging
pendant, e [pɑ̃dɑ̃, -ɑ̃t] adj hanging (out); (Admin, Jur) pending ▷ nm counterpart; matching piece ▷ prép (au cours de) during; (indique la durée) for; **faire ~ à** to match; to be the counterpart of; **~ que** while; **~s d'oreilles** drop ou pendant earrings
pendentif [pɑ̃dɑ̃tif] nm pendant
penderie [pɑ̃dʀi] nf wardrobe; (placard) walk-in cupboard
pendre [pɑ̃dʀ] vt, vi to hang; **se ~ (à)** (se suicider) to hang o.s. (on); **~ à** to hang (down) from; **~ qch à** (mur) to hang sth (up) on; (plafond) to hang sth (up) from; **se ~ à** (se suspendre) to hang from
pendule [pɑ̃dyl] nf clock ▷ nm pendulum
pénétrer [penetʀe] vi to come ou get in ▷ vt to penetrate; **~ dans** to enter; (froid, projectile) to penetrate; (: air, eau) to come into, get into; (mystère, secret) to fathom; **se ~ de qch** to get sth firmly set in one's mind
pénible [penibl] adj (astreignant) hard; (affligeant) painful; (personne, caractère) tiresome; **il m'est ~ de ...** I'm sorry to ...
péniblement [peniblәmã] adv with difficulty
péniche [peniʃ] nf barge; **~ de débarquement** landing craft inv
pénicilline [penisilin] nf penicillin
péninsule [penɛ̃syl] nf peninsula
pénis [penis] nm penis

p

pénitence [penitãs] *nf* (*repentir*) penitence; (*peine*) penance; (*punition, châtiment*) punishment; **mettre un enfant en ~** = to make a child stand in the corner; **faire ~** to do a penance

pénitencier [penitãsje] *nm* prison, penitentiary (US)

pénombre [penɔ̃br] *nf* (*faible clarté*) half-light; (*obscurité*) darkness

pensée [pãse] *nf* thought; (*démarche, doctrine*) thinking *no pl*; (*Bot*) pansy; **se représenter qch par la ~** to conjure up a mental picture of sth; **en ~** in one's mind

penser [pãse] *vi* to think ▷ *vt* to think; (*concevoir: problème, machine*) to think out; **~ à** (*prévoir*) to think of; (*songer à: ami, vacances*) to think of *ou* about; (*réfléchir à: problème, offre*): **~ à qch** to think about sth, think sth over; **~ à faire qch** to think of doing sth; **~ faire qch** to be thinking of doing sth, intend to do sth; **faire ~ à** to remind one of; **n'y pensons plus** let's forget it; **vous n'y pensez pas!** don't let it bother you!; **sans ~ à mal** without meaning any harm; **je le pense aussi** I think so too; **je pense que oui/non** I think so/don't think so

pensif, -ive [pãsif, -iv] *adj* pensive, thoughtful

pension [pãsjɔ̃] *nf* (*allocation*) pension; (*prix du logement*) board and lodging, bed and board; (*maison particulière*) boarding house; (*hôtel*) guesthouse, hotel; (*école*) boarding school; **prendre ~ chez** to take board and lodging at; **prendre qn en ~** to take sb (in) as a lodger; **mettre en ~** to send to boarding school; **~ alimentaire** (*d'étudiant*) living allowance; (*de divorcée*) maintenance allowance; alimony; **~ complète** full board; **~ de famille** boarding house, guesthouse; **~ de guerre/d'invalidité** war/disablement pension

pensionnaire [pãsjɔnɛr] *nm/f* (*Scol*) boarder; guest

pensionnat [pãsjɔna] *nm* boarding school

pente [pãt] *nf* slope; **en ~** *adj* sloping

Pentecôte [pãtkot] *nf:* **la ~** Whitsun (Brit), Pentecost; (*dimanche*) Whitsunday (Brit); **lundi de ~** Whit Monday (Brit)

pénurie [penyri] *nf* shortage; **~ de main-d'œuvre** undermanning

pépé [pepe] *nm* (*fam*) grandad

pépin [pepɛ̃] *nm* (*Bot: graine*) pip; (*fam: ennui*) snag, hitch; (*: parapluie*) brolly (Brit), umbrella

pépinière [pepinjɛr] *nf* nursery; (*fig*) nest, breeding-ground

perçant, e [pɛrsã, -ãt] *adj* (*vue, regard, yeux*) sharp, keen; (*cri, voix*) piercing, shrill

percée [pɛrse] *nf* (*trouée*) opening; (*Mil, Comm: fig*) breakthrough; (*Sport*) break

perce-neige [pɛrsanɛʒ] *nm ou f inv* snowdrop

percepteur [pɛrsɛptœr, tris], **-trice** *nm/f* tax collector

perception [pɛrsɛpsjɔ̃] *nf* perception; (*d'impôts etc*) collection; (*bureau*) tax (collector's) office

percer [pɛrse] *vt* to pierce; (*ouverture etc*) to make; (*mystère, énigme*) to penetrate ▷ *vi* to come through; (*réussir*) to break through; **~ une dent** to cut a tooth

perceuse [pɛrsøz] *nf* drill; **~ à percussion** hammer drill

percevoir [pɛrsəvwar] *vt* (*distinguer*) to perceive, detect; (*taxe, impôt*) to collect; (*revenu, indemnité*) to receive

perche [pɛrʃ] *nf* (*Zool*) perch; (*bâton*) pole; **~ à son** (sound) boom

percher [pɛrʃe] *vt* to perch; **~ qch sur** to perch sth on; **se percher** *vi* (*oiseau*) to perch

perchoir [pɛrʃwar] *nm* perch; (*fig*) presidency of the French National Assembly

perçois *etc* [pɛrswa] *vb voir* **percevoir**

percolateur [pɛrkɔlatœr] *nm* percolator

perçu, e [pɛrsy] *pp de* **percevoir**

percussion [pɛrkysjɔ̃] *nf* percussion

percuter [pɛrkyte] *vt* to strike; (*véhicule*) to crash into ▷ *vi:* **~ contre** to crash into

perdant, e [pɛrdã, -ãt] *nm/f* loser ▷ *adj* losing

perdre [pɛrdr] *vt* to lose; (*gaspiller: temps, argent*) to waste; (*: occasion*) to waste, miss; (*personne: moralement etc*) to ruin ▷ *vi* to lose; (*sur une vente etc*) to lose out; (*récipient*) to leak; **se perdre** *vi* (*s'égarer*) to get lost, lose one's way; (*fig: se gâter*) to go to waste; (*disparaître*) to disappear, vanish; **il ne perd rien pour attendre** it can wait, it'll keep; **je me suis perdu** (*et je le suis encore*) I'm lost; (*et je ne le suis plus*) I got lost

perdrix [pɛrdri] *nf* partridge

perdu, e [pɛrdy] *pp de* **perdre** ▷ *adj* (*enfant, cause, objet*) lost; (*isolé*) out-of-the-way; (*Comm: emballage*) non-returnable; (*récolte etc*) ruined; (*malade*): **il est ~** there's no hope left for him; **à vos moments ~s** in your spare time

père [pɛr] *nm* father; **pères** *nmpl* (*ancêtres*) forefathers; **de ~ en fils** from father to son; **~ de famille** father; family man; **mon ~** (*Rel*) Father; **le ~ Noël** Father Christmas

perfection [pɛrfɛksjɔ̃] *nf* perfection; **à la ~** *adv* to perfection

perfectionné, e [pɛrfɛksjɔne] *adj* sophisticated

perfectionner [pɛrfɛksjɔne] *vt* to improve, perfect; **se ~ en anglais** to improve one's English

perforer [pɛrfɔre] *vt* to perforate, punch a hole *ou* holes in; (*ticket, bande, carte*) to punch

performant, e [pɛrfɔrmã, -ãt] *adj* (*Écon: produit, entreprise*) high-return *cpd*; (*Tech*): **très ~** (*appareil, machine*) high-performance *cpd*

perfusion [pɛrfyzjɔ̃] *nf* perfusion; **faire une ~ à qn** to put sb on a drip

péricliter [periklite] *vi* to go downhill

péril [peril] *nm* peril; **au ~ de sa vie** at the risk of his life; **à ses risques et ~s** at his (*ou* her) own risk

périmé, e [peʀime] *adj* (out)dated; (*Admin*) out-of-date, expired

périmètre [peʀimetʀ] *nm* perimeter

période [peʀjɔd] *nf* period

périodique [peʀjɔdik] *adj* (*phases*) periodic; (*publication*) periodical; (*Math: fraction*) recurring ▷ *nm* periodical; (*Presse*) periodical; **serviette** ~ sanitary towel (*Brit*) *ou* napkin (*US*)

péripéties [peʀipesi] *nfpl* events, episodes

périphérique [peʀifeʀik] *adj* (*quartiers*) outlying; (*Anat, Tech*) peripheral; (*station de radio*) operating from a neighbouring country ▷ *nm* (*Inform*) peripheral; (*Auto*): **(boulevard)** ~ ring road (*Brit*), beltway (*US*)

périple [peʀipl] *nm* journey

périr [peʀiʀ] *vi* to die, perish

périssable [peʀisabl] *adj* perishable

perle [peʀl] *nf* pearl; (*de plastique, métal, sueur*) bead; (*personne, chose*) gem, treasure; (*erreur*) gem, howler

permanence [peʀmanãs] *nf* permanence; (*local*) (duty) office, strike headquarters; (*service des urgences*) emergency service; (*Scol*) study room; **assurer une** ~ (*service public, bureaux*) to operate *ou* maintain a basic service; **être de** ~ to be on call *ou* duty; **en** ~ *adv* (*toujours*) permanently; (*continûment*) continuously

permanent, e [peʀmanã, -ãt] *adj* permanent; (*spectacle*) continuous; (*armée, comité*) standing ▷ *nf* perm ▷ *nm/f* (*d'un syndicat, parti*) paid official

perméable [peʀmeabl] *adj* (*terrain*) permeable; ~ **à** (*fig*) receptive *ou* open to

permettre [peʀmetʀ] *vt* to allow, permit; ~ **à qn de faire/qch** to allow sb to do/sth; **se** ~ **de faire qch** to take the liberty of doing sth; **permettez!** excuse me!

permis, e [peʀmi, -iz] *pp de* **permettre** ▷ *nm* permit, licence (*Brit*), license (*US*); ~ **de chasse** hunting permit; ~ **(de conduire)** (driving) licence (*Brit*), (driver's) license (*US*); ~ **de construire** planning permission (*Brit*), building permit (*US*); ~ **d'inhumer** burial certificate; ~ **poids lourds** ≈ HGV (driving) licence (*Brit*), ≈ class E (driver's) license (*US*); ~ **de séjour** residence permit; ~ **de travail** work permit

permission [peʀmisjɔ̃] *nf* permission; (*Mil*) leave; (: *papier*) pass; **en** ~ on leave; **avoir la** ~ **de faire** to have permission to do, be allowed to do

permuter [peʀmyte] *vt* to change around, permutate ▷ *vi* to change, swap

Pérou [peʀu] *nm*: **le** ~ Peru

perpétuel, le [peʀpetɥel] *adj* perpetual; (*Admin etc*) permanent; for life

perpétuité [peʀpetɥite] *nf*: **à** ~ *adj, adv* for life; **être condamné à** ~ to be sentenced to life imprisonment, receive a life sentence

perplexe [peʀpleks] *adj* perplexed, puzzled

perquisitionner [peʀkizisjɔne] *vi* to carry out a search

perron [peʀɔ̃] *nm* steps *pl* (*in front of mansion etc*)

perroquet [peʀɔke] *nm* parrot

perruche [peʀyʃ] *nf* budgerigar (*Brit*), budgie (*Brit*), parakeet (*US*)

perruque [peʀyk] *nf* wig

persan, e [peʀsã, -an] *adj* Persian ▷ *nm* (*Ling*) Persian

persécuter [peʀsekyte] *vt* to persecute

persévérer [peʀseveʀe] *vi* to persevere; ~ **à croire que** to continue to believe that

persiennes [peʀsjen] *nfpl* (slatted) shutters

persil [peʀsi] *nm* parsley

Persique [peʀsik] *adj*: **le golfe** ~ the (Persian) Gulf

persistant, e [peʀsistã, -ãt] *adj* persistent; (*feuilles*) evergreen; **à feuillage** ~ evergreen

persister [peʀsiste] *vi* to persist; ~ **à faire qch** to persist in doing sth

personnage [peʀsɔnaʒ] *nm* (*notable*) personality; figure; (*individu*) character, individual; (*Théât: de roman, film*) character; (*Peinture*) figure

personnalité [peʀsɔnalite] *nf* personality; (*personnage*) prominent figure

personne [peʀsɔn] *nf* person ▷ *pron* nobody, no one; (*avec négation en anglais*) anybody, anyone; **personnes** *nfpl* people *pl*; **il n'y a** ~ there's nobody in *ou* there, there isn't anybody in *ou* there; **10 euros par** ~ 10 euros per person *ou* a head; **en** ~ personally, in person; ~ **âgée** elderly person; ~ **à charge** (*Jur*) dependent; ~ **morale** *ou* **civile** (*Jur*) legal entity

personnel, le [peʀsɔnel] *adj* personal; (*égoïste: personne*) selfish, self-centred; (*idée, opinion*): **j'ai des idées ~les à ce sujet** I have my own ideas about that ▷ *nm* personnel, staff; **service du** ~ personnel department

personnellement [peʀsɔnelmã] *adv* personally

perspective [peʀspektiv] *nf* (*Art*) perspective; (*vue, coup d'œil*) view; (*point de vue*) viewpoint, angle; (*chose escomptée, envisagée*) prospect; **en** ~ in prospect

perspicace [peʀspikas] *adj* clear-sighted, gifted with *ou* showing) insight

perspicacité [peʀspikasite] *nf* insight, perspicacity

persuader [peʀsɥade] *vt*: ~ **qn (de/de faire)** to persuade sb (of/to do); **j'en suis persuadé** I'm quite sure *ou* convinced (of it)

persuasif, -ive [peʀsɥazif, -iv] *adj* persuasive

perte [peʀt] *nf* loss; (*de temps*) waste; (*fig: morale*) ruin; **pertes** *nfpl* losses; **à** ~ (*Comm*) at a loss; **à** ~ **de vue** as far as the eye can (*ou* could) see; (*fig*) interminably; **en pure** ~ for absolutely nothing; **en** ~ **de vitesse** (*fig*) to be losing momentum; **avec** ~ **et fracas**

forcibly; **~ de chaleur** heat loss; **~ sèche** dead loss; **~s blanches** (vaginal) discharge sg

pertinemment [pɛrtinamɑ̃] adv to the point; (savoir) perfectly well, full well

pertinent, e [pɛrtinɑ̃, -ɑ̃t] adj (remarque) apt, pertinent, relevant; (analyse) discerning, judicious

perturbation [pɛrtyrbasjɔ̃] nf (dans un service public) disruption; (agitation, trouble) perturbation; **~ (atmosphérique)** atmospheric disturbance

perturber [pɛrtyrbe] vt to disrupt; (Psych) to perturb, disturb

pervers, e [pɛrvɛr, -ɛrs] adj perverted, depraved; (malfaisant) perverse

pervertir [pɛrvɛrtir] vt to pervert

pesant, e [pəzɑ̃, -ɑ̃t] adj heavy; (fig: présence) burdensome ▷ nm: **valoir son ~ de** to be worth one's weight in

pèse-personne [pɛzpɛrsɔn] nm (bathroom) scales pl

peser [pəze] vt to weigh; (considérer, comparer) to weigh up ▷ vi to be heavy; (fig: avoir de l'importance) to carry weight; **~ sur** (levier, bouton) to press, push; (fig: accabler) to lie heavy on; (: influencer) to influence; **~ à qn** to weigh heavy on sb

pessimisme [pesimism] nm pessimism

pessimiste [pesimist] adj pessimistic ▷ nm/f pessimist

peste [pɛst] nf plague; (fig) pest, nuisance

pester [pɛste] vi: **~ contre** to curse

pétale [petal] nm petal

pétanque [petɑ̃k] nf type of bowls; see note

⬤ PÉTANQUE

Pétanque is a version of the game of "boules", played on a hard surfaces. Standing with their feet together, players throw steel bowls at a wooden jack. Pétanque originated in the South of France and is still very much associated with that area.

---

pétarader [petarade] vi to backfire

pétard [petar] nm (feu d'artifice) banger (Brit), firecracker; (de cotillon) cracker; (Rail) detonator

péter [pete] vi (fam: casser, sauter) to burst; to bust; (fam!) to fart (!)

pétillant, e [petijɑ̃, -ɑ̃t] adj (eau) sparkling

pétiller [petije] vi (flamme, bois) to crackle; (mousse, champagne) to bubble; (pierre, métal) to glisten; (yeux) to sparkle; (fig): **~ d'esprit** to sparkle with wit

petit, e [pəti, -it] adj (gén) small; (avec nuance affective) little; (main, objet, colline, en âge: enfant) small, little; (mince, fin: personne, taille, pluie) slight; (voyage) short, little; (bruit etc) faint, slight; (mesquin) mean; (peu important) minor ▷ nm/f (petit enfant) little one, child; **petits** nmpl (d'un animal) young pl; **faire des**

~s to have kittens (ou puppies etc); **en ~** in miniature; **mon ~** son; little one; **ma ~e** dear; little one; **pauvre ~** poor little thing; **la classe des ~s** the infant class; **pour ~s et grands** for children and adults; **les tout-~s** the little ones, the tiny tots; **à ~** bit by bit, gradually; **~(e) ami/e** boyfriend/girlfriend; **les ~es annonces** the small ads; **~ déjeuner** breakfast; **~ ~ doigt** little finger; **le ~ écran** the small screen; **~ four** petit four; **~ pain** (bread) roll; **~e monnaie** small change; **~e vérole** smallpox; **~s pois** petit pois pl, garden peas; **~es gens** people of modest means

petite-fille (pl **petites-filles**) [pətitfij] nf granddaughter

petit-fils (pl **petits-fils**) [pətifis] nm grandson

pétition [petisjɔ̃] nf petition; **faire signer une ~** to get up a petition

petits-enfants [pətizɑ̃fɑ̃] nmpl grandchildren

petit-suisse (pl **petits-suisses**) [pətisɥis] nm small individual pot of cream cheese

pétrin [petrɛ̃] nm kneading-trough; (fig): **dans le ~** in a jam ou fix

pétrir [petrir] vt to knead

pétrole [petrɔl] nm oil; (aussi: **~ lampant**: pour lampe, réchaud etc) paraffin (Brit), kerosene (US)

pétrolier, -ière [petrɔlje, -jɛr] adj oil cpd; (pays) oil-producing ▷ nm (navire) oil tanker; (financier) oilman; (technicien) petroleum engineer

P et T sigle fpl = postes et télécommunications

 MOT-CLÉ

peu [pø] adv **1** (modifiant verbe, adjectif, adverbe): **il boit peu** he doesn't drink (very) much; **il est peu bavard** he's not very talkative; **peu avant/après** shortly before/afterwards; **pour peu qu'il fasse** if he should do, if by any chance he does

2 (modifiant nom): **peu de: peu de gens/d'arbres** few ou not (very) many people/trees; **il a peu d'espoir** he hasn't (got) much hope, he has little hope; **pour peu de temps** for (only) a short while; **à peu de frais** for very little cost

3: **peu à peu** little by little; **à peu près** just about, more or less; **à peu près 10 kg/10 euros** approximately 10 kg/10 euros

▷ nm **1**: **le peu de gens qui** the few people who; **le peu de sable qui** what little sand, the little sand which

2: **un peu** a little; **un petit peu** a little bit; **un peu d'espoir** a little hope; **elle est un peu bavarde** she's rather talkative; **un peu plus de** slightly more than; **un peu moins de** slightly less than; (avec pluriel) slightly fewer than; **pour un peu il ...**, **un peu plus et il ...** he very nearly ou all but ...; **essayez un peu!** have a go!, just try it!

▷ pron: **peu le savent** few know (it); **avant ou**

sous peu shortly, before long; **depuis peu** for a short *ou* little while; *(au passé)* a short *ou* little while ago; **de peu** (only) just; **c'est peu de chose** it's nothing; **il est de peu mon cadet** he's just a little *ou* bit younger than me

peuple [pœpl] *nm* people; *(masse)*: **un ~ de vacanciers** a crowd of holiday-makers; **il y a du ~** there are a lot of people

peupler [pœple] *vt (pays, région)* to populate; *(étang)* to stock; *(hommes, poissons)* to inhabit; *(fig: imagination, rêves)* to fill; **se peupler** *vi (ville, région)* to become populated; *(fig: s'animer)* to fill (up), be filled

peuplier [pøplije] *nm* poplar (tree)

peur [pœr] *nf* fear; **avoir ~ (de/de faire/que)** to be frightened *ou* afraid (of/of doing/that); **prendre ~** to take fright; **faire ~ à** to frighten; **de ~ de/que** for fear of/that; **j'ai ~ qu'il ne soit trop tard** I'm afraid it might be too late; **j'ai ~ qu'il (ne) vienne (pas)** I'm afraid he may (not) come

peureux, -euse [pœrø, -øz] *adj* fearful, timorous

peut [pø] *vb voir* **pouvoir**

peut-être [pøtɛtr] *adv* perhaps, maybe; **~ que** perhaps, maybe; **~ bien qu'il fera/est** he may well do/be

phare [faʁ] *nm (en mer)* lighthouse; *(d'aéroport)* beacon; *(de véhicule)* headlight, headlamp *(Brit)* ▷ *adj*: **produit ~** leading product; **se mettre en ~s, mettre ses ~s** to put on one's headlights; **~s de recul** reversing *(Brit) ou* back-up *(US)* lights

pharmacie [farmasi] *nf (science)* pharmacology; *(magasin)* chemist's *(Brit)*, pharmacy; *(officine)* dispensary; *(produits)* pharmaceuticals *pl*; *(armoire)* medicine chest *ou* cupboard, first-aid cupboard

pharmacien, ne [farmasjɛ̃, -ɛn] *nm/f* pharmacist, chemist *(Brit)*

phénomène [fenɔmɛn] *nm* phenomenon; *(monstre)* freak

philatélie [filateli] *nf* philately, stamp collecting

philosophe [filɔzɔf] *nm/f* philosopher ▷ *adj* philosophical

philosophie [filɔzɔfi] *nf* philosophy

phobie [fɔbi] *nf* phobia

phonétique [fɔnetik] *adj* phonetic ▷ *nf* phonetics *sg*

phoque [fɔk] *nm* seal; *(fourrure)* sealskin

phosphorescent, e [fɔsfɔʁesɑ̃, -ɑ̃t] *adj* luminous

photo [fɔto] *nf (photographie)* photo ▷ *adj*: **appareil/pellicule ~** camera/film; **en ~** in *ou* on a photo; **prendre en ~** to take a photo of; **aimer la/faire de la ~** to like taking/take photos; **~ en couleurs** colour photo; **~ d'identité** passport photo

photocopie [fɔtɔkɔpi] *nf (procédé)* photocopying; *(document)* photocopy

photocopier [fɔtɔkɔpje] *vt* to photocopy

photocopieur [fɔtɔkɔpjœʁ] *nm*, **photocopieuse** [fɔtɔkɔpjøz] *nf* (photo) copier

photographe [fɔtɔɡʁaf] *nm/f* photographer

photographie [fɔtɔɡʁafi] *nf (procédé, technique)* photography; *(cliché)* photograph; **faire de la ~** to do photography as a hobby; *(comme métier)* to be a photographer

photographier [fɔtɔɡʁafje] *vt* to photograph, take

phrase [fʁaz] *nf (Ling)* sentence; *(propos, Mus)* phrase; **phrases** *nfpl (péj)* flowery language *sg*

physicien, ne [fizisjɛ̃, -ɛn] *nm/f* physicist

physionomie [fizjɔnɔmi] *nf* face; *(d'un paysage etc)* physiognomy

physique [fizik] *adj* physical ▷ *nm* physique ▷ *nf* physics *sg*; **au ~** physically

physiquement [fizikmɑ̃] *adv* physically

piailler [pjaje] *vi* to squawk

pianiste [pjanist] *nm/f* pianist

piano [pjano] *nm* piano; **~ à queue** grand piano

pianoter [pjanɔte] *vi* to tinkle away (at the piano); *(tapoter)*: **~ sur** to drum one's fingers on

pic [pik] *nm (instrument)* pick(axe); *(montagne)* peak; *(Zool)* woodpecker; **à ~** *adv* vertically; *(fig: tomber, arriver)* just at the right time; **couler à ~** *(bateau)* to go straight down; **~ à glace** ice pick

pichet [piʃɛ] *nm* jug

picorer [pikɔʁe] *vt* to peck

picoter [pikɔte] *vt (oiseau)* to peck ▷ *vi (irriter)* to smart, prickle

pie [pi] *nf* magpie; *(fig)* chatterbox ▷ *adj inv*: **cheval ~** piebald; **vache ~** black and white cow

pièce [pjɛs] *nf (d'un logement)* room; *(Théât)* play; *(de mécanisme, machine)* part; *(de monnaie)* coin; *(Couture)* patch; *(document)* document; *(de drap, fragment, d'une collection)* piece; *(de bétail)* head; **mettre en ~s** to smash to pieces; **deux euros ~** two euros each; **vendre à la ~** to sell separately *ou* individually; **travailler/payer à la ~** to do piecework/pay piece rate; **de toutes ~s: c'est inventé de toutes pièces** it's a complete fabrication; **un maillot une ~** a one-piece swimsuit; **un deux-~s cuisine** a two-room(ed) flat *(Brit) ou* apartment *(US)* with kitchen; **tout d'une ~** *(personne: franc)* blunt; (: *sans souplesse)* inflexible; **~ à conviction** exhibit; **~ d'eau** ornamental lake *ou* pond; **~ d'identité: avez-vous une pièce d'identité?** have you got any (means of) identification?; **~ jointe** *(Inform)* attachment; **~ montée** tiered cake; **~ de rechange** spare (part); **~ de résistance** pièce de résistance; *(plat)* main dish; **~s détachées** spares, (spare) parts; **en ~s détachées** *(à monter)* in kit form; **~s justificatives** supporting documents

P

pied [pje] nm foot; (de verre) stem; (de table) leg; (de lampe) base; (plante) plant; **~s nus** barefoot; **à ~** on foot; **à ~ sec** without getting one's feet wet; **à ~ d'œuvre** ready to start (work); **au ~ de la lettre** literally; **au ~ levé** at a moment's notice; **de ~ en cap** from head to foot; **en ~** (portrait) full-length; **avoir ~** to be able to touch the bottom, not to be out of one's depth; **avoir le ~ marin** to be a good sailor; **perdre ~** to lose one's footing; (fig) to get out of one's depth; **sur ~** (Agr) on the stalk, uncut; (debout, rétabli) up and about; **mettre sur ~** (entreprise) to set up; **mettre à ~** to suspend; to lay off; **mettre qn au ~ du mur** to get sb with his (ou her) back to the wall; **sur le ~ de guerre** ready for action; **sur un ~ d'égalité** on an equal footing; **sur ~ d'intervention** on stand-by; **faire du ~ à qn** (prévenir) to give sb a (warning) kick; (galamment) to play footsie with sb; **mettre les ~s quelque part** to set foot somewhere; **faire des ~s et des mains** (fig) to move heaven and earth, pull out all the stops; **c'est le ~!** (fam) it's brilliant!; **mettre les ~s dans le plat** (fam) to put one's foot in it; **il se débrouille comme un ~** (fam) he's completely useless; **se lever du bon ~/du ~ gauche** to get out of bed on the right/wrong side; **~ de lit** footboard; **~ de nez: faire un pied de nez à** to thumb one's nose at; **~ de vigne** vine

pied-noir (pl **pieds-noirs**) [pjenwaʀ] nm Algerian-born Frenchman

piège [pjɛʒ] nm trap; **prendre au ~** to trap

piéger [pjeʒe] vt (animal, fig) to trap; (avec une bombe) to booby-trap; **lettre/voiture piégée** letter-/car-bomb

piercing [pjɛʀsiŋ] nm piercing

pierre [pjɛʀ] nf stone; **première ~** (d'un édifice) foundation stone; **mur de ~s sèches** drystone wall; **faire d'une ~ deux coups** to kill two birds with one stone; **~ à briquet** flint; **~ fine** semiprecious stone; **~ ponce** pumice stone; **~ de taille** freestone no pl; **~ tombale** tombstone, gravestone; **~ de touche** touchstone

pierreries [pjɛʀʀi] nfpl gems, precious stones

piétiner [pjetine] vi (trépigner) to stamp (one's foot); (marquer le pas) to stand about; (fig) to be at a standstill ▷ vt to trample on

piéton, ne [pjetɔ̃, -ɔn] nm/f pedestrian ▷ adj pedestrian cpd

piétonnier, -ière [pjetɔnje, -jɛʀ] adj pedestrian cpd

pieu, x [pjø] nm (piquet) post; (pointu) stake; (fam: lit) bed

pieuvre [pjœvʀ] nf octopus

pieux, -euse [pjø, -øz] adj pious

piffer [pife] vt (fam): **je ne peux pas le ~** I can't stand him

pigeon [piʒɔ̃] nm pigeon; **~ voyageur** homing pigeon

piger [piʒe] vi (fam) to get it ▷ vt (fam) to get, understand

pigiste [piʒist] nm/f (typographe) typesetter on piecework; (journaliste) freelance journalist (paid by the line)

pignon [piɲɔ̃] nm (de mur) gable; (d'engrenage) cog(wheel), gearwheel; (graine) pine kernel; **avoir ~ sur rue** (fig) to have a prosperous business

pile [pil] nf (tas, pilier) pile; (Élec) battery ▷ adj: **le côté ~** tails ▷ adv (net, brusquement) dead; (à temps, à point nommé) just at the right time; **à deux heures ~** at two on the dot; **jouer à ~ ou face** to toss up (for it); **~ ou face?** heads or tails?

piler [pile] vt to crush, pound

pilier [pilje] nm (colonne, support) pillar; (personne) mainstay; (Rugby) prop (forward)

piller [pije] vt to pillage, plunder, loot

pilote [pilɔt] nm pilot; (de char, voiture) driver ▷ adj pilot cpd; **usine/ferme ~** experimental factory/farm; **~ de chasse/d'essai/de ligne** fighter/test/airline pilot; **~ de course** racing driver

piloter [pilɔte] vt (navire) to pilot; (avion) to fly; (automobile) to drive; (fig): **~ qn** to guide sb round

pilule [pilyl] nf pill; **prendre la ~** to be on the pill; **~ du lendemain** morning-after pill

piment [pimɑ̃] nm (Bot) pepper, capsicum; (fig) spice, piquancy; **~ rouge** (Culin) chilli

pimenté, e [pimɑ̃te] adj (plat) hot and spicy

pimpant, e [pɛ̃pɑ̃, -ɑ̃t] adj spruce

pin [pɛ̃] nm pine (tree); (bois) pine(wood)

pinard [pinaʀ] nm (fam) (cheap) wine, plonk (Brit)

pince [pɛ̃s] nf (outil) pliers pl; (de homard, crabe) pincer, claw; (Couture: pli) dart; **~ à sucre/glace** sugar/ice tongs pl; **~ à épiler** tweezers pl; **~ à linge** clothes peg (Brit) ou pin (US); **~ universelle** (universal) pliers pl; **~s de cycliste** bicycle clips

pincé, e [pɛ̃se] adj (air) stiff; (mince: bouche) pinched ▷ nf: **une ~e de** a pinch of

pinceau, x [pɛ̃so] nm (paint)brush

pincer [pɛ̃se] vt to pinch; (Mus: cordes) to pluck; (Couture) to dart, put darts in; (fam) to nab; **se ~ le doigt** to squeeze ou nip one's finger; **se ~ le nez** to hold one's nose

pinède [pinɛd] nf pinewood, pine forest

pingouin [pɛ̃gwɛ̃] nm penguin

ping-pong [piŋpɔ̃g] nm table tennis

pingre [pɛ̃gʀ] adj niggardly

pinson [pɛ̃sɔ̃] nm chaffinch

pintade [pɛ̃tad] nf guinea-fowl

pioche [pjɔʃ] nf pickaxe

piocher [pjɔʃe] vt to dig up (with a pickaxe); (fam) to swot (Brit) ou grind (US) at; **~ dans** to dig into

pion, ne [pjɔ̃, pjɔn] nm/f (Scol: péj) student paid to supervise schoolchildren ▷ nm (Échecs) pawn; (Dames) piece, draught (Brit), checker (US)

pionnier [pjɔnje] nm pioneer

pipe [pip] nf pipe; **fumer la** ou **une ~** to smoke a pipe; **~ de bruyère** briar pipe

pipeau, x [pipo] nm (reed-)pipe

piquant, e [pikã, -ãt] adj (barbe, rosier etc) prickly; (saveur, sauce) hot, pungent; (fig: description, style) racy; (: mordant, caustique) biting ▷ nm (épine) thorn, prickle; (de hérisson) quill, spine; (fig) spiciness, spice

pique [pik] nf (arme) pike; (fig): **envoyer** ou **lancer des ~s à qn** to make cutting remarks to sb ▷ nm (Cartes: couleur) spades pl; (: carte) spade

pique-nique [piknik] nm picnic

pique-niquer [piknike] vi to (have a) picnic

piquer [pike] vt (percer) to prick; (Méd) to give an injection to; (: animal blessé etc) to put to sleep; (insecte, fumée, ortie) to sting; (moustique) to bite; (: poivre) to burn; (: froid) to bite; (Couture) to machine (stitch); (intérêt etc) to arouse; (fam: prendre) to pick up; (: voler) to pinch; (: arrêter) to nab; (planter): **~ qch dans** to stick sth into; (fixer): **~ qch à** ou **sur** to pin sth onto ▷ vi (oiseau, avion) to go into a dive; (saveur) to be pungent; to be sour; **se piquer** (avec une aiguille) to prick o.s.; (se faire une piqûre) to inject o.s.; (se vexer) to get annoyed; **se ~ de faire** to pride o.s. on doing; **~ sur** to swoop down on; to head straight for; **~ du nez** (avion) to go into a nose-dive; **~ une tête** (plonger) to dive headfirst; **~ un galop/un cent mètres** to break into a gallop/put on a sprint; **~ une crise** to throw a fit; **~ au vif** (fig) to sting

piquet [pikɛ] nm (pieu) post, stake; (de tente) peg; **mettre un élève au ~** to make a pupil stand in the corner; **~ de grève** (strike) picket; **~ d'incendie** fire-fighting squad

piqûre [pikyʀ] nf (d'épingle) prick; (d'ortie) sting; (de moustique) bite; (Méd) injection, shot (US); (Couture) (straight) stitch; straight stitching; (de ver) hole; (tache) spot of mildew; **faire une ~ à qn** to give sb an injection

pirate [piʀat] adj pirate cpd ▷ nm pirate; (fig: escroc) crook, shark; (Inform) hacker; **~ de l'air** hijacker

pirater [piʀate] vi (Inform) to hack ▷ vt (Inform) to hack into

pire [piʀ] adj (comparatif) worse; (superlatif): **le (la) ~ ...** the worst ... ▷ nm: **le ~ (de)** the worst (of); **au ~** at (the very) worst

pis [pi] nm (de vache) udder; (pire): **le ~** the worst ▷ adj, adv worse; **qui ~ est** what is worse; **au ~ aller** if the worst comes to the worst, at worst; **de mal en ~** from bad to worse

piscine [pisin] nf (swimming) pool; **~ couverte** indoor (swimming) pool

pissenlit [pisɑ̃li] nm dandelion

pistache [pistaʃ] nf pistachio (nut)

piste [pist] nf (d'un animal, sentier) track, trail; (indice) lead; (de stade, de magnétophone) track; (de cirque) ring; (de danse) floor; (de patinage)

rink; (de ski) run; (Aviat) runway; **~ cavalière** bridle path; **~ cyclable** cycle track, bikeway (US); **~ sonore** sound track

pistolet [pistolɛ] nm (arme) pistol, gun; (à peinture) spray gun; **~ à bouchon/air comprimé** popgun/airgun; **~ à eau** water pistol

pistolet-mitrailleur (pl **pistolets-mitrailleurs**) [pistolɛmitʀajœʀ] nm submachine gun

piston [pistɔ̃] nm (Tech) piston; (Mus) valve; (fig: appui) string-pulling; **avoir du ~** (fam) to have friends in the right places

pistonner [pistone] vt (candidat) to pull strings for

piteux, -euse [pitø, -øz] adj pitiful, sorry (avant le nom); **en ~ état** in a sorry state

pitié [pitje] nf pity; **sans ~** adj pitiless, merciless; **faire ~** to inspire pity; **il me fait ~** I pity him, I feel sorry for him; **avoir ~ de** (compassion) to pity, feel sorry for; (merci) to have pity ou mercy on; **par ~!** for pity's sake!

pitoyable [pitwajabl] adj pitiful

pitre [pitʀ] nm clown

pitrerie [pitʀəʀi] nf tomfoolery no pl

pittoresque [pitɔʀɛsk] adj picturesque; (expression, détail) colourful (Brit), colorful (US)

pivot [pivo] nm pivot; (d'une dent) post

pivoter [pivɔte] vi (fauteuil) to swivel; (porte) to revolve; **~ sur ses talons** to swing round

pizza [pidza] nf pizza

PJ sigle f (= police judiciaire) ≈ CID (Brit), ≈ FBI (US) ▷ sigle fpl (= pièces jointes) encl

placard [plakaʀ] nm (armoire) cupboard; (affiche) poster, notice; (Typo) galley; **~ publicitaire** display advertisement

place [plas] nf (emplacement, situation, classement) place; (de ville, village) square; (Écon): **~ financière/boursière** money/stock market; (espace libre) room, space; (de parking) space; (siège: de train, cinéma, voiture) seat; (prix: au cinéma etc) price; (: dans un bus, taxi) fare; (emploi) job; **en ~** (mettre) in its place; **de ~ en ~**, **par ~s** here and there, in places; **sur ~** on the spot; **faire ~ à** to give way to; **faire de la ~ à** to make room for; **ça prend de la ~** it takes up a lot of room ou space; **prendre ~** to take one's place; **remettre qn à sa ~** to put sb in his (ou her) place; **ne pas rester ou tenir en ~** to be always on the go; **à la ~ de** in place of, instead of; **à votre ~ ...** if I were you ...; **se mettre à la ~ de qn** to put o.s. in sb's place ou in sb's shoes; **une quatre ~s** (Auto) a four-seater; **il y a 20 ~s assises/debout** there are 20 seats/there is standing room for 20; **~ forte** fortified town; **~ d'honneur** place (ou seat) of honour (Brit) ou honor (US)

placé, e [plase] adj (Hippisme) placed; **haut ~** (fig) high-ranking; **être bien/mal ~** to be well/badly placed; (spectateur) to have a good/ bad seat; **être bien/mal ~ pour faire** to be in/not to be in a position to do; **il est bien ~ pour le savoir** he is in a position to know

placement [plasmã] nm placing; (Finance) investment; **agence** ou **bureau de ~** employment agency

placer [plase] vt to place, put; (convive, spectateur) to seat; (capital, argent) to place, invest; (dans la conversation) to put ou get in; **~ qn chez** to get sb a job at (ou with); **se ~ au premier rang** to go and stand (ou sit) in the first row

plafond [plafɔ̃] nm ceiling

plage [plaʒ] nf beach; (station) (seaside) resort; (fig) band, bracket; (de disque) track, band; **~ arrière** (Auto) parcel ou back shelf

plagiat [plaʒja] nm plagiarism

plaid [plɛd] nm (tartan) car rug, lap robe (US)

plaider [plede] vi (avocat) to plead; (plaignant) to go to court, litigate ▷ vt to plead; **~ pour** (fig) to speak for

plaidoyer [pledwaje] nm (Jur) speech for the defence (Brit) ou defense (US); (fig) plea

plaie [plɛ] nf wound

plaignant, e [plɛɲɑ̃, -ɑ̃t] vb voir **plaindre** ▷ nm/f plaintiff

plaindre [plɛ̃dʀ] vt to pity, feel sorry for; **se plaindre** vi (gémir) to moan; (protester, rouspéter): **se ~ (à qn) (de)** to complain (to sb) (about); (souffrir): **se ~ de** to complain of

plaine [plɛn] nf plain

plain-pied [plɛ̃pje]: **de ~** adv at street-level; (fig) straight; **de ~ (avec)** on the same level (as)

plaint, e [plɛ̃, -ɛ̃t] pp de **plaindre** ▷ nf (gémissement) moan, groan; (doléance) complaint; **porter ~e** to lodge a complaint

plaire [plɛʀ] vi to be a success, be successful; to please; **à:** **cela me plaît** I like it; **ça plaît beaucoup aux jeunes** it's very popular with young people; **essayer de ~ à qn** (en étant serviable etc) to try and please sb; **elle plaît aux hommes** she's a success with men, men like her; **se ~ quelque part** to like being somewhere, like it somewhere; **se ~ à faire** to take pleasure in doing; **ce qu'il vous plaira** what(ever) you like ou wish; **s'il vous plaît, s'il te plaît** please

plaisance [plɛzɑ̃s] nf (aussi: **navigation de ~**) (pleasure) sailing, yachting

plaisant, e [plɛzɑ̃, -ɑ̃t] adj pleasant; (histoire, anecdote) amusing

plaisanter [plɛzɑ̃te] vi to joke ▷ vt (personne) to tease, make fun of; **pour ~** for a joke; **on ne plaisante pas avec cela** that's no joking matter; **tu plaisantes!** you're joking ou kidding!

plaisanterie [plɛzɑ̃tʀi] nf joke; joking no pl

plaise etc [plɛz] vb voir **plaire**

plaisir [pleziʀ] nm pleasure; **faire ~ à qn** (délibérément) to be nice to sb, please sb; (cadeau, nouvelle etc): **ça me fait ~** I'm delighted ou very pleased with this; **j'espère que ça te fera ~** I hope you'll like it; **prendre ~ à/à faire** to take pleasure in/in doing; **j'ai**

le ~ de ... it is with great pleasure that I ...; **M. et Mme X ont le ~ de vous faire part de ...** M. and Mme X are pleased to announce ...; **se faire un ~ de faire qch** to be (only too) pleased to do sth; **faites-moi le ~ de ...** would you mind ..., would you be kind enough to ...; **à ~** freely; for the sake of it; **au ~ (de vous revoir)** (I hope to) see you again; **pour le** ou **pour son** ou **par ~** for pleasure

plaît [plɛ] vb voir **plaire**

plan, e [plɑ̃, -an] adj flat ▷ nm plan; (Géom) plane; (fig) level, plane; (Ciné) shot; **au premier/second ~** in the foreground/middle distance; **à l'arrière ~** in the background; **mettre qch au premier ~** (fig) to consider sth to be of primary importance; **sur le ~ sexuel** sexually, as far as sex is concerned; **laisser/rester en ~** to abandon/be abandoned; **~ d'action** plan of action; **~ directeur** (Écon) master plan; **~ d'eau** lake; pond; **~ de travail** work-top, work surface; **~ de vol** (Aviat) flight plan

planche [plɑ̃ʃ] nf (pièce de bois) plank, (wooden) board; (illustration) plate; (de salades, radis, poireaux) bed; (d'un plongeoir) (diving) board; **les ~s** (Théât) the boards; **en ~s** adj wooden; **faire la ~** (dans l'eau) to float on one's back; **avoir du pain sur la ~** to have one's work cut out; **~ à découper** chopping board; **~ à dessin** drawing board; **~ à pain** breadboard; **~ à repasser** ironing board; **~ (à roulettes)** (planche) skateboard; (sport) skateboarding; **~ de salut** (fig) sheet anchor; **~ à voile** (planche) windsurfer, sailboard; (sport) windsurfing

plancher [plɑ̃ʃe] nm floor; (planches) floorboards pl; (fig) minimum level ▷ vi to work hard

planer [plane] vi (oiseau, avion) to glide; (fumée, vapeur) to float, hover; (drogué) to be (on a) high; (fam: rêveur) to have one's head in the clouds; **~ sur** (fig: danger) to hang over; to hover above

planète [planɛt] nf planet

planeur [planœʀ] nm glider

planification [planifikasjɔ̃] nf (economic) planning

planifier [planifje] vt to plan

planning [planiŋ] nm programme (Brit), program (US), schedule; **~ familial** family planning

planque [plɑ̃k] nf (fam: combine, filon) cushy (Brit) ou easy number; (: cachette) hideout

plant [plɑ̃] nm seedling, young plant

plante [plɑ̃t] nf plant; **~ d'appartement** house ou pot plant; **~ du pied** sole (of the foot); **~ verte** house plant

planter [plɑ̃te] vt (plante) to plant; (enfoncer) to hammer ou drive in; (tente) to put up, pitch; (drapeau, échelle, décors) to put up; (fam: mettre) to dump; (: abandonner): **~ là** to ditch; **se planter** vi (fam: se tromper) to get it wrong;

(ordinateur) to crash; **~ qch dans** to hammer ou drive sth into; to stick sth into; **se ~ dans** to sink into; to get stuck in; **se ~ devant** to plant o.s. in front of

plantureux, -euse [plɑ̃tyʀø, -øz] adj (repas) copious, lavish; (femme) buxom

plaque [plak] nf plate; (de verre) sheet; (de verglas, d'eczéma) patch; (dentaire) plaque; (avec inscription) plaque; **~ (minéralogique** ou **de police** ou **d'immatriculation)** number (Brit) ou license (US) plate; **~ de beurre** slab of butter; **~ chauffante** hotplate; **~ de chocolat** bar of chocolate; **~ de cuisson** hob; **~ d'identité** identity disc; **~ tournante** (fig) centre (Brit), center (US)

plaqué, e [plake] adj: **~ or/argent** gold-/silver-plated ▷ nm: **~ or/argent** gold/silver plate; **~ acajou** with a mahogany veneer

plaquer [plake] vt (bijou) to plate; (bois) to veneer; (aplatir): **~ qch sur/contre** to make sth stick ou cling to; (Rugby) to bring down; (fam: laisser tomber) to drop, ditch; **se ~ contre** to flatten o.s. against; **~ qn contre** to pin sb to

plaquette [plakɛt] nf tablet; (de chocolat) bar; (de beurre) slab, packet; (livre) small volume; (Méd: de pilules, gélules) pack, packet; **~ de frein** (Auto) brake pad

plastique [plastik] adj plastic ▷ nm plastic ▷ nf plastic arts pl; (d'une statue) modelling

plastiquer [plastike] vt to blow up

plat, e [pla, -at] adj flat; (fade: vin) flat-tasting, insipid; (personne, livre) dull; (style) flat, dull ▷ nm (récipient, Culin) dish; (d'un repas) course; **le premier ~** the first course; (partie plate) **le ~ de la main** the flat of the hand; (: d'une route) flat (part); **à ~ ventre** adv face down; (tomber) flat on one's face; **à ~** adj (pneu, batterie) flat; (fam: fatigué) dead beat, tired out; **~ cuisiné** pre-cooked meal (ou dish); **~ du jour** dish of the day; **~ principal** ou **de résistance** main course; **~s préparés** convenience food(s)

platane [platan] nm plane tree

plateau, x [plato] nm (support) tray; (d'une table) top; (d'une balance) pan; (Géo) plateau; (de tourne-disques) turntable; (Ciné) set; (TV): **nous avons deux journalistes sur le ~ ce soir** we have two journalists with us tonight; **~ à fromages** cheeseboard

plate-bande (pl **plates-bandes**) [platbɑ̃d] nf flower bed

plate-forme (pl **plates-formes**) [platfɔʀm] nf platform; **~ de forage/pétrolière** drilling/oil rig

platine [platin] nm platinum ▷ nf (d'un tourne-disque) turntable; **~ disque/cassette** record/cassette deck; **~ laser** ou **compact-disc** compact disc (player)

plâtre [plɑtʀ] nm (matériau) plaster; (statue) plaster statue; (Méd) plaster cast; **plâtres** nmpl plasterwork sg; **avoir un bras dans le ~** to have an arm in plaster

plein, e [plɛ̃, -ɛn] adj full; (porte, roue) solid; (chienne, jument) big (with young) ▷ nm: **faire le ~ (d'essence)** to fill up (with petrol (Brit) ou gas (US)) ▷ prép: **avoir de l'argent ~ les poches** to have loads of money; **~ de** full of; **avoir les mains ~es** to have one's hands full; **à ~es mains** (ramasser) in handfuls; (empoigner) firmly; **à ~ régime** at maximum revs; (fig) at full speed; **à ~ temps** full-time; **en ~ air** in the open air; **jeux en ~ air** outdoor games; **en ~e mer** on the open sea; **en ~ soleil** in direct sunlight; **en ~e nuit/rue** in the middle of the night/street; **en ~ milieu** right in the middle; **en ~ jour** in broad daylight; **les ~s** the downstrokes (in handwriting); **faire le ~ des voix** to get the maximum number of votes possible; **en ~ sur** right on; **en avoir ~ le dos** (fam) to have had it up to here

pleurer [plœʀe] vi to cry; (yeux) to water ▷ vt to mourn (for); **~ sur** vt to lament (over), bemoan; **~ de rire** to laugh till one cries

pleurnicher [plœʀniʃe] vi to snivel, whine

pleurs [plœʀ] nmpl: **en ~** in tears

pleut [plø] vb voir **pleuvoir**

pleuvait etc [pløvɛ] vb voir **pleuvoir**

pleuvoir [pløvwaʀ] vb impers to rain ▷ vi (fig): **~ (sur)** (coups) to rain down; (critiques, invitations) to shower down; **il pleut** it's raining; **il pleut des cordes** ou **à verse** ou **à torrents** it's pouring (down), it's raining cats and dogs

pli [pli] nm fold; (de jupe) pleat; (de pantalon) crease; (aussi: **faux ~**) crease; (enveloppe) envelope; (lettre) letter; (Cartes) trick; **prendre le ~ de faire** to get into the habit of doing; **ça ne fait un ~!** don't you worry!; **~ d'aisance** inverted pleat

pliant, e [plijɑ̃, -ɑ̃t] adj folding ▷ nm folding stool, campstool

plier [plije] vt to fold; (pour ranger) to fold up; (table pliante) to fold down; (genou, bras) to bend ▷ vi to bend; (fig) to yield; **se ~ à** to submit to; **~ bagages** (fig) to pack up (and go)

plinthe [plɛ̃t] nf skirting board

plisser [plise] vt (chiffonner: papier, étoffe) to crease; (rider: yeux) to screw up; (front) to furrow, wrinkle; (: bouche) to pucker; (jupe) to put pleats in; **se plisser** vi (vêtement, étoffe) to crease

plomb [plɔ̃] nm (métal) lead; (d'une cartouche) (lead) shot; (Pêche) sinker; (sceau) (lead) seal; (Élec) fuse; **de ~ (soleil)** blazing; **sans ~ (essence)** unleaded; **sommeil de ~** heavy ou very deep sleep; **mettre à ~** to plumb

plombage [plɔ̃baʒ] nm (de dent) filling

plomberie [plɔ̃bʀi] nf plumbing

plombier [plɔ̃bje] nm plumber

plonge [plɔ̃ʒ] nf: **faire la ~** to be a washer-up (Brit) ou dishwasher (person)

plongeant, e [plɔ̃ʒɑ̃, -ɑ̃t] adj (vue) from above; (tir, décolleté) plunging

plongée [plɔ̃ʒe] nf (Sport) diving no pl; (: sans scaphandre) skin diving; (de sous-marin) submersion, dive; (de sous-marin) submerged; (prise de vue) high angle; **~ sous-marine** diving

plongeoir [plɔ̃ʒwaʀ] nm diving board

plongeon [plɔ̃ʒɔ̃] nm dive

plonger [plɔ̃ʒe] vi to dive ▷ vt: **~ qch dans** to plunge sth into; **~ dans un sommeil profond** to sink straight into a deep sleep; **~ qn dans l'embarras** to throw sb into a state of confusion; **se ~ dans** (études, lecture) to bury ou immerse o.s. in

plongeur, -euse [plɔ̃ʒœʀ, -øz] nm/f diver; (de café) washer-up (Brit), dishwasher (person)

ployer [plwaje] vt to bend ▷ vi to bend; (plancher) to sag

plu [ply] pp de **plaire**; **pleuvoir**

pluie [plɥi] nf rain; (averse, ondée): **une ~ brève** a shower; (fig): **~ de** shower of; **une ~ fine** fine rain; **retomber en ~** to shower down; **sous la ~** in the rain

plume [plym] nf feather; (pour écrire) (pen) nib; (fig) pen; **dessin à la ~** pen and ink drawing

plupart [plypaʀ]: **la ~** pron the majority, most (of them); **la ~ des** most, the majority of; **la ~ du temps/d'entre nous** most of the time/of us; **pour la ~** adv for the most part, mostly

pluriel [plyʀjɛl] nm plural; **au ~** in the plural

plus¹ [ply] vb voir **plaire**

○ MOT-CLÉ

plus² [ply] adv 1 (forme négative): **ne ... plus** no more, no longer; **je n'ai plus d'argent** I've got no more money ou no money left; **il ne travaille plus** he's no longer working, he doesn't work any more

2 [ply, plyz] (+voyelle: comparatif) more, ...+er; (superlatif): **le plus** the most, the ...+est; **plus grand/intelligent (que)** bigger/more intelligent (than); **le plus grand/intelligent** the biggest/most intelligent; **tout au plus** at the very most

3 [plys, plyz] (+voyelle: davantage) more; **il travaille plus (que)** he works more (than); **plus il travaille, plus il est heureux** the more he works, the happier he is; **plus de pain** more bread; **plus de 10 personnes/trois heures/quatre kilos** more than ou over 10 people/three hours/four kilos; **trois heures de plus que** three hours more than; **plus de minuit** after ou past midnight; **de plus** what's more, moreover; **il a trois ans de plus que moi** he's three years older than me; **trois kilos en plus** three kilos more; **en plus de** in addition to; **de plus en plus** more and more; **en plus de cela ...** what is more ...; **plus ou moins** more or less; **ni plus ni moins** no more, no less; **sans plus** (but) no

more than that, (but) that's all; **qui plus est** what is more

▷ prép [plys]: **quatre plus deux** four plus two

plusieurs [plyzjœʀ] adj, pron several; **ils sont ~** there are several of them

plus-value [plyvaly] nf (d'un bien) appreciation; (bénéfice) capital gain; (budgétaire) surplus

plut [ply] vb voir **plaire**; **pleuvoir**

plutôt [plyto] adv rather; **je ferais ~ ceci** I'd rather ou sooner do this; **fais ~ comme ça** try this way instead; **~ que (de) faire** rather than ou instead of doing

pluvieux, -euse [plyvjø, -øz] adj rainy, wet

PME sigle fpl (= petites et moyennes entreprises) small businesses

PMU sigle m (= pari mutuel urbain) (café) betting agency; see note

● **PMU**
●
● The PMU ("pari mutuel urbain") is a
● Government-regulated network of
● betting counters run from bars
● displaying the PMU sign or online.
● Punters buy fixed-price tickets predicting
● winners or finishing positions in horse
● races. The traditional bet is the "tiercé", a
● triple bet, although other multiple bets
● ("quarté" and so on) are becoming
● increasingly popular.

PNB sigle m (= produit national brut) GNP

pneu [pnø] nm (de roue) tyre (Brit), tire (US); (message) letter sent by pneumatic tube

pneumonie [pnømɔni] nf pneumonia

poche [pɔʃ] nf pocket; (déformation): **faire une/des ~(s)** to bag; (sous les yeux) bag, pouch; (Zool) pouch ▷ nm (livre de poche) (pocket-size) paperback; **de ~** pocket cpd; **en être de sa ~** to be out of pocket; **c'est dans la ~** it's in the bag; **argent de ~** pocket money

pocher [pɔʃe] vt (Culin) to poach; (Art) to sketch ▷ vi (vêtement) to bag

pochette [pɔʃɛt] nf (de timbres) wallet, envelope; (d'aiguilles etc) case; (sac: de femme) clutch bag, purse; (: d'homme) bag; (sur veston) breast pocket; (mouchoir) breast pocket handkerchief; **~ d'allumettes** book of matches; **~ de disque** record sleeve; **~ surprise** lucky bag

podcast [pɔdkast] nm (Inform) podcast

podcaster [pɔdkaste] vi (Inform) to podcast

poêle [pwal] nm stove ▷ nf: **~ (à frire)** frying pan

poème [pɔɛm] nm poem

poésie [pɔezi] nf (poème) poem; (art): **la ~** poetry

poète [pɔɛt] nm poet; (fig) dreamer ▷ adj poetic

poids [pwa] *nm* weight; (*Sport*) shot; **vendre au ~** to sell by weight; **de ~** *adj* (*argument etc*) weighty; **perdre/prendre du ~** to lose/put on weight; **faire le ~** (*fig*) to measure up; **~ plume/mouche/coq/moyen** (*Boxe*) feather/fly/bantam/middleweight; **~ et haltères** weight lifting *sg*; **~ lourd** (*Boxe*) heavyweight; (*camion: aussi*: **PL**) (big) lorry (*Brit*), truck (*US*); (: *Admin*) large goods vehicle (*Brit*), truck (*US*); **~ mort** dead weight; **~ utile** net weight

poignant, e [pwaɲɑ̃, -ɑ̃t] *adj* poignant, harrowing

poignard [pwaɲaʀ] *nm* dagger

poignarder [pwaɲaʀde] *vt* to stab, knife

poigne [pwaɲ] *nf* grip; (*fig*) firm-handedness; **à ~** firm-handed; **avoir de la ~** (*fig*) to rule with a firm hand

poignée [pwaɲe] *nf* (*de sel etc, fig*) handful; (*de couvercle, porte*) handle; **~ de main** handshake

poignet [pwaɲɛ] *nm* (*Anat*) wrist; (*de chemise*) cuff

poil [pwal] *nm* (*Anat*) hair; (*de pinceau, brosse*) bristle; (*de tapis, tissu*) strand; (*pelage*) coat; (*ensemble des poils*): **avoir du ~ sur la poitrine** to have hair(s) on one's chest, have a hairy chest; **à ~** *adj* (*fam*) starkers; **au ~** *adj* (*fam*) hunky-dory; **de tout ~** of all kinds; **être de bon/mauvais ~** to be in a good/bad mood; **~ à gratter** itching powder

poilu, e [pwaly] *adj* hairy

poinçon [pwɛ̃sɔ̃] *nm* awl; bodkin; (*marque*) hallmark

poinçonner [pwɛ̃sɔne] *vt* (*marchandise*) to stamp; (*bijou etc*) to hallmark; (*billet, ticket*) to punch, clip

poing [pwɛ̃] *nm* fist; **coup de ~** punch; **dormir à ~s fermés** to sleep soundly

point [pwɛ̃] *nm* (*marque, signe*) dot; (: *de ponctuation*) full stop, period (*US*); (*moment, de score etc, fig: question*) point; (*endroit*) spot; (*Couture, Tricot*) stitch ▷ *adv* = **pas**; **ne ... ~** not (at all); **faire le ~** (*Navig*) to take a bearing; (*fig*) to take stock of (the situation); **faire le ~ sur** to review; **en tout ~** in every respect; **sur le ~ de faire** (just) about to do; **au ~ que, à tel ~ que** so much so that; **mettre au ~** (*mécanisme, procédé*) to develop; (*appareil photo*) to focus; (*affaire*) to settle; **à ~** (*Culin*) just right; (: *viande*) medium; **à ~ (nommé)** just at the right time; **~ de croix/tige/chaînette** (*Couture*) cross/stem/chain stitch; **~ mousse/jersey** (*Tricot*) garter/stocking stitch; **~ de départ/d'arrivée/d'arrêt** departure/arrival/stopping point; **~ chaud** (*Mil, Pol*) hot spot; **~ de chute** landing place; (*fig*) stopping-off point; **deux ~s** colon; **~ (de côté)** stitch (*pain*); **~ culminant** summit; (*fig*) height, climax; **~ d'eau** spring, water point; **~ d'exclamation** exclamation mark; **~ faible** weak spot; **~ final** full stop, period (*US*); **~ d'interrogation** question mark; **~ mort** (*Finance*) break-even point; **au ~ mort** (*Auto*)

in neutral; (*affaire, entreprise*) at a standstill; **~ noir** (*sur le visage*) blackhead; (*Auto*) accident black spot; **~ de non-retour** point of no return; **~ de repère** landmark; (*dans le temps*) point of reference; **~ de vente** retail outlet; **~ de vue** viewpoint; (*fig: opinion*) point of view; **du ~ de vue de** from the point of view of; **~s cardinaux** points of the compass, cardinal points; **~s de suspension** suspension points

pointe [pwɛ̃t] *nf* point; (*de la côte*) headland; (*allusion*) dig; sally; (*clou*) tack; (*fig*): **une ~ d'ail/d'accent** a touch of garlic/of an accent; **pointes** *nfpl* (*Danse*) points, point shoes; **être à la ~ de** (*fig*) to be in the forefront of; **faire ou pousser une ~ jusqu'à ...** to press on as far as ...; **sur la ~ des pieds** on tiptoe; **en ~** *adv* (*tailler*) into a point ▷ *adj* pointed, tapered; **de ~** *adj* (*technique etc*) leading; (*vitesse*) maximum, top; **heures/jours de ~** peak hours/days; **faire du 180 en ~** (*Auto*) to have a top *ou* maximum speed of 180; **faire des ~s** (*Danse*) to dance on points; **~ d'asperge** asparagus tip; **~ de courant** surge (of current); **~ de vitesse** burst of speed

pointer [pwɛ̃te] *vt* (*cocher*) to tick off; (*employés etc*) to check in; (*diriger: canon, longue-vue, doigt*): **~ vers qch, ~ sur qch** to point at sth; (*Mus: note*) to dot ▷ *vi* (*employé*) to clock in ou on; (*pousses*) to come through; (*jour*) to break; **~ les oreilles** (*chien*) to prick up its ears

pointeur, -euse [pwɛ̃tœʀ, -øz] *nf* timeclock ▷ *nm* (*Inform*) cursor

pointillé [pwɛ̃tije] *nm* (*trait*) dotted line; (*Art*) stippling *no pl*

pointilleux, -euse [pwɛ̃tijø, -øz] *adj* particular, pernickety

pointu, e [pwɛ̃ty] *adj* pointed; (*clou*) sharp; (*voix*) shrill; (*analyse*) precise

pointure [pwɛ̃tyʀ] *nf* size

point-virgule (*pl* **points-virgules**) [pwɛ̃viʀgyl] *nm* semi-colon

poire [pwaʀ] *nf* pear; (*fam: péj*) mug; **~ électrique** (*pear-shaped*) switch; **~ à injections** syringe

poireau, x [pwaʀo] *nm* leek

poireauter [pwaʀote] *vi* (*fam*) to hang about (waiting)

poirier [pwaʀje] *nm* pear tree; (*Sport*): **faire le ~** to do a headstand

pois [pwa] *nm* (*Bot*) pea; (*sur une étoffe*) dot, spot; **à ~** (*cravate etc*) spotted, polka-dot *cpd*; **~ chiche** chickpea; **~ de senteur** sweet pea; **~ cassés** split peas

poison [pwazɔ̃] *nm* poison

poisse [pwas] *nf* rotten luck

poisseux, -euse [pwasø, -øz] *adj* sticky

poisson [pwasɔ̃] *nm* fish *gen inv*; (*Astrol*): **les P~s** (*signe*) Pisces, the Fish; **être des P~s** to be Pisces; **pêcher ou prendre du ~ ou des ~s** to fish; **~ d'avril** April fool; (*blague*) April fool's day trick; *see note*; **~ rouge** goldfish

P

POISSON D'AVRIL

The traditional April Fools' Day prank in France involves attaching a cut-out paper fish, known as a "poisson d'avril", to the back of one's victim, without being caught.

poissonnerie [pwasɔnʀi] *nf* fishmonger's (Brit), fish store (US)

poissonnier, -ière [pwasɔnje, -jɛʀ] *nm/f* fishmonger (Brit), fish merchant (US) ▷ *nf* (*ustensile*) fish kettle

poitrine [pwatʀin] *nf* (*Anat*) chest; (*seins*) bust, bosom; (*Culin*) breast; **~ de bœuf** brisket

poivre [pwavʀ] *nm* pepper; **~ en grains/moulu** whole/ground pepper; **~ de cayenne** cayenne (pepper); **~ et sel** *adj* (*cheveux*) pepper-and-salt

poivron [pwavʀɔ̃] *nm* pepper, capsicum; **~ vert/rouge** green/red pepper

polaire [pɔlɛʀ] *adj* polar

polar [pɔlaʀ] (*fam*) *nm* detective novel

pôle [pol] *nm* (*Géo, Élec*) pole; **le ~ Nord/Sud** the North/South Pole; **~ d'attraction** (*fig*) centre of attraction

poli, e [pɔli] *adj* polite; (*lisse*) smooth; polished

police [pɔlis] *nf* police; (*discipline*): **assurer la ~ de** *ou* **dans** to keep order in; **peine de simple ~** sentence given by a magistrate's or police court; **~ (d'assurance)** (insurance) policy; **~ (de caractères)** (*Typo, Inform*) font, typeface; **~ judiciaire (PJ)** ≈ Criminal Investigation Department (CID) (Brit), ≈ Federal Bureau of Investigation (FBI) (US); **~ des mœurs** ≈ vice squad; **~ secours** ≈ emergency services *pl* (Brit), ≈ paramedics *pl* (US)

policier, -ière [pɔlisje, -jɛʀ] *adj* police *cpd* ▷ *nm* policeman; (*aussi*: **roman ~**) detective novel

polio [pɔljo] *nf* (*aussi*: **~myélite**) polio ▷ *nm/f* (*aussi*: **~myélitique**) polio patient *ou* case

poliomyélite [pɔljɔmjelit] *nf* poliomyelitis

poliomyélitique [pɔljɔmjelitik] *nm/f* polio patient *ou* case

polir [pɔliʀ] *vt* to polish

polisson, ne [pɔlisɔ̃, -ɔn] *adj* naughty

politesse [pɔlitɛs] *nf* politeness; **politesses** *nfpl* (exchange of) courtesies; **rendre une ~ à qn** to return sb's favour (Brit) *ou* favor (US)

politicien, ne [pɔlitisjɛ̃, -ɛn] *adj* political ▷ *nm/f* (*péj*) politician

politique [pɔlitik] *adj* political ▷ *nf* (*science, activité*) politics *sg*; (*principes, tactique*) policy, policies *pl* ▷ *nm* (*politicien*) politician; **~ étrangère/intérieure** foreign/domestic policy

politiquement [pɔlitikmɑ̃] *adv* politically; **~ correct** politically correct

pollen [pɔlɛn] *nm* pollen

polluant, e [pɔlɥɑ̃, -ɑ̃t] *adj* polluting ▷ *nm* polluting agent, pollutant; **non ~** non-polluting

polluer [pɔlɥe] *vt* to pollute

pollution [pɔlysjɔ̃] *nf* pollution

polo [pɔlo] *nm* (*sport*) polo; (*tricot*) polo shirt

Pologne [pɔlɔɲ] *nf*: **la ~** Poland

polonais, e [pɔlɔnɛ, -ɛz] *adj* Polish ▷ *nm* (*Ling*) Polish ▷ *nm/f*: **P~, e** Pole

poltron, ne [pɔltʀɔ̃, -ɔn] *adj* cowardly

polycopier [pɔlikɔpje] *vt* to duplicate

Polynésie [pɔlinezi] *nf*: **la ~** Polynesia; **la ~ française** French Polynesia

polyvalent, e [pɔlivalɑ̃, -ɑ̃t] *adj* (*vaccin*) polyvalent; (*personne*) versatile; (*rôle*) varied; (*salle*) multi-purpose ▷ *nm* ≈ tax inspector

pommade [pɔmad] *nf* ointment, cream

pomme [pɔm] *nf* (*Bot*) apple; (*boule décorative*) knob; (*pomme de terre*): **steak ~s (frites)** steak and chips (Brit) *ou* (French) fries (US); **tomber dans les ~s** (*fam*) to pass out; **~ d'Adam** Adam's apple; **~s allumettes** French fries (thin-cut); **~ d'arrosoir** (sprinkler) rose; **~ de pin** pine *ou* fir cone; **~ de terre** potato; **~s vapeur** boiled potatoes

pommeau, x [pɔmo] *nm* (*boule*) knob; (*de selle*) pommel

pommette [pɔmɛt] *nf* cheekbone

pommier [pɔmje] *nm* apple tree

pompe [pɔ̃p] *nf* pump; (*faste*) pomp (and ceremony); **~ à eau/essence** water/petrol pump; **~ à huile** oil pump; **~ à incendie** fire engine (*apparatus*); **~s funèbres** undertaker's *sg*, funeral parlour *sg* (Brit), mortician's *sg* (US)

pomper [pɔ̃pe] *vt* to pump; (*évacuer*) to pump out; (*aspirer*) to pump up; (*absorber*) to soak up ▷ *vi* to pump

pompeux, -euse [pɔ̃pø, -øz] *adj* pompous

pompier [pɔ̃pje] *nm* fireman ▷ *adj m* (*style*) pretentious, pompous

pompiste [pɔ̃pist] *nm/f* petrol (Brit) *ou* gas (US) pump attendant

poncer [pɔ̃se] *vt* to sand (down)

ponctuation [pɔ̃ktɥasjɔ̃] *nf* punctuation

ponctuel, le [pɔ̃ktɥɛl] *adj* (*à l'heure, Tech*) punctual; (*fig: opération etc*) one-off, single; (*scrupuleux*) punctilious, meticulous

pondéré, e [pɔ̃deʀe] *adj* level-headed, composed

pondre [pɔ̃dʀ] *vt* to lay; (*fig*) to produce ▷ *vi* to lay

poney [pɔnɛ] *nm* pony

pont [pɔ̃] *nm* bridge; (*Auto*): **~ arrière/avant** rear/front axle; (*Navig*) deck; **faire le ~** to take the extra day off; *see note*; **faire un ~ d'or à qn** to offer sb a fortune to take a job; **~ aérien** airlift; **~ basculant** bascule bridge; **~ d'envol** flight deck; **~ élévateur** hydraulic ramp; **~ de graissage** ramp (in garage); **~ à péage** tollbridge; **~ roulant** travelling crane; **~ suspendu** suspension bridge; **~ tournant** swing bridge; **P~s et Chaussées** highways department

pont-levis (*pl* **ponts-levis**) [pɔ̃lvi] *nm*
drawbridge

pop [pɔp] *adj inv* pop ▷ *nm*: **le ~** pop (music)

populace [pɔpylas] *nf* (*péj*) rabble

populaire [pɔpylɛʀ] *adj* popular;
(*manifestation*) mass *cpd*, of the people;
(*milieux, clientèle*) working-class; (*Ling: mot etc*)
used by the lower classes (of society)

popularité [pɔpylaʀite] *nf* popularity

population [pɔpylasjɔ̃] *nf* population;
~ active/agricole working/farming
population

populeux, -euse [pɔpylø, -øz] *adj* densely
populated

porc [pɔʀ] *nm* (*Zool*) pig; (*Culin*) pork; (*peau*)
pigskin

porcelaine [pɔʀsəlɛn] *nf* (*substance*)
porcelain, china; (*objet*) piece of china(ware)

porc-épic (*pl* **porcs-épics**) [pɔʀkepik] *nm*
porcupine

porche [pɔʀʃ] *nm* porch

porcherie [pɔʀʃəʀi] *nf* pigsty

pore [pɔʀ] *nm* pore

porno [pɔʀno] *adj* porno ▷ *nm* porn

port [pɔʀ] *nm* (*Navig*) harbour (*Brit*), harbor
(*US*), port; (*ville, Inform*) port; (*de l'uniforme etc*)
wearing; (*pour lettre*) postage; (*pour colis, aussi:
posture*) carriage; **~ de commerce/de pêche**
commercial/fishing port; **arriver à bon ~** to
arrive safe and sound; **~ d'arme** (*Jur*) carrying
of a firearm; **~ d'attache** (*Navig*) port of
registry; (*fig*) home base; **~ d'escale** port of
call; **~ franc** free port; **~ payé** postage paid

portable [pɔʀtabl] *adj* (*vêtement*) wearable;
(*portatif*) portable; (*téléphone*) mobile (*Brit*),
cell(phone) (*US*) ▷ *nm* (*Inform*) laptop
(computer); (*téléphone*) mobile (phone) (*Brit*),
cell(phone) (*US*)

portail [pɔʀtaj] *nm* gate; (*de cathédrale*) portal

portant, e [pɔʀtɑ̃, -ɑ̃t] *adj* (*murs*) structural,
supporting; (*roues*) running; **bien/mal ~** in
good/poor health

portatif, -ive [pɔʀtatif, -iv] *adj* portable

porte [pɔʀt] *nf* door; (*de ville, forteresse, Ski*)
gate; **mettre à la ~** to throw out; **prendre la
~** to leave, go away; **à ma/sa ~** (*tout près*) on
my/his (*ou* her) doorstep;
~ (d'embarquement) (*Aviat*) (departure)
gate; **~ d'entrée** front door; **~ à ~** *nm* door-to-
door selling; **~ de secours** emergency exit;
~ de service service entrance

porté, e [pɔʀte] *adj*: **être ~ à faire qch** to be
apt to do sth, tend to do sth; **être ~ sur qch** to
be partial to sth

porte-avions [pɔʀtavjɔ̃] *nm inv* aircraft carrier

porte-bagages [pɔʀtbagaʒ] *nm inv* luggage
rack (*ou* basket *etc*)

porte-bonheur [pɔʀtbɔnœʀ] *nm inv* lucky
charm

porte-clés, porte-clefs [pɔʀtəkle] *nm inv*
key ring

porte-documents [pɔʀtdɔkymɑ̃] *nm inv*
attaché *ou* document case

portée [pɔʀte] *nf* (*d'une arme*) range; (*fig:
importance*) impact, import; (: *capacités*) scope,
capability; (*de chatte etc*) litter; (*Mus*) stave,
staff; **à hors de ~ (de)** within/out of reach
(of); **à ~ de (la) main** within (arm's) reach; **à
~ de voix** within earshot; **à la ~ de qn** (*fig*) at
sb's level, within sb's capabilities; **à la ~ de
toutes les bourses** to suit every pocket,
within everyone's means

porte-fenêtre (*pl* **portes-fenêtres**) [pɔʀtfə
nɛtʀ] *nf* French window

portefeuille [pɔʀtəfœj] *nm* wallet; (*Pol,
Bourse*) portfolio; **faire un lit en ~** to make an
apple-pie bed

portemanteau, x [pɔʀtmɑ̃to] *nm* coat rack;
(*cintre*) coat hanger

porte-monnaie [pɔʀtmɔnɛ] *nm inv* purse

porte-parole [pɔʀtpaʀɔl] *nm inv*
spokesperson

porter [pɔʀte] *vt* (*charge ou sac etc, aussi: fœtus*)
to carry; (*sur soi: vêtement, barbe, bague*) to wear;
(*fig: responsabilité etc*) to bear, carry; (*inscription,
marque, titre, patronyme: arbre: fruits, fleurs*) to
bear; (*coup*) to deal; (*attention*) to turn;
(*jugement*) to pass; (*apporter*): **~ qch quelque
part/à qn** to take sth somewhere/to sb;
(*inscrire*): **~ qch sur** to put sth down on; to
enter sth in ▷ *vi* (*voix, regard, canon*) to carry;
(*coup, argument*) to hit home; **se porter** *vi* (*se
sentir*): **se ~ bien/mal** to be well/unwell;
(*aller*): **se ~ vers** to go towards; **~ sur** (*peser*) to
rest on; (*accent*) to fall on; (*conférence etc*) to
concern; (*heurter*) to strike; **être porté à faire**
to be apt *ou* inclined to do; **elle portait le
nom de Rosalie** she was called Rosalie; **~ qn
au pouvoir** to bring sb to power; **se ~ bonheur
à qn** to bring sb luck; **~ qn à croire** to lead sb
to believe; **~ son âge** to look one's age; **~ un
toast** to drink a toast; **~ l'argent au crédit
d'un compte** to credit an account with some
money; **se ~ partie civile** to associate in a court
action with the public prosecutor; **se ~ garant de
qch** to guarantee sth, vouch for sth; **se ~
candidat à la députation ≈** to stand for
Parliament (*Brit*), ≈ run for Congress (*US*); **se
faire ~ malade** to report sick; **~ la main à
son chapeau** to raise one's hand to one's
hat; **~ son effort sur** to direct one's efforts
towards; **~ un fait à la connaissance de qn**
to bring a fact to sb's attention *ou* notice

porteur, -euse [pɔʀtœʀ, -øz] adj (Comm) strong, promising; (nouvelle, chèque etc): **être ~ de** to be the bearer of ▷ nm/f (de messages) bearer ▷ nm (de bagages) porter; (Comm: de chèque) bearer; (: d'actions) holder; **(avion) gros ~** wide-bodied aircraft, jumbo (jet)

porte-voix [pɔʀtəvwa] nm inv megaphone, loudhailer (Brit)

portier [pɔʀtje] nm doorman, commissionnaire (Brit)

portière [pɔʀtjɛʀ] nf door

portillon [pɔʀtijɔ̃] nm gate

portion [pɔʀsjɔ̃] nf (part) portion, share; (partie) portion, section

porto [pɔʀto] nm port (wine)

portrait [pɔʀtʀɛ] nm portrait; (photographie) photograph; (fig): **elle est le ~ de sa mère** she's the image of her mother

portrait-robot [pɔʀtʀɛʀɔbo] nm Identikit® ou Photo-fit® (Brit) picture

portuaire [pɔʀtɥɛʀ] adj port cpd, harbour cpd (Brit), harbor cpd (US)

portugais, e [pɔʀtɥɡɛ, -ɛz] adj Portuguese ▷ nm (Ling) Portuguese ▷ nm/f: **P~, e** Portuguese

Portugal [pɔʀtɥɡal] nm: **le ~** Portugal

pose [poz] nf (de moquette) laying; (de rideaux, papier peint) hanging; (attitude, d'un modèle) pose; (Photo) exposure

posé, e [poze] adj calm, unruffled

poser [poze] vt (déposer): **~ qch (sur)/qn à** to put sth down (on)/drop sb at; (placer): **~ qch sur/quelque part** to put sth on/somewhere; (installer: moquette, carrelage) to lay; (rideaux, papier peint) to hang; (Math: chiffre) to put (down); (question) to ask; (principe, conditions) to lay ou set down; (problème) to formulate; (difficulté) to pose; (personne: mettre en valeur) to give standing to ▷ vi (modèle) to pose; to sit; **se poser** vi (oiseau, avion) to land; (question) to arise; **se ~ en** to pass o.s off as, pose as; **~ son ou un regard sur qn/qch** to turn one's gaze on sb/sth; **~ sa candidature à un poste** to apply for a post; (Pol) to put o.s up for election

positif, -ive [pozitif, -iv] adj positive

position [pozisjɔ̃] nf position; **prendre ~** (fig) to take a stand

posologie [pozɔlɔʒi] nf directions pl for use, dosage

posséder [posede] vt to own, possess; (qualité, talent) to have, possess; (bien connaître: métier, langue) to have mastered, have a thorough knowledge of; (sexuellement, aussi: suj: colère) to possess; (fam: duper) to take in

possession [posesjɔ̃] nf ownership no pl; possession; (aussi: **être/entrer en/prendre ~ de qch**) to be in/take possession of sth

possibilité [posibilite] nf possibility; **possibilités** nfpl (moyens) means; (potentiel) potential sg; **avoir la ~ de faire** to be in a position to do; to have the opportunity to do

possible [posibl] adj possible; (projet, entreprise) feasible ▷ nm: **faire son ~** to do all one can, do one's utmost; **(ce n'est) pas ~!** impossible!; **le plus/moins de livres ~** as many/few books as possible; **le plus vite ~** as quickly as possible; **dès que ~** as soon as possible; **gentil etc au ~** as nice etc as it is possible to be

postal, e, -aux [pɔstal, -o] adj postal, post office cpd; **sac ~** mailbag, postbag

poste[1] [pɔst] nf (service) post, postal service; (administration, bureau) post office; **mettre à la ~** to post; **~ restante (PR)** poste restante (Brit), general delivery (US); **postes** nfpl post office sg; **P~s télécommunications et télédiffusion (PTT)** postal and telecommunications service; **agent ou employé des ~s** post office worker

poste[2] [pɔst] nm (fonction, Mil) post; (Tél) extension; (de radio etc) set; (de budget) item; **~ de commandement (PC)** (Mil etc) headquarters; **~ de contrôle** checkpoint; **~ de douane** customs post; **~ émetteur** transmitting set; **~ d'essence** filling station; **~ d'incendie** fire point; **~ de péage** tollgate; **~ de pilotage** cockpit, flight deck; **~ (de police)** police station; **~ de radio** radio set; **~ de secours** first-aid post; **~ de télévision** television set; **~ de travail** work station

poster vt [pɔste] to post ▷ nm [pɔstɛʀ] poster; **se poster** to position o.s

postérieur, e [pɔsteʀjœʀ] adj (date) later; (partie) back ▷ nm (fam) behind

posthume [pɔstym] adj posthumous

postulant, e [pɔstylɑ̃, -ɑ̃t] nm/f (candidat) applicant; (Rel) postulant

postuler [pɔstyle] vt (emploi) to apply for, put in for ▷ vi: **~ à ou pour un emploi** to apply for a job

posture [pɔstyʀ] nf posture, position; (fig) position

pot [po] nm (en verre) jar; (en terre) pot; (en plastique, carton) carton; (en métal) tin; (fam: chance) luck; **avoir du ~** to be lucky; **boire ou prendre un ~** (fam) to have a drink; **petit ~ (pour bébé)** (jar of) baby food; **découvrir le ~ aux roses** to find out what's been going on; **~ catalytique** catalytic converter; **~ (de chambre)** (chamber)pot; **~ d'échappement** exhaust pipe; **~ de fleurs** plant pot, flowerpot; (plante) pot plant; **~ à tabac** tobacco jar

potable [pɔtabl] adj (fig: boisson) drinkable; (: travail, devoir) decent; **eau (non) ~** (not) drinking water

potage [pɔtaʒ] nm soup

potager, -ère [pɔtaʒe, -ɛʀ] adj (plante) edible, vegetable cpd; **(jardin) ~** kitchen ou vegetable garden

pot-au-feu [pɔtofø] nm inv (beef) stew; (viande) stewing beef ▷ adj (fam: personne) stay-at-home

pot-de-vin (pl **pots-de-vin**) [podvɛ̃] nm bribe

pote [pɔt] nm (fam) mate (Brit), pal

poteau, x [pɔto] nm post; ~ **de départ/ arrivée** starting/finishing post; ~ **(d'exécution)** execution post, stake; ~ **indicateur** signpost; ~ **télégraphique** telegraph pole; ~**x (de but)** goal-posts

potelé, e [pɔtle] adj plump, chubby

potence [pɔtɑ̃s] nf gallows sg; **en** ~ T-shaped

potentiel, le [pɔtɑ̃sjɛl] adj, nm potential

poterie [pɔtʀi] nf (fabrication) pottery; (objet) piece of pottery

potier, -ière [pɔtje, jɛʀ] nm/f potter

potins [pɔtɛ̃] nmpl gossip sg

potiron [pɔtiʀɔ̃] nm pumpkin

pou, x [pu] nm louse

poubelle [pubɛl] nf (dust)bin

pouce [pus] nm thumb; **se tourner** ou **se rouler les** ~**s** (fig) to twiddle one's thumbs; **manger sur le** ~ to eat on the run, snatch something to eat

poudre [pudʀ] nf powder; (fard) (face) powder; (explosif) gunpowder; **en** ~: **café en poudre** instant coffee; **savon en** ~ soap powder; **lait en** ~ dried ou powdered milk; ~ **à canon** gunpowder; ~ **à éternuer** sneezing powder; ~ **à récurer** scouring powder; ~ **de riz** face powder

poudreux, -euse [pudʀø, -øz] adj dusty; (neige) powdery, powder cpd

poudrier [pudʀije] nm (powder) compact

pouffer [pufe] vi: ~ **(de rire)** to burst out laughing

poulailler [pulaje] nm henhouse; (Théât): **le** ~ the gods sg

poulain [pulɛ̃] nm foal; (fig) protégé

poule [pul] nf (Zool) hen; (Culin) (boiling) fowl; (Sport) (round-robin) tournament; (Rugby) group; (fam) bird (Brit), chick, broad (US); (prostituée) tart; ~ **d'eau** moorhen; ~ **mouillée** coward; ~ **pondeuse** laying hen, layer; ~ **au riz** chicken and rice

poulet [pulɛ] nm chicken; (fam) cop

poulie [puli] nf pulley

pouls [pu] nm pulse; (Anat): **prendre le** ~ **de qn** to take sb's pulse

poumon [pumɔ̃] nm lung; ~ **d'acier** ou **artificiel** iron ou artificial lung

poupe [pup] nf stern; **en** ~ astern

poupée [pupe] nf doll; **jouer à la** ~ to play with one's doll (ou dolls); **de** ~ (très petit): **jardin de** ~ doll's garden, pocket-handkerchief-sized garden

pouponnière [pupɔnjɛʀ] nf crèche, day nursery

pour [puʀ] prép for ▷ nm: **le** ~ **et le contre** the pros and cons; ~ **faire** (so as) to do, in order to do; ~ **avoir fait** for having done; ~ **que** so that, in order that; **fermé** ~ **(cause de) travaux** closed for refurbishment ou alterations; **c'est** ~ **ça que ...** that's why ...; ~ **quoi faire?** what for?; ~ **moi** (à mon avis, pour ma part) for

my part, personally; ~ **riche qu'il soit** rich though he may be; ~ **20 euros d'essence** 20 euros' worth of petrol; ~ **cent** per cent; ~ **ce qui est de** as for; **y être** ~ **quelque chose** to have something to do with it

pourboire [puʀbwaʀ] nm tip

pourcentage [puʀsɑ̃taʒ] nm percentage; **travailler au** ~ to work on commission

pourchasser [puʀʃase] vt to pursue

pourparlers [puʀpaʀle] nmpl talks, negotiations; **être en** ~ **avec** to be having talks with

pourpre [puʀpʀ] adj crimson

pourquoi [puʀkwa] adv, conj why ▷ nm inv: **le** ~ **(de)** the reason (for)

pourrai etc [puʀe] vb voir **pouvoir**

pourri, e [puʀi] adj rotten; (roche, pierre) crumbling; (temps, climat) filthy, foul ▷ nm: **sentir le** ~ to smell rotten

pourriel [puʀjɛl] nm (Inform) spam

pourrir [puʀiʀ] vi to rot; (fruit) to go rotten ou bad; (fig: situation) to deteriorate ▷ vt to rot; (fig: corrompre: personne) to corrupt; (: gâter: enfant) to spoil thoroughly

pourriture [puʀityʀ] nf rot

pourrons etc [puʀɔ̃] vb voir **pouvoir**

poursuite [puʀsɥit] nf pursuit, chase; **poursuites** nfpl (Jur) legal proceedings; **(course)** ~ track race; (fig) chase

poursuivre [puʀsɥivʀ] vt to pursue, chase (after); (relancer) to hound, harry; (obséder) to haunt; (Jur) to bring proceedings against, prosecute; (: au civil) to sue; (but) to strive towards; (voyage, études) to carry on with, continue ▷ vi to carry on, go on; **se poursuivre** vi to go on, continue

pourtant [puʀtɑ̃] adv yet; **mais** ~ but nevertheless, but even so; **c'est** ~ **facile** (and) yet it's easy

pourtour [puʀtuʀ] nm perimeter

pourvoir [puʀvwaʀ] nm (Comm) supply ▷ vt: ~ **qch/qn de** to equip sth/sb with ▷ vi: ~ **à** to provide for; (emploi) to fill; **se pourvoir** vi (Jur): **se** ~ **en cassation** to take one's case to the Court of Appeal

pourvoyeur, -euse [puʀvwajœʀ, -øz] nm/f supplier

pourvu, e [puʀvy] pp de **pourvoir** ▷ adj: ~ **de** equipped with; ~ **que** conj (si) provided that, so long as; (espérons que) let's hope (that)

pousse [pus] nf growth; (bourgeon) shoot

poussé, e [puse] adj sophisticated, advanced; (moteur) souped-up

poussée [puse] nf thrust; (coup) push; (Méd: d'acné) eruption; (fig: prix) upsurge

pousser [puse] vt to push; (acculer) to drive sb to do sth; (moteur, voiture) to drive hard; (émettre: cri etc) to give; (stimuler: élève) to urge on; to drive hard; (poursuivre: études, discussion) to carry on; (inciter): ~ **qn à faire qch** (inciter) to urge ou press sb to do sth; (acculer) ▷ vi to push; (croître) to grow; (aller): ~ **plus loin** to push on a bit further; **se pousser** vi to move over; **faire ~** (plante) to grow; **~ le dévouement** etc **jusqu'à ...** to take devotion etc as far as ...

poussette [puset] nf (voiture d'enfant) pushchair (Brit), stroller (US)

poussière [pusjɛʀ] nf dust; (grain) speck of dust; **et des ~s** (fig) and a bit; **~ de charbon** coaldust

poussiéreux, -euse [pusjeʀø, -øz] adj dusty

poussin [pusɛ̃] nm chick

poutre [putʀ] nf beam; (en fer, ciment armé) girder; **~s apparentes** exposed beams

⊙ MOT-CLÉ

pouvoir [puvwaʀ] nm power; (Pol: dirigeants): **le pouvoir** those in power; **les pouvoirs publics** the authorities; **avoir pouvoir de faire** (autorisation) to have (the) authority to do; (droit) to have the right to do; **pouvoir absolu** absolute power; **pouvoir absorbant** absorbency; **pouvoir d'achat** purchasing power; **pouvoir calorifique** calorific value ▷ vb semi-aux 1 (être en état de) can, be able to; **je ne peux pas le réparer** I can't ou I am not able to repair it; **déçu de ne pas pouvoir le faire** disappointed not to be able to do it 2 (avoir la permission) can, may, be allowed to; **vous pouvez aller au cinéma** you can ou may go to the pictures 3 (probabilité, hypothèse) may, might, could; **il a pu avoir un accident** he may ou might ou could have had an accident; **il aurait pu le dire!** he might ou could have said (so)! 4 (expressions): **tu ne peux pas savoir!** you have no idea!; **tu peux le dire!** you can say that again! ▷ vb impers may, might, could; **il peut arriver que** it may ou might ou could happen that; **il pourrait pleuvoir** it might rain ▷ vt 1 can, be able to; **j'ai fait tout ce que j'ai pu** I did all I could; **je n'en peux plus** (épuisé) I'm exhausted; (à bout) I can't take any more 2 (vb+adj ou adv comparatif): **je me porte ou ne peux mieux** I'm absolutely fine, I couldn't be better; **elle est on ne peut plus gentille** she couldn't be nicer, she's as nice as can be **se pouvoir** vi: **il se peut que** it may ou might be that; **cela se pourrait** that's quite possible

prairie [pʀeʀi] nf meadow

praline [pʀalin] nf (bonbon) sugared almond; (au chocolat) praline

praticable [pʀatikabl] adj (route etc) passable, practicable; (projet) practicable

pratiquant, e [pʀatikã, -ãt] adj practising (Brit), practicing (US) ▷ nm/f (regular) churchgoer

pratique [pʀatik] nf practice ▷ adj practical; (commode: horaire etc) convenient; (: outil)

handy, useful; **dans la ~** in (actual) practice; **mettre en ~** to put into practice

pratiquement [pʀatikmã] adv (dans la pratique) in practice; (pour ainsi dire) practically, virtually

pratiquer [pʀatike] vt to practise (Brit), practice (US); (l'équitation, la pêche) to go in for; (le golf, football) to play; (appliquer: méthode, théorie) to apply; (intervention, opération) to carry out; (ouverture, abri) to make ▷ vi (Rel) to be a churchgoer

pré [pʀe] nm meadow

préalable [pʀealabl] adj preliminary; **condition ~ (de)** precondition (for), prerequisite (for); **sans avis ~** without prior ou previous notice; **au ~** first, beforehand

préambule [pʀeãbyl] nm preamble; (fig) prelude; **sans ~** straight away

préau, x [pʀeo] nm (d'une cour d'école) covered playground; (d'un monastère, d'une prison) inner courtyard

préavis [pʀeavi] nm notice; **~ de congé** notice; **communication avec ~** (Tél) personal ou person-to-person call

précaution [pʀekosjɔ̃] nf precaution; **avec ~** cautiously; **prendre des** ou **ses ~s** to take precautions; **par ~** as a precaution; **pour plus de ~** to be on the safe side; **~s oratoires** carefully phrased remarks

précédemment [pʀesedamã] adv before, previously

précédent, e [pʀesedã, -ãt] adj previous ▷ nm precedent; **sans ~** unprecedented; **le jour ~** the day before, the previous day

précéder [pʀesede] vt to precede; (marcher ou rouler devant) to be in front of; (arriver avant) to get ahead of

précepteur, -trice [pʀeseptœʀ, -tʀis] nm/f (private) tutor

prêcher [pʀeʃe] vt, vi to preach

précieux, -euse [pʀesjø, -øz] adj precious; (collaborateur, conseils) invaluable; (style, écrivain) précieux, precious

précipice [pʀesipis] nm drop, chasm; (fig) abyss; **au bord du ~** at the edge of the precipice

précipitamment [pʀesipitamã] adv hurriedly, hastily

précipitation [pʀesipitasjɔ̃] nf (hâte) haste; **~s (atmosphériques)** precipitation sg

précipité, e [pʀesipite] adj (respiration) fast; (pas) hurried; (départ) hasty

précipiter [pʀesipite] vt (faire tomber): **~ qn/ qch du haut de** to throw ou hurl sb/sth off ou from; (hâter: marche) to quicken; (: départ) to hasten; **se précipiter** vi (événements) to move faster; (respiration) to speed up; **se ~ sur/vers** to rush at/towards; **se ~ au-devant de qn** to throw o.s. before sb

précis, e [pʀesi, -iz] adj precise; (tir, mesures) accurate, precise; **à 4 heures ~es** at 4 o'clock sharp ▷ nm handbook

précisément [presizemã] *adv* precisely; **ma vie n'est pas ~ distrayante** my life is not exactly entertaining

préciser [presize] *vt* (*expliquer*) to be more specific about, clarify; (*spécifier*) to state, specify; **se préciser** *vi* to become clear(er)

précision [presizjõ] *nf* precision; accuracy; (*détail*) point *ou* detail (*made clear or to be clarified*); **précisions** *nfpl* further details

précoce [prekɔs] *adj* early; (*enfant*) precocious; (*calvitie*) premature

préconçu, e [prekõsy] *adj* preconceived

préconiser [prekɔnize] *vt* to advocate

prédécesseur [predesesœr] *nm* predecessor

prédilection [predilɛksjõ] *nf*: **avoir une ~ pour** to be partial to; **de ~ favourite** (*Brit*), favorite (*US*)

prédire [predir] *vt* to predict

prédominer [predɔmine] *vi* to predominate; (*avis*) to prevail

préface [prefas] *nf* preface

préfecture [prefektyr] *nf* prefecture; *see note*; **~ de police** police headquarters

> ● **PRÉFECTURE**
> ●
> ● The *préfecture* is the administrative
> ● headquarters of the "département". The
> ● "préfet", a senior civil servant appointed
> ● by the government, is responsible for
> ● putting government policy into practice.
> ● France's 27 regions, each comprising a
> ● number of "départements", also have a
> ● "préfet de région".

préférable [preferabl] *adj* preferable

préféré, e [prefere] *adj, nm/f* favourite (*Brit*), favorite (*US*)

préférence [preferãs] *nf* preference; **de ~** preferably; **de** *ou* **par ~ à** in preference to, rather than; **donner la ~ à qn** to give preference to sb; **par ordre de ~** in order of preference; **obtenir la ~ sur** to have preference over

préférer [prefere] *vt*: **~ qn/qch (à)** to prefer sb/sth (to), like sb/sth better (than); **~ faire** to prefer to do; **je préférerais du thé** I would rather have tea, I'd prefer tea

préfet [prefɛ] *nm* prefect; **~ de police** ≈ Chief Constable (*Brit*), ≈ Police Commissioner (*US*)

préhistorique [preistɔrik] *adj* prehistoric

préjudice [preʒydis] *nm* (*matériel*) loss; (*moral*) harm *no pl*; **porter ~ à** to harm, be detrimental to; **au ~ de** at the expense of

préjugé [preʒyʒe] *nm* prejudice; **avoir un ~ contre** to be prejudiced against; **bénéficier d'un ~ favorable** to be viewed favourably

préjuger [preʒyʒe]: **~ de** *vt* to prejudge

prélasser [prelase]: **se prélasser** *vi* to lounge

prélèvement [prelɛvmã] *nm* (*montant*) deduction; withdrawal; **faire un ~ de sang** to take a blood sample

prélever [prelve] *vt* (*échantillon*) to take; **~ (sur)** (*argent*) to deduct (from); (: *sur son compte*) to withdraw (from)

prématuré, e [prematyre] *adj* premature; (*retraite*) early ▷ *nm* premature baby

premier, -ière [prəmje, -jɛr] *adj* first; (*rang*) front; (*branche, marche, grade*) bottom; (*fig: fondamental*) basic; prime; (*en importance*) first, foremost ▷ *nm* (*premier étage*) first (*Brit*) *ou* second (*US*) floor ▷ *nf* (*Auto*) first (gear); (*Rail, Aviat etc*) first class; (*Scol*) year 12 (*Brit*), eleventh grade (*US*); (*Théât*) first night; (*Ciné*) première; (*exploit*) first; **au ~ abord** at first sight; **au** *ou* **du ~ coup** at the first attempt *ou* go; **de ~ ordre** first-class, first-rate; **de première qualité, de ~ choix** best *ou* top quality; **de première importance** of the highest importance; **de première nécessité** absolutely essential; **le ~ venu** the first person to come along; **jeune ~** leading man; **le ~ de l'an** New Year's Day; **enfant du ~ lit** child of a first marriage; **en ~ lieu** in the first place; **~ âge** (*d'un enfant*) the first three months (of life); **P~ Ministre** Prime Minister

premièrement [prəmjɛrmã] *adv* firstly

prémonition [premɔnisjõ] *nf* premonition

prémunir [premynir]: **se prémunir** *vi*: **se ~ contre** to protect o.s. from, guard against

prenant, e [prənã, -ãt] *vb voir* **prendre** ▷ *adj* absorbing, engrossing

prénatal, e [prenatal] *adj* (*Méd*) antenatal; (*allocation*) maternity *cpd*

prendre [prãdr] *vt* to take; (*repas*) to have; (*aller chercher*) to get, fetch; (*se procurer*) to get; (*réserver: place*) to book; (*acquérir: du poids, de la valeur*) to put on, gain; (*malfaiteur, poisson*) to catch; (*passager*) to pick up; (*personnel, aussi: couleur, goût*) to take on; (*locataire*) to take in; (*traiter: enfant, problème*) to handle; (*voix, ton*) to put on; (*prélever: pourcentage, argent*) to take off; (*ôter*): **~ qch à** to take sth from; (*coincer*): **se les doigts dans** to get one's fingers caught in ▷ *vi* (*liquide, ciment*) to set; (*greffe, vaccin*) to take; (*mensonge*) to be successful; (*feu: foyer*) to go; (: *incendie*) to start; (*allumette*) to light; (*se diriger*): **~ à gauche** to turn (to the) left; **~ froid** to catch cold; **~ son origine** *ou* **sa source** (*mot, rivière*) to have its source; **~ qn pour** to take sb for; **se ~ pour** to think one is; **~ sur soi de faire qch** to take it upon o.s. to do sth; **~ qn en sympathie/horreur** to get to like/ loathe sb; **à tout ~** all things considered; **s'en ~ à** (*agresser*) to set about; (*passer sa colère sur*) to take it out on; (*critiquer*) to attack; (*remettre en question*) to challenge; **se ~ d'amitié/ d'affection pour** to befriend/become fond of; **s'y ~** (*procéder*) to set about it; **s'y ~ à l'avance** to see to it in advance; **s'y ~ à deux fois** to try twice, make two attempts

preneur [prənœr] *nm*: **être ~** to be willing to buy; **trouver ~** to find a buyer

preniez [prənje] *vb voir* **prendre**

P

prenne *etc* [pʀɛn] *vb voir* **prendre**
prénom [pʀenɔ̃] *nm* first name
préoccupation [pʀeɔkypasjɔ̃] *nf* (*souci*) concern; (*idée fixe*) preoccupation
préoccuper [pʀeɔkype] *vt* (*tourmenter, tracasser*) to concern; (*absorber, obséder*) to preoccupy; **se ~ de qch** to be concerned about sth; to show concern about sth
préparatifs [pʀepaʀatif] *nmpl* preparations
préparation [pʀepaʀasjɔ̃] *nf* preparation; (*Scol*) piece of homework
préparer [pʀepaʀe] *vt* to prepare; (*café, repas*) to make; (*examen*) to prepare for; (*voyage, entreprise*) to plan; **se préparer** *vi* (*orage, tragédie*) to brew, be in the air; **se ~ (à qch/à faire)** to prepare (o.s.) ou get ready (for sth/to do); **~ qch à qn** (*surprise etc*) to have sth in store for sb; **~ qn à qch** (*nouvelle etc*) to prepare sb for sth
prépondérant, e [pʀepɔ̃deʀɑ̃, -ɑ̃t] *adj* major, dominating; **voix ~e** casting vote
préposé, e [pʀepoze] *adj*: **~ à** in charge of ▷ *nm/f* (*gén: employé*) employee; (*Admin: facteur*) postman/woman (*Brit*), mailman/woman (*US*); (*de la douane etc*) official; (*de vestiaire*) attendant
préposition [pʀepozisjɔ̃] *nf* preposition
près [pʀɛ] *adv* near, close; **~ de** *prép* near (to), close to; (*environ*) nearly, almost; **~ d'ici** near here; **de ~** *adv* closely; **à cinq kg ~** to within about five kg; **à cela ~ que** apart from the fact that; **je ne suis pas ~ de lui pardonner** I'm nowhere near ready to forgive him; **on n'est pas à un jour ~** one day (either way) won't make much difference, we're not going to quibble over the odd day; **il n'est pas à 10 minutes ~** he can spare 10 minutes
présage [pʀezaʒ] *nm* omen
présager [pʀezaʒe] *vt* (*prévoir*) to foresee; (*annoncer*) to portend
presbyte [pʀɛsbit] *adj* long-sighted (*Brit*), far-sighted (*US*)
presbytère [pʀɛsbitɛʀ] *nm* presbytery
prescription [pʀɛskʀipsjɔ̃] *nf* (*instruction*) order, instruction; (*Méd, Jur*) prescription
prescrire [pʀɛskʀiʀ] *vt* to prescribe; **se prescrire** *vi* (*Jur*) to lapse
présence [pʀezɑ̃s] *nf* presence; (*au bureau etc*) attendance; **en ~** face to face; **en ~ de** in (the) presence of; (*fig*) in the face of; **faire acte de ~** to put in a token appearance; **~ d'esprit** presence of mind
présent, e [pʀezɑ̃, -ɑ̃t] *adj, nm* present; (*Admin, Comm*): **la ~e lettre/loi** this letter/law ▷ *nm/f*: **les ~s** (*personnes*) those present ▷ *nf* (*Comm: lettre*): **la ~e** this letter; **à ~** now, at present; **dès à ~** here and now; **jusqu'à ~** up till now, until now; **à ~ que** now that
présentation [pʀezɑ̃tasjɔ̃] *nf* presentation; (*de nouveau venu*) introduction; (*allure*) appearance; **faire les ~s** to do the introductions

présenter [pʀezɑ̃te] *vt* to present; (*invité, candidat*) to introduce; (*félicitations, condoléances*) to offer; (*montrer: billet, pièce d'identité*) to show, produce; (*faire inscrire: candidat*) to put forward; (*soumettre*) to submit; **~ qn à** to introduce sb to ▷ *vi*: **~ mal/bien** to have an unattractive/a pleasing appearance; **se présenter** *vi* (*sur convocation*) to report, come; (*se faire connaître*) to come forward; (*à une élection*) to stand; (*occasion*) to arise; **se ~ à un examen** to sit an exam; **se ~ bien/mal** to look good/not too good; **je vous présente Nadine** this is Nadine
préservatif [pʀezɛʀvatif] *nm* condom, sheath
préserver [pʀezɛʀve] *vt*: **~ de** (*protéger*) to protect from; (*sauver*) to save from
président [pʀezidɑ̃] *nm* (*Pol*) president; (*d'une assemblée, Comm*) chairman; **~ directeur général (PDG)** chairman and managing director (*Brit*), chairman and president (*US*); **~ du jury** (*Jur*) foreman of the jury; (*d'examen*) chief examiner
présidentiel, le [pʀezidɑ̃sjɛl] *adj* presidential; **présidentielles** *nfpl* presidential election(s)
présider [pʀezide] *vt* to preside over; (*dîner*) to be the guest of honour (*Brit*) ou honor (*US*) at; **~ à** *vt* to direct; to govern
présomptueux, -euse [pʀezɔ̃ptɥø, -øz] *adj* presumptuous
presque [pʀɛsk] *adv* almost, nearly; **~ rien** hardly anything; **~ pas** hardly (at all); **~ pas de** hardly any; **personne, ou ~** next to nobody, hardly anyone; **la ~ totalité (de)** almost ou nearly all
presqu'île [pʀɛskil] *nf* peninsula
pressant, e [pʀɛsɑ̃, -ɑ̃t] *adj* urgent; (*personne*) insistent; **se faire ~** to become insistent
presse [pʀɛs] *nf* press; (*affluence*): **heures de ~** busy times; **sous ~** gone to press; **mettre sous ~** to send to press; **avoir une bonne/mauvaise ~** to have a good/bad press; **~ féminine** women's magazines *pl*; **~ d'information** quality newspapers *pl*
pressé, e [pʀese] *adj* in a hurry; (*air*) hurried; (*besogne*) urgent ▷ *nm*: **aller au plus ~** to see to first things first; **être ~ de faire qch** to be in a hurry to do sth; **orange ~e** freshly squeezed orange juice
pressentiment [pʀesɑ̃timɑ̃] *nm* foreboding, premonition
pressentir [pʀesɑ̃tiʀ] *vt* to sense; (*prendre contact avec*) to approach
presse-papiers [pʀɛspapje] *nm inv* paperweight
presser [pʀese] *vt* (*fruit, éponge*) to squeeze; (*interrupteur, bouton*) to press, push; (*allure, affaire*) to speed up; (*débiteur etc*) to press; (*inciter*): **~ qn de faire** to urge ou press sb to do ▷ *vi* to be urgent; **se presser** *vi* (*se hâter*) to hurry (up); (*se grouper*) to crowd; **rien ne presse**

there's no hurry; **se ~ contre qn** to squeeze up against sb; **le temps presse** there's not much time; **~ le pas** to quicken one's step; **~ qn entre ses bras** to squeeze sb tight

pressing [pʀesiŋ] nm (repassage) steam-pressing; (magasin) dry-cleaner's

pression [pʀesjɔ̃] nf pressure; (bouton) press stud (Brit), snap fastener; (fam: bière) draught beer; **faire ~ sur** to put pressure on; **sous ~** pressurized, under pressure; (fig) keyed up; **~ artérielle** blood pressure

prestance [pʀestɑ̃s] nf presence, imposing bearing

prestataire [pʀestatɛʀ] nm/f person receiving benefits; (Comm): **~ de services** provider of services

prestation [pʀestasjɔ̃] nf (allocation) benefit; (d'une assurance) cover no pl; (d'une entreprise) service provided; (d'un joueur, artiste) performance; **~ de serment** taking the oath; **~ de service** provision of a service; **~s familiales** = child benefit

prestidigitateur, -trice [pʀestidiʒitatœʀ, -tʀis] nm/f conjurer

prestige [pʀestiʒ] nm prestige

prestigieux, -euse [pʀestiʒjø, -øz] adj prestigious

présumer [pʀezyme] vt: **~ que** to presume ou assume that; **~ de** to overrate; **~ qn coupable** to presume sb guilty

prêt, e [pʀɛ, pʀɛt] adj ready ▷ nm lending no pl; (somme prêtée) loan; **~ à faire** ready to do; **~ à tout** ready for anything; **~ sur gages** pawnbroking no pl

prêt-à-porter (pl prêts-à-porter) [pʀɛtapɔʀte] nm ready-to-wear ou off-the-peg (Brit) clothes pl

prétendre [pʀetɑ̃dʀ] vt (affirmer): **~ que** to claim that; (avoir l'intention de): **~ faire qch** to mean ou intend to do sth; **~ à** vt (droit, titre) to lay claim to

prétendu, e [pʀetɑ̃dy] adj (supposé) so-called

prétentieux, -euse [pʀetɑ̃sjø, -øz] adj pretentious

prétention [pʀetɑ̃sjɔ̃] nf pretentiousness; (exigence, ambition) claim; **sans ~** unpretentious

prêter [pʀete] vt (livres, argent): **~ qch (à)** to lend sth (to); (supposer): **~ à qn** (caractère, propos) to attribute to sb ▷ vi: **se prêter** (tissu, cuir) to give; **~ à** (commentaires etc) to be open to, give rise to; **se ~ à** to lend o.s. (ou itself) to; (manigances etc) to go along with; **~ assistance à** to give help to; **~ attention** to pay attention; **~ serment** to take the oath; **~ l'oreille** to listen

prétexte [pʀetɛkst] nm pretext, excuse; **sous aucun ~** on no account; **sous (le) ~ que/de** on the pretext that/of

prétexter [pʀetɛkste] vt to give as a pretext ou an excuse

prêtre [pʀɛtʀ] nm priest

preuve [pʀœv] nf proof; (indice) proof, evidence no pl; **jusqu'à ~ du contraire** until proved otherwise; **faire ~ de** to show; **faire ses ~s** to prove o.s. (ou itself); **~ matérielle** material evidence

prévaloir [pʀevalwaʀ] vi to prevail; **se ~ de** vt to take advantage of; (tirer vanité de) to pride o.s. on

prévenant, e [pʀevnɑ̃, -ɑ̃t] adj thoughtful, kind

prévenir [pʀevniʀ] vt (éviter: catastrophe etc) to avoid, prevent; (anticiper: désirs, besoins) to anticipate; **~ qn (de)** (avertir) to warn sb (about); (informer) to tell ou inform sb (about); **~ qn contre** (influencer) to prejudice sb against

préventif, -ive [pʀevɑ̃tif, -iv] adj preventive

prévention [pʀevɑ̃sjɔ̃] nf prevention; (préjugé) prejudice; (Jur) custody, detention; **~ routière** road safety

prévenu, e [pʀevny] nm/f (Jur) defendant, accused

prévision [pʀevizjɔ̃] nf: **~s** predictions; (météorologiques, économiques) forecast sg; **en ~ de** in anticipation of; **~s météorologiques** ou **du temps** weather forecast sg

prévoir [pʀevwaʀ] vt (deviner) to foresee; (s'attendre à) to expect, reckon on; (prévenir) to anticipate; (organiser: voyage etc) to plan; (préparer, réserver) to allow; **prévu pour quatre personnes** designed for four people; **prévu pour 10 h** scheduled for 10 o'clock; **comme prévu** as planned

prévoyant, e [pʀevwajɑ̃, -ɑ̃t] vb voir **prévoir** ▷ adj gifted with (ou showing) foresight, far-sighted

prévu, e [pʀevy] pp de **prévoir**

prier [pʀije] vi to pray ▷ vt (Dieu) to pray to; (implorer) to beg; (demander): **~ qn de faire** to ask sb to do; (inviter): **~ qn à dîner** to invite sb to dinner; **se faire ~** to need coaxing ou persuading; **je vous en prie** (allez-y) please do; (de rien) don't mention it; **je vous prie de faire** please (would you) do

prière [pʀijɛʀ] nf prayer; (demande instante) plea, entreaty; **"~ de faire ..."** "please do ..."

primaire [pʀimɛʀ] adj primary; (péj: personne) simple-minded; (: idées) simplistic ▷ nm (Scol) primary education

prime [pʀim] nf (bonification) bonus; (subside) allowance; (Comm: cadeau) free gift; (Assurances, Bourse) premium ▷ adj: **de ~ abord** at first glance; **~ de risque** danger money no pl; **~ de transport** travel allowance

primer [pʀime] vt (l'emporter sur) to prevail over; (récompenser) to award a prize to ▷ vi to dominate, prevail

primeur [pʀimœʀ] nf: **avoir la ~ de** to be the first to hear (ou see etc); **primeurs** nfpl (fruits, légumes) early fruits and vegetables; **marchand de ~** greengrocer (Brit), produce dealer (US)

primevère [primvɛʀ] nf primrose

primitif, -ive [primitif, -iv] adj primitive; (*originel*) original ▷ nm/f primitive

primordial, e, -aux [primɔʀdjal, -o] adj essential, primordial

prince [pʀɛ̃s] nm prince; ~ **charmant** Prince Charming; ~ **de Galles** nm inv (*tissu*) check cloth; ~ **héritier** crown prince

princesse [pʀɛ̃sɛs] nf princess

principal, e, -aux [pʀɛ̃sipal, -o] adj principal, main ▷ nm (*Scol*) head (teacher) (*Brit*), principal (*US*); (*essentiel*) main thing ▷ nf (*Ling*): ~e main clause

principe [pʀɛ̃sip] nm principle; **partir du** ~ **que** to work on the principle ou assumption that; **pour le** ~ on principle, for the sake of it; **de** ~ adj (*hostilité*) automatic; (*accord*) in principle; **par** ~ on principle; **en** ~ (*habituellement*) as a rule; (*théoriquement*) in principle

printemps [pʀɛ̃tɑ̃] nm spring; **au** ~ in spring

priorité [pʀijɔʀite] nf priority; (*Auto*): **avoir la** ~ **(sur)** to have right of way (over); ~ **à droite** right of way to vehicles coming from the right; **en** ~ as a (matter of) priority

pris, e [pʀi, pʀiz] pp de **prendre** ▷ adj (*place*) taken; (*billets*) sold; (*journée, mains*) full; (*personne*) busy; (*crème, ciment*) set; (*Méd: enflammé*): **avoir le nez/la gorge ~(e)** to have a stuffy nose/a bad throat; (*saisi*): **être ~ de peur/de fatigue/de panique** to be stricken with fear/overcome with fatigue/panic-stricken

prise [pʀiz] nf (*d'une ville*) capture; (*Pêche, Chasse*) catch; (*de judo ou catch, point d'appui ou pour empoigner*) hold; (*Élec: fiche*) plug; (*: femelle*) socket; (*: au mur*) point; **en** ~ (*Auto*) in gear; **être aux ~s avec** to be grappling with; to be battling with; **lâcher** ~ to let go; **donner** ~ **à** (*fig*) to give rise to; **avoir** ~ **sur qn** to have a hold over sb; ~ **en charge** (*taxe*) pick-up charge; (*par la sécurité sociale*) *undertaking to reimburse costs*; ~ **de contact** initial meeting, first contact; ~ **de courant** power point; ~ **d'eau** water (supply) point; tap; ~ **multiple** adaptor; ~ **d'otages** hostage-taking; ~ **à partie** (*Jur*) action against a judge; ~ **péritel** SCART socket; ~ **de sang** blood test; ~ **de son** sound recording; ~ **de tabac** pinch of snuff; ~ **de terre** earth; ~ **de vue** (*photo*) shot; (*action*): ~ **de vue(s)** filming, shooting

priser [pʀize] vt (*tabac, héroïne*) to take; (*estimer*) to prize, value ▷ vi to take snuff

prison [pʀizɔ̃] nf prison; **aller/être en** ~ to go/be in prison ou jail; **faire de la** ~ to serve time; **être condamné à cinq ans de** ~ to be sentenced to five years' imprisonment ou five years in prison

prisonnier, -ière [pʀizɔnje, -jɛʀ] nm/f prisoner ▷ adj captive; **faire qn** ~ to take sb prisoner

prit [pʀi] vb voir **prendre**

privé, e [pʀive] adj private; (*en punition*): **tu es** ~ **de télé!** no TV for you!; (*dépourvu*): ~ **de** without, lacking ▷ nm (*Comm*) private sector; **en** ~, **dans le** ~ in private

priver [pʀive] vt: ~ **qn de** to deprive sb of; **se** ~ **de** to go ou do without; **ne pas se** ~ **de faire** not to refrain from doing

privilège [pʀivilɛʒ] nm privilege

prix [pʀi] nm (*valeur*) price; (*récompense, Scol*) prize; **mettre à** ~ to set a reserve (*Brit*) ou an upset (*US*) price on; **au** ~ **fort** at a very high price; **acheter qch à** ~ **d'or** to pay a (small) fortune for sth; **hors de** ~ exorbitantly priced; **à aucun** ~ not at any price; **à tout** ~ at all costs; **grand** ~ (*Sport*) Grand Prix; ~ **d'achat/de vente/de revient** purchasing/ selling/cost price; ~ **conseillé** manufacturer's recommended price (MRP)

probable [pʀɔbabl] adj likely, probable

probablement [pʀɔbabləmɑ̃] adv probably

probant, e [pʀɔbɑ̃, -ɑ̃t] adj convincing

problème [pʀɔblɛm] nm problem

procédé [pʀɔsede] nm (*méthode*) process; (*comportement*) behaviour no pl (*Brit*), behavior no pl (*US*)

procéder [pʀɔsede] vi to proceed; (*moralement*) to behave; ~ **à** vt to carry out

procès [pʀɔsɛ] nm (*Jur*) trial; (*: poursuites*) proceedings pl; **être en** ~ **avec** to be involved in a lawsuit with; **faire le** ~ **de qn/qch** (*fig*) to put sb/sth on trial; **sans autre forme de** ~ without further ado

processus [pʀɔsesys] nm process

procès-verbal, -aux [pʀɔsɛvɛʀbal, -o] nm (*constat*) statement; (*aussi: PV*): **avoir un** ~ to get a parking ticket; to be booked; (*de réunion*) minutes pl

prochain, e [pʀɔʃɛ̃, -ɛn] adj next; (*proche: départ, arrivée*) impending; near ▷ nm fellow man; **la ~e fois/semaine ~e** next time/week; **à la ~e!** (*fam*): **à la ~e fois** see you!, till the next time!; **un ~ jour** (some day) soon

prochainement [pʀɔʃɛnmɑ̃] adv soon, shortly

proche [pʀɔʃ] adj nearby; (*dans le temps*) imminent; close at hand; (*parent, ami*) close; **proches** nmpl (*parents*) close relatives, next of kin; (*amis*): **l'un de ses ~s** one of those close to him (ou her); **être** ~ (**de**) to be near, be close (to); **de** ~ **en** ~ gradually

proclamer [pʀɔklame] vt to proclaim; (*résultat d'un examen*) to announce

procuration [pʀɔkyʀasjɔ̃] nf proxy; power of attorney; **voter par** ~ to vote by proxy

procurer [pʀɔkyʀe] vt (*fournir*): ~ **qch à qn** to get ou obtain sth for sb; (*causer: plaisir etc*): ~ **qch à qn** to bring ou give sb sth; **se procurer** vt to get

procureur [pʀɔkyʀœʀ] nm public prosecutor; ~ **général** public prosecutor (in appeal court)

prodige [pʀɔdiʒ] nm (*miracle, merveille*) marvel, wonder; (*personne*) prodigy

prodiguer [pʀɔdige] vt (argent, biens) to be lavish with; (soins, attentions): **~ qch à qn** to lavish sth on sb

producteur, -trice [pʀɔdyktœʀ, -tʀis] adj: **~ de blé** wheat-producing; (Ciné): **société productrice** film ou movie company ▷ nm/f producer

productif, -ive [pʀɔdyktif, -iv] adj productive

production [pʀɔdyksjɔ̃] nf (gén) production; (rendement) output; (produits) products pl, goods pl; (œuvres): **la ~ dramatique du XVIIe siècle** the plays of the 17th century

productivité [pʀɔdyktivite] nf productivity

produire [pʀɔdɥiʀ] vt, vi to produce; **se produire** vi (acteur) to perform, appear; (événement) to happen, occur

produit, e [pʀɔdɥi, -it] pp de **produire** ▷ nm (gén) product; **~ chimique** chemical; **~ d'entretien** cleaning product; **~ national brut (PNB)** gross national product (GNP); **~ net** net profit; **~ pour la vaisselle** washing-up (Brit) ou dish-washing (US) liquid; **~ des ventes** income from sales; **~s agricoles** farm produce sg; **~s alimentaires** foodstuffs; **~s de beauté** beauty products, cosmetics

prof [pʀɔf] nm (fam: = professeur) teacher; professor; lecturer

profane [pʀɔfan] adj (Rel) secular; (ignorant, non initié) uninitiated ▷ nm/f layman

proférer [pʀɔfeʀe] vt to utter

professeur, e [pʀɔfesœʀ] nm/f teacher; (titulaire d'une chaire) professor; **~ (de faculté)** (university) lecturer

profession [pʀɔfesjɔ̃] nf (libérale) profession; (gén) occupation; **faire ~ de** (opinion, religion) to profess; **de ~** by profession; **"sans ~"** "unemployed"; (femme mariée) "housewife"

professionnel, le [pʀɔfesjɔnɛl] adj professional ▷ nm/f professional; (ouvrier qualifié) skilled worker

profil [pʀɔfil] nm profile; (d'une voiture) line, contour; **de ~** in profile

profit [pʀɔfi] nm (avantage) benefit, advantage; (Comm, Finance) profit; **au ~ de** in aid of; **tirer** ou **retirer ~ de** to profit from; **mettre à ~** to take advantage of; to turn to good account; **~s et pertes** (Comm) profit and loss(es)

profitable [pʀɔfitabl] adj (utile) beneficial; (lucratif) profitable

profiter [pʀɔfite] vi: **~ de** (situation, occasion) to take advantage of; (vacances, jeunesse etc) to make the most of; **~ de ce que ...** to take advantage of the fact that ...; **~ à** to be of benefit to, benefit; to be profitable to

profond, e [pʀɔfɔ̃, -ɔ̃d] adj deep; (méditation, mépris) profound; **peu ~** (eau, vallée, puits) shallow; (coupure) superficial; **au plus ~ de** in the depths of, at the (very) bottom of; **la France ~e** the heartlands of France

profondément [pʀɔfɔ̃demɑ̃] adv deeply; profoundly; **il dort ~** he is sound asleep

profondeur [pʀɔfɔ̃dœʀ] nf depth; **l'eau a quelle ~?** how deep is the water?

progéniture [pʀɔʒenityʀ] nf offspring inv

programme [pʀɔgʀam] nm programme (Brit), program (US); (TV, Radio) program(me)s pl; (Scol) syllabus, curriculum; (Inform) program; **au ~ de ce soir** (TV) among tonight's program(me)s

programmer [pʀɔgʀame] vt (TV, Radio) to put on, show; (organiser, prévoir: émission) to schedule; (Inform) to program

programmeur, -euse [pʀɔgʀamœʀ, -øz] nm/f (computer) programmer

progrès [pʀɔgʀɛ] nm progress no pl; **faire des/ être en ~** to make/be making progress

progresser [pʀɔgʀese] vi to progress; (troupes etc) to make headway ou progress

progressif, -ive [pʀɔgʀesif, -iv] adj progressive

prohiber [pʀɔibe] vt to prohibit, ban

proie [pʀwa] nf prey no pl; **être la ~ de** to fall prey to; **être en ~ à** (doutes, sentiment) to be prey to; (douleur, mal) to be suffering

projecteur [pʀɔʒɛktœʀ] nm projector; (de théâtre, cirque) spotlight

projectile [pʀɔʒɛktil] nm missile; (d'arme) projectile, bullet (ou shell etc)

projection [pʀɔʒɛksjɔ̃] nf projection; (séance) showing; **conférence avec ~s** lecture with slides (ou a film)

projet [pʀɔʒɛ] nm plan; (ébauche) draft; **faire des ~s** to make plans; **~ de loi** bill

projeter [pʀɔʒte] vt (envisager) to plan; (film, photos) to project; (passer) to show; (ombre, lueur) to throw, cast, project; (jeter) to throw up (ou off ou out); **~ de faire qch** to plan to do sth

prolétaire [pʀɔletɛʀ] adj, nm/f proletarian

prolongement [pʀɔlɔ̃ʒmɑ̃] nm extension; **prolongements** nmpl (fig) repercussions, effects; **dans le ~ de** running on from

prolonger [pʀɔlɔ̃ʒe] vt (débat, séjour) to prolong; (délai, billet, rue) to extend; (chose) to be a continuation ou an extension of; **se prolonger** vi to go on

promenade [pʀɔmnad] nf walk (ou drive ou ride); **faire une ~** to go for a walk; **une ~ (à pied)/en voiture/à vélo** a walk/drive/ (bicycle) ride

promener [pʀɔmne] vt (personne, chien) to take out for a walk; (fig) to carry around; to trail round; (doigts, regard): **~ qch sur** to run sth over; **se promener** vi (à pied) to go for (ou be out for) a walk; (en voiture) to go for (ou be out for) a drive; (fig): **se ~ sur** to wander over

promesse [pʀɔmɛs] nf promise; **~ d'achat** commitment to buy

promettre [pʀɔmɛtʀ] vt to promise ▷ vi (récolte, arbre) to look promising; (enfant, musicien) to be promising; **se ~ de faire** to resolve ou mean to do; **~ à qn de faire** to promise sb that one will do

P

promiscuité [pʀɔmiskɥite] nf crowding; lack of privacy

promontoire [pʀɔmɔ̃twaʀ] nm headland

promoteur, -trice [pʀɔmɔtœʀ, -tʀis] nm/f (*instigateur*) instigator, promoter; ~ **(immobilier)** property developer (*Brit*), real estate promoter (*US*)

promotion [pʀɔmɔsjɔ̃] nf (*avancement*) promotion; (*Scol*) year (*Brit*), class; **en ~** (*Comm*) on promotion, on (special) offer

promouvoir [pʀɔmuvwaʀ] vt to promote

prompt, e [pʀɔ̃, pʀɔ̃t] adj swift, rapid; (*intervention, changement*) sudden; ~ **à faire qch** quick to do sth

prôner [pʀone] vt (*louer*) to laud, extol; (*préconiser*) to advocate, commend

pronom [pʀɔnɔ̃] nm pronoun

prononcer [pʀɔnɔ̃se] vt (*son, mot, jugement*) to pronounce; (*dire*) to utter; (*discours*) to deliver ▷ vi (*Jur*) to deliver ou give a verdict; ~ **bien/mal** to have good/poor pronunciation; **se prononcer** vi to be pronounced; **se ~ (sur)** (*se décider*) to reach a decision (on ou about), give a verdict (on); **se ~ contre** to come down against; **ça se prononce comment?** how do you pronounce this?

prononciation [pʀɔnɔ̃sjasjɔ̃] nf pronunciation

pronostic [pʀɔnɔstik] nm (*Méd*) prognosis; (*fig: aussi*: **~s**) forecast

propagande [pʀɔpagɑ̃d] nf propaganda; **faire de la ~ pour qch** to plug ou push sth

propager [pʀɔpaʒe] vt to spread; **se propager** vi to spread; (*Physique*) to be propagated

prophète [pʀɔfɛt], **prophétesse** [pʀɔfetɛs] nm/f prophet(ess)

prophétie [pʀɔfesi] nf prophecy

propice [pʀɔpis] adj favourable (*Brit*), favorable (*US*)

proportion [pʀɔpɔʀsjɔ̃] nf proportion; **il n'y a aucune ~ entre le prix demandé et le prix réel** the asking price bears no relation to the real price; **à ~ de** proportionally to, in proportion to; **en ~ (de)** in proportion (to); **hors de ~** out of proportion; **toute(s) ~(s) gardée(s)** making due allowance(s)

propos [pʀɔpo] nm (*paroles*) talk no pl, remark; (*intention, but*) intention, aim; (*sujet*): **à quel ~?** what about?; **à ~ de** about, regarding; **à tout ~** for no reason at all; **à ce ~** on that subject, in this connection; **à ~** adv by the way; (*opportunément*) (just) at the right moment; **hors de ~, mal à ~** adv at the wrong moment

proposer [pʀɔpoze] vt (*loi, motion*) to propose; (*suggérer*): ~ **qch (à qn)/de faire** to suggest sth (to sb)/doing, propose sth (to sb)/(to) do; (*offrir*): ~ **qch à qn/de faire** to offer sb sth/to do; (*candidat*) to nominate, put forward; **se ~ (pour faire)** to offer one's services (to do); **se ~ de faire** to intend ou propose to do

proposition [pʀɔpozisjɔ̃] nf suggestion; proposal; offer; (*Ling*) clause; **sur la ~ de** at the suggestion of; **~ de loi** private bill

propre [pʀɔpʀ] adj clean; (*net*) neat, tidy; (*qui ne salit pas: chien, chat*) house-trained; (: *enfant*) toilet-trained; (*fig: honnête*) honest; (*possessif*) own; (*sens*) literal; (*particulier*): ~ **à** peculiar to, characteristic of; (*approprié*): ~ **à** suitable ou appropriate for; (*de nature à*): ~ **à faire** likely to do, that will do ▷ nm: **recopier au ~** to make a fair copy of; (*particularité*): **le ~ de** the peculiarity of, the distinctive feature of; **au ~** (*Ling*) literally; **appartenir à qn en ~** to belong to sb (exclusively); ~ **à rien** nm/f (*péj*) good-for-nothing

proprement [pʀɔpʀəmɑ̃] adv (*avec propreté*) cleanly; neatly, tidily; **à ~ parler** strictly speaking; **le village ~ dit** the actual village, the village itself

propreté [pʀɔpʀəte] nf cleanliness, cleanness; neatness, tidiness

propriétaire [pʀɔpʀijetɛʀ] nm/f owner; (*d'hôtel etc*) proprietor(-tress), owner; (*pour le locataire*) landlord(-lady); ~ **(immobilier)** house-owner; householder; ~ **récoltant** grower; ~ **(terrien)** landowner

propriété [pʀɔpʀijete] nf (*droit*) ownership; (*objet, immeuble etc*) property gen no pl; (*villa*) residence, property; (*terres*) property gen no pl, land gen no pl; (*qualité, Chimie, Math*) property; (*correction*) appropriateness, suitability; ~ **artistique et littéraire** artistic and literary copyright; ~ **industrielle** patent rights pl

propulser [pʀɔpylse] vt (*missile*) to propel; (*projeter*) to hurl, fling

proroger [pʀɔʀɔʒe] vt to put back, defer; (*prolonger*) to extend; (*assemblée*) to adjourn, prorogue

proscrire [pʀɔskʀiʀ] vt (*bannir*) to banish; (*interdire*) to ban, prohibit

prose [pʀoz] nf prose (*style*)

prospecter [pʀɔspɛkte] vt to prospect; (*Comm*) to canvass

prospectus [pʀɔspɛktys] nm (*feuille*) leaflet; (*dépliant*) brochure, leaflet

prospère [pʀɔspɛʀ] adj prosperous; (*santé, entreprise*) thriving, flourishing

prospérer [pʀɔspeʀe] vi to thrive

prosterner [pʀɔstɛʀne]: **se prosterner** vi to bow low, prostrate o.s

prostituée [pʀɔstitɥe] nf prostitute

prostitution [pʀɔstitysjɔ̃] nf prostitution

protecteur, -trice [pʀɔtɛktœʀ, -tʀis] adj protective; (*air, ton: péj*) patronizing ▷ nm/f (*défenseur*) protector; (*des arts*) patron

protection [pʀɔtɛksjɔ̃] nf protection; (*d'un personnage influent: aide*) patronage; **écran de ~** protective screen; ~ **civile** state-financed civilian rescue service; ~ **maternelle et infantile (PMI)** social service concerned with child welfare

protéger [pʀɔteʒe] vt to protect; (*aider, patronner: personne, arts*) to be a patron of;

(: *carrière*) to further; **se ~ de/contre** to protect o.s. from

protège-slip [pʀɔtɛʒslip] *nm* panty liner

protéine [pʀɔtein] *nf* protein

protestant, e [pʀɔtɛstɑ̃, -ɑ̃t] *adj, nm/f* Protestant

protestation [pʀɔtɛstasjɔ̃] *nf* (*plainte*) protest; (*déclaration*) protestation, profession

protester [pʀɔtɛste] *vi*: **~ (contre)** to protest (against *ou* about); **~ de** (*son innocence, sa loyauté*) to protest

prothèse [pʀɔtɛz] *nf* artificial limb, prosthesis; **~ dentaire** (*appareil*) denture; (*science*) dental engineering

protocole [pʀɔtɔkɔl] *nm* protocol; (*fig*) etiquette; **~ d'accord** draft treaty; **~ opératoire** (*Méd*) operating procedure

proue [pʀu] *nf* bow(s *pl*), prow

prouesse [pʀuɛs] *nf* feat

prouver [pʀuve] *vt* to prove

provenance [pʀɔvnɑ̃s] *nf* origin; (*de mot, coutume*) source; **avion en ~ de** plane (arriving) from

provenir [pʀɔvniʀ]: **~ de** *vt* to come from; (*résulter de*) to be due to, be the result of

proverbe [pʀɔvɛʀb] *nm* proverb

province [pʀɔvɛ̃s] *nf* province

proviseur [pʀɔvizœʀ] *nm* ≈ head (teacher) (*Brit*), ≈ principal (*US*)

provision [pʀɔvizjɔ̃] *nf* (*réserve*) stock, supply; (*avance: à un avocat, avoué*) retainer, retaining fee; (*Comm*) funds *pl* (in account); reserve; **provisions** *nfpl* (*vivres*) provisions, food *no pl*; **faire ~ de** to stock up with; **placard** *ou* **armoire à ~s** food cupboard

provisoire [pʀɔvizwaʀ] *adj* temporary; (*Jur*) provisional; **mise en liberté ~** release on bail

provisoirement [pʀɔvizwaʀmɑ̃] *adv* temporarily, for the time being

provocant, e [pʀɔvɔkɑ̃, -ɑ̃t] *adj* provocative

provoquer [pʀɔvɔke] *vt* (*défier*) to provoke; (*causer*) to cause, bring about; (*: curiosité*) to arouse, give rise to; (*: aveux*) to prompt, elicit; (*inciter*): **~ qn à** to incite sb to

proxénète [pʀɔksenɛt] *nm* procurer

proximité [pʀɔksimite] *nf* nearness, closeness, proximity; (*dans le temps*) imminence, closeness; **à ~** near *ou* close by; **à ~ de** near (to), close to

prudemment [pʀydamɑ̃] *adv* (*voir prudent*) carefully; cautiously; prudently; wisely, sensibly

prudence [pʀydɑ̃s] *nf* carefulness; caution; prudence; **avec ~** carefully; cautiously; wisely; **par (mesure de) ~** as a precaution

prudent, e [pʀydɑ̃, -ɑ̃t] *adj* (*pas téméraire*) careful, cautious, prudent; (*: en général*) safety-conscious; (*sage, conseillé*) wise, sensible; (*réservé*) cautious; **c'est plus ~** it's wiser; **ce n'est pas ~** it's risky; it's not sensible; **soyez ~** take care, be careful

prune [pʀyn] *nf* plum

pruneau, x [pʀyno] *nm* prune

prunelle [pʀynɛl] *nf* pupil; (*œil*) eye; (*Bot*) sloe; (*eau de vie*) sloe gin

prunier [pʀynje] *nm* plum tree

PS *sigle m* = **parti socialiste**; (= *post-scriptum*) PS

psaume [psom] *nm* psalm

pseudonyme [psødɔnim] *nm* (*gén*) fictitious name; (*d'écrivain*) pseudonym, pen name; (*de comédien*) stage name

psychanalyse [psikanaliz] *nf* psychoanalysis

psychiatre [psikjatʀ] *nm/f* psychiatrist

psychiatrique [psikjatʀik] *adj* psychiatric; (*hôpital*) mental, psychiatric

psychique [psiʃik] *adj* psychological

psychologie [psikɔlɔʒi] *nf* psychology

psychologique [psikɔlɔʒik] *adj* psychological

psychologue [psikɔlɔg] *nm/f* psychologist; **être ~** (*fig*) to be a good psychologist

pu [py] *pp de* **pouvoir**

puanteur [pɥɑ̃tœʀ] *nf* stink, stench

pub [pyb] *nf* (*fam*: = *publicité*): **la ~** advertising

public, -ique [pyblik] *adj* public; (*école, instruction*) state *cpd*; (*scrutin*) open ▷ *nm* public; (*assistance*) audience; **en ~** in public; **le grand ~** the general public

publicitaire [pyblisitɛʀ] *adj* advertising *cpd*; (*film, voiture*) publicity *cpd*; (*vente*) promotional ▷ *nm* adman; **rédacteur ~** copywriter

publicité [pyblisite] *nf* (*méthode, profession*) advertising; (*annonce*) advertisement; (*révélations*) publicity

publier [pyblije] *vt* to publish; (*nouvelle*) to publicize, make public

publipostage [pyblipɔstaʒ] *nm* mailshot, (mass) mailing

publique [pyblik] *adj f voir* **public**

puce [pys] *nf* flea; (*Inform*) chip; **carte à ~** smart card; (*marché aux*) **~s** flea market *sg*; **mettre la ~ à l'oreille de qn** to give sb something to think about

pudeur [pydœʀ] *nf* modesty

pudique [pydik] *adj* (*chaste*) modest; (*discret*) discreet

puer [pɥe] (*péj*) *vi* to stink ▷ *vt* to stink of, reek of

puéricultrice [pɥeʀikyltʀis] *nf* ≈ paediatric nurse

puéril, e [pɥeʀil] *adj* childish

puis [pɥi] *vb voir* **pouvoir** ▷ *adv* (*ensuite*) then; (*dans une énumération*) next; (*en outre*): **et ~** and (then); **et ~ (après** *ou* **quoi?)** so (what?)

puiser [pɥize] *vt*: **~ (dans)** to draw (from); **~ dans qch** to dip into sth

puisque [pɥisk] *conj* since; (*valeur intensive*): **~ je te le dis!** I'm telling you!

puissance [pɥisɑ̃s] *nf* power; **en ~** *adj* potential; **deux (à la) ~ cinq** two to the power (of) five

puissant, e [pɥisɑ̃, -ɑ̃t] *adj* powerful

puisse etc [pɥis] vb voir **pouvoir**

puits [pɥi] nm well; ~ **artésien** artesian well; ~ **de mine** mine shaft; ~ **de science** fount of knowledge

pull [pyl], **pull-over** [pylɔvœʀ] nm sweater, jumper (Brit)

pulluler [pylyle] vi to swarm; (fig: erreurs) to abound, proliferate

pulpe [pylp] nf pulp

pulvérisateur [pylveʀizatœʀ] nm spray

pulvériser [pylveʀize] vt (solide) to pulverize; (liquide) to spray; (fig: anéantir: adversaire) to pulverize; (: record) to smash, shatter; (: argument) to demolish

punaise [pynɛz] nf (Zool) bug; (clou) drawing pin (Brit), thumb tack (US)

punch [pɔ̃ʃ] nm (boisson) punch [pœnʃ] (Boxe) punching ability; (fig) punch

punir [pyniʀ] vt to punish; ~ **qn de qch** to punish sb for sth

punition [pynisjɔ̃] nf punishment

pupille [pypij] nf (Anat) pupil ▷ nm/f (enfant) ward; ~ **de l'État** child in care; ~ **de la Nation** war orphan

pupitre [pypitʀ] nm (Scol) desk; (Rel) lectern; (de chef d'orchestre) rostrum; ~ **de commande** control panel

pur, e [pyʀ] adj pure; (vin) undiluted; (whisky) neat; (intentions) honourable (Brit), honorable (US) ▷ nm (personne) hard-liner; **en ~e perte** fruitlessly, to no avail; **c'est de la folie ~e** it's sheer madness

purée [pyʀe] nf: ~ **(de pommes de terre)** ≈ mashed potatoes pl; ~ **de marrons** chestnut purée; ~ **de pois** (fig) peasoup(er)

purement [pyʀmɑ̃] adv purely

purgatoire [pyʀgatwaʀ] nm purgatory

purger [pyʀʒe] vt (radiateur) to flush (out), drain; (circuit hydraulique) to bleed; (Méd, Pol) to purge; (Jur: peine) to serve

purin [pyʀɛ̃] nm liquid manure

pur-sang [pyʀsɑ̃] nm inv thoroughbred, pure-bred

pus [py] vb voir **pouvoir** ▷ nm pus

putain [pytɛ̃] nf (fam!) whore (!); **ce/cette ~ de ...** this bloody (Brit) ou goddamn (US) ... (!)

puzzle [pœzl] nm jigsaw (puzzle)

PV sigle m = **procès-verbal**

pyjama [piʒama] nm pyjamas pl (Brit), pajamas pl (US)

pyramide [piʀamid] nf pyramid

Pyrénées [piʀene] nfpl: **les ~** the Pyrenees

QI sigle m (= quotient intellectuel) IQ

quadragénaire [kadʀaʒenɛʀ] nm/f (de quarante ans) forty-year-old; (de quarante à cinquante ans) man/woman in his/her forties

quadriller [kadʀije] vt (papier) to mark out in squares; (Police: ville, région etc) to keep under tight control, be positioned throughout

quadruple [k(w)adʀypl] nm: **le ~ de** four times as much as

quadruplés, -ées [k(w)adʀyple] nm/fpl quadruplets, quads

quai [ke] nm (de port) quay; (de gare) platform; (de cours d'eau, canal) embankment; **être à ~** (navire) to be alongside; (train) to be in the station; **le Q~ d'Orsay** offices of the French Ministry for Foreign Affairs; **le Q~ des Orfèvres** central police headquarters

qualification [kalifikasjɔ̃] nf qualification

qualifié, e [kalifje] adj qualified; (main d'œuvre) skilled

qualifier [kalifje] vt to qualify; (appeler): ~ **qch/qn de** to describe sth/sb as; **se qualifier** vi (Sport) to qualify; **être qualifié pour** to be qualified for

qualité [kalite] nf quality; (titre, fonction) position; **en ~ de** in one's capacity as; **ès ~s** in an official capacity; **avoir ~ pour** to have authority to; **de ~** adj quality cpd; **rapport ~-prix** value (for money)

quand [kɑ̃] conj, adv when; ~ **je serai riche** when I'm rich; ~ **même** (cependant, pourtant) nevertheless; (tout de même) all the same;

~ même, il exagère! really, he overdoes it!; **~ bien même** even though

quant [kɑ̃]: **~ à** prép (pour ce qui est de) as for, as to; (au sujet de) regarding

quant-à-soi [kɑ̃taswa] nm: **rester sur son ~** to remain aloof

quantité [kɑ̃tite] nf quantity, amount; (Science) quantity; (grand nombre): **une** ou **des ~(s) de** a great deal of, a lot of; **en grande ~** in large quantities; **en ~s industrielles** in vast amounts; **du travail en ~** a great deal of work; **~ de** many

quarantaine [kaʀɑ̃tɛn] nf (isolement) quarantine; (âge): **avoir la ~** to be around forty; (nombre): **une ~ (de)** forty or so, about forty; **mettre en ~** to put into quarantine; (fig) to send to Coventry (Brit), ostracize

quarante [kaʀɑ̃t] num forty

quart [kaʀ] nm (fraction) quarter; (surveillance) watch; (partie): **un ~ de poulet/fromage** a chicken quarter/a quarter of a cheese; **un ~ de beurre** a quarter kilo of butter, ≈ a half pound of butter; **un ~ de vin** a quarter litre of wine; **une livre un ~** ou **et ~** one and a quarter pounds; **le ~ de** a quarter of; **~ d'heure** quarter of an hour; **deux heures et** ou **un ~** (a) quarter past two, (a) quarter after two (US); **il est le ~** it's (a) quarter past ou after (US); **une heure moins le ~** (a) quarter to one, (a) quarter of one (US); **il est moins le ~** it's (a) quarter to; **être/prendre le ~** to keep/take the watch; **~ de tour** quarter turn; **au ~ de tour** (fig) straight off; **~s de finale** (Sport) quarter finals

quartier [kaʀtje] nm (de ville) district, area; (de bœuf, de la lune) quarter; (de fruit, fromage) piece; **quartiers** nmpl (Mil, Blason) quarters; **cinéma/salle de ~** local cinema/hall; **avoir ~ libre** to be free; (Mil) to have leave from barracks; **ne pas faire de ~** to spare no one, give no quarter; **~ commerçant/résidentiel** shopping/residential area; **~ général (QG)** headquarters (HQ)

quartz [kwaʀts] nm quartz

quasi [kazi] adv almost, nearly ▷ préfixe: **~-certitude** near certainty

quasiment [kazimɑ̃] adv almost, (very) nearly; **~ jamais** hardly ever

quatorze [katɔʀz] num fourteen

quatorzième [katɔʀzjɛm] num fourteenth

quatre [katʀ] num four; **à ~ pattes** on all fours; **tiré à ~ épingles** dressed up to the nines; **faire les ~ cent coups** to be a bit wild; **se mettre en ~ pour qn** to go out of one's way for sb; **~ à ~** (monter, descendre) four at a time; **à ~ mains** (fraction) four-handed

quatre-vingt-dix [katʀəvɛ̃dis] num ninety

quatre-vingts [katʀəvɛ̃] num eighty

quatre-vingt-un num eighty-one

quatrième [katʀijɛm] num fourth ▷ nf (Scol) year 9 (Brit), eighth grade (US)

quatuor [kwatyɔʀ] nm quartet(te)

 MOT-CLÉ

que [kə] conj **1** (introduisant complétive) that; **il sait que tu es là** he knows (that) you're here; **je veux que tu acceptes** I want you to accept; **il a dit que oui** he said he would (ou it was etc) **2** (reprise d'autres conjonctions): **quand il rentrera et qu'il aura mangé** when he gets back and (when) he has eaten; **si vous y allez ou que vous …** if you go there or if you … **3** (en tête de phrase: hypothèse, souhait etc): **qu'il le veuille ou non** whether he likes it or not; **qu'il fasse ce qu'il voudra!** let him do as he pleases! **4** (but): **tenez-le qu'il ne tombe pas** hold it so (that) it doesn't fall **5** (après comparatif) than; as; voir aussi **plus**; **aussi; autant** etc **6** (seulement): **ne … que** only; **il ne boit que de l'eau** he only drinks water **7** (temps): **elle venait à peine de sortir qu'il se mit à pleuvoir** she had just gone out when it started to rain, no sooner had she gone out than it started to rain; **il y a quatre ans qu'il est parti** it is four years since he left, he left four years ago ▷ adv (exclamation): **qu'il** ou **qu'est-ce qu'il est bête/court vite!** he's so silly!/he runs so fast!; **que de livres!** what a lot of books! ▷ pron **1** (relatif: personne) whom; (: chose) that, which; **l'homme que je vois** the man (whom) I see; **le livre que tu vois** the book (that ou which) you see; **un jour que j'étais …** a day when I was .. **2** (interrogatif) what; **que fais-tu?, qu'est-ce que tu fais?** what are you doing?; **qu'est-ce que c'est?** what is it?, what's that?; **que faire?** what can one do?; **que préfères-tu, celui-ci ou celui-là?** which (one) do you prefer, this one or that one?

Québec [kebɛk] n (ville) Quebec ▷ nm: **le ~** Quebec (Province)

québécois, e [kebekwa, -waz] adj Quebec cpd ▷ nm (Ling) Quebec French ▷ nm/f: **Q~, e** Quebecois, Quebec(k)er

 MOT-CLÉ

quel, quelle [kɛl] adj **1** (interrogatif: personne) who; (: chose) what; which; **quel est cet homme?** who is this man?; **quel est ce livre?** what is this book?; **quel livre/homme?** what book/man?; (parmi un certain choix) which book/man?; **quels acteurs préférez-vous?** which actors do you prefer?; **dans quels pays êtes-vous allé?** which ou what countries did you go to? **2** (exclamatif): **quelle surprise/coïncidence!** what a surprise/coincidence! **3**: **quel(le) que soit le coupable** whoever is guilty; **quel que soit votre avis** whatever your opinion (may be)

q

quelconque [kɛlkɔ̃k] *adj* (*médiocre: repas*) indifferent, poor; (*sans attrait*) ordinary, plain; (*indéfini*): **un ami/prétexte** ~ some friend/pretext or other; **un livre** ~ **suffira** any book will do; **pour une raison** ~ for some reason (or other)

 MOT-CLÉ

quelque [kɛlk] *adj* **1** (*au singulier*) some; (*au pluriel*) a few, some; (*tournure interrogative*) any; **quelque espoir** some hope; **il a quelques amis** he has a few *ou* some friends; **a-t-il quelques amis?** does he have any friends?; **les quelques livres qui** the few books which; **20 kg et quelque(s)** a bit over 20 kg; **il habite à quelque distance d'ici** he lives some distance *ou* way (away) from here **2**: **quelque ... que** whatever, whichever; **quelque livre qu'il choisisse** whatever (*ou* whichever) book he chooses; **par quelque temps qu'il fasse** whatever the weather **3**: **quelque chose** something; (*tournure interrogative*) anything; **quelque chose d'autre** something else; anything else; **y être pour quelque chose** to have something to do with it; **faire quelque chose à qn** to have an effect on sb, do something to sb; **quelque part** somewhere; anywhere; **en quelque sorte** as it were
▷ *adv* **1** (*environ*): **quelque 100 mètres** some 100 metres **2**: **quelque peu** rather, somewhat

quelquefois [kɛlkəfwa] *adv* sometimes
quelques-uns, -unes [kɛlkəzœ̃, -yn] *pron* some, a few; ~ **des lecteurs** some of the readers
quelqu'un [kɛlkœ̃] *pron* someone, somebody; (*tournure interrogative ou négative* +) anyone *ou* anybody; ~ **d'autre** someone *ou* somebody else; anybody else
quémander [kemɑ̃de] *vt* to beg for
qu'en dira-t-on [kɑ̃diratɔ̃] *nm inv*: **le** ~ gossip, what people say
querelle [kərɛl] *nf* quarrel; **chercher** ~ **à qn** to pick a quarrel with sb
quereller [kərele]: **se quereller** *vi* to quarrel
qu'est-ce que [kɛskə] *vb + conj voir* **que**
qu'est-ce qui [kɛski] *vb + conj voir* **qui**
question [kɛstjɔ̃] *nf* (*gén*) question; (*fig*) matter; issue; **il a été** ~ **de** we (*ou* they) spoke about; **il est** ~ **de les emprisonner** there's talk of them being jailed; **c'est une** ~ **de temps** it's a matter *ou* question of time; **de quoi est-il** ~? what is it about?; **il n'en est pas** ~ there's no question of it; **en** ~ in question; **hors de** ~ out of the question; **je ne me suis jamais posé la** ~ I've never thought about it; **(re)mettre en** ~ (*autorité, science*) to question; **poser la** ~ **de confiance** (*Pol*) to ask for a vote of confidence; ~ **piège** (*d'apparence facile*) trick question; (*pour nuire*) loaded question; ~ **subsidiaire** tiebreaker

questionnaire [kɛstjɔnɛʀ] *nm* questionnaire
questionner [kɛstjɔne] *vt* to question
quête [kɛt] *nf* (*collecte*) collection; (*recherche*) quest, search; **faire la** ~ (*à l'église*) to take the collection; (*artiste*) to pass the hat round; **se mettre en** ~ **de qch** to go in search of sth
quetsche [kwɛtʃ] *nf* damson
queue [kø] *nf* tail; (*fig: du classement*) bottom; (: *de poêle*) handle; (: *de fruit, feuille*) stalk; (: *de train, colonne, file*) rear; (*file: de personnes*) queue (Brit), line (US); **en** ~ (**de train**) at the rear (of the train); **faire la** ~ to queue (up) (Brit), line up (US); **se mettre à la** ~ to join the queue *ou* line; **histoire sans** ~ **ni tête** cock and bull story; **à la** ~ **leu leu** in single file; (*fig*) one after the other; ~ **de cheval** ponytail; ~ **de poisson: faire une queue de poisson à qn** (*Auto*) to cut in front of sb; **finir en** ~ **de poisson** (*film*) to come to an abrupt end

 MOT-CLÉ

qui [ki] *pron* **1** (*interrogatif: personne*) who; (*avec préposition*) whom; (*chose, animal*) which, that; (*interrogatif indirect: sujet*): **je me demande** ~ **est là?** I wonder who is there?; (*objet*): **elle ne sait à** ~ **se plaindre** she doesn't know who to complain to *ou* to whom to complain; (: *chose*): **qu'est-ce** ~ **est sur la table?** what is on the table?; ~ **est-ce** ~? who?; ~ **est-ce que?** who?; **à** ~ **est ce sac?** whose bag is this?; **à** ~ **parlais-tu?** who were you talking to?, to whom were you talking?; **chez** ~ **allez-vous?** whose house are you going to?
2 (*relatif: personne*) who; (+*prép*) whom; **l'ami de** ~ **je vous ai parlé** the friend I told you about; **la dame chez** ~ **je suis allé** the lady whose house I went to
3 (*sans antécédent*): **amenez** ~ **vous voulez** bring who you like; ~ **que ce soit** whoever it may be

quiche [kiʃ] *nf* quiche; ~ **lorraine** quiche Lorraine
quiconque [kikɔ̃k] *pron* (*celui qui*) whoever, anyone who; (*n'importe qui, personne*) anyone, anybody
quiétude [kjetyd] *nf* (*d'un lieu*) quiet, tranquillity; (*d'une personne*) peace (of mind), serenity; **en toute** ~ in complete peace; (*mentale*) with complete peace of mind
quille [kij] *nf* bowling, skittle (Brit); (*Navig: d'un bateau*) keel; (**jeu de**) ~**s** skittles *sg* (Brit), bowling (US)
quincaillerie [kɛ̃kajʀi] *nf* (*ustensiles, métier*) hardware, ironmongery (Brit); (*magasin*) hardware shop *ou* store (US), ironmonger's (Brit)
quincaillier, -ière [kɛ̃kaje, -jɛʀ] *nm/f* hardware dealer, ironmonger (Brit)
quinquagénaire [kɛ̃kaʒenɛʀ] *nm/f* (*de cinquante ans*) fifty-year old; (*de cinquante à soixante ans*) man/woman in his/her fifties

quinquennat [kɛ̃kena] *nm five year term of office (of French President)*

quintal, -aux [kɛ̃tal, -o] *nm* quintal (100 kg)

quinte [kɛ̃t] *nf:* ~ **(de toux)** coughing fit

quintuple [kɛ̃typl] *nm:* **le ~ de** five times as much as

quintuplés, -ées [kɛ̃typle] *nm/fpl* quintuplets, quins

quinzaine [kɛ̃zɛn] *nf:* **une ~ (de)** about fifteen, fifteen or so; **une ~ (de jours)** (*deux semaines*) a fortnight (*Brit*), two weeks; **~ publicitaire** *ou* **commerciale** (two-week) sale

quinze [kɛ̃z] *num* fifteen; **demain en ~** a fortnight (*Brit*) *ou* two weeks tomorrow; **dans ~ jours** in a fortnight('s time) (*Brit*), in two weeks(' time)

quinzième [kɛ̃zjɛm] *num* fifteenth

quittance [kitɑ̃s] *nf* (*reçu*) receipt; (*facture*) bill

quitte [kit] *adj:* **être ~ envers qn** to be no longer in sb's debt; (*fig*) to be quits with sb; **être ~ de** (*obligation*) to be clear of; **en être ~ à bon compte** to have got off lightly; **~ à faire** even if it means doing; **~ ou double** (*jeu*) double or quits; (*fig*): **c'est du ~ ou double** it's a big risk

quitter [kite] *vt* to leave; (*espoir, illusion*) to give up; (*vêtement*) to take off; **se quitter** *vi* (*couples, interlocuteurs*) to part; **ne quittez pas** (*au téléphone*) hold the line; **ne pas ~ qn d'une semelle** to stick to sb like glue

qui-vive [kiviv] *nm inv:* **être sur le ~** to be on the alert

quoi [kwa] *pron interrog* what; **~ de neuf?** what's new?; **~?** (*qu'est-ce que tu dis?*) what?; (*avec prép*): **à ~ tu penses?** what are you thinking about?; **de ~ parlez-vous?** what are you talking about?; **à ~ bon?** what's the use? ▷ *pron rel:* **as-tu de ~ écrire?** do you have anything to write with?; **il n'a pas de ~ l'acheter** he can't afford it, he hasn't got the money to buy it; **il y a de ~ être fier** that's something to be proud of; **il n'y a pas de ~** (*please*) don't mention it; **il n'y a pas de ~ rire** there's nothing to laugh about ▷ *pron* (*locutions*): **~ qu'il arrive** whatever happens; **~ qu'il en soit** be that as it may; **~ que ce soit** anything at all; **en ~ puis-je vous aider?** how can I help you?; **et puis ~ encore!** what(ever) next!; **~ faire?** what's to be done?; **sans ~** (*ou sinon*) otherwise ▷ *excl* what!

quoique [kwak] *conj* (al)though

quote-part [kɔtpaʀ] *nf* share

quotidien, ne [kɔtidjɛ̃, -ɛn] *adj* (*journalier*) daily; (*banal*) ordinary, everyday ▷ *nm* (*journal*) daily (paper); (*vie quotidienne*) daily life, day-to-day existence; **les grands ~s** the big (national) dailies

quotidiennement [kɔtidjɛnmɑ̃] *adv* daily, every day

r

rab [ʀab], **rabiot** [ʀabjo] (*fam*) *nm* (*nourriture*) extra, more; **est-ce qu'il y a du ~?** are there any seconds?

rabâcher [ʀabɑʃe] *vi* to harp on ▷ *vt* to keep on repeating

rabais [ʀabɛ] *nm* reduction, discount; **au ~** at a reduction *ou* discount

rabaisser [ʀabese] *vt* (*rabattre: prix*) to reduce; (*dénigrer*) to belittle

Rabat [ʀaba(t)] *n* Rabat

rabat-joie [ʀabaʒwa] *nm/f inv* killjoy (*Brit*), spoilsport

rabattre [ʀabatʀ] *vt* (*couvercle, siège*) to pull down; (*col*) to turn down; (*couture*) to stitch down; (*gibier*) to drive; (*somme d'un prix*) to deduct, take off; (*orgueil, prétentions*) to humble; (*Tricot*) to decrease; (*déduire*) to reduce; **se rabattre** *vi* (*bords, couvercle*) to fall shut; (*véhicule, coureur*) to cut in; **se ~ sur** (*accepter*) to fall back on

rabbin [ʀabɛ̃] *nm* rabbi

râblé, e [ʀable] *adj* broad-backed, stocky

rabot [ʀabo] *nm* plane

rabougri, e [ʀabugʀi] *adj* stunted

rabrouer [ʀabʀue] *vt* to snub, rebuff

racaille [ʀakaj] *nf* (*péj*) rabble, riffraff

raccommoder [ʀakɔmɔde] *vt* to mend, repair; (*chaussette etc*) to darn; (*fam: réconcilier: amis, ménage*) to bring together again; **se ~ (avec)** (*fam*) to patch it up (with)

r

raccompagner [Rakɔ̃paɲe] *vt* to take *ou* see back

raccord [Rakɔʀ] *nm* link; ~ **de maçonnerie** pointing *no pl*; ~ **de peinture** join; (*retouche*) touch-up

raccorder [Rakɔʀde] *vt* to join (up), link up; (*pont etc*) to connect, link; **se ~ à** to join up with; (*fig: se rattacher à*) to tie in with; ~ **au réseau du téléphone** to connect to the telephone service

raccourci [Rakuʀsi] *nm* short cut; **en ~** in brief

raccourcir [Rakuʀsiʀ] *vt* to shorten ▷ *vi* (*vêtement*) to shrink; (*jours*) to grow shorter, draw in

raccrocher [Rakʀoʃe] *vt* (*tableau, vêtement*) to hang back up; (*récepteur*) to put down; (*fig: affaire*) to save ▷ *vi* (*Tél*) to hang up, ring off; **se ~ à** *vt* to cling to, hang on to; **ne raccrochez pas** (*Tél*) hold on, don't hang up

race [Ras] *nf* race; (*d'animaux, fig: espèce*) breed; (*ascendance, origine*) stock, race; **de ~** *adj* purebred, pedigree

rachat [Raʃa] *nm* buying; (*du même objet*) buying back; redemption; atonement

racheter [Raʃte] *vt* (*article perdu*) to buy another; (*davantage*): ~ **du lait/trois œufs** to buy more milk/another three eggs *ou* three more eggs; (*après avoir vendu*) to buy back; (*d'occasion*) to buy; (*Comm: part, firme*) to buy up; (: *pension, rente*) to redeem; (*Rel: pécheur*) to redeem; (: *péché*) to atone for, expiate; (*mauvaise conduite, oubli, défaut*) to make up for; **se racheter** (*Rel*) to redeem o.s.; (*gén*) to make amends, make up for it

racial, e, -aux [Rasjal, -o] *adj* racial

racine [Rasin] *nf* root; (*fig: attache*) roots *pl*; ~ **carrée/cubique** square/cube root; **prendre ~** (*fig*) to take root; to put down roots

racisme [Rasism] *nm* racism

raciste [Rasist] *adj, nm/f* racist

racket [Raket] *nm* racketeering *no pl*

raclée [Rakle] *nf* (*fam*) hiding, thrashing

racler [Rakle] *vt* (*os, plat*) to scrape; (*tache, boue*) to scrape off; (*fig: instrument*) to scrape on; (*chose: frotter contre*) to scrape (against); **se ~ la gorge** to clear one's throat

racoler [Rakole] *vt* (*attirer: prostituée*) to solicit; (: *parti, marchand*) to tout for; (*attraper*) to pick up

racontars [Rakɔ̃taʀ] *nmpl* stories, gossip *sg*

raconter [Rakɔ̃te] *vt*: ~ (**à qn**) (*décrire*) to relate (to sb), tell (sb) about; (*dire*) to tell (sb); ~ **une histoire** to tell a story

racorni, e [Rakɔʀni] *adj* hard(ened)

radar [Radaʀ] *nm* radar; ~ (*automatique*) (*Auto*) speed camera; **système ~** radar system; **écran ~** radar screen

rade [Rad] *nf* (*natural*) harbour; **en ~ de Toulon** in Toulon harbour; **rester en ~** (*fig*) to be left stranded

radeau, x [Rado] *nm* raft; ~ **de sauvetage** life raft

radiateur [Radjatœʀ] *nm* radiator, heater; (*Auto*) radiator; ~ **électrique/à gaz** electric/gas heater *ou* fire

radiation [Radjasjɔ̃] *nf* (*d'un nom etc*) striking off *no pl*; (*Physique*) radiation

radical, e, -aux [Radikal, -o] *adj* radical ▷ *nm* (*Ling*) stem; (*Math*) root sign; (*Pol*) radical

radier [Radje] *vt* to strike off

radieux, -euse [Radjø, -øz] *adj* (*visage, personne*) radiant; (*journée, soleil*) brilliant, glorious

radin, e [Radɛ̃, -in] *adj* (*fam*) stingy

radio [Radjo] *nf* radio; (*Méd*) X-ray ▷ *nm* (*personne*) radio operator; **à la ~** on the radio; **avoir la ~** to have a radio; **passer à la ~** to be on the radio; **se faire faire une ~/une ~ des poumons** to have an X-ray/a chest X-ray

radioactif, -ive [Radjoaktif, -iv] *adj* radioactive

radiocassette [Radjokaset] *nf* cassette radio

radiodiffuser [Radjodifyze] *vt* to broadcast

radiographie [Radjɔgʀafi] *nf* radiography; (*photo*) X-ray photograph, radiograph

radiophonique [Radjofɔnik] *adj* radio *cpd*; **programme/émission/jeu ~** radio programme/broadcast/game

radio-réveil [Radjoʀevɛj] (*pl* **radios-réveils**) *nm* radio alarm (clock)

radis [Radi] *nm* radish; ~ **noir** horseradish *no pl*

radoter [Radɔte] *vi* to ramble on

radoucir [Radusiʀ]: **se radoucir** *vi* (*se réchauffer*) to become milder; (*se calmer*) to calm down; to soften

rafale [Rafal] *nf* (*vent*) gust of wind); (*de balles, d'applaudissements*) burst; ~ **de mitrailleuse** burst of machine-gun fire

raffermir [Rafɛʀmiʀ] *vt*, **se raffermir** *vi* (*tissu, muscle*) to firm up; (*fig*) to strengthen

raffiner [Rafine] *vt* to refine

raffinerie [Rafinʀi] *nf* refinery

raffoler [Rafɔle]: ~ **de** *vt* to be very keen on

rafistoler [Rafistɔle] *vt* (*fam*) to patch up

rafle [Rɑfl] *nf* (*de police*) roundup, raid

rafler [Rɑfle] *vt* (*fam*) to swipe, nick

rafraîchir [Rafʀeʃiʀ] *vt* (*atmosphère, température*) to cool (down); (*aussi*: **mettre à ~**) to chill; (*air, eau*) to freshen up; (: *boisson*) to refresh; (*fig: rénover*) to brighten up ▷ *vi*: **mettre du vin/une boisson à ~** to chill wine/a drink; **se rafraîchir** (*temps*) to grow cooler; (*en se lavant*) to freshen up; (*personne: en buvant etc*) to refresh o.s.; ~ **la mémoire à qn** to refresh sb's memory

rafraîchissant, e [Rafʀeʃisɑ̃, -ɑ̃t] *adj* refreshing

rafraîchissement [Rafʀeʃismɑ̃] *nm* cooling; (*boisson*) cool drink; **rafraîchissements** *nmpl* (*boissons, fruits etc*) refreshments

rage [Rɑʒ] *nf* (*Méd*): **la ~** rabies; (*fureur*) rage, fury; **faire ~** to rage; ~ **de dents** (*raging*) toothache

ragot [rago] nm (fam) malicious gossip no pl

ragoût [ragu] nm (plat) stew

raide [rɛd] adj (tendu) taut, tight; (escarpé) steep; (droit: cheveux) straight; (ankylosé, dur, guindé) stiff; (fam: cher) steep, stiff; (: sans argent) flat broke; (osé, licencieux) daring ▷ adv (en pente) steeply; ~ **mort** stone dead

raideur [rɛdœr] nf steepness; (rigidité) stiffness; **avec** ~ (répondre) stiffly, abruptly

raidir [redir] vt (muscles) to stiffen; (câble) to pull taut, tighten; **se raidir** vi to stiffen; to become taut; (personne: se crisper) to tense up; (: se préparer moralement) to brace o.s.; (fig: devenir intransigeant) to harden

raie [rɛ] nf (Zool) skate, ray; (rayure) stripe; (des cheveux) parting

raifort [rɛfɔr] nm horseradish

rail [raj] nm (barre d'acier) rail; (chemins de fer) railways pl (Brit), railroads pl (US); **les ~s** (la voie ferrée) the rails, the track sg; **par** ~ by rail; ~ **conducteur** live ou conductor rail

railler [raje] vt to scoff at, jeer at

rainure [renyr] nf groove; slot

raisin [rɛzɛ̃] nm (aussi: ~s) grapes pl; (variété): ~ **blanc/noir** white (ou green)/black grape; ~ **muscat** muscat grape; ~**s secs** raisins

raison [rɛzɔ̃] nf reason; **avoir** ~ to be right; **donner** ~ **à qn** (personne) to agree with sb; (fait) to prove sb right; **avoir** ~ **de qn/qch** to get the better of sb/sth; **se faire une** ~ to learn to live with it; **perdre la** ~ to become insane; (fig) to take leave of one's senses; **recouvrer la** ~ to come to one's senses; **ramener qn à la** ~ to make sb see sense; **demander** ~ **à qn de** (affront etc) to demand satisfaction from sb for; **entendre** ~ to listen to reason, see reason; **plus que de** ~ too much, more than is reasonable; ~ **de plus** all the more reason; **à plus forte** ~ all the more so; **sans** ~ for no reason; **en** ~ **de** (à cause de) because of; (à proportion de) in proportion to; **à** ~ **de** at the rate of; ~ **d'État** reason of state; ~ **d'être** raison d'être; ~ **sociale** corporate name

raisonnable [rɛzɔnabl] adj reasonable, sensible

raisonnement [rɛzɔnmã] nm reasoning; arguing; argument

raisonner [rɛzɔne] vi (penser) to reason; (argumenter, discuter) to argue ▷ vt (personne) to reason with; (attitude: justifier) to reason out; **se raisonner** to reason with oneself

rajeunir [raʒœnir] vt (coiffure, robe): ~ **qn** to make sb look younger; (cure etc) to rejuvenate; (fig: rafraîchir) to brighten up; (: moderniser) to give a new look to; (: en recrutant) to inject new blood into ▷ vi (personne) to become (ou look) younger; (entreprise, quartier) to be modernized

rajouter [raʒute] vt (commentaire) to add; ~ **du sel/un œuf** to add some more salt/another egg; ~ **que** to add that; **en** ~ to lay it on thick

rajuster [raʒyste] vt (vêtement) to straighten, tidy; (salaires) to adjust; (machine) to readjust; **se rajuster** to tidy ou straighten o.s. up

ralenti [ralãti] nm: **au** ~ (Ciné) in slow motion; (fig) at a slower pace; **tourner au** ~ (Auto) to tick over, idle

ralentir [ralãtir] vt, vi, **se ralentir** vi to slow down

râler [rale] vi to groan; (fam) to grouse, moan (and groan)

rallier [ralje] vt (rassembler) to rally; (rejoindre) to rejoin; (gagner à sa cause) to win over; **se** ~ **à** (avis) to come over ou round to

rallonge [ralɔ̃ʒ] nf (de table) (extra) leaf; (argent etc) extra no pl; (Élec) extension (cable ou flex); (fig: de crédit etc) extension

rallonger [ralɔ̃ʒe] vt to lengthen

rallye [rali] nm rally; (Pol) march

ramassage [ramasaʒ] nm: ~ **scolaire** school bus service

ramassé, e [ramase] adj (trapu) squat, stocky; (concis: expression etc) compact

ramasser [ramase] vt (objet tombé ou par terre: fam) to pick up; (recueillir: copies, ordures) to collect; (récolter) to gather; (: pommes de terre) to lift; **se ramasser** vi (sur soi-même) to huddle up; to crouch

ramassis [ramasi] nm (péj: de voyous) bunch; (: de choses) jumble

rambarde [rɑ̃bard] nf guardrail

rame [ram] nf (aviron) oar; (de métro) train; (de papier) ream; ~ **de haricots** bean support; **faire force de** ~**s** to row hard

rameau, x [ramo] nm (small) branch; (fig) branch; **les R~x** (Rel) Palm Sunday sg

ramener [ramne] vt to bring back; (reconduire) to take back; (rabattre: couverture, visière): ~ **qch sur** to pull sth back over; ~ **qch à** (réduire à, Math) to reduce sth to; ~ **qn à la vie/raison** to bring sb back to life/bring sb to his (ou her) senses; **se ramener** vi (fam) to roll ou turn up; **se** ~ **à** (se réduire à) to come ou boil down to

ramer [rame] vi to row

ramollir [ramɔlir] vt to soften; **se ramollir** vi (os, tissus) to get (ou go) soft; (beurre, asphalte) to soften

ramoner [ramɔne] vt (cheminée) to sweep; (pipe) to clean

rampe [rɑ̃p] nf (d'escalier) banister(s pl); (dans un garage, d'un terrain) ramp; (Théât): **la** ~ the footlights pl; (lampes: lumineuse, de balisage) floodlights pl; **passer la** ~ (toucher le public) to get across to the audience; ~ **de lancement** launching pad

ramper [rɑ̃pe] vi (reptile, animal) to crawl; (plante) to creep

rancard [rɑ̃kar] nm (fam) date; tip

rancart [rɑ̃kar] nm: **mettre au** ~ (article, projet) to scrap; (personne) to put on the scrapheap

rance [rɑ̃s] adj rancid

r

rancœur [ʀɑ̃kœʀ] nf rancour (Brit), rancor (US), resentment

rançon [ʀɑ̃sɔ̃] nf ransom; (fig): **la ~ du succès** etc the price of success etc

rancune [ʀɑ̃kyn] nf grudge, rancour (Brit), rancor (US); **garder ~ à qn (de qch)** to bear sb a grudge (for sth); **sans ~!** no hard feelings!

rancunier, -ière [ʀɑ̃kynje, -jɛʀ] adj vindictive, spiteful

randonnée [ʀɑ̃dɔne] nf ride; (à pied) walk, ramble; (en montagne) hike, hiking no pl; **la ~** (activité) hiking, walking; **une ~ à cheval** a pony trek

rang [ʀɑ̃] nm (rangée) row; (de perles) row, string, rope; (grade, condition sociale, classement) rank; **rangs** nmpl (Mil) ranks; **se mettre en ~s/sur un ~** to form rows/a line; **sur trois ~s** (lined up) three deep; **se mettre en ~s par quatre** to form fours ou rows of four; **se ranger sur les ~s** (fig) to get into the running; **au premier ~** in the first row; (fig) ranking first; **rentrer dans le ~** to get into line; **au ~ de** (au nombre de) among (the ranks of); **avoir ~ de** to hold the rank of

rangé, e [ʀɑ̃ʒe] adj (vie) well-ordered; (sérieux: personne) orderly, steady

rangée [ʀɑ̃ʒe] nf row

ranger [ʀɑ̃ʒe] vt (classer, grouper) to order, arrange; (mettre à sa place) to put away; (voiture dans la rue) to park; (mettre de l'ordre dans) to tidy up; (arranger, disposer: en cercle etc) to arrange; (fig: classer): **~ qn/qch parmi** to rank sb/sth among; **se ranger** vi (se placer, se disposer: autour d'une table etc) to take one's place, sit round; (véhicule, conducteur: s'écarter) to pull over ou in; (: s'arrêter) to pull in; (piéton) to step aside; (s'assagir) to settle down; **se ~ à** (avis) to come round to, fall in with

ranimer [ʀanime] vt (personne évanouie) to bring round; (revigorer: forces, courage) to restore; (réconforter: troupes etc) to kindle new life in; (douleur, souvenir) to revive; (feu) to rekindle

rap [ʀap] nm rap (music)

rapace [ʀapas] nm bird of prey ▷ adj (péj) rapacious, grasping; **~ diurne/nocturne** diurnal/nocturnal bird of prey

râpe [ʀɑp] nf (Culin) grater; (à bois) rasp

râper [ʀɑpe] vt (Culin) to grate; (gratter, râcler) to rasp

rapetisser [ʀaptise] vt: **~ qch** to shorten sth; to make sth look smaller ▷ vi, **se rapetisser** vi to shrink

rapide [ʀapid] adj fast; (prompt: intelligence, coup d'œil, mouvement) quick ▷ nm express (train); (de cours d'eau) rapid

rapidement [ʀapidmɑ̃] adv fast; quickly

rapiécer [ʀapjese] vt to patch

rappel [ʀapɛl] nm (d'un ambassadeur, Mil) recall; (Théât) curtain call; (Méd: vaccination) booster; (Admin: de salaire) back pay no pl; (d'une aventure, d'un nom) reminder; (de limitation de vitesse: sur écriteau) speed limit sign (reminder); (Tech) return; (Navig) sitting out; (Alpinisme: aussi: **~ de corde**) abseiling no pl, roping down no pl; abseil; **~ à l'ordre** call to order

rappeler [ʀaple] vt (pour faire revenir, retéléphoner) to call back; (ambassadeur, Mil) to recall; (acteur) to call back (onto the stage); (faire se souvenir): **~ qch à qn** to remind sb of sth; **se rappeler** vt (se souvenir de) to remember, recall; **~ qn à la vie** to bring sb back to life; **~ qn à la décence** to recall sb to a sense of decency; **ça rappelle la Provence** it's reminiscent of Provence, it reminds you of Provence; **se ~ que...** to remember that...

rapport [ʀapɔʀ] nm (compte rendu) report; (profit) yield, return; revenue; (lien, analogie) relationship; (corrélation) connection; (proportion: Math, Tech) ratio; **rapports** nmpl (entre personnes, pays) relations; **avoir ~ à** to have something to do with, concern; **être en ~ avec** (idée de corrélation) to be related to; **être/se mettre en ~ avec qn** to be/get in touch with sb; **par ~ à** (comparé à) in relation to; (à propos de) with regard to; **sous le ~ de** from the point of view of; **sous tous (les) ~s** in all respects; **~s (sexuels)** (sexual) intercourse sg; **~ qualité-prix** value (for money)

rapporter [ʀapɔʀte] vt (rendre, ramener) to bring back; (apporter davantage) to bring more; (Couture) to sew on; (investissement) to yield; (: activité) to bring in; (relater) to report; (Jur: annuler) to revoke ▷ vi (investissement) to give a good return ou yield; (activité) to be very profitable; (péj: moucharder) to tell; **~ qch à** (fig: rattacher) to relate sth to; **se ~ à** (correspondre à) to relate to; **s'en ~ à** to rely on

rapporteur, -euse [ʀapɔʀtœʀ, -øz] nm/f (de procès, commission) reporter; (péj) telltale ▷ nm (Géom) protractor

rapprochement [ʀapʀɔʃmɑ̃] nm (réconciliation: de nations, familles) reconciliation; (analogie, rapport) parallel

rapprocher [ʀapʀɔʃe] vt (chaise d'une table): **~ qch (de)** to bring sth closer (to); (deux objets) to bring closer together; (réunir: ennemis, partis etc) to bring together; (comparer) to establish a parallel between; **se rapprocher** vi to draw closer ou nearer; (fig: familles, pays) to come together; to come closer together; **se ~ de** to come closer to; (présenter une analogie avec) to be close to

rapt [ʀapt] nm abduction

raquette [ʀakɛt] nf (de tennis) racket; (de ping-pong) bat; (à neige) snowshoe

rare [ʀɑʀ] adj rare; (main-d'œuvre, denrées) scarce; (cheveux, herbe) sparse; **il est ~ que** it's rare that, it's unusual that; **se faire ~** to become scarce; (fig: personne) to make oneself scarce

rarement [ʀaʀmɑ̃] adv rarely, seldom

ras, e [ʀɑ, ʀɑz] adj (tête, cheveux) close-cropped; (poil, herbe) short; (mesure, cuillère) level ▷ *adv* short; **faire table ~e** to make a clean sweep; **en ~e campagne** in open country; **à ~ bords** to the brim; **au ~ de** level with; **en avoir ~ le bol** (*fam*) to be fed up; **~ du cou** *adj* (*pull, robe*) crew-neck

rasade [ʀazad] *nf* glassful

raser [ʀaze] *vt* (*barbe, cheveux*) to shave off; (*menton, personne*) to shave; (*fam: ennuyer*) to bore; (*démolir*) to raze (to the ground); (*frôler*) to graze, skim; **se raser** *vi* to shave; (*fam*) to be bored (to tears)

rasoir [ʀazwaʀ] *nm* razor; **~ électrique** electric shaver *ou* razor; **~ mécanique** *ou* **de sûreté** safety razor

rassasier [ʀasazje] *vt* to satisfy; **être rassasié** (*dégoûté*) to be sated; to have had more than enough

rassemblement [ʀasɑ̃bləmɑ̃] *nm* (*groupe*) gathering; (*Pol*) union; association; (*Mil*): **le ~** parade

rassembler [ʀasɑ̃ble] *vt* (*réunir*) to assemble, gather; (*regrouper, amasser: documents, notes*) to gather together, collect; **se rassembler** *vi* to gather; **~ ses idées/ses esprits/son courage** to collect one's thoughts/gather one's wits/screw up one's courage

rassis, e [ʀasi, -iz] *adj* (*pain*) stale

rassurer [ʀasyʀe] *vt* to reassure; **se rassurer** *vi* to be reassured; **rassure-toi** don't worry

rat [ʀa] *nm* rat; **~ d'hôtel** hotel thief; **~ musqué** muskrat

rate [ʀat] *nf* female rat; (*Anat*) spleen

raté, e [ʀate] *adj* (*tentative*) unsuccessful, failed ▷ *nm/f* (*personne*) failure ▷ *nm* misfiring *no pl*

râteau, x [ʀato] *nm* rake

rater [ʀate] *vi* (*ne pas partir: coup de feu*) to fail to go off; (*affaire, projet etc*) to go wrong, fail ▷ *vt* (*cible, train, occasion*) to miss; (*démonstration, plat*) to spoil; (*examen*) to fail; **~ son coup** to fail, not to bring it off

ration [ʀasjɔ̃] *nf* ration; (*fig*) share; **~ alimentaire** food intake

ratisser [ʀatise] *vt* (*allée*) to rake; (*feuilles*) to rake up; (*armée, police*) to comb; **~ large** to cast one's net wide

RATP *sigle f* (= *Régie autonome des transports parisiens*) Paris transport authority

rattacher [ʀataʃe] *vt* (*animal, cheveux*) to tie up again; (*incorporer: Admin etc*): **~ qch à** to join sth to, unite sth with; (*fig: relier*): **~ qch à** to link sth with, relate sth to; (: *lier*): **~ qn à** to bind *ou* tie sb to; **se ~ à** (*fig: avoir un lien avec*) to be linked (*ou* connected) with

rattrapage [ʀatʀapaʒ] *nm* (*Scol*) remedial classes *pl*; (*Écon*) catching up

rattraper [ʀatʀape] *vt* (*fugitif*) to recapture; (*retenir, empêcher de tomber*) to catch (hold of); (*atteindre, rejoindre*) to catch up with; (*réparer: erreur*) to make up for; **se rattraper** *vi* (*regagner: du temps*) to make up for lost time; (: *de l'argent etc*) to make good one's losses;

(*réparer une gaffe etc*) to make up for it; **se ~ (à)** (*se raccrocher*) to stop o.s. falling (by catching hold of); **~ son retard/le temps perdu** to make up (for) lost time

rature [ʀatyʀ] *nf* deletion, erasure

rauque [ʀok] *adj* raucous; (*voix*) hoarse

ravages [ʀavaʒ] *nmpl* ravages; **faire des ~** to wreak havoc; (*fig: séducteur*) to break hearts

ravaler [ʀavale] *vt* (*mur, façade*) to restore; (*déprécier*) to lower; (*avaler de nouveau*) to swallow again; **~ sa colère/son dégoût** to stifle one's anger/swallow one's distaste

ravi, e [ʀavi] *adj* delighted; **être ~ de/que** to be delighted with/that

ravigoter [ʀavigɔte] *vt* (*fam*) to buck up

ravin [ʀavɛ̃] *nm* gully, ravine

ravir [ʀaviʀ] *vt* (*enchanter*) to delight; (*enlever*): **~ qch à qn** to rob sb of sth; **à ~** *adv* delightfully, beautifully; **être beau à ~** to be ravishingly beautiful

raviser [ʀavize]: **se raviser** *vi* to change one's mind

ravissant, e [ʀavisɑ̃, -ɑ̃t] *adj* delightful

ravisseur, -euse [ʀavisœʀ, -øz] *nm/f* abductor, kidnapper

ravitaillement [ʀavitajmɑ̃] *nm* resupplying; refuelling; (*provisions*) supplies *pl*; **aller au ~** to go for fresh supplies; **~ en vol** (*Aviat*) in-flight refuelling

ravitailler [ʀavitaje] *vt* (*en vivres, munitions*) to provide with fresh supplies; (*véhicule*) to refuel; **se ravitailler** *vi* to get fresh supplies

raviver [ʀavive] *vt* (*feu*) to rekindle, revive; (*douleur*) to revive; (*couleurs*) to brighten up

rayé, e [ʀeje] *adj* (*à rayures*) striped; (*éraflé*) scratched

rayer [ʀeje] *vt* (*érafler*) to scratch; (*barrer*) to cross *ou* score out; (*d'une liste: radier*) to cross *ou* strike off

rayon [ʀejɔ̃] *nm* (*de soleil etc*) ray; (*Géom*) radius; (*de roue*) spoke; (*étagère*) shelf; (*de grand magasin*) department; (*fig: domaine*) responsibility, concern; (*de ruche*) (honey) comb; **dans un ~ de** within a radius of; **rayons** *nmpl* (*radiothérapie*) radiation; **~ d'action** range; **~ de braquage** (*Auto*) turning circle; **~ laser** laser beam; **~ de soleil** sunbeam, ray of sunlight *ou* sunshine; **~s X** X-rays

rayonnement [ʀejɔnmɑ̃] *nm* radiation; (*fig: éclat*) radiance; (*influence: d'une culture*) influence

rayonner [ʀejɔne] *vi* (*chaleur, énergie*) to radiate; (*fig: émotion*) to shine forth; (: *visage, personne*) to be radiant; (*avenues, axes*) to radiate; (*touriste*) to go touring (*from one base*)

rayure [ʀejyʀ] *nf* (*motif*) stripe; (*éraflure*) scratch; (*rainure, d'un fusil*) groove; **à ~s** striped

raz-de-marée [ʀadmaʀe] *nm inv* tidal wave

ré [ʀe] *nm* (*Mus*) D; (*en chantant la gamme*) re

réacteur [ʀeaktœʀ] *nm* jet engine; **~ nucléaire** nuclear reactor

r

réaction [ʀeaksjɔ̃] nf reaction; **par ~** jet-propelled; **avion/moteur à ~** jet (plane)/jet engine; **~ en chaîne** chain reaction

réadapter [ʀeadapte] vt to readjust; (Méd) to rehabilitate; **se ~ (à)** vi to readjust (to)

réagir [ʀeaʒiʀ] vi to react

réalisateur, -trice [ʀealizatœʀ, -tʀis] nm/f (TV, Ciné) director

réalisation [ʀealizasjɔ̃] nf carrying out; realization; fulfilment; achievement; (Ciné) production; (œuvre) production, work; (création) creation; **en cours de ~** under way

réaliser [ʀealize] vt (projet, opération) to carry out, realize; (rêve, souhait) to realize, fulfil; (exploit) to achieve; (achat, vente) to make; (film) to produce; (se rendre compte de, Comm: bien, capital) to realize; **se réaliser** vi to be realized

réaliste [ʀealist] adj realistic; (peintre, roman) realist ▷ nm/f realist

réalité [ʀealite] nf reality; **en ~** in (actual) fact; **dans la ~** in reality; **~ virtuelle** virtual reality

réanimation [ʀeanimasjɔ̃] nf resuscitation; **service de ~** intensive care unit

rébarbatif, -ive [ʀebaʀbatif, -iv] adj forbidding; (style) off-putting (Brit), crabbed

rebattu, e [ʀəbaty] adj hackneyed

rebelle [ʀəbɛl] nm/f rebel ▷ adj (troupes) rebel; (enfant) rebellious; (mèche etc) unruly; **~ à qch** unamenable to sth; **~ à faire** unwilling to do

rebeller [ʀəbele]: **se rebeller** vi to rebel

rebondi, e [ʀəbɔ̃di] adj (ventre) rounded; (joues) chubby, well-rounded

rebondir [ʀəbɔ̃diʀ] vi (ballon: au sol) to bounce; (: contre un mur) to rebound; (fig: procès, action, conversation) to get moving again, be suddenly revived

rebondissement [ʀəbɔ̃dismɑ̃] nm new development

rebord [ʀəbɔʀ] nm edge; **le ~ de la fenêtre** the windowsill

rebours [ʀəbuʀ]: **à ~** adv the wrong way

rebrousser [ʀəbʀuse] vt (cheveux, poils) to brush back, brush up; **~ chemin** to turn back

rebut [ʀəby] nm: **mettre au ~** to scrap, discard

rebutant, e [ʀəbytɑ̃, -ɑ̃t] adj (travail, démarche) off-putting, disagreeable

rebuter [ʀəbyte] vt to put off

récalcitrant, e [ʀekalsitʀɑ̃, -ɑ̃t] adj refractory, recalcitrant

recaler [ʀəkale] vt (Scol) to fail

récapituler [ʀekapityle] vt to recapitulate; (résumer) to sum up

receler [ʀəsəle] vt (produit d'un vol) to receive; (malfaiteur) to harbour; (fig) to conceal

receleur, -euse [ʀəsəlœʀ, -øz] nm/f receiver

récemment [ʀesamɑ̃] adv recently

recensement [ʀəsɑ̃smɑ̃] nm census; inventory

recenser [ʀəsɑ̃se] vt (population) to take a census of; (inventorier) to make an inventory of; (dénombrer) to list

récent, e [ʀesɑ̃, -ɑ̃t] adj recent

récépissé [ʀesepise] nm receipt

récepteur, -trice [ʀeseptœʀ, -tʀis] adj receiving ▷ nm receiver; **~ (de radio)** radio set ou receiver

réception [ʀesepsjɔ̃] nf receiving no pl; (d'une marchandise, commande) receipt; (accueil) reception, welcome; (bureau) reception (desk); (réunion mondaine) reception, party; (pièces) reception rooms pl; (Sport: après un saut) landing; (du ballon) catching no pl; **jour/heures de ~** day/hours for receiving visitors (ou students etc)

réceptionniste [ʀesepsjɔnist] nm/f receptionist

recette [ʀəsɛt] nf (Culin) recipe; (fig) formula, recipe; (Comm) takings pl; (Admin: bureau) tax ou revenue office; **recettes** nfpl (Comm: rentrées) receipts; **faire ~** (spectacle, exposition) to be a winner

receveur, -euse [ʀəsəvœʀ, -øz] nm/f (des contributions) tax collector; (des postes) postmaster/mistress; (d'autobus) conductor/conductress; (Méd: de sang, organe) recipient

recevoir [ʀəsəvwaʀ] vt to receive; (lettre, prime) to receive, get; (client, patient, représentant) to see; (jour, soleil: pièce) to get; (Scol: candidat) to pass ▷ vi to receive visitors; to give parties; to see patients etc; **se recevoir** vi (athlète) to land; **~ qn à dîner** to invite sb to dinner; **il reçoit de huit à 10** he's at home from eight to 10, he will see visitors from eight to 10; (docteur, dentiste etc) he sees patients from eight to 10; **être reçu** (à un examen) to pass; **être bien/mal reçu** to be well/badly received

rechange [ʀəʃɑ̃ʒ]: **de ~** adj (pièces, roue) spare; (fig: solution) alternative; **des vêtements de ~** a change of clothes

réchapper [ʀeʃape]: **~ de ou à** vt (accident, maladie) to come through; **va-t-il en ~?** is he going to get over it?, is he going to come through (it)?

recharge [ʀəʃaʀʒ] nf refill

rechargeable [ʀəʃaʀʒabl] adj (stylo etc) refillable; rechargeable

recharger [ʀəʃaʀʒe] vt (camion, fusil, appareil photo) to reload; (briquet, stylo) to refill; (batterie) to recharge

réchaud [ʀeʃo] nm (portable) stove, plate-warmer

réchauffer [ʀeʃofe] vt (plat) to reheat; (mains, personne) to warm; **se réchauffer** vi (température) to get warmer; (personne) to warm o.s. (up); **se ~ les doigts** to warm (up) one's fingers

rêche [ʀɛʃ] adj rough

recherche [ʀəʃɛʀʃ] nf (action): **la ~ de** the search for; (raffinement) affectedness, studied elegance; (scientifique etc): **la ~** research;

recherches *nfpl* (*de la police*) investigations; (*scientifiques*) research *sg*; **être/se mettre à la ~ de** to be/go in search of

recherché, e [ʀəʃɛʀʃe] *adj* (*rare, demandé*) much sought-after; (*entouré: acteur, femme*) in demand; (*raffiné*) studied, affected; (*tenue*) elegant

rechercher [ʀəʃɛʀʃe] *vt* (*objet égaré, personne*) to look for, search for; (*témoins, coupable, main-d'œuvre*) to look for; (*causes d'un phénomène, nouveau procédé*) to try to find; (*bonheur etc, l'amitié de qn*) to seek; **"~ et remplacer"** (*Inform*) "find and replace"

rechigner [ʀəʃiɲe] *vi*: **~ (à)** to balk (at)

rechute [ʀəʃyt] *nf* (*Méd*) relapse; (*dans le péché, le vice*) lapse; **faire une ~** to have a relapse

récidiver [ʀesidive] *vi* to commit a second (*ou* subsequent) offence; (*fig*) to do it again

récif [ʀesif] *nm* reef

récipient [ʀesipjã] *nm* container

réciproque [ʀesipʀɔk] *adj* reciprocal ▷ *nf*: **la ~** (*l'inverse*) the converse

récit [ʀesi] *nm* (*action de narrer*) telling; (*conte, histoire*) story

récital [ʀesital] *nm* recital

réciter [ʀesite] *vt* to recite

réclamation [ʀeklamasjõ] *nf* complaint; **réclamations** *nfpl* (*bureau*) complaints department *sg*

réclame [ʀeklam] *nf*: **la ~** advertising; **une ~** an ad(vertisement), an advert (*Brit*); **faire de la ~ (pour qch/qn)** to advertise (sth/sb); **article en ~** special offer

réclamer [ʀeklame] *vt* (*aide, nourriture etc*) to ask for; (*revendiquer: dû, part, indemnité*) to claim, demand; (*nécessiter*) to demand, require ▷ *vi* to complain; **se ~ de** to give as one's authority; to claim filiation with

réclusion [ʀeklyzjõ] *nf* imprisonment; **~ à perpétuité** life imprisonment

recoin [ʀəkwɛ̃] *nm* nook, corner; (*fig*) hidden recess

reçois *etc* [ʀəswa] *vb voir* **recevoir**

récolte [ʀekɔlt] *nf* harvesting, gathering; (*produits*) harvest, crop; (*fig*) crop, collection; (: *d'observations*) findings

récolter [ʀekɔlte] *vt* to harvest, gather (in); (*fig*) to get

recommandé [ʀəkɔmãde] *nm* (*méthode etc*) recommended; (*Postes*): **en ~** by registered mail

recommander [ʀəkɔmãde] *vt* to recommend; (*qualités etc*) to commend; (*Postes*) to register; **~ qch à qn** to recommend sth to sb; **~ à qn de faire** to recommend sb to do; **~ qn auprès de qn** *ou* **à qn** to recommend sb to sb; **il est recommandé de faire ...** it is recommended that one does ...; **se ~ à qn** to commend o.s. to sb; **se ~ de qn** to give sb's name as a reference

recommencer [ʀəkɔmãse] *vt* (*reprendre: lutte, séance*) to resume, start again; (*refaire: travail, explications*) to start afresh, start (over) again;

(*récidiver: erreur*) to make again ▷ *vi* to start again; (*récidiver*) to do it again; **~ à faire** to start doing again; **ne recommence pas!** don't do that again!

récompense [ʀekõpãs] *nf* reward; (*prix*) award; **recevoir qch en ~** to get sth as a reward, be rewarded with sth

récompenser [ʀekõpãse] *vt*: **~ qn (de** *ou* **pour)** to reward sb (for)

réconcilier [ʀekõsilje] *vt* to reconcile; **~ avec qn** to reconcile sb with sb; **~ qn avec qch** to reconcile sb to sth; **se réconcilier (avec)** to be reconciled (with)

reconduire [ʀəkõdɥiʀ] *vt* (*raccompagner*) to take *ou* see back; (: *à la porte*) to show out; (: *à son domicile*) to see home, take home; (*Jur, Pol*: *renouveler*) to renew

réconfort [ʀekõfɔʀ] *nm* comfort

réconforter [ʀekõfɔʀte] *vt* (*consoler*) to comfort; (*revigorer*) to fortify

reconnaissance [ʀəkɔnɛsãs] *nf* (*action de reconnaître*) recognition; acknowledgement; (*gratitude*) gratitude, gratefulness; (*Mil*) reconnaissance, recce; **en ~** (*Mil*) on reconnaissance; **~ de dette** acknowledgement of a debt, IOU

reconnaissant, e [ʀəkɔnɛsã, -ãt] *vb voir* **reconnaître** ▷ *adj* grateful; **je vous serais ~ de bien vouloir** I should be most grateful if you would (kindly)

reconnaître [ʀəkɔnɛtʀ] *vt* to recognize; (*Mil*: *lieu*) to reconnoitre; (*Jur*: *enfant, dette, droit*) to acknowledge; **~ que** to admit *ou* acknowledge that; **~ qn/qch à** (*l'identifier grâce à*) to recognize sb/sth by; **~ à qn: je lui reconnais certaines qualités** I recognize certain qualities in him; **se ~ quelque part** (*s'y retrouver*) to find one's way around (a place)

reconnu, e [ʀ(ə)kɔny] *pp de* **reconnaître** ▷ *adj* (*indiscuté, connu*) recognized

reconstituant, e [ʀəkõstitɥã, -ãt] *adj* (*régime*) strength-building ▷ *nm* tonic, pick-me-up

reconstituer [ʀəkõstitɥe] *vt* (*monument ancien*) to recreate, build a replica of; (*fresque, vase brisé*) to piece together, reconstitute; (*événement, accident*) to reconstruct; (*fortune, patrimoine*) to rebuild; (*Bio*: *tissus etc*) to regenerate

reconstruction [ʀəkõstʀyksjõ] *nf* rebuilding, reconstruction

reconstruire [ʀəkõstʀɥiʀ] *vt* to rebuild, reconstruct

reconvertir [ʀəkõvɛʀtiʀ] *vt* (*usine*) to reconvert; (*personnel, troupes etc*) to redeploy; **se ~ dans** (*un métier, une branche*) to move into, be redeployed into

record [ʀəkɔʀ] *nm, adj* record; **~ du monde** world record

recoupement [ʀəkupmã] *nm*: **faire un ~** *ou* **des ~s** to cross-check; **par ~** by cross-checking

recouper [Rəkupe] vt (tranche) to cut again; (vêtement) to recut ▷ vi (Cartes) to cut again; **se recouper** vi (témoignages) to tie ou match up

recourber [RəkuRbe] vt (branche, tige de métal) to bend; **se recourber** vi to curve (up), bend (up)

recourir [RəkuRiR] vi (courir de nouveau) to run again; (refaire une course) to race again; ~ **à** vt (ami, agence) to turn ou appeal to; (force, ruse, emprunt) to resort to, have recourse to

recours [RəkuR] vb voir **recourir** ▷ nm (Jur) appeal; **avoir** ~ **à** = **recourir à**; **en dernier** ~ as a last resort; **sans** ~ final; with no way out; ~ **en grâce** plea for clemency (ou pardon)

recouvrer [RəkuvRe] vt (vue, santé etc) to recover, regain; (impôts) to collect; (créance) to recover

recouvrir [RəkuvRiR] vt (couvrir à nouveau) to re-cover; (couvrir entièrement: aussi fig) to cover; (cacher, masquer) to conceal, hide; **se recouvrir** (se superposer) to overlap

récréation [RekReasjɔ̃] nf recreation, entertainment; (Scol) break

récrier [RekRije]: **se récrier** vi to exclaim

récriminations [RekRiminasjɔ̃] nfpl remonstrations, complaints

recroqueviller [RəkRɔkvije]: **se recroqueviller** vi (feuilles) to curl ou shrivel up; (personne) to huddle up

recru, e [RəkRy] adj: ~ **de fatigue** exhausted ▷ nf recruit

recrudescence [RəkRydesɑ̃s] nf fresh outbreak

recruter [RəkRyte] vt to recruit

rectangle [Rɛktɑ̃gl] nm rectangle

rectangulaire [Rɛktɑ̃gylɛR] adj rectangular

rectificatif, -ive [Rɛktifikatif, -iv] adj corrected ▷ nm correction

rectifier [Rɛktifje] vt (tracé, virage) to straighten; (calcul, adresse) to correct; (erreur, faute) to rectify, put right

rectiligne [Rɛktilin] adj straight; (Géom) rectilinear

recto [Rɛkto] nm front (of a sheet of paper); ~ **verso** on both sides (of the page)

reçu, e [Rəsy] pp de **recevoir** ▷ adj (candidat) successful; (admis, consacré) accepted ▷ nm (Comm) receipt

recueil [Rəkœj] nm collection

recueillir [Rəkœjir] vt to collect; (voix, suffrages) to win; (accueillir: réfugiés, chat) to take in; **se recueillir** vi to gather one's thoughts; to meditate

recul [Rəkyl] nm retreat; recession; (déclin) decline; (éloignement) distance; (d'arme à feu) recoil, kick; **avoir un mouvement de** ~ to recoil, start back; **prendre du** ~ to stand back; **être en** ~ to be on the decline; **avec le** ~ with the passing of time, in retrospect

reculé, e [Rəkyle] adj remote

reculer [Rəkyle] vi to move back, back away; (Auto) to reverse, back (up); (fig: civilisation, épidémie) to (be on the) decline; (: se dérober) to shrink back ▷ vt to move back; (véhicule) to reverse, back (up); (fig: possibilités, limites) to extend; (: date, décision) to postpone; ~ **devant** (danger, difficulté) to shrink from; ~ **pour mieux sauter** (fig) to postpone the evil day

reculons [Rəkylɔ̃]: **à** ~ adv backwards

récupérer [RekypeRe] vt (rentrer en possession de) to recover, get back; (: forces) to recover; (déchets etc) to salvage (for reprocessing); (remplacer: journée, heures de travail) to make up; (délinquant etc) to rehabilitate; (Pol) to bring into line ▷ vi to recover

récurer [RekyRe] vt to scour; **poudre à** ~ scouring powder

reçus etc [Rəsy] vb voir **recevoir**

récuser [Rekyze] vt to challenge; **se récuser** to decline to give an opinion

recyclage [Rəsiklaʒ] nm recycling; **centre de** ~ recycling centre

recycler [Rəsikle] vt (Scol) to reorientate; (employés) to retrain; (matériau) to recycle; **se recycler** vi to retrain; to go on a retraining course

rédacteur, -trice [RedaktœR, -tRis] nm/f (journaliste) writer; subeditor; (d'ouvrage de référence) editor, compiler; ~ **en chef** chief editor; ~ **publicitaire** copywriter

rédaction [Redaksjɔ̃] nf writing; (rédacteurs) editorial staff; (bureau) editorial office(s); (Scol: devoir) essay, composition

redemander [Rədmɑ̃de] vt (renseignement) to ask again for; (nourriture): ~ **de** to ask for more (ou another); (objet prêté): ~ **qch** to ask for sth back

redescendre [Rədesɑ̃dR] vi (à nouveau) to go back down; (après la montée) to go down (again) ▷ vt (pente etc) to go down

redevance [Rədvɑ̃s] nf (Tél) rental charge; (TV) licence (Brit) ou license (US) fee

rédiger [Rediʒe] vt to write; (contrat) to draw up

redire [RədiR] vt to repeat; **trouver à** ~ **à** to find fault with

redonner [Rədɔne] vt (restituer) to give back, return; (du courage, des forces) to restore

redoubler [Rəduble] vi (tempête, violence) to intensify, get even stronger ou fiercer etc; (Scol) to repeat a year ▷ vt (Scol: classe) to repeat; (Ling: lettre) to double; **le vent redouble de violence** the wind is blowing twice as hard; ~ **de patience/prudence** to be doubly patient/careful

redoutable [Rədutabl] adj formidable, fearsome

redouter [Rədute] vt to fear; (appréhender) to dread; ~ **de faire** to dread doing

redressement [RədRɛsmɑ̃] nm (économique) recovery; (de l'économie etc) putting right; **maison de** ~ reformatory; ~ **fiscal** repayment of back taxes

redresser [RədRese] vt (arbre, mât) to set upright, right; (pièce tordue) to straighten out; (Aviat, Auto) to straighten up; (situation, économie) to put right; **se redresser** vi (objet penché) to right itself; to straighten up; (personne) to sit (ou stand) up; to stand up straight; (fig: pays, situation) to recover; ~ **(les roues)** (Auto) to straighten up

réduction [Redyksjɔ̃] nf reduction; **en** ~ adv in miniature, scaled-down

réduire [Reduiʀ] vt (gén, Culin, Math) to reduce; (prix, dépenses) to cut, reduce; (carte) to scale down; (Méd: fracture) to set; ~ **qn/qch à** to reduce sb/sth to; **se** ~ **à** (revenir à) to boil down to; **se** ~ **en** (se transformer en) to be reduced to; **en être réduit à** to be reduced to

réduit, e [Redui, -it] pp de **réduire** ▷ adj (prix, tarif, échelle) reduced; (mécanisme) scaled-down; (vitesse) reduced ▷ nm tiny room; recess

rééducation [Reedykasjɔ̃] nf (d'un membre) re-education; (de délinquants, d'un blessé) rehabilitation; ~ **de la parole** speech therapy; **centre de** ~ physiotherapy ou physical therapy (US) centre

réel, le [Reɛl] adj real ▷ nm: **le** ~ reality

réellement [Reɛlmã] adv really

réexpédier [Reekspedje] vt (à l'envoyeur) to return, send back; (au destinataire) to send on, forward

refaire [RəfɛR] vt (faire de nouveau, recommencer) to do again; (sport) to take up again; (réparer, restaurer) to do up; **se refaire** vi (en argent) to make up one's losses; **se** ~ **une santé** to recuperate; **se** ~ **à qch** (se réhabituer à) to get used to sth again

réfection [Refɛksjɔ̃] nf repair; **en** ~ under repair

réfectoire [Refɛktwaʀ] nm refectory

référence [Referãs] nf reference; **références** nfpl (recommandations) reference sg; **faire** ~ **à** to refer to; **ouvrage de** ~ reference work; **ce n'est pas une** ~ (fig) that's no recommendation

référer [Refere]: **se** ~ **à** vt to refer to; **en** ~ **à qn** to refer the matter to sb

refermer [RəfɛRme] vt to close again, shut again; **se refermer** vi (porte) to close ou shut (again)

refiler [Rəfile] vt (fam): ~ **qch à qn** to palm (Brit) ou fob sth off on sb; to pass sth on to sb

réfléchi, e [Refleʃi] adj (caractère) thoughtful; (action) well-thought-out; (Ling) reflexive; **c'est tout** ~ my mind's made up

réfléchir [RefleʃiR] vt to reflect ▷ vi to think; ~ **à** ou **sur** to think about; **c'est tout réfléchi** my mind's made up

reflet [Rəflɛ] nm reflection; (sur l'eau etc) sheen no pl, glint; **reflets** nmpl gleam sg

refléter [Rəflete] vt to reflect; **se refléter** vi to be reflected

réflexe [Reflɛks] adj, nm reflex; ~ **conditionné** conditioned reflex

réflexion [Refleksjɔ̃] nf (de la lumière etc, pensée) reflection; (fait de penser) thought; (remarque) remark; **réflexions** nfpl (méditations) thought sg, reflection sg; **sans** ~ without thinking; ~ **faite, à la** ~, **après** ~ on reflection; **délai de** ~ cooling-off period; **groupe de** ~ think tank

réflexologie [Refleksɔlɔʒi] nf reflexology

refluer [Rəflye] vi to flow back; (foule) to surge back

reflux [Rəfly] nm (de la mer) ebb; (fig) backward surge

réforme [RefɔRm] nf reform; (Mil) declaration of unfitness for service; discharge (on health grounds); (Rel): **la R~** the Reformation

réformer [RefɔRme] vt to reform; (Mil: recrue) to declare unfit for service; (: soldat) to discharge, invalid out; (matériel) to scrap

refouler [Rəfule] vt (envahisseurs) to drive back, repulse; (liquide, larmes) to force back; (fig) to suppress; (Psych: désir, colère) to repress

refrain [Rəfrɛ̃] nm (Mus) refrain, chorus; (air, fig) tune

refréner, réfréner [Rəfrene, Refrene] vt to curb, check

réfrigérateur [RefriʒeRatœR] nm refrigerator; ~-**congélateur** fridge-freezer

refroidir [Rəfrwadiʀ] vt to cool; (fig) to have a cooling effect on; (personne) to put off ▷ vi to cool (down); **se refroidir** vi (prendre froid) to catch a chill; (temps) to get cooler ou colder; (fig: ardeur) to cool (off)

refroidissement [Rəfrwadismã] nm cooling; (grippe etc) chill

refuge [Rəfyʒ] nm refuge; (pour piétons) (traffic) island; **demander** ~ **à qn** to ask sb for refuge

réfugié, e [Refyʒje] adj, nm/f refugee

réfugier [Refyʒje]: **se réfugier** vi to take refuge

refus [Rəfy] nm refusal; **ce n'est pas de** ~ I won't say no, it's very welcome

refuser [Rəfyze] vt to refuse; (Scol: candidat) to fail ▷ vi to refuse; ~ **qch à qn/de faire** to refuse sb sth/to do; ~ **du monde** to have to turn people away; **se** ~ **à qch** ou **à faire qch** to refuse to do sth; **il ne se refuse rien** he doesn't stint himself; **se** ~ **à qn** to refuse sb

réfuter [Refyte] vt to refute

regagner [Rəɡaɲe] vt (argent, faveur) to win back; (lieu) to get back to; ~ **le temps perdu** to make up for lost time; ~ **du terrain** to regain ground

regain [Rəɡɛ̃] nm (herbe) second crop of hay; (renouveau): ~ **de qch** renewed sth

régal [Reɡal] nm treat; **un** ~ **pour les yeux** a pleasure ou delight to look at

régaler [Reɡale] vt: ~ **qn** to treat sb to a delicious meal; ~ **qn de** to treat sb to; **se régaler** vi to have a delicious meal; (fig) to enjoy o.s

regard [RəɡaR] nm (coup d'œil) look, glance; (expression) look (in one's eye); **parcourir/menacer du** ~ to cast an eye over/look threateningly at; **au ~ de** (loi, morale) from the point of view of; **en ~** (vis à vis) opposite; **en ~ de** in comparison with

regardant, e [ʀəgaʀdɑ̃, -ɑ̃t] adj: **très/peu ~ (sur)** quite fussy/very free (about); (économe) very tight-fisted/quite generous (with)

regarder [ʀəgaʀde] vt (examiner, observer, lire) to look at; (film, télévision, match) to watch; (envisager: situation, avenir) to view; (considérer: son intérêt etc) to be concerned with; (être orienté vers): **~ (vers)** to face; (concerner) to concern ▷ vi to look; **~ à** vt (dépense, qualité, détails) to be fussy ou over; **~ à faire** to hesitate to do; **dépenser sans ~** to spend freely; **ne pas ~ à la dépense** to spare no expense; **~ qn/qch comme** to regard sb/sth as; **~ (qch) dans le dictionnaire** to look (sth up) in the dictionary; **~ par la fenêtre** to look out of the window; **cela me regarde** it concerns me, it's my business

régie [ʀeʒi] nf (Comm, Industrie) state-owned company; (Théât, Ciné) production; (Radio, TV) control room; **~ de l'État** state control

regimber [ʀəʒɛ̃be] vi to balk, jib

régime [ʀeʒim] nm (Pol Géo) régime; (Admin: carcéral, fiscal etc) system; (Méd) diet; (Tech) (engine) speed; (fig) rate, pace; (de bananes, dattes) bunch; **se mettre au/suivre un ~** to go on/be on a diet; **~ sans sel** salt-free diet; **à bas/haut ~** (Auto) at low/high revs; **à plein ~** flat out, at full speed; **~ matrimonial** marriage settlement

régiment [ʀeʒimɑ̃] nm (Mil: unité) regiment; (fig: fam): **un ~ de** an army of; **un copain de ~** a pal from military service ou (one's) army days

région [ʀeʒjɔ̃] nf region; **la ~ parisienne** the Paris area

régional, e, -aux [ʀeʒjɔnal, -o] adj regional

régir [ʀeʒiʀ] vt to govern

régisseur [ʀeʒisœʀ] nm (d'un domaine) steward; (Ciné, TV) assistant director; (Théât) stage manager

registre [ʀəʒistʀ] nm (livre) register; logbook; ledger; (Mus, Ling) register; (d'orgue) stop; **~ de comptabilité** ledger; **~ de l'état civil** register of births, marriages and deaths

réglage [ʀeglaʒ] nm (d'une machine) adjustment; (d'un moteur) tuning

réglé, e [ʀegle] adj well-ordered; stable, steady; (papier) ruled; (arrangé) settled

règle [ʀegl] nf (instrument) ruler; (loi, prescription) rule; **règles** nfpl (Physiol) period sg; **avoir pour ~ de** to make it a rule that ou to; **en ~** (papiers d'identité) in order; **être/se mettre en ~** to be/put o.s. straight with the authorities; **en ~ générale** as a (general) rule; **être la ~** to be the rule; **être de ~** to be usual; **~ à calcul** slide rule; **~ de trois** (Math) rule of three

règlement [ʀeglamɑ̃] nm settling; (paiement) settlement; (arrêté) regulation; (règles, statuts)

regulations pl, rules pl; **~ à la commande** cash with order; **~ de compte(s)** settling of scores; **~ en espèces/par chèque** payment in cash/by cheque; **~ intérieur** (Scol) school rules pl; (Admin) by-laws pl; **~ judiciaire** compulsory liquidation

réglementaire [ʀeglamɑ̃tɛʀ] adj conforming to the regulations; (tenue, uniforme) regulation cpd

réglementation [ʀeglamɑ̃tasjɔ̃] nf regulation, control; (règlements) regulations pl

réglementer [ʀeglamɑ̃te] vt to regulate, control

régler [ʀegle] vt (mécanisme, machine) to regulate, adjust; (moteur) to tune; (thermostat etc) to set, adjust; (emploi du temps etc) to organize, plan; (question, conflit, facture, dette) to settle; (fournisseur) to settle up with, pay; (papier) to rule; **~ qch sur** to model sth on; **~ son compte** to sort sb out, settle sb; **~ un compte** to settle a score with sb

réglisse [ʀeglis] nf ou m liquorice; **bâton de ~** liquorice stick

règne [ʀɛɲ] nm (d'un roi etc, fig) reign; (Bio): **le ~ végétal/animal** the vegetable/animal kingdom

régner [ʀeɲe] vi (roi) to rule, reign; (fig) to reign

regorger [ʀəgɔʀʒe] vi to overflow; **~ de** to overflow with, be bursting with

regret [ʀəgʀɛ] nm regret; **à ~** with regret; **avec ~** regretfully; **sans ~** with no regrets; **être au ~ de devoir/ne pas pouvoir faire** to regret to have to/that one is unable to do; **j'ai le ~ de vous informer que …** I regret to inform you that …

regrettable [ʀəgʀetabl] adj regrettable

regretter [ʀəgʀete] vt to regret; (personne) to miss; **~ d'avoir fait** to regret doing; **~ que** to regret that, be sorry that; **non, je regrette** no, I'm sorry

regrouper [ʀəgʀupe] vt (grouper) to group together; (contenir) to include, comprise; **se regrouper** vi to gather (together)

régulier, -ière [ʀegylje, -jɛʀ] adj (gén) regular; (vitesse, qualité) steady; (répartition, pression) even; (Transports: ligne, service) scheduled, regular; (légal, réglementaire) lawful, in order; (fam: correct) straight, on the level

régulièrement [ʀegyljɛʀmɑ̃] adv regularly; steadily; evenly; normally

rehausser [ʀəose] vt (relever) to heighten, raise; (fig: souligner) to set off, enhance

rein [ʀɛ̃] nm kidney; **reins** nmpl (dos) back sg; **avoir mal aux ~s** to have backache; **~ artificiel** kidney machine

reine [ʀɛn] nf queen

reine-claude [ʀɛnklod] nf greengage

réinscriptible [ʀeɛ̃skʀiptibl] adj (CD, DVD) rewritable

réinsertion [ʀeɛ̃sɛʀsjɔ̃] nf (de délinquant) reintegration, rehabilitation

réintégrer [ʀeɛ̃tegʀe] vt (lieu) to return to; (fonctionnaire) to reinstate

rejaillir [ʀəʒajiʀ] vi to splash up; **~ sur** to splash up onto; (fig: scandale) to rebound on; (: gloire) to be reflected on; to fall upon

rejet [ʀəʒɛ] nm (action, aussi Méd) rejection; (Poésie) enjambement, rejet; (Bot) shoot

rejeter [ʀəʒte] vt (relancer) to throw back; (vomir) to bring ou throw up; (écarter) to reject; (déverser) to transfer, rejet, discharge; (reporter): **~ un mot à la fin d'une phrase** to transpose a word to the end of a sentence; **se ~ sur qch** (accepter faute de mieux) to fall back on sth; **~ la tête/les épaules en arrière** to throw one's head/pull one's shoulders back; **~ la responsabilité de qch sur qn** to lay the responsibility for sth at sb's door

rejoindre [ʀəʒwɛ̃dʀ] vt (famille, régiment) to rejoin, return to; (lieu) to get (back) to; (route etc) to meet, join; (rattraper) to catch up (with); **se rejoindre** vi to meet; **je te rejoins au café** I'll see ou meet you at the café

réjouir [ʀeʒwiʀ] vt to delight; **se réjouir** vi to be delighted; **se ~ de qch/de faire** to be delighted about sth/to do; **se ~ que** to be delighted that

réjouissances [ʀeʒwisɑ̃s] nfpl (joie) rejoicing sg; (fête) festivities, merry-making sg

relâche [ʀəlɑʃ]: **faire ~** vi (navire) to put into port; (Ciné) to be closed; **c'est le jour de ~** (Ciné) it's closed today; **sans ~** adv without respite ou a break

relâché, e [ʀəlɑʃe] adj loose, lax

relâcher [ʀəlɑʃe] vt (ressort, prisonnier) to release; (étreinte, cordes) to loosen; (discipline) to relax ▷ vi (Navig) to put into port; **se relâcher** vi to loosen; (discipline) to become slack ou lax; (élève etc) to slacken off

relais [ʀəlɛ] nm (Sport): **(course de) ~** relay (race); (Radio, TV) relay; (intermédiaire) go-between; **équipe de ~** shift team; (Sport) relay team; **prendre le ~ (de)** to take over (from); **~ de poste** post house, coaching inn; **~ routier** ≈ transport café (Brit), ≈ truck stop (US)

relancer [ʀəlɑ̃se] vt (balle) to throw back (again); (moteur) to restart; (fig) to boost, revive; (personne): **~ qn** to pester sb; to get on to sb again

relatif, -ive [ʀəlatif, -iv] adj relative

relation [ʀəlasjɔ̃] nf (récit) account, report; (rapport) relation(ship); (connaissance) acquaintance; **relations** nfpl (rapports) relations; relationship; (connaissances) connections; **être/entrer en ~(s) avec** to be in contact ou be dealing/get in contact with; **mettre qn en ~(s) avec** to put sb in touch with; **~s internationales** international relations; **~s publiques** public relations; **~s (sexuelles)** sexual relations, (sexual) intercourse sg

relaxer [ʀəlakse] vt to relax; (Jur) to discharge; **se relaxer** vi to relax

relayer [ʀəleje] vt (collaborateur, coureur etc) to relieve, take over from; (Radio, TV) to relay; **se relayer** vi (dans une activité) to take it in turns

reléguer [ʀəlege] vt to relegate; **~ au second plan** to push into the background

relent [ʀəlɑ̃], **relents** nm(pl) stench sg

relevé, e [ʀəlve] adj (bord de chapeau) turned-up; (manches) rolled-up; (fig: style) elevated; (: sauce) highly-seasoned ▷ nm (lecture) reading; (de cotes) plotting; (liste) statement; list; (facture) account; **~ bancaire** ou **de compte** bank statement; **~ d'identité bancaire (RIB)** (bank) account number

relève [ʀəlɛv] nf (personne) relief; (équipe) relief team (ou troops pl); **prendre la ~** to take over

relever [ʀəlve] vt (statue, meuble) to stand up again; (personne tombée) to help up; (vitre, plafond, niveau de vie) to raise; (pays, économie, entreprise) to put back on its feet; (col) to turn up; (style, conversation) to elevate; (plat, sauce) to season; (sentinelle, équipe) to relieve; (souligner: fautes, points) to pick out; (constater: traces etc) to find, pick up; (répliquer à: remarque) to react to, reply to; (: défi) to accept, take up; (noter: adresse etc) to take down, note; (: plan) to sketch; (: cotes etc) to plot; (compteur) to read; (ramasser: cahiers, copies) to collect, take in ▷ vi (jupe, bord) to ride up; **~ de** vt (maladie) to be recovering from; (être du ressort de) to be a matter for; (Admin: dépendre de) to come under; (fig) to pertain to; **se relever** vi (se remettre debout) to get up; (fig): **se ~ (de)** to recover (from); **~ qn de** (vœux) to release sb from; (fonctions) to relieve sb of; **~ la tête** to look up; to hold up one's head

relief [ʀəljɛf] nm relief; (de pneu) tread pattern; **reliefs** nmpl (restes) remains; **en ~** in relief; (photographie) three-dimensional; **mettre en ~** (fig) to bring out, highlight

relier [ʀəlje] vt to link up; (livre) to bind; **~ qch à** to link sth to; **livre relié cuir** leather-bound book

religieux, -euse [ʀəliʒjø, -øz] adj religious ▷ nm monk ▷ nf nun; (gâteau) cream bun

religion [ʀəliʒjɔ̃] nf religion; (piété, dévotion) faith; **entrer en ~** to take one's vows

relire [ʀəliʀ] vt (à nouveau) to reread, read again; (vérifier) to read over; **se relire** to read through what one has written

reliure [ʀəljyʀ] nf binding; (art, métier): **la ~** book-binding

relooker [ʀəluke] vt: **~ qn** to give sb a makeover

reluire [ʀəlɥiʀ] vi to gleam

remanier [ʀəmanje] vt to reshape, recast; (Pol) to reshuffle

remarquable [ʀəmaʀkabl] adj remarkable

remarque [ʀəmaʀk] nf remark; (écrite) note

remarquer [ʀəmaʀke] vt (voir) to notice; (dire): **~ que** to remark that; **se ~** vi to be noticeable; **se faire ~** to draw attention to o.s.; **faire ~ (à qn) que** to point out (to sb) that; **faire ~ qch (à qn)** to point sth out (to sb); **remarquez, ...** mark you, ..., mind you, ...

rembourrer [ʀɑ̃buʀe] vt to stuff; (dossier, vêtement, souliers) to pad

remboursement [ʀɑ̃buʀsəmɑ̃] nm (de dette, d'emprunt) repayment; (de frais) refund; **envoi contre ~** cash on delivery

rembourser [ʀɑ̃buʀse] vt to pay back, repay; (frais, billet etc) to refund; **se faire ~** to get a refund

remède [ʀəmɛd] nm (médicament) medicine; (traitement, fig) remedy, cure; **trouver un ~ à** (Méd, fig) to find a cure for

remémorer [ʀəmemɔʀe]: **se remémorer** vt to recall, recollect

remerciements [ʀəmɛʀsimɑ̃] nmpl thanks; **(avec) tous mes ~** (with) grateful ou many thanks

remercier [ʀəmɛʀsje] vt to thank; (congédier) to dismiss; **~ qn de/d'avoir fait** to thank sb for/for having done; **non, je vous remercie** no thank you

remettre [ʀəmɛtʀ] vt (vêtement): **~ qch** to put sth back on, put sth on again; (replacer): **~ qch quelque part** to put sth back somewhere; (ajouter): **~ du sel/un sucre** to add more salt/another lump of sugar; (rétablir: personne): **~ qn** to set sb back on his (ou her) feet; (rendre, restituer): **~ qch à qn** to give sth back to sb, return sth to sb; (donner, confier: paquet, argent): **~ qch à qn** to hand sth over to sb, deliver sth to sb; (prix, décoration): **~ qch à qn** (donner: lettre, clé etc) to hand over sth to sb; (: prix, décoration) to present sb with sth; (ajourner): **~ qch (à)** to postpone sth ou put sth off (until); **se remettre** vi to get better, recover; **se ~ de** to recover from, get over; **s'en ~ à** to leave it (up) to; **se ~ à faire/qch** to start doing/sth again; **~ une pendule à l'heure** to put a clock right; **~ un moteur/une machine en marche** to get an engine/a machine going again; **~ en état/en ordre** to repair/sort out; **~ en cause/question** to challenge/question again; **~ sa démission** to hand in one's notice; **~ qch à neuf** to make sth as good as new; **~ qn à sa place** (fig) to put sb in his (ou her) place

remis, e [ʀəmi, -iz] pp de remettre ▷ nf delivery; presentation; (rabais) discount; (local) shed; **~e en marche/en ordre** starting up again/sorting out; **~e en cause/question** calling into question/challenging; **~e de fonds** remittance; **~e en jeu** (Football) throw-in; **~e à neuf** restoration; **~e de peine** remission of sentence; **~e des prix** prize-giving

remontant [ʀəmɔ̃tɑ̃] nm tonic, pick-me-up

remonte-pente [ʀəmɔ̃tpɑ̃t] nm ski lift, (ski) tow

remonter [ʀəmɔ̃te] vi (à nouveau) to go back up; (à cheval) to remount; (après une descente) to go up (again); (prix, température) to go up again; (en voiture) to get back in; (jupe) to ride up ▷ vt (pente) to go up; (fleuve) to sail (ou swim etc) up; up; (col) to turn up; (manches, pantalon) to roll up; (niveau, limite) to raise; (fig: personne) to buck up; (moteur, meuble) to put back together, reassemble; (garde-robe etc) to renew, replenish; (montre, mécanisme) to wind up; **~ le moral à qn** to raise sb's spirits; **~ à** (dater de) to date ou go back to; **~ en voiture** to get back into the car

remontrance [ʀəmɔ̃tʀɑ̃s] nf reproof, reprimand

remontrer [ʀəmɔ̃tʀe] vt (montrer de nouveau): **~ qch (à qn)** to show sth again (to sb); (fig): **en ~ à** to prove one's superiority over

remords [ʀəmɔʀ] nm remorse no pl; **avoir des ~** to feel remorse, be conscience-stricken

remorque [ʀəmɔʀk] nf trailer; **prendre/être en ~** to tow/be on tow; **être à la ~** (fig) to tag along (behind)

remorquer [ʀəmɔʀke] vt to tow

remorqueur [ʀəmɔʀkœʀ] nm tug(boat)

remous [ʀəmu] nm (d'un navire) (back)wash no pl; (de rivière) swirl, eddy pl; (fig) stir sg

remparts [ʀɑ̃paʀ] nmpl walls, ramparts

remplaçant, e [ʀɑ̃plasɑ̃, -ɑ̃t] nm/f replacement, substitute, stand-in; (Théât) understudy; (Scol) supply (Brit) ou substitute (US) teacher

remplacement [ʀɑ̃plasmɑ̃] nm replacement; (job) replacement work no pl; (suppléance: Scol) supply (Brit) ou substitute (US) teacher; **assurer le ~ de qn** (remplaçant) to stand in ou substitute for sb; **faire des ~s** (professeur) to do supply ou substitute teaching; (médecin) to do locum work; (secrétaire) to temp

remplacer [ʀɑ̃plase] vt to replace; (prendre temporairement la place de) to stand in for; (tenir lieu de) to take the place of, act as a substitute for; **~ qch/qn par** to replace sth/sb with

rempli, e [ʀɑ̃pli] adj (emploi du temps) full, busy; **~ de** full of, filled with

remplir [ʀɑ̃pliʀ] vt to fill (up); (questionnaire) to fill out ou up; (obligations, fonction, condition) to fulfil; **se remplir** vi to fill up; **~ qch de** to fill sth with

remporter [ʀɑ̃pɔʀte] vt (marchandise) to take away; (fig) to win, achieve

remuant, e [ʀəmyɑ̃, -ɑ̃t] adj restless

remue-ménage [ʀəmymenaʒ] nm inv commotion

remuer [ʀəmye] vt to move; (café, sauce) to stir ▷ vi to move; (fig: opposants) to show signs of unrest; **se remuer** vi to move; (se démener) to stir o.s.; (fam: s'activer) to get a move on

rémunérer [ʀemyneʀe] vt to remunerate, pay

renard [ʀənaʀ] nm fox

renchérir [ʀɑ̃ʃeʀiʀ] vi to become more expensive; (fig): **~ (sur)** (en paroles) to add something (to)

rencontre [RãkõtR] *nf* (*de cours d'eau*) confluence; (*de véhicules*) collision; (*entrevue, congrès, match etc*) meeting; (*imprévue*) encounter; **faire la ~ de qn** to meet sb; **aller à la ~ de qn** to go and meet sb; **amours de ~** casual love affairs

rencontrer [RãkõtRe] *vt* to meet; (*mot, expression*) to come across; (*difficultés*) to meet with; **se rencontrer** *vi* to meet; (*véhicules*) to collide

rendement [Rãdmã] *nm* (*d'un travailleur, d'une machine*) output; (*d'une culture, d'un champ*) yield; (*d'un investissement*) return; **à plein ~** at full capacity

rendez-vous [Rãdevu] *nm* (*rencontre*) appointment; (: *d'amoureux*) date; (*lieu*) meeting place; **donner ~ à qn** to arrange to meet sb; **recevoir sur ~** to have an appointment system; **fixer un ~ à qn** to give sb an appointment; **avoir/prendre ~ (avec)** to have/make an appointment (with); **prendre ~ chez le médecin** to make an appointment with the doctor; **~ spatial** *ou* **orbital** docking (in space)

rendre [RãdR] *vt* (*livre, argent etc*) to give back, return; (*otages, visite, politesse, invitation, Jur: verdict*) to return; (*honneurs*) to pay; (*sang, aliments*) to bring up; (*exprimer, traduire*) to render; (*jugement*) to pronounce, render; (*faire devenir*): **~ qn célèbre/qch possible** to make sb famous/sth possible; **se rendre** *vi* (*capituler*) to surrender, give o.s. up; (*aller*): **se ~ quelque part** to go somewhere; **se ~ à** (*arguments etc*) to bow to; (*ordres*) to comply with; **se ~ compte de qch** to realize sth; **~ la vue/la santé à qn** to restore sb's sight/health; **~ la liberté à qn** to set sb free; **~ la monnaie** to give change; **se ~ insupportable/malade** to become unbearable/make o.s. ill

rênes [Rɛn] *nfpl* reins

renfermé, e [RãfɛRme] *adj* (*fig*) withdrawn ▷ *nm*: **sentir le ~** to smell stuffy

renfermer [RãfɛRme] *vt* to contain; **se renfermer (sur soi-même)** to withdraw into o.s

renflouer [Rãflue] *vt* to refloat; (*fig*) to set back on its (*ou* his/her *etc*) feet (again)

renfoncement [Rãfõsmã] *nm* recess

renforcer [RãfɔRse] *vt* to reinforce; **~ qn dans ses opinions** to confirm sb's opinion

renfort [RãfɔR] **~s** *nmpl* reinforcements; **en ~** as a back-up; **à grand ~ de** with a great deal of

renfrogné, e [Rãfrɔɲe] *adj* sullen, scowling

rengaine [Rãgɛn] *nf* (*péj*) old tune

renier [Rənje] *vt* (*parents*) to disown, repudiate; (*engagements*) to go back on; (*foi*) to renounce

renifler [Rənifle] *vi* to sniff ▷ *vt* (*tabac*) to sniff up; (*odeur*) to sniff

renne [Rɛn] *nm* reindeer *inv*

renom [Rənõ] *nm* reputation; (*célébrité*) renown; **vin de grand ~** celebrated *ou* highly renowned wine

renommé, e [Rən(ə)nɔme] *adj* celebrated, renowned ▷ *nf* fame

renoncer [Rənõse] *vi*: **~ à** *vt* to give up; **~ à faire** to give up the idea of doing; **j'y renonce!** I give up!

renouer [Rənwe] *vt* (*cravate etc*) to retie; (*fig: conversation, liaison*) to renew, resume; **~ avec** (*tradition*) to revive; (*habitude*) to take up again; **~ avec qn** to take up with sb again

renouvelable [Rən(ə)nuvlabl] *adj* (*contrat, bail, énergie*) renewable; (*expérience*) which can be renewed

renouveler [Rənuvle] *vt* to renew; (*exploit, méfait*) to repeat; **se renouveler** *vi* (*incident*) to recur, happen again, be repeated; (*cellules etc*) to be renewed *ou* replaced; (*artiste, écrivain*) to try something new

renouvellement [Rən(ə)nuvelmã] *nm* renewal; recurrence

rénover [Renɔve] *vt* (*immeuble*) to renovate, do up; (*meuble*) to restore; (*enseignement*) to reform; (*quartier*) to redevelop

renseignement [Rãsɛɲmã] *nm* information *no pl*, piece of information; (*Mil*) intelligence *no pl*; **prendre des ~s sur** to make inquiries about, ask for information about; (*guichet des*) **~s** information desk; (*service des*) **~s** (*Tél*) directory inquiries (*Brit*), information (*US*); **service de ~s** (*Mil*) intelligence service; **les ~s généraux** = the secret police

renseigner [Rãseɲe] *vt*: **~ qn (sur)** to give information to sb (about); **se renseigner** *vi* to ask for information, make inquiries

rentabilité [Rãtabilite] *nf* profitability; cost-effectiveness; (*d'un investissement*) return; **seuil de ~** break-even point

rentable [Rãtabl] *adj* profitable; cost-effective

rente [Rãt] *nf* income; (*pension*) pension; (*titre*) government stock *ou* bond; **~ viagère** life annuity

rentrée [RãtRe] *nf*: **~ (d'argent)** cash *no pl* coming in; **la ~ (des classes** *ou* **scolaire)** the start of the new school year; **la ~ (parlementaire)** the reopening *ou* reassembly of parliament; *see note*; **faire sa ~** (*artiste, acteur*) to make a comeback

RENTRÉE

La rentrée (des classes) in September each year has wider connotations than just the start of the new school year. It is also the time when political and social life picks up again after the long summer break, and so marks an important point in the French calendar.

rentrer [RãtRe] *vi* (*entrer de nouveau*) to go (*ou* come) back in; (*entrer*) to go (*ou* come) in;

(revenir chez soi) to go (ou come) (back) home; (air, clou: pénétrer) to go in; (revenu, argent) to come in ▷ vt (foins) to bring in; (véhicule) to put away; (chemise dans pantalon etc) to tuck in; (griffes) to draw in; (train d'atterrissage) to raise; (fig: larmes, colère etc) to hold back; ~ **le ventre** to pull in one's stomach; ~ **dans** to go to (ou come) back into; to go (ou come) into; (famille, patrie) to go back ou return to; (heurter) to crash into; (appartenir à) to be included in; (: catégorie etc) to fall into; ~ **dans l'ordre** to get back to normal; ~ **dans ses frais** to recover one's expenses (ou initial outlay)

renverse [ʀɑ̃vɛʀs]: **à la** ~ adv backwards

renverser [ʀɑ̃vɛʀse] vt (faire tomber: chaise, verre) to knock over, overturn; (piéton) to knock down; (liquide, contenu) to spill, upset; (retourner: verre, image) to turn upside down, invert; (: ordre des mots etc) to reverse; (fig: gouvernement etc) to overthrow; (stupéfier) to bowl over, stagger; **se renverser** vi (verre, vase) to fall over; to overturn; (contenu) to spill; **se ~ (en arrière)** to lean back; ~ **la tête/le corps (en arrière)** to tip one's head back/throw oneself back; ~ **la vapeur** (fig) to change course

renvoi [ʀɑ̃vwa] nm (d'employé) dismissal; return; reflection; postponement; (d'élève) expulsion; (référence) cross-reference; (éructation) belch

renvoyer [ʀɑ̃vwaje] vt to send back; (congédier) to dismiss; (Tennis) to return; (élève: définitivement) to expel; (lumière) to reflect; (son) to echo; (ajourner): ~ **qch (à)** to postpone sth (until); ~ **qch à qn** (rendre) to return sth to sb; ~ **qn à** (fig) to refer sb to

repaire [ʀəpɛʀ] nm den

répandre [ʀepɑ̃dʀ] vt (renverser) to spill; (étaler, diffuser) to spread; (lumière) to shed; (chaleur, odeur) to give off; **se répandre** vi to spill; to spread; **se ~ en** (injures etc) to pour out

répandu, e [ʀepɑ̃dy] pp de **répandre** ▷ adj (opinion, usage) widespread

réparateur, -trice [ʀepaʀatœʀ, -tʀis] nm/f repairer

réparation [ʀepaʀasjɔ̃] nf repairing no pl, repair; **en ~** (machine etc) under repair; **demander à qn ~ de** (offense etc) to ask sb to make amends for

réparer [ʀepaʀe] vt to repair; (fig: offense) to make up for, atone for; (: oubli, erreur) to put right

repartie [ʀəpaʀti] nf retort; **avoir de la ~** to be quick at repartee

repartir [ʀəpaʀtiʀ] vi to set off again; (voyageur) to leave again; (fig) to get going again, pick up again; ~ **à zéro** to start from scratch (again)

répartir [ʀepaʀtiʀ] vt (pour attribuer) to share out; (pour disperser, disposer) to divide up; (poids, chaleur) to distribute; (étaler: dans le temps): ~ **sur** to spread over; (classer, diviser): ~ **en** to

divide into, split up into; **se répartir** vt (travail, rôles) to share out between themselves

répartition [ʀepaʀtisjɔ̃] nf sharing out; dividing up; (des richesses etc) distribution

repas [ʀəpɑ] nm meal; **à l'heure des** ~ at mealtimes

repassage [ʀəpɑsaʒ] nm ironing

repasser [ʀəpɑse] vi to come (ou go) back ▷ vt (vêtement, tissu) to iron; (examen) to retake, resit; (film) to show again; (lame) to sharpen; (leçon, rôle: revoir) to go over (again); (plat, pain): ~ **qch à qn** to pass sth back to sb

repêcher [ʀəpeʃe] vt (noyé) to recover the body of, fish out; (fam: candidat) to pass (by inflating marks); to give a second chance to

repentir [ʀəpɑ̃tiʀ] nm repentance; **se repentir** vi to repent; **se ~ d'avoir fait qch** (regretter) to regret having done sth

répercussions [ʀepɛʀkysjɔ̃] nfpl repercussions

répercuter [ʀepɛʀkyte] vt (réfléchir, renvoyer: son, voix) to reflect; (faire transmettre: consignes, charges etc) to pass on; **se répercuter** vi (bruit) to reverberate; (fig): **se ~ sur** to have repercussions on

repère [ʀəpɛʀ] nm mark; (monument etc) landmark; (**point de**) ~ point of reference

repérer [ʀəpeʀe] vt (erreur, connaissance) to spot; (abri, ennemi) to locate; **se repérer** vi to get one's bearings; **se faire ~** to be spotted

répertoire [ʀepɛʀtwaʀ] nm (liste) (alphabetical) list; (carnet) index notebook; (Inform) directory; (de carnet) thumb index; (indicateur) directory, index; (d'un théâtre, artiste) repertoire

répéter [ʀepete] vt to repeat; (préparer: leçon) ▷ aussi vi to learn, go over; (Théât) to rehearse; **se répéter** (redire) to repeat o.s.; (se reproduire) to be repeated, recur

répétition [ʀepetisjɔ̃] nf repetition; (Théât) rehearsal; **répétitions** nfpl (leçons) private coaching sg; **armes à** ~ repeater weapons; ~ **générale** final dress rehearsal

répit [ʀepi] nm respite; **sans** ~ without letting up

replier [ʀəplije] vt (rabattre) to fold down ou over; **se replier** vi (armée) to withdraw, fall back; **se ~ sur soi-même** to withdraw into oneself

réplique [ʀeplik] nf (repartie, fig) reply; (objection) retort; (Théât) line; (copie) replica; **donner la ~ à** to play opposite; **sans** ~ adj no-nonsense; irrefutable

répliquer [ʀeplike] vi to reply; (avec impertinence) to answer back; (riposter) to retaliate

répondeur [ʀepɔ̃dœʀ] nm: ~ **(automatique)** (Tél) answering machine

répondre [ʀepɔ̃dʀ] vi to answer, reply; (freins, mécanisme) to respond; ~ **à** vt to reply to, answer; (avec impertinence): ~ **à qn** to answer sb back; (invitation, convocation) to reply to;

(*affection, salut*) to return; (*provocation: mécanisme etc*) to respond to; (*correspondre à: besoin*) to answer; (*: conditions*) to meet; (*: description*) to match; **~ que** to answer ou reply that; **~ de** to answer for

réponse [repɔ̃s] *nf* answer, reply; **avec ~ payée** (*Postes*) reply-paid, post-paid (US); **avoir ~ à tout** to have an answer for everything; **en ~ à** in reply to; **carte-/ bulletin-~** reply card/slip

reportage [rəpɔrtaʒ] *nm* (*bref*) report; (*écrit: documentaire*) story; article; (*en direct*) commentary; (*genre, activité*) **le ~** reporting

reporter¹ [rəpɔrtɛr] *nm* reporter

reporter² [rəpɔrte] *vt* (*total*): **~ qch sur** to carry sth forward ou over to; (*ajourner*): **~ qch (à)** to postpone sth (until); (*transférer*): **~ qch sur** to transfer sth to; **se ~ à** (*époque*) to think back to; (*document*) to refer to

repos [rəpo] *nm* rest; (*fig*) peace (and quiet); (*mental*) peace of mind; (*Mil*): **~!** (*stand*) at ease!; **en ~** at rest; **au ~** at rest; (*soldat*) at ease; **de tout ~** safe; **ce n'est pas de tout ~!** it's no picnic!

reposant, e [r(ə)pozɑ̃, -ɑ̃t] *adj* restful; (*sommeil*) refreshing

reposer [rəpoze] *vt* (*verre, livre*) to put down; (*rideaux, carreaux*) to put back; (*délasser*) to rest; (*problème*) to reformulate ▷ *vi* (*liquide, pâte*) to settle, rest; **laisser ~** (*pâte*) to leave to stand; (*personne*) **ici repose ...** here lies ...; **~ sur** to be built on; (*fig*) to rest on; **se reposer** *vi* to rest; **se ~ sur qn** to rely on sb

repoussant, e [rəpusɑ̃, -ɑ̃t] *adj* repulsive

repousser [rəpuse] *vi* to grow again ▷ *vt* to repel, repulse; (*offre*) to turn down, reject; (*tiroir, personne*) to push back; (*différer*) to put back

reprendre [rəprɑ̃dr] *vt* (*prisonnier, ville*) to recapture; (*objet prêté, donné*) to take back; (*chercher*): **je viendrai te ~ à 4 h** I'll come and fetch you ou I'll come back for you at 4; (*se resservir de*): **~ du pain/un œuf** to take (*ou eat*) more bread/another egg; (*Comm: article usagé*) to take back; to take in part exchange; (*firme, entreprise*) to take over; (*travail, promenade*) to resume; (*emprunter: argument, idée*) to take up, use; (*refaire: article etc*) to go over again; (*jupe etc*) to alter; (*émission, pièce*) to put on again; (*réprimander*) to tell off; (*corriger*) to correct ▷ *vi* (*classes, pluie*) to start (up) again; (*activités, travaux, combats*) to resume, start (up) again; (*affaires, industrie*) to pick up; (*dire*): **reprit-il** he went on; **se reprendre** (*se ressaisir*) to recover, pull o.s. together; **s'y ~** to make another attempt; **~ des forces** to recover one's strength; **~ courage** to take new heart; **~ ses habitudes/sa liberté** to get back into one's old habits/regain one's freedom; **~ la route** to resume one's journey, set off again; **~ connaissance** to come to, regain consciousness; **~ haleine** ou **son souffle** to

get one's breath back; **~ la parole** to speak again

représailles [rəprezaj] *nfpl* reprisals, retaliation *sg*

représentant, e [rəprezɑ̃tɑ̃, -ɑ̃t] *nm/f* representative

représentation [rəprezɑ̃tasjɔ̃] *nf* representation; (*spectacle*) performing; (*symbole, image*) representation; (*spectacle*) performance; (*Comm*): **la ~ commerciale** travelling; sales representation; **frais de ~** (*d'un diplomate*) entertainment allowance

représenter [rəprezɑ̃te] *vt* to represent; (*donner: pièce, opéra*) to perform; **se représenter** *vt* (*se figurer*) to imagine; to visualize ▷ *vi*: **se ~ à** (*Pol*) to stand ou run again at; (*Scol*) to resit

répression [represjɔ̃] *nf voir* **réprimer** suppression; repression; (*Pol*): **la ~** repression; **mesures de ~** repressive measures

réprimer [reprime] *vt* (*émotions*) to suppress; (*peuple etc*) repress

repris, e [rəpri, -iz] *pp de* **reprendre** ▷ *nm*: **~ de justice** ex-prisoner, ex-convict

reprise [rəpriz] *nf* (*recommencement*) resumption; (*économique*) recovery; (*TV*) repeat; (*Ciné*) rerun; (*Boxe etc*) round; (*Auto*) acceleration *no pl*; (*Comm*) trade-in, part exchange; (*de location*) *sum asked for any extras or improvements made to the property*; (*raccommodage*) darn; mend; **la ~ des hostilités** the resumption of hostilities; **à plusieurs ~s** on several occasions, several times

repriser [rəprize] *vt* (*chaussette, lainage*) to darn; (*tissu*) to mend; **aiguille/coton à ~** darning needle/thread

reproche [rəprɔʃ] *nm* (*remontrance*) reproach; **ton/air de ~** reproachful tone/look; **faire des ~s à qn** to reproach sb; **faire ~ à qn de qch** to reproach sb for sth; **sans ~(s)** beyond ou above reproach

reprocher [rəprɔʃe] *vt*: **~ qch à qn** to reproach ou blame sb for sth; **~ qch à** (*machine, théorie*) to have sth against; **se ~ qch/d'avoir fait qch** to blame o.s. for sth/for doing sth

reproduction [rəprɔdyksjɔ̃] *nf* reproduction; **~ interdite** all rights (of reproduction) reserved

reproduire [rəprɔdɥir] *vt* to reproduce; **se reproduire** *vi* (*Bio*) to reproduce; (*recommencer*) to recur, re-occur

réprouver [repruve] *vt* to reprove

reptile [rɛptil] *nm* reptile

repu, e [rəpy] *adj* satisfied, sated

république [repyblik] *nf* republic; **R~ arabe du Yémen** Yemen Arab Republic; **R~ Centrafricaine** Central African Republic; **R~ de Corée** South Korea; **R~ dominicaine** Dominican Republic; **R~ d'Irlande** Irish Republic, Eire; **R~ populaire de Chine** People's Republic of China; **R~ populaire**

démocratique de Corée Democratic People's Republic of Korea; **R~ populaire du Yémen** People's Democratic Republic of Yemen

répugnant, e [Repynɑ̃, -ɑ̃t] adj repulsive, loathsome

répugner [Repyɲe]: **~ à** vt: **~ à qn** to repel ou disgust sb; **~ à faire** to be loath ou reluctant to do

réputation [Repytasjɔ̃] nf reputation; **avoir la ~ d'être ...** to have a reputation for being ...; **connaître qn/qch de ~** to know sb/ sth by repute; **de ~ mondiale** world-renowned

réputé, e [Repyte] adj renowned; **être ~ pour** to have a reputation for, be renowned for

requérir [RəkeriR] vt (nécessiter) to require, call for; (au nom de la loi) to call upon; (Jur: peine) to call for, demand

requête [Rəkɛt] nf request, petition; (Jur) petition

requin [Rəkɛ̃] nm shark

requis, e [Rəki, -iz] pp de **requérir** ▷ adj required

RER sigle m (= Réseau express régional) Greater Paris high-speed train service

rescapé, e [Rɛskape] nm/f survivor

rescousse [Rɛskus] nf: **aller à la ~ de qn** to go to sb's aid ou rescue; **appeler qn à la ~** to call on sb for help

réseau, x [Rezo] nm network

réservation [RezɛRvasjɔ̃] nf reservation; booking

réserve [RezɛRv] nf (retenue) reserve; (entrepôt) storeroom; (restriction, aussi: d'Indiens) reservation; (de pêche, chasse) preserve; (restrictions) **faire des ~s** to have reservations; **officier de ~** reserve officer; **sous toutes ~s** with all reserve; (dire) with reservations; **sous ~ de** subject to; **sans ~** adv unreservedly; **en ~** in reserve; **de ~** (provisions etc) in reserve

réservé, e [RezɛRve] adj (discret) reserved; (chasse, pêche) private; **~ à ou pour** reserved for

réserver [RezɛRve] vt (gén) to reserve; (chambre, billet etc) to book, reserve; (mettre de côté, garder): **~ qch pour ou à** to keep ou save sth for; **~ qch à qn** to reserve (ou book) sth for sb; (fig: destiner) to have sth in store for sb; **se ~ le droit de faire** to reserve the right to do

réservoir [RezɛRvwaR] nm tank

résidence [Rezidɑ̃s] nf residence; **~ principale/secondaire** main/second home; **~ universitaire** hall of residence (Brit), dormitory (US); **(en) ~ surveillée** (under) house arrest

résidentiel, le [Rezidɑ̃sjɛl] adj residential

résider [Rezide] vi: **~ à ou dans ou en** to reside in; **~ dans** (fig) to lie in

résidu [Rezidy] nm residue no pl

résigner [Reziɲe] vt to relinquish, resign; **se résigner** vi: **se ~ (à qch/à faire)** to resign o.s. (to sth/doing)

résilier [Rezilje] vt to terminate

résistance [Rezistɑ̃s] nf resistance; (de réchaud, bouilloire: fil) element

résistant, e [Rezistɑ̃, -ɑ̃t] adj (personne) robust, tough; (matériau) strong, hard-wearing ▷ nm/f (patriote) Resistance worker ou fighter

résister [Reziste] vi to resist; **~ à** vt (assaut, tentation) to resist; (effort, souffrance) to withstand; (matériau, plante) to withstand, stand up to; (personne: désobéir à) to stand up to, oppose

résolu, e [Rezɔly] pp de **résoudre** ▷ adj (ferme) resolute; **être ~ à qch/faire** to be set upon sth/doing

résolution [Rezɔlysjɔ̃] nf solving; (fermeté, décision, Inform) resolution; (d'un problème) solution; **prendre la ~ de** to make a resolution to

résolvais etc [Rezɔlvɛ] vb voir **résoudre**

résonner [Rezɔne] vi (cloche, pas) to reverberate, resound; (salle) to be resonant; **~ de** to resound with

résorber [RezɔRbe]: **se résorber** vi (Méd) to be resorbed; (fig) to be absorbed

résoudre [RezudR] vt to solve; **~ qn à faire qch** to get sb to make up his (ou her) mind to do sth; **~ de faire** to resolve to do; **se ~ à faire** to bring o.s. to do

respect [Rɛspɛ] nm respect; **tenir en ~** to keep at bay; **présenter ses ~s à qn** to pay one's respects to sb

respecter [Rɛspɛkte] vt to respect; **faire ~** to enforce; **le lexicographe qui se respecte** (fig) any self-respecting lexicographer

respectueux, -euse [Rɛspɛktɥø, -øz] adj respectful; **~ de** respectful of

respiration [RɛspiRasjɔ̃] nf breathing no pl; **faire une ~ complète** to breathe in and out; **retenir sa ~** to hold one's breath; **~ artificielle** artificial respiration

respirer [RɛspiRe] vi to breathe; (fig: se reposer) to get one's breath, have a break; (: être soulagé) to breathe again ▷ vt to breathe (in), inhale; (manifester: santé, calme etc) to exude

resplendir [Rɛsplɑ̃diR] vi to shine; (fig): **~ (de)** to be radiant (with)

responsabilité [Rɛspɔ̃sabilite] nf responsibility; (légale) liability; **refuser la ~ de** to deny responsibility (ou liability) for; **prendre ses ~s** to assume responsibility for one's actions; **~ civile** civil liability; **~ pénale/morale/collective** criminal/moral/collective responsibility

responsable [Rɛspɔ̃sabl] adj responsible ▷ nm/f (personne coupable) person responsible; (du ravitaillement etc) person in charge; (de parti, syndicat) official; **~ de** responsible for; (légalement: de dégâts etc) liable for; (chargé de) in charge of, responsible for

resquiller [Rɛskije] vi (au cinéma, au stade) to get in on the sly; (dans le train) to fiddle a free ride

ressaisir [ʀəseziʀ]: **se ressaisir** vi to regain one's self-control; (équipe sportive) to rally

ressasser [ʀəsase] vt (remâcher) to keep turning over; (redire) to keep trotting out

ressemblance [ʀəsɑ̃blɑ̃s] nf (visuelle) resemblance, similarity, likeness; (: Art) likeness; (analogie, trait commun) similarity

ressemblant, e [ʀəsɑ̃blɑ̃, -ɑ̃t] adj (portrait) lifelike, true to life

ressembler [ʀəsɑ̃ble]: **~ à** vt to be like, resemble; (visuellement) to look like; **se ressembler** vi to be (ou look) alike

ressemeler [ʀəsəmle] vt to (re)sole

ressentiment [ʀəsɑ̃timɑ̃] nm resentment

ressentir [ʀəsɑ̃tiʀ] vt to feel; **se ~ de** to feel (ou show) the effects of

resserrer [ʀəseʀe] vt (pores) to close; (nœud, boulon) to tighten (up); (fig: liens) to strengthen; **se resserrer** vi (route, vallée) to narrow; (liens) to strengthen; **se ~ (autour de)** to draw closer (around), to close in (on)

resservir [ʀəseʀviʀ] vi to do ou serve again ▷ vt: **~ qch (à qn)** to serve sth up again (to sb); **~ de qch (à qn)** to give (sb) a second helping of sth; **~ qn (d'un plat)** to give sb a second helping of a dish; **se ~ de** (plat) to take a second helping of; (outil etc) to use again

ressort [ʀəsɔʀ] vb voir **ressortir** ▷ nm (pièce) spring; (force morale) spirit; (recours): **en dernier ~** as a last resort; (compétence): **être du ~ de** to fall within the competence of

ressortir [ʀəsɔʀtiʀ] vi to go (ou come) out (again); (contraster) to stand out; **~ de** (résulter de): **il ressort de ceci que** it emerges from this that; **~ à** (Jur) to come under the jurisdiction of; (Admin) to be the concern of; **faire ~** (fig: souligner) to bring out

ressortissant, e [ʀəsɔʀtisɑ̃, -ɑ̃t] nm/f national

ressource [ʀəsuʀs] nf: **avoir la ~ de** to have the possibility of; **ressources** nfpl resources; (fig) possibilities; **leur seule ~ était de** the only course open to them was to; **~s d'énergie** energy resources

ressusciter [ʀesysite] vt to resuscitate, restore to life; (fig) to revive, bring back ▷ vi to rise (from the dead); (fig: pays) to come back to life

restant, e [ʀɛstɑ̃, -ɑ̃t] adj remaining ▷ nm: **le ~ (de)** the remainder (of); **un ~ de** (de trop) some leftover; (fig: vestige): **un ~ de** a remnant ou last trace of

restaurant [ʀɛstɔʀɑ̃] nm restaurant; **manger au ~** to eat out; **~ d'entreprise** staff canteen ou cafeteria (US); **~ universitaire (RU)** university refectory ou cafeteria (US)

restauration [ʀɛstɔʀasjɔ̃] nf restoration; (hôtellerie) catering; **~ rapide** fast food

restaurer [ʀɛstɔʀe] vt to restore; **se restaurer** vi to have something to eat

reste [ʀɛst] nm (restant): **le ~ (de)** the rest (of); (de trop): **un ~ (de)** some leftover; (vestige): **un**

~ de a remnant ou last trace of; (Math) remainder; **restes** nmpl leftovers; (d'une cité etc, dépouille mortelle) remains; **avoir du temps de ~** to have time to spare; **ne voulant pas être en ~** not wishing to be outdone; **partir sans attendre** ou **demander son ~** (fig) to leave without waiting to hear more; **du ~, au ~** adv besides, moreover; **pour le ~, quant au ~** adv as for the rest

rester [ʀɛste] vi (dans un lieu, un état, une position) to stay, remain; (subsister) to remain, be left; (durer) to last, live on ▷ vb impers: **il reste du pain/deux œufs** there's some bread/there are two eggs left (over); **il reste du temps/10 minutes** there's some time/there are 10 minutes left; **il me reste assez de temps** I have enough time left; **il ne me reste plus qu'à ...** I've just got to ...; **voilà tout ce qui (me) reste** that's all I've got left; **ce qui reste à faire** what remains to be done; **ce qui me reste à faire** what remains for me to do; (il) **reste à savoir/établir si ...** it remains to be seen/established if ou whether ...; **il n'en reste pas moins que ...** it's nevertheless a fact that ...; **en ~ à** (stade, menaces) to go no further than, only go as far as; **restons-en là** let's leave it at that; **sur une impression** to retain an impression; **y ~:** **il a failli y rester** he nearly met his end

restituer [ʀɛstitɥe] vt (objet, somme): **~ qch (à qn)** to return ou restore sth (to sb); (énergie) to release; (son) to reproduce

restreindre [ʀɛstʀɛ̃dʀ] vt to restrict, limit; **se restreindre** (dans ses dépenses etc) to cut down; (champ de recherches) to narrow

restriction [ʀɛstʀiksjɔ̃] nf restriction; (condition) qualification; **restrictions** nfpl (mentales) reservations; **sans ~** adv unreservedly

résultat [ʀezylta] nm result; (conséquence) outcome no pl, result; (d'élection etc) results pl; **résultats** nmpl (d'une enquête) findings; **~s sportifs** sports results

résulter [ʀezylte]: **~ de** vt to result from, be the result of; **il résulte de ceci que ...** the result of this is that ...

résumé [ʀezyme] nm summary, résumé; **faire le ~ de** to summarize; **en ~** adv in brief; (pour conclure) to sum up

résumer [ʀezyme] vt (texte) to summarize; (récapituler) to sum up; (fig) to epitomize, typify; **se résumer** vi (personne) to sum up (one's ideas); **se ~ à** to come down to

résurrection [ʀezyʀɛksjɔ̃] nf resurrection; (fig) revival

rétablir [ʀetabliʀ] vt to restore, re-establish; (personne: traitement): **~ qn** to restore sb to health, help sb recover; (Admin): **~ qn dans son emploi/ses droits** to reinstate sb in his post/restore sb's rights; **se rétablir** vi (guérir) to recover; *(silence, calme)* to return, be restored; *(Gym etc)*: **se ~ (sur)** to pull o.s. up (onto)

rétablissement [retablismɑ̃] *nm* restoring; *(guérison)* recovery; pull-up

retaper [ʀətape] *vt (maison, voiture etc)* to do up; *(fam: revigorer)* to buck up; *(redactylographier)* to retype

retard [ʀətaʀ] *nm (d'une personne attendue)* lateness *no pl; (sur l'horaire, un programme, une échéance)* delay; *(fig: scolaire, mental etc)* learning difficulty; **être en ~** *(pays)* to be backward; *(dans paiement, travail)* to be behind; **en ~ (de deux heures)** (two hours) late; **désolé d'être en ~** sorry I'm late; **avoir un ~ de deux km** *(Sport)* to be two km behind; **rattraper son ~** to catch up; **avoir du ~** to be late; *(sur un programme)* to be behind (schedule); **prendre du ~** *(train, avion)* to be delayed; *(montre)* to lose (time); **sans ~** *adv* without delay; **à l'allumage** *(Auto)* retarded spark; **~ scolaire** learning difficulty

retardataire [ʀətaʀdatɛʀ] *adj* late; *(idées)* backward ▷ *nm/f* latecomer; child with a learning difficulty

retardement [ʀətaʀdəmɑ̃]: **à ~** *adj* delayed action *cpd*; **bombe à ~** time bomb

retarder [ʀətaʀde] *vt* to delay; *(sur un horaire)*: **~ qn (d'une heure)** to delay sb (an hour); *(sur un programme)*: **~ qn (de trois mois)** to set sb back *ou* delay sb three (months); *(départ, date)*: **~ qch (de deux jours)** to put sth back (two days), delay sth (for *ou* by two days); *(horloge)* to put back ▷ *vi (montre)* to be slow; *(: habituellement)* to lose (time); **je retarde (d'une heure)** I'm (an hour) slow

retenir [ʀətniʀ] *vt (garder, retarder)* to keep, detain; *(maintenir: objet qui glisse, fig: colère, larmes, rire)* to hold back; *(: objet suspendu)* to hold; *(: chaleur, odeur)* to retain; *(fig: empêcher d'agir)*: **~ qn (de faire)** to hold sb back (from doing); *(se rappeler)* to retain; *(réserver)* to reserve; *(accepter)* to accept; *(prélever)*: **~ qch (sur)** to deduct sth (from); **se retenir** *vi (euphémisme)* to hold on; *(se raccrocher)*: **se ~ à** to hold onto; *(se contenir)*: **se ~ de faire** to restrain o.s. from doing; **~ son souffle** *ou* **haleine** to hold one's breath; **~ qn à dîner** to ask sb to stay for dinner; **je pose trois et je retiens deux** put down three and carry two

retentir [ʀətɑ̃tiʀ] *vi* to ring out; *(salle)*: **~ de** to ring *ou* resound with; **~ sur** *vt (fig)* to have an effect upon

retentissant, e [ʀətɑ̃tisɑ̃, -ɑ̃t] *adj* resounding; *(fig)* impact-making

retentissement [ʀətɑ̃tismɑ̃] *nm (retombées)* repercussions *pl*; effect, impact

retenu, e [ʀətny] *pp de* **retenir** ▷ *adj (place)* reserved; *(personne: empêché)* held up; *(propos: contenu, discret)* restrained ▷ *nf (prélèvement)* deduction; *(Math)* number to carry over; *(Scol)* detention; *(modération)* (self-)restraint; *(réserve)* reserve, reticence; *(Auto)* tailback

réticence [retisɑ̃s] *nf* reticence *no pl*, reluctance *no pl*; **sans ~** without hesitation

réticent, e [retisɑ̃, -ɑ̃t] *adj* reticent, reluctant

rétine [retin] *nf* retina

retiré, e [ʀətiʀe] *adj (solitaire)* secluded; *(éloigné)* remote

retirer [ʀətiʀe] *vt (argent, plainte)* to withdraw; *(vêtement, lunettes)* to take off, remove; *(enlever)*: **~ qch à qn** to take sth from sb; *(extraire)*: **~ qn/qch de** to take sb away from/ sth out of, remove sb/sth from; *(reprendre: bagages, billets)* to collect, pick up; **~ des avantages de** to derive advantages from; **se retirer** *vi (partir, reculer)* to withdraw; *(prendre sa retraite)* to retire; **se ~ de** to withdraw from; to retire from

retombées [ʀətɔ̃be] *nfpl (radioactives)* fallout *sg; (fig)* fallout; spin-offs

retomber [ʀətɔ̃be] *vi (à nouveau)* to fall again; *(rechuter)*: **~ malade/dans l'erreur** to fall ill again/fall back into error; *(atterrir: après un saut etc)* to land; *(tomber, redescendre)* to fall back; *(pendre)* to fall, hang (down); *(échoir)*: **~ sur qn** to fall on sb

rétorquer [ʀetɔʀke] *vt*: **~ (à qn) que** to retort (to sb) that

retouche [ʀətuʃ] *nf* touching up *no pl; (sur vêtement)* alteration; **faire une ~** *ou* **des ~s à** to touch up

retoucher [ʀətuʃe] *vt (photographie, tableau)* to touch up; *(texte, vêtement)* to alter

retour [ʀətuʀ] *nm* return; **au ~** *(en arrivant)* when we *(ou* they *etc)* get *(ou* got) back; *(en route)* on the way back; **pendant le ~** on the way *ou* journey back; **à mon/ton ~** on my/ your return; **au ~ de** on the return of; **être de ~ (de)** to be back (from); **de ~ à .../chez moi** back at .../back home; **quand serons-nous de ~?** when do we get back?; **en ~** *adv* in return; **par ~ du courrier** by return of post; **par un juste ~ des choses** by a favourable twist of fate; **match ~** return match; **~ en arrière** *(Ciné)* flashback; *(mesure)* backward step; **~ de bâton** kickback; **~ de chariot** carriage return; **à l'envoyeur** *(Postes)* return to sender; **~ de flamme** backfire; **~ (automatique) à la ligne** *(Inform)* wordwrap; **~ de manivelle** *(fig)* backfire; **~ offensif** renewed attack; **~ aux sources** *(fig)* return to basics

retourner [ʀətuʀne] *vt (dans l'autre sens: matelas, crêpe)* to turn (over); *(: caisse)* to turn upside down; *(: sac, vêtement)* to turn inside out; *(fig: argument)* to turn back; *(en remuant: terre, sol, foin)* to turn over; *(émouvoir: personne)* to shake; *(renvoyer, restituer)*: **~ qch à qn** to return sth to sb ▷ *vi (aller, revenir)*: **~ quelque part/à** to go back *ou* return somewhere/to; **~ à** *(état, activité)* to return to, go back to; **se retourner** *vi* to turn over; *(tourner la tête)* to turn round; **s'en ~** to go back; **se ~ contre**

(fig) to turn against; **savoir de quoi il retourne** to know what it is all about; ~ **sa veste** *(fig)* to turn one's coat; ~ **en arrière** *ou* **sur ses pas** to turn back, retrace one's steps; ~ **aux sources** to go back to basics

retrait [ʀətʀɛ] *nm (d'argent)* withdrawal; collection; *(rétrécissement)* shrinkage; **en** ~ *adj* set back; **écrire en** ~ to indent; ~ **du permis (de conduire)** disqualification from driving *(Brit)*, revocation of driver's license *(US)*

retraite [ʀətʀɛt] *nf (d'une armée, Rel, refuge)* retreat; *(d'un employé)* retirement; *(revenu)* (retirement) pension; **être/mettre à la** ~ to be retired/pension off *ou* retire; **prendre sa** ~ to retire; ~ **anticipée** early retirement; ~ **aux flambeaux** torchlight tattoo

retraité, e [ʀətʀete] *adj* retired ▷ *nm/f (old age)* pensioner

retrancher [ʀətʀɑ̃ʃe] *vt (passage, détails)* to take out, remove; *(nombre, détails)* to take ou deduct sth from; *(couper)* to cut off; **se** ~ **derrière/dans** to entrench o.s. behind/in; *(fig)* to take refuge behind/in

retransmettre [ʀətʀɑ̃smɛtʀ] *vt (Radio)* to broadcast, relay; *(TV)* to show

rétrécir [ʀetʀesiʀ] *vt (vêtement)* to take in ▷ *vi* to shrink; **se rétrécir** *vi (route, vallée)* to narrow

rétribution [ʀetʀibysjɔ̃] *nf* payment

rétro [ʀetʀo] *adj inv* old-style ▷ *nm (rétroviseur)* (rear-view) mirror; **la mode** ~ the nostalgia vogue

rétrograde [ʀetʀɔgʀad] *adj* reactionary, backward-looking

rétroprojecteur [ʀetʀopʀɔʒɛktœʀ] *nm* overhead projector

rétrospectif, -ive [ʀetʀɔspɛktif, -iv] *adj, nf (Art)* retrospective; *(Ciné)* season, retrospective

rétrospectivement [ʀetʀɔspɛktivmɑ̃] *adv* in retrospect

retrousser [ʀətʀuse] *vt* to roll up; *(fig: nez)* to wrinkle; *(: lèvres)* to curl

retrouvailles [ʀətʀuvaj] *nfpl* reunion *sg*

retrouver [ʀətʀuve] *vt (fugitif, objet perdu)* to find; *(occasion)* to find again; *(calme, santé)* to regain; *(reconnaître: expression, style)* to recognize; *(revoir)* to see again; *(rejoindre)* to meet (again), join; **se retrouver** *vi* to meet; *(s'orienter)* to find one's way; **se** ~ **quelque part** to find o.s. somewhere; to end up somewhere; **se** ~ **seul/sans argent** to find o.s. alone/with no money; **se** ~ **dans** *(calculs, dossiers, désordre)* to make sense of; **s'y** ~ *(y voir clair)* to make sense of it; *(rentrer dans ses frais)* to break even

rétroviseur [ʀetʀɔvizœʀ] *nm* (rear-view) mirror

retweet [ʀətwit] *nm (Inform: Twitter)* retweet

retweeter [ʀətwite] *vt (Inform: Twitter)* to retweet

réunion [ʀeynjɔ̃] *nf* bringing together; joining; *(séance)* meeting

réunir [ʀeyniʀ] *vt (convoquer)* to call together; *(rassembler)* to gather together; *(inviter: amis, famille)* to have round, have in; *(cumuler: qualités etc)* to combine; *(rapprocher: ennemis)* to bring together (again), reunite; *(rattacher: parties)* to join (together); **se réunir** *vi (se rencontrer)* to meet; *(s'allier)* to unite

réussi, e [ʀeysi] *adj* successful

réussir [ʀeysiʀ] *vi* to succeed, be successful; *(à un examen)* to pass; *(plante, culture)* to thrive, do well ▷ *vt* to make a success of; to bring off; ~ **à faire** to succeed in doing; ~ **à qn** to go right for sb; *(être bénéfique à)* to agree with sb; **le travail/le mariage lui réussit** work/ married life agrees with him

réussite [ʀeysit] *nf* success; *(Cartes)* patience

revaloir [ʀəvalwaʀ] *vt*: **je vous revaudrai cela** I'll repay you some day; *(en mal)* I'll pay you back for this

revanche [ʀəvɑ̃ʃ] *nf* revenge; *(sport)* revenge match; **prendre sa** ~ **(sur)** to take one's revenge (on); **en** ~ *(par contre)* on the other hand; *(en compensation)* in return

rêve [ʀɛv] *nm* dream; *(activité psychique)*: **le** ~ dreaming; **de** ~ dream *cpd*; **faire un** ~ to have a dream; ~ **éveillé** daydreaming *no pl*, daydream

revêche [ʀəvɛʃ] *adj* surly, sour-tempered

réveil [ʀevɛj] *nm (d'un dormeur)* waking up *no pl*; *(fig)* awakening; *(pendule)* alarm (clock); **au** ~ when I *(ou you etc)* wake *(ou woke)* up, on waking (up); **sonner le** ~ *(Mil)* to sound the reveille

réveille-matin [ʀevɛjmatɛ̃] *nm inv* alarm clock

réveiller [ʀeveje] *vt (personne)* to wake up; *(fig)* to awaken, revive; **se réveiller** *vi* to wake up; *(fig)* to be revived, reawaken

réveillon [ʀevɛjɔ̃] *nm* Christmas Eve; *(de la Saint-Sylvestre)* New Year's Eve; Christmas Eve *(ou New Year's Eve)* party ou dinner

réveillonner [ʀevɛjɔne] *vi* to celebrate Christmas Eve *(ou New Year's Eve)*

révélateur, -trice [ʀevelatœʀ, -tʀis] *adj*: ~ **(de qch)** revealing (sth) ▷ *nm (Photo)* developer

révéler [ʀevele] *vt (gén)* to reveal; *(divulguer)* to disclose, reveal; *(dénoter)* to reveal, show; *(faire connaître au public)*: ~ **qn/qch** to make sb/ sth widely known, bring sb/sth to the public's notice; **se révéler** *vi* to be revealed, reveal itself; **se** ~ **facile/faux** to prove (to be) easy/false; **se** ~ **cruel/un allié sûr** to show o.s. to be cruel/a trustworthy ally

revenant, e [ʀəvnɑ̃, -ɑ̃t] *nm/f* ghost

revendeur, -euse [ʀəvɑ̃dœʀ, -øz] *nm/f (détaillant)* retailer; *(d'occasions)* secondhand dealer; *(de drogue)* (drug-)dealer

revendication [ʀəvɑ̃dikasjɔ̃] *nf* claim, demand; **journée de** ~ day of action (in support of one's claims)

revendiquer [ʀəvɑ̃dike] *vt* to claim, demand; *(responsabilité)* to claim ▷ *vi* to agitate in favour of one's claims

revendre [ʀəvɑ̃dʀ] vt (d'occasion) to resell; (détailler) to sell; (vendre davantage de): **~ du sucre/un foulard/deux bagues** to sell more sugar/another scarf/another two rings; **à ~** adv (en abondance) to spare

revenir [ʀəvniʀ] vi to come back; (Culin): **faire ~** to brown; (coûter): **~ cher/à 100 euros (à qn)** to cost (sb) a lot/100 euros; **~ à** (reprendre: études, projet) to return to, go back to; (équivaloir à) to amount to; **~ à qn** (rumeur, nouvelle) to get back to sb, reach sb's ears; (part, honneur) to go to sb, be sb's; (souvenir, nom) to come back to sb; **~ de** (fig: maladie, étonnement) to recover from; **~ sur** (question, sujet) to go back over; (engagement) to go back on; **~ à la charge** to return to the attack; **~ à soi** to come round; **n'en pas ~**: **je n'en reviens** I can't get over it; **~ sur ses pas** to retrace one's steps; **cela revient à dire que/au même** it amounts to saying that/to the same thing; **~ de loin** (fig) to have been at death's door

revenu, e [ʀəvny] pp de **revenir** ▷ nm income; (de l'État) revenue; (d'un capital) yield; **revenus** nmpl income sg; **~ national brut** gross national income

rêver [ʀeve] vi, vt to dream; (rêvasser) to (day) dream; **~ de** (voir en rêve) to dream of ou about; **~ de qch/de faire** to dream of sth/of doing; **~ à** to dream of

réverbère [ʀeveʀbɛʀ] nm street lamp ou light

réverbérer [ʀeveʀbeʀe] vt to reflect

révérence [ʀeveʀɑ̃s] nf (vénération) reverence; (salut: d'homme) bow; (: de femme) curtsey

rêverie [ʀɛvʀi] nf daydreaming no pl, daydream

revers [ʀəvɛʀ] nm (de feuille, main) back; (d'étoffe) wrong side; (de pièce, médaille) back, reverse; (Tennis, Ping-Pong) backhand; (de veston) lapel; (de pantalon) turn-up; (fig: échec) setback; **~ de fortune** reverse of fortune; **d'un ~ de main** with the back of one's hand; **le ~ de la médaille** (fig) the other side of the coin; **prendre à ~** (Mil) to take from the rear

revêtement [ʀəvɛtmɑ̃] nm (de paroi) facing; (des sols) flooring; (de chaussée) surface; (de tuyau etc: enduit) coating

revêtir [ʀəvetiʀ] vt (habit) to don, put on; (prendre: importance, apparence) to take on; **~ qn de** to dress sb in; (fig) to endow ou invest sb with; **~ qch de** to cover sth with; (fig) to cloak sth in; **~ d'un visa** to append a visa to

rêveur, -euse [ʀɛvœʀ, -øz] adj dreamy ▷ nm/f dreamer

revient [ʀəvjɛ̃] vb voir **revenir** ▷ nm: **prix de ~** cost price

revigorer [ʀəviɡɔʀe] vt (air frais) to invigorate, brace up; (repas, boisson) to revive, buck up

revirement [ʀəviʀmɑ̃] nm change of mind; (d'une situation) reversal

réviser [ʀevize] vt (texte, Scol: matière) to revise; (comptes) to audit; (machine, installation, moteur) to overhaul, service; (Jur: procès) to review

révision [ʀevizjɔ̃] nf revision; auditing no pl; (de voiture) overhaul, servicing no pl; review; **conseil de ~** (Mil) recruiting board; **faire ses ~s** (Scol) to do one's revision (Brit), revise (Brit), review (US); **la ~ des 10 000 km** (Auto) the 10,000 km service

revivre [ʀəvivʀ] vi (reprendre des forces) to come alive again; (traditions) to be revived ▷ vt (épreuve, moment) to relive; **faire ~** (mode, institution, usage) to bring back to life

revoir [ʀəvwaʀ] vt to see again; (réviser) to revise (Brit), review (US) ▷ nm: **au ~** goodbye; **dire au ~ à qn** to say goodbye to sb; **se revoir** (amis) to meet (again), see each other again

révoltant, e [ʀevɔltɑ̃, -ɑ̃t] adj revolting, appalling

révolte [ʀevɔlt] nf rebellion, revolt

révolter [ʀevɔlte] vt to revolt, outrage; **se révolter** vi: **se ~ (contre)** to rebel (against); **se ~ (à)** to be outraged (by)

révolu, e [ʀevɔly] adj past; (Admin): **âgé de 18 ans ~s** over 18 years of age; **après trois ans ~s** when three full years have passed

révolution [ʀevɔlysjɔ̃] nf revolution; **être en ~** (pays etc) to be in revolt; **la ~ industrielle** the industrial revolution

révolutionnaire [ʀevɔlysjɔnɛʀ] adj, nm/f revolutionary

revolver [ʀevɔlvɛʀ] nm gun; (à barillet) revolver

révoquer [ʀevɔke] vt (fonctionnaire) to dismiss, remove from office; (arrêt, contrat) to revoke

revu, e [ʀəvy] pp de **revoir** ▷ nf (inventaire, examen) review; (Mil: défilé) review, march past; (: inspection) inspection, review; (périodique) review, magazine; (pièce satirique) revue; (de music-hall) variety show; **passer en ~** to review, inspect; (fig: mentalement) to review, to go through; **~ de (la) presse** press review

rez-de-chaussée [ʀedʃose] nm inv ground floor

RF sigle f = **République française**

Rhin [ʀɛ̃] nm: **le ~** the Rhine

rhinocéros [ʀinɔseʀɔs] nm rhinoceros

Rhône [ʀon] nm: **le ~** the Rhone

rhubarbe [ʀybaʀb] nf rhubarb

rhum [ʀɔm] nm rum

rhumatisme [ʀymatism] nm rheumatism no pl

rhume [ʀym] nm cold; **~ de cerveau** head cold; **le ~ des foins** hay fever

ri [ʀi] pp de **rire**

riant, e [ʀjɑ̃, -ɑ̃t] vb voir **rire** ▷ adj smiling, cheerful; (campagne, paysage) pleasant

ricaner [ʀikane] vi (avec méchanceté) to snigger; (bêtement, avec gêne) to giggle

riche [ʀiʃ] adj (gén) rich; (personne, pays) rich, wealthy; **~ en** rich in; **~ de** full of; rich in

richesse [Riʃɛs] nf wealth; (fig: de sol, musée etc) richness; **richesses** nfpl (ressources, argent) wealth sg; (fig: trésors) treasures; **~ en vitamines** high vitamin content

ricochet [Rikoʃɛ] nm rebound; bounce; **faire ~** to draw/open the curtains; **bounce**; (fig) to rebound; **faire des ~s** to skip stones; **par ~** adv on the rebound; (fig) as an indirect result

rictus [Riktys] nm grin, (snarling) grimace

ride [Rid] nf wrinkle; (fig) ripple

rideau, x [Rido] nm curtain; **tirer/ouvrir les ~x** to draw/open the curtains; **~ de fer** metal shutter; (Pol): **le ~ de fer** the Iron Curtain

rider [Ride] vt to wrinkle; (fig) to ripple, ruffle the surface of; **se rider** vi to become wrinkled

ridicule [Ridikyl] adj ridiculous ▷ nm ridiculousness no pl; **le ~** ridicule; (travers: gén pl) absurdities pl; **tourner en ~** to ridicule

ridiculiser [Ridikylize] vt to ridicule; **se ridiculiser** vi to make a fool of o.s

O MOT-CLÉ

rien [Rjɛ̃] pron 1: **(ne) ... rien** nothing; (tournure négative) anything; **qu'est-ce que vous avez? — rien** what have you got? — nothing; **il n'a rien dit/fait** he said/did nothing, he hasn't said/done anything; **n'avoir peur de rien** to be afraid ou frightened of nothing, not to be afraid ou frightened of anything; **il n'a rien** (n'est pas blessé) he's all right; **ça ne fait rien** it doesn't matter; **il n'y est pour rien** he's got nothing to do with it
2 (quelque chose): **a-t-il jamais rien fait pour nous?** has he ever done anything for us?
3: **rien de: rien d'intéressant** nothing interesting; **rien d'autre** nothing else; **rien du tout** nothing at all; **il n'a rien d'un champion** he's no champion, there's nothing of the champion about him
4: **rien que** just, only; nothing but; **rien que pour lui faire plaisir** only ou just to please him; **rien que la vérité** nothing but the truth; **rien que cela** that alone
▷ excl: **de rien!** not at all!, don't mention it!; **il n'en est rien!** nothing of the sort!; **rien à faire!** it's no good!, it's no use!
▷ nm: **un petit rien** (cadeau) a little something; **des riens** trivia pl; **un rien de** a hint of; **en un rien de temps** in no time at all; **avoir peur d'un rien** to be frightened of the slightest thing

rieur, -euse [RjœR, -øz] adj cheerful

rigide [Riʒid] adj stiff; (fig) rigid; (moralement) strict

rigole [Rigol] nf (conduit) channel; (filet d'eau) rivulet

rigoler [Rigole] vi (rire) to laugh; (s'amuser) to have (some) fun; (plaisanter) to be joking ou kidding

rigolo, rigolote [Rigolo, -ɔt] adj (fam) funny ▷ nm/f comic; (péj) fraud, phoney

rigoureusement [RiguRøzmɑ̃] adv rigorously; **~ vrai/interdit** strictly true/forbidden

rigoureux, -euse [RiguRø, -øz] adj (morale) rigorous, strict; (personne) stern, strict; (climat, châtiment) rigorous, harsh, severe; (interdiction, neutralité) strict; (preuves, analyse, méthode) rigorous

rigueur [RigœR] nf rigour (Brit), rigor (US); strictness; harshness; **"tenue de soirée de ~"** "evening dress (to be worn)"; **être de ~** to be the usual thing, be the rule; **à la ~** at a pinch; possibly; **tenir ~ à qn de qch** to hold sth against sb

rillettes [Rijɛt] nfpl ≈ potted meat sg (made from pork or goose)

rime [Rim] nf rhyme; **n'avoir ni ~ ni raison** to have neither rhyme nor reason

rinçage [Rɛ̃saʒ] nm rinsing (out); (opération) rinse

rincer [Rɛ̃se] vt to rinse; (récipient) to rinse out; **se ~ la bouche** to rinse one's mouth out

ring [Riŋ] nm (boxing) ring; **monter sur le ~** (aussi fig) to enter the ring; (: faire carrière de boxeur) to take up boxing

ringard, e [RɛɡaR, -aRd] adj (péj) old-fashioned

rions [Rjɔ̃] vb voir **rire**

riposter [Riposte] vi to retaliate ▷ vt: **~ que** to retort that; **~ à** vt to counter; to reply to

ripper [Ripe] vt (Inform) to rip

rire [RiR] vi to laugh; (se divertir) to have fun; (plaisanter) to joke ▷ nm laugh; **le ~** laughter; **~ de** vt to laugh at; **se ~ de** to make light of; **tu veux ~!** you must be joking!; **~ aux éclats/aux larmes** to roar with laughter/laugh until one cries; **~ jaune** to force oneself to laugh; **~ sous cape** to laugh up one's sleeve; **~ au nez de qn** to laugh in sb's face; **pour ~** (pas sérieusement) for a joke ou a laugh

risée [Rize] nf: **être la ~ de** to be the laughing stock of

risible [Rizibl] adj laughable, ridiculous

risque [Risk] nm risk; **le ~** danger; **l'attrait du ~** the lure of danger; **prendre des ~s** to take risks; **à ses ~s et périls** at his own risk; **au ~ de** at the risk of; **~ d'incendie** fire risk; **~ calculé** calculated risk

risqué, e [Riske] adj risky; (plaisanterie) risqué, daring

risquer [Riske] vt to risk; (allusion, question) to venture, hazard; **tu risques qu'on te renvoie** you risk being dismissed; **ça ne risque rien** it's quite safe; **~ de: il risque de se tuer** he could get ou risks getting himself killed; **il a risqué de se tuer** he almost got himself killed; **ce qui risque de se produire** what might ou could well happen; **il ne risque pas de recommencer** there's no chance of him doing that again; **se risquer:**

se ~ dans (s'aventurer) to venture into; **se ~ à faire** (tenter) to dare to do; **~ le tout pour le tout** to risk the lot

rissoler [Risɔle] vi, vt: **(faire) ~** to brown

ristourne [Risturn] nf rebate; discount

rite [Rit] nm rite; (fig) ritual

rivage [Rivaʒ] nm shore

rival, e, -aux [Rival, -o] adj, nm/f rival; **sans ~** adj unrivalled

rivaliser [Rivalize] vi: **~ avec** to rival, vie with; (être comparable) to hold its own against, compare with; **~ avec qn de** (élégance etc) to vie with ou rival sb in

rivalité [Rivalite] nf rivalry

rive [Riv] nf shore; (de fleuve) bank

riverain, e [Rivrɛ̃, -ɛn] adj riverside cpd; lakeside cpd; roadside cpd ▷ nm/f riverside (ou lakeside) resident; (d'une route) local ou roadside resident

rivet [Rivɛ] nm rivet

rivière [Rivjɛr] nf river; **~ de diamants** diamond rivière

rixe [Riks] nf brawl, scuffle

riz [Ri] nm rice; **~ au lait** ≈ rice pudding

rizière [Rizjɛr] nf paddy field

RMI sigle m (= revenu minimum d'insertion) ≈ income support (Brit), ≈ welfare (US)

RN sigle f = **route nationale**

robe [Rɔb] nf dress; (de juge, d'ecclésiastique) robe; (de professeur) gown; (pelage) coat; **~ de soirée/de mariée** evening/wedding dress; **~ de baptême** christening robe; **~ de chambre** dressing gown; **~ de grossesse** maternity dress

robinet [Rɔbinɛ] nm tap (Brit), faucet (US); **~ du gaz** gas tap; **~ mélangeur** mixer tap

robot [Rɔbo] nm robot; **~ de cuisine** food processor

robuste [Rɔbyst] adj robust, sturdy

robustesse [Rɔbystɛs] nf robustness, sturdiness

roc [Rɔk] nm rock

rocade [Rɔkad] nf (Auto) bypass

rocaille [Rɔkaj] nf (pierres) loose stones pl; (terrain) rocky ou stony ground; (jardin) rockery, rock garden ▷ adj (style) rocaille

roche [Rɔʃ] nf rock

rocher [Rɔʃe] nm rock; (Anat) petrosal bone

rocheux, -euse [Rɔʃø, -øz] adj rocky; **les (montagnes) Rocheuses** the Rockies, the Rocky Mountains

rock [Rɔk] **rock and roll** [Rɔkɛnrɔl] nm (musique) rock(-'n'-roll); (danse) rock

rodage [Rɔdaʒ] nm running in (Brit), breaking in (US); **en ~** (Auto) running ou breaking in

roder [Rɔde] vt (moteur, voiture) to run in (Brit), break in (US); **~ un spectacle** to iron out the initial problems of a show

rôder [Rode] vi to roam ou wander about; (de façon suspecte) to lurk (about ou around)

rôdeur, -euse [RodœR, -øz] nm/f prowler

rogne [Rɔɲ] nf: **être en ~** to be mad ou in a temper; **se mettre en ~** to get mad ou in a temper

rogner [Rɔɲe] vt to trim; (fig) to whittle down; **~ sur** (fig) to cut down ou back on

rognons [Rɔɲɔ̃] nmpl kidneys

roi [Rwa] nm king; **les R~s mages** the Three Wise Men, the Magi; **le jour** ou **la fête des R~s, les R~s** Twelfth Night; see note

● FÊTE DES ROIS

● The fête des Rois is celebrated on 6 January.
● Figurines representing the Three Wise
● Men are traditionally added to the
● Christmas crib ("crèche") and people eat
● "galette des Rois", a flat cake in which a
● porcelain charm ("la fève") is hidden.
● Whoever finds the charm is king or
● queen for the day and can choose a
● partner.

rôle [Rol] nm role; (contribution) part

rollers [RɔlœR] nmpl Rollerblades®

romain, e [Rɔmɛ̃, -ɛn] adj Roman ▷ nm/f: **R~, e** Roman ▷ nf (Culin) cos (lettuce)

roman, e [Rɔmɑ̃, -an] adj (Archit) Romanesque; (Ling) Romance cpd, Romanic ▷ nm novel; **~ d'amour** love story; **~ d'espionnage** spy novel ou story; **~ noir** thriller; **~ policier** detective novel

romance [Rɔmɑ̃s] nf ballad

romancer [Rɔmɑ̃se] vt to romanticize

romancier, -ière [Rɔmɑ̃sje, -jɛR] nm/f novelist

romanesque [Rɔmanɛsk] adj (fantastique) fantastic; (amours, aventures) storybook cpd; (sentimental: personne) romantic; (Littérature) novelistic

roman-feuilleton (pl **romans-feuilletons**) [Rɔmɑ̃fœjtɔ̃] nm serialized novel

romanichel, le [Rɔmaniʃɛl] nm/f gipsy

romantique [Rɔmɑ̃tik] adj romantic

romarin [Rɔmarɛ̃] nm rosemary

Rome [Rɔm] n Rome

rompre [Rɔ̃pr] vt to break; (entretien, fiançailles) to break off ▷ vi (fiancés) to break it off; **se rompre** vi to break; (Méd) to burst, rupture; **se ~ les os** ou **le cou** to break one's neck; **~ avec** to break with; **à tout ~** adv wildly; **applaudir à tout ~** to bring down the house, applaud wildly; **~ la glace** (fig) to break the ice; **rompez (les rangs)!** (Mil) dismiss!, fall out!

rompu, e [Rɔ̃py] pp de **rompre** ▷ adj (fourbu) exhausted, worn out; **~ à** with wide experience of; inured to

ronce [Rɔ̃s] nf (Bot) bramble branch; (Menuiserie): **~ de noyer** burr walnut; **ronces** nfpl brambles, thorns

ronchonner [Rɔ̃ʃɔne] vi (fam) to grouse, grouch

rond, e [ʀɔ̃, ʀɔ̃d] adj round; (joues, mollets) well-rounded; (fam: ivre) tight; (sincère, décidé): **être ~ en affaires** to be on the level in business, do an honest deal ▷ nm (cercle) ring; (fam: sou): **je n'ai plus un ~** I haven't a penny left ▷ nf (gén: de surveillance) rounds pl, patrol; (danse) round (dance); (Mus) semibreve (Brit), whole note (US) ▷ adv: **tourner ~** (moteur) to run smoothly; **ça ne tourne pas ~** (fig) there's something not quite right about it; **pour faire un compte ~** to make (it) a round figure, to round (it) off; **avoir le dos ~** to be round-shouldered; (s'asseoir, danser) in a ring; **à la ~e** (alentour): **à 10 km à la ~e** for 10 km round; (à chacun son tour): **passer qch à la ~e** to pass sth (a)round; **faire des ~s de jambe** to bow and scrape; **~ de serviette** napkin ring

rondelet, te [ʀɔ̃dlɛ, -ɛt] adj plump; (fig: somme) tidy; (: bourse) well-lined, fat

rondelle [ʀɔ̃dɛl] nf (Tech) washer; (tranche) slice, round

rondement [ʀɔ̃dmɑ̃] adv (avec décision) briskly; (loyalement) frankly

rondin [ʀɔ̃dɛ̃] nm log

rond-point (pl ronds-points) [ʀɔ̃pwɛ̃] nm roundabout (Brit), traffic circle (US)

ronflant, e [ʀɔ̃flɑ̃, -ɑ̃t] adj (péj) high-flown, grand

ronflement [ʀɔ̃fləmɑ̃] nm snore, snoring no pl

ronfler [ʀɔ̃fle] vi to snore; (moteur, poêle) to hum; (: plus fort) to roar

ronger [ʀɔ̃ʒe] vt to gnaw (at); (vers, rouille) to eat into; **~ son frein** to champ (at) the bit; (fig): **se ~ de souci, se ~ les sangs** to worry o.s. sick, fret; **se ~ les ongles** to bite one's nails

rongeur, -euse [ʀɔ̃ʒœʀ, -øz] nm/f rodent

ronronner [ʀɔ̃ʀɔne] vi to purr

rosace [ʀozas] nf (vitrail) rose window, rosace; (motif: de plafond etc) rose

rosbif [ʀɔsbif] nm: **du ~** roasting beef; (cuit) roast beef; **un ~** a joint of (roasting) beef

rose [ʀoz] nf rose; (vitrail) rose window ▷ adj pink; **~ bonbon** adj inv candy pink; **~ des vents** compass card

rosé, e [ʀoze] adj pinkish; (vin) ~ rosé (wine)

roseau, x [ʀozo] nm reed

rosée [ʀoze] adj f voir **rosé** ▷ nf dew; **goutte de ~** dewdrop

rosette [ʀozɛt] nf rosette (gen of the Légion d'honneur)

rosier [ʀozje] nm rosebush, rose tree

rosse [ʀɔs] nf (péj: cheval) nag ▷ adj nasty, vicious

rossignol [ʀɔsiɲɔl] nm (Zool) nightingale; (crochet) picklock

rot [ʀo] nm belch; (de bébé) burp

rotatif, -ive [ʀɔtatif, -iv] adj rotary ▷ nf rotary press

rotation [ʀɔtasjɔ̃] nf rotation; (fig) rotation, swap-around; (renouvellement) turnover; **par ~** on a rota (Brit) ou rotation (US) basis; **~ des cultures** crop rotation; **~ des stocks** stock turnover

roter [ʀɔte] vi (fam) to burp, belch

rôti [ʀoti] nm: **du ~** roasting meat; (cuit) roast meat; **un ~ de bœuf/porc** a joint of beef/pork

rotin [ʀɔtɛ̃] nm rattan (cane); **fauteuil en ~** cane (arm)chair

rôtir [ʀotiʀ] vt (aussi: **faire ~**) to roast ▷ vi to roast; **se ~ au soleil** to bask in the sun

rôtisserie [ʀotisʀi] nf (restaurant) steakhouse; (comptoir, magasin) roast meat counter (ou shop); (traiteur) roast meat shop

rôtissoire [ʀotiswaʀ] nf (roasting) spit

rotule [ʀotyl] nf kneecap, patella

roturier, -ière [ʀotyʀje, -jɛʀ] nm/f commoner

rouage [ʀwaʒ] nm cog(wheel), gearwheel; (de montre) part; (fig) cog; **rouages** nmpl (fig) internal structure sg; **les ~s de l'État** the wheels of State

roucouler [ʀukule] vi to coo; (fig: péj) to warble; (: amoureux) to bill and coo

roue [ʀu] nf wheel; **faire la ~** (paon) to spread ou fan its tail; (Gym) to do a cartwheel; **descendre en ~ libre** to freewheel ou coast down; **pousser à la ~** to put one's shoulder to the wheel; **grande ~** (à la foire) big wheel; **~ à aubes** paddle wheel; **~ dentée** cogwheel; **~ de secours** spare wheel

roué, e [ʀwe] adj wily

rouer [ʀwe] vt: **~ qn de coups** to give sb a thrashing

rouge [ʀuʒ] adj, nm/f red ▷ nm red; (fard) rouge; (vin) ~ red wine; **passer au ~** (signal) to go red; (automobiliste) to go through a red light; **porter au ~** (métal) to bring to red heat; **sur la liste ~** (Tél) ex-directory (Brit), unlisted (US); **~ de honte/colère** red with shame/anger; **se fâcher tout/voir ~** to blow one's top/see red; **~ à joue** blusher; **~ (à lèvres)** lipstick

rouge-gorge [ʀuʒgɔʀʒ] nm robin (redbreast)

rougeole [ʀuʒɔl] nf measles sg

rougeoyer [ʀuʒwaje] vi to glow red

rouget [ʀuʒɛ] nm mullet

rougeur [ʀuʒœʀ] nf redness; (du visage) red face; **rougeurs** nfpl (Méd) red blotches

rougir [ʀuʒiʀ] vi to turn red; (de honte, timidité) to blush, flush; (de plaisir, colère) to flush; (fraise, tomate) to go ou turn red; (ciel) to redden

rouille [ʀuj] adj inv rust-coloured, rusty ▷ nf rust; (Culin) spicy (Provençal) sauce served with fish dishes

rouillé, e [ʀuje] adj rusty

rouiller [ʀuje] vt to rust ▷ vi to rust, go rusty; **se rouiller** vi to rust; (fig: mentalement) to become rusty; (: physiquement) to grow stiff

roulant, e [ʀulɑ̃, -ɑ̃t] adj (meuble) on wheels; (surface, trottoir, tapis) moving; **matériel ~** (Rail) rolling stock; **escalier ~** = escalator; **personnel ~** (Rail) train crews pl

rouleau, x [Rulo] nm (de papier, tissu, pièces de monnaie, Sport) roll; (de machine à écrire) roller, platen; (à mise en plis, à peinture, vague) roller; **être au bout du ~** (fig) to be at the end of the line; **~ compresseur** steamroller; **~ à pâtisserie** rolling pin; **~ de pellicule** roll of film

roulement [Rulmã] nm (bruit) rumbling no pl, rumble; (rotation) rotation; turnover; (: de capitaux) circulation; **par ~** on a rota (Brit) ou rotation (US) basis; **~ (à billes)** ball bearings pl; **~ de tambour** drum roll; **~ d'yeux** roll(ing) of the eyes

rouler [Rule] vt to roll; (papier, tapis) to roll up; (Culin: pâte) to roll out; (fam: duper) to do, con ▷ vi (bille, boule) to roll; (voiture, train) to go, run; (automobiliste) to drive; (cycliste) to ride; (bateau) to roll; (tonnerre) to rumble, roll; (dégringoler): **~ en bas de** to roll down; **~ sur** (conversation) to turn on; **se ~ dans** (boue) to roll in; (couverture) to roll o.s. (up) in; **~ dans la farine** (fam) to con; **~ les épaules/hanches** to sway one's shoulders/wiggle one's hips; **~ les "r"** to roll one's r's; **~ sur l'or** to be rolling in money, be rolling in it; **~ (sa bosse)** to go places

roulette [Rulɛt] nf (de table, fauteuil) castor; (de dentiste) drill; (de pâtissier) pastry wheel; (jeu): **la ~** roulette; **à ~s** on castors; **la ~ russe** Russian roulette; **ça a marché comme sur des ~s** (fam) it went off very smoothly

roulis [Ruli] nm roll(ing)

roulotte [Rulɔt] nf caravan

roumain, e [Rumɛ̃, -ɛn] adj Rumanian, Romanian ▷ nm (Ling) Rumanian, Romanian ▷ nm/f: **R~, e** Rumanian, Romanian

Roumanie [Rumani] nf: **la ~** Rumania, Romania

rouquin, e [Rukɛ̃, -in] nm/f (péj) redhead

rouspéter [Ruspete] vi (fam) to moan, grouse

rousse [Rus] adj f voir **roux**

roussir [RusiR] vt to scorch ▷ vi (feuilles) to go ou turn brown; (Culin): **faire ~** to brown

route [Rut] nf road; (fig: chemin) way; (itinéraire, parcours) route; (fig: voie) road, path; **par (la) ~** by road; **il y a trois heures de ~** it's a three-hour ride ou journey; **en ~** adv on the way; **en ~!** let's go!; **en cours de ~** en route; **mettre en ~** to start up; **se mettre en ~** to set off; **faire ~ vers** to head towards; **faire fausse ~** (fig) to be on the wrong track; **~ nationale (RN)** ≈ A-road (Brit), ≈ state highway (US)

routeur [RutœR] nm (Inform) router

routier, -ière [Rutje, -jɛR] adj road cpd ▷ nm (camionneur) (long-distance) lorry (Brit) ou truck driver; (restaurant) ≈ transport café (Brit), ≈ truck stop (US); (scout) ≈ rover; (cycliste) road racer ▷ nf (voiture) touring car; **vieux ~** old stager; **carte routière** road map

routine [Rutin] nf routine; **visite/contrôle de ~** routine visit/check

routinier, -ière [Rutinje, -jɛR] adj (péj: travail) humdrum, routine; (: personne) addicted to routine

rouvrir [RuvRiR] vt, vi to reopen, open again; **se rouvrir** vi (blessure) to open up again

roux, rousse [Ru, Rus] adj red; (personne) red-haired ▷ nm/f redhead ▷ nm (Culin) roux

royal, e, -aux [Rwajal, -o] adj royal; (fig) fit for a king, princely; blissful; thorough

royaume [Rwajom] nm kingdom; (fig) realm; **le ~ des cieux** the kingdom of heaven

Royaume-Uni [Rwajomyni] nm: **le ~** the United Kingdom

royauté [Rwajote] nf (dignité) kingship; (régime) monarchy

ruban [Rybã] nm (gén) ribbon; (pour ourlet, couture) binding; (de téléscripteur etc) tape; (d'acier) strip; **~ adhésif** adhesive tape; **~ carbone** carbon ribbon

rubéole [Rybeɔl] nf German measles sg, rubella

rubis [Rybi] nm ruby; (Horlogerie) jewel; **payer ~ sur l'ongle** to pay cash on the nail

rubrique [RybRik] nf (titre, catégorie) heading, rubric; (Presse: article) column

ruche [Ryʃ] nf hive

rude [Ryd] adj (barbe, toile) rough; (métier, tâche) hard, tough; (climat) severe, harsh; (bourru) harsh, rough; (fruste: manières) rugged, tough; (fam: fameux) jolly good; **être mis à ~ épreuve** to be put through the mill

rudement [Rydmã] adv (tomber, frapper) hard; (traiter, reprocher) harshly; (fam: très) terribly; (: beaucoup) terribly hard

rudimentaire [RydimãtɛR] adj rudimentary, basic

rudiments [Rydimã] nmpl rudiments; basic knowledge sg; basic principles; **avoir des ~ d'anglais** to have a smattering of English

rudoyer [Rydwaje] vt to treat harshly

rue [Ry] nf street; **être/jeter qn à la ~** to be on the streets/throw sb out onto the street

ruée [Rɥe] nf rush; **la ~ vers l'or** the gold rush

ruelle [Rɥɛl] nf alley(way)

ruer [Rɥe] vi (cheval) to kick out; **se ruer** vi: **se ~ sur** to pounce on; **se ~ vers/dans/hors de** to rush ou dash towards/into/out of; **~ dans les brancards** to become rebellious

rugby [Rygbi] nm rugby (football); **~ à treize/quinze** rugby league/union

rugir [RyʒiR] vi to roar

rugueux, -euse [Rygø, -øz] adj rough

ruine [Rɥin] nf ruin; **ruines** nfpl ruins; **tomber en ~** to fall into ruin(s)

ruiner [Rɥine] vt to ruin

ruineux, -euse [Rɥinø, -øz] adj terribly expensive to buy (ou run), ruinous; extravagant

ruisseau, x [Rɥiso] nm stream, brook; (caniveau) gutter; (fig): **~x de larmes/sang** floods of tears/streams of blood

ruisseler [ʀɥisle] vi to stream; ~ **(d'eau)** to be streaming (with water); ~ **de lumière** to stream with light

rumeur [ʀymœʀ] nf (bruit confus) rumbling; hubbub no pl; (protestation) murmur(ing); (nouvelle) rumour (Brit), rumor (US)

ruminer [ʀymine] vt (herbe) to ruminate; (fig) to ruminate on ou over, chew over ▷ vi (vache) to chew the cud, ruminate

rupture [ʀyptyʀ] nf (de câble, digue) breaking; (de tendon) rupture, tearing; (de négociations etc) breakdown; (de contrat) breach; (dans continuité) break; (séparation, désunion) break-up, split; **en ~ de ban** at odds with authority; **en ~ de stock** (Comm) out of stock

rural, e, -aux [ʀyʀal, -o] adj rural, country cpd ▷ nmpl: **les ruraux** country people

ruse [ʀyz] nf: **la ~** cunning, craftiness; (pour tromper) trickery; **une ~** a trick, a ruse; **par ~** by trickery

rusé, e [ʀyze] adj cunning, crafty

russe [ʀys] adj Russian ▷ nm (Ling) Russian ▷ nm/f: **R~** Russian

Russie [ʀysi] nf: **la ~** Russia; **la ~ blanche** White Russia; **la ~ soviétique** Soviet Russia

rustine [ʀystin] nf repair patch (for bicycle inner tube)

rustique [ʀystik] adj rustic; (plante) hardy

rustre [ʀystʀ] nm boor

rutilant, e [ʀytilɑ̃, -ɑ̃t] adj gleaming

rythme [ʀitm] nm rhythm; (vitesse) rate; (: de la vie) pace, tempo; **au ~ de 10 par jour** at the rate of 10 a day

rythmé, e [ʀitme] adj rhythmic(al)

---

s' [s] pron voir **se**

SA sigle f = **société anonyme**; (= Son Altesse) HH

sa [sa] adj possessif voir **son**

sable [sabl] nm sand; ~**s mouvants** quicksand(s)

sablé [sable] adj (allée) sandy ▷ nm shortbread biscuit; **pâte ~e** (Culin) shortbread dough

sabler [sable] vt to sand; (contre le verglas) to grit; ~ **le champagne** to drink champagne

sablier [sablije] nm hourglass; (de cuisine) egg timer

sablonneux, -euse [sablɔnø, -øz] adj sandy

saborder [sabɔʀde] vt (navire) to scuttle; (fig) to wind up, shut down

sabot [sabo] nm clog; (de cheval, bœuf) hoof; ~ **(de Denver)** (wheel) clamp; ~ **de frein** brake shoe

saboter [sabɔte] vt (travail, morceau de musique) to botch, make a mess of; (machine, installation, négociation etc) to sabotage

sac [sak] nm bag; (à charbon etc) sack; (pillage) sack(ing); **mettre à ~** to sack; ~ **à provisions/ de voyage** shopping/travelling bag; ~ **de couchage** sleeping bag; ~ **à dos** rucksack; ~ **à main** handbag; ~ **de plage** beach bag

saccadé, e [sakade] adj jerky; (respiration) spasmodic

saccager [sakaʒe] vt (piller) to sack, lay waste; (dévaster) to create havoc in, wreck

saccharine [sakaʀin] nf saccharin(e)

sacerdoce [sasɛʀdɔs] nm priesthood; (fig) calling, vocation

sache etc [saʃ] vb voir **savoir**

sachet [saʃɛ] nm (small) bag; (de lavande, poudre, shampooing) sachet; **thé en ~s** tea bags; **~ de thé** tea bag; **du potage en ~** packet soup

sacoche [sakɔʃ] nf (gén) bag; (de bicyclette) saddlebag; (du facteur) (post)bag; (d'outils) toolbag

sacquer [sake] vt (fam: candidat, employé) to sack; (: réprimander, mal noter) to plough

sacre [sakʀ] nm coronation; consecration

sacré, e [sakʀe] adj sacred; (fam: satané) blasted; (: fameux): **un ~ ...** a heck of a ...; (Anat) sacral

sacrement [sakʀəmɑ̃] nm sacrament; **les derniers ~s** the last rites

sacrifice [sakʀifis] nm sacrifice; **faire le ~ de** to sacrifice

sacrifier [sakʀifje] vt to sacrifice; **~ à** vt to conform to; **se sacrifier** to sacrifice o.s; **articles sacrifiés** (Comm) items sold at rock-bottom ou give-away prices

sacristie [sakʀisti] nf sacristy; (culte protestant) vestry

sadique [sadik] adj sadistic ▷ nm/f sadist

safran [safʀɑ̃] nm saffron

sage [saʒ] adj wise; (enfant) good ▷ nm wise man; sage

sage-femme [saʒfam] nf midwife

sagesse [saʒɛs] nf wisdom

Sagittaire [saʒiteʀ] nm: **le ~** Sagittarius, the Archer; **être du ~** to be Sagittarius

Sahara [saaʀa] nm: **le ~** the Sahara (Desert); **le ~ occidental** (pays) Western Sahara

saignant, e [sɛɲɑ̃, -ɑ̃t] adj (viande) rare; (blessure, plaie) bleeding

saignée [seɲe] nf (Méd) bleeding no pl, bloodletting no pl; (Anat): **la ~ du bras** the bend of the arm; (fig: Mil) heavy losses pl; (: prélèvement) savage cut

saigner [seɲe] vi to bleed ▷ vt to bleed; (animal) to bleed to death; **~ qn à blanc** (fig) to bleed sb white; **~ du nez** to have a nosebleed

saillie [saji] nf (sur un mur etc) projection; (trait d'esprit) witticism; (accouplement) covering, serving; **faire ~** to project, stick out; **en ~, formant ~** projecting, overhanging

saillir [sajiʀ] vi to project, stick out; (veine, muscle) to bulge ▷ vt (Élevage) to cover, serve

sain, e [sɛ̃, sɛn] adj healthy; (dents, constitution) healthy, sound; (lectures) wholesome; **~ et sauf** safe and sound, unharmed; **~ d'esprit** sound in mind, sane

saindoux [sɛ̃du] nm lard

saint, e [sɛ̃, sɛ̃t] adj holy; (fig) saintly ▷ nm/f saint; **la S-e Vierge** the Blessed Virgin

Saint-Esprit [sɛ̃tɛspʀi] nm: **le ~** the Holy Spirit ou Ghost

sainteté [sɛ̃tte] nf holiness; saintliness

Saint-Sylvestre [sɛ̃silvɛstʀ] nf: **la ~** New Year's Eve

sais etc [sɛ] vb voir **savoir**

saisie [sezi] nf seizure; **à ~** (texte) being keyed; **~ (de données)** (data) capture

saisir [seziʀ] vt to take hold of, grab; (fig: occasion) to seize; (comprendre) to grasp; (entendre) to get, catch; (émotions) to take hold of, come over; (Inform) to capture, keyboard; (Culin) to fry quickly; (Jur: biens, publication) to seize; (: juridiction): **~ un tribunal d'une affaire** to submit ou refer a case to a court; **se ~ de** vt to seize; **être saisi** (frappé de) to be overcome

saisissant, e [sezisɑ̃, -ɑ̃t] adj startling, striking; (froid) biting

saison [sezɔ̃] nf season; **la belle/mauvaise ~** the summer/winter months; **être de ~** to be in season; **en/hors ~** in/out of season; **haute/basse/morte ~** high/low/slack season; **la ~ des pluies/des amours** the rainy/mating season

saisonnier, -ière [sezɔnje, -jɛʀ] adj seasonal ▷ nm (travailleur) seasonal worker; (vacancier) seasonal holidaymaker

sait [sɛ] vb voir **savoir**

salade [salad] nf (Bot) lettuce etc (generic term); (Culin) (green) salad; (fam: confusion) tangle, muddle; **salades** nfpl (fam): **raconter des ~s** to tell tales (fam); **haricots en ~** bean salad; **~ composée** mixed salad; **~ de concombres** cucumber salad; **~ de fruits** fruit salad; **~ niçoise** salade niçoise; **~ russe** Russian salad; **~ de tomates** tomato salad; **~ verte** green salad

saladier [saladje] nm (salad) bowl

salaire [salɛʀ] nm (annuel, mensuel) salary; (hebdomadaire, journalier) pay, wages pl; (fig) reward; **~ de base** basic salary (ou wage); **~ de misère** starvation wage; **~ minimum interprofessionnel de croissance (SMIC)** index-linked guaranteed minimum wage

salami [salami] nm salami no pl, salami sausage

salarié, e [salaʀje] adj salaried; wage-earning ▷ nm/f salaried employee; wage-earner

salaud [salo] nm (fam!) sod (!), bastard (!)

sale [sal] adj dirty, filthy; (fig: mauvais: avant le nom) nasty

salé, e [sale] adj (liquide, saveur, mer, goût) salty; (Culin: amandes, beurre etc) salted; (: gâteaux) savoury; (fig: grivois) spicy, juicy; (: note, facture) steep, stiff ▷ nm (porc salé) salt pork; **petit ~** boiling bacon

saler [sale] vt to salt

saleté [salte] nf (état) dirtiness; (crasse) dirt, filth; (tache etc) dirt no pl, something dirty, dirty mark; (fig: tour) filthy trick; (: chose sans valeur) rubbish no pl; (: obscénité) filth no pl; (: microbe etc) bug; **vivre dans la ~** to live in squalor

salière [saljɛʀ] nf saltcellar

salin, e [salɛ̃, -in] adj saline ▷ nf saltworks sg

salir [saliʀ] vt to (make) dirty; (fig) to soil the reputation of; **se salir** vi to get dirty

salissant, e [salisɑ̃, -ɑ̃t] adj (tissu) which shows the dirt; (métier) dirty, messy

salle [sal] *nf* room; (*d'hôpital*) ward; (*de restaurant*) dining room; (*d'un cinéma*) auditorium; (*: public*) audience; **faire ~ comble** to have a full house; **~ d'armes** (*pour l'escrime*) arms room; **~ d'attente** waiting room; **~ de bain(s)** bathroom; **~ de bal** ballroom; **~ de cinéma** cinema; **~ de classe** classroom; **~ commune** (*d'hôpital*) ward; **~ concert** concert hall; **~ de consultation** consulting room (*Brit*), office (*US*); **~ de danse** dance hall; **~ de douches** shower-room; **~ d'eau** shower-room; **~ d'embarquement** (*à l'aéroport*) departure lounge; **~ d'exposition** showroom; **~ de jeux** games room; (*pour enfants*) playroom; **~ des machines** engine room; **~ à manger** dining room; (*mobilier*) dining room suite; **~ obscure** cinema (*Brit*), movie theater (*US*); **~ d'opération** (*d'hôpital*) operating theatre; **~ des professeurs** staffroom; **~ de projection** film theatre; **~ de séjour** living room; **~ de spectacle** theatre; cinema; **~ des ventes** saleroom

salon [salɔ̃] *nm* lounge, sitting room; (*mobilier*) lounge suite; (*exposition*) exhibition, show; (*mondain, littéraire*) salon; **~ de coiffure** hairdressing salon; **~ de discussion** (*Inform*) chatroom; **~ de thé** tearoom

salope [salɔp] *nf* (*fam!*) bitch (!)

saloperie [salɔpʀi] *nf* (*fam!*) filth *no pl*; (*action*) dirty trick; (*chose sans valeur*) rubbish *no pl*

salopette [salɔpɛt] *nf* dungarees *pl*; (*d'ouvrier*) overall(s)

salsifis [salsifi] *nm* salsify, oyster plant

salubre [salybʀ] *adj* healthy, salubrious

saluer [salɥe] *vt* (*pour dire bonjour, fig*) to greet; (*pour dire au revoir*) to take one's leave; (*Mil*) to salute

salut [saly] *nm* (*sauvegarde*) safety; (*Rel*) salvation; (*geste*) wave; (*parole*) greeting; (*Mil*) salute ▷ *excl* (*fam: pour dire bonjour*) hi (there); (*: pour dire au revoir*) see you!, bye!

salutations [salytasjɔ̃] *nfpl* greetings; **recevez mes ~ distinguées** *ou* **respectueuses** yours faithfully

samedi [samdi] *nm* Saturday; *voir aussi* **lundi**

SAMU [samy] *sigle m* (= *service d'assistance médicale d'urgence*) ≈ ambulance (service) (*Brit*), ≈ paramedics (*US*)

sanction [sãksjɔ̃] *nf* sanction; (*fig*) penalty; **prendre des ~s contre** to impose sanctions on

sanctionner [sãksjɔne] *vt* (*loi, usage*) to sanction; (*punir*) to punish

sandale [sãdal] *nf* sandal; **~s à lanières** strappy sandals

sandwich [sãdwitʃ] *nm* sandwich; **pris en ~** sandwiched

sang [sã] *nm* blood; **en ~** covered in blood; **jusqu'au ~** (*mordre, pincer*) till the blood comes; **se faire du mauvais ~** to fret, get in a state

sang-froid [sãfʀwa] *nm* calm, sangfroid; **garder/perdre/reprendre son ~** to keep/ lose/regain one's cool; **de ~** in cold blood

sanglant, e [sãglã, -ãt] *adj* bloody, covered in blood; (*combat*) bloody; (*fig: reproche, affront*) cruel

sangle [sãgl] *nf* strap; **sangles** *nfpl* (*pour lit etc*) webbing *sg*

sanglier [sãglije] *nm* (wild) boar

sanglot [sãglo] *nm* sob

sangloter [sãglɔte] *vi* to sob

sangsue [sãsy] *nf* leech

sanguin, e [sãgɛ̃, -in] *adj* blood *cpd*; (*fig*) fiery ▷ *nf* blood orange; (*Art*) red pencil drawing

sanguinaire [sãginɛʀ] *adj* (*animal, personne*) bloodthirsty; (*lutte*) bloody

sanitaire [sanitɛʀ] *adj* health *cpd*; **sanitaires** *nmpl* (*salle de bain et w.-c.*) bathroom *sg*; **installation/appareil ~** bathroom plumbing/appliance

sans [sã] *prép* without; **~ qu'il s'en aperçoive** without him *ou* his noticing; **~ scrupules** unscrupulous; **~ manches** sleeveless; **un pull ~ manches** a sleeveless jumper; **~ faute** without fail; **~ arrêt** without a break; **~ ça** (*fam*) otherwise

sans-abri [sãzabri] *nmpl* homeless

sans-emploi [sãzãplwa] *nm/f inv* unemployed person; **les ~** the unemployed

sans-gêne [sãʒɛn] *adj inv* inconsiderate ▷ *nm inv* (*attitude*) lack of consideration

santé [sãte] *nf* health; **avoir une ~ de fer** to be bursting with health; **être en bonne ~** to be in good health, be healthy; **boire à la ~ de qn** to drink (to) sb's health; **"à la ~ de"** "here's to"; **à ta** *ou* **votre ~!** cheers!; **service de ~** (*dans un port etc*) quarantine service; **la ~ publique** public health

saoudien, ne [saudjɛ̃, -ɛn] *adj* Saudi (Arabian) ▷ *nm/f*: **S~, ne** Saudi (Arabian)

saoul, e [su, sul] *adj* = **soûl, e**

saper [sape] *vt* to undermine, sap; **se saper** *vi* (*fam*) to dress

sapeur-pompier [sapœʀpɔ̃pje] *nm* fireman

saphir [safiʀ] *nm* sapphire; (*d'électrophone*) needle, sapphire

sapin [sapɛ̃] *nm* fir (tree); (*bois*) fir; **~ de Noël** Christmas tree

sarcastique [saʀkastik] *adj* sarcastic

sarcler [saʀkle] *vt* to weed

Sardaigne [saʀdɛɲ] *nf*: **la ~** Sardinia

sardine [saʀdin] *nf* sardine; **~s à l'huile** sardines in oil

SARL [saʀl] *sigle f* (= *société à responsabilité limitée*) ≈ plc (*Brit*), ≈ Inc. (*US*)

sarrasin [saʀazɛ̃] *nm* buckwheat

sas [sas] *nm* (*de sous-marin, d'engin spatial*) airlock; (*d'écluse*) lock

satané, e [satane] *adj* (*fam*) confounded

satellite [satelit] *nm* satellite; **pays ~** satellite country

satin [satɛ̃] *nm* satin

satire [satiʀ] *nf* satire; **faire la ~ de** to satirize

satirique [satiʀik] *adj* satirical

satisfaction [satisfaksjɔ̃] nf satisfaction; **à ma grande ~** to my great satisfaction; **obtenir ~** to obtain ou get satisfaction (to); **donner ~ (à)** to give satisfaction (to)

satisfaire [satisfɛʀ] vt to satisfy; **se satisfaire de** to be satisfied ou content with; **~ à** vt (*engagement*) to fulfil; (*revendications, conditions*) to meet, satisfy

satisfaisant, e [satisfəzɑ̃, -ɑ̃t] vb voir **satisfaire** ▷ adj (*acceptable*) satisfactory; (*qui fait plaisir*) satisfying

satisfait, e [satisfɛ, -ɛt] pp de **satisfaire** ▷ adj satisfied; **~ de** happy ou satisfied with

saturer [satyʀe] vt to saturate; **~ qn/qch de** to saturate sb/sth with

sauce [sos] nf sauce; (*avec un rôti*) gravy; **en ~** in a sauce; **~ blanche** white sauce; **~ chasseur** sauce chasseur; **~ tomate** tomato sauce

saucière [sosjɛʀ] nf sauceboat; gravy boat

saucisse [sosis] nf sausage

saucisson [sosisɔ̃] nm (*slicing*) sausage; **~ à l'ail** garlic sausage

sauf¹ [sof] prép except; **~ si** (*à moins que*) unless; **~ avis contraire** unless you hear to the contrary; **~ empêchement** barring (any) problems; **~ erreur** if I'm not mistaken; **~ imprévu** unless anything unforeseen arises, barring accidents

sauf², sauve [sof, sov] adj unharmed, unhurt; (*fig: honneur*) intact, saved; **laisser la vie sauve à qn** to spare sb's life

sauge [soʒ] nf sage

saugrenu, e [soɡʀəny] adj preposterous, ludicrous

saule [sol] nm willow (tree); **~ pleureur** weeping willow

saumon [somɔ̃] nm salmon inv ▷ adj inv salmon (pink)

saumure [somyʀ] nf brine

saupoudrer [supudʀe] vt: **~ qch de** to sprinkle sth with

saur [sɔʀ] adj m: **hareng ~** smoked ou red herring, kipper

saurai etc [sɔʀe] vb voir **savoir**

saut [so] nm jump; (*discipline sportive*) jumping; **faire un ~** to (make a) jump ou leap; **faire un ~ chez qn** to pop over to sb's (place); **au ~ du lit** on getting out of bed; **~ en hauteur/longueur** high/long jump; **~ à la corde** skipping; **~ de page/ligne** (Inform) page/line break; **~ en parachute** parachuting no pl; **~ à la perche** pole vaulting; **~ à l'élastique** bungee jumping; **~ périlleux** somersault

saute [sot] nf: **~ de vent/température** sudden change of wind direction/in the temperature; **avoir des ~s d'humeur** to have sudden changes of mood

sauter [sote] vi to jump, leap; (*exploser*) to blow up, explode; (: *fusibles*) to blow; (*se rompre*) to snap, burst; (*se détacher*) to pop out

(*ou off*) ▷ vt to jump (over), leap (over); (*fig: omettre*) to skip, miss (out); **faire ~** to blow up; to burst open; (Culin) to sauté; **~ à pieds joints/à cloche-pied** to make a standing jump/to hop; **~ en parachute** to make a parachute jump; **~ à la corde** to skip; **~ de joie** to jump for joy; **~ de colère** to be hopping with rage ou hopping mad; **~ au cou de qn** to fly into sb's arms; **~ sur une occasion** to jump at an opportunity; **~ aux yeux** to be quite obvious; **~ au plafond** (*fig*) to hit the roof

sauterelle [sotʀɛl] nf grasshopper

sautiller [sotije] vi (*oiseau*) to hop; (*enfant*) to skip

sauvage [sovaʒ] adj (*gén*) wild; (*peuplade*) savage; (*farouche*) unsociable; (*barbare*) wild, savage; (*non officiel*) unauthorized, unofficial; **faire du camping ~** to camp in the wild ▷ nm/f savage; (*timide*) unsociable type, recluse

sauve [sov] adj f voir **sauf**

sauvegarde [sovgaʀd] nf safeguard; **sous la ~ de** under the protection of; **disquette/ fichier de ~** (Inform) backup disk/file

sauvegarder [sovgaʀde] vt to safeguard; (Inform: *enregistrer*) to save; (: *copier*) to back up

sauve-qui-peut [sovkipø] nm inv stampede, mad rush ▷ excl run for your life!

sauver [sove] vt to save; (*porter secours à*) to rescue; (*récupérer*) to salvage, rescue; **se sauver** vi (*s'enfuir*) to run away; (*fam: partir*) to be off; **~ qn de** to save sb from; **~ la vie à qn** to save sb's life; **~ les apparences** to keep up appearances

sauvetage [sovtaʒ] nm rescue; **~ en montagne** mountain rescue; **ceinture de ~** lifebelt (Brit), life preserver (US); **brassière** ou **gilet de ~** lifejacket (Brit), life preserver (US)

sauveteur [sovtœʀ] nm rescuer

sauvette [sovɛt] nf: **à la ~** adv (*vendre*) without authorization; (*se marier etc*) hastily, hurriedly; **vente à la ~** (unauthorized) street trading, (street) peddling

sauveur [sovœʀ] nm saviour (Brit), savior (US)

savais etc [savɛ] vb voir **savoir**

savamment [savamɑ̃] adv (*avec érudition*) learnedly; (*habilement*) skilfully, cleverly

savant, e [savɑ̃, -ɑ̃t] adj scholarly, learned; (*calé*) clever ▷ nm scientist; **animal ~** performing animal

saveur [savœʀ] nf flavour (Brit), flavor (US); (*fig*) savour (Brit), savor (US)

savoir [savwaʀ] vt to know; (*être capable de*): **il sait nager** he knows how to swim, he can swim ▷ nm knowledge; **se savoir** vi (*être connu*) to be known; **se ~ malade/incurable** to know that one is ill/incurably ill; **il est petit: tu ne peux pas ~!** you won't believe how small he is!; **vous n'êtes pas sans ~ que** you are not ou will not be unaware of the fact that; **je crois ~ que ...**

I believe that ..., I think I know that ...; **je n'en sais rien** I (really) don't know; **à ~ (que)** that is, namely; **faire ~ qch à qn** to let sb know sth, inform sb about sth; **pas que je sache** not as far as I know; **sans le ~** *adv* unknowingly, unwittingly; **en ~ long** to know a lot

savon [savɔ̃] *nm* (*produit*) soap; (*morceau*) bar *ou* tablet of soap; (*fam*): **passer un ~ à qn** to give sb a good dressing-down

savonner [savɔne] *vt* to soap

savonnette [savɔnɛt] *nf* bar of soap

savons [savɔ̃] *vb voir* **savoir**

savourer [savuʀe] *vt* to savour (*Brit*), savor (*US*)

savoureux, -euse [savuʀø, -øz] *adj* tasty; (*fig: anecdote*) spicy, juicy

saxo [saksɔ], **saxophone** [saksɔfɔn] *nm* sax(ophone)

scabreux, -euse [skabʀø, -øz] *adj* risky; (*indécent*) improper, shocking

scandale [skɑ̃dal] *nm* scandal; **faire un ~** (*scène*) to make a scene; (*Jur*) create a disturbance; **faire ~** to scandalize people; **au grand ~ de ...** to the great indignation of ...

scandaleux, -euse [skɑ̃dalø, -øz] *adj* scandalous, outrageous

scandinave [skɑ̃dinav] *adj* Scandinavian ⊳ *nm/f*: **S~** Scandinavian

Scandinavie [skɑ̃dinavi] *nf*: **la ~** Scandinavia

scaphandre [skafɑ̃dʀ] *nm* (*de plongeur*) diving suit; (*de cosmonaute*) spacesuit; **~ autonome** aqualung

scarabée [skaʀabe] *nm* beetle

scarlatine [skaʀlatin] *nf* scarlet fever

scarole [skaʀɔl] *nf* endive

sceau, x [so] *nm* seal; (*fig*) stamp, mark; **sous le ~ du secret** under the seal of secrecy

scélérat, e [selera, -at] *nm/f* villain, blackguard ⊳ *adj* villainous, blackguardly

sceller [sele] *vt* to seal

scénario [senaʀjo] *nm* (*Ciné*) screenplay, script; (*: idée, plan*) scenario; (*fig*) pattern; scenario

scène [sɛn] *nf* (*gén*) scene; (*estrade, fig: théâtre*) stage; **entrer en ~** to come on stage; **mettre en ~** (*Théât*) to stage; (*Ciné*) to direct; (*fig*) to present, introduce; **sur le devant de la ~** (*en pleine actualité*) in the forefront; **porter à la ~** to adapt for the stage; **faire une ~ (à qn)** to make a scene (with sb); **~ de ménage** domestic fight *ou* scene

sceptique [sɛptik] *adj* sceptical ⊳ *nm/f* sceptic

schéma [ʃema] *nm* (*diagramme*) diagram, sketch; (*fig*) outline

schématique [ʃematik] *adj* diagrammatic(al), schematic; (*fig*) oversimplified

sciatique [sjatik] *adj*: **nerf ~** sciatic nerve ⊳ *nf* sciatica

scie [si] *nf* saw; (*fam: rengaine*) catch-tune; (*: personne*) bore; **~ à bois** wood saw; **~ circulaire** circular saw; **~ à découper** fretsaw; **~ à métaux** hacksaw; **~ sauteuse** jigsaw

sciemment [sjamɑ̃] *adv* knowingly, wittingly

science [sjɑ̃s] *nf* science; (*savoir*) knowledge; (*savoir-faire*) art, skill; **~s économiques** economics; **~s humaines/sociales** social sciences; **~s naturelles** (*Scol*) natural science *sg*, biology *sg*; **~s po** political science *ou* studies *pl*

science-fiction [sjɑ̃sfiksjɔ̃] *nf* science fiction

scientifique [sjɑ̃tifik] *adj* scientific ⊳ *nm/f* (*savant*) scientist; (*étudiant*) science student

scier [sje] *vt* to saw; (*retrancher*) to saw off

scierie [siʀi] *nf* sawmill

scinder [sɛ̃de] *vt*, **se scinder** *vi* to split (up)

scintiller [sɛ̃tije] *vi* to sparkle; (*étoile*) to twinkle

scission [sisjɔ̃] *nf* split

sciure [sjyʀ] *nf*: **~ (de bois)** sawdust

sclérose [skleroz] *nf* sclerosis; (*fig*) ossification; **~ en plaques (SEP)** multiple sclerosis (MS)

scolaire [skɔlɛʀ] *adj* school *cpd*; (*péj*) schoolish; **l'année ~** the school year; (*à l'université*) the academic year; **en âge ~** of school age

scolariser [skɔlaʀize] *vt* to provide with schooling (*ou* schools)

scolarité [skɔlaʀite] *nf* schooling; **frais de ~** school fees (*Brit*), tuition (*US*)

scooter [skutœʀ] *nm* (motor) scooter

score [skɔʀ] *nm* score; (*électoral etc*) result

scorpion [skɔʀpjɔ̃] *nm* (*signe*): **le S~** Scorpio, the Scorpion; **être du S~** to be Scorpio

scotch [skɔtʃ] *nm* (*whisky*) scotch, whisky; **S~®** (*adhésif*) Sellotape® (*Brit*), Scotch tape® (*US*)

scout, e [skut] *adj, nm* scout

script [skʀipt] *nm* (*écriture*) printing; (*Ciné*) (shooting) script

scrupule [skʀypyl] *nm* scruple; **être sans ~s** to be unscrupulous; **se faire un ~ de qch** to have scruples *ou* qualms about doing sth

scruter [skʀyte] *vt* to scrutinize, search; (*l'obscurité*) to peer into; (*motifs, comportement*) to examine, scrutinize

scrutin [skʀytɛ̃] *nm* (*vote*) ballot; (*ensemble des opérations*) poll; **~ proportionnel/majoritaire** election on a proportional/majority basis; **~ à deux tours** poll with two ballots *ou* rounds; **~ de liste** list system

sculpter [skylte] *vt* to sculpt; (*érosion*) to carve

sculpteur [skyltœʀ] *nm* sculptor

sculpture [skyltyʀ] *nf* sculpture; **~ sur bois** wood carving

SDF *sigle m* (= *sans domicile fixe*) homeless person; **les ~** the homeless

○ **MOT-CLÉ**

se, s' [sə, s] pron 1 (emploi réfléchi) oneself; (: masc) himself; (: fém) herself; (: sujet non humain) itself; (: pl) themselves; **se voir comme l'on est** to see o.s. as one is; **se savonner** to soap o.s.

2 (réciproque) one another, each other; **ils s'aiment** they love one another ou each other

3 (passif): **cela se répare facilement** it is easily repaired

4 (possessif): **se casser la jambe/se laver les mains** to break one's leg/wash one's hands

séance [seɑ̃s] nf (d'assemblée, récréative) meeting, session; (de tribunal) sitting, session; (musicale, Ciné, Théât) performance; **ouvrir/lever la ~** to open/close the meeting; **~ tenante** forthwith

seau, x [so] nm bucket, pail; **~ à glace** ice bucket

sec, sèche [sɛk, sɛʃ] adj dry; (raisins, figues) dried; (cœur, personne: insensible) hard, cold; (maigre, décharné) spare, lean; (réponse, ton) sharp, curt; (démarrage) sharp, sudden ⊳ nm: **tenir au ~** to keep in a dry place ⊳ adv hard; (démarrer) sharply; **boire ~** to be a heavy drinker; **je le bois ~** I drink it straight ou neat; **à pied ~** without getting one's feet wet; **à ~** adj (puits) dried up; (à court d'argent) broke

sécateur [sekatœʀ] nm secateurs pl (Brit), shears pl, pair of secateurs ou shears

sèche [sɛʃ] adj f voir **sec** ⊳ nf (fam) cigarette, fag (Brit)

sèche-cheveux [sɛʃʃəvø] nm inv hair-drier

sèche-linge [sɛʃlɛ̃ʒ] nm inv tumble dryer

sèchement [sɛʃmɑ̃] adv (frapper etc) sharply; (répliquer etc) drily, sharply

sécher [seʃe] vt to dry; (dessécher: peau, blé) to dry (out); (: étang) to dry up; (bois) to season; (fam: classe, cours) to skip, miss ⊳ vi to dry; to dry up; to dry out; (fam: candidat) to be stumped; **se sécher** (après le bain) to dry o.s.

sécheresse [seʃʀɛs] nf dryness; (absence de pluie) drought

séchoir [seʃwaʀ] nm drier

second, e [səgɔ̃, -ɔ̃d] adj second ⊳ nm (assistant) second in command; (étage) second floor (Brit), third floor (US); (Navig) first mate ⊳ nf (Scol) ≈ year 11 (Brit), ≈ tenth grade (US); (Aviat, Rail etc) second class; **en ~** (en second rang) in second place; **voyager en ~e** to travel second-class; **doué de ~e vue** having (the gift of) second sight; **trouver son ~ souffle** (Sport, fig) to get one's second wind; **être dans un état ~** to be in a daze (ou trance); **de ~e main** second-hand

secondaire [səgɔ̃dɛʀ] adj secondary

seconder [səgɔ̃de] vt to assist; (favoriser) to back

secouer [səkwe] vt to shake; (passagers) to rock; (traumatiser) to shake (up); **se secouer**

(chien) to shake itself; (fam: se démener) to shake o.s. up; **~ la poussière d'un tapis** to shake the dust off a carpet; **~ la tête** to shake one's head

secourir [səkuʀiʀ] vt (aller sauver) to (go and) rescue; (prodiguer des soins à) to help, assist; (venir en aide à) to assist, aid

secourisme [səkuʀism] nm (premiers soins) first aid; (sauvetage) life saving

secouriste [səkuʀist] nm/f first-aid worker

secours [səkuʀ] vb voir **secourir** ⊳ nm help, aid, assistance ⊳ nmpl aid sg; **cela lui a été d'un grand ~** this was a great help to him; **au ~!** help!; **appeler au ~** to shout ou call for help; **appeler qn à son ~** to call sb to one's assistance; **porter ~ à qn** to give sb assistance, help sb; **les premiers ~** first aid sg; **le ~ en montagne** mountain rescue

● **ÉQUIPES DE SECOURS**

Emergency phone numbers can be dialled free from public phones. For the police ("la police") dial 17; for medical services ("le SAMU") dial 15; for the fire brigade ("les sapeurs pompiers"), dial 18.

secousse [səkus] nf jolt, bump; (électrique) shock; (fig: psychologique) jolt, shock; **~ sismique** ou **tellurique** earth tremor

secret, -ète [səkʀɛ, -ɛt] adj secret; (fig: renfermé) reticent, reserved ⊳ nm secret; (discrétion absolue): **le ~** secrecy; **en ~** in secret, secretly; **au ~** in solitary confinement; **~ de fabrication** trade secret; **~ professionnel** professional secrecy

secrétaire [səkʀetɛʀ] nm/f secretary ⊳ nm (meuble) writing desk, secretaire; **~ d'ambassade** embassy secretary; **~ de direction** private ou personal secretary; **~ d'État** ≈ junior minister; **~ général (SG)** Secretary-General; (Comm) company secretary; **~ de mairie** town clerk; **~ médicale** medical secretary; **~ de rédaction** sub-editor

secrétariat [s(ə)kʀetaʀja] nm (profession) secretarial work; (bureau: d'entreprise, d'école) (secretary's) office; (: d'organisation internationale) secretariat; (Pol etc: fonction) secretaryship, office of Secretary

secteur [sɛktœʀ] nm sector; (Admin) district; (Élec): **branché sur le ~** plugged into the mains (supply); **fonctionne sur pile et ~** battery or mains operated; **le ~ privé/public** (Écon) the private/public sector; **le ~ primaire/tertiaire** the primary/tertiary sector

section [sɛksjɔ̃] nf section; (de parcours d'autobus) fare stage; (Mil: unité) platoon; **~ rythmique** rhythm section

sectionner [sɛksjɔne] vt to sever; **se sectionner** vi to be severed

sécu [seky] nf (fam: = sécurité sociale) ≈ dole (Brit), ≈ Welfare (US)

séculaire [sekylɛʀ] adj secular; (très vieux) age-old

sécuriser [sekyʀize] vt to give a sense of security to

sécurité [sekyʀite] nf (absence de troubles) security; (absence de danger) safety; **impression de ~** sense of security; **la ~ internationale** international security; **système de ~** security (ou safety) system; **être en ~** to be safe; **la ~ de l'emploi** job security; **la ~ routière** road safety; **la ~ sociale** ≈ (the) Social Security (Brit), ≈ (the) Welfare (US)

sédentaire [sedɑ̃tɛʀ] adj sedentary

séduction [sedyksjɔ̃] nf seduction; (charme, attrait) appeal, charm

séduire [sedɥiʀ] vt to charm; (femme: abuser de) to seduce; (chose) to appeal to

séduisant, e [sedɥizɑ̃, -ɑ̃t] vb voir **séduire** ▷ adj (femme) seductive; (homme, offre) very attractive

ségrégation [segʀegasjɔ̃] nf segregation

seigle [sɛɡl] nm rye

seigneur [sɛɲœʀ] nm lord; **le S~** the Lord

sein [sɛ̃] nm breast; (entrailles) womb; **au ~ de** prép (équipe, institution) within; (flots, bonheur) in the midst of; **donner le ~ à** (bébé) to feed (at the breast); to breast-feed; **nourrir au ~** to breast-feed

séisme [seism] nm earthquake

seize [sɛz] num sixteen

seizième [sɛzjɛm] num sixteenth

séjour [seʒuʀ] nm stay; (pièce) living room

séjourner [seʒuʀne] vi to stay

sel [sɛl] nm salt; (fig) wit; (piquant) spice; **~ de cuisine/de table** cooking/table salt; **~ gemme** rock salt; **~s de bain** bathsalts

sélection [seleksjɔ̃] nf selection; **faire/opérer une ~** to make a selection from among; **épreuve de ~** (Sport) trial (for selection); **~ naturelle** natural selection; **~ professionnelle** professional recruitment

sélectionner [seleksjone] vt to select

self [sɛlf] nm (fam) self-service

self-service [sɛlfsɛʀvis] adj self-service ▷ nm self-service (restaurant); (magasin) self-service shop

selle [sɛl] nf saddle; **selles** nfpl (Méd) stools; **aller à la ~** (Méd) to have a bowel movement; **se mettre en ~** to mount, get into the saddle

seller [sele] vt to saddle

sellette [sɛlɛt] nf: **être sur la ~** to be on the carpet (fig)

selon [səlɔ̃] prép according to; (en se conformant à) in accordance with; **~ moi** as I see it; **~ que** according to, depending on whether

semaine [səmɛn] nf week; (salaire) week's wages ou pay, weekly wages ou pay; **en ~** during the week, on weekdays; **à la petite ~** from day to day; **la ~ sainte** Holy Week

semblable [sɑ̃blabl] adj similar; (de ce genre): **de ~s mésaventures** such mishaps ▷ nm fellow creature ou man; **~ à** similar to, like

semblant [sɑ̃blɑ̃] nm: **un ~ de vérité** a semblance of truth; **faire ~ (de faire)** to pretend (to do)

sembler [sɑ̃ble] vb copule to seem ▷ vb impers: **il semble (bien) que/inutile de** it (really) seems ou appears that/useless to; **il me semble (bien) que** it (really) seems to me that, I (really) think that; **il me semble le connaître** I think ou I've a feeling I know him; **~ être** to seem to be; **comme bon lui semble** as he sees fit; **me semble-t-il, à ce qu'il me semble** it seems to me, to my mind

semelle [səmɛl] nf sole; (intérieure) insole, inner sole; **battre la ~** to stamp one's feet (to keep them warm); (fig) to hang around (waiting); **~s compensées** platform soles

semence [səmɑ̃s] nf (graine) seed; (clou) tack

semer [səme] vt to sow; (fig: éparpiller) to scatter; (: confusion) to spread; (fam: poursuivants) to lose, shake off; **la discorde parmi** to sow discord among; **semé de** (difficultés) riddled with

semestre [səmɛstʀ] nm half-year; (Scol) semester

séminaire [seminɛʀ] nm seminar; (Rel) seminary

semi-remorque [səmiʀəmɔʀk] nf trailer ▷ nm articulated lorry (Brit), semi(trailer) (US)

semoule [səmul] nf semolina; **~ de riz** ground rice

sempiternel, le [sɛ̃pitɛʀnɛl] adj eternal, never-ending

sénat [sena] nm senate; see note

SÉNAT

The Sénat is the upper house of the French parliament and is housed in the Palais du Luxembourg in Paris. One-third of its members, "sénateurs" are elected for a nine-year term every three years by an electoral college consisting of the "députés" and other elected representatives. The Sénat has a wide range of powers but can be overridden by the lower house, the "Assemblée nationale" in case of dispute.

sénateur [senatœʀ] nm senator

Sénégal [senegal] nm: **le ~** Senegal

sens [sɑ̃s] vb voir **sentir** ▷ nm [sɑ̃s] (Physiol, instinct) sense; (signification) meaning, sense; (direction) direction, way ▷ nmpl (sensualité) senses; **reprendre ses ~** to regain consciousness; **avoir le ~ des affaires/de la mesure** to have business sense/a sense of moderation; **ça n'a pas de ~** that doesn't make (any) sense; **en dépit du bon ~**

contrary to all good sense; **tomber sous le ~** to stand to reason, be perfectly obvious; **en un ~, dans un ~** in a way; **en ce ~ que** in the sense that; **à mon ~** to my mind; **dans le ~ des aiguilles d'une montre** clockwise; **dans le ~ contraire des aiguilles d'une montre** anticlockwise; **dans le ~ de la longueur/largeur** lengthways/widthways; **dans le mauvais ~** (*aller*) the wrong way; in the wrong direction; **bon ~** good sense; **~ commun** common sense; **~ dessus dessous** upside down; **~ interdit, ~ unique** one-way street

sensass [sãsas] *adj* (*fam*) fantastic

sensation [sãsasjõ] *nf* sensation; **faire ~** to cause a sensation, create a stir; **à ~** (*péj*) sensational

sensationnel, le [sãsasjɔnɛl] *adj* sensational, fantastic

sensé, e [sãse] *adj* sensible

sensibiliser [sãsibilize] *vt* to sensitize; **~ qn (à)** to make sb sensitive (to)

sensibilité [sãsibilite] *nf* sensitivity; (*affectivité, émotivité*) sensitivity, sensibility

sensible [sãsibl] *adj* sensitive; (*aux sens*) perceptible; (*appréciable: différence, progrès*) appreciable, noticeable; (*quartier*) problem *cpd*; **~ à** sensitive to

sensiblement [sãsibləmã] *adv* (*notablement*) appreciably, noticeably; (*à peu près*): **ils ont ~ le même poids** they weigh approximately the same

sensiblerie [sãsibləri] *nf* sentimentality; squeamishness

sensuel, le [sãsɥɛl] *adj* (*personne*) sensual; (*musique*) sensuous

sentence [sãtãs] *nf* (*jugement*) sentence; (*adage*) maxim

sentier [sãtje] *nm* path

sentiment [sãtimã] *nm* feeling; (*conscience, impression*): **avoir le ~ de/que** to be aware of/ have the feeling that; **recevez mes ~s respectueux** (*personne nommée*) yours sincerely; (*personne non nommée*) yours faithfully; **faire du ~** (*péj*) to be sentimental; **si vous me prenez par les ~s** if you appeal to my feelings

sentimental, e, -aux [sãtimãtal, -o] *adj* sentimental; (*vie, aventure*) love *cpd*

sentinelle [sãtinɛl] *nf* sentry; **en ~** standing guard; (*soldat: en faction*) on sentry duty

sentir [sãtir] *vt* (*par l'odorat*) to smell; (*par le goût*) to taste; (*au toucher, fig*) to feel; (*répandre une odeur de*) to smell of; (: *ressemblance*) to smell like; (*avoir la saveur de*) to taste of; to taste like; (*fig: dénoter, annoncer*) to be indicative of; to smack of; to foreshadow ▷ *vi* to smell; **~ mauvais** to smell bad; **se ~ bien** to feel good; **se ~ mal** (*être indisposé*) to feel unwell *ou* ill; **se ~ le courage/la force de faire** to feel brave/strong enough to do; **ne plus se ~ de joie** to be beside o.s. with joy; **il**

ne peut pas le ~ (*fam*) he can't stand him; **je ne me sens pas bien** I don't feel well

séparation [separasjõ] *nf* separation; (*cloison*) division, partition; **~ de biens** division of property (*in marriage settlement*); **~ de corps** legal separation

séparé, e [separe] *adj* (*appartements, pouvoirs*) separate; (*époux*) separated; **~ de** separate from; separated from

séparément [separemã] *adv* separately

séparer [separe] *vt* (*gén*) to separate; (*désunir: divergences etc*) to divide; to drive apart; (: *différences, obstacles*) to stand between; (*détacher*): **~ qch de** to pull sth (off) from; (*dissocier*) to distinguish between; (*diviser*): **~ qch par** to divide sth (up) with; **~ une pièce en deux** to divide a room into two; **se séparer** *vi* (*époux*) to separate, part; (*prendre congé: amis etc*) to part, leave each other; (*adversaires*) to separate; (*se diviser: route, tige etc*) to divide; (*se détacher*): **se ~ (de)** to split off (from); to come off; **se ~ de** (*époux*) to separate *ou* part from; (*employé, objet personnel*) to part with

sept [sɛt] *num* seven

septante [sɛptãt] *num* (*Belgique, Suisse*) seventy

septembre [sɛptãbr] *nm* September; *voir aussi* **juillet**

septennat [sɛptena] *nm* seven-year term (of office)

septentrional, e, -aux [sɛptãtrijɔnal, -o] *adj* northern

septicémie [sɛptisemi] *nf* blood poisoning, septicaemia

septième [sɛtjɛm] *num* seventh; **être au ~ ciel** to be on cloud nine

septique [sɛptik] *adj*: **fosse ~** septic tank

sépulture [sepyltyr] *nf* burial; (*tombeau*) burial place, grave

séquelles [sekɛl] *nfpl* after-effects; (*fig*) aftermath *sg*; consequences

séquestrer [sekɛstre] *vt* (*personne*) to confine illegally; (*biens*) to impound

serai *etc* [səre] *vb voir* **être**

serbe [sɛrb] *adj* Serbian ▷ *nm* (*Ling*) Serbian ▷ *nm/f*

Serbie [sɛrbi] *nf*: **la ~** Serbia

serein, e [sərɛ̃, -ɛn] *adj* serene; (*jugement*) dispassionate

serez [səre] *vb voir* **être**

sergent [sɛrʒã] *nm* sergeant

série [seri] *nf* (*de questions, d'accidents, TV*) series *inv*; (*de clés, casseroles, outils*) set; (*catégorie: Sport*) rank; class; **en ~** in quick succession; (*Comm*) mass *cpd*; **de ~** *adj* (*voiture*) standard; **hors ~** (*Comm*) custom-built; (*fig*) outstanding; **imprimante ~** (*Inform*) serial printer; **soldes de fin de ~s** end of line special offers; **~ noire** *nm* (crime) thriller ▷ *nf* (*suite de malheurs*) run of bad luck

sérieusement [serjøzmã] *adv* seriously; reliably; responsibly; **il parle ~** he's serious, he means it; **~?** are you serious?, do you mean it?

sérieux, -euse [serjø, -øz] *adj* serious; (*élève, employé*) reliable, responsible; (*client, maison*) reliable, dependable; (*offre, proposition*) genuine, serious; (*grave, sévère*) serious, solemn; (*maladie, situation*) serious, grave; (*important*) considerable ▷ *nm* seriousness; (*d'une entreprise etc*) reliability; **ce n'est pas ~** (*raisonnable*) that's not on; **garder son ~** to keep a straight face; **manquer de ~** not to be very responsible (*ou* reliable); **prendre qch/qn au ~** to take sth/sb seriously

serin [sərɛ̃] *nm* canary

seringue [sərɛ̃g] *nf* syringe

serions *etc* [sərjɔ̃] *vb voir* **être**

serment [sɛrmɑ̃] *nm* (*juré*) oath; (*promesse*) pledge, vow; **prêter ~** to take the *ou* an oath; **faire le ~ de** to take a vow to, swear to; **sous ~** on *ou* under oath

sermon [sɛrmɔ̃] *nm* sermon; (*péj*) sermon, lecture

séronégatif, -ive [seronegatif, -iv] *adj* HIV negative

séropositif, -ive [seropozitif, -iv] *adj* HIV positive

serpent [sɛrpɑ̃] *nm* snake; **~ à sonnettes** rattlesnake; **~ monétaire (européen)** (European) monetary snake

serpenter [sɛrpɑ̃te] *vi* to wind

serpillière [sɛrpijɛr] *nf* floorcloth

serre [sɛr] *nf* (*Agr*) greenhouse; **serres** *nfpl* (*griffes*) claws, talons; **~ chaude** hothouse; **~ froide** unheated greenhouse

serré, e [sere] *adj* (*tissu*) closely woven; (*réseau, ligne*) close; (*écriture*) close; (*habits*) tight; (*fig: lutte, match*) tight, close-fought; (*passagers etc*) (tightly) packed; (*café*) strong ▷ *adv*: **jouer ~** to play it close, play a close game; **écrire ~** to write a cramped hand; **avoir la gorge ~e** to have a lump in one's throat; **avoir le cœur ~** to have a heavy heart

serrer [sere] *vt* (*tenir*) to grip *ou* hold tight; (*comprimer, coincer*) to squeeze; (*poings, mâchoires*) to clench; (*vêtement*) to be too tight for; to fit tightly; (*rapprocher*) to close up, move closer together; (*ceinture, nœud, frein, vis*) to tighten ▷ *vi*: **~ à droite** to keep to the right; to move into the right-hand lane; **se serrer** (*se rapprocher*) to squeeze up; **se ~ contre qn** to huddle up to sb; **se ~ les coudes** to stick together, back one another up; **se ~ la ceinture** to tighten one's belt; **~ la main à qn** to shake sb's hand; **~ qn dans ses bras** to hug sb, clasp sb in one's arms; **~ la gorge à qn** (*chagrin*) to bring a lump to sb's throat; **~ les dents** to clench *ou* grit one's teeth; **~ qn de près** to follow close behind sb; **~ le trottoir** to hug the kerb; **~ sa droite** to keep well to the right; **~ la vis à qn** to crack down harder on sb; **~ les rangs** to close ranks

serrure [seryr] *nf* lock

serrurier [seryrje] *nm* locksmith

sers, sert [sɛr] *vb voir* **servir**

servante [sɛrvɑ̃t] *nf* (maid)servant

serveur, -euse [sɛrvœr, -øz] *nm/f* waiter/ waitress ▷ *nm* (*Inform*) server ▷ *adj*: **centre ~** (*Inform*) service centre

serviable [sɛrvjabl] *adj* obliging, willing to help

service [sɛrvis] *nm* (*gén*) service; (*série de repas*): **premier ~** first sitting; (*pourboire*) service (charge); (*assortiment de vaisselle*) set, service; (*linge de table*) set; (*bureau: de la vente etc*) department, section; (*travail*): **pendant le ~** on duty; **services** *nmpl* (*travail, Écon*) services, inclusive/exclusive of service; **faire le ~** to serve; **être en ~ chez qn** (*domestique*) to be in sb's service; **être au ~ de** (*patron, patrie*) to be in the service of; **être au ~ de qn** (*collaborateur, voiture*) to be at sb's service; **porte de ~** tradesman's entrance; **rendre ~ à** to help; **il aime rendre ~** he likes to help; **rendre un ~ à qn** to do sb a favour; (*objet: s'avérer utile*) to come in useful *ou* handy for sb; **heures de ~** hours of duty; **être de ~** to be on duty; **reprendre du ~** to get back into action; **avoir 25 ans de ~** to have completed 25 years' service; **être/mettre en ~** to be in/put into service *ou* operation; **~ compris/non compris** service included/not included; **hors ~** not in use; out of order; **~ à thé/café** tea/coffee set *ou* service; **~ après-vente (SAV)** after-sales service; **en ~ commandé** on an official assignment; **~ funèbre** funeral service; **~ militaire** military service; *see note*; **~ d'ordre** police (*ou* stewards) in charge of maintaining order; **~s publics** public services, (public) utilities; **~s secrets** secret service *sg*; **~s sociaux** social services

● **SERVICE MILITAIRE**
●
● Until 1997, French men over the age of 18
● who were passed as fit, and who were
● not in full-time higher education, were
● required to do ten months' *service*
● *militaire*. Conscientious objectors were
● required to do two years' community
● service.
●
● Since 1997, military service has been
● suspended in France. However, all 16-
● and 17-year-olds, both male and female,
● are required to attend a compulsory
● one-day training course, the "JDC"
● ("journée défense et citoyenneté"),
● which covers basic information on the
● principles and organization of defence
● in France, and also advises on career
● opportunities in the military and in the
● voluntary sector. Young people must
● attend the training day before their
● eighteenth birthday.

serviette [sɛʀvjɛt] nf (de table) (table) napkin, serviette; (de toilette) towel; (porte-documents) briefcase; ~ **éponge** terry towel; ~ **hygiénique** sanitary towel

servir [sɛʀviʀ] vt (gén) to serve; (dîneur: au restaurant) to wait on; (client: au magasin) to serve, attend to; (fig: aider): ~ **qn** to aid sb; to serve sb's interests; to stand sb in good stead; (Comm: rente) to pay ▷ vi (Tennis) to serve; (Cartes) to deal; (être militaire) to serve; ~ **qch à qn** to serve sb with sth, help sb to sth; **qu'est-ce que je vous sers?** what can I get you?; **se servir** vi (prendre d'un plat) to help o.s.; (s'approvisionner): **vous êtes servi?** are you being served?; **sers-toi!** help yourself!; **se ~ chez** to shop at; **se ~ de** (plat) to help o.s. to; (voiture, outil, relations) to use; ~ **à qn** (diplôme, livre) to be of use to sb; **ça m'a servi pour faire** it was useful to me when I did; I used it to do; ~ **à qch/à faire** (outil etc) to be used for sth/for doing; **ça peut** ~ it may come in handy; **à quoi cela sert-il (de faire)?** what's the use (of doing)?; **ça ne sert à rien** it's no use; ~ **(à qn) de ...** to serve as ... (for sb); ~ **à dîner (à qn)** to serve dinner (to sb)

serviteur [sɛʀvitœʀ] nm servant

ses [se] adj possessif voir **son**

set [sɛt] nm set; (napperon) placemat; ~ **de table** set of placemats

seuil [sœj] nm doorstep; (fig) threshold; **sur le ~ de la maison** in the doorway of his house, on his doorstep; **au ~ de** (fig) on the threshold ou brink ou edge of; ~ **de rentabilité** (Comm) breakeven point

seul, e [sœl] adj (sans compagnie) alone; (avec nuance affective: isolé) lonely; (unique): **un ~ livre** only one book, a single book; **le ~ livre** the only book; ~ **ce livre, ce livre ~** this book alone, only this book; **d'un ~ coup** (soudainement) all at once; (à la fois) at one blow ▷ adv (vivre) alone, on one's own; **parler tout ~** to talk to oneself; **faire qch (tout) ~** to do sth (all) on one's own ou (all) by oneself ▷ nm, nf: **il en reste un(e) ~(e)** there's only one left; **pas un(e) ~(e)** not a single; **à lui (tout) ~** single-handed, on his own; ~ **à ~** in private; **se sentir** ~ to feel lonely

seulement [sœlmɑ̃] adv only; (pas davantage): ~ **cinq, cinq** ~ only five; (exclusivement): ~ **eux** only them, them alone; (pas avant): ~ **hier/à 10h** only yesterday/at 10 o'clock; (mais, toutefois): **il consent,** ~ **il demande des garanties** he agrees, only he wants guarantees; **non** ~ **... mais aussi** ou **encore** not only ... but also

sève [sɛv] nf sap

sévère [sevɛʀ] adj severe

sévices [sevis] nmpl (physical) cruelty sg, ill treatment sg

sévir [seviʀ] vi (punir) to use harsh measures, crack down; (fléau) to rage, be rampant; ~ **contre** (abus) to deal ruthlessly with, crack down on

sevrer [səvʀe] vt to wean; (fig): ~ **qn de** to deprive sb of

sexe [sɛks] nm sex; (organe mâle) member

sexuel, le [sɛksɥɛl] adj sexual; **acte** ~ sex act

seyant, e [sɛjɑ̃, -ɑ̃t] adj becoming

shampooing [ʃɑ̃pwɛ̃] nm shampoo; **se faire un** ~ to shampoo one's hair; ~ **colorant** (colour) rinse; ~ **traitant** medicated shampoo

Shetland [ʃɛtlɑ̃d] n: **les îles** ~ the Shetland Islands, Shetland

shopping [ʃɔpiŋ] nm: **faire du** ~ to go shopping

short [ʃɔʀt] nm (pair of) shorts pl

 MOT-CLÉ

si [si] nm (Mus) B; (en chantant la gamme) ti ▷ adv **1** (oui) yes; **"Paul n'est pas venu"** — **"si!"** "Paul hasn't come" — "Yes he has!"; **je vous assure que si** I assure you he did/ she is etc

2 (tellement) so; **si gentil/rapidement** so kind/fast; **(tant et) si bien que** so much so that; **si rapide qu'il soit** however fast he may be

▷ conj if; **si tu veux** if you want; **je me demande si** I wonder if ou whether; **si j'étais toi** if I were you; **si seulement** if only; **si ce n'est que** apart from; **une des plus belles, si ce n'est la plus belle** one of the most beautiful, if not THE most beautiful; **s'il est aimable, eux par contre ...** while ou whereas he's nice, they (on the other hand) ...

Sicile [sisil] nf: **la** ~ Sicily

sida [sida] nm (= syndrome immuno-déficitaire acquis) AIDS sg

sidéré, e [sideʀe] adj staggered

sidérurgie [sideʀyʀʒi] nf steel industry

siècle [sjɛkl] nm century; (époque): **le** ~ **des lumières/de l'atome** the age of enlightenment/atomic age; (Rel): **le** ~ the world

siège [sjɛʒ] nm seat; (d'entreprise) head office; (d'organisation) headquarters pl; (Mil) siege; **lever le** ~ to raise the siege; **mettre le** ~ **devant** to besiege; **présentation par le** ~ (Méd) breech presentation; ~ **avant/arrière** (Auto) front/back seat; ~ **baquet** bucket seat; ~ **social** registered office

siéger [sjeʒe] vi (assemblée, tribunal) to sit; (résider, se trouver) to lie, be located

sien, ne [sjɛ̃, sjɛn] pron: **le(la)** ~**(ne), les** ~**s(~nes)** (d'un homme) his; (d'une femme) hers; (d'une chose) its; **y mettre du** ~ to pull one's weight; **faire des ~nes** (fam) to be up to one's (usual) tricks; **les** ~**s** (sa famille) one's family

sieste [sjɛst] nf (afternoon) snooze ou nap, siesta; **faire la** ~ to have a snooze ou nap

sifflement [sifləmɑ̃] *nm* whistle, whistling *no pl*; wheezing *no pl*; hissing *no pl*

siffler [sifle] *vi* (*gén*) to whistle; (*avec un sifflet*) to blow (on) one's whistle; (*en respirant*) to wheeze; (*serpent, vapeur*) to hiss ▷ *vt* (*chanson*) to whistle; (*chien etc*) to whistle for; (*fille*) to whistle at; (*pièce, orateur*) to hiss, boo; (*faute*) to blow one's whistle at; (*fin du match, départ*) to blow one's whistle for; (*fam: verre, bouteille*) to guzzle, knock back (Brit)

sifflet [siflε] *nm* whistle; **sifflets** *nmpl* (*de mécontentement*) whistles, boos; **coup de ~** whistle

siffloter [siflɔte] *vi, vt* to whistle

sigle [sigl] *nm* acronym, (set of) initials *pl*

signal, -aux [siɲal, -o] *nm* (*signe convenu, appareil*) signal; (*indice, écriteau*) sign; **donner le ~ de** to give the signal for; **~ d'alarme** alarm signal; **~ d'alerte/de détresse** warning/distress signal; **~ horaire** time signal; **~ optique/sonore** warning light/sound; visual/acoustic signal; **signaux (lumineux)** (*Auto*) traffic signals; **signaux routiers** road signs; (*lumineux*) traffic lights

signalement [siɲalmɑ̃] *nm* description, particulars *pl*

signaler [siɲale] *vt* to indicate; to announce; (*vol, perte*) to report; (*personne: faire un signe*) to signal; (*être l'indice de*) to indicate; (*faire remarquer*): **~ qch à qn/à qn que** to point out sth to sb/to sb that; (*appeler l'attention sur*): **~ qn à la police** to bring sb to the notice of the police; **se ~ par** to distinguish o.s. by; **se ~ à l'attention de qn** to attract sb's attention

signature [siɲatyʀ] *nf* signature; (*action*) signing

signe [siɲ] *nm* sign; (*Typo*) mark; **ne pas donner ~ de vie** to give no sign of life; **c'est bon ~** it's a good sign; **c'est ~ que** it's a sign that; **faire un ~ de la main/tête** to give a sign with one's hand/shake one's head; **faire ~ à qn** (*fig: contacter*) to get in touch with sb; **faire ~ à qn d'entrer** to motion (to) sb to come in; **en ~ de** as a sign *ou* mark of; **le ~ de la croix** the sign of the Cross; **~ de ponctuation** punctuation mark; **~ du zodiaque** sign of the zodiac; **~s particuliers** distinguishing marks

signer [siɲe] *vt* to sign; **se signer** *vi* to cross o.s

significatif, -ive [siɲifikatif, -iv] *adj* significant

signification [siɲifikasjɔ̃] *nf* meaning

signifier [siɲifje] *vt* (*vouloir dire*) to mean, signify; (*faire connaître*): **~ qch (à qn)** to make sth known (to sb); (*Jur*): **~ qch à qn** to serve notice of sth on sb

silence [silɑ̃s] *nm* silence; (*Mus*) rest; **garder le ~ (sur qch)** to keep silent (about sth), say nothing (about sth); **passer sous ~** to pass over (in silence); **réduire au ~** to silence

silencieux, -euse [silɑ̃sjø, -øz] *adj* quiet, silent ▷ *nm* silencer (Brit), muffler (US)

silex [silεks] *nm* flint

silhouette [silwεt] *nf* outline, silhouette; (*lignes, contour*) outline; (*figure*) figure

silicium [silisjɔm] *nm* silicon; **plaquette de ~** silicon chip

sillage [sijaʒ] *nm* wake; (*fig*) trail; **dans le ~ de** (*fig*) in the wake of

sillon [sijɔ̃] *nm* (*d'un champ*) furrow; (*de disque*) groove

sillonner [sijɔne] *vt* (*creuser*) to furrow; (*traverser*) to criss-cross, cross

simagrées [simagʀe] *nfpl* fuss *sg*; airs and graces

similaire [similεʀ] *adj* similar

similicuir [similikɥiʀ] *nm* imitation leather

similitude [similityd] *nf* similarity

simple [sɛ̃pl] *adj* (*gén*) simple; (*non multiple*) single; **simples** *nmpl* (*Méd*) medicinal plants; **~ messieurs/dames** *nm* (*Tennis*) men's/ladies' singles *sg*; **un ~ particulier** an ordinary citizen; **une ~ formalité** a mere formality; **cela varie du ~ au double** it can double, it can double the price *etc*; **dans le plus ~ appareil** in one's birthday suit; **~ course** *adj* single; **~ d'esprit** *nm/f* simpleton; **~ soldat** private

simplicité [sɛ̃plisite] *nf* simplicity; **en toute ~** quite simply

simplifier [sɛ̃plifje] *vt* to simplify

simulacre [simylakʀ] *nm* enactment; (*péj*): **un ~ de** a pretence of, a sham

simuler [simyle] *vt* to sham, simulate

simultané, e [simyltane] *adj* simultaneous

sincère [sɛ̃sεʀ] *adj* sincere; genuine; heartfelt; **mes ~s condoléances** my deepest sympathy

sincèrement [sɛ̃sεʀmɑ̃] *adv* sincerely; genuinely

sincérité [sɛ̃seʀite] *nf* sincerity; **en toute ~** in all sincerity

sine qua non [sinekwanɔn] *adj*: **condition ~** indispensable condition

Singapour [sɛ̃gapuʀ] *nm* Singapore

singe [sɛ̃ʒ] *nm* monkey; (*de grande taille*) ape

singer [sɛ̃ʒe] *vt* to ape, mimic

singeries [sɛ̃ʒʀi] *nfpl* antics; (*simagrées*) airs and graces

singulariser [sɛ̃gylaʀize] *vt* to mark out; **se singulariser** *vi* to call attention to o.s.

singularité [sɛ̃gylaʀite] *nf* peculiarity

singulier, -ière [sɛ̃gylje, -jεʀ] *adj* remarkable, singular; (*Ling*) singular ▷ *nm* singular

sinistre [sinistʀ] *adj* sinister; (*intensif*): **un ~ imbécile** an incredible idiot ▷ *nm* (*incendie*) blaze; (*catastrophe*) disaster; (*Assurances*) damage (*giving rise to a claim*)

sinistré, e [sinistʀe] *adj* disaster-stricken ▷ *nm/f* disaster victim

sinon [sinɔ̃] *conj* (*autrement, sans quoi*) otherwise, or else; (*sauf*) except, other than; (*si ce n'est*) if not

sinueux, -euse [sinɥø, -øz] *adj* winding; (*fig*) tortuous

S

sinus [sinys] *nm* (*Anat*) sinus; (*Géom*) sine

sinusite [sinyzit] *nf* sinusitis, sinus infection

siphon [sifɔ̃] *nm* (*tube, d'eau gazeuse*) siphon; (*d'évier etc*) U-bend

sirène [siʀɛn] *nf* siren; **~ d'alarme** fire alarm; (*pendant la guerre*) air-raid siren

sirop [siʀo] *nm* (*à diluer: de fruit etc*) syrup, cordial (*Brit*); (*boisson*) fruit drink; (*pharmaceutique*) syrup, mixture; **~ de menthe** mint syrup *ou* cordial; **~ contre la toux** cough syrup *ou* mixture

siroter [siʀote] *vt* to sip

sismique [sismik] *adj* seismic

site [sit] *nm* (*paysage, environnement*) setting; (*d'une ville etc: emplacement*) site; **~ (pittoresque)** beauty spot; **~s touristiques** places of interest; **~s naturels/historiques** natural/historic sites; **~ web** (*Inform*) website

sitôt [sito] *adv*: **~ parti** as soon as he *etc* had left; **~ après** straight after; **pas de ~** not for a long time; **~ (après) que** as soon as

situation [sitɥasjɔ̃] *nf* (*gén*) situation; (*d'un édifice, d'une ville*) situation, position; (*emplacement*) location; **être en ~ de faire qch** to be in a position to do sth; **~ de famille** marital status

situé, e [sitɥe] *adj*: **bien ~** well situated, in a good location; **~ à/près de** situated at/near

situer [sitɥe] *vt* to site, situate; (*en pensée*) to set, place; **se situer** *vi*: **se ~ à/près de** to be situated at/near

six [sis] *num* six

sixième [sizjɛm] *num* sixth ▷ *nf*: **en ~** (*Scol: classe*) year 7 (*Brit*), sixth grade (*US*)

skaï® [skaj] *nm* ≈ Leatherette®

skate [sket], **skate-board** [sketbɔrd] *nm* (*sport*) skateboarding; (*planche*) skateboard

ski [ski] *nm* (*objet*) ski; (*sport*) skiing; **faire du ~** to ski; **~ alpin** Alpine skiing; **~ court** short ski; **~ évolutif** short ski method; **~ de fond** cross-country skiing; **~ nautique** water-skiing; **~ de piste** downhill skiing; **~ de randonnée** cross-country skiing

skier [skje] *vi* to ski

skieur, -euse [skjœr, -øz] *nm/f* skier

slip [slip] *nm* (*sous-vêtement*) underpants *pl*, pants *pl* (*Brit*), briefs *pl*; (*de bain: d'homme*) trunks *pl*; (: *du bikini*) (bikini) briefs *pl*

slogan [slɔɡɑ̃] *nm* slogan

Slovaquie [slɔvaki] *nf*: **la ~** Slovakia

SMIC [smik] *sigle m* = **salaire minimum interprofessionnel de croissance** *see note*

⬤ **SMIC**
⬤
⬤ In France, the *SMIC* ("salaire minimum
⬤ interprofessionnel de croissance") is the
⬤ minimum hourly rate which workers
⬤ over the age of 18 must legally be paid. It
⬤ is index-linked and is raised each time
⬤ the cost of living rises by 2 per cent.

smicard, e [smikar, -ard] *nm/f* minimum wage earner

smoking [smɔkiŋ] *nm* dinner *ou* evening suit

SMS *sigle m* (= *short message service*) (*service*) SMS; (*message*) text (message)

SNC *abr* = **service non compris**

SNCF *sigle f* (= *Société nationale des chemins de fer français*) French railways

snob [snɔb] *adj* snobbish ▷ *nm/f* snob

snobisme [snɔbism] *nm* snobbery, snobbishness

sobre [sɔbr] *adj* (*personne*) temperate, abstemious; (*élégance, style*) restrained, sober; **~ de** (*gestes, compliments*) sparing of

sobriquet [sɔbrikɛ] *nm* nickname

social, e, -aux [sɔsjal, -o] *adj* social

socialisme [sɔsjalism] *nm* socialism

socialiste [sɔsjalist] *adj, nm/f* socialist

société [sɔsjete] *nf* society; (*d'abeilles, de fourmis*) colony; (*sportive*) club; (*Comm*) company; **la bonne ~** polite society; **se plaire dans la ~ de** to enjoy the society of; **l'archipel de la S~** the Society Islands; **la ~ d'abondance/de consommation** the affluent/consumer society; **~ par actions** joint stock company; **~ anonyme (SA)** ≈ limited company (Ltd) (*Brit*), ≈ incorporated company (Inc.) (*US*); **~ d'investissement à capital variable (SICAV)** ≈ investment trust (*Brit*), ≈ mutual fund (*US*); **~ à responsabilité limitée (SARL)** *type of limited liability company* (*with non-negotiable shares*); **~ savante** learned society; **~ de services** service company

sociologie [sɔsjɔlɔʒi] *nf* sociology

socle [sɔkl] *nm* (*de colonne, statue*) plinth, pedestal; (*de lampe*) base

socquette [sɔkɛt] *nf* ankle sock

sœur [sœr] *nf* sister; (*religieuse*) nun, sister; **~ Élisabeth** (*Rel*) Sister Elizabeth; **~ de lait** foster sister

soi [swa] *pron* oneself; **en ~** (*intrinsèquement*) in itself; **cela va de ~** that *ou* it goes without saying, it stands to reason

soi-disant [swadizɑ̃] *adj inv* so-called ▷ *adv* supposedly

soie [swa] *nf* silk; (*de porc, sanglier: poil*) bristle

soierie [swari] *nf* (*industrie*) silk trade; (*tissu*) silk

soif [swaf] *nf* thirst; (*fig*): **~ de** thirst *ou* craving for; **avoir ~** to be thirsty; **donner ~ à qn** to make sb thirsty

soigné, e [swaɲe] *adj* (*tenue*) well-groomed, neat; (*travail*) careful, meticulous; (*fam*) whopping; stiff

soigner [swaɲe] *vt* (*malade, maladie: docteur*) to treat; (: *infirmière, mère*) to nurse, look after; (*blessé*) to tend; (*travail, détails*) to take care over; (*jardin, chevelure, invités*) to look after

soigneux, -euse [swaɲø, -øz] *adj* (*propre*) tidy, neat; (*méticuleux*) painstaking, careful; **~ de** careful with

soi-même [swamɛm] *pron* oneself

soin [swɛ̃] nm (application) care; (propreté, ordre) tidiness, neatness; (responsabilité): **le ~ de qch** the care of sth; **soins** nmpl (à un malade, blessé) treatment sg, medical attention sg; (attentions, prévenance) care and attention sg; (hygiène) care sg; **~s de la chevelure/de beauté** hair/beauty care; **~s du corps/ménage** care of one's body/the home; **avoir ou prendre ~ de** to take care of, look after; **avoir ou prendre ~ de faire** to take care to do; **faire qch avec (grand) ~** to do sth (very) carefully; **sans ~** adj careless; untidy; **les premiers ~s** first aid sg; **aux bons ~s de** c/o, care of; **être aux petits ~s pour qn** to wait on sb hand and foot, see to sb's every need; **confier qn aux ~s de qn** to hand sb over to sb's care

soir [swar] nm, adv evening; **le ~** in the evening(s); **ce ~** this evening, tonight; **à ce ~!** see you this evening (ou tonight)!; **la veille au ~** the previous evening; **sept/dix heures du ~** seven in the evening/ten at night; **le repas/journal du ~** the evening meal/newspaper; **dimanche ~** Sunday evening; **hier ~** yesterday evening; **demain ~** tomorrow evening, tomorrow night

soirée [sware] nf evening; (réception) party; **donner en ~** (film, pièce) to give an evening performance of

soit [swa] vb voir **être** ▷ conj (à savoir) namely, to wit; (ou): **~ ... ~** either ... or ▷ adv so be it, very well; **~ un triangle ABC** let ABC be a triangle; **~ que ... que ou ou que** whether ... or whether

soixantaine [swasɑ̃tɛn] nf: **une ~ (de)** sixty or so, about sixty; **avoir la ~** (âge) to be around sixty

soixante [swasɑ̃t] num sixty

soixante-dix [swasɑ̃tdis] num seventy

soja [sɔʒa] nm soya; (graines) soya beans pl; **germes de ~** beansprouts

sol [sɔl] nm ground; (de logement) floor; (revêtement) flooring no pl; (territoire, Agr, Géo) soil; (Mus) G; (: en chantant la gamme) so(h)

solaire [sɔlɛr] adj (énergie etc) solar; (crème etc) sun cpd

soldat [sɔlda] nm soldier; **S~ inconnu** Unknown Warrior ou Soldier; **~ de plomb** tin ou toy soldier

solde [sɔld] nf pay ▷ nm (Comm) balance; **soldes** nmpl ou nfpl (Comm) sales; (articles) sale goods; **à la ~ de qn** (péj) in sb's pay; **~ créditeur/débiteur** credit/debit balance; **~ à payer** balance outstanding; **en ~** at sale price; **aux ~s** at the sales

solder [sɔlde] vt (compte) to settle; (marchandise) to sell at sale price, sell off; **se ~ par** (fig) to end in; **article soldé (à) 10 euros** item reduced to 10 euros

sole [sɔl] nf sole inv (fish)

soleil [sɔlɛj] nm sun; (lumière) sun(light); (temps ensoleillé) sun(shine); (feu d'artifice) Catherine wheel; (d'acrobate) grand circle; (Bot) sunflower; **il y a ou il fait du ~** it's sunny; **au ~** in the sun; **en plein ~** in full sun; **le ~ levant/couchant** the rising/setting sun; **le ~ de minuit** the midnight sun

solennel, le [sɔlanɛl] adj solemn; ceremonial

solfège [sɔlfɛʒ] nm rudiments pl of music; (exercices) ear training no pl

solidaire [sɔlidɛr] adj: **être ~s** (personnes) to show solidarity, stand ou stick together; (pièces mécaniques) interdependent; (Jur: engagement) binding on all parties; (: débiteurs) jointly liable; **être ~ de** (collègues) to stand by; (mécanisme) to be bound up with, be dependent on

solidarité [sɔlidarite] nf (entre personnes) solidarity; (de mécanisme, phénomènes) interdependence; **par ~ (avec)** (cesser le travail etc) in sympathy (with)

solide [sɔlid] adj solid; (mur, maison, meuble) solid, sturdy; (connaissances, argument) sound; (personne) robust, sturdy; (estomac) strong ▷ nm solid; **avoir les reins ~s** (fig) to be in a good financial position; to have sound financial backing

soliste [sɔlist] nm/f soloist

solitaire [sɔlitɛr] adj (sans compagnie) solitary, lonely; (isolé) solitary, isolated, lone; (lieu) lonely ▷ nm/f (ermite) recluse; (fig: ours) loner ▷ nm (diamant, jeu) solitaire

solitude [sɔlityd] nf loneliness; (paix) solitude

solive [sɔliv] nf joist

solliciter [sɔlisite] vt (personne) to appeal to; (emploi, faveur) to seek; (moteur) to prompt; (occupations, attractions etc): **~ qn** to appeal to sb's curiosity etc; to entice sb; to make demands on sb's time; **~ qn de faire** to appeal to sb ou request sb to do

sollicitude [sɔlisityd] nf concern

soluble [sɔlybl] adj (sucre, cachet) soluble; (problème etc) soluble, solvable

solution [sɔlysjɔ̃] nf solution; **~ de continuité** gap, break; **~ de facilité** easy way out

solvable [sɔlvabl] adj solvent

sombre [sɔ̃br] adj dark; (fig) sombre, gloomy; (sinistre) awful, dreadful

sombrer [sɔ̃bre] vi (bateau) to sink, go down; **~ corps et biens** to go down with all hands; **~ dans** (misère, désespoir) to sink into

sommaire [sɔmɛr] adj (simple) basic; (expéditif) summary ▷ nm summary; **faire le ~ de** to make a summary of, summarize; **exécution ~** summary execution

sommation [sɔmasjɔ̃] nf (Jur) summons sg; (avant de faire feu) warning

somme [sɔm] nf (Math) sum; (fig) amount; (argent) sum, amount ▷ nm: **faire un ~** to have a (short) nap; **faire la ~ de** to add up; **en ~, ~ toute** adv all in all

sommeil [sɔmɛj] nm sleep; **avoir ~** to be sleepy; **avoir le ~ léger** to be a light sleeper; **en ~** (fig) dormant

sommeiller [sɔmeje] vi to doze; (fig) to lie dormant

sommer [sɔme] vt: ~ **qn de faire** to command ou order sb to do; (Jur) to summon sb to do

sommes [sɔm] vb voir **être** voir aussi **somme**

sommet [sɔme] nm top; (d'une montagne) summit, top; (fig: de la perfection, gloire) height; (Géom: d'angle) vertex; (conférence) summit (conference)

sommier [sɔmje] nm bed base, bedspring (US); (Admin: registre) register; ~ **à ressorts** (interior sprung) divan base (Brit), box spring (US); ~ **à lattes** slatted bed base

somnambule [sɔmnãbyl] nm/f sleepwalker

somnifère [sɔmnifɛʀ] nm sleeping drug; (comprimé) sleeping pill ou tablet

somnoler [sɔmnɔle] vi to doze

somptueux, -euse [sɔptɥø, -øz] adj sumptuous; (cadeau) lavish

son¹ [sɔ̃], **sa** [sa] (pl **ses**) [se] adj possessif (antécédent humain mâle) his; (: femelle) her; (: valeur indéfinie) one's, his/her; (: non humain) its; voir **il**

son² [sɔ̃] nm sound; (de blé etc) bran; ~ **et lumière** adj inv son et lumière

sondage [sɔ̃daʒ] nm (de terrain) boring, drilling; (de mer, atmosphère) sounding; probe; (enquête) survey, sounding out of opinion; ~ **(d'opinion)** (opinion) poll

sonde [sɔ̃d] nf (Navig) lead ou sounding line; (Météorologie) sonde; (Méd) probe; catheter; (d'alimentation) feeding tube; (Tech) borer, driller; (de forage, sondage) drill; (pour fouiller etc) probe; ~ **à avalanche** pole (for probing snow and locating victims); ~ **spatiale** probe

sonder [sɔ̃de] vt (Navig) to sound; (atmosphère, plaie, bagages etc) to probe; (Tech) to bore, drill; (fig: personne) to sound out; (: opinion) to probe; ~ **le terrain** (fig) to see how the land lies

songe [sɔ̃ʒ] nm dream

songer [sɔ̃ʒe] vi to dream; ~ **à** (rêver à) to think over, muse over; (penser à) to think of; (envisager) to contemplate, think of, consider; ~ **que** to consider that; to think that

songeur, -euse [sɔ̃ʒœʀ, -øz] adj pensive; **ça me laisse** ~ that makes me wonder

sonnant, -ât [sɔnã, -ãt] adj: **en espèces ~es et trébuchantes** in coin of the realm; **à huit heures ~es** on the stroke of eight

sonné, e [sɔne] adj (fam) cracked; (passé): **il est midi** ~ it's gone twelve; **il a quarante ans bien ~s** he's well into his forties

sonner [sɔne] vi (retentir) to ring; (donner une impression) to sound ▷ vt (cloche) to ring; (glas, tocsin) to sound; (portier, infirmière) to ring for; (messe) to ring the bell for; (fam: choc, coup) to knock out; ~ **du clairon** to sound the bugle; ~ **bien/mal/creux** to sound good/bad/hollow; ~ **faux** (instrument) to sound out of tune; (rire) to ring false; ~ **les heures** to strike the hours; **minuit vient de** ~ midnight has

just struck; ~ **chez qn** to ring sb's doorbell, ring at sb's door

sonnerie [sɔnʀi] nf (son) ringing; (sonnette) bell; (mécanisme d'horloge) striking mechanism; (de portable) ringtone; ~ **d'alarme** alarm bell; ~ **de clairon** bugle call

sonnette [sɔnɛt] nf bell; ~ **d'alarme** alarm bell; ~ **de nuit** night-bell

sono [sɔno] nf (= sonorisation) PA (system); (d'une discothèque) sound system

sonore [sɔnɔʀ] adj (voix) sonorous, ringing; (salle, métal) resonant; (ondes, film, signal) sound cpd; (Ling) voiced; **effets ~s** sound effects

sonorisation [sɔnɔʀizasjɔ̃] nf (équipement: de salle de conférences) public address system, P.A. system; (: de discothèque) sound system

sonorité [sɔnɔʀite] nf (de piano, violon) tone; (de voix, mot) sonority; (d'une salle) resonance; acoustics pl

sont [sɔ̃] vb voir **être**

sophistiqué, e [sɔfistike] adj sophisticated

sorbet [sɔʀbe] nm water ice, sorbet

sorcellerie [sɔʀsɛlʀi] nf witchcraft no pl, sorcery no pl

sorcier, -ière [sɔʀsje, -jɛʀ] nm/f sorcerer/witch ou sorceress ▷ adj: **ce n'est pas** ~ (fam) it's as easy as pie

sordide [sɔʀdid] adj (lieu) squalid; (action) sordid

sornettes [sɔʀnɛt] nfpl twaddle sg

sort [sɔʀ] vb voir **sortir** ▷ nm (fortune, destinée) fate; (condition, situation) lot; (magique): **jeter un** ~ to cast a spell; **un coup du** ~ a blow dealt by fate; **le** ~ **en est jeté** the die is cast; **tirer au** ~ to draw lots; **tirer qch au** ~ to draw lots for sth

sorte [sɔʀt] vb voir **sortir** ▷ nf sort, kind; **une** ~ **de** a sort of; **de la** ~ adv in that way; **en quelque** ~ in a way; **de** ~ **à** so as to, in order to; **de (telle)** ~ **que, en** ~ **que** (de manière que) so that; (si bien que) so much so that; **faire en** ~ **que** to see to it that

sortie [sɔʀti] nf (issue) way out, exit; (Mil) sortie; (fig: verbale) outburst, sally; (: parole incongrue) odd remark; (d'un gaz, de l'eau) outlet; (promenade) outing; (le soir: au restaurant etc) night out; (de produits) export; (de capitaux) outflow; (Comm: somme): ~**s** items of expenditure; outgoings; (Inform) output; (d'imprimante) printout; (Comm: d'un disque) release; (: d'un livre) publication; (: d'un modèle) launching; ~ **à** ~ as he went out ou left; **à la** ~ **de l'école/l'usine** (moment) after school/work; when school/the factory comes out; (lieu) at the school/factory gates; **à la** ~ **de ce nouveau modèle** when this new model comes (ou came) out, when they bring (ou brought) out this new model; ~ **de bain** (vêtement) bathrobe; **"~ de camions"** "vehicle exit"; ~ **papier** hard copy; ~ **de secours** emergency exit

sortilège [sɔʀtilɛʒ] nm (magic) spell
sortir [sɔʀtiʀ] vi (gén) to come out; (partir, se promener, aller au spectacle etc) to go out; (bourgeon, plante, numéro gagnant) to come up ▷ vt (gén) to take out; (produit, ouvrage, modèle) to bring out; (fam: dire: boniments, incongruités) to come out with; (Inform) to output; (: sur papier) to print out; (fam: expulser) to throw out ▷ nm: **au ~ de l'hiver/l'enfance** as winter/childhood nears its end; **~ qch de** to take sth out of; **~ qn d'embarras** to get sb out of trouble; **~ avec qn** to be going out with sb; **~ de** (gén) to leave; (endroit) to go (ou come) out of, leave; (rainure etc) to come out of; (maladie) to get over; (époque) to get through; (cadre, compétence) to be outside; (provenir de: famille etc) to come from; **~ de table** to leave the table; **~ du système** (Inform) to log out; **~ de ses gonds** (fig) to fly off the handle; **se ~ de** (affaire, situation) to get out of; **s'en ~** (malade) to pull through; (d'une difficulté etc) to come through all right; to get through, be able to manage
sosie [sɔzi] nm double
sot, sotte [so, sɔt] adj silly, foolish ▷ nm/f fool
sottise [sɔtiz] nf silliness no pl, foolishness no pl; (propos, acte) silly ou foolish thing (to do ou say)
sou [su] nm: **près de ses ~s** tight-fisted; **sans le ~** penniless; **~ à ~** penny by penny; **pas un ~ de bon sens** not a scrap ou an ounce of good sense; **de quatre ~s** worthless
soubresaut [subʀəso] nm (de peur etc) start; (cahot: d'un véhicule) jolt
souche [suʃ] nf (d'arbre) stump; (de carnet) counterfoil (Brit), stub; **dormir comme une ~** to sleep like a log; **de vieille ~** of old stock
souci [susi] nm (inquiétude) worry; (préoccupation) concern; (Bot) marigold; **se faire du ~** to worry; **avoir (le) ~ de** to have concern for; **par ~ de** for the sake of, out of concern for
soucier [susje]: **se ~ de** vt to care about
soucieux, -euse [susjø, -øz] adj concerned, worried; **~ de** concerned about; **peu ~ de/que** caring little about/whether
soucoupe [sukup] nf saucer; **~ volante** flying saucer
soudain, e [sudɛ̃, -ɛn] adj (douleur, mort) sudden ▷ adv suddenly, all of a sudden
Soudan [sudɑ̃] nm: **le ~** Sudan
soude [sud] nf soda
souder [sude] vt (avec fil à souder) to solder; (par soudure autogène) to weld; (fig) to bind ou knit together; to fuse (together); **se souder** vi (os) to knit (together)
soudoyer [sudwaje] vt (péj) to bribe, buy over
soudure [sudyʀ] nf soldering; welding; (joint) soldered joint; weld; **faire la ~** (Comm) to fill a gap; (fig: assurer une transition) to bridge the gap

souffert, e [sufɛʀ, -ɛʀt] pp de **souffrir**
souffle [sufl] nm (en expirant) breath; (en soufflant) puff, blow; (respiration) breathing; (d'explosion, de ventilateur) blast; (du vent) blowing; (fig) inspiration; **retenir son ~** to hold one's breath; **avoir du/manquer de ~** to have a lot of puff/be short of breath; **être à bout de ~** to be out of breath; **avoir le ~ court** to be short-winded; **un ~ d'air** ou **de vent** a breath of air, a puff of wind; **~ au cœur** (Méd) heart murmur
soufflé, e [sufle] adj (Culin) souffléd; (fam: ahuri, stupéfié) staggered ▷ nm (Culin) soufflé
souffler [sufle] vi (gén) to blow; (haleter) to puff (and blow) ▷ vt (feu, bougie) to blow out; (chasser: poussière etc) to blow away; (Tech: verre) to blow; (explosion) to destroy (with its blast); (dire): **~ qch à qn** to whisper sth to sb; (fam: voler): **~ qch à qn** to pinch sth from sb; **~ son rôle à qn** to prompt sb; **ne pas ~ mot** not to breathe a word; **laisser ~ qn** (fig) to give sb a breather
soufflet [sufle] nm (instrument) bellows pl; (entre wagons) vestibule; (Couture) gusset; (gifle) slap (in the face)
souffleur, -euse [suflœʀ, -øz] nm/f (Théât) prompter; (Tech) glass-blower
souffrance [sufʀɑ̃s] nf suffering; **en ~** (marchandise) awaiting delivery; (affaire) pending
souffrant, e [sufʀɑ̃, -ɑ̃t] adj unwell
souffre-douleur [sufʀədulœʀ] nm inv whipping boy (Brit), butt, underdog
souffrir [sufʀiʀ] vi to suffer; (éprouver des douleurs) to be in pain ▷ vt to suffer, endure; (supporter) to bear, stand; (admettre: exception etc) to allow ou admit of; **~ de** (maladie, froid) to suffer from; **~ des dents** to have trouble with one's teeth; **ne pas pouvoir ~ qch/qn ...** not to be able to endure ou bear sth/that ...; **elle ne peut pas le ~** she can't stand ou bear him; **faire ~ qn** (personne) to make sb suffer; (: dents, blessure etc) to hurt sb
soufre [sufʀ] nm sulphur (Brit), sulfur (US)
souhait [swɛ] nm wish; **tous nos ~s de** good wishes ou our best wishes for; **tous nos ~s pour la nouvelle année** (our) best wishes for the New Year; **riche etc à ~** as rich etc as one could wish; **à vos ~s!** bless you!
souhaitable [swɛtabl] adj desirable
souhaiter [swete] vt to wish for; **~ le bonjour à qn** to bid sb good day; **~ la bonne année à qn** to wish sb a happy New Year; **~ que** to hope that; **il est à ~ que** it is to be hoped that
souiller [suje] vt to dirty, soil; (fig) to sully, tarnish
soûl, e [su, sul] adj drunk; (fig): **~ de musique/plaisirs** drunk with music/pleasure ▷ nm: **tout son ~** to one's heart's content
soulagement [sulaʒmɑ̃] nm relief

soulager [sulaʒe] vt to relieve; **~ qn de** to relieve sb of

soûler [sule] vt: **~ qn** to get sb drunk; (boisson) to make sb drunk; (fig) to make sb's head spin ou reel; **se soûler** vi to get drunk; **se ~ de** (fig) to intoxicate o.s with

soulever [sulve] vt to lift; (vagues, poussière) to send up; (peuple) to stir up (to revolt); (enthousiasme) to arouse; (question, débat, protestations, difficultés) to raise; **se soulever** vi (peuple) to rise up; (personne couchée) to lift o.s. up; (couvercle etc) to lift; **cela me soulève le cœur** it makes me feel sick

soulier [sulje] nm shoe; **~s bas** low-heeled shoes; **~s plats/à talons** flat/heeled shoes

souligner [suliɲe] vt to underline; (fig) to emphasize, stress

soumettre [sumɛtʀ] vt (pays) to subject, subjugate; (rebelles) to put down, subdue; **~ qn/qch à** to subject sb/sth to; **~ qch à qn** (projet etc) to submit sth to sb; **se ~ (à)** (se rendre, obéir) to submit (to); **se ~ à** (formalités etc) to submit to; (régime etc) to submit o.s. to

soumis, e [sumi, -iz] pp de **soumettre** ⊳ adj submissive; **revenus ~ à l'impôt** taxable income

soumission [sumisjɔ̃] nf (voir se soumettre) submission; (docilité) submissiveness; (Comm) tender

soupape [supap] nf valve; **~ de sûreté** safety valve

soupçon [supsɔ̃] nm suspicion; (petite quantité): **un ~ de** a hint ou touch of; **avoir ~ de** to suspect; **au dessus de tout ~** above (all) suspicion

soupçonner [supsɔne] vt to suspect; **~ qn de qch/d'être** to suspect sb of sth/of being

soupçonneux, -euse [supsɔnø, -øz] adj suspicious

soupe [sup] nf soup; **~ au lait** adj inv quick-tempered; **~ à l'oignon/de poisson** onion/fish soup; **~ populaire** soup kitchen

souper [supe] vi to have supper ⊳ nm supper; **avoir soupé de** (fam) to be sick and tired of

soupeser [supəze] vt to weigh in one's hand(s), feel the weight of; (fig) to weigh up

soupière [supjɛʀ] nf (soup) tureen

soupir [supiʀ] nm sigh; (Mus) crotchet rest (Brit), quarter note rest (US); **rendre le dernier ~** to breathe one's last; **pousser un ~ de soulagement** to heave a sigh of relief

soupirail, -aux [supiʀaj, -o] nm (small) basement window

soupirer [supiʀe] vi to sigh; **~ après qch** to yearn for sth

souple [supl] adj supple; (col) soft; (fig: règlement, caractère) flexible; (: démarche, taille) lithe, supple

souplesse [suplɛs] nf suppleness; (de caractère) flexibility

source [suʀs] nf (point d'eau) spring; (d'un cours d'eau, fig) source; **prendre sa ~ à/dans** (cours

d'eau) to have its source at/in; **tenir qch de bonne ~/de ~ sûre** to have sth on good authority/from a reliable source; **~ thermale/d'eau minérale** hot ou thermal/mineral spring

sourcil [suʀsij] nm (eye)brow

sourciller [suʀsije] vi: **sans ~** without turning a hair ou batting an eyelid

sourd, e [suʀ, suʀd] adj deaf; (bruit, voix) muffled; (couleur) muted; (douleur) dull; (lutte) silent, hidden; (Ling) voiceless ⊳ nm/f deaf person; **être ~ à** to be deaf to; **faire la ~e oreille** to turn a deaf ear

sourdine [suʀdin] nf (Mus) mute; **en ~** adv softly, quietly; **mettre une ~ à** (fig) to tone down

sourd-muet, sourde-muette [suʀmɥɛ, suʀdmɥɛt] nm/f person with a speech and hearing impairment

souriant, e [suʀjɑ̃, -ɑ̃t] vb voir **sourire** ⊳ adj cheerful

souricière [suʀisjɛʀ] nf mousetrap; (fig) trap

sourire [suʀiʀ] nm smile ⊳ vi to smile; **~ à qn** to smile at sb; (fig: plaire à) to appeal to sb; (: chance) to smile on sb; **faire un ~ à qn** to give sb a smile; **garder le ~** to keep smiling

souris [suʀi] nf (aussi Inform) mouse

sournois, e [suʀnwa, -waz] adj deceitful, underhand

sous [su] prép (gén) under; **~ la pluie/le soleil** in the rain/sunshine; **~ mes yeux** before my eyes; **~ terre** adj, adv underground; **~ vide** adj, adv vacuum-packed; **~ l'influence/l'action de** under the influence of/by the action of; **~ antibiotiques/perfusion** on antibiotics/a drip; **~ cet angle/ce rapport** from this angle/in this respect; **~ peu** adv shortly, before long

sous-bois [subwa] nm inv undergrowth

souscrire [suskʀiʀ]: **~ à** vt to subscribe to

sous-directeur, -trice [sudiʀɛktœʀ, -tʀis] nm/f assistant manager/manageress, submanager/manageress

sous-entendre [suzɑ̃tɑ̃dʀ] vt to imply, infer

sous-entendu, e [suzɑ̃tɑ̃dy] adj implied; (Ling) understood ⊳ nm innuendo, insinuation

sous-estimer [suzɛstime] vt to underestimate

sous-jacent, e [suʒasɑ̃, -ɑ̃t] adj underlying

sous-louer [sulwe] vt to sublet

sous-marin, e [sumaʀɛ̃, -in] adj (flore, volcan) submarine; (navigation, pêche, explosif) underwater ⊳ nm submarine

sous-officier [suzɔfisje] nm ≈ non-commissioned officer (NCO)

sous-produit [supʀɔdɥi] nm by-product; (fig: péj) pale imitation

sous-pull [supul] nm thin poloneck sweater

soussigné, e [susiɲe] adj: **je ~** I the undersigned

sous-sol [susɔl] nm basement; (Géo) subsoil

sous-titre [sutitʀ] nm subtitle

soustraction [sustʀaksjɔ̃] nf subtraction

soustraire [sustʀɛʀ] vt to subtract, take away; (*dérober*) **qch à qn** to remove sth from sb; **~ qn à** (*danger*) to shield sb from; **se ~ à** (*autorité, obligation, devoir*) to elude, escape from

sous-traitant [sutʀɛtɑ̃] nm subcontractor

sous-traiter [sutʀete] vt, vi to subcontract

sous-vêtement [suvɛtmɑ̃] nm undergarment, item of underwear; **sous-vêtements** nmpl underwear sg

soutane [sutan] nf cassock, soutane

soute [sut] nf hold; **~ à bagages** baggage hold

soutenir [sutniʀ] vt to support; (*assaut, choc, regard*) to stand up to, withstand; (*intérêt, effort*) to keep up; (*assurer*) **~ que** to maintain that; **se soutenir** (*dans l'eau etc*) to hold o.s. up; (*être soutenable: point de vue*) to be tenable; (*s'aider mutuellement*) to stand by each other; **~ la comparaison avec** to bear ou stand comparison with; **~ le regard de qn** to be able to look sb in the face

soutenu, e [sutny] pp de **soutenir** ▷ adj (*efforts*) sustained, unflagging; (*style*) elevated; (*couleur*) strong

souterrain, e [sutɛʀɛ̃, -ɛn] adj underground; (*fig*) subterranean ▷ nm underground passage

soutien [sutjɛ̃] nm support; **apporter son ~ à** to lend one's support to; **~ de famille** breadwinner

soutien-gorge (*pl* **soutiens-gorge**) [sutjɛ̃gɔʀʒ] nm bra; (*de maillot de bain*) top

soutirer [sutiʀe] vt: **~ qch à qn** to squeeze ou get sth out of sb

souvenir [suvniʀ] nm (*réminiscence*) memory; (*cadeau*) souvenir, keepsake; (*de voyage*) souvenir ▷ vb: **se ~ de** vt to remember; **se ~ que** to remember that; **garder le ~ de** to retain the memory of; **en ~ de** in memory ou remembrance of; **avec mes affectueux/meilleurs ~s, ...** with love from, .../regards, ...

souvent [suvɑ̃] adv often; **peu ~** seldom, infrequently; **le plus ~** more often than not, most often

souverain, e [suvʀɛ̃, -ɛn] adj sovereign; (*fig: mépris*) supreme ▷ nm/f sovereign, monarch

soyeux, -euse [swajø, -øz] adj silky

soyons etc [swajɔ̃] vb voir **être**

spacieux, -euse [spasjø, -øz] adj spacious; roomy

spaghettis [spageti] nmpl spaghetti sg

sparadrap [spaʀadʀa] nm adhesive ou sticking (*Brit*) plaster, bandaid® (*US*)

spatial, e, -aux [spasjal, -o] adj (*Aviat*) space cpd; (*Psych*) spatial

speaker, ine [spikœʀ, -kʀin] nm/f announcer

spécial, e, -aux [spesjal, -o] adj special; (*bizarre*) peculiar

spécialement [spesjalmɑ̃] adv especially, particularly; (*tout exprès*) specially; **pas ~** not particularly

spécialiser [spesjalize]: **se spécialiser** vi to specialize

spécialiste [spesjalist] nm/f specialist

spécialité [spesjalite] nf speciality; (*Scol*) special field; **~ pharmaceutique** patent medicine

spécifier [spesifje] vt to specify, state

spécimen [spesimɛn] nm specimen; (*revue etc*) specimen ou sample copy

spectacle [spɛktakl] nm (*tableau, scène*) sight; (*représentation*) show; (*industrie*) show business, entertainment; **se donner en ~** (*péj*) to make a spectacle ou an exhibition of o.s; **pièce/revue à grand ~** spectacular (play/revue); **au ~ de ...** at the sight of ...

spectaculaire [spɛktakylɛʀ] adj spectacular

spectateur, -trice [spɛktatœʀ, -tʀis] nm/f (*Ciné etc*) member of the audience; (*Sport*) spectator; (*d'un événement*) onlooker, witness

spéculer [spekyle] vi to speculate; **~ sur** (*Comm*) to speculate in; (*réfléchir*) to speculate on; (*tabler sur*) to bank ou rely on

spéléologie [speleolɔʒi] nf (*étude*) speleology; (*activité*) potholing

sperme [spɛʀm] nm semen, sperm

sphère [sfɛʀ] nf sphere

spirale [spiʀal] nf spiral; **en ~** in a spiral

spirituel, le [spiʀitɥɛl] adj spiritual; (*fin, piquant*) witty; **musique ~le** sacred music; **concert ~** concert of sacred music

splendide [splɑ̃did] adj splendid, magnificent

sponsoriser [spɔ̃sɔʀize] vt to sponsor

spontané, e [spɔ̃tane] adj spontaneous

spontanéité [spɔ̃taneite] nf spontaneity

sport [spɔʀ] nm sport ▷ adj inv (*vêtement*) casual; (*fair-play*) sporting; **faire du ~** to do sport; **~ individuel/d'équipe** individual/team sport; **~ de combat** combative sport; **~s d'hiver** winter sports

sportif, -ive [spɔʀtif, -iv] adj (*journal, association, épreuve*) sports cpd; (*allure, démarche*) athletic; (*attitude, esprit*) sporting; **les résultats ~s** the sports results

spot [spɔt] nm (*lampe*) spot(light); (*annonce*): **~ (publicitaire)** commercial (*break*)

square [skwaʀ] nm public garden(s)

squelette [skəlɛt] nm skeleton

squelettique [skəletik] adj scrawny; (*fig*) skimpy

SRAS [sʀas] sigle m (= *syndrome respiratoire aigu sévère*) SARS

Sri Lanka [sʀilɑ̃ka] nm: **le ~** Sri Lanka

stabiliser [stabilize] vt to stabilize; (*terrain*) to consolidate

stable [stabl] adj stable, steady

stade [stad] nm (*Sport*) stadium; (*phase, niveau*) stage

stage [staʒ] nm training period; (*cours*) training course; (*d'avocat stagiaire*) articles pl;

S

~ en entreprise work experience placement; **~ de formation (professionnelle)** vocational (training) course; **~ de perfectionnement** advanced training course

stagiaire [staʒjɛʀ] nm/f, adj trainee (cpd)

stagner [stagne] vi to stagnate

stalle [stal] nf stall, box

stand [stɑ̃d] nm (d'exposition) stand; (de foire) stall; **~ de tir** (à la foire, Sport) shooting range; **~ de ravitaillement** pit

standard [stɑ̃daʀ] adj inv standard ▷ nm (type, norme) standard; (téléphonique) switchboard

standardiste [stɑ̃daʀdist] nm/f switchboard operator

standing [stɑ̃diŋ] nm standing; **de grand ~** luxury; **immeuble de grand ~** block of luxury flats (Brit), condo(minium) (US)

starter [staʀtɛʀ] nm (Auto) choke; (Sport: personne) starter; **mettre le ~** to pull out the choke

station [stasjɔ̃] nf station; (de bus) stop; (de villégiature) resort; (posture): **la ~ debout** standing, an upright posture; **~ balnéaire** seaside resort; **~ de graissage** lubrication bay; **~ de lavage** carwash; **~ de ski** ski resort; **~ de sports d'hiver** winter sports resort; **~ de taxis** taxi rank (Brit) ou stand (US); **~ thermale** thermal spa; **~ de travail** workstation

stationnement [stasjɔnmɑ̃] nm parking; **zone de ~ interdit** no parking area; **~ alterné** parking on alternate sides

stationner [stasjɔne] vi to park

station-service [stasjɔ̃sɛʀvis] nf service station

statistique [statistik] nf (science) statistics sg; (rapport, étude) statistic ▷ adj statistical; **statistiques** nfpl (données) statistics pl

statue [staty] nf statue

statu quo [statykwo] nm status quo

statut [staty] nm status; **statuts** nmpl (Jur, Admin) statutes

statutaire [statytɛʀ] adj statutory

Sté abr (= société) soc

steak [stɛk] nm steak; **~ haché** hamburger

sténo [stenɔ] nf (aussi: **~graphie**) shorthand; **prendre en ~** to take down in shorthand

sténographie [stenɔgʀafi] nf shorthand; **prendre en ~** to take down in shorthand

stéréo nf (aussi: **~phonie**) stereo; **émission en ~** stereo broadcast ▷ adj (aussi: **~phonique**) stereo

stéréophonie [steʀeɔfɔni] nf stereo(phony); **émission en ~** stereo broadcast

stéréophonique [steʀeɔfɔnik] adj stereo(phonic)

stérile [steʀil] adj sterile; (terre) barren; (fig) fruitless, futile

stérilet [steʀilɛ] nm coil, loop

stériliser [steʀilize] vt to sterilize

stigmates [stigmat] nmpl scars, marks; (Rel) stigmata pl

stimulant, e [stimylɑ̃, -ɑ̃t] adj stimulating ▷ nm (Méd) stimulant; (fig) stimulus, incentive

stimuler [stimyle] vt to stimulate

stipuler [stipyle] vt to stipulate, specify

stock [stɔk] nm stock; **en ~** in stock

stocker [stɔke] vt to stock; (déchets) to store

stop [stɔp] nm (Auto: écriteau) stop sign; (: signal) brake-light; (dans un télégramme) stop ▷ excl stop!; **faire du ~** (fam) to hitch(hike)

stopper [stɔpe] vt to stop, halt; (Couture) to mend ▷ vi to stop, halt

store [stɔʀ] nm blind; (de magasin) shade, awning

strabisme [stʀabism] nm squint(ing)

strapontin [stʀapɔ̃tɛ̃] nm jump ou foldaway seat

Strasbourg [stʀazbuʀ] n Strasbourg

stratégie [stʀateʒi] nf strategy

stratégique [stʀateʒik] adj strategic

stress [stʀɛs] nm inv stress

stressant, e [stʀɛsɑ̃, -ɑ̃t] adj stressful

stresser [stʀɛse] vt to stress, cause stress in; **~ qn** to make sb (feel) tense

strict, e [stʀikt] adj strict; (tenue, décor) severe, plain; **son droit le plus ~** his most basic right; **dans la plus ~e intimité** strictly in private; **le ~ nécessaire/minimum** the bare essentials/minimum

strident, e [stʀidɑ̃, -ɑ̃t] adj shrill, strident

strophe [stʀɔf] nf verse, stanza

structure [stʀyktyʀ] nf structure; **~s d'accueil/touristiques** reception/tourist facilities

studieux, -euse [stydjø, -øz] adj (élève) studious; (vacances) study cpd

studio [stydjo] nm (logement) studio flat (Brit) ou apartment (US); (d'artiste, TV etc) studio

stupéfait, e [stypefɛ, -ɛt] adj astonished

stupéfiant, e [stypefjɑ̃, -ɑ̃t] adj (étonnant) stunning, astonishing ▷ nm (Méd) drug, narcotic

stupéfier [stypefje] vt to stupefy; (étonner) to stun, astonish

stupeur [stypœʀ] nf (inertie, insensibilité) stupor; (étonnement) astonishment, amazement

stupide [stypid] adj stupid; (hébété) stunned

stupidité [stypidite] nf stupidity no pl; (parole, acte) stupid thing (to say ou do)

style [stil] nm style; **meuble/robe de ~** piece of period furniture/period dress; **~ de vie** lifestyle

stylé, e [stile] adj well-trained

styliste [stilist] nm/f designer; stylist

stylo [stilo] nm: **~ (à encre)** (fountain) pen; **~ (à) bille** ballpoint pen

su, e [sy] pp de **savoir** ▷ nm: **au su de** with the knowledge of

suave [sɥav] adj (odeur) sweet; (voix) suave, smooth; (coloris) soft, mellow

subalterne [sybaltɛʀn] adj (employé, officier)

junior; (*rôle*) subordinate, subsidiary ▷ *nm/f* subordinate, inferior

subconscient [sybkɔ̃sjɑ̃] *nm* subconscious

subir [sybiʀ] *vt* (*affront, dégâts, mauvais traitements*) to suffer; (*influence, charme*) to be under, be subjected to; (*traitement, opération, châtiment*) to undergo; (*personne*) to suffer, be subjected to

subit, e [sybi, -it] *adj* sudden

subitement [sybitmɑ̃] *adv* suddenly, all of a sudden

subjectif, -ive [sybʒɛktif, -iv] *adj* subjective

subjonctif [sybʒɔ̃ktif] *nm* subjunctive

subjuguer [sybʒyge] *vt* to subjugate

submerger [sybmɛʀʒe] *vt* to submerge; (*foule*) to engulf; (*fig*) to overwhelm

subordonné, e [sybɔʀdɔne] *adj, nm/f* subordinate; ~ **à** (*personne*) subordinate to; (*résultats etc*) subject to, depending on

subrepticement [sybʀɛptismɑ̃] *adv* surreptitiously

subside [sypsid] *nm* grant

subsidiaire [sypsidjɛʀ] *adj* subsidiary; **question** ~ deciding question

subsister [sybziste] *vi* (*rester*) to remain, subsist; (*vivre*) to live; (*survivre*) to live on

substance [sypstɑ̃s] *nf* substance; **en** ~ in substance

substituer [sypstitɥe] *vt*: ~ **qn/qch à** to substitute sb/sth for; **se** ~ **à qn** (*représenter*) to substitute for sb; (*évincer*) to substitute o.s. for sb

substitut [sypstity] *nm* (*Jur*) deputy public prosecutor; (*succédané*) substitute

subterfuge [syptɛʀfyʒ] *nm* subterfuge

subtil, e [syptil] *adj* subtle

subtiliser [syptilize] *vt*: ~ **qch** (**à qn**) to spirit sth away (from sb)

subvenir [sybvəniʀ]: ~ **à** *vt* to meet

subvention [sybvɑ̃sjɔ̃] *nf* subsidy, grant

subventionner [sybvɑ̃sjɔne] *vt* to subsidize

suc [syk] *nm* (*Bot*) sap; (*de viande, fruit*) juice; **~s gastriques** gastric juices

succédané [syksedane] *nm* substitute

succéder [syksede]: ~ **à** *vt* (*directeur, roi etc*) to succeed; (*venir après: dans une série*) to follow, succeed; **se succéder** *vi* (*accidents, années*) to follow one another

succès [syksɛ] *nm* success; **avec** ~ successfully; **sans** ~ unsuccessfully; **avoir du** ~ to be a success, be successful; **à** ~ successful; **livre à** ~ bestseller; ~ **de librairie** bestseller; ~ (**féminins**) conquests

successeur [syksesœʀ] *nm* successor

successif, -ive [syksesif, -iv] *adj* successive

succession [syksesjɔ̃] *nf* (*série, Pol*) succession; (*Jur: patrimoine*) estate, inheritance; **prendre la** ~ **de** (*directeur*) to succeed, take over from; (*entreprise*) to take over

succomber [sykɔ̃be] *vi* to die, succumb; (*fig*): ~ **à** to succumb to, give way to

succulent, e [sykylɑ̃, -ɑ̃t] *adj* delicious

succursale [sykyʀsal] *nf* branch; **magasin à ~s multiples** chain *ou* multiple store

sucer [syse] *vt* to suck

sucette [sysɛt] *nf* (*bonbon*) lollipop; (*de bébé*) dummy (*Brit*), comforter, pacifier (*US*)

sucre [sykʀ] *nm* (*substance*) sugar; (*morceau*) lump of sugar, sugar lump *ou* cube; ~ **de canne/betterave** cane/beet sugar; ~ **en morceaux/cristallisé/en poudre** lump *ou* cube/granulated/caster sugar; ~ **glace** icing sugar (*Brit*), confectioner's sugar (*US*); ~ **d'orge** barley sugar

sucré, e [sykʀe] *adj* (*produit alimentaire*) sweetened; (*au goût*) sweet; (*péj*) sugary, honeyed

sucrer [sykʀe] *vt* (*thé, café*) to sweeten, put sugar in; ~ **qn** to put sugar in sb's tea (*ou* coffee *etc*); **se sucrer** to help o.s. to sugar, have some sugar; (*fam*) to line one's pocket(s)

sucrerie [sykʀəʀi] *nf* (*usine*) sugar refinery; **sucreries** *nfpl* (*bonbons*) sweets, sweet things

sucrier, -ière [sykʀije, -jɛʀ] *adj* (*industrie*) sugar *cpd*; (*région*) sugar-producing ▷ *nm* (*fabricant*) sugar producer; (*récipient*) sugar bowl *ou* basin

sud [syd] *nm*: **le** ~ the south ▷ *adj inv* south; (*côte*) south, southern; **au** ~ (*situation*) in the south; (*direction*) to the south; **au** ~ **de** (to the) south of

sud-africain, e [sydafʀikɛ̃, -ɛn] *adj* South African ▷ *nm/f*: **Sud-Africain, e** South African

sud-américain, e [sydameʀikɛ̃, -ɛn] *adj* South American ▷ *nm/f*: **Sud-Américain, e** South American

sud-est [sydɛst] *nm, adj inv* south-east

sud-ouest [sydwɛst] *nm, adj inv* south-west

Suède [sɥɛd] *nf*: **la** ~ Sweden

suédois, e [sɥedwa, -waz] *adj* Swedish ▷ *nm* (*Ling*) Swedish ▷ *nm/f*: **S~, e** Swede

suer [sɥe] *vi* to sweat; (*suinter*) to ooze ▷ *vt* (*fig*) to exude; ~ **à grosses gouttes** to sweat profusely

sueur [sɥœʀ] *nf* sweat; **en** ~ sweating, in a sweat; **avoir des ~s froides** to be in a cold sweat

suffire [syfiʀ] *vi* (*être assez*): ~ (**à qn/pour qch/ pour faire**) to be enough *ou* sufficient (for sb/for sth/to do); (*satisfaire*): **cela lui suffit** he's content with this, this is enough for him; **se suffire** *vi* to be self-sufficient; **cela suffit pour les irriter/qu'ils se fâchent** it's enough to annoy them/for them to get angry; **il suffit d'une négligence/qu'on oublie pour que ...** it only takes one act of carelessness/one only needs to forget for ...; **ça suffit!** that's enough!, that'll do!

suffisamment [syfizamɑ̃] *adv* sufficiently, enough; ~ **de** sufficient, enough

suffisant, e [syfizɑ̃, -ɑ̃t] *adj* (*temps, ressources*) sufficient; (*résultats*) satisfactory; (*vaniteux*) self-important, bumptious

s

suffixe [syfiks] nm suffix

suffoquer [syfɔke] vt to choke, suffocate; (*stupéfier*) to stagger, astound ▷ vi to choke, suffocate; **~ de colère/d'indignation** to choke with anger/indignation

suffrage [syfraʒ] nm (Pol: *voix*) vote; (*: méthode*): **~ universel/direct/indirect** universal/direct/indirect suffrage; (*du public etc*) approval no pl; **~s exprimés** valid votes

suggérer [sygʒere] vt to suggest; **~ que/de faire** to suggest that/doing

suggestion [sygʒestjɔ̃] nf suggestion

suicide [sɥisid] nm suicide ▷ adj: **opération ~** suicide mission

suicider [sɥiside]: **se suicider** vi to commit suicide

suie [sɥi] nf soot

suinter [sɥɛ̃te] vi to ooze

suis [sɥi] vb voir **être**; **suivre**

suisse [sɥis] adj Swiss ▷ nm (*bedeau*) ≈ verger ▷ nm/f: **S~** Swiss pl inv ▷ nf: **la S~** Switzerland; **la S~ romande/allemande** French-speaking/German-speaking Switzerland; **~ romand** Swiss French

Suissesse [sɥises] nf Swiss (woman ou girl)

suite [sɥit] nf (*continuation: d'énumération etc*) rest, remainder; (*: de feuilleton*) continuation; (*: second film etc sur le même thème*) sequel; (*série: de maisons, succès*): **une ~ de** a series ou succession of; (*Math*) series sg; (*conséquence*) result; (*ordre, liaison logique*) coherence; (*appartement, Mus*) suite; (*escorte*) retinue, suite; **suites** nfpl (*d'une maladie etc*) effects; **prendre la ~ de** (*directeur etc*) to succeed, take over from; **faire ~ à** to follow; (*faisant*) **~ à votre lettre du** further to your letter of the; **sans ~** adj incoherent, disjointed ▷ adv incoherently, disjointedly; **de ~** adv (*d'affilée*) in succession; (*immédiatement*) at once; **par la ~** afterwards, subsequently; **à la ~** adv one after the other; **à la ~ de** (*derrière*) behind; (*en conséquence de*) following; **par ~ de** owing to, as a result of; **avoir de la ~ dans les idées** to show great singleness of purpose; **attendre la ~ des événements** to (wait and see) what happens

suivant, e [sɥivɑ̃, -ɑ̃t] vb voir **suivre** ▷ adj next, following; (*ci-après*): **l'exercice ~** the following exercise ▷ prép (*selon*) according to; **~ que** according to whether; **au ~!** next!

suivi, e [sɥivi] pp de **suivre** ▷ adj (*régulier*) regular; (*Comm: article*) in general production; (*effort, qualité*) consistent; (*cohérent*) coherent ▷ nm follow-up; **très/peu ~** (*cours*) well-/poorly-attended; (*mode*) widely/not widely adopted; (*feuilleton etc*) widely/not widely followed

suivre [sɥivr] vt (*gén*) to follow; (*Scol: cours*) to attend; (*: leçon*) to follow, attend to; (*: programme*) to keep up with; (*Comm: article*) to continue to stock ▷ vi to follow; (*élève:*

écouter) to attend, pay attention; (*: assimiler le programme*) to keep up, follow; **se suivre** vi (*accidents, personnes, voitures etc*) to follow one after the other; (*raisonnement*) to be coherent; **~ des yeux** to follow with one's eyes; **faire ~** (*lettre*) to forward; **~ son cours** (*enquête etc*) to run ou take its course; **"à ~"** "to be continued"

sujet, te [syʒɛ, -ɛt] adj: **être ~ à** (*accidents*) to be prone to; (*vertige etc*) to be liable ou subject to ▷ nm/f (*d'un souverain*) subject ▷ nm subject; **un ~ de dispute/discorde/mécontentement** a cause for argument/dissension/dissatisfaction; **c'est à quel ~?** what is it about?; **avoir ~ de se plaindre** to have cause for complaint; **au ~ de** prép about; **~ à caution** adj questionable; **~ de conversation** topic ou subject of conversation; **~ d'examen** (*Scol*) examination question; examination paper; **~ d'expérience** (*Bio etc*) experimental subject

summum [sɔmɔm] nm: **le ~ de** the height of

super [sypɛr] adj inv great, fantastic ▷ nm (= *supercarburant*) ≈ 4-star (Brit), ≈ premium (US)

superbe [sypɛrb] adj magnificent, superb ▷ nf arrogance

supercherie [sypɛrʃəri] nf trick, trickery no pl; (*fraude*) fraud

supérette [sypɛret] nf minimarket

superficie [sypɛrfisi] nf (*surface*) area; (*fig*) surface

superficiel, le [sypɛrfisjel] adj superficial

superflu, e [sypɛrfly] adj superfluous ▷ nm: **le ~** the superfluous

supérieur, e [sypɛrjœr] adj (*lèvre, étages, classes*) upper; (*plus élevé: température, niveau*): **~ (à)** higher (than); (*meilleur: qualité, produit*): **~ (à)** superior (to); (*excellent, hautain*) superior ▷ nm/f superior; **Mère ~e** Mother Superior; **à l'étage ~** on the next floor up; **en nombre ~** superior in number

supériorité [sypɛrjɔrite] nf superiority

superlatif [sypɛrlatif] nm superlative

supermarché [sypɛrmarʃe] nm supermarket

superposer [sypɛrpoze] vt to superpose; (*meubles, caisses*) to stack; (*faire chevaucher*) to superimpose; **se superposer** (*images, souvenirs*) to be superimposed; **lits superposés** bunk beds

superproduction [sypɛrprɔdyksjɔ̃] nf (*film*) spectacular

superpuissance [sypɛrpɥisɑ̃s] nf superpower

superstitieux, -euse [sypɛrstisjø, -øz] adj superstitious

superviser [sypɛrvize] vt to supervise

supplanter [syplɑ̃te] vt to supplant

suppléance [sypleɑ̃s] nf (*poste*) supply post (Brit), substitute teacher's post (US)

suppléant, e [sypleɑ̃, -ɑ̃t] adj (*juge, fonctionnaire*) deputy cpd; (*professeur*) supply cpd

(Brit), substitute cpd (US) ▷ nm/f deputy; (professeur) supply ou substitute teacher; **médecin** ~ locum

suppléer [syplee] vt (ajouter: mot manquant etc) to supply, provide; (compenser: lacune) to fill in; (: défaut) to make up for; (remplacer: professeur) to stand in for; (: juge) to deputize for; ~ **à** vt to make up for; to substitute for

supplément [syplemɑ̃] nm supplement; **un ~ de travail** extra ou additional work; **un ~ de frites** etc an extra portion of chips etc; **un ~ de 10 euros** a supplement of 10 euros, an extra ou additional 10 euros; **ceci est en ~** (au menu etc) this is extra, there is an extra charge for this; **le vin est en ~** = wine is extra; **payer un ~** to pay an additional charge; **~ d'information** additional information

supplémentaire [syplemɑ̃tɛʀ] adj additional, further; (train, bus) relief cpd, extra

supplication [syplikasjɔ̃] nf (Rel) supplication; **supplications** nfpl (adjurations) pleas, entreaties

supplice [syplis] nm (peine corporelle) torture no pl; form of torture; (douleur physique, morale) torture, agony; **être au ~** to be in agony

supplier [syplije] vt to implore, beseech

support [sypɔʀ] nm support; (pour livre, outils) stand; **~ audio-visuel** audio-visual aid; **~ publicitaire** advertising medium

supportable [sypɔʀtabl] adj (douleur, température) bearable; (procédé, conduite) tolerable

supporter[1] [sypɔʀtɛʀ] nm supporter, fan

supporter[2] [sypɔʀte] vt [sypɔʀte] (poids, poussée, Sport: concurrent, équipe) to support; (conséquences, épreuve) to bear, endure; (défauts, personne) to tolerate, put up with; (chose: chaleur etc) to withstand; (personne: chaleur, vin) to take

supposer [sypoze] vt to suppose; (impliquer) to presuppose; **en supposant** ou **à ~ que** supposing (that)

suppositoire [sypozitwaʀ] nm suppository

suppression [sypʀesjɔ̃] nf (voir supprimer) removal; deletion; cancellation; suppression

supprimer [sypʀime] vt (cloison, cause, anxiété) to remove; (clause, mot) to delete; (congés, service d'autobus etc) to cancel; (publication, article) to suppress; (emplois, privilèges, témoin gênant) to do away with; **~ qch à qn** to deprive sb of sth

suprême [sypʀɛm] adj supreme

 MOT-CLÉ

sur[1] [syʀ] prép **1** (position) on; (pardessus) over; (au-dessus) above; **pose-le sur la table** put it on the table; **je n'ai pas d'argent sur moi** I haven't any money on me
2 (direction) towards; **en allant sur Paris** going towards Paris; **sur votre droite** on ou

to your right
3 (à propos de) on, about; **un livre/une conférence sur Balzac** a book/lecture on ou about Balzac
4 (proportion, mesures) out of; by; **un sur 10** one in 10; (Scol) one out of 10; **sur 20, deux sont venus** out of 20, two came; **4 m sur 2** 4 m by 2; **avoir accident sur accident** to have one accident after another
5 (cause) **sur sa recommandation** on ou at his recommendation; **sur son invitation** at his invitation
6: **sur ce** adv whereupon; **sur ce, il faut que je vous quitte** and now I must leave you

sur[2], **e** [syʀ] adj sour

sûr, e [syʀ] adj sure, certain; (digne de confiance) reliable; (sans danger) safe; **peu ~** unreliable; **~ de qch** sure ou certain of sth; **être ~ de qn** to be sure of sb; **~ et certain** absolutely certain; **~ de soi** self-assured, self-confident; **le plus ~ est** the safest thing is to

surcharge [syʀʃaʀʒ] nf (de passagers, marchandises) excess load; (de détails, d'ornements) overabundance, excess; (correction) alteration; (Postes) surcharge; **prendre des passagers en ~** to take on excess ou extra passengers; **~ de bagages** excess luggage; **~ de travail** extra work

surcharger [syʀʃaʀʒe] vt to overload; (timbre-poste) to surcharge; (décoration) to overdo

surchoix [syʀʃwa] adj inv top-quality

surclasser [syʀklase] vt to outclass

surcroît [syʀkʀwa] nm: **~ de qch** additional sth; **par ou de ~** moreover; **en ~** in addition

surdité [syʀdite] nf deafness; **atteint de ~ totale** profoundly deaf

surélever [syʀɛlve] vt to raise, heighten

sûrement [syʀmɑ̃] adv reliably; (sans risques) safely, securely; (certainement) certainly; **~ pas** certainly not

surenchère [syʀɑ̃ʃɛʀ] nf (aux enchères) higher bid; (sur prix fixe) overbid; (fig) overstatement; outbidding tactics pl; **~ de violence** build-up of violence; **~ électorale** political (ou electoral) one-upmanship

surenchérir [syʀɑ̃ʃeʀiʀ] vi to bid higher; to raise one's bid; (fig) to try and outbid each other

surent [syʀ] vb voir **savoir**

surestimer [syʀɛstime] vt (tableau) to overvalue; (possibilité, personne) to overestimate

sûreté [syʀte] nf (voir sûr: exactitude: de renseignements etc) reliability; (sécurité) safety; (d'un geste) steadiness; (Jur) guaranty; surety; **mettre en ~** to put in a safe place; **pour plus de ~** as an extra precaution; **to be on the safe side; la ~ de l'État** State security; **la S~ (nationale)** division du Ministère de l'Intérieur heading all police forces except the gendarmerie and the Paris préfecture de police

S

surf [sœrf] nm surfing; **faire du ~** to go surfing

surface [syrfas] nf surface; (*superficie*) surface area; **une grande ~** a supermarket; **faire ~** to surface; **en ~** adv near the surface; (*fig*) superficially; **la pièce fait 100 m² de ~** the room has a surface area of 100m²; **~ de réparation** (*Sport*) penalty area; **~ porteuse** *ou* **de sustentation** (*Aviat*) aerofoil

surfait, e [syrfɛ, -ɛt] adj overrated

surfer [sœrfe] vi to surf; **~ sur Internet** to surf *ou* browse the Internet

surgelé, e [syrʒəle] adj (deep-)frozen ▷ nm: **les ~s** (deep-)frozen food

surgir [syrʒir] vi (*personne, véhicule*) to appear suddenly; (*jaillir*) to shoot up; (*montagne etc*) to rise up, loom up; (*fig: problème, conflit*) to arise

surhumain, e [syrymɛ̃, -ɛn] adj superhuman

sur-le-champ [syrləʃɑ̃] adv immediately

surlendemain [syrlɑ̃dmɛ̃] nm: **le ~ (soir)** two days later (in the evening); **le ~ de** two days after

surmenage [syrmənaʒ] nm overwork; **le ~ intellectuel** mental fatigue

surmener [syrməne] vt, **se surmener** vi to overwork

surmonter [syrmɔ̃te] vt (*coupole etc*) to surmount, top; (*vaincre*) to overcome, surmount; (*être au-dessus de*) to top

surnaturel, le [syrnatyrɛl] adj, nm supernatural

surnom [syrnɔ̃] nm nickname

surnombre [syrnɔ̃br] nm: **être en ~** to be too many (*ou* one too many)

surpeuplé, e [syrpœple] adj overpopulated

surplace [syrplas] nm: **faire du ~** to mark time

surplomber [syrplɔ̃be] vi to be overhanging ▷ vt to overhang; (*dominer*) to tower above

surplus [syrply] nm (*Comm*) surplus; (*reste*): **~ de bois** wood left over; **au ~** moreover; **~ américains** American army surplus *sg*

surprenant, e [syrprənɑ̃, -ɑ̃t] vb voir **surprendre** ▷ adj amazing

surprendre [syrprɑ̃dr] vt (*étonner, prendre à l'improviste*) to amaze, surprise; (*secret*) to discover; (*tomber sur: intrus etc*) to catch; (*fig*) to detect; to chance *ou* happen upon; (*clin d'œil*) to intercept; (*conversation*) to overhear; (*orage, nuit etc*) to catch out, take by surprise; **~ la vigilance/bonne foi de qn** to catch sb out/ betray sb's good faith; **se ~ à faire** to catch *ou* find o.s. doing

surpris, e [syrpri, -iz] pp de **surprendre** ▷ adj: **~ (de/que)** amazed *ou* surprised (at/that)

surprise [syrpriz] nf surprise; **faire une ~ à qn** to give sb a surprise; **voyage sans ~s** uneventful journey; **par ~** adv by surprise

surprise-partie [syrprizparti] nf party

sursaut [syrso] nm start, jump; **~ de** (*énergie, indignation*) sudden fit *ou* burst of; **en ~** adv with a start

sursauter [syrsote] vi to (give a) start, jump

sursis [syrsi] nm (*Jur: gén*) suspended sentence; (*à l'exécution capitale, aussi fig*) reprieve; (*Mil*): **~ (d'appel** *ou* **d'incorporation)** deferment; **condamné à cinq mois (de prison) avec ~** given a five-month suspended (prison) sentence

surtaxe [syrtaks] nf surcharge

surtout [syrtu] adv (*avant tout, d'abord*) above all; (*spécialement, particulièrement*) especially; **il aime le sport, ~ le football** he likes sport, especially football; **cet été, il a ~ fait de la pêche** this summer he went fishing more than anything (else); **~ pas d'histoires!** no fuss now!; **~, ne dites rien!** whatever you do – don't say anything!; **~ pas!** certainly not, definitely not!; **~ que ...** especially as ...

surveillance [syrvejɑ̃s] nf watch; (*Police, Mil*) surveillance; **sous ~ médicale** under medical supervision; **la ~ du territoire** internal security; voir aussi **DST**

surveillant, e [syrvejɑ̃, -ɑ̃t] nm/f (*de prison*) warder; (*Scol*) monitor; (*de travaux*) supervisor, overseer

surveiller [syrveje] vt (*enfant, élèves, bagages*) to watch, keep an eye on; (*malade*) to watch over; (*prisonnier, suspect*) to keep (a) watch on; (*territoire, bâtiment*) to (keep) watch over; (*travaux, cuisson*) to supervise; (*Scol: examen*) to invigilate; **se surveiller** to keep a check *ou* watch on o.s.; **~ son langage/sa ligne** to watch one's language/figure

survenir [syrvənir] vi (*incident, retards*) to occur, arise; (*événement*) to take place; (*personne*) to appear, arrive

survêt [syrvɛt], **survêtement** [syrvɛtmɑ̃] nm tracksuit (*Brit*), sweat suit (*US*)

survie [syrvi] nf survival; (*Rel*) afterlife; **équipement de ~** survival equipment; **une ~ de quelques mois** a few more months of life

survivant, e [syrvivɑ̃, -ɑ̃t] vb voir **survivre** ▷ nm/f survivor

survivre [syrvivr] vi to survive; **~ à** vt (*accident etc*) to survive; (*personne*) to outlive; **la victime a peu de chance de ~** the victim has little hope of survival

survoler [syrvɔle] vt to fly over; (*fig: livre*) to skim through; (*: question, problèmes*) to skim over

survolté, e [syrvɔlte] adj (*Élec*) stepped up, boosted; (*fig*) worked up

sus [sy(s)]: **en ~ de** prép in addition to, over and above; **en ~** adv in addition; **~ à** excl: **~ au tyran!** at the tyrant! ▷ vb [sy] voir **savoir**

susceptible [sysɛptibl] adj touchy, sensitive; **~ d'amélioration** *ou* **d'être amélioré** that can be improved, open to improvement; **~ de faire** (*capacité*) able to do; (*probabilité*) liable to do

susciter [sysite] vt (*admiration*) to arouse; (*obstacles, ennuis*): **~ (à qn)** to create (for sb)

suspect, e [syspɛ(kt), -ɛkt] adj suspicious;

(témoignage, opinions, vin etc) suspect ▷ *nm/f* suspect; **peu ~ de** most unlikely to be suspected of

suspecter [syspɛkte] *vt* to suspect; *(honnêteté de qn)* to question, have one's suspicions about; **~ qn d'être/d'avoir fait qch** to suspect sb of being/having done sth

suspendre [syspãdʀ] *vt (accrocher: vêtement)*: **~ qch (à)** to hang sth up (on); *(fixer: lustre etc)*: **~ qch à** to hang sth from; *(interrompre, démettre)* to suspend; *(remettre)* to defer; **se ~ à** to hang from

suspendu, e [syspãdy] *pp de* **suspendre** ▷ *adj (accroché)*: **~ à** hanging on (ou from); *(perché)*: **~ au-dessus de** suspended over; *(Auto)*: **bien/mal ~** with good/poor suspension; **être ~ aux lèvres de qn** to hang upon sb's every word

suspens [syspã]: **en ~** *adv (affaire)* in abeyance; **tenir en ~** to keep in suspense

suspense [syspãs] *nm* suspense

suspension [syspãsjõ] *nf* suspension; deferment; *(Auto)* suspension; *(lustre)* pendant light fitting; **en ~** in suspension, suspended; **~ d'audience** adjournment

sut [sy] *vb voir* **savoir**

suture [sytyʀ] *nf*: **point de ~** stitch

svelte [svɛlt] *adj* slender, svelte

SVP *sigle (= s'il vous plaît)* please

sweat [swit] *nm (fam)* sweatshirt

sweat-shirt [switʃœʀt] *(pl* **sweat-shirts**) *nm* sweatshirt

syllabe [silab] *nf* syllable

symbole [sɛ̃bɔl] *nm* symbol

symbolique [sɛ̃bɔlik] *adj* symbolic; *(geste, offrande)* token *cpd*; *(salaire, dommages-intérêts)* nominal

symboliser [sɛ̃bɔlize] *vt* to symbolize

symétrique [simetʀik] *adj* symmetrical

sympa [sɛ̃pa] *adj inv (fam: = sympathique)* nice; friendly; good; **sois ~, prête-le moi** be a pal and lend it to me

sympathie [sɛ̃pati] *nf (inclination)* liking; *(affinité)* fellow feeling; *(condoléances)* sympathy; **accueillir avec ~** *(projet)* to receive favourably; **avoir de la ~ pour qn** to like sb, have a liking for sb; **témoignages de ~** expressions of sympathy; **croyez à toute ma ~** you have my deepest sympathy

sympathique [sɛ̃patik] *adj (personne, figure)* nice, friendly, likeable; *(geste)* friendly; *(livre)* good; *(déjeuner)* nice; *(réunion, endroit)* pleasant, nice

sympathisant, e [sɛ̃patizã, -ãt] *nm/f* sympathizer

sympathiser [sɛ̃patize] *vi (voisins etc: s'entendre)* to get on (Brit) *ou* along (US) (well); *(: se fréquenter)* to socialize, see each other; **~ avec** to get on *ou* along (well) with, to see, socialize with

symphonie [sɛ̃fɔni] *nf* symphony

symptôme [sɛ̃ptom] *nm* symptom

synagogue [sinagɔg] *nf* synagogue

syncope [sɛ̃kɔp] *nf (Méd)* blackout; *(Mus)* syncopation; **tomber en ~** to faint, pass out

syndic [sɛ̃dik] *nm* managing agent

syndical, e, -aux [sɛ̃dikal, -o] *adj* (trade-)union *cpd*; **centrale ~e** group of affiliated trade unions

syndicaliste [sɛ̃dikalist] *nm/f* trade unionist

syndicat [sɛ̃dika] *nm (d'ouvriers, employés)* (trade(s)) union; *(autre association d'intérêts)* union, association; **~ d'initiative (SI)** tourist office *ou* bureau; **~ patronal** employers' syndicate, federation of employers; **~ de propriétaires** association of property owners

syndiqué, e [sɛ̃dike] *adj* belonging to a (trade) union; **non ~** non-union

syndiquer [sɛ̃dike]: **se syndiquer** *vi* to form a trade union; *(adhérer)* to join a trade union

synonyme [sinɔnim] *adj* synonymous ▷ *nm* synonym; **~ de** synonymous with

syntaxe [sɛ̃taks] *nf* syntax

synthèse [sɛ̃tɛz] *nf* synthesis; **faire la ~ de** to synthesize

synthétique [sɛ̃tetik] *adj* synthetic

Syrie [siʀi] *nf*: **la ~** Syria

systématique [sistematik] *adj* systematic

système [sistɛm] *nm* system; **le ~ D** resourcefulness; **~ décimal** decimal system; **~ expert** expert system; **~ d'exploitation** *(Inform)* operating system; **~ immunitaire** immune system; **~ métrique** metric system; **~ solaire** solar system

S

t' [t] *pron voir* **te**

ta [ta] *adj poss voir* **ton**

tabac [taba] *nm* tobacco; (*aussi:* **débit** *ou* **bureau de ~**) tobacconist's (shop) ▷ *adj inv:* (*couleur*) ~ buff, tobacco *cpd;* **passer qn à ~** to beat sb up; **faire un ~** (*fam*) to be a big hit; **~ blond/brun** light/dark tobacco; **~ gris** shag; **à priser** snuff

tabagisme [tabaʒism] *nm* nicotine addiction; **~ passif** passive smoking

tabasser [tabase] *vt* to beat up

table [tabl] *nf* table; **avoir une bonne ~** to keep a good table; **à ~!** dinner *etc* is ready!; **se mettre à ~** to sit down to eat; (*fig: fam*) to come clean; **mettre** *ou* **dresser/desservir la ~** to lay *ou* set/clear the table; **faire ~ rase de** to make a clean sweep of; **~ à repasser** ironing board; **~ basse** coffee table; **~ de cuisson** (*à l'électricité*) hob, hotplate; (*au gaz*) hob, gas ring; **~ d'écoute** wire-tapping set; **~ d'harmonie** sounding board; **~ d'hôte** set menu; **~ de lecture** turntable; **~ des matières** (table of) contents *pl;* **~ de multiplication** multiplication table; **~ des négociations** negotiating table; **~ de nuit** *ou* **de chevet** bedside table; **~ d'orientation** viewpoint indicator; **~ ronde** (*débat*) round table; **~ roulante** (tea) trolley (*Brit*), tea wagon (*US*); **~ de toilette** washstand; **~ traçante** (*Inform*) plotter

tableau, x [tablo] *nm* (*Art*) painting; (*reproduction, fig*) picture; (*panneau*) board; (*schéma*) table, chart; **~ blanc** whiteboard; **~ blanc interactif** interactive whiteboard; **~ d'affichage** notice board; **~ de bord** dashboard; (*Aviat*) instrument panel; **~ de chasse** tally; **~ de contrôle** console, control panel; **~ de maître** masterpiece; **~ noir** blackboard

tabler [table] *vi:* **~ sur** to count *ou* bank on

tablette [tablet] *nf* (*planche*) shelf; **~ de chocolat** bar of chocolate

tableur [tablœr] *nm* (*Inform*) spreadsheet

tablier [tablije] *nm* apron; (*de pont*) roadway; (*de cheminée*) (flue-)shutter

tabou, e [tabu] *adj, nm* taboo

tabouret [taburɛ] *nm* stool

tac [tak] *nm:* **du ~ au ~** tit for tat

tache [taʃ] *nf* (*saleté*) stain, mark; (*Art, de couleur, lumière*) spot; splash, patch; **faire ~ d'huile** to spread, gain ground; **~ de rousseur** *ou* **de son** freckle; **~ de vin** (*sur la peau*) strawberry mark

tâche [taʃ] *nf* task; **travailler à la ~** to do piecework

tacher [taʃe] *vt* to stain, mark; (*fig*) to sully, stain; **se tacher** *vi* (*fruits*) to become marked

tâcher [taʃe] *vi:* **~ de faire** to try to do, endeavour (*Brit*) *ou* endeavor (*US*) to do

tacheté, e [taʃte] *adj:* **~ de** speckled *ou* spotted with

tacot [tako] *nm* (*péj: voiture*) banger (*Brit*), clunker (*US*)

tact [takt] *nm* tact; **avoir du ~** to be tactful, have tact

tactique [taktik] *adj* tactical ▷ *nf* (*technique*) tactics *nsg;* (*plan*) tactic

taie [tɛ] *nf:* **~ (d'oreiller)** pillowslip, pillowcase

taille [taj] *nf* cutting; (*d'arbre*) pruning; (*milieu du corps*) waist; (*hauteur*) height; (*grandeur*) size; **de ~ à faire** capable of doing; **de ~** *adj* sizeable; **quelle ~ faites-vous?** what size are you?

taille-crayon, taille-crayons [tajkrɛjɔ̃] *nm inv* pencil sharpener

tailler [taje] *vt* (*pierre, diamant*) to cut; (*arbre, plante*) to prune; (*crayon*) to sharpen; **se tailler** *vt* (*ongles, barbe*) to trim, cut; (*fig: réputation*) to gain, win ▷ *vi* (*fam: s'enfuir*) to beat it; **~ dans** (*chair, bois*) to cut into; **~ grand/petit** to be on the large/small side

tailleur [tajœr] *nm* (*couturier*) tailor; (*vêtement*) suit, costume; **en ~** (*assis*) cross-legged; **~ de diamants** diamond-cutter

taillis [taji] *nm* copse

taire [tɛr] *vt* to keep to o.s., conceal ▷ *vi:* **faire ~ qn** to make sb be quiet; (*fig*) to silence sb; **se taire** *vi* (*s'arrêter de parler*) to fall silent, stop talking; (*ne pas parler*) to be silent *ou* quiet; (*s'abstenir de s'exprimer*) to keep quiet; (*bruit, voix*) to disappear; **tais-toi!, taisez-vous!** be quiet!

Taiwan [tajwan] *nf* Taiwan

talc [talk] *nm* talc, talcum powder

talent [talɑ̃] *nm* talent; **avoir du ~** to be talented, have talent

talkie-walkie [tɔkiwɔki] *nm* walkie-talkie

taloche [talɔʃ] *nf (fam: claque)* slap; *(Tech)* plaster float

talon [talɔ̃] *nm* heel; *(de chèque, billet)* stub, counterfoil *(Brit)*; **~s plats/aiguilles** flat/stiletto heels; **être sur les ~s de qn** to be on sb's heels; **tourner les ~s** to turn on one's heel; **montrer les ~s** *(fig)* to show a clean pair of heels

talonner [talɔne] *vt* to follow hard behind; *(fig)* to hound; *(Rugby)* to heel

talus [taly] *nm* embankment; **~ de remblai/déblai** embankment/excavation slope

tambour [tɑ̃buʀ] *nm (Mus, also Tech)* drum; *(musicien)* drummer; *(porte)* revolving door(s *pl*); **sans ~ ni trompette** unobtrusively

tambourin [tɑ̃buʀɛ̃] *nm* tambourine

tambouriner [tɑ̃buʀine] *vi:* **~ contre** to drum against *ou* on

tamis [tami] *nm* sieve

Tamise [tamiz] *nf:* **la ~** the Thames

tamisé, e [tamize] *adj (fig)* subdued, soft

tampon [tɑ̃pɔ̃] *nm* stamp; *(aussi:* **~ hygiénique** *ou* **périodique)** tampon; *(amortisseur, Inform: aussi:* **mémoire ~)** buffer; *(bouchon)* plug, stopper; *(cachet, timbre)* stamp; *(Chimie)* buffer; **~ buvard** blotter; **~ encreur** inking pad; **~ (à récurer)** scouring pad

tamponner [tɑ̃pɔne] *vt (timbres)* to stamp; *(heurter)* to crash *ou* ram into; *(essuyer)* to mop up; **se tamponner** *(voitures)* to crash (into each other)

tamponneuse [tɑ̃pɔnøz] *adj f:* **autos ~s** dodgems, bumper cars

tandem [tɑ̃dɛm] *nm* tandem; *(fig)* duo, pair

tandis [tɑ̃di]: **~ que** *conj* while

tanguer [tɑ̃ge] *vi* to pitch (and toss)

tanière [tanjɛʀ] *nf* lair, den

tankini [tɑ̃kini] *nm* tankini

tanné, e [tane] *adj* weather-beaten

tanner [tane] *vt* to tan

tant [tɑ̃] *adv* so much; **~ de** *(sable, eau)* so much; *(gens, livres)* so many; **~ que** *conj* as long as; **~ que** *(comparatif)* as much as; **~ mieux** that's great; *(avec une certaine réserve)* so much the better; **~ mieux pour lui** good for him; **~ pis** too bad; *(conciliant)* never mind; **un ~ soit peu** *(un peu)* a little bit; *(même un peu)* (even) remotely; **~ bien que mal** as well as can be expected; **~ s'en faut** far from it, not by a long way

tante [tɑ̃t] *nf* aunt

tantôt [tɑ̃to] *adv (parfois):* **~ ... ~** now ... now; *(cet après-midi)* this afternoon

taon [tɑ̃] *nm* horsefly, gadfly

tapage [tapaʒ] *nm* uproar, din; *(fig)* fuss, row; **~ nocturne** *(Jur)* disturbance of the peace *(at night)*

tapageur, -euse [tapaʒœʀ, -øz] *adj (bruyant: enfants etc)* noisy; *(voyant: toilette)* loud, flashy; *(publicité)* obtrusive

tape [tap] *nf* slap

tape-à-l'œil [tapalœj] *adj inv* flashy, showy

taper [tape] *vt (personne)* to clout; *(porte)* to

bang, slam; *(enfant)* to slap; *(dactylographier)* to type (out); *(Inform)* to key(board); *(fam: emprunter):* **~ qn de 10 euros** to touch sb for 10 euros, cadge 10 euros off sb ▷ *vi (soleil)* to beat down; **se taper** *vt (fam: travail)* to get landed with; *(: boire, manger)* to down; **~ sur qn** to thump sb; *(fig)* to run sb down; **~ sur qch** *(clou etc)* to hit sth; *(table etc)* to bang on sth; **~ à** *(porte etc)* to knock on; **~ dans** *(se servir)* to dig into; **~ des mains/pieds** to clap one's hands/stamp one's feet; **~ (à la machine)** to type

tapi, e [tapi] *adj:* **~ dans/derrière** *(blotti)* crouching *ou* cowering in/behind; *(caché)* hidden away in/behind

tapis [tapi] *nm* carpet; *(petit)* rug; *(de table)* cloth; **mettre sur le ~** *(fig)* to bring up for discussion; **aller au ~** *(Boxe)* to go down; **envoyer au ~** *(Boxe)* to floor; **~ roulant** conveyor belt; *(pour piétons)* moving walkway; *(pour bagages)* carousel; **~ de sol** *(de tente)* groundsheet; **~ de souris** *(Inform)* mouse mat

tapisser [tapise] *vt (avec du papier peint)* to paper; *(recouvrir):* **~ qch (de)** to cover sth (with)

tapisserie [tapisʀi] *nf (tenture, broderie)* tapestry; *(: travail)* tapestry-making; *(: ouvrage)* tapestry work; *(papier peint)* wallpaper; *(fig):* **faire ~** to sit out, be a wallflower

tapissier, -ière [tapisje, -jɛʀ] *nm/f:* **~-décorateur** interior decorator

tapoter [tapɔte] *vt (joue, main)* to pat; *(objet)* to tap

taquin, e [takɛ̃, -in] *adj* teasing

taquiner [takine] *vt* to tease

tarabiscoté, e [taʀabiskɔte] *adj* over-ornate, fussy

tard [taʀ] *adv* late; **au plus ~** at the latest; **plus ~** later (on) ▷ *nm:* **sur le ~** *(à une heure avancée)* late in the day; *(vers la fin de la vie)* late in life; **il est trop ~** it's too late

tarder [taʀde] *vi (chose)* to be a long time coming; *(personne):* **~ à faire** to delay doing; **il me tarde d'être** I am longing to be; **sans (plus) ~** without (further) delay

tardif, -ive [taʀdif, -iv] *adj (heure, repas, fruit)* late; *(talent, goût)* late in developing

taré, e [taʀe] *nm/f* cretin

tarif [taʀif] *nm:* **~ des consommations** price list; **~s postaux/douaniers** postal/customs rates; **~ des taxis** taxi fares; **~ plein/réduit** *(train)* full/reduced fare; *(téléphone)* peak/off-peak rate; **voyager à plein ~/à ~ réduit** to travel at full/reduced fare

tarir [taʀiʀ] *vi* to dry up, run dry ▷ *vt* to dry up

tarte [taʀt] *nf* tart; **~ aux pommes/à la crème** apple/custard tart; **~ Tatin** ≈ apple upside-down tart

tartine [taʀtin] *nf* slice of bread (and butter *(ou* jam)); **~ de miel** slice of bread and honey; **~ beurrée** slice of bread and butter

tartiner [taʁtine] vt to spread; **fromage à ~** cheese spread

tartre [taʁtʁ] nm (des dents) tartar; (de chaudière) fur, scale

tas [ta] nm heap, pile; (fig): **un ~ de** heaps of, lots of; **en ~** in a heap ou pile; **dans le ~** (fig) in the crowd; among them; **formé sur le ~** trained on the job

tasse [tas] nf cup; **boire la ~** (en se baignant) to swallow a mouthful; **~ à café/thé** coffee/ teacup

tassé, e [tase] adj: **bien ~** (café etc) strong

tasser [tase] vt (terre, neige) to pack down; (entasser): **~ qch dans** to cram sth into; **se tasser** vi (se serrer) to squeeze up; (s'affaisser) to settle; (personne: avec l'âge) to shrink; (fig) to sort itself out, settle down

tâter [tate] vt to feel; (fig) to try out; **~ de** (prison etc) to have a taste of; **se tâter** (hésiter) to be in two minds; **~ le terrain** (fig) to test the ground

tatillon, ne [tatijɔ̃, -ɔn] adj pernickety

tâtonnement [tatɔnmã] nm: **par ~s** (fig) by trial and error

tâtonner [tatɔne] vi to grope one's way along; (fig) to grope around (in the dark)

tâtons [tatɔ̃]: **à ~** adv: chercher/avancer à ~ to grope around for/grope one's way forward

tatouage [tatwaʒ] nm tattooing; (dessin) tattoo

tatouer [tatwe] vt to tattoo

taudis [todi] nm hovel, slum

taule [tol] nf (fam) nick (Brit), jail

taupe [top] nf mole; (peau) moleskin

taureau, x [tɔʁo] nm bull; (signe): **le T~** Taurus, the Bull; **être du T~** to be Taurus

tauromachie [tɔʁɔmaʃi] nf bullfighting

taux [to] nm rate; (d'alcool): level; **~ d'escompte** discount rate; **~ d'intérêt** interest rate; **~ de mortalité** mortality rate

taxe [taks] nf tax; (douanière) duty; **toutes ~s comprises (TTC)** inclusive of tax; **la boutique hors ~** the duty-free shop; **~ de base** (Tél) unit charge; **~ de séjour** tourist tax; **~ à ou sur la valeur ajoutée (TVA)** value added tax (VAT)

taxer [takse] vt (personne) to tax; (produit) to put a tax on, tax; **~ qn de qch** (qualifier) to call sb sth; (accuser) to accuse sb of sth, tax sb with sth

taxi [taksi] nm taxi; (chauffeur: fam) taxi driver

Tchécoslovaquie [tʃekɔslɔvaki] nf: **la ~** Czechoslovakia

tchèque [tʃɛk] adj Czech ▷ nm (Ling) Czech ▷ nm/f: **T~** Czech; **la République ~** the Czech Republic

Tchétchénie [tʃetʃeni] nf: **la ~** Chechnya

te, t' [tə] pron you; (réfléchi) yourself

technicien, ne [tɛknisjɛ̃, -ɛn] nm/f technician

technico-commercial, e, -aux [tɛknikokɔmɛʁsjal, -o] adj: **agent ~** sales technician

technique [tɛknik] adj technical ▷ nf technique

techniquement [tɛknikmã] adv technically

techno [tɛkno] nf (fam: Mus): **la (musique) ~** techno (music); (fam) = **technologie**

technologie [tɛknɔlɔʒi] nf technology

technologique [tɛknɔlɔʒik] adj technological

teck [tɛk] nm teak

tee-shirt [tiʃœʁt] nm T-shirt, tee-shirt

teindre [tɛ̃dʁ] vt to dye; **se ~ (les cheveux)** to dye one's hair

teint, e [tɛ̃, tɛ̃t] pp de **teindre** ▷ adj dyed ▷ nm (du visage: permanent) complexion, colouring (Brit), coloring (US); (momentané) colour (Brit), color (US) ▷ nf shade, colour, color; (fig: petite dose): **une ~e de** a hint of; **grand ~** adj inv colourfast; **bon ~** adj inv (couleur) fast; (tissu) colourfast; (personne) staunch, firm

teinté, e [tɛ̃te] adj (verres) tinted; (bois) stained; **~ acajou** mahogany-stained; **~ de** (fig) tinged with

teinter [tɛ̃te] vt (verre) to tint; (bois) to stain; (fig: d'ironie etc) to tinge

teinture [tɛ̃tyʁ] nf dyeing; (substance) dye; (Méd): **~ d'iode** tincture of iodine

teinturerie [tɛ̃tyʁʁi] nf dry cleaner's

teinturier, -ière [tɛ̃tyʁje, -jɛʁ] nm/f dry cleaner

tel, telle [tɛl] adj (pareil) such; (comme): **~ un/ des ...** like a/like ...; (indéfini) such-and-such a, a given; **venez ~ jour** come on such-and-such a day; (intensif): **un ~/de ~s ...** such (a)/ such ...; **rien de ~** nothing like it, no such thing; **~ que** conj like, such as; **~ quel** as it is ou stands (ou was etc)

télé [tele] nf (fam: télévision) TV, telly (Brit); **à la ~** on TV ou telly

télécabine [telekabin] nm, nf (benne) cable car

télécarte [telekaʁt] nf phonecard

téléchargeable [teleʃaʁʒabl] adj downloadable

téléchargement [teleʃaʁʒemã] nm (action) downloading; (fichier) download

télécharger [teleʃaʁʒe] vt (Inform) to download

télécommande [telekɔmãd] nf remote control

télécopie [telekɔpi] nf fax, telefax

télécopieur [telekɔpjœʁ] nm fax (machine)

télédistribution [teledistʁibysjɔ̃] nf cable TV

téléférique [telefeʁik] nm = **téléphérique**

télégramme [telegʁam] nm telegram

télégraphier [telegʁafje] vt to telegraph, cable

téléguider [telegide] vt to operate by remote control, radio-control

téléjournal, -aux [teleʒuʁnal, -o] nm television news magazine programme

télématique [telematik] nf telematics nsg ▷ adj telematic

téléobjectif [teleɔbʒɛktif] nm telephoto lens nsg

télépathie [telepati] nf telepathy

téléphérique [teleferik] nm cable-car

téléphone [telefɔn] nm telephone; **avoir le ~** to be on the (tele)phone; **au ~** on the phone; **~ arabe** bush telegraph; **~ à carte** cardphone; **~ avec appareil photo** cameraphone; **~ mobile** ou **portable** mobile (phone) (Brit), cell (phone) (US); **~ rouge** hotline; **~ sans fil** cordless (tele)phone

téléphoner [telefɔne] vt to telephone ▷ vi to telephone; to make a phone call; **~ à** to phone, ring up, call up

téléphonie [telefɔni] nf telephony

téléphonique [telefɔnik] adj (tele)phone cpd, phone cpd; **cabine ~** call box (Brit), (tele) phone box (Brit) ou booth; **conversation/ appel ~** (tele)phone conversation/call

téléréalité [telerealite] nf reality TV

télescope [teleskɔp] nm telescope

télescoper [teleskɔpe] vt to smash up; **se télescoper** (véhicules) to concertina, crash into each other

téléscripteur [teleskriptœr] nm teleprinter

télésiège [telesjɛʒ] nm telesales

téléski [teleski] nm ski-tow; **~ à archets** T-bar tow; **~ à perche** button lift

téléspectateur, -trice [telespɛktatœr, -tris] nm/f (television) viewer

télétravail nm telecommuting

télévente [televãt] nf telesales

téléviseur [televizœr] nm television set

télévision [televizjɔ̃] nf television; (**poste de) ~** television (set); **avoir la ~** to have a television; **à la ~** on television; **~ numérique** digital TV; **~ par câble/satellite** cable/ satellite television

télex [telɛks] nm telex

telle [tɛl] adj f voir **tel**

tellement [tɛlmɑ̃] adv (tant) so much; (si) so; **~ plus grand (que)** so much bigger (than); **~ de** (sable, eau) so much; (gens, livres) so many; **il s'est endormi ~ il était fatigué** he was so tired (that) he fell asleep; **pas ~** not really; **pas ~ fort/lentement** not (all) that strong/ slowly; **il ne mange pas ~** he doesn't eat (all that) much

téméraire [temerer] adj reckless, rash

témérité [temerite] nf recklessness, rashness

témoignage [temwaɲaʒ] nm (Jur: déclaration) testimony no pl, evidence no pl; (: faits) evidence no pl; (gén: rapport, récit) account; (fig: token, mark; (geste) expression

témoigner [temwaɲe] vt (manifester: intérêt, gratitude) to show ▷ vi (Jur) to testify, give evidence; **~ que** (Jur) to testify that; (fig: démontrer) to reveal that, testify to the fact that; **~ de** vt (confirmer) to bear witness to, testify to

témoin [temwɛ̃] nm witness; (fig) testimony; (Sport) baton; (Constr) telltale ▷ adj control cpd, test cpd; **le fait que ...** (as) witness the fact that ...; **appartement-~** show flat (Brit), model apartment (US); **être ~ de** (voir) to

witness; **prendre à ~** to call to witness; **~ à charge** witness for the prosecution; **~ de connexion** (Inform) cookie; **T~ de Jehovah** Jehovah's Witness; **~ de moralité** character reference; **~ oculaire** eyewitness

tempe [tɑ̃p] nf (Anat) temple

tempérament [tɑ̃peramɑ̃] nm temperament, disposition; (santé) constitution; **à ~** (vente) on deferred (payment) terms; (achat) by instalments, hire purchase cpd; **avoir du ~** to be hot-blooded

température [tɑ̃peratyr] nf temperature; **prendre la ~ de** to take the temperature of; (fig) to gauge the feeling of; **avoir** ou **faire de la ~** to be running ou have a temperature

tempéré, e [tɑ̃pere] adj temperate

tempête [tɑ̃pɛt] nf storm; **~ de sable/neige** sand/snowstorm; **vent de ~** gale

temple [tɑ̃pl] nm temple; (protestant) church

temporaire [tɑ̃pɔrer] adj temporary

temps [tɑ̃] nm (atmosphérique) weather; (durée) time; (époque) time, times pl; (Ling) tense; (Mus) beat; (Tech) stroke; **~ de chien** (fam) rotten weather; **quel ~ fait-il?** what's the weather like?; **il fait beau/mauvais ~** the weather is fine/bad; **avoir le ~/tout le ~/ juste le ~** to have time/plenty of time/just enough time; **les ~ changent/sont durs** times are changing/hard; **avoir fait son ~** (fig) to have had its (ou his ou etc) day; **en ~ de paix/guerre** in peacetime/wartime; **en ~ utile** ou **voulu** in due time ou course; **ces derniers ~** lately; **dans quelque ~** in a (little) while; **de ~ en ~, de ~ à autre** from time to time, now and again; **en même ~** at the same time; **à ~** (partir, arriver) in time; **à ~ complet, à plein ~** adv, adj full-time; **à ~ partiel, à mi-~** adv, adj part-time; **dans le ~** at one time; **de tout ~** always; **du ~ que** at the time when; **du ou au ~ où** at the time when, in the days when; **dans le** ou **du** ou **au ~ où** at the time when; **pendant ce ~** in the meantime; **~ d'accès** (Inform) access time; **~ d'arrêt** pause, halt; **~ libre** free ou spare time; **~ mort** (Sport) stoppage (time); (Comm) slack period; **~ partagé** (Inform) time-sharing; **~ réel** (Inform) real time

tenable [tənabl] adj bearable

tenace [tənas] adj tenacious, persistent

tenailler [tənaje] vt (fig) to torment, torture

tenailles [tənaj] nfpl pincers

tenais etc [t(ə)nɛ] vb voir **tenir**

tenancier, -ière [tənɑ̃sje, -jɛr] nm/f (d'hôtel, de bistro) manager/manageress

tenant, e [tənɑ̃, -ɑ̃t] adj f voir **séance** ▷ nm/f (Sport): **~ du titre** title-holder ▷ nm: **d'un seul ~** in one piece; **les ~s et les aboutissants** (fig) the ins and outs

tendance [tɑ̃dɑ̃s] nf (opinions) leanings pl, sympathies pl; (inclination) tendency; (évolution) trend; **à la hausse/baisse** upward/downward trend; **avoir ~ à** to have a tendency to, tend to

tendeur [tɑ̃dœʀ] nm (de vélo) chain-adjuster; (de câble) wire-strainer; (de tente) runner; (attache) elastic strap

tendre [tɑ̃dʀ] adj (viande, légumes) tender; (bois, roche, couleur) soft; (affectueux) tender, loving ▷ vt (élastique, peau) to stretch, draw tight; (corde) to tighten; (muscle) to tense; (donner): ~ **qch à qn** to hold sth out to sb; (offrir) to offer sb sth; (fig: piège) to set, lay; (tapisserie): **tendu de soie** hung with silk, with silk hangings; **se tendre** vi (corde) to tighten; (relations) to become strained; ~ **à qch/à faire** to tend towards sth/to do; ~ **l'oreille** to prick up one's ears; ~ **la main/le bras** to hold out one's hand/stretch out one's arm; ~ **la perche à qn** (fig) to throw sb a line

tendrement [tɑ̃dʀəmɑ̃] adv tenderly, lovingly

tendresse [tɑ̃dʀɛs] nf tenderness; **tendresses** nfpl (caresses etc) tenderness no pl, caresses

tendu, e [tɑ̃dy] pp de **tendre** ▷ adj (corde) tight; (muscles) tensed; (relations) strained

ténèbres [tenɛbʀ] nfpl darkness nsg

teneur [tənœʀ] nf content, substance; (d'une lettre) terms pl, content; ~ **en cuivre** copper content

tenir [təniʀ] vt to hold; (magasin, hôtel) to run; (promesse) to keep ▷ vi to hold; (neige, gel) to last; (survivre) to survive; **se tenir** vi (avoir lieu) to be held, take place; (être: personne) to stand; **se ~ droit** to stand up (ou sit up) straight; **bien se ~** to behave well; **se ~ à qch** to hold on to sth; **s'en ~ à qch** to confine o.s. to sth; to stick to sth; ~ **à** vt (personne, objet) to be attached to, care about (ou for); (réputation) to care about; (avoir pour cause) to be due to, stem from; ~ **à faire** to want to do, be keen to do; ~ **à ce que qn fasse qch** to be anxious that sb should do sth; ~ **de** vt to partake of; (ressembler à) to take after; **ça ne tient qu'à lui** it is entirely up to him; ~ **qn pour** to take sb for; ~ **qch de qn** (histoire) to have heard ou learnt sth from sb; (qualité, défaut) to have inherited ou got sth from sb; ~ **dans** to fit into; ~ **compte de qch** to take sth into account; ~ **les comptes** to keep the books; ~ **un rôle** to play a part; ~ **de la place** to take up space ou room; ~ **l'alcool** to be able to hold a drink; ~ **le coup** to hold out; ~ **bon** to stand ou hold fast; ~ **trois jours/deux mois** (résister) to hold out ou last three days/two months; ~ **au chaud/à l'abri** to keep hot/under shelter ou cover; **un manteau qui tient chaud** a warm coat; ~ **prêt** to have ready; ~ **sa langue** (fig) to hold one's tongue; **tiens** (ou **tenez**), **voilà le stylo** there's the pen!; **tiens, Alain!** look, here's Alain!; **tiens?** (surprise) really?; **tiens-toi bien!** (pour informer) brace yourself!, take a deep breath!

tennis [tenis] nm tennis; (aussi: **court de ~**) tennis court ▷ nmpl ou fpl (aussi: **chaussures**

de ~) tennis ou gym shoes; ~ **de table** table tennis

tennisman [tenisman] nm tennis player

tension [tɑ̃sjɔ̃] nf tension; (fig: des relations, de la situation) tension; (: concentration, effort) strain; (Méd) blood pressure; **faire** ou **avoir de la ~** to have high blood pressure; ~ **nerveuse/raciale** nervous/racial tension

tentation [tɑ̃tasjɔ̃] nf temptation

tentative [tɑ̃tativ] nf attempt, bid; ~ **d'évasion** escape bid; ~ **de suicide** suicide attempt

tente [tɑ̃t] nf tent; ~ **à oxygène** oxygen tent

tenter [tɑ̃te] vt (éprouver, attirer) to tempt; (essayer): ~ **qch/de faire** to attempt ou try sth/ to do; **être tenté de** to be tempted to; ~ **sa chance** to try one's luck

tenture [tɑ̃tyʀ] nf hanging

tenu, e [təny] pp de **tenir** ▷ adj (maison, comptes): **bien** ~ well-kept; (obligé): ~ **de faire** under an obligation to do ▷ nf (action de tenir) running; keeping; holding; (vêtements) clothes pl, gear; (allure) dress no pl, appearance; (comportement) manners pl, behaviour (Brit), behavior (US); (d'une maison) upkeep; **être en** ~**e** to be dressed (up); **se mettre en** ~**e** to dress (up); **en grande** ~**e** in full dress; **en petite** ~**e** scantily dressed ou clad; **avoir de la** ~**e** to have good manners; (journal) to have a high standard; ~**e de combat** combat gear ou dress; ~**e de pompier** fireman's uniform; ~**e de route** (Auto) road-holding; ~**e de soirée** evening dress; ~**e de sport/voyage** sports/travelling clothes pl ou gear no pl

TER abr m (= Train Express Régional) local train

ter [tɛʀ] adj: **16** = **16b ou B**

térébenthine [teʀebɑ̃tin] nf: (**essence de**) ~ (oil of) turpentine

tergal® [tɛʀgal] nm Terylene®

terme [tɛʀm] nm term; (fin) end; **être en bons/mauvais** ~**s avec qn** to be on good/bad terms with sb; **vente/achat à** ~ (Comm) forward sale/purchase; **au** ~ **de** at the end of; **en d'autres** ~**s** in other words; **moyen** ~ (solution intermédiaire) middle course; **à court/ long** ~ adj short-/long-term ou -range ▷ adv in the short/long term; **à** ~ adj (Méd) full-term ▷ adv sooner or later, eventually; (Méd) at term; **avant** ~ (Méd) ▷ adj premature ▷ adv prematurely; **mettre un** ~ **à** to put an end ou a stop to; **toucher à son** ~ to be nearing its end

terminaison [tɛʀminɛzɔ̃] nf (Ling) ending

terminal, e, -aux [tɛʀminal, -o] adj (partie, phase) final; (Méd) terminal ▷ nm terminal ▷ nf (Scol) ≈ year 13 (Brit), ≈ twelfth grade (US)

terminer [tɛʀmine] vt to end; (travail, repas) to finish; **se terminer** vi to end; **se ~ par** to end with

terne [tɛʀn] adj dull

ternir [tɛʀniʀ] vt to dull; (fig) to sully, tarnish; **se ternir** vi to become dull

terrain [teʀɛ̃] nm (sol, fig) ground; (Comm: étendue de terre) land no pl; (parcelle) plot (of land); (: à bâtir) site; **sur le ~** (fig) on the field; **~ de football/rugby** football/rugby pitch (Brit) ou field (US); **~ d'atterrissage** landing strip; **~ d'aviation** airfield; **~ de camping** campsite; **un ~ d'entente** an area of agreement; **~ de golf** golf course; **~ de jeu** (pour les petits) playground; (Sport) games field; **~ de sport** sports ground; **~ vague** waste ground no pl

terrasse [teʀas] nf terrace; (de café) pavement area, terrasse; **à la ~** (café) outside

terrasser [teʀase] vt (adversaire) to floor, bring down; (maladie etc) to lay low

terre [teʀ] nf (gén, aussi Élec) earth; (substance) soil, earth; (opposé à mer) land no pl; (contrée) land; **terres** nfpl (terrains) lands, land nsg; **travail de la ~** work on the land; **en ~** (pipe, poterie) clay cpd; **mettre en ~** (plante etc) to plant; (personne: enterrer) to bury; **à** ou **par ~** (mettre, être, s'asseoir) on the ground (ou floor); (jeter, tomber) to the ground, down; **~ à ~** adj inv down-to-earth, matter-of-fact; **la T~ Adélie** Adélie Coast ou Land; **~ de bruyère** (heath-) peat; **~ cuite** earthenware; terracotta; **la ~ ferme** dry land, terra firma; **la T~ de Feu** Tierra del Fuego; **~ glaise** clay; **la T~ promise** the Promised Land; **la T~ Sainte** the Holy Land

terreau [teʀo] nm compost

terre-plein [teʀplɛ̃] nm platform; (sur chaussée) central reservation

terrer [teʀe]: **se terrer** vi to hide away; to go to ground

terrestre [teʀɛstʀ] adj (surface) earth's, of the earth; (Bot, Zool, Mil) land cpd; (Rel) earthly, worldly

terreur [teʀœʀ] nf terror no pl, fear

terrible [teʀibl] adj terrible, dreadful; (fam: fantastique) terrific; **pas ~** nothing special

terrien, ne [teʀjɛ̃, -ɛn] adj: **propriétaire ~** landowner ▷ nm/f countryman/woman, man/woman of the soil; (non martien etc) earthling; (non marin) landsman

terrier [teʀje] nm burrow, hole; (chien) terrier

terrifier [teʀifje] vt to terrify

terrine [teʀin] nf (récipient) terrine; (Culin) pâté

territoire [teʀitwaʀ] nm territory; **T~ des Afars et des Issas** French Territory of Afars and Issas

terroir [teʀwaʀ] nm (Agr) soil; (région) region; **accent du ~** country ou rural accent

terroriser [teʀɔʀize] vt to terrorize

terrorisme [teʀɔʀism] nm terrorism

terroriste [teʀɔʀist] nm/f terrorist

tertiaire [teʀsjɛʀ] adj tertiary ▷ nm (Écon) tertiary sector, service industries pl

tertre [teʀtʀ] nm hillock, mound

tes [te] adj poss voir **ton**

tesson [tesɔ̃] nm: **~ de bouteille** piece of broken bottle

test [tɛst] nm test; **~ de grossesse** pregnancy test

testament [tɛstamɑ̃] nm (Jur) will; (fig) legacy; (Rel): **T~** Testament; **faire son ~** to make one's will

tester [tɛste] vt to test

testicule [tɛstikyl] nm testicle

tétanos [tetanos] nm tetanus

têtard [tɛtaʀ] nm tadpole

tête [tɛt] nf head; (cheveux) hair no pl; (visage) face; (longueur): **gagner d'une (courte) ~** to win by a (short) head; (Football) header; **de ~** adj (wagon etc) front cpd; (concurrent) leading ▷ adv (calculer) in one's head, mentally; **par ~** (par personne) per head; **se mettre en ~ que** to get it into one's head that; **se mettre en ~ de faire** to take it into one's head to do; **prendre la ~ de qch** to take the lead in sth; **perdre la ~** (fig: s'affoler) to lose one's head; (: devenir fou) to go off one's head; **ça ne va pas, la ~?** (fam) are you crazy?; **tenir ~ à qn** to stand up to ou defy sb; **la ~ en bas** with one's head down; **la ~ la première** (tomber) head-first; **la ~ basse** hanging one's head; **avoir la ~ dure** (fig) to be thickheaded; **faire une ~** (Football) to head the ball; **faire la ~** (fig) to sulk; **en ~** (Sport) in the lead; at the front ou head; **à la ~ de** at the head of; **à ~ reposée** in a more leisurely moment; **n'en faire qu'à sa ~** to do as one pleases; **en avoir par-dessus la ~** to be fed up; **en ~ à ~** in private, alone together; **de la ~ aux pieds** from head to toe; **~ d'affiche** (Théât etc) top of the bill; **~ de bétail** head inv of cattle; **~ brûlée** desperado; **~ chercheuse** homing device; **~ d'enregistrement** recording head; **~ d'impression** printhead; **~ de lecture** (playback) head; **~ de ligne** (Transports) start of the line; **~ de liste** (Pol) chief candidate; **~ de mort** skull and crossbones; **~ de pont** (Mil) bridge- ou beachhead; **~ de série** (Tennis) seeded player, seed; **~ de Turc** (fig) whipping boy (Brit), butt; **~ de veau** (Culin) calf's head

tête-à-queue [tɛtakø] nm inv: **faire un ~** to spin round

tête-à-tête [tɛtatɛt] nm inv: **en ~** in private, alone together

téter [tete] vt: **~ (sa mère)** to suck at one's mother's breast, feed

tétine [tetin] nf teat; (sucette) dummy (Brit), pacifier (US)

têtu, e [tety] adj stubborn, pigheaded

texte [tɛkst] nm text; (morceau choisi) passage; (Scol: d'un devoir) subject, topic; **apprendre son ~** (Théât) to learn one's lines; **un ~ de loi** the wording of a law

textile [tɛkstil] adj textile cpd ▷ nm textile; (industrie) textile industry

Texto® [tɛksto] nm text (message)

texto [tɛksto] (fam) adj word for word

texture [tɛkstyʀ] nf texture; (fig: d'un texte, livre) feel

t

TGV sigle m = **train à grande vitesse**

thaïlandais, e [tailɑ̃dɛ, -ɛz] adj Thai ▷ nm/f:
T~, e Thai

Thaïlande [tailɑ̃d] nf: **la ~** Thailand

thé [te] nm tea; (réunion) tea party; **prendre
le ~** to have tea; **~ au lait/citron** tea with
milk/lemon; **faire du ~** to make the tea

théâtral, e, -aux [teatral, -o] adj theatrical

théâtre [teatr] nm theatre; (techniques, genre)
drama, theatre; (activité) stage, theatre;
(œuvres) plays pl, dramatic works pl; (fig: lieu):
le ~ de the scene of; (péj) histrionics pl,
playacting; **faire du ~** (en professionnel) to be
on the stage; (en amateur) to act; **~ filmé**
filmed stage productions pl

théière [tejɛr] nf teapot

thème [tɛm] nm theme; (Scol: traduction)
prose (composition); **~ astral** birth chart

théologie [teɔlɔʒi] nf theology

théorie [teɔri] nf theory; **en ~** in theory

théorique [teɔrik] adj theoretical

thérapie [terapi] nf therapy; **~ de groupe**
group therapy

thermal, e, -aux [tɛrmal, -o] adj thermal;
station ~e spa; **cure ~e** water cure

thermes [tɛrm] nmpl thermal baths;
(romains) thermae pl

thermomètre [tɛrmɔmɛtr] nm
thermometer

thermos® [tɛrmɔs] nm ou nf: (bouteille) **~**
vacuum ou Thermos® flask (Brit) ou bottle (US)

thermostat [tɛrmɔsta] nm thermostat

thèse [tɛz] nf thesis

thon [tɔ̃] nm tuna (fish)

thym [tɛ̃] nm thyme

Tibet [tibɛ] nm: **le ~** Tibet

tibia [tibja] nm shin; (os) shinbone, tibia

TIC sigle fpl (= technologies de l'information et de la
communication) ICT sg

tic [tik] nm tic, (nervous) twitch; (de langage
etc) mannerism

ticket [tikɛ] nm ticket; **~ de caisse** till receipt;
~ modérateur patient's contribution towards
medical costs; **~ de quai** platform ticket;
~ repas luncheon voucher

tic-tac [tiktak] nm inv tick-tock

tiède [tjɛd] adj (bière etc) lukewarm; (thé, café
etc) tepid; (bain, accueil, sentiment) lukewarm;
(vent, air) mild, warm ▷ adv: **boire ~** to drink
things lukewarm

tiédir [tjedir] vi (se réchauffer) to grow warmer;
(refroidir) to cool

tien, tienne [tjɛ̃, tjɛn] pron: **le ~ (la ~ne), les
~s (~nes)** yours; **à la ~ne!** cheers!

tiens [tjɛ̃] vb, excl voir **tenir**

tierce [tjɛrs] adj f, nf voir **tiers**

tiercé [tjɛrse] nm system of forecast betting giving
first three horses

tiers, tierce [tjɛr, tjɛrs] adj third ▷ nm (Jur)
third party; (fraction) third ▷ nf (Mus) third;
(Cartes) tierce; **une tierce personne** a third
party; **assurance au ~** third-party insurance;

le ~ monde the third world; **~ payant** direct
payment by insurers of medical expenses;
~ provisionnel interim payment of tax

tifs [tif] (fam) nmpl hair

tige [tiʒ] nf stem; (baguette) rod

tignasse [tiɲas] nf (péj) shock ou mop of hair

tigre [tigr] nm tiger

tigré, e [tigre] adj (rayé) striped; (tacheté)
spotted; (chat) tabby

tigresse [tigrɛs] nf tigress

tilleul [tijœl] nm lime (tree), linden (tree);
(boisson) lime(-blossom) tea

timbale [tɛ̃bal] nf (metal) tumbler; **timbales**
nfpl (Mus) timpani, kettledrums

timbre [tɛ̃br] nm (tampon) stamp; (aussi:
~-poste) (postage) stamp; (cachet de la poste)
postmark; (sonnette) bell; (Mus: de voix,
instrument) timbre, tone; **~ anti-tabac**
nicotine patch; **~ dateur** date stamp

timbré, e [tɛ̃bre] adj (enveloppe) stamped;
(voix) resonant; (fam: fou) cracked, nuts

timide [timid] adj (emprunté) shy, timid;
(timoré) timid, timorous

timidement [timidmɑ̃] adv shyly; timidly

timidité [timidite] nf shyness; timidity

tintamarre [tɛ̃tamar] nm din, uproar

tinter [tɛ̃te] vi to ring, chime; (argent, clés) to
jingle

tique [tik] nf tick (insect)

tir [tir] nm (sport) shooting; (fait ou manière de
tirer) firing no pl; (Football) shot; (rafale) fire;
(stand) shooting gallery; **~ d'obus/de
mitraillette** shell/machine gun fire; **~ à
l'arc** archery; **~ de barrage** barrage fire; **~ au
fusil** (rifle) shooting; **~ au pigeon** (d'argile)
clay pigeon shooting

tirage [tiraʒ] nm (action) printing; (Photo)
print; (Inform) printout; (de journal) circulation;
(de livre) (print-)run; edition; (de cheminée)
draught (Brit), draft (US); (de loterie) draw; (fig:
désaccord) friction; **~ au sort** drawing lots

tirailler [tiraje] vt to pull at, tug at; (fig) to
gnaw at ▷ vi to fire at random

tire [tir] nf: **vol à la ~** pickpocketing

tiré, e [tire] adj (visage, traits) drawn ▷ nm
(Comm) drawee; **~ par les cheveux** far-
fetched; **~ à part** off-print

tire-au-flanc [tiroflɑ̃] nm inv (péj) skiver

tire-bouchon [tirbuʃɔ̃] nm corkscrew

tirelire [tirlir] nf moneybox

tirer [tire] vt (gén) to pull; (extraire): **~ qch de**
to take ou pull sth out of; to get sth out of; to
extract sth from; (tracer: ligne, trait) to draw,
trace; (fermer: volet, store, trappe) to pull to,
close; (: rideau) to draw; (choisir: carte,
conclusion, aussi Comm: chèque) to draw; (en
faisant feu: balle, coup) to fire; (: animal) to
shoot; (journal, livre, photo) to print; (Football:
corner etc) to take ▷ vi (faire feu) to fire; (faire du
tir, Football) to shoot; (cheminée) to draw; **se
tirer** vi (fam) to push off; (aussi: **s'en ~**: éviter le
pire) to get off; (survivre) to pull through; (se

débrouiller) to manage; **~ sur** (*corde, poignée*) to pull on ou at; (*faire feu sur*) to shoot ou fire at; (*pipe*) to draw on; (*fig: avoisiner*) to verge ou border on; **~ six mètres** (*Navig*) to draw six metres of water; **~ son nom de** to take ou get its name from; **~ la langue** to stick out one's tongue; **~ qn de** (*embarras etc*) to help ou get sb out of; **~ à l'arc/la carabine** to shoot with a bow and arrow/with a rifle; **~ en longueur** to drag on; **à sa fin** to be drawing to an end; **~ qch au clair** to clear sth up; **~ au sort** to draw lots; **~ parti de** to take advantage of; **~ profit de** to profit from; **~ les cartes** to read ou tell the cards

tiret [tiʀɛ] nm dash; (*en fin de ligne*) hyphen

tireur [tiʀœʀ] nm gunman; (*Comm*) drawer; **bon ~** good shot; **~ d'élite** marksman; **~ de cartes** fortuneteller

tiroir [tiʀwaʀ] nm drawer

tiroir-caisse [tiʀwaʀkɛs] nm till

tisane [tizan] nf herb tea

tisonnier [tizɔnje] nm poker

tisser [tise] vt to weave

tisserand, e [tisʀɑ̃, -ɑ̃d] nm/f weaver

tissu¹ [tisy] nm fabric, material, cloth no pl; (*fig*) fabric; (*Anat, Bio*) tissue; **~ de mensonges** web of lies

tissu², e [tisy] adj: **~ de** woven through with

tissu-éponge [tisyepɔ̃ʒ] nm (terry) towelling no pl

titre [titʀ] nm (*gén*) title; (*de journal*) headline; (*diplôme*) qualification; (*Comm*) security; (*Chimie*) titre; **en ~** (*champion, responsable*) official, recognized; **à juste ~** with just cause, rightly; **à quel ~?** on what grounds?; **à aucun ~** on no account; **au même ~ (que)** in the same way (as); **au ~ de la coopération** etc in the name of cooperation etc; **à ~ d'exemple** as an ou by way of an example; **à ~ exceptionnel** exceptionally; **à ~ d'information** for (your) information; **à ~ gracieux** free of charge; **à ~ d'essai** on a trial basis; **à ~ privé** in a private capacity; **~ courant** running head; **~ de propriété** title deed; **~ de transport** ticket

tituber [titybe] vi to stagger ou reel (along)

titulaire [tityleʀ] adj (*Admin*) appointed, with tenure ▷ nm/f (*Admin*) incumbent; (*de permis*) holder; **être ~ de** (*diplôme, permis*) to hold

TNT sigle m (= *Trinitrotoluène*) TNT ▷ sigle f (= *Télévision numérique terrestre*) digital television

toast [tost] nm slice ou piece of toast; (*de bienvenue*) (welcoming) toast; **porter un ~ à qn** to propose ou drink a toast to sb

toboggan [tɔbɔɡɑ̃] nm toboggan; (*jeu*) slide; (*Auto*) flyover (*Brit*), overpass (*US*); **~ de secours** (*Aviat*) escape chute

toc [tɔk] nm: **en ~** imitation cpd ▷ excl: **~, ~** knock knock

tocsin [tɔksɛ̃] nm alarm (bell)

toge [tɔʒ] nf toga; (*de juge*) gown

tohu-bohu [tɔybɔy] nm (*désordre*) confusion; (*tumulte*) commotion

toi [twa] pron you; **~, tu l'as fait?** did YOU do it?

toile [twal] nf (*matériau*) cloth no pl; (*bâche*) piece of canvas; (*tableau*) canvas; **grosse ~** canvas; **de** ou **en ~** (*pantalon*) cotton; (*sac*) canvas; **tisser sa ~** (*araignée*) to spin its web; **~ d'araignée** spider's web; (*au plafond etc: à enlever*) cobweb; **la T~** (*Internet*) the Web; **~ cirée** oilcloth; **~ émeri** emery cloth; **~ de fond** (*fig*) backdrop; **~ de jute** hessian; **~ de lin** linen; **~ de tente** canvas

toilette [twalɛt] nf wash; (*s'habiller et se préparer*) getting ready, washing and dressing; (*habits*) outfit; dress no pl; **toilettes** nfpl toilet nsg; **les ~s des dames/messieurs** the ladies'/gents' (toilets) (*Brit*), the ladies'/men's (rest)room (*US*); **faire sa ~** to have a wash, get washed; **faire la ~ de** (*animal*) to groom; (*voiture etc*) to clean, wash; (*texte*) to tidy up; **articles de ~** toiletries; **~ intime** personal hygiene

toi-même [twamɛm] pron yourself

toiser [twaze] vt to eye up and down

toison [twazɔ̃] nf (*de mouton*) fleece; (*cheveux*) mane

toit [twa] nm roof; **~ ouvrant** sun roof

toiture [twatyʀ] nf roof

Tokyo [tɔkjo] n Tokyo

tôle [tol] nf sheet metal no pl; (*plaque*) steel (ou iron) sheet; **tôles** nfpl (*carrosserie*) bodywork nsg (*Brit*), body nsg; panels; **~ d'acier** sheet steel no pl; **~ ondulée** corrugated iron

tolérable [tɔleʀabl] adj tolerable, bearable

tolérant, e [tɔleʀɑ̃, -ɑ̃t] adj tolerant

tolérer [tɔleʀe] vt to tolerate; (*Admin: hors taxe etc*) to allow

tollé [tɔle] nm: **un ~ (de protestations)** a general outcry

tomate [tɔmat] nf tomato; **~s farcies** stuffed tomatoes

tombe [tɔ̃b] nf (*sépulture*) grave; (*avec monument*) tomb

tombeau, x [tɔ̃bo] nm tomb; **à ~ ouvert** at breakneck speed

tombée [tɔ̃be] nf: **à la ~ du jour** ou **de la nuit** at the close of day, at nightfall

tomber [tɔ̃be] vi to fall; (*fièvre, vent*) to drop ▷ vt: **~ la veste** to slip off one's jacket; **laisser ~** (*objet*) to drop; (*personne*) to let down; (*activité*) to give up; **laisse ~!** forget it!; **faire ~** to knock over; **~ sur** vt (*rencontrer*) to come across; (*attaquer*) to set about; **~ de fatigue/sommeil** to drop from exhaustion/be falling asleep on one's feet; **~ à l'eau** (*fig: projet etc*) to fall through; **~ en panne** to break down; **~ juste** (*opération, calcul*) to come out right; **~ en ruine** to fall into ruins; **ça tombe bien/mal** (*fig*) that's come at the right/wrong time; **il est bien/mal tombé** (*fig*) he's been lucky/unlucky

tombola [tɔ̃bɔla] nf raffle

tome [tɔm] nm volume

ton¹, ta (*pl* **tes**) [tɔ̃, ta, te] *adj poss* your

ton² [tɔ̃] *nm* (*gén*) tone; (*Mus*) key; (*couleur*) shade, tone; (*de la voix: hauteur*) pitch; **donner le ~** to set the tone; **élever** *ou* **hausser le ~** to raise one's voice; **de bon ~** in good taste; **si vous le prenez sur ce ~** if you're going to take it like that; **~ sur ~** in matching shades

tonalité [tɔnalite] *nf* (*au téléphone*) dialling tone; (*Mus*) tonality; (*: ton*) key; (*fig*) tone

tondeuse [tɔ̃døz] *nf* (*à gazon*) (lawn)mower; (*du coiffeur*) clippers *pl*; (*pour la tonte*) shears *pl*

tondre [tɔ̃dʀ] *vt* (*pelouse, herbe*) to mow; (*haie*) to cut, clip; (*mouton, toison*) to shear; (*cheveux*) to crop

tongs [tɔ̃g] *nfpl* flip-flops (Brit), thongs (US)

tonifier [tɔnifje] *vt* (*air, eau*) to invigorate; (*peau, organisme*) to tone up

tonique [tɔnik] *adj* fortifying; (*personne*) dynamic ⊳ *nm, nf* tonic

tonne [tɔn] *nf* metric ton, tonne

tonneau, x [tɔno] *nm* (*à vin, cidre*) barrel; (*Navig*) ton; **faire des ~x** (*voiture, avion*) to roll over

tonnelle [tɔnɛl] *nf* bower, arbour (Brit), arbor (US)

tonner [tɔne] *vi* to thunder; (*parler avec véhémence*): **~ contre qn/qch** to inveigh against sb/sth; **il tonne** it is thundering, there's some thunder

tonnerre [tɔnɛʀ] *nm* thunder; **coup de ~** (*fig*) thunderbolt, bolt from the blue; **un ~ d'applaudissements** thunderous applause; **du ~** *adj* (*fam*) terrific

tonte [tɔ̃t] *nf* shearing

tonton [tɔ̃tɔ̃] *nm* uncle

tonus [tɔnys] *nm* energy; (*des muscles*) tone; (*d'une personne*) dynamism

top [tɔp] *nm*: **au troisième ~** at the third stroke ⊳ *adj*: **~ secret** top secret ⊳ *excl* go!

topinambour [tɔpinɑ̃buʀ] *nm* Jerusalem artichoke

topo [tɔpo] *nm* (*discours, exposé*) talk; (*fam*) spiel

toque [tɔk] *nf* (*de fourrure*) fur hat; **~ de jockey/juge** jockey's/judge's cap; **~ de cuisinier** chef's hat

toqué, e [tɔke] *adj* (*fam*) touched, cracked

torche [tɔʀʃ] *nf* torch; **se mettre en ~** (*parachute*) to candle

torchon [tɔʀʃɔ̃] *nm* cloth, duster; (*à vaisselle*) tea towel *ou* cloth

tordre [tɔʀdʀ] *vt* (*chiffon*) to wring; (*barre, fig: visage*) to twist; **se tordre** *vi* (*barre*) to bend; (*roue*) to twist, buckle; (*ver, serpent*) to writhe; **se ~ le poignet/la cheville** to twist one's wrist/ankle; **se ~ de douleur/rire** to writhe in pain/be doubled up with laughter

tordu, e [tɔʀdy] *pp de* **tordre** ⊳ *adj* (*fig*) warped, twisted; (*fig*) crazy

tornade [tɔʀnad] *nf* tornado

torpille [tɔʀpij] *nf* torpedo

torréfier [tɔʀefje] *vt* to roast

torrent [tɔʀɑ̃] *nm* torrent, mountain stream; (*fig*): **un ~ de** a torrent *ou* flood of; **il pleut à ~s** the rain is lashing down

torsade [tɔʀsad] *nf* twist; (*Archit*) cable moulding (Brit) *ou* molding (US); **un pull à ~s** a cable sweater

torse [tɔʀs] *nm* chest; (*Anat, Sculpture*) torso; (*poitrine*) chest; **~ nu** stripped to the waist

tort [tɔʀ] *nm* (*défaut*) fault; (*préjudice*) wrong *no pl*; **torts** *nmpl* (*Jur*) fault *nsg*; **avoir ~** to be wrong; **être dans son ~** to be in the wrong; **donner ~ à qn** to lay the blame on sb; (*fig*) to prove sb wrong; **causer du ~ à** to harm; to be harmful *ou* detrimental to; **en ~** in the wrong, at fault; **à ~** wrongly; **à ~ ou à raison** rightly or wrongly; **à ~ et à travers** wildly

torticolis [tɔʀtikɔli] *nm* stiff neck

tortiller [tɔʀtije] *vt* (*corde, mouchoir*) to twist; (*doigts*) to twiddle; (*moustache*) to twirl; **se tortiller** *vi* to wriggle, squirm; (*en dansant*) to wiggle

tortionnaire [tɔʀsjɔnɛʀ] *nm* torturer

tortue [tɔʀty] *nf* tortoise; (*fig*) slowcoach (Brit), slowpoke (US); (*d'eau douce*) terrapin; (*d'eau de mer*) turtle

tortueux, -euse [tɔʀtɥø, -øz] *adj* (*rue*) twisting; (*fig*) tortuous

torture [tɔʀtyʀ] *nf* torture

torturer [tɔʀtyʀe] *vt* to torture; (*fig*) to torment

tôt [to] *adv* early; **~ ou tard** sooner or later; **si ~** so early; (*déjà*) so soon; **au plus ~** at the earliest, as soon as possible; **plus ~** earlier; **il eut ~ fait de faire ...** he soon did ...

total, e, -aux [tɔtal, -o] *adj, nm* total; **au ~** in total *ou* all; (*fig*) all in all, on the whole; **faire le ~** to work out the total

totalement [tɔtalmɑ̃] *adv* totally, completely

totaliser [tɔtalize] *vt* to total (up)

totalitaire [tɔtalitɛʀ] *adj* totalitarian

totalité [tɔtalite] *nf*: **la ~ de**: **la totalité des élèves** all (of) the pupils; **la ~ de la population/classe** the whole population/class; **en ~** entirely

toubib [tubib] *nm* (*fam*) doctor

touchant, e [tuʃɑ̃, -ɑ̃t] *adj* touching

touche [tuʃ] *nf* (*de piano, de machine à écrire*) key; (*de violon*) fingerboard; (*de télécommande etc*) key, button; (*de téléphone*) button; (*Peinture etc*) stroke, touch; (*fig: de couleur, nostalgie*) touch, hint; (*Rugby*) line-out; (*Football: aussi:* **remise en ~**) throw-in; (*aussi:* **ligne de ~**) touch-line; (*Escrime*) hit; **en ~** in (*ou* into) touch; **avoir une drôle de ~** to look a sight; **~ de commande/de fonction/de retour** (*Inform*) control/function/return key; **~ dièse** (*de téléphone, clavier*) hash key; **~ à effleurement** *ou* **sensitive** touch-sensitive control *ou* key

toucher [tuʃe] *nm* touch ⊳ *vt* to touch; (*palper*) to feel; (*atteindre: d'un coup de feu etc*) to hit; (*affecter*) to touch, affect; (*concerner*) to concern, affect; (*contacter*) to reach, contact; (*recevoir: récompense*) to receive, get; (*: salaire*) to draw, get; (*chèque*) to cash; (*aborder: problème,*

sujet) to touch on; **au ~** to the touch; by the
feel; **se toucher** (*être en contact*) to touch; **~ à** to
touch; (*modifier*) to touch, tamper *ou* meddle
with; (*traiter de, concerner*) to have to do with,
concern; **je vais lui en ~ un mot** I'll have a
word with him about it; **~ au but** (*fig*) to near
one's goal; **~ à sa fin** to be drawing to a close

touffe [tuf] *nf* tuft

touffu, e [tufy] *adj* thick, dense; (*fig*)
complex, involved

toujours [tuʒuʀ] *adv* always; (*encore*) still;
(*constamment*) forever; **depuis ~** always;
essaie ~ (you can) try anyway; **pour ~**
forever; **~ est-il que** the fact remains that;
~ plus more and more

toupet [tupɛ] *nm* quiff (*Brit*), tuft; (*fam*)
nerve, cheek (*Brit*)

toupie [tupi] *nf* (spinning) top

tour [tuʀ] *nf* tower; (*immeuble*) high-rise
block (*Brit*) *ou* building (*US*), tower block (*Brit*);
(*Échecs*) castle, rook ▷ *nm* (*excursion: à pied*)
stroll, walk; (: *en voiture etc*) run, ride; (: *plus
long*) trip; (*Sport: aussi:* **~ de piste**) lap; (*d'être
servi ou de jouer etc, tournure, de vis ou clef*) turn;
(*de roue etc*) revolution; (*circonférence*): **de 3 m
de ~** 3 m round, with a circumference *ou*
girth of 3 m; (*Pol: aussi:* **~ de scrutin**) ballot;
(*ruse, de prestidigitation, de cartes*) trick; (*de potier*)
wheel; (*à bois, métaux*) lathe; **faire le ~ de** to
go (a)round; (*à pied*) to walk (a)round; (*fig*) to
review; **faire le ~ de l'Europe** to tour Europe;
faire un ~ to go for a walk; (*en voiture etc*) to go
for a ride; **faire 2 ~s** to go (a)round twice;
(*hélice etc*) to turn *ou* revolve twice; **fermer à
double ~** vi to double-lock the door; **c'est au
~ de Renée** it's Renée's turn; **à ~ de rôle, ~ à
~ in** turn; **à ~ de bras** with all one's strength;
(*fig*) non-stop, relentlessly; **~ de taille/tête**
nm waist/head measurement; **~ de chant**
nm song recital; **~ de contrôle** *nf* control
tower; **la ~ Eiffel** the Eiffel Tower; **le T~ de
France** the Tour de France; *see note;* **~ de
force** *nm* tour de force; **~ de garde** *nm* spell
of duty; **un 33 ~s** an LP; **un 45 ~s** a single;
~ d'horizon *nm* (*fig*) general survey; **~ de lit**
nm valance; **~ de main** *nm* dexterity, knack;
en un ~ de main (as) quick as a flash; **~ de
passe-passe** *nm* trick, sleight of hand; **~ de
reins** *nm* sprained back

● TOUR DE FRANCE

The *Tour de France* is an annual road race for
professional cyclists. It takes about three
weeks to complete and is divided into
daily stages, or "étapes" of approximately
175km (110 miles) over terrain of varying
levels of difficulty. The leading cyclist
wears a yellow jersey, the "maillot jaune".
The route varies; it is not usually confined
to France but always ends in Paris. In
addition, there are a number of time trials.

tourbe [tuʀb] *nf* peat

tourbillon [tuʀbijɔ̃] *nm* whirlwind; (*d'eau*)
whirlpool; (*fig*) whirl, swirl

tourbillonner [tuʀbijɔne] *vi* to whirl, swirl;
(*objet, personne*) to whirl *ou* twirl round

tourelle [tuʀɛl] *nf* turret

tourisme [tuʀism] *nm* tourism; **agence de ~**
tourist agency; **avion/voiture de ~** private
plane/car; **faire du ~** to go touring; (*en ville*)
to go sightseeing

touriste [tuʀist] *nm/f* tourist

touristique [tuʀistik] *adj* tourist *cpd*; (*région*)
touristic (*péj*), with tourist appeal

tourment [tuʀmɑ̃] *nm* torment

tourmenter [tuʀmɑ̃te] *vt* to torment; **se
tourmenter** *vi* to fret, worry o.s.

tournage [tuʀnaʒ] *nm* (*d'un film*) shooting

tournant, e [tuʀnɑ̃, -ɑ̃t] *adj* (*feu, scène*)
revolving; (*chemin*) winding; (*escalier*) spiral
cpd; (*mouvement*) circling ▷ *nm* (*de route*) bend
(*Brit*), curve (*US*); (*fig*) turning point; *voir*
plaque; grève

tournebroche [tuʀnəbʀɔʃ] *nm* roasting spit

tourne-disque [tuʀnədisk] *nm* record player

tournée [tuʀne] *nf* (*du facteur etc*) round;
(*d'artiste, politicien*) tour; (*au café*) round (*of
drinks*); **faire la ~ de** to go (a)round

tournemain [tuʀnəmɛ̃]: **en un ~** *adv* in a flash

tourner [tuʀne] *vt* to turn; (*sauce, mélange*) to
stir; (*contourner*) to get (a)round; (*Ciné: faire les
prises de vues*) to shoot; (*produire*) to make ▷ *vi*
to turn; (*moteur*) to run; (*compteur*) to tick
away; (*lait etc*) to turn (sour); (*fig: chance, vie*)
to turn out; **se tourner** *vi* to turn (a)round;
se ~ vers to turn to; to turn towards; **bien ~**
to turn out well; **mal ~** to go wrong; **~ autour
de** to go (a)round; (*planète*) to revolve (a)
round; (*péj*) to hang (a)round; **~ autour du
pot** (*fig*) to go (a)round in circles; **~ à/en** to
turn into; **~ à la pluie/au rouge** to turn
rainy/red; **~ en ridicule** to ridicule; **le dos à**
(*mouvement*) to turn one's back on; (*position*) to
have one's back to; **~ court** to come to a
sudden end; **se ~ les pouces** to twiddle one's
thumbs; **~ la tête** to look away; **~ la tête à qn**
(*fig*) to go to sb's head; **~ de l'œil** to pass out;
~ la page (*fig*) to turn the page

tournesol [tuʀnəsɔl] *nm* sunflower

tournevis [tuʀnəvis] *nm* screwdriver

tourniquet [tuʀnikɛ] *nm* (*pour arroser*)
sprinkler; (*portillon*) turnstile; (*présentoir*)
revolving stand, spinner; (*Chirurgie*) tourniquet

tournoi [tuʀnwa] *nm* tournament

tournoyer [tuʀnwaje] *vi* (*oiseau*) to wheel (a)
round; (*fumée*) to swirl (a)round

tournure [tuʀnyʀ] *nf* (*Ling: syntaxe*) turn of
phrase; form; (: *d'une phrase*) phrasing;
(*évolution*): **la ~ de qch** the way sth is
developing; (*aspect*): **la ~ de** the look of; **la ~
des événements** the turn of events;
prendre ~ to take shape; **~ d'esprit** turn *ou*
cast of mind

t

tourte [tuʀt] *nf* pie
tourterelle [tuʀtəʀɛl] *nf* turtledove
tous [*adj* tu, *pron* tus] *adj, pron voir* **tout**
Toussaint [tusɛ̃] *nf*: **la ~** All Saints' Day; *see note*

● **TOUSSAINT**
●
● *La Toussaint*, 1 November, or All Saints' Day,
● is a public holiday in France. People
● traditionally visit the graves of friends
● and relatives to lay chrysanthemums on
● them.

tousser [tuse] *vi* to cough

 MOT-CLÉ

tout, e [tu, tut] (*mpl* **tous**, *fpl* **toutes**) *adj* **1**
(*avec article singulier*) all; **tout le lait** all the
milk; **toute la nuit** all night, the whole
night; **tout le livre** the whole book; **tout un
pain** a whole loaf; **tout le temps** all the
time, the whole time; **c'est tout le
contraire** it's quite the opposite; **c'est toute
une affaire** *ou* **histoire** it's quite a business,
it's a whole rigmarole
2 (*avec article pluriel*) every; all; **tous les livres**
all the books; **toutes les nuits** every night;
toutes les fois every time; **toutes les trois/
deux semaines** every third/other *ou* second
week, every three/two weeks; **tous les deux**
both *ou* each of us (*ou* them *ou* you); **toutes
les trois** all three of us (*ou* them *ou* you)
3 (*sans article*): **à tout âge** at any age; **pour
toute nourriture, il avait …** his only food
was …; **de tous côtés, de toutes parts** from
everywhere, from every side
▷ *pron* everything, all; **il a tout fait** he's done
everything; **je les vois tous** I can see them
all *ou* all of them; **nous y sommes tous allés**
all of us went, we all went; **c'est tout** that's
all; **en tout** in all; **en tout et pour tout** all
in all; **tout ce qu'il sait** all he knows; **c'était
tout ce qu'il y a de chic** it was the last word
ou the ultimate in chic
▷ *nm* whole; **le tout** all of it (*ou* them); **le
tout est de …** the main thing is to …; **pas du
tout** not at all; **elle a tout d'une mère/
d'une intrigante** she's a real *ou* true
mother/schemer; **du tout au tout** utterly
▷ *adv* **1** (*très, complètement*) very; **tout près** *ou* **à
côté** very near; **le tout premier** the very
first; **tout seul** all alone; **il était tout rouge**
he was really *ou* all red; **parler tout bas** to
speak very quietly; **le livre tout entier** the
whole book; **tout en haut** right at the top;
tout droit straight ahead
2: **tout en** while; **tout en travaillant** while
working, as he *etc* works
3: **tout d'abord** first of all; **tout à coup**
suddenly; **tout à fait** absolutely; **tout à fait!**
exactly!; **tout à l'heure** a short while ago;

(*futur*) in a short while, shortly; **à tout à
l'heure!** see you later!; **il répondit tout
court que non** he just answered no (and
that was all); **tout de même** all the same;
tout le monde everybody; **tout ou rien** all
or nothing; **tout simplement** quite simply;
tout de suite immediately, straight away

toutefois [tutfwa] *adv* however
toutes [tut] *adj, pron voir* **tout**
tout-terrain [tuteʀɛ̃] *adj*: **vélo ~** mountain
bike; **véhicule ~** four-wheel drive
toux [tu] *nf* cough
toxicomane [tɔksikɔman] *nm/f* drug addict
toxique [tɔksik] *adj* toxic, poisonous
trac [tʀak] *nm* (*aux examens*) nerves *pl*; (*Théât*)
stage fright; **avoir le ~** (*aux examens*) to get an
attack of nerves; (*Théât*) to have stage fright;
tout à ~ all of a sudden
tracasser [tʀakase] *vt* to worry, bother;
(*harceler*) to harass; **se tracasser** *vi* to worry
(o.s.), fret
trace [tʀas] *nf* (*empreintes*) tracks *pl*; (*marques,
aussi fig*) mark; (*restes, vestige*) trace; (*indice*)
sign; (*aussi*: **suivre à la ~**) to track; **~s de pas**
footprints
tracé [tʀase] *nm* (*contour*) line; (*plan*) layout
tracer [tʀase] *vt* to draw; (*mot*) to trace; (*piste*)
to open up; (*fig: chemin*) to show
tract [tʀakt] *nm* tract, pamphlet; (*publicitaire*)
handout
tractations [tʀaktasjɔ̃] *nfpl* dealings,
bargaining *nsg*
tracteur [tʀaktœʀ] *nm* tractor
traction [tʀaksjɔ̃] *nf* traction; (*Gym*) pull-up;
~ avant/arrière front-wheel/rear-wheel drive;
~ électrique electric(al) traction *ou* haulage
tradition [tʀadisjɔ̃] *nf* tradition
traditionnel, le [tʀadisjɔnɛl] *adj* traditional
traducteur, -trice [tʀadyktœʀ, -tʀis] *nm/f*
translator
traduction [tʀadyksjɔ̃] *nf* translation
traduire [tʀaduiʀ] *vt* to translate; (*exprimer*)
to convey, render; **se ~ par** to find expression
in; **~ en français** to translate into French;
~ en justice to bring before the courts
trafic [tʀafik] *nm* traffic; **~ d'armes** arms
dealing; **~ de drogue** drug peddling
trafiquant, e [tʀafikɑ̃, -ɑ̃t] *nm/f* trafficker;
(*d'armes*) dealer
trafiquer [tʀafike] *vt* (*péj: vin*) to doctor;
(*moteur, document*) to tamper with ▷ *vi* to
traffic, be engaged in trafficking
tragédie [tʀaʒedi] *nf* tragedy
tragique [tʀaʒik] *adj* tragic ▷ *nm*: **prendre
qch au ~** to make a tragedy out of sth
trahir [tʀaiʀ] *vt* to betray; (*fig*) to give away,
reveal; **se trahir** to betray o.s., give o.s. away
trahison [tʀaizɔ̃] *nf* betrayal; (*Jur*) treason
train [tʀɛ̃] *nm* (*Rail*) train; (*allure*) pace; (*fig:
ensemble*) set; **être en ~ de faire qch** to be
doing sth; **mettre qch en ~** to get sth under

way; **mettre qn en ~** to put sb in good spirits; **se mettre en ~** (*commencer*) to get started; (*faire de la gymnastique*) to warm up; **se sentir en ~** to feel in good form; **aller bon ~** to make good progress; **~ avant/arrière** front-wheel/rear-wheel axle unit; **~ à grande vitesse (TGV)** high-speed train; **~ d'atterrissage** undercarriage; **~ autos-couchettes** car-sleeper train; **~ électrique** (*jouet*) (electric) train set; **~ de pneus** set of tyres *ou* tires; **~ de vie** style of living

traîne [tʀɛn] *nf* (*de robe*) train; **être à la ~** to be in tow; (*en arrière*) to lag behind; (*en désordre*) to be lying around

traîneau, x [tʀɛno] *nm* sleigh, sledge

traînée [tʀɛne] *nf* streak, trail; (*péj*) slut (!)

traîner [tʀɛne] *vt* (*remorque*) to pull; (*enfant, chien*) to drag *ou* trail along; (*maladie*): **il traîne un rhume depuis l'hiver** he has a cold which has been dragging on since winter ▷ *vi* (*robe, manteau*) to trail; (*être en désordre*) to lie around; (*marcher lentement*) to dawdle (along); (*vagabonder*) to hang about; (*agir lentement*) to idle about; (*durer*) to drag on; **se traîner** *vi* (*ramper*) to crawl along; (*marcher avec difficulté*) to drag o.s. along; (*durer*) to drag on; **se ~ par terre** to crawl (on the ground); **~ qn au cinéma** to drag sb to the cinema; **~ les pieds** to drag one's feet; **~ par terre** to trail on the ground; **~ en longueur** to drag out

train-train [tʀɛ̃tʀɛ̃] *nm* humdrum routine

traire [tʀɛʀ] *vt* to milk

trait, e [tʀɛ, -ɛt] *pp de* **traire** ▷ *nm* (*ligne*) line; (*de dessin*) stroke; (*caractéristique*) feature, trait; (*flèche*) dart, arrow; shaft; **traits** *nmpl* (*du visage*) features; **d'un ~** (*boire*) in one gulp; **de ~** *adj* (*animal*) draught (*Brit*), draft (*US*); **avoir ~ à** to concern; **~ pour ~** line for line; **~ de caractère** characteristic, trait; **~ d'esprit** flash of wit; **~ de génie** brainwave; **~ d'union** hyphen; (*fig*) link

traitant, e [tʀɛtɑ̃, -ɑ̃t] *adj*: **votre médecin ~** your usual *ou* family doctor; **shampooing ~** medicated shampoo; **crème ~e** conditioning cream, conditioner

traite [tʀɛt] *nf* (*Comm*) draft; (*Agr*) milking; (*trajet*) stretch; **d'une (seule) ~** without stopping (once); **la ~ des noirs** the slave trade; **la ~ des blanches** the white slave trade

traité [tʀɛte] *nm* treaty

traitement [tʀɛtmɑ̃] *nm* treatment; processing; (*salaire*) salary; **suivre un ~** to undergo treatment; **mauvais ~** ill-treatment; **~ de données** *ou* **de l'information** (*Inform*) data processing; **~ hormono-supplétif** hormone replacement therapy; **~ par lots** (*Inform*) batch processing; **~ de texte** (*Inform*) word processing; (*logiciel*) word processing package

traiter [tʀɛte] *vt* (*gén*) to treat; (*Tech: matériaux*) to process, treat; (*Inform*) to process; (*affaire*) to deal with, handle;

(*qualifier*): **~ qn d'idiot** to call sb a fool ▷ *vi* to deal; **~ de** *vt* to deal with; **bien/mal ~** to treat well/ill-treat

traiteur [tʀɛtœʀ] *nm* caterer

traître, -esse [tʀɛtʀ, -tʀɛs] *adj* (*dangereux*) treacherous ▷ *nm* traitor; **prendre qn en ~** to make an insidious attack on sb

trajectoire [tʀaʒɛktwaʀ] *nf* trajectory, path

trajet [tʀaʒɛ] *nm* (*parcours, voyage*) journey; (*itinéraire*) route; (*fig*) path, course; (*distance à parcourir*) distance; **il y a une heure de ~** the journey takes one hour

trame [tʀam] *nf* (*de tissu*) weft; (*fig*) framework; texture; (*Typo*) screen

tramer [tʀame] *vt* to plot, hatch

trampoline [tʀɑ̃pɔlin], **trampolino** [tʀɑ̃pɔlino] *nm* trampoline; (*Sport*) trampolining

tramway [tʀamwɛ] *nm* tram(way); (*voiture*) tram(car) (*Brit*), streetcar (*US*)

tranchant, e [tʀɑ̃ʃɑ̃, -ɑ̃t] *adj* sharp; (*fig: personne*) peremptory; (*: couleurs*) striking ▷ *nm* (*d'un couteau*) cutting edge; (*de la main*) edge; **à double ~** (*argument, procédé*) double-edged

tranche [tʀɑ̃ʃ] *nf* (*morceau*) slice; (*arête*) edge; (*partie*) section; (*série*) block; (*d'impôts, revenus etc*) bracket; (*loterie*) issue; **~ d'âge/de salaires** age/wage bracket; **~ (de silicium)** wafer

tranché, e [tʀɑ̃ʃe] *adj* (*couleurs*) distinct, sharply contrasted; (*opinions*) clear-cut, definite ▷ *nf* trench

trancher [tʀɑ̃ʃe] *vt* to cut, sever; (*fig: résoudre*) to settle ▷ *vi* to be decisive; (*entre deux choses*) to settle the argument; **~ avec** to contrast sharply with

tranquille [tʀɑ̃kil] *adj* calm, quiet; (*enfant, élève*) quiet; (*rassuré*) easy in one's mind, with one's mind at rest; **se tenir ~** (*enfant*) to be quiet; **avoir la conscience ~** to have an easy conscience; **laisse-moi/laisse-ça ~** leave me/ it alone

tranquillisant, e [tʀɑ̃kiliza, -ɑ̃t] *adj* (*nouvelle*) reassuring ▷ *nm* tranquillizer

tranquillité [tʀɑ̃kilite] *nf* quietness, peace (and quiet); **en toute ~** with complete peace of mind; **~ d'esprit** peace of mind

transat [tʀɑ̃zat] *nm* deckchair ▷ *nf* = **course transatlantique**

transborder [tʀɑ̃sbɔʀde] *vt* to tran(s)ship

transcription [tʀɑ̃skʀipsjɔ̃] *nf* transcription

transférer [tʀɑ̃sfeʀe] *vt* to transfer

transfert [tʀɑ̃sfɛʀ] *nm* transfer

transformation [tʀɑ̃sfɔʀmasjɔ̃] *nf* change, alteration; (*radicale*) transformation; (*Rugby*) conversion; **transformations** *nfpl* (*travaux*) alterations; **industries de ~** processing industries

transformer [tʀɑ̃sfɔʀme] *vt* to change; (*radicalement*) to transform, alter ("*alter*" *implique un changement moins radical*); (*vêtement*) alter; (matière première, appartement, Rugby) to convert; ~ **en** to transform into; to turn into; to convert into; **se transformer** vi to be transformed; to alter

transfusion [trɑ̃sfyzjɔ̃] nf: ~ **sanguine** blood transfusion

transgénique [trɑ̃sʒenik] adj transgenic

transgresser [trɑ̃sgrese] vt to contravene, disobey

transi, e [trɑ̃zi] adj numb (with cold), chilled to the bone

transiger [trɑ̃ziʒe] vi to compromise, come to an agreement; ~ **sur** ou **avec qch** to compromise on sth

transistor [trɑ̃zistɔr] nm transistor

transit [trɑ̃zit] nm transit; **de** ~ transit cpd; **en** ~ in transit

transiter [trɑ̃zite] vi to pass in transit

transitif, -ive [trɑ̃zitif, -iv] adj transitive

transition [trɑ̃zisjɔ̃] nf transition; **de** ~ transitional

transitoire [trɑ̃zitwar] adj (mesure, gouvernement) transitional, provisional; (fugitif) transient

translucide [trɑ̃slysid] adj translucent

transmettre [trɑ̃smɛtr] vt (passer): ~ **qch à qn** to pass sth on to sb; (Tech, Tél, Méd) to transmit; (TV, Radio: retransmettre) to broadcast

transmission [trɑ̃smisjɔ̃] nf transmission, passing on; (Auto) transmission; **transmissions** nfpl (Mil) ≈ signals corps nsg; ~ **de données** (Inform) data transmission; ~ **de pensée** thought transmission

transparent, e [trɑ̃sparɑ̃, -ɑ̃t] adj transparent

transpercer [trɑ̃spɛrse] vt (froid, pluie) to go through, pierce; (balle) to go through

transpiration [trɑ̃spirasjɔ̃] nf perspiration

transpirer [trɑ̃spire] vi to perspire; (information, nouvelle) to come to light

transplantation [trɑ̃splɑ̃tasjɔ̃] nf transplant

transplanter [trɑ̃splɑ̃te] vt (Méd, Bot) to transplant; (personne) to uproot, move

transport [trɑ̃spɔr] nm transport; (émotions): ~ **de colère** fit of rage; ~ **de joie** transport of delight; ~ **de voyageurs/marchandises** passenger/goods transportation; ~**s en commun** public transport nsg; ~**s routiers** haulage (Brit), trucking (US)

transporter [trɑ̃spɔrte] vt to carry, move; (Comm) to transport, convey; (fig): ~ **qn (de joie)** to send sb into raptures; **se** ~ **quelque part** (fig) to let one's imagination carry one away (somewhere)

transporteur [trɑ̃spɔrtœr] nm haulage contractor (Brit), trucker (US)

transvaser [trɑ̃svaze] vt to decant

transversal, e, -aux [trɑ̃svɛrsal, -o] adj transverse, cross(-); (route etc) cross-country; (mur, chemin, rue) running at right angles;

(Auto): **axe** ~ main cross-country road (Brit) ou highway (US); **coupe** ~**e** cross section

trapèze [trapɛz] nm (Géom) trapezium; (au cirque) trapeze

trappe [trap] nf (de cave, grenier) trap door; (piège) trap

trapu, e [trapy] adj squat, stocky

traquenard [traknar] nm trap

traquer [trake] vt to track down; (harceler) to hound

traumatiser [tromatize] vt to traumatize

travail, -aux [travaj, -o] nm (gén) work; (tâche, métier) work no pl, job; (Écon, Méd) labour (Brit), labor (US); (Inform) job ▷ nmpl (de réparation, agricoles etc) work nsg; (sur route) roadworks; (de construction) building (work) nsg; **être/entrer en** ~ (Méd) to be in/go into labour; **être sans** ~ (employé) to be out of work, be unemployed; ~ **d'intérêt général (TIG)** ≈ community service; ~ **(au) noir** moonlighting; ~ **posté** shiftwork; **travaux des champs** farmwork nsg; **travaux dirigés (TD)** (Scol) supervised practical work nsg; **travaux forcés** hard labour nsg; **travaux manuels** (Scol) handicrafts; **travaux ménagers** housework nsg; **travaux pratiques (TP)** (gén) practical work; (en laboratoire) lab work (Brit), lab (US); **travaux publics (TP)** ≈ public works nsg

travailler [travaje] vi to work; (bois) to warp ▷ vt (bois, métal) to work; (pâte) to knead; (objet d'art, discipline, fig: influencer) to work on; **cela le travaille** it is on his mind; ~ **la terre** to work the land; ~ **son piano** to do one's piano practice; ~ **à** to work on; (fig: contribuer à) to work towards; ~ **à faire** to endeavour (Brit) ou endeavor (US) to do

travailleur, -euse [travajœr, -øz] adj hard-working ▷ nm/f worker; ~ **de force** labourer (Brit), laborer (US); ~ **intellectuel** non-manual worker; ~ **social** social worker; **travailleuse familiale** home help

travailliste [travajist] adj ≈ Labour cpd ▷ nm/f member of the Labour party

travaux [travo] nmpl voir **travail**

travers [travɛr] nm fault, failing; **en** ~ **(de)** across; **au** ~ **(de)** through; **de** ~ adj (nez, bouche) crooked; (chapeau) askew ▷ adv sideways; (fig) the wrong way; **à** ~ through; **regarder de** ~ (fig) to look askance at; **comprendre de** ~ to misunderstand

traverse [travɛrs] nf (de voie ferrée) sleeper; **chemin de** ~ shortcut

traversée [traverse] nf crossing

traverser [traverse] vt (gén) to cross; (ville, tunnel, aussi: percer, fig) to go through; (ligne, trait) to run across

traversin [traversɛ̃] nm bolster

travesti [travesti] nm (comme mode de vie) transvestite; (artiste de cabaret) female impersonator, drag artist; (costume) fancy dress

trébucher [trebyʃe] vi: ~ **(sur)** to stumble (over), trip (over)

trèfle [tʀɛfl] nm (Bot) clover; (Cartes: couleur) clubs pl; (: carte) club; ~ **à quatre feuilles** four-leaf clover

treille [tʀɛj] nf (tonnelle) vine arbour (Brit) ou arbor (US); (vigne) climbing vine

treillis [tʀeji] nm (métallique) wire-mesh; (toile) canvas; (Mil: tenue) combat uniform; (pantalon) combat trousers pl

treize [tʀɛz] num thirteen

treizième [tʀɛzjɛm] num thirteenth; see note

● **TREIZIÈME MOIS**

● The treizième mois is an end-of-year bonus
● roughly corresponding to one month's
● salary. For many employees it is a
● standard part of their salary package.

tréma [tʀema] nm diaeresis

tremblement [tʀɑ̃bləmɑ̃] nm trembling no pl, shaking no pl, shivering no pl; ~ **de terre** earthquake

trembler [tʀɑ̃ble] vi to tremble, shake; ~ **de** (froid, fièvre) to shiver ou tremble with; (peur) to shake ou tremble with; ~ **pour qn** to fear for sb

trémousser [tʀemuse]: **se trémousser** vi to jig about, wriggle about

trempe [tʀɑ̃p] nf (fig): **de cette/sa** ~ of this/ his calibre (Brit) ou caliber (US)

trempé, e [tʀɑ̃pe] adj soaking (wet), drenched; (Tech): **acier** ~ tempered steel

tremper [tʀɑ̃pe] vt to soak, drench; (aussi: **faire** ~, **mettre à** ~) to soak; (plonger): ~ **qch dans** to dip sth in(to) ▷ vi to soak; (fig): ~ **dans** to be involved ou have a hand in; **se tremper** vi to have a quick dip; **se faire** ~ to get soaked ou drenched

trempette [tʀɑ̃pɛt] nf: **faire** ~ to go paddling

tremplin [tʀɑ̃plɛ̃] nm springboard; (Ski) ski jump

trentaine [tʀɑ̃tɛn] nf (âge): **avoir la** ~ to be around thirty; **une** ~ **(de)** thirty or so, about thirty

trente [tʀɑ̃t] num thirty; **voir** ~-**six chandelles** (fig) to see stars; **être/se mettre sur son** ~ **et un** to be wearing/put on one's Sunday best; ~-**trois tours** nm long-playing record, LP

trentième [tʀɑ̃tjɛm] num thirtieth

trépidant, e [tʀepidɑ̃, -ɑ̃t] adj (fig: rythme) pulsating; (: vie) hectic

trépied [tʀepje] nm (d'appareil) tripod; (meuble) trivet

trépigner [tʀepiɲe] vi to stamp (one's feet)

très [tʀɛ] adv very; ~ **beau/bien** very beautiful/well; ~ **critiqué** much criticized; ~ **industrialisé** highly industrialized; **j'ai** ~ **faim** I'm very hungry

trésor [tʀezɔʀ] nm treasure; (Admin) finances pl; (d'une organisation) funds pl; ~ **(public) (TP)** public revenue; (service) public revenue office

trésorerie [tʀezɔʀʀi] nf (fonds) funds pl; (gestion) accounts pl; (bureaux) accounts department; (poste) treasurership; **difficultés de** ~ cash problems, shortage of cash ou funds; ~ **générale (TG)** local government finance office

trésorier, -ière [tʀezɔʀje, -jɛʀ] nm/f treasurer

tressaillir [tʀesajiʀ] vi (de peur etc) to shiver, shudder; (de joie) to quiver

tressauter [tʀesote] vi to start, jump

tresse [tʀɛs] nf (de cheveux) braid, plait; (cordon, galon) braid

tresser [tʀese] vt (cheveux) to braid, plait; (fil, jonc) to plait; (corbeille) to weave; (corde) to twist

tréteau, x [tʀeto] nm trestle; **les** ~**x** (fig: Théât) the boards

treuil [tʀœj] nm winch

trêve [tʀɛv] nf (Mil, Pol) truce; (fig) respite; **sans** ~ unremittingly; ~ **de ...** enough of this ...; **les États de la T**~ the Trucial States

tri [tʀi] nm (voir trier) sorting (out) no pl; selection; screening; (Inform) sort; (Postes: action) sorting; **faire le** ~ **(de)** to sort out; **le (bureau de)** ~ (Postes) the sorting office

triangle [tʀijɑ̃gl] nm triangle; ~ **isocèle/ équilatéral** isosceles/equilateral triangle; ~ **rectangle** right-angled triangle

triangulaire [tʀijɑ̃gylɛʀ] adj triangular

tribord [tʀibɔʀ] nm: **à** ~ to starboard, on the starboard side

tribu [tʀiby] nf tribe

tribunal, -aux [tʀibynal, -o] nm (Jur) court; (Mil) tribunal; ~ **de police/pour enfants** police/juvenile court; ~ **d'instance (TI)** ≈ magistrates' court (Brit), ≈ district court (US); ~ **de grande instance (TGI)** ≈ High Court (Brit), ≈ Supreme Court (US)

tribune [tʀibyn] nf (estrade) platform, rostrum; (débat) forum; (d'église, de tribunal) gallery; (de stade) stand; ~ **libre** (Presse) opinion column

tribut [tʀiby] nm tribute

tributaire [tʀibytɛʀ] adj: **être** ~ **de** to be dependent on; (Géo) to be a tributary of

tricher [tʀiʃe] vi to cheat

tricheur, -euse [tʀiʃœʀ, -øz] nm/f cheat

tricolore [tʀikɔlɔʀ] adj three-coloured (Brit), three-colored (US); (français: drapeau) red, white and blue; (: équipe etc) French

tricot [tʀiko] nm (technique, ouvrage) knitting no pl; (tissu) knitted fabric; (vêtement) jersey, sweater; ~ **de corps**, ~ **de peau** vest (Brit), undershirt (US)

tricoter [tʀikɔte] vt to knit; **machine/ aiguille à** ~ knitting machine/needle (Brit) ou pin (US)

trictrac [tʀiktʀak] nm backgammon

tricycle [tʀisikl] nm tricycle

triennal, e, -aux [tʀienal, -o] adj (prix, foire, élection) three-yearly; (charge, mandat, plan) three-year

trier [tʀije] vt (classer) to sort (out); (choisir) to select; (visiteurs) to screen; (Postes, Inform, fruits) to sort

trimestre [tʀimɛstʀ] nm (Scol) term; (Comm) quarter

trimestriel, le [tʀimɛstʀijɛl] adj quarterly; (Scol) end-of-term

tringle [tʀɛ̃gl] nf rod

trinquer [tʀɛ̃ke] vi to clink glasses; (fam) to cop it; **~ à qch/la santé de qn** to drink to sth/sb

triomphe [tʀijɔ̃f] nm triumph; **être reçu/porté en ~** to be given a triumphant welcome/be carried shoulder-high in triumph

triompher [tʀijɔ̃fe] vi to triumph, win; **~ de** to triumph over, overcome

tripes [tʀip] nfpl (Culin) tripe nsg; (fam) guts

triple [tʀipl] adj (à trois éléments) triple; (trois fois plus grand) treble ▷ nm: **le ~ (de)** (comparaison) three times as much (as); **en ~ exemplaire** in triplicate; **~ saut** (Sport) triple jump

tripler [tʀiple] vi, vt to triple, treble, increase threefold

triplés, -ées [tʀiple] nm/fpl triplets

tripoter [tʀipɔte] vt to fiddle with, finger ▷ vi (fam) to rummage about

triste [tʀist] adj sad; (couleur, temps, journée) dreary; (péj): **personnage/affaire** sorry individual/affair; **c'est pas ~!** (fam) it's something else!

tristesse [tʀistɛs] nf sadness

trivial, e, -aux [tʀivjal, -o] adj coarse, crude; (commun) mundane

troc [tʀɔk] nm (Écon) barter; (transaction) exchange, swap

troène [tʀɔɛn] nm privet

trognon [tʀɔɲɔ̃] nm (de fruit) core; (de légume) stalk

trois [tʀwɑ] num three

troisième [tʀwazjɛm] num third ▷ nf (Scol) year 10 (Brit), ninth grade (US); **le ~ âge** (période de vie) one's retirement years; (personnes âgées) senior citizens pl

trois quarts [tʀwɑkaʀ] nmpl: **les ~ de** three-quarters of

trombe [tʀɔ̃b] nf waterspout; **des ~s d'eau** a downpour; **en ~** (arriver, passer) like a whirlwind

trombone [tʀɔ̃bɔn] nm (Mus) trombone; (de bureau) paper clip; **~ à coulisse** slide trombone

trompe [tʀɔ̃p] nf (d'éléphant) trunk; (Mus) trumpet, horn; **~ d'Eustache** Eustachian tube; **~s utérines** Fallopian tubes

tromper [tʀɔ̃pe] vt to deceive; (fig: espoir, attente) to disappoint; (vigilance, poursuivants) to elude; **se tromper** vi to make a mistake, be mistaken; **se ~ de voiture/jour** to take the wrong car/get the day wrong; **se ~ de 3 cm/20 euros** to be out by 3 cm/20 euros

tromperie [tʀɔ̃pʀi] nf deception, trickery no pl

trompette [tʀɔ̃pɛt] nf trumpet; **en ~** (nez) turned-up

trompeur, -euse [tʀɔ̃pœʀ, -øz] adj deceptive, misleading

tronc [tʀɔ̃] nm (Bot, Anat) trunk; (d'église) collection box; **~ d'arbre** tree trunk; **~ commun** (Scol) common-core syllabus; **~ de cône** truncated cone

tronçon [tʀɔ̃sɔ̃] nm section

tronçonner [tʀɔ̃sɔne] vt (arbre) to saw up; (pierre) to cut up

tronçonneuse [tʀɔ̃sɔnøz] nf chainsaw

trône [tʀon] nm throne; **monter sur le ~** to ascend the throne

trop [tʀo] adv too; (avec verbe) too much; (aussi: **~ nombreux**) too many; (aussi: **~ souvent**) too often; (aussi: **~ peu (nombreux)**) too few; **~ longtemps** (for) too long; **~ de** (nombre) too many; (quantité) too much; **de ~, en ~:** **des livres en trop** a few books too many, a few extra books; **du lait en ~** too much milk; **trois livres/cinq euros de ~** three books too many/five euros too much; **ça coûte ~ cher** it's too expensive

tropical, e, -aux [tʀɔpikal, -o] adj tropical

tropique [tʀɔpik] nm tropic; **tropiques** nmpl tropics; **~ du Cancer/Capricorne** Tropic of Cancer/Capricorn

trop-plein [tʀoplɛ̃] nm (tuyau) overflow ou outlet (pipe); (liquide) overflow

troquer [tʀɔke] vt: **~ qch contre** to barter ou trade sth for; (fig) to swap sth for

trot [tʀo] nm trot; **aller au ~** to trot along; **partir au ~** to set off at a trot

trotter [tʀɔte] vi to trot; (fig) to scamper along (ou about)

trotteuse [tʀɔtøz] nf (de montre) second hand

trottinette [tʀɔtinɛt] nf (child's) scooter

trottoir [tʀɔtwaʀ] nm pavement (Brit), sidewalk (US); **faire le ~** (péj) to walk the streets; **~ roulant** moving walkway, travellator

trou [tʀu] nm hole; (fig) gap; (Comm) deficit; **~ d'aération** (air) vent; **~ d'air** air pocket; **~ de mémoire** blank, lapse of memory; **~ noir** black hole; **~ de la serrure** keyhole

troublant, e [tʀublɑ̃, -ɑ̃t] adj disturbing

trouble [tʀubl] adj (liquide) cloudy; (image, photo) blurred; (mémoire) indistinct, hazy; (affaire) shady, murky ▷ adv indistinctly; **voir ~** to have blurred vision ▷ nm (désarroi) distress, agitation; (émoi sensuel) turmoil, agitation; (embarras) confusion; (zizanie) unrest, discord; **troubles** nmpl (Pol) disturbances, troubles, unrest nsg; (Méd) trouble nsg, disorders; **~s de la personnalité** personality problems; **~s de la vision** eye trouble

trouble-fête [tʀublfɛt] nm/f inv spoilsport

troubler [tʀuble] vt (embarrasser) to confuse, disconcert; (émouvoir) to agitate; to disturb; to perturb; (perturber: ordre etc) to disrupt, disturb; (*liquide*) to make cloudy; (*intriguer*) to bother; **se troubler** *vi* (*personne*) to become flustered *ou* confused; **~ l'ordre public** to cause a breach of the peace

trouer [tʀue] *vt* to make a hole (*ou* holes) in; (*fig*) to pierce

trouille [tʀuj] *nf* (*fam*): **avoir la ~** to be scared stiff, be scared out of one's wits

troupe [tʀup] *nf* (*Mil*) troop; (*groupe*) troop, group; **la ~** (*Mil: l'armée*) the army; (: *les simples soldats*) the troops *pl*; **~ de théâtre**) (theatrical) company; **~s de choc** shock troops

troupeau, x [tʀupo] *nm* (*de moutons*) flock; (*de vaches*) herd

trousse [tʀus] *nf* case, kit; (*d'écolier*) pencil case; (*de docteur*) instrument case; **aux ~s de** (*fig*) on the heels *ou* tail of; **~ à outils** toolkit; **~ de toilette** toilet bag

trousseau, x [tʀuso] *nm* (*de mariée*) trousseau; **~ de clefs** bunch of keys

trouvaille [tʀuvaj] *nf* find; (*fig: idée, expression etc*) brainwave

trouver [tʀuve] *vt* to find; (*rendre visite*): **aller/ venir ~ qn** to go/come and see sb; **je trouve que** I find *ou* think that; **~ à boire/critiquer** to find something to drink/criticize; **~ asile/ refuge** to find refuge/shelter; **se trouver** *vi* (*être*) to be; (*être soudain*) to find o.s.; **se ~ être/ avoir** to happen to be/have; **il se trouve que** it happens that, it turns out that; **se ~ bien** to feel well; **se ~ mal** to pass out

truand [tʀyɑ̃] *nm* villain, crook

truander [tʀyɑ̃de] *vi* (*fam*) to cheat, do ▷ *vt*: **se faire ~** to be swindled

truc [tʀyk] *nm* (*astuce*) way, device; (*de cinéma, prestidigitateur*) trick effect; (*chose*) thing; (*machin*) thingumajig, whatsit (*Brit*); **avoir le ~** to have the knack; **c'est pas son** (*ou* **mon** *etc*) **~** (*fam*) it's not really his (*ou* my *etc*) thing

truelle [tʀyɛl] *nf* trowel

truffe [tʀyf] *nf* (*Culin*) truffle; (*nez*) nose

truffé, e [tʀyfe] *adj* (*Culin*) garnished with truffles; **~ de** (*fig: citations*) peppered with; (*fautes*) riddled with; (*pièges*) bristling with

truie [tʀɥi] *nf* sow

truite [tʀɥit] *nf* trout *inv*

truquage [tʀykaʒ] *nm* fixing; (*Ciné*) special effects *pl*

truquer [tʀyke] *vt* (*élections, serrure, dés*) to fix; (*Ciné*) to use special effects in

TSVP *abr* (= *tournez s'il vous plaît*) PTO

TTC *abr* (= *toutes taxes comprises*) inclusive of tax

tu¹ [ty] *pron* you ▷ *nm*: **employer le tu** to use the "tu" form

tu², e [ty] *pp de* **taire**

tuba [tyba] *nm* (*Mus*) tuba; (*Sport*) snorkel

tube [tyb] *nm* tube; (*de canalisation, métallique etc*) pipe; (*chanson, disque*) hit song *ou* record; **~ digestif** alimentary canal, digestive tract; **~ à essai** test tube

tuberculose [tybɛʀkyloz] *nf* tuberculosis, TB

tuer [tɥe] *vt* to kill; **se tuer** (*se suicider*) to kill

o.s.; (*dans un accident*) to be killed; **se ~ au travail** (*fig*) to work o.s. to death

tuerie [tyʀi] *nf* slaughter *no pl*, massacre

tue-tête [tytɛt]: **à ~** *adv* at the top of one's voice

tueur [tɥœʀ] *nm* killer; **~ à gages** hired killer

tuile [tɥil] *nf* tile; (*fam*) spot of bad luck, blow

tulipe [tylip] *nf* tulip

tuméfié, e [tymefje] *adj* puffy, swollen

tumeur [tymœʀ] *nf* growth, tumour (*Brit*), tumor (*US*)

tumulte [tymylt] *nm* commotion, hubbub

tumultueux, -euse [tymyltɥø, -øz] *adj* stormy, turbulent

tunique [tynik] *nf* tunic; (*de femme*) smock, tunic

Tunis [tynis] *n* Tunis

Tunisie [tynizi] *nf*: **la ~** Tunisia

tunisien, ne [tynizjɛ̃, -ɛn] *adj* Tunisian ▷ *nm/f*: **T~, ne** Tunisian

tunnel [tynɛl] *nm* tunnel; **le ~ sous la Manche** the Channel Tunnel

turbulences [tyʀbylɑ̃s] *nfpl* (*Aviat*) turbulence *sg*

turbulent, e [tyʀbylɑ̃, -ɑ̃t] *adj* boisterous, unruly

turc, turque [tyʀk] *adj* Turkish; (*w.-c.*) seatless ▷ *nm* (*Ling*) Turkish ▷ *nm/f*: **T~, Turque** Turk/Turkish woman; **à la turque** *adv* (*assis*) cross-legged

turf [tyʀf] *nm* racing

turfiste [tyʀfist] *nm/f* racegoer

Turquie [tyʀki] *nf*: **la ~** Turkey

turquoise [tyʀkwaz] *nf, adj inv* turquoise

tus *etc* [ty] *vb voir* **taire**

tutelle [tytɛl] *nf* (*Jur*) guardianship; (*Pol*) trusteeship; **sous la ~ de** (*fig*) under the supervision of

tuteur, -trice [tytœʀ, -tʀis] *nm/f* (*Jur*) guardian; (*de plante*) stake, support

tutoyer [tytwaje] *vt*: **~ qn** to address sb as "tu"

tuyau, x [tɥijo] *nm* pipe; (*flexible*) tube; (*fam: conseil*) tip; (: *mise au courant*) gen *no pl*; **~ d'arrosage** hosepipe; **~ d'échappement** exhaust pipe; **~ d'incendie** fire hose

tuyauterie [tɥijotʀi] *nf* piping *no pl*

TVA *sigle f* (= *taxe à ou sur la valeur ajoutée*) VAT

TVHD *abr f* (= *télévision haute-définition*) HDTV

tweet [twit] *nm* (*Inform: Twitter*) tweet

tweeter [twite] *vt* (*Inform: Twitter*) to tweet

tympan [tɛ̃pɑ̃] *nm* (*Anat*) eardrum

type [tip] *nm* type; (*personne, chose: représentant*) classic example, epitome; (*fam*) chap, guy ▷ *adj* typical, standard; **avoir le ~ nordique** to be Nordic-looking

typé, e [tipe] *adj* ethnic (*euph*)

typique [tipik] *adj* typical

tyran [tiʀɑ̃] *nm* tyrant

tyrannique [tiʀanik] *adj* tyrannical

tzigane [dzigan] *adj* gipsy, tzigane ▷ *nm/f* (Hungarian) gipsy, Tzigane

t

u

UEM *sigle f* (= *Union économique et monétaire*) EMU

ulcère [ylsɛʀ] *nm* ulcer; ~ **à l'estomac** stomach ulcer

ulcérer [ylseʀe] *vt* (*Méd*) to ulcerate; (*fig*) to sicken, appal

ultérieur, e [ylteʀjœʀ] *adj* later, subsequent; **remis à une date ~e** postponed to a later date

ultérieurement [ylteʀjœʀmɑ̃] *adv* later, subsequently

ultime [yltim] *adj* final

UMP *sigle f* (= *Union pour un mouvement populaire*) *political party*

 MOT-CLÉ

un, une [œ̃, yn] *art indéf* a; (*devant voyelle*) an; **un garçon/vieillard** a boy/an old man; **une fille** a girl
▷ *pron* one; **l'un des meilleurs** one of the best; **l'un ..., l'autre** (the) one ..., the other; **les uns ..., les autres** some ..., others; **l'un et l'autre** both (of them); **l'un ou l'autre** either (of them); **l'un l'autre, les uns les autres** each other, one another; **pas un seul** not a single one; **un par un** one by one
▷ *num* one; **une pomme seulement** one apple only, just one apple
▷ *nf:* **la une** (*Presse*) the front page

unanime [ynanim] *adj* unanimous; **ils sont ~s (à penser que)** they are unanimous (in thinking that)

unanimité [ynanimite] *nf* unanimity; **à l'~** unanimously; **faire l'~** to be approved unanimously

uni, e [yni] *adj* (*ton, tissu*) plain; (*surface*) smooth, even; (*famille*) close(-knit); (*pays*) united

unifier [ynifje] *vt* to unite, unify; (*systèmes*) to standardize, unify; **s'unifier** *vi* to become united

uniforme [ynifɔʀm] *adj* (*mouvement*) regular, uniform; (*surface, ton*) even; (*objets, maisons*) uniform; (*fig: vie, conduite*) unchanging ▷ *nm* uniform; **être sous l'~** (*Mil*) to be serving

uniformiser [ynifɔʀmize] *vt* to make uniform; (*systèmes*) to standardize

union [ynjɔ̃] *nf* union; ~ **conjugale** union of marriage; ~ **de consommateurs** consumers' association; ~ **libre** free love; **vivre en ~ libre** (*en concubinage*) to cohabit; **U~ européenne** European Union; **l'U~ des Républiques socialistes soviétiques (URSS)** the Union of Soviet Socialist Republics (USSR); **l'U~ soviétique** the Soviet Union

unique [ynik] *adj* (*seul*) only; (*le même*): **un prix/système ~** a single price/system; (*exceptionnel*) unique; **ménage à salaire ~** one-salary family; **route à voie ~** single-lane road; **fils/fille ~** only son/daughter, only child; **sens ~** one-way street; ~ **en France** the only one of its kind in France

uniquement [ynikmɑ̃] *adv* only, solely; (*juste*) only, merely

unir [yniʀ] *vt* (*nations*) to unite; (*éléments, couleurs*) to combine; (*en mariage*) to unite, join together; ~ **qch à** to unite sth with; to combine sth with; **s'unir** *vi* to unite; (*en mariage*) to be joined together; **s'~ à** *ou* **avec** to unite with

unitaire [yniteʀ] *adj* unitary; (*Pol*) unitarian; **prix ~** unit price

unité [ynite] *nf* (*harmonie, cohésion*) unity; (*Comm, Mil, de mesure, Math*) unit; ~ **centrale** central processing unit; ~ **de valeur** (*university*) course, credit

univers [ynivɛʀ] *nm* universe

universel, le [ynivɛʀsɛl] *adj* universal; (*esprit*) all-embracing

universitaire [ynivɛʀsiteʀ] *adj* university *cpd*; (*diplôme, études*) academic, university *cpd* ▷ *nm/f* academic

université [ynivɛʀsite] *nf* university

urbain, e [yʀbɛ̃, -ɛn] *adj* urban, city *cpd*, town *cpd*; (*poli*) urbane

urbanisme [yʀbanism] *nm* town planning

urgence [yʀʒɑ̃s] *nf* urgency; (*Méd etc*) emergency; **d'~** *adj* emergency *cpd* ▷ *adv* as a matter of urgency; **en cas d'~** in case of emergency; **service des ~s** emergency service

urgent, e [yʀʒɑ̃, -ɑ̃t] *adj* urgent

urine [yʀin] *nf* urine

urinoir [yʀinwaʀ] *nm* (*public*) urinal

urne [yʀn] nf (électorale) ballot box; (vase) urn; **aller aux ~s** (voter) to go to the polls

urticaire [yʀtikɛʀ] nf nettle rash, urticaria

us [ys] nmpl: **us et coutumes** (habits and) customs

USA sigle mpl (= United States of America) USA

usage [yzaʒ] nm (emploi, utilisation) use; (coutume) custom; (éducation) (good) manners pl, (good) breeding; (Ling): l'~ usage; **faire ~ de** (pouvoir, droit) to exercise; **avoir l'~ de** to have the use of; **à l'~** adv with use; **à l'~ de** (pour) for (use of); **en ~** in use; **hors d'~** out of service; **à ~ interne** (Méd) to be taken (internally); **à ~ externe** (Méd) for external use only

usagé, e [yzaʒe] adj (usé) worn; (d'occasion) used

usager, -ère [yzaʒe, -ɛʀ] nm/f user

usé, e [yze] adj worn (down ou out ou away); ruined; (banal: argument etc) hackneyed

user [yze] vt (outil) to wear down; (vêtement) to wear out; (matière) to wear away; (consommer: charbon etc) to use; (fig: santé) to ruin; (: personne) to wear out; **s'user** vi to wear; (tissu, vêtement) to wear out; (fig) to decline; **s'~ à la tâche** to wear o.s. out with work; **~ de** vt (moyen, procédé) to use, employ; (droit) to exercise

usine [yzin] nf factory; **~ atomique** nuclear power plant; **~ à gaz** gasworks sg; **~ marémotrice** tidal power station

usité, e [yzite] adj in common use, common; **peu ~** rarely used

ustensile [ystãsil] nm implement; **~ de cuisine** kitchen utensil

usuel, le [yzɥɛl] adj everyday, common

usure [yzyʀ] nf wear; worn state; (de l'usurier) usury; **avoir qn à l'~** to wear sb down; **~ normale** fair wear and tear

utérus [yteʀys] nm uterus, womb

utile [ytil] adj useful; **~ à qn/qch** of use to sb/sth

utilisation [ytilizasjɔ̃] nf use

utiliser [ytilize] vt to use

utilitaire [ytilitɛʀ] adj utilitarian; (objets) practical ▷ nm (Inform) utility

utilité [ytilite] nf usefulness no pl; use; **jouer les ~s** (Théât) to play bit parts; **reconnu d'~ publique** state-approved; **c'est d'une grande ~** it's extremely useful; **il n'y a aucune ~ à ...** there's no use in ...; **de peu d'~** of little use ou help

utopie [ytopi] nf (idée, conception) utopian idea ou view; (société etc idéale) utopia

V

va [va] vb voir **aller**

vacance [vakãs] nf (Admin) vacancy; **vacances** nfpl holiday(s) pl (Brit), vacation sg (US); **les grandes ~s** the summer holidays ou vacation; **prendre des/ses ~s** to take a holiday ou vacation/one's holiday(s) ou vacation; **aller en ~s** to go on holiday ou vacation

vacancier, -ière [vakãsje, -jɛʀ] nm/f holidaymaker (Brit), vacationer (US)

vacant, e [vakã, -ãt] adj vacant

vacarme [vakaʀm] nm row, din

vaccin [vaksɛ̃] nm vaccine; (opération) vaccination

vaccination [vaksinasjɔ̃] nf vaccination

vacciner [vaksine] vt to vaccinate; (fig) to make immune; **être vacciné** (fig) to be immune

vache [vaʃ] nf (Zool) cow; (cuir) cowhide ▷ adj (fam) rotten, mean; **~ à eau** (canvas) water bag; **(manger de la) ~ enragée** (to go through) hard times; **~ à lait** (péj) mug, sucker; **~ laitière** dairy cow; **période des ~s maigres** lean times pl, lean period

vachement [vaʃmã] adv (fam) damned, really

vacherie [vaʃʀi] nf (fam) meanness no pl; (action) dirty trick; (propos) nasty remark

vaciller [vasije] vi to sway, wobble; (bougie, lumière) to flicker; (fig) to be failing, falter; **~ dans ses réponses** to falter in one's replies; **~ dans ses résolutions** to waver in one's resolutions

v

va-et-vient [vaevjɛ̃] *nm inv* (*de pièce mobile*) to and fro (*ou* up and down) movement; (*de personnes, véhicules*) comings and goings *pl*, to-ings and fro-ings *pl*; (*Élec*) two-way switch

vagabond, e [vagabɔ̃, -ɔ̃d] *adj* wandering; (*imagination*) roaming, roving ▷ *nm* (*rôdeur*) tramp, vagrant; (*voyageur*) wanderer

vagabonder [vagabɔ̃de] *vi* to roam, wander

vagin [vaʒɛ̃] *nm* vagina

vague [vag] *nf* wave ▷ *adj* vague; (*regard*) faraway; (*manteau, robe*) loose(-fitting); (*quelconque*): **un ~ bureau/cousin** some office/cousin or other ▷ *nm*: **être dans le ~** to be rather in the dark; **rester dans le ~** to keep things rather vague; **regarder dans le ~** to gaze into space; **~ à l'âme** *nm* vague melancholy; **~ d'assaut** *nf* (*Mil*) wave of assault; **~ de chaleur** *nf* heatwave; **~ de fond** *nf* ground swell; **~ de froid** *nf* cold spell

vaillant, e [vajɑ̃, -ɑ̃t] *adj* (*courageux*) brave, gallant; (*robuste*) vigorous, hale and hearty; **n'avoir plus un sou ~** to be penniless

vaille [vaj] *vb voir* **valoir**

vain, e [vɛ̃, vɛn] *adj* vain; **en ~** *adv* in vain

vaincre [vɛ̃kʀ] *vt* to defeat; (*fig*) to conquer, overcome

vaincu, e [vɛ̃ky] *pp de* **vaincre** ▷ *nm/f* defeated party

vainqueur [vɛ̃kœʀ] *nm* victor; (*Sport*) winner ▷ *adj m* victorious

vais [vɛ] *vb voir* **aller**

vaisseau, x [veso] *nm* (*Anat*) vessel; (*Navig*) ship, vessel; **~ spatial** spaceship

vaisselier [vesəlje] *nm* dresser

vaisselle [vesɛl] *nf* (*service*) crockery; (*plats etc à laver*) dishes *pl*; **faire la ~** to do the washing-up (*Brit*) *ou* the dishes

val [val] (*pl* **vaux** *ou* **vals**) *nm* valley

valable [valabl] *adj* valid; (*acceptable*) decent, worthwhile

valent *etc* [val] *vb voir* **valoir**

valet [valɛ] *nm* valet; (*péj*) lackey; (*Cartes*) jack, knave (*Brit*); **~ de chambre** manservant, valet; **~ de ferme** farmhand; **~ de pied** footman

valeur [valœʀ] *nf* (*gén*) value; (*mérite*) merit; (*Comm*: *titre*) security; **valeurs** *nfpl* (*morales*) values; **mettre en ~** (*bien*) to exploit; (*terrain, région*) to develop; (*fig*) to highlight; to show off to advantage; **avoir de la ~** to be valuable; **prendre de la ~** to go up *ou* gain in value; **sans ~** worthless; **~ absolue** absolute value; **~ d'échange** exchange value; **~ nominale** face value; **~s mobilières** transferable securities

valide [valid] *adj* (*en bonne santé*) fit, well; (*indemne*) able-bodied, fit; (*valable*) valid

valider [valide] *vt* to validate

valions *etc* [valjɔ̃] *vb voir* **valoir**

valise [valiz] *nf* (suit)case; **faire sa ~** to pack one's (suit)case; **la ~ (diplomatique)** the diplomatic bag

vallée [vale] *nf* valley

vallon [valɔ̃] *nm* small valley

vallonné, e [valɔne] *adj* undulating

valoir [valwaʀ] *vi* (*être valable*) to hold, apply ▷ *vt* (*prix, valeur, effort*) to be worth; (*causer*): **~ qch à qn** to earn sb sth; **se valoir** to be of equal merit; (*péj*) to be two of a kind; **faire ~** (*droits, prérogatives*) to assert; (*domaine, capitaux*) to exploit; **faire ~ que** to point out that; **se faire ~** to make the most of o.s.; **à ~ on** account; **à ~ sur** to be deducted from; **vaille que vaille** somehow or other; **cela ne me dit rien qui vaille** I don't like the look of it at all; **ce climat ne me vaut rien** this climate doesn't suit me; **~ la peine** to be worth the trouble, be worth it; **~ mieux: il vaut mieux se taire** it's better to say nothing; **il vaut mieux que je fasse/comme ceci** it's better if I do/like this; **ça ne vaut rien** it's worthless; **que vaut ce candidat?** how good is this applicant?

valse [vals] *nf* waltz; **c'est la ~ des étiquettes** the prices don't stay the same from one moment to the next

valu, e [valy] *pp de* **valoir**

vandalisme [vɑ̃dalism] *nm* vandalism

vanille [vanij] *nf* vanilla; **glace à la ~** vanilla ice cream

vanité [vanite] *nf* vanity

vaniteux, -euse [vanitø, -øz] *adj* vain, conceited

vanne [van] *nf* gate; (*fam*: *remarque*) dig, (nasty) crack; **lancer une ~ à qn** to have a go at sb (*Brit*), knock sb

vannerie [vanʀi] *nf* basketwork

vantard, e [vɑ̃taʀ, -aʀd] *adj* boastful

vanter [vɑ̃te] *vt* to speak highly of, praise; **se vanter** *vi* to boast, brag; **se ~ de** to pride o.s. on; (*péj*) to boast of

vapeur [vapœʀ] *nf* steam; (*émanation*) vapour (*Brit*), vapor (*US*), fumes *pl*; (*brouillard, buée*) haze; **vapeurs** *nfpl* (*bouffées*) vapours, vapors; **à ~** steam-powered, steam *cpd*; **à toute ~** full steam ahead; (*fig*) at full tilt; **renverser la ~** to reverse engines; (*fig*) to backtrack, backpedal; **cuit à la ~** steamed

vaporeux, -euse [vapoʀø, -øz] *adj* (*flou*) hazy, misty; (*léger*) filmy, gossamer *cpd*

vaporisateur [vapoʀizatœʀ] *nm* spray

vaporiser [vapoʀize] *vt* (*Chimie*) to vaporize; (*parfum etc*) to spray

varappe [vaʀap] *nf* rock climbing

vareuse [vaʀøz] *nf* (*blouson*) pea jacket; (*d'uniforme*) tunic

variable [vaʀjabl] *adj* variable; (*temps, humeur*) changeable; (*Tech*: *à plusieurs positions etc*) adaptable; (*Ling*) inflectional; (*divers*: *résultats*) varied, various ▷ *nf* (*Inform, Math*) variable

varice [vaʀis] *nf* varicose vein

varicelle [vaʀisɛl] *nf* chickenpox

varié, e [vaʀje] *adj* varied; (*divers*) various; **hors-d'œuvre ~s** selection of hors d'œuvres

varier [varje] vi to vary; (temps, humeur) to change ▷ vt to vary

variété [varjete] nf variety; **spectacle de ~s** variety show

variole [varjɔl] nf smallpox

Varsovie [varsɔvi] n Warsaw

vas [va] vb voir **aller**; **~-y!** [vazi] go on!

vase [vaz] nm vase ▷ nf silt, mud; **en ~ clos** in isolation; **~ de nuit** chamberpot; **~s communicants** communicating vessels

vaseux, -euse [vazø, -øz] adj silty, muddy; (fig: confus) woolly, hazy; (: fatigué) peaky; (: étourdi) woozy

vasistas [vazistas] nm fanlight

vaste [vast] adj vast, immense

vaudrai etc [vodʀe] vb voir **valoir**

vaurien, ne [vɔʀjɛ̃, -ɛn] nm/f good-for-nothing, guttersnipe

vaut [vo] vb voir **valoir**

vautour [votuʀ] nm vulture

vautrer [votʀe]: **se vautrer** vi: **se ~ dans** to wallow in; **se ~ sur** to sprawl on

vaux [vo] pl de **val** ▷ vb voir **valoir**

va-vite [vavit]: **à la ~** adv in a rush

VDQS sigle m (= vin délimité de qualité supérieure) label guaranteeing quality of wine

veau, x [vo] nm (Zool) calf; (Culin) veal; (peau) calfskin; **tuer le ~ gras** to kill the fatted calf

vécu, e [veky] pp de **vivre** ▷ adj real(-life)

vedette [vədɛt] nf (artiste etc) star; (canot) patrol boat; (police) launch; **avoir la ~** to top the bill, get star billing; **mettre qn en ~** (Ciné etc) to give sb the starring role; (fig) to push sb into the limelight; **voler la ~ à qn** to steal the show from sb

végétal, e, -aux [veʒetal, -o] adj vegetable ▷ nm vegetable, plant

végétalien, ne [veʒetaljɛ̃, -ɛn] adj, nm/f vegan

végétarien, ne [veʒetaʀjɛ̃, -ɛn] adj, nm/f vegetarian

végétation [veʒetasjɔ̃] nf vegetation; **végétations** nfpl (Méd) adenoids

véhicule [veikyl] nm vehicle; **~ utilitaire** commercial vehicle

veille [vɛj] nf (garde) watch; (Psych) wakefulness; (jour): **la ~** the day before, the previous day; **la ~ au soir** the previous evening; **la ~ de** the day before; **la ~ de Noël** Christmas Eve; **la ~ du jour de l'An** New Year's Eve; **à la ~ de** on the eve of; **l'état de ~** the waking state

veillée [veje] nf (soirée) evening; (réunion) evening gathering; **~ d'armes** night before combat; (fig) vigil; **~ (funèbre)** wake; **~ (mortuaire)** watch

veiller [veje] vi (rester debout) to stay ou sit up; (ne pas dormir) to be awake; (être de garde) to be on watch; (être vigilant) to be watchful ▷ vt (malade, mort) to watch over, sit up with; **à** vt to attend to, see to; **~ à ce que** to make sure that, see to it that; **~ sur** vt to keep a watch ou an eye on

veilleur [vɛjœʀ] nm: **~ de nuit** night watchman

veilleuse [vɛjøz] nf (lampe) night light; (Auto) sidelight; (flamme) pilot light; **en ~** adj (lampe) dimmed; (fig: affaire) shelved, set aside

veinard, e [venaʀ, -aʀd] nm/f (fam) lucky devil

veine [vɛn] nf (Anat, du bois etc) vein; (filon) vein, seam; (fam: chance): **avoir de la ~** to be lucky; (inspiration) inspiration

véliplanchiste [veliplɑ̃ʃist] nm/f windsurfer

vélo [velo] nm bike, cycle; **faire du ~** to go cycling

vélomoteur [velomotœʀ] nm moped

velours [v(ə)luʀ] nm velvet; **~ côtelé** corduroy

velouté, e [vəlute] adj (au toucher) velvety; (à la vue) soft, mellow; (au goût) smooth, mellow ▷ nm: **~ d'asperges/de tomates** cream of asparagus/tomato soup

velu, e [vəly] adj hairy

venais etc [vənɛ] vb voir **venir**

venaison [vənɛzɔ̃] nf venison

vendange [vɑ̃dɑ̃ʒ] nf (opération, période: aussi: **~s**) grape harvest; (raisins) grape crop, grapes pl

vendanger [vɑ̃dɑ̃ʒe] vi to harvest the grapes

vendeur, -euse [vɑ̃dœʀ, -øz] nm/f (de magasin) shop ou sales assistant (Brit), sales clerk (US); (Comm) salesman/woman ▷ nm (Jur) vendor, seller; **~ de journaux** newspaper seller

vendre [vɑ̃dʀ] vt to sell; **~ qch à qn** to sell sb sth; **cela se vend à la douzaine** these are sold by the dozen; **"à ~"** "for sale"

vendredi [vɑ̃dʀədi] nm Friday; **V~ saint** Good Friday; voir aussi **lundi**

vénéneux, -euse [venenø, -øz] adj poisonous

vénérien, ne [venerjɛ̃, -ɛn] adj venereal

vengeance [vɑ̃ʒɑ̃s] nf vengeance no pl, revenge no pl; (acte) act of vengeance ou revenge

venger [vɑ̃ʒe] vt to avenge; **se venger** vi to avenge o.s.; (par rancune) to take revenge; **se ~ de qch** to avenge o.s. for sth; to take one's revenge for sth; **se ~ de qn** to take revenge on sb; **se ~ sur** to wreak vengeance upon; to take revenge on ou through; to take it out on

venimeux, -euse [vənimø, -øz] adj poisonous, venomous; (fig: haineux) venomous, vicious

venin [vənɛ̃] nm venom, poison; (fig) venom

venir [v(ə)niʀ] vi to come; **~ de** to come from; **~ de faire: je viens d'y aller/de le voir** I've just been there/seen him; **s'il vient à pleuvoir** if it should rain, if it happens to rain; **~ à faire: j'en viens à croire que** I am coming to believe that; **où veux-tu en ~?** what are you getting at?; **il en est venu à mendier** he has been reduced to begging; **en ~ aux mains** to come to blows; **les années/**

générations à ~ the years/generations to come; **il me vient une idée** an idea has just occurred to me; **il me vient des soupçons** I'm beginning to be suspicious; **je te vois ~** I know what you're after; **faire ~** (*docteur, plombier*) to call (out); **d'où vient que ...?** how is it that ...?; **~ au monde** to come into the world

vent [vɑ̃] *nm* wind; **il y a du ~** it's windy; **c'est du ~** it's all hot air; **au ~** to windward; **sous le ~** to leeward; **avoir le ~ debout/ arrière** to head into the wind/have the wind astern; **dans le ~** (*fam*) trendy; **prendre le ~** (*fig*) to see which way the wind blows; **avoir ~ de** to get wind of; **contre ~s et marées** come hell or high water

vente [vɑ̃t] *nf* sale; **la ~** (*activité*) selling; (*secteur*) sales *pl*; **mettre en ~** to put on sale; (*objets personnels*) to put up for sale; **~ aux enchères** auction sale; **~ de charité** jumble (*Brit*) *ou* rummage (*US*) sale; **~ par correspondance (VPC)** mail-order selling

venteux, -euse [vɑ̃tø, -øz] *adj* windswept, windy

ventilateur [vɑ̃tilatœʀ] *nm* fan

ventiler [vɑ̃tile] *vt* to ventilate; (*total, statistiques*) to break down

ventouse [vɑ̃tuz] *nf* (*ampoule*) cupping glass; (*de caoutchouc*) suction pad; (*Zool*) sucker

ventre [vɑ̃tʀ] *nm* (*Anat*) stomach; (*fig*) belly; **prendre du ~** to be getting a paunch; **avoir mal au ~** to have (a) stomach ache

ventriloque [vɑ̃tʀilɔk] *nm/f* ventriloquist

venu, e [v(ə)ny] *pp de* venir ▷ *adj*: **être mal ~ à** *ou* **de faire** to have no grounds for doing, be in no position to do; **mal ~** ill-timed, unwelcome; **bien ~** timely, welcome ▷ *nf* coming

ver [vɛʀ] *nm* worm; (*des fruits etc*) maggot; (*du bois*) woodworm *no pl*; **~ blanc** May beetle grub; **~ luisant** glow-worm; **~ à soie** silkworm; **~ solitaire** tapeworm; **~ de terre** earthworm

verbaliser [vɛʀbalize] *vi* (*Police*) to book *ou* report an offender; (*Psych*) to verbalize

verbe [vɛʀb] *nm* (*Ling*) verb; (*voix*): **avoir le ~ sonore** to have a sonorous tone (of voice); (*expression*): **la magie du ~** the magic of language *ou* the Word; (*Rel*): **le V~** the Word

verdâtre [vɛʀdɑtʀ] *adj* greenish

verdict [vɛʀdik(t)] *nm* verdict

verdir [vɛʀdiʀ] *vi, vt* to turn green

verdure [vɛʀdyʀ] *nf* (*arbres, feuillages*) greenery; (*légumes verts*) green vegetables *pl*, greens *pl*

véreux, -euse [veʀø, -øz] *adj* worm-eaten; (*malhonnête*) shady, corrupt

verge [vɛʀʒ] *nf* (*Anat*) penis; (*baguette*) stick, cane

verger [vɛʀʒe] *nm* orchard

verglacé, e [vɛʀglase] *adj* icy, iced-over

verglas [vɛʀglɑ] *nm* (black) ice

vergogne [vɛʀgɔɲ]: **sans ~** *adv* shamelessly

véridique [veʀidik] *adj* truthful

vérification [veʀifikasjɔ̃] *nf* checking *no pl*, check; **~ d'identité** identity check

vérifier [veʀifje] *vt* to check; (*corroborer*) to confirm, bear out; **se vérifier** *vi* to be confirmed *ou* verified

véritable [veʀitabl] *adj* real; (*ami, amour*) true; **un ~ désastre** an absolute disaster

vérité [veʀite] *nf* truth; (*d'un portrait*) lifelikeness; (*sincérité*) truthfulness, sincerity; **en ~, à la ~** to tell the truth

verlan [vɛʀlɑ̃] *nm* (back) slang; *see note*

● **VERLAN**
●
● *Verlan* is a form of slang popularized in
● the 1950's. It consists of inverting a
● word's syllables, the term *verlan* itself
● coming from "l'envers" ("à l'envers" =
● back to front). Typical examples are
● "féca" ("café"), "ripou" ("pourri"),
● "meuf" ("femme"), and "beur" ("Arabe").

---

vermeil, le [vɛʀmɛj] *adj* bright red, ruby red ▷ *nm* (*substance*) vermeil

vermine [vɛʀmin] *nf* vermin *pl*

vermoulu, e [vɛʀmuly] *adj* worm-eaten, with woodworm

verni, e [vɛʀni] *adj* varnished; glazed; (*fam*) lucky; **cuir ~** patent leather; **souliers ~s** patent (leather) shoes

vernir [vɛʀniʀ] *vt* (*bois, tableau, ongles*) to varnish; (*poterie*) to glaze

vernis [vɛʀni] *nm* (*enduit*) varnish; glaze; (*fig*) veneer; **~ à ongles** nail varnish (*Brit*) *ou* polish

vernissage [vɛʀnisaʒ] *nm* varnishing; glazing; (*d'une exposition*) preview

vérole [veʀɔl] *nf* (*variole*) smallpox; (*fam: syphilis*) pox

verrai *etc* [veʀe] *vb voir* **voir**

verre [vɛʀ] *nm* glass; (*de lunettes*) lens *sg*; **verres** *nmpl* (*lunettes*) glasses; **boire** *ou* **prendre un ~** to have a drink; **~ à vin/à liqueur** wine/liqueur glass; **~ à dents** tooth mug; **~ dépoli** frosted glass; **~ de lampe** lamp glass *ou* chimney; **~ de montre** watch glass; **~ à pied** stemmed glass; **~s de contact** contact lenses; **~s fumés** tinted lenses

verrerie [vɛʀʀi] *nf* (*fabrique*) glassworks *sg*; (*activité*) glass-making, glass-working; (*objets*) glassware

verrière [vɛʀjɛʀ] *nf* (*grand vitrage*) window; (*toit vitré*) glass roof

verrons *etc* [vɛʀɔ̃] *vb voir* **voir**

verrou [vɛʀu] *nm* (*targette*) bolt; (*fig*) constriction; **mettre le ~** to bolt the door; **mettre qn sous les ~s** to put sb behind bars

verrouillage [vɛʀujaʒ] *nm* (*dispositif*) locking mechanism; (*Auto*): **~ central** *ou* **centralisé** central locking

verrouiller [veʀuje] vt to bolt; to lock; (*Mil: brèche*) to close

verrue [veʀy] nf wart; (*plantaire*) verruca; (*fig*) eyesore

vers [veʀ] nm line ▷ nmpl (*poésie*) verse sg ▷ prép (*en direction de*) toward(s); (*près de*) around (about); (*temporel*) about, around

versant [veʀsɑ̃] nm slopes pl, side

versatile [veʀsatil] adj fickle, changeable

verse [veʀs]: **à ~** adv: **il pleut à ~** it's pouring (with rain)

Verseau [veʀso] nm: **le ~** Aquarius, the water-carrier; **être du ~** to be Aquarius

versement [veʀsəmɑ̃] nm payment; (*sur un compte*) deposit, remittance; **en trois ~s** in three instalments

verser [veʀse] vt (*liquide, grains*) to pour; (*larmes, sang*) to shed; (*argent*) to pay; (*soldat: affecter*): **~ qn dans** to assign sb to ▷ vi (*véhicule*) to overturn; (*fig*): **~ dans** to lapse into; **~ sur un compte** to pay into an account

verset [veʀse] nm verse; versicle

version [veʀsjɔ̃] nf version; (*Scol*) translation (*into the mother tongue*); **film en ~ originale** film in the original language

verso [veʀso] nm back; **voir au ~** see over(leaf)

vert, e [veʀ, veʀt] adj green; (*vin*) young; (*vigoureux*) sprightly; (*cru*) forthright ▷ nm green; **dire des ~es (et des pas mûres)** to say some pretty spicy things; **il en a vu des ~es** to've seen a thing or two; **~ bouteille** adj inv bottle-green; **~ d'eau** adj inv sea-green; **~ pomme** adj inv apple-green; **les V~s** (*Pol*) the Greens

vertèbre [veʀtɛbʀ] nf vertebra

vertement [veʀtəmɑ̃] adv (*réprimander*) sharply

vertical, e, -aux [veʀtikal, -o] adj, nf vertical; **à la ~e** adv vertically

verticalement [veʀtikalmɑ̃] adv vertically

vertige [veʀtiʒ] nm (*peur du vide*) vertigo; (*étourdissement*) dizzy spell; (*fig*) fever; **ça me donne le ~** it makes me dizzy; (*fig*) it makes my head spin ou reel

vertigineux, -euse [veʀtiʒinø, -øz] adj (*hausse, vitesse*) breathtaking; (*altitude, gorge*) breathtakingly high (*ou deep*)

vertu [veʀty] nf virtue; **une ~** a saint, a paragon of virtue; **avoir la ~ de faire** to have the virtue of doing; **en ~ de** prép in accordance with

vertueux, -euse [veʀtɥø, -øz] adj virtuous

verve [veʀv] nf witty eloquence; **être en ~** to be in brilliant form

verveine [veʀvɛn] nf (*Bot*) verbena, vervain; (*infusion*) verbena tea

vésicule [vezikyl] nf vesicle; **~ biliaire** gall-bladder

vessie [vesi] nf bladder

veste [vɛst] nf jacket; **~ droite/croisée** single-/double-breasted jacket; **retourner sa ~** (*fig*) to change one's colours

vestiaire [vɛstjɛʀ] nm (*au théâtre etc*) cloakroom; (*de stade etc*) changing-room (*Brit*), locker-room (*US*); (*métallique*): **(armoire) ~** locker

vestibule [vɛstibyl] nm hall

vestige [vɛstiʒ] nm (*objet*) relic; (*fragment*) trace; (*fig*) remnant, vestige; **vestiges** nmpl (*d'une ville*) remains; (*d'une civilisation, du passé*) remnants, relics

vestimentaire [vɛstimɑ̃tɛʀ] adj (*dépenses*) clothing; (*détail*) of dress; (*élégance*) sartorial; **dépenses ~s** clothing expenditure

veston [vɛstɔ̃] nm jacket

vêtement [vɛtmɑ̃] nm garment, item of clothing; (*Comm*): **le ~** the clothing industry; **vêtements** nmpl clothes; **~s de sport** sportswear sg, sports clothes

vétérinaire [veteʀinɛʀ] adj veterinary ▷ nm/f vet, veterinary surgeon (*Brit*), veterinarian (*US*)

vêtir [vetiʀ] vt to clothe, dress; **se vêtir** to dress (o.s.)

veto [veto] nm veto; **droit de ~** right of veto; **mettre** ou **opposer un ~ à** to veto

vêtu, e [vety] pp de **vêtir** ▷ adj: **~ de** dressed in, wearing; **chaudement ~** warmly dressed

vétuste [vetyst] adj ancient, timeworn

veuf, veuve [vœf, vœv] adj widowed ▷ nm widower ▷ nf widow

veuille [vœj], **veuillez** etc [vœje] vb voir **vouloir**

veule [vøl] adj spineless

veuve [vœv] adj f, nf voir **veuf**

veux [vø] vb voir **vouloir**

vexant, e [vɛksɑ̃, -ɑ̃t] adj (*contrariant*) annoying; (*blessant*) upsetting

vexation [vɛksasjɔ̃] nf humiliation

vexations [vɛksasjɔ̃] nfpl humiliations

vexer [vɛkse] vt to hurt, upset; **se vexer** vi to be offended, get upset

viable [vjabl] adj viable; (*économie, industrie etc*) sustainable

viaduc [vjadyk] nm viaduct

viager, -ère [vjaʒe, -ɛʀ] adj: **rente viagère** life annuity ▷ nm: **mettre en ~** to sell in return for a life annuity

viande [vjɑ̃d] nf meat; **je ne mange pas de ~** I don't eat meat

vibrer [vibʀe] vi to vibrate; (*son, voix*) to be vibrant; (*fig*) to be stirred; **faire ~** to (cause to) vibrate; to stir, thrill

vice [vis] nm vice; (*défaut*) fault; **~ caché** (*Comm*) latent ou inherent defect; **~ de forme** legal flaw ou irregularity

vichy [viʃi] nm (*toile*) gingham; (*eau*) Vichy water; **carottes V~** boiled carrots

vicié, e [visje] adj (*air*) polluted, tainted; (*Jur*) invalidated

vicieux, -euse [visjø, -øz] adj (*pervers*) dirty(-minded); (*méchant*) nasty; (*fautif*) incorrect, wrong ▷ nm/f lecher

vicinal, e, -aux [visinal, -o] adj: **chemin ~** byroad, byway

v

victime [viktim] *nf* victim; (*d'accident*) casualty; **être (la) ~ de** to be the victim of; **être ~ d'une attaque/d'un accident** to suffer a stroke/be involved in an accident
victoire [viktwar] *nf* victory
victuailles [viktчaj] *nfpl* provisions
vidange [vidɑ̃ʒ] *nf* (*d'un fossé, réservoir*) emptying; (*Auto*) oil change; (*de lavabo: bonde*) waste outlet; **vidanges** *nfpl* (*matières*) sewage *sg*; **faire la ~** (*Auto*) to change the oil, do an oil change; **tuyau de ~** drainage pipe
vidanger [vidɑ̃ʒe] *vt* to empty; **faire ~ la voiture** to have the oil changed in one's car
vide [vid] *adj* empty ⊳ *nm* (*Physique*) vacuum; (*espace*) (empty) space, gap; (*sous soi: dans une falaise etc*) drop; (*futilité, néant*) void; **~ de** empty of; (*de sens etc*) devoid of; **sous ~** *adv* in a vacuum; **emballé sous ~** vacuum-packed; **regarder dans le ~** to stare into space; **avoir peur du ~** to be afraid of heights; **parler dans le ~** to waste one's breath; **faire le ~** (*dans son esprit*) to make one's mind go blank; **faire le ~ autour de qn** to isolate sb; **emballé sous ~** vacuum packed; **à ~** *adv* (*sans occupants*) empty; (*sans charge*) unladen; (*Tech*) without gripping ou being in gear
vidéo [video] *nf, adj inv* video; **cassette ~** video cassette; **~ inverse** reverse video
vidéoclip [videoklip] *nm* music video
vidéoclub [videoklœb] *nm* video club
vidéoconférence [videokɔ̃f] *nf* videoconference
vide-ordures [vidɔʀdyʀ] *nm inv* (rubbish) chute
vidéothèque [videotek] *nf* video library
vide-poches [vidpɔʃ] *nm inv* tidy; (*Auto*) glove compartment
vider [vide] *vt* to empty; (*Culin: volaille, poisson*) to gut, clean out; (*régler: querelle*) to settle; (*fatiguer*) to wear out; (*fam: expulser*) to throw out, chuck out; **se vider** *vi* to empty; **~ les lieux** to quit ou vacate the premises
videur [vidœr] *nm* (*de boîte de nuit*) bouncer
vie [vi] *nf* life; **être en ~** to be alive; **sans ~** lifeless; **à ~** for life; **membre à ~** life member; **dans la ~ courante** in everyday life; **avoir la ~ dure** to have nine lives; to die hard; **mener la ~ dure à qn** to make life a misery for sb; **que faites-vous dans la ~?** what do you do?
vieil [vjɛj] *adj m voir* **vieux**
vieillard [vjɛjaʀ] *nm* old man; **les ~s** old people, the elderly
vieille [vjɛj] *adj f, nf voir* **vieux**
vieilleries [vjɛjʀi] *nfpl* old things ou stuff *sg*
vieillesse [vjɛjɛs] *nf* old age; (*vieillards*): **la ~** the old *pl*, the elderly *pl*
vieillir [vjejiʀ] *vi* (*prendre de l'âge*) to grow old; (*population, vin*) to age; (*doctrine, auteur*) to become dated ⊳ *vt* to age; **il a beaucoup vieilli** he has aged a lot; **se vieillir** to make o.s. older
vieillissement [vjejismɑ̃] *nm* growing old; ageing

Vienne [vjɛn] *n* (*en Autriche*) Vienna
vienne [vjɛn], **viens** *etc* [vjɛ̃] *vb voir* **venir**
viens [vjɛ̃] *vb voir* **venir**
vierge [vjɛʀʒ] *adj* virgin; (*film*) blank; (*page*) clean, blank; (*jeune fille*): **être ~** to be a virgin ⊳ *nf* virgin; (*signe*): **la V~** Virgo, the Virgin; **être de la V~** to be Virgo; **~ de** (*sans*) free from, unsullied by
Viêtnam, Vietnam [vjetnam] *nm*: **le ~** Vietnam; **le ~ du Nord/du Sud** North/South Vietnam
vietnamien, ne [vjɛtnamjɛ̃, -ɛn] *adj* Vietnamese ⊳ *nm* (*Ling*) Vietnamese ⊳ *nm/f*: **V~, ne** Vietnamese; **V~, ne du Nord/Sud** North/South Vietnamese
vieux, vieil, vieille [vjø, vjɛj] *adj* old ⊳ *nm/f* old man/woman ⊳ *nmpl*: **les ~** old people; (*fam: parents*) the old folk ou ones; **un petit ~** a little old man; **mon ~/ma vieille** (*fam*) old man/girl; **pauvre ~** poor old soul; **prendre un coup de ~** to put years on; **se faire ~** to make o.s. look older; **un ~ de la vieille** one of the old brigade; **~ garçon** *nm* bachelor; **~ jeu** *adj inv* old-fashioned; **~ rose** *adj inv* old rose; **vieil or** *adj inv* old gold; **vieille fille** *nf* spinster (*péj*)
vif, vive [vif, viv] *adj* (*animé*) lively; (*alerte*) sharp, quick; (*brusque*) sharp, brusque; (*aigu*) sharp; (*lumière, couleur*) brilliant; (*air*) crisp; (*vent, émotion*) keen; (*froid*) bitter; (*fort: regret, déception*) great, deep; (*vivant*): **brûlé ~** burnt alive; **eau vive** running water; **de vive voix** personally; **avoir l'esprit ~** to be quick-witted; **piquer qn au ~** to cut sb to the quick; **tailler dans le ~** to cut into the living flesh; **à ~** (*plaie*) open; **avoir les nerfs à ~** to be on edge; **sur le ~** (*Art*) from life; **entrer dans le ~ du sujet** to get to the very heart of the matter
vigne [viɲ] *nf* (*plante*) vine; (*plantation*) vineyard; **~ vierge** Virginia creeper
vigneron [viɲʀɔ̃] *nm* wine grower
vignette [viɲɛt] *nf* (*motif*) vignette; (*de marque*) manufacturer's label ou seal; (*petite illustration*) (small) illustration; (*Admin*) ≈ (road) tax disc (Brit), ≈ license plate sticker (US); (*: sur médicament*) price label (*on medicines for reimbursement by Social Security*)
vignoble [viɲɔbl] *nm* (*plantation*) vineyard; (*vignes d'une région*) vineyards *pl*
vigoureux, -euse [viguʀø, -øz] *adj* vigorous, robust
vigueur [vigœr] *nf* vigour (Brit), vigor (US); **être/entrer en ~** to be in/come into force; **en ~** current
vil, e [vil] *adj* vile, base; **à ~ prix** at a very low price
vilain, e [vilɛ̃, -ɛn] *adj* (*laid*) ugly; (*affaire, blessure*) nasty; (*pas sage: enfant*) naughty ⊳ *nm* (*paysan*) villein, villain; **ça va tourner au ~** things are going to turn nasty; **~ mot** bad word

villa [vila] *nf* (detached) house; **~ en
multipropriété** time-share villa
village [vilaʒ] *nm* village; **~ de toile** tent
village; **~ de vacances** holiday village
villageois, e [vilaʒwa, -waz] *adj* village *cpd*
▷ *nm/f* villager
ville [vil] *nf* town; (*importante*) city;
(*administration*): **la ~** ≈ the Corporation, ≈ the
(town) council; **aller en ~** to go to town;
habiter en ~ to live in town; **~ jumelée** twin
town; **~ d'eaux** spa; **~ nouvelle** new town
villégiature [vileʒjatyʀ] *nf* (*séjour*) holiday;
(*lieu*) (holiday) resort
vin [vɛ̃] *nm* wine; **avoir le ~ gai/triste** to get
happy/miserable after a few drinks; **~ blanc/
rosé/rouge** white/rosé/red wine; **~
d'honneur** reception (*with wine and snacks*);
~ de messe altar wine; **~ ordinaire** *ou* **de
table** table wine; **~ de pays** local wine; *voir
aussi* **AOC**; **VDQS**
vinaigre [vinɛgʀ] *nm* vinegar; **tourner au ~**
(*fig*) to turn sour; **~ de vin/d'alcool** wine/
spirit vinegar
vinaigrette [vinɛgʀɛt] *nf* vinaigrette,
French dressing
vindicatif, -ive [vɛ̃dikatif, -iv] *adj* vindictive
vineux, -euse [vinø, -øz] *adj* win(e)y
vingt [vɛ̃, vɛ̃t] (*2nd pron used when followed by
a vowel*) *num* twenty; **~-quatre heures sur
~-quatre** twenty-four hours a day, round
the clock
vingtaine [vɛ̃tɛn] *nf*: **une ~ (de)** around
twenty, twenty or so
vingtième [vɛ̃tjɛm] *num* twentieth
vinicole [vinikɔl] *adj* (*production*) wine *cpd*;
(*région*) wine-growing
vins *etc* [vɛ̃] *vb voir* **venir**
vinyle [vinil] *nm* vinyl
viol [vjɔl] *nm* (*d'une femme*) rape; (*d'un lieu sacré*)
violation
violacé, e [vjɔlase] *adj* purplish, mauvish
violemment [vjɔlamɑ̃] *adv* violently
violence [vjɔlɑ̃s] *nf* violence; **violences** *nfpl*
acts of violence; **faire ~ à qn** to do violence to
sb; **se faire ~** to force o.s
violent, e [vjɔlɑ̃, -ɑ̃t] *adj* violent; (*remède*)
drastic; (*besoin, désir*) intense, urgent
violer [vjɔle] *vt* (*femme*) to rape; (*sépulture*) to
desecrate, violate; (*loi, traité*) to violate
violet, te [vjɔlɛ, -ɛt] *adj, nm* purple, mauve
▷ *nf* (*fleur*) violet
violon [vjɔlɔ̃] *nm* violin; (*dans la musique folklorique
etc*) fiddle; (*fam: prison*) lock-up; **premier ~**
first violin; **~ d'Ingres** (artistic) hobby
violoncelle [vjɔlɔ̃sɛl] *nm* cello
violoniste [vjɔlɔnist] *nm/f* violinist, violin-
player; (*folklorique etc*) fiddler
vipère [vipɛʀ] *nf* viper, adder
virage [viʀaʒ] *nm* (*d'un véhicule*) turn; (*d'une
route, piste*) bend; (*Chimie*) change in colour
(Brit) *ou* color (US); (*de cuti-réaction*) positive
reaction; (*Photo*) toning; (*fig: Pol*) about-turn;

prendre un ~ to go into a bend, take a bend;
~ sans visibilité blind bend
viral, e, -aux [viʀal, -o] *adj* (*aussi Inform*) viral
virée [viʀe] *nf* (*courte*) walk; (: *à pied*) walk,
(*longue*) trip; hike, walking tour
virement [viʀmɑ̃] *nm* (*Comm*) transfer;
~ bancaire (bank) credit transfer, ≈ (bank)
giro transfer (Brit); **~ postal** Post office credit
transfer, ≈ Girobank® transfer (Brit)
virent [viʀ] *vb voir* **voir**
virer [viʀe] *vt* (*Comm*): **~ qch (sur)** to transfer
sth (into); (*Photo*) to tone; (*fam: renvoyer*) to
sack, boot out ▷ *vi* to turn; (*Chimie*) to change
colour (Brit) *ou* color (US); (*cuti-réaction*) to
come up positive; (*Photo*) to tone; **~ au bleu**
to turn blue; **~ de bord** to tack; (*fig*) to change
tack; **~ sur l'aile** to bank
virevolter [viʀvɔlte] *vi* to twirl around
virgule [viʀgyl] *nf* comma; (*Math*) point;
quatre ~ deux four point two; **~ flottante**
floating decimal
viril, e [viʀil] *adj* (*propre à l'homme*) masculine;
(*énergique, courageux*) manly, virile
virtuel, le [viʀtɥɛl] *adj* potential; (*théorique*)
virtual
virtuose [viʀtɥoz] *nm/f* (*Mus*) virtuoso; (*gén*)
master
virus [viʀys] *nm* virus
vis *vb* [vi] *voir* **voir**; **vivre** ▷ *nf* [vis] screw; **~ à
tête plate/ronde** flat-headed/round-headed
screw; **~ platinées** (*Auto*) (contact) points;
~ sans fin worm, endless screw
visa [viza] *nm* (*sceau*) stamp; (*validation de
passeport*) visa; **~ de censure** (censor's)
certificate
visage [vizaʒ] *nm* face; **à ~ découvert**
(*franchement*) openly
vis-à-vis [vizavi] *adv* face to face ▷ *nm* person
opposite; house *etc* opposite; **~ de** *prép*
opposite; (*fig*) towards, vis-à-vis; **en ~** facing
ou opposite each other; **sans ~** (*immeuble*) with
an open outlook
viscéral, e, -aux [viseʀal, -o] *adj* (*fig*) deep-
seated, deep-rooted
visée [vize] *nf* (*avec une arme*) aiming; (*Arpentage*)
sighting; **visées** *nfpl* (*intentions*) designs; **avoir
des ~s sur qn/qch** to have designs on sb/sth
viser [vize] *vi* to aim ▷ *vt* to aim at; (*concerner*)
to be aimed *ou* directed at; (*apposer un visa sur*)
to stamp, visa; **~ à qch/faire** to aim at sth/at
doing *ou* to do
viseur [vizœʀ] *nm* (*d'arme*) sights *pl*; (*Photo*)
viewfinder
visibilité [vizibilite] *nf* visibility; **sans ~**
(*pilotage, virage*) blind *cpd*
visible [vizibl] *adj* visible; (*disponible*): **est-il ~?**
can he see me?, will he see visitors?
visière [vizjɛʀ] *nf* (*de casquette*) peak; (*qui
s'attache*) eyeshade
vision [vizjɔ̃] *nf* vision; (*sens*) (eye)sight,
vision; (*fait de voir*): **la ~ de** the sight of;
première ~ (*Ciné*) first showing

V

visionneuse [vizjɔnøz] nf viewer
visiophone [vizjɔfɔn] nm videophone
visite [vizit] nf visit; (*visiteur*) visitor; (*touristique: d'un musée etc*) tour; (*Comm: de représentant*) call; (*expertise, d'inspection*) inspection; (*médicale, à domicile*) visit, call; ~ **médicale** medical examination; (*Mil: d'entrée*) medicals pl; (: *quotidienne*) sick parade; ~ **accompagnée** ou **guidée** guided tour; **faire une ~ à qn** to call on sb, pay sb a visit; **rendre ~ à qn** to visit sb, pay sb a visit; **être en ~ (chez qn)** to be visiting (sb); **avoir de la ~** to have visitors; **heures de ~** (*hôpital, prison*) visiting hours; **le droit de ~** (*Jur: aux enfants*) right of access, access; ~ **de douane** customs inspection ou examination; ~ **guidée** guided tour
visiter [vizite] vt to visit; (*musée, ville*) to visit, go round
visiteur, -euse [vizitœR, -øz] nm/f visitor; ~ **des douanes** customs inspector; ~ **médical** medical rep(resentative); ~ **de prison** prison visitor
vison [vizɔ̃] nm mink
visser [vise] vt: ~ **qch** (*fixer, serrer*) to screw sth on
visuel, le [vizyɛl] adj visual
vit [vi] vb voir **vivre**; **voir**
vital, e, -aux [vital, -o] adj vital
vitamine [vitamin] nf vitamin
vite [vit] adv (*rapidement*) quickly, fast; (*sans délai*) quickly; soon; ~! quick!; **faire ~** (*agir rapidement*) to act fast; (*se dépêcher*) to be quick; **ce sera ~ fini** this will soon be finished; **viens ~** come quick(ly)
vitesse [vites] nf speed; (*Auto: dispositif*) gear; **faire de la ~** to drive fast ou at speed; **prendre qn de ~** to outstrip sb, get ahead of sb; **prendre de la ~** to pick up ou gather speed; **à toute ~** at full ou top speed; **en perte de ~** (*avion*) losing lift; (*fig*) losing momentum; **changer de ~** (*Auto*) to change gear; ~ **acquise** acquired momentum; ~ **de croisière** cruising speed; ~ **de pointe** top speed; ~ **du son** speed of sound; **en ~** quickly

LIMITE DE VITESSE

- The speed limit in France is 50 km/h in
- built-up areas, 90 km/h on main roads
- (80 km/h when it is raining), 110 km/h on
- 4-lane roads with central reservations,
- and 130 km/h on motorways (110 km/h
- when it is raining).

viticole [vitikɔl] adj (*industrie*) wine cpd; (*région*) wine-growing
viticulteur [vitikyltœR] nm wine grower
vitrage [vitRaʒ] nm (*cloison*) glass partition; (*toit*) glass roof; (*rideau*) net curtain; **double ~** double glazing
vitrail, -aux [vitRaj, -o] nm stained-glass window

vitre [vitR] nf (*window*) pane; (*de portière, voiture*) window
vitré, e [vitRe] adj glass cpd
vitrer [vitRe] vt to glaze
vitreux, -euse [vitRø, -øz] adj vitreous; (*terne*) glassy
vitrine [vitRin] nf (*devanture*) (shop) window; (*étalage*) display; (*petite armoire*) display cabinet; **en ~** in the window, on display; ~ **publicitaire** display case, showcase
vivable [vivabl] adj (*personne*) livable-with; (*maison*) fit to live in
vivace adj (*vivas*) (*arbre, plante*) hardy; (*fig*) enduring ▷ adv [vivatʃe] (*Mus*) vivace
vivacité [vivasite] nf (*voir vif*) liveliness, vivacity; sharpness; brilliance
vivant, e [vivɑ̃, -ɑ̃t] vb voir **vivre** ▷ adj (*qui vit*) living, alive; (*animé*) lively; (*preuve, exemple*) living; (*langue*) modern ▷ nm: **du ~ de qn** in sb's lifetime; **les ~s et les morts** the living and the dead
vive [viv] adj f voir **vif** ▷ vb voir **vivre** ▷ excl: ~ **le roi!** long live the king!; ~ **les vacances!** hurrah for the holidays!
vivement [vivmɑ̃] adv vivaciously; sharply ▷ excl: ~ **les vacances!** I can't wait for the holidays!, roll on the holidays!
vivier [vivje] nm (*au restaurant etc*) fish tank; (*étang*) fishpond
vivifiant, e [vivifjɑ̃, -ɑ̃t] adj invigorating
vivions [vivjɔ̃] vb voir **vivre**
vivoter [vivɔte] vi (*personne*) to scrape a living, get by; (*fig: affaire etc*) to struggle along
vivre [vivR] vi, vt to live ▷ nm: **le ~ et le logement** board and lodging; **vivres** nmpl provisions, food supplies; **il vit encore** he is still alive; **se laisser ~** to take life as it comes; **ne plus ~** (*être anxieux*) to live on one's nerves; **il a vécu** (*eu une vie aventureuse*) he has seen life; **ce régime a vécu** this regime has had its day; **être facile à ~** to be easy to get on with; **faire ~ qn** (*pourvoir à sa subsistance*) to provide (a living) for sb; ~ **mal** (*chichement*) to have a meagre existence; ~ **de** (*salaire etc*) to live on
vlan [vlɑ̃] excl wham!, bang!
VO sigle f (*Ciné: = version originale*): **voir un film en VO** to see a film in its original language
vocable [vɔkabl] nm term
vocabulaire [vɔkabylɛR] nm vocabulary
vocation [vɔkasjɔ̃] nf vocation, calling; **avoir la ~** to have a vocation
vociférer [vɔsifere] vi, vt to scream
vœu, x [vø] nm wish; (*à Dieu*) vow; **faire ~ de** to take a vow of; **avec tous nos ~x** with every good wish ou our best wishes; **meilleurs ~x** best wishes; (*sur une carte*) "Season's Greetings"; ~**x de bonheur** best wishes for your future happiness; ~**x de bonne année** best wishes for the New Year
vogue [vɔg] nf fashion, vogue; **en ~** in fashion, in vogue
voguer [vɔge] vi to sail

voici [vwasi] *prép* (*pour introduire, désigner*) here is; (+*sg*) here are; (+*pl*): **et ~ que ...** and now he (*ou* he) ...; **il est parti ~ trois ans** he left three years ago; **une semaine que je l'ai vue** it's a week since I've seen her; **me ~** here I am; *voir aussi* **voilà**

voie [vwa] *vb voir* ▷ *nf* way; (*Rail*) track, line; (*Auto*) lane; **par ~ buccale** *ou* **orale** orally; **par ~ rectale** rectally; **suivre la ~ hiérarchique** to go through official channels; **ouvrir/montrer la ~** to open up/ show the way; **être en bonne ~** to be shaping *ou* going well; **mettre qn sur la ~** to put sb on the right track; **être en ~ d'achèvement/de rénovation** to be nearing completion/in the process of renovation; **à ~ étroite** narrow-gauge; **à ~ unique** single-track; **route à deux/trois ~s** two-/three-lane road; **par la ~ aérienne/maritime** by air/ sea; **~ d'eau** (*Navig*) leak; **~ express** expressway; **~ de fait** (*Jur*) assault (and battery); **~ ferrée** track; railway line (*Brit*), railroad (*US*); **par ~ ferrée** by rail, by railroad; **~ de garage** (*Rail*) siding; **la ~ lactée** the Milky Way; **~ navigable** waterway; **~ prioritaire** (*Auto*) road with right of way; **~ privée** private road; **la ~ publique** the public highway

voilà [vwala] *prép* (*en désignant*) there is; (+*sg*) there are; (+*pl*): **les ~** *ou* **voici** here *ou* there they are; **en ~** *ou* **voici un** here's one, there's one; **voici mon frère et ~ ma sœur** this is my brother and that's my sister; **~** *ou* **voici deux ans** two years ago; **~** *ou* **voici deux ans que** it's two years since; **et ~!** there we are!; **~ tout** that's all; **"~** *ou* **voici"** (*en offrant etc*) "there *ou* here you are"; **tiens! ~ Paul** look! there's Paul

voile [vwal] *nm* veil; (*tissu léger*) net ▷ *nf* sail; (*sport*) sailing; **prendre le ~** to take the veil; **mettre à la ~** to make way under sail; **~ du palais** *nm* soft palate, velum; **~ au poumon** *nm* shadow on the lung

voiler [vwale] *vt* to veil; (*Photo*) to fog; (*fausser: roue*) to buckle; (*: bois*) to warp; **se voiler** *vi* (*lune, regard*) to mist over; (*ciel*) to grow hazy; (*voix*) to become husky; (*roue, disque*) to buckle; (*planche*) to warp; **se ~ la face** to hide one's face

voilier [vwalje] *nm* sailing ship; (*de plaisance*) sailing boat

voilure [vwalyʀ] *nf* (*de voilier*) sails *pl*; (*d'avion*) aerofoils *pl* (*Brit*), airfoils *pl* (*US*); (*de parachute*) canopy

voir [vwaʀ] *vi, vt* to see; **se voir; se ~ critiquer/transformer** to be criticized/ transformed; **cela se voit** (*cela arrive*) it happens; (*c'est visible*) that's obvious, it shows; **~ à faire qch** to see to it that sth is done; **~ loin** (*fig*) to be far-sighted; **~ venir** (*fig*) to wait and see; **faire ~ qch à qn** to show sb sth; **en faire ~ à qn** (*fig*) to give sb a hard time; **ne pas pouvoir ~ qn** (*fig*) not to be able to stand sb; **regardez ~** just look; **montrez ~** show (me); **dites ~** tell me; **voyons!** let's see now; (*indignation etc*) come (along) now!; **c'est à ~!** we'll see!; **c'est ce qu'on va ~!** we'll see about that!; **avoir quelque chose à ~ avec** to have something to do with; **ça n'a rien à ~ avec lui** that has nothing to do with him

voire [vwaʀ] *adv* indeed; nay; or even

voisin, e [vwazɛ̃, -in] *adj* (*proche*) neighbouring (*Brit*), neighboring (*US*); (*contigu*) next; (*ressemblant*) connected ▷ *nm/f* neighbo(u)r; (*de table, de dortoir etc*) person next to me (*ou* him etc); **~ de palier** neighbo(u)r across the landing (*Brit*) *ou* hall (*US*)

voisinage [vwazinaʒ] *nm* (*proximité*) proximity; (*environs*) vicinity; (*quartier, voisins*) neighbourhood (*Brit*), neighborhood (*US*); **relations de bon ~** neighbo(u)rly terms

voiture [vwatyʀ] *nf* car; (*wagon*) coach, carriage; **en ~!** all aboard!; **~ à bras** handcart; **~ d'enfant** pram (*Brit*), baby carriage (*US*); **~ d'infirme** invalid carriage; **~ de course** racing car; **~ de sport** sports car

voix [vwa] *nf* voice; (*Pol*) vote; **la ~ de la conscience/raison** the voice of conscience/ reason; **à haute ~** aloud; **à ~ basse** in a low voice; **faire la grosse ~** to speak gruffly; **avoir de la ~** to have a good voice; **rester sans ~** to be speechless; **~ de basse/ténor** *etc* bass/tenor *etc* voice; **à deux/quatre ~** (*Mus*) in two/four parts; **avoir ~ au chapitre** to have a say in the matter; **mettre aux ~** to put to the vote; **~ off** voice-over

vol [vɔl] *nm* (*mode de locomotion*) flying; (*trajet, voyage, groupe d'oiseaux*) flight; (*mode d'appropriation*) theft, stealing; (*larcin*) theft; **à ~ d'oiseau** as the crow flies; **au ~: attraper qch au vol** to catch sth as it flies past; **saisir une remarque au ~** to pick up a passing remark; **prendre son ~** to take flight; **de haut ~** (*fig*) of the highest order; **en ~** in flight; **~ avec effraction** breaking and entering *no pl*, break-in; **~ à l'étalage** shoplifting *no pl*; **~ libre** hang-gliding; **~ à main armée** armed robbery; **~ de nuit** night flight; **~ régulier** scheduled flight; **~ plané** (*Aviat*) glide, gliding *no pl*; **~ à la tire** pickpocketing *no pl*; **~ à voile** gliding

volage [vɔlaʒ] *adj* fickle

volaille [vɔlaj] *nf* (*oiseaux*) poultry *pl*; (*viande*) poultry *no pl*; (*oiseau*) fowl

volant, e [vɔlɑ̃, -ɑ̃t] *adj voir* **feuille** *etc* ▷ *nm* (*d'automobile*) (steering) wheel; (*de commande*) wheel; (*objet lancé*) shuttlecock; (*jeu*) battledore and shuttlecock; (*bande de tissu*) flounce; (*feuillet détachable*) tear-off portion; **le personnel ~, les ~s** (*Aviat*) the flight staff; **~ de sécurité** (*fig*) reserve, margin, safeguard

volcan [vɔlkɑ̃] *nm* volcano; (*fig: personne*) hothead

volée [vɔle] nf (groupe d'oiseaux) flight, flock; (Tennis) volley; ~ **de coups/de flèches** volley of blows/arrows; **à la ~: rattraper à la volée** to catch in midair; **lancer à la ~** to fling about; **semer à la ~** (to sow) broadcast; **à toute ~** (sonner les cloches) vigorously; (lancer un projectile) with full force; **de haute ~** (fig) of the highest order

voler [vɔle] vi (avion, oiseau, fig) to fly; (voleur) to steal ▷ vt (objet) to steal; (personne) to rob; **~ en éclats** to smash to smithereens; **~ de ses propres ailes** (fig) to stand on one's own two feet; **~ au vent** to fly in the wind; **~ qch à qn** to steal sth from sb; **on m'a volé mon portefeuille** my wallet (Brit) ou billfold (US) has been stolen; **il ne l'a pas volé!** he asked for it!

volet [vɔle] nm (de fenêtre) shutter; (Aviat) flap; (de feuillet, document) section; (fig: d'un plan) facet; **trié sur le ~** hand-picked

voleur, -euse [vɔlœʀ, -øz] nm/f thief ▷ adj thieving; **"au ~!"** "stop thief!"

volière [vɔljɛʀ] nf aviary

volley [vɔle], **volley-ball** [vɔlɛbɔl] nm volleyball

volontaire [vɔlɔ̃tɛʀ] adj (acte, activité) voluntary; (délibéré) deliberate; (caractère, personne: décidé) self-willed ▷ nm/f volunteer

volonté [vɔlɔ̃te] nf (faculté de vouloir) will; (énergie, fermeté) will(power); (souhait, désir) wish; **se servir/boire à ~** to take/drink as much as one likes; **bonne ~** goodwill, willingness; **mauvaise ~** lack of goodwill, unwillingness

volontiers [vɔlɔ̃tje] adv (de bonne grâce) willingly; (avec plaisir) willingly, gladly; (habituellement, souvent) readily, willingly; **"~"** "with pleasure", "I'd be glad to"

volt [vɔlt] nm volt

volte-face [vɔltəfas] nf inv about-turn; (fig) about-turn, U-turn; **faire ~** to do an about-turn; to do a U-turn

voltige [vɔltiʒ] nf (Équitation) trick riding; (au cirque) acrobatics sg; (Aviat) (aerial) acrobatics sg; **numéro de haute ~** acrobatic act

voltiger [vɔltiʒe] vi to flutter (about)

volubile [vɔlybil] adj voluble

volume [vɔlym] nm volume; (Géom: solide) solid

volumineux, -euse [vɔlyminø, -øz] adj voluminous, bulky

volupté [vɔlypte] nf sensual delight ou pleasure

vomi [vɔmi] nm vomit

vomir [vɔmiʀ] vi to vomit, be sick ▷ vt to vomit, bring up; (fig) to belch out, spew out; (exécrer) to loathe, abhor

vomissements [vɔmismɑ̃] nmpl (action) vomiting no pl; **des ~** vomit sg

vont [vɔ̃] vb voir **aller**

vorace [vɔʀas] adj voracious

vos [vo] adj poss voir **votre**

vote [vɔt] nm vote; **~ par correspondance/procuration** postal/proxy vote; **~ à main levée** vote by show of hands; **~ secret**, **~ à bulletins secrets** secret ballot

voter [vɔte] vi to vote ▷ vt (loi, décision) to vote for

votre [vɔtʀ] (pl **vos** [vo]) adj poss your

vôtre [votʀ] pron: **le ~**, **la ~**, **les ~s** yours; **les ~s** (fig) your family ou folks; **à la ~** (toast) your (good) health!

voudrai etc [vudʀe] vb voir **vouloir**

voué, e [vwe] adj: **~ à** doomed to, destined for

vouer [vwe] vt: **~ qch à** (Dieu/un saint) to dedicate sth to; **~ sa vie/son temps à** (étude, cause etc) to devote one's life/time to; **~ une haine/amitié éternelle à qn** to vow undying hatred/friendship to sb

⭘ MOT-CLÉ

vouloir [vulwaʀ] nm: **le bon vouloir de qn** sb's goodwill; sb's pleasure
▷ vt **1** (exiger, désirer) to want; **vouloir faire/que qn fasse** to want to do/sb to do; **voulez-vous du thé?** would you like ou do you want some tea?; **vouloir qch à qn** to wish sth for sb; **que me veut-il?** what does he want with me?; **que veux-tu que je te dise?** what do you want me to say?; **sans le vouloir** (involontairement) without meaning to, unintentionally; **je voudrais ceci/faire** I would ou I'd like this/to do; **le hasard a voulu que ...** as fate would have it, ...; **la tradition veut que ...** tradition demands that ...; **... qui se veut moderne** ... which purports to be modern

2 (consentir): **je veux bien** (bonne volonté) I'll be happy to; (concession) fair enough, that's fine; **oui, si on veut** (en quelque sorte) yes, if you like; **comme tu veux** as you wish; (en quelque sorte) if you like; **veuillez attendre** please wait; **veuillez agréer ...** (formule épistolaire) yours faithfully

3: **en vouloir** (être ambitieux) to be out to win; **en vouloir à qn** to bear sb a grudge; **je lui en veux d'avoir fait ça** I resent his having done that; **s'en vouloir (de)** to be annoyed with o.s. (for); **il en veut à mon argent** he's after my money

4: **vouloir de** to want; **l'entreprise ne veut plus de lui** the firm doesn't want him any more; **elle ne veut pas de son aide** she doesn't want his help

5: **vouloir dire** to mean

voulu, e [vuly] pp de **vouloir** ▷ adj (requis) required, requisite; (délibéré) deliberate, intentional

vous [vu] pron you; (objet indirect) (to) you; (réfléchi: sg) yourself; (: pl) yourselves; (réciproque) each other ▷ nm: **employer le ~** (vouvoyer) to use the "vous" form; **~-même** yourself; **~-mêmes** yourselves

voûte [vut] *nf* vault; **la ~ céleste** the vault of heaven; **~ du palais** (*Anat*) roof of the mouth; **~ plantaire** arch (of the foot)

voûter [vute] *vt* (*Archit*) to arch, vault; **se voûter** *vi* (*dos, personne*) to become stooped

vouvoyer [vuvwaje] *vt*: **~ qn** to address sb as "vous"

voyage [vwajaʒ] *nm* journey, trip; (*fait de voyager*): **le ~** travel(ling); **partir/être en ~** to go off/be away on a journey *ou* trip; **faire un ~** to go on *ou* make a trip *ou* journey; **faire bon ~** to have a good journey; **les gens du ~** travelling people; **~ d'agrément/d'affaires** pleasure/business trip; **~ de noces** honeymoon; **~ organisé** package tour

voyager [vwajaʒe] *vi* to travel

voyageur, -euse [vwajaʒœʀ, -øz] *nm/f* traveller; (*passager*) passenger ▷ *adj* (*tempérament*) nomadic, wayfaring; **~ (de commerce)** commercial traveller

voyant, e [vwajɑ̃, -ɑ̃t] *adj* (*couleur*) loud, gaudy ▷ *nm/f* (*personne qui voit*) sighted person ▷ *nm* (*signal*) (warning) light ▷ *nf* clairvoyant

voyelle [vwajɛl] *nf* vowel

voyons *etc* [vwajɔ̃] *vb voir* **voir**

voyou [vwaju] *nm* lout, hoodlum; (*enfant*) guttersnipe

vrac [vʀak]: **en ~** *adv* loose; (*Comm*) in bulk

vrai, e [vʀɛ] *adj* (*véridique: récit, faits*) true; (*non factice, authentique*) real ▷ *nm*: **le ~** the truth; **à ~ dire** to tell the truth; **il est ~ que** it is true that; **être dans le ~** to be right

vraiment [vʀɛmɑ̃] *adv* really

vraisemblable [vʀɛsɑ̃blabl] *adj* (*plausible*) likely; (*excuse*) plausible; (*probable*) likely, probable

vraisemblablement [vʀɛsɑ̃blabləmɑ̃] *adv* in all likelihood, very likely

vraisemblance [vʀɛsɑ̃blɑ̃s] *nf* likelihood, plausibility; (*romanesque*) verisimilitude; **selon toute ~** in all likelihood

vrille [vʀij] *nf* (*de plante*) tendril; (*outil*) gimlet; (*spirale*) spiral; (*Aviat*) spin

vrombir [vʀɔ̃biʀ] *vi* to hum

VRP *sigle m* (= *voyageur, représentant, placier*) (sales) rep (*fam*)

VTT *sigle m* (= *vélo tout-terrain*) mountain bike

vu¹ [vy] *prép* (*en raison de*) in view of; **vu que** in view of the fact that

vu², e¹ [vy] *pp de* **voir** ▷ *adj*: **bien/mal vu** (*personne*) well/poorly thought of; (*conduite*) good/bad form ▷ *nm*: **au vu et au su de tous** openly and publicly; **ni vu ni connu** what the eye doesn't see ...!, no one will be any the wiser; **c'est tout vu** it's a foregone conclusion

vue² [vy] *nf* (*fait de voir*): **la ~ de** the sight of; (*sens, faculté*) (eye)sight; (*panorama, image, photo*) view; (*spectacle*) sight; **vues** *nfpl* (*idées*) views; (*dessein*) designs; **perdre la ~** to lose one's (eye)sight; **perdre de ~** to lose sight of; **à la ~ de tous** in full view of everybody; **hors de ~** out of sight; **à première ~** at first sight; **connaître de ~** to know by sight; **à ~** (*Comm*) at sight; **tirer à ~** to shoot on sight; **à ~ d'œil** *adv* visibly; (*à première vue*) at a quick glance; **avoir ~ sur** to have a view of; **en ~** (*visible*) in sight; (*Comm: célèbre*) in the public eye; **avoir qch en ~** (*intentions*) to have one's sights on sth; **en ~ de faire** with the intention of doing, with a view to doing; **~ d'ensemble** overall view; **~ de l'esprit** theoretical view

vulgaire [vylgɛʀ] *adj* (*grossier*) vulgar, coarse; (*trivial*) commonplace, mundane; (*péj: quelconque*): **de ~s touristes/chaises de cuisine** common tourists/kitchen chairs; (*Bot, Zool: non latin*) common

vulgariser [vylgaʀize] *vt* to popularize

vulnérable [vylneʀabl] *adj* vulnerable

V

W   X

wagon [vagɔ̃] *nm* (*de voyageurs*) carriage; (*de marchandises*) truck, wagon
wagon-lit (*pl* **wagons-lits**) [vagɔ̃li] *nm* sleeper, sleeping car
wagon-restaurant (*pl* **wagons-restaurants**) [vagɔ̃ʀɛstɔʀɑ̃] *nm* restaurant *ou* dining car
wallon, ne [walɔ̃, -ɔn] *adj* Walloon ▷ *nm* (*Ling*) Walloon ▷ *nm/f*: **W-, ne** Walloon
waters [watɛʀ] *nmpl* toilet *sg*, loo *sg* (*Brit*)
watt [wat] *nm* watt
WC [vese] *nmpl* toilet *sg*, lavatory *sg*
Web [wɛb] *nm inv*: **le ~** (World Wide) Web
webcam [wɛbkam] *nf* webcam
webmaster [-mastœʀ], **webmestre** [-mɛstʀ] *nm/f* webmaster
week-end [wikɛnd] *nm* weekend
western [wɛstɛʀn] *nm* western
whisky (*pl* **whiskies**) [wiski] *nm* whisky
widget [widʒɛt] *nm* (*Inform*) widget
wifi [wifi] *nm inv* wifi
WWW *sigle m* (= *World Wide Web*) WWW

xénophobe [gzenɔfɔb] *adj* xenophobic ▷ *nm/f* xenophobe
xérès [gzeʀɛs] *nm* sherry
xylophone [gzilɔfɔn] *nm* xylophone

Y Z

y [i] *adv* (*à cet endroit*) there; (*dessus*) on it (*ou* them); (*dedans*) in it (*ou* them) ▷ *pron* (about *ou* on *ou* of) it (*vérifier la syntaxe du verbe employé*); **j'y pense** I'm thinking about it; **ça y est!** that's it!; *voir aussi* **aller; avoir**

yacht [jɔt] *nm* yacht

yaourt [jauʀt] *nm* yogurt; **~ nature/aux fruits** plain/fruit yogurt

yeux [jø] *nmpl de* **œil**

yoga [jɔga] *nm* yoga

yoghourt [jɔguʀt] *nm* = **yaourt**

yougoslave [jugɔslav] *adj* Yugoslav(ian) ▷ *nm/f:* **Y~** Yugoslav(ian)

Yougoslavie [jugɔslavi] *nf:* **la ~** Yugoslavia; **l'ex-~** the former Yugoslavia

zapper [zape] *vi* to zap

zapping [zapiŋ] *nm:* **faire du ~** to flick through the channels

zébré, e [zebʀe] *adj* striped, streaked

zèbre [zɛbʀ] *nm* (*Zool*) zebra

zélé, e [zele] *adj* zealous

zèle [zɛl] *nm* zeal, diligence, assiduousness; **faire du ~** (*péj*) to be over-zealous

zéro [zeʀo] *nm* zero, nought (*Brit*); **au-dessous de ~** below zero (Centigrade), below freezing; **partir ~** to start from scratch; **réduire à ~** to reduce to nothing; **trois (buts) à ~** three (goals) to nil

zeste [zɛst] *nm* peel, zest; **un ~ de citron** a piece of lemon peel

zézayer [zezeje] *vi* to have a lisp

zigzag [zigzag] *nm* zigzag

zigzaguer [zigzage] *vi* to zigzag (along)

Zimbabwe [zimbabwe] *nm:* **le ~** Zimbabwe

zinc [zɛ̃g] *nm* (*Chimie*) zinc; (*comptoir*) bar, counter

zipper [zipe] *vt* (*Inform*) to zip

zizanie [zizani] *nf:* **semer la ~** to stir up ill-feeling

zizi [zizi] *nm* (*fam*) willy (*Brit*), peter (*US*)

zodiaque [zɔdjak] *nm* zodiac

zona [zona] *nm* shingles *sg*

zone [zon] *nf* zone, area; (*quartiers pauvres*): **la ~** the slums; **de seconde ~** (*fig*) second-rate; **~ d'action** (*Mil*) sphere of activity; **~ bleue** ≈ restricted parking area; **~ d'extension** *ou* **d'urbanisation** urban development area;

~ **franche** free zone; ~ **industrielle (ZI)**
industrial estate; ~ **piétonne** pedestrian
precinct; ~ **résidentielle** residential area;
~ **tampon** buffer zone
zoo [zoo] *nm* zoo
zoologie [zɔɔlɔʒi] *nf* zoology
zoologique [zɔɔlɔʒik] *adj* zoological
zut [zyt] *excl* dash (it)! (*Brit*), nuts! (*US*)

A, a¹ [eɪ] n (letter) A, a m; (Scol: mark) A; (Mus) la m; **A for Andrew, A for Able** (US) A comme Anatole; **A shares** npl (Brit Stock Exchange) actions fpl prioritaires

○ KEYWORD

a² [eɪ, ə] (before vowel and silent h **an**) indef art **1** un(e); **a book** un livre; **an apple** une pomme; **she's a doctor** elle est médecin
2 (instead of the number "one") un(e); **a year ago** il y a un an; **a hundred/thousand** etc **pounds** cent/mille etc livres
3 (in expressing ratios, prices etc): **three a day/week** trois par jour/semaine; **10 km an hour** 10 km à l'heure; **£5 a person** 5£ par personne; **30p a kilo** 30p le kilo

A2 n (Brit: Scol) deuxième partie de l'examen équivalent au baccalauréat
A.A. n abbr (Brit: = Automobile Association) ≈ ACF m; (US: = Associate in/of Arts) diplôme universitaire; (= Alcoholics Anonymous) AA; (= anti-aircraft) AA
A.A.A. n abbr (= American Automobile Association) ≈ ACF m; (Brit) = **Amateur Athletics Association**
aback [ə'bæk] adv: **to be taken ~** être décontenancé(e)
abandon [ə'bændən] vt abandonner ▷ n abandon m; **to ~ ship** évacuer le navire
abate [ə'beɪt] vi s'apaiser, se calmer
abattoir ['æbətwɑːʳ] n (Brit) abattoir m

abbey ['æbɪ] n abbaye f
abbot ['æbət] n père supérieur
abbreviation [əbriːvɪ'eɪʃən] n abréviation f
abdicate ['æbdɪkeɪt] vt, vi abdiquer
abdomen ['æbdəmən] n abdomen m
abduct [æb'dʌkt] vt enlever
aberration [æbə'reɪʃən] n anomalie f; **in a moment of mental ~** dans un moment d'égarement
abide [ə'baɪd] vt souffrir, supporter; **I can't ~ it/him** je ne le supporte pas; **abide by** vt fus observer, respecter
ability [ə'bɪlɪtɪ] n compétence f; capacité f; (skill) talent m; **to the best of my ~** de mon mieux
abject ['æbdʒekt] adj (poverty) sordide; (coward) méprisable; **an ~ apology** les excuses les plus plates
ablaze [ə'bleɪz] adj en feu, en flammes; **~ with light** resplendissant de lumière
able ['eɪbl] adj compétent(e); **to be ~ to do sth** pouvoir faire qch, être capable de faire qch
able-bodied ['eɪbl'bɔdɪd] adj robuste; **~ seaman** (Brit) matelot breveté
ably ['eɪblɪ] adv avec compétence or talent, habilement
abnormal [æb'nɔːməl] adj anormal(e)
aboard [ə'bɔːd] adv à bord ▷ prep à bord de; (train) dans
abode [ə'bəud] n (old) demeure f; (Law): **of no fixed ~** sans domicile fixe
abolish [ə'bɔlɪʃ] vt abolir
abolition [æbə'lɪʃən] n abolition f
aborigine [æbə'rɪdʒɪnɪ] n aborigène m/f
abort [ə'bɔːt] vt (Med) faire avorter; (Comput, fig) abandonner
abortion [ə'bɔːʃən] n avortement m; **to have an ~** se faire avorter
abortive [ə'bɔːtɪv] adj manqué(e)

○ KEYWORD

about [ə'baut] adv **1** (approximately) environ, à peu près; **about a hundred/thousand** etc environ cent/mille etc, une centaine (de)/un millier (de) etc; **it takes about 10 hours** ça prend environ or à peu près 10 heures; **at about 2 o'clock** vers 2 heures; **I've just about finished** j'ai presque fini
2 (referring to place) çà et là, de-ci de-là; **to run about** courir çà et là; **to walk about** se promener, aller et venir; **is Paul about?** (Brit) est-ce que Paul est là?; **it's about here** c'est par ici, c'est dans les parages; **they left all their things lying about** ils ont laissé traîner toutes leurs affaires
3: **to be about to do sth** être sur le point de faire qch; **I'm not about to do all that for nothing** (inf) je ne vais quand même pas faire tout ça pour rien
4 (opposite): **it's the other way about** (Brit) c'est l'inverse

▷ *prep* **1** (*relating to*) au sujet de, à propos de;
a book about London un livre sur Londres;
what is it about? de quoi s'agit-il?; **we
talked about it** nous en avons parlé; **do
something about it!** faites quelque chose!;
what *or* **how about doing this?** et si nous
faisions ceci?
2 (*referring to place*) dans; **to walk about the
town** se promener dans la ville

above [ə'bʌv] *adv* au-dessus ▷ *prep* au-dessus
de; (*more than*) plus de; **mentioned ~**
mentionné ci-dessus; **costing ~ £10** coûtant
plus de 10 livres; **~ all** par-dessus tout,
surtout
aboveboard [ə'bʌv'bɔːd] *adj* franc/franche,
loyal(e); honnête
abrasive [ə'breɪzɪv] *adj* abrasif(-ive); (*fig*)
caustique, agressif(-ive)
abreast [ə'brest] *adv* de front; **to keep ~ of** se
tenir au courant de
abroad [ə'brɔːd] *adv* à l'étranger; **there is
a rumour ~ that ...** (*fig*) le bruit court
que ...
abrupt [ə'brʌpt] *adj* (*steep, blunt*) abrupt(e);
(*sudden, gruff*) brusque
abruptly [ə'brʌptlɪ] *adv* (*speak, end*)
brusquement
abscess ['æbsɪs] *n* abcès *m*
absence ['æbsəns] *n* absence *f*; **in the ~ of**
(*person*) en l'absence de; (*thing*) faute de
absent ['æbsənt] *adj* absent(e); **~ without
leave (AWOL)** (*Mil*) en absence irrégulière
absentee [æbsən'tiː] *n* absent(e)
absent-minded ['æbsənt'maɪndɪd] *adj*
distrait(e)
absolute ['æbsəluːt] *adj* absolu(e)
absolutely [æbsə'luːtlɪ] *adv* absolument
absolve [əb'zɔlv] *vt*: **to ~ sb (from)** (*sin etc*)
absoudre qn (de); **to ~ sb from** (*oath*) délier
qn de
absorb [əb'zɔːb] *vt* absorber; **to be ~ed in a
book** être plongé(e) dans un livre
absorbent cotton [əb'zɔːbənt-] *n* (*US*) coton
m hydrophile
absorbing [əb'zɔːbɪŋ] *adj* absorbant(e); (*book,
film etc*) captivant(e)
abstain [əb'steɪn] *vi*: **to ~ (from)** s'abstenir
(de)
abstract ['æbstrækt] *adj* abstrait(e) ▷ *n*
(*summary*) résumé *m* ▷ *vt* [æb'strækt] extraire
absurd [əb'sɜːd] *adj* absurde
abundance [ə'bʌndəns] *n* abondance *f*
abundant [ə'bʌndənt] *adj* abondant(e)
abuse *n* [ə'bjuːs] (*insults*) insultes *fpl*, injures
fpl; (*ill-treatment*) mauvais traitements *mpl*;
(*of power etc*) abus *m* ▷ *vt* [ə'bjuːz] (*insult*)
insulter; (*ill-treat*) malmener; (*power etc*)
abuser de; **to be open to ~** se prêter à des
abus
abusive [ə'bjuːsɪv] *adj* grossier(-ière),
injurieux(-euse)

abysmal [ə'bɪzməl] *adj* exécrable; (*ignorance
etc*) sans bornes
abyss [ə'bɪs] *n* abîme *m*, gouffre *m*
AC *n abbr* (*US*) = **athletic club**
academic [ækə'demɪk] *adj* universitaire;
(*person: scholarly*) intellectuel(-le); (*pej: issue*)
oiseux(-euse), purement théorique ▷ *n*
universitaire *m/f*; **~ freedom** liberté *f*
académique
academic year *n* (*University*) année *f*
universitaire; (*Scol*) année scolaire
academy [ə'kædəmɪ] *n* (*learned body*)
académie *f*; (*school*) collège *m*; **military/
naval ~** école militaire/navale; **~ of music**
conservatoire *m*
accelerate [æk'seləreɪt] *vt, vi* accélérer
acceleration [ækselə'reɪʃən] *n* accélération *f*
accelerator [æk'seləreɪtəʳ] *n* (*Brit*)
accélérateur *m*
accent ['æksent] *n* accent *m*
accept [ək'sept] *vt* accepter
acceptable [ək'septəbl] *adj* acceptable
acceptance [ək'septəns] *n* acceptation *f*; **to
meet with general ~** être favorablement
accueilli par tous
access ['ækses] *n* accès *m* ▷ *vt* (*Comput*)
accéder à; **to have ~ to** (*information, library etc*)
avoir accès à, pouvoir utiliser *or* consulter;
(*person*) avoir accès auprès de; **the burglars
gained ~ through a window** les
cambrioleurs sont entrés par une fenêtre
accessible [æk'sesəbl] *adj* accessible
accessory [æk'sesərɪ] *n* accessoire *m*; **toilet
accessories** (*Brit*) articles *mpl* de toilette; **~ to**
(*Law*) accessoire à
accident ['æksɪdənt] *n* accident *m*; (*chance*)
hasard *m*; **to meet with** *or* **to have an ~** avoir
un accident; **I've had an ~** j'ai eu un
accident; **~s at work** accidents du travail;
by ~ (*by chance*) par hasard; (*not deliberately*)
accidentellement
accidental [æksɪ'dentl] *adj* accidentel(le)
accidentally [æksɪ'dentəlɪ] *adv*
accidentellement
Accident and Emergency Department *n*
(*Brit*) service *m* des urgences
accident insurance *n* assurance *f* accident
accident-prone ['æksɪdənt'prəun] *adj*
sujet(te) aux accidents
acclaim [ə'kleɪm] *vt* acclamer ▷ *n*
acclamations *fpl*
accommodate [ə'kɔmədeɪt] *vt* loger,
recevoir; (*oblige, help*) obliger; (*car etc*)
contenir; (*adapt*): **to ~ one's plans to** adapter
ses projets à
accommodating [ə'kɔmədeɪtɪŋ] *adj*
obligeant(e), arrangeant(e)
accommodation, (*US*) **accommodations**
[əkɔmə'deɪʃən(z)] *n(pl)* logement *m*; **he's
found ~** il a trouvé à se loger; **"~ to let"** (*Brit*)
"appartement *or* studio *etc* à louer"; **they
have ~ for 500** ils peuvent recevoir 500

personnes, il y a de la place pour 500 personnes; **the hall has seating ~ for 600** (Brit) la salle contient 600 places assises

accompaniment [əˈkʌmpənɪmənt] n accompagnement m

accompany [əˈkʌmpənɪ] vt accompagner

accomplice [əˈkʌmplɪs] n complice m/f

accomplish [əˈkʌmplɪʃ] vt accomplir

accomplishment [əˈkʌmplɪʃmənt] n (skill: gen pl) talent m; (completion) accomplissement m; (achievement) réussite f

accord [əˈkɔːd] n accord m ▷ vt accorder; **of his own ~** de son plein gré; **with one ~** d'un commun accord

accordance [əˈkɔːdəns] n: **in ~ with** conformément à

according [əˈkɔːdɪŋ]: **~ to** prep selon; **~ to plan** comme prévu

accordingly [əˈkɔːdɪŋlɪ] adv (appropriately) en conséquence; (as a result) par conséquent

accordion [əˈkɔːdɪən] n accordéon m

account [əˈkaunt] n (Comm) compte m; (report) compte rendu, récit m; **accounts** npl (Comm: records) comptabilité f, comptes; **"~ payee only"** (Brit) "chèque non endossable"; **to keep an ~ of** noter; **to bring sb to ~ for sth/for having done sth** amener qn à rendre compte de qch/d'avoir fait qch; **by all ~s** au dire de tous; **of little ~** de peu d'importance; **of no ~** sans importance; **on ~** en acompte; **to buy sth on ~** acheter qch à crédit; **on no ~** en aucun cas; **on ~ of** à cause de; **to take into ~, take ~ of** tenir compte de; **account for** vt fus (explain) expliquer, rendre compte de; (represent) représenter; **all the children were ~ed for** aucun enfant ne manquait; **four people are still not ~ed for** on n'a toujours pas retrouvé quatre personnes

accountable [əˈkauntəbl] adj: **~ (for/to)** responsable (de/devant)

accountancy [əˈkauntənsɪ] n comptabilité f

accountant [əˈkauntənt] n comptable m/f

account number n numéro m de compte

accrue [əˈkruː] vi s'accroître; (mount up) s'accumuler; **to ~ to** s'ajouter à; **~d interest** intérêt couru

accumulate [əˈkjuːmjuleɪt] vt accumuler, amasser ▷ vi s'accumuler, s'amasser

accuracy [ˈækjurəsɪ] n exactitude f, précision f

accurate [ˈækjurɪt] adj exact(e), précis(e); (device) précis

accurately [ˈækjurɪtlɪ] adv avec précision

accusation [ækjuˈzeɪʃən] n accusation f

accuse [əˈkjuːz] vt: **to ~ sb (of sth)** accuser qn (de qch)

accused [əˈkjuːzd] n (Law) accusé(e)

accustom [əˈkʌstəm] vt accoutumer, habituer; **to ~ o.s. to sth** s'habituer à qch

accustomed [əˈkʌstəmd] adj (usual) habituel(le); **~ to** habitué(e) or accoutumé(e) à

ace [eɪs] n as m; **within an ~ of** (Brit) à deux doigts or un cheveu de

ache [eɪk] n mal m, douleur f ▷ vi (be sore) faire mal, être douloureux(-euse); (yearn): **to ~ to do sth** mourir d'envie de faire qch; **I've got stomach ~** or (US) **a stomach ~** j'ai mal à l'estomac; **my head ~s** j'ai mal à la tête; **I'm aching all over** j'ai mal partout

achieve [əˈtʃiːv] vt (aim) atteindre; (victory, success) remporter, obtenir; (task) accomplir

achievement [əˈtʃiːvmənt] n exploit m, réussite f; (of aims) réalisation f

acid [ˈæsɪd] adj, n acide (m)

acid rain n pluies fpl acides

acknowledge [əkˈnɔlɪdʒ] vt (also: **~ receipt of**) accuser réception de; (fact) reconnaître

acknowledgement [əkˈnɔlɪdʒmənt] n (of letter) accusé m de réception; **acknowledgements** (in book) remerciements mpl

acne [ˈæknɪ] n acné m

acorn [ˈeɪkɔːn] n gland m

acoustic [əˈkuːstɪk] adj acoustique

acoustics [əˈkuːstɪks] n, npl acoustique f

acquaint [əˈkweɪnt] vt: **to ~ sb with sth** mettre qn au courant de qch; **to be ~ed with** (person) connaître; (fact) savoir

acquaintance [əˈkweɪntəns] n connaissance f; **to make sb's ~** faire la connaissance de qn

acquire [əˈkwaɪə*] vt acquérir

acquisition [ækwɪˈzɪʃən] n acquisition f

acquit [əˈkwɪt] vt acquitter; **to ~ o.s. well** s'en tirer très honorablement

acre [ˈeɪkə*] n acre f (= 4047 m²)

acrid [ˈækrɪd] adj (smell) âcre; (fig) mordant(e)

acrobat [ˈækrəbæt] n acrobate m/f

acronym [ˈækrənɪm] n acronyme m

across [əˈkrɔs] prep (on the other side) de l'autre côté de; (crosswise) en travers de ▷ adv de l'autre côté; en travers; **to walk ~ (the road)** traverser (la route); **to run/swim ~** traverser en courant/à la nage; **to take sb ~ the road** faire traverser la route à qn; **a road ~ the wood** une route qui traverse le bois; **the lake is 12 km ~** le lac fait 12 km de large; **~ from** en face de; **to get sth ~ (to sb)** faire comprendre qch (à qn)

acrylic [əˈkrɪlɪk] adj, n acrylique (m)

act [ækt] n acte m, action f; (Theat: part of play) acte; (: of performer) numéro m; (Law) loi f ▷ vi agir; (Theat) jouer; (pretend) jouer la comédie ▷ vt (role) jouer, tenir; **~ of God** (Law) catastrophe naturelle; **to catch sb in the ~** prendre qn sur le fait or en flagrant délit; **it's only an ~** c'est du cinéma; **to ~ Hamlet** (Brit) tenir or jouer le rôle d'Hamlet; **to ~ the fool** (Brit) faire l'idiot; **to ~ as** servir de; **it ~s as a deterrent** cela a un effet dissuasif; **~ing in my capacity as chairman, I ... am** en ma qualité de président, je ...; **act on** vt: **to ~ on sth** agir sur la base de qch; **act out** vt (event) raconter en mimant; (*fantasies*) réaliser; **act up** (*inf*) *vi* (*person*) se conduire mal; (*knee, back, injury*) jouer des tours; (*machine*) être capricieux(-ieuse)

acting ['æktɪŋ] *adj* suppléant(e), par intérim ▷ *n* (*of actor*) jeu *m*; (*activity*): **to do some ~** faire du théâtre (*or* du cinéma); **he is the ~ manager** il remplace (provisoirement) le directeur

action ['ækʃən] *n* action *f*; (*Mil*) combat(s) *m*(*pl*); (*Law*) procès *m*, action en justice ▷ *vt* (*Comm*) mettre en œuvre; **to bring an ~ against sb** (*Law*) poursuivre qn en justice, intenter un procès contre qn; **killed in ~** (*Mil*) tué au champ d'honneur; **out of ~** hors de combat; (*machine etc*) hors d'usage; **to take ~** agir, prendre des mesures; **to put a plan into ~** mettre un projet à exécution

action replay *n* (*Brit TV*) ralenti *m*

activate ['æktɪveɪt] *vt* (*mechanism*) actionner, faire fonctionner; (*Chem, Physics*) activer

active ['æktɪv] *adj* actif(-ive); (*volcano*) en activité; **to play an ~ part in** jouer un rôle actif dans

actively ['æktɪvlɪ] *adv* activement; (*discourage*) vivement

activist ['æktɪvɪst] *n* activiste *m/f*

activity [æk'tɪvɪtɪ] *n* activité *f*

activity holiday *n* vacances actives

actor ['æktə'] *n* acteur *m*

actress ['æktrɪs] *n* actrice *f*

actual ['æktjuəl] *adj* réel(le), véritable; (*emphatic use*) lui-même/elle-même

actually ['æktjuəlɪ] *adv* réellement, véritablement; (*in fact*) en fait

acupuncture ['ækjupʌŋktʃə'] *n* acuponcture *f*

acute [ə'kju:t] *adj* aigu(ë); (*mind, observer*) pénétrant(e)

A.D. *adv abbr* (= *Anno Domini*) ap. J.-C. ▷ *n abbr* (*US Mil*) = **active duty**

ad [æd] *n abbr* = **advertisement**

adamant ['ædəmənt] *adj* inflexible

adapt [ə'dæpt] *vt* adapter ▷ *vi*: **to ~ (to)** s'adapter (à)

adaptable [ə'dæptəbl] *adj* (*device*) adaptable; (*person*) qui s'adapte facilement

adapter, adaptor [ə'dæptə'] *n* (*Elec*) adaptateur *m*; (*for several plugs*) prise *f* multiple

add [æd] *vt* ajouter; (*figures: also*: **to ~ up**) additionner ▷ *vi*: **to ~ to** (*increase*) ajouter à, accroître ▷ *n* (*Internet*): **thanks for the ~** merci pour l'ajout; **add on** *vt* ajouter ▷ *vi* (*fig*): **it doesn't ~ up** cela ne rime à rien; **add up to** *vt fus* (*Math*) s'élever à; (*fig: mean*) signifier; **it doesn't ~ up to much** ça n'est pas grand'chose

adder ['ædə'] *n* vipère *f*

addict ['ædɪkt] *n* toxicomane *m/f*; (*fig*) fanatique *m/f*; **heroin ~** héroïnomane *m/f*; **drug ~** drogué(e) *m/f*

addicted [ə'dɪktɪd] *adj*: **to be ~ to** (*drink, drugs*) être adonné(e) à; (*fig: football etc*) être un(e) fanatique de

addiction [ə'dɪkʃən] *n* (*Med*) dépendance *f*

addictive [ə'dɪktɪv] *adj* qui crée une dépendance

addition [ə'dɪʃən] *n* (*adding up*) addition *f*; (*thing added*) ajout *m*; **in ~** de plus, de surcroît; **in ~ to** en plus de

additional [ə'dɪʃənl] *adj* supplémentaire

additive ['ædɪtɪv] *n* additif *m*

address [ə'drɛs] *n* adresse *f*; (*talk*) discours *m*, allocution *f* ▷ *vt* adresser; (*speak to*) s'adresser à; **my ~ is ...** mon adresse, c'est ...; **form of ~** titre *m*; **what form of ~ do you use for ...?** comment s'adresse-t-on à ...?; **to ~ (o.s. to) sth** (*problem, issue*) aborder qch; **absolute/relative ~** (*Comput*) adresse absolue/relative

address book *n* carnet *m* d'adresses

adept ['ædɛpt] *adj*: **~ at** expert(e) à *or* en

adequate ['ædɪkwɪt] *adj* (*enough*) suffisant(e); (*satisfactory*) satisfaisant(e); **to feel ~ to the task** se sentir à la hauteur de la tâche

adhere [əd'hɪə'] *vi*: **to ~ to** adhérer à; (*fig: rule, decision*) se tenir à

adhesive [əd'hi:zɪv] *adj* adhésif(-ive) ▷ *n* adhésif *m*

adhesive tape *n* (*Brit*) ruban *m* adhésif; (*US Med*) sparadrap *m*

ad hoc [æd'hɔk] *adj* (*decision*) de circonstance; (*committee*) ad hoc

adjacent [ə'dʒeɪsənt] *adj* adjacent(e), contigu(ë); **~ to** adjacent à

adjective ['ædʒɛktɪv] *n* adjectif *m*

adjoining [ə'dʒɔɪnɪŋ] *adj* voisin(e), adjacent(e), attenant(e) ▷ *prep* voisin de, adjacent à

adjourn [ə'dʒə:n] *vt* ajourner ▷ *vi* suspendre la séance; lever la séance; clore la session; (*go*) se retirer; **to ~ a meeting till the following week** reporter une réunion à la semaine suivante; **they ~ed to the pub** (*Brit inf*) ils ont filé au pub

adjust [ə'dʒʌst] *vt* (*machine*) ajuster, régler; (*prices, wages*) rajuster ▷ *vi*: **to ~ (to)** s'adapter (à)

adjustable [ə'dʒʌstəbl] *adj* réglable

adjustment [ə'dʒʌstmənt] *n* (*of machine*) ajustage *m*, réglage *m*; (*of prices, wages*) rajustement *m*; (*of person*) adaptation *f*

administer [əd'mɪnɪstə'] *vt* administrer; (*justice*) rendre

administration [ədmɪnɪs'treɪʃən] *n* (*management*) administration *f*; (*government*) gouvernement *m*

administrative [əd'mɪnɪstrətɪv] *adj* administratif(-ive)

administrator [əd'mɪnɪstreɪtə^r] n
administrateur(-trice)

admiral ['ædmərəl] n amiral m

Admiralty ['ædmərəltɪ] n (Brit: also: ~ **Board**)
ministère m de la Marine

admiration [ædmə'reɪʃən] n admiration f

admire [əd'maɪə^r] vt admirer

admirer [əd'maɪərə^r] n (fan)
admirateur(-trice)

admission [əd'mɪʃən] n admission f; (to
exhibition, night club etc) entrée f; (confession)
aveu m; "**~ free**", "**free ~**" "entrée libre"; **by
his own ~** de son propre aveu

admission charge n droits mpl d'admission

admit [əd'mɪt] vt laisser entrer; admettre;
(agree) reconnaître, admettre; (crime)
reconnaître avoir commis; "**children not
~ted**" "entrée interdite aux enfants"; **this
ticket ~s two** ce billet est valable pour deux
personnes; **I must ~ that ...** je dois admettre
or reconnaître que ...; **admit of** vt fus
admettre, permettre; **admit to** vt fus
reconnaître, avouer

admittance [əd'mɪtəns] n admission f,
(droit m d')entrée f; "**no ~**" "défense d'entrer"

admittedly [əd'mɪtɪdlɪ] adv il faut en
convenir

ado [ə'du:] n: **without (any) more ~** sans plus
de cérémonies

adolescence [ædəu'lɛsns] n adolescence f

adolescent [ædəu'lɛsnt] adj, n adolescent(e)

adopt [ə'dɔpt] vt adopter

adopted [ə'dɔptɪd] adj adoptif(-ive),
adopté(e)

adoption [ə'dɔpʃən] n adoption f

adore [ə'dɔ:^r] vt adorer

adorn [ə'dɔ:n] vt orner

Adriatic [eɪdrɪ'ætɪk], **Adriatic Sea** n: **the ~
(Sea)** la mer Adriatique, l'Adriatique f

adrift [ə'drɪft] adv à la dérive; **to come ~** (boat)
aller à la dérive; (wire, rope, fastening etc) se
défaire

ADSL n abbr (= asymmetric digital subscriber line)
ADSL m

adult ['ædʌlt] n adulte m/f ▷ adj (grown-up)
adulte; (for adults) pour adultes

adult education n éducation f des adultes

adultery [ə'dʌltərɪ] n adultère m

advance [əd'vɑ:ns] n avance f ▷ vt avancer
▷ vi s'avancer; **in ~** en avance, d'avance; **to
make ~s to sb** (gen) faire des propositions à
qn; (amorously) faire des avances à qn;
~ booking location f; **~ notice, ~ warning**
préavis m; (verbal) avertissement m; **do I need
to book in ~?** est-ce qu'il faut réserver à
l'avance?

advanced [əd'vɑ:nst] adj avancé(e); (Scol:
studies) supérieur(e); **~ in years** d'un âge
avancé

advantage [əd'vɑ:ntɪdʒ] n (also Tennis)
avantage m; **to take ~ of** (person) exploiter;
(opportunity) profiter de; **it's to our ~** c'est à

notre intérêt; **it's to our ~ to ...** nous avons
intérêt à ...

advent [ədvənt] n avènement m, venue f; **A~**
(Rel) avent m

adventure [əd'vɛntʃə^r] n aventure f

adventurous [əd'vɛntʃərəs] adj
aventureux(-euse)

adverb ['ædvə:b] n adverbe m

adversary ['ædvəsərɪ] n adversaire m/f

adverse ['ædvə:s] adj adverse; (effect)
négatif(-ive); (weather, publicity) mauvais(e);
(wind) contraire; **~ to** hostile à; **in ~
circumstances** dans l'adversité

advert ['ædvə:t] n abbr (Brit) = **advertisement**

advertise ['ædvətaɪz] vi faire de la publicité
or de la réclame; (in classified ads etc) mettre
une annonce ▷ vt faire de la publicité or de la
réclame pour; (in classified ads etc) mettre une
annonce pour vendre; **to ~ for** (staff) recruter
par (voie d')annonce

advertisement [əd'və:tɪsmənt] n publicité
f, réclame f; (in classified ads etc) annonce f

advertiser ['ædvətaɪzə^r] n annonceur m

advertising ['ædvətaɪzɪŋ] n publicité f

advice [əd'vaɪs] n conseils mpl; (notification)
avis m; **a piece of ~** un conseil; **to ask (sb)
for ~** demander conseil (à qn); **to take legal ~**
consulter un avocat

advisable [əd'vaɪzəbl] adj recommandable,
indiqué(e)

advise [əd'vaɪz] vt conseiller; **to ~ sb of sth**
aviser or informer qn de qch; **to ~ against
sth/doing sth** déconseiller qch/conseiller de
ne pas faire qch; **you would be well/ill ~d to
go** vous feriez mieux d'y aller/de ne pas y
aller, vous auriez intérêt à y aller/à ne pas y
aller

adviser, advisor [əd'vaɪzə^r] n
conseiller(-ère)

advisory [əd'vaɪzərɪ] adj consultatif(-ive); **in
an ~ capacity** à titre consultatif

advocate n ['ædvəkɪt] (lawyer) avocat
(plaidant); (upholder) défenseur m, avocat(e)
▷ vt ['ædvəkeɪt] recommander, prôner; **to be
an ~ of** être partisan(e) de

Aegean [i:'dʒi:ən] n, adj: **the ~ (Sea)** la mer
Égée, l'Égée f

aerial ['ɛərɪəl] n antenne f ▷ adj aérien(ne)

aerobics [ɛə'rəubɪks] n aérobic m

aeroplane ['ɛərəpleɪn] n (Brit) avion m

aerosol ['ɛərəsɔl] n aérosol m

aesthetic [ɪs'θɛtɪk] adj esthétique

afar [ə'fɑ:^r] adv: **from ~** de loin

affair [ə'fɛə^r] n affaire f; (also: **love ~**) liaison f;
aventure f; **affairs** (business) affaires f

affect [ə'fɛkt] vt affecter; (subj: disease)
atteindre

affected [ə'fɛktɪd] adj affecté(e)

affection [ə'fɛkʃən] n affection f

affectionate [ə'fɛkʃənɪt] adj
affectueux(-euse)

affinity [ə'fɪnɪtɪ] n affinité f

afflict [əˈflɪkt] vt affliger

affluence [ˈæfluəns] n aisance f, opulence f

affluent [ˈæfluənt] adj opulent(e); (person, family, surroundings) aisé(e), riche; **the ~ society** la société d'abondance

afford [əˈfɔːd] vt (goods etc) avoir les moyens d'acheter or d'entretenir; (behaviour) se permettre; (provide) fournir, procurer; **can we ~ a car?** avons-nous de quoi acheter or les moyens d'acheter une voiture?; **I can't ~ the time** je n'ai vraiment pas le temps

affordable [əˈfɔːdəbl] adj abordable

Afghanistan [æfˈɡænɪstæn] n Afghanistan m

afloat [əˈfləut] adj à flot ▷ adv: **to stay ~** surnager; **to keep/get a business ~** maintenir à flot/lancer une affaire

afoot [əˈfut] adv: **there is something ~** il se prépare quelque chose

afraid [əˈfreɪd] adj effrayé(e); **to be ~ of** or **to** avoir peur de; **I am ~ that** je crains que + sub; **I'm ~ so/not** oui/non, malheureusement

Africa [ˈæfrɪkə] n Afrique f

African [ˈæfrɪkən] adj africain(e) ▷ n Africain(e)

African-American [ˈæfrɪkənəˈmɛrɪkən] adj afro-américain(e) ▷ n Afro-Américain(e)

after [ˈɑːftəʳ] prep, adv après ▷ conj après que, après avoir or être + pp; **~ dinner** après (le) dîner; **the day ~ tomorrow** après-demain; **it's quarter ~ two** (US) il est deux heures et quart; **~ having done/~ he left** après avoir fait/après son départ; **to name sb ~ sb** donner à qn le nom de qn; **to ask ~ sb** demander des nouvelles de qn; **what/who are you ~?** que/qui cherchez-vous?; **the police are ~ him** la police est à ses trousses; **~ you!** après vous!; **~ all** après tout

after-effects [ˈɑːftərɪfɛkts] npl (of disaster, radiation, drink etc) répercussions fpl; (of illness) séquelles fpl, suites fpl

aftermath [ˈɑːftəmɑːθ] n conséquences fpl; **in the ~ of** dans les mois ou années etc qui suivirent, au lendemain de

afternoon [ˈɑːftəˈnuːn] n après-midi m or f; **good ~!** bonjour!; (goodbye) au revoir!

afters [ˈɑːftəz] n (Brit inf: dessert) dessert m

after-sales service [ˈɑːftəˈseɪlz-] n service m après-vente, SAV m

after-shave [ˈɑːftəʃeɪv], **after-shave lotion** n lotion f après-rasage

aftersun [ˈɑːftəsʌn], **aftersun cream, aftersun lotion** n après-soleil m inv

afterthought [ˈɑːftəθɔːt] n: **I had an ~** il m'est venu une idée après coup

afterwards [ˈɑːftəwədz], (US) **afterward** [ˈɑːftəwəd] adv après

again [əˈɡɛn] adv de nouveau, encore (une fois); **to do sth ~** refaire qch; **not ... ~** ne ... plus; **~ and ~** à plusieurs reprises; **he's opened it ~** il l'a rouvert, il l'a de nouveau or il l'a encore ouvert; **now and ~** de temps à autre

against [əˈɡɛnst] prep contre; (compared to) par rapport à; **~ a blue background** sur un fond bleu; **(as) ~** (Brit) contre

age [eɪdʒ] n âge m ▷ vt, vi vieillir; **what ~ is he?** quel âge a-t-il?; **he is 20 years of ~** il a 20 ans; **under ~** mineur(e); **to come of ~** atteindre sa majorité; **it's been ~s since I saw you** ça fait une éternité que je ne t'ai pas vu

aged [ˈeɪdʒd] adj âgé(e); **~ 10** âgé de 10 ans ▷ npl [ˈeɪdʒɪd]: **the ~** les personnes âgées

age group n tranche f d'âge; **the 40 to 50 ~** la tranche d'âge des 40 à 50 ans

age limit n limite f d'âge

agency [ˈeɪdʒənsɪ] n agence f; **through** or **by the ~ of** par l'entremise or l'action de

agenda [əˈdʒɛndə] n ordre m du jour; **on the ~** à l'ordre du jour

agent [ˈeɪdʒənt] n agent m; (firm) concessionnaire m

aggravate [ˈæɡrəveɪt] vt (situation) aggraver; (annoy) exaspérer, agacer

aggression [əˈɡrɛʃən] n agression f

aggressive [əˈɡrɛsɪv] adj agressif(-ive)

agile [ˈædʒaɪl] adj agile

agitate [ˈædʒɪteɪt] vt rendre inquiet(-ète) or agité(e) ▷ vi faire de l'agitation (politique); **to ~ for** faire campagne pour

AGM n abbr (= annual general meeting) AG f

ago [əˈɡəu] adv: **two days ~** il y a deux jours; **not long ~** il n'y a pas longtemps; **as long as 1960 ~** déjà en 1960; **how long ~?** il y a combien de temps (de cela)?

agony [ˈæɡənɪ] n (pain) douleur f atroce; (distress) angoisse f; **to be in ~** souffrir le martyre

agree [əˈɡriː] vt (price) convenir de ▷ vi: **to ~ with** (person) être d'accord avec; (statements etc) concorder avec; (Ling) s'accorder avec; **to ~ to do** accepter de or consentir à faire; **to ~ to sth** consentir à qch; **to ~ that** (admit) convenir or reconnaître que; **it was ~d that ...** il a été convenu que ...; **they ~ on this** ils sont d'accord sur ce point; **they ~d on going/a price** ils se mirent d'accord pour y aller/sur un prix; **garlic doesn't ~ with me** je ne supporte pas l'ail

agreeable [əˈɡriːəbl] adj (pleasant) agréable; (willing) consentant(e), d'accord; **are you ~ to this?** est-ce que vous êtes d'accord?

agreed [əˈɡriːd] adj (time, place) convenu(e); **to be ~** être d'accord

agreement [əˈɡriːmənt] n accord m; **in ~** d'accord; **by mutual ~** d'un commun accord

agricultural [æɡrɪˈkʌltʃərəl] adj agricole

agriculture [ˈæɡrɪkʌltʃəʳ] n agriculture f

aground [əˈɡraund] adv: **to run ~** s'échouer

ahead [əˈhɛd] adv en avant; devant; **go right** or **straight ~** (direction) allez tout droit; **go ~!** (permission) allez-y!; **~ of** devant; (fig: schedule etc) en avance sur; **~ of time** en avance; **they were (right) ~ of us** ils nous précédaient (de peu), ils étaient (juste) devant nous

aid [eɪd] *n* aide *f*; (*device*) appareil *m* ▷ *vt* aider; **with the ~ of** avec l'aide de; **in ~ of** en faveur de; **to ~ and abet** (*Law*) se faire le complice de

aide [eɪd] *n* (*person*) assistant(e)

AIDS [eɪdz] *n abbr* (= *acquired immune* (or *immuno-*) *deficiency syndrome*) SIDA *m*

ailing ['eɪlɪŋ] *adj* (*person*) souffreteux(euse); (*economy*) malade

ailment ['eɪlmənt] *n* affection *f*

aim [eɪm] *vt*: **to ~ sth (at)** (*gun, camera*) braquer or pointer qch (sur); (*missile*) lancer qch (à or contre or en direction de); (*remark, blow*) destiner or adresser qch (à) ▷ *vi* (*also*: **to take ~**) viser ▷ *n* (*objective*) but *m*; (*skill*): **his ~ is bad** il vise mal; **to ~ at** viser; (*fig*) viser (à); avoir pour but or ambition; **to ~ to do** avoir l'intention de faire

aimless ['eɪmlɪs] *adj* sans but

ain't [eɪnt] (*inf*) = **am not; aren't; isn't**

air [ɛəʳ] *n* air *m* ▷ *vt* aérer; (*idea, grievance, views*) mettre sur le tapis; (*knowledge*) faire étalage de ▷ *cpd* (*currents, attack etc*) aérien(ne); **to throw sth into the ~** (*ball etc*) jeter qch en l'air; **by ~** par avion; **to be on the ~** (*Radio, TV: programme*) être diffusé(e); (*: station*) émettre

airbag ['ɛəbæg] *n* airbag *m*

airbed ['ɛəbɛd] *n* (*Brit*) matelas *m* pneumatique

airborne ['ɛəbɔːn] *adj* (*plane*) en vol; (*troops*) aéroporté(e); (*particles*) dans l'air; **as soon as the plane was ~** dès que l'avion eut décollé

air-conditioned ['ɛəkənˈdɪʃənd] *adj* climatisé(e), à air conditionné

air conditioning [-kənˈdɪʃnɪŋ] *n* climatisation *f*

aircraft ['ɛəkrɑːft] *n inv* avion *m*

aircraft carrier *n* porte-avions *m inv*

airfield ['ɛəfiːld] *n* terrain *m* d'aviation

Air Force *n* Armée *f* de l'air

air freshener [-ˈfrɛʃnəʳ] *n* désodorisant *m*

airgun ['ɛəgʌn] *n*: fusil *m* à air comprimé

air hostess *n* (*Brit*) hôtesse *f* de l'air

airing cupboard *n* (*Brit*) placard qui contient la chaudière et dans lequel on met le linge à sécher

air letter *n* (*Brit*) aérogramme *m*

airlift ['ɛəlɪft] *n* pont aérien

airline ['ɛəlaɪn] *n* ligne aérienne, compagnie aérienne

airliner ['ɛəlaɪnəʳ] *n* avion *m* de ligne

airmail ['ɛəmeɪl] *n*: **by ~** par avion

air mile *n* air mile *m*

airplane ['ɛəpleɪn] *n* (*US*) avion *m*

airport ['ɛəpɔːt] *n* aéroport *m*

air raid *n* attaque aérienne

airsick ['ɛəsɪk] *adj*: **to be ~** avoir le mal de l'air

airspace ['ɛəspeɪs] *n* espace *m* aérien

airstrip ['ɛəstrɪp] *n* terrain *m* d'atterrissage

air terminal *n* aérogare *f*

airtight ['ɛətaɪt] *adj* hermétique

air-traffic controller *n* aiguilleur *m* du ciel

airy ['ɛərɪ] *adj* bien aéré(e); (*manners*) dégagé(e)

aisle [aɪl] *n* (*of church: central*) allée *f* centrale; (*: side*) nef *f* latérale, bas-côté *m*; (*in theatre, supermarket*) allée; (*on plane*) couloir *m*

aisle seat *n* place *f* côté couloir

ajar [əˈdʒɑːʳ] *adj* entrouvert(e)

akin [əˈkɪn] *adj*: **~ to** semblable à, du même ordre que

à la carte [ælæˈkɑːt] *adv* à la carte

alarm [əˈlɑːm] *n* alarme *f* ▷ *vt* alarmer

alarm call *n* coup *m* de fil pour réveiller; **could I have an ~ at 7 am, please?** pouvez-vous me réveiller à 7 heures, s'il vous plaît?

alarm clock *n* réveille-matin *m inv*, réveil *m*

alarmed [əˈlɑːmd] *adj* (*frightened*) alarmé(e); (*protected by an alarm*) protégé(e) par un système d'alarme; **to become ~** prendre peur

alarming [əˈlɑːmɪŋ] *adj* alarmant(e)

alas [əˈlæs] *excl* hélas

Albania [ælˈbeɪnɪə] *n* Albanie *f*

albeit [ɔːlˈbiːɪt] *conj* bien que + *sub*, encore que + *sub*

album ['ælbəm] *n* album *m*

alcohol ['ælkəhɔl] *n* alcool *m*

alcohol-free ['ælkəhɔlfriː] *adj* sans alcool

alcoholic [ælkəˈhɔlɪk] *adj, n* alcoolique (*m/f*)

alcove ['ælkəuv] *n* alcôve *f*

ale [eɪl] *n* bière *f*

alert [əˈləːt] *adj* alerte, vif/vive; (*watchful*) vigilant(e) ▷ *n* alerte *f* ▷ *vt* alerter; **to ~ sb (to sth)** attirer l'attention de qn (sur qch); **to ~ sb to the dangers of sth** avertir qn des dangers de qch; **on the ~** sur le qui-vive; (*Mil*) en état d'alerte

A level *n abbr* (*Brit: = Advanced level*) ≈ baccalauréat *m*

algebra ['ældʒɪbrə] *n* algèbre *m*

Algeria [ælˈdʒɪərɪə] *n* Algérie *f*

Algerian [ælˈdʒɪərɪən] *adj* algérien(ne) ▷ *n* Algérien(ne)

Algiers [ælˈdʒɪəz] *n* Alger

alias ['eɪlɪəs] *adv* alias ▷ *n* faux nom, nom d'emprunt

alibi ['ælɪbaɪ] *n* alibi *m*

alien ['eɪlɪən] *n* (*from abroad*) étranger(-ère); (*from outer space*) extraterrestre ▷ *adj*: **~ (to)** étranger(-ère) (à)

alienate ['eɪlɪəneɪt] *vt* aliéner; (*subj: person*) s'aliéner

alight [əˈlaɪt] *adj, adv* en feu ▷ *vi* mettre pied à terre; (*passenger*) descendre; (*bird*) se poser

align [əˈlaɪn] *vt* aligner

alike [əˈlaɪk] *adj* semblable, pareil(le) ▷ *adv* de même; **to look ~** se ressembler

alimony ['ælɪmənɪ] *n* (*payment*) pension *f* alimentaire

alive [əˈlaɪv] *adj* vivant(e); (*active*) plein(e) de vie; **~ with** grouillant(e) de; **~ to** sensible à

◯ KEYWORD

all [ɔːl] *adj* (*singular*) tout(e); (*plural*) tous/toutes; **all day** toute la journée; **all night** toute la nuit; **all men** tous les hommes; **all**

five tous les cinq; **all the food** toute la nourriture; **all the books** tous les livres; **all the time** tout le temps; **all his life** toute sa vie ▷ *pron* **1** tout; **I ate it all, I ate all of it** j'ai tout mangé; **all of us went** nous y sommes tous allés; **all of the boys went** tous les garçons y sont allés; **is that all?** c'est tout?; *(in shop)* ce sera tout?

2 *(in phrases)*: **above all** surtout, par-dessus tout; **after all** après tout; **at all: not at all** *(in answer to question)* pas du tout; *(in answer to thanks)* je vous en prie!; **I'm not at all tired** je ne suis pas du tout fatigué(e); **anything at all will do** n'importe quoi fera l'affaire; **all in all** tout bien considéré, en fin de compte ▷ *adv*: **all alone** tout(e) seul(e); **it's not as hard as all that** ce n'est pas si difficile que ça; **all the more/the better** d'autant plus/ mieux; **all but** presque, pratiquement; **to be all in** *(Brit inf)* être complètement à plat; **the score is 2 all** le score est de 2 partout

Allah ['ælə] *n* Allah *m*
allegation [ælɪ'geɪʃən] *n* allégation *f*
allege [ə'ledʒ] *vt* alléguer, prétendre; **he is -d to have said** il aurait dit
alleged [ə'ledʒd] *adj* prétendu(e)
allegedly [ə'ledʒɪdlɪ] *adv* à ce que l'on prétend, paraît-il
allegiance [ə'liːdʒəns] *n* fidélité *f*, obéissance *f*
allergic [ə'ləːdʒɪk] *adj*: ~ **to** allergique à; **I'm ~ to penicillin** je suis allergique à la pénicilline
allergy ['ælədʒɪ] *n* allergie *f*
alleviate [ə'liːvɪeɪt] *vt* soulager, adoucir
alley ['ælɪ] *n* ruelle *f*; *(in garden)* allée *f*
alliance [ə'laɪəns] *n* alliance *f*
allied ['ælaɪd] *adj* allié(e)
alligator ['ælɪgeɪtə^r] *n* alligator *m*
all-in ['ɔːlɪn] *adj, adv* *(Brit: charge)* tout compris
all-night ['ɔːl'naɪt] *adj* ouvert(e) or qui dure toute la nuit
allocate ['æləkeɪt] *vt* *(share out)* répartir, distribuer; **to ~ sth to** *(duties)* assigner or attribuer qch à; *(sum, time)* allouer qch à; **to ~ sth for** affecter qch à
allot [ə'lɔt] *vt* *(share out)* répartir, distribuer; **to ~ sth to** *(time)* allouer qch à; *(duties)* assigner qch à; **in the ~ted time** dans le temps imparti
allotment [ə'lɔtmənt] *n* *(share)* part *f*; *(garden)* lopin *m* de terre *(loué à la municipalité)*
all-out ['ɔːlaut] *adj* *(effort etc)* total(e)
allow [ə'lau] *vt* *(practice, behaviour)* permettre, autoriser; *(sum to spend etc)* accorder, allouer; *(sum, time estimated)* compter, prévoir; *(claim, goal)* admettre; *(concede)*: **to ~ that** convenir que; **to ~ sb to do** permettre à qn de faire, autoriser qn à faire; **he is ~ed to ...** on lui permet de ...; **smoking is not ~ed** il est interdit de fumer; **we must ~ three days for**

the journey il faut compter trois jours pour le voyage; **allow for** *vt fus* tenir compte de
allowance [ə'lauəns] *n* *(money received)* allocation *f*; *(: from parent etc)* subside *m*; *(: for expenses)* indemnité *f*; *(US: pocket money)* argent *m* de poche; *(Tax)* somme *f* déductible du revenu imposable, abattement *m*; **to make ~s for** *(person)* essayer de comprendre; *(thing)* tenir compte de
alloy ['ælɔɪ] *n* alliage *m*
all right *adv* *(feel, work)* bien; *(as answer)* d'accord
all-rounder [ɔːl'raundə^r] *n* *(Brit)*: **to be a good ~** être doué(e) en tout
all-time ['ɔːl'taɪm] *adj* *(record)* sans précédent, absolu(e)
ally ['ælaɪ] *n* allié *m* ▷ *vt* [ə'laɪ]: **to ~ o.s. with** s'allier avec
almighty [ɔːl'maɪtɪ] *adj* tout(e)-puissant(e); *(tremendous)* énorme
almond ['ɑːmənd] *n* amande *f*
almost ['ɔːlməust] *adv* presque; **he ~ fell** il a failli tomber
alone [ə'ləun] *adj, adv* seul(e); **to leave sb ~** laisser qn tranquille; **to leave sth ~** ne pas toucher à qch; **let ~ ...** sans parler de ...; encore moins ...
along [ə'lɔŋ] *prep* le long de ▷ *adv*: **is he coming ~ with us?** vient-il avec nous?; **he was hopping/limping ~** il venait or avançait en sautillant/boitant; **~ with** avec, en plus de; *(person)* en compagnie de; **all ~** *(all the time)* depuis le début
alongside [ə'lɔŋ'saɪd] *prep* *(along)* le long de; *(beside)* à côté de ▷ *adv* bord à bord; côte à côte; **we brought our boat ~** *(of a pier, shore etc)* nous avons accosté
aloof [ə'luːf] *adj* distant(e) ▷ *adv* à distance, à l'écart; **to stand ~** se tenir à l'écart or à distance
aloud [ə'laud] *adv* à haute voix
alphabet ['ælfəbet] *n* alphabet *m*
alphabetical [ælfə'betɪkl] *adj* alphabétique; **in ~ order** par ordre alphabétique
alpine ['ælpaɪn] *adj* alpin(e), alpestre; **~ hut** cabane *f* or refuge *m* de montagne; **~ pasture** pâturage *m* (de montagne); **~ skiing** ski alpin
Alps [ælps] *npl*: **the ~** les Alpes *fpl*
already [ɔːl'redɪ] *adv* déjà
alright ['ɔːl'raɪt] *adv* *(Brit)* = **all right**
Alsatian [æl'seɪʃən] *adj* alsacien(ne), d'Alsace ▷ *n* Alsacien(ne); *(Brit: dog)* berger allemand
also ['ɔːlsəu] *adv* aussi
altar ['ɔltə^r] *n* autel *m*
alter ['ɔltə^r] *vt, vi* changer
alteration [ɔltə'reɪʃən] *n* changement *m*, modification *f*; **alterations** *npl* *(Sewing)* retouches *fpl*; *(Archit)* modifications *fpl*; **timetable subject to ~** horaires sujets à modifications
alternate *adj* [ɔl'təːnɪt] alterné(e), alternant(e), alternatif(-ive); *(US)*

= **alternative** ▷ vi ['ɔltə:neɪt] alterner; **to ~ with** alterner avec; **on ~ days** un jour sur deux, tous les deux jours

alternative [ɔl'tə:nətɪv] adj (solution, plan) autre, de remplacement; (energy) doux/douce; (lifestyle) parallèle ▷ n (choice) alternative f; (other possibility) autre possibilité f; **~ medicine** médecine alternative, médecine douce

alternatively [ɔl'tə:nətɪvlɪ] adv: **~ one could ...** une autre or l'autre solution serait de ...

alternator ['ɔltə:neɪtəʳ] n (Aut) alternateur m

although [ɔːl'ðəu] conj bien que + sub

altitude ['æltɪtjuːd] n altitude f

alto ['æltəu] n (female) contralto m; (male) haute-contre f

altogether [ɔːltə'ɡɛðəʳ] adv entièrement, tout à fait; (on the whole) tout compte fait; (in all) en tout; **how much is that ~?** ça fait combien en tout?

aluminium [ælju'mɪnɪəm], (US) **aluminum** [ə'lu:mɪnəm] n aluminium m

always ['ɔːlweɪz] adv toujours

Alzheimer's ['æltshaɪməz], **Alzheimer's disease** n maladie f d'Alzheimer

AM abbr = **amplitude modulation** ▷ n abbr (= Assembly Member) député m au Parlement gallois

am [æm] vb see **be**

a.m. adv abbr (= ante meridiem) du matin

amalgamate [ə'mælɡəmeɪt] vt, vi fusionner

amass [ə'mæs] vt amasser

amateur ['æmətəʳ] n amateur m ▷ adj (Sport) amateur inv; **~ dramatics** le théâtre amateur

amateurish ['æmətərɪʃ] adj (pej) d'amateur, un peu amateur

amaze [ə'meɪz] vt stupéfier; **to be ~d (at)** être stupéfait(e) (de)

amazed [ə'meɪzd] adj stupéfait(e)

amazement [ə'meɪzmənt] n surprise f, étonnement m

amazing [ə'meɪzɪŋ] adj étonnant(e), incroyable; (bargain, offer) exceptionnel(le)

Amazon ['æməzən] n (Geo, Mythology) Amazone f ▷ cpd amazonien(ne), de l'Amazone; **the ~ basin** le bassin de l'Amazone; **the ~ jungle** la forêt amazonienne

ambassador [æm'bæsədəʳ] n ambassadeur m

amber ['æmbəʳ] n ambre m; **at ~** (Brit Aut) à l'orange

ambiguous [æm'bɪɡjuəs] adj ambigu(ë)

ambition [æm'bɪʃən] n ambition f

ambitious [æm'bɪʃəs] adj ambitieux(-euse)

ambulance ['æmbjuləns] n ambulance f; **call an ~!** appelez une ambulance!

ambush ['æmbuʃ] n embuscade f ▷ vt tendre une embuscade à

amen ['ɑ:'mɛn] excl amen

amenable [ə'mi:nəbl] adj: **~ to** (advice etc) disposé(e) à écouter or suivre; **~ to the law** responsable devant la loi

amend [ə'mɛnd] vt (law) amender; (text) corriger; (habits) réformer ▷ vi s'amender, se corriger; **to make ~s** réparer ses torts, faire amende honorable

amendment [ə'mɛndmənt] n (to law) amendement m; (to text) correction f

amenities [ə'mi:nɪtɪz] npl aménagements mpl, équipements mpl

America [ə'mɛrɪkə] n Amérique f

American [ə'mɛrɪkən] adj américain(e) ▷ n Américain(e)

American football n (Brit) football m américain

amiable ['eɪmɪəbl] adj aimable, affable

amicable ['æmɪkəbl] adj amical(e); (Law) à l'amiable

amid [ə'mɪd], **amidst** [ə'mɪdst] prep parmi, au milieu de

amiss [ə'mɪs] adj, adv: **there's something ~** il y a quelque chose qui ne va pas or qui cloche; **to take sth ~** prendre qch mal or de travers

ammonia [ə'məunɪə] n (gas) ammoniac m; (liquid) ammoniaque f

ammunition [æmju'nɪʃən] n munitions fpl; (fig) arguments mpl

amnesty ['æmnɪstɪ] n amnistie f; **to grant an ~ to** accorder une amnistie à

amok [ə'mɔk] adv: **to run ~** être pris(e) d'un accès de folie furieuse

among [ə'mʌŋ], **amongst** [ə'mʌŋst] prep parmi, entre

amorous ['æmərəs] adj amoureux(-euse)

amount [ə'maunt] n (sum of money) somme f; (total) montant m; (quantity) quantité f; nombre m ▷ vi: **to ~ to** (total) s'élever à; (be same as) équivaloir à, revenir à; **this ~s to a refusal** cela équivaut à un refus; **the total ~** (of money) le montant total

amp [æmp], **ampère** ['æmpɛəʳ] n ampère m; **a 13 ~ plug** une fiche de 13 A

ample ['æmpl] adj ample, spacieux(-euse); (enough): **this is ~** c'est largement suffisant; **to have ~ time/room** avoir bien assez de temps/place, avoir largement le temps/la place

amplifier ['æmplɪfaɪəʳ] n amplificateur m

amputate ['æmpjuteɪt] vt amputer

Amtrak ['æmtræk] (US) n société mixte de transports ferroviaires interurbains pour voyageurs

amuse [ə'mju:z] vt amuser; **to ~ o.s. with sth/by doing sth** se divertir avec qch/à faire qch; **to be ~d at** être amusé par; **he was not ~d** il n'a pas apprécié

amusement [ə'mju:zmənt] n amusement m; (pastime) distraction f

amusement arcade n salle f de jeu

amusement park n parc m d'attractions

amusing [ə'mju:zɪŋ] adj amusant(e), divertissant(e)

an [æn, ən, n] indef art see **a**

anaemia, (US) **anemia** [ə'ni:mɪə] n anémie f

anaemic, (US) **anemic** [ə'ni:mɪk] adj anémique

anaesthetic, (US) **anesthetic** [ænɪs'θɛtɪk] *adj, n* anesthésique *m*; **under the** ~ sous anesthésie; **local/general** ~ anesthésie locale/générale

analogue, analog ['ænəlɒɡ] *adj* (*watch, computer*) analogique

analogy [ə'nælədʒɪ] *n* analogie *f*; **to draw an** ~ **between** établir une analogie entre

analyse, (US) **analyze** [ænəlaɪz] *vt* analyser

analysis (*pl* **analyses**) [ə'næləsɪs, -siːz] *n* analyse *f*; **in the last** ~ en dernière analyse

analyst ['ænəlɪst] *n* (*political analyst etc*) analyste *m/f*; (US) psychanalyste *m/f*

analyze ['ænəlaɪz] *vt* (US) = **analyse**

anarchist ['ænəkɪst] *adj, n* anarchiste (*m/f*)

anarchy ['ænəkɪ] *n* anarchie *f*

anatomy [ə'nætəmɪ] *n* anatomie *f*

ancestor ['ænsɪstə^r] *n* ancêtre *m*, aïeul *m*

anchor ['æŋkə^r] *n* ancre *f* ▷ *vi* (*also*: **to drop** ~) jeter l'ancre, mouiller ▷ *vt* mettre à l'ancre; (*fig*): **to** ~ **sth to** fixer qch à; **to weigh** ~ lever l'ancre

anchovy ['æntʃəvɪ] *n* anchois *m*

ancient ['eɪnʃənt] *adj* ancien(ne), antique; (*person*) d'un âge vénérable; (*car*) antédiluvien(ne); ~ **monument** monument *m* historique

ancillary [æn'sɪlərɪ] *adj* auxiliaire

and [ænd] *conj* et; ~ **so on** et ainsi de suite; **try** ~ **come** tâchez de venir; **come** ~ **sit here** venez vous asseoir ici; **he talked** ~ **talked** il a parlé pendant des heures; **better** ~ **better** de mieux en mieux; **more** ~ **more** de plus en plus

Andorra [æn'dɔːrə] *n* (principauté *f* d')Andorre *f*

anemia *etc* [ə'niːmɪə] *n* (US) = **anaemia** *etc*

anesthetic [ænɪs'θɛtɪk] *n, adj* (US) = **anaesthetic**

anew [ə'njuː] *adv* à nouveau

angel ['eɪndʒəl] *n* ange *m*

anger ['æŋɡə^r] *n* colère *f* ▷ *vt* mettre en colère, irriter

angina [æn'dʒaɪnə] *n* angine *f* de poitrine

angle ['æŋɡl] *n* angle *m* ▷ *vi*: **to** ~ **for** (*trout*) pêcher; (*compliments*) chercher, quêter; **from their** ~ de leur point de vue

angler ['æŋɡlə^r] *n* pêcheur(-euse) à la ligne

Anglican ['æŋɡlɪkən] *adj, n* anglican(e)

angling ['æŋɡlɪŋ] *n* pêche *f* à la ligne

Anglo- ['æŋɡləu] *prefix* anglo(-)

angrily ['æŋɡrɪlɪ] *adv* avec colère

angry ['æŋɡrɪ] *adj* en colère, furieux(-euse); (*wound*) enflammé(e); **to be** ~ **with sb/at sth** être furieux contre qn/de qch; **to get** ~ se fâcher, se mettre en colère; **to make sb** ~ mettre qn en colère

anguish ['æŋɡwɪʃ] *n* angoisse *f*

animal ['ænɪməl] *n* animal *m* ▷ *adj* animal(e)

animate *vt* ['ænɪmeɪt] animer ▷ *adj* ['ænɪmɪt] animé(e), vivant(e)

animated ['ænɪmeɪtɪd] *adj* animé(e)

animation [ænɪ'meɪʃən] *n* (*of person*) entrain *m*; (*of street, Cine*) animation *f*

aniseed ['ænɪsiːd] *n* anis *m*

ankle ['æŋkl] *n* cheville *f*

ankle socks *npl* socquettes *fpl*

annex ['ænɛks] *n* (Brit: *also*: **~e**) annexe *f* ▷ *vt* [ə'nɛks] annexer

anniversary [ænɪ'vəːsərɪ] *n* anniversaire *m*

announce [ə'nauns] *vt* annoncer; (*birth, death*) faire part de; **he ~d that he wasn't going** il a déclaré qu'il n'irait pas

announcement [ə'naunsmənt] *n* annonce *f*; (*for births etc*: *in newspaper*) avis *m* de faire-part; (: *letter, card*) faire-part *m*; **I'd like to make an** ~ j'ai une communication à faire

announcer [ə'naunsə^r] *n* (Radio, TV: *between programmes*) speaker(ine); (: *in a programme*) présentateur(-trice)

annoy [ə'nɔɪ] *vt* agacer, ennuyer, contrarier; **to be ~ed (at sth/with sb)** être en colère or irrité (contre qch/qn); **don't get ~ed!** ne vous fâchez pas!

annoyance [ə'nɔɪəns] *n* mécontentement *m*, contrariété *f*

annoying [ə'nɔɪɪŋ] *adj* agaçant(e), contrariant(e)

annual ['ænjuəl] *adj* annuel(le) ▷ *n* (Bot) plante annuelle; (*book*) album *m*

annually ['ænjuəlɪ] *adv* annuellement

annul [ə'nʌl] *vt* annuler; (*law*) abroger

annum ['ænəm] *n see* **per**

anonymous [ə'nɒnɪməs] *adj* anonyme; **to remain** ~ garder l'anonymat

anorak ['ænəræk] *n* anorak *m*

anorexia [ænə'rɛksɪə] *n* (*also*: ~ **nervosa**) anorexie *f*

anorexic [ænə'rɛksɪk] *adj, n* anorexique (*m/f*)

another [ə'nʌðə^r] *adj*: ~ **book** (*one more*) un autre livre, encore un livre, un livre de plus; (*a different one*) un autre livre ▷ *pron* un(e) autre, encore un(e), un(e) de plus; ~ **drink?** encore un verre?; **in** ~ **five years** dans cinq ans; *see also* **one**

answer ['ɑːnsə^r] *n* réponse *f*; (*to problem*) solution *f* ▷ *vi* répondre ▷ *vt* (*reply to*) répondre à; (*problem*) résoudre; (*prayer*) exaucer; **in** ~ **to your letter** suite à or en réponse à votre lettre; **to** ~ **the phone** répondre (au téléphone); **to** ~ **the bell** or **the door** aller or venir ouvrir (la porte); **answer back** *vi* répondre, répliquer; **answer for** *vt fus* répondre de, se porter garant de; (*crime, one's actions*) répondre de; **answer to** *vt fus* (*description*) répondre or correspondre à

answerable ['ɑːnsərəbl] *adj*: ~ **(to sb/for sth)** responsable (devant qn/de qch); **I am** ~ **to no-one** je n'ai de comptes à rendre à personne

answering machine ['ɑːnsərɪŋ-] *n* répondeur *m*

answerphone ['ɑːnsəfəun] *n* (*esp Brit*) répondeur *m* (téléphonique)

ant [ænt] n fourmi f
antagonism [æn'tægənɪzəm] n antagonisme m
antagonize [æn'tægənaɪz] vt éveiller l'hostilité de, contrarier
Antarctic [ænt'ɑːktɪk] adj antarctique, austral(e) ▷ n: **the ~** l'Antarctique m
antelope [ˈæntɪləʊp] n antilope f
antenatal [ˈæntɪ'neɪtl] adj prénatal(e)
antenatal clinic n service m de consultation prénatale
antenna (pl **antennae**) [æn'tɛnə, -niː] n antenne f
anthem [ˈænθəm] n motet m; **national ~** hymne national
anthology [æn'θɒlədʒɪ] n anthologie f
anthrax [ˈænθræks] n anthrax m
anthropology [ænθrə'pɒlədʒɪ] n anthropologie f
anti [ˈæntɪ] prefix anti-
anti-aircraft [ˈæntɪ'ɛəkrɑːft] adj antiaérien(ne)
antibiotic [ˈæntɪbaɪ'ɒtɪk] adj, n antibiotique m
antibody [ˈæntɪbɒdɪ] n anticorps m
anticipate [æn'tɪsɪpeɪt] vt s'attendre à, prévoir; (wishes, request) aller au devant de, devancer; **this is worse than I ~d** c'est pire que je ne pensais; **as ~d** comme prévu
anticipation [æntɪsɪ'peɪʃən] n attente f; **thanking you in ~** en vous remerciant d'avance, avec mes remerciements anticipés
anticlimax [ˈæntɪ'klaɪmæks] n déception f
anticlockwise [ˈæntɪ'klɒkwaɪz] (Brit) adv dans le sens inverse des aiguilles d'une montre
antics [ˈæntɪks] npl singeries fpl
antidepressant [ˈæntɪdɪ'prɛsnt] n antidépresseur m
antidote [ˈæntɪdəʊt] n antidote m, contrepoison m
antifreeze [ˈæntɪfriːz] n antigel m
anti-globalization [æntɪgləʊbəlaɪ'zeɪʃən] n antimondialisation f
antihistamine [æntɪ'hɪstəmɪn] n antihistaminique m
antiperspirant [ˈæntɪ'pəːspɪrənt] n déodorant m
antiquated [ˈæntɪkweɪtɪd] adj vieilli(e), suranné(e), vieillot(te)
antique [æn'tiːk] n (ornament) objet m d'art ancien; (furniture) meuble ancien ▷ adj ancien(ne); (pre-mediaeval) antique
antique dealer n antiquaire m/f
antique shop n magasin m d'antiquités
anti-Semitism [ˈæntɪ'sɛmɪtɪzəm] n antisémitisme m
antiseptic [æntɪ'sɛptɪk] adj, n antiseptique (m)
antisocial [ˈæntɪ'səʊʃəl] adj (unfriendly) peu liant(e), insociable; (against society) antisocial(e)
antiviral [ˈæntɪvaɪərəl] adj (Med) antiviral

antivirus [æntɪ'vaɪrəs] adj (Comput) antivirus inv; **~ software** (logiciel m) antivirus
antlers [ˈæntləz] npl bois mpl, ramure f
anvil [ˈænvɪl] n enclume f
anxiety [æŋ'zaɪətɪ] n anxiété f; (keenness): **~ to do** grand désir or impatience f de faire
anxious [ˈæŋkʃəs] adj (très) inquiet(-ète); (always worried) anxieux(-euse); (worrying) angoissant(e); (keen): **~ to do/that** qui tient beaucoup à faire/à ce que + sub; impatient(e) de faire/que + sub; **I'm very ~ about you** je me fais beaucoup de souci pour toi

 KEYWORD

any [ˈɛnɪ] adj **1** (in questions etc: singular) du, de l', de la; (: plural) des; **do you have any butter/children/ink?** avez-vous du beurre/des enfants/de l'encre?
2 (with negative) de, d'; **I don't have any money/books** je n'ai pas d'argent/de livres; **without any difficulty** sans la moindre difficulté
3 (no matter which) n'importe quel(le); (each and every) tout(e), chaque; **choose any book you like** vous pouvez choisir n'importe quel livre; **any teacher you ask will tell you** n'importe quel professeur vous le dira
4 (in phrases): **in any case** de toute façon; **any day now** d'un jour à l'autre; **at any moment** à tout moment, d'un instant à l'autre; **at any rate** en tout cas; **any time** n'importe quand; **he might come (at) any time** il pourrait venir n'importe quand; **come (at) any time** venez quand vous voulez
▷ pron **1** (in questions etc) en; **have you got any?** est-ce que vous en avez?; **can any of you sing?** est-ce que parmi vous il y en a qui savent chanter?
2 (with negative) en; **I don't have any (of them)** je n'en ai pas, je n'en ai aucun
3 (no matter which one(s)) n'importe lequel (or laquelle); (anybody) n'importe qui; **take any of those books (you like)** vous pouvez prendre n'importe lequel de ces livres
▷ adv **1** (in questions etc): **do you want any more soup/sandwiches?** voulez-vous encore de la soupe/des sandwichs?; **are you feeling any better?** est-ce que vous vous sentez mieux?
2 (with negative): **I can't hear him any more** je ne l'entends plus; **don't wait any longer** n'attendez pas plus longtemps

anybody [ˈɛnɪbɒdɪ] pron n'importe qui; (in interrogative sentences) quelqu'un; (in negative sentences): **I don't see ~** je ne vois personne; **if ~ should phone ...** si quelqu'un téléphone ...
anyhow [ˈɛnɪhaʊ] adv quoi qu'il en soit; (haphazardly) n'importe comment; **do it ~ you like** faites-le comme vous voulez; **she leaves things just ~** elle laisse tout traîner; **I shall go ~** j'irai de toute façon

anyone ['ɛnɪwʌn] *pron* = **anybody**

anything ['ɛnɪθɪŋ] *pron* (*no matter what*) n'importe quoi; (*in questions*) quelque chose; (*with negative*) ne ... rien; **I don't want** ~ je ne veux rien; **can you see ~?** tu vois quelque chose?; **if ~ happens to me ...** s'il m'arrive quoi que ce soit ...; **you can say ~ you like** vous pouvez dire ce que vous voulez; ~ **will do** n'importe quoi fera l'affaire; **he'll eat** ~ il mange de tout; ~ **else?** (*in shop*) avec ceci?; **it can cost ~ between £15 and £20** (*Brit*) ça peut coûter dans les 15 à 20 livres

anytime ['ɛnɪtaɪm] *adv* (*at any moment*) d'un moment à l'autre; (*whenever*) n'importe quand

anyway ['ɛnɪweɪ] *adv* de toute façon; ~, **I couldn't come even if I wanted to** de toute façon, je ne pouvais pas venir même si je le voulais; **I shall go** ~ j'irai quand même; **why are you phoning,** ~? au fait, pourquoi tu me téléphones?

anywhere ['ɛnɪwɛəʳ] *adv* n'importe où; (*in interrogative sentences*) quelque part; (*in negative sentences*): **I can't see him** ~ je ne le vois nulle part; **can you see him** ~? tu le vois quelque part?; **put the books down** ~ pose les livres n'importe où; ~ **in the world** (*no matter where*) n'importe où dans le monde

apart [ə'pɑːt] *adv* (*to one side*) à part; de côté; à l'écart; (*separately*) séparément; **to take/pull** ~ démonter; **10 miles/a long way** ~ à 10 miles/très éloignés l'un de l'autre; **they are living** ~ ils vivent séparés; ~ **from** *prep* à part, excepté

apartheid [ə'pɑːteɪt] *n* apartheid *m*

apartment [ə'pɑːtmənt] *n* (*US*) appartement *m*, logement *m*; (*room*) chambre *f*

apartment building *n* (*US*) immeuble *m*; maison divisée en appartements

apathy ['æpəθɪ] *n* apathie *f*, indifférence *f*

ape [eɪp] *n* (grand) singe ▷ *vt* singer

aperitif [ə'pɛrɪtɪf] *n* apéritif *m*

aperture ['æpətʃuəʳ] *n* orifice *m*, ouverture *f*; (*Phot*) ouverture (du diaphragme)

APEX ['eɪpɛks] *n abbr* (*Aviat*: = *advance purchase excursion*) APEX *m*

apex ['eɪpɛks] *n* sommet *m*

apologetic [əpɔlə'dʒɛtɪk] *adj* (*tone, letter*) d'excuse; **to be very ~ about** s'excuser vivement de

apologize [ə'pɔlədʒaɪz] *vi*: **to ~ (for sth to sb)** s'excuser (de qch auprès de qn), présenter des excuses (à qn pour qch)

apology [ə'pɔlədʒɪ] *n* excuses *fpl*; **to send one's apologies** envoyer une lettre *or* un mot d'excuse, s'excuser (de ne pas pouvoir venir); **please accept my apologies** vous voudrez bien m'excuser

apostle [ə'pɔsl] *n* apôtre *m*

apostrophe [ə'pɔstrəfɪ] *n* apostrophe *f*

app *n abbr* (*Comput*) = **application**

appal, (*US*) **appall** [ə'pɔːl] *vt* consterner, atterrer; horrifier

appalling [ə'pɔːlɪŋ] *adj* épouvantable; (*stupidity*) consternant(e); **she's an ~ cook** c'est une très mauvaise cuisinière

apparatus [æpə'reɪtəs] *n* appareil *m*, dispositif *m*; (*in gymnasium*) agrès *mpl*

apparel [ə'pærl] *n* (*US*) habillement *m*, confection *f*

apparent [ə'pærənt] *adj* apparent(e); **it is ~ that** il est évident que

apparently [ə'pærəntlɪ] *adv* apparemment

appeal [ə'piːl] *vi* (*Law*) faire *or* interjeter appel ▷ *n* (*Law*) appel *m*; (*request*) appel; prière *f*; (*charm*) attrait *m*, charme *m*; **to ~ for** demander (instamment); implorer; **to ~ to** (*beg*) faire appel à; (*be attractive*) plaire à; **to ~ to sb for mercy** implorer la pitié de qn, prier *or* adjurer qn d'avoir pitié; **it doesn't ~ to me** cela ne m'attire pas; **right of ~** droit *m* de recours

appealing [ə'piːlɪŋ] *adj* (*attractive*) attrayant(e); (*touching*) attendrissant(e)

appear [ə'pɪəʳ] *vi* apparaître, se montrer; (*Law*) comparaître; (*publication*) paraître, sortir, être publié(e); (*seem*) paraître, sembler; **it would ~ that** il semble que; **to ~ in Hamlet** jouer dans Hamlet; **to ~ on TV** passer à la télé

appearance [ə'pɪərəns] *n* apparition *f*; parution *f*; (*look, aspect*) apparence *f*, aspect *m*; **to put in** *or* **make an ~** faire acte de présence; (*Theat*): **by order of ~** par ordre d'entrée en scène; **to keep up ~s** sauver les apparences; **to all ~s** selon toute apparence

appease [ə'piːz] *vt* apaiser, calmer

appendices [ə'pɛndɪsiːz] *npl of* **appendix**

appendicitis [əpɛndɪ'saɪtɪs] *n* appendicite *f*

appendix (*pl* **appendices**) [ə'pɛndɪks, -siːz] *n* appendice *m*; **to have one's ~ out** se faire opérer de l'appendicite

appetite ['æpɪtaɪt] *n* appétit *m*; **that walk has given me an ~** cette promenade m'a ouvert l'appétit

appetizer ['æpɪtaɪzəʳ] *n* (*food*) amuse-gueule *m*; (*drink*) apéritif *m*

applaud [ə'plɔːd] *vt, vi* applaudir

applause [ə'plɔːz] *n* applaudissements *mpl*

apple ['æpl] *n* pomme *f*; (*also*: ~ **tree**) pommier *m*; **it's the ~ of my eye** j'y tiens comme à la prunelle de mes yeux

apple pie *n* tarte *f* aux pommes

appliance [ə'plaɪəns] *n* appareil *m*; **electrical ~s** l'électroménager *m*

applicable [ə'plɪkəbl] *adj* applicable; **the law is ~ from January** la loi entre en vigueur au mois de janvier; **to be ~ to** (*relevant*) valoir pour

applicant ['æplɪkənt] *n*: ~ **(for)** (*Admin: for benefit etc*) demandeur(-euse) (de); (*for post*) candidat(e) à(l')

application [æplɪ'keɪʃən] *n* application *f*; (*for a job, a grant etc*) demande *f*; candidature *f*;

(*Comput*) application f, (logiciel m) applicatif m; **on ~** sur demande

application form n formulaire m de demande

applied [ə'plaɪd] adj appliqué(e); **~ arts** npl arts décoratifs

apply [ə'plaɪ] vt: **to ~ (to)** (*paint, ointment*) appliquer (sur); (*law, etc*) appliquer (à) ▷ vi: **to ~ to** (*ask*) s'adresser à; (*be suitable for, relevant to*) s'appliquer à, être valable pour; **to ~ (for)** (*permit, grant*) faire une demande (en vue d'obtenir); (*job*) poser sa candidature (pour), faire une demande d'emploi (concernant); **to ~ the brakes** actionner les freins, freiner; **to ~ o.s. to** s'appliquer à

appoint [ə'pɔɪnt] vt (*to post*) nommer, engager; (*date, place*) fixer, désigner

appointment [ə'pɔɪntmənt] n (*to post*) nomination f; (*job*) poste m; (*arrangement to meet*) rendez-vous m; **to have an ~** avoir un rendez-vous; **to make an ~ (with)** prendre rendez-vous (avec); **I'd like to make an ~** je voudrais prendre rendez-vous; **"~s (vacant)"** (*Press*) "offres d'emploi"; **by ~** sur rendez-vous

appraisal [ə'preɪzl] n évaluation f

appreciate [ə'priːʃɪeɪt] vt (*like*) apprécier, faire cas de; (*be grateful for*) être reconnaissant(e) de; (*assess*) évaluer; (*be aware of*) comprendre, se rendre compte de ▷ vi (*Finance*) prendre de la valeur; **I ~ your help** je vous remercie pour votre aide

appreciation [əpriːʃɪ'eɪʃən] n appréciation f; (*gratitude*) reconnaissance f; (*Finance*) hausse f, valorisation f

appreciative [ə'priːʃɪətɪv] adj (*person*) sensible; (*comment*) élogieux(-euse)

apprehension [æprɪ'henʃən] n appréhension f, inquiétude f

apprehensive [æprɪ'hensɪv] adj inquiet(-ète), appréhensif(-ive)

apprentice [ə'prentɪs] n apprenti m ▷ vt: **to be ~d to** être en apprentissage chez

apprenticeship [ə'prentɪʃɪp] n apprentissage m; **to serve one's ~** faire son apprentissage

approach [ə'prəʊtʃ] vi approcher ▷ vt (*come near*) approcher de; (*ask, apply to*) s'adresser à; (*subject, passer-by*) aborder ▷ n approche f; accès m, abord m; démarche f (*auprès de qn*); (*intellectual*) démarche f; **to ~ sb about sth** aller or venir voir qn pour qch

approachable [ə'prəʊtʃəbl] adj accessible

appropriate adj [ə'prəʊprɪɪt] (*tool etc*) qui convient, approprié(e); (*moment, remark*) opportun(e) ▷ vt [ə'prəʊprɪeɪt] (*take*) s'approprier; (*allot*): **to ~ sth for** affecter qch à; **~ for** or **to** approprié à; **it would not be ~ for me to comment** il ne me serait pas approprié de commenter

approval [ə'pruːvl] n approbation f; **to meet with sb's ~** (*proposal etc*) recueillir l'assentiment de qn; **on ~** (*Comm*) à l'examen

approve [ə'pruːv] vt approuver; **approve of** vt fus (*thing*) approuver; (*person*): **they don't ~ of her** ils n'ont pas bonne opinion d'elle

approximate [ə'prɒksɪmɪt] adj approximatif(-ive) ▷ vt [ə'prɒksɪmeɪt] se rapprocher de; être proche de

approximately [ə'prɒksɪmətlɪ] adv approximativement

Apr. abbr = **April**

apricot ['eɪprɪkɒt] n abricot m

April ['eɪprəl] n avril m; **~ fool!** poisson d'avril!; *see also* **July**

April Fools' Day n le premier avril; *voir article*

● **APRIL FOOLS' DAY**
●
● *April Fools' Day* est le 1er avril, à l'occasion
● duquel on fait des farces de toutes sortes.
● Les victimes de ces farces sont les "April
● fools". Traditionnellement, on n'est
● censé faire des farces que jusqu'à midi.

apron ['eɪprən] n tablier m; (*Aviat*) aire f de stationnement

apt [æpt] adj (*suitable*) approprié(e); (*able*): **~ (at)** doué(e) (pour); apte (à); (*likely*): **~ to do** susceptible de faire; ayant tendance à faire

aquarium [ə'kwɛərɪəm] n aquarium m

Aquarius [ə'kwɛərɪəs] n le Verseau; **to be ~** être du Verseau

Arab ['ærəb] n Arabe m/f ▷ adj arabe

Arabia [ə'reɪbɪə] n Arabie f

Arabian [ə'reɪbɪən] adj arabe

Arabic ['ærəbɪk] adj, n arabe (m)

arbitrary ['ɑːbɪtrərɪ] adj arbitraire

arbitration [ɑːbɪ'treɪʃən] n arbitrage m; **the dispute went to ~** le litige a été soumis à arbitrage

arc [ɑːk] n arc m

arcade [ɑː'keɪd] n arcade f; (*passage with shops*) passage m, galerie f; (*with games*) salle f de jeu

arch [ɑːtʃ] n arche f; (*of foot*) cambrure f, voûte f plantaire ▷ vt arquer, cambrer ▷ adj malicieux(-euse) ▷ prefix: **~(-)** achevé(e); par excellence; **pointed ~** ogive f

archaeologist [ɑːkɪ'ɒlədʒɪst] n archéologue m/f

archaeology, (US) **archeology** [ɑːkɪ'ɒlədʒɪ] n archéologie f

archbishop [ɑːtʃ'bɪʃəp] n archevêque m

archeology [ɑːkɪ'ɒlədʒɪ] n = **archaeology**

archery ['ɑːtʃərɪ] n tir m à l'arc

architect ['ɑːkɪtɛkt] n architecte m

architectural [ɑːkɪ'tɛktʃərəl] adj architectural(e)

architecture ['ɑːkɪtɛktʃə'] n architecture f

archive ['ɑːkaɪv] n (*often pl*) archives fpl

archives ['ɑːkaɪvz] npl archives fpl

Arctic ['ɑːktɪk] adj arctique ▷ n: **the ~** l'Arctique m

ardent ['ɑːdənt] adj fervent(e)

are [ɑːʳ] vb *see* **be**

area ['ɛərɪə] n (Geom) superficie f; (zone) région f; (: smaller) secteur m; (in room) coin m; (knowledge, research) domaine m; **the London ~** la région Londonienne

area code (US) n (Tel) indicatif m de zone

arena [ə'riːnə] n arène f

aren't [ɑːnt] = **are not**

Argentina [ɑːdʒən'tiːnə] n Argentine f

Argentinian [ɑːdʒən'tɪnɪən] adj argentin(e) ▷ n Argentin(e)

arguably ['ɑːgjuəblɪ] adv: **it is ~ ...** on peut soutenir que c'est ...

argue ['ɑːgjuː] vi (quarrel) se disputer; (reason) argumenter ▷ vt (debate: case, matter) débattre; **to ~ about sth (with sb)** se disputer (avec qn) au sujet de qch; **to ~ that** objecter or alléguer que, donner comme argument que

argument ['ɑːgjumənt] n (quarrel) dispute f, discussion f; (reasons) argument m; (debate) discussion, controverse f; **~ for/against** argument pour/contre

argumentative [ɑːgju'mentətɪv] adj ergoteur(-euse), raisonneur(-euse)

Aries ['ɛərɪz] n le Bélier; **to be ~** être du Bélier

arise (pt **arose**, pp **arisen**) [ə'raɪz, ə'rəʊz, ə'rɪzn] vi survenir, se présenter; **to ~ from** résulter de; **should the need ~** en cas de besoin

aristocrat ['ærɪstəkræt] n aristocrate m/f

arithmetic [ə'rɪθmətɪk] n arithmétique f

ark [ɑːk] n: **Noah's A~** l'Arche f de Noé

arm [ɑːm] n bras m ▷ vt armer; **arms** npl (weapons, Heraldry) armes fpl; **~ in ~** bras dessus bras dessous

armaments ['ɑːməmənts] npl (weapons) armement m

armchair ['ɑːmtʃɛəʳ] n fauteuil m

armed [ɑːmd] adj armé(e)

armed forces npl: **the ~** les forces armées

armed robbery n vol m à main armée

armour, (US) **armor** ['ɑːməʳ] n armure f; (also: **~-plating**) blindage m; (Mil: tanks) blindés mpl

armoured car, (US) **armored car** ['ɑːməd-] n véhicule blindé

armpit ['ɑːmpɪt] n aisselle f

armrest ['ɑːmrest] n accoudoir m

army ['ɑːmɪ] n armée f

A road n (Brit) ≈ route nationale

aroma [ə'rəʊmə] n arôme m

aromatherapy [ərəʊmə'θerəpɪ] n aromathérapie f

arose [ə'rəʊz] pt of **arise**

around [ə'raʊnd] adv (tout) autour; (nearby) dans les parages ▷ prep autour de; (near) près de; (fig: about) environ; (: date, time) vers; **is he ~?** est-il dans les parages or là?

arouse [ə'raʊz] vt (sleeper) éveiller; (curiosity, passions) éveiller, susciter; (anger) exciter

arrange [ə'reɪndʒ] vt arranger; (programme) arrêter, convenir de ▷ vi: **we have ~d for a** car to pick you up nous avons prévu qu'une voiture vienne vous prendre; **it was ~d that ...** il a été convenu que ..., il a été décidé que ...; **to ~ to do sth** prévoir de faire qch

arrangement [ə'reɪndʒmənt] n arrangement m; **to come to an ~ (with sb)** se mettre d'accord (avec qn); **home deliveries by ~** livraison à domicile sur demande; **arrangements** npl (plans etc) arrangements mpl, dispositions fpl; **I'll make ~s for you to be met** je vous enverrai chercher

array [ə'reɪ] n (of objects) déploiement m, étalage m; (Math, Comput) tableau m

arrears [ə'rɪəz] npl arriéré m; **to be in ~ with one's rent** devoir un arriéré de loyer, être en retard pour le paiement de son loyer

arrest [ə'rest] vt arrêter; (sb's attention) retenir, attirer ▷ n arrestation f; **under ~** en état d'arrestation

arrival [ə'raɪvl] n arrivée f; (Comm) arrivage m; (person) arrivant(e); **new ~** nouveau venu/ nouvelle venue; (baby) nouveau-né(e)

arrive [ə'raɪv] vi arriver; **arrive at** vt fus (decision, solution) parvenir à

arrogance ['ærəgəns] n arrogance f

arrogant ['ærəgənt] adj arrogant(e)

arrow ['ærəʊ] n flèche f

arse [ɑːs] n (Brit inf!) cul m (!)

arson ['ɑːsn] n incendie criminel

art [ɑːt] n art m; (craft) métier m; **work of ~** œuvre f d'art; **Arts** npl (Scol) les lettres fpl

art college n école f des beaux-arts

artery ['ɑːtərɪ] n artère f

art gallery n musée m d'art; (saleroom) galerie f de peinture

arthritis [ɑː'θraɪtɪs] n arthrite f

artichoke ['ɑːtɪtʃəʊk] n artichaut m; **Jerusalem ~** topinambour m

article ['ɑːtɪkl] n article m; (Brit Law: training): **articles** npl ≈ stage m; **~s of clothing** vêtements mpl

articulate adj [ɑː'tɪkjulɪt] (person) qui s'exprime clairement et aisément; (speech) bien articulé(e), prononcé(e) clairement ▷ vi [ɑː'tɪkjuleɪt] articuler, parler distinctement ▷ vt articuler

articulated lorry [ɑː'tɪkjuleɪtɪd-] n (Brit) (camion m) semi-remorque m

artificial [ɑːtɪ'fɪʃəl] adj artificiel(le)

artificial respiration n respiration artificielle

artist ['ɑːtɪst] n artiste m/f

artistic [ɑː'tɪstɪk] adj artistique

artistry ['ɑːtɪstrɪ] n art m, talent m

art school n ≈ école f des beaux-arts

 KEYWORD

as [æz] conj **1** (time: moment) comme, alors que; à mesure que; (: duration) tandis que; **he came in as I was leaving** il est arrivé comme je partais; **as the years went by** à mesure que les années passaient; **as from tomorrow** à partir de demain

2 (since, because) comme, puisque; **he left early as he had to be home by 10** comme il or puisqu'il devait être de retour avant 10h, il est parti de bonne heure

3 (referring to manner, way) comme; **do as you wish** faites comme vous voudrez; **as she said** comme elle disait

▷ adv **1** (in comparisons): **as big as** aussi grand que; **twice as big as** deux fois plus grand que; **big as it is** si grand que ce soit; **much as I like them, I …** je les aime bien, mais je …; **as much** or **many as** autant que; **as much money/many books as** autant d'argent/de livres que; **as soon as** dès que

2 (concerning): **as for** or **to that** quant à cela, pour ce qui est de cela

3: **as if** or **though** comme si; **he looked as if he was ill** il avait l'air d'être malade; see also **long**; **such**; **well**

▷ prep (in the capacity of) en tant que, en qualité de; **he works as a driver** il travaille comme chauffeur; **as chairman of the company, he …** en tant que président de la société, il …; **dressed up as a cowboy** déguisé en cowboy; **he gave me it as a present** il me l'a offert, il m'en a fait cadeau

a.s.a.p. abbr = **as soon as possible**

asbestos [æz'bɛstəs] n asbeste m, amiante m

ascend [ə'sɛnd] vt gravir

ascent [ə'sɛnt] n (climb) ascension f

ascertain [æsə'teɪn] vt s'assurer de, vérifier; établir

ash [æʃ] n (dust) cendre f; (also: ~ **tree**) frêne m

ashamed [ə'ʃeɪmd] adj honteux(-euse), confus(e); **to be ~ of** avoir honte de; **to be ~ (of o.s.) for having done** avoir honte d'avoir fait

ashore [ə'ʃɔːʳ] adv à terre; **to go ~** aller à terre, débarquer

ashtray [æʃtreɪ] n cendrier m

Ash Wednesday n mercredi m des Cendres

Asia [ˈeɪʃə] n Asie f

Asian [ˈeɪʃən] n (from Asia) Asiatique m/f; (Brit: from Indian subcontinent) Indo-Pakistanais(-e) ▷ adj asiatique; indo-pakistanais(-e)

aside [ə'saɪd] adv de côté; à l'écart ▷ n aparté m; ~ **from** prep à part, excepté

ask [ɑːsk] vt (inquire) demander; (invite) inviter; **to ~ sb sth/to do sth** demander à qn qch/de faire qch; **to ~ sb the time** demander l'heure à qn; **to ~ sb about sth** questionner qn au sujet de qch; se renseigner auprès de qn au sujet de qch; **to ~ about the price** s'informer du prix, se renseigner au sujet du prix; **to ~ (sb) a question** poser une question (à qn); **to ~ sb out to dinner** inviter qn au restaurant; **ask after** vt fus demander des nouvelles de; **ask for** vt fus demander; **it's just ~ing for trouble** or **for it** ce serait chercher des ennuis

asking price [ˈɑːskɪŋ-] n prix demandé

asleep [ə'sliːp] adj endormi(e); **to be ~** dormir, être endormi; **to fall ~** s'endormir

AS level n abbr (= Advanced Subsidiary level) première partie de l'examen équivalent au baccalauréat

asparagus [əsˈpærəgəs] n asperges fpl

aspect [ˈæspɛkt] n aspect m; (direction in which a building etc faces) orientation f, exposition f

aspire [əsˈpaɪəʳ] vi: **to ~ to** aspirer à

aspirin [ˈæsprɪn] n aspirine f

ass [æs] n âne m; (inf) imbécile m/f; (US inf!) cul m (!)

assailant [ə'seɪlənt] n agresseur m; assaillant m

assassin [ə'sæsɪn] n assassin m

assassinate [ə'sæsɪneɪt] vt assassiner

assassination [əsæsɪ'neɪʃən] n assassinat m

assault [ə'sɔːlt] n (Mil) assaut m; (gen: attack) agression f; (Law): ~ **(and battery)** voies fpl de fait, coups mpl et blessures fpl ▷ vt attaquer; (sexually) violenter

assemble [ə'sɛmbl] vt assembler ▷ vi s'assembler, se rassembler

assembly [ə'sɛmblɪ] n (meeting) rassemblement m; (parliament) assemblée f; (construction) assemblage m

assembly line n chaîne f de montage

assent [ə'sɛnt] n assentiment m, consentement m ▷ vi: **to ~ (to sth)** donner son assentiment (à qch), consentir (à qch)

assert [ə'səːt] vt affirmer, déclarer; établir; (authority) faire valoir; (innocence) protester de; **to ~ o.s.** s'imposer

assertion [ə'səːʃən] n assertion f, affirmation f

assess [ə'sɛs] vt évaluer, estimer; (tax, damages) établir or fixer le montant de; (property etc: for tax) calculer la valeur imposable de; (person) juger la valeur de

assessment [ə'sɛsmənt] n évaluation f, estimation f; (of tax) fixation f; (of property) calcul m de la valeur imposable; (judgment): ~ **(of)** jugement m or opinion f (sur)

assessor [ə'sɛsəʳ] n expert m (en matière d'impôt et d'assurance)

asset [ˈæsɛt] n avantage m, atout m; (person) atout; **assets** npl (Comm) capital m; avoir(s) m(pl); actif m

assign [ə'saɪn] vt (date) fixer, arrêter; **to ~ sth to** (task) assigner qch à; (resources) affecter qch à; (cause, meaning) attribuer qch à

assignment [ə'saɪnmənt] n (task) mission f; (homework) devoir m

assist [ə'sɪst] vt aider, assister; (injured person etc) secourir

assistance [ə'sɪstəns] n aide f, assistance f; secours mpl

assistant [ə'sɪstənt] n assistant(e), adjoint(e); (Brit: also: **shop ~**) vendeur(-euse)

associate [adj, n ə'səʊʃɪɪt, vb ə'səʊʃɪeɪt] adj, n associé(e) ▷ vt associer ▷ vi: **to ~ with sb**

fréquenter qn; **~ director** directeur adjoint; **~d company** société affiliée

association [əsəusɪ'eɪʃən] n association f; **in ~ with** en collaboration avec

assorted [ə'sɔ:tɪd] adj assorti(e); **in ~ sizes** en plusieurs tailles

assortment [ə'sɔ:tmənt] n assortiment m; (of people) mélange m

assume [ə'sju:m] vt supposer; (responsibilities etc) assumer; (attitude, name) prendre, adopter

assumption [ə'sʌmpʃən] n supposition f, hypothèse f; (of power) assomption f, prise f; **on the ~ that** dans l'hypothèse où; (on condition that) à condition que

assurance [ə'fuərəns] n assurance f; **I can give you no ~s** je ne peux rien vous garantir

assure [ə'fuər] vt assurer

asterisk ['æstərɪsk] n astérisque m

asthma ['æsmə] n asthme m

astonish [ə'stɔnɪʃ] vt étonner, stupéfier

astonished [ə'stɔnɪʃt] adj étonné(e); **to be ~ at** être étonné(e) de

astonishing [ə'stɔnɪʃɪŋ] adj étonnant(e), stupéfiant(e); **I find it ~ that ...** je trouve incroyable que ... + sub

astonishment [ə'stɔnɪʃmənt] n (grand) étonnement m, stupéfaction f

astound [ə'staund] vt stupéfier, sidérer

astray [ə'streɪ] adv: **to go ~** s'égarer; (fig) quitter le droit chemin; **to lead ~** (morally) détourner du droit chemin; **to go ~ in one's calculations** faire fausse route dans ses calculs

astride [ə'straɪd] adv à cheval ▷ prep à cheval sur

astrology [əs'trɔlədʒɪ] n astrologie f

astronaut ['æstrənɔ:t] n astronaute m/f

astronomer [əs'trɔnəmər] n astronome m

astronomical [æstrə'nɔmɪkl] adj astronomique

astronomy [əs'trɔnəmɪ] n astronomie f

astute [əs'tju:t] adj astucieux(-euse), malin(-igne)

asylum [ə'saɪləm] n asile m; **to seek political ~** demander l'asile politique

asylum seeker [-si:kər] n demandeur(-euse) d'asile

KEYWORD

at [æt] prep **1** (referring to position, direction) à; **at the top** au sommet; **at home/school** à la maison or chez soi/à l'école; **at the baker's** à la boulangerie, chez le boulanger; **to look at sth** regarder qch

2 (referring to time): **at 4 o'clock** à 4 heures; **at Christmas** à Noël; **at night** la nuit; **at times** par moments, parfois

3 (referring to rates, speed etc) à; **at £1 a kilo** une livre le kilo; **two at a time** deux à la fois; **at 50 km/h** à 50 km/h; **at full speed** à toute vitesse

4 (referring to manner): **at a stroke** d'un seul coup; **at peace** en paix

5 (referring to activity): **to be at work** (in the office etc) être au travail; (working) travailler; **to play at cowboys** jouer aux cowboys; **to be good at sth** être bon en qch

6 (referring to cause): **shocked/surprised/annoyed at sth** choqué par/étonné de/agacé par qch; **I went at his suggestion** j'y suis allé sur son conseil

7 (@ symbol) arobase f

ate [eɪt] pt of **eat**

atheist ['eɪθɪɪst] n athée m/f

Athens ['æθɪnz] n Athènes

athlete ['æθli:t] n athlète m/f

athletic [æθ'lɛtɪk] adj athlétique

athletics [æθ'lɛtɪks] n athlétisme m

Atlantic [ət'læntɪk] adj atlantique ▷ n: **the ~ (Ocean)** l'(océan m) Atlantique m

atlas ['ætləs] n atlas m

A.T.M. n abbr (= Automated Telling Machine) guichet m automatique

atmosphere ['ætməsfɪər] n (air) atmosphère f; (fig: of place etc) atmosphère, ambiance f

atom ['ætəm] n atome m

atom bomb n bombe f atomique

atomic [ə'tɔmɪk] adj atomique

atomic bomb n bombe f atomique

atomizer ['ætəmaɪzər] n atomiseur m

atone [ə'təun] vi: **to ~ for** expier, racheter

atrocious [ə'trəuʃəs] adj (very bad) atroce, exécrable

atrocity [ə'trɔsɪtɪ] n atrocité f

attach [ə'tætʃ] vt (gen) attacher; (document, letter) joindre; (employee, troops) affecter; **to be ~ed to sb/sth** (to like) être attaché à qn/qch; **to ~ a file to an email** joindre un fichier à un e-mail; **the ~ed letter** la lettre ci-jointe

attaché case [ə'tæʃeɪ-] n mallette f, attaché-case m

attachment [ə'tætʃmənt] n (tool) accessoire m; (Comput) fichier m joint; (love): **~ (to)** affection f (pour), attachement m (à)

attack [ə'tæk] vt attaquer; (task etc) s'attaquer à ▷ n attaque f; **heart ~** crise f cardiaque

attacker [ə'tækər] n attaquant m; agresseur m

attain [ə'teɪn] vt (also: **to ~ to**) parvenir à, atteindre; (knowledge) acquérir

attempt [ə'tɛmpt] n tentative f ▷ vt essayer, tenter; **~ed theft** etc (Law) tentative de vol etc; **to make an ~ on sb's life** attenter à la vie de qn; **he made no ~ to help** il n'a rien fait pour m'aider or l'aider etc

attempted [ə'tɛmptɪd] adj: **~ murder/suicide** tentative f de meurtre/suicide

attend [ə'tɛnd] vt (course) suivre; (meeting, talk) assister à; (school, church) aller à, fréquenter; (patient) soigner, s'occuper de; **to ~ (up)on** servir; être au service de; **attend to** vt fus (needs, affairs etc) s'occuper de; (customer) s'occuper de, servir

attendance [ə'tɛndəns] n (being present) présence f; (people present) assistance f

attendant [ə'tɛndənt] n employé(e); gardien(ne) ▷ adj concomitant(e), qui accompagne or s'ensuit

attention [ə'tɛnʃən] n attention f; **attentions** attentions fpl, prévenances fpl ▷ excl (Mil) garde-à-vous!; **at ~** (Mil) au garde-à-vous!; **for the ~ of** (Admin) à l'attention de; **it has come to my ~ that ...** je constate que ...

attentive [ə'tɛntɪv] adj attentif(-ive); (kind) prévenant(e)

attest [ə'tɛst] vi: **to ~ to** témoigner de attester (de)

attic ['ætɪk] n grenier m, combles mpl

attitude ['ætɪtjuːd] n (behaviour) attitude f, manière f; (posture) pose f, attitude; (view): **~ (to)** attitude (envers)

attorney [ə'təːnɪ] n (US: lawyer) avocat m; (having proxy) mandataire m; **power of ~** procuration f

Attorney General n (Brit) ≈ procureur général; (US) ≈ garde m des Sceaux, ministre m de la Justice

attract [ə'trækt] vt attirer

attraction [ə'trækʃən] n (gen pl: pleasant things) attraction f, attrait m; (Physics) attraction; (fig: towards sb, sth) attirance f

attractive [ə'træktɪv] adj séduisant(e), attrayant(e)

attribute n ['ætrɪbjuːt] attribut m ▷ vt [ə'trɪbjuːt]: **to ~ sth to** attribuer qch à

attrition [ə'trɪʃən] n: **war of ~** guerre f d'usure

aubergine ['əubəʒiːn] n aubergine f

auburn ['ɔːbən] adj auburn inv, châtain roux inv

auction ['ɔːkʃən] n (also: **sale by ~**) vente f aux enchères ▷ vt (also: **to sell by ~**) vendre aux enchères; (also: **to put up for ~**) mettre aux enchères

auctioneer [ɔːkʃə'nɪər] n commissaire-priseur m

audible ['ɔːdɪbl] adj audible

audience ['ɔːdɪəns] n (people) assistance f, public m; (on radio) auditeurs mpl; (at theatre) spectateurs mpl; (interview) audience f

audiovisual [ɔːdɪəu'vɪzjuəl] adj audiovisuel(le); **~ aids** supports or moyens audiovisuels

audit ['ɔːdɪt] n vérification f des comptes, apurement m ▷ vt vérifier, apurer

audition [ɔː'dɪʃən] n audition f ▷ vi auditionner

auditor ['ɔːdɪtər] n vérificateur m des comptes

auditorium [ɔːdɪ'tɔːrɪəm] n auditorium m, salle f de concert or de spectacle

Aug. abbr = **August**

augur ['ɔːgər] vt (be a sign of) présager, annoncer ▷ vi: **it ~s well** c'est bon signe or de bon augure, cela s'annonce bien

August ['ɔːgəst] n août m; see also **July**

august [ɔː'gʌst] adj majestueux(-euse), imposant(e)

aunt [aːnt] n tante f

auntie, aunty ['aːntɪ] n diminutive of **aunt**

au pair ['əu'pɛər] n (also: **~ girl**) jeune fille f au pair

aura ['ɔːrə] n atmosphère f; (of person) aura f

auspicious [ɔːs'pɪʃəs] adj de bon augure, propice

austerity [ɔs'tɛrɪtɪ] n austérité f

Australia [ɔs'treɪlɪə] n Australie f

Australian [ɔs'treɪlɪən] adj australien(ne) ▷ n Australien(ne)

Austria ['ɔstrɪə] n Autriche f

Austrian ['ɔstrɪən] adj autrichien(ne) ▷ n Autrichien(ne)

authentic [ɔː'θɛntɪk] adj authentique

author ['ɔːθər] n auteur m

authoritarian [ɔːθɔrɪ'tɛərɪən] adj autoritaire

authoritative [ɔː'θɔrɪtətɪv] adj (account) digne de foi; (study, treatise) qui fait autorité; (manner) autoritaire

authority [ɔː'θɔrɪtɪ] n autorité f; (permission) autorisation (formelle); **the authorities** les autorités fpl, l'administration f; **to have ~ to do sth** être habilité à faire qch

authorize ['ɔːθəraɪz] vt autoriser

auto ['ɔːtəu] n (US) auto f, voiture f

autobiography [ɔːtəbaɪ'ɔgrəfɪ] n autobiographie f

autograph ['ɔːtəgrɑːf] n autographe m ▷ vt signer, dédicacer

automated ['ɔːtəmeɪtɪd] adj automatisé(e)

automatic [ɔːtə'mætɪk] adj automatique ▷ n (gun) automatique m; (washing machine) lave-linge m automatique; (car) voiture f à transmission automatique

automatically [ɔːtə'mætɪklɪ] adv automatiquement

automation [ɔːtə'meɪʃən] n automatisation f

automobile ['ɔːtəməbiːl] n (US) automobile f

autonomous [ɔː'tɔnəməs] adj autonome

autonomy [ɔː'tɔnəmɪ] n autonomie f

autumn ['ɔːtəm] n automne m

auxiliary [ɔːg'zɪlɪərɪ] adj, n auxiliaire (m/f)

avail [ə'veɪl] vt: **to ~ o.s. of** user de; profiter de ▷ n: **to no ~** sans résultat, en vain, en pure perte

availability [əveɪlə'bɪlɪtɪ] n disponibilité f

available [ə'veɪləbl] adj disponible; **every ~ means** tous les moyens possibles or à sa (or notre etc) disposition; **is the manager ~?** est-ce que le directeur peut (me) recevoir?; (on phone) pourrais-je parler au directeur?; **to make sth ~ to sb** mettre qch à la disposition de qn

avalanche ['ævəlɑːnʃ] n avalanche f

Ave. abbr = **avenue**

avenge [ə'vɛndʒ] vt venger

avenue ['ævənjuː] n avenue f; (fig) moyen m

average ['ævərɪdʒ] n moyenne f ▷ adj moyen(ne) ▷ vt (a certain figure) atteindre or faire etc en moyenne; **on ~** en moyenne; **above/below (the) ~** au-dessus/en-dessous de la moyenne; **average out** vi: **to ~ out at** représenter en moyenne, donner une moyenne de

averse [ə'vɜːs] adj: **to be ~ to sth/doing** éprouver une forte répugnance envers qch/à faire; **I wouldn't be ~ to a drink** un petit verre ne serait pas de refus, je ne dirais pas non à un petit verre

avert [ə'vɜːt] vt (danger) prévenir, écarter; (one's eyes) détourner

aviary ['eɪvɪərɪ] n volière f

avid ['ævɪd] adj avide

avocado [ævə'kɑːdəu] n (Brit: also: ~ **pear**) avocat m

avoid [ə'vɔɪd] vt éviter

await [ə'weɪt] vt attendre; **~ing attention/delivery** (Comm) en souffrance; **long ~ed** tant attendu(e)

awake [ə'weɪk] (pt **awoke**) [ə'wəuk] (pp **awoken**) [ə'wəukən] adj éveillé(e); (fig) en éveil ▷ vt éveiller ▷ vi s'éveiller; **~ to** conscient de; **to be ~** être réveillé(e); **he was still ~** il ne dormait pas encore

awakening [ə'weɪknɪŋ] n réveil m

award [ə'wɔːd] n (for bravery) récompense f; (prize) prix m; (Law: damages) dommages-intérêts mpl ▷ vt (prize) décerner; (Law: damages) accorder

aware [ə'weər] adj: **~ of** (conscious) conscient(e) de; (informed) au courant de; **to become ~ of/that** prendre conscience de/que; se rendre compte de/que; **politically/socially ~** sensibilisé(e) aux or ayant pris conscience des problèmes politiques/sociaux; **I am fully ~ that** je me rends parfaitement compte que

awareness [ə'weənɪs] n conscience f, connaissance f; **to develop people's ~ (of)** sensibiliser le public (à)

away [ə'weɪ] adv (au) loin; (movement): **she went ~** elle est partie ▷ adj (not in, not here) absent(e); **far ~** (au) loin; **two kilometres ~** à (une distance de) deux kilomètres, à deux kilomètres de distance; **two hours ~ by car** à deux heures de voiture or de route; **the holiday was two weeks ~** il restait deux semaines jusqu'aux vacances; **~ from** loin de; **he's ~ for a week** il est parti (pour) une semaine; **he's ~ in Milan** il est (parti) à Milan; **to take sth ~ from sb** prendre qch à qn; **to take sth ~ from sth** (subtract) ôter qch de qch; **to work/pedal ~** travailler/pédaller à cœur joie; **to fade ~** (colour) s'estomper; (sound) s'affaiblir

away game n (Sport) match m à l'extérieur

awe [ɔː] n respect mêlé de crainte, effroi mêlé d'admiration

awe-inspiring ['ɔːɪnspaɪərɪŋ], **awesome** ['ɔːsəm] adj impressionnant(e)

awesome ['ɔːsəm] (US) adj (inf: excellent) génial(e)

awful ['ɔːfəl] adj affreux(-euse); **an ~ lot of** énormément de

awfully ['ɔːfəlɪ] adv (very) terriblement, vraiment

awkward ['ɔːkwəd] adj (clumsy) gauche, maladroit(e); (inconvenient) peu pratique; (embarrassing) gênant; **I can't talk just now, it's a bit ~** je ne peux pas parler tout de suite, c'est un peu difficile

awning ['ɔːnɪŋ] n (of tent) auvent m; (of shop) store m; (of hotel etc) marquise f (de toile)

awoke [ə'wəuk] pt of **awake**

awoken [ə'wəukən] pp of **awake**

axe, (US) **ax** [æks] n hache f ▷ vt (employee) renvoyer; (project etc) abandonner; (jobs) supprimer; **to have an ~ to grind** (fig) prêcher pour son saint

axes ['æksiːz] npl of **axis**

axis (pl **axes**) ['æksɪs, -siːz] n axe m

axle ['æksl] n (also: ~-**tree**) essieu m

ay, aye [aɪ] excl (yes) oui ▷ n: **the ay(e)s** les oui

azalea [ə'zeɪlɪə] n azalée f

B, b [bi:] *n* (*letter*) B, b *m*; (*Scol: mark*) B; (*Mus*): **B** si *m*; **B for Benjamin**, (*US*) **B for Baker** B comme Berthe; **B road** *n* (*Brit Aut*) route départementale

B.A. *abbr* = **British Academy**; (*Scol*) = **Bachelor of Arts**

babble ['bæbl] *vi* babiller ▷ *n* babillage *m*

baby ['beɪbɪ] *n* bébé *m*

baby carriage *n* (*US*) voiture *f* d'enfant

baby food *n* aliments *mpl* pour bébé(s)

baby-sit ['beɪbɪsɪt] *vi* garder les enfants

baby-sitter ['beɪbɪsɪtəʳ] *n* baby-sitter *m/f*

baby wipe *n* lingette *f* (*pour bébé*)

bachelor ['bætʃələʳ] *n* célibataire *m*; **B~ of Arts/Science (BA/BSc)** ≈ licencié(e) ès or en lettres/sciences; **B~ of Arts/Science degree (BA/BSc)** ≈ licence *f* ès or en lettres/sciences; *voir article*

back [bæk] *n* (*of person, horse*) dos *m*; (*of hand*) dos, revers *m*; (*of house*) derrière *m*; (*of car, train*) arrière *m*; (*of chair*) dossier *m*; (*of page*) verso *m*; (*of crowd*): **can the people at the ~ hear me properly?** est-ce que les gens du fond peuvent m'entendre?; (*Football*) arrière *m*; **to have one's ~ to the wall** (*fig*) être au pied du mur; **to break the ~ of a job** (*Brit*) faire le gros d'un travail; **~ to front** à l'envers ▷ *vt* (*financially*) soutenir (financièrement); (*candidate: also:* **~ up**) soutenir, appuyer; (*horse: at races*) parier or miser sur; (*car*) (faire) reculer ▷ *vi* reculer; (*car etc*) faire marche arrière ▷ *adj* (in compounds) de derrière, à l'arrière; **~ seat/ wheel** (*Aut*) siège *m*/roue *f* arrière *inv*; **~ payments/rent** arriéré *m* de paiements/ loyer; **~ garden/room** jardin/pièce sur l'arrière; **to take a ~ seat** (*fig*) se contenter d'un second rôle, être relégué(e) au second plan ▷ *adv* (*not forward*) en arrière; (*returned*): **he's ~** il est rentré, il est de retour; **when will you be ~?** quand seras-tu de retour?; **he ran ~** il est revenu en courant; (*restitution*): **throw the ball ~** renvoie la balle; **can I have it ~?** puis-je le ravoir?, peux-tu me le rendre?; (*again*): **he called ~** il a rappelé; **back down** *vi* rabattre de ses prétentions; **back on to** *vt fus*: **the house ~s on to the golf course** la maison donne derrière sur le terrain de golf; **back out** *vi* (*of promise*) se dédire; **back up** *vt* (*person*) soutenir; (*Comput*) faire une copie de sauvegarde de

backache ['bækeɪk] *n* mal *m* au dos

backbencher ['bæk'bentʃəʳ] (*Brit*) *n* membre du parlement sans portefeuille

backbone ['bækbəʊn] *n* colonne vertébrale, épine dorsale; **he's the ~ of the organization** c'est sur lui que repose l'organisation

backdate [bæk'deɪt] *vt* (*letter*) antidater; **~d pay rise** augmentation *f* avec effet rétroactif

back door *n* porte *f* de derrière

backfire [bæk'faɪəʳ] *vi* (*Aut*) pétarader; (*plans*) mal tourner

backgammon ['bækgæmən] *n* trictrac *m*

background ['bækgraʊnd] *n* arrière-plan *m*; (*of events*) situation *f*, conjoncture *f*; (*basic knowledge*) éléments *mpl* de base; (*experience*) formation *f* ▷ *cpd* (*noise, music*) de fond; **~ reading** lecture(s) générale(s) (sur un sujet); **family ~** milieu familial

backhand ['bækhænd] *n* (*Tennis: also:* **~ stroke**) revers *m*

backhander ['bæk'hændəʳ] *n* (*Brit: bribe*) pot-de-vin *m*

backing ['bækɪŋ] *n* (*fig*) soutien *m*, appui *m*; (*Comm*) soutien (financier); (*Mus*) accompagnement *m*

backlash ['bæklæʃ] *n* contre-coup *m*, répercussion *f*

backlog ['bæklɔg] *n*: **~ of work** travail *m* en retard

back number *n* (*of magazine etc*) vieux numéro

backpack ['bækpæk] *n* sac *m* à dos

backpacker ['bækpækəʳ] *n* randonneur(-euse)

back pain *n* mal *m* de dos

back pay *n* rappel *m* de salaire

backside ['bæksaɪd] *n* (*inf*) derrière *m*, postérieur *m*

backslash ['bækslæʃ] *n* barre oblique inversée

backstage [bæk'steɪdʒ] *adv* dans les coulisses

backstroke ['bækstrəuk] n dos crawlé

backup ['bækʌp] adj (train, plane) supplémentaire, de réserve; (Comput) de sauvegarde ▷ n (support) appui m, soutien m; (Comput: also: **~ file**) sauvegarde f

backward ['bækwəd] adj (movement) en arrière; (measure) rétrograde; (person, country) arriéré(e), attardé(e); (shy) hésitant(e); **~ and forward movement** mouvement de va-et-vient

backwards ['bækwədz] adv (move, go) en arrière; (read a list) à l'envers, à rebours; (fall) à la renverse; (walk) à reculons; (in time) en arrière, vers le passé; **to know sth ~** or (US) **~ and forwards** (inf) connaître qch sur le bout des doigts

backwater ['bækwɔːtəʳ] n (fig) coin reculé; bled perdu

backyard [bæk'jɑːd] n arrière-cour f

bacon ['beɪkən] n bacon m, lard m

bacteria [bæk'tɪərɪə] npl bactéries fpl

bad [bæd] adj mauvais(e); (child) vilain(e); (mistake, accident) grave; (meat, food) gâté(e), avarié(e); **his ~ leg** sa jambe malade; **to go ~** (meat, food) se gâter; (milk) tourner; **to have a ~ time of it** traverser une mauvaise passe; **I feel ~ about it** (guilty) j'ai un peu mauvaise conscience; **~ debt** créance douteuse; **in ~ faith** de mauvaise foi

bade [bæd] pt of **bid**

badge [bædʒ] n insigne m; (of policeman) plaque f; (stick-on, sew-on) badge m

badger ['bædʒəʳ] n blaireau m ▷ vt harceler

badly ['bædlɪ] adv (work, dress etc) mal; **to reflect ~ on sb** donner une mauvaise image de qn; **~ wounded** grièvement blessé; **he needs it ~** il en a absolument besoin; **things are going ~** les choses vont mal; **~ off** adj, adv dans la gêne

bad-mannered ['bæd'mænəd] adj mal élevé(e)

badminton ['bædmɪntən] n badminton m

bad-tempered ['bæd'tɛmpəd] adj (by nature) ayant mauvais caractère; (on one occasion) de mauvaise humeur

baffle ['bæfl] vt (puzzle) déconcerter

bag [bæg] n sac m; (of hunter) gibecière f, chasse f ▷ vt (inf: take) empocher; s'approprier; (Tech) mettre en sacs; **~s of** (inf: lots of) des tas de; **to pack one's ~s** faire ses valises or bagages; **~s under the eyes** poches fpl sous les yeux

baggage ['bægɪdʒ] n bagages mpl

baggage allowance n franchise f de bagages

baggage reclaim n (at airport) livraison f des bagages

baggy ['bægɪ] adj avachi(e), qui fait des poches

bagpipes ['bægpaɪps] npl cornemuse f

bail [beɪl] n caution f ▷ vt (prisoner: also:

grant ~ to) mettre en liberté sous caution; (boat: also: **~ out**) écoper; **to be released on ~** être libéré(e) sous caution; see **bale**; **bail out** vt (prisoner) payer la caution de

bailiff ['beɪlɪf] n huissier m

bait [beɪt] n appât m ▷ vt appâter; (fig: tease) tourmenter

bake [beɪk] vt (faire) cuire au four ▷ vi (bread etc) cuire (au four); (make cakes etc) faire de la pâtisserie

baked beans [beɪkt-] npl haricots blancs à la sauce tomate

baked potato n pomme f de terre en robe des champs

baker ['beɪkəʳ] n boulanger m

bakery ['beɪkərɪ] n boulangerie f; boulangerie industrielle

baking ['beɪkɪŋ] n (process) cuisson f

baking powder n levure f (chimique)

balance ['bæləns] n équilibre m; (Comm: sum) solde m; (remainder) reste m; (scales) balance f ▷ vt mettre or faire tenir en équilibre; (pros and cons) peser; (budget) équilibrer; (account) balancer; (compensate) compenser, contrebalancer; **~ of trade/payments** balance commerciale/des comptes or paiements; **~ carried forward** solde m à reporter; **~ brought forward** solde reporté; **to ~ the books** arrêter les comptes, dresser le bilan

balanced ['bælənst] adj (personality, diet) équilibré(e); (report) objectif(-ive)

balance sheet n bilan m

balcony ['bælkənɪ] n balcon m; **do you have a room with a ~?** avez-vous une chambre avec balcon?

bald [bɔːld] adj chauve; (tyre) lisse

bale [beɪl] n balle f, ballot m; **bale out** vi (of a plane) sauter en parachute ▷ vt (Naut: water, boat) écoper

ball [bɔːl] n boule f; (football) ballon m; (for tennis, golf) balle f; (dance) bal m; **to play ~** jouer au ballon (or à la balle); (fig) coopérer; **to be on the ~** (fig: competent) être à la hauteur; (: alert) être éveillé(e), être vif/vive; **to start the ~ rolling** (fig) commencer; **the ~ is in their court** (fig) la balle est dans leur camp

ballast ['bæləst] n lest m

ball bearings n roulement m à billes

ballerina [bælə'riːnə] n ballerine f

ballet ['bæleɪ] n ballet m; (art) danse f (classique)

ballet dancer n danseur(-euse) de ballet

ballet shoe n chausson m de danse

balloon [bə'luːn] n ballon m; (in comic strip) bulle f ▷ vi gonfler

ballot ['bælət] n scrutin m

ballot paper n bulletin m de vote

ballpoint ['bɔːlpɔɪnt], **ballpoint pen** n stylo m à bille

ballroom ['bɔːlrum] n salle f de bal

Baltic ['bɔːltɪk] *adj, n*: **the ~ (Sea)** la (mer) Baltique

bamboo [bæm'buː] *n* bambou *m*

ban [bæn] *n* interdiction *f* ▷ *vt* interdire; **he was ~ned from driving** (*Brit*) on lui a retiré le permis (de conduire)

banana [bə'nɑːnə] *n* banane *f*

band [bænd] *n* bande *f*; (*at a dance*) orchestre *m*; (*Mil*) musique *f*, fanfare *f*; **band together** *vi* se liguer

bandage ['bændɪdʒ] *n* bandage *m*, pansement *m* ▷ *vt* (*wound, leg*) mettre un pansement *or* un bandage sur; (*person*) mettre un pansement *or* un bandage à

Band-Aid® ['bændeɪd] *n* (*US*) pansement adhésif

B. & B. *n abbr* = **bed and breakfast**

bandit ['bændɪt] *n* bandit *m*

bandy-legged ['bændɪ'legɪd] *adj* aux jambes arquées

bang [bæŋ] *n* détonation *f*; (*of door*) claquement *m*; (*blow*) coup (violent) ▷ *vt* frapper (violemment); (*door*) claquer ▷ *vi* détoner; claquer ▷ *adv*: **to be ~ on time** (*Brit inf*) être à l'heure pile; **to ~ at the door** cogner à la porte; **to ~ into sth** se cogner contre qch

Bangladesh [bæŋglə'deʃ] *n* Bangladesh *m*

Bangladeshi [bæŋglə'deʃɪ] *adj* du Bangladesh ▷ *n* habitant(e) du Bangladesh

bangle ['bæŋgl] *n* bracelet *m*

bangs [bæŋz] *npl* (*US: fringe*) frange *f*

banish ['bænɪʃ] *vt* bannir

banister ['bænɪstəʳ] *n*, **banisters** ['bænɪstəz] *npl* rampe *f* (d'escalier)

banjo (*pl* **banjoes** *or* **banjos**) ['bændʒəʊ] *n* banjo *m*

bank [bæŋk] *n* banque *f*; (*of river, lake*) bord *m*, rive *f*; (*of earth*) talus *m*, remblai *m* ▷ *vi* (*Aviat*) virer sur l'aile; (*Comm*): **they ~ with Pitt's** leur banque *or* banquier est Pitt's; **bank on** *vt fus* miser *or* tabler sur

bank account *n* compte *m* en banque

bank balance *n* solde *m* bancaire

bank card *n* (*Brit*) carte *f* d'identité bancaire

bank charges *npl* (*Brit*) frais *mpl* de banque

banker ['bæŋkəʳ] *n* banquier *m*; **~'s card** (*Brit*) carte *f* d'identité bancaire; **~'s order** (*Brit*) ordre *m* de virement

bank holiday *n* (*Brit*) jour férié (*où les banques sont fermées*); *voir article*

● **BANK HOLIDAY**
●
● Le terme *bank holiday* s'applique au
● Royaume-Uni aux jours fériés pendant
● lesquels banques et commerces sont
● fermés. Les principaux *bank holidays* à part
● Noël et Pâques se situent au mois de mai
● et fin août, et contrairement aux pays de
● tradition catholique, ne coïncident pas
● nécessairement avec une fête religieuse.

banking ['bæŋkɪŋ] *n* opérations *fpl* bancaires; profession *f* de banquier

bank manager *n* directeur *m* d'agence (bancaire)

banknote ['bæŋknəʊt] *n* billet *m* de banque

bank rate *n* taux *m* de l'escompte

bankrupt ['bæŋkrʌpt] *n* failli(e) *◁ adj* en faillite; **to go ~** faire faillite

bankruptcy ['bæŋkrʌptsɪ] *n* faillite *f*

bank statement *n* relevé *m* de compte

banner ['bænəʳ] *n* bannière *f*

bannister ['bænɪstəʳ] *n*, **bannisters** ['bænɪstəz] *npl* = **banister**; **banisters**

banquet ['bæŋkwɪt] *n* banquet *m*, festin *m*

baptism ['bæptɪzəm] *n* baptême *m*

baptize [bæp'taɪz] *vt* baptiser

bar [bɑːʳ] *n* (*pub*) bar *m*; (*counter*) comptoir *m*, bar; (*rod: of metal etc*) barre *f*; (*of window etc*) barreau *m*; (*of chocolate*) tablette *f*, plaque *f*; (*fig: obstacle*) obstacle *m*; (*prohibition*) mesure *f* d'exclusion; (*Mus*) mesure *f* ▷ *vt* (*road*) barrer; (*window*) munir de barreaux; (*person*) exclure; (*activity*) interdire; **~ of soap** savonnette *f*; **behind ~s** (*prisoner*) derrière les barreaux; **the B~** (*Law*) le barreau; **~ none** sans exception

barbaric [bɑː'bærɪk] *adj* barbare

barbecue ['bɑːbɪkjuː] *n* barbecue *m*

barbed wire ['bɑːbd-] *n* fil *m* de fer barbelé

barber ['bɑːbəʳ] *n* coiffeur *m* (pour hommes)

barber's ['bɑːbəz], **barber's shop**, (*US*) **barber shop** *n* salon *m* de coiffure (pour hommes); **to go to the ~** aller chez le coiffeur

bar code *n* code *m* à barres, code-barre *m*

bare [bɛəʳ] *adj* nu(e) ▷ *vt* mettre à nu, dénuder; (*teeth*) montrer; **the ~ essentials** le strict nécessaire

bareback ['bɛəbæk] *adv* à cru, sans selle

barefaced ['bɛəfeɪst] *adj* impudent(e), effronté(e)

barefoot ['bɛəfut] *adj, adv* nu-pieds, (les) pieds nus

barely ['bɛəlɪ] *adv* à peine

bargain ['bɑːgɪn] *n* (*transaction*) marché *m*; (*good buy*) affaire *f*, occasion *f* ▷ *vi* (*haggle*) marchander; (*negotiate*) négocier, traiter; **into the ~** par-dessus le marché; **bargain for** *vt fus* (*inf*): **he got more than he ~ed for!** il en a eu pour son argent!

barge [bɑːdʒ] *n* péniche *f*; **barge in** *vi* (*walk in*) faire irruption; (*interrupt talk*) intervenir mal à propos; **barge into** *vt fus* rentrer dans

bark [bɑːk] *n* (*of tree*) écorce *f*; (*of dog*) aboiement *m* ▷ *vi* aboyer

barley ['bɑːlɪ] *n* orge *f*

barley sugar *n* sucre *m* d'orge

barmaid ['bɑːmeɪd] *n* serveuse *f* (de bar), barmaid *f*

barman ['bɑːmən] (*irreg*) *n* serveur *m* (de bar), barman *m*

bar meal *n* repas *m* de bistrot; **to go for a ~** aller manger au bistrot

barn [bɑːn] *n* grange *f*

barometer [bəˈrɒmɪtə*] n baromètre m

baron [ˈbærən] n baron m; **the press/oil ~s** les magnats mpl ou barons mpl de la presse/du pétrole

baroness [ˈbærənɪs] n baronne f

barracks [ˈbærəks] npl caserne f

barrage [ˈbærɑːʒ] n (Mil) tir m de barrage; (dam) barrage m; (of criticism) feu m

barrel [ˈbærəl] n tonneau m; (of gun) canon m

barren [ˈbærən] adj stérile; (hills) aride

barrette [bəˈret] (US) n barrette f

barricade [bærɪˈkeɪd] n barricade f ▷ vt barricader

barrier [ˈbærɪə*] n barrière f; (Brit: also: **crash ~**) rail m de sécurité

barring [ˈbɑːrɪŋ] prep sauf

barrister [ˈbærɪstə*] n (Brit) avocat (plaidant); voir article

barrow [ˈbærəʊ] n (cart) charrette f à bras

bartender [ˈbɑːtɛndə*] n (US) serveur m (de bar), barman m

barter [ˈbɑːtə*] n échange m, troc m ▷ vt: **to ~ sth for** échanger qch contre

base [beɪs] n base f ▷ vt (troops): **to be ~d at** être basé(e) à; (opinion, belief): **to ~ sth on** baser ou fonder qch sur ▷ adj vil(e), bas(se); **coffee-~d** à base de café; **a Paris-~d firm** une maison opérant de Paris ou dont le siège est à Paris; **I'm ~d in London** je suis basé(e) à Londres

baseball [ˈbeɪsbɔːl] n base-ball m

baseball cap n casquette f de base-ball

Basel [ˈbɑːl] n = **Basle**

basement [ˈbeɪsmənt] n sous-sol m

bases [ˈbeɪsɪz] npl of **basis** [ˈbeɪsɪz] npl of **base**

bash [bæʃ] vt (inf) frapper, cogner ▷ n: **I'll have a ~ (at it)** (Brit inf) je vais essayer un coup; **-ed in** adj enfoncé(e), défoncé(e); **bash up** vt (inf: car) bousiller; (: Brit: person) tabasser

bashful [ˈbæʃful] adj timide; modeste

basic [ˈbeɪsɪk] adj (precautions, rules) élémentaire; (principles, research) fondamental(e); (vocabulary, salary) de base; (minimal) réduit(e) au minimum, rudimentaire

basically [ˈbeɪsɪklɪ] adv (in fact) en fait; (essentially) fondamentalement

basics [ˈbeɪsɪks] npl: **the ~** l'essentiel m

basil [ˈbæzl] n basilic m

basin [ˈbeɪsn] n (vessel, also Geo) cuvette f, bassin m; (Brit: for food) bol m; (: bigger) saladier m; (also: **wash~**) lavabo m

basis (pl **bases**) [ˈbeɪsɪs, -siːz] n base f; **on a part-time/trial ~** à temps partiel/à l'essai; **on the ~ of what you've said** d'après ou compte tenu de ce que vous dites

bask [bɑːsk] vi: **to ~ in the sun** se chauffer au soleil

basket [ˈbɑːskɪt] n corbeille f; (with handle) panier m

basketball [ˈbɑːskɪtbɔːl] n basket-ball m

Basle [bɑːl] n Bâle

Basque [bæsk] adj basque ▷ n Basque m/f; **the ~ Country** le Pays basque

bass [beɪs] n (Mus) basse f

bass drum n grosse caisse f

bassoon [bəˈsuːn] n basson m

bastard [ˈbɑːstəd] n enfant naturel(le), bâtard(e); (inf!) salaud m (!)

bat [bæt] n chauve-souris f; (for baseball etc) batte f; (Brit: for table tennis) raquette f ▷ vt: **he didn't ~ an eyelid** il n'a pas sourcillé ou bronché; **off one's own ~** de sa propre initiative

batch [bætʃ] n (of bread) fournée f; (of papers) liasse f; (of applicants, letters) paquet m; (of work) monceau m; (of goods) lot m

bated [ˈbeɪtɪd] adj: **with ~ breath** en retenant son souffle

bath (pl **baths**) [bɑːθ, bɑːðz] n bain m; (bathtub) baignoire f ▷ vt baigner, donner un bain à; **to have a ~** prendre un bain; see also **baths**

bathe [beɪð] vi se baigner ▷ vt baigner; (wound etc) laver

bathing [ˈbeɪðɪŋ] n baignade f

bathing costume, (US) **bathing suit** n maillot m (de bain)

bathrobe [ˈbɑːθrəʊb] n peignoir m de bain

bathroom [ˈbɑːθrum] n salle f de bains

baths [bɑːðz] npl (Brit: also: **swimming ~**) piscine f

bath towel n serviette f de bain

bathtub [ˈbɑːθtʌb] n baignoire f

baton [ˈbætən] n bâton m; (Mus) baguette f; (club) matraque f

batter [ˈbætə*] vt battre ▷ n pâte f à frire

battered [ˈbætəd] adj (hat, pan) cabossé(e); **~ wife/child** épouse/enfant maltraité(e) ou martyr(e)

battery [ˈbætəri] n (for torch, radio) pile f; (Aut, Mil) batterie f

battery farming n élevage m en batterie

battle [ˈbætl] n bataille f, combat m ▷ vi se battre, lutter; **that's half the ~** (fig) c'est déjà bien; **it's a** ou **we're fighting a losing ~** (fig) c'est perdu d'avance, c'est peine perdue

battlefield [ˈbætlfiːld] n champ m de bataille

battleship [ˈbætlʃɪp] n cuirassé m

Bavaria [bəˈvɛərɪə] n Bavière f

bawl [bɔːl] vi hurler, brailler

bay [beɪ] n (of sea) baie f; (Brit: for parking) place f de stationnement; (: for loading) aire f de chargement; (horse) bai(e) m/f; **B~ of Biscay** golfe m de Gascogne; **to hold sb at ~** tenir qn à distance ou en échec

bay leaf n laurier m

bazaar [bəˈzɑː*] n (shop, market) bazar m; (sale) vente f de charité

BBC n abbr (= British Broadcasting Corporation) office de la radiodiffusion et télévision britannique

B.C. adv abbr (= before Christ) av. J.-C. ▷ abbr (Canada) = **British Columbia**

b

○ KEYWORD

be [biː] (*pt* was *or* were, *pp* been) *aux vb* **1** (*with present participle: forming continuous tenses*): **what are you doing?** que faites-vous?; **they're coming tomorrow** ils viennent demain; **I've been waiting for you for 2 hours** je t'attends depuis 2 heures

2 (*with pp: forming passives*) être; **to be killed** être tué(e); **the box had been opened** la boîte avait été ouverte; **he was nowhere to be seen** on ne le voyait nulle part

3 (*in tag questions*): **it was fun, wasn't it?** c'était drôle, n'est-ce pas?; **he's good-looking, isn't he?** il est beau, n'est-ce pas?; **she's back, is she?** elle est rentrée, n'est-ce pas *or* alors?

4 (*+to +infinitive*): **the house is to be sold** (*necessity*) la maison doit être vendue; (*future*) la maison va être vendue; **he's not to open it** il ne doit pas l'ouvrir; **am I to understand that …?** dois-je comprendre que …?; **he was to have come yesterday** il devait venir hier

5 (*possibility, supposition*): **if I were you, I …** à votre place, je …, si j'étais vous, je …

▷ *vb + complement* **1** (*gen*) être; **I'm English** je suis anglais(e); **I'm tired** je suis fatigué(e); **I'm hot/cold** j'ai chaud/froid; **he's a doctor** il est médecin; **be careful/good/quiet!** faites attention/soyez sages/taisez-vous!; **2 and 2 are 4** 2 et 2 font 4

2 (*of health*) aller; **how are you?** comment allez-vous?; **I'm better now** je vais mieux maintenant; **he's fine now** il va bien maintenant; **he's very ill** il est très malade

3 (*of age*) avoir; **how old are you?** quel âge avez-vous?; **I'm sixteen (years old)** j'ai seize ans

4 (*cost*) coûter; **how much was the meal?** combien a coûté le repas?; **that'll be £5, please** ça fera 5 livres, s'il vous plaît; **this shirt is £17** cette chemise coûte 17 livres

▷ *vi* **1** (*exist, occur etc*) être, exister; **the prettiest girl that ever was** la fille la plus jolie qui ait jamais existé; **is there a God?** y a-t-il un dieu?; **be that as it may** quoi qu'il en soit; **so be it** soit

2 (*referring to place*) être, se trouver; **I won't be here tomorrow** je ne serai pas là demain; **Edinburgh is in Scotland** Édimbourg est *or* se trouve en Écosse

3 (*referring to movement*) aller; **where have you been?** où êtes-vous allé(s)?

▷ *impers vb* **1** (*referring to time*) être; **it's 5 o'clock** il est 5 heures; **it's the 28th of April** c'est le 28 avril

2 (*referring to distance*): **it's 10 km to the village** le village est à 10 km

3 (*referring to the weather*) faire; **it's too hot/cold** il fait trop chaud/froid; **it's windy today** il y a du vent aujourd'hui

4 (*emphatic*): **it's me/the postman** c'est moi/le facteur; **it was Maria who paid the bill** c'est Maria qui a payé la note

beach [biːtʃ] *n* plage *f* ▷ *vt* échouer
beacon ['biːkən] *n* (*lighthouse*) fanal *m*; (*marker*) balise *f*; (*also*: **radio ~**) radiophare *m*
bead [biːd] *n* perle *f*; (*of dew, sweat*) goutte *f*; **beads** *npl* (*necklace*) collier *m*
beak [biːk] *n* bec *m*
beaker ['biːkəʳ] *n* gobelet *m*
beam [biːm] *n* (*Archit*) poutre *f*; (*of light*) rayon *m*; (*Radio*) faisceau *m* radio ▷ *vi* rayonner; **to drive on full** *or* **main** *or* (*US*) **high ~** rouler en pleins phares
bean [biːn] *n* haricot *m*; (*of coffee*) grain *m*
beansprouts ['biːnsprauts] *npl* pousses *fpl* *or* germes *mpl* de soja
bear [bɛəʳ] (*pt* bore, *pp* borne) [bɔːʳ, bɔːn] *n* ours *m*; (*Stock Exchange*) baissier *m* ▷ *vt* porter; (*endure*) supporter; (*traces, signs*) porter; (*Comm: interest*) rapporter ▷ *vi*: **to ~ right/left** obliquer à droite/gauche, se diriger vers la droite/gauche; **to ~ the responsibility of** assumer la responsabilité de; **to ~ comparison with** soutenir la comparaison avec; **I can't ~ him** je ne peux pas le supporter *or* souffrir; **to bring pressure to ~ on sb** faire pression sur qn; **bear out** *vt* (*theory, suspicion*) confirmer; **bear up** *vi* supporter, tenir le coup; **he bore up well** il a tenu le coup; **bear with** *vt fus* (*sb's moods, temper*) supporter; **~ with me a minute** un moment, s'il vous plaît
beard [biəd] *n* barbe *f*
bearded ['biədɪd] *adj* barbu(e)
bearer ['bɛərəʳ] *n* porteur *m*; (*of passport etc*) titulaire *m/f*
bearing ['bɛərɪŋ] *n* maintien *m*, allure *f*; (*connection*) rapport *m*; (*Tech*): (**ball) bearings** *npl* roulement *m* (à billes); **to take a ~** faire le point; **to find one's ~s** s'orienter
beast [biːst] *n* bête *f*; (*inf: person*) brute *f*
beastly ['biːstlɪ] *adj* infect(e)
beat [biːt] *n* battement *m*; (*Mus*) temps *m*, mesure *f*; (*of policeman*) ronde *f* ▷ *vt, vi* (*pt* beat, *pp* beaten) battre; **off the ~ en track** hors des chemins *or* sentiers battus; **to ~ it** (*inf*) ficher le camp; **to ~ about the bush** tourner autour du pot; **that ~s everything!** c'est le comble!; **beat down** *vt* (*door*) enfoncer; (*price*) faire baisser; (*seller*) faire descendre ▷ *vi* (*rain*) tambouriner; (*sun*) taper; **beat off** *vt* repousser; **beat up** *vt* (*eggs*) battre; (*inf: person*) tabasser
beating ['biːtɪŋ] *n* raclée *f*
beautiful ['bjuːtɪful] *adj* beau/belle
beautifully ['bjuːtɪflɪ] *adv* admirablement
beauty ['bjuːtɪ] *n* beauté *f*; **the ~ of it is that …** le plus beau, c'est que …
beauty parlour, (*US*) **beauty parlor** *n* institut *m* de beauté
beauty salon *n* institut *m* de beauté

beauty spot n (on skin) grain m de beauté; (Brit Tourism) site naturel (d'une grande beauté)
beaver ['biːvəʳ] n castor m
became [bɪˈkeɪm] pt of **become**
because [bɪˈkɒz] conj parce que; ~ of prep à cause de
beck [bek] n: **to be at sb's** ~ **and call** être à l'entière disposition de qn
beckon ['bekən] vt (also: ~ **to**) faire signe (de venir) à
become [bɪˈkʌm] vi devenir; **to** ~ **fat/thin** grossir/maigrir; **to** ~ **angry** se mettre en colère; **it became known that** on apprit que; **what has** ~ **of him?** qu'est-il devenu?
becoming [bɪˈkʌmɪŋ] adj (behaviour) convenable, bienséant(e); (clothes) seyant(e)
bed [bed] n lit m; (of flowers) parterre m; (of coal, clay) couche f; (of sea, lake) fond m; **to go to** ~ aller se coucher; **bed down** vi se coucher
bed and breakfast n (terms) chambre et petit déjeuner; (place) ≈ chambre f d'hôte; voir article

● **BED AND BREAKFAST**

● Un bed and breakfast est une petite pension
● dans une maison particulière ou une
● ferme où l'on peut louer une chambre
● avec petit déjeuner compris pour un prix
● modique par rapport à ce que l'on paierait
● dans un hôtel. Ces établissements sont
● communément appelés "B & B", et sont
● signalés par une pancarte dans le jardin
● ou au-dessus de la porte.

bedclothes ['bedkləʊðz] npl couvertures fpl et draps mpl
bedding ['bedɪŋ] n literie f
bed linen n draps mpl de lit (et taies fpl d'oreillers), literie f
bedraggled [bɪˈdrægld] adj dépenaillé(e), les vêtements en désordre
bedridden ['bedrɪdn] adj cloué(e) au lit
bedroom ['bedrum] n chambre f (à coucher)
bedside ['bedsaɪd] n: **at sb's** ~ au chevet de qn ▷ cpd (book, lamp) de chevet
bedside lamp n lampe f de chevet
bedside table n table f de chevet
bedsit ['bedsɪt], **bedsitter** ['bedsɪtəʳ] n (Brit) chambre meublée, studio m
bedspread ['bedspred] n couvre-lit m, dessus-de-lit m
bedtime ['bedtaɪm] n: **it's** ~ c'est l'heure de se coucher
bee [biː] n abeille f; **to have a** ~ **in one's bonnet (about sth)** être obnubilé(e) (par qch)
beech [biːtʃ] n hêtre m
beef [biːf] n bœuf m; **roast** ~ rosbif m; **beef up** vt (inf: support) renforcer; (: essay) étoffer

beefburger ['biːfbəːgəʳ] n hamburger m
beehive ['biːhaɪv] n ruche f
beeline ['biːlaɪn] n: **to make a** ~ **for** se diriger tout droit vers
been [biːn] pp of **be**
beer [bɪəʳ] n bière f
beer garden n (Brit) jardin m d'un pub (où l'on peut emmener ses consommations)
beet [biːt] n (vegetable) betterave f; (US: also: **red** ~) betterave (potagère)
beetle ['biːtl] n scarabée m, coléoptère m
beetroot ['biːtruːt] n (Brit) betterave f
before [bɪˈfɔːʳ] prep (of time) avant; (of space) devant ▷ conj avant que + sub; avant de ▷ adv avant; ~ **going** avant de partir; ~ **she goes** avant qu'elle (ne) parte; **the** ~ la semaine précédente or d'avant; **I've seen it** ~ je l'ai déjà vu; **I've never seen it** ~ c'est la première fois que je le vois
beforehand [bɪˈfɔːhænd] adv au préalable, à l'avance
beg [beg] vi mendier ▷ vt mendier; (favour) quémander, solliciter; (forgiveness, mercy etc) demander; (entreat) supplier; **to** ~ **sb to do sth** supplier qn de faire qch; **I** ~ **your pardon** (apologising) excusez-moi; (: not hearing) pardon?; **that** ~**s the question of** ... cela soulève la question de ..., cela suppose réglée la question de ...; see also **pardon**
began [bɪˈgæn] pt of **begin**
beggar ['begəʳ] n (also: ~**-man, ~-woman**) mendiant(e)
begin [bɪˈgɪn] (pt **began**, pp **begun**) [bɪˈgɪn, -ˈgæn, -ˈgʌn] vt, vi commencer; **to** ~ **doing** or **to do sth** commencer à faire qch; ~**ning (from) Monday** à partir de lundi; **I can't** ~ **to thank you** je ne saurais vous remercier; **to** ~ **with** d'abord, pour commencer
beginner [bɪˈgɪnəʳ] n débutant(e)
beginning [bɪˈgɪnɪŋ] n commencement m, début m; **right from the** ~ dès le début
begun [bɪˈgʌn] pp of **begin**
behalf [bɪˈhɑːf] n: **on** ~ **of**, (US) **in** ~ **of** (representing) de la part de; au nom de; (for benefit of) pour le compte de; **on my/his** ~ de ma/sa part
behave [bɪˈheɪv] vi se conduire, se comporter; (well: also: ~ **o.s.**) se conduire bien or comme il faut
behaviour, (US) **behavior** [bɪˈheɪvjəʳ] n comportement m, conduite f
behead [bɪˈhed] vt décapiter
behind [bɪˈhaɪnd] prep derrière; (time) en retard sur; (supporting): **to be** ~ **sb** soutenir qn ▷ adv derrière; en retard ▷ n derrière m; ~ **the scenes** dans les coulisses; **to leave sth** ~ (forget) oublier de prendre qch; **to be** ~ (schedule) **with sth** être en retard dans qch
behold [bɪˈhəʊld] vt (irreg like: **hold**) apercevoir, voir
beige [beɪʒ] adj beige
Beijing ['beɪˈdʒɪŋ] n Pékin

being ['biːɪŋ] n être m; **to come into ~**
prendre naissance

Beirut [beɪ'ruːt] n Beyrouth

Belarus [bɛlə'rʊs] n Biélorussie f, Bélarus m

belated [bɪ'leɪtɪd] adj tardif(-ive)

belch [bɛltʃ] vi avoir un renvoi, roter ▷ vt
(also: **~ out**: smoke etc) vomir, cracher

Belgian ['bɛldʒən] adj belge, de Belgique ▷ n
Belge m/f

Belgium ['bɛldʒəm] n Belgique f

belie [bɪ'laɪ] vt démentir; (give false impression
of) occulter

belief [bɪ'liːf] n (opinion) conviction f; (trust,
faith) foi f; (acceptance as true) croyance f; **it's
beyond ~** c'est incroyable; **in the ~ that** dans
l'idée que

believe [bɪ'liːv] vt, vi croire, estimer; **to ~ in**
(God) croire en; (ghosts, method) croire à; **I
don't ~ in corporal punishment** je ne suis
pas partisan des châtiments corporels; **he is
~d to be abroad** il serait à l'étranger

believer [bɪ'liːvəʳ] n (in idea, activity)
partisan(e); **~ in** partisan(e) de; (Rel)
croyant(e)

belittle [bɪ'lɪtl] vt déprécier, rabaisser

bell [bɛl] n cloche f; (small) clochette f,
grelot m; (on door) sonnette f; (electric)
sonnerie f; **that rings a ~** (fig) cela me
rappelle qch

bellboy ['bɛlbɔɪ], (US) **bellhop** ['bɛlhɔp] n
groom m, chasseur m

belligerent [bɪ'lɪdʒərənt] adj (at war)
belligérant(e); (fig) agressif(-ive)

bellow ['bɛləu] vi (bull) meugler; (person)
brailler ▷ vt (orders) hurler

bell pepper n (esp US) poivron m

belly ['bɛlɪ] n ventre m

belly button (inf) n nombril m

belong [bɪ'lɔŋ] vi: **to ~ to** appartenir à; (club
etc) faire partie de; **this book ~s here** ce livre
va ici, la place de ce livre est ici

belongings [bɪ'lɔŋɪŋz] npl affaires fpl,
possessions fpl; **personal ~** effets personnels

beloved [bɪ'lʌvɪd] adj (bien-)aimé(e), chéri(e)
▷ n bien-aimé(e)

below [bɪ'ləu] prep sous, au-dessous de ▷ adv
en dessous, en contre-bas; **see ~** voir plus bas
or plus loin or ci-dessous; **temperatures ~
normal** températures inférieures à la
normale

belt [bɛlt] n ceinture f; (Tech) courroie f ▷ vt
(thrash) donner une raclée à ▷ vi (Brit inf) filer
(à toutes jambes); **industrial ~** zone
industrielle; **belt out** vt (song) chanter à tue-
tête or à pleins poumons; **belt up** vi (Brit inf)
la boucler

beltway ['bɛltweɪ] n (US Aut) route f de
ceinture; (: motorway) périphérique m

bemused [bɪ'mjuːzd] adj médusé(e)

bench [bɛntʃ] n banc m; (in workshop) établi m;
the B~ (Law: judges) la magistrature, la Cour

bend [bɛnd] (pt, pp **bent** [bɛnt]) vt courber;

(leg, arm) plier ▷ vi se courber ▷ n (Brit: in road)
virage m, tournant m; (in pipe, river) coude m;
bend down vi se baisser; **bend over** vi se
pencher

beneath [bɪ'niːθ] prep sous, au-dessous de;
(unworthy of) indigne de ▷ adv dessous,
au-dessous, en bas

benefactor ['bɛnɪfæktəʳ] n bienfaiteur m

beneficial [bɛnɪ'fɪʃəl] adj: **~ (to)** salutaire
(pour), bénéfique (à)

benefit ['bɛnɪfɪt] n avantage m, profit m;
(allowance of money) allocation f ▷ vt faire du
bien à, profiter à ▷ vi: **he'll ~ from it** cela lui
fera du bien, il y gagnera or s'en trouvera
bien

Benelux ['bɛnɪlʌks] n Bénélux m

benevolent [bɪ'nɛvələnt] adj bienveillant(e)

benign [bɪ'naɪn] adj (person, smile)
bienveillant(e), affable; (Med) bénin(-igne)

bent [bɛnt] pt, pp of **bend** ▷ n inclination f,
penchant m ▷ adj (wire, pipe) coudé(e); (inf:
dishonest) véreux(-euse); **to be ~ on** être
résolu(e) à

bequest [bɪ'kwɛst] n legs m

bereaved [bɪ'riːvd] n: **the ~** la famille du
disparu ▷ adj endeuillé(e)

beret ['bɛreɪ] n béret m

Berlin [bəː'lɪn] n Berlin; **East/West ~** Berlin
Est/Ouest

berm [bəːm] n (US Aut) accotement m

Bermuda [bəː'mjuːdə] n Bermudes fpl

Bern [bəːn] n Berne

berry ['bɛrɪ] n baie f

berserk [bə'səːk] adj: **to go ~** être pris(e)
d'une rage incontrôlable; se déchaîner

berth [bəːθ] n (bed) couchette f; (for ship)
poste m d'amarrage, mouillage m ▷ vi (in
harbour) venir à quai; (at anchor) mouiller; **to
give sb a wide ~** (fig) éviter qn

beseech (pt, pp **besought**) [bɪ'siːtʃ, -'sɔːt] vt
implorer, supplier

beset (pt, pp **beset**) [bɪ'sɛt] vt assaillir ▷ adj:
~ with semé(e) de

beside [bɪ'saɪd] prep à côté de; (compared with)
par rapport à; **that's ~ the point** ça n'a rien à
voir; **to be ~ o.s. (with anger)** être hors de
soi

besides [bɪ'saɪdz] adv en outre, de plus ▷ prep
en plus de; (except) excepté

besiege [bɪ'siːdʒ] vt (town) assiéger; (fig)
assaillir

best [bɛst] adj meilleur(e) ▷ adv le mieux;
the ~ part of (quantity) le plus clair de, la plus
grande partie de; **at ~** au mieux; **to make the
~ of sth** s'accommoder de qch (du mieux que
l'on peut); **to do one's ~** faire de son mieux;
to the ~ of my knowledge pour autant que
je sache; **to the ~ of my ability** du mieux
que je pourrai; **he's not exactly patient at
the ~ of times** il n'est jamais spécialement
patient; **the ~ thing to do is ...** le mieux,
c'est de ...

best-before date n date f de limite
d'utilisation or de consommation
best man (irreg) n garçon m d'honneur
bestow [bɪ'stəu] vt accorder; (title) conférer
bestseller ['best'selər] n best-seller m,
succès m de librairie
bet [bet] n pari m ▷ vt, vi (pt, pp **bet** or **betted**)
parier; **it's a safe ~** (fig) il y a de fortes
chances; **to ~ sb sth** parier qch à qn
betray [bɪ'treɪ] vt trahir
better ['betər] adj meilleur(e) ▷ adv mieux
▷ vt améliorer ▷ n: **to get the ~ of** triompher
de, l'emporter sur; **a change for the ~** une
amélioration; **I had ~ go** il faut que je m'en
aille; **you had ~ do it** vous feriez mieux de
le faire; **he thought ~ of it** il s'est ravisé;
to get ~ (Med) aller mieux; (improve)
s'améliorer; **that's ~!** c'est mieux!; **~ off** adj
plus à l'aise financièrement; (fig): **you'd
be ~ off this way** vous vous en trouveriez
mieux ainsi, ce serait mieux or plus
pratique ainsi
betting ['betɪŋ] n paris mpl
betting shop n (Brit) bureau m de paris
between [bɪ'twiːn] prep entre ▷ adv au
milieu, dans l'intervalle; **the road ~ here
and London** la route d'ici à Londres; **we only
had 5 ~ us** nous n'en avions que 5 en tout
beverage ['bevərɪdʒ] n boisson f (gén sans
alcool)
beware [bɪ'wɛər] vt, vi: **to ~ (of)** prendre garde
(à); **"~ of the dog"** "(attention) chien
méchant"
bewildered [bɪ'wɪldəd] adj dérouté(e),
ahuri(e)
beyond [bɪ'jɔnd] prep (in space, time) au-delà
de; (exceeding) au-dessus de ▷ adv au-delà;
~ doubt hors de doute; **~ repair** irréparable
bias [baɪəs] n (prejudice) préjugé m, parti pris;
(preference) prévention f
biased, biassed ['baɪəst] adj partial(e),
montrant un parti pris; **to be bias(s)ed
against** avoir un préjugé contre
bib [bɪb] n bavoir m, bavette f
Bible ['baɪbl] n Bible f
bicarbonate of soda [baɪ'kɑːbənɪt-] n
bicarbonate m de soude
biceps ['baɪseps] n biceps m
bicker ['bɪkər] vi se chamailler
bicycle ['baɪsɪkl] n bicyclette f
bicycle pump n pompe f à vélo
bid [bɪd] n offre f; (at auction) enchère f;
(attempt) tentative f ▷ vi (pt, pp **bid**) faire une
enchère or offre ▷ vt (pt **bade**) [bæd] (pp
bidden) ['bɪdn] faire une enchère or offre de;
to ~ sb good day souhaiter le bonjour à qn
bidder ['bɪdər] n: **the highest ~** le plus
offrant
bidding ['bɪdɪŋ] n enchères fpl
bide [baɪd] vt: **to ~ one's time** attendre son
heure
bidet ['biːdeɪ] n bidet m

bifocals [baɪ'fəuklz] npl lunettes fpl à double
foyer
big [bɪg] adj (in height: person, building, tree)
grand(e); (in bulk, amount: person, parcel, book)
gros(se); **to do things in a ~ way** faire les
choses en grand
Big Apple n voir article

⬤ **BIG APPLE**
⬤
⬤ Si l'on sait que The Big Apple désigne la
⬤ ville de New York ("apple" est en réalité
⬤ un terme d'argot signifiant "grande
⬤ ville"), on connaît moins les surnoms
⬤ donnés aux autres grandes villes
⬤ américaines. Chicago est surnommée
⬤ "Windy City" à cause des rafales
⬤ soufflant du lac Michigan, La Nouvelle-
⬤ Orléans doit son sobriquet de "Big Easy"
⬤ à son style de vie décontracté, et
⬤ l'industrie automobile a donné à Detroit
⬤ son surnom de "Motown".

bigheaded ['bɪg'hɛdɪd] adj
prétentieux(-euse)
bigot ['bɪgət] n fanatique m/f, sectaire m/f
bigoted ['bɪgətɪd] adj fanatique, sectaire
bigotry ['bɪgətrɪ] n fanatisme m,
sectarisme m
big toe n gros orteil
big top n grand chapiteau
bike [baɪk] n vélo m, bécane f
bike lane n piste f cyclable
bikini [bɪ'kiːnɪ] n bikini m
bilateral [baɪ'lætərl] adj bilatéral(e)
bilingual [baɪ'lɪŋgwəl] adj bilingue
bill [bɪl] n note f, facture f; (in restaurant)
addition f, note f; (Pol) projet m de loi; (US:
banknote) billet m (de banque); (notice) affiche
f; (of bird) bec m; (Theat): **on the ~** à l'affiche
▷ vt (item) facturer; (customer) remettre la
facture à; **may I have the ~ please?** (est-ce
que je peux avoir) l'addition, s'il vous plaît?;
put it on my ~ mettez-le sur mon compte;
"post no ~s" "défense d'afficher"; **to fit** or
fill the ~ (fig) faire l'affaire; **~ of exchange**
lettre f de change; **~ of lading**
connaissement m; **~ of sale** contrat m de
vente
billboard ['bɪlbɔːd] (US) n panneau m
d'affichage
billet ['bɪlɪt] n cantonnement m (chez
l'habitant) ▷ vt (troops) cantonner
billfold ['bɪlfəuld] n (US) portefeuille m
billiards ['bɪljədz] n (jeu m de) billard m
billion ['bɪljən] n (Brit) billion m (million de
millions); (US) milliard m
bimbo ['bɪmbəu] n (inf) ravissante idiote f
bin [bɪn] n boîte f; (Brit: also: **dust-, litter ~**)
poubelle f; (for coal) coffre m
bind (pt, pp **bound**) [baɪnd, baund] vt
attacher; (book) relier; (oblige) obliger,

contraindre ▷ n (inf: nuisance) scie f; **bind over** vt (Law) mettre en liberté conditionnelle; **bind up** vt (wound) panser; **to be bound up in** (work, research etc) être complètement absorbé par, être accroché par; **to be bound up with** (person) être accroché à

binding ['baɪndɪŋ] n (of book) reliure f ▷ adj (contract) qui constitue une obligation

binge [bɪndʒ] n (inf): **to go on a ~** faire la bringue

bingo ['bɪŋɡəʊ] n sorte de jeu de loto pratiqué dans des établissements publics

binoculars [bɪ'nɔkjuləz] npl jumelles fpl

biochemistry [baɪə'kɛmɪstrɪ] n biochimie f

biodegradable ['baɪəʊdɪ'ɡreɪdəbl] adj biodégradable

biofuel ['baɪəʊfjuəl] n biocarburant m

biography [baɪ'ɔɡrəfɪ] n biographie f

biological [baɪə'lɔdʒɪkl] adj biologique

biology [baɪ'ɔlədʒɪ] n biologie f

biometric [baɪə'mɛtrɪk] adj biométrique

bipolar [baɪ'pəʊlə'] adj bipolaire

birch [bəːtʃ] n bouleau m

bird [bəːd] n oiseau m; (Brit inf: girl) nana f

bird flu n grippe f aviaire

bird of prey n oiseau m de proie

bird's-eye view ['bəːdzaɪ-] n vue f à vol d'oiseau; (fig) vue d'ensemble or générale

bird watcher [-wɔtʃə'] n ornithologue m/f amateur

birdwatching ['bəːdwɔtʃɪŋ] n ornithologie f (d'amateur)

Biro® ['baɪərəʊ] n stylo m à bille

birth [bəːθ] n naissance f; **to give ~ to** donner naissance à, mettre au monde; (subj: animal) mettre bas

birth certificate n acte m de naissance

birth control n (policy) limitation f des naissances; (methods) méthode(s) contraceptive(s)

birthday ['bəːθdeɪ] n anniversaire m ▷ cpd (cake, card etc) d'anniversaire

birthmark ['bəːθmaːk] n envie f, tache f de vin

birthplace ['bəːθpleɪs] n lieu m de naissance

birth rate n (taux m de) natalité f

biscuit ['bɪskɪt] n (Brit) biscuit m; (US) petit pain au lait

bisect [baɪ'sɛkt] vt couper or diviser en deux

bishop ['bɪʃəp] n évêque m; (Chess) fou m

bistro ['biːstrəʊ] n petit restaurant m, bistrot m

bit [bɪt] pt of **bite** ▷ n morceau m; (Comput) bit m, élément m binaire; (of tool) mèche f; (of horse) mors m; **a ~ of** un peu de; **a ~ mad/dangerous** un peu fou/risqué; **~ by ~** petit à petit; **to come to ~s** (break) tomber en morceaux, se déglinguer; **bring all your ~s and pieces** apporte toutes tes affaires; **to do one's ~** y mettre du sien

bitch [bɪtʃ] n (dog) chienne f; (offensive) salope f (!), garce f

bite [baɪt] vt, vi (pt **bit**, pp **bitten**) [bɪt, 'bɪtn] mordre; (insect) piquer ▷ n morsure f; (insect bite) piqûre f; (mouthful) bouchée f; **let's have a ~ (to eat)** mangeons un morceau; **to ~ one's nails** se ronger les ongles

bitten ['bɪtn] pp of **bite**

bitter ['bɪtə'] adj amer(-ère); (criticism) cinglant(e); (icy: weather, wind) glacial(e) ▷ n (Brit: beer) bière f (à forte teneur en houblon); **to the ~ end** jusqu'au bout

bitterness ['bɪtənɪs] n amertume f; goût amer

bizarre [bɪ'zɑː'] adj bizarre

black [blæk] adj noir(e) ▷ n (colour) noir ▷ vt (shoes) cirer; (Brit Industry) boycotter; **to give sb a ~ eye** pocher l'œil à qn, faire un œil au beurre noir à qn; **there it is in ~ and white** (fig) c'est écrit noir sur blanc; **to be in the ~** (in credit) avoir un compte créditeur; **~ and blue** (bruised) couvert(e) de bleus; **black out** vi (faint) s'évanouir

blackberry ['blækbərɪ] n mûre f

blackbird ['blækbəːd] n merle m

blackboard ['blækbɔːd] n tableau noir

black coffee n café noir

blackcurrant ['blæk'kʌrənt] n cassis m

blacken ['blækn] vt noircir

black ice n verglas m

blackleg ['blæklɛɡ] n (Brit) briseur m de grève, jaune m

blacklist ['blæklɪst] n liste noire ▷ vt mettre sur la liste noire

blackmail ['blækmeɪl] n chantage m ▷ vt faire chanter, soumettre au chantage

black market n marché noir

blackout ['blækaʊt] n panne f d'électricité; (in wartime) black-out m; (TV) interruption f d'émission; (fainting) syncope f

black pepper n poivre noir

black pudding n boudin (noir)

Black Sea n: **the ~** la mer Noire

black sheep n brebis galeuse

blacksmith ['blæksmɪθ] n forgeron m

black spot n (Aut) point noir

bladder ['blædə'] n vessie f

blade [bleɪd] n lame f; (of oar) plat m; (of propeller) pale f; **a ~ of grass** un brin d'herbe

blame [bleɪm] n faute f, blâme m ▷ vt: **to ~ sb/sth for sth** attribuer à qn/qch la responsabilité de qch; reprocher qch à qn/qch; **who's to ~?** qui est le fautif or coupable or responsable?; **I'm not to ~** ce n'est pas ma faute

bland [blænd] adj affable; (taste, food) doux/douce, fade

blank [blæŋk] adj blanc/blanche; (look) sans expression, dénué(e) d'expression ▷ n espace m vide, blanc m; (cartridge) cartouche f à blanc; **his mind was a ~** il avait la tête vide; **we drew a ~** (fig) nous n'avons abouti à rien

blanket ['blæŋkɪt] n couverture f; (of snow, cloud) couche f ▷ adj (statement, agreement) global(e), de portée générale; **to give ~ cover** (*insurance policy*) couvrir tous les risques

blare [blɛəʳ] vi (*brass band, horns, radio*) beugler

blast [blɑːst] n explosion f; (*shock wave*) souffle m; (*of air, steam*) bouffée f ▷ vt faire sauter *or* exploser ▷ *excl* (*Brit inf*) zut!; **(at) full ~** (*play music etc*) à plein volume; **blast off** vi (*Space*) décoller

blast-off ['blɑːstɔf] n (*Space*) lancement m

blatant ['bleɪtənt] adj flagrant(e), criant(e)

blaze [bleɪz] n (*fire*) incendie m; (*flames: of fire, sun etc*) embrasement m; (: *in hearth*) flamme f, flambée f; (*fig*) flamboiement m ▷ vi (*fire*) flamber; (*fig*) flamboyer, resplendir ▷ vt: **to ~ a trail** (*fig*) montrer la voie; **in a ~ of publicity** à grand renfort de publicité

blazer ['bleɪzəʳ] n blazer m

bleach [bliːtʃ] n (*also*: **household ~**) eau f de Javel ▷ vt (*linen*) blanchir

bleached [bliːtʃt] adj (*hair*) oxygéné(e), décoloré(e)

bleachers ['bliːtʃəz] npl (*US Sport*) gradins mpl (*en plein soleil*)

bleak [bliːk] adj morne, désolé(e); (*weather*) triste, maussade; (*smile*) lugubre; (*prospect, future*) morose

bleat [bliːt] n bêlement m ▷ vi bêler

bled [bled] pt, pp of **bleed**

bleed (*pt, pp* **bled**) [bliːd, bled] vt saigner; (*brakes, radiator*) purger ▷ vi saigner; **my nose is ~ing** je saigne du nez

bleeper ['bliːpəʳ] n (*of doctor etc*) bip m

blemish ['blɛmɪʃ] n défaut m; (*on reputation*) tache f

blend [blend] n mélange m ▷ vt mélanger ▷ vi (*colours etc: also*: **~ in**) se mélanger, se fondre, s'allier

blender ['blendəʳ] n (*Culin*) mixeur m

bless (*pt, pp* **blessed** *or* **blest**) [bles, blest] vt bénir; **to be ~ed with** avoir le bonheur de jouir de *or* d'avoir; **~ you!** (*after sneeze*) à tes souhaits!

blessing ['blɛsɪŋ] n bénédiction f; (*godsend*) bienfait m; **to count one's ~s** s'estimer heureux; **it was a ~ in disguise** c'est un bien pour un mal

blew [bluː] pt of **blow**

blight [blaɪt] n (*of plants*) rouille f ▷ vt (*hopes etc*) anéantir, briser

blimey ['blaɪmɪ] excl (*Brit inf*) mince alors!

blind [blaɪnd] adj aveugle ▷ n (*for window*) store m ▷ vt aveugler; **to turn a ~ eye (on** *or* **to)** fermer les yeux (sur); **~ people** les aveugles mpl

blind alley n impasse f

blind corner n (*Brit*) virage m sans visibilité

blindfold ['blaɪndfəuld] n bandeau m ▷ adj, adv les yeux bandés ▷ vt bander les yeux à

blindly ['blaɪndlɪ] adv aveuglément

blindness ['blaɪndnɪs] n cécité f; (*fig*) aveuglement m

blind spot n (*Aut etc*) angle m aveugle; (*fig*) angle mort

blink [blɪŋk] vi cligner des yeux; (*light*) clignoter ▷ n: **the TV's on the ~** (*inf*) la télé ne va pas tarder à nous lâcher

blinkers ['blɪŋkəz] npl œillères fpl

bliss [blɪs] n félicité f, bonheur m sans mélange

blister ['blɪstəʳ] n (*on skin*) ampoule f, cloque f; (*on paintwork*) boursouflure f ▷ vi (*paint*) se boursoufler, se cloquer

blizzard ['blɪzəd] n blizzard m, tempête f de neige

bloated ['bləutɪd] adj (*face*) bouffi(e); (*stomach, person*) gonflé(e)

blob [blɔb] n (*drop*) goutte f; (*stain, spot*) tache f

block [blɔk] n bloc m; (*in pipes*) obstruction f; (*toy*) cube m; (*of buildings*) pâté m (de maisons) ▷ vt bloquer; (*fig*) faire obstacle à; (*Comput*) grouper; **the sink is ~ed** l'évier est bouché; **~ of flats** (*Brit*) immeuble (locatif); **3 ~s from here** à trois rues d'ici; **mental ~** blocage m; **~ and tackle** (*Tech*) palan m; **block up** vt boucher

blockade [blɔ'keɪd] n blocus m ▷ vt faire le blocus de

blockage ['blɔkɪdʒ] n obstruction f

blockbuster ['blɔkbʌstəʳ] n (*film, book*) grand succès

block capitals npl majuscules fpl d'imprimerie

block letters npl majuscules fpl

blog [blɔg] n blog m, blogue m ▷ vi bloguer

blogger ['blɔgəʳ] (*inf*) n (*person*) blogueur(-euse) m/f

blogging ['blɔgɪŋ] n blogging m

bloke [bləuk] n (*Brit inf*) type m

blond, blonde [blɔnd] adj, n blond(e)

blood [blʌd] n sang m

blood donor n donneur(-euse) de sang

blood group n groupe sanguin

bloodhound ['blʌdhaund] n limier m

blood poisoning n empoisonnement m du sang

blood pressure n tension (artérielle); **to have high/low ~** faire de l'hypertension/l'hypotension

bloodshed ['blʌdʃɛd] n effusion f de sang, carnage m

bloodshot ['blʌdʃɔt] adj: **~ eyes** yeux injectés de sang

blood sports npl sports mpl sanguinaires

bloodstream ['blʌdstriːm] n sang m, système sanguin

blood test n analyse f de sang

bloodthirsty ['blʌdθəːstɪ] adj sanguinaire

blood transfusion n transfusion f de sang

blood type n groupe sanguin

blood vessel n vaisseau sanguin

bloody ['blʌdɪ] adj sanglant(e); (*Brit inf!*): **this ~ ...** ce foutu ..., ce putain de ... (!) ▷ adv:

~ **strong/good** (Brit: inf!) vachement or sacrément fort/bon

bloody-minded ['blʌdɪ'maɪndɪd] adj (Brit inf) contrariant(e), obstiné(e)

bloom [blu:m] n fleur f; (fig) épanouissement m ⊳ vi être en fleur; (fig) s'épanouir; être florissant(e)

blossom ['blɔsəm] n fleur(s) f(pl) ⊳ vi être en fleurs; (fig) s'épanouir; **to ~ into** (fig) devenir

blot [blɔt] n tache f ⊳ vt tacher; (ink) sécher; **to be a ~ on the landscape** gâcher le paysage; **to ~ one's copy book** (fig) faire un impair; **blot out** vt (memories) effacer; (view) cacher, masquer; (nation, city) annihiler

blotchy ['blɔtʃɪ] adj (complexion) couvert(e) de marbrures

blotting paper ['blɔtɪŋ-] n buvard m

blouse [blauz] n (feminine garment) chemisier m, corsage m

blow [bləu] (pt blew, pp blown) [blu:, bləun] n coup m ⊳ vi souffler ⊳ vt (glass) souffler; (instrument) jouer de; (fuse) faire sauter; **to ~ one's nose** se moucher; **to ~ a whistle** siffler; **to come to ~s** en venir aux coups; **blow away** vi s'envoler ⊳ vt chasser, faire s'envoler; **blow down** vt faire tomber, renverser; **blow off** vi s'envoler ⊳ vt (hat) emporter; (ship): **to ~ off course** faire dévier; **blow out** vi (fire, flame) s'éteindre; (tyre) éclater; (fuse) sauter; **blow over** vi s'apaiser; **blow up** vi exploser, sauter ⊳ vt faire sauter; (tyre) gonfler; (Phot) agrandir

blow-dry ['bləudraɪ] n (hairstyle) brushing m ⊳ vt faire un brushing à

blowlamp ['bləulæmp] n (Brit) chalumeau m

blown [bləun] pp of **blow**

blow-out ['bləuaut] n (of tyre) éclatement m; (Brit: inf: big meal) gueuleton m

blowtorch ['bləutɔ:tʃ] n chalumeau m

blue [blu:] adj bleu(e); (depressed) triste; ~ **film/joke** film m/histoire f pornographique; **(only) once in a ~ moon** tous les trente-six du mois; **out of the ~** (fig) à l'improviste, sans qu'on s'y attende

bluebell ['blu:bɛl] n jacinthe f des bois

blueberry ['blu:bərɪ] n myrtille f, airelle f

bluebottle ['blu:bɔtl] n mouche f à viande

blue cheese n (fromage) bleu m

blueprint ['blu:prɪnt] n bleu m; (fig) projet m, plan directeur

blues [blu:z] npl: **the ~** (Mus) le blues; **to have the ~** (inf: feeling) avoir le cafard

bluff [blʌf] vi bluffer ⊳ n bluff m; (cliff) promontoire m, falaise f ⊳ adj (person) bourru(e), brusque; **to call sb's ~** mettre qn au défi d'exécuter ses menaces

blunder ['blʌndər] n gaffe f, bévue f ⊳ vi faire une gaffe or une bévue; **to ~ into sb/sth** buter contre qn/qch

blunt [blʌnt] adj (knife) émoussé(e), peu tranchant(e); (pencil) mal taillé(e); (person) brusque, ne mâchant pas ses mots ⊳ vt

émousser; ~ **instrument** (Law) instrument contondant

blur [blə:r] n (shape): **to become a ~** devenir flou ⊳ vt brouiller, rendre flou(e)

blurred [blə:d] adj flou(e)

blush [blʌʃ] vi rougir ⊳ n rougeur f

blusher ['blʌʃər] n rouge m à joues

blustery ['blʌstərɪ] adj (weather) à bourrasques

boar [bɔ:r] n sanglier m

board [bɔ:d] n (wooden) planche f; (on wall) panneau m; (for chess etc) plateau m; (cardboard) carton m; (committee) conseil m, comité m; (in firm) conseil d'administration; (Naut, Aviat): **on ~** à bord ⊳ vt (ship) monter à bord de; (train) monter dans; **full ~** (Brit) pension complète; **half ~** (Brit) demi-pension f; ~ **and lodging** n chambre f avec pension; **with ~ and lodging** logé nourri; **above ~** (fig) régulier(-ère); **across the ~** (fig: adv) systématiquement; (: adj) de portée générale; **to go by the ~** (hopes, principles) être abandonné(e); (be unimportant) compter pour rien, n'avoir aucune importance; **board up** vt (door) condamner (au moyen de planches, de tôle)

boarder ['bɔ:dər] n pensionnaire m/f; (Scol) interne m/f, pensionnaire

board game n jeu m de société

boarding card ['bɔ:dɪŋ-] n (Aviat, Naut) carte f d'embarquement

boarding house ['bɔ:dɪŋ-] n pension f

boarding pass ['bɔ:dɪŋ-] n (Brit) = **boarding card**

boarding school ['bɔ:dɪŋ-] n internat m, pensionnat m

board room n salle f du conseil d'administration

boast [bəust] vi: **to ~ (about or of)** se vanter (de) ⊳ vt s'enorgueillir de ⊳ n vantardise f; sujet m d'orgueil or de fierté

boat [bəut] n bateau m; (small) canot m; barque f; **to go by ~** aller en bateau; **to be in the same ~** (fig) être logé à la même enseigne

bob [bɔb] vi (boat, cork on water): **also: ~ up and down**) danser, se balancer ⊳ n (Brit inf) = **shilling; bob up** vi surgir or apparaître brusquement

bobby ['bɔbɪ] n (Brit inf) = agent m (de police)

bobby pin ['bɔbɪ-] n (US) pince f à cheveux

bobsleigh ['bɔbsleɪ] n bob m

bode [bəud] vi: **to ~ well/ill (for)** être de bon/mauvais augure (pour)

bodily ['bɔdɪlɪ] adj corporel(le); (pain, comfort) physique; (needs) matériel(le) ⊳ adv (carry, lift) dans ses bras

body ['bɔdɪ] n corps m; (of car) carrosserie f; (of plane) fuselage m; (also: ~ **stocking**) body m, justaucorps m; (fig: society) organe m, organisme m; (: quantity) ensemble m, masse f; (of wine) corps m; **ruling ~** organe directeur; **in a ~** en masse, ensemble; (speak) comme un seul et même homme

body-building ['bɒdıbıldıŋ] n body-
building m, culturisme m
bodyguard ['bɒdıgɑːd] n garde m du corps
bodywork ['bɒdıwəːk] n carrosserie f
bog [bɒg] n tourbière f ▷ vt: **to get ~ged
down (in)** (fig) s'enliser (dans)
bogus ['bəugəs] adj bidon inv; fantôme
boil [bɔıl] vt (faire) bouillir ▷ vi bouillir ▷ n
(Med) furoncle m; **to come to the** or (US) **a ~**
bouillir; **to bring to the** or (US) **a ~** porter à
ébullition; **boil down** vi (fig): **to ~ down** to se
réduire or ramener à; **boil over** vi déborder
boiled egg n œuf m à la coque
boiler ['bɔılər] n chaudière f
boiling ['bɔılıŋ] adj: **I'm ~ (hot)** (inf) je crève
de chaud
boiling point n point m d'ébullition
boisterous ['bɔıstərəs] adj bruyant(e),
tapageur(-euse)
bold [bəuld] adj hardi(e), audacieux(-euse);
(pej) effronté(e); (outline, colour) franc/franche,
tranché(e), marqué(e)
bollard ['bɒləd] n (Naut) bitte f d'amarrage;
(Brit Aut) borne lumineuse or de signalisation
bolt [bəult] n verrou m; (with nut) boulon m
▷ adv: **~ upright** droit(e) comme un piquet
▷ vt (door) verrouiller; (food) engloutir ▷ vi se
sauver, filer (comme une flèche); **a ~ from
the blue** (horse) s'emballer; (fig) un coup de
tonnerre dans un ciel bleu
bomb [bɒm] n bombe f ▷ vt bombarder
bombard [bɒm'bɑːd] vt bombarder
bomb disposal n: **~ unit** section f de
déminage; **~ expert** artificier m
bomber ['bɒmər] n caporal m d'artillerie;
(Aviat) bombardier m; (terrorist) poseur m de
bombes
bombing ['bɒmıŋ] n bombardement m
bomb scare n alerte f à la bombe
bombshell ['bɒmʃel] n obus m; (fig) bombe f
bond [bɒnd] n lien m; (binding promise)
engagement m, obligation f; (Finance)
obligation; **bonds** npl (chains) chaînes fpl; **in
~** (of goods) en entrepôt
bondage ['bɒndıdʒ] n esclavage m
bone [bəun] n os m; (of fish) arête f ▷ vt
désosser; ôter les arêtes de
bone-dry ['bəun'draı] adj absolument sec/
sèche
bone idle adj fainéant(e)
bone marrow n moelle osseuse
bonfire ['bɒnfaıər] n feu m (de joie); (for
rubbish) feu
bonnet ['bɒnıt] n bonnet m; (Brit: of car)
capot m
bonus ['bəunəs] n (money) prime f; (advantage)
avantage m
bony ['bəunı] adj (arm, face: Med: tissue)
osseux(-euse); (thin: person) squelettique;
(meat) plein(e) d'os; (fish) plein d'arêtes
boo [buː] excl hou!, peuh! ▷ vt huer
▷ n huée f

booby trap ['buːbı-] n guet-apens m
book [buk] n livre m; (of stamps, tickets etc)
carnet m; (Comm): **books** npl comptes mpl,
comptabilité f ▷ vt (ticket) prendre; (seat,
room) réserver; (driver) dresser un procès-
verbal à; (football player) prendre le nom de,
donner un carton à; **I ~ed a table in the
name of ...** j'ai réservé une table au nom de
...; **to keep the ~s** tenir la comptabilité; **by
the ~** à la lettre, selon les règles; **to throw
the ~ at sb** passer un savon à qn; **book in** vi
(Brit: at hotel) prendre sa chambre; **book up** vt
réserver; **all seats are ~ed up** tout est pris,
c'est complet; **the hotel is ~ed up** l'hôtel
est complet
bookcase ['bukkeıs] n bibliothèque f (meuble)
booking ['bukıŋ] n (Brit) réservation f;
I confirmed my ~ by fax/email j'ai
confirmé ma réservation par fax/
e-mail
booking office n (Brit) bureau m de location
book-keeping ['buk'kiːpıŋ] n comptabilité f
booklet ['buklıt] n brochure f
bookmaker ['bukmeıkər] n bookmaker m
bookmark ['bukmɑːk] n (for book) marque-
page m; (Comput) signet m
bookseller ['bukselər] n libraire m/f
bookshelf ['bukʃelf] n (single) étagère f
(à livres); (bookcase) bibliothèque f;
bookshelves rayons mpl (de bibliothèque)
bookshop ['bukʃɒp], **bookstore** ['bukstɔːʳ] n
librairie f
book store n = bookshop
boom [buːm] n (noise) grondement m; (in
prices, population) forte augmentation; (busy
period) boom m, vague f de prospérité ▷ vi
gronder; prospérer
boon [buːn] n bénédiction f, grand avantage
boost [buːst] n stimulant m, remontant m
▷ vt stimuler; **to give a ~ to sb's spirits** or **to
sb** remonter le moral à qn
booster ['buːstər] n (TV) amplificateur m
(de signal); (Elec) survolteur m; (also:
~ rocket) booster m; (Med: vaccine) rappel m
boot [buːt] n botte f; (for hiking) chaussure f
(de marche); (ankle boot) bottine f; (Brit: of car)
coffre m ▷ vt (Comput) lancer, mettre en
route; **to ~** (in addition) par-dessus le marché,
en plus; **to give sb the ~** (inf) flanquer qn
dehors, virer qn
booth [buːð] n (at fair) baraque (foraine); (of
telephone etc) cabine f; (also: **voting ~**) isoloir m
booze [buːz] (inf) n boissons fpl alcooliques,
alcool m ▷ vi boire, picoler
border ['bɔːdər] n bordure f; bord m; (of a
country) frontière f; **the B~s** la région frontière
entre l'Écosse et l'Angleterre; **border on** vt fus être
voisin(e) de, toucher à
borderline ['bɔːdəlaın] n (fig) ligne f de
démarcation ▷ adj: **~ case** cas m limite
bore [bɔːʳ] pt of **bear** ▷ vt (person) ennuyer,
raser; (hole) percer; (well, tunnel) creuser ▷ n

(person) raseur(-euse); (boring thing) barbe f; (of gun) calibre m

bored ['bɔːd] adj: **to be ~** s'ennuyer; **he's ~ to tears** or **to death** or **stiff** il s'ennuie à mourir

boredom ['bɔːdəm] n ennui m

boring ['bɔːrɪŋ] adj ennuyeux(-euse)

born [bɔːn] adj: **to be ~** naître; **I was ~ in 1960** je suis né en 1960; **~ blind** aveugle de naissance; **a ~ comedian** un comédien-né

borne [bɔːn] pp of **bear**

borough ['bʌrə] n municipalité f

borrow ['bɔrəʊ] vt: **to ~ sth (from sb)** emprunter qch (à qn); **may I ~ your car?** est-ce que je peux vous emprunter votre voiture?

Bosnian ['bɔznɪən] adj bosniaque, bosnien(ne) ▷ n Bosniaque m/f, Bosnien(ne)

bosom ['buzəm] n poitrine f; (fig) sein m

boss [bɔs] n patron(ne) ▷ vt (also: **~ about, ~ around**) mener à la baguette

bossy ['bɔsɪ] adj autoritaire

bosun ['bəʊsn] n maître m d'équipage

botany ['bɔtənɪ] n botanique f

botch [bɔtʃ] vt (also: **~ up**) saboter, bâcler

both [bəʊθ] adj les deux, l'un(e) et l'autre ▷ pron: **~ (of them)** les deux, tous/toutes (les) deux, l'un(e) et l'autre; **~ of us went, we ~ went** nous y sommes allés tous les deux ▷ adv: **~ A and B** A et B; **they sell ~ the fabric and the finished curtains** ils vendent (et) le tissu et les rideaux (finis), ils vendent à la fois le tissu et les rideaux (finis)

bother ['bɔðər] vt (worry) tracasser; (needle, bait) importuner, ennuyer; (disturb) déranger ▷ vi (also: **~ o.s.**) se tracasser, se faire du souci ▷ n (trouble) ennui m; **it is a ~ to have to do** c'est vraiment ennuyeux d'avoir à faire ▷ excl zut!; **to ~ doing** prendre la peine de faire; **I'm sorry to ~ you** excusez-moi de vous déranger; **please don't ~** ne vous dérangez pas; **don't ~** ce n'est pas la peine; **it's no ~** aucun problème

bottle ['bɔtl] n bouteille f; (baby's) biberon m; (of perfume, medicine) flacon m ▷ vt mettre en bouteille(s); **~ of wine/milk** bouteille de vin/lait; **wine/milk ~** bouteille à vin/lait; **bottle up** vt refouler, contenir

bottle bank n conteneur m (de bouteilles)

bottleneck ['bɔtlnɛk] n (in traffic) bouchon m; (in production) goulet m d'étranglement

bottle-opener ['bɔtləʊpnər] n ouvre-bouteille m

bottom ['bɔtəm] n (of container, sea etc) fond m; (buttocks) derrière m; (of page, list) bas m; (of chair) siège m; (of mountain, tree, hill) pied m ▷ adj (shelf, step) du bas; **to get to the ~ of sth** (fig) découvrir le fin fond de qch

bough [baʊ] n branche f, rameau m

bought [bɔːt] pt, pp of **buy**

boulder ['bəʊldər] n gros rocher (gén lisse, arrondi)

bounce [baʊns] vi (ball) rebondir; (cheque) être refusé (étant sans provision); (also: **to ~ forward/out etc**) bondir, s'élancer ▷ vt faire rebondir ▷ n (rebound) rebond m; **he's got plenty of ~** (fig) il est plein d'entrain or d'allant

bouncer ['baʊnsər] n (inf: at dance, club) videur m

bound [baʊnd] pt, pp of **bind** ▷ n (gen pl) limite f; (leap) bond m ▷ vi (leap) bondir ▷ vt (limit) borner ▷ adj: **to be ~ to do sth** (obliged) être obligé(e) or avoir obligation de faire qch; **he's ~ to fail** (likely) il est sûr d'échouer, son échec est inévitable or assuré; **~ by** (law, regulation) engagé(e) par; **~ for** à destination de; **out of ~s** dont l'accès est interdit

boundary ['baʊndrɪ] n frontière f

bouquet ['bʊkeɪ] n bouquet m

bourbon ['bʊəbən] n (US: also: **~ whiskey**) bourbon m

bout [baʊt] n période f; (of malaria etc) accès m, crise f, attaque f; (Boxing etc) combat m, match m

boutique [buːˈtiːk] n boutique f

bow¹ [bəʊ] n nœud m; (weapon) arc m; (Mus) archet m

bow² [baʊ] n (with body) révérence f, inclination f (du buste or corps); (Naut: also: **~s**) proue f ▷ vi faire une révérence, s'incliner; (yield): **to ~ to** or **before** s'incliner devant, se soumettre à; **to ~ to the inevitable** accepter l'inévitable or l'inéluctable

bowels [baʊəlz] npl intestins mpl; (fig) entrailles fpl

bowl [bəʊl] n (for eating) bol m; (for washing) cuvette f; (ball) boule f; (of pipe) fourneau m ▷ vi (Cricket) lancer (la balle); **bowl over** vt (fig) renverser

bow-legged ['bəʊˈlɛgɪd] adj aux jambes arquées

bowler ['bəʊlər] n joueur m de boules; (Cricket) lanceur m (de la balle); (Brit: also: **~ hat**) (chapeau m) melon m

bowling ['bəʊlɪŋ] n (game) jeu m de boules, jeu de quilles

bowling alley n bowling m

bowling green n terrain m de boules (gazonné et carré)

bowls [bəʊlz] n (jeu m de) boules fpl

bow tie [baʊ-] n nœud m papillon

box [bɔks] n boîte f; (also: **cardboard ~**) carton m; (crate) caisse f; (Theat) loge f ▷ vt mettre en boîte; (Sport) boxer avec ▷ vi boxer, faire de la boxe

boxer ['bɔksər] n (person) boxeur m; (dog) boxer m

boxer shorts npl caleçon m

boxing ['bɔksɪŋ] n (sport) boxe f

Boxing Day n (Brit) le lendemain de Noël; voir article

● **BOXING DAY**

Boxing Day est le lendemain de Noël, férié
en Grande-Bretagne. Ce nom vient d'une
coutume du XIXe siècle qui consistait à
donner des cadeaux de Noël (dans des
boîtes) à ses employés etc le 26 décembre.

boxing gloves *npl* gants *mpl* de boxe
boxing ring *n* ring *m*
box office *n* bureau *m* de location
box room *n* débarras *m*; chambrette *f*
boy [bɔɪ] *n* garçon *m*
boy band *n* boys band *m*
boycott ['bɔɪkɔt] *n* boycottage *m* ▷ *vt*
boycotter
boyfriend ['bɔɪfrɛnd] *n* (petit) ami
boyish ['bɔɪɪʃ] *adj* d'enfant, de garçon; **to
look ~** (*man: appear youthful*) faire jeune
BR *abbr* = **British Rail**
bra [brɑː] *n* soutien-gorge *m*
brace [breɪs] *n* (*support*) attache *f*, agrafe *f*;
(*Brit: also:* **~s**: *on teeth*) appareil *m* (dentaire);
(*tool*) vilebrequin *m*; (*Typ: also:* **~ bracket**)
accolade *f* ▷ *vt* (*support*) consolider, soutenir;
braces *npl* (*Brit: for trousers*) bretelles *fpl*; **to ~
o.s.** (*fig*) se préparer mentalement
bracelet ['breɪslɪt] *n* bracelet *m*
bracing ['breɪsɪŋ] *adj* tonifiant(e), tonique
bracket ['brækɪt] *n* (*Tech*) tasseau *m*, support
m; (*group*) classe *f*, tranche *f*; (*also:* **brace ~**)
accolade *f*; (*also:* **round ~**) parenthèse *f*; (*also:*
square ~) crochet *m* ▷ *vt* mettre entre
parenthèses; (*fig: also:* **~ together**) regrouper;
income ~ tranche *f* des revenus; **in ~s** entre
parenthèses or crochets
brag [bræg] *vi* se vanter
braid [breɪd] *n* (*trimming*) galon *m*; (*of hair*)
tresse *f*, natte *f*
brain [breɪn] *n* cerveau *m*; **brains** *npl* (*intellect,
food*) cervelle *f*; **he's got ~s** il est intelligent
brainwash ['breɪnwɔʃ] *vt* faire subir un
lavage de cerveau à
brainwave ['breɪnweɪv] *n* idée *f* de génie
brainy ['breɪnɪ] *adj* intelligent(e), doué(e)
braise [breɪz] *vt* braiser
brake [breɪk] *n* frein *m* ▷ *vt, vi* freiner
brake light *n* feu *m* de stop
bran [bræn] *n* son *m*
branch [brɑːntʃ] *n* branche *f*; (*Comm*)
succursale *f*; (*of bank*) agence *f*; (*of association*)
section locale ▷ *vi* bifurquer; **branch off** *vi*
(*road*) bifurquer; **branch out** *vi* diversifier ses
activités; **to ~ out into** étendre ses activités à
brand [brænd] *n* marque (commerciale) ▷ *vt*
(*cattle*) marquer (au fer rouge); (*fig: pej*): **to ~
sb a communist** *etc* traiter or qualifier qn de
communiste *etc*
brand name *n* nom *m* de marque
brand-new ['brænd'njuː] *adj* tout(e) neuf/
neuve, flambant neuf/neuve
brandy ['brændɪ] *n* cognac *m*, fine *f*

brash [bræʃ] *adj* effronté(e)
brass [brɑːs] *n* cuivre *m* (jaune), laiton *m*; **the
~** (*Mus*) les cuivres
brass band *n* fanfare *f*
brat [bræt] *n* (*pej*) mioche *m/f*, môme *m/f*
brave [breɪv] *adj* courageux(-euse), brave ▷ *n*
guerrier indien ▷ *vt* braver, affronter
bravery ['breɪvərɪ] *n* bravoure *f*, courage *m*
brawl [brɔːl] *n* rixe *f*, bagarre *f* ▷ *vi* se bagarrer
brazen ['breɪzn] *adj* impudent(e), effronté(e)
▷ *vt*: **to ~ it out** payer d'effronterie, crâner
brazier ['breɪzɪər] *n* brasero *m*
Brazil [brə'zɪl] *n* Brésil *m*
Brazilian [brə'zɪljən] *adj* brésilien(ne) ▷ *n*
Brésilien(ne)
breach [briːtʃ] *vt* ouvrir une brèche dans ▷ *n*
(*gap*) brèche *f*; (*estrangement*) brouille *f*;
(*breaking*): **~ of contract** rupture *f* de contrat;
~ of the peace attentat *m* à l'ordre public;
~ of trust abus *m* de confiance
bread [brɛd] *n* pain *m*; (*inf: money*) fric *m*;
~ and butter *n* tartines (beurrées); (*fig*)
subsistance *f*; **to earn one's daily ~** gagner
son pain; **to know which side one's ~ is
buttered (on)** savoir où est son avantage or
intérêt
breadbin ['brɛdbɪn] *n* (*Brit*) boîte *f* or huche *f* à
pain
breadbox ['brɛdbɔks] *n* (*US*) boîte *f* or huche *f*
à pain
breadcrumbs ['brɛdkrʌmz] *npl* miettes *fpl* de
pain; (*Culin*) chapelure *f*, panure *f*
breadline ['brɛdlaɪn] *n*: **to be on the ~** être
sans le sou or dans l'indigence
breadth [brɛtθ] *n* largeur *f*
breadwinner ['brɛdwɪnər] *n* soutien *m* de
famille
break [breɪk] (*pt* broke, *pp* broken) [brəuk,
'brəukən] *vt* casser, briser; (*promise*) rompre;
(*law*) violer ▷ *vi* se casser, se briser; (*weather*)
tourner; (*storm*) éclater; (*day*) se lever ▷ *n*
(*gap*) brèche *f*; (*fracture*) cassure *f*; (*rest*)
interruption *f*, arrêt *m*; (: *short*) pause *f*; (: *at
school*) récréation *f*; (*chance*) chance *f*, occasion
f favorable; **to ~ one's leg** *etc* se casser la
jambe *etc*; **to ~ a record** battre un record; **to ~
the news to sb** annoncer la nouvelle à qn; **to
~ with sb** rompre avec qn; **to ~ even** *vi*
rentrer dans ses frais; **to ~ free** or **loose** *vi* se
dégager, s'échapper; **to take a ~** (*few minutes*)
faire une pause, s'arrêter cinq minutes;
(*holiday*) prendre un peu de repos; **without a
~** sans interruption, sans arrêt; **break down**
vt (*door etc*) enfoncer; (*resistance*) venir à bout
de; (*figures, data*) décomposer, analyser ▷ *vi*
s'effondrer; (*Med*) faire une dépression
(nerveuse); (*Aut*) tomber en panne; **my car
has broken down** ma voiture est en panne;
break in *vt* (*horse etc*) dresser ▷ *vi* (*burglar*)
entrer par effraction; (*interrupt*) interrompre;
break into *vt fus* (*house*) s'introduire or
pénétrer par effraction dans; **break off** *vi*

(speaker) s'interrompre; (branch) se rompre
▷ vt (talks, engagement) rompre; **break open** vt
(door etc) forcer, fracturer; **break out** vi
éclater, se déclarer; (prisoner) s'évader; **to ~
out in spots** se couvrir de boutons; **break
through** vi: **the sun broke through** le soleil
a fait son apparition ▷ vt fus (defences, barrier)
franchir; (crowd) se frayer un passage à
travers; **break up** vi (partnership) cesser,
prendre fin; (marriage) se briser; (crowd,
meeting) se séparer; (ship) se disloquer; (Scol:
pupils) être en vacances; (line) couper; **the
line's** or **you're ~ing up** ça coupe ▷ vt
fracasser, casser; (fight etc) interrompre, faire
cesser; (marriage) désunir

breakage ['breɪkɪdʒ] n casse f; **to pay for ~s**
payer la casse

breakdown ['breɪkdaʊn] n (Aut) panne f; (in
communications, marriage) rupture f; (Med: also:
nervous ~) dépression (nerveuse); (of figures)
ventilation f, répartition f

breakdown truck, (US) **breakdown van** n
dépanneuse f

breaker ['breɪkəʳ] n brisant m

breakfast ['brɛkfəst] n petit déjeuner m;
what time is ~? le petit déjeuner est à quelle
heure?

break-in ['breɪkɪn] n cambriolage m

breaking and entering n (Law) effraction f

breakthrough ['breɪkθruː] n percée f

breakwater ['breɪkwɔːtəʳ] n brise-lames m
inv, digue f

breast [brɛst] n (of woman) sein m; (chest)
poitrine f; (of chicken, turkey) blanc m

breast-feed ['brɛstfiːd] vt, vi (irreg like: **feed**)
allaiter

breast-stroke ['brɛststrəʊk] n brasse f

breath [brɛθ] n haleine f, souffle m; **to go out
for a ~ of air** sortir prendre l'air; **to take a
deep ~** respirer à fond; **out of ~** à bout de
souffle, essoufflé(e)

Breathalyser® ['brɛθəlaɪzəʳ] (Brit) n
alcootest m

breathe [briːð] vt, vi respirer; **I won't ~ a
word about it** je n'en soufflerai pas mot, je
n'en dirai rien à personne; **breathe in** vi
inspirer ▷ vt aspirer; **breathe out** vt, vi
expirer

breather ['briːðəʳ] n moment m de repos or de
répit

breathing ['briːðɪŋ] n respiration f

breathless ['brɛθlɪs] adj essoufflé(e),
haletant(e), oppressé(e); **~ with excitement**
le souffle coupé par l'émotion

breathtaking ['brɛθteɪkɪŋ] adj stupéfiant(e),
à vous couper le souffle

breath test n alcootest m

bred [brɛd] pt, pp of **breed**

breed [briːd] (pt, pp **bred**) [brɛd] vt élever,
faire l'élevage de; (fig: hate, suspicion)
engendrer ▷ vi se reproduire ▷ n race f,
variété f

breeding ['briːdɪŋ] n reproduction f;
élevage m; (upbringing) éducation f

breeze [briːz] n brise f

breezy ['briːzɪ] adj (day, weather)
venteux(-euse); (manner) désinvolte; (person)
jovial(e)

brevity ['brɛvɪtɪ] n brièveté f

brew [bruː] vt (tea) faire infuser; (beer)
brasser; (plot) tramer, préparer ▷ vi (tea)
infuser; (beer) fermenter; (fig) se préparer,
couver

brewery ['bruːərɪ] n brasserie f (fabrique)

bribe [braɪb] n pot-de-vin m ▷ vt acheter;
soudoyer; **to ~ sb to do sth** soudoyer qn pour
qu'il fasse qch

bribery ['braɪbərɪ] n corruption f

bric-a-brac ['brɪkəbræk] n bric-à-brac m

brick [brɪk] n brique f

bricklayer ['brɪkleɪəʳ] n maçon m

bridal ['braɪdl] adj nuptial(e); **~ party** noce f

bride [braɪd] n mariée f, épouse f

bridegroom ['braɪdgruːm] n marié m,
époux m

bridesmaid ['braɪdzmeɪd] n demoiselle f
d'honneur

bridge [brɪdʒ] n pont m; (Naut) passerelle f (de
commandement); (of nose) arête f; (Cards,
Dentistry) bridge m ▷ vt (river) construire un
pont sur; (gap) combler

bridle ['braɪdl] n bride f ▷ vt refréner, mettre
la bride à; (horse) brider

bridle path n piste or allée cavalière

brief [briːf] adj bref/brève ▷ n (Law) dossier m,
cause f; (gen) tâche f ▷ vt mettre au courant;
(Mil) donner des instructions à; **briefs** npl
slip m; **in ~ ...** (en) bref ...

briefcase ['briːfkeɪs] n serviette f;
porte-documents m inv

briefing ['briːfɪŋ] n instructions fpl; (Press)
briefing m

briefly ['briːflɪ] adv brièvement; (visit) en
coup de vent; **to glimpse ~** entrevoir

brigadier [brɪgə'dɪəʳ] n brigadier général

bright [braɪt] adj brillant(e); (room, weather)
clair(e); (person: clever) intelligent(e), doué(e);
(: cheerful) gai(e); (idea) génial(e); (colour) vif/
vive; **to look on the ~ side** regarder le bon
côté des choses

brighten ['braɪtn] (also: **~ up**) vt (room)
éclaircir; égayer ▷ vi s'éclaircir; (person)
retrouver un peu de sa gaieté

brilliance ['brɪljəns] n éclat m; (fig: of person)
brio m

brilliant ['brɪljənt] adj brillant(e); (light,
sunshine) éclatant(e); (inf: great) super

brim [brɪm] n bord m

brine [braɪn] n eau salée; (Culin) saumure f

bring (pt, pp **brought**) [brɪŋ, brɔːt] vt (thing)
apporter; (person) amener; **to ~ sth to an end**
mettre fin à qch; **I can't ~ myself to fire
him** je ne peux me résoudre à le mettre à la
porte; **bring about** vt provoquer, entraîner;

bring back vt rapporter; (*person*) ramener; **bring down** vt (*lower*) abaisser; (*shoot down*) abattre; (*government*) faire s'effondrer; **bring forward** vt avancer; (*Book-keeping*) reporter; **bring in** vt (*person*) faire entrer; (*object*) rentrer; (Pol: *legislation*) introduire; (Law: *verdict*) rendre; (*produce: income*) rapporter; **bring off** vt (*task, plan*) réussir, mener à bien; (*deal*) mener à bien; **bring on** vt (*illness, attack*) provoquer; (*player, substitute*) amener; **bring out** vt sortir; (*meaning*) faire ressortir, mettre en relief; (*new product, book*) sortir; **bring round, bring to** vt (*unconscious person*) ranimer; **bring up** vt élever; (*carry up*) monter; (*question*) soulever; (*food: vomit*) vomir, rendre

brink [brɪŋk] n bord m; **on the ~ of doing** sur le point de faire, à deux doigts de faire; **she was on the ~ of tears** elle était au bord des larmes

brisk [brɪsk] adj vif/vive; (*abrupt*) brusque; (*trade etc*) actif(-ive); **to go for a ~ walk** se promener d'un bon pas; **business is ~** les affaires marchent (bien)

bristle ['brɪsl] n poil m ▷ vi se hérisser; **bristling with** hérissé(e) de

Brit [brɪt] n abbr (inf: = British person) Britannique m/f

Britain ['brɪtən] n (also: **Great ~**) la Grande-Bretagne; **in ~** en Grande-Bretagne

British ['brɪtɪʃ] adj britannique ▷ npl: **the ~** les Britanniques mpl

British Isles npl: **the ~** les îles fpl Britanniques

British Rail n compagnie ferroviaire britannique, ≈ SNCF

Briton ['brɪtən] n Britannique m/f

Brittany ['brɪtənɪ] n Bretagne f

brittle ['brɪtl] adj cassant(e), fragile

broach [brəʊtʃ] vt (*subject*) aborder

B road n (Brit) ≈ route départementale

broad [brɔːd] adj large; (*distinction*) général(e); (*accent*) prononcé(e) ▷ n (US inf) nana f; **~ hint** allusion transparente; **in ~ daylight** en plein jour; **the ~ outlines** les grandes lignes

broadband ['brɔːdbænd] n transmission f à haut débit

broad bean n fève f

broadcast ['brɔːdkɑːst] (pt, pp **broadcast**) n émission f ▷ vt (*Radio*) radiodiffuser; (TV) téléviser ▷ vi émettre

broaden ['brɔːdn] vt élargir; **to ~ one's mind** élargir ses horizons ▷ vi s'élargir

broadly ['brɔːdlɪ] adv en gros, généralement

broad-minded ['brɔːd'maɪndɪd] adj large d'esprit

broccoli ['brɔkəlɪ] n brocoli m

brochure ['brəʊʃjʊər] n prospectus m, dépliant m

broil [brɔɪl] (US) vt rôtir

broke [brəʊk] pt of **break** ▷ adj (inf) fauché(e); **to go ~** (*business*) faire faillite

broken ['brəʊkn] pp of **break** ▷ adj (*stick, leg etc*) cassé(e); (*machine: also: ~ down*) fichu(e); (*promise, vow*) rompu(e); **a ~ marriage** un couple dissocié; **a ~ home** un foyer désuni; **in ~ French/English** dans un français/anglais approximatif or hésitant

broken-hearted ['brəʊkn'hɑːtɪd] adj (ayant) le cœur brisé

broker ['brəʊkər] n courtier m

brolly ['brɔlɪ] n (Brit inf) pépin m, parapluie m

bronchitis [brɔŋ'kaɪtɪs] n bronchite f

bronze [brɔnz] n bronze m

brooch [brəʊtʃ] n broche f

brood [bruːd] n couvée f ▷ vi (*hen, storm*) couver; (*person*) méditer (sombrement), ruminer

broom [brum] n balai m; (Bot) genêt m

broomstick ['brumstɪk] n manche m à balai

Bros. abbr (Comm: = brothers) Frères

broth [brɔθ] n bouillon m de viande et de légumes

brothel ['brɔθl] n maison close, bordel m

brother ['brʌðər] n frère m

brother-in-law ['brʌðərɪn'lɔː] n beau-frère m

brought [brɔːt] pt, pp of **bring**

brow [brau] n front m; (*rare: gen: eyebrow*) sourcil m; (*of hill*) sommet m

brown [braun] adj brun(e), marron inv; (*hair*) châtain inv; (*tanned*) bronzé(e); (*rice, bread, flour*) complet(-ète) ▷ n (*colour*) brun m, marron m ▷ vt brunir; (Culin) faire dorer, faire roussir; **to go ~** (*person*) bronzer; (*leaves*) jaunir

brown bread n pain m bis

Brownie ['braunɪ] n jeannette f éclaireuse (cadette)

brown paper n papier m d'emballage, papier kraft

brown rice n riz m complet

brown sugar n cassonade f

browse [brauz] vi (*in shop*) regarder (*sans acheter*); (*among books*) bouquiner, feuilleter les livres; (*animal*) paître; **to ~ through a book** feuilleter un livre

browser [brauzər] n (Comput) navigateur m

bruise [bruːz] n bleu m, ecchymose f, contusion f ▷ vt contusionner, meurtrir ▷ vi (*fruit*) se taler, se meurtrir; **to ~ one's arm** se faire un bleu au bras

brunette [bruː'nɛt] n (femme) brune

brunt [brʌnt] n: **the ~ of** (*attack, criticism etc*) le plus gros de

brush [brʌʃ] n brosse f; (*for painting*) pinceau m; (*for shaving*) blaireau m; (*quarrel*) accrochage m, prise f de bec ▷ vt brosser; (*also: ~ past, ~ against*) effleurer, frôler; **to have a ~ with sb** s'accrocher avec qn; **to have a ~ with the police** avoir maille à partir avec la police; **brush aside** vt écarter, balayer; **brush up** vt (*knowledge*) rafraîchir, réviser

brushwood ['brʌʃwud] n broussailles fpl, taillis m

Brussels ['brʌslz] n Bruxelles

Brussels sprout n chou m de Bruxelles

brutal ['bru:tl] adj brutal(e)

brute [bru:t] n brute f ▷ adj: **by ~ force** par la force

B.Sc. n abbr = **Bachelor of Science**

BSE n abbr (= bovine spongiform encephalopathy) ESB f, BSE f

bubble ['bʌbl] n bulle f ▷ vi bouillonner, faire des bulles; (sparkle, fig) pétiller

bubble bath n bain moussant

bubble gum n chewing-gum m

bubblejet printer ['bʌbldʒet-] n imprimante f à bulle d'encre

buck [bʌk] n mâle m (d'un lapin, lièvre, daim etc); (US inf) dollar m ▷ vi ruer, lancer une ruade; **to pass the ~ (to sb)** se décharger de la responsabilité (sur qn); **buck up** vi (cheer up) reprendre du poil de la bête, se remonter ▷ vt: **to ~ one's ideas up** se reprendre

bucket ['bʌkɪt] n seau m ▷ vi (Brit inf): **the rain is ~ing (down)** il pleut à verse

Buckingham Palace ['bʌkɪŋhəm-] n le palais de Buckingham; voir article

> ● **BUCKINGHAM PALACE**
> ●
> ● Buckingham Palace est la résidence officielle
> ● londonienne du souverain britannique
> ● depuis 1762. Construit en 1703, il fut à
> ● l'origine le palais du duc de Buckingham.
> ● Il a été partiellement reconstruit au
> ● début du XXe siècle.

buckle ['bʌkl] n boucle f ▷ vt (belt etc) boucler, attacher ▷ vi (warp) tordre, gauchir; (: wheel) se voiler; **buckle down** vi s'y mettre

bud [bʌd] n bourgeon m; (of flower) bouton m ▷ vi bourgeonner; (flower) éclore

Buddhism ['budɪzəm] n bouddhisme m

Buddhist ['budɪst] adj bouddhiste ▷ n Bouddhiste m/f

budding ['bʌdɪŋ] adj (flower) en bouton; (poet etc) en herbe; (passion etc) naissant(e)

buddy ['bʌdɪ] n (US) copain m

budge [bʌdʒ] vt faire bouger ▷ vi bouger

budgerigar ['bʌdʒərɪga:ʳ] n perruche f

budget ['bʌdʒɪt] n budget m ▷ vi: **to ~ for sth** inscrire qch au budget; **I'm on a tight ~** je dois faire attention à mon budget

budgie ['bʌdʒɪ] n = **budgerigar**

buff [bʌf] adj (couleur f) chamois m ▷ n (inf: enthusiast) mordu(e)

buffalo (pl buffalo or buffaloes) ['bʌfələu] n (Brit) buffle m; (US) bison m

buffer ['bʌfəʳ] n tampon m; (Comput) mémoire f tampon ▷ vti (Comput) mettre en mémoire tampon

buffering ['bʌfərɪŋ] n (Comput) mise f en mémoire tampon

buffet n ['bufei] (food Brit: bar) buffet m ▷ vt ['bʌfit] gifler, frapper; secouer, ébranler

buffet car n (Brit Rail) voiture-bar f

bug [bʌg] n (bedbug etc) punaise f; (esp US: any insect) insecte m, bestiole f; (fig: germ) virus m, microbe m; (spy device) dispositif m d'écoute (électronique), micro clandestin; (Comput: of program) erreur f; (: of equipment) défaut m ▷ vt (room) poser des micros dans; (inf: annoy) embêter; **I've got the travel ~** (fig) j'ai le virus du voyage

buggy ['bʌgɪ] n poussette f

bugle ['bju:gl] n clairon m

build [bɪld] n (of person) carrure f, charpente f ▷ vt (pt, pp **built**) construire, bâtir; **build on** vt fus (fig) tirer parti de, partir de; **build up** vt accumuler, amasser; (business) développer; (reputation) bâtir

builder ['bɪldəʳ] n entrepreneur m

building ['bɪldɪŋ] n (trade) construction f; (structure) bâtiment m, construction; (: residential, offices) immeuble m

building site n chantier m (de construction)

building society n (Brit) société f de crédit immobilier; voir article

> ● **BUILDING SOCIETY**
> ●
> ● Une building society est une mutuelle dont
> ● les épargnants et emprunteurs sont les
> ● propriétaires. Ces mutuelles offrent deux
> ● services principaux: on peut y avoir un
> ● compte d'épargne duquel on peut retirer
> ● son argent sur demande ou moyennant
> ● un court préavis et on peut également y
> ● faire des emprunts à long terme, par
> ● exemple pour acheter une maison. Les
> ● building societies ont eu jusqu'en 1985 le
> ● quasi-monopole des comptes d'épargne
> ● et des prêts immobiliers, mais les
> ● banques ont maintenant une part
> ● importante de ce marché.

built [bɪlt] pt, pp of **build**

built-in ['bɪlt'ɪn] adj (cupboard) encastré(e); (device) incorporé(e); intégré(e)

built-up ['bɪlt'ʌp] adj: **~ area** agglomération (urbaine); zone urbanisée

bulb [bʌlb] n (Bot) bulbe m, oignon m; (Elec) ampoule f

Bulgaria [bʌl'geərɪə] n Bulgarie f

Bulgarian [bʌl'geərɪən] adj bulgare ▷ n Bulgare m/f; (Ling) bulgare m

bulge [bʌldʒ] n renflement m, gonflement m; (in birth rate, sales) brusque augmentation f ▷ vi faire saillie; présenter un renflement; (pocket, file): **to be bulging with** être plein(e) à craquer de

bulimia [bə'lɪmɪə] n boulimie f

bulimic [bju:'lɪmɪk] adj, n boulimique m/f

bulk [bʌlk] n masse f, volume m; **in ~** (Comm) en gros, en vrac; **the ~ of** la plus grande or grosse partie de

bulky ['bʌlkɪ] adj volumineux(-euse), encombrant(e)

bull [bul] n taureau m; (male elephant, whale) mâle m; (Stock Exchange) haussier m; (Rel) bulle f

bulldog ['buldɒg] n bouledogue m

bulldozer ['buldəuzə'] n bulldozer m

bullet ['bulɪt] n balle f (de fusil etc)

bulletin ['bulɪtɪn] n bulletin m, communiqué m; (also: **news ~**) (bulletin d')informations fpl

bulletin board n (Comput) messagerie f (électronique)

bulletproof ['bulɪtpruːf] adj à l'épreuve des balles; **~ vest** gilet m pare-balles

bullfight ['bulfaɪt] n corrida f, course f de taureaux

bullfighter ['bulfaɪtə'] n torero m

bullfighting ['bulfaɪtɪŋ] n tauromachie f

bullion ['buljən] n or m or argent m en lingots

bullock ['bulək] n bœuf m

bullring ['bulrɪŋ] n arène f

bull's-eye ['bulzaɪ] n centre m (de la cible)

bully ['bulɪ] n brute f, tyran m ▷ vt tyranniser, rudoyer; (frighten) intimider

bum [bʌm] n (inf: Brit: backside) derrière m; (: esp US: tramp) vagabond(e), traîne-savates m/f inv; (: idler) glandeur m; **bum around** vi (inf) vagabonder

bumblebee ['bʌmblbiː] n bourdon m

bump [bʌmp] n (blow) coup m, choc m; (jolt) cahot m; (on road etc, on head) bosse f ▷ vt heurter, cogner; (car) emboutir; **bump along** vi avancer en cahotant; **bump into** vt fus rentrer dans, tamponner; (inf: meet) tomber sur

bumper ['bʌmpə'] n pare-chocs m inv ▷ adj: **~ crop/harvest** récolte/moisson exceptionnelle

bumper cars npl (US) autos tamponneuses

bumpy ['bʌmpɪ] adj (road) cahoteux(-euse); **it was a ~ flight/ride** on a été secoués dans l'avion/la voiture

bun [bʌn] n (cake) petit gâteau; (bread) petit pain au lait; (of hair) chignon m

bunch [bʌntʃ] n (of flowers) bouquet m; (of keys) trousseau m; (of bananas) régime m; (of people) groupe m; **bunches** npl (in hair) couettes fpl; **~ of grapes** grappe f de raisin

bundle ['bʌndl] n paquet m ▷ vt (also: **~ up**) faire un paquet de; (put): **to ~ sth/sb into** fourrer or enfourner qch/qn dans; **bundle off** vt (person) faire sortir (en toute hâte); expédier; **bundle out** vt éjecter, sortir (sans ménagements)

bungalow ['bʌŋgələu] n bungalow m

bungee jumping ['bʌndʒiː'dʒʌmpɪŋ] n saut m à l'élastique

bungle ['bʌŋgl] vt bâcler, gâcher

bunion ['bʌnjən] n oignon m (au pied)

bunk [bʌŋk] n couchette f; (Brit inf): **to do a ~** mettre les bouts or les voiles; **bunk off** vi (Brit inf: Scol) sécher (les cours); **I'll ~ off at 3 o'clock this afternoon** je vais mettre les bouts or les voiles à 3 heures cet après-midi

bunk beds npl lits superposés

bunker ['bʌŋkə'] n (coal store) soute f à charbon; (Mil, Golf) bunker m

bunny ['bʌnɪ] n (also: **~ rabbit**) lapin m

bunting ['bʌntɪŋ] n pavoisement m, drapeaux mpl

buoy [bɔɪ] n bouée f; **buoy up** vt faire flotter; (fig) soutenir, épauler

buoyant ['bɔɪənt] adj (ship) flottable; (carefree) gai(e), plein(e) d'entrain; (Comm: market, economy) actif(-ive); (: prices, currency) soutenu(e)

burden ['bəːdn] n fardeau m, charge f ▷ vt charger; (oppress) accabler, surcharger; **to be a ~ to sb** être un fardeau pour qn

bureau (pl **bureaux**) ['bjuərəu, -z] n (Brit: writing desk) bureau m, secrétaire m; (US: chest of drawers) commode f; (office) bureau, office m

bureaucracy [bjuə'rɔkrəsɪ] n bureaucratie f

bureaucrat ['bjuərəkræt] n bureaucrate m/f, rond-de-cuir m

bureau de change [-də'ʃɑ̃ʒ] (pl **bureaux de change**) n bureau m de change

bureaux ['bjuərəuz] npl of **bureau**

burger ['bəːgə'] n hamburger m

burglar ['bəːglə'] n cambrioleur m

burglar alarm n sonnerie f d'alarme

burglary ['bəːglərɪ] n cambriolage m

Burgundy ['bəːgəndɪ] n Bourgogne f

burial ['berɪəl] n enterrement m

burly ['bəːlɪ] adj de forte carrure, costaud(e)

Burma ['bəːmə] n Birmanie f; see also **Myanmar**

burn [bəːn] vt, vi (pt, pp **burned** or **burnt**) [bəːnt] brûler ▷ n brûlure f; **the cigarette ~t a hole in her dress** la cigarette a fait un trou dans sa robe; **I've ~t myself!** je me suis brûlé(e)!; **burn down** vt incendier, détruire par le feu; **burn out** vt (writer etc): **to ~ o.s. out** s'user (à force de travailler)

burner ['bəːnə'] n brûleur m

burning ['bəːnɪŋ] adj (building, forest) en flammes; (issue, question) brûlant(e); (ambition) dévorant(e)

Burns' Night [bəːnz-] n fête écossaise à la mémoire du poète Robert Burns; voir article

● **BURNS' NIGHT**
●
● Burns' Night est une fête qui a lieu le 25
● janvier, à la mémoire du poète écossais
● Robert Burns (1759-1796), à l'occasion de
● laquelle les Écossais partout dans le
● monde organisent un souper, en général
● arrosé de whisky. Le plat principal est
● toujours le haggis, servi avec de la purée
● de pommes de terre et de la purée de

rutabagas. On apporte le haggis au son
des cornemuses et au cours du repas on
lit des poèmes de Burns et on chante ses
chansons.

burnt [bəːnt] *pt, pp of* **burn**

burp [bəːp] (*inf*) *n* rot m ▷ *vi* roter

burrow ['bʌrəu] *n* terrier m ▷ *vt* creuser ▷ *vi*
(*rabbit*) creuser un terrier; (*rummage*) fouiller

bursary ['bəːsərɪ] *n* (*Brit*) bourse f (d'études)

burst [bəːst] (*pt, pp* **burst**) *vt* faire éclater;
(*river: banks etc*) rompre ▷ *vi* éclater; (*tyre*)
crever ▷ *n* explosion f; (*also: ~ pipe*) fuite f
(*due à une rupture*); **a ~ of enthusiasm/energy**
un accès d'enthousiasme/d'énergie; **~ of
laughter** éclat m de rire; **a ~ of applause** une
salve d'applaudissements; **a ~ of gunfire** une
rafale de tir; **a ~ of speed** une pointe de
vitesse; **~ blood vessel** rupture f de vaisseau
sanguin; **the river has ~ its banks** le cours
d'eau est sorti de son lit; **to ~ into flames**
s'enflammer soudainement; **to ~ out
laughing** éclater de rire; **to ~ into tears**
fondre en larmes; **to ~ open** *vi* s'ouvrir
violemment *or* soudainement; **to be ~ing
with** (*container*) être plein(e) (à craquer) de,
regorger de; (*fig*) être débordant(e) de; **burst
into** *vt fus* (*room etc*) faire irruption dans;
burst out of *vt fus* sortir précipitamment de

bury ['bɛrɪ] *vt* enterrer; **to ~ one's face in
one's hands** se couvrir le visage de ses
mains; **to ~ one's head in the sand** (*fig*)
pratiquer la politique de l'autruche; **to ~ the
hatchet** (*fig*) enterrer la hache de guerre

bus (*pl* **buses**) [bʌs, 'bʌsɪz] *n* (auto)bus m

bus conductor *n* receveur(-euse) m/f de bus

bush [buʃ] *n* buisson m; (*scrub land*) brousse f;
to beat about the ~ tourner autour du pot

bushy ['buʃɪ] *adj* broussailleux(-euse),
touffu(e)

busily ['bɪzɪlɪ] *adv*: **to be ~ doing sth**
s'affairer à faire qch

business ['bɪznɪs] *n* (*matter, firm*) affaire f;
(*trading*) affaires fpl; (*job, duty*) travail m; **to be
away on ~** être en voyage d'affaires; **I'm here on ~** je suis là pour affaires; **he's in
the insurance ~** il est dans les assurances;
to do ~ with sb traiter avec qn; **it's none of
my ~** cela ne me regarde pas, ce ne sont pas
mes affaires; **he means ~** il ne plaisante pas,
il est sérieux

business class *n* (*on plane*) classe f affaires

businesslike ['bɪznɪslaɪk] *adj* sérieux(-euse),
efficace

businessman ['bɪznɪsmən] (*irreg*) *n*
homme m d'affaires

business trip *n* voyage m d'affaires

businesswoman ['bɪznɪswumən] (*irreg*) *n*
femme f d'affaires

busker ['bʌskəʳ] *n* (*Brit*) artiste ambulant(e)

bus pass *n* carte f de bus

bus shelter *n* abribus m

bus station *n* gare routière

bus stop *n* arrêt m d'autobus

bust [bʌst] *n* buste m; (*measurement*) tour m de
poitrine ▷ *adj* (*inf: broken*) fichu(e), fini(e) ▷ *vt*
(*inf: Police: arrest*) pincer; **to go ~** faire faillite

bustle ['bʌsl] *n* remue-ménage m,
affairement m ▷ *vi* s'affairer, se démener

bustling ['bʌslɪŋ] *adj* (*person*) affairé(e); (*town*)
très animé(e)

busy ['bɪzɪ] *adj* occupé(e); (*shop, street*) très
fréquenté(e); (*US: telephone, line*) occupé ▷ *vt*:
to ~ o.s. s'occuper; **he's a ~ man** (*normally*)
c'est un homme très pris; (*temporarily*) il est
très pris

busybody ['bɪzɪbɔdɪ] *n* mouche f du coche,
âme f charitable

busy signal *n* (US) tonalité f occupé *inv*

KEYWORD

but [bʌt] *conj* mais; **I'd love to come, but I'm
busy** j'aimerais venir mais je suis occupé;
he's not English but French il n'est pas
anglais mais français; **but that's far too
expensive!** mais c'est bien trop cher!
▷ *prep* (*apart from, except*) sauf, excepté;
nothing but rien d'autre que; **we've had
nothing but trouble** nous n'avons eu que
des ennuis; **no-one but him** can do it lui
seul peut le faire; **who but a lunatic would
do such a thing?** qui sinon un fou ferait une
chose pareille?; **but for you/your help** sans
toi/ton aide; **anything but that** tout sauf *or*
excepté ça, tout mais pas ça; **the last but
one** (*Brit*) l'avant-dernier(-ère)
▷ *adv* (*just, only*) ne ... que; **she's but a child**
elle n'est qu'une enfant; **had I but known** si
seulement j'avais su; **I can but try** je peux
toujours essayer; **all but finished**
pratiquement terminé; **anything but
finished** tout sauf fini, très loin d'être fini

butcher ['butʃəʳ] *n* boucher m ▷ *vt* massacrer;
(*cattle etc for meat*) tuer

butcher's ['butʃəz], **butcher's shop** *n*
boucherie f

butler ['bʌtləʳ] *n* maître m d'hôtel

butt [bʌt] *n* (*cask*) gros tonneau; (*thick end*)
(gros) bout; (*of gun*) crosse f; (*of cigarette*)
mégot m; (*Brit fig: target*) cible f ▷ *vt* donner
un coup de tête à; **butt in** *vi* (*interrupt*)
interrompre

butter ['bʌtəʳ] *n* beurre m ▷ *vt* beurrer

buttercup ['bʌtəkʌp] *n* bouton m d'or

butterfly ['bʌtəflaɪ] *n* papillon m; (*Swimming:
also: ~ stroke*) brasse f papillon

buttocks ['bʌtəks] *npl* fesses fpl

button ['bʌtn] *n* bouton m; (US: *badge*) pin m
▷ *vt* (*also: ~ up*) boutonner ▷ *vi* se boutonner

buttress ['bʌtrɪs] *n* contrefort m

buy [baɪ] (*pt, pp* **bought**) [bɔːt] *vt* acheter;
(*Comm: company*) (r)acheter ▷ *n* achat m; **that**

was a good/bad ~ c'était un bon/mauvais achat; **to ~ sb sth/sth from sb** acheter qch à qn; **to ~ sb a drink** offrir un verre *or* à boire à qn; **can I ~ you a drink?** je vous offre un verre?; **where can I ~ some postcards?** où est-ce que je peux acheter des cartes postales?; **buy back** *vt* racheter; **buy in** *vt* (Brit: *goods*) acheter, faire venir; **buy into** *vt fus* (Brit Comm) acheter des actions de; **buy off** *vt* (*bribe*) acheter; **buy out** *vt* (*partner*) désintéresser; (*business*) racheter; **buy up** *vt* acheter en bloc, rafler

buyer ['baɪəᵊ] *n* acheteur(-euse) *m/f*; **~'s market** marché *m* favorable aux acheteurs

buzz [bʌz] *n* bourdonnement *m*; (*inf: phone call*): **to give sb a ~** passer un coup de fil à qn ▷ *vi* bourdonner ▷ *vt* (*call on intercom*) appeler; (*with buzzer*) sonner; (Aviat: *plane, building*) raser; **my head is ~ing** j'ai la tête qui bourdonne; **buzz off** *vi* (*inf*) s'en aller, ficher le camp

buzzer ['bʌzəᵊ] *n* timbre *m* électrique

buzz word *n* (*inf*) mot *m* à la mode *or* dans le vent

 KEYWORD

by [baɪ] *prep* **1** (*referring to cause, agent*) par, de; **killed by lightning** tué par la foudre; **surrounded by a fence** entouré d'une barrière; **a painting by Picasso** un tableau de Picasso

2 (*referring to method, manner, means*): **by bus/car** en autobus/voiture; **by train** par le *or* en train; **to pay by cheque** payer par chèque; **by moonlight/candlelight** à la lueur de la lune/d'une bougie; **by saving hard, he ...** à force d'économiser, il ...

3 (*via, through*) par; **we came by Dover** nous sommes venus par Douvres

4 (*close to, past*) à côté de; **the house by the school** la maison à côté de l'école; **a holiday by the sea** des vacances au bord de la mer; **she sat by his bed** elle était assise à son chevet; **she went by me** elle est passée à côté de moi; **I go by the post office every day** je passe devant la poste tous les jours

5 (*with time: not later than*) avant; (*: during*): **by daylight** à la lumière du jour; **by night** la nuit, de nuit; **by 4 o'clock** avant 4 heures; **by this time tomorrow** d'ici demain à la même heure; **by the time I got here it was too late** lorsque je suis arrivé il était déjà trop tard

6 (*amount*) à; **by the kilo/metre** au kilo/au mètre; **paid by the hour** payé à l'heure; **to increase** *etc* **by the hour** augmenter *etc* d'heure en heure

7 (Math: *measure*): **to divide/multiply by 3** diviser/multiplier par 3; **a room 3 metres by 4** une pièce de 3 mètres sur 4; **it's broader by a metre** c'est plus large d'un mètre; **the**

bullet missed him by inches la balle est passée à quelques centimètres de lui; **one by one** un à un; **little by little** petit à petit, peu à peu

8 (*according to*) d'après, selon; **it's 3 o'clock by my watch** il est 3 heures à ma montre; **it's all right by me** je n'ai rien contre

9: **(all) by oneself** *etc* tout(e) seul(e) ▷ *adv* **1** *see* **go**; **pass** *etc* **2**: **by and by** un peu plus tard, bientôt; **by and large** dans l'ensemble

bye ['baɪ], **bye-bye** ['baɪ'baɪ] *excl* au revoir!, salut!

bye-law ['baɪlɔ:] *n* = **by-law**

by-election ['baɪɪlɛkʃən] *n* (Brit) élection (législative) partielle

bygone ['baɪgɔn] *adj* passé(e) ▷ *n*: **let ~s be ~s** passons l'éponge, oublions le passé

by-law ['baɪlɔ:] *n* arrêté municipal

bypass ['baɪpɑ:s] *n* rocade *f*; (Med) pontage *m* ▷ *vt* éviter

by-product ['baɪprɔdʌkt] *n* sous-produit *m*, dérivé *m*; (*fig*) conséquence *f* secondaire, retombée *f*

bystander ['baɪstændəᵊ] *n* spectateur(-trice), badaud(e)

byte [baɪt] *n* (Comput) octet *m*

byword ['baɪwə:d] *n*: **to be a ~ for** être synonyme de (*fig*)

C¹, c¹ [siː] n (letter) C, c m; (Scol: mark) C; (Mus): **C do** m; **C for Charlie** C comme Célestin

C² abbr (= Celsius, centigrade) C

c² abbr (= century) s.; (= circa) v.; (US etc) = **cent(s)**

CA n abbr = **Central America**; (Brit) = **chartered accountant** ▷ abbr (US) = **California**

cab [kæb] n taxi m; (of train, truck) cabine f; (horse-drawn) fiacre m

cabaret ['kæbəreɪ] n attractions fpl; (show) spectacle m de cabaret

cabbage ['kæbɪdʒ] n chou m

cabin ['kæbɪn] n (house) cabane f, hutte f; (on ship) cabine f; (on plane) compartiment m

cabin crew n (Aviat) équipage m

cabin cruiser n yacht m (à moteur)

cabinet ['kæbɪnɪt] n (Pol) cabinet m; (furniture) petit meuble à tiroirs et rayons; (also: **display ~**) vitrine f, petite armoire vitrée

cabinet minister n ministre m (membre du cabinet)

cable ['keɪbl] n câble m ▷ vt câbler, télégraphier

cable car n téléphérique m

cable television n télévision f par câble

cache [kæʃ] n cachette f; **a ~ of food** etc un dépôt secret de provisions etc, une cachette contenant des provisions etc

cackle ['kækl] vi caqueter

cactus (pl cacti) ['kæktəs, -taɪ] n cactus m

cadet [kə'dɛt] n (Mil) élève m officier; **police ~** élève agent de police

cadge [kædʒ] vt (inf) se faire donner; **to ~ a meal (off sb)** se faire inviter à manger (par qn)

Caesarean, (US) **Cesarean** [siːˈzɛərɪən] adj: **~ (section)** césarienne f

café ['kæfeɪ] n ≈ café(-restaurant) m (sans alcool)

cafeteria [kæfɪ'tɪərɪə] n cafétéria f

caffeine ['kæfiːn] n caféine f

cage [keɪdʒ] n cage f ▷ vt mettre en cage

cagey ['keɪdʒɪ] adj (inf) réticent(e), méfiant(e)

cagoule [kə'guːl] n K-way® m

Cairo ['kaɪərəʊ] n le Caire

cajole [kə'dʒəʊl] vt couvrir de flatteries or de gentillesses

cake [keɪk] n gâteau m; **~ of soap** savonnette f; **it's a piece of ~** (inf) c'est un jeu d'enfant; **he wants to have his ~ and eat it (too)** (fig) il veut tout avoir

caked [keɪkt] adj: **~ with** raidi(e) par, couvert(e) d'une croûte de

calcium ['kælsɪəm] n calcium m

calculate ['kælkjuleɪt] vt calculer; (estimate: chances, effect) évaluer; **calculate on** vt fus: **to ~ on sth/on doing sth** compter sur qch/ faire qch

calculation [kælkju'leɪʃən] n calcul m

calculator ['kælkjuleɪtər] n machine f à calculer, calculatrice f

calendar ['kæləndər] n calendrier m

calendar year n année civile

calf (pl calves) [kɑːf, kɑːvz] n (of cow) veau m; (of other animals) petit m; (also: **~-skin**) veau m, vachette f; (Anat) mollet m

calibre, (US) **caliber** ['kælɪbər] n calibre m

call [kɔːl] vt (gen, also Tel) appeler; (announce: flight) annoncer; (meeting) convoquer; (strike) lancer ▷ vi appeler; (visit: also: **~ in, ~ round**) passer ▷ n (shout) appel m, cri m; (summons: for flight etc, fig: lure) appel; (visit) visite f; (also: **telephone ~**) coup m de téléphone; communication f; **to be on ~** être de permanence; **to be ~ed** s'appeler; **she's ~ed Suzanne** elle s'appelle Suzanne; **who is ~ing?** (Tel) qui est à l'appareil?; **London ~ing** (Radio) ici Londres; **please give me a ~ at 7** appelez-moi à 7 heures; **to make a ~** téléphoner, passer un coup de fil; **can I make a ~ from here?** est-ce que je peux téléphoner d'ici?; **to pay a ~ on sb** rendre visite à qn, passer voir qn; **there's not much ~ for these items** ces articles ne sont pas très demandés; **call at** vt fus (ship) faire escale à; (train) s'arrêter à; **call back** vi (return) repasser; (Tel) rappeler ▷ vt (Tel) rappeler; **can you ~ back later?** pouvez-vous rappeler plus tard?; **call for** vt fus (demand) demander; (fetch) passer prendre; **call in** vt (doctor, expert, police) appeler, faire venir; **call off** vt annuler; **the strike was ~ed off** l'ordre de grève a été rapporté; **call on** vt fus (visit) rendre visite à, passer voir; (request): **to ~ on**

sb to do inviter qn à faire; **call out** vi pousser un cri or des cris ▷ vt (doctor, police, troops) appeler; **call up** vt (Mil) appeler, mobiliser; (Tel) appeler

call box ['kɔːlbɒks] n (Brit) cabine f téléphonique

call centre, (US) **call center** n centre m d'appels

caller ['kɔːlər] n (Tel) personne f qui appelle; (visitor) visiteur m; **hold the line, ~!** (Tel) ne quittez pas, Monsieur (or Madame)!

call girl n call-girl f

call-in ['kɔːlɪn] n (US Radio, TV) programme m à ligne ouverte

calling ['kɔːlɪŋ] n vocation f; (trade, occupation) état m

calling card n (US) carte f de visite

callous ['kæləs] adj dur(e), insensible

calm [kɑːm] adj calme ▷ n calme m ▷ vt calmer, apaiser; **calm down** vi se calmer, s'apaiser ▷ vt calmer, apaiser

calmly ['kɑːmlɪ] adv calmement, avec calme

Calor gas® ['kælər-] n (Brit) butane m, butagaz® m

calorie ['kælərɪ] n calorie f; **low ~ product** produit m pauvre en calories

calves [kɑːvz] npl of **calf**

camber ['kæmbər] n (of road) bombement m

Cambodia [kæm'bəudɪə] n Cambodge m

camcorder ['kæmkɔːdər] n caméscope m

came [keɪm] pt of **come**

camel ['kæməl] n chameau m

camera ['kæmərə] n appareil photo m; (Cine, TV) caméra f; **digital ~** appareil numérique; **in ~** à huis clos, en privé

cameraman ['kæmərəmæn] (irreg) n caméraman m

camera phone n téléphone m avec appareil photo

camouflage ['kæməflɑːʒ] n camouflage m ▷ vt camoufler

camp [kæmp] n camp m ▷ vi camper ▷ adj (man) efféminé(e)

campaign [kæm'peɪn] n (Mil, Pol) campagne f (also fig) faire campagne; **to ~ for/ against** militer pour/contre

campaigner [kæm'peɪnər] n: **~ for** partisan(e) de; **~ against** opposant(e) à

camp bed ['kæmp'bed] n (Brit) lit m de camp

camper ['kæmpər] n campeur(-euse); (vehicle) camping-car m

camping ['kæmpɪŋ] n camping m; **to go ~** faire du camping

camping gas® n butane m

campsite ['kæmpsaɪt] n (terrain m de) camping m

campus ['kæmpəs] n campus m

can¹ [kæn] n (of milk, oil, water) bidon m; (tin) boîte f (de conserve) ▷ vt mettre en conserve; **a ~ of beer** une canette de bière; **he had to carry the ~** (Brit inf) on lui a fait porter le chapeau; see also **keyword**

⭕ KEYWORD

can² [kæn] (negative **cannot** or **can't**, conditional and pt **could**) aux vb **1** (be able to) pouvoir; **you can do it if you try** vous pouvez le faire si vous essayez; **I can't hear you** je ne t'entends pas

2 (know how to) savoir; **I can swim/play tennis/drive** je sais nager/jouer au tennis/ conduire; **can you speak French?** parlez-vous français?

3 (may) pouvoir; **can I use your phone?** puis-je me servir de votre téléphone?

4 (expressing disbelief, puzzlement etc): **it can't be true!** ce n'est pas possible!; **what CAN he want?** qu'est-ce qu'il peut bien vouloir?

5 (expressing possibility, suggestion etc): **he could be in the library** il est peut-être dans la bibliothèque; **she could have been delayed** il se peut qu'elle ait été retardée; **they could have forgotten** ils ont pu oublier

---

Canada ['kænədə] n Canada m

Canadian [kə'neɪdɪən] adj canadien(ne) ▷ n Canadien(ne)

canal [kə'næl] n canal m

canary [kə'nɛərɪ] n canari m, serin m

cancel ['kænsəl] vt annuler; (train) supprimer; (party, appointment) décommander; (cross out) barrer, rayer; (stamp) oblitérer; (cheque) faire opposition à; **I would like to ~ my booking** je voudrais annuler ma réservation; **cancel out** vt annuler; **they ~ each other out** ils s'annulent

cancellation [kænsə'leɪʃən] n annulation f; suppression f; oblitération f; (Tourism) réservation annulée, client etc qui s'est décommandé

Cancer ['kænsər] n (Astrology) le Cancer; **to be ~** être du Cancer

cancer ['kænsər] n cancer m

candid ['kændɪd] adj (très) franc/franche, sincère

candidate ['kændɪdeɪt] n candidat(e)

candle ['kændl] n bougie f; (of tallow) chandelle f; (in church) cierge m

candlelight ['kændllaɪt] n: **by ~** à la lumière d'une bougie; (dinner) aux chandelles

candlestick ['kændlstɪk] n (also: **candle holder**) bougeoir m; (bigger, ornate) chandelier m

candour, (US) **candor** ['kændər] n (grande) franchise f, sincérité f

candy ['kændɪ] n sucre candi; (US) bonbon m

candy bar (US) n barre f chocolatée

candyfloss ['kændɪflɒs] n (Brit) barbe f à papa

cane [keɪn] n canne f; (for baskets, chairs etc) rotin m ▷ vt (Brit Scol) administrer des coups de bâton à

canister ['kænɪstər] n boîte f (gén en métal); (of gas) bombe f

cannabis ['kænəbis] n (drug) cannabis m; (cannabis plant) chanvre indien

canned ['kænd] adj (food) en boîte, en conserve; (inf: music) enregistré(e); (Brit inf: drunk) bourré(e); (US inf: worker) mis(e) à la porte

cannon (pl cannon or cannons) ['kænən] n (gun) canon m

cannot ['kænɔt] = **can not**

canoe [kə'nuː] n pirogue f; (Sport) canoë m

canoeing [kə'nuːɪŋ] n (sport) canoë m

canon ['kænən] n (clergyman) chanoine m; (standard) canon m

can-opener [-'əupnəʳ] n ouvre-boîte m

canopy ['kænəpɪ] n baldaquin m; dais m

can't [kɑːnt] = **can not**

canteen [kæn'tiːn] n (eating place) cantine f; (Brit: of cutlery) ménagère f

canter ['kæntəʳ] n petit galop ▷ vi aller au petit galop

canvas ['kænvəs] n (gen) toile f; **under ~** (camping) sous la tente; (Naut) toutes voiles dehors

canvass ['kænvəs] vi (Pol): **to ~ for** faire campagne pour ▷ vt (Pol: district) faire la tournée électorale dans; (: person) solliciter le suffrage de; (Comm: district) prospecter; (citizens, opinions) sonder

canyon ['kænjən] n cañon m, gorge f (profonde)

cap [kæp] n casquette f; (for swimming) bonnet m de bain; (of pen) capuchon m; (of bottle) capsule f; (Brit: contraceptive: also: **Dutch ~**) diaphragme m; (Football) sélection f pour l'équipe nationale ▷ vt capsuler; (outdo) surpasser; (put limit on) plafonner; **~ped with** coiffé(e) de; **and to ~ it all, he ...** (Brit) pour couronner le tout, il ...

capability [keɪpə'bɪlɪtɪ] n aptitude f, capacité f

capable ['keɪpəbl] adj capable; **~ of** (interpretation etc) susceptible de

capacity [kə'pæsɪtɪ] n (of container) capacité f, contenance f; (ability) aptitude f; **filled to ~** plein(e); **in his ~ as** en sa qualité de; **in an advisory ~** à titre consultatif; **to work at full ~** travailler à plein rendement

cape [keɪp] n (garment) cape f; (Geo) cap m

caper ['keɪpəʳ] n (Culin: gen pl) câpre f; (prank) farce f

capital ['kæpɪtl] n (also: **~ city**) capitale f; (money) capital m; (also: **~ letter**) majuscule f

capital gains tax n impôt m sur les plus-values

capitalism ['kæpɪtəlɪzəm] n capitalisme m

capitalist ['kæpɪtəlɪst] adj, n capitaliste m/f

capitalize ['kæpɪtəlaɪz] vt (provide with capital) financer; **capitalize on** vt fus (fig) profiter de

capital punishment n peine capitale

Capitol ['kæpɪtl] n: **the ~** le Capitole; voir article

Capricorn ['kæprɪkɔːn] n le Capricorne; **to be ~** être du Capricorne

capsize [kæp'saɪz] vt faire chavirer ▷ vi chavirer

capsule ['kæpsjuːl] n capsule f

captain ['kæptɪn] n capitaine m ▷ vt commander, être le capitaine de

caption ['kæpʃən] n légende f

captive ['kæptɪv] adj, n captif(-ive)

captivity [kæp'tɪvɪtɪ] n captivité f

capture ['kæptʃəʳ] vt (prisoner, animal) capturer; (town) prendre; (attention) capter; (Comput) saisir ▷ n capture f; (of data) saisie f de données

car [kɑːʳ] n voiture f, auto f; (US Rail) wagon m, voiture; **by ~** en voiture

carafe [kə'ræf] n carafe f

caramel ['kærəməl] n caramel m

carat ['kærət] n carat m; **18 ~ gold** or m à 18 carats

caravan ['kærəvæn] n caravane f

caravan site n (Brit) camping m pour caravanes

carbohydrate [kɑːbəu'haɪdreɪt] n hydrate m de carbone; (food) féculent m

carbon ['kɑːbən] n carbone m

carbon dioxide [-daɪ'ɔksaɪd] n gaz m carbonique, dioxyde m de carbone

carbon footprint n empreinte f carbone

carbon monoxide [-mɔ'nɔksaɪd] n oxyde m de carbone

carbon-neutral [kɑːbn'njuːtrəl] adj neutre en carbone

carbon paper n papier m carbone

car boot sale n voir article

carburettor, (US) **carburetor** [kɑː'bjuːretəʳ] n carburateur m

card [kɑːd] n carte f; (material) carton m; (membership card) carte d'adhérent; **to play ~s** jouer aux cartes

cardboard ['kɑːdbɔːd] n carton m

card game n jeu m de cartes

cardiac ['kɑːdɪæk] adj cardiaque

cardigan ['kɑːdɪgən] n cardigan m

cardinal ['kɑːdɪnl] adj cardinal(e); (importance) capital(e) ▷ n cardinal m

card index n fichier m (alphabétique)

cardphone ['kɑːdfəʊn] n téléphone m à carte (magnétique)

care [keəʳ] n soin m, attention f; (worry) souci m ▷ vi: **to ~ about** (feel interest for) se soucier de, s'intéresser à; (person: love) être attaché(e) à; **in sb's ~** à la garde de qn, confié à qn; **~ of** (on letter) chez; **"with ~"** "fragile"; **to take ~ (to do)** faire attention (à faire); **to take ~ of** vt s'occuper de; **the child has been taken into ~** l'enfant a été placé en institution; **would you ~ to/for ...?** voulez-vous ...?; **I wouldn't ~ to do it** je n'aimerais pas le faire; **I don't ~** ça m'est bien égal, peu m'importe; **I couldn't ~ less** cela m'est complètement égal, je m'en fiche complètement; **care for** vt fus s'occuper de; (like) aimer

career [kə'rɪəʳ] n carrière f ▷ vi (also: **~ along**) aller à toute allure

career woman irreg n femme ambitieuse

carefree ['keəfriː] adj sans souci, insouciant(e)

careful ['keəful] adj soigneux(-euse); (cautious) prudent(e); **(be) ~!** (fais) attention!; **to be ~ with one's money** regarder à la dépense

carefully ['keəfəlɪ] adv avec soin, soigneusement; prudemment

caregiver ['keəgɪvəʳ] (US) n (professional) travailleur social; (unpaid) personne qui s'occupe d'un proche qui est malade

careless ['keəlɪs] adj négligent(e); (heedless) insouciant(e)

carelessness ['keəlɪsnɪs] n manque m de soin, négligence f; insouciance f

carer ['keərəʳ] n (professional) travailleur social; (unpaid) personne qui s'occupe d'un proche qui est malade

caress [kə'rɛs] n caresse f ▷ vt caresser

caretaker ['keəteɪkəʳ] n gardien(ne), concierge m/f

car-ferry ['kɑːferɪ] n (on sea) ferry(-boat) m; (on river) bac m

cargo (pl **cargoes**) ['kɑːgəʊ] n cargaison f, chargement m

car hire n (Brit) location f de voitures

Caribbean [kærɪ'biːən] adj, n: **the ~ (Sea)** la mer des Antilles or des Caraïbes

caring ['keərɪŋ] adj (person) bienveillant(e); (society, organization) humanitaire

carnation [kɑː'neɪʃən] n œillet m

carnival ['kɑːnɪvl] n (public celebration) carnaval m; (US: funfair) fête foraine

carol ['kærəl] n: **(Christmas) ~** chant m de Noël

carousel [kærə'sel] n (for luggage) carrousel m; (US) manège m

carp [kɑːp] n (fish) carpe f; **carp at** vt fus critiquer

car park (Brit) n parking m, parc m de stationnement

carpenter ['kɑːpɪntəʳ] n charpentier m; (joiner) menuisier m

carpentry ['kɑːpɪntrɪ] n charpenterie f, métier m de charpentier; (woodwork: at school etc) menuiserie f

carpet ['kɑːpɪt] n tapis m ▷ vt recouvrir (d'un tapis); **fitted ~** (Brit) moquette f

carpet sweeper [-'swiːpəʳ] n balai m mécanique

car phone n téléphone m de voiture

car rental n (US) location f de voitures

carriage ['kærɪdʒ] n (Brit Rail) wagon m; (horse-drawn) voiture f; (of goods) transport m; (: cost) port m; (of typewriter) chariot m; (bearing) maintien m, port m; **~ forward** port dû; **~ free** franco de port; **~ paid** (en) port payé

carriageway ['kærɪdʒweɪ] n (Brit: part of road) chaussée f

carrier ['kærɪəʳ] n transporteur m, camionneur m; (company) entreprise f de transport; (Med) porteur(-euse); (Naut) porte-avions m inv

carrier bag n (Brit) sac m en papier or en plastique

carrot ['kærət] n carotte f

carry ['kærɪ] vt (subj: person) porter; (: vehicle) transporter; (a motion, bill) voter, adopter; (Math: figure) retenir; (Comm: interest) rapporter; (involve: responsibilities etc) comporter, impliquer; (Med: disease) être porteur de ▷ vi (sound) porter; **to get carried away** (fig) s'emballer, s'enthousiasmer; **this loan carries 10% interest** ce prêt est à 10% (d'intérêt); **carry forward** vt (gen, Book-keeping) reporter; **carry on** vi (continue) continuer; (inf: make a fuss) faire des histoires ▷ vt (conduct: business) diriger; (: conversation) entretenir; (continue: business, conversation) continuer; **to ~ on with sth/doing** continuer qch/à faire; **carry out** vt (orders) exécuter; (investigation) effectuer; (idea, threat) mettre à exécution

carrycot ['kærɪkɔt] n (Brit) porte-bébé m

carry-on ['kærɪ'ɔn] n (inf: fuss) histoires fpl; (: annoying behaviour) cirque m, cinéma m

cart [kɑːt] n charrette f ▷ vt (inf) transporter

carton ['kɑːtən] n (box) carton m; (of yogurt) pot m (en carton); (of cigarettes) cartouche f

cartoon [kɑː'tuːn] n (Press) dessin m (humoristique); (satirical) caricature f; (comic strip) bande dessinée; (Cine) dessin animé

cartridge ['kɑːtrɪdʒ] n (for gun, pen) cartouche f; (for camera) chargeur m; (music tape) cassette f; (of record player) cellule f

carve [kɑːv] vt (meat: also: **~ up**) découper; (wood, stone) tailler, sculpter

carving ['kɑːvɪŋ] n (in wood etc) sculpture f

carving knife n couteau m à découper

car wash n station f de lavage (de voitures)

case [keɪs] n cas m; (Law) affaire f, procès m; (box) caisse f, boîte f; (for glasses) étui m; (Brit: also: **suit~**) valise f; (Typ): **lower/upper ~**

minuscule f/majuscule f; **to have a good ~** avoir de bons arguments; **there's a strong ~ for reform** il y aurait lieu d'engager une réforme; **in ~ of** en cas de; **in ~ he** au cas où il; **just in ~** à tout hasard; **in any ~** en tout cas, de toute façon

cash [kæʃ] n argent m; (Comm) (argent m) liquide m, numéraire m; liquidités fpl; (: in payment) argent comptant, espèces fpl ▷ vt encaisser; **to pay (in) ~** payer (en argent) comptant or en espèces; **~ with order/on delivery** (Comm) payable or paiement à la commande/livraison; **to be short of ~** être à court d'argent; **I haven't got any ~** je n'ai pas de liquide; **cash in** vt (insurance policy etc) toucher; **cash in on** vt fus profiter de

cashback ['kæʃbæk] n (discount) remise f; (at supermarket etc) retrait m (à la caisse)

cashbook ['kæʃbuk] n livre m de caisse

cash card n carte f de retrait

cash desk n (Brit) caisse f

cash dispenser n distributeur m automatique de billets

cashew [kæ'ʃu:] n (also: **~ nut**) noix f de cajou

cashier [kæ'ʃɪər] n caissier(-ère) ▷ vt (Mil) destituer, casser

cashmere ['kæʃmɪər] n cachemire m

cash point n distributeur m automatique de billets

cash register n caisse enregistreuse

casing ['keɪsɪŋ] n revêtement (protecteur), enveloppe (protectrice)

casino [kə'si:nəu] n casino m

casket ['kɑ:skɪt] n coffret m; (US: coffin) cercueil m

casserole ['kæsərəul] n (pot) cocotte f; (food) ragoût m (en cocotte)

cassette [kæ'sɛt] n cassette f

cassette player n lecteur m de cassettes

cassette recorder n magnétophone m à cassettes

cast [kɑ:st] (vb: pt, pp **cast**) vt (throw) jeter; (shadow: lit) projeter; (: fig) jeter; (glance) jeter; (shed) perdre; se dépouiller de; (metal) couler, fondre ▷ n (Theat) distribution f; (mould) moule m; (also: **plaster ~**) plâtre m; **to ~ sb as Hamlet** attribuer à qn le rôle d'Hamlet; **to ~ one's vote** voter, exprimer son suffrage; **to ~ doubt on** jeter un doute sur; **cast aside** vt (reject) rejeter; **cast off** vi (Naut) larguer les amarres; (Knitting) arrêter les mailles ▷ vt (Knitting) arrêter; **cast on** (Knitting) monter ▷ vi monter les mailles

castanets [kæstə'nɛts] npl castagnettes fpl

castaway ['kɑ:stəweɪ] n naufragé(e)

caster sugar ['kɑ:stə-] n (Brit) sucre m semoule

casting vote ['kɑ:stɪŋ-] n (Brit) voix f prépondérante (pour départager)

cast-iron ['kɑ:staɪən] adj (lit) de or en fonte; (fig: will) de fer; (alibi) en béton

cast iron n fonte f

castle ['kɑ:sl] n château m; (fortress) château-fort m; (Chess) tour f

castor ['kɑ:stər] n (wheel) roulette f

castor oil n huile f de ricin

castrate [kæs'treɪt] vt châtrer

casual ['kæʒjul] adj (by chance) de hasard, fait(e) au hasard, fortuit(e); (irregular: work etc) temporaire; (unconcerned) désinvolte; **~ wear** vêtements mpl sport inv

casually ['kæʒjulɪ] adv avec désinvolture, négligemment; (by chance) fortuitement

casualty ['kæʒjultɪ] n accidenté(e), blessé(e); (dead) victime f, mort(e); (Brit: Med: department) urgences fpl; **heavy casualties** lourdes pertes

cat [kæt] n chat m

Catalan ['kætəlæn] adj catalan(e)

catalogue, (US) **catalog** ['kætəlɔg] n catalogue m ▷ vt cataloguer

catalyst ['kætəlɪst] n catalyseur m

catalytic converter [kætə'lɪtɪkkən'və:tər] n pot m catalytique

catapult ['kætəpʌlt] n lance-pierres m inv, fronde f; (Hist) catapulte f

cataract ['kætərækt] n (also Med) cataracte f

catarrh [kə'tɑ:r] n rhume m chronique, catarrhe f

catastrophe [kə'tæstrəfɪ] n catastrophe f

catch [kætʃ] (pt, pp **caught**) [kɔ:t] vt (ball, train, thief, cold) attraper; (person: by surprise) prendre, surprendre; (understand) saisir; (get entangled) accrocher ▷ vi (fire) prendre; (get entangled) s'accrocher ▷ n (fish etc) prise f; (thief etc) capture f; (hidden problem) attrape f; (Tech) loquet m; cliquet m; **to ~ sb's attention** or **eye** attirer l'attention de qn; **to ~ fire** prendre feu; **to ~ sight of** apercevoir; **to play ~** jouer à chat; (with ball) jouer à attraper le ballon; **catch on** vi (become popular) prendre; (understand): **to ~ on (to sth)** saisir (qch); **catch out** vt (Brit: fig: with trick question) prendre en défaut; **catch up** vi (with work) se rattraper, combler son retard ▷ vt (also: **~ up with**) rattraper

catching ['kætʃɪŋ] adj (Med) contagieux(-euse)

catchment area ['kætʃmənt-] n (Brit Scol) aire f de recrutement; (Geo) bassin m hydrographique

catch phrase n slogan m, expression toute faite

catchy ['kætʃɪ] adj (tune) facile à retenir

category ['kætɪgərɪ] n catégorie f

cater ['keɪtər] vi: **to ~ for** (Brit: needs) satisfaire, pourvoir à; (: readers, consumers) s'adresser à, pourvoir aux besoins de; (Comm: parties etc) préparer des repas pour

caterer ['keɪtərər] n traiteur m; fournisseur m

catering ['keɪtərɪŋ] n restauration f; approvisionnement m, ravitaillement m

caterpillar ['kætəpɪlər] n chenille f ▷ cpd (vehicle) à chenille; **~ track** n chenille f

cathedral [kə'θi:drəl] n cathédrale f
Catholic ['kæθəlɪk] (Rel) adj catholique ▷ n
catholique m/f
catholic ['kæθəlɪk] adj (wide-ranging)
éclectique; universel(le); libéral(e)
cattle ['kætl] npl bétail m, bestiaux mpl
catty ['kætɪ] adj méchant(e)
catwalk ['kætwɔ:k] n passerelle f; (for models)
podium m (de défilé de mode)
caucus ['kɔːkəs] n (US Pol) comité électoral
(pour désigner des candidats); voir article;
(Brit Pol: group) comité local (d'un parti politique)

- **CAUCUS**
-
- Un caucus aux États-Unis est une réunion
- restreinte des principaux dirigeants d'un
- parti politique, précédant souvent une
- assemblée générale, dans le but de
- choisir des candidats ou de définir une
- ligne d'action. Par extension, ce terme
- désigne également l'état-major d'un
- parti politique.

caught [kɔːt] pt, pp of **catch**
cauliflower ['kɔlɪflauə'] n chou-fleur m
cause [kɔːz] n cause f ▷ vt causer; **there is no
~ for concern** il n'y a pas lieu de s'inquiéter;
to ~ sth to be done faire faire qch; **to ~ sb to
do sth** faire faire qch à qn
caution ['kɔːʃən] n prudence f; (warning)
avertissement m ▷ vt avertir, donner un
avertissement à
cautious ['kɔːʃəs] adj prudent(e)
cavalry ['kævəlrɪ] n cavalerie f
cave [keɪv] n caverne f, grotte f ▷ vi: **to go
caving** faire de la spéléo(logie); **cave in** vi
(roof etc) s'effondrer
caveman ['keɪvmæn] irreg n homme m des
cavernes
caviar, caviare ['kævɪɑːʳ] n caviar m
cavity ['kævɪtɪ] n cavité f; (Med) carie f
CB n abbr (= Citizens' Band (Radio)) CB f; (Brit:
= Companion of (the Order of) the Bath) titre
honorifique
CBI n abbr (= Confederation of British Industry)
≈ MEDEF m (= Mouvement des entreprises de France)
cc abbr (= cubic centimetre) cm³; (on letter etc)
= **carbon copy**
CCTV n abbr = **closed-circuit television**
CD n abbr (= compact disc) CD m; (Mil: Brit) = **Civil
Defence (Corps)**; (: US) = **Civil Defense** ▷ abbr
(Brit: = Corps Diplomatique) CD
CD burner n graveur m de CD
CD player n platine f laser
CD-ROM [si:di:'rɔm] n abbr (= compact disc read-
only memory) CD-ROM m inv
CD writer n graveur m de CD
cease [si:s] vt, vi cesser
ceasefire ['si:sfaɪə'] n cessez-le-feu m
ceaseless ['si:slɪs] adj incessant(e),
continuel(le)

cedar ['si:də'] n cèdre m
ceilidh ['keɪlɪ] n bal m folklorique écossais or
irlandais
ceiling ['si:lɪŋ] n (also fig) plafond m
celebrate ['selɪbreɪt] vt, vi célébrer
celebrated ['selɪbreɪtɪd] adj célèbre
celebration [selɪ'breɪʃən] n célébration f
celebrity [sɪ'lebrɪtɪ] n célébrité f
celery ['selərɪ] n céleri m (en branches)
cell [sel] n (gen) cellule f; (Elec) élément m
(de pile)
cellar ['selə'] n cave f
cello ['tʃeləu] n violoncelle m
Cellophane® ['seləfeɪn] n cellophane® f
cellphone ['selfəun] n téléphone m)
portable m, mobile m
Celsius ['selsɪəs] adj Celsius inv
Celt [kelt, selt] n Celte m/f
Celtic ['keltɪk, 'seltɪk] adj celte, celtique ▷ n
(Ling) celtique m
cement [sə'ment] n ciment m ▷ vt cimenter
cement mixer n bétonnière f
cemetery ['semɪtrɪ] n cimetière m
censor ['sensə'] n censeur m ▷ vt censurer
censorship ['sensəʃɪp] n censure f
censure ['sensə'] vt blâmer, critiquer
census ['sensəs] n recensement m
cent [sent] n (unit of dollar, euro) cent m (= un
centième du dollar, de l'euro); see also **per**
centenary [sen'ti:nərɪ], (US) **centennial**
[sen'tenɪəl] n centenaire m
center ['sentə'] n, vt (US) = **centre**
centigrade ['sentɪgreɪd] adj centigrade
centimetre, (US) **centimeter** ['sentɪmi:tə']
n centimètre m
centipede ['sentɪpi:d] n mille-pattes m inv
central ['sentrəl] adj central(e)
Central America n Amérique centrale
central heating n chauffage central
central reservation n (Brit Aut) terre-plein
central
centre, (US) **center** ['sentə'] n centre m ▷ vt
centrer; (Phot) cadrer; (concentrate): **to ~ (on)**
centrer (sur)
centre-forward ['sentə'fɔ:wəd] n (Sport)
avant-centre m
centre-half ['sentə'hɑ:f] n (Sport)
demi-centre m
century ['sentjurɪ] n siècle m; **in the
twentieth ~** au vingtième siècle
CEO n abbr (US) = **chief executive officer**
ceramic [sɪ'ræmɪk] adj céramique
cereal ['si:rɪəl] n céréale f
ceremony ['serɪmənɪ] n cérémonie f; **to
stand on ~** faire des façons
certain ['sə:tən] adj certain(e); **to make ~ of**
s'assurer de; **for ~** certainement, sûrement
certainly ['sə:tənlɪ] adv certainement
certainty ['sə:təntɪ] n certitude f
certificate [sə'tɪfɪkɪt] n certificat m
certify ['sə:tɪfaɪ] vt certifier; (award diploma to)
conférer un diplôme etc à; (declare insane)

déclarer malade mental(e) ⊳ *vi*: **to ~ to** attester

cervical ['sə:vɪkl] *adj*: ~ **cancer** cancer *m* du col de l'utérus; ~ **smear** frottis vaginal

cervix ['sə:vɪks] *n* col *m* de l'utérus

cf. *abbr* (= *compare*) cf., voir

CFC *n abbr* (= *chlorofluorocarbon*) CFC *m*

ch. *abbr* (= *chapter*) chap

chafe [tʃeɪf] *vt* irriter, frotter contre ⊳ *vi* (*fig*): **to ~ against** se rebiffer contre, regimber contre

chain [tʃeɪn] *n* (*gen*) chaîne *f* ⊳ *vt* (*also*: ~ **up**) enchaîner, attacher (avec une chaîne)

chain reaction *n* réaction *f* en chaîne

chain-smoke ['tʃeɪnsməʊk] *vi* fumer cigarette sur cigarette

chain store *n* magasin *m* à succursales multiples

chair [tʃeəʳ] *n* chaise *f*; (*armchair*) fauteuil *m*; (*of university*) chaire *f*; (*of meeting*) présidence *f* ⊳ *vt* (*meeting*) présider; **the ~** (US: *electric chair*) la chaise électrique

chairlift ['tʃeəlɪft] *n* télésiège *m*

chairman ['tʃeəmən] *irreg n* président *m*

chairperson ['tʃeəpə:sn] *irreg n* président(e)

chairwoman ['tʃeəwʊmən] *n* présidente *f*

chalet ['ʃæleɪ] *n* chalet *m*

chalk [tʃɔ:k] *n* craie *f*; **chalk up** *vt* écrire à la craie; (*fig*: *success etc*) remporter

challenge ['tʃælɪndʒ] *n* défi *m* ⊳ *vt* défier; (*statement, right*) mettre en question, contester; **to ~ sb to a fight/game** inviter qn à se battre/à jouer (*sous forme d'un défi*); **to ~ sb to do** mettre qn au défi de faire

challenging ['tʃælɪndʒɪŋ] *adj* (*task, career*) qui représente un défi *or* une gageure; (*tone, look*) de défi, provocateur(-trice)

chamber ['tʃeɪmbəʳ] *n* chambre *f*; (*Brit Law*: *gen pl*) cabinet *m*; ~ **of commerce** chambre de commerce

chambermaid ['tʃeɪmbəmeɪd] *n* femme *f* de chambre

chamber music *n* musique *f* de chambre

champagne [ʃæm'peɪn] *n* champagne *m*

champion ['tʃæmpɪən] *n* (*also of cause*) champion(ne) ⊳ *vt* défendre

championship ['tʃæmpɪənʃɪp] *n* championnat *m*

chance [tʃɑ:ns] *n* (*luck*) hasard *m*; (*opportunity*) occasion *f*, possibilité *f*; (*hope, likelihood*) chance *f*; (*risk*) risque *m* ⊳ *vt* (*risk*) risquer; (*happen*): **to ~ to do** faire par hasard ⊳ *adj* fortuit(e), de hasard; **there is little ~ of his coming** il est peu probable *or* il y a peu de chances qu'il vienne; **to take a ~** prendre un risque; **it's the ~ of a lifetime** c'est une occasion unique; **by ~** par hasard; **to ~ doing sth** se risquer à faire qch; **to ~ it** risquer le coup, essayer; **chance on, chance upon** *vt fus* (*person*) tomber sur, rencontrer par hasard; (*thing*) trouver par hasard

chancellor ['tʃɑ:nsələʳ] *n* chancelier *m*

Chancellor of the Exchequer [-ɪks'tʃekəʳ] (Brit) *n* chancelier *m* de l'Échiquier

chandelier [ʃændə'lɪəʳ] *n* lustre *m*

change [tʃeɪndʒ] *vt* (*alter, replace; Comm: money*) changer; (*switch, substitute: hands, trains, clothes, one's name etc*) changer de; (*transform*): **to ~ sb into** changer *or* transformer qn en ⊳ *vi* (*gen*) changer; (*change clothes*) se changer; (*be transformed*): **to ~ into** se changer *or* transformer en ⊳ *n* changement *m*; (*money*) monnaie *f*; **to ~ gear** (*Aut*) changer de vitesse; **to ~ one's mind** changer d'avis; **she ~d into an old skirt** elle (s'est changée et) a enfilé une vieille jupe; **a ~ of clothes** des vêtements de rechange; **for a ~** pour changer; **small ~** petite monnaie; **to give sb ~ for** *or* **of £10** faire à qn la monnaie de 10 livres; **do you have ~ for £10?** vous avez la monnaie de 10 livres?; **where can I ~ some money?** où est-ce que je peux changer de l'argent?; **keep the ~!** gardez la monnaie!; **change over** *vi* (*swap*) échanger; (*change: drivers etc*) changer; (*change sides: players etc*) changer de côté; **to ~ over from sth to sth** passer de qch à qch

changeable ['tʃeɪndʒəbl] *adj* (*weather*) variable; (*person*) d'humeur changeante

change machine *n* distributeur *m* de monnaie

changeover ['tʃeɪndʒəʊvəʳ] *n* (*to new system*) changement *m*, passage *m*

changing ['tʃeɪndʒɪŋ] *adj* changeant(e)

changing room *n* (Brit: *in shop*) salon *m* d'essayage; (: *Sport*) vestiaire *m*

channel ['tʃænl] *n* (TV) chaîne *f*; (*waveband, groove, fig: medium*) canal *m*; (*of river, sea*) chenal *m* ⊳ *vt* canaliser; (*fig: interest, energies*): **to ~ into** diriger vers; **through the usual ~s** en suivant la filière habituelle; **green/red ~** (Customs) couloir *m* *or* sortie *f* "rien à déclarer"/"marchandises à déclarer"; **the (English) C~** la Manche

channel-hopping ['tʃænl'hɔpɪŋ] *n* (TV) zapping *m*

Channel Islands *npl*: **the ~** les îles *fpl* Anglo-Normandes

Channel Tunnel *n*: **the ~** le tunnel sous la Manche

chant [tʃɑ:nt] *n* chant *m*; mélopée *f*; (Rel) psalmodie *f* ⊳ *vt* chanter, scander; psalmodier

chaos ['keɪɔs] *n* chaos *m*

chaotic [keɪ'ɔtɪk] *adj* chaotique

chap [tʃæp] *n* (Brit inf: *man*) type *m*; (*term of address*): **old ~** mon vieux ⊳ *vt* (*skin*) gercer, crevasser

chapel ['tʃæpl] *n* chapelle *f*

chaplain ['tʃæplɪn] *n* aumônier *m*

chapped [tʃæpt] *adj* (*skin, lips*) gercé(e)

chapter ['tʃæptəʳ] *n* chapitre *m*

char [tʃɑ:ʳ] *vt* (*burn*) carboniser ⊳ *vi* (Brit: *cleaner*) faire des ménages ⊳ *n* (Brit) = **charlady**

character ['kærɪktər] n caractère m; (in novel, film) personnage m; (eccentric person) numéro m, phénomène m; **a person of good ~** une personne bien

characteristic ['kærɪktə'rɪstɪk] adj, n caractéristique (f)

characterize ['kærɪktəraɪz] vt caractériser; **to ~ (as)** définir (comme)

charcoal ['tʃɑ:kəul] n charbon m de bois; (Art) charbon

charge [tʃɑ:dʒ] n (accusation) accusation f; (Law) inculpation f; (cost) prix (demandé); (of gun, battery, Mil: attack) charge f ▷ vt (gun, battery, Mil: enemy) charger; (customer, sum) faire payer ▷ vi (gen with: up, along etc) foncer; **charges** npl (costs) frais mpl; (Brit Tel): **to reverse the ~s** téléphoner en PCV; **bank/labour ~s** frais mpl de banque/main-d'œuvre; **is there a ~?** doit-on payer?; **there's no ~** c'est gratuit, on ne fait pas payer; **extra ~** supplément m; **to take ~ of** se charger de; **to be in ~ of** être responsable de, s'occuper de; **to ~ in/out** entrer/sortir en trombe; **to ~ down/up** dévaler/ grimper à toute allure; **to ~ sb (with)** (Law) inculper qn (de); **to have ~ of sb** avoir la charge de qn; **they ~d us £10 for the meal** ils nous ont fait payer le repas 10 livres, ils nous ont compté 10 livres pour le repas; **how much do you ~ for this repair?** combien demandez-vous pour cette réparation?; **to ~ an expense (up) to sb** mettre une dépense sur le compte de qn; **~ it to my account** facturez-le sur mon compte

charge card n carte f de client (émise par un grand magasin)

charger ['tʃɑ:dʒər] n (also: **battery ~**) chargeur m; (old: warhorse) cheval m de bataille

charismatic [kærɪz'mætɪk] adj charismatique

charity ['tʃærɪtɪ] n charité f; (organization) institution f charitable or de bienfaisance, œuvre f (de charité)

charity shop n (Brit) boutique vendant des articles d'occasion au profit d'une organisation caritative

charm [tʃɑ:m] n charme m; (on bracelet) breloque f ▷ vt charmer, enchanter

charming ['tʃɑ:mɪŋ] adj charmant(e)

chart [tʃɑ:t] n tableau m, diagramme m; graphique m; (map) carte marine; (weather chart) carte f du temps ▷ vt dresser or établir la carte de; (sales, progress) établir la courbe de; **charts** npl (Mus) hit-parade m; **to be in the ~s** (record, pop group) figurer au hit-parade

charter ['tʃɑ:tər] vt (plane) affréter ▷ n (document) charte f; **on ~** (plane) affrété(e)

chartered accountant ['tʃɑ:təd-] n (Brit) expert-comptable m

charter flight n charter m

chase [tʃeɪs] vt poursuivre, pourchasser; (also: **~ away**) chasser ▷ n poursuite f,

chasse f; **chase down** vt (US) = **chase up**; **chase up** vt (Brit: person) relancer; (: information) rechercher

chasm ['kæzəm] n gouffre m, abîme m

chat [tʃæt] vi (also: **have a ~**) bavarder, causer; (on Internet) chatter ▷ n conversation f; (on Internet) chat m; **chat up** vt (Brit inf: girl) baratiner

chat room n (Internet) salon m de discussion

chat show n (Brit) talk-show m

chatter ['tʃætər] vi (person) bavarder, papoter ▷ n bavardage m, papotage m; **my teeth are ~ing** je claque des dents

chatterbox ['tʃætəbɒks] n moulin m à paroles, babillard(e)

chatty ['tʃætɪ] adj (style) familier(-ière); (person) enclin(e) à bavarder or au papotage

chauffeur ['ʃəufər] n chauffeur m (de maître)

chauvinist ['ʃəuvɪnɪst] n (also: **male ~**) phallocrate m, macho m; (nationalist) chauvin(e)

cheap [tʃi:p] adj bon marché inv, pas cher/chère; (reduced: ticket) à prix réduit; (: fare) réduit(e); (joke) facile, d'un goût douteux; (poor quality) à bon marché, de qualité médiocre ▷ adv à bon marché, pas cher; **~er** adj moins cher/chère; **can you recommend a ~ hotel/restaurant, please?** pourriez-vous m'indiquer un hôtel/restaurant bon marché?

cheap day return n billet m d'aller et retour réduit (valable pour la journée)

cheaply ['tʃi:plɪ] adv à bon marché, à bon compte

cheat [tʃi:t] vi tricher; (in exam) copier ▷ vt tromper, duper; (rob): **to ~ sb out of sth** escroquer qch à qn ▷ n tricheur(-euse) m/f; escroc m; (trick) duperie f, tromperie f; **cheat on** vt fus tromper

Chechnya [tʃɪtʃ'njɑ:] n Tchétchénie f

check [tʃɛk] vt vérifier; (passport, ticket) contrôler; (halt) enrayer; (restrain) maîtriser ▷ vi (official etc) se renseigner ▷ n vérification f; contrôle m; (curb) frein m; (Brit: bill) addition f; (US) = cheque; (pattern: gen pl) carreaux mpl ▷ adj (also: **~ed**: pattern, cloth) à carreaux; **to ~ with sb** demander à qn; **to keep a ~ on sb/sth** surveiller qn/qch; **check in** vi (in hotel) remplir sa fiche (d'hôtel); (at airport) se présenter à l'enregistrement ▷ vt (luggage) (faire) enregistrer; **check off** vt (tick off) cocher; **check out** vi (in hotel) régler sa note ▷ vt (luggage) retirer; (investigate: story) vérifier; (person) prendre des renseignements sur; **check up** vi: **to ~ up (on sth)** vérifier (qch); **to ~ up on sb** se renseigner sur le compte de qn

checkbook ['tʃɛkbuk] n (US) = chequebook

checked [tʃɛkt] adj (pattern, cloth) à carreaux

checkered ['tʃɛkəd] adj (US) = chequered

checkers ['tʃɛkəz] n (US) jeu m de dames

check-in ['tʃɛkɪn] n (also: **~ desk**: at airport) enregistrement m

checking account ['tʃɛkɪŋ-] n (US) compte courant

checklist ['tʃɛklɪst] n liste f de contrôle

checkmate ['tʃɛkmeɪt] n échec et mat m

checkout ['tʃɛkaut] n (in supermarket) caisse f

checkpoint ['tʃɛkpɔɪnt] n contrôle m

checkroom ['tʃɛkru:m] n (US) consigne f

checkup ['tʃɛkʌp] n (Med) examen médical, check-up m

cheddar ['tʃɛdəʳ] n (also: **~ cheese**) cheddar m

cheek [tʃi:k] n joue f; (impudence) toupet m, culot m; **what a ~!** quel toupet!

cheekbone ['tʃi:kbəun] n pommette f

cheeky ['tʃi:kɪ] adj effronté(e), culotté(e)

cheep [tʃi:p] n (of bird) piaulement m ▷ vi piauler

cheer [tʃɪəʳ] vt acclamer, applaudir; (gladden) réjouir, réconforter ▷ vi applaudir ▷ n (gen pl) acclamations fpl, applaudissements mpl; bravos mpl, hourras mpl; **~s!** à la vôtre!; **cheer on** vt encourager (par des cris etc); **cheer up** vi se dérider, reprendre courage ▷ vt remonter le moral à or de, dérider, égayer

cheerful ['tʃɪəful] adj gai(e), joyeux(-euse)

cheerio ['tʃɪərɪ'əu] excl (Brit) salut!, au revoir!

cheerleader ['tʃɪəli:dəʳ] n membre d'un groupe de majorettes qui chantent et dansent pour soutenir leur équipe pendant les matchs de football américain

cheese [tʃi:z] n fromage m

cheeseboard ['tʃi:zbɔ:d] n plateau m à fromages; (with cheese on it) plateau m de fromages

cheeseburger ['tʃi:zbə:gəʳ] n cheeseburger m

cheesecake ['tʃi:zkeɪk] n tarte f au fromage

cheetah ['tʃi:tə] n guépard m

chef [ʃɛf] n chef (cuisinier)

chemical ['kɛmɪkl] adj chimique ▷ n produit m chimique

chemist ['kɛmɪst] n (Brit: pharmacist) pharmacien(ne); (scientist) chimiste m/f

chemistry ['kɛmɪstrɪ] n chimie f

chemist's ['kɛmɪsts], **chemist's shop** n (Brit) pharmacie f

cheque, (US) **check** [tʃɛk] n chèque m; **to pay by ~** payer par chèque

chequebook, (US) **checkbook** ['tʃɛkbuk] n chéquier m, carnet m de chèques

cheque card n (Brit) carte f (d'identité) bancaire

chequered, (US) **checkered** ['tʃɛkəd] adj (fig) varié(e)

cherish ['tʃɛrɪʃ] vt chérir; (hope etc) entretenir

cherry ['tʃɛrɪ] n cerise f; (also: **~ tree**) cerisier m

chess [tʃɛs] n échecs mpl

chessboard ['tʃɛsbɔ:d] n échiquier m

chest [tʃɛst] n poitrine f; (box) coffre m, caisse f; **to get sth off one's ~** (inf) vider son sac

chestnut ['tʃɛsnʌt] n châtaigne f; (also: **~ tree**) châtaignier m; (colour) châtain m ▷ adj (hair) châtain inv; (horse) alezan

chest of drawers n commode f

chew [tʃu:] vt mâcher

chewing gum ['tʃu:ɪŋ-] n chewing-gum m

chic [ʃi:k] adj chic inv, élégant(e)

chick [tʃɪk] n poussin m; (inf) pépée f

chicken ['tʃɪkɪn] n poulet m; (inf: coward) poule mouillée; **chicken out** vi (inf) se dégonfler

chickenpox ['tʃɪkɪnpɔks] n varicelle f

chickpea ['tʃɪkpi:] n pois m chiche

chicory ['tʃɪkərɪ] n chicorée f; (salad) endive f

chief [tʃi:f] n chef m ▷ adj principal(e); **C~ of Staff** (Mil) chef d'État-major

chief executive, (US) **chief executive officer** n directeur(-trice) général(e)

chiefly ['tʃi:flɪ] adv principalement, surtout

chiffon ['ʃɪfɔn] n mousseline f de soie

chilblain ['tʃɪlbleɪn] n engelure f

child (pl **children**) [tʃaɪld, 'tʃɪldrən] n enfant m/f

child abuse n maltraitance f d'enfants; (sexual) abus mpl sexuels sur des enfants

child benefit n (Brit) ≈ allocations familiales

childbirth ['tʃaɪldbə:θ] n accouchement m

childcare ['tʃaɪldkɛəʳ] n (for working parents) garde f des enfants (pour les parents qui travaillent)

childhood ['tʃaɪldhud] n enfance f

childish ['tʃaɪldɪʃ] adj puéril(e), enfantin(e)

childlike ['tʃaɪldlaɪk] adj innocent(e), pur(e)

child minder n (Brit) garde f d'enfants

children ['tʃɪldrən] npl of **child**

Chile ['tʃɪlɪ] n Chili m

chill [tʃɪl] n (of water) froid m; (of air) fraîcheur f; (Med) refroidissement m, coup m de froid ▷ adj froid(e), glacial(e) ▷ vt (person) faire frissonner; refroidir; (Culin) mettre au frais, rafraîchir; **"serve ~ed"** "à servir frais"; **chill out** vi (inf: esp US) se relaxer

chilli, **chili** ['tʃɪlɪ] n piment m (rouge)

chilly ['tʃɪlɪ] adj froid(e), glacé(e); (sensitive to cold) frileux(-euse); **to feel ~** avoir froid

chime [tʃaɪm] n carillon m ▷ vi carillonner, sonner

chimney ['tʃɪmnɪ] n cheminée f

chimney sweep n ramoneur m

chimpanzee [tʃɪmpæn'zi:] n chimpanzé m

chin [tʃɪn] n menton m

China ['tʃaɪnə] n Chine f

china ['tʃaɪnə] n (material) porcelaine f; (crockery) (vaisselle f en) porcelaine

Chinese [tʃaɪ'ni:z] adj chinois(e) ▷ n (pl inv) Chinois(e); (Ling) chinois m

chink [tʃɪŋk] n (opening) fente f, fissure f; (noise) tintement m

chip [tʃɪp] n (gen pl: Culin: Brit) frite f; (: US: also: **potato ~**) chip m; (of wood) copeau m; (of glass, stone) éclat m; (also: **micro~**) puce f; (in gambling) fiche f ▷ vt (cup, plate) ébrécher; **when the ~s are down** (fig) au moment critique; **chip in** vi (inf) mettre son grain de sel

chip shop n (Brit) friterie f; voir article

chiropodist [kɪˈrɔpədɪst] n (Brit) pédicure m/f

chirp [tʃəːp] n pépiement m, gazouillis m; (of crickets) stridulation f ▷ vi pépier, gazouiller; chanter, striduler

chisel [ˈtʃɪzl] n ciseau m

chit [tʃɪt] n mot m, note f

chitchat [ˈtʃɪttʃæt] n bavardage m, papotage m

chivalry [ˈʃɪvəlrɪ] n chevalerie f; esprit m chevaleresque

chives [tʃaɪvz] npl ciboulette f, civette f

chlorine [ˈklɔːriːn] n chlore m

choc-ice [ˈtʃɔkaɪs] n (Brit) esquimau® m

chock-a-block [ˈtʃɔkəˈblɔk], **chock-full** [tʃɔkˈful] adj plein(e) à craquer

chocolate [ˈtʃɔklɪt] n chocolat m

choice [tʃɔɪs] n choix m ▷ adj de choix; **by** or **from ~** par choix; **a wide ~** un grand choix

choir [ˈkwaɪəʳ] n chœur m, chorale f

choirboy [ˈkwaɪəbɔɪ] n jeune choriste m, petit chanteur

choke [tʃəuk] vi étouffer ▷ vt étrangler; étouffer; (block) boucher, obstruer ▷ n (Aut) starter m

cholesterol [kəˈlɛstərɔl] n cholestérol m

choose (pt **chose**, pp **chosen**) [tʃuːz, tʃəuz, ˈtʃəuzn] vt choisir ▷ vi: **to ~ between** choisir entre; **to ~ from** choisir parmi; **to ~ to do** décider de faire, juger bon de faire

choosy [ˈtʃuːzɪ] adj: **to be ~** (faire le) difficile

chop [tʃɔp] vt (wood) couper (à la hache); (Culin: also: **~ up**) couper (fin), émincer, hacher (en morceaux) ▷ n coup m (de hache, du tranchant de la main); (Culin) côtelette f; **to get the ~** (Brit inf: project) tomber à l'eau; (: person: be sacked) se faire renvoyer; **chop down** vt (tree) abattre; **chop off** vt trancher

chopper [ˈtʃɔpəʳ] n (helicopter) hélicoptère m, hélico m

choppy [ˈtʃɔpɪ] adj (sea) un peu agité(e)

chopsticks [ˈtʃɔpstɪks] npl baguettes fpl

chord [kɔːd] n (Mus) accord m

chore [tʃɔːʳ] n travail m de routine; **household ~s** travaux mpl du ménage

chortle [ˈtʃɔːtl] vi glousser

chorus [ˈkɔːrəs] n chœur m; (repeated part of song, also fig) refrain m

chose [tʃəuz] pt of **choose**

chosen [ˈtʃəuzn] pp of **choose**

chowder [ˈtʃaudəʳ] n soupe f de poisson

Christ [kraɪst] n Christ m

christen [ˈkrɪsn] vt baptiser

christening [ˈkrɪsnɪŋ] n baptême m

Christian [ˈkrɪstɪən] adj, n chrétien(ne)

Christianity [krɪstɪˈænɪtɪ] n christianisme m

Christian name n prénom m

Christmas [ˈkrɪsməs] n Noël m or f; **happy** or **merry ~!** joyeux Noël!

Christmas card n carte f de Noël

Christmas carol n chant m de Noël

Christmas Day n le jour de Noël

Christmas Eve n la veille de Noël; la nuit de Noël

Christmas pudding n (esp Brit) Christmas m pudding

Christmas tree n arbre m de Noël

chrome [krəum] n chrome m

chromium [ˈkrəumɪəm] n chrome m; (also: **~ plating**) chromage m

chronic [ˈkrɔnɪk] adj chronique; (fig: liar, smoker) invétéré(e)

chronicle [ˈkrɔnɪkl] n chronique f

chronological [krɔnəˈlɔdʒɪkl] adj chronologique

chrysanthemum [krɪˈsænθəməm] n chrysanthème m

chubby [ˈtʃʌbɪ] adj potelé(e), rondelet(te)

chuck [tʃʌk] vt (inf) lancer, jeter; (Brit: also: **~ up**: job) lâcher; (: person) plaquer; **chuck out** vt (inf: person) flanquer dehors or à la porte; (: rubbish etc) jeter

chuckle [ˈtʃʌkl] vi glousser

chug [tʃʌg] vi faire teuf-teuf; souffler

chum [tʃʌm] n copain/copine

chunk [tʃʌŋk] n gros morceau; (of bread) quignon m

church [tʃəːtʃ] n église f; **the C~ of England** l'Église anglicane

churchyard [ˈtʃəːtʃjɑːd] n cimetière m

churn [tʃəːn] n (for butter) baratte f; (also: **milk ~**) (grand) bidon à lait; **churn out** vt débiter

chute [ʃuːt] n goulotte f; (also: **rubbish ~**) vide-ordures m inv; (Brit: children's slide) toboggan m

chutney [ˈtʃʌtnɪ] n chutney m

CIA n abbr (= Central Intelligence Agency) CIA f

CID n abbr (= Criminal Investigation Department) ≈ P.J. f

cider [ˈsaɪdəʳ] n cidre m

cigar [sɪˈgɑːʳ] n cigare m

cigarette [sɪgəˈrɛt] n cigarette f

cigarette case n étui m à cigarettes

cigarette end n mégot m

cigarette lighter n briquet m

Cinderella [sɪndəˈrɛlə] n Cendrillon

cine-camera [ˈsɪnɪˈkæmərə] n (Brit) caméra f

cinema ['sɪnəmə] n cinéma m

cinnamon ['sɪnəmən] n cannelle f

circle ['sɜːkl] n cercle m; (in cinema) balcon m ▷ vi faire or décrire des cercles ▷ vt (surround) entourer, encercler; (move round) faire le tour de, tourner autour de

circuit ['sɜːkɪt] n circuit m; (lap) tour m

circuitous [sɜː'kjuːɪtəs] adj indirect(e), qui fait un détour

circular ['sɜːkjulər] adj circulaire ▷ n circulaire f; (as advertisement) prospectus m

circulate ['sɜːkjuleɪt] vi circuler ▷ vt faire circuler

circulation [sɜːkju'leɪʃən] n circulation f; (of newspaper) tirage m

circumflex ['sɜːkəmfleks] n (also: ~ **accent**) accent m circonflexe

circumstances ['sɜːkəmstənsɪz] npl circonstances fpl; (financial condition) moyens mpl, situation financière; **in** or **under the ~** dans ces conditions; **under no ~** en aucun cas, sous aucun prétexte

circus ['sɜːkəs] n cirque m; (also: **C~**: in place names) place f

CIS n abbr (= Commonwealth of Independent States) CEI f

cistern ['sɪstən] n réservoir m (d'eau); (in toilet) réservoir de la chasse d'eau

cite [saɪt] vt citer

citizen ['sɪtɪzn] n (Pol) citoyen(ne); (resident): **the ~s of this town** les habitants de cette ville

citizenship ['sɪtɪznʃɪp] n citoyenneté f; (Brit: Scol) ≈ éducation f civique

citrus fruits ['sɪtrəs-] npl agrumes mpl

city ['sɪtɪ] n (grande) ville f; **the C~** la Cité de Londres (centre des affaires)

city centre n centre ville m

city technology college n (Brit) établissement m d'enseignement technologique (situé dans un quartier défavorisé)

civic ['sɪvɪk] adj civique; (authorities) municipal(e)

civic centre n (Brit) centre administratif (municipal)

civil ['sɪvɪl] adj civil(e); (polite) poli(e), civil(e)

civil engineer n ingénieur civil

civilian [sɪ'vɪlɪən] adj, n civil(e)

civilization [sɪvɪlaɪ'zeɪʃən] n civilisation f

civilized ['sɪvɪlaɪzd] adj civilisé(e); (fig) où règnent les bonnes manières, empreint(e) d'une courtoisie de bon ton

civil law n code civil; (study) droit civil

civil rights npl droits mpl civiques

civil servant n fonctionnaire m/f

Civil Service n fonction publique, administration f

civil war n guerre civile

CJD n abbr (= Creutzfeldt-Jakob disease) MCJ f

clad [klæd] adj: ~ **(in)** habillé(e) de, vêtu(e) de

claim [kleɪm] vt (rights etc) revendiquer; (compensation) réclamer; (assert) déclarer,

prétendre ▷ vi (for insurance) faire une déclaration de sinistre ▷ n revendication f; prétention f; (right) droit m; (for expenses) note f de frais; **(insurance)** ~ demande f d'indemnisation, déclaration f de sinistre; **to put in a ~ for** (pay rise etc) demander

claimant ['kleɪmənt] n (Admin, Law) requérant(e)

claim form n (gen) formulaire m de demande

clairvoyant [kleə'vɔɪənt] n voyant(e), extra-lucide m/f

clam [klæm] n palourde f; **clam up** vi (inf) la boucler

clamber ['klæmbər] vi grimper, se hisser

clammy ['klæmɪ] adj humide et froid(e) (au toucher), moite

clamour, (US) **clamor** ['klæmər] n (noise) clameurs fpl; (protest) protestations bruyantes ▷ vi: **to ~ for sth** réclamer qch à grands cris

clamp [klæmp] n crampon m; (on workbench) valet m; (on car) sabot m de Denver ▷ vt attacher; (car) mettre un sabot à; **clamp down on** vt fus sévir contre, prendre des mesures draconiennes à l'égard de

clan [klæn] n clan m

clang [klæŋ] n bruit m or fracas m métallique ▷ vi émettre un bruit or fracas métallique

clap [klæp] vi applaudir ▷ vt: **to ~ (one's hands)** battre des mains ▷ n claquement m; tape f; **a ~ of thunder** un coup de tonnerre

clapping ['klæpɪŋ] n applaudissements mpl

claret ['klærət] n (vin m de) bordeaux m (rouge)

clarify ['klærɪfaɪ] vt clarifier

clarinet [klærɪ'net] n clarinette f

clarity ['klærɪtɪ] n clarté f

clash [klæʃ] n (sound) choc m, fracas m; (with police) affrontement m; (fig) conflit m ▷ vi se heurter; être or entrer en conflit; (colours) jurer; (dates, events) tomber en même temps

clasp [klɑːsp] n (of necklace, bag) fermoir m ▷ vt serrer, étreindre

class [klɑːs] n (gen) classe f; (group, category) catégorie f ▷ vt classer, classifier

classic ['klæsɪk] adj classique ▷ n (author, work) classique m; (race etc) classique f

classical ['klæsɪkl] adj classique

classification [klæsɪfɪ'keɪʃən] n classification f

classified ['klæsɪfaɪd] adj (information) secret(-ète); ~ **ads** petites annonces

classify ['klæsɪfaɪ] vt classifier, classer

classmate ['klɑːsmeɪt] n camarade m/f de classe

classroom ['klɑːsrum] n (salle f de) classe f

classroom assistant n assistant(-e) d'éducation

classy ['klɑːsɪ] (inf) adj classe (inf)

clatter ['klætər] n cliquetis m ▷ vi cliqueter

clause [klɔːz] n clause f; (Ling) proposition f

claustrophobic [klɔ:strə'fəubɪk] *adj* (*person*) claustrophobe; (*place*) où l'on se sent claustrophobe

claw [klɔ:] *n* griffe *f*; (*of bird of prey*) serre *f*; (*of lobster*) pince *f* ▷ *vt* griffer; déchirer

clay [kleɪ] *n* argile *f*

clean [kli:n] *adj* propre; (*clear, smooth*) net(te); (*record, reputation*) sans tache; (*joke, story*) correct(e) ▷ *vt* nettoyer ▷ *adv*: **he ~ forgot** il a complètement oublié; **to come ~** (*inf: admit guilt*) se mettre à table; **to ~ one's teeth** se laver les dents; **~ driving licence** *or* (*US*) **record** permis où n'est portée aucune indication de contravention; **clean off** *vt* enlever; **clean out** *vt* nettoyer (à fond); **clean up** *vt* nettoyer; (*fig*) remettre de l'ordre dans ▷ *vi* (*fig: make profit*): **to ~ up on** faire son beurre avec

clean-cut [kli:n'kʌt] *adj* (*man*) soigné; (*situation etc*) bien délimité(e), net(te), clair(e)

cleaner ['kli:nər] *n* (*person*) nettoyeur(-euse), femme *f* de ménage; (*also: dry ~*) teinturier(-ière); (*product*) détachant *m*

cleaner's ['kli:nəz] *n* (*also: dry ~*) teinturier *m*

cleaning ['kli:nɪŋ] *n* nettoyage *m*

cleanliness ['klɛnlɪnɪs] *n* propreté *f*

cleanse [klɛnz] *vt* nettoyer; purifier

cleanser ['klɛnzər] *n* détergent *m*; (*for face*) démaquillant *m*

clean-shaven ['kli:n'ʃeɪvn] *adj* rasé(e) de près

cleansing department ['klɛnzɪŋ-] *n* (*Brit*) service *m* de voirie

clear [klɪər] *adj* clair(e); (*glass, plastic*) transparent(e); (*road, way*) libre, dégagé(e); (*profit, majority*) net(te); (*conscience*) tranquille; (*skin*) frais/fraîche; (*sky*) dégagé(e) ▷ *vt* (*road*) dégager, déblayer; (*table*) débarrasser; (*room etc: of people*) faire évacuer; (*woodland*) défricher; (*cheque*) compenser; (*Comm: goods*) liquider; (*Law: suspect*) innocenter; (*obstacle*) franchir *or* sauter sans heurter ▷ *vi* (*weather*) s'éclaircir; (*fog*) se dissiper ▷ *adv*: **~ of** à distance de, à l'écart de ▷ *n*: **to be in the ~** (*out of debt*) être dégagé(e) de toute dette; (*out of suspicion*) être lavé(e) de tout soupçon; (*out of danger*) être hors de danger; **to ~ the table** débarrasser la table, desservir; **to ~ one's throat** s'éclaircir la gorge; **to ~ a profit** faire un bénéfice net; **to make o.s. ~** se faire bien comprendre; **to make it ~ to sb that ...** bien faire comprendre à qn que ...; **I have a ~ day tomorrow** (*Brit*) je n'ai rien de prévu demain; **to keep ~ of sb/sth** éviter qn/qch; **clear away** *vt* (*things, clothes etc*) enlever, retirer; **to ~ away the dishes** débarrasser la table; **clear off** *vi* (*inf: leave*) dégager; **clear up** *vi* s'éclaircir, se dissiper ▷ *vt* ranger, mettre en ordre; (*mystery*) éclaircir, résoudre

clearance ['klɪərəns] *n* (*removal*) déblayage *m*; (*free space*) dégagement *m*; (*permission*) autorisation *f*

clear-cut ['klɪə'kʌt] *adj* précis(e), nettement défini(e)

clearing ['klɪərɪŋ] *n* (*in forest*) clairière *f*; (*Brit Banking*) compensation *f*, clearing *m*

clearing bank *n* (*Brit*) banque *f* qui appartient à une chambre de compensation

clearly ['klɪəlɪ] *adv* clairement; (*obviously*) de toute évidence

clearway ['klɪəweɪ] *n* (*Brit*) route *f* à stationnement interdit

clef [klɛf] *n* (*Mus*) clé *f*

cleft [klɛft] *n* (*in rock*) crevasse *f*, fissure *f*

clementine ['klɛməntaɪn] *n* clémentine *f*

clench [klɛntʃ] *vt* serrer

clergy ['klə:dʒɪ] *n* clergé *m*

clergyman ['klə:dʒɪmən] *irreg n* ecclésiastique *m*

clerical ['klɛrɪkl] *adj* de bureau, d'employé de bureau; (*Rel*) clérical(e), du clergé

clerk [klɑ:k, (*US*) klə:rk] *n* (*Brit*) employé(e) de bureau; (*US: salesman/woman*) vendeur(-euse); **C~ of Court** (*Law*) greffier *m* (du tribunal)

clever ['klɛvər] *adj* (*intelligent*) intelligent(e); (*skilful*) habile, adroit(e); (*device, arrangement*) ingénieux(-euse), astucieux(-euse)

cliché ['kli:ʃeɪ] *n* cliché *m*

click [klɪk] *vi* faire un bruit sec *or* un déclic; (*Comput*) cliquer ▷ *vt*: **to ~ one's tongue** faire claquer sa langue; **to ~ one's heels** claquer des talons; **to ~ on an icon** cliquer sur une icône

client ['klaɪənt] *n* client(e)

cliff [klɪf] *n* falaise *f*

climate ['klaɪmɪt] *n* climat *m*

climate change *n* changement *m* climatique

climax ['klaɪmæks] *n* apogée *m*, point culminant; (*sexual*) orgasme *m*

climb [klaɪm] *vi* grimper, monter; (*plane*) prendre de l'altitude ▷ *vt* (*stairs*) monter; (*mountain*) escalader; (*tree*) grimper à ▷ *n* montée *f*, escalade *f*; **to ~ over a wall** passer par dessus un mur; **climb down** *vi* (re)descendre; (*Brit fig*) rabattre de ses prétentions

climb-down ['klaɪmdaun] *n* (*Brit*) reculade *f*

climber ['klaɪmər] *n* (*also: rock ~*) grimpeur(-euse), varappeur(-euse); (*plant*) plante grimpante

climbing ['klaɪmɪŋ] *n* (*also: rock ~*) escalade *f*, varappe *f*

clinch [klɪntʃ] *vt* (*deal*) conclure, sceller

cling (*pt, pp* **clung**) [klɪŋ, klʌŋ] *vi*: **to ~ (to)** se cramponner (à), s'accrocher (à); (*clothes*) coller (à)

Clingfilm® ['klɪŋfɪlm] *n* film *m* alimentaire

clinic ['klɪnɪk] *n* clinique *f*; centre médical; (*session: Med*) consultation(s) *f(pl)*, séance(s) *f(pl)*; (*Sport*) séance(s) de perfectionnement

clinical ['klɪnɪkl] *adj* clinique; (*fig*) froid(e)

clink [klɪŋk] *vi* tinter, cliqueter

clip [klɪp] n (for hair) barrette f; (also: **paper ~**) trombone m; (Brit: also: **bulldog ~**) pince f de bureau; (holding hose etc) collier m or bague f (métallique) de serrage; (TV, Cine) clip m ▷ vt (also: **~ together**: papers) attacher; (hair, nails) couper; (hedge) tailler

clippers ['klɪpəz] npl tondeuse f; (also: **nail ~**) coupe-ongles m inv

clipping ['klɪpɪŋ] n (from newspaper) coupure f de journal

cloak [kləuk] n grande cape ▷ vt (fig) masquer, cacher

cloakroom ['kləukrum] n (for coats etc) vestiaire m; (Brit: W.C.) toilettes fpl

clock [klɒk] n (large) horloge f; (small) pendule f; **round the ~** (work etc) vingt-quatre heures sur vingt-quatre; **to sleep round the ~** or **the ~ round** faire le tour du cadran; **30,000 on the ~** (Brit Aut) 30 000 milles au compteur; **to work against the ~** faire la course contre la montre; **clock in** or **on** (Brit) vi (with card) pointer (en arrivant); (start work) commencer à travailler; **clock off** or **out** (Brit) vi (with card) pointer (en partant); (leave work) quitter le travail; **clock up** vt (miles, hours etc) faire

clockwise ['klɒkwaɪz] adv dans le sens des aiguilles d'une montre

clockwork ['klɒkwə:k] n rouages mpl, mécanisme m; (of clock) mouvement m (d'horlogerie) ▷ adj (toy, train) mécanique

clog [klɒg] n sabot m ▷ vt boucher, encrasser ▷ vi (also: **~ up**) se boucher, s'encrasser

cloister ['klɔɪstə^r] n cloître m

clone [kləun] n clone m ▷ vt cloner

close¹ [kləus] adj (near): **~ (to)** près (de), proche (de); (writing, texture) serré(e); (contact, link, watch) étroit(e); (examination) attentif(-ive), minutieux(-euse); (contest) très serré(e); (weather) lourd(e), étouffant(e); (room) mal aéré(e) ▷ adv près, à proximité; **~ to** prep près de; **~ by, ~ at hand** adv tout près; **how ~ is Edinburgh to Glasgow?** combien de kilomètres y-a-t-il entre Édimbourg et Glasgow?; **a ~ friend** un ami intime; **to have a ~ shave** (fig) l'échapper belle; **at ~ quarters** tout près, à côté

close² [kləuz] vt fermer; (bargain, deal) conclure ▷ vi (shop etc) fermer; (lid, door etc) se fermer; (end) se terminer, se conclure ▷ n (end) conclusion f; **to bring sth to a ~** mettre fin à qch; **what time do you ~?** à quelle heure fermez-vous?; **close down** vt, vi fermer (définitivement); **close in** vi (hunters) approcher; (night, fog) tomber; **the days are closing in** les jours raccourcissent; **to ~ in on sb** cerner qn; **close off** vt (area) boucler

closed [kləuzd] adj (shop etc) fermé(e); (road) fermé à la circulation

closed shop n organisation f qui n'admet que des travailleurs syndiqués

close-knit ['kləus'nɪt] adj (family, community) très uni(e)

closely ['kləuslɪ] adv (examine, watch) de près; **we are ~ related** nous sommes proches parents; **a ~ guarded secret** un secret bien gardé

closet ['klɒzɪt] n (cupboard) placard m, réduit m

close-up ['kləusʌp] n gros plan

closing time n heure f de fermeture

closure ['kləuʒə^r] n fermeture f

clot [klɒt] n (of blood, milk) caillot m; (inf: person) ballot m ▷ vi (blood) former des caillots; (: external bleeding) se coaguler

cloth [klɒθ] n (material) tissu m, étoffe f; (Brit: also: **tea ~**) torchon m; lavette f; (also: **table~**) nappe f

clothe [kləuð] vt habiller, vêtir

clothes [kləuðz] npl vêtements mpl, habits mpl; **to put one's ~ on** s'habiller; **to take one's ~ off** enlever ses vêtements

clothes brush n brosse f à habits

clothes line n corde f (à linge)

clothes peg, (US) **clothes pin** n pince f à linge

clothing ['kləuðɪŋ] n = **clothes**

cloud [klaud] n nuage m ▷ vt (liquid) troubler; **to ~ the issue** brouiller les cartes; **every ~ has a silver lining** (proverb) à quelque chose malheur est bon (proverbe); **cloud over** vi se couvrir; (fig) s'assombrir

cloudburst ['klaudbə:st] n violente averse

cloudy ['klaudɪ] adj nuageux(-euse), couvert(e); (liquid) trouble

clout [klaut] n (blow) taloche f; (fig) pouvoir m ▷ vt flanquer une taloche à

clove [kləuv] n clou m de girofle; **a ~ of garlic** une gousse d'ail

clover ['kləuvə^r] n trèfle m

clown [klaun] n clown m ▷ vi (also: **~ about, ~ around**) faire le clown

cloying ['klɔɪɪŋ] adj (taste, smell) écœurant(e)

club [klʌb] n (society) club m; (weapon) massue f, matraque f; (also: **golf ~**) club ▷ vt matraquer ▷ vi: **to ~ together** s'associer; **clubs** npl (Cards) trèfle m

club class n (Aviat) classe f club

clubhouse ['klʌbhaus] n pavillon m

cluck [klʌk] vi glousser

clue [klu:] n indice m; (in crosswords) définition f; **I haven't a ~** je n'en ai pas la moindre idée

clump [klʌmp] n: **~ of trees** bouquet m d'arbres

clumsy ['klʌmzɪ] adj (person) gauche, maladroit(e); (object) malcommode, peu maniable

clung [klʌŋ] pt, pp of **cling**

cluster ['klʌstə^r] n (petit) groupe m; (of flowers) grappe f ▷ vi se rassembler

clutch [klʌtʃ] n (Aut) embrayage m; (grasp): **~es** étreinte f, prise f ▷ vt (grasp) agripper; (hold tightly) serrer fort; (hold on to) se cramponner à

clutter ['klʌtə^r] vt (also: **~ up**) encombrer ▷ n désordre m, fouillis m

cm *abbr* (= *centimetre*) cm

CND *n abbr* = **Campaign for Nuclear Disarmament**

Co. *abbr* = **company, county**

c/o *abbr* (= *care of*) c/o, aux bons soins de

coach [kəutʃ] *n* (*bus*) autocar *m*; (*horse-drawn*) diligence *f*; (*of train*) voiture *f*, wagon *m*; (*Sport: trainer*) entraîneur(-euse); (*school: tutor*) répétiteur(-trice) ▷ *vt* (*Sport*) entraîner; (*student*) donner des leçons particulières à

coach station (*Brit*) *n* gare routière

coach trip *n* excursion *f* en car

coal [kəul] *n* charbon *m*

coal face *n* front *m* de taille

coalfield [ˈkəulfiːld] *n* bassin houiller

coalition [kəuəˈlɪʃən] *n* coalition *f*

coalman [ˈkəulmən] *irreg n* charbonnier *m*, marchand *m* de charbon

coal mine *n* mine *f* de charbon

coarse [kɔːs] *adj* grossier(-ère), rude; (*vulgar*) vulgaire

coast [kəust] *n* côte *f* ▷ *vi* (*car, cycle*) descendre en roue libre

coastal [ˈkəustl] *adj* côtier(-ère)

coastguard [ˈkəustgɑːd] *n* garde-côte *m*

coastline [ˈkəustlaɪn] *n* côte *f*, littoral *m*

coat [kəut] *n* manteau *m*; (*of animal*) pelage *m*, poil *m*; (*of paint*) couche *f* ▷ *vt* couvrir, enduire; **~ of arms** blason *m*, armoiries *fpl*

coat hanger *n* cintre *m*

coating [ˈkəutɪŋ] *n* couche *f*, enduit *m*

coax [kəuks] *vt* persuader par des cajoleries

cob [kɔb] *n* see **corn**

cobbled [ˈkɔbld] *adj* pavé(e)

cobbler [ˈkɔblə] *n* cordonnier *m*

cobbles, cobblestones [ˈkɔblz, ˈkɔblstəunz] *npl* pavés (ronds)

cobweb [ˈkɔbwɛb] *n* toile *f* d'araignée

cocaine [kəˈkeɪn] *n* cocaïne *f*

cock [kɔk] *n* (*rooster*) coq *m*; (*male bird*) mâle *m* ▷ *vt* (*gun*) armer; **to ~ one's ears** (*fig*) dresser l'oreille

cockerel [ˈkɔkərl] *n* jeune coq *m*

cockle [ˈkɔkl] *n* coque *f*

cockney [ˈkɔknɪ] *n* cockney *m/f* (*habitant des quartiers populaires de l'East End de Londres*), ≈ faubourien(ne)

cockpit [ˈkɔkpɪt] *n* (*in aircraft*) poste *m* de pilotage, cockpit *m*

cockroach [ˈkɔkrəutʃ] *n* cafard *m*, cancrelat *m*

cocktail [ˈkɔkteɪl] *n* cocktail *m*; **prawn ~**, (*US*) **shrimp ~** cocktail de crevettes

cocktail cabinet *n* (*meuble-*)bar *m*

cocktail party *n* cocktail *m*

cocoa [ˈkəukəu] *n* cacao *m*

coconut [ˈkəukənʌt] *n* noix *f* de coco

C.O.D. *abbr* = **cash on delivery**; (*US*) = **collect on delivery**

cod [kɔd] *n* morue fraîche, cabillaud *m*

code [kəud] *n* code *m*; (*Tel: area code*) indicatif *m*; **~ of behaviour** règles *fpl* de conduite; **~ of practice** déontologie *f*

cod-liver oil [ˈkɔdlɪvər-] *n* huile *f* de foie de morue

coeducational [ˈkəuɛdjuˈkeɪʃənl] *adj* mixte

coercion [kəuˈəːʃən] *n* contrainte *f*

coffee [ˈkɔfɪ] *n* café *m*; **white ~**, (*US*) **~ with cream** (café-)crème *m*

coffee bar *n* (*Brit*) café *m*

coffee bean *n* grain *m* de café

coffee break *n* pause-café *f*

coffee maker *n* cafetière *f*

coffeepot [ˈkɔfɪpɔt] *n* cafetière *f*

coffee shop *n* café *m*

coffee table *n* (petite) table basse

coffin [ˈkɔfɪn] *n* cercueil *m*

cog [kɔg] *n* (*wheel*) roue dentée; (*tooth*) dent *f* (d'engrenage)

cogent [ˈkəudʒənt] *adj* puissant(e), convaincant(e)

cognac [ˈkɔnjæk] *n* cognac *m*

coherent [kəuˈhɪərənt] *adj* cohérent(e)

coil [kɔɪl] *n* rouleau *m*, bobine *f*; (*one loop*) anneau *m*, spire *f*; (*of smoke*) volute *f*; (*contraceptive*) stérilet *m* ▷ *vt* enrouler

coin [kɔɪn] *n* pièce *f* (de monnaie) ▷ *vt* (*word*) inventer

coinage [ˈkɔɪnɪdʒ] *n* monnaie *f*, système *m* monétaire

coinbox [ˈkɔɪnbɔks] *n* (*Brit*) cabine *f* téléphonique

coincide [kəuɪnˈsaɪd] *vi* coïncider

coincidence [kəuˈɪnsɪdəns] *n* coïncidence *f*

Coke® [kəuk] *n* coca *m*

coke [kəuk] *n* (*coal*) coke *m*

colander [ˈkɔləndə] *n* passoire *f* (à légumes)

cold [kəuld] *adj* froid(e) ▷ *n* froid *m*; (*Med*) rhume *m*; **it's ~** il fait froid; **to be ~** (*person*) avoir froid; **to catch ~** prendre *or* attraper froid; **to catch a ~** s'enrhumer, attraper un rhume; **in ~ blood** de sang-froid; **to have ~ feet** avoir froid aux pieds; (*fig*) avoir la frousse *or* la trouille; **to give sb the ~ shoulder** battre froid à qn

cold sore *n* bouton *m* de fièvre

coleslaw [ˈkəulslɔː] *n* sorte de salade de chou cru

colic [ˈkɔlɪk] *n* colique(s) *f(pl)*

collaborate [kəˈlæbəreɪt] *vi* collaborer

collapse [kəˈlæps] *vi* s'effondrer, s'écrouler; (*Med*) avoir un malaise ▷ *n* effondrement *m*, écroulement *m*; (*of government*) chute *f*

collapsible [kəˈlæpsəbl] *adj* pliant(e), télescopique

collar [ˈkɔlə] *n* (*of coat, shirt*) col *m*; (*for dog*) collier *m*; (*Tech*) collier, bague *f* ▷ *vt* (*inf: person*) pincer

collarbone [ˈkɔləbəun] *n* clavicule *f*

collateral [kɔˈlætərl] *n* nantissement *m*

colleague [ˈkɔliːg] *n* collègue *m/f*

collect [kəˈlɛkt] *vt* rassembler; (*pick up*) ramasser; (*as a hobby*) collectionner; (*Brit: call for*) (passer) prendre; (*mail*) faire la levée de, ramasser; (*money owed*) encaisser; (*donations, subscriptions*) recueillir ▷ *vi* (*people*) se rassembler; (*dust, dirt*) s'amasser; **to ~ one's thoughts** réfléchir, réunir ses idées; **~ on delivery (COD)** (*US Comm*) payable *or* paiement *or* paiement à la livraison; **to call ~** (*US Tel*) téléphoner en PCV

collection [kə'lɛkʃən] *n* collection *f*; (*of mail*) levée *f*; (*for money*) collecte *f*, quête *f*

collective [kə'lɛktɪv] *adj* collectif(-ive) ▷ *n* collectif *m*

collector [kə'lɛktə'] *n* collectionneur *m*; (*of taxes*) percepteur *m*; (*of rent, cash*) encaisseur *m*; **~'s item** *or* **piece** pièce *f* de collection

college ['kɔlɪdʒ] *n* collège *m*; (*of technology, agriculture etc*) institut *m*; **to go to ~** faire des études supérieures; **~ of education** ≈ école normale

collide [kə'laɪd] *vi*: **to ~ (with)** entrer en collision (avec)

colliery ['kɔlɪərɪ] *n* (*Brit*) mine *f* de charbon, houillère *f*

collision [kə'lɪʒən] *n* collision *f*, heurt *m*; **to be on a ~ course** aller droit à la collision; (*fig*) aller vers l'affrontement

colloquial [kə'ləʊkwɪəl] *adj* familier(-ère)

cologne [kə'ləʊn] *n* (*also*: **eau de ~**) eau *f* de cologne

colon ['kəʊlən] *n* (*sign*) deux-points *mpl*; (*Med*) côlon *m*

colonel ['kə:nl] *n* colonel *m*

colonial [kə'ləʊnɪəl] *adj* colonial(e)

colony ['kɔlənɪ] *n* colonie *f*

colour, (*US*) **color** ['kʌlə'] *n* couleur *f* ▷ *vt* colorer; (*dye*) teindre; (*paint*) peindre; (*with crayons*) colorier; (*news*) fausser, exagérer ▷ *vi* (*blush*) rougir ▷ *cpd* (*film, photograph, television*) en couleur; **colours** *npl* (*of party, club*) couleurs *fpl*; **I'd like a different ~** je le voudrais dans un autre coloris; **colour in** *vt* colorier

colour bar, (*US*) **color bar** *n* discrimination raciale (*dans un établissement etc*)

colour-blind, (*US*) **color-blind** ['kʌləblaɪnd] *adj* daltonien(ne)

coloured, (*US*) **colored** ['kʌləd] *adj* coloré(e); (*photo*) en couleur

colour film, (*US*) **color film** *n* (*for camera*) pellicule *f* (en) couleur

colourful, (*US*) **colorful** ['kʌləful] *adj* coloré(e), vif/vive; (*personality*) pittoresque, haut(e) en couleurs

colouring, (*US*) **coloring** ['kʌlərɪŋ] *n* colorant *m*; (*complexion*) teint *m*

colour scheme, (*US*) **color scheme** *n* combinaison *f* de(s) couleur(s)

colour television, (*US*) **color television** *n* télévision *f* (en) couleur

colt [kəʊlt] *n* poulain *m*

column ['kɔləm] *n* colonne *f*; (*fashion column, sports column etc*) rubrique *f*; **the editorial ~** l'éditorial *m*

columnist ['kɔləmnɪst] *n* rédacteur(-trice) d'une rubrique

coma ['kəʊmə] *n* coma *m*

comb [kəʊm] *n* peigne *m* ▷ *vt* (*hair*) peigner; (*area*) ratisser, passer au peigne fin

combat ['kɔmbæt] *n* combat *m* ▷ *vt* combattre, lutter contre

combination [kɔmbɪ'neɪʃən] *n* (*gen*) combinaison *f*

combine [kəm'baɪn] *vt* combiner ▷ *vi* s'associer; (*Chem*) se combiner ▷ *n* ['kɔmbaɪn] association *f*; (*Econ*) trust *m*; (*also*: **~ harvester**) moissonneuse-batteuse (-lieuse) *f*; **to ~ sth with sth** (*one quality with another*) joindre *ou* allier qch à qch; **a ~d effort** un effort conjugué

combine harvester *n* moissonneuse-batteuse(-lieuse) *f*

KEYWORD

come (*pt* **came**, *pp* **come**) [kʌm, keɪm] *vi* **1** (*movement towards*) venir; **to come running** arriver en courant; **he's come here to work** il est venu ici pour travailler; **come with me** suivez-moi; **to come into sight** *or* **view** apparaître

2 (*arrive*) arriver; **to come home** rentrer (chez soi *or* à la maison); **we've just come from Paris** nous arrivons de Paris; **coming!** j'arrive!

3 (*reach*): **to come to** (*decision etc*) parvenir à, arriver à; **the bill came to £40** la note s'est élevée à 40 livres; **if it comes to it** s'il le faut, dans le pire des cas

4 (*occur*): **an idea came to me** il m'est venu une idée; **what might come of it** ce qui pourrait en résulter, ce qui pourrait advenir *or* se produire

5 (*be, become*): **to come loose/undone** se défaire/desserrer; **I've come to like him** j'ai fini par bien l'aimer

6 (*inf: sexually*) jouir

come about *vi* se produire, arriver

come across *vt fus* rencontrer par hasard, tomber sur

▷ *vi*: **to come across well/badly** faire une bonne/mauvaise impression

come along *vi* (*Brit: pupil, work*) faire des progrès, avancer; **come along!** viens!; allons!, allez!

come apart *vi* s'en aller en morceaux; se détacher

come away *vi* partir, s'en aller; (*become detached*) se détacher

come back *vi* revenir; (*reply*): **can I come back to you on that one?** est-ce qu'on peut revenir là-dessus plus tard?

come by *vt fus* (*acquire*) obtenir, se procurer

come down *vi* descendre; (*prices*) baisser; (*buildings*) s'écrouler; (*: be demolished*) être démoli(e)

come forward *vi* s'avancer; (*make o.s. known*) se présenter, s'annoncer

come from vt fus (source) venir de; (place) venir de, être originaire de

come in vi entrer; (train) arriver; (fashion) entrer en vogue; (on deal etc) participer

come in for vt fus (criticism etc) être l'objet de

come into vt fus (money) hériter de

come off vi (button) se détacher; (attempt) réussir

come on vi (lights, electricity) s'allumer; (central heating) se mettre en marche; (pupil, work, project) faire des progrès, avancer; **come on!** viens!; allons!, allez!

come out vi sortir; (sun) se montrer; (book) paraître; (stain) s'enlever; (strike) cesser le travail, se mettre en grève

come over vt fus: **I don't know what's come over him!** je ne sais pas ce qui lui a pris!

come round vi (after faint, operation) revenir à soi, reprendre connaissance

come through vi (survive) s'en sortir; (telephone call): **the call came through** l'appel est bien parvenu

come to vi revenir à soi
▷ vt (add up to: amount): **how much does it come to?** ça fait combien?

come under vt fus (heading) se trouver sous; (influence) subir

come up vi monter; (sun) se lever; (problem) se poser; (event) survenir; (in conversation) être soulevé

come up against vt fus (resistance, difficulties) rencontrer

come upon vt fus tomber sur

come up to vt fus arriver à; **the film didn't come up to our expectations** le film nous a déçu

come up with vt fus (money) fournir; **he came up with an idea** il a eu une idée, il a proposé quelque chose

comeback ['kʌmbæk] n (Theat) rentrée f; (reaction) réaction f; (response) réponse f

comedian [kə'miːdɪən] n (comic) comique m; (Theat) comédien m

comedy ['kɒmɪdɪ] n comédie f; (humour) comique m

comet ['kɒmɪt] n comète f

comeuppance [kʌm'ʌpəns] n: **to get one's ~** recevoir ce qu'on mérite

comfort ['kʌmfət] n confort m, bien-être m; (solace) consolation f, réconfort m ▷ vt consoler, réconforter

comfortable ['kʌmfətəbl] adj confortable; (person) à l'aise; (financially) aisé(e); (patient) dont l'état est stationnaire; **I don't feel very ~ about it** cela m'inquiète un peu

comfortably ['kʌmfətəblɪ] adv (sit) confortablement; (live) à l'aise

comfort station n (US) toilettes fpl

comic ['kɒmɪk] adj (also: **~al**) comique ▷ n (person) comique m; (Brit: magazine: for children)

comic book (US) n (for children) magazine m de bandes dessinées or de BD; (: for adults) illustré m

comic strip n bande dessinée

coming ['kʌmɪŋ] n arrivée f ▷ adj (next) prochain(e); (future) à venir; **in the ~ weeks** dans les prochaines semaines

comma ['kɒmə] n virgule f

command [kə'mɑːnd] n ordre m, commandement m; (Mil: authority) commandement m; (mastery) maîtrise f; (Comput) commande f ▷ vt (troops) commander; (be able to get) (pouvoir) disposer de, avoir à sa disposition; (deserve) avoir droit à; **to ~ sb to do** donner l'ordre or commander à qn de faire; **to have/take ~ of** avoir/prendre le commandement de; **to have at one's ~** (money, resources etc) disposer de

commandeer [kɒmən'dɪər] vt réquisitionner (par la force)

commander [kə'mɑːndər] n chef m; (Mil) commandant m

commando [kə'mɑːndəu] n commando m; membre m d'un commando

commemorate [kə'mɛməreɪt] vt commémorer

commence [kə'mɛns] vt, vi commencer

commend [kə'mɛnd] vt louer; (recommend) recommander

commensurate [kə'mɛnʃərɪt] adj: **~ with/to** en rapport avec/selon

comment ['kɒmɛnt] n commentaire m ▷ vi faire des remarques or commentaires; **to ~ on** faire des remarques sur; **to ~ that** faire remarquer que; **"no ~"** "je n'ai rien à déclarer"

commentary ['kɒməntərɪ] n commentaire m; (Sport) reportage m (en direct)

commentator ['kɒmənteɪtər] n commentateur m; (Sport) reporter m

commerce ['kɒməːs] n commerce m

commercial [kə'məːʃəl] adj commercial(e) ▷ n (Radio, TV) annonce f publicitaire, spot m (publicitaire)

commercial break n (Radio, TV) spot m (publicitaire)

commiserate [kə'mɪzəreɪt] vi: **to ~ with sb** témoigner de la sympathie pour qn

commission [kə'mɪʃən] n (committee, fee) commission f; (order for work of art etc) commande f ▷ vt (Mil) nommer (à un commandement); (work of art) commander, charger un artiste de l'exécution de; **out of ~** (Naut) hors de service; (machine) hors service; **I get 10% ~** je reçois une commission de 10%; **~ of inquiry** (Brit) commission d'enquête

commissionaire [kəmɪʃə'nɛər] n (Brit: at shop, cinema etc) portier m (en uniforme)

commissioner [kə'mɪʃənər] n membre m d'une commission; (Police) préfet m (de police)

commit [kə'mɪt] vt (act) commettre; (resources) consacrer; (to sb's care) confier (à); **to ~ o.s. (to do)** s'engager (à faire); **to ~ suicide** se suicider; **to ~ to writing** coucher par écrit; **to ~ sb for trial** traduire qn en justice

commitment [kə'mɪtmənt] n engagement m; (obligation) responsabilité(s) (fpl)

committee [kə'mɪtɪ] n comité m; commission f; **to be on a ~** siéger dans un comité or une commission

commodity [kə'mɔdɪtɪ] n produit m, marchandise f, article m; (food) denrée f

common ['kɔmən] adj (gen) commun(e); (usual) courant(e) ▷ n terrain communal; **in ~** en commun; **in ~ use** d'un usage courant; **it's ~ knowledge that** il est bien connu or notoire que; **for the ~ good** pour le bien de tous, dans l'intérêt général

commoner ['kɔmənər] n roturier(-ière)

common law n droit coutumier

commonly ['kɔmənlɪ] adv communément, généralement; couramment

Common Market n Marché commun

commonplace ['kɔmənpleɪs] adj banal(e), ordinaire

common room n salle commune; (Scol) salle des professeurs

Commons ['kɔmənz] npl (Brit Pol): **the (House of) ~** la chambre des Communes

common sense n bon sens

Commonwealth ['kɔmənwelθ] n: **the ~** le Commonwealth; voir article

commotion [kə'məʊʃən] n désordre m, tumulte m

communal ['kɔmju:nl] adj (life) communautaire; (for common use) commun(e)

commune ['kɔmju:n] n (group) communauté f ▷ vi [kə'mju:n]: **to ~ with** (nature) converser intimement avec; communier avec

communicate [kə'mju:nɪkeɪt] vt communiquer, transmettre ▷ vi: **to ~ (with)** communiquer (avec)

communication [kəmju:nɪ'keɪʃən] n communication f

communication cord n (Brit) sonnette f d'alarme

communion [kə'mju:nɪən] n (also: **Holy C~**) communion f

communism ['kɔmjunɪzəm] n communisme m

communist ['kɔmjunɪst] adj, n communiste m/f

community [kə'mju:nɪtɪ] n communauté f

community centre, (US) **community center** n foyer socio-éducatif, centre m de loisirs

community chest n (US) fonds commun

community service n ≈ travail m d'intérêt général, TIG m

commutation ticket [kɔmju'teɪʃən-] n (US) carte f d'abonnement

commute [kə'mju:t] vi faire le trajet journalier (de son domicile à un lieu de travail assez éloigné) ▷ vt (Law) commuer; (Math: terms etc) opérer la commutation de

commuter [kə'mju:tər] n banlieusard(e) (qui fait un trajet journalier pour se rendre à son travail)

compact adj [kəm'pækt] compact(e) ▷ n ['kɔmpækt] contrat m, entente f; (also: **powder ~**) poudrier m

compact disc n disque compact

compact disc player n lecteur m de disques compacts

companion [kəm'pænjən] n compagnon/compagne

companionship [kəm'pænjənʃɪp] n camaraderie f

company ['kʌmpənɪ] n (also Comm, Mil, Theat) compagnie f; **he's good ~** il est d'une compagnie agréable; **we have ~** nous avons de la visite; **to keep sb ~** tenir compagnie à qn; **to part ~ with** se séparer de; **Smith and C~** Smith et Compagnie

company car n voiture f de fonction

company director n administrateur(-trice)

company secretary n (Brit Comm) secrétaire général (d'une société)

comparable ['kɔmpərəbl] adj comparable

comparative [kəm'pærətɪv] adj (study) comparatif(-ive); (relative) relatif(-ive)

comparatively [kəm'pærətɪvlɪ] adv (relatively) relativement

compare [kəm'peər] vt: **to ~ sth/sb with or to** comparer qch/qn avec or à ▷ vi: **to ~ (with)** se comparer (à); être comparable (à); **how do the prices ~?** comment sont les prix?, est-ce que les prix sont comparables?; **~d with or to** par rapport à

comparison [kəm'pærɪsn] n comparaison f; **in ~ (with)** en comparaison (de)

compartment [kəm'pɑ:tmənt] n (also Rail) compartiment m; **a non-smoking ~** un compartiment non-fumeurs

compass ['kʌmpəs] n boussole f; **compasses** npl (Math) compas m; **within the ~ of** dans les limites de

compassion [kəm'pæʃən] n compassion f, humanité f

compassionate [kəm'pæʃənɪt] adj accessible à la compassion, au cœur charitable et bienveillant; **on ~ grounds** pour raisons personnelles de famille

compatible [kəm'pætɪbl] adj compatible

compel [kəm'pel] vt contraindre, obliger

compelling [kəm'pelɪŋ] adj (fig: argument) irrésistible

compensate ['kɔmpənseɪt] vt indemniser, dédommager ▷ vi: **to ~ for** compenser

compensation [kɔmpən'seɪʃən] n compensation f; (money) dédommagement m, indemnité f

compere ['kɔmpeər] n présentateur(-trice), animateur(-trice)

compete [kəm'pi:t] vi (*take part*) concourir; (*vie*): **to ~ (with)** rivaliser (avec), faire concurrence (à)

competent ['kɒmpɪtənt] adj compétent(e), capable

competition [kɒmpɪ'tɪʃən] n (*contest*) compétition f, concours m; (*Econ*) concurrence f; **in ~ with** en concurrence avec

competitive [kəm'petɪtɪv] adj (*Econ*) concurrentiel(le); (*sports*) de compétition; (*person*) qui a l'esprit de compétition

competitor [kəm'petɪtər] n concurrent(e)

complacency [kəm'pleɪsnsɪ] n contentement m de soi, autosatisfaction f

complacent [kəm'pleɪsnt] adj (*trop*) content(e) de soi

complain [kəm'pleɪn] vi: **to ~ (about)** se plaindre (de); (*in shop etc*) réclamer (au sujet de); **complain of** vt fus (*Med*) se plaindre de

complaint [kəm'pleɪnt] n plainte f; (*in shop etc*) réclamation f; (*Med*) affection f

complement ['kɒmplɪmənt] n complément m; (*esp of ship's crew etc*) effectif complet ▷ vt (*enhance*) compléter

complementary [kɒmplɪ'mentərɪ] adj complémentaire

complete [kəm'pli:t] adj complet(-ète); (*finished*) achevé(e) ▷ vt achever, parachever; (*set, group*) compléter; (*a form*) remplir

completely [kəm'pli:tlɪ] adv complètement

completion [kəm'pli:ʃən] n achèvement m; (*of contract*) exécution f; **to be nearing ~** être presque terminé

complex ['kɒmpleks] adj complexe ▷ n (*Psych, buildings etc*) complexe m

complexion [kəm'plekʃən] n (*of face*) teint m; (*of event etc*) aspect m, caractère m

compliance [kəm'plaɪəns] n (*submission*) docilité f; (*agreement*): **~ with** le fait de se conformer à; **in ~ with** en conformité avec, conformément à

complicate ['kɒmplɪkeɪt] vt compliquer

complicated ['kɒmplɪkeɪtɪd] adj compliqué(e)

complication [kɒmplɪ'keɪʃən] n complication f

compliment n ['kɒmplɪmənt] compliment m ▷ vt ['kɒmplɪment] complimenter; **compliments** npl compliments mpl, hommages mpl; vœux mpl; **to pay sb a ~** faire or adresser un compliment à qn; **to ~ sb (on sth/on doing sth)** féliciter qn (pour qch/de faire qch)

complimentary [kɒmplɪ'mentərɪ] adj flatteur(-euse); (*free*) à titre gracieux

complimentary ticket n billet m de faveur

comply [kəm'plaɪ] vi: **to ~ with** se soumettre à, se conformer à

component [kəm'pəunənt] adj composant(e), constituant(e) ▷ n composant m, élément m

compose [kəm'pəuz] vt composer; (*form*): **to be ~d of** se composer de; **to ~ o.s.** se calmer, se maîtriser; **to ~ one's features** prendre une contenance

composed [kəm'pəuzd] adj calme, posé(e)

composer [kəm'pəuzər] n (*Mus*) compositeur m

composition [kɒmpə'zɪʃən] n composition f

composure [kəm'pəuʒər] n calme m, maîtrise f de soi

compound ['kɒmpaund] n (*Chem, Ling*) composé m; (*enclosure*) enclos m, enceinte f ▷ adj composé(e); (*fracture*) compliqué(e) ▷ vt [kəm'paund] (*fig: problem etc*) aggraver

compound fracture n fracture compliquée

compound interest n intérêt composé

comprehend [kɒmprɪ'hend] vt comprendre

comprehension [kɒmprɪ'henʃən] n compréhension f

comprehensive [kɒmprɪ'hensɪv] adj (*très*) complet(-ète); **~ policy** (*Insurance*) assurance f tous risques

comprehensive [kɒmprɪ'hensɪv], **comprehensive school** n (*Brit*) école secondaire non sélective avec libre circulation d'une section à l'autre, ≈ CES m

compress vt [kəm'pres] comprimer; (*text, information*) condenser ▷ n ['kɒmpres] (*Med*) compresse f

comprise [kəm'praɪz] vt (*also*: **be ~d of**) comprendre; (*constitute*) constituer, représenter

compromise ['kɒmprəmaɪz] n compromis m ▷ vt compromettre ▷ vi transiger, accepter un compromis ▷ cpd (*decision, solution*) de compromis

compulsion [kəm'pʌlʃən] n contrainte f, force f; **under ~** sous la contrainte

compulsive [kəm'pʌlsɪv] adj (*Psych*) compulsif(-ive); (*book, film etc*) captivant(e); **he's a ~ smoker** c'est un fumeur invétéré

compulsory [kəm'pʌlsərɪ] adj obligatoire

computer [kəm'pju:tər] n ordinateur m; (*mechanical*) calculatrice f

computer game n jeu m vidéo

computer-generated [kəm'pju:tə-'dʒenəreɪtɪd] adj de synthèse

computerize [kəm'pju:təraɪz] vt (*data*) traiter par ordinateur; (*system, office*) informatiser

computer programmer n programmeur(-euse)

computer programming n programmation f

computer science n informatique f

computer studies npl informatique f

computing [kəm'pju:tɪŋ] n informatique f

comrade ['kɒmrɪd] n camarade m/f

con [kɒn] vt duper; (*cheat*) escroquer ▷ n escroquerie f; **to ~ sb into doing sth** tromper qn pour lui faire faire qch

conceal [kən'si:l] vt cacher, dissimuler

concede [kən'siːd] vt concéder ▷ vi céder
conceit [kən'siːt] n vanité f, suffisance f, prétention f
conceited [kən'siːtɪd] adj vaniteux(-euse), suffisant(e)
conceive [kən'siːv] vt, vi concevoir; **to ~ of sth/of doing sth** imaginer qch/de faire qch
concentrate ['kɔnsəntreɪt] vi se concentrer ▷ vt concentrer
concentration [kɔnsən'treɪʃən] n concentration f
concentration camp n camp m de concentration
concept ['kɔnsɛpt] n concept m
concern [kən'səːn] n affaire f (Comm) entreprise f, firme f; (anxiety) inquiétude f, souci m ▷ vt (worry) inquiéter; (involve) concerner; (relate to) se rapporter à; **to be ~ed (about)** s'inquiéter (de), être inquiet(-ète) (au sujet de); **"to whom it may ~"** "à qui de droit"; **as far as I am ~ed** en ce qui me concerne; **to be ~ed with** (person: involved with) s'occuper de; **the department ~ed** (under discussion) le service en question; (involved) le service concerné
concerning [kən'səːnɪŋ] prep en ce qui concerne, à propos de
concert ['kɔnsət] n concert m; **in ~** à l'unisson, en chœur; ensemble
concerted [kən'səːtɪd] adj concerté(e)
concert hall n salle f de concert
concerto [kən'tʃəːtəu] n concerto m
concession [kən'sɛʃən] n (compromise) concession f; (reduced price) réduction f; **tax ~** dégrèvement fiscal; **"-s"** tarif réduit
concise [kən'saɪs] adj concis(e)
conclude [kən'kluːd] vt conclure ▷ vi (speaker) conclure; (events): **to ~ (with)** se terminer (par)
conclusion [kən'kluːʒən] n conclusion f; **to come to the ~ that** (en) conclure que
conclusive [kən'kluːsɪv] adj concluant(e), définitif(-ive)
concoct [kən'kɔkt] vt confectionner, composer
concoction [kən'kɔkʃən] n (food, drink) mélange m
concourse ['kɔnkɔːs] n (hall) hall m, salle f des pas perdus; (crowd) affluence f; multitude f
concrete ['kɔnkriːt] n béton m ▷ adj concret(-ète); (Constr) en béton
concur [kən'kəːr] vi être d'accord
concurrently [kən'kʌrntlɪ] adv simultanément
concussion [kən'kʌʃən] n (Med) commotion (cérébrale)
condemn [kən'dɛm] vt condamner
condensation [kɔndɛn'seɪʃən] n condensation f
condense [kən'dɛns] vi se condenser ▷ vt condenser

condensed milk [kən'dɛnst-] n lait concentré (sucré)
condition [kən'dɪʃən] n condition f; (disease) maladie f ▷ vt déterminer, conditionner; **in good/poor ~** en bon/mauvais état; **a heart ~** une maladie cardiaque; **weather ~s** conditions fpl météorologiques; **on ~ that** à condition que + sub, à condition de
conditional [kən'dɪʃənl] adj conditionnel(le); **to be ~ upon** dépendre de
conditioner [kən'dɪʃənər] n (for hair) baume démêlant; (for fabrics) assouplissant m
condo ['kɔndəu] n (US inf) = **condominium**
condolences [kən'dəulənsɪz] npl condoléances fpl
condom ['kɔndəm] n préservatif m
condominium [kɔndə'mɪnɪəm] n (US: building) immeuble m (en copropriété); (: rooms) appartement m (dans un immeuble en copropriété)
condone [kən'dəun] vt fermer les yeux sur, approuver (tacitement)
conducive [kən'djuːsɪv] adj: **~ to** favorable à, qui contribue à
conduct n ['kɔndʌkt] conduite f ▷ vt [kə n'dʌkt] conduire; (manage) mener, diriger; (Mus) diriger; **to ~ o.s.** se conduire, se comporter
conductor [kən'dʌktər] n (of orchestra) chef m d'orchestre; (on bus) receveur m; (US: on train) chef m de train; (Elec) conducteur m
conductress [kən'dʌktrɪs] n (on bus) receveuse f
cone [kəun] n cône m; (for ice-cream) cornet m; (Bot) pomme f de pin, cône
confectioner [kən'fɛkʃənər] n (of cakes) pâtissier(-ière); (of sweets) confiseur(-euse); **~'s (shop)** confiserie(-pâtisserie) f
confectionery [kən'fɛkʃənrɪ] n (sweets) confiserie f; (cakes) pâtisserie f
confer [kən'fəːr] vt: **to ~ sth on** conférer qch à ▷ vi conférer, s'entretenir; **to ~ (with sb about sth)** s'entretenir (de qch avec qn)
conference ['kɔnfərns] n conférence f; **to be in ~** être en réunion or en conférence
confess [kən'fɛs] vt confesser, avouer ▷ vi (admit sth) avouer; (Rel) se confesser
confession [kən'fɛʃən] n confession f
confetti [kən'fɛtɪ] n confettis mpl
confide [kən'faɪd] vi: **to ~ in** s'ouvrir à, se confier à
confidence ['kɔnfɪdns] n confiance f; (also: **self-~**) assurance f, confiance en soi; (secret) confidence f; **to have (every) ~ that** être certain que; **motion of no ~** motion f de censure; **in ~** (speak, write) en confidence, confidentiellement; **to tell sb sth in strict ~** dire qch à qn en toute confidence
confidence trick n escroquerie f
confident ['kɔnfɪdənt] adj (self-assured) sûr(e) de soi; (sure) sûr

confidential [kɒnfɪ'dɛnʃəl] adj
confidentiel(le); (secretary) particulier(-ère)
confine [kən'faɪn] vt limiter, borner; (shut up)
confiner, enfermer; **to ~ o.s. to doing sth/to
sth** se contenter de faire qch/se limiter à qch
confined [kən'faɪnd] adj (space) restreint(e),
réduit(e)
confinement [kən'faɪnmənt] n
emprisonnement m, détention f; (Mil)
consigne f (au quartier); (Med)
accouchement m
confines ['kɒnfaɪnz] npl confins mpl,
bornes fpl
confirm [kən'fə:m] vt (report, Rel) confirmer;
(appointment) ratifier
confirmation [kɒnfə'meɪʃən] n
confirmation f; ratification f
confirmed [kən'fə:md] adj invétéré(e),
incorrigible
confiscate ['kɒnfɪskeɪt] vt confisquer
conflict n ['kɒnflɪkt] conflit m, lutte f ▷ vi
[kən'flɪkt] être or entrer en conflit; (opinions)
s'opposer, se heurter
conflicting [kən'flɪktɪŋ] adj contradictoire
conform [kən'fɔ:m] vi: **to ~ (to)** se
conformer (à)
confound [kən'faʊnd] vt confondre; (amaze)
rendre perplexe
confront [kən'frʌnt] vt (two people)
confronter; (enemy, danger) affronter, faire
face à; (problem) faire face à
confrontation [kɒnfrən'teɪʃən] n
confrontation f
confuse [kən'fju:z] vt (person) troubler;
(situation) embrouiller; (one thing with another)
confondre
confused [kən'fju:zd] adj (person) dérouté(e),
désorienté(e); (situation) embrouillé(e)
confusing [kən'fju:zɪŋ] adj peu clair(e),
déroutant(e)
confusion [kən'fju:ʒən] n confusion f
congeal [kən'dʒi:l] vi (oil) se figer; (blood) se
coaguler
congenial [kən'dʒi:nɪəl] adj sympathique,
agréable
congested [kən'dʒɛstɪd] adj (Med)
congestionné(e); (fig) surpeuplé(e);
congestionné; bloqué(e); (telephone lines)
encombré(e)
congestion [kən'dʒɛstʃən] n (Med)
congestion f; (fig: traffic) encombrement m
congratulate [kən'grætjuleɪt] vt: **to ~ sb
(on)** féliciter qn (de)
congratulations [kəngrætjʊ'leɪʃənz] npl:
~ (on) félicitations fpl (pour) ▷ excl: **~!** (toutes
mes) félicitations!
congregate ['kɒŋgrɪgeɪt] vi se rassembler,
se réunir
congregation [kɒŋgrɪ'geɪʃən] n assemblée f
(des fidèles)
congress ['kɒŋgrɛs] n congrès m; (Pol):
C~ Congrès m; voir article

● **CONGRESS**
●
● Le Congress est le parlement des États-
● Unis. Il comprend la "House of
● Representatives" et le "Senate".
● Représentants et sénateurs sont élus au
● suffrage universel direct. Le Congrès se
● réunit au "Capitol", à Washington.

congressman ['kɒŋgrɛsmən] irreg n membre
m du Congrès
congresswoman ['kɒŋgrɛswʊmən] irreg n
membre m du Congrès
conifer ['kɒnɪfəʳ] n conifère m
conjugate ['kɒndʒugeɪt] vt conjuguer
conjugation [kɒndʒə'geɪʃən] n
conjugaison f
conjunction [kən'dʒʌŋkʃən] n conjonction f;
in ~ with (conjointement) avec
conjunctivitis [kəndʒʌŋktɪ'vaɪtɪs] n
conjonctivite f
conjure ['kʌndʒəʳ] vt faire apparaître (par la
prestidigitation); [kən'dʒuə] conjurer,
supplier ▷ vi faire des tours de passe-passe;
conjure up vt (ghost, spirit) faire apparaître;
(memories) évoquer
conjurer ['kʌndʒərəʳ] n prestidigitateur m,
illusionniste m/f
conman ['kɒnmæn] irreg n escroc m
connect [kə'nɛkt] vt joindre, relier; (Elec)
connecter; (Tel: caller) mettre en connexion;
(: subscriber) brancher; (fig) établir un rapport
entre, faire un rapprochement entre ▷ vi
(train): **to ~ with** assurer la correspondance
avec; **to be ~ed with** avoir un rapport avec;
(have dealings with) avoir des rapports avec,
être en relation avec; **I am trying to ~ you**
(Tel) j'essaie d'obtenir votre communication
connecting flight n (vol m de)
correspondance f
connection [kə'nɛkʃən] n relation f, lien m;
(Elec) connexion f; (Tel) communication f;
(train etc) correspondance f; **in ~ with** à propos
de; **what is the ~ between them?** quel est le
lien entre eux?; **business ~s** relations
d'affaires; **to miss/get one's ~** (train etc)
rater/avoir sa correspondance
connive [kə'naɪv] vi: **to ~ at** se faire le
complice de
conquer ['kɒŋkəʳ] vt conquérir; (feelings)
vaincre, surmonter
conquest ['kɒŋkwest] n conquête f
cons [kɒnz] npl see **convenience**; **pro**
conscience ['kɒnʃəns] n conscience f; **in all ~**
en conscience
conscientious [kɒnʃɪ'ɛnʃəs] adj
consciencieux(-euse); (scruple, objection) de
conscience
conscious ['kɒnʃəs] adj conscient(e);
(deliberate: insult, error) délibéré(e); **to
become ~ of sth/that** prendre conscience
de qch/que

consciousness ['kɒnʃəsnɪs] n conscience f; (Med) connaissance f; **to lose/regain ~** perdre/reprendre connaissance

conscript ['kɒnskrɪpt] n conscrit m

consecutive [kən'sekjʊtɪv] adj consécutif(-ive); **on three ~ occasions** trois fois de suite

consensus [kən'sensəs] n consensus m; **the ~ (of opinion)** le consensus (d'opinion)

consent [kən'sent] n consentement m ▷ vi: **to ~ (to)** consentir (à); **age of ~** âge nubile (légal); **by common ~** d'un commun accord

consequence ['kɒnsɪkwəns] n suites fpl, conséquence f; (significance) importance f; **in ~** en conséquence, par conséquent

consequently ['kɒnsɪkwəntlɪ] adv par conséquent, donc

conservation [kɒnsə'veɪʃən] n préservation f, protection f; (also: **nature ~**) défense f de l'environnement; **energy ~** économies fpl d'énergie

conservative [kən'sɜːvətɪv] adj conservateur(-trice); (cautious) prudent(e)

Conservative [kən'sɜːvətɪv] adj, n (Brit Pol) conservateur(-trice); **the ~ Party** le parti conservateur

conservatory [kən'sɜːvətrɪ] n (room) jardin m d'hiver; (Mus) conservatoire m

conserve [kən'sɜːv] vt conserver, préserver; (supplies, energy) économiser ▷ n confiture f, conserve f (de fruits)

consider [kən'sɪdəʳ] vt (study) considérer, réfléchir à; (take into account) penser à, prendre en considération; (regard, judge) considérer, estimer; **to ~ doing sth** envisager de faire qch; **~ yourself lucky** estimez-vous heureux; **all things ~ed** (toute) réflexion faite

considerable [kən'sɪdərəbl] adj considérable

considerably [kən'sɪdərəblɪ] adv nettement

considerate [kən'sɪdərɪt] adj prévenant(e), plein(e) d'égards

consideration [kənsɪdə'reɪʃən] n considération f; (reward) rétribution f, rémunération f; **out of ~ for** par égard pour; **under ~** à l'étude; **my first ~ is my family** ma famille passe avant tout le reste

considering [kən'sɪdərɪŋ] prep: **~ (that)** étant donné (que)

consign [kən'saɪn] vt expédier, livrer

consignment [kən'saɪnmənt] n arrivage m, envoi m

consist [kən'sɪst] vi: **to ~ of** consister en, se composer de

consistency [kən'sɪstənsɪ] n (thickness) consistance f; (fig) cohérence f

consistent [kən'sɪstənt] adj logique, cohérent(e); **~ with** compatible avec, en accord avec

consolation [kɒnsə'leɪʃən] n consolation f

console¹ [kən'səʊl] vt consoler

console² ['kɒnsəʊl] n console f

consonant ['kɒnsənənt] n consonne f

conspicuous [kən'spɪkjʊəs] adj voyant(e), qui attire l'attention; **to make o.s. ~** se faire remarquer

conspiracy [kən'spɪrəsɪ] n conspiration f, complot m

constable ['kʌnstəbl] n (Brit) ≈ agent m de police, gendarme m; **chief ~** ≈ préfet m de police

constabulary [kən'stæbjʊlərɪ] n ≈ police f, gendarmerie f

constant ['kɒnstənt] adj constant(e); incessant(e)

constantly ['kɒnstəntlɪ] adv constamment, sans cesse

constipated ['kɒnstɪpeɪtɪd] adj constipé(e)

constipation [kɒnstɪ'peɪʃən] n constipation f

constituency [kən'stɪtjuənsɪ] n (Pol: area) circonscription électorale; (: electors) électorat m; voir article

● **CONSTITUENCY**
●
● Une constituency est à la fois une région qui
● élit un député au parlement et
● l'ensemble des électeurs dans cette
● région. En Grande-Bretagne, les députés
● font régulièrement des "permanences"
● dans leur circonscription électorale lors
● desquelles les électeurs peuvent venir les
● voir pour parler de leurs problèmes de
● logement etc.

constituent [kən'stɪtjuənt] n électeur(-trice); (part) élément constitutif, composant m

constitute ['kɒnstɪtjuːt] vt constituer

constitution [kɒnstɪ'tjuːʃən] n constitution f

constitutional [kɒnstɪ'tjuːʃənl] adj constitutionnel(le)

constraint [kən'streɪnt] n contrainte f; (embarrassment) gêne f

construct [kən'strʌkt] vt construire

construction [kən'strʌkʃən] n construction f; (fig: interpretation) interprétation f; **under ~** (building etc) en construction

constructive [kən'strʌktɪv] adj constructif(-ive)

consul ['kɒnsl] n consul m

consulate ['kɒnsjʊlɪt] n consulat m

consult [kən'sʌlt] vt consulter; **to ~ sb (about sth)** consulter qn (à propos de qch)

consultant [kən'sʌltənt] n (Med) médecin consultant; (other specialist) consultant m, (expert-)conseil m ▷ cpd: **~ engineer** n ingénieur-conseil m; **~ paediatrician** n pédiatre m; **legal/management ~** conseiller m juridique/en gestion

consultation [kɒnsəl'teɪʃən] n consultation f; **in ~ with** en consultation avec

consulting room [kən'sʌltɪŋ-] n (Brit)
cabinet m de consultation

consume [kən'sju:m] vt consommer; (subj:
flames, hatred, desire) consumer; **to be ~d with
hatred** être dévoré par la haine; **to be ~d
with desire** brûler de désir

consumer [kən'sju:məʳ] n
consommateur(-trice); (of electricity, gas etc)
usager m

consumer goods npl biens mpl de
consommation

consumer society n société f de
consommation

consummate ['kɒnsʌmeɪt] vt consommer

consumption [kən'sʌmpʃən] n
consommation f; **not fit for human ~** non
comestible

cont. abbr (= continued) suite

contact ['kɒntækt] n contact m; (person)
connaissance f, relation f ▷ vt se mettre en
contact or en rapport avec; **to be in ~ with
sb/sth** être en contact avec qn/qch;
business ~s relations fpl d'affaires,
contacts mpl

contact lenses npl verres mpl de contact

contagious [kən'teɪdʒəs] adj
contagieux(-euse)

contain [kən'teɪn] vt contenir; **to ~ o.s.** se
contenir, se maîtriser

container [kən'teɪnəʳ] n récipient m; (for
shipping etc) conteneur m

contaminate [kən'tæmɪneɪt] vt contaminer

cont'd abbr (= continued) suite

contemplate ['kɒntəmpleɪt] vt contempler;
(consider) envisager

contemporary [kən'tempərəri] adj
contemporain(e); (design, wallpaper) moderne
▷ n contemporain(e)

contempt [kən'tempt] n mépris m,
dédain m; **~ of court** (Law) outrage m à
l'autorité de la justice

contemptuous [kən'temptjuəs] adj
dédaigneux(-euse), méprisant(e)

contend [kən'tend] vt: **to ~ that** soutenir or
prétendre que ▷ vi: **to ~ with** (compete)
rivaliser avec; (struggle) lutter avec; **to have
to ~ with** (be faced with) avoir affaire à, être
aux prises avec

contender [kən'tendəʳ] n prétendant(e);
candidat(e)

content [kən'tent] adj content(e), satisfait(e)
▷ vt contenter, satisfaire ▷ n ['kɒntent]
contenu m; (of fat, moisture) teneur f;
contents npl (of container etc) contenu m; **(table of) ~s**
table f des matières; **to be ~ with** se
contenter de; **to ~ o.s. with sth/with doing
sth** se contenter de qch/de faire qch

contented [kən'tentɪd] adj content(e),
satisfait(e)

contention [kən'tenʃən] n dispute f,
contestation f; (argument) assertion f,
affirmation f; **bone of ~** sujet m de discorde

contest n ['kɒntest] combat m, lutte f;
(competition) concours m ▷ vt [kən'test]
contester, discuter; (compete for) disputer;
(Law) attaquer

contestant [kən'testənt] n concurrent(e);
(in fight) adversaire m/f

context ['kɒntekst] n contexte m; **in/out of ~**
dans le/hors contexte

continent ['kɒntɪnənt] n continent m; **the
C~** (Brit) l'Europe continentale; **on the C~** en
Europe (continentale)

continental [kɒntɪ'nentl] adj continental(e)
▷ n (Brit) Européen(ne) (continental(e))

continental breakfast n café (or thé)
complet

continental quilt n (Brit) couette f

contingency [kən'tɪndʒənsɪ] n éventualité f,
événement imprévu

continual [kən'tɪnjuəl] adj continuel(le)

continually [kən'tɪnjuəlɪ] adv
continuellement, sans cesse

continuation [kəntɪnju'eɪʃən] n
continuation f; (after interruption) reprise f;
(of story) suite f

continue [kən'tɪnju:] vi continuer ▷ vt
continuer; (start again) reprendre; **to be ~d**
(story) à suivre; **~d on page 10** suite page 10

continuity [kɒntɪ'njuːɪtɪ] n continuité f;
(TV) enchaînement m; (Cine) script m

continuous [kən'tɪnjuəs] adj continu(e),
permanent(e); (Ling) progressif(-ive);
~ performance (Cine) séance permanente;
~ stationery (Comput) papier m en continu

continuous assessment (Brit) n contrôle
continu

continuously [kən'tɪnjuəslɪ] adv (repeatedly)
continuellement; (uninterruptedly) sans
interruption

contort [kən'tɔ:t] vt tordre, crisper

contour ['kɒntuəʳ] n contour m, profil m;
(also: **~ line**) courbe f de niveau

contraband ['kɒntrəbænd] n contrebande f
▷ adj de contrebande

contraception [kɒntrə'sepʃən] n
contraception f

contraceptive [kɒntrə'septɪv] adj
contraceptif(-ive), anticonceptionnel(le) ▷ n
contraceptif m

contract n ['kɒntrækt] contrat m ▷ cpd (price,
date) contractuel(le); (work) à forfait ▷ vi [kə
n'trækt] (become smaller) se contracter, se
resserrer ▷ vt contracter; (Comm): **to ~ to do
sth** s'engager (par contrat) à faire qch; **~ of
employment/service** contrat de travail/de
service; **contract in** vi s'engager (par
contrat); (Brit Admin) s'affilier au régime de
retraite complémentaire; **contract out** vi
se dégager; (Brit Admin) opter pour la non-
affiliation au régime de retraite
complémentaire

contraction [kən'trækʃən] n contraction f;
(Ling) forme contractée

contractor [kən'træktəʳ] n entrepreneur m
contradict [kɒntrə'dɪkt] vt contredire; (be contrary to) démentir, être en contradiction avec
contradiction [kɒntrə'dɪkʃən] n contradiction f; **to be in ~ with** contredire, être en contradiction avec
contraflow ['kɒntrəfləu] n (Aut): **~ lane** voie f à contresens; **there's a ~ system in operation on ...** une voie a été mise en sens inverse sur ...
contraption [kən'træpʃən] n (pej) machin m, truc m
contrary¹ ['kɒntrəri] adj contraire, opposé(e) ▷ n contraire m; **on the ~** au contraire; **unless you hear to the ~** sauf avis contraire; **~ to what we thought** contrairement à ce que nous pensions
contrary² [kən'trɛəri] adj (perverse) contrariant(e), entêté(e)
contrast n ['kɒntrɑːst] contraste m ▷ vt [kən'trɑːst] mettre en contraste, contraster; **in ~ to** or **with** contrairement à, par opposition à
contravene [kɒntrə'viːn] vt enfreindre, violer, contrevenir à
contribute [kən'trɪbjuːt] vi contribuer ▷ vt: **to ~ £10/an article to** donner 10 livres/un article à; **to ~ to** (gen) contribuer à; (newspaper) collaborer à; (discussion) prendre part à
contribution [kɒntrɪ'bjuːʃən] n contribution f; (Brit: for social security) cotisation f; (to publication) article m
contributor [kən'trɪbjutəʳ] n (to newspaper) collaborateur(-trice); (of money, goods) donateur(-trice)
contrive [kən'traɪv] vt combiner, inventer ▷ vi: **to ~ to do** s'arranger pour faire, trouver le moyen de faire
control [kən'trəul] vt (process, machinery) commander; (temper) maîtriser; (disease) enrayer; (check) contrôler ▷ n maîtrise f; (power) autorité f; **controls** npl (of machine etc) commandes fpl; (on radio) boutons mpl de réglage; **to take ~ of** se rendre maître de; (Comm) acquérir une participation majoritaire dans; **to be in ~ of** être maître de, maîtriser; (in charge of) être responsable de; **to ~ o.s.** se contrôler; **everything is under ~** j'ai (or il a etc) la situation en main; **the car went out of ~** j'ai (or il a etc) perdu le contrôle du véhicule; **beyond our ~** indépendant(e) de notre volonté
control panel n (on aircraft, ship, TV etc) tableau m de commandes
control room n (Naut Mil) salle f des commandes; (Radio, TV) régie f
control tower n (Aviat) tour f de contrôle
controversial [kɒntrə'vəːʃl] adj discutable, controversé(e)
controversy ['kɒntrəvəːsɪ] n controverse f, polémique f

convalesce [kɒnvə'lɛs] vi relever de maladie, se remettre (d'une maladie)
convector [kən'vɛktəʳ] n radiateur m à convection, appareil m de chauffage par convection
convene [kən'viːn] vt convoquer, assembler ▷ vi se réunir, s'assembler
convenience [kən'viːnɪəns] n commodité f; **at your ~** quand or comme cela vous convient; **at your earliest ~** (Comm) dans les meilleurs délais, le plus tôt possible; **all modern ~s, all mod cons** (Brit) avec tout le confort moderne, tout confort
convenient [kən'viːnɪənt] adj commode; **if it is ~ to you** si cela vous convient, si cela ne vous dérange pas
convent ['kɒnvənt] n couvent m
convention [kən'vɛnʃən] n convention f; (custom) usage m
conventional [kən'vɛnʃənl] adj conventionnel(le)
convent school n couvent m
conversant [kən'vəːsnt] adj: **to be ~ with** s'y connaître en; être au courant de
conversation [kɒnvə'seɪʃən] n conversation f
converse ['kɒnvəːs] n contraire m, inverse m ▷ vi [kən'vəːs]: **to ~ (with sb about sth)** s'entretenir (avec qn de qch)
conversely [kɒn'vəːslɪ] adv inversement, réciproquement
conversion [kən'vəːʃən] n conversion f; (Brit: of house) transformation f, aménagement m; (Rugby) transformation f
convert vt [kən'vəːt] (Rel, Comm) convertir; (alter) transformer; (house) aménager; (Rugby) transformer ▷ n ['kɒnvəːt] converti(e)
convertible [kən'vəːtəbl] adj convertible ▷ n (voiture f) décapotable f
convey [kən'veɪ] vt transporter; (thanks) transmettre; (idea) communiquer
conveyor belt [kən'veɪəʳ-] n convoyeur m, tapis roulant
convict vt [kən'vɪkt] déclarer (or reconnaître) coupable ▷ n ['kɒnvɪkt] forçat m, convict m
conviction [kən'vɪkʃən] n (Law) condamnation f; (belief) conviction f
convince [kən'vɪns] vt convaincre, persuader; **to ~ sb (of sth/that)** persuader qn (de qch/que)
convinced [kən'vɪnst] adj: **~ of/that** convaincu(e) de/que
convincing [kən'vɪnsɪŋ] adj persuasif(-ive), convaincant(e)
convoluted ['kɒnvəluːtɪd] adj (shape) tarabiscoté(e); (argument) compliqué(e)
convoy ['kɒnvɔɪ] n convoi m
convulse [kən'vʌls] vt ébranler; **to be ~d with laughter** se tordre de rire
cook [kuk] vt (faire) cuire ▷ vi cuire; (person) faire la cuisine ▷ n cuisinier(-ière); **cook up** vt (inf: excuse, story) inventer

cookbook ['kukbuk] n livre m de cuisine

cooker ['kukə'] n cuisinière f

cookery ['kukərı] n cuisine f

cookery book n (Brit) = **cookbook**

cookie ['kukı] n (US) biscuit m, petit gâteau sec; (Comput) cookie m, témien m de connexion

cooking ['kukɪŋ] n ▷ cpd (apples, chocolate) à cuire; (utensils, salt) de cuisine

cool [ku:l] adj frais/fraîche; (not afraid) calme; (unfriendly) froid(e); (impertinent) effronté(e); (inf: trendy) cool inv (inf); (: great) super inv (inf) ▷ vt, vi rafraîchir, refroidir; **it's ~** (weather) il fait frais; **to keep sth ~** or **in a ~ place** garder or conserver qch au frais; **cool down** vi refroidir; (fig: person, situation) se calmer; **cool off** vi (become calmer) se calmer; (lose enthusiasm) perdre son enthousiasme

coop [ku:p] n poulailler m ▷ vt: **to ~ up** (fig) cloîtrer, enfermer

cooperate [kəu'ɒpəreɪt] vi coopérer, collaborer

cooperation [kəuɒpə'reɪʃən] n coopération f, collaboration f

cooperative [kəu'ɒpərətɪv] adj coopératif(-ive) ▷ n coopérative f

coordinate vt [kəu'ɔ:dɪneɪt] coordonner ▷ n [kəu'ɔdnət] (Math) coordonnée f; **coordinates** npl (clothes) ensemble m, coordonnés mpl

co-ownership ['kəu'əunəʃɪp] n copropriété f

cop [kɒp] n (inf) flic m

cope [kəup] vi s'en sortir, tenir le coup; **to ~ with** (problem) faire face à; (take care of) s'occuper de

copper ['kɒpə'] n cuivre m; (Brit: inf: policeman) flic m; **coppers** npl petite monnaie

copy ['kɒpı] n copie f; (book etc) exemplaire m; (material: for printing) copie ▷ vt copier; (imitate) imiter; **rough ~** (gen) premier jet; (Scol) brouillon m; **fair ~** version définitive; propre m; **to make good ~** (Press) faire un bon sujet d'article; **copy out** vt copier

copyright ['kɒpıraıt] n droit m d'auteur, copyright m; **~ reserved** tous droits (de reproduction) réservés

coral ['kɒrəl] n corail m

cord [kɔ:d] n corde f; (fabric) velours côtelé; whipcord m; corde f; (Elec) cordon m (d'alimentation), fil m (électrique); **cords** npl (trousers) pantalon m de velours côtelé

cordial ['kɔ:dıəl] adj cordial(e), chaleureux(-euse) ▷ n sirop m; cordial m

cordless ['kɔ:dlıs] adj sans fil

cordon ['kɔ:dn] n cordon m; **cordon off** vt (area) interdire l'accès à; (crowd) tenir à l'écart

corduroy ['kɔ:dərɔı] n velours côtelé

core [kɔ:'] n (of fruit) trognon m, cœur m; (Tech: also of earth) noyau m; (of nuclear reactor, fig: of problem etc) cœur ▷ vt enlever le trognon or le cœur de; **rotten to the ~** complètement pourri

coriander [kɒrı'ændə'] n coriandre f

cork [kɔ:k] n (material) liège m; (of bottle) bouchon m

corkscrew ['kɔ:kskru:] n tire-bouchon m

corn [kɔ:n] n (Brit: wheat) blé m; (US: maize) maïs m; (on foot) cor m; **~ on the cob** (Culin) épi m de maïs au naturel

corned beef ['kɔ:nd-] n corned-beef m

corner ['kɔ:nə'] n coin m; (in road) tournant m, virage m; (Football: also: **~ kick**) corner m ▷ vt (trap: prey) acculer; (fig) coincer; (Comm: market) accaparer ▷ vi prendre un virage; **to cut ~s** (fig) prendre des raccourcis

corner shop (Brit) n magasin m du coin

cornerstone ['kɔ:nəstəun] n pierre f angulaire

cornet ['kɔ:nıt] n (Mus) cornet m à pistons; (Brit: of ice-cream) cornet (de glace)

cornflakes ['kɔ:nfleıks] npl cornflakes mpl

cornflour ['kɔ:nflauə'] n (Brit) farine f de maïs, maïzena® f

cornstarch ['kɔ:nsta:tʃ] n (US) farine f de maïs, maïzena® f

Cornwall ['kɔ:nwəl] n Cornouailles f

corny ['kɔ:nı] adj (inf) rebattu(e), galvaudé(e)

coronary ['kɒrənərı] n: **~ (thrombosis)** infarctus m (du myocarde), thrombose f coronaire

coronation [kɒrə'neıʃən] n couronnement m

coroner ['kɒrənə'] n coroner m, officier de police judiciaire chargé de déterminer les causes d'un décès

corporal ['kɔ:pərl] n caporal m, brigadier m ▷ adj: **~ punishment** châtiment corporel

corporate ['kɔ:pərıt] adj (action, ownership) en commun; (Comm) de la société

corporation [kɔ:pə'reıʃən] n (of town) municipalité f, conseil municipal; (Comm) société f

corps [kɔ:'] (pl **corps** [kɔ:z]) n corps m; **the diplomatic ~** le corps diplomatique; **the press ~** la presse

corpse [kɔ:ps] n cadavre m

correct [kə'rekt] adj (accurate) correct(e), exact(e); (proper) correct, convenable ▷ vt corriger; **you are ~** vous avez raison

correction [kə'rekʃən] n correction f

correspond [kɒrıs'pɒnd] vi correspondre; **to ~ to sth** (be equivalent to) correspondre à qch

correspondence [kɒrıs'pɒndəns] n correspondance f

correspondence course n cours m par correspondance

correspondent [kɒrıs'pɒndənt] n correspondant(e)

corresponding [kɒrıs'pɒndıŋ] adj correspondant(e)

corridor ['kɒrıdɔ:'] n couloir m, corridor m

corrode [kə'rəud] vt corroder, ronger ▷ vi se corroder

corrugated ['kɒrəgeıtıd] adj plissé(e); ondulé(e)

corrugated iron n tôle ondulée

corrupt [kə'rʌpt] *adj* corrompu(e); (*Comput*) altéré(e) ▷ *vt* corrompre; (*Comput*) altérer; **~ practices** (*dishonesty, bribery*) malversation *f*

corruption [kə'rʌpfən] *n* corruption *f*; (*Comput*) altération *f* (de données)

Corsica ['kɔːsɪkə] *n* Corse *f*

cosmetic [kɔz'metɪk] *n* produit *m* de beauté, cosmétique *m* ▷ *adj* (*preparation*) cosmétique; (*fig: reforms*) symbolique, superficiel(le)

cosmetic surgery *n* chirurgie *f* esthétique

cosmopolitan [kɔzmə'pɔlɪtn] *adj* cosmopolite

cost [kɔst] (*pt, pp* **cost**) *n* coût *m* ▷ *vi* coûter ▷ *vt* établir *or* calculer le prix de revient de; **costs** *npl* (*Comm*) frais *mpl*; (*Law*) dépens *mpl*; **how much does it ~?** combien ça coûte?; **it ~s £5/too much** cela coûte 5 livres/trop cher; **what will it ~ to have it repaired?** combien cela coûtera de faire réparer?; **to ~ sb time/effort** demander du temps/un effort à qn; **it ~ him his life/job** ça lui a coûté la vie/son emploi; **at all ~s** coûte que coûte, à tout prix

co-star ['kəʊstɑːʳ] *n* partenaire *m/f*

cost-effective [kɔstɪ'fektɪv] *adj* rentable

costly ['kɔstlɪ] *adj* coûteux(-euse)

cost of living ['kɔstəv'lɪvɪŋ] *n* coût *m* de la vie ▷ *adj*: **~ allowance** indemnité *f* de vie chère; **~ index** indice *m* du coût de la vie

cost price *n* (*Brit*) prix coûtant *or* de revient

costume ['kɔstjuːm] *n* costume *m*; (*lady's suit*) tailleur *m*; (*Brit: also: swimming ~*) maillot *m* (de bain)

costume jewellery *n* bijoux *mpl* de fantaisie

cosy, (*US*) **cozy** ['kəʊzɪ] *adj* (*room, bed*) douillet(te); (*scarf, gloves*) bien chaud(e); (*atmosphere*) chaleureux(-euse); **to be ~** (*person*) être bien (au chaud)

cot [kɔt] *n* (*Brit: child's*) lit *m* d'enfant, petit lit; (*US: campbed*) lit de camp

cottage ['kɔtɪdʒ] *n* petite maison (à la campagne), cottage *m*

cottage cheese *n* fromage blanc (*maigre*)

cotton ['kɔtn] *n* coton *m*; (*thread*) fil *m* (de coton); **~ dress** *etc* robe *etc* en *or* de coton; **cotton on** *vi* (*inf*): **to ~ on (to sth)** piger (qch)

cotton bud (*Brit*) *n* coton-tige® *m*

cotton candy (*US*) *n* barbe *f* à papa

cotton wool *n* (*Brit*) ouate *f*, coton *m* hydrophile

couch [kautʃ] *n* canapé *m*; divan *m*; (*doctor's*) table *f* d'examen; (*psychiatrist's*) divan ▷ *vt* formuler, exprimer

couchette [kuː'ʃet] *n* couchette *f*

cough [kɔf] *vi* tousser ▷ *n* toux *f*; **I've got a ~** j'ai la toux

cough mixture, cough syrup *n* sirop *m* pour la toux

cough sweet *n* pastille *f* pour *or* contre la toux

could [kud] *pt of* **can²**

couldn't ['kudnt] = **could not**

council ['kaunsl] *n* conseil *m*; **city** *or* **town ~** conseil municipal; **C~ of Europe** Conseil de l'Europe

council estate *n* (*Brit*) (quartier *m* or zone *f* de) logements loués à/par la municipalité

council house *n* (*Brit*) maison *f* (à loyer modéré) louée par la municipalité

councillor, (*US*) **councilor** ['kaunslər] *n* conseiller(-ère)

council tax *n* (*Brit*) impôts locaux

counsel ['kaunsl] *n* conseil *m*; (*lawyer*) avocat(e) ▷ *vt*: **to ~ (sb to do sth)** conseiller (à qn de faire qch); **~ for the defence/the prosecution** (avocat de la) défense/ avocat du ministère public

counselling, (*US*) **counseling** ['kaunslɪŋ] *n* (*Psych*) aide psychosociale

counsellor, (*US*) **counselor** ['kaunslər] *n* conseiller(-ère); (*US Law*) avocat *m*

count [kaunt] *vt, vi* compter ▷ *n* compte *m*; (*nobleman*) comte *m*; **to ~ (up) to 10** compter jusqu'à 10; **to keep ~ of sth** tenir le compte de qch; **not ~ing the children** sans compter les enfants; **10 ~ing him** 10 avec lui, 10 en le comptant; **to ~ the cost of** établir le coût de; **it ~s for very little** cela n'a pas beaucoup d'importance; **~ yourself lucky** estimez-vous heureux; **count in** *vt* (*inf*): **to ~ sb in on sth** inclure qn dans qch; **count on** *vt fus* compter sur; **to ~ on doing sth** compter faire qch; **count up** *vt* compter, additionner

countdown ['kauntdaun] *n* compte *m* à rebours

countenance ['kauntɪnəns] *n* expression *f* ▷ *vt* approuver

counter ['kauntəʳ] *n* comptoir *m*; (*in post office, bank*) guichet *m*; (*in game*) jeton *m* ▷ *vt* aller à l'encontre de, opposer; (*blow*) parer ▷ *adv*: **~ to** à l'encontre de; contrairement à; **to buy under the ~** (*fig*) acheter sous le manteau or en sous-main; **to ~ sth with sth/ by doing sth** contrer *or* riposter à qch par qch/en faisant qch

counteract ['kauntər'ækt] *vt* neutraliser, contrebalancer

counterclockwise ['kauntə'klɔkwaɪz] (*US*) *adv* en sens inverse des aiguilles d'une montre

counterfeit ['kauntəfɪt] *n* faux *m*, contrefaçon *f* ▷ *vt* contrefaire ▷ *adj* faux/ fausse

counterfoil ['kauntəfɔɪl] *n* talon *m*, souche *f*

counterpart ['kauntəpɑːt] *n* (*of document etc*) double *m*; (*of person*) homologue *m/f*

countess ['kauntɪs] *n* comtesse *f*

countless ['kauntlɪs] *adj* innombrable

country ['kʌntrɪ] *n* pays *m*; (*native land*) patrie *f*; (*as opposed to town*) campagne *f*; (*region*) région *f*, pays; **in the ~** à la campagne; **mountainous ~** pays de montagne, région montagneuse

country and western, country and western music n musique f country

country dancing n (Brit) danse f folklorique

country house n manoir m, (petit) château

countryman ['kʌntrɪmən] irreg n (national) compatriote m; (rural) habitant m de la campagne, campagnard m

countryside ['kʌntrɪsaɪd] n campagne f

county ['kaʊntɪ] n comté m

coup [kuː] (pl coups) [kuːz] n (achievement) beau coup; (also: ~ d'état) coup d'État

couple ['kʌpl] n couple m ▷ vt (carriages) atteler; (ideas, names) associer; **a ~ of** (two) deux; (a few) deux ou trois

coupon ['kuːpɒn] n (voucher) bon m de réduction; (detachable form) coupon m détachable, coupon-réponse m; (Finance) coupon

courage ['kʌrɪdʒ] n courage m

courageous [kə'reɪdʒəs] adj courageux(-euse)

courgette [kʊə'ʒet] n (Brit) courgette f

courier ['kʊrɪəʳ] n messager m, courrier m; (for tourists) accompagnateur(-trice)

course [kɔːs] n cours m; (of ship) route f; (for golf) terrain m; (part of meal) plat m; **first ~** entrée f; **of ~** adv bien sûr; **(no,) of ~ not!** bien sûr que non!, évidemment que non!; **in the ~ of** au cours de; **in the ~ of the next few days** au cours des prochains jours; **in due ~** en temps utile or voulu; **~ (of action)** parti m, ligne f de conduite; **the best ~ would be to ...** le mieux serait de ...; **we have no other ~ but to ...** nous n'avons pas d'autre solution que de ...; **~ of lectures** série f de conférences; **~ of treatment** (Med) traitement m

court [kɔːt] n cour f; (Law) cour, tribunal m; (Tennis) court m ▷ vt (woman) courtiser, faire la cour à; (fig: favour, popularity) rechercher; (: death, disaster) courir après, flirter avec; **out of ~** (Law: settle) à l'amiable; **to take to ~** actionner or poursuivre en justice; **~ of appeal** cour d'appel

courteous ['kɜːtɪəs] adj courtois(e), poli(e)

courtesy ['kɜːtəsɪ] n courtoisie f, politesse f; **(by) ~ of** avec l'aimable autorisation de

courtesy bus, courtesy coach n navette gratuite

court-house ['kɔːthaʊs] n (US) palais m de justice

courtier ['kɔːtɪəʳ] n courtisan m, dame f de cour

court martial (pl courts martial) n cour martiale, conseil m de guerre

courtroom ['kɔːtrʊm] n salle f de tribunal

courtyard ['kɔːtjɑːd] n cour f

cousin ['kʌzn] n cousin(e); **first ~** cousin(e) germain(e)

cove [kəʊv] n petite baie, anse f

covenant ['kʌvənənt] n contrat m, engagement m ▷ vt: **to ~ £200 per year to a**

charity s'engager à verser 200 livres par an à une œuvre de bienfaisance

cover ['kʌvəʳ] vt couvrir; (Press: report on) faire un reportage sur; (feelings, mistake) cacher; (include) englober; (discuss) traiter ▷ n (of book, Comm) couverture f; (of pan) couvercle m; (over furniture) housse f; (shelter) abri m; **covers** npl (on bed) couvertures; **to take ~** se mettre à l'abri; **under ~** à l'abri; **under ~ of darkness** à la faveur de la nuit; **under separate ~** (Comm) sous pli séparé; **£10 will ~ everything** 10 livres suffiront (pour tout payer); **cover up** vt (person, object): **to ~ up (with)** couvrir (de); (fig: truth, facts) occulter ▷ vi: **to ~ up for sb** (fig) couvrir qn

coverage ['kʌvərɪdʒ] n (in media) reportage m; (Insurance) couverture f

cover charge n couvert m (supplément à payer)

covering ['kʌvərɪŋ] n couverture f, enveloppe f

covering letter, (US) **cover letter** n lettre explicative

cover note n (Insurance) police f provisoire

covert ['kʌvət] adj (threat) voilé(e), caché(e); (attack) indirect(e); (glance) furtif(-ive)

cover-up ['kʌvərʌp] n tentative f pour étouffer une affaire

covet ['kʌvɪt] vt convoiter

cow [kaʊ] n vache f ▷ cpd femelle ▷ vt effrayer, intimider

coward ['kaʊəd] n lâche m/f

cowardice ['kaʊədɪs] n lâcheté f

cowardly ['kaʊədlɪ] adj lâche

cowboy ['kaʊbɔɪ] n cow-boy m

cower ['kaʊəʳ] vi se recroqueviller; trembler

coy [kɔɪ] adj faussement effarouché(e) or timide

cozy ['kəʊzɪ] adj (US) = **cosy**

CPA n abbr (US) = **certified public accountant**

crab [kræb] n crabe m

crab apple n pomme f sauvage

crack [kræk] n (split) fente f, fissure f; (in cup, bone) fêlure f; (in wall) lézarde f; (noise) craquement m, coup (sec); (joke) plaisanterie f; (inf: attempt): **to have a ~ (at sth)** essayer (qch); (Drugs) crack m ▷ vt fendre, fissurer; fêler; lézarder; (whip) faire claquer; (nut) casser; (problem) résoudre, trouver la clef de; (code) déchiffrer ▷ cpd (athlete) de première classe, d'élite; **to ~ jokes** (inf) raconter des blagues; **to get ~ing** (inf) s'y mettre, se magner; **crack down on** vt fus (crime) sévir contre, réprimer; (spending) mettre un frein à; **crack up** vi être au bout de son rouleau, flancher

cracked [krækt] adj (cup, bone) fêlé(e); (broken) cassé(e); (wall) lézardé(e); (surface) craquelé(e); (inf) toqué(e), timbré(e)

cracker ['krækəʳ] n (also: **Christmas ~**) pétard m; (biscuit) biscuit (salé), craquelin m; **a ~ of a ...** (Brit inf) un(e) ... formidable; **he's ~** (Brit inf) il est cinglé

crackle ['krækl] vi crépiter, grésiller

cradle ['kreɪdl] n berceau m ▷ vt (child) bercer; (object) tenir dans ses bras

craft [krɑːft] n métier (artisanal); (cunning) ruse f, astuce f; (boat: pl inv) embarcation f, barque f; (plane: pl inv) appareil m

craftsman (irreg) ['krɑːftsmən] irreg n artisan m ouvrier (qualifié)

craftsmanship ['krɑːftsmənʃɪp] n métier m, habileté f

crafty ['krɑːftɪ] adj rusé(e), malin(-igne), astucieux(-euse)

crag [kræg] n rocher escarpé

cram [kræm] vt (fill): **to ~ sth with** bourrer qch de; (put): **to ~ sth into** fourrer qch dans ▷ vi (for exams) bachoter

cramp [kræmp] n crampe f ▷ vt gêner, entraver; **I've got ~ in my leg** j'ai une crampe à la jambe

cramped [kræmpt] adj à l'étroit, très serré(e)

cranberry ['krænbərɪ] n canneberge f

crane [kreɪn] n grue f ▷ vt, vi: **to ~ forward, to ~ one's neck** allonger le cou

crank [kræŋk] n manivelle f; (person) excentrique m/f

cranny ['krænɪ] n see **nook**

crap [kræp] n (inf!: nonsense) conneries fpl (!); (: excrement) merde f (!); **the party was ~** la fête était merdique (!); **to have a ~** chier (!)

crash [kræʃ] n (noise) fracas m; (of car, plane) collision f; (of business) faillite f; (Stock Exchange) krach m ▷ vt (plane) écraser ▷ vi (plane) s'écraser; (two cars) se percuter, s'emboutir; (business) s'effondrer; **to ~ into** se jeter or se fracasser contre; **he ~ed the car into a wall** il s'est écrasé contre un mur avec sa voiture

crash course n cours intensif

crash helmet n casque (protecteur)

crash landing n atterrissage forcé or en catastrophe

crate [kreɪt] n cageot m; (for bottles) caisse f

cravat [krə'væt] n foulard (noué autour du cou)

crave [kreɪv] vt, vi: **to ~ (for)** désirer violemment, avoir un besoin physiologique de, avoir une envie irrésistible de

crawl [krɔːl] vi ramper; (vehicle) avancer au pas ▷ n (Swimming) crawl m; **to ~ on one's hands and knees** aller à quatre pattes; **to ~ to sb** (inf) faire de la lèche à qn

crayfish ['kreɪfɪʃ] n (pl inv: freshwater) écrevisse f; (saltwater) langoustine f

crayon ['kreɪən] n crayon m (de couleur)

craze [kreɪz] n engouement m

crazy ['kreɪzɪ] adj fou/folle; **to go ~** devenir fou; **to be ~ about sb/sth** (inf) être fou de qn/qch

creak [kriːk] vi (hinge) grincer; (floor, shoes) craquer

cream [kriːm] n crème f ▷ adj (colour) crème inv; **whipped ~** crème fouettée; **cream off** vt (fig) prélever

cream cake n (petit) gâteau à la crème

cream cheese n fromage m à la crème, fromage blanc

creamy ['kriːmɪ] adj crémeux(-euse)

crease [kriːs] n pli m ▷ vt froisser, chiffonner ▷ vi se froisser, se chiffonner

create [kriː'eɪt] vt créer; (impression, fuss) faire

creation [kriː'eɪʃən] n création f

creative [kriː'eɪtɪv] adj créatif(-ive)

creator [kriː'eɪtər] n créateur(-trice)

creature ['kriːtʃər] n créature f

crèche [krɛʃ] n garderie f, crèche f

credence ['kriːdns] n croyance f, foi f

credentials [krɪ'dɛnʃlz] npl (references) références fpl; (identity papers) pièce f d'identité; (letters of reference) pièces justificatives

credibility [krɛdɪ'bɪlɪtɪ] n crédibilité f

credible ['krɛdɪbl] adj digne de foi, crédible

credit ['krɛdɪt] n crédit m; (recognition) honneur m; (Scol) unité f de valeur ▷ vt (Comm) créditer; (believe: also: **give ~ to**) ajouter foi à, croire; **credits** npl (Cine) générique m; **to be in ~** (person, bank account) être créditeur(-trice); **on ~** à crédit; **to one's ~** à son honneur; à son actif; **to take the ~ for** s'attribuer le mérite de; **it does him ~** cela lui fait honneur; **to ~ sb with** (fig) prêter or attribuer à qn; **to ~ £5 to sb** créditer (le compte de) qn de 5 livres

credit card n carte f de crédit; **do you take ~s?** acceptez-vous les cartes de crédit?

credit crunch n crise f du crédit

creditor ['krɛdɪtər] n créancier(-ière)

creed [kriːd] n croyance f, credo m, principes mpl

creek [kriːk] n (inlet) crique f, anse f; (US: stream) ruisseau m, petit cours d'eau

creep (pt, pp **crept**) [kriːp, krɛpt] vi ramper; (silently) se faufiler, se glisser; (plant) grimper ▷ n (inf: flatterer) lèche-botte m; **he's a ~** c'est un type puant; **it gives me the ~s** cela me fait froid dans le dos; **to ~ up on sb** s'approcher furtivement de qn

creeper ['kriːpər] n plante grimpante

creepy ['kriːpɪ] adj (frightening) qui fait frissonner, qui donne la chair de poule

cremate [krɪ'meɪt] vt incinérer

crematorium (pl **crematoria**) [krɛmə'tɔːrɪəm, -'tɔːrɪə] n four m crématoire

crepe [kreɪp] n crêpe m

crepe bandage n (Brit) bande f Velpeau®

crept [krɛpt] pt, pp of **creep**

crescent ['krɛsnt] n croissant m; (street) rue f (en arc de cercle)

cress [krɛs] n cresson m

crest [krɛst] n crête f; (of helmet) cimier m; (of coat of arms) timbre m

crestfallen ['krɛstfɔːlən] adj déconfit(e), découragé(e)

Crete ['kriːt] n Crète f

crevice ['krɛvɪs] n fissure f, lézarde f, fente f

crew [kruː] n équipage m; (Cine) équipe f (de tournage); (gang) bande f

crew-cut ['kruːkʌt] n: **to have a ~** avoir les cheveux en brosse

crew-neck ['kruːnɛk] n col ras

crib [krɪb] n lit m d'enfant; (for baby) berceau m ▷ vt (inf) copier

crick [krɪk] n crampe f; **~ in the neck** torticolis m

cricket ['krɪkɪt] n (insect) grillon m, cri-cri m inv; (game) cricket m

cricketer ['krɪkɪtə^r] n joueur m de cricket

crime [kraɪm] n crime m; **minor ~** délit mineur, infraction mineure

criminal ['krɪmɪnl] adj, n criminel(le)

crimson ['krɪmzn] adj cramoisi(e)

cringe [krɪndʒ] vi avoir un mouvement de recul; (fig) s'humilier, ramper

crinkle ['krɪŋkl] vt froisser, chiffonner

cripple ['krɪpl] n (inf!) boiteux(-euse), infirme m/f ▷ vt (person) estropier, paralyser; (ship, plane) immobiliser; (production, exports) paralyser; **~d with rheumatism** perclus(e) de rhumatismes

crisis (pl **crises**) ['kraɪsɪs, -siːz] n crise f

crisp [krɪsp] adj croquant(e); (weather) vif, vive; (manner etc) brusque

crisps [krɪsps] (Brit) npl (pommes fpl) chips fpl

crispy ['krɪspɪ] adj croustillant(e)

crisscross ['krɪskrɔs] adj entrecroisé(e), en croisillons ▷ vt sillonner; **~ pattern** croisillons mpl

criterion (pl **criteria**) [kraɪˈtɪərɪən, -ˈtɪərɪə] n critère m

critic ['krɪtɪk] n critique m/f

critical ['krɪtɪkl] adj critique; **to be ~ of sb/sth** critiquer qn/qch

critically ['krɪtɪklɪ] adv (examine) d'un œil critique; (speak) sévèrement; **~ ill** gravement malade

criticism ['krɪtɪsɪzəm] n critique f

criticize ['krɪtɪsaɪz] vt critiquer

croak [krəuk] vi (frog) coasser; (raven) croasser

Croat ['krəuæt] adj, n = **Croatian**

Croatia [krəuˈeɪʃə] n Croatie f

Croatian [krəuˈeɪʃən] adj croate ▷ n Croate m/f; (Ling) croate m

crochet ['krəuʃeɪ] n travail m au crochet

crockery ['krɔkərɪ] n vaisselle f

crocodile ['krɔkədaɪl] n crocodile m

crocus ['krəukəs] n crocus m

croft [krɔft] n (Brit) petite ferme f

croissant ['krwasā] n croissant m

crony ['krəunɪ] n copain/copine

crook [kruk] n escroc m; (of shepherd) houlette f

crooked ['krukɪd] adj courbé(e), tordu(e); (action) malhonnête

crop [krɔp] n (produce) culture f; (amount produced) récolte f; (riding crop) cravache f; (of bird) jabot m ▷ vt (hair) tondre; (animals: grass) brouter; **crop up** vi surgir, se présenter, survenir

cross [krɔs] n croix f; (Biol) croisement m ▷ vt (street etc) traverser; (arms, legs, Biol) croiser; (cheque) barrer; (thwart: person, plan) contrarier ▷ vi: **the boat ~es from ... to ...** le bateau fait la traversée de ... à ... ▷ adj en colère, fâché(e); **to ~ o.s.** se signer, faire le signe de (la) croix; **we have a ~ed line** (Brit: on telephone) il y a des interférences; **they've got their lines ~ed** (fig) il y a un malentendu entre eux; **to be/get ~ with sb (about sth)** être en colère/(se) fâcher contre qn (à propos de qch); **cross off** or **out** vt barrer, rayer; **cross over** vi traverser

crossbar ['krɔsbɑː^r] n barre transversale

cross-Channel ferry ['krɔsˈtʃænl-] n ferry m qui fait la traversée de la Manche

cross-country ['krɔsˈkʌntrɪ], **cross-country race** n cross(-country) m

cross-examine ['krɔsɪgˈzæmɪn] vt (Law) faire subir un examen contradictoire à

cross-eyed ['krɔsaɪd] adj qui louche

crossfire ['krɔsfaɪə^r] n feux croisés

crossing ['krɔsɪŋ] n croisement m, carrefour m; (sea passage) traversée f; (also: **pedestrian ~**) passage clouté; **how long does the ~ take?** combien de temps dure la traversée?

crossing guard (US) n contractuel qui fait traverser la rue aux enfants

cross-purposes ['krɔsˈpəːpəsɪz] npl: **to be at ~ with sb** comprendre qn de travers; **we're (talking) at ~** on ne parle pas de la même chose

cross-reference ['krɔsˈrɛfrəns] n renvoi m, référence f

crossroads ['krɔsrəudz] n carrefour m

cross section n (Biol) coupe transversale; (in population) échantillon m

crosswalk ['krɔswɔːk] n (US) passage clouté

crosswind ['krɔswɪnd] n vent m de travers

crossword ['krɔswəːd] n mots mpl croisés

crotch [krɔtʃ] n (of garment) entrejambe m; (Anat) entrecuisse m

crouch [krautʃ] vi s'accroupir; (hide) se tapir; (before springing) se ramasser

crouton ['kruːtɔn] n croûton m

crow [krəu] n (bird) corneille f; (of cock) chant m du coq, cocorico m ▷ vi (cock) chanter; (fig) pavoiser, chanter victoire

crowbar ['krəubɑː^r] n levier m

crowd [kraud] n foule f ▷ vt bourrer, remplir ▷ vi affluer, s'attrouper, s'entasser; **~s of people** une foule de gens

crowded ['kraudɪd] adj bondé(e), plein(e); **~ with** plein de

crown [kraun] n couronne f; (of head) sommet m de la tête, calotte crânienne; (of hat) fond m; (of hill) sommet m ▷ vt (also tooth) couronner

crown jewels npl joyaux mpl de la Couronne

crow's-feet ['krəʊzfiːt] npl pattes fpl d'oie (fig)

crucial ['kruːʃl] adj crucial(e), décisif(-ive); (also: **~ to**) essentiel(le) à

crucifix ['kruːsɪfɪks] n crucifix m

crucifixion [kruːsɪ'fɪkʃən] n crucifiement m, crucifixion f

crude [kruːd] adj (materials) brut(e); non raffiné(e); (basic) rudimentaire, sommaire; (vulgar) cru(e), grossier(-ière) ▷ n (also: **~ oil**) (pétrole m) brut m

cruel ['kruəl] adj cruel(le)

cruelty ['kruəltɪ] n cruauté f

cruise [kruːz] n croisière f ▷ vi (ship) croiser; (car) rouler; (aircraft) voler; (taxi) être en maraude

cruiser ['kruːzə'] n croiseur m

crumb [krʌm] n miette f

crumble ['krʌmbl] vt émietter ▷ vi s'émietter; (plaster etc) s'effriter; (land, earth) s'ébouler; (building) s'écrouler, crouler; (fig) s'effondrer

crumbly ['krʌmblɪ] adj friable

crumpet ['krʌmpɪt] n petite crêpe (épaisse)

crumple ['krʌmpl] vt froisser, friper

crunch [krʌntʃ] vt croquer; (underfoot) faire craquer, écraser; faire crisser ▷ n (fig) instant m or moment m critique, moment de vérité

crunchy ['krʌntʃɪ] adj croquant(e), croustillant(e)

crusade [kruː'seɪd] n croisade f ▷ vi (fig): **to ~ for/against** partir en croisade pour/contre

crush [krʌʃ] n (crowd) foule f, cohue f; (love): **to have a ~ on sb** avoir le béguin pour qn; (drink): **lemon ~** citron pressé ▷ vt écraser; (crumple) froisser; (grind, break up: garlic, ice) piler; (: grapes) presser; (hopes) anéantir

crust [krʌst] n croûte f

crusty ['krʌstɪ] adj (bread) croustillant(e); (inf: person) revêche, bourru(e); (: remark) irrité(e)

crutch [krʌtʃ] n béquille f; (Tech) support m; (also: **crotch**) entrejambe m

crux [krʌks] n point crucial

cry [kraɪ] vi pleurer; (shout: also: **~ out**) crier ▷ n cri m; **why are you ~ing?** pourquoi pleures-tu?; **to ~ for help** appeler à l'aide; **she had a good ~** elle a pleuré un bon coup; **it's a far ~ from ...** (fig) on est loin de ...; **cry off** vi se dédire; se décommander; **cry out** vi (call out, shout) pousser un cri ▷ vt crier

cryptic ['krɪptɪk] adj énigmatique

crystal ['krɪstl] n cristal m

crystal-clear ['krɪstl'klɪə'] adj clair(e) comme de l'eau de roche

CSA n abbr = **Confederate States of America**; (Brit: = Child Support Agency) organisme pour la protection des enfants de parents séparés, qui contrôle le versement des pensions alimentaires.

CTC n abbr (Brit) = **city technology college**

cub [kʌb] n petit m (d'un animal); (also: **~ scout**) louveteau m

Cuba ['kjuːbə] n Cuba m

cube [kjuːb] n cube m ▷ vt (Math) élever au cube

cubic ['kjuːbɪk] adj cubique; **~ metre** etc mètre m etc cube; **~ capacity** (Aut) cylindrée f

cubicle ['kjuːbɪkl] n (in hospital) box m; (at pool) cabine f

cuckoo ['kukuː] n coucou m

cuckoo clock n (pendule f à) coucou m

cucumber ['kjuːkʌmbə'] n concombre m

cuddle ['kʌdl] vt câliner, caresser ▷ vi se blottir l'un contre l'autre

cue [kjuː] n queue f de billard; (Theat etc) signal m

cuff [kʌf] n (Brit: of shirt, coat etc) poignet m, manchette f; (US: on trousers) revers m; (blow) gifle f ▷ vt gifler; **off the ~** adv à l'improviste

cufflinks ['kʌflɪŋks] n boutons m de manchette

cuisine [kwɪ'ziːn] n cuisine f, art m culinaire

cul-de-sac ['kʌldəsæk] n cul-de-sac m, impasse f

cull [kʌl] vt sélectionner; (kill selectively) pratiquer l'abattage sélectif de ▷ n (of animals) abattage sélectif

culminate ['kʌlmɪneɪt] vi: **to ~ in** finir or se terminer par; (lead to) mener à

culmination [kʌlmɪ'neɪʃən] n point culminant

culottes [kjuː'lɔts] npl jupe-culotte f

culprit ['kʌlprɪt] n coupable m/f

cult [kʌlt] n culte m

cultivate ['kʌltɪveɪt] vt (also fig) cultiver

cultivation [kʌltɪ'veɪʃən] n culture f

cultural ['kʌltʃərəl] adj culturel(le)

culture ['kʌltʃə'] n (also fig) culture f

cultured ['kʌltʃəd] adj cultivé(e) (fig)

cumbersome ['kʌmbəsəm] adj encombrant(e), embarrassant(e)

cumin ['kʌmɪn] n (spice) cumin m

cunning ['kʌnɪŋ] n ruse f, astuce f ▷ adj rusé(e), malin(-igne); (clever: device, idea) astucieux(-euse)

cup [kʌp] n tasse f; (prize, event) coupe f; (of bra) bonnet m; **a ~ of tea** une tasse de thé

cupboard ['kʌbəd] n placard m

cup final n (Brit Football) finale f de la coupe

cup tie ['kʌptaɪ] n (Brit Football) match m de coupe

curate ['kjuərɪt] n vicaire m

curator [kjuə'reɪtə'] n conservateur m (d'un musée etc)

curb [kəːb] vt refréner, mettre un frein à; (expenditure) limiter, juguler ▷ n (fig) frein m; (US) bord m du trottoir

curdle ['kəːdl] vi (se) cailler

cure [kjuə'] vt guérir; (Culin: salt) saler; (: smoke) fumer; (: dry) sécher ▷ n remède m; **to be ~d of sth** être guéri de qch

curfew ['kəːfjuː] n couvre-feu m

curiosity [kjuərɪ'ɔsɪtɪ] n curiosité f

curious ['kjuərɪəs] adj curieux(-euse); **I'm ~ about him** il m'intrigue

curl [kəːl] n boucle f (de cheveux); (of smoke etc) volute f ▷ vt, vi boucler; (tightly) friser; **curl up** vi s'enrouler; (person) se pelotonner

curler [ˈkəːləʳ] n bigoudi m, rouleau m; (Sport) joueur(-euse) de curling

curly [ˈkəːlɪ] adj bouclé(e); (tightly curled) frisé(e)

currant [ˈkʌrnt] n raisin m de Corinthe, raisin sec; (fruit) groseille f

currency [ˈkʌrnsɪ] n monnaie f; **foreign ~** devises étrangères, monnaie étrangère; **to gain ~** (fig) s'accréditer

current [ˈkʌrnt] n courant m ▷ adj (common) courant(e); (tendency, price, event) actuel(le); **direct/alternating ~** (Elec) courant continu/ alternatif; **the ~ issue of a magazine** le dernier numéro d'un magazine; **in ~ use** d'usage courant

current account n (Brit) compte courant

current affairs npl (questions fpl d')actualité f

currently [ˈkʌrntlɪ] adv actuellement

curriculum (pl **curriculums** or **curricula**) [kəˈrɪkjuləm, -lə] n programme m d'études

curriculum vitae [-ˈviːtaɪ] n curriculum vitae (CV) m

curry [ˈkʌrɪ] n curry m ▷ vt: **to ~ favour with** chercher à gagner la faveur or à s'attirer les bonnes grâces de; **chicken ~** curry de poulet, poulet m au curry

curry powder n poudre f de curry

curse [kəːs] vi jurer, blasphémer ▷ vt maudire ▷ n (spell) malédiction f; (problem, scourge) fléau m; (swearword) juron m

cursor [ˈkəːsəʳ] n (Comput) curseur m

cursory [ˈkəːsərɪ] adj superficiel(le), hâtif(-ive)

curt [kəːt] adj brusque, sec(-sèche)

curtail [kəːˈteɪl] vt (visit etc) écourter; (expenses etc) réduire

curtain [ˈkəːtn] n rideau m; **to draw the ~s** (together) fermer or tirer les rideaux; (apart) ouvrir les rideaux

curtsey, curtsy [ˈkəːtsɪ] n révérence f ▷ vi faire une révérence

curve [kəːv] n courbe f; (in the road) tournant m, virage m ▷ vt courber ▷ vi se courber; (road) faire une courbe

curved [kəːvd] adj courbe

cushion [ˈkuʃən] n coussin m ▷ vt (seat) rembourrer; (fall, shock) amortir

custard [ˈkʌstəd] n (for pouring) crème anglaise

custody [ˈkʌstədɪ] n (of child) garde f; (for offenders) détention préventive; **to take sb into ~** placer qn en détention préventive; **in the ~ of** sous la garde de

custom [ˈkʌstəm] n coutume f, usage m; (Law) droit coutumier, coutume f; (Comm) clientèle f

customary [ˈkʌstəmərɪ] adj habituel(le); **it is ~ to do it** l'usage veut qu'on le fasse

customer [ˈkʌstəməʳ] n client(e); **he's an awkward ~** (inf) ce n'est pas quelqu'un de facile

customized [ˈkʌstəmaɪzd] adj personnalisé(e); (car etc) construit(e) sur commande

custom-made [ˈkʌstəmˈmeɪd] adj (clothes) fait(e) sur mesure; (other goods: also: **custom-built**) hors série, fait(e) sur commande

customs [ˈkʌstəmz] npl douane f; **to go through (the) ~** passer la douane

customs officer n douanier m

cut [kʌt] (pt, pp **cut**) vt couper; (meat) découper; (shape, make) tailler; couper; creuser; graver; (reduce) réduire; (inf: lecture, appointment) manquer ▷ vt couper; (intersect) se couper ▷ n (gen) coupure f; (of clothes) coupe f; (of jewel) taille f; (in salary etc) réduction f; (of meat) morceau m; **to ~ teeth** (baby) faire ses dents; **to ~ a tooth** percer une dent; **to ~ one's finger** se couper le doigt; **to get one's hair ~** se faire couper les cheveux; **I've ~ myself** je me suis coupé; **to ~ sth short** couper court à qch; **to ~ sb dead** ignorer (complètement) qn; **cut back** vt (plants) tailler; (production, expenditure) réduire; **cut down** vt (tree) abattre; (reduce) réduire; **to ~ sb down to size** (fig) remettre qn à sa place; **cut down on** vt fus réduire; **cut in** vi (interrupt: conversation): **to ~ in (on)** couper la parole (à); (Aut) faire une queue de poisson; **cut off** vt (gen) couper; (fig) isoler; **we've been ~ off** (Tel) nous avons été coupés; **cut out** vt (picture etc) découper; (remove) supprimer; **cut up** vt découper

cutback [ˈkʌtbæk] n réduction f

cute [kjuːt] adj mignon(ne), adorable; (clever) rusé(e), astucieux(-euse)

cutlery [ˈkʌtlərɪ] n couverts mpl; (trade) coutellerie f

cutlet [ˈkʌtlɪt] n côtelette f

cutout [ˈkʌtaut] n coupe-circuit m inv; (paper figure) découpage m

cut-price [ˈkʌtˈpraɪs], (US) **cut-rate** [ˈkʌtˈreɪt] adj au rabais, à prix réduit

cut-throat [ˈkʌtθrəut] n assassin m ▷ adj: **~ competition** concurrence f sauvage

cutting [ˈkʌtɪŋ] adj tranchant(e), coupant(e); (fig) cinglant(e) ▷ n (Brit: from newspaper) coupure f (de journal); (from plant) bouture f; (Rail) tranchée f; (Cine) montage m

CV n abbr = **curriculum vitae**

cwt abbr = **hundredweight**

cyanide [ˈsaɪənaɪd] n cyanure m

cyberspace [ˈsaɪbəspeɪs] n cyberespace m

cycle [ˈsaɪkl] n cycle m; (bicycle) bicyclette f, vélo m ▷ vi faire de la bicyclette

cycle hire n location f de vélos

cycle lane, cycle path n piste f cyclable

cycling [ˈsaɪklɪŋ] n cyclisme m; **to go on a ~ holiday** (Brit) faire du cyclotourisme

cyclist [ˈsaɪklɪst] n cycliste m/f

cyclone [ˈsaɪkləun] n cyclone m

cygnet [ˈsɪgnɪt] n jeune cygne m

cylinder [ˈsɪlɪndəʳ] n cylindre m

cymbals ['sɪmblz] *npl* cymbales *fpl*
cynic ['sɪnɪk] *n* cynique *m/f*
cynical ['sɪnɪkl] *adj* cynique
cynicism ['sɪnɪsɪzəm] *n* cynisme *m*
Cypriot ['sɪprɪət] *adj* cypriote, chypriote ▷ *n* Cypriote *m/f*, Chypriote *m/f*
Cyprus ['saɪprəs] *n* Chypre *f*
cyst [sɪst] *n* kyste *m*
cystitis [sɪs'taɪtɪs] *n* cystite *f*
czar [zɑːʳ] *n* tsar *m*
Czech [tʃɛk] *adj* tchèque ▷ *n* Tchèque *m/f*; (Ling) tchèque *m*
Czechoslovak [tʃɛkə'sləuvæk] *adj, n* = **Czechoslovakian**
Czechoslovakia [tʃɛkəslə'vækɪə] *n* Tchécoslovaquie *f*
Czechoslovakian [tʃɛkəslə'vækɪən] *adj* tchécoslovaque ▷ *n* Tchécoslovaque *m/f*
Czech Republic *n*: **the ~** la République tchèque

D¹, d¹ [diː] *n* (*letter*) D, d *m*; (*Mus*): **D** ré *m*; **D for David**, (US) **D for Dog** D comme Désirée
D² *abbr* (US Pol) = **democrat**; **democratic**
d² *abbr* (Brit: *old*) = **penny**
dab [dæb] *vt* (*eyes, wound*) tamponner; (*paint, cream*) appliquer (par petites touches *or* rapidement); **a ~ of paint** un petit coup de peinture
dabble ['dæbl] *vi*: **to ~ in** faire *or* se mêler *or* s'occuper un peu de
dad, daddy [dæd, 'dædɪ] *n* papa *m*
daffodil ['dæfədɪl] *n* jonquille *f*
daft [dɑːft] *adj* (*inf*) idiot(e), stupide; **to be ~ about** être toqué(e) *or* mordu(e) de
dagger ['dægəʳ] *n* poignard *m*; **to be at ~s drawn with sb** être à couteaux tirés avec qn; **to look ~s at sb** foudroyer qn du regard
daily ['deɪlɪ] *adj* quotidien(ne), journalier(-ière) ▷ *n* quotidien *m*; (*Brit*: *servant*) femme *f* de ménage (*à la journée*) ▷ *adv* tous les jours; **twice ~** deux fois par jour
dainty ['deɪntɪ] *adj* délicat(e), mignon(ne)
dairy ['dɛərɪ] *n* (*shop*) crémerie *f*, laiterie *f*; (*on farm*) laiterie ▷ *adj* laitier(-ière)
dairy produce *n* produits laitiers
dairy products *npl* produits laitier
daisy ['deɪzɪ] *n* pâquerette *f*
dale [deɪl] *n* vallon *m*
dam [dæm] *n* (*wall*) barrage *m*; (*water*) réservoir *m*, lac *m* de retenue ▷ *vt* endiguer
damage ['dæmɪdʒ] *n* dégâts *mpl*, dommages *mpl*; (*fig*) tort *m* ▷ *vt* endommager, abîmer;

(fig) faire du tort à; **damages** *npl (Law)* dommages-intérêts *mpl*; **to pay £5000 in ~s** payer 5000 livres de dommages- intérêts; **~ to property** dégâts matériels

damn [dæm] *vt* condamner; *(curse)* maudire ▷ *n (inf)*: **I don't give a ~** je m'en fous ▷ *adj (inf: also: ~ed)*: **this ~** ... ce sacré or foutu ...; **~ (it)!** zut!

damning ['dæmɪŋ] *adj (evidence)* accablant(e)

damp [dæmp] *adj* humide ▷ *n* humidité *f* ▷ *vt (also: ~en: cloth, rag)* humecter; *(: enthusiasm etc)* refroidir

damson ['dæmzən] *n* prune *f* de Damas

dance [dɑːns] *n* danse *f*; *(ball)* bal *m* ▷ *vi* danser; **to ~ about** sautiller, gambader

dance floor *n* piste *f* de danse

dance hall *n* salle *f* de bal, dancing *m*

dancer ['dɑːnsər] *n* danseur(-euse)

dancing ['dɑːnsɪŋ] *n* danse *f*

dandelion ['dændɪlaɪən] *n* pissenlit *m*

dandruff ['dændrəf] *n* pellicules *fpl*

D & T *n abbr (Brit: Scol)* = **design and technology**

Dane [deɪn] *n* Danois(e)

danger ['deɪndʒər] *n* danger *m*; **~!** *(on sign)* danger!; **there is a ~ of fire** il y a (un) risque d'incendie; **in ~** en danger; **he was in ~ of falling** il risquait de tomber; **out of ~** hors de danger

dangerous ['deɪndʒrəs] *adj* dangereux(-euse)

dangle ['dæŋgl] *vt* balancer; *(fig)* faire miroiter ▷ *vi* pendre, se balancer

Danish ['deɪnɪʃ] *adj* danois(e) ▷ *n (Ling)* danois *m*

dare [dɛər] *vt*: **to ~ sb to do** défier qn or mettre qn au défi de faire ▷ *vi*: **to ~ (to) do sth** oser faire qch; **I ~n't tell him** *(Brit)* je n'ose pas le lui dire; **I ~ say he'll turn up** il est probable qu'il viendra

daring ['dɛərɪŋ] *adj* hardi(e), audacieux(-euse) ▷ *n* audace *f*, hardiesse *f*

dark [dɑːk] *adj (night, room)* obscur(e), sombre; *(colour, complexion)* foncé(e), sombre; *(fig)* sombre ▷ *n*: **in the ~** dans le noir; **to be in the ~ about** *(fig)* ignorer tout de; **after ~** après la tombée de la nuit; **it is/is getting ~** il fait nuit/commence à faire nuit

darken ['dɑːkn] *vt* obscurcir, assombrir ▷ *vi* s'obscurcir, s'assombrir

dark glasses *npl* lunettes noires

darkness ['dɑːknɪs] *n* obscurité *f*

darkroom ['dɑːkrʊm] *n* chambre noire

darling ['dɑːlɪŋ] *adj, n* chéri(e)

darn [dɑːn] *vt* repriser

dart [dɑːt] *n* fléchette *f*; *(in sewing)* pince *f* ▷ *vi*: **to ~ towards** *(also:* **make a ~ towards**) se précipiter or s'élancer vers; **to ~ away/along** partir/passer comme une flèche

dartboard ['dɑːtbɔːd] *n* cible *f* (de jeu de fléchettes)

darts [dɑːts] *n* jeu *m* de fléchettes

dash [dæʃ] *n (sign)* tiret *m*; *(small quantity)* goutte *f*, larme *f* ▷ *vt (throw)* jeter or lancer violemment; *(hopes)* anéantir ▷ *vi*: **to ~ towards** *(also:* **make a ~ towards**) se précipiter or se ruer vers; **a ~ of soda** un peu d'eau gazeuse; **dash away** *vi* partir à toute allure; **dash off** *vi* = **dash away**

dashboard ['dæʃbɔːd] *n (Aut)* tableau *m* de bord

dashing ['dæʃɪŋ] *adj* fringant(e)

data ['deɪtə] *npl* données *fpl*

database ['deɪtəbeɪs] *n* base *f* de données

data processing *n* traitement *m* des données

date [deɪt] *n* date *f*; *(with sb)* rendez-vous *m*; *(fruit)* datte *f* ▷ *vt* dater; *(person)* sortir avec; **what's the ~ today?** quelle date sommes-nous aujourd'hui?; **~ of birth** date de naissance; **closing ~** date de clôture; **to ~** *adv* à ce jour; **out of ~** périmé(e); **up to ~** à la page, mis(e) à jour, moderne; **to bring up to ~** *(correspondence, information)* mettre à jour; *(method)* moderniser; *(person)* mettre au courant; **letter ~d 5th July** or *(US)* **July 5th** lettre (datée) du 5 juillet

dated ['deɪtɪd] *adj* démodé(e)

date rape *n* viol *m* (à l'issue d'un rendez-vous *galant*)

daub [dɔːb] *vt* barbouiller

daughter ['dɔːtər] *n* fille *f*

daughter-in-law ['dɔːtərɪnlɔː] *n* belle-fille *f*, bru *f*

daunting ['dɔːntɪŋ] *adj* décourageant(e), intimidant(e)

dawdle ['dɔːdl] *vi* traîner, lambiner; **to ~ over one's work** traînasser or lambiner sur son travail

dawn [dɔːn] *n* aube *f*, aurore *f* ▷ *vi (day)* se lever, poindre; *(fig)* naître, se faire jour; **at ~** à l'aube; **from ~ to dusk** du matin au soir; **it ~ed on him that** ... il lui vint à l'esprit que ...

day [deɪ] *n* jour *m*; *(as duration)* journée *f*; *(period of time, age)* époque *f*, temps *m*; **the ~ before** la veille, le jour précédent; **the ~ after, the following ~** le lendemain, le jour suivant; **the ~ before yester-** avant-hier; **the ~ after tomorrow** après-demain; **(on) the ~ that** ... le jour où ...; **~ by ~** jour après jour; **by ~** de jour; **paid by the ~** payé(e) à la journée; **these ~s, in the present ~** de nos jours, à l'heure actuelle

daybreak ['deɪbreɪk] *n* point *m* du jour

day-care centre ['deɪkɛə-] *n (for elderly etc)* centre *m* d'accueil de jour; *(for children)* garderie *f*

daydream ['deɪdriːm] *n* rêverie *f* ▷ *vi* rêver (tout éveillé)

daylight ['deɪlaɪt] *n* (lumière *f* du) jour *m*

day return *n (Brit)* billet *m* d'aller-retour *(valable pour la journée)*

daytime ['deɪtaɪm] *n* jour *m*, journée *f*

day-to-day ['deɪtə'deɪ] adj (routine, expenses) journalier(-ière); **on a ~ basis** au jour le jour

day trip n excursion f (d'une journée)

daze [deɪz] vt (drug) hébéter; (blow) étourdir ▷ n: **in a ~** hébété(e), étourdi(e)

dazed [deɪzd] adj abruti(e)

dazzle ['dæzl] vt éblouir, aveugler

dazzling ['dæzlɪŋ] adj (light) aveuglant(e), éblouissant(e); (fig) éblouissant(e)

DC abbr (Elec) = **direct current**; (US) = **District of Columbia**

D-day ['di:deɪ] n le jour J

dead [dɛd] adj mort(e); (numb) engourdi(e), insensible; (battery) à plat ▷ adv (completely) absolument, complètement; (exactly) juste; **the dead** npl les morts; **he was shot ~** il a été tué d'un coup de revolver; **~ on time** à l'heure pile; **~ tired** éreinté(e), complètement fourbu(e); **to stop ~** s'arrêter pile or net; **the line is ~** (Tel) la ligne est coupée

deaden [dɛdn] vt (blow, sound) amortir; (make numb) endormir, rendre insensible

dead end n impasse f

dead heat n (Sport): **to finish in a ~** terminer ex aequo

deadline ['dɛdlaɪn] n date f or heure f limite; **to work to a ~** avoir des délais stricts à respecter

deadlock ['dɛdlɔk] n impasse f (fig)

dead loss n (inf): **to be a ~** (person) n'être bon/bonne à rien; (thing) ne rien valoir

deadly ['dɛdlɪ] adj mortel(le); (weapon) meurtrier(-ière); **~ dull** mortellement ennuyeux

deadpan ['dɛdpæn] adj impassible; (humour) pince-sans-rire inv

Dead Sea n: **the ~** la mer Morte

deaf [dɛf] adj sourd(e); **to turn a ~ ear to sth** faire la sourde oreille à qch

deafen ['dɛfn] vt rendre sourd(e); (fig) assourdir

deafening ['dɛfnɪŋ] adj assourdissant(e)

deaf-mute ['dɛfmju:t] n (inf!) sourd/e-muet/te

deafness ['dɛfnɪs] n surdité f

deal [di:l] n affaire f, marché m ▷ vt (pt, pp **dealt**) [dɛlt] (blow) porter; (cards) donner, distribuer; **to strike a ~ with sb** faire or conclure un marché avec qn; **it's a ~!** (inf) marché conclu!, tope-là!, topez-là!; **he got a bad ~ from them** ils ont mal agi envers lui; **he got a fair ~ from them** ils ont agi loyalement envers lui; **a good ~** (a lot) beaucoup; **a good ~ of, a great ~ of** beaucoup de, énormément de; **deal in** vt fus (Comm) faire le commerce de, être dans le commerce de; **deal with** vt fus (Comm) traiter avec; (handle) s'occuper or se charger de; (be about: book etc) traiter de

dealer ['di:lə^r] n (Comm) marchand m; (Cards) donneur m

dealings ['di:lɪŋz] npl (in goods, shares) opérations fpl, transactions fpl; (relations) relations fpl, rapports mpl

dealt [dɛlt] pt, pp of **deal**

dean [di:n] n (Rel, Brit Scol) doyen m; (US Scol) conseiller principal/conseillère principale d'éducation

dear [dɪə^r] adj cher/chère; (expensive) cher, coûteux(-euse) ▷ n: **my ~** mon cher/ma chère ▷ excl: **~ me!** mon Dieu!; **D~ Sir/Madam** (in letter) Monsieur/Madame; **D~ Mr/Mrs X** Cher Monsieur/Chère Madame X

dearly ['dɪəlɪ] adv (love) tendrement; (pay) cher

death [dɛθ] n mort f; (Admin) décès m

death certificate n acte m de décès

deathly ['dɛθlɪ] adj de mort ▷ adv comme la mort

death penalty n peine f de mort

death rate n taux m de mortalité

death sentence n condamnation f à mort

death toll n nombre m de morts

debase [dɪ'beɪs] vt (currency) déprécier, dévaloriser; (person) abaisser, avilir

debatable [dɪ'beɪtəbl] adj discutable, contestable; **it is ~ whether ...** il est douteux que ...

debate [dɪ'beɪt] n discussion f, débat m ▷ vt discuter, débattre ▷ vi (consider): **to ~ whether** se demander si

debit ['dɛbɪt] n débit m ▷ vt: **to ~ a sum to sb** or **to sb's account** porter une somme au débit de qn, débiter qn d'une somme

debit card n carte f de paiement

debris ['dɛbri:] n débris mpl, décombres mpl

debt [dɛt] n dette f; **to be in ~** avoir des dettes, être endetté(e); **bad ~** créance f irrécouvrable

debtor ['dɛtə^r] n débiteur(-trice)

debug [di:'bʌg] vt (Comput) déboguer

debut ['deɪbju:] n début(s) m(pl)

Dec. abbr (= December) déc

decade ['dɛkeɪd] n décennie f, décade f

decadence ['dɛkədəns] n décadence f

decaf ['di:kæf] n (inf) déca m

decaffeinated [dɪ'kæfɪneɪtɪd] adj décaféiné(e)

decanter [dɪ'kæntə^r] n carafe f

decay [dɪ'keɪ] n (of food, wood etc) décomposition f, pourriture f; (of building) délabrement m; (fig) déclin m; (also: **tooth ~**) carie f (dentaire) ▷ vi (rot) se décomposer, pourrir; (: teeth) se carier; (fig: city, district, building) se délabrer; (: civilization) décliner; (: system) tomber en ruine

deceased [dɪ'si:st] n: **the ~** le/la défunt(e)

deceit [dɪ'si:t] n tromperie f, supercherie f

deceitful [dɪ'si:tful] adj trompeur(-euse)

deceive [dɪ'si:v] vt tromper; **to ~ o.s.** s'abuser

December [dɪ'sɛmbə^r] n décembre m; see also **July**

decency ['di:sənsɪ] n décence f

decent ['di:sənt] adj (proper) décent(e), convenable; **they were very ~ about it** ils se sont montrés très chics

deception [dɪ'sɛpʃən] n tromperie f

deceptive [dɪ'sɛptɪv] adj trompeur(-euse)

decide [dɪ'saɪd] vt (subj: person) décider; (question, argument) trancher, régler ▷ vi se décider, décider; **to ~ on** décider, se décider pour; **to ~ on doing** décider de faire; **to ~ against doing** décider de ne pas faire

decided [dɪ'saɪdɪd] adj (resolute) résolu(e), décidé(e); (clear, definite) net(te), marqué(e)

decidedly [dɪ'saɪdɪdlɪ] adv résolument; incontestablement, nettement

deciduous [dɪ'sɪdjuəs] adj à feuilles caduques

decimal ['dɛsɪməl] adj décimal(e) ▷ n décimale f; **to three ~ places** (jusqu')à la troisième décimale

decimal point n ≈ virgule f

decipher [dɪ'saɪfər] vt déchiffrer

decision [dɪ'sɪʒən] n décision f; **to make a ~** prendre une décision

decisive [dɪ'saɪsɪv] adj décisif(-ive); (influence) décisif, déterminant(e); (manner, person) décidé(e), catégorique; (reply) ferme, catégorique

deck [dɛk] n (Naut) pont m; (of cards) jeu m; (record deck) platine f; (of bus): **top ~** impériale f; **to go up on ~** monter sur le pont; **below ~** dans l'entrepont

deckchair ['dɛktʃɛər] n chaise longue

declaration [dɛklə'reɪʃən] n déclaration f

declare [dɪ'klɛər] vt déclarer

decline [dɪ'klaɪn] n (decay) déclin m; (lessening) baisse f ▷ vt refuser, décliner ▷ vi décliner; (business) baisser; **~ in living standards** baisse du niveau de vie; **to ~ to do sth** refuser (poliment) de faire qch

decoder [di:'kəudər] n (Comput, TV) décodeur m

decorate ['dɛkəreɪt] vt (adorn, give a medal to) décorer; (paint and paper) peindre et tapisser

decoration [dɛkə'reɪʃən] n (medal etc, adornment) décoration f

decorator ['dɛkəreɪtər] n peintre m en bâtiment

decoy ['di:kɔɪ] n piège m; **they used him as a ~ for the enemy** ils se sont servis de lui pour attirer l'ennemi

decrease n ['di:kri:s] diminution f ▷ vt, vi [di:'kri:s] diminuer; **to be on the ~** diminuer, être en diminution

decree [dɪ'kri:] n (Pol, Rel) décret m; (Law) arrêt m, jugement m ▷ vt: **to ~ (that)** décréter (que), ordonner (que); **~ absolute** jugement définitif (de divorce); **~ nisi** jugement provisoire de divorce

dedicate ['dɛdɪkeɪt] vt consacrer; (book etc) dédier

dedicated ['dɛdɪkeɪtɪd] adj (person) dévoué(e); (Comput) spécialisé(e), dédié(e); **~ word processor** station f de traitement de texte

dedication [dɛdɪ'keɪʃən] n (devotion) dévouement m; (in book) dédicace f

deduce [dɪ'dju:s] vt déduire, conclure

deduct [dɪ'dʌkt] vt: **to ~ sth (from)** déduire qch (de), retrancher qch (de); (from wage etc) prélever qch (sur), retenir qch (sur)

deduction [dɪ'dʌkʃən] n (deducting) déduction f; (from wage etc) prélèvement m, retenue f

deed [di:d] n action f, acte m; (Law) acte notarié, contrat m; **~ of covenant** (acte m de) donation f

deem [di:m] vt (formal) juger, estimer; **to ~ it wise to do** juger bon de faire

deep [di:p] adj (water, sigh, sorrow, thoughts) profond(e); (voice) grave ▷ adv: **~ in snow** recouvert(e) d'une épaisse couche de neige; **spectators stood 20 ~** il y avait 20 rangs de spectateurs; **knee-~ in water** dans l'eau jusqu'aux genoux; **4 metres ~** de 4 mètres de profondeur; **how ~ is the water?** l'eau a quelle profondeur?; **he took a ~ breath** il inspira profondément, il prit son souffle

deepen [di:pn] vt (hole) approfondir ▷ vi s'approfondir; (darkness) s'épaissir

deepfreeze ['di:p'fri:z] n congélateur m ▷ vt surgeler

deep-fry ['di:p'fraɪ] vt faire frire (dans une friteuse)

deeply ['di:plɪ] adv profondément; (dig) en profondeur; (regret, interested) vivement

deep-sea ['di:p'si:] adj: **~ diver** plongeur sous-marin; **~ diving** plongée sous-marine; **~ fishing** pêche hauturière

deep-seated ['di:p'si:tɪd] adj (belief) profondément enraciné(e)

deer [dɪər] n pl inv: **the ~** les cervidés mpl; (Zool): **(red) ~** cerf m; **(fallow) ~** daim m; **(roe) ~** chevreuil m

deerskin ['dɪəskɪn] n peau f de daim

deface [dɪ'feɪs] vt dégrader; barbouiller; rendre illisible

default [dɪ'fɔ:lt] vi (Law) faire défaut; (gen) manquer à ses engagements ▷ n (Comput: also: **~ value**) valeur f par défaut; **by ~** (Law) par défaut, par contumace; (Sport) par forfait; **to ~ on a debt** ne pas s'acquitter d'une dette

defeat [dɪ'fi:t] n défaite f ▷ vt (team, opponents) battre; (fig: plans, efforts) faire échouer

defect n ['di:fɛkt] défaut m ▷ vi [dɪ'fɛkt]: **to ~ to the enemy/the West** passer à l'ennemi/l'Ouest; **physical ~** malformation f, vice m de conformation; **mental ~** anomalie or déficience mentale

defective [dɪ'fɛktɪv] adj défectueux(-euse)

defence, (US) **defense** [dɪ'fɛns] n défense f; **in ~ of** pour défendre; **witness for the ~** témoin m à décharge; **the Ministry of D~**,

(US) **the Department of Defense** le ministère de la Défense nationale

defenceless [dɪ'fɛnslɪs] *adj* sans défense

defend [dɪ'fɛnd] *vt* défendre; (*decision, action, opinion*) justifier, défendre

defendant [dɪ'fɛndənt] *n* défendeur(-deresse); (*in criminal case*) accusé(e), prévenu(e)

defender [dɪ'fɛndə^r] *n* défenseur *m*

defense [dɪ'fɛns] *n* (US) = **defence**

defensive [dɪ'fɛnsɪv] *adj* défensif(-ive) ⊳ *n* défensive *f*; **on the ~** sur la défensive

defer [dɪ'fə:^r] *vt* (*postpone*) différer, ajourner ⊳ *vi* (*submit*): **to ~ to sb/sth** déférer à qn/qch, s'en remettre à qn/qch

defiance [dɪ'faɪəns] *n* défi *m*; **in ~ of** au mépris de

defiant [dɪ'faɪənt] *adj* provocant(e), de défi; (*person*) rebelle, intraitable

deficiency [dɪ'fɪʃənsɪ] *n* (*lack*) insuffisance *f*; (*: Med*) carence *f*; (*flaw*) faiblesse *f*; (*Comm*) déficit *m*, découvert *m*

deficient [dɪ'fɪʃənt] *adj* (*inadequate*) insuffisant(e); (*defective*) défectueux(-euse); **to be ~ in** manquer de

deficit ['dɛfɪsɪt] *n* déficit *m*

define [dɪ'faɪn] *vt* définir

definite ['dɛfɪnɪt] *adj* (*fixed*) défini(e), (*bien*) déterminé(e); (*clear, obvious*) net(te), manifeste; (*Ling*) défini(e); (*certain*) sûr(e); **he was ~ about it** il a été catégorique; il était sûr de son fait

definitely ['dɛfɪnɪtlɪ] *adv* sans aucun doute

definition [dɛfɪ'nɪʃən] *n* définition *f*; (*clearness*) netteté *f*

deflate [di:'fleɪt] *vt* dégonfler; (*pompous person*) rabattre le caquet à; (*Econ*) provoquer la déflation de; (*: prices*) faire tomber *or* baisser

deflect [dɪ'flɛkt] *vt* détourner, faire dévier

deformed [dɪ'fɔ:md] *adj* difforme

defraud [dɪ'frɔ:d] *vt* frauder; **to ~ sb of sth** soutirer qch malhonnêtement à qn; escroquer qch à qn; frustrer qn de qch

defrost [di:'frɔst] *vt* (*fridge*) dégivrer; (*frozen food*) décongeler

deft [dɛft] *adj* adroit(e), preste

defunct [dɪ'fʌŋkt] *adj* défunt(e)

defuse [di:'fju:z] *vt* désamorcer

defy [dɪ'faɪ] *vt* défier; (*efforts etc*) résister à; **it defies description** cela défie toute description

degenerate *vi* [dɪ'dʒɛnəreɪt] dégénérer ⊳ *adj* [dɪ'dʒɛnərət] dégénéré(e)

degree [dɪ'gri:] *n* degré *m*; (*Scol*) diplôme *m* (universitaire); **10 ~s below (zero)** 10 degrés au-dessous de zéro; **a (first) ~ in maths** (*Brit*) une licence en maths; **a considerable ~ of risk** une part importante de facteur *or* élément de risque; **by ~s** (*gradually*) par degrés; **to some ~, to a certain ~** jusqu'à un certain point, dans une certaine mesure

dehydrated [di:haɪ'dreɪtɪd] *adj* déshydraté(e); (*milk, eggs*) en poudre

de-ice ['di:'aɪs] *vt* (*windscreen*) dégivrer

de-icer ['di:'aɪsə^r] *n* dégivreur *m*

deign [deɪn] *vi*: **to ~ to do** daigner faire

dejected [dɪ'dʒɛktɪd] *adj* abattu(e), déprimé(e)

delay [dɪ'leɪ] *vt* (*journey, operation*) retarder, différer; (*traveller, train*) retarder; (*payment*) différer ⊳ *vi* s'attarder ⊳ *n* délai *m*, retard *m*; **to be ~ed** être en retard; **without ~** sans délai, sans tarder

delectable [dɪ'lɛktəbl] *adj* délicieux(-euse)

delegate *n* ['dɛlɪgɪt] délégué(e) ⊳ *vt* ['dɛlɪgeɪt] déléguer; **to ~ sth to sb/sb to do sth** déléguer qch à qn/qn pour faire qch

delete [dɪ'li:t] *vt* rayer, supprimer; (*Comput*) effacer

deli ['dɛlɪ] *n* épicerie fine

deliberate *adj* [dɪ'lɪbərɪt] (*intentional*) délibéré(e); (*slow*) mesuré(e) ⊳ *vi* [dɪ'lɪbəreɪt] délibérer, réfléchir

deliberately [dɪ'lɪbərɪtlɪ] *adv* (*on purpose*) exprès, délibérément

delicacy ['dɛlɪkəsɪ] *n* délicatesse *f*; (*choice food*) mets fin *or* délicat, friandise *f*

delicate ['dɛlɪkɪt] *adj* délicat(e)

delicatessen [dɛlɪkə'tɛsn] *n* épicerie fine

delicious [dɪ'lɪʃəs] *adj* délicieux(-euse), exquis(e)

delight [dɪ'laɪt] *n* (grande) joie, grand plaisir ⊳ *vt* enchanter; **she's a ~ to work with** c'est un plaisir de travailler avec elle; **a ~ to the eyes** un régal *or* plaisir pour les yeux; **to take ~ in** prendre grand plaisir à; **to be the ~ of** faire les délices *or* la joie de

delighted [dɪ'laɪtɪd] *adj*: **~ (at *or* with sth)** ravi(e) (de qch); **to be ~ to do sth/that** être enchanté(e) *or* ravi(e) de faire qch/que; **I'd be ~** j'en serais enchanté *or* ravi

delightful [dɪ'laɪtful] *adj* (*person*) absolument charmant(e), adorable; (*meal, evening*) merveilleux(-euse)

delinquent [dɪ'lɪŋkwənt] *adj, n* délinquant(e)

delirious [dɪ'lɪrɪəs] *adj* (*Med: fig*) délirant(e); **to be ~** délirer

deliver [dɪ'lɪvə^r] *vt* (*mail*) distribuer; (*goods*) livrer; (*message*) remettre; (*speech*) prononcer; (*warning, ultimatum*) lancer; (*free*) délivrer; (*Med: baby*) mettre au monde; (*: woman*) accoucher; **to ~ the goods** (*fig*) tenir ses promesses

delivery [dɪ'lɪvərɪ] *n* (*of mail*) distribution *f*; (*of goods*) livraison *f*; (*of speaker*) élocution *f*; (*Med*) accouchement *m*; **to take ~ of** prendre livraison de

delude [dɪ'lu:d] *vt* tromper, leurrer; **to ~ o.s.** se leurrer, se faire des illusions

delusion [dɪ'lu:ʒən] *n* illusion *f*; **to have ~s of grandeur** être un peu mégalomane

de luxe [də'lʌks] *adj* de luxe

delve [dɛlv] vi: **to ~ into** fouiller dans

demand [dɪˈmɑːnd] vt réclamer, exiger; (need) exiger, requérir ▷ n exigence f; (claim) revendication f; (Econ) demande f; **to ~ sth (from** or **of sb)** exiger qch (de qn), réclamer qch (à qn); **in ~** demandé(e), recherché(e); **on ~** sur demande

demanding [dɪˈmɑːndɪŋ] adj (person) exigeant(e); (work) astreignant(e)

demean [dɪˈmiːn] vt: **to ~ o.s.** s'abaisser

demeanour, (US) **demeanor** [dɪˈmiːnəʳ] n comportement m; maintien m

demented [dɪˈmɛntɪd] adj dément(e), fou/folle

demise [dɪˈmaɪz] n décès m

demister [diːˈmɪstəʳ] n (Brit Aut) dispositif m anti-buée inv

demo [ˈdɛməu] n abbr (inf: = demonstration) (protest) manif f; (Comput) démonstration f

democracy [dɪˈmɔkrəsɪ] n démocratie f

democrat [ˈdɛməkræt] n démocrate m/f

democratic [dɛməˈkrætɪk] adj démocratique; **the D~ Party** (US) le parti démocrate

demolish [dɪˈmɔlɪʃ] vt démolir

demolition [dɛməˈlɪʃən] n démolition f

demon [ˈdiːmən] n démon m ▷ cpd: **a ~ squash player** un crack en squash; **a ~ driver** un fou du volant

demonstrate [ˈdɛmənstreɪt] vt démontrer, prouver; (show) faire une démonstration de ▷ vi: **to ~ (for/against)** manifester (en faveur de/contre)

demonstration [dɛmənˈstreɪʃən] n démonstration f; (Pol etc) manifestation f; **to hold a ~** (Pol etc) organiser une manifestation, manifester

demonstrator [ˈdɛmənstreɪtəʳ] n (Pol etc) manifestant(e); (Comm: sales person) vendeur(-euse); (: car, computer etc) modèle m de démonstration

demote [dɪˈməut] vt rétrograder

demure [dɪˈmjuəʳ] adj sage, réservé(e), d'une modestie affectée

den [dɛn] n (of lion) tanière f; (room) repaire m

denial [dɪˈnaɪəl] n (of accusation) démenti m; (of rights, guilt, truth) dénégation f

denim [ˈdɛnɪm] n jean m; **denims** npl (blue-)jeans mpl

Denmark [ˈdɛnmɑːk] n Danemark m

denomination [dɪnɔmɪˈneɪʃən] n (money) valeur f; (Rel) confession f; culte m

denounce [dɪˈnauns] vt dénoncer

dense [dɛns] adj dense; (inf: stupid) obtus(e), dur(e) or lent(e) à la comprenette

densely [ˈdɛnslɪ] adv: **~ wooded** couvert(e) d'épaisses forêts; **~ populated** à forte densité (de population), très peuplé(e)

density [ˈdɛnsɪtɪ] n densité f

dent [dɛnt] n bosse f ▷ vt (also: **make a ~ in**) cabosser; **to make a ~ in** (fig) entamer

dental [ˈdɛntl] adj dentaire

dental floss [-flɔs] n fil m dentaire

dental surgeon n (chirurgien(ne)) dentiste

dental surgery n cabinet m de dentiste

dentist [ˈdɛntɪst] n dentiste m/f; **~'s surgery** (Brit) cabinet m de dentiste

dentures [ˈdɛntʃəz] npl dentier msg

deny [dɪˈnaɪ] vt nier; (refuse) refuser; (disown) renier; **he denies having said it** il nie l'avoir dit

deodorant [diːˈəudərənt] n désodorisant m, déodorant m

depart [dɪˈpɑːt] vi partir; **to ~ from** (leave) quitter, partir de; (fig: differ from) s'écarter de

department [dɪˈpɑːtmənt] n (Comm) rayon m; (Scol) section f; (Pol) ministère m, département m; **that's not my ~** (fig) ce n'est pas mon domaine or ma compétence, ce n'est pas mon rayon; **D~ of State** (US) Département d'État

department store n grand magasin

departure [dɪˈpɑːtʃəʳ] n départ m; (fig): **~ from** écart m par rapport à; **a new ~** une nouvelle voie

departure lounge n salle f de départ

depend [dɪˈpɛnd] vi: **to ~ (up)on** dépendre de; (rely on) compter sur; (financially) dépendre (financièrement) de, être à la charge de; **it ~s** cela dépend; **~ing on the result ...** selon le résultat ...

dependable [dɪˈpɛndəbl] adj sûr(e), digne de confiance

dependant [dɪˈpɛndənt] n personne f à charge

dependent [dɪˈpɛndənt] adj: **to be ~ (on)** dépendre (de) ▷ n = **dependant**

depict [dɪˈpɪkt] vt (in picture) représenter; (in words) (dé)peindre, décrire

depleted [dɪˈpliːtɪd] adj (considérablement) réduit(e) or diminué(e)

deport [dɪˈpɔːt] vt déporter, expulser

deposit [dɪˈpɔzɪt] n (Chem, Comm, Geo) dépôt m; (of ore, oil) gisement m; (part payment) arrhes fpl, acompte m; (on bottle etc) consigne f; (for hired goods etc) cautionnement m, garantie f ▷ vt déposer; (valuables) mettre or laisser en dépôt; **to put down a ~ of £50** verser 50 livres d'arrhes or d'acompte; laisser 50 livres en garantie

deposit account n compte m sur livret

depot [ˈdɛpəu] n dépôt m; (US: Rail) gare f

depreciate [dɪˈpriːʃɪeɪt] vt déprécier ▷ vi se déprécier, se dévaloriser

depress [dɪˈprɛs] vt déprimer; (press down) appuyer sur, abaisser; (wages etc) faire baisser

depressed [dɪˈprɛst] adj (person) déprimé(e), abattu(e); (area) en déclin, touché(e) par le sous-emploi; (Comm: market, trade) maussade; **to get ~** se démoraliser, se laisser abattre

depressing [dɪˈprɛsɪŋ] adj déprimant(e)

depression [dɪˈprɛʃən] n (Econ) dépression f

deprivation [dɛprɪˈveɪʃən] n privation f; (loss) perte f

deprive [dɪˈpraɪv] vt: **to ~ sb of** priver qn de

deprived [dɪˈpraɪvd] adj déshérité(e)

dept. abbr (= department) dép, dépt

depth [dɛpθ] n profondeur f; **in the ~s of** au fond de; au cœur de; au plus profond de; **to be in the ~s of despair** être au plus profond du désespoir; **at a ~ of 3 metres** à 3 mètres de profondeur; **to be out of one's ~** (Brit: swimmer) ne plus avoir pied; (fig) être dépassé(e), nager; **to study sth in ~** étudier qch en profondeur

deputize [ˈdɛpjʊtaɪz] vi: **to ~ for** assurer l'intérim de

deputy [ˈdɛpjʊtɪ] n (replacement) suppléant m, intérimaire m/f; (second in command) adjoint(e); (Pol) député m; (US: also: **~ sheriff**) shérif adjoint ▷ adj: **~ chairman** vice-président m; **~ head** (Scol) directeur(-trice) adjoint(e), sous-directeur(-trice); **~ leader** (Brit Pol) vice-président(e), secrétaire adjoint(e)

derail [dɪˈreɪl] vt faire dérailler; **to be ~ed** dérailler

deranged [dɪˈreɪndʒd] adj: **to be (mentally) ~** avoir le cerveau dérangé

derby [ˈdəːrbɪ] n (US) (chapeau m) melon m

derelict [ˈdɛrɪlɪkt] adj abandonné(e), à l'abandon

derisory [dɪˈraɪsərɪ] adj (sum) dérisoire; (smile, person) moqueur(-euse), railleur(-euse)

derive [dɪˈraɪv] vt: **to ~ sth from** tirer qch de; trouver qch dans ▷ vi: **to ~ from** provenir de, dériver de

derogatory [dɪˈrɔgətərɪ] adj désobligeant(e), péjoratif(-ive)

descend [dɪˈsɛnd] vt, vi descendre; **to ~ from** descendre de, être issu(e) de; **to ~ to** s'abaisser à; **in ~ing order of importance** par ordre d'importance décroissante; **descend on** vt fus (enemy, angry person) tomber or sauter sur; (misfortune) s'abattre sur; (gloom, silence) envahir; **visitors ~ed (up)on us** des gens sont arrivés chez nous à l'improviste

descendant [dɪˈsɛndənt] n descendant(e)

descent [dɪˈsɛnt] n descente f; (origin) origine f

describe [dɪsˈkraɪb] vt décrire

description [dɪsˈkrɪpʃən] n description f; (sort) sorte f, espèce f; **of every ~** de toutes sortes

desecrate [ˈdɛsɪkreɪt] vt profaner

desert [ˈdɛzət] n désert m ▷ vt [dɪˈzəːt] déserter, abandonner ▷ vi (Mil) déserter

deserted [dɪˈzəːtɪd] adj désert(e)

deserter [dɪˈzəːtəʳ] n déserteur m

desertion [dɪˈzəːʃən] n désertion f

desert island n île déserte

deserve [dɪˈzəːv] vt mériter

deserving [dɪˈzəːvɪŋ] adj (person) méritant(e); (action, cause) méritoire

design [dɪˈzaɪn] n (sketch) plan m, dessin m; (layout, shape) conception f, ligne f; (pattern) dessin, motif(s) m(pl); (of dress, car) modèle m; (art) design m, stylisme m; (intention) dessein m ▷ vt dessiner; (plan) concevoir; **to have ~s on** avoir des visées sur; **well-~ed** adj bien conçu(e); **industrial ~** esthétique industrielle

design and technology n (Brit: Scol) technologie f

designate vt [ˈdɛzɪgneɪt] désigner ▷ adj [ˈdɛzɪgnɪt] désigné(e)

designer [dɪˈzaɪnəʳ] n (Archit, Art) dessinateur(-trice); (Industry) concepteur m, designer m; (Fashion) styliste m/f

desirable [dɪˈzaɪərəbl] adj (property, location, purchase) attrayant(e); **it is ~ that** il est souhaitable que

desire [dɪˈzaɪəʳ] n désir m ▷ vt désirer, vouloir; **to ~ to do sth/that** désirer faire qch/que

desk [dɛsk] n (in office) bureau m; (for pupil) pupitre m; (Brit: in shop, restaurant) caisse f; (in hotel, at airport) réception f

desk-top publishing [ˈdɛsktɔp-] n publication assistée par ordinateur, PAO f

desolate [ˈdɛsəlɪt] adj désolé(e)

despair [dɪsˈpɛəʳ] n désespoir m ▷ vi: **to ~ of** désespérer de; **to be in ~** être au désespoir

despatch [dɪsˈpætʃ] n, vt = dispatch

desperate [ˈdɛspərɪt] adj désespéré(e); (fugitive) prêt(e) à tout; (measures) désespéré, extrême; **to be ~ for sth/to do sth** avoir désespérément besoin de qch/de faire qch; **we are getting ~** nous commençons à désespérer

desperately [ˈdɛspərɪtlɪ] adv désespérément; (very) terriblement, extrêmement; **~ ill** très gravement malade

desperation [dɛspəˈreɪʃən] n désespoir m; **in (sheer) ~** en désespoir de cause

despicable [dɪsˈpɪkəbl] adj méprisable

despise [dɪsˈpaɪz] vt mépriser, dédaigner

despite [dɪsˈpaɪt] prep malgré, en dépit de

despondent [dɪsˈpɔndənt] adj découragé(e), abattu(e)

dessert [dɪˈzəːt] n dessert m

dessertspoon [dɪˈzəːtspuːn] n cuiller f à dessert

destination [dɛstɪˈneɪʃən] n destination f

destined [ˈdɛstɪnd] adj: **to be ~ to do sth** être destiné(e) à faire qch; **~ for London** à destination de Londres

destiny [ˈdɛstɪnɪ] n destinée f, destin m

destitute [ˈdɛstɪtjuːt] adj indigent(e), dans le dénuement; **~ of** dépourvu(e) or dénué(e) de

destroy [dɪsˈtrɔɪ] vt détruire; (injured horse) abattre; (dog) faire piquer

destroyer [dɪsˈtrɔɪəʳ] n (Naut) contre-torpilleur m

destruction [dɪsˈtrʌkʃən] n destruction f

destructive [dɪsˈtrʌktɪv] adj destructeur(-trice)

detach [dɪ'tætʃ] vt détacher
detached [dɪ'tætʃt] adj (attitude) détaché(e)
detached house n pavillon m maison(nette)
(individuelle)
detachment [dɪ'tætʃmənt] n (Mil)
détachement m; (fig) détachement,
indifférence f
detail ['di:teɪl] n détail m; (Mil) détachement
m ▷ vt raconter en détail, énumérer; (Mil): to
~ sb (for) affecter qn (à), détacher qn (pour);
in ~ en détail; to go into ~(s) entrer dans les
détails
detailed ['di:teɪld] adj détaillé(e)
detain [dɪ'teɪn] vt retenir; (in captivity)
détenir; (in hospital) hospitaliser
detect [dɪ'tɛkt] vt déceler, percevoir; (Med,
Police) dépister; (Mil, Radar, Tech) détecter
detection [dɪ'tɛkʃən] n découverte f; (Med,
Police) dépistage m; (Mil, Radar, Tech) détection
f; to escape ~ échapper aux recherches,
éviter d'être découvert(e); (mistake) passer
inaperçu(e); crime ~ le dépistage des criminels
detective [dɪ'tɛktɪv] n agent m de la sûreté,
policier m; private ~ détective privé
detective story n roman policier
detention [dɪ'tɛnʃən] n détention f; (Scol)
retenue f, consigne f
deter [dɪ'tə:ʳ] vt dissuader
detergent [dɪ'tə:dʒənt] n détersif m,
détergent m
deteriorate [dɪ'tɪərɪəreɪt] vi se détériorer, se
dégrader
determination [dɪtə:mɪ'neɪʃən] n
détermination f
determine [dɪ'tə:mɪn] vt déterminer; to ~ to
do résoudre de faire, se déterminer à faire
determined [dɪ'tə:mɪnd] adj (person)
déterminé(e), décidé(e); (quantity) déterminé,
établi(e); (effort) très gros(se); ~ to do bien
décidé à faire
deterrent [dɪ'tɛrənt] n effet m de dissuasion;
force f de dissuasion; to act as a ~ avoir un
effet dissuasif
detest [dɪ'tɛst] vt détester, avoir horreur de
detonate ['dɛtəneɪt] vi exploser ▷ vt faire
exploser or détoner
detour ['di:tuəʳ] n détour m; (US Aut: diversion)
déviation f
detox ['di:tɔks] vi se détoxifier ▷ vt (body)
détoxifier ▷ n détox f
detract [dɪ'trækt] vt: to ~ from (quality, pleasure)
diminuer; (reputation) porter atteinte à
detriment ['dɛtrɪmənt] n: to the ~ of au
détriment de, au préjudice de; without ~ to
sans porter atteinte or préjudice à, sans
conséquences fâcheuses pour
detrimental [dɛtrɪ'mɛntl] adj: ~ to
préjudiciable or nuisible à
devaluation [dɪvælju'eɪʃən] n dévaluation f
devastate ['dɛvəsteɪt] vt dévaster; he was ~d
by the news cette nouvelle lui a porté un
coup terrible

devastating ['dɛvəsteɪtɪŋ] adj
dévastateur(-trice); (news) accablant(e)
develop [dɪ'vɛləp] vt (gen) développer;
(disease) commencer à souffrir de; (habit)
contracter; (resources) mettre en valeur,
exploiter; (land) aménager ▷ vi se
développer; (situation, disease: evolve) évoluer;
(facts, symptoms: appear) se manifester, se
produire; can you ~ this film? pouvez-vous
développer cette pellicule?; to ~ a taste for
sth prendre goût à qch; to ~ into devenir
developer [dɪ'vɛləpəʳ] n (Phot) révélateur m;
(of land) promoteur m; (also: property ~)
promoteur immobilier
developing country [dɪ'vɛləpɪŋ-] n pays m
en voie de développement
development [dɪ'vɛləpmənt] n
développement m; (of land) exploitation f;
(new fact, event) rebondissement m, fait(s)
nouveau(x)
device [dɪ'vaɪs] n (scheme) moyen m,
expédient m; (apparatus) appareil m,
dispositif m; explosive ~ engin explosif
devil ['dɛvl] n diable m; démon m
devious ['di:vɪəs] adj (means) détourné(e);
(person) sournois(e), dissimulé(e)
devise [dɪ'vaɪz] vt imaginer, concevoir
devoid [dɪ'vɔɪd] adj: ~ of dépourvu(e) de,
dénué(e) de
devolution [di:və'lu:ʃən] n (Pol)
décentralisation f
devote [dɪ'vəut] vt: to ~ sth to consacrer
qch à
devoted [dɪ'vəutɪd] adj dévoué(e); to be ~ to
être dévoué(e) or très attaché(e) à; (book etc)
être consacré(e) à
devotee [dɛvəu'ti:] n (Rel) adepte m/f; (Mus,
Sport) fervent(e)
devotion [dɪ'vəuʃən] n dévouement m,
attachement m; (Rel) dévotion f, piété f
devour [dɪ'vauəʳ] vt dévorer
devout [dɪ'vaut] adj pieux(-euse), dévot(e)
dew [dju:] n rosée f
diabetes [daɪə'bi:ti:z] n diabète m
diabetic [daɪə'bɛtɪk] n diabétique m/f ▷ adj
(person) diabétique; (chocolate, jam) pour
diabétiques
diabolical [daɪə'bɔlɪkl] adj diabolique; (inf:
dreadful) infernal(e), atroce
diagnose [daɪəg'nəuz] vt diagnostiquer
diagnosis (pl **diagnoses**) [daɪəg'nəusɪs, -si:z]
n diagnostic m
diagonal [daɪ'ægənl] adj diagonal(e) ▷ n
diagonale f
diagram ['daɪəgræm] n diagramme m,
schéma m
dial ['daɪəl] n cadran m ▷ vt (number) faire,
composer; to ~ a wrong number faire un
faux numéro; can I ~ London direct? puis-je
or est-ce que je peux avoir Londres par
l'automatique?
dialect ['daɪəlɛkt] n dialecte m

dialling code ['daɪəlɪŋ-], (US) **dial code** n indicatif m (téléphonique); **what's the ~ for Paris?** quel est l'indicatif de Paris?

dialling tone ['daɪəlɪŋ-], (US) **dial tone** n tonalité f

dialogue, (US) **dialog** ['daɪəlɒg] n dialogue m

diameter [daɪˈæmɪtəʳ] n diamètre m

diamond ['daɪəmənd] n diamant m; (shape) losange m; **diamonds** npl (Cards) carreau m

diaper ['daɪəpəʳ] n (US) couche f

diaphragm ['daɪəfræm] n diaphragme m

diarrhoea, (US) **diarrhea** [daɪəˈriːə] n diarrhée f

diary ['daɪərɪ] n (daily account) journal m; (book) agenda m; **to keep a ~** tenir un journal

dice [daɪs] n (pl inv) dé m ⊳ vt (Culin) couper en dés or en cubes

dictate vt [dɪkˈteɪt] dicter ⊳ vi: **to ~ to** (person) imposer sa volonté à, régenter; **I won't be ~d to** je n'ai d'ordres à recevoir de personne ⊳ n ['dɪkteɪt] injonction f

dictation [dɪkˈteɪʃən] n dictée f; **at ~ speed** à une vitesse de dictée

dictator [dɪkˈteɪtəʳ] n dictateur m

dictatorship [dɪkˈteɪtəʃɪp] n dictature f

dictionary ['dɪkʃənrɪ] n dictionnaire m

did [dɪd] pt of **do**

didn't ['dɪdnt] = **did not**

die [daɪ] n (pl **dice**) dé m; (pl **dies**) coin m; matrice f; étampe f ⊳ vi mourir; **to ~ of or from** mourir de; **to be dying** être mourant(e); **to be dying for sth** avoir une envie folle de qch; **to be dying to do sth** mourir d'envie de faire qch; **die away** vi s'éteindre; **die down** vi se calmer, s'apaiser; **die out** vi disparaître, s'éteindre

diesel ['diːzl] n (vehicle) diesel m; (also: ~ **oil**) carburant m diesel, gas-oil m

diesel engine n moteur m diesel

diet ['daɪət] n alimentation f; (restricted food) régime m ⊳ vi (also: **be on a ~**) suivre un régime; **to live on a ~ of** se nourrir de

differ ['dɪfəʳ] vi: **to ~ from sth** (be different) être différent(e) de qch, différer de qch; **to ~ from sb over sth** ne pas être d'accord avec qn au sujet de qch

difference ['dɪfrəns] n différence f; (quarrel) différend m, désaccord m; **it makes no ~ to me** cela m'est égal, cela m'est indifférent; **to settle one's ~s** résoudre la situation

different ['dɪfrənt] adj différent(e)

differentiate [dɪfəˈrenʃɪeɪt] vt différencier ⊳ vi se différencier; **to ~ between** faire une différence entre

differently ['dɪfrəntlɪ] adv différemment

difficult ['dɪfɪkəlt] adj difficile; **~ to understand** difficile à comprendre

difficulty ['dɪfɪkəltɪ] n difficulté f; **to have difficulties with** avoir des ennuis or problèmes avec; **to be in ~** avoir des difficultés, avoir des problèmes

dig [dɪg] vt (pt, pp **dug**) [dʌg] (hole) creuser; (garden) bêcher ⊳ n (prod) coup m de coude; (fig: remark) coup de griffe or de patte; (Archaeology) fouille f; **to ~ into** (snow, soil) creuser; **to ~ into one's pockets for sth** fouiller dans ses poches pour chercher or prendre qch; **to ~ one's nails into** enfoncer ses ongles dans; **dig in** vi (also: ~ **o.s. in**: Mil) se retrancher; (: fig) tenir bon, se braquer; (inf: eat) attaquer (un repas or un plat etc) ⊳ vt (compost) bien mélanger à la bêche; (knife, claw) enfoncer; **to ~ in one's heels** (fig) se braquer, se buter; **dig out** vt (survivors, car from snow) sortir or dégager (à coups de pelles or pioches); **dig up** vt déterrer

digest vt [daɪˈdʒest] digérer ⊳ n ['daɪdʒest] sommaire m, résumé m

digestion [dɪˈdʒestʃən] n digestion f

digit ['dɪdʒɪt] n (number) chiffre m (de 0 à 9); (finger) doigt m

digital ['dɪdʒɪtl] adj (system, recording, radio) numérique, digital(e); (watch) à affichage numérique or digital

digital camera n appareil m photo numérique

digital TV n télévision f numérique

dignified ['dɪgnɪfaɪd] adj digne

dignity ['dɪgnɪtɪ] n dignité f

digress [daɪˈgres] vi: **to ~ from** s'écarter de, s'éloigner de

digs [dɪgz] npl (Brit inf) piaule f, chambre meublée

dilapidated [dɪˈlæpɪdeɪtɪd] adj délabré(e)

dilemma [daɪˈlemə] n dilemme m; **to be in a ~** être pris dans un dilemme

diligent ['dɪlɪdʒənt] adj appliqué(e), assidu(e)

dill [dɪl] n aneth m

dilute [daɪˈluːt] vt diluer ⊳ adj dilué(e)

dim [dɪm] adj (light, eyesight) faible; (memory, outline) vague, indécis(e); (room) sombre; (inf: stupid) borné(e), obtus(e) ⊳ vt (light) réduire, baisser; (US Aut) mettre en code, baisser; **to take a ~ view of sth** voir qch d'un mauvais œil

dime [daɪm] n (US) pièce f de 10 cents

dimension [daɪˈmenʃən] n dimension f

diminish [dɪˈmɪnɪʃ] vt, vi diminuer

diminutive [dɪˈmɪnjutɪv] adj minuscule, tout(e) petit(e) ⊳ n (Ling) diminutif m

dimmer ['dɪməʳ] n (also: ~ **switch**) variateur m; **dimmers** npl (US Aut: dipped headlights) phares mpl, code inv; (parking lights) feux mpl de position

dimple ['dɪmpl] n fossette f

din [dɪn] n vacarme m ⊳ vt: **to ~ sth into sb** (inf) enfoncer qch dans la tête or la caboche de qn

dine [daɪn] vi dîner

diner ['daɪnəʳ] n (person) dîneur(-euse); (Rail) = **dining car**; (US: eating place) petit restaurant

dinghy ['dɪŋɡɪ] n youyou m; (inflatable) canot m pneumatique; (also: **sailing ~**) voilier m, dériveur m

dingy ['dɪndʒɪ] adj miteux(-euse), minable

dining car ['daɪnɪŋ-] n (Brit) voiture-restaurant f, wagon-restaurant m

dining room ['daɪnɪŋ-] n salle f à manger

dining table [daɪnɪŋ-] n table f de (la) salle à manger

dinner ['dɪnəʳ] n (evening meal) dîner m; (lunch) déjeuner m; (public) banquet m; **~'s ready!** à table!

dinner jacket n smoking m

dinner party n dîner m

dinner time n (evening) heure f du dîner; (midday) heure du déjeuner

dinosaur ['daɪnəsɔ:ʳ] n dinosaure m

dip [dɪp] n (slope) déclivité f; (in sea) baignade f, bain m; (Culin) = sauce f ▷ vt tremper, plonger; (Brit Aut: lights) mettre en code, baisser ▷ vi plonger

diploma [dɪ'pləumə] n diplôme m

diplomacy [dɪ'pləuməsɪ] n diplomatie f

diplomat ['dɪpləmæt] n diplomate m

diplomatic [dɪplə'mætɪk] adj diplomatique; **to break off ~ relations (with)** rompre les relations diplomatiques (avec)

dipstick ['dɪpstɪk] n (Brit Aut) jauge f de niveau d'huile

dipswitch ['dɪpswɪtʃ] n (Brit Aut) commutateur m de code

dire [daɪəʳ] adj (poverty) extrême; (awful) affreux(-euse)

direct [daɪ'rɛkt] adj direct(e); (manner, person) direct, franc/franche ▷ vt (tell way) diriger, orienter; (letter, remark) adresser; (Cine, TV) réaliser; (Theat) mettre en scène; (order): **to ~ sb to do sth** ordonner à qn de faire qch ▷ adv directement; **can you ~ me to ...?** pouvez-vous m'indiquer le chemin de ...?

direct debit n (Brit Banking) prélèvement m automatique

direction [dɪ'rɛkʃən] n direction f; (Theat) mise f en scène; (Cine, TV) réalisation f; **directions** npl (to a place) indications fpl; **~s for use** mode m d'emploi; **to ask for ~s** demander sa route or son chemin; **sense of ~** sens m de l'orientation; **in the ~ of** dans la direction de, vers

directly [dɪ'rɛktlɪ] adv (in straight line) directement, tout droit; (at once) tout de suite, immédiatement

director [dɪ'rɛktəʳ] n directeur m; (board member) administrateur m; (Theat) metteur en scène; (Cine, TV) réalisateur(-trice); **D~ of Public Prosecutions** (Brit) ≈ procureur général

directory [dɪ'rɛktərɪ] n annuaire m; (also: **street ~**) indicateur m de rues; (also: **trade ~**) annuaire du commerce; (Comput) répertoire m

directory enquiries, (US) **directory assistance** n (Tel: service) renseignements mpl

dirt [də:t] n saleté f; (mud) boue f; **to treat sb like ~** traiter qn comme un chien

dirt-cheap ['də:t'tʃi:p] adj (ne) coûtant presque rien

dirty ['də:tɪ] adj sale; (joke) cochon(ne) ▷ vt salir; **~ story** histoire cochonne; **~ trick** coup tordu

disability [dɪsə'bɪlɪtɪ] n invalidité f, infirmité f

disabled [dɪs'eɪbld] adj handicapé(e); (maimed) mutilé(e); (through illness, old age) impotent(e)

disadvantage [dɪsəd'vɑ:ntɪdʒ] n désavantage m, inconvénient m

disagree [dɪsə'gri:] vi (differ) ne pas concorder; (be against, think otherwise): **to ~ (with)** ne pas être d'accord (avec); **garlic ~s with me** l'ail ne me convient pas, je ne supporte pas l'ail

disagreeable [dɪsə'gri:əbl] adj désagréable

disagreement [dɪsə'gri:mənt] n désaccord m, différend m

disallow [dɪsə'lau] vt rejeter, désavouer; (Brit Football: goal) refuser

disappear [dɪsə'pɪəʳ] vi disparaître

disappearance [dɪsə'pɪərəns] n disparition f

disappoint [dɪsə'pɔɪnt] vt décevoir

disappointed [dɪsə'pɔɪntɪd] adj déçu(e)

disappointing [dɪsə'pɔɪntɪŋ] adj décevant(e)

disappointment [dɪsə'pɔɪntmənt] n déception f

disapproval [dɪsə'pru:vəl] n désapprobation f

disapprove [dɪsə'pru:v] vi: **to ~ of** désapprouver

disarm [dɪs'ɑ:m] vt désarmer

disarmament [dɪs'ɑ:məmənt] n désarmement m

disarray [dɪsə'reɪ] n désordre m, confusion f; **in ~** (troops) en déroute; (thoughts) embrouillé(e); (clothes) en désordre; **to throw into ~** semer la confusion or le désordre dans (or parmi)

disaster [dɪ'zɑ:stəʳ] n catastrophe f, désastre m

disastrous [dɪ'zɑ:strəs] adj désastreux(-euse)

disband [dɪs'bænd] vt démobiliser; disperser ▷ vi se séparer; se disperser

disbelief ['dɪsbə'li:f] n incrédulité f; **in ~** avec incrédulité

disc [dɪsk] n disque m; (Comput) = **disk**

discard [dɪs'kɑ:d] vt (old things) se débarrasser de, mettre au rencart or au rebut; (fig) écarter, renoncer à

discern [dɪ'sə:n] vt discerner, distinguer

discerning [dɪ'sə:nɪŋ] adj judicieux(-euse), perspicace

discharge vt [dɪs'tʃɑːdʒ] (duties) s'acquitter de; (settle: debt) s'acquitter de, régler; (waste etc) déverser; décharger; (Elec, Med) émettre; (patient) renvoyer (chez lui); (employee, soldier) congédier, licencier; (defendant) relaxer, élargir ⊳ n ['dɪstʃɑːdʒ] (Elec, Med) émission f; (also: **vaginal ~**) pertes blanches; (dismissal) renvoi m; licenciement m; élargissement m; **to ~ one's gun** faire feu; **~d bankrupt** failli(e), réhabilité(e)

discipline ['dɪsɪplɪn] n discipline f ⊳ vt discipliner; (punish) punir; **to ~ o.s. to do sth** s'imposer or s'astreindre à une discipline pour faire qch

disc jockey n disque-jockey m (DJ)

disclaim [dɪs'kleɪm] vt désavouer, dénier

disclose [dɪs'kləuz] vt révéler, divulguer

disclosure [dɪs'kləuʒəʳ] n révélation f, divulgation f

disco ['dɪskəu] n abbr discothèque f

discoloured, (US) **discolored** [dɪs'kʌləd] adj décoloré(e), jauni(e)

discomfort [dɪs'kʌmfət] n malaise m, gêne f; (lack of comfort) manque m de confort

disconcert [dɪskən'səːt] vt déconcerter, décontenancer

disconnect [dɪskə'nɛkt] vt détacher; (Elec, Radio) débrancher; (gas, water) couper

discontent [dɪskən'tɛnt] n mécontentement m

discontented [dɪskən'tɛntɪd] adj mécontent(e)

discontinue [dɪskən'tɪnjuː] vt cesser, interrompre; **"~d"** (Comm) "fin de série"

discord ['dɪskɔːd] n discorde f, dissension f; (Mus) dissonance f

discount n ['dɪskaunt] remise f, rabais m ⊳ vt [dɪs'kaunt] (report etc) ne pas tenir compte de; **to give sb a ~ on sth** faire une remise or un rabais à qn sur qch; **~ for cash** escompte f au comptant; **at a ~** avec une remise or réduction, au rabais

discourage [dɪs'kʌrɪdʒ] vt décourager; (dissuade, deter) dissuader, décourager

discover [dɪs'kʌvəʳ] vt découvrir

discovery [dɪs'kʌvərɪ] n découverte f

discredit [dɪs'krɛdɪt] vt (idea) mettre en doute; (person) discréditer ⊳ n discrédit m

discreet [dɪs'kriːt] adj discret(-ète)

discrepancy [dɪs'krɛpənsɪ] n divergence f, contradiction f

discretion [dɪs'krɛʃən] n discrétion f; **at the ~ of** à la discrétion de; **use your own ~** à vous de juger

discriminate [dɪs'krɪmɪneɪt] vi: **to ~ between** établir une distinction entre, faire la différence entre; **to ~ against** pratiquer une discrimination contre

discriminating [dɪs'krɪmɪneɪtɪŋ] adj qui a du discernement

discrimination [dɪskrɪmɪ'neɪʃən] n discrimination f; (judgment) discernement m;

racial/sexual ~ discrimination raciale/ sexuelle

discuss [dɪ'skʌs] vt discuter de; (debate) discuter

discussion [dɪ'skʌʃən] n discussion f; **under ~** en discussion

disdain [dɪs'deɪn] n dédain m

disease [dɪ'ziːz] n maladie f

disembark [dɪsɪm'bɑːk] vt, vi débarquer

disentangle [dɪsɪn'tæŋgl] vt démêler

disfigure [dɪs'fɪgəʳ] vt défigurer

disgrace [dɪs'greɪs] n honte f; (disfavour) disgrâce f ⊳ vt déshonorer, couvrir de honte

disgraceful [dɪs'greɪsful] adj scandaleux(-euse), honteux(-euse)

disgruntled [dɪs'grʌntld] adj mécontent(e)

disguise [dɪs'gaɪz] n déguisement m ⊳ vt déguiser; (voice) déguiser, contrefaire; (feelings etc) masquer, dissimuler; **in ~** déguisé(e); **to ~ o.s. as** se déguiser en; **there's no disguising the fact that ...** on ne peut pas se dissimuler que ...

disgust [dɪs'gʌst] n dégoût m, aversion f ⊳ vt dégoûter, écœurer

disgusted [dɪs'gʌstɪd] adj dégoûté(e), écœuré(e)

disgusting [dɪs'gʌstɪŋ] adj dégoûtant(e), révoltant(e)

dish [dɪʃ] n plat m; **to do** or **wash the ~es** faire la vaisselle; **dish out** vt distribuer; **dish up** vt servir; (facts, statistics) sortir, débiter

dishcloth ['dɪʃklɔθ] n (for drying) torchon m; (for washing) lavette f

dishearten [dɪs'hɑːtn] vt décourager

dishevelled, (US) **disheveled** [dɪ'ʃɛvəld] adj ébouriffé(e), décoiffé(e), débraillé(e)

dishonest [dɪs'ɔnɪst] adj malhonnête

dishonour, (US) **dishonor** [dɪs'ɔnəʳ] n déshonneur m

dishonourable, (US) **dishonorable** [dɪs'ɔnərəbl] adj déshonorant(e)

dishtowel ['dɪʃtauəl] n (US) torchon m (à vaisselle)

dishwasher ['dɪʃwɔʃəʳ] n lave-vaisselle m; (person) plongeur(-euse)

disillusion [dɪsɪ'luːʒən] vt désabuser, désenchanter ⊳ n désenchantement m; **to become ~ed (with)** perdre ses illusions (en ce qui concerne)

disinfect [dɪsɪn'fɛkt] vt désinfecter

disinfectant [dɪsɪn'fɛktənt] n désinfectant m

disintegrate [dɪs'ɪntɪgreɪt] vi se désintégrer

disinterested [dɪs'ɪntrəstɪd] adj désintéressé(e)

disjointed [dɪs'dʒɔɪntɪd] adj décousu(e), incohérent(e)

disk [dɪsk] n (Comput) disquette f; **single-/ double-sided ~** disquette une face/double face

disk drive n lecteur m de disquette

diskette [dɪs'kɛt] n (Comput) disquette f

dislike [dɪs'laɪk] *n* aversion *f*, antipathie *f* ▷ *vt* ne pas aimer; **to take a ~ to sb/sth** prendre qn/qch en grippe; **I ~ the idea** l'idée me déplaît

dislocate ['dɪsləkeɪt] *vt* disloquer, déboîter; *(services etc)* désorganiser; **he has ~d his shoulder** il s'est disloqué l'épaule

dislodge [dɪs'lɒdʒ] *vt* déplacer, faire bouger; *(enemy)* déloger

disloyal [dɪs'lɔɪəl] *adj* déloyal(e)

dismal ['dɪzml] *adj (gloomy)* lugubre, maussade; *(very bad)* lamentable

dismantle [dɪs'mæntl] *vt* démonter; *(fort, warship)* démanteler

dismay [dɪs'meɪ] *n* consternation *f* ▷ *vt* consterner; **much to my ~** à ma grande consternation, à ma grande inquiétude

dismiss [dɪs'mɪs] *vt* congédier, renvoyer; *(idea)* écarter; *(Law)* rejeter ▷ *vi (Mil)* rompre les rangs

dismissal [dɪs'mɪsl] *n* renvoi *m*

dismount [dɪs'maunt] *vi* mettre pied à terre

disobedient [dɪsə'biːdɪənt] *adj* désobéissant(e), indiscipliné(e)

disobey [dɪsə'beɪ] *vt* désobéir à; *(rule)* transgresser, enfreindre

disorder [dɪs'ɔːdəʳ] *n* désordre *m*; *(rioting)* désordres *mpl*; *(Med)* troubles *mpl*

disorderly [dɪs'ɔːdəlɪ] *adj (room)* en désordre; *(behaviour, retreat, crowd)* désordonné(e)

disorganized [dɪs'ɔːgənaɪzd] *adj* désorganisé(e)

disorientated [dɪs'ɔːrɪenteɪtɪd] *adj* désorienté(e)

disown [dɪs'əun] *vt* renier

disparaging [dɪs'pærɪdʒɪŋ] *adj* désobligeant(e); **to be ~ about sb/sth** faire des remarques désobligeantes sur qn/qch

dispassionate [dɪs'pæʃənət] *adj* calme, froid(e), impartial(e), objectif(-ive)

dispatch [dɪs'pætʃ] *vt* expédier, envoyer; *(deal with: business)* régler, en finir avec ▷ *n* envoi *m*, expédition *f*; *(Mil, Press)* dépêche *f*

dispel [dɪs'pɛl] *vt* dissiper, chasser

dispense [dɪs'pɛns] *vt* distribuer, administrer; *(medicine)* préparer (et vendre); **to ~ sb from** dispenser qn de; **dispense with** *vt fus* se passer de; *(make unnecessary)* rendre superflu(e)

dispenser [dɪs'pɛnsəʳ] *n (device)* distributeur *m*

dispensing chemist [dɪs'pɛnsɪŋ-] *n (Brit)* pharmacie *f*

disperse [dɪs'pəːs] *vt* disperser; *(knowledge)* disséminer ▷ *vi* se disperser

dispirited [dɪs'pɪrɪtɪd] *adj* découragé(e), déprimé(e)

displace [dɪs'pleɪs] *vt* déplacer

display [dɪs'pleɪ] *n (of goods)* étalage *m*; affichage *m*; *(Comput: information)* visualisation *f*; *(: device)* visuel *m*; *(of feeling)* manifestation *f*; *(pej)* ostentation *f*; *(show,* spectacle*)* spectacle *m*; *(military display)* parade *f* militaire ▷ *vt* montrer; *(goods)* mettre à l'étalage, exposer; *(results, departure times)* afficher; *(pej)* faire étalage de; **on ~** *(exhibits)* exposé(e), exhibé(e); *(goods)* à l'étalage

displease [dɪs'pliːz] *vt* mécontenter, contrarier; **~d with** mécontent(e) de

displeasure [dɪs'plɛʒəʳ] *n* mécontentement *m*

disposable [dɪs'pəuzəbl] *adj (pack etc)* jetable; *(income)* disponible; **~ nappy** *(Brit)* couche *f* à jeter, couche-culotte *f*

disposal [dɪs'pəuzl] *n (of rubbish)* évacuation *f*, destruction *f*; *(of property etc: by selling)* vente *f*; *(: by giving away)* cession *f*; *(availability, arrangement)* disposition *f*; **at one's ~** à sa disposition; **to put sth at sb's ~** mettre qch à la disposition de qn

dispose [dɪs'pəuz] *vt* disposer ▷ *vi*: **to ~ of** *(time, money)* disposer de; *(unwanted goods)* se débarrasser de, se défaire de; *(Comm: stock)* écouler, vendre; *(problem)* expédier

disposed [dɪs'pəuzd] *adj*: **~ to do** disposé(e) à faire

disposition [dɪspə'zɪʃən] *n* disposition *f*; *(temperament)* naturel *m*

disproportionate [dɪsprə'pɔːʃənət] *adj* disproportionné(e)

disprove [dɪs'pruːv] *vt* réfuter

dispute [dɪs'pjuːt] *n* discussion *f*; *(also:* **industrial ~**) conflit *m* ▷ *vt (question)* contester; *(matter)* discuter; *(victory)* disputer; **to be in** *or* **under ~** *(matter)* être en discussion; *(territory)* être contesté(e)

disqualify [dɪs'kwɒlɪfaɪ] *vt (Sport)* disqualifier; **to ~ sb for sth/from doing** *(status, situation)* rendre qn inapte à qch/à faire; *(authority)* signifier à qn l'interdiction de faire; **to ~ sb (from driving)** *(Brit)* retirer à qn son permis (de conduire)

disquiet [dɪs'kwaɪət] *n* inquiétude *f*, trouble *m*

disregard [dɪsrɪ'gɑːd] *vt* ne pas tenir compte de ▷ *n (indifference)*: **~ (for)** *(feelings)* indifférence *f* (pour), insensibilité *f* (à); *(danger, money)* mépris *m* (pour)

disrepair [dɪsrɪ'pɛəʳ] *n* mauvais état; **to fall into ~** *(building)* tomber en ruine; *(street)* se dégrader

disreputable [dɪs'rɛpjutəbl] *adj (person)* de mauvaise réputation, peu recommandable; *(behaviour)* déshonorant(e); *(area)* mal famé(e), louche

disrespectful [dɪsrɪ'spɛktful] *adj* irrespectueux(-euse)

disrupt [dɪs'rʌpt] *vt (plans, meeting, lesson)* perturber, déranger

disruption [dɪs'rʌpʃən] *n* perturbation *f*, dérangement *m*

dissatisfaction [dɪssætɪs'fækʃən] *n* mécontentement *m*, insatisfaction *f*

dissatisfied [dɪsˈsætɪsfaɪd] *adj*: ~ **(with)** insatisfait(e) (de)

dissect [dɪˈsɛkt] *vt* disséquer; *(fig)* disséquer, éplucher

dissent [dɪˈsɛnt] *n* dissentiment *m*, différence *f* d'opinion

dissertation [dɪsəˈteɪʃən] *n* (*Scol*) mémoire *m*

disservice [dɪsˈsəːvɪs] *n*: **to do sb a** ~ rendre un mauvais service à qn; desservir qn

dissimilar [dɪˈsɪmɪləʳ] *adj*: ~ **(to)** dissemblable (à), différent(e) (de)

dissipate [ˈdɪsɪpeɪt] *vt* dissiper; (*energy, efforts*) disperser

dissolute [ˈdɪsəluːt] *adj* débauché(e), dissolu(e)

dissolve [dɪˈzɒlv] *vt* dissoudre ▷ *vi* se dissoudre, fondre; *(fig)* disparaître; **to ~ in(to) tears** fondre en larmes

distance [ˈdɪstns] *n* distance *f*; **what's the ~ to London?** à quelle distance se trouve Londres?; **it's within walking ~** on peut y aller à pied; **in the ~** au loin

distant [ˈdɪstnt] *adj* lointain(e), éloigné(e); (*manner*) distant(e), froid(e)

distaste [dɪsˈteɪst] *n* dégoût *m*

distasteful [dɪsˈteɪstful] *adj* déplaisant(e), désagréable

distended [dɪsˈtɛndɪd] *adj* (*stomach*) dilaté(e)

distil, (*US*) **distill** [dɪsˈtɪl] *vt* distiller

distillery [dɪsˈtɪlərɪ] *n* distillerie *f*

distinct [dɪsˈtɪŋkt] *adj* distinct(e); (*clear*) marqué(e); **as ~ from** par opposition à, en contraste avec

distinction [dɪsˈtɪŋkʃən] *n* distinction *f*; (*in exam*) mention *f* très bien; **to draw a ~ between** faire une distinction entre; **a writer of ~** un écrivain réputé

distinctive [dɪsˈtɪŋktɪv] *adj* distinctif(-ive)

distinguish [dɪsˈtɪŋgwɪʃ] *vt* distinguer ▷ *vi*: **to ~ between** (*concepts*) distinguer entre, faire une distinction entre; **to ~ o.s.** se distinguer

distinguished [dɪsˈtɪŋgwɪʃt] *adj* (*eminent, refined*) distingué(e); (*career*) remarquable, brillant(e)

distinguishing [dɪsˈtɪŋgwɪʃɪŋ] *adj* (*feature*) distinctif(-ive), caractéristique

distort [dɪsˈtɔːt] *vt* déformer

distract [dɪsˈtrækt] *vt* distraire, déranger

distracted [dɪsˈtræktɪd] *adj* (*not concentrating*) distrait(e); (*worried*) affolé(e)

distraction [dɪsˈtrækʃən] *n* distraction *f*, dérangement *m*; **to drive sb to ~** rendre qn fou/folle

distraught [dɪsˈtrɔːt] *adj* éperdu(e)

distress [dɪsˈtrɛs] *n* détresse *f*; (*pain*) douleur *f* ▷ *vt* affliger; **in ~** (*ship*) en perdition; (*plane*) en détresse; **~ed area** (*Brit*) zone sinistrée

distressing [dɪsˈtrɛsɪŋ] *adj* douloureux(-euse), pénible, affligeant(e)

distribute [dɪsˈtrɪbuːt] *vt* distribuer

distribution [dɪstrɪˈbjuːʃən] *n* distribution *f*

distributor [dɪsˈtrɪbjutəʳ] *n* (*gen: Tech*) distributeur *m*; (*Comm*) concessionnaire *m/f*

district [ˈdɪstrɪkt] *n* (*of country*) région *f*; (*of town*) quartier *m*; (*Admin*) district *m*

district attorney *n* (*US*) ≈ procureur *m* de la République

district nurse *n* (*Brit*) infirmière visiteuse

distrust [dɪsˈtrʌst] *n* méfiance *f*, doute *m* ▷ *vt* se méfier de

disturb [dɪsˈtəːb] *vt* troubler; (*inconvenience*) déranger; **sorry to ~ you** excusez-moi de vous déranger

disturbance [dɪsˈtəːbəns] *n* dérangement *m*; (*political etc*) troubles *mpl*; (*by drunks etc*) tapage *m*; **to cause a ~** troubler l'ordre public; **~ of the peace** (*Law*) tapage injurieux ou nocturne

disturbed [dɪsˈtəːbd] *adj* (*worried, upset*) agité(e), troublé(e); **to be emotionally ~** avoir des problèmes affectifs

disturbing [dɪsˈtəːbɪŋ] *adj* troublant(e), inquiétant(e)

disuse [dɪsˈjuːs] *n*: **to fall into ~** tomber en désuétude

disused [dɪsˈjuːzd] *adj* désaffecté(e)

ditch [dɪtʃ] *n* fossé *m*; (*for irrigation*) rigole *f* ▷ *vt* (*inf*) abandonner; (*person*) plaquer

dither [ˈdɪðəʳ] *vi* hésiter

ditto [ˈdɪtəu] *adv* idem

dive [daɪv] *n* plongeon *m*; (*of submarine*) plongée *f*; (*Aviat*) piqué *m*; (*pej: café, bar etc*) bouge *m* ▷ *vi* plonger; **to ~ into** (*bag etc*) plonger la main dans; (*place*) se précipiter dans

diver [ˈdaɪvəʳ] *n* plongeur *m*

diverse [daɪˈvəːs] *adj* divers(e)

diversion [daɪˈvəːʃən] *n* (*Brit Aut*) déviation *f*; (*distraction, Mil*) diversion *f*

diversity [daɪˈvəːsɪtɪ] *n* diversité *f*, variété *f*

divert [daɪˈvəːt] *vt* (*Brit: traffic*) dévier; (*plane*) dérouter; (*train, river*) détourner; (*amuse*) divertir

divide [dɪˈvaɪd] *vt* diviser; (*separate*) séparer ▷ *vi* se diviser; **to ~ (between** *or* **among)** répartir *or* diviser (entre); **40 ~d by 5** 40 divisé par 5; **divide out** *vt*: **to ~ out (between** *or* **among)** distribuer *or* répartir (entre)

divided highway (*US*) *n* route *f* à quatre voies

dividend [ˈdɪvɪdɛnd] *n* dividende *m*

divine [dɪˈvaɪn] *adj* divin(e) ▷ *vt* (*future*) prédire; (*truth*) deviner, entrevoir; (*water, metal*) détecter la présence de (*par l'intermédiaire de la radiesthésie*)

diving [ˈdaɪvɪŋ] *n* plongée (sous-marine)

diving board *n* plongeoir *m*

divinity [dɪˈvɪnɪtɪ] *n* divinité *f*; (*as study*) théologie *f*

division [dɪˈvɪʒən] *n* division *f*; (*Brit: Football*) division *f*; (*separation*) séparation *f*; (*Comm*) service *m*; (*Brit: Pol*) vote *m*; (*also*: ~ **of labour**) division du travail

divorce [dɪ'vɔːs] n divorce m ▷ vt divorcer
d'avec
divorced [dɪ'vɔːst] adj divorcé(e)
divorcee [dɪvɔː'siː] n divorcé(e)
DIY adj, n abbr (Brit) = **do-it-yourself**
dizzy ['dɪzɪ] adj (height) vertigineux(-euse);
to make sb ~ donner le vertige à qn; **I feel ~**
la tête me tourne, j'ai la tête qui tourne
DJ n abbr = **disc jockey**
DNA n abbr (= deoxyribonucleic acid) ADN m
DNA fingerprinting [-'fɪŋɡəprɪntɪŋ] n
technique f des empreintes génétiques
do abbr (= ditto) d

 KEYWORD

do [duː] (pt did, pp done) n (inf: party etc)
soirée f, fête f, (: formal gathering) réception f
▷ vb **1** (in negative constructions) non traduit;
I don't understand je ne comprends pas
2 (to form questions) non traduit; **didn't you
know?** vous ne le saviez pas?; **what do you
think?** qu'en pensez-vous?; **why didn't you
come?** pourquoi n'êtes-vous
pas venu?
3 (for emphasis, in polite expressions): **people do
make mistakes sometimes** on peut
toujours se tromper; **she does seem rather
late** je trouve qu'elle est bien en retard; **do
sit down/help yourself** asseyez-vous/
servez-vous je vous en prie; **do take care!**
faites bien attention à vous!; **I DO wish I
could go** j'aimerais tant y aller; **but I DO
like it!** mais si, je l'aime!
4 (used to avoid repeating vb): **she swims better
than I do** elle nage mieux que moi; **do you
agree? — yes, I do/no I don't** vous êtes
d'accord? — oui/non; **she lives in Glasgow
— so do I** elle habite Glasgow — moi aussi;
he didn't like it and neither did we il n'a
pas aimé ça, et nous non plus; **who broke it?
— I did** qui l'a cassé? — c'est moi; **he asked
me to help him and I did** il m'a demandé de
l'aider, et c'est ce que j'ai fait
5 (in question tags): **you like him, don't you?**
vous l'aimez bien, n'est-ce pas?; **he laughed,
didn't he?** il a ri, n'est-ce pas?; **I don't know
him, do I?** je ne crois pas le connaître
▷ vt **1** (gen: carry out, perform etc) faire; (visit: city,
museum) faire, visiter; **what are you doing
tonight?** qu'est-ce que vous faites ce soir?;
what do you do? (job) que faites-vous dans
la vie?; **what did he do with the cat?**
qu'a-t-il fait du chat?; **what can I do for
you?** que puis-je faire pour vous?; **to do the
cooking/washing-up** faire la cuisine/
la vaisselle; **to do one's teeth/hair/nails**
se brosser les dents/se coiffer/se faire les
ongles
2 (Aut etc: distance) faire; (: speed) faire du;
we've done 200 km already nous avons déjà
fait 200 km; **the car was doing 100** la

voiture faisait du 100 (à l'heure); **he can do
100 in that car** il peut faire du 100 (à
l'heure) dans cette voiture-là
▷ vi **1** (act, behave) faire; **do as I do** faites
comme moi
2 (get on, fare) marcher; **the firm is doing
well** l'entreprise marche bien; **he's doing
well/badly at school** ça marche bien/
mal pour lui à l'école; **how do you do?**
comment allez-vous?; (on being introduced)
enchanté(e)!
3 (suit) aller; **will it do?** est-ce que ça ira?
4 (be sufficient) suffire, aller; **will £10 do?** est-
ce que 10 livres suffiront?; **that'll do** ça
suffit, ça ira; **that'll do!** (in annoyance) ça va or
suffit comme ça!; **to make do (with)** se
contenter (de)
do away with vt fus abolir; (kill) supprimer
do for vt fus (Brit inf: clean for) faire le ménage
chez
do up vt (laces, dress) attacher; (buttons)
boutonner; (zip) fermer; (renovate: room)
refaire; (: house) remettre à neuf; **to do o.s.
up** se faire beau/belle
do with vt fus (need): **I could do with a
drink/some help** quelque chose à boire/un
peu d'aide ne serait pas de refus; **it could do
with a wash** ça ne lui ferait pas de mal d'être
lavé; (be connected with): **that has nothing to
do with you** cela ne vous concerne pas; **I
won't have anything to do with it** je ne
veux pas m'en mêler; **what has that got to
do with it?** quel est le rapport?, qu'est-ce que
cela vient faire là-dedans?
do without vi s'en passer; **if you're late for
tea then you'll do without** si vous êtes en
retard pour le dîner il faudra vous en passer
▷ vt fus se passer de; **I can do without a car**
je peux me passer de voiture

dock [dɔk] n dock m; (wharf) quai m; (Law)
banc m des accusés ▷ vi se mettre à quai;
(Space) s'arrimer ▷ vt: **they ~ed a third of
his wages** ils lui ont retenu or décompté un
tiers de son salaire; **docks** npl (Naut) docks
docker ['dɔkə'] n docker m
dockyard ['dɔkjɑːd] n chantier m de
construction navale
doctor ['dɔktə'] n médecin m, docteur m;
(PhD etc) docteur ▷ vt (cat) couper; (interfere
with: food) altérer; (: drink) frelater; (: text,
document) arranger; **~'s office** (US) cabinet m
de consultation; **call a ~!** appelez un docteur
or un médecin!
Doctor of Philosophy n (degree) doctorat m;
(person) titulaire m/f d'un doctorat
document ['dɔkjumənt] n document m ▷ vt
['dɔkjument] documenter
documentary [dɔkju'mentərɪ] adj, n
documentaire (m)
documentation [dɔkjumən'teɪʃən] n
documentation f

dodge [dɔdʒ] n truc m; combine f ▷ vt esquiver, éviter ▷ vi faire un saut de côté; (Sport) faire une esquive; **to ~ out of the way** s'esquiver; **to ~ through the traffic** se faufiler or faire de savantes manœuvres entre les voitures

dodgems ['dɔdʒəmz] npl (Brit) autos tamponneuses

dodgy ['dɔdʒɪ] adj (inf: uncertain) douteux(-euse); (: shady) louche

doe [dəu] n (deer) biche f; (rabbit) lapine f

does [dʌz] vb see **do**

doesn't ['dʌznt] = **does not**

dog [dɔg] n chien(ne) ▷ vt (follow closely) suivre de près, ne pas lâcher d'une semelle; (fig: memory etc) poursuivre, harceler; **to go to the ~s** (nation etc) aller à vau-l'eau

dog collar n collier m de chien; (fig) faux-col m d'ecclésiastique

dog-eared ['dɔgɪəd] adj corné(e)

dogged ['dɔgɪd] adj obstiné(e), opiniâtre

doggy bag ['dɔgɪ-] n petit sac pour emporter les restes

dogsbody ['dɔgzbɔdɪ] n (Brit) bonne f à tout faire, tâcheron m

doings ['duɪŋz] npl activités fpl

do-it-yourself ['duːɪtjɔːˈself] n bricolage m

doldrums ['dɔldrəmz] npl: **to be in the ~** avoir le cafard; être dans le marasme

dole [dəul] n (Brit: payment) allocation f de chômage; **on the ~** au chômage; **dole out** vt donner au compte-goutte

doll [dɔl] n poupée f; **doll up** vt: **to ~ o.s. up** se faire beau/belle

dollar ['dɔləʳ] n dollar m

dolphin ['dɔlfɪn] n dauphin m

dome [dəum] n dôme m

domestic [dəˈmɛstɪk] adj (duty, happiness) familial(e); (policy, affairs, flight) intérieur(e); (news) national(e); (animal) domestique

domesticated [dəˈmɛstɪkeɪtɪd] adj domestiqué(e); (pej) d'intérieur; **he's very ~** il participe volontiers aux tâches ménagères; question ménage, il est très organisé

dominant ['dɔmɪnənt] adj dominant(e)

dominate ['dɔmɪneɪt] vt dominer

domineering [dɔmɪˈnɪərɪŋ] adj dominateur(-trice), autoritaire

dominion [dəˈmɪnɪən] n domination f; territoire m; dominion m

domino ['dɔmɪnəu] (pl **dominoes**) n domino m

dominoes ['dɔmɪnəuz] n (game) dominos mpl

don [dɔn] n (Brit) professeur m d'université ▷ vt revêtir

donate [dəˈneɪt] vt faire don de, donner

donation [dəˈneɪʃən] n donation f, don m

done [dʌn] pp of **do**

donkey ['dɔŋkɪ] n âne m

donor ['dəunəʳ] n (of blood etc) donneur(-euse); (to charity) donateur(-trice)

donor card n carte f de don d'organes

don't [dəunt] = **do not**

donut ['dəunʌt] (US) n = **doughnut**

doodle ['duːdl] n griffonnage m, gribouillage m ▷ vi griffonner, gribouiller

doom [duːm] n (fate) destin m; (ruin) ruine f ▷ vt: **to be ~ed to failure** être voué(e) à l'échec

door [dɔːʳ] n porte f; (Rail, car) portière f; **to go from ~ to ~** aller de porte en porte

doorbell ['dɔːbɛl] n sonnette f

door handle n poignée f de porte; (of car) poignée de portière

doorknob ['dɔːnɔb] n poignée f or bouton m de porte

doorman ['dɔːmən] irreg n (in hotel) portier m; (in block of flats) concierge m

doormat ['dɔːmæt] n paillasson m

doorstep ['dɔːstɛp] n pas m de (la) porte, seuil m

doorway ['dɔːweɪ] n (embrasure f de) porte f

dope [dəup] n (inf: drug) drogue f; (: person) andouille f; (: information) tuyaux mpl, rancards mpl ▷ vt (horse etc) doper

dormant ['dɔːmənt] adj assoupi(e), en veilleuse; (rule, law) inappliqué(e)

dormitory ['dɔːmɪtrɪ] n (Brit) dortoir m; (US: hall of residence) résidence f universitaire

dormouse (pl **dormice**) ['dɔːmaus, -maɪs] n loir m

DOS [dɔs] n abbr (= disk operating system) DOS m

dosage ['dəusɪdʒ] n dose f; dosage m; (on label) posologie f

dose [dəus] n dose f; (Brit: bout) attaque f ▷ vt: **to ~ o.s.** se bourrer de médicaments; **a ~ of flu** une belle or bonne grippe

dosh [dɔʃ] (inf) n fric m

doss house ['dɔs-] n (Brit) asile m de nuit

dot [dɔt] n point m; (on material) pois m ▷ vt: **~ted with** parsemé(e) de; **on the ~** à l'heure tapante

dotcom [dɔtˈkɔm] n point com m, pointcom m

dotted line ['dɔtɪd-] n ligne pointillée; (Aut) ligne discontinue; **to sign on the ~** signer à l'endroit indiqué or sur la ligne pointillée; (fig) donner son consentement

double ['dʌbl] adj double ▷ adv (fold) en deux; (twice): **to cost ~ (sth)** coûter le double (de qch) or deux fois plus (que qch) ▷ n double m; (Cine) doublure f ▷ vt doubler; (fold) plier en deux ▷ vi doubler; (have two uses): **to ~ as** servir aussi de; **~ five two six (5526)** (Brit Tel) cinquante-cinq – vingt-six; **it's spelt with a ~ "l"** ça s'écrit avec deux "l"; **on the ~, at the ~** au pas de course; **double back** vi (person) revenir sur ses pas; **double up** vi (bend over) se courber, se plier; (share room) partager la chambre

double bass n contrebasse f

double bed n grand lit

double-breasted ['dʌblˈbrɛstɪd] adj croisé(e)

double-check ['dʌbl'tʃɛk] vt, vi revérifier

double-click ['dʌbl'klɪk] vi (Comput) double-cliquer

double-cross ['dʌbl'krɔs] vt doubler, trahir

double-decker ['dʌbl'dɛkə^r] n autobus m à impériale

double glazing n (Brit) double vitrage m

double room n chambre f pour deux

doubles ['dʌblz] n (Tennis) double m

double yellow lines npl (Brit: Aut) double bande jaune marquant l'interdiction de stationner

doubly ['dʌblɪ] adv doublement, deux fois plus

doubt [daut] n doute m ▷ vt douter de; **no ~** sans doute; **without (a) ~** sans aucun doute; **beyond ~** adv indubitablement ▷ adj indubitable; **to ~ that** douter que + sub; **I ~ it very much** j'en doute fort

doubtful ['dautful] adj douteux(-euse); (person) incertain(e); **to be ~ about sth** avoir des doutes sur qch, ne pas être convaincu de qch; **I'm a bit ~** je n'en suis pas certain or sûr

doubtless ['dautlɪs] adv sans doute, sûrement

dough [dəu] n pâte f; (inf: money) fric m, pognon m

doughnut ['dəunʌt], (US) **donut** n beignet m

dove [dʌv] n colombe f

Dover ['dəuvə^r] n Douvres

dovetail ['dʌvteɪl] n: **~ joint** assemblage m à queue d'aronde ▷ vi (fig) concorder

dowdy ['daudɪ] adj démodé(e), mal fagoté(e)

down [daun] n (fluff) duvet m; (hill) colline (dénudée) ▷ adv en bas, vers le bas; (on the ground) par terre ▷ prep en bas de; (along) le long de ▷ vt (enemy) abattre; (inf: drink) siffler; **to fall ~** tomber; **she's going ~ to Bristol** elle descend à Bristol; **to write sth ~** écrire qch; **~ there** là-bas (en bas), là au fond; **~ here** ici en bas; **the price of meat is ~** le prix de la viande a baissé; **I've got it ~ in my diary** c'est inscrit dans mon agenda; **to pay £2 ~** verser 2 livres d'arrhes or en acompte; **England is two goals ~** l'Angleterre a deux buts de retard; **to walk ~ a hill** descendre une colline; **to run ~ the street** descendre la rue en courant; **to ~ tools** (Brit) cesser le travail; **~ with X!** à bas X!

down-and-out ['daunəndaut] n (tramp) clochard(e)

down-at-heel ['daunət'hiːl] adj (fig) miteux(-euse)

downcast ['daunkɑːst] adj démoralisé(e)

downfall ['daunfɔːl] n chute f; ruine f

downhearted ['daun'hɑːtɪd] adj découragé(e)

downhill ['daun'hɪl] adv (face, look) en aval, vers l'aval; (roll, go) vers le bas, en bas ▷ n (Ski: also: **~ race**) descente f; **to go ~** descendre; (business) péricliter, aller à vau-l'eau

Downing Street ['daunɪŋ-] n (Brit): **10 ~** résidence du Premier ministre; voir article

download ['daunləud] n téléchargement m ▷ vt (Comput) télécharger

downloadable [daun'ləudəbl] adj (Comput) téléchargeable

down payment n acompte m

downpour ['daunpɔː^r] n pluie torrentielle, déluge m

downright ['daunraɪt] adj (lie etc) effronté(e); (refusal) catégorique

downsize [daun'saɪz] vt réduire l'effectif de

Down's syndrome [daunz-] n mongolisme m, trisomie f; **a ~ baby** un bébé mongolien or trisomique

downstairs ['daun'stɛəz] adv (on or to ground floor) au rez-de-chaussée; (on or to floor below) à l'étage inférieur; **to come ~, to go ~** descendre (l'escalier)

downstream ['daunstriːm] adv en aval

down-to-earth ['dauntu'ə:θ] adj terre à terre inv

downtown ['daun'taun] adv en ville ▷ adj (US): **~ Chicago** le centre commerçant de Chicago

down under adv en Australie or Nouvelle Zélande

downward ['daunwəd] adj, adv vers le bas; **a ~ trend** une tendance à la baisse, une diminution progressive

downwards ['daunwədz] adv vers le bas

dowry ['daurɪ] n dot f

doz. abbr = **dozen**

doze [dəuz] vi sommeiller; **doze off** vi s'assoupir

dozen ['dʌzn] n douzaine f; **a ~ books** une douzaine de livres; **80p a ~** 80p la douzaine; **~s of** des centaines de

Dr. abbr (= doctor) Dr; (in street names) = **drive**

drab [dræb] adj terne, morne

draft [drɑːft] n (of letter, school work) brouillon m; (of literary work) ébauche f; (of contract, document) version f préliminaire; (Comm) traite f; (US Mil) contingent m; (: call-up) conscription f ▷ vt faire le brouillon de; (document, report) rédiger une version préliminaire de; (Mil: send) détacher; see also **draught**

drag [dræg] vt traîner; (river) draguer ▷ vi traîner ▷ n (Aviat, Naut) résistance f; (inf) casse-pieds m/f; (women's clothing): **in ~** (en) travesti; **to ~ and drop** (Comput) glisser-poser; **drag away** vt: **to ~ away (from)** arracher or emmener de force (de); **drag on** vi s'éterniser

dragon ['drægn] n dragon m
dragonfly ['drægənflaɪ] n libellule f
drain [dreɪn] n égout m; (on resources) saignée f ▷ vt (land, marshes) drainer, assécher; (vegetables) égoutter; (reservoir etc) vider ▷ vi (water) s'écouler; **to feel ~ed (of energy or emotion)** être miné(e)
drainage ['dreɪnɪdʒ] n (system) système m d'égouts; (act) drainage m
draining board ['dreɪnɪŋ-], (US) **drainboard** ['dreɪnbɔːd] n égouttoir m
drainpipe ['dreɪnpaɪp] n tuyau m d'écoulement
drama ['drɑːmə] n (art) théâtre m, art m dramatique; (play) pièce f, (event) drame m
dramatic [drə'mætɪk] adj (Theat) dramatique; (impressive) spectaculaire
dramatist ['dræmətɪst] n auteur m dramatique
dramatize ['dræmətaɪz] vt (events etc) dramatiser; (adapt) adapter pour la télévision (or pour l'écran)
drank [dræŋk] pt of **drink**
drape [dreɪp] vt draper; **drapes** npl (US) rideaux mpl
drastic ['dræstɪk] adj (measures) d'urgence, énergique; (change) radical(e)
draught, (US) **draft** [drɑːft] n courant m d'air; (of chimney) tirage m; (Naut) tirant m d'eau; **on ~** (beer) à la pression
draught beer n bière f (à la) pression
draughtboard ['drɑːftbɔːd] n (Brit) damier m
draughts [drɑːfts] n (Brit: game) (jeu m de) dames fpl
draughtsman, (US) **draftsman** ['drɑːftsmən] irreg n dessinateur(-trice) (industriel(le))
draw [drɔː] (vb: pt **drew**, pp **drawn**) [druː, drɔːn] vt tirer; (picture) dessiner; (attract) attirer; (line, circle) tracer; (money) retirer; (wages) toucher; (comparison, distinction): **to ~ (between)** faire (entre) ▷ vi (Sport) faire match nul ▷ n match nul; (lottery) loterie f; (: picking of ticket) tirage m au sort; **to ~ to a close** toucher à or tirer à sa fin; **to ~ near** vi s'approcher; approcher; **draw back** vi (move back): **to ~ back (from)** reculer (devant); **draw in** vi (Brit: car) s'arrêter le long du trottoir; (: train) entrer en gare or dans la station; **draw on** vt (resources) faire appel à; (imagination, person) avoir recours à, faire appel à; **draw out** vi (lengthen) s'allonger ▷ vt (money) retirer; **draw up** vi (stop) s'arrêter ▷ vt (document) établir, dresser; (plan) formuler, dessiner; (chair) approcher
drawback ['drɔːbæk] n inconvénient m, désavantage m
drawbridge ['drɔːbrɪdʒ] n pont-levis m
drawer [drɔːᵉ] n tiroir m; ['drɔːə'] (of cheque) tireur m
drawing ['drɔːɪŋ] n dessin m

drawing board n planche f à dessin
drawing pin n (Brit) punaise f
drawing room n salon m
drawl [drɔːl] n accent traînant
drawn [drɔːn] pp of **draw** ▷ adj (haggard) tiré(e), crispé(e)
dread [drɛd] n épouvante f, effroi m ▷ vt redouter, appréhender
dreadful ['drɛdful] adj épouvantable, affreux(-euse)
dream [driːm] n rêve m ▷ vt, vi (pt, pp **dreamed** or **dreamt**) [drɛmt] rêver; **to have a ~ about sb/sth** rêver à qn/qch; **sweet ~s!** faites de beaux rêves!; **dream up** vt inventer
dreamer ['driːmə'] n rêveur(-euse)
dreamt [drɛmt] pt, pp of **dream**
dreamy ['driːmɪ] adj (absent-minded) rêveur(-euse)
dreary ['drɪərɪ] adj triste; monotone
dredge [drɛdʒ] vt draguer; **dredge up** vt draguer; (fig: unpleasant facts) (faire) ressortir
dregs [drɛgz] npl lie f
drench [drɛntʃ] vt tremper; **~ed to the skin** trempé(e) jusqu'aux os
dress [drɛs] n robe f; (clothing) habillement m, tenue f ▷ vt habiller; (wound) panser; (food) préparer ▷ vi: **she ~es very well** elle s'habille très bien; **to ~, to get ~ed** s'habiller; **to ~ a shop window** faire l'étalage or la vitrine; **dress up** vi s'habiller; (in fancy dress) se déguiser
dress circle n (Brit) premier balcon
dresser ['drɛsə'] n (Theat) habilleur(-euse); (also: **window ~**) étalagiste m/f; (furniture) vaisselier m; (: US) coiffeuse f, commode f
dressing ['drɛsɪŋ] n (Med) pansement m; (Culin) sauce f, assaisonnement m
dressing gown n (Brit) robe f de chambre
dressing room n (Theat) loge f, (Sport) vestiaire m
dressing table n coiffeuse f
dressmaker ['drɛsmeɪkə'] n couturière f
dress rehearsal n (répétition f) générale f
drew [druː] pt of **draw**
dribble ['drɪbl] vi tomber goutte à goutte; (baby) baver ▷ vt (ball) dribbler
dried [draɪd] adj (fruit, beans) sec/sèche; (eggs, milk) en poudre
drier ['draɪə'] n = **dryer**
drift [drɪft] n (of current etc) force f, direction f; (of sand etc) amoncellement m; (of snow) rafale f; coulée f; (: on ground) congère f; (general meaning) sens général ▷ vi (boat) aller à la dérive, dériver; (sand, snow) s'amonceler, s'entasser; **to let things ~** laisser les choses aller à la dérive; **to ~ apart** (friends, lovers) s'éloigner l'un de l'autre; **I get or catch your ~** je vois en gros ce que vous voulez dire
driftwood ['drɪftwud] n bois flotté
drill [drɪl] n perceuse f; (bit) foret m; (of dentist) roulette f, fraise f; (Mil) exercice m ▷ vt percer; (troops) entraîner; (pupils: in grammar)

faire faire des exercices à ▷ *vi (for oil)* faire un
or des forage(s)

drink [drɪŋk] *n* boisson *f*; *(alcoholic)* verre *m*
▷ *vt, vi (pt* **drank**, *pp* **drunk**) [dræŋk, drʌŋk]
boire; **to have a ~** boire quelque chose, boire
un verre; **a ~ of water** un verre d'eau; **would
you like a ~?** tu veux boire quelque chose?;
we had ~s before lunch on a pris l'apéritif;
drink in *vt (fresh air)* inspirer profondément;
(story) avaler, ne pas perdre une miette de;
(sight) se remplir la vue de

drink-driving ['drɪŋk'draɪvɪŋ] *n* conduite *f*
en état d'ivresse

drinker ['drɪŋkə'] *n* buveur(-euse)

drinking water *n* eau *f* potable

drip [drɪp] *n (drop)* goutte *f*; *(sound: of water etc)*
bruit *m* de l'eau qui tombe goutte à goutte;
(Med: device) goutte-à-goutte *m inv*; (: *liquid)*
perfusion *f*; *(inf: person)* lavette *f*, nouille *f* ▷ *vi*
tomber goutte à goutte; *(tap)* goutter;
(washing) s'égoutter; *(wall)* suinter

drip-dry ['drɪp'draɪ] *adj (shirt)* sans repassage

dripping ['drɪpɪŋ] *n* graisse *f* de rôti ▷ *adj*:
~ wet trempé(e)

drive [draɪv] *n (pt* **drove**, *pp* **driven**) [drəuv,
'drɪvn] *n* promenade *f* or trajet *m* en voiture;
(also: **~way**) allée *f*; *(energy)* dynamisme *m*,
énergie *f*; *(Psych)* besoin *m*; pulsion *f*; *(push)*
effort (concerté); campagne *f*; *(Sport)* drive *m*;
(Tech) entraînement *m*; traction *f*;
transmission *f*; *(Comput: also:* **disk ~**) lecteur
m de disquette ▷ *vt* conduire; *(nail)* enfoncer;
(push) chasser, pousser; *(Tech: motor)*
actionner; entraîner ▷ *vi (be at the wheel)*
conduire; *(travel by car)* aller en voiture; **to go
for a ~** aller faire une promenade en voiture;
it's 3 hours' ~ from London Londres est à
3 heures de route; **left-/right-hand ~** *(Aut)*
conduite *f* à gauche/droite; **front-/rear-
wheel ~** *(Aut)* traction *f* avant/arrière; **to ~ sb
to (do) sth** pousser or conduire qn à (faire)
qch; **to ~ sb mad** rendre qn fou/folle; **drive
at** *vt fus (fig: intend, mean)* vouloir dire, en
venir à; **drive on** *vi* poursuivre sa route,
continuer; *(after stopping)* reprendre sa route,
repartir ▷ *vt (incite, encourage)* inciter; **drive
out** *vt (force out)* chasser

drive-by ['draɪvbaɪ] *n (also:* **~ shooting**)
tentative d'assassinat par coups de feu tirés d'une
voiture

drive-in ['draɪvɪn] *adj, n (esp US)* drive-in *m*

drivel ['drɪvl] *n (inf)* idioties *fpl*,
imbécillités *fpl*

driven ['drɪvn] *pp of* **drive**

driver ['draɪvə'] *n* conducteur(-trice); *(of taxi,
bus)* chauffeur *m*

driver's license *n (US)* permis *m* de conduire

driveway ['draɪvweɪ] *n* allée *f*

driving ['draɪvɪŋ] *adj:* **~ rain** *n* pluie battante
▷ *n* conduite *f*

driving instructor *n* moniteur *m* d'auto-
école

driving lesson *n* leçon *f* de conduite

driving licence *n (Brit)* permis *m* de conduire

driving school *n* auto-école *f*

driving test *n* examen *m* du permis de
conduite

drizzle ['drɪzl] *n* bruine *f*, crachin *m* ▷ *vi*
bruiner

drool [dru:l] *vi* baver; **to ~ over sb/sth** *(fig)*
baver d'admiration or être en extase devant
qn/qch

droop [dru:p] *vi (flower)* commencer à se
faner; *(shoulders, head)* tomber

drop [drɔp] *n (of liquid)* goutte *f*; *(fall)* baisse *f*;
(: *in salary)* réduction *f*; *(also:* **parachute ~**)
saut *m*; *(of cliff)* dénivellation *f*; à-pic *m* ▷ *vt*
laisser tomber; *(voice, eyes, price)* baisser;
(passenger) déposer ▷ *vi (wind, temperature, price,
voice)* tomber; *(numbers, attendance)* diminuer;
drops *npl (Med)* gouttes; **cough ~s** pastilles
fpl pour la toux; **a ~ of 10%** une baisse or
réduction de 10%; **to ~ anchor** jeter l'ancre;
to ~ sb a line mettre un mot à qn; **drop in** *vi*
(inf: visit): **to ~ in (on)** faire un saut (chez),
passer (chez); **drop off** *vi (sleep)* s'assoupir
▷ *vt (passenger)* déposer; **to ~ sb off** déposer
qn; **drop out** *vi (withdraw)* se retirer; *(student
etc)* abandonner, décrocher

dropout ['drɔpaut] *n (from society)*
marginal(e); *(from university)* drop-out *m/f*,
dropé(e)

dropper ['drɔpə'] *n (Med etc)* compte-gouttes
m inv

droppings ['drɔpɪŋz] *npl* crottes *fpl*

drought [draut] *n* sécheresse *f*

drove [drəuv] *pt of* **drive** ▷ *n:* **~s of people**
une foule de gens

drown [draun] *vt* noyer; *(also:* **~ out**: *sound)*
couvrir, étouffer ▷ *vi* se noyer

drowsy ['drauzɪ] *adj* somnolent(e)

drug [drʌg] *n* médicament *m*; *(narcotic)*
drogue *f* ▷ *vt* droguer; **to be on ~s** se droguer;
he's on ~s il se drogue; *(Med)* il est sous
médication

drug addict *n* toxicomane *m/f*

drug dealer *n* revendeur(-euse) de drogue

druggist ['drʌgɪst] *n (US)* pharmacien(ne)-
droguiste

drugstore ['drʌgstɔ:'] *n (US)* pharmacie-
droguerie *f*, drugstore *m*

drum [drʌm] *n* tambour *m*; *(for oil, petrol)*
bidon *m* ▷ *vt:* **to ~ one's fingers on the
table** pianoter or tambouriner sur la table;
drums *npl (Mus)* batterie *f*; **drum up** *vt*
(enthusiasm, support) susciter, rallier

drummer ['drʌmə'] *n* (joueur *m* de)
tambour *m*

drunk [drʌŋk] *pp of* **drink** ▷ *adj* ivre, soûl(e)
▷ *n (also:* **~ard**) ivrogne *m/f*; **to get ~** s'enivrer,
se soûler

drunken ['drʌŋkən] *adj* ivre, soûl(e); *(rage,
stupor)* ivrogne, d'ivrogne; **~ driving** conduite
f en état d'ivresse

dry [draɪ] *adj* sec/sèche; *(day)* sans pluie; *(humour)* pince-sans-rire; *(uninteresting)* aride, rébarbatif(-ive) ▷ *vt* sécher; *(clothes)* faire sécher ▷ *vi* sécher; **on ~ land** sur la terre ferme; **to ~ one's hands/hair/eyes** se sécher les mains/les cheveux/les yeux; **dry off** *vi, vt* sécher; **dry up** *vi (river, supplies)* se tarir; *(: speaker)* sécher, rester sec

dry-cleaner's ['draɪ'kliːnəz] *n* teinturerie *f*

dry-cleaning ['draɪ'kliːnɪŋ] *n (process)* nettoyage *m* à sec

dryer ['draɪə'] *n (tumble-dryer)* sèche-linge *m inv; (for hair)* sèche-cheveux *m inv*

dryness ['draɪnɪs] *n* sécheresse *f*

dry rot *n* pourriture sèche *(du bois)*

DSS *n abbr (Brit)* = **Department of Social Security**

DTP *n abbr (= desktop publishing)* PAO *f*

dual ['djuəl] *adj* double

dual carriageway *n (Brit)* route *f* à quatre voies

dual-purpose ['djuəl'pə:pəs] *adj* à double emploi

dubbed [dʌbd] *adj (Cine)* doublé(e); *(nicknamed)* surnommé(e)

dubious ['dju:bɪəs] *adj* hésitant(e), incertain(e); *(reputation, company)* douteux(-euse); *(also:* **I'm very ~ about it)** j'ai des doutes sur la question, je n'en suis pas sûr du tout

duchess ['dʌtʃɪs] *n* duchesse *f*

duck [dʌk] *n* canard *m* ▷ *vi* se baisser vivement, baisser subitement la tête ▷ *vt* plonger dans l'eau

duckling ['dʌklɪŋ] *n* caneton *m*

duct [dʌkt] *n* conduite *f*, canalisation *f; (Anat)* conduit *m*

dud [dʌd] *n (shell)* obus non éclaté; *(object, tool):* **it's a ~** c'est de la camelote, ça ne marche pas ▷ *adj (Brit: cheque)* sans provision; *(: note, coin)* faux/fausse

due [dju:] *adj (money, payment)* dû/due; *(expected)* attendu(e); *(fitting)* qui convient ▷ *n* dû *m* ▷ *adv:* ~ **north** droit vers le nord; **dues** *npl (for club, union)* cotisation *f; (in harbour)* droits *mpl* (de port); ~ **to** *(because of)* en raison de; *(caused by)* dû à; **in ~ course** en temps utile *or* voulu; *(in the end)* finalement; **the rent is ~ on the 30th** il faut payer le loyer le 30; **the train is ~ at 8 a.m.** le train est attendu à 8 h; **she is ~ back tomorrow** elle doit rentrer demain; **he is ~ £10** on lui doit 10 livres; **I am ~ 6 days' leave** j'ai droit à 6 jours de congé; **to give sb his** *or* **her ~** être juste envers qn

duel ['djuəl] *n* duel *m*

duet [dju:'ɛt] *n* duo *m*

duffel bag, duffle bag ['dʌfl-] *n* sac marin

duffel coat, duffle coat ['dʌfl-] *n* duffel-coat *m*

dug [dʌg] *pt, pp of* **dig**

duke [dju:k] *n* duc *m*

dull [dʌl] *adj (boring)* ennuyeux(-euse); *(slow)* borné(e); *(not bright)* morne, terne; *(sound, pain)* sourd(e); *(weather, day)* gris(e), maussade; *(blade)* émoussé(e) ▷ *vt (pain, grief)* atténuer; *(mind, senses)* engourdir

duly ['dju:lɪ] *adv (on time)* en temps voulu; *(as expected)* comme il se doit

dumb [dʌm] *adj (stupid)* bête; **to be struck ~** *(fig)* rester abasourdi(e), être sidéré(e)

dumbfounded [dʌm'faundɪd] *adj* sidéré(e)

dummy ['dʌmɪ] *n (tailor's model)* mannequin *m; (mock-up)* factice *m*, maquette *f; (Sport)* feinte *f; (Brit: for baby)* tétine *f* ▷ *adj* faux/fausse, factice

dump [dʌmp] *n* tas *m* d'ordures; *(also:* **rubbish ~)** décharge (publique); *(Mil)* dépôt *m; (Comput)* listage *m* (de la mémoire); *(inf: place)* trou *m* ▷ *vt (put down)* déposer; déverser; *(get rid of)* se débarrasser de; *(Comput)* lister; *(Comm: goods)* vendre à perte *(sur le marché extérieur);* **to be (down) in the ~s** *(inf)* avoir le cafard, broyer du noir

dumpling ['dʌmplɪŋ] *n* boulette *f* (de pâte)

dumpy ['dʌmpɪ] *adj* courtaud(e), boulot(te)

dunce [dʌns] *n* âne *m*, cancre *m*

dune [dju:n] *n* dune *f*

dung [dʌŋ] *n* fumier *m*

dungarees [dʌŋgə'ri:z] *npl* bleu(s) *m(pl); (for child, woman)* salopette *f*

dungeon ['dʌndʒən] *n* cachot *m*

duplex ['dju:plɛks] *n (US: also:* ~ **apartment)** duplex *m*

duplicate *n* ['dju:plɪkət] double *m*, copie exacte; *(copy of letter etc)* duplicata *m* ▷ *adj (copy)* en double ▷ *vt* ['dju:plɪkeɪt] faire un double de; *(on machine)* polycopier; **in ~** en deux exemplaires, en double; ~ **key** double *m* de la *(or* d'une) clé

durable ['djuərəbl] *adj* durable; *(clothes, metal)* résistant(e), solide

duration [djuə'reɪʃən] *n* durée *f*

during ['djuərɪŋ] *prep* pendant, au cours de

dusk [dʌsk] *n* crépuscule *m*

dust [dʌst] *n* poussière *f* ▷ *vt (furniture)* essuyer, épousseter; *(cake etc):* **to ~ with** saupoudrer de; **dust off** *vt (also fig)* dépoussiérer

dustbin ['dʌstbɪn] *n (Brit)* poubelle *f*

duster ['dʌstə'] *n* chiffon *m*

dustman ['dʌstmən] *irreg n (Brit)* boueux *m*, éboueur *m*

dustpan ['dʌstpæn] *n* pelle *f* à poussière

dusty ['dʌstɪ] *adj* poussiéreux(-euse)

Dutch [dʌtʃ] *adj* hollandais(e), néerlandais(e) ▷ *n (Ling)* hollandais *m*, néerlandais *m* ▷ *adv:* **to go ~** *or* **dutch** *(inf)* partager les frais; **the Dutch** *npl* les Hollandais, les Néerlandais

Dutchman ['dʌtʃmən] *irreg n* Hollandais *m*

Dutchwoman ['dʌtʃwumən] *irreg n* Hollandaise *f*

duty ['dju:tɪ] n devoir m; (tax) droit m, taxe f; **duties** npl fonctions fpl; **to make it one's ~ to do sth** se faire un devoir de faire qch; **to pay ~ on sth** payer un droit or une taxe sur qch; **on ~** de service; (at night etc) de garde; **off ~** libre, pas de service or de garde

duty-free ['dju:tɪ'fri:] adj exempté(e) de douane, hors-taxe; **~ shop** boutique f hors-taxe

duvet ['du:veɪ] n (Brit) couette f

DVD n abbr (= digital versatile or video disc) DVD m

DVD burner n graveur m de DVD

DVD player n lecteur m de DVD

DVD writer n graveur m de DVD

dwarf (pl **dwarves**) [dwɔ:f, dwɔ:vz] n (pej) nain(e) ▷ vt écraser

dwell (pt, pp **dwelt**) [dwɛl, dwɛlt] vi demeurer; **dwell on** vt fus s'étendre sur

dwelt [dwɛlt] pt, pp of **dwell**

dwindle ['dwɪndl] vi diminuer, décroître

dye [daɪ] n teinture f ▷ vt teindre; **hair ~** teinture pour les cheveux

dying ['daɪɪŋ] adj mourant(e), agonisant(e)

dyke [daɪk] n (embankment) digue f

dynamic [daɪ'næmɪk] adj dynamique

dynamite ['daɪnəmaɪt] n dynamite f ▷ vt dynamiter, faire sauter à la dynamite

dynamo ['daɪnəməʊ] n dynamo f

dyslexia [dɪs'lɛksɪə] n dyslexie f

dyslexic [dɪs'lɛksɪk] adj, n dyslexique m/f

E¹, e [i:] n (letter) E, e m; (Mus): **E** mi m; **E for Edward**, (US) **E for Easy** E comme Eugène

E² abbr (= east) E ▷ n abbr (Drugs) = **ecstasy**

each [i:tʃ] adj chaque ▷ pron chacun(e); **~ one** chacun(e); **~ other** l'un l'autre; **they hate ~ other** ils se détestent (mutuellement); **you are jealous of ~ other** vous êtes jaloux l'un de l'autre; **~ day** chaque jour, tous les jours; **they have 2 books ~** ils ont 2 livres chacun; **they cost £5 ~** ils coûtent 5 livres (la) pièce; **~ of us** chacun(e) de nous

eager ['i:gə'] adj (person, buyer) empressé(e); (lover) ardent(e), passionné(e); (keen: pupil, worker) enthousiaste; **to be ~ to do sth** (impatient) brûler de faire qch; (keen) désirer vivement faire qch; **to be ~ for** (event) désirer vivement; (vengeance, affection, information) être avide de

eagle ['i:gl] n aigle m

ear [ɪə'] n oreille f; (of corn) épi m; **up to one's ~s in debt** endetté(e) jusqu'au cou

earache ['ɪəreɪk] n mal m aux oreilles

eardrum ['ɪədrʌm] n tympan m

earl [ə:l] n comte m

earlier ['ə:lɪə'] adj (date etc) plus rapproché(e); (edition etc) plus ancien(ne), antérieur(e) ▷ adv plus tôt

early ['ə:lɪ] adv tôt, de bonne heure; (ahead of time) en avance; (near the beginning) au début ▷ adj précoce, qui se manifeste (or se fait) tôt or de bonne heure; (Christians, settlers) premier(-ière); (reply) rapide; (death) prématuré(e); (*work*) de jeunesse; **to have an ~ night/start** se coucher/partir tôt *or* de bonne heure; **take the ~ train** prenez le premier train; **in the ~ or ~ in the spring/19th century** au début *or* commencement du printemps/19ème siècle; **you're ~!** tu es en avance!; **~ in the morning** tôt le matin; **she's in her ~ forties** elle a un peu plus de quarante ans *or* de la quarantaine; **at your earliest convenience** (*Comm*) dans les meilleurs délais

early retirement *n* retraite anticipée

earmark ['ɪəmɑ:k] *vt*: **to ~ sth for** réserver *or* destiner qch à

earn [ə:n] *vt* gagner; (*Comm*: *yield*) rapporter; **to ~ one's living** gagner sa vie; **this ~ed him much praise, he ~ed much praise for this** ceci lui a valu de nombreux éloges; **he's ~ed his rest/reward** il mérite *or* a bien mérité *or* a bien gagné son repos/sa récompense

earnest ['ə:nɪst] *adj* sérieux(-euse) ▷ *n* (*also*: **~ money**) acompte *m*, arrhes *fpl*; **in ~** *adv* sérieusement, pour de bon

earnings ['ə:nɪŋz] *npl* salaire *m*; gains *mpl*; (*of company etc*) profits *mpl*, bénéfices *mpl*

earphones ['ɪəfəunz] *npl* écouteurs *mpl*

earplugs ['ɪəplʌgz] *npl* boules *fpl* Quiès®; (*to keep out water*) protège-tympans *mpl*

earring ['ɪərɪŋ] *n* boucle *f* d'oreille

earshot ['ɪəʃɔt] *n*: **out of/within ~** hors de portée/à portée de voix

earth [ə:θ] *n* (*gen, also Brit Elec*) terre *f*; (*of fox etc*) terrier *m* ▷ *vt* (*Brit Elec*) relier à la terre

earthenware ['ə:θnwɛə'] *n* poterie *f*; faïence *f* ▷ *adj* de *or* en faïence

earthquake ['ə:θkweɪk] *n* tremblement *m* de terre, séisme *m*

earthy ['ə:θɪ] *adj* (*fig*) terre à terre *inv*, truculent(e)

ease [i:z] *n* facilité *f*, aisance *f*; (*comfort*) bien-être *m* ▷ *vt* (*soothe*: *mind*) tranquilliser; (*reduce*: *pain, problem*) atténuer; (: *tension*) réduire; (*loosen*) relâcher, détendre; (*help pass*): **to ~ sth in/out** faire pénétrer/sortir qch délicatement *or* avec douceur, faciliter la pénétration/la sortie de qch ▷ *vi* (*situation*) se détendre; **with ~** sans difficulté, aisément; **life of ~** vie oisive; **~ at ~** à l'aise; (*Mil*) au repos; **ease off, ease up** *vi* diminuer; (*slow down*) ralentir; (*relax*) se détendre

easel ['i:zl] *n* chevalet *m*

easily ['i:zɪlɪ] *adv* facilement; (*by far*) de loin

east [i:st] *n* est *m* ▷ *adj* (*wind*) d'est; (*side*) est *inv* ▷ *adv* à l'est, vers l'est; **the E~** l'Orient *m*; (*Pol*) les pays *mpl* de l'Est

eastbound ['i:stbaund] *adj* en direction de l'est; (*carriageway*) est *inv*

Easter ['i:stə'] *n* Pâques *fpl* ▷ *adj* (*holidays*) de Pâques, pascal(e)

Easter egg *n* œuf *m* de Pâques

easterly ['i:stəlɪ] *adj* d'est

eastern ['i:stən] *adj* de l'est, oriental(e);

E~ Europe l'Europe de l'Est; **the E~ bloc** (*Pol*) les pays *mpl* de l'est

Easter Sunday *n* le dimanche de Pâques

eastward ['i:stwəd], **eastwards** ['i:stwədz] *adv* vers l'est, à l'est

easy ['i:zɪ] *adj* facile; (*manner*) aisé(e) ▷ *adv*: **to take it** *or* **things ~** (*rest*) ne pas se fatiguer; (*not worry*) ne pas (trop) s'en faire; **to have an ~ life** avoir la vie facile; **payment on ~ terms** (*Comm*) facilités *fpl* de paiement; **that's easier said than done** c'est plus facile à dire qu'à faire, c'est vite dit; **I'm ~** (*inf*) ça m'est égal

easy chair *n* fauteuil *m*

easy-going ['i:zɪ'gəuɪŋ] *adj* accommodant(e), facile à vivre

eat (*pt* **ate**, *pp* **eaten**) [i:t, eɪt, 'i:tn] *vt, vi* manger; **can we have something to ~?** est-ce qu'on peut manger quelque chose?; **eat away** *vt* (*sea*) saper, éroder; (*acid*) ronger, corroder; **eat away at, eat into** *vt fus* ronger, attaquer; **eat out** *vi* manger au restaurant; **eat up** *vt* (*food*) finir (de manger); **it ~s up electricity** ça bouffe du courant, ça consomme beaucoup d'électricité

eaten ['i:tn] *pp of* **eat**

eaves [i:vz] *npl* avant-toit *m*

eavesdrop ['i:vzdrɔp] *vi*: **to ~ (on)** écouter de façon indiscrète

ebb [ɛb] *n* reflux *m* ▷ *vi* refluer; (*fig*: *also*: **~ away**) décliner; **the ~ and flow** le flux et le reflux; **to be at a low ~** (*fig*) être bien bas(se), ne pas aller bien fort

ebony ['ɛbənɪ] *n* ébène *f*

e-book ['i:buk] *n* livre *m* électronique

e-business ['i:bɪznɪs] *n* (*company*) entreprise *f* électronique; (*commerce*) commerce *m* électronique

ECB *n abbr* (= *European Central Bank*) BCE *f* (= *Banque centrale européenne*)

eccentric [ɪk'sɛntrɪk] *adj, n* excentrique *m/f*

echo ['ɛkəu] (*pl* **echoes**) *n* écho *m* ▷ *vt* répéter; faire chorus avec ▷ *vi* résonner; faire écho

e-cigarette [i:sɪgəret] *n* cigarette *f* électronique

eclipse [ɪ'klɪps] *n* éclipse *f* ▷ *vt* éclipser

eco-friendly [i:kəu'frɛndlɪ] *adj* non nuisible à *or* qui ne nuit pas à l'environnement

ecological [i:kə'lɔdʒɪkəl] *adj* écologique

ecology [ɪ'kɔlədʒɪ] *n* écologie *f*

e-commerce [i:kɔmə:s] *n* commerce *m* électronique

economic [i:kə'nɔmɪk] *adj* économique; (*profitable*) rentable

economical [i:kə'nɔmɪkl] *adj* économique; (*person*) économe

economics [i:kə'nɔmɪks] *n* (*Scol*) économie *f* politique ▷ *npl* (*of project etc*) côté *m* or aspect *m* économique

economist [ɪ'kɔnəmɪst] *n* économiste *m/f*

economize [ɪ'kɔnəmaɪz] *vi* économiser, faire des économies

economy [ɪ'kɔnəmɪ] n économie f;
economies of scale économies d'échelle
economy class n (Aviat) classe f touriste
economy class syndrome n syndrome m
de la classe économique
economy size n taille f économique
ecstasy ['ɛkstəsɪ] n extase f; (Drugs) ecstasy
m; **to go into ecstasies over** s'extasier sur
ecstatic [ɛks'tætɪk] adj extatique, en extase
eczema ['ɛksɪmə] n eczéma m
edge [ɛdʒ] n bord m; (of knife etc) tranchant m,
fil m ⊳ vt border ⊳ vi: **to ~ forward** avancer
petit à petit; **to ~ away from** s'éloigner
furtivement de; **on ~** (fig) crispé(e), tendu(e);
to have the ~ on (fig) l'emporter (de justesse)
sur, être légèrement meilleur que
edgeways ['ɛdʒweɪz] adv latéralement; **he
couldn't get a word in ~** il ne pouvait pas
placer un mot
edgy ['ɛdʒɪ] adj crispé(e), tendu(e)
edible ['ɛdɪbl] adj comestible; (meal)
mangeable
Edinburgh ['ɛdɪnbərə] n Édimbourg; voir
article

● **EDINBURGH FESTIVAL**
●
● Le Festival d'Édimbourg, qui se tient
● chaque année durant trois semaines au
● mois d'août, est l'un des grands festivals
● européens. Il est réputé pour son
● programme officiel mais aussi pour son
● festival "off" (the Fringe) qui propose des
● spectacles aussi bien traditionnels que
● résolument d'avant-garde. Pendant la
● durée du Festival se tient par ailleurs, sur
● l'esplanade du château, un grand
● spectacle de musique militaire, le
● "Military Tattoo".

edit ['ɛdɪt] vt (text, book) éditer; (report)
préparer; (film) monter; (broadcast) réaliser;
(magazine) diriger; (newspaper) être le
rédacteur or la rédactrice en chef de
edition [ɪ'dɪʃən] n édition f
editor ['ɛdɪtə'] n (of newspaper)
rédacteur(-trice), rédacteur(-trice) en chef;
(of sb's work) éditeur(-trice); (also: **film ~**)
monteur(-euse); **political/ foreign ~**
rédacteur politique/au service étranger
editorial [ɛdɪ'tɔːrɪəl] adj de la rédaction,
éditorial(e) ⊳ n éditorial m; **the ~ staff** la
rédaction
educate ['ɛdjukeɪt] vt (teach) instruire; (bring
up) éduquer; **~d at ...** qui a fait ses études à ...
educated ['ɛdjukeɪtɪd] adj (person) cultivé(e)
education [ɛdju'keɪʃən] n éducation f;
(studies) études fpl; (teaching) enseignement m,
instruction f; (at university: subject etc)
pédagogie f; **primary** or (US) **elementary/
secondary ~** instruction f primaire/
secondaire

educational [ɛdju'keɪʃənl] adj pédagogique;
(institution) scolaire; (useful) instructif(-ive);
(game, toy) éducatif(-ive); **~ technology**
technologie f de l'enseignement
eel [iːl] n anguille f
eerie ['ɪərɪ] adj inquiétant(e), spectral(e),
surnaturel(le)
effect [ɪ'fɛkt] n effet m ⊳ vt effectuer;
effects npl (Theat) effets mpl; (property) effets,
affaires fpl; **to take ~** (Law) entrer en vigueur,
prendre effet; (drug) agir, faire son effet; **to
put into ~** (plan) mettre en application or à
exécution; **to have an ~ on sb/sth** avoir or
produire un effet sur qn/qch; **in ~** en fait;
his letter is to the ~ that ... sa lettre nous
apprend que ...
effective [ɪ'fɛktɪv] adj efficace; (striking:
display, outfit) frappant(e), qui produit or fait
de l'effet; (actual) véritable; **to become ~**
(Law) entrer en vigueur, prendre effet; **~ date**
date f d'effet or d'entrée en vigueur
effectively [ɪ'fɛktɪvlɪ] adv efficacement;
(strikingly) d'une manière frappante, avec
beaucoup d'effet; (in reality) effectivement,
en fait
effectiveness [ɪ'fɛktɪvnɪs] n efficacité f
effeminate [ɪ'fɛmɪnɪt] adj efféminé(e)
effervescent [ɛfə'vɛsnt] adj effervescent(e)
efficiency [ɪ'fɪʃənsɪ] n efficacité f; (of machine,
car) rendement m
efficient [ɪ'fɪʃənt] adj efficace; (machine, car)
d'un bon rendement
efficiently [ɪ'fɪʃəntlɪ] adv efficacement
effort ['ɛfət] n effort m; **to make an ~ to do
sth** faire or fournir un effort pour faire qch
effortless ['ɛfətlɪs] adj sans effort, aisé(e);
(achievement) facile
effusive [ɪ'fjuːsɪv] adj (person) expansif(-ive);
(welcome) chaleureux(-euse)
e.g. adv abbr (= exempli gratia) par exemple,
p. ex.
egg [ɛg] n œuf m; **hard-boiled/soft-boiled ~**
œuf dur/à la coque; **egg on** vt pousser
eggcup ['ɛgkʌp] n coquetier m
egg plant ['ɛgplaːnt] (US) n aubergine f
eggshell ['ɛgʃɛl] n coquille f d'œuf ⊳ adj
(colour) blanc cassé inv
egg white n blanc m d'œuf
egg yolk n jaune m d'œuf
ego ['iːgəu] n (self-esteem) amour-propre m;
(Psych) moi m
egotism ['ɛgəutɪzəm] n égotisme m
egotist ['ɛgəutɪst] n égocentrique m/f
Egypt ['iːdʒɪpt] n Égypte f
Egyptian [ɪ'dʒɪpʃən] adj égyptien(ne) ⊳ n
Égyptien(ne)
eiderdown ['aɪdədaun] n édredon m
Eiffel Tower ['aɪfəl-] n tour f Eiffel
eight [eɪt] num huit
eighteen [eɪ'tiːn] num dix-huit
eighteenth [eɪ'tiːnθ] num dix-huitième
eighth [eɪtθ] num huitième

eightieth ['eɪtɪɪθ] *num* quatre-vingtième

eighty ['eɪtɪ] *num* quatre-vingt(s)

Eire ['ɛərə] *n* République *f* d'Irlande

either ['aɪðər] *adj* l'un ou l'autre; (*both, each*) chaque ▷ *pron*: ~ **(of them)** l'un ou l'autre ▷ *adv* non plus ▷ *conj*: ~ **good or bad** ou bon ou mauvais, soit bon soit mauvais; **I haven't seen ~ one or the other** je n'ai vu ni l'un ni l'autre; **on ~ side** de chaque côté; **I don't like ~** je n'aime ni l'un ni l'autre; **no, I don't ~** moi non plus; **which bike do you want? — ~ will do** quel vélo voulez-vous? — n'importe lequel; **answer with ~ yes or no** répondez par oui ou par non

eject [ɪ'dʒɛkt] *vt* (*tenant etc*) expulser; (*object*) éjecter ▷ *vi* (*pilot*) s'éjecter

elaborate *adj* [ɪ'læbərɪt] compliqué(e), recherché(e), minutieux(-euse) ▷ *vt* [ɪ'læbəreɪt] élaborer ▷ *vi* entrer dans les détails

elastic [ɪ'læstɪk] *adj, n* élastique (*m*)

elastic band *n* (*Brit*) élastique *m*

elated [ɪ'leɪtɪd] *adj* transporté(e) de joie

elation [ɪ'leɪʃən] *n* (grande) joie, allégresse *f*

elbow ['ɛlbəu] *n* coude *m* ▷ *vt*: **to ~ one's way through the crowd** se frayer un passage à travers la foule (en jouant des coudes)

elder ['ɛldər] *adj* aîné(e) ▷ *n* (*tree*) sureau *m*; **one's ~s** ses aînés

elderly ['ɛldəlɪ] *adj* âgé(e); **~ people** les personnes âgées

eldest ['ɛldɪst] *adj, n*: **the ~ (child)** l'aîné(e) (des enfants)

elect [ɪ'lɛkt] *vt* élire; (*choose*): **to ~ to do** choisir de faire ▷ *adj*: **the president ~** le président désigné

election [ɪ'lɛkʃən] *n* élection *f*; **to hold an ~** procéder à une élection

electioneering [ɪlɛkʃə'nɪərɪŋ] *n* propagande électorale, manœuvres électorales

elector [ɪ'lɛktər] *n* électeur(-trice)

electoral [ɪ'lɛktərəl] *adj* électoral(e)

electorate [ɪ'lɛktərɪt] *n* électorat *m*

electric [ɪ'lɛktrɪk] *adj* électrique

electrical [ɪ'lɛktrɪkl] *adj* électrique

electric blanket *n* couverture chauffante

electric fire *n* (*Brit*) radiateur *m* électrique

electrician [ɪlɛk'trɪʃən] *n* électricien *m*

electricity [ɪlɛk'trɪsɪtɪ] *n* électricité *f*; **to switch on/off the ~** rétablir/couper le courant

electric shock *n* choc *m* or décharge *f* électrique

electrify [ɪ'lɛktrɪfaɪ] *vt* (*Rail*) électrifier; (*audience*) électriser

electronic [ɪlɛk'trɔnɪk] *adj* électronique

electronic mail *n* courrier *m* électronique

electronics [ɪlɛk'trɔnɪks] *n* électronique *f*

elegance ['ɛlɪgəns] *n* élégance *f*

elegant ['ɛlɪgənt] *adj* élégant(e)

element ['ɛlɪmənt] *n* (*gen*) élément *m*; (*of heater, kettle etc*) résistance *f*

elementary [ɛlɪ'mɛntərɪ] *adj* élémentaire; (*school, education*) primaire

elementary school *n* (*US*) école *f* primaire; *voir article*

● **ELEMENTARY SCHOOL**
●
● Aux États-Unis et au Canada, une
● *elementary school* (également appelée
● "grade school" ou "grammar school" aux
● États-Unis) est une école publique où les
● enfants passent les six à huit premières
● années de leur scolarité.

elephant ['ɛlɪfənt] *n* éléphant *m*

elevate ['ɛlɪveɪt] *vt* élever

elevation [ɛlɪ'veɪʃən] *n* élévation *f*; (*height*) altitude *f*

elevator ['ɛlɪveɪtər] *n* (*in warehouse etc*) élévateur *m*, monte-charge *m inv*; (*US: lift*) ascenseur *m*

eleven [ɪ'lɛvn] *num* onze

elevenses [ɪ'lɛvnzɪz] *npl* (*Brit*) ≈ pause-café *f*

eleventh [ɪ'lɛvnθ] *num* onzième; **at the ~ hour** (*fig*) à la dernière minute

elicit [ɪ'lɪsɪt] *vt*: **to ~ (from)** obtenir (de); tirer (de)

eligible ['ɛlɪdʒəbl] *adj* éligible; (*for membership*) admissible; **an ~ young man** un beau parti; **to be ~ for sth** remplir les conditions requises pour qch; **~ for a pension** ayant droit à la retraite

eliminate [ɪ'lɪmɪneɪt] *vt* éliminer

elm [ɛlm] *n* orme *m*

elongated ['i:lɔŋgeɪtɪd] *adj* étiré(e), allongé(e)

elope [ɪ'ləup] *vi* (*lovers*) s'enfuir (ensemble)

eloquent ['ɛləkwənt] *adj* éloquent(e)

else [ɛls] *adv* d'autre; **something ~** quelque chose d'autre, autre chose; **somewhere ~** ailleurs, autre part; **everywhere ~** partout ailleurs; **everyone ~** tous les autres; **nothing ~** rien d'autre; **is there anything ~ I can do?** est-ce que je peux faire quelque chose d'autre?; **where ~?** à quel autre endroit?; **little ~** pas grand-chose d'autre

elsewhere [ɛls'wɛər] *adv* ailleurs, autre part

elude [ɪ'lu:d] *vt* échapper à; (*question*) éluder

elusive [ɪ'lu:sɪv] *adj* insaisissable; (*answer*) évasif(-ive)

emaciated [ɪ'meɪsɪeɪtɪd] *adj* émacié(e), décharné(e)

email ['i:meɪl] *n abbr* (= *electronic mail*) (e-)mail *m*, courriel *m* ▷ *vt*: **to ~ sb** envoyer un (e-)mail *or* un courriel à qn

email account *n* compte *m* (e-)mail

email address *n* adresse *f* (e-)mail *or* électronique

emancipate [ɪ'mænsɪpeɪt] *vt* émanciper

embankment [ɪm'bæŋkmənt] *n* (*of road, railway*) remblai *m*, talus *m*; (*of river*) berge *f*, quai *m*; (*dyke*) digue *f*

embargo [ɪmˈbɑːgəʊ] (pl **embargoes**) n (Comm, Naut) embargo m; (prohibition) interdiction f ▷ vt frapper d'embargo, mettre l'embargo sur; **to put an ~ on sth** mettre l'embargo sur qch

embark [ɪmˈbɑːk] vi embarquer; **to ~ on** (s')embarquer à bord de or sur ▷ vt embarquer; **to ~ on** (journey etc) commencer, entreprendre; (fig) se lancer or s'embarquer dans

embarkation [ɛmbɑːˈkeɪʃən] n embarquement m

embarrass [ɪmˈbærəs] vt embarrasser, gêner

embarrassed [ɪmˈbærəst] adj gêné(e); **to be ~** être gêné(e)

embarrassing [ɪmˈbærəsɪŋ] adj gênant(e), embarrassant(e)

embarrassment [ɪmˈbærəsmənt] n embarras m, gêne f; (embarrassing thing, person) source f d'embarras

embassy [ˈɛmbəsɪ] n ambassade f; **the French E~** l'ambassade de France

embellish [ɪmˈbɛlɪʃ] vt embellir; enjoliver

embers [ˈɛmbəz] npl braise f

embezzle [ɪmˈbɛzl] vt détourner

embezzlement [ɪmˈbɛzlmənt] n détournement m (de fonds)

embitter [ɪmˈbɪtər] vt aigrir; envenimer

embody [ɪmˈbɒdɪ] vt (features) réunir, comprendre; (ideas) formuler, exprimer

embossed [ɪmˈbɒst] adj repoussé(e), gaufré(e); **~ with** où figure(nt) en relief

embrace [ɪmˈbreɪs] vt embrasser, étreindre; (include) embrasser, couvrir, comprendre ▷ vi s'embrasser, s'étreindre ▷ n étreinte f

embroider [ɪmˈbrɔɪdər] vt broder; (fig: story) enjoliver

embroidery [ɪmˈbrɔɪdərɪ] n broderie f

embryo [ˈɛmbrɪəʊ] n (also fig) embryon m

emerald [ˈɛmərəld] n émeraude f

emerge [ɪˈmɜːdʒ] vi apparaître; (from room, car) surgir; (from sleep, imprisonment) sortir; **it ~s that** (Brit) il ressort que

emergency [ɪˈmɜːdʒənsɪ] n (crisis) cas m d'urgence; (Med) urgence f; **in an ~** en cas d'urgence; **state of ~** état m d'urgence

emergency brake n (US) frein m à main

emergency exit n sortie f de secours

emergency landing n atterrissage forcé

emergency room n (US: Med) urgences fpl

emergency services npl: **the ~** (fire, police, ambulance) les services mpl d'urgence

emery board [ˈɛmərɪ-] n lime f à ongles (en carton émerisé)

emigrate [ˈɛmɪgreɪt] vi émigrer

emigration [ɛmɪˈgreɪʃən] n émigration f

eminent [ˈɛmɪnənt] adj éminent(e)

emissions [ɪˈmɪʃənz] npl émissions fpl

emit [ɪˈmɪt] vt émettre

emoticon [ɪˈməʊtɪkən] n (Comput) émoticone m

emotion [ɪˈməʊʃən] n sentiment m; (as opposed to reason) émotion f, sentiments

emotional [ɪˈməʊʃənl] adj (person) émotif(-ive), très sensible; (needs) affectif(-ive); (scene) émouvant(e); (tone, speech) qui fait appel aux sentiments

emotive [ɪˈməʊtɪv] adj émotif(-ive); **~ power** capacité f d'émouvoir or de toucher

emperor [ˈɛmpərər] n empereur m

emphasis (pl **emphases**) [ˈɛmfəsɪs, -siːz] n accent m; **to lay** or **place ~ on sth** (fig) mettre l'accent sur, insister sur; **the ~ is on reading** la lecture tient une place primordiale, on accorde une importance particulière à la lecture

emphasize [ˈɛmfəsaɪz] vt (syllable, word, point) appuyer or insister sur; (feature) souligner, accentuer

emphatic [ɛmˈfætɪk] adj (strong) énergique, vigoureux(-euse); (unambiguous, clear) catégorique

empire [ˈɛmpaɪər] n empire m

employ [ɪmˈplɔɪ] vt employer; **he's ~ed in a bank** il est employé de banque, il travaille dans une banque

employee [ɪmplɔɪˈiː] n employé(e)

employer [ɪmˈplɔɪər] n employeur(-euse)

employment [ɪmˈplɔɪmənt] n emploi m; **to find ~** trouver un emploi or du travail; **without ~** au chômage, sans emploi; **place of ~** lieu m de travail

employment agency n agence f or bureau m de placement

empower [ɪmˈpaʊər] vt: **to ~ sb to do** autoriser or habiliter qn à faire

empress [ˈɛmprɪs] n impératrice f

emptiness [ˈɛmptɪnɪs] n vide m; (of area) aspect m désertique

empty [ˈɛmptɪ] adj vide; (street, area) désert(e); (threat, promise) en l'air, vain(e) ▷ n (bottle) bouteille f vide ▷ vt vider; (liquid) s'écouler; **on an ~ stomach** à jeun; **to ~ into** (river) se jeter dans, se déverser dans

empty-handed [ˈɛmptɪˈhændɪd] adj les mains vides

EMU n abbr (= European Monetary Union) UME f

emulate [ˈɛmjuleɪt] vt rivaliser avec, imiter

emulsion [ɪˈmʌlʃən] n émulsion f; (also: ~ paint) peinture mate

enable [ɪˈneɪbl] vt: **to ~ sb to do** permettre à qn de faire, donner à qn la possibilité de faire

enamel [ɪˈnæməl] n émail m; (also: ~ paint) (peinture f) laque f

enchant [ɪnˈtʃɑːnt] vt enchanter

enchanting [ɪnˈtʃɑːntɪŋ] adj ravissant(e), enchanteur(-eresse)

encl. abbr (on letters etc: = enclosed) ci-joint(e); (= enclosure) PJ f

enclose [ɪnˈkləʊz] vt (land) clôturer; (space, object) entourer; (letter etc): **to ~ (with)** joindre (à); **please find ~d** veuillez trouver ci-joint

enclosure [ɪnˈkləʊzəᵉ] n enceinte f; (in letter etc) annexe f

encompass [ɪnˈkʌmpəs] vt encercler, entourer; (include) contenir, inclure

encore [ɔŋˈkɔːᵉ] excl, n bis (m)

encounter [ɪnˈkaʊntəᵉ] n rencontre f ▷ vt rencontrer

encourage [ɪnˈkʌrɪdʒ] vt encourager; (industry, growth) favoriser; **to ~ sb to do sth** encourager qn à faire qch

encouragement [ɪnˈkʌrɪdʒmənt] n encouragement m

encouraging [ɪnˈkʌrɪdʒɪŋ] adj encourageant(e)

encroach [ɪnˈkrəʊtʃ] vi: **to ~ (up)on** empiéter sur

encyclopaedia, encyclopedia [ɛnsaɪkləʊˈpiːdɪə] n encyclopédie f

end [ɛnd] n fin f; (of table, street, rope etc) bout m, extrémité f; (of pointed object) pointe f; (of town) bout m; (Sport) côté m ▷ vt terminer; (also: **bring to an ~, put an ~ to**) mettre fin à ▷ vi se terminer, finir; **from ~ to ~** d'un bout à l'autre; **to come to an ~** prendre fin; **to be at an ~** être fini(e), être terminé(e); **in the ~** finalement; **on ~** (object) debout, dressé(e); **to stand on ~** (hair) se dresser sur la tête; **for 5 hours on ~** durant 5 heures d'affilée or de suite; **for hours on ~** pendant des heures (et des heures); **at the ~ of the day** (Brit fig) en fin de compte; **to this ~, with this ~ in view** à cette fin, dans ce but; **end up** vi: **to ~ up in** (condition) finir or se terminer par; (place) finir or aboutir à

endanger [ɪnˈdeɪndʒəᵉ] vt mettre en danger; **an ~ed species** une espèce en voie de disparition

endearing [ɪnˈdɪərɪŋ] adj attachant(e)

endeavour, (US) **endeavor** [ɪnˈdɛvəᵉ] n effort m; (attempt) tentative f ▷ vt: **to ~ to do** tenter or s'efforcer de faire

ending [ˈɛndɪŋ] n dénouement m, conclusion f; (Ling) terminaison f

endive [ˈɛndaɪv] n (curly) chicorée f; (smooth, flat) endive f

endless [ˈɛndlɪs] adj sans fin, interminable; (patience, resources) inépuisable, sans limites; (possibilities) illimité(e)

endorse [ɪnˈdɔːs] vt (cheque) endosser; (approve) appuyer, approuver, sanctionner

endorsement [ɪnˈdɔːsmənt] n (approval) appui m, aval m; (signature) endossement m; (Brit: on driving licence) contravention f (portée au permis de conduire)

endurance [ɪnˈdjuərəns] n endurance f

endure [ɪnˈdjuəᵉ] vt (bear) supporter, endurer ▷ vi (last) durer

enemy [ˈɛnəmɪ] adj, n ennemi(e); **to make an ~ of sb** se faire un(e) ennemi(e) de qn, se mettre qn à dos

energetic [ɛnəˈdʒɛtɪk] adj énergique; (activity) très actif(-ive), qui fait se

dépenser (physiquement)

energy [ˈɛnədʒɪ] n énergie f; **Department of E~** ministère m de l'Énergie

enforce [ɪnˈfɔːs] vt (law) appliquer, faire respecter

engage [ɪnˈgeɪdʒ] vt engager; (Mil) engager le combat avec; (lawyer) prendre ▷ vi (Tech) s'enclencher, s'engrener; **to ~ in** se lancer dans; **to ~ sb in conversation** engager la conversation avec qn

engaged [ɪnˈgeɪdʒd] adj (Brit: busy, in use) occupé(e); (betrothed) fiancé(e); **to get ~** se fiancer; **the line's ~** la ligne est occupée; **he is ~ in research/a survey** il fait de la recherche/une enquête

engaged tone n (Brit Tel) tonalité f occupé inv

engagement [ɪnˈgeɪdʒmənt] n (undertaking) obligation f, engagement m; (appointment) rendez-vous m inv; (to marry) fiançailles fpl; (Mil) combat m; **I have a previous ~** j'ai déjà un rendez-vous, je suis déjà pris(e)

engagement ring n bague f de fiançailles

engaging [ɪnˈgeɪdʒɪŋ] adj engageant(e), attirant(e)

engine [ˈɛndʒɪn] n (Aut) moteur m; (Rail) locomotive f

engine driver n (Brit: of train) mécanicien m

engineer [ɛndʒɪˈnɪəᵉ] n ingénieur m; (Brit: repairer) dépanneur m; (Navy, US Rail) mécanicien m; **civil/mechanical ~** ingénieur des Travaux Publics or des Ponts et Chaussées/mécanicien

engineering [ɛndʒɪˈnɪərɪŋ] n engineering m, ingénierie f; (of bridges, ships) génie m; (of machine) mécanique f ▷ cpd: **~ works** or **factory** atelier m de construction mécanique

England [ˈɪŋglənd] n Angleterre f

English [ˈɪŋglɪʃ] adj anglais(e) ▷ n (Ling) anglais m; **the ~** npl les Anglais; **an ~ speaker** un anglophone

English Channel n: **the ~** la Manche

Englishman [ˈɪŋglɪʃmən] irreg n Anglais m

Englishwoman [ˈɪŋglɪʃwumən] irreg n Anglaise f

engrave [ɪnˈgreɪv] vt graver

engraving [ɪnˈgreɪvɪŋ] n gravure f

engrossed [ɪnˈgrəust] adj: **~ in** absorbé(e) par, plongé(e) dans

engulf [ɪnˈgʌlf] vt engloutir

enhance [ɪnˈhɑːns] vt (position) rehausser, mettre en valeur; (position) améliorer; (reputation) accroître

enjoy [ɪnˈdʒɔɪ] vt aimer, prendre plaisir à; (have benefit of: health, fortune) jouir de; (: success) connaître; **to ~ o.s.** s'amuser

enjoyable [ɪnˈdʒɔɪəbl] adj agréable

enjoyment [ɪnˈdʒɔɪmənt] n plaisir m

enlarge [ɪnˈlɑːdʒ] vt accroître; (Phot) agrandir ▷ vi: **to ~ on** (subject) s'étendre sur

enlargement [ɪnˈlɑːdʒmənt] n (Phot) agrandissement m

enlighten [ɪnˈlaɪtn] vt éclairer

enlightened [ɪn'laɪtnd] *adj* éclairé(e)
enlightenment [ɪn'laɪtnmənt] *n*
édification *f*; éclaircissements *mpl*; (*Hist*):
the E~ = le Siècle des lumières
enlist [ɪn'lɪst] *vt* recruter; (*support*) s'assurer
▷ *vi* s'engager; **~ed man** (*US Mil*) simple
soldat *m*
enmity ['ɛnmɪtɪ] *n* inimitié *f*
enormous [ɪ'nɔːməs] *adj* énorme
enough [ɪ'nʌf] *adj*: **~ time/books** assez *or*
suffisamment de temps/livres ▷ *adv*: **big ~**
assez *or* suffisamment grand ▷ *pron*: **have**
you got ~? (en) avez-vous assez?; **will five be**
~? est-ce que cinq suffiront?, est-ce qu'il y en
aura assez avec cinq?; **~ to eat** assez à
manger; **that's ~!** ça suffit!, assez!; **that's ~,**
thanks cela suffit *or* c'est assez, merci; **I've**
had ~! je n'en peux plus!; **I've had ~ of him**
j'en ai assez de lui; **he has not worked ~** il
n'a pas assez *or* suffisamment travaillé, il n'a
pas travaillé assez *or* suffisamment; **~!** assez!,
ça suffit!; **it's hot ~ (as it is)!** il fait assez
chaud comme ça!; **he was kind ~ to lend me**
the money il a eu la gentillesse de me prêter
l'argent; **... which, funnily** *or* **oddly ~** ... qui,
chose curieuse, ...
enquire [ɪn'kwaɪə'] *vt*, *vi* = **inquire**
enquiry [ɪn'kwaɪərɪ] *n* = **inquiry**
enrage [ɪn'reɪdʒ] *vt* mettre en fureur *or* en
rage, rendre furieux(-euse)
enrich [ɪn'rɪtʃ] *vt* enrichir
enrol, (*US*) **enroll** [ɪn'rəul] *vt* inscrire ▷ *vi*
s'inscrire
enrolment, (*US*) **enrollment** [ɪn'rəulmənt]
n inscription *f*
en route [ɔn'ruːt] *adv* en route, en chemin;
~ for *or* **to** en route vers, à destination de
en suite ['ɔnswiːt] *adj*: **with ~ bathroom**
avec salle de bains en attenante
ensure [ɪn'ʃuə'] *vt* assurer, garantir; **to ~ that**
s'assurer que
entail [ɪn'teɪl] *vt* entraîner, nécessiter
entangle [ɪn'tæŋgl] *vt* emmêler,
embrouiller; **to become ~d in sth** (*fig*) se
laisser entraîner *or* empêtrer dans qch
enter ['ɛntə'] *vt* (*room*) entrer dans,
pénétrer dans; (*club, army*) entrer à;
(*profession*) embrasser; (*competition*) s'inscrire
à *or* pour; (*sb for a competition*) (faire) inscrire;
(*write down*) inscrire, noter; (*Comput*) entrer,
introduire ▷ *vi* entrer; **enter for** *vt fus*
s'inscrire à, se présenter pour *or* à; **enter**
into *vt fus* (*explanation*) se lancer dans;
(*negotiations*) entamer; (*debate*) prendre part à;
(*agreement*) conclure; **enter on** *vt fus*
commencer; **enter up** *vt* inscrire; **enter**
upon *vt fus* = **enter on**
enterprise ['ɛntəpraɪz] *n* (*company,*
undertaking) entreprise *f*; (*initiative*) (esprit *m*
d')initiative *f*; **free ~** libre entreprise;
private ~ entreprise privée
enterprising ['ɛntəpraɪzɪŋ] *adj*

entreprenant(e), dynamique; (*scheme*)
audacieux(-euse)
entertain [ɛntə'teɪn] *vt* amuser, distraire;
(*invite*) recevoir (à dîner); (*idea, plan*) envisager
entertainer [ɛntə'teɪnə'] *n* artiste *m/f* de
variétés
entertaining [ɛntə'teɪnɪŋ] *adj* amusant(e),
distrayant(e) ▷ *n*: **to do a lot of ~** beaucoup
recevoir
entertainment [ɛntə'teɪnmənt] *n*
(*amusement*) distraction *f*, divertissement *m*,
amusement *m*; (*show*) spectacle *m*
enthralled [ɪn'θrɔːld] *adj* captivé(e)
enthusiasm [ɪn'θuːzɪæzəm] *n*
enthousiasme *m*
enthusiast [ɪn'θuːzɪæst] *n* enthousiaste *m/f*;
a jazz etc ~ un fervent *or* passionné du jazz *etc*
enthusiastic [ɪnθuːzɪ'æstɪk] *adj*
enthousiaste; **to be ~ about** être
enthousiasmé(e) par
entire [ɪn'taɪə'] *adj* (tout) entier(-ère)
entirely [ɪn'taɪəlɪ] *adv* entièrement,
complètement
entirety [ɪn'taɪərətɪ] *n*: **in its ~** dans sa
totalité
entitle [ɪn'taɪtl] *vt* (*allow*): **to ~ sb to do**
donner (le) droit à qn de faire; **to ~ sb to sth**
donner droit à qch à qn
entitled [ɪn'taɪtld] *adj* (*book*) intitulé(e); **to be**
~ to do avoir le droit de faire
entrance *n* ['ɛntrns] entrée *f* ▷ *vt* [ɪn'trɑːns]
enchanter, ravir; **where's the ~?** où est
l'entrée?; **to gain ~ to** (*university etc*) être
admis à
entrance examination *n* examen *m*
d'entrée *or* d'admission
entrance fee *n* (*to museum etc*) prix *m*
d'entrée; (*to join club etc*) droit *m* d'inscription
entrance ramp *n* (*US Aut*) bretelle *f* d'accès
entrant ['ɛntrnt] *n* (*in race etc*) participant(e),
concurrent(e); (*Brit: in exam*) candidat(e)
entrenched [ɛn'trɛntʃt] *adj* retranché(e)
entrepreneur ['ɔntrəprə'nəː'] *n*
entrepreneur *m*
entrust [ɪn'trʌst] *vt*: **to ~ sth to** confier qch à
entry ['ɛntrɪ] *n* entrée *f*; (*in register, diary*)
inscription *f*; (*in ledger*) écriture *f*; **"no ~"**
"défense d'entrer", "entrée interdite"; (*Aut*)
"sens interdit"; **single/double ~ book-**
keeping comptabilité *f* en partie simple/
double
entry form *n* feuille *f* d'inscription
entry phone *n* (*Brit*) interphone *m* (*à l'entrée*
d'un immeuble)
envelop [ɪn'vɛləp] *vt* envelopper
envelope ['ɛnvələup] *n* enveloppe *f*
envious ['ɛnvɪəs] *adj* envieux(-euse)
environment [ɪn'vaɪərnmənt] *n* (*social,*
moral) milieu *m*; (*natural world*): **the ~**
l'environnement *m*; **Department of the E~**
(*Brit*) ministère de l'Équipement et de l'Aménagement
du territoire

environmental [ɪnvaɪərn'mɛntl] adj (of surroundings) du milieu; (issue, disaster) écologique; **~ studies** (in school etc) écologie f

environmentally [ɪnvaɪərn'mɛntlɪ] adv: **~ sound/friendly** qui ne nuit pas à l'environnement

envisage [ɪn'vɪzɪdʒ] vt (imagine) envisager; (foresee) prévoir

envoy ['ɛnvɔɪ] n envoyé(e); (diplomat) ministre m plénipotentiaire

envy ['ɛnvɪ] n envie f ▷ vt envier; **to ~ sb sth** envier qch à qn

epic ['ɛpɪk] n épopée f ▷ adj épique

epidemic [ɛpɪ'dɛmɪk] n épidémie f

epilepsy ['ɛpɪlɛpsɪ] n épilepsie f

epileptic [ɛpɪ'lɛptɪk] adj, n épileptique m/f

epileptic fit [ɛpɪ'lɛptɪk-] n crise f d'épilepsie

episode ['ɛpɪsəud] n épisode m

epitome [ɪ'pɪtəmɪ] n (fig) quintessence f, type m

epitomize [ɪ'pɪtəmaɪz] vt (fig) illustrer, incarner

equal ['i:kwl] adj égal(e) ▷ n égal(e) ▷ vt égaler; **~ to** (task) à la hauteur de; **~ to doing** de taille à or capable de faire

equality [i:'kwɔlɪtɪ] n égalité f

equalize ['i:kwəlaɪz] vt, vi (Sport) égaliser

equally ['i:kwəlɪ] adv également; (share) en parts égales; (treat) de la même façon; (pay) autant; (just as) tout aussi; **they are ~ clever** ils sont tout aussi intelligents

equanimity [ɛkwə'nɪmɪtɪ] n égalité f d'humeur

equate [ɪ'kweɪt] vt: **to ~ sth with** comparer qch à; assimiler qch à; **to ~ sth to** mettre qch en équation avec; égaler qch à

equation [ɪ'kweɪʃən] n (Math) équation f

equator [ɪ'kweɪtə'] n équateur m

equilibrium [i:kwɪ'lɪbrɪəm] n équilibre m

equip [ɪ'kwɪp] vt équiper; **to ~ sb/sth with** équiper or munir qn/qch de; **he is well ~ped for the job** il a les compétences or les qualités requises pour ce travail

equipment [ɪ'kwɪpmənt] n équipement m; (electrical etc) appareillage m, installation f

equities ['ɛkwɪtɪz] npl (Brit Comm) actions cotées en Bourse

equivalent [ɪ'kwɪvəlnt] adj équivalent(e) ▷ n équivalent m; **to be ~ to** équivaloir à, être équivalent(e) à

ER abbr (Brit: = Elizabeth Regina) la reine Élisabeth; (US: Med: = emergency room) urgences fpl

era ['ɪərə] n ère f, époque f

eradicate [ɪ'rædɪkeɪt] vt éliminer

erase [ɪ'reɪz] vt effacer

eraser [ɪ'reɪzə'] n gomme f

e-reader ['i:ri:də'] n liseuse f

erect [ɪ'rɛkt] adj droit(e) ▷ vt construire; (monument) ériger, élever; (tent etc) dresser

erection [ɪ'rɛkʃən] n (Physiol) érection f; (of building) construction f; (of machinery etc) installation f

ERM n abbr (= Exchange Rate Mechanism) mécanisme m des taux de change

erode [ɪ'rəud] vt éroder; (metal) ronger

erosion [ɪ'rəuʒən] n érosion f

erotic [ɪ'rɔtɪk] adj érotique

errand ['ɛrnd] n course f, commission f; **to run ~s** faire des courses; **~ of mercy** mission f de charité, acte m charitable

erratic [ɪ'rætɪk] adj irrégulier(-ière), inconstant(e)

error ['ɛrə'] n erreur f; **typing/spelling ~** faute f de frappe/d'orthographe; **in ~** par erreur, par méprise; **~s and omissions excepted** sauf erreur ou omission

erupt [ɪ'rʌpt] vi entrer en éruption; (fig) éclater, exploser

eruption [ɪ'rʌpʃən] n éruption f; (of anger, violence) explosion f

escalate ['ɛskəleɪt] vi s'intensifier; (costs) monter en flèche

escalator ['ɛskəleɪtə'] n escalier roulant

escapade [ɛskə'peɪd] n fredaine f; équipée f

escape [ɪ'skeɪp] n évasion f, fuite f; (of gas etc) fuite; (Tech) échappement m ▷ vi s'échapper, fuir; (from jail) s'évader; (fig) s'en tirer, en réchapper; (leak) fuir; s'échapper ▷ vt échapper à; **to ~ from** (person) échapper à; (place) s'échapper de; (fig) fuir; **to ~ to** (another place) fuir à, s'enfuir à; **to ~ to safety** se réfugier dans or gagner un endroit sûr; **to ~ notice** passer inaperçu(e); **his name ~s me** son nom m'échappe

escapism [ɪ'skeɪpɪzəm] n évasion f (fig)

escort vt [ɪ'skɔ:t] escorter ▷ n ['ɛskɔ:t] (Mil) escorte f; (to dance etc): **her ~** son compagnon or cavalier; **his ~** sa compagne

Eskimo ['ɛskɪməu] adj esquimau(de), eskimo ▷ n Esquimau(de); (Ling) esquimau m

especially [ɪ'spɛʃlɪ] adv (particularly) particulièrement; (above all) surtout

espionage ['ɛspɪənɑ:ʒ] n espionnage m

Esquire [ɪ'skwaɪə'] n (Brit: abbr **Esq.**): **J. Brown, ~** Monsieur J. Brown

essay ['ɛseɪ] n (Scol) dissertation f; (Literature) essai m; (attempt) tentative f

essence ['ɛsns] n essence f; (Culin) extrait m; **in ~** en substance; **speed is of the ~** l'essentiel, c'est la rapidité

essential [ɪ'sɛnʃl] adj essentiel(le); (basic) fondamental(e); **essentials** npl éléments essentiels; **it is ~ that** il est essentiel or primordial que

essentially [ɪ'sɛnʃlɪ] adv essentiellement

establish [ɪ'stæblɪʃ] vt établir; (business) fonder, créer; (one's power etc) asseoir, affermir

established [ɪ'stæblɪʃt] adj bien établi(e)

establishment [ɪ'stæblɪʃmənt] n établissement m; (founding) création f; (institution) établissement m; **the E~** les pouvoirs établis; l'ordre établi

estate [ɪ'steɪt] n (land) domaine m, propriété f; (Law) biens mpl, succession f; (Brit: also: **housing ~**) lotissement m

estate agent n (Brit) agent immobilier

estate car n (Brit) break m

esteem [ɪ'stiːm] n estime f ⊳ vt estimer; apprécier; **to hold sb in high ~** tenir qn en haute estime

esthetic [ɪs'θɛtɪk] adj (US) = **aesthetic**

estimate n ['ɛstɪmət] estimation f; (Comm) devis m vt ['ɛstɪmeɪt] estimer ⊳ vi (Brit Comm): **to ~ for** estimer, faire une estimation de; (bid for) faire un devis pour; **to give sb an ~ of** faire or donner un devis à qn pour; **at a rough ~** approximativement

estimation [ɛstɪ'meɪʃən] n opinion f; estime f; **in my ~** à mon avis, selon moi

estranged [ɪs'treɪndʒd] adj (couple) séparé(e); (husband, wife) dont on s'est séparé(e)

etc abbr (= et cetera) etc

eternal [ɪ'təːnl] adj éternel(le)

eternity [ɪ'təːnɪtɪ] n éternité f

ethical ['ɛθɪkl] adj moral(e)

ethics ['ɛθɪks] n éthique f ⊳ npl moralité f

Ethiopia [iːθɪ'əʊpɪə] n Éthiopie f

ethnic ['ɛθnɪk] adj ethnique; (clothes, food) folklorique, exotique, propre aux minorités ethniques non-occidentales

ethnic minority n minorité f ethnique

ethos ['iːθɒs] n (système m de) valeurs fpl

e-ticket ['iːtɪkɪt] n billet m électronique

etiquette ['ɛtɪkɛt] n convenances fpl, étiquette f

EU n abbr (= European Union) UE f

euro ['juərəu] n (currency) euro m

Euroland ['juərəulænd] n Euroland m

Europe ['juərəp] n Europe f

European [juərə'piːən] adj européen(ne) ⊳ n Européen(ne)

European Community n Communauté européenne

European Union n Union européenne

Eurostar® ['juərəustɑːʳ] n Eurostar® m

evacuate [ɪ'vækjueɪt] vt évacuer

evade [ɪ'veɪd] vt échapper à; (question etc) éluder; (duties) se dérober à

evaluate [ɪ'væljueɪt] vt évaluer

evaporate [ɪ'væpəreɪt] vi s'évaporer; (fig: hopes, fear) s'envoler; (anger) se dissiper ⊳ vt faire évaporer

evaporated milk [ɪ'væpəreɪtɪd-] n lait condensé (non sucré)

evasion [ɪ'veɪʒən] n dérobade f; (excuse) faux-fuyant m

eve [iːv] n: **on the ~ of** à la veille de

even ['iːvn] adj (level, smooth) régulier(-ière); (equal) égal(e); (number) pair(e) ⊳ adv même; **~ if** même si +indic; **~ though** quand (bien) même + cond, alors même que + cond; **~ more** encore plus; **~ faster** encore plus vite; **~ so** quand même; **not ~** pas même; **~ he was there** même lui était là; **~ on Sundays**

même le dimanche; **to break ~** s'y retrouver, équilibrer ses comptes; **to get ~ with sb** prendre sa revanche sur qn; **even out** vi s'égaliser

evening ['iːvnɪŋ] n soir m; (as duration, event) soirée f; **in the ~** le soir; **this ~** ce soir; **tomorrow/yesterday ~** demain/hier soir

evening class n cours m du soir

evening dress n (man's) tenue f de soirée, smoking m; (woman's) robe f de soirée

event [ɪ'vɛnt] n événement m; (Sport) épreuve f; **in the course of ~s** par la suite; **in the ~ of** en cas de; **in the ~** en réalité, en fait; **at all ~s**, (Brit) **in any ~** en tout cas, de toute manière

eventful [ɪ'vɛntful] adj mouvementé(e)

eventual [ɪ'vɛntʃuəl] adj final(e)

eventuality [ɪvɛntʃu'ælɪtɪ] n possibilité f, éventualité f

eventually [ɪ'vɛntʃuəlɪ] adv finalement

ever ['ɛvəʳ] adv jamais; (at all times) toujours; (in questions): **why ~ not?** mais enfin, pourquoi pas?; **the best ~** le meilleur qu'on ait jamais vu; **have you ~ seen it?** l'as-tu déjà vu?, as-tu eu l'occasion or t'est-il arrivé de le voir?; **did you ~ meet him?** est-ce qu'il vous est arrivé de le rencontrer?; **have you ~ been there?** y êtes-vous déjà allé?; **for ~** pour toujours; **hardly ~** ne ... presque jamais; **~ since** (as adv) depuis; (as conj) depuis que; **~ so pretty** si joli; **thank you ~ so much** merci mille fois

evergreen ['ɛvəgriːn] n arbre m à feuilles persistantes

everlasting [ɛvə'lɑːstɪŋ] adj éternel(le)

 KEYWORD

every ['ɛvrɪ] adj **1** (each) chaque; **every one of them** tous (sans exception); **every shop in town was closed** tous les magasins en ville étaient fermés

2 (all possible) tous/toutes les; **I gave you every assistance** j'ai fait tout mon possible pour vous aider; **I have every confidence in him** j'ai entièrement or pleinement confiance en lui; **we wish you every success** nous vous souhaitons beaucoup de succès

3 (showing recurrence) tous les; **every day** tous les jours, chaque jour; **every other car** une voiture sur deux; **every other/third day** tous les deux/trois jours; **every now and then** de temps en temps

everybody ['ɛvrɪbɒdɪ] pron = **everyone**

everyday ['ɛvrɪdeɪ] adj (expression) courant(e), d'usage courant; (use) courant; (clothes, life) de tous les jours; (occurrence, problem) quotidien(ne)

everyone ['ɛvrɪwʌn] pron tout le monde, tous pl; **~ knows about it** tout le monde le sait; **~ else** tous les autres

everything ['ɛvrɪθɪŋ] *pron* tout; **~ is ready** tout est prêt; **he did ~ possible** il a fait tout son possible

everywhere ['ɛvrɪwɛəʳ] *adv* partout; **~ you go you meet ...** où qu'on aille on rencontre ...

evict [ɪ'vɪkt] *vt* expulser

eviction [ɪ'vɪkʃən] *n* expulsion *f*

evidence ['ɛvɪdns] *n* (*proof*) preuve(s) *f(pl)*; (*of witness*) témoignage *m*; (*sign*) signe *m*; **to show ~** donner des signes de; **to give ~** témoigner, déposer; **in ~** (*obvious*) en évidence; en vue

evident ['ɛvɪdnt] *adj* évident(e)

evidently ['ɛvɪdntlɪ] *adv* de toute évidence; (*apparently*) apparemment

evil ['iːvl] *adj* mauvais(e) ▷ *n* mal *m*

evoke [ɪ'vəuk] *vt* évoquer; (*admiration*) susciter

evolution [iːvə'luːʃən] *n* évolution *f*

evolve [ɪ'vɔlv] *vt* élaborer ▷ *vi* évoluer, se transformer

ewe [juː] *n* brebis *f*

ex [ɛks] *n* (*inf*): **my ex** mon ex

ex- [ɛks] *prefix* (*former: husband, president etc*) ex-; (*out of*): **the price ~works** le prix départ usine

exact [ɪg'zækt] *adj* exact(e) ▷ *vt*: **to ~ sth (from)** (*signature, confession*) extorquer qch (à); (*apology*) exiger qch (de)

exacting [ɪg'zæktɪŋ] *adj* exigeant(e); (*work*) fatigant(e)

exactly [ɪg'zæktlɪ] *adv* exactement; **~!** parfaitement!, précisément!

exaggerate [ɪg'zædʒəreɪt] *vt, vi* exagérer

exaggeration [ɪgzædʒə'reɪʃən] *n* exagération *f*

exalted [ɪg'zɔːltɪd] *adj* (*rank*) élevé(e); (*person*) haut placé(e); (*elated*) exalté(e)

exam [ɪg'zæm] *n abbr* (*Scol*) = **examination**

examination [ɪgzæmɪ'neɪʃən] *n* (*Scol, Med*) examen *m*; **to take** or **sit an ~** (*Brit*) passer un examen; **the matter is under ~** la question est à l'examen

examine [ɪg'zæmɪn] *vt* (*gen*) examiner; (*Scol, Law: person*) interroger; (*inspect: machine, premises*) inspecter; (*passport*) contrôler; (*luggage*) fouiller

examiner [ɪg'zæmɪnəʳ] *n* examinateur(-trice)

example [ɪg'zɑːmpl] *n* exemple *m*; **for ~** par exemple; **to set a good/bad ~** donner le bon/mauvais exemple

exasperate [ɪg'zɑːspəreɪt] *vt* exaspérer, agacer

exasperated [ɪg'zɑːspəreɪtɪd] *adj* exaspéré(e)

exasperation [ɪgzɑːspə'reɪʃən] *n* exaspération *f*, irritation *f*

excavate ['ɛkskəveɪt] *vt* (*site*) fouiller, excaver; (*object*) mettre au jour

excavation [ɛkskə'veɪʃən] *n* excavation *f*

exceed [ɪk'siːd] *vt* dépasser; (*one's powers*) outrepasser

exceedingly [ɪk'siːdɪŋlɪ] *adv* extrêmement

excel [ɪk'sɛl] *vi* exceller ▷ *vt* surpasser; **to ~ o.s.** se surpasser

excellence ['ɛksələns] *n* excellence *f*

excellent ['ɛksələnt] *adj* excellent(e)

except [ɪk'sɛpt] *prep* (*also:* **~ for, ~ing**) sauf, excepté, à l'exception de ▷ *vt* excepter; **~ if/ when** sauf si/quand; **~ that** excepté que, si ce n'est que

exception [ɪk'sɛpʃən] *n* exception *f*; **to take ~ to** s'offusquer de; **with the ~ of** à l'exception de

exceptional [ɪk'sɛpʃənl] *adj* exceptionnel(le)

exceptionally [ɪk'sɛpʃənəlɪ] *adv* exceptionnellement

excerpt ['ɛksəːpt] *n* extrait *m*

excess [ɪk'sɛs] *n* excès *m*; **in ~ of** plus de

excess baggage *n* excédent *m* de bagages

excess fare *n* supplément *m*

excessive [ɪk'sɛsɪv] *adj* excessif(-ive)

exchange [ɪks'tʃeɪndʒ] *n* échange *m*; (*also:* **telephone ~**) central *m* ▷ *vt*: **to ~ (for)** échanger (contre); **could I ~ this, please?** est-ce que je peux échanger ceci, s'il vous plaît?; **in ~ for** en échange de; **foreign ~** (*Comm*) change *m*

exchange rate *n* taux *m* de change

excise *n* ['ɛksaɪz] taxe *f* ▷ *vt* [ɛk'saɪz] exciser

excite [ɪk'saɪt] *vt* exciter

excited [ɪk'saɪtəd] *adj* (tout/toute) excité(e); **to get ~** s'exciter

excitement [ɪk'saɪtmənt] *n* excitation *f*

exciting [ɪk'saɪtɪŋ] *adj* passionnant(e)

exclaim [ɪk'skleɪm] *vi* s'exclamer

exclamation [ɛksklə'meɪʃən] *n* exclamation *f*

exclamation mark, (US) **exclamation point** *n* point *m* d'exclamation

exclude [ɪk'skluːd] *vt* exclure

excluding [ɪk'skluːdɪŋ] *prep*: **~ VAT** la TVA non comprise

exclusion [ɪk'skluːʒən] *n* exclusion *f*; **to the ~ of** à l'exclusion de

exclusion zone *n* zone interdite

exclusive [ɪk'skluːsɪv] *adj* exclusif(-ive); (*club, district*) sélect(e); (*item of news*) en exclusivité ▷ *adv* (*Comm*) exclusivement, non inclus; **~ of VAT** TVA non comprise; **~ of postage** (les) frais de poste non compris; **from 1st to 15th March ~** du 1er au 15 mars exclusivement *or* exclu; **~ rights** (*Comm*) exclusivité *f*

exclusively [ɪk'skluːsɪvlɪ] *adv* exclusivement

excruciating [ɪk'skruːʃɪeɪtɪŋ] *adj* (*pain*) atroce, déchirant(e); (*embarrassing*) pénible

excursion [ɪk'skəːʃən] *n* excursion *f*

excuse *n* [ɪk'skjuːs] excuse *f* ▷ *vt* [ɪk'skjuːz] (*forgive*) excuser; (*justify*) excuser, justifier; **to ~ sb from** (*activity*) dispenser qn de; **~ me!** excusez-moi!, pardon!; **now if you will ~ me, ...** maintenant, si vous (le) permettez ...; **to make ~s for sb** trouver des excuses à qn; **to ~ o.s. for sth/for doing sth** s'excuser de/d'avoir fait qch

ex-directory [ˈeksdɪˈrektərɪ] *adj* (Brit) sur la liste rouge

execute [ˈeksɪkjuːt] *vt* exécuter

execution [eksɪˈkjuːʃən] *n* exécution *f*

executive [ɪgˈzekjutɪv] *n* (person) cadre *m*; (managing group) bureau *m*; (Pol) exécutif *m* ▷ *adj* exécutif(-ive); (position, job) de cadre; (secretary) de direction; (offices) de la direction; (car, plane) de fonction

exemplify [ɪgˈzemplɪfaɪ] *vt* illustrer

exempt [ɪgˈzempt] *adj*: ~ **from** exempté(e) *or* dispensé(e) de ▷ *vt*: **to ~ sb from** exempter *or* dispenser qn de

exercise [ˈeksəsaɪz] *n* exercice *m* ▷ *vt* exercer; (patience etc) faire preuve de; (dog) promener ▷ *vi* (also: **to take ~**) prendre de l'exercice

exercise book *n* cahier *m*

exert [ɪgˈzəːt] *vt* exercer, employer; (strength, force) employer; **to ~ o.s.** se dépenser

exertion [ɪgˈzəːʃən] *n* effort *m*

exhale [eksˈheɪl] *vt* (breathe out) expirer; exhaler ▷ *vi* expirer

exhaust [ɪgˈzɔːst] *n* (also: ~ **fumes**) gaz *mpl* d'échappement; (also: ~ **pipe**) tuyau *m* d'échappement ▷ *vt* épuiser; **to ~ o.s.** s'épuiser

exhausted [ɪgˈzɔːstɪd] *adj* épuisé(e)

exhaustion [ɪgˈzɔːstʃən] *n* épuisement *m*; **nervous ~** fatigue nerveuse

exhaustive [ɪgˈzɔːstɪv] *adj* très complet(-ète)

exhibit [ɪgˈzɪbɪt] *n* (Art) objet exposé, pièce exposée; (Law) pièce à conviction ▷ *vt* (Art) exposer; (courage, skill) faire preuve de

exhibition [eksɪˈbɪʃən] *n* exposition *f*; ~ **of temper** manifestation *f* de colère

exhilarating [ɪgˈzɪləreɪtɪŋ] *adj* grisant(e), stimulant(e)

ex-husband [ˈeksˈhazbənd] *n* ex-mari *m*

exile [ˈeksaɪl] *n* exil *m*; (person) exilé(e) ▷ *vt* exiler; **in ~** en exil

exist [ɪgˈzɪst] *vi* exister

existence [ɪgˈzɪstəns] *n* existence *f*; **to be in ~** exister

existing [ɪgˈzɪstɪŋ] *adj* (laws) existant(e); (system, regime) actuel(le)

exit [ˈeksɪt] *n* sortie *f* ▷ *vi* (Comput, Theat) sortir; **where's the ~?** où est la sortie?

exit poll *n* sondage *m* (fait à la sortie de l'isoloir)

exit ramp *n* (US Aut) bretelle *f* d'accès

exodus [ˈeksədəs] *n* exode *m*

exonerate [ɪgˈzɔnəreɪt] *vt*: **to ~ from** disculper de

exotic [ɪgˈzɔtɪk] *adj* exotique

expand [ɪkˈspænd] *vt* (area) agrandir; (quantity) accroître; (influence etc) étendre ▷ *vi* (population, production) s'accroître; (trade, etc) se développer; (gas, metal) se dilater; **to ~ on** (notes, story etc) développer

expanse [ɪkˈspæns] *n* étendue *f*

expansion [ɪkˈspænʃən] *n* (territorial, economic) expansion *f*; (of trade, influence etc) développement *m*; (of production)

accroissement *m*; (of population) croissance *f*; (of gas, metal) expansion, dilatation *f*

expect [ɪkˈspekt] *vt* (anticipate) s'attendre à, s'attendre à ce que + *sub*; (count on) compter sur, escompter; (hope for) espérer; (require) demander, exiger; (suppose) supposer; (await: also baby) attendre ▷ *vi*: **to be ~ing** (pregnant woman) être enceinte; **to ~ sb to do** (anticipate) s'attendre à ce que qn fasse; (demand) attendre de qn qu'il fasse; **to ~ to do sth** penser *or* compter faire qch, s'attendre à faire qch; **as ~ed** comme prévu; **I ~ so** je crois que oui, je crois bien

expectancy [ɪksˈpektənsɪ] *n* attente *f*; **life ~** espérance *f* de vie

expectant [ɪksˈpektənt] *adj* qui attend (quelque chose); ~ **mother** future maman

expectation [ekspekˈteɪʃən] *n* (hope) attente *f*, espérance(s) *f(pl)*; (belief) attente; **in ~ of** dans l'attente de, en prévision de; **against** *or* **contrary to all ~(s)** contre toute attente, contrairement à ce qu'on attendait; **to come** *or* **live up to sb's ~s** répondre à l'attente *or* aux espérances de qn

expedient [ɪksˈpiːdɪənt] *adj* indiqué(e), opportun(e), commode ▷ *n* expédient *m*

expedition [ekspəˈdɪʃən] *n* expédition *f*

expel [ɪksˈpel] *vt* chasser, expulser; (Scol) renvoyer, exclure

expend [ɪksˈpend] *vt* consacrer; (use up) dépenser

expenditure [ɪksˈpendɪtʃəʳ] *n* (act of spending) dépense *f*; (money spent) dépenses *fpl*

expense [ɪksˈpens] *n* (high cost) coût *m*; (spending) dépense *f*, frais *mpl*; **expenses** *npl* frais *mpl*; dépenses; **to go to the ~ of** faire la dépense de; **at great/little ~** à grands/peu de frais; **at the ~ of** aux frais de; (fig) aux dépens de

expense account *n* (note *f* de) frais *mpl*

expensive [ɪksˈpensɪv] *adj* cher/chère, coûteux(-euse); **to be ~** coûter cher; **it's too ~** ça coûte trop cher; ~ **tastes** goûts *mpl* de luxe

experience [ɪksˈspɪərɪəns] *n* expérience *f* ▷ *vt* connaître; (feeling) éprouver; **to know by ~** savoir par expérience

experienced [ɪksˈspɪərɪənst] *adj* expérimenté(e)

experiment [ɪksˈsperɪmənt] *n* expérience *f* ▷ *vi* faire une expérience; **to ~ with** expérimenter; **to perform** *or* **carry out an ~** faire une expérience; **as an ~** à titre d'expérience

experimental [ɪkssperɪˈmentl] *adj* expérimental(e)

expert [ˈekspəːt] *adj* expert(e) ▷ *n* expert *m*; ~ **in** *or* **at doing sth** spécialiste de qch; **an ~ on sth** un spécialiste de qch; ~ **witness** (Law) expert *m*

expertise [ekspəːˈtiːz] *n* (grande) compétence *f*

expire [ɪksˈspaɪəʳ] *vi* expirer

expiry [ɪkˈspaɪərɪ] n expiration f
expiry date n date f d'expiration; (on label) à utiliser avant ...
explain [ɪkˈspleɪn] vt expliquer; **explain away** vt justifier, excuser
explanation [ɛkspləˈneɪʃən] n explication f; **to find an ~ for sth** trouver une explication à qch
explanatory [ɪkˈsplænətrɪ] adj explicatif(-ive)
explicit [ɪkˈsplɪsɪt] adj explicite; (definite) formel(le)
explode [ɪkˈspləʊd] vi exploser ▷ vt faire exploser; (fig: theory) démolir; **to ~ a myth** détruire un mythe
exploit n [ˈɛksplɔɪt] exploit m ▷ vt [ɪkˈsplɔɪt] exploiter
exploitation [ɛksplɔɪˈteɪʃən] n exploitation f
exploratory [ɪkˈsplɔrətrɪ] adj (fig: talks) préliminaire; **~ operation** (Med) intervention f (à visée) exploratrice
explore [ɪkˈsplɔːʳ] vt explorer; (possibilities) étudier, examiner
explorer [ɪkˈsplɔːrəʳ] n explorateur(-trice)
explosion [ɪkˈspləʊʒən] n explosion f
explosive [ɪkˈspləʊsɪv] adj explosif(-ive) ▷ n explosif m
exponent [ɪkˈspəʊnənt] n (of school of thought etc) interprète m, représentant m; (Math) exposant m
export vt [ɛkˈspɔːt] exporter ▷ n [ˈɛks   pɔːt] exportation f ▷ cpd [ˈɛksp ɔːt] d'exportation
exporter [ɛkˈspɔːtəʳ] n exportateur m
expose [ɪkˈspəʊz] vt exposer; (unmask) démasquer, dévoiler; **to ~ o.s.** (Law) commettre un outrage à la pudeur
exposed [ɪkˈspəʊzd] adj (land, house) exposé(e); (Elec: wire) à nu; (pipe, beam) apparent(e)
exposure [ɪkˈspəʊʒəʳ] n exposition f; (publicity) couverture f; (Phot: speed) (temps m de) pose f; (: shot) pose; **suffering from ~** (Med) souffrant des effets du froid et de l'épuisement; **to die of ~** (Med) mourir de froid
exposure meter n posemètre m
express [ɪkˈsprɛs] adj (definite) formel(le), exprès(-esse); (Brit: letter etc) exprès inv ▷ n (train) rapide m ▷ adv (send) exprès ▷ vt exprimer; **to ~ o.s.** s'exprimer
expression [ɪkˈsprɛʃən] n expression f
expressly [ɪkˈsprɛslɪ] adv expressément, formellement
expressway [ɪkˈsprɛsweɪ] n (US) voie f express (à plusieurs files)
exquisite [ɛkˈskwɪzɪt] adj exquis(e)
extend [ɪkˈstɛnd] vt (visit, street) prolonger; (deadline) reporter, remettre; (building) agrandir; (offer) présenter, offrir; (Comm: credit) accorder; (hand, arm) tendre ▷ vi (land) s'étendre

extension [ɪkˈstɛnʃən] n (of visit, street) prolongation f; (of building) agrandissement m; (building) annexe f; (to wire, table) rallonge f; (telephone: in offices) poste m; (: in private house) téléphone m supplémentaire; **~ 3718** (Tel) poste 3718
extension cable, extension lead n (Elec) rallonge f
extensive [ɪkˈstɛnsɪv] adj étendu(e), vaste; (damage, alterations) considérable; (inquiries) approfondi(e); (use) largement répandu(e)
extensively [ɪkˈstɛnsɪvlɪ] adv (altered, damaged etc) considérablement; **he's travelled ~** il a beaucoup voyagé
extent [ɪkˈstɛnt] n étendue f; (degree: of damage, loss) importance f; **to some ~** dans une certaine mesure; **to a certain ~** dans une certaine mesure, jusqu'à un certain point; **to a large ~** en grande partie; **to the ~ of ...** au point de ...; **to what ~?** dans quelle mesure?, jusqu'à quel point?; **to such an ~ that ...** à tel point que ...
extenuating [ɪkˈstɛnjueɪtɪŋ] adj: **~ circumstances** circonstances atténuantes
exterior [ɛkˈstɪərɪəʳ] adj extérieur(e) ▷ n extérieur m
external [ɛkˈstəːnl] adj externe ▷ n: **the ~s** les apparences fpl; **for ~ use only** (Med) à usage externe
extinct [ɪkˈstɪŋkt] adj (volcano) éteint(e); (species) disparu(e)
extinction [ɪkˈstɪŋkʃən] n extinction f
extinguish [ɪkˈstɪŋgwɪʃ] vt éteindre
extort [ɪkˈstɔːt] vt: **to ~ sth (from)** extorquer qch (à)
extortionate [ɪkˈstɔːʃnɪt] adj exorbitant(e)
extra [ˈɛkstrə] adj supplémentaire, de plus ▷ adv (in addition) en plus ▷ n supplément m; (perk) à-coté m; (Cine, Theat) figurant(e); **wine will cost ~** le vin sera en supplément; **~ large sizes** très grandes tailles
extract vt [ɪkˈstrækt] extraire; (tooth) arracher; (money, promise) soutirer ▷ n [ˈɛkstrækt] extrait m
extracurricular [ˈɛkstrəkəˈrɪkjuləʳ] adj (Scol) parascolaire
extradite [ˈɛkstrədaɪt] vt extrader
extramarital [ˈɛkstrəˈmærɪtl] adj extraconjugal(e)
extramural [ˈɛkstrəˈmjuərl] adj hors-faculté inv
extraordinary [ɪkˈstrɔːdnrɪ] adj extraordinaire; **the ~ thing is that ...** le plus étrange or étonnant c'est que ...
extravagance [ɪkˈstrævəgəns] n (excessive spending) prodigalités fpl; (thing bought) folie f, dépense excessive
extravagant [ɪkˈstrævəgənt] adj extravagant(e); (in spending: person) prodigue, dépensier(-ière); (: tastes) dispendieux(-euse)
extreme [ɪkˈstriːm] adj, n extrême (m); **the ~ left/right** (Pol) l'extrême gauche f/droite f; **~s**

of temperature différences *fpl* extrêmes de
  température
extremely [ɪk'striːmlɪ] *adv* extrêmement
extremist [ɪk'striːmɪst] *adj, n* extrémiste *m/f*
extricate ['ɛkstrɪkeɪt] *vt*: **to ~ sth (from)**
  dégager qch (de)
extrovert ['ɛkstrəvɜːt] *n* extraverti(e)
ex-wife ['ɛkswaɪf] *n* ex-femme *f*
eye [aɪ] *n* œil *m*; (*of needle*) trou *m*, chas *m* ▷ *vt*
  examiner; **as far as the ~ can see** à perte de
  vue; **to keep an ~ on** surveiller; **to have an ~
  for sth** avoir l'œil pour qch; **in the public ~**
  en vue; **with an ~ to doing sth** (*Brit*) en vue
  de faire qch; **there's more to this than
  meets the ~** ce n'est pas aussi simple que
  cela paraît
eyeball ['aɪbɔːl] *n* globe *m* oculaire
eyebrow ['aɪbrau] *n* sourcil *m*
eye drops ['aɪdrɔps] *npl* gouttes *fpl* pour les
  yeux
eyelash ['aɪlæʃ] *n* cil *m*
eyelid ['aɪlɪd] *n* paupière *f*
eyeliner ['aɪlaɪnər] *n* eye-liner *m*
eye-opener ['aɪəupnər] *n* révélation *f*
eye shadow ['aɪʃædəu] *n* ombre *f* à paupières
eyesight ['aɪsaɪt] *n* vue *f*
eyesore ['aɪsɔːr] *n* horreur *f*, chose *f* qui
  dépare *or* enlaidit
eye witness *n* témoin *m* oculaire

f

F¹, f [ɛf] *n* (*letter*) F, f *m*; (*Mus*): **F** fa *m*; **F for
  Frederick**, (*US*) **F for Fox** F comme François
F² *abbr* (= *Fahrenheit*) F
fable ['feɪbl] *n* fable *f*
fabric ['fæbrɪk] *n* tissu *m* ▷ *cpd*: **~ ribbon**
  (*for typewriter*) ruban *m* (en) tissu
fabulous ['fæbjuləs] *adj* fabuleux(-euse);
  (*inf: super*) formidable, sensationnel(le)
face [feɪs] *n* visage *m*, figure *f*; (*expression*)
  air *m*; grimace *f*; (*of clock*) cadran *m*; (*of cliff*)
  paroi *f*; (*of mountain*) face *f*; (*of building*)
  façade *f*; (*side, surface*) face *f* ▷ *vt* faire face à;
  (*facts etc*) accepter; **~ down** (*person*) à plat
  ventre; (*card*) face en dessous; **to lose/save ~**
  perdre/sauver la face; **to pull a ~** faire une
  grimace; **in the ~ of** (*difficulties etc*) face à,
  devant; **on the ~ of it** à première vue; **~ to ~**
  face à face; **face up to** *vt fus* faire face à,
  affronter
face cloth *n* (*Brit*) gant *m* de toilette
face cream *n* crème *f* pour le visage
face lift *n* lifting *m*; (*of façade etc*)
  ravalement *m*, retapage *m*
face pack *n* (*Brit*) masque *m* (de beauté)
face powder *n* poudre *f* (pour le visage)
face value ['feɪs'væljuː] *n* (*of coin*) valeur
  nominale; **to take sth at ~** (*fig*) prendre qch
  pour argent comptant
facial ['feɪʃl] *adj* facial(e) ▷ *n* soin complet du
  visage
facilitate [fə'sɪlɪteɪt] *vt* faciliter
facilities [fə'sɪlɪtɪz] *npl* installations *fpl*,

équipement m; **credit ~** facilités de paiement

facility [fəˈsɪlɪtɪ] n facilité f

facing [ˈfeɪsɪŋ] prep face à, en face de ▷ n (of wall etc) revêtement m; (Sewing) revers m

facsimile [fækˈsɪmɪlɪ] n (exact replica) facsimilé m; (also: **~ machine**) télécopieur m; (transmitted document) télécopie f

fact [fækt] n fait m; **in ~** en fait; **to know for a ~ that ...** savoir pertinemment que ...

faction [ˈfækʃən] n faction f

factor [ˈfæktər] n facteur m; (of sun cream) indice m (de protection); (Comm) factor m, société f d'affacturage; (: agent) dépositaire m/f ▷ vi faire du factoring; **safety ~** facteur de sécurité; **I'd like a ~ 15 suntan lotion** je voudrais une crème solaire d'indice 15

factory [ˈfæktərɪ] n usine f, fabrique f

factual [ˈfæktjuəl] adj basé(e) sur les faits

faculty [ˈfækəltɪ] n faculté f; (US: teaching staff) corps enseignant

fad [fæd] n (personal) manie f; (craze) engouement m

fade [feɪd] vi se décolorer, passer; (light, sound) s'affaiblir, disparaître; (flower) se faner; **fade away** vi (sound) s'affaiblir; **fade in** vt (picture) ouvrir en fondu; (sound) monter progressivement; **fade out** vt (picture) fermer en fondu; (sound) baisser progressivement

fag [fæg] n (Brit inf: cigarette) clope f; (: chore): **what a ~!** quelle corvée!; (US inf!: homosexual) pédé m

Fahrenheit [ˈfɑːrənhaɪt] n Fahrenheit m inv

fail [feɪl] vt (exam) échouer à; (candidate) recaler; (subj: courage, memory) faire défaut à ▷ vi échouer; (supplies) manquer; (eyesight, health, light: also: **be ~ing**) baisser, s'affaiblir; (brakes) lâcher; **to ~ to do sth** (neglect) négliger de or ne pas faire qch; (be unable) ne pas arriver or parvenir à faire qch; **without ~** à coup sûr; sans faute

failing [ˈfeɪlɪŋ] n défaut m ▷ prep faute de; **~ that** à défaut, sinon

failure [ˈfeɪljər] n échec m; (person) raté(e); (mechanical etc) défaillance f; **his ~ to turn up** le fait de n'être pas venu or qu'il ne soit pas venu

faint [feɪnt] adj faible; (recollection) vague; (mark) à peine visible; (smell, breeze, trace) léger(-ère) ▷ n évanouissement m ▷ vi s'évanouir; **to feel ~** défaillir

faintest [ˈfeɪntɪst] adj: **I haven't the ~ idea** je n'en ai pas la moindre idée

faintly [ˈfeɪntlɪ] adv faiblement; (vaguely) vaguement

fair [fɛər] adj équitable, juste; (reasonable) correct(e), honnête; (hair) blond(e); (skin, complexion) pâle, blanc/blanche; (weather) beau/belle; (good enough) assez bon(ne); (sizeable) considérable ▷ adv: **to play ~** jouer franc jeu ▷ n foire f; (Brit: funfair) fête f (foraine); (also: **trade ~**) foire(-exposition)

commerciale; **it's not ~!** ce n'est pas juste!; **a ~ amount of** une quantité considérable de

fairground [ˈfɛəgraund] n champ m de foire

fair-haired [fɛəˈhɛəd] adj (person) aux cheveux clairs, blond(e)

fairly [ˈfɛəlɪ] adv (justly) équitablement; (quite) assez; **I'm ~ sure** j'en suis quasiment or presque sûr

fairness [ˈfɛənɪs] n (of trial etc) justice f, équité f; (of person) sens m de la justice; **in all ~** en toute justice

fair trade n commerce m équitable

fairway [ˈfɛəweɪ] n (Golf) fairway m

fairy [ˈfɛərɪ] n fée f

fairy tale n conte m de fées

faith [feɪθ] n foi f; (trust) confiance f; (sect) culte m, religion f; **to have ~ in sb/sth** avoir confiance en qn/qch

faithful [ˈfeɪθful] adj fidèle

faithfully [ˈfeɪθfəlɪ] adv fidèlement; **yours ~** (Brit: in letters) veuillez agréer l'expression de mes salutations les plus distinguées

fake [feɪk] n (painting etc) faux m; (photo) trucage m; (person) imposteur m ▷ adj faux/fausse ▷ vt (emotions) simuler; (painting) faire un faux de; (photo) truquer; (story) fabriquer; **his illness is a ~** sa maladie est une comédie or de la simulation

falcon [ˈfɔːlkən] n faucon m

fall [fɔːl] n chute f; (decrease) baisse f; (US: autumn) automne m ▷ vi (pt fell, pp fallen) [fɛl, ˈfɔːlən] tomber; (price, temperature, dollar) baisser; **falls** npl (waterfall) chute f d'eau, cascade f; **to ~ flat** vi (on one's face) tomber de tout son long, s'étaler; (joke) tomber à plat; (plan) échouer; **to ~ short of** (sb's expectations) ne pas répondre à; **a ~ of snow** (Brit) une chute de neige; **fall apart** vi (object) tomber en morceaux; (inf: emotionally) craquer; **fall back** vi reculer, se retirer; **fall back on** vt fus se rabattre sur; **to have something to ~ back on** (money etc) avoir quelque chose en réserve; (job etc) avoir une solution de rechange; **fall behind** vi prendre du retard; **fall down** vi (person) tomber; (building) s'effondrer, s'écrouler; **fall for** vt fus (trick) se laisser prendre à; (person) tomber amoureux(-euse) de; **fall in** vi s'effondrer; (Mil) se mettre en rangs; **fall in with** vt fus (sb's plans etc) accepter; **fall off** vi tomber; (diminish) baisser, diminuer; **fall out** vi (friends etc) se brouiller; (hair, teeth) tomber; **fall over** vi tomber (par terre); **fall through** vi (plan, project) tomber à l'eau

fallacy [ˈfæləsɪ] n erreur f, illusion f

fallen [ˈfɔːlən] pp of **fall**

fallout [ˈfɔːlaut] n retombées (radioactives)

fallow [ˈfæləu] adj en jachère; en friche

false [fɔːls] adj faux/fausse; **under ~ pretences** sous un faux prétexte

false alarm n fausse alerte

false teeth npl (Brit) fausses dents, dentier m
falter ['fɔːltər] vi chanceler, vaciller
fame [feɪm] n renommée f, renom m
familiar [fəˈmɪlɪər] adj familier(-ière); **to be ~ with sth** connaître qch; **to make o.s. ~ with sth** se familiariser avec qch; **to be on ~ terms with sb** bien connaître qn
familiarize [fəˈmɪlɪəraɪz] vt familiariser; **to ~ o.s. with** se familiariser avec
family ['fæmɪlɪ] n famille f
family doctor n médecin m de famille
family planning n planning familial
famine ['fæmɪn] n famine f
famished ['fæmɪʃt] adj affamé(e); **I'm ~!** (inf) je meurs de faim!
famous ['feɪməs] adj célèbre
famously ['feɪməslɪ] adv (get on) fameusement, à merveille
fan [fæn] n (folding) éventail m; (Elec) ventilateur m; (person) fan m, admirateur(-trice); (Sport) supporter m/f ▷ vt éventer; (fire, quarrel) attiser; **fan out** vi se déployer (en éventail)
fanatic [fəˈnætɪk] n fanatique m/f
fan belt n courroie f de ventilateur
fan club n fan-club m
fancy ['fænsɪ] n (whim) fantaisie f, envie f; (imagination) imagination f ▷ adj (luxury) de luxe; (elaborate: jewellery, packaging) fantaisie inv; (showy) tape-à-l'œil inv; (pretentious: words) recherché(e) ▷ vt (feel like, want) avoir envie de; (imagine) imaginer; **to take a ~ to** se prendre d'affection pour; s'enticher de; **it took** or **caught my ~** ça m'a plu; **when the ~ takes him** quand ça lui prend; **to ~ that ... se figurer** or **s'imaginer que ...; he fancies her** elle lui plaît
fancy dress n déguisement m, travesti m
fancy-dress ball [fænsɪˈdres-] n bal masqué or costumé
fang [fæŋ] n croc m; (of snake) crochet m
fan heater n (Brit) radiateur soufflant
fantasize ['fæntəsaɪz] vi fantasmer
fantastic [fænˈtæstɪk] adj fantastique
fantasy ['fæntəsɪ] n imagination f, fantaisie f; (unreality) fantasme m
fanzine ['fænziːn] n fanzine m
FAQ n abbr (= frequently asked question) FAQ f inv, faq f inv ▷ abbr (= free alongside quay) FLQ
far [fɑːr] adj (distant) lointain(e), éloigné(e) ▷ adv loin; **the ~ side/end** l'autre côté/bout; **the ~ left/right** (Pol) l'extrême gauche f/ droite f; **is it ~ to London?** est-ce qu'on est loin de Londres?; **it's not ~ (from here)** ce n'est pas loin (d'ici); **~ away, ~ off** au loin, dans le lointain; **~ better** beaucoup mieux; **~ from** loin de; **by ~** de loin, de beaucoup; **as ~ back as the 13th century** dès le 13e siècle; **go as ~ as the bridge** allez jusqu'au pont; **as ~ as I know** pour autant que je sache; **how ~ is it to ...?** combien y a-t-il jusqu'à ...?; **as ~ as**

possible dans la mesure du possible; **how ~ have you got with your work?** où en êtes-vous dans votre travail?
faraway ['fɑːrəweɪ] adj lointain(e); (look) absent(e)
farce [fɑːs] n farce f
fare [feər] n (on trains, buses) prix m du billet; (in taxi) prix de la course; (passenger in taxi) client m; (food) table f, chère f ▷ vi se débrouiller; **half ~** demi-tarif; **full ~** plein tarif
Far East n: **the ~** l'Extrême-Orient m
farewell [feəˈwɛl] excl, n adieu m ▷ cpd (party etc) d'adieux
farm [fɑːm] n ferme f ▷ vt cultiver; **farm out** vt (work etc) distribuer
farmer ['fɑːmər] n fermier(-ière), cultivateur(-trice)
farmhand ['fɑːmhænd] n ouvrier(-ière) agricole
farmhouse ['fɑːmhaus] n (maison f de) ferme f
farming ['fɑːmɪŋ] n agriculture f; (of animals) élevage m; **intensive ~** culture intensive; **sheep ~** élevage du mouton
farmland ['fɑːmlænd] n terres cultivées or arables
farm worker n = farmhand
farmyard ['fɑːmjɑːd] n cour f de ferme
far-reaching [fɑːˈriːtʃɪŋ] adj d'une grande portée
fart [fɑːt] (inf!) n pet m ▷ vi péter
farther ['fɑːðər] adv plus loin ▷ adj plus éloigné(e), plus lointain(e)
farthest ['fɑːðɪst] superlative of **far**
fascinate ['fæsɪneɪt] vt fasciner, captiver
fascinating ['fæsɪneɪtɪŋ] adj fascinant(e)
fascination [fæsɪˈneɪʃən] n fascination f
fascism ['fæʃɪzəm] n fascisme m
fascist ['fæʃɪst] adj, n fasciste m/f
fashion ['fæʃən] n mode f; (manner) façon f, manière f ▷ vt façonner; **in ~** à la mode; **out of ~** démodé(e); **in the Greek ~** à la grecque; **after a ~** (finish, manage etc) tant bien que mal
fashionable ['fæʃnəbl] adj à la mode
fashion show n défilé m de mannequins or de mode
fast [fɑːst] adj rapide; (clock): **to be ~** avancer; (dye, colour) grand or bon teint inv ▷ adv vite, rapidement; (stuck, held) solidement ▷ n jeûne m ▷ vi jeûner; **my watch is 5 minutes ~** ma montre avance de 5 minutes; **~ asleep** profondément endormi; **as ~ as I can** aussi vite que je peux; **to make a boat ~** (Brit) amarrer un bateau
fasten ['fɑːsn] vt attacher, fixer; (coat) attacher, fermer ▷ vi se fermer, s'attacher; **fasten on, fasten upon** vt fus (idea) se cramponner à
fastener ['fɑːsnər], **fastening** ['fɑːsnɪŋ] n fermeture f, attache f; (Brit: zip fastener) fermeture éclair® inv or à glissière

fast food n fast food m, restauration f rapide

fastidious [fæsˈtɪdɪəs] adj exigeant(e), difficile

fat [fæt] adj gros(se) ▷ n graisse f; (on meat) gras m; (for cooking) matière grasse; **to live off the ~ of the land** vivre grassement

fatal [ˈfeɪtl] adj (mistake) fatal(e); (injury) mortel(le)

fatality [fəˈtælɪtɪ] n (road death etc) victime f, décès m

fatally [ˈfeɪtəlɪ] adv fatalement; (injured) mortellement

fate [feɪt] n destin m; (of person) sort m; **to meet one's ~** trouver la mort

fateful [ˈfeɪtful] adj fatidique

father [ˈfɑːðəʳ] n père m

Father Christmas n le Père Noël

father-in-law [ˈfɑːðərənlɔː] n beau-père m

fatherly [ˈfɑːðəlɪ] adj paternel(le)

fathom [ˈfæðəm] n brasse f (= 1828 mm) ▷ vt (mystery) sonder, pénétrer

fatigue [fəˈtiːg] n fatigue f; (Mil) corvée f; **metal ~** fatigue du métal

fatten [ˈfætn] vt, vi engraisser

fattening [ˈfætnɪŋ] adj (food) qui fait grossir; **chocolate is ~** le chocolat fait grossir

fatty [ˈfætɪ] adj (food) gras(se) ▷ n (inf) gros/grosse

fatuous [ˈfætjuəs] adj stupide

faucet [ˈfɔːsɪt] n (US) robinet m

fault [fɔːlt] n faute f; (defect) défaut m; (Geo) faille f ▷ vt trouver des défauts à, prendre en défaut; **it's my ~** c'est de ma faute; **to find ~ with** trouver à redire or à critiquer à; **at ~** fautif(-ive), coupable; **to a ~** à l'excès

faulty [ˈfɔːltɪ] adj défectueux(-euse)

fauna [ˈfɔːnə] n faune f

favour, (US) **favor** [ˈfeɪvəʳ] n faveur f; (help) service m ▷ vt (proposition) être en faveur de; (pupil etc) favoriser; (team, horse) donner gagnant; **to do sb a ~** rendre un service à qn; **in ~ of** en faveur de; **to be in ~ of sth/of doing sth** être partisan de qch/de faire qch; **to find ~ with sb** trouver grâce aux yeux de qn

favourable, (US) **favorable** [ˈfeɪvrəbl] adj favorable; (price) avantageux(-euse)

favourite, (US) **favorite** [ˈfeɪvrɪt] adj, n favori(te)

fawn [fɔːn] n (deer) faon m ▷ adj (also: **~-coloured**) fauve ▷ vi: **to ~ (up)on** flatter servilement

fax [fæks] n (document) télécopie f; (machine) télécopieur m ▷ vt envoyer par télécopie

FBI n abbr (US: = Federal Bureau of Investigation) FBI m

fear [fɪəʳ] n crainte f, peur f ▷ vt craindre ▷ vi: **to ~ for** craindre pour; **to ~ that** craindre que; **~ of heights** vertige m; **for ~ of** de peur que + sub or de + infinitive

fearful [ˈfɪəful] adj craintif(-ive); (sight, noise) affreux(-euse), épouvantable; **to be ~ of** avoir peur de, craindre

fearless [ˈfɪəlɪs] adj intrépide, sans peur

feasible [ˈfiːzəbl] adj faisable, réalisable

feast [fiːst] n festin m, banquet m; (Rel: also: **~ day**) fête f ▷ vi festoyer; **to ~ on** se régaler de

feat [fiːt] n exploit m, prouesse f

feather [ˈfɛðəʳ] n plume f ▷ vt: **to ~ one's nest** (fig) faire sa pelote ▷ cpd (bed etc) de plumes

feature [ˈfiːtʃəʳ] n caractéristique f; (article) chronique f, rubrique f ▷ vt (film) avoir pour vedette(s) ▷ vi figurer (en bonne place); **features** npl (of face) traits mpl; **a (special) ~ on sth/sb** un reportage sur qch/qn; **it ~d prominently in ...** cela a figuré en bonne place sur or dans ...

feature film n long métrage

Feb. abbr (= February) fév

February [ˈfɛbruərɪ] n février m; see also **July**

fed [fɛd] pt, pp of **feed**

federal [ˈfɛdərəl] adj fédéral(e)

federation [fɛdəˈreɪʃən] n fédération f

fed up [fɛdˈʌp] adj: **to be ~ (with)** en avoir marre or plein le dos (de)

fee [fiː] n rémunération f; (of doctor, lawyer) honoraires mpl; (of school, college etc) frais mpl de scolarité; (for examination) droits mpl; **entrance/membership ~** droit d'entrée/d'inscription; **for a small ~** pour une somme modique

feeble [ˈfiːbl] adj faible; (attempt, excuse) pauvre; (joke) piteux(-euse)

feed [fiːd] n (of baby) tétée f; (of animal) nourriture f, pâture f; (on printer) mécanisme m d'alimentation ▷ vt (pt, pp **fed**) (person) nourrir; (Brit: baby: breastfeed) allaiter; (: with bottle) donner le biberon à; (horse etc) donner à manger à; (machine) alimenter; (data etc): **to ~ sth into** enregistrer qch dans; **feed back** vt (results) donner en retour; **feed on** vt fus se nourrir de

feedback [ˈfiːdbæk] n (Elec) effet m Larsen; (from person) réactions fpl

feel [fiːl] n (sensation) sensation f; (impression) impression f ▷ vt (pt, pp **felt**) [fɛlt] (touch) toucher; (explore) tâter, palper; (cold, pain) sentir; (grief, anger) ressentir, éprouver; (think, believe): **to ~ (that)** trouver que; **I ~ that you ought to do it** il me semble que vous devriez le faire; **to ~ hungry/cold** avoir faim/froid; **to ~ lonely/better** se sentir seul/mieux; **I don't ~ well** je ne me sens pas bien; **to ~ sorry for** avoir pitié de; **it ~s soft** c'est doux au toucher; **it ~s colder here** je trouve qu'il fait plus froid ici; **it ~s like velvet** on dirait du velours, ça ressemble au velours; **to ~ like** (want) avoir envie de; **to ~ about or around** fouiller, tâtonner; **to get the ~ of sth** (fig) s'habituer à qch

feeler ['fiːlə'] n (of insect) antenne f; (fig):
  to put out a ~ or **~s** tâter le terrain
feeling ['fiːlɪŋ] n (physical) sensation f;
  (emotion, impression) sentiment m; **to hurt sb's
  ~s** froisser qn; **~s ran high about it** cela a
  déchaîné les passions; **what are your ~s
  about the matter?** quel est votre sentiment
  sur cette question?; **my ~ is that ...** j'estime
  que ...; **I have a ~ that ...** j'ai l'impression
  que ...
feet [fiːt] npl of **foot**
feign [feɪn] vt feindre, simuler
fell [fɛl] pt of **fall** ▷ vt (tree) abattre ▷ n
  (Brit: mountain) montagne f; (: moorland):
  the ~s la lande ▷ adj: **with one ~ blow** d'un
  seul coup
fellow ['fɛləu] n type m; (comrade)
  compagnon m; (of learned society) membre m;
  (of university) universitaire m/f (membre du
  conseil) ▷ cpd: **their ~ prisoners/students**
  leurs camarades prisonniers/étudiants;
  his ~ workers ses collègues mpl (de travail)
fellow citizen n concitoyen(ne)
fellow countryman irreg n compatriote m
fellow men npl semblables mpl
fellowship ['fɛləuʃɪp] n (society) association f;
  (comradeship) amitié f, camaraderie f; (Scol)
  sorte de bourse universitaire
felony ['fɛlənɪ] n crime m, forfait m
felt [fɛlt] pt, pp of **feel** ▷ n feutre m
felt-tip ['fɛlttɪp-] n (also: **~ pen**) stylo-feutre m
female ['fiːmeɪl] n (Zool) femelle f; (pej:
  woman) bonne femme ▷ adj (Biol, Elec)
  femelle; (sex, character) féminin(e); (vote etc)
  des femmes; (child etc) du sexe féminin;
  male and ~ students étudiants et
  étudiantes
feminine ['fɛmɪnɪn] adj féminin(e) ▷ n
  féminin m
feminist ['fɛmɪnɪst] n féministe m/f
fence [fɛns] n barrière f; (Sport) obstacle m;
  (inf: person) receleur(-euse) ▷ vt (also: **~ in**)
  clôturer ▷ vi faire de l'escrime; **to sit on
  the ~** (fig) ne pas se mouiller
fencing ['fɛnsɪŋ] n (sport) escrime m
fend [fɛnd] vi: **to ~ for o.s.** se débrouiller
  (tout seul); **fend off** vt (attack etc) parer;
  (questions) éluder
fender ['fɛndə'] n garde-feu m inv; (on boat)
  défense f; (US: of car) aile f
fennel ['fɛnl] n fenouil m
ferment vi [fə'mɛnt] fermenter ▷ n ['fəːmɛnt]
  (fig) agitation f, effervescence f
fern [fəːn] n fougère f
ferocious [fə'rəuʃəs] adj féroce
ferret ['fɛrɪt] n furet m; **ferret about, ferret
  around** vi fureter; **ferret out** vt dénicher
ferry ['fɛrɪ] n (small) bac m; (large: also: **~boat**)
  ferry(-boat m) m ▷ vt transporter; **to ~ sth/sb
  across** or **over** faire traverser qch/qn
fertile ['fəːtaɪl] adj fertile; (Biol) fécond(e);
  ~ period période f de fécondité

fertilize [fəːtɪlaɪz] vt fertiliser; (Biol)
  féconder
fertilizer ['fəːtɪlaɪzə'] n engrais m
fester ['fɛstə'] vi suppurer
festival ['fɛstɪvəl] n (Rel) fête f; (Art, Mus)
  festival m
festive ['fɛstɪv] adj de fête; **the ~ season**
  (Brit: Christmas) la période des fêtes
festivities [fɛs'tɪvɪtɪz] npl réjouissances fpl
festoon [fɛs'tuːn] vt: **to ~ with** orner de
fetch [fɛtʃ] vt aller chercher; (Brit: sell for)
  rapporter; **how much did it ~?** ça a atteint
  quel prix?; **fetch up** vi (Brit) se retrouver
fête [feɪt] n fête f, kermesse f
fetus ['fiːtəs] n (US) = **foetus**
feud [fjuːd] n querelle f, dispute f ▷ vi se
  quereller, se disputer; **a family ~** une
  querelle de famille
fever ['fiːvə'] n fièvre f; **he has a ~** il a de la
  fièvre
feverish ['fiːvərɪʃ] adj fiévreux(-euse), fébrile
few [fjuː] adj (not many) peu de ▷ pron peu;
  ~ succeed il y en a peu qui réussissent,
  (bien) peu réussissent; **they were ~** ils
  étaient peu (nombreux), il y en avait peu;
  a ~ (as adj) quelques; (as pron) quelques-
  uns(-unes); **I know a ~** j'en connais
  quelques-uns; **quite a ~ ...** adj un certain
  nombre de ..., pas mal de ...; **in the next ~
  days** dans les jours qui viennent; **in the past
  ~ days** ces derniers jours; **every ~ days/
  months** tous les deux ou trois jours/mois;
  a ~ more ... encore quelques ..., quelques ...
  de plus
fewer ['fjuːə'] adj moins de ▷ pron moins;
  they are ~ now il y en a moins maintenant,
  ils sont moins (nombreux) maintenant
fewest ['fjuːɪst] adj le moins nombreux
fiancé [fɪ'ɑːŋseɪ] n fiancé m
fiancée [fɪ'ɑːŋseɪ] n fiancée f
fiasco [fɪ'æskəu] n fiasco m
fib [fɪb] n bobard m
fibre, (US) **fiber** ['faɪbə'] n fibre f
fibreglass, Fiberglass® (US) ['faɪbəglɑːs] n
  fibre f de verre
fickle ['fɪkl] adj inconstant(e), volage,
  capricieux(-euse)
fiction ['fɪkʃən] n romans mpl, littérature f
  romanesque; (invention) fiction f
fictional ['fɪkʃənl] adj fictif(-ive)
fictitious [fɪk'tɪʃəs] adj fictif(-ive),
  imaginaire
fiddle ['fɪdl] n (Mus) violon m; (cheating)
  combine f, escroquerie f ▷ vt (Brit: accounts)
  falsifier, maquiller; **tax ~** fraude fiscale,
  combine f pour échapper au fisc; **to work a ~**
  trafcoter; **fiddle with** vt fus tripoter
fidelity [fɪ'dɛlɪtɪ] n fidélité f
fidget ['fɪdʒɪt] vi se trémousser, remuer
field [fiːld] n champ m; (fig) domaine m,
  champ; (Sport: ground) terrain m; (Comput)
  champ, zone f; **to lead the ~** (Sport, Comm)

dominer; **the children had a ~ day** (fig)
c'était un grand jour pour les enfants

field marshal n maréchal m

fieldwork ['fi:ldwə:k] n travaux mpl
pratiques (or recherches fpl) sur le terrain

fiend [fi:nd] n démon m

fierce [fɪəs] adj (look, animal) féroce, sauvage;
(wind, attack, person) (très) violent(e); (fighting,
enemy) acharné(e)

fiery ['faɪərɪ] adj ardent(e), brûlant(e),
fougueux(-euse)

fifteen [fɪf'ti:n] num quinze

fifteenth [fɪf'ti:nθ] num quinzième

fifth [fɪfθ] num cinquième

fiftieth ['fɪftɪɪθ] num cinquantième

fifty ['fɪftɪ] num cinquante

fifty-fifty ['fɪftɪ'fɪftɪ] adv moitié-moitié; **to
share ~ with sb** partager moitié-moitié avec
qn ▷ adj: **to have a ~ chance (of success)**
avoir une chance sur deux (de réussir)

fig [fɪg] n figue f

fight [faɪt] (pt, pp **fought**) [fɔ:t] n (between
persons) bagarre f; (argument) dispute f; (Mil)
combat m; (against cancer etc) lutte f ▷ vt se
battre contre; (cancer, alcoholism, emotion)
combattre, lutter contre; (election) se
présenter à; (Law: case) défendre ▷ vi se
battre; (argue) se disputer; (fig): **to ~ (for/
against)** lutter (pour/contre); **fight back** vi
rendre les coups; (after illness) reprendre le
dessus ▷ vt (tears) réprimer; **fight off** vt
repousser; (disease, sleep, urge) lutter contre

fighter ['faɪtə'] n lutteur m; (fig: plane)
chasseur m

fighting ['faɪtɪŋ] n combats mpl; (brawls)
bagarres fpl

figment ['fɪgmənt] n: **a ~ of the
imagination** une invention

figurative ['fɪgjurətɪv] adj figuré(e)

figure ['fɪgə'] n (Drawing, Geom) figure f;
(number) chiffre m; (body, outline) silhouette f;
(person's shape) ligne f, formes fpl; (person)
personnage m ▷ vt (US: think) supposer ▷ vi
(appear) figurer; (US: make sense) s'expliquer;
public ~ personnalité f; **~ of speech** figure f
de rhétorique; **figure on** vt fus (US): **to ~ on
doing** compter faire; **figure out** vt
(understand) arriver à comprendre; (plan)
calculer

figurehead ['fɪgəhɛd] n (Naut) figure f de
proue; (pej) prête-nom m

file [faɪl] n (tool) lime f; (dossier) dossier m;
(folder) dossier, chemise f; (: binder) classeur m;
(Comput) fichier m; (row) file f ▷ vt (nails, wood)
limer; (papers) classer; (Law: claim) faire
enregistrer; déposer ▷ vi: **to ~ in/out**
entrer/sortir l'un derrière l'autre; **to ~ past** défiler
devant; **to ~ a suit against sb** (Law) intenter
un procès à qn

filing cabinet n classeur m (meuble)

Filipino [fɪlɪ'pi:nəu] adj philippin(e) ▷ n
(person) Philippin(e); (Ling) tagalog m

fill [fɪl] vt remplir; (vacancy) pourvoir à ▷ n: **to
eat one's ~** manger à sa faim; **to ~ with**
remplir de; **fill in** vt (hole) boucher; (form)
remplir; (details, report) compléter; **fill out**
vt (form, receipt) remplir; **fill up** vt remplir ▷ vi
(Aut) faire le plein; **~ it up, please** (Aut) le
plein, s'il vous plaît

fillet ['fɪlɪt] n filet m ▷ vt préparer en filets

fillet steak n filet m de bœuf, tournedos m

filling ['fɪlɪŋ] n (Culin) garniture f, farce f;
(for tooth) plombage m

filling station n station-service f, station f
d'essence

film [fɪlm] n film m; (Phot) pellicule f, film;
(of powder, liquid) couche f, pellicule ▷ vt
(scene) filmer ▷ vi tourner; **I'd like a
36-exposure ~** je voudrais une pellicule
de 36 poses

film star n vedette f de cinéma

filter ['fɪltə'] n filtre m ▷ vt filtrer

filter lane n (Brit Aut: at traffic lights) voie f de
dégagement; (: on motorway) voie f de sortie

filter tip n bout m filtre

filth [fɪlθ] n saleté f

filthy ['fɪlθɪ] adj sale, dégoûtant(e); (language)
ordurier(-ière), grossier(-ière)

fin [fɪn] n (of fish) nageoire f; (of shark)
aileron m; (of diver) palme f

final ['faɪnl] adj final(e), dernier(-ière);
(decision, answer) définitif(-ive) ▷ n (Brit Sport)
finale f; **finals** npl (Scol) examens mpl de
dernière année; (US Sport) finale f; **~ demand**
(on invoice etc) dernier rappel

finale [fɪ'nɑ:lɪ] n finale m

finalist ['faɪnəlɪst] n (Sport) finaliste m/f

finalize ['faɪnəlaɪz] vt mettre au point

finally ['faɪnəlɪ] adv (eventually) enfin,
finalement; (lastly) en dernier lieu;
(irrevocably) définitivement

finance [faɪ'næns] n finance f ▷ vt financer;
finances npl finances fpl

financial [faɪ'nænʃəl] adj financier(-ière);
~ statement bilan m, exercice financier

financial year n année f budgétaire

find [faɪnd] vt (pt, pp **found**) [faund] trouver;
(lost object) retrouver ▷ n trouvaille f,
découverte f; **to ~ sb guilty** (Law) déclarer qn
coupable; **to ~ (some) difficulty in doing
sth** avoir du mal à faire qch; **find out** vt se
renseigner sur; (truth, secret) découvrir;
(person) démasquer ▷ vi: **to ~ out about**
(make enquiries) se renseigner sur; (by chance)
apprendre

findings ['faɪndɪŋz] npl (Law) conclusions fpl,
verdict m; (of report) constatations fpl

fine [faɪn] adj (weather) beau/belle; (excellent)
excellent(e); (thin, subtle, not coarse) fin(e);
(acceptable) bien inv ▷ adv (well) très bien;
(small) fin, finement ▷ n (Law) amende f;
contravention f ▷ vt (Law) condamner à une
amende; donner une contravention à; **he's ~**
il va bien; **the weather is ~** il fait beau;

you're doing ~ c'est bien, vous vous débrouillez bien; **to cut it** ~ calculer un peu juste

fine arts *npl* beaux-arts *mpl*

finery ['faɪnərɪ] *n* parure *f*

finger ['fɪŋgər] *n* doigt *m* ▷ *vt* palper, toucher; **index** ~ index *m*

fingernail ['fɪŋgəneɪl] *n* ongle *m* (de la main)

fingerprint ['fɪŋgəprɪnt] *n* empreinte digitale ▷ *vt* (*person*) prendre les empreintes digitales de

fingertip ['fɪŋgətɪp] *n* bout *m* du doigt; (*fig*): **to have sth at one's ~s** avoir qch à sa disposition; (*knowledge*) savoir qch sur le bout du doigt

finish ['fɪnɪʃ] *n* fin *f*; (*Sport*) arrivée *f*; (*polish etc*) finition *f* ▷ *vt* finir, terminer ▷ *vi* finir, se terminer; (*session*) s'achever; **to ~ doing sth** finir de faire qch; **to ~ third** arriver or terminer troisième; **when does the show ~?** quand est-ce que le spectacle se termine?; **finish off** *vt* finir, terminer; (*kill*) achever; **finish up** *vi*, *vt* finir

finishing line ['fɪnɪʃɪŋ-] *n* ligne *f* d'arrivée

finite ['faɪnaɪt] *adj* fini(e); (*verb*) conjugué(e)

Finland ['fɪnlənd] *n* Finlande *f*

Finn [fɪn] *n* Finnois(e), Finlandais(e)

Finnish ['fɪnɪʃ] *adj* finnois(e), finlandais(e) ▷ *n* (*Ling*) finnois *m*

fir [fəːr] *n* sapin *m*

fire ['faɪər] *n* feu *m*; (*accidental*) incendie *m*; (*heater*) radiateur *m* ▷ *vt* (*discharge*): **to ~ a gun** tirer un coup de feu; (*fig: interest*) enflammer, animer; (*inf: dismiss*) mettre à la porte, renvoyer ▷ *vi* (*shoot*) tirer, faire feu ▷ *cpd*: **~ hazard, ~ risk: that's a fire hazard** or **risk** cela présente un risque d'incendie; **~!** au feu!; **on ~** en feu; **to set ~ to sth, set sth on ~** mettre le feu à qch; **insured against ~** assuré contre l'incendie

fire alarm *n* avertisseur *m* d'incendie

firearm ['faɪərɑːm] *n* arme *f* à feu

fire brigade *n* (*régiment m de sapeurs-*) pompiers *mpl*

fire department *n* (*US*) = **fire brigade**

fire engine *n* (*Brit*) pompe *f* à incendie

fire escape *n* escalier *m* de secours

fire exit *n* issue *f* or sortie *f* de secours

fire extinguisher *n* extincteur *m*

fireman *irreg* ['faɪəmən] *n* pompier *m*

fireplace ['faɪəpleɪs] *n* cheminée *f*

fireside ['faɪəsaɪd] *n* foyer *m*, coin *m* du feu

fire station *n* caserne *f* de pompiers

fire truck *n* (*US*) = **fire engine**

firewall ['faɪəwɔːl] *n* (*Internet*) pare-feu *m*

firewood ['faɪəwud] *n* bois *m* de chauffage

fireworks ['faɪəwəːks] *npl* (*display*) feu(x) *m(pl)* d'artifice

firing squad *n* peloton *m* d'exécution

firm [fəːm] *adj* ferme ▷ *n* compagnie *f*, firme *f*; **it is my ~ belief that ...** je crois fermement que ...

firmly ['fəːmlɪ] *adv* fermement

first [fəːst] *adj* premier(-ière) ▷ *adv* (*before other people*) le premier, la première; (*before other things*) en premier, d'abord; (*when listing reasons etc*) en premier lieu, premièrement; (*in the beginning*) au début ▷ *n* (*person: in race*) premier(-ière); (*Aut*) première *f*; **the ~ of January** le premier janvier; **at ~** au commencement, au début; **~ of all** tout d'abord, pour commencer; **in the ~ instance** en premier lieu; **I'll do it ~ thing tomorrow** je le ferai tout de suite demain matin

first aid *n* premiers secours or soins

first-aid kit [fəːst'eɪd-] *n* trousse *f* à pharmacie

first-class ['fəːst'klɑːs] *adj* (*ticket etc*) de première classe; (*excellent*) excellent(e), exceptionnel(le); (*post*) en tarif prioritaire

first-hand ['fəːst'hænd] *adj* de première main

first lady *n* (*US*) femme *f* du président

firstly ['fəːstlɪ] *adv* premièrement, en premier lieu

first name *n* prénom *m*

first-rate ['fəːst'reɪt] *adj* excellent(e)

fiscal ['fɪskl] *adj* fiscal(e)

fiscal year *n* exercice financier

fish [fɪʃ] *n* (*pl inv*) poisson *m*; poissons *mpl* ▷ *vt*, *vi* pêcher; **to ~ a river** pêcher dans une rivière; **~ and chips** poisson frit et frites

fisherman *irreg* ['fɪʃəmən] *n* pêcheur *m*

fish farm *n* établissement *m* piscicole

fish fingers *npl* (*Brit*) bâtonnets *mpl* de poisson (congelés)

fishing ['fɪʃɪŋ] *n* pêche *f*; **to go ~** aller à la pêche

fishing boat *n* barque *f* de pêche

fishing line *n* ligne *f* (de pêche)

fishing rod *n* canne *f* à pêche

fishing tackle *n* attirail *m* de pêche

fishmonger ['fɪʃmʌŋgər] *n* (*Brit*) marchand *m* de poisson

fishmonger's ['fɪʃmʌŋgəz], **fishmonger's shop** *n* (*Brit*) poissonnerie *f*

fish slice *n* (*Brit*) pelle *f* à poisson

fish sticks *npl* (*US*) = **fish fingers**

fishy ['fɪʃɪ] *adj* (*inf*) suspect(e), louche

fist [fɪst] *n* poing *m*

fit [fɪt] *adj* (*Med, Sport*) en (bonne) forme; (*proper*) convenable; approprié(e) ▷ *vt* (*subj: clothes*) aller à; (*adjust*) ajuster; (*put in, attach*) installer, poser; adapter; (*equip*) équiper, garnir, munir; (*suit*) convenir à ▷ *vi* (*clothes*) aller; (*parts*) s'adapter; (*in space, gap*) entrer, s'adapter ▷ *n* (*Med*) accès *m*, crise *f*; (*of anger*) accès; (*of hysterics, jealousy*) crise; **~ to** (*ready to*) en état de; **~ for** (*worthy*) digne de; (*capable*) apte à; **to keep ~** se maintenir en forme; **this dress is a tight/good ~** cette robe est un peu juste/(me) va très bien; **a ~ of coughing** une quinte de toux; **to have a ~**

(*Med*) faire or avoir une crise; (*inf*) piquer une crise; **by ~s and starts** par à-coups; **fit in** vi (*add up*) cadrer; (*integrate*) s'intégrer; (*to new situation*) s'adapter; **fit out** vt (*Brit: also: ~ up*) équiper

fitful ['fɪtful] *adj* intermittent(e)

fitment ['fɪtmənt] *n* meuble encastré, élément *m*

fitness ['fɪtnɪs] *n* (*Med*) forme f physique; (*of remark*) à-propos *m*, justesse f

fitted ['fɪtɪd] *adj* (*jacket, shirt*) ajusté(e)

fitted carpet ['fɪtɪd-] *n* moquette f

fitted kitchen ['fɪtɪd-] *n* (*Brit*) cuisine équipée

fitted sheet ['fɪtɪd-] *n* drap-housse *m*

fitter ['fɪtə'] *n* monteur *m*; (*Dressmaking*) essayeur(-euse)

fitting ['fɪtɪŋ] *adj* approprié(e) ▷ *n* (*of dress*) essayage *m*; (*of piece of equipment*) pose f, installation f

fitting room *n* (*in shop*) cabine f d'essayage

fittings ['fɪtɪŋz] *npl* installations fpl

five [faɪv] *num* cinq

fiver ['faɪvə'] *n* (*inf: Brit*) billet *m* de cinq livres; (*: US*) billet de cinq dollars

fix [fɪks] vt (*date, amount etc*) fixer; (*sort out*) arranger; (*mend*) réparer; (*make ready: meal, drink*) préparer; (*inf: game etc*) truquer ▷ *n*: **to be in a ~** être dans le pétrin; **fix up** vt (*meeting*) arranger; **to ~ sb up with sth** faire avoir qch à qn

fixation [fɪk'seɪʃən] *n* (*Psych*) fixation f; (*fig*) obsession f

fixed [fɪkst] *adj* (*prices etc*) fixe; **there's a ~ charge** il y a un prix forfaitaire; **how are you ~ for money?** (*inf*) question fric, ça va?

fixture ['fɪkstʃə'] *n* installation f (fixe); (*Sport*) rencontre f (au programme)

fizzy ['fɪzɪ] *adj* pétillant(e), gazeux(-euse)

flabbergasted ['flæbəgɑːstɪd] *adj* sidéré(e), ahuri(e)

flabby ['flæbɪ] *adj* mou/molle

flag [flæg] *n* drapeau *m*; (*also: ~stone*) dalle f ▷ vi faiblir; fléchir; **~ of convenience** pavillon *m* de complaisance; **flag down** vt héler, faire signe (de s'arrêter) à

flagpole ['flægpəul] *n* mât *m*

flagship ['flægʃɪp] *n* vaisseau *m* amiral; (*fig*) produit *m* vedette

flair [flɛə'] *n* flair *m*

flak [flæk] *n* (*Mil*) tir antiaérien; (*inf: criticism*) critiques fpl

flake [fleɪk] *n* (*of rust, paint*) écaille f; (*of snow, soap powder*) flocon *m* ▷ vi (*also: ~ off*) s'écailler

flamboyant [flæm'bɔɪənt] *adj* flamboyant(e), éclatant(e); (*person*) haut(e) en couleur

flame [fleɪm] *n* flamme f

flamingo [flə'mɪŋɡəu] *n* flamant *m* (rose)

flammable ['flæməbl] *adj* inflammable

flan [flæn] *n* (*Brit*) tarte f

flank [flæŋk] *n* flanc *m* ▷ vt flanquer

flannel ['flænl] *n* (*Brit: also:* **face ~**) gant *m* de toilette; (*fabric*) flanelle f; (*Brit inf*) baratin *m*; **flannels** *npl* pantalon *m* de flanelle

flap [flæp] *n* (*of pocket, envelope*) rabat *m* ▷ vt (*wings*) battre (de) ▷ vi (*sail, flag*) claquer; (*inf: also:* **be in a ~**) paniquer

flare [flɛə'] *n* (*signal*) signal lumineux; (*Mil*) fusée éclairante; (*in skirt etc*) évasement *m*; **flares** *npl* (*trousers*) pantalon *m* à pattes d'éléphant; **flare up** vi s'embraser; (*fig: person*) se mettre en colère, s'emporter; (*: revolt*) éclater

flash [flæʃ] *n* éclair *m*; (*also:* **news ~**) flash *m* (d'information); (*Phot*) flash ▷ vt (*switch on*) allumer (brièvement); (*direct*): **to ~ sth at** braquer qch sur; (*flaunt*) étaler, exhiber; (*send: message*) câbler; (*smile*) lancer ▷ vi briller; jeter des éclairs; (*light on ambulance etc*) clignoter; **a ~ of lightning** un éclair; **in a ~** en un clin d'œil; **to ~ one's headlights** faire un appel de phares; **he ~ed by** or **past** il passa (devant nous) comme un éclair

flashback ['flæʃbæk] *n* flashback *m*, retour *m* en arrière

flashbulb ['flæʃbʌlb] *n* ampoule f de flash

flashcube ['flæʃkjuːb] *n* cube-flash *m*

flashlight ['flæʃlaɪt] *n* lampe f de poche

flashy ['flæʃɪ] *adj* (*pej*) tape-à-l'œil inv, tapageur(-euse)

flask [flɑːsk] *n* flacon *m*, bouteille f; (*Chem*) ballon *m*; (*also:* **vacuum ~**) bouteille f thermos®

flat [flæt] *adj* plat(e); (*tyre*) dégonflé(e), à plat; (*beer*) éventé(e); (*battery*) à plat; (*denial*) catégorique; (*Mus*) bémol inv; (*: voice*) faux/ fausse ▷ *n* (*Brit: apartment*) appartement *m*; (*Aut*) crevaison f, pneu crevé; (*Mus*) bémol *m*; **~ out** (*work*) sans relâche; (*race*) à fond; **~ rate of pay** (*Comm*) salaire *m* fixe

flatly ['flætlɪ] *adv* catégoriquement

flatten ['flætn] vt (*also:* **~ out**) aplatir; (*crop*) coucher; (*house, city*) raser

flatter ['flætə'] vt flatter

flattering ['flætərɪŋ] *adj* flatteur(-euse); (*clothes etc*) seyant(e)

flattery ['flætərɪ] *n* flatterie f

flaunt [flɔːnt] vt faire étalage de

flavour, (*US*) **flavor** ['fleɪvə'] *n* goût *m*, saveur f; (*of ice cream etc*) parfum *m* ▷ vt parfumer, aromatiser; **vanilla-~ed** à l'arôme de vanille, vanillé(e); **what ~s do you have?** quels parfums avez-vous?; **to give** or **add ~ to** donner du goût à, relever

flavouring, (*US*) **flavoring** ['fleɪvərɪŋ] *n* arôme *m* (synthétique)

flaw [flɔː] *n* défaut *m*

flawless ['flɔːlɪs] *adj* sans défaut

flax [flæks] *n* lin *m*

flea [fliː] *n* puce f

flea market *n* marché *m* aux puces

fleck [flɛk] *n* (*of dust*) particule f; (*of mud, paint, colour*) tacheture f, moucheture f ▷ vt tacher, éclabousser; **brown ~ed with white** brun moucheté de blanc

fled [flɛd] *pt, pp of* **flee**

flee (*pt, pp* **fled**) [fliː, flɛd] *vt* fuir, s'enfuir de ▷ *vi* fuir, s'enfuir

fleece [fliːs] *n* (*of sheep*) toison *f*; (*top*) (laine *f*) polaire ▷ *vt* (*inf*) voler, filouter

fleet [fliːt] *n* flotte *f*; (*of lorries, cars etc*) parc *m*; convoi *m*

fleeting ['fliːtɪŋ] *adj* fugace, fugitif(-ive); (*visit*) très bref/brève

Flemish ['flɛmɪʃ] *adj* flamand(e) ▷ *n* (*Ling*) flamand *m*; **the ~** *npl* les Flamands

flesh [flɛʃ] *n* chair *f*

flesh wound [-wuːnd] *n* blessure superficielle

flew [fluː] *pt of* **fly**

flex [flɛks] *n* fil *m* or câble *m* électrique (souple) ▷ *vt* (*knee*) fléchir; (*muscles*) bander

flexibility [flɛksɪ'bɪlɪtɪ] *n* flexibilité *f*

flexible ['flɛksəbl] *adj* flexible; (*person, schedule*) souple

flexitime ['flɛksɪtaɪm], (*US*) **flextime** ['flɛkstaɪm] *n* horaire *m* variable or à la carte

flick [flɪk] *n* petit coup; (*with finger*) chiquenaude *f* ▷ *vt* donner un petit coup à; (*switch*) appuyer sur; **flick through** *vt fus* feuilleter

flicker ['flɪkə'] *vi* (*light, flame*) vaciller ▷ *n* vacillement *m*; **a ~ of light** une brève lueur

flier ['flaɪə'] *n* aviateur *m*

flies [flaɪz] *npl of* **fly**

flight [flaɪt] *n* vol *m*; (*escape*) fuite *f*; (*also:* **~ of steps**) escalier *m*; **to take ~** prendre la fuite; **to put to ~** mettre en fuite

flight attendant *n* steward *m*, hôtesse *f* de l'air

flight deck *n* (*Aviat*) poste *m* de pilotage; (*Naut*) pont *m* d'envol

flimsy ['flɪmzɪ] *adj* peu solide; (*clothes*) trop léger(-ère); (*excuse*) pauvre, mince

flinch [flɪntʃ] *vi* tressaillir; **to ~ from** se dérober à, reculer devant

fling [flɪŋ] *vt* (*pt, pp* **flung**) [flʌŋ] jeter, lancer ▷ *n* (*love affair*) brève liaison, passade *f*

flint [flɪnt] *n* silex *m*; (*in lighter*) pierre *f* (à briquet)

flip [flɪp] *n* chiquenaude *f* ▷ *vt* (*throw*) donner une chiquenaude à; (*switch*) appuyer sur; (*US: pancake*) faire sauter; **to ~ sth over** retourner qch ▷ *vi*: **to ~ for sth** (*US*) jouer qch à pile ou face; **flip through** *vt fus* feuilleter

flip-flops ['flɪpflɔps] *npl* (*esp Brit*) tongs *fpl*

flippant ['flɪpənt] *adj* désinvolte, irrévérencieux(-euse)

flipper ['flɪpə'] *n* (*of animal*) nageoire *f*; (*for swimmer*) palme *f*

flirt [fləːt] *vi* flirter ▷ *n* flirteur(-euse)

float [fləut] *n* flotteur *m*; (*in procession*) char *m*; (*sum of money*) réserve *f* ▷ *vi* flotter; (*bather*) flotter, faire la planche ▷ *vt* faire flotter; (*loan, business, idea*) lancer

flock [flɔk] *n* (*of sheep*) troupeau *m*; (*of birds*) vol *m*; (*of people*) foule *f*

flog [flɔg] *vt* fouetter

flood [flʌd] *n* inondation *f*; (*of letters, refugees etc*) flot *m* ▷ *vt* inonder; (*Aut: carburettor*) noyer ▷ *vi* (*place*) être inondé; (*people*): **to ~ into** envahir; **to ~ the market** (*Comm*) inonder le marché; **in ~** en crue

flooding ['flʌdɪŋ] *n* inondation *f*

floodlight ['flʌdlaɪt] *n* projecteur *m* ▷ *vt* éclairer aux projecteurs, illuminer

floor [flɔː'] *n* sol *m*; (*storey*) étage *m*; (*of sea, valley*) fond *m*; (*fig: at meeting*): **the ~** l'assemblée *f*, les membres *mpl* de l'assemblée ▷ *vt* (*knock down*) terrasser; (*baffle*) désorienter; **on the ~** par terre; **ground ~**, (*US*) **first ~** rez-de-chaussée *m*; **first ~**, (*US*) **second ~** premier étage; **top ~** dernier étage; **what ~ is it on?** c'est à quel étage?; **to have the ~** (*speaker*) avoir la parole

floorboard ['flɔːbɔːd] *n* planche *f* (du plancher)

flooring ['flɔːrɪŋ] *n* sol *m*; (*wooden*) plancher *m*; (*material to make floor*) matériau(x) *m(pl)* pour planchers; (*covering*) revêtement *m* de sol

floor show *n* spectacle *m* de variétés

flop [flɔp] *n* fiasco *m* ▷ *vi* (*fail*) faire fiasco; (*fall*) s'affaler, s'effondrer

floppy ['flɔpɪ] *adj* lâche, flottant(e) ▷ *n* (*Comput: also:* **~ disk**) disquette *f*; **~ hat** chapeau *m* à bords flottants

flora ['flɔːrə] *n* flore *f*

floral ['flɔːrl] *adj* floral(e); (*dress*) à fleurs

florid ['flɔrɪd] *adj* (*complexion*) fleuri(e); (*style*) plein(e) de fioritures

florist ['flɔrɪst] *n* fleuriste *m/f*

florist's ['flɔrɪsts], **florist's shop** *n* magasin *m* or boutique *f* de fleuriste

flotation [fləu'teɪʃən] *n* (*of shares*) émission *f*; (*of company*) lancement *m* (en Bourse)

flounder ['flaundə'] *n* (*Zool*) flet *m* ▷ *vi* patauger

flour ['flauə'] *n* farine *f*

flourish ['flʌrɪʃ] *vi* prospérer ▷ *n* (*gesture*) moulinet (*decoration*) fioriture *f*; (*of trumpets*) fanfare *f*

flout [flaut] *vt* se moquer de, faire fi de

flow [fləu] *n* (*of water, traffic etc*) écoulement *m*; (*tide, influx*) flux *m*; (*of orders, letters etc*) flot *m*; (*of blood, Elec*) circulation *f*; (*of river*) courant *m* ▷ *vi* couler; (*traffic*) s'écouler; (*robes, hair*) flotter

flow chart, flow diagram *n* organigramme *m*

flower ['flauə'] *n* fleur *f* ▷ *vi* fleurir; **in ~** en fleur

flower bed *n* plate-bande *f*

flowerpot ['flauəpɔt] *n* pot *m* (à fleurs)

flowery ['flauərɪ] *adj* fleuri(e)

flown [fləun] *pp of* **fly**

fl. oz. *abbr* = **fluid ounce**

flu [fluː] *n* grippe *f*

fluctuate ['flʌktjueɪt] vi varier, fluctuer

fluent ['fluːənt] adj (speech, style) coulant(e), aisé(e); **he's a ~ speaker/reader** il s'exprime/lit avec aisance or facilité; **he speaks ~ French, he's ~ in French** il parle le français couramment

fluff [flʌf] n duvet m; (on jacket, carpet) peluche f

fluffy ['flʌfɪ] adj duveteux(-euse); (jacket, carpet) pelucheux(-euse); (toy) en peluche

fluid ['fluːɪd] n fluide m; (in diet) liquide m
▷ adj fluide

fluid ounce n (Brit) = 0.028 l; 0.05 pints

fluke [fluːk] n coup m de veine

flung [flʌŋ] pt, pp of **fling**

fluorescent [fluəˈrɛsnt] adj fluorescent(e)

fluoride ['fluəraɪd] n fluor m

flurry ['flʌrɪ] n (of snow) rafale f, bourrasque f; **a ~ of activity** un affairement soudain; **a ~ of excitement** une excitation soudaine

flush [flʌʃ] n (on face) rougeur f; (fig: of youth etc) éclat m; (of blood) afflux m ▷ vt nettoyer à grande eau; (also: **~ out**) débusquer ▷ vi rougir ▷ adj (inf) en fonds; (level): **~ with** au ras de, de niveau avec; **to ~ the toilet** tirer la chasse (d'eau); **hot ~es** (Med) bouffées fpl de chaleur

flushed ['flʌʃt] adj (tout(e)) rouge

flustered ['flʌstəd] adj énervé(e)

flute [fluːt] n flûte f

flutter ['flʌtər] n (of panic, excitement) agitation f; (of wings) battement m ▷ vi (bird) battre des ailes, voleter; (person) aller et venir dans une grande agitation

flux [flʌks] n: **in a state of ~** fluctuant sans cesse

fly [flaɪ] (pt **flew**, pp **flown**) [fluː, fləun] n (insect) mouche f; (on trousers: also: **flies**) braguette f ▷ vt (plane) piloter; (passengers, cargo) transporter (par avion); (distance) parcourir ▷ vi voler; (passengers) aller en avion; (escape) s'enfuir, fuir; (flag) se déployer; **to ~ open** s'ouvrir brusquement; **to ~ off the handle** s'énerver, s'emporter; **fly away, fly off** vi s'envoler; **fly in** vi (plane) atterrir; **he flew in yesterday** il est arrivé hier (par avion); **fly out** vi partir (par avion)

fly-drive ['flaɪdraɪv] n formule f avion plus voiture

flying ['flaɪɪŋ] n (activity) aviation f; (action) vol m ▷ adj: **~ visit** visite f éclair inv; **with ~ colours** haut la main; **he doesn't like ~** il n'aime pas voyager en avion

flying saucer n soucoupe volante

flying start n: **to get off to a ~** faire un excellent départ

flyover ['flaɪəuvər] n (Brit: overpass) pont routier, saut-de-mouton m (Canada)

flysheet ['flaɪʃiːt] n (for tent) double toit m

FM abbr (Brit Mil) = **field marshal**; (Radio: = frequency modulation) FM

foal [fəul] n poulain m

foam [fəum] n écume f; (on beer) mousse f; (also: **~ rubber**) caoutchouc m mousse; (also: **plastic ~**) mousse cellulaire or de plastique ▷ vi (liquid) écumer; (soapy water) mousser

fob [fɔb] n (also: **watch ~**) chaîne f, ruban m ▷ vt: **to ~ sb off with sth** refiler qch à qn

focal point n foyer m; (fig) centre m de l'attention, point focal

focus ['fəukəs] n (pl **focuses**) foyer m; (of interest) centre m ▷ vt (field glasses etc) mettre au point; (light rays) faire converger ▷ vi: **to ~ (on)** (with camera) régler la mise au point (sur); (with eyes) fixer son regard (sur); (fig: concentrate) se concentrer; **out of/in ~** (picture) flou(e)/net(te); (camera) pas au point/au point

fodder ['fɔdər] n fourrage m

foe [fəu] n ennemi m

foetus, (US) **fetus** ['fiːtəs] n fœtus m

fog [fɔg] n brouillard m

foggy ['fɔgɪ] adj: **it's ~** il y a du brouillard

fog lamp, (US) **fog light** n (Aut) phare m anti-brouillard

foil [fɔɪl] vt déjouer, contrecarrer ▷ n feuille f de métal; (kitchen foil) papier m d'alu(minium); (Fencing) fleuret m; **to act as a ~ to** (fig) servir de repoussoir or de faire-valoir à

fold [fəuld] n (bend, crease) pli m; (Agr) parc m à moutons; (fig) bercail m ▷ vt plier; **to ~ one's arms** croiser les bras; **fold up** vi (map etc) se plier, se replier; (business) fermer boutique ▷ vt (map etc) plier, replier

folder ['fəuldər] n (for papers) chemise f; (: binder) classeur m; (brochure) dépliant m; (Comput) dossier m

folding ['fəuldɪŋ] adj (chair, bed) pliant(e)

foliage ['fəuliɪdʒ] n feuillage m

folk [fəuk] npl gens mpl ▷ cpd folklorique; **folks** npl (inf: parents) famille f, parents mpl

folklore ['fəuklɔːr] n folklore m

folk music n musique f folklorique; (contemporary) musique folk, folk m

folk song ['fəuksɔŋ] n chanson f folklorique; (contemporary) chanson folk inv

follow ['fɔləu] vt suivre; (on Twitter) s'abonner aux tweets de; ▷ vi suivre; (result) s'ensuivre; **to ~ sb's advice** suivre les conseils de qn; **I don't quite ~ you** je ne vous suis plus; **to ~ in sb's footsteps** emboîter le pas à qn; (fig) suivre les traces de qn; **it ~s that …** il s'ensuit que …; **to ~ suit** (fig) faire de même; **follow out** vt (idea, plan) poursuivre, mener à terme; **follow through** vt = **follow out**; **follow up** vt (victory) tirer parti de; (letter, offer) donner suite à; (case) suivre

follower ['fɔləuər] n disciple m/f, partisan(e)

following ['fɔləuɪŋ] adj suivant(e) ▷ n partisans mpl, disciples mpl

follow-up ['fɔləuʌp] n suite f; (on file, case) suivi m

folly | 432

folly ['fɒlɪ] *n* inconscience *f*; sottise *f*; (*building*) folie *f*

fond [fɒnd] *adj* (*memory, look*) tendre, affectueux(-euse); (*hopes, dreams*) un peu fou/ folle; **to be ~ of** aimer beaucoup

fondle ['fɒndl] *vt* caresser

font [fɒnt] *n* (*Rel*) fonts baptismaux; (*Typ*) police *f* de caractères

food [fuːd] *n* nourriture *f*

food mixer *n* mixeur *m*

food poisoning *n* intoxication *f* alimentaire

food processor *n* robot *m* de cuisine

food stamp *n* (*US*) bon *m* de nourriture (*pour indigents*)

foodstuffs ['fuːdstʌfs] *npl* denrées *fpl* alimentaires

fool [fuːl] *n* idiot(e); (*Hist: of king*) bouffon *m*, fou *m*; (*Culin*) mousse *f* de fruits ▷ *vt* berner, duper ▷ *vi* (*also:* **~ around**) faire l'idiot or l'imbécile; **to make a ~ of sb** (*ridicule*) ridiculiser qn; (*trick*) avoir or duper qn; **to make a ~ of o.s.** se couvrir de ridicule; **you can't ~ me** vous (ne) me la ferez pas, on (ne) me la fait pas; **fool about, fool around** *vi* (*pej: waste time*) traînailler, glandouiller; (*: behave foolishly*) faire l'idiot or l'imbécile

foolhardy ['fuːlhɑːdɪ] *adj* téméraire, imprudent(e)

foolish ['fuːlɪʃ] *adj* idiot(e), stupide; (*rash*) imprudent(e)

foolproof ['fuːlpruːf] *adj* (*plan etc*) infaillible

foot [fut] (*pl* **feet**) [fut, fiːt] *n* pied *m*; (*of animal*) patte *f*; (*measure*) pied *m* (= 30.48 cm; 12 inches) ▷ *vt* (*bill*) casquer, payer; **on ~** à pied; **to find one's feet** (*fig*) s'acclimater; **to put one's ~ down** (*Aut*) appuyer sur le champignon; (*say no*) s'imposer

footage ['futɪdʒ] *n* (*Cine: length*) ≈ métrage *m*; (*: material*) séquences *fpl*

foot-and-mouth [futənd'mauθ], **foot-and-mouth disease** *n* fièvre aphteuse

football ['futbɔːl] *n* (*ball*) ballon *m* (de football); (*sport: Brit*) football *m*; (*: US*) football américain

footballer ['futbɔːləʳ] *n* (*Brit*) = **football player**

football match *n* (*Brit*) match *m* de foot(ball)

football player *n* footballeur(-euse), joueur(-euse) de football; (*US*) joueur(-euse) de football américain

football pools *npl* (*US*) ≈ loto *m* sportif, ≈ pronostics *mpl* (sur les matchs de football)

footbrake ['futbreɪk] *n* frein *m* à pédale

footbridge ['futbrɪdʒ] *n* passerelle *f*

foothills ['futhɪlz] *npl* contreforts *mpl*

foothold ['futhəuld] *n* prise *f* (de pied)

footing ['futɪŋ] *n* (*fig*) position *f*; **to lose one's ~** perdre pied; **on an equal ~** sur pied d'égalité

footlights ['futlaɪts] *npl* rampe *f*

footnote ['futnəut] *n* note *f* (en bas de page)

footpath ['futpɑːθ] *n* sentier *m*; (*in street*) trottoir *m*

footprint ['futprɪnt] *n* trace *f* (de pied)

footstep ['futstɛp] *n* pas *m*

footwear ['futwɛəʳ] *n* chaussures *fpl*

 KEYWORD

for [fɔːʳ] *prep* **1** (*indicating destination, intention, purpose*) pour; **the train for London** le train pour (or à destination de) Londres; **he left for Rome** il est parti pour Rome; **he went for the paper** il est allé chercher le journal; **is this for me?** c'est pour moi?; **it's time for lunch** c'est l'heure du déjeuner; **what's it for?** ça sert à quoi?; **what for?** (*why*) pourquoi?; (*to what end*) pour quoi faire?, à quoi bon?; **for sale** à vendre; **to pray for peace** prier pour la paix

2 (*on behalf of, representing*) pour; **the MP for Hove** le député de Hove; **to work for sb/sth** travailler pour qn/qch; **I'll ask him for you** je vais lui demander pour toi; **G for George** G comme Georges

3 (*because of*) pour; **for this reason** pour cette raison; **for fear of being criticized** de peur d'être critiqué

4 (*with regard to*) pour; **it's cold for July** il fait froid pour juillet; **a gift for languages** un don pour les langues

5 (*in exchange for*): **I sold it for £5** je l'ai vendu 5 livres; **to pay 50 pence for a ticket** payer un billet 50 pence

6 (*in favour of*) pour; **are you for or against us?** êtes-vous pour ou contre nous?; **I'm all for it** je suis tout à fait pour; **vote for X** votez pour X

7 (*referring to distance*) pendant, sur; **there are roadworks for 5 km** il y a des travaux sur or pendant 5 km; **we walked for miles** nous avons marché pendant des kilomètres

8 (*referring to time*) pendant; depuis; pour; **he was away for 2 years** il a été absent pendant 2 ans; **she will be away for a month** elle sera absente (pendant) un mois; **it hasn't rained for 3 weeks** ça fait 3 semaines qu'il ne pleut pas, il ne pleut pas depuis 3 semaines; **I have known her for years** je la connais depuis des années; **can you do it for tomorrow?** est-ce que tu peux le faire pour demain?

9 (*with infinitive clauses*): **it is not for me to decide** ce n'est pas à moi de décider; **it would be best for you to leave** le mieux serait que vous partiez; **there is still time for you to do it** vous avez encore le temps de le faire; **for this to be possible ...** pour que cela soit possible ..

10 (*in spite of*): **for all that** malgré cela, néanmoins; **for all his work/efforts** malgré tout son travail/tous ses efforts; **for all his complaints, he's very fond of her** il a beau

se plaindre, il l'aime beaucoup
▷ *conj* (*since, as: formal*) car

forage ['fɔrɪdʒ] *n* fourrage *m* ▷ *vi* fourrager, fouiller

foray ['fɔreɪ] *n* incursion *f*

forbid (*pt* **forbad** *or* **forbade**, *pp* **forbidden**) [fə'bɪd, -'bæd, -'bɪdn] *vt* défendre, interdire; **to ~ sb to do** défendre *or* interdire à qn de faire

forbidden [fə'bɪdn] *adj* défendu(e)

forbidding [fə'bɪdɪŋ] *adj* d'aspect *or* d'allure sévère *or* sombre

force [fɔːs] *n* force *f* ▷ *vt* forcer; (*push*) pousser (de force); **Forces** *npl*: **the F~s** (*Brit Mil*) les forces armées; **to ~ o.s. to do** se forcer à faire; **to ~ sb to do sth** forcer qn à faire qch; **in ~** (*being used: rule, law, prices*) en vigueur; (*in large numbers*) en force; **to come into ~** entrer en vigueur; **a ~ 5 wind** un vent de force 5; **the sales ~** (*Comm*) la force de vente; **to join ~s** unir ses forces; **force back** *vt* (*crowd, enemy*) repousser; (*tears*) refouler; **force down** *vt* (*food*) se forcer à manger

forced [fɔːst] *adj* forcé(e)

force-feed ['fɔːsfiːd] *vt* nourrir de force

forceful ['fɔːsful] *adj* énergique

forcibly ['fɔːsəblɪ] *adv* par la force, de force; (*vigorously*) énergiquement

ford [fɔːd] *n* gué *m* ▷ *vt* passer à gué

fore [fɔːʳ] *n*: **to the ~** en évidence; **to come to the ~** se faire remarquer

forearm ['fɔːrɑːm] *n* avant-bras *m inv*

foreboding [fɔː'bəudɪŋ] *n* pressentiment *m* (néfaste)

forecast ['fɔːkɑːst] *n* prévision *f*; (*also: weather ~*) prévisions *fpl* météorologiques, météo *f* ▷ *vt* (*irreg like: cast*) prévoir

forecourt ['fɔːkɔːt] *n* (*of garage*) devant *m*

forefinger ['fɔːfɪŋgəʳ] *n* index *m*

forefront ['fɔːfrʌnt] *n*: **in the ~ of** au premier rang *or* plan de

foregone ['fɔːgɔn] *adj*: **it's a ~ conclusion** c'est à prévoir, c'est couru d'avance

foreground ['fɔːgraund] *n* premier plan ▷ *cpd* (*Comput*) prioritaire

forehead ['fɔrɪd] *n* front *m*

foreign ['fɔrɪn] *adj* étranger(-ère); (*trade*) extérieur(e); (*travel*) à l'étranger

foreign currency *n* devises étrangères

foreigner ['fɔrɪnəʳ] *n* étranger(-ère)

foreign exchange *n* (*system*) change *m*; (*money*) devises *fpl*

Foreign Office *n* (*Brit*) ministère *m* des Affaires étrangères

Foreign Secretary *n* (*Brit*) ministre *m* des Affaires étrangères

foreleg ['fɔːleg] *n* patte *f* de devant, jambe antérieure

foreman *irreg* ['fɔːmən] *n* (*in construction*) contremaître *m*; (*Law: of jury*) président *m* (du jury)

foremost ['fɔːməust] *adj* le/la plus en vue, premier(-ière) ▷ *adv*: **first and ~** avant tout, tout d'abord

forename ['fɔːneɪm] *n* prénom *m*

forensic [fə'rensɪk] *adj*: **~ medicine** médecine légale; **~ expert** expert *m* de la police, expert légiste

forerunner ['fɔːrʌnəʳ] *n* précurseur *m*

foresee (*pt* **foresaw**, *pp* **foreseen**) [fɔː'siː, -'sɔː, -'siːn] *vt* prévoir

foreseeable [fɔː'siːəbl] *adj* prévisible

foreseen [fɔː'siːn] *pp of* **foresee**

foreshadow [fɔː'ʃædəu] *vt* présager, annoncer, laisser prévoir

foresight ['fɔːsaɪt] *n* prévoyance *f*

forest ['fɔrɪst] *n* forêt *f*

forestry ['fɔrɪstrɪ] *n* sylviculture *f*

foretaste ['fɔːteɪst] *n* avant-goût *m*

foretell (*pt, pp* **foretold**) [fɔː'tel, -'təuld] *vt* prédire

foretold [fɔː'təuld] *pt, pp of* **foretell**

forever [fə'revəʳ] *adv* pour toujours; (*fig: endlessly*) continuellement

foreword ['fɔːwəːd] *n* avant-propos *m inv*

forfeit ['fɔːfɪt] *n* prix *m*, rançon *f* ▷ *vt* perdre; (*one's life, health*) payer de

forgave [fə'geɪv] *pt of* **forgive**

forge [fɔːdʒ] *n* forge *f* ▷ *vt* (*signature*) contrefaire; (*wrought iron*) forger; **to ~ documents/a will** fabriquer de faux papiers/un faux testament; **to ~ money** (*Brit*) fabriquer de la fausse monnaie; **forge ahead** *vi* pousser de l'avant, prendre de l'avance

forged [fɔːdʒd] *adj* faux/fausse

forger ['fɔːdʒəʳ] *n* faussaire *m*

forgery ['fɔːdʒərɪ] *n* faux *m*, contrefaçon *f*

forget (*pt* **forgot**, *pp* **forgotten**) [fə'get, -'gɔt, -'gɔtn] *vt, vi* oublier; **to ~ to do sth** oublier de faire qch; **to ~ about sth** (*accidentally*) oublier qch; (*on purpose*) ne plus penser à qch; **I've forgotten my key/passport** j'ai oublié ma clé/mon passeport

forgetful [fə'getful] *adj* distrait(e), étourdi(e); **~ of** oublieux(-euse) de

forget-me-not [fə'getmɪnɔt] *n* myosotis *m*

forgive (*pt* **forgave**, *pp* **forgiven**) [fə'gɪv, -'geɪv, -'gɪvn] *vt* pardonner; **to ~ sb for sth/ for doing sth** pardonner qch à qn/à qn de faire qch

forgiveness [fə'gɪvnɪs] *n* pardon *m*

forgo (*pt* **forwent**, *pp* **forgone**) [fɔː'gəu, -'went, -'gɔn] *vt* = **forego**

forgot [fə'gɔt] *pt of* **forget**

forgotten [fə'gɔtn] *pp of* **forget**

fork [fɔːk] *n* (*for eating*) fourchette *f*; (*for gardening*) fourche *f*; (*of roads*) bifurcation *f*; (*of railways*) embranchement *m* ▷ *vi* (*road*) bifurquer; **fork out** (*inf: pay*) *vt* allonger, se fendre de ▷ *vi* casquer

fork-lift truck ['fɔːklɪft-] n chariot élévateur

forlorn [fə'lɔːn] adj (person) délaissé(e); (deserted) abandonné(e); (hope, attempt) désespéré(e)

form [fɔːm] n forme f; (Scol) classe f; (questionnaire) formulaire m ▷ vt former; (habit) contracter; **in the ~ of** sous forme de; **to ~ part of sth** faire partie de qch; **to be on good ~** (Sport: fig) être en forme; **on top ~** en pleine forme

formal ['fɔːməl] adj (offer, receipt) en bonne et due forme; (person) cérémonieux(-euse), à cheval sur les convenances; (occasion, dinner) officiel(le); (garden) à la française; (Art, Philosophy) formel(le); (clothes) de soirée

formality [fɔː'mælɪtɪ] n formalité f, cérémonie(s) f(pl)

formally ['fɔːməlɪ] adv officiellement; formellement; cérémonieusement

format ['fɔːmæt] n format m ▷ vt (Comput) formater

formation [fɔː'meɪʃən] n formation f

formative ['fɔːmətɪv] adj: **~ years** années fpl d'apprentissage (fig) or de formation (d'un enfant, d'un adolescent)

former ['fɔːmə'] adj ancien(ne); (before n) précédent(e); **the ~ ... the latter** le premier ... le second, celui-là ... celui-ci; **the ~ president** l'ex-président; **the ~ Yugoslavia/ Soviet Union** l'ex Yougoslavie/Union Soviétique

formerly ['fɔːməlɪ] adv autrefois

formidable ['fɔːmɪdəbl] adj redoutable

formula ['fɔːmjulə] n formule f; **F~ One** (Aut) Formule une

forsake (pt **forsook**, pp **forsaken**) [fə'seɪk, -'suk, -'seɪkən] vt abandonner

fort [fɔːt] n fort m; **to hold the ~** (fig) assurer la permanence

forte ['fɔːtɪ] n (point) fort m

forth [fɔːθ] adv en avant; **to go back and ~** aller et venir; **and so ~** et ainsi de suite

forthcoming [fɔːθ'kʌmɪŋ] adj qui va paraître or avoir lieu prochainement; (character) ouvert(e), communicatif(-ive); (available) disponible

forthright ['fɔːθraɪt] adj franc/franche, direct(e)

forthwith ['fɔːθ'wɪθ] adv sur le champ

fortieth ['fɔːtɪɪθ] num quarantième

fortify ['fɔːtɪfaɪ] vt (city) fortifier; (person) remonter

fortitude ['fɔːtɪtjuːd] n courage m, force f d'âme

fortnight ['fɔːtnaɪt] n (Brit) quinzaine f, quinze jours mpl; **it's a ~ since ...** il y a quinze jours que ...

fortnightly ['fɔːtnaɪtlɪ] adj bimensuel(le) ▷ adv tous les quinze jours

fortress ['fɔːtrɪs] n forteresse f

fortunate ['fɔːtʃənɪt] adj heureux(-euse); (person) chanceux(-euse); **to be ~** avoir de la

chance; **it is ~ that** c'est une chance que, il est heureux que

fortunately ['fɔːtʃənɪtlɪ] adv heureusement, par bonheur

fortune ['fɔːtʃən] n chance f; (wealth) fortune f; **to make a ~** faire fortune

fortune-teller ['fɔːtʃəntɛlə'] n diseuse f de bonne aventure

forty ['fɔːtɪ] num quarante

forum ['fɔːrəm] n forum m, tribune f

forward ['fɔːwəd] adj (movement, position) en avant, vers l'avant; (not shy) effronté(e); (in time) en avance; (Comm: delivery, sales, exchange) à terme ▷ adv (also: **~s**) en avant ▷ n (Sport) avant m ▷ vt (letter) faire suivre; (parcel, goods) expédier; (fig) promouvoir, favoriser; **to look ~ to sth** attendre qch avec impatience; **to move ~** avancer; **"please ~"** "prière de faire suivre"; **~ planning** planification f à long terme

forwarding address n adresse f de réexpédition

forward slash n barre f oblique

fossil ['fɔsl] adj, n fossile m; **~ fuel** combustible m fossile

foster ['fɔstə'] vt (encourage) encourager, favoriser; (child) élever (sans adopter)

foster child n enfant élevé dans une famille d'accueil

foster parent n parent qui élève un enfant sans l'adopter

fought [fɔːt] pt, pp of **fight**

foul [faul] adj (weather, smell, food) infect(e); (language) ordurier(-ière); (deed) infâme ▷ n (Football) faute f ▷ vt (dirty) salir, encrasser; (football player) commettre une faute sur; (entangle: anchor, propeller) emmêler; **he's got a ~ temper** il a un caractère de chien

foul play n (Sport) jeu déloyal; (Law) acte criminel; **~ is not suspected** la mort (or l'incendie etc) n'a pas de causes suspectes, on écarte l'hypothèse d'un meurtre (or d'un acte criminel)

found [faund] pt, pp of **find** ▷ vt (establish) fonder

foundation [faun'deɪʃən] n (act) fondation f; (base) fondement m; (also: **~ cream**) fond m de teint; **foundations** npl (of building) fondations fpl; **to lay the ~s** (fig) poser les fondements

founder ['faundə'] n fondateur m ▷ vi couler, sombrer

foundry ['faundrɪ] n fonderie f

fountain ['fauntɪn] n fontaine f

fountain pen n stylo m (à encre)

four [fɔː'] num quatre; **on all ~s** à quatre pattes

four-letter word ['fɔːlɛtə-] n obscénité f, gros mot

four-poster ['fɔː'pəustə'] n (also: **~ bed**) lit m à baldaquin

fourteen ['fɔː'tiːn] num quatorze

fourteenth ['fɔː'tiːnθ] num quatorzième

fourth ['fɔːθ] *num* quatrième ▷ *n* (*Aut: also:* **~ gear**) quatrième *f*

four-wheel drive ['fɔːwiːl-] *n* (*Aut: car*) voiture *f* à quatre roues motrices; **with ~** à quatre roues motrices

fowl [faul] *n* volaille *f*

fox [fɒks] *n* renard *m* ▷ *vt* mystifier

foyer ['fɔɪeɪ] *n* (*in hotel*) vestibule *m*; (*Theat*) foyer *m*

fracking ['frækɪŋ] *n* fracturation *f* hydraulique

fraction ['frækʃən] *n* fraction *f*

fracture ['fræktʃəʳ] *n* fracture *f* ▷ *vt* fracturer

fragile ['frædʒaɪl] *adj* fragile

fragment ['frægmənt] *n* fragment *m*

fragrance ['freɪɡrəns] *n* parfum *m*

fragrant ['freɪɡrənt] *adj* parfumé(e), odorant(e)

frail [freɪl] *adj* fragile, délicat(e); (*person*) frêle

frame [freɪm] *n* (*of building*) charpente *f*; (*of human, animal*) charpente, ossature *f*; (*of picture*) cadre *m*; (*of door, window*) encadrement *m*, chambranle *m*; (*of spectacles: also:* **~s**) monture *f* ▷ *vt* (*picture*) encadrer; (*theory, plan*) construire, élaborer; **to ~ sb** (*inf*) monter un coup contre qn; **~ of mind** disposition *f* d'esprit

framework ['freɪmwəːk] *n* structure *f*

France [frɑːns] *n* la France; **in ~** en France

franchise ['fræntʃaɪz] *n* (*Pol*) droit *m* de vote; (*Comm*) franchise *f*

frank [fræŋk] *adj* franc/franche ▷ *vt* (*letter*) affranchir

frankly ['fræŋklɪ] *adv* franchement

frantic ['fræntɪk] *adj* (*hectic*) frénétique; (*need, desire*) effréné(e); (*distraught*) hors de soi

fraternity [frə'təːnɪtɪ] *n* (*in club*) communauté *f*, confrérie *f*; (*spirit*) fraternité *f*

fraud [frɔːd] *n* supercherie *f*, fraude *f*, tromperie *f*; (*person*) imposteur *m*

fraught [frɔːt] *adj* (*tense*) très tendu(e); (*: situation*) pénible; **~ with** (*difficulties etc*) chargé(e), plein(e) de

fray [freɪ] *n* bagarre *f*; (*Mil*) combat *m* ▷ *vt* effilocher ▷ *vi* s'effilocher; **tempers were ~ed** les gens commençaient à s'énerver; **her nerves were ~ed** elle était à bout de nerfs

freak [friːk] *n* (*eccentric person*) phénomène *m*; (*unusual event*) hasard *m* extraordinaire; (*pej: fanatic*): **health food ~** fana *m/f* or obsédé(e) de l'alimentation saine ▷ *adj* (*storm*) exceptionnel(le); (*accident*) bizarre; **freak out** *vi* (*inf: drop out*) se marginaliser; (*: on drugs*) se défoncer

freckle ['frɛkl] *n* tache *f* de rousseur

free [friː] *adj* libre; (*gratis*) gratuit(e); (*liberal*) généreux(-euse), large ▷ *vt* (*prisoner etc*) libérer; (*jammed object or person*) dégager; **is this seat ~?** la place est libre?; **to give sb a ~ hand** donner carte blanche à qn; **~ and easy** sans façon, décontracté(e); **admission ~** entrée libre; **~ (of charge)** gratuitement

freedom ['friːdəm] *n* liberté *f*

Freefone® ['friːfəun] *n* numéro vert

free-for-all ['friːfərɔːl] *n* mêlée générale

free gift *n* prime *f*

freehold ['friːhəuld] *n* propriété foncière libre

free kick *n* (*Sport*) coup franc

freelance ['friːlɑːns] *adj* (*journalist etc*) indépendant(e), free-lance *inv*; (*work*) en free-lance ▷ *adv* en free-lance

freely ['friːlɪ] *adv* librement; (*liberally*) libéralement

freemason ['friːmeɪsn] *n* franc-maçon *m*

Freepost® ['friːpəust] *n* (*Brit*) port payé

free-range ['friː'reɪndʒ] *adj* (*egg*) de ferme; (*chicken*) fermier

free trade *n* libre-échange *m*

freeway ['friːweɪ] *n* (*US*) autoroute *f*

free will *n* libre arbitre *m*; **of one's own ~** de son plein gré

freeze [friːz] (*pt* **froze**, *pp* **frozen**) [frəuz, 'frəuzn] *vi* geler ▷ *vt* geler; (*food*) congeler; (*prices, salaries*) bloquer, geler ▷ *n* gel *m*; (*of prices, salaries*) blocage *m*; **freeze over** *vi* (*river*) geler; (*windscreen*) se couvrir de givre or de glace; **freeze up** *vi* geler

freeze-dried ['friːzdraɪd] *adj* lyophilisé(e)

freezer ['friːzəʳ] *n* congélateur *m*

freezing ['friːzɪŋ] *adj*: **~ (cold)** (*room etc*) glacial(e); (*person, hands*) gelé(e), glacé(e) ▷ *n*: **3 degrees below ~** 3 degrés au-dessous de zéro; **it's ~** il fait un froid glacial

freezing point *n* point *m* de congélation

freight [freɪt] *n* (*goods*) fret *m*, cargaison *f*; (*money charged*) fret, prix *m* du transport; **~ forward** port dû; **~ inward** port payé par le destinataire

freight train *n* (*US*) train *m* de marchandises

French [frɛntʃ] *adj* français(e) ▷ *n* (*Ling*) français *m*; **the ~** *npl* les Français; **what's the ~ (word) for ...?** comment dit-on ... en français?

French bean *n* (*Brit*) haricot vert

French bread *n* pain *m* français

French dressing *n* (*Culin*) vinaigrette *f*

French fried potatoes, French fries (*US*) *npl* (pommes de terre *fpl*) frites *fpl*

French horn *n* (*Mus*) cor *m* (d'harmonie)

French kiss *n* baiser profond

French loaf *n* ≈ pain *m*, ≈ parisien *m*

Frenchman *irreg* ['frɛntʃmən] *n* Français *m*

French stick *n* ≈ baguette *f*

French window *n* porte-fenêtre *f*

Frenchwoman *irreg* ['frɛntʃwumən] *n* Française *f*

frenzy ['frɛnzɪ] *n* frénésie *f*

frequency ['friːkwənsɪ] *n* fréquence *f*

frequent *adj* ['friːkwənt] fréquent(e) ▷ *vt* [frɪ'kwɛnt] fréquenter

frequently ['friːkwəntlɪ] *adv* fréquemment

fresh [frɛʃ] *adj* frais/fraîche; (*new*) nouveau/nouvelle; (*cheeky*) familier(-ière), culotté(e); **to make a ~ start** prendre un nouveau départ

freshen ['freʃən] vi (wind, air) fraîchir; **freshen up** vi faire un brin de toilette

fresher ['freʃəʳ] n (Brit University: inf) bizuth m, étudiant(e) de première année

freshly ['freʃlɪ] adv nouvellement, récemment

freshman (US) irreg ['freʃmən] n = **fresher**

freshness ['freʃnɪs] n fraîcheur f

freshwater ['freʃwɔːtəʳ] adj (fish) d'eau douce

fret [fret] vi s'agiter, se tracasser

friar ['fraɪəʳ] n moine m, frère m

friction ['frɪkʃən] n friction f, frottement m

Friday ['fraɪdɪ] n vendredi m; see also **Tuesday**

fridge [frɪdʒ] n (Brit) frigo m, frigidaire® m

fried [fraɪd] pt, pp of **fry** ▷ adj frit(e); ~ **egg** œuf m sur le plat

friend [frend] n ami(e) f ▷ vt (Internet) ajouter comme ami(e); **to make ~s with** se lier (d'amitié) avec

friendly ['frendlɪ] adj amical(e); (kind) sympathique, gentil(le); (place) accueillant(e); (Pol: country) ami(e) ▷ n (also: ~ **match**) match amical; **to be ~ with** être ami(e) avec; **to be ~ to** être bien disposé(e) à l'égard de

friendship ['frendʃɪp] n amitié f

fries [fraɪz] (esp US) npl = **chips**

frieze [friːz] n frise f, bordure f

frigate ['frɪgɪt] n (Naut: modern) frégate f

fright [fraɪt] n peur f, effroi m; **to give sb a ~** faire peur à qn; **to take ~** prendre peur, s'effrayer; **she looks a ~** elle a l'air d'un épouvantail

frighten ['fraɪtn] vt effrayer, faire peur à; **frighten away, frighten off** vt (birds, children etc) faire fuir, effaroucher

frightened ['fraɪtnd] adj: **to be ~ (of)** avoir peur (de)

frightening ['fraɪtnɪŋ] adj effrayant(e)

frightful ['fraɪtful] adj affreux(-euse)

frigid ['frɪdʒɪd] adj frigide

frill [frɪl] n (of dress) volant m; (of shirt) jabot m; **without ~s** (fig) sans manières

fringe [frɪndʒ] n (Brit: of hair) frange f; (edge: of forest etc) bordure f; (fig): **on the ~** en marge

fringe benefits npl avantages sociaux or en nature

Frisbee® ['frɪzbɪ] n Frisbee® m

frisk [frɪsk] vt fouiller

fritter ['frɪtəʳ] n beignet m; **fritter away** vt gaspiller

frivolous ['frɪvələs] adj frivole

frizzy ['frɪzɪ] adj crépu(e)

fro [frəu] adv see **to**

frock [frɔk] n robe f

frog [frɔg] n grenouille f; **to have a ~ in one's throat** avoir un chat dans la gorge

frogman irreg ['frɔgmən] n homme-grenouille m

frolic ['frɔlɪk] n ébats mpl ▷ vi folâtrer, batifoler

○ **KEYWORD**

from [frɔm] prep **1** (indicating starting place, origin etc) de; **where do you come from?, where are you from?** d'où venez-vous?; **where has he come from?** d'où arrive-t-il?; **from London to Paris** de Londres à Paris; **to escape from sb/sth** échapper à qn/qch; **a letter/telephone call from my sister** une lettre/un appel de ma sœur; **to drink from the bottle** boire à (même) la bouteille; **tell him from me that ...** dites-lui de ma part que ...

2 (indicating time) (à partir) de; **from one o'clock to** or **until** or **till two** d'une heure à deux heures; **from January (on)** à partir de janvier

3 (indicating distance) de; **the hotel is one kilometre from the beach** l'hôtel est à un kilomètre de la plage

4 (indicating price, number etc) de; **prices range from £10 to £50** les prix varient entre 10 livres et 50 livres; **the interest rate was increased from 9% to 10%** le taux d'intérêt est passé de 9% à 10%

5 (indicating difference) de; **he can't tell red from green** il ne peut pas distinguer le rouge du vert; **to be different from sb/sth** être différent de qn/qch

6 (because of, on the basis of): **from what he says** d'après ce qu'il dit; **weak from hunger** affaibli par la faim

front [frʌnt] n (of house, dress) devant m; (of coach, train) avant m; (of book) couverture f; (promenade: also: **sea ~**) bord m de mer; (Mil, Pol, Meteorology) front m; (fig: appearances) contenance f, façade f ▷ adj de devant; (page, row) premier(-ière); (seat, wheel) avant inv ▷ vi: **to ~ onto sth** donner sur qch; **in ~ (of)** devant

frontage ['frʌntɪdʒ] n façade f; (of shop) devanture f

front door n porte f d'entrée; (of car) portière f avant

frontier ['frʌntɪəʳ] n frontière f

front page n première page

front room n (Brit) pièce f de devant, salon m

front-wheel drive ['frʌntwiːl-] n traction f avant

frost [frɔst] n gel m, gelée f; (also: **hoar~**) givre m

frostbite ['frɔstbaɪt] n gelures fpl

frosted ['frɔstɪd] adj (glass) dépoli(e); (esp US: cake) glacé(e)

frosting ['frɔstɪŋ] n (esp US: on cake) glaçage m

frosty ['frɔstɪ] adj (window) couvert(e) de givre; (weather, welcome) glacial(e)

froth [frɔθ] n mousse f; écume f

frown [fraun] n froncement m de sourcils ▷ vi froncer les sourcils; **frown on** vt (fig) désapprouver

froze [frəuz] *pt of* **freeze**

frozen ['frəuzn] *pp of* **freeze** ▷ *adj (food)* congelé(e); *(very cold: person: Comm: assets)* gelé(e)

fruit [fru:t] *n (pl inv)* fruit *m*

fruiterer ['fru:tərər] *n* fruitier *m*, marchand(e) de fruits; **~'s (shop)** fruiterie *f*

fruitful ['fru:tful] *adj* fructueux(-euse); *(plant, soil)* fécond(e)

fruition [fru:'ɪʃən] *n*: **to come to ~** se réaliser

fruit juice *n* jus *m* de fruit

fruit machine *n (Brit)* machine *f* à sous

fruit salad *n* salade *f* de fruits

frustrate [frʌs'treɪt] *vt* frustrer; *(plot, plans)* faire échouer

frustrated [frʌs'treɪtɪd] *adj* frustré(e)

fry *(pt, pp* **fried**) [fraɪ, -d] *vt* (faire) frire ▷ *n*: **small ~** le menu fretin

frying pan ['fraɪɪŋ-] *n* poêle *f* (à frire)

ft. *abbr* = **foot; feet**

fudge [fʌdʒ] *n (Culin)* sorte de confiserie à base de sucre, de beurre et de lait ▷ *vt (issue, problem)* esquiver

fuel ['fjuəl] *n (for heating)* combustible *m*; *(for engine)* carburant *m*

fuel oil *n* mazout *m*

fuel poverty *n* pauvreté *f* énergétique

fuel tank *n* cuve *f* à mazout, citerne *f*; *(in vehicle)* réservoir *m* de or à carburant

fugitive ['fju:dʒɪtɪv] *n* fugitif(-ive)

fulfil, *(US)* **fulfill** [ful'fɪl] *vt (function, condition)* remplir; *(order)* exécuter; *(wish, desire)* satisfaire, réaliser

fulfilment, *(US)* **fulfillment** [ful'fɪlmənt] *n (of wishes)* réalisation *f*

full [ful] *adj* plein(e); *(details, hotel, bus)* complet(-ète); *(price)* fort(e), normal(e); *(busy: day)* chargé(e); *(skirt)* ample, large ▷ *adv*: **to know ~ well that** savoir fort bien que; **~ (up)** *(hotel etc)* complet(-ète); **I'm ~ (up)** j'ai bien mangé; **~ employment/fare** plein emploi/tarif; **a ~ two hours** deux bonnes heures; **at ~ speed** à toute vitesse; **in ~** *(reproduce, quote, pay)* intégralement; *(write name etc)* en toutes lettres

full-length [ful'leŋθ] *adj (portrait)* en pied; *(coat)* long(ue); **~ film** long métrage

full moon *n* pleine lune

full-scale ['fulskeɪl] *adj (model)* grandeur nature *inv*; *(search, retreat)* complet(-ète), total(e)

full stop *n* point *m*

full-time ['ful'taɪm] *adj, adv (work)* à plein temps ▷ *n (Sport)* fin *f* du match

fully ['fulɪ] *adv* entièrement, complètement; *(at least)*: **~ as big** au moins aussi grand

fully-fledged ['fulɪ'fledʒd] *adj (teacher, barrister)* diplômé(e); *(citizen, member)* à part entière

fumble ['fʌmbl] *vi* fouiller, tâtonner ▷ *vt (ball)* mal réceptionner, cafouiller; **fumble**

with *vt fus* tripoter

fume [fju:m] *vi (rage)* rager

fumes [fju:mz] *npl* vapeurs *fpl*, émanations *fpl*, gaz *mpl*

fun [fʌn] *n* amusement *m*, divertissement *m*; **to have ~** s'amuser; **for ~** pour rire; **it's not much ~** ce n'est pas très drôle *or* amusant; **to make ~ of** se moquer de

function ['fʌŋkʃən] *n* fonction *f*; *(reception, dinner)* cérémonie *f*, soirée officielle ▷ *vi* fonctionner; **to ~ as** faire office de

functional ['fʌŋkʃənl] *adj* fonctionnel(le)

fund [fʌnd] *n* caisse *f*, fonds *m*; *(source, store)* source *f*, mine *f*; **funds** *npl (money)* fonds *mpl*

fundamental [fʌndə'mɛntl] *adj* fondamental(e); **fundamentals** *npl* principes *mpl* de base

funeral ['fju:nərəl] *n* enterrement *m*, obsèques *fpl (more formal occasion)*

funeral director *n* entrepreneur *m* des pompes funèbres

funeral parlour *n (Brit)* dépôt *m* mortuaire

funeral service *n* service *m* funèbre

funfair ['fʌnfɛər] *n (Brit)* fête (foraine)

fungus *(pl* **fungi**) ['fʌŋgəs, -gaɪ] *n* champignon *m*; *(mould)* moisissure *f*

funnel ['fʌnl] *n* entonnoir *m*; *(of ship)* cheminée *f*

funny ['fʌnɪ] *adj* amusant(e), drôle; *(strange)* curieux(-euse), bizarre

fur [fə:r] *n* fourrure *f*; *(Brit: in kettle etc)* (dépôt *m* de) tartre *m*

fur coat *n* manteau *m* de fourrure

furious ['fjuərɪəs] *adj* furieux(-euse); *(effort)* acharné(e); **to be ~ with sb** être dans une fureur noire contre qn

furlong ['fə:lɔŋ] *n* = 201.17 m *(terme d'hippisme)*

furnace ['fə:nɪs] *n* fourneau *m*

furnish ['fə:nɪʃ] *vt* meubler; *(supply)* fournir; **~ed flat** *or (US)* **apartment** meublé *m*

furnishings ['fə:nɪʃɪŋz] *npl* mobilier *m*, articles *mpl* d'ameublement

furniture ['fə:nɪtʃər] *n* meubles *mpl*, mobilier *m*; **piece of ~** meuble *m*

furrow ['fʌrəu] *n* sillon *m*

furry ['fə:rɪ] *adj (animal)* à fourrure; *(toy)* en peluche

further ['fə:ðər] *adj* supplémentaire, autre; nouveau/nouvelle ▷ *adv* plus loin; *(more)* davantage; *(moreover)* de plus ▷ *vt* faire avancer *or* progresser, promouvoir; **how much ~ is it?** quelle distance *or* combien reste-t-il à parcourir?; **until ~ notice** jusqu'à nouvel ordre *or* avis; **~ to your letter of ...** *(Comm)* suite à votre lettre du ...

further education *n* enseignement *m* postscolaire *(recyclage, formation professionnelle)*

furthermore [fə:ðə'mɔːr] *adv* de plus, en outre

furthest ['fə:ðɪst] *superlative of* **far**

fury ['fjuərɪ] *n* fureur *f*

fuse, (US) **fuze** [fju:z] n fusible m; (for bomb etc) amorce f, détonateur m ▷ vt, vi (metal) fondre; (fig) fusionner; (Brit: Elec): **to ~ the lights** faire sauter les fusibles or les plombs; **a ~ has blown** un fusible a sauté

fuse box n boîte f à fusibles

fusion ['fju:ʒən] n fusion f

fuss [fʌs] n (anxiety, excitement) chichis mpl, façons fpl; (commotion) tapage m; (complaining, trouble) histoire(s) f(pl) ▷ vi faire des histoires ▷ vt (person) embêter; **to make a ~** faire des façons (or des histoires); **to make a ~ of sb** dorloter qn; **fuss over** vt fus (person) dorloter

fussy ['fʌsɪ] adj (person) tatillon(ne), difficile, chichiteux(-euse); (dress, style) tarabiscoté(e); **I'm not ~** (inf) ça m'est égal

future ['fju:tʃə'] adj futur(e) ▷ n avenir m; (Ling) futur m; **futures** npl (Comm) opérations fpl à terme; **in (the) ~** à l'avenir; **in the near/immediate ~** dans un avenir proche/immédiat

fuze [fju:z] n, vt, vi (US) = **fuse**

fuzzy ['fʌzɪ] adj (Phot) flou(e); (hair) crépu(e)

FYI abbr = **for your information**

g

G¹, g [dʒi:] n (letter) G, g m; (Mus): **G** sol m; **G for George** G comme Gaston

G² n abbr (Brit Scol: = good) b (= bien); (US Cine: = general (audience)) ≈ tous publics; (Pol: = G8) G8 m

g. abbr (= gram) g; (= gravity) g

gabble ['gæbl] vi bredouiller; jacasser

gable ['geɪbl] n pignon m

gadget ['gædʒɪt] n gadget m

Gaelic ['geɪlɪk] adj, n (Ling) gaélique (m)

gag [gæg] n (on mouth) bâillon m; (joke) gag m ▷ vt (prisoner etc) bâillonner ▷ vi (choke) étouffer

gaiety ['geɪɪtɪ] n gaieté f

gain [geɪn] n (improvement) gain m; (profit) gain, profit m ▷ vt gagner ▷ vi (watch) avancer; **to ~ from/by** gagner de/à; **to ~ on sb** (catch up) rattraper qn; **to ~ 3lbs (in weight)** prendre 3 livres; **to ~ ground** gagner du terrain

gal. abbr = **gallon**

gala ['gɑ:lə] n gala m; **swimming ~** grand concours de natation

galaxy ['gæləksɪ] n galaxie f

gale [geɪl] n coup m de vent; **~ force 10** vent m de force 10

gallant ['gælənt] adj vaillant(e), brave; (towards ladies) empressé(e), galant(e)

gall bladder ['gɔ:l-] n vésicule f biliaire

gallery ['gælərɪ] n galerie f; (also: **art ~**) musée m; (: private) galerie; (for spectators) tribune f; (: in theatre) dernier balcon

gallon ['gæln] n gallon m (Brit = 4.543 l; US = 3.785 l), = 8 pints

gallop ['gæləp] n galop m ▷ vi galoper; **~ing inflation** inflation galopante

gallows ['gæləʊz] n potence f

gallstone ['gɔ:lstəʊn] n calcul m (biliaire)

galore [gə'lɔ:ʳ] adv en abondance, à gogo

Gambia ['gæmbɪə] n Gambie f

gambit ['gæmbɪt] n (fig): **(opening) ~** manœuvre f stratégique

gamble ['gæmbl] n pari m, risque calculé ▷ vt, vi jouer; **to ~ on the Stock Exchange** jouer en or à la Bourse; **to ~ on** (fig) miser sur

gambler ['gæmbləʳ] n joueur m

gambling ['gæmblɪŋ] n jeu m

game [geɪm] n jeu m; (event) match m; (of tennis, chess, cards) partie f; (Hunting) gibier m ▷ adj brave; (willing): **to be ~ (for)** être prêt(e) (à or pour); **a ~ of football/tennis** une partie de football/tennis; **big ~** gros gibier; **games** npl (Scol) sport m; (sport event) jeux

gamekeeper ['geɪmkiːpəʳ] n garde-chasse m

gamer ['geɪməʳ] n joueur(-euse) de jeux vidéos

games console ['geɪmz-] n console f de jeux vidéo

game show ['geɪmʃəʊ] n jeu télévisé

gaming ['geɪmɪŋ] n (video games) jeux mpl vidéos

gammon ['gæmən] n (bacon) quartier m de lard fumé; (ham) jambon fumé or salé

gamut ['gæmət] n gamme f

gang [gæŋ] n bande f, groupe m; (of workmen) équipe f; **gang up** vi: **to ~ up on sb** se liguer contre qn

gangster ['gæŋstəʳ] n gangster m, bandit m

gangway ['gæŋweɪ] n passerelle f; (Brit: of bus) couloir central

gaol [dʒeɪl] n, vt (Brit) = **jail**

gap [gæp] n trou m; (in time) intervalle m; (fig) lacune f; vide m; (difference): **~ (between)** écart m (entre)

gape [geɪp] vi (person) être or rester bouche bée; (hole, shirt) être ouvert(e)

gaping ['geɪpɪŋ] adj (hole) béant(e)

gap year n année que certains étudiants prennent pour voyager ou pour travailler avant d'entrer à l'université

garage ['gæra:ʒ] n garage m

garage sale n vide-grenier m

garbage ['ga:bɪdʒ] n (US: rubbish) ordures fpl, détritus mpl; (inf: nonsense) âneries fpl

garbage can n (US) poubelle f, boîte f à ordures

garbage collector n (US) éboueur m

garbled ['ga:bld] adj déformé(e), faussé(e)

garden ['ga:dn] n jardin m ▷ vi jardiner; **gardens** npl (public) jardin public; (private) parc m

garden centre (Brit) n pépinière f, jardinerie f

gardener ['ga:dnəʳ] n jardinier m

gardening ['ga:dnɪŋ] n jardinage m

gargle ['ga:gl] vi se gargariser ▷ n gargarisme m

garish ['geərɪʃ] adj criard(e), voyant(e)

garland ['ga:lənd] n guirlande f; couronne f

garlic ['ga:lɪk] n ail m

garment ['ga:mənt] n vêtement m

garnish ['ga:nɪʃ] (Culin) vt garnir ▷ n décoration f

garrison ['gærɪsn] n garnison f ▷ vt mettre en garnison, stationner

garter ['ga:təʳ] n jarretière f; (US: suspender) jarretelle f

gas [gæs] n gaz m; (used as anaesthetic): **to be given ~** se faire endormir; (US: gasoline) essence f ▷ vt asphyxier; (Mil) gazer; **I can smell ~** ça sent le gaz

gas cooker n (Brit) cuisinière f à gaz

gas cylinder n bouteille f de gaz

gas fire n (Brit) radiateur m à gaz

gash [gæʃ] n entaille f; (on face) balafre f ▷ vt tailler; balafrer

gasket ['gæskɪt] n (Aut) joint m de culasse

gas mask n masque m à gaz

gas meter n compteur m à gaz

gasoline ['gæsəliːn] n (US) essence f

gasp [ga:sp] n halètement m; (of shock etc): **she gave a small ~ of pain** la douleur lui coupa le souffle ▷ vi haleter; (fig) avoir le souffle coupé; **gasp out** vt (say) dire dans un souffle or d'une voix entrecoupée

gas pedal n (US) accélérateur m

gas ring n brûleur m

gas station n (US) station-service f

gas tank n (US Aut) réservoir m d'essence

gas tap n bouton m (de cuisinière à gaz); (on pipe) robinet m à gaz

gastric ['gæstrɪk] adj gastrique

gate [geɪt] n (of garden) portail m; (of field, at level crossing) barrière f; (of building, town, at airport) porte f; (of lock) vanne f

gateau (pl gateaux) ['gætəʊ, -z] n gros gâteau m à la crème

gatecrash ['geɪtkræʃ] vt s'introduire sans invitation dans

gateway ['geɪtweɪ] n porte f

gather ['gæðəʳ] vt (flowers, fruit) cueillir; (pick up) ramasser; (assemble: objects) rassembler; (: people) réunir; (: information) recueillir; (understand) comprendre; (Sewing) froncer ▷ vi (assemble) se rassembler; (dust) s'amasser; (clouds) s'amonceler; **to ~ (from/that)** conclure or déduire (de/que); **as far as I can ~** d'après ce que je comprends; **to ~ speed** prendre de la vitesse

gathering ['gæðərɪŋ] n rassemblement m

gaudy ['gɔ:dɪ] adj voyant(e)

gauge [geɪdʒ] n (standard measure) calibre m; (Rail) écartement m; (instrument) jauge f ▷ vt jauger; (fig: sb's capabilities, character) juger de; **to ~ the right moment** calculer le moment propice; **petrol ~**, (US) **gas ~** jauge d'essence

gaunt [gɔ:nt] *adj* décharné(e); *(grim, desolate)* désolé(e)

gauntlet ['gɔ:ntlɪt] *n (fig)*: **to throw down the ~** jeter le gant; **to run the ~ through an angry crowd** se frayer un passage à travers une foule hostile *or* entre deux haies de manifestants *etc* hostiles

gauze [gɔ:z] *n* gaze *f*

gave [geɪv] *pt of* **give**

gay [geɪ] *adj* homosexuel(le); *(slightly old-fashioned: cheerful)* gai(e), réjoui(e); *(colour)* gai, vif/vive

gaze [geɪz] *n* regard *m* fixe ▷ *vi*: **to ~ at** *vt* fixer du regard

gazump [gə'zʌmp] *vi (Brit)* revenir sur une *promesse de vente* pour accepter un prix plus élevé

GB *abbr* = **Great Britain**

GCE *n abbr (Brit)* = **General Certificate of Education**

GCSE *n abbr (Brit: = General Certificate of Secondary Education)* examen passé à l'âge de 16 ans sanctionnant les connaissances de l'élève; **she's got eight ~s** elle a réussi dans huit matières aux épreuves du GCSE

gear [gɪə'] *n* matériel *m*, équipement *m*; *(Tech)* engrenage *m*; *(Aut)* vitesse *f* ▷ *vt (fig: adapt)* adapter; **top** *or (US)* **high/low ~** quatrième *(or* cinquième)/première vitesse; **in ~** en prise; **out of ~** au point mort; **our service is ~ed to meet the needs of the disabled** notre service répond de façon spécifique aux besoins des handicapés; **gear up** *vi*: **to ~ up (to do)** se préparer (à faire)

gear box *n* boîte *f* de vitesse

gear lever *n* levier *m* de vitesse

gear shift *(US) n* = **gear lever**

gear stick *(Brit) n* = **gear lever**

geese [gi:s] *npl of* **goose**

gel [dʒɛl] *n* gelée *f*; *(Chem)* colloïde *m*

gem [dʒɛm] *n* pierre précieuse

Gemini ['dʒɛmɪnaɪ] *n* les Gémeaux *mpl*; **to be ~** être des Gémeaux

gender ['dʒɛndə'] *n* genre *m*; *(person's sex)* sexe *m*

gene [dʒi:n] *n (Biol)* gène *m*

general ['dʒɛnərl] *n* général *m* ▷ *adj* général(e); **in ~** en général; **the ~ public** le grand public; **~ audit** *(Comm)* vérification annuelle

general anaesthetic, *(US)* **general anesthetic** *n* anesthésie générale

general delivery *n* poste restante

general election *n* élection(s) législative(s)

generalize ['dʒɛnrəlaɪz] *vi* généraliser

general knowledge *n* connaissances générales

generally ['dʒɛnrəlɪ] *adv* généralement

general practitioner *n* généraliste *m/f*

general store *n* épicerie *f*

generate ['dʒɛnəreɪt] *vt* engendrer; *(electricity)* produire

generation [dʒɛnə'reɪʃən] *n* génération *f*; *(of electricity etc)* production *f*

generator ['dʒɛnəreɪtə'] *n* générateur *m*

generosity [dʒɛnə'rɒsɪtɪ] *n* générosité *f*

generous ['dʒɛnərəs] *adj* généreux(-euse); *(copious)* copieux(-euse)

genetic [dʒɪ'nɛtɪk] *adj* génétique; **~ engineering** ingénierie *m* génétique; **~ fingerprinting** système *m* d'empreinte génétique

genetically modified *adj (food etc)* génétiquement modifié(e)

genetics [dʒɪ'nɛtɪks] *n* génétique *f*

Geneva [dʒɪ'ni:və] *n* Genève; **Lake ~** le lac Léman

genial ['dʒi:nɪəl] *adj* cordial(e), chaleureux(-euse); *(climate)* clément(e)

genitals ['dʒɛnɪtlz] *npl* organes génitaux

genius ['dʒi:nɪəs] *n* génie *m*

genome ['dʒi:nəum] *n* génome *m*

gent [dʒɛnt] *n abbr (Brit inf)* = **gentleman**

genteel [dʒɛn'ti:l] *adj* de bon ton, distingué(e)

gentle ['dʒɛntl] *adj* doux/douce; *(breeze, touch)* léger(-ère)

gentleman *irreg* ['dʒɛntlmən] *n* monsieur *m*; *(well-bred man)* gentleman *m*; **~'s agreement** gentleman's agreement *m*

gently ['dʒɛntlɪ] *adv* doucement

gentry ['dʒɛntrɪ] *n* petite noblesse

gents [dʒɛnts] *n* W.-C. *mpl* (pour hommes)

genuine ['dʒɛnjuɪn] *adj* véritable, authentique; *(person, emotion)* sincère

genuinely ['dʒɛnjuɪnlɪ] *adv* sincèrement, vraiment

geographic [dʒɪə'græfɪk], **geographical** [dʒɪə'græfɪkl] *adj* géographique

geography [dʒɪ'ɒgrəfɪ] *n* géographie *f*

geology [dʒɪ'ɒlədʒɪ] *n* géologie *f*

geometric [dʒɪə'mɛtrɪk], **geometrical** [dʒɪə'mɛtrɪkl] *adj* géométrique

geometry [dʒɪ'ɒmətrɪ] *n* géométrie *f*

geranium [dʒɪ'reɪnɪəm] *n* géranium *m*

geriatric [dʒɛrɪ'ætrɪk] *adj* gériatrique ▷ *n* patient(e) gériatrique

germ [dʒə:m] *n (Med)* microbe *m*; *(Biol: fig)* germe *m*

German ['dʒə:mən] *adj* allemand(e) ▷ *n* Allemand(e); *(Ling)* allemand *m*

German measles *n* rubéole *f*

Germany ['dʒə:mənɪ] *n* Allemagne *f*

gesture ['dʒɛstjə'] *n* geste *m*; **as a ~ of friendship** en témoignage d'amitié

KEYWORD

get [gɛt] *(pt, pp* **got**, *US: pp* **gotten)** *vi* **1** *(become, be)* devenir; **to get old/tired** devenir vieux/fatigué, vieillir/se fatiguer; **to get drunk** s'enivrer; **to get ready/washed/shaved** *etc* se préparer/laver/raser *etc*; **to get killed** se faire tuer; **to get dirty** se salir; **to get married** se marier; **when do I get paid?**

quand est-ce que je serai payé?; **it's getting late** il se fait tard

2 (*go*): **to get to/from** aller à/de; **to get home** rentrer chez soi; **how did you get here?** comment es-tu arrivé ici?; **he got across the bridge/under the fence** il a traversé le pont/est passé au-dessous de la barrière

3 (*begin*) commencer *or* se mettre à; **to get to know sb** apprendre à connaître qn; **I'm getting to like him** je commence à l'apprécier; **let's get going** *or* **started** allons-y

4 (*modal aux vb*): **you've got to do it** il faut que vous le fassiez; **I've got to tell the police** je dois le dire à la police

▷ *vt* **1**: **to get sth done** (*do*) faire qch; (*have done*) faire faire qch; **to get sth/sb ready** préparer qch/qn; **to get one's hair cut** se faire couper les cheveux; **to get the car going** *or* **to go** (faire) démarrer la voiture; **to get sb to do sth** faire faire qch à qn; **to get sb drunk** enivrer qn

2 (*obtain*: *money, permission, results*) obtenir, avoir; (*buy*) acheter; (*find*: *job, flat*) trouver; (*fetch*: *person, doctor, object*) aller chercher; **to get sth for sb** procurer qch à qn; **get me Mr Jones, please** (*on phone*) passez-moi Mr Jones, s'il vous plaît; **can I get you a drink?** est-ce que je peux vous servir à boire?

3 (*receive*: *present, letter*) recevoir, avoir; (*acquire*: *reputation*) avoir; (*prize*) obtenir; **what did you get for your birthday?** qu'est-ce que tu as eu pour ton anniversaire?; **how much did you get for the painting?** combien avez-vous vendu le tableau?

4 (*catch*) prendre, saisir, attraper; (*hit*: *target etc*) atteindre; **to get sb by the arm/throat** prendre *or* saisir *or* attraper qn par le bras/à la gorge; **get him!** arrête-le!; **the bullet got him in the leg** il a pris la balle dans la jambe; **he really gets me!** il me porte sur les nerfs!

5 (*take, move*): **to get sth to sb** faire parvenir qch à qn; **do you think we'll get it through the door?** on arrivera à le faire passer par la porte?; **I'll get you there somehow** je me débrouillerai pour t'y emmener

6 (*catch, take*: *plane, bus etc*) prendre; **where do I get the train for Birmingham?** où prend-on le train pour Birmingham?

7 (*understand*) comprendre, saisir; (*hear*) entendre; **I've got it!** j'ai compris!; **I don't get your meaning** je ne vois *or* comprends pas ce que vous voulez dire; **I didn't get your name** je n'ai pas entendu votre nom

8 (*have, possess*): **to have got** avoir; **how many have you got?** vous en avez combien?

9 (*illness*) avoir; **I've got a cold** j'ai le rhume; **she got pneumonia and died** elle a fait une pneumonie et elle en est morte

get about *vi* se déplacer; (*news*) se répandre

get across *vt*: **to get across (to)** (*message, meaning*) faire passer (à)

▷ *vi*: **to get across (to)** (*speaker*) se faire comprendre (par)

get along *vi* (*agree*) s'entendre; (*depart*) s'en aller; (*manage*) = **get by**

get at *vt fus* (*attack*) s'en prendre à; (*reach*) attraper, atteindre; **what are you getting at?** à quoi voulez-vous en venir?

get away *vi* partir, s'en aller; (*escape*) s'échapper

get away with *vt fus* (*punishment*) en être quitte pour; (*crime etc*) se faire pardonner

get back *vi* (*return*) rentrer

▷ *vt* récupérer, recouvrer; **to get back to** (*start again*) retourner *or* revenir à; (*contact again*) recontacter; **when do we get back?** quand serons-nous de retour?

get back at *vt fus* (*inf*): **to get back at sb** rendre la monnaie de sa pièce à qn

get by *vi* (*pass*) passer; (*manage*) se débrouiller; **I can get by in Dutch** je me débrouille en hollandais

get down *vi*, *vt fus* descendre

▷ *vt* descendre; (*depress*) déprimer

get down to *vt fus* (*work*) se mettre à (faire); **to get down to business** passer aux choses sérieuses

get in *vi* entrer; (*arrive home*) rentrer; (*train*) arriver

▷ *vt* (*bring in*: *harvest*) rentrer; (: *coal*) faire rentrer; (: *supplies*) faire des provisions de

get into *vt fus* entrer dans; (*car, train etc*) monter dans; (*clothes*) mettre, enfiler, endosser; **to get into bed/a rage** se mettre au lit/en colère

get off *vi* (*from train etc*) descendre; (*depart*: *person, car*) s'en aller; (*escape*) s'en tirer

▷ *vt* (*remove*: *clothes, stain*) enlever; (*send off*) expédier; (*have as leave*: *day, time*): **we got 2 days off** nous avons eu 2 jours de congé

▷ *vt fus* (*train, bus*) descendre de; **where do I get off?** où est-ce que je dois descendre?; **to get off to a good start** (*fig*) prendre un bon départ

get on *vi* (*at exam etc*) se débrouiller; (*agree*): **to get on (with)** s'entendre (avec); **how are you getting on?** comment ça va?

▷ *vt fus* monter dans; (*horse*) monter sur

get on to *vt fus* (*Brit*: *deal with*: *problem*) s'occuper de; (*contact*: *person*) contacter

get out *vi* sortir; (*of vehicle*) descendre; (*news etc*) s'ébruiter

▷ *vt* sortir

get out of *vt fus* sortir de; (*duty etc*) échapper à, se soustraire à

get over *vt fus* (*illness*) se remettre de

▷ *vt* (*communicate*: *idea etc*) communiquer; (*finish*): **let's get it over (with)** finissons-en

get round *vi*: **to get round to doing sth** se mettre (finalement) à faire qch

▷ *vt fus* contourner; (*fig*: *person*) entortiller

get through vi (Tel) avoir la communication; **to get through to sb** atteindre qn
▷ vt fus (finish: work, book) finir, terminer
get together vi se réunir
▷ vt rassembler
get up vi (rise) se lever
▷ vt fus monter
get up to vt fus (reach) arriver à; (prank etc) faire

getaway ['gɛtəweɪ] n fuite f
geyser ['giːzəʳ] n chauffe-eau m inv; (Geo) geyser m
Ghana ['gɑːnə] n Ghana m
ghastly ['gɑːstlɪ] adj atroce, horrible; (pale) livide, blême
gherkin ['gəːkɪn] n cornichon m
ghetto ['gɛtəu] n ghetto m
ghetto blaster [-blɑːstəʳ] n (inf) gros radiocassette
ghost [gəust] n fantôme m, revenant m ▷ vt (sb else's book) écrire
giant ['dʒaɪənt] n géant(e) ▷ adj géant(e), énorme; ~ (size) packet paquet géant
gibberish ['dʒɪbərɪʃ] n charabia m
giblets ['dʒɪblɪts] npl abats mpl
Gibraltar [dʒɪ'brɔːltəʳ] n Gibraltar m
giddy ['gɪdɪ] adj (dizzy): **to be** (or **feel**) ~ avoir le vertige; (height) vertigineux(-euse); (thoughtless) sot(te), étourdi(e)
gift [gɪft] n cadeau m, présent m; (donation, talent) don m; (Comm: also: **free ~**) cadeau(-réclame) m; **to have a ~ for sth** avoir des dons pour or le don de qch
gifted ['gɪftɪd] adj doué(e)
gift shop, (US) **gift store** n boutique f de cadeaux
gift token, gift voucher n chèque-cadeau m
gig [gɪg] n (inf: concert) concert m
gigabyte ['dʒɪgəbaɪt] n gigaoctet m
gigantic [dʒaɪ'gæntɪk] adj gigantesque
giggle ['gɪgl] vi pouffer, ricaner sottement ▷ n petit rire sot, ricanement m
gill [dʒɪl] n (measure) = 0.25 pints (Brit = 0.148 l; US = 0.118 l)
gills [gɪlz] npl (of fish) ouïes fpl, branchies fpl
gilt [gɪlt] n dorure f ▷ adj doré(e)
gilt-edged ['gɪltɛdʒd] adj (stocks, securities) de premier ordre
gimmick ['gɪmɪk] n truc m; **sales ~** offre promotionnelle
gin [dʒɪn] n gin m
ginger ['dʒɪndʒəʳ] n gingembre m; **ginger up** vt secouer; animer
ginger ale, ginger beer n boisson gazeuse au gingembre
gingerbread ['dʒɪndʒəbrɛd] n pain m d'épices
gingerly ['dʒɪndʒəlɪ] adv avec précaution
gipsy ['dʒɪpsɪ] n = **gypsy**
giraffe [dʒɪ'rɑːf] n girafe f

girder ['gəːdəʳ] n poutrelle f
girl [gəːl] n fille f, fillette f; (young unmarried woman) jeune fille; (daughter) fille; **an English ~** une jeune Anglaise; **a little English ~** une petite Anglaise
girl band n girls band m
girlfriend ['gəːlfrɛnd] n (of girl) amie f; (of boy) petite amie
Girl Guide n (Brit) éclaireuse f; (Roman Catholic) guide f
girlish ['gəːlɪʃ] adj de jeune fille
Girl Scout n (US) = **Girl Guide**
giro ['dʒaɪrəu] n (bank giro) virement m bancaire; (post office giro) mandat m
gist [dʒɪst] n essentiel m
give [gɪv] (pt **gave**, pp **given**) [geɪv, 'gɪvn] n (of fabric) élasticité f ▷ vt donner ▷ vi (break) céder; (stretch: fabric) se prêter; **to ~ sb sth**, **~ sth to sb** donner qch à qn; (gift) offrir qch à qn; (message) transmettre qch à qn; **to ~ sb a call/kiss** appeler/embrasser qn; **how much did you ~ for it?** combien (l')avez-vous payé?; **12 o'clock, ~ or take a few minutes** midi, à quelques minutes près; **to ~ way** céder; (Brit Aut) donner la priorité; **give away** vt donner; (give free) faire cadeau de; (betray) donner, trahir; (disclose) révéler; (bride) conduire à l'autel; **give back** vt rendre; **give in** vi céder ▷ vt donner; **give off** vt dégager; **give out** vt (food etc) distribuer; (news) annoncer ▷ vi (be exhausted: supplies) s'épuiser; (fail) lâcher; **give up** vi renoncer ▷ vt renoncer à; **to ~ up smoking** arrêter de fumer; **to ~ o.s. up** se rendre
given ['gɪvn] pp of **give** ▷ adj (fixed: time, amount) donné(e), déterminé(e) ▷ conj: **~ the circumstances ...** étant donné les circonstances ..., vu les circonstances ...; **~ that ...** étant donné que ...
glacier ['glæsɪəʳ] n glacier m
glad [glæd] adj content(e); **to be ~ about sth/ that** être heureux(-euse) or bien content de qch/que; **I was ~ of his help** j'étais bien content de (pouvoir compter sur) son aide or qu'il m'aide
gladly ['glædlɪ] adv volontiers
glamorous ['glæmərəs] adj (person) séduisant(e); (job) prestigieux(-euse)
glamour, (US) **glamor** ['glæməʳ] n éclat m, prestige m
glance [glɑːns] n coup m d'œil ▷ vi: **to ~ at** jeter un coup d'œil à; **glance off** vt fus (bullet) ricocher sur
glancing ['glɑːnsɪŋ] adj (blow) oblique
gland [glænd] n glande f
glare [glɛəʳ] n (of anger) regard furieux; (of light) lumière éblouissante; (of publicity) feux mpl ▷ vi briller d'un éclat aveuglant; **to ~ at** lancer un regard or des regards furieux à
glaring ['glɛərɪŋ] adj (mistake) criant(e), qui saute aux yeux

glass [glɑːs] n verre m; (also: **looking ~**) miroir m; **glasses** npl (spectacles) lunettes fpl

glasshouse ['glɑːshaus] n serre f

glassware ['glɑːsweər] n verrerie f

glaze [gleɪz] vt (door) vitrer; (pottery) vernir; (Culin) glacer ▷ n vernis m; (Culin) glaçage m

glazed [gleɪzd] adj (eye) vitreux(-euse); (pottery) verni(e); (tiles) vitrifié(e)

glazier ['gleɪzɪər] n vitrier m

gleam [gliːm] n lueur f ▷ vi luire, briller; **a ~ of hope** une lueur d'espoir

glean [gliːn] vt (information) recueillir

glee [gliː] n joie f

glen [glɛn] n vallée f

glib [glɪb] adj qui a du bagou; facile

glide [glaɪd] vi glisser; (Aviat, bird) planer ▷ n glissement m; vol plané

glider ['glaɪdər] n (Aviat) planeur m

gliding ['glaɪdɪŋ] n (Aviat) vol m à voile

glimmer ['glɪmər] vi luire ▷ n lueur f

glimpse [glɪmps] n vision passagère, aperçu m ▷ vt entrevoir, apercevoir; **to catch a ~ of** entrevoir

glint [glɪnt] n éclair m ▷ vi étinceler

glisten ['glɪsn] vi briller, luire

glitter ['glɪtər] vi scintiller, briller ▷ n scintillement m

gloat [gləut] vi: **to ~ (over)** jubiler (à propos de)

global ['gləubl] adj (world-wide) mondial(e); (overall) global(e)

globalization [gləubəlaɪz'eɪʃən] n mondialisation f

global warming [-'wɔːmɪŋ] n réchauffement m de la planète

globe [gləub] n globe m

gloom [gluːm] n obscurité f; (sadness) tristesse f, mélancolie f

gloomy ['gluːmɪ] adj (person) morose; (place, outlook) sombre; **to feel ~** avoir or se faire des idées noires

glorious ['glɔːrɪəs] adj glorieux(-euse); (beautiful) splendide

glory ['glɔːrɪ] n gloire f; splendeur f ▷ vi: **to ~ in** se glorifier de

gloss [glɒs] n (shine) brillant m, vernis m; (also: **~ paint**) peinture brillante or laquée; **gloss over** vt fus glisser sur

glossary ['glɒsərɪ] n glossaire m, lexique m

glossy ['glɒsɪ] adj brillant(e), luisant(e) ▷ n (also: **~ magazine**) revue f de luxe

glove [glʌv] n gant m

glove compartment n (Aut) boîte f à gants, vide-poches m inv

glow [gləu] vi rougeoyer; (face) rayonner; (eyes) briller ▷ n rougeoiement m

glower ['glauər] vi lancer des regards mauvais

glucose ['gluːkəus] n glucose m

glue [gluː] n colle f ▷ vt coller

glum [glʌm] adj maussade, morose

glut [glʌt] n surabondance f ▷ vt rassasier; (market) encombrer

glutton ['glʌtn] n glouton(ne); **a ~ for work** un bourreau de travail

GM abbr (= genetically modified) génétiquement modifié(e)

gm abbr (= gram) g

GM crop n culture f OGM

GMO n abbr (= genetically modified organism) OGM m

GMT abbr (= Greenwich Mean Time) GMT

gnat [næt] n moucheron m

gnaw [nɔː] vt ronger

go [gəu] (pt **went**, pp **gone**) [wɛnt, gɒn] vi aller; (depart) partir, s'en aller; (work) marcher; (break) céder; (time) passer; (be sold): **to go for £10** se vendre 10 livres; (become): **to go pale/mouldy** pâlir/moisir ▷ n (pl **goes**); **to have a go (at)** essayer (de faire); **to be on the go** être en mouvement; **whose go is it?** à qui est-ce de jouer?; **to go by car/on foot** aller en voiture/à pied; **he's going to do it** il va le faire, il est sur le point de le faire; **to go for a walk** aller se promener; **to go dancing/shopping** aller danser/faire les courses; **to go looking for sb/sth** aller or partir à la recherche de qn/qch; **to go to sleep** s'endormir; **to go and see sb, go to see sb** aller voir qn; **how is it going?** comment ça marche?; **how did it go?** comment est-ce que ça s'est passé?; **to go round the back/by the shop** passer par derrière/devant le magasin; **my voice has gone** j'ai une extinction de voix; **the cake is all gone** il n'y a plus de gâteau; **I'll take whatever is going** (Brit) je prendrai ce qu'il y a (or ce que vous avez); **... to go** (US: food) ... à emporter; **go about** vi (also: **go around**) aller çà et là; (rumour) se répandre ▷ vt fus: **how do I go about this?** comment dois-je m'y prendre (pour faire ceci)?; **to go about one's business** s'occuper de ses affaires; **go after** vt fus (pursue) poursuivre, courir après; (job, record etc) essayer d'obtenir; **go against** vt fus (be unfavourable to) être défavorable à; (be contrary to) être contraire à; **go ahead** vi (make progress) avancer; (take place) avoir lieu; (get going) y aller; **go along** vi aller, avancer ▷ vt fus longer, parcourir; **as you go along (with your work)** au fur et à mesure (de votre travail); **to go along with** (accompany) accompagner; (agree with: idea) être d'accord sur; (: person) suivre; **go away** vi partir, s'en aller; **go back** vi rentrer; revenir; (go again) retourner; **go back on** vt fus (promise) revenir sur; **go by** vi (years, time) passer, s'écouler ▷ vt fus s'en tenir à; (believe) en croire; **go down** vi descendre; (number, price, amount) baisser; (ship) couler; (sun) se coucher ▷ vt fus descendre; **that should go down well with him** (fig) ça devrait lui plaire; **go for** vt fus (fetch) aller chercher; (like) aimer; (attack) s'en prendre à; attaquer; **go in** vi entrer;

go in for vt fus (competition) se présenter à; (like) aimer; **go into** vt fus entrer dans; (investigate) étudier, examiner; (embark on) se lancer dans; **go off** vi partir, s'en aller; (food) se gâter; (milk) tourner; (bomb) sauter; (alarm clock) sonner; (alarm) se déclencher; (lights etc) s'éteindre; (event) se dérouler ▷ vt fus ne plus aimer, ne plus avoir envie de; **the gun went off** le coup est parti; **to go off to sleep** s'endormir; **the party went off well** la fête s'est bien passée or était très réussie; **go on** vi continuer; (happen) se passer; (lights) s'allumer ▷ vt fus (be guided by: evidence etc) se fonder sur; **to go on doing** continuer à faire; **what's going on here?** qu'est-ce qui se passe ici?; **go on at** vt fus (nag) tomber sur le dos de; **go on with** vt fus poursuivre, continuer; **go out** vi sortir; (fire, light) s'éteindre; (tide) descendre; **to go out with sb** sortir avec qn; **go over** vi (ship) chavirer ▷ vt fus (check) revoir, vérifier; **to go over sth in one's mind** repasser qch dans son esprit; **go past** vt fus: **to go past sth** passer devant qch; **go round** vi (circulate: news, rumour) circuler; (revolve) tourner; (suffice) suffire (pour tout le monde); (visit): **to go round to sb's** passer chez qn, aller chez qn; (make a detour): **to go round (by)** faire un détour (par); **go through** vt fus (town etc) traverser; (search through) fouiller; (suffer) subir; (examine: list, book) lire or regarder en détail, éplucher; (perform: lesson) réciter; (: formalities) remplir; (: programme) exécuter; **go through with** vt fus (plan, crime) aller jusqu'au bout de; **go under** vi (sink: also fig) couler; (: person) succomber; **go up** vi monter; (price) augmenter ▷ vt fus gravir; (also: **go up in flames**) flamber, s'enflammer brusquement; **go with** vt fus aller avec; **go without** vt fus se passer de

goad [gəud] vt aiguillonner

go-ahead ['gəuəhed] adj dynamique, entreprenant(e) ▷ n feu vert

goal [gəul] n but m

goalkeeper ['gəulkiːpəʳ] n gardien m de but

goal-post ['gəulpəust] n poteau m de but

goat [gəut] n chèvre f

gobble ['gɔbl] vt (also: **~ down, ~ up**) engloutir

go-between ['gəubitwiːn] n médiateur m

god [gɔd] n dieu m; **G~** Dieu

godchild ['gɔdtʃaɪld] n filleul(e)

goddaughter ['gɔddɔːtəʳ] n filleule f

goddess ['gɔdɪs] n déesse f

godfather ['gɔdfɑːðəʳ] n parrain m

god-forsaken ['gɔdfəseɪkən] adj maudit(e)

godmother ['gɔdmʌðəʳ] n marraine f

godsend ['gɔdsend] n aubaine f

godson ['gɔdsʌn] n filleul m

goggles ['gɔglz] npl (for skiing etc) lunettes (protectrices); (for swimming) lunettes de piscine

going ['gəuɪŋ] n (conditions) état m du terrain ▷ adj: **the ~ rate** le tarif (en vigueur); **a ~ concern** une affaire prospère; **it was slow ~** les progrès étaient lents, ça n'avançait pas vite

gold [gəuld] n or m ▷ adj en or; (reserves) d'or

golden ['gəuldən] adj (made of gold) en or; (gold in colour) doré(e)

goldfish ['gəuldfɪʃ] n poisson m rouge

goldmine ['gəuldmaɪn] n mine f d'or

gold-plated ['gəuld'pleɪtɪd] adj plaqué(e) or inv

goldsmith ['gəuldsmɪθ] n orfèvre m

golf [gɔlf] n golf m

golf ball n balle f de golf; (on typewriter) boule f

golf club n club m de golf; (stick) club m, crosse f de golf

golf course n terrain m de golf

golfer ['gɔlfəʳ] n joueur(-euse) de golf

gone [gɔn] pp of **go** ▷ adj parti(e)

gong [gɔŋ] n gong m

good [gud] adj bon(ne); (kind) gentil(le); (child) sage; (weather) beau/belle ▷ n bien m; **goods** npl marchandise f, articles mpl; (Comm etc) marchandises; **~!** bon!, très bien!; **to be ~ at** être bon en; **to be ~ for** être bon pour; **it's ~ for you** c'est bon pour vous; **it's a ~ thing you were there** heureusement que vous étiez là; **she is ~ with children/her hands** elle sait bien s'occuper des enfants/sait se servir de ses mains; **to feel ~** se sentir bien; **it's ~ to see you** ça me fait plaisir de vous voir, je suis content de vous voir; **he's up to no ~** il prépare quelque mauvais coup; **it's no ~ complaining** cela ne sert à rien de se plaindre; **to make ~** (deficit) combler; (losses) compenser; **for the common ~** dans l'intérêt commun; **for ~** (for ever) pour de bon, une fois pour toutes; **would you be ~ enough to ...?** auriez-vous la bonté or l'amabilité de ...?; **that's very ~ of you** c'est très gentil de votre part; **is this any ~?** (will it do?) est-ce que ceci fera l'affaire?, est-ce que cela peut vous rendre service?; (what's it like?) qu'est-ce que ça vaut?; **~s and chattels** biens mpl et effets mpl; **a ~ deal (of)** beaucoup (de); **a ~ many** beaucoup (de); **~ morning/afternoon!** bonjour!; **~ evening!** bonsoir!; **~ night!** bonsoir!; (on going to bed) bonne nuit!

goodbye [gud'baɪ] excl au revoir!; **to say ~ to sb** dire au revoir à qn

Good Friday n Vendredi saint

good-looking ['gud'lukɪŋ] adj beau/belle, bien inv

good-natured ['gud'neɪtʃəd] adj (person) qui a un bon naturel; (discussion) enjoué(e)

goodness ['gudnɪs] n (of person) bonté f; **for ~ sake!** je vous en prie!; **~ gracious!** mon Dieu!

goods train n (Brit) train m de marchandises

goodwill [gud'wɪl] n bonne volonté f; (Comm) réputation f (auprès de la clientèle)

goose (pl **geese**) [guːs, giːs] n oie f

gooseberry ['guzbərɪ] n groseille f à maquereau; **to play ~** (Brit) tenir la chandelle

goose bumps, goose pimples npl chair f
de poule
gooseflesh ['guːsfleʃ] n, **goosepimples**
['guːspɪmplz] npl chair f de poule
gore [gɔːʳ] vt encorner ▷ n sang m
gorge [gɔːdʒ] n gorge f ▷ vt: **to ~ o.s. (on)** se
gorger (de)
gorgeous ['gɔːdʒəs] adj splendide, superbe
gorilla [gə'rɪlə] n gorille m
gorse [gɔːs] n ajoncs mpl
gory ['gɔːrɪ] adj sanglant(e)
gosh [gɔʃ] (inf) excl mince alors!
go-slow ['gəu'sləu] n (Brit) grève perlée
gospel ['gɔspl] n évangile m
gossip ['gɔsɪp] n (chat) bavardages mpl;
(malicious) commérage m, cancans mpl;
(person) commère f ▷ vi bavarder; cancaner,
faire des commérages; **a piece of ~** un ragot,
un racontar
gossip column n (Press) échos mpl
got [gɔt] pt, pp of **get**
gotten ['gɔtn] (US) pp of **get**
gourmet ['guəmeɪ] n gourmet m,
gastronome m/f
gout [gaut] n goutte f
govern ['gʌvən] vt (gen: Ling) gouverner;
(influence) déterminer
governess ['gʌvənɪs] n gouvernante f
government ['gʌvnmənt] n gouvernement m;
(Brit: ministers) ministère m ▷ cpd de l'État
governor ['gʌvənəʳ] n (of colony, state, bank)
gouverneur m; (of school, hospital etc)
administrateur(-trice); (Brit: of prison)
directeur(-trice)
gown [gaun] n robe f; (of teacher, Brit: of judge)
toge f
GP n abbr (Med) = **general practitioner; who's
your GP?** qui est votre médecin traitant?
GPS n abbr (= global positioning system) GPS m
grab [græb] vt saisir, empoigner; (property,
power) se saisir de ▷ vi: **to ~ at** essayer de
saisir
grace [greɪs] n grâce f ▷ vt (honour) honorer;
(adorn) orner; **5 days'** ~ un répit de 5 jours; **to
say ~** dire le bénédicité; (after meal) dire les
grâces; **with a good/bad ~** de bonne/
mauvaise grâce; **his sense of humour is his
saving ~** il se rachète par son sens de
l'humour
graceful ['greɪsful] adj gracieux(-euse),
élégant(e)
gracious ['greɪʃəs] adj (kind) charmant(e),
bienveillant(e); (elegant) plein(e) d'élégance,
d'une grande élégance; (formal: pardon etc)
miséricordieux(-euse) ▷ excl: **(good) ~!** mon
Dieu!
grade [greɪd] n (Comm: quality) qualité f; (size)
calibre m; (type) catégorie f; (in hierarchy) grade
m, échelon m; (Scol) note f; (US: school class)
classe f; (: gradient) pente f ▷ vt classer; (by
size) calibrer; graduer; **to make the ~** (fig)
réussir

grade crossing n (US) passage m à niveau
grade school n (US) école f primaire
gradient ['greɪdɪənt] n inclinaison f, pente f;
(Geom) gradient m
gradual ['grædjuəl] adj graduel(le),
progressif(-ive)
gradually ['grædjuəlɪ] adv peu à peu,
graduellement
graduate n ['grædjuɪt] diplômé(e)
d'université; (US: of high school) diplômé(e)
de fin d'études ▷ vi ['grædjueɪt] obtenir un
diplôme d'université (or de fin d'études)
graduation [grædju'eɪʃən] n cérémonie f de
remise des diplômes
graffiti [grə'fiːtɪ] npl graffiti mpl
graft [grɑːft] n (Agr, Med) greffe f; (bribery)
corruption f ▷ vt greffer; **hard ~** (Brit: inf)
boulot acharné
grain [greɪn] n (single piece) grain m; (no pl:
cereals) céréales fpl; (US: corn) blé m; (of wood)
fibre f; **it goes against the ~** cela va à
l'encontre de sa (or ma etc) nature
gram [græm] n gramme m
grammar ['græməʳ] n grammaire f
grammar school n (Brit) ≈ lycée m
grammatical [grə'mætɪkl] adj
grammatical(e)
gramme [græm] n = **gram**
gran [græn] n (inf) n (Brit) mamie f (inf), mémé f
(inf); **my ~** (young child speaking) ma mamie or
mémé; (older child or adult speaking) ma grand-
mère
grand [grænd] adj magnifique, splendide;
(terrific) magnifique, formidable; (gesture etc)
noble ▷ n (inf: thousand) mille livres fpl (or
dollars mpl)
grandad ['grændæd] (inf) n = **granddad**
grandchild (pl **grandchildren**) ['græntʃaɪld,
'græntʃɪldrən] n petit-fils m, petite-fille f;
grandchildren npl petits-enfants
granddad ['grændæd] n (inf) papy m (inf),
papi m (inf), pépé m (inf); **my ~** (young child
speaking) mon papy or papi or pépé; (older child
or adult speaking) mon grand-père
granddaughter ['grændɔːtəʳ] n petite-fille f
grandfather ['grændfɑːðəʳ] n grand-père m
grandma ['grænmɑː] n (inf) = **gran**
grandmother ['grænmʌðəʳ] n grand-mère f
grandpa ['grænpɑː] n (inf) = **granddad**
grandparents ['grændpeərənts] npl grands-
parents mpl
grand piano n piano m à queue
Grand Prix ['grɑ̃'priː] n (Aut) grand prix
automobile
grandson ['grænsʌn] n petit-fils m
grandstand ['grændstænd] n (Sport)
tribune f
granite ['grænɪt] n granit m
granny ['grænɪ] n (inf) = **gran**
grant [grɑːnt] vt accorder; (a request) accéder
à; (admit) concéder ▷ n (Scol) bourse f; (Admin)
subside m, subvention f; **to take sth for ~ed**

considérer qch comme acquis; **to take sb for ~ed** considérer qn comme faisant partie du décor; **to ~ that** admettre que

granulated ['grænjuleɪtɪd] *adj*: **~ sugar** sucre *m* en poudre

grape [greɪp] *n* raisin *m*; **a bunch of ~s** une grappe de raisin

grapefruit ['greɪpfruːt] *n* pamplemousse *m*

graph [grɑːf] *n* graphique *m*, courbe *f*

graphic ['græfɪk] *adj* graphique; (*vivid*) vivant(e)

graphics ['græfɪks] *n* (*art*) arts *mpl* graphiques; (*process*) graphisme *m* ▷ *npl* (*drawings*) illustrations *fpl*

grapple ['græpl] *vi*: **to ~ with** être aux prises avec

grasp [grɑːsp] *vt* saisir, empoigner; (*understand*) saisir, comprendre ▷ *n* (*grip*) prise *f*; (*fig*) compréhension *f*, connaissance *f*; **to have sth within one's ~** avoir qch à sa portée; **to have a good ~ of sth** (*fig*) bien comprendre qch; **grasp at** *vt fus* (*rope etc*) essayer de saisir; (*fig: opportunity*) sauter sur

grasping ['grɑːspɪŋ] *adj* avide

grass [grɑːs] *n* herbe *f*; (*lawn*) gazon *m*; (*Brit inf: informer*) mouchard(e); (: *ex-terrorist*) balanceur(-euse)

grasshopper ['grɑːshɒpəʳ] *n* sauterelle *f*

grass roots *npl* (*fig*) base *f*

grate [greɪt] *n* grille *f* de cheminée ▷ *vi* grincer ▷ *vt* (*Culin*) râper

grateful ['greɪtful] *adj* reconnaissant(e)

grater ['greɪtəʳ] *n* râpe *f*

gratifying ['grætɪfaɪɪŋ] *adj* agréable, satisfaisant(e)

grating ['greɪtɪŋ] *n* (*iron bars*) grille *f* ▷ *adj* (*noise*) grinçant(e)

gratitude ['grætɪtjuːd] *n* gratitude *f*

gratuity [grə'tjuːɪtɪ] *n* pourboire *m*

grave [greɪv] *n* tombe *f* ▷ *adj* grave, sérieux(-euse)

gravel ['grævl] *n* gravier *m*

gravestone ['greɪvstəun] *n* pierre tombale

graveyard ['greɪvjɑːd] *n* cimetière *m*

gravity ['grævɪtɪ] *n* (*Physics*) gravité *f*; pesanteur *f*; (*seriousness*) gravité, sérieux *m*

gravy ['greɪvɪ] *n* jus *m* (de viande), sauce *f* (au jus de viande)

gray [greɪ] *adj* (*US*) = **grey**

graze [greɪz] *vi* paître, brouter ▷ *vt* (*touch lightly*) frôler, effleurer; (*scrape*) écorcher ▷ *n* écorchure *f*

grease [griːs] *n* (*fat*) graisse *f*; (*lubricant*) lubrifiant *m* ▷ *vt* graisser; lubrifier; **to ~ the skids** (*US: fig*) huiler les rouages

greaseproof paper ['griːspruːf-] *n* (*Brit*) papier sulfurisé

greasy ['griːsɪ] *adj* gras(se), graisseux(-euse); (*hands, clothes*) graisseux; (*Brit: road, surface*) glissant(e)

great [greɪt] *adj* grand(e); (*heat, pain etc*) très fort(e), intense; (*inf*) formidable; **they're ~**

friends ils sont très amis, ce sont de grands amis; **we had a ~ time** nous nous sommes bien amusés; **it was ~!** c'était fantastique ou super!; **the ~ thing is that ...** ce qu'il y a de vraiment bien c'est que ...

Great Britain *n* Grande-Bretagne *f*

great-grandfather [greɪt'grænfɑːðəʳ] *n* arrière-grand-père *m*

great-grandmother [greɪt'grænmʌðəʳ] *n* arrière-grand-mère *f*

greatly ['greɪtlɪ] *adv* très, grandement; (*with verbs*) beaucoup

greatness ['greɪtnɪs] *n* grandeur *f*

Greece [griːs] *n* Grèce *f*

greed [griːd] *n* (*also*: **~iness**) avidité *f*; (*for food*) gourmandise *f*

greedy ['griːdɪ] *adj* avide; (*for food*) gourmand(e)

Greek [griːk] *adj* grec/grecque ▷ *n* Grec/ Grecque; (*Ling*) grec *m*; **ancient/modern ~** grec classique/moderne

green [griːn] *adj* vert(e); (*inexperienced*) (bien) jeune, naïf(-ive); (*ecological: product etc*) écologique ▷ *n* (*colour*) vert *m*; (*on golf course*) green *m*; (*stretch of grass*) pelouse *f*; (*also*: **village ~**) ≈ place *f* du village; **greens** *npl* (*vegetables*) légumes verts; **to have ~ fingers** *or* (*US*) **a ~ thumb** (*fig*) avoir le pouce vert; **G-** (*Pol*) écologiste *m/f*; **the G~ Party** le parti écologiste

green belt *n* (*round town*) ceinture verte

green card *n* (*Aut*) carte verte; (*US: work permit*) permis *m* de travail

greenery ['griːnərɪ] *n* verdure *f*

greengage ['griːngeɪdʒ] *n* reine-claude *f*

greengrocer ['griːngrəusəʳ] *n* (*Brit*) marchand *m* de fruits et légumes

greengrocer's ['griːngrəusəʳ], **greengrocer's shop** *n* magasin *m* de fruits et légumes

greenhouse ['griːnhaus] *n* serre *f*

greenhouse effect *n*: **the ~** l'effet *m* de serre

greenhouse gas *n* gaz *m* contribuant à l'effet de serre

greenish ['griːnɪʃ] *adj* verdâtre

Greenland ['griːnlənd] *n* Groenland *m*

green salad *n* salade verte

green tax *n* écotaxe *f*

greet [griːt] *vt* accueillir

greeting ['griːtɪŋ] *n* salutation *f*; **Christmas/ birthday ~s** souhaits *mpl* de Noël/de bon anniversaire

greeting card, greetings card *n* carte *f* de vœux

gregarious [grə'gɛərɪəs] *adj* grégaire; sociable

grenade [grə'neɪd] *n* (*also*: **hand ~**) grenade *f*

grew [gruː] *pt of* **grow**

grey, (*US*) **gray** [greɪ] *adj* gris(e); (*dismal*) sombre; **to go ~** (commencer à) grisonner

grey-haired, (*US*) **gray-haired** [greɪ'hɛəd] *adj* aux cheveux gris

greyhound ['greɪhaund] *n* lévrier *m*

grid [grɪd] n grille f; (Elec) réseau m; (US Aut) intersection f (matérialisée par des marques au sol)

gridlock ['grɪdlɔk] n (traffic jam) embouteillage m

gridlocked ['grɪdlɔkt] adj: **to be ~** (roads) être bloqué par un embouteillage; (talks etc) être suspendu

grief [gri:f] n chagrin m, douleur f; **to come to ~** (plan) échouer; (person) avoir un malheur

grievance ['gri:vəns] n doléance f, grief m; (cause for complaint) grief

grieve [gri:v] vi avoir du chagrin; se désoler ▷ vt faire de la peine à, affliger; **to ~ for sb** pleurer qn; **to ~ at** se désoler de; pleurer

grievous ['gri:vəs] adj grave, cruel(le); **~ bodily harm** (Law) coups mpl et blessures fpl

grill [grɪl] n (on cooker) gril m; (also: **mixed ~**) grillade(s) f(pl); (also: **~room**) rôtisserie f ▷ vt (Brit) griller; (inf: question) interroger longuement, cuisiner

grille [grɪl] n grillage m; (Aut) calandre f

grillroom ['grɪlrum] n rôtisserie f

grim [grɪm] adj sinistre, lugubre; (serious, stern) sévère

grimace [grɪ'meɪs] n grimace f ▷ vi grimacer, faire une grimace

grime [graɪm] n crasse f

grin [grɪn] n large sourire m ▷ vi sourire; **to ~ (at)** faire un grand sourire (à)

grind [graɪnd] (pt, pp ground) [graund] vt écraser; (coffee, pepper etc) moudre; (US: meat) hacher; (make sharp) aiguiser; (polish: gem, lens) polir ▷ vi (car gears) grincer ▷ n (work) corvée f; **to ~ one's teeth** grincer des dents; **to ~ to a halt** (vehicle) s'arrêter dans un grincement de freins; (fig) s'arrêter, s'immobiliser; **the daily ~** (inf) le train-train quotidien

grip [grɪp] n (handclasp) poigne f; (control) prise f; (handle) poignée f; (holdall) sac m de voyage ▷ vt saisir, empoigner; (viewer, reader) captiver; **to come to ~s with** se colleter avec, en venir aux prises avec; **to ~ the road** (Aut) adhérer à la route; **to lose one's ~** lâcher prise; (fig) perdre les pédales, être dépassé(e)

gripping ['grɪpɪŋ] adj prenant(e), palpitant(e)

grisly ['grɪzlɪ] adj sinistre, macabre

gristle ['grɪsl] n cartilage m (de poulet etc)

grit [grɪt] n gravillon m; (courage) cran m ▷ vt (road) sabler; **to ~ one's teeth** serrer les dents; **to have a piece of ~ in one's eye** avoir une poussière ou saleté dans l'œil

grits [grɪts] npl (US) gruau m de maïs

groan [grəun] n (of pain) gémissement m; (of disapproval, dismay) grognement m ▷ vi gémir; grogner

grocer ['grəusə'] n épicier m

groceries ['grəusərɪz] npl provisions fpl

grocer's ['grəusəz], **grocer's shop, grocery** ['grəusərɪ] n épicerie f

groin [grɔɪn] n aine f

groom [gru:m] n (for horses) palefrenier m; (also: **bride~**) marié m ▷ vt (horse) panser; (fig): **to ~ sb for** former qn pour

groove [gru:v] n sillon m, rainure f

grope [grəup] vi tâtonner; **to ~ for** chercher à tâtons

gross [grəus] adj grossier(-ière); (Comm) brut(e) ▷ n pl inv (twelve dozen) grosse f ▷ vt (Comm): **to ~ £500,000** gagner 500 000 livres avant impôt

grossly ['grəuslɪ] adv (greatly) très, grandement

grotesque [grə'tɛsk] adj grotesque

grotto ['grɔtəu] n grotte f

grotty ['grɔtɪ] adj (Brit inf) minable

ground [graund] pt, pp of **grind** ▷ n sol m, terre f; (land) terrain m, terres fpl; (Sport) terrain; (reason: gen pl) raison f; (US: also: **~ wire**) terre f ▷ vt (plane) empêcher de décoller, retenir au sol; (US Elec) équiper d'une prise de terre, mettre à la terre ▷ vi (ship) s'échouer ▷ adj (coffee etc) moulu(e); (US: meat) haché(e); **grounds** npl (gardens etc) parc m, domaine m; (of coffee) marc m; **on the ~, to the ~** par terre; **below ~** sous terre; **to gain/lose ~** gagner/perdre du terrain; **common ~** terrain d'entente; **he covered a lot of ~ in his lecture** sa conférence a traité un grand nombre de questions ou la question en profondeur

ground cloth n (US) = **groundsheet**

ground floor n (Brit) rez-de-chaussée m

grounding ['graundɪŋ] n (in education) connaissances fpl de base

groundless ['graundlɪs] adj sans fondement

groundsheet ['graundʃi:t] n (Brit) tapis m de sol

ground staff n équipage m au sol

groundwork ['graundwə:k] n préparation f

group [gru:p] n groupe m ▷ vt (also: **~ together**) grouper ▷ vi (also: **~ together**) se grouper

grouse [graus] n pl inv (bird) grouse f (sorte de coq de bruyère) ▷ vi (complain) rouspéter, râler

grove [grəuv] n bosquet m

grovel ['grɔvl] vi (fig): **to ~ (before)** ramper (devant)

grow (pt **grew**, pp **grown**) [grəu, gru:, grəun] vi (plant) pousser, croître; (person) grandir; (increase) augmenter, se développer; (become) devenir; **to ~ rich/weak** s'enrichir/s'affaiblir ▷ vt cultiver, faire pousser; (hair, beard) laisser pousser; **grow apart** vi (fig) se détacher (l'un de l'autre); **grow away from** vt fus (fig) s'éloigner de; **grow on** vt fus: **that painting is ~ing on me** je finirai par aimer ce tableau; **grow out of** vt fus (clothes) devenir trop grand pour; (habit) perdre (avec le temps); **he'll ~ out of it** ça lui passera; **grow up** vi grandir

grower ['grəuə'] n producteur m; (Agr) cultivateur(-trice)

growing ['grəuɪŋ] adj (fear, amount)

croissant(e), grandissant(e); **~ pains** (Med) fièvre f de croissance; (fig) difficultés fpl de croissance

growl [graul] vi grogner

grown [grəun] pp of **grow** ▷ adj adulte

grown-up [grəun'ʌp] n adulte m/f, grande personne

growth [grəuθ] n croissance f, développement m; (what has grown) pousse f, poussée f; (Med) grosseur f, tumeur f

grub [grʌb] n larve f; (inf: food) bouffe f

grubby ['grʌbɪ] adj crasseux(-euse)

grudge [grʌdʒ] n rancune f ▷ vt: **to ~ sb sth** (in giving) donner qch à qn à contre-cœur; (resent) reprocher qch à qn; **to bear sb a ~ (for)** garder rancune or en vouloir à qn (de); **he ~s spending** il rechigne à dépenser

gruelling, (US) **grueling** ['gruəlɪŋ] adj exténuant(e)

gruesome ['gru:səm] adj horrible

gruff [grʌf] adj bourru(e)

grumble ['grʌmbl] vi rouspéter, ronchonner

grumpy ['grʌmpɪ] adj grincheux(-euse)

grunt [grʌnt] vi grogner ▷ n grognement m

G-string ['dʒiː:strɪŋ] n (garment) cache-sexe m inv

guarantee [gærən'tiː] n garantie f ▷ vt garantir; **he can't ~ (that) he'll come** il n'est pas absolument certain de pouvoir venir

guard [gɑːd] n garde f, surveillance f; (squad: Boxing, Fencing) garde f; (one man) garde m; (Brit Rail) chef m de train; (safety device: on machine) dispositif m de sûreté; (also: **fire~**) garde-feu m inv ▷ vt garder, surveiller; (protect): **to ~ sb/sth (against** or **from)** protéger qn/qch (contre); **to be on one's ~** (fig) être sur ses gardes; **guard against** vi: **to ~ against doing sth** se garder de faire qch

guarded ['gɑːdɪd] adj (fig) prudent(e)

guardian ['gɑːdɪən] n gardien(ne); (of minor) tuteur(-trice)

guard's van ['gɑːdz-] n (Brit Rail) fourgon m

guerrilla [gə'rɪlə] n guérillero m

guess [gɛs] vi deviner ▷ vt deviner; (estimate) évaluer; (US) croire, penser ▷ n supposition f, hypothèse f; **to take** or **have a ~** essayer de deviner; **to keep sb ~ing** laisser qn dans le doute or l'incertitude, tenir qn en haleine

guesswork ['gɛswəːk] n hypothèse f; **I got the answer by ~** j'ai deviné la réponse

guest [gɛst] n invité(e); (in hotel) client(e); **be my ~** faites comme chez vous

guest house ['gɛsthaus] n pension f

guest room n chambre f d'amis

guffaw [gʌ'fɔː] n gros rire ▷ vi pouffer de rire

guidance ['gaɪdəns] n (advice) conseils mpl; **under the ~ of** conseillé(e) or encadré(e) par, sous la conduite de; **vocational ~** orientation professionnelle; **marriage ~** conseils conjugaux

guide [gaɪd] n (person) guide m/f; (book) guide m; (also: **Girl G~**) éclaireuse f; (Roman Catholic) guide f ▷ vt guider; **to be ~d by sb/ sth** se laisser guider par qn/qch; **is there an English-speaking ~?** est-ce que l'un des guides parle anglais?

guidebook ['gaɪdbuk] n guide m; **do you have a ~ in English?** est-ce que vous avez un guide en anglais?

guide dog n chien m d'aveugle

guided tour n visite guidée; **what time does the ~ start?** la visite guidée commence à quelle heure?

guidelines ['gaɪdlaɪnz] npl (advice) instructions générales, conseils mpl

guild [gɪld] n (Hist) corporation f; (sharing interests) cercle m, association f

guillotine ['gɪləti:n] n guillotine f; (for paper) massicot m

guilt [gɪlt] n culpabilité f

guilty ['gɪltɪ] adj coupable; **to plead ~/not ~** plaider coupable/non coupable; **to feel ~ about doing sth** avoir mauvaise conscience à faire qch

guinea pig ['gɪnɪ-] n cobaye m

guise [gaɪz] n aspect m, apparence f

guitar [gɪ'tɑːʳ] n guitare f

guitarist [gɪ'tɑːrɪst] n guitariste m/f

gulf [gʌlf] n golfe m; (abyss) gouffre m; **the (Persian) G~** le golfe Persique

gull [gʌl] n mouette f

gullible ['gʌlɪbl] adj crédule

gully ['gʌlɪ] n ravin m; ravine f; couloir m

gulp [gʌlp] vi avaler sa salive; (from emotion) avoir la gorge serrée, s'étrangler ▷ vt (also: **~ down**) avaler ▷ n (of drink) gorgée f; **at one ~** d'un seul coup

gum [gʌm] n (Anat) gencive f; (glue) colle f; (sweet) boule f de gomme; (also: **chewing-~**) chewing-gum m ▷ vt coller

gumboots ['gʌmbu:ts] npl (Brit) bottes fpl en caoutchouc

gun [gʌn] n (small) revolver m, pistolet m; (rifle) fusil m, carabine f; (cannon) canon m ▷ vt (also: **~ down**) abattre; **to stick to one's ~s** (fig) ne pas en démordre

gunboat ['gʌnbəut] n canonnière f

gunfire ['gʌnfaɪəʳ] n fusillade f

gunman irreg ['gʌnmən] n bandit armé

gunpoint ['gʌnpɔɪnt] n: **at ~** sous la menace du pistolet (or fusil)

gunpowder ['gʌnpaudəʳ] n poudre f à canon

gunshot ['gʌnʃɔt] n coup m de feu; **within ~** à portée de fusil

gurgle ['gəːgl] n gargouillis m ▷ vi gargouiller

gush [gʌʃ] n jaillissement m, jet m ▷ vi jaillir; (fig) se répandre en effusions

gust [gʌst] n (of wind) rafale f; (of smoke) bouffée f

gusto ['gʌstəu] n enthousiasme m

gut [gʌt] n intestin m, boyau m; (Mus etc) boyau m ▷ vt (poultry, fish) vider; (building) ne laisser que les murs de; **guts** npl (Anat) boyaux mpl; (inf: courage) cran m; **to hate sb's**

~s ne pas pouvoir voir qn en peinture or sentir qn

gutter ['gʌtər] n (of roof) gouttière f; (in street) caniveau m; (fig) ruisseau m

guy [gaɪ] n (inf: man) type m; (also: ~rope) corde f; (figure) effigie de Guy Fawkes

Guy Fawkes' Night [gaɪ'fɔːks-] n voir article

guzzle ['gʌzl] vi s'empiffrer ▷ vt avaler gloutonnement

gym [dʒɪm] n (also: **gymnasium**) gymnase m; (also: **gymnastics**) gym f

gymnasium [dʒɪm'neɪzɪəm] n gymnase m

gymnast ['dʒɪmnæst] n gymnaste m/f

gymnastics [dʒɪm'næstɪks] n, npl gymnastique f

gym shoes npl chaussures fpl de gym(nastique)

gynaecologist, (US) **gynecologist** [gaɪnɪ'kɔlədʒɪst] n gynécologue m/f

gypsy ['dʒɪpsɪ] n gitan(e), bohémien(ne) ▷ cpd: ~ **caravan** n roulotte f

haberdashery [hæbə'dæʃərɪ] n (Brit) mercerie f

habit ['hæbɪt] n habitude f; (costume: Rel) habit m; (for riding) tenue f d'équitation; **to get out of/into the ~ of doing sth** perdre/prendre l'habitude de faire qch

habitat ['hæbɪtæt] n habitat m

habitual [hə'bɪtjuəl] adj habituel(le); (drinker, liar) invétéré(e)

hack [hæk] vt hacher, tailler ▷ n (cut) entaille f; (blow) coup m; (pej: writer) nègre m; (old horse) canasson m

hacker ['hækər] n (Comput) pirate m (informatique); (: enthusiast) passionné(e) m/f des ordinateurs

hackneyed ['hæknɪd] adj usé(e), rebattu(e)

had [hæd] pt, pp of have

haddock (pl haddock or haddocks) ['hædək] n églefin m; **smoked ~** haddock m

hadn't ['hædnt] = had not

haemorrhage, (US) **hemorrhage** ['hemərɪdʒ] n hémorragie f

haemorrhoids, (US) **hemorrhoids** ['hemərɔɪdz] npl hémorroïdes fpl

haggle ['hægl] vi marchander; **to ~ over** chicaner sur

Hague [heɪg] n: **The ~** La Haye

hail [heɪl] n grêle f ▷ vt (call) héler; (greet) acclamer ▷ vi grêler; (originate): **he ~s from Scotland** il est originaire d'Écosse

hailstone ['heɪlstəun] n grêlon m

hair [hɛə^r] n cheveux mpl; (on body) poils mpl, pilosité f; (of animal) pelage m; (single hair: on head) cheveu m; (: on body, of animal) poil m; **to do one's ~** se coiffer

hairband ['hɛəbænd] n (elasticated) bandeau m; (plastic) serre-tête m

hairbrush ['hɛəbrʌʃ] n brosse f à cheveux

haircut ['hɛəkʌt] n coupe f (de cheveux)

hairdo ['hɛəduː] n coiffure f

hairdresser ['hɛədrɛsə^r] n coiffeur(-euse)

hairdresser's ['hɛədrɛsəz] n salon m de coiffure, coiffeur m

hair dryer ['hɛədraɪə^r] n sèche-cheveux m, séchoir m

hair gel n gel m pour cheveux

hairgrip ['hɛəgrɪp] n pince f à cheveux

hairnet ['hɛənɛt] n résille f

hairpiece ['hɛəpiːs] n postiche m

hairpin ['hɛəpɪn] n épingle f à cheveux

hairpin bend, (US) **hairpin curve** n virage m en épingle à cheveux

hair-raising ['hɛəreɪzɪŋ] adj à (vous) faire dresser les cheveux sur la tête

hair removing cream n crème f dépilatoire

hair spray n laque f (pour les cheveux)

hairstyle ['hɛəstaɪl] n coiffure f

hairy ['hɛərɪ] adj poilu(e), chevelu(e); (inf: frightening) effrayant(e)

hake (pl **hake** or **hakes**) [heɪk] n colin m, merlu m

half [hɑːf] n (pl **halves**) [hɑːvz] moitié f; (of beer: also: **~ pint**) ≈ demi m; (Rail, bus: also: **~ fare**) demi-tarif m; (Sport: of match) mi-temps f; (: of ground) moitié (du terrain) ▷ adj demi(e) ▷ adv (à) moitié, à demi; **~ an hour** une demi-heure; **~ a dozen** une demi-douzaine; **~ a pound** une demi-livre, ≈ 250 g; **two and a ~** deux et demi; **a week and a ~** une semaine et demie; **~ (of it)** la moitié; **~ (of)** la moitié de; **~ the amount of** la moitié de; **to cut sth in ~** couper qch en deux; **~ past three** trois heures et demie; **~ empty/closed** à moitié vide/fermé; **to go halves (with sb)** se mettre de moitié avec qn

half board n (Brit: in hotel) demi-pension f

half-brother ['hɑːfbrʌðə^r] n demi-frère m

half-caste ['hɑːfkɑːst] n (inf!) métis(se)

half day n demi-journée f

half fare n demi-tarif m

half-hearted ['hɑːf'hɑːtɪd] adj tiède, sans enthousiasme

half-hour ['hɑːf'auə^r] n demi-heure f

half-mast ['hɑːf'mɑːst] n: **at ~** (flag) en berne, à mi-mât

halfpenny ['heɪpnɪ] n demi-penny m

half-price ['hɑːf'praɪs] adj à moitié prix ▷ adv (also: **at ~**) à moitié prix

half term n (Brit Scol) vacances fpl (de demi-trimestre)

half-time ['hɑːf'taɪm] n mi-temps f

halfway ['hɑːf'weɪ] adv à mi-chemin; **to meet sb ~** (fig) parvenir à un compromis avec

qn; **~ through sth** au milieu de qch

hall [hɔːl] n salle f; (entrance way: big) hall m; (small) entrée f; (US: corridor) couloir m; (mansion) château m, manoir m

hallmark ['hɔːlmɑːk] n poinçon m; (fig) marque f

hallo [hə'ləu] excl = **hello**

hall of residence n (Brit) pavillon m or résidence f universitaire

Hallowe'en, Halloween ['hæləu'iːn] n veille f de la Toussaint; voir article

● **HALLOWE'EN**
●
● Selon la tradition, Hallowe'en est la nuit
● des fantômes et des sorcières. En Écosse
● et aux États-Unis surtout (et de plus en
● plus en Angleterre) les enfants, pour fêter
● Hallowe'en, se déguisent ce soir-là et ils
● vont ainsi de porte en porte en
● demandant de petits cadeaux
● (du chocolat, etc).

hallucination [həluːsɪ'neɪʃən] n hallucination f

hallway ['hɔːlweɪ] n (entrance) vestibule m; (corridor) couloir m

halo ['heɪləu] n (of saint etc) auréole f; (of sun) halo m

halt [hɔːlt] n halte f, arrêt m ▷ vt faire arrêter; (progress etc) interrompre ▷ vi faire halte, s'arrêter; **to call a ~ to sth** (fig) mettre fin à qch

halve [hɑːv] vt (apple etc) partager or diviser en deux; (reduce by half) réduire de moitié

halves [hɑːvz] npl of **half**

ham [hæm] n jambon m; (inf: also: **radio ~**) radio-amateur m; (also: **~ actor**) cabotin(e)

hamburger ['hæmbəːgə^r] n hamburger m

hamlet ['hæmlɪt] n hameau m

hammer ['hæmə^r] n marteau m ▷ vt (nail) enfoncer; (fig) éreinter, démolir ▷ vi (at door) frapper à coups redoublés; **to ~ a point home to sb** faire rentrer qch dans la tête de qn; **hammer out** vt (metal) étendre au marteau; (fig: solution) élaborer

hammock ['hæmək] n hamac m

hamper ['hæmpə^r] vt gêner ▷ n panier m (d'osier)

hamster ['hæmstə^r] n hamster m

hamstring ['hæmstrɪŋ] n (Anat) tendon m du jarret

hand [hænd] n main f; (of clock) aiguille f; (handwriting) écriture f; (at cards) jeu m; (measurement: of horse) paume f; (worker) ouvrier(-ière) ▷ vt passer, donner; **to give sb a ~** donner un coup de main à qn; **at ~** à portée de la main; **in ~** (situation) en main; (work) en cours; **we have the situation in ~** nous avons la situation bien en main; **to be on ~** (person) être disponible; (emergency services) se tenir prêt(e) (à intervenir); **to ~**

(information etc) sous la main, à portée de la main; **to force sb's ~** forcer la main à qn; **to have a free ~** avoir carte blanche; **to have sth in one's ~** tenir qch à la main; **on the one ~ ..., on the other ~** d'une part ..., d'autre part ...; **hand down** vt passer; (tradition, heirloom) transmettre; (US: sentence, verdict) prononcer; **hand in** vt remettre; **hand out** vt distribuer; **hand over** vt remettre; (powers etc) transmettre; **hand round** vt (Brit: information) faire circuler; (: chocolates etc) faire passer

handbag ['hændbæg] n sac m à main
hand baggage n = **hand luggage**
handbook ['hændbuk] n manuel m
handbrake ['hændbreɪk] n frein m à main
handcuffs ['hændkʌfs] npl menottes fpl
handful ['hændful] n poignée f
handicap ['hændɪkæp] n handicap m ▷ vt handicaper; **mentally/physically ~ped** (pej) handicapé(e) mentalement/physiquement
handicraft ['hændɪkrɑːft] n travail m d'artisanat, technique artisanale
handiwork ['hændɪwəːk] n ouvrage m; **this looks like his ~** (pej) ça a tout l'air d'être son œuvre
handkerchief ['hæŋkətʃɪf] n mouchoir m
handle ['hændl] n (of door etc) poignée f; (of cup etc) anse f; (of knife etc) manche m; (of saucepan) queue f; (for winding) manivelle f ▷ vt toucher, manier; (deal with) s'occuper de; (treat: people) prendre; **"~ with care"** "fragile"; **to fly off the ~** s'énerver
handlebar ['hændlbɑːʳ] n, **handlebars** ['hændlbɑːz] npl guidon m
hand luggage ['hændlʌɡɪdʒ] n bagages mpl à main; **one item of ~** un bagage à main
handmade ['hænd'meɪd] adj fait(e) à la main
handout ['hændaut] n (money) aide f, don m; (leaflet) prospectus m; (press handout) communiqué m de presse; (at lecture) polycopié m
handrail ['hændreɪl] n (on staircase etc) rampe f, main courante
handset ['hændset] n (Tel) combiné m
hands-free ['hændz'friː] adj mains libres inv ▷ n (also: **~ kit**) kit m mains libres inv
handshake ['hændʃeɪk] n poignée f de main; (Comput) établissement m de la liaison
handsome ['hænsəm] adj beau/belle; (gift) généreux(-euse); (profit) considérable
handwriting ['hændraɪtɪŋ] n écriture f
handy ['hændɪ] adj (person) adroit(e); (close at hand) sous la main; (convenient) pratique; **to come in ~** être (or s'avérer) utile
hang (pt, pp hung) [hæŋ, hʌŋ] vt accrocher; (criminal) (pt, pp hanged) pendre ▷ vi pendre; (hair, drapery) tomber ▷ to: **to get the ~ of (doing) sth** (inf) attraper le coup pour faire qch; **hang about, hang around** vi flâner, traîner; **hang back** vi (hesitate): **to ~ back**

(from doing) être réticent(e) (pour faire); **hang down** vi pendre; **hang on** vi (wait) attendre ▷ vt fus (depend on) dépendre de; **to ~ on to** (keep hold of) ne pas lâcher; (keep) garder; **hang out** vt (washing) étendre (dehors) ▷ vi pendre; (inf: live) habiter, percher; (: spend time) traîner; **hang round** vi = **hang around**; **hang together** vi (argument etc) se tenir, être cohérent(e); **hang up** vi (Tel) raccrocher ▷ vt (coat, painting etc) accrocher, suspendre; **to ~ up on sb** (Tel) raccrocher au nez de qn

hangar ['hæŋəʳ] n hangar m
hanger ['hæŋəʳ] n cintre m, portemanteau m
hanger-on [hæŋər'ɔn] n parasite m
hang-gliding ['hæŋglaɪdɪŋ] n vol m libre or sur aile delta
hangover ['hæŋəuvəʳ] n (after drinking) gueule f de bois
hang-up ['hæŋʌp] n complexe m
hanker ['hæŋkəʳ] vi: **to ~ after** avoir envie de
hankie, hanky ['hæŋkɪ] n abbr = **handkerchief**
haphazard [hæp'hæzəd] adj fait(e) au hasard, fait(e) au petit bonheur
happen ['hæpən] vi arriver, se passer, se produire; **what's ~ing?** que se passe-t-il?; **she ~ed to be free** il s'est trouvé (or se trouvait) qu'elle était libre; **if anything ~ed to him** s'il lui arrivait quoi que ce soit; **as it ~s** justement; **happen on, happen upon** vt fus tomber sur
happening ['hæpnɪŋ] n événement m
happily ['hæpɪlɪ] adv heureusement; (cheerfully) joyeusement
happiness ['hæpɪnɪs] n bonheur m
happy ['hæpɪ] adj heureux(-euse); **~ with** (arrangements etc) satisfait(e) de; **to be ~ to do** faire volontiers; **yes, I'd be ~ to** oui, avec plaisir or (bien) volontiers; **~ birthday!** bon anniversaire!; **~ Christmas/New Year!** joyeux Noël/bonne année!
happy-go-lucky ['hæpɪgəu'lʌkɪ] adj insouciant(e)
happy hour n l'heure f de l'apéritif, heure pendant laquelle les consommations sont à prix réduit
harass ['hærəs] vt accabler, tourmenter
harassment ['hærəsmənt] n tracasseries fpl; **sexual ~** harcèlement sexuel
harbour, (US) **harbor** ['hɑːbəʳ] n port m ▷ vt héberger, abriter; (hopes, suspicions) entretenir; **to ~ a grudge against sb** en vouloir à qn
hard [hɑːd] adj dur(e); (question, problem) difficile; (facts, evidence) concret(-ète) ▷ adv (work) dur; (think, try) sérieusement; **to look ~ at** regarder fixement; (thing) regarder de près; **to drink ~** boire sec; **~ luck!** pas de veine!; **no ~ feelings!** sans rancune!; **to be ~ of hearing** être dur(e) d'oreille; **to be done by** être traité(e) injustement; **to be ~ on sb** être dur(e) avec qn; **I find it ~ to believe that ...** je n'arrive pas à croire que ...

h

hardback ['hɑːdbæk] n livre relié
hardboard ['hɑːdbɔːd] n Isorel® m
hard cash n espèces fpl
hard disk n (Comput) disque dur
harden ['hɑːdn] vt durcir; (steel) tremper; (fig) endurcir ▷ vi (substance) durcir
hard-headed ['hɑːd'hedɪd] adj réaliste; décidé(e)
hard labour n travaux forcés
hardly ['hɑːdlɪ] adv (scarcely) à peine; (harshly) durement; **it's ~ the case** ce n'est guère le cas; **~ anywhere/ever** presque nulle part/jamais; **I can ~ believe it** j'ai du mal à le croire
hardship ['hɑːdʃɪp] n (difficulties) épreuves fpl; (deprivation) privations fpl
hard shoulder n (Brit Aut) accotement stabilisé
hard-up [hɑːd'ʌp] adj (inf) fauché(e)
hardware ['hɑːdwɛə'] n quincaillerie f; (Comput, Mil) matériel m
hardware shop, (US) **hardware store** n quincaillerie f
hard-wearing [hɑːd'wɛərɪŋ] adj solide
hard-working [hɑːd'wɜːkɪŋ] adj travailleur(-euse), consciencieux(-euse)
hardy ['hɑːdɪ] adj robuste; (plant) résistant(e) au gel
hare [hɛə'] n lièvre m
hare-brained ['hɛəbreɪnd] adj farfelu(e), écervelé(e)
harm [hɑːm] n mal m; (wrong) tort m ▷ vt (person) faire du mal ou du tort à; (thing) endommager; **to mean no ~** ne pas avoir de mauvaises intentions; **there's no ~ in trying** on peut toujours essayer; **out of ~'s way** à l'abri du danger, en lieu sûr
harmful ['hɑːmful] adj nuisible
harmless ['hɑːmlɪs] adj inoffensif(-ive)
harmony ['hɑːmənɪ] n harmonie f
harness ['hɑːnɪs] n harnais m ▷ vt (horse) harnacher; (resources) exploiter
harp [hɑːp] n harpe f ▷ vi: **to ~ on about** revenir toujours sur
harrowing ['hærəʊɪŋ] adj déchirant(e)
harsh [hɑːʃ] adj (hard) dur(e); (severe) sévère; (rough: surface) rugueux(-euse); (unpleasant: sound) discordant(e); (: light) cru(e); (: taste) âpre
harvest ['hɑːvɪst] n (of corn) moisson f; (of fruit) récolte f; (of grapes) vendange f ▷ vi, vt moissonner; récolter; vendanger
has [hæz] vb see **have**
hash [hæʃ] n (Culin) hachis m; (fig: mess) gâchis m
hashtag ['hæʃtæg] n (on Twitter) mot-dièse m
hasn't ['hæznt] = **has not**
hassle ['hæsl] n (inf: fuss) histoire(s) f(pl)
haste [heɪst] n hâte f, précipitation f; **in ~** à la hâte, précipitamment
hasten ['heɪsn] vt hâter, accélérer ▷ vi se hâter, s'empresser; **I ~ to add that …** je m'empresse d'ajouter que …

hastily ['heɪstɪlɪ] adv à la hâte; (leave) précipitamment
hasty ['heɪstɪ] adj (decision, action) hâtif(-ive); (departure, escape) précipité(e)
hat [hæt] n chapeau m
hatch [hætʃ] n (Naut: also: **~way**) écoutille f; (Brit: also: **service ~**) passe-plats m inv ▷ vi éclore ▷ vt faire éclore; (fig: scheme) tramer, ourdir
hatchback ['hætʃbæk] n (Aut) modèle m avec hayon arrière
hatchet ['hætʃɪt] n hachette f
hate [heɪt] vt haïr, détester ▷ n haine f; **to ~ to do** or **doing** détester faire; **I ~ to trouble you, but …** désolé de vous déranger, mais …
hateful ['heɪtful] adj odieux(-euse), détestable
hatred ['heɪtrɪd] n haine f
haughty ['hɔːtɪ] adj hautain(e), arrogant(e)
haul [hɔːl] vt traîner, tirer; (by lorry) camionner; (Naut) haler ▷ n (of fish) prise f; (of stolen goods etc) butin m
haulage ['hɔːlɪdʒ] n transport routier
haulier ['hɔːlɪə'], (US) **hauler** ['hɔːlə'] n transporteur (routier), camionneur m
haunch [hɔːntʃ] n hanche f; **~ of venison** cuissot m de chevreuil
haunt [hɔːnt] vt (subj: ghost, fear) hanter; (: person) fréquenter ▷ n repaire m
haunted ['hɔːntɪd] adj (castle etc) hanté(e); (look) égaré(e), hagard(e)

○ **KEYWORD**

have [hæv] (pt, pp **had**) aux vb **1** (gen) avoir; être; **to have eaten/slept** avoir mangé/dormi; **to have arrived/gone** être arrivé(e)/allé(e); **he has been promoted** il a eu une promotion; **having finished** or **when he had finished, he left** quand il a eu fini, il est parti; **we'd already eaten** nous avions déjà mangé
2 (in tag questions): **you've done it, haven't you?** vous l'avez fait, n'est-ce pas?
3 (in short answers and questions): **no I haven't!/yes we have!** mais non!/mais si!; **so I have!** ah oui!, oui c'est vrai!; **I've been there before, have you?** j'y suis déjà allé, et vous?
▷ modal aux vb (be obliged): **to have (got) to do sth** devoir faire qch, être obligé(e) de faire qch; **she has (got) to do it** elle doit le faire, il faut qu'elle le fasse; **you haven't to tell her** vous n'êtes pas obligé de le lui dire; (must not) ne le lui dites surtout pas; **do you have to book?** il faut réserver?
▷ vt **1** (possess) avoir; **he has (got) blue eyes/dark hair** il a les yeux bleus/les cheveux bruns
2 (referring to meals etc): **to have breakfast** prendre le petit déjeuner; **to have dinner/lunch** dîner/déjeuner; **to have a drink** prendre un verre; **to have a cigarette** fumer une cigarette

3 (*receive*) avoir, recevoir; (*obtain*) avoir; **may I have your address?** puis-je avoir votre adresse?; **you can have it for £5** vous pouvez l'avoir pour 5 livres; **I must have it for tomorrow** il me le faut pour demain; **to have a baby** avoir un bébé

4 (*maintain, allow*): **I won't have it!** ça ne se passera pas comme ça!; **we can't have that** nous ne tolérerons pas ça

5 (*by sb else*): **to have sth done** faire faire qch; **to have one's hair cut** se faire couper les cheveux; **to have sb do sth** faire faire qch à qn

6 (*experience, suffer*) avoir; **to have a cold/flu** avoir un rhume/la grippe; **to have an operation** se faire opérer; **she had her bag stolen** elle s'est fait voler son sac

7 (*+noun*): **to have a swim/walk** nager/se promener; **to have a bath/shower** prendre un bain/une douche; **let's have a look** regardons; **to have a meeting** se réunir; **to have a party** organiser une fête; **let me have a try** laissez-moi essayer

8 (*inf: dupe*) avoir; **he's been had** il s'est fait avoir or rouler

have out vt: **to have it out with sb** (*settle a problem etc*) s'expliquer (franchement) avec qn

haven ['heivn] n port m; (*fig*) havre m
haven't ['hævnt] = **have not**
havoc ['hævək] n ravages mpl, dégâts mpl; **to play ~ with** (*fig*) désorganiser complètement; détraquer
Hawaii [hə'waːi:] n (îles fpl) Hawaï m
hawk [hɔːk] n faucon m ▷ vt (*goods for sale*) colporter
hawthorn ['hɔːθɔːn] n aubépine f
hay [hei] n foin m
hay fever n rhume m des foins
haystack ['heistæk] n meule f de foin
haywire ['heiwaiəʳ] adj (*inf*): **to go ~** perdre la tête; mal tourner
hazard ['hæzəd] n (*risk*) danger m, risque m; (*chance*) hasard m, chance f ▷ vt risquer, hasarder; **to be a health/fire ~** présenter un risque pour la santé/d'incendie; **to ~ a guess** émettre or hasarder une hypothèse
hazardous ['hæzədəs] adj hasardeux(-euse), risqué(e)
hazard warning lights npl (*Aut*) feux mpl de détresse
haze [heiz] n brume f
hazel ['heizl] n (*tree*) noisetier m ▷ adj (*eyes*) noisette inv
hazelnut ['heizlnʌt] n noisette f
hazy ['heizi] adj brumeux(-euse); (*idea*) vague; (*photograph*) flou(e)
HD abbr (= high definition) HD (= haute définition)
HDTV n abbr (= high definition television) TVHD f (= télévision haute-définition)
he [hiː] pron il; **it is he who ...** c'est lui qui ...; **here he is** le voici; **he-bear** etc ours etc mâle

head [hɛd] n tête f; (*leader*) chef m; (*of school*) directeur(-trice); (*of secondary school*) proviseur m ▷ vt (*list*) être en tête de; (*group, company*) être à la tête de; **heads** pl (*on coin*) (le côté) face; **~s or tails** pile ou face; **~ first** la tête la première; **~ over heels in love** follement or éperdument amoureux(-euse); **to ~ the ball** faire une tête; **10 euros a** or **per ~** 10 euros par personne; **to sit at the ~ of the table** présider la tablée; **to have a ~ for business** avoir des dispositions pour les affaires; **to have no ~ for heights** être sujet(te) au vertige; **to come to a ~** (*fig: situation etc*) devenir critique; **head for** vt fus se diriger vers; (*disaster*) aller à; **head off** vt (*threat, danger*) détourner
headache ['hɛdeik] n mal m de tête; **to have a ~** avoir mal à la tête
headdress ['hɛddrɛs] n coiffure f
heading ['hɛdiŋ] n titre m; (*subject title*) rubrique f
headlamp ['hɛdlæmp] (*Brit*) n = **headlight**
headland ['hɛdlənd] n promontoire m, cap m
headlight ['hɛdlait] n phare m
headline ['hɛdlain] n titre m
headlong ['hɛdlɔŋ] adv (*fall*) la tête la première; (*rush*) tête baissée
headmaster [hɛd'mɑːstəʳ] n directeur m, proviseur m
headmistress [hɛd'mistris] n directrice f
head office n siège m, bureau m central
head-on [hɛd'ɔn] adj (*collision*) de plein fouet
headphones ['hɛdfəunz] npl casque m (à écouteurs)
headquarters ['hɛdkwɔːtəz] npl (*of business*) bureau or siège central; (*Mil*) quartier général
headrest ['hɛdrɛst] n appui-tête m
headroom ['hɛdrum] n (*in car*) hauteur f de plafond; (*under bridge*) hauteur limite; dégagement m
headscarf (pl **headscarves**) ['hɛdskɑːf, -skɑːvz] n foulard m
headset ['hɛdsɛt] n = **headphones**
headstrong ['hɛdstrɔŋ] adj têtu(e), entêté(e)
headteacher [hɛd'tiːtʃəʳ] n directeur(-trice); (*of secondary school*) proviseur m
head waiter n maître m d'hôtel
headway ['hɛdwei] n: **to make ~** avancer, faire des progrès
headwind ['hɛdwind] n vent m contraire
heady ['hɛdi] adj capiteux(-euse), enivrant(e)
heal [hiːl] vt, vi guérir
health [hɛlθ] n santé f; **Department of H~** (*Brit, US*) ≈ ministère m de la Santé
health care n services médicaux
health centre n (*Brit*) centre m de santé
health food n aliment(s) naturel(s)
health food shop n magasin m diététique
Health Service n: **the ~** (*Brit*) ≈ la Sécurité Sociale
healthy ['hɛlθi] adj (*person*) en bonne santé; (*climate, food, attitude etc*) sain(e)

h

heap [hi:p] n tas m, monceau m ▷ vt (also: ~ up) entasser, amonceler; **she ~ed her plate with cakes** elle a chargé son assiette de gâteaux; **~s (of)** (inf: lots) des tas (de); **to ~ favours/praise/gifts** etc **on sb** combler qn de faveurs/d'éloges/de cadeaux etc

hear (pt, pp **heard**) [hɪəʳ, hə:d] vt entendre; (news) apprendre; (lecture) assister à, écouter ▷ vi entendre; **to ~ about** entendre parler de; (have news of) avoir des nouvelles de; **did you ~ about the move?** tu es au courant du déménagement?; **to ~ from sb** recevoir des nouvelles de qn; **I've never ~d of that book** je n'ai jamais entendu parler de ce livre; **hear out** vt écouter jusqu'au bout

heard [hə:d] pt, pp of **hear**

hearing ['hɪərɪŋ] n (sense) ouïe f; (of witnesses) audition f; (of a case) audience f; (of committee) séance f; **to give sb a ~** (Brit) écouter ce que qn a à dire

hearing aid n appareil m acoustique

hearsay ['hɪəseɪ] n on-dit mpl, rumeurs fpl; **by ~** adv par ouï-dire

hearse [hə:s] n corbillard m

heart [ha:t] n cœur m; **hearts** npl (Cards) cœur; **at ~** au fond; **by ~** (learn, know) par cœur; **to have a weak ~** avoir le cœur malade, avoir des problèmes de cœur; **to lose/take ~** perdre/prendre courage; **to set one's ~ on sth/on doing sth** vouloir absolument qch/faire qch; **the ~ of the matter** le fond du problème

heart attack n crise f cardiaque

heartbeat ['ha:tbi:t] n battement m de cœur

heartbreaking ['ha:tbreikiŋ] adj navrant(e), déchirant(e)

heartbroken ['ha:tbrəukən] adj: **to be ~** avoir beaucoup de chagrin

heartburn ['ha:tbə:n] n brûlures fpl d'estomac

heart disease n maladie f cardiaque

heart failure n (Med) arrêt m du cœur

heartfelt ['ha:tfelt] adj sincère

hearth [ha:θ] n foyer m, cheminée f

heartily ['ha:tɪlɪ] adv chaleureusement; (laugh) de bon cœur; (eat) de bon appétit; **to agree ~** être entièrement d'accord; **to be ~ sick of** (Brit) en avoir ras le bol de

heartless ['ha:tlɪs] adj (person) sans cœur, insensible; (treatment) cruel(le)

hearty ['ha:tɪ] adj chaleureux(-euse); (appetite) solide; (dislike) cordial(e); (meal) copieux(-euse)

heat [hi:t] n chaleur f; (fig) ardeur f; feu m; (Sport: also: **qualifying ~**) éliminatoire f; (Zool): **in** or **on** ~ (Brit) en chaleur ▷ vt chauffer; **heat up** vi (liquid) chauffer; (room) se réchauffer ▷ vt réchauffer

heated ['hi:tɪd] adj chauffé(e); (fig) passionné(e), échauffé(e), excité(e)

heater ['hi:təʳ] n appareil m de chauffage; radiateur m; (in car) chauffage m; (water heater) chauffe-eau m

heath [hi:θ] n (Brit) lande f

heather ['hɛðəʳ] n bruyère f

heating ['hi:tɪŋ] n chauffage m

heatstroke ['hi:tstrəuk] n coup m de chaleur

heatwave ['hi:tweɪv] n vague f de chaleur

heave [hi:v] vt soulever (avec effort) ▷ vi se soulever; (retch) avoir des haut-le-cœur ▷ n (push) poussée f; **to ~ a sigh** pousser un gros soupir

heaven ['hɛvn] n ciel m, paradis m; (fig) paradis; **~ forbid!** surtout pas!; **thank ~!** Dieu merci!; **for ~'s sake!** (pleading) je vous en prie!; (protesting) mince alors!

heavenly ['hɛvnlɪ] adj céleste, divin(e)

heavily ['hɛvɪlɪ] adv lourdement; (drink, smoke) beaucoup; (sleep, sigh) profondément

heavy ['hɛvɪ] adj lourd(e); (work, rain, user, eater) gros(se); (drinker, smoker) grand(e); (schedule, week) chargé(e); **it's too ~** c'est trop lourd; **it's ~ going** ça ne va pas tout seul, c'est pénible

heavy goods vehicle n (Brit) poids lourd m

heavyweight ['hɛvɪweɪt] n (Sport) poids lourd

Hebrew ['hi:bru:] adj hébraïque ▷ n (Ling) hébreu m

Hebrides ['hɛbrɪdi:z] npl: **the ~** les Hébrides fpl

heckle ['hɛkl] vt interpeller (un orateur)

hectare ['hɛktɑ:ʳ] n (Brit) hectare m

hectic ['hɛktɪk] adj (schedule) très chargé(e); (day) mouvementé(e); (activity) fiévreux(-euse); (lifestyle) trépidant(e)

he'd [hi:d] = he would; he had

hedge [hɛdʒ] n haie f ▷ vi se dérober ▷ vt: **to ~ one's bets** (fig) se couvrir; **as a ~ against inflation** pour se prémunir contre l'inflation; **hedge in** vt entourer d'une haie

hedgehog ['hɛdʒhɔg] n hérisson m

heed [hi:d] vt (also: **take ~ of**) tenir compte de, prendre garde à

heedless ['hi:dlɪs] adj insouciant(e)

heel [hi:l] n (of person) talon m ▷ vt (shoe) retalonner; **to bring to ~** (dog) faire venir à ses pieds; (fig: person) rappeler à l'ordre; **to take to one's ~s** prendre ses jambes à son cou

hefty ['hɛftɪ] adj (person) costaud(e); (parcel) lourd(e); (piece, price) gros(se)

heifer ['hɛfəʳ] n génisse f

height [haɪt] n (of person) taille f, grandeur f; (of object) hauteur f; (of plane, mountain) altitude f; (high ground) hauteur, éminence f; (fig: of glory, fame, power) sommet m; (: of luxury, stupidity) comble m; **at the ~ of summer** au cœur de l'été; **what ~ are you?** combien mesurez-vous?, quelle est votre taille?; **of average ~** de taille moyenne; **to be afraid of ~s** être sujet(te) au vertige; **it's the ~ of fashion** c'est le dernier cri

heighten ['haɪtn] vt hausser, surélever; (fig) augmenter

heir [ɛəʳ] n héritier m

heiress ['ɛəres] n héritière f

heirloom ['ɛəlu:m] n meuble m (or bijou m or tableau m) de famille

held [held] pt, pp of **hold**

helicopter ['helɪkɒptər] n hélicoptère m

hell [hel] n enfer m; **a ~ of a ...** (inf) un(e) sacré(e) ...; **oh ~!** (inf) merde!

he'll [hi:l] = **he will; he shall**

hellish ['helɪʃ] adj infernal(e)

hello [hə'ləu] excl bonjour!; (to attract attention) hé!; (surprise) tiens!

helm [helm] n (Naut) barre f

helmet ['helmɪt] n casque m

help [help] n aide f; (cleaner etc) femme f de ménage; (assistant etc) employé(e) f ▷ vt aider; **~!** au secours!; **~ yourself** servez-vous; **can you ~ me?** pouvez-vous m'aider?; **can I ~ you?** (in shop) vous désirez?; **with the ~ of** (person) avec l'aide de; (tool etc) à l'aide de; **to be of ~ to sb** être utile à qn; **to ~ sb (to) do sth** aider qn à faire qch; **I can't ~ saying** je ne peux pas m'empêcher de dire; **he can't ~ it** il n'y peut rien; **help out** vi aider ▷ vt: **to ~ sb out** aider qn

helper ['helpər] n aide m/f, assistant(e)

helpful ['helpful] adj serviable, obligeant(e); (useful) utile

helping ['helpɪŋ] n portion f

helpless ['helplɪs] adj impuissant(e); (baby) sans défense

helpline ['helplaɪn] n service m d'assistance téléphonique; (free) ≈ numéro vert

hem [hem] n ourlet m ▷ vt ourler; **hem in** vt cerner; **to feel ~med in** (fig) avoir l'impression d'étouffer, se sentir oppressé(e) or écrasé(e)

hemisphere ['hemɪsfɪər] n hémisphère m

hemorrhage ['hemərɪdʒ] n (US) = **haemorrhage**

hemorrhoids ['hemərɔɪdz] npl (US) = **haemorrhoids**

hen [hen] n poule f; (female bird) femelle f

hence [hens] adv (therefore) d'où, de là; **2 years ~** d'ici 2 ans

henceforth ['hensfɔ:θ] adv dorénavant

hen night, hen party n soirée f entre filles (avant le mariage de l'une d'elles)

hepatitis [hepə'taɪtɪs] n hépatite f

her [hə:r] pron (direct) la, l' + vowel or h mute; (indirect) lui; (stressed, after prep) elle ▷ adj son/sa, ses pl; **I see ~** je la vois; **give ~ a book** donne-lui un livre; **after ~** après elle; see also **me; my**

herald ['herəld] n héraut m ▷ vt annoncer

heraldry ['herəldrɪ] n héraldique f; (coat of arms) blason m

herb [hə:b] n herbe f; **herbs** npl fines herbes

herbal ['hə:bl] adj à base de plantes

herbal tea n tisane f

herd [hə:d] n troupeau m; (of wild animals, swine) troupeau, troupe f ▷ vt (drive: animals, people) mener, conduire; (gather) rassembler; **~ed together** parqués (comme du bétail)

here [hɪər] adv ici; (time) alors ▷ excl tiens!, tenez!; **~!** (present) présent!; **~ is, ~ are** voici; **~'s my sister** voici ma sœur; **~ he/she is** le/la voici; **~ she comes** la voici qui vient; **come ~!** viens ici!; **~ and there** ici et là

hereafter [hɪər'ɑ:ftər] adv après, plus tard; ci-après ▷ n: **the ~** l'au-delà m

hereby [hɪə'baɪ] adv (in letter) par la présente

hereditary [hɪ'redɪtrɪ] adj héréditaire

heresy ['herəsɪ] n hérésie f

heritage ['herɪtɪdʒ] n héritage m, patrimoine m; **our national ~** notre patrimoine national

hermit ['hə:mɪt] n ermite m

hernia ['hə:nɪə] n hernie f

hero ['hɪərəu] (pl **heroes**) n héros m

heroic [hɪ'rəuɪk] adj héroïque

heroin ['herəuɪn] n héroïne f (drogue)

heroine ['herəuɪn] n héroïne f (femme)

heron ['herən] n héron m

herring ['herɪŋ] n hareng m

hers [hə:z] pron le/la sien(ne), les siens/ siennes; **a friend of ~** un(e) ami(e) à elle, un(e) de ses ami(e)s; see also **mine[1]**

herself [hə:'self] pron (reflexive) se; (emphatic) elle-même; (after prep) elle; see also **oneself**

he's [hi:z] = **he is; he has**

hesitant ['hezɪtənt] adj hésitant(e), indécis(e); **to be ~ about doing sth** hésiter à faire qch

hesitate ['hezɪteɪt] vi: **to ~ (about/to do)** hésiter (sur/à faire)

hesitation [hezɪ'teɪʃən] n hésitation f; **I have no ~ in saying (that) ...** je n'hésiterais pas à dire (que) ...

heterosexual ['hetərəu'seksjuəl] adj, n hétérosexuel(le)

hexagon ['heksəgən] n hexagone m

hey [heɪ] excl hé!

heyday ['heɪdeɪ] n: **the ~ of** l'âge m d'or de, les beaux jours de

HGV n abbr = **heavy goods vehicle**

hi [haɪ] excl salut!; (to attract attention) hé!

hiatus [haɪ'eɪtəs] n trou m, lacune f; (Ling) hiatus m

hibernate ['haɪbəneɪt] vi hiberner

hiccough, hiccup ['hɪkʌp] vi hoqueter ▷ n hoquet m; **to have (the) ~s** avoir le hoquet

hid [hɪd] pt of **hide**

hidden ['hɪdn] pp of **hide** ▷ adj: **there are no ~ extras** absolument tout est compris dans le prix; **~ agenda** intentions non déclarées

hide [haɪd] (pt **hid**, pp **hidden**) [hɪd, 'hɪdn] n (skin) peau f ▷ vt cacher; (feelings, truth) dissimuler; **to ~ sth from sb** cacher qch à qn ▷ vi: **to ~ (from sb)** se cacher (de qn)

hide-and-seek ['haɪdən'si:k] n cache-cache m

hideous ['hɪdɪəs] adj hideux(-euse), atroce

hiding ['haɪdɪŋ] n (beating) correction f, volée f de coups; **to be in ~** (concealed) se tenir caché(e)

hierarchy ['haɪərɑːkɪ] n hiérarchie f
hi-fi ['haɪfaɪ] adj, n abbr (= high fidelity)
hi-fi f inv
high [haɪ] adj haut(e); (speed, respect, number)
grand(e); (price) élevé(e); (wind) fort(e),
violent(e); (voice) aigu(ë); (inf: person: on drugs)
défoncé(e), fait(e); (: on drink) soûl(e),
bourré(e); (Brit Culin: meat, game) faisandé(e);
(: spoilt) avarié(e) ▷ adv haut, en haut ▷ n
(weather) zone f de haute pression; **exports
have reached a new ~** les exportations ont
atteint un nouveau record; **20 m ~** haut(e) de
20 m; **to pay a ~ price for sth** payer cher
pour qch; **~ in the air** haut dans le ciel
highbrow ['haɪbraʊ] adj, n intellectuel(le)
highchair ['haɪtʃɛə²] n (child's) chaise haute
high-class ['haɪ'klɑːs] adj (neighbourhood, hotel)
chic inv, de grand standing; (performance etc)
de haut niveau
higher education n études supérieures
high-handed [haɪ'hændɪd] adj très
autoritaire; très cavalier(-ière)
high-heeled [haɪ'hiːld] adj à hauts talons
high heels npl talons hauts, hauts talons
high jump n (Sport) saut m en hauteur
highlands ['haɪləndz] npl région
montagneuse; **the H~** (in Scotland) les
Highlands mpl
highlight ['haɪlaɪt] n (fig: of event) point
culminant ▷ vt (emphasize) faire ressortir,
souligner; **highlights** npl (in hair) reflets mpl
highlighter ['haɪlaɪtə²] n (pen) surligneur
(lumineux)
highly ['haɪlɪ] adv extrêmement, très;
(unlikely) fort; (recommended, skilled, qualified)
hautement; **~ paid** très bien payé(e); **to
speak ~ of** dire beaucoup de bien de
highly strung adj nerveux(-euse), toujours
tendu(e)
highness ['haɪnɪs] n hauteur f; **His/Her H~**
son Altesse f
high-pitched [haɪ'pɪtʃt] adj aigu(ë)
high-rise ['haɪraɪz] n (also: **~ block,
~ building**) tour f (d'habitation)
high school n lycée m; (US) établissement m
d'enseignement supérieur; voir article

○ **HIGH SCHOOL**
○
○ Une high school est un établissement
○ d'enseignement secondaire. Aux États-
○ Unis, il y a la "Junior High School", qui
○ correspond au collège, et la "Senior High
○ School", qui correspond au lycée. En
○ Grande-Bretagne, c'est un nom que l'on
○ donne parfois aux écoles secondaires;
○ voir "elementary school".

high season n (Brit) haute saison
high street n (Brit) grand-rue f
high-tech ['haɪ'tɛk] (inf) adj de pointe
highway ['haɪweɪ] n (Brit) route f; (US) route

nationale; **the information ~** l'autoroute f
de l'information
Highway Code n (Brit) code m de la route
hijack ['haɪdʒæk] vt détourner (par la force) ▷ n
(also: **~ing**) détournement m (d'avion)
hijacker ['haɪdʒækə²] n auteur m d'un
détournement d'avion, pirate m de l'air
hike [haɪk] vi faire des excursions à pied ▷ n
excursion f à pied, randonnée f; (inf: in prices
etc) augmentation f ▷ vt (inf) augmenter
hiker ['haɪkə²] n promeneur(-euse),
excursionniste m/f
hiking ['haɪkɪŋ] n excursions fpl à pied,
randonnée f
hilarious [hɪ'lɛərɪəs] adj (behaviour, event)
désopilant(e)
hill [hɪl] n colline f; (fairly high) montagne f;
(on road) côte f
hillside ['hɪlsaɪd] n (flanc m de) coteau m
hill walking ['hɪl'wɔːkɪŋ] n randonnée f
de basse montagne
hilly ['hɪlɪ] adj vallonné(e),
montagneux(-euse); (road) à fortes côtes
hilt [hɪlt] n (of sword) garde f; **to the ~** (fig:
support) à fond
him [hɪm] pron (direct) le, l' + vowel or h mute;
(stressed, indirect, after prep) lui; **I see ~** je le vois;
give ~ a book donne-lui un livre; **after ~**
après lui; see also **me**
himself [hɪm'sɛlf] pron (reflexive) se;
(emphatic) lui-même; (after prep) lui; see
also **oneself**
hind [haɪnd] adj de derrière ▷ n biche f
hinder ['hɪndə²] vt gêner; (delay) retarder;
(prevent): **to ~ sb from doing** empêcher qn de
faire
hindrance ['hɪndrəns] n gêne f, obstacle m
hindsight ['haɪndsaɪt] n bon sens après
coup; **with (the benefit of) ~** avec du recul,
rétrospectivement
Hindu ['hɪnduː] n Hindou(e)
Hinduism ['hɪnduɪzəm] n (Rel)
hindouisme m
hinge [hɪndʒ] n charnière f ▷ vi (fig): **to ~ on**
dépendre de
hint [hɪnt] n allusion f; (advice) conseil m;
(clue) indication f ▷ vt: **to ~ that** insinuer que
▷ vi: **to ~ at** faire une allusion à; **to drop a ~**
faire une allusion or insinuation; **give me a ~**
(clue) mettez-moi sur la voie, donnez-moi
une indication
hip [hɪp] n hanche f; (Bot) fruit m de
l'églantier or du rosier
hippie, hippy ['hɪpɪ] n hippie m/f
hippo ['hɪpəʊ] (pl hippos) n hippopotame m
hippopotamus [hɪpə'pɒtəməs]
(pl hippopotamuses or hippopotami
[hɪpə'pɒtəmaɪ]) n hippopotame m
hippy ['hɪpɪ] n = **hippie**
hire ['haɪə²] vt (Brit: car, equipment) louer;
(worker) embaucher, engager ▷ n location f;
for ~ à louer; (taxi) libre; **on ~** en location;

I'd like to ~ a car je voudrais louer une voiture; **hire out** vt louer

hire car, hired car ['haɪəd-] n (Brit) voiture f de location

hire purchase n (Brit) achat m (or vente f) à tempérament or crédit; **to buy sth on ~** acheter qch en location-vente

his [hɪz] pron le/la sien(ne), les siens/siennes ▷ adj son/sa, ses pl; **this is** ~ c'est à lui, c'est le sien; **a friend of** ~ un(e) de ses ami(e)s, un(e) ami(e) à lui; see also **mine'** see also **my**

Hispanic [hɪs'pænɪk] adj (in US) hispano-américain(e) ▷ n Hispano-Américain(e)

hiss [hɪs] vi siffler ▷ n sifflement m

historian [hɪ'stɔːrɪən] n historien(ne)

historic [hɪ'stɔrɪk], **historical** [hɪ'stɔrɪkl] adj historique

history ['hɪstərɪ] n histoire f; **medical ~** (of patient) passé médical

hit [hɪt] vt (pt, pp **hit**) frapper; (knock against) cogner; (reach: target) atteindre, toucher; (collide with: car) entrer en collision avec, heurter; (fig: affect) toucher; (find) tomber sur ▷ n coup m; (success) coup réussi; succès m; (song) chanson f à succès, tube m; (to website) visite f; (on search engine) résultat m de recherche; **to ~ it off with sb** bien s'entendre avec qn; **to ~ the headlines** être à la une des journaux; **to ~ the road** (inf) se mettre en route; **hit back** vi: **to ~ back at sb** prendre sa revanche sur qn; **hit on** vt fus (answer) trouver (par hasard); (solution) tomber sur (par hasard); **hit out at** vt fus envoyer un coup à; (fig) attaquer; **hit upon** vt fus = **hit on**

hit-and-run driver ['hɪtænd'rʌn-] n chauffard m

hitch [hɪtʃ] vt (fasten) accrocher, attacher; (also: ~ **up**) remonter d'une saccade ▷ vi faire de l'autostop ▷ n (knot) nœud m; (difficulty) anicroche f, contretemps m; **to ~ a lift** faire du stop; **technical ~** incident m technique; **hitch up** vt (horse, cart) atteler; see also **hitch**

hitch-hike ['hɪtʃhaɪk] vi faire de l'auto-stop

hitch-hiker ['hɪtʃhaɪkəʳ] n auto-stoppeur(-euse)

hitch-hiking ['hɪtʃhaɪkɪŋ] n auto-stop m, stop m (inf)

hi-tech ['haɪ'tɛk] adj de pointe ▷ n high-tech m

hitherto [hɪðə'tuː] adv jusqu'ici, jusqu'à présent

hitman ['hɪtmæn] irreg n (inf) tueur m à gages

HIV n abbr (= human immunodeficiency virus) HIV m, VIH m; **~-negative/positive** séronégatif(-ive)/positif(-ive)

hive [haɪv] n ruche f; **the shop was a ~ of activity** (fig) le magasin était une véritable ruche; **hive off** vt (inf) mettre à part, séparer

HMS abbr (Brit) = **His or Her Majesty's Ship**

hoard [hɔːd] n (of food) provisions fpl, réserves fpl; (of money) trésor m ▷ vt amasser

hoarding ['hɔːdɪŋ] n (Brit) panneau m d'affichage or publicitaire

hoarse [hɔːs] adj enroué(e)

hoax [həʊks] n canular m

hob [hɔb] n plaque chauffante

hobble ['hɔbl] vi boitiller

hobby ['hɔbɪ] n passe-temps favori

hobo ['həʊbəʊ] n (US) vagabond m

hockey ['hɔkɪ] n hockey m

hockey stick n crosse f de hockey

hog [hɔg] n porc (châtré) ▷ vt (fig) accaparer; **to go the whole ~** aller jusqu'au bout

Hogmanay [hɔgmə'neɪ] n réveillon m du jour de l'An, Saint-Sylvestre f; voir article

● HOGMANAY
●
● La Saint-Sylvestre ou "New Year's Eve"
● se nomme Hogmanay en Écosse. En cette
● occasion, la famille et les amis se
● réunissent pour entendre sonner les
● douze coups de minuit et pour fêter le
● "first-footing", une coutume qui veut
● qu'on se rende chez ses amis et voisins
● en apportant quelque chose à boire (du
● whisky en général) et un morceau de
● charbon en gage de prospérité pour la
● nouvelle année.

hoist [hɔɪst] n palan m ▷ vt hisser

hold [həʊld] (pt, pp **held**) [hɛld] vt tenir; (contain) contenir; (meeting) tenir; (keep back) retenir; (believe) maintenir, considérer; (possess) avoir; détenir ▷ vi (withstand pressure) tenir (bon); (be valid) valoir; (on telephone) attendre ▷ n prise f; (find) influence f; (Naut) cale f; **to catch or get (a) ~ of** saisir; **to get ~ of** (find) trouver; **to get ~ of o.s.** se contrôler; ~ **the line!** (Tel) ne quittez pas!; **to ~ one's own** (fig) (bien) se défendre; **to ~ office** (Pol) avoir un portefeuille; **to ~ firm or fast** tenir bon; **he ~s the view that ...** il pense or estime que ..., d'après lui ...; **to ~ sb responsible for sth** tenir qn pour responsable de qch; **hold back** vt retenir; (secret) cacher; **to ~ sb back from doing sth** empêcher qn de faire qch; **hold down** vt (person) maintenir à terre; (job) occuper; **hold forth** vi pérorer; **hold off** vt tenir à distance ▷ vi: **if the rain ~s off** s'il ne pleut pas, s'il ne se met pas à pleuvoir; **hold on** vi tenir bon; (wait) attendre; ~ **on!** (Tel) ne quittez pas!; **to ~ on to sth** (grasp) se cramponner à qch; (keep) conserver or garder qch; **hold out** vt offrir ▷ vi (resist): **to ~ out (against)** résister (devant), tenir bon (devant); **hold over** vt (meeting etc) ajourner, reporter; **hold up** vt (raise) lever; (support) soutenir; (delay) retarder; (: traffic) ralentir; (rob) braquer

holdall ['həʊldɔːl] n (Brit) fourre-tout m inv

holder ['həʊldəʳ] n (container) support m; (of ticket, record) détenteur(-trice); (of office, title, passport etc) titulaire m/f

holding ['həʊldɪŋ] n (share) intérêts mpl; (farm) ferme f

hold-up ['həʊldʌp] n (robbery) hold-up m; (delay) retard m; (Brit: in traffic) embouteillage m

hole [həʊl] n trou m ▷ vt trouer, faire un trou dans; ~ **in the heart** (Med) communication f interventriculaire; **to pick ~s (in)** (fig) chercher des poux (dans); **hole up** vi se terrer

holiday ['hɒlədɪ] n (Brit: vacation) vacances fpl; (day off) jour m de congé; (public) jour férié; **to be on ~** être en vacances; **I'm here on ~** je suis ici en vacances; **tomorrow is a ~** demain c'est fête, on a congé demain

holiday camp n (Brit: for children) colonie f de vacances; (also: **holiday centre**) camp m de vacances

holiday home n (rented) location f de vacances; (owned) résidence f secondaire

holiday job n (Brit) boulot m (inf) de vacances

holiday-maker ['hɒlədɪmeɪkəʳ] n (Brit) vacancier(-ière)

holiday resort n centre m de villégiature or de vacances

Holland ['hɒlənd] n Hollande f

hollow ['hɒləʊ] adj creux(-euse); (fig) faux/ fausse ▷ n creux m; (in land) dépression f (de terrain), cuvette f ▷ vt: **to ~ out** creuser, évider

holly ['hɒlɪ] n houx m

holocaust ['hɒləkɔ:st] n holocauste m

holster ['həʊlstəʳ] n étui m de revolver

holy ['həʊlɪ] adj saint(e); (bread, water) bénit(e); (ground) sacré(e)

Holy Ghost, Holy Spirit n Saint-Esprit m

homage ['hɒmɪdʒ] n hommage m; **to pay ~ to** rendre hommage à

home [həʊm] n foyer m, maison f; (country) pays natal, patrie f; (institution) maison ▷ adj de famille; (Econ, Pol) national(e), intérieur(e); (Sport: team) qui reçoit; (: match, win) sur leur (or notre) terrain ▷ adv chez soi, à la maison; au pays natal; (right in: nail etc) à fond; **at ~** chez soi, à la maison; **to go (or come) ~** rentrer (chez soi), rentrer à la maison (or au pays); **I'm going ~ on Tuesday** je rentre mardi; **make yourself at ~** faites comme chez vous; **near my ~** près de chez moi; **home in on** vt fus (missile) se diriger automatiquement vers or sur

home address n domicile permanent

homeland ['həʊmlænd] n patrie f

homeless ['həʊmlɪs] adj sans foyer, sans abri; **the homeless** npl les sans-abri mpl

homely ['həʊmlɪ] adj (plain) simple, sans prétention; (welcoming) accueillant(e)

home-made [həʊm'meɪd] adj fait(e) à la maison

home match n match m à domicile

Home Office n (Brit) ministère m de l'Intérieur

homeopathy etc [həʊmɪ'ɒpəθɪ] (US) n = **homoeopathy** etc

home owner ['həʊməʊnəʳ] n propriétaire occupant

home page n (Comput) page f d'accueil

home rule n autonomie f

Home Secretary n (Brit) ministre m de l'Intérieur

homesick ['həʊmsɪk] adj: **to be ~** avoir le mal du pays; (missing one's family) s'ennuyer de sa famille

home town n ville natale

homeward ['həʊmwəd] adj (journey) du retour ▷ adv = **homewards**

homework ['həʊmwə:k] n devoirs mpl

homicide ['hɒmɪsaɪd] n (US) homicide m

homoeopathic, (US) **homeopathic** [həʊmɪə'pæθɪk] adj (medicine) homéopathique; (doctor) homéopathe

homoeopathy, (US) **homeopathy** [həʊmɪ'ɒpəθɪ] n homéopathie f

homogeneous [hɒməʊ'dʒi:nɪəs] adj homogène

homosexual [hɒməʊ'sɛksjuəl] adj, n homosexuel(le)

honest ['ɒnɪst] adj honnête; (sincere) franc/ franche; **to be quite ~ with you** ... à dire vrai ...

honestly ['ɒnɪstlɪ] adv honnêtement; franchement

honesty ['ɒnɪstɪ] n honnêteté f

honey ['hʌnɪ] n miel m; (inf: darling) chéri(e)

honeycomb ['hʌnɪkəʊm] n rayon m de miel; (pattern) nid m d'abeilles, motif alvéolé ▷ vt (fig): **to ~ with** cribler de

honeymoon ['hʌnɪmu:n] n lune f de miel, voyage m de noces; **we're on ~** nous sommes en voyage de noces

honeysuckle ['hʌnɪsʌkl] n chèvrefeuille m

Hong Kong ['hɒŋ'kɒŋ] n Hong Kong

honk [hɒŋk] n (Aut) coup m de klaxon ▷ vi klaxonner

honorary ['ɒnərərɪ] adj honoraire; (duty, title) honorifique; **~ degree** diplôme m honoris causa

honour, (US) **honor** ['ɒnəʳ] vt honorer ▷ n honneur m; **in ~ of** l'honneur de; **to graduate with ~s** obtenir sa licence avec mention

honourable, (US) **honorable** ['ɒnərəbl] adj honorable

honours degree ['ɒnəz-] n (Scol) ≈ licence f avec mention

hood [hʊd] n capuchon m; (of cooker) hotte f; (Brit Aut) capote f; (US Aut) capot m; (inf) truand m

hoodie ['hʊdɪ] n (top) sweat m à capuche

hoof (pl hoofs or hooves) [hu:f, hu:vz] n sabot m

hook [huk] n crochet m; (on dress) agrafe f; (for fishing) hameçon m ▷ vt accrocher; (dress) agrafer; **off the ~** (Tel) décroché; **~ and eye** agrafe; **by ~ or by crook** de gré ou de force, coûte que coûte; **to be ~ed (on)** (inf) être accroché(e) (par); (person) être dingue (de); **hook up** vt (Radio, TV etc) faire un duplex entre

hooligan ['hu:lɪɡən] n voyou m

hoop [hu:p] n cerceau m; (of barrel) cercle m

hoot [hu:t] vi (Brit: Aut) klaxonner; (siren) mugir; (owl) hululer ▷ vt (jeer at) huer ▷ n huée f; coup m de klaxon; mugissement m; hululement m; **to ~ with laughter** rire aux éclats

hooter ['hu:tə'] n (Brit Aut) klaxon m; (Naut, factory) sirène f

Hoover® ['hu:və'] n (Brit) aspirateur m ▷ vt: **to hoover** (room) passer l'aspirateur dans; (carpet) passer l'aspirateur sur

hooves [hu:vz] npl of **hoof**

hop [hɔp] vi sauter; (on one foot) sauter à cloche-pied; (bird) sautiller ▷ n saut m

hope [həup] vt, vi espérer ▷ n espoir m; **I ~ so** je l'espère; **I ~ not** j'espère que non

hopeful ['həupful] adj (person) plein(e) d'espoir; (situation) prometteur(-euse), encourageant(e); **I'm ~ that she'll manage to come** j'ai bon espoir qu'elle pourra venir

hopefully ['həupfulɪ] adv (expectantly) avec espoir, avec optimisme; (one hopes) avec un peu de chance; **~, they'll come back** espérons bien qu'ils reviendront

hopeless ['həuplɪs] adj désespéré(e), sans espoir; (useless) nul(le)

hops [hɔps] npl houblon m

horizon [hə'raɪzn] n horizon m

horizontal [hɔrɪ'zɔntl] adj horizontal(e)

hormone ['hɔ:məun] n hormone f

horn [hɔ:n] n corne f; (Mus) cor m; (Aut) klaxon m

hornet ['hɔ:nɪt] n frelon m

horoscope ['hɔrəskəup] n horoscope m

horrendous [hə'rɛndəs] adj horrible, affreux(-euse)

horrible ['hɔrɪbl] adj horrible, affreux(-euse)

horrid ['hɔrɪd] adj (person) détestable; (weather, place, smell) épouvantable

horrific [hɔ'rɪfɪk] adj horrible

horrify ['hɔrɪfaɪ] vt horrifier

horrifying ['hɔrɪfaɪɪŋ] adj horrifiant(e)

horror ['hɔrə'] n horreur f

horror film n film m d'épouvante

hors d'œuvre [ɔ:'də:vrə] n hors d'œuvre m

horse [hɔ:s] n cheval m

horseback ['hɔ:sbæk]: **on ~** adj, adv à cheval

horse chestnut n (nut) marron m (d'Inde); (tree) marronnier m (d'Inde)

horseman ['hɔ:smən] irreg n cavalier m

horsepower ['hɔ:spauə'] n puissance f (en chevaux); (unit) cheval-vapeur m (CV)

horse-racing ['hɔ:sreɪsɪŋ] n courses fpl de chevaux

horseradish ['hɔ:srædɪʃ] n raifort m

horse riding n (Brit) équitation f

horseshoe ['hɔ:sʃu:] n fer m à cheval

hose [həuz] n (also: **~pipe**) tuyau m; (also: **garden ~**) tuyau d'arrosage; **hose down** vt laver au jet

hosepipe ['həuzpaɪp] n tuyau m; (in garden) tuyau d'arrosage; (for fire) tuyau d'incendie

hospitable ['hɔspɪtəbl] adj hospitalier(-ière)

hospital ['hɔspɪtl] n hôpital m; **in ~**, (US) **in the ~** à l'hôpital; **where's the nearest ~?** où est l'hôpital le plus proche?

hospitality [hɔspɪ'tælɪtɪ] n hospitalité f

host [həust] n hôte m; (in hotel etc) patron m; (TV, Radio) présentateur(-trice), animateur(-trice); (large number): **a ~ of** une foule de; (Rel) hostie f ▷ vt (TV programme) présenter, animer

hostage ['hɔstɪdʒ] n otage m

hostel ['hɔstl] n foyer m; (also: **youth ~**) auberge f de jeunesse

hostess ['həustɪs] n hôtesse f; (Brit: also: **air ~**) hôtesse de l'air; (TV, Radio) présentatrice f; (in nightclub) entraîneuse f

hostile ['hɔstaɪl] adj hostile

hostility [hɔ'stɪlɪtɪ] n hostilité f

hot [hɔt] adj chaud(e); (as opposed to only warm) très chaud; (spicy) fort(e); (fig: contest) acharné(e); (topic) brûlant(e); (temper) violent(e), passionné(e); **to be ~** (person) avoir chaud; (thing) être (très) chaud; (weather) faire chaud; **hot up** (Brit inf) vi (situation) devenir tendu(e); (party) s'animer ▷ vt (pace) accélérer, forcer; (engine) gonfler

hotbed ['hɔtbɛd] n (fig) foyer m, pépinière f

hot dog n hot-dog m

hotel [həu'tɛl] n hôtel m

hothouse ['hɔthaus] n serre chaude

hotline ['hɔtlaɪn] n (Pol) téléphone m rouge, ligne directe

hotly ['hɔtlɪ] adv passionnément, violemment

hotplate ['hɔtpleɪt] n (on cooker) plaque chauffante

hotpot ['hɔtpɔt] n (Brit Culin) ragoût m

hotspot ['hɔtspɔt] n (Comput: also: **wireless ~**) borne f wifi, hotspot m

hot-water bottle [hɔt'wɔ:tə-] n bouillotte f

hound [haund] vt poursuivre avec acharnement ▷ n chien courant; **the ~s** la meute

hour ['auə'] n heure f; **at 30 miles an ~** ≈ à 50 km à l'heure; **lunch ~** heure du déjeuner; **to pay sb by the ~** payer qn à l'heure

hourly ['auəlɪ] adj toutes les heures; (rate) horaire; **~ paid** adj payé(e) à l'heure

house (pl **houses**) [haus, 'hauzɪz] n maison f; (Pol) chambre f; (Theat) salle f; auditoire m ▷ vt [hauz] (person) loger, héberger; **at (or to)**

my ~ chez moi; **the H~ of Commons/of Lords** (Brit) la Chambre des communes/des lords; voir article; **the H~ (of Representatives)** (US) la Chambre des représentants; voir article; **on the ~** (fig) aux frais de la maison

house arrest n assignation f à domicile

houseboat ['hausbəut] n bateau (aménagé en habitation)

housebound ['hausbaund] adj confiné(e) chez soi

housebreaking ['hausbreikıŋ] n cambriolage m (avec effraction)

household ['haushəuld] n (Admin etc) ménage m; (people) famille f, maisonnée f; **~ name** nom connu de tout le monde

householder ['haushəuldə^r] n propriétaire m/f; (head of house) chef m de famille

housekeeper ['hauski:pə^r] n gouvernante f

housekeeping ['hauski:pıŋ] n (work) ménage m; (also: **~ money**) argent m du ménage; (Comput) gestion f (des disques)

house-warming ['hauswɔ:mıŋ] n (also: **~ party**) pendaison f de crémaillère

housewife (irreg) ['hauswaıf] n ménagère f; femme f au foyer

house wine n cuvée f maison or du patron

housework ['hauswə:k] n (travaux mpl du) ménage m

housing ['hauzıŋ] n logement m ▷ cpd (problem, shortage) de or du logement

housing development, housing estate (Brit) n (blocks of flats) cité f; (houses) lotissement m

hovel ['hɔvl] n taudis m

hover ['hɔvə^r] vi planer; **to ~ round sb** rôder or tourner autour de qn

hovercraft ['hɔvəkra:ft] n aéroglisseur m, hovercraft m

how [hau] adv comment; **~ are you?** comment allez-vous?; **~ do you do?** bonjour; (on being introduced) enchanté(e); **~ far is it to ...?** combien y a-t-il jusqu'à ...?; **~ long have you been here?** depuis combien de temps êtes-vous là?; **~ lovely/awful!** que or comme c'est joli/affreux!; **~ many/much?** combien?; **~ much time/many people?** combien de temps/gens?; **~ much does it cost?** ça coûte combien?; **~ old are you?** quel âge avez-vous?; **~ tall is he?** combien mesure-t-il?; **~ is school?** ça va à l'école?; **~ was the film?** comment était le film?; **~'s life?** (inf) comment ça va?; **~ about a drink?** si on buvait quelque chose?; **~ is that ...?** comment se fait-il que ... + sub?

however [hau'evə^r] conj pourtant, cependant ▷ adv de quelque façon or manière que + sub; (+ adjective) quelque or si ... que + sub; (in questions) comment; **~ I do it** de quelque manière que je m'y prenne; **~ cold it is** même s'il fait très froid; **~ did you do it?** comment y êtes-vous donc arrivé?

howl [haul] n hurlement m ▷ vi hurler; (wind) mugir

H.P. n abbr (Brit) = **hire purchase**

h.p. abbr (Aut) = **horsepower**

HQ n abbr (= headquarters) QG m

hr abbr (= hour) h

hrs abbr (= hours) h

HTML n abbr (= hypertext markup language) HTML m

hub [hʌb] n (of wheel) moyeu m; (fig) centre m, foyer m

hubcap [hʌbkæp] n (Aut) enjoliveur m

huddle ['hʌdl] vi: **to ~ together** se blottir les uns contre les autres

hue [hju:] n teinte f, nuance f; **~ and cry** n tollé (général), clameur f

huff [hʌf] n: **in a ~** fâché(e); **to take the ~** prendre la mouche

hug [hʌg] vt serrer dans ses bras; (shore, kerb) serrer ▷ n étreinte f; **to give sb a ~** serrer qn dans ses bras

huge [hju:dʒ] adj énorme, immense

hulk [hʌlk] n (ship) vieux rafiot; (car, building) carcasse f; (person) mastodonte m, malabar m

hull [hʌl] n (of ship) coque f; (of nuts) coque; (of peas) cosse f

hullo [hə'ləu] excl = **hello**

hum [hʌm] vt (tune) fredonner ▷ vi fredonner; (insect) bourdonner; (plane, tool) vrombir ▷ n fredonnement m; bourdonnement m; vrombissement m

human ['hju:mən] adj humain(e) ▷ n (also: **~ being**) être humain

humane [hju:'meın] adj humain(e), humanitaire

humanitarian [hju:mænı'tɛərıən] adj humanitaire

humanity [hju:'mænıtı] n humanité f

human rights npl droits mpl de l'homme

humble ['hʌmbl] adj humble, modeste ▷ vt humilier

humdrum ['hʌmdrʌm] adj monotone, routinier(-ière)

humid ['hju:mıd] adj humide

humidity [hju:'mıdıtı] n humidité f

humiliate [hju:'mılıeıt] vt humilier

humiliating [hju:'mılıeıtıŋ] adj humiliant(e)

humiliation [hju:mılı'eıʃən] n humiliation f

hummus ['huməs] n houm(m)ous m

humorous ['hju:mərəs] adj humoristique; (person) plein(e) d'humour

humour, (US) **humor** ['hju:mə^r] n humour m; (mood) humeur f ▷ vt (person) faire plaisir à; se prêter aux caprices de; **sense of ~** sens m de l'humour; **to be in a good/bad ~** être de bonne/mauvaise humeur

hump [hʌmp] n bosse f

hunch [hʌntʃ] n bosse f; (premonition) intuition f; **I have a ~ that** j'ai (comme une vague) idée que

hunchback ['hʌntʃbæk] n bossu(e)

hunched [hʌntʃt] *adj* arrondi(e), voûté(e)

hundred ['hʌndrəd] *num* cent; **about a ~ people** une centaine de personnes; **~s of** des centaines de; **I'm a ~ per cent sure** j'en suis absolument certain

hundredth ['hʌndrɪdθ] *num* centième

hundredweight ['hʌndrɪdweɪt] *n* (Brit) =50.8 kg; 112 lb; (US) = 45.3 kg; 100 lb

hung [hʌŋ] *pt, pp of* **hang**

Hungarian [hʌŋˈgɛərɪən] *adj* hongrois(e) ▷ *n* Hongrois(e); (Ling) hongrois *m*

Hungary ['hʌŋgərɪ] *n* Hongrie *f*

hunger ['hʌŋgəʳ] *n* faim *f* ▷ *vi:* **to ~ for** avoir faim de, désirer ardemment

hungry ['hʌŋgrɪ] *adj* affamé(e); **to be ~** avoir faim; **~ for** (fig) avide de

hunk [hʌŋk] *n* gros morceau; (inf: man) beau mec

hunt [hʌnt] *vt* (seek) chercher; (criminal) pourchasser; (Sport) chasser ▷ *vi* (search): **to ~ for** chercher (partout); (Sport) chasser ▷ *n* (Sport) chasse *f*; **hunt down** *vt* pourchasser

hunter ['hʌntəʳ] *n* chasseur *m*; (Brit: horse) cheval *m* de chasse

hunting ['hʌntɪŋ] *n* chasse *f*

hurdle ['həːdl] *n* (for fences) claie *f*; (Sport) haie *f*; (fig) obstacle *m*

hurl [həːl] *vt* lancer (avec violence); (abuse, insults) lancer

hurrah, hurray [hu'rɑː, hu'reɪ] *excl* hourra!

hurricane ['hʌrɪkən] *n* ouragan *m*

hurried ['hʌrɪd] *adj* pressé(e), précipité(e); (work) fait(e) à la hâte

hurriedly ['hʌrɪdlɪ] *adv* précipitamment, à la hâte

hurry ['hʌrɪ] *n* hâte *f*, précipitation *f* ▷ *vi* se presser, se dépêcher ▷ *vt* (person) faire presser, faire se dépêcher; (work) presser; **to be in a ~** être pressé(e); **to do sth in a ~** faire qch en vitesse; **to ~ in/out** entrer/sortir précipitamment; **to ~ home** se dépêcher de rentrer; **hurry along** *vi* marcher d'un pas pressé; **hurry away, hurry off** *vi* partir précipitamment; **hurry up** *vi* se dépêcher

hurt [həːt] (pt, pp **hurt**) *vt* (cause pain to) faire mal à; (injure, fig) blesser; (damage: business, interests etc) nuire à; faire du tort à ▷ *vi* faire mal ▷ *adj* blessé(e); **my arm ~s** j'ai mal au bras; **I - my arm** je me suis fait mal au bras; **to - o.s.** se faire mal; **where does it ~?** où avez-vous mal?, où est-ce que ça vous fait mal?

hurtful ['həːtful] *adj* (remark) blessant(e)

hurtle ['həːtl] *vt* lancer (de toutes ses forces) ▷ *vi:* **to ~ past** passer en trombe; **to ~ down** dégringoler

husband ['hʌzbənd] *n* mari *m*

hush [hʌʃ] *n* calme *m*, silence *m* ▷ *vt* faire taire; **~!** chut!; **hush up** *vt* (fact) étouffer

husk [hʌsk] *n* (of wheat) balle *f*; (of rice, maize) enveloppe *f*; (of peas) cosse *f*

husky ['hʌskɪ] *adj* (voice) rauque; (burly)

costaud(e) ▷ *n* chien *m* esquimau or de traîneau

hustle ['hʌsl] *vt* pousser, bousculer ▷ *n* bousculade *f*; **~ and bustle** *n* tourbillon *m* (d'activité)

hut [hʌt] *n* hutte *f*; (shed) cabane *f*

hutch [hʌtʃ] *n* clapier *m*

hyacinth ['haɪəsɪnθ] *n* jacinthe *f*

hydrant ['haɪdrənt] *n* prise *f* d'eau; (also: **fire ~**) bouche *f* d'incendie

hydraulic [haɪ'drɔːlɪk] *adj* hydraulique

hydroelectric ['haɪdrəuɪ'lɛktrɪk] *adj* hydro-électrique

hydrofoil ['haɪdrəfɔɪl] *n* hydrofoil *m*

hydrogen ['haɪdrədʒən] *n* hydrogène *m*

hyena [haɪ'iːnə] *n* hyène *f*

hygiene ['haɪdʒiːn] *n* hygiène *f*

hygienic [haɪ'dʒiːnɪk] *adj* hygiénique

hymn [hɪm] *n* hymne *m*; cantique *m*

hype [haɪp] *n* (inf) matraquage *m* publicitaire or médiatique

hyperlink ['haɪpəlɪŋk] *n* hyperlien *m*

hypermarket ['haɪpəmɑːkɪt] (Brit) *n* hypermarché *m*

hypertext ['haɪpətɛkst] *n* (Comput) hypertexte *m*

hyphen ['haɪfn] *n* trait *m* d'union

hypnotize ['hɪpnətaɪz] *vt* hypnotiser

hypocrisy [hɪ'pɔkrɪsɪ] *n* hypocrisie *f*

hypocrite ['hɪpəkrɪt] *n* hypocrite *m/f*

hypocritical [hɪpə'krɪtɪkl] *adj* hypocrite

hypothesis (pl **hypotheses**) [haɪ'pɔθɪsɪs, -siːz] *n* hypothèse *f*

hysterical [hɪ'stɛrɪkl] *adj* hystérique; (funny) hilarant(e); **to become ~** avoir une crise de nerfs

hysterics [hɪ'stɛrɪks] *npl* (violente) crise de nerfs; (laughter) crise de rire; **to be in/have ~** (anger, panic) avoir une crise de nerfs; (laughter) attraper un fou rire

h

I¹, i [aɪ] n (letter) I, i m; **I for Isaac,** (US) **I for Item** I comme Irma

I² [aɪ] pron je; (before vowel) j'; (stressed) moi ▷ abbr (= island, isle) I

ice [aɪs] n glace f; (on road) verglas m ▷ vt (cake) glacer; (drink) faire rafraîchir ▷ vi (also: **~ over**) geler; (also: **~ up**) se givrer; **to put sth on ~** (fig) mettre qch en attente

iceberg ['aɪsbɜːg] n iceberg m; **the tip of the ~** (also fig) la partie émergée de l'iceberg

icebox ['aɪsbɔks] n (US) réfrigérateur m; (Brit) compartiment m à glace; (insulated box) glacière f

ice cream n glace f

ice cube n glaçon m

iced [aɪst] adj (drink) frappé(e); (coffee, tea, also cake) glacé(e)

ice hockey n hockey m sur glace

Iceland ['aɪslənd] n Islande f

Icelander ['aɪsləndə'] n Islandais(e)

Icelandic [aɪs'lændɪk] adj islandais(e) ▷ n (Ling) islandais m

ice lolly n (Brit) esquimau m

ice rink n patinoire f

ice skating ['aɪsskeɪtɪŋ] n patinage m (sur glace)

icicle ['aɪsɪkl] n glaçon m (naturel)

icing ['aɪsɪŋ] n (Aviat etc) givrage m; (Culin) glaçage m

icing sugar n (Brit) sucre m glace

icon ['aɪkɔn] n icône f

ICT n abbr (Brit: Scol: = information and communications technology) TIC fpl

icy ['aɪsɪ] adj glacé(e); (road) verglacé(e); (weather, temperature) glacial(e)

I'd [aɪd] = **I would; I had**

ID card n carte f d'identité

idea [aɪ'dɪə] n idée f; **good ~!** bonne idée!; **to have an ~ that ...** avoir idée que ...; **I have no ~** je n'ai pas la moindre idée

ideal [aɪ'dɪəl] n idéal m ▷ adj idéal(e)

ideally [aɪ'dɪəlɪ] adv (preferably) dans l'idéal; (perfectly): **he is ~ suited to the job** il est parfait pour ce poste; **~ the book should have ...** l'idéal serait que le livre ait ...

identical [aɪ'dɛntɪkl] adj identique

identification [aɪdɛntɪfɪ'keɪʃən] n identification f; **means of ~** pièce f d'identité

identify [aɪ'dɛntɪfaɪ] vt identifier ▷ vi: **to ~ with** s'identifier à

Identikit® [aɪ'dɛntɪkɪt] n: **~ (picture)** portrait-robot m

identity [aɪ'dɛntɪtɪ] n identité f

identity card n carte f d'identité

identity theft n usurpation f d'identité

ideology [aɪdɪ'ɔlədʒɪ] n idéologie f

idiom ['ɪdɪəm] n (language) langue f, idiome m; (phrase) expression f idiomatique; (style) style m

idiosyncrasy [ɪdɪəu'sɪŋkrəsɪ] n particularité f, caractéristique f

idiot ['ɪdɪət] n idiot(e), imbécile m/f

idiotic [ɪdɪ'ɔtɪk] adj idiot(e), bête, stupide

idle ['aɪdl] adj (doing nothing) sans occupation, désœuvré(e); (lazy) oisif(-ive), paresseux(-euse); (unemployed) au chômage; (machinery) au repos; (question, pleasures) vain(e), futile ▷ vi (engine) tourner au ralenti; **to lie ~** être arrêté, ne pas fonctionner; **idle away** vt: **to ~ away one's time** passer son temps à ne rien faire

idol ['aɪdl] n idole f

idolize ['aɪdəlaɪz] vt idolâtrer, adorer

idyllic [ɪ'dɪlɪk] adj idyllique

i.e. abbr (= id est: that is) c. à d., c'est-à-dire

if [ɪf] conj si ▷ n: **there are a lot of ifs and buts** il y a beaucoup de si mpl et de mais mpl; **I'd be pleased if you could do it** je serais très heureux si vous pouviez le faire; **if necessary** si nécessaire, le cas échéant; **if so** si c'est le cas; **if not** sinon; **if only I could!** si seulement je pouvais!; **if only he were here** si seulement il était là; **if only to show him my gratitude** ne serait-ce que pour lui témoigner ma gratitude; see also **as;** even

ignite [ɪg'naɪt] vt mettre le feu à, enflammer ▷ vi s'enflammer

ignition [ɪg'nɪʃən] n (Aut) allumage m; **to switch on/off the ~** mettre/couper le contact

ignition key n (Aut) clé f de contact

ignorance ['ɪgnərəns] n ignorance f; **to keep**

sb in ~ of sth tenir qn dans l'ignorance de qch
ignorant ['ɪgnərənt] *adj* ignorant(e); **to be ~ of** (*subject*) ne rien connaître en; (*events*) ne pas être au courant de
ignore [ɪg'nɔːʳ] *vt* ne tenir aucun compte de; (*mistake*) ne pas relever; (*person: pretend to not see*) faire semblant de ne pas reconnaître; (: *pay no attention to*) ignorer
ill [ɪl] *adj* (*sick*) malade; (*bad*) mauvais(e) ▷ *n* mal *m* ▷ *adv:* **to speak/think ~ of sb** dire/penser du mal de qn; **to be taken ~** tomber malade
I'll [aɪl] = **I will; I shall**
ill-advised [ɪləd'vaɪzd] *adj* (*decision*) peu judicieux(-euse); (*person*) malavisé(e)
ill-at-ease [ɪlət'iːz] *adj* mal à l'aise
illegal [ɪ'liːgl] *adj* illégal(e)
illegible [ɪ'lɛdʒɪbl] *adj* illisible
illegitimate [ɪlɪ'dʒɪtɪmət] *adj* illégitime
ill-fated [ɪl'feɪtɪd] *adj* malheureux(-euse); (*day*) néfaste
ill feeling *n* ressentiment *m*, rancune *f*
ill health *n* mauvaise santé
illiterate [ɪ'lɪtərət] *adj* illettré(e); (*letter*) plein(e) de fautes
ill-mannered [ɪl'mænəd] *adj* impoli(e), grossier(-ière)
illness ['ɪlnɪs] *n* maladie *f*
ill-treat [ɪl'triːt] *vt* maltraiter
illuminate [ɪ'luːmɪneɪt] *vt* (*room, street*) éclairer; (*for special effect*) illuminer; **~d sign** enseigne lumineuse
illumination [ɪluːmɪ'neɪʃən] *n* éclairage *m*; illumination *f*
illusion [ɪ'luːʒən] *n* illusion *f*; **to be under the ~ that** avoir l'illusion que
illustrate ['ɪləstreɪt] *vt* illustrer
illustration [ɪlə'streɪʃən] *n* illustration *f*
ill will *n* malveillance *f*
IM *n abbr* (= *instant messaging*) messagerie *f* instantanée ▷ *vt* envoyer un message instantané à
I'm [aɪm] = **I am**
image ['ɪmɪdʒ] *n* image *f*; (*public face*) image de marque
imagery ['ɪmɪdʒərɪ] *n* images *fpl*
imaginary [ɪ'mædʒɪnərɪ] *adj* imaginaire
imagination [ɪmædʒɪ'neɪʃən] *n* imagination *f*
imaginative [ɪ'mædʒɪnətɪv] *adj* imaginatif(-ive); (*person*) plein(e) d'imagination
imagine [ɪ'mædʒɪn] *vt* s'imaginer; (*suppose*) imaginer, supposer
imam [ɪ'mɑːm] *n* imam *m*
imbalance [ɪm'bæləns] *n* déséquilibre *m*
imitate ['ɪmɪteɪt] *vt* imiter
imitation [ɪmɪ'teɪʃən] *n* imitation *f*
immaculate [ɪ'mækjulət] *adj* impeccable; (*Rel*) immaculé(e)
immaterial [ɪmə'tɪərɪəl] *adj* sans importance, insignifiant(e)

immature [ɪmə'tjuəʳ] *adj* (*fruit*) qui n'est pas mûr(e); (*person*) qui manque de maturité
immediate [ɪ'miːdɪət] *adj* immédiat(e)
immediately [ɪ'miːdɪətlɪ] *adv* (*at once*) immédiatement; **~ next to** juste à côté de
immense [ɪ'mɛns] *adj* immense, énorme
immerse [ɪ'məːs] *vt* immerger, plonger; **to ~ sth in** plonger qch dans; **to be ~d in** (*fig*) être plongé dans
immersion heater [ɪ'məːʃən-] *n* (*Brit*) chauffe-eau *m* électrique
immigrant ['ɪmɪgrənt] *n* immigrant(e); (*already established*) immigré(e)
immigration [ɪmɪ'greɪʃən] *n* immigration *f*
imminent ['ɪmɪnənt] *adj* imminent(e)
immoral [ɪ'mɔrl] *adj* immoral(e)
immortal [ɪ'mɔːtl] *adj, n* immortel(le)
immune [ɪ'mjuːn] *adj:* **~ (to)** immunisé(e) (contre)
immune system *n* système *m* immunitaire
immunity [ɪ'mjuːnɪtɪ] *n* immunité *f*; **diplomatic ~** immunité diplomatique
immunize ['ɪmjunaɪz] *vt* immuniser
impact ['ɪmpækt] *n* choc *m*, impact *m*; (*fig*) impact
impair [ɪm'pɛəʳ] *vt* détériorer, diminuer
impart [ɪm'pɑːt] *vt* (*make known*) communiquer, transmettre; (*bestow*) confier, donner
impartial [ɪm'pɑːʃl] *adj* impartial(e)
impassable [ɪm'pɑːsəbl] *adj* infranchissable; (*road*) impraticable
impassive [ɪm'pæsɪv] *adj* impassible
impatience [ɪm'peɪʃəns] *n* impatience *f*
impatient [ɪm'peɪʃənt] *adj* impatient(e); **to get** *or* **grow ~** s'impatienter
impatiently [ɪm'peɪʃəntlɪ] *adv* avec impatience
impeccable [ɪm'pɛkəbl] *adj* impeccable, parfait(e)
impede [ɪm'piːd] *vt* gêner
impediment [ɪm'pɛdɪmənt] *n* obstacle *m*; (*also:* **speech ~**) défaut *m* d'élocution
impending [ɪm'pɛndɪŋ] *adj* imminent(e)
imperative [ɪm'pɛrətɪv] *adj* nécessaire; (*need*) urgent(e), pressant(e); (*tone*) impérieux(-euse) ▷ *n* (*Ling*) impératif *m*
imperfect [ɪm'pəːfɪkt] *adj* imparfait(e); (*goods etc*) défectueux(-euse) ▷ *n* (*Ling: also:* **~ tense**) imparfait *m*
imperial [ɪm'pɪərɪəl] *adj* impérial(e); (*Brit: measure*) légal(e)
impersonal [ɪm'pəːsənl] *adj* impersonnel(le)
impersonate [ɪm'pəːsəneɪt] *vt* se faire passer pour; (*Theat*) imiter
impertinent [ɪm'pəːtɪnənt] *adj* impertinent(e), insolent(e)
impervious [ɪm'pəːvɪəs] *adj* imperméable; (*fig*): **~ to** insensible à; inaccessible à
impetuous [ɪm'pɛtjuəs] *adj* impétueux(-euse), fougueux(-euse)

impetus ['ɪmpɪtəs] n impulsion f; (of runner)
élan m

impinge [ɪm'pɪndʒ]: **to ~ on** vt fus (person)
affecter, toucher; (rights) empiéter sur

implant [ɪm'plɑ:nt] vt (Med) implanter; (fig:
idea, principle) inculquer

implement n ['ɪmplɪmənt] outil m,
instrument m; (for cooking) ustensile m ▷ vt
['ɪmplɪment] exécuter, mettre à effet

implicate ['ɪmplɪkeɪt] vt impliquer,
compromettre

implication [ɪmplɪ'keɪʃən] n implication f;
by ~ indirectement

implicit [ɪm'plɪsɪt] adj implicite; (complete)
absolu(e), sans réserve

imply [ɪm'plaɪ] vt (hint) suggérer, laisser
entendre; (mean) indiquer, supposer

impolite [ɪmpə'laɪt] adj impoli(e)

import vt [ɪm'pɔ:t] importer ▷ n ['ɪmpɔ:t]
(Comm) importation f; (meaning) portée f,
signification f ▷ cpd ['ɪmpɔ:t] (duty, licence etc)
d'importation

importance [ɪm'pɔ:tns] n importance f;
to be of great/little ~ avoir beaucoup/peu
d'importance

important [ɪm'pɔ:tnt] adj important(e); **it is
~ that** il importe que, il est important que;
it's not ~ c'est sans importance, ce n'est pas
important

importer [ɪm'pɔ:tər] n importateur(-trice)

impose [ɪm'pəuz] vt imposer ▷ vi: **to ~ on sb**
abuser de la gentillesse de qn

imposing [ɪm'pəuzɪŋ] adj imposant(e),
impressionnant(e)

imposition [ɪmpə'zɪʃən] n (of tax etc)
imposition f; **to be an ~ on** (person) abuser de
la gentillesse or la bonté de

impossible [ɪm'pɔsɪbl] adj impossible; **it is ~
for me to leave** il m'est impossible de partir

impotent ['ɪmpətnt] adj impuissant(e)

impound [ɪm'paund] vt confisquer, saisir

impoverished [ɪm'pɔvərɪʃt] adj pauvre,
appauvri(e)

impractical [ɪm'præktɪkl] adj pas pratique;
(person) qui manque d'esprit pratique

impregnable [ɪm'prɛgnəbl] adj (fortress)
imprenable; (fig) inattaquable, irréfutable

impress [ɪm'prɛs] vt impressionner, faire
impression sur; (mark) imprimer, marquer;
to ~ sth on sb faire bien comprendre qch
à qn

impressed [ɪm'prɛst] adj impressionné(e)

impression [ɪm'prɛʃən] n impression f;
(of stamp, seal) empreinte f; (imitation)
imitation f; **to make a good/bad ~ on sb**
faire bonne/mauvaise impression sur qn;
to be under the ~ that avoir l'impression
que

impressionist [ɪm'prɛʃənɪst] n
impressionniste m/f

impressive [ɪm'prɛsɪv] adj
impressionnant(e)

imprint ['ɪmprɪnt] n empreinte f; (Publishing)
notice f; (: label) nom m (de collection or
d'éditeur)

imprison [ɪm'prɪzn] vt emprisonner, mettre
en prison

imprisonment [ɪm'prɪznmənt] n
emprisonnement m; (period): **to sentence sb
to 10 years' ~** condamner qn à 10 ans de
prison

improbable [ɪm'prɔbəbl] adj improbable;
(excuse) peu plausible

improper [ɪm'prɔpər] adj (wrong) incorrect(e);
(unsuitable) déplacé(e), de mauvais goût;
(indecent) indécent(e); (dishonest)
malhonnête

improve [ɪm'pru:v] vt améliorer ▷ vi
s'améliorer; (pupil etc) faire des progrès;
improve on, improve upon vt fus (offer)
enchérir sur

improvement [ɪm'pru:vmənt] n
amélioration f; (of pupil etc) progrès m; **to
make ~s to** apporter des améliorations à

improvise ['ɪmprəvaɪz] vt, vi improviser

impudent ['ɪmpjudnt] adj impudent(e)

impulse ['ɪmpʌls] n impulsion f; **on ~**
impulsivement, sur un coup de tête

impulsive [ɪm'pʌlsɪv] adj impulsif(-ive)

🔵 **KEYWORD**

in [ɪn] prep **1** (indicating place, position) dans;
in the house/the fridge dans la maison/
le frigo; **in the garden** dans le or au jardin;
in town en ville; **in the country** à la
campagne; **in school** à l'école; **in here/
there** ici/là

2 (with place names: of town, region, country): **in
London** à Londres; **in England** en
Angleterre; **in Japan** au Japon; **in the
United States** aux États-Unis

3 (indicating time: during): **in spring** au
printemps; **in summer** en été; **in May/2005**
en mai/2005; **in the afternoon** (dans)
l'après-midi; **at 4 o'clock in the afternoon**
à 4 heures de l'après-midi

4 (indicating time: in the space of) en; (: future)
dans; **I did it in 3 hours/days** je l'ai fait en
3 heures/jours; **I'll see you in 2 weeks** or **in
2 weeks' time** je te verrai dans 2 semaines;
once in a hundred years une fois tous les
cent ans

5 (indicating manner etc) à; **in a loud/soft voice**
à voix haute/basse; **in pencil** au crayon; **in
writing** par écrit; **in French** en français; **to
pay in dollars** payer en dollars; **the boy in
the blue shirt** le garçon à or avec la chemise
bleue

6 (indicating circumstances): **in the sun** au
soleil; **in the shade** à l'ombre; **in the rain**
sous la pluie; **a change in policy** un
changement de politique

7 (indicating mood, state): **in tears** en larmes;

in anger sous le coup de la colère; **in despair** au désespoir; **in good condition** en bon état; **to live in luxury** vivre dans le luxe
8 (*with ratios, numbers*): **1 in 10 households, 1 household in 10** 1 ménage sur 10; **20 pence in the pound** 20 pence par livre sterling; **they lined up in twos** ils se mirent en rangs (deux) par deux; **in hundreds** par centaines
9 (*referring to people, works*) chez; **the disease is common in children** c'est une maladie courante chez les enfants; **in (the works of) Dickens** chez Dickens, dans (l'œuvre de) Dickens
10 (*indicating profession etc*) dans; **to be in teaching** être dans l'enseignement
11 (*after superlative*) de; **the best pupil in the class** le meilleur élève de la classe
12 (*with present participle*): **in saying this** en disant ceci
▷ *adv*: **to be in** (*person: at home, work*) être là; (*train, ship, plane*) être arrivé(e); (*in fashion*) être à la mode; **to ask sb in** inviter qn à entrer; **to run/limp etc in** entrer en courant/boitant etc; **their party is in** leur parti est au pouvoir
▷ *n*: **the ins and outs (of)** (*of proposal, situation etc*) les tenants et aboutissants (de)

in. *abbr* = **inch; inches**
inability [ɪnə'bɪlɪtɪ] *n* incapacité *f*; **~ to pay** incapacité de payer
inaccurate [ɪn'ækjurət] *adj* inexact(e); (*person*) qui manque de précision
inadequate [ɪn'ædɪkwət] *adj* insuffisant(e), inadéquat(e)
inadvertently [ɪnəd'vɜ:ntlɪ] *adv* par mégarde
inadvisable [ɪnəd'vaɪzəbl] *adj* à déconseiller; **it is ~ to** il est déconseillé de
inane [ɪ'neɪn] *adj* inepte, stupide
inanimate [ɪn'ænɪmət] *adj* inanimé(e)
inappropriate [ɪnə'prəʊprɪət] *adj* inopportun(e), mal à propos; (*word, expression*) impropre
inarticulate [ɪnɑ:'tɪkjulət] *adj* (*person*) qui s'exprime mal; (*speech*) indistinct(e)
inasmuch [ɪnəz'mʌtʃ] *adv*: **~ as** vu que, en ce sens que
inaugurate [ɪ'nɔːgjureɪt] *vt* inaugurer; (*president, official*) investir de ses fonctions
inauguration [ɪnɔːgju'reɪʃən] *n* inauguration *f*; investiture *f*
inborn [ɪn'bɔːn] *adj* (*feeling*) inné(e); (*defect*) congénital(e)
inbred [ɪn'bred] *adj* inné(e), naturel(le); (*family*) consanguin(e)
Inc. *abbr* = **incorporated**
incapable [ɪn'keɪpəbl] *adj*: **~ (of)** incapable (de)
incapacitate [ɪnkə'pæsɪteɪt] *vt*: **to ~ sb from doing** rendre qn incapable de faire
incense *n* ['ɪnsens] encens *m* ▷ *vt* [ɪn'sens] (*anger*) mettre en colère

incentive [ɪn'sentɪv] *n* encouragement *m*, raison *f* de se donner de la peine
incessant [ɪn'sesnt] *adj* incessant(e)
incessantly [ɪn'sesntlɪ] *adv* sans cesse, constamment
inch [ɪntʃ] *n* pouce *m* (=25 mm; 12 in a foot); **within an ~ of** à deux doigts de; **he wouldn't give an ~** (*fig*) il n'a pas voulu céder d'un pouce; **inch forward** *vi* avancer petit à petit
incidence ['ɪnsɪdns] *n* (*of crime, disease*) fréquence *f*
incident ['ɪnsɪdnt] *n* incident *m*; (*in book*) péripétie *f*
incidental [ɪnsɪ'dentl] *adj* accessoire; (*unplanned*) accidentel(le); **~ to** qui accompagne; **~ expenses** faux frais *mpl*
incidentally [ɪnsɪ'dentəlɪ] *adv* (*by the way*) à propos
inclination [ɪnklɪ'neɪʃən] *n* inclination *f*; (*desire*) envie *f*
incline *n* ['ɪnklaɪn] pente *f*, plan incliné ▷ *vt* [ɪn'klaɪn] incliner ▷ *vi* (*surface*) s'incliner; **to ~ to** avoir tendance à; **to be ~d to do** (*want to*) être enclin(e) à faire; (*have a tendency to do*) avoir tendance à faire; **to be well ~d towards sb** être bien disposé(e) à l'égard de qn
include [ɪn'kluːd] *vt* inclure, comprendre; **service is/is not ~d** le service est compris/n'est pas compris
including [ɪn'kluːdɪŋ] *prep* y compris; **~ service** service compris
inclusion [ɪn'kluːʒən] *n* inclusion *f*
inclusive [ɪn'kluːsɪv] *adj* inclus(e), compris(e); **~ of tax** taxes comprises; **£50 ~ of all surcharges** 50 livres tous frais compris
income ['ɪnkʌm] *n* revenu *m*; (*from property etc*) rentes *fpl*; **gross/net ~** revenu brut/net; **~ and expenditure account** compte *m* de recettes et de dépenses
income support *n* (*Brit*) ≈ revenu *m* minimum d'insertion, RMI *m*
income tax *n* impôt *m* sur le revenu
incoming ['ɪnkʌmɪŋ] *adj* (*passengers, mail*) à l'arrivée; (*government, tenant*) nouveau/nouvelle; **~ tide** marée montante
incompatible [ɪnkəm'pætɪbl] *adj* incompatible
incompetence [ɪn'kɒmpɪtns] *n* incompétence *f*, incapacité *f*
incompetent [ɪn'kɒmpɪtnt] *adj* incompétent(e), incapable
incomplete [ɪnkəm'pliːt] *adj* incomplet(-ète)
incongruous [ɪn'kɒŋgruəs] *adj* peu approprié(e); (*remark, act*) incongru(e), déplacé(e)
inconsiderate [ɪnkən'sɪdərət] *adj* (*action*) inconsidéré(e); (*person*) qui manque d'égards
inconsistency [ɪnkən'sɪstənsɪ] *n* (*of actions etc*) inconséquence *f*; (*of work*) irrégularité *f*; (*of statement etc*) incohérence *f*

inconsistent [ɪnkən'sɪstnt] adj qui manque de constance; (work) irrégulier(-ière); (statement) peu cohérent(e); **~ with** en contradiction avec

inconspicuous [ɪnkən'spɪkjuəs] adj qui passe inaperçu(e); (colour, dress) discret(-ète); **to make o.s. ~** ne pas se faire remarquer

inconvenience [ɪnkən'viːnjəns] n inconvénient m; (trouble) dérangement m ▷ vt déranger; **don't ~ yourself** ne vous dérangez pas

inconvenient [ɪnkən'viːnjənt] adj malcommode; (time, place) mal choisi(e), qui ne convient pas; (visitor) importun(e); **that time is very ~ for me** c'est un moment qui ne me convient pas du tout

incorporate [ɪn'kɔːpəreɪt] vt incorporer; (contain) contenir ▷ vi fusionner; (two firms) se constituer en société

incorporated [ɪn'kɔːpəreɪtɪd] adj: **~ company** (US) ≈ société f anonyme

incorrect [ɪnkə'rɛkt] adj incorrect(e); (opinion, statement) inexact(e)

increase n ['ɪnkriːs] augmentation f ▷ vi, vt [ɪn'kriːs] augmenter; **an ~ of 5%** une augmentation de 5%; **to be on the ~** être en augmentation

increasing [ɪn'kriːsɪŋ] adj croissant(e)

increasingly [ɪn'kriːsɪŋlɪ] adv de plus en plus

incredible [ɪn'krɛdɪbl] adj incroyable

incredibly [ɪn'krɛdɪblɪ] adv incroyablement

incubator ['ɪnkjubeɪtəʳ] n incubateur m; (for babies) couveuse f

incumbent [ɪn'kʌmbənt] adj: **it is ~ on him to ...** il lui appartient de ... ▷ n titulaire m/f

incur [ɪn'kəːʳ] vt (expenses) encourir; (anger, risk) s'exposer à; (debt) contracter; (loss) subir

indebted [ɪn'dɛtɪd] adj: **to be ~ to sb (for)** être redevable à qn (de)

indecent [ɪn'diːsnt] adj indécent(e), inconvenant(e)

indecent assault n (Brit) attentat m à la pudeur

indecent exposure n outrage m public à la pudeur

indecisive [ɪndɪ'saɪsɪv] adj indécis(e); (discussion) peu concluant(e)

indeed [ɪn'diːd] adv (confirming, agreeing) en effet, effectivement; (for emphasis) vraiment; (furthermore) d'ailleurs; **yes ~!** certainement!

indefinitely [ɪn'dɛfɪnɪtlɪ] adv (wait) indéfiniment; (speak) vaguement, avec imprécision

indemnity [ɪn'dɛmnɪtɪ] n (insurance) assurance f, garantie f; (compensation) indemnité f

independence [ɪndɪ'pɛndns] n indépendance f

Independence Day n (US) fête de l'Indépendance américaine; voir article

● **INDEPENDENCE DAY**

L'*Independence Day* est la fête nationale aux États-Unis, le 4 juillet. Il commémore l'adoption de la déclaration d'Indépendance, en 1776, écrite par Thomas Jefferson et proclamant la séparation des 13 colonies américaines de la Grande-Bretagne.

independent [ɪndɪ'pɛndnt] adj indépendant(e); (radio) libre; **to become ~** s'affranchir

independent school n (Brit) école privée

index ['ɪndɛks] n (pl **indexes**) (in book) index m; (: in library etc) catalogue m; (pl **indices**) ['ɪndɪsiːz] (ratio, sign) indice m

index card n fiche f

index finger n index m

index-linked ['ɪndɛks'lɪŋkt], (US) **indexed** ['ɪndɛkst] adj indexé(e) (sur le coût de la vie etc)

India ['ɪndɪə] n Inde f

Indian ['ɪndɪən] adj indien(ne) ▷ n Indien(ne); (American) **~** Indien(ne) (d'Amérique)

Indian Ocean n: **the ~** l'océan Indien

indicate ['ɪndɪkeɪt] vt indiquer ▷ vi (Brit Aut): **to ~ left/right** mettre son clignotant à gauche/à droite

indication [ɪndɪ'keɪʃən] n indication f, signe m

indicative [ɪn'dɪkətɪv] adj indicatif(-ive); **to be ~ of sth** être symptomatique de qch ▷ n (Ling) indicatif m

indicator ['ɪndɪkeɪtəʳ] n (sign) indicateur m; (Aut) clignotant m

indices ['ɪndɪsiːz] npl of **index**

indict [ɪn'daɪt] vt accuser

indictment [ɪn'daɪtmənt] n accusation f

indifference [ɪn'dɪfrəns] n indifférence f

indifferent [ɪn'dɪfrənt] adj indifférent(e); (poor) médiocre, quelconque

indigenous [ɪn'dɪdʒɪnəs] adj indigène

indigestion [ɪndɪ'dʒɛstʃən] n indigestion f, mauvaise digestion

indignant [ɪn'dɪgnənt] adj: **~ (at sth/ with sb)** indigné(e) (de qch/contre qn)

indignity [ɪn'dɪgnɪtɪ] n indignité f, affront m

indirect [ɪndɪ'rɛkt] adj indirect(e)

indiscreet [ɪndɪ'skriːt] adj indiscret(-ète); (rash) imprudent(e)

indiscriminate [ɪndɪ'skrɪmɪnət] adj (person) qui manque de discernement; (admiration) aveugle; (killings) commis(e) au hasard

indispensable [ɪndɪ'spɛnsəbl] adj indispensable

indisputable [ɪndɪ'spjuːtəbl] adj incontestable, indiscutable

individual [ɪndɪ'vɪdjuəl] n individu m ▷ adj individuel(le); (characteristic) particulier(-ière), original(e)

individually [ɪndɪ'vɪdjuəlɪ] *adv* individuellement

indoctrination [ɪndɔktrɪ'neɪʃən] *n* endoctrinement *m*

Indonesia [ɪndə'niːzɪə] *n* Indonésie *f*

indoor ['ɪndɔːʳ] *adj* d'intérieur; *(plant)* d'appartement; *(swimming pool)* couvert(e); *(sport, games)* pratiqué(e) en salle

indoors [ɪn'dɔːz] *adv* à l'intérieur; *(at home)* à la maison

induce [ɪn'djuːs] *vt (persuade)* persuader; *(bring about)* provoquer; *(labour)* déclencher; **to ~ sb to do sth** inciter or pousser qn à faire qch

inducement [ɪn'djuːsmənt] *n* incitation *f*; *(incentive)* but *m*; *(pej: bribe)* pot-de-vin *m*

indulge [ɪn'dʌldʒ] *vt (whim)* céder à, satisfaire; *(child)* gâter ▷ *vi*: **to ~ in sth** *(luxury)* s'offrir qch, se permettre qch; *(fantasies etc)* se livrer à qch

indulgence [ɪn'dʌldʒəns] *n* fantaisie *f* (que l'on s'offre); *(leniency)* indulgence *f*

indulgent [ɪn'dʌldʒənt] *adj* indulgent(e)

industrial [ɪn'dʌstrɪəl] *adj* industriel(le); *(injury)* du travail; *(dispute)* ouvrier(-ière)

industrial action *n* action revendicative

industrial estate *n (Brit)* zone industrielle

industrialist [ɪn'dʌstrɪəlɪst] *n* industriel *m*

industrial park *n (US)* zone industrielle

industrious [ɪn'dʌstrɪəs] *adj* travailleur(-euse)

industry ['ɪndəstrɪ] *n* industrie *f*; *(diligence)* zèle *m*, application *f*

inebriated [ɪ'niːbrɪeɪtɪd] *adj* ivre

inedible [ɪn'edɪbl] *adj* immangeable; *(plant etc)* non comestible

ineffective [ɪnɪ'fektɪv], **ineffectual** [ɪnɪ'fektʃuəl] *adj* inefficace; incompétent(e)

inefficient [ɪnɪ'fɪʃənt] *adj* inefficace

inequality [ɪnɪ'kwɔlɪtɪ] *n* inégalité *f*

inescapable [ɪnɪ'skeɪpəbl] *adj* inéluctable, inévitable

inevitable [ɪn'evɪtəbl] *adj* inévitable

inevitably [ɪn'evɪtəblɪ] *adv* inévitablement, fatalement

inexpensive [ɪnɪk'spɛnsɪv] *adj* bon marché *inv*

inexperienced [ɪnɪk'spɪərɪənst] *adj* inexpérimenté(e); **to be ~ in sth** manquer d'expérience dans qch

inexplicable [ɪnɪk'splɪkəbl] *adj* inexplicable

infallible [ɪn'fælɪbl] *adj* infaillible

infamous ['ɪnfəməs] *adj* infâme, abominable

infancy ['ɪnfənsɪ] *n* petite enfance, bas âge; *(fig)* enfance, débuts *mpl*

infant ['ɪnfənt] *n (baby)* nourrisson *m*; *(young child)* petit(e) enfant

infantry ['ɪnfəntrɪ] *n* infanterie *f*

infant school *n (Brit)* classes *fpl* préparatoires *(entre 5 et 7 ans)*

infatuated [ɪn'fætjueɪtɪd] *adj*: **~ with** entiché(e) de; **to become ~ (with sb)** s'enticher (de qn)

infatuation [ɪnfætju'eɪʃən] *n* toquade *f*; engouement *m*

infect [ɪn'fekt] *vt (wound)* infecter; *(person, blood)* contaminer; *(fig: pej)* corrompre; **~ed with** *(illness)* atteint(e) de; **to become ~ed** *(wound)* s'infecter

infection [ɪn'fekʃən] *n* infection *f*; *(contagion)* contagion *f*

infectious [ɪn'fekʃəs] *adj* infectieux(-euse); *(also fig)* contagieux(-euse)

infer [ɪn'fəːʳ] *vt*: **to ~ (from)** conclure (de), déduire (de)

inferior [ɪn'fɪərɪəʳ] *adj* inférieur(e); *(goods)* de qualité inférieure ▷ *n* inférieur(e); *(in rank)* subalterne *m/f*; **to feel ~** avoir un sentiment d'infériorité

inferiority [ɪnfɪərɪ'ɔrɪtɪ] *n* infériorité *f*

infertile [ɪn'fəːtaɪl] *adj* stérile

infertility [ɪnfəː'tɪlɪtɪ] *n* infertilité *f*, stérilité *f*

infested [ɪn'festɪd] *adj*: **~ (with)** infesté(e) (de)

in-fighting ['ɪnfaɪtɪŋ] *n* querelles *fpl* internes

infinite ['ɪnfɪnɪt] *adj* infini(e); *(time, money)* illimité(e)

infinitely ['ɪnfɪnɪtlɪ] *adv* infiniment

infinitive [ɪn'fɪnɪtɪv] *n* infinitif *m*

infinity [ɪn'fɪnɪtɪ] *n* infinité *f*; *(also Math)* infini *m*

infirmary [ɪn'fəːmərɪ] *n* hôpital *m*; *(in school, factory)* infirmerie *f*

inflamed [ɪn'fleɪmd] *adj* enflammé(e)

inflammable [ɪn'flæməbl] *adj (Brit)* inflammable

inflammation [ɪnflə'meɪʃən] *n* inflammation *f*

inflatable [ɪn'fleɪtəbl] *adj* gonflable

inflate [ɪn'fleɪt] *vt (tyre, balloon)* gonfler; *(fig: exaggerate)* grossir, gonfler; *(: increase)* gonfler

inflation [ɪn'fleɪʃən] *n (Econ)* inflation *f*

inflationary [ɪn'fleɪʃənərɪ] *adj* inflationniste

inflexible [ɪn'flɛksɪbl] *adj* inflexible, rigide

inflict [ɪn'flɪkt] *vt*: **to ~ on** infliger à

influence ['ɪnfluəns] *n* influence *f* ▷ *vt* influencer; **under the ~** sous l'effet de; **under the ~ of alcohol** en état d'ébriété

influential [ɪnflu'ɛnʃl] *adj* influent(e)

influenza [ɪnflu'ɛnzə] *n* grippe *f*

influx ['ɪnflʌks] *n* afflux *m*

info *(inf)* ['ɪnfəu] *n (= information)* renseignements *mpl*

infomercial ['ɪnfəuməːʃl] *(US) n (for product)* publi-information *f*; *(Pol) émission où un candidat présente son programme* électoral

inform [ɪn'fɔːm] *vt*: **to ~ sb (of)** informer or avertir qn (de) ▷ *vi*: **to ~ on sb** dénoncer qn, informer contre qn; **to ~ sb about** renseigner qn sur, mettre qn au courant de

informal [ɪn'fɔːml] *adj (person, manner, party)* simple, sans cérémonie; *(visit, discussion)* dénué(e) de formalités; *(announcement, invitation)* non officiel(le); *(colloquial)* familier(-ère); **"dress ~"** "tenue de ville"

informality [ɪnfɔː'mælɪtɪ] n simplicité f,
absence f de cérémonie; caractère non officiel
informant [ɪn'fɔːmənt] n
informateur(-trice)
information [ɪnfə'meɪʃən] n information(s)
f(pl); renseignements mpl; (knowledge)
connaissances fpl; **to get ~ on** se renseigner
sur; **a piece of ~** un renseignement; **for
your ~** à titre d'information
information desk n accueil m
information office n bureau m de
renseignements
information technology n informatique f
informative [ɪn'fɔːmətɪv] adj instructif(-ive)
informer [ɪn'fɔːmər] n dénonciateur(-trice);
(also: **police ~**) indicateur(-trice)
infra-red [ɪnfrə'rɛd] adj infrarouge
infrastructure ['ɪnfrəstrʌktʃər] n
infrastructure f
infrequent [ɪn'friːkwənt] adj peu
fréquent(e), rare
infringe [ɪn'frɪndʒ] vt enfreindre ▷ vi: **to ~ on**
empiéter sur
infringement [ɪn'frɪndʒmənt] n: **~ (of)**
infraction f (à)
infuriate [ɪn'fjuərɪeɪt] vt mettre en fureur
infuriating [ɪn'fjuərɪeɪtɪŋ] adj exaspérant(e)
ingenious [ɪn'dʒiːnjəs] adj ingénieux(-euse)
ingenuity [ɪndʒɪ'njuːɪtɪ] n ingéniosité f
ingenuous [ɪn'dʒɛnjuəs] adj franc/franche,
ouvert(e)
ingot ['ɪŋɡət] n lingot m
ingrained [ɪn'ɡreɪnd] adj enraciné(e)
ingratiate [ɪn'ɡreɪʃɪeɪt] vt: **to ~ o.s. with**
s'insinuer dans les bonnes grâces de, se faire
bien voir de
ingredient [ɪn'ɡriːdɪənt] n ingrédient m; (fig)
élément m
inhabit [ɪn'hæbɪt] vt habiter
inhabitant [ɪn'hæbɪtnt] n habitant(e)
inhale [ɪn'heɪl] vt inhaler; (perfume) respirer;
(smoke) avaler ▷ vi (breathe in) aspirer; (in
smoking) avaler la fumée
inhaler [ɪn'heɪlər] n inhalateur m
inherent [ɪn'hɪərənt] adj: **~ (in or to)**
inhérent(e) (à)
inherit [ɪn'hɛrɪt] vt hériter (de)
inheritance [ɪn'hɛrɪtəns] n héritage m; (fig):
the situation that was his ~ as president
la situation dont il a hérité en tant que
président; **law of ~** droit m de la succession
inhibit [ɪn'hɪbɪt] vt (Psych) inhiber; (growth)
freiner; **to ~ sb from doing** empêcher qn de
retenir qn de faire
inhibition [ɪnhɪ'bɪʃən] n inhibition f
inhuman [ɪn'hjuːmən] adj inhumain(e)
initial [ɪ'nɪʃl] adj initial(e) ▷ n initiale f ▷ vt
parafer; **initials** npl initiales fpl; (as signature)
parafe m
initially [ɪ'nɪʃəlɪ] adv initialement, au début
initiate [ɪ'nɪʃɪeɪt] vt (start) entreprendre;
amorcer; (enterprise) lancer; (person) initier;

to ~ sb into a secret initier qn à un secret;
to ~ proceedings against sb (Law) intenter
une action à qn, engager des poursuites
contre qn
initiative [ɪ'nɪʃətɪv] n initiative f; **to take
the ~** prendre l'initiative
inject [ɪn'dʒɛkt] vt (liquid, fig: money) injecter;
(person): **to ~ sb with sth** faire une piqûre de
qch à qn
injection [ɪn'dʒɛkʃən] n injection f, piqûre f;
to have an ~ se faire faire une piqûre
injure ['ɪndʒər] vt blesser; (wrong) faire du tort
à; (damage: reputation etc) compromettre;
(feelings) heurter; **to ~ o.s.** se blesser
injured ['ɪndʒəd] adj (person, leg etc) blessé(e);
(tone, feelings) offensé(e); **~ party** (Law) partie
lésée
injury ['ɪndʒərɪ] n blessure f; (wrong) tort m;
to escape without ~ s'en sortir sain et sauf
injury time n (Sport) arrêts mpl de jeu
injustice [ɪn'dʒʌstɪs] n injustice f; **you do me
an ~** vous êtes injuste envers moi
ink [ɪŋk] n encre f
ink-jet printer ['ɪŋkdʒɛt-] n imprimante f
à jet d'encre
inkling ['ɪŋklɪŋ] n soupçon m, vague idée f
inlaid ['ɪnleɪd] adj incrusté(e); (table etc)
marqueté(e)
inland adj ['ɪnlənd] intérieur(e) ▷ adv
[ɪn'lænd] à l'intérieur, dans les terres;
~ waterways canaux mpl et rivières fpl
Inland Revenue n (Brit) fisc m
in-laws ['ɪnlɔːz] npl beaux-parents mpl; belle
famille
inlet ['ɪnlɛt] n (Geo) crique f
inmate ['ɪnmeɪt] n (in prison) détenu(e);
(in asylum) interné(e)
inn [ɪn] n auberge f
innate [ɪ'neɪt] adj inné(e)
inner ['ɪnər] adj intérieur(e)
inner city n centre m urbain (souffrant souvent
de délabrement, d'embouteillages etc)
inner-city ['ɪnə'sɪtɪ] adj (schools, problems) de
quartiers déshérités
inner tube n (of tyre) chambre f à air
inning ['ɪnɪŋ] n (US: Baseball) tour m de batte;
innings n (Cricket) tour de batte; (Brit fig):
he has had a good ~ il (en) a bien profité
innocence ['ɪnəsns] n innocence f
innocent ['ɪnəsnt] adj innocent(e)
innocuous [ɪ'nɔkjuəs] adj inoffensif(-ive)
innovation [ɪnəu'veɪʃən] n innovation f
innovative ['ɪnəu'veɪtɪv] adj novateur(-trice);
(product) innovant(e)
innuendo [ɪnju'ɛndəu] (pl **innuendoes**) n
insinuation f, allusion (malveillante)
innumerable [ɪ'njuːmrəbl] adj innombrable
in-patient ['ɪnpeɪʃənt] n malade
hospitalisé(e)
input ['ɪnput] n (contribution) contribution f;
(resources) ressources fpl; (Elec) énergie f,
puissance f; (of machine) consommation f;

(*Comput*) entrée f (de données); (: *data*) données fpl ▷ vt (*Comput*) introduire, entrer

inquest [ˈɪnkwɛst] n enquête (criminelle); (*coroner's*) enquête judiciaire

inquire [ɪnˈkwaɪəʳ] vi demander ▷ vt demander, s'informer de; **to ~ about** s'informer de, se renseigner sur; **to ~ when/where/whether** demander quand/où/si; **inquire after** vt fus demander des nouvelles de; **inquire into** vt fus faire une enquête sur

inquiry [ɪnˈkwaɪərɪ] n demande f de renseignements; (*Law*) enquête f, investigation f; **"inquiries"** "renseignements"; **to hold an ~ into sth** enquêter sur qch

inquisitive [ɪnˈkwɪzɪtɪv] adj curieux(-euse)

ins. abbr = **inches**

insane [ɪnˈseɪn] adj fou/folle; (*Med*) aliéné(e)

insanity [ɪnˈsænɪtɪ] n folie f; (*Med*) aliénation (mentale)

inscription [ɪnˈskrɪpʃən] n inscription f; (*in book*) dédicace f

inscrutable [ɪnˈskruːtəbl] adj impénétrable

insect [ˈɪnsɛkt] n insecte m

insecticide [ɪnˈsɛktɪsaɪd] n insecticide m

insect repellent n crème f anti-insectes

insecure [ɪnsɪˈkjuəʳ] adj (*person*) anxieux(-euse); (*job*) précaire; (*building etc*) peu sûr(e)

insecurity [ɪnsɪˈkjuərɪtɪ] n insécurité f

insensitive [ɪnˈsɛnsɪtɪv] adj insensible

insert vt [ɪnˈsəːt] insérer ▷ n [ˈɪnsəːt] insertion f

insertion [ɪnˈsəːʃən] n insertion f

in-service [ˈɪnˈsəːvɪs] adj (*training*) continu(e); (*course*) d'initiation; de perfectionnement; de recyclage

inshore adj [ˈɪnʃɔːʳ] côtier(-ière) ▷ adv [ɪnˈʃɔːʳ] près de la côte; vers la côte

inside [ˈɪnsaɪd] n intérieur m; (*of road: Brit*) côté m gauche (*de la route*); (: *US, Europe etc*) côté droit (*de la route*) ▷ adj intérieur(e) ▷ adv à l'intérieur, dedans ▷ prep à l'intérieur de; (*of time*): **~ 10 minutes** en moins de 10 minutes; **insides** npl (*inf*) intestins mpl; **~ information** renseignements mpl à la source; **~ story** histoire racontée par un témoin; **to go ~** rentrer

inside lane n (*Aut: in Britain*) voie f de gauche; (: *in US, Europe*) voie f de droite

inside out adv à l'envers; (*know*) à fond; **to turn sth ~** retourner qch

insider dealing, insider trading n (*Stock Exchange*) délit m d'initiés

insight [ˈɪnsaɪt] n perspicacité f; (*glimpse, idea*) aperçu m; **to gain (an) ~ into** parvenir à comprendre

insignificant [ɪnsɪɡˈnɪfɪknt] adj insignifiant(e)

insincere [ɪnsɪnˈsɪəʳ] adj hypocrite

insinuate [ɪnˈsɪnjueɪt] vt insinuer

insist [ɪnˈsɪst] vi insister; **to ~ on doing** insister pour faire; **to ~ on sth** exiger qch; **to ~ that** insister pour que + sub; (*claim*) maintenir or soutenir que

insistent [ɪnˈsɪstənt] adj insistant(e), pressant(e); (*noise, action*) ininterrompu(e)

insole [ˈɪnsəul] n semelle intérieure; (*fixed part of shoe*) première f

insolent [ˈɪnsələnt] adj insolent(e)

insolvent [ɪnˈsɔlvənt] adj insolvable; (*bankrupt*) en faillite

insomnia [ɪnˈsɔmnɪə] n insomnie f

inspect [ɪnˈspɛkt] vt inspecter; (*Brit: ticket*) contrôler

inspection [ɪnˈspɛkʃən] n inspection f; (*Brit: of tickets*) contrôle m

inspector [ɪnˈspɛktəʳ] n inspecteur(-trice); (*Brit: on buses, trains*) contrôleur(-euse)

inspiration [ɪnspəˈreɪʃən] n inspiration f

inspire [ɪnˈspaɪəʳ] vt inspirer

inspiring [ɪnˈspaɪərɪŋ] adj inspirant(e)

instability [ɪnstəˈbɪlɪtɪ] n instabilité f

install, (US) instal [ɪnˈstɔːl] vt installer

installation [ɪnstəˈleɪʃən] n installation f

instalment, (US) installment [ɪnˈstɔːlmənt] n (*payment*) acompte m, versement partiel; (*of TV serial etc*) épisode m; **in ~s** (*pay*) à tempérament; (*receive*) en plusieurs fois

instance [ˈɪnstəns] n exemple m; **for ~** par exemple; **in many ~s** dans bien des cas; **in that ~** dans ce cas; **in the first ~** tout d'abord, en premier lieu

instant [ˈɪnstənt] n instant m ▷ adj immédiat(e), urgent(e); (*coffee, food*) instantané(e), en poudre; **the 10th ~** le 10 courant

instantly [ˈɪnstəntlɪ] adv immédiatement, tout de suite

instant messaging n messagerie f instantanée

instead [ɪnˈstɛd] adv au lieu de cela; **~ of** au lieu de; **~ of sb** à la place de qn

instep [ˈɪnstɛp] n cou-de-pied m; (*of shoe*) cambrure f

instigate [ˈɪnstɪɡeɪt] vt (*rebellion, strike, crime*) inciter à; (*new ideas etc*) susciter

instil [ɪnˈstɪl] vt: **to ~ (into)** inculquer (à); (*courage*) insuffler (à)

instinct [ˈɪnstɪŋkt] n instinct m

instinctive [ɪnˈstɪŋktɪv] adj instinctif(-ive)

institute [ˈɪnstɪtjuːt] n institut m ▷ vt instituer, établir; (*inquiry*) ouvrir; (*proceedings*) entamer

institution [ɪnstɪˈtjuːʃən] n institution f; (*school*) établissement m (scolaire); (*for care*) établissement (psychiatrique etc)

instruct [ɪnˈstrʌkt] vt instruire, former; **to ~ sb in sth** enseigner qch à qn; **to ~ sb to do** charger qn or ordonner à qn de faire

instruction [ɪnˈstrʌkʃən] n instruction f; **instructions** npl (*orders*) directives fpl; **~s for use** mode m d'emploi

instructor [ɪn'strʌktə'] n professeur m; (for skiing, driving) moniteur m

instrument ['ɪnstrumənt] n instrument m

instrumental [ɪnstru'mɛntl] adj (Mus) instrumental(e); **to be ~ in sth/in doing sth** contribuer à qch/à faire qch

instrument panel n tableau m de bord

insufficient [ɪnsə'fɪʃənt] adj insuffisant(e)

insular ['ɪnsjulə'] adj insulaire; (outlook) étroit(e); (person) aux vues étroites

insulate ['ɪnsjuleɪt] vt isoler; (against sound) insonoriser

insulation [ɪnsju'leɪʃən] n isolation f; (against sound) insonorisation f

insulin ['ɪnsjulɪn] n insuline f

insult n ['ɪnsʌlt] insulte f, affront m ▷ vt [ɪn'sʌlt] insulter, faire un affront à

insulting [ɪn'sʌltɪŋ] adj insultant(e), injurieux(-euse)

insurance [ɪn'ʃuərəns] n assurance f; **fire/ life** ~ assurance-incendie/-vie; **to take out ~ (against)** s'assurer (contre)

insurance company n compagnie f or société f d'assurances

insurance policy n police f d'assurance

insure [ɪn'ʃuə'] vt assurer; **to ~ (o.s.) against** (fig) parer à; **to ~ sb/sb's life** assurer qn/la vie de qn; **to be ~d for £5000** être assuré(e) pour 5000 livres

intact [ɪn'tækt] adj intact(e)

intake ['ɪnteɪk] n (Tech) admission f; (consumption) consommation f; (Brit Scol): **an ~ of 200 a year** 200 admissions par an

integral ['ɪntɪɡrəl] adj (whole) intégral(e); (part) intégrant(e)

integrate ['ɪntɪɡreɪt] vt intégrer ▷ vi s'intégrer

integrity [ɪn'tɛɡrɪtɪ] n intégrité f

intellect ['ɪntəlɛkt] n intelligence f

intellectual [ɪntə'lɛktjuəl] adj, n intellectuel(le)

intelligence [ɪn'tɛlɪdʒəns] n intelligence f; (Mil) informations fpl, renseignements mpl

Intelligence Service n services mpl de renseignements

intelligent [ɪn'tɛlɪdʒənt] adj intelligent(e)

intend [ɪn'tɛnd] vt (gift etc): **to ~ sth for** destiner qch à; **to ~ to do** avoir l'intention de faire

intense [ɪn'tɛns] adj intense; (person) véhément(e)

intensely [ɪn'tɛnslɪ] adv intensément; (moving) profondément

intensify [ɪn'tɛnsɪfaɪ] vt intensifier

intensity [ɪn'tɛnsɪtɪ] n intensité f

intensive [ɪn'tɛnsɪv] adj intensif(-ive)

intensive care n: **to be in ~** être en réanimation

intensive care unit n service m de réanimation

intent [ɪn'tɛnt] n intention f ▷ adj attentif(-ive), absorbé(e); **to all ~s and**

purposes en fait, pratiquement; **to be ~ on doing sth** être (bien) décidé à faire qch

intention [ɪn'tɛnʃən] n intention f

intentional [ɪn'tɛnʃənl] adj intentionnel(le), délibéré(e)

intently [ɪn'tɛntlɪ] adv attentivement

interact [ɪntər'ækt] vi avoir une action réciproque; (people) communiquer

interaction [ɪntər'ækʃən] n interaction f

interactive [ɪntər'æktɪv] adj (group) interactif(-ive); (Comput) interactif, conversationnel(le)

intercept [ɪntə'sɛpt] vt intercepter; (person) arrêter au passage

interchange n (exchange) échange m; (on motorway) échangeur m ▷ vt [ɪntə'tʃeɪndʒ] échanger; mettre à la place l'un(e) de l'autre

interchangeable [ɪntə'tʃeɪndʒəbl] adj interchangeable

intercom ['ɪntəkɔm] n interphone m

intercourse ['ɪntəkɔːs] n rapports mpl; **sexual ~** rapports sexuels

interest ['ɪntrɪst] n intérêt m; (Comm: stake, share) participation f, intérêts mpl ▷ vt intéresser; **compound/simple ~** intérêt composé/simple; **British ~s in the Middle East** les intérêts britanniques au Moyen-Orient; **his main ~ is ...** ce qui l'intéresse le plus est ...

interested ['ɪntrɪstɪd] adj intéressé(e); **to be ~ in sth** s'intéresser à qch; **I'm ~ in going** ça m'intéresse d'y aller

interesting ['ɪntrɪstɪŋ] adj intéressant(e)

interest rate n taux m d'intérêt

interface ['ɪntəfeɪs] n (Comput) interface f

interfere [ɪntə'fɪə'] vi: **to ~ in** (quarrel) s'immiscer dans; (other people's business) se mêler de; **to ~ with** (object) tripoter, toucher à; (plans) contrecarrer; (duty) être en conflit avec; **don't ~** mêlez-vous de vos affaires

interference [ɪntə'fɪərəns] n (gen) ingérence f; (Physics) interférence f; (Radio, TV) parasites mpl

interim ['ɪntərɪm] adj provisoire; (post) intérimaire ▷ n: **in the ~** dans l'intérim

interior [ɪn'tɪərɪə'] n intérieur m ▷ adj intérieur(e); (minister, department) de l'intérieur

interior decorator, interior designer n décorateur(-trice) d'intérieur

interior design n architecture f d'intérieur

interjection [ɪntə'dʒɛkʃən] n interjection f

interlock [ɪntə'lɔk] vi s'enclencher ▷ vt enclencher

interlude ['ɪntəluːd] n intervalle m; (Theat) intermède m

intermediate [ɪntə'miːdɪət] adj intermédiaire; (Scol: course, level) moyen(ne)

intermission [ɪntə'mɪʃən] n pause f; (Theat, Cine) entracte m

intern vt [ɪnˈtɜːn] interner ▷ n [ˈɪntɜːn] (US) interne m/f

internal [ɪnˈtɜːnl] adj interne; (dispute, reform etc) intérieur(e); **~ injuries** lésions fpl internes

internally [ɪnˈtɜːnəlɪ] adv intérieurement; **"not to be taken ~"** "pour usage externe"

Internal Revenue Service n (US) fisc m

international [ɪntəˈnæʃənl] adj international(e) ▷ n (Brit Sport) international m

Internet [ˈɪntənet] n: **the ~** l'Internet m

Internet café n cybercafé m

Internet Service Provider n fournisseur m d'accès à Internet

Internet user n internaute m/f

interplay [ˈɪntəpleɪ] n effet m réciproque, jeu m

interpret [ɪnˈtɜːprɪt] vt interpréter ▷ vi servir d'interprète

interpretation [ɪntɜːprɪˈteɪʃən] n interprétation f

interpreter [ɪnˈtɜːprɪtər] n interprète m/f; **could you act as an ~ for us?** pourriez-vous nous servir d'interprète?

interrelated [ɪntərɪˈleɪtɪd] adj en corrélation, en rapport étroit

interrogate [ɪnˈtɛrəugeɪt] vt interroger; (suspect etc) soumettre à un interrogatoire

interrogation [ɪntɛrəuˈgeɪʃən] n interrogation f; (by police) interrogatoire m

interrogative [ɪntəˈrɔgətɪv] adj interrogateur(-trice) ▷ n (Ling) interrogatif m

interrupt [ɪntəˈrʌpt] vt, vi interrompre

interruption [ɪntəˈrʌpʃən] n interruption f

intersect [ɪntəˈsekt] vt couper, croiser; (Math) intersecter ▷ vi se croiser, se couper; s'intersecter

intersection [ɪntəˈsekʃən] n intersection f; (of roads) croisement m

intersperse [ɪntəˈspɜːs] vt: **to ~ with** parsemer de

interstate [ˈɪntəsteɪt] (US) n autoroute f (qui relie plusieurs États)

intertwine [ɪntəˈtwaɪn] vt entrelacer ▷ vi s'entrelacer

interval [ˈɪntəvl] n intervalle m; (Brit: Theat) entracte m; (: Sport) mi-temps f; **bright ~s** (in weather) éclaircies fpl; **at ~s** par intervalles

intervene [ɪntəˈviːn] vi (time) s'écouler (entre-temps); (event) survenir; (person) intervenir

intervention [ɪntəˈvenʃən] n intervention f

interview [ˈɪntəvjuː] n (Radio, TV) interview f; (for job) entrevue f ▷ vt interviewer, avoir une entrevue avec

interviewer [ˈɪntəvjuːər] n (Radio, TV) interviewer m

intestine [ɪnˈtestɪn] n intestin m; **large ~** gros intestin; **small ~** intestin grêle

intimacy [ˈɪntɪməsɪ] n intimité f

intimate adj [ˈɪntɪmət] intime; (friendship) profond(e); (knowledge) approfondi(e) ▷ vt [ˈɪntɪmeɪt] suggérer, laisser entendre; (announce) faire savoir

intimidate [ɪnˈtɪmɪdeɪt] vt intimider

intimidating [ɪnˈtɪmɪdeɪtɪŋ] adj intimidant(e)

into [ˈɪntu] prep dans; **~ pieces/French** en morceaux/français; **to change pounds ~ dollars** changer des livres en dollars; **3 ~ 9 goes 3** 9 divisé par 3 donne 3; **she's ~ opera** c'est une passionnée d'opéra

intolerant [ɪnˈtɔlərnt] adj: **~ (of)** intolérant(e) (de); (Med) intolérant (à)

intoxicated [ɪnˈtɔksɪkeɪtɪd] adj ivre

intractable [ɪnˈtræktəbl] adj (child, temper) indocile, insoumis(e); (problem) insoluble; (illness) incurable

intranet [ˈɪntrənet] n intranet m

intransitive [ɪnˈtrænsɪtɪv] adj intransitif(-ive)

intravenous [ɪntrəˈviːnəs] adj intraveineux(-euse)

in-tray [ˈɪntreɪ] n courrier m "arrivée"

intricate [ˈɪntrɪkət] adj complexe, compliqué(e)

intrigue [ɪnˈtriːg] n intrigue f ▷ vt intriguer ▷ vi intriguer, comploter

intriguing [ɪnˈtriːgɪŋ] adj fascinant(e)

intrinsic [ɪnˈtrɪnsɪk] adj intrinsèque

introduce [ɪntrəˈdjuːs] vt introduire; (TV show etc) présenter; **to ~ sb (to sb)** présenter qn (à qn); **to ~ sb to** (pastime, technique) initier qn à; **may I ~ ...?** je vous présente ...

introduction [ɪntrəˈdʌkʃən] n introduction f; (of person) présentation f; (to new experience) initiation f; **a letter of ~** une lettre de recommandation

introductory [ɪntrəˈdʌktərɪ] adj préliminaire, introductif(-ive); **~ remarks** remarques fpl liminaires; **an ~ offer** une offre de lancement

intrude [ɪnˈtruːd] vi (person) être importun(e); **to ~ on** or **into** (conversation etc) s'immiscer dans; **am I intruding?** est-ce que je vous dérange?

intruder [ɪnˈtruːdər] n intrus(e)

intuition [ɪntjuːˈɪʃən] n intuition f

inundate [ˈɪnʌndeɪt] vt: **to ~ with** inonder de

invade [ɪnˈveɪd] vt envahir

invalid n [ˈɪnvəlɪd] malade m/f; (with disability) invalide m/f ▷ adj [ɪnˈvælɪd] (not valid) invalide, non valide

invaluable [ɪnˈvæljuəbl] adj inestimable, inappréciable

invariably [ɪnˈvɛərɪəblɪ] adv invariablement; **she is ~ late** elle est toujours en retard

invasion [ɪnˈveɪʒən] n invasion f

invent [ɪnˈvent] vt inventer

invention [ɪnˈvenʃən] n invention f

inventive [ɪnˈventɪv] adj inventif(-ive)

inventor [ɪnˈvɛntə^r] n inventeur(-trice)
inventory [ˈɪnvəntrɪ] n inventaire m
invert [ɪnˈvəːt] vt intervertir; (cup, object) retourner
inverted commas [ɪnˈvəːtɪd-] npl (Brit) guillemets mpl
invest [ɪnˈvɛst] vt investir; (endow): **to ~ sb with sth** conférer qch à qn ▷ vi faire un investissement, investir; **to ~ in** placer de l'argent or investir dans; (fig: acquire) s'offrir, faire l'acquisition de
investigate [ɪnˈvɛstɪɡeɪt] vt étudier, examiner; (crime) faire une enquête sur
investigation [ɪnvɛstɪˈɡeɪʃən] n examen m; (of crime) enquête f, investigation f
investigator [ɪnˈvɛstɪɡeɪtə^r] n investigateur(-trice); **private ~** détective privé
investment [ɪnˈvɛstmənt] n investissement m, placement m
investor [ɪnˈvɛstə^r] n épargnant(e); (shareholder) actionnaire m/f
invigilator [ɪnˈvɪdʒɪleɪtə^r] n (Brit) surveillant m (d'examen)
invigorating [ɪnˈvɪɡəreɪtɪŋ] adj vivifiant(e), stimulant(e)
invisible [ɪnˈvɪzɪbl] adj invisible
invitation [ɪnvɪˈteɪʃən] n invitation f; **by ~ only** sur invitation; **at sb's ~** à la demande de qn
invite [ɪnˈvaɪt] vt inviter; (opinions etc) demander; (trouble) chercher; **to ~ sb (to do)** inviter qn (à faire); **to ~ sb to dinner** inviter qn à dîner; **invite out** vt inviter (à sortir); **invite over** vt inviter (chez soi)
inviting [ɪnˈvaɪtɪŋ] adj engageant(e), attrayant(e); (gesture) encourageant(e)
invoice [ˈɪnvɔɪs] n facture f ▷ vt facturer; **to ~ sb for goods** facturer des marchandises à qn
involuntary [ɪnˈvɔləntrɪ] adj involontaire
involve [ɪnˈvɔlv] vt (entail) impliquer; (concern) concerner; (require) nécessiter; **to ~ sb in** (theft etc) impliquer qn dans; (activity, meeting) faire participer qn à
involved [ɪnˈvɔlvd] adj (complicated) complexe; **to be ~ in** (take part) participer à; (be engrossed) être plongé(e) dans; **to feel ~** se sentir concerné(e); **to become ~** (in love etc) s'engager
involvement [ɪnˈvɔlvmənt] n (personal role) rôle m; (participation) participation f; (enthusiasm) enthousiasme m; (of resources, funds) mise f en jeu
inward [ˈɪnwəd] adj (movement) vers l'intérieur; (thought, feeling) profond(e), intime ▷ adv = **inwards**
inwards [ˈɪnwədz] adv vers l'intérieur
I/O abbr (Comput: = input/output) E/S
iodine [ˈaɪəudiːn] n iode m
IOM abbr = **Isle of Man**
iota [aɪˈəutə] n (fig) brin m, grain m

IOU n abbr (= I owe you) reconnaissance f de dette
iPod® [ˈaɪpɒd] n iPod® m
IQ n abbr (= intelligence quotient) Q.I. m
IRA n abbr (= Irish Republican Army) IRA f; (US) = **individual retirement account**
Iran [ɪˈrɑːn] n Iran m
Iranian [ɪˈreɪnɪən] adj iranien(ne) ▷ n Iranien(ne); (Ling) iranien m
Iraq [ɪˈrɑːk] n Irak m
Iraqi [ɪˈrɑːkɪ] adj irakien(ne) ▷ n Irakien(ne)
irate [aɪˈreɪt] adj courroucé(e)
Ireland [ˈaɪələnd] n Irlande f; **Republic of ~** République f d'Irlande
iris, irises [ˈaɪrɪs, -ɪz] n iris m
Irish [ˈaɪrɪʃ] adj irlandais(e) ▷ npl: **the ~** les Irlandais ▷ n (Ling) irlandais m; **the Irish** npl les Irlandais
Irishman [ˈaɪrɪʃmən] irreg n Irlandais m
Irish Sea n: **the ~** la mer d'Irlande
Irishwoman [ˈaɪrɪʃwumən] irreg n Irlandaise f
iron [ˈaɪən] n fer m; (for clothes) fer m à repasser ▷ adj de or en fer ▷ vt (clothes) repasser; **irons** npl (chains) fers mpl, chaînes fpl; **iron out** vt (crease) faire disparaître au fer; (fig) aplanir; faire disparaître
ironic [aɪˈrɔnɪk], **ironical** [aɪˈrɔnɪkl] adj ironique
ironically [aɪˈrɔnɪklɪ] adv ironiquement
ironing [ˈaɪənɪŋ] n (activity) repassage m; (clothes: ironed) linge repassé; (: to be ironed) linge à repasser
ironing board n planche f à repasser
ironmonger [ˈaɪənmʌŋɡə^r] n (Brit) quincaillier m; **~'s (shop)** quincaillerie f
irony [ˈaɪrənɪ] n ironie f
irrational [ɪˈræʃənl] adj irrationnel(le); (person) qui n'est pas rationnel
irregular [ɪˈreɡjulə^r] adj irrégulier(-ière); (surface) inégal(e); (action, event) peu orthodoxe
irrelevant [ɪˈrɛləvənt] adj sans rapport, hors de propos
irresistible [ɪrɪˈzɪstɪbl] adj irrésistible
irrespective [ɪrɪˈspɛktɪv]: **~ of** prep sans tenir compte de
irresponsible [ɪrɪˈspɒnsɪbl] adj (act) irréfléchi(e); (person) qui n'a pas le sens des responsabilités
irrigate [ˈɪrɪɡeɪt] vt irriguer
irrigation [ɪrɪˈɡeɪʃən] n irrigation f
irritable [ˈɪrɪtəbl] adj irritable
irritate [ˈɪrɪteɪt] vt irriter
irritating [ˈɪrɪteɪtɪŋ] adj irritant(e)
irritation [ɪrɪˈteɪʃən] n irritation f
IRS n abbr (US) = **Internal Revenue Service**
is [ɪz] vb see **be**
ISDN n abbr (= Integrated Services Digital Network) RNIS m
Islam [ˈɪzlɑːm] n Islam m
Islamic [ɪzˈlɑːmɪk] adj islamique;

~ fundamentalists intégristes *mpl* musulmans

island ['aɪlənd] *n* île *f*; *(also:* **traffic ~)** refuge *m* (pour piétons)

islander ['aɪləndər] *n* habitant(e) d'une île, insulaire *m/f*

isle [aɪl] *n* île *f*

isn't ['ɪznt] = **is not**

isolate ['aɪsəleɪt] *vt* isoler

isolated ['aɪsəleɪtɪd] *adj* isolé(e)

isolation [aɪsə'leɪʃən] *n* isolement *m*

ISP *n abbr* = **Internet Service Provider**

Israel ['ɪzreɪl] *n* Israël *m*

Israeli [ɪz'reɪlɪ] *adj* israélien(ne) ▷ *n* Israélien(ne)

issue ['ɪʃuː] *n* question *f*, problème *m*; *(outcome)* résultat *m*, issue *f*; *(of banknotes)* émission *f*; *(of newspaper)* numéro *m*; *(of book)* publication *f*, parution *f*; *(offspring)* descendance *f* ▷ *vt* *(rations, equipment)* distribuer; *(orders)* donner; *(statement)* publier, faire; *(certificate, passport)* délivrer; *(book)* faire paraître; publier; *(banknotes, cheques, stamps)* émettre, mettre en circulation ▷ *vi*: **to ~ from** provenir de; **at ~** en jeu, en cause; **to avoid the ~** éluder le problème; **to take ~ with sb (over sth)** exprimer son désaccord avec qn (sur qch); **to make an ~ of sth** faire de qch un problème; **to confuse** *or* **obscure the ~** embrouiller la question

IT *n abbr* = **information technology**

 KEYWORD

it [ɪt] *pron* **1** *(specific: subject)* il/elle; *(: direct object)* le/la, l'; *(: indirect object)* lui; **it's on the table** c'est *or* il *(or* elle) est sur la table; **I can't find it** je n'arrive pas à le trouver; **give it to me** donne-le-moi

2 *(after prep)*: **about/from/of it** en; **I spoke to him about it** je lui en ai parlé; **what did you learn from it?** qu'est-ce que vous en avez retiré?; **I'm proud of it** j'en suis fier; **I've come from it** j'en viens; **in/to it** y; **put the book in it** mettez-y le livre; **it's on it** c'est dessus; **he agreed to it** il y a consenti; **did you go to it?** *(party, concert etc)* est-ce que vous y êtes allé(s)?; **above it, over it** (au-)dessus; **below it, under it** (en-)dessous; **in front of/ behind it** devant/derrière

3 *(impersonal)* il; ce, cela, ça; **it's raining** il pleut; **it's Friday tomorrow** demain, c'est vendredi *or* nous sommes, vendredi; **it's 6 o'clock** il est 6 heures; **how far is it? — it's 10 miles** c'est loin? — c'est à 10 miles; **it's 2 hours by train** c'est à 2 heures de train; **who is it? — it's me** qui est-ce? — c'est moi

Italian [ɪ'tæljən] *adj* italien(ne) ▷ *n* Italien(ne); *(Ling)* italien *m*

italic [ɪ'tælɪk] *adj* italique

italics [ɪ'tælɪks] *npl* italique *m*

Italy ['ɪtəlɪ] *n* Italie *f*

itch [ɪtʃ] *n* démangeaison *f* ▷ *vi* *(person)* éprouver des démangeaisons; *(part of body)* démanger; **I'm ~ing to do** l'envie me démange de faire

itchy ['ɪtʃɪ] *adj* qui démange; **my back is ~** j'ai le dos qui me démange

it'd ['ɪtd] = **it would; it had**

item ['aɪtəm] *n* *(gen)* article *m*; *(on agenda)* question *f*, point *m*; *(in programme)* numéro *m*; *(also:* **news ~)** nouvelle *f*; **~s of clothing** articles vestimentaires

itemize ['aɪtəmaɪz] *vt* détailler, spécifier

itinerary [aɪ'tɪnərərɪ] *n* itinéraire *m*

it'll ['ɪtl] = **it will; it shall**

its [ɪts] *adj* son/sa, ses *pl* ▷ *pron* le/la sien(ne), les siens/siennes

it's [ɪts] = **it is; it has**

itself [ɪt'self] *pron* *(reflexive)* se; *(emphatic)* lui-même/elle-même

ITV *n abbr* (Brit: = *Independent Television*) chaîne de télévision commerciale

IUD *n abbr* = **intra-uterine device**

I've [aɪv] = **I have**

ivory ['aɪvərɪ] *n* ivoire *m*

ivy ['aɪvɪ] *n* lierre *m*

J

jab [dʒæb] *vt*: **to ~ sth into** enfoncer *or* planter qch dans ▷ *n* coup *m*; (*Med*: *inf*) piqûre *f*

jack [dʒæk] *n* (*Aut*) cric *m*; (*Bowls*) cochonnet *m*; (*Cards*) valet *m*; **jack in** *vt* (*inf*) laisser tomber; **jack up** *vt* soulever (au cric)

jackal ['dʒækl] *n* chacal *m*

jacket ['dʒækɪt] *n* veste *f*, veston *m*; (*of boiler etc*) enveloppe *f*; (*of book*) couverture *f*, jaquette *f*

jacket potato *n* pomme *f* de terre en robe des champs

jackknife ['dʒæknaɪf] *n* couteau *m* de poche ▷ *vi*: **the lorry ~d** la remorque (du camion) s'est mise en travers

jack plug *n* (*Brit*) jack *m*

jackpot ['dʒækpɒt] *n* gros lot

Jacuzzi® [dʒə'ku:zɪ] *n* jacuzzi® *m*

jaded ['dʒeɪdɪd] *adj* éreinté(e), fatigué(e)

jagged ['dʒægɪd] *adj* dentelé(e)

jail [dʒeɪl] *n* prison *f* ▷ *vt* emprisonner, mettre en prison

jail sentence *n* peine *f* de prison

jam [dʒæm] *n* confiture *f*; (*of shoppers etc*) cohue *f*; (*also*: **traffic ~**) embouteillage *m* ▷ *vt* (*passage etc*) encombrer, obstruer; (*mechanism, drawer etc*) bloquer, coincer; (*Radio*) brouiller ▷ *vi* (*mechanism, sliding part*) se coincer, se bloquer; (*gun*) s'enrayer; **to be in a ~** (*inf*) être dans le pétrin; **to get sb out of a ~** (*inf*) sortir qn du pétrin; **to ~ sth into** (*stuff*) entasser *or* comprimer qch dans; (*thrust*) enfoncer qch

dans; **the telephone lines are ~med** les lignes (téléphoniques) sont encombrées

Jamaica [dʒə'meɪkə] *n* Jamaïque *f*

jam jar *n* pot *m* à confiture

jammed [dʒæmd] *adj* (*window etc*) coincé(e)

jam-packed [dʒæm'pækt] *adj*: ~ **(with)** bourré(e) (de)

jangle ['dʒæŋgl] *vi* cliqueter

janitor ['dʒænɪtə^r] *n* (*caretaker*) concierge *m*

January ['dʒænjuərɪ] *n* janvier *m*; *see also* **July**

Japan [dʒə'pæn] *n* Japon *m*

Japanese [dʒæpə'ni:z] *adj* japonais(e) ▷ *n pl inv* Japonais(e); (*Ling*) japonais *m*

jar [dʒɑ:^r] *n* (*stone, earthenware*) pot *m*; (*glass*) bocal *m* ▷ *vi* (*sound*) produire un son grinçant *or* discordant; (*colours etc*) détonner, jurer ▷ *vt* (*shake*) ébranler, secouer

jargon ['dʒɑ:gən] *n* jargon *m*

jaundice ['dʒɔ:ndɪs] *n* jaunisse *f*

javelin ['dʒævlɪn] *n* javelot *m*

jaw [dʒɔ:] *n* mâchoire *f*

jay [dʒeɪ] *n* geai *m*

jaywalker ['dʒeɪwɔ:kə^r] *n* piéton indiscipliné

jazz [dʒæz] *n* jazz *m*; **jazz up** *vt* animer, égayer

jealous ['dʒeləs] *adj* jaloux(-ouse)

jealousy ['dʒeləsɪ] *n* jalousie *f*

jeans [dʒi:nz] *npl* jean *m*

jeer [dʒɪə^r] *vi*: **to ~ (at)** huer; se moquer cruellement (de), railler

Jehovah's Witness [dʒɪ'həuvəz-] *n* témoin *m* de Jéhovah

Jello® ['dʒeləu] (US) *n* gelée *f*

jelly ['dʒelɪ] *n* (*dessert*) gelée *f*; (US: *jam*) confiture *f*

jellyfish ['dʒelɪfɪʃ] *n* méduse *f*

jeopardize ['dʒepədaɪz] *vt* mettre en danger *or* péril

jeopardy ['dʒepədɪ] *n*: **in ~** en danger *or* péril

jerk [dʒə:k] *n* secousse *f*, saccade *f*; (*of muscle*) spasme *m*; (*inf*) pauvre type *m* ▷ *vt* (*shake*) donner une secousse à; (*pull*) tirer brusquement ▷ *vi* (*vehicles*) cahoter

jersey ['dʒə:zɪ] *n* tricot *m*; (*fabric*) jersey *m*

Jesus ['dʒi:zəs] *n* Jésus *m*; ~ **Christ** Jésus-Christ

jet [dʒet] *n* (*of gas, liquid*) jet *m*; (*Aut*) gicleur *m*; (*Aviat*) avion *m* à réaction, jet *m*

jet-black ['dʒet'blæk] *adj* (d'un noir) de jais

jet engine *n* moteur *m* à réaction

jet lag *n* décalage *m* horaire

jet-ski *vi* faire du jet-ski *or* scooter des mers

jettison ['dʒetɪsn] *vt* jeter par-dessus bord

jetty ['dʒetɪ] *n* jetée *f*, digue *f*

Jew [dʒu:] *n* Juif *m*

jewel ['dʒu:əl] *n* bijou *m*, joyau *m*; (*in watch*) rubis *m*

jeweller, (US) **jeweler** ['dʒu:ələ^r] *n* bijoutier(-ière), joaillier *m*

jeweller's, **jeweller's shop** *n* (*Brit*) bijouterie *f*, joaillerie *f*

jewellery, (US) **jewelry** ['dʒu:əlrɪ] *n* bijoux *mpl*

Jewess ['dʒuːɪs] n (infl) Juive f

Jewish ['dʒuːɪʃ] adj juif/juive

jibe [dʒaɪb] n sarcasme m

jiffy ['dʒɪfɪ] n (inf): **in a ~** en un clin d'œil

jigsaw ['dʒɪgsɔː] n (also: **~ puzzle**) puzzle m; (tool) scie sauteuse

jilt [dʒɪlt] vt laisser tomber, plaquer

jingle ['dʒɪŋgl] n (advertising jingle) couplet m publicitaire ▷ vi cliqueter, tinter

jinx [dʒɪŋks] n (inf) (mauvais) sort

jitters ['dʒɪtəz] npl (inf): **to get the ~** avoir la trouille or la frousse

job [dʒɔb] n (chore, task) travail m, tâche f; (employment) emploi m, poste m, place f; **a part-time/full-time ~** un emploi à temps partiel/à plein temps; **he's only doing his ~** il fait son boulot; **it's a good ~ that ...** c'est heureux or c'est une chance que ... +sub; **just the ~!** (c'est) juste or exactement ce qu'il faut!

job centre ['dʒɔbsɛntər] (Brit) n ≈ ANPE f, ≈ Agence nationale pour l'emploi

jobless ['dʒɔblɪs] adj sans travail, au chômage ▷ npl: **the ~** les sans-emploi m inv, les chômeurs mpl

jockey ['dʒɔkɪ] n jockey m ▷ vi: **to ~ for position** manœuvrer pour être bien placé

jog [dʒɔg] vt secouer ▷ vi (Sport) faire du jogging; **to ~ along** cahoter; trotter; **to ~ sb's memory** rafraîchir la mémoire de qn

jogging ['dʒɔgɪŋ] n jogging m

join [dʒɔɪn] vt (put together) unir, assembler; (become member of) s'inscrire à; (meet) rejoindre, retrouver; (queue) se joindre à ▷ vi (roads, rivers) se rejoindre, se rencontrer ▷ n raccord m; **will you ~ us for dinner?** vous dînerez bien avec nous?; **I'll ~ you later** je vous rejoindrai plus tard; **to ~ forces (with)** s'associer (à); **join in** vi se mettre de la partie ▷ vt fus se mêler à; **join up** vi (meet) se rejoindre; (Mil) s'engager

joiner ['dʒɔɪnər] (Brit) n menuisier m

joint [dʒɔɪnt] n (Tech) jointure f, joint m; (Anat) articulation f, jointure f; (Brit Culin) rôti m; (inf: place) boîte f; (of cannabis) joint ▷ adj commun(e); (committee) mixte, paritaire; (winner) ex aequo; **~ responsibility** coresponsabilité f

joint account n compte joint

jointly ['dʒɔɪntlɪ] adv ensemble, en commun

joke [dʒəuk] n plaisanterie f; (also: **practical ~**) farce f ▷ vi plaisanter; **to play a ~ on** jouer un tour à, faire une farce à

joker ['dʒəukər] n plaisantin m, blagueur(-euse); (Cards) joker m

jolly ['dʒɔlɪ] adj gai(e), enjoué(e); (enjoyable) amusant(e), plaisant(e) ▷ adv (Brit inf) rudement, drôlement ▷ vt (Brit): **to ~ sb along** amadouer qn, convaincre or entraîner qn à force d'encouragements; **~ good!** (Brit) formidable!

jolt [dʒəult] n cahot m, secousse f; (shock) choc m ▷ vt cahoter, secouer

Jordan ['dʒɔːdən] n (country) Jordanie f; (river) Jourdain m

jostle ['dʒɔsl] vt bousculer, pousser ▷ vi jouer des coudes

jot [dʒɔt] n: **not one ~** pas un brin; **jot down** vt inscrire rapidement, noter

jotter ['dʒɔtər] n (Brit) cahier m (de brouillon); bloc-notes m

journal ['dʒəːnl] n journal m

journalism ['dʒəːnəlɪzəm] n journalisme m

journalist ['dʒəːnəlɪst] n journaliste m/f

journey ['dʒəːnɪ] n voyage m; (distance covered) trajet m ▷ vi voyager; **the ~ takes two hours** le trajet dure deux heures; **a 5-hour ~** un voyage de 5 heures; **how was your ~?** votre voyage s'est bien passé?

joy [dʒɔɪ] n joie f

joyful ['dʒɔɪful], **joyous** ['dʒɔɪəs] adj joyeux(-euse)

joyrider ['dʒɔɪraɪdər] n voleur(-euse) de voiture (qui fait une virée dans le véhicule volé)

joy stick ['dʒɔɪstɪk] n (Aviat) manche m à balai; (Comput) manche à balai, manette f (de jeu)

JP n abbr = **Justice of the Peace**

Jr abbr = **junior**

jubilant ['dʒuːbɪlnt] adj triomphant(e), réjoui(e)

judge [dʒʌdʒ] n juge m ▷ vt juger; (estimate: weight, size etc) apprécier; (consider) estimer ▷ vi: **judging or to ~ by his expression** d'après son expression; **as far as I can ~** autant que je puisse en juger

judgment, judgement ['dʒʌdʒmənt] n jugement m; (punishment) châtiment m; **in my ~** à mon avis; **to pass ~ on** (Law) prononcer un jugement (sur)

judicial [dʒuː'dɪʃl] adj judiciaire; (fair) impartial(e)

judiciary [dʒuː'dɪʃɪərɪ] n (pouvoir m) judiciaire m

judo ['dʒuːdəu] n judo m

jug [dʒʌg] n pot m, cruche f

juggernaut ['dʒʌgənɔːt] n (Brit: huge truck) mastodonte m

juggle ['dʒʌgl] vi jongler

juggler ['dʒʌglər] n jongleur m

juice [dʒuːs] n jus m; (inf: petrol): **we've run out of ~** c'est la panne sèche

juicy ['dʒuːsɪ] adj juteux(-euse)

jukebox ['dʒuːkbɔks] n juke-box m

July [dʒuː'laɪ] n juillet m; **the first of ~** le premier juillet; **(on) the eleventh of ~** le onze juillet; **in the month of ~** au mois de juillet; **at the beginning/end of ~** au début/ à la fin (du mois) de juillet, début/fin juillet; **in the middle of ~** au milieu (du mois) de juillet, à la mi-juillet; **during ~** pendant le mois de juillet; **in ~ of next year** en juillet de l'année prochaine; **each** or **every ~** tous les ans or chaque année en juillet; **~ was wet this year** il a beaucoup plu cette année en juillet

jumble ['dʒʌmbl] n fouillis m ▷ vt (also: **~ up, ~ together**) mélanger, brouiller

jumble sale n (Brit) vente f de charité; voir article

> **JUMBLE SALE**
>
> Les jumble sales ont lieu dans les églises,
> salles des fêtes ou halls d'écoles, et l'on
> y vend des articles de toutes sortes,
> en général bon marché et surtout
> d'occasion, pour collecter des fonds pour
> une œuvre de charité, une école (par
> exemple, pour acheter des ordinateurs,
> ou encore une église (pour réparer un
> toit etc).

jumbo ['dʒʌmbəu] adj (also: **~ jet**) (avion) gros porteur (à réaction); **~ size** format maxi or extra-grand

jump [dʒʌmp] vi sauter, bondir; (with fear etc) sursauter; (increase) monter en flèche ▷ vt sauter, franchir ▷ n saut m, bond m; (with fear etc) sursaut m; (fence) obstacle m; **to ~ the queue** (Brit) passer avant son tour; **jump about** vi sautiller; **jump at** vt fus (fig) sauter sur; **he ~ed at the offer** il s'est empressé d'accepter la proposition; **jump down** vi sauter (pour descendre); **jump up** vi se lever (d'un bond)

jumper ['dʒʌmpər] n (Brit: pullover) pull-over m; (US: pinafore dress) robe-chasuble f; (Sport) sauteur(-euse)

jump leads, (US) **jumper cables** npl câbles mpl de démarrage

jumpy ['dʒʌmpɪ] adj nerveux(-euse), agité(e)

Jun. abbr = **June**; **junior**

junction ['dʒʌŋkʃən] n (Brit: of roads) carrefour m; (of rails) embranchement m

juncture ['dʒʌŋktʃər] n: **at this ~** à ce moment-là, sur ces entrefaites

June [dʒuːn] n juin m; see also **July**

jungle ['dʒʌŋgl] n jungle f

junior ['dʒuːnɪər] adj, n: **he's ~ to me (by two years), he's my ~ (by two years)** il est mon cadet (de deux ans), il est plus jeune que moi (de deux ans); **he's ~ to me** (seniority) il est en dessous de moi (dans la hiérarchie), j'ai plus d'ancienneté que lui

junior high school n (US) ≈ collège m d'enseignement secondaire; see also **high school**

junior school n (Brit) école f primaire

junk [dʒʌŋk] n (rubbish) camelote f; (cheap goods) bric-à-brac m inv; (ship) jonque f ▷ vt (inf) abandonner, mettre au rancart

junk food n snacks vite prêts (sans valeur nutritive)

junkie ['dʒʌŋkɪ] n (inf) junkie m, drogué(e)

junk mail n prospectus mpl; (Comput) messages mpl publicitaires

junk shop n (boutique f de) brocanteur m

Junr abbr = **junior**

Jupiter ['dʒuːpɪtər] n (planet) Jupiter f

jurisdiction [dʒuərɪs'dɪkʃən] n juridiction f; **it falls** or **comes within/outside our ~** cela est/n'est pas de notre compétence or ressort

juror ['dʒuərər] n juré m

jury ['dʒuərɪ] n jury m

just [dʒʌst] adj juste ▷ adv: **he's ~ done it/ left** il vient de le faire/partir; **~ as I expected** exactement or précisément comme je m'y attendais; **~ right/two o'clock** exactement or juste ce qu'il faut/deux heures; **we were ~ going** nous partions; **I was ~ about to phone** j'allais téléphoner; **~ as he was leaving** au moment or à l'instant précis où il partait; **~ before/enough/here** juste avant/ assez/là; **it's ~ me/a mistake** ce n'est que moi/(rien) qu'une erreur; **~ missed/caught** manqué/attrapé de justesse; **~ listen to this!** écoutez un peu ça!; **~ ask someone the way** vous n'avez qu'à demander votre chemin à quelqu'un; **it's ~ as good** c'est (vraiment) aussi bon; **she's ~ as clever as you** elle est tout aussi intelligente que vous; **it's ~ as well that you (...** heureusement que vous ...); **not ~ now** pas tout de suite; **~ a minute!, ~ one moment!** un instant (s'il vous plaît)!

justice ['dʒʌstɪs] n justice f; (US: judge) juge m de la Cour suprême; **Lord Chief J~** (Brit) premier président de la cour d'appel; **this photo doesn't do you ~** cette photo ne vous avantage pas

Justice of the Peace n juge m de paix

justification [dʒʌstɪfɪ'keɪʃən] n justification f

justify ['dʒʌstɪfaɪ] vt justifier; **to be justified in doing sth** être en droit de faire qch

jut [dʒʌt] vi (also: **~ out**) dépasser, faire saillie

juvenile ['dʒuːvənaɪl] adj juvénile; (court, books) pour enfants ▷ n adolescent(e)

K

K, k [keɪ] *n* (*letter*) K, k *m*; **K for King** K comme Kléber ▷ *abbr* (= *one thousand*) K; (*Brit:* = *Knight*) titre honorifique

kangaroo [kæŋɡə'ruː] *n* kangourou *m*

karaoke [kɑːrə'əʊkɪ] *n* karaoké *m*

karate [kə'rɑːtɪ] *n* karaté *m*

kebab [kə'bæb] *n* kebab *m*

keel [kiːl] *n* quille *f*; **on an even ~** (*fig*) à flot; **keel over** *vi* (*Naut*) chavirer, dessaler; (*person*) tomber dans les pommes

keen [kiːn] *adj* (*eager*) plein(e) d'enthousiasme; (*interest, desire, competition*) vif/vive; (*eye, intelligence*) pénétrant(e); (*edge*) effilé(e); **to be ~ to do** *or* **on doing sth** désirer vivement faire qch, tenir beaucoup à faire qch; **to be ~ on sth/sb** aimer beaucoup qch/qn; **I'm not ~ on going** je ne suis pas chaud pour y aller, je n'ai pas très envie d'y aller

keep [kiːp] (*pt, pp* **kept**) [kɛpt] *vt* (*retain, preserve*) garder; (*hold back*) retenir; (*shop, accounts, promise, diary*) tenir; (*support*) entretenir, assurer la subsistance de; (*a promise*) tenir; (*chickens, bees, pigs etc*) élever ▷ *vi* (*food*) se conserver; (*remain: in a certain state or place*) rester ▷ *n* (*of castle*) donjon *m*; (*food etc*): **enough for his ~** assez pour (assurer) sa subsistance; **to ~ doing sth** (*continue*) continuer à faire qch; (*repeatedly*) ne pas arrêter de faire qch; **to ~ sb from doing/sth from happening** empêcher qn de faire *or* que qn (ne) fasse/que qch (n')arrive; **to ~ sb happy/a place tidy** faire que qn soit content/ qu'un endroit reste propre; **to ~ sb waiting** faire attendre qn; **to ~ an appointment** ne pas manquer un rendez-vous; **to ~ a record of sth** prendre note de qch; **to ~ sth to o.s.** garder qch pour soi, tenir qch secret; **to ~ sth from sb** cacher qch à qn; **to ~ time** (*clock*) être à l'heure, ne pas retarder; **for ~s** (*inf*) pour de bon, pour toujours; **keep away** *vt*: **to ~ sth/ sb away from sb** tenir qch/qn éloigné de qn ▷ *vi*: **to ~ away (from)** ne pas s'approcher (de); **keep back** *vt* (*crowds, tears, money*) retenir; (*conceal: information*): **to ~ sth back from sb** cacher qch à qn ▷ *vi* rester en arrière; **keep down** *vt* (*control: prices, spending*) empêcher d'augmenter, limiter; (*retain: food*) garder ▷ *vi* (*person*) rester assis(e); rester par terre; **keep in** *vt* (*invalid, child*) garder à la maison; (*Scol*) consigner ▷ *vi* (*inf*): **to ~ in with sb** rester en bons termes avec qn; **keep off** *vt* (*dog, person*) éloigner ▷ *vi* ne pas s'approcher; **if the rain ~s off** s'il ne pleut pas; **~ your hands off!** pas touche! (*inf*); **"~ off the grass"** "pelouse interdite"; **keep on** *vi* continuer; **to ~ on doing** continuer à faire; **don't ~ on about it!** arrête (d'en parler)!; **keep out** *vt* empêcher d'entrer ▷ *vi* (*stay out*) rester en dehors; **"~ out"** "défense d'entrer"; **keep up** *vi* (*fig: in comprehension*) suivre ▷ *vt* continuer, maintenir; **to ~ up with sb** (*in work etc*) se maintenir au même niveau que qn; (*in race etc*) aller aussi vite que qn

keeper ['kiːpəʳ] *n* gardien(ne)

keep-fit ['kiːp'fɪt] *n* gymnastique *f* (d'entretien)

keeping ['kiːpɪŋ] *n* (*care*) garde *f*; **in ~ with** en harmonie avec

keepsake ['kiːpseɪk] *n* souvenir *m*

kennel ['kɛnl] *n* niche *f*; **kennels** *npl* (*for boarding*) chenil *m*

Kenya ['kɛnjə] *n* Kenya *m*

kept [kɛpt] *pt, pp of* **keep**

kerb [kəːb] *n* (*Brit*) bordure *f* du trottoir

kernel ['kəːnl] *n* amande *f*; (*fig*) noyau *m*

kerosene ['kɛrəsiːn] *n* kérosène *m*

ketchup ['kɛtʃəp] *n* ketchup *m*

kettle ['kɛtl] *n* bouilloire *f*

key [kiː] *n* (*gen, Mus*) clé *f*; (*of piano, typewriter*) touche *f*; (*on map*) légende *f* ▷ *adj* (*factor, role, area*) clé *inv* ▷ *cpd* (-)clé ▷ *vt* (*also:* **~ in:** *text*) saisir; **can I have my ~?** je peux avoir ma clé?; **a ~ issue** un problème fondamental

keyboard ['kiːbɔːd] *n* clavier *m* ▷ *vt* (*text*) saisir

keyed up [kiːd'ʌp] *adj*: **to be (all) ~** être surexcité(e)

keyhole ['kiːhəʊl] *n* trou *m* de la serrure

keyhole surgery *n* chirurgie très minutieuse où l'incision est minimale

keynote ['kiːnəʊt] *n* (*Mus*) tonique *f*; (*fig*) note dominante

keyring ['kiːrɪŋ] *n* porte-clés *m*

kg abbr (= kilogram) K
khaki ['kɑːkɪ] adj, n kaki m
kick [kɪk] vt donner un coup de pied à ⊳ vi (horse) ruer ⊳ n coup m de pied; (of rifle) recul m; (inf: thrill): **he does it for ~s** il le fait parce que ça l'excite, il le fait pour le plaisir; **to ~ the habit** (inf) arrêter; **kick around** vi (inf) traîner; **kick off** vi (Sport) donner le coup d'envoi
kick-off ['kɪkɔf] n (Sport) coup m d'envoi
kid [kɪd] n (inf: child) gamin(e), gosse m/f; (animal, leather) chevreau m ⊳ vi (inf) plaisanter, blaguer
kidnap ['kɪdnæp] vt enlever, kidnapper
kidnapper ['kɪdnæpə'] n ravisseur(-euse)
kidnapping ['kɪdnæpɪŋ] n enlèvement m
kidney ['kɪdnɪ] n (Anat) rein m; (Culin) rognon m
kidney bean n haricot m rouge
kill [kɪl] vt tuer; (fig) faire échouer; détruire; supprimer ⊳ n mise f à mort; **to ~ time** tuer le temps; **kill off** vt exterminer; (fig) éliminer
killer ['kɪlə'] n tueur(-euse); (murderer) meurtrier(-ière)
killing ['kɪlɪŋ] n meurtre m; (of group of people) tuerie f, massacre m; (inf): **to make a ~** se remplir les poches, réussir un beau coup ⊳ adj (inf) tordant(e)
killjoy ['kɪldʒɔɪ] n rabat-joie m inv
kiln [kɪln] n four m
kilo ['kiːləu] n kilo m
kilobyte ['kiːləubaɪt] n (Comput) kilo-octet m
kilogram, kilogramme ['kɪləugræm] n kilogramme m
kilometre, (US) **kilometer** ['kɪləmiːtə'] n kilomètre m
kilowatt ['kɪləuwɔt] n kilowatt m
kilt [kɪlt] n kilt m
kin [kɪn] n see **next-of-kin**
kind [kaɪnd] adj gentil(le), aimable ⊳ n sorte f, espèce f; (species) genre m; **would you be ~ enough to ...?, would you be so ~ as to ...?** auriez-vous la gentillesse ou l'obligeance de ...?; **it's very ~ of you (to do)** c'est très aimable à vous (de faire); **to be two of a ~** se ressembler; **in ~** (Comm) en nature; (fig): **to repay sb in ~** rendre la pareille à qn; **~ of** (inf: rather) plutôt; **a ~ of** une sorte de; **what ~ of ...?** quelle sorte de ...?
kindergarten ['kɪndəgɑːtn] n jardin m d'enfants
kind-hearted [kaɪnd'hɑːtɪd] adj bon/bonne
kindle ['kɪndl] vt allumer, enflammer
kindly ['kaɪndlɪ] adj bienveillant(e), plein(e) de gentillesse ⊳ adv avec bonté; **will you ~ ...** auriez-vous la bonté ou l'obligeance de ...; **he didn't take it ~** il l'a mal pris
kindness ['kaɪndnɪs] n (quality) bonté f, gentillesse f
king [kɪŋ] n roi m
kingdom ['kɪŋdəm] n royaume m

kingfisher ['kɪŋfɪʃə'] n martin-pêcheur m
king-size ['kɪŋsaɪz], **king-sized** ['kɪŋsaɪzd] adj (cigarette) (format) extra-long/longue
king-size bed, king-sized bed n grand lit (de 1,95 m de large)
kiosk ['kiːɔsk] n kiosque m; (Brit: also: **telephone ~**) cabine f (téléphonique); (also: **newspaper ~**) kiosque à journaux
kipper ['kɪpə'] n hareng fumé et salé
kiss [kɪs] n baiser m ⊳ vt embrasser; **to ~ (each other)** s'embrasser; **to ~ sb goodbye** dire au revoir à qn en l'embrassant
kiss of life n (Brit) bouche à bouche m
kit [kɪt] n équipement m, matériel m; (set of tools etc) trousse f; (for assembly) kit m; **tool ~** nécessaire m à outils; **kit out** vt (Brit) équiper
kitchen ['kɪtʃɪn] n cuisine f
kitchen sink n évier m
kite [kaɪt] n (toy) cerf-volant m; (Zool) milan m
kitten ['kɪtn] n petit chat, chaton m
kitty ['kɪtɪ] n (money) cagnotte f
kiwi ['kiːwiː] n (also: **~ fruit**) kiwi m
km abbr (= kilometre) km
km/h abbr (= kilometres per hour) km/h
knack [næk] n: **to have the ~ (of doing)** avoir le coup (pour faire); **there's a ~** il y a un coup à prendre ou une combine
knapsack ['næpsæk] n musette f
knead [niːd] vt pétrir
knee [niː] n genou m
kneecap ['niːkæp] n rotule f ⊳ vt tirer un coup de feu dans la rotule de
kneel (pt, pp **knelt**) [niːl, nɛlt] vi (also: **~ down**) s'agenouiller
knelt [nɛlt] pt, pp of **kneel**
knew [njuː] pt of **know**
knickers ['nɪkəz] npl (Brit) culotte f (de femme)
knife (pl **knives**) [naɪf, naɪvz] n couteau m ⊳ vt poignarder, frapper d'un coup de couteau; **~, fork and spoon** couvert m
knight [naɪt] n chevalier m; (Chess) cavalier m
knighthood ['naɪthud] n chevalerie f; (title): **to get a ~** être fait chevalier
knit [nɪt] vt tricoter; (fig): **to ~ together** unir ⊳ vi tricoter; (broken bones) se ressouder; **to ~ one's brows** froncer les sourcils
knitting ['nɪtɪŋ] n tricot m
knitting needle n aiguille f à tricoter
knitwear ['nɪtwɛə'] n tricots mpl, lainages mpl
knives [naɪvz] npl of **knife**
knob [nɔb] n bouton m; (Brit): **a ~ of butter** une noix de beurre
knock [nɔk] vt frapper; (bump into) heurter; (make: hole etc): **to ~ a hole in** faire un trou dans, trouer; (force: nail etc): **to ~ a nail into** enfoncer un clou dans; (fig: col) dénigrer ⊳ vi (engine) cogner; (at door etc): **to ~ at/on** frapper à/sur ⊳ n coup m; **he ~ed at the door** il frappa à la porte, **knock down** vt renverser; (price) réduire; **knock off** vi (inf: finish) s'arrêter (de travailler) ⊳ vt (vase, object) faire

tomber; (inf: steal) piquer; (fig: from price etc):
to ~ off £10 faire une remise de 10 livres;
knock out vt assommer; (Boxing) mettre
k.-o.; (in competition) éliminer; knock over vt
(object) faire tomber; (pedestrian) renverser
knocker ['nɔkər] n (on door) heurtoir m
knockout ['nɔkaut] n (Boxing) knock-out m,
K.-O. m; ~ competition (Brit) compétition f
avec épreuves éliminatoires
knot [nɔt] n (gen) nœud m ▷ vt nouer; to tie
a ~ faire un nœud
know [nəu] vt (pt knew, pp known) [njuː, nə
un] savoir; (person, place) connaître; to ~ that
savoir que; to ~ how to do savoir faire; to ~
how to swim savoir nager; to ~ about/of sth
(event) être au courant de qch; (subject)
connaître qch; to get to ~ sth (fact)
apprendre qch; (place) apprendre à connaître
qch; I don't ~ je ne sais pas; I don't ~ him je
ne le connais pas; do you ~ where I can ...?
savez-vous où je peux ...?; to ~ right from
wrong savoir distinguer le bon du mauvais;
as far as I ~ ... à ma connaissance ..., autant
que je sache ...
know-all ['nəuɔːl] n (US) = know-it-all
know-how ['nəuhau] n savoir-faire m,
technique f, compétence f
knowing ['nəuɪŋ] adj (look etc) entendu(e)
knowingly ['nəuɪŋlɪ] adv (on purpose)
sciemment; (smile, look) d'un air entendu
know-it-all ['nəuɪtɔːl] n (US) = know-all
knowledge ['nɔlɪdʒ] n connaissance f;
(learning) connaissances, savoir m; to have no
~ of ignorer; not to my ~ pas à ma
connaissance; without my ~ à mon insu;
to have a working ~ of French se
débrouiller en français; it is common ~ that
... chacun sait que ...; it has come to my ~
that ... j'ai appris que ...
knowledgeable ['nɔlɪdʒəbl] adj bien
informé(e)
known [nəun] pp of know ▷ adj (thief, facts)
notoire; (expert) célèbre
knuckle ['nʌkl] n articulation f (des
phalanges), jointure f; knuckle down vi (inf)
s'y mettre; knuckle under vi (inf) céder
koala [kəu'ɑːlə] n (also: ~ bear) koala m
Koran [kɔ'rɑːn] n Coran m
Korea [kə'rɪə] n Corée f; North/South ~ Corée
du Nord/Sud
Korean [kə'rɪən] adj coréen(ne) ▷ n
Coréen(ne)
kosher ['kəuʃər] adj kascher inv
Kosovar, Kosovan ['kɔsəvɑːr, 'kɔsəvən] adj
kosovar(e)
Kosovo ['kɔsɔvəu] n Kosovo m
Kuwait [ku'weɪt] n Koweït m

L¹, l [ɛl] n (letter) L, l m; L for Lucy, (US) L for
Love L comme Louis
L² abbr (= lake, large) L; (= left) g; (Brit Aut:
= learner) signale un conducteur débutant
l. abbr (= litre) l
lab [læb] n abbr (= laboratory) labo m
label ['leɪbl] n étiquette f; (brand: of record)
marque f ▷ vt étiqueter; to ~ sb a ... qualifier
qn de ...
labor etc ['leɪbər] (US) n = labour etc
laboratory [lə'bɔrətərɪ] n laboratoire m
Labor Day n (US, Canada) fête f du travail
(le premier lundi de septembre); voir article

LABOR DAY

Labor Day aux États-Unis et au Canada est
fixée au premier lundi de septembre.
Instituée par le Congrès en 1894 après
avoir été réclamée par les mouvements
ouvriers pendant douze ans, elle a perdu
une grande partie de son caractère
politique pour devenir un jour férié assez
ordinaire et l'occasion de partir pour un
long week-end avant la rentrée des classes.

labor union n (US) syndicat m
Labour ['leɪbər] n (Brit Pol: also: the ~ Party)
le parti travailliste, les travaillistes mpl
labour, (US) labor ['leɪbər] n (work) travail m;
(workforce) main-d'œuvre f; (Med) travail,
accouchement m ▷ vi: to ~ (at) travailler dur

(à), peiner (sur) ▷ vt: **to ~ a point** insister sur un point; **in ~** (Med) en travail

laboured, (US) **labored** ['leɪbəd] adj lourd(e), laborieux(-euse); (breathing) difficile, pénible; (style) lourd, embarrassé(e)

labourer, (US) **laborer** ['leɪbərər] n manœuvre m; **farm ~** ouvrier m agricole

lace [leɪs] n dentelle f; (of shoe etc) lacet m ▷ vt (shoe: also: **~ up**) lacer; (drink) arroser, corser

lack [læk] n manque m ▷ vt manquer de; **through** or **for ~ of** faute de, par manque de; **to be ~ing** manquer, faire défaut; **to be ~ing in** manquer de

lacquer ['lækər] n laque f

lacy ['leɪsɪ] adj (made of lace) en dentelle; (like lace) comme de la dentelle, qui ressemble à de la dentelle

lad [læd] n garçon m, gars m; (Brit: in stable etc) lad m

ladder ['lædər] n échelle f; (Brit: in tights) maille filée ▷ vt, vi (Brit: tights) filer

laden ['leɪdn] adj: **~ (with)** chargé(e) (de); **fully ~** (truck, ship) en pleine charge

ladle ['leɪdl] n louche f

lady ['leɪdɪ] n dame f; **"ladies and gentlemen ..."** "Mesdames (et) Messieurs ..."; **young ~** jeune fille f; (married) jeune femme f; **L~ Smith** lady Smith; **the ladies' (room)** les toilettes fpl des dames; **a ~ doctor** une doctoresse, une femme médecin

ladybird ['leɪdɪbəːd], (US) **ladybug** ['leɪdɪbʌg] n coccinelle f

ladylike ['leɪdɪlaɪk] adj distingué(e)

ladyship ['leɪdɪʃɪp] n: **your L~** Madame la comtesse (or duchesse etc)

lag [læg] n retard m ▷ vi (also: **~ behind**) rester en arrière, traîner; (fig) rester à la traîne ▷ vt (pipes) calorifuger

lager ['lɑːgər] n bière blonde

lagoon [lə'guːn] n lagune f

laid [leɪd] pt, pp of **lay**

laid back adj (inf) relaxe, décontracté(e)

laid up adj alité(e)

lain [leɪn] pp of **lie**

lake [leɪk] n lac m

lamb [læm] n agneau m

lamb chop n côtelette f d'agneau

lame [leɪm] adj (also fig) boiteux(-euse); **~ duck** (fig) canard m boiteux

lament [lə'mɛnt] n lamentation f ▷ vt pleurer, se lamenter sur

laminated ['læmɪneɪtɪd] adj laminé(e); (windscreen) (en verre) feuilleté

lamp [læmp] n lampe f

lamppost ['læmppəust] n (Brit) réverbère m

lampshade ['læmpʃeɪd] n abat-jour m inv

lance [lɑːns] n lance f ▷ vt (Med) inciser

land [lænd] n (as opposed to sea) terre f (ferme); (country) pays m; (soil) terre; (piece of land) terrain m; (estate) terre(s), domaine(s) m(pl) ▷ vi (from ship) débarquer; (Aviat) atterrir; (fig: fall) (re) tomber ▷ vt (passengers, goods) débarquer;

(obtain) décrocher; **to go/travel by ~** se déplacer par voie de terre; **to own ~** être propriétaire foncier; **to ~ on one's feet** (also fig) retomber sur ses pieds; **to ~ sb with sth** (inf) coller qch à qn; **land up** vi atterrir, (finir par) se retrouver

landfill site ['lændfɪl-] n centre m d'enfouissement des déchets

landing ['lændɪŋ] n (from ship) débarquement m; (Aviat) atterrissage m; (of staircase) palier m

landing card n carte f de débarquement

landing strip n piste f d'atterrissage

landlady ['lændleɪdɪ] n propriétaire f, logeuse f; (of pub) patronne f

landline ['lændlaɪn] n ligne f fixe

landlocked ['lændlɔkt] adj entouré(e) de terre(s), sans accès à la mer

landlord ['lændlɔːd] n propriétaire m, logeur m; (of pub etc) patron m

landmark ['lændmɑːk] n (point m de) repère m; **to be a ~** (fig) faire date or époque

landowner ['lændəunər] n propriétaire foncier or terrien

landscape ['lænskeɪp] n paysage m

landscape architect, landscape gardener n paysagiste m/f

landslide ['lændslaɪd] n (Geo) glissement m (de terrain); (fig: Pol) raz-de-marée (électoral)

lane [leɪn] n (in country) chemin m; (in town) ruelle f; (Aut: of road) voie f; (: line of traffic) file f; (in race) couloir m; **shipping ~** route f maritime or de navigation

language ['læŋgwɪdʒ] n langue f; (way one speaks) langage m; **what ~s do you speak?** quelles langues parlez-vous?; **bad ~** grossièretés fpl, langage grossier

language laboratory n laboratoire m de langues

language school n école f de langue

lank [læŋk] adj (hair) raide et terne

lanky ['læŋkɪ] adj grand(e) et maigre, efflanqué(e)

lantern ['læntn] n lanterne f

lap [læp] n (of track) tour m (de piste); (of body): **in** or **on one's ~** sur les genoux ▷ vt (also: **~ up**) laper ▷ vi (waves) clapoter; **lap up** vt (fig) boire comme du petit-lait, se gargariser de; (: lies etc) gober

lapel [lə'pɛl] n revers m

Lapland ['læplænd] n Laponie f

lapse [læps] n défaillance f, erreur f; (in behaviour) écart m (de conduite) ▷ vi (Law) cesser d'être en vigueur; (contract) expirer; (pass) être périmé; (subscription) prendre fin; **to ~ into bad habits** prendre de mauvaises habitudes; ~ **of time** laps m de temps, intervalle m; **a ~ of memory** un trou de mémoire

laptop ['læptɔp], **laptop computer** n (ordinateur m) portable m

larceny ['lɑːsənɪ] n vol m

larch [lɑːtʃ] n mélèze m

lard [lɑːd] n saindoux m

larder ['lɑːdər] n garde-manger m inv

large [lɑːdʒ] adj grand(e); (person, animal) gros/grosse; **to make ~r** agrandir; **a ~ number of people** beaucoup de gens; **by and ~** en général; **on a ~ scale** sur une grande échelle; **at ~** (free) en liberté; (generally) en général; pour la plupart; see also **by**

largely [lɑːdʒli] adv en grande partie; (principally) surtout

large-scale [lɑːdʒ'skeɪl] adj (map, drawing etc) à grande échelle; (fig) important(e)

lark [lɑːk] n (bird) alouette f; (joke) blague f, farce f; **lark about** vi faire l'idiot, rigoler

laryngitis [lærɪn'dʒaɪtɪs] n laryngite f

lasagne [lə'zænjə] n lasagne f

laser [leɪzə'] n laser m

laser printer n imprimante f laser

lash [læʃ] n coup m de fouet; (also: **eye~**) cil m ▷ vt fouetter; (tie) attacher; **lash down** vt attacher; amarrer; arrimer ▷ vi (rain) tomber avec violence; **lash out** vi: **to ~ out (at or against sb/sth)** attaquer violemment (qn/qch); **to ~ out (on sth)** (inf: spend) se fendre (de qch)

lass [læs] (Brit) n (jeune) fille f

lasso [læ'suː] n lasso m ▷ vt prendre au lasso

last [lɑːst] adj dernier(-ière) ▷ adv en dernier; (most recently) la dernière fois; (finally) finalement ▷ vi durer; **~ week** la semaine dernière; **~ night** (evening) hier soir; (night) la nuit dernière; **at ~** enfin; **~ but one** avant-dernier(-ière); **the ~ time** la dernière fois; **it ~s (for) 2 hours** ça dure 2 heures

last-ditch [lɑːst'dɪtʃ] adj ultime, désespéré(e)

lasting [lɑːstɪŋ] adj durable

lastly [lɑːstlɪ] adv en dernier lieu, pour finir

last-minute [lɑːst'mɪnɪt] adj de dernière minute

latch [lætʃ] n loquet m; **latch onto** vt fus (cling to: person, group) s'accrocher à; (idea) se mettre en tête

late [leɪt] adj (not on time) en retard; (far on in day etc) tardif(-ive); (: edition, delivery) dernier(-ière); (recent) récent(e), dernier; (former) ancien(ne); (dead) défunt(e) ▷ adv tard; (behind time, schedule) en retard; **to be ~** avoir du retard; **to be 10 minutes ~** avoir 10 minutes de retard; **sorry I'm ~** désolé d'être en retard; **it's too ~** il est trop tard; **to work ~** travailler tard; **~ in life** sur le tard, à un âge avancé; **of ~** dernièrement; **in ~ May** vers la fin du mois de mai, fin mai; **the ~ Mr X** feu M. X

latecomer [leɪtkʌmə'] n retardataire m/f

lately [leɪtlɪ] adv récemment

later [leɪtə'] adj (date etc) ultérieur(e); (version etc) plus récent(e) ▷ adv plus tard; **~ on today** plus tard dans la journée

latest [leɪtɪst] adj tout(e) dernier(-ière); **the ~ news** les dernières nouvelles; **at the ~** au plus tard

lathe [leɪð] n tour m

lather [lɑːðə'] n mousse f (de savon) ▷ vt savonner ▷ vi mousser

Latin [lætɪn] n latin m ▷ adj latin(e)

Latin America n Amérique latine

Latin American adj latino-américain(e), d'Amérique latine ▷ n Latino-Américain(e)

latitude [lætɪtjuːd] n (also fig) latitude f

latter [lætə'] adj deuxième, dernier(-ière) ▷ n: **the ~** ce dernier, celui-ci

latterly [lætəlɪ] adv dernièrement, récemment

laudable [lɔːdəbl] adj louable

laugh [lɑːf] n rire m ▷ vi rire; **(to do sth) for a ~** (faire qch) pour rire; **laugh at** vt fus se moquer de; (joke) rire de; **laugh off** vt écarter or rejeter par une plaisanterie or par une boutade

laughable [lɑːfəbl] adj risible, ridicule

laughing stock n: **the ~** la risée de

laughter [lɑːftə'] n rire m; (of several people) rires mpl

launch [lɔːntʃ] n lancement m; (boat) chaloupe f; (also: **motor ~**) vedette f ▷ vt (ship, rocket, plan) lancer; **launch into** vt fus se lancer dans; **launch out** vi: **to ~ out (into)** se lancer (dans)

launder [lɔːndə'] vt laver; (fig: money) blanchir

Launderette® [lɔːn'drɛt], (US) **Laundromat®** [lɔːndrəmæt] n laverie f (automatique)

laundry [lɔːndrɪ] n (clothes) linge m; (business) blanchisserie f; (room) buanderie f; **to do the ~** faire la lessive

laurel [lɔrl] n laurier m; **to rest on one's ~s** se reposer sur ses lauriers

lava [lɑːvə] n lave f

lavatory [lævətərɪ] n toilettes fpl

lavender [lævəndə'] n lavande f

lavish [lævɪʃ] adj (amount) copieux(-euse); (meal) somptueux(-euse); (hospitality) généreux(-euse); (person: giving freely): **~ with** prodigue de ▷ vt: **to ~ sth on sb** prodiguer qch à qn; (money) dépenser qch sans compter pour qn

law [lɔː] n loi f; (science) droit m; **against the ~** contraire à la loi; **to study ~** faire du droit; **to go to ~** (Brit) avoir recours à la justice; **~ and order** n l'ordre public

law-abiding [lɔːəbaɪdɪŋ] adj respectueux(-euse) des lois

law court n tribunal m, cour f de justice

lawful [lɔːful] adj légal(e), permis(e)

lawless [lɔːlɪs] adj (action) illégal(e); (place) sans loi

lawn [lɔːn] n pelouse f

lawnmower [lɔːnməuə'] n tondeuse f à gazon

lawn tennis n tennis m

law school n faculté f de droit

lawsuit [lɔːsuːt] n procès m; **to bring a ~ against** engager des poursuites contre

lawyer [lɔːjə'] n (consultant, with company) juriste m; (for sales, wills etc) ≈ notaire m; (partner, in court) ≈ avocat m

lax [læks] *adj* relâché(e)
laxative ['læksətɪv] *n* laxatif *m*
lay [leɪ] *pt of* **lie** ▷ *adj* laïque; (*not expert*)
profane ▷ *vt* (*pt, pp* **laid**) [leɪd] poser, mettre;
(*eggs*) pondre; (*trap*) tendre; (*plans*) élaborer;
to ~ the table mettre la table; **to ~ the facts/
one's proposals before sb** présenter les
faits/ses propositions à qn; **to get laid** (*inf!*)
baiser (!), se faire baiser (!); **lay aside, lay by**
vt mettre de côté; **lay down** *vt* poser; (*rules
etc*) établir; **to ~ down the law** (*fig*) faire la
loi; **lay in** *vt* accumuler, s'approvisionner
en; **lay into** *vi* (*inf: attack*) tomber sur; (: *scold*)
passer une engueulade à; **lay off** *vt* (*workers*)
licencier; **lay on** *vt* (*water, gas*) mettre,
installer; (*provide: meal etc*) fournir; (*paint*)
étaler; **lay out** *vt* (*design*) dessiner, concevoir;
(*display*) disposer; (*spend*) dépenser; **lay up** *vt*
(*store*) amasser; (*car*) remiser; (*ship*) désarmer;
(*illness*) forcer à s'aliter
layabout ['leɪəbaut] *n* fainéant(e)
lay-by ['leɪbaɪ] *n* (*Brit*) aire *f* de stationnement
(sur le bas-côté)
layer ['leɪəʳ] *n* couche *f*
layman ['leɪmən] *irreg n* (*Rel*) laïque *m*; (*non-
expert*) profane *m*
layout ['leɪaut] *n* disposition *f*, plan *m*,
agencement *m*; (*Press*) mise *f* en page
laze [leɪz] *vi* paresser
lazy ['leɪzɪ] *adj* paresseux(-euse)
lb. *abbr* (*weight*) = **pound**
lead¹ [liːd] (*pt, pp* **led**) [led] *n* (*front position*)
tête *f*; (*distance, time ahead*) avance *f*; (*clue*) piste
f; (*to battery*) raccord *m*; (*Elec*) fil *m*; (*for dog*)
laisse *f*; (*Theat*) rôle principal ▷ *vt* (*guide*)
mener, conduire; (*induce*) amener; (*be leader
of*) être à la tête de; (*Sport*) être en tête de;
(*orchestra: Brit*) être le premier violon de; (: *US*)
diriger ▷ *vi* (*Sport*) mener, être en tête; **to ~**
(*road, pipe*) mener à, conduire à; (*result in*)
conduire à; aboutir à; **to ~ sb astray**
détourner qn du droit chemin; **to be in the ~**
(*Sport: in race*) mener, être en tête; (: *in match*)
mener (à la marque); **to take the ~** (*Sport*)
passer en tête, prendre la tête; mener; (*fig*)
prendre l'initiative; **to ~ sb to believe that
...** amener qn à croire que ...; **to ~ sb to do
sth** amener qn à faire qch; **to ~ the way**
montrer le chemin; **lead away** *vt* emmener;
lead back *vt* ramener; **lead off** *vi* (*in game etc*)
commencer; **lead on** *vt* (*tease*) faire
marcher; **to ~ sb on to** (*induce*) amener qn à;
lead up to *vt* conduire à; (*in conversation*) en
venir à
lead² [led] *n* (*metal*) plomb *m*; (*in pencil*) mine *f*
leaded petrol *n* essence *f* au plomb
leaden ['ledn] *adj* de or en plomb
leader ['liːdəʳ] *n* (*of team*) chef *m*; (*of party etc*)
dirigeant(e), leader *m*; (*Sport: in league*) leader;
(: *in race*) coureur *m* de tête; (*in newspaper*)
éditorial *m*; **they are ~s in their field** (*fig*) ils
sont à la pointe du progrès dans leur

domaine; **the L~ of the House** (*Brit*) le chef
de la majorité ministérielle
leadership ['liːdəʃɪp] *n* (*position*) direction *f*;
under the ~ of ... sous la direction de ...;
qualities of ~ qualités *fpl* de chef or de
meneur
lead-free ['ledfriː] *adj* sans plomb
leading ['liːdɪŋ] *adj* de premier plan; (*main*)
principal(e); (*in race*) de tête; **a ~ question**
une question tendancieuse; **~ role** rôle
prépondérant or de premier plan
leading lady *n* (*Theat*) vedette (féminine)
leading light *n* (*person*) sommité *f*,
personnalité *f* de premier plan
leading man *irreg n* (*Theat*) vedette
(masculine)
lead singer [liːd-] *n* (*in pop group*) (chanteur *m*)
vedette *f*
leaf (*pl* **leaves**) [liːf, liːvz] *n* feuille *f*; (*of table*)
rallonge *f*; **to turn over a new ~** (*fig*) changer
de conduite or d'existence; **to take a ~ out of
sb's book** (*fig*) prendre exemple sur qn; **leaf
through** *vt* (*book*) feuilleter
leaflet ['liːflɪt] *n* prospectus *m*, brochure *f*;
(*Pol, Rel*) tract *m*
league [liːg] *n* ligue *f*; (*Football*) championnat *m*;
(*measure*) lieue *f*; **to be in ~ with** avoir partie
liée avec, être de mèche avec
leak [liːk] *n* (*out: also fig*) fuite *f*; (*in*)
infiltration *f* ▷ *vi* (*pipe, liquid etc*) fuir; (*shoes*)
prendre l'eau; (*ship*) faire eau ▷ *vt* (*liquid*)
répandre; (*information*) divulguer; **leak out** *vi*
fuir; (*information*) être divulgué(e)
lean [liːn] (*pt, pp* **leaned** or **leant**) [lent] *adj*
maigre ▷ *n* (*of meat*) maigre *m* ▷ *vt*: **to ~ sth
on** appuyer qch sur ▷ *vi* (*slope*) pencher; (*rest*):
to ~ against s'appuyer contre; être appuyé(e)
contre; **to ~ on** s'appuyer sur; **lean back** *vi* se
pencher en arrière; **lean forward** *vi* se
pencher en avant; **lean out** *vi*: **to ~ out (of)**
se pencher au dehors (de); **lean over** *vi* se
pencher
leaning ['liːnɪŋ] *adj* penché(e) ▷ *n*:
~ (towards) penchant *m* (pour); **the L~
Tower of Pisa** la tour penchée de Pise
leant [lent] *pt, pp of* **lean**
leap [liːp] *n* bond *m*, saut *m* ▷ *vi* (*pt, pp* **leaped**
or **leapt**) [lept] bondir, sauter; **to ~ at an
offer** saisir une offre; **leap up** *vi* (*person*) faire
un bond; se lever d'un bond
leapfrog ['liːpfrɒg] *n* jeu *m* de saute-mouton
leapt [lept] *pt, pp of* **leap**
leap year *n* année *f* bissextile
learn (*pt, pp* **learned** or **learnt**) [lɜːn, -t] *vt, vi*
apprendre; **to ~ (how) to do sth** apprendre
à faire qch; **we were sorry to ~ that ...** nous
avons appris avec regret que ...; **to ~ about
sth** (*Scol*) étudier qch; (*hear, read*) apprendre
qch
learned ['lɜːnɪd] *adj* érudit(e), savant(e)
learner ['lɜːnəʳ] *n* débutant(e); (*Brit: also:
~ driver*) (conducteur(-trice)) débutant(e)

learning ['ləːnɪŋ] n savoir m

learnt [ləːnt] pp of **learn**

lease [liːs] n bail m ▷ vt louer à bail; **on ~** en location; **lease back** vt vendre en cession-bail

leash [liːʃ] n laisse f

least [liːst] adj: **the ~** (+noun) le/la plus petit(e), le/la moindre; (smallest amount of) le moins de ▷ pron: **(the)** ~ le moins ▷ adv (+verb) le moins; (+adj): **the ~** le/la moins; **~ money** le moins d'argent; **the ~ expensive** le/la moins cher/chère; **the ~ possible effort** le moins d'effort possible; **at ~** au moins; (or rather) du moins; **you could at ~ have written** tu aurais au moins pu écrire; **not in the ~** pas le moins du monde

leather ['lɛðər] n cuir m ▷ cpd en or de cuir; **~ goods** maroquinerie f

leave [liːv] (pt, pp **left**) [lɛft] vt laisser; (go away from) quitter; (forget) oublier ▷ vi partir, s'en aller ▷ n (time off) congé m; (Mil, also: consent) permission f; **what time does the train/bus ~?** le train/le bus part à quelle heure?; **to ~ sth to sb** (money etc) laisser qch à qn; **to be left** rester; **there's some milk left over** il reste du lait; **to ~ school** quitter l'école, terminer sa scolarité; **~ it to me!** laissez-moi faire!, je m'en occupe!; **on ~** en permission; **to take one's ~ of** prendre congé de; **~ of absence** n congé exceptionnel; (Mil) permission spéciale; **leave behind** vt (also fig) laisser; (opponent in race) distancer; (forget) laisser, oublier; **leave off** vt (cover, lid, heating) ne pas (re)mettre; (light) ne pas (r)allumer, laisser éteint(e); (Brit inf: stop): **to ~ off (doing sth)** s'arrêter (de faire qch); **leave on** vt (cover, coat etc) garder, ne pas enlever; (lid) laisser dessus; (light, fire, cooker) laisser allumé(e); **leave out** vt oublier, omettre

leaves [liːvz] npl of **leaf**

Lebanon ['lɛbənən] n Liban m

lecherous ['lɛtʃərəs] adj lubrique

lecture ['lɛktʃər] n conférence f; (Scol) cours (magistral) ▷ vi donner des cours; enseigner ▷ vt (scold) sermonner, réprimander; **to ~ on** faire un cours (or son cours) sur; **to give a ~ (on)** faire une conférence (sur), faire un cours (sur)

lecture hall n amphithéâtre m

lecturer ['lɛktʃərər] n (speaker) conférencier(-ière) m; (Brit: at university) professeur m/f d'université), prof m/f de fac (inf); **assistant ~** (Brit) ≈ assistant(e); **senior ~** (Brit) ≈ chargé(e) d'enseignement

lecture theatre n = **lecture hall**

led [lɛd] pt, pp of **lead**[1]

ledge [lɛdʒ] n (of window, on wall) rebord m; (of mountain) saillie f, corniche f

ledger ['lɛdʒər] n registre m, grand livre

leech [liːtʃ] n sangsue f

leek [liːk] n poireau m

leer [lɪər] vi: **to ~ at sb** regarder qn d'un air mauvais or concupiscent, lorgner qn

leeway ['liːweɪ] n (fig): **to make up ~** rattraper son retard; **to have some ~** avoir une certaine liberté d'action

left [lɛft] pt, pp of **leave** ▷ adj gauche ▷ adv à gauche ▷ n gauche f; **there are two ~** il en reste deux; **on the ~, to the ~** à gauche; **the L~** (Pol) la gauche

left-hand ['lɛfthænd] adj: **the ~ side** la gauche, le côté gauche

left-hand drive ['lɛfthænd-] n (Brit) conduite f à gauche; (vehicle) véhicule m avec la conduite à gauche

left-handed [lɛft'hændɪd] adj gaucher(-ère); (scissors etc) pour gauchers

left-luggage [lɛft'lʌgɪdʒ], **left-luggage office** n (Brit) consigne f

left-luggage locker [lɛft'lʌgɪdʒ-] n (Brit) (casier m à) consigne f automatique

left-overs ['lɛftəʊvəz] npl restes mpl

left wing n (Mil, Sport) aile f gauche; (Pol) gauche f

left-wing ['lɛft'wɪŋ] adj (Pol) de gauche

leg [lɛg] n jambe f; (of animal) patte f; (of furniture) pied m; (Culin: of chicken) cuisse f; (of journey) étape f; **1st/2nd ~** (Sport) match m aller/retour; (of journey) 1ère/2ème étape; **~ of lamb** (Culin) gigot m d'agneau; **to stretch one's ~s** se dégourdir les jambes

legacy ['lɛgəsɪ] n (also fig) héritage m, legs m

legal ['liːgl] adj (permitted by law) légal(e); (relating to law) juridique; **to take ~ action** or **proceedings against sb** poursuivre qn en justice

legal holiday (US) n jour férié

legalize ['liːgəlaɪz] vt légaliser

legally ['liːgəlɪ] adv légalement; **~ binding** juridiquement contraignant(e)

legal tender n monnaie légale

legend ['lɛdʒənd] n légende f

legendary ['lɛdʒəndərɪ] adj légendaire

leggings ['lɛgɪŋz] npl caleçon m

legible ['lɛdʒəbl] adj lisible

legislation [lɛdʒɪs'leɪʃən] n législation f; **a piece of ~** un texte de loi

legislative ['lɛdʒɪslətɪv] adj législatif(-ive)

legislature ['lɛdʒɪslətʃər] n corps législatif

legitimate [lɪ'dʒɪtɪmət] adj légitime

leg-room ['lɛgruːm] n place f pour les jambes

leisure ['lɛʒər] n (free time) temps libre, loisirs mpl; **at ~** (tout) à loisir; **at your ~** (later) à tête reposée

leisure centre n (Brit) centre m de loisirs

leisurely ['lɛʒəlɪ] adj tranquille, fait(e) sans se presser

lemon ['lɛmən] n citron m

lemonade [lɛmə'neɪd] n (fizzy) limonade f

lemon tea n thé m au citron

lend (pt, pp **lent**) [lɛnd, lɛnt] vt: **to ~ sth (to sb)** prêter qch (à qn); **could you ~ me some money?** pourriez-vous me prêter de l'argent?; **to ~ a hand** donner un coup de main

length [lɛŋθ] n longueur f; (section: of road, pipe etc) morceau m, bout m; **~ of time** durée f; **what ~ is it?** quelle longueur fait-il?; **it is 2 metres ~** cela fait 2 mètres de long; **to fall full ~** tomber de tout son long; **at ~** (at last) enfin, à la fin; (lengthily) longuement; **to go to any ~(s) to do sth** faire n'importe quoi pour faire qch, ne reculer devant rien pour faire qch

lengthen [lɛŋθn] vt allonger, prolonger ▷ vi s'allonger

lengthways [lɛŋθweɪz] adv dans le sens de la longueur, en long

lengthy [lɛŋθɪ] adj (très) long/longue

lenient [liːnɪənt] adj indulgent(e), clément(e)

lens [lɛnz] n lentille f; (of spectacles) verre m; (of camera) objectif m

Lent [lɛnt] n carême m

lent [lɛnt] pt, pp of **lend**

lentil [lɛntl] n lentille f

Leo [liːəu] n le Lion; **to be ~** être du Lion

leopard [lɛpəd] n léopard m

leotard [liːətɑːd] n justaucorps m

leprosy [lɛprəsɪ] n lèpre f

lesbian [lɛzbɪən] n lesbienne f ▷ adj lesbien(ne)

less [lɛs] adj moins de ▷ pron, adv moins ▷ prep: **~ tax/10% discount** avant impôt/ moins 10% de remise; **~ than that/you** moins que cela/vous; **~ than half** moins de la moitié; **~ than one/a kilo/3 metres** moins de un/d'un kilo/de 3 mètres; **~ than ever** moins que jamais; **~ and ~** de moins en moins; **the ~ he works** ... moins il travaille ...

lessen [lɛsn] vi diminuer, s'amoindrir, s'atténuer ▷ vt diminuer, réduire, atténuer

lesser [lɛsə^r] adj moindre; **to a ~ extent** or **degree** à un degré moindre

lesson [lɛsn] n leçon f; **a maths ~** une leçon or un cours de maths; **to give ~s in** donner des cours de; **to teach sb a ~** (fig) donner une bonne leçon à qn; **it taught him a ~** (fig) cela lui a servi de leçon

let [lɛt] (pt, pp **let**) vt laisser; (Brit: lease) louer; **to ~ sb do sth** laisser qn faire qch; **to ~ sb know sth** faire savoir qch à qn, prévenir qn de qch; **he ~ me go** il m'a laissé partir; **~ the water boil and** ... faites bouillir l'eau et ...; **to ~ go** lâcher prise; **to ~ go of sth, to ~ sth go** lâcher qch; **~'s go** allons-y; **~ him come** qu'il vienne; **"to ~"** (Brit) "à louer"; **let down** vt (lower) baisser; (dress) rallonger; (hair) défaire; (Brit: tyre) dégonfler; (disappoint) décevoir; **let go** vi lâcher prise ▷ vt lâcher; **let in** vt laisser entrer; (visitor etc) faire entrer; **what have you ~ yourself in for?** à quoi t'es-tu engagé?; **let off** vt (allow to leave) laisser partir; (not punish) ne pas punir; (taxi driver, bus driver) déposer; (firework etc) faire

partir; (bomb) faire exploser; (smell etc) dégager; **to ~ off steam** (fig: inf) se défouler, décharger sa rate or bile; **let on** vi (inf): **to ~ on that** .... révéler que ..., dire que ...; **let out** vt laisser sortir; (dress) élargir; (scream) laisser échapper; (Brit: rent out) louer; **let up** vi diminuer, s'arrêter

lethal [liːθl] adj mortel(le), fatal(e); (weapon) meurtrier(-ère)

letter [lɛtə^r] n lettre f; **letters** npl (Literature) lettres; **small/capital ~** minuscule f/ majuscule f; **~ of credit** lettre f de crédit

letter bomb n lettre piégée

letterbox [lɛtəbɔks] n (Brit) boîte f aux or à lettres

lettering [lɛtərɪŋ] n lettres fpl; caractères mpl

lettuce [lɛtɪs] n laitue f, salade f

let-up [lɛtʌp] n répit m, détente f

leukaemia, (US) **leukemia** [luːˈkiːmɪə] n leucémie f

level [lɛvl] adj (flat) plat(e), plan(e), uni(e); (horizontal) horizontal ▷ n niveau m; (flat place) terrain plat; (also: **spirit ~**) niveau à bulle ▷ vt niveler, aplanir; (gun) pointer, braquer; (accusation): **to ~ (against)** lancer or porter (contre) ▷ vi (inf): **to ~ with sb** être franc/franche avec qn; **"A" ~s** npl (Brit) ≈ baccalauréat m; **"O" ~s** npl (Brit: formerly) examens passés à l'âge de 16 ans sanctionnant les connaissances de l'élève, ≈ brevet m des collèges; **a ~ spoonful** (Culin) une cuillerée rase; **to be ~ with** être au même niveau que; **to draw ~ with** (team) arriver à égalité de points avec, égaliser avec; arriver au même classement que; (runner, car) arriver à la hauteur de, rattraper; **on the ~** à l'horizontale; (fig: honest) régulier(-ière); **level off, level out** vi (prices etc) se stabiliser ▷ vt (ground) aplanir, niveler

level crossing n (Brit) passage m à niveau

level-headed [lɛvlˈhɛdɪd] adj équilibré(e)

lever [liːvə^r] n levier m ▷ vt: **to ~ up/out** soulever/extraire au moyen d'un levier

leverage [liːvərɪdʒ] n (influence): **~ (on** or **with)** prise f (sur)

levy [lɛvɪ] n taxe f, impôt m ▷ vt (tax) lever; (fine) infliger

lewd [luːd] adj obscène, lubrique

liability [laɪəˈbɪlɪtɪ] n responsabilité f; (handicap) handicap m

liable [laɪəbl] adj (subject): **~ to** sujet(te) à, passible de; (responsible): **~ (for)** responsable (de); (likely): **~ to do** susceptible de faire; **to be ~ to do** être passible d'une amende

liaise [liːˈeɪz] vi: **to ~ with** assurer la liaison avec

liaison [liːˈeɪzɔn] n liaison f

liar [laɪə^r] n menteur(-euse)

libel [laɪbl] n diffamation f; (document) écrit m diffamatoire ▷ vt diffamer

liberal [lɪbərl] adj libéral(e); (generous): **~ with** prodigue de, généreux(-euse) avec ▷ n: **L~** (Pol) libéral(e)

Liberal Democrat n (*Brit*) libéral(e)-démocrate m/f

liberate ['lɪbəreɪt] vt libérer

liberation [lɪbə'reɪʃən] n libération f

liberty ['lɪbətɪ] n liberté f; **to be at ~** (*criminal*) être en liberté; **at ~ to do** libre de faire; **to take the ~ of** prendre la liberté de, se permettre de

Libra ['liːbrə] n la Balance; **to be ~** être de la Balance

librarian [laɪ'brɛərɪən] n bibliothécaire m/f

library ['laɪbrərɪ] n bibliothèque f

libretto [lɪ'brɛtəu] n livret m

Libya ['lɪbɪə] n Libye f

lice [laɪs] npl of **louse**

licence, (*US*) **license** ['laɪsns] n autorisation f, permis m; (*Comm*) licence f; (*Radio, TV*) redevance f; (*also*: **driving ~**: *US*: *also*: **driver's license**) permis m (de conduire); (*excessive freedom*) licence f; **import ~** licence d'importation; **produced under ~** fabriqué(e) sous licence

licence number n (*Brit Aut*) numéro m d'immatriculation

license ['laɪsns] n (*US*) = **licence** ▷ vt donner une licence à; (*car*) acheter la vignette de; délivrer la vignette de

licensed ['laɪsnst] adj (*for alcohol*) patenté(e) pour la vente des spiritueux, qui a une patente de débit de boissons; (*car*) muni(e) de la vignette

license plate n (*US Aut*) plaque f minéralogique

licensing hours (*Brit*) npl heures fpl d'ouvertures (*des pubs*)

lick [lɪk] vt lécher; (*inf: defeat*) écraser, flanquer une piquette or raclée à ▷ n coup m de langue; **a ~ of paint** un petit coup de peinture; **to ~ one's lips** (*fig*) se frotter les mains

licorice ['lɪkərɪs] n = **liquorice**

lid [lɪd] n couvercle m; (*eyelid*) paupière f; **to take the ~ off sth** (*fig*) exposer or étaler qch au grand jour

lie [laɪ] n mensonge m ▷ vi (*pt, pp* **lied**) (*tell lies*) mentir; (*pt* **lay**, *pp* **lain**) [leɪ, leɪn] (*rest*) être étendu(e) or allongé(e) or couché(e); (*in grave*) être enterré(e), reposer; (*object: be situated*) se trouver, être; **to ~ low** (*fig*) se cacher, rester caché(e); **to tell ~s** mentir; **lie about, lie around** vi (*things*) traîner; (*Brit: person*) traînasser, flemmarder; **lie back** vi se renverser en arrière; **lie down** vi se coucher, s'étendre; **lie up** vi (*hide*) se cacher

Liechtenstein ['lɪktənstaɪn] n Liechtenstein m

lie-down ['laɪdaun] n (*Brit*): **to have a ~** s'allonger, se reposer

lie-in ['laɪɪn] n (*Brit*): **to have a ~** faire la grasse matinée

lieutenant [lɛf'tɛnənt, *US*: luː'tɛnənt] n lieutenant m

life (*pl* **lives**) [laɪf, laɪvz] n vie f; **to come to ~** (*fig*) s'animer ▷ cpd de vie; de la vie; à vie; **true-to ~** réaliste, fidèle à la réalité; **to paint from ~** peindre d'après nature; **to be sent to prison for ~** être condamné(e) (à la réclusion criminelle) à perpétuité; **country/city ~** la vie à la campagne/à la ville

life assurance n (*Brit*) = **life insurance**

lifebelt ['laɪfbɛlt] n (*Brit*) bouée f de sauvetage

lifeboat ['laɪfbəut] n canot m or chaloupe f de sauvetage

lifebuoy ['laɪfbɔɪ] n bouée f de sauvetage

lifeguard ['laɪfgɑːd] n surveillant m de baignade

life insurance n assurance-vie f

life jacket n gilet m or ceinture f de sauvetage

lifeless ['laɪflɪs] adj sans vie, inanimé(e); (*dull*) qui manque de vie or de vigueur

lifelike ['laɪflaɪk] adj qui semble vrai(e) or vivant(e), ressemblant(e); (*painting*) réaliste

lifelong ['laɪflɔŋ] adj de toute une vie, de toujours

life preserver [-prɪ'zə:vər] n (*US*) gilet m or ceinture f de sauvetage

life-saving ['laɪfseɪvɪŋ] n sauvetage m

life sentence n condamnation f à vie or à perpétuité

life-size ['laɪfsaɪz], **life-sized** ['laɪfsaɪzd] adj grandeur nature inv

life span n (durée f de) vie f

lifestyle ['laɪfstaɪl] n style m de vie

life-support system n (*Med*) respirateur artificiel

lifetime ['laɪftaɪm] n: **in his ~** de son vivant; **the chance of a ~** la chance de ma (or sa etc) vie, une occasion unique

lift [lɪft] vt soulever, lever; (*end*) supprimer, lever; (*steal*) prendre, voler ▷ vi (*fog*) se lever ▷ n (*Brit: elevator*) ascenseur m; **to give sb a ~** (*Brit*) emmener or prendre qn en voiture; **can you give me a ~ to the station?** pouvez-vous m'emmener à la gare?; **lift off** vi (*rocket, helicopter*) décoller; **lift out** vt sortir; (*troops, evacuees etc*) évacuer par avion or hélicoptère; **lift up** vt soulever

lift-off ['lɪftɔf] n décollage m

light [laɪt] n lumière f; (*daylight*) lumière, jour m; (*lamp*) lampe f; (*Aut: rear light*) feu m; (: *headlamp*) phare m; (*for cigarette etc*): **have you got a ~?** avez-vous du feu? ▷ vt (*pt, pp* **lighted** or **lit**) [lɪt] (*candle, cigarette, fire*) allumer; (*room*) éclairer ▷ adj (*room, colour*) clair(e); (*not heavy, also fig*) léger(-ère); (*not strenuous*) peu fatigant(e) ▷ adv (*travel*) avec peu de bagages; **lights** npl (*traffic lights*) feux mpl; **to turn the ~ on/off** allumer/éteindre; **to cast** or **shed** or **throw ~ on** éclaircir; **to come to ~** être dévoilé(e) or découvert(e); **in the ~ of** à la lumière de; étant donné; **to make ~ of sth** (*fig*) prendre qch à la légère, faire peu de cas de qch; **light up** vi s'allumer; (*face*) s'éclairer; (*smoke*) allumer une cigarette or une pipe *etc* ▷ *vt* (*illuminate*) éclairer, illuminer

light bulb *n* ampoule *f*

lighten ['laɪtn] *vi* s'éclairer ▷ *vt* (*light up*) éclairer; (*make lighter*) éclaircir; (*make less heavy*) alléger

lighter ['laɪtəʳ] *n* (*also*: **cigarette ~**) briquet *m*; (: *in car*) allume-cigare *m inv*; (*boat*) péniche *f*

light-headed [laɪt'hɛdɪd] *adj* étourdi(e), écervelé(e)

light-hearted [laɪt'hɑːtɪd] *adj* gai(e), joyeux(-euse), enjoué(e)

lighthouse ['laɪthaus] *n* phare *m*

lighting ['laɪtɪŋ] *n* éclairage *m*; (*in theatre*) éclairages

lightly ['laɪtlɪ] *adv* légèrement; **to get off ~** s'en tirer à bon compte

lightness ['laɪtnɪs] *n* clarté *f*; (*in weight*) légèreté *f*

lightning ['laɪtnɪŋ] *n* foudre *f*; (*flash*) éclair *m*

lightning conductor, (US) **lightning rod** *n* paratonnerre *m*

light pen *n* crayon *m* optique

lightweight ['laɪtweɪt] *adj* (*suit*) léger(-ère) ▷ *n* (*Boxing*) poids léger

like [laɪk] *vt* aimer (bien) ▷ *prep* comme ▷ *adj* semblable, pareil(le) ▷ *n*: **the ~** un(e) pareil(le) or semblable; le/la pareil(le); (*pej*) (d')autres du même genre or acabit; **his ~s and dislikes** ses goûts *mpl* or préférences *fpl*; **I would ~**, **I'd ~** je voudrais, j'aimerais; **would you ~ a coffee?** voulez-vous du café?; **to be/look ~ sb/sth** ressembler à qn/qch; **what's he ~?** comment est-il?; **what's the weather ~?** quel temps fait-il?; **what does it look ~?** de quoi est-ce que ça a l'air?; **what does it taste ~?** quel goût est-ce que ça a?; **that's just ~ him** c'est bien de lui, ça lui ressemble; **something ~ that** quelque chose comme ça; **do it ~ this** fais-le comme ceci; **I feel ~ a drink** je boirais bien quelque chose; **if you ~** si vous voulez; **it's nothing ~ ...** ce n'est pas du tout comme ...; **there's nothing ~ ...** il n'y a rien de tel que ...

likeable ['laɪkəbl] *adj* sympathique, agréable

likelihood ['laɪklɪhud] *n* probabilité *f*; **in all ~** selon toute vraisemblance

likely ['laɪklɪ] *adj* (*result, outcome*) probable; (*excuse*) plausible; **he's ~ to leave** il va sûrement partir, il risque fort de partir; **not ~!** (*inf*) pas de danger!

likeness ['laɪknɪs] *n* ressemblance *f*

likewise ['laɪkwaɪz] *adv* de même, pareillement

liking ['laɪkɪŋ] *n* (*for person*) affection *f*; (*for thing*) penchant *m*, goût *m*; **to take a ~ to sb** se prendre d'amitié pour qn; **to be to sb's ~** être au goût de qn, plaire à qn

lilac ['laɪlək] *n* lilas *m* ▷ *adj* lilas *inv*

Lilo® ['laɪləu] *n* matelas *m* pneumatique

lily ['lɪlɪ] *n* lis *m*; **~ of the valley** muguet *m*

limb [lɪm] *n* membre *m*; **to be out on a ~** (*fig*) être isolé(e)

limber ['lɪmbəʳ]: **to ~ up** *vi* se dégourdir, se mettre en train

limbo ['lɪmbəu] *n*: **to be in ~** (*fig*) être tombé(e) dans l'oubli

lime [laɪm] *n* (*tree*) tilleul *m*; (*fruit*) citron vert, lime *f*; (*Geo*) chaux *f*

limelight ['laɪmlaɪt] *n*: **in the ~** (*fig*) en vedette, au premier plan

limerick ['lɪmərɪk] *n* petit poème humoristique

limestone ['laɪmstəun] *n* pierre *f* à chaux; (*Geo*) calcaire *m*

limit ['lɪmɪt] *n* limite *f* ▷ *vt* limiter; **weight/speed ~** limite de poids/de vitesse

limited ['lɪmɪtɪd] *adj* limité(e), restreint(e); **~ edition** édition *f* à tirage limité; **to be ~ to** se limiter à, ne concerner que

limited company, limited liability company *n* (*Brit*) ≈ société *f* anonyme

limousine ['lɪməzi:n] *n* limousine *f*

limp [lɪmp] *n*: **to have a ~** boiter ▷ *vi* boiter ▷ *adj* mou/molle

limpet ['lɪmpɪt] *n* patelle *f*; **like a ~** (*fig*) comme une ventouse

line [laɪn] *n* (*gen*) ligne *f*; (*stroke*) trait *m*; (*wrinkle*) ride *f*; (*rope*) corde *f*; (*wire*) fil *m*; (*of poem*) vers *m*; (*row, series*) rangée *f*; (*of people*) file *f*, queue *f*; (*railway track*) voie *f*; (*Comm*: *series of goods*) article(s) *m(pl)*, ligne de produits; (*work*) métier *m* ▷ *vt*: **to ~ (with)** (*clothes*) doubler (de); (*box*) garnir or tapisser (de); (*subj*: *trees, crowd*) border; **to stand in ~** (US) faire la queue; **to cut in ~** (US) passer avant son tour; **in his ~ of business** dans sa partie, dans son rayon; **on the right ~s** sur la bonne voie; **a new ~ in cosmetics** une nouvelle ligne de produits de beauté; **hold the ~ please** (*Brit Tel*) ne quittez pas; **to be in ~ for sth** (*fig*) être en lice pour qch; **in ~ with** en accord avec, en conformité avec; **in a ~** aligné(e); **to bring sth into ~ with sth** aligner qch sur qch; **to draw the ~ at (doing) sth** (*fig*) se refuser à (faire) qch; ne pas tolérer or admettre (qu'on fasse) qch; **to take the ~ that ...** être d'avis or de l'opinion que ...; **line up** *vi* s'aligner, se mettre en rang(s); (*in queue*) faire la queue ▷ *vt* aligner; (*event*) prévoir; (*find*) trouver; **to have sb/sth ~d up** avoir qn/qch en vue or de prévu(e)

linear ['lɪnɪəʳ] *adj* linéaire

lined [laɪnd] *adj* (*paper*) réglé(e); (*face*) marqué(e), ridé(e); (*clothes*) doublé(e)

linen ['lɪnɪn] *n* linge *m* (de corps or de maison); (*cloth*) lin *m*

liner ['laɪnəʳ] *n* (*ship*) paquebot *m* de ligne; (*for bin*) sac-poubelle *m*

linesman ['laɪnzmən] *irreg n* (*Tennis*) juge *m* de ligne; (*Football*) juge de touche

line-up ['laɪnʌp] *n* (US: *queue*) file *f*; (*also*: **police ~**) parade *f* d'identification; (*Sport*) (composition *f* de l')équipe *f*

linger ['lɪŋgəʳ] *vi* s'attarder; traîner; (*smell, tradition*) persister

lingerie ['lænʒəriː] n lingerie f

linguist ['lɪŋgwɪst] n linguiste m/f; **to be a good ~** être doué(e) pour les langues

linguistic [lɪŋ'gwɪstɪk] adj linguistique

linguistics [lɪŋ'gwɪstɪks] n linguistique f

lining ['laɪnɪŋ] n doublure f; (Tech) revêtement m; (: of brakes) garniture f

link [lɪŋk] n (connection) lien m, rapport m; (Internet) lien; (of a chain) maillon m ▷ vt relier, lier, unir; **links** npl (Golf) (terrain m de) golf m; **rail ~** liaison f ferroviaire; **link up** vt relier ▷ vi (people) se rejoindre; (companies etc) s'associer

lino ['laɪnəu] n = **linoleum**

linoleum [lɪ'nəuliəm] n linoléum m

lion ['laɪən] n lion m

lioness ['laɪənɪs] n lionne f

lip [lɪp] n lèvre f; (of cup etc) rebord m; (insolence) insolences fpl

liposuction ['lɪpəusʌkʃən] n liposuccion f

lip-read ['lɪpriːd] vi (irreg like: **read**) lire sur les lèvres

lip salve [-sælv] n pommade f pour les lèvres, pommade rosat

lip service n: **to pay ~ to sth** ne reconnaître le mérite de qch que pour la forme or qu'en paroles

lipstick ['lɪpstɪk] n rouge m à lèvres

liqueur [lɪ'kjuəʳ] n liqueur f

liquid ['lɪkwɪd] n liquide m ▷ adj liquide

liquidize ['lɪkwɪdaɪz] vt (Brit Culin) passer au mixer

liquidizer ['lɪkwɪdaɪzəʳ] n (Brit Culin) mixer m

liquor ['lɪkəʳ] n spiritueux m, alcool m

liquorice ['lɪkərɪʃ] n (Brit) réglisse m

liquor store (US) n magasin m de vins et spiritueux

Lisbon ['lɪzbən] n Lisbonne

lisp [lɪsp] n zézaiement m ▷ vi zézayer

list [lɪst] n liste f; (of ship) inclinaison f ▷ vt (write down) inscrire; (make list of) faire la liste de; (enumerate) énumérer; (Comput) lister ▷ vi (ship) gîter, donner de la bande; **shopping ~** liste des courses

listed building ['lɪstɪd-] n (Archit) monument classé

listen ['lɪsn] vi écouter; **to ~ to** écouter

listener ['lɪsnəʳ] n auditeur(-trice)

listless ['lɪstlɪs] adj indolent(e), apathique

lit [lɪt] pt, pp of **light**

liter ['liːtəʳ] n (US) = **litre**

literacy ['lɪtərəsɪ] n degré m d'alphabétisation, fait m de savoir lire et écrire; (Brit: Scol) enseignement m de la lecture et de l'écriture

literal ['lɪtərl] adj littéral(e)

literally ['lɪtrəlɪ] adv littéralement; (really) réellement

literary ['lɪtərərɪ] adj littéraire

literate ['lɪtərət] adj qui sait lire et écrire; (educated) instruit(e)

literature ['lɪtrɪtʃəʳ] n littérature f; (brochures etc) copie f publicitaire, prospectus mpl

lithe [laɪð] adj agile, souple

litigation [lɪtɪ'geɪʃən] n litige m; contentieux m

litre, (US) **liter** ['liːtəʳ] n litre m

litter ['lɪtəʳ] n (rubbish) détritus mpl; (dirtier) ordures fpl; (young animals) portée f ▷ vt éparpiller; laisser des détritus dans; **~ed with** jonché(e) de, couvert(e) de

litter bin n (Brit) poubelle f

little ['lɪtl] adj (small) petit(e); (not much): **~ milk** peu de lait ▷ adv peu; **a ~** un peu (de); **a ~ milk** un peu de lait; **a ~ bit** un peu; **for a ~ while** pendant un petit moment; **with difficulty** sans trop de difficulté; **as ~ as possible** le moins possible; **by ~** petit à petit, peu à peu; **to make ~ of** faire peu de cas de

little finger n auriculaire m, petit doigt

live¹ [laɪv] adj (animal) vivant(e), en vie; (wire) sous tension; (broadcast) (transmis(e)) en direct; (issue) d'actualité, brûlant(e); (unexploded) non explosé(e); **~ ammunition** munitions fpl de combat

live² [lɪv] vi vivre; (reside) vivre, habiter; **to ~ in London** habiter (à) Londres; **where do you ~?** où habitez-vous?; **live down** vt faire oublier (avec le temps); **live in** vi être logé(e) et nourri(e); être interne; **live off** vt (land, fish etc) vivre de; (pej: parents etc) vivre aux crochets de; **live on** vt fus (food) vivre de ▷ vi survivre; **to ~ on £50 a week** vivre avec 50 livres par semaine; **live out** vi (Brit: students) être externe ▷ vt: **to ~ out one's days** or **life** passer sa vie; **live together** vi vivre ensemble, cohabiter; **live up** vt: **to ~ it up** (inf) faire la fête; mener la grande vie; **live up to** vt fus se montrer à la hauteur de

livelihood ['laɪvlɪhud] n moyens mpl d'existence

lively ['laɪvlɪ] adj vif/vive, plein(e) d'entrain; (place, book) vivant(e)

liven up ['laɪvn-] vt (room etc) égayer; (discussion, evening) animer ▷ vi s'animer

liver ['lɪvəʳ] n foie m

lives [laɪvz] npl of **life**

livestock ['laɪvstɔk] n cheptel m, bétail m

livid ['lɪvɪd] adj livide, blafard(e); (furious) furieux(-euse), furibond(e)

living ['lɪvɪŋ] adj vivant(e), en vie ▷ n: **to earn** or **make a ~** gagner sa vie; **within ~ memory** de mémoire d'homme

living conditions npl conditions fpl de vie

living room n salle f de séjour

living standards npl niveau m de vie

living wage n salaire m permettant de vivre (décemment)

lizard ['lɪzəd] n lézard m

load [ləud] n (weight) poids m; (thing carried) chargement m, charge f; (Elec, Tech) charge ▷ vt: **to ~ (with)** (also: **~ up**) lorry, ship) charger (de); (gun, camera) charger (avec); (Comput) charger; **a ~ of, ~s of** (fig) un or des tas de, des masses de; **to talk a ~ of rubbish** (inf) dire des bêtises

loaded ['ləʊdɪd] adj (dice) pipé(e); (question) insidieux(-euse); (inf: rich) bourré(e) de fric; (: drunk) bourré

loaf (pl **loaves**) [ləʊf, ləʊvz] n pain m, miche f ▷ vi (also: **~ about, ~ around**) fainéanter, traîner

loan [ləʊn] n prêt m ▷ vt prêter; **on ~** prêté(e), en prêt; **public ~** emprunt public

loath [ləʊθ] adj: **to be ~ to do** répugner à faire

loathe [ləʊð] vt détester, avoir en horreur

loaves [ləʊvz] npl of **loaf**

lobby ['lɒbɪ] n hall m, entrée f; (Pol) groupe m de pression, lobby m ▷ vt faire pression sur

lobster ['lɒbstər] n homard m

local ['ləʊkl] adj local(e) ▷ n (Brit: pub) pub m or café m du coin; **the locals** npl les gens mpl du pays or du coin

local anaesthetic, (US) **local anesthetic** n anesthésie locale

local authority n collectivité locale, municipalité f

local call n (Tel) communication urbaine

local government n administration locale or municipale

locality [ləʊ'kælɪtɪ] n région f, environs mpl; (position) lieu m

locally ['ləʊkəlɪ] adv localement; dans les environs or la région

locate [ləʊ'keɪt] vt (find) trouver, repérer; (situate) situer; **to be ~d in** être situé à or en

location [ləʊ'keɪʃən] n emplacement m; **on ~** (Cine) en extérieur

loch [lɒx] n lac m, loch m

lock [lɒk] n (of door, box) serrure f; (of canal) écluse f; (of hair) mèche f, boucle f ▷ vt (with key) fermer à clé; (immobilize) bloquer ▷ vi (door etc) fermer à clé; (wheels) se bloquer; **~ stock and barrel** (fig) en bloc; **on full ~** (Brit Aut) le volant tourné à fond; **lock away** vt (valuables) mettre sous clé; (criminal) mettre sous les verrous, enfermer; **lock in** vt enfermer; **lock out** vt enfermer dehors; (on purpose) mettre à la porte; (: workers) lock-outer; **lock up** vt (person) enfermer; (house) fermer à clé ▷ vi tout fermer (à clé)

locker ['lɒkər] n casier m; (in station) consigne f automatique

locker-room ['lɒkəruːm] (US) n (Sport) vestiaire m

locket ['lɒkɪt] n médaillon m

locksmith ['lɒksmɪθ] n serrurier m

lock-up ['lɒkʌp] n (prison) prison f; (cell) cellule f provisoire; (also: **~ garage**) box m

locomotive [ləʊkə'məʊtɪv] n locomotive f

locum ['ləʊkəm] n (Med) suppléant(e) de médecin etc

lodge [lɒdʒ] n pavillon m (de gardien); (also: **hunting ~**) pavillon de chasse; (Freemasonry) loge f ▷ vi (person): **to ~ with** être logé(e) chez,

être en pension chez; (bullet) se loger ▷ vt (appeal etc) présenter; déposer; **to ~ a complaint** porter plainte; **to ~ (itself) in/ between** se loger dans/entre

lodger ['lɒdʒər] n locataire m/f; (with room and meals) pensionnaire m/f

lodging ['lɒdʒɪŋ] n logement m; see also **board**

lodgings ['lɒdʒɪŋz] npl chambre f, meublé m

loft [lɒft] n grenier m; (apartment) grenier aménagé m (en appartement) (gén dans ancien entrepôt ou fabrique)

lofty ['lɒftɪ] adj élevé(e); (haughty) hautain(e); (sentiments, aims) noble

log [lɒg] n (of wood) bûche f; (Naut) livre m or journal m de bord; (of car) ≈ carte grise ▷ n abbr (= logarithm) log m ▷ vt enregistrer; **log in, log on** vi (Comput) ouvrir une session, entrer dans le système; **log off, log out** vi (Comput) clore une session, sortir du système

logbook ['lɒgbʊk] n (Naut) livre m or journal m de bord; (Aviat) carnet m de vol; (of lorry driver) carnet de route; (of movement of goods etc) registre m; (of car) ≈ carte grise

loggerheads ['lɒgəhedz] npl: **at ~ (with)** à couteaux tirés (avec)

logic ['lɒdʒɪk] n logique f

logical ['lɒdʒɪkl] adj logique

login ['lɒgɪn] n (Comput) identifiant m

logo ['ləʊgəʊ] n logo m

loin [lɔɪn] n (Culin) filet m, longe f; **loins** npl reins mpl

Loire [lwaː] n: **the (River) ~** la Loire

loiter ['lɔɪtər] vi s'attarder; **to ~ (about)** traîner, musarder; (pej) rôder

loll [lɒl] vi (also: **~ about**) se prélasser, fainéanter

lollipop ['lɒlɪpɒp] n sucette f

lollipop man/lady (Brit) irreg n contractuel(le) qui fait traverser la rue aux enfants; voir article

● **LOLLIPOP MEN/LADIES**

● Les **lollipop men/ladies** sont employés pour
● aider les enfants à traverser la rue à
● proximité des écoles à l'heure où ils
● entrent en classe et à la sortie. On les
● repère facilement à cause de leur long
● ciré jaune et ils portent une pancarte
● ronde pour faire signe aux
● automobilistes de s'arrêter. On les
● appelle ainsi car la forme circulaire
● de cette pancarte rappelle une sucette.

lolly ['lɒlɪ] n (inf: ice) esquimau m; (: lollipop) sucette f; (: money) fric m

London ['lʌndən] n Londres

Londoner ['lʌndənər] n Londonien(ne)

lone [ləʊn] adj solitaire

loneliness ['ləʊnlɪnɪs] n solitude f, isolement m

lonely ['ləʊnlɪ] adj seul(e); (childhood etc) solitaire; (place) solitaire, isolé(e)

long [lɔŋ] *adj* long/longue ▷ *adv* longtemps ▷ *n*: **the ~ and the short of it is that ...** (*fig*) le fin mot de l'histoire c'est que ... ▷ *vi*: **to ~ for sth/to do sth** avoir très envie de qch/de faire qch, attendre qch avec impatience/ attendre avec impatience de faire qch; **he had ~ understood that ...** il avait compris depuis longtemps que ...; **how ~ is this river/course?** quelle est la longueur de ce fleuve/la durée de ce cours?; **6 metres ~** (long) de 6 mètres; **6 months ~** qui dure 6 mois, de 6 mois; **all night ~** toute la nuit; **he no ~er comes** il ne vient plus; **I can't stand it any ~er** je ne peux plus le supporter; **~ before** longtemps avant; **before ~** (+ *future*) avant peu, dans peu de temps; (+ *past*) peu de temps après; **~ ago** il y a longtemps; **don't be ~!** fais vite!, dépêche-toi!; **I shan't be ~** je n'en ai pas pour longtemps; **at ~ last** enfin; **in the ~ run** à la longue; finalement; **so** or **as ~ as** à condition que + *sub*

long-distance [lɔŋ'dɪstəns] *adj* (*race*) de fond; (*call*) interurbain(e)

longer ['lɔŋgər] *adv see* **long**

longhand ['lɔŋhænd] *n* écriture normale or courante

long-haul ['lɔŋhɔ:l] *adj* (*flight*) long-courrier

longing ['lɔŋɪŋ] *n* désir *m*, envie *f*; (*nostalgia*) nostalgie *f* ▷ *adj* plein(e) d'envie or de nostalgie

longitude ['lɔŋgɪtju:d] *n* longitude *f*

long jump *n* saut *m* en longueur

long-life [lɔŋ'laɪf] *adj* (*batteries etc*) longue durée *m*; (*milk*) longue conservation

long-lost ['lɔŋlɒst] *adj* perdu(e) depuis longtemps

long-range ['lɔŋ'reɪndʒ] *adj* à longue portée; (*weather forecast*) à long terme

long-sighted ['lɔŋ'saɪtɪd] *adj* (*Brit*) presbyte; (*fig*) prévoyant(e)

long-standing ['lɔŋ'stændɪŋ] *adj* de longue date

long-suffering [lɔŋ'sʌfərɪŋ] *adj* empreint(e) d'une patience résignée; extrêmement patient(e)

long-term ['lɔŋtə:m] *adj* à long terme

long wave *n* (*Radio*) grandes ondes, ondes longues

long-winded [lɔŋ'wɪndɪd] *adj* intarissable, interminable

loo [lu:] *n* (*Brit inf*) w.-c *mpl*, petit coin

look [lʊk] *vi* regarder; (*seem*) sembler, paraître, avoir l'air; (*building etc*): **to ~ south/ on to the sea** donner au sud/sur la mer ▷ *n* regard *m*; (*appearance*) air *m*, allure *f*, aspect *m*; **looks** *npl* (*good looks*) physique *m*, beauté *f*; **to ~ like** ressembler à; **it ~s like him** on dirait que c'est lui; **it ~s about 4 metres long** je dirais que ça fait 4 mètres de long; **it ~s all right to me** ça me paraît bien; **to have a ~** regarder; **to have a ~ at sth** jeter un coup d'œil à qch; **to have a ~ for sth** chercher qch;

to ~ ahead regarder devant soi; (*fig*) envisager l'avenir; **~ (here)!** (*annoyance*) écoutez!; **look after** *vt fus* s'occuper de, prendre soin de; (*luggage etc: watch over*) garder, surveiller; **look around** *vi* regarder autour de soi; **look at** *vt fus* regarder; (*problem etc*) examiner; **look back** *vi*: **to ~ back at sth/sb** se retourner pour regarder qch/qn; **to ~ back on** (*event, period*) évoquer, repenser à; **look down on** *vt fus* (*fig*) regarder de haut, dédaigner; **look for** *vt fus* chercher; **we're ~ing for a hotel/restaurant** nous cherchons un hôtel/restaurant; **look forward to** *vt fus* attendre avec impatience; **I'm not ~ing forward to it** cette perspective ne me réjouit guère; **~ing forward to hearing from you** (*in letter*) dans l'attente de vous lire; **look in** *vi*: **to ~ in on sb** passer voir qn; **look into** *vt fus* (*matter, possibility*) examiner, étudier; **look on** *vi* regarder (en spectateur); **look out** *vi* (*beware*): **to ~ out (for)** prendre garde (à), faire attention (à); **~ out!** attention!; **look out for** *vt fus* (*seek*) être à la recherche de; (*try to spot*) guetter; **look over** *vt* (*essay*) jeter un coup d'œil à; (*town, building*) visiter (rapidement); (*person*) jeter un coup d'œil à; examiner de la tête aux pieds; **look round** *vt fus* (*house, shop*) faire le tour de ▷ *vi* (*turn*) regarder derrière soi, se retourner; **to ~ round for sth** chercher qch; **look through** *vt fus* (*papers, book*) examiner; (: *briefly*) parcourir; (*telescope*) regarder à travers; **look to** *vt fus* veiller à; (*rely on*) compter sur; **look up** *vi* lever les yeux; (*improve*) s'améliorer ▷ *vt* (*word*) chercher; (*friend*) passer voir; **look up to** *vt fus* avoir du respect pour

lookout ['lʊkaʊt] *n* (*tower etc*) poste *m* de guet; (*person*) guetteur *m*; **to be on the ~ (for)** guetter

loom [lu:m] *n* métier *m* à tisser ▷ *vi* (*also*: **~ up**) surgir; (*event*) paraître imminent(e); (*threaten*) menacer

loony ['lu:nɪ] *adj* (*inf*) timbré(e), cinglé(e)

loop [lu:p] *n* boucle *f*; (*contraceptive*) stérilet *m* ▷ *vt*: **to ~ sth round sth** passer qch autour de qch

loophole ['lu:phəʊl] *n* (*fig*) porte *f* de sortie; échappatoire *f*

loose [lu:s] *adj* (*knot, screw*) desserré(e); (*stone*) branlant(e); (*clothes*) vague, ample, lâche; (*hair*) dénoué(e), épars(e); (*not firmly fixed*) pas solide; (*animal*) en liberté, échappé(e); (*life*) dissolu(e); (*morals, discipline*) relâché(e); (*thinking*) peu rigoureux(-euse), vague; (*translation*) approximatif(-ive) ▷ *n*: **to be on the ~** être en liberté ▷ *vt* (*free: animal*) lâcher; (: *prisoner*) relâcher, libérer; (*slacken*) détendre, relâcher; desserrer; défaire; donner du mou a; donner du ballant à; (*Brit: arrow*) tirer; **~ connection** (*Elec*) mauvais contact; **to be at a ~ end** or (*US*) **at ~ ends** (*fig*) ne pas trop

savoir quoi faire; **to tie up ~ ends** (*fig*) mettre au point *or* régler les derniers détails
loose change *n* petite monnaie
loose chippings [-'tʃɪpɪŋz] *npl* (*on road*) gravillons *mpl*
loosely ['luːslɪ] *adv* sans serrer; (*imprecisely*) approximativement
loosen ['luːsn] *vt* desserrer, relâcher, défaire; **loosen up** *vi* (*before game*) s'échauffer; (*inf: relax*) se détendre, se laisser aller
loot [luːt] *n* butin *m* ▷ *vt* piller
lop-sided ['lɔp'saɪdɪd] *adj* de travers, asymétrique
lord [lɔːd] *n* seigneur *m*; **L- Smith** lord Smith; **the L-** (*Rel*) le Seigneur; **my L-** (*to noble*) Monsieur le comte/le baron; (*to judge*) Monsieur le juge; (*to bishop*) Monseigneur; **good L-!** mon Dieu!
Lords ['lɔːdz] *npl* (*Brit: Pol*): **the (House of) ~** (*Brit*) la Chambre des Lords
lordship ['lɔːdʃɪp] *n* (*Brit*): **your L-** Monsieur le comte (*or* le baron *or* le Juge)
lore [lɔːʳ] *n* tradition(s) *f(pl)*
lorry ['lɔrɪ] *n* (*Brit*) camion *m*
lorry driver *n* (*Brit*) camionneur *m*, routier *m*
lose (*pt, pp* **lost**) [luːz, lɔst] *vt* perdre; (*opportunity*) manquer, perdre; (*pursuers*) distancer, semer ▷ *vi* perdre; **I've lost my wallet/passport** j'ai perdu mon portefeuille/passeport; **to ~ (time)** (*clock*) retarder; **to ~ no time (in doing sth)** ne pas perdre de temps (à faire qch); **to get lost** *vi* (*person*) se perdre; **my watch has got lost** ma montre est perdue; **lose out** *vi* être perdant(e)
loser ['luːzəʳ] *n* perdant(e); **to be a good/bad ~** être beau/mauvais joueur
loss [lɔs] *n* perte *f*; **to cut one's ~es** limiter les dégâts; **to make a ~** enregistrer une perte; **to sell sth at a ~** vendre qch à perte; **to be at a ~** être perplexe *or* embarrassé(e); **to be at a ~ to do** se trouver incapable de faire
lost [lɔst] *pt, pp of* **lose** ▷ *adj* perdu(e); **to get ~** *vi* se perdre; **I'm ~** je me suis perdu(e); **~ in thought** perdu dans ses pensées; **~ and found property** *n* (*US*) objets trouvés; **~ and found** *n* (*US*) (bureau *m* des) objets trouvés
lost property *n* (*Brit*) objets trouvés; **~ office** *or* **department** (bureau *m* des) objets trouvés
lot [lɔt] *n* (*at auctions, set*) lot *m*; (*destiny*) sort *m*, destinée *f*; **the ~** (*everything*) le tout; (*everyone*) tous *mpl*, toutes *fpl*; **a ~** beaucoup; **a ~ of** beaucoup de; **~s of** des tas de; **to draw ~s (for sth)** tirer (qch) au sort
lotion ['ləuʃən] *n* lotion *f*
lottery ['lɔtərɪ] *n* loterie *f*
loud [laud] *adj* bruyant(e), sonore; (*voice*) fort(e); (*condemnation etc*) vigoureux(-euse); (*gaudy*) voyant(e), tapageur(-euse) ▷ *adv* (*speak etc*) fort; **out ~** tout haut
loud-hailer [laud'heɪləʳ] *n* porte-voix *m inv*

loudly ['laudlɪ] *adv* fort, bruyamment
loudspeaker [laud'spiːkəʳ] *n* haut-parleur *m*
lounge [laundʒ] *n* salon *m*; (*of airport*) salle *f*; (*Brit: also*: **~ bar**) (salle de) café *m or* bar *m* ▷ *vi* (*also*: **~ about, ~ around**) se prélasser, paresser
lounge suit *n* (*Brit*) complet *m*; (: *on invitation*) "tenue de ville"
louse (*before pl* **lice**) [laus, laɪs] *n* pou *m*; **louse up** [lauz-] *vt* (*inf*) gâcher
lousy ['lauzɪ] (*inf*) *adj* (*bad quality*) infect(e), moche; **I feel ~** je suis mal fichu(e)
lout [laut] *n* rustre *m*, butor *m*
lovable ['lʌvəbl] *adj* très sympathique; adorable
love [lʌv] *n* amour *m* ▷ *vt* aimer; (*caringly, kindly*) aimer beaucoup; **I ~ chocolate** j'adore le chocolat; **to ~ to do** aimer beaucoup *or* adorer faire; **I'd ~ to come** cela me ferait très plaisir (de venir); **"15 ~"** (*Tennis*) "15 à rien *or* zéro"; **to be/fall in ~ with** être/tomber amoureux(-euse) de; **to make ~** faire l'amour; **~ at first sight** le coup de foudre; **to send one's ~ to sb** adresser ses amitiés à qn; **~ from Anne, ~,** Anne affectueusement, Anne; **I ~ you** je t'aime
love affair *n* liaison (amoureuse)
love life *n* vie sentimentale
lovely ['lʌvlɪ] *adj* (*pretty*) ravissant(e); (*friend, wife*) charmant(e); (*holiday, surprise*) très agréable, merveilleux(-euse); **we had a ~ time** c'était vraiment très bien, nous avons eu beaucoup de plaisir
lover ['lʌvəʳ] *n* amant *m*; (*person in love*) amoureux(-euse); (*amateur*): **a ~ of** un(e) ami(e) de, un(e) amoureux(-euse) de
loving ['lʌvɪŋ] *adj* affectueux(-euse), tendre, aimant(e)
low [ləu] *adj* bas/basse; (*quality*) mauvais(e), inférieur(e) ▷ *adv* bas ▷ *n* (*Meteorology*) dépression *f* ▷ *vi* (*cow*) mugir; **to feel ~** se sentir déprimé(e); **he's very ~** (*ill*) il est bien bas *or* très affaibli; **to turn (down)** ~ *vt* baisser; **to be ~ on** (*supplies etc*) être à court de; **to reach a new ~** *or* **an all-time ~** tomber au niveau le plus bas
low-alcohol [ləu'ælkəhɔl] *adj* à faible teneur en alcool, peu alcoolisé(e)
low-calorie ['ləu'kælərɪ] *adj* hypocalorique
low-cut ['ləukʌt] *adj* (*dress*) décolleté(e)
lower *adj* ['ləuəʳ] inférieur(e) ▷ *vt* ['ləuəʳ] baisser; (*resistance*) diminuer ▷ *vi* ['lauəʳ] (*person*): **to ~ at sb** jeter un regard mauvais *or* noir à qn; (*sky, clouds*) être menaçant(e); **to ~ o.s. to** s'abaisser à
lower sixth (*Brit*) *n* (*Scol*) première *f*
low-fat ['ləu'fæt] *adj* maigre
lowland, lowlands ['ləulənd(z)] *n(pl)* plaine(s) *f(pl)*
lowly ['ləulɪ] *adj* humble, modeste
loyal ['lɔɪəl] *adj* loyal(e), fidèle
loyalty ['lɔɪəltɪ] *n* loyauté *f*, fidélité *f*

loyalty card n carte f de fidélité
lozenge ['lɒzɪndʒ] n (Med) pastille f; (Geom) losange m
L-plates ['ɛlpleɪts] npl (Brit) plaques fpl (obligatoires) d'apprenti conducteur
Lt abbr (= lieutenant) Lt.
Ltd abbr (Comm: company: = limited) ≈ S.A.
lubricant ['lu:brɪkənt] n lubrifiant m
lubricate ['lu:brɪkeɪt] vt lubrifier, graisser
luck [lʌk] n chance f; **bad ~** malchance f, malheur m; **to be in ~** avoir de la chance; **to be out of ~** ne pas avoir de chance; **good ~!** bonne chance!; **bad** or **hard ~!** pas de chance!
luckily ['lʌkɪlɪ] adv heureusement, par bonheur
lucky ['lʌkɪ] adj (person) qui a de la chance; (coincidence) heureux(-euse); (number etc) qui porte bonheur
lucrative ['lu:krətɪv] adj lucratif(-ive), rentable, qui rapporte
ludicrous ['lu:dɪkrəs] adj ridicule, absurde
lug [lʌg] vt traîner, tirer
luggage ['lʌgɪdʒ] n bagages mpl; **our ~ hasn't arrived** nos bagages ne sont pas arrivés; **could you send someone to collect our ~?** pourriez-vous envoyer quelqu'un chercher nos bagages?
luggage rack n (in train) porte-bagages m inv; (: made of string) filet m à bagages; (on car) galerie f
lukewarm ['lu:kwɔ:m] adj tiède
lull [lʌl] n accalmie f; (in conversation) pause f ▷ vt: **to ~ sb to sleep** bercer qn pour qu'il s'endorme; **to be ~ed into a false sense of security** s'endormir dans une fausse sécurité
lullaby ['lʌləbaɪ] n berceuse f
lumbago [lʌm'beɪgəu] n lumbago m
lumber ['lʌmbər] n (wood) bois m de charpente; (junk) bric-à-brac m inv ▷ vt (Brit inf): **to ~ sb with sth/sb** coller or refiler qch/qn à qn ▷ vi (also: **~ about, ~ along**) marcher pesamment
lumberjack ['lʌmbədʒæk] n bûcheron m
luminous ['lu:mɪnəs] adj lumineux(-euse)
lump [lʌmp] n morceau m; (in sauce) grumeau m; (swelling) grosseur f ▷ vt (also: **~ together**) réunir, mettre en tas
lump sum n somme globale or forfaitaire
lumpy ['lʌmpɪ] adj (sauce) qui a des grumeaux; (bed) défoncé(e), peu confortable
lunar ['lu:nər] adj lunaire
lunatic ['lu:nətɪk] n (inf!) fou/folle, dément(e) ▷ adj fou/folle, dément(e)
lunch [lʌntʃ] n déjeuner m ▷ vi déjeuner; **it is his ~ hour** c'est l'heure où il déjeune; **to invite sb to** or **for ~** inviter qn à déjeuner
lunch break, lunch hour n pause f de midi, heure f du déjeuner
luncheon ['lʌntʃən] n déjeuner m
luncheon meat n sorte de saucisson

luncheon voucher n chèque-repas m, ticket-repas m
lunchtime ['lʌntʃtaɪm] n: **it's ~** c'est l'heure du déjeuner
lung [lʌŋ] n poumon m
lunge [lʌndʒ] vi (also: **~ forward**) faire un mouvement brusque en avant; **to ~ at sb** envoyer or assener un coup à qn
lurch [lə:tʃ] vi vaciller, tituber ▷ n écart m brusque, embardée f; **to leave sb in the ~** laisser qn se débrouiller or se dépêtrer tout(e) seul(e)
lure [luər] n (attraction) attrait m, charme m; (in hunting) appât m, leurre m ▷ vt attirer or persuader par la ruse
lurid ['luərɪd] adj affreux(-euse), atroce
lurk [lə:k] vi se tapir, se cacher
luscious ['lʌʃəs] adj succulent(e), appétissant(e)
lush [lʌʃ] adj luxuriant(e)
lust [lʌst] n (sexual) désir (sexuel); (Rel) luxure f; (fig): **~ for** soif f de; **lust after** vt fus convoiter, désirer
lusty ['lʌstɪ] adj vigoureux(-euse), robuste
Luxembourg ['lʌksəmbə:g] n Luxembourg m
luxurious [lʌg'zjuərɪəs] adj luxueux(-euse)
luxury ['lʌkʃərɪ] n luxe m ▷ cpd de luxe
Lycra® ['laɪkrə] n Lycra® m
lying ['laɪɪŋ] n mensonge(s) m(pl) ▷ adj (statement, story) mensonger(-ère), faux/fausse; (person) menteur(-euse)
Lyons ['ljɔ̃] n Lyon
lyric ['lɪrɪk] adj lyrique
lyrical ['lɪrɪkl] adj lyrique
lyrics ['lɪrɪks] npl (of song) paroles fpl

m

m. *abbr* (= metre) m; (= million) M; (= mile) mi

M.A. *n abbr* (Scol) = **Master of Arts** ▷ *abbr* (US) = **military academy**; (US) = **Massachusetts**

ma [mɑː] (inf) *n* maman *f*

mac [mæk] *n* (Brit) imper(méable *m*) *m*

macaroni [mækə'rəʊnɪ] *n* macaronis *mpl*

Macedonia [mæsɪ'dəʊnɪə] *n* Macédoine *f*

Macedonian [mæsɪ'dəʊnɪən] *adj* macédonien(ne) ▷ *n* Macédonien(ne); (Ling) macédonien *m*

machine [mə'ʃiːn] *n* machine *f* ▷ *vt* (dress etc) coudre à la machine; (Tech) usiner

machine gun *n* mitrailleuse *f*

machine language *n* (Comput) langage *m* machine

machinery [mə'ʃiːnərɪ] *n* machinerie *f*, machines *fpl*; (fig) mécanisme(s) *m(pl)*

machine washable *adj* (garment) lavable en machine

macho ['mætʃəʊ] *adj* macho *inv*

mackerel ['mækrl] *n* (pl inv) maquereau *m*

mackintosh ['mækɪntɒʃ] *n* (Brit) imperméable *m*

mad [mæd] *adj* fou/folle; (foolish) insensé(e); (angry) furieux(-euse); **to go ~** devenir fou; **to be ~ (keen) about** or **on sth** (inf) être follement passionné de qch, être fou de qch

Madagascar [mædə'gæskəʳ] *n* Madagascar *m*

madam ['mædəm] *n* madame *f*; **yes ~** oui Madame; **M~ Chairman** Madame la Présidente

mad cow disease *n* maladie *f* des vaches folles

madden ['mædn] *vt* exaspérer

made [meɪd] *pt, pp of* **make**

Madeira [mə'dɪərə] *n* (Geo) Madère *f*; (wine) madère *m*

made-to-measure ['meɪdtə'mɛʒəʳ] *adj* (Brit) fait(e) sur mesure

made-up ['meɪdʌp] *adj* (story) inventé(e), fabriqué(e)

madly ['mædlɪ] *adv* follement; **~ in love** éperdument amoureux(-euse)

madman ['mædmən] *irreg n* fou *m*, aliéné *m*

madness ['mædnɪs] *n* folie *f*

Madrid [mə'drɪd] *n* Madrid

Mafia ['mæfɪə] *n* maf(f)ia *f*

mag [mæg] *n abbr* (Brit inf: = magazine) magazine *m*

magazine [mægə'ziːn] *n* (Press) magazine *m*, revue *f*; (Radio, TV) magazine; (Mil: store) dépôt *m*, arsenal *m*; (of firearm) magasin *m*

maggot ['mægət] *n* ver *m*, asticot *m*

magic ['mædʒɪk] *n* magie *f* ▷ *adj* magique

magical ['mædʒɪkl] *adj* magique; (experience, evening) merveilleux(-euse)

magician [mə'dʒɪʃən] *n* magicien(ne)

magistrate ['mædʒɪstreɪt] *n* magistrat *m*; juge *m*; **~s' court** (Brit) ≈ tribunal *m* d'instance

magnet ['mægnɪt] *n* aimant *m*

magnetic [mæg'nɛtɪk] *adj* magnétique

magnificent [mæg'nɪfɪsnt] *adj* superbe, magnifique; (splendid: robe, building) somptueux(-euse), magnifique

magnify ['mægnɪfaɪ] *vt* grossir; (sound) amplifier

magnifying glass ['mægnɪfaɪɪŋ-] *n* loupe *f*

magnitude ['mægnɪtjuːd] *n* ampleur *f*

magpie ['mægpaɪ] *n* pie *f*

mahogany [mə'hɔgənɪ] *n* acajou *m* ▷ *cpd* en (bois d')acajou

maid [meɪd] *n* bonne *f*; (in hotel) femme *f* de chambre; **old ~** (pej) vieille fille

maiden ['meɪdn] *n* jeune fille *f* ▷ *adj* (aunt etc) non mariée; (speech, voyage) inaugural(e)

maiden name *n* nom *m* de jeune fille

mail [meɪl] *n* poste *f*; (letters) courrier *m* ▷ *vt* envoyer (par la poste); **by ~** par la poste

mailbox ['meɪlbɔks] *n* (US: also Comput) boîte *f* aux lettres

mailing list ['meɪlɪŋ-] *n* liste *f* d'adresses

mailman ['meɪlmæn] *irreg n* (US) facteur *m*

mail-order ['meɪlɔːdəʳ] *n* vente *f* or achat *m* par correspondance ▷ *cpd*: **~ firm** or **house** maison *f* de vente par correspondance

maim [meɪm] *vt* mutiler

main [meɪn] *adj* principal(e) ▷ *n* (pipe) conduite principale, canalisation *f*; **the ~s** (Elec) le secteur; **the ~ thing** l'essentiel *m*; **in the ~** dans l'ensemble

main course *n* (Culin) plat *m* de résistance

mainframe ['meɪnfreɪm] n (also: **~ computer**) (gros) ordinateur, unité centrale

mainland ['meɪnlənd] n continent m

mainly ['meɪnlɪ] adv principalement, surtout

main road n grand axe, route nationale

mainstay ['meɪnsteɪ] n (fig) pilier m

mainstream ['meɪnstriːm] n (fig) courant principal

main street n rue f principale

maintain [meɪn'teɪn] vt entretenir; (continue) maintenir, préserver; (affirm) soutenir; **to ~ that ...** soutenir que ...

maintenance ['meɪntənəns] n entretien m; (Law: alimony) pension f alimentaire

maisonette [meɪzə'nɛt] n (Brit) appartement m en duplex

maize [meɪz] n (Brit) maïs m

majestic [mə'dʒɛstɪk] adj majestueux(-euse)

majesty ['mædʒɪstɪ] n majesté f; (title): **Your M~** Votre Majesté

major ['meɪdʒəʳ] n (Mil) commandant m ▷ adj (important) important(e); (most important) principal(e); (Mus) majeur(e) ▷ vi (US Scol): **to ~ (in)** se spécialiser (en); **a ~ operation** (Med) une grosse opération

Majorca [mə'jɔːkə] n Majorque f

majority [mə'dʒɔrɪtɪ] n majorité f ▷ cpd (verdict, holding) majoritaire

make [meɪk] vt (pt, pp made) [meɪd] faire; (manufacture) faire, fabriquer; (earn) gagner; (decision) prendre; (friend) se faire; (speech) faire, prononcer; (cause to be): **to ~ sb sad** etc rendre qn triste etc; (force): **to ~ sb do sth** obliger qn à faire qch, faire faire qch à qn; (equal): **2 and 2 ~ 4** 2 et 2 font 4 ▷ n (manufacture) fabrication f; (brand) marque f; **to ~ the bed** faire le lit; **to ~ a fool of sb** (ridicule) ridiculiser qn; (trick) avoir ou duper qn; **to ~ a profit** faire un ou des bénéfice(s); **to ~ a loss** essuyer une perte; **to ~ it** (in time etc) y arriver; (succeed) réussir; **what time do you ~ it?** quelle heure avez-vous?; **I ~ it £249** d'après mes calculs ça fait 249 livres; **to be made of** être en; **to ~ good** vi (succeed) faire son chemin, réussir ▷ vt (deficit) combler; (losses) compenser; **to ~ do with** se contenter de; se débrouiller avec; **make for** vt fus (place) se diriger vers; **make off** vi filer; **make out** vt (write out: cheque) faire; (decipher) déchiffrer; (understand) comprendre; (see) distinguer; (claim, imply) prétendre, vouloir faire croire; **to ~ out a case for sth** présenter des arguments solides en faveur de qch; **make over** vt (assign): **to ~ over (to)** céder (à), transférer (au nom de); **make up** vt (invent) inventer, imaginer; (constitute) constituer; (parcel, bed) faire ▷ vi se réconcilier; (with cosmetics) se maquiller, se farder; **to be made up of** se composer de; **make up for** vt fus compenser; (lost time) rattraper

make-believe ['meɪkbɪliːv] n: **a world of ~** un monde de chimères ou d'illusions; **it's**

just ~ c'est de la fantaisie; c'est une illusion

makeover ['meɪkəuvəʳ] n (by beautician) soins mpl de maquillage; (change of image) changement m d'image; **to give sb a ~** relooker qn

maker ['meɪkəʳ] n fabricant m; (of film, programme) réalisateur(-trice)

makeshift ['meɪkʃɪft] adj provisoire, improvisé(e)

make-up ['meɪkʌp] n maquillage m

making ['meɪkɪŋ] n (fig): **in the ~** en formation ou gestation; **to have the ~s of** (actor, athlete) avoir l'étoffe de

malaria [mə'lɛərɪə] n malaria f, paludisme m

Malaysia [mə'leɪzɪə] n Malaisie f

male [meɪl] n (Biol, Elec) mâle m ▷ adj (sex, attitude) masculin(e); (animal) mâle; (child etc) du sexe masculin; **~ and female students** étudiants et étudiantes

malevolent [mə'lɛvələnt] adj malveillant(e)

malfunction [mæl'fʌŋkʃən] n fonctionnement défectueux

malice ['mælɪs] n méchanceté f, malveillance f

malicious [mə'lɪʃəs] adj méchant(e), malveillant(e); (Law) avec intention criminelle

malignant [mə'lɪgnənt] adj (Med) malin(-igne)

mall [mɔːl] n (also: **shopping ~**) centre commercial

mallet ['mælɪt] n maillet m

malnutrition [mælnjuːˈtrɪʃən] n malnutrition f

malpractice [mælˈpræktɪs] n faute professionnelle; négligence f

malt [mɔːlt] n malt m ▷ cpd (whisky) pur malt

Malta ['mɔːltə] n Malte f

Maltese [mɔːlˈtiːz] adj maltais(e) ▷ n (pl inv) Maltais(e); (Ling) maltais m

mammal ['mæml] n mammifère m

mammoth ['mæməθ] n mammouth m ▷ adj géant(e), monstre

man (pl **men**) [mæn, mɛn] n homme m; (Sport) joueur m; (Chess) pièce f; (Draughts) pion m ▷ vt (Naut: ship) garnir d'hommes; (machine) assurer le fonctionnement de; (Mil: gun) servir; (: post) être de service à; **an old ~** un vieillard; **~ and wife** mari et femme

manage ['mænɪdʒ] vi se débrouiller; (succeed) y arriver, réussir ▷ vt (business) gérer; (team, operation) diriger; (control: ship) manier, manœuvrer; (: person) savoir s'y prendre avec; (device, things to do, carry etc) arriver à se débrouiller avec, s'en tirer avec; **to ~ to do** se débrouiller pour faire; (succeed) réussir à faire

manageable ['mænɪdʒəbl] adj maniable; (task etc) faisable; (number) raisonnable

management ['mænɪdʒmənt] n (running) administration f, direction f; (people in charge: of business, firm) dirigeants mpl, cadres mpl; (: of hotel, shop, theatre) direction; **"under new ~"**

m

"changement de gérant", "changement de propriétaire"

manager ['mænɪdʒəʳ] n (of business) directeur m; (of institution etc) administrateur m; (of department, unit) responsable m/f, chef m; (of hotel etc) gérant m; (Sport) manager m; (of artist) impresario m; **sales ~** responsable or chef des ventes

manageress [mænɪdʒə'rɛs] n directrice f; (of hotel etc) gérante f

managerial [mænɪ'dʒɪərɪəl] adj directorial(e); (skills) de cadre, de gestion; **~ staff** cadres mpl

managing director ['mænɪdʒɪŋ-] n directeur général

mandarin ['mændərɪn] n (also: **~ orange**) mandarine f; (person) mandarin m

mandate ['mændeɪt] n mandat m

mandatory ['mændətərɪ] adj obligatoire; (powers etc) mandataire

mane [meɪn] n crinière f

maneuver [mə'nu:vəʳ] (US) n = **manoeuvre**

manfully ['mænfəlɪ] adv vaillamment

mangetout ['mɔnʒ'tu:] n mange-tout m inv

mangle ['mæŋgl] vt déchiqueter; mutiler ▷ n essoreuse f; calandre f

mango (pl **mangoes**) ['mæŋgəu] n mangue f

mangy ['meɪndʒɪ] adj galeux(-euse)

manhandle ['mænhændl] vt (mistreat) maltraiter, malmener; (move by hand) manutentionner

manhole ['mænhəul] n trou m d'homme

manhood ['mænhud] n (age) âge m d'homme; (manliness) virilité f

man-hour ['mænauəʳ] n heure-homme f, heure f de main-d'œuvre

manhunt ['mænhʌnt] n chasse f à l'homme

mania ['meɪnɪə] n manie f

maniac ['meɪnɪæk] n maniaque m/f; (fig) fou/folle

manic ['mænɪk] adj maniaque

manicure ['mænɪkjuəʳ] n manucure f ▷ vt (person) faire les mains à

manifest ['mænɪfɛst] vt manifester ▷ adj manifeste, évident(e) ▷ n (Aviat, Naut) manifeste m

manifesto [mænɪ'fɛstəu] n (Pol) manifeste m

manipulate [mə'nɪpjuleɪt] vt manipuler; (system, situation) exploiter

mankind [mæn'kaɪnd] n humanité f, genre humain

manly ['mænlɪ] adj viril(e)

man-made ['mæn'meɪd] adj artificiel(le); (fibre) synthétique

manner ['mænəʳ] n manière f, façon f; (behaviour) attitude f, comportement m; **manners** npl: (**good**) **~s** (bonnes) manières; **bad ~s** mauvaises manières; **all ~ of** toutes sortes de

mannerism ['mænərɪzəm] n particularité f de langage (or de comportement), tic m

manoeuvre, (US) **maneuver** [mə'nu:vəʳ] vt

(move) manœuvrer; (manipulate: person) manipuler; (: situation) exploiter ▷ vi manœuvre f; **to ~ sb into doing sth** manipuler qn pour lui faire faire qch

manor ['mænəʳ] n (also: **~ house**) manoir m

manpower ['mænpauəʳ] n main-d'œuvre f

mansion ['mænʃən] n château m, manoir m

manslaughter ['mænslɔ:təʳ] n homicide m involontaire

mantelpiece ['mæntlpi:s] n cheminée f

manual ['mænjuəl] adj manuel(le) ▷ n manuel m

manufacture [mænju'fæktʃəʳ] vt fabriquer ▷ n fabrication f

manufacturer [mænju'fæktʃərəʳ] n fabricant m

manure [mə'njuəʳ] n fumier m; (artificial) engrais m

manuscript ['mænjuskrɪpt] n manuscrit m

many ['mɛnɪ] adj beaucoup de, de nombreux(-euses) ▷ pron beaucoup, un grand nombre; **how ~?** combien?; **a great ~** un grand nombre (de); **too ~ difficulties** trop de difficultés; **twice as ~** deux fois plus; **~ a ...** bien des ..., plus d'un(e) ...

map [mæp] n carte f; (of town) plan m ▷ vt dresser la carte de; **can you show it to me on the ~?** pouvez-vous me l'indiquer sur la carte?; **map out** vt tracer; (fig: task) planifier; (career, holiday) organiser, préparer (à l'avance); (: essay) faire le plan de

maple ['meɪpl] n érable m

mar [mɑ:ʳ] vt gâcher, gâter

marathon ['mærəθən] n marathon m ▷ adj: **a ~ session** une séance-marathon

marble ['mɑ:bl] n marbre m; (toy) bille f; **marbles** npl (game) billes

March [mɑ:tʃ] n mars m; see also **July**

march [mɑ:tʃ] vi marcher au pas; (demonstrators) défiler ▷ n marche f; (demonstration) manifestation f; **to ~ out of/ into** etc sortir de/entrer dans etc (de manière décidée ou impulsive)

mare [mɛəʳ] n jument f

margarine [mɑ:dʒə'ri:n] n margarine f

margin ['mɑ:dʒɪn] n marge f

marginal ['mɑ:dʒɪnl] adj marginal(e); **~ seat** (Pol) siège disputé

marginally ['mɑ:dʒɪnəlɪ] adv très légèrement, sensiblement

marigold ['mærɪgəuld] n souci m

marijuana [mærɪ'wɑ:nə] n marijuana f

marina [mə'ri:nə] n marina f

marinade n [mærɪ'neɪd] marinade f ▷ vt ['mærɪneɪd] = **marinate**

marinate ['mærɪneɪt] vt (faire) mariner

marine [mə'ri:n] adj marin(e) ▷ n fusilier marin; (US) marine m

marital ['mærɪtl] adj matrimonial(e)

marital status n situation f de famille

maritime ['mærɪtaɪm] adj maritime

marjoram ['mɑ:dʒərəm] n marjolaine f

mark [mɑːk] n marque f; (of skid etc) trace f; (Brit Scol) note f; (Sport) cible f; (currency) mark m; (Brit Tech): **M~ 2/3** 2ème/3ème série f or version f; (oven temperature): **(gas) ~ 4** thermostat m 4 ▷ vt (also Sport) marquer; (stain) tacher; (Brit Scol) corriger, noter; (also: **punctuation ~s**) signes mpl de ponctuation; **to ~ time** marquer le pas; **to be quick off the ~ (in doing)** (fig) ne pas perdre de temps (pour faire); **up to the ~** (in efficiency) à la hauteur; **mark down** vt (prices, goods) démarquer, réduire le prix de; **mark off** vt (tick off) cocher, pointer; **mark out** vt désigner; **mark up** vt (price) majorer

marked [mɑːkt] adj (obvious) marqué(e), net(te)

marker ['mɑːkəʳ] n (sign) jalon m; (bookmark) signet m

market ['mɑːkɪt] n marché m ▷ vt (Comm) commercialiser; **to be on the ~** être sur le marché; **on the open ~** en vente libre; **to play the ~** jouer à la or spéculer en Bourse

market garden n (Brit) jardin maraîcher

marketing ['mɑːkɪtɪŋ] n marketing m

marketplace ['mɑːkɪtpleɪs] n place f du marché; (Comm) marché m

market research n étude f de marché

marksman ['mɑːksmən] irreg n tireur m d'élite

marmalade ['mɑːməleɪd] n confiture f d'oranges

maroon [məˈruːn] vt: **to be ~ed** être abandonné(e); (fig) être bloqué(e) ▷ adj (colour) bordeaux inv

marquee [mɑːˈkiː] n chapiteau m

marriage ['mærɪdʒ] n mariage m

marriage certificate n extrait m d'acte de mariage

married ['mærɪd] adj marié(e); (life, love) conjugal(e)

marrow ['mærəu] n (of bone) moelle f; (vegetable) courge f

marry ['mærɪ] vt épouser, se marier avec; (subj: father, priest etc) marier ▷ vi (also: **get married**) se marier

Mars [mɑːz] n (planet) Mars f

Marseilles [mɑːˈseɪ] n Marseille

marsh [mɑːʃ] n marais m, marécage m

marshal ['mɑːʃl] n maréchal m; (US: fire, police) ≈ capitaine m; (for demonstration, meeting) membre m du service d'ordre ▷ vt rassembler

marshy ['mɑːʃɪ] adj marécageux(-euse)

martyr ['mɑːtəʳ] n martyr(e) ▷ vt martyriser

martyrdom ['mɑːtədəm] n martyre m

marvel ['mɑːvl] n merveille f ▷ vi: **to ~ (at)** s'émerveiller (de)

marvellous, (US) **marvelous** ['mɑːvləs] adj merveilleux(-euse)

Marxism ['mɑːksɪzəm] n marxisme m

Marxist ['mɑːksɪst] adj, n marxiste (m/f)

marzipan ['mɑːzɪpæn] n pâte f d'amandes

mascara [mæsˈkɑːrə] n mascara m

mascot ['mæskət] n mascotte f

masculine ['mæskjulɪn] adj masculin(e) ▷ n masculin m

mash [mæʃ] vt (Culin) faire une purée de

mashed potato n, **mashed potatoes** npl purée f de pommes de terre

mask [mɑːsk] n masque m ▷ vt masquer

mason ['meɪsn] n (also: **stone~**) maçon m; (also: **free~**) franc-maçon m

masonry ['meɪsnrɪ] n maçonnerie f

masquerade [mæskəˈreɪd] n bal masqué; (fig) mascarade f ▷ vi: **to ~ as** se faire passer pour

mass [mæs] n multitude f, masse f; (Physics) masse; (Rel) messe f ▷ cpd (communication) de masse; (unemployment) massif(-ive) ▷ vi se masser; **masses** npl: **the ~es** les masses; **~es of** (inf) des tas de; **to go to ~** aller à la messe

massacre ['mæsəkəʳ] n massacre m ▷ vt massacrer

massage ['mæsɑːʒ] n massage m ▷ vt masser

massive ['mæsɪv] adj énorme, massif(-ive)

mass media npl mass-media mpl

mass-produce ['mæsprəˈdjuːs] vt fabriquer en série

mass production n fabrication f en série

mast [mɑːst] n mât m; (Radio, TV) pylône m

master ['mɑːstəʳ] n maître m; (in secondary school) professeur m; (in primary school) instituteur m; (title for boys): **M~ X** Monsieur X ▷ vt maîtriser; (learn) apprendre à fond; (understand) posséder parfaitement or à fond; **~ of ceremonies (MC)** n maître des cérémonies; **M~ of Arts/Science (MA/MSc)** n ≈ titulaire m/f d'une maîtrise (en lettres/science); **M~ of Arts/Science degree (MA/MSc)** n ≈ maîtrise f

masterly ['mɑːstəlɪ] adj magistral(e)

mastermind ['mɑːstəmaɪnd] n esprit supérieur ▷ vt diriger, être le cerveau de

masterpiece ['mɑːstəpiːs] n chef-d'œuvre m

master plan n stratégie f d'ensemble

mastery ['mɑːstərɪ] n maîtrise f; connaissance parfaite

masturbate ['mæstəbeɪt] vi se masturber

mat [mæt] n petit tapis; (also: **door~**) paillasson m; (also: **table~**) set m de table ▷ adj = **matt**

match [mætʃ] n allumette f; (game) match m, partie f; (fig) égal(e); mariage m; parti m ▷ vt (also: **~ up**) assortir; (go well with) aller bien avec, s'assortir à; (equal) égaler, valoir ▷ vi être assorti(e); **to be a good ~** être bien assorti(e); **match up** vt assortir

matchbox ['mætʃbɔks] n boîte f d'allumettes

matching ['mætʃɪŋ] adj assorti(e)

mate [meɪt] n camarade m/f de travail; (inf) copain/copine; (animal) partenaire m/f, mâle/femelle; (in merchant navy) second m ▷ vi s'accoupler ▷ vt accoupler

material [məˈtɪərɪəl] n (substance) matière f, matériau m; (cloth) tissu m, étoffe f; (information, data) données fpl ▷ adj matériel(le); (*relevant: evidence*) pertinent(e); (*important*) essentiel(le); **materials** *npl* (*equipment*) matériaux *mpl*; **reading** ~ de quoi lire, de la lecture

materialize [mə'tɪərɪəlaɪz] *vi* se matérialiser, se réaliser

maternal [mə'təːnl] *adj* maternel(le)

maternity [mə'təːnɪtɪ] *n* maternité *f* ▷ *cpd* de maternité, de grossesse

maternity dress *n* robe *f* de grossesse

maternity hospital *n* maternité *f*

maternity leave *n* congé *m* de maternité

math [mæθ] *n* (*US*: = *mathematics*) maths *fpl*

mathematical [mæθə'mætɪkl] *adj* mathématique

mathematician [mæθəmə'tɪʃən] *n* mathématicien(ne)

mathematics [mæθə'mætɪks] *n* mathématiques *fpl*

maths [mæθs] *n abbr* (*Brit*: = *mathematics*) maths *fpl*

matinée ['mætɪneɪ] *n* matinée *f*

mating call *n* appel *m* du mâle

matrices ['meɪtrɪsiːz] *npl of* **matrix**

matriculation [mətrɪkju'leɪʃən] *n* inscription *f*

matrimonial [mætrɪ'məunɪəl] *adj* matrimonial(e), conjugal(e)

matrimony ['mætrɪmənɪ] *n* mariage *m*

matrix (*pl* **matrices**) ['meɪtrɪks, 'meɪtrɪsiːz] *n* matrice *f*

matron ['meɪtrən] *n* (*in hospital*) infirmière-chef *f*; (*in school*) infirmière *f*

matt [mæt] *adj* mat(e)

matted ['mætɪd] *adj* emmêlé(e)

matter ['mætə^r] *n* question *f*; (*Physics*) matière *f*, substance *f*; (*content*) contenu *m*, fond *m*; (*Med: pus*) pus *m* ▷ *vi* importer; **matters** *npl* (*affairs, situation*) la situation; **it doesn't** ~ cela n'a pas d'importance; (*I don't mind*) cela ne fait rien; **what's the ~?** qu'est-ce qu'il y a?, qu'est-ce qui ne va pas?; **no** ~ **what** quoi qu'il arrive; **that's another** ~ c'est une autre affaire; **as a** ~ **of course** tout naturellement; **as a** ~ **of fact** en fait; **it's a** ~ **of habit** c'est une question d'habitude; **printed** ~ imprimés *mpl*; **reading** ~ (*Brit*) de quoi lire, de la lecture

matter-of-fact ['mætərəv'fækt] *adj* terre à terre, neutre

mattress ['mætrɪs] *n* matelas *m*

mature [mə'tjuə^r] *adj* mûr(e); (*cheese*) fait(e); (*wine*) arrive(e) à maturité ▷ *vi* mûrir; (*cheese, wine*) se faire

mature student *n* étudiant(e) plus âgé(e) que la moyenne

maturity [mə'tjuərɪtɪ] *n* maturité *f*

maul [mɔːl] *vt* lacérer

mauve [məuv] *adj* mauve

max *abbr* = **maximum**

maximize ['mæksɪmaɪz] *vt* (*profits etc, chances*) maximiser

maximum ['mæksɪməm] (*pl* **maxima**) ['mæksɪmə] *adj* maximum ▷ *n* maximum *m*

May [meɪ] *n* mai *m*; *see also* **July**

may [meɪ] (*conditional* **might**) *vi* (*indicating possibility*): **he** ~ **come** il se peut qu'il vienne; (*be allowed to*): ~ **I smoke?** puis-je fumer?; (*wishes*): ~ **God bless you!** (que) Dieu vous bénisse!; ~ **I sit here?** vous permettez que je m'assoie ici?; **he might be there** il pourrait bien y être, il se pourrait qu'il y soit; **you** ~ **as well go** vous feriez aussi bien d'y aller; **I might as well go** je ferais aussi bien d'y aller, autant y aller; **you might like to try** vous pourriez (peut-être) essayer

maybe ['meɪbiː] *adv* peut-être; ~ **he'll** ... peut-être qu'il ...; ~ **not** peut-être pas

May Day *n* le Premier mai

mayday ['meɪdeɪ] *n* S.O.S *m*

mayhem ['meɪhem] *n* grabuge *m*

mayonnaise [meɪə'neɪz] *n* mayonnaise *f*

mayor [meə^r] *n* maire *m*

mayoress ['meəres] *n* (*female mayor*) maire *m*; (*wife of mayor*) épouse *f* du maire

maze [meɪz] *n* labyrinthe *m*, dédale *m*

MD *n abbr* (= *Doctor of Medicine*) titre universitaire; (*Comm*) = **managing director**

me [miː] *pron* me, m' + *vowel or h mute*; (*stressed, after prep*) moi; **it's me** c'est moi; **he heard me** il m'a entendu; **give me a book** donnez-moi un livre; **it's for me** c'est pour moi

meadow ['medəu] *n* prairie *f*, pré *m*

meagre, (*US*) **meager** ['miːgə^r] *adj* maigre

meal [miːl] *n* repas *m*; (*flour*) farine *f*; **to go out for a** ~ sortir manger

mealtime ['miːltaɪm] *n* heure *f* du repas

mean [miːn] *adj* (*with money*) avare, radin(e); (*unkind*) mesquin(e), méchant(e); (*shabby*) misérable; (*US inf: animal*) méchant, vicieux(-euse); (: *person*) vache; (*average*) moyen(ne) ▷ *vt* (*pt, pp* **meant**) [ment] (*signify*) signifier, vouloir dire; (*refer to*) faire allusion à, parler de; (*intend*): **to** ~ **to do** avoir l'intention de faire ▷ *n* moyenne *f*; **means** *npl* (*way, money*) moyens *mpl*; **by** ~**s of** (*instrument*) au moyen de; **by all** ~**s** je vous en prie; **to be** ~**t for** être destiné(e) à; **do you** ~ **it?** vous êtes sérieux?; **what do you** ~? que voulez-vous dire?

meander [mɪ'ændə^r] *vi* faire des méandres; (*fig*) flâner

meaning ['miːnɪŋ] *n* signification *f*, sens *m*

meaningful ['miːnɪŋful] *adj* significatif(-ive); (*relationship*) valable

meaningless ['miːnɪŋlɪs] *adj* dénué(e) de sens

meanness ['miːnnɪs] *n* avarice *f*; mesquinerie *f*

meant [ment] *pt, pp of* **mean**

meantime ['miːntaɪm] *adv* (*also*: **in the** ~) pendant ce temps

meanwhile ['miːnwaɪl] *adv* = **meantime**

measles ['miːzlz] *n* rougeole *f*

measure ['mɛʒər] vt, vi mesurer ▷ n mesure f; (ruler) règle (graduée); **a litre ~** un litre; **some ~ of success** un certain succès; **to take ~s to do sth** prendre des mesures pour faire qch; **measure up** vi: **to ~ up (to)** être à la hauteur (de)

measurements ['mɛʒəməntz] npl mesures fpl; **chest/hip ~** tour m de poitrine/hanches; **to take sb's ~** prendre les mesures de qn

meat [miːt] n viande f; **I don't eat ~** je ne mange pas de viande; **cold ~s** (Brit) viandes froides; **crab ~** crabe f

meatball ['miːtbɔːl] n boulette f de viande

Mecca ['mɛkə] n la Mecque; (fig): **a ~ (for)** la Mecque (de)

mechanic [mɪ'kænɪk] n mécanicien m; **can you send a ~?** pouvez-vous nous envoyer un mécanicien?

mechanical [mɪ'kænɪkl] adj mécanique

mechanics [mə'kænɪks] n mécanique f ▷ npl mécanisme m

mechanism ['mɛkənɪzəm] n mécanisme m

medal ['mɛdl] n médaille f

medallion [mɪ'dælɪən] n médaillon m

medallist, (US) **medalist** ['mɛdlɪst] n (Sport) médaillé(e)

meddle ['mɛdl] vi: **to ~ in** se mêler de, s'occuper de; **to ~ with** toucher à

media ['miːdɪə] npl media mpl ▷ npl of **medium**

mediaeval [mɛdɪ'iːvl] adj = medieval

median ['miːdɪən] n (US: also: **~ strip**) bande médiane

mediate ['miːdɪeɪt] vi servir d'intermédiaire

Medicaid ['mɛdɪkeɪd] n (US) assistance médicale aux indigents

medical ['mɛdɪkl] adj médical(e) ▷ n (also: **~ examination**) visite médicale; (private) examen médical

medical certificate n certificat médical

Medicare ['mɛdɪkɛər] n (US) régime d'assurance maladie

medicated ['mɛdɪkeɪtɪd] adj traitant(e), médicamenteux(-euse)

medication [mɛdɪ'keɪʃən] n (drugs etc) médication f

medicine ['mɛdsɪn] n médecine f; (drug) médicament m

medieval [mɛdɪ'iːvl] adj médiéval(e)

mediocre [miːdɪ'əukər] adj médiocre

meditate ['mɛdɪteɪt] vi: **to ~ (on)** méditer (sur)

meditation [mɛdɪ'teɪʃən] n méditation f

Mediterranean [mɛdɪtə'reɪnɪən] adj méditerranéen(ne); **the ~ (Sea)** la (mer) Méditerranée

medium ['miːdɪəm] adj moyen(ne) ▷ n (pl **media**) (means) moyen m; (pl **mediums**) (person) médium m; **the happy ~** le juste milieu

medium-sized ['miːdɪəm'saɪzd] adj de taille moyenne

medium wave n (Radio) ondes moyennes, petites ondes

medley ['mɛdlɪ] n mélange m

meek [miːk] adj doux/douce, humble

meet (pt, pp **met**) [miːt, mɛt] vt rencontrer; (by arrangement) retrouver, rejoindre; (for the first time) faire la connaissance de; (go and fetch): **I'll ~ you at the station** j'irai te chercher à la gare; (opponent, danger, problem) faire face à; (requirements) satisfaire à, répondre à; (bill, expenses) régler, honorer ▷ vi (friends) se rencontrer; se retrouver; (in session) se réunir; (join: lines, roads) se joindre ▷ n (Brit Hunting) rendez-vous m de chasse; (US Sport) rencontre f, meeting m; **pleased to ~ you!** enchanté!; **nice ~ing you** ravi d'avoir fait votre connaissance; **meet up** vi: **to ~ up with sb** rencontrer qn; (become friends) (difficulty) rencontrer; **to ~ with success** être couronné(e) de succès

meeting ['miːtɪŋ] n (of group of people) réunion f; (between individuals) rendez-vous m; (formal) assemblée f; (Sport: rally) rencontre, meeting m; (interview) entrevue f; **she's at** or **in a ~** (Comm) elle est en réunion; **to call a ~** convoquer une réunion

meeting place n lieu m de (la) réunion; (for appointment) lieu de rendez-vous

mega ['mɛgə] (inf) adv: **he's ~ rich** il est hyper-riche

megabyte ['mɛgəbaɪt] n (Comput) méga-octet m

megaphone ['mɛgəfəun] n porte-voix m inv

megapixel ['mɛgəpɪksl] n mégapixel m

meh [mɛ] excl bof

melancholy ['mɛlənkəlɪ] n mélancolie f ▷ adj mélancolique

mellow ['mɛləu] adj velouté(e), doux/douce; (colour) riche et profond(e); (fruit) mûr(e) ▷ vi (person) s'adoucir

melody ['mɛlədɪ] n mélodie f

melon ['mɛlən] n melon m

melt [mɛlt] vi fondre; (become soft) s'amollir; (fig) s'attendrir ▷ vt faire fondre; **melt away** vi fondre complètement; **melt down** vt fondre

meltdown ['mɛltdaun] n fusion f (du cœur d'un réacteur nucléaire)

melting pot ['mɛltɪŋ-] n (fig) creuset m; **to be in the ~** être encore en discussion

member ['mɛmbər] n membre m; (of club, political party) membre, adhérent(e) ▷ cpd: **~ country/state** n pays m/état m membre

membership ['mɛmbəʃɪp] n (becoming a member) adhésion f; admission f; (being a member) qualité f de membre, fait m d'être membre; (members) membres mpl, adhérents mpl; (number of members) nombre m des membres ou adhérents

membership card n carte f de membre

memento [mə'mɛntəu] n souvenir m

memo ['mɛməu] n note f (de service)

memoir ['mɛmwɑːʳ] n mémoire m, étude f;
memoirs npl mémoires

memorable ['mɛmərəbl] adj mémorable

memorandum (pl **memoranda**)
[mɛmə'rændəm, -də] n note f (de service);
(Diplomacy) mémorandum m

memorial [mɪ'mɔːrɪəl] n mémorial m ▷ adj
commémoratif(-ive)

memorize ['mɛməraɪz] vt apprendre or
retenir par cœur

memory ['mɛmərɪ] n (also Comput) mémoire f;
(recollection) souvenir m; **to have a good/bad ~**
avoir une bonne/mauvaise mémoire; **loss of**
~ perte f de mémoire; **in ~ of** à la mémoire de

memory card n (for digital camera) carte f
mémoire

memory stick n (Comput: flash pen) clé f USB;
(: card) carte f mémoire

men [mɛn] npl of **man**

menace ['mɛnɪs] n menace f; (inf: nuisance)
peste f, plaie f ▷ vt menacer; **a public ~** un
danger public

menacing ['mɛnɪsɪŋ] adj menaçant(e)

mend [mɛnd] vt réparer; (darn)
raccommoder, repriser ▷ n reprise f; **on the ~**
en voie de guérison; **to ~ one's ways**
s'amender

mending ['mɛndɪŋ] n raccommodages mpl

menial ['miːnɪəl] adj de domestique,
inférieur(e); subalterne

meningitis [mɛnɪn'dʒaɪtɪs] n méningite f

menopause ['mɛnəupɔːz] n ménopause f

men's room (US) n: **the ~** les toilettes fpl pour
hommes

menstruation [mɛnstru'eɪʃən] n
menstruation f

menswear ['mɛnzwɛəʳ] n vêtements mpl
d'hommes

mental ['mɛntl] adj mental(e); **~ illness**
maladie mentale

mental hospital n hôpital m psychiatrique

mentality [mɛn'tælɪtɪ] n mentalité f

mentally ['mɛntlɪ] adv: **to be ~ handicapped**
(pej) être handicapé(e) mental(e); **~ ill people**
les malades mentaux

menthol ['mɛnθɔl] n menthol m

mention ['mɛnʃən] n mention f ▷ vt
mentionner, faire mention de; **don't ~ it!**
je vous en prie, il n'y a pas de quoi!; **I need**
hardly ~ that ... est-il besoin de rappeler
que ...?; **not to ~ ..., without ~ing ...** sans
parler de ..., sans compter ...

menu ['mɛnjuː] n (set menu, Comput) menu m;
(list of dishes) carte f; **could we see the ~?**
est-ce qu'on peut voir la carte?

MEP n abbr = **Member of the European**
Parliament

mercenary ['məːsɪnərɪ] adj (person)
intéressé(e), mercenaire ▷ n mercenaire m

merchandise ['məːtʃəndaɪz] n
marchandises fpl ▷ vt commercialiser

merchant ['məːtʃənt] n négociant m,
marchand m; **timber/wine ~** négociant en
bois/vins, marchand de bois/vins

merchant bank n (Brit) banque f d'affaires

merchant navy, (US) **merchant marine** n
marine marchande

merciful ['məːsɪful] adj
miséricordieux(-euse), clément(e)

merciless ['məːsɪlɪs] adj impitoyable, sans
pitié

mercury ['məːkjurɪ] n mercure m

mercy ['məːsɪ] n pitié f, merci f; (Rel)
miséricorde f; **to have ~ on sb** avoir pitié de
qn; **at the ~ of** à la merci de

mere [mɪəʳ] adj simple; (chance) pur(e); **a ~**
two hours seulement deux heures

merely ['mɪəlɪ] adv simplement, purement

merge [məːdʒ] vt unir; (Comput) fusionner,
interclasser ▷ vi (colours, shapes, sounds) se
mêler; (roads) se joindre; (Comm) fusionner

merger ['məːdʒəʳ] n (Comm) fusion f

meringue [mə'ræŋ] n meringue f

merit ['mɛrɪt] n mérite m, valeur f ▷ vt
mériter

mermaid ['məːmeɪd] n sirène f

merry ['mɛrɪ] adj gai(e); **M~ Christmas!**
joyeux Noël!

merry-go-round ['mɛrɪgəuraund] n
manège m

mesh [mɛʃ] n mailles fpl ▷ vi (gears)
s'engrener; **wire ~** grillage m (métallique),
treillis m (métallique)

mesmerize ['mɛzməraɪz] vt hypnotiser;
fasciner

mess [mɛs] n désordre m, fouillis m, pagaille f;
(muddle: of life) gâchis m; (: of economy) pagaille f;
(dirt) saleté f; (Mil) mess m, cantine f; **to be**
(in) a ~ être en désordre; **to be/get o.s. in a ~**
(fig) être/se mettre dans le pétrin; **mess**
about or **around** (inf) vi perdre son temps;
mess about or **around with** vt fus (inf)
chambarder, tripoter; **mess up** vt (dirty)
salir; (spoil) gâcher; **mess with** (inf) vt fus
(challenge, confront) se frotter à; (interfere with)
toucher à

message ['mɛsɪdʒ] n message m; **can I leave**
a ~? est-ce que je peux laisser un message?;
are there any ~s for me? est-ce que j'ai des
messages?; **to get the ~** (fig: inf) saisir, piger

messenger ['mɛsɪndʒəʳ] n messager m

Messrs, Messrs. ['mɛsəz] abbr (on letters:
= messieurs) MM

messy ['mɛsɪ] adj (dirty) sale; (untidy) en
désordre

met [mɛt] pt, pp of **meet** ▷ adj abbr
(= meteorological) météo-inv

metabolism [mɛ'tæbəlɪzəm] n
métabolisme m

metal ['mɛtl] n métal m ▷ cpd en métal ▷ vt
empierrer

metallic [mɛ'tælɪk] adj métallique

metaphor ['mɛtəfəʳ] n métaphore f

meteor ['miːtɪəʳ] n météore m

meteorite ['miːtɪəraɪt] n météorite m or f

meteorology [miːtɪə'rɔlədʒɪ] n météorologie f

meter ['miːtər] n (instrument) compteur m; (also: **parking ~**) parc(o)mètre m; (US: unit) = **metre** ▷ vt (US Post) affranchir à la machine

method ['mɛθəd] n méthode f; **~ of payment** mode m or modalité f de paiement

methodical [mɪ'θɔdɪkl] adj méthodique

Methodist ['mɛθədɪst] adj, n méthodiste (m/f)

methylated spirit ['mɛθɪleɪtɪd-] n (Brit: also: **meths**) alcool m à brûler

meticulous [mɛ'tɪkjuləs] adj méticuleux(-euse)

metre, (US) **meter** ['miːtər] n mètre m

metric ['mɛtrɪk] adj métrique; **to go ~** adopter le système métrique

metro ['mɛtrəu] n métro m

metropolitan [mɛtrə'pɔlɪtən] adj métropolitain(e); **the M~ Police** (Brit) la police londonienne

mettle ['mɛtl] n courage m

mew [mjuː] vi (cat) miauler

mews [mjuːz] n (Brit): **~ cottage** maisonnette aménagée dans une ancienne écurie ou remise

Mexican ['mɛksɪkən] adj mexicain(e) ▷ n Mexicain(e)

Mexico ['mɛksɪkəu] n Mexique m

mg abbr (= milligram) mg

miaow [miː'au] vi miauler

mice [maɪs] npl of **mouse**

micro ['maɪkrəu] n (also: **~computer**) micro(-ordinateur m) m

micro... [maɪkrəu] prefix micro...

microchip ['maɪkrəutʃɪp] n (Elec) puce f

microcomputer ['maɪkrəukəm'pjuːtər] n micro-ordinateur m

microphone ['maɪkrəfəun] n microphone m

microscope ['maɪkrəskəup] n microscope m; **under the ~** au microscope

mid [mɪd] adj: **~ May** la mi-mai; **~ afternoon** le milieu de l'après-midi; **in ~ air** en plein ciel; **he's in his ~ thirties** il a dans les trente-cinq ans

midday [mɪd'deɪ] n midi m

middle ['mɪdl] n milieu m; (waist) ceinture f, taille f ▷ adj du milieu; (average) moyen(ne); **in the ~ of the night** au milieu de la nuit; **I'm in the ~ of reading it** je suis (justement) en train de le lire

middle-aged [mɪdl'eɪdʒd] adj d'un certain âge, ni vieux ni jeune; (pej: values, outlook) conventionnel(le), rassis(e)

Middle Ages npl: **the ~** le moyen âge

middle-class [mɪdl'klɑːs] adj bourgeois(e)

middle class n, **middle classes** npl: **the ~(es)** ≈ les classes moyennes

Middle East n: **the ~** le Proche-Orient, le Moyen-Orient

middleman ['mɪdlmæn] irreg n intermédiaire m

middle name n second prénom

middle-of-the-road ['mɪdləvðə'rəud] adj (policy) modéré(e), du juste milieu; (music etc) plutôt classique, assez traditionnel(le)

middle school n (US) école pour les enfants de 12 à 14 ans, ≈ collège m; (Brit) école pour les enfants de 8 à 14 ans

middleweight ['mɪdlweɪt] n (Boxing) poids moyen

middling ['mɪdlɪŋ] adj moyen(ne)

midge [mɪdʒ] n moucheron m

midget ['mɪdʒɪt] n (pej) nain(e) ▷ adj minuscule

Midlands ['mɪdləndz] npl comtés du centre de l'Angleterre

midnight ['mɪdnaɪt] n minuit m; **at ~** à minuit

midriff ['mɪdrɪf] n estomac m, taille f

midst [mɪdst] n: **in the ~ of** au milieu de

midsummer [mɪd'sʌmər] n milieu m de l'été

midway [mɪd'weɪ] adj, adv: **~ (between)** à mi-chemin (entre); **~ through ...** au milieu de ..., en plein(e) ...

midweek [mɪd'wiːk] adj du milieu de la semaine ▷ adv au milieu de la semaine, en pleine semaine

midwife (pl **midwives**) ['mɪdwaɪf, -vz] n sage-femme f

midwinter [mɪd'wɪntər] n milieu m de l'hiver

might [maɪt] vb see **may** ▷ n puissance f, force f

mighty ['maɪtɪ] adj puissant(e) ▷ adv (inf) rudement

migraine ['miːgreɪn] n migraine f

migrant ['maɪgrənt] n (bird, animal) migrateur m; (person) migrant(e); nomade m/f ▷ adj migrateur(-trice); migrant(e); nomade; (worker) saisonnier(-ière)

migrate [maɪ'greɪt] vi migrer

migration [maɪ'greɪʃən] n migration f

mike [maɪk] n abbr (= microphone) micro m

mild [maɪld] adj doux/douce; (reproach, infection) léger(-ère); (illness) bénin(-igne); (interest) modéré(e); (taste) peu relevé(e) ▷ n bière légère

mildly ['maɪldlɪ] adv doucement; légèrement; **to put it ~** (inf) c'est le moins qu'on puisse dire

mile [maɪl] n mil(l)e m (= 1609 m); **to do 30 ~s per gallon** ≈ faire 9, 4 litres aux cent

mileage ['maɪlɪdʒ] n distance f en milles, ≈ kilométrage m

mileometer [maɪ'lɔmɪtər] n compteur m kilométrique

milestone ['maɪlstəun] n borne f; (fig) jalon m

militant ['mɪlɪtnt] adj, n militant(e)

military ['mɪlɪtərɪ] adj militaire ▷ n: **the ~** l'armée f, les militaires mpl

militia [mɪ'lɪʃə] n milice f

milk [mɪlk] n lait m ▷ vt (cow) traire; (fig: person) dépouiller, plumer; (: situation) exploiter à fond

milk chocolate n chocolat m au lait
milkman ['mɪlkmən] irreg n laitier m
milk shake n milk-shake m
milky ['mɪlkɪ] adj (drink) au lait; (colour) laiteux(-euse)
Milky Way n Voie lactée
mill [mɪl] n moulin m; (factory) usine f, fabrique f; (spinning mill) filature f; (flour mill) minoterie f; (steel mill) aciérie f ▷ vt moudre, broyer ▷ vi (also: ~ about) grouiller
millennium (pl **millenniums** or **millennia**) [mɪˈlenɪəm, -ˈlenɪə] n millénaire m
millennium bug n bogue m or bug m de l'an 2000
miller ['mɪlər] n meunier m
milli... ['mɪlɪ] prefix milli...
milligram, milligramme ['mɪlɪgræm] n milligramme m
millilitre, (US) **milliliter** ['mɪlɪliːtər] n millilitre m
millimetre, (US) **millimeter** ['mɪlɪmiːtər] n millimètre m
million ['mɪljən] n million m; **a ~ pounds** un million de livres sterling
millionaire [mɪljəˈnɛər] n millionnaire m
millionth [ˈmɪljənθ] num millionième
milometer [maɪˈlɒmɪtər] n = **mileometer**
mime [maɪm] n mime m ▷ vt, vi mimer
mimic ['mɪmɪk] n imitateur(-trice) ▷ vt, vi imiter, contrefaire
min. abbr (= minute(s)) mn.; (= minimum) min.
mince [mɪns] vt hacher ▷ vi (in walking) marcher à petits pas maniérés ▷ n (Brit Culin) viande hachée, hachis m; **he does not ~ (his) words** il ne mâche pas ses mots
mincemeat ['mɪnsmiːt] n hachis de fruits secs utilisés en pâtisserie; (US) viande hachée, hachis m
mince pie n sorte de tarte aux fruits secs
mincer ['mɪnsər] n hachoir m
mind [maɪnd] n esprit m ▷ vt (attend to, look after) s'occuper de; (be careful) faire attention à; (object to): **I don't ~ the noise** je ne crains pas le bruit, le bruit ne me dérange pas; **it is on my ~** cela me préoccupe; **to change one's ~** changer d'avis; **to be in two ~s about sth** (Brit) être indécis(e) or irrésolu(e) en ce qui concerne qch; **to my ~** à mon avis, selon moi; **to be out of one's ~** ne plus avoir toute sa raison; **to keep sth in ~** ne pas oublier qch; **to bear sth in ~** tenir compte de qch; **to have sb/sth in ~** avoir qn/qch en tête; **to have in ~ to do** avoir l'intention de faire; **it went right out of my ~** ça m'est complètement sorti de la tête; **to bring** or **call sth to ~** se rappeler qch; **to make up one's ~** se décider; **do you ~ if ...?** est-ce que cela vous gêne si ...?; **I don't ~** cela ne me dérange pas; (don't care) ça m'est égal; **~ you, ...** remarquez, ...; **never ~** ça ne fait rien; (don't worry) ne vous en faîtes pas; **"~ the step"** "attention à la marche"

minder ['maɪndər] n (child minder) gardienne f; (bodyguard) ange gardien (fig)
mindful ['maɪndful] adj: **~ of** attentif(-ive), soucieux(-euse) de
mindless ['maɪndlɪs] adj irréfléchi(e); (violence, crime) insensé(e); (boring: job) idiot(e)
mine¹ [maɪn] pron le/la mien(ne), les miens/miennes; **a friend of ~** un de mes amis, un ami à moi; **this book is ~** ce livre est à moi
mine² [maɪn] n mine f ▷ vt (coal) extraire; (ship, beach) miner
minefield ['maɪnfiːld] n champ m de mines
miner ['maɪnər] n mineur m
mineral ['mɪnərəl] adj minéral(e) ▷ n minéral m; **minerals** npl (Brit: soft drinks) boissons gazeuses (sucrées)
mineral water n eau minérale
mingle ['mɪŋgl] vt mêler, mélanger ▷ vi: **to ~ with** se mêler à
miniature ['mɪnətʃər] adj (en) miniature ▷ n miniature f
minibar ['mɪnɪbɑːr] n minibar m
minibus ['mɪnɪbʌs] n minibus m
minicab ['mɪnɪkæb] n (Brit) taxi m indépendant
minimal ['mɪnɪml] adj minimal(e)
minimize ['mɪnɪmaɪz] vt (reduce) réduire au minimum; (play down) minimiser
minimum ['mɪnɪməm] n (pl **minima** ['mɪnɪmə]) minimum m ▷ adj minimum; **to reduce to a ~** réduire au minimum
mining ['maɪnɪŋ] n exploitation minière ▷ adj minier(-ière); de mineurs
miniskirt ['mɪnɪskəːt] n mini-jupe f
minister ['mɪnɪstər] n (Brit Pol) ministre m; (Rel) pasteur m ▷ vi: **to ~ to sb** donner ses soins à qn; **to ~ to sb's needs** pourvoir aux besoins de qn
ministerial [mɪnɪsˈtɪərɪəl] adj (Brit Pol) ministériel(le)
ministry ['mɪnɪstrɪ] n (Brit Pol) ministère m; (Rel): **to go into the ~** devenir pasteur
mink [mɪŋk] n vison m
minor ['maɪnər] adj petit(e), de peu d'importance; (Mus, poet, problem) mineur(e) ▷ n (Law) mineur(e)
minority [maɪˈnɒrɪtɪ] n minorité f; **to be in a ~** être en minorité
mint [mɪnt] n (plant) menthe f; (sweet) bonbon m à la menthe ▷ vt (coins) battre; **the (Royal) M~, the (US) M~** ≈ l'hôtel m de la Monnaie; **in ~ condition** à l'état de neuf
minus ['maɪnəs] n (also: **~ sign**) signe m moins ▷ prep moins; **12 ~ 6 equals 6** 12 moins 6 égal 6; **~ 24°C** moins 24°C
minute¹ n ['mɪnɪt] minute f; (official record) procès-verbal m, compte rendu; **minutes** npl (of meeting) procès-verbal m, compte rendu; **it is 5 ~s past 3** il est 3 heures 5; **wait a ~!** (attendez) un instant!; **at the last ~** à la dernière minute; **up to the ~** (fashion) dernier cri; (news) de dernière minute; (machine, technology) de pointe

minute² adj [maɪ'njuːt] minuscule; (detailed) minutieux(-euse); **in ~ detail** par le menu
miracle ['mɪrəkl] n miracle m
miraculous [mɪ'rækjʊləs] adj miraculeux(-euse)
mirage ['mɪrɑːʒ] n mirage m
mirror ['mɪrə'] n miroir m, glace f; (in car) rétroviseur m ▷ vt refléter
mirth [mɜːθ] n gaieté f
misadventure [mɪsəd'ventʃə'] n mésaventure f; **death by ~** (Brit) décès accidentel
misapprehension ['mɪsæprɪ'henʃən] n malentendu m, méprise f
misappropriate [mɪsə'prəʊprɪeɪt] vt détourner
misbehave [mɪsbɪ'heɪv] vi mal se conduire
misc. abbr = **miscellaneous**
miscalculate [mɪs'kælkjʊleɪt] vt mal calculer
miscarriage ['mɪskærɪdʒ] n (Med) fausse couche; **~ of justice** erreur f judiciaire
miscellaneous [mɪsɪ'leɪnɪəs] adj (items, expenses) divers(es); (selection) varié(e)
mischief ['mɪstʃɪf] n (naughtiness) sottises fpl; (fun) farce f; (playfulness) espièglerie f; (harm) mal m, dommage m; (maliciousness) méchanceté f
mischievous ['mɪstʃɪvəs] adj (playful, naughty) coquin(e), espiègle; (harmful) méchant(e)
misconception ['mɪskən'sepʃən] n idée fausse
misconduct [mɪs'kɒndʌkt] n inconduite f; **professional ~** faute professionnelle
misdemeanour, (US) **misdemeanor** [mɪsdɪ'miːnə'] n écart m de conduite; infraction f
miser ['maɪzə'] n avare m/f
miserable ['mɪzərəbl] adj (person, expression) malheureux(-euse); (conditions) misérable; (weather) maussade; (offer, donation) minable; (failure) pitoyable; **to feel ~** avoir le cafard
miserly ['maɪzəlɪ] adj avare
misery ['mɪzərɪ] n (unhappiness) tristesse f; (pain) souffrances fpl; (wretchedness) misère f
misfire [mɪs'faɪə'] vi rater; (car engine) avoir des ratés
misfit ['mɪsfɪt] n (person) inadapté(e)
misfortune [mɪs'fɔːtʃən] n malchance f, malheur m
misgiving [mɪs'gɪvɪŋ] n (apprehension) craintes fpl; **to have ~s about sth** avoir des doutes quant à qch
misguided [mɪs'gaɪdɪd] adj malavisé(e)
mishandle [mɪs'hændl] vt (treat roughly) malmener; (mismanage) mal s'y prendre pour faire or résoudre etc
mishap ['mɪshæp] n mésaventure f
misinform [mɪsɪn'fɔːm] vt mal renseigner
misinterpret [mɪsɪn'tə:prɪt] vt mal interpréter
misjudge [mɪs'dʒʌdʒ] vt méjuger, se méprendre sur le compte de

mislay [mɪs'leɪ] vt (irreg like: **lay**) égarer
mislead [mɪs'liːd] vt (irreg like: **lead**) induire en erreur
misleading [mɪs'liːdɪŋ] adj trompeur(-euse)
mismanage [mɪs'mænɪdʒ] vt mal gérer; mal s'y prendre pour faire or résoudre etc
misplace [mɪs'pleɪs] vt égarer; **to be ~d** (trust etc) être mal placé(e)
misprint ['mɪsprɪnt] n faute f d'impression
misrepresent [mɪsreprɪ'zent] vt présenter sous un faux jour
Miss [mɪs] n Mademoiselle; **Dear ~ Smith** Chère Mademoiselle Smith
miss [mɪs] vt (fail to get, attend, see) manquer, rater; (appointment, class) manquer; (escape, avoid) échapper à, éviter; (notice loss of: money etc) s'apercevoir de l'absence de; (regret the absence of): **I ~ him/it** il/cela me manque ▷ vi manquer ▷ n (shot) coup manqué; **we ~ed our train** nous avons raté notre train; **the bus just ~ed the wall** le bus a évité le mur de justesse; **you're ~ing the point** vous êtes à côté de la question; **you can't ~ it** vous ne pouvez pas vous tromper; **miss out** vt (Brit) oublier; **miss out on** vt fus (fun, party) rater, manquer; (chance, bargain) laisser passer
misshapen [mɪs'ʃeɪpən] adj difforme
missile ['mɪsaɪl] n (Aviat) missile m; (object thrown) projectile m
missing ['mɪsɪŋ] adj manquant(e); (after escape, disaster: person) disparu(e); **to go ~** disparaître; **~ person** personne disparue, disparu(e); **~ in action** (Mil) porté(e) disparu(e)
mission ['mɪʃən] n mission f; **on a ~ to sb** en mission auprès de qn
missionary ['mɪʃənrɪ] n missionnaire m/f
mission statement n déclaration f d'intention
misspell ['mɪs'spel] vt (irreg like: **spell**) mal orthographier
mist [mɪst] n brume f ▷ vi (also: **~ over**, **~ up**) devenir brumeux(-euse); (Brit: windows) s'embuer
mistake [mɪs'teɪk] n erreur f, faute f ▷ vt (irreg like: **take**) (meaning) mal comprendre; (intentions) se méprendre sur; **to ~ for** prendre pour; **by ~** par erreur, par inadvertance; **to make a ~** (in writing) faire une faute; (in calculating etc) faire une erreur; **there must be some ~** il doit y avoir une erreur, se tromper; **to make a ~ about sb/sth** se tromper sur le compte de qn/sur qch
mistaken [mɪs'teɪkən] pp of **mistake** ▷ adj (idea etc) erroné(e); **to be ~** faire erreur, se tromper
mister ['mɪstə'] n (inf) Monsieur m; see **Mr**
mistletoe ['mɪsltəʊ] n gui m
mistook [mɪs'tʊk] pt of **mistake**
mistress ['mɪstrɪs] n maîtresse f; (Brit: in primary school) institutrice f; (: in secondary school) professeur m

mistrust [mɪs'trʌst] vt se méfier de ▷ n:
~ **(of)** méfiance f (à l'égard de)

misty ['mɪstɪ] adj brumeux(-euse); (glasses,
window) embué(e)

misunderstand [mɪsʌndə'stænd] vt, vi (irreg
like: **stand**) mal comprendre

misunderstanding ['mɪsʌndə'stændɪŋ] n
méprise f, malentendu m; **there's been a** ~
il y a eu un malentendu

misunderstood [mɪsʌndə'stud] pt, pp of
misunderstand ▷ adj (person) incompris(e)

misuse n [mɪs'ju:s] mauvais emploi; (of
power) abus m ▷ vt [mɪs'ju:z] mal employer;
abuser de

mitigate ['mɪtɪɡeɪt] vt atténuer; **mitigating
circumstances** circonstances atténuantes

mitt ['mɪt], **mitten** ['mɪtn] n moufle f;
(fingerless) mitaine f

mix [mɪks] vt mélanger; (sauce, drink etc)
préparer ▷ vi se mélanger; (socialize): **he
doesn't ~ well** il est peu sociable ▷ n
mélange m; **to ~ sth with sth** mélanger qch
à qch; **to ~ business with pleasure** unir
l'utile à l'agréable; **cake ~** préparation f pour
gâteau; **mix in** vt incorporer, mélanger; **mix
up** vt mélanger; (confuse) confondre; **to be
~ed up in sth** être mêlé(e) à qch or
impliqué(e) dans qch

mixed [mɪkst] adj (feelings, reactions)
contradictoire; (school, marriage) mixte

mixed grill n (Brit) assortiment m de grillades

mixed salad n salade f de crudités

mixed-up [mɪkst'ʌp] adj (person)
désorienté(e), embrouillé(e)

mixer ['mɪksər] n (for food) batteur m, mixeur
m; (drink) boisson gazeuse (servant à couper un
alcool); (person): **he is a good** ~ il est très
sociable

mixture ['mɪkstʃər] n assortiment m,
mélange m; (Med) préparation f

mix-up ['mɪksʌp] n: **there was a** ~ il y a eu
confusion

ml abbr (= millilitre(s)) ml

mm abbr (= millimetre) mm

moan [məun] n gémissement m ▷ vi gémir;
(inf: complain): **to ~ (about)** se plaindre (de)

moat [məut] n fossé m, douves fpl

mob [mɔb] n foule f; (disorderly) cohue f; (pej):
the ~ la populace ▷ vt assaillir

mobile ['məubaɪl] adj mobile ▷ n (Art) mobile
m; (Brit inf: mobile phone) (téléphone m)
portable m, mobile m; **applicants must be ~**
(Brit) les candidats devront être prêts à
accepter tout déplacement

mobile home n caravane f

mobile phone n (téléphone m) portable m,
mobile m

mobility [məu'bɪlɪtɪ] n mobilité f

mobilize ['məubɪlaɪz] vt, vi mobiliser

mock [mɔk] vt ridiculiser; (laugh at) se
moquer de ▷ adj faux/fausse; **mocks** npl
(Brit: Scol) examens blancs

mockery ['mɔkərɪ] n moquerie f, raillerie f;
to make a ~ of ridiculiser, tourner en
dérision

mock-up ['mɔkʌp] n maquette f

mod [mɔd] adj see **convenience**

mod cons ['mɔd'kɔnz] npl abbr (Brit) = **modern
conveniences**; see **convenience**

mode [məud] n mode m; (of transport)
moyen m

model ['mɔdl] n modèle m; (person: for fashion)
mannequin m; (: for artist) modèle ▷ vt (with
clay etc) modeler ▷ vi travailler comme
mannequin ▷ adj (railway: toy) modèle réduit
inv; (child, factory) modèle; **to ~ clothes**
présenter des vêtements; **to ~ o.s. on** imiter;
to ~ sb/sth on modeler qn/qch sur

modem ['məudɛm] n modem m

moderate [adj [n 'mɔdərət, vb 'mɔdəreɪt] adj
modéré(e); (amount, change) peu important(e)
▷ n (Pol) modéré(e) ▷ vi se modérer, se calmer
▷ vt modérer

moderation [mɔdə'reɪʃən] n modération f,
mesure f; **in** ~ à dose raisonnable, pris(e) or
pratiqué(e) modérément

modern ['mɔdən] adj moderne

modernize ['mɔdənaɪz] vt moderniser

modern languages npl langues vivantes

modest ['mɔdɪst] adj modeste

modesty ['mɔdɪstɪ] n modestie f

modification [mɔdɪfɪ'keɪʃən] n modification
f; **to make ~s** faire or apporter des
modifications

modify ['mɔdɪfaɪ] vt modifier

module ['mɔdju:l] n module m

mogul ['məuɡl] n (fig) nabab m; (Ski) bosse f

mohair ['məuhɛər] n mohair m

Mohammed [mə'hæmɛd] n Mahomet m

moist [mɔɪst] adj humide, moite

moisten ['mɔɪsn] vt humecter, mouiller
légèrement

moisture ['mɔɪstʃər] n humidité f; (on glass)
buée f

moisturizer ['mɔɪstʃəraɪzər] n crème
hydratante

molar ['məulər] n molaire f

molasses [məu'læsɪz] n mélasse f

mold etc [məuld] (US) n = **mould** etc

mole [məul] n (animal, spy) taupe f; (spot) grain
m de beauté

molecule ['mɔlɪkju:l] n molécule f

molest [məu'lest] vt (assault sexually) attenter
à la pudeur de; (attack) molester; (harass)
tracasser

mollycoddle ['mɔlɪkɔdl] vt chouchouter,
couver

molt [məult] vi (US) = **moult**

molten ['məultən] adj fondu(e); (rock) en
fusion

mom [mɔm] n (US) = **mum**

moment ['məumənt] n moment m,
instant m; (importance) importance f; **at the** ~
en ce moment; **for the** ~ pour l'instant; **in**

a ~ dans un instant; **"one ~ please"** (Tel)
"ne quittez pas"

momentarily ['məumntrɪlɪ] adv
momentanément; (US: soon) bientôt

momentary ['məumntərɪ] adj
momentané(e), passager(-ère)

momentous [məu'mɛntəs] adj
important(e), capital(e)

momentum [məu'mɛntəm] n élan m,
vitesse acquise; (fig) dynamique f; **to gather
~** prendre de la vitesse; (fig) gagner du terrain

mommy ['mɔmɪ] n (US: mother) maman f

Monaco ['mɔnəkəu] n Monaco f

monarch ['mɔnək] n monarque m

monarchy ['mɔnəkɪ] n monarchie f

monastery ['mɔnəstərɪ] n monastère m

Monday ['mʌndɪ] n lundi m; see also **Tuesday**

monetary ['mʌnɪtərɪ] adj monétaire

money ['mʌnɪ] n argent m; **to make ~** (person)
gagner de l'argent; (business) rapporter; **I've
got no ~ left** je n'ai plus d'argent, je n'ai
plus un sou

money belt n ceinture-portefeuille f

money order n mandat m

money-spinner ['mʌnɪspɪnəʳ] n (inf) mine f
d'or (fig)

mongrel ['mʌŋgrəl] n (dog) bâtard m

monitor ['mɔnɪtəʳ] n (TV, Comput) écran m,
moniteur m; (Brit Scol) chef m de classe; (US
Scol) surveillant m (d'examen); ▷ vt contrôler;
(foreign station) être à l'écoute de; (progress)
suivre de près

monk [mʌŋk] n moine m

monkey ['mʌŋkɪ] n singe m

monkey nut n (Brit) cacahuète f

monologue ['mɔnəlɔg] n monologue m

monopoly [mə'nɔpəlɪ] n monopole m;
Monopolies and Mergers Commission
(Brit) commission britannique d'enquête sur les
monopoles

monosodium glutamate [mɔnə'səudɪəm
'glu:təmeɪt] n glutamate m de sodium

monotone ['mɔnətəun] n ton m (or voix f)
monocorde; **to speak in a ~** parler sur un ton
monocorde

monotonous [mə'nɔtənəs] adj monotone

monsoon [mɔn'su:n] n mousson f

monster ['mɔnstəʳ] n monstre m

monstrous ['mɔnstrəs] adj (huge)
gigantesque; (atrocious) monstrueux(-euse),
atroce

month [mʌnθ] n mois m; **every ~** tous les
mois; **300 dollars a ~** 300 dollars par mois

monthly ['mʌnθlɪ] adj mensuel(le) ▷ adv
mensuellement; ▷ n (magazine) mensuel m,
publication mensuelle; **twice ~** deux fois par
mois

Montreal [mɔntrɪ'ɔ:l] n Montréal m

monument ['mɔnjumənt] n monument m

moo [mu:] vi meugler, beugler

mood [mu:d] n humeur f, disposition f; **to be
in a good/bad ~** être de bonne/mauvaise

humeur; **to be in the ~ for** être d'humeur à,
avoir envie de

moody ['mu:dɪ] adj (variable) d'humeur
changeante, lunatique; (sullen) morose,
maussade

moon [mu:n] n lune f

moonlight ['mu:nlaɪt] n clair m de lune ▷ vi
travailler au noir

moonlighting ['mu:nlaɪtɪŋ] n travail m au
noir

moonlit ['mu:nlɪt] adj éclairé(e) par la lune;
a ~ night une nuit de lune

moor [muəʳ] n lande f ▷ vt (ship) amarrer ▷ vi
mouiller

moorland ['muələnd] n lande f

moose [mu:s] n (pl inv) élan m

mop [mɔp] n balai m à laver; (for dishes) lavette
f à vaisselle ▷ vt éponger, essuyer; **~ of hair**
tignasse f; **mop up** vt éponger

mope [məup] vi avoir le cafard, se
morfondre; **mope about, mope around** vi
broyer du noir, se morfondre

moped ['məupɛd] n cyclomoteur m

moral ['mɔrl] adj moral(e) ▷ n morale f;
morals npl moralité f

morale [mɔ'rɑ:l] n moral m

morality [mə'rælɪtɪ] n moralité f

morass [mə'ræs] n marais m, marécage m

morbid ['mɔ:bɪd] adj morbide

KEYWORD

more [mɔ:ʳ] adj **1** (greater in number etc) plus (de),
davantage (de); **more people/work (than)**
plus de gens/de travail (que)
2 (additional) encore (de); **do you want (some)
more tea?** voulez-vous encore du thé?; **is
there any more wine?** reste-t-il du vin?;
I have no or **I don't have any more money**
je n'ai plus d'argent; **it'll take a few more
weeks** ça prendra encore quelques semaines
▷ pron plus, davantage; **more than 10** plus de
10; **it cost more than we expected** cela a
coûté plus que prévu; **I want more** j'en veux
plus or davantage; **is there any more?** est-ce
qu'il en reste?; **there's no more** il n'y en a
plus; **a little more** un peu plus; **many/much
more** beaucoup plus, bien davantage
▷ adv plus; **more dangerous/easily (than)**
plus dangereux/facilement (que); **more and
more expensive** de plus en plus cher; **more
or less** plus ou moins; **more than ever** plus
que jamais; **once more** encore une fois,
une fois de plus; **and what's more ...** et de
plus ..., et qui plus est ...

moreover [mɔ:'rəuvəʳ] adv de plus

morgue [mɔ:g] n morgue f

morning ['mɔ:nɪŋ] n matin m; (as duration)
matinée f ▷ cpd matinal(e); (paper) du matin;
in the ~ le matin; **7 o'clock in the ~** 7 heures
du matin; **this ~** ce matin

m

morning sickness *n* nausées matinales
Moroccan [məˈrɔkən] *adj* marocain(e) ▷ *n* Marocain(e)
Morocco [məˈrɔkəʊ] *n* Maroc *m*
moron [ˈmɔːrɔn] *n* (*pej*) idiot(e), minus *m/f*
morphine [ˈmɔːfiːn] *n* morphine *f*
morris dancing [ˈmɔrɪs-] *n* (*Brit*) *danses folkloriques anglaises; voir article*

● **MORRIS DANCING**
●
● Le *morris dancing* est une danse folklorique
● anglaise traditionnellement réservée
● aux hommes. Habillés tout en blanc et
● portant des clochettes, ils exécutent
● différentes figures avec des mouchoirs et
● de longs bâtons. Cette danse est très
● populaire dans les fêtes de village.

Morse [mɔːs] *n* (*also*: **~ code**) morse *m*
morsel [ˈmɔːsl] *n* bouchée *f*
mortal [ˈmɔːtl] *adj*, *n* mortel(le)
mortar [ˈmɔːtəʳ] *n* mortier *m*
mortgage [ˈmɔːɡɪdʒ] *n* hypothèque *f*; (*loan*) prêt *m* (*or* crédit *m*) hypothécaire ▷ *vt* hypothéquer; **to take out a ~** prendre une hypothèque, faire un emprunt
mortgage company *n* (*US*) société *f* de crédit immobilier
mortician [mɔːˈtɪʃən] *n* (*US*) entrepreneur *m* de pompes funèbres
mortified [ˈmɔːtɪfaɪd] *adj* mort(e) de honte
mortuary [ˈmɔːtjuərɪ] *n* morgue *f*
mosaic [məʊˈzeɪɪk] *n* mosaïque *f*
Moscow [ˈmɔskəʊ] *n* Moscou
Moslem [ˈmɔzləm] *adj*, *n* = **Muslim**
mosque [mɔsk] *n* mosquée *f*
mosquito (*pl* **mosquitoes**) [mɔsˈkiːtəʊ] *n* moustique *m*
moss [mɔs] *n* mousse *f*
most [məʊst] *adj* (*majority of*) la plupart de; (*greatest amount of*) le plus de ▷ *pron* la plupart ▷ *adv* le plus; (*very*) très, extrêmement; **the ~** le plus; **~ fish** la plupart des poissons; **the ~ beautiful woman in the world** la plus belle femme du monde; **~ of** (*with plural*) la plupart de; (*with singular*) la plus grande partie de; **~ of them** la plupart d'entre eux; **~ of the time** la plupart du temps; **I saw ~** (*a lot but not all*) j'en ai vu la plupart; (*more than anyone else*) c'est moi qui en ai vu le plus; **at the (very) ~** au plus; **to make the ~ of** profiter au maximum de
mostly [ˈməʊstlɪ] *adv* (*chiefly*) surtout, principalement; (*usually*) généralement
MOT *n abbr* (*Brit*: = *Ministry of Transport*): **the ~ (test)** *visite technique (annuelle) obligatoire des véhicules à moteur*
motel [məʊˈtɛl] *n* motel *m*
moth [mɔθ] *n* papillon *m* de nuit; (*in clothes*) mite *f*
mother [ˈmʌðəʳ] *n* mère *f* ▷ *vt* (*pamper, protect*) dorloter

motherhood [ˈmʌðəhud] *n* maternité *f*
mother-in-law [ˈmʌðərɪnlɔː] *n* belle-mère *f*
motherly [ˈmʌðəlɪ] *adj* maternel(le)
mother-of-pearl [ˈmʌðərəvˈpəːl] *n* nacre *f*
Mother's Day *n* fête *f* des Mères
mother-to-be [ˈmʌðətəˈbiː] *n* future maman
mother tongue *n* langue maternelle
motif [məʊˈtiːf] *n* motif *m*
motion [ˈməʊʃən] *n* mouvement *m*; (*gesture*) geste *m*; (*at meeting*) motion *f*; (*Brit*: *also*: **bowel ~**) selles *fpl* ▷ *vt*, *vi*: **to ~ (to) sb to do** faire signe à qn de faire; **to be in ~** (*vehicle*) être en marche; **to set in ~** mettre en marche; **to go through the ~s of doing sth** (*fig*) faire qch machinalement *or* sans conviction
motionless [ˈməʊʃənlɪs] *adj* immobile, sans mouvement
motion picture *n* film *m*
motivate [ˈməʊtɪveɪt] *vt* motiver
motivated [ˈməʊtɪveɪtɪd] *adj* motivé(e)
motivation [məʊtɪˈveɪʃən] *n* motivation *f*
motive [ˈməʊtɪv] *n* motif *m*, mobile *m* ▷ *adj* moteur(-trice); **from the best (of) ~s** avec les meilleures intentions (du monde)
motley [ˈmɔtlɪ] *adj* hétéroclite; bigarré(e), bariolé(e)
motor [ˈməʊtəʳ] *n* moteur *m*; (*Brit inf*: *vehicle*) auto *f* ▷ *adj* moteur(-trice)
motorbike [ˈməʊtəbaɪk] *n* moto *f*
motorboat [ˈməʊtəbəʊt] *n* bateau *m* à moteur
motorcar [ˈməʊtəkɑː] *n* (*Brit*) automobile *f*
motorcycle [ˈməʊtəsaɪkl] *n* moto *f*
motorcycle racing *n* course *f* de motos
motorcyclist [ˈməʊtəsaɪklɪst] *n* motocycliste *m/f*
motoring [ˈməʊtərɪŋ] (*Brit*) *n* tourisme *m* automobile ▷ *adj* (*accident*) de voiture, de la route; **~ holiday** vacances *fpl* en voiture; **~ offence** infraction *f* au code de la route
motorist [ˈməʊtərɪst] *n* automobiliste *m/f*
motor mechanic *n* mécanicien *m* garagiste
motor racing *n* (*Brit*) course *f* automobile
motor trade *n* secteur *m* de l'automobile
motorway [ˈməʊtəweɪ] *n* (*Brit*) autoroute *f*
mottled [ˈmɔtld] *adj* tacheté(e), marbré(e)
motto (*pl* **mottoes**) [ˈmɔtəʊ] *n* devise *f*
mould, (*US*) **mold** [məʊld] *n* moule *m*; (*mildew*) moisissure *f* ▷ *vt* mouler, modeler; (*fig*) façonner
mouldy, (*US*) **moldy** [ˈməʊldɪ] *adj* moisi(e); (*smell*) de moisi
moult, (*US*) **molt** [məʊlt] *vi* muer
mound [maund] *n* monticule *m*, tertre *m*
mount [maunt] *n* (*hill*) mont *m*, montagne *f*; (*horse*) monture *f*; (*for picture*) carton *m* de montage; (*for jewel etc*) monture ▷ *vt* monter; (*horse*) monter à; (*bike*) monter sur; (*exhibition*) organiser, monter; (*picture*) monter sur carton; (*stamp*) coller dans un album ▷ *vi* (*inflation, tension*) augmenter; **mount up** *vi*

s'élever, monter; *(bills, problems, savings)* s'accumuler

mountain ['mauntɪn] *n* montagne *f* ▷ *cpd* de (la) montagne; **to make a ~ out of a molehill** *(fig)* se faire une montagne d'un rien

mountain bike *n* VTT *m*, vélo *m* tout terrain

mountaineer [maunti'nɪəʳ] *n* alpiniste *m/f*

mountaineering [maunti'nɪərɪŋ] *n* alpinisme *m*; **to go ~** faire de l'alpinisme

mountainous ['mauntɪnəs] *adj* montagneux(-euse)

mountain range *n* chaîne *f* de montagnes

mountain rescue team *n* colonne *f* de secours

mountainside ['mauntɪnsaɪd] *n* flanc *m* or versant *m* de la montagne

mourn [mɔːn] *vt* pleurer ▷ *vi*: **to ~ for sb** pleurer qn; **to ~ for sth** se lamenter sur qch

mourner ['mɔːnəʳ] *n* parent(e) or ami(e) du défunt; personne *f* en deuil or venue rendre hommage au défunt

mourning ['mɔːnɪŋ] *n* deuil *m* ▷ *cpd (dress)* de deuil; **in ~** en deuil

mouse *(pl* **mice)** [maus, maɪs] *n (also Comput)* souris *f*

mouse mat *n (Comput)* tapis *m* de souris

mousetrap ['maustræp] *n* souricière *f*

moussaka [mu'sɑːkə] *n* moussaka *f*

mousse [muːs] *n* mousse *f*

moustache [məs'tɑːʃ], *(US)* **mustache** ['mʌstæʃ] *n* moustache(s) *f(pl)*

mousy ['mausɪ] *adj (person)* effacé(e); *(hair)* d'un châtain terne

mouth [mauθ, *pl* mauðz] *n* bouche *f*; *(of dog, cat)* gueule *f*; *(of river)* embouchure *f*; *(of hole, cave)* ouverture *f*; *(of bottle)* goulot *m*; *(opening)* orifice *m*

mouthful ['mauθful] *n* bouchée *f*

mouth organ *n* harmonica *m*

mouthpiece ['mauθpiːs] *n (of musical instrument)* bec *m*, embouchure *f*; *(spokesperson)* porte-parole *m inv*

mouthwash ['mauθwɔʃ] *n* eau *f* dentifrice

mouth-watering ['mauθwɔːtərɪŋ] *adj* qui met l'eau à la bouche

movable ['muːvəbl] *adj* mobile

move [muːv] *n (movement)* mouvement *m*; *(in game)* coup *m*; *(: turn to play)* tour *m*; *(change of house)* déménagement *m*; *(change of job)* changement *m* d'emploi ▷ *vt* déplacer, bouger; *(emotionally)* émouvoir; *(Pol: resolution etc)* proposer ▷ *vi* bouger, remuer; *(traffic)* circuler; *(also: ~ house)* déménager; *(in game)* jouer; **can you ~ your car, please?** pouvez-vous déplacer votre voiture, s'il vous plaît?; **to ~ towards** se diriger vers; **to ~ sb to do sth** pousser or inciter qn à faire qch; **to get a ~ on** se dépêcher, se remuer; **move about, move around** *vi (fidget)* remuer; *(travel)* voyager, se déplacer; **move along** *vi* se pousser; **move away** *vi* s'en aller,

s'éloigner; **move back** *vi* revenir, retourner; **move forward** *vi* avancer ▷ *vt* avancer; *(people)* faire avancer; **move in** *vi (to a house)* emménager; *(police, soldiers)* intervenir; **move off** *vi* s'éloigner, s'en aller; **move on** *vi* se remettre en route ▷ *vt (onlookers)* faire circuler; **move out** *vi (of house)* déménager; **move over** *vi* se pousser, se déplacer; **move up** *vi* avancer; *(employee)* avoir de l'avancement; *(pupil)* passer dans la classe supérieure

moveable ['muːvəbl] *adj* = **movable**

movement ['muːvmənt] *n* mouvement *m*; **~ (of the bowels)** *(Med)* selles *fpl*

movie ['muːvɪ] *n* film *m*; **movies** *npl*: **the ~s** le cinéma

movie theater *(US) n* cinéma *m*

moving ['muːvɪŋ] *adj* en mouvement; *(touching)* émouvant(e) ▷ *n (US)* déménagement *m*

mow *(pt* **mowed,** *pp* **mowed** or **mown)** [məu, -d, -n] *vt* faucher; *(lawn)* tondre; **mow down** *vt* faucher

mower ['məuəʳ] *n (also:* **lawn~)** tondeuse *f* à gazon

mown [məun] *pp of* **mow**

Mozambique [məuzəm'biːk] *n* Mozambique *m*

MP *n abbr (= Military Police)* PM; *(Brit)* = **Member of Parliament**; *(Canada)* = **Mounted Police**

MP3 *n* mp3 *m*

MP3 player *n* baladeur *m* numérique, lecteur *m* mp3

mpg *n abbr (= miles per gallon)* (30 mpg = 9,4 l. aux 100 km)

m.p.h. *abbr (= miles per hour)* (60 mph = 96 km/h)

Mr, *(US)* **Mr.** ['mɪstəʳ] *n*: **Mr X** Monsieur X, M. X

Mrs, *(US)* **Mrs.** ['mɪsɪz] *n*: **~ X** Madame X, Mme X

Ms, *(US)* **Ms.** [mɪz] *n (Miss or Mrs)*: **Ms X** Madame X, Mme X; *voir article*

> **Ms**
>
> Ms est un titre utilisé à la place de "Mrs" (Mme) ou de "Miss" (Mlle) pour éviter la distinction traditionnelle entre femmes mariées et femmes non mariées.

MSc *n abbr* = **Master of Science**

MSP *n abbr (= Member of the Scottish Parliament)* député *m* au Parlement écossais

Mt *abbr (Geo:* = *mount)* Mt

much [mʌtʃ] *adj* beaucoup de ▷ *adv, n or pron* beaucoup; **~ milk** beaucoup de lait; **we don't have ~ time** nous n'avons pas beaucoup de temps; **how ~ is it?** combien est-ce que ça coûte?; **it's not ~** ce n'est pas beaucoup; **too ~** trop (de); **so ~** tant (de); **I like it very/so ~** j'aime beaucoup/tellement ça; **as ~ as** autant de; **thank you very ~** merci beaucoup; **that's**

~ better c'est beaucoup mieux; **~ to my amazement ...** à mon grand étonnement ...
muck [mʌk] n (mud) boue f; (dirt) ordures fpl;
muck about vi (inf) faire l'imbécile; (: waste time) traînasser; (: tinker) bricoler; tripoter;
muck in vi (Brit inf) donner un coup de main;
muck out vt (stable) nettoyer; **muck up** vt (inf: ruin) gâcher, esquinter; (: dirty) salir; (: exam, interview) se planter à
mucky ['mʌkɪ] adj (dirty) boueux(-euse), sale
mucus ['mjuːkəs] n mucus m
mud [mʌd] n boue f
muddle ['mʌdl] n (mess) pagaille f, fouillis m; (mix-up) confusion f ▷ vt (also: **~ up**) brouiller, embrouiller; **to be in a ~** (person) ne plus savoir où l'on en est; **to get in a ~** (while explaining etc) s'embrouiller; **muddle along** vi aller son chemin tant bien que mal; **muddle through** vi se débrouiller
muddy ['mʌdɪ] adj boueux(-euse)
mudguard ['mʌdgɑːd] n garde-boue m inv
muesli ['mjuːzlɪ] n muesli m
muffin ['mʌfɪn] n (roll) petit pain rond et plat; (cake) petit gâteau au chocolat ou aux fruits
muffle ['mʌfl] vt (sound) assourdir, étouffer; (against cold) emmitoufler
muffled ['mʌfld] adj étouffé(e), voilé(e)
muffler ['mʌfləʳ] n (scarf) cache-nez m inv; (US Aut) silencieux m
mug [mʌg] n (cup) tasse f (sans soucoupe); (: for beer) chope f; (inf: face) bouille f; (: fool) poire f ▷ vt (assault) agresser; **it's a ~'s game** (Brit) c'est bon pour les imbéciles; **mug up** vt (Brit inf: also: **~ up on**) bosser, bûcher
mugger ['mʌgəʳ] n agresseur m
mugging ['mʌgɪŋ] n agression f
muggy ['mʌgɪ] adj lourd(e), moite
mule [mjuːl] n mule f
multicoloured, (US) **multicolored** ['mʌltɪkʌləd] adj multicolore
multi-level ['mʌltɪlevl] adj (US) = **multistorey**
multimedia ['mʌltɪ'miːdɪə] adj multimédia inv
multinational [mʌltɪ'næʃənl] n multinationale f ▷ adj multinational(e)
multiple ['mʌltɪpl] adj multiple ▷ n multiple m; (Brit: also: **~ store**) magasin m à succursales (multiples)
multiple choice, **multiple choice test** n QCM m, questionnaire m à choix multiple
multiple sclerosis [-sklɪ'rəusɪs] n sclérose f en plaques
multiplex ['mʌltɪpleks], **multiplex cinema** n (cinéma m) multisalles m
multiplication [mʌltɪplɪ'keɪʃən] n multiplication f
multiply ['mʌltɪplaɪ] vt multiplier ▷ vi se multiplier
multistorey ['mʌltɪ'stɔːrɪ] adj (Brit: building) à étages; (: car park) à étages or niveaux multiples

mum [mʌm] n (Brit) maman f ▷ adj: **to keep ~** ne pas souffler mot; **~'s the word!** motus et bouche cousue!
mumble ['mʌmbl] vt, vi marmotter, marmonner
mummy ['mʌmɪ] n (Brit: mother) maman f; (embalmed) momie f
mumps [mʌmps] n oreillons mpl
munch [mʌntʃ] vt, vi mâcher
mundane [mʌn'deɪn] adj banal(e), terre à terre inv
municipal [mjuː'nɪsɪpl] adj municipal(e)
mural ['mjuərl] n peinture murale
murder ['məːdəʳ] n meurtre m, assassinat m ▷ vt assassiner; **to commit ~** commettre un meurtre
murderer ['məːdərəʳ] n meurtrier m, assassin m
murderous ['məːdərəs] adj meurtrier(-ière)
murky ['məːkɪ] adj sombre, ténébreux(-euse); (water) trouble
murmur ['məːməʳ] n murmure m ▷ vt, vi murmurer; **heart ~** (Med) souffle m au cœur
muscle ['mʌsl] n muscle m; (fig) force f; **muscle in** vi s'imposer, s'immiscer
muscular ['mʌskjuləʳ] adj musculaire; (person, arm) musclé(e)
muse [mjuːz] vi méditer, songer ▷ n muse f
museum [mjuː'zɪəm] n musée m
mushroom ['mʌʃrum] n champignon m ▷ vi (fig) pousser comme un (or des) champignon(s)
music ['mjuːzɪk] n musique f
musical ['mjuːzɪkl] adj musical(e); (person) musicien(ne) ▷ n (show) comédie musicale
musical instrument n instrument m de musique
music centre n chaîne compacte
musician [mjuː'zɪʃən] n musicien(ne)
Muslim ['mʌzlɪm] adj, n musulman(e)
muslin ['mʌzlɪn] n mousseline f
mussel ['mʌsl] n moule f
must [mʌst] aux vb (obligation): **I ~ do it** je dois le faire, il faut que je le fasse; (probability): **he ~ be there by now** il doit y être maintenant, il y est probablement maintenant; (suggestion, invitation): **you ~ come and see me** il faut que vous veniez me voir ▷ n nécessité f, impératif m; **it's a ~** c'est indispensable; **I ~ have made a mistake** j'ai dû me tromper
mustache ['mʌstæʃ] n (US) = **moustache**
mustard ['mʌstəd] n moutarde f
muster ['mʌstəʳ] vt rassembler; (also: **~ up**: strength, courage) rassembler
mustn't ['mʌsnt] = **must not**
mute [mjuːt] adj muet(te)
muted ['mjuːtɪd] adj (noise) sourd(e), assourdi(e); (criticism) voilé(e); (Mus) en sourdine; (: trumpet) bouché(e)
mutilate ['mjuːtɪleɪt] vt mutiler
mutiny ['mjuːtɪnɪ] n mutinerie f ▷ vi se mutiner

mutter ['mʌtər] *vt, vi* marmonner,
marmotter

mutton ['mʌtn] *n* mouton *m*

mutual ['mju:tʃuəl] *adj* mutuel(le),
réciproque; (*benefit, interest*) commun(e)

mutually ['mju:tʃuəlɪ] *adv* mutuellement,
réciproquement

muzzle ['mʌzl] *n* museau *m*; (*protective device*)
muselière *f*; (*of gun*) gueule *f* ▷ *vt* museler

my [maɪ] *adj* mon/ma, mes *pl*; **my house/car/
gloves** ma maison/ma voiture/mes gants;
I've washed my hair/cut my finger je me
suis lavé les cheveux/coupé le doigt; **is this
my pen or yours?** c'est mon stylo ou c'est le
vôtre?

myself [maɪ'sɛlf] *pron* (*reflexive*) me; (*emphatic*)
moi-même; (*after prep*) moi; *see also* **oneself**

mysterious [mɪs'tɪərɪəs] *adj*
mystérieux(-euse)

mystery ['mɪstərɪ] *n* mystère *m*

mystical ['mɪstɪkl] *adj* mystique

mystify ['mɪstɪfaɪ] *vt* (*deliberately*) mystifier;
(*puzzle*) ébahir

myth [mɪθ] *n* mythe *m*

mythology [mɪ'θɒlədʒɪ] *n* mythologie *f*

n/a *abbr* (= *not applicable*) n.a.; (*Comm etc*)
= **no account**

naff [næf] (*Brit: inf*) *adj* nul(le)

nag [næg] *vt* (*scold*) être toujours après,
reprendre sans arrêt ▷ *n* (*pej: horse*)
canasson *m*; (*person*): **she's an awful ~** elle est
constamment après lui (*or* eux *etc*), elle est
très casse-pieds

nagging ['nægɪŋ] *adj* (*doubt, pain*)
persistant(e) ▷ *n* remarques continuelles

nail [neɪl] *n* (*human*) ongle *m*; (*metal*) clou *m*
▷ *vt* clouer; **to ~ sth to sth** clouer qch à qch;
to ~ sb down to a date/price contraindre qn
à accepter *or* donner une date/un prix; **to pay
cash on the ~** (*Brit*) payer rubis sur l'ongle

nailbrush ['neɪlbrʌʃ] *n* brosse *f* à ongles

nailfile ['neɪlfaɪl] *n* lime *f* à ongles

nail polish *n* vernis *m* à ongles

nail polish remover *n* dissolvant *m*

nail scissors *npl* ciseaux *mpl* à ongles

nail varnish *n* (*Brit*) = **nail polish**

naïve [naɪ'iːv] *adj* naïf(-ïve)

naked ['neɪkɪd] *adj* nu(e); **with the ~ eye** à
l'œil nu

name [neɪm] *n* nom *m*; (*reputation*)
réputation *f* ▷ *vt* nommer; (*identify: accomplice
etc*) citer; (*price, date*) fixer, donner; **by ~** par
son nom; de nom; **in the ~ of** au nom de;
what's your ~? comment vous appelez-
vous?, quel est votre nom?; **my ~ is Peter**
je m'appelle Peter; **to take sb's ~ and
address** relever l'identité de qn *or* les nom et

adresse de qn; **to make a ~ for o.s.** se faire
un nom; **to get (o.s.) a bad ~** se faire une
mauvaise réputation; **to call sb ~s** traiter qn
de tous les noms

nameless ['neɪmlɪs] *adj* sans nom; (*witness,
contributor*) anonyme

namely ['neɪmlɪ] *adv* à savoir

namesake ['neɪmseɪk] *n* homonyme *m*

nanny ['nænɪ] *n* bonne *f* d'enfants

nap [næp] *n* (*sleep*) (petit) somme ▷ *vi*: **to be
caught ~ping** être pris(e) à l'improviste *or*
en défaut

nape [neɪp] *n*: **~ of the neck** nuque *f*

napkin ['næpkɪn] *n* serviette *f* (de table)

nappy ['næpɪ] *n* (Brit) couche *f*

nappy rash *n*: **to have ~** avoir les fesses
rouges

narcissus (*pl* **narcissi**) [nɑː'sɪsəs, -saɪ] *n*
narcisse *m*

narcotic [nɑː'kɔtɪk] *n* (Med) narcotique *m*

narcotics [nɑː'kɔtɪkz] *npl* (*illegal drugs*)
stupéfiants *mpl*

narrative ['nærətɪv] *n* récit *m* ▷ *adj*
narratif(-ive)

narrator [nə'reɪtər] *n* narrateur(-trice)

narrow ['nærəʊ] *adj* étroit(e); (fig)
restreint(e), limité(e) ▷ *vi* (*road*) devenir plus
étroit, se rétrécir; (*gap, difference*) se réduire;
to have a ~ escape l'échapper belle; **narrow
down** *vt* restreindre

narrowly ['nærəʊlɪ] *adv*: **he ~ missed
injury/the tree** il a failli se blesser/rentrer
dans l'arbre; **he only ~ missed the target** il
a manqué la cible de peu *or* de justesse

narrow-minded [nærəʊ'maɪndɪd] *adj* à
l'esprit étroit, borné(e); (*attitude*) borné(e)

nasal ['neɪzl] *adj* nasal(e)

nasty ['nɑːstɪ] *adj* (*person: malicious*)
méchant(e); (: *rude*) très désagréable; (*smell*)
dégoûtant(e); (*wound, situation*) mauvais(e),
vilain(e); (*weather*) affreux(-euse); **to turn ~**
(*situation*) mal tourner; (*weather*) se gâter;
(*person*) devenir méchant; **it's a ~ business**
c'est une sale affaire

nation ['neɪʃən] *n* nation *f*

national ['næʃənl] *adj* national(e) ▷ *n* (*abroad*)
ressortissant(e); (*when home*) national(e)

national anthem *n* hymne national

national dress *n* costume national

National Health Service *n* (Brit) *service
national de santé*, ≈ Sécurité Sociale

National Insurance *n* (Brit) ≈ Sécurité
Sociale

nationalism ['næʃnəlɪzəm] *n*
nationalisme *m*

nationalist ['næʃnəlɪst] *adj, n*
nationaliste *m/f*

nationality [næʃə'nælɪtɪ] *n* nationalité *f*

nationalize ['næʃnəlaɪz] *vt* nationaliser

nationally ['næʃnəlɪ] *adv* du point de vue
national; dans le pays entier

national park *n* parc national

National Trust *n* (Brit) ≈ Caisse *f* nationale
des monuments historiques et des sites;
voir article

⬤ **NATIONAL TRUST**
⬤
⬤ Le *National Trust* est un organisme
⬤ indépendant, à but non lucratif, dont la
⬤ mission est de protéger et de mettre en
⬤ valeur les monuments et les sites
⬤ britanniques en raison de leur intérêt
⬤ historique ou de leur beauté naturelle.

nationwide ['neɪʃənwaɪd] *adj* s'étendant à
l'ensemble du pays; (*problem*) à l'échelle du
pays entier ▷ *adv* à travers *or* dans tout le pays

native ['neɪtɪv] *n* habitant(e) du pays,
autochtone *m/f*; (*in colonies*) indigène *m/f* ▷ *adj*
du pays, indigène; (*country*) natal(e);
(*language*) maternel(le); (*ability*) inné(e); **a ~ of
Russia** une personne originaire de Russie;
a ~ speaker of French une personne de
langue maternelle française

Native American *n* Indien(ne) d'Amérique
▷ *adj* amérindien(ne)

native speaker *n* locuteur natif; *see also*
native

NATO ['neɪtəʊ] *n abbr* (= *North Atlantic Treaty
Organization*) OTAN *f*

natural ['nætʃrəl] *adj* naturel(le); **to die of ~
causes** mourir d'une mort naturelle

natural gas *n* gaz naturel

natural history *n* histoire naturelle

naturalist ['nætʃrəlɪst] *n* naturaliste *m/f*

naturally ['nætʃrəlɪ] *adv* naturellement

natural resources *npl* ressources naturelles

nature ['neɪtʃər] *n* nature *f*; **by ~** par
tempérament, de nature; **documents of a
confidential ~** documents à caractère
confidentiel

nature reserve *n* (Brit) réserve naturelle

naught [nɔːt] *n* = **nought**

naughty ['nɔːtɪ] *adj* (*child*) vilain(e), pas sage;
(*story, film*) grivois(e)

nausea ['nɔːsɪə] *n* nausée *f*

naval ['neɪvl] *adj* naval(e)

naval officer *n* officier *m* de marine

nave [neɪv] *n* nef *f*

navel ['neɪvl] *n* nombril *m*

navigate ['nævɪgeɪt] *vt* (*steer*) diriger, piloter
▷ *vi* naviguer; (*Aut*) indiquer la route à suivre

navigation [nævɪ'geɪʃən] *n* navigation *f*

navvy ['nævɪ] *n* (Brit) terrassier *m*

navy ['neɪvɪ] *n* marine *f*; **Department of the
N~** (US) ministère *m* de la Marine

navy-blue ['neɪvɪ'bluː] *adj* bleu marine *inv*

Nazi ['nɑːtsɪ] *adj* nazi(e) ▷ *n* Nazi(e)

NB *abbr* (= *nota bene*) NB; (Canada) = **New
Brunswick**

near [nɪər] *adj* proche ▷ *adv* près ▷ *prep* (*also:*
~ to) près de ▷ *vt* approcher de; **~ here/there**
près d'ici/non loin de là; **£25,000 or ~est**

offer (Brit) 25 000 livres à débattre; **in the ~ future** dans un proche avenir; **to come ~** vi s'approcher

nearby ['nɪə'baɪ] adj proche ▷ adv tout près, à proximité

nearly ['nɪəlɪ] adv presque; **I ~ fell** j'ai failli tomber; **it's not ~ big enough** ce n'est vraiment pas assez grand, c'est loin d'être assez grand

near miss n collision évitée de justesse; (when aiming) coup manqué de peu or de justesse

nearside ['nɪəsaɪd] (Aut) n (right-hand drive) côté m gauche; (left-hand drive) côté droit ▷ adj de gauche; de droite

near-sighted [nɪə'saɪtɪd] adj myope

neat [niːt] adj (person, work) soigné(e); (room etc) bien tenu(e) or rangé(e); (solution, plan) habile; (spirits) pur(e); **I drink it ~** je le bois sec or sans eau

neatly ['niːtlɪ] adv avec soin or ordre; (skilfully) habilement

necessarily ['nɛsɪsrɪlɪ] adv nécessairement; **not ~** pas nécessairement or forcément

necessary ['nɛsɪsrɪ] adj nécessaire; **if ~** si besoin est, le cas échéant

necessity [nɪ'sɛsɪtɪ] n nécessité f; chose nécessaire or essentielle; **in case of ~** en cas d'urgence

neck [nɛk] n cou m; (of horse, garment) encolure f; (of bottle) goulot m ▷ vi (inf) se peloter; **~ and ~** à égalité; **to stick one's ~ out** (inf) se mouiller

necklace ['nɛklɪs] n collier m

neckline ['nɛklaɪn] n encolure f

necktie ['nɛktaɪ] n (esp US) cravate f

nectarine ['nɛktərɪn] n brugnon m, nectarine f

need [niːd] n besoin m ▷ vt avoir besoin de; **to ~ to do** devoir faire; avoir besoin de faire; **you don't ~ to go** vous n'avez pas besoin or vous n'êtes pas obligé de partir; **a signature is ~ed** il faut une signature; **to be in ~ of** or **have ~ of** avoir besoin de; **£10 will meet my immediate ~s** 10 livres suffiront pour mes besoins immédiats; **in case of ~** en cas de besoin, au besoin; **there's no ~ to do ....** il n'y a pas lieu de faire ..., il n'est pas nécessaire de faire ...; **there's no ~ for that** ce n'est pas la peine, cela n'est pas nécessaire

needle ['niːdl] n aiguille f; (on record player) saphir m ▷ vt (inf) asticoter, tourmenter

needless ['niːdlɪs] adj inutile; **~ to say, ...** inutile de dire que ...

needlework ['niːdlwəːk] n (activity) travaux mpl d'aiguille; (object) ouvrage m

needn't ['niːdnt] = need not

needy ['niːdɪ] adj nécessiteux(-euse)

negative ['nɛgətɪv] n (Phot, Elec) négatif m; (Ling) terme m de négation ▷ adj négatif(-ive); **to answer in the ~** répondre par la négative

neglect [nɪ'glɛkt] vt négliger; (garden) ne pas entretenir; (duty) manquer à ▷ n (of person, duty, garden) manque m de négligence; (state of ~) abandon m; **to ~ to do sth** négliger or omettre de faire qch; **to ~ one's appearance** se négliger

neglected [nɪ'glɛktɪd] adj négligé(e), à l'abandon

negligee ['nɛglɪʒeɪ] n déshabillé m

negotiate [nɪ'gəʊʃɪeɪt] vi négocier ▷ vt négocier; (Comm) négocier; (obstacle) franchir, négocier; (bend in road) négocier; **to ~ with sb for sth** négocier avec qn en vue d'obtenir qch

negotiation [nɪgəʊʃɪ'eɪʃən] n négociation f, pourparlers mpl; **to enter into ~s with sb** engager des négociations avec qn

negotiator [nɪ'gəʊʃɪeɪtəʳ] n négociateur(-trice)

neigh [neɪ] vi hennir

neighbour, neighbor (US) ['neɪbəʳ] n voisin(e)

neighbourhood, neighborhood (US) ['neɪbəhud] n (place) quartier m; (people) voisinage m

neighbouring, neighboring (US) ['neɪbə rɪŋ] adj voisin(e), avoisinant(e)

neighbourly, neighborly (US) ['neɪbəlɪ] adj obligeant(e); (relations) de bon voisinage

neither ['naɪðəʳ] adj, pron aucun(e) (des deux), ni l'un(e) ni l'autre ▷ conj: **~ do I** moi non plus; **I didn't move and ~ did Claude** je n'ai pas bougé, (et) Claude non plus ▷ adv: **~ good nor bad** ni bon ni mauvais; **~ did I refuse** (et or mais) je n'ai pas non plus refusé; **~ of them** ni l'un ni l'autre

neon ['niːɔn] n néon m

neon light n lampe f au néon

Nepal [nɪ'pɔːl] n Népal m

nephew ['nɛvjuː] n neveu m

nerve [nəːv] n nerf m; (bravery) sang-froid m, courage m; (cheek) aplomb m, toupet m; **nerves** npl (nervousness) nervosité f; **he gets on my ~s** il m'énerve; **to have a fit of ~s** avoir le trac; **to lose one's ~** (self-confidence) perdre son sang-froid

nerve-racking ['nəː'vrækɪŋ] adj angoissant(e)

nervous ['nəːvəs] adj nerveux(-euse); (anxious) inquiet(-ète), plein(e) d'appréhension; (timid) intimidé(e)

nervous breakdown n dépression nerveuse

nest [nɛst] n nid m ▷ vi (se) nicher, faire son nid; **~ of tables** table f gigogne

nest egg n (fig) bas m de laine, magot m

nestle ['nɛsl] vi se blottir

Net [nɛt] n (Comput): **the ~** (Internet) le Net

net [nɛt] n filet m; (fabric) tulle f ▷ adj net(te) ▷ vt (fish etc) prendre au filet; (money: person) toucher; (: deal, sale) rapporter; **~ of tax** d'impôt; **he earns £10,000 ~ per year** il gagne 10 000 livres net par an

netball ['nɛtbɔːl] n netball m
Netherlands ['nɛðələndz] npl: **the ~** les Pays-Bas mpl
nett [nɛt] adj = **net**
netting ['nɛtɪŋ] n (for fence etc) treillis m, grillage m; (fabric) voile m
nettle ['nɛtl] n ortie f
network ['nɛtwəːk] n réseau m ▷ vt (Radio, TV) diffuser sur l'ensemble du réseau; (computers) interconnecter; **there's no ~ coverage here** (Tel) il n'y a pas de réseau ici
neurotic [njuə'rɔtɪk] adj, n névrosé(e)
neuter ['njuːtə'] adj neutre ▷ n neutre m ▷ vt (cat etc) châtrer, couper
neutral ['njuːtrəl] adj neutre ▷ n (Aut) point mort
neutralize ['njuːtrəlaɪz] vt neutraliser
never ['nɛvə'] adv (ne ...) jamais; **I ~ went** je n'y suis pas allé; **I've ~ been to Spain** je ne suis jamais allé en Espagne; **~ again** plus jamais; **~ in my life** jamais de ma vie; see also **mind**
never-ending [nɛvər'ɛndɪŋ] adj interminable
nevertheless [nɛvəðə'lɛs] adv néanmoins, malgré tout
new [njuː] adj nouveau/nouvelle; (brand new) neuf/neuve; **as good as ~** comme neuf
New Age n New Age m
newbie ['njuːbɪ] n (beginner) newbie mf; (on forum) nouveau/-elle)
newborn ['njuːbɔːn] adj nouveau-né(e)
newcomer ['njuːkʌmə'] n nouveau venu/ nouvelle venue
new-fangled ['njuːfæŋgld] adj (pej) ultramoderne (et farfelu(e))
new-found ['njuːfaund] adj de fraîche date; (friend) nouveau/nouvelle
newly ['njuːlɪ] adv nouvellement, récemment
newly-weds ['njuːlɪwɛdz] npl jeunes mariés mpl
news [njuːz] n nouvelle(s) f(pl); (Radio, TV) informations fpl, actualités fpl; **a piece of ~** une nouvelle; **good/bad ~** bonne/mauvaise nouvelle; **financial ~** (Press, Radio, TV) page financière
news agency n agence f de presse
newsagent ['njuːzeɪdʒənt] n (Brit) marchand m de journaux
newscaster ['njuːzkɑːstə'] n (Radio, TV) présentateur(-trice)
news flash n flash m d'information
newsletter ['njuːzlɛtə'] n bulletin m
newspaper ['njuːzpeɪpə'] n journal m; **daily ~** quotidien m; **weekly ~** hebdomadaire m
newsprint ['njuːzprɪnt] n papier m (de) journal
newsreader ['njuːzriːdə'] n = **newscaster**
newsreel ['njuːzriːl] n actualités (filmées)
news stand n kiosque m à journaux
newt [njuːt] n triton m

New Year n Nouvel An; **Happy ~!** Bonne Année!; **to wish sb a happy ~** souhaiter la Bonne Année à qn
New Year's Day n le jour de l'An
New Year's Eve n la Saint-Sylvestre
New York [-'jɔːk] n New York; (also: **~ State**) New York m
New Zealand [-'ziːlənd] n Nouvelle-Zélande f ▷ adj néo-zélandais(e)
New Zealander [-'ziːləndə'] n Néo-Zélandais(e)
next [nɛkst] adj (in time) prochain(e); (seat, room) voisin(e), d'à côté; (meeting, bus stop) suivant(e) ▷ adv la fois suivante; la prochaine fois; (afterwards) ensuite; **~ to** prep à côté de; **~ to nothing** presque rien; **~ time** adv la prochaine fois; **the ~ day** le lendemain, le jour suivant or d'après; **~ week** la semaine prochaine; **the ~ week** la semaine suivante; **~ year** l'année prochaine; **"turn to the ~ page"** "voir page suivante"; **~ please!** (at doctor's etc) au suivant!; **who's ~?** c'est à qui?; **the week after ~** dans deux semaines; **when do we meet ~?** quand nous revoyons-nous?
next door adv à côté ▷ adj (neighbour) d'à côté
next-of-kin ['nɛkstəv'kɪn] n parent m le plus proche
NHS n abbr (Brit) = **National Health Service**
nib [nɪb] n (of pen) (bec m de) plume f
nibble ['nɪbl] vt grignoter
nice [naɪs] adj (holiday, trip, taste) agréable; (flat, picture) joli(e); (person) gentil(le); (distinction, point) subtil(e)
nicely ['naɪslɪ] adv agréablement; joliment; gentiment; subtilement; **that will do ~** ce sera parfait
niceties ['naɪsɪtɪz] npl subtilités fpl
niche [niːʃ] n (Archit) niche f
nick [nɪk] n (indentation) encoche f; (wound) entaille f; (Brit inf): **in good ~** en bon état ▷ vt (cut): **to ~ o.s.** se couper; (inf: steal) faucher, piquer; (: Brit: arrest) choper, pincer; **in the ~ of time** juste à temps
nickel ['nɪkl] n nickel m; (US) pièce f de 5 cents
nickname ['nɪkneɪm] n surnom m ▷ vt surnommer
nicotine ['nɪkətiːn] n nicotine f
nicotine patch n timbre m anti-tabac, patch m
niece [niːs] n nièce f
Nigeria [naɪ'dʒɪərɪə] n Nigéria m or f
niggling ['nɪglɪŋ] adj taillon(ne); (detail) insignifiant(e); (doubt, pain) persistant(e)
night [naɪt] n nuit f; (evening) soir m; **at ~** la nuit; **by ~** de nuit; **in the ~**, **during the ~** pendant la nuit; **last ~** (evening) hier soir; (night-time) la nuit dernière; **the ~ before last** avant-hier soir
nightcap ['naɪtkæp] n boisson prise avant le coucher
night club n boîte f de nuit

nightdress ['naɪtdrɛs] *n* chemise *f* de nuit
nightfall ['naɪtfɔ:l] *n* tombée *f* de la nuit
nightie ['naɪtɪ] *n* chemise *f* de nuit
nightingale ['naɪtɪŋgeɪl] *n* rossignol *m*
nightlife ['naɪtlaɪf] *n* vie *f* nocturne
nightly ['naɪtlɪ] *adj* (*news*) nocturne ▷ *adv* (*every evening*) tous les soirs;
(*every night*) toutes les nuits
nightmare ['naɪtmɛəʳ] *n* cauchemar *m*
night porter *n* gardien *m* de nuit, concierge *m* de service la nuit
night school *n* cours *mpl* du soir
night shift ['naɪtʃɪft] *n* équipe *f* de nuit
night-time ['naɪttaɪm] *n* nuit *f*
night watchman *irreg n* veilleur *m* de nuit; poste *m* de nuit
nil [nɪl] *n* rien *m*; (*Brit Sport*) zéro *m*
Nile [naɪl] *n*: **the ~** le Nil
nimble ['nɪmbl] *adj* agile
nine [naɪn] *num* neuf
nineteen [naɪn'ti:n] *num* dix-neuf
nineteenth [naɪn'ti:nθ] *num* dix-neuvième
ninetieth ['naɪntɪɪθ] *num* quatre-vingt-dixième
ninety ['naɪntɪ] *num* quatre-vingt-dix
ninth [naɪnθ] *num* neuvième
nip [nɪp] *vt* pincer ▷ *vi* (*Brit inf*): **to ~ out/down/up** sortir/descendre/monter en vitesse ▷ *n* pincement *m*; (*drink*) petit verre;
to ~ into a shop faire un saut dans un magasin
nipple ['nɪpl] *n* (*Anat*) mamelon *m*, bout *m* du sein
nitrogen ['naɪtrədʒən] *n* azote *m*

◯ KEYWORD

no [nəʊ] (*pl* **noes**) *adv* (*opposite of "yes"*) non;
are you coming? — no (I'm not) est-ce que vous venez? — non; **would you like some more? — no thank you** vous en voulez encore? — non merci
▷ *adj* (*not any*) pas de, (ne ...) aucun(e);
I have no money/books je n'ai pas d'argent/de livres; **no student would have done it** aucun étudiant ne l'aurait fait; **"no smoking"** "défense de fumer"; **"no dogs"** "les chiens ne sont pas admis"
▷ *n* non *m*; **I won't take no for an answer** il n'est pas question de refuser

nobility [nəʊ'bɪlɪtɪ] *n* noblesse *f*
noble ['nəʊbl] *adj* noble
nobody ['nəʊbədɪ] *pron* (ne ...) personne
nod [nɒd] *vi* faire un signe de (la) tête (*affirmatif ou amical*); (*sleep*) somnoler ▷ *vt*:
to ~ one's head faire un signe de (la) tête; (*in agreement*) faire signe que oui ▷ *n* signe *m* de (la) tête; **they ~ded their agreement** ils ont acquiescé d'un signe de la tête; **nod off** *vi* s'assoupir
noise [nɔɪz] *n* bruit *m*; **I can't sleep for the ~**

je n'arrive pas à dormir à cause du bruit
noisy ['nɔɪzɪ] *adj* bruyant(e)
nominal ['nɒmɪnl] *adj* (*rent, fee*) symbolique;
(*value*) nominal(e)
nominate ['nɒmɪneɪt] *vt* (*propose*) proposer;
(*appoint*) nommer
nomination [nɒmɪ'neɪʃən] *n* nomination *f*
nominee [nɒmɪ'ni:] *n* candidat agréé;
personne nommée
non- [nɒn] *prefix* non-
nonalcoholic [nɒnælkə'hɒlɪk] *adj* non alcoolisé(e)
noncommittal [nɒnkə'mɪtl] *adj* évasif(-ive)
nondescript ['nɒndɪskrɪpt] *adj* quelconque, indéfinissable
none [nʌn] *pron* aucun(e); **~ of you** aucun d'entre vous, personne parmi vous; **I have ~** je n'en ai pas; **I have ~ left** je n'en ai plus; **~ at all** (*not one*) aucun(e); **how much milk? — ~ at all** combien de lait? — pas du tout;
he's ~ the worse for it il ne s'en porte pas plus mal
nonentity [nɒ'nɛntɪtɪ] *n* personne insignifiante
nonetheless ['nʌnðə'lɛs] *adv* néanmoins
nonexistent [nɒnɪg'zɪstənt] *adj* inexistant(e)
non-fiction [nɒn'fɪkʃən] *n* littérature *f* non romanesque
nonplussed [nɒn'plʌst] *adj* perplexe
nonsense ['nɒnsəns] *n* absurdités *fpl*, idioties *fpl*; **~! ne dites pas d'idioties!; it is ~ to say that ...** il est absurde de dire que ....
non-smoker ['nɒn'sməʊkəʳ] *n* non-fumeur *m*
non-smoking ['nɒn'sməʊkɪŋ] *adj* non-fumeur
non-stick ['nɒn'stɪk] *adj* qui n'attache pas
nonstop ['nɒn'stɒp] *adj* direct(e), sans arrêt (*or escale*) ▷ *adv* sans arrêt
noodles ['nu:dlz] *npl* nouilles *fpl*
nook [nʊk] *n*: **~s and crannies** recoins *mpl*
noon [nu:n] *n* midi *m*
no-one ['nəʊwʌn] *pron* = **nobody**
noose [nu:s] *n* nœud coulant; (*hangman's*) corde *f*
nor [nɔːʳ] *conj* = **neither** ▷ *adv see* **neither**
norm [nɔ:m] *n* norme *f*
normal ['nɔ:ml] *adj* normal(e) ▷ *n*: **to return to ~** redevenir normal(e)
normally ['nɔ:məlɪ] *adv* normalement
Normandy ['nɔ:məndɪ] *n* Normandie *f*
north [nɔ:θ] *n* nord *m* ▷ *adj* nord *inv*; (*wind*) du nord ▷ *adv* au *or* vers le nord
North Africa *n* Afrique *f* du Nord
North African *adj* nord-africain(e), d'Afrique du Nord ▷ *n* Nord-Africain(e)
North America *n* Amérique *f* du Nord
North American *n* Nord-Américain(e) ▷ *adj* nord-américain(e), d'Amérique du Nord
northbound ['nɔ:θbaʊnd] *adj* (*traffic*) en direction du nord; (*carriageway*) nord *inv*

n

north-east [nɔːθ'iːst] n nord-est m
northerly ['nɔːðəlɪ] adj (wind, direction) du
nord
northern ['nɔːðən] adj du nord,
septentrional(e)
Northern Ireland n Irlande f du Nord
North Korea n Corée f du Nord
North Pole n: the ~ le pôle Nord
North Sea n: the ~ la mer du Nord
northward ['nɔːθwəd], **northwards**
['nɔːθwədz] adv vers le nord
north-west [nɔːθ'west] n nord-ouest m
Norway ['nɔːweɪ] n Norvège f
Norwegian [nɔː'wiːdʒən] adj norvégien(ne)
▷ n Norvégien(ne); (Ling) norvégien m
nose [nəuz] n nez m; (of dog, cat) museau m;
(fig) flair m ▷ vi (also: ~ one's way) avancer
précautionneusement; **to pay through the
~ (for sth)** (inf) payer un prix excessif (pour
qch); **nose about, nose around** vi fouiner or
fureter (partout)
nosebleed ['nəuzbliːd] n saignement m de nez
nose-dive ['nəuzdaɪv] n (descente f en)
piqué m
nosey ['nəuzɪ] adj (inf) curieux(-euse)
nostalgia [nɔs'tældʒɪə] n nostalgie f
nostalgic [nɔs'tældʒɪk] adj nostalgique
nostril ['nɔstrɪl] n narine f; (of horse) naseau m
nosy ['nəuzɪ] (inf) adj = **nosey**
not [nɔt] adv (ne ...) pas; **he is ~ or isn't here** il
n'est pas ici; **you must ~ or mustn't do that**
tu ne dois pas faire ça; **I hope ~** j'espère que
non; **~ at all** pas du tout; (after thanks) de rien;
it's too late, isn't it? c'est trop tard, n'est-ce
pas?; **~ yet/now** pas encore/maintenant; see
also **only**
notable ['nəutəbl] adj notable
notably ['nəutəblɪ] adv (particularly) en
particulier; (markedly) spécialement
notary ['nəutərɪ] n (also: ~ public) notaire m
notch [nɔtʃ] n encoche f; **notch up** vt (score)
marquer; (victory) remporter
note [nəut] n note f; (letter) mot m; (banknote)
billet m ▷ vt (also: ~ down) noter;
constater; **just a quick ~ to let you know ...**
juste un mot pour vous dire ...; **to take ~s**
prendre des notes; **to compare ~s** (fig)
échanger des (or leurs etc) impressions; **to
take ~ of** prendre note de; **a person of ~** une
personne éminente
notebook ['nəutbuk] n carnet m; (for
shorthand etc) bloc-notes m
noted ['nəutɪd] adj réputé(e)
notepad ['nəutpæd] n bloc-notes m
notepaper ['nəutpeɪpə'] n papier m à lettres
nothing ['nʌθɪŋ] n rien m; **he does ~** il ne fait
rien; **~ new** rien de nouveau; **for ~** (free) pour
rien, gratuitement; (in vain) pour rien; **~ at
all** rien du tout; **~ much** pas grand-chose
notice ['nəutɪs] n (announcement, warning)
avis m; (of leaving) congé m; (Brit: review: of play
etc) critique f, compte rendu m ▷ vt

remarquer, s'apercevoir de; **without ~** sans
préavis; **advance ~** préavis m; **to give sb ~ of
sth** notifier qn de qch; **at short ~** dans un
délai très court; **until further ~** jusqu'à
nouvel ordre; **to give ~, hand in one's ~**
(employee) donner sa démission,
démissionner; **to take ~ of** prêter attention
à; **to bring sth to sb's ~** porter qch à la
connaissance de qn; **it has come to my ~
that ...** on m'a signalé que ...; **to escape or
avoid ~** (essayer de) passer inaperçu or ne pas
se faire remarquer
noticeable ['nəutɪsəbl] adj visible
notice board n (Brit) panneau m d'affichage
notify ['nəutɪfaɪ] vt: **to ~ sth to sb** notifier
qch à qn; **to ~ sb of sth** avertir qn de qch
notion ['nəuʃən] n idée f; (concept) notion f;
notions npl (US: haberdashery) mercerie f
notorious [nəu'tɔːrɪəs] adj notoire (souvent en
mal)
notwithstanding [nɔtwɪθ'stændɪŋ] adv
néanmoins ▷ prep en dépit de
nought [nɔːt] n zéro m
noun [naun] n nom m
nourish ['nʌrɪʃ] vt nourrir
nourishing ['nʌrɪʃɪŋ] adj nourrissant(e)
nourishment ['nʌrɪʃmənt] n nourriture f
Nov. abbr (= November)
novel ['nɔvl] n roman m ▷ adj nouveau/
nouvelle, original(e)
novelist ['nɔvəlɪst] n romancier m
novelty ['nɔvəltɪ] n nouveauté f
November [nəu'vɛmbə'] n novembre m;
see also **July**
novice ['nɔvɪs] n novice m/f
now [nau] adv maintenant ▷ conj: **~ (that)**
maintenant (que); **right ~** tout de suite; **by ~**
à l'heure qu'il est; **just ~: that's the fashion
just now** c'est la mode en ce moment or
maintenant; **I saw her just ~** je viens de la
voir, je l'ai vue à l'instant; **I'll read it just ~**
je vais le lire à l'instant or dès maintenant;
~ and then, ~ and again de temps en temps;
from ~ on dorénavant; **in 3 days from ~** dans
or d'ici trois jours; **between ~ and Monday**
d'ici (à) lundi; **that's all for ~** c'est tout pour
l'instant
nowadays ['nauədeɪz] adv de nos jours
nowhere ['nəuwɛə'] adv (ne ...) nulle part;
~ else nulle part ailleurs
nozzle ['nɔzl] n (of hose) jet m, lance f; (of
vacuum cleaner) suceur m
nr abbr (Brit) = **near**
nuclear ['njuːklɪə'] adj nucléaire
nucleus (pl **nuclei**) ['njuːklɪəs, 'njuːklɪaɪ] n
noyau m
nude [njuːd] adj nu(e) ▷ n (Art) nu m; **in the ~**
(tout(e)) nu(e)
nudge [nʌdʒ] vt donner un (petit) coup de
coude à
nudist ['njuːdɪst] n nudiste m/f
nudity ['njuːdɪtɪ] n nudité f

nuisance ['nju:sns] n: **it's a** ~ c'est (très) ennuyeux or gênant; **he's a** ~ il est assommant or casse-pieds; **what a** ~! quelle barbe!

null [nʌl] adj: ~ **and void** nul(le) et non avenu(e)

numb [nʌm] adj engourdi(e); (with fear) paralysé(e) ▷ vt engourdir; ~ **with cold** engourdi(e) par le froid, transi(e) (de froid); ~ **with fear** transi de peur, paralysé(e) par la peur

number ['nʌmbəʳ] n nombre m; (numeral) chiffre m; (of house, car, telephone, newspaper) numéro m ▷ vt numéroter; (amount to) compter; **a** ~ **of** un certain nombre de; **they were seven in** ~ ils étaient (au nombre de) sept; **to be** ~**ed among** compter parmi; **the staff** ~**s 20** le nombre d'employés s'élève à or est de 20; **wrong** ~ (Tel) mauvais numéro

number plate n (Brit Aut) plaque f minéralogique or d'immatriculation

Number Ten n (Brit: 10 Downing Street) résidence du Premier ministre

numeral ['nju:mərəl] n chiffre m

numerate ['nju:mərɪt] adj (Brit): **to be** ~ avoir des notions d'arithmétique

numerical [nju:'merɪkl] adj numérique

numerous ['nju:mərəs] adj nombreux(-euse)

nun [nʌn] n religieuse f, sœur f

nurse [nəːs] n infirmière f; (also: ~**maid**) bonne f d'enfants ▷ vt (patient, cold) soigner; (baby: Brit) bercer (dans ses bras); (: US) allaiter, nourrir; (hope) nourrir

nursery ['nəːsərɪ] n (room) nursery f; (institution) crèche f, garderie f; (for plants) pépinière f

nursery rhyme n comptine f, chansonnette f pour enfants

nursery school n école maternelle

nursery slope n (Brit Ski) piste f pour débutants

nursing ['nəːsɪŋ] n (profession) profession f d'infirmière; (care) soins mpl ▷ adj (mother) qui allaite

nursing home n clinique f; (for convalescence) maison f de convalescence or de repos; (for old people) maison de retraite

nurture ['nəːtʃəʳ] vt élever

nut [nʌt] n (of metal) écrou m; (fruit: walnut) noix f; (: hazelnut) noisette f; (: peanut) cacahuète f (terme générique en anglais) ▷ adj (chocolate etc) aux noisettes; **he's** ~**s** (inf) il est dingue

nutcrackers ['nʌtkrækəz] npl casse-noix m inv, casse-noisette(s) m

nutmeg ['nʌtmeg] n (noix f) muscade f

nutrient ['nju:trɪənt] adj nutritif(-ive) ▷ n substance nutritive

nutrition [nju:'trɪʃən] n nutrition f, alimentation f

nutritious [nju:'trɪʃəs] adj nutritif(-ive), nourrissant(e)

nuts [nʌts] (inf) adj dingue

nutshell ['nʌtʃel] n coquille f de noix; **in a** ~ en un mot

nutter ['nʌtəʳ] (Brit: inf) n: **he's a complete** ~ il est complètement cinglé

NVQ n abbr (Brit) = **National Vocational Qualification**

nylon ['naɪlɔn] n nylon m ▷ adj de or en nylon; **nylons** npl bas mpl nylon

n

O

oak [əuk] n chêne m ▷ cpd de or en (bois de) chêne

O.A.P. n abbr (Brit) = **old age pensioner**

oar [ɔːʳ] n aviron m, rame f; **to put** or **shove one's ~ in** (fig: inf) mettre son grain de sel

oasis (pl **oases**) [əu'eɪsɪs, əu'eɪsiːz] n oasis f

oath [əuθ] n serment m; (swear word) juron m; **to take the ~** prêter serment; **on** (Brit) or **under ~** sous serment, assermenté(e)

oatmeal ['əutmiːl] n flocons mpl d'avoine

oats [əuts] n avoine f

obedience [ə'biːdiəns] n obéissance f; **in ~ to** conformément à

obedient [ə'biːdiənt] adj obéissant(e); **to be ~ to sb/sth** obéir à qn/qch

obese [əu'biːs] adj obèse

obesity [əu'biːsɪtɪ] n obésité f

obey [ə'beɪ] vt obéir à; (instructions, regulations) se conformer à ▷ vi obéir

obituary [ə'bɪtjuərɪ] n nécrologie f

object n ['ɔbdʒɪkt] objet m; (purpose) but m, objet; (Ling) complément m d'objet ▷ vi [ə b'dʒɛkt]: **to ~** (attitude) désapprouver; (proposal) protester contre, élever une objection contre; **I ~!** je proteste!; **he ~ed that** ... il a fait valoir or a objecté que ...; **do you ~ to my smoking?** est-ce que cela vous gêne si je fume?; **what's the ~ of doing that?** quel est l'intérêt de faire cela?; **money is no ~** l'argent n'est pas un problème

objection [əb'dʒɛkʃən] n objection f; (drawback) inconvénient m; **if you have no ~** si vous n'y voyez pas d'inconvénient; **to make** or **raise an ~** élever une objection

objectionable [əb'dʒɛkʃənəbl] adj très désagréable; choquant(e)

objective [əb'dʒɛktɪv] n objectif m ▷ adj objectif(-ive)

obligation [ɔblɪ'geɪʃən] n obligation f, devoir m; (debt) dette f (de reconnaissance); **"without ~"** "sans engagement"

obligatory [ə'blɪgətərɪ] adj obligatoire

oblige [ə'blaɪdʒ] vt (force): **to ~ sb to do** obliger or forcer qn à faire; (do a favour) rendre service à, obliger; **to be ~d to sb for sth** être obligé(e) à qn de qch; **anything to ~!** (inf) (toujours prêt à rendre) service!

obliging [ə'blaɪdʒɪŋ] adj obligeant(e), serviable

oblique [ə'bliːk] adj oblique; (allusion) indirect(e) ▷ n (Brit Typ): **~ (stroke)** barre f oblique

obliterate [ə'blɪtəreɪt] vt effacer

oblivion [ə'blɪvɪən] n oubli m

oblivious [ə'blɪvɪəs] adj: **~ of** oublieux(-euse) de

oblong ['ɔblɔŋ] adj oblong(ue) ▷ n rectangle m

obnoxious [əb'nɔkʃəs] adj odieux(-euse); (smell) nauséabond(e)

oboe ['əubəu] n hautbois m

obscene [əb'siːn] adj obscène

obscure [əb'skjuəʳ] adj obscur(e) ▷ vt obscurcir; (hide: sun) cacher

observant [əb'zəːvnt] adj observateur(-trice)

observation [ɔbzə'veɪʃən] n observation f; (by police etc) surveillance f

observatory [əb'zəːvətrɪ] n observatoire m

observe [əb'zəːv] vt observer; (remark) faire observer or remarquer

observer [əb'zəːvəʳ] n observateur(-trice)

obsess [əb'sɛs] vt obséder; **to be ~ed by** or **with sb/sth** être obsédé(e) par qn/qch

obsession [əb'sɛʃən] n obsession f

obsessive [əb'sɛsɪv] adj obsédant(e)

obsolete ['ɔbsəliːt] adj dépassé(e), périmé(e)

obstacle ['ɔbstəkl] n obstacle m

obstacle race n course f d'obstacles

obstinate ['ɔbstɪnɪt] adj obstiné(e); (pain, cold) persistant(e)

obstruct [əb'strʌkt] vt (block) boucher, obstruer; (halt) arrêter; (hinder) entraver

obstruction [əb'strʌkʃən] n obstruction f; (to plan, progress) obstacle m

obtain [əb'teɪn] vt obtenir ▷ vi avoir cours

obvious ['ɔbvɪəs] adj évident(e), manifeste

obviously ['ɔbvɪəslɪ] adv manifestement; (of course): **~, he ... or he ~ ...** il est bien évident qu'il ...; **~!** bien sûr!; **~ not!** évidemment pas!, bien sûr que non!

occasion [ə'keɪʒən] n occasion f; (event) événement m ▷ vt occasionner, causer; **on that ~** à cette occasion; **to rise to the ~** se montrer à la hauteur de la situation

occasional [əˈkeɪʒənl] *adj* pris(e) (or fait(e) *etc*) de temps en temps; (*worker, spending*) occasionnel(le)

occasionally [əˈkeɪʒənəlɪ] *adv* de temps en temps, quelquefois; **very ~** (*assez*) rarement

occult [ɔˈkʌlt] *adj* occulte ▷ *n*: **the ~** le surnaturel

occupant [ˈɔkjupənt] *n* occupant *m*

occupation [ɔkjuˈpeɪʃən] *n* occupation *f*; (*job*) métier *m*, profession *f*; **unfit for ~** (*house*) impropre à l'habitation

occupational hazard *n* risque *m* du métier

occupier [ˈɔkjupaɪə*ʳ*] *n* occupant(e)

occupy [ˈɔkjupaɪ] *vt* occuper; **to ~ o.s. with** or **by doing** s'occuper à faire; **to be occupied with** être occupé avec qch

occur [əˈkə:*ʳ*] *vi* se produire; (*difficulty, opportunity*) se présenter; (*phenomenon, error*) se rencontrer; **to ~ to sb** venir à l'esprit de qn

occurrence [əˈkʌrəns] *n* (*existence*) présence *f*, existence *f*; (*event*) cas *m*, fait *m*

ocean [ˈəuʃən] *n* océan *m*; **~s of** (*inf*) des masses de

o'clock [əˈklɔk] *adv*: **it is 5 ~** il est 5 heures

OCR *n abbr* = **optical character reader**; **optical character recognition**

Oct. *abbr* (= **October**) oct

October [ɔkˈtəubə*ʳ*] *n* octobre *m*; *see also* **July**

octopus [ˈɔktəpəs] *n* pieuvre *f*

odd [ɔd] *adj* (*strange*) bizarre, curieux(-euse); (*number*) impair(e); (*left over*) qui reste, en plus; (*not of a set*) dépareillé(e); **60~** 60 et quelques; **at ~ times** de temps en temps; **the ~ one out** l'exception *f*

oddity [ˈɔdɪtɪ] *n* bizarrerie *f*; (*person*) excentrique *m/f*

odd-job man [ɔdˈdʒɔb-] *irreg n* homme *m* à tout faire

odd jobs *npl* petits travaux divers

oddly [ˈɔdlɪ] *adv* bizarrement, curieusement

oddments [ˈɔdmənts] *npl* (*Brit Comm*) fins *fpl* de série

odds [ɔdz] *npl* (*in betting*) cote *f*; **the ~ are against his coming** il y a peu de chances qu'il vienne; **it makes no ~** cela n'a pas d'importance; **to succeed against all the ~** réussir contre toute attente; **~ and ends** de petites choses; **at ~** en désaccord

odometer [ɔˈdɔmɪtə*ʳ*] *n* (*US*) odomètre *m*

odour, odor (*US*) [ˈəudə*ʳ*] *n* odeur *f*

KEYWORD

of [ɔv, əv] *prep* **1** (*gen*) de; **a friend of ours** un de nos amis; **a boy of 10** un garçon de 10 ans; **that was kind of you** c'était gentil de votre part

2 (*expressing quantity, amount, dates etc*) de; **a kilo of flour** un kilo de farine; **how much of this do you need?** combien vous en faut-il?; **there were three of them** (*people*) ils étaient 3; (*objects*) il y en avait 3; **three of us went**

3 d'entre nous y sont allé(e)s; **the 5th of July** le 5 juillet; **a quarter of 4** (*US*) 4 heures moins le quart

3 (*from, out of*) en, de; **a statue of marble** une statue de or en marbre; **made of wood** (fait) en bois

off [ɔf] *adj, adv* (*engine*) coupé(e); (*light, TV*) éteint(e); (*tap*) fermé(e); (*Brit: food*) mauvais(e), avancé(e); (: *milk*) tourné(e); (*absent*) absent(e); (*cancelled*) annulé(e); (*removed*): **the lid was ~** le couvercle était retiré or n'était pas mis; (*away*): **to run/drive ~** partir en courant/en voiture ▷ *prep* de; **to be ~** (*to leave*) partir, s'en aller; **I must be ~** il faut que je file; **to be ~ sick** être absent pour cause de maladie; **a day ~** un jour de congé; **to have an ~ day** n'être pas en forme; **he had his coat ~** il avait enlevé son manteau; **the hook is ~** le crochet s'est détaché; le crochet n'est pas mis; **10% ~** (*Comm*) 10% de rabais; **5 km ~ (the road)** à 5 km de la route; **~ the coast** au large de la côte; **a house ~ the main road** une maison à l'écart de la grand-route; **it's a long way ~** c'est loin (d'ici); **I'm ~ meat** je ne mange plus de viande; je n'aime plus la viande; **on the ~ chance** à tout hasard; **to be well/badly ~** être bien/mal loti; (*financially*) être aisé/dans la gêne; **~ and on, on and ~** de temps à autre; **I'm afraid the chicken is ~** (*Brit: not available*) je regrette, il n'y a plus de poulet; **that's a bit ~** (*fig: inf*) c'est un peu fort

offal [ˈɔfl] *n* (*Culin*) abats *mpl*

off-colour [ˈɔfˈkʌlə*ʳ*] *adj* (*Brit: ill*) malade, mal fichu(e); **to feel ~** être mal fichu

offence, (*US*) **offense** [əˈfens] *n* (*crime*) délit *m*, infraction *f*; **to give ~ to** blesser, offenser; **to take ~ at** se vexer de, s'offenser de; **to commit an ~** commettre une infraction

offend [əˈfend] *vt* (*person*) offenser, blesser ▷ *vi*: **to ~ against** (*law, rule*) contrevenir à, enfreindre

offender [əˈfendə*ʳ*] *n* délinquant(e); (*against regulations*) contrevenant(e)

offense [əˈfens] *n* (*US*) = **offence**

offensive [əˈfensɪv] *adj* offensant(e), choquant(e); (*smell etc*) très déplaisant(e); (*weapon*) offensif(-ive) ▷ *n* (*Mil*) offensive *f*

offer [ˈɔfə*ʳ*] *n* offre *f*, proposition *f* ▷ *vt* offrir, proposer; **to make an ~ for sth** faire une offre pour qch; **to ~ sth to sb**, **~ sb sth** offrir qch à qn; **to ~ to do sth** proposer de faire qch; **"on ~"** (*Comm*) "en promotion"

offering [ˈɔfərɪŋ] *n* offrande *f*

offhand [ˈɔfˈhænd] *adj* désinvolte ▷ *adv* spontanément; **I can't tell you ~** je ne peux pas vous le dire comme ça

office [ˈɔfɪs] *n* (*place*) bureau *m*; (*position*) charge *f*, fonction *f*; **doctor's ~** (*US*) cabinet (*médical*); **to take ~** entrer en fonctions; **through his good ~s** (*fig*) grâce à ses bons

o

offices; **O~ of Fair Trading** (Brit) *organisme de protection contre les pratiques commerciales abusives*
office automation n bureautique f
office block, (US) **office building** n immeuble m de bureaux
office hours npl heures fpl de bureau; (US Med) heures de consultation
officer ['ɒfɪsə'] n (Mil etc) officier m; (also: **police ~**) agent m (de police); (of organization) membre m du bureau directeur
office worker n employé(e) de bureau
official [ə'fɪʃl] adj (authorized) officiel(le) ▷ n officiel m; (civil servant) fonctionnaire m/f; (of railways, post office, town hall) employé(e)
officiate [ə'fɪʃɪeɪt] vi (Rel) officier; **to ~ as Mayor** exercer les fonctions de maire; **to ~ at a marriage** célébrer un mariage
officious [ə'fɪʃəs] adj trop empressé(e)
offing ['ɒfɪŋ] n: **in the ~** (fig) en perspective
off-licence ['ɒflaɪsns] n (Brit: shop) débit m de vins et de spiritueux
off-line [ɒf'laɪn] adj (Comput) (en mode) autonome; (: switched off) non connecté(e)
off-peak [ɒf'piːk] adj aux heures creuses; (electricity, ticket) au tarif heures creuses
off-putting ['ɒfputɪŋ] adj (Brit: remark) rébarbatif(-ive); (person) rebutant(e), peu engageant(e)
off-road vehicle ['ɒfrəud-] n véhicule m tout-terrain
off-season ['ɒf'siːzn] adj, adv hors-saison inv
offset ['ɒfset] vt (irreg like: **set**) (counteract) contrebalancer, compenser ▷ n (also: **~ printing**) offset m
offshoot ['ɒfʃuːt] n (fig) ramification f, antenne f; (: of discussion etc) conséquence f
offshore [ɒf'ʃɔː'] adj (breeze) de terre; (island) proche du littoral; (fishing) côtier(-ière); **~ oilfield** gisement m pétrolifère en mer
offside ['ɒf'saɪd] n (Aut: with right-hand drive) côté droit; (: with left-hand drive) côté gauche ▷ adj (Sport) hors jeu; (Aut: in Britain) de droite; (: in US, Europe) de gauche
offspring ['ɒfsprɪŋ] n progéniture f
offstage [ɒf'steɪdʒ] adv dans les coulisses
off-the-peg ['ɒfðə'pɛg], (US) **off-the-rack** ['ɒfðə'ræk] adv en prêt-à-porter
off-white ['ɒfwaɪt] adj blanc cassé inv
often ['ɒfn] adv souvent; **how ~ do you go?** vous y allez tous les combien?; **every so ~** de temps en temps, de temps à autre; **as ~ as not** la plupart du temps
Ofwat ['ɒfwɒt] n abbr (Brit: = Office of Water Services) organisme qui surveille les activités des compagnies des eaux
oh [əu] excl ô!, oh!, ah!
oil [ɔɪl] n huile f; (petroleum) pétrole m; (for central heating) mazout m ▷ vt (machine) graisser
oilcan ['ɔɪlkæn] n burette f de graissage; (for storing) bidon m à huile

oilfield ['ɔɪlfiːld] n gisement m de pétrole
oil filter n (Aut) filtre m à huile
oil painting n peinture f à l'huile
oil refinery n raffinerie f de pétrole
oil rig n derrick m; (at sea) plate-forme pétrolière
oil slick n nappe f de mazout
oil tanker n (ship) pétrolier m; (truck) camion-citerne m
oil well n puits m de pétrole
oily ['ɔɪlɪ] adj huileux(-euse); (food) gras(se)
ointment ['ɔɪntmənt] n onguent m
O.K., okay ['əu'keɪ] (inf) excl d'accord! ▷ vt approuver, donner son accord à ▷ n: **to give sth one's ~** donner son accord à qch ▷ adj (not bad) pas mal, en règle; en bon état; sain et sauf; acceptable; **is it ~?, are you ~?** ça va?; **are you ~ for money?** ça va or ira question argent?; **it's ~ with** or **by me** ça me va, c'est d'accord en ce qui me concerne
old [əuld] adj vieux/vieille; (person) vieux, âgé(e); (former) ancien(ne), vieux; **how ~ are you?** quel âge avez-vous?; **he's 10 years ~** il a 10 ans, il est âgé de 10 ans; **~er brother/sister** frère/sœur aîné(e); **any ~ thing will do** n'importe quoi fera l'affaire
old age n vieillesse f
old-age pensioner n (Brit) retraité(e)
old-fashioned ['əuld'fæʃnd] adj démodé(e); (person) vieux jeu inv
old people's home n (esp Brit) maison f de retraite
olive ['ɒlɪv] n (fruit) olive f; (tree) olivier m ▷ adj (also: **~-green**) (vert) olive inv
olive oil n huile f d'olive
Olympic [əu'lɪmpɪk] adj olympique; **the ~ Games, the ~s** les Jeux mpl olympiques
omelette, omelet ['ɒmlɪt] n omelette f; **ham/cheese omelet(te)** omelette au jambon/fromage
omen ['əumən] n présage m
ominous ['ɒmɪnəs] adj menaçant(e), inquiétant(e); (event) de mauvais augure
omit [əu'mɪt] vt omettre; **to ~ to do sth** négliger de faire qch

⊙ KEYWORD

on [ɒn] prep **1** (indicating position) sur; **on the table** sur la table; **on the wall** sur le or au mur; **on the left** à gauche; **I haven't any money on me** je n'ai pas d'argent sur moi
2 (indicating means, method, condition etc): **on foot** à pied; **on the train/plane** (be) dans le train/l'avion; (go) en train/avion; **on the telephone/radio/television** au téléphone/à la radio/à la télévision; **to be on drugs** se droguer; **on holiday**, Brit **on vacation** (US) en vacances; **on the continent** sur le continent
3 (referring to time): **on Friday** vendredi; **on Fridays** le vendredi; **on June 20th** le 20 juin; **a week on Friday** vendredi en huit; **on arrival**

à l'arrivée; **on seeing this** en voyant cela
4 (*about, concerning*) sur, de; **a book on Balzac/
physics** un livre sur Balzac/de physique
5 (*at the expense of*): **this round is on me** c'est
ma tournée
▷ *adv* **1** (*referring to dress*): **to have one's coat
on** avoir (mis) son manteau; **to put one's
coat on** mettre son manteau; **what's she
got on?** qu'est-ce qu'elle porte?
2 (*referring to covering*): **screw the lid on
tightly** vissez bien le couvercle
3 (*further, continuously*): **to walk** *etc* **on**
continuer à marcher *etc*; **on and off** de temps
à autre; **from that day on** depuis ce jour
▷ *adj* **1** (*in operation: machine*) en marche;
(: *radio, TV, light*) allumé(e); (: *tap, gas*)
ouvert(e); (: *brakes*) mis(e); **is the meeting
still on?** (*not cancelled*) est-ce que la réunion a
bien lieu?; **it was well on in the evening**
c'était tard dans la soirée; **when is this film
on?** quand passe ce film?
2 (*inf*): **that's not on!** (*not acceptable*) cela ne se
fait pas!; (*not possible*) pas question!

once [wʌns] *adv* une fois; (*formerly*) autrefois
▷ *conj* une fois que + *sub*; **~ he had left/it was
done** une fois qu'il fut parti/que ce fut
terminé; **at ~** tout de suite, immédiatement;
(*simultaneously*) à la fois; **all at ~** *adv* tout d'un
coup; **~ a week** une fois par semaine; **~ more**
encore une fois; **I knew him ~** je l'ai connu
autrefois; **~ and for all** une fois pour toutes;
~ upon a time there was … il y avait une
fois …, il était une fois …

oncoming ['ɒnkʌmɪŋ] *adj* (*traffic*) venant en
sens inverse

 KEYWORD

one [wʌn] *num* un(e); **one hundred and fifty**
cent cinquante; **one by one** un(e) à *or* par
un(e); **one day** un jour
▷ *adj* **1** (*sole*) seul(e), unique; **the one book
which** l'unique *or* le seul livre qui; **the one
man who** le seul (homme) qui
2 (*same*): **they came in the one car** ils
sont venus dans la même voiture
▷ *pron* **1**: **this one** celui-ci/celle-ci; **that one**
celui-là/celle-là; **I've already got one/a red
one** j'en ai déjà un(e)/un(e) rouge; **which
one do you want?** lequel voulez-vous?
2: **one another** l'un(e) l'autre; **to look at
one another** se regarder
3 (*impersonal*) on; **one never knows** on ne sait
jamais; **to cut one's finger** se couper le
doigt; **one needs to eat** il faut manger
4 (*phrases*): **to be one up on sb** avoir
l'avantage sur qn; **to be at one (with sb)** être
d'accord (avec qn)

one-day excursion ['wʌndeɪ-] *n* (US) billet *m*
d'aller-retour (valable pour la journée)

one-man ['wʌn'mæn] *adj* (*business*) dirigé(e)
etc par un seul homme
one-man band *n* homme-orchestre *m*
one-off [wʌn'ɒf] *n* (*Brit inf*) exemplaire *m*
unique ▷ *adj* unique
oneself [wʌn'sɛlf] *pron* se; (*after prep, also
emphatic*) soi-même; **to hurt ~** se faire mal; **to
keep sth for ~** garder qch pour soi; **to talk
to ~** se parler à soi-même; **by ~** tout seul
one-shot [wʌn'ʃɒt] (US) *n* = **one-off**
one-sided [wʌn'saɪdɪd] *adj* (*argument, decision*)
unilatéral(e); (*judgment, account*) partial(e);
(*contest*) inégal(e)
one-to-one ['wʌntəwʌn] *adj* (*relationship*)
univoque
one-way ['wʌnweɪ] *adj* (*street, traffic*) à sens
unique
ongoing ['ɒngəʊɪŋ] *adj* en cours; (*relationship*)
suivi(e)
onion ['ʌnjən] *n* oignon *m*
on-line ['ɒnlaɪn] *adj* (*Comput*) en ligne;
(: *switched on*) connecté(e)
onlooker ['ɒnlʊkəʳ] *n* spectateur(-trice)
only ['əʊnlɪ] *adv* seulement ▷ *adj* seul(e),
unique ▷ *conj* seulement, mais; **an ~ child**
un enfant unique; **not ~ … but also** non
seulement … mais aussi; **I ~ took one** j'en ai
seulement pris un, je n'en ai pris qu'un;
I saw her ~ yesterday je l'ai vue hier encore;
I'd be ~ too pleased to help je ne serais que
trop content de vous aider; **I would come,
~ I'm very busy** je viendrais bien mais j'ai
beaucoup à faire
on-screen [ɒn'skriːn] *adj* à l'écran
onset ['ɒnsɛt] *n* début *m*; (*of winter, old age*)
approche *f*
onshore ['ɒnʃɔːʳ] *adj* (*wind*) du large
onslaught ['ɒnslɔːt] *n* attaque *f*, assaut *m*
onto ['ɒntʊ] *prep* = **on to**
onward ['ɒnwəd], **onwards** ['ɒnwədz] *adv*
(*move*) en avant; **from that time ~s** à partir
de ce moment
oops [ʊps] *excl* houp!; **~-a-daisy!** houp-là!
ooze [uːz] *vi* suinter
opaque [əʊ'peɪk] *adj* opaque
OPEC ['əʊpɛk] *n abbr* (= *Organization of Petroleum-
Exporting Countries*) OPEP *f*
open ['əʊpn] *adj* ouvert(e); (*car*) découvert(e);
(*road, view*) dégagé(e); (*meeting*) public(-ique);
(*admiration*) manifeste; (*question*) non résolu(e);
(*enemy*) déclaré(e) ▷ *vt* ouvrir ▷ *vi* (*flower, eyes,
door, debate*) s'ouvrir; (*shop, bank, museum*)
ouvrir; (*book etc: commence*) commencer,
débuter; **is it ~ to public?** est-ce ouvert au
public?; **what time do you ~?** à quelle heure
ouvrez-vous?; **in the ~ (air)** en plein air; **the
~ sea** le large; **~ ground** (*among trees*) clairière
f; (*waste ground*) terrain *m* vague; **to have an ~
mind (on sth)** avoir l'esprit ouvert (sur qch);
open on to *vt fus* (*room, door*) donner sur;
open out *vt* ouvrir ▷ *vi* s'ouvrir; **open up** *vt*
ouvrir; (*blocked road*) dégager ▷ *vi* s'ouvrir

o

open-air [əupn'ɛəʳ] *adj* en plein air
opening ['əupnɪŋ] *n* ouverture *f*; (*opportunity*) occasion *f*; (*work*) débouché *m*; (*job*) poste vacant
opening hours *npl* heures *fpl* d'ouverture
open learning *n enseignement universitaire à la carte, notamment par correspondance*; (*distance learning*) télé-enseignement *m*
openly ['əupnlɪ] *adv* ouvertement
open-minded [əupn'maɪndɪd] *adj* à l'esprit ouvert
open-necked ['əupnnɛkt] *adj* à col ouvert
open-plan ['əupn'plæn] *adj* sans cloisons
Open University *n* (*Brit*) *cours universitaires par correspondance*; *voir article*

> ○ **OPEN UNIVERSITY**
> ○
> ○ L'*Open University* a été fondée en 1969.
> ○ L'enseignement comprend des cours
> ○ (certaines plages horaires sont réservées
> ○ à cet effet à la télévision et à la radio), des
> ○ devoirs qui sont envoyés par l'étudiant à
> ○ son directeur ou sa directrice d'études, et
> ○ un séjour obligatoire en université d'été.
> ○ Il faut préparer un certain nombre
> ○ d'unités de valeur pendant une période
> ○ de temps déterminée et obtenir la
> ○ moyenne à un certain nombre d'entre
> ○ elles pour recevoir le diplôme visé.

opera ['ɔpərə] *n* opéra *m*
opera house *n* opéra *m*
opera singer *n* chanteur(-euse) d'opéra
operate ['ɔpəreɪt] *vt* (*machine*) faire marcher, faire fonctionner; (*system*) pratiquer ▷ *vi* fonctionner; (*drug*) faire effet; **to ~ on sb (for)** (*Med*) opérer qn (de)
operatic [ɔpə'rætɪk] *adj* d'opéra
operating ['ɔpəreɪtɪŋ] *adj* (*Comm: costs, profit*) d'exploitation; (*Med*): **~ table** table *f* d'opération
operating room *n* (*US: Med*) salle *f* d'opération
operating theatre *n* (*Brit: Med*) salle *f* d'opération
operation [ɔpə'reɪʃən] *n* opération *f*; (*of machine*) fonctionnement *m*; **to have an ~ (for)** se faire opérer (de); **to be in ~** (*machine*) être en service; (*system*) être en vigueur
operational [ɔpə'reɪʃənl] *adj* opérationnel(le); (*ready for use*) en état de marche; **when the service is fully ~** lorsque le service fonctionnera pleinement
operative ['ɔpərətɪv] *adj* (*measure*) en vigueur ▷ *n* (*in factory*) ouvrier(-ière); **the ~ word** le mot clef
operator ['ɔpəreɪtəʳ] *n* (*of machine*) opérateur(-trice); (*Tel*) téléphoniste *m/f*
opinion [ə'pɪnjən] *n* opinion *f*, avis *m*; **in my ~** à mon avis; **to seek a second ~** demander un deuxième avis

opinionated [ə'pɪnjəneɪtɪd] *adj* aux idées bien arrêtées
opinion poll *n* sondage *m* d'opinion
opponent [ə'pəunənt] *n* adversaire *m/f*
opportunity [ɔpə'tjuːnɪtɪ] *n* occasion *f*; **to take the ~ to do** or **of doing** profiter de l'occasion pour faire
oppose [ə'pəuz] *vt* s'opposer à; **to be ~d to sth** être opposé(e) à qch; **as ~d to** par opposition à
opposing [ə'pəuzɪŋ] *adj* (*side*) opposé(e)
opposite ['ɔpəzɪt] *adj* opposé(e); (*house etc*) d'en face ▷ *adv* en face ▷ *prep* en face de ▷ *n* opposé *m*, contraire *m*; (*of word*) contraire; **"see ~ page"** "voir ci-contre"
opposition [ɔpə'zɪʃən] *n* opposition *f*
oppress [ə'prɛs] *vt* opprimer
oppressive [ə'prɛsɪv] *adj* oppressif(-ive)
opt [ɔpt] *vi*: **to ~ for** opter pour; **to ~ to do** choisir de faire; **opt out** *vi* (*school, hospital*) devenir autonome; (*health service*) devenir privé(e); **to ~ out of** choisir de ne pas participer à or de ne pas faire
optical ['ɔptɪkl] *adj* optique; (*instrument*) d'optique
optical character reader *n* lecteur *m* optique
optical character recognition *n* lecture *f* optique
optician [ɔp'tɪʃən] *n* opticien(ne)
optimism ['ɔptɪmɪzəm] *n* optimisme *m*
optimist ['ɔptɪmɪst] *n* optimiste *m/f*
optimistic [ɔptɪ'mɪstɪk] *adj* optimiste
optimum ['ɔptɪməm] *adj* optimum
option ['ɔpʃən] *n* choix *m*, option *f*; (*Scol*) matière *f* à option; (*Comm*) option; **to keep one's ~s open** (*fig*) ne pas s'engager; **I have no ~** je n'ai pas le choix
optional ['ɔpʃənl] *adj* facultatif(-ive); (*Comm*) en option; **~ extras** accessoires *mpl* en option, options *fpl*
or [ɔːʳ] *conj* ou; (*with negative*): **he hasn't seen or heard anything** il n'a rien vu ni entendu; **or else** sinon; ou bien
oral ['ɔːrəl] *adj* oral(e) ▷ *n* oral *m*
orange ['ɔrɪndʒ] *n* (*fruit*) orange *f* ▷ *adj* orange *inv*
orange juice *n* jus *m* d'orange
orbit ['ɔːbɪt] *n* orbite *f* ▷ *vt* graviter autour de; **to be in/go into ~ (round)** être/entrer en orbite (autour de)
orchard ['ɔːtʃəd] *n* verger *m*; **apple ~** verger de pommiers
orchestra ['ɔːkɪstrə] *n* orchestre *m*; (*US: seating*) (fauteuils *mpl* d')orchestre
orchid ['ɔːkɪd] *n* orchidée *f*
ordain [ɔː'deɪn] *vt* (*Rel*) ordonner; (*decide*) décréter
ordeal [ɔː'diːl] *n* épreuve *f*
order ['ɔːdəʳ] *n* ordre *m*; (*Comm*) commande *f* ▷ *vt* ordonner; (*Comm*) commander; **in ~** en ordre; (*of document*) en règle; **out of ~** (*not in*

correct order) en désordre; (machine) hors service; (telephone) en dérangement; **a machine in working ~** une machine en état de marche; **in ~ of size** par ordre de grandeur; **in ~ to do/ that** pour faire/que + sub; **to place an ~ for sth with sb** commander qch auprès de qn, passer commande de qch à qn; **could I ~ now, please?** je peux commander, s'il vous plaît?; **to be on ~** être en commande; **made to ~** fait sur commande; **to be under ~s to do sth** avoir ordre de faire qch; **a point of ~** un point de procédure; **to the ~ of** (Banking) à l'ordre de; **to ~ sb to do** ordonner à qn de faire

order form n bon m de commande

orderly ['ɔːdəlɪ] n (Mil) ordonnance f; (Med) garçon m de salle ▷ adj (room) en ordre; (mind) méthodique; (person) qui a de l'ordre

ordinary ['ɔːdnrɪ] adj ordinaire, normal(e); (pej) ordinaire, quelconque; **out of the ~** exceptionnel(le)

Ordnance Survey map n (Brit) ≈ carte f d'État-major

ore [ɔːʳ] n minerai m

oregano [ɒrɪ'gɑːnəʊ] n origan m

organ ['ɔːgən] n organe m; (Mus) orgue m, orgues fpl

organic [ɔː'gænɪk] adj organique; (crops etc) biologique, naturel(le)

organism ['ɔːgənɪzəm] n organisme m

organization [ɔːgənaɪ'zeɪʃən] n organisation f

organize ['ɔːgənaɪz] vt organiser; **to get ~d** s'organiser

organized ['ɔːgənaɪzd] adj (planned) organisé(e); (efficient) bien organisé

organizer ['ɔːgənaɪzəʳ] n organisateur(-trice)

orgasm ['ɔːgæzəm] n orgasme m

orgy ['ɔːdʒɪ] n orgie f

Orient ['ɔːrɪənt] n: **the ~** l'Orient m

oriental [ɔːrɪ'entl] adj oriental(e) ▷ n Oriental(e)

orientation [ɔːrɪen'teɪʃən] n (attitudes) tendance f; (in job) orientation f; (of building) orientation, exposition f

origin ['ɒrɪdʒɪn] n origine f; **country of ~** pays m d'origine

original [ə'rɪdʒɪnl] adj original(e); (earliest) originel(le) ▷ n original m

originally [ə'rɪdʒɪnəlɪ] adv (at first) à l'origine

originate [ə'rɪdʒɪneɪt] vi: **to ~ from** être originaire de; (suggestion) provenir de; **to ~ in** (custom) prendre naissance dans, avoir son origine dans

Orkney ['ɔːknɪ] n (also: **the ~s, the ~ Islands**) les Orcades fpl

ornament ['ɔːnəmənt] n ornement m; (trinket) bibelot m

ornamental [ɔːnə'mentl] adj décoratif(-ive); (garden) d'agrément

ornate [ɔː'neɪt] adj très orné(e)

orphan ['ɔːfn] n orphelin(e) ▷ vt: **to be ~ed** devenir orphelin

orthodox ['ɔːθədɒks] adj orthodoxe

orthopaedic, (US) **orthopedic** [ɔːθə'piːdɪk] adj orthopédique

ostensibly [ɒs'tensɪblɪ] adv en apparence

ostentatious [ɒsten'teɪʃəs] adj prétentieux(-euse); ostentatoire

osteopath ['ɒstɪəpæθ] n ostéopathe m/f

ostracize ['ɒstrəsaɪz] vt frapper d'ostracisme

ostrich ['ɒstrɪtʃ] n autruche f

other ['ʌðəʳ] adj autre ▷ pron: **the ~ (one)** l'autre; **~s** (other people) d'autres ▷ adv: **~ than** autrement que; à part; **some actor or ~** un certain acteur, je ne sais quel acteur; **somebody or ~** quelqu'un; **some ~ people have still to arrive** on attend encore quelques personnes; **the ~ day** l'autre jour; **the car was none ~ than John's** la voiture n'était autre que celle de John

otherwise ['ʌðəwaɪz] adv, conj autrement; **an ~ good piece of work** par ailleurs, un beau travail

Ottawa ['ɒtəwə] n Ottawa

otter ['ɒtəʳ] n loutre f

ouch [autʃ] excl aïe!

ought (pt **ought**) [ɔːt] aux vb: **I ~ to do it** je devrais le faire, il faudrait que je le fasse; **this ~ to have been corrected** cela aurait dû être corrigé; **he ~ to win** (probability) il devrait gagner; **you ~ to go and see it** vous devriez aller le voir

ounce [auns] n once f (28.35g; 16 in a pound)

our ['auəʳ] adj notre, nos pl; see also **my**

ours [auəz] pron le/la nôtre, les nôtres; see also **mine**¹

ourselves [auə'selvz] pron pl (reflexive, after preposition) nous; (emphatic) nous-mêmes; **we did it (all) by ~** nous avons fait ça tous seuls; see also **oneself**

oust [aust] vt évincer

out [aut] adv dehors; (published, not at home etc) sorti(e); (light, fire) éteint(e); (on strike) en grève ▷ vt: **to ~ sb** révéler l'homosexualité de qn; **~ here** ici; **~ there** là-bas; **he's ~** (absent) il est sorti; (unconscious) il est sans connaissance; **to be ~ in one's calculations** s'être trompé dans ses calculs; **to run/back etc ~** sortir en courant/en reculant etc; **to be ~ and ab~** or (US) **around again** être de nouveau sur pied; **before the week was ~** avant la fin de la semaine; **the journey ~** l'aller m; **the boat was 10 km ~** le bateau était à 10 km du rivage; **~ loud** adv à haute voix; **~ of** prep (outside) en dehors de; (because of: anger etc) par; (from among): **10 ~ of 10** 10 sur 10; (without): **~ of petrol** sans essence, à court d'essence; **made ~ of wood** en or de bois; **~ of order** (machine) en panne; (Tel: line) en dérangement; **~ of stock** (Comm: article) épuisé(e); (: shop) en rupture de stock

out-and-out ['autəndaut] adj véritable

outback ['autbæk] n campagne isolée; (in Australia) intérieur m

outboard ['autbɔːd] n: ~ **(motor)** (moteur m) hors-bord m

outbound ['autbaund] adj: ~ **(from/for)** en partance (de/pour)

outbreak ['autbreɪk] n (of violence) éruption f, explosion f; (of disease) de nombreux cas; **the ~ of war south of the border** la guerre qui s'est déclarée au sud de la frontière

outburst ['autbɜːst] n explosion f, accès m

outcast ['autkɑːst] n exilé(e); (socially) paria m

outcome ['autkʌm] n issue f, résultat m

outcrop ['autkrɔp] n affleurement m

outcry ['autkraɪ] n tollé (général)

outdated [aut'deɪtɪd] adj démodé(e)

outdo [aut'duː] vt (irreg like: **do**) surpasser

outdoor [aut'dɔːʳ] adj de or en plein air

outdoors [aut'dɔːz] adv dehors; au grand air

outer ['autəʳ] adj extérieur(e); ~ **suburbs** grande banlieue

outer space n espace m cosmique

outfit ['autfɪt] n équipement m; (clothes) tenue f; (inf: Comm) organisation f, boîte f

outgoing ['autgəuɪŋ] adj (president, tenant) sortant(e); (character) ouvert(e), extraverti(e)

outgoings ['autgəuɪŋz] npl (Brit: expenses) dépenses fpl

outgrow [aut'grəu] vt (irreg like: **grow**) (clothes) devenir trop grand(e) pour

outhouse ['authaus] n appentis m, remise f

outing ['autɪŋ] n sortie f; excursion f

outlaw ['autlɔː] n hors-la-loi m inv ▷ vt (person) mettre hors la loi; (practice) proscrire

outlay ['autleɪ] n dépenses fpl; (investment) mise f de fonds

outlet ['autlet] n (for liquid etc) issue f, sortie f; (for emotion) exutoire m; (for goods) débouché m; (also: **retail ~**) point m de vente; (US: Elec) prise f de courant

outline ['autlaɪn] n (shape) contour m; (summary) esquisse f, grandes lignes ▷ vt (fig: theory, plan) exposer à grands traits

outlive [aut'lɪv] vt survivre à

outlook ['autluk] n perspective f; (point of view) attitude f

outlying ['autlaɪɪŋ] adj écarté(e)

outmoded [aut'məudɪd] adj démodé(e); dépassé(e)

outnumber [aut'nʌmbəʳ] vt surpasser en nombre

out-of-date [autəv'deɪt] adj (passport, ticket) périmé(e); (theory, idea) dépassé(e); (custom) désuet(-ète); (clothes) démodé(e)

out-of-doors [autəv'dɔːz] adv = **outdoors**

out-of-the-way ['autəvðə'weɪ] adj loin de tout; (fig) insolite

out-of-town [autəv'taun] adj (shopping centre etc) en périphérie

outpatient ['autpeɪʃənt] n malade m/f en consultation externe

outpost ['autpəust] n avant-poste m

output ['autput] n rendement m, production f; (Comput) sortie f ▷ vt (Comput) sortir

outrage ['autreɪdʒ] n (anger) indignation f; (violent act) atrocité f, acte m de violence; (scandal) scandale m ▷ vt outrager

outrageous [aut'reɪdʒəs] adj atroce; (scandalous) scandaleux(-euse)

outright adv [aut'raɪt] complètement; (deny, refuse) catégoriquement; (ask) carrément; (kill) sur le coup ▷ adj ['autraɪt] complet(-ète); catégorique

outset ['autset] n début m

outside [aut'saɪd] n extérieur m ▷ adj extérieur(e); (remote, unlikely): **an ~ chance** une (très) faible chance ▷ adv (au) dehors, à l'extérieur ▷ prep hors de, à l'extérieur de; (in front of) devant; **at the ~** (fig) au plus or maximum; ~ **left/right** n (Football) ailier gauche/droit

outside lane n (Aut: in Britain) voie f de droite; (: in US, Europe) voie de gauche

outside line n (Tel) ligne extérieure

outsider [aut'saɪdəʳ] n (in race etc) outsider m; (stranger) étranger(-ère)

outsize ['autsaɪz] adj énorme; (clothes) grande taille inv

outskirts ['autskɜːts] npl faubourgs mpl

outspoken [aut'spəukən] adj très franc/ franche

outstanding [aut'stændɪŋ] adj remarquable, exceptionnel(le); (unfinished: work, business) en suspens, en souffrance; (debt) impayé(e); (problem) non réglé(e); **your account is still ~** vous n'avez pas encore tout remboursé

outstay [aut'steɪ] vt: **to ~ one's welcome** abuser de l'hospitalité de son hôte

outstretched [aut'stretʃt] adj (hand) tendu(e); (body) étendu(e)

outstrip [aut'strɪp] vt (also fig) dépasser

out-tray ['auttreɪ] n courrier m "départ"

outward ['autwəd] adj (sign, appearances) extérieur(e); (journey) (d')aller

outwards ['autwədz] adv (esp Brit) = **outward**

outweigh [aut'weɪ] vt l'emporter sur

outwit [aut'wɪt] vt se montrer plus malin que

oval ['əuvl] adj, n ovale m

Oval Office n (US: Pol) voir article

⬤ **OVAL OFFICE**
⬤
⬤
⬤ L'Oval Office est le bureau personnel du
⬤ président des États-Unis à la Maison-
⬤ Blanche, ainsi appelé du fait de sa forme
⬤ ovale. Par extension, ce terme désigne la
⬤ présidence elle-même.

ovary ['əuvərɪ] n ovaire m

oven ['ʌvn] n four m

oven glove n gant m de cuisine

ovenproof ['ʌvnpruːf] adj allant au four

oven-ready ['ʌvnredɪ] adj prêt(e) à cuire

over ['əuvəʳ] adv (par-)dessus; (excessively) trop ▷ adj (or adv) (finished) fini(e), terminé(e); (too much) en plus ▷ *prep* sur; par-dessus; *(above)* au-dessus de; *(on the other side of)* de l'autre côté de; *(more than)* plus de; *(during)* pendant; *(about, concerning)*: **they fell out ~ money/her** ils se sont brouillés pour des questions d'argent/à cause d'elle; **~ here** ici; **~ there** là-bas; **all ~** *(everywhere)* partout; *(finished)* fini(e); **~ and ~ (again)** à plusieurs reprises; **~ and above** en plus de; **to ask sb ~** inviter qn (à passer); **to go ~ to sb's** passer chez qn; **to fall ~** tomber; **to turn sth ~** retourner qch; **now ~ to our Paris correspondent** nous passons l'antenne à notre correspondant à Paris; **the world ~** dans le monde entier; **she's not ~ intelligent** *(Brit)* elle n'est pas particulièrement intelligente

overall ['əʊvərɔːl] *adj (length)* total(e); *(study, impression)* d'ensemble ▷ *n (Brit)* blouse f ▷ *adv* [əʊvər'ɔːl] dans l'ensemble, en général; **overalls** *npl (boiler suit)* bleus *mpl* (de travail)

overawe [əʊvər'ɔː] *vt* impressionner

overbalance [əʊvə'bæləns] *vi* basculer

overboard ['əʊvəbɔːd] *adv (Naut)* par-dessus bord; **to go ~ for sth** *(fig)* s'emballer (pour qch)

overbook [əʊvə'buk] *vi* faire du surbooking

overcame [əʊvə'keɪm] *pt of* **overcome**

overcast ['əʊvəkɑːst] *adj* couvert(e)

overcharge [əʊvə'tʃɑːdʒ] *vt*: **to ~ sb for sth** faire payer qch trop cher à qn

overcoat ['əʊvəkəʊt] *n* pardessus *m*

overcome [əʊvə'kʌm] *vt (irreg like:* **come**) *(defeat)* triompher de; *(difficulty)* surmonter ▷ *adj (emotionally)* bouleversé(e); **~ with grief** accablé(e) de douleur

overcrowded [əʊvə'kraʊdɪd] *adj* bondé(e); *(city, country)* surpeuplé(e)

overdo [əʊvə'duː] *vt (irreg like:* **do**) exagérer; *(overcook)* trop cuire; **to ~ it, to ~ things** *(work too hard)* en faire trop, se surmener

overdone [əʊvə'dʌn] *adj (vegetables, steak)* trop cuit(e)

overdose ['əʊvədəʊs] *n* dose excessive

overdraft ['əʊvədrɑːft] *n* découvert *m*

overdrawn [əʊvə'drɔːn] *adj (account)* à découvert

overdue [əʊvə'djuː] *adj* en retard; *(bill)* impayé(e); *(change)* qui tarde; **that change was long ~** ce changement n'avait que trop tardé

overestimate [əʊvər'ɛstɪmeɪt] *vt* surestimer

overflow *vi* [əʊvə'fləʊ] déborder ▷ *n* ['əʊvəfləʊ] trop-plein *m*; *(also:* **~ pipe**) tuyau *m* d'écoulement, trop-plein *m*

overgrown [əʊvə'grəʊn] *adj (garden)* envahi(e) par la végétation; **he's just an ~ schoolboy** *(fig)* c'est un écolier attardé

overhaul *vt* [əʊvə'hɔːl] réviser ▷ *n* ['əʊvəhɔːl] révision f

overhead [*adv* əʊvə'hɛd, *adj, n* 'əʊvəhɛd] *adv* au-dessus ▷ *adj* aérien(ne); *(lighting)* vertical(e) ▷ *n (US)* = **overheads**

overhead projector *n* rétroprojecteur *m*

overheads ['əʊvəhɛdz] *npl (Brit)* frais généraux

overhear [əʊvə'hɪər] *vt (irreg like:* **hear**) entendre (par hasard)

overheat [əʊvə'hiːt] *vi* devenir surchauffé(e); *(engine)* chauffer

overjoyed [əʊvə'dʒɔɪd] *adj* ravi(e), enchanté(e)

overland ['əʊvəlænd] *adj, adv* par voie de terre

overlap *vi* [əʊvə'læp] se chevaucher ▷ *n* ['əʊvəlæp] chevauchement *m*

overleaf [əʊvə'liːf] *adv* au verso

overload [əʊvə'ləʊd] *vt* surcharger

overlook [əʊvə'luk] *vt (have view of)* donner sur; *(miss)* oublier, négliger; *(forgive)* fermer les yeux sur

overnight *adv* [əʊvə'naɪt] *(happen)* durant la nuit; *(fig)* soudain ▷ *adj* ['əʊvənaɪt] d'une *(or* de*)* nuit; soudain(e); **to stay ~ (with sb)** passer la nuit (chez qn); **he stayed there ~** il y a passé la nuit; **if you travel ~ ...** si tu fais le voyage de nuit ...; **he'll be away ~** il ne rentrera pas ce soir

overnight bag *n* nécessaire *m* de voyage

overpass ['əʊvəpɑːs] *n (US: for cars)* pont autoroutier; *(: for pedestrians)* passerelle f, pont *m*

overpower [əʊvə'paʊər] *vt* vaincre; *(fig)* accabler

overpowering [əʊvə'paʊərɪŋ] *adj* irrésistible; *(heat, stench)* suffocant(e)

overrate [əʊvə'reɪt] *vt* surestimer

overreact [əʊvəriː'ækt] *vi* réagir de façon excessive

override [əʊvə'raɪd] *vt (irreg like:* **ride**) *(order, objection)* passer outre à; *(decision)* annuler

overriding [əʊvə'raɪdɪŋ] *adj* prépondérant(e)

overrule [əʊvə'ruːl] *vt (decision)* annuler; *(claim)* rejeter; *(person)* rejeter l'avis de

overrun [əʊvə'rʌn] *vt (irreg like:* **run**) *(Mil: country etc)* occuper; *(time limit etc)* dépasser ▷ *vi* dépasser le temps imparti; **the town is ~ with tourists** la ville est envahie de touristes

overseas [əʊvə'siːz] *adv* outre-mer; *(abroad)* à l'étranger ▷ *adj (trade)* extérieur(e); *(visitor)* étranger(-ère)

oversee [əʊvə'siː] *vt (irreg like:* **see**) surveiller

overshadow [əʊvə'ʃædəʊ] *vt (fig)* éclipser

oversight ['əʊvəsaɪt] *n* omission f, oubli *m*; **due to an ~** par la suite d'une inadvertance

oversleep [əʊvə'sliːp] *vi (irreg like:* **sleep**) se réveiller (trop) tard

overspend [əʊvə'spɛnd] *vi (irreg like:* **spend**) dépenser de trop; **we have overspent by 5,000 dollars** nous avons dépassé notre budget de 5 000 dollars, nous avons dépensé 5 000 dollars de trop

overstep [əʊvə'stɛp] *vt*: **to ~ the mark** dépasser la mesure

overt [əu'və:t] *adj* non dissimulé(e)

overtake [əuvə'teɪk] *vt* (*irreg like*: **take**) dépasser; (*Brit*: *Aut*) dépasser, doubler

overthrow [əuvə'θrəu] *vt* (*irreg like*: **throw**) (*government*) renverser

overtime ['əuvətaɪm] *n* heures *fpl* supplémentaires; **to do** *or* **work ~** faire des heures supplémentaires

overtone ['əuvətəun] *n* (*also*: **~s**) note *f*, sous-entendus *mpl*

overtook [əuvə'tuk] *pt of* **overtake**

overture ['əuvətʃuər] *n* (*Mus*, *fig*) ouverture *f*

overturn [əuvə'tə:n] *vt* renverser; (*decision*, *plan*) annuler ▷ *vi* se retourner

overweight [əuvə'weɪt] *adj* (*person*) trop gros(se); (*luggage*) trop lourd(e)

overwhelm [əuvə'welm] *vt* (*subj*: *emotion*) accabler, submerger; (*enemy*, *opponent*) écraser

overwhelming [əuvə'welmɪŋ] *adj* (*victory*, *defeat*) écrasant(e); (*desire*) irrésistible; **one's ~ impression is of heat** on a une impression dominante de chaleur

overwrought [əuvə'rɔ:t] *adj* excédé(e)

owe [əu] *vt* devoir; **to ~ sb sth**, **to ~ sth to sb** devoir qch à qn; **how much do I ~ you?** combien est-ce que je vous dois?

owing to ['əuɪŋtu:] *prep* à cause de, en raison de

owl [aul] *n* hibou *m*

own [əun] *vt* posséder ▷ *vi* (*Brit*): **to ~ to sth** reconnaître *or* avouer qch; **to ~ to having done sth** avouer avoir fait qch ▷ *adj* propre; **a room of my ~** une chambre à moi, ma propre chambre; **can I have it for my (very) ~?** puis-je l'avoir pour moi (tout) seul?; **to get one's ~ back** prendre sa revanche; **on one's ~** tout(e) seul(e); **to come into one's ~** trouver sa voie; trouver sa justification; **own up** *vi* avouer

owner ['əunər] *n* propriétaire *m/f*

ownership ['əunəʃɪp] *n* possession *f*; **it's under new ~** (*shop etc*) il y a eu un changement de propriétaire

ox (*pl* **oxen**) [ɔks, 'ɔksn] *n* bœuf *m*

Oxbridge ['ɔksbrɪdʒ] *n* (*Brit*) *les universités d'Oxford et de Cambridge*; *voir article*

● **OXBRIDGE**
●
● *Oxbridge*, nom formé à partir des mots
● Ox(ford) et (Cam)bridge, s'utilise pour
● parler de ces deux universités comme
● formant un tout, dans la mesure où elles
● sont toutes deux les universités
● britanniques les plus prestigieuses et
● mondialement connues.

oxen ['ɔksən] *npl of* **ox**

oxtail ['ɔksteɪl] *n*: **~ soup** soupe *f* à la queue de bœuf

oxygen ['ɔksɪdʒən] *n* oxygène *m*

oyster ['ɔɪstər] *n* huître *f*

oz. *abbr* = **ounce; ounces**

ozone ['əuzəun] *n* ozone *m*

ozone friendly ['əuzəunfrendlɪ] *adj* qui n'attaque pas *or* qui préserve la couche d'ozone

ozone hole *n* trou *m* d'ozone

ozone layer *n* couche *f* d'ozone

p

p *abbr* (= *page*) p; (*Brit*) = **penny; pence**

P.A. *n abbr* = **personal assistant; public address system** ▷ *abbr* (*US*) = **Pennsylvania**

pa [pɑː] *n* (*inf*) papa *m*

p.a. *abbr* = **per annum**

pace [peɪs] *n* pas *m*; (*speed*) allure *f*; vitesse *f* ▷ *vi*: **to ~ up and down** faire les cent pas; **to keep ~ with** aller à la même vitesse que; (*events*) se tenir au courant de; **to set the ~** (*running*) donner l'allure; (*fig*) donner le ton; **to put sb through his ~s** (*fig*) mettre qn à l'épreuve

pacemaker ['peɪsmeɪkəʳ] *n* (*Med*) stimulateur *m* cardiaque; (*Sport: also:* **pacesetter**) meneur(-euse) de train

Pacific [pə'sɪfɪk] *n*: **the ~ (Ocean)** le Pacifique, l'océan *m* Pacifique

pacifier ['pæsɪfaɪəʳ] *n* (*US: dummy*) tétine *f*

pack [pæk] *n* paquet *m*; (*bundle*) ballot *m*; (*of hounds*) meute *f*; (*of thieves, wolves etc*) bande *f*; (*of cards*) jeu *m*; (*US: of cigarettes*) paquet; (*back pack*) sac *m* à dos ▷ *vt* (*goods*) empaqueter, emballer; (*in suitcase etc*) emballer; (*box*) remplir; (*cram*) entasser; (*press down*) tasser; damer; (*Comput*) grouper, tasser ▷ *vi*: **to ~ (one's bags)** faire ses bagages; **to ~ into** (*room, stadium*) s'entasser dans; **to send sb ~ing** (*inf*) envoyer promener qn; **pack in** (*Brit inf*) *vi* (*machine*) tomber en panne ▷ *vt* (*boyfriend*) plaquer; **~ it in!** laisse tomber!; **pack off** *vt*: **to ~ sb off to** expédier qn à; **pack up** *vi* (*Brit inf: machine*) tomber en panne; (*: person*) se tirer ▷ *vt* (*belongings*) ranger; (*goods, presents*) empaqueter, emballer

package ['pækɪdʒ] *n* paquet *m*; (*of goods*) emballage *m*, conditionnement *m*; (*also:* **~ deal**: *agreement*) marché global; (*: purchase*) forfait *m*; (*Comput*) progiciel *m* ▷ *vt* (*goods*) conditionner

package holiday *n* (*Brit*) vacances organisées

package tour *n* voyage organisé

packaging ['pækɪdʒɪŋ] *n* (*wrapping materials*) emballage *m*; (*of goods*) conditionnement *m*

packed [pækt] *adj* (*crowded*) bondé(e)

packed lunch (*Brit*) *n* repas froid

packet ['pækɪt] *n* paquet *m*

packing ['pækɪŋ] *n* emballage *m*

packing case *n* caisse *f* (d'emballage)

pact [pækt] *n* pacte *m*, traité *m*

pad [pæd] *n* bloc(-notes *m*) *m*; (*to prevent friction*) tampon *m*; (*for inking*) tampon *m* encreur; (*inf: flat*) piaule *f* ▷ *vt* rembourrer ▷ *vi*: **to ~ in/about** *etc* entrer/aller et venir *etc* à pas feutrés

padded ['pædɪd] *adj* (*jacket*) matelassé(e); (*bra*) rembourré(e); **~ cell** cellule capitonnée

padding ['pædɪŋ] *n* rembourrage *m*; (*fig*) délayage *m*

paddle ['pædl] *n* (*oar*) pagaie *f*; (*US: for table tennis*) raquette *f* de ping-pong ▷ *vi* (*with feet*) barboter, faire trempette ▷ *vt*: **to ~ a canoe** *etc* pagayer

paddling pool ['pædlɪŋ-] *n* petit bassin

paddock ['pædək] *n* enclos *m*; (*Racing*) paddock *m*

padlock ['pædlɔk] *n* cadenas *m* ▷ *vt* cadenasser

paediatrics, (*US*) **pediatrics** [piːdɪ'ætrɪks] *n* pédiatrie *f*

paedophile, pedophile (*US*) ['piːdəʊfaɪl] *n* pédophile *m*

pagan ['peɪgən] *adj, n* païen(ne)

page [peɪdʒ] *n* (*of book*) page *f*; (*also:* **~ boy**) groom *m*, chasseur *m*; (*at wedding*) garçon *m* d'honneur ▷ *vt* (*in hotel etc*) (faire) appeler

pageant ['pædʒənt] *n* spectacle *m* historique; grande cérémonie

pageantry ['pædʒəntrɪ] *n* apparat *m*, pompe *f*

pager ['peɪdʒəʳ] *n* bip *m* (*inf*), Alphapage® *m*

paid [peɪd] *pt, pp of* **pay** ▷ *adj* (*work, official*) rémunéré(e); (*holiday*) payé(e); **to put ~ to** (*Brit*) mettre fin à, mettre par terre

pail [peɪl] *n* seau *m*

pain [peɪn] *n* douleur *f*; (*inf: nuisance*) plaie *f*; **to be in ~** souffrir, avoir mal; **to have a ~ in** avoir mal à *or* une douleur *or* dans; **to take ~s to do** se donner du mal pour faire; **on ~ of death** sous peine de mort

pained ['peɪnd] *adj* peiné(e), chagrin(e)

painful ['peɪnful] *adj* douloureux(-euse); (*difficult*) difficile, pénible

painfully ['peɪnfəlɪ] *adv* (*fig: very*) terriblement

p

painkiller ['peɪnkɪlə'] n calmant m, analgésique m

painless ['peɪnlɪs] adj indolore

painstaking ['peɪnzteɪkɪŋ] adj (person) soigneux(-euse); (work) soigné(e)

paint [peɪnt] n peinture f ▷ vt peindre; (fig) dépeindre; **to ~ the door blue** peindre la porte en bleu; **to ~ in oils** faire de la peinture à l'huile

paintbrush ['peɪntbrʌʃ] n pinceau m

painter ['peɪntə'] n peintre m

painting ['peɪntɪŋ] n peinture f; (picture) tableau m

paintwork ['peɪntwə:k] n (Brit) peintures fpl; (: of car) peinture f

pair [peə'] n (of shoes, gloves etc) paire f; (of people) couple m; (twosome) duo m; **~ of scissors** (paire de) ciseaux mpl; **~ of trousers** pantalon m; **pair off** vi se mettre par deux

pajamas [pə'dʒɑːməz] npl (US) pyjama(s) m(pl)

Pakistan [pɑːkɪ'stɑːn] n Pakistan m

Pakistani [pɑːkɪ'stɑːnɪ] adj pakistanais(e) ▷ n Pakistanais(e)

pal [pæl] n (inf) copain/copine

palace ['pæləs] n palais m

palatable ['pælɪtəbl] adj bon/bonne, agréable au goût

palate ['pælɪt] n palais m (Anat)

pale [peɪl] adj pâle ▷ vi pâlir ▷ n: **to be beyond the ~** être au ban de la société; **to grow** or **turn ~** (person) pâlir; **~ blue** adj bleu pâle inv; **to ~ into insignificance (beside)** perdre beaucoup d'importance (par rapport à)

Palestine ['pælɪstaɪn] n Palestine f

Palestinian [pælɪs'tɪnɪən] adj palestinien(ne) ▷ n Palestinien(ne)

palette ['pælɪt] n palette f

pall [pɔːl] n (of smoke) voile m ▷ vi: **to ~ (on)** devenir lassant (pour)

pallet ['pælɪt] n (for goods) palette f

pallid ['pælɪd] adj blême

palm [pɑːm] n (Anat) paume f; (also: **~ tree**) palmier m; (leaf, symbol) palme f ▷ vt: **to ~ sth off on sb** (inf) refiler qch à qn

Palm Sunday n le dimanche des Rameaux

paltry ['pɔːltrɪ] adj dérisoire; piètre

pamper ['pæmpə'] vt gâter, dorloter

pamphlet ['pæmflət] n brochure f; (political etc) tract m

pan [pæn] n (also: **sauce~**) casserole f; (also: **frying ~**) poêle f; (of lavatory) cuvette f ▷ vi (Cine) faire un panoramique ▷ vt (inf: book, film) éreinter; **to ~ for gold** laver du sable aurifère

pancake ['pænkeɪk] n crêpe f

panda ['pændə] n panda m

pandemic [pæn'dɛmɪk] n pandémie f

pandemonium [pændɪ'məʊnɪəm] n tohu-bohu m

pander ['pændə'] vi: **to ~** flatter bassement; obéir servilement à

pane [peɪn] n carreau m (de fenêtre), vitre f

panel ['pænl] n (of wood, cloth etc) panneau m; (Radio, TV) panel m, invités mpl; (for interview, exams) jury m; (official: of experts) table ronde, comité m

panelling, paneling (US) ['pænəlɪŋ] n boiseries fpl

pang [pæŋ] n: **~s of remorse** pincements mpl de remords; **~s of hunger/conscience** tiraillements mpl d'estomac/de la conscience

panhandler ['pænhændlə'] n (US inf) mendiant(e)

panic ['pænɪk] n panique f, affolement m ▷ vi s'affoler, paniquer

panicky ['pænɪkɪ] adj (person) qui panique or s'affole facilement

panic-stricken ['pænɪkstrɪkən] adj affolé(e)

panorama [pænə'rɑːmə] n panorama m

pansy ['pænzɪ] n (Bot) pensée f; (inf!) tapette f, pédé m

pant [pænt] vi haleter

panther ['pænθə'] n panthère f

panties ['pæntɪz] npl slip m, culotte f

pantihose ['pæntɪhəʊz] n (US) collant m

pantomime ['pæntəmaɪm] n (Brit) spectacle m de Noël; voir article

---

◉ **PANTOMIME**
◉
◉ Une *pantomime* (à ne pas confondre avec
◉ le mot tel qu'on l'utilise en français,
◉ que l'on appelle également de façon
◉ familière "panto", est un genre de farce
◉ où le personnage principal est souvent
◉ un jeune garçon et où il y a toujours une
◉ "dame", c'est-à-dire une vieille femme
◉ jouée par un homme, et un méchant.
◉ La plupart du temps, l'histoire est basée
◉ sur un conte de fées comme Cendrillon
◉ ou Le Chat botté, et le public est
◉ encouragé à participer en prévenant le
◉ héros d'un danger imminent. Ce genre
◉ de spectacle, qui s'adresse surtout aux
◉ enfants, vise également un public
◉ d'adultes au travers des nombreuses
◉ plaisanteries faisant allusion à des faits
◉ d'actualité.

---

pantry ['pæntrɪ] n garde-manger m inv; (room) office m

pants [pænts] n (Brit: woman's) culotte f, slip m; (: man's) slip, caleçon m; (US: trousers) pantalon m

pantyhose ['pæntɪhəʊz] (US) npl collant m

paper ['peɪpə'] n papier m; (also: **wall~**) papier peint; (also: **news~**) journal m; (academic essay) article m; (exam) épreuve écrite ▷ adj en or de papier ▷ vt tapisser (de papier peint); **papers** npl (also: **identity ~s**) papiers mpl (d'identité); **a piece of ~** (odd bit) un bout de papier; (sheet) une feuille de papier; **to put sth down on ~** mettre qch par écrit

paperback ['peɪpəbæk] n livre broché or non relié; (small) livre m de poche ▷ adj: **~ edition** édition brochée

paper bag n sac m en papier

paper clip n trombone m

paper handkerchief, paper hankie n (inf) mouchoir m en papier

paper shop n (Brit) marchand m de journaux

paperweight ['peɪpəweɪt] n presse-papiers m inv

paperwork ['peɪpəwə:k] n papiers mpl; (pej) paperasserie f

paprika ['pæprɪkə] n paprika m

par [pɑːʳ] n pair m; (Golf) normale f du parcours; **on a ~ with** à égalité avec, au même niveau que; **at ~** au pair; **above/below ~** au-dessus/au-dessous du pair; **to feel below** or **under** or **not up to ~** ne pas se sentir en forme

paracetamol [pærə'si:təmɔl] (Brit) n paracétamol m

parachute ['pærəʃuːt] n parachute m ▷ vi sauter en parachute

parade [pə'reɪd] n défilé m; (inspection) revue f; (street) boulevard m ▷ vt (fig) faire étalage de ▷ vi défiler; **a fashion ~** (Brit) un défilé de mode

paradise ['pærədaɪs] n paradis m

paradox ['pærədɔks] n paradoxe m

paradoxically [pærə'dɔksɪklɪ] adv paradoxalement

paraffin ['pærəfɪn] n (Brit): **~ (oil)** pétrole (lampant); **liquid ~** huile f de paraffine

paragon ['pærəgən] n parangon m

paragraph ['pærəgrɑːf] n paragraphe m; **to begin a new ~** aller à la ligne

parallel ['pærəlel] adj: **~ (with** or **to)** parallèle (à); (fig) analogue (à) ▷ n (line) parallèle f; (fig, Geo) parallèle m

paralysed ['pærəlaɪzd] adj paralysé(e)

paralysis (pl **paralyses**) [pə'rælɪsɪs, -siːz] n paralysie f

paralyze ['pærəlaɪz] vt paralyser

paramedic [pærə'medɪk] n auxiliaire m/f médical(e)

paramount ['pærəmaunt] adj: **of ~ importance** de la plus haute or grande importance

paranoid ['pærənɔɪd] adj (Psych) paranoïaque; (neurotic) paranoïde

paraphernalia [pærəfə'neɪlɪə] n attirail m, affaires fpl

parasite ['pærəsaɪt] n parasite m

parasol ['pærəsɔl] n ombrelle f; (at café etc) parasol m

paratrooper ['pærətruːpəʳ] n parachutiste m (soldat)

parcel ['pɑːsl] n paquet m, colis m ▷ vt (also: **~ up**) empaqueter; **parcel out** vt répartir

parchment ['pɑːtʃmənt] n parchemin m

pardon ['pɑːdn] n pardon m; (Law) grâce f ▷ vt pardonner à; (Law) gracier; **~!** pardon!; **~ me!** (after burping etc) excusez-moi!; **I beg your ~!** (I'm sorry) pardon!, je suis désolé!; **(I beg your) ~?,** (US) **~ me?** (what did you say?) pardon?

parent ['peərənt] n (father) père m; (mother) mère f; **parents** npl parents mpl

parental [pə'rentl] adj parental(e), des parents

Paris ['pærɪs] n Paris

parish ['pærɪʃ] n paroisse f; (Brit: civil) ≈ commune f ▷ adj paroissial(e)

Parisian [pə'rɪzɪən] adj parisien(ne), de Paris ▷ n Parisien(ne)

park [pɑːk] n parc m, jardin public ▷ vt garer ▷ vi se garer; **can I ~ here?** est-ce que je peux me garer ici?

parking ['pɑːkɪŋ] n stationnement m; **"no ~"** "stationnement interdit"

parking lot n (US) parking m, parc m de stationnement

parking meter n parc(o)mètre m

parking ticket n P.-V. m

parkway ['pɑːkweɪ] n (US) route f express (en site vert ou aménagé)

parliament ['pɑːləmənt] n parlement m

parliamentary [pɑːlə'mentərɪ] adj parlementaire

parlour, (US) **parlor** ['pɑːləʳ] n salon m

Parmesan [pɑːmɪ'zæn] n (also: **~ cheese**) Parmesan m

parochial [pə'rəukɪəl] adj paroissial(e); (pej) à l'esprit de clocher

parole [pə'rəul] n: **on ~** en liberté conditionnelle

parrot ['pærət] n perroquet m

parry ['pærɪ] vt esquiver, parer à

parsley ['pɑːslɪ] n persil m

parsnip ['pɑːsnɪp] n panais m

parson ['pɑːsn] n ecclésiastique m; (Church of England) pasteur m

part [pɑːt] n partie f; (of machine) pièce f; (Theat) rôle m; (Mus) voix f; partie; (of serial) épisode m; (US: in hair) raie f ▷ adj partiel(le) ▷ adv = **partly** ▷ vt séparer ▷ vi (people) se séparer; (crowd) s'ouvrir; (roads) se diviser; **to take ~ in** participer à, prendre part à; **to take sb's ~** prendre le parti de qn, prendre parti pour qn; **on his ~** de sa part; **for my ~** en ce qui me concerne; **for the most ~** en grande partie; dans la plupart des cas; **for the better ~ of the day** pendant la plus grande partie de la journée; **to be ~ and parcel of** faire partie de; **in ~** en partie; **to take sth in good/bad ~** prendre qch du bon/mauvais côté; **part with** vt fus (person) se séparer de; (possessions) se défaire de

part exchange n (Brit): **in ~** en reprise

partial ['pɑːʃl] adj (incomplete) partiel(le); (unjust) partial(e); **to be ~ to** aimer, avoir un faible pour

participant [pɑːˈtɪsɪpənt] n (in competition, campaign) participant(e)

participate [pɑːˈtɪsɪpeɪt] vi: **to ~ (in)** participer (à), prendre part (à)

participation [pɑːtɪsɪˈpeɪʃən] n participation f

participle [ˈpɑːtɪsɪpl] n participe m

particle [ˈpɑːtɪkl] n particule f; (of dust) grain m

particular [pəˈtɪkjuləʳ] adj (specific) particulier(-ière); (special) particulier, spécial(e); (fussy) difficile, exigeant(e); (careful) méticuleux(-euse); **in ~** en particulier, surtout

particularly [pəˈtɪkjuləlɪ] adv particulièrement; (in particular) en particulier

particulars [pəˈtɪkjuləz] npl détails mpl; (information) renseignements mpl

parting [ˈpɑːtɪŋ] n séparation f; (Brit: in hair) raie f ▷ adj d'adieu; **his ~ shot was ...** il lança en partant ....

partisan [pɑːtɪˈzæn] n partisan(e) ▷ adj partisan(e); de parti

partition [pɑːˈtɪʃən] n (Pol) partition f, division f; (wall) cloison f

partly [ˈpɑːtlɪ] adv en partie, partiellement

partner [ˈpɑːtnəʳ] n (Comm) associé(e); (Sport) partenaire m/f; (spouse) conjoint(e); (lover) ami(e); (at dance) cavalier(-ière) ▷ vt être l'associé or le partenaire or le cavalier de

partnership [ˈpɑːtnəʃɪp] n association f; **to go into ~ (with), form a ~ (with)** s'associer (avec)

partridge [ˈpɑːtrɪdʒ] n perdrix f

part-time [ˈpɑːtˈtaɪm] adj, adv à mi-temps, à temps partiel

party [ˈpɑːtɪ] n (Pol) parti m; (celebration) fête f; (: formal) réception f; (: in evening) soirée f; (team) équipe f; (group) groupe m; (Law) partie f; **dinner ~** dîner m; **to give** or **throw a ~** donner une réception; **we're having a ~ next Saturday** nous organisons une soirée or réunion entre amis samedi prochain; **it's for our son's birthday** - c'est pour la fête (or le goûter) d'anniversaire de notre garçon; **to be a ~ to a crime** être impliqué(e) dans un crime

party dress n robe habillée

pass [pɑːs] vt (time, object) passer; (place) passer devant; (friend) croiser; (exam) être reçu(e) à, réussir; (candidate) admettre; (overtake) dépasser; (approve) approuver, accepter; (law) promulguer ▷ vi passer; (Scol) être reçu(e) or admis(e), réussir ▷ n (permit) laissez-passer m inv; (membership card) carte f d'accès or d'abonnement; (in mountains) col m; (Sport) passe f; (Scol: also: **~ mark**): **to get a ~** être reçu(e) (sans mention); **to ~ sb sth** passer qch à qn; **could you ~ the salt/oil, please?** pouvez-vous me passer le sel/l'huile, s'il vous plaît?; **she could ~ for 25** on lui donnerait 25 ans; **to ~ sth through a ring** etc

(faire) passer qch dans un anneau etc; **could you ~ the vegetables round?** pourriez-vous faire passer les légumes?; **things have come to a pretty ~** (Brit) voilà où on en est!; **to make a ~ at sb** (inf) faire des avances à qn; **pass away** vi mourir; **pass by** vi passer ▷ vt (ignore) négliger; **pass down** vt (customs, inheritance) transmettre; **pass on** vi (die) s'éteindre, décéder ▷ vt (hand on): **to ~ on (to)** transmettre (à); (: illness) passer (à); (: price rises) répercuter (sur); **pass out** vi s'évanouir; (Brit Mil) sortir (d'une école militaire); **pass over** vt (ignore) passer sous silence; **pass up** vt (opportunity) laisser passer

passable [ˈpɑːsəbl] adj (road) praticable; (work) acceptable

passage [ˈpæsɪdʒ] n (also: **~way**) couloir m; (gen, in book) passage m; (by boat) traversée f

passbook [ˈpɑːsbuk] n livret m

passenger [ˈpæsɪndʒəʳ] n passager(-ère)

passer-by [pɑːsəˈbaɪ] n passant(e)

passing [ˈpɑːsɪŋ] adj (fig) passager(-ère); **in ~** en passant

passing place n (Aut) aire f de croisement

passion [ˈpæʃən] n passion f; **to have a ~ for sth** avoir la passion de qch

passionate [ˈpæʃənɪt] adj passionné(e)

passion fruit n fruit m de la passion

passive [ˈpæsɪv] adj (also Ling) passif(-ive)

passive smoking n tabagisme passif

Passover [ˈpɑːsəuvəʳ] n Pâque juive

passport [ˈpɑːspɔːt] n passeport m

passport control n contrôle m des passeports

passport office n bureau m de délivrance des passeports

password [ˈpɑːswɜːd] n mot m de passe

past [pɑːst] prep (in front of) devant; (further than) au delà de, plus loin que; après; (later than) après ▷ adv: **to run ~** passer en courant ▷ adj passé(e); (president etc) ancien(ne) ▷ n passé m; **he's ~ forty** il a dépassé la quarantaine, il a plus de or passé quarante ans; **ten/quarter ~ eight** huit heures dix/un or et quart; **it's ~ midnight** il est plus de minuit, il est passé minuit; **he ran ~ me** il m'a dépassé en courant, il a passé devant moi en courant; **for the ~ few/3 days** depuis quelques/3 jours; ces derniers/3 derniers jours; **in the ~** (gen) dans le temps, autrefois; (Ling) au passé; **I'm ~ caring** je ne m'en fais plus; **to be ~ it** (Brit inf: person) avoir passé l'âge

pasta [ˈpæstə] n pâtes fpl

paste [peɪst] n pâte f; (Culin: meat) pâté m (à tartiner); (: tomato) purée f, concentré m; (glue) colle f (de pâte); (jewellery) strass m ▷ vt coller

pastel [ˈpæstl] adj pastel inv ▷ n (Art: pencil) (crayon m) pastel m; (: drawing) (dessin m au) pastel; (colour) ton m pastel inv

pasteurized [ˈpæstəraɪzd] adj pasteurisé(e)

pastille ['pæstl] *n* pastille *f*

pastime ['pɑːstaɪm] *n* passe-temps *m inv*, distraction *f*

pastor ['pɑːstər] *n* pasteur *m*

pastry ['peɪstrɪ] *n* pâte *f*; (*cake*) pâtisserie *f*

pasture ['pɑːstʃər] *n* pâturage *m*

pasty[1] *n* ['pæstɪ] petit pâté (en croûte)

pasty[2] ['peɪstɪ] *adj* pâteux(-euse); (*complexion*) terreux(-euse)

pat [pæt] *vt* donner une petite tape à; (*dog*) caresser ▷ *n:* **a ~ of butter** une noisette de beurre; **to give sb/o.s. a ~ on the back** (*fig*) congratuler qn/se congratuler; **he knows it (off) ~**, (*US*) **he has it down** ~ il sait cela sur le bout des doigts

patch [pætʃ] *n* (*of material*) pièce *f*; (*eye patch*) cache *m*; (*spot*) tache *f*; (*of land*) parcelle *f*; (*on tyre*) rustine *f* ▷ *vt* (*clothes*) rapiécer; **a bad** ~ (*Brit*) une période difficile; **patch up** *vt* réparer

patchy ['pætʃɪ] *adj* inégal(e); (*incomplete*) fragmentaire

pâté ['pæteɪ] *n* pâté *m*, terrine *f*

patent ['peɪtnt, (*US*) 'pætnt] *n* brevet *m* (d'invention) ▷ *vt* faire breveter ▷ *adj* patent(e), manifeste

patent leather *n* cuir verni

paternal [pə'tɜːnl] *adj* paternel(le)

paternity leave [pə'tɜːnɪtɪ-] *n* congé *m* de paternité

path [pɑːθ] *n* chemin *m*, sentier *m*; (*in garden*) allée *f*; (*of planet*) course *f*; (*of missile*) trajectoire *f*

pathetic [pə'θetɪk] *adj* (*pitiful*) pitoyable; (*very bad*) lamentable, minable; (*moving*) pathétique

pathological [pæθə'lɔdʒɪkl] *adj* pathologique

pathway ['pɑːθweɪ] *n* chemin *m*, sentier *m*; (*in garden*) allée *f*

patience ['peɪʃns] *n* patience *f*; (*Brit: Cards*) réussite *f*; **to lose (one's)** ~ perdre patience

patient ['peɪʃnt] *n* malade *m/f*; (*of dentist etc*) patient(e) ▷ *adj* patient(e)

patio ['pætɪəʊ] *n* patio *m*

patriotic [pætrɪ'ɔtɪk] *adj* patriotique; (*person*) patriote

patrol [pə'trəʊl] *n* patrouille *f* ▷ *vt* patrouiller dans; **to be on** ~ être de patrouille

patrol car *n* voiture *f* de police

patrolman [pə'trəʊlmən] *irreg n* (*US*) agent *m* de police

patron ['peɪtrən] *n* (*in shop*) client(e); (*of charity*) patron(ne); ~ **of the arts** mécène *m*

patronize ['pætrənaɪz] *vt* être (un) client *or* un habitué de; (*fig*) traiter avec condescendance

patronizing ['pætrənaɪzɪŋ] *adj* condescendant(e)

patter ['pætər] *n* crépitement *m*, tapotement *m*; (*sales talk*) boniment *m* ▷ *vi* crépiter, tapoter

pattern ['pætən] *n* modèle *m*; (*Sewing*) patron *m*; (*design*) motif *m*; (*sample*) échantillon *m*; **behaviour** ~ mode *m* de comportement

patterned ['pætənd] *adj* à motifs

pauper ['pɔːpər] *n* indigent(e); ~'s **grave** fosse commune

pause [pɔːz] *n* pause *f*, arrêt *m*; (*Mus*) silence *m* ▷ *vi* faire une pause, s'arrêter; **to ~ for breath** reprendre son souffle; (*fig*) faire une pause

pave [peɪv] *vt* paver, daller; **to ~ the way for** ouvrir la voie à

pavement ['peɪvmənt] *n* (*Brit*) trottoir *m*; (*US*) chaussée *f*

pavilion [pə'vɪlɪən] *n* pavillon *m*; tente *f*; (*Sport*) stand *m*

paving ['peɪvɪŋ] *n* (*material*) pavé *m*, dalle *f*; (*area*) pavage *m*, dallage *m*

paving stone *n* pavé *m*

paw [pɔː] *n* patte *f* ▷ *vt* donner un coup de patte à; (*person: pej*) tripoter

pawn [pɔːn] *n* gage *m*; (*Chess, also fig*) pion *m* ▷ *vt* mettre en gage

pawnbroker ['pɔːnbrəʊkər] *n* prêteur *m* sur gages

pawnshop ['pɔːnʃɔp] *n* mont-de-piété *m*

pay [peɪ] *n* (*pt, pp* **paid**) [peɪd] *n* salaire *m*; (*of manual worker*) paie *f* ▷ *vt* payer; (*be profitable to: also fig*) rapporter à ▷ *vi* payer; (*be profitable*) être rentable; **how much did you ~ for it?** combien l'avez-vous payé?, vous l'avez payé combien?; **I paid £5 for that ticket** j'ai payé ce billet 5 livres; **can I ~ by credit card?** est-ce que je peux payer par carte de crédit?; **to ~ one's way** payer sa part; (*company*) couvrir ses frais; **to ~ dividends** (*fig*) porter ses fruits, s'avérer rentable; **it won't ~ you to do that** vous ne gagnerez rien à faire cela; **to ~ attention (to)** prêter attention (à); **to ~ sb a visit** rendre visite à qn; **to ~ one's respects to sb** présenter ses respects à qn; **pay back** *vt* rembourser; **pay for** *vt fus* payer; **pay in** *vt* verser; **pay off** *vt* (*debts*) régler, acquitter; (*person*) rembourser; (*workers*) licencier ▷ *vi* (*scheme, decision*) se révéler payant(e); **to ~ sth off in instalments** payer qch à tempérament; **pay out** *vt* (*money*) payer, sortir de sa poche; (*rope*) laisser filer; **pay up** *vt* (*debts*) régler; (*amount*) payer

payable ['peɪəbl] *adj* payable; **to make a cheque ~ to sb** établir un chèque à l'ordre de qn

pay-as-you-go [peɪəzjə'gəʊ] *adj* (*mobile phone*) à carte prépayée

payday *n* jour *m* de paie

payee [peɪ'iː] *n* bénéficiaire *m/f*

pay envelope *n* (*US*) paie *f*

payment ['peɪmənt] *n* paiement *m*; (*of bill*) règlement *m*; (*of deposit, cheque*) versement *m*; **advance** ~ (*part sum*) acompte *m*; (*total sum*) paiement anticipé; **deferred** ~, ~ **by**

p

instalments paiement par versements échelonnés; **monthly ~** mensualité f; **in ~ for, in ~ of** en règlement de; **on ~ of £5** pour 5 livres

payout ['peɪaʊt] n (from insurance) dédommagement m; (in competition) prix m

pay packet n (Brit) paie f

pay phone n cabine f téléphonique, téléphone public

pay raise n (US) = **pay rise**

pay rise n (Brit) augmentation f (de salaire)

payroll ['peɪrəʊl] n registre m du personnel; **to be on a firm's ~** être employé par une entreprise

pay slip n (Brit) bulletin m de paie, feuille f de paie

pay television n chaînes fpl payantes

PC n abbr = **personal computer**; (Brit) = **police constable** ⊳ adj abbr = **politically correct** ⊳ abbr (Brit) = **Privy Councillor**

p.c. abbr = **per cent; postcard**

pcm n abbr (= per calender month) par mois

PDA n abbr (= personal digital assistant) agenda m électronique

PE n abbr (= physical education) EPS f ⊳ abbr (Canada) = **Prince Edward Island**

pea [pi:] n (petit) pois

peace [pi:s] n paix f; (calm) calme m, tranquillité f; **to be ~ with sb/sth** être en paix avec qn/qch; **to keep the ~** (policeman) assurer le maintien de l'ordre; (citizen) ne pas troubler l'ordre

peaceful ['pi:sful] adj paisible, calme

peach [pi:tʃ] n pêche f

peacock ['pi:kɔk] n paon m

peak [pi:k] n (mountain) pic m, cime f; (of cap) visière f; (fig: highest level) maximum m; (: of career, fame) apogée m

peak hours npl heures fpl d'affluence or de pointe

peal [pi:l] n (of bells) carillon m; **~s of laughter** éclats mpl de rire

peanut ['pi:nʌt] n arachide f, cacahuète f

peanut butter n beurre m de cacahuète

pear [pɛər] n poire f

pearl [pə:l] n perle f

peasant ['pɛznt] n paysan(ne)

peat [pi:t] n tourbe f

pebble ['pɛbl] n galet m, caillou m

peck [pɛk] vt (also: **~ at**) donner un coup de bec à; (food) picorer ⊳ n coup m de bec; (kiss) bécot m

pecking order ['pɛkɪŋ-] n ordre m hiérarchique

peckish ['pɛkɪʃ] adj (Brit inf): **I feel ~** je mangerais bien quelque chose, j'ai la dent

peculiar [pɪ'kju:lɪər] adj (odd) étrange, bizarre, curieux(-euse); (particular) particulier(-ière); **~ to** particulier à

pedal ['pɛdl] n pédale f ⊳ vi pédaler

pedantic [pɪ'dæntɪk] adj pédant(e)

peddler ['pɛdlər] n colporteur m; camelot m

pedestal ['pɛdəstl] n piédestal m

pedestrian [pɪ'dɛstrɪən] n piéton m ⊳ adj piétonnier(-ière); (fig) prosaïque, terre à terre inv

pedestrian crossing n (Brit) passage clouté

pedestrianized [pɪ'dɛstrɪənaɪzd] adj: **a ~ street** une rue piétonne

pedestrian precinct, (US) **pedestrian zone** n (Brit) zone piétonne

pediatrics [pi:dɪ'ætrɪks] n (US) = **paediatrics**

pedigree ['pɛdɪgri:] n ascendance f; (of animal) pedigree m ⊳ cpd (animal) de race

pedophile ['pi:dəʊfaɪl] (US) n = **paedophile**

pee [pi:] vi (inf) faire pipi, pisser

peek [pi:k] vi jeter un coup d'œil (furtif)

peel [pi:l] n pelure f, épluchure f; (of orange, lemon) écorce f ⊳ vt peler, éplucher ⊳ vi (paint etc) s'écailler; (wallpaper) se décoller; (skin) peler; **peel back** vt décoller

peep [pi:p] n (Brit: look) coup d'œil furtif; (sound) pépiement m ⊳ vi (Brit) jeter un coup d'œil (furtif); **peep out** vi (Brit) se montrer (furtivement)

peephole ['pi:phəʊl] n judas m

peer [pɪər] vi: **to ~ at** regarder attentivement, scruter ⊳ n (noble) pair m; (equal) pair, égal(e)

peerage ['pɪərɪdʒ] n pairie f

peeved ['pi:vd] adj irrité(e), ennuyé(e)

peg [pɛg] n cheville f; (for coat etc) patère f; (Brit: also: **clothes ~**) pince f à linge ⊳ vt (clothes) accrocher; (Brit: groundsheet) fixer (avec des piquets); (fig: prices, wages) contrôler, stabiliser

Pekinese, Pekingese [pi:kɪ'ni:z] n pékinois m

pelican ['pɛlɪkən] n pélican m

pelican crossing n (Brit Aut) feu m à commande manuelle

pellet ['pɛlɪt] n boulette f; (of lead) plomb m

pelt [pɛlt] vt: **to ~ sb (with)** bombarder qn (de) ⊳ vi (rain) tomber à seaux; (inf: run) courir à toutes jambes ⊳ n peau f

pelvis ['pɛlvɪs] n bassin m

pen [pɛn] n (for writing) stylo m; (for sheep) parc m; (US inf: prison) taule f; **to put ~ to paper** prendre la plume

penal ['pi:nl] adj pénal(e)

penalize ['pi:nəlaɪz] vt pénaliser; (fig) désavantager

penalty ['pɛnltɪ] n pénalité f; sanction f; (fine) amende f; (Sport) pénalisation f; (also: **~ kick**: Football) penalty m; (: Rugby) pénalité f; **to pay the ~ for** être pénalisé(e) pour

penance ['pɛnəns] n pénitence f

pence [pɛns] npl of **penny**

pencil ['pɛnsl] n crayon m; **pencil in** vt noter provisoirement

pencil case n trousse f (d'écolier)

pencil sharpener n taille-crayon(s) m inv

pendant ['pɛndnt] n pendentif m

pending ['pɛndɪŋ] prep en attendant ⊳ adj en suspens

pendulum ['pɛndjuləm] n pendule m; (of clock) balancier m

penetrate ['pɛnɪtreɪt] vt pénétrer dans; (enemy territory) entrer en; (sexually) pénétrer

pen friend n (Brit) correspondant(e)

penguin ['pɛŋgwɪn] n pingouin m

penicillin [pɛnɪ'sɪlɪn] n pénicilline f

peninsula [pə'nɪnsjulə] n péninsule f

penis ['piːnɪs] n pénis m, verge f

penitentiary [pɛnɪ'tɛnʃərɪ] n (US) prison f

penknife ['pɛnnaɪf] n canif m

pen name n nom m de plume, pseudonyme m

penniless ['pɛnɪlɪs] adj sans le sou

penny (pl **pennies** or **pence**) ['pɛnɪ, 'pɛnɪz, pɛns] n (Brit) penny m; (US) cent m

pen pal n correspondant(e)

pension ['pɛnʃən] n (from company) retraite f; (Mil) pension f; **pension off** vt mettre à la retraite

pensioner ['pɛnʃənər] n (Brit) retraité(e)

pension fund n caisse f de retraite

pension plan n plan m de retraite

pentagon ['pɛntəgən] n pentagone m; **the P-** (US Pol) le Pentagone; voir article

● **PENTAGON**
●
● Le *Pentagon* est le nom donné aux bureaux
● du ministère de la Défense américain,
● situés à Arlington en Virginie, à cause de
● la forme pentagonale du bâtiment dans
● lequel ils se trouvent. Par extension, ce
● terme est également utilisé en parlant
● du ministère lui-même.

pentathlon [pɛn'tæθlən] n pentathlon m

Pentecost ['pɛntɪkɔst] n Pentecôte f

penthouse ['pɛnthaus] n appartement m (de luxe) en attique

pent-up ['pɛntʌp] adj (feelings) refoulé(e)

penultimate [pɪ'nʌltɪmət] adj pénultième, avant-dernier(-ière)

people ['piːpl] npl gens mpl; personnes fpl; (inhabitants) population f; (Pol) peuple m ▷ n (nation, race) peuple m ▷ vt peupler; **I know ~ who ...** je connais des gens qui ...; **the room was full of ~** la salle était pleine de monde or de gens; **several ~ came** plusieurs personnes sont venues; **say that ...** on dit or les gens disent que ...; **old ~** les personnes âgées; **young ~** les jeunes; **a man of the ~** un homme du peuple

pepper ['pɛpər] n poivre m; (vegetable) poivron m ▷ vt (Culin) poivrer

pepper mill n moulin m à poivre

peppermint ['pɛpəmɪnt] n (plant) menthe poivrée; (sweet) pastille f de menthe

pep talk ['pɛptɔːk] n (inf) (petit) discours d'encouragement

per [pəːr] prep par; **~ hour** (miles etc) à l'heure; (fee) (de) l'heure; **~ kilo** etc le kilo etc; **~ day/~son** par jour/personne; **~ annum** par an; **as ~ your instructions** conformément à vos instructions

perceive [pə'siːv] vt percevoir; (notice) remarquer, s'apercevoir de

per cent adv pour cent; **a 20 ~ discount** une réduction de 20 pour cent

percentage [pə'sɛntɪdʒ] n pourcentage m; **on a ~ basis** au pourcentage

perception [pə'sɛpʃən] n perception f; (insight) sensibilité f

perceptive [pə'sɛptɪv] adj (remark, person) perspicace

perch [pəːtʃ] n (fish) perche f; (for bird) perchoir m ▷ vi (se) percher

percolator ['pəːkəleɪtər] n percolateur m; cafetière f électrique

percussion [pə'kʌʃən] n percussion f

perennial [pə'rɛnɪəl] adj perpétuel(le); (Bot) vivace ▷ n (Bot) (plante f) vivace f, plante pluriannuelle

perfect ['pəːfɪkt] adj parfait(e) ▷ n (also: **~ tense**) parfait m ▷ vt [pə'fɛkt] (technique, skill, work of art) parfaire; (method, plan) mettre au point; **he's a ~ stranger to me** il m'est totalement inconnu

perfection [pə'fɛkʃən] n perfection f

perfectly ['pəːfɪktlɪ] adv parfaitement; **I'm ~ happy with the situation** cette situation me convient parfaitement; **you know ~ well** vous le savez très bien

perforate ['pəːfəreɪt] vt perforer, percer

perforation [pəːfə'reɪʃən] n perforation f; (line of holes) pointillé m

perform [pə'fɔːm] vt (carry out) exécuter, remplir; (concert etc) jouer, donner ▷ vi (actor, musician) jouer; (machine, car) marcher, fonctionner; (company, economy): **to ~ well/badly** produire de bons/mauvais résultats

performance [pə'fɔːməns] n représentation f, spectacle m; (of an artist) interprétation f; (Sport: of car, engine) performance f; (of company, economy) résultats mpl; **the team put up a good ~** l'équipe a bien joué

performer [pə'fɔːmər] n artiste m/f

perfume ['pəːfjuːm] n parfum m ▷ vt parfumer

perhaps [pə'hæps] adv peut-être; **~ he'll ...** peut-être qu'il ...; **~ so/not** peut-être que oui/que non

peril ['pɛrɪl] n péril m

perimeter [pə'rɪmɪtər] n périmètre m

period ['pɪərɪəd] n période f; (Hist) époque f; (Scol) cours m; (full stop) point m; (Med) règles fpl ▷ adj (costume, furniture) d'époque; **for a ~ of three weeks** pour (une période de) trois semaines; **the holiday ~** (Brit) la période des vacances

periodical [pɪərɪ'ɔdɪkl] adj périodique ▷ n périodique m

periodically [pɪərɪˈɒdɪklɪ] *adv*
périodiquement

peripheral [pəˈrɪfərəl] *adj* périphérique ▷ *n*
(*Comput*) périphérique *m*

perish [ˈperɪʃ] *vi* périr, mourir; (*decay*) se
détériorer

perishable [ˈperɪʃəbl] *adj* périssable

perjury [ˈpəːdʒərɪ] *n* (*Law: in court*)
faux témoignage; (*breach of oath*)
parjure *m*

perk [pəːk] *n* (*inf*) avantage *m*, à-côté *m*; **perk
up** *vi* (*inf: cheer up*) se ragaillardir

perky [ˈpəːkɪ] *adj* (*cheerful*) guilleret(te), gai(e)

perm [pəːm] *n* (*for hair*) permanente *f* ▷ *vt*: **to
have one's hair ~ed** se faire faire une
permanente

permanent [ˈpəːmənənt] *adj* permanent(e);
(*job, position*) permanent, fixe; (*dye, ink*)
indélébile; **I'm not ~ here** je ne suis pas ici à
titre définitif; **~ address** adresse habituelle

permanently [ˈpəːmənəntlɪ] *adv* de façon
permanente; (*move abroad*) définitivement;
(*open, closed*) en permanence; (*tired, unhappy*)
constamment

permeate [ˈpəːmɪeɪt] *vi* s'infiltrer ▷ *vt*
s'infiltrer dans; pénétrer

permissible [pəˈmɪsɪbl] *adj* permis(e),
acceptable

permission [pəˈmɪʃən] *n* permission *f*,
autorisation *f*; **to give sb ~ to do sth** donner
à qn la permission de faire qch

permissive [pəˈmɪsɪv] *adj* tolérant(e); **the ~
society** la société de tolérance

permit *n* [ˈpəːmɪt] permis *m*; (*entrance pass*)
autorisation *f*, laissez-passer *m*; (*for goods*)
licence *f* ▷ *vt* [pəˈmɪt] permettre; **to ~ sb to
do** autoriser qn à faire, permettre à qn de
faire; **weather ~ting** si le temps le permet

perpendicular [pəːpənˈdɪkjʊləʳ] *adj, n*
perpendiculaire *f*

perplex [pəˈpleks] *vt* (*person*) rendre perplexe;
(*complicate*) embrouiller

persecute [ˈpəːsɪkjuːt] *vt* persécuter

persecution [pəːsɪˈkjuːʃən] *n* persécution *f*

persevere [pəːsɪˈvɪəʳ] *vi* persévérer

Persian [ˈpəːʃən] *adj* persan(e) ▷ *n* (*Ling*)
persan *m*; **the ~ Gulf** le golfe Persique

persist [pəˈsɪst] *vi* **to ~ (in doing)** persister
(à faire), s'obstiner (à faire)

persistent [pəˈsɪstənt] *adj* persistant(e),
tenace; (*lateness, rain*) persistant; **~ offender**
(*Law*) multirécidiviste *m/f*

person [ˈpəːsn] *n* personne *f*; **in ~** en
personne; **on** *or* **about one's ~** sur soi; **~ to ~
call** (*Tel*) appel *m* avec préavis

personal [ˈpəːsnl] *adj* personnel(le);
~ belongings, ~ effects effets personnels;
~ hygiene hygiène *f* intime; **a ~ interview**
un entretien

personal assistant *n* secrétaire
personnel(le)

personal column *n* annonces personnelles

personal computer *n* ordinateur
individuel, PC *m*

personality [pəːsəˈnælɪtɪ] *n* personnalité *f*

personally [ˈpəːsnlɪ] *adv* personnellement;
to take sth ~ se sentir visé(e) par qch

personal organizer *n* agenda (personnel);
(*electronic*) agenda électronique

personal stereo *n* Walkman® *m*,
baladeur *m*

personnel [pəːsəˈnel] *n* personnel *m*

perspective [pəˈspektɪv] *n* perspective *f*; **to
get sth into ~** ramener qch à sa juste mesure

perspex® [ˈpəːspeks] *n* (*Brit*) Plexiglas® *m*

perspiration [pəːspɪˈreɪʃən] *n* transpiration *f*

persuade [pəˈsweɪd] *vt*: **to ~ sb to do sth**
persuader qn de faire qch, amener *or* décider
qn à faire qch; **to ~ sb of sth/that** persuader
qn de qch/que

persuasion [pəˈsweɪʒən] *n* persuasion *f*;
(*creed*) conviction *f*

persuasive [pəˈsweɪsɪv] *adj* persuasif(-ive)

perverse [pəˈvəːs] *adj* pervers(e); (*contrary*)
entêté(e), contrariant(e)

pervert *n* [ˈpəːvəːt] perverti(e) ▷ *vt* [pəˈvəːt]
pervertir; (*words*) déformer

pessimism [ˈpesɪmɪzəm] *n* pessimisme *m*

pessimist [ˈpesɪmɪst] *n* pessimiste *m/f*

pessimistic [pesɪˈmɪstɪk] *adj* pessimiste

pest [pest] *n* animal *m* (*or* insecte *m*) nuisible;
(*fig*) fléau *m*

pester [ˈpestəʳ] *vt* importuner, harceler

pesticide [ˈpestɪsaɪd] *n* pesticide *m*

pet [pet] *n* animal familier; (*favourite*)
chouchou *m* ▷ *cpd* (*favourite*) favori(e) ▷ *vt*
choyer; (*stroke*) caresser, câliner ▷ *vi* (*inf*) se
peloter; **~ lion** *etc* lion *etc* apprivoisé;
teacher's ~ chouchou *m* du professeur;
~ hate bête noire

petal [ˈpetl] *n* pétale *m*

peter [ˈpiːtəʳ]: **to ~ out** *vi* s'épuiser; s'affaiblir

petite [pəˈtiːt] *adj* menu(e)

petition [pəˈtɪʃən] *n* pétition *f* ▷ *vi*: **to ~ for
divorce** demander le divorce

petrified [ˈpetrɪfaɪd] *adj* (*fig*) mort(e) de peur

petrol [ˈpetrəl] *n* (*Brit*) essence *f*; **I've run out
of ~** je suis en panne d'essence

petrol can *n* (*Brit*) bidon *m* à essence

petroleum [pəˈtrəʊlɪəm] *n* pétrole *m*

petrol pump *n* (*Brit: in car, at garage*) pompe *f*
à essence

petrol station *n* (*Brit*) station-service *f*

petrol tank *n* (*Brit*) réservoir *m* d'essence

petticoat [ˈpetɪkəʊt] *n* jupon *m*

petty [ˈpetɪ] *adj* (*mean*) mesquin(e);
(*unimportant*) insignifiant(e), sans
importance

petty cash *n* caisse *f* des dépenses courantes,
petite caisse

petty officer *n* second-maître *m*

petulant [ˈpetjʊlənt] *adj* irritable

pew [pjuː] *n* banc *m* (d'église)

pewter ['pju:tə^r] n étain m
phantom ['fæntəm] n fantôme m; (vision) fantasme m
pharmacist ['fɑ:məsɪst] n pharmacien(ne)
pharmacy ['fɑ:məsɪ] n pharmacie f
phase [feɪz] n phase f, période f; **phase in** vt introduire progressivement; **phase out** vt supprimer progressivement
Ph.D. abbr = **Doctor of Philosophy**
pheasant ['fɛznt] n faisan m
phenomena [fə'nɔmɪnə] npl of **phenomenon**
phenomenal [fɪ'nɔmɪnl] adj phénoménal(e)
phenomenon (pl **phenomena**) [fə'nɔmɪnən, -nə] n phénomène m
Philippines ['fɪlɪpi:nz] npl (also: **Philippine Islands**): **the** ~ les Philippines fpl
philosopher [fɪ'lɔsəfə^r] n philosophe m
philosophical [fɪlə'sɔfɪkl] adj philosophique
philosophy [fɪ'lɔsəfɪ] n philosophie f
phlegm [flɛm] n flegme m
phobia ['fəubjə] n phobie f
phone [fəun] n téléphone m ▷ vt téléphoner à ▷ vi téléphoner; **to be on the** ~ avoir le téléphone; (be calling) être au téléphone; **phone back** vt, vi rappeler; **phone up** vt téléphoner à ▷ vi téléphoner
phone bill n facture f de téléphone
phone book n annuaire m
phone box, (US) **phone booth** n cabine f téléphonique
phone call n coup m de fil or de téléphone
phonecard ['fəunkɑ:d] n télécarte f
phone-in ['fəunɪn] n (Brit Radio, TV) programme m à ligne ouverte
phone number n numéro m de téléphone
phonetics [fə'nɛtɪks] n phonétique f
phoney ['fəunɪ] adj faux/fausse, factice; (person) pas franc/franche ▷ n (person) charlatan m; fumiste m/f
photo ['fəutəu] n photo f; **to take a** ~ **of** prendre en photo
photo album n album m de photos
photocopier ['fəutəukɔpɪə^r] n copieur m
photocopy ['fəutəukɔpɪ] n photocopie f ▷ vt photocopier
photograph ['fəutəgræf] n photographie f ▷ vt photographier; **to take a** ~ **of sb** prendre qn en photo
photographer [fə'tɔgrəfə^r] n photographe m/f
photography [fə'tɔgrəfɪ] n photographie f
phrase [freɪz] n expression f; (Ling) locution f ▷ vt exprimer; (letter) rédiger
phrase book n recueil m d'expressions (pour touristes)
physical ['fɪzɪkl] adj physique; ~ **examination** examen médical; ~ **exercises** gymnastique f
physical education n éducation f physique
physically ['fɪzɪklɪ] adv physiquement
physician [fɪ'zɪʃən] n médecin m
physicist ['fɪzɪsɪst] n physicien(ne)

physics ['fɪzɪks] n physique f
physiotherapist [fɪzɪəu'θerəpɪst] n kinésithérapeute m/f
physiotherapy [fɪzɪəu'θerəpɪ] n kinésithérapie f
physique [fɪ'zi:k] n (appearance) physique m; (health etc) constitution f
pianist ['pi:ənɪst] n pianiste m/f
piano [pɪ'ænəu] n piano m
pick [pɪk] n (tool: also: ~-**axe**) pic m, pioche f ▷ vt choisir; (gather) cueillir; (remove) prendre; (lock) forcer; (scab, spot) gratter, écorcher; **take your** ~ faites votre choix; **the** ~ **of** le/la meilleur(e) de; **to** ~ **a bone** ronger un os; **to** ~ **one's nose** se mettre les doigts dans le nez; **to** ~ **one's teeth** se curer les dents; **to** ~ **sb's brains** faire appel aux lumières de qn; **to** ~ **pockets** pratiquer le vol à la tire; **to** ~ **a quarrel with sb** chercher noise à qn; **pick at** vt fus: **to** ~ **at one's food** manger du bout des dents, chipoter; **pick off** vt (kill) (viser soigneusement et) abattre; **pick on** vt fus (person) harceler; **pick out** vt choisir; (distinguish) distinguer; **pick up** vi (improve) remonter, s'améliorer ▷ vt ramasser; (telephone) décrocher; (collect) passer prendre; (Aut: give lift to) prendre; (learn) apprendre; (Radio) capter; **to** ~ **up speed** prendre de la vitesse; **to** ~ **o.s. up** se relever; **to** ~ **up where one left off** reprendre là où l'on s'est arrêté
picket ['pɪkɪt] n (in strike) gréviste m/f participant à un piquet de grève; piquet m de grève ▷ vt mettre un piquet de grève devant
pickle ['pɪkl] n (also: ~**s**: as condiment) pickles mpl ▷ vt conserver dans le vinaigre or dans de la saumure; **in a** ~ (fig) dans le pétrin
pickpocket ['pɪkpɔkɪt] n pickpocket m
pick-up ['pɪkʌp] n (also: ~ **truck**) pick-up m inv; (Brit: on record player) bras m pick-up
picnic ['pɪknɪk] n pique-nique m ▷ vi pique-niquer
picnic area n aire f de pique-nique
picture ['pɪktʃə^r] n (also TV) image f; (painting) peinture f, tableau m; (photograph) photo(graphie) f; (drawing) dessin m; (film) film m; (fig: description) description f ▷ vt (imagine) se représenter; (describe) dépeindre, représenter; **pictures** npl: **the** ~**s** (Brit) le cinéma; **to take a** ~ **of sb/sth** prendre qn/qch en photo; **would you take a** ~ **of us, please?** pourriez-vous nous prendre en photo, s'il vous plaît?; **the overall** ~ le tableau d'ensemble; **to put sb in the** ~ mettre qn au courant
picture book n livre m d'images
picture frame n cadre m
picture messaging n picture messaging m, messagerie f d'images
picturesque [pɪktʃə'rɛsk] adj pittoresque
pie [paɪ] n (of meat) tourte f; (of fruit) tarte f; (of meat) pâté m en croûte

piece [piːs] n morceau m; (of land) parcelle f; (item): **a ~ of furniture/advice** un meuble/conseil; (Draughts) pion m ▷ vt: **to ~ together** rassembler; **in ~s** (broken) en morceaux, en miettes; (not yet assembled) en pièces détachées; **to take to ~s** démonter; **in one ~** (object) intact(e); **to get back all in one ~** (person) rentrer sain et sauf; **a 10p ~** (Brit) une pièce de 10p; **~ by ~** morceau par morceau; **a six~ band** un orchestre de six musiciens; **to say one's ~** réciter son morceau

piecemeal [ˈpiːsmiːl] adv par bouts

piecework [ˈpiːswɜːk] n travail m aux pièces or à la pièce

pie chart n graphique m à secteurs, camembert m

pier [pɪər] n jetée f; (of bridge etc) pile f

pierce [pɪəs] vt percer, transpercer; **to have one's ears ~d** se faire percer les oreilles

pierced [pɪəst] adj (ears) percé(e)

pig [pɪg] n cochon m, porc m; (pej: unkind person) mufle m; (: greedy person) goinfre m

pigeon [ˈpɪdʒən] n pigeon m

pigeonhole [ˈpɪdʒənhəʊl] n casier m

piggy bank [ˈpɪgɪ-] n tirelire f

pigheaded [ˈpɪgˈhedɪd] adj entêté(e), têtu(e)

piglet [ˈpɪglɪt] n petit cochon, porcelet m

pigskin [ˈpɪgskɪn] n (peau f de) porc m

pigsty [ˈpɪgstaɪ] n porcherie f

pigtail [ˈpɪgteɪl] n natte f, tresse f

pike [paɪk] n (spear) pique f; (fish) brochet m

pilchard [ˈpɪltʃəd] n pilchard m (sorte de sardine)

pile [paɪl] n (pillar, of books) pile f; (heap) tas m; (of carpet) épaisseur f; **in a ~** en tas; **pile on** vt: **to ~ it on** (inf) exagérer; **pile up** vi (accumulate) s'entasser, s'accumuler ▷ vt (put in heap) empiler, entasser; (accumulate) accumuler

piles [paɪlz] npl hémorroïdes fpl

pile-up [ˈpaɪlʌp] n (Aut) télescopage m, collision f en série

pilfering [ˈpɪlfərɪŋ] n chapardage m

pilgrim [ˈpɪlgrɪm] n pèlerin m; voir article

● **PILGRIM FATHERS**
●
● Les Pilgrim Fathers ("Pères pèlerins") sont
● un groupe de puritains qui quittèrent
● l'Angleterre en 1620 pour fuir les
● persécutions religieuses. Ayant traversé
● l'Atlantique à bord du "Mayflower", ils
● fondèrent New Plymouth en Nouvelle-
● Angleterre, dans ce qui est aujourd'hui le
● Massachusetts. Ces Pères pèlerins sont
● considérés comme les fondateurs des
● États-Unis, et l'on commémore chaque
● année, le jour de "Thanksgiving",
● la réussite de leur première récolte.

pilgrimage [ˈpɪlgrɪmɪdʒ] n pèlerinage m

pill [pɪl] n pilule f; **the ~** la pilule; **to be on the ~** prendre la pilule

pillage [ˈpɪlɪdʒ] vt piller

pillar [ˈpɪlər] n pilier m

pillar box n (Brit) boîte f aux lettres (publique)

pillion [ˈpɪljən] n (of motor cycle) siège m arrière; **to ride ~** être derrière; (on horse) être en croupe

pillow [ˈpɪləʊ] n oreiller m

pillowcase [ˈpɪləʊkeɪs], **pillowslip** [ˈpɪləʊslɪp] n taie f d'oreiller

pilot [ˈpaɪlət] n pilote m ▷ cpd (scheme etc) pilote, expérimental(e) ▷ vt piloter

pilot light n veilleuse f

pimp [pɪmp] n souteneur m, maquereau m

pimple [ˈpɪmpl] n bouton m

PIN n abbr (= personal identification number) code m confidentiel

pin [pɪn] n épingle f; (Tech) cheville f; (Brit: drawing pin) punaise f; (in grenade) goupille f; (Brit Elec: of plug) broche f ▷ vt épingler; **~s and needles** fourmis fpl; **to ~ sb against/to** clouer qn contre/à; **to ~ sb down** (fig) coincer qn; **to ~ sth on sb** (fig) mettre qch sur le dos de qn; **pin down** vt (fig): **to ~ sb down** obliger qn à répondre; **there's something strange here but I can't quite ~ it down** il y a quelque chose d'étrange ici, mais je n'arrive pas exactement à savoir quoi

pinafore [ˈpɪnəfɔːr] n tablier m

pinball [ˈpɪnbɔːl] n flipper m

pincers [ˈpɪnsəz] npl tenailles fpl

pinch [pɪntʃ] n pincement m; (of salt etc) pincée f ▷ vt pincer; (inf: steal) piquer, chiper ▷ vi (shoe) serrer; **at a ~** à la rigueur; **to feel the ~** (fig) se ressentir des restrictions (or de la récession etc)

pincushion [ˈpɪnkʊʃən] n pelote f à épingles

pine [paɪn] n (also: **~ tree**) pin m ▷ vi: **to ~ for** aspirer à, désirer ardemment; **pine away** vi dépérir

pineapple [ˈpaɪnæpl] n ananas m

ping [pɪŋ] n (noise) tintement m

ping-pong® [ˈpɪŋpɔŋ] n ping-pong® m

pink [pɪŋk] adj rose ▷ n (colour) rose m; (Bot) œillet m, mignardise f

pinpoint [ˈpɪnpɔɪnt] vt indiquer (avec précision)

pint [paɪnt] n pinte f (Brit = 0,57 l; US = 0,47 l); (Brit inf) ≈ demi-m, ≈ pot m

pioneer [paɪəˈnɪər] n explorateur(-trice); (early settler) pionnier m; (fig) pionnier, précurseur m ▷ vt être un pionnier de

pious [ˈpaɪəs] adj pieux(-euse)

pip [pɪp] n (seed) pépin m; **pips** npl: **the ~s** (Brit: time signal on radio) le top

pipe [paɪp] n tuyau m, conduite f; (for smoking) pipe f; (Mus) pipeau m ▷ vt amener par tuyau; **pipes** npl (also: **bag~s**) cornemuse f; **pipe down** vi (inf) se taire

pipe cleaner n cure-pipe m

pipe dream n chimère f, utopie f

pipeline [ˈpaɪplaɪn] n (for gas) gazoduc m,

pipeline *m*; (*for oil*) oléoduc *m*, pipeline; **it is in the ~** (*fig*) c'est en route, ça va se faire

piper ['paɪpə'] *n* (*flautist*) joueur(-euse) de pipeau; (*of bagpipes*) joueur(-euse) de cornemuse

piping ['paɪpɪŋ] *adv*: **~ hot** très chaud(e)

pique [piːk] *n* dépit *m*

pirate ['paɪərət] *n* pirate *m* ▷ *vt* (*CD, video, book*) pirater

pirated ['paɪərətɪd] *adj* pirate

Pisces ['paɪsiːz] *n* les Poissons *mpl*; **to be ~** être des Poissons

piss [pɪs] *vi* (*inf!*) pisser (!); **~ off!** tire-toi! (!)

pissed [pɪst] *adj* (*inf!*) (*Brit: drunk*) bourré(e); (*US: angry*) furieux(-euse)

pistol ['pɪstl] *n* pistolet *m*

piston ['pɪstən] *n* piston *m*

pit [pɪt] *n* trou *m*, fosse *f*; (*also*: **coal ~**) puits *m* de mine; (*also*: **orchestra ~**) fosse d'orchestre; (*US: fruit stone*) noyau *m* ▷ *vt*: **to ~ sb against sb** opposer qn à qn; **to ~ o.s.** *or* **one's wits against** se mesurer à; **pits** *npl* (*in motor racing*) aire *f* de service

pitch [pɪtʃ] *n* (*Brit Sport*) terrain *m*; (*throw*) lancement *m*; (*Mus*) ton *m*; (*of voice*) hauteur *f*; (*fig: degree*) degré *m*; (*also*: **sales ~**) baratin *m*, boniment *m*; (*Naut*) tangage *m*; (*tar*) poix *f* ▷ *vt* (*throw*) lancer; (*tent*) dresser; (*set: price, message*) adapter, positionner ▷ *vi* (*Naut*) tanguer; (*fall*): **to ~ into/off** tomber dans/de; **to be ~ed forward** être projeté(e) en avant; **at this ~** à ce rythme

pitch-black ['pɪtʃ'blæk] *adj* noir(e) comme poix

pitched battle [pɪtʃt-] *n* bataille rangée

pitfall ['pɪtfɔːl] *n* trappe *f*, piège *m*

pith [pɪθ] *n* (*of plant*) moelle *f*; (*of orange etc*) intérieur *m* de l'écorce; (*fig*) essence *f*; vigueur *f*

pithy ['pɪθɪ] *adj* piquant(e); vigoureux(-euse)

pitiful ['pɪtɪful] *adj* (*touching*) pitoyable; (*contemptible*) lamentable

pitiless ['pɪtɪlɪs] *adj* impitoyable

pittance ['pɪtns] *n* salaire *m* de misère

pity ['pɪtɪ] *n* pitié *f* ▷ *vt* plaindre; **what a ~!** quel dommage!; **it is a ~ that you can't come** c'est dommage que vous ne puissiez venir; **to have** *or* **take ~ on sb** avoir pitié de qn

pizza ['piːtsə] *n* pizza *f*

placard ['plækɑːd] *n* affiche *f*; (*in march*) pancarte *f*

placate [plə'keɪt] *vt* apaiser, calmer

place [pleɪs] *n* endroit *m*, lieu *m*; (*proper position, job, rank, seat*) place *f*; (*house*) maison *f*, logement *m*; (*in street names*): **Laurel ~** = rue des Lauriers; (*home*): **at/to his ~** chez lui ▷ *vt* (*position*) placer, mettre; (*identify*) situer; reconnaître; **to take ~** avoir lieu; (*occur*) se produire; **to take sb's ~** remplacer qn; **to change ~s with sb** changer de place avec qn; **from ~ to ~** d'un endroit à l'autre; **all over**

the ~ partout; **out of ~** (*not suitable*) déplacé(e), inopportun(e); **I feel out of ~ here** je ne me sens pas à ma place ici; **in the first ~** d'abord, en premier; **to put sb in his ~** (*fig*) remettre qn à sa place; **he's going ~s** (*fig: inf*) il fait son chemin; **it is not my ~ to do it** ce n'est pas à moi de le faire; **to ~ an order with sb (for)** (*Comm*) passer commande à qn (de); **to be ~d** (*in race, exam*) se placer; **how are you ~d next week?** comment ça se présente pour la semaine prochaine?

place mat *n* set *m* de table; (*in linen etc*) napperon *m*

placement ['pleɪsmənt] *n* placement *m*; (*during studies*) stage *m*

placid ['plæsɪd] *adj* placide

plague [pleɪg] *n* fléau *m*; (*Med*) peste *f* ▷ *vt* (*fig*) tourmenter; **to ~ sb with questions** harceler qn de questions

plaice [pleɪs] *n* (*pl inv*) carrelet *m*

plaid [plæd] *n* tissu écossais

plain [pleɪn] *adj* (*in one colour*) uni(e); (*clear*) clair(e), évident(e); (*simple*) simple, ordinaire; (*frank*) franc/franche; (*not handsome*) quelconque, ordinaire; (*cigarette*) sans filtre; (*without seasoning etc*) nature *inv* ▷ *adv* franchement, carrément ▷ *n* plaine *f*; **in ~ clothes** (*police*) en civil; **to make sth ~ to sb** faire clairement comprendre qch à qn

plain chocolate *n* chocolat *m* à croquer

plainly ['pleɪnlɪ] *adv* clairement; (*frankly*) carrément, sans détours

plaintiff ['pleɪntɪf] *n* plaignant(e)

plait [plæt] *n* tresse *f*, natte *f* ▷ *vt* tresser, natter

plan [plæn] *n* plan *m*; (*scheme*) projet *m* ▷ *vt* (*think in advance*) projeter; (*prepare*) organiser ▷ *vi* faire des projets; **to ~ to do** projeter de faire; **how long do you ~ to stay?** combien de temps comptez-vous rester?

plane [pleɪn] *n* (*Aviat*) avion *m*; (*also*: **~ tree**) platane *m*; (*tool*) rabot *m*; (*Art, Math etc*) plan *m*; (*fig*) niveau *m*, plan *m* ▷ *adj* plan(e); plat(e) ▷ *vt* (*with tool*) raboter

planet ['plænɪt] *n* planète *f*

plank [plæŋk] *n* planche *f*; (*Pol*) point *m* d'un programme

planner ['plænə'] *n* planificateur(-trice); (*chart*) planning *m*; **town** *or* (*US*) **city ~** urbaniste *m/f*

planning ['plænɪŋ] *n* planification *f*; **family ~** planning familial

planning permission *n* (*Brit*) permis *m* de construire

plant [plɑːnt] *n* plante *f*; (*machinery*) matériel *m*; (*factory*) usine *f* ▷ *vt* planter; (*bomb*) déposer, poser; (*microphone, evidence*) cacher

plantation [plæn'teɪʃən] *n* plantation *f*

plaque [plæk] *n* plaque *f*

P

plaster ['plɑːstə^r] n plâtre m; (also: ~ **of Paris**) plâtre à mouler; (Brit: also: **sticking ~**) pansement adhésif ▷ vt plâtrer; (cover): **to ~ with** couvrir de; **in ~** (Brit: leg etc) dans le plâtre

plaster cast n (Med) plâtre m; (model, statue) moule m

plastered ['plɑːstəd] adj (inf) soûl(e)

plastic ['plæstɪk] n plastique m ▷ adj (made of plastic) en plastique; (flexible) plastique, malléable; (art) plastique

plastic bag n sac m en plastique

plasticine® ['plæstɪsiːn] n pâte f à modeler

plastic surgery n chirurgie f esthétique

plate [pleɪt] n (dish) assiette f; (sheet of metal, on door: Phot) plaque f; (Typ) cliché m; (in book) gravure f; (dental) dentier m; (Aut: number plate) plaque minéralogique; **gold/silver ~** (dishes) vaisselle f d'or/d'argent

plateau (pl **plateaus** or **plateaux**) ['plætəu, -z] n plateau m

plate glass n verre m à vitre, vitre f

platform ['plætfɔːm] n (at meeting) tribune f; (Brit: of bus) plate-forme f; (stage) estrade f; (Rail) quai m; (Pol) plateforme f; **the train leaves from ~ 7** le train part de la voie 7

platinum ['plætɪnəm] n platine m

platoon [plə'tuːn] n peloton m

platter ['plætə^r] n plat m

plausible ['plɔːzɪbl] adj plausible; (person) convaincant(e)

play [pleɪ] n jeu m; (Theat) pièce f (de théâtre) ▷ vt (game) jouer à; (team, opponent) jouer contre; (instrument) jouer de; (part, piece of music, note) jouer; (CD etc) passer ▷ vi jouer; **to bring** or **call into ~** faire entrer en jeu; **~ on words** jeu de mots; **to ~ safe** ne prendre aucun risque; **to ~ a trick on sb** jouer un tour à qn; **they're ~ing at soldiers** ils jouent aux soldats; **to ~ for time** (fig) chercher à gagner du temps; **to ~ into sb's hands** (fig) faire le jeu de qn; **play about, play around** vi (person) s'amuser; **play along** vi (fig): **to ~ along with** (person) entrer dans le jeu de ▷ vt (fig): **to ~ sb along** faire marcher qn; **play back** vt repasser, réécouter; **play down** vt minimiser; **play on** vt fus (sb's feelings, credulity) jouer sur; **to ~ on sb's nerves** porter sur les nerfs de qn; **play up** vi (cause trouble) faire des siennes

playboy ['pleɪbɔɪ] n playboy m

player ['pleɪə^r] n joueur(-euse); (Theat) acteur(-trice); (Mus) musicien(ne)

playful ['pleɪful] adj enjoué(e)

playground ['pleɪgraund] n cour f de récréation; (in park) aire f de jeux

playgroup ['pleɪgruːp] n garderie f

playing card ['pleɪɪŋ-] n carte f à jouer

playing field ['pleɪɪŋ-] n terrain m de sport

playmate ['pleɪmeɪt] n camarade m/f, copain/copine

play-off ['pleɪɔf] n (Sport) belle f

playpen ['pleɪpɛn] n parc m (pour bébé)

playschool ['pleɪskuːl] n = **playgroup**

plaything ['pleɪθɪŋ] n jouet m

playtime ['pleɪtaɪm] n (Scol) récréation f

playwright ['pleɪraɪt] n dramaturge m

plc abbr (Brit: = public limited company) ≈ SARL f

plea [pliː] n (request) appel m; (excuse) excuse f; (Law) défense f

plead [pliːd] vt plaider; (give as excuse) invoquer ▷ vi (Law) plaider; (beg): **to ~ with sb (for sth)** implorer qn (d'accorder qch); **to ~ for sth** implorer qn; **to ~ guilty/not guilty** plaider coupable/non coupable

pleasant ['plɛznt] adj agréable

pleasantry ['plɛzntrɪ] n (joke) plaisanterie f; **pleasantries** npl (polite remarks) civilités fpl

please [pliːz] excl s'il te (or vous) plaît ▷ vt plaire à ▷ vi (think fit): **do as you ~** faites comme il vous plaira; **my bill, ~** l'addition, s'il vous plaît; **~ don't cry!** je t'en prie, ne pleure pas!; **~ yourself!** (inf) (faites) comme vous voulez!

pleased [pliːzd] adj: **~ (with)** content(e) (de); **~ to meet you** enchanté (de faire votre connaissance); **we are ~ to inform you that ...** nous sommes heureux de vous annoncer que ...

pleasing ['pliːzɪŋ] adj plaisant(e), qui fait plaisir

pleasure ['plɛʒə^r] n plaisir m; **"it's a ~"** "je vous en prie"; **with ~** avec plaisir; **is this trip for business or ~?** est-ce un voyage d'affaires ou d'agrément?

pleat [pliːt] n pli m

pledge [plɛdʒ] n gage m; (promise) promesse f ▷ vt engager; promettre; **to ~ support for sb** s'engager à soutenir qn; **to ~ sb to secrecy** faire promettre à qn de garder le secret

plentiful ['plɛntɪful] adj abondant(e), copieux(-euse)

plenty ['plɛntɪ] n abondance f; **~ of** beaucoup de; (sufficient) (bien) assez de; **we've got ~ of time** nous avons largement le temps

pliable ['plaɪəbl] adj flexible; (person) malléable

pliers ['plaɪəz] npl pinces fpl

plight [plaɪt] n situation f critique

plimsolls ['plɪmsəlz] npl (Brit) (chaussures fpl) tennis fpl

plinth [plɪnθ] n socle m

PLO n abbr (= Palestine Liberation Organization) OLP f

plod [plɔd] vi avancer péniblement; (fig) peiner

plonk [plɔŋk] (inf) n (Brit: wine) pinard m, piquette f ▷ vt: **to ~ sth down** poser brusquement qch

plot [plɔt] n complot m, conspiration f; (of story, play) intrigue f; (of land) lot m de terrain, lopin m ▷ vt (mark out) tracer point par point; (Naut) pointer; (make graph of) faire le graphique de; (conspire) comploter ▷ vi comploter; **a vegetable ~** (Brit) un carré de légumes

plough, plow (US) [plaʊ] n charrue f ▷ vt (earth) labourer; **to ~ money into** investir dans; **plough back** vt (Comm) réinvestir; **plough through** vt fus (snow etc) avancer péniblement dans

ploughman, plowman (US) ['plaʊmən] irreg n laboureur m

plow [plaʊ] (US) n = **plough**

ploy [plɔɪ] n stratagème m

pls abbr (= please) SVP m

pluck [plʌk] vt (fruit) cueillir; (musical instrument) pincer; (bird) plumer ▷ n courage m, cran m; **to ~ one's eyebrows** s'épiler les sourcils; **to ~ up courage** prendre son courage à deux mains

plug [plʌg] n (stopper) bouchon m, bonde f; (Elec) prise f de courant; (Aut: also: **spark(ing) ~**) bougie f ▷ vt (hole) boucher; (inf: advertise) faire du battage pour, matraquer; **to give sb/ sth a ~** (inf) faire de la pub pour qn/qch; **plug in** vt (Elec) brancher ▷ vi (Elec) se brancher

plughole ['plʌghəʊl] n (Brit) trou m (d'écoulement)

plum [plʌm] n (fruit) prune f ▷ adj: **~ job** (inf) travail m en or

plumb [plʌm] adj vertical(e) ▷ n plomb m ▷ adv (exactly) en plein ▷ vt sonder; **plumb in** vt (washing machine) faire le raccordement de

plumber ['plʌmə^r] n plombier m

plumbing ['plʌmɪŋ] n (trade) plomberie f; (piping) tuyauterie f

plummet ['plʌmɪt] vi (person, object) plonger; (sales, prices) dégringoler

plump [plʌmp] adj rondelet(te), dodu(e), bien en chair ▷ vt: **to ~ sth (down) on** laisser tomber qch lourdement sur; **plump for** vt fus (inf: choose) se décider pour; **plump up** vt (cushion) battre (pour lui redonner forme)

plunder ['plʌndə^r] n pillage m ▷ vt piller

plunge [plʌndʒ] n plongeon m; (fig) chute f ▷ vt plonger ▷ vi (fall) tomber, dégringoler; (dive) plonger; **to take the ~** se jeter à l'eau

plunging ['plʌndʒɪŋ] adj (neckline) plongeant(e)

pluperfect [pluː'pə:fɪkt] n (Ling) plus-que-parfait m

plural ['plʊərl] adj pluriel(le) ▷ n pluriel m

plus [plʌs] n (also: **~ sign**) signe m plus; (advantage) atout m ▷ prep plus; **ten/twenty ~** plus de dix/vingt; **it's a ~** c'est un atout

plush [plʌʃ] adj somptueux(-euse) ▷ n peluche f

ply [plaɪ] n (of wool) fil m; (of wood) feuille f, épaisseur f ▷ vt (tool) manier; (a trade) exercer ▷ vi (ship) faire la navette; **three ~ (wool)** laine f trois fils; **to ~ sb with drink** donner continuellement à boire à qn

plywood ['plaɪwʊd] n contreplaqué m

P.M. n abbr (Brit) = **prime minister**

p.m. adv abbr (= post meridiem) de l'après-midi

PMS n abbr (= premenstrual syndrome) syndrome prémenstruel

PMT n abbr (= premenstrual tension) syndrome prémenstruel

pneumatic [njuː'mætɪk] adj pneumatique

pneumatic drill [njuː'mætɪk-] n marteau-piqueur m

pneumonia [njuː'məʊnɪə] n pneumonie f

poach [pəʊtʃ] vt (cook) pocher; (steal) pêcher (or chasser) sans permis ▷ vi braconner

poached [pəʊtʃt] adj (egg) poché(e)

poacher ['pəʊtʃə^r] n braconnier m

P.O. Box n abbr = **post office box**

pocket ['pɔkɪt] n poche f ▷ vt empocher; **to be (£5) out of ~** (Brit) en être de sa poche (pour 5 livres)

pocketbook ['pɔkɪtbʊk] n (notebook) carnet m; (US: wallet) portefeuille m; (: handbag) sac m à main

pocket knife n canif m

pocket money n argent m de poche

pod [pɔd] n cosse f ▷ vt écosser

podcast ['pɔdkɑːst] n podcast m ▷ vi podcaster

podgy ['pɔdʒɪ] adj rondelet(te)

podiatrist [pɔ'diːətrɪst] n (US) pédicure m/f

podium ['pəʊdɪəm] n podium m

poem ['pəʊɪm] n poème m

poet ['pəʊɪt] n poète m

poetic [pəʊ'ɛtɪk] adj poétique

poetry ['pəʊɪtrɪ] n poésie f

poignant ['pɔɪnjənt] adj poignant(e); (sharp) vif/vive

point [pɔɪnt] n (Geom, Scol, Sport, on scale) point m; (tip) pointe f; (in time) moment m; (in space) endroit m; (subject, idea) point, sujet m; (purpose) but m; (also: **decimal ~**): **2 ~ 3 (2.3)** 2 virgule 3 (2,3); (Brit Elec: also: **power ~**) prise f (de courant) ▷ vt (show) indiquer; (wall, window) jointoyer; (gun etc): **to ~ sth at** braquer or diriger qch sur ▷ vi: **to ~ at** montrer du doigt; **points** npl (Aut) vis platinées; (Rail) aiguillage m; **good ~s** qualités fpl; **the train stops at Carlisle and all ~s south** le train dessert Carlisle et toutes les gares vers le sud; **to make a ~** faire une remarque; **to make a ~ of doing sth** ne pas manquer de faire qch; **to make one's ~** se faire comprendre; **to get/ miss the ~** comprendre/ne pas comprendre; **to come to the ~** en venir au fait; **when it comes to the ~** le moment venu; **there's no ~ (in doing)** cela ne sert à rien (de faire); **to be on the ~ of doing sth** être sur le point de faire qch; **that's the whole ~!** précisément!; **to be beside the ~** être à côté de la question; **you've got a ~ there!** (c'est) juste!; **in ~ of fact** en fait, en réalité; **~ of departure** (also fig) point de départ; **~ of order** point de procédure; **~ of sale** (Comm) point de vente; **to ~ sth** (fig) signaler; **point out** vt (show) montrer, indiquer; (mention) faire remarquer, souligner

p

point-blank ['pɔɪnt'blæŋk] adv (fig)
catégoriquement; (also: **at ~ range**) à bout
portant ▷ adj (fig) catégorique
pointed ['pɔɪntɪd] adj (shape) pointu(e);
(remark) plein(e) de sous-entendus
pointer ['pɔɪntə'] n (stick) baguette f; (needle)
aiguille f; (dog) chien m d'arrêt; (clue)
indication f; (advice) tuyau m
pointless ['pɔɪntlɪs] adj inutile, vain(e)
point of view n point m de vue
poise [pɔɪz] n (balance) équilibre m; (of head,
body) port m; (calmness) calme m ▷ vt placer en
équilibre; **to be ~d for** (fig) être prêt à
poison ['pɔɪzn] n poison m ▷ vt empoisonner
poisonous ['pɔɪznəs] adj (snake)
venimeux(-euse); (substance, plant)
vénéneux(-euse); (fumes) toxique; (fig)
pernicieux(-euse)
poke [pəʊk] vt (fire) tisonner; (jab with finger,
stick etc) piquer; pousser du doigt; (put): **to ~
sth in(to)** fourrer or enfoncer qch dans ▷ n
(jab) (petit) coup; (to fire) coup m de tisonnier;
to ~ fun at sb se moquer de qn; **poke about**
vi fureter; **poke out** vi (stick out) sortir ▷ vt:
to ~ one's head out of the window passer
la tête par la fenêtre
poker ['pəʊkə'] n tisonnier m; (Cards) poker m
poky ['pəʊkɪ] adj exigu(ë)
Poland ['pəʊlənd] n Pologne f
polar ['pəʊlə'] adj polaire
polar bear n ours blanc
Pole [pəʊl] n Polonais(e)
pole [pəʊl] n (of wood) mât m, perche f; (Elec)
poteau m; (Geo) pôle m
pole bean n (US) haricot m (à rames)
pole vault ['pəʊlvɔːlt] n saut m à la perche
police [pə'liːs] npl police f ▷ vt maintenir
l'ordre dans; **a large number of ~ were hurt**
de nombreux policiers ont été blessés
police car n voiture f de police
police constable n (Brit) agent m de police
police force n police f, forces fpl de l'ordre
policeman [pə'liːsmən] irreg n agent m de
police, policier m
police officer n agent m de police
police station n commissariat m de police
policewoman [pə'liːswʊmən] irreg n femme-
agent f
policy ['pɔlɪsɪ] n politique f; (also: **insurance
~**) police f (d'assurance); (of newspaper,
company) politique générale; **to take out a ~**
(Insurance) souscrire une police d'assurance
polio ['pəʊlɪəʊ] n polio f
Polish ['pəʊlɪʃ] adj polonais(e) ▷ n (Ling)
polonais m
polish ['pɔlɪʃ] n (for shoes) cirage m; (for floor)
cire f, encaustique f; (for nails) vernis m; (shine)
éclat m, poli m; (fig: refinement) raffinement m
▷ vt (put polish on: shoes, wood) cirer; (make shiny)
astiquer, faire briller; (fig: improve)
perfectionner; **polish off** vt (work) expédier;
(food) liquider

polished ['pɔlɪʃt] adj (fig) raffiné(e)
polite [pə'laɪt] adj poli(e); **it's not ~ to do
that** ça ne se fait pas
politely [pə'laɪtlɪ] adv poliment
politeness [pə'laɪtnɪs] n politesse f
political [pə'lɪtɪkl] adj politique
politically [pə'lɪtɪklɪ] adv politiquement;
~ correct politiquement correct(e)
politician [pɔlɪ'tɪʃən] n homme/femme
politique, politicien(ne)
politics ['pɔlɪtɪks] n politique f
poll [pəʊl] n scrutin m, vote m; (also: **opinion
~**) sondage m (d'opinion) ▷ vt (votes) obtenir;
to go to the ~s (voters) aller aux urnes;
(government) tenir des élections
pollen ['pɔlən] n pollen m
polling day n (Brit) jour m des élections
polling station n (Brit) bureau m de vote
pollute [pə'luːt] vt polluer
pollution [pə'luːʃən] n pollution f
polo ['pəʊləʊ] n polo m
polo-neck ['pəʊləʊnɛk] adj à col roulé ▷ n
(sweater) pull m à col roulé
polo shirt n polo m
polyester [pɔlɪ'ɛstə'] n polyester m
polystyrene [pɔlɪ'staɪriːn] n polystyrène m
polythene ['pɔlɪθiːn] n (Brit)
polyéthylène m
polythene bag n sac m en plastique
pomegranate ['pɔmɪgrænɪt] n grenade f
pomp [pɔmp] n pompe f, faste f, apparat m
pompous ['pɔmpəs] adj pompeux(-euse)
pond [pɔnd] n étang m; (stagnant) mare f
ponder ['pɔndə'] vi réfléchir ▷ vt considérer,
peser
ponderous ['pɔndərəs] adj pesant(e),
lourd(e)
pong [pɔŋ] (Brit inf) n puanteur f ▷ vi
schlinguer
pony ['pəʊnɪ] n poney m
ponytail ['pəʊnɪteɪl] n queue f de cheval
pony trekking [-trɛkɪŋ] n (Brit) randonnée f
équestre or à cheval
poodle ['puːdl] n caniche m
pool [puːl] n (of rain) flaque f; (pond) mare f;
(artificial) bassin m; (also: **swimming ~**)
piscine f; (sth shared) fonds commun; (money
at cards) cagnotte f; (billiards) poule f; (Comm:
consortium) pool m; (US: monopoly trust) trust m
▷ vt mettre en commun; **pools** npl (football)
= loto sportif; **typing ~**, (US) **secretary ~** pool
m dactylographique; **to do the (football) ~s**
(Brit) = jouer au loto sportif; see also **football
pools**
poor [puə'] adj pauvre; (mediocre) médiocre,
faible, mauvais(e) ▷ npl: **the ~** les pauvres
mpl
poorly ['puəlɪ] adv pauvrement,
médiocrement ▷ adj souffrant(e), malade
pop [pɔp] n (noise) bruit sec; (Mus) musique f
pop; (inf: drink) soda m; (US inf: father) papa m
▷ vt (put) fourrer, mettre (rapidement) ▷ vi

éclater; (*cork*) sauter; **she ~ped her head out of the window** elle passa la tête par la fenêtre; **pop in** vi entrer en passant; **pop out** vi sortir; **pop up** vi apparaître, surgir

popcorn ['pɒpkɔ:n] *n* pop-corn *m*

pope [pəup] *n* pape *m*

poplar ['pɒplə'] *n* peuplier *m*

popper ['pɒpə'] *n* (*Brit*) bouton-pression *m*

poppy ['pɒpɪ] *n* (*wild*) coquelicot *m*; (*cultivated*) pavot *m*

Popsicle® ['pɒpsɪkl] *n* (*US*) esquimau *m* (*glace*)

pop star *n* pop star *f*

popular ['pɒpjulə'] *adj* populaire; (*fashionable*) à la mode; **to be ~ (with)** (*person*) avoir du succès (auprès de); (*decision*) être bien accueilli(e) (par)

popularity [pɒpju'lærɪtɪ] *n* popularité *f*

population [pɒpju'leɪʃən] *n* population *f*

pop-up *adj* (*Comput: menu, window*) pop up *inv* ⊳ *n* pop up *m inv*, fenêtre *f* pop up

porcelain ['pɔ:slɪn] *n* porcelaine *f*

porch [pɔ:tʃ] *n* porche *m*; (*US*) véranda *f*

porcupine ['pɔ:kjupaɪn] *n* porc-épic *m*

pore [pɔ:'] *n* pore *m* ⊳ *vi*: **to ~ over** s'absorber dans, être plongé(e) dans

pork [pɔ:k] *n* porc *m*

pork chop *n* côte *f* de porc

pork pie *n* pâté *m* de porc en croûte

porn [pɔ:n] *adj* (*inf*) porno ⊳ *n* (*inf*) porno *m*

pornographic [pɔ:nə'græfɪk] *adj* pornographique

pornography [pɔ:'nɒgrəfɪ] *n* pornographie *f*

porpoise ['pɔ:pəs] *n* marsouin *m*

porridge ['pɒrɪdʒ] *n* porridge *m*

port [pɔ:t] *n* (*harbour*) port *m*; (*opening in ship*) sabord *m*; (*Naut: left side*) bâbord *m*; (*wine*) porto *m*; (*Comput*) port *m*, accès *m* ⊳ *cpd* portuaire, du port; **to ~** (*Naut*) à bâbord; **~ of call** (port d')escale *f*

portable ['pɔ:təbl] *adj* portatif(-ive)

porter ['pɔ:tə'] *n* (*for luggage*) porteur *m*; (*doorkeeper*) gardien(ne); portier *m*

portfolio [pɔ:t'fəuljəu] *n* portefeuille *m*; (*of artist*) portfolio *m*

porthole ['pɔ:thəul] *n* hublot *m*

portion ['pɔ:ʃən] *n* portion *f*, part *f*

portrait ['pɔ:treɪt] *n* portrait *m*

portray [pɔ:'treɪ] *vt* faire le portrait de; (*in writing*) dépeindre, représenter; (*subj: actor*) jouer

Portugal ['pɔ:tjugl] *n* Portugal *m*

Portuguese [pɔ:tju'gi:z] *adj* portugais(e) ⊳ *n* (*pl inv*) Portugais(e); (*Ling*) portugais *m*

pose [pəuz] *n* pose *f* ⊳ *vi* poser; (*pretend*): **to ~ as** se faire passer pour ⊳ *vt* (*problem*) créer; **to strike a ~** poser (pour la galerie)

posh [pɒʃ] *adj* (*inf*) chic *inv*; **to talk ~** parler d'une manière affectée

position [pə'zɪʃən] *n* position *f*; (*job, situation*) situation *f* ⊳ *vt* mettre en place or en

position; **to be in a ~ to do sth** être en mesure de faire qch

positive ['pɒzɪtɪv] *adj* positif(-ive); (*certain*) sûr(e), certain(e); (*definite*) formel(le), catégorique; (*clear*) indéniable, réel(le)

positively ['pɒzɪtɪvlɪ] *adv* (*affirmatively, enthusiastically*) de façon positive; (*inf: really*) carrément; **to think ~** être positif(-ive)

possess [pə'zɛs] *vt* posséder; **like one ~ed** comme un fou; **whatever can have ~ed you?** qu'est-ce qui vous a pris?

possession [pə'zɛʃən] *n* possession *f*; **possessions** *npl* (*belongings*) affaires *fpl*; **to take ~ of sth** prendre possession de qch

possessive [pə'zɛsɪv] *adj* possessif(-ive)

possibility [pɒsɪ'bɪlɪtɪ] *n* possibilité *f*; (*event*) éventualité *f*; **he's a ~ for the part** c'est un candidat possible pour le rôle

possible ['pɒsɪbl] *adj* possible; (*solution*) envisageable, éventuel(le); **it is ~ to do it** il est possible de le faire; **as far as ~** dans la mesure du possible, autant que possible; **if ~** si possible; **as big as ~** aussi gros que possible

possibly ['pɒsɪblɪ] *adv* (*perhaps*) peut-être; **if you ~ can** si cela vous est possible; **I cannot ~ come** il m'est impossible de venir

post [pəust] *n* (*Brit: mail*) poste *f*; (: *collection*) levée *f*; (: *letters, delivery*) courrier *m*; (*job, situation*) poste *m*; (*pole*) poteau *m*; (*trading post*) comptoir *m* (*commercial*); (*on internet forum*) billet *m*, post *m* ⊳ *vt* (*to internet*) poster; (*Brit: send by post, Mil*) poster; (: *appoint*): **to ~** affecter à; (*notice*) afficher; **by ~** (*Brit*) par la poste; **by return of ~** (*Brit*) par retour du courrier; **where can I ~ these cards?** où est-ce que je peux poster ces cartes postales?; **to keep sb ~ed** tenir qn au courant

postage ['pəustɪdʒ] *n* tarifs *mpl* d'affranchissement; **~ paid** port payé; **~ prepaid** (*US*) franco (de port)

postal ['pəustl] *adj* postal(e)

postal order *n* mandat(-poste *m*) *m*

postbox ['pəustbɒks] *n* (*Brit*) boîte *f* aux lettres (*publique*)

postcard ['pəustkɑ:d] *n* carte postale

postcode ['pəustkəud] *n* (*Brit*) code postal

poster ['pəustə'] *n* affiche *f*

poste restante ['pəust'rɛstɑ̃:nt] *n* (*Brit*) poste restante

postgraduate ['pəust'grædjuət] *n* ≈ étudiant(e) de troisième cycle

posthumous ['pɒstjuməs] *adj* posthume

postman ['pəustmən] (*Brit*) *irreg n* facteur *m*

postmark ['pəustmɑ:k] *n* cachet *m* (de la poste)

post-mortem [pəust'mɔ:təm] *n* autopsie *f*

post office *n* (*building*) poste *f*; (*organization*): **the Post Office** les postes *fpl*

post office box *n* boîte postale

postpone [pəs'pəun] *vt* remettre (à plus tard), reculer

P

posture ['pɒstʃə^r] n posture f; (fig) attitude f
▷ vi poser

postwar [pəust'wɔ:^r] adj d'après-guerre

postwoman [pəust'wumən] (Brit) irreg n
factrice f

posy ['pəuzɪ] n petit bouquet

pot [pɒt] n (for cooking) marmite f; casserole f;
(teapot) théière f; (for coffee) cafetière f; (for
plants, jam) pot m; (piece of pottery) poterie f;
(inf: marijuana) herbe f ▷ vt (plant) mettre en
pot; **to go to ~** (inf) aller à vau-l'eau; **~s of**
(Brit inf) beaucoup de, plein de

potato (pl potatoes) [pə'teɪtəu] n pomme f
de terre

potato peeler n épluche-légumes m

potent ['pəutnt] adj puissant(e); (drink)
fort(e), très alcoolisé(e); (man) viril

potential [pə'tɛnʃl] adj potentiel(le) ▷ n
potentiel m; **to have ~** être
prometteur(-euse); ouvrir des possibilités

pothole ['pɒthəul] n (in road) nid m de poule;
(Brit: underground) gouffre m, caverne f

potholing ['pɒthəulɪŋ] n (Brit): **to go ~** faire
de la spéléologie

potluck [pɒt'lʌk] n: **to take ~** tenter sa
chance

pot plant n plante f d'appartement

potted ['pɒtɪd] adj (food) en conserve; (plant)
en pot; (fig: shortened) abrégé(e)

potter ['pɒtə^r] n potier m ▷ vi (Brit): **to ~
around** or **about** bricoler; **~'s wheel** tour m
de potier

pottery ['pɒtərɪ] n poterie f; **a piece of ~** une
poterie

potty ['pɒtɪ] adj (Brit inf: mad) dingue ▷ n
(child's) pot m

pouch [pautʃ] n (Zool) poche f; (for tobacco)
blague f; (for money) bourse f

poultry ['pəultrɪ] n volaille f

pounce [pauns] vi: **to ~ (on)** bondir (sur),
fondre (sur) ▷ n bond m, attaque f

pound [paund] n livre f (weight = 453g, 16 ounces;
money = 100 pence); (for dogs, cars) fourrière f ▷ vt
(beat) bourrer de coups, marteler; (crush)
piler, pulvériser; (with guns) pilonner ▷ vi
(heart) battre violemment, taper; **half a ~ (of)**
une demi-livre (de); **a five-~ note** un billet de
cinq livres

pound sterling n livre f sterling

pour [pɔ:^r] vt verser ▷ vi couler à flots; (rain)
pleuvoir à verse; **to ~ sb a drink** verser or
servir à boire à qn; **to come ~ing in** (water)
entrer à flots; (letters) arriver par milliers;
(cars, people) affluer; **pour away, pour off** vt
vider; **pour in** vi (people) affluer, se précipiter;
(news, letters) arriver en masse; **pour out** vi
(people) sortir en masse ▷ vt vider; (fig)
déverser; (serve: a drink) verser

pouring ['pɔ:rɪŋ] adj: **~ rain** pluie
torrentielle

pout [paut] n moue f ▷ vi faire la moue

poverty ['pɒvətɪ] n pauvreté f, misère f

poverty-stricken ['pɒvətɪstrɪkn] adj pauvre,
déshérité(e)

powder ['paudə^r] n poudre f ▷ vt poudrer; **to
~ one's nose** se poudrer; (euphemism) aller à la
salle de bain

powder compact n poudrier m

powdered milk n lait m en poudre

powder room n toilettes fpl (pour dames)

power ['pauə^r] n (strength, nation) puissance f,
force f; (ability, Pol: of party, leader) pouvoir m;
(Math) puissance; (of speech, thought) faculté f;
(Elec) courant m ▷ vt faire marcher,
actionner; **to do all in one's ~ to help sb**
faire tout ce qui est en son pouvoir pour aider
qn; **the world ~s** les grandes puissances; **to
be in ~** être au pouvoir

power cut n (Brit) coupure f de courant

powered ['pauəd] adj: **~ by** actionné(e) par,
fonctionnant à; **nuclear-~ submarine** sous-
marin m (à propulsion) nucléaire

power failure n panne f de courant

powerful ['pauəful] adj puissant(e);
(performance etc) très fort(e)

powerless ['pauəlɪs] adj impuissant(e)

power point n (Brit) prise f de courant

power station n centrale f électrique

power struggle n lutte f pour le pouvoir

p.p. abbr (= per procurationem: by proxy) p.p.

PR n abbr = **proportional representation**;
public relations ▷ abbr (US) = **Puerto Rico**

practical ['præktɪkl] adj pratique

practicality [præktɪ'kælɪtɪ] n (of plan)
aspect m pratique; (of person) sens m pratique;
practicalities npl détails mpl pratiques

practical joke n farce f

practically ['præktɪklɪ] adv (almost)
pratiquement

practice ['præktɪs] n pratique f; (of profession)
exercice m; (at football etc) entraînement m;
(business) cabinet m; clientèle f ▷ vt, vi (US)
= **practise**; **in ~** (in reality) en pratique; **out of ~**
rouillé(e); **2 hours' piano ~** 2 heures de
travail or d'exercices au piano; **target ~**
exercices de tir; **it's common ~** c'est courant,
ça se fait couramment; **to put sth into ~**
mettre qch en pratique

practise, (US) **practice** ['præktɪs] vt (work at:
piano, backhand etc) s'exercer à, travailler; (train
for: sport) s'entraîner à; (a sport, religion, method)
pratiquer; (profession) exercer ▷ vi s'exercer,
travailler; (train) s'entraîner; (lawyer, doctor)
exercer; **to ~ for a match** s'entraîner pour
un match

practising, (US) **practicing** ['præktɪsɪŋ] adj
(Christian etc) pratiquant(e); (lawyer) en
exercice; (homosexual) déclaré

practitioner [præk'tɪʃənə^r] n praticien(ne)

pragmatic [præg'mætɪk] adj pragmatique

prairie ['prɛərɪ] n savane f; (US): **the ~s** la
Prairie

praise [preɪz] n éloge(s) m(pl), louange(s) f(pl)
▷ vt louer, faire l'éloge de

praiseworthy ['preɪzwəːðɪ] adj digne de louanges

pram [præm] n (Brit) landau m, voiture f d'enfant

prance [prɑːns] vi (horse) caracoler

prank [præŋk] n farce f

prawn [prɔːn] n crevette f (rose)

prawn cocktail n cocktail m de crevettes

pray [preɪ] vi prier

prayer [prɛəʳ] n prière f

preach [priːtʃ] vi, vt prêcher; **to ~ at sb** faire la morale à qn

preacher ['priːtʃəʳ] n prédicateur m; (US: clergyman) pasteur m

precarious [prɪ'kɛərɪəs] adj précaire

precaution [prɪ'kɔːʃən] n précaution f

precede [prɪ'siːd] vt, vi précéder

precedent ['prɛsɪdənt] n précédent m; **to establish** or **set a ~** créer un précédent

preceding [prɪ'siːdɪŋ] adj qui précède (or précédait)

precinct ['priːsɪŋkt] n (round cathedral) pourtour m, enceinte f; (US: district) circonscription f, arrondissement m; **precincts** npl (neighbourhood) alentours mpl, environs mpl; **pedestrian ~** (Brit) zone piétonnière; **shopping ~** (Brit) centre commercial

precious ['prɛʃəs] adj précieux(-euse) ▷ adv (inf): **~ little** or **few** fort peu; **your ~ dog** (ironic) ton chien chéri, ton chéri chien

precipitate [prɪ'sɪpɪtɪt] adj (hasty) précipité(e) ▷ vt [prɪ'sɪpɪteɪt] précipiter

precise [prɪ'saɪs] adj précis(e)

precisely [prɪ'saɪslɪ] adv précisément

precision [prɪ'sɪʒən] n précision f

precocious [prɪ'kəʊʃəs] adj précoce

precondition ['priːkən'dɪʃən] n condition f nécessaire

predator ['prɛdətəʳ] n prédateur m, rapace m

predecessor ['priːdɪsɛsəʳ] n prédécesseur m

predicament [prɪ'dɪkəmənt] n situation f difficile

predict [prɪ'dɪkt] vt prédire

predictable [prɪ'dɪktəbl] adj prévisible

prediction [prɪ'dɪkʃən] n prédiction f

predominantly [prɪ'dɔmɪnəntlɪ] adv en majeure partie; (especially) surtout

pre-empt [priː'ɛmt] vt (Brit) acquérir par droit de préemption; (fig) anticiper sur; **to ~ the issue** conclure avant même d'ouvrir les débats

preen [priːn] vt: **to ~ itself** (bird) se lisser les plumes; **to ~ o.s.** s'admirer

prefab ['priːfæb] n abbr (= prefabricated building) bâtiment préfabriqué

preface ['prɛfəs] n préface f

prefect ['priːfɛkt] n (Brit: in school) élève chargé de certaines fonctions de discipline; (in France) préfet m

prefer [prɪ'fəːʳ] vt préférer; (Law): **to ~ charges** procéder à une inculpation; **to ~ coffee to tea** préférer le café au thé; **to ~ doing** or **to do sth** préférer faire qch

preferable ['prɛfrəbl] adj préférable

preferably ['prɛfrəblɪ] adv de préférence

preference ['prɛfrəns] n préférence f; **in ~ to sth** plutôt que qch, de préférence à qch

preferential [prɛfə'rɛnʃəl] adj préférentiel(le); **~ treatment** traitement m de faveur

prefix ['priːfɪks] n préfixe m

pregnancy ['prɛgnənsɪ] n grossesse f

pregnant ['prɛgnənt] adj enceinte adj f; (animal) pleine; **3 months ~** enceinte de 3 mois

prehistoric ['priːhɪs'tɔrɪk] adj préhistorique

prejudice ['prɛdʒudɪs] n préjugé m; (harm) tort m, préjudice m ▷ vt porter préjudice à; (bias): **to ~ sb in favour of/against** prévenir qn en faveur de/contre; **racial ~** préjugés raciaux

prejudiced ['prɛdʒudɪst] adj (person) plein(e) de préjugés; (in a matter) partial(e); (view) préconçu(e), partial(e); **to be ~ against sb/ sth** avoir un parti-pris contre qn/qch; **to be racially ~** avoir des préjugés raciaux

preliminary [prɪ'lɪmɪnərɪ] adj préliminaire

prelude ['prɛljuːd] n prélude m

premarital ['priː'mærɪtl] adj avant le mariage; **~ contract** contrat m de mariage

premature ['prɛmətʃuəʳ] adj prématuré(e); **to be ~ (in doing sth)** aller un peu (trop) vite (en faisant qch)

premier ['prɛmɪəʳ] adj premier(-ière), principal(e) ▷ n (Pol: Prime Minister) premier ministre; (Pol: President) chef m de l'État

premiere ['prɛmɪɛəʳ] n première f

Premier League n première division

premise ['prɛmɪs] n prémisse f

premises ['prɛmɪsɪz] npl locaux mpl; **on the ~** sur les lieux; sur place; **business ~** locaux commerciaux

premium ['priːmɪəm] n prime f; **to be at a ~** (fig: housing etc) être très demandé(e), être rarissime; **to sell at a ~** (shares) vendre au-dessus du pair

premium bond n (Brit) obligation f à prime, bon m à lots

premonition [prɛmə'nɪʃən] n prémonition f

preoccupied [priː'ɔkjupaɪd] adj préoccupé(e)

prep [prɛp] adj abbr: **~ school** = **preparatory school** ▷ n abbr (Scol: = preparation) étude f

prepaid [priː'peɪd] adj payé(e) d'avance

preparation [prɛpə'reɪʃən] n préparation f; **preparations** npl (for trip, war) préparatifs mpl; **in ~ for** en vue de

preparatory [prɪ'pærətərɪ] adj préparatoire; **~ to sth/to doing sth** en prévision de qch/ avant de faire qch

preparatory school n (Brit) école primaire privée; (US) lycée privé; voir article

P

● PREPARATORY SCHOOL
●
●

En Grande-Bretagne, une *preparatory school* – ou, plus familièrement, une *prep school* – est une école payante qui prépare les enfants de 7 à 13 ans aux "public schools".

prepare [prɪˈpɛəʳ] vt préparer ▷ vi: **to ~ for** se préparer à

prepared [prɪˈpɛəd] adj: **~ for** préparé(e) à; **~ to** prêt(e) à

preposition [prɛpəˈzɪʃən] n préposition f

preposterous [prɪˈpɔstərəs] adj ridicule, absurde

prep school n = **preparatory school**

prerequisite [priːˈrɛkwɪzɪt] n condition f préalable

presbyterian [prɛzbɪˈtɪərɪən] adj, n presbytérien(ne)

preschool [ˈpriːˈskuːl] adj préscolaire; (*child*) d'âge préscolaire

prescribe [prɪˈskraɪb] vt prescrire; **~d books** (*Brit Scol*) œuvres fpl au programme

prescription [prɪˈskrɪpʃən] n prescription f; (*Med*) ordonnance f; (: *medicine*) médicament m (obtenu sur ordonnance); **to make up** or (*US*) **fill a ~** faire une ordonnance; **could you write me a ~?** pouvez-vous me faire une ordonnance?; **"only available on ~"** "uniquement sur ordonnance"

presence [ˈprɛzns] n présence f; **in sb's ~** en présence de qn; **~ of mind** présence d'esprit

present [ˈprɛznt] adj présent(e); (*current*) présent, actuel(le) ▷ n cadeau m; (*actuality, also: ~ tense*) présent m ▷ vt [prɪˈzɛnt] présenter; (*prize, medal*) remettre; (*give*): **to ~ sb with sth** offrir qch à qn; **to be ~ at** assister à; **those ~** les présents; **at ~** en ce moment; **to give sb a ~** offrir un cadeau à qn; **to ~ sb (to sb)** présenter qn (à qn)

presentable [prɪˈzɛntəbl] adj présentable

presentation [prɛznˈteɪʃən] n présentation f; (*gift*) cadeau m, présent m; (*ceremony*) remise f du cadeau (or de la médaille *etc*); **on ~ of** (*voucher etc*) sur présentation de

present-day [ˈprɛzntdeɪ] adj contemporain(e), actuel(le)

presenter [prɪˈzɛntəʳ] n (*Brit Radio, TV*) présentateur(-trice)

presently [ˈprɛzntlɪ] adv (*soon*) tout à l'heure, bientôt; (*with verb in past*) peu après; (*at present*) en ce moment; (*US: now*) maintenant

preservation [prɛzəˈveɪʃən] n préservation f, conservation f

preservative [prɪˈzəːvətɪv] n agent m de conservation

preserve [prɪˈzəːv] vt (*keep safe*) préserver, protéger; (*maintain*) conserver, garder; (*food*) mettre en conserve ▷ n (*for game, fish*) réserve f; (*often pl: jam*) confiture f; (: *fruit*) fruits mpl en conserve

preside [prɪˈzaɪd] vi présider

president [ˈprɛzɪdənt] n président(e); (*US: of company*) président-directeur général, PDG m

presidential [prɛzɪˈdɛnʃl] adj présidentiel(le)

press [prɛs] n (*tool, machine, newspapers*) presse f; (*for wine*) pressoir m; (*crowd*) cohue f, foule f ▷ vt (*push*) appuyer sur; (*squeeze*) presser, serrer; (*clothes: iron*) repasser; (*pursue*) talonner; (*insist*): **to ~ sth on sb** presser qn d'accepter qch; (*urge, entreat*): **to ~ sb to do** or **into doing sth** pousser qn à faire qch ▷ vi appuyer, peser; se presser; **we are ~ed for time** le temps nous manque; **to ~ for sth** faire pression pour obtenir qch; **to ~ sb for an answer** presser qn de répondre; **to ~ charges against sb** (*Law*) engager des poursuites contre qn; **to go to ~** aller à l'impression; **to be in the ~** (*being printed*) être sous presse; (*in the newspapers*) être dans le journal; **press ahead** vi = **press on**; **press on** vi continuer

press conference n conférence f de presse

pressing [ˈprɛsɪŋ] adj urgent(e), pressant(e) ▷ n repassage m

press stud n (*Brit*) bouton-pression m

press-up [ˈprɛsʌp] n (*Brit*) traction f

pressure [ˈprɛʃəʳ] n (*stress*) tension f ▷ vt = **to put pressure on**; **to put ~ on sb (to do sth)** faire pression sur qn (pour qu'il fasse qch)

pressure cooker n cocotte-minute® f

pressure gauge n manomètre m

pressure group n groupe m de pression

prestige [prɛsˈtiːʒ] n prestige m

prestigious [prɛsˈtɪdʒəs] adj prestigieux(-euse)

presumably [prɪˈzjuːməblɪ] adv vraisemblablement; **~ he did it** c'est sans doute lui (qui a fait cela)

presume [prɪˈzjuːm] vt présumer, supposer; **to ~ to do** (*dare*) se permettre de faire

pretence, (*US*) **pretense** [prɪˈtɛns] n (*claim*) prétention f; (*pretext*) prétexte m; **she is devoid of all ~** elle n'est pas du tout prétentieuse; **to make a ~ of doing** faire semblant de faire; **on** or **under the ~ of doing sth** sous prétexte de faire qch; **under false ~s** sous des prétextes fallacieux

pretend [prɪˈtɛnd] vt (*feign*) feindre, simuler ▷ vi (*feign*) faire semblant; (*claim*): **to ~ to sth** prétendre à qch; **to ~ to do** faire semblant de faire

pretense [prɪˈtɛns] n (*US*) = **pretence**

pretentious [prɪˈtɛnʃəs] adj prétentieux(-euse)

pretext [ˈpriːtɛkst] n prétexte m; **on** or **under the ~ of doing sth** sous prétexte de faire qch

pretty [ˈprɪtɪ] adj joli(e) ▷ adv assez

prevail [prɪˈveɪl] vi (*win*) l'emporter, prévaloir; (*be usual*) avoir cours; (*persuade*): **to ~ (up)on sb to do** persuader qn de faire

prevailing [prɪ'veɪlɪŋ] *adj* (*widespread*) courant(e), répandu(e); (*wind*) dominant(e)

prevalent ['prɛvələnt] *adj* répandu(e), courant(e); (*fashion*) en vogue

prevent [prɪ'vɛnt] *vt*: **to ~ (from doing)** empêcher (de faire)

preventative [prɪ'vɛntətɪv] *adj* préventif(-ive)

prevention [prɪ'vɛnʃən] *n* prévention *f*

preventive [prɪ'vɛntɪv] *adj* préventif(-ive)

preview ['pri:vju:] *n* (*of film*) avant-première *f*; (*fig*) aperçu *m*

previous ['pri:vɪəs] *adj* (*last*) précédent(e); (*earlier*) antérieur(e); (*question, experience*) préalable; **I have a ~ engagement** je suis déjà pris(e); **~ to doing** avant de faire

previously ['pri:vɪəslɪ] *adv* précédemment, auparavant

prewar [pri:'wɔ:ʳ] *adj* d'avant-guerre

prey [preɪ] *n* proie *f* ▷ *vi*: **to ~ on** s'attaquer à; **it was ~ing on his mind** ça le rongeait *or* minait

price [praɪs] *n* prix *m*; (*Betting: odds*) cote *f* ▷ *vt* (*goods*) fixer le prix de; tarifer; **what is the ~ of ...?** combien coûte ...?, quel est le prix de ...?; **to go up** *or* **rise in ~** augmenter; **to put a ~ on sth** chiffrer qch; **to be ~d out of the market** (*article*) être trop cher pour soutenir la concurrence; (*producer, nation*) ne pas pouvoir soutenir la concurrence; **what ~ his promises now?** que valent maintenant toutes ses promesses?; **he regained his freedom, but at a ~** il a retrouvé sa liberté, mais cela lui a coûté cher

priceless ['praɪslɪs] *adj* sans prix, inestimable; (*inf: amusing*) impayable

price list *n* tarif *m*

prick [prɪk] *n* (*sting*) piqûre *f*; (*inf!*) bitte *f* (!); connard *m* (!) ▷ *vt* piquer; **to ~ up one's ears** dresser *or* tendre l'oreille

prickle ['prɪkl] *n* (*of plant*) épine *f*; (*sensation*) picotement *m*

prickly ['prɪklɪ] *adj* piquant(e), épineux(-euse); (*fig: person*) irritable

prickly heat *n* fièvre *f* miliaire

pride [praɪd] *n* (*feeling proud*) fierté *f*; (*pej*) orgueil *m*; (*self-esteem*) amour-propre *m* ▷ *vt*: **to ~ o.s. on** se flatter de; s'enorgueillir de; **to take (a) ~ in** être (très) fier(-ère) de; **to take a ~ in doing** mettre sa fierté à faire; **to have ~ of place** (*Brit*) avoir la place d'honneur

priest [pri:st] *n* prêtre *m*

priesthood ['pri:sthud] *n* prêtrise *f*, sacerdoce *m*

prim [prɪm] *adj* collet monté *inv*, guindé(e)

primarily ['praɪmərɪlɪ] *adv* principalement, essentiellement

primary ['praɪmərɪ] *adj* primaire; (*first in importance*) premier(-ière), primordial(e) ▷ *n* (*US: election*) (élection *f*) primaire *f*

primary school *n* (*Brit*) école *f* primaire; *voir article*

◉ **PRIMARY SCHOOL**

◉
◉ Les *primary schools* en Grande-Bretagne
◉ accueillent les enfants de 5 à 11 ans.
◉ Elles marquent le début du cycle scolaire
◉ obligatoire et elles comprennent deux
◉ sections: la section des petits ("infant
◉ school") et la section des grands ("junior
◉ school"); voir "secondary school".

prime [praɪm] *adj* primordial(e), fondamental(e); (*excellent*) excellent(e) ▷ *vt* (*gun, pump*) amorcer; (*fig*) mettre au courant ▷ *n*: **in the ~ of life** dans la fleur de l'âge

Prime Minister *n* Premier ministre

primeval [praɪ'mi:vl] *adj* primitif(-ive)

primitive ['prɪmɪtɪv] *adj* primitif(-ive)

primrose ['prɪmrəuz] *n* primevère *f*

primus® ['praɪməs], **primus® stove** *n* (*Brit*) réchaud *m* de camping

prince [prɪns] *n* prince *m*

princess [prɪn'sɛs] *n* princesse *f*

principal ['prɪnsɪpl] *adj* principal(e) ▷ *n* (*head teacher*) directeur *m*, principal *m*; (*in play*) rôle principal; (*money*) principal *m*

principally ['prɪnsɪplɪ] *adv* principalement

principle ['prɪnsɪpl] *n* principe *m*; **in ~** en principe; **on ~** par principe

print [prɪnt] *n* (*mark*) empreinte *f*; (*letters*) caractères *mpl*; (*fabric*) imprimé *m*; (*Art*) gravure *f*, estampe *f*; (*Phot*) épreuve *f* ▷ *vt* imprimer; (*publish*) publier; (*write in capitals*) écrire en majuscules; **out of ~** épuisé(e); **print out** *vt* (*Comput*) imprimer

printed matter ['prɪntɪd-] *n* imprimés *mpl*

printer ['prɪntəʳ] *n* (*machine*) imprimante *f*; (*person*) imprimeur *m*

printing ['prɪntɪŋ] *n* impression *f*

printout ['prɪntaut] *n* (*Comput*) sortie *f* imprimante

prior ['praɪəʳ] *adj* antérieur(e), précédent(e); (*more important*) prioritaire ▷ *n* (*Rel*) prieur *m* ▷ *adv*: **~ to doing** avant de faire; **without ~ notice** sans préavis; **to have a ~ claim to sth** avoir priorité pour qch

priority [praɪ'ɔrɪtɪ] *n* priorité *f*; **to have** *or* **take ~ over sth/sb** avoir la priorité sur qch/sb

prise [praɪz] *vt*: **to ~ open** forcer

prison ['prɪzn] *n* prison *f* ▷ *cpd* pénitentiaire

prisoner ['prɪznəʳ] *n* prisonnier(-ière); **the ~ at the bar** l'accusé(e); **to take sb ~** faire qn prisonnier

prisoner of war *n* prisonnier(-ière) de guerre

pristine ['prɪsti:n] *adj* virginal(e)

privacy ['prɪvəsɪ] *n* intimité *f*, solitude *f*

private ['praɪvɪt] *adj* (*not public*) privé(e); (*personal*) personnel(le); (*house, car, lesson*) particulier(-ière); (*quiet: place*) tranquille ▷ *n* soldat *m* de deuxième classe; **"~"** (*on envelope*) "personnelle"; (*on door*) "privé"; **in ~** en privé;

in (his) ~ **life** dans sa vie privée; **he is a very ~ person** il est très secret; **to be in ~ practice** être médecin (*or* dentiste *etc*) non conventionné; ~ **hearing** (*Law*) audience f à huis-clos

private detective n détective privé
private enterprise n entreprise privée
privately ['praɪvtlɪ] adv en privé; (*within oneself*) intérieurement
private property n propriété privée
private school n école privée
privatize ['praɪvətaɪz] vt privatiser
privet ['prɪvɪt] n troène m
privilege ['prɪvɪlɪdʒ] n privilège m
privy ['prɪvɪ] adj: **to be ~ to** être au courant de
prize [praɪz] n prix m ▷ adj (*example, idiot*) parfait(e); (*bull, novel*) primé(e) ▷ vt priser, faire grand cas de
prize-giving ['praɪzɡɪvɪŋ] n distribution f des prix
prizewinner ['praɪzwɪnəʳ] n gagnant(e)
pro [prəʊ] n (*inf: Sport*) professionnel(le) ▷ prep pro; **pros** npl: **the ~s and cons** le pour et le contre
probability [prɔbə'bɪlɪtɪ] n probabilité f; **in all ~** très probablement
probable ['prɔbəbl] adj probable; **it is ~/ hardly ~ that** ... il est probable/peu probable que ...
probably ['prɔbəblɪ] adv probablement
probation [prə'beɪʃən] n (*in employment*) (période f d') essai m; (*Law*) liberté surveillée; (*Rel*) noviciat m, probation f; **on ~** (*employee*) à l'essai; (*Law*) en liberté surveillée
probe [prəʊb] n (*Med, Space*) sonde f; (*enquiry*) enquête f, investigation f ▷ vt sonder, explorer
problem ['prɔbləm] n problème m; **to have ~s with the car** avoir des ennuis avec la voiture; **what's the ~?** qu'y a-t-il?, quel est le problème?; **I had no ~ in finding her** je n'ai pas eu de mal à la trouver; **no ~!** pas de problème!
procedure [prə'siːdʒəʳ] n (*Admin, Law*) procédure f; (*method*) marche f à suivre, façon f de procéder
proceed [prə'siːd] vi (*go forward*) avancer; (*act*) procéder; (*continue*): **to ~ (with)** continuer, poursuivre; **to ~** aller à; passer à; **to ~ to do** se mettre à faire; **I am not sure how to ~** je ne sais pas exactement comment m'y prendre; **to ~ against sb** (*Law*) intenter des poursuites contre qn
proceedings [prə'siːdɪŋz] npl (*measures*) mesures fpl; (*Law: against sb*) poursuites fpl; (*meeting*) réunion f, séance f; (*records*) compte rendu; actes mpl
proceeds ['prəʊsiːdz] npl produit m, recette f
process ['prəʊsɛs] n processus m; (*method*) procédé m ▷ vt traiter ▷ vi [prə'sɛs] (*Brit formal: go in procession*) défiler; **in ~** en cours;

we are in the ~ of doing nous sommes en train de faire
processing ['prəʊsɛsɪŋ] n traitement m
procession [prə'sɛʃən] n défilé m, cortège m; **funeral ~** (*on foot*) cortège funèbre; (*in cars*) convoi m mortuaire
proclaim [prə'kleɪm] vt déclarer, proclamer
procrastinate [prəʊ'kræstɪneɪt] vi faire traîner les choses, vouloir tout remettre au lendemain
procure [prə'kjʊəʳ] vt (*for o.s.*) se procurer; (*for sb*) procurer
prod [prɔd] vt pousser ▷ n (*push, jab*) petit coup, poussée f
prodigal ['prɔdɪɡl] adj prodigue
prodigy ['prɔdɪdʒɪ] n prodige m
produce n ['prɔdjuːs] (*Agr*) produits mpl ▷ vt [prə'djuːs] (*show*) présenter; (*cause*) provoquer, causer; (*Theat*) monter, mettre en scène; (*TV: programme*) réaliser; (*: play, film*) mettre en scène; (*Radio: programme*) réaliser; (*: play*) mettre en ondes
producer [prə'djuːsəʳ] n (*Theat*) metteur m en scène; (*Agr, Comm, Cine*) producteur m; (*TV: of programme*) réalisateur m; (*: of play, film*) metteur en scène; (*Radio: of programme*) réalisateur; (*: of play*) metteur en ondes
product ['prɔdʌkt] n produit m
production [prə'dʌkʃən] n production f; (*Theat*) mise f en scène; **to put into ~** (*goods*) entreprendre la fabrication de
production line n chaîne f (de fabrication)
productive [prə'dʌktɪv] adj productif(-ive)
productivity [prɔdʌk'tɪvɪtɪ] n productivité f
Prof. [prɔf] abbr (= *professor*) Prof
profession [prə'fɛʃən] n profession f; **the ~s** les professions libérales
professional [prə'fɛʃənl] n professionnel(le) ▷ adj professionnel(le); (*work*) de professionnel; **he's a ~ man** il exerce une profession libérale; **to take ~ advice** consulter un spécialiste
professionally [prə'fɛʃnəlɪ] adv professionnellement; (*Sport: play*) en professionnel; **I only know him ~** je n'ai avec lui que des relations de travail
professor [prə'fɛsəʳ] n professeur m (titulaire d'une chaire); (*US: teacher*) professeur m
proficiency [prə'fɪʃənsɪ] n compétence f, aptitude f
profile ['prəʊfaɪl] n profil m; **to keep a high/ low ~** (*fig*) rester *or* être très en évidence/ discret(-ète)
profit ['prɔfɪt] n (*from trading*) bénéfice m; (*advantage*) profit m ▷ vi: **to ~ (by *or* from)** profiter (de); **~ and loss account** compte m de profits et pertes; **to make a ~** faire un *or* des bénéfice(s); **to sell sth at a ~** vendre qch à profit
profitable ['prɔfɪtəbl] adj lucratif(-ive), rentable; (*fig: beneficial*) avantageux(-euse); (*: meeting*) fructueux(-euse)

profound [prə'faund] *adj* profond(e)
profusely [prə'fju:slɪ] *adv* abondamment;
(*thank etc*) avec effusion
prognosis [prɒg'nəusɪs] (*pl* **prognoses**) *n*
pronostic *m*
programme, (US) **program** ['prəugræm] *n*
(*Comput: also Brit*) programme *m*; (*Radio, TV*)
émission *f* ▷ *vt* programmer
programmer ['prəugræmə'] *n*
programmeur(-euse)
programming, (US) **programing**
['prəugræmɪŋ] *n* programmation *f*
progress *n* ['prəugrɛs] progrès *m(pl)* ▷ *vi*
[prə'grɛs] progresser, avancer; **in ~** en cours;
to make ~ progresser, faire des progrès, être
en progrès; **as the match ~ed** au fur et à
mesure que la partie avançait
progressive [prə'grɛsɪv] *adj* progressif(-ive);
(*person*) progressiste
prohibit [prə'hɪbɪt] *vt* interdire, défendre;
to ~ sb from doing sth défendre *or* interdire
à qn de faire qch; **"smoking ~ed"** "défense
de fumer"
project [*n* 'prɔdʒɛkt, *vb* prə'dʒɛkt] *n* (*plan*)
projet *m*, plan *m*; (*venture*) opération *f*,
entreprise *f*; (*Scol: research*) étude *f*, dossier *m*
▷ *vt* projeter ▷ *vi* (*stick out*) faire saillie,
s'avancer
projection [prə'dʒɛkʃən] *n* projection *f*;
(*overhang*) saillie *f*
projector [prə'dʒɛktə'] *n* (*Cine etc*)
projecteur *m*
prolific [prə'lɪfɪk] *adj* prolifique
prolong [prə'lɒŋ] *vt* prolonger
prom [prɒm] *n abbr* = **promenade**;
promenade concert; (*US: ball*) bal *m*
d'étudiants; **the P~s** série de concerts de musique
classique; voir article

> ● **PROM**
> ●
> ● En Grande-Bretagne, un *promenade concert*
> ● ou *prom* est un concert de musique
> ● classique, ainsi appelé car, à l'origine,
> ● le public restait debout et se promenait
> ● au lieu de rester assis. De nos jours, une
> ● partie du public reste debout, mais il y
> ● a également des places assises (plus
> ● chères). Les *Proms* les plus connus sont
> ● les Proms londoniens. La dernière séance
> ● (the "Last Night of the Proms") est un
> ● grand événement médiatique où se
> ● jouent des airs traditionnels et
> ● patriotiques.
> ●
> ● Aux États-Unis et au Canada, le *prom* ou
> ● *promenade* est un bal organisé par le lycée.

promenade [prɒmə'nɑːd] *n* (*by sea*)
esplanade *f*, promenade *f*
promenade concert *n* concert *m* (de
musique classique)

prominent ['prɒmɪnənt] *adj* (*standing out*)
proéminent(e); (*important*) important(e);
he is ~ in the field of ... il est très connu
dans le domaine de ...
promiscuous [prə'mɪskjuəs] *adj* (*sexually*) de
mœurs légères
promise ['prɒmɪs] *n* promesse *f* ▷ *vt, vi*
promettre; **to make sb a ~** faire une
promesse à qn; **a young man of ~** un jeune
homme plein d'avenir; **to ~ well** *vi*
promettre
promising ['prɒmɪsɪŋ] *adj* prometteur(-euse)
promote [prə'məut] *vt* promouvoir; (*venture,
event*) organiser, mettre sur pied; (*new product*)
lancer; **the team was ~d to the second
division** (*Brit Football*) l'équipe est montée en
2e division
promoter [prə'məutə'] *n* (*of event*)
organisateur(-trice)
promotion [prə'məuʃən] *n* promotion *f*
prompt [prɒmpt] *adj* rapide ▷ *n* (*Comput*)
message *m* (de guidage) ▷ *vt* inciter; (*cause*)
entraîner, provoquer; (*Theat*) souffler (son
rôle *or* ses répliques) à; **they're very ~**
(*punctual*) ils sont ponctuels; **at 8 o'clock ~**
à 8 heures précises; **he was ~ to accept** il a
tout de suite accepté; **to ~ sb to do** inciter *or*
pousser qn à faire
promptly ['prɒmptlɪ] *adv* (*quickly*)
rapidement, sans délai; (*on time*)
ponctuellement
prone [prəun] *adj* (*lying*) couché(e) (face
contre terre); (*liable*): **~ to** enclin(e) à; **to be ~
to illness** être facilement malade; **to be ~ to
an illness** être sujet à une maladie; **she is ~
to burst into tears if ...** elle a tendance à
tomber en larmes si ...
prong [prɒŋ] *n* pointe *f*; (*of fork*) dent *f*
pronoun ['prəunaun] *n* pronom *m*
pronounce [prə'nauns] *vt* prononcer ▷ *vi*: **to
~ (up)on** se prononcer sur; **how do you ~ it?**
comment est-ce que ça se prononce?; **they ~d
him unfit to drive** ils l'ont déclaré inapte à
la conduite
pronunciation [prənʌnsɪ'eɪʃən] *n*
prononciation *f*
proof [pruːf] *n* preuve *f*; (*test, of book, Phot*)
épreuve *f*; (*of alcohol*) degré *m* ▷ *adj*: **~ against**
à l'épreuve de ▷ *vt* (*Brit: tent, anorak*)
imperméabiliser; **to be 70°** ≈ titrer 40
degrés
prop [prɒp] *n* support *m*, étai *m*; (*fig*) soutien
m ▷ *vt* (*also*: **~ up**) étayer, soutenir; **props** *npl*
accessoires *mpl*; (*lean*): **to ~ sth against**
appuyer qch contre *or* à
propaganda [prɒpə'gændə] *n* propagande *f*
propel [prə'pɛl] *vt* propulser, faire avancer
propeller [prə'pɛlə'] *n* hélice *f*
propensity [prə'pɛnsɪtɪ] *n* propension *f*
proper ['prɒpə'] *adj* (*suited, right*) approprié(e),
bon/bonne; (*seemly*) correct(e), convenable;
(*authentic*) vrai(e), véritable; (*inf: real*) fini(e),

p

vrai(e); *(referring to place)*: **the village ~**
le village proprement dit; **to go through
the ~ channels** *(Admin)* passer par la voie
officielle

properly ['prɒpəlɪ] *adv* correctement,
convenablement; *(really)* bel et bien

proper noun *n* nom *m* propre

property ['prɒpətɪ] *n (possessions)* biens *mpl*;
(house etc) propriété *f*; *(land)* terres *fpl*,
domaine *m*; *(Chem etc: quality)* propriété *f*;
it's their ~ cela leur appartient, c'est leur
propriété

prophecy ['prɒfɪsɪ] *n* prophétie *f*

prophesy ['prɒfɪsaɪ] *vt* prédire ▷ *vi*
prophétiser

prophet ['prɒfɪt] *n* prophète *m*

proportion [prə'pɔ:ʃən] *n* proportion *f*;
(share) part *f*; partie *f* ▷ *vt* proportionner;
proportions *npl (size)* dimensions *fpl*; **to be
in/out of ~ to** *or* **with sth** être à la mesure
de/hors de proportion avec qch; **to see sth
in ~** *(fig)* ramener qch à de justes proportions

proportional [prə'pɔ:ʃənl], **proportionate**
[prə'pɔ:ʃənɪt] *adj* proportionnel(le)

proposal [prə'pəuzl] *n* proposition *f*, offre *f*;
(plan) projet *m*; *(of marriage)* demande *f* en
mariage

propose [prə'pəuz] *vt* proposer, suggérer;
(have in mind): **to ~ sth/to do** *or* **doing sth**
envisager qch/de faire qch ▷ *vi* faire sa
demande en mariage; **to ~ to do** avoir
l'intention de faire

proposition [prɒpə'zɪʃən] *n* proposition *f*; **to
make sb a ~** faire une proposition à qn

proprietor [prə'praɪətə'] *n* propriétaire *m/f*

propriety [prə'praɪətɪ] *n (seemliness)*
bienséance *f*, convenance *f*

prose [prəuz] *n* prose *f*; *(Scol: translation)*
thème *m*

prosecute ['prɒsɪkju:t] *vt* poursuivre

prosecution [prɒsɪ'kju:ʃən] *n* poursuites *fpl*
judiciaires; *(accusing side: in criminal case)*
accusation *f*; *(: in civil case)* la partie
plaignante

prosecutor ['prɒsɪkju:tə'] *n (lawyer)*
procureur *m*; *(also:* **public ~**) ministère public;
(US: plaintiff) plaignant(e)

prospect [*n* 'prɒspɛkt] *n* perspective *f*; *(hope)*
espoir *m*, chances *fpl* ▷ *vt, vi* [prə'spɛkt]
prospecter; **prospects** *npl (for work etc)*
possibilités *fpl* d'avenir, débouchés *mpl*; **we
are faced with the ~ of leaving** nous
risquons de devoir partir; **there is every ~ of
an early victory** tout laisse prévoir une
victoire rapide

prospecting [prə'spɛktɪŋ] *n* prospection *f*

prospective [prə'spɛktɪv] *adj (possible)*
éventuel(le); *(future)* futur(e)

prospectus [prə'spɛktəs] *n* prospectus *m*

prosper ['prɒspə'] *vi* prospérer

prosperity [prɒ'spɛrɪtɪ] *n* prospérité *f*

prosperous ['prɒspərəs] *adj* prospère

prostitute ['prɒstɪtju:t] *n* prostituée *f*;
male ~ prostitué *m*

protect [prə'tɛkt] *vt* protéger

protection [prə'tɛkʃən] *n* protection *f*; **to be
under sb's ~** être sous la protection de qn

protective [prə'tɛktɪv] *adj* protecteur(-trice);
(clothing) de protection; **~ custody** *(Law)*
détention préventive

protein ['prəuti:n] *n* protéine *f*

protest [*n* 'prəutɛst, *vb* prə'tɛst] *n*
protestation *f* ▷ *vi*: **to ~ against/about**
protester contre/à propos de ▷ *vt* protester
de; **to ~ (that)** protester que

Protestant ['prɒtɪstənt] *adj, n* protestant(e)

protester, protestor [prə'tɛstə'] *n (in
demonstration)* manifestant(e)

protracted [prə'træktɪd] *adj* prolongé(e)

protractor [prə'træktə'] *n (Geom)*
rapporteur *m*

protrude [prə'tru:d] *vi* avancer, dépasser

proud [praud] *adj* fier(-ère); *(pej)*
orgueilleux(-euse); **to be ~ to do sth** être fier
de faire qch; **to do sb ~** *(inf)* faire honneur
à qn; **to do o.s. ~** *(inf)* ne se priver de rien

prove [pru:v] *vt* prouver, démontrer ▷ *vi*:
to ~ correct *etc* s'avérer juste *etc*; **to ~ o.s.**
montrer ce dont on est capable; **to ~ o.s./
itself (to be) useful** *etc* se montrer *or* se
révéler utile *etc*; **he was ~d right in the end**
il s'est avéré qu'il avait raison

proverb ['prɒvə:b] *n* proverbe *m*

provide [prə'vaɪd] *vt* fournir; **to ~ sb with
sth** fournir qch à qn; **to be ~d with** *(person)*
disposer de; *(thing)* être équipé(e) *or*
muni(e) de; **provide for** *vt fus (person)*
subvenir aux besoins de; *(future event)*
prévoir

provided [prə'vaɪdɪd] *conj*: **~ (that)** à
condition que + *sub*

providing [prə'vaɪdɪŋ] *conj* à condition
que + *sub*

province ['prɒvɪns] *n* province *f*; *(fig)*
domaine *m*

provincial [prə'vɪnʃəl] *adj* provincial(e)

provision [prə'vɪʒən] *n (supply)* provision *f*;
(supplying) fourniture *f*; approvisionnement *m*;
(stipulation) disposition *f*; **provisions** *npl (food)*
provisions *fpl*; **to make ~ for** *(one's future)*
assurer; *(one's family)* assurer l'avenir de;
there's no ~ for this in the contract
le contrat ne prévoit pas cela

provisional [prə'vɪʒənl] *adj* provisoire ▷ *n*:
P~ *(Irish Pol)* Provisional *m (membre de la
tendance activiste de l'IRA)*

proviso [prə'vaɪzəu] *n* condition *f*; **with the ~
that** à la condition (expresse) que

provocative [prə'vɒkətɪv] *adj*
provocateur(-trice), provocant(e)

provoke [prə'vəuk] *vt* provoquer; **to ~ sb to
sth/to do** *or* **into doing sth** pousser qn à
qch/à faire qch

prowess ['prauɪs] *n* prouesse *f*

prowl [praul] vi (also: ~ **about**, ~ **around**) rôder ▷ n: **to be on the ~** rôder

prowler ['praulə'] n rôdeur(-euse)

proximity [prɔk'sɪmɪtɪ] n proximité f

proxy ['prɔksɪ] n procuration f; **by ~** par procuration

prudent ['pru:dnt] adj prudent(e)

prune [pru:n] n pruneau m ▷ vt élaguer

pry [praɪ] vi: **to ~ into** fourrer son nez dans

PS n abbr (= postscript) PS m

psalm [sɑ:m] n psaume m

pseudonym ['sju:dənɪm] n pseudonyme m

PSHE n abbr (Brit: Scol: = personal, social and health education) cours d'éducation personnelle, sanitaire et sociale préparant à la vie adulte

psyche ['saɪkɪ] n psychisme m

psychiatric [saɪkɪ'ætrɪk] adj psychiatrique

psychiatrist [saɪ'kaɪətrɪst] n psychiatre m/f

psychic ['saɪkɪk] adj (also: ~**al**) (méta) psychique; (person) doué(e) de télépathie or d'un sixième sens

psychoanalysis (pl **psychoanalyses**) [saɪkəuə'nælɪsɪs, -siːz] n psychanalyse f

psychoanalyst [saɪkəu'ænəlɪst] n psychanalyste m/f

psychological [saɪkə'lɔdʒɪkl] adj psychologique

psychologist [saɪ'kɔlədʒɪst] n psychologue m/f

psychology [saɪ'kɔlədʒɪ] n psychologie f

psychotherapy [saɪkəu'θerəpɪ] n psychothérapie f

pt abbr = **pint**; **pints**; **point**; **points**

PTO abbr (= please turn over) TSVP

PTV abbr (US) = **pay television**

pub [pʌb] n abbr (= public house) pub m

puberty ['pju:bətɪ] n puberté f

public ['pʌblɪk] adj public(-ique) ▷ n public m; **in ~** en public; **the general ~** le grand public; **to be ~ knowledge** être de notoriété publique; **to go ~** (Comm) être coté(e) en Bourse; **to make ~** rendre public

public address system n (système m de) sonorisation f, sono f (col)

publican ['pʌblɪkən] n patron m or gérant m de pub

publication [pʌblɪ'keɪʃən] n publication f

public company n société f anonyme

public convenience n (Brit) toilettes fpl

public holiday n (Brit) jour férié

public house n (Brit) pub m

publicity [pʌb'lɪsɪtɪ] n publicité f

publicize ['pʌblɪsaɪz] vt (make known) faire connaître, rendre public; (advertise) faire de la publicité pour

public limited company n ≈ société f anonyme (SA) (cotée en Bourse)

publicly ['pʌblɪklɪ] adv publiquement, en public

public opinion n opinion publique

public relations n or npl relations publiques (RP)

public school n (Brit) école privée; (US) école publique; voir article

● **PUBLIC SCHOOL**
●
● Une public school est un établissement
● d'enseignement secondaire privé.
● Bon nombre d'entre elles sont des
● pensionnats. Beaucoup ont également
● une école primaire qui leur est rattachée
● (une "prep" ou "preparatory school")
● pour préparer les élèves à l'école
● secondaire. Ces écoles sont en général
● prestigieuses, et les frais de scolarité sont
● très élevés dans les plus connues
● (Westminster, Eton, Harrow). Beaucoup
● d'élèves vont ensuite à l'université,
● et un grand nombre entre à Oxford ou
● à Cambridge. Les grands industriels,
● les députés et les hauts fonctionnaires
● sortent souvent de ces écoles.
● Aux États-Unis, le terme "public school"
● désigne tout simplement une école
● publique gratuite.

public-spirited [pʌblɪk'spɪrɪtɪd] adj qui fait preuve de civisme

public transport, (US) **public transportation** n transports mpl en commun

publish ['pʌblɪʃ] vt publier

publisher ['pʌblɪʃə'] n éditeur m

publishing ['pʌblɪʃɪŋ] n (industry) édition f; (of a book) publication f

pub lunch n repas m de bistrot

pucker ['pʌkə'] vt plisser

pudding ['pudɪŋ] n (Brit: dessert) dessert m, entremets m; (sweet dish) pudding m, gâteau m; (sausage) boudin m; **rice ~** ≈ riz m au lait; **black ~**, (US) **blood ~** boudin (noir)

puddle ['pʌdl] n flaque f d'eau

puff [pʌf] n bouffée f ▷ vt: **to ~ one's pipe** tirer sur sa pipe; (also: ~ **out**: sails, cheeks) gonfler ▷ vi sortir par bouffées; (pant) haleter; **to ~ out smoke** envoyer des bouffées de fumée

puff pastry, (US) **puff paste** n pâte feuilletée

puffy ['pʌfɪ] adj bouffi(e), boursouflé(e)

pull [pul] n (tug): **to give sth a ~** tirer sur qch; (of moon, magnet, the sea etc) attraction f; (fig) influence f ▷ vt tirer; (trigger) presser; (strain: muscle, tendon) se claquer ▷ vi tirer; **to ~ a face** faire une grimace; **to ~ to pieces** mettre en morceaux; **to ~ one's punches** (also fig) ménager son adversaire; **to ~ one's weight** y mettre du sien; **to ~ o.s. together** se ressaisir; **to ~ sb's leg** (fig) faire marcher qn; **to ~ strings (for sb)** intervenir (en faveur de qn); **pull about** vt (Brit: handle roughly: object) maltraiter; (: person) malmener; **pull apart** vt séparer; (break) mettre en pièces, démantibuler; **pull away** vi (vehicle: move off) partir; (draw back) s'éloigner; **pull back** vi (lever etc) tirer sur; (curtains) ouvrir ▷ vi (refrain) s'abstenir; (Mil: withdraw) se retirer; **pull down** vt baisser, abaisser; (house) démolir; (tree) abattre; **pull in** vi (Aut) se ranger; (Rail) entrer en gare; **pull off** vt enlever, ôter; (deal etc) conclure; **pull out** vi démarrer, partir; (withdraw) se retirer; (Aut: come out of line) déboîter ▷ vt (from bag, pocket) sortir; (remove) arracher; (withdraw) retirer; **pull over** vi (Aut) se ranger; **pull round** vi (unconscious person) revenir à soi; (sick person) se rétablir; **pull through** vi s'en sortir; **pull up** vi (stop) s'arrêter ▷ vt remonter; (uproot) déraciner, arracher; (stop) arrêter

pulley ['pulɪ] n poulie f

pullover ['puləuvə'] n pull-over m, tricot m

pulp [pʌlp] n (of fruit) pulpe f; (for paper) pâte f à papier; (pej: also: ~ **magazines** etc) presse f à sensation or de bas étage; **to reduce sth to (a) ~** réduire qch en purée

pulpit ['pulpɪt] n chaire f

pulsate [pʌl'seɪt] vi battre, palpiter; (music) vibrer

pulse [pʌls] n (of blood) pouls m; (of heart) battement m; (of music, engine) vibrations fpl; **pulses** npl (Culin) légumineuses fpl; **to feel** or **take sb's ~** prendre le pouls à qn

puma ['pjuːmə] n puma m

pump [pʌmp] n pompe f; (shoe) escarpin m ▷ vt pomper; (fig: inf) faire parler; **to ~ sb for information** essayer de soutirer des renseignements à qn; **pump up** vt gonfler

pumpkin ['pʌmpkɪn] n potiron m, citrouille f

pun [pʌn] n jeu m de mots, calembour m

punch [pʌntʃ] n (blow) coup m de poing; (fig: force) vivacité f, mordant m; (tool) poinçon m; (drink) punch m ▷ vt (make a hole in) poinçonner, perforer; (hit) **to ~ sb/sth** donner un coup de poing à qn/sur qch; **to ~ a hole (in)** faire un trou (dans); **punch in** vi (US) pointer (en arrivant); **punch out** vi (US) pointer (en partant)

punch line n (of joke) conclusion f

punch-up ['pʌntʃʌp] n (Brit inf) bagarre f

punctual ['pʌŋktjuəl] adj ponctuel(le)

punctuation [pʌŋktju'eɪʃən] n ponctuation f

puncture ['pʌŋktʃə'] n (Aut) crevaison f ▷ vt crever; **I have a ~** (Aut) j'ai (un pneu) crevé

pundit ['pʌndɪt] n individu m qui pontifie, pontife m

pungent ['pʌndʒənt] adj piquant(e); (fig) mordant(e), caustique

punish ['pʌnɪʃ] vt punir; **to ~ sb for sth/for doing sth** punir qn de qch/d'avoir fait qch

punishment ['pʌnɪʃmənt] n punition f, châtiment m; (fig: inf): **to take a lot of ~** (boxer) encaisser; (car, person etc) être mis(e) à dure épreuve

punk [pʌŋk] n (person: also: ~ **rocker**) punk m/f; (music: also: ~ **rock**) le punk; (US inf: hoodlum) voyou m

punt [pʌnt] n (boat) bachot m; (Irish) livre irlandaise ▷ vi (Brit: bet) parier

punter ['pʌntə'] n (Brit: gambler) parieur(-euse); (: inf) Monsieur m tout le monde; type m

puny ['pjuːnɪ] adj chétif(-ive)

pup [pʌp] n chiot m

pupil ['pjuːpl] n élève m/f; (of eye) pupille f

puppet ['pʌpɪt] n marionnette f, pantin m

puppy ['pʌpɪ] n chiot m, petit chien

purchase ['pəːtʃɪs] n achat m; (grip) prise f ▷ vt acheter; **to get a ~ on** trouver appui sur

purchaser ['pəːtʃɪsə'] n acheteur(-euse)

pure [pjuə'] adj pur(e); **a ~ wool jumper** un pull en pure laine; **~ and simple** pur(e) et simple

purely ['pjuəlɪ] adv purement

purge [pəːdʒ] n (Med) purge f; (Pol) épuration f, purge ▷ vt purger; (fig) épurer, purger

purify ['pjuərɪfaɪ] vt purifier, épurer

purity ['pjuərɪtɪ] n pureté f

purple ['pəːpl] adj violet(te); (face) cramoisi(e)

purpose ['pəːpəs] n intention f, but m; **on ~** exprès; **for illustrative ~s** à titre d'illustration; **for teaching ~s** dans un but pédagogique; **for the ~s of this meeting** pour cette réunion; **to no ~** en pure perte

purposeful ['pəːpəsful] adj déterminé(e), résolu(e)

purr [pəː'] n ronronnement m ▷ vi ronronner

purse [pəːs] n (Brit: for money) porte-monnaie m inv, bourse f; (US: handbag) sac m (à main) ▷ vt serrer, pincer

purser ['pəːsə'] n (Naut) commissaire m du bord

pursue [pə'sjuː] vt poursuivre; (pleasures) rechercher; (inquiry, matter) approfondir

pursuit [pə'sjuːt] n poursuite f; (occupation) occupation f, activité f; **scientific ~s** recherches fpl scientifiques; **in (the) ~ of sth** à la recherche de qch

pus [pʌs] n pus m

push [puʃ] n poussée f; (effort) gros effort; (drive) énergie f ▷ vt pousser; (button) appuyer sur; (thrust): **to ~ sth (into)** enfoncer qch (dans); (fig: product) mettre en avant, faire de la publicité pour ▷ vi pousser; appuyer; **to ~ a door open/shut** pousser une porte (pour l'ouvrir/pour la fermer); **"~"** (on door) "pousser"; (on bell) "appuyer"; **to ~ for** (better pay, conditions) réclamer; **to be ~ed for time/ money** être à court de temps/d'argent; **she is ~ing fifty** (inf) elle frise la cinquantaine; **at a ~** (Brit inf) à la limite, à la rigueur; **push aside** vt écarter; **push in** vi s'introduire de force; **push off** vi (inf) filer, ficher le camp; **push on** vi (continue) continuer; **push over** vt renverser; **push through** vt (measure) faire

voter ▷ vi (in crowd) se frayer un chemin;
push up vt (total, prices) faire monter
pushchair ['puʃtʃeəʳ] n (Brit) poussette f
pusher ['puʃəʳ] n (also: **drug ~**)
revendeur(-euse) (de drogue),
ravitailleur(-euse) (en drogue)
pushover ['puʃəuvəʳ] n (inf): **it's a ~** c'est un
jeu d'enfant
push-up ['puʃʌp] n (US) traction f
pushy ['puʃɪ] adj (pej) arriviste
pussy ['pusɪ], **pussy-cat** n (inf) minet m
put (pt, pp **put**) [put] vt mettre; (place) poser,
placer; (say) dire, exprimer; (a question) poser;
(case, view) exposer, présenter; (estimate)
estimer; **to ~ sb in a good/bad mood** mettre
qn de bonne/mauvaise humeur; **to ~ sb to
bed** mettre qn au lit, coucher qn; **to ~ sb to a
lot of trouble** déranger qn; **how shall I ~ it?**
comment dirais-je?, comment dire?; **to ~ a
lot of time into sth** passer beaucoup de
temps à qch; **to ~ money on a horse** miser
sur un cheval; **I ~ it to you that ...** (Brit) je
(vous) suggère que ..., je suis d'avis que ...;
to stay ~ ne pas bouger; **put about** vi (Naut)
virer de bord ▷ vt (rumour) faire courir; **put
across** vt (ideas etc) communiquer; faire
comprendre; **put aside** vt mettre de côté;
put away vt (store) ranger; **put back** vt
(replace) remettre, replacer; (postpone)
remettre; (delay, watch, clock) retarder; **this
will ~ us back ten years** cela nous ramènera
dix ans en arrière; **put by** vt (money) mettre
de côté, économiser; **put down** vt (parcel etc)
poser, déposer; (pay) verser; (in writing) mettre
par écrit, inscrire; (suppress: revolt etc)
réprimer, écraser; (attribute) attribuer;
(animal) abattre; (cat, dog) faire piquer; **put
forward** vt (ideas) avancer, proposer; (date,
watch, clock) avancer; **put in** vt (gas, electricity)
installer; (complaint) soumettre; (time, effort)
consacrer; **put in for** vt fus (job) poser sa
candidature pour; (promotion) solliciter; **put
off** vt (light etc) éteindre; (postpone) remettre
à plus tard, ajourner; (discourage) dissuader;
put on vt (clothes, lipstick, CD) mettre; (light etc)
allumer; (play etc) monter; (extra bus, train etc)
mettre en service; (food, meal: provide) servir;
(: cook) mettre à cuire or à chauffer; (weight)
prendre; (assume: accent, manner) prendre;
(: airs) se donner, prendre; (inf: tease) faire
marcher; (inform, indicate): **to ~ sb on to sb/
sth** indiquer qn/qch à qn; **to ~ the brakes on**
freiner; **put out** vt (take outside) mettre
dehors; (one's hand) tendre; (news, rumour)
faire courir, répandre; (light etc) éteindre;
(person: inconvenience) déranger, gêner; (Brit:
dislocate) se démettre ▷ vi (Naut): **to ~ out to
sea** prendre le large; **to ~ out from
Plymouth** quitter Plymouth; **put through**
vt (Tel: caller) mettre en communication;
(: call) passer; (plan) faire accepter; **~ me
through to Miss Blair** passez-moi Miss

Blair; **put together** vt mettre ensemble;
(assemble: furniture) monter, assembler; (meal)
préparer; **put up** vt (raise) lever, relever,
remonter; (pin up) afficher; (hang) accrocher;
(build) construire, ériger; (tent) monter;
(umbrella) ouvrir; (increase) augmenter;
(accommodate) loger; (incite): **to ~ sb up to
doing sth** pousser qn à faire qch; **to ~ sth up
for sale** mettre qch en vente; **put upon** vt fus:
to be ~ upon (imposed on) se laisser faire; **put
up with** vt fus supporter
putt [pʌt] vt, vi putter ▷ n putt m
putting green ['pʌtɪŋ-] n green m
putty ['pʌtɪ] n mastic m
put-up ['putʌp] adj: **~ job** coup monté
puzzle ['pʌzl] n énigme f, mystère m; (game)
jeu m, casse-tête m; (jigsaw) puzzle m; (also:
crossword ~) mots croisés ▷ vt intriguer,
rendre perplexe ▷ vi se creuser la tête; **to ~
over** chercher à comprendre
puzzled ['pʌzld] adj perplexe; **to be ~ about
sth** être perplexe au sujet de qch
puzzling ['pʌzlɪŋ] adj déconcertant(e),
inexplicable
pyjamas [pɪ'dʒɑːməz] npl (Brit) pyjama m;
a pair of ~ un pyjama
pylon ['paɪlən] n pylône m
pyramid ['pɪrəmɪd] n pyramide f
Pyrenees [pɪrə'niːz] npl Pyrénées fpl

p

q

quack [kwæk] n (of duck) coin-coin m inv;
(pej: doctor) charlatan m ▷ vi faire coin-coin
quad [kwɒd] n abbr = **quadruplet**; **quadrangle**
quadrangle ['kwɒdræŋgl] n (Math)
quadrilatère m; (courtyard: abbr: quad) cour f
quadruple [kwɒ'dru:pl] adj, n quadruple m
▷ vt, vi quadrupler
quadruplet [kwɒ'dru:plɪt] n quadruplé(e)
quail [kweɪl] n (Zool) caille f ▷ vi: **to ~ at** or
before reculer devant
quaint [kweɪnt] adj bizarre; (old-fashioned)
désuet(-ète); (picturesque) au charme vieillot,
pittoresque
quake [kweɪk] vi trembler ▷ n abbr
= **earthquake**
qualification [kwɒlɪfɪ'keɪʃən] n (often pl:
degree etc) diplôme m; (training)
qualification(s) f(pl); (ability) compétence(s)
f(pl); (limitation) réserve f, restriction f; **what
are your ~s?** qu'avez-vous comme
diplômes?; quelles sont vos qualifications?
qualified ['kwɒlɪfaɪd] adj (trained) qualifié(e);
(professionally) diplômé(e); (fit, competent)
compétent(e), qualifié(e); (limited)
conditionnel(le); **it was a ~ success** ce fut un
succès mitigé; **~ for/to do** qui a les diplômes
requis pour/pour faire; qualifié pour/pour
faire
qualify ['kwɒlɪfaɪ] vt qualifier; (modify)
atténuer, nuancer; (limit: statement) apporter
des réserves à ▷ vi: **to ~ (as)** obtenir son
diplôme (de); **to ~ (for)** remplir les
conditions requises (pour); (Sport) se
qualifier (pour)
quality ['kwɒlɪtɪ] n qualité f ▷ cpd de qualité;
of good/poor ~ de bonne/mauvaise qualité
quality press n (Brit): **the ~** la presse
d'information; voir article

● **QUALITY PRESS**
●
● La quality press ou les "quality (news)
● papers" englobent les journaux sérieux,
● quotidiens ou hebdomadaires, par
● opposition aux journaux populaires
● ("tabloid press"). Ces journaux visent un
● public qui souhaite des informations
● détaillées sur un éventail très vaste de
● sujets et qui est prêt à consacrer
● beaucoup de temps à leur lecture.
● Les "quality newspapers" sont en
● général de grand format.

quality time n moments privilégiés
qualm [kwɑ:m] n doute m; scrupule m;
to have ~s about sth avoir des doutes
sur qch; éprouver des scrupules à propos
de qch
quandary ['kwɒndrɪ] n: **in a ~** devant un
dilemme, dans l'embarras
quantify ['kwɒntɪfaɪ] vt quantifier
quantity ['kwɒntɪtɪ] n quantité f; **in ~** en
grande quantité
quantity surveyor n (Brit) métreur
vérificateur
quarantine ['kwɒrntiːn] n quarantaine f
quarrel ['kwɒrl] n querelle f, dispute f ▷ vi se
disputer, se quereller; **to have a ~ with sb** se
quereller avec qn; **I've no ~ with him** je n'ai
rien contre lui; **I can't ~ with that** je ne vois
rien à redire à cela
quarry ['kwɒrɪ] n (for stone) carrière f; (animal)
proie f, gibier m ▷ vt (marble etc) extraire
quart [kwɔːt] n ≈ litre m
quarter ['kwɔːtəʳ] n quart m; (of year)
trimestre m; (district) quartier m; (US, Canada:
25 cents) (pièce f de) vingt-cinq cents mpl ▷ vt
partager en quartiers or en quatre; (Mil)
caserner, cantonner; **quarters** npl
logement m; (Mil) quartiers mpl,
cantonnement m; **a ~ of an hour** un quart
d'heure; **it's a ~ to 3**, (US) **it's a ~ of 3** il est
3 heures moins le quart; **it's a ~ past 3**, (US)
it's a ~ after 3 il est 3 heures et quart; **from
all ~s** de tous côtés
quarter final n quart m de finale
quarterly ['kwɔːtəlɪ] adj trimestriel(le) ▷ adv
tous les trois mois ▷ n (Press) revue
trimestrielle
quartet, quartette [kwɔː'tɛt] n quatuor m;
(jazz players) quartette m
quartz [kwɔːts] n quartz m ▷ cpd de or en
quartz; (watch, clock) à quartz
quash [kwɒʃ] vt (verdict) annuler, casser

quaver ['kweɪvə'] n (Brit Mus) croche f ▷ vi trembler

quay [kiː] n (also: **~side**) quai m

queasy ['kwiːzɪ] adj (stomach) délicat(e); **to feel ~** avoir mal au cœur

Quebec [kwɪ'bɛk] n (city) Québec; (province) Québec m

queen [kwiːn] n (gen) reine f; (Cards etc) dame f

queen mother n reine mère f

queer [kwɪə'] adj étrange, curieux(-euse); (suspicious) louche; (Brit: sick): **I feel ~** je ne me sens pas bien ▷ n (inf: highly offensive) homosexuel m

quell [kwɛl] vt réprimer, étouffer

quench [kwɛntʃ] vt (flames) éteindre; **to ~ one's thirst** se désaltérer

query ['kwɪərɪ] n question f; (doubt) doute m; (question mark) point m d'interrogation ▷ vt (disagree with, dispute) mettre en doute, questionner

quest [kwɛst] n recherche f, quête f

question ['kwɛstʃən] n question f ▷ vt (person) interroger; (plan, idea) mettre en question ou en doute; **to ask sb a ~, to put a ~ to sb** poser une question à qn; **to bring** ou **call sth into ~** remettre qch en question; **the ~ is ...** la question est de savoir ...; **it's a ~ of doing** il s'agit de faire; **there's some ~ of doing** il est question de faire; **beyond ~** sans aucun doute; **out of the ~** hors de question

questionable ['kwɛstʃənəbl] adj discutable

question mark n point m d'interrogation

questionnaire [kwɛstʃə'nɛə'] n questionnaire m

queue [kjuː] (Brit) n queue f, file f ▷ vi (also: **~ up**) faire la queue; **to jump the ~** passer avant son tour

quibble ['kwɪbl] vi ergoter, chicaner

quiche [kiːʃ] n quiche f

quick [kwɪk] adj rapide; (reply) prompt(e), rapide; (mind) vif/vive; (agile) agile, vif/vive ▷ adv vite, rapidement ▷ n: **cut to the ~** (fig) touché(e) au vif; **be ~!** dépêche-toi!; **to be ~ to act** agir tout de suite

quicken ['kwɪkən] vt accélérer, presser; (rouse) stimuler ▷ vi s'accélérer, devenir plus rapide

quickly ['kwɪklɪ] adv (fast) vite, rapidement; (immediately) tout de suite

quicksand ['kwɪksænd] n sables mouvants

quick-witted [kwɪk'wɪtɪd] adj à l'esprit vif

quid [kwɪd] n pl inv (Brit inf) livre f

quiet ['kwaɪət] adj tranquille, calme; (not noisy: engine) silencieux(-euse); (reserved) réservé(e); (voice) bas(se); (not busy: day, business) calme; (ceremony, colour) discret(-ète) ▷ n tranquillité f, calme m; (silence) silence m ▷ vt, vi (US) = **quieten; keep ~!** tais-toi!; **on the ~** en secret, discrètement; **I'll have a ~ word with him** je lui en parlerai discrètement

quieten ['kwaɪətn] (also: **~ down**) vi se calmer, s'apaiser ▷ vt calmer, apaiser

quietly ['kwaɪətlɪ] adv tranquillement; (silently) silencieusement; (discreetly) discrètement

quietness ['kwaɪətnɪs] n tranquillité f, calme m; silence m

quilt [kwɪlt] n édredon m; (continental quilt) couette f

quin [kwɪn] n abbr = **quintuplet**

quintuplet [kwɪn'tjuːplɪt] n quintuplé(e)

quip [kwɪp] n remarque piquante ou spirituelle, pointe f ▷ vt: **... he quipped ...** lança-t-il

quirk [kwəːk] n bizarrerie f; **by some ~ of fate** par un caprice du hasard

quirky ['kwəːkɪ] adj singulier(-ère)

quit [kwɪt] (pt, pp **quit** ou **quitted**) vt quitter ▷ vi (give up) abandonner, renoncer; (resign) démissionner; **to ~ doing** arrêter de faire; **~ stalling!** (US inf) arrête de te dérober!; **notice to ~** (Brit) congé m (signifié au locataire)

quite [kwaɪt] adv (rather) assez, plutôt; (entirely) complètement, tout à fait; **~ new** plutôt neuf; tout à fait neuf; **she's ~ pretty** elle est plutôt jolie; **I ~ understand** je comprends très bien; **~ a few of them** un assez grand nombre d'entre eux; **that's not ~ right** ce n'est pas tout à fait juste; **not ~ as many as last time** pas tout à fait autant que la dernière fois; **~ (so)!** exactement!

quits [kwɪts] adj: **~ (with)** quitte (envers); **let's call it ~** restons-en là

quiver ['kwɪvə'] vi trembler, frémir ▷ n (for arrows) carquois m

quiz [kwɪz] n (on TV) jeu-concours m (télévisé); (in magazine etc) test m de connaissances ▷ vt interroger

quizzical ['kwɪzɪkl] adj narquois(e)

quota ['kwəʊtə] n quota m

quotation [kwəʊ'teɪʃən] n citation f; (of shares etc) cote f, cours m; (estimate) devis m

quotation marks npl guillemets mpl

quote [kwəʊt] n citation f; (estimate) devis m ▷ vt (sentence, author) citer; (price) donner, soumettre; (shares) coter ▷ vi: **to ~ from** citer; **to ~ for a job** établir un devis pour des travaux; **quotes** npl (inverted commas) guillemets mpl; **in ~s** entre guillemets; **~ ... unquote** (in dictation) ouvrez les guillemets ... fermez les guillemets

r

Rabat [rə'bɑːt] n Rabat
rabbi ['ræbaɪ] n rabbin m
rabbit ['ræbɪt] n lapin m ▷ vi: **to ~ (on)** (Brit) parler à n'en plus finir
rabbit hutch n clapier m
rabble ['ræbl] n (pej) populace f
rabies ['reɪbiːz] n rage f
RAC n abbr (Brit: = Royal Automobile Club) ≈ ACF m
raccoon, racoon [rə'kuːn] n raton m laveur
race [reɪs] n (species) race f; (competition, rush) course f ▷ vt (person) faire la course avec; (horse) faire courir; (engine) emballer ▷ vi (compete) faire la course, courir; (hurry) aller à toute vitesse, courir; (engine) s'emballer; (pulse) battre très vite; **the human ~** la race humaine; **to ~ in/out** etc entrer/sortir etc à toute vitesse
race car n (US) = **racing car**
race car driver n (US) = **racing driver**
racecourse ['reɪskɔːs] n champ m de courses
racehorse ['reɪshɔːs] n cheval m de course
racer ['reɪsə*] n (bike) vélo m de course
racetrack ['reɪstræk] n piste f
racial ['reɪʃl] adj racial(e)
racing ['reɪsɪŋ] n courses fpl
racing car n (Brit) voiture f de course
racing driver n (Brit) pilote m de course
racism ['reɪsɪzəm] n racisme m
racist ['reɪsɪst] adj, n raciste m/f
rack [ræk] n (for guns, tools) râtelier m; (for clothes) portant m; (for bottles) casier m; (also:

luggage ~) filet m à bagages; (also: **roof ~**) galerie f; (also: **dish ~**) égouttoir m ▷ vt tourmenter; **magazine ~** porte-revues m inv; **shoe ~** étagère f à chaussures; **toast ~** porte-toast m; **to ~ one's brains** se creuser la cervelle; **to go to ~ and ruin** (building) tomber en ruine; (business) péricliter; **rack up** vt accumuler
racket ['rækɪt] n (for tennis) raquette f; (noise) tapage m, vacarme m; (swindle) escroquerie f; (organized crime) racket m
racquet ['rækɪt] n raquette f
racy ['reɪsɪ] adj plein(e) de verve, osé(e)
radar ['reɪdɑː*] n radar m ▷ cpd radar inv
radial ['reɪdɪəl] adj (also: **~-ply**) à carcasse radiale
radiant ['reɪdɪənt] adj rayonnant(e); (Physics) radiant(e)
radiate ['reɪdɪeɪt] vt (heat) émettre, dégager ▷ vi (lines) rayonner
radiation [reɪdɪ'eɪʃən] n rayonnement m; (radioactive) radiation f
radiator ['reɪdɪeɪtə*] n radiateur m
radical ['rædɪkl] adj radical(e)
radii ['reɪdɪaɪ] npl of radius
radio ['reɪdɪəu] n radio f ▷ vi: **to ~ to sb** envoyer un message radio à qn ▷ vt (information) transmettre par radio; (one's position) signaler par radio; (person) appeler par radio; **on the ~** à la radio
radioactive ['reɪdɪəu'æktɪv] adj radioactif(-ive)
radio cassette n radiocassette m
radio-controlled ['reɪdɪəukən'trəuld] adj radioguidé(e)
radio station n station f de radio
radish ['rædɪʃ] n radis m
radius (pl radii) ['reɪdɪəs, -ɪaɪ] n rayon m; (Anat) radius m; **within a ~ of 50 miles** dans un rayon de 50 milles
RAF n abbr (Brit) = **Royal Air Force**
raffle ['ræfl] n tombola f ▷ vt mettre comme lot dans une tombola
raft [rɑːft] n (craft: also: **life ~**) radeau m; (logs) train m de flottage
rafter ['rɑːftə*] n chevron m
rag [ræg] n chiffon m; (pej: newspaper) feuille f, torchon m; (for charity) attractions organisées par les étudiants au profit d'œuvres de charité ▷ vt (Brit) chahuter, mettre en boîte; **rags** npl haillons mpl; **in ~s** (person) en haillons; (clothes) en lambeaux
rag doll n poupée f de chiffon
rage [reɪdʒ] n (fury) rage f, fureur f ▷ vi (person) être fou/folle de rage; (storm) faire rage, être déchaîné(e); **to fly into a ~** se mettre en rage; **it's all the ~** cela fait fureur
ragged ['rægɪd] adj (edge) inégal(e), qui accroche; (clothes) en loques; (cuff) effiloché(e); (appearance) déguenillé(e)
raid [reɪd] n (Mil) raid m; (criminal) hold-up m inv; (by police) descente f, rafle f ▷ vt faire un

raid sur or un hold-up dans or une
descente dans

rail [reɪl] n (on stair) rampe f; (on bridge, balcony)
balustrade f; (of ship) bastingage m; (for train)
rail m; **rails** npl rails mpl, voie ferrée; **by** ~ en
train, par le train

railcard ['reɪlkɑːd] n (Brit) carte f de chemin
de fer; **young person's** ~ carte f jeune

railing ['reɪlɪŋ] n, **railings** ['reɪlɪŋz] npl
grille f

railway ['reɪlweɪ], (US) **railroad** ['reɪlrəʊd] n
chemin m de fer; (track) voie ferrée

railway line n (Brit) ligne f de chemin de fer;
(track) voie ferrée

railwayman ['reɪlweɪmən] irreg n
cheminot m

railway station n (Brit) gare f

rain [reɪn] n pluie f ▷ vi pleuvoir; **in the** ~
sous la pluie; **it's ~ing** il pleut; **it's ~ing cats
and dogs** il pleut à torrents

rainbow ['reɪnbəʊ] n arc-en-ciel m

raincoat ['reɪnkəʊt] n imperméable m

raindrop ['reɪndrɒp] n goutte f de pluie

rainfall ['reɪnfɔːl] n chute f de pluie;
(measurement) hauteur f des précipitations

rainforest ['reɪnfɒrɪst] n forêt tropicale

rainy ['reɪnɪ] adj pluvieux(-euse)

raise [reɪz] n augmentation f ▷ vt (lift) lever;
hausser; (end: siege, embargo) lever; (build)
ériger; (increase) augmenter; (morale)
remonter; (standards) améliorer; (a protest,
doubt) provoquer, causer; (a question) soulever;
(cattle, family) élever; (crop) faire pousser;
(army, funds) rassembler; (loan) obtenir; **to** ~
one's glass to sb/sth porter un toast en
l'honneur de qn/qch; **to** ~ **one's voice** élever
la voix; **to** ~ **sb's hopes** donner de l'espoir à
qn; **to** ~ **a laugh/a smile** faire rire/sourire

raisin ['reɪzn] n raisin sec

rake [reɪk] n (tool) râteau m; (person) débauché
m ▷ vt (garden) ratisser; (fire) tisonner; (with
machine gun) balayer ▷ vi: **to** ~ **through** (fig:
search) fouiller (dans)

rally ['rælɪ] n (Pol etc) meeting m,
rassemblement m; (Aut) rallye m; (Tennis)
échange m ▷ vt rassembler, rallier; (support)
gagner ▷ vi se rallier; (sick person) aller mieux;
(Stock Exchange) reprendre; **rally round** vi
venir en aide ▷ vt fus se rallier à; venir
en aide à

RAM [ræm] n abbr (Comput: = random access
memory) mémoire vive

ram [ræm] n bélier m ▷ vt (push) enfoncer;
(soil) tasser; (crash into: vehicle) emboutir;
(: lamppost etc) percuter; (in battle) éperonner

Ramadan [ræmə'dæn] n Ramadan m

ramble ['ræmbl] n randonnée f ▷ vi (walk)
se promener, faire une randonnée; (pej: also:
~ **on**) discourir, pérorer

rambler ['ræmblə²] n promeneur(-euse),
randonneur(-euse); (Bot) rosier grimpant

rambling ['ræmblɪŋ] adj (speech) décousu(e);

(house) plein(e) de coins et de recoins; (Bot)
grimpant(e)

ramp [ræmp] n (incline) rampe f; (Aut)
dénivellation f; (in garage) pont m; **on/off** ~
(US Aut) bretelle f d'accès

rampage ['ræmpeɪdʒ] n: **to be on the** ~ se
déchaîner ▷ vi [ræm'peɪdʒ]: **they went
rampaging through the town** ils ont
envahi les rues et ont tout saccagé sur leur
passage

rampant ['ræmpənt] adj (disease etc) qui sévit

ram raiding [-reɪdɪŋ] n pillage d'un magasin en
enfonçant la vitrine avec une voiture volée

ramshackle ['ræmʃækl] adj (house)
délabré(e); (car etc) déglingué(e)

ran [ræn] pt of **run**

ranch [rɑːntʃ] n ranch m

rancher ['rɑːntʃə²] n (owner) propriétaire m de
ranch; (ranch hand) cowboy m

rancid ['rænsɪd] adj rance

rancour, (US) **rancor** ['ræŋkə²] n rancune f,
rancœur f

random ['rændəm] adj fait(e) or établi(e) au
hasard; (Comput, Math) aléatoire ▷ n: **at** ~ au
hasard

random access memory n (Comput)
mémoire vive, RAM f

randy ['rændɪ] adj (Brit inf) excité(e); lubrique

rang [ræŋ] pt of **ring**

range [reɪndʒ] n (of mountains) chaîne f; (of
missile, voice) portée f; (of products) choix m,
gamme f; (also: **shooting** ~) champ m de tir;
(: indoor) stand m de tir; (also: **kitchen** ~)
fourneau m (de cuisine) ▷ vt (place) mettre en
rang, placer; (roam) parcourir ▷ vi: **to** ~ **over**
couvrir; **to** ~ **from ... to** aller de ... à; **price** ~
éventail m des prix; **do you have anything
else in this price** ~? avez-vous autre chose
dans ces prix?; **within (firing)** ~ à portée
(de tir); **~d left/right** (text) justifié à
gauche/à droite

ranger ['reɪndʒə²] n garde m forestier

rank [ræŋk] n rang m; (Mil) grade m; (Brit:
also: **taxi** ~) station f de taxis ▷ vi: **to** ~ **among**
compter or se classer parmi ▷ vt: **I** ~ **him
sixth** je le place sixième ▷ adj (smell)
nauséabond(e); (hypocrisy, injustice etc)
flagrant(e); **he's a** ~ **outsider** il n'est
vraiment pas dans la course; **the** ~**s** (Mil) la
troupe; **the** ~ **and file** (fig) la masse, la base;
to close ~**s** (Mil: fig) serrer les rangs

ransack ['rænsæk] vt fouiller (à fond);
(plunder) piller

ransom ['rænsəm] n rançon f; **to hold sb to** ~
(fig) exercer un chantage sur qn

rant [rænt] vi fulminer

rap [ræp] n petit coup sec; tape f; (music) rap m
▷ vt (door) frapper sur or à; (table etc) taper sur

rape [reɪp] n viol m; (Bot) colza m ▷ vt violer

rape oil, rapeseed oil ['reɪp(siːd)-] n huile f
de colza

rapid ['ræpɪd] adj rapide

rapidly ['ræpɪdlɪ] adv rapidement

rapids ['ræpɪdz] npl (Geo) rapides mpl

rapist ['reɪpɪst] n auteur m d'un viol

rapport [ræ'pɔː] n entente f

rapturous ['ræptʃərəs] adj extasié(e); frénétique

rare [reə^r] adj rare; (Culin: steak) saignant(e)

rarely ['reəlɪ] adv rarement

raring ['reərɪŋ] adj: **to be ~ to go** (inf) être très impatient(e) de commencer

rascal ['rɑːskl] n vaurien m

rash [ræʃ] adj imprudent(e), irréfléchi(e) ⊳ n (Med) rougeur f, éruption f; (of events) série f (noire); **to come out in a ~** avoir une éruption

rasher ['ræʃə^r] n fine tranche (de lard)

raspberry ['rɑːzbərɪ] n framboise f

raspberry bush n framboisier m

rasping ['rɑːspɪŋ] adj: **~ noise** grincement m

rat [ræt] n rat m

rate [reɪt] n (ratio) taux m, pourcentage m; (speed) vitesse f, rythme m; (price) tarif m ⊳ vt (price) évaluer, estimer; (people) classer; (deserve) mériter; **rates** npl (Brit: property tax) impôts locaux; **to ~ sb/sth among** classer qn/ qch comme; **to ~ sb/sth among** classer qn/ qch parmi; **to ~ sb/sth highly** avoir une haute opinion de qn/qch; **at a ~ of 60 kph** à une vitesse de 60 km/h; **at any ~** en tout cas; **~ of exchange** taux or cours m du change; **~ of flow** débit m; **~ of return** (taux de) rendement m; **pulse ~** fréquence f des pulsations

rateable value ['reɪtəbl-] n (Brit) valeur locative imposable

ratepayer ['reɪtpeɪə^r] n (Brit) contribuable m/f (payant les impôts locaux)

rather ['rɑːðə^r] adv (somewhat) assez, plutôt; (to some extent) un peu; **it's ~ expensive** c'est assez cher; (too much) c'est un peu cher; **there's ~ a lot** il y en a beaucoup; **I would** or **I'd ~ go** j'aimerais mieux or je préférerais partir; **I had ~ go** il vaudrait mieux que je parte; **I'd ~ not leave** j'aimerais mieux ne pas partir; **or ~** (more accurately) ou plutôt; **I ~ think he won't come** je crois bien qu'il ne viendra pas

rating ['reɪtɪŋ] n (assessment) évaluation f; (score) classement m; (Finance) cote f; (Naut: category) classe f; (: sailor: Brit) matelot m; **ratings** npl (Radio) indice(s) m(pl) d'écoute; (TV) Audimat® m

ratio ['reɪʃɪəu] n proportion f; **in the ~ of 100 to 1** dans la proportion de 100 contre 1

ration ['ræʃən] n ration f ⊳ vt rationner; **rations** npl (food) vivres mpl

rational ['ræʃənl] adj raisonnable, sensé(e); (solution, reasoning) logique; (Med: person) lucide

rationale [ræʃə'nɑːl] n raisonnement m; justification f

rationalize ['ræʃnəlaɪz] vt rationaliser;

(conduct) essayer d'expliquer or de motiver

rat race n foire f d'empoigne

rattle ['rætl] n (of door, window) battement m; (of coins, chain) cliquetis m; (of train, engine) bruit m de ferraille; (for baby) hochet m; (of sports fan) crécelle f ⊳ vi cliqueter; (car, bus): **to ~ along** rouler en faisant un bruit de ferraille ⊳ vt agiter (bruyamment); (inf: disconcert) déconcertancer; (: annoy) embêter

rattlesnake ['rætlsneɪk] n serpent m à sonnettes

raucous ['rɔːkəs] adj rauque

rave [reɪv] vi (in anger) s'emporter; (with enthusiasm) s'extasier; (Med) délirer ⊳ n (inf: party) rave f, soirée f techno ⊳ adj (scene, culture, music) rave, techno ⊳ cpd: **~ review** (inf) critique f dithyrambique

raven ['reɪvən] n grand corbeau

ravenous ['rævənəs] adj affamé(e)

ravine [rə'viːn] n ravin m

raving ['reɪvɪŋ] adj: **he's ~ mad** il est complètement cinglé

ravishing ['rævɪʃɪŋ] adj enchanteur(-eresse)

raw [rɔː] adj (uncooked) cru(e); (not processed) brut(e); (sore) à vif, irrité(e); (inexperienced) inexpérimenté(e); (weather, day) froid(e) et humide; **~ deal** (inf: bad bargain) sale coup m; (: unfair treatment): **to get a ~ deal** être traité(e) injustement; **~ materials** matières premières

raw material n matière première

ray [reɪ] n rayon m; **~ of hope** lueur f d'espoir

raze [reɪz] vt (also: **~ to the ground**) raser

razor ['reɪzə^r] n rasoir m

razor blade n lame f de rasoir

Rd abbr = **road**

RE n abbr (Brit: = religious education) instruction réligieuse; (Brit Mil) = **Royal Engineers**

re [riː] prep concernant

reach [riːtʃ] n portée f, atteinte f; (of river etc) étendue f ⊳ vt atteindre, arriver à; (conclusion, decision) parvenir à ⊳ vi s'étendre; (stretch out hand): **to ~ up/down** etc (for sth) lever/ baisser etc le bras (pour prendre qch); **to ~ sb by phone** joindre qn par téléphone; **out of/ within ~** (object) hors de/à portée; **within easy ~ (of)** (place) à proximité (de), proche (de); **reach out** vt tendre ⊳ vi: **to ~ out (for)** allonger le bras (pour prendre)

react [riː'ækt] vi réagir

reaction [riː'ækʃən] n réaction f

reactor [riː'æktə^r] n réacteur m

read (pt, pp **read**) [riːd, rɛd] vi lire ⊳ vt lire; (understand) comprendre, interpréter; (study) étudier; (meter) relever; (subj: instrument etc) indiquer, marquer; **to take sth as ~** (fig) considérer qch comme accepté; **do you ~ me?** (Tel) est-ce que vous me recevez?; **read out** vt lire à haute voix; **read over** vt relire; **read through** vt (quickly) parcourir; (thoroughly) lire jusqu'au bout; **read up** vt, **read up on** vt fus étudier

readable ['riːdəbl] *adj* facile *or* agréable à lire
reader ['riːdər] *n* lecteur(-trice); (*book*) livre *m* de lecture; (*Brit: at university*) maître *m* de conférences
readership ['riːdəʃɪp] *n* (*of paper etc*) (nombre *m* de) lecteurs *mpl*
readily ['redɪlɪ] *adv* volontiers, avec empressement; (*easily*) facilement
readiness ['redɪnɪs] *n* empressement *m*; **in ~** (*prepared*) prêt(e)
reading ['riːdɪŋ] *n* lecture *f*; (*understanding*) interprétation *f*; (*on instrument*) indications *fpl*
ready ['redɪ] *adj* prêt(e); (*willing*) prêt, disposé(e); (*quick*) prompt(e); (*available*) disponible ▷ *n*: **at the ~** (*Mil*) prêt à faire feu; (*fig*) tout(e) prêt(e); **~ for use** prêt à l'emploi; **to be ~ to do sth** être prêt à faire qch; **when will my photos be ~?** quand est-ce que mes photos seront prêtes?; **to get ~** (*as vi*) se préparer; (*as vt*) préparer
ready-cooked ['redɪkʊkd] *adj* précuit(e)
ready-made ['redɪmeɪd] *adj* tout(e) faite(e)
ready-to-wear ['redɪtə'wɛər] *adj* (en) prêt-à-porter
real [rɪəl] *adj* (*world, life*) réel(le); (*genuine*) véritable; (*proper*) vrai(e) ▷ *adv* (*US inf: very*) vraiment; **in ~ life** dans la réalité
real ale *n* bière traditionnelle
real estate *n* biens fonciers *or* immobiliers
realistic [rɪə'lɪstɪk] *adj* réaliste
reality [riːˈælɪtɪ] *n* réalité *f*; **in ~** en réalité, en fait
reality TV *n* téléréalité *f*
realization [rɪəlarˈzeɪʃən] *n* (*awareness*) prise *f* de conscience; (*fulfilment: also: of asset*) réalisation *f*
realize ['rɪəlaɪz] *vt* (*understand*) se rendre compte de, prendre conscience de; (*a project, Comm: asset*) réaliser
really ['rɪəlɪ] *adv* vraiment; **~?** vraiment?, c'est vrai?
realm [relm] *n* royaume *m*; (*fig*) domaine *m*
realtor ['rɪəltɔːr] *n* (*US*) agent immobilier
reap [riːp] *vt* moissonner; (*fig*) récolter
reappear [riːə'pɪər] *vi* réapparaître, reparaître
rear [rɪər] *adj* de derrière, arrière *inv*; (*Aut: wheel etc*) arrière ▷ *n* arrière *m*, derrière *m* ▷ *vt* (*cattle, family*) élever ▷ *vi* (*also: ~ up: animal*) se cabrer
rearguard ['rɪəgɑːd] *n* arrière-garde *f*
rearrange [riːə'reɪndʒ] *vt* réarranger
rear-view mirror *n* (*Aut*) rétroviseur *m*
rear-wheel drive *n* (*Aut*) traction *f* arrière
reason ['riːzn] *n* raison *f* ▷ *vi*: **to ~ with sb** raisonner qn, faire entendre raison à qn; **the ~ for/why** la raison de/pour laquelle; **to have ~ to think** avoir lieu de penser; **it stands to ~ that** il va sans dire que; **she claims with good ~ that ...** elle affirme à juste titre que ...; **all the more ~ why** raison

de plus pour + *infinitive or* pour que + *sub*; **within ~** dans les limites du raisonnable
reasonable ['riːznəbl] *adj* raisonnable; (*not bad*) acceptable
reasonably ['riːznəblɪ] *adv* (*behave*) raisonnablement; (*fairly*) assez; **one can ~ assume that ...** on est fondé à *or* il est permis de supposer que ...
reasoning ['riːznɪŋ] *n* raisonnement *m*
reassurance [riːə'ʃuərəns] *n* (*factual*) assurance *f*, garantie *f*; (*emotional*) réconfort *m*
reassure [riːə'ʃuər] *vt* rassurer; **to ~ sb of** donner à qn l'assurance répétée de
rebate ['riːbeɪt] *n* (*on product*) rabais *m*; (*on tax etc*) dégrèvement *m*; (*repayment*) remboursement *m*
rebel *n* ['rebl] rebelle *m/f* ▷ *vi* [rɪ'bel] se rebeller, se révolter
rebellion [rɪ'beljən] *n* rébellion *f*, révolte *f*
rebellious [rɪ'beljəs] *adj* rebelle
rebound *vi* [rɪ'baund] (*ball*) rebondir ▷ *n* ['riːbaund] rebond *m*
rebuff [rɪ'bʌf] *n* rebuffade *f* ▷ *vt* repousser
rebuild [riːˈbɪld] *vt* (*irreg like:* **build**) reconstruire
rebuke [rɪ'bjuːk] *n* réprimande *f*, reproche *m* ▷ *vt* réprimander
rebut [rɪ'bʌt] *vt* réfuter
recall *vt* [rɪ'kɔːl] rappeler; (*remember*) se rappeler, se souvenir de ▷ *n* ['riːkɔl] rappel *m*; (*ability to remember*) mémoire *f*; **beyond ~** *adj* irrévocable
recant [rɪ'kænt] *vi* se rétracter; (*Rel*) abjurer
recap ['riːkæp] *n* récapitulation *f* ▷ *vt, vi* récapituler
recede [rɪ'siːd] *vi* s'éloigner, reculer
receding [rɪ'siːdɪŋ] *adj* (*forehead, chin*) fuyant(e); **~ hairline** front dégarni
receipt [rɪ'siːt] *n* (*document*) reçu *m*; (*for parcel etc*) accusé *m* de réception; (*act of receiving*) réception *f*; **receipts** *npl* (*Comm*) recettes *fpl*; **to acknowledge ~ of** accuser réception de; **we are in ~ of ...** nous avons bien reçu ...; **can I have a ~, please?** je peux avoir un reçu, s'il vous plaît?
receive [rɪ'siːv] *vt* recevoir; (*guest*) recevoir, accueillir; **"~d with thanks"** (*Comm*) "pour acquit"; **R~d Pronunciation** *voir article*

RECEIVED PRONUNCIATION

En Grande-Bretagne, la *Received Pronunciation* ou "RP" est une prononciation de la langue anglaise qui, récemment encore, était surtout associée à l'aristocratie et à la bourgeoisie, mais qui maintenant est en général considérée comme la prononciation correcte.

receiver [rɪ'siːvər] *n* (*Tel*) récepteur *m*, combiné *m*; (*Radio*) récepteur; (*of stolen goods*) receleur m; (for bankruptcies) administrateur m judiciaire

recent ['riːsnt] adj récent(e); **in ~ years** au cours de ces dernières années

recently ['riːsntlɪ] adv récemment; **as ~ as** pas plus tard que; **until ~** jusqu'à il y a peu de temps encore

receptacle [rɪ'sɛptɪkl] n récipient m

reception [rɪ'sɛpʃən] n réception f; (welcome) accueil m, réception

reception desk n réception f

receptionist [rɪ'sɛpʃənɪst] n réceptionniste m/f

recess [rɪ'sɛs] n (in room) renfoncement m; (for bed) alcôve f; (secret place) recoin m; (Pol etc: holiday) vacances fpl; (US Law: short break) suspension f d'audience; (Scol: esp US) récréation f

recession [rɪ'sɛʃən] n (Econ) récession f

recharge [riː'tʃɑːdʒ] vt (battery) recharger

recipe ['rɛsɪpɪ] n recette f

recipient [rɪ'sɪpɪənt] n (of payment) bénéficiaire m/f; (of letter) destinataire m/f

recital [rɪ'saɪtl] n récital m

recite [rɪ'saɪt] vt (poem) réciter; (complaints etc) énumérer

reckless ['rɛkləs] adj (driver etc) imprudent(e); (spender etc) insouciant(e)

reckon ['rɛkən] vt (count) calculer, compter; (consider) considérer, estimer; (think): **I ~ (that) ...** je pense (que) ..., j'estime (que) ... ▷ vi: **he is somebody to be ~ed with** il ne faut pas le sous-estimer; **to ~ without sb/ sth** ne pas tenir compte de qn/qch; **reckon on** vt fus compter sur, s'attendre à

reckoning ['rɛknɪŋ] n compte m, calcul m; estimation f; **the day of ~** le jour du Jugement

reclaim [rɪ'kleɪm] vt (land: from sea) assécher; (: from forest) défricher; (: with fertilizer) amender; (demand back) réclamer (le remboursement or la restitution de); (waste materials) récupérer

recline [rɪ'klaɪn] vi être allongé(e) or étendu(e)

reclining [rɪ'klaɪnɪŋ] adj (seat) à dossier réglable

recluse [rɪ'kluːs] n reclus(e), ermite m

recognition [rɛkəg'nɪʃən] n reconnaissance f; **in ~ of** en reconnaissance de; **to gain ~** être reconnu(e); **transformed beyond ~** méconnaissable

recognizable ['rɛkəgnaɪzəbl] adj: **~ (by)** reconnaissable (à)

recognize ['rɛkəgnaɪz] vt: **to ~ (by/as)** reconnaître (à/comme étant)

recoil [rɪ'kɔɪl] vi (person): **to ~ (from)** reculer (devant) ▷ n (of gun) recul m

recollect [rɛkə'lɛkt] vt se rappeler, se souvenir de

recollection [rɛkə'lɛkʃən] n souvenir m;

to the best of my ~ autant que je m'en souvienne

recommend [rɛkə'mɛnd] vt recommander; **can you ~ a good restaurant?** pouvez-vous me conseiller un bon restaurant?; **she has a lot to ~ her** elle a beaucoup de choses en sa faveur

recommendation [rɛkəmɛn'deɪʃən] n recommandation f

reconcile ['rɛkənsaɪl] vt (two people) réconcilier; (two facts) concilier, accorder; **to ~ o.s. to** se résigner à

recondition [riː'kən'dɪʃən] vt remettre à neuf; réviser entièrement

reconnoitre, (US) **reconnoiter** [rɛkə'nɔɪtər] (Mil) vt reconnaître ▷ vi faire une reconnaissance

reconsider [riː'kən'sɪdər] vt reconsidérer

reconstruct [riː'kən'strʌkt] vt (building) reconstruire; (crime, system) reconstituer

record n ['rɛkɔːd] rapport m, récit m; (of meeting etc) procès-verbal m; (register) registre m; (file) dossier m; (Comput) article m; (also: **police ~**) casier m judiciaire; (Mus: disc) disque m; (Sport) record m ▷ adj record inv ▷ vt [rɪ'kɔːd] (set down) noter; (relate) rapporter; (Mus: song etc) enregistrer; **public ~s** archives fpl; **to keep a ~ of** noter; **to keep the ~ straight** (fig) mettre les choses au point; **he is on ~ as saying that ...** il a déclaré en public que ...; **Italy's excellent ~** les excellents résultats obtenus par l'Italie; **off the ~** adj officieux(-euse) ▷ adv officieusement; **in ~ time** dans un temps record

record card n (in file) fiche f

recorded delivery [rɪ'kɔːdɪd-] n (Brit Post): **to send sth ~** ≈ envoyer qch en recommandé

recorded delivery letter [rɪ'kɔːdɪd-] n (Brit Post) ≈ lettre recommandée

recorder [rɪ'kɔːdər] n (Law) avocat nommé à la fonction de juge; (Mus) flûte f à bec

record holder n (Sport) détenteur(-trice) du record

recording [rɪ'kɔːdɪŋ] n (Mus) enregistrement m

record player n tourne-disque m

recount [rɪ'kaʊnt] vt raconter

re-count n ['riːkaʊnt] (Pol: of votes) nouveau décompte (des suffrages) ▷ vt [riː'kaʊnt] recompter

recoup [rɪ'kuːp] vt: **to ~ one's losses** récupérer ce qu'on a perdu, se refaire

recourse [rɪ'kɔːs] n recours m; expédient m; **to have ~ to** recourir à, avoir recours à

recover [rɪ'kʌvər] vt récupérer ▷ vi (from illness) se rétablir; (from shock) se remettre; (country) se redresser

recovery [rɪ'kʌvərɪ] n récupération f; rétablissement m; (Econ) redressement m

recreate [riː'krɪ'eɪt] vt recréer

recreation [rɛkrɪˈeɪʃən] n (leisure) récréation f, détente f

recreational [rɛkrɪˈeɪʃənl] adj pour la détente, récréatif(-ive)

recreational drug [rɛkrɪˈeɪʃənl-] n drogue récréative

recreational vehicle [rɛkrɪˈeɪʃənl-] n (US) camping-car m

recruit [rɪˈkruːt] n recrue f ▷ vt recruter

recruitment [rɪˈkruːtmənt] n recrutement m

rectangle [ˈrɛktæŋgl] n rectangle m

rectangular [rɛkˈtæŋgjʊləʳ] adj rectangulaire

rectify [ˈrɛktɪfaɪ] vt (error) rectifier, corriger; (omission) réparer

rector [ˈrɛktəʳ] n (Rel) pasteur m; (in Scottish universities) personnalité élue par les étudiants pour les représenter

recuperate [rɪˈkjuːpəreɪt] vi (from illness) se rétablir

recur [rɪˈkəːʳ] vi se reproduire; (idea, opportunity) se retrouver; (symptoms) réapparaître

recurrence [rɪˈkəːrns] n répétition f; réapparition f

recurrent [rɪˈkəːrnt] adj périodique, fréquent(e)

recurring [rɪˈkəːrɪŋ] adj (problem) périodique, fréquent(e); (Math) périodique

recyclable [riːˈsaɪkləbl] adj recyclable

recycle [riːˈsaɪkl] vt, vi recycler

recycling [riːˈsaɪklɪŋ] n recyclage m

red [rɛd] n rouge m; (Pol: pej) rouge m/f ▷ adj rouge; (hair) roux/rousse; **in the ~** (account) à découvert; (business) en déficit

red carpet treatment n réception f en grande pompe

Red Cross n Croix-Rouge f

redcurrant [ˈrɛdkʌrənt] n groseille f (rouge)

redden [ˈrɛdn] vt, vi rougir

redecorate [riːˈdɛkəreɪt] vt refaire à neuf, repeindre et retapisser

redeem [rɪˈdiːm] vt (debt) rembourser; (sth in pawn) dégager; (fig, also Rel) racheter

redeeming [rɪˈdiːmɪŋ] adj (feature) qui sauve, qui rachète (le reste)

redeploy [riːdɪˈplɔɪ] vt (Mil) redéployer; (staff, resources) reconvertir

red-haired [rɛdˈhɛəd] adj roux/rousse

red-handed [rɛdˈhændɪd] adj: **to be caught ~** être pris(e) en flagrant délit or la main dans le sac

redhead [ˈrɛdhɛd] n roux/rousse

red herring n (fig) diversion f, fausse piste

red-hot [rɛdˈhɔt] adj chauffé(e) au rouge, brûlant(e)

redirect [riːdaɪˈrɛkt] vt (mail) faire suivre

red light n: **to go through a ~** (Aut) brûler un feu rouge

red-light district [ˈrɛdlaɪt-] n quartier mal famé

red meat n viande f rouge

redo [riːˈduː] vt (irreg like: do) refaire

redress [rɪˈdrɛs] n réparation f ▷ vt redresser; **to ~ the balance** rétablir l'équilibre

Red Sea n: **the ~** la mer Rouge

redskin [ˈrɛdskɪn] n (inf!) Peau-Rouge m/f

red tape n (fig) paperasserie (administrative)

reduce [rɪˈdjuːs] vt réduire; (lower) abaisser; **"~ speed now"** (Aut) "ralentir"; **to ~ sth by/ to** réduire qch de/à; **to ~ sb to tears** faire pleurer qn

reduced [rɪˈdjuːst] adj réduit(e); **"greatly ~ prices"** "gros rabais"; **at a ~ price** (goods) au rabais; (ticket etc) à prix réduit

reduction [rɪˈdʌkʃən] n réduction f; (of price) baisse f; (discount) rabais m; réduction; **is there a ~ for children/students?** y a-t-il une réduction pour les enfants/les étudiants?

redundancy [rɪˈdʌndənsɪ] n (Brit) licenciement m, mise f au chômage; **compulsory ~** licenciement; **voluntary ~** départ m volontaire

redundant [rɪˈdʌndnt] adj (Brit: worker) licencié(e), mis(e) au chômage; (detail, object) superflu(e); **to be made ~** (worker) être licencié, être mis au chômage

reed [riːd] n (Bot) roseau m; (Mus: of clarinet etc) anche f

reef [riːf] n (at sea) récif m, écueil m

reek [riːk] vi: **to ~ (of)** puer, empester

reel [riːl] n bobine f; (Tech) dévidoir m; (Fishing) moulinet m; (Cine) bande f; (dance) quadrille écossais ▷ vt (Tech) bobiner; (also: **~ up**) enrouler ▷ vi (sway) chanceler; **my head is ~ing** j'ai la tête qui tourne; **reel in** vt (fish, line) ramener; **reel off** vt (say) énumérer, débiter

ref [rɛf] n abbr (inf: = referee) arbitre m

refectory [rɪˈfɛktərɪ] n réfectoire m

refer [rɪˈfəːʳ] vt: **to ~ sth to** (dispute, decision) soumettre qch à; **to ~ sb to** (inquirer, patient) adresser qn à; (reader: to text) renvoyer qn à ▷ vi: **to ~ to** (allude to) parler de, faire allusion à; (consult) se reporter à; (apply to) s'appliquer à; **~ring to your letter** (Comm) en réponse à votre lettre; **he ~red me to the manager** il m'a dit de m'adresser au directeur

referee [rɛfəˈriː] n arbitre m; (Tennis) juge-arbitre m; (Brit: for job application) répondant(e) ▷ vt arbitrer

reference [ˈrɛfrəns] n référence f, renvoi m; (mention) allusion f, mention f; (for job application: letter) références; lettre f de recommandation; (: person) répondant(e); **with ~ to** en ce qui concerne; (Comm: in letter) me référant à; **"please quote this ~"** (Comm) "prière de rappeler cette référence"

reference book n ouvrage m de référence

reference number n (Comm) numéro m de référence

refill vt [riːˈfɪl] remplir à nouveau; (pen, lighter etc) recharger ▷ n [ˈriːfɪl] (for pen etc) recharge f

refine [rɪ'faɪn] vt (sugar, oil) raffiner; (taste) affiner; (idea, theory) peaufiner

refined [rɪ'faɪnd] adj (person, taste) raffiné(e)

refinery [rɪ'faɪnərɪ] n raffinerie f

reflect [rɪ'flɛkt] vt (light, image) réfléchir, refléter; (fig) refléter ▷ vi (think) réfléchir, méditer; **it ~s badly on him** cela le discrédite; **it ~s well on him** c'est tout à son honneur

reflection [rɪ'flɛkʃən] n réflexion f; (image) reflet m; (criticism): ~ **on** critique f de; atteinte f à; **on ~** réflexion faite

reflex ['ri:flɛks] adj, n réflexe (m)

reflexive [rɪ'flɛksɪv] adj (Ling) réfléchi(e)

reform [rɪ'fɔ:m] n réforme f ▷ vt réformer

reformatory [rɪ'fɔ:mətərɪ] n (US) centre m d'éducation surveillée

refrain [rɪ'freɪn] vi: **to ~ from doing** s'abstenir de faire ▷ n refrain m

refresh [rɪ'frɛʃ] vt rafraîchir; (subj: food, sleep etc) redonner des forces à

refresher course [rɪ'frɛʃə-] n (Brit) cours m de recyclage

refreshing [rɪ'frɛʃɪŋ] adj (drink) rafraîchissant(e); (sleep) réparateur(-trice); (fact, idea etc) qui réjouit par son originalité or sa rareté

refreshment [rɪ'frɛʃmənt] n: **for some ~** (eating) pour se restaurer or sustenter; **in need of ~** (resting etc) ayant besoin de refaire ses forces

refreshments [rɪ'frɛʃmənts] npl rafraîchissements mpl

refrigerator [rɪ'frɪdʒəreɪtər] n réfrigérateur m, frigidaire m

refuel [ri:'fjuəl] vt ravitailler en carburant ▷ vi se ravitailler en carburant

refuge ['rɛfju:dʒ] n refuge m; **to take ~ in** se réfugier dans

refugee [rɛfju'dʒi:] n réfugié(e)

refund n ['ri:fʌnd] remboursement m ▷ vt [rɪ'fʌnd] rembourser

refurbish [ri:'fə:bɪʃ] vt remettre à neuf

refusal [rɪ'fju:zəl] n refus m; **to have first ~ on sth** avoir droit de préemption sur qch

refuse¹ ['rɛfju:s] n ordures fpl, détritus mpl

refuse² [rɪ'fju:z] vt, vi refuser; **to ~ to do sth** refuser de faire qch

refuse collection n ramassage m d'ordures

regain [rɪ'geɪn] vt (lost ground) regagner; (strength) retrouver

regal ['ri:gl] adj royal(e)

regard [rɪ'gɑ:d] n respect m, estime f, considération f ▷ vt considérer; **to give one's ~s to** faire ses amitiés à; **"with kindest ~s"** "bien amicalement"; **as ~s, with ~ to** en ce qui concerne

regarding [rɪ'gɑ:dɪŋ] prep en ce qui concerne

regardless [rɪ'gɑ:dlɪs] adv quand même; ~ **of** sans se soucier de

regenerate [rɪ'dʒɛnəreɪt] vt régénérer ▷ vi se régénérer

reggae ['rɛgeɪ] n reggae m

régime [reɪ'ʒi:m] n régime m

regiment n ['rɛdʒɪmənt] n régiment m ▷ vt ['rɛdʒɪment] imposer une discipline trop stricte à

regimental [rɛdʒɪ'mɛntl] adj d'un régiment

region ['ri:dʒən] n région f; **in the ~ of** (fig) aux alentours de

regional ['ri:dʒənl] adj régional(e)

register ['rɛdʒɪstər] n registre m; (also: **electoral ~**) liste électorale ▷ vt enregistrer, inscrire; (birth) déclarer; (vehicle) immatriculer; (luggage) enregistrer; (letter) envoyer en recommandé; (subj: instrument) marquer ▷ vi s'inscrire; (at hotel) signer le registre; (make impression) être (bien) compris(e); **to ~ for a course** s'inscrire à un cours; **to ~ a protest** protester

registered ['rɛdʒɪstəd] adj (design) déposé(e); (Brit: letter) recommandé(e); (student, voter) inscrit(e)

registered trademark n marque déposée

registrar ['rɛdʒɪstrɑ:r] n officier m de l'état civil; secrétaire m/f général

registration [rɛdʒɪs'treɪʃən] n (act) enregistrement m; (of student) inscription f; (Brit Aut: also: ~ **number**) numéro m d'immatriculation

registry ['rɛdʒɪstrɪ] n bureau m de l'enregistrement

registry office ['rɛdʒɪstrɪ-] n (Brit) bureau m de l'état civil; **to get married in a ~** se marier à la mairie

regret [rɪ'grɛt] n regret m ▷ vt regretter; **to ~ that** regretter que + sub; **we ~ to inform you that ...** nous sommes au regret de vous informer que ...

regretfully [rɪ'grɛtfəlɪ] adv à or avec regret

regrettable [rɪ'grɛtəbl] adj regrettable, fâcheux(-euse)

regular ['rɛgjulər] adj régulier(-ière); (usual) habituel(le), normal(e); (listener, reader) fidèle; (soldier) de métier; (Comm: size) ordinaire ▷ n (client etc) habitué(e)

regularly ['rɛgjuləlɪ] adv régulièrement

regulate ['rɛgjuleɪt] vt régler

regulation [rɛgju'leɪʃən] n (rule) règlement m; (adjustment) réglage m ▷ cpd réglementaire

rehabilitation ['ri:əbɪlɪ'teɪʃən] n (of offender) réhabilitation f; (of addict) réadaptation f; (of disabled) rééducation f, réadaptation f

rehearsal [rɪ'hə:səl] n répétition f; **dress ~** (répétition) générale f

rehearse [rɪ'hə:s] vt répéter

reign [reɪn] n règne m ▷ vi régner

reimburse [ri:ɪm'bə:s] vt rembourser

rein [reɪn] n (for horse) rêne f; **to give sb free ~** (fig) donner carte blanche à qn

reincarnation [ri:ɪnkɑ:'neɪʃən] n réincarnation f

reindeer ['reɪndɪər] n (pl inv) renne m

reinforce [riːɪnˈfɔːs] vt renforcer

reinforced concrete [riːɪnˈfɔːst-] n béton armé

reinforcement [riːɪnˈfɔːsmənt] n (action) renforcement m

reinforcements [riːɪnˈfɔːsmənts] npl (Mil) renfort(s) m(pl)

reinstate [riːɪnˈsteɪt] vt rétablir, réintégrer

reject n [ˈriːdʒɛkt] (Comm) article m de rebut ▷ vt [rɪˈdʒɛkt] refuser; (Comm: goods) mettre au rebut; (idea) rejeter

rejection [rɪˈdʒɛkʃən] n rejet m, refus m

rejoice [rɪˈdʒɔɪs] vi: **to ~ (at** or **over)** se réjouir (de)

rejuvenate [rɪˈdʒuːvəneɪt] vt rajeunir

relapse [rɪˈlæps] n (Med) rechute f

relate [rɪˈleɪt] vt (tell) raconter; (connect) établir un rapport entre ▷ vi: **to ~ to** (connect) se rapporter à; **to ~ to sb** (interact) entretenir des rapports avec qn

related [rɪˈleɪtɪd] adj apparenté(e); **~ to** (subject) lié(e) à

relating to [rɪˈleɪtɪŋ-] prep concernant

relation [rɪˈleɪʃən] n (person) parent(e); (link) rapport m, lien m; **relations** npl (relatives) famille f; **diplomatic/international ~s** relations diplomatiques/internationales; **in ~ to** en ce qui concerne; par rapport à; **to bear no ~ to** être sans rapport avec

relationship [rɪˈleɪʃənʃɪp] n rapport m, lien m; (personal ties) relations fpl, rapports; (also: **family ~**) lien de parenté; (affair) liaison f; **they have a good ~** ils s'entendent bien

relative [ˈrɛlətɪv] n parent(e) ▷ adj relatif(-ive); (respective) respectif(-ive); **all her ~s** toute sa famille

relatively [ˈrɛlətɪvlɪ] adv relativement

relax [rɪˈlæks] vi (muscle) se relâcher; (person: unwind) se détendre; (calm down) se calmer ▷ vt relâcher; (mind, person) détendre

relaxation [riːlækˈseɪʃən] n relâchement m; (of mind) détente f; (recreation) détente, délassement m; (entertainment) distraction f

relaxed [rɪˈlækst] adj relâché(e); détendu(e)

relaxing [rɪˈlæksɪŋ] adj délassant(e)

relay [ˈriːleɪ] n (Sport) course f de relais ▷ vt (message) retransmettre, relayer

release [rɪˈliːs] n (from prison, obligation) libération f; (of gas etc) émission f; (of film etc) sortie f; (new recording) disque m; (device) déclencheur m ▷ vt (prisoner) libérer; (book, film) sortir; (report, news) rendre public, publier; (gas etc) émettre, dégager; (free: from wreckage etc) dégager; (Tech: catch, spring etc) déclencher; (let go: person, animal) relâcher; (: hand, object) lâcher; (: grip, brake) desserrer; **to ~ one's grip** or **hold** lâcher prise; **to ~ the clutch** (Aut) débrayer

relegate [ˈrɛləgeɪt] vt reléguer; (Brit Sport): **to be ~d** descendre dans une division inférieure

relent [rɪˈlɛnt] vi se laisser fléchir

relentless [rɪˈlɛntlɪs] adj implacable; (non-stop) continuel(le)

relevant [ˈrɛləvənt] adj (question) pertinent(e); (corresponding) approprié(e); (fact) significatif(-ive); (information) utile; **~ to** ayant rapport à, approprié à

reliable [rɪˈlaɪəbl] adj (person, firm) sérieux(-euse), fiable; (method, machine) fiable; (news, information) sûr(e)

reliably [rɪˈlaɪəblɪ] adv: **to be ~ informed** savoir de source sûre

reliance [rɪˈlaɪəns] n: **~ (on)** (trust) confiance f (en); (dependence) besoin m (de), dépendance f (de)

relic [ˈrɛlɪk] n (Rel) relique f; (of the past) vestige m

relief [rɪˈliːf] n (from pain, anxiety) soulagement m; (help, supplies) secours m(pl); (of guard) relève f; (Art, Geo) relief m; **by way of light ~** pour faire diversion

relieve [rɪˈliːv] vt (pain, patient) soulager; (fear, worry) dissiper; (bring help) secourir; (take over from: gen) relayer; (: guard) relever; **to ~ sb of sth** débarrasser qn de qch; **to ~ sb of his command** (Mil) relever qn de ses fonctions; **to ~ o.s.** (euphemism) se soulager, faire ses besoins

relieved [rɪˈliːvd] adj soulagé(e); **to be ~ that ...** être soulagé que ...; **I'm ~ to hear it** je suis soulagé de l'entendre

religion [rɪˈlɪdʒən] n religion f

religious [rɪˈlɪdʒəs] adj religieux(-euse); (book) de piété

religious education n instruction religieuse

relinquish [rɪˈlɪŋkwɪʃ] vt abandonner; (plan, habit) renoncer à

relish [ˈrɛlɪʃ] n (Culin) condiment m; (enjoyment) délectation f ▷ vt (food etc) savourer; **to ~ doing** se délecter à faire

relocate [riːləʊˈkeɪt] vt (business) transférer ▷ vi se transférer, s'installer or s'établir ailleurs; **to ~ in** (déménager et) s'installer or s'établir à, se transférer à

reluctance [rɪˈlʌktəns] n répugnance f

reluctant [rɪˈlʌktənt] adj peu disposé(e), qui hésite; **to be ~ to do sth** hésiter à faire qch

reluctantly [rɪˈlʌktəntlɪ] adv à contrecœur, sans enthousiasme

rely on [rɪˈlaɪ-] vt fus (be dependent on) dépendre de; (trust) compter sur

remain [rɪˈmeɪn] vi rester; **to ~ silent** garder le silence; **I ~, yours faithfully** (Brit: in letters) je vous prie d'agréer, Monsieur etc l'assurance de mes sentiments distingués

remainder [rɪˈmeɪndər] n reste m; (Comm) fin f de série

remaining [rɪˈmeɪnɪŋ] adj qui reste

remains [rɪˈmeɪnz] npl restes mpl

remake [ˈriːmeɪk] n (Cine) remake m

r

remand [rɪ'mɑ:nd] n: **on ~** en détention préventive ▷ vt: **to be ~ed in custody** être placé(e) en détention préventive

remark [rɪ'mɑ:k] n remarque f, observation f ▷ vt (faire) remarquer, dire; (notice) remarquer; **to ~ on sth** faire une or des remarque(s) sur qch

remarkable [rɪ'mɑ:kəbl] adj remarquable

remarkably [rɪ'mɑ:kəblɪ] adv remarquablement

remarry [ri:'mærɪ] vi se remarier

remedial [rɪ'mi:dɪəl] adj (tuition, classes) de rattrapage

remedy ['rɛmədɪ] n: **~ (for)** remède m (contre or à) ▷ vt remédier à

remember [rɪ'mɛmbə^r] vt se rappeler, se souvenir de; (send greetings): **~ me to him** saluez-le de ma part; **I ~ seeing it, I ~ having seen it** je me rappelle l'avoir vu or que je l'ai vu; **she ~ed to do it** elle a pensé à le faire; **~ me to your wife** rappelez-moi au bon souvenir de votre femme

remembrance [rɪ'mɛmbrəns] n souvenir m; mémoire f

Remembrance Day n (Brit) ≈ (le jour de) l'Armistice m, ≈ le 11 novembre; voir article

○ **REMEMBRANCE DAY**

○ Remembrance Day ou Remembrance Sunday est
○ le dimanche le plus proche du 11
○ novembre, jour où la Première Guerre
○ mondiale a officiellement pris fin. Il rend
○ hommage aux victimes des deux guerres
○ mondiales. À cette occasion, on observe
○ deux minutes de silence à 11h, heure de la
○ signature de l'armistice avec l'Allemagne
○ en 1918; certaines membres de la famille
○ royale et du gouvernement déposent des
○ gerbes de coquelicots au cénotaphe de
○ Whitehall, et des couronnes sont placées
○ sur les monuments aux morts dans toute
○ la Grande-Bretagne; par ailleurs, les gens
○ portent des coquelicots artificiels
○ fabriqués et vendus par des membres de
○ la légion britannique blessés au combat,
○ au profit des blessés de guerre et de leur
○ famille.

remind [rɪ'maɪnd] vt: **to ~ sb of sth** rappeler qch à qn; **to ~ sb to do** faire penser à qn à faire, rappeler à qn qu'il doit faire; **that ~s me!** j'y pense!

reminder [rɪ'maɪndə^r] n (Comm: letter) rappel m; (note etc) pense-bête m; (souvenir) souvenir m

reminisce [rɛmɪ'nɪs] vi: **to ~ (about)** évoquer ses souvenirs (de)

reminiscent [rɛmɪ'nɪsnt] adj: **~ of** qui rappelle, qui fait penser à

remiss [rɪ'mɪs] adj négligent(e); **it was ~ of me** c'était une négligence de ma part

remission [rɪ'mɪʃən] n rémission f; (of debt, sentence) remise f; (of fee) exemption f

remit [rɪ'mɪt] vt (send: money) envoyer

remittance [rɪ'mɪtns] n envoi m, paiement m

remnant ['rɛmnənt] n reste m, restant m; (of cloth) coupon m; **remnants** npl (Comm) fins fpl de série

remorse [rɪ'mɔ:s] n remords m

remorseful [rɪ'mɔ:sful] adj plein(e) de remords

remorseless [rɪ'mɔ:slɪs] adj (fig) impitoyable

remote [rɪ'məut] adj éloigné(e), lointain(e); (person) distant(e); (possibility) vague; **there is a ~ possibility that ...** il est tout juste possible que ...

remote control n télécommande f

remotely [rɪ'məutlɪ] adv au loin; (slightly) très vaguement

remould ['ri:məuld] n (Brit: tyre) pneu m rechapé

removable [rɪ'mu:vəbl] adj (detachable) amovible

removal [rɪ'mu:vəl] n (taking away) enlèvement m; suppression f; (Brit: from house) déménagement m; (from office: dismissal) renvoi m; (of stain) nettoyage m; (Med) ablation f

removal man irreg n (Brit) déménageur m

removal van n (Brit) camion m de déménagement

remove [rɪ'mu:v] vt enlever, retirer; (employee) renvoyer; (stain) faire partir; (abuse) supprimer; (doubt) chasser; **first cousin once ~d** cousin(e) au deuxième degré

Renaissance [rɪ'neɪsɑ̃s] n: **the ~** la Renaissance

rename [ri:'neɪm] vt rebaptiser

render ['rɛndə^r] vt rendre; (Culin: fat) clarifier

rendering ['rɛndərɪŋ] n (Mus etc) interprétation f

rendezvous ['rɔndɪvu:] n rendez-vous m inv ▷ vi opérer une jonction, se rejoindre; **to ~ with sb** rejoindre qn

renew [rɪ'nju:] vt renouveler; (negotiations) reprendre; (acquaintance) renouer

renewable [rɪ'nju:əbl] adj (energy) renouvelable; **~s** énergies renouvelables

renewal [rɪ'nju:əl] n renouvellement m; reprise f

renounce [rɪ'nauns] vt renoncer à; (disown) renier

renovate ['rɛnəveɪt] vt rénover; (work of art) restaurer

renown [rɪ'naun] n renommée f

renowned [rɪ'naund] adj renommé(e)

rent [rɛnt] pt, pp of **rend** ▷ n loyer m ▷ vt louer; (car, TV) louer, prendre en location; (also: **~ out**) louer; (car, TV) louer, donner en location

rental ['rɛntl] n (for television, car) (prix m de) location f

reorganize [ri:'ɔ:gənaɪz] vt réorganiser

rep [rɛp] *n abbr* (*Comm*) = **representative**; (*Theat*) = **repertory**

repair [rɪˈpɛəʳ] *n* réparation *f* ▷ *vt* réparer; **in good/bad** ~ en bon/mauvais état; **under** ~ en réparation; **where can I get this ~ed?** où est-ce que je peux faire réparer ceci?

repair kit *n* trousse *f* de réparations

repatriate [riːˈpætrɪeɪt] *vt* rapatrier

repay [riːˈpeɪ] *vt* (*irreg like*: **pay**) (*money, creditor*) rembourser; (*sb's efforts*) récompenser

repayment [riːˈpeɪmənt] *n* remboursement *m*; récompense *f*

repeal [rɪˈpiːl] *n* (*of law*) abrogation *f*; (*of sentence*) annulation *f* ▷ *vt* abroger; annuler

repeat [rɪˈpiːt] *n* (*Radio, TV*) reprise *f* ▷ *vt* répéter; (*pattern*) reproduire; (*promise, attack, also Comm: order*) renouveler; (*Scol: a class*) redoubler ▷ *vi* répéter; **can you ~ that, please?** pouvez-vous répéter, s'il vous plaît?

repeatedly [rɪˈpiːtɪdlɪ] *adv* souvent, à plusieurs reprises

repeat prescription *n* (*Brit*): **I'd like a ~** je voudrais renouveler mon ordonnance

repel [rɪˈpɛl] *vt* repousser

repellent [rɪˈpɛlənt] *adj* repoussant(e) ▷ *n*: **insect ~** insectifuge *m*; **moth ~** produit *m* antimite(s)

repent [rɪˈpɛnt] *vi*: **to ~ (of)** se repentir (de)

repentance [rɪˈpɛntəns] *n* repentir *m*

repercussions [riːpəˈkʌʃənz] *npl* répercussions *fpl*

repertory [ˈrɛpətərɪ] *n* (*also*: **~ theatre**) théâtre *m* de répertoire

repetition [rɛpɪˈtɪʃən] *n* répétition *f*

repetitive [rɪˈpɛtɪtɪv] *adj* (*movement, work*) répétitif(-ive); (*speech*) plein(e) de redites

replace [rɪˈpleɪs] *vt* (*put back*) remettre, replacer; (*take the place of*) remplacer; (*Tel*): **"~ the receiver"** "raccrochez"

replacement [rɪˈpleɪsmənt] *n* replacement *m*; (*substitution*) remplacement *m*; (*person*) remplaçant(e)

replay [ˈriːpleɪ] *n* (*of match*) match rejoué; (*of tape, film*) répétition *f*

replenish [rɪˈplɛnɪʃ] *vt* (*glass*) remplir (de nouveau); (*stock etc*) réapprovisionner

replica [ˈrɛplɪkə] *n* réplique *f*, copie exacte

reply [rɪˈplaɪ] *n* réponse *f* ▷ *vi* répondre; **in ~ (to)** en réponse (à); **there's no ~** (*Tel*) ça ne répond pas

report [rɪˈpɔːt] *n* rapport *m*; (*Press etc*) reportage *m*; (*Brit: also*: **school ~**) bulletin *m* (scolaire); (*of gun*) détonation *f* ▷ *vt* rapporter, faire un compte rendu de; (*Press etc*) faire un reportage sur; (*notify: accident*) signaler; (: *culprit*) dénoncer ▷ *vi* (*make a report*) faire un rapport; (*for newspaper*) faire un reportage (sur); **I'd like to ~ a theft** je voudrais signaler un vol; (*present o.s.*): **to ~ (to sb)** se présenter (chez qn); **it is ~ed that** on dit *or* annonce que; **it is ~ed from Berlin that** on nous apprend de Berlin que

report card *n* (*US, Scottish*) bulletin *m* (scolaire)

reportedly [rɪˈpɔːtɪdlɪ] *adv*: **she is ~ living in Spain** elle habiterait en Espagne; **he ~ told them to ...** il leur aurait dit de ...

reporter [rɪˈpɔːtəʳ] *n* reporter *m*

repose [rɪˈpəuz] *n*: **in ~** en *or* au repos

represent [rɛprɪˈzɛnt] *vt* représenter; (*view, belief*) présenter, expliquer; (*describe*): **to ~ sth as** présenter *or* décrire qch comme; **to ~ to sb that** expliquer à qn que

representation [rɛprɪzɛnˈteɪʃən] *n* représentation *f*; **representations** *npl* (*protest*) démarche *f*

representative [rɛprɪˈzɛntətɪv] *n* représentant(e); (*Comm*) représentant(e) (de commerce); (*US Pol*) député *m* ▷ *adj* représentatif(-ive), caractéristique

repress [rɪˈprɛs] *vt* réprimer

repression [rɪˈprɛʃən] *n* répression *f*

reprieve [rɪˈpriːv] *n* (*Law*) grâce *f*; (*fig*) sursis *m*, délai *m* ▷ *vt* gracier; accorder un sursis *or* un délai à

reprimand [ˈrɛprɪmɑːnd] *n* réprimande *f* ▷ *vt* réprimander

reprisal [rɪˈpraɪzl] *n* représailles *fpl*; **to take ~s** user de représailles

reproach [rɪˈprəutʃ] *n* reproche *m* ▷ *vt*: **to ~ sb with sth** reprocher qch à qn; **beyond ~** irréprochable

reproachful [rɪˈprəutʃful] *adj* de reproche

reproduce [riːprəˈdjuːs] *vt* reproduire ▷ *vi* se reproduire

reproduction [riːprəˈdʌkʃən] *n* reproduction *f*

reproof [rɪˈpruːf] *n* reproche *m*

reptile [ˈrɛptaɪl] *n* reptile *m*

republic [rɪˈpʌblɪk] *n* république *f*

republican [rɪˈpʌblɪkən] *adj, n* républicain(e)

repudiate [rɪˈpjuːdɪeɪt] *vt* (*ally, behaviour*) désavouer; (*accusation*) rejeter; (*wife*) répudier

repulsive [rɪˈpʌlsɪv] *adj* repoussant(e), répulsif(-ive)

reputable [ˈrɛpjutəbl] *adj* de bonne réputation; (*occupation*) honorable

reputation [rɛpjuˈteɪʃən] *n* réputation *f*; **to have a ~ for** être réputé(e) pour; **he has a ~ for being awkward** il a la réputation de ne pas être commode

reputed [rɪˈpjuːtɪd] *adj* réputé(e); **he is ~ to be rich/intelligent** *etc* on dit qu'il est riche/intelligent *etc*

reputedly [rɪˈpjuːtɪdlɪ] *adv* d'après ce qu'on dit

request [rɪˈkwɛst] *n* demande *f*; (*formal*) requête *f* ▷ *vt*: **to ~ (of *or* from sb)** demander (à qn); **at the ~ of** à la demande de

request stop *n* (*Brit: for bus*) arrêt facultatif

require [rɪˈkwaɪəʳ] *vt* (*need: subj: person*) avoir besoin de; (: *thing, situation*) nécessiter, demander; (*want*) exiger; (*order*): **to ~ sb to do sth/sth of sb** exiger que qn fasse qch/qch

de qn; **if ~d** s'il le faut; **what qualifications
are ~d?** quelles sont les qualifications
requises?; **~d by law** requis par la loi
requirement [rɪ'kwaɪəmənt] *n* (*need*)
exigence *f*; besoin *m*; (*condition*) condition *f*
(*requise*)
requisition [rɛkwɪ'zɪʃən] *n*: ~ **(for)** demande *f*
(de) ▷ *vt* (*Mil*) réquisitionner
resat [ri:'sæt] *pt, pp* of **resit**
rescue ['rɛskju:] *n* (*from accident*) sauvetage *m*;
(*help*) secours *mpl* ▷ *vt* sauver; **to come to
sb's ~** venir au secours de qn
rescue party *n* équipe *f* de sauvetage
rescuer ['rɛskjuəʳ] *n* sauveteur *m*
research [rɪ'sə:tʃ] *n* recherche(s) *f(pl)* ▷ *vt*
faire des recherches sur ▷ *vi*: **to ~ (into sth)**
faire des recherches (sur qch); **a piece of ~** un
travail de recherche; **~ and development
(R & D)** recherche-développement (R-D)
resemblance [rɪ'zɛmbləns] *n* ressemblance *f*;
to bear a strong ~ to ressembler beaucoup à
resemble [rɪ'zɛmbl] *vt* ressembler à
resent [rɪ'zɛnt] *vt* éprouver du ressentiment
de, être contrarié(e) par
resentful [rɪ'zɛntful] *adj* irrité(e), plein(e) de
ressentiment
resentment [rɪ'zɛntmənt] *n* ressentiment *m*
reservation [rɛzə'veɪʃən] *n* (*booking*)
réservation *f*; (*doubt, protected area*) réserve *f*;
(*Brit Aut: also:* **central ~**) bande médiane; **to
make a ~ (in an hotel/a restaurant/on a
plane)** réserver *or* retenir une chambre/une
table/une place; **with ~s** (*doubts*) avec
certaines réserves
reservation desk *n* (US: in hotel) réception *f*
reserve [rɪ'zə:v] *n* réserve *f*; (*Sport*)
remplaçant(e) ▷ *vt* (*seats etc*) réserver, retenir;
reserves *npl* (*Mil*) réservistes *mpl*; **in ~** en
réserve
reserved [rɪ'zə:vd] *adj* réservé(e)
reservoir ['rɛzəvwɑ:ʳ] *n* réservoir *m*
reshuffle ['ri:'ʃʌfl] *n*: **Cabinet ~** (*Pol*)
remaniement ministériel
residence ['rɛzɪdəns] *n* résidence *f*; **to take
up ~** s'installer; **in ~** (*queen etc*) en résidence;
(*doctor*) résidant(e)
residence permit *n* (Brit) permis *m* de séjour
resident ['rɛzɪdənt] *n* (*of country*) résident(e);
(*of area, house*) habitant(e); (*in hotel*)
pensionnaire ▷ *adj* résidant(e)
residential [rɛzɪ'dɛnʃəl] *adj* de résidence;
(*area*) résidentiel(le); (*course*) avec
hébergement sur place
residential school *n* internat *m*
residue ['rɛzɪdju:] *n* reste *m*; (*Chem, Physics*)
résidu *m*
resign [rɪ'zaɪn] *vt* (*one's post*) se démettre de
▷ *vi* démissionner; **to ~ o.s. to** (*endure*) se
résigner à
resignation [rɛzɪg'neɪʃən] *n* (*from post*)
démission *f*; (*state of mind*) résignation *f*;
to tender one's ~ donner sa démission

resigned [rɪ'zaɪnd] *adj* résigné(e)
resilient [rɪ'zɪlɪənt] *adj* (*person*) qui réagit, qui
a du ressort
resin ['rɛzɪn] *n* résine *f*
resist [rɪ'zɪst] *vt* résister à
resistance [rɪ'zɪstəns] *n* résistance *f*
resit *vt* [ri:'sɪt] (Brit pt, pp **resat**) (*exam*) repasser
▷ *n* ['ri:sɪt] deuxième session *f* (*d'un examen*)
resolution [rɛzə'lu:ʃən] *n* résolution *f*;
to make a ~ prendre une résolution
resolve [rɪ'zɔlv] *n* résolution *f* ▷ *vt* (*decide*):
to ~ to do résoudre *or* décider de faire;
(*problem*) résoudre
resort [rɪ'zɔ:t] *n* (*seaside town*) station *f*
balnéaire; (*for skiing*) station de ski; (*recourse*)
recours *m* ▷ *vi*: **to ~ to** avoir recours à; **in the
last ~** en dernier ressort
resounding [rɪ'zaundɪŋ] *adj* retentissant(e)
resource [rɪ'sɔ:s] *n* ressource *f*; **resources** *npl*
ressources; **natural ~s** ressources naturelles;
to leave sb to his (*or* **her**) **own ~s** (*fig*) livrer
qn à lui-même (*or* elle-même)
resourceful [rɪ'sɔ:sful] *adj* ingénieux(-euse),
débrouillard(e)
respect [rɪs'pɛkt] *n* respect *m*; (*point, detail*):
in some ~s à certains égards ▷ *vt* respecter;
respects *npl* respects, hommages *mpl*; **to
have** *or* **show ~ for sb/sth** respecter qn/qch;
out of ~ for par respect pour; **with ~ to** en ce
qui concerne; **in ~ of** sous le rapport de,
quant à; **in this ~** sous ce rapport, à cet égard;
with due ~ I ... malgré le respect que je vous
dois, je ...
respectable [rɪs'pɛktəbl] *adj* respectable;
(*quite good: result etc*) honorable; (*player*) assez
bon/bonne
respectful [rɪs'pɛktful] *adj*
respectueux(-euse)
respective [rɪs'pɛktɪv] *adj* respectif(-ive)
respectively [rɪs'pɛktɪvlɪ] *adv*
respectivement
respite ['rɛspaɪt] *n* répit *m*
respond [rɪs'pɔnd] *vi* répondre; (*react*) réagir
response [rɪs'pɔns] *n* réponse *f*; (*reaction*)
réaction *f*; **in ~ to** en réponse à
responsibility [rɪspɔnsɪ'bɪlɪtɪ] *n*
responsabilité *f*; **to take ~ for sth/sb**
accepter la responsabilité de qch/d'être
responsable de qn
responsible [rɪs'pɔnsɪbl] *adj* (*liable*): **~ (for)**
responsable (de); (*person*) digne de confiance;
(*job*) qui comporte des responsabilités; **to be
~ to sb (for sth)** être responsable devant qn
(de qch)
responsibly [rɪs'pɔnsɪblɪ] *adv* avec sérieux
responsive [rɪs'pɔnsɪv] *adj* (*student, audience*)
réceptif(-ive); (*brakes, steering*) sensible
rest [rɛst] *n* repos *m*; (*stop*) arrêt *m*, pause *f*;
(*Mus*) silence *m*; (*support*) support *m*, appui *m*;
(*remainder*) reste *m*, restant *m* ▷ *vi* se reposer;
(*be supported*): **to ~ on** appuyer *or* reposer sur;
(*remain*) rester ▷ *vt* (*lean*): **to ~ sth on/against**

appuyer qch sur/contre; **the ~ of them** les autres; **to set sb's mind at ~** tranquilliser qn; **it ~s with him to** c'est à lui de; **~ assured that ...** soyez assuré que ...

restaurant ['restərɔ̃] n restaurant m

restaurant car n (Brit Rail) wagon-restaurant m

restful ['restful] adj reposant(e)

restive ['restiv] adj agité(e), impatient(e); (horse) rétif(-ive)

restless ['restlis] adj agité(e); **to get ~** s'impatienter

restoration [restə'reɪʃən] n (of building) restauration f; (of stolen goods) restitution f

restore [rɪ'stɔːᵊ] vt (building) restaurer; (sth stolen) restituer; (peace, health) rétablir; **to ~ to** (former state) ramener à

restrain [rɪs'treɪn] vt (feeling) contenir; (person): **to ~ (from doing)** retenir (de faire)

restrained [rɪs'treɪnd] adj (style) sobre; (manner) mesuré(e)

restraint [rɪs'treɪnt] n (restriction) contrainte f; (moderation) retenue f; (of style) sobriété f; **wage ~** limitations salariales

restrict [rɪs'trɪkt] vt restreindre, limiter

restriction [rɪs'trɪkʃən] n restriction f, limitation f

rest room n (US) toilettes fpl

restructure [riː'strʌktʃəᵊ] vt restructurer

result [rɪ'zʌlt] n résultat m ▷ vi: **to ~ (from)** résulter (de); **to ~ in** aboutir à, se terminer par; **as ~ it is too expensive** il en résulte que c'est trop cher; **as a ~ of** à la suite de

resume [rɪ'zjuːm] vt (work, journey) reprendre; (sum up) résumer ▷ vi (work etc) reprendre

résumé ['reɪzjuːmeɪ] n (summary) résumé m; (US: curriculum vitae) curriculum vitae m inv

resumption [rɪ'zʌmpʃən] n reprise f

resurgence [rɪ'səːdʒəns] n réapparition f

resurrection [rezə'rekʃən] n résurrection f

resuscitate [rɪ'sʌsɪteɪt] vt (Med) réanimer

retail ['riːteɪl] n (vente f au) détail m ▷ adj de or au détail ▷ adv au détail ▷ vt vendre au détail ▷ vi: **to ~ at 10 euros** se vendre au détail à 10 euros

retailer ['riːteɪləᵊ] n détaillant(e)

retail price n prix m de détail

retain [rɪ'teɪn] vt (keep) garder, conserver; (employ) engager

retainer [rɪ'teɪnəᵊ] n (servant) serviteur m; (fee) acompte m, provision f

retaliate [rɪ'tælɪeɪt] vi: **to ~ (against)** se venger (de); **to ~ (on sb)** rendre la pareille (à qn)

retaliation [rɪtælɪ'eɪʃən] n représailles fpl, vengeance f; **in ~ for** en représailles pour

retarded [rɪ'taːdɪd] adj (!) retardé(e)

retch [retʃ] vi avoir des haut-le-cœur

retentive [rɪ'tentɪv] adj: **~ memory** excellente mémoire

retina ['retɪnə] n rétine f

retire [rɪ'taɪəᵊ] vi (give up work) prendre sa retraite; (withdraw) se retirer, partir; (go to bed) (aller) se coucher

retired [rɪ'taɪəd] adj (person) retraité(e)

retirement [rɪ'taɪəmənt] n retraite f

retiring [rɪ'taɪərɪŋ] adj (person) réservé(e); (chairman etc) sortant(e)

retort [rɪ'tɔːt] n (reply) riposte f; (container) cornue f ▷ vi riposter

retrace [riː'treɪs] vt reconstituer; **to ~ one's steps** revenir sur ses pas

retract [rɪ'trækt] vt (statement, claws) rétracter; (undercarriage, aerial) rentrer, escamoter ▷ vi se rétracter; rentrer

retrain [riː'treɪn] vt recycler ▷ vi se recycler

retread vt [riː'tred] (Aut: tyre) rechaper ▷ n ['riːtred] pneu rechapé

retreat [rɪ'triːt] n retraite f ▷ vi battre en retraite; (flood) reculer; **to beat a hasty ~** (fig) partir avec précipitation

retribution [retrɪ'bjuːʃən] n châtiment m

retrieval [rɪ'triːvəl] n récupération f; réparation f; recherche f et extraction f

retrieve [rɪ'triːv] vt (sth lost) récupérer; (situation, honour) sauver; (error, loss) réparer; (Comput) rechercher

retriever [rɪ'triːvəᵊ] n chien m d'arrêt

retrospect ['retrəspekt] n: **in ~** rétrospectivement, après coup

retrospective [retrə'spektɪv] adj rétrospectif(-ive); (law) rétroactif(-ive) ▷ n (Art) rétrospective f

return [rɪ'təːn] n (going or coming back) retour m; (of sth stolen etc) restitution f; (recompense) récompense f; (Finance: from land, shares) rapport m; (report) relevé m, rapport ▷ cpd (journey) de retour; (Brit: ticket) aller et retour; (match) retour ▷ vi (person etc: come back) revenir; (: go back) retourner ▷ vt rendre; (bring back) rapporter; (send back) renvoyer; (put back) remettre; (Pol: candidate) élire; **returns** npl (Comm) recettes fpl; (Finance) bénéfices mpl; (: returned goods) marchandises renvoyées; **many happy ~s (of the day)!** bon anniversaire!; **by ~ (of post)** par retour (du courrier); **in ~ (for)** en échange (de); **a ~ (ticket) for ...** un billet aller et retour pour ...

return ticket n (esp Brit) billet m aller-retour

retweet [riː'twiːt] (on Twitter) vt retweeter ▷ n retweet m

reunion [riː'juːnɪən] n réunion f

reunite [riːjuː'naɪt] vt réunir

reuse [riː'juːz] vt réutiliser

rev [rev] n abbr (= revolution) (Aut) tour m ▷ vt (also: ~ up) emballer ▷ vi (also: ~ up) s'emballer

revamp [riː'væmp] vt (house) retaper; (firm) réorganiser

reveal [rɪ'viːl] vt (make known) révéler; (display) laisser voir

revealing [rɪ'viːlɪŋ] adj révélateur(-trice); (dress) au décolleté généreux or suggestif

revel ['revl] vi: **to ~ in sth/in doing** se délecter de qch/à faire

revelation [revə'leɪʃən] n révélation f

r

revenge [rɪ'vendʒ] n vengeance f; (in game etc) revanche f ▷ vt venger; **to take ~ (on)** se venger (sur)

revenue ['revənjuː] n revenu m

reverberate [rɪ'vəːbəreɪt] vi (sound) retentir, se répercuter; (light) se réverbérer

reverence ['revərəns] n vénération f, révérence f

Reverend ['revərənd] adj vénérable; (in titles): **the ~ John Smith** (Anglican) le révérend John Smith; (Catholic) l'abbé (John) Smith; (Protestant) le pasteur (John) Smith

reversal [rɪ'vəːsl] n (of opinion) revirement m; (of order) renversement m; (of direction) changement m

reverse [rɪ'vəːs] n contraire m, opposé m; (back) dos m, envers m; (of paper) verso m; (of coin) revers m; (Aut: also: **~ gear**) marche f arrière ▷ adj (order, direction) opposé(e), inverse ▷ vt (order, position) changer, inverser; (direction, policy) changer complètement de; (decision) annuler; (roles) renverser; (car) faire marche arrière avec; (Law: judgment) réformer ▷ vi (Brit Aut) faire marche arrière; **to go into ~** faire marche arrière; **in ~ order** en ordre inverse

reversing lights [rɪ'vəːsɪŋ-] npl (Brit Aut) feux mpl de marche arrière or de recul

revert [rɪ'vəːt] vi: **to ~ to** revenir à, retourner à

review [rɪ'vjuː] n revue f; (of book, film) critique f; (of situation, policy) examen m, bilan m; (US: examination) examen ▷ vt passer en revue; faire la critique de; examiner; **to come under ~** être révisé(e)

reviewer [rɪ'vjuːəʳ] n critique m

revise [rɪ'vaɪz] vt réviser, modifier; (manuscript) revoir, corriger ▷ vi (study) réviser; **~d edition** édition revue et corrigée

revision [rɪ'vɪʒən] n révision f; (revised version) version corrigée

revival [rɪ'vaɪvəl] n reprise f; (recovery) rétablissement m; (of faith) renouveau m

revive [rɪ'vaɪv] vt (person) ranimer; (custom) rétablir; (economy) relancer; (hope, courage) raviver, faire renaître; (play, fashion) reprendre ▷ vi (person) reprendre connaissance; (: from ill health) se rétablir; (hope etc) renaître; (activity) reprendre

revoke [rɪ'vəuk] vt révoquer; (promise, decision) revenir sur

revolt [rɪ'vəult] n révolte f ▷ vi se révolter, se rebeller ▷ vt révolter, dégoûter

revolting [rɪ'vəultɪŋ] adj dégoûtant(e)

revolution [revə'luːʃən] n révolution f; (of wheel etc) tour m, révolution f

revolutionary [revə'luːʃənrɪ] adj, n révolutionnaire (m/f)

revolve [rɪ'vɔlv] vi tourner

revolver [rɪ'vɔlvəʳ] n revolver m

revolving [rɪ'vɔlvɪŋ] adj (chair) pivotant(e); (light) tournant(e)

revolving door n (porte f à) tambour m

revulsion [rɪ'vʌlʃən] n dégoût m, répugnance f

reward [rɪ'wɔːd] n récompense f ▷ vt: **to ~ (for)** récompenser (de)

rewarding [rɪ'wɔːdɪŋ] adj (fig) qui (en) vaut la peine, gratifiant(e); **financially ~** financièrement intéressant(e)

rewind [riː'waɪnd] vt (irreg like: **wind**) (watch) remonter; (tape) réembobiner

rewire [riː'waɪəʳ] vt (house) refaire l'installation électrique de

rewritable [riː'raɪtəbl] adj (CD, DVD) réinscriptible

rewrite [riː'raɪt] (pt **rewrote**, pp **rewritten**) vt récrire

rheumatism ['ruːmətɪzəm] n rhumatisme m

Rhine [raɪn] n: **the (River) ~** le Rhin

rhinoceros [raɪ'nɔsərəs] n rhinocéros m

rhubarb ['ruːbɑːb] n rhubarbe f

rhyme [raɪm] n rime f; (verse) vers mpl ▷ vi: **to ~ (with)** rimer (avec); **without ~ or reason** sans rime ni raison

rhythm ['rɪðm] n rythme m

rib [rɪb] n (Anat) côte f ▷ vt (mock) taquiner

ribbon ['rɪbən] n ruban m; **in ~s** (torn) en lambeaux

rice [raɪs] n riz m

rice pudding n riz m au lait

rich [rɪtʃ] adj riche; (gift, clothes) somptueux(-euse); **the ~** npl les riches mpl; **riches** npl richesses fpl; **to be ~ in sth** être riche en qch

richly ['rɪtʃlɪ] adv richement; (deserved, earned) largement, grandement

rickets ['rɪkɪts] n rachitisme m

rid [rɪd] (pt, pp **rid**) vt: **to ~ sb of** débarrasser qn de; **to get ~ of** se débarrasser de

riddle ['rɪdl] n (puzzle) énigme f ▷ vt: **to be ~d with** être criblé(e) de; (fig) être en proie à

ride [raɪd] (pt **rode**, pp **ridden**) [rəud, 'rɪdn] n promenade f, tour m; (distance covered) trajet m ▷ vi (as sport) monter (à cheval), faire du cheval; (go somewhere: on horse, bicycle) aller (à cheval or bicyclette etc); (travel: on bicycle, motor cycle, bus) rouler ▷ vt (a horse) monter; (distance) parcourir, faire; **we rode all day/all the way** nous sommes restés toute la journée en selle/avons fait tout le chemin en selle or à cheval; **to ~ a horse/bicycle** monter à cheval/à bicyclette; **can you ~ a bike?** est-ce que tu sais monter à bicyclette?; **to ~ at anchor** (Naut) être à l'ancre; **horse/car ~** promenade or tour à cheval/en voiture; **to go for a ~** faire une promenade (en voiture or à bicyclette etc); **to take sb for a ~** (fig) faire marcher qn; (cheat) rouler qn; **ride out** vt: **to ~ out the storm** (fig) surmonter les difficultés

rider ['raɪdəʳ] n cavalier(-ière); (in race) jockey m; (on bicycle) cycliste m/f; (on *motorcycle*) motocycliste *m/f*; (*in document*) annexe *f*, clause additionnelle

ridge [rɪdʒ] *n* (*of hill*) faîte *m*; (*of roof, mountain*) arête *f*; (*on object*) strie *f*

ridicule ['rɪdɪkjuːl] *n* ridicule *m*; dérision *f* ▷ *vt* ridiculiser, tourner en dérision; **to hold sb/sth up to ~** tourner qn/qch en ridicule

ridiculous [rɪ'dɪkjʊləs] *adj* ridicule

riding ['raɪdɪŋ] *n* équitation *f*

riding school *n* manège *m*, école *f* d'équitation

rife [raɪf] *adj* répandu(e); **~ with** abondant(e) en

riffraff ['rɪfræf] *n* racaille *f*

rifle ['raɪfl] *n* fusil *m* (à canon rayé) ▷ *vt* vider, dévaliser; **rifle through** *vt fus* fouiller dans

rifle range *n* champ *m* de tir; (*indoor*) stand *m* de tir

rift [rɪft] *n* fente *f*, fissure *f*; (*fig: disagreement*) désaccord *m*

rig [rɪg] *n* (*also*: **oil ~**: *on land*) derrick *m*; (*: at sea*) plate-forme pétrolière ▷ *vt* (*election etc*) truquer; **rig out** *vt* (*Brit*) habiller; (*: pej*) fringuer, attifer; **rig up** *vt* arranger, faire avec des moyens de fortune

rigging ['rɪgɪŋ] *n* (*Naut*) gréement *m*

right [raɪt] *adj* (*true*) juste, exact(e); (*correct*) bon/bonne; (*suitable*) approprié(e), convenable; (*just*) juste, équitable; (*morally good*) bien *inv*; (*not left*) droit(e) ▷ *n* (*moral good*) bien *m*; (*title, claim*) droit *m*; (*not left*) droite *f* ▷ *adv* (*answer*) correctement; (*treat*) bien, comme il faut; (*not on the left*) à droite ▷ *vt* redresser ▷ *excl* bon!; **rights** *npl* (*Comm*) droits *mpl*; **the ~ time** (*precise*) l'heure exacte; (*not wrong*) la bonne heure; **do you have the ~ time?** avez-vous l'heure juste *or* exacte?; **to be ~** (*person*) avoir raison; (*answer*) être juste *or* correct(e); **to get sth ~** ne pas se tromper sur qch; **let's get it ~ this time!** essayons de ne pas nous tromper cette fois-ci!; **you did the ~ thing** vous avez bien fait; **to put a mistake ~** (*Brit*) rectifier une erreur; **by ~s** en toute justice; **on the ~** à droite; **~ and wrong** le bien et le mal; **to be in the ~** avoir raison; **film ~s** droits d'adaptation cinématographique; **~ now** en ce moment même; (*immediately*) tout de suite; **~ before/after** juste avant/après; **~ against the wall** tout contre le mur; **~ ahead** tout droit; droit devant; **~ in the middle** en plein milieu; **~ away** immédiatement; **to go ~ to the end of sth** aller jusqu'au bout de qch

right angle *n* (*Math*) angle droit

righteous ['raɪtʃəs] *adj* droit(e), vertueux(-euse); (*anger*) justifié(e)

rightful ['raɪtful] *adj* (*heir*) légitime

right-hand ['raɪthænd] *adj*: **the ~ side** la droite

right-hand drive *n* (*Brit*) conduite *f* à droite; (*vehicle*) véhicule *m* avec la conduite à droite

right-handed [raɪt'hændɪd] *adj* (*person*) droitier(-ière)

right-hand man ['raɪthænd-] *irreg n* bras droit (*fig*)

rightly ['raɪtlɪ] *adv* bien, correctement; (*with reason*) à juste titre; **if I remember ~** (*Brit*) si je me souviens bien

right of way *n* (*on path etc*) droit *m* de passage; (*Aut*) priorité *f*

right wing *n* (*Mil, Sport*) aile droite; (*Pol*) droite *f*

right-wing [raɪt'wɪŋ] *adj* (*Pol*) de droite

rigid ['rɪdʒɪd] *adj* rigide; (*principle, control*) strict(e)

rigmarole ['rɪgmərəul] *n* galimatias *m*, comédie *f*

rigorous ['rɪgərəs] *adj* rigoureux(-euse)

rile [raɪl] *vt* agacer

rim [rɪm] *n* bord *m*; (*of spectacles*) monture *f*; (*of wheel*) jante *f*

rind [raɪnd] *n* (*of bacon*) couenne *f*; (*of lemon etc*) écorce *f*, zeste *m*; (*of cheese*) croûte *f*

ring [rɪŋ] (*pt* **rang**, *pp* **rung**) [ræŋ, rʌŋ] *n* anneau *m*; (*on finger*) bague *f*; (*also*: **wedding ~**) alliance *f*; (*for napkin*) rond *m*; (*of people, objects*) cercle *m*; (*of spies*) réseau *m*; (*of smoke etc*) rond *m*; (*arena*) piste *f*, arène *f*; (*for boxing*) ring *m*; (*sound of bell*) sonnerie *f*; (*telephone call*) coup *m* de téléphone ▷ *vi* (*telephone, bell*) sonner; (*person: by telephone*) téléphoner; (*ears*) bourdonner; (*also*: **~ out**: *voice, words*) retentir ▷ *vt* (*Brit Tel*: *also*: **~ up**) téléphoner à, appeler; **to ~ the bell** sonner; **to give sb a ~** (*Tel*) passer un coup de téléphone *or* de fil à qn; **that has the ~ of truth about it** cela sonne vrai; **the name doesn't ~ a bell (with me)** ce nom ne me dit rien; **ring back** *vt, vi* (*Brit Tel*) rappeler; **ring off** *vi* (*Brit Tel*) raccrocher; **ring up** (*Brit*) *vt* (*Tel*) téléphoner à, appeler

ring binder *n* classeur *m* à anneaux

ringing ['rɪŋɪŋ] *n* (*of bell*) tintement *m*; (*louder: also*: **of telephone**) sonnerie *f*; (*in ears*) bourdonnement *m*

ringing tone *n* (*Brit Tel*) tonalité *f* d'appel

ringleader ['rɪŋliːdəʳ] *n* (*of gang*) chef *m*, meneur *m*

ringlets ['rɪŋlɪts] *npl* anglaises *fpl*

ring road *n* (*Brit*) rocade *f*; (*motorway*) périphérique *m*

ringtone ['rɪŋtəun] *n* (*on mobile*) sonnerie *f* (*de téléphone portable*)

rink [rɪŋk] *n* (*also*: **ice ~**) patinoire *f*; (*for roller-skating*) skating *m*

rinse [rɪns] *n* rinçage *m* ▷ *vt* rincer

riot ['raɪət] *n* émeute *f*, bagarres *fpl* ▷ *vi* (*demonstrators*) manifester avec violence; (*population*) se soulever, se révolter; **a ~ of colours** une débauche *or* orgie de couleurs; **to run ~** se déchaîner

riotous ['raɪətəs] *adj* tapageur(-euse); tordant(e)

rip [rɪp] *n* déchirure *f* ▷ *vt* déchirer ▷ *vi* se déchirer; **rip off** *vt* (*inf: cheat*) arnaquer; **rip up** *vt* déchirer

ripcord ['rɪpkɔːd] n poignée f d'ouverture
ripe [raɪp] adj (fruit) mûr(e); (cheese) fait(e)
ripen ['raɪpn] vt mûrir ▷ vi mûrir; se faire
rip-off ['rɪpɔf] n (inf): **it's a ~!** c'est du vol manifeste!, c'est de l'arnaque!
ripple ['rɪpl] n ride f, ondulation f; (of applause, laughter) cascade f ▷ vi se rider, onduler ▷ vt rider, faire onduler
rise [raɪz] n (slope) côte f, pente f; (hill) élévation f; (increase: in wages: Brit) augmentation f; (: in prices, temperature) hausse f, augmentation f; (fig: to power etc) ascension f ▷ vi (pt **rose**, pp **risen**) [rəuz, rɪzn] s'élever, monter; (prices, numbers) augmenter, monter; (waters, river) monter; (sun, wind, person: from chair, bed) se lever; (also: ~ **up**: tower, building) s'élever; (: rebel) se révolter; se rebeller; (in rank) s'élever; ~ **to power** être au pouvoir; **to give ~ to** donner lieu à; **to ~ to the occasion** se montrer à la hauteur
risen ['rɪzn] pp of **rise**
rising ['raɪzɪŋ] adj (increasing: number, prices) en hausse; (tide) montant(e); (sun, moon) levant(e) ▷ n (uprising) soulèvement m, insurrection f
risk [rɪsk] n risque m, danger m; (deliberate) risque ▷ vt risquer; **to take or run the ~ of doing** courir le risque de faire; **at ~** en danger; **at one's own ~** à ses risques et périls; **it's a fire/health ~** cela présente un risque d'incendie/pour la santé; **I'll ~ it** je vais risquer le coup
risky ['rɪskɪ] adj risqué(e)
rissole ['rɪsəul] n croquette f
rite [raɪt] n rite m; **the last ~s** les derniers sacrements
ritual ['rɪtjuəl] adj rituel(le) ▷ n rituel m
rival ['raɪvl] n rival(e); (in business) concurrent(e) ▷ adj rival(e); qui fait concurrence ▷ vt (match) égaler; (compete with) être en concurrence avec; **to ~ sb/sth in** rivaliser avec qn/qch de
rivalry ['raɪvlrɪ] n rivalité f; (in business) concurrence f
river ['rɪvəʳ] n rivière f; (major: also fig) fleuve m ▷ cpd (port, traffic) fluvial(e); **up/down** ~ en amont/aval
riverbank ['rɪvəbæŋk] n rive f, berge f
riverbed ['rɪvəbed] n lit m (de rivière or de fleuve)
rivet ['rɪvɪt] n rivet m ▷ vt riveter; (fig) river, fixer
Riviera [rɪvɪ'eərə] n: **the (French) ~** la Côte d'Azur; **the Italian ~** la Riviera (italienne)
road [rəud] n route f; (in town) rue f; (fig) chemin, voie f ▷ cpd (accident) de la route; **main ~** grande route; **major/minor ~** route principale or à priorité/voie secondaire; **it takes four hours by ~** il y a quatre heures de route; **which ~ do I take for ...?** quelle route dois-je prendre pour aller à ...?; **"~ up"** (Brit) "attention travaux"

road accident n accident m de la circulation
roadblock ['rəudblɔk] n barrage routier
roadhog ['rəudhɔg] n chauffard m
road map n carte routière
road rage n comportement très agressif de certains usagers de la route
road safety n sécurité routière
roadside ['rəudsaɪd] n bord m de la route, bas-côté m ▷ cpd (situé(e) etc) au bord de la route; **by the ~** au bord de la route
road sign ['rəudsaɪn] n panneau m de signalisation
road tax n (Brit Aut) taxe f sur les automobiles
roadway ['rəudweɪ] n chaussée f
roadworks ['rəudwəːks] npl travaux mpl (de réfection des routes)
roadworthy ['rəudwəːðɪ] adj en bon état de marche
roam [rəum] vi errer, vagabonder ▷ vt parcourir, errer par
roar [rɔːʳ] n rugissement m; (of crowd) hurlements mpl; (of vehicle, thunder, storm) grondement m ▷ vi rugir; hurler; gronder; **to ~ with laughter** rire à gorge déployée
roast [rəust] n rôti m ▷ vt (meat) (faire) rôtir; (coffee) griller, torréfier
roast beef n rôti m de bœuf, rosbif m
rob [rɔb] vt (person) voler; (bank) dévaliser; **to ~ sb of sth** voler or dérober qch à qn; (fig: deprive) priver qn de qch
robber ['rɔbəʳ] n bandit m, voleur m
robbery ['rɔbərɪ] n vol m
robe [rəub] n (for ceremony etc) robe f; (also: **bath~**) peignoir m; (US: rug) couverture f ▷ vt revêtir (d'une robe)
robin ['rɔbɪn] n rouge-gorge m
robot ['rəubɔt] n robot m
robust [rəu'bʌst] adj robuste; (material, appetite) solide
rock [rɔk] n (substance) roche f, roc m; (boulder) rocher m, roche; (US: small stone) caillou m; (Brit: sweet) ≈ sucre m d'orge ▷ vt (swing gently: cradle) balancer; (: child) bercer; (shake) ébranler, secouer ▷ vi se balancer, être ébranlé(e) or secoué(e); **on the ~s** (drink) avec des glaçons; (ship) sur les écueils; (marriage etc) en train de craquer; **to ~ the boat** (fig) jouer les trouble-fête
rock and roll n rock (and roll) m, rock'n'roll m
rock-bottom ['rɔk'bɔtəm] n (fig) niveau le plus bas ▷ adj (fig: prices) sacrifié(e); **to reach or touch ~** (price, person) tomber au plus bas
rock climbing n varappe f
rockery ['rɔkərɪ] n (jardin m de) rocaille f
rocket ['rɔkɪt] n fusée f; (Mil) fusée, roquette f; (Culin) roquette f ▷ vi (prices) monter en flèche
rocking chair ['rɔkɪŋ-] n fauteuil m à bascule
rocking horse ['rɔkɪŋ-] n cheval m à bascule
rocky ['rɔkɪ] adj (hill) rocheux(-euse); (path) rocailleux(-euse); (unsteady: table) branlant(e)
rod [rɔd] n (metallic) tringle f; (Tech) tige f; (wooden) baguette f; (also: **fishing ~**) canne f à pêche

rode [rəud] *pt of* **ride**

rodent ['rəudnt] *n* rongeur *m*

rodeo ['rəudɪəu] *n* rodéo *m*

roe [rəu] *n* (*species: also:* **~ deer**) chevreuil *m*; (*of fish: also:* **hard ~**) œufs *mpl* de poisson; **soft ~** laitance *f*

rogue [rəug] *n* coquin(e)

role [rəul] *n* rôle *m*

role-model ['rəulmɔdl] *n* modèle *m* à émuler

role play, role playing *n* jeu *m* de rôle

roll [rəul] *n* rouleau *m*; (*of banknotes*) liasse *f*; (*also:* **bread ~**) petit pain; (*register*) liste *f*; (*sound: of drums etc*) roulement *m*; (*movement: of ship*) roulis *m* ▷ *vt* rouler; (*also:* **~ up**: *string*) enrouler; (*also:* **~ out**: *pastry*) étendre au rouleau, abaisser ▷ *vi* rouler; (*wheel*) tourner; **cheese ~** ≈ sandwich *m* au fromage (*dans un petit pain*); **roll about, roll around** *vi* rouler çà et là; (*person*) se rouler par terre; **roll by** *vi* (*time*) s'écouler, passer; **roll in** *vi* (*mail, cash*) affluer; **roll over** *vi* se retourner; **roll up** *vi* (*inf: arrive*) arriver, s'amener ▷ *vt* (*carpet, cloth, map*) rouler; (*sleeves*) retrousser; **to ~ o.s. up into a ball** se rouler en boule

roll call *n* appel *m*

roller ['rəulə*r*] *n* rouleau *m*; (*wheel*) roulette *f*; (*for road*) rouleau compresseur; (*for hair*) bigoudi *m*

Rollerblades® ['rəulableɪdz] *npl* patins *mpl* en ligne

roller coaster *n* montagnes *fpl* russes

roller skates *npl* patins *mpl* à roulettes

roller-skating ['rəuləskeɪtɪŋ] *n* patin *m* à roulettes; **to go ~** faire du patin à roulettes

rolling ['rəulɪŋ] *adj* (*landscape*) onduleux(-euse)

rolling pin *n* rouleau *m* à pâtisserie

rolling stock *n* (*Rail*) matériel roulant

ROM [rɔm] *n abbr* (*Comput: = read-only memory*) mémoire morte, ROM *f*

Roman ['rəumən] *adj* romain(e) ▷ *n* Romain(e)

Roman Catholic *adj, n* catholique (*m/f*)

romance [rə'mæns] *n* (*love affair*) idylle *f*; (*charm*) poésie *f*; (*novel*) roman *m* à l'eau de rose

Romania [rəu'meɪnɪə] *n* = **Rumania**

Romanian [rəu'meɪnɪən] *adj, n see* **Rumanian**

Roman numeral *n* chiffre romain

romantic [rə'mæntɪk] *adj* romantique; (*novel, attachment*) sentimental(e)

Rome [rəum] *n* Rome

romp [rɔmp] *n* jeux bruyants ▷ *vi* (*also:* **~ about**) s'ébattre, jouer bruyamment; **to ~ home** (*horse*) arriver bon premier

rompers ['rɔmpəz] *npl* barboteuse *f*

roof [ru:f] *n* toit *m*; (*of tunnel, cave*) plafond *m* ▷ *vt* couvrir (d'un toit); **the ~ of the mouth** la voûte du palais

roofing ['ru:fɪŋ] *n* toiture *f*

roof rack *n* (*Aut*) galerie *f*

rook [ruk] *n* (*bird*) freux *m*; (*Chess*) tour *f* ▷ *vt* (*inf: cheat*) rouler, escroquer

room [ru:m] *n* (*in house*) pièce *f*; (*also:* **bed~**) chambre *f* (à coucher); (*in school etc*) salle *f*; (*space*) place *f*; **rooms** *npl* (*lodging*) meublé *m*; **"~s to let"**, (*US*) **"~s for rent"** "chambres à louer"; **is there ~ for this?** est-ce qu'il y a de la place pour ceci?; **to make ~ for sb** faire de la place à qn; **there is ~ for improvement** on peut faire mieux

rooming house ['ru:mɪŋ-] *n* (*US*) maison *f* de rapport

roommate ['ru:mmeɪt] *n* camarade *m/f* de chambre

room service *n* service *m* des chambres (*dans un hôtel*)

roomy ['ru:mɪ] *adj* spacieux(-euse); (*garment*) ample

roost [ru:st] *n* juchoir *m* ▷ *vi* se jucher

rooster ['ru:stə*r*] *n* coq *m*

root [ru:t] *n* (*Bot, Math*) racine *f*; (*fig: of problem*) origine *f*, fond *m* ▷ *vi* (*plant*) s'enraciner; **to take ~** (*plant, idea*) prendre racine; **root about** *vi* (*fig*) fouiller, chercher; **root for** *vt fus* (*inf*) applaudir; **root out** *vt* extirper

rope [rəup] *n* corde *f*; (*Naut*) cordage *m* ▷ *vt* (*box*) corder; (*tie up or together*) attacher; (*climbers: also:* **~ together**) encorder; (*area: also:* **~ off**) interdire l'accès de; (*: divide off*) séparer; **to ~ sb in** (*fig*) embringuer qn; **to know the ~s** (*fig*) être au courant, connaître les ficelles

rosary ['rəuzərɪ] *n* chapelet *m*

rose [rəuz] *pt of* **rise** ▷ *n* rose *f*; (*also:* **~bush**) rosier *m*; (*on watering can*) pomme *f* ▷ *adj* rose

rosé ['rəuzeɪ] *n* rosé *m*

rosebud ['rəuzbʌd] *n* bouton *m* de rose

rosemary ['rəuzmərɪ] *n* romarin *m*

roster ['rɔstə*r*] *n*: **duty ~** tableau *m* de service

rostrum ['rɔstrəm] *n* tribune *f* (*pour un orateur etc*)

rosy ['rəuzɪ] *adj* rose; **a ~ future** un bel avenir

rot [rɔt] *n* (*decay*) pourriture *f*; (*fig: pej: nonsense*) idioties *fpl*, balivernes *fpl* ▷ *vt, vi* pourrir; **to stop the ~** (*Brit fig*) rétablir la situation; **dry ~** pourriture sèche (*du bois*); **wet ~** pourriture (du bois)

rota ['rəutə] *n* liste *f*, tableau *m* de service; **on a ~ basis** par roulement

rotary ['rəutərɪ] *adj* rotatif(-ive)

rotate [rəu'teɪt] *vt* (*revolve*) faire tourner; (*change round: crops*) alterner; (*: jobs*) faire à tour de rôle ▷ *vi* (*revolve*) tourner

rotating [rəu'teɪtɪŋ] *adj* (*movement*) tournant(e)

rotten ['rɔtn] *adj* (*decayed*) pourri(e); (*dishonest*) corrompu(e); (*inf: bad*) mauvais(e), moche; **to feel ~** (*ill*) être mal fichu(e)

rotund [rəu'tʌnd] *adj* rondelet(te); arrondi(e)

rough [rʌf] *adj* (*cloth, skin*) rêche, rugueux(-euse); (*terrain*) accidenté(e); (*path*) rocailleux(-euse); (*voice*) rauque, rude;

r

(*person, manner: coarse*) rude, fruste; (*: violent*) brutal(e); (*district, weather*) mauvais(e); (*sea*) houleux(-euse); (*plan*) ébauché(e); (*guess*) approximatif(-ive) ▷ *n* (*Golf*) rough *m* ▷ *vt*: **to ~ it** vivre à la dure; **the sea is ~ today** la mer est agitée aujourd'hui; **to have a ~ time (of it)** en voir de dures; **~ estimate** approximation *f*; **to play ~** jouer avec brutalité; **to sleep ~** (*Brit*) coucher à la dure; **to feel ~** (*Brit*) être mal fichu(e); **rough out** *vt* (*draft*) ébaucher

roughage ['rʌfɪdʒ] *n* fibres *fpl* diététiques

rough-and-ready ['rʌfən'redɪ] *adj* (*accommodation, method*) rudimentaire

rough copy, rough draft *n* brouillon *m*

roughly ['rʌflɪ] *adv* (*handle*) rudement, brutalement; (*speak*) avec brusquerie; (*make*) grossièrement; (*approximately*) à peu près, en gros; **~ speaking** en gros

roulette [ru:'lɛt] *n* roulette *f*

Roumania *etc* [ru:'meɪnɪə] *n* = **Romania** *etc*

round [raund] *adj* rond(e) ▷ *n* rond *m*, cercle *m*; (*Brit: of toast*) tranche *f*; (*duty: of policeman, milkman etc*) tournée *f*; (*: of doctor*) visites *fpl*; (*game: of cards, in competition*) partie *f*; (*Boxing*) round *m*; (*of talks*) série *f* ▷ *vt* (*corner*) tourner; (*bend*) prendre; (*cape*) doubler ▷ *prep* autour de ▷ *adv*: **right ~, all ~** tout autour; **in ~ figures** en chiffres ronds; **to go the ~s** (*disease, story*) circuler; **the daily ~** (*fig*) la routine quotidienne; **~ of ammunition** cartouche *f*; **~ of applause** applaudissements *mpl*; **~ of drinks** tournée *f*; **~ of sandwiches** (*Brit*) sandwich *m*; **the long way ~** (par) le chemin le plus long; **all (the) year ~** toute l'année; **it's just ~ the corner** c'est juste après le coin; (*fig*) c'est tout près; **to ask sb ~** inviter qn (chez soi); **I'll be ~ at 6 o'clock** je serai là à 6 heures; **to go ~** faire le tour *or* un détour; **to go ~ to sb's (house)** aller chez qn; **to go ~ an obstacle** contourner un obstacle; **go ~ the back** passez par derrière; **to go ~ a house** visiter une maison, faire le tour d'une maison; **enough to go ~** assez pour tout le monde; **she arrived ~ (about) noon** (*Brit*) elle est arrivée vers midi; **~ the clock** 24 heures sur 24; **round off** *vt* (*speech etc*) terminer; **round up** *vt* rassembler; (*criminals*) effectuer une rafle de; (*prices*) arrondir (au chiffre supérieur)

roundabout ['raundəbaut] *n* (*Brit Aut*) rond-point *m* (à sens giratoire); (*at fair*) manège *m* (de chevaux de bois) ▷ *adj* (*route, means*) détourné(e)

rounders ['raundəz] *npl* (*game*) ≈ balle *f* au camp

roundly ['raundlɪ] *adv* (*fig*) tout net, carrément

round trip *n* (voyage *m*) aller et retour *m*

roundup ['raundʌp] *n* rassemblement *m*; (*of criminals*) rafle *f*; **a ~ of the latest news** un rappel des derniers événements

rouse [rauz] *vt* (*wake up*) réveiller; (*stir up*) susciter, provoquer; (*interest*) éveiller; (*suspicions*) susciter, éveiller

rousing ['rauzɪŋ] *adj* (*welcome*) enthousiaste

route [ru:t] *n* itinéraire *m*; (*of bus*) parcours *m*; (*of trade, shipping*) route *f*; **"all ~s"** (*Aut*) "toutes directions"; **the best ~ to London** le meilleur itinéraire pour aller à Londres

router ['ru:tə', (*US*) 'rautə'] *n* (*Comput*) routeur *m*

routine [ru:'ti:n] *adj* (*work*) ordinaire, courant(e); (*procedure*) d'usage ▷ *n* (*habits*) habitudes *fpl*; (*pej*) train-train *m*; (*Theat*) numéro *m*; **daily ~** occupations journalières

row[1] [rəu] *n* (*line*) rangée *f*; (*of people, seats, Knitting*) rang *m*; (*behind one another: of cars, people*) file *f* ▷ *vi* (*in boat*) ramer; (*as sport*) faire de l'aviron ▷ *vt* (*boat*) faire aller à la rame *or* à l'aviron; **in a ~** (*fig*) d'affilée

row[2] [rau] *n* (*noise*) vacarme *m*; (*dispute*) dispute *f*, querelle *f*; (*scolding*) réprimande *f*, savon *m* ▷ *vi* (*also*: **to have a ~**) se disputer, se quereller

rowboat ['rəubəut] *n* (*US*) canot *m* (à rames)

rowdy ['raudɪ] *adj* chahuteur(-euse); bagarreur(-euse); *n* voyou *m*

rowing ['rəuɪŋ] *n* canotage *m*; (*as sport*) aviron *m*

rowing boat *n* (*Brit*) canot *m* (à rames)

royal ['rɔɪəl] *adj* royal(e)

Royal Air Force *n* (*Brit*) armée de l'air britannique

royalty ['rɔɪəltɪ] *n* (*royal persons*) (membres *mpl* de la) famille royale; (*payment: to author*) droits *mpl* d'auteur; (*: to inventor*) royalties *fpl*

rpm *abbr* (= *revolutions per minute*) t/mn (= = *tours/minute*)

R.S.V.P. *abbr* (= *répondez s'il vous plaît*) RSVP

Rt. Hon. *abbr* (*Brit*: = *Right Honourable*) titre donné aux députés de la Chambre des communes

rub [rʌb] *n* (*with cloth*) coup *m* de chiffon *or* de torchon; (*on person*) friction *f*; **to give sth a ~** donner un coup de chiffon *or* de torchon à qch ▷ *vt* frotter; (*person*) frictionner; (*hands*) se frotter; **to ~ sb up** (*Brit*) *or* **to ~ sb** (*US*) **the wrong way** prendre qn à rebrousse-poil; **rub down** *vt* (*body*) frictionner; (*horse*) bouchonner; **rub in** *vt* (*ointment*) faire pénétrer; **rub off** *vi* partir; **to ~ off on** déteindre sur; **rub out** *vt* effacer ▷ *vi* s'effacer

rubber ['rʌbə'] *n* caoutchouc *m*; (*Brit: eraser*) gomme *f* (à effacer)

rubber band *n* élastique *m*

rubber gloves *npl* gants *mpl* en caoutchouc

rubber plant *n* caoutchouc *m* (*plante verte*)

rubbish ['rʌbɪʃ] *n* (*from household*) ordures *fpl*; (*fig: pej*) choses *fpl* sans valeur; camelote *f*; (*nonsense*) bêtises *fpl*, idioties *fpl* ▷ *vt* (*Brit inf*) dénigrer, rabaisser; **what you've just said is ~** tu viens de dire une bêtise

rubbish bin *n* (*Brit*) boîte *f* à ordures, poubelle *f*

rubbish dump *n* (*Brit*: *in town*) décharge publique, dépotoir *m*

rubble ['rʌbl] n décombres mpl; (smaller) gravats mpl; (Constr) blocage m

ruby ['ru:bɪ] n rubis m

rucksack ['rʌksæk] n sac m à dos

rudder ['rʌdə'] n gouvernail m

ruddy ['rʌdɪ] adj (face) coloré(e); (inf: damned) sacré(e), fichu(e)

rude [ru:d] adj (impolite: person) impoli(e); (: word, manners) grossier(-ière); (shocking) indécent(e), inconvenant(e); **to be ~ to sb** être grossier envers qn

ruffle ['rʌfl] vt (hair) ébouriffer; (clothes) chiffonner; (water) agiter; (fig: person) émouvoir, faire perdre son flegme à; **to get ~d** s'énerver

rug [rʌg] n petit tapis; (Brit: blanket) couverture f

rugby ['rʌgbɪ] n (also: **~ football**) rugby m

rugged ['rʌgɪd] adj (landscape) accidenté(e); (features, character) rude; (determination) farouche

ruin ['ru:ɪn] n ruine f ▷ vt ruiner; (spoil: clothes) abîmer; (: event) gâcher; **ruins** npl (of building) ruine(s); **in ~** en ruine

rule [ru:l] n règle f; (regulation) règlement m; (government) autorité f, gouvernement m; (dominion etc): **under British ~** sous l'autorité britannique ▷ vt (country) gouverner; (person) dominer; (decide) décider ▷ vi commander; décider; (Law): **to ~ against/in favour of/on** statuer contre/en faveur de/sur; **to ~ that** (umpire, judge etc) décider que; **it's against the ~s** c'est contraire au règlement; **by ~ of thumb** à vue de nez; **as a ~** normalement, en règle générale; **rule out** vt exclure; **murder cannot be ~d out** l'hypothèse d'un meurtre ne peut être exclue

ruled [ru:ld] adj (paper) réglé(e)

ruler ['ru:lə'] n (sovereign) souverain(e); (leader) chef m (d'État); (for measuring) règle f

ruling ['ru:lɪŋ] adj (party) au pouvoir; (class) dirigeant(e) ▷ n (Law) décision f

rum [rʌm] n rhum m ▷ adj (Brit inf) bizarre

Rumania [ru:'meɪnɪə] n Roumanie f

Rumanian [ru:'meɪnɪən] adj roumain(e) ▷ n Roumain(e); (Ling) roumain m

rumble ['rʌmbl] n grondement m; (of stomach, pipe) gargouillement m ▷ vi gronder; (stomach, pipe) gargouiller

rummage ['rʌmɪdʒ] vi fouiller

rumour, (US) **rumor** ['ru:mə'] n rumeur f, bruit m (qui court) ▷ vt: **it is ~ed that** le bruit court que

rump [rʌmp] n (of animal) croupe f

rump steak n romsteck m

rumpus ['rʌmpəs] n (inf) tapage m, chahut m; (quarrel) prise f de bec; **to kick up a ~** faire toute une histoire

run [rʌn] (pt **ran**, pp **run**) [ræn, rʌn] n (race) course f; (outing) tour m or promenade f (en voiture); (distance travelled) parcours m, trajet m; (series) suite f, série f; (Theat) série de représentations; (Ski) piste f; (Cricket, Baseball) point m; (in tights, stockings) maille filée, échelle f ▷ vt (business) diriger; (competition, course) organiser; (hotel, house) tenir; (race) participer à; (Comput: program) exécuter; (force through: rope, pipe): **to ~ sth through** faire passer qch à travers; (to pass: hand, finger): **to ~ sth over** promener or passer qch sur; (water, bath) faire couler; (Press: feature) publier ▷ vi courir; (pass: road etc) passer; (work: machine, factory) marcher; (bus, train) circuler; (continue: play) se jouer, être à l'affiche; (: contract) être valide or en vigueur; (slide: drawer etc) glisser; (flow: river, bath, nose) couler; (colours, washing) déteindre; (in election) être candidat, se présenter; **at a ~** au pas de course; **to go for a ~** aller courir or faire un peu de course à pied; (in car) faire un tour or une promenade (en voiture); **to break into a ~** se mettre à courir; **a ~ of luck** une série de coups de chance; **to have the ~ of sb's house** avoir la maison de qn à sa disposition; **there was a ~ on** (meat, tickets) les gens se sont rués sur; **in the long ~** à la longue, à longue échéance; **in the short ~** à brève échéance, à court terme; **on the ~** en fuite; **to make a ~ for it** s'enfuir; **I'll ~ you to the station** je vais vous emmener or conduire à la gare; **to ~ errands** faire des commissions; **the train ~s between Gatwick and Victoria** le train assure le service entre Gatwick et Victoria; **the bus ~s every 20 minutes** il y a un autobus toutes les 20 minutes; **it's very cheap to ~** (car, machine) c'est très économique; **to ~ on petrol** or (US) **gas/on diesel/off batteries** marcher à l'essence/au diesel/sur piles; **to ~ for president** être candidat à la présidence; **to ~ a risk** courir un risque; **their losses ran into millions** leurs pertes se sont élevées à plusieurs millions; **to be ~ off one's feet** (Brit) ne plus savoir où donner de la tête; **run about** vi (children) courir çà et là; **run across** vt fus (find) trouver par hasard; **run after** vt fus (to catch up) courir après; (chase) poursuivre; **run around** vi = **run about**; **run away** vi s'enfuir; **run down** vi (clock) s'arrêter (faute d'avoir été remonté) ▷ vt (Aut: knock over) renverser; (Brit: reduce: production) réduire progressivement; (: factory/shop) réduire progressivement la production/l'activité de; (: criticize) critiquer, dénigrer; **to be ~ down** (tired) être fatigué(e) or à plat; **run in** vt (Brit: car) roder; **run into** vt fus (meet: person) rencontrer par hasard; (: trouble) se heurter à; (collide with) heurter; **to ~ into debt** contracter des dettes; **run off** vi s'enfuir ▷ vt (water) laisser s'écouler; (copies) tirer; **run out** vi (person) sortir en courant; (liquid) couler; (lease) expirer; (money) être épuisé(e); **run out of** vt fus se trouver à court de; **I've ~ out of petrol** or (US)

gas je suis en panne d'essence; **run over** vt (*Aut*) écraser ▷ vt fus (*revise*) revoir, reprendre; **run through** vt fus (*recap*) reprendre, revoir; (*play*) répéter; **run up** vi: **to ~ up against** (*difficulties*) se heurter à ▷ vt: **to ~ up a debt** s'endetter

runaway ['rʌnəweɪ] adj (*horse*) emballé(e); (*truck*) fou/folle; (*person*) fugitif(-ive); (*child*) fugueur(-euse); (*inflation*) galopant(e)

rung [rʌŋ] pp of **ring** ▷ n (*of ladder*) barreau m

runner ['rʌnəʳ] n (*in race: person*) coureur(-euse); (: *horse*) partant m; (*on sledge*) patin m; (*for drawer etc*) coulisseau m; (*carpet: in hall etc*) chemin m

runner bean n (*Brit*) haricot m (à rames)

runner-up [rʌnərʌp] n second(e)

running ['rʌnɪŋ] n (*in race etc*) course f; (*of business, organization*) direction f, gestion f; (*of event*) organisation f; (*of machine etc*) marche f, fonctionnement m ▷ adj (*water*) courant(e); (*commentary*) suivi(e); **6 days ~** 6 jours de suite; **to be in/out of the ~ for sth** être/ne pas être sur les rangs pour qch

running commentary n commentaire détaillé

running costs npl (*of business*) frais mpl de gestion; (*of car*): **the ~ are high** elle revient cher

runny ['rʌnɪ] adj qui coule

run-of-the-mill ['rʌnəvðə'mɪl] adj ordinaire, banal(e)

runt [rʌnt] n avorton m

run-up ['rʌnʌp] n (*Brit*): **~ to sth** période f précédant qch

runway ['rʌnweɪ] n (*Aviat*) piste f (d'envol or d'atterrissage)

rupture ['rʌptʃəʳ] n (*Med*) hernie f ▷ vt: **to ~ o.s.** se donner une hernie

rural ['ruərl] adj rural(e)

rush [rʌʃ] n course précipitée; (*of crowd, Comm: sudden demand*) ruée f; (*hurry*) hâte f; (*of anger, joy*) accès m; (*current*) flot m; (*Bot*) jonc m; (*for chair*) paille f ▷ vt (*hurry*) transporter or envoyer d'urgence; (*attack: town etc*) prendre d'assaut; (*Brit inf: overcharge*) estamper; faire payer ▷ vi se précipiter; **don't ~ me!** laissez-moi le temps de souffler!; **to ~ sth off** (*do quickly*) faire qch à la hâte; (*send*) envoyer qch d'urgence; **is there any ~ for this?** est-ce urgent?; **we've had a ~ of orders** nous avons reçu une avalanche de commandes; **I'm in a ~ (to do)** je suis vraiment pressé (de faire); **gold ~** ruée vers l'or; **rush through** vt fus (*work*) exécuter à la hâte ▷ vt (*Comm: order*) exécuter d'urgence

rush hour n heures fpl de pointe or d'affluence

rusk [rʌsk] n biscotte f

Russia ['rʌʃə] n Russie f

Russian ['rʌʃən] adj russe ▷ n Russe m/f; (*Ling*) russe m

rust [rʌst] n rouille f ▷ vi rouiller

rustic ['rʌstɪk] adj rustique ▷ n (*pej*) rustaud(e)

rustle ['rʌsl] vi bruire, produire un bruissement ▷ vt (*paper*) froisser; (*US: cattle*) voler

rustproof ['rʌstpruːf] adj inoxydable

rusty ['rʌstɪ] adj rouillé(e)

rut [rʌt] n ornière f; (*Zool*) rut m; **to be in a ~** (*fig*) suivre l'ornière, s'encroûter

ruthless ['ruːθlɪs] adj sans pitié, impitoyable

RV abbr (= revised version) traduction anglaise de la Bible de 1885 ▷ n abbr (*US*) = **recreational vehicle**

rye [raɪ] n seigle m

S

Sabbath ['sæbəθ] n (Jewish) sabbat m; (Christian) dimanche m

sabotage ['sæbətɑ:ʒ] n sabotage m ▷ vt saboter

saccharin, saccharine ['sækərɪn] n saccharine f

sachet ['sæʃeɪ] n sachet m

sack [sæk] n (bag) sac m ▷ vt (dismiss) renvoyer, mettre à la porte; (plunder) piller, mettre à sac; **to give sb the ~** renvoyer qn, mettre qn à la porte; **to get the ~** être renvoyé(e) or mis(e) à la porte

sacking ['sækɪŋ] n toile f à sac; (dismissal) renvoi m

sacrament ['sækrəmənt] n sacrement m

sacred ['seɪkrɪd] adj sacré(e)

sacrifice ['sækrɪfaɪs] n sacrifice m ▷ vt sacrifier; **to make ~s (for sb)** se sacrifier or faire des sacrifices (pour qn)

sad [sæd] adj (unhappy) triste; (deplorable) triste, fâcheux(-euse); (inf: pathetic: thing) triste, lamentable; (: person) minable

saddle ['sædl] n selle f ▷ vt (horse) seller; **to be ~d with sth** (inf) avoir qch sur les bras

saddlebag ['sædlbæg] n sacoche f

sadistic [sə'dɪstɪk] adj sadique

sadly ['sædlɪ] adv tristement; (unfortunately) malheureusement; (seriously) fort

sadness ['sædnɪs] n tristesse f

s.a.e. n abbr (Brit: = stamped addressed envelope) enveloppe affranchie pour la réponse

safari [sə'fɑ:rɪ] n safari m

safe [seɪf] adj (out of danger) hors de danger, en sécurité; (not dangerous) sans danger; (cautious) prudent(e); (sure: bet) assuré(e) ▷ n coffre-fort m; **~ from** à l'abri de; **~ and sound** sain(e) et sauf/sauve; **(just) to be on the ~ side** pour plus de sûreté, par précaution; **to play ~** ne prendre aucun risque; **it is ~ to say that …** on peut dire sans crainte que …; **~ journey!** bon voyage!

safe-conduct [seɪf'kɔndʌkt] n sauf-conduit m

safe-deposit ['seɪfdɪpɔzɪt] n (vault) dépôt m de coffres-forts; (box) coffre-fort m

safeguard ['seɪfgɑ:d] n sauvegarde f, protection f ▷ vt sauvegarder, protéger

safekeeping ['seɪf'ki:pɪŋ] n bonne garde

safely ['seɪflɪ] adv (assume, say) sans risque d'erreur; (drive, arrive) sans accident; **I can ~ say …** je peux dire à coup sûr …

safe sex n rapports sexuels protégés

safety ['seɪftɪ] n sécurité f; **~ first!** la sécurité d'abord!

safety belt n ceinture f de sécurité

safety pin n épingle f de sûreté or de nourrice

safety valve n soupape f de sûreté

saffron ['sæfrən] n safran m

sag [sæg] vi s'affaisser, fléchir; (hem, breasts) pendre

sage [seɪdʒ] n (herb) sauge f; (person) sage m

Sagittarius [sædʒɪ'tɛərɪəs] n le Sagittaire; **to be ~** être du Sagittaire

Sahara [sə'hɑ:rə] n: **the ~ (Desert)** le désert du Sahara m

said [sɛd] pt, pp of **say**

sail [seɪl] n (on boat) voile f; (trip): **to go for a ~** faire un tour en bateau ▷ vt (boat) manœuvrer, piloter ▷ vi (travel: ship) avancer, naviguer; (: passenger) aller or se rendre (en bateau); (set off) partir, prendre la mer; (Sport) faire de la voile; **they ~ed into Le Havre** ils sont entrés dans le port du Havre; **sail through** vi, vt fus (fig) réussir haut la main

sailboat ['seɪlbəut] n (US) bateau m à voiles, voilier m

sailing ['seɪlɪŋ] n (Sport) voile f; **to go ~** faire de la voile

sailing boat n bateau m à voiles, voilier m

sailing ship n grand voilier

sailor ['seɪlə'] n marin m, matelot m

saint [seɪnt] n saint(e)

sake [seɪk] n: **for the ~ of** (out of concern for) pour (l'amour de), dans l'intérêt de; (out of consideration for) par égard pour; (in order to achieve) pour plus de, par souci de; **arguing for arguing's ~** discuter pour (le plaisir de) discuter; **for heaven's ~!** pour l'amour du ciel!; **for the ~ of argument** à titre d'exemple

salad ['sæləd] n salade f; **tomato ~** salade de tomates

salad bowl n saladier m

salad cream n (Brit) (sorte f de) mayonnaise f
salad dressing n vinaigrette f
salami [sə'lɑːmɪ] n salami m
salary ['sælərɪ] n salaire m, traitement m
sale [seɪl] n vente f; (at reduced prices) soldes
mpl; **sales** npl (total amount sold) chiffre m de
ventes; **"for ~"** "à vendre"; **on ~** en vente; **on
~ or return** vendu(e) avec faculté de retour;
closing-down or **liquidation ~** (US)
liquidation f (avant fermeture); **~ and lease
back** n cession-bail f
saleroom ['seɪlruːm] n salle f des ventes
sales assistant, (US) **sales clerk** n
vendeur(-euse)
salesman ['seɪlzmən] irreg n (in shop)
vendeur m; (representative) représentant m
de commerce
salesperson ['seɪlzpɜːsn] irreg n (in shop)
vendeur(-euse)
sales rep n (Comm) représentant(e) m/f
saleswoman ['seɪlzwʊmən] irreg n (in shop)
vendeuse f
saline ['seɪlaɪn] adj salin(e)
saliva [sə'laɪvə] n salive f
salmon ['sæmən] n (pl inv) saumon m
salon ['sælɔn] n salon m
saloon [sə'luːn] n (US) bar m; (Brit Aut)
berline f; (ship's lounge) salon m
salt [sɔːlt] n sel m ▷ vt saler ▷ cpd de sel;
(Culin) salé(e); **an old ~** un vieux loup de mer;
salt away vt mettre de côté
salt cellar n salière f
saltwater ['sɔːlt'wɔːtəʳ] adj (fish etc) (d'eau)
de mer
salty ['sɔːltɪ] adj salé(e)
salute [sə'luːt] n salut m; (of guns) salve f ▷ vt
saluer
salvage ['sælvɪdʒ] n (saving) sauvetage m;
(things saved) biens sauvés or récupérés ▷ vt
sauver, récupérer
salvation [sæl'veɪʃən] n salut m
Salvation Army [sæl'veɪʃən-] n Armée f
du Salut
same [seɪm] adj même ▷ pron: **the ~** le/la
même, les mêmes; **the ~ book as** le même
livre que; **on the ~ day** le même jour; **at the ~
time** en même temps; (yet) néanmoins; **all
or just the ~** tout de même, quand même;
they're one and the ~ (person/thing) c'est une
seule et même personne/chose; **to do the ~**
faire de même, en faire autant; **to do the ~
as sb** faire comme qn; **and the ~ to you!** et à
vous de même!; (after insult) toi-même!;
~ here! moi aussi!; **the ~ again!** (in bar etc)
la même chose!
sample ['sɑːmpl] n échantillon m; (Med)
prélèvement m ▷ vt (food, wine) goûter; **to
take a ~** prélever un échantillon; **free ~**
échantillon gratuit
sanction ['sæŋkʃən] n approbation f,
sanction f ▷ vt cautionner, sanctionner;
sanctions npl (Pol) sanctions f; **to impose**

economic ~s on or **against** prendre des
sanctions économiques contre
sanctity ['sæŋktɪtɪ] n sainteté f, caractère m
sacré
sanctuary ['sæŋktjʊərɪ] n (holy place)
sanctuaire m; (refuge) asile m; (for wildlife)
réserve f
sand [sænd] n sable m ▷ vt sabler; (also:
~ down: wood etc) poncer
sandal ['sændl] n sandale f
sandbox ['sændbɔks] n (US: for children) tas m
de sable
sand castle ['sændkɑːsl] n château m de
sable
sand dune n dune f de sable
sandpaper ['sændpeɪpəʳ] n papier m
de verre
sandpit ['sændpɪt] n (Brit: for children) tas m de
sable
sands [sændz] npl plage f (de sable)
sandstone ['sændstəʊn] n grès m
sandwich ['sændwɪtʃ] n sandwich m ▷ vt
(also: **~ in**) intercaler; **~ed between** pris en
sandwich entre; **cheese/ham ~** sandwich au
fromage/jambon
sandwich course n (Brit) cours m de
formation professionnelle
sandy ['sændɪ] adj sablonneux(-euse);
couvert(e) de sable; (colour) sable inv, blond
roux inv
sane [seɪn] adj (person) sain(e) d'esprit;
(outlook) sensé(e), sain(e)
sang [sæŋ] pt of **sing**
sanitary ['sænɪtərɪ] adj (system, arrangements)
sanitaire; (clean) hygiénique
sanitary towel, (US) **sanitary napkin**
['sænɪtərɪ-] n serviette f hygiénique
sanitation [sænɪ'teɪʃən] n (in house)
installations fpl sanitaires; (in town)
système m sanitaire
sanitation department n (US) service m
de voirie
sanity ['sænɪtɪ] n santé mentale; (common
sense) bon sens
sank [sæŋk] pt of **sink**
Santa Claus [sæntə'klɔːz] n le Père Noël
sap [sæp] n (of plants) sève f ▷ vt (strength)
saper, miner
sapling ['sæplɪŋ] n jeune arbre m
sapphire ['sæfaɪəʳ] n saphir m
sarcasm ['sɑːkæzm] n sarcasme m, raillerie f
sarcastic [sɑː'kæstɪk] adj sarcastique
sardine [sɑː'diːn] n sardine f
Sardinia [sɑː'dɪnɪə] n Sardaigne f
SASE n abbr (US: = self-addressed stamped envelope)
enveloppe affranchie pour la réponse
sash [sæʃ] n écharpe f
sat [sæt] pt, pp of **sit**
Sat. abbr (= Saturday) sa
satchel ['sætʃl] n cartable m
satellite ['sætəlaɪt] adj, n satellite m
satellite dish n antenne f parabolique

satellite navigation system n système m de navigation par satellite

satellite television n télévision f par satellite

satin ['sætɪn] n satin m ▷ adj en or de satin, satiné(e); **with a ~ finish** satiné(e)

satire ['sætaɪəʳ] n satire f

satisfaction [sætɪs'fækʃən] n satisfaction f

satisfactory [sætɪs'fæktərɪ] adj satisfaisant(e)

satisfied ['sætɪsfaɪd] adj satisfait(e); **to be ~ with sth** être satisfait de qch

satisfy ['sætɪsfaɪ] vt satisfaire, contenter; (convince) convaincre, persuader; **to ~ the requirements** remplir les conditions; **to ~ sb/o.s. of sth** convaincre qn (que); **to ~ o.s. of sth** vérifier qch, s'assurer de qch

satisfying ['sætɪsfaɪɪŋ] adj satisfaisant(e)

Saturday ['sætədɪ] n samedi m; see also **Tuesday**

sauce [sɔːs] n sauce f

saucepan ['sɔːspən] n casserole f

saucer ['sɔːsəʳ] n soucoupe f

Saudi Arabia n Arabie f Saoudite

Saudi (Arabian) ['saudi] adj saoudien(ne) ▷ n Saoudien(ne)

sauna ['sɔːnə] n sauna m

saunter ['sɔːntəʳ] vi: **to ~ to** aller en flânant or se balader jusqu'à

sausage ['sɔsɪdʒ] n saucisse f; (salami etc) saucisson m

sausage roll n friand m

sautéed ['sauteɪd] adj sauté(e)

savage ['sævɪdʒ] adj (cruel, fierce) brutal(e), féroce; (primitive) primitif(-ive), sauvage ▷ n sauvage m/f ▷ vt attaquer férocement

save [seɪv] vt (person, belongings) sauver; (money) mettre de côté, économiser; (time) (faire) gagner, (keep) garder; (Comput) sauvegarder; (Sport: stop) arrêter; (avoid: trouble) éviter ▷ vi (also: ~ **up**) mettre de l'argent de côté ▷ n (Sport) arrêt m (du ballon) ▷ prep sauf, à l'exception de; **it will ~ me an hour** ça me fera gagner une heure; **to ~ face** sauver la face; **God ~ the Queen!** vive la Reine!

saving ['seɪvɪŋ] n économie f ▷ adj: **the ~ grace of** ce qui rachète; **savings** npl économies fpl; **to make ~s** faire des économies

savings account n compte m d'épargne

savings and loan association (US) n ≈ société f de crédit immobilier

savings bank n caisse f d'épargne

saviour, (US) **savior** ['seɪvjəʳ] n sauveur m

savour, (US) **savor** ['seɪvəʳ] n saveur f, goût m ▷ vt savourer

savoury, (US) **savory** ['seɪvərɪ] adj savoureux(-euse); (dish: not sweet) salé(e)

saw [sɔː] pt of **see** ▷ n (tool) scie f ▷ vt (pt **sawed**, pp **sawed** or **sawn**) [sɔːn] scier; **to ~ sth up** débiter qch à la scie

sawdust ['sɔːdʌst] n sciure f

sawmill ['sɔːmɪl] n scierie f

sawn [sɔːn] pp of **saw**

sawn-off ['sɔːnɔf], (US) **sawed-off** ['sɔːdɔf] adj: **~ shotgun** carabine f à canon scié

sax [sæks] (inf) n saxo m

saxophone ['sæksəfəun] n saxophone m

say [seɪ] n: **to have one's ~** dire ce qu'on a à dire ▷ vt (pt, pp **said**) [sɛd] dire; **to have a ~** avoir voix au chapitre; **could you ~ that again?** pourriez-vous répéter ce que vous venez de dire?; **to ~ yes/no** dire oui/non; **she said (that) I was to give you this** elle m'a chargé de vous remettre ceci; **my watch ~s 3 o'clock** ma montre indique 3 heures, il est 3 heures à ma montre; **shall we ~ Tuesday?** disons mardi?; **that doesn't ~ much for him** ce n'est pas vraiment à son honneur; **when all is said and done** en fin de compte, en définitive; **there is something or a lot to be said for it** cela a des avantages; **that is to ~** c'est-à-dire; **to ~ nothing of** sans compter; **~ that ...** mettons or disons que ...; **that goes without ~ing** cela va sans dire, cela va de soi

saying ['seɪɪŋ] n dicton m, proverbe m

scab [skæb] n croûte f; (pej) jaune m

scaffold ['skæfəld] n échafaud m

scaffolding ['skæfəldɪŋ] n échafaudage m

scald [skɔːld] n brûlure f ▷ vt ébouillanter

scale [skeɪl] n (of fish) écaille f; (Mus) gamme f; (of ruler, thermometer etc) graduation f, échelle f (graduée); (of salaries, fees etc) barème m; (of map, also size, extent) échelle f ▷ vt (mountain) escalader; (fish) écailler; **scales** npl balance f; (larger) bascule f; (also: **bathroom ~s**) pèse-personne m inv; **pay ~** échelle des salaires; **~ of charges** tableau m des tarifs; **on a large ~** sur une grande échelle, en grand; **to draw sth to ~** dessiner qch à l'échelle; **small-~ model** modèle réduit; **scale down** vt réduire

scallion ['skæljən] n oignon m; (US: salad onion) ciboule f; (: shallot) échalote f; (: leek) poireau m

scallop ['skɔləp] n coquille f Saint-Jacques; (Sewing) feston m

scalp [skælp] n cuir chevelu ▷ vt scalper

scalpel ['skælpl] n scalpel m

scam [skæm] n (inf) arnaque f

scampi ['skæmpɪ] npl langoustines (frites), scampi mpl

scan [skæn] vt (examine) scruter, examiner; (glance at quickly) parcourir; (poetry) scander; (TV, Radar) balayer ▷ n (Med) scanographie f

scandal ['skændl] n scandale m; (gossip) ragots mpl

Scandinavia [skændɪ'neɪvɪə] n Scandinavie f

Scandinavian [skændɪ'neɪvɪən] adj scandinave ▷ n Scandinave m/f

scanner ['skænəʳ] n (Radar, Med) scanner m, scanographe m; (Comput) scanner

scant [skænt] adj insuffisant(e)

S

scanty ['skæntɪ] *adj* peu abondant(e),
insuffisant(e), maigre

scapegoat ['skeɪpgəʊt] *n* bouc *m* émissaire

scar [skɑ:ʳ] *n* cicatrice *f* ▷ *vt* laisser une
cicatrice *or* une marque à

scarce [skɛəs] *adj* rare, peu abondant(e); **to
make o.s. ~** (*inf*) se sauver

scarcely ['skɛəslɪ] *adv* à peine, presque pas;
~ anybody pratiquement personne; **I can ~
believe it** j'ai du mal à le croire

scarcity ['skɛəsɪtɪ] *n* rareté *f*, manque *m*,
pénurie *f*

scare [skɛəʳ] *n* peur *f*, panique *f* ▷ *vt* effrayer,
faire peur à; **to ~ sb stiff** faire une peur bleue
à qn; **bomb ~ alerte** *f* à la bombe; **scare away,
scare off** *vt* faire fuir

scarecrow ['skɛəkrəʊ] *n* épouvantail *m*

scared ['skɛəd] *adj*: **to be ~** avoir peur

scarf (*pl* **scarves**) [skɑ:f, skɑ:vz] *n* (*long*)
écharpe *f*; (*square*) foulard *m*

scarlet ['skɑ:lɪt] *adj* écarlate

scarlet fever *n* scarlatine *f*

scarves [skɑ:vz] *npl of* **scarf**

scary ['skɛərɪ] *adj* (*inf*) effrayant(e); (*film*) qui
fait peur

scathing ['skeɪðɪŋ] *adj* cinglant(e), acerbe;
to be ~ about sth être très critique vis-à-vis
de qch

scatter ['skætəʳ] *vt* éparpiller, répandre;
(*crowd*) disperser ▷ *vi* se disperser

scatterbrained ['skætəbreɪnd] *adj*
écervelé(e), étourdi(e)

scavenger ['skævəndʒəʳ] *n* éboueur *m*

scenario [sɪ'nɑ:rɪəʊ] *n* scénario *m*

scene [si:n] *n* (*Theat, fig etc*) scène *f*; (*of crime,
accident*) lieu(x) *m*(*pl*), endroit *m*; (*sight, view*)
spectacle *m*, vue *f*; **behind the ~s** (*also fig*)
dans les coulisses; **to make a ~** (*inf*: *fuss*) faire
une scène *or* toute une histoire; **to appear on
the ~** (*also fig*) faire son apparition, arriver;
the political ~ la situation politique

scenery ['si:nərɪ] *n* (*Theat*) décor(s) *m*(*pl*);
(*landscape*) paysage *m*

scenic ['si:nɪk] *adj* scénique; offrant de beaux
paysages *or* panoramas

scent [sɛnt] *n* parfum *m*, odeur *f*; (*fig: track*)
piste *f*; (*sense of smell*) odorat *m* ▷ *vt* parfumer;
(*smell: also fig*) flairer; (*also*: **to put** *or* **throw sb
off the ~**: *fig*) mettre qn sur une mauvaise
piste

sceptical, (*US*) **skeptical** ['skɛptɪkl] *adj*
sceptique

schedule ['ʃɛdju:l, *US*: 'skɛdju:l] *n*
programme *m*, plan *m*; (*of trains*) horaire *m*;
(*of prices etc*) barème *m*, tarif *m* ▷ *vt* prévoir;
as ~d comme prévu; **on ~** à l'heure (prévue);
à la date prévue; **to be ahead of/behind ~**
avoir de l'avance/du retard; **we are working
to a very tight ~** notre programme de travail
est très serré *or* intense; **everything went
according to ~** tout s'est passé comme prévu

scheduled flight *n* vol régulier

scheme [ski:m] *n* plan *m*, projet *m*; (*method*)
procédé *m*; (*plot*) complot *m*, combine *f*;
(*arrangement*) arrangement *m*, classification *f*;
(*pension scheme etc*) régime *m* ▷ *vt, vi*
comploter, manigancer; **colour ~**
combinaison *f* de(s) couleurs

scheming ['ski:mɪŋ] *adj* rusé(e), intrigant(e)
▷ *n* manigances *fpl*, intrigues *fpl*

schizophrenic [skɪtsə'frɛnɪk] *adj*
schizophrène

scholar ['skɔləʳ] *n* érudit(e); (*pupil*)
boursier(-ère)

scholarship ['skɔləʃɪp] *n* érudition *f*; (*grant*)
bourse *f* (d'études)

school [sku:l] *n* (*gen*) école *f*; (*secondary school*)
collège *m*; lycée *m*; (*in university*) faculté *f*; (*US:
university*) université *f*; (*of fish*) banc *m* ▷ *cpd*
scolaire ▷ *vt* (*animal*) dresser

schoolbook ['sku:lbʊk] *n* livre *m* scolaire *or*
de classe

schoolboy ['sku:lbɔɪ] *n* écolier *m*; (*at secondary
school*) collégien *m*; lycéen *m*

schoolchildren ['sku:ltʃɪldrən] *npl* écoliers
mpl; (*at secondary school*) collégiens *mpl*;
lycéens *mpl*

schoolgirl ['sku:lgə:l] *n* écolière *f*; (*at
secondary school*) collégienne *f*; lycéenne *f*

schooling ['sku:lɪŋ] *n* instruction *f*, études *fpl*

schoolmaster ['sku:lmɑ:stəʳ] *n* (*primary*)
instituteur *m*; (*secondary*) professeur *m*

schoolmistress ['sku:lmɪstrɪs] *n* (*primary*)
institutrice *f*; (*secondary*) professeur *m*

schoolteacher ['sku:lti:tʃəʳ] *n* (*primary*)
instituteur(-trice); (*secondary*) professeur *m*

science ['saɪəns] *n* science *f*; **the ~s** les
sciences; (*Scol*) les matières *fpl* scientifiques

science fiction *n* science-fiction *f*

scientific [saɪən'tɪfɪk] *adj* scientifique

scientist ['saɪəntɪst] *n* scientifique *m/f*;
(*eminent*) savant *m*

sci-fi ['saɪfaɪ] *n abbr* (*inf*: = *science fiction*) SF *f*

scissors ['sɪzəz] *npl* ciseaux *mpl*; **a pair of ~**
une paire de ciseaux

scoff [skɔf] *vt* (*Brit inf: eat*) avaler, bouffer ▷ *vi*:
to ~ (at) (*mock*) se moquer (de)

scold [skəʊld] *vt* gronder, attraper,
réprimander

scone [skɔn] *n* sorte de petit pain rond au lait

scoop [sku:p] *n* pelle *f* (à main); (*for ice cream*)
boule *f* à glace; (*Press*) reportage exclusif *or* à
sensation; **scoop out** *vt* évider, creuser;
scoop up *vt* ramasser

scooter ['sku:təʳ] *n* (*motor cycle*) scooter *m*;
(*toy*) trottinette *f*

scope [skəʊp] *n* (*capacity: of plan, undertaking*)
portée *f*, envergure *f*; (: *of person*) compétence
f, capacités *fpl*; (*opportunity*) possibilités *fpl*;
within the ~ of dans les limites de; **there is
plenty of ~ for improvement** (*Brit*) cela
pourrait être beaucoup mieux

scorch [skɔ:tʃ] *vt* (*clothes*) brûler (légèrement),
roussir; (*earth, grass*) dessécher, brûler

scorching ['skɔːtʃɪŋ] *adj* torride, brûlant(e)

score [skɔːʳ] *n* score *m*, décompte *m* des points; (*Mus*) partition *f* ▷ *vt* (*goal, point*) marquer; (*success*) remporter; (*cut: leather, wood, card*) entailler, inciser ▷ *vi* marquer des points; (*Football*) marquer un but; (*keep score*) compter les points; **on that ~** sur ce chapitre, à cet égard; **to have an old ~ to settle with sb** (*fig*) avoir un (vieux) compte à régler avec qn; **a ~ of** (*twenty*) vingt; **~s of** (*fig*) des tas de; **to ~ 6 out of 10** obtenir 6 sur 10; **score out** *vt* rayer, barrer, biffer

scoreboard ['skɔːbɔːd] *n* tableau *m*

scorer ['skɔːrəʳ] *n* (*Football*) auteur *m* du but; buteur *m*; (*keeping score*) marqueur *m*

scorn [skɔːn] *n* mépris *m*, dédain *m* ▷ *vt* mépriser, dédaigner

Scorpio ['skɔːpɪəu] *n* le Scorpion; **to be ~** être du Scorpion

scorpion ['skɔːpɪən] *n* scorpion *m*

Scot [skɔt] *n* Écossais(e)

Scotch [skɔtʃ] *n* whisky *m*, scotch *m*

scotch [skɔtʃ] *vt* faire échouer; enrayer; étouffer

Scotch tape® (*US*) *n* scotch® *m*, ruban adhésif

scot-free ['skɔt'friː] *adj*: **to get off ~** s'en tirer sans être puni(e); s'en sortir indemne

Scotland ['skɔtlənd] *n* Écosse *f*

Scots [skɔts] *adj* écossais(e)

Scotsman ['skɔtsmən] *irreg n* Écossais *m*

Scotswoman ['skɔtswumən] *irreg n* Écossaise *f*

Scottish ['skɔtɪʃ] *adj* écossais(e); **the ~ National Party** le parti national écossais; **the ~ Parliament** le Parlement écossais

scoundrel ['skaundrl] *n* vaurien *m*

scour ['skauəʳ] *vt* (*clean*) récurer; frotter; décaper; (*search*) battre, parcourir

scout [skaut] *n* (*Mil*) éclaireur *m*; (*also*: **boy ~**) scout *m*; **girl ~** (*US*) guide *f*; **scout around** *vi* chercher

scowl [skaul] *vi* se renfrogner, avoir l'air maussade; **to ~ at** regarder de travers

scrabble ['skræbl] *vi* (*claw*): **to ~ (at)** gratter; **to ~ about** *or* **around for sth** chercher qch à tâtons ▷ *n*: **S~**® Scrabble® *m*

scram [skræm] *vi* (*inf*) ficher le camp

scramble ['skræmbl] *n* (*rush*) bousculade *f*, ruée *f* ▷ *vi* grimper/descendre tant bien que mal; **to ~ for** se bousculer *or* se disputer pour (avoir); **to go scrambling** (*Sport*) faire du trial

scrambled eggs ['skræmbld-] *npl* œufs brouillés

scrap [skræp] *n* bout *m*, morceau *m*; (*fight*) bagarre *f*; (*also*: **~ iron**) ferraille *f* ▷ *vt* jeter, mettre au rebut; (*fig*) abandonner, laisser tomber ▷ *vi* se bagarrer; **scraps** *npl* (*waste*) déchets *mpl*; **to sell sth for ~** vendre qch à la casse *or* à la ferraille

scrapbook ['skræpbuk] *n* album *m*

scrap dealer *n* marchand *m* de ferraille

scrape [skreɪp] *vt, vi* gratter, racler ▷ *n*: **to get into a ~** s'attirer des ennuis; **scrape through** *vi* (*exam etc*) réussir de justesse; **scrape together** *vt* (*money*) racler ses fonds de tiroir pour réunir

scrap heap *n* tas *m* de ferraille; (*fig*): **on the ~** au rancart *or* rebut

scrap merchant *n* (*Brit*) marchand *m* de ferraille

scrap paper *n* papier *m* brouillon

scratch [skrætʃ] *n* égratignure *f*, rayure *f*; (*on paint*) éraflure *f*; (*from claw*) coup *m* de griffe ▷ *adj*: **~ team** équipe de fortune *or* improvisée ▷ *vt* (*rub*) (se) gratter; (*record*) rayer; (*paint etc*) érafler; (*with claw, nail*) griffer; (*Comput*) effacer ▷ *vi* (se) gratter; **to start from ~** partir de zéro; **to be up to ~** être à la hauteur

scratch card *n* carte *f* à gratter

scrawl [skrɔːl] *n* gribouillage *m* ▷ *vi* gribouiller

scrawny ['skrɔːnɪ] *adj* décharné(e)

scream [skriːm] *n* cri perçant, hurlement *m* ▷ *vi* crier, hurler; **to be a ~** (*inf*) être impayable; **to ~ at sb to do sth** crier *or* hurler à qn de faire qch

screech [skriːtʃ] *n* cri strident, hurlement *m*; (*of tyres, brakes*) crissement *m*, grincement *m* ▷ *vi* hurler; crisser, grincer

screen [skriːn] *n* écran *m*; (*in room*) paravent *m*; (*Cine, TV*) écran; (*fig*) écran, rideau *m* ▷ *vt* masquer, cacher; (*from the wind etc*) abriter, protéger; (*film*) projeter; (*candidates etc*) filtrer; (*for illness*): **to ~ sb for sth** faire subir un test de dépistage de qch à qn

screening ['skriːnɪŋ] *n* (*of film*) projection *f*; (*Med*) test *m* (*or* tests) de dépistage; (*for security*) filtrage *m*

screenplay ['skriːnpleɪ] *n* scénario *m*

screen saver *n* (*Comput*) économiseur *m* d'écran

screenshot ['skriːnʃɔt] *n* (*Comput*) capture *f* d'écran

screw [skruː] *n* vis *f*; (*propeller*) hélice *f* ▷ *vt* (*also*: **~ in**) visser; (*inf!*: *woman*) baiser (!); **to ~ sth to the wall** visser qch au mur; **to have one's head ~ed on** (*fig*) avoir la tête sur les épaules; **screw up** *vt* (*paper etc*) froisser; (*inf*: *ruin*) bousiller; **to ~ up one's eyes** se plisser les yeux; **to ~ up one's face** faire la grimace

screwdriver ['skruːdraɪvəʳ] *n* tournevis *m*

scribble ['skrɪbl] *n* gribouillage *m* ▷ *vt* gribouiller, griffonner; **to ~ sth down** griffonner qch

script [skrɪpt] *n* (*Cine etc*) scénario *m*, texte *m*; (*in exam*) copie *f*; (*writing*) (écriture *f*) script *m*

Scripture ['skrɪptʃəʳ] *n* Écriture sainte

scroll [skrəul] *n* rouleau *m* ▷ *vt* (*Comput*) faire défiler (sur l'écran)

scrounge [skraundʒ] (*inf*) *vt*: **to ~ sth (off** *or* **from sb)** se faire payer qch (par qn), emprunter qch (à qn) ▷ *vi*: **to ~ on sb** vivre aux crochets de qn

s

scrounger ['skraundʒəʳ] n parasite m

scrub [skrʌb] n (clean) nettoyage m (à la brosse); (land) broussailles fpl ▷ vt (floor) nettoyer à la brosse; (pan) récurer; (washing) frotter; (reject) annuler

scruff [skrʌf] n: **by the ~ of the neck** par la peau du cou

scruffy ['skrʌfɪ] adj débraillé(e)

scrum [skrʌm], **scrummage** ['skrʌmɪdʒ] n mêlée f

scruple ['skru:pl] n scrupule m; **to have no ~s about doing sth** n'avoir aucun scrupule à faire qch

scrutiny ['skru:tɪnɪ] n examen minutieux; **under the ~ of sb** sous la surveillance de qn

scuba diving ['sku:bə-] n plongée sous-marine

scuff [skʌf] vt érafler

scuffle ['skʌfl] n échauffourée f, rixe f

sculptor ['skʌlptəʳ] n sculpteur m

sculpture ['skʌlptʃəʳ] n sculpture f

scum [skʌm] n écume f, mousse f; (pej: people) rebut m, lie f

scurry ['skʌrɪ] vi filer à toute allure; **to ~ off** détaler, se sauver

scuttle ['skʌtl] n (Naut) écoutille f; (also: **coal ~**) seau m (à charbon) ▷ vt (ship) saborder ▷ vi (scamper): **to ~ away, ~ off** détaler

scythe [saɪð] n faux f

sea [si:] n mer f ▷ cpd marin(e), de (la) mer, maritime; **on the ~** (boat) en mer; (town) au bord de la mer; **by the ~** (holiday, town) au bord de la mer; **by ~** par mer, en bateau; **out to ~** au large; (out) **at ~** en mer; **heavy** or **rough ~(s)** grosse mer, mer agitée; **a ~ of faces** (fig) une multitude de visages; **to be all at ~** (fig) nager complètement

seaboard ['si:bɔ:d] n côte f

seafood ['si:fu:d] n fruits mpl de mer

sea front ['si:frʌnt] n bord m de mer

seagoing ['si:gəuɪŋ] adj (ship) de haute mer

seagull ['si:gʌl] n mouette f

seal [si:l] n (animal) phoque m; (stamp) sceau m, cachet m; (impression) cachet, estampille f ▷ vt sceller; (envelope) coller; (: with seal) cacheter; (decide: sb's fate) décider (de); (: bargain) conclure; **~ of approval** approbation f; **seal off** vt (close) condamner; (forbid entry to) interdire l'accès de

sea level n niveau m de la mer

sea lion n lion m de mer

seam [si:m] n couture f; (of coal) veine f, filon m; **the hall was bursting at the ~s** la salle était pleine à craquer

seaman ['si:mən] irreg n marin m

seance ['seɪɔns] n séance f de spiritisme

seaplane ['si:pleɪn] n hydravion m

search [sə:tʃ] n (for person, thing, Comput) recherche(s) f(pl); (of drawer, pockets) fouille f; (Law: at sb's home) perquisition f ▷ vt fouiller; (examine) examiner minutieusement; scruter ▷ vi: **to ~ for** chercher; **in ~ of** à la recherche

de; **search through** vt fus fouiller

search engine n (Comput) moteur m de recherche

searching ['sə:tʃɪŋ] adj (look, question) pénétrant(e); (examination) minutieux(-euse)

searchlight ['sə:tʃlaɪt] n projecteur m

search party n expédition f de secours

search warrant n mandat m de perquisition

seashore ['si:ʃɔ:ʳ] n rivage m, plage f, bord m de (la) mer; **on the ~** sur le rivage

seasick ['si:sɪk] adj: **to be ~** avoir le mal de mer

seaside ['si:saɪd] n bord m de mer

seaside resort n station f balnéaire

season ['si:zn] n saison f ▷ vt assaisonner, relever; **to be in/out of ~** être/ne pas être de saison; **the busy ~** (for shops) la période de pointe; (for hotels etc) la pleine saison; **the open ~** (Hunting) la saison de la chasse

seasonal ['si:znl] adj saisonnier(-ière)

seasoned ['si:znd] adj (wood) séché(e); (fig: worker, actor, troops) expérimenté(e); **a ~ campaigner** un vieux militant, un vétéran

seasoning ['si:znɪŋ] n assaisonnement m

season ticket n carte f d'abonnement

seat [si:t] n siège m; (in bus, train: place) place f; (Parliament) siège; (buttocks) postérieur m; (of trousers) fond m ▷ vt faire asseoir, placer; (have room for) avoir des places assises pour, pouvoir accueillir; **are there any ~s left?** est-ce qu'il reste des places?; **to take one's ~** prendre place; **to be ~ed** être assis; **please be ~ed** veuillez vous asseoir

seat belt n ceinture f de sécurité

seating ['si:tɪŋ] n sièges fpl, places assises

sea water n eau f de mer

seaweed ['si:wi:d] n algues fpl

seaworthy ['si:wə:ðɪ] adj en état de naviguer

sec. abbr (= second) sec

secluded [sɪ'klu:dɪd] adj retiré(e), à l'écart

seclusion [sɪ'klu:ʒən] n solitude f

second¹ ['sɛkənd] num deuxième, second(e) ▷ adv (in race etc) en seconde position ▷ n (unit of time) seconde f; (Aut: also: **~ gear**) seconde; (in series, position) deuxième m/f, second(e); (Comm: imperfect) article m de second choix; (Brit Scol) ≈ licence f avec mention ▷ vt (motion) appuyer; **seconds** npl (inf: food) rab m (inf); **Charles the S~** Charles II; **just a ~!** une seconde!, un instant!; (stopping sb) pas si vite!; **~ floor** (Brit) deuxième (étage) m; (US) premier (étage) m; **to ask for a ~ opinion** (Med) demander l'avis d'un autre médecin

second² [sɪ'kɔnd] vt (employee) détacher, mettre en détachement

secondary ['sɛkəndərɪ] adj secondaire

secondary school n (age 11 to 15) collège m; (age 15 to 18) lycée m

second-class ['sɛkənd'klɑ:s] adj de deuxième classe; (Rail) de seconde (classe); (Post) au tarif réduit; (pej) de qualité inférieure ▷ adv (Rail) en seconde; (Post) au tarif réduit; **~ citizen** citoyen(ne) de deuxième classe

second hand n (on clock) trotteuse f

secondhand ['sɛkənd'hænd] adj d'occasion; (information) de seconde main ▷ adv (buy) d'occasion; **to hear sth ~** apprendre qch indirectement

secondly ['sɛkəndlɪ] adv deuxièmement; **firstly ... ~ ...** d'abord ... ensuite ... or de plus ...

secondment [sɪ'kɔndmənt] n (Brit) détachement m

second-rate ['sɛkənd'reɪt] adj de deuxième ordre, de qualité inférieure

second thoughts npl: **to have ~** changer d'avis; **on ~** or **thought** (US) à la réflexion

secrecy ['si:krəsɪ] n secret m; **in ~** en secret

secret ['si:krɪt] adj secret(-ète) ▷ n secret m; **in ~** adv en secret, secrètement, en cachette; **to keep sth ~ from sb** cacher qch à qn, ne pas révéler qch à qn; **to make no ~ of sth** ne pas cacher qch; **keep it ~** n'en parle à personne

secretary ['sɛkrətrɪ] n secrétaire m/f; (Comm) secrétaire général; **S~ of State** (US Pol) ≈ ministre m des Affaires étrangères; **S~ of State (for)** (Brit Pol) ministre m (de)

secretive ['si:krətɪv] adj réservé(e); (pej) cachottier(-ière), dissimulé(e)

secretly ['si:krɪtlɪ] adv en secret, secrètement, en cachette

secret service n services secrets

sect [sɛkt] n secte f

sectarian [sɛk'tɛərɪən] adj sectaire

section ['sɛkʃən] n section f; (department) section; (Comm) rayon m; (of document) section, article m, paragraphe m; (cut) coupe f ▷ vt sectionner; **the business** etc **~** (Press) la page des affaires etc

sector ['sɛktə*r*] n secteur m

secular ['sɛkjulə*r*] adj laïque

secure [sɪ'kjuə*r*] adj (free from anxiety) sans inquiétude, sécurisé(e); (firmly fixed) solide, bien attaché(e) (or fermé(e) etc); (in safe place) en lieu sûr, en sûreté ▷ vt (fix) fixer, attacher; (get) obtenir, se procurer; (Comm: loan) garantir; **to make sth ~** bien fixer or attacher qch; **to ~ sth for sb** obtenir qch pour qn, procurer qch à qn

security [sɪ'kjuərɪtɪ] n sécurité f, mesures fpl de sécurité; (for loan) caution f, garantie f; **securities** npl (Stock Exchange) valeurs fpl, titres mpl; **to increase** or **tighten ~** renforcer les mesures de sécurité; **~ of tenure** stabilité f d'un emploi, titularisation f

security guard n garde chargé de la sécurité; (transporting money) convoyeur m de fonds

sedan [sə'dæn] n (US Aut) berline f

sedate [sɪ'deɪt] adj calme; posé(e) ▷ vt donner des sédatifs à

sedative ['sɛdɪtɪv] n calmant m, sédatif m

seduce [sɪ'dju:s] vt séduire

seduction [sɪ'dʌkʃən] n séduction f

seductive [sɪ'dʌktɪv] adj séduisant(e); (smile) séducteur(-trice); (fig: offer) alléchant(e)

see [si:] (pt saw, pp seen) [sɔ:, si:n] vt (gen) voir; (accompany): **to ~ sb to the door** reconduire or raccompagner qn jusqu'à la porte ▷ vi voir ▷ n évêché m; (ensure) veiller à ce que + sub, faire en sorte que + sub, s'assurer que; **there was nobody to be ~n** il n'y avait pas un chat; **let me ~** (show me) fais(-moi) voir; (let me think) voyons (un peu); **to go and ~ sb** aller voir qn; **~ for yourself** voyez vous-même; **I don't know what she ~s in him** je ne sais pas ce qu'elle lui trouve; **as far as I can ~** pour autant que je puisse en juger; **~ you!** au revoir!, à bientôt!; **~ you soon/later/tomorrow!** à bientôt/plus tard/demain!; **see about** vt fus (deal with) s'occuper de; **see off** vt accompagner (à l'aéroport etc); **see out** vt (take to door) raccompagner à la porte; **see through** vt mener à bonne fin ▷ vt fus voir clair dans; **see to** vt fus s'occuper de, se charger de

seed [si:d] n graine f; (fig) germe m; (Tennis etc) tête f de série; **to go to ~** (plant) monter en graine; (fig) se laisser aller

seedling ['si:dlɪŋ] n jeune plant m, semis m

seedy ['si:dɪ] adj (shabby) minable, miteux(-euse)

seeing ['si:ɪŋ] conj: **~ (that)** vu que, étant donné que

seek [si:k] (pt, pp sought) [sɔ:t] vt chercher, rechercher; **to ~ advice/help from sb** demander conseil/de l'aide à qn; **seek out** vt (person) chercher

seem [si:m] vi sembler, paraître; **there ~s to be ...** il semble qu'il y a ..., on dirait qu'il y a ...; **it ~s (that) ...** il semble que ...; **what ~s to be the trouble?** qu'est-ce qui ne va pas?

seemingly ['si:mɪŋlɪ] adv apparemment

seen [si:n] pp of **see**

seep [si:p] vi suinter, filtrer

seesaw ['si:sɔ:] n (jeu m de) bascule f

seethe [si:ð] vi être en effervescence; **to ~ with anger** bouillir de colère

see-through ['si:θru:] adj transparent(e)

segment ['sɛgmənt] n segment m; (of orange) quartier m

segregate ['sɛgrɪgeɪt] vt séparer, isoler

Seine [seɪn] n: **the (River) ~** la Seine

seize [si:z] vt (grasp) saisir, attraper; (take possession of) s'emparer de; (opportunity) saisir; (Law) saisir; **seize on** vt fus saisir, sauter sur; **seize up** vi (Tech) se gripper; **seize upon** vt fus = **seize on**

seizure ['si:ʒə*r*] n (Med) crise f, attaque f; (of power) prise f; (Law) saisie f

seldom ['sɛldəm] adv rarement

select [sɪ'lɛkt] adj choisi(e), d'élite; (hotel, restaurant, club) chic inv, sélect inv ▷ vt

S

sélectionner, choisir; **a ~ few** quelques privilégiés

selection [sɪ'lekʃən] n sélection f, choix m

selective [sɪ'lektɪv] adj sélectif(-ive); (school) à recrutement sélectif

self (pl **selves**) [self, selvz] n: **the ~** le moi inv ▷ prefix auto-

self-assured [selfə'ʃuəd] adj sûr(e) de soi, plein(e) d'assurance

self-catering [self'keɪtərɪŋ] adj (Brit: flat) avec cuisine, où l'on peut faire sa cuisine; (: holiday) en appartement (or chalet etc) loué

self-centred, (US) **self-centered** [self'sentəd] adj égocentrique

self-confidence [self'kɒnfɪdns] n confiance f en soi

self-confident [self'kɒnfɪdnt] adj sûr(e) de soi, plein(e) d'assurance

self-conscious [self'kɒnʃəs] adj timide, qui manque d'assurance

self-contained [selfkən'teɪnd] adj (Brit: flat) avec entrée particulière, indépendant(e)

self-control [selfkən'trəul] n maîtrise f de soi

self-defence, (US) **self-defense** [selfdɪ'fens] n autodéfense f; (Law) légitime défense f

self-discipline [self'dɪsɪplɪn] n discipline personnelle

self-drive [self'draɪv] adj (Brit): **~ car** voiture f de location

self-employed [selfɪm'plɔɪd] adj qui travaille à son compte

self-esteem [selfɪ'stiːm] n amour-propre m

self-evident [self'evɪdnt] adj évident(e), qui va de soi

self-harm [self'hɑːm] vi s'automutiler

self-governing [self'gʌvənɪŋ] adj autonome

self-indulgent [selfɪn'dʌldʒənt] adj qui ne se refuse rien

self-interest [self'ɪntrɪst] n intérêt personnel

selfish ['selfɪʃ] adj égoïste

selfishness ['selfɪʃnɪs] n égoïsme m

selfless ['selflɪs] adj désintéressé(e)

self-pity [self'pɪtɪ] n apitoiement m sur soi-même

self-possessed [selfpə'zest] adj assuré(e)

self-preservation ['selfprezə'veɪʃən] n instinct m de conservation

self-raising [self'reɪzɪŋ], (US) **self-rising** [self'raɪzɪŋ] adj: **~ flour** farine f pour gâteaux (avec levure incorporée)

self-respect [selfrɪs'pekt] n respect m de soi, amour-propre m

self-righteous [self'raɪtʃəs] adj satisfait(e) de soi, pharisaïque

self-sacrifice [self'sækrɪfaɪs] n abnégation f

self-satisfied [self'sætɪsfaɪd] adj content(e) de soi, suffisant(e)

self-service [self'səːvɪs] adj, n libre-service (m), self-service (m)

self-sufficient [selfsə'fɪʃənt] adj indépendant(e)

self-taught [self'tɔːt] adj autodidacte

sell (pt, pp **sold**) [sel, səuld] vt vendre ▷ vi se vendre; **to ~ at or for 10 euros** se vendre 10 euros; **to ~ sb an idea** (fig) faire accepter une idée à qn; **sell off** vt liquider; **sell out** vi: **to ~ out (of sth)** (use up stock) vendre tout son stock (de qch); **to ~ out (to)** (Comm) vendre son fonds or son affaire (à) ▷ vt vendre tout son stock de; **the tickets are all sold out** il ne reste plus de billets; **sell up** vi vendre son fonds or son affaire

sell-by date ['selbaɪ-] n date f limite de vente

seller ['selər] n vendeur(-euse), marchand(e); **~'s market** marché m à la hausse

selling price ['selɪŋ-] n prix m de vente

Sellotape® ['seləuteɪp] n (Brit) scotch® m

selves [selvz] npl of **self**

semblance ['semblns] n semblant m

semen ['siːmən] n sperme m

semester [sɪ'mestər] n (esp US) semestre m

semi... ['semɪ] prefix semi-, demi-; à demi, à moitié ▷ n: **semi = semidetached house**

semicircle ['semɪsəːkl] n demi-cercle m

semicolon [semɪ'kəulən] n point-virgule m

semidetached [semɪd'tætʃt], **semidetached house** n (Brit) maison jumelée or jumelle

semi-final [semɪ'faɪnl] n demi-finale f

seminar ['semɪnɑːr] n séminaire m

seminary ['semɪnərɪ] n (Rel: for priests) séminaire m

semiskilled [semɪ'skɪld] adj: **~ worker** ouvrier(-ière) spécialisé(e)

semi-skimmed ['semɪ'skɪmd] adj demi-écrémé(e)

senate ['senɪt] n sénat m; (US): **the S~** le Sénat; voir article

○ **SENATE**
○
○ Le Senate est la chambre haute du
○ "Congress", le parlement des États-Unis.
○ Il est composé de 100 sénateurs, 2 par
○ État, élus au suffrage universel direct
○ tous les 6 ans, un tiers d'entre eux étant
○ renouvelé tous les 2 ans.

senator ['senətər] n sénateur m

send (pt, pp **sent**) [send, sent] vt envoyer; **to ~ by post** or (US) **mail** envoyer or expédier par la poste; **to ~ sb for sth** envoyer qn chercher qch; **to ~ word that ...** faire dire que ...; **she ~s (you) her love** elle vous adresse ses amitiés; **to ~ sb to Coventry** (Brit) mettre qn en quarantaine; **to ~ sb to sleep** endormir qn; **to ~ sb into fits of laughter** faire rire qn aux éclats; **to ~ sth flying** envoyer valser qch; **send away** vt (letter, goods) envoyer, expédier; **send away for** vt fus commander par correspondance, se faire envoyer; **send back** vt renvoyer; **send for** vt fus envoyer chercher; faire venir; (by post) se faire envoyer, commander par correspondance; **send in** vt (report, application, resignation) remettre; **send off** vt (goods) envoyer, expédier; (Brit Sport: player) expulser or renvoyer du terrain; **send on** vt (Brit: letter) faire suivre; (luggage etc: in advance) (faire) expédier à l'avance; **send out** vt (invitation) envoyer (par la poste); (emit: light, heat, signal) émettre; **send round** vt (letter, document etc) faire circuler; **send up** vt (person, price) faire monter; (Brit: parody) mettre en boîte, parodier

sender ['sɛndə'] n expéditeur(-trice)

send-off ['sɛndɔf] n: **a good ~** des adieux chaleureux

senile ['siːnaɪl] adj sénile

senior ['siːnɪə'] adj (older) aîné(e), plus âgé(e); (high-ranking) de haut niveau; (of higher rank): **to be ~ to sb** être le supérieur de qn ▷ n (older): **she is 15 years his ~** elle est son aînée de 15 ans, elle est plus âgée que lui de 15 ans; (in service) personne f qui a plus d'ancienneté; **P. Jones ~** P. Jones père

senior citizen n personne f du troisième âge

senior high school n (US) = lycée m

seniority [siːnɪ'ɔːrɪtɪ] n priorité f d'âge, ancienneté f; (in rank) supériorité f (hiérarchique)

sensation [sɛn'seɪʃən] n sensation f; **to create a ~** faire sensation

sensational [sɛn'seɪʃənl] adj qui fait sensation; (marvellous) sensationnel(le)

sense [sɛns] n sens m; (feeling) sentiment m; (meaning) sens, signification f; (wisdom) bon sens ▷ vt sentir, pressentir; **senses** npl raison f; **it makes ~** c'est logique; **there is no ~ in (doing) that** cela n'a pas de sens; **to come to one's ~s** (regain consciousness) reprendre conscience; (become reasonable) revenir à la raison; **to take leave of one's ~s** perdre la tête

senseless ['sɛnslɪs] adj insensé(e), stupide; (unconscious) sans connaissance

sense of humour, (US) **sense of humor** n sens m de l'humour

sensible ['sɛnsɪbl] adj sensé(e), raisonnable; (shoes etc) pratique

sensitive ['sɛnsɪtɪv] adj: **~ (to)** sensible (à); **he is very ~ about it** c'est un point très sensible (chez lui)

sensual ['sɛnsjuəl] adj sensuel(le)

sensuous ['sɛnsjuəs] adj voluptueux(-euse), sensuel(le)

sent [sɛnt] pt, pp of **send**

sentence ['sɛntns] n (Ling) phrase f; (Law: judgment) condamnation f, sentence f; (: punishment) peine f ▷ vt: **to ~ sb to death/to 5 years** condamner qn à mort/à 5 ans; **to pass ~ on sb** prononcer une peine contre qn

sentiment ['sɛntɪmənt] n sentiment m; (opinion) opinion f, avis m

sentimental [sɛntɪ'mɛntl] adj sentimental(e)

sentry ['sɛntrɪ] n sentinelle f, factionnaire m

separate [adj 'sɛprɪt, vb 'sɛpəreɪt] adj séparé(e); (organization) indépendant(e); (day, occasion, issue) différent(e) ▷ vt séparer; (distinguish) distinguer ▷ vi se séparer; **~ from** distinct(e) de; **under ~ cover** (Comm) sous pli séparé; **to ~ into** diviser en

separately ['sɛprɪtlɪ] adv séparément

separates ['sɛprɪts] npl (clothes) coordonnés mpl

separation [sɛpə'reɪʃən] n séparation f

September [sɛp'tɛmbə'] n septembre m; see also **July**

septic ['sɛptɪk] adj septique; (wound) infecté(e); **to go ~** s'infecter

septic tank n fosse f septique

sequel ['siːkwl] n conséquence f; séquelles fpl; (of story) suite f

sequence ['siːkwəns] n ordre m, suite f; (in film) séquence f; (dance) numéro m; **in ~** par ordre, dans l'ordre, les uns après les autres; **~ of tenses** concordance f des temps

sequin ['siːkwɪn] n paillette f

Serb [səːb] adj, n = **Serbian**

Serbia ['səːbɪə] n Serbie f

Serbian ['səːbɪən] adj serbe ▷ n Serbe m/f; (Ling) serbe m

serene [sɪ'riːn] adj serein(e), calme, paisible

sergeant ['sɑːdʒənt] n sergent m; (Police) brigadier m

serial ['sɪərɪəl] n feuilleton m ▷ adj (Comput: interface, printer) série inv; (: access) séquentiel(le)

serial killer n meurtrier m tuant en série

serial number n numéro m de série

series ['sɪərɪz] n série f; (Publishing) collection f

serious ['sɪərɪəs] adj sérieux(-euse); (accident etc) grave; **are you ~ (about it)?** parlez-vous sérieusement?

seriously ['sɪərɪəslɪ] adv sérieusement; (hurt) gravement; **~ rich/difficult** (inf: extremely) drôlement riche/difficile; **to take sth/sb ~** prendre qch/qn au sérieux

sermon ['səːmən] n sermon m

serrated [sɪ'reɪtɪd] adj en dents de scie

servant ['səːvənt] n domestique m/f; (fig) serviteur/servante

serve [səːv] vt (employer etc) servir, être au service de; (purpose) servir à; (customer, food, meal) servir; (subj: train) desservir; (apprenticeship) faire, accomplir; (prison term) faire; purger ▷ vi (Tennis) servir; (be useful): **to ~ as/for/to do** servir de/à/à faire ▷ n (Tennis) service m; **are you being ~d?** est-ce qu'on s'occupe de vous?; **to ~ on a committee/jury** faire partie d'un comité/jury; **it ~s him right** c'est bien fait pour lui; **it ~s my purpose** cela fait mon affaire; **serve out, serve up** vt (food) servir

server [səːvə'] n (Comput) serveur m

service ['səːvɪs] n (gen) service m; (Aut) révision f; (Rel) office m ▷ vt (car etc) réviser;

services npl (Econ: tertiary sector) (secteur m) tertiaire m, secteur des services; (Brit: on motorway) station-service f; (Mil): **the S~s** npl les forces armées; **to be of ~ to sb, to do sb a ~** rendre service à qn; **~ included/not included** service compris/non compris; **to put one's car in for ~** donner sa voiture à réviser; **dinner ~** service de table

serviceable ['sə:vɪsəbl] adj pratique, commode

service area n (on motorway) aire f de services

service charge n (Brit) service m

serviceman ['sə:vɪsmən] irreg n militaire m

service station n station-service f

serviette [sə:vɪ'ɛt] n (Brit) serviette f (de table)

session ['sɛʃən] n (sitting) séance f; (Scol) année f scolaire (or universitaire); **to be in ~** siéger, être en session or en séance

set [sɛt] (pt, pp **set**) n série f, assortiment m; (of tools etc) jeu m; (Radio, TV) poste m; (Tennis) set m; (group of people) cercle m, milieu m; (Cine) plateau m; (Theat: stage) scène f; (: scenery) décor m; (Math) ensemble m; (Hairdressing) mise f en plis ▷ adj (fixed) fixe, déterminé(e); (ready) prêt(e) ▷ vt (place) mettre, poser, placer; (fix, establish) fixer; (: record) établir; (assign: task, homework) donner; (exam) composer; (adjust) régler; (decide: rules etc) fixer, choisir; (Typ) composer ▷ vi (sun) se coucher; (jam, jelly, concrete) prendre; (bone) se ressouder; **to be ~ on doing** être résolu(e) à faire; **to be all ~ to do** être (fin) prêt(e) pour faire; **to be (dead) ~ against** être (totalement) opposé à; **he's ~ in his ways** il n'est pas très souple, il tient à ses habitudes; **to ~ to music** mettre en musique; **to ~ on fire** mettre le feu à; **to ~ free** libérer; **to ~ sth going** déclencher qch; **to ~ the alarm clock for seven o'clock** mettre le réveil à sonner à sept heures; **to ~ sail** partir, prendre la mer; **a ~ phrase** une expression toute faite, une locution; **a ~ of false teeth** un dentier; **a ~ of dining-room furniture** une salle à manger; **set about** vt fus (task) entreprendre, se mettre à; **to ~ about doing sth** se mettre à faire qch; **set aside** vt mettre de côté; (time) garder; **set back** vt (in time) **to ~ back (by)** retarder (de); (place): **a house ~ back from the road** une maison située en retrait de la route; **set down** vt (subj: bus, train) déposer; **set in** vi (infection, bad weather) s'installer; (complications) survenir, surgir; **the rain has ~ in for the day** c'est parti pour qu'il pleuve toute la journée; **set off** vi se mettre en route, partir ▷ vt (bomb) faire exploser; (cause to start) déclencher; (show up well) mettre en valeur, faire valoir; **set out** vi: **to ~ out (from)** partir (de) ▷ vt (arrange) disposer; (state) présenter, exposer; **to ~ out to do** entreprendre de faire; avoir pour but or intention de faire; **set up** vt (organization)

fonder, créer; (monument) ériger; **to ~ up shop** (fig) s'établir, s'installer

setback ['sɛtbæk] n (hitch) revers m, contretemps m; (in health) rechute f

set menu n menu m

settee [sɛ'ti:] n canapé m

setting ['sɛtɪŋ] n cadre m; (of jewel) monture f; (position: of controls) réglage m

settle ['sɛtl] vt (argument, matter, account) régler; (problem) résoudre; (Med: calm) calmer; (colonize: land) coloniser ▷ vi (bird, dust etc) se poser; (sediment) se déposer; **to ~ to sth** se mettre sérieusement à qch; **to ~ for sth** accepter qch, se contenter de qch; **to ~ on sth** opter or se décider pour qch; **that's ~d then** alors, c'est d'accord!; **to ~ one's stomach** calmer des maux d'estomac; **settle down** vi (get comfortable) s'installer; (become calmer) se calmer; se ranger; **settle in** vi s'installer; **settle up** vi: **to ~ up with sb** régler (ce que l'on doit à) qn

settlement ['sɛtlmənt] n (payment) règlement m; (agreement) accord m; (colony) colonie f; (village etc) village m, hameau m; **in ~ of our account** (Comm) en règlement de notre compte

settler ['sɛtlə'] n colon m

setup ['sɛtʌp] n (arrangement) manière f dont les choses sont organisées; (situation) situation f, allure f des choses

seven ['sɛvn] num sept

seventeen [sɛvn'ti:n] num dix-sept

seventeenth [sɛvn'ti:nθ] num dix-septième

seventh ['sɛvnθ] num septième

seventieth ['sɛvntɪɪθ] num soixante-dixième

seventy ['sɛvntɪ] num soixante-dix

sever ['sɛvə'] vt couper, trancher; (relations) rompre

several ['sɛvərl] adj, pron plusieurs pl; **~ of us** plusieurs d'entre nous; **~ times** plusieurs fois

severance ['sɛvərəns] n (of relations) rupture f

severance pay n indemnité f de licenciement

severe [sɪ'vɪə'] adj (stern) sévère, strict(e); (serious) grave, sérieux(-euse); (hard) rigoureux(-euse), dur(e); (plain) sévère, austère

severity [sɪ'vɛrɪtɪ] n sévérité f; gravité f; rigueur f

sew (pt **sewed**, pp **sewn**) [səu, səud, səun] vt, vi coudre; **sew up** vt (re)coudre; **it is all ~n up** (fig) c'est dans le sac or dans la poche

sewage ['su:ɪdʒ] n vidange(s) f(pl)

sewer ['su:ə'] n égout m

sewing ['səuɪŋ] n couture f; (item(s)) ouvrage m

sewing machine n machine f à coudre

sewn [səun] pp of **sew**

sex [sɛks] n sexe m; **to have ~ with** avoir des rapports (sexuels) avec

sexism ['sɛksɪzəm] n sexisme m

sexist ['sɛksɪst] adj sexiste

sexual ['sɛksjuəl] adj sexuel(le); **~ assault** attentat m à la pudeur; **~ harassment** harcèlement sexuel

sexual intercourse n rapports sexuels

sexuality [sɛksju'ælɪtɪ] n sexualité f

sexy ['sɛksɪ] adj sexy inv

shabby ['ʃæbɪ] adj miteux(-euse); (behaviour) mesquin(e), méprisable

shack [ʃæk] n cabane f, hutte f

shackles ['ʃæklz] npl chaînes fpl, entraves fpl

shade [ʃeɪd] n ombre f; (for lamp) abat-jour m inv; (of colour) nuance f, ton m; (US: window shade) store m; (small quantity): **a ~ of** un soupçon de ▷ vt abriter du soleil, ombrager; **shades** npl (US: sunglasses) lunettes fpl de soleil; **in the ~** à l'ombre; **a ~ smaller** un tout petit peu plus petit

shadow ['ʃædəu] n ombre f ▷ vt (follow) filer; **without** or **beyond a ~ of** doubt sans l'ombre d'un doute

shadow cabinet n (Brit Pol) cabinet parallèle formé par le parti qui n'est pas au pouvoir

shadowy ['ʃædəu] adj ombragé(e); (dim) vague, indistinct(e)

shady ['ʃeɪdɪ] adj ombragé(e); (fig: dishonest) louche, véreux(-euse)

shaft [ʃɑːft] n (of arrow, spear) hampe f; (Aut, Tech) arbre m; (of mine) puits m; (of lift) cage f; (of light) rayon m, trait m; **ventilator ~** conduit m d'aération or de ventilation

shaggy ['ʃægɪ] adj hirsute; en broussaille

shake [ʃeɪk] (pt **shook**, pp **shaken**) [ʃuk, 'ʃeɪkn] vt secouer; (bottle, cocktail) agiter; (house, confidence) ébranler ▷ vi trembler ▷ n secousse f; **to ~ one's head** (in refusal etc) dire or faire non de la tête; (in dismay) secouer la tête; **to ~ hands with sb** serrer la main à qn; **shake off** vt secouer; (pursuer) se débarrasser de; **shake up** vt secouer

shaky ['ʃeɪkɪ] adj (hand, voice) tremblant(e); (building) branlant(e), peu solide; (memory) chancelant(e); (knowledge) incertain(e)

shall [ʃæl] aux vb: **I ~ go** j'irai; **~ I open the door?** j'ouvre la porte?; **I'll get the coffee, ~ I?** je vais chercher le café, d'accord?

shallow ['ʃæləu] adj peu profond(e); (fig) superficiel(le), qui manque de profondeur

sham [ʃæm] n frime f; (jewellery, furniture) imitation f ▷ adj feint(e), simulé(e) ▷ vt feindre, simuler

shambles ['ʃæmblz] n confusion f, pagaïe f, fouillis m; **the economy is (in) a complete ~** l'économie est dans la confusion la plus totale

shame [ʃeɪm] n honte f ▷ vt faire honte à; **it is a ~ (that/to do)** c'est dommage (que + sub/de faire); **what a ~!** quel dommage!; **to put sb/sth to ~** (fig) faire honte à qn/qch

shameful ['ʃeɪmful] adj honteux(-euse), scandaleux(-euse)

shameless ['ʃeɪmlɪs] adj éhonté(e), effronté(e); (immodest) impudique

shampoo [ʃæm'puː] n shampooing m ▷ vt faire un shampooing à; **~ and set** shampooing et mise f en plis

shamrock ['ʃæmrɔk] n trèfle m (emblème national de l'Irlande)

shandy ['ʃændɪ] n bière panachée

shan't [ʃɑːnt] = **shall not**

shantytown ['ʃæntɪtaun] n bidonville m

shape [ʃeɪp] n forme f ▷ vt façonner, modeler; (clay, stone) donner forme à; (statement) formuler; (sb's ideas, character) former; (sb's course of events) influer sur le cours de ▷ vi (also: **~ up**: events) prendre tournure; (: person) faire des progrès, s'en sortir; **to take ~** prendre forme or tournure; **in the ~ of a heart** en forme de cœur; **I can't bear gardening in any ~ or form** je déteste le jardinage sous quelque forme que ce soit; **to get o.s. into ~** (re)trouver la forme

-shaped [ʃeɪpt] suffix: **heart~** en forme de cœur

shapeless ['ʃeɪplɪs] adj informe, sans forme

shapely ['ʃeɪplɪ] adj bien proportionné(e), beau/belle

share [ʃɛəʳ] n (thing received, contribution) part f; (Comm) action f ▷ vt partager; (have in common) avoir en commun; **to ~ out** (among or between) partager (entre); **to ~ in** (joy, sorrow) prendre part à; (profits) participer à, avoir part à; (work) partager

shareholder ['ʃɛəhəuldəʳ] n (Brit) actionnaire m/f

shark [ʃɑːk] n requin m

sharp [ʃɑːp] adj (razor, knife) tranchant(e), bien aiguisé(e); (point, voice) aigu(ë); (nose, chin) pointu(e); (outline, increase) net(te); (curve, bend) brusque; (cold, pain) vif/vive; (taste) piquant(e), âcre; (Mus) dièse; (person: quick-witted) vif/vive, éveillé(e); (: unscrupulous) malhonnête ▷ n (Mus) dièse m ▷ adv: **at 2 o'clock ~** à 2 heures pile or tapantes; **turn ~ left** tournez immédiatement à gauche; **to be ~ with sb** être brusque avec qn; **look ~!** dépêche-toi!

sharpen ['ʃɑːpn] vt aiguiser; (pencil) tailler; (fig) aviver

sharpener ['ʃɑːpnəʳ] n (also: **pencil ~**) taille-crayon(s) m inv; (also: **knife ~**) aiguisoir m

sharp-eyed [ʃɑːp'aɪd] adj à qui rien n'échappe

sharply ['ʃɑːplɪ] adv (turn, stop) brusquement; (stand out) nettement; (criticize, retort) sèchement, vertement

shatter ['ʃætəʳ] vt fracasser, briser, faire voler en éclats; (fig: upset) bouleverser; (: ruin) briser, ruiner ▷ vi voler en éclats, se briser, fracasser

shattered ['ʃætəd] adj (overwhelmed, grief-stricken) bouleversé(e); (inf: exhausted) éreinté(e)

s

shave [ʃeɪv] vt raser ▷ vi se raser ▷ n: **to have a ~** se raser

shaver [ʃeɪvəʳ] n (*also*: **electric ~**) rasoir m électrique

shaving [ʃeɪvɪŋ] n (*action*) rasage m

shaving brush n blaireau m

shaving cream n crème f à raser

shaving foam n mousse f à raser

shavings [ʃeɪvɪŋz] npl (*of wood etc*) copeaux mpl

shawl [ʃɔːl] n châle m

she [ʃiː] pron elle; **there ~ is** la voilà; **she-elephant** etc éléphant m etc femelle

sheaf (*pl* **sheaves**) [ʃiːf, ʃiːvz] n gerbe f

shear [ʃɪəʳ] vt (*pt* **sheared**, *pp* **sheared** or **shorn**) [ʃɔːn] (*sheep*) tondre; **shear off** vt (*branch*) élaguer

shears [ʃɪəz] npl (*for hedge*) cisaille(s) f(pl)

sheath [ʃiːθ] n gaine f, fourreau m, étui m; (*contraceptive*) préservatif m

shed [ʃed] n remise f, resserre f; (*Industry, Rail*) hangar m ▷ vt (*pt, pp* **shed**) (*leaves, fur etc*) perdre; (*tears*) verser, répandre; (*workers*) congédier; **to ~ light on** (*problem, mystery*) faire la lumière sur

she'd [ʃiːd] = **she had**; **she would**

sheen [ʃiːn] n lustre m

sheep [ʃiːp] n (*pl inv*) mouton m

sheepdog [ʃiːpdɔg] n chien m de berger

sheepskin [ʃiːpskɪn] n peau f de mouton

sheer [ʃɪəʳ] adj (*utter*) pur(e), pur et simple; (*steep*) à pic, abrupt(e); (*almost transparent*) extrêmement fin(e) ▷ adv à pic, abruptement; **by ~ chance** par pur hasard

sheet [ʃiːt] n (*on bed*) drap m; (*of paper*) feuille f; (*of glass, metal etc*) feuille f, plaque f

sheik, sheikh [ʃeɪk] n cheik m

shelf (*pl* **shelves**) [ʃelf, ʃelvz] n étagère f, rayon m; **set of shelves** rayonnage m

shell [ʃel] n (*on beach*) coquillage m; (*of egg, nut etc*) coquille f; (*explosive*) obus m; (*of building*) carcasse f ▷ vt (*crab, prawn etc*) décortiquer; (*peas*) écosser; (*Mil*) bombarder (d'obus); **shell out** vi (*inf*): **to ~ out (for)** casquer (pour)

she'll [ʃiːl] = **she will**; **she shall**

shellfish [ʃelfɪʃ] n (*pl inv*: *crab etc*) crustacé m; (: *scallop etc*) coquillage m ▷ npl (*as food*) fruits mpl de mer

shell suit n survêtement m

shelter [ʃeltəʳ] n abri m, refuge m ▷ vt abriter, protéger; (*give lodging to*) donner asile à ▷ vi s'abriter, se mettre à l'abri; **to take ~ (from)** s'abriter (de)

sheltered [ʃeltəd] adj (*life*) retiré(e), à l'abri des soucis; (*spot*) abrité(e)

sheltered housing n foyers mpl (*pour personnes âgées ou handicapées*)

shelve [ʃelv] vt (*fig*) mettre en suspens or en sommeil

shelves [ʃelvz] npl of **shelf**

shelving [ʃelvɪŋ] n (*shelves*) rayonnage(s) m(pl)

shepherd [ʃepəd] n berger m ▷ vt (*guide*) guider, escorter

shepherd's pie [ʃepədz-] n ≈ hachis m Parmentier

sheriff [ʃerɪf] (US) n shérif m

sherry [ʃerɪ] n xérès m, sherry m

she's [ʃiːz] = **she is**; **she has**

Shetland [ʃetlənd] n (*also*: **the ~s, the ~ Isles** or **Islands**) les îles fpl Shetland

shield [ʃiːld] n bouclier m; (*protection*) écran m de protection ▷ vt: **to ~ (from)** protéger (de or contre)

shift [ʃɪft] n (*change*) changement m; (*work period*) période f de travail; (*of workers*) équipe f, poste m ▷ vt déplacer, changer de place; (*remove*) enlever ▷ vi changer de place, bouger; **the wind has ~ed to the south** le vent a tourné au sud; **a ~ in demand** (*Comm*) un déplacement de la demande

shift work n travail m par roulement; **to do ~** travailler par roulement

shifty [ʃɪftɪ] adj sournois(e); (*eyes*) fuyant(e)

shimmer [ʃɪməʳ] n miroitement m, chatoiement m ▷ vi miroiter, chatoyer

shin [ʃɪn] n tibia m ▷ vi: **to ~ up/down a tree** grimper dans un/descendre d'un arbre

shine [ʃaɪn] (*pt, pp* **shone**) [ʃɔn] n éclat m, brillant m ▷ vi briller ▷ vt (*torch*): **to ~ on** braquer sur; (*polish*) (*pt, pp* **shined**) faire briller or reluire

shingle [ʃɪŋgl] n (*on beach*) galets mpl; (*on roof*) bardeau m

shingles [ʃɪŋglz] n (*Med*) zona m

shiny [ʃaɪnɪ] adj brillant(e)

ship [ʃɪp] n bateau m; (*large*) navire m ▷ vt transporter (par mer); (*send*) expédier (par mer); (*load*) charger, embarquer; **on board ~** à bord

shipbuilding [ʃɪpbɪldɪŋ] n construction navale

shipment [ʃɪpmənt] n cargaison f

shipping [ʃɪpɪŋ] n (*ships*) navires mpl; (*traffic*) navigation f; (*the industry*) industrie navale; (*transport*) transport m

shipwreck [ʃɪprek] n épave f; (*event*) naufrage m ▷ vt: **to be ~ed** faire naufrage

shipyard [ʃɪpjaːd] n chantier naval

shire [ʃaɪəʳ] n (*Brit*) comté m

shirt [ʃəːt] n chemise f; (*woman's*) chemisier m; **in ~ sleeves** en bras de chemise

shit [ʃɪt] excl (*inf!*) merde (!)

shiver [ʃɪvəʳ] n frisson m ▷ vi frissonner

shoal [ʃəul] n (*of fish*) banc m

shock [ʃɔk] n (*impact*) choc m, heurt m; (*Elec*) secousse f, décharge f; (*emotional*) choc; (*Med*) commotion f, choc ▷ vt (*scandalize*) choquer, scandaliser; (*upset*) bouleverser; **suffering from ~** (*Med*) commotionné(e); **it gave us a ~** ça nous a fait un choc; **it came as a ~ to hear that ...** nous avons appris avec stupeur que ...

shock absorber [-əbzɔːbəʳ] n amortisseur m

shocking ['ʃɔkɪŋ] *adj* (*outrageous*) choquant(e), scandaleux(-euse); (*awful*) épouvantable

shoddy ['ʃɔdɪ] *adj* de mauvaise qualité, mal fait(e)

shoe [ʃuː] *n* chaussure *f*, soulier *m*; (*also:* **horse~**) fer *m* à cheval; (*also:* **brake ~**) mâchoire *f* de frein ▷ *vt* (*pt, pp* **shod**) [ʃɔd] (*horse*) ferrer

shoelace ['ʃuːleɪs] *n* lacet *m* (de soulier)

shoe polish *n* cirage *m*

shoeshop ['ʃuːʃɔp] *n* magasin *m* de chaussures

shoestring ['ʃuːstrɪŋ] *n*: **on a ~** (*fig*) avec un budget dérisoire; avec des moyens très restreints

shone [ʃɔn] *pt, pp of* **shine**

shook [ʃuk] *pt of* **shake**

shoot [ʃuːt] (*pt, pp* **shot**) [ʃɔt] *n* (*on branch, seedling*) pousse *f*; (*shooting party*) partie *f* de chasse ▷ *vt* (*game: hunt*) chasser; (*: aim at*) tirer; (*: kill*) abattre; (*person*) blesser/tuer d'un coup de fusil (or de revolver); (*execute*) fusiller; (*arrow*) tirer; (*gun*) tirer un coup de; (*Cine*) tourner ▷ *vi* (*with gun, bow*): **to ~ (at)** tirer (sur); (*Football*) shooter, tirer; **to ~ past sb** passer en flèche devant qn; **to ~ in/out** entrer/sortir comme une flèche; **shoot down** *vt* (*plane*) abattre; **shoot up** *vi* (*fig: prices etc*) monter en flèche

shooting ['ʃuːtɪŋ] *n* (*shots*) coups *mpl* de feu; (*attack*) fusillade *f*; (*murder*) homicide *m* (*à l'aide d'une arme à feu*); (*Hunting*) chasse *f*; (*Cine*) tournage *m*

shooting star *n* étoile filante

shop [ʃɔp] *n* magasin *m*; (*workshop*) atelier *m* ▷ *vi* (*also:* **go ~ping**) faire ses courses or ses achats; **repair ~** atelier de réparations; **to talk ~** (*fig*) parler boutique; **shop around** *vi* faire le tour des magasins (pour comparer les prix); (*fig*) se renseigner avant de choisir or décider

shop assistant *n* (*Brit*) vendeur(-euse)

shop floor *n* (*Brit: fig*) ouvriers *mpl*

shopkeeper ['ʃɔpkiːpəʳ] *n* marchand(e), commerçant(e)

shoplifting ['ʃɔplɪftɪŋ] *n* vol *m* à l'étalage

shopper ['ʃɔpəʳ] *n* personne *f* qui fait ses courses, acheteur(-euse)

shopping ['ʃɔpɪŋ] *n* (*goods*) achats *mpl*, provisions *fpl*

shopping bag *n* sac *m* (à provisions)

shopping centre, (*US*) **shopping center** *n* centre commercial

shopping mall *n* centre commercial

shopping trolley *n* (*Brit*) Caddie® *m*

shop-soiled ['ʃɔpsɔɪld] *adj* défraîchi(e), qui a fait la vitrine

shop window *n* vitrine *f*

shore [ʃɔːʳ] *n* (*of sea, lake*) rivage *m*, rive *f* ▷ *vt*: **to ~ (up)** étayer; **on ~** à terre

shorn [ʃɔːn] *pp of* **shear** ▷ *adj*: **~ of** dépouillé(e) de

short [ʃɔːt] *adj* (*not long*) court(e); (*soon finished*) court, bref/brève; (*person, step*) petit(e); (*curt*) brusque, sec/sèche; (*insufficient*) insuffisant(e) ▷ *n* (*also:* **~ film**) court métrage; (*Elec*) court-circuit *m*; **to be ~ of sth** être à court de or manquer de qch; **to be in ~ supply** manquer, être difficile à trouver; **I'm 3 ~** il m'en manque 3; **in ~** bref; en bref; **~ of doing** à moins de faire; **everything ~ of** tout sauf; **it is ~ for** c'est l'abréviation or le diminutif de; **a ~ time ago** il y a peu de temps; **in the ~ term** à court terme; **to cut ~** (*speech, visit*) abréger, écourter; (*person*) couper la parole à; **to fall ~ of** ne pas être à la hauteur de; **to run ~ of** arriver à court de, venir à manquer de; **to stop ~** s'arrêter net; **to stop ~ of** ne pas aller jusqu'à

shortage ['ʃɔːtɪdʒ] *n* manque *m*, pénurie *f*

shortbread ['ʃɔːtbrɛd] *n* ≈ sablé *m*

short-change [ʃɔːt'tʃeɪndʒ] *vt*: **to ~ sb** ne pas rendre assez à qn

short-circuit [ʃɔːt'səːkɪt] *n* court-circuit *m* ▷ *vt* court-circuiter ▷ *vi* se mettre en court-circuit

shortcoming ['ʃɔːtkʌmɪŋ] *n* défaut *m*

shortcrust pastry ['ʃɔːtkrʌst-], **short pastry** *n* (*Brit*) pâte brisée

shortcut ['ʃɔːtkʌt] *n* raccourci *m*

shorten ['ʃɔːtn] *vt* raccourcir; (*text, visit*) abréger

shortfall ['ʃɔːtfɔːl] *n* déficit *m*

shorthand ['ʃɔːthænd] *n* (*Brit*) sténo(graphie) *f*; **to take sth down in ~** prendre qch en sténo

shorthand typist *n* (*Brit*) sténodactylo *m/f*

shortlist ['ʃɔːtlɪst] *n* (*Brit: for job*) liste *f* des candidats sélectionnés

short-lived ['ʃɔːt'lɪvd] *adj* de courte durée

shortly ['ʃɔːtlɪ] *adv* bientôt, sous peu

short notice *n*: **at ~** au dernier moment

shorts [ʃɔːts] *npl*: **(a pair of) ~** un short

short-sighted [ʃɔːt'saɪtɪd] *adj* (*Brit*) myope; (*fig*) qui manque de clairvoyance

short-sleeved [ʃɔːt'sliːvd] *adj* à manches courtes

short-staffed [ʃɔːt'stɑːft] *adj* à court de personnel

short-stay [ʃɔːt'steɪ] *adj* (*car park*) de courte durée

short story *n* nouvelle *f*

short-tempered [ʃɔːt'tɛmpəd] *adj* qui s'emporte facilement

short-term ['ʃɔːttəːm] *adj* (*effect*) à court terme

short wave *n* (*Radio*) ondes courtes

shot [ʃɔt] *pt, pp of* **shoot** ▷ *n* coup *m* (de feu); (*shotgun pellets*) plombs *mpl*; (*try*) coup, essai *m*; (*injection*) piqûre *f*; (*Phot*) photo *f*; **to be a good/poor ~** (*person*) tirer bien/mal; **to fire a ~ at sb/sth** tirer sur qn/qch; **to have a ~ at (doing) sth** essayer de faire qch; **like a ~** comme une flèche; (*very readily*) sans hésiter;

s

to get ~ of sb/sth (inf) se débarrasser de qn/qch; **a big ~** (inf) un gros bonnet

shotgun ['ʃɒtɡʌn] n fusil m de chasse

should [ʃʊd] aux vb: **I ~ go now** je devrais partir maintenant; **he ~ be there now** il devrait être arrivé maintenant; **I ~ go if I were you** si j'étais vous j'irais; **I ~ like to** volontiers, j'aimerais bien; **~ he phone ...** si jamais il téléphone ...

shoulder ['ʃəʊldə'] n épaule f; (Brit: of road): **hard ~** accotement m ⊳ vt (fig) endosser, se charger de; **to look over one's ~** regarder derrière soi (en tournant la tête); **to rub ~s with sb** (fig) côtoyer qn; **to give sb the cold ~** (fig) battre froid à qn

shoulder bag n sac m à bandoulière

shoulder blade n omoplate f

shouldn't ['ʃʊdnt] = **should not**

shout [ʃaʊt] n cri m ⊳ vt crier ⊳ vi crier, pousser des cris; **to give sb a ~** appeler qn; **shout down** vt huer

shouting ['ʃaʊtɪŋ] n cris mpl

shove [ʃʌv] vt pousser; (inf: put): **to ~ sth in** fourrer or ficher qch dans ⊳ n poussée f; **he ~d me out of the way** il m'a écarté en me poussant; **shove off** vi (Naut) pousser au large; (fig: col) ficher le camp

shovel ['ʃʌvl] n pelle f ⊳ vt pelleter, enlever (or enfourner) à la pelle

show [ʃəʊ] (pt **showed**, pp **shown**) [ʃəʊn] n (of emotion) manifestation f, démonstration f; (semblance) semblant m, apparence f; (exhibition) exposition f, salon m; (Theat, TV) spectacle m; (Cine) séance f ⊳ vt montrer; (film) passer; (courage etc) faire preuve de, manifester; (exhibit) exposer ⊳ vi se voir, être visible; **can you ~ me where it is, please?** pouvez-vous me montrer où c'est?; **to ask for a ~ of hands** demander que l'on vote à main levée; **to be on ~** être exposé(e); **it's just for ~** c'est juste pour l'effet; **who's running the ~ here?** (inf) qui est-ce qui commande ici?; **to ~ sb to his seat/to the door** accompagner qn jusqu'à sa place/la porte; **to ~ a profit/loss** (Comm) indiquer un bénéfice/une perte; **it just goes to ~ that ...** ça prouve bien que ...; **show in** vt faire entrer; **show off** vi (pej) crâner ⊳ vt (display) faire valoir; (pej) faire étalage de; **show out** vt reconduire à la porte; **show up** vi (stand out) ressortir; (inf: turn up) se montrer ⊳ vt démontrer; (unmask) démasquer, dénoncer; (flaw) faire ressortir

show business n le monde du spectacle

showdown ['ʃəʊdaʊn] n épreuve f de force

shower ['ʃaʊə'] n (for washing) douche f; (rain) averse f; (of stones etc) pluie f, grêle f; (US: party) réunion organisée pour la remise de cadeaux ⊳ vi prendre une douche, se doucher ⊳ vt: **to ~ sb with** (gifts etc) combler qn de; (abuse etc) accabler qn de; (missiles) bombarder qn de; **to have** or **take a ~** prendre une douche, se doucher

shower cap n bonnet m de douche

shower gel n gel m douche

showerproof ['ʃaʊəpru:f] adj imperméable

showing ['ʃəʊɪŋ] n (of film) projection f

show jumping [-dʒʌmpɪŋ] n concours m hippique

shown [ʃəʊn] pp of **show**

show-off ['ʃəʊɒf] n (inf: person) crâneur(-euse), m'as-tu-vu(e)

showpiece ['ʃəʊpi:s] n (of exhibition etc) joyau m, clou m; **that hospital is a ~** cet hôpital est un modèle du genre

showroom ['ʃəʊrum] n magasin m or salle f d'exposition

shrank [ʃræŋk] pt of **shrink**

shrapnel ['ʃræpnl] n éclats mpl d'obus

shred [ʃred] n (gen pl) lambeau m, petit morceau m; (fig: of truth, evidence) parcelle f ⊳ vt mettre en lambeaux, déchirer; (documents) détruire; (Culin: grate) râper; (: lettuce etc) couper en lanières

shredder ['ʃredə'] n (for vegetables) râpeur m; (for documents, papers) déchiqueteuse f

shrewd [ʃru:d] adj astucieux(-euse), perspicace; (business person) habile

shriek [ʃri:k] n cri perçant or aigu, hurlement m ⊳ vt, vi hurler, crier

shrill [ʃrɪl] adj perçant(e), aigu(ë), strident(e)

shrimp [ʃrɪmp] n crevette grise

shrine [ʃraɪn] n châsse f; (place) lieu m de pèlerinage

shrink (pt **shrank**, pp **shrunk**) [ʃrɪŋk, ʃræŋk, ʃrʌŋk] vi rétrécir; (fig) diminuer; (also: **~ away**) reculer ⊳ vt (wool) (faire) rétrécir ⊳ n (inf: pej) psychanalyste m/f; **to ~ from (doing) sth** reculer devant (la pensée de faire) qch

shrink-wrap ['ʃrɪŋkræp] vt emballer sous film plastique

shrivel ['ʃrɪvl] (also: **~ up**) vt ratatiner, flétrir ⊳ vi se ratatiner, se flétrir

shroud [ʃraʊd] n linceul m ⊳ vt: **~ed in mystery** enveloppé(e) de mystère

Shrove Tuesday ['ʃrəʊv-] n (le) Mardi gras

shrub [ʃrʌb] n arbuste m

shrubbery ['ʃrʌbərɪ] n massif m d'arbustes

shrug [ʃrʌg] n haussement m d'épaules ⊳ vt, vi: **to ~ (one's shoulders)** hausser les épaules; **shrug off** vt faire fi de; (cold, illness) se débarrasser de

shrunk [ʃrʌŋk] pp of **shrink**

shudder ['ʃʌdə'] n frisson m, frémissement m ⊳ vi frissonner, frémir

shuffle ['ʃʌfl] vt (cards) battre; **to ~ (one's feet)** traîner les pieds

shun [ʃʌn] vt éviter, fuir

shunt [ʃʌnt] vt (Rail: direct) aiguiller; (: divert) détourner ⊳ vi: **to ~ (to and fro)** faire la navette

shut (pt, pp **shut**) [ʃʌt] vt fermer ⊳ vi (se) fermer; **shut down** vt fermer définitivement; (machine) arrêter ⊳ vi fermer définitivement; **shut off** vt couper, arrêter;

shut out vt (person, cold) empêcher d'entrer; (noise) éviter d'entendre; (block: view) boucher; (: memory of sth) chasser de son esprit; **shut up** vi (inf: keep quiet) se taire ▷ vt (close) fermer; (silence) faire taire

shutter ['ʃʌtə'] n volet m; (Phot) obturateur m

shuttle ['ʃʌtl] n navette f; (also: ~ service) (service m de) navette f ▷ vi (vehicle, person) faire la navette ▷ vt (passengers) transporter par un système de navette

shuttlecock ['ʃʌtlkɔk] n volant m (de badminton)

shuttle diplomacy n navettes fpl diplomatiques

shy [ʃaɪ] adj timide; **to fight ~ of** se dérober devant; **to be ~ of doing sth** hésiter à faire qch, ne pas oser faire qch ▷ vi: **to ~ away from doing sth** craindre de faire qch

Siberia [saɪˈbɪərɪə] n Sibérie f

siblings ['sɪblɪŋz] npl (formal) frères et sœurs mpl (de mêmes parents)

Sicily ['sɪsɪlɪ] n Sicile f

sick [sɪk] adj (ill) malade; (Brit: vomiting): **to be ~** vomir; (humour) noir(e), macabre; **to feel ~** avoir envie de vomir, avoir mal au cœur; **to fall ~** tomber malade; **to be (off) ~** être absent(e) pour cause de maladie; **a ~ person** un(e) malade; **to be ~ of** (fig) en avoir assez de

sick bay n infirmerie f

sicken ['sɪkn] vt écœurer ▷ vi: **to be ~ing for sth** (cold, flu etc) couver qch

sickening ['sɪknɪŋ] adj (fig) écœurant(e), révoltant(e)

sickle ['sɪkl] n faucille f

sick leave n congé m de maladie

sickly ['sɪklɪ] adj maladif(-ive), souffreteux(-euse); (causing nausea) écœurant(e)

sickness ['sɪknɪs] n maladie f; (vomiting) vomissement(s) m(pl)

sick note n (from parents) mot m d'absence; (from doctor) certificat médical

sick pay n indemnité f de maladie (versée par l'employeur)

side [saɪd] n côté m; (of animal) flanc m; (of lake, road) bord m; (of mountain) versant m; (fig: aspect) côté, aspect m; (team: Sport) équipe f; (TV: channel) chaîne f ▷ adj (door, entrance) latéral(e) ▷ vi: **to ~ with sb** prendre le parti de qn, se ranger du côté de qn; **by the ~ of** au bord de; **~ by ~** côte à côte; **the right/wrong ~** le bon/mauvais côté, l'endroit/l'envers m; **they are on our ~** ils sont avec nous; **from all ~s** de tous côtés; **to rock from ~ to ~** se balancer; **to take ~s (with)** prendre parti (pour); **a ~ of beef** ≈ un quartier de bœuf

sideboard ['saɪdbɔːd] n buffet m

sideboards (Brit) ['saɪdbɔːdz], **sideburns** ['saɪdbəːnz] npl (whiskers) pattes fpl

side drum n (Mus) tambour plat, caisse claire

side effect n effet m secondaire

sidelight ['saɪdlaɪt] n (Aut) veilleuse f

sideline ['saɪdlaɪn] n (Sport) (ligne f de) touche f; (fig) activité f secondaire

sidelong ['saɪdlɔŋ] adj: **to give sb a ~ glance** regarder qn du coin de l'œil

side order n garniture f

side road n petite route, route transversale

sideshow ['saɪdʃəu] n attraction f

sidestep ['saɪdstɛp] vt (question) éluder; (problem) éviter ▷ vi (Boxing etc) esquiver

side street n rue transversale

sidetrack ['saɪdtræk] vt (fig) faire dévier de son sujet

sidewalk ['saɪdwɔːk] n (US) trottoir m

sideways ['saɪdweɪz] adv de côté

siding ['saɪdɪŋ] n (Rail) voie f de garage

siege [siːdʒ] n siège m; **to lay ~ to** assiéger

sieve [sɪv] n tamis m, passoire f ▷ vt tamiser, passer (au tamis)

sift [sɪft] vt passer au tamis or au crible; (fig) passer au crible ▷ vi (fig): **to ~ through** passer en revue

sigh [saɪ] n soupir m ▷ vi soupirer, pousser un soupir

sight [saɪt] n (faculty) vue f; (spectacle) spectacle m; (on gun) mire f ▷ vt apercevoir; **in ~** visible; (fig) en vue; **out of ~** hors de vue; **at ~** (Comm) à vue; **at first ~** à première vue, au premier abord; **I know her by ~** je la connais de vue; **to catch ~ of sb/sth** apercevoir qn/qch; **to lose ~ of sb/sth** perdre qn/qch de vue; **to set one's ~s on sth** jeter son dévolu sur qch

sightseeing ['saɪtsiːɪŋ] n tourisme m; **to go ~** faire du tourisme

sign [saɪn] n (gen) signe m; (with hand etc) signe, geste m; (notice) panneau m, écriteau m; (also: road ~) panneau de signalisation ▷ vt signer; **as a ~ of** en signe de; **it's a good/bad ~** c'est bon/mauvais signe; **plus/minus ~** signe plus/moins; **there's no ~ of a change of mind** rien ne laisse présager un revirement; **he was showing ~s of improvement** il commençait visiblement à faire des progrès; **to ~ one's name** signer; **where do I ~?** où dois-je signer?; **sign away** vt (rights etc) renoncer officiellement à; **sign for** vt fus (item) signer le reçu pour; **sign in** vi signer le registre (en arrivant); **sign off** vi (Radio, TV) terminer l'émission; **sign on** vi (Mil) s'engager; (Brit: as unemployed) s'inscrire au chômage; (enrol) s'inscrire ▷ vt (Mil) engager; (employee) embaucher; **to ~ on for a course** s'inscrire pour un cours; **sign out** vi signer le registre (en partant); **sign over** vt: **to ~ sth over to sb** céder qch par écrit à qn; **sign up** vi (Mil) s'engager ▷ vi (Mil) s'engager; (for course) s'inscrire

signal ['sɪgnl] n signal m ▷ vi (Aut) mettre son clignotant ▷ vt (person) faire signe à; (message) communiquer par signaux; **to ~ a**

left/right turn (*Aut*) indiquer *or* signaler que l'on tourne à gauche/droite; **to ~ to sb (to do sth)** faire signe à qn (de faire qch)

signalman ['sɪɡnlmən] *n* (*Rail*) aiguilleur *m*

signature ['sɪɡnətʃəʳ] *n* signature *f*

signature tune *n* indicatif musical

signet ring ['sɪɡnət-] *n* chevalière *f*

significance [sɪɡ'nɪfɪkəns] *n* signification *f*; importance *f*; **that is of no ~** ceci n'a pas d'importance

significant [sɪɡ'nɪfɪkənt] *adj* significatif(-ive); (*important*) important(e), considérable

signify ['sɪɡnɪfaɪ] *vt* signifier

sign language *n* langage *m* par signes

signpost ['saɪnpəust] *n* poteau indicateur

Sikh [siːk] *adj, n* Sikh *m/f*

silence ['saɪlns] *n* silence *m* ⊳ *vt* faire taire, réduire au silence

silencer ['saɪlənsəʳ] *n* (*Brit: on gun, Aut*) silencieux *m*

silent ['saɪlnt] *adj* silencieux(-euse); (*film*) muet(te); **to keep** *or* **remain ~** garder le silence, ne rien dire

silent partner *n* (*Comm*) bailleur *m* de fonds, commanditaire *m*

silhouette [sɪluː'ɛt] *n* silhouette *f* ⊳ *vt*: **~d against** se profilant sur, se découpant contre

silicon chip ['sɪlɪkən-] *n* puce *f* électronique

silk [sɪlk] *n* soie *f* ⊳ *cpd* de *or* en soie

silky ['sɪlkɪ] *adj* soyeux(-euse)

silly ['sɪlɪ] *adj* stupide, sot(te), bête; **to do something ~** faire une bêtise

silt [sɪlt] *n* vase *f*; limon *m*

silver ['sɪlvəʳ] *n* argent *m*; (*money*) monnaie *f* (en pièces d'argent); (*also:* **~ware**) argenterie *f* ⊳ *adj* (*made of silver*) d'argent, en argent; (*in colour*) argenté(e); (*car*) gris métallisé *inv*

silver-plated [sɪlvə'pleɪtɪd] *adj* plaqué(e) argent

silversmith ['sɪlvəsmɪθ] *n* orfèvre *m/f*

silvery ['sɪlvrɪ] *adj* argenté(e)

SIM card ['sɪm-] *abbr* (*Tel*) carte *f* SIM

similar ['sɪmɪləʳ] *adj*: **~ (to)** semblable (à)

similarity [sɪmɪ'lærɪtɪ] *n* ressemblance *f*, similarité *f*

similarly ['sɪmɪləlɪ] *adv* de la même façon, de même

simmer ['sɪməʳ] *vi* cuire à feu doux, mijoter; **simmer down** *vi* (*fig: inf*) se calmer

simple ['sɪmpl] *adj* simple; **the ~ truth** la vérité pure et simple

simplicity [sɪm'plɪsɪtɪ] *n* simplicité *f*

simplify ['sɪmplɪfaɪ] *vt* simplifier

simply ['sɪmplɪ] *adv* simplement; (*without fuss*) avec simplicité; (*absolutely*) absolument

simulate ['sɪmjuleɪt] *vt* simuler, feindre

simultaneous [sɪməl'teɪnɪəs] *adj* simultané(e)

simultaneously [sɪməl'teɪnɪəslɪ] *adv* simultanément

sin [sɪn] *n* péché *m* ⊳ *vi* pécher

since [sɪns] *adv, prep* depuis *f* ⊳ *conj* (*time*) depuis que; (*because*) puisque, étant donné que, comme; **~ then, ever ~** depuis ce moment-là; **~ Monday** depuis lundi; (*ever*) **~ I arrived** depuis mon arrivée, depuis que je suis arrivé

sincere [sɪn'sɪəʳ] *adj* sincère

sincerely [sɪn'sɪəlɪ] *adv* sincèrement; **Yours ~** (*at end of letter*) veuillez agréer, Monsieur (*or* Madame) l'expression de mes sentiments distingués *or* les meilleurs

sincerity [sɪn'sɛrɪtɪ] *n* sincérité *f*

sinew ['sɪnjuː] *n* tendon *m*; **sinews** *npl* muscles *mpl*

sing (*pt* **sang**, *pp* **sung**) [sɪŋ, sæŋ, sʌŋ] *vt, vi* chanter

Singapore [sɪŋɡə'pɔːʳ] *n* Singapour *m*

singe [sɪndʒ] *vt* brûler légèrement; (*clothes*) roussir

singer ['sɪŋəʳ] *n* chanteur(-euse)

singing ['sɪŋɪŋ] *n* (*of person, bird*) chant *m*; façon *f* de chanter; (*of kettle, bullet, in ears*) sifflement *m*

single ['sɪŋɡl] *adj* seul(e), unique; (*unmarried*) célibataire; (*not double*) simple ⊳ *n* (*Brit: also:* **~ ticket**) aller *m* (simple); (*record*) 45 tours *m*; **singles** *npl* (*Tennis*) simple *m*; (*US: single people*) célibataires *m/fpl*; **not a ~ one was left** il n'en est pas resté un(e), seul(e); **every ~ day** chaque jour sans exception; **single out** *vt* choisir; (*distinguish*) distinguer

single bed *n* lit *m* d'une personne *or* à une place

single-breasted ['sɪŋɡlbrɛstɪd] *adj* droit(e)

single file *n*: **in ~** en file indienne

single-handed ['sɪŋɡl'hændɪd] *adv* tout(e) seul(e), sans (aucune) aide

single-minded ['sɪŋɡl'maɪndɪd] *adj* résolu(e), tenace

single parent *n* parent unique (*or* célibataire); **single-parent family** famille monoparentale

single room *n* chambre *f* à un lit *or* pour une personne

single-track road [sɪŋɡl'træk-] *n* route *f* à voie unique

singly ['sɪŋɡlɪ] *adv* séparément

singular ['sɪŋɡjuləʳ] *adj* singulier(-ière); (*odd*) singulier, étrange; (*outstanding*) remarquable; (*Ling*) (au) singulier, du singulier ⊳ *n* (*Ling*) singulier *m*; **in the feminine ~** au féminin singulier

sinister ['sɪnɪstəʳ] *adj* sinistre

sink [sɪŋk] (*pt* **sank**, *pp* **sunk**) [sæŋk, sʌŋk] *n* évier *m*; (*washbasin*) lavabo *m* ⊳ *vt* (*ship*) (faire) couler, faire sombrer; (*foundations*) creuser; (*piles etc*): **to ~ sth into** enfoncer qch dans ⊳ *vi* couler, sombrer; (*ground etc*) s'affaisser; **to ~ into sth** (*chair*) s'enfoncer dans qch; **he sank into a chair/the mud** il s'est enfoncé dans un fauteuil/la boue; **a ~ing feeling** un serrement de cœur; **sink in** vi s'enfoncer, pénétrer; (*explanation*) rentrer (*inf*), être compris; **it took a long time to ~ in** il a fallu longtemps pour que ça rentre

sinner ['sɪnə'] n pécheur(-eresse)

sinus ['saɪnəs] n (*Anat*) sinus m inv

sip [sɪp] n petite gorgée ▷ vt boire à petites gorgées

siphon ['saɪfən] n siphon m ▷ vt (*also*: **~ off**) siphonner; (: *fig*: *funds*) transférer; (: *illegally*) détourner

sir [sə'] n monsieur m; **S~ John Smith** sir John Smith; **yes ~** oui Monsieur; **Dear S~** (*in letter*) Monsieur

siren ['saɪərn] n sirène f

sirloin ['sə:lɔɪn] n (*also*: **~ steak**) aloyau m

sissy ['sɪsɪ] n (*inf*: *coward*) poule mouillée

sister ['sɪstə'] n sœur f; (*nun*) religieuse f, (bonne) sœur; (*Brit*: *nurse*) infirmière f en chef ▷ cpd: **~ organization** organisation f sœur; **~ ship** sister(-)ship m

sister-in-law ['sɪstərɪnlɔ:] n belle-sœur f

sit (*pt*, *pp* **sat**) [sɪt, sæt] vi s'asseoir; (*be sitting*) être assis(e); (*assembly*) être en séance, siéger; (*for painter*) poser; (*dress etc*) tomber ▷ vt (*exam*) passer, se présenter à; **to ~ tight** ne pas bouger; **sit about, sit around** vi être assis(e) or rester à ne rien faire; **sit back** vi (*in seat*) bien s'installer, se carrer; **sit down** vi s'asseoir; **to be ~ting down** être assis(e); **sit in** vi: **to ~ in on a discussion** assister à une discussion; **sit on** vt fus (*jury*, *committee*) faire partie de; **sit up** vi s'asseoir; (*straight*) se redresser; (*not go to bed*) rester debout, ne pas se coucher

sitcom ['sɪtkɔm] n abbr (*TV*: = *situation comedy*) sitcom f, comédie f de situation

site [saɪt] n emplacement m, site m; (*also*: **building ~**) chantier m ▷ vt placer

sit-in ['sɪtɪn] n (*demonstration*) sit-in m inv, occupation f de locaux

sitting ['sɪtɪŋ] n (*of assembly etc*) séance f; (*in canteen*) service m

sitting room n salon m

situated ['sɪtjueɪtɪd] adj situé(e)

situation [sɪtju'eɪʃən] n situation f; **"~s vacant/wanted"** (*Brit*) "offres/demandes d'emploi"

six [sɪks] num six

sixteen [sɪks'ti:n] num seize

sixteenth [sɪks'ti:nθ] num seizième

sixth ['sɪksθ] num sixième ▷ n: **the upper/ lower ~** (*Brit Scol*) la terminale/la première

sixth form n (*Brit*) ≈ classes fpl de première et de terminale

sixth-form college n lycée n'ayant que des classes de première et de terminale

sixtieth ['sɪkstɪθ] num soixantième

sixty ['sɪkstɪ] num soixante

size [saɪz] n dimensions fpl; (*of person*) taille f; (*of clothing*) taille f; (*of shoes*) pointure f; (*of estate*, *area*) étendue f; (*of problem*) ampleur f;

(*of company*) importance f; (*glue*) colle f; **I take ~ 14** (*of dress etc*) ≈ je prends du 42 or la taille 42; **the small/large ~** (*of soap powder etc*) le petit/ grand modèle; **it's the ~ of ...** c'est de la taille (or grosseur) de ..., c'est grand (or gros) comme ...; **cut to ~** découpé(e) aux dimensions voulues; **size up** vt juger, jauger

sizeable ['saɪzəbl] adj (*object*, *building*, *estate*) assez grand(e); (*amount*, *problem*, *majority*) assez important(e)

sizzle ['sɪzl] vi grésiller

skate [skeɪt] n patin m; (*fish*: *pl inv*) raie f ▷ vi patiner; **skate over, skate around** vt (*problem*, *issue*) éluder

skateboard ['skeɪtbɔ:d] n skateboard m, planche f à roulettes

skateboarding ['skeɪtbɔ:dɪŋ] n skateboard m

skater ['skeɪtə'] n patineur(-euse)

skating ['skeɪtɪŋ] n patinage m

skating rink n patinoire f

skeleton ['skɛlɪtn] n squelette m; (*outline*) schéma m

skeleton staff n effectifs réduits

skeptical ['skɛptɪkl] (*US*) adj = **sceptical**

sketch [skɛtʃ] n (*drawing*) croquis m, esquisse f; (*outline plan*) aperçu m; (*Theat*) sketch m, saynète f ▷ vt esquisser, faire un croquis or une esquisse de; (*plan etc*) esquisser

sketch book n carnet m à dessin

sketchy ['skɛtʃɪ] adj incomplet(-ète), fragmentaire

skewer ['skju:ə'] n brochette f

ski [ski:] n ski m ▷ vi skier, faire du ski

ski boot n chaussure f de ski

skid [skɪd] n dérapage m ▷ vi déraper; **to go into a ~** déraper

skier ['ski:ə'] n skieur(-euse)

skiing ['ski:ɪŋ] n ski m; **to go ~** (aller) faire du ski

ski jump n (*ramp*) tremplin m; (*event*) saut m à skis

skilful, (*US*) **skillful** ['skɪlful] adj habile, adroit(e)

ski lift n remonte-pente m inv

skill [skɪl] n (*ability*) habileté f, adresse f, talent m; (*requiring training*) compétences fpl

skilled [skɪld] adj habile, adroit(e); (*worker*) qualifié(e)

skim [skɪm] vt (*milk*) écrémer; (*soup*) écumer; (*glide over*) raser, effleurer ▷ vi: **to ~ through** (*fig*) parcourir

skimmed milk [skɪmd-], (*US*) **skim milk** n lait écrémé

skimp [skɪmp] vt (*work*) bâcler, faire à la va-vite; (*cloth etc*) lésiner sur

skimpy ['skɪmpɪ] adj étriqué(e); maigre

skin [skɪn] n peau f ▷ vt (*fruit etc*) éplucher; (*animal*) écorcher; **wet or soaked to the ~** trempé(e) jusqu'aux os

skin cancer n cancer m de la peau

skin-deep ['skɪn'di:p] adj superficiel(le)

S

skin diving n plongée sous-marine
skinhead ['skɪnhɛd] n skinhead m
skinny ['skɪnɪ] adj maigre, maigrichon(ne)
skintight ['skɪntaɪt] adj (dress etc) collant(e),
ajusté(e)
skip [skɪp] n petit bond or saut; (Brit: container)
benne f ▷ vi gambader, sautiller; (with rope)
sauter à la corde ▷ vt (pass over) sauter; **to ~
school** (esp US) faire l'école buissonnière
ski pass n forfait-skieur(s) m
ski pole n bâton m de ski
skipper ['skɪpər] n (Naut, Sport) capitaine m;
(in race) skipper m ▷ vt (boat) commander;
(team) être le chef de
skipping rope ['skɪpɪŋ-], (US) **skip rope** n
corde f à sauter
skirmish ['skəːmɪʃ] n escarmouche f,
accrochage m
skirt [skəːt] n jupe f ▷ vt longer, contourner
skirting board ['skəːtɪŋ-] n (Brit) plinthe f
ski slope n piste f de ski
ski suit n combinaison f de ski
ski tow n = **ski lift**
skittle ['skɪtl] n quille f; **skittles** (game) (jeu m
de) quilles fpl
skive [skaɪv] vi (Brit inf) tirer au flanc
skull [skʌl] n crâne m
skunk [skʌŋk] n mouffette f; (fur) sconse m
sky [skaɪ] n ciel m; **to praise sb to the skies**
porter qn aux nues
skylight ['skaɪlaɪt] n lucarne f
skyscraper ['skaɪskreɪpər] n gratte-ciel m inv
slab [slæb] n plaque f; (of stone) dalle f; (of
wood) bloc m; (of meat, cheese) tranche épaisse
slack [slæk] adj (loose) lâche, desserré(e);
(slow) stagnant(e); (careless) négligent(e), peu
sérieux(-euse) or consciencieux(-euse);
(Comm: market) peu actif(-ive); (: demand)
faible; (period) creux(-euse) ▷ n (in rope etc)
mou m; **business is ~** les affaires vont mal
slacken ['slækn] (also: ~ **off**) vi ralentir,
diminuer ▷ vt relâcher
slacks [slæks] npl pantalon m
slag heap n crassier m
slag off (Brit: inf) vt dire du mal de
slain [sleɪn] pp of **slay**
slam [slæm] vt (door) (faire) claquer; (throw)
jeter violemment, flanquer; (inf: criticize)
éreinter, démolir ▷ vi claquer
slander ['slɑːndər] n calomnie f; (Law)
diffamation f ▷ vt calomnier; diffamer
slang [slæŋ] n argot m
slant [slɑːnt] n inclinaison f; (fig) angle m,
point m de vue
slanted ['slɑːntɪd] adj tendancieux(-euse)
slanting ['slɑːntɪŋ] adj en pente, incliné(e);
couché(e)
slap [slæp] n claque f, gifle f; (on the back)
tape f ▷ vt donner une claque or une gifle
(or une tape) à; (paint) appliquer
rapidement ▷ adv (directly) tout droit,
en plein

slapdash ['slæpdæʃ] adj (work) fait(e) sans
soin or à la va-vite; (person) insouciant(e),
négligent(e)
slapstick ['slæpstɪk] n (comedy) grosse farce
(style tarte à la crème)
slap-up ['slæpʌp] adj (Brit): **a ~ meal** un repas
extra or fameux
slash [slæʃ] vt entailler, taillader; (fig: prices)
casser
slat [slæt] n (of wood) latte f, lame f
slate [sleɪt] n ardoise f ▷ vt (fig: criticize)
éreinter, démolir
slaughter ['slɔːtər] n carnage m, massacre m;
(of animals) abattage m ▷ vt (animal) abattre;
(people) massacrer
slaughterhouse ['slɔːtəhaus] n abattoir m
Slav [slɑːv] adj slave
slave [sleɪv] n esclave m/f ▷ vi (also: ~ **away**)
trimer, travailler comme un forçat; **to ~
(away) at sth/at doing sth** se tuer à qch/à
faire qch
slavery ['sleɪvərɪ] n esclavage m
slay (pt **slew**, pp **slain**) [sleɪ, sluː, sleɪn] vt
(literary) tuer
sleazy ['sliːzɪ] adj miteux(-euse), minable
sled [slɛd] (US) = **sledge**
sledge [slɛdʒ] n luge f
sledgehammer ['slɛdʒhæmər] n marteau m
de forgeron
sleek [sliːk] adj (hair, fur) brillant(e),
luisant(e); (car, boat) aux lignes pures or
élégantes
sleep [sliːp] n sommeil m ▷ vi (pt, pp **slept**)
[slɛpt] dormir; (spend night) dormir, coucher
▷ vt: **we can ~ 4** on peut coucher or loger 4
personnes; **to go to ~** s'endormir; **to have a
good night's ~** passer une bonne nuit; **to
put to ~** (patient) endormir; (animal:
euphemism: kill) piquer; **to ~ lightly** avoir le
sommeil léger; **to ~ with sb** (have sex) coucher
avec qn; **sleep around** vi coucher à droite et
à gauche; **sleep in** vi (oversleep) se réveiller
trop tard; (on purpose) faire la grasse matinée;
sleep together vi (have sex) coucher
ensemble
sleeper ['sliːpər] n (person) dormeur(-euse);
(Brit Rail: on track) traverse f; (: train)
train-couchettes m; (: carriage)
wagon-lits m, voiture-lits f; (: berth)
couchette f
sleeping bag ['sliːpɪŋ-] n sac m de couchage
sleeping car ['sliːpɪŋ-] n wagon-lits m,
voiture-lits f
sleeping partner ['sliːpɪŋ-] n (Brit Comm)
= **silent partner**
sleeping pill ['sliːpɪŋ-] n somnifère m
sleepless ['sliːplɪs] adj: **a ~ night** une nuit
blanche
sleepover ['sliːpəuvər] n nuit f chez un
copain or une copine; **we're having a ~ at
Jo's** nous allons passer la nuit chez Jo
sleepwalk ['sliːpwɔːk] vi marcher en dormant

sleepwalker ['sliːpwɔːkəʳ] *n* somnambule *m/f*

sleepy ['sliːpɪ] *adj* qui a envie de dormir; *(fig)* endormi(e); **to be** *or* **feel ~** avoir sommeil, avoir envie de dormir

sleet [sliːt] *n* neige fondue

sleeve [sliːv] *n* manche *f*; *(of record)* pochette *f*

sleeveless ['sliːvlɪs] *adj (garment)* sans manches

sleigh [sleɪ] *n* traîneau *m*

sleight [slaɪt] *n*: **~ of hand** tour *m* de passe-passe

slender ['slɛndəʳ] *adj* svelte, mince; *(fig)* faible, ténu(e)

slept [slɛpt] *pt, pp* of **sleep**

slew [sluː] *vi (also:* **~ round)** virer, pivoter ▷ *pt* of **slay**

slice [slaɪs] *n* tranche *f*; *(round)* rondelle *f*; *(utensil)* spatule *f*; *(also:* **fish ~)** pelle *f* à poisson ▷ *vt* couper en tranches *(or* en rondelles); **~d bread** pain *m* en tranches

slick [slɪk] *adj (skilful)* bien ficelé(e); *(salesperson)* qui a du bagout, mielleux(-euse) ▷ *n (also:* **oil ~)** nappe *f* de pétrole, marée noire

slide [slaɪd] *(pt, pp* **slid)** [slɪd] *n (in playground)* toboggan *m*; *(Phot)* diapositive *f*; *(Brit: also:* **hair ~)** barrette *f*; *(microscope slide)* lame *f*) porte-objet *m*; *(in prices)* chute *f*, baisse *f* ▷ *vt* (faire) glisser ▷ *vi* glisser; **to let things ~** *(fig)* laisser les choses aller à la dérive

sliding ['slaɪdɪŋ] *adj (door)* coulissant(e); **~ roof** *(Aut)* toit ouvrant

sliding scale *n* échelle *f* mobile

slight [slaɪt] *adj (slim)* mince, menu(e); *(frail)* frêle; *(trivial)* faible, insignifiant(e); *(small)* petit(e), léger(-ère) *(before n)* ▷ *n* offense *f*, affront *m* ▷ *vt (offend)* blesser, offenser; **the ~est** le *(or* la) moindre; **not in the ~est** pas le moins du monde, pas du tout

slightly ['slaɪtlɪ] *adv* légèrement, un peu; **~ built** fluet(te)

slim [slɪm] *adj* mince ▷ *vi* maigrir; *(diet)* suivre un régime amaigrissant

slime [slaɪm] *n* vase *f*; substance visqueuse

slimming ['slɪmɪŋ] *n* amaigrissement *m* ▷ *adj (diet, pills)* amaigrissant(e), pour maigrir; *(food)* qui ne fait pas grossir

slimy ['slaɪmɪ] *adj* visqueux(-euse), gluant(e); *(covered with mud)* vaseux(-euse)

sling [slɪŋ] *n (Med)* écharpe *f*; *(for baby)* porte-bébé *m*; *(weapon)* fronde *f*, lance-pierre *m* ▷ *vt (pt* **slung,** *pp* [slʌŋ]) lancer, jeter; **to have one's arm in a ~** avoir le bras en écharpe

slip [slɪp] *n* faux pas *m*; *(mistake)* erreur *f*, bévue *f*; *(underskirt)* combinaison *f*; *(of paper)* petite feuille, fiche *f* ▷ *vt (slide)* glisser ▷ *vi (slide)* glisser; *(decline)* baisser; *(move smoothly)*: **to ~ into/out of** se glisser *or* se faufiler dans/hors de; **to let a chance ~ by** laisser passer une occasion; **to ~ sth on/off** enfiler/enlever qch; **it ~ped from her hand** cela lui a glissé des mains; **to give sb the ~** fausser

compagnie à qn; **a ~ of the tongue** un lapsus; **slip away** *vi* s'esquiver; **slip in** *vt* glisser; **slip out** *vi* sortir; *(slip out)* glisser; **slip up** *vi* faire une erreur, gaffer

slipped disc [slɪpt-] *n* déplacement *m* de vertèbre

slipper ['slɪpəʳ] *n* pantoufle *f*

slippery ['slɪpərɪ] *adj* glissant(e); *(fig: person)* insaisissable

slip road *n (Brit: to motorway)* bretelle *f* d'accès

slip-up ['slɪpʌp] *n* bévue *f*

slipway ['slɪpweɪ] *n* cale *f* (de construction *or* de lancement)

slit [slɪt] *n* fente *f*; *(cut)* incision *f*; *(tear)* déchirure *f* ▷ *vt (pt, pp* **slit)** fendre; couper, inciser; déchirer; **to ~ sb's throat** trancher la gorge à qn

slither ['slɪðəʳ] *vi* glisser, déraper

sliver ['slɪvəʳ] *n (of glass, wood)* éclat *m*; *(of cheese, sausage)* petit morceau

slob [slɔb] *n (inf)* rustaud(e)

slog [slɔg] *n (Brit: effort)* gros effort; *(: work)* tâche fastidieuse ▷ *vi* travailler très dur

slogan ['sləʊgən] *n* slogan *m*

slope [sləʊp] *n* pente *f*, côte *f*; *(side of mountain)* versant *m*; *(slant)* inclinaison *f* ▷ *vi*: **to ~ down** être *or* descendre en pente; **to ~ up** monter

sloping ['sləʊpɪŋ] *adj* en pente, incliné(e); *(handwriting)* penché(e)

sloppy ['slɔpɪ] *adj (work)* peu soigné(e), bâclé(e); *(appearance)* négligé(e), débraillé(e); *(film etc)* sentimental(e)

slot [slɔt] *n* fente *f*; *(fig: in timetable, Radio, TV)* créneau *m*, plage *f* ▷ *vt*: **to ~ sth into** encastrer *or* insérer qch dans ▷ *vi*: **to ~ into** s'encastrer *or* s'insérer dans

sloth [sləʊθ] *n (vice)* paresse *f*; *(Zool)* paresseux *m*

slot machine *n (Brit: vending machine)* distributeur *m* (automatique), machine *f* à sous; *(for gambling)* appareil *m* *or* machine à sous

slouch [slaʊtʃ] *vi* avoir le dos rond, être voûté(e); **slouch about, slouch around** *vi* traîner à ne rien faire

Slovakia [sləʊ'vækɪə] *n* Slovaquie *f*

Slovene [sləʊ'viːn] *adj* slovène ▷ *n* Slovène *m/f*; *(Ling)* slovène *m*

Slovenia [sləʊ'viːnɪə] *n* Slovénie *f*

Slovenian [sləʊ'viːnɪən] *adj, n* = **Slovene**

slovenly ['slʌvənlɪ] *adj* sale, débraillé(e), négligé(e)

slow [sləʊ] *adj* lent(e); *(watch)*: **to be ~** retarder ▷ *adv* lentement ▷ *vt, vi* ralentir; **"~"** *(road sign)* "ralentir"; **at a ~ speed** à petite vitesse; **to be ~ to act/decide** être lent à agir/décider; **my watch is 20 minutes ~** ma montre retarde de 20 minutes; **business is ~** les affaires marchent au ralenti; **to go ~** *(driver)* rouler lentement; *(in industrial dispute)* faire la grève perlée; **slow down** *vi* ralentir

S

slowly ['sləʊlɪ] adv lentement
slow motion n: **in ~** au ralenti
sludge [slʌdʒ] n boue f
slug [slʌg] n limace f; (bullet) balle f
sluggish ['slʌgɪʃ] adj (person) mou/molle,
lent(e); (stream, engine, trading) lent(e);
(business, sales) stagnant(e)
sluice [slu:s] n écluse f; (also: **~ gate**) vanne f
▷ vt: **to ~ down** or **out** laver à grande eau
slum [slʌm] n (house) taudis m; **slums** npl
(area) quartiers mpl pauvres
slump [slʌmp] n baisse soudaine,
effondrement m; (Econ) crise f ▷ vi
s'effondrer, s'affaisser
slung [slʌŋ] pt, pp of **sling**
slur [slə:ʳ] n bredouillement m; (smear):
~ (on) atteinte f (à); insinuation f (contre)
▷ vt mal articuler; **to be a ~ on** porter
atteinte à
slush [slʌʃ] n neige fondue
slut [slʌt] n (inf!) souillon f
sly [slaɪ] adj (person) rusé(e); (smile, expression,
remark) sournois(e); **on the ~** en cachette
smack [smæk] n (slap) tape f; (on face) gifle f
▷ vt donner une tape à; (on face) gifler; (on
bottom) donner la fessée à ▷ vi: **to ~ of** avoir
des relents de, sentir ▷ adv (inf): **it fell ~ in
the middle** c'est tombé en plein milieu or en
plein dedans; **to ~ one's lips** se lécher les
babines
small [smɔ:l] adj petit(e); (letter) minuscule
▷ n: **the ~ of the back** le creux des reins; **to
get** or **grow ~er** diminuer; **to make ~er**
(amount, income) diminuer; (object, garment)
rapetisser; **a ~ shopkeeper** un petit
commerçant
small ads npl (Brit) petites annonces
small change n petite or menue monnaie
smallholder ['smɔ:lhəʊldəʳ] n (Brit) petit
cultivateur
small hours npl: **in the ~** au petit matin
smallpox ['smɔ:lpɔks] n variole f
small talk n menus propos
smart [smɑ:t] adj élégant(e), chic inv; (clever)
intelligent(e), (pej) futé(e); (quick) vif/vive,
prompt(e) ▷ vi faire mal, brûler; **the ~ set** le
beau monde; **to look ~** être élégant(e); **my
eyes are ~ing** j'ai les yeux irrités or qui me
piquent
smart card ['smɑ:t'kɑ:d] n carte f à puce
smarten up ['smɑ:tn-] vi devenir plus
élégant(e), se faire beau/belle ▷ vt rendre
plus élégant(e)
smart phone n smartphone m
smash [smæʃ] n (also: **~-up**) collision f,
accident m; (Mus) succès foudroyant; (sound)
fracas m ▷ vt casser, briser, fracasser;
(opponent) écraser; (hopes) ruiner, détruire;
(Sport: record) pulvériser ▷ vi se briser, se
fracasser; s'écraser; **smash up** vt (car)
bousiller; (room) tout casser dans
smashing ['smæʃɪŋ] adj (inf) formidable

smattering ['smætərɪŋ] n: **a ~ of** quelques
notions de
smear [smɪəʳ] n (stain) tache f; (mark) trace f;
(Med) frottis m; (insult) calomnie f ▷ vt
enduire; (make dirty) salir; (fig) porter atteinte
à; **his hands were ~ed with oil/ink** il avait
les mains maculées de cambouis/d'encre
smear campaign n campagne f de
dénigrement
smear test n (Brit Med) frottis m
smell [smɛl] (pt, pp **smelt** or **smelled**) [smɛlt,
smɛld] n odeur f; (sense) odorat m ▷ vt sentir
▷ vi (pej) sentir mauvais; (food etc): **to ~ (of)**
sentir; **it ~s good** ça sent bon
smelly ['smɛlɪ] adj qui sent mauvais,
malodorant(e)
smelt [smɛlt] pt, pp of **smell** ▷ vt (ore) fondre
smile [smaɪl] n sourire m ▷ vi sourire
smirk [smə:k] n petit sourire suffisant or
affecté
smock [smɔk] n blouse f, sarrau m
smog [smɔg] n brouillard mêlé de fumée
smoke [sməʊk] n fumée f ▷ vt, vi fumer; **to
have a ~** fumer une cigarette; **do you ~?** est-
ce que vous fumez?; **do you mind if I ~?** ça ne
vous dérange pas que je fume?; **to go up in ~**
(house etc) brûler; (fig) partir en fumée
smoke alarm n détecteur m de fumée
smoked ['sməʊkt] adj (bacon, glass) fumé(e)
smoker ['sməʊkəʳ] n (person) fumeur(-euse);
(Rail) wagon m fumeurs
smoke screen n rideau m or écran m de
fumée; (fig) paravent m
smoking ['sməʊkɪŋ] n: **"no ~"** (sign) "défense
de fumer"; **to give up ~** arrêter de fumer
smoking compartment, (US) **smoking
car** n wagon m fumeurs
smoky ['sməʊkɪ] adj enfumé(e); (taste)
fumé(e)
smolder ['sməʊldəʳ] vi (US) = **smoulder**
smooth [smu:ð] adj lisse; (sauce)
onctueux(-euse); (flavour, whisky)
moelleux(-euse); (cigarette) doux/douce;
(movement) régulier(-ière), sans à-coups or
heurts; (landing, takeoff) en douceur; (flight)
sans secousses; (pej: person)
doucereux(-euse), mielleux(-euse) ▷ vt (also:
~ out) lisser, défroisser; (creases, difficulties)
faire disparaître; **smooth over** vt: **to ~
things over** (fig) arranger les choses
smother ['smʌðəʳ] vt étouffer
smoulder, (US) **smolder** ['sməʊldəʳ] vi
couver
SMS n abbr (= short message service) SMS m
SMS message n (message m) SMS m
smudge [smʌdʒ] n tache f, bavure f ▷ vt salir,
maculer
smug [smʌg] adj suffisant(e), content(e) de soi
smuggle ['smʌgl] vt passer en contrebande or
en fraude; **to ~ in/out** (goods etc) faire entrer/
sortir clandestinement or en fraude
smuggler ['smʌgləʳ] n contrebandier(-ière)

smuggling ['smʌglɪŋ] n contrebande f
smutty ['smʌtɪ] adj (fig) grossier(-ière), obscène
snack [snæk] n casse-croûte m inv; **to have a ~** prendre un en-cas, manger quelque chose (de léger)
snack bar n snack(-bar) m
snag [snæg] n inconvénient m, difficulté f
snail [sneɪl] n escargot m
snake [sneɪk] n serpent m
snap [snæp] n (sound) claquement m, bruit sec; (photograph) photo f, instantané m; (game) sorte de jeu de bataille ▷ adj subit(e), fait(e) sans réfléchir ▷ vt (fingers) faire claquer; (break) casser net; (photograph) prendre un instantané de ▷ vi se casser net or avec un bruit sec; (fig: person) craquer; (speak sharply) parler d'un ton brusque; **to ~ open/shut** s'ouvrir ou se refermer brusquement; **to ~ one's fingers at** (fig) se moquer de; **a cold ~** (of weather) un refroidissement soudain de la température; **snap at** vt fus (subj: dog) essayer de mordre; **snap off** vt (break) casser net; **snap up** vt sauter sur, saisir
snappy ['snæpɪ] adj prompt(e); (slogan) qui a du punch; **make it ~!** (inf: hurry up) grouille-toi!, magne-toi!
snapshot ['snæpʃɔt] n photo f, instantané m
snare [snɛə'] n piège m ▷ vt attraper, prendre au piège
snarl [snɑːl] n grondement m or grognement m féroce ▷ vi gronder ▷ vt: **to get ~ed up** (wool, plans) s'emmêler; (traffic) se bloquer
snatch [snætʃ] n (fig) vol m; (small amount): **~es of** des fragments mpl or bribes fpl de ▷ vt saisir (d'un geste vif); (steal) voler ▷ vi: **don't ~!** doucement!; **to ~ a sandwich** manger or avaler un sandwich à la hâte; **to ~ some sleep** arriver à dormir un peu; **snatch up** vt saisir, s'emparer de
sneak [sniːk] (US pt **snuck**) vi: **to ~ in/out** entrer/sortir furtivement or à la dérobée ▷ vt: **to ~ a look at sth** regarder furtivement qch ▷ n (inf: pej: informer) faux jeton; **to ~ up on sb** s'approcher de qn sans faire de bruit
sneakers ['sniːkəz] npl tennis mpl, baskets fpl
sneer [snɪə'] n ricanement m ▷ vi ricaner, sourire d'un air sarcastique; **to ~ at sb/sth** se moquer de qn/qch avec mépris
sneeze [sniːz] n éternuement m ▷ vi éternuer
sniff [snɪf] n reniflement m ▷ vi renifler ▷ vt renifler, flairer; (glue, drug) sniffer, respirer; **sniff at** vt fus: **it's not to be ~ed at** il ne faut pas cracher dessus, ce n'est pas à dédaigner
snigger ['snɪgə'] n ricanement m; rire moqueur ▷ vi ricaner
snip [snɪp] n (cut) entaille f; (piece) petit bout; (Brit: inf: bargain) (bonne) occasion or affaire ▷ vt couper
sniper ['snaɪpə'] n (marksman) tireur embusqué

snippet ['snɪpɪt] n bribes fpl
snob [snɔb] n snob m/f
snobbish ['snɔbɪʃ] adj snob inv
snooker ['snuːkə'] n sorte de jeu de billard
snoop [snuːp] vi: **to ~ on sb** espionner qn; **to ~ about** fureter
snooze [snuːz] n petit somme ▷ vi faire un petit somme
snore [snɔː'] vi ronfler ▷ n ronflement m
snorkel ['snɔːkl] n (of swimmer) tuba m
snort [snɔːt] n grognement m ▷ vi grogner; (horse) renâcler ▷ vt (inf: drugs) sniffer
snout [snaʊt] n museau m
snow [snəʊ] n neige f ▷ vi neiger ▷ vt: **to be ~ed under with work** être débordé(e) de travail
snowball ['snəʊbɔːl] n boule f de neige
snowbound ['snəʊbaʊnd] adj enneigé(e), bloqué(e) par la neige
snowdrift ['snəʊdrɪft] n congère f
snowdrop ['snəʊdrɔp] n perce-neige m
snowfall ['snəʊfɔːl] n chute f de neige
snowflake ['snəʊfleɪk] n flocon m de neige
snowman ['snəʊmæn] irreg n bonhomme m de neige
snowplough, (US) **snowplow** ['snəʊplaʊ] n chasse-neige m inv
snowshoe ['snəʊʃuː] n raquette f (pour la neige)
snowstorm ['snəʊstɔːm] n tempête f de neige
snub [snʌb] vt repousser, snober ▷ n rebuffade f
snub-nosed [snʌb'nəʊzd] adj au nez retroussé
snuck [snʌk] (US) pt, pp of **sneak**
snuff [snʌf] n tabac m à priser ▷ vt (also: **~ out**: candle) moucher
snug [snʌg] adj douillet(te), confortable; (person) bien au chaud; **it's a ~ fit** c'est bien ajusté(e)
snuggle ['snʌgl] vi: **to ~ down in bed/up to sb** se pelotonner dans son lit/contre qn

 KEYWORD

so [səʊ] adv **1** (thus, likewise) ainsi, de cette façon; **if so** si oui; **so do or have I** moi aussi; **it's 5 o'clock — so it is!** il est 5 heures — en effet! or c'est vrai!; **I hope/think so** je l'espère/le crois; **so far** jusqu'ici, jusqu'à maintenant; (in past) jusque-là; **quite so!** exactement!, c'est bien ça!; **even so** quand même, tout de même
2 (in comparisons etc: to such a degree) si, tellement; **so big (that)** si or tellement grand (que); **she's not so clever as her brother** elle n'est pas aussi intelligente que son frère
3: **so much** adj, adv tant (de); **I've got so much work** j'ai tant de travail; **I love you so much** je vous aime tant; **so many** tant (de)
4 (phrases): **10 or so** à peu près or environ 10; **so long!** (inf: goodbye) au revoir!, à un de ces

S

jours!; **so to speak** pour ainsi dire; **so (what)?** (inf) (bon) et alors?, et après?
▷ *conj* **1** (*expressing purpose*): **so as to do** pour faire, afin de faire; **so (that)** pour que or afin que + *sub*
2 (*expressing result*) donc, par conséquent; **so that** si bien que, de (telle) sorte que; **so that's the reason!** c'est donc (pour) ça!; **so you see, I could have gone** alors tu vois, j'aurais pu y aller

soak [səuk] *vt* faire or laisser tremper; (*drench*) tremper ▷ *vi* tremper; **to be ~ed through** être trempé jusqu'aux os; **soak in** *vi* pénétrer, être absorbé(e); **soak up** *vt* absorber

soaking ['səukıŋ] *adj* (*also*: **~ wet**) trempé(e)

so-and-so ['səuənsəu] *n* (*somebody*) un(e) tel(le)

soap [səup] *n* savon *m*

soapflakes ['səupfleıks] *npl* paillettes *fpl* de savon

soap opera *n* feuilleton télévisé (*quotidienneté réaliste ou embellie*)

soap powder *n* lessive *f*, détergent *m*

soapy ['səupı] *adj* savonneux(-euse)

soar [sɔːˈ] *vi* monter (en flèche), s'élancer; (*building*) s'élancer; **~ing prices** prix qui grimpent

sob [sɔb] *n* sanglot *m* ▷ *vi* sangloter

sober ['səubəˈ] *adj* qui n'est pas (or plus) ivre; (*serious*) sérieux(-euse), sensé(e); (*moderate*) mesuré(e); (*colour, style*) sobre, discret(-ète); **sober up** *vt* dégriser ▷ *vi* se dégriser

so-called ['səu'kɔːld] *adj* soi-disant *inv*

soccer ['sɔkəˈ] *n* football *m*

sociable ['səuʃəbl] *adj* sociable

social ['səuʃl] *adj* social(e); (*sociable*) sociable ▷ *n* (petite) fête

social club *n* amicale *f*, foyer *m*

socialism ['səuʃəlɪzəm] *n* socialisme *m*

socialist ['səuʃəlɪst] *adj*, *n* socialiste (*m/f*)

socialize ['səuʃəlaɪz] *vi* voir or rencontrer des gens, se faire des amis; **to ~ with** (*meet often*) fréquenter; (*get to know*) lier connaissance or parler avec

social life *n* vie sociale; **how's your ~?** est-ce que tu sors beaucoup?

socially ['səuʃəlı] *adv* socialement, en société

social media *npl* médias *mpl* sociaux

social networking [-'netwə:kıŋ] *n* réseaux *mpl* sociaux

social security *n* aide sociale

social services *npl* services sociaux

social work *n* assistance sociale

social worker *n* assistant(e) sociale(e)

society [sə'saıətı] *n* société *f*; (*club*) société, association *f*; (*also*: **high ~**) (haute) société, grand monde ▷ *cpd* (*party*) mondain(e)

sociology [səusı'ɔlədʒı] *n* sociologie *f*

sock [sɔk] *n* chaussette *f* ▷ *vt* (*inf*: *hit*) flanquer un coup à; **to pull one's ~s up** (*fig*) se secouer (les puces)

socket ['sɔkıt] *n* cavité *f*; (*Elec*: *also*: **wall ~**) prise *f* de courant; (: *for light bulb*) douille *f*

sod [sɔd] *n* (*of earth*) motte *f*; (*Brit inf!*) con *m* (!), salaud *m* (!); **sod off** *vi*: **~ off!** (*Brit inf!*) fous le camp!, va te faire foutre! (!)

soda ['səudə] *n* (*Chem*) soude *f*; (*also*: **~ water**) eau *f* de Seltz; (*US*: *also*: **~ pop**) soda *m*

sodium ['səudıəm] *n* sodium *m*

sofa ['səufə] *n* sofa *m*, canapé *m*

sofa bed *n* canapé-lit *m*

soft [sɔft] *adj* (*not rough*) doux/douce; (*not hard*) doux, mou/molle; (*not loud*) doux, léger(-ère); (*kind*) doux, gentil(le); (*weak*) indulgent(e); (*stupid*) stupide, débile

soft drink *n* boisson non alcoolisée

soft drugs *npl* drogues douces

soften ['sɔfn] *vt* (r)amollir; (*fig*) adoucir ▷ *vi* se ramollir; (*fig*) s'adoucir

softly ['sɔftlı] *adv* doucement; (*touch*) légèrement; (*kiss*) tendrement

softness ['sɔftnıs] *n* douceur *f*

software ['sɔftwɛəˈ] *n* (*Comput*) logiciel *m*, software *m*

soggy ['sɔgı] *adj* (*clothes*) trempé(e); (*ground*) détrempé(e)

soil [sɔıl] *n* (*earth*) sol *m*, terre *f* ▷ *vt* salir; (*fig*) souiller

solar ['səuləˈ] *adj* solaire

solar panel *n* panneau *m* solaire

solar power *n* énergie *f* solaire

solar system *n* système *m* solaire

sold [səuld] *pt*, *pp* of **sell**

solder ['səuldəˈ] *vt* souder (*au fil à souder*) ▷ *n* soudure *f*

soldier ['səuldʒəˈ] *n* soldat *m*, militaire *m* ▷ *vi*: **to ~ on** persévérer, s'accrocher; **toy ~** petit soldat

sold out *adj* (*Comm*) épuisé(e)

sole [səul] *n* (*of foot*) plante *f*; (*of shoe*) semelle *f*; (*fish*: *pl inv*) sole *f* ▷ *adj* seul(e), unique; **the ~ reason** la seule et unique raison

solely ['səullı] *adv* seulement, uniquement; **I will hold you ~ responsible** je vous en tiendrai pour seul responsable

solemn ['sɔləm] *adj* solennel(le); (*person*) sérieux(-euse), grave

sole trader *n* (*Comm*) chef *m* d'entreprise individuelle

solicit [sə'lısıt] *vt* (*request*) solliciter ▷ *vi* (*prostitute*) racoler

solicitor [sə'lısıtəˈ] *n* (*Brit*: *for wills etc*) ≈ notaire *m*; (: *in court*) ≈ avocat *m*

solid ['sɔlıd] *adj* (*strong, sound, reliable*: *not liquid*) solide; (*not hollow*: *mass*) compact(e); (: *metal, rock, wood*) massif(-ive); (*meal*) consistant(e), substantiel(le); (*vote*) unanime ▷ *n* solide *m*; **to be on ~ ground** être sur la terre ferme; (*fig*) être en terrain sûr; **we waited two ~ hours** nous avons attendu deux heures entières

solidarity [sɔlı'dærıtı] *n* solidarité *f*

solitary ['sɔlɪtərɪ] *adj* solitaire

solitary confinement *n* (*Law*) isolement *m* (cellulaire)

solitude ['sɔlɪtjuːd] *n* solitude *f*

solo ['səuləu] *n* solo *m* ⊳ *adv* (*fly*) en solitaire

soloist ['səuləuɪst] *n* soliste *m/f*

soluble ['sɔljubl] *adj* soluble

solution [sə'luːʃən] *n* solution *f*

solve [sɔlv] *vt* résoudre

solvent ['sɔlvənt] *adj* (*Comm*) solvable ⊳ *n* (*Chem*) (dis)solvant *m*

sombre, (US) **somber** ['sɔmbə^r] *adj* sombre, morne

 KEYWORD

some [sʌm] *adj* **1** (*a certain amount or number of*): **some tea/water/ice cream** du thé/de l'eau/de la glace; **some children/apples** des enfants/pommes; **I've got some money but not much** j'ai de l'argent mais pas beaucoup

2 (*certain: in contrasts*): **some people say that ...** il y a des gens qui disent que ...; **some films were excellent, but most were mediocre** certains films étaient excellents, mais la plupart étaient médiocres

3 (*unspecified*): **some woman was asking for you** il y avait une dame qui vous demandait; **he was asking for some book (or other)** il demandait un livre quelconque; **some day** un de ces jours; **some day next week** un jour la semaine prochaine; **after some time** après un certain temps; **at some length** assez longuement; **in some form or other** sous une forme ou une autre, sous une forme quelconque

⊳ *pron* **1** (*a certain number*) quelques-un(e)s, certain(e)s; **I've got some** (*books etc*) j'en ai (quelques-uns); **some (of them) have been sold** certains ont été vendus

2 (*a certain amount*) un peu; **I've got some** (*money, milk*) j'en ai (un peu); **would you like some?** est-ce que vous en voulez?, en voulez-vous?; **could I have some of that cheese?** pourrais-je avoir un peu de ce fromage?; **I've read some of the book** j'ai lu une partie du livre

⊳ *adv*: **some 10 people** quelque 10 personnes, 10 personnes environ

somebody ['sʌmbədɪ] *pron* = **someone**

somehow ['sʌmhau] *adv* d'une façon ou d'une autre; (*for some reason*) pour une raison ou une autre

someone ['sʌmwʌn] *pron* quelqu'un; **~ or other** quelqu'un, je ne sais qui

someplace ['sʌmpleɪs] *adv* (*US*) = **somewhere**

somersault ['sʌməsɔːlt] *n* culbute *f*, saut périlleux ⊳ *vi* faire la culbute *or* un saut périlleux; (*car*) faire un tonneau

something ['sʌmθɪŋ] *pron* quelque chose *m*; **~ interesting** quelque chose d'intéressant; **~ to do** quelque chose à faire; **he's ~ like me** il est un peu comme moi; **it's ~ of a problem** il y a là un problème

sometime ['sʌmtaɪm] *adv* (*in future*) un de ces jours, un jour ou l'autre; (*in past*): **~ last month** au cours du mois dernier

sometimes ['sʌmtaɪmz] *adv* quelquefois, parfois

somewhat ['sʌmwɔt] *adv* quelque peu, un peu

somewhere ['sʌmwɛə^r] *adv* quelque part; **~ else** ailleurs, autre part

son [sʌn] *n* fils *m*

song [sɔŋ] *n* chanson *f*; (*of bird*) chant *m*

son-in-law ['sʌnɪnlɔː] *n* gendre *m*, beau-fils *m*

soon [suːn] *adv* bientôt; (*early*) tôt; **~ afterwards** peu après; **quite ~** sous peu; **how ~ can you do it?** combien de temps vous faut-il pour le faire, au plus pressé?; **how ~ can you come back?** quand *or* dans combien de temps pouvez-vous revenir, au plus tôt?; **see you ~!** à bientôt!; *see also* **as**

sooner ['suːnə^r] *adv* (*time*) plus tôt; (*preference*): **I would ~ do that** j'aimerais autant *or* je préférerais faire ça; **~ or later** tôt ou tard; **no ~ said than done** sitôt dit, sitôt fait; **the ~ the better** le plus tôt sera le mieux; **no ~ had we left than ...** à peine étions-nous partis que ...

soot [sut] *n* suie *f*

soothe [suːð] *vt* calmer, apaiser

sophisticated [sə'fɪstɪkeɪtɪd] *adj* raffiné(e), sophistiqué(e); (*machinery*) hautement perfectionné(e), très complexe; (*system etc*) très perfectionné(e), sophistiqué

sophomore ['sɔfəmɔː^r] *n* (*US*) étudiant(e) de seconde année

sopping ['sɔpɪŋ] *adj* (*also: ~ wet*) tout(e) trempé(e)

soppy ['sɔpɪ] *adj* (*pej*) sentimental(e)

soprano [sə'prɑːnəu] *n* (*voice*) soprano *m*; (*singer*) soprano *m/f*

sorbet ['sɔːbeɪ] *n* sorbet *m*

sorcerer ['sɔːsərə^r] *n* sorcier *m*

sordid ['sɔːdɪd] *adj* sordide

sore [sɔː^r] *adj* (*painful*) douloureux(-euse), sensible; (*offended*) contrarié(e), vexé(e) ⊳ *n* plaie *f*; **to have a ~ throat** avoir mal à la gorge; **it's a ~ point** (*fig*) c'est un point délicat

sorely ['sɔːlɪ] *adv* (*tempted*) fortement

sorrow ['sɔrəu] *n* peine *f*, chagrin *m*

sorry ['sɔrɪ] *adj* désolé(e); (*condition, excuse, tale*) triste, déplorable; (*sight*) désolant(e); **~!** pardon!, excusez-moi!; **~?** pardon?; **to feel ~ for sb** plaindre qn; **I'm ~ to hear that ...** je suis désolé(e) *or* navré(e) d'apprendre que ...; **to be ~ about sth** regretter qch

sort [sɔːt] n genre m, espèce f, sorte f; (make: of coffee, car etc) marque f ▷ vt (also: ~ **out**: select which to keep) trier; (classify) classer; (tidy) ranger; (letters etc) trier; (Comput) trier; **what ~ do you want?** quelle sorte or quel genre voulez-vous?; **what ~ of car?** quelle marque de voiture?; **I'll do nothing of the ~!** je ne ferai rien de tel!; **it's ~ of awkward** (inf) c'est plutôt gênant; **sort out** vt (problem) résoudre, régler

sorting office ['sɔːtɪŋ-] n (Post) bureau m de tri

SOS n SOS m

so-so ['səʊsəʊ] adv comme ci comme ça

sought [sɔːt] pt, pp of **seek**

soul [səʊl] n âme f; **the poor ~ had nowhere to sleep** le pauvre n'avait nulle part où dormir; **I didn't see a ~** je n'ai vu (absolument) personne

soulful ['səʊlful] adj plein(e) de sentiment

sound [saʊnd] adj (healthy) en bonne santé, sain(e); (safe, not damaged) solide, en bon état; (reliable, not superficial) sérieux(-euse), solide; (sensible) sensé(e) ▷ adv: ~ **asleep** profondément endormi(e) ▷ n (noise, volume) son m; (louder) bruit m; (Geo) détroit m, bras m de mer ▷ vt (alarm) sonner; (also: ~ **out**: opinions) sonder ▷ vi sonner, retentir; (fig: seem) sembler (être); **to be of ~ mind** être sain(e) d'esprit; **I don't like the ~ of it** ça ne me dit rien qui vaille; **to ~ one's horn** (Aut) klaxonner, actionner son avertisseur; **to ~ like** ressembler à; **it ~s as if** ... il semblerait que ..., j'ai l'impression que ...; **sound off** vi (inf): **to ~ off (about)** la ramener (sur)

sound barrier n mur m du son

sound bite n phrase toute faite (pour être citée dans les médias)

sound effects npl bruitage m

soundly ['saʊndlɪ] adv (sleep) profondément; (beat) complètement, à plate couture

soundproof ['saʊndpruːf] vt insonoriser ▷ adj insonorisé(e)

soundtrack ['saʊndtræk] n (of film) bande f sonore

soup [suːp] n soupe f, potage m; **in the ~** (fig) dans le pétrin

soup plate n assiette creuse or à soupe

soupspoon ['suːpspuːn] n cuiller f à soupe

sour ['saʊər] adj aigre, acide; (milk) tourné(e), aigre; (fig) acerbe, aigre; revêche; **to go** or **turn ~** (milk, wine) tourner; (fig: relationship, plans) mal tourner; **it's ~ grapes** c'est du dépit

source [sɔːs] n source f; **I have it from a reliable ~ that** je sais de source sûre que

south [saʊθ] n sud m ▷ adj sud inv; (wind) du sud ▷ adv au sud, vers le sud; **(to the) ~ of** au sud de; **to travel ~** aller en direction du sud

South Africa n Afrique f du Sud

South African adj sud-africain(e) ▷ n Sud-Africain(e)

South America n Amérique f du Sud

South American adj sud-américain(e) ▷ n Sud-Américain(e)

southbound ['saʊθbaʊnd] adj en direction du sud; (carriageway) sud inv

south-east [saʊθ'iːst] n sud-est m

southerly ['sʌðəlɪ] adj du sud; au sud

southern ['sʌðən] adj (du) sud; méridional(e); (with a ~ aspect) orienté(e) or exposé(e) au sud; **the ~ hemisphere** l'hémisphère sud or austral

South Korea n Corée f du Sud

South of France n: **the ~ le** Sud de la France, le Midi

South Pole n Pôle m Sud

South Wales n sud m du Pays de Galles

southward ['saʊθwəd], **southwards** ['saʊθwədz] adv vers le sud

south-west [saʊθ'wɛst] n sud-ouest m

souvenir [suːvə'nɪər] n souvenir m (objet)

sovereign ['sɔvrɪn] adj, n souverain(e)

soviet ['səʊvɪət] adj soviétique

sow¹ [səʊ] (pt **sowed**, pp **sown**) [səʊn] vt semer

sow² [saʊ] truie f

soya ['sɔɪə], (US) **soy** [sɔɪ] n: ~ **bean** graine f de soja; ~ **sauce** sauce f au soja

spa [spaː] n (town) station thermale; (US: also: **health ~**) établissement m de cure de rajeunissement

space [speɪs] n (gen) espace m; (room) place f; espace; (length of time) laps m de temps ▷ cpd spatial(e) ▷ vt (also: ~ **out**) espacer; **to clear a ~ for sth** faire de la place pour qch; **in a confined ~** dans un espace réduit or restreint; **in a short ~ of time** dans peu de temps; **(with)in the ~ of an hour** en l'espace d'une heure

spacecraft ['speɪskrɑːft] n engin or vaisseau spatial

spaceman ['speɪsmæn] irreg n astronaute m, cosmonaute m

spaceship ['speɪsʃɪp] n = **spacecraft**

spacing ['speɪsɪŋ] n espacement m; **single/double ~** (Typ etc) interligne m simple/double

spacious ['speɪʃəs] adj spacieux(-euse), grand(e)

spade [speɪd] n (tool) bêche f, pelle f; (child's) pelle; **spades** npl (Cards) pique m

spaghetti [spə'gɛtɪ] n spaghetti mpl

Spain [speɪn] n Espagne f

spam [spæm] n (Comput) pourriel m

span [spæn] n (of bird, plane) envergure f; (of arch) portée f; (in time) espace m de temps, durée f ▷ vt enjamber, franchir; (fig) couvrir, embrasser

Spaniard ['spænjəd] n Espagnol(e)

spaniel ['spænjəl] n épagneul m

Spanish ['spænɪʃ] adj espagnol(e), d'Espagne ▷ n (Ling) espagnol m; **the Spanish** npl les Espagnols; ~ **omelette** omelette f à l'espagnole

spank [spæŋk] vt donner une fessée à

spanner ['spænə'] n (Brit) clé f (de mécanicien)

spare [spɛə'] adj de réserve, de rechange; (surplus) de or en trop, de reste ▷ n (part) pièce f de rechange, pièce détachée ▷ vt (do without) se passer de; (afford to give) donner, accorder, passer; (not hurt) épargner; (not use) ménager; **to ~** (surplus) en surplus, de trop; **there are 2 going** ~ (Brit) il y en a 2 de disponible; **to ~ no expense** ne pas reculer devant la dépense; **can you ~ the time?** est-ce que vous avez le temps?; **there is no time to ~** il n'y a pas de temps à perdre; **I've a few minutes to ~** je dispose de quelques minutes

spare part n pièce f de rechange, pièce détachée

spare room n chambre f d'ami

spare time n moments mpl de loisir

spare tyre, (US) **spare tire** n (Aut) pneu m de rechange

spare wheel n (Aut) roue f de secours

sparingly ['spɛərɪŋlɪ] adv avec modération

spark [spɑ:k] n étincelle f; (fig) étincelle, lueur f

sparkle ['spɑ:kl] n scintillement m, étincellement m, éclat m ▷ vi étinceler, scintiller; (bubble) pétiller

sparkling ['spɑ:klɪŋ] adj étincelant(e), scintillant(e); (wine) mousseux(-euse), pétillant(e); (water) pétillant(e), gazeux(-euse)

spark plug n bougie f

sparrow ['spærəu] n moineau m

sparse [spɑ:s] adj clairsemé(e)

spartan ['spɑ:tən] adj (fig) spartiate

spasm ['spæzəm] n (Med) spasme m; (fig) accès m

spasmodic [spæz'mɔdɪk] adj (fig) intermittent(e)

spastic ['spæstɪk] n (old: pej) handicapé(e) moteur

spat [spæt] pt, pp of **spit** ▷ n (US) prise f de bec

spate [speɪt] n (fig): **~ of** avalanche f or torrent m de; **in ~** (river) en crue

spatula ['spætjulə] n spatule f

spawn [spɔ:n] vt pondre; (pej) engendrer ▷ vi frayer ▷ n frai m

speak (pt **spoke**, pp **spoken**) [spi:k, spəuk, 'spəukn] vt (language) parler; (truth) dire ▷ vi parler; (make a speech) prendre la parole; **to ~ to sb/of** or **about sth** parler à qn/de qch; **I don't ~ French** je ne parle pas français; **do you ~ English?** parlez-vous anglais?; **can I ~ to ...?** est-ce que je peux parler à ...?; **~ing!** (on telephone) c'est moi-même!; **to ~ one's mind** dire ce que l'on pense; **it ~s for itself** c'est évident; **~ up!** parle plus fort!; **he has no money to ~ of** il n'a pas d'argent; **speak for** vt fus: **to ~ for sb** parler pour qn; **that picture is already spoken for** (in shop) ce tableau est déjà réservé

speaker ['spi:kə'] n (in public) orateur m; (also: **loud~**) haut-parleur m; (for stereo etc) baffle m, enceinte f; (Pol): **the S~** (Brit) le président de la Chambre des communes or des représentants; (US) le président de la Chambre; **are you a Welsh ~?** parlez-vous gallois?

spear [spɪə'] n lance f ▷ vt transpercer

spearhead ['spɪəhɛd] n fer m de lance; (Mil) colonne f d'attaque ▷ vt (attack etc) mener

spec [spɛk] n (Brit inf): **on ~** à tout hasard; **to buy on ~** acheter avec l'espoir de faire une bonne affaire

special ['spɛʃl] adj spécial(e) ▷ n (train) train spécial; **take ~ care** soyez particulièrement prudents; **nothing ~** rien de spécial; **today's ~** (at restaurant) le plat du jour

special delivery n (Post): **by ~** en express

special effects npl (Cine) effets spéciaux

specialist ['spɛʃəlɪst] n spécialiste m/f; **heart ~** cardiologue m/f

speciality [spɛʃɪ'ælɪtɪ] n (Brit) spécialité f

specialize ['spɛʃəlaɪz] vi: **to ~ (in)** se spécialiser (dans)

specially ['spɛʃlɪ] adv spécialement, particulièrement

special needs npl (Brit) difficultés fpl d'apprentissage scolaire

special offer n (Comm) réclame f

special school n (Brit) établissement m d'enseignement spécialisé

specialty ['spɛʃəltɪ] n (US) = **speciality**

species ['spi:ʃi:z] n (pl inv) espèce f

specific [spə'sɪfɪk] adj (not vague) précis(e), explicite; (particular) particulier(-ière); (Bot, Chem etc) spécifique; **to be ~ to** être particulier à, être le or un caractère (or les caractères) spécifique(s) de

specifically [spə'sɪfɪklɪ] adv explicitement, précisément; (intend, ask, design) expressément, spécialement; (exclusively) exclusivement, spécifiquement

specification [spɛsɪfɪ'keɪʃən] n spécification f; stipulation f; **specifications** npl (of car, building etc) spécification

specify ['spɛsɪfaɪ] vt spécifier, préciser; **unless otherwise specified** sauf indication contraire

specimen ['spɛsɪmən] n spécimen m, échantillon m; (Med: of blood) prélèvement m; (: of urine) échantillon m

speck [spɛk] n petite tache, petit point; (particle) grain m

speckled ['spɛkld] adj tacheté(e), moucheté(e)

specs [spɛks] npl (inf) lunettes fpl

spectacle ['spɛktəkl] n spectacle m; **spectacles** npl (Brit) lunettes fpl

spectacular [spɛk'tækjulə'] adj spectaculaire ▷ n (Cine etc) superproduction f

spectator [spɛk'teɪtə'] n spectateur(-trice)

spectrum (pl **spectra**) ['spɛktrəm, -rə] n spectre m; (fig) gamme f

S

speculate ['spɛkjuleɪt] vi spéculer; (try to guess): **to ~ about** s'interroger sur

speculation [spɛkju'leɪʃən] n spéculation f; conjectures fpl

sped [spɛd] pt, pp of **speed**

speech [spiːtʃ] n (faculty) parole f; (talk) discours m, allocution f; (manner of speaking) façon f de parler, langage m; (language) langage m; (enunciation) élocution f

speechless ['spiːtʃlɪs] adj muet(te)

speed [spiːd] n vitesse f; (promptness) rapidité f ▷ vi (pt, pp **sped**) (Aut: exceed speed limit) faire un excès de vitesse; **to ~ along/by** etc aller/passer etc à toute vitesse; **at ~** (Brit) rapidement; **at ~ of 70 km/h** à une vitesse de 70 km/h; **shorthand/typing ~s** nombre m de mots à la minute en sténographie/ dactylographie; **a five-~ gearbox** une boîte cinq vitesses; **speed up** (pt, pp **speeded up**) vi aller plus vite, accélérer ▷ vt accélérer

speedboat ['spiːdbəut] n vedette f, hors-bord m inv

speed camera n radar m automatique

speedily ['spiːdɪlɪ] adv rapidement, promptement

speeding ['spiːdɪŋ] n (Aut) excès m de vitesse

speed limit n limitation f de vitesse, vitesse maximale permise

speedometer [spɪ'dɔmɪtər] n compteur m (de vitesse)

speedway n (Sport) piste f de vitesse pour motos; (also: **~ racing**) épreuve(s) f(pl) de vitesse de motos

speedy ['spiːdɪ] adj rapide, prompt(e)

spell [spɛl] n (also: **magic ~**) sortilège m, charme m; (period of time) (courte) période f ▷ vt (pt, pp **spelt** or **spelled**) [spɛlt, spɛld] (in writing) écrire, orthographier; (aloud) épeler; (fig) signifier; **to cast a ~ on sb** jeter un sort à qn; **he can't ~** il fait des fautes d'orthographe; **how do you ~ your name?** comment écrivez-vous votre nom?; **can you ~ it for me?** pouvez-vous me l'épeler?; **spell out** vt (explain): **to ~ sth out for sb** expliquer qch clairement à qn

spellbound ['spɛlbaund] adj envoûté(e), subjugué(e)

spellchecker ['spɛltʃɛkər] n (Comput) correcteur m or vérificateur m orthographique

spelling ['spɛlɪŋ] n orthographe f

spelt [spɛlt] pt, pp of **spell**

spend (pt, pp **spent**) [spɛnd, spɛnt] vt (money) dépenser; (time, life) passer; (devote) consacrer; **to ~ time/money/effort on sth** consacrer du temps/de l'argent/de l'énergie à qch

spending ['spɛndɪŋ] n dépenses fpl; **government ~** les dépenses publiques

spendthrift ['spɛndθrɪft] n dépensier(-ière)

spent [spɛnt] pt, pp of **spend** ▷ adj (patience)

épuisé(e), à bout; (cartridge, bullets) vide; **~ matches** vieilles allumettes

sperm [spəːm] n spermatozoïde m; (semen) sperme m

sphere [sfɪər] n sphère f; (fig) sphère, domaine m

spice [spaɪs] n épice f ▷ vt épicer

spicy ['spaɪsɪ] adj épicé(e), relevé(e); (fig) piquant(e)

spider ['spaɪdər] n araignée f; **~'s web** toile f d'araignée

spike [spaɪk] n pointe f; (Elec) pointe de tension; (Bot) épi m; **spikes** npl (Sport) chaussures fpl à pointes

spill (pt, pp **spilt** or **spilled**) [spɪl, -t, -d] vt renverser; répandre ▷ vi se répandre; **to ~ the beans** (inf) vendre la mèche; (: confess) lâcher le morceau; **spill out** vi sortir à flots, se répandre; **spill over** vi déborder

spilt [spɪlt] pt, pp of **spill**

spin [spɪn] (pt, pp **spun**) [spʌn] n (revolution of wheel) tour m; (Aviat) (chute f en) vrille f; (trip in car) petit tour, balade f; (on ball) effet m ▷ vt (wool etc) filer; (wheel) faire tourner; (Brit: clothes) essorer ▷ vi (turn) tourner, tournoyer; **to ~ a yarn** débiter une longue histoire; **to ~ a coin** (Brit) jouer à pile ou face; **spin out** vt faire durer

spinach ['spɪnɪtʃ] n épinard m; (as food) épinards mpl

spinal ['spaɪnl] adj vertébral(e), spinal(e)

spinal cord n moelle épinière

spin doctor n (inf) personne employée pour présenter un parti politique sous un jour favorable

spin-dryer [spɪn'draɪər] n (Brit) essoreuse f

spine [spaɪn] n colonne vertébrale; (thorn) épine f, piquant m

spineless ['spaɪnlɪs] adj invertébré(e); (fig) mou/molle, sans caractère

spinning ['spɪnɪŋ] n (of thread) filage m; (by machine) filature f

spinning top n toupie f

spin-off ['spɪnɔf] n sous-produit m; avantage inattendu

spinster ['spɪnstər] n célibataire f; vieille fille

spiral ['spaɪərl] n spirale f ▷ adj en spirale ▷ vi (fig: prices etc) monter en flèche; **the inflationary ~** la spirale inflationniste

spiral staircase n escalier m en colimaçon

spire ['spaɪər] n flèche f, aiguille f

spirit ['spɪrɪt] n (soul) esprit m, âme f; (ghost) esprit, revenant m; (mood) esprit, état m d'esprit; (courage) courage m, énergie f; **spirits** npl (drink) spiritueux mpl, alcool m; **in good ~s** de bonne humeur; **in low ~s** démoralisé(e); **community ~** solidarité f; **public ~** civisme m

spirited ['spɪrɪtɪd] adj vif/vive, fougueux(-euse), plein(e) d'allant

spiritual ['spɪrɪtjuəl] adj spirituel(le); (religious) religieux(-euse) ▷ n (also: **Negro ~**) spiritual m

spit [spɪt] n (for roasting) broche f; (spittle) crachat m; (saliva) salive f ▷ vi (pt, pp **spat**) [spæt] cracher; (sound) crépiter; (rain) crachiner

spite [spaɪt] n rancune f, dépit m ▷ vt contrarier, vexer; **in ~ of** en dépit de, malgré

spiteful ['spaɪtful] adj malveillant(e), rancunier(-ière)

spittle ['spɪtl] n salive f; bave f; crachat m

splash [splæʃ] n (sound) plouf m; (of colour) tache f ▷ vt éclabousser ▷ vi (also: **~ about**) barboter, patauger; **splash out** vi (Brit) faire une folie

spleen [spli:n] n (Anat) rate f

splendid ['splɛndɪd] adj splendide, superbe, magnifique

splint [splɪnt] n attelle f, éclisse f

splinter ['splɪntə^r] n (wood) écharde f; (metal) éclat m ▷ vi (wood) se fendre; (glass) se briser

split [splɪt] (pt, pp **split**) n fente f, déchirure f; (fig: Pol) scission f ▷ vt fendre, déchirer; (party) diviser; (work, profits) partager, répartir ▷ vi (break) se fendre, se briser; (divide) se diviser; **let's ~ the difference** coupons la poire en deux; **to do the ~s** faire le grand écart; **split up** vi (couple) se séparer, rompre; (meeting) se disperser

spoil (pt, pp **spoiled** or **spoilt**) [spɔɪl, -d, -t] vt (damage) abîmer; (mar) gâcher; (child) gâter; (ballot paper) rendre nul ▷ vi: **to be ~ing for a fight** chercher la bagarre

spoils [spɔɪlz] npl butin m

spoilsport ['spɔɪlspɔ:t] n trouble-fête m/f inv, rabat-joie m inv

spoilt [spɔɪlt] pt, pp of **spoil** ▷ adj (child) gâté(e); (ballot paper) nul(le)

spoke [spəuk] pt of **speak** ▷ n rayon m

spoken ['spəukn] pp of **speak**

spokesman ['spəuksmən] irreg n porte-parole m inv

spokesperson ['spəukspə:sn] irreg n porte-parole m inv

spokeswoman ['spəukswumən] (irreg) n porte-parole m inv

sponge [spʌndʒ] n éponge f; (Culin: also: **~ cake**) ≈ biscuit m de Savoie ▷ vt éponger ▷ vi: **to ~ off** or **on** vivre aux crochets de

sponge bag n (Brit) trousse f de toilette

sponsor ['spɔnsə^r] n (Radio, TV, Sport) sponsor m; (for application) parrain m, marraine f; (Brit: for fund-raising event) donateur(-trice) ▷ vt (programme, competition etc) parrainer, patronner, sponsoriser; (Pol: bill) présenter; (new member) parrainer; (fund-raiser) faire un don à; **I -ed him at 3p a mile** (in fund-raising race) je me suis engagé à lui donner 3p par mile

sponsorship ['spɔnsəʃɪp] n sponsoring m; patronage m, parrainage m; dons mpl

spontaneous [spɔn'teɪnɪəs] adj spontané(e)

spooky ['spu:kɪ] adj (inf) qui donne la chair de poule

spool [spu:l] n bobine f

spoon [spu:n] n cuiller f

spoon-feed ['spu:nfi:d] vt nourrir à la cuiller; (fig) mâcher le travail à

spoonful ['spu:nful] n cuillerée f

sport [spɔ:t] n sport m; (amusement) divertissement m; (person) chic type m/chic fille f ▷ vt (wear) arborer; **indoor/outdoor ~s** sports en salle/de plein air; **to say sth in ~** dire qch pour rire

sporting ['spɔ:tɪŋ] adj sportif(-ive); **to give sb a ~ chance** donner sa chance à qn

sport jacket n (US) = **sports jacket**

sports car n voiture f de sport

sports centre (Brit) n centre sportif

sports jacket n (Brit) veste f de sport

sportsman ['spɔ:tsmən] irreg n sportif m

sportsmanship ['spɔ:tsmənʃɪp] n esprit sportif, sportivité f

sports utility vehicle n véhicule m de loisirs (de type SUV)

sportswear ['spɔ:tswɛə^r] n vêtements mpl de sport

sportswoman ['spɔ:tswumən] irreg n sportive f

sporty ['spɔ:tɪ] adj sportif(-ive)

spot [spɔt] n tache f; (dot: on pattern) pois m; (pimple) bouton m; (place) endroit m, coin m; (also: **~ advertisement**) message m publicitaire; (small amount): **a ~ of** un peu de ▷ vt (notice) apercevoir, repérer; **on the ~** (notice) sur place, sur les lieux; (immediately) sur le champ; **to put sb on the ~** (fig) mettre qn dans l'embarras; **to come out in ~s** se couvrir de boutons, avoir une éruption de boutons

spot check n contrôle intermittent

spotless ['spɔtlɪs] adj immaculé(e)

spotlight ['spɔtlaɪt] n projecteur m; (Aut) phare m auxiliaire

spotted ['spɔtɪd] adj tacheté(e), moucheté(e); à pois; **~ with** tacheté(e) de

spotty ['spɔtɪ] adj (face) boutonneux(-euse)

spouse [spauz] n époux/épouse

spout [spaut] n (of jug) bec m; (of liquid) jet m ▷ vi jaillir

sprain [spreɪn] n entorse f, foulure f ▷ vt: **to ~ one's ankle** se fouler or se tordre la cheville

sprang [spræŋ] pt of **spring**

sprawl [sprɔ:l] vi s'étaler ▷ n: **urban ~** expansion urbaine; **to send sb ~ing** envoyer qn rouler par terre

spray [spreɪ] n jet m (en fines gouttelettes); (from sea) embruns mpl; (aerosol) vaporisateur m, bombe f; (for garden) pulvérisateur m; (of flowers) petit bouquet ▷ vt vaporiser, pulvériser; (crops) traiter ▷ cpd (deodorant etc) en bombe or atomiseur

spread [sprɛd] (pt, pp **spread**) n (distribution) répartition f; (Culin) pâte f à tartiner; (inf: meal) festin m; (Press, Typ: two pages) double page f ▷ vt (paste, contents) étendre, étaler;

(*rumour, disease*) répandre, propager; (*repayments*) échelonner, étaler; (*wealth*) répartir ▷ vi s'étendre; se répandre; se propager; (*stain*) s'étaler; **middle-age ~** embonpoint *m* (pris avec l'âge); **spread out** vi (*people*) se disperser

spread-eagled ['spredi:gld] *adj*: **to be** *or* **lie ~** être étendu(e) bras et jambes écartés

spreadsheet ['spredʃi:t] *n* (*Comput*) tableur *m*

spree [spri:] *n*: **to go on a ~** faire la fête

sprightly ['spraitli] *adj* alerte

spring [sprɪŋ] (*pt* **sprang**, *pp* **sprung**) [spræŋ, sprʌŋ] *n* (*season*) printemps *m*; (*leap*) bond *m*, saut *m*; (*coiled metal*) ressort *m*; (*bounciness*) élasticité *f*; (*of water*) source *f* ▷ vi bondir, sauter ▷ **to ~ a leak** (*pipe etc*) se mettre à fuir; **he sprang the news on me** il m'a annoncé la nouvelle de but en blanc; **in ~, in the ~** au printemps; **to ~ from** provenir de; **to ~ into action** passer à l'action; **to walk with a ~ in one's step** marcher d'un pas souple; **spring up** vi (*problem*) se présenter, surgir; (*plant, buildings*) surgir de terre

springboard ['sprɪŋbɔːd] *n* tremplin *m*

spring-clean [sprɪŋ'kliːn] *n* (*also:* **~ing**) grand nettoyage de printemps

spring onion *n* (*Brit*) ciboule *f*, cive *f*

springtime ['sprɪŋtaɪm] *n* printemps *m*

sprinkle ['sprɪŋkl] *vt* (*pour*) répandre; verser; **to ~ water** *etc* **on, ~ with water** *etc* asperger d'eau *etc*; **to ~ sugar** *etc* **on, ~ with sugar** *etc* saupoudrer de sucre *etc*; **~d with** (*fig*) parsemé(e) de

sprinkler ['sprɪŋklə'] *n* (*for lawn etc*) arroseur *m*; (*to put out fire*) diffuseur *m* d'extincteur automatique d'incendie

sprint [sprɪnt] *n* sprint *m* ▷ vi courir à toute vitesse; (*Sport*) sprinter

sprinter ['sprɪntə'] *n* sprinteur(-euse)

sprout [spraut] *vi* germer, pousser

sprouts [sprauts] *npl* (*also:* **Brussels ~**) choux *mpl* de Bruxelles

spruce [spruːs] *n* épicéa *m* ▷ *adj* net(te), pimpant(e); **spruce up** *vt* (*smarten up: room etc*) apprêter; **to ~ o.s. up** se faire beau/belle

sprung [sprʌŋ] *pp of* **spring**

spun [spʌn] *pt, pp of* **spin**

spur [spəː'] *n* éperon *m*; (*fig*) aiguillon *m* ▷ vt (*also:* **~ on**) éperonner; aiguillonner; **on the ~ of the moment** sous l'impulsion du moment

spurious ['spjuəriəs] *adj* faux/fausse

spurn [spəːn] *vt* repousser avec mépris

spurt [spəːt] *n* jet *m*; (*of blood*) jaillissement *m*; (*of energy*) regain *m*, sursaut *m* ▷ vi jaillir, gicler; **to put in** *or* **on a ~** (*runner*) piquer un sprint; (*fig: in work etc*) donner un coup de collier

spy [spaɪ] *n* espion(ne) ▷ vi: **to ~ on** espionner, épier ▷ vt (*see*) apercevoir ▷ *cpd* (*film, story*) d'espionnage

spying ['spaɪɪŋ] *n* espionnage *m*

sq. *abbr* (*Math etc*) = **square**

squabble ['skwɔbl] *n* querelle *f*, chamaillerie *f* ▷ vi se chamailler

squad [skwɔd] *n* (*Mil, Police*) escouade *f*, groupe *m*; (*Football*) contingent *m*; **flying ~** (*Police*) brigade volante

squadron ['skwɔdrn] *n* (*Mil*) escadron *m*; (*Aviat, Naut*) escadrille *f*

squalid ['skwɔlid] *adj* sordide, ignoble

squall [skwɔːl] *n* rafale *f*, bourrasque *f*

squalor ['skwɔlə'] *n* conditions *fpl* sordides

squander ['skwɔndə'] *vt* gaspiller, dilapider

square [skwɛə'] *n* carré *m*; (*in town*) place *f*; (*US: block of houses*) îlot *m*, pâté *m* de maisons; (*instrument*) équerre *f* ▷ *adj* carré(e); (*honest*) honnête, régulier(-ière); (*inf: ideas, tastes*) vieux jeu *inv*, qui retarde ▷ vt (*arrange*) régler; arranger; (*Math*) élever au carré; (*reconcile*) concilier ▷ vi (*agree*) cadrer, s'accorder; **all ~** quitte; à égalité; **a ~ meal** un repas convenable; **2 metres ~** (de) 2 mètres sur 2; **1 ~ metre** 1 mètre carré; **we're back to ~ one** (*fig*) on se retrouve à la case départ; **square up** vi (*Brit: settle*) régler; **to ~ up with sb** régler ses comptes avec qn

squarely ['skwɛəlɪ] *adv* carrément; (*honestly, fairly*) honnêtement, équitablement

square root *n* racine carrée

squash [skwɔʃ] *n* (*Brit: drink*): **lemon/orange ~** citronnade *f*/orangeade *f*; (*Sport*) squash *m*; (*US: vegetable*) courge *f* ▷ vt écraser

squat [skwɔt] *adj* petit(e) et épais(se), ramassé(e) ▷ vi (*also:* **~ down**) s'accroupir; (*on property*) squatter, squattériser

squatter ['skwɔtə'] *n* squatter *m*

squeak [skwiːk] *n* (*of hinge, wheel etc*) grincement *m*; (*of shoes*) craquement *m*; (*of mouse etc*) petit cri aigu ▷ vi (*hinge, wheel*) grincer; (*mouse*) pousser un petit cri

squeal [skwiːl] *vi* pousser un *or* des cri(s) aigu(s) *or* perçant(s); (*brakes*) grincer

squeamish ['skwiːmɪʃ] *adj* facilement dégoûté(e); facilement scandalisé(e)

squeeze [skwiːz] *n* pression *f*; (*also:* **credit ~**) encadrement *m* du crédit, restrictions *fpl* de crédit ▷ vt presser; (*hand, arm*) serrer ▷ vi: **to ~ past/under sth** se glisser avec (beaucoup de) difficulté devant/sous qch; **a ~ of lemon** quelques gouttes de citron; **squeeze out** vt exprimer; (*fig*) soutirer

squelch [skwɛltʃ] *vi* faire un bruit de succion; patauger

squid [skwɪd] *n* calmar *m*

squiggle ['skwɪgl] *n* gribouillis *m*

squint [skwɪnt] *vi* loucher ▷ *n*: **he has a ~** il louche, il souffre de strabisme; **to ~ at sth** regarder qch du coin de l'œil; (*quickly*) jeter un coup d'œil à qch

squirm [skwəːm] *vi* se tortiller

squirrel ['skwɪrəl] *n* écureuil *m*

squirt [skwəːt] *n* jet *m* ▷ vi jaillir, gicler ▷ vt faire gicler

Sr abbr = **senior**; (Rel) = **sister**
Sri Lanka [srɪ'læŋkə] n Sri Lanka m
St abbr = **saint**; **street**
stab [stæb] n (with knife etc) coup m (de couteau etc); (of pain) lancée f; (inf: try): **to have a ~ at (doing) sth** s'essayer à (faire) qch ▷ vt poignarder; **to ~ sb to death** tuer qn à coups de couteau
stability [stə'bɪlɪtɪ] n stabilité f
stable ['steɪbl] n écurie f ▷ adj stable; **riding ~s** centre m d'équitation
stack [stæk] n tas m, pile f ▷ vt empiler, entasser; **there's ~s of time** (Brit inf) on a tout le temps
stadium ['steɪdɪəm] n stade m
staff [stɑːf] n (work force) personnel m; (Brit Scol: also: **teaching ~**) professeurs mpl, enseignants mpl, personnel enseignant; (servants) domestiques mpl; (Mil) état-major m; (stick) perche f, bâton m ▷ vt pourvoir en personnel
stag [stæg] n cerf m; (Brit Stock Exchange) loup m
stage [steɪdʒ] n scène f; (platform) estrade f; (point) étape f, stade m; (profession): **the ~** le théâtre ▷ vt (play) monter, mettre en scène; (demonstration) organiser; (fig: recovery etc) effectuer; **in ~s** par étapes, par degrés; **to go through a difficult ~** traverser une période difficile; **in the early ~s** au début; **in the final ~s** à la fin
stagecoach ['steɪdʒkəʊtʃ] n diligence f
stage manager n régisseur m
stagger ['stægə'] vi chanceler, tituber ▷ vt (person: amaze) stupéfier; bouleverser; (hours, holidays) étaler, échelonner
staggering ['stægərɪŋ] adj (amazing) stupéfiant(e), renversant(e)
stagnant ['stægnənt] adj stagnant(e)
stagnate [stæg'neɪt] vi stagner, croupir
stag night, stag party n enterrement m de vie de garçon
staid [steɪd] adj posé(e), rassis(e)
stain [steɪn] n tache f; (colouring) colorant m ▷ vt tacher; (wood) teindre
stained glass [steɪnd-] n (decorative) verre coloré; (in church) vitraux mpl; **~ window** vitrail m
stainless ['steɪnlɪs] adj (steel) inoxydable
stainless steel n inox m, acier m inoxydable
stain remover n détachant m
stair [steə'] n (step) marche f
staircase ['steəkeɪs] n = **stairway**
stairs [steəz] npl escalier m; **on the ~** dans l'escalier
stairway ['steəweɪ] n escalier m
stake [steɪk] n pieu m, poteau m; (Comm: interest) intérêts mpl; (Betting) enjeu m ▷ vt risquer, jouer; (also: **~ out**: area) marquer, délimiter; **to be at ~** être en jeu; **to have a ~ in sth** avoir des intérêts (en jeu) dans qch; **to ~ a claim (to sth)** revendiquer (qch)

stale [steɪl] adj (bread) rassis(e); (food) pas frais/fraîche; (beer) éventé(e); (smell) de renfermé; (air) confiné(e)
stalemate ['steɪlmeɪt] n pat m; (fig) impasse f
stall [stɔːl] n (Brit: in street, market etc) éventaire m, étal m; (in stable) stalle f ▷ vt (Aut) caler; (fig: delay) retarder ▷ vi (Aut) caler; (fig) essayer de gagner du temps; **stalls** npl (Brit: in cinema, theatre) orchestre m; **a newspaper/ flower ~** un kiosque à journaux/de fleuriste
stallion ['stæljən] n étalon m (cheval)
stamina ['stæmɪnə] n vigueur f, endurance f
stammer ['stæmə'] n bégaiement m ▷ vi bégayer
stamp [stæmp] n timbre m; (also: **rubber ~**) tampon m; (mark, also fig) empreinte f; (on document) cachet m ▷ vi (also: **~ one's foot**) taper du pied ▷ vt (letter) timbrer; (with rubber stamp) tamponner; **stamp out** vt (fire) piétiner; (crime) éradiquer; (opposition) éliminer
stamp album n album m de timbres(-poste)
stamp collecting [-kəlektɪŋ] n philatélie f
stamped addressed envelope n (Brit) enveloppe affranchie pour la réponse
stampede [stæm'piːd] n ruée f; (of cattle) débandade f
stance [stæns] n position f
stand [stænd] (pt, pp **stood**) [stud] n (position) position f; (for taxis) station f (de taxis); (Mil) résistance f; (structure) guéridon m; support m; (Comm) étalage m, stand m; (Sport: also: **~s**) tribune f; (also: **music ~**) pupitre m ▷ vi être or se tenir (debout); (rise) se lever, se mettre debout; (be placed) se trouver; (remain: offer etc) rester valable ▷ vt (place) mettre, poser; (tolerate, withstand) supporter; (treat, invite) offrir, payer; **to make a ~** prendre position; **to take a ~ on an issue** prendre position sur un problème; **to ~ for parliament** (Brit) se présenter aux élections (comme candidat à la députation); **to ~ guard** or **watch** (Mil) monter la garde; **it ~s to reason** c'est logique; cela va de soi; **as things ~** dans l'état actuel des choses; **to ~ sb a drink/meal** payer à boire/à manger à qn; **I can't ~ him** je ne peux pas le voir; **stand aside** vi s'écarter; **stand back** vi (move back) reculer, s'écarter; **stand by** vi (be ready) se tenir prêt(e) ▷ vt fus (opinion) s'en tenir à; (person) ne pas abandonner, soutenir; **stand down** vi (withdraw) se retirer; (Law) renoncer à ses droits; **stand for** vt fus (signify) représenter, signifier; (tolerate) supporter, tolérer; **stand in for** vt fus remplacer; **stand out** vi (be prominent) ressortir; **stand up** vi (rise) se lever, se mettre debout; **stand up for** vt fus défendre; **stand up to** vt fus tenir tête à, résister à
standard ['stændəd] n (norm) norme f, étalon m; (level) niveau m (voulu); (criterion)

critère m; (flag) étendard m ▷ adj (size etc) ordinaire, normal(e); (model, feature) standard inv; (practice) courant(e); (text) de base; **standards** npl (morals) morale f, principes mpl; **to be** or **come up to** ~ être du niveau voulu or à la hauteur; **to apply a double** ~ avoir or appliquer deux poids deux mesures

standard lamp n (Brit) lampadaire m

standard of living n niveau m de vie

stand-by ['stændbaɪ] n remplaçant(e) ▷ adj (provisions) de réserve; **to be on** ~ se tenir prêt(e) (à intervenir); (doctor) être de garde

stand-by ticket n (Aviat) billet m stand-by

stand-in ['stændɪn] n remplaçant(e); (Cine) doublure f

standing ['stændɪŋ] adj debout inv; (permanent) permanent(e); (rule) immuable; (army) de métier; (grievance) constant(e), de longue date ▷ n réputation f, rang m, standing m; (duration): **of 6 months'** ~ qui dure depuis 6 mois; **of many years'** ~ qui dure or existe depuis longtemps; **he was given a** ~ **ovation** on s'est levé pour l'acclamer; **it's a** ~ **joke** c'est un vieux sujet de plaisanterie; **a man of some** ~ un homme estimé

standing order n (Brit: at bank) virement m automatique, prélèvement m bancaire; **standing orders** npl (Mil) règlement m

standing room n places fpl debout

standpoint ['stændpɔɪnt] n point m de vue

standstill ['stændstɪl] n: **at a** ~ à l'arrêt; (fig) au point mort; **to come to a** ~ s'immobiliser, s'arrêter

stank [stæŋk] pt of **stink**

staple ['steɪpl] n (for papers) agrafe f; (chief product) produit m de base ▷ adj (food, crop, industry etc) de base principal(e) ▷ vt agrafer

stapler ['steɪplə'] n agrafeuse f

star [stɑ:'] n étoile f; (celebrity) vedette f ▷ vi: **to** ~ **(in)** être la vedette (de) ▷ vt (Cine) avoir pour vedette; **4-~ hotel** hôtel m 4 étoiles; **2-~ petrol** (Brit) essence f ordinaire; **4-~ petrol** (Brit) super m; **stars** npl: **the ~s** (Astrology) l'horoscope m

starboard ['stɑ:bəd] n tribord m; **to** ~ à tribord

starch [stɑ:tʃ] n amidon m; (in food) fécule f

stardom ['stɑ:dəm] n célébrité f

stare [stɛə'] n regard m fixe ▷ vi: **to** ~ **at** regarder fixement

starfish ['stɑ:fɪʃ] n étoile f de mer

stark [stɑ:k] adj (bleak) désolé(e), morne; (simplicity, colour) austère; (reality, poverty) nu(e) ▷ adv: ~ **naked** complètement nu(e)

starling ['stɑ:lɪŋ] n étourneau m

starry ['stɑ:rɪ] adj étoilé(e)

starry-eyed [stɑ:rɪ'aɪd] adj (innocent) ingénu(e)

start [stɑ:t] n commencement m, début m; (of race) départ m; (sudden movement) sursaut m; (advantage) avance f, avantage m ▷ vt

commencer; (cause: fight) déclencher; (rumour) donner naissance à; (fashion) lancer; (found: business, newspaper) lancer, créer; (engine) mettre en marche ▷ vi (begin) commencer; (begin journey) partir, se mettre en route; (jump) sursauter; **when does the film** ~? à quelle heure est-ce que le film commence?; **at** ~ au début; **for a** ~ d'abord, pour commencer; **to make an early** ~ partir or commencer de bonne heure; **to** ~ **doing** or **to do sth** se mettre à faire qch; **to** ~ **(off) with** ... (firstly) d'abord ...; (at the beginning) au commencement ...; **start off** vi commencer; (leave) partir; **start out** vi (begin) commencer; (set out) partir; **start over** vi (US) recommencer; **start up** vi commencer; (car) démarrer ▷ vt (fight) déclencher; (business) créer; (car) mettre en marche

starter ['stɑ:tə'] n (Aut) démarreur m; (Sport: official) starter m; (: runner, horse) partant m; (Brit Culin) entrée f

starting point ['stɑ:tɪŋ-] n point m de départ

startle ['stɑ:tl] vt faire sursauter; donner un choc à

startling ['stɑ:tlɪŋ] adj surprenant(e), saisissant(e)

starvation [stɑ:'veɪʃən] n faim f, famine f; **to die of** ~ mourir de faim or d'inanition

starve [stɑ:v] vi mourir de faim ▷ vt laisser mourir de faim; **I'm starving** je meurs de faim

state [steɪt] n état m; (Pol) État; (pomp): **in** ~ en grande pompe ▷ vt (declare) déclarer, affirmer; (specify) indiquer, spécifier; **States** npl: **the S~s** les États-Unis; **to be in a** ~ être dans tous ses états; ~ **of emergency** état d'urgence; ~ **of mind** état d'esprit; **the** ~ **of the art** l'état actuel de la technologie (or des connaissances)

stately ['steɪtlɪ] adj majestueux(-euse), imposant(e)

stately home n manoir m or château m (ouvert au public)

statement ['steɪtmənt] n déclaration f; (Law) déposition f; (Econ) relevé m; **official** ~ communiqué officiel; ~ **of account, bank** ~ relevé de compte

state school n école publique

statesman ['steɪtsmən] irreg n homme m d'État

static ['stætɪk] n (Radio) parasites mpl; (also: ~ **electricity**) électricité f statique ▷ adj statique

station ['steɪʃən] n gare f; (also: **police** ~) poste m or commissariat m (de police); (Mil) poste m (militaire); (rank) condition f, rang m ▷ vt placer, poster; **action** ~**s** postes de combat; **to be** ~**ed in** (Mil) être en garnison à

stationary ['steɪʃnərɪ] adj à l'arrêt, immobile

stationer ['steɪʃənə'] n papetier(-ière)

stationer's, stationer's shop n (Brit) papeterie f

stationery ['steɪʃnərɪ] n papier m à lettres, petit matériel de bureau

station wagon n (US) break m

statistic [stə'tɪstɪk] n statistique f

statistics [stə'tɪstɪks] n (science) statistique f

statue ['stætjuː] n statue f

stature ['stætʃə^r] n stature f; (fig) envergure f

status ['steɪtəs] n position f, situation f; (prestige) prestige m; (Admin, official position) statut m

status quo [-'kwəʊ] n: **the ~** le statu quo

status symbol n marque f de standing, signe extérieur de richesse

statute ['stætjuːt] n loi f; **statutes** npl (of club etc) statuts mpl

statutory ['stætjutrɪ] adj statutaire, prévu(e) par un article de loi; **~ meeting** assemblée constitutive or statutaire

staunch [stɔːntʃ] adj sûr(e), loyal(e) ▷ vt étancher

stay [steɪ] n (period of time) séjour m; (Law): **~ of execution** sursis m à statuer ▷ vi rester; (reside) loger; (spend some time) séjourner; **to ~ put** ne pas bouger; **to ~ with friends** loger chez des amis; **to ~ the night** passer la nuit; **stay away** vi (from person, building) ne pas s'approcher; (from event) ne pas venir; **stay behind** vi rester en arrière; **stay in** vi (at home) rester à la maison; **stay on** vi rester; **stay out** vi (of house) ne pas rentrer; (strikers) rester en grève; **stay up** vi (at night) ne pas se coucher

staying power ['steɪɪŋ-] n endurance f

stead [sted] n (Brit): **in sb's ~** à la place de qn; **to stand sb in good ~** être très utile or servir beaucoup à qn

steadfast ['stedfɑːst] adj ferme, résolu(e)

steadily ['stedɪlɪ] adv (regularly) progressivement; (firmly) fermement; (walk) d'un pas ferme; (fixedly: look) sans détourner les yeux

steady ['stedɪ] adj stable, solide, ferme; (regular) constant(e), régulier(-ière); (person) calme, pondéré(e) ▷ vt assurer, stabiliser; (nerves) calmer; (voice) assurer; **a ~ boyfriend** un petit ami; **to ~ oneself** reprendre son aplomb

steak [steɪk] n (meat) bifteck m, steak m; (fish, pork) tranche f

steal (pt **stole**, pp **stolen**) [stiːl, stəʊl, 'stəʊln] vt, vi voler; (move) se déplacer furtivement; **my wallet has been stolen** on m'a volé mon portefeuille; **steal away, steal off** vi s'esquiver

stealth [stelθ] n: **by ~** furtivement

steam [stiːm] n vapeur f ▷ vt passer à la vapeur; (Culin) cuire à la vapeur ▷ vi fumer; (ship): **to ~ along** filer; **under one's own ~** (fig) par ses propres moyens; **to run out of ~** (fig: person) caler; être à bout; **to let off ~** (fig: inf) se défouler; **steam up** vi (window) se couvrir de buée; **to get ~ed up about sth** (fig: inf) s'exciter à propos de qch

steam engine n locomotive f à vapeur

steamer ['stiːmə^r] n (bateau m à) vapeur m; (Culin) ≈ couscoussier m

steamship ['stiːmʃɪp] n = **steamer**

steamy ['stiːmɪ] adj humide; (window) embué(e); (sexy) torride

steel [stiːl] n acier m ▷ cpd d'acier

steelworks ['stiːlwəːks] n aciérie f

steep [stiːp] adj raide, escarpé(e); (price) très élevé(e), excessif(-ive) ▷ vt (faire) tremper

steeple ['stiːpl] n clocher m

steer [stɪə^r] n bœuf m ▷ vt diriger; (boat) gouverner; (lead: person) guider, conduire ▷ vi tenir le gouvernail; **to ~ clear of sb/sth** (fig) éviter qn/qch

steering ['stɪərɪŋ] n (Aut) conduite f

steering wheel n volant m

stem [stem] n (of plant) tige f; (of leaf, fruit) queue f; (of glass) pied m ▷ vt contenir, endiguer; (attack, spread of disease) juguler; **stem from** vt fus provenir de, découler de

stench [stentʃ] n puanteur f

stencil ['stensl] n stencil m; pochoir m ▷ vt polycopier

stenographer [stɛ'nɔgrəfə^r] n (US) sténographe m/f

step [step] n pas m; (stair) marche f; (action) mesure f, disposition f ▷ vi: **to ~ forward/back** faire un pas en avant/arrière, avancer/reculer; **steps** npl (Brit) = **stepladder**; **~ by ~** pas à pas; (fig) petit à petit; **to be in/out of ~ (with)** (fig) aller dans le sens (de)/être déphasé(e) (par rapport à); **step down** vi (fig) se retirer, se désister; **step in** vi (fig) intervenir; **step off** vt fus descendre de; **step over** vt fus enjamber; **step up** vt (production, sales) augmenter; (campaign, efforts) intensifier

stepbrother ['stepbrʌðə^r] n demi-frère m

stepchild ['steptʃaɪld] (pl **stepchildren**) n beau-fils m, belle-fille f

stepdaughter ['stepdɔːtə^r] n belle-fille f

stepfather ['stepfɑːðə^r] n beau-père m

stepladder ['steplædə^r] n (Brit) escabeau m

stepmother ['stepmʌðə^r] n belle-mère f

stepping stone ['stepɪŋ-] n pierre f de gué; (fig) tremplin m

stepsister ['stepsɪstə^r] n demi-sœur f

stepson ['stepsʌn] n beau-fils m

stereo ['stɪərɪəʊ] n (sound) stéréo f; (hi-fi) chaîne f stéréo ▷ adj (also: **~phonic**) stéréo(phonique); **in ~** en stéréo

stereotype ['stɪərɪətaɪp] n stéréotype m ▷ vt stéréotyper

sterile ['steraɪl] adj stérile

sterilize ['sterɪlaɪz] vt stériliser

sterling ['stəːlɪŋ] adj sterling inv; (silver) de bon aloi, fin(e); (fig) à toute épreuve, excellent(e) ▷ n (currency) livre f sterling inv; **a pound ~** une livre sterling

stern [stəːn] adj sévère ▷ n (Naut) arrière m, poupe f

s

steroid ['stɪərɔɪd] n stéroïde m

stew [stju:] n ragoût m ▷ vt, vi cuire à la casserole; **~ed tea** thé trop infusé; **~ed fruit** fruits cuits or en compote

steward ['stju:əd] n (Aviat, Naut, Rail) steward m; (in club etc) intendant m; (also: **shop ~**) délégué syndical

stewardess ['stju:ədes] n hôtesse f

stick [stɪk] (pt, pp **stuck**) [stʌk] n bâton m; (for walking) canne f; (of chalk etc) morceau m ▷ vt (glue) coller; (thrust): **to ~ sth into** piquer or planter or enfoncer qch dans; (inf: put) mettre, fourrer; (: tolerate) supporter ▷ vi (adhere) tenir, coller; (remain) rester; (get jammed: door, lift) se bloquer; **to get hold of the wrong end of the ~** (Brit fig) comprendre de travers; **to ~ to** (one's promise) s'en tenir à; (principles) rester fidèle à; **stick around** vi (inf) rester (dans les parages); **stick out** vi dépasser, sortir ▷ vt: **to ~ it out** (inf) tenir le coup; **stick up** vi dépasser, sortir; **stick up for** vt fus défendre

sticker ['stɪkə'] n auto-collant m

sticking plaster ['stɪkɪŋ-] n sparadrap m, pansement adhésif

stick insect n phasme m

stick shift n (US Aut) levier m de vitesses

stick-up ['stɪkʌp] n (inf) braquage m, hold-up m

sticky ['stɪkɪ] adj poisseux(-euse); (label) adhésif(-ive); (fig: situation) délicat(e)

stiff [stɪf] adj (gen) raide, rigide; (door, brush) dur(e); (difficult) difficile, ardu(e); (cold) froid(e), distant(e); (strong, high) fort(e), élevé(e) ▷ adv: **to be bored/scared/frozen ~** s'ennuyer à mourir/être mort(e) de peur/ froid; **to be** or **feel ~** (person) avoir des courbatures; **to have a ~ back** avoir mal au dos; **~ upper lip** (Brit: fig) flegme m (typiquement britannique)

stiffen ['stɪfn] vt raidir, renforcer ▷ vi se raidir; se durcir

stiff neck n torticolis m

stifle ['staɪfl] vt étouffer, réprimer

stifling ['staɪflɪŋ] adj (heat) suffocant(e)

stigma ['stɪgmə] (Bot, Med, Rel) (pl **stigmata**) ['stɪgˈmɑ:tə] (fig), **stigmas** n stigmate m

stile [staɪl] n échalier m

stiletto [stɪˈletəu] n (Brit: also: **~ heel**) talon m aiguille

still [stɪl] adj (motionless) immobile; (calm) calme, tranquille; (Brit: mineral water etc) non gazeux(-euse) ▷ adv (up to this time) encore, toujours; (even) encore; (nonetheless) quand même, tout de même ▷ n (Cine) photo f; **to stand ~** rester immobile, ne pas bouger; **keep ~!** ne bouge pas!; **he ~ hasn't arrived** il n'est pas encore arrivé, il n'est toujours pas arrivé

stillborn ['stɪlbɔ:n] adj mort-né(e)

still life n nature morte

stilt [stɪlt] n échasse f; (pile) pilotis m

stilted ['stɪltɪd] adj guindé(e), emprunté(e)

stimulate ['stɪmjuleɪt] vt stimuler

stimulus (pl **stimuli**) ['stɪmjuləs, 'stɪmjulaɪ] n stimulant m; (Biol, Psych) stimulus m

sting [stɪŋ] n piqûre f; (organ) dard m; (inf: confidence trick) arnaque m ▷ vt, vi (pt, pp **stung**) [stʌn] piquer; **my eyes are ~ing** j'ai les yeux qui piquent

stingy ['stɪndʒɪ] adj avare, pingre, chiche

stink [stɪŋk] n puanteur f ▷ vi (pt **stank**, pp **stunk**) [stæŋk, stʌŋk] puer, empester

stinking ['stɪŋkɪŋ] adj (fig: inf) infect(e); **~ rich** bourré(e) de pognon

stint [stɪnt] n part f de travail ▷ vi: **to ~ on** lésiner sur, être chiche de

stir [stə:'] n agitation f, sensation f ▷ vt remuer ▷ vi remuer, bouger; **to give sth a ~** remuer qch; **to cause a ~** faire sensation; **stir up** vt exciter; (trouble) fomenter, provoquer

stir-fry ['stə:'fraɪ] vt faire sauter ▷ n: **vegetable ~** légumes sautés à la poêle

stirrup ['stɪrəp] n étrier m

stitch [stɪtʃ] n (Sewing) point m; (Knitting) maille f; (Med) point de suture; (pain) point de côté n ▷ vt coudre, piquer; (Med) suturer

stoat [stəut] n hermine f (avec son pelage d'été)

stock [stɔk] n réserve f, provision f; (Comm) stock m; (Agr) cheptel m, bétail m; (Culin) bouillon m; (Finance) valeurs fpl, titres mpl; (Rail: also: **rolling ~**) matériel roulant; (descent, origin) souche f ▷ adj (fig: reply etc) courant(e); classique ▷ vt (have in stock) avoir, vendre; **well-~ed** bien approvisionné(e) or fourni(e); **in ~** en stock, en magasin; **out of ~** épuisé(e); **to take ~** (fig) faire le point; **~s and shares** valeurs (mobilières), titres; **government ~** fonds publics; **stock up** vi: **to ~ up (with)** s'approvisionner (en)

stockbroker ['stɔkbrəukə'] n agent m de change

stock cube n (Brit Culin) bouillon-cube m

stock exchange n Bourse f (des valeurs)

stockholder ['stɔkhəuldə'] n (US) actionnaire m/f

stocking ['stɔkɪŋ] n bas m

stock market n Bourse f, marché financier

stockpile ['stɔkpaɪl] n stock m, réserve f ▷ vt stocker, accumuler

stocktaking ['stɔkteɪkɪŋ] n (Brit Comm) inventaire m

stocky ['stɔkɪ] adj trapu(e), râblé(e)

stodgy ['stɔdʒɪ] adj bourratif(-ive), lourd(e)

stoke [stəuk] vt garnir, entretenir; chauffer

stole [stəul] pt of **steal** ▷ n étole f

stolen ['stəuln] pp of **steal**

stomach ['stʌmək] n estomac m; (abdomen) ventre m ▷ vt supporter, digérer

stomachache ['stʌməkeɪk] n mal m à l'estomac or au ventre

stone [stəun] n pierre f; (pebble) caillou m, galet m; (in fruit) noyau m; (Med) calcul m; (Brit: weight) = 6.348 kg; 14 pounds ▷ cpd de or en pierre ▷ vt (person) lancer des pierres sur, lapider; (fruit) dénoyauter; **within a ~'s throw of the station** à deux pas de la gare

stone-cold ['stəun'kəuld] adj complètement froid(e)

stone-deaf ['stəun'dɛf] adj sourd(e) comme un pot

stonework ['stəunwə:k] n maçonnerie f

stood [stud] pt, pp of **stand**

stool [stu:l] n tabouret m

stoop [stu:p] vi (also: **have a ~**) être voûté(e); (also: **~ down**: bend) se baisser, se courber; (fig): **to ~ to sth/doing sth** s'abaisser jusqu'à qch/jusqu'à faire qch

stop [stɔp] n arrêt m; (short stay) halte f; (in punctuation) point m ▷ vt arrêter; (break off) interrompre; (also: **put a ~ to**) mettre fin à; (prevent) empêcher ▷ vi s'arrêter; (rain, noise etc) cesser, s'arrêter; **could you ~ here/at the corner?** arrêtez-vous ici/au coin, s'il vous plaît; **to ~ doing sth** cesser or arrêter de faire qch; **to ~ sb (from) doing sth** empêcher qn de faire qch; **to ~ dead** vi s'arrêter net; **~ it!** arrête!; **stop by** vi s'arrêter (au passage); **stop off** vi faire une courte halte; **stop up** vt (hole) boucher

stopgap ['stɔpgæp] n (person) bouche-trou m; (also: **~ measure**) mesure f intérimaire

stopover ['stɔpəuvə'] n halte f; (Aviat) escale f

stoppage ['stɔpɪdʒ] n arrêt m; (of pay) retenue f; (strike) arrêt m de travail; (obstruction) obstruction f

stopper ['stɔpə'] n bouchon m

stop press n nouvelles fpl de dernière heure

stopwatch ['stɔpwɔtʃ] n chronomètre m

storage ['stɔ:rɪdʒ] n emmagasinage m; (of nuclear waste etc) stockage m; (in house) rangement m; (Comput) mise f en mémoire or réserve

storage heater n (Brit) radiateur m électrique par accumulation

store [stɔ:'] n (stock) provision f, réserve f; (depot) entrepôt m; (Brit: large shop) grand magasin; (US: shop) magasin m ▷ vt emmagasiner; (nuclear waste etc) stocker; (information) enregistrer; (in filing system) classer, ranger; (Comput) mettre en mémoire; **stores** npl (food) provisions; **who knows what is in ~ for us?** qui sait ce que l'avenir nous réserve or ce qui nous attend?; **to set great/little ~ by sth** faire grand cas/peu de cas de qch; **store up** vt mettre en réserve, emmagasiner

storekeeper ['stɔ:ki:pə'] n (US) commerçant(e)

storeroom ['stɔ:ru:m] n réserve f, magasin m

storey, (US) **story** ['stɔ:rɪ] n étage m

stork [stɔ:k] n cigogne f

storm [stɔ:m] n tempête f; (thunderstorm) orage m ▷ vi (fig) fulminer ▷ vt prendre d'assaut

stormy ['stɔ:mɪ] adj orageux(-euse)

story ['stɔ:rɪ] n histoire f; récit m; (Press: article) article m; (: subject) affaire f; (US) = **storey**

storybook ['stɔ:rɪbuk] n livre m d'histoires or de contes

stout [staut] adj (strong) solide; (brave) intrépide; (fat) gros(se), corpulent(e) ▷ n bière brune

stove [stəuv] n (for cooking) fourneau m; (: small) réchaud m; (for heating) poêle m; **gas/electric ~** (cooker) cuisinière f à gaz/électrique

stow [stəu] vt ranger; cacher

stowaway ['stəuəwei] n passager(-ère) clandestin(e)

straddle ['strædl] vt enjamber, être à cheval sur

straggle ['strægl] vi être (or marcher) en désordre; **~d along the coast** disséminé(e) tout au long de la côte

straight [streit] adj droit(e); (hair) raide; (frank) honnête, franc/franche; (simple) simple; (Theat: part, play) sérieux(-euse); (inf: heterosexual) hétéro inv ▷ adv (tout) droit; (drink) sec, sans eau ▷ n: **the ~** (Sport) la ligne droite; **to put** or **get ~** mettre en ordre, mettre de l'ordre dans; (fig) mettre au clair; **let's get this ~** mettons les choses au point; **10 ~ wins** 10 victoires d'affilée; **to go ~ home** rentrer directement à la maison; **~ away, ~ off** (at once) tout de suite; **~ off, ~ out** sans hésiter

straighten ['streitn] vt ajuster; (bed) arranger; **straighten out** vt (fig) débrouiller; **to ~ things out** arranger les choses; **straighten up** vi (stand up) se redresser; (tidy) ranger

straighteners ['streitnəz] npl (for hair) lisseur msg

straight-faced [streit'feist] adj impassible ▷ adv en gardant son sérieux

straightforward [streit'fɔ:wəd] adj simple; (frank) honnête, direct(e)

strain [strein] n (Tech) tension f; pression f; (physical) effort m; (mental) tension (nerveuse); (Med) entorse f; (streak, trace) tendance f; élément m; (breed: of plants) variété f; (: of animals) race f; (of virus) souche f ▷ vt (stretch) tendre fortement; (fig: resources etc) mettre à rude épreuve, grever; (hurt: back etc) se faire mal à; (filter) passer, filtrer; (vegetables) égoutter ▷ vi peiner, fournir un gros effort; **strains** npl (Mus) accords mpl, accents mpl; **he's been under a lot of ~** il a traversé des moments difficiles, il est très éprouvé nerveusement

strained [streind] adj (muscle) froissé(e); (laugh etc) forcé(e), contraint(e); (relations) tendu(e)

strainer ['streinə'] n passoire f

strait [streit] n (Geo) détroit m; **straits** npl: **to be in dire ~s** (fig) avoir de sérieux ennuis

straitjacket ['streitdʒækit] n camisole f de force

strait-laced [streɪt'leɪst] *adj* collet monté *inv*
strand [strænd] *n* (*of thread*) fil *m*, brin *m*; (*of rope*) toron *m*; (*of hair*) mèche *f* ▷ *vt* (*boat*) échouer
stranded ['strændɪd] *adj* en rade, en plan
strange [streɪndʒ] *adj* (*not known*) inconnu(e); (*odd*) étrange, bizarre
strangely ['streɪndʒlɪ] *adv* étrangement, bizarrement; *see also* **enough**
stranger ['streɪndʒəʳ] *n* (*unknown*) inconnu(e); (*from somewhere else*) étranger(-ère); **I'm a ~ here** je ne suis pas d'ici
strangle ['stræŋgl] *vt* étrangler
stranglehold ['stræŋglhəʊld] *n* (*fig*) emprise totale, mainmise *f*
strap [stræp] *n* lanière *f*, courroie *f*, sangle *f*; (*of slip, dress*) bretelle *f* ▷ *vt* attacher (avec une courroie *etc*)
strappy ['stræpɪ] *adj* (*dress*) à bretelles; (*sandals*) à lanières
strategic [strə'tiːdʒɪk] *adj* stratégique
strategy ['strætɪdʒɪ] *n* stratégie *f*
straw [strɔː] *n* paille *f*; **that's the last ~!** ça c'est le comble!
strawberry ['strɔːbərɪ] *n* fraise *f*; (*plant*) fraisier *m*
stray [streɪ] *adj* (*animal*) perdu(e), errant(e); (*scattered*) isolé(e) ▷ *vi* s'égarer; **~ bullet** balle perdue
streak [striːk] *n* bande *f*, filet *m*; (*in hair*) raie *f*; (*fig: of madness etc*): **a ~ of** une or des tendance(s) à ▷ *vt* zébrer, strier ▷ *vi*: **to ~ past** passer à toute allure; **to have ~s in one's hair** s'être fait faire des mèches; **a winning/losing ~** une bonne/mauvaise série or période
stream [striːm] *n* (*brook*) ruisseau *m*; (*current*) courant *m*, flot *m*; (*of people*) défilé *m* ininterrompu, flot ▷ *vt* (*Scol*) répartir par niveau ▷ *vi* ruisseler; **to ~ in/out** entrer/ sortir à flots; **against the ~** à contre courant; **on ~** (*new power plant etc*) en service
streamer ['striːməʳ] *n* serpentin *m*, banderole *f*
streamlined ['striːmlaɪnd] *adj* (*Aviat*) fuselé(e), profilé(e); (*Aut*) aérodynamique; (*fig*) rationalisé(e)
street [striːt] *n* rue *f*; **the back ~s** les quartiers pauvres; **to be on the ~s** (*homeless*) être à la rue or sans abri
streetcar ['striːtkɑːʳ] *n* (*US*) tramway *m*
street lamp *n* réverbère *m*
street light *n* réverbère *m*
street map, street plan *n* plan *m* des rues
streetwise ['striːtwaɪz] *adj* (*inf*) futé(e), réaliste
strength [streŋθ] *n* force *f*; (*of girder, knot etc*) solidité *f*; (*of chemical solution*) titre *m*; (*of wine*) degré *m* d'alcool; **on the ~ of** en vertu de; **at full ~** au grand complet; **below ~** à effectifs réduits

strengthen ['streŋθn] *vt* renforcer; (*muscle*) fortifier; (*building, Econ*) consolider
strenuous ['strenjuəs] *adj* vigoureux(-euse), énergique; (*tiring*) ardu(e), fatigant(e)
stress [stres] *n* (*force, pressure*) pression *f*; (*mental strain*) tension (nerveuse), stress *m*; (*accent*) accent *m*; (*emphasis*) insistance *f* ▷ *vt* insister sur, souligner; (*syllable*) accentuer; **to lay great ~ on sth** insister beaucoup sur qch; **to be under ~** être stressé(e)
stressed [strest] *adj* (*tense*) stressé(e); (*syllable*) accentué(e)
stressful ['stresful] *adj* (*job*) stressant(e)
stretch [stretʃ] *n* (*of sand etc*) étendue *f*; (*of time*) période *f* ▷ *vi* s'étirer; (*extend*): **to ~ to** or **as far as** s'étendre jusqu'à; (*be enough: money, food*): **to ~ to** aller pour ▷ *vt* tendre, étirer; (*spread*) étendre; (*fig*) pousser (au maximum); **at a ~** d'affilée; **to ~ a muscle** se distendre un muscle; **to ~ one's legs** se dégourdir les jambes; **stretch out** *vi* s'étendre ▷ *vt* (*arm etc*) allonger, tendre; (*to spread*) étendre; **to ~ out for sth** allonger la main pour prendre qch
stretcher ['stretʃəʳ] *n* brancard *m*, civière *f*
stretchy ['stretʃɪ] *adj* élastique
strewn [struːn] *adj*: **~ with** jonché(e) de
stricken ['strɪkən] *adj* très éprouvé(e); dévasté(e); (*ship*) très endommagé(e); **~ with** frappé(e) or atteint(e) de
strict [strɪkt] *adj* strict(e); **in ~ confidence** tout à fait confidentiellement
strictly ['strɪktlɪ] *adv* strictement; **~ confidential** strictement confidentiel(le); **~ speaking** à strictement parler
stride [straɪd] *n* grand pas, enjambée *f* ▷ *vi* (*pt* **strode**) [strəʊd] marcher à grands pas; **to take in one's ~** (*fig: changes etc*) accepter sans sourciller
strife [straɪf] *n* conflit *m*, dissensions *fpl*
strike [straɪk] (*pt, pp* **struck**) [strʌk] *n* grève *f*; (*of oil etc*) découverte *f*; (*attack*) raid *m* ▷ *vt* frapper; (*oil etc*) trouver, découvrir; (*make: agreement, deal*) conclure ▷ *vi* faire grève; (*attack*) attaquer; (*clock*) sonner; **to go on** or **come out on ~** se mettre en grève, faire grève; **to ~ a match** frotter une allumette; **to ~ a balance** (*fig*) trouver un juste milieu; **strike back** *vi* (*Mil, fig*) contre-attaquer; **strike down** *vt* (*fig*) terrasser; **strike off** *vt* (*from list*) rayer; (: *doctor etc*) radier; **strike out** *vt* rayer; **strike up** *vt* (*Mus*) se mettre à jouer; **to ~ up a friendship with** se lier d'amitié avec
striker ['straɪkəʳ] *n* gréviste *m/f*; (*Sport*) buteur *m*
striking ['straɪkɪŋ] *adj* frappant(e), saisissant(e); (*attractive*) éblouissant(e)
string [strɪŋ] *n* ficelle *f*, fil *m*; (*row: of beads*) rang *m*; (: *of onions, excuses*) chapelet *m*; (: *of people, cars*) file *f*; (*Mus*) corde *f*; (*Comput*) chaîne *f* ▷ *vt* (*pt, pp* **strung**) [strʌŋ]: **to ~ out**

échelonner; **to ~ together** enchaîner; **the strings** npl (Mus) les instruments mpl à cordes; **to pull ~s** (fig) faire jouer le piston; **to get a job by pulling ~s** obtenir un emploi en faisant jouer le piston; **with no ~s attached** (fig) sans conditions

stringed instrument, string instrument [strɪŋ(d)-] n (Mus) instrument m à cordes

stringent ['strɪndʒənt] adj rigoureux(-euse); (need) impérieux(-euse)

strip [strɪp] n bande f; (Sport) tenue f ▷ vt (undress) déshabiller; (paint) décaper; (fig) dégarnir, dépouiller; (also: **~ down**: machine) démonter ▷ vi se déshabiller; **wearing the Celtic ~** en tenue du Celtic; **strip off** vt (paint etc) décaper ▷ vi (person) se déshabiller

strip cartoon n bande dessinée
stripe [straɪp] n raie f, rayure f; (Mil) galon m
striped ['straɪpt] adj rayé(e), à rayures
stripper ['strɪpər] n strip-teaseuse f
strip-search ['strɪpsɑːtʃ] n fouille corporelle (en faisant déshabiller la personne) ▷ vt: **to ~ sb** fouiller qn (en le faisant se déshabiller)
stripy ['straɪpɪ] adj rayé(e)
strive (pt strove, pp striven) [straɪv, strəuv, 'strɪvn] vi: **to ~ to do/for sth** s'efforcer de faire/d'obtenir qch
strode [strəud] pt of **stride**
stroke [strəuk] n coup m; (Med) attaque f; (caress) caresse f; (Swimming: style) (sorte f de) nage f; (of piston) course f ▷ vt caresser; **at a ~** d'un (seul) coup; **on the ~ of 5** à 5 heures sonnantes; **a ~ of luck** un coup de chance; **a 2-~ engine** un moteur à 2 temps
stroll [strəul] n petite promenade ▷ vi flâner, se promener nonchalamment; **to go for a ~** aller se promener or faire un tour
stroller ['strəulər] n (US: for child) poussette f
strong [strɒŋ] adj (gen) fort(e); (healthy) vigoureux(-euse); (heart, nerves) solide; (distaste, desire) vif/vive; (drugs, chemicals) puissant(e) ▷ adv: **to be going ~** (company) marcher bien; (person) être toujours solide; **they are 50 ~** ils sont au nombre de 50
stronghold ['strɒŋhəuld] n forteresse f, fort m; (fig) bastion m
strongly ['strɒŋlɪ] adv fortement, avec force; vigoureusement; solidement; **I feel ~ about it** c'est une question qui me tient particulièrement à cœur; (negatively) j'y suis profondément opposé(e)
strongroom ['strɒŋruːm] n chambre forte
strove [strəuv] pt of **strive**
struck [strʌk] pt, pp of **strike**
structural ['strʌktʃrəl] adj structural(e); (Constr) de construction; affectant les parties portantes
structure ['strʌktʃər] n structure f; (building) construction f
struggle ['strʌgl] n lutte f ▷ vi lutter, se battre; **to have a ~ to do sth** avoir beaucoup de mal à faire qch

strum [strʌm] vt (guitar) gratter de
strung [strʌŋ] pt, pp of **string**
strut [strʌt] n étai m, support m ▷ vi se pavaner
stub [stʌb] n (of cigarette) bout m, mégot m; (of ticket etc) talon m ▷ vt: **to ~ one's toe (on sth)** se heurter le doigt de pied (contre qch); **stub out** vt écraser
stubble ['stʌbl] n chaume m; (on chin) barbe f de plusieurs jours
stubborn ['stʌbən] adj têtu(e), obstiné(e), opiniâtre
stuck [stʌk] pt, pp of **stick** ▷ adj (jammed) bloqué(e), coincé(e); **to get ~** se bloquer or coincer
stuck-up [stʌk'ʌp] adj prétentieux(-euse)
stud [stʌd] n (on boots etc) clou m; (collar stud) bouton m de col; (earring) petite boucle d'oreille; (of horses: also: **~ farm**) écurie f, haras m; (also: **~ horse**) étalon m ▷ vt (fig): **~ded with** parsemé(e) or criblé(e) de
student ['stjuːdənt] n étudiant(e) ▷ adj (life) estudiantin(e), étudiant(e), d'étudiant; (residence, restaurant) universitaire; (loan, movement) étudiant, universitaire d'étudiant; **law/medical ~** étudiant en droit/ médecine
student driver n (US) (conducteur(-trice)) débutant(e)
students' union n (Brit: association) ≈ union f des étudiants; (: building) ≈ foyer m des étudiants
studio ['stjuːdɪəu] n studio m, atelier m; (TV etc) studio
studio flat, (US) **studio apartment** n studio m
studious ['stjuːdɪəs] adj studieux(-euse), appliqué(e); (studied) étudié(e)
studiously ['stjuːdɪəslɪ] adv (carefully) soigneusement
study ['stʌdɪ] n étude f; (room) bureau m ▷ vt étudier; (examine) examiner ▷ vi étudier, faire ses études; **to make a ~ of sth** étudier qch, faire une étude de qch; **to ~ for an exam** préparer un examen
stuff [stʌf] n (gen) chose(s) f(pl), truc m; (belongings) affaires fpl, trucs m; (substance) substance f ▷ vt rembourrer; (Culin) farcir; (inf: push) fourrer; (animal: for exhibition) empailler; **my nose is ~ed up** j'ai le nez bouché; **get ~ed!** (inf!) va te faire foutre! (!); **~ed toy** jouet m en peluche
stuffing ['stʌfɪŋ] n bourre f, rembourrage m; (Culin) farce f
stuffy ['stʌfɪ] adj (room) mal ventilé(e) or aéré(e); (ideas) vieux jeu inv
stumble ['stʌmbl] vi trébucher; **to ~ across** or **on** (fig) tomber sur
stumbling block ['stʌmblɪŋ-] n pierre f d'achoppement
stump [stʌmp] n souche f; (of limb) moignon m ▷ vt: **to be ~ed** sécher, ne pas savoir que répondre

s

stun [stʌn] vt (blow) étourdir; (news) abasourdir, stupéfier

stung [stʌŋ] pt, pp of **sting**

stunk [stʌŋk] pp of **stink**

stunned [stʌnd] adj assommé(e); (fig) sidéré(e)

stunning ['stʌnɪŋ] adj (beautiful) étourdissant(e); (news etc) stupéfiant(e)

stunt [stʌnt] n tour m de force; (in film) cascade f, acrobatie f; (publicity) truc m publicitaire; (Aviat) acrobatie f ▷ vt retarder, arrêter

stuntman ['stʌntmæn] irreg n cascadeur m

stupendous [stju:'pɛndəs] adj prodigieux(-euse), fantastique

stupid ['stju:pɪd] adj stupide, bête

stupidity [stju:'pɪdɪtɪ] n stupidité f, bêtise f

sturdy ['stə:dɪ] adj (person, plant) robuste, vigoureux(-euse); (object) solide

stutter ['stʌtə'] n bégaiement m ▷ vi bégayer

sty [staɪ] n (of pigs) porcherie f

stye [staɪ] n (Med) orgelet m

style [staɪl] n style m; (of dress etc) genre m; (distinction) allure f, cachet m, style; (design) modèle m; **in the latest ~** à la dernière mode; **hair ~** coiffure f

stylish ['staɪlɪʃ] adj élégant(e), chic inv

stylist ['staɪlɪst] n (hair stylist) coiffeur(-euse); (literary stylist) styliste m/f

stylus (pl **styli** or **styluses**) ['staɪləs, -laɪ] n (of record player) pointe f de lecture

suave [swɑ:v] adj doucereux(-euse), onctueux(-euse)

sub... [sʌb] prefix sub..., sous-

subconscious [sʌb'kɒnʃəs] adj subconscient(e) ▷ n subconscient m

subcontract n ['sʌb'kɒntrækt] contrat m de sous-traitance ▷ vt [sʌbkən'trækt] sous-traiter

subdue [səb'dju:] vt subjuguer, soumettre

subdued [səb'dju:d] adj contenu(e), atténué(e); (light) tamisé(e); (person) qui a perdu de son entrain

subject n ['sʌbdʒɪkt] sujet m; (Scol) matière f ▷ vt [səb'dʒɛkt]: **to ~** soumettre à; exposer à; **to be ~ to** (law) être soumis(e) à; (disease) être sujet(te) à; **~ to confirmation in writing** sous réserve de confirmation écrite; **to change the ~** changer de conversation

subjective [səb'dʒɛktɪv] adj subjectif(-ive)

subject matter n sujet m; (content) contenu m

subjunctive [səb'dʒʌŋktɪv] adj subjonctif(-ive) ▷ n subjonctif m

sublet [sʌb'lɛt] vt sous-louer

submarine [sʌbmə'ri:n] n sous-marin m

submerge [səb'mə:dʒ] vt submerger; immerger ▷ vi plonger

submission [səb'mɪʃən] n soumission f; (to committee etc) présentation f

submissive [səb'mɪsɪv] adj soumis(e)

submit [səb'mɪt] vt soumettre ▷ vi se soumettre

subnormal [sʌb'nɔ:ml] adj au-dessous de la normale; (person) arriéré(e)

subordinate [sə'bɔ:dɪnət] adj (junior) subalterne; (Grammar) subordonné(e) ▷ n subordonné(e)

subpoena [səb'pi:nə] (Law) n citation f, assignation f ▷ vt citer or assigner (à comparaître)

subscribe [səb'skraɪb] vi cotiser; **to ~ to** (opinion, fund) souscrire à; (newspaper) s'abonner à; être abonné(e) à

subscriber [səb'skraɪbə'] n (to periodical, telephone) abonné(e)

subscription [səb'skrɪpʃən] n (to fund) souscription f; (to magazine etc) abonnement m; (membership dues) cotisation f; **to take out a ~ to** s'abonner à

subsequent ['sʌbsɪkwənt] adj ultérieur(e), suivant(e); **~ to** prep à la suite de

subsequently ['sʌbsɪkwəntlɪ] adv par la suite

subside [səb'saɪd] vi (land) s'affaisser; (flood) baisser; (wind, feelings) tomber

subsidence [səb'saɪdns] n affaissement m

subsidiary [səb'sɪdɪərɪ] adj subsidiaire; accessoire; (Brit Scol: subject) complémentaire ▷ n filiale f

subsidize ['sʌbsɪdaɪz] vt subventionner

subsidy ['sʌbsɪdɪ] n subvention f

substance ['sʌbstəns] n substance f; (fig) essentiel m; **a man of ~** un homme jouissant d'une certaine fortune; **to lack ~** être plutôt mince (fig)

substantial [səb'stænʃl] adj substantiel(le); (fig) important(e)

substantially [səb'stænʃəlɪ] adv considérablement; en grande partie

substantiate [səb'stænʃɪeɪt] vt étayer, fournir des preuves à l'appui de

substitute ['sʌbstɪtju:t] n (person) remplaçant(e); (thing) succédané m ▷ vt: **to ~ sth/sb for** substituer qch/qn à, remplacer par qch/qn

substitution [sʌbstɪ'tju:ʃən] n substitution f

subterranean [sʌbtə'reɪnɪən] adj souterrain(e)

subtitled ['sʌbtaɪtld] adj sous-titré(e)

subtitles ['sʌbtaɪtlz] npl (Cine) sous-titres mpl

subtle ['sʌtl] adj subtil(e)

subtotal [sʌb'təʊtl] n total partiel

subtract [səb'trækt] vt soustraire, retrancher

subtraction [səb'trækʃən] n soustraction f

suburb ['sʌbə:b] n faubourg m; **the ~s** la banlieue

suburban [sə'bə:bən] adj de banlieue, suburbain(e)

suburbia [sə'bə:bɪə] n la banlieue

subway ['sʌbweɪ] n (Brit: underpass) passage souterrain; (US: railway) métro m

succeed [sək'si:d] vi réussir ▷ vt succéder à;
to ~ in doing réussir à faire

succeeding [sək'si:dɪŋ] adj suivant(e), qui
suit (or suivent or suivront etc)

success [sək'sɛs] n succès m; réussite f

successful [sək'sɛsful] adj qui a du succès;
(candidate) choisi(e), agréé(e); (business)
prospère, qui réussit; (attempt) couronné(e)
de succès; **to be ~ (in doing)** réussir (à faire)

successfully [sək'sɛsfəlɪ] adv avec succès

succession [sək'sɛʃən] n succession f; **in ~**
successivement; **3 years in ~** 3 ans de suite

successive [sək'sɛsɪv] adj successif(-ive);
on 3 ~ days 3 jours de suite or consécutifs

successor [sək'sɛsə^r] n successeur m

succumb [sə'kʌm] vi succomber

such [sʌtʃ] adj tel/telle; (of that kind): **~ a book**
un livre de ce genre or pareil, un tel livre;
(so much): **~ courage** un tel courage ▷ adv si;
~ books des livres de ce genre or pareils, de
tels livres; **~ a long trip** un si long voyage;
~ good books de si bons livres; **~ a long trip
that** un voyage si or tellement long que;
~ a lot of tellement or tant de; **making ~ a
noise that** faisant un tel bruit que or
tellement de bruit que; **~ a long time ago** il y
a si or tellement longtemps; **~ as** (like) tel/
telle que, comme; **a noise ~ as to** un bruit de
nature à; **~ books as I have** les quelques
livres que j'ai; **as ~** adv en tant que tel/telle,
à proprement parler

such-and-such [sʌtʃənsʌtʃ] adj tel ou tel/
telle ou telle

suck [sʌk] vt sucer; (breast, bottle) téter; (pump,
machine) aspirer

sucker ['sʌkə^r] n (Bot, Zool, Tech) ventouse f;
(inf) naïf(-ïve), poire f

suction ['sʌkʃən] n succion f

Sudan [su'dɑ:n] n Soudan m

sudden ['sʌdn] adj soudain(e), subit(e); **all
of a ~** tout à coup

suddenly ['sʌdnlɪ] adv brusquement, tout à
coup, soudain

sudoku [su'dəuku:] n sudoku m

suds [sʌdz] npl eau savonneuse

sue [su:] vt poursuivre en justice, intenter un
procès à ▷ vi: **to ~ (for)** intenter un procès
(pour); **to ~ for divorce** engager une
procédure de divorce; **to ~ sb for damages**
poursuivre qn en dommages-intérêts

suede [sweɪd] n daim m, cuir suédé ▷ cpd de
daim

suet [suɪt] n graisse f de rognon or de bœuf

suffer ['sʌfə^r] vt souffrir, subir; (bear) tolérer,
supporter, subir ▷ vi souffrir; **to ~ from**
(illness) souffrir de, avoir; **to ~ from the
effects of alcohol/a fall** se ressentir des
effets de l'alcool/des conséquences d'une
chute

sufferer ['sʌfərə^r] n malade m/f; victime m/f

suffering ['sʌfərɪŋ] n souffrance(s) f(pl)

suffice [sə'faɪs] vi suffire

sufficient [sə'fɪʃənt] adj suffisant(e);
~ money suffisamment d'argent

sufficiently [sə'fɪʃəntlɪ] adv suffisamment,
assez

suffocate ['sʌfəkeɪt] vi suffoquer; étouffer

sugar ['ʃugə^r] n sucre m ▷ vt sucrer

sugar beet n betterave sucrière

sugar cane n canne f à sucre

suggest [sə'dʒɛst] vt suggérer, proposer;
(indicate) sembler indiquer; **what do you ~ I
do?** que vous me suggérez de faire?

suggestion [sə'dʒɛstʃən] n suggestion f

suicide ['suɪsaɪd] n suicide m; **to commit ~** se
suicider; **~ bombing** attentat m suicide; see
also **commit**

suicide bomber n kamikaze m/f

suit [su:t] n (man's) costume m, complet m;
(woman's) tailleur m, ensemble m; (Cards)
couleur f; (lawsuit) procès m ▷ vt (subj: clothes,
hairstyle) aller à; (be convenient for) convenir à;
(adapt): **to ~ sth to** adapter or approprier qch
à; **to be ~ed to sth** (suitable for) être adapté(e)
or approprié(e) à qch; **well ~ed** (couple) faits
l'un pour l'autre, très bien assortis; **to bring
a ~ against sb** intenter un procès contre qn;
to follow ~ (fig) faire de même

suitable ['su:təbl] adj qui convient;
approprié(e), adéquat(e); **would tomorrow
be ~?** est-ce que demain vous conviendrait?;
we found somebody ~ nous avons trouvé la
personne qu'il nous faut

suitably ['su:təblɪ] adv comme il se doit (or se
devait etc), convenablement

suitcase ['su:tkeɪs] n valise f

suite [swi:t] n (of rooms, also Mus) suite f;
(furniture): **bedroom/dining room ~**
(ensemble m de) chambre f à coucher/salle f
à manger; **a three-piece ~** un salon (canapé
et deux fauteuils)

suitor ['su:tə^r] n soupirant m, prétendant m

sulfur ['sʌlfə^r] (US) n = **sulphur**

sulk [sʌlk] vi bouder

sulky ['sʌlkɪ] adj boudeur(-euse), maussade

sullen ['sʌlən] adj renfrogné(e), maussade;
morne

sulphur, (US) **sulfur** ['sʌlfə^r] n soufre m

sultana [sʌl'tɑ:nə] n (fruit) raisin (sec) de
Smyrne

sultry ['sʌltrɪ] adj étouffant(e)

sum [sʌm] n somme f; (Scol etc) calcul m; **sum
up** vt résumer; (evaluate rapidly) récapituler
▷ vi résumer

summarize ['sʌməraɪz] vt résumer

summary ['sʌmərɪ] n résumé m ▷ adj (justice)
sommaire

summer ['sʌmə^r] n été m ▷ cpd d'été,
estival(e); **in (the) ~** en été, pendant l'été

summer holidays npl grandes vacances

summerhouse ['sʌməhaus] n (in garden)
pavillon m

summertime ['sʌmətaɪm] n (season) été m

summer time n (by clock) heure f d'été

summit ['sʌmɪt] n sommet m; (also: ~ **conference**) (conférence f au) sommet m

summon ['sʌmən] vt appeler, convoquer; **to ~ a witness** citer or assigner un témoin; **summon up** vt rassembler, faire appel à

summons ['sʌmənz] n citation f, assignation f ▷ vt citer, assigner; **to serve a ~ on sb** remettre une assignation à qn

Sun. abbr (= Sunday)

sun [sʌn] n soleil m; **in the ~** au soleil; **to catch the ~** prendre le soleil; **everything under the ~** absolument tout

sunbathe ['sʌnbeɪð] vi prendre un bain de soleil

sunbed ['sʌnbed] n lit pliant; (with sun lamp) lit à ultra-violets

sunblock ['sʌnblɔk] n écran m total

sunburn ['sʌnbə:n] n coup m de soleil

sunburned ['sʌnbə:nd], **sunburnt** ['sʌnbə:nt] adj bronzé(e), hâlé(e); (painfully) brûlé(e) par le soleil

Sunday ['sʌndɪ] n dimanche m; see also **Tuesday**

Sunday school n ≈ catéchisme m

sundial ['sʌndaɪəl] n cadran m solaire

sundown ['sʌndaun] n coucher m du soleil

sundries ['sʌndrɪz] npl articles divers

sundry ['sʌndrɪ] adj divers(e), différent(e); **all and ~** tout le monde, n'importe qui

sunflower ['sʌnflauə'] n tournesol m

sung [sʌŋ] pp of **sing**

sunglasses ['sʌnglɑ:sɪz] npl lunettes fpl de soleil

sunk [sʌŋk] pp of **sink**

sunlight ['sʌnlaɪt] n (lumière f du) soleil m

sunlit ['sʌnlɪt] adj ensoleillé(e)

sun lounger n chaise longue

sunny ['sʌnɪ] adj ensoleillé(e); (fig) épanoui(e), radieux(-euse); **it is ~** il fait (du) soleil, il y a du soleil

sunrise ['sʌnraɪz] n lever m du soleil

sun roof n (Aut) toit ouvrant

sunscreen ['sʌnskri:n] n crème f solaire

sunset ['sʌnset] n coucher m du soleil

sunshade ['sʌnʃeɪd] n (lady's) ombrelle f; (over table) parasol m

sunshine ['sʌnʃaɪn] n (lumière f du) soleil m

sunstroke ['sʌnstrəuk] n insolation f, coup m de soleil

suntan ['sʌntæn] n bronzage m

suntan lotion n lotion f or lait m solaire

suntan oil n huile f solaire

super ['su:pə'] adj (inf) formidable

superannuation [su:pərænju'eɪʃən] n cotisations fpl pour la pension

superb [su:'pə:b] adj superbe, magnifique

supercilious [su:pə'sɪlɪəs] adj hautain(e), dédaigneux(-euse)

superficial [su:pə'fɪʃəl] adj superficiel(le)

superimpose ['su:pərɪm'pəuz] vt superposer

superintendent [su:pərɪn'tendənt] n directeur(-trice); (Police) ≈ commissaire m

superior [su'pɪərɪə'] adj supérieur(e); (Comm: goods, quality) de qualité supérieure; (smug) condescendant(e), méprisant(e) ▷ n supérieur(e); **Mother S~** (Rel) Mère supérieure

superiority [supɪərɪ'ɔrɪtɪ] n supériorité f

superlative [su'pə:lətɪv] adj sans pareil(le), suprême ▷ n (Ling) superlatif m

superman ['su:pəmæn] irreg n surhomme m

supermarket ['su:pəmɑ:kɪt] n supermarché m

supernatural [su:pə'nætʃərəl] adj surnaturel(le) ▷ n: **the ~** le surnaturel

superpower ['su:pəpauə'] n (Pol) superpuissance f

supersede [su:pə'si:d] vt remplacer, supplanter

superstition [su:pə'stɪʃən] n superstition f

superstitious [su:pə'stɪʃəs] adj superstitieux(-euse)

superstore ['su:pəstɔ:'] n (Brit) hypermarché m, grande surface

supervise ['su:pəvaɪz] vt (children etc) surveiller; (organization, work) diriger

supervision [su:pə'vɪʒən] n surveillance f; (monitoring) contrôle m; (management) direction f; **under medical ~** sous contrôle du médecin

supervisor ['su:pəvaɪzə'] n surveillant(e); (in shop) chef m de rayon; (Scol) directeur(-trice) de thèse

supper ['sʌpə'] n dîner m; (late) souper m; **to have ~** dîner; souper

supple ['sʌpl] adj souple

supplement n ['sʌplɪmənt] supplément m ▷ vt [sʌplɪ'ment] ajouter à, compléter

supplementary [sʌplɪ'mentərɪ] adj supplémentaire

supplementary benefit n (Brit) allocation f supplémentaire d'aide sociale

supplier [sə'plaɪə'] n fournisseur m

supply [sə'plaɪ] vt (provide) fournir; (equip): **to ~ (with)** approvisionner or ravitailler (en); fournir (en); (system, machine): **to ~ sth (with sth)** alimenter qch (en qch); (a need) répondre à ▷ n provision f, réserve f; (supplying) approvisionnement m; (Tech) alimentation f; **supplies** npl (food) vivres mpl; (Mil) subsistances fpl; **office supplies** fournitures fpl de bureau; **to be in short ~** être rare, manquer; **the electricity/water/gas ~** l'alimentation f en électricité/eau/gaz; **~ and demand** l'offre f et la demande; **it comes supplied with an adaptor** il (or elle) est pourvu(e) d'un adaptateur

supply teacher n (Brit) suppléant(e)

support [sə'pɔ:t] n (moral, financial etc) soutien m, appui m; (Tech) support m, soutien ▷ vt soutenir, supporter; (financially) subvenir aux besoins de; (uphold) être pour, être partisan de, appuyer; (Sport: team) être pour; **to ~ o.s.** (financially) gagner sa vie

supporter [sə'pɔːtəʳ] n (Pol etc) partisan(e); (Sport) supporter m

suppose [sə'pəuz] vt, vi supposer; imaginer; **to be ~d to do/be** être censé(e) faire/être; **I don't ~ she'll come** je suppose qu'elle ne viendra pas, cela m'étonnerait qu'elle vienne

supposedly [sə'pəuzɪdlɪ] adv soi-disant

supposing [sə'pəuzɪŋ] conj si, à supposer que + sub

suppress [sə'pres] vt (revolt, feeling) réprimer; (information) faire disparaître; (scandal, yawn) étouffer

supreme [su'priːm] adj suprême

surcharge [ˈsəːtʃɑːdʒ] n surcharge f; (extra tax) surtaxe f

sure [ʃuəʳ] adj (gen) sûr(e); (definite, convinced) sûr, certain(e) ▷ adv (inf: US): **that ~ is pretty, that's ~ pretty** c'est drôlement joli(e); **~!** (of course) bien sûr!; **~ enough** effectivement; **I'm not ~ how/why/when** je ne sais pas très bien comment/pourquoi/quand; **to be ~ of o.s.** être sûr de soi; **to make ~ of sth/that** s'assurer de qch/que, vérifier qch/que

surely [ˈʃuəlɪ] adv sûrement; certainement; **~ you don't mean that!** vous ne parlez pas sérieusement!

surf [səːf] n (waves) ressac m ▷ vt: **to ~ the Net** surfer sur Internet, surfer sur le net

surface [ˈsəːfɪs] n surface f ▷ vt (road) poser un revêtement sur ▷ vi remonter à la surface; (fig) faire surface; **on the ~** (fig) au premier abord; **by ~ mail** par voie de terre; (by sea) par voie maritime

surface mail n courrier m par voie de terre (or maritime)

surfboard [ˈsəːfbɔːd] n planche f de surf

surfeit [ˈsəːfɪt] n: **a ~ of** un excès de; une indigestion de

surfer [ˈsəːfəʳ] n (in sea) surfeur(-euse); **web** or **net ~** internaute m/f

surfing [ˈsəːfɪŋ] n surf m

surge [səːdʒ] n (of emotion) vague f; (Elec) pointe f de courant ▷ vi déferler; **to ~ forward** se précipiter (en avant)

surgeon [ˈsəːdʒən] n chirurgien m

surgery [ˈsəːdʒərɪ] n chirurgie f; (Brit: room) cabinet m (de consultation); (also: **~ hours**) heures fpl de consultation; (of MP etc) permanence f (où le député etc reçoit les électeurs etc); **to undergo ~** être opéré(e)

surgical [ˈsəːdʒɪkl] adj chirurgical(e)

surgical spirit n (Brit) alcool m à 90°

surname [ˈsəːneɪm] n nom m de famille

surpass [səːˈpɑːs] vt surpasser, dépasser

surplus [ˈsəːpləs] n surplus m, excédent m ▷ adj en surplus, de trop; (Comm) excédentaire; **it is ~ to our requirements** cela dépasse nos besoins; **~ stock** surplus m

surprise [sə'praɪz] n (gen) surprise f; (astonishment) étonnement m ▷ vt surprendre, étonner; **to take by ~** (person) prendre au dépourvu; (Mil: town, fort) prendre par surprise

surprised [sə'praɪzd] adj (look, smile) surpris(e), étonné(e); **to be ~** être surpris

surprising [sə'praɪzɪŋ] adj surprenant(e), étonnant(e)

surprisingly [sə'praɪzɪŋlɪ] adv (easy, helpful) étonnamment, étrangement; (somewhat) ~, **he agreed** curieusement, il a accepté

surrender [sə'rendəʳ] n reddition f, capitulation f ▷ vi se rendre, capituler ▷ vt (claim, right) renoncer à

surreptitious [sʌrəp'tɪʃəs] adj subreptice, furtif(-ive)

surrogate [ˈsʌrəgɪt] n (Brit: substitute) substitut m ▷ adj de substitution, de remplacement; **a food ~** un succédané alimentaire; **~ coffee** ersatz m or succédané m de café

surrogate mother n mère porteuse or de substitution

surround [sə'raund] vt entourer; (Mil etc) encercler

surrounding [sə'raundɪŋ] adj environnant(e)

surroundings [sə'raundɪŋz] npl environs mpl, alentours mpl

surveillance [səːˈveɪləns] n surveillance f

survey n [ˈsəːveɪ] enquête f, étude f; (in house buying etc) inspection f, (rapport m d') expertise f; (of land) levé m; (comprehensive view: of situation etc) vue f d'ensemble ▷ vt [səːˈveɪ] (situation) passer en revue; (examine carefully) inspecter; (building) expertiser; (land) faire le levé de; (look at) embrasser du regard

surveyor [səːˈveɪəʳ] n (of building) expert m; (of land) (arpenteur m) géomètre m

survival [sə'vaɪvl] n survie f; (relic) vestige m ▷ cpd (course, kit) de survie

survive [sə'vaɪv] vi survivre; (custom etc) subsister ▷ vt (accident etc) survivre à, réchapper de; (person) survivre à

survivor [sə'vaɪvəʳ] n survivant(e)

susceptible [sə'septəbl] adj: **~ (to)** sensible (à); (disease) prédisposé(e) (à)

suspect adj, n [ˈsʌspekt] suspect(e) ▷ vt [səs'pekt] soupçonner, suspecter

suspend [səs'pend] vt suspendre

suspended sentence [səs'pendɪd-] n (Law) condamnation f avec sursis

suspender belt [səs'pendə-] n (Brit) porte-jarretelles m inv

suspenders [səs'pendəz] npl (Brit) jarretelles fpl; (US) bretelles fpl

suspense [səs'pens] n attente f, incertitude f; (in film etc) suspense m; **to keep sb in ~** tenir qn en suspens, laisser qn dans l'incertitude

suspension [səs'penʃən] n (gen, Aut) suspension f; (of driving licence) retrait m provisoire

suspension bridge n pont suspendu

suspicion [səs'pɪʃən] n soupçon(s) m(pl); **to be under ~** être considéré(e) comme suspect(e), être suspecté(e); **arrested on ~ of murder** arrêté sur présomption de meurtre

suspicious [səs'pɪʃəs] adj (suspecting) soupçonneux(-euse), méfiant(e); (causing suspicion) suspect(e); **to be ~ of or about sb/ sth** avoir des doutes à propos de qn/sur qch, trouver qn/qch suspect(e)

sustain [səs'teɪn] vt soutenir; supporter; corroborer; (subj: food) nourrir, donner des forces à; (damage) subir; (injury) recevoir

sustainable [səs'teɪnəbl] adj (rate, growth) qui peut être maintenu(e); (development) durable

sustained [səs'teɪnd] adj (effort) soutenu(e), prolongé(e)

sustenance ['sʌstɪnəns] n nourriture f; moyens mpl de subsistance

SUV n abbr (esp US: = sports utility vehicle) SUV m, véhicule m de loisirs

swab [swɔb] n (Med) tampon m; prélèvement m ▷ vt (Naut: also: **~ down**) nettoyer

swagger ['swægəʳ] vi plastronner, parader

swallow ['swɔləu] n (bird) hirondelle f; (of food etc) gorgée f ▷ vt avaler; (fig: story) gober; **swallow up** vt engloutir

swam [swæm] pt of **swim**

swamp [swɔmp] n marais m, marécage m ▷ vt submerger

swan [swɔn] n cygne m

swap [swɔp] n échange m, troc m ▷ vt: **to ~ (for)** échanger (contre), troquer (contre)

swarm [swɔːm] n essaim m ▷ vi (bees) essaimer; (people) grouiller; **to be ~ing with** grouiller de

swastika ['swɔstɪkə] n croix gammée

swat [swɔt] vt écraser ▷ n (Brit: also: **fly ~**) tapette f

sway [sweɪ] vi se balancer, osciller; tanguer ▷ vt (influence) influencer ▷ n (rule, power): **~ (over)** emprise f (sur); **to hold ~ over sb** avoir de l'emprise sur qn

swear [sweəʳ] (pt **swore**, pp **sworn**) [swɔːʳ, swɔːn] vt, vi jurer; **to ~ to sth** jurer de qch; **to ~ an oath** prêter serment; **swear in** vt assermenter

swearword ['sweəwəːd] n gros mot, juron m

sweat [swet] n sueur f, transpiration f ▷ vi suer; **in a ~** en sueur

sweater ['swetəʳ] n tricot m, pull m

sweatshirt ['swetʃəːt] n sweat-shirt m

sweaty ['swetɪ] adj en sueur, moite or mouillé(e) de sueur

Swede [swiːd] n Suédois(e)

swede [swiːd] n (Brit) rutabaga m

Sweden ['swiːdn] n Suède f

Swedish ['swiːdɪʃ] adj suédois(e) ▷ n (Ling) suédois m

sweep [swiːp] (pt, pp **swept**) [swept] n coup m de balai; (curve) grande courbe; (range) champ m; (also: **chimney ~**) ramoneur m ▷ vt

balayer; (subj: current) emporter; (subj: fashion, craze) se répandre dans ▷ vi avancer majestueusement or rapidement; s'élancer; s'étendre; **sweep away** vt balayer; entraîner; emporter; **sweep past** vi passer majestueusement or rapidement; **sweep up** vt, vi balayer

sweeping ['swiːpɪŋ] adj (gesture) large; circulaire; (changes, reforms) radical(e); **a ~ statement** une généralisation hâtive

sweet [swiːt] n (Brit: pudding) dessert m; (candy) bonbon m ▷ adj doux/douce; (not savoury) sucré(e); (fresh) frais/fraîche, pur(e); (kind) gentil(le); (baby) mignon(ne) ▷ adv: **to smell ~** sentir bon; **to taste ~** avoir un goût sucré; **~ and sour** adj aigre-doux/douce

sweetcorn ['swiːtkɔːn] n maïs doux

sweeten ['swiːtn] vt sucrer; (fig) adoucir

sweetener ['swiːtnəʳ] n (Culin) édulcorant m

sweetheart ['swiːthaːt] n amoureux(-euse)

sweetness ['swiːtnɪs] n douceur f; (of taste) goût sucré

sweet pea n pois m de senteur

sweetshop ['swiːtʃɔp] n (Brit) confiserie f

swell [swel] (pt **swelled**, pp **swollen** or **swelled**) ['swəulən] n (of sea) houle f ▷ adj (US: inf: excellent) chouette ▷ vt (increase) grossir, augmenter ▷ vi (increase) grossir, augmenter; (sound) s'enfler; (Med: also: **~ up**) enfler

swelling ['swelɪŋ] n (Med) enflure f; (: lump) grosseur f

sweltering ['sweltərɪŋ] adj étouffant(e), oppressant(e)

swept [swept] pt, pp of **sweep**

swerve [swəːv] vi (to avoid obstacle) faire une embardée or un écart; (off the road) dévier

swift [swɪft] n (bird) martinet m ▷ adj rapide, prompt(e)

swig [swɪg] n (inf: drink) lampée f

swill [swɪl] n pâtée f ▷ vt (also: **~ out, ~ down**) laver à grande eau

swim [swɪm] (pt **swam**, pp **swum**) [swæm, swʌm] n: **to go for a ~** aller nager or se baigner ▷ vi nager; (Sport) faire de la natation; (fig: head, room) tourner ▷ vt traverser (à la nage); (distance) faire (à la nage); **to ~ a length** nager une longueur; **to go ~ming** aller nager

swimmer ['swɪməʳ] n nageur(-euse)

swimming ['swɪmɪŋ] n nage f, natation f

swimming cap n bonnet m de bain

swimming costume n (Brit) maillot m (de bain)

swimming pool n piscine f

swimming trunks npl maillot m de bain

swimsuit ['swɪmsuːt] n maillot m (de bain)

swindle ['swɪndl] n escroquerie f ▷ vt escroquer

swine [swaɪn] n (pl inv) pourceau m, porc m; (inf!) salaud m (!)

swine flu n grippe f porcine

swing [swɪŋ] (pt, pp **swung**) [swʌŋ] n (in

playground) balançoire f; (movement) balancement m, oscillations fpl; (change in opinion etc) (Mus) swing m; rythme m ▷ vt balancer, faire osciller; (also: ~ round) tourner, faire virer ▷ vi se balancer, osciller; (also: ~ round) virer, tourner; **a ~ to the left** (Pol) un revirement en faveur de la gauche; **to be in full ~** battre son plein; **to get into the ~ of things** se mettre dans le bain; **the road ~s south** la route prend la direction sud

swing bridge n pont tournant

swing door n (Brit) porte battante

swingeing ['swɪndʒɪŋ] adj (Brit) écrasant(e); considérable

swipe [swaɪp] n grand coup; gifle f ▷ vt (hit) frapper à toute volée; gifler; (inf: steal) piquer; (credit card etc) faire passer (dans la machine)

swipe card n carte f magnétique

swirl [swə:l] n tourbillon m ▷ vi tourbillonner, tournoyer

Swiss [swɪs] adj suisse ▷ n (pl inv) Suisse(-esse)

switch [swɪtʃ] n (for light, radio etc) bouton m; (change) changement m, revirement m ▷ vt (change) changer; (exchange) intervertir; (invert): **to ~ (round or over)** changer de place; **switch off** vt éteindre; (engine, machine) arrêter; **could you ~ off the light?** pouvez-vous éteindre la lumière?; **switch on** vt allumer; (engine, machine) mettre en marche; (Brit: water supply) ouvrir

switchboard ['swɪtʃbɔ:d] n (Tel) standard m

Switzerland ['swɪtsələnd] n Suisse f

swivel ['swɪvl] vt (also: ~ round) pivoter, tourner

swollen ['swəulən] pp of **swell** ▷ adj (ankle etc) enflé(e)

swoon [swu:n] vi se pâmer

swoop [swu:p] n (by police etc) rafle f, descente f; (of bird etc) descente f en piqué ▷ vi (bird: also: ~ down) descendre en piqué, piquer

swop [swɔp] n, vt = **swap**

sword [sɔ:d] n épée f

swordfish ['sɔ:dfɪʃ] n espadon m

swore [swɔ:r] pt of **swear**

sworn [swɔ:n] pp of **swear** ▷ adj (statement, evidence) donné(e) sous serment; (enemy) juré(e)

swot [swɔt] vt, vi bûcher, potasser

swum [swʌm] pp of **swim**

swung [swʌŋ] pt, pp of **swing**

syllable ['sɪləbl] n syllabe f

syllabus ['sɪləbəs] n programme m; **on the ~** au programme

symbol ['sɪmbl] n symbole m

symbolic [sɪm'bɔlɪk], **symbolical** [sɪm'bɔlɪkl] adj symbolique

symmetrical [sɪ'mɛtrɪkl] adj symétrique

symmetry ['sɪmɪtrɪ] n symétrie f

sympathetic [sɪmpə'θɛtɪk] adj (showing pity) compatissant(e); (understanding) bienveillant(e), compréhensif(-ive); **~ towards** bien disposé(e) envers

sympathize ['sɪmpəθaɪz] vi: **to ~ with sb** plaindre qn; (in grief) s'associer à la douleur de qn; **to ~ with sth** comprendre qch

sympathizer ['sɪmpəθaɪzər] n (Pol) sympathisant(e)

sympathy ['sɪmpəθɪ] n (pity) compassion f; **sympathies** npl (support) soutien m; **in ~ with** en accord avec; (strike) en or par solidarité avec; **with our deepest ~** en vous priant d'accepter nos sincères condoléances

symphony ['sɪmfənɪ] n symphonie f

symptom ['sɪmptəm] n symptôme m; indice m

synagogue ['sɪnəgɔg] n synagogue f

syndicate ['sɪndɪkɪt] n syndicat m, coopérative f; (Press) agence f de presse

syndrome ['sɪndrəum] n syndrome m

synonym ['sɪnənɪm] n synonyme m

synopsis (pl **synopses**) [sɪ'nɔpsɪs, -si:z] n résumé m, synopsis m or f

synthetic [sɪn'θɛtɪk] adj synthétique ▷ n matière f synthétique; **synthetics** npl textiles artificiels

syphon ['saɪfən] n, vb = **siphon**

Syria ['sɪrɪə] n Syrie f

syringe [sɪ'rɪndʒ] n seringue f

syrup ['sɪrəp] n sirop m; (Brit: also: **golden ~**) mélasse raffinée

system ['sɪstəm] n système m; (order) méthode f; (Anat) organisme m

systematic [sɪstə'mætɪk] adj systématique; méthodique

system disk n (Comput) disque m système

systems analyst n analyste-programmeur m/f

S

t

ta [tɑ:] *excl (Brit inf)* merci!

tab [tæb] *n (loop on coat etc)* attache *f; (label)* étiquette *f; (on drinks can etc)* languette *f;* **to keep ~s on** *(fig)* surveiller

tabby ['tæbɪ] *n (also:* **~ cat**) chat(te) tigré(e)

table ['teɪbl] *n* table *f ▷ vt (Brit: motion etc)* présenter; **to lay** *or* **set the ~** mettre le couvert *or* la table; **to clear the ~** débarrasser la table; **league ~** *(Brit Football, Rugby)* classement *m* (du championnat); **~ of contents** table des matières

tablecloth ['teɪblklɔθ] *n* nappe *f*

table d'hôte [tɑ:bl'dəut] *adj (meal)* à prix fixe

table lamp *n* lampe décorative *or* de table

tablemat ['teɪblmæt] *n (for plate)* napperon *m*, set *m; (for hot dish)* dessous-de-plat *m inv*

tablespoon ['teɪblspu:n] *n* cuiller *f* de service; *(also:* **~ful:** *as measurement)* cuillerée *f* à soupe

tablet ['tæblɪt] *n (Med)* comprimé *m; (: for sucking)* pastille *f; (of stone)* plaque *f; ~ of soap* *(Brit)* savonnette *f; (Comput)* tablette *f* (tactile)

table tennis *n* ping-pong *m*, tennis *m* de table

table wine *n* vin *m* de table

tabloid ['tæblɔɪd] *n (newspaper)* quotidien *m* populaire; *voir article*

⬤ **TABLOID PRESS**
⬤
⬤ Le terme *tabloid press* désigne les journaux
⬤ populaires de demi-format où l'on trouve
⬤ beaucoup de photos et qui adoptent un

⬤ style très concis. Ce type de journaux vise
⬤ des lecteurs s'intéressant aux faits divers
⬤ ayant un parfum de scandale; voir
⬤ "quality press"

taboo [tə'bu:] *adj, n* tabou *(m)*

tack [tæk] *n (nail)* petit clou; *(stitch)* point *m* de bâti; *(Naut)* bord *m*, bordée *f; (fig)* direction *f ▷ vt (nail)* clouer; *(sew)* bâtir ▷ *vi (Naut)* tirer un *or* des bord(s); **to change ~** virer de bord; **on the wrong ~** *(fig)* sur la mauvaise voie; **to ~ sth on to (the end of) sth** *(of letter, book)* rajouter qch à la fin de qch

tackle ['tækl] *n* matériel *m*, équipement *m; (for lifting)* appareil *m* de levage; *(Football, Rugby)* plaquage *m ▷ vt (difficulty, animal, burglar)* s'attaquer à; *(person: challenge)* s'expliquer avec; *(Football, Rugby)* plaquer

tacky ['tækɪ] *adj* collant(e); *(paint)* pas sec/sèche; *(inf: shabby)* moche; *(pej: poor-quality)* minable; *(: showing bad taste)* ringard(e)

tact [tækt] *n* tact *m*

tactful ['tæktful] *adj* plein(e) de tact

tactical ['tæktɪkl] *adj* tactique; **~ error** erreur *f* de tactique

tactics ['tæktɪks] *n, npl* tactique *f*

tactless ['tæktlɪs] *adj* qui manque de tact

tadpole ['tædpəul] *n* têtard *m*

taffy ['tæfɪ] *n (US) (bonbon m au)* caramel *m*

tag [tæg] *n* étiquette *f;* **price/name ~** étiquette (portant le prix/le nom); **tag along** *vi* suivre

tail [teɪl] *n* queue *f; (of shirt)* pan *m ▷ vt (follow)* suivre, filer; **tails** *npl (suit)* habit *m;* **to turn ~** se sauver à toutes jambes; *see also* **head; tail away, tail off** *vi (in size, quality etc)* baisser peu à peu

tailback ['teɪlbæk] *n (Brit)* bouchon *m*

tail end *n* bout *m*, fin *f*

tailgate ['teɪlgeɪt] *n (Aut)* hayon *m* arrière

tailor ['teɪlə^r] *n* tailleur *m (artisan) ▷ vt:* **to ~ sth (to)** adapter qch exactement (à); **~'s (shop)** (boutique *f* de) tailleur *m*

tailoring ['teɪlərɪŋ] *n (cut)* coupe *f*

tailor-made ['teɪlə'meɪd] *adj* fait(e) sur mesure; *(fig)* conçu(e) spécialement

tailwind ['teɪlwɪnd] *n* vent *m* arrière inv

tainted ['teɪntɪd] *adj (food)* gâté(e); *(water, air)* infecté(e); *(fig)* souillé(e)

Taiwan ['taɪ'wɑ:n] *n* Taïwan *(no article)*

Taiwanese [taɪwə'ni:z] *adj* taïwanais(e) ▷ *n inv* Taïwanais(e)

take [teɪk] *(pt* **took**, *pp* **taken**) [tuk, 'teɪkn] *vt* prendre; *(gain: prize)* remporter; *(require: effort, courage)* demander; *(tolerate)* accepter, supporter; *(hold: passengers etc)* contenir; *(accompany)* emmener, accompagner; *(bring, carry)* apporter, emporter; *(exam)* passer, se présenter à; *(conduct: meeting)* présider ▷ *vi (dye, fire etc)* prendre ▷ *n (Cine)* prise *f* de vues; **to ~ sth from** *(drawer etc)* prendre qch dans; *(person)* prendre qch à; **I ~ it that** je suppose que; **I took him for a doctor** je l'ai pris pour un docteur; **to ~ sb's hand** prendre qn par la main; **to ~ for a walk** (child, dog) emmener promener; **to be ~n ill** tomber malade; **to ~ it upon o.s. to do sth** prendre sur soi de faire qch; **to ~ the first (street) on the left** prenez la première à gauche; **it won't ~ long** ça ne prendra pas longtemps; **I was quite ~n with her/it** elle/cela m'a beaucoup plu; **take after** vt fus ressembler à; **take apart** vt démonter; **take away** vt (carry off) emporter; (remove) enlever; (subtract) soustraire ▷ **to ~ away from** diminuer; **take back** vt (return) rendre, rapporter; (one's words) retirer; **take down** vt (building) démolir; (dismantle: scaffolding) démonter; (letter etc) prendre, écrire; **take in** vt (deceive) tromper, rouler; (understand) comprendre, saisir; (include) couvrir, inclure; (lodger) prendre; (orphan, stray dog) recueillir; (dress, waistband) reprendre; **take off** vi (Aviat) décoller ▷ vt (remove) enlever; (imitate) imiter, pasticher; **take on** vt (work) accepter, se charger de; (employee) prendre, embaucher; (opponent) accepter de se battre contre; **take out** vt sortir; (remove) enlever; (invite) sortir avec; (licence) prendre, se procurer; **to ~ sth out of** enlever qch de; (out of drawer etc) prendre qch dans; **don't ~ it out on me!** ne t'en prends pas à moi!; **to ~ sb out to a restaurant** emmener qn au restaurant; **take over** vt (business) reprendre ▷ vi: **to ~ over from sb** prendre la relève de qn; **take to** vt fus (person) se prendre d'amitié pour; (activity) prendre goût à; **to ~ to doing sth** prendre l'habitude de faire qch; **take up** vt (one's story) reprendre; (dress) raccourcir; (occupy: time, space) prendre, occuper; (engage in: hobby etc) se mettre à; (accept: offer, challenge) accepter; (absorb: liquids) absorber ▷ vi: **to ~ up with sb** se lier d'amitié avec qn

takeaway ['teɪkəweɪ] (Brit) adj (food) à emporter ▷ n (shop, restaurant) ≈ magasin m qui vend des plats à emporter

taken ['teɪkən] pp of **take**

takeoff ['teɪkɒf] n (Aviat) décollage m

takeout ['teɪkaʊt] adj, n (US) = **takeaway**

takeover ['teɪkəʊvə^r] n (Comm) rachat m

takings ['teɪkɪŋz] npl (Comm) recette f

talc [tælk] n (also: **~um powder**) talc m

tale [teɪl] n (story) conte m, histoire f; (account) récit m; (pej) histoire; **to tell ~s** (fig) rapporter

talent ['tælənt] n talent m, don m

talented ['tæləntɪd] adj doué(e), plein(e) de talent

talk [tɔːk] n (a speech) causerie f, exposé m; (conversation) discussion f; (interview) entretien m, propos mpl; (gossip) racontars mpl (péj) ▷ vi parler; (chatter) bavarder; **talks** npl (Pol etc) entretiens mpl; conférence f; **to give a ~** faire un exposé; **to ~ about** parler de; (converse) s'entretenir or parler de; **~ing of films, have**

you seen ...? à propos de films, as-tu vu ...?; **to ~ sb out of/into doing** persuader qn de ne pas faire/de faire; **to ~ shop** parler métier or affaires; **talk over** vt discuter (de)

talkative ['tɔːkətɪv] adj bavard(e)

talk show n (TV, Radio) émission-débat f

tall [tɔːl] adj (person) grand(e); (building, tree) haut(e); **to be 6 feet ~** ≈ mesurer 1 mètre 80; **how ~ are you?** combien mesurez-vous?

tall story n histoire f invraisemblable

tally ['tælɪ] n compte m ▷ vi: **to ~ (with)** correspondre (à); **to keep a ~ of sth** tenir le compte de qch

talon ['tælən] n griffe f; (of eagle) serre f

tambourine [tæmbə'riːn] n tambourin m

tame [teɪm] adj apprivoisé(e); (fig: story, style) insipide

tamper ['tæmpə^r] vi: **to ~ with** toucher à (en cachette ou sans permission)

tampon ['tæmpən] n tampon m hygiénique or périodique

tan [tæn] n (also: **sun~**) bronzage m ▷ vt, vi bronzer, brunir ▷ adj (colour) marron clair inv; **to get a ~** bronzer

tandem ['tændəm] n tandem m

tang [tæŋ] n odeur (or saveur) piquante

tangent ['tændʒənt] n (Math) tangente f; **to go off at a ~** (fig) partir dans une digression

tangerine [tændʒə'riːn] n mandarine f

tangle ['tæŋgl] n enchevêtrement m ▷ vt enchevêtrer; **to get in(to) a ~** s'emmêler

tank [tæŋk] n réservoir m; (for processing) cuve f; (for fish) aquarium m; (Mil) char m d'assaut, tank m

tanker ['tæŋkə^r] n (ship) pétrolier m, tanker m; (truck) camion-citerne m; (Rail) wagon-citerne m

tankini [tæn'kiːnɪ] n tankini m

tanned [tænd] adj bronzé(e)

tantalizing ['tæntəlaɪzɪŋ] adj (smell) extrêmement appétissant(e); (offer) terriblement tentant(e)

tantamount ['tæntəmaʊnt] adj: **~ to** qui équivaut à

tantrum ['tæntrəm] n accès m de colère; **to throw a ~** piquer une colère

Tanzania [tænzə'nɪə] n Tanzanie f

tap [tæp] n (on sink etc) robinet m; (gentle blow) petite tape ▷ vt frapper or taper légèrement; (resources) exploiter, utiliser; (telephone) mettre sur écoute; **on ~** (beer) en tonneau; (fig: resources) disponible

tap dancing ['tæpdɑːnsɪŋ] n claquettes fpl

tape [teɪp] n (for tying) ruban m; (also: **magnetic ~**) bande f (magnétique); (cassette) cassette f; (sticky) Scotch® m ▷ vt (record) enregistrer (au magnétoscope or sur cassette); (stick) coller avec du Scotch®; **on ~** (song etc) enregistré(e)

tape deck n platine f d'enregistrement

tape measure n mètre m à ruban

taper ['teɪpə^r] n cierge m ▷ vi s'effiler

t

tape recorder n magnétophone m

tapestry ['tæpɪstrɪ] n tapisserie f

tar [tɑː] n goudron m; **low-/middle-~ cigarettes** cigarettes fpl à faible/moyenne teneur en goudron

target ['tɑːgɪt] n cible f; (fig: objective) objectif m; **to be on ~** (project) progresser comme prévu

tariff ['tærɪf] n (Comm) tarif m; (taxes) tarif douanier

tarmac ['tɑːmæk] n (Brit: on road) macadam m; (Aviat) aire f d'envol ▷ vt (Brit) goudronner

tarnish ['tɑːnɪʃ] vt ternir

tarpaulin [tɑːˈpɔːlɪn] n bâche goudronnée

tarragon ['tærəgən] n estragon m

tart [tɑːt] n (Culin) tarte f; (Brit inf: pej: prostitute) poule f ▷ adj (flavour) âpre, aigrelet(te); **tart up** vt (inf): **to ~ o.s. up** se faire beau/belle; (: pej) s'attifer

tartan ['tɑːtn] n tartan m ▷ adj écossais(e)

tartar ['tɑːtəʳ] n (on teeth) tartre m

tartar sauce, tartare sauce n sauce f tartare

task [tɑːsk] n tâche f; **to take to ~** prendre à partie

task force n (Mil, Police) détachement spécial

tassel ['tæsl] n gland m; pompon m

taste [teɪst] n goût m; (fig: glimpse, idea) idée f, aperçu m ▷ vt goûter ▷ vi: **to ~ of** (fish etc) avoir le or un goût de; **it ~s like fish** ça a un or le goût de poisson, on dirait du poisson; **what does it ~ like?** quel goût ça a?; **you can ~ the garlic (in it)** on sent bien l'ail; **to have a ~ of sth** goûter (à) qch; **can I have a ~?** je peux goûter?; **to have a ~ for sth** aimer qch, avoir un penchant pour qch; **to be in good/ bad or poor ~** être de bon/mauvais goût

tasteful ['teɪstful] adj de bon goût

tasteless ['teɪstlɪs] adj (food) insipide; (remark) de mauvais goût

tasty ['teɪstɪ] adj savoureux(-euse), délicieux(-euse)

tatters ['tætəz] npl: **in ~** (also: **tattered**) en lambeaux

tattoo [təˈtuː] n tatouage m; (spectacle) parade f militaire ▷ vt tatouer

tatty ['tætɪ] adj (Brit inf) défraîchi(e), en piteux état

taught [tɔːt] pt, pp of **teach**

taunt [tɔːnt] n raillerie f ▷ vt railler

Taurus ['tɔːrəs] n le Taureau; **to be ~** être du Taureau

taut [tɔːt] adj tendu(e)

tax [tæks] n (on goods etc) taxe f; (on income) impôts mpl, contributions fpl ▷ vt taxer; imposer; (fig: patience etc) mettre à l'épreuve; **before/after ~** avant/après l'impôt; **free of ~** exonéré(e) d'impôt

taxable ['tæksəbl] adj (income) imposable

taxation [tækˈseɪʃən] n taxation f; impôts mpl, contributions fpl; **system of ~** système fiscal

tax avoidance n évasion fiscale

tax disc n (Brit Aut) vignette f (automobile)

tax evasion n fraude fiscale

tax-free ['tæksfriː] adj exempt(e) d'impôts

taxi ['tæksɪ] n taxi m ▷ vi (Aviat) rouler (lentement) au sol

taxi driver n chauffeur m de taxi

taxi rank, (Brit) taxi stand n station f de taxis

tax payer [-peɪəʳ] n contribuable m/f

tax relief n dégrèvement or allègement fiscal, réduction f d'impôt

tax return n déclaration f d'impôts or de revenus

TB n abbr = **tuberculosis**

tbc abbr = **to be confirmed**

tea [tiː] n thé m; (Brit: snack: for children) goûter m; **high ~** (Brit) collation combinant goûter et dîner

tea bag n sachet m de thé

tea break n (Brit) pause-thé f

teach (pt, pp **taught**) [tiːtʃ, tɔːt] vt: **to ~ sb sth, to ~ sth to sb** apprendre qch à qn; (in school etc) enseigner qch à qn ▷ vi enseigner; **it taught him a lesson** (fig) ça lui a servi de leçon

teacher ['tiːtʃəʳ] n (in secondary school) professeur m; (in primary school) instituteur(-trice); **French ~** professeur de français

teaching ['tiːtʃɪŋ] n enseignement m

tea cosy n couvre-théière m

teacup ['tiːkʌp] n tasse f à thé

teak [tiːk] n teck m ▷ adj en or de teck

tea leaves npl feuilles fpl de thé

team [tiːm] n équipe f; (of animals) attelage m; **team up** vi: **to ~ up (with)** faire équipe (avec)

teamwork ['tiːmwəːk] n travail m d'équipe

teapot ['tiːpɔt] n théière f

tear¹ ['tɪəʳ] n larme f; **in ~s** en larmes; **to burst into ~s** fondre en larmes

tear² [tɛəʳ] (pt **tore**, pp **torn**) [tɔːʳ, tɔːn] n déchirure f ▷ vt déchirer ▷ vi se déchirer; **to ~ to pieces** or **to bits** or **to shreds** mettre en pièces; (fig) démolir; **tear along** vi (rush) aller à toute vitesse; **tear apart** vt (also fig) déchirer; **tear away** vt: **to ~ o.s. away (from sth)** (fig) s'arracher (de qch); **tear down** vt (building, statue) démolir; (poster, flag) arracher; **tear off** vt (sheet of paper etc) arracher; (one's clothes) enlever à toute vitesse; **tear out** vt (sheet of paper, cheque) arracher; **tear up** vt (sheet of paper etc) déchirer, mettre en morceaux or pièces

tearful ['tɪəful] adj larmoyant(e)

tear gas ['tɪə-] n gaz m lacrymogène

tearoom ['tiːruːm] n salon m de thé

tease [tiːz] n taquin(e) ▷ vt taquiner; (unkindly) tourmenter

tea set n service m à thé

teaspoon ['tiːspuːn] n petite cuiller f; (also: **~ful**: as measurement) ≈ cuillerée f à café

teat [ti:t] n tétine f
teatime ['ti:taɪm] n l'heure f du thé
tea towel n (Brit) torchon m (à vaisselle)
technical ['tɛknɪkl] adj technique
technicality [tɛknɪ'kælɪtɪ] n technicité f; (detail) détail m technique; **on a legal ~** à cause de (or grâce à) l'application à la lettre d'une subtilité juridique; pour vice de forme
technically ['tɛknɪklɪ] adv techniquement; (strictly speaking) en théorie, en principe
technician [tɛk'nɪʃən] n technicien(ne)
technique [tɛk'ni:k] n technique f
techno ['tɛknəu] n (Mus) techno f
technological [tɛknə'lɔdʒɪkl] adj technologique
technology [tɛk'nɔlədʒɪ] n technologie f
teddy ['tɛdɪ], **teddy bear** n ours m (en peluche)
tedious ['ti:dɪəs] adj fastidieux(-euse)
tee [ti:] n (Golf) tee m
teem [ti:m] vi: **to ~ (with)** grouiller (de); **it is ~ing (with rain)** il pleut à torrents
teen [ti:n] adj = **teenage** ⊳ n (US) = **teenager**
teenage ['ti:neɪdʒ] adj (fashions etc) pour jeunes, pour adolescents; (child) qui est adolescent(e)
teenager ['ti:neɪdʒər] n adolescent(e)
teens [ti:nz] npl: **to be in one's ~** être adolescent(e)
tee-shirt ['ti:ʃə:t] n = **T-shirt**
teeter ['ti:tər] vi chanceler, vaciller
teeth [ti:θ] npl of **tooth**
teethe [ti:ð] vi percer ses dents
teething troubles ['ti:ðɪŋ-] npl (fig) difficultés initiales
teetotal ['ti:'təutl] adj (person) qui ne boit jamais d'alcool
telecommunications ['tɛlɪkəmju:nɪ'keɪʃənz] n télécommunications fpl
teleconferencing [tɛlɪ'kɔnfərənsɪŋ] n téléconférence(s) f(pl)
telegram ['tɛlɪgræm] n télégramme m
telegraph ['tɛlɪgrɑ:f] n télégraphe m
telegraph pole ['tɛlɪgrɑ:f-] n poteau m télégraphique
telephone ['tɛlɪfəun] n téléphone m ⊳ vt (person) téléphoner à; (message) téléphoner; **to have a ~** (Brit), **to be on the ~** (subscriber) être abonné(e) au téléphone; **to be on the ~** (be speaking) être au téléphone
telephone book n = **telephone directory**
telephone booth n, (Brit) **telephone box** n cabine f téléphonique
telephone call n appel m téléphonique
telephone directory n annuaire m (du téléphone)
telephone number n numéro m de téléphone
telephonist [tə'lɛfənɪst] n (Brit) téléphoniste m/f
telesales ['tɛlɪseɪlz] npl télévente f

telescope ['tɛlɪskəup] n télescope m ⊳ vi se télescoper ⊳ vt télescoper
televise ['tɛlɪvaɪz] vt téléviser
television ['tɛlɪvɪʒən] n télévision f; **on ~** à la télévision
television programme n émission f de télévision
television set n poste m de télévision, téléviseur m
telex ['tɛlɛks] n télex m ⊳ vt (message) envoyer par télex; (person) envoyer un télex à ⊳ vi envoyer un télex
tell (pt, pp **told**) [tɛl, təuld] vt dire; (relate: story) raconter; (distinguish): **to ~ sth from** distinguer qch de ⊳ vi (talk): **to ~ of** parler de; (have effect) se faire sentir, se voir; **to ~ sb to do** dire à qn de faire; **to ~ sb about sth** (place, object etc) parler de qch à qn; (what happened etc) raconter qch à qn; **to ~ the time** (know how to) savoir lire l'heure; **can you ~ me the time?** pourriez-vous me dire l'heure?; **(I) ~ you what, …** écoute, …; **I can't ~ them apart** je n'arrive pas à les distinguer; **tell off** vt réprimander, gronder; **tell on** vt fus (inform against) dénoncer, rapporter contre
teller ['tɛlər] n (in bank) caissier(-ière)
telling ['tɛlɪŋ] adj (remark, detail) révélateur(-trice)
telltale ['tɛlteɪl] n rapporteur(-euse) ⊳ adj (sign) éloquent(e), révélateur(-trice)
telly ['tɛlɪ] n abbr (Brit inf: = television) télé f
temp [tɛmp] n (Brit: = temporary worker) intérimaire m/f ⊳ vi travailler comme intérimaire
temper ['tɛmpər] n (nature) caractère m; (mood) humeur f; (fit of anger) colère f ⊳ vt (moderate) tempérer, adoucir; **to be in a ~** être en colère; **to lose one's ~** se mettre en colère; **to keep one's ~** rester calme
temperament ['tɛmprəmənt] n (nature) tempérament m
temperamental [tɛmprə'mɛntl] adj capricieux(-euse)
temperate ['tɛmprət] adj modéré(e); (climate) tempéré(e)
temperature ['tɛmprətʃər] n température f; **to have** or **run a ~** avoir de la fièvre
temple ['tɛmpl] n (building) temple m; (Anat) tempe f
temporary ['tɛmpərərɪ] adj temporaire, provisoire; (job, worker) temporaire; **~ secretary** (secrétaire f) intérimaire f; **a ~ teacher** un professeur remplaçant or suppléant
tempt [tɛmpt] vt tenter; **to ~ sb into doing** induire qn à faire; **to be ~ed to do sth** être tenté(e) de faire qch
temptation [tɛmp'teɪʃən] n tentation f
tempting ['tɛmptɪŋ] adj tentant(e); (food) appétissant(e)
ten [tɛn] num dix ⊳ n: **~s of thousands** des dizaines fpl de milliers

t

tenacity [tə'næsɪtɪ] n ténacité f

tenancy ['tɛnənsɪ] n location f; état m de locataire

tenant ['tɛnənt] n locataire m/f

tend [tɛnd] vt s'occuper de; (sick etc) soigner ▷ vi: **to ~ to do** avoir tendance à faire; (colour): **to ~ to** tirer sur

tendency ['tɛndənsɪ] n tendance f

tender ['tɛndə^r] adj tendre; (delicate) délicat(e); (sore) sensible; (affectionate) tendre, doux/douce ▷ n (Comm: offer) soumission f; (money): **legal ~** cours légal ▷ vt offrir; **to ~ one's resignation** donner sa démission; **to put in a ~ (for)** faire une soumission (pour); **to put work out to ~** (Brit) mettre un contrat en adjudication

tendon ['tɛndən] n tendon m

tenement ['tɛnəmənt] n immeuble m (de rapport)

tenner ['tɛnə^r] n (Brit inf) billet m de dix livres

tennis ['tɛnɪs] n tennis m ▷ cpd (club, match, racket, player) de tennis

tennis ball n balle f de tennis

tennis court n (court m de) tennis m

tennis match n match m de tennis

tennis player n joueur(-euse) de tennis

tennis racket n raquette f de tennis

tennis shoes npl (chaussures fpl de) tennis mpl

tenor ['tɛnə^r] n (Mus) ténor m; (of speech etc) sens général

tenpin bowling ['tɛnpɪn-] n (Brit) bowling m (à 10 quilles)

tense [tɛns] adj tendu(e); (person) tendu, crispé(e) ▷ n (Ling) temps m ▷ vt (tighten: muscles) tendre

tension ['tɛnʃən] n tension f

tent [tɛnt] n tente f

tentative ['tɛntətɪv] adj timide, hésitant(e); (conclusion) provisoire

tenterhooks ['tɛntəhuks] npl: **on ~** sur des charbons ardents

tenth [tɛnθ] num dixième

tent peg n piquet m de tente

tent pole n montant m de tente

tenuous ['tɛnjuəs] adj ténu(e)

tenure ['tɛnjuə^r] n (of property) bail m; (of job) période f de jouissance; statut m de titulaire

tepid ['tɛpɪd] adj tiède

term [tə:m] n (limit) terme m; (word) terme, mot m; (Scol) trimestre m; (Law) session f ▷ vt appeler; **terms** npl (conditions) conditions fpl; (Comm) tarif m; **~ of imprisonment** peine f de prison; **his ~ of office** la période où il était en fonction; **in the short/long ~** à court/long terme; **"easy ~s"** (Comm) "facilités de paiement"; **to come to ~s with** (problem) faire face à; **to be on good ~s with** bien s'entendre avec, être en bons termes avec

terminal ['tə:mɪnl] adj terminal(e); (disease) dans sa phase terminale; (patient) incurable ▷ n (Elec) borne f; (for oil, ore etc, also Comput) terminal m; (also: **air ~**) aérogare f; (Brit: also: **coach ~**) gare routière

terminally ['tə:mɪnlɪ] adv: **to be ~ ill** être condamné(e)

terminate ['tə:mɪneɪt] vt mettre fin à; (pregnancy) interrompre ▷ vi: **to ~ in** finir en or par

termini ['tə:mɪnaɪ] npl of **terminus**

terminology [tə:mɪ'nɔlədʒɪ] n terminologie f

terminus (pl **termini**) ['tə:mɪnəs, 'tə:mɪnaɪ] n terminus m inv

terrace ['tɛrəs] n terrasse f; (Brit: row of houses) rangée f de maisons (attenantes les unes aux autres); **the ~s** (Brit Sport) les gradins mpl

terraced ['tɛrəst] adj (garden) en terrasses; (in a row: house) attenant(e) aux maisons voisines

terracotta [tɛrə'kɔtə] n terre cuite

terrain [tɛ'reɪn] n terrain m (sol)

terrestrial [tɪ'rɛstrɪəl] adj terrestre

terrible ['tɛrɪbl] adj terrible, atroce; (weather, work) affreux(-euse), épouvantable

terribly ['tɛrɪblɪ] adv terriblement; (very badly) affreusement mal

terrier ['tɛrɪə^r] n terrier m (chien)

terrific [tə'rɪfɪk] adj (very great) fantastique, incroyable, terrible; (wonderful) formidable, sensationnel(le)

terrified ['tɛrɪfaɪd] adj terrifié(e); **to be ~ of sth** avoir très peur de qch

terrify ['tɛrɪfaɪ] vt terrifier

terrifying ['tɛrɪfaɪɪŋ] adj terrifiant(e)

territorial [tɛrɪ'tɔ:rɪəl] adj territorial(e)

territory ['tɛrɪtərɪ] n territoire m

terror ['tɛrə^r] n terreur f

terrorism ['tɛrərɪzəm] n terrorisme m

terrorist ['tɛrərɪst] n terroriste m/f

terrorist attack n attentat m terroriste

test [tɛst] n (trial, check) essai m; (: of goods in factory) contrôle m; (of courage etc) épreuve f; (Med) examen m; (Chem) analyse f; (exam: of intelligence etc) test m (d'aptitude); (Scol) interrogation f de contrôle; (also: **driving ~**) (examen du) permis m de conduire ▷ vt essayer; contrôler; mettre à l'épreuve; examiner; analyser; tester; faire subir une interrogation à; **to put sth to the ~** mettre qch à l'épreuve

testament ['tɛstəmənt] n testament m; **the Old/New T~** l'Ancien/le Nouveau Testament

testicle ['tɛstɪkl] n testicule m

testify ['tɛstɪfaɪ] vi (Law) témoigner, déposer; **to ~ to sth** (Law) attester qch; (gen) témoigner de qch

testimony ['tɛstɪmənɪ] n (Law) témoignage m, déposition f

test match n (Cricket, Rugby) match international

test tube n éprouvette f

tetanus ['tɛtənəs] n tétanos m

tether ['tɛðə'] vt attacher ▷ n: **at the end of one's ~** à bout (de patience)

text [tɛkst] n texte m; (on mobile phone) SMS m inv, texto® m ▷ vt (inf) envoyer un SMS or texto® à

textbook ['tɛkstbuk] n manuel m

textile ['tɛkstaɪl] n textile m

text message n SMS m inv, texto® m

text messaging [-'mɛsɪdʒɪŋ] n messagerie textuelle

texture ['tɛkstʃə'] n texture f; (of skin, paper etc) grain m

Thai [taɪ] adj thaïlandais(e) ▷ n Thaïlandais(e); (Ling) thaï m

Thailand ['taɪlænd] n Thaïlande f

Thames [tɛmz] n: **the (River) ~** la Tamise

than [ðæn, ðən] conj que; (with numerals): **more ~ 10/once** plus de 10/d'une fois; **I have more/less ~ you** j'en ai plus/moins que toi; **she has more apples ~ pears** elle a plus de pommes que de poires; **it is better to phone ~ to write** il vaut mieux téléphoner (plutôt) qu'écrire; **she is older ~ you think** elle est plus âgée que tu le crois; **no sooner did he leave ~ the phone rang** il venait de partir quand le téléphone a sonné

thank [θæŋk] vt remercier, dire merci à; **thanks** npl remerciements mpl ▷ excl merci!; **~ you (very much)** merci (beaucoup); **~ heavens, ~ God** Dieu merci; **~s to** prep grâce à

thankful ['θæŋkful] adj: **~ (for)** reconnaissant(e) (de); **~ for/that** (relieved) soulagé(e) de/que

thankfully ['θæŋkfəlɪ] adv avec reconnaissance; avec soulagement; (fortunately) heureusement; **~ there were few victims** il y eut fort heureusement peu de victimes

thankless ['θæŋklɪs] adj ingrat(e)

Thanksgiving ['θæŋksgɪvɪŋ], **Thanksgiving Day** n jour m d'action de grâce; voir article

● **THANKSGIVING (DAY)**
●
● *Thanksgiving (Day)* est un jour de congé aux
● États-Unis, le quatrième jeudi du mois de
● novembre, commémorant la bonne récolte
● que les Pèlerins venus de Grande-Bretagne
● ont eu en 1621; traditionnellement,
● c'était un jour où l'on remerciait Dieu et
● où l'on organisait un grand festin. Une
● fête semblable, mais qui n'a aucun
● rapport avec les Pères Pèlerins, a lieu au
● Canada le deuxième lundi d'octobre.

 KEYWORD

that [ðæt] adj (demonstrative) (pl **those**) ce, cet + vowel or h mute, cette f; **that man/woman/ book** cet homme/cette femme/ce livre; (not this) cet homme-là/cette femme-là/ce livre-là; **that one** celui-là/celle-là

▷ pron **1** (demonstrative) (pl **those**) ce; (not this one) cela, ça; (that one) celui/celle; **who's that?** qui est-ce que c'est?; **what's that?** qu'est-ce que c'est?; **is that you?** c'est toi?; **I prefer this to that** je préfère ceci à cela or ça; **that's what he said** c'est or voilà ce qu'il a dit; **will you eat all that?** tu vas manger tout ça?; **that is (to say)** c'est-à-dire, à savoir; **at or with that, he ...** là-dessus, il ...; **do it like that** fais-le comme ça

2 (relative: subject) qui; (: object) que; (: after prep) lequel/laquelle, lesquels/lesquelles pl; **the book that I read** le livre que j'ai lu; **the books that are in the library** les livres qui sont dans la bibliothèque; **all that I have** tout ce que j'ai; **the box that I put it in** la boîte dans laquelle je l'ai mis; **the people that I spoke to** les gens auxquels or à qui j'ai parlé; **not that I know of** pas à ma connaissance

3 (relative: of time) où; **the day that he came** le jour où il est venu

▷ conj que; **he thought that I was ill** il pensait que j'étais malade

▷ adv (demonstrative): **I don't like it that much** ça ne me plaît pas tant que ça; **I didn't know it was that bad** je ne savais pas que c'était si or aussi mauvais; **that high** aussi haut; si haut; **it's about that high** c'est à peu près de cette hauteur

thatched [θætʃt] adj (roof) de chaume; **~ cottage** chaumière f

thaw [θɔː] n dégel m ▷ vi (ice) fondre; (food) dégeler ▷ vt (food) (faire) dégeler; **it's ~ing** (weather) il dégèle

KEYWORD

the [ðiː, ðə] def art **1** (gen) le, la f, l' + vowel or h mute, les pl (NB: à + le(s) = **au(x)**; de + le = **du**; de + les = **des**); **the boy/girl/ink** le garçon/la fille/l'encre; **the children** les enfants; **the history of the world** l'histoire du monde; **give it to the postman** donne-le au facteur; **to play the piano/flute** jouer du piano/de la flûte

2 (+ adj to form n) le, la f, l' + vowel or h mute, les pl; **the rich and the poor** les riches et les pauvres; **to attempt the impossible** tenter l'impossible

3 (in titles): **Elizabeth the First** Elisabeth première; **Peter the Great** Pierre le Grand

4 (in comparisons): **the more he works, the more he earns** plus il travaille, plus il gagne de l'argent; **the sooner the better** le plus tôt sera le mieux

theatre, (US) **theater** ['θɪətə'] n théâtre m; (also: **lecture ~**) amphithéâtre m, amphi m (inf); (Med: also: **operating ~**) salle f d'opération

t

theatre-goer, (US) **theater-goer**
['θɪətəɡəʊə^r] n habitué(e) du théâtre
theatrical [θɪˈætrɪkl] adj théâtral(e); **~ company** troupe f de théâtre
theft [θeft] n vol m (larcin)
their [ðɛə^r] adj leur, leurs pl; see also **my**
theirs [ðɛəz] pron le/la leur, les leurs; **it is ~** c'est à eux; **a friend of ~** un de leurs amis; see also **mine'**
them [ðɛm, ðəm] pron (direct) les; (indirect) leur; (stressed, after prep) eux/elles; **I see ~** je les vois; **give ~ the book** donne-leur le livre; **give me a few of ~** donnez m'en quelques uns (or quelques unes); see also **me**
theme [θiːm] n thème m
theme park n parc m à thème
theme song n chanson principale
themselves [ðəmˈsɛlvz] pl pron (reflexive) se; (emphatic, after prep) eux-mêmes/elles-mêmes; **between ~** entre eux/elles; see also **oneself**
then [ðɛn] adv (at that time) alors, à ce moment-là; (next) puis, ensuite; (and also) et puis ▷ conj (therefore) alors, dans ce cas ▷ adj: **the ~ president** le président d'alors or de l'époque; **by ~** (past) à ce moment-là; (future) d'ici là; **from ~ on** dès lors; **before ~** avant; **until ~** jusqu'à ce moment-là, jusque-là; **and ~ what?** et puis après?; **what do you want me to do ~?** (afterwards) que veux-tu que je fasse ensuite?; (in that case) bon alors, qu'est-ce que je fais?
theology [θɪˈɔlədʒɪ] n théologie f
theoretical [θɪəˈrɛtɪkl] adj théorique
theory ['θɪərɪ] n théorie f
therapist ['θɛrəpɪst] n thérapeute m/f
therapy ['θɛrəpɪ] n thérapie f

◯ KEYWORD

there [ðɛə^r] adv **1**: **there is**, **there are** il y a; **there are 3 of them** (people, things) il y en a 3; **there is no-one here/no bread left** il n'y a personne/il n'y a plus de pain; **there has been an accident** il y a eu un accident **2** (referring to place) là, là-bas; **it's there** c'est là(-bas); **in/on/up/down there** là-dedans/là-dessus/là-haut/en bas; **he went there on Friday** il y est allé vendredi; **to go there and back** faire l'aller-retour; **I want that book there** je veux ce livre-là; **there he is!** le voilà! **3**: **there, there** (esp to child) allons, allons!

thereabouts ['ðɛərə'baʊts] adv (place) par là, près de là; (amount) environ, à peu près
thereafter [ðɛərˈɑːftə^r] adv par la suite
thereby ['ðɛəbaɪ] adv ainsi
therefore ['ðɛəfɔː^r] adv donc, par conséquent
there's ['ðɛəz] = **there is**; **there has**
thermal ['θəːml] adj thermique; **~ paper/ printer** papier m/imprimante f thermique; **~ underwear** sous-vêtements mpl en Thermolactyl®

thermometer [θəˈmɔmɪtə^r] n thermomètre m
Thermos® ['θəːməs] n (also: **~ flask**) thermos® m or f inv
thermostat ['θəːməʊstæt] n thermostat m
thesaurus [θɪˈsɔːrəs] n dictionnaire m synonymique
these [ðiːz] pl pron ceux-ci/celles-ci ▷ pl adj ces; (not those): **~ books** ces livres-ci
thesis (pl **theses**) ['θiːsɪs, 'θiːsiːz] n thèse f
they [ðeɪ] pl pron ils/elles; (stressed) eux/elles; **~ say that ...** (it is said that) on dit que ...
they'd [ðeɪd] = **they had**; **they would**
they'll [ðeɪl] = **they shall**; **they will**
they're [ðɛə^r] = **they are**
they've [ðeɪv] = **they have**
thick [θɪk] adj épais(se); (crowd) dense; (stupid) bête, borné(e) ▷ n: **in the ~ of** au beau milieu de, en plein cœur de; **it's 20 cm ~** ça a 20 cm d'épaisseur
thicken ['θɪkn] vi s'épaissir ▷ vt (sauce etc) épaissir
thickness ['θɪknɪs] n épaisseur f
thickset [θɪkˈsɛt] adj trapu(e), costaud(e)
thief (pl **thieves**) [θiːf, θiːvz] n voleur(-euse)
thigh [θaɪ] n cuisse f
thimble ['θɪmbl] n dé m (à coudre)
thin [θɪn] adj mince; (skinny) maigre; (soup) peu épais(se); (hair, crowd) clairsemé(e); (fog) léger(-ère) ▷ vt (hair) éclaircir; (also: **~ down**: sauce, paint) délayer ▷ vi (fog) s'éclaircir; (also: **~ out**: crowd) se disperser; **his hair is ~ning** il se dégarnit
thing [θɪŋ] n chose f; (object) objet m; (contraption) truc m; **things** npl (belongings) affaires fpl; **first ~ (in the morning)** à la première heure, tout de suite (le matin); **last ~ (at night)**, **he ...** juste avant de se coucher, il ...; **the ~ is ...** c'est que ...; **for one ~** d'abord; **the best ~ would be to** le mieux serait de; **how are ~s?** comment ça va?; **to have a ~ about** (be obsessed by) être obsédé(e) par; (hate) détester; **poor ~!** le (or la) pauvre!
think (pt, pp **thought**) [θɪŋk, θɔːt] vi penser, réfléchir ▷ vt penser, croire; (imagine) s'imaginer; **to ~ of** penser à; **what do you ~ of it?** qu'en pensez-vous?; **what did you ~ of them?** qu'avez-vous pensé d'eux?; **to ~ about sth/sb** penser à qch/qn; **I'll ~ about it** je vais y réfléchir; **to ~ of doing** avoir l'idée de faire; **I ~ so/not** je crois or pense que oui/ non; **to ~ well of** avoir une haute opinion de; **~ again!** attention, réfléchis bien!; **to ~ aloud** penser tout haut; **think out** vt (plan) bien réfléchir à; (solution) trouver; **think over** vt bien réfléchir à; **I'd like to ~ things over** (offer, suggestion) j'aimerais bien y réfléchir un peu; **think through** vt étudier dans tous les détails; **think up** vt inventer, trouver
think tank n groupe m de réflexion
thinly ['θɪnlɪ] adv (cut) en tranches fines; (spread) en couche mince

third [θəːd] *num* troisième ▷ *n* troisième *m/f*; (*fraction*) tiers *m*; (*Aut*) troisième (vitesse) *f*; (*Brit Scol*: *degree*) ≈ licence *f* avec mention passable; **a ~ of** le tiers de

thirdly ['θəːdlɪ] *adv* troisièmement

third party insurance *n* (*Brit*) assurance *f* au tiers

third-rate ['θəːd'reɪt] *adj* de qualité médiocre

Third World *n*: **the ~** le Tiers-Monde

thirst [θəːst] *n* soif *f*

thirsty ['θəːstɪ] *adj* qui a soif, assoiffé(e); (*work*) qui donne soif; **to be ~** avoir soif

thirteen [θəː'tiːn] *num* treize

thirteenth [θəː'tiːnθ] *num* treizième

thirtieth ['θəːtɪɪθ] *num* trentième

thirty ['θəːtɪ] *num* trente

○ **KEYWORD**

this [ðɪs] *adj* (*demonstrative*) (*pl* **these**) ce, cet + vowel or h mute, cette *f*; **this man/woman/book** cet homme/cette femme/ce livre; (*not that*) cet homme-ci/cette femme-ci/ce livre-ci; **this one** celui-ci/celle-ci; **this time** cette fois-ci; **this time last year** l'année dernière à la même époque; **this way** (*in this direction*) par ici; (*in this fashion*) de cette façon, ainsi
▷ *pron* (*demonstrative*) (*pl* **these**) ce; (*not that one*) celui-ci/celle-ci, ceci; **who's this?** qui est-ce?; **what's this?** qu'est-ce que c'est?; **I prefer this to that** je préfère ceci à cela; **they were talking of this and that** ils parlaient de choses et d'autres; **this is where I live** c'est ici que j'habite; **this is what he said** voici ce qu'il a dit; **this is Mr Brown** (*in introductions*) je vous présente Mr Brown; (*in photo*) c'est Mr Brown; (*on telephone*) ici Mr Brown
▷ *adv* (*demonstrative*): **it was about this big** c'était à peu près de cette grandeur or grand comme ça; **I didn't know it was this bad** je ne savais pas que c'était si or aussi mauvais

thistle ['θɪsl] *n* chardon *m*

thorn [θɔːn] *n* épine *f*

thorough ['θʌrə] *adj* (*search*) minutieux(-euse); (*knowledge, research*) approfondi(e); (*work, person*) consciencieux(-euse); (*cleaning*) à fond

thoroughbred ['θʌrəbred] *n* (*horse*) pur-sang *m inv*

thoroughfare ['θʌrəfɛər] *n* rue *f*; **"no ~"** (*Brit*) "passage interdit"

thoroughly ['θʌrəlɪ] *adv* (*search*) minutieusement; (*study*) en profondeur; (*clean*) à fond; (*very*) tout à fait; **he ~ agreed** il était tout à fait d'accord

those [ðəuz] *pl pron* ceux-là/celles-là ▷ *pl adj* ces; (*not these*): **~ books** ces livres-là

though [ðəu] *conj* bien que + *sub*, quoique + *sub* ▷ *adv* pourtant; **even ~** quand bien même + *conditional*; **it's not easy, ~** pourtant, ce n'est pas facile

thought [θɔːt] *pt, pp of* **think** ▷ *n* pensée *f*; (*idea*) idée *f*; (*opinion*) avis *m*; (*intention*) intention *f*; **after much ~** après mûre réflexion; **I've just had a ~** je viens de penser à quelque chose; **to give sth some ~** réfléchir à qch

thoughtful ['θɔːtful] *adj* (*deep in thought*) pensif(-ive); (*serious*) réfléchi(e); (*considerate*) prévenant(e)

thoughtless ['θɔːtlɪs] *adj* qui manque de considération

thousand ['θauzənd] *num* mille; **one ~** mille; **two ~** deux mille; **~s of** des milliers de

thousandth ['θauzəntθ] *num* millième

thrash [θræʃ] *vt* rouer de coups; (*as punishment*) donner une correction à; (*inf: defeat*) battre à plate(s) couture(s); **thrash about** *vi* se débattre; **thrash out** *vt* débattre de

thread [θred] *n* fil *m*; (*of screw*) pas *m*, filetage *m* ▷ *vt* (*needle*) enfiler; **to ~ one's way between** se faufiler entre

threadbare ['θredbɛər] *adj* râpé(e), élimé(e)

threat [θret] *n* menace *f*; **to be under ~ of** être menacé(e) de

threaten ['θretn] *vi* (*storm*) menacer ▷ *vt*: **to ~ sb with sth/to do** menacer qn de qch/de faire

threatening ['θretnɪŋ] *adj* menaçant(e)

three [θriː] *num* trois

three-dimensional [θriːdɪ'menʃənl] *adj* à trois dimensions; (*film*) en relief

three-piece suit ['θriːpiːs-] *n* complet *m* (avec gilet)

three-piece suite *n* salon *m* (canapé et deux fauteuils)

three-ply [θriː'plaɪ] *adj* (*wood*) à trois épaisseurs; (*wool*) trois fils *inv*

three-quarters [θriː'kwɔːtəz] *npl* trois-quarts *mpl*; **~ full** aux trois-quarts plein

threshold ['θreʃhəuld] *n* seuil *m*; **to be on the ~ of** (*fig*) être au seuil de

threw [θruː] *pt of* **throw**

thrifty ['θrɪftɪ] *adj* économe

thrill [θrɪl] *n* (*excitement*) émotion *f*, sensation forte; (*shudder*) frisson *m* ▷ *vi* tressaillir, frissonner ▷ *vt* (*audience*) électriser

thrilled [θrɪld] *adj*: **~ (with)** ravi(e) de

thriller ['θrɪlər] *n* film *m* (or roman *m* or pièce *f*) à suspense

thrilling ['θrɪlɪŋ] *adj* (*book, play etc*) saisissant(e); (*news, discovery*) excitant(e)

thrive (*pt* **thrived** *or* **throve**, *pp* **thrived** *or* **thriven**) [θraɪv, θrəuv, 'θrɪvn] *vi* pousser *or* se développer bien; (*business*) prospérer; **he ~s on it** cela lui réussit

thriving ['θraɪvɪŋ] *adj* vigoureux(-euse); (*business, community*) prospère

throat [θrəut] *n* gorge *f*; **to have a sore ~** avoir mal à la gorge

throb [θrɔb] *n* (*of heart*) pulsation *f*; (*of engine*) vibration *f*; (*of pain*) élancement *m* ▷ *vi* (*heart*)

t

palpiter; (*engine*) vibrer; (*pain*) lanciner; (*wound*) causer des élancements; **my head is ~bing** j'ai des élancements dans la tête

throes [θrəʊz] *npl*: **in the ~ of** au beau milieu de; en proie à; **in the ~ of death** à l'agonie

throne [θrəʊn] *n* trône *m*

throng [θrɒŋ] *n* foule *f* ▷ *vt* se presser dans

throttle ['θrɒtl] *n* (*Aut*) accélérateur *m* ▷ *vt* étrangler

through [θruː] *prep* à travers; (*time*) pendant, durant; (*by means of*) par, par l'intermédiaire de; (*owing to*) à cause de ▷ *adj* (*ticket, train, passage*) direct(e) ▷ *adv* à travers; (**from**) **Monday ~ Friday** (*US*) de lundi à vendredi; **to let sb ~** laisser passer qn; **to put sb ~ to sb** (*Tel*) passer qn à qn; **to be ~** (*Brit*: : *Tel*) avoir la communication; (*esp US*: *have finished*) avoir fini; **"no ~ traffic"** (*US*) "passage interdit"; **"no ~ road"** (*Brit*) "impasse"

throughout [θruː'aʊt] *prep* (*place*) partout dans; (*time*) durant tout(e) le/la ▷ *adv* partout

throw [θrəʊ] *n* jet *m*; (*Sport*) lancer *m* ▷ *vt* (*pt* **threw**, *pp* **thrown**) [θruː, θrəʊn] lancer, jeter; (*Sport*) lancer; (*rider*) désarçonner; (*fig*) décontenancer; (*pottery*) tourner; **to ~ a party** donner une réception; **throw about**; **throw around** *vt* (*litter etc*) éparpiller; **throw away** *vt* jeter; (*money*) gaspiller; **throw in** *vt* (*Sport*: *ball*) remettre en jeu; (*include*) ajouter; **throw off** *vt* se débarrasser de; **throw out** *vt* jeter; (*reject*) rejeter; (*person*) mettre à la porte; **throw together** *vt* (*clothes, meal etc*) assembler à la hâte; (*essay*) bâcler; **throw up** *vi* vomir

throwaway ['θrəʊəweɪ] *adj* à jeter

throw-in ['θrəʊɪn] *n* (*Sport*) remise *f* en jeu

thrown [θrəʊn] *pp* of **throw**

thru [θruː] (*US*) *prep* = **through**

thrush [θrʌʃ] *n* (*Zool*) grive *f*; (*Med*: *esp in children*) muguet *m*; (: *in women*: *Brit*) muguet vaginal

thrust [θrʌst] *n* (*Tech*) poussée *f* ▷ *vt* (*pt, pp* **thrust**) pousser brusquement; (*push in*) enfoncer

thud [θʌd] *n* bruit sourd

thug [θʌg] *n* voyou *m*

thumb [θʌm] *n* (*Anat*) pouce *m* ▷ *vt* (*book*) feuilleter; **to ~ a lift** faire de l'auto-stop, arrêter une voiture; **to give sb/sth the ~s up/~s down** donner/refuser de donner le feu vert à qn/qch; **thumb through** *vt* (*book*) feuilleter

thumbtack ['θʌmtæk] *n* (*US*) punaise *f* (*clou*)

thump [θʌmp] *n* grand coup; (*sound*) bruit sourd ▷ *vt* cogner sur ▷ *vi* cogner, frapper

thunder ['θʌndə'] *n* tonnerre *m* ▷ *vi* tonner; (*train etc*): **to ~ past** passer dans un grondement or un bruit de tonnerre

thunderbolt ['θʌndəbəʊlt] *n* foudre *f*

thunderclap ['θʌndəklæp] *n* coup *m* de tonnerre

thunderstorm ['θʌndəstɔːm] *n* orage *m*

thundery ['θʌndərɪ] *adj* orageux(-euse)

Thursday ['θɜːzdɪ] *n* jeudi *m*; *see also* **Tuesday**

thus [ðʌs] *adv* ainsi

thwart [θwɔːt] *vt* contrecarrer

thyme [taɪm] *n* thym *m*

tiara [tɪ'ɑːrə] *n* (*woman's*) diadème *m*

Tibet [tɪ'bɛt] *n* Tibet *m*

tick [tɪk] *n* (*sound: of clock*) tic-tac *m*; (*mark*) coche *f*; (*Zool*) tique *f*; (*Brit inf*): **in a ~** dans un instant; (*Brit inf*: *credit*): **to buy sth on ~** acheter qch à crédit ▷ *vi* faire tic-tac ▷ *vt* (*item on list*) cocher; **to put a ~ against sth** cocher qch; **tick off** *vt* (*item on list*) cocher; (*person*) réprimander, attraper; **tick over** *vi* (*Brit*: *engine*) tourner au ralenti; (: *fig*) aller or marcher doucement

ticket ['tɪkɪt] *n* billet *m*; (*for bus, tube*) ticket *m*; (*in shop*: *on goods*) étiquette *f*; (: *from cash register*) reçu *m*, ticket; (*for library*) carte *f*; (*also*: **parking ~**) contravention *f*, p.-v. *m*; (*US Pol*) liste électorale (*soutenue par un parti*); **to get a (parking) ~** (*Aut*) attraper une contravention (pour stationnement illégal)

ticket barrier *n* (*Brit*: *Rail*) portillon *m* automatique

ticket collector *n* contrôleur(-euse)

ticket inspector *n* contrôleur(-euse)

ticket machine *n* billetterie *f* automatique

ticket office *n* guichet *m*, bureau *m* de vente des billets

tickle ['tɪkl] *n* chatouillement *m* ▷ *vi* chatouiller ▷ *vt* chatouiller; (*fig*) plaire à; faire rire

ticklish ['tɪklɪʃ] *adj* (*person*) chatouilleux(-euse); (*which tickles: blanket*) qui chatouille; (: *cough*) qui irrite; (*problem*) épineux(-euse)

tidal ['taɪdl] *adj* à marée

tidal wave *n* raz-de-marée *m inv*

tidbit ['tɪdbɪt] *n* (*esp US*) = **titbit**

tiddlywinks ['tɪdlɪwɪŋks] *n* jeu *m* de puce

tide [taɪd] *n* marée *f*; (*fig*: *of events*) cours *m* ▷ *vt*: **to ~ sb over** dépanner qn; **high/low ~** marée haute/basse

tidy ['taɪdɪ] *adj* (*room*) bien rangé(e); (*dress, work*) net/nette, soigné(e); (*person*) ordonné(e), qui a de l'ordre; (: *in character*) soigneux(-euse); (*mind*) méthodique ▷ *vt* (*also*: **~ up**) ranger; **to ~ o.s. up** s'arranger

tie [taɪ] *n* (*string etc*) cordon *m*; (*Brit*: *also*: **neck~**) cravate *f*; (*fig*: *link*) lien *m*; (*Sport*: *draw*) égalité *f* de points; (*match*) nul; (: *match*) rencontre *f*; (*US Rail*) traverse *f* ▷ *vt* (*parcel*) attacher; (*ribbon*) nouer ▷ *vi* (*Sport*) faire match nul; finir à égalité de points; **"black/ white ~"** "smoking/habit de rigueur"; **family ~s** liens de famille; **to ~ sth in a bow** faire un nœud à or avec qch; **to ~ a knot in sth** faire un nœud à qch; **tie down** *vt* attacher; (*fig*): **to ~ sb down to** contraindre qn à accepter; **to feel ~d down** (*by relationship*) se sentir coincé(e); **tie in** vi: **to ~ in (with)** (correspond) correspondre (à); **tie on** vt (Brit: label etc) attacher (avec une ficelle); **tie up** vt (parcel) ficeler; (dog, boat) attacher; (prisoner) ligoter; (arrangements) conclure; **to be ~d up** (busy) être pris(e) or occupé(e)

tier [tɪər] n gradin m; (of cake) étage m

tiger ['taɪgər] n tigre m

tight [taɪt] adj (rope) tendu(e), raide; (clothes) étroit(e), très juste; (budget, programme, bend) serré(e); (control) strict(e), sévère; (inf: drunk) ivre, rond(e) ▷ adv (squeeze) très fort; (shut) à bloc, hermétiquement; **to be packed ~** (suitcase) être bourré(e); (people) être serré(e); **hold ~!** accrochez-vous bien!

tighten ['taɪtn] vt (rope) tendre; (screw) resserrer; (control) renforcer ▷ vi se tendre; se resserrer

tightfisted [taɪt'fɪstɪd] adj avare

tightly ['taɪtlɪ] adv (grasp) bien, très fort

tightrope ['taɪtrəup] n corde f raide

tights [taɪts] npl (Brit) collant m

tile [taɪl] n (on roof) tuile f; (on wall or floor) carreau m ▷ vt (floor, bathroom etc) carreler

tiled [taɪld] adj en tuiles; carrelé(e)

till [tɪl] n caisse (enregistreuse) ▷ vt (land) cultiver ▷ prep, conj = **until**

tiller ['tɪlər] n (Naut) barre f (du gouvernail)

tilt [tɪlt] vt pencher, incliner ▷ vi pencher, être incliné(e) ▷ n (slope) inclinaison f; **to wear one's hat at a ~** porter son chapeau incliné sur le côté; **(at) full ~** à toute vitesse

timber ['tɪmbər] n (material) bois m de construction; (trees) arbres mpl

time [taɪm] n temps m; (epoch: often pl) époque f, temps; (by clock) heure f; (moment) moment m; (occasion, also Math) fois f; (Mus) mesure f ▷ vt (race) chronométrer; (programme) minuter; (visit) fixer; (remark etc) choisir le moment de; **a long ~** un long moment, longtemps; **four at a ~** quatre à la fois; **for the ~ being** pour le moment; **from ~ to ~** de temps en temps; **~ after ~, ~ and again** bien des fois; **at ~s** parfois; **in ~** (soon enough) à temps; (after some time) avec le temps, à la longue; (Mus) en mesure; **in a week's ~** dans une semaine; **in no ~** en un rien de temps; **any ~** n'importe quand; **on ~** à l'heure; **to be 30 minutes behind/ahead of ~** avoir 30 minutes de retard/d'avance; **by the ~ he arrived** quand il est arrivé, le temps qu'il arrive + sub; **5 ~s 5** 5 fois 5; **what ~ is it?** quelle heure est-il?; **what ~ do you make it?** quelle heure avez-vous?; **what ~ is the museum/shop open?** à quelle heure ouvre le musée/magasin?; **to have a good ~** bien s'amuser; **we** (or **they** etc) **had a hard ~** ça a été difficile or pénible; **~'s up!** c'est l'heure!; **I've no ~ for it** (fig) cela m'agace; **he'll do it in his own (good) ~** (without being hurried) il le fera quand il en aura le temps; **he'll do it in** or (US) **on his own ~** (out of working hours) il le

fera à ses heures perdues; **to be behind the ~s** retarder (sur son temps)

time bomb n bombe f à retardement

time lag n (Brit) décalage m; (: in travel) décalage horaire

timeless ['taɪmlɪs] adj éternel(le)

time limit n limite f de temps, délai m

timely ['taɪmlɪ] adj opportun(e)

time off n temps m libre

timer ['taɪmər] n (in kitchen) compte-minutes m inv; (Tech) minuteur m

timescale ['taɪmskeɪl] n délais mpl

time-share ['taɪmʃɛər] n (in kitchen) maison f/ appartement m en multipropriété

time switch n (Brit) minuteur m; (: for lighting) minuterie f

timetable ['taɪmteɪbl] n (Rail) (indicateur m) horaire m; (Scol) emploi m du temps; (programme of events etc) programme m

time zone n fuseau m horaire

timid ['tɪmɪd] adj timide; (easily scared) peureux(-euse)

timing ['taɪmɪŋ] n minutage m; (Sport) chronométrage m; **the ~ of his resignation** le moment choisi pour sa démission

timpani ['tɪmpənɪ] npl timbales fpl

tin [tɪn] n étain m; (also: **~ plate**) fer-blanc m; (Brit: can) boîte f (de conserve); (: for baking) moule m (à gâteau); (for storage) boîte f; **a ~ of paint** un pot de peinture

tinfoil ['tɪnfɔɪl] n papier m d'étain or d'aluminium

tinge [tɪndʒ] n nuance f ▷ vt: **~d with** teinté(e) de

tingle ['tɪŋgl] n picotement m; frisson m ▷ vi picoter; (person) avoir des picotements

tinker ['tɪŋkər] n rétameur ambulant; (inf!: gipsy) romanichel m; **tinker with** vt fus bricoler, rafistoler

tinkle ['tɪŋkl] vi tinter ▷ n (inf): **to give sb a ~** passer un coup de fil à qn

tinned [tɪnd] adj (Brit: food) en boîte, en conserve

tin opener [-'əupnər] n (Brit) ouvre-boîte(s) m

tinsel ['tɪnsl] n guirlandes fpl de Noël (argentées)

tint [tɪnt] n teinte f; (for hair) shampooing colorant ▷ vt (hair) faire un shampooing colorant à

tinted ['tɪntɪd] adj (hair) teint(e); (spectacles, glass) teinté(e)

tiny ['taɪnɪ] adj minuscule

tip [tɪp] n (end) bout m; (protective: on umbrella etc) embout m; (gratuity) pourboire m; (Brit: for coal) terril m; (Brit: for rubbish) décharge f; (advice) tuyau m ▷ vt (waiter) donner un pourboire à; (tilt) incliner; (overturn: also: **~ over**) renverser; (empty: also: **~ out**) déverser; (predict: winner etc) pronostiquer; **he ~ped out the contents of the box** il a vidé le contenu de la boîte; **how much**

should I ~? combien de pourboire est-ce qu'il faut laisser?; **tip off** vt prévenir, avertir

tip-off ['tɪpɔf] n (hint) tuyau m

tipped ['tɪpt] adj (Brit: cigarette) (à bout) filtre inv; **steel-~** à bout métallique, à embout de métal

tipsy ['tɪpsɪ] adj un peu ivre, éméché(e)

tiptoe ['tɪptəu] n: **on ~** sur la pointe des pieds

tiptop ['tɪptɔp] adj: **in ~ condition** en excellent état

tire ['taɪəʳ] n (US) = **tyre** ▷ vt fatiguer ▷ vi se fatiguer; **tire out** vt épuiser

tired ['taɪəd] adj fatigué(e); **to be/feel/look ~** être/se sentir/avoir l'air fatigué; **to be ~ of** en avoir assez de, être las/lasse de

tireless ['taɪəlɪs] adj infatigable, inlassable

tire pressure (US) = **tyre pressure**

tiresome ['taɪəsəm] adj ennuyeux(-euse)

tiring ['taɪərɪŋ] adj fatigant(e)

tissue ['tɪʃuː] n tissu m; (paper handkerchief) mouchoir m en papier, kleenex® m

tissue paper n papier m de soie

tit [tɪt] n (bird) mésange f; (inf: breast) nichon m; **to give ~ for tat** rendre coup pour coup

titbit ['tɪtbɪt] n (food) friandise f; (before meal) amuse-gueule m inv; (news) potin m

title ['taɪtl] n titre m; (Law: right): **~ (to)** droit m (à)

title deed n (Law) titre (constitutif) de propriété

title role n rôle principal

T-junction ['tiː'dʒʌŋkʃən] n croisement m en T

TM n abbr = **trademark; transcendental meditation**

 KEYWORD

to [tuː, tə] prep (with noun/pronoun) **1** (direction) à; (towards) vers; envers; **to go to France/ Portugal/London/school** aller en France/au Portugal/à Londres/à l'école; **to go to Claude's/the doctor's** aller chez Claude/le docteur; **the road to Edinburgh** la route d'Édimbourg

2 (as far as) (jusqu')à; **to count to 10** compter jusqu'à 10; **from 40 to 50 people** de 40 à 50 personnes

3 (with expressions of time): **a quarter to 5** 5 heures moins le quart; **it's twenty to 3** il est 3 heures moins vingt

4 (for, of) de; **the key to the front door** la clé de la porte d'entrée; **a letter to his wife** une lettre (adressée) à sa femme

5 (expressing indirect object) à; **to give sth to sb** donner qch à qn; **to talk to sb** parler à qn; **it belongs to him** cela lui appartient, c'est à lui; **to be a danger to sb** être dangereux(-euse) pour qn

6 (in relation to) à; **3 goals to 2** (buts) à 2; **30 miles to the gallon** ≈ 9,4 litres aux cent (km)

7 (purpose, result): **to come to sb's aid** venir au secours de qn, porter secours à qn; **to sentence sb to death** condamner qn à mort; **to my surprise** à ma grande surprise

▷ prep (with vb) **1** (simple infinitive): **to go/eat** aller/manger

2 (following another vb): **to want/try/start to do** vouloir/essayer de/commencer à faire

3 (with vb omitted): **I don't want to** je ne veux pas

4 (purpose, result) pour; **I did it to help you** je l'ai fait pour vous aider

5 (equivalent to relative clause): **I have things to do** j'ai des choses à faire; **the main thing is to try** l'important est d'essayer

6 (after adjective etc): **ready to go** prêt(e) à partir; **too old/young to ...** trop vieux/jeune pour ...

▷ adv: **push/pull the door to** tirez/poussez la porte to; **to go to and fro** aller et venir

toad [təud] n crapaud m

toadstool ['təudstuːl] n champignon (vénéneux)

toast [təust] n (Culin) pain grillé, toast m; (drink, speech) toast m; (drink to) porter un toast à; **a piece** or **slice of ~** un toast

toaster ['təustəʳ] n grille-pain m inv

tobacco [tə'bækəu] n tabac m; **pipe ~** tabac à pipe

tobacconist [tə'bækənɪst] n marchand(e) de tabac; **~'s (shop)** (bureau m de) tabac m

toboggan [tə'bɔgən] n toboggan m; (child's) luge f

today [tə'deɪ] adv, n (also fig) aujourd'hui (m); **what day is it ~?** quel jour sommes-nous aujourd'hui?; **what date is it ~?** quelle est la date aujourd'hui?; **~ is the 4th of March** aujourd'hui nous sommes le 4 mars; **a week ago** - il y a huit jours aujourd'hui

toddler ['tɔdləʳ] n enfant m/f qui commence à marcher, bambin m

toe [təu] n doigt m de pied, orteil m; (of shoe) bout m ▷ vt: **to the line** (fig) obéir, se conformer; **big ~** gros orteil; **little ~** petit orteil

toenail ['təuneɪl] n ongle m de l'orteil

toffee ['tɔfɪ] n caramel m

toffee apple n (Brit) pomme caramélisée

together [tə'gɛðəʳ] adv ensemble; (at same time) en même temps; **~ with** prep avec

toil [tɔɪl] n dur travail, labeur m ▷ vi travailler dur; peiner

toilet ['tɔɪlət] n (Brit: lavatory) toilettes fpl, cabinets mpl ▷ cpd (bag, soap etc) de toilette; **to go to the ~** aller aux toilettes; **where's the ~?** où sont les toilettes?

toilet bag n (Brit) nécessaire m de toilette

toilet paper n papier m hygiénique

toiletries ['tɔɪlətrɪz] npl articles mpl de toilette

toilet roll n rouleau m de papier hygiénique

token ['təukən] n (sign) marque f, témoignage m; (metal disc) jeton m; (voucher) bon m, coupon m ▷ adj (fee, strike) symbolique; **by the same ~** (fig) de même; **book/record ~** (Brit) chèque-livre/-disque m

Tokyo ['təukjəu] n Tokyo

told [təuld] pt, pp of **tell**

tolerable ['tɔlərəbl] adj (bearable) tolérable; (fairly good) passable

tolerant ['tɔlərnt] adj: ~ **(of)** tolérant(e) (à l'égard de)

tolerate ['tɔləreɪt] vt supporter; (Med., Tech) tolérer

toll [təul] n (tax, charge) péage m ▷ vi (bell) sonner; **the accident ~ on the roads** le nombre des victimes de la route

toll call n (US Tel) appel m (à) longue distance

toll-free ['təul'fri:] adj (US) gratuit(e) ▷ adv gratuitement

tomato [tə'mɑ:təu] (pl **tomatoes**) n tomate f

tomato sauce n sauce f tomate

tomb [tu:m] n tombe f

tomboy ['tɔmbɔɪ] n garçon manqué

tombstone ['tu:mstəun] n pierre tombale

tomcat ['tɔmkæt] n matou m

tomorrow [tə'mɔrəu] adv, n (also fig) demain (m); **the day after ~** après-demain; **a week ~** demain en huit; **~ morning** demain matin

ton [tʌn] n tonne f (Brit: = 1016 kg; US = 907 kg; metric = 1000 kg); (Naut: also: **register ~**) tonneau m (= 2.83 cu.m.); **~s of** (inf) des tas de

tone [təun] n ton m; (of radio, Brit Tel) tonalité f ▷ vi (also: ~ **in**) s'harmoniser; **tone down** vt (colour, criticism) adoucir; (sound) baisser; **tone up** vt (muscles) tonifier

tone-deaf ['təun'dɛf] adj qui n'a pas d'oreille

tongs [tɔŋz] npl pinces fpl; (for coal) pincettes fpl; (for hair) fer m à friser

tongue [tʌŋ] n langue f; **~ in cheek** adv ironiquement

tongue-tied ['tʌŋtaɪd] adj (fig) muet(te)

tonic ['tɔnɪk] n (Med) tonique m; (Mus) tonique f; (also: ~ **water**) Schweppes® m

tonight [tə'naɪt] adv, n cette nuit; (this evening) ce soir; **(I'll) see you ~!** à ce soir!

tonne [tʌn] n (Brit: metric ton) tonne f

tonsil ['tɔnsl] n amygdale f; **to have one's ~s out** se faire opérer des amygdales

tonsillitis [tɔnsɪ'laɪtɪs] n amygdalite f; **to have ~** avoir une angine or une amygdalite

too [tu:] adv (excessively) trop; (also) aussi; **it's ~ sweet** c'est trop sucré; **I went ~** moi aussi, j'y suis allé; **~ much** (as adv) trop; (as adj) trop de; **~ many** adj trop de; **~ bad!** tant pis!

took [tuk] pt of **take**

tool [tu:l] n outil m; (fig) instrument m ▷ vt travailler, ouvrager

tool box n boîte f à outils

tool kit n trousse f à outils

toot [tu:t] n coup m de sifflet (or de klaxon) ▷ vi siffler; (with car-horn) klaxonner

tooth (pl **teeth**) [tu:θ, ti:θ] n (Anat, Tech) dent f; **to have a ~ out** or (US) **pulled** se faire arracher une dent; **to brush one's teeth** se laver les dents; **by the skin of one's teeth** (fig) de justesse

toothache ['tu:θeɪk] n mal m de dents; **to have ~** avoir mal aux dents

toothbrush ['tu:θbrʌʃ] n brosse f à dents

toothpaste ['tu:θpeɪst] n (pâte f) dentifrice m

toothpick ['tu:θpɪk] n cure-dent m

top [tɔp] n (of mountain, head) sommet m; (of page, ladder) haut m; (of list, queue) commencement m; (of box, cupboard, table) dessus m; (lid: of box, jar) couvercle m; (: of bottle) bouchon m; (toy) toupie f; (Dress: blouse etc) haut; (: of pyjamas) veste f ▷ adj du haut; (in rank) premier(-ière); (best) meilleur(e) ▷ vt (exceed) dépasser; (be first in) être en tête de; **the ~ of the milk** (Brit) la crème du lait; **at the ~ of the stairs/page/street** en haut de l'escalier/de la page/de la rue; **from ~ to bottom** de fond en comble; **on ~ of** sur; (in addition to) en plus de; **from ~ to toe** (Brit) de la tête aux pieds; **at the ~ of the list** en tête de liste; **at the ~ of one's voice** à tue-tête; **at ~ speed** à toute vitesse; **over the ~** (inf: behaviour etc) qui dépasse les limites; **top up**, (US) **top off** vt (bottle) remplir; (salary) compléter; **to ~ up one's mobile (phone)** recharger son compte

top floor n dernier étage

top hat n haut-de-forme m

top-heavy [tɔp'hɛvɪ] adj (object) trop lourd(e) du haut

topic ['tɔpɪk] n sujet m, thème m

topical ['tɔpɪkl] adj d'actualité

topless ['tɔplɪs] adj (bather etc) aux seins nus; **~ swimsuit** monokini m

top-level ['tɔplɛvl] adj (talks) à l'échelon le plus élevé

topmost ['tɔpməust] adj le/la plus haut(e)

topping ['tɔpɪŋ] n (Culin) couche de crème, fromage etc qui recouvre un plat

topple ['tɔpl] vt renverser, faire tomber ▷ vi basculer; tomber

top-secret ['tɔp'si:krɪt] adj ultra-secret(-ète)

topsy-turvy ['tɔpsɪ'tə:vɪ] adj, adv sens dessus-dessous

top-up ['tɔpʌp] n (for mobile phone) recharge f, minutes fpl; **would you like a ~?** je vous en remets or rajoute?

top-up card n (for mobile phone) recharge f

torch [tɔ:tʃ] n torche f; (Brit: electric) lampe f de poche

tore [tɔ:ʳ] pt of **tear²**

torment n ['tɔ:mɛnt] tourment m ▷ vt [tɔ:'mɛnt] tourmenter; (fig: annoy) agacer

torn [tɔ:n] pp of **tear²** ▷ adj: **~ between** (fig) tiraillé(e) entre

tornado [tɔ:'neɪdəu] (pl **tornadoes**) n tornade f

torpedo [tɔːˈpiːdəu] (pl **torpedoes**) n
torpille f

torrent [ˈtɔrnt] n torrent m

torrential [tɔˈrɛnʃl] adj torrentiel(le)

tortoise [ˈtɔːtəs] n tortue f

tortoiseshell [ˈtɔːtəʃɛl] adj en écaille

torture [ˈtɔːtʃər] n torture f ▷ vt torturer

Tory [ˈtɔːrɪ] adj, n (Brit Pol) tory m/f,
conservateur(-trice)

toss [tɔs] vt lancer, jeter; (Brit: pancake) faire
sauter; (head) rejeter en arrière ▷ vi: **to ~ up
for sth** (Brit) jouer qch à pile ou face ▷ n
(movement: of head etc) mouvement soudain;
(of coin) tirage m à pile ou face; **to ~ a coin**
jouer à pile ou face; **to ~ and turn** (in bed) se
tourner et se retourner; **to win/lose the ~**
gagner/perdre à pile ou face; (Sport) gagner/
perdre le tirage au sort

tot [tɔt] n (Brit: drink) petit verre; (child)
bambin m; **tot up** vt (Brit: figures)
additionner

total [ˈtəutl] adj total(e) ▷ n total m ▷ vt
(add up) faire le total de, additionner;
(amount to) s'élever à; **in ~** au total

totalitarian [təutælɪˈtɛərɪən] adj totalitaire

totally [ˈtəutəlɪ] adv totalement

totter [ˈtɔtər] vi chanceler; (object, government)
être chancelant(e)

touch [tʌtʃ] n contact m, toucher m; (sense,
skill: of pianist etc) toucher; (fig: note, also
Football) touche f ▷ vt (gen) toucher; (tamper
with) toucher à; **the personal ~** la petite note
personnelle; **to put the finishing ~es to sth**
mettre la dernière main à qch; **a ~ of** (fig) un
petit peu de; une touche de; **in ~ with** en
contact or rapport avec; **to get in ~ with**
prendre contact avec; **I'll be in ~** je resterai
en contact; **to lose ~** (friends) se perdre de vue;
to be out of ~ with events ne pas être au
courant de ce qui se passe; **touch down** vi
(Aviat) atterrir; (on sea) amerrir; **touch on** vt
fus (topic) effleurer, toucher; **touch up** vt
(paint) retoucher

touch-and-go [ˈtʌtʃənˈɡəu] adj incertain(e);
it was ~ whether we did it nous avons failli
ne pas le faire

touchdown [ˈtʌtʃdaun] n (Aviat)
atterrissage m; (on sea) amerrissage m;
(US Football) essai m

touched [tʌtʃt] adj (moved) touché(e); (inf)
cinglé(e)

touching [ˈtʌtʃɪŋ] adj touchant(e),
attendrissant(e)

touchline [ˈtʌtʃlaɪn] n (Sport) (ligne f de)
touche f

touch screen n (Tech) écran tactile; **~ mobile**
(téléphone) portable m à écran tactile;
~ technology technologie f à écran tactile

touch-sensitive [ˈtʌtʃsɛnsɪtɪv] adj (keypad)
à effleurement; (screen) tactile

touchy [ˈtʌtʃɪ] adj (person) susceptible

tough [tʌf] adj dur(e); (resistant) résistant(e),

solide; (meat) dur, coriace; (firm) inflexible;
(journey) pénible; (task, problem, situation)
difficile; (rough) dur ▷ n (gangster etc) dur m;
~ luck! pas de chance!; tant pis!

toughen [ˈtʌfn] vt rendre plus dur(e) (or plus
résistant(e) or plus solide)

toupee [ˈtuːpeɪ] n postiche m

tour [ˈtuər] n voyage m; (also: **package ~**)
voyage organisé; (of town, museum) tour m,
visite f; (by band) tournée f ▷ vt visiter; **to go
on a ~ of** (museum, region) visiter; **to go on ~**
partir en tournée

tour guide n (person) guide m/f

tourism [ˈtuərɪzm] n tourisme m

tourist [ˈtuərɪst] n touriste m/f ▷ adv (travel)
en classe touriste ▷ cpd touristique; **the ~
trade** le tourisme

tourist office n syndicat m d'initiative

tournament [ˈtuənəmənt] n tournoi m

tour operator n (Brit) organisateur m de
voyages, tour-opérateur m

tousled [ˈtauzld] adj (hair) ébouriffé(e)

tout [taut] vi: **to ~ for** essayer de raccrocher,
racoler; **to ~ sth (around)** (Brit) essayer de
placer or (re)vendre qch ▷ n (Brit: ticket tout)
revendeur de billets

tow [təu] n: **to give sb a ~** (Aut) remorquer qn
▷ vt remorquer; (caravan, trailer) tracter;
"on ~", (US) **"in ~"** (Aut) "véhicule en
remorque"; **tow away** vt (subj: police)
emmener à la fourrière; (: breakdown service)
remorquer

toward [təˈwɔːd], **towards** [təˈwɔːdz] prep
vers; (of attitude) envers, à l'égard de; (of
purpose) pour; **~(s) noon/the end of the year**
vers midi/la fin de l'année; **to feel friendly
~(s) sb** être bien disposé envers qn

towel [ˈtauəl] n serviette f (de toilette); (also:
tea ~) torchon m; **to throw in the ~** (fig) jeter
l'éponge

towelling [ˈtauəlɪŋ] n (fabric) tissu-éponge m

towel rail, (US) **towel rack** n
porte-serviettes m inv

tower [ˈtauər] n tour f ▷ vi (building, mountain)
se dresser (majestueusement); **to ~ above** or
over sb/sth dominer qn/qch

tower block n (Brit) tour f (d'habitation)

towering [ˈtauərɪŋ] adj très haut(e),
imposant(e)

town [taun] n ville f; **to go to ~** aller en ville;
(fig) y mettre le paquet; **in the ~** dans la ville,
en ville; **to be out of ~** (person) être en
déplacement

town centre n (Brit) centre m de la ville,
centre-ville m

town council n conseil municipal

town hall n ≈ mairie f

town plan n plan m de ville

town planning n urbanisme m

towrope [ˈtəurəup] n (câble m de) remorque f

tow truck n (US) dépanneuse f

toxic [ˈtɔksɪk] adj toxique

toxic asset n (Econ) actif m toxique
toy [tɔɪ] n jouet m; **toy with** vt fus jouer avec; (idea) caresser
toyshop ['tɔɪʃɔp] n magasin m de jouets
trace [treɪs] n trace f ▷ vt (draw) tracer, dessiner; (follow) suivre la trace de; (locate) retrouver; **without ~** (disappear) sans laisser de traces; **there was no ~ of it** il n'y en avait pas trace
tracing paper ['treɪsɪŋ-] n papier-calque m
track [træk] n (mark) trace f; (path: gen) chemin m, piste f; (: of bullet etc) trajectoire f; (: of suspect, animal) piste f; (Rail) voie ferrée, rails mpl; (on tape, Comput, Sport) piste; (on CD) piste f; (on record) plage f ▷ vt suivre la trace or la piste de; **to keep ~ of** suivre; **to be on the right ~** (fig) être sur la bonne voie; **track down** vt (prey) trouver et capturer; (sth lost) finir par retrouver
tracksuit ['træksu:t] n survêtement m
tract [trækt] n (Geo) étendue f, zone f; (pamphlet) tract m; **respiratory ~** (Anat) système m respiratoire
traction ['trækʃən] n traction f
tractor ['træktə'] n tracteur m
trade [treɪd] n commerce m; (skill, job) métier m ▷ vi faire du commerce ▷ vt (exchange): **to ~ sth (for sth)** échanger qch (contre qch); **to ~ with/in** faire du commerce avec/le commerce de; **foreign ~** commerce extérieur; **trade in** vt (old car etc) faire reprendre
trade fair n foire(-exposition) commerciale
trade-in price n prix m à la reprise
trademark ['treɪdmɑːk] n marque f de fabrique
trade name n marque déposée
trader ['treɪdə'] n commerçant(e), négociant(e)
tradesman ['treɪdzmən] irreg (shopkeeper) commerçant m; (skilled worker) ouvrier qualifié
trade union n syndicat m
trade unionist [-'ju:njənɪst] n syndicaliste m/f
trading ['treɪdɪŋ] n affaires fpl, commerce m
tradition [trə'dɪʃən] n tradition f; **traditions** npl coutumes fpl, traditions
traditional [trə'dɪʃənl] adj traditionnel(le)
traffic ['træfɪk] n trafic m; (cars) circulation f ▷ vi: **to ~ in** (pej: liquor, drugs) faire le trafic de
traffic calming [-'kɑːmɪŋ] n ralentissement m de la circulation
traffic circle n (US) rond-point m
traffic island n refuge m (pour piétons)
traffic jam n embouteillage m
traffic lights npl feux mpl (de signalisation)
traffic warden n contractuel(le)
tragedy ['trædʒədɪ] n tragédie f
tragic ['trædʒɪk] adj tragique
trail [treɪl] n (tracks) trace f, piste f; (path) chemin m, piste; (of smoke etc) traînée f ▷ vt

(drag) traîner, tirer; (follow) suivre ▷ vi traîner; (in game, contest) être en retard; **to be on sb's ~** être sur la piste de qn; **trail away**, **trail off** vi (sound, voice) s'évanouir; (interest) disparaître; **trail behind** vi traîner, être à la traîne
trailer ['treɪlə'] n (Aut) remorque f; (US) caravane f; (Cine) bande-annonce f
trailer truck n (US) (camion m) semi-remorque m
train [treɪn] n train m; (in underground) rame f; (of dress) traîne f; (Brit: series): **~ of events** série f d'événements ▷ vt (apprentice, doctor etc) former; (Sport) entraîner; (dog) dresser; (memory) exercer; (point: gun etc): **to ~ sth on** braquer qch sur ▷ vi recevoir sa formation; (Sport) s'entraîner; **one's ~ of thought** le fil de sa pensée; **to go by ~** voyager par le train or en train; **what time does the ~ from Paris get in?** à quelle heure arrive le train de Paris?; **is this the ~ for ...?** c'est bien le train pour ...?; **to ~ sb to do sth** apprendre à qn à faire qch; (employee) former qn à faire qch
trained [treɪnd] adj qualifié(e), qui a reçu une formation; dressé(e)
trainee [treɪ'niː] n stagiaire m/f; (in trade) apprenti(e)
trainer ['treɪnə'] n (Sport) entraîneur(-euse); (of dogs etc) dresseur(-euse); **trainers** npl (shoes) chaussures fpl de sport
training ['treɪnɪŋ] n formation f; (Sport) entraînement m; (of dog etc) dressage m; **in ~** (Sport) à l'entraînement; (fit) en forme
training college n école professionnelle; (for teachers) ≈ école normale
training course n cours m de formation professionnelle
training shoes npl chaussures fpl de sport
trait [treɪt] n trait m (de caractère)
traitor ['treɪtə'] n traître m
tram [træm] n (Brit: also: **~car**) tram(way) m
tramp [træmp] n (person) vagabond(e), clochard(e); (inf: pej: woman): **to be a ~** être coureuse ▷ vi marcher d'un pas lourd ▷ vt (walk through: town, streets) parcourir à pied
trample ['træmpl] vt: **to ~ (underfoot)** piétiner; (fig) bafouer
trampoline ['træmpəliːn] n trampoline m
tranquil ['træŋkwɪl] adj tranquille
tranquillizer, (US) **tranquilizer** ['træŋkwɪlaɪzə'] n (Med) tranquillisant m
transact [træn'zækt] vt (business) traiter
transaction [træn'zækʃən] n transaction f; **transactions** npl (minutes) actes mpl; **cash ~** transaction au comptant
transatlantic ['trænzət'læntɪk] adj transatlantique
transcript ['trænskrɪpt] n transcription f (texte)
transfer n ['trænsfə'] (gen, also Sport) transfert m; (Pol: of power) passation f;

(of money) virement m; (picture, design) décalcomanie f; (: stick-on) autocollant m ▷ vt [træns'fɜːʳ] transférer; passer; virer; décalquer; **to ~ the charges** (Brit Tel) téléphoner en P.C.V.; **by bank ~** par virement bancaire

transfer desk n (Aviat) guichet m de transit

transform [træns'fɔːm] vt transformer

transformation [trænsfə'meɪʃən] n transformation f

transfusion [træns'fjuːʒən] n transfusion f

transient ['trænzɪənt] adj transitoire, éphémère

transistor [træn'zɪstəʳ] n (Elec: also: ~ radio) transistor m

transit ['trænzɪt] n: **in ~** en transit

transition [træn'zɪʃən] n transition f

transitive ['trænzɪtɪv] adj (Ling) transitif(-ive)

transit lounge n (Aviat) salle f de transit

translate [trænz'leɪt] vt: **to ~ (from/into)** traduire (du/en); **can you ~ this for me?** pouvez-vous me traduire ceci?

translation [trænz'leɪʃən] n traduction f; (Scol: as opposed to prose) version f

translator [trænz'leɪtəʳ] n traducteur(-trice)

transmission [trænz'mɪʃən] n transmission f

transmit [trænz'mɪt] vt transmettre; (Radio, TV) émettre

transmitter [trænz'mɪtəʳ] n émetteur m

transparency [træns'pɛərnsɪ] n (Brit Phot) diapositive f

transparent [træns'pærnt] adj transparent(e)

transpire [træns'paɪəʳ] vi (become known): **it finally ~d that ...** on a finalement appris que ...; (happen) arriver

transplant vt [træns'plaːnt] transplanter; (seedlings) repiquer ▷ n ['trænsplaːnt] (Med) transplantation f; **to have a heart ~** subir une greffe du cœur

transport n ['trænspɔːt] transport m ▷ vt [træns'pɔːt] transporter; **public ~** transports en commun; **Department of T~** (Brit) ministère m des Transports

transportation [trænspɔːˈteɪʃən] n (moyen m de) transport m; (of prisoners) transportation f; **Department of T~** (US) ministère m des Transports ≈

transport café n (Brit) ≈ routier m

transvestite [trænz'vɛstaɪt] n travesti(e)

trap [træp] n (snare, trick) piège m; (carriage) cabriolet m ▷ vt prendre au piège; (immobilize) bloquer; (confine) coincer; **to set** or **lay a ~ (for sb)** tendre un piège (à qn); **to shut one's ~** (inf) la fermer

trap door n trappe f

trapeze [trə'piːz] n trapèze m

trappings ['træpɪŋz] npl ornements mpl; attributs mpl

trash [træʃ] n (pej: goods) camelote f; (: nonsense) sottises fpl; (US: rubbish) ordures fpl

trash can n (US) poubelle f

trashy ['træʃɪ] adj (inf) de camelote, qui ne vaut rien

trauma ['trɔːmə] n traumatisme m

traumatic [trɔːˈmætɪk] adj traumatisant(e)

travel ['trævl] n voyage(s) m(pl) ▷ vi voyager; (move) aller, se déplacer; (news, sound) se propager ▷ vt (distance) parcourir; **this wine doesn't ~ well** ce vin voyage mal

travel agency n agence f de voyages

travel agent n agent m de voyages

travel insurance n assurance-voyage f

traveller, (US) **traveler** ['trævləʳ] n voyageur(-euse); (Comm) représentant m de commerce

traveller's cheque, (US) **traveler's check** n chèque m de voyage

travelling, (US) **traveling** ['trævlɪŋ] n voyage(s) m(pl) ▷ adj (circus, exhibition) ambulant(e) ▷ cpd (bag, clock) de voyage; (expenses) de déplacement

travel-sick ['trævlsɪk] adj: **to get ~** avoir le mal de la route (or de mer or de l'air)

travel sickness n mal m de la route (or de mer or de l'air)

trawler ['trɔːləʳ] n chalutier m

tray [treɪ] n (for carrying) plateau m; (on desk) corbeille f

treacherous ['trɛtʃərəs] adj traître(sse); (ground, tide) dont il faut se méfier; **road conditions are ~** l'état des routes est dangereux

treacle ['triːkl] n mélasse f

tread [trɛd] n (step) pas m; (sound) bruit m de pas; (of tyre) chape f, bande f de roulement ▷ vi (pt trod, pp trodden) [trɔd, 'trɔdn] marcher; **tread on** vt fus marcher sur

treason ['triːzn] n trahison f

treasure ['trɛʒəʳ] n trésor m ▷ vt (value) tenir beaucoup à; (store) conserver précieusement

treasurer ['trɛʒərəʳ] n trésorier(-ière)

treasury ['trɛʒərɪ] n trésorerie f; **the T~**, (US) **the T~ Department** ≈ le ministère des Finances

treat [triːt] n petit cadeau, petite surprise ▷ vt traiter; **it was a ~** ça m'a (or nous a etc) vraiment fait plaisir; **to ~ sb to sth** offrir qch à qn; **to ~ sth as a joke** prendre qch à la plaisanterie

treatment ['triːtmənt] n traitement m; **to have ~ for sth** (Med) suivre un traitement pour qch

treaty ['triːtɪ] n traité m

treble ['trɛbl] adj triple ▷ n (Mus) soprano m ▷ vt, vi tripler

treble clef n clé f de sol

tree [triː] n arbre m

trek [trɛk] n (long walk) randonnée f; (tiring walk) longue marche, trotte f ▷ vi (as holiday) faire de la randonnée

tremble ['trɛmbl] vi trembler

tremendous [trɪ'mɛndəs] adj (enormous) énorme; (excellent) formidable, fantastique

tremor ['trɛməʳ] n tremblement m; (also: **earth ~**) secousse f sismique

trench [trɛntʃ] n tranchée f

trend [trɛnd] n (tendency) tendance f; (of events) cours m; (fashion) mode f; **~ towards/away from doing** tendance à faire/à ne pas faire; **to set the ~** donner le ton; **to set a ~** lancer une mode

trendy ['trɛndɪ] adj (idea, person) dans le vent; (clothes) dernier cri inv

trespass ['trɛspəs] vi: **to ~ on** s'introduire sans permission dans; (fig) empiéter sur; **"no ~ing"** "propriété privée", "défense d'entrer"

trestle ['trɛsl] n tréteau m

trial ['traɪəl] n (Law) procès m, jugement m; (test: of machine etc) essai m; (worry) souci m; **trials** npl (unpleasant experiences) épreuves fpl; (Sport) épreuves éliminatoires; **horse ~s** concours m hippique; **~ by jury** jugement par jury; **to be sent for ~** être traduit(e) en justice; **to be on ~** passer en jugement; **by ~ and error** par tâtonnements

trial period n période f d'essai

triangle ['traɪæŋgl] n (Math, Mus) triangle m

triangular [traɪ'æŋgjuləʳ] adj triangulaire

tribe [traɪb] n tribu f

tribesman ['traɪbzmən] n membre m de la tribu

tribunal [traɪ'bjuːnl] n tribunal m

tributary ['trɪbjutərɪ] n (river) affluent m

tribute ['trɪbjuːt] n tribut m, hommage m; **to pay ~ to** rendre hommage à

trick [trɪk] n (magic) tour m; (joke, prank) tour, farce f; (skill, knack) astuce f; (Cards) levée f ▷ vt attraper, rouler; **to play a ~ on sb** jouer un tour à qn; **to ~ sb into doing sth** persuader qn par la ruse de faire qch; **to ~ sb out of sth** obtenir qch de qn par la ruse; **it's a ~ of the light** c'est une illusion d'optique causée par la lumière; **that should do the ~** (fam) ça devrait faire l'affaire

trickery ['trɪkərɪ] n ruse f

trickle ['trɪkl] n (of water etc) filet m ▷ vi couler en un filet or goutte à goutte; **to ~ in/out** (people) entrer/sortir par petits groupes

tricky ['trɪkɪ] adj difficile, délicat(e)

tricycle ['traɪsɪkl] n tricycle m

trifle ['traɪfl] n bagatelle f; (Culin) ≈ diplomate m ▷ adv: **a ~ long** un peu long ▷ vi: **to ~ with** traiter à la légère

trifling ['traɪflɪŋ] adj insignifiant(e)

trigger ['trɪgəʳ] n (of gun) gâchette f; **trigger off** vt déclencher

trim [trɪm] adj net(te); (house, garden) bien tenu(e); (figure) svelte ▷ n (haircut etc) légère coupe; (embellishment) finitions fpl; (on car) garnitures fpl ▷ vt (cut) couper légèrement; (decorate): **to ~ (with)** décorer (de); (Naut: a

sail) gréer; **to keep in (good) ~** maintenir en (bon) état

trimmings ['trɪmɪŋz] npl décorations fpl; (extras: gen Culin) garniture f

trinket ['trɪŋkɪt] n bibelot m; (piece of jewellery) colifichet m

trio ['triːəu] n trio m

trip [trɪp] n voyage m; (excursion) excursion f; (stumble) faux pas ▷ vi faire un faux pas, trébucher; (go lightly) marcher d'un pas léger; **on a ~** en voyage; **trip up** vi trébucher ▷ vt faire un croc-en-jambe à

tripe [traɪp] n (Culin) tripes fpl; (pej: rubbish) idioties fpl

triple ['trɪpl] adj triple ▷ adv: **~ the distance/ the speed** trois fois la distance/la vitesse

triplets ['trɪplɪts] npl triplés(-ées)

triplicate ['trɪplɪkət] n: **in ~** en trois exemplaires

tripod ['traɪpɔd] n trépied m

trite [traɪt] adj banal(e)

triumph ['traɪʌmf] n triomphe m ▷ vi: **to ~ (over)** triompher (de)

triumphant [traɪ'ʌmfənt] adj triomphant(e)

trivia ['trɪvɪə] npl futilités fpl

trivial ['trɪvɪəl] adj insignifiant(e); (commonplace) banal(e)

trod [trɔd] pt of **tread**

trodden ['trɔdn] pp of **tread**

trolley ['trɔlɪ] n chariot m

trombone [trɔm'bəun] n trombone m

troop [truːp] n bande f, groupe m ▷ vi: **to ~ in/ out** entrer/sortir en groupe; **troops** npl (Mil) troupes fpl; (: men) hommes mpl, soldats mpl; **~ing the colour** (Brit: ceremony) le salut au drapeau

trophy ['trəufɪ] n trophée m

tropic ['trɔpɪk] n tropique m; **in the ~s** sous les tropiques; **T~ of Cancer/Capricorn** tropique du Cancer/Capricorne

tropical ['trɔpɪkl] adj tropical(e)

trot [trɔt] n trot m ▷ vi trotter; **on the ~** (Brit: fig) d'affilée; **trot out** vt (excuse, reason) débiter; (names, facts) réciter les uns après les autres

trouble ['trʌbl] n difficulté(s) f(pl), problème(s) m(pl); (worry) ennuis mpl, soucis mpl; (bother, effort) peine f; (Pol) conflit(s) m(pl), troubles mpl; (Med): **stomach** etc **~** troubles gastriques etc ▷ vt (disturb) déranger, gêner; (worry) inquiéter ▷ vi: **to ~ to do** prendre la peine de faire; **troubles** npl (Pol etc) troubles; (personal) ennuis, soucis; **to be in ~** avoir des ennuis; (ship, climber etc) être en difficulté; **to have ~ doing sth** avoir du mal à faire qch; **to go to the ~ of doing** se donner le mal de faire; **it's no ~!** je vous en prie!; **please don't ~ yourself** je vous en prie, ne vous dérangez pas!; **the ~ is ...** le problème, c'est que ...; **what's the ~?** qu'est-ce qui ne va pas?

troubled ['trʌbld] adj (person) inquiet(-ète); (times, life) agité(e)

t

troublemaker ['trʌblmeɪkəʳ] n élément perturbateur, fauteur m de troubles

troubleshooter ['trʌblʃuːtəʳ] n (in conflict) conciliateur m

troublesome ['trʌblsəm] adj (child) fatigant(e), difficile; (cough) gênant(e)

trough [trɔf] n (also: **drinking ~**) abreuvoir m; (also: **feeding ~**) auge f; (depression) creux m; (channel) chenal m; **~ of low pressure** (Meteorology) dépression f

trousers ['traʊzəz] npl pantalon m; **short ~** (Brit) culottes courtes

trout [traʊt] n (pl inv) truite f

trowel ['traʊəl] n (garden tool) truelle f; (garden tool) déplantoir m

truant ['truənt] n: **to play ~** (Brit) faire l'école buissonnière

truce [truːs] n trêve f

truck [trʌk] n camion m; (Rail) wagon m à plate-forme; (for luggage) chariot m (à bagages)

truck driver n camionneur m

truck farm n (US) jardin maraîcher

true [truː] adj vrai(e); (accurate) exact(e); (genuine) vrai, véritable; (faithful) fidèle; (wall) d'aplomb; (beam) droit(e); (wheel) dans l'axe; **to come ~** se réaliser; **~ to life** réaliste

truffle ['trʌfl] n truffe f

truly ['truːlɪ] adv vraiment, réellement; (truthfully) sans mentir; (faithfully) fidèlement; **yours ~** (in letter) je vous prie d'agréer, Monsieur (or Madame etc), l'expression de mes sentiments respectueux

trump [trʌmp] n atout m; **to turn up ~s** (fig) faire des miracles

trumpet ['trʌmpɪt] n trompette f

truncheon ['trʌntʃən] n bâton m (d'agent de police); matraque f

trundle ['trʌndl] vt, vi: **to ~ along** rouler bruyamment

trunk [trʌŋk] n (of tree, person) tronc m; (of elephant) trompe f; (case) malle f; (US Aut) coffre m; **trunks** npl (also: **swimming ~s**) maillot m or slip m de bain

truss [trʌs] n (Med) bandage m herniaire ▷ vt: **to ~ (up)** (Culin) brider

trust [trʌst] n confiance f; (responsibility): **to place sth in sb's ~** confier la responsabilité de qch à qn; (Law) fidéicommis m; (Comm) trust m ▷ vt (rely on) avoir confiance en; (entrust): **to ~ sth to sb** confier qch à qn; (hope): **to ~ (that)** espérer (que); **to take sth on ~** accepter qch les yeux fermés; **in ~** (Law) par fidéicommis

trusted ['trʌstɪd] adj en qui l'on a confiance

trustee [trʌsˈtiː] n (Law) fidéicommissaire m/f; (of school etc) administrateur(-trice)

trustful ['trʌstful] adj confiant(e)

trustworthy ['trʌstwəːðɪ] adj digne de confiance

truth [truːθ, pl truːðz] n vérité f

truthful ['truːθful] adj (person) qui dit la vérité; (answer) sincère; (description) exact(e), vrai(e)

try [traɪ] n essai m, tentative f; (Rugby) essai ▷ vt (attempt) essayer, tenter; (test: sth new: also: **~ out**) essayer, tester; (Law: person) juger; (strain) éprouver ▷ vi essayer; **to ~ to do** essayer de faire; (seek) chercher à faire; **to ~ one's (very) best** or **one's (very) hardest** faire de son mieux; **to give sth a ~** essayer qch; **try on** vt (clothes) essayer; **to ~ it on** (fig) tenter le coup, bluffer; **try out** vt essayer, mettre à l'essai

trying ['traɪɪŋ] adj pénible

T-shirt ['tiːʃəːt] n tee-shirt m

T-square ['tiːskwɛəʳ] n équerre f en T

tsunami [tsʊˈnɑːmɪ] n tsunami m

tub [tʌb] n cuve f; (for washing clothes) baquet m; (bath) baignoire f

tubby ['tʌbɪ] adj rondelet(te)

tube [tjuːb] n tube m; (Brit: underground) métro m; (for tyre) chambre f à air; (inf: television): **the ~** la télé

tuberculosis [tjubəˈkjuːləʊsɪs] n tuberculose f

tube station n (Brit) station f de métro

TUC n abbr (Brit: = Trades Union Congress) confédération f des syndicats britanniques

tuck [tʌk] n (Sewing) pli m, rempli m ▷ vt (put) mettre; **tuck away** vt cacher, ranger; (money) mettre de côté; (building): **to be ~ed away** être caché(e); **tuck in** vt rentrer; (child) border ▷ vi (eat) manger de bon appétit; attaquer le repas; **tuck up** vt (child) border

tuck shop n (Brit Scol) boutique f à provisions

Tuesday ['tjuːzdɪ] n mardi m; (the date) **today is ~ 23rd March** nous sommes aujourd'hui le mardi 23 mars; **on ~** mardi; **on ~s** le mardi; **every ~** tous les mardis, chaque mardi; **every other ~** un mardi sur deux; **last/next ~** mardi dernier/prochain; **~ next** mardi qui vient; **the following ~** le mardi suivant; **a week/fortnight on ~**, **~ week/fortnight** mardi en huit/quinze; **the ~ before last** l'autre mardi; **the ~ after next** mardi en huit; **~ morning/lunchtime/afternoon/evening** mardi matin/midi/après-midi/soir; **~ night** mardi soir; (overnight) la nuit de mardi (à mercredi); **~'s newspaper** le journal de mardi

tuft [tʌft] n touffe f

tug [tʌg] n (ship) remorqueur m ▷ vt tirer (sur)

tug-of-war [tʌgəvˈwɔːʳ] n lutte f à la corde

tuition [tjuːˈɪʃən] n (Brit: lessons) leçons fpl; (: private) cours particuliers; (US: fees) frais mpl de scolarité

tulip ['tjuːlɪp] n tulipe f

tumble ['tʌmbl] n (fall) chute f, culbute f ▷ vi tomber, dégringoler; (somersault) faire une or des culbute(s) ▷ vt renverser, faire tomber; **to ~ to sth** (inf) réaliser qch

tumbledown ['tʌmbldaʊn] adj délabré(e)

tumble dryer n (Brit) séchoir m (à linge) à air chaud

tumbler ['tʌmblə'] n verre (droit), gobelet m

tummy ['tʌmɪ] n (inf) ventre m

tumour, (US) **tumor** ['tjuːmə'] n tumeur f

tuna ['tjuːnə] n (pl inv: also: ~ **fish**) thon m

tune [tjuːn] n (melody) air m ▷ vt (Mus) accorder; (Radio, TV, Aut) régler, mettre au point; **to be in/out of ~** (instrument) être accordé/désaccordé; (singer) chanter juste/faux; **she was robbed to the ~ of £30,000** (fig) on lui a volé la jolie somme de 10 000 livres; **tune in** vi (Radio, TV): **to ~ in (to)** se mettre à l'écoute (de); **tune up** vi (musician) accorder son instrument

tuneful ['tjuːnful] adj mélodieux(-euse)

tuner ['tjuːnə'] n (radio set) tuner m; **piano ~** accordeur m de pianos

tunic ['tjuːnɪk] n tunique f

Tunis ['tjuːnɪs] n Tunis

Tunisia [tjuːˈnɪzɪə] n Tunisie f

Tunisian [tjuːˈnɪzɪən] adj tunisien(ne) ▷ n Tunisien(ne)

tunnel ['tʌnl] n tunnel m; (in mine) galerie f ▷ vi creuser un tunnel (or une galerie)

turbulence ['tɜːbjʊləns] n (Aviat) turbulence f

tureen [təˈriːn] n soupière f

turf [tɜːf] n gazon m; (clod) motte f (de gazon) ▷ vt gazonner; **the T~** le turf, les courses fpl; **turf out** vt (inf) jeter; jeter dehors

Turk [tɜːk] n Turc/Turque

Turkey ['tɜːkɪ] n Turquie f

turkey ['tɜːkɪ] n dindon m, dinde f

Turkish ['tɜːkɪʃ] adj turc/turque ▷ n (Ling) turc m

turmoil ['tɜːmɔɪl] n trouble m, bouleversement m

turn [tɜːn] n tour m; (in road) tournant m; (tendency: of mind, events) tournure f; (performance) numéro m; (Med) crise f, attaque f ▷ vt tourner; (collar, steak) retourner; (age) atteindre; (shape: wood, metal) tourner; (milk) faire tourner; (change): **to ~ sth into** changer qch en ▷ vi (object, wind, milk) tourner; (person: look back) se (re)tourner; (reverse direction) faire demi-tour; (change) changer; (become) devenir; **to ~ into** se changer en, se transformer en; **a good ~** service; **a bad ~** un mauvais tour; **it gave me quite a ~** ça m'a fait un coup; **"no left ~"** (Aut) "défense de tourner à gauche"; **~ left/right at the next junction** tournez à gauche/droite au prochain carrefour; **it's your ~** c'est (à) votre tour; **in ~** à son tour; **to take ~s** se relayer; **to take ~s at** faire à tour de rôle; **at the ~ of the year/century** à la fin de l'année/du siècle; **to take a ~ for the worse** (situation, events) empirer; **his health** or **he has taken a ~ for the worse** son état s'est aggravé; **turn about** vi faire demi-tour; faire un demi-tour; **turn around** vi (person) se retourner ▷ vt (object) tourner; **turn away** vi se détourner, tourner la tête ▷ vt (reject: person) renvoyer; (: business) refuser; **turn back** vi revenir, faire demi-tour; **turn down** vt (refuse) rejeter, refuser; (reduce) baisser; (fold) rabattre; **turn in** vi (inf: go to bed) aller se coucher ▷ vt (fold) rentrer; **turn off** vi (from road) tourner ▷ vt (light, radio etc) éteindre; (tap) fermer; (engine) arrêter; **I can't ~ the heating off** je n'arrive pas à éteindre le chauffage; **turn on** vt (light, radio etc) allumer; (tap) ouvrir; (engine) mettre en marche; **I can't ~ the heating on** je n'arrive pas à allumer le chauffage; **turn out** vt (light, gas) éteindre; (produce: goods, novel, good pupils) produire ▷ vi (voters, troops) se présenter; **to ~ out to be ...** s'avérer ..., se révéler ...; **turn over** vi (person) se retourner ▷ vt (object) retourner; (page) tourner; **turn round** vi faire demi-tour; (rotate) tourner; **turn to** vt fus: **to ~ to sb** s'adresser à qn; **turn up** vi (person) arriver, se pointer (inf); (lost object) être retrouvé(e) ▷ vt (collar) remonter; (radio, heater) mettre plus fort

turning ['tɜːnɪŋ] n (in road) tournant m; **the first ~ on the right** la première (rue or route) à droite

turning point n (fig) tournant m, moment décisif

turnip ['tɜːnɪp] n navet m

turnout ['tɜːnaʊt] n (nombre m de personnes dans l')assistance f; (of voters) taux m de participation

turnover ['tɜːnəʊvə'] n (Comm: amount of money) chiffre m d'affaires; (: of goods) roulement m; (of staff) renouvellement m, changement m ▷ vt (Culin) sorte de chausson; **there is a rapid ~ in staff** le personnel change souvent

turnpike ['tɜːnpaɪk] n (US) autoroute f à péage

turnstile ['tɜːnstaɪl] n tourniquet m (d'entrée)

turntable ['tɜːnteɪbl] n (on record player) platine f

turn-up ['tɜːnʌp] n (Brit: on trousers) revers m

turpentine ['tɜːpəntaɪn] n (also: **turps**) (essence f de) térébenthine f

turquoise ['tɜːkwɔɪz] n (stone) turquoise f ▷ adj turquoise inv

turret ['tʌrɪt] n tourelle f

turtle ['tɜːtl] n tortue marine

turtleneck ['tɜːtlnɛk], **turtleneck sweater** n pullover m à col montant

tusk [tʌsk] n défense f (d'éléphant)

tutor ['tjuːtə'] n (Brit Scol: in college) directeur(-trice) d'études; (private teacher) précepteur(-trice)

tutorial [tjuːˈtɔːrɪəl] n (Scol) (séance f de) travaux mpl pratiques

tuxedo [tʌkˈsiːdəu] n (US) smoking m

TV [tiː'viː] *n abbr* (= *television*) télé *f*, TV *f*

twang [twæŋ] *n* (*of instrument*) son vibrant; (*of voice*) ton nasillard ▷ *vi* vibrer ▷ *vt* (*guitar*) pincer les cordes de

tweed [twiːd] *n* tweed *m*

tweet [twiːt] (*on Twitter*) *n* tweet *m* ▷ *vt* tweeter

tweezers [twiːzəz] *npl* pince *f* à épiler

twelfth [twɛlfθ] *num* douzième

twelve [twɛlv] *num* douze; **at ~ (o'clock)** à midi; (*midnight*) à minuit

twentieth [twɛntɪɪθ] *num* vingtième

twenty [twɛntɪ] *num* vingt

twice [twaɪs] *adv* deux fois; **~ as much** deux fois plus; **~ a week** deux fois par semaine; **she is ~ your age** elle a deux fois ton âge

twiddle [twɪdl] *vt, vi*: **to ~ (with) sth** tripoter qch; **to ~ one's thumbs** (*fig*) se tourner les pouces

twig [twɪg] *n* brindille *f* ▷ *vt, vi* (*inf*) piger

twilight [twaɪlaɪt] *n* crépuscule *m*; (*morning*) aube *f*; **in the ~** dans la pénombre

twin [twɪn] *adj, n* jumeau(-elle) ▷ *vt* jumeler

twin-bedded room [twɪn'bɛdɪd-] *n* = **twin room**

twin beds *npl* lits *mpl* jumeaux

twine [twaɪn] *n* ficelle *f* ▷ *vi* (*plant*) s'enrouler

twinge [twɪndʒ] *n* (*of pain*) élancement *m*; (*of conscience*) remords *m*

twinkle [twɪŋkl] *n* scintillement *m*; pétillement *m* ▷ *vi* scintiller; (*eyes*) pétiller

twin room *n* chambre *f* à deux lits

twirl [twəːl] *n* tournoiement *m* ▷ *vt* faire tournoyer ▷ *vi* tournoyer

twist [twɪst] *n* torsion *f*, tour *m*; (*in wire, flex*) tortillon *m*; (*bend: in road*) tournant *m*; (*in story*) coup *m* de théâtre ▷ *vt* tordre; (*weave*) entortiller; (*roll around*) enrouler; (*fig*) déformer ▷ *vi* s'entortiller; s'enrouler; (*road, river*) serpenter; **to ~ one's ankle/wrist** (*Med*) se tordre la cheville/le poignet

twit [twɪt] *n* (*inf*) crétin(e)

twitch [twɪtʃ] *n* (*pull*) coup sec, saccade *f*; (*nervous*) tic *m* ▷ *vi* se convulser; avoir un tic

two [tuː] *num* deux; **~ by ~, in ~s** par deux; **to put ~ and ~ together** (*fig*) faire le rapprochement

two-door [tuː'dɔː] *adj* (*Aut*) à deux portes

two-faced [tuː'feɪst] *adj* (*pej: person*) faux/ fausse

twofold [tuː'fəuld] *adv*: **to increase ~** doubler ▷ *adj* (*increase*) de cent pour cent; (*reply*) en deux parties

two-piece [tuː'piːs] *n* (*also: ~ suit*) (costume *m*) deux-pièces *m inv*; (*also: ~ swimsuit*) (maillot *m* de bain) deux-pièces

twosome [tuːsəm] *n* (*people*) couple *m*

two-way [tuː'weɪ] *adj* (*traffic*) dans les deux sens; **~ radio** émetteur-récepteur *m*

tycoon [taɪ'kuːn] *n*: **(business) ~** gros homme d'affaires

type [taɪp] *n* (*category*) genre *m*, espèce *f*; (*model*) modèle *m*; (*example*) type *m*; (*Typ*) type, caractère *m* ▷ *vt* (*letter etc*) taper (à la machine); **what ~ do you want?** quel genre voulez-vous?; **in bold/italic ~** en caractères gras/en italiques

typecast [taɪpkaːst] *adj* condamné(e) à toujours jouer le même rôle

typeface [taɪpfeɪs] *n* police *f* (de caractères)

typescript [taɪpskrɪpt] *n* texte dactylographié

typewriter [taɪpraɪtə] *n* machine *f* à écrire

typewritten [taɪprɪtn] *adj* dactylographié(e)

typhoid [taɪfɔɪd] *n* typhoïde *f*

typhoon [taɪ'fuːn] *n* typhon *m*

typical [tɪpɪkl] *adj* typique, caractéristique

typically [tɪpɪklɪ] *adv* (*as usual*) comme d'habitude; (*characteristically*) typiquement

typing [taɪpɪŋ] *n* dactylo(graphie) *f*

typist [taɪpɪst] *n* dactylo *m/f*

tyrant [taɪrənt] *n* tyran *m*

tyre, (*US*) **tire** [taɪə] *n* pneu *m*

tyre pressure *n* (*Brit*) pression *f* (de gonflage)

u

U-bend ['ʌlbɛnd] *n* (*Brit Aut*) coude *m*, virage *m* en épingle à cheveux; (*in pipe*) coude

ubiquitous [ju:'bɪkwɪtəs] *adj* doué(e) d'ubiquité, omniprésent(e)

udder ['ʌdər] *n* pis *m*, mamelle *f*

UFO ['ju:fəu] *n abbr* (= *unidentified flying object*) ovni *m*

Uganda [ju:'gændə] *n* Ouganda *m*

ugh [ə:h] *excl* pouah!

ugly ['ʌglɪ] *adj* laid(e), vilain(e); (*fig*) répugnant(e)

UHT *adj abbr* (= *ultra-heat treated*); **~ milk** lait *m* UHT *or* longue conservation

UK *n abbr* = **United Kingdom**

ulcer ['ʌlsər] *n* ulcère *m*; **mouth ~** aphte *f*

Ulster ['ʌlstər] *n* Ulster *m*

ulterior [ʌl'tɪərɪər] *adj* ultérieur(e); **~ motive** arrière-pensée *f*

ultimate ['ʌltɪmət] *adj* ultime, final(e); (*authority*) suprême ▷ *n*: **the ~ in luxury** le summum du luxe

ultimately ['ʌltɪmətlɪ] *adv* (*at last*) en fin de compte; (*fundamentally*) finalement; (*eventually*) par la suite

ultimatum (*pl* **ultimatums** *or* **ultimata**) [ʌltɪ'meɪtəm, -tə] *n* ultimatum *m*

ultrasound ['ʌltrəsaund] *n* (*Med*) ultrason *m*

ultraviolet ['ʌltrə'vaɪəlɪt] *adj* ultraviolet(te)

umbilical [ʌmbɪ'laɪkl] *adj*: **~ cord** cordon ombilical

umbrella [ʌm'brɛlə] *n* parapluie *m*; (*for sun*) parasol *m*; (*fig*): **under the ~ of** sous les auspices de; chapeauté(e) par

umpire ['ʌmpaɪər] *n* arbitre *m*; (*Tennis*) juge *m* de chaise ▷ *vt* arbitrer

umpteen [ʌmp'ti:n] *adj* je ne sais combien de; **for the umpteeth time** pour la nième fois

UN *n abbr* = **United Nations**

unable [ʌn'eɪbl] *adj*: **to be ~ to** ne (pas) pouvoir, être dans l'impossibilité de; (*not capable*) être incapable de

unacceptable [ʌnək'sɛptəbl] *adj* (*behaviour*) inadmissible; (*price, proposal*) inacceptable

unaccompanied [ʌnə'kʌmpənɪd] *adj* (*child, lady*) non accompagné(e); (*singing, song*) sans accompagnement

unaccustomed [ʌnə'kʌstəmd] *adj* inaccoutumé(e), inhabituel(le); **to be ~ to sth** ne pas avoir l'habitude de qch

unanimous [ju:'nænɪməs] *adj* unanime

unanimously [ju:'nænɪməslɪ] *adv* à l'unanimité

unarmed [ʌn'ɑ:md] *adj* (*person*) non armé(e); (*combat*) sans armes

unattached [ʌnə'tætʃt] *adj* libre, sans attaches

unattended [ʌnə'tɛndɪd] *adj* (*car, child, luggage*) sans surveillance

unattractive [ʌnə'træktɪv] *adj* peu attrayant(e); (*character*) peu sympathique

unauthorized [ʌn'ɔ:θəraɪzd] *adj* non autorisé(e), sans autorisation

unavailable [ʌnə'veɪləbl] *adj* (*article, room, book*) (qui n'est) pas disponible; (*person*) (qui n'est) pas libre

unavoidable [ʌnə'vɔɪdəbl] *adj* inévitable

unaware [ʌnə'wɛər] *adj*: **to be ~ of** ignorer, ne pas savoir, être inconscient(e) de

unawares [ʌnə'wɛəz] *adv* à l'improviste, au dépourvu

unbalanced [ʌn'bælənst] *adj* déséquilibré(e)

unbearable [ʌn'bɛərəbl] *adj* insupportable

unbeatable [ʌn'bi:təbl] *adj* imbattable

unbeknown [ʌnbɪ'nəun], **unbeknownst** [ʌnbɪ'nəunst] *adv*: **~ to** à l'insu de

unbelievable [ʌnbɪ'li:vəbl] *adj* incroyable

unbend [ʌn'bɛnd] (*irreg like*: **bend**) *vi* se détendre ▷ *vt* (*wire*) redresser, détordre

unbiased, unbiassed [ʌn'baɪəst] *adj* impartial(e)

unborn [ʌn'bɔ:n] *adj* à naître

unbreakable [ʌn'breɪkəbl] *adj* incassable

unbroken [ʌn'brəukn] *adj* intact(e); (*line*) continu(e); (*record*) non battu(e)

unbutton [ʌn'bʌtn] *vt* déboutonner

uncalled-for [ʌn'kɔ:ldfɔ:ʳ] *adj* déplacé(e), injustifié(e)

uncanny [ʌn'kænɪ] *adj* étrange, troublant(e)

unceremonious [ʌnsɛrɪ'məunɪəs] *adj* (*abrupt, rude*) brusque

uncertain [ʌn'sə:tn] *adj* incertain(e); (*hesitant*) hésitant(e); **we were ~ whether ...** nous ne savions pas vraiment si ...; **in no ~ terms** sans équivoque possible

uncertainty [ʌn'sɜːtnti] n incertitude f, doutes mpl

unchanged [ʌn'tʃeɪndʒd] adj inchangé(e)

uncivilized [ʌn'sɪvɪlaɪzd] adj non civilisé(e); (fig) barbare

uncle ['ʌŋkl] n oncle m

unclear [ʌn'klɪəʳ] adj (qui n'est) pas clair(e) or évident(e); **I'm still ~ about what I'm supposed to do** je ne sais pas encore exactement ce que je dois faire

uncomfortable [ʌn'kʌmfətəbl] adj inconfortable, peu confortable; (uneasy) mal à l'aise, gêné(e); (situation) désagréable

uncommon [ʌn'kɔmən] adj rare, singulier(-ière), peu commun(e)

uncompromising [ʌn'kɔmprəmaɪzɪŋ] adj intransigeant(e), inflexible

unconcerned [ʌnkən'sɜːnd] adj (unworried): **to be ~ (about)** ne pas s'inquiéter (de)

unconditional [ʌnkən'dɪʃənl] adj sans conditions

unconscious [ʌn'kɔnʃəs] adj sans connaissance, évanoui(e); (unaware): **~ (of)** inconscient(e) (de) ▷ n: **the ~** l'inconscient m; **to knock sb ~** assommer qn

unconsciously [ʌn'kɔnʃəslɪ] adv inconsciemment

uncontrollable [ʌnkən'trəʊləbl] adj (child, dog) indiscipliné(e); (temper, laughter) irrépressible

unconventional [ʌnkən'vɛnʃənl] adj peu conventionnel(le)

uncouth [ʌn'kuːθ] adj grossier(-ière), fruste

uncover [ʌn'kʌvəʳ] vt découvrir

undecided [ʌndɪ'saɪdɪd] adj indécis(e), irrésolu(e)

undeniable [ʌndɪ'naɪəbl] adj indéniable, incontestable

under ['ʌndəʳ] prep sous; (less than) (de) moins de; au-dessous de; (according to) selon, en vertu de ▷ adv au-dessous; en dessous; **from ~ sth** de dessous or de sous qch; **~ there** là-dessous; **in ~ 2 hours** en moins de 2 heures; **~ anaesthetic** sous anesthésie; **~ discussion** en discussion; **~ the circumstances** étant donné les circonstances; **~ repair** en (cours de) réparation

underage [ʌndər'eɪdʒ] adj qui n'a pas l'âge réglementaire

undercarriage ['ʌndəkærɪdʒ] n (Brit Aviat) train m d'atterrissage

undercharge [ʌndə'tʃɑːdʒ] vt ne pas faire payer assez à

undercoat ['ʌndəkəʊt] n (paint) couche f de fond

undercover [ʌndə'kʌvəʳ] adj secret(-ète), clandestin(e)

undercurrent ['ʌndəkʌrnt] n courant sous-jacent

undercut [ʌndə'kʌt] vt (irreg like: cut) vendre moins cher que

underdog ['ʌndədɔg] n opprimé m

underdone [ʌndə'dʌn] adj (Culin) saignant(e); (: pej) pas assez cuit(e)

underestimate ['ʌndər'ɛstɪmeɪt] vt sous-estimer, mésestimer

underfed [ʌndə'fɛd] adj sous-alimenté(e)

underfoot [ʌndə'fut] adv sous les pieds

undergo [ʌndə'gəʊ] vt (irreg like: go) subir; (treatment) suivre; **the car is ~ing repairs** la voiture est en réparation

undergraduate [ʌndə'grædjuɪt] n étudiant(e) (qui prépare la licence) ▷ cpd: **~ courses** cours mpl préparant à la licence

underground ['ʌndəgraund] adj souterrain(e); (fig) clandestin(e) ▷ n (Brit: railway) métro m; (Pol) clandestinité f

undergrowth ['ʌndəgrəʊθ] n broussailles fpl, sous-bois m

underhand [ʌndə'hænd], **underhanded** [ʌndə'hændɪd] adj (fig) sournois(e), en dessous

underlie [ʌndə'laɪ] vt (irreg like: lie) être à la base de; **the underlying cause** la cause sous-jacente

underline [ʌndə'laɪn] vt souligner

undermine [ʌndə'maɪn] vt saper, miner

underneath [ʌndə'niːθ] adv (en) dessous ▷ prep sous, au-dessous de

underpaid [ʌndə'peɪd] adj sous-payé(e)

underpants ['ʌndəpænts] npl caleçon m, slip m

underpass ['ʌndəpɑːs] n (Brit: for pedestrians) passage souterrain; (: for cars) passage inférieur

underprivileged [ʌndə'prɪvɪlɪdʒd] adj défavorisé(e)

underrate [ʌndə'reɪt] vt sous-estimer, mésestimer

underscore [ʌndə'skɔːʳ] vt souligner

undershirt ['ʌndəʃɜːt] n (US) tricot m de corps

undershorts ['ʌndəʃɔːts] npl (US) caleçon m, slip m

underside ['ʌndəsaɪd] n dessous m

underskirt ['ʌndəskɜːt] n (Brit) jupon m

understand [ʌndə'stænd] vt, vi (irreg like: stand) comprendre; **I don't ~** je ne comprends pas; **I ~ that ...** je me suis laissé dire que ..., je crois comprendre que ...; **to make o.s. understood** se faire comprendre

understandable [ʌndə'stændəbl] adj compréhensible

understanding [ʌndə'stændɪŋ] adj compréhensif(-ive) ▷ n compréhension f; (agreement) accord m; **to come to an ~ with sb** s'entendre avec qn; **on the ~ that ...** à condition que ...

understatement ['ʌndəsteɪtmənt] n: **that's an ~** c'est (bien) peu dire, le terme est faible

understood [ʌndə'stud] pt, pp of **understand** ▷ adj entendu(e); (implied) sous-entendu(e)

understudy ['ʌndəstʌdɪ] n doublure f

undertake [ʌndə'teɪk] vt (irreg like: take) (job,

task) entreprendre; (*duty*) se charger de; **to ~ to do sth** s'engager à faire qch

undertaker ['ʌndəteɪkə'] *n* (*Brit*) entrepreneur *m* des pompes funèbres, croque-mort *m*

undertaking ['ʌndəteɪkɪŋ] *n* entreprise *f*; (*promise*) promesse *f*

undertone ['ʌndətəʊn] *n* (*low voice*): **in an ~** à mi-voix; (*of criticism etc*) nuance cachée

underwater [ʌndə'wɔːtə'] *adv* sous l'eau ▷ *adj* sous-marin(e)

underway [ʌndə'weɪ] *adj*: **to be ~** (*meeting, investigation*) être en cours

underwear ['ʌndəweə'] *n* sous-vêtements *mpl*; (*women's only*) dessous *mpl*

underwent [ʌndə'went] *pt of* **undergo**

underworld ['ʌndəwə:ld] *n* (*of crime*) milieu *m*, pègre *f*

underwrite [ʌndə'raɪt] *vt* (*Finance*) garantir; (*Insurance*) souscrire

undesirable [ʌndɪ'zaɪərəbl] *adj* peu souhaitable; (*person, effect*) indésirable

undies ['ʌndɪz] *npl* (*inf*) dessous *mpl*, lingerie *f*

undiplomatic ['ʌndɪplə'mætɪk] *adj* peu diplomatique, maladroit(e)

undisputed ['ʌndɪs'pjuːtɪd] *adj* incontesté(e)

undo [ʌn'duː] *vt* (*irreg like*: **do**) défaire

undoing [ʌn'duːɪŋ] *n* ruine *f*, perte *f*

undone [ʌn'dʌn] *pp of* **undo** ▷ *adj*: **to come ~** se défaire

undoubted [ʌn'dautɪd] *adj* indubitable, certain(e)

undoubtedly [ʌn'dautɪdlɪ] *adv* sans aucun doute

undress [ʌn'dres] *vi* se déshabiller ▷ *vt* déshabiller

undue [ʌn'djuː] *adj* indu(e), excessif(-ive)

undulating ['ʌndjuleɪtɪŋ] *adj* ondoyant(e), onduleux(-euse)

unduly [ʌn'djuːlɪ] *adv* trop, excessivement

unearth [ʌn'ə:θ] *vt* déterrer; (*fig*) dénicher

unearthly [ʌn'ə:θlɪ] *adj* surnaturel(le); (*hour*) indu(e), impossible

uneasy [ʌn'iːzɪ] *adj* mal à l'aise, gêné(e); (*worried*) inquiet(-ète); (*feeling*) désagréable; (*peace, truce*) fragile; **to feel ~ about doing sth** se sentir mal à l'aise à l'idée de faire qch

uneconomic ['ʌniːkə'nɔmɪk],

uneconomical ['ʌniːkə'nɔmɪkl] *adj* peu économique; peu rentable

uneducated [ʌn'edjukeɪtɪd] *adj* sans éducation

unemployed [ʌnɪm'plɔɪd] *adj* sans travail, au chômage ▷ *n*: **the ~** les chômeurs *mpl*

unemployment [ʌnɪm'plɔɪmənt] *n* chômage *m*

unemployment benefit, (*US*) **unemployment compensation** *n* allocation *f* de chômage

unending [ʌn'endɪŋ] *adj* interminable

unequal [ʌn'iːkwəl] *adj* inégal(e)

unerring [ʌn'ə:rɪŋ] *adj* infaillible, sûr(e)

uneven [ʌn'iːvn] *adj* inégal(e); (*quality, work*) irrégulier(-ière)

unexpected [ʌnɪk'spektɪd] *adj* inattendu(e), imprévu(e)

unexpectedly [ʌnɪk'spektɪdlɪ] *adv* (*succeed*) contre toute attente; (*arrive*) à l'improviste

unfailing [ʌn'feɪlɪŋ] *adj* inépuisable; infaillible

unfair [ʌn'feə'] *adj*: **~ (to)** injuste (envers); **it's ~ that ...** il n'est pas juste que ...

unfaithful [ʌn'feɪθful] *adj* infidèle

unfamiliar [ʌnfə'mɪliə'] *adj* étrange, inconnu(e); **to be ~ with sth** mal connaître qch

unfashionable [ʌn'fæʃnəbl] *adj* (*clothes*) démodé(e); (*place*) peu chic *inv*; (*district*) déshérité(e), pas à la mode

unfasten [ʌn'fɑːsn] *vt* défaire; (*belt, necklace*) détacher; (*open*) ouvrir

unfavourable, (*US*) **unfavorable** [ʌn'feɪvrəbl] *adj* défavorable

unfeeling [ʌn'fiːlɪŋ] *adj* insensible, dur(e)

unfinished [ʌn'fɪnɪʃt] *adj* inachevé(e)

unfit [ʌn'fɪt] *adj* (*physically*: *ill*) en mauvaise santé; (: *out of condition*) pas en forme; (*incompetent*): **~ (for)** impropre (à); (*work, service*) inapte (à)

unfold [ʌn'fəʊld] *vt* déplier; (*fig*) révéler, exposer ▷ *vi* se dérouler

unforeseen ['ʌnfɔː'siːn] *adj* imprévu(e)

unforgettable [ʌnfə'getəbl] *adj* inoubliable

unfortunate [ʌn'fɔːtʃnət] *adj* malheureux(-euse); (*event, remark*) malencontreux(-euse)

unfortunately [ʌn'fɔːtʃnətlɪ] *adv* malheureusement

unfounded [ʌn'faundɪd] *adj* sans fondement

unfriendly [ʌn'frendlɪ] *adj* peu aimable, froid(e), inamical(e)

unfurnished [ʌn'fə:nɪʃt] *adj* non meublé(e)

ungainly [ʌn'geɪnlɪ] *adj* gauche, dégingandé(e)

ungodly [ʌn'gɔdlɪ] *adj* impie; **at an ~ hour** à une heure indue

ungrateful [ʌn'greɪtful] *adj* qui manque de reconnaissance, ingrat(e)

unhappiness [ʌn'hæpɪnɪs] *n* tristesse *f*, peine *f*

unhappy [ʌn'hæpɪ] *adj* triste, malheureux(-euse); (*unfortunate*: *remark etc*) malheureux(-euse); (*not pleased*): **~ with** mécontent(e) de, peu satisfait(e) de

unharmed [ʌn'hɑːmd] *adj* indemne, sain(e) et sauf/sauve

UNHCR *n abbr* (= *United Nations High Commission for Refugees*) HCR *m*

unhealthy [ʌn'helθɪ] *adj* (*gen*) malsain(e); (*person*) maladif(-ive)

unheard-of [ʌn'hə:dɔv] *adj* inouï(e), sans précédent

unhelpful [ʌn'helpful] *adj* (*person*) peu serviable; (*advice*) peu utile

u

unhurt [ʌn'hɜːt] *adj* indemne, sain(e) et sauf/sauve

unidentified [ʌnaɪ'dɛntɪfaɪd] *adj* non identifié(e); *see also* **UFO**

uniform ['juːnɪfɔːm] *n* uniforme *m* ▷ *adj* uniforme

unify ['juːnɪfaɪ] *vt* unifier

unimportant [ʌnɪm'pɔːtənt] *adj* sans importance

uninhabited [ʌnɪn'hæbɪtɪd] *adj* inhabité(e)

unintentional [ʌnɪn'tɛnʃənəl] *adj* involontaire

union ['juːnjən] *n* union *f*; (*also*: **trade ~**) syndicat *m* ▷ *cpd* du syndicat, syndical(e)

Union Jack *n* drapeau *du Royaume-Uni*

unique [juː'niːk] *adj* unique

unisex ['juːnɪsɛks] *adj* unisexe

unison ['juːnɪsn] *n*: **in ~** à l'unisson, en chœur

unit ['juːnɪt] *n* unité *f*; (*section: of furniture etc*) élément *m*, bloc *m*; (*team, squad*) groupe *m*, service *m*; **production ~** atelier *m* de fabrication; **kitchen ~** élément de cuisine; **sink ~** bloc-évier *m*

unite [juː'naɪt] *vt* unir ▷ *vi* s'unir

united [juː'naɪtɪd] *adj* uni(e); (*country, party*) unifié(e); (*efforts*) conjugué(e)

United Kingdom *n* Royaume-Uni *m*

United Nations, United Nations Organization *n* (Organisation *f* des) Nations unies

United States, United States of America *n* États-Unis *mpl*

unit trust *n* (Brit Comm) fonds commun de placement, FCP *m*

unity ['juːnɪtɪ] *n* unité *f*

universal [juːnɪ'vɜːsl] *adj* universel(le)

universe ['juːnɪvɜːs] *n* univers *m*

university [juːnɪ'vɜːsɪtɪ] *n* université *f* ▷ *cpd* (*student, professor*) d'université; (*education, year, degree*) universitaire

unjust [ʌn'dʒʌst] *adj* injuste

unkempt [ʌn'kɛmpt] *adj* mal tenu(e), débraillé(e); mal peigné(e)

unkind [ʌn'kaɪnd] *adj* peu gentil(le), méchant(e)

unknown [ʌn'nəun] *adj* inconnu(e); **~ to me** sans que je le sache; **~ quantity** (Math, fig) inconnue *f*

unlawful [ʌn'lɔːful] *adj* illégal(e)

unleaded [ʌn'lɛdɪd] *n* (*also*: **~ petrol**) essence *f* sans plomb

unleash [ʌn'liːʃ] *vt* détacher; (*fig*) déchaîner, déclencher

unless [ʌn'lɛs] *conj*: **~ he leaves** à moins qu'il (ne) parte; **~ we leave** à moins de partir, à moins que nous (ne) partions; **~ otherwise stated** sauf indication contraire; **~ I am mistaken** si je ne me trompe

unlike [ʌn'laɪk] *adj* dissemblable, différent(e) ▷ *prep* à la différence de, contrairement à

unlikely [ʌn'laɪklɪ] *adj* (*result, event*) improbable; (*explanation*) invraisemblable

unlimited [ʌn'lɪmɪtɪd] *adj* illimité(e)

unlisted ['ʌn'lɪstɪd] *adj* (US Tel) sur la liste rouge; (Stock Exchange) non coté(e) en Bourse

unload [ʌn'ləud] *vt* décharger

unlock [ʌn'lɔk] *vt* ouvrir

unlucky [ʌn'lʌkɪ] *adj* (*person*) malchanceux(-euse); (*object, number*) qui porte malheur; **to be ~** (*person*) ne pas avoir de chance

unmarried [ʌn'mærɪd] *adj* célibataire

unmistakable, unmistakeable [ʌnmɪs'teɪkəbl] *adj* indubitable; qu'on ne peut pas ne pas reconnaître

unmitigated [ʌn'mɪtɪɡeɪtɪd] *adj* non mitigé(e), absolu(e), pur(e)

unnatural [ʌn'nætʃrəl] *adj* non naturel(le); (*perversion*) contre nature

unnecessary [ʌn'nɛsəsərɪ] *adj* inutile, superflu(e)

unnoticed [ʌn'nəutɪst] *adj* inaperçu(e); **to go ~** passer inaperçu

UNO ['juːnəu] *n abbr* = **United Nations Organization**

unobtainable [ʌnəb'teɪnəbl] *adj* (Tel) impossible à obtenir

unobtrusive [ʌnəb'truːsɪv] *adj* discret(-ète)

unofficial [ʌnə'fɪʃl] *adj* (*news*) officieux(-euse), non officiel(le); (*strike*) ≈ sauvage

unorthodox [ʌn'ɔːθədɔks] *adj* peu orthodoxe

unpack [ʌn'pæk] *vi* défaire sa valise, déballer ses affaires ▷ *vt* (*suitcase*) défaire; (*belongings*) déballer

unpaid [ʌn'peɪd] *adj* (*bill*) impayé(e); (*holiday*) non-payé(e), sans salaire; (*work*) non rétribué(e); (*worker*) bénévole

unpalatable [ʌn'pælətəbl] *adj* (*truth*) désagréable (à entendre)

unparalleled [ʌn'pærəlɛld] *adj* incomparable, sans égal

unpleasant [ʌn'plɛznt] *adj* déplaisant(e), désagréable

unplug [ʌn'plʌɡ] *vt* débrancher

unpopular [ʌn'pɔpjulə*] *adj* impopulaire; **to make o.s. ~ (with)** se rendre impopulaire (auprès de)

unprecedented [ʌn'prɛsɪdɛntɪd] *adj* sans précédent

unpredictable [ʌnprɪ'dɪktəbl] *adj* imprévisible

unprofessional [ʌnprə'fɛʃənl] *adj* (*conduct*) contraire à la déontologie

UNPROFOR [ʌn'prəufɔː*] *n abbr* (= United Nations Protection Force) FORPRONU *f*

unprotected ['ʌnprə'tɛktɪd] *adj* (*sex*) non protégé(e)

unqualified [ʌn'kwɔlɪfaɪd] *adj* (*teacher*) non diplômé(e), sans titres; (*success*) sans réserve, total(e); (*disaster*) total(e)

unquestionably [ʌn'kwɛstʃənəblɪ] *adv* incontestablement

unravel [ʌn'rævl] *vt* démêler

unreal [ʌnˈrɪəl] *adj* irréel(le); (*extraordinary*) incroyable

unrealistic [ˈʌnrɪəˈlɪstɪk] *adj* (*idea*) irréaliste; (*estimate*) peu réaliste

unreasonable [ʌnˈriːznəbl] *adj* qui n'est pas raisonnable; **to make ~ demands on sb** exiger trop de qn

unrelated [ʌnrɪˈleɪtɪd] *adj* sans rapport; (*people*) sans lien de parenté

unreliable [ʌnrɪˈlaɪəbl] *adj* sur qui (*or* quoi) on ne peut pas compter, peu fiable

unremitting [ʌnrɪˈmɪtɪŋ] *adj* inlassable, infatigable, acharné(e)

unreservedly [ʌnrɪˈzəːvɪdlɪ] *adv* sans réserve

unrest [ʌnˈrest] *n* agitation *f*, troubles *mpl*

unroll [ʌnˈrəʊl] *vt* dérouler

unruly [ʌnˈruːlɪ] *adj* indiscipliné(e)

unsafe [ʌnˈseɪf] *adj* (*in danger*) en danger; (*journey, car*) dangereux(-euse); (*method*) hasardeux(-euse); **~ to drink/eat** non potable/comestible

unsaid [ʌnˈsed] *adj*: **to leave sth ~** passer qch sous silence

unsatisfactory [ˈʌnsætɪsˈfæktərɪ] *adj* peu satisfaisant(e), qui laisse à désirer

unsavoury, (*US*) **unsavory** [ʌnˈseɪvərɪ] *adj* (*fig*) peu recommandable, répugnant(e)

unscathed [ʌnˈskeɪðd] *adj* indemne

unscrew [ʌnˈskruː] *vt* dévisser

unscrupulous [ʌnˈskruːpjuləs] *adj* sans scrupules

unsettled [ʌnˈsetld] *adj* (*restless*) perturbé(e); (*unpredictable*) instable; incertain(e); (*not finalized*) non résolu(e)

unsettling [ʌnˈsetlɪŋ] *adj* qui a un effet perturbateur

unshaven [ʌnˈʃeɪvn] *adj* non *or* mal rasé(e)

unsightly [ʌnˈsaɪtlɪ] *adj* disgracieux(-euse), laid(e)

unskilled [ʌnˈskɪld] *adj*: **~ worker** manœuvre *m*

unspeakable [ʌnˈspiːkəbl] *adj* indicible; (*awful*) innommable

unspoiled [ˈʌnˈspɔɪld], **unspoilt** [ˈʌnˈspɔɪlt] *adj* (*place*) non dégradé(e)

unstable [ʌnˈsteɪbl] *adj* instable

unsteady [ʌnˈstedɪ] *adj* mal assuré(e), chancelant(e), instable

unstuck [ʌnˈstʌk] *adj*: **to come ~** se décoller; (*fig*) faire fiasco

unsuccessful [ʌnsəkˈsesful] *adj* (*attempt*) infructueux(-euse); (*writer, proposal*) qui n'a pas de succès; (*marriage*) malheureux(-euse), qui ne réussit pas; **to be ~** (*in attempting sth*) ne pas réussir; ne pas avoir de succès; (*application*) ne pas être retenu(e)

unsuitable [ʌnˈsuːtəbl] *adj* qui ne convient pas, peu approprié(e); (*time*) inopportun(e)

unsure [ʌnˈʃʊər] *adj* pas sûr(e); **to be ~ of o.s.** ne pas être sûr de soi, manquer de confiance en soi

unsuspecting [ʌnsəˈspektɪŋ] *adj* qui ne se méfie pas

unsympathetic [ˈʌnsɪmpəˈθetɪk] *adj* hostile; (*unpleasant*) antipathique; **~ to** indifférent(e) à

untapped [ʌnˈtæpt] *adj* (*resources*) inexploité(e)

unthinkable [ʌnˈθɪŋkəbl] *adj* impensable, inconcevable

untidy [ʌnˈtaɪdɪ] *adj* (*room*) en désordre; (*appearance, person*) débraillé(e); (*person: in character*) sans ordre, désordonné; débraillé; (*work*) peu soigné(e)

untie [ʌnˈtaɪ] *vt* (*knot, parcel*) défaire; (*prisoner, dog*) détacher

until [ənˈtɪl] *prep* jusqu'à; (*after negative*) avant ▷ *conj* jusqu'à ce que + *sub*, en attendant que + *sub*; (*in past, after negative*) avant que + *sub*; **~ he comes** jusqu'à ce qu'il vienne, jusqu'à son arrivée; **~ now** jusqu'à présent, jusqu'ici; **~ then** jusque-là; **from morning ~ night** du matin au soir *or* jusqu'au soir

untimely [ʌnˈtaɪmlɪ] *adj* inopportun(e); (*death*) prématuré(e)

untold [ʌnˈtəʊld] *adj* incalculable; indescriptible

untoward [ʌntəˈwɔːd] *adj* fâcheux(-euse), malencontreux(-euse)

untrue [ʌnˈtruː] *adj* (*statement*) faux/fausse

unused[1] [ʌnˈjuːzd] *adj* (*new*) neuf/neuve

unused[2] [ʌnˈjuːst] *adj*: **to be ~ to sth/to doing sth** ne pas avoir l'habitude de qch/de faire qch

unusual [ʌnˈjuːʒuəl] *adj* insolite, exceptionnel(le), rare

unusually [ʌnˈjuːʒuəlɪ] *adv* exceptionnellement, particulièrement

unveil [ʌnˈveɪl] *vt* dévoiler

unwanted [ʌnˈwɒntɪd] *adj* (*child, pregnancy*) non désiré(e); (*clothes etc*) à donner

unwelcome [ʌnˈwelkəm] *adj* importun(e); **to feel ~** se sentir de trop

unwell [ʌnˈwel] *adj* indisposé(e), souffrant(e); **to feel ~** ne pas se sentir bien

unwieldy [ʌnˈwiːldɪ] *adj* difficile à manier

unwilling [ʌnˈwɪlɪŋ] *adj*: **to be ~ to do** ne pas vouloir faire

unwillingly [ʌnˈwɪlɪŋlɪ] *adv* à contrecœur, contre son gré

unwind [ʌnˈwaɪnd] (*irreg like*: **wind**) *vt* dérouler ▷ *vi* (*relax*) se détendre

unwise [ʌnˈwaɪz] *adj* imprudent(e), peu judicieux(-euse)

unwitting [ʌnˈwɪtɪŋ] *adj* involontaire

unwittingly [ʌnˈwɪtɪŋlɪ] *adv* involontairement

unworkable [ʌnˈwəːkəbl] *adj* (*plan etc*) inexploitable

unworthy [ʌnˈwəːðɪ] *adj* indigne

unwrap [ʌnˈræp] *vt* défaire; ouvrir

unwritten [ʌnˈrɪtn] *adj* (*agreement*) tacite

unzip [ʌnˈzɪp] *vt* ouvrir (la fermeture éclair de); (*Comput*) dézipper

u

KEYWORD

up [ʌp] *prep*: **he went up the stairs/the hill** il a monté l'escalier/la colline; **the cat was up a tree** le chat était dans un arbre; **they live further up the street** ils habitent plus haut dans la rue; **go up that road and turn left** remontez la rue et tournez à gauche
▷ *vi* (*inf*): **she upped and left** elle a fichu le camp sans plus attendre
▷ *adv* **1** en haut; en l'air; (*upwards, higher*): **up in the sky/the mountains** (là-haut) dans le ciel/les montagnes; **put it a bit higher up** mettez-le un peu plus haut; **to stand up** (*get up*) se lever, se mettre debout; (*be standing*) être debout; **up there** là-haut; **up above** au-dessus; **"this side up"** "haut"
2: **to be up** (*out of bed*) être levé(e); (*prices*) avoir augmenté or monté; (*finished*): **when the year was up** à la fin de l'année; **time's up** c'est l'heure
3: **up to** (*as far as*) jusqu'à; **up to now** jusqu'à présent
4: **to be up to** (*depending on*): **it's up to you** c'est à vous de décider; (*equal to*): **he's not up to it** (*job, task etc*) il n'en est pas capable; (*inf: be doing*): **what is he up to?** qu'est-ce qu'il peut bien faire?
5 (*phrases*): **he's well up in** or **on …** (*Brit: knowledgeable*) il s'y connaît en …; **up with Leeds United!** vive Leeds United!; **what's up?** (*inf*) qu'est-ce qui ne va pas?; **what's up with him?** (*inf*) qu'est-ce qui lui arrive?
▷ *n*: **ups and downs** hauts et bas *mpl*

up-and-coming [ʌpənd'kʌmɪŋ] *adj* plein(e) d'avenir *or* de promesses
upbringing ['ʌpbrɪŋɪŋ] *n* éducation *f*
update [ʌp'deɪt] *vt* mettre à jour
upfront [ʌp'frʌnt] *adj* (*open*) franc/franche ▷ *adv* (*pay*) d'avance; **to be ~ about sth** ne rien cacher de qch
upgrade [ʌp'greɪd] *vt* (*person*) promouvoir; (*job*) revaloriser; (*property, equipment*) moderniser
upheaval [ʌp'hiːvl] *n* bouleversement *m*; (*in room*) branle-bas *m*; (*event*) crise *f*
uphill [ʌp'hɪl] *adj* qui monte; (*fig: task*) difficile, pénible ▷ *adv* (*face, look*) en amont, vers l'amont; (*go, move*) vers le haut, en haut; **to go ~** monter
uphold [ʌp'həʊld] *vt* (*irreg like:* **hold**) maintenir; soutenir
upholstery [ʌp'həʊlstəri] *n* rembourrage *m*; (*cover*) tissu *m* d'ameublement; (*of car*) garniture *f*
upkeep ['ʌpkiːp] *n* entretien *m*
upmarket [ʌp'maːkɪt] *adj* (*product*) haut de gamme *inv*; (*area*) chic *inv*
upon [ə'pɔn] *prep* sur
upper ['ʌpəʳ] *adj* supérieur(e); du dessus ▷ *n* (*of shoe*) empeigne *f*

upper class *n*: **the ~** ≈ la haute bourgeoisie
upper-class [ʌpə'klɑːs] *adj* de la haute société, aristocratique; (*district*) élégant(e), huppé(e); (*accent, attitude*) caractéristique des classes supérieures
upper hand *n*: **to have the ~** avoir le dessus
uppermost ['ʌpəməʊst] *adj* le/la plus haut(e), en dessus; **it was ~ in my mind** j'y pensais avant tout autre chose
upper sixth *n* terminale *f*
upright ['ʌpraɪt] *adj* droit(e); (*fig*) droit, honnête ▷ *n* montant *m*
uprising ['ʌpraɪzɪŋ] *n* soulèvement *m*, insurrection *f*
uproar ['ʌprɔːʳ] *n* tumulte *m*, vacarme *m*; (*protests*) protestations *fpl*
uproot [ʌp'ruːt] *vt* déraciner
upset *n* ['ʌpset] dérangement *m* ▷ *vt* [ʌp'set] (*irreg like:* **set**) (*glass etc*) renverser; (*plan*) déranger; (*person: offend*) contrarier; (*: grieve*) faire de la peine à; bouleverser ▷ *adj* [ʌp'set] contrarié(e); peiné(e); (*stomach*) détraqué(e), dérangé(e); **to get ~** (*sad*) devenir triste; (*offended*) se vexer; **to have a stomach ~** (*Brit*) avoir une indigestion
upshot ['ʌpʃɔt] *n* résultat *m*; **the ~ of it all was that …** il a résulté de tout cela que …
upside down ['ʌpsaɪd-] *adv* à l'envers; **to turn sth ~** (*fig: place*) mettre sens dessus dessous
upstairs [ʌp'steəz] *adv* en haut ▷ *adj* (*room*) du dessus, d'en haut ▷ *n*: **the ~** l'étage *m*; **there's no ~** il n'y a pas d'étage
upstart ['ʌpstɑːt] *n* parvenu(e)
upstream [ʌp'striːm] *adv* en amont
uptake ['ʌpteɪk] *n*: **he is quick/slow on the ~** il comprend vite/est lent à comprendre
uptight [ʌp'taɪt] *adj* (*inf*) très tendu(e), crispé(e)
up-to-date ['ʌptə'deɪt] *adj* moderne; (*information*) très récent(e)
upturn ['ʌptəːn] *n* (*in economy*) reprise *f*
upward ['ʌpwəd] *adj* ascendant(e); vers le haut ▷ *adv* vers le haut; (*more than*): **~ of** plus de; **and ~** et plus, et au-dessus
upwards ['ʌpwədz] *adv* vers le haut; (*more than*): **~ of** plus de; **and ~** et plus, et au-dessus
uranium [juə'reɪnɪəm] *n* uranium *m*
Uranus [juə'reɪnəs] *n* Uranus *f*
urban ['əːbən] *adj* urbain(e)
urban clearway *n* rue *f* à stationnement interdit
urbane [əː'beɪn] *adj* urbain(e), courtois(e)
urchin ['əːtʃɪn] *n* gosse *m*, garnement *m*
urge [əːdʒ] *n* besoin (impératif), envie (pressante) ▷ *vt* (*caution etc*) recommander avec insistance; (*person*): **to ~ sb to do** exhorter qn à faire, pousser qn à faire, recommander vivement à qn de faire; **urge on** *vt* pousser, presser
urgency ['əːdʒənsi] *n* urgence *f*; (*of tone*) insistance *f*

urgent ['ə:dʒənt] *adj* urgent(e); (*plea, tone*) pressant(e)

urinal ['juərınl] *n* (Brit: *place*) urinoir *m*

urinate ['juərıneıt] *vi* uriner

urine ['juərın] *n* urine *f*

URL *abbr* (= *uniform resource locator*) URL *f*

urn [ə:n] *n* urne *f*; (*also:* **tea ~**) fontaine *f* à thé

US *n abbr* = **United States**

us [ʌs] *pron* nous; *see also* **me**

USA *n abbr* = **United States of America**; (*Mil*) = **United States Army**

USB stick *n* clé *f* USB

use *n* [ju:s] emploi *m*, utilisation *f*; usage *m*; (*usefulness*) utilité *f* ▷ *vt* [ju:z] se servir de, utiliser, employer; **in ~** en usage; **out of ~** hors d'usage; **to be of ~** servir, être utile; **to make ~ of sth** utiliser qch; **ready for ~** prêt à l'emploi; **it's no ~** ça ne sert à rien; **to have the ~ of** avoir l'usage de; **what's this ~d for?** à quoi est-ce que ça sert?; **she ~d to do it** elle le faisait (autrefois), elle avait coutume de le faire; **to be ~d to** avoir l'habitude de, être habitué(e) à; **to get ~d to** s'habituer à; **use up** *vt* finir, épuiser; (*food*) consommer

used [ju:zd] *adj* (*car*) d'occasion

useful ['ju:sful] *adj* utile; **to come in ~** être utile

usefulness ['ju:sfəlnıs] *n* utilité *f*

useless ['ju:slıs] *adj* inutile; (*inf: person*) nul(le)

user ['ju:zə*ʳ*] *n* utilisateur(-trice), usager *m*

user-friendly ['ju:zə'frɛndlı] *adj* convivial(e), facile d'emploi

username ['ju:zəneım] *n* (*Comput*) nom *m* d'utilisateur

usher ['ʌʃə*ʳ*] *n* placeur *m* ▷ *vt*: **to ~ sb in** faire entrer qn

usherette [ʌʃə'rɛt] *n* (*in cinema*) ouvreuse *f*

usual ['ju:ʒuəl] *adj* habituel(le); **as ~** comme d'habitude

usually ['ju:ʒuəlı] *adv* d'habitude, d'ordinaire

utensil [ju:'tɛnsl] *n* ustensile *m*; **kitchen ~s** batterie *f* de cuisine

uterus ['ju:tərəs] *n* utérus *m*

utility [ju:'tılıtı] *n* utilité *f*; (*also:* **public ~**) service public

utility room *n* buanderie *f*

utilize ['ju:tılaız] *vt* utiliser; (*make good use of*) exploiter

utmost ['ʌtməust] *adj* extrême, le/la plus grand(e) ▷ *n*: **to do one's ~** faire tout son possible; **of the ~ importance** d'une importance capitale, de la plus haute importance

utter ['ʌtə*ʳ*] *adj* total(e), complet(-ète) ▷ *vt* prononcer, proférer; (*sounds*) émettre

utterance ['ʌtrns] *n* paroles *fpl*

utterly ['ʌtəlı] *adv* complètement, totalement

U-turn ['ju:'tə:n] *n* demi-tour *m*; (*fig*) volte-face *f inv*

v. *abbr* (= *verse*) v.; (= *vide*) v.; (= *versus*) vs; (= *volt*) V

vacancy ['veıkənsı] *n* (Brit: *job*) poste vacant; (*room*) chambre *f* disponible; **"no vacancies"** "complet"

vacant ['veıkənt] *adj* (*post*) vacant(e); (*seat etc*) libre, disponible; (*expression*) distrait(e)

vacate [və'keıt] *vt* quitter

vacation [və'keıʃən] *n* (*esp US*) vacances *fpl*; **to take a ~** prendre des vacances; **on ~** en vacances

vacationer [və'keıʃənə*ʳ*], (US) **vacationist** [və'keıʃənıst] *n* vacancier(-ière)

vaccinate ['væksıneıt] *vt* vacciner

vaccination [væksı'neıʃən] *n* vaccination *f*

vaccine ['væksi:n] *n* vaccin *m*

vacuum ['vækjum] *n* vide *m*

vacuum cleaner *n* aspirateur *m*

vacuum-packed ['vækjumpækt] *adj* emballé(e) sous vide

vagina [və'dʒaınə] *n* vagin *m*

vagrant ['veıgrənt] *n* vagabond(e), mendiant(e)

vague [veıg] *adj* vague, imprécis(e); (*blurred: photo, memory*) flou(e); **I haven't the ~st idea** je n'en ai pas la moindre idée

vaguely ['veıglı] *adv* vaguement

vain [veın] *adj* (*useless*) vain(e); (*conceited*) vaniteux(-euse); **in ~** en vain

valentine ['væləntaın] *n* (*also:* **~ card**) carte *f* de la Saint-Valentin

Valentine's Day ['væləntaınz-] *n* Saint-Valentin *f*

V

valiant ['væliənt] *adj* vaillant(e),
courageux(-euse)

valid ['vælɪd] *adj* (*document*) valide, valable;
(*excuse*) valable

valley ['væli] *n* vallée *f*

valour, (US) **valor** ['vælə^r] *n* courage *m*

valuable ['væljuəbl] *adj* (*jewel*) de grande
valeur; (*time*, *help*) précieux(-euse)

valuables ['væljuəblz] *npl* objets *mpl* de
valeur

valuation [vælju'eɪʃən] *n* évaluation *f*,
expertise *f*

value ['vælju:] *n* valeur *f* ▷ *vt* (*fix price*)
évaluer, expertiser; (*appreciate*) apprécier;
(*cherish*) tenir à; **values** *npl* (*principles*)
valeurs *fpl*; **you get good ~ (for money) in
that shop** vous en avez pour votre argent
dans ce magasin; **to lose (in) ~** (*currency*)
baisser; (*property*) se déprécier; **to gain (in) ~**
(*currency*) monter; (*property*) prendre de la
valeur; **to be of great ~ to sb** (*fig*) être très
utile à qn

value added tax [-'ædɪd-] *n* (*Brit*) taxe *f* à la
valeur ajoutée

valued ['vælju:d] *adj* (*appreciated*) estimé(e)

valve [vælv] *n* (*in machine*) soupape *f*; (*on tyre*)
valve *f*; (*in radio*) lampe *f*; (*Med*) valve, valvule *f*

vampire ['væmpaɪə^r] *n* vampire *m*

van [væn] *n* (*Aut*) camionnette *f*; (*Brit Rail*)
fourgon *m*

vandal ['vændl] *n* vandale *m/f*

vandalism ['vændəlɪzəm] *n* vandalisme *m*

vandalize ['vændəlaɪz] *vt* saccager

vanguard ['vænɡɑ:d] *n* avant-garde *m*

vanilla [və'nɪlə] *n* vanille *f* ▷ *cpd* (*ice cream*) à la
vanille

vanish ['vænɪʃ] *vi* disparaître

vanity ['vænɪtɪ] *n* vanité *f*

vantage ['vɑ:ntɪdʒ] *n*: **~ point** bonne
position

vapour, (US) **vapor** ['veɪpə^r] *n* vapeur *f*;
(*on window*) buée *f*

variable ['veərɪəbl] *adj* variable; (*mood*)
changeant(e) ▷ *n* variable *f*

variance ['veərɪəns] *n*: **to be at ~ (with)** être
en désaccord (avec); (*facts*) être en
contradiction (avec)

variant ['veərɪənt] *n* variante *f*

variation [veərɪ'eɪʃən] *n* variation *f*; (*in
opinion*) changement *m*

varicose ['værɪkəus] *adj*: **~ veins** varices *fpl*

varied ['veərɪd] *adj* varié(e), divers(e)

variety [və'raɪətɪ] *n* variété *f*; (*quantity*)
nombre *m*, quantité *f*; **a wide ~ of ...** une
quantité or un grand nombre de ...
(différent(e)s or divers(es)); **for a ~ of
reasons** pour diverses raisons

variety show *n* (spectacle *m* de) variétés *fpl*

various ['veərɪəs] *adj* divers(e), différent(e);
(*several*) divers, plusieurs; **at ~ times** (*different*)
en diverses occasions; (*several*) à plusieurs
reprises

varnish ['vɑ:nɪʃ] *n* vernis *m*; (*for nails*) vernis
(à ongles) ▷ *vt* vernir; **to ~ one's nails** se
vernir les ongles

vary ['veərɪ] *vt*, *vi* varier, changer; **to ~ with** or
according to varier selon

vase [vɑ:z] *n* vase *m*

Vaseline® ['væsɪli:n] *n* vaseline *f*

vast [vɑ:st] *adj* vaste, immense; (*amount*,
success) énorme

VAT [væt] *n abbr* (*Brit*: = *value added tax*) TVA *f*

vat [væt] *n* cuve *f*

vault [vɔ:lt] *n* (*of roof*) voûte *f*; (*tomb*) caveau *m*;
(*in bank*) salle *f* des coffres; chambre forte;
(*jump*) saut *m* ▷ *vt* (*also*: **~ over**) sauter (d'un
bond)

vaunted ['vɔ:ntɪd] *adj*: **much-~** tant
célébré(e)

VCR *n abbr* = **video cassette recorder**

VD *n abbr* = **venereal disease**

VDU *n abbr* = **visual display unit**

veal [vi:l] *n* veau *m*

veer [vɪə^r] *vi* tourner; (*car*, *ship*) virer

vegan ['vi:ɡən] *n* végétalien(ne)

vegeburger ['vedʒɪbə:ɡə^r] *n* burger
végétarien

vegetable ['vedʒtəbl] *n* légume *m* ▷ *adj*
végétal(e)

vegetarian [vedʒɪ'teərɪən] *adj*, *n*
végétarien(ne); **do you have any ~ dishes?**
avez-vous des plats végétariens?

vegetation [vedʒɪ'teɪʃən] *n* végétation *f*

vehement ['vi:ɪmənt] *adj* violent(e),
impétueux(-euse); (*impassioned*) ardent(e)

vehicle ['vi:ɪkl] *n* véhicule *m*

veil [veɪl] *n* voile *m* ▷ *vt* voiler; **under a ~ of
secrecy** (*fig*) dans le plus grand secret

vein [veɪn] *n* veine *f*; (*on leaf*) nervure *f*; (*fig*:
mood) esprit *m*

Velcro® ['velkrəu] *n* velcro® *m*

velocity [vɪ'lɔsɪtɪ] *n* vitesse *f*, vélocité *f*

velvet ['velvɪt] *n* velours *m*

vending machine ['vendɪŋ-] *n* distributeur
m automatique

vendor ['vendə^r] *n* vendeur(-euse); **street ~**
marchand ambulant

veneer [və'nɪə^r] *n* placage *m* de bois; (*fig*)
vernis *m*

venereal [vɪ'nɪərɪəl] *adj*: **~ disease** maladie
vénérienne

Venetian blind [vɪ'ni:ʃən-] *n* store vénitien

vengeance ['vendʒəns] *n* vengeance *f*; **with
a ~** (*fig*) vraiment, pour de bon

venison ['venɪsn] *n* venaison *f*

venom ['venəm] *n* venin *m*

vent [vent] *n* conduit *m* d'aération; (*in dress*,
jacket) fente *f* ▷ *vt* (*fig*: *one's feelings*) donner
libre cours à

ventilation [ventɪ'leɪʃən] *n* ventilation *f*,
aération *f*

ventilator ['ventɪleɪtə^r] *n* ventilateur *m*

ventriloquist [ven'trɪləkwɪst] *n*
ventriloque *m/f*

venture ['vɛntʃəʳ] n entreprise f ▷ vt risquer, hasarder ▷ vi s'aventurer, se risquer; **a business ~** une entreprise commerciale; **to ~ to do sth** se risquer à faire qch

venue ['vɛnjuː] n lieu m; (of conference etc) lieu de la réunion (or manifestation etc); (of match) lieu de la rencontre

Venus ['viːnəs] n (planet) Vénus f

verb [vəːb] n verbe m

verbal ['vəːbl] adj verbal(e); (translation) littéral(e)

verbatim [vəː'beɪtɪm] adj, adv mot pour mot

verdict ['vəːdɪkt] n verdict m; **~ of guilty/not guilty** verdict de culpabilité/de non-culpabilité

verge [vəːdʒ] n bord m; **"soft ~s"** (Brit) "accotements non stabilisés"; **on the ~ of doing** sur le point de faire; **verge on** vt fus approcher de

verify ['vɛrɪfaɪ] vt vérifier

vermin ['vəːmɪn] npl animaux mpl nuisibles; (insects) vermine f

vermouth ['vəːməθ] n vermouth m

versatile ['vəːsətaɪl] adj polyvalent(e)

verse [vəːs] n vers mpl; (stanza) strophe f; (in Bible) verset m; **in ~** en vers

version ['vəːʃən] n version f

versus ['vəːsəs] prep contre

vertical ['vəːtɪkl] adj vertical(e) ▷ n verticale f

vertigo ['vəːtɪɡəu] n vertige m; **to suffer from ~** avoir des vertiges

verve [vəːv] n brio m; enthousiasme m

very ['vɛrɪ] adv très ▷ adj: **the ~ book which** le livre même que; **the ~ thought (of it) ...** rien que d'y penser ...; **at the ~ end** tout à la fin; **the ~ last** le tout dernier; **at the ~ least** au moins; **~ well** très bien; **~ little** très peu; **~ much** beaucoup

vessel ['vɛsl] n (Anat, Naut) vaisseau m; (container) récipient m; see also **blood**

vest [vɛst] n (Brit: underwear) tricot m de corps; (US: waistcoat) gilet m ▷ vt: **to ~ sb with sth, to ~ sth in sb** investir qn de qch

vested interest n: **to have a ~ in doing** avoir tout intérêt à faire; **vested interests** npl (Comm) droits acquis

vet [vɛt] n abbr (Brit: = veterinary surgeon) vétérinaire m/f; (US: = veteran) ancien(ne) combattant(e) ▷ vt examiner minutieusement; (text) revoir; (candidate) se renseigner soigneusement sur, soumettre à une enquête approfondie

veteran ['vɛtərn] n vétéran m; (also: **war ~**) ancien combattant ▷ adj: **she's a ~ campaigner for ...** cela fait très longtemps qu'elle lutte pour ...

veterinary surgeon ['vɛtrɪnərɪ-] (Brit) n vétérinaire m/f

veto ['viːtəu] n (pl vetoes) veto m ▷ vt opposer son veto à; **to put a ~ on** mettre (or opposer) son veto à

vex [vɛks] vt fâcher, contrarier

vexed [vɛkst] adj (question) controversé(e)

via ['vaɪə] prep par, via

viable ['vaɪəbl] adj viable

vibrate [vaɪ'breɪt] vi: **to ~ (with)** vibrer (de); (resound) retentir (de)

vibration [vaɪ'breɪʃən] n vibration f

vicar ['vɪkəʳ] n pasteur m (de l'Église anglicane)

vicarage ['vɪkərɪdʒ] n presbytère m

vicarious [vɪ'kɛərɪəs] adj (pleasure, experience) indirect(e)

vice [vaɪs] n (evil) vice m; (Tech) étau m

vice- [vaɪs] prefix vice-

vice-chairman [vaɪs'tʃɛəmən] irreg n vice-président(e)

vice squad n ≈ brigade mondaine

vice versa ['vaɪsɪ'vəːsə] adv vice versa

vicinity [vɪ'sɪnɪtɪ] n environs mpl, alentours mpl

vicious ['vɪʃəs] adj (remark) cruel(le); méchant(e); (blow) brutal(e); (dog) méchant(e), dangereux(-euse); **a ~ circle** un cercle vicieux

victim ['vɪktɪm] n victime f; **to be the ~ of** être victime de

victor ['vɪktəʳ] n vainqueur m

Victorian [vɪk'tɔːrɪən] adj victorien(ne)

victorious [vɪk'tɔːrɪəs] adj victorieux(-euse)

victory ['vɪktərɪ] n victoire f; **to win a ~ over sb** remporter une victoire sur qn

video ['vɪdɪəu] n (video film) vidéo f; (also: **~ cassette**) vidéocassette f; (also: **~ cassette recorder**) magnétoscope m ▷ vt (with recorder) enregistrer; (with camera) filmer ▷ cpd vidéo inv

video camera n caméra f vidéo inv

video cassette recorder n = **video recorder**

video game n jeu m vidéo inv

videophone n vidéophone m

video recorder n magnétoscope m

video shop n vidéoclub m

video tape n bande f vidéo inv; (cassette) vidéocassette f

video wall n mur m d'images vidéo

vie [vaɪ] vi: **to ~ with** lutter avec, rivaliser avec

Vienna [vɪ'ɛnə] n Vienne

Vietnam, Viet Nam ['vjɛt'næm] n Viêt-nam or Vietnam m

Vietnamese [vjɛtnə'miːz] adj vietnamien(ne) ▷ n (pl inv) Vietnamien(ne); (Ling) vietnamien m

view [vjuː] n vue f; (opinion) avis m, vue ▷ vt voir, regarder; (situation) considérer; (house) visiter; **on ~** (in museum etc) exposé(e); **in full ~ of sb** sous les yeux de qn; **to be within ~ (of sth)** être à portée de vue (de qch); **an overall ~ of the situation** une vue d'ensemble de la situation; **in my ~** à mon avis; **in ~ of the fact that** étant donné que; **with a ~ to doing sth** dans l'intention de faire qch

viewer ['vjuːəʳ] n (viewfinder) viseur m; (small projector) visionneuse f; (TV) téléspectateur(-trice)

V

viewfinder ['vjuːfaɪndə^r] n viseur m
viewpoint ['vjuːpɔɪnt] n point m de vue
vigilant ['vɪdʒɪlənt] adj vigilant(e)
vigorous ['vɪgərəs] adj vigoureux(-euse)
vile [vaɪl] adj (action) vil(e); (smell, food)
abominable; (temper) massacrant(e)
villa ['vɪlə] n villa f
village ['vɪlɪdʒ] n village m
villager ['vɪlɪdʒə^r] n villageois(e)
villain ['vɪlən] n (scoundrel) scélérat m; (Brit:
criminal) bandit m; (in novel etc) traître m
vinaigrette [vɪneɪ'grɛt] n vinaigrette f
vindicate ['vɪndɪkeɪt] vt défendre avec
succès; justifier
vindictive [vɪn'dɪktɪv] adj vindicatif(-ive),
rancunier(-ière)
vine [vaɪn] n vigne f; (climbing plant) plante
grimpante
vinegar ['vɪnɪgə^r] n vinaigre m
vineyard ['vɪnjɑːd] n vignoble m
vintage ['vɪntɪdʒ] n (year) année f, millésime m
▷ cpd (car) d'époque; (wine) de grand cru; **the
1970** le millésime 1970
vinyl ['vaɪnl] n vinyle m
viola [vɪ'əʊlə] n alto m
violate ['vaɪəleɪt] vt violer
violation [vaɪə'leɪʃən] n violation f; **in ~ of**
(rule, law) en infraction à, en violation de
violence ['vaɪələns] n violence f; (Pol etc)
incidents violents
violent ['vaɪələnt] adj violent(e); **a ~ dislike
of sb/sth** une aversion profonde pour
qn/qch
violet ['vaɪələt] adj (colour) violet(te) ▷ n
(plant) violette f
violin [vaɪə'lɪn] n violon m
violinist [vaɪə'lɪnɪst] n violoniste m/f
VIP n abbr (= very important person) VIP m
viral ['vaɪərəl] adj (also Comput) viral
virgin ['vəːdʒɪn] n vierge f ▷ adj vierge; **she is
a ~** elle est vierge; **the Blessed V~** la Sainte
Vierge
Virgo ['vəːgəʊ] n la Vierge; **to be ~** être de la
Vierge
virile ['vɪraɪl] adj viril(e)
virtual ['vəːtjuəl] adj (Comput, Physics)
virtuel(le); (in effect): **it's a ~ impossibility**
c'est quasiment impossible; **the ~ leader** le
chef dans la pratique
virtually ['vəːtjuəlɪ] adv (almost)
pratiquement; **it is ~ impossible** c'est
quasiment impossible
virtual reality n (Comput) réalité virtuelle
virtue ['vəːtjuː] n vertu f; (advantage) mérite m,
avantage m; **by ~ of** en vertu or raison de
virtuous ['vəːtjuəs] adj vertueux(-euse)
virus ['vaɪərəs] n (Med, Comput) virus m
visa ['viːzə] n visa m
vise [vaɪs] n (US Tech) = vice
visibility [vɪzɪ'bɪlɪtɪ] n visibilité f
visible ['vɪzəbl] adj visible; **~ exports/imports**
exportations/importations fpl visibles

vision ['vɪʒən] n (sight) vue f, vision f; (foresight,
in dream) vision
visit ['vɪzɪt] n visite f; (stay) séjour m ▷ vt
(person: US: also: **~ with**) rendre visite à; (place)
visiter; **on a private/official ~** en visite
privée/officielle
visiting hours npl heures fpl de visite
visitor ['vɪzɪtə^r] n visiteur(-euse); (to one's
house) invité(e); (in hotel) client(e)
visitor centre, visitor center (US) n hall m
or centre m d'accueil
visor ['vaɪzə^r] n visière f
vista ['vɪstə] n vue f, perspective f
visual ['vɪzjuəl] adj visuel(le)
visual aid n support visuel (pour
l'enseignement)
visual display unit n console f de
visualisation, visuel m
visualize ['vɪzjuəlaɪz] vt se représenter;
(foresee) prévoir
visually-impaired ['vɪzjuəlɪɪm'pɛəd] adj
malvoyant(e)
vital ['vaɪtl] adj vital(e); **of ~ importance
(to sb/sth)** d'une importance capitale
(pour qn/qch)
vitality [vaɪ'tælɪtɪ] n vitalité f
vitally ['vaɪtəlɪ] adv extrêmement
vital statistics npl (of population) statistiques
fpl démographiques; (inf: woman's)
mensurations fpl
vitamin ['vɪtəmɪn] n vitamine f
vivacious [vɪ'veɪʃəs] adj animé(e), qui a de
la vivacité
vivid ['vɪvɪd] adj (account) frappant(e),
vivant(e); (light, imagination) vif/vive
vividly ['vɪvɪdlɪ] adv (describe) d'une manière
vivante; (remember) de façon précise
V-neck ['viːnɛk] n décolleté m en V
vocabulary [vəu'kæbjulərɪ] n vocabulaire m
vocal ['vəukl] adj vocal(e); (articulate) qui
n'hésite pas à s'exprimer, qui sait faire
entendre ses opinions; **vocals** npl voix fpl
vocal cords npl cordes vocales
vocation [vəu'keɪʃən] n vocation f
vocational [vəu'keɪʃənl] adj
professionnel(le); **~ guidance/training**
orientation/formation professionnelle
vociferous [və'sɪfərəs] adj bruyant(e)
vodka ['vɔdkə] n vodka f
vogue [vəug] n mode f; (popularity) vogue f;
to be in ~ être en vogue or à la mode
voice [vɔɪs] n voix f; (opinion) avis m ▷ vt
(opinion) exprimer, formuler; **in a loud/soft ~**
à voix haute/basse; **to give ~ to** exprimer
voice mail n (system) messagerie f vocale,
boîte f vocale; (device) répondeur m
void [vɔɪd] n vide m ▷ adj (invalid) nul(le);
(empty): **~ of** vide de, dépourvu(e) de
volatile ['vɔlətaɪl] adj volatil(e); (fig: person)
versatile; (: situation) explosif(-ive)
volcano (pl **volcanoes**) [vɔl'keɪnəʊ] n
volcan m

volition [vəˈlɪʃən] n: **of one's own** ~ de son propre gré

volley [ˈvɒlɪ] n (of gunfire) salve f; (of stones etc) pluie f, volée f; (Tennis etc) volée

volleyball [ˈvɒlɪbɔːl] n volley(-ball) m

volt [vəʊlt] n volt m

voltage [ˈvəʊltɪdʒ] n tension f, voltage m; **high/low** ~ haute/basse tension

volume [ˈvɒljuːm] n volume m; (of tank) capacité f; ~ **one/two** (of book) tome un/deux; **his expression spoke** ~**s** son expression en disait long

voluntarily [ˈvɒləntrɪlɪ] adv volontairement; bénévolement

voluntary [ˈvɒləntərɪ] adj volontaire; (unpaid) bénévole

volunteer [vɒlənˈtɪər] n volontaire m/f ▷ vt (information) donner spontanément ▷ vi (Mil) s'engager comme volontaire; **to** ~ **to do** se proposer pour faire

vomit [ˈvɒmɪt] n vomissure f ▷ vt, vi vomir

vote [vəʊt] n vote m, suffrage m; (votes cast) voix f, vote; (franchise) droit m de vote ▷ vt (bill) voter; (chairman) élire; (propose): **to** ~ **that** proposer que + sub ▷ vi voter; **to put sth to the** ~, **to take a** ~ **on sth** mettre qch aux voix, procéder à un vote sur qch; **to** ~ **for or in favour of/against** vote pour/contre; **to** ~ **to do sth** voter en faveur de faire qch; ~ **of censure** motion f de censure; ~ **of thanks** discours m de remerciement

voter [ˈvəʊtər] n électeur(-trice)

voting [ˈvəʊtɪŋ] n scrutin m, vote m

vouch [vaʊtʃ] : **to** ~ **for** vt fus se porter garant de

voucher [ˈvaʊtʃər] n (for meal, petrol, gift) bon m; (receipt) reçu m; **travel** ~ bon m de transport

vow [vaʊ] n vœu m, serment m ▷ vi jurer; **to take** or **make a** ~ **to do sth** faire le vœu de faire qch

vowel [ˈvaʊəl] n voyelle f

voyage [ˈvɔɪdʒ] n voyage m par mer, traversée f; (by spacecraft) voyage

vulgar [ˈvʌlɡər] adj vulgaire

vulnerable [ˈvʌlnərəbl] adj vulnérable

vulture [ˈvʌltʃər] n vautour m

W

wad [wɒd] n (of cotton wool, paper) tampon m; (of banknotes etc) liasse f

waddle [ˈwɒdl] vi se dandiner

wade [weɪd] vi: **to** ~ **through** marcher dans, patauger dans; (fig: book) venir à bout de ▷ vt passer à gué

wafer [ˈweɪfər] n (Culin) gaufrette f; (Rel) pain m d'hostie; (Comput) tranche f (de silicium)

waffle [ˈwɒfl] n (Culin) gaufre f; (inf) rabâchage m; remplissage m ▷ vi parler pour ne rien dire; faire du remplissage

waft [wɒft] vt porter ▷ vi flotter

wag [wæɡ] vt agiter, remuer ▷ vi remuer; **the dog** ~**ged its tail** le chien a remué la queue

wage [weɪdʒ] n (also: ~**s**) salaire m, paye f ▷ vt: **to** ~ **war** faire la guerre; **a day's** ~**s** un jour de salaire

wage earner [-əːnər] n salarié(e); (breadwinner) soutien m de famille

wage packet n (Brit) (enveloppe f de) paye f

wager [ˈweɪdʒər] n pari m ▷ vt parier

wagon, waggon [ˈwæɡən] n (horse-drawn) chariot m; (Brit Rail) wagon m (de marchandises)

wail [weɪl] n gémissement m; (of siren) hurlement m ▷ vi gémir; (siren) hurler

waist [weɪst] n taille f, ceinture f

waistcoat [ˈweɪskəʊt] n (Brit) gilet m

waistline [ˈweɪstlaɪn] n (tour m de) taille f

wait [weɪt] n attente f ▷ vi attendre; **to** ~ **for sb/sth** attendre qn/qch; **to keep sb** ~**ing**

faire attendre qn; **~ for me, please** attendez-moi, s'il vous plaît; **~ a minute!** un instant!; **"repairs while you ~"** "réparations minute"; **I can't ~ to ...** (fig) je meurs d'envie de ...; **to lie in ~ for** guetter; **wait behind** vi rester (à attendre); **wait on** vt fus servir; **wait up** vi attendre, ne pas se coucher; **don't ~ up for me** ne m'attendez pas pour aller vous coucher

waiter ['weɪtəʳ] n garçon m (de café), serveur m

waiting ['weɪtɪŋ] n: **"no ~"** (Brit Aut) "stationnement interdit"

waiting list n liste f d'attente

waiting room n salle f d'attente

waitress ['weɪtrɪs] n serveuse f

waive [weɪv] vt renoncer à, abandonner

wake [weɪk] (pt **woke** or **waked**, pp **woken** or **waked**) [wəʊk, 'wəʊkn] vt (also: **~ up**) réveiller ▷ vi (also: **~ up**) se réveiller ▷ n (for dead person) veillée f mortuaire; (Naut) sillage m; **to ~ up to sth** (fig) se rendre compte de qch; **in the ~ of** (fig) à la suite de; **to follow in sb's ~** (fig) marcher sur les traces de qn

Wales [weɪlz] n pays m de Galles; **the Prince of ~** le prince de Galles

walk [wɔːk] n promenade f; (short) petit tour; (gait) démarche f; (path) chemin m; (in park etc) allée f; (pace): **at a quick ~** d'un pas rapide ▷ vi marcher; (for pleasure, exercise) se promener ▷ vt (distance) faire à pied; (dog) promener; **10 minutes' ~ from** à 10 minutes de marche de; **to go for a ~** se promener; faire un tour; **from all ~s of life** de toutes conditions sociales; **I'll ~ you home** je vais vous raccompagner chez vous; **walk out** vi (go out) sortir; (as protest) partir (en signe de protestation); (strike) se mettre en grève; **to ~ out on sb** quitter qn

walker ['wɔːkəʳ] n (person) marcheur(-euse)

walkie-talkie ['wɔːkɪ'tɔːkɪ] n talkie-walkie m

walking ['wɔːkɪŋ] n marche f à pied; **it's within ~ distance** on peut y aller à pied

walking shoes npl chaussures fpl de marche

walking stick n canne f

Walkman® ['wɔːkmən] n Walkman® m

walkout ['wɔːkaut] n (of workers) grève-surprise f

walkover ['wɔːkəuvəʳ] n (inf) victoire f or examen m etc facile

walkway ['wɔːkweɪ] n promenade f, cheminement piéton

wall [wɔːl] n mur m; (of tunnel, cave) paroi f; **to go to the ~** (fig: firm etc) faire faillite; **wall in** vt (garden etc) entourer d'un mur

walled [wɔːld] adj (city) fortifié(e)

wallet ['wɔlɪt] n portefeuille m; **I can't find my ~** je ne retrouve plus mon portefeuille

wallflower ['wɔːlflauəʳ] n giroflée f; **to be a ~** (fig) faire tapisserie

wallow ['wɔləu] vi se vautrer; **to ~ in one's grief** se complaire à sa douleur

wallpaper ['wɔːlpeɪpəʳ] n papier peint ▷ vt tapisser

walnut ['wɔːlnʌt] n noix f; (tree, wood) noyer m

walrus (pl **walrus** or **walruses**) ['wɔːlrəs] n morse m

waltz [wɔːlts] n valse f ▷ vi valser

wand [wɔnd] n (also: **magic ~**) baguette f (magique)

wander ['wɔndəʳ] vi (person) errer, aller sans but; (thoughts) vagabonder; (river) serpenter ▷ vt errer dans

wane [weɪn] vi (moon) décroître; (reputation) décliner

wangle ['wæŋgl] (Brit inf) vt se débrouiller pour avoir; carotter ▷ n combine f, magouille f

want [wɔnt] vt vouloir; (need) avoir besoin de; (lack) manquer de ▷ n (poverty) pauvreté f, besoin m; **wants** npl (needs) besoins mpl; **to ~ to do** vouloir faire; **to ~ sb to do** vouloir que qn fasse; **you're ~ed on the phone** on vous demande au téléphone; **"cook ~ed"** "on demande un cuisinier"; **for ~ of** par manque de, faute de

wanted ['wɔntɪd] adj (criminal) recherché(e) par la police

wanting ['wɔntɪŋ] adj: **to be ~ (in)** manquer (de); **to be found ~** ne pas être à la hauteur

war [wɔːʳ] n guerre f; **to go to ~** se mettre en guerre; **to make ~ (on)** faire la guerre (à)

ward [wɔːd] n (in hospital) salle f; (Pol) section électorale; (Law: child: also: **~ of court**) pupille m/f; **ward off** vt parer, éviter

warden ['wɔːdn] n (Brit: of institution) directeur(-trice); (of park, game reserve) gardien(ne); (Brit: also: **traffic ~**) contractuel(le); (of youth hostel) responsable m/f

warder ['wɔːdəʳ] n (Brit) gardien m de prison

wardrobe ['wɔːdrəub] n (cupboard) armoire f; (clothes) garde-robe f; (Theat) costumes mpl

warehouse ['wɛəhaus] n entrepôt m

wares [wɛəz] npl marchandises fpl

warfare ['wɔːfɛəʳ] n guerre f

warhead ['wɔːhɛd] n (Mil) ogive f

warily ['wɛərɪlɪ] adv avec prudence, avec précaution

warm [wɔːm] adj chaud(e); (person, thanks, welcome, applause) chaleureux(-euse); (supporter) ardent(e), enthousiaste; **it's ~** il fait chaud; **I'm ~** j'ai chaud; **to keep sth ~** tenir qch au chaud; **with my ~est thanks/congratulations** avec mes remerciements/mes félicitations les plus sincères; **warm up** vi (person, room) se réchauffer; (water) chauffer; (athlete, discussion) s'échauffer ▷ vt (food) (faire) réchauffer; (water) (faire) chauffer; (engine) faire chauffer

warm-hearted [wɔːm'hɑːtɪd] adj affectueux(-euse)

warmly ['wɔːmlɪ] adv (dress) chaudement; (thank, welcome) chaleureusement

warmth [wɔːmθ] n chaleur f
warn [wɔːn] vt avertir, prévenir; **to ~ sb (not) to do** conseiller à qn de (ne pas) faire
warning ['wɔːnɪŋ] n avertissement m; (notice) avis m; (signal) avertisseur m; **without (any) ~** (suddenly) inopinément; (without notifying) sans prévenir; **gale ~** (Meteorology) avis de grand vent
warning light n avertisseur lumineux
warning triangle n (Aut) triangle m de présignalisation
warp [wɔːp] n (Textiles) chaîne f ▷ vi (wood) travailler, se voiler or gauchir ▷ vt voiler; (fig) pervertir
warrant ['wɔrnt] n (guarantee) garantie f; (Law: to arrest) mandat m d'arrêt; (: to search) mandat de perquisition ▷ vt (justify, merit) justifier
warranty ['wɔrəntɪ] n garantie f; **under ~** (Comm) sous garantie
warren ['wɔrən] n (of rabbits) terriers mpl, garenne f
warrior ['wɔrɪəʳ] n guerrier(-ière)
Warsaw ['wɔːsɔː] n Varsovie
warship ['wɔːʃɪp] n navire m de guerre
wart [wɔːt] n verrue f
wartime ['wɔːtaɪm] n: **in ~** en temps de guerre
wary ['wɛərɪ] adj prudent(e); **to be ~ about or of doing sth** hésiter beaucoup à faire qch
was [wɔz] pt of **be**
wash [wɔʃ] vt laver; (sweep, carry: sea etc) emporter, entraîner; (: ashore) rejeter ▷ vi se laver; (sea): **to ~ over/against sth** inonder/baigner qch ▷ n (paint) badigeon m; (clothes) lessive f; (washing programme) lavage m; (of ship) sillage m; **to give sth a ~** laver qch; **to have a ~** se laver, faire sa toilette; **he was ~ed overboard** il a été emporté par une vague; **wash away** vt (stain) enlever au lavage; (subj: river etc) emporter; **wash down** vt laver; laver à grande eau; **wash off** vi partir au lavage; **wash up** vi (Brit) faire la vaisselle; (US: have a wash) se débarbouiller
washable ['wɔʃəbl] adj lavable
washbasin ['wɔʃbeɪsn] n lavabo m
washer ['wɔʃəʳ] n (Tech) rondelle f, joint m
washing ['wɔʃɪŋ] n (Brit: linen etc: dirty) linge m; (: clean) lessive f
washing line n (Brit) corde f à linge
washing machine n machine f à laver
washing powder n (Brit) lessive f (en poudre)
Washington ['wɔʃɪŋtən] n (city, state) Washington m
washing-up [wɔʃɪŋ'ʌp] n (Brit) vaisselle f
washing-up liquid n (Brit) produit m pour la vaisselle
wash-out ['wɔʃaut] n (inf) désastre m
washroom ['wɔʃrum] n (US) toilettes fpl
wasn't ['wɔznt] = **was not**
wasp [wɔsp] n guêpe f

wastage ['weɪstɪdʒ] n gaspillage m; (in manufacturing, transport etc) déchet m
waste [weɪst] n gaspillage m; (of time) perte f; (rubbish) déchets mpl; (also: **household ~**) ordures fpl ▷ adj (energy, heat) perdu(e); (food) inutilisé(e); (land, ground: in city) à l'abandon; (: in country) inculte, en friche; (leftover): **~ material** déchets ▷ vt gaspiller; (time, opportunity) perdre; **wastes** npl étendue f désertique; **it's a ~ of money** c'est de l'argent jeté en l'air; **to go to ~** être gaspillé(e); **to lay ~** (destroy) dévaster; **waste away** vi dépérir
waste disposal, waste disposal unit n (Brit) broyeur m d'ordures
wasteful ['weɪstful] adj gaspilleur(-euse); (process) peu économique
waste ground n (Brit) terrain m vague
wastepaper basket ['weɪstpeɪpə-] n corbeille f à papier
watch [wɔtʃ] n montre f; (act of watching) surveillance f; (guard: Mil) sentinelle f; (: Naut) homme m de quart; (Naut: spell of duty) quart m ▷ vt (look at) observer; (: match, programme) regarder; (spy on, guard) surveiller; (be careful of) faire attention à ▷ vi regarder; (keep guard) monter la garde; **to keep a close ~ on sb/sth** surveiller qn/qch de près; **to keep ~** faire le guet; **~ what you're doing** fais attention à ce que tu fais; **watch out** vi faire attention
watchdog ['wɔtʃdɔg] n chien m de garde; (fig) gardien(ne)
watchful ['wɔtʃful] adj attentif(-ive), vigilant(e)
watchmaker ['wɔtʃmeɪkəʳ] n horloger(-ère)
watchman ['wɔtʃmən] irreg n gardien m; (also: **night ~**) veilleur m de nuit
watch strap ['wɔtʃstræp] n bracelet m de montre
water ['wɔːtəʳ] n eau f ▷ vt (plant, garden) arroser ▷ vi (eyes) larmoyer; **a drink of ~** un verre d'eau; **in British ~s** dans les eaux territoriales Britanniques; **to pass ~** uriner; **to make sb's mouth ~** mettre l'eau à la bouche de qn; **water down** vt (milk etc) couper avec de l'eau; (fig: story) édulcorer
watercolour, (US) watercolor ['wɔːtəkʌləʳ] n aquarelle f; **watercolours** npl couleurs fpl pour aquarelle
watercress ['wɔːtəkrɛs] n cresson m (de fontaine)
waterfall ['wɔːtəfɔːl] n chute f d'eau
water heater n chauffe-eau m
watering can ['wɔːtərɪŋ-] n arrosoir m
water lily n nénuphar m
waterline ['wɔːtəlaɪn] n (Naut) ligne f de flottaison
waterlogged ['wɔːtəlɔgd] adj détrempé(e); imbibé(e) d'eau
water main n canalisation f d'eau
watermelon ['wɔːtəmɛlən] n pastèque f

W

waterproof ['wɔ:təpru:f] adj imperméable

watershed ['wɔ:təʃed] n (Geo) ligne f de partage des eaux; (fig) moment m critique, point décisif

water-skiing ['wɔ:təski:ɪŋ] n ski m nautique

watertight ['wɔ:tətaɪt] adj étanche

waterway ['wɔ:təweɪ] n cours m d'eau navigable

waterworks ['wɔ:təwə:ks] npl station f hydraulique

watery ['wɔ:tərɪ] adj (colour) délavé(e); (coffee) trop faible

watt [wɔt] n watt m

wave [weɪv] n vague f; (of hand) geste m, signe m; (Radio) onde f; (in hair) ondulation f; (fig: of enthusiasm, strikes etc) vague ▷ vi faire signe de la main; (flag) flotter au vent; (grass) ondoyer ▷ vt (handkerchief) agiter; (stick) brandir; (hair) onduler; **short/medium ~** (Radio) ondes courtes/moyennes; **long ~** (Radio) grandes ondes; **the new ~** (Cine, Mus) la nouvelle vague; **to ~ goodbye to sb** dire au revoir de la main à qn; **wave aside, wave away** vt (fig: suggestion, objection) rejeter, repousser; (: doubts) chasser; **to ~ sb aside** faire signe à qn de s'écarter

wavelength ['weɪvleŋθ] n longueur f d'ondes

waver ['weɪvər] vi vaciller; (voice) trembler; (person) hésiter

wavy ['weɪvɪ] adj (hair, surface) ondulé(e); (line) onduleux(-euse)

wax [wæks] n cire f; (for skis) fart m ▷ vt cirer; (car) lustrer; (skis) farter ▷ vi (moon) croître

waxworks ['wækswə:ks] npl personnages mpl de cire; musée m de cire

way [weɪ] n chemin m, voie f; (path, access) passage m; (distance) distance f; (direction) chemin, direction f; (manner) façon f, manière f; (habit) habitude f, façon; (condition) état m; **which ~? — this ~/that ~** par où or de quel côté? — par ici/par là; **to crawl one's ~ to ...** ramper jusqu'à ...; **to lie one's ~ out of it** s'en sortir par un mensonge; **to lose one's ~** perdre son chemin; **on the ~ (to)** en route (pour); **to be on one's ~** être en route; **to be in the ~** bloquer le passage; (fig) gêner; **to keep out of sb's ~** éviter qn; **it's a long ~ away** c'est loin d'ici; **the village is rather out of the ~** le village est plutôt à l'écart or isolé; **to go out of one's ~ to do** (fig) se donner beaucoup de mal pour faire; **to be under ~** (work, project) être en cours; **to make ~ (for sb/sth)** faire place (à qn/qch), s'écarter pour laisser passer (qn/qch); **to get one's own ~** arriver à ses fins; **put it the right ~ up** (Brit) mettez-le dans le bon sens; **to be the wrong ~ round** être à l'envers, ne pas être dans le bon sens; **he's in a bad ~** il va mal; **in a ~** dans un sens, d'une manière; **by the ~** à propos; **in some ~s** à certains égards; **d'un côté**; **in the ~ of** en fait de, comme; **by ~ of** (through) en passant

par, via; (as a sort of) en guise de; **"~ in"** (Brit) "entrée"; **"~ out"** (Brit) "sortie"; **the ~ back** le chemin du retour; **this ~ and that** par-ci par-là; **"give ~"** (Brit Aut) "cédez la priorité"; **no ~!** (inf) pas question!

waylay [weɪ'leɪ] vt (irreg like: **lay**) attaquer; (fig): **I got waylaid** quelqu'un m'a accroché

wayward ['weɪwəd] adj capricieux(-euse), entêté(e)

W.C. n abbr (Brit: = water closet) w.-c. mpl, waters mpl

we [wi:] pl pron nous

weak [wi:k] adj faible; (health) fragile; (beam etc) peu solide; (tea, coffee) léger(-ère); **to grow ~(er)** s'affaiblir, faiblir

weaken ['wi:kn] vi faiblir ▷ vt affaiblir

weakling ['wi:klɪŋ] n gringalet m; faible m/f

weakness ['wi:knɪs] n faiblesse f; (fault) point m faible

wealth [welθ] n (money, resources) richesse(s) f(pl); (of details) profusion f

wealthy ['welθɪ] adj riche

wean [wi:n] vt sevrer

weapon ['wepən] n arme f; **~s of mass destruction** armes fpl de destruction massive

wear [weər] (pt **wore**, pp **worn**) [wɔ:r, wɔ:n] n (use) usage m; (deterioration through use) usure f ▷ vt (clothes) porter; (put on) mettre; (beard etc) avoir; (damage: through use) user ▷ vi (last) faire de l'usage; (rub etc through) s'user; **sports/baby~** vêtements mpl de sport/pour bébés; **evening ~** tenue f de soirée; **~ and tear** usure f; **to ~ a hole in sth** faire (à la longue) un trou dans qch; **wear away** vt user, ronger ▷ vi s'user, être rongé(e); **wear down** vt user; (strength) épuiser; **wear off** vi disparaître; **wear on** vi se poursuivre; passer; **wear out** vt user; (person, strength) épuiser

weary ['wɪərɪ] adj (tired) épuisé(e); (dispirited) las/lasse; abattu(e) ▷ vt lasser ▷ vi: **to ~ of** se lasser de

weasel ['wi:zl] n (Zool) belette f

weather ['weðər] n temps m ▷ vt (wood) faire mûrir; (storm: lit, fig) essuyer; (crisis) survivre à; **what's the ~ like?** quel temps fait-il?; **under the ~** (fig: ill) mal fichu(e)

weather-beaten ['weðəbi:tn] adj (person) hâlé(e); (building) dégradé(e) par les intempéries

weather forecast n prévisions fpl météorologiques, météo f

weatherman ['weðəmæn] irreg n météorologue m

weather vane [-veɪn] n = **weather cock**

weave (pt **wove**, pp **woven**) [wi:v, wəuv, 'wəuvn] vt (cloth) tisser; (basket) tresser ▷ vi (fig) (pt, pp **weaved**) (move in and out) se faufiler

weaver ['wi:vər] n tisserand(e)

web [web] n (of spider) toile f; (on duck's foot) palmure f; (fig) tissu m; (Comput): **the (World-Wide) W~** le Web

web address n adresse f Web
webcam ['wɛbkæm] n webcam f
weblog ['wɛblɒg] n blog m, blogue m
web page n (Comput) page f Web
website ['wɛbsaɪt] n (Comput) site m web
wed [wɛd] (pt, pp **wedded**) vt épouser ▷ vi se marier ▷ n: **the newly--s** les jeunes mariés
we'd [wiːd] = **we had**; **we would**
wedding ['wɛdɪŋ] n mariage m
wedding anniversary n anniversaire m de mariage; **silver/golden ~** noces fpl d'argent/d'or
wedding day n jour m du mariage
wedding dress n robe f de mariée
wedding ring n alliance f
wedge [wɛdʒ] n (of wood etc) coin m; (under door etc) cale f; (of cake) part f ▷ vt (fix) caler; (push) enfoncer, coincer
Wednesday ['wɛdnzdɪ] n mercredi m; see also **Tuesday**
wee [wiː] adj (Scottish) petit(e); tout(e) petit(e)
weed [wiːd] n mauvaise herbe ▷ vt désherber; **weed out** vt éliminer
weedkiller ['wiːdkɪləʳ] n désherbant m
weedy ['wiːdɪ] adj (man) gringalet
week [wiːk] n semaine f; **once/twice a ~** une fois/deux fois par semaine; **in two ~s' time** dans quinze jours; **a ~ today/on Tuesday** aujourd'hui/mardi en huit
weekday ['wiːkdeɪ] n jour m de semaine; (Comm) jour ouvrable; **on ~s** en semaine
weekend [wiːk'ɛnd] n week-end m
weekly ['wiːklɪ] adv une fois par semaine, chaque semaine ▷ adj, n hebdomadaire (m)
weep [wiːp] (pt, pp **wept**) [wɛpt] vi (person) pleurer; (Med: wound etc) suinter
weeping willow ['wiːpɪŋ-] n saule pleureur
weigh [weɪ] vt, vi peser; **to ~ anchor** lever l'ancre; **to ~ the pros and cons** peser le pour et le contre; **weigh down** vt (branch) faire plier; (fig: with worry) accabler; **weigh out** vt (goods) peser; **weigh up** vt examiner
weight [weɪt] n poids m ▷ vt alourdir; (fig: factor) pondérer; **sold by ~** vendu au poids; **to put on/lose ~** grossir/maigrir; **~s and measures** poids et mesures
weighting ['weɪtɪŋ] n: **~ allowance** indemnité f de résidence
weightlifter ['weɪtlɪftəʳ] n haltérophile m
weightlifting ['weɪtlɪftɪŋ] n haltérophilie f
weighty ['weɪtɪ] adj lourd(e)
weir [wɪəʳ] n barrage m
weird [wɪəd] adj bizarre; (eerie) surnaturel(le)
welcome ['wɛlkəm] adj bienvenu(e) ▷ n accueil m ▷ vt accueillir; (also: **bid ~**) souhaiter la bienvenue à; (be glad of) se réjouir de; **to be ~** être le/la bienvenu(e); **to make sb ~** faire bon accueil à qn; **you're ~ to try** vous pouvez essayer si vous voulez; **you're ~!** (after thanks) de rien, il n'y a pas de quoi
weld [wɛld] n soudure f ▷ vt souder

welder ['wɛldəʳ] n (person) soudeur m
welfare ['wɛlfɛəʳ] n (wellbeing) bien-être m; (social aid) assistance sociale
welfare state n État-providence m
well [wɛl] n puits m ▷ adv bien ▷ adj: **to be ~** aller bien ▷ excl eh bien!; (resignation) enfin!; (relief also) bon!; **~ done!** bravo!; **I don't feel ~** je ne me sens pas bien; **get ~ soon!** remets-toi vite!; **to do ~** bien réussir; (business) prospérer; **to think ~ of sb** penser du bien de qn; **as ~** (in addition) aussi, également; **you might as ~ tell me** tu ferais aussi bien de me le dire; **as ~ as** aussi bien que or de; en plus de; **~, as I was saying ...** donc, comme je disais ...; **well up** vi (tears, emotions) monter
we'll [wiːl] = **we will**; **we shall**
well-behaved ['wɛlbɪ'heɪvd] adj sage, obéissant(e)
well-being ['wɛl'biːɪŋ] n bien-être m
well-built ['wɛl'bɪlt] adj (house) bien construit(e); (person) bien bâti(e)
well-deserved ['wɛldɪ'zəːvd] adj (bien) mérité(e)
well-dressed ['wɛl'drɛst] adj bien habillé(e), bien vêtu(e)
well-groomed ['-'gruːmd] adj très soigné(e)
well-heeled ['wɛl'hiːld] adj (inf: wealthy) fortuné(e), riche
wellies ['wɛlɪz] (inf) npl (Brit) = **wellingtons**
wellingtons ['wɛlɪŋtənz] npl (also: **wellington boots**) bottes fpl en caoutchouc
well-known ['wɛl'nəun] adj (person) bien connu(e)
well-mannered ['wɛl'mænəd] adj bien élevé(e)
well-meaning ['wɛl'miːnɪŋ] adj bien intentionné(e)
well-off ['wɛl'ɔf] adj aisé(e), assez riche
well-paid [wɛl'peɪd] adj bien payé(e)
well-read ['wɛl'rɛd] adj cultivé(e)
well-to-do ['wɛltə'duː] adj aisé(e), assez riche
well-wisher ['wɛlwɪʃəʳ] n ami(e), admirateur(-trice); **scores of ~s had gathered** de nombreux amis et admirateurs s'étaient rassemblés; **letters from ~s** des lettres d'encouragement
Welsh [wɛlʃ] adj gallois(e) ▷ n (Ling) gallois m; **the Welsh** npl (people) les Gallois
Welsh Assembly n Parlement gallois
Welshman ['wɛlʃmən] irreg n Gallois m
Welshwoman ['wɛlʃwumən] irreg n Galloise f
went [wɛnt] pt of **go**
wept [wɛpt] pt, pp of **weep**
were [wəːʳ] pt of **be**
we're [wɪəʳ] = **we are**
weren't [wəːnt] = **were not**
west [wɛst] n ouest m ▷ adj (wind) d'ouest; (side) ouest inv ▷ adv à or vers l'ouest; **the W~** l'Occident m, l'Ouest

westbound ['wɛstbaund] adj en direction de l'ouest; (carriageway) ouest inv

westerly ['wɛstəlɪ] adj (situation) à l'ouest; (wind) d'ouest

western ['wɛstən] adj occidental(e), de or à l'ouest ▷ n (Cine) western m

West Indian adj antillais(e) ▷ n Antillais(e)

West Indies [-'ɪndɪz] npl Antilles fpl

westward ['wɛstwəd], **westwards** ['wɛstwədz] adv vers l'ouest

wet [wɛt] adj mouillé(e); (damp) humide; (soaked: also: ~ **through**) trempé(e); (rainy) pluvieux(-euse) ▷ vt: **to ~ one's pants** or **o.s.** mouiller sa culotte, faire pipi dans sa culotte; **to get ~** se mouiller; **"~ paint"** "attention peinture fraîche"

wetsuit ['wɛtsuːt] n combinaison f de plongée

we've [wiːv] = **we have**

whack [wæk] vt donner un grand coup à

whale [weɪl] n (Zool) baleine f

wharf (pl **wharves**) [wɔːf, wɔːvz] n quai m

○ **KEYWORD**

what [wɔt] adj **1** (in questions) quel(le); **what size is he?** quelle taille fait-il?; **what colour is it?** de quelle couleur est-ce?; **what books do you need?** quels livres vous faut-il?
2 (in exclamations): **what a mess!** quel désordre!; **what a fool I am!** que je suis bête!
▷ pron **1** (interrogative) que; de/à/en etc quoi; **what are you doing?** que faites-vous?, qu'est-ce que vous faites?; **what is happening?** qu'est-ce qui se passe?, que se passe-t-il?; **what are you talking about?** de quoi parlez-vous?; **what are you thinking about?** à quoi pensez-vous?; **what is it called?** comment est-ce que ça s'appelle?; **what about me?** et moi?; **what about doing ...?** et si on faisait ...?
2 (relative: subject) ce qui; (: direct object) ce que; (: indirect object) ce à quoi, ce dont; **I saw what you did/was on the table** j'ai vu ce que vous avez fait/ce qui était sur la table; **tell me what you remember** dites-moi ce dont vous vous souvenez; **what I want is a cup of tea** ce que je veux, c'est une tasse de thé
▷ excl (disbelieving) quoi!, comment!

whatever [wɔt'ɛvər] adj: **take ~ book you prefer** prenez le livre que vous préférez, peu importe lequel; **~ book you take** quel que soit le livre que vous preniez ▷ pron: **do ~ is necessary** faites (tout) ce qui est nécessaire; **~ happens** quoi qu'il arrive; **no reason ~** or **whatsoever** pas la moindre raison; **nothing ~** or **whatsoever** rien du tout

whatsoever [wɔtsəʊ'ɛvər] adj see **whatever**

wheat [wiːt] n blé m, froment m

wheedle ['wiːdl] vt: **to ~ sb into doing sth** cajoler or enjôler qn pour qu'il fasse qch; **to ~**

sth out of sb obtenir qch de qn par des cajoleries

wheel [wiːl] n roue f; (Aut: also: **steering ~**) volant m; (Naut) gouvernail m ▷ vt (pram etc) pousser, rouler ▷ vi (birds) tournoyer; (also: ~ **round**: person) se retourner, faire volte-face

wheelbarrow ['wiːlbærəʊ] n brouette f

wheelchair ['wiːltʃɛər] n fauteuil roulant

wheel clamp n (Aut) sabot m (de Denver)

wheeze [wiːz] n respiration bruyante (d'asthmatique) ▷ vi respirer bruyamment

○ **KEYWORD**

when [wɛn] adv quand; **when did he go?** quand est-ce qu'il est parti?
▷ conj **1** (at, during, after the time that) quand, lorsque; **she was reading when I came in** elle lisait quand or lorsque je suis entré
2 (on, at which): **on the day when I met him** le jour où je l'ai rencontré
3 (whereas) alors que; **I thought I was wrong when in fact I was right** j'ai cru que j'avais tort alors qu'en fait j'avais raison

whenever [wɛn'ɛvər] adv quand donc ▷ conj quand; (every time that) chaque fois que; **I go ~ I can** j'y vais quand or chaque fois que je le peux

where [wɛər] adv, conj où; **this is ~** c'est là que; **~ are you from?** d'où venez vous?

whereabouts ['wɛərəbauts] adv où donc ▷ n: **nobody knows his ~** personne ne sait où il se trouve

whereas [wɛər'æz] conj alors que

whereby [wɛə'baɪ] adv (formal) par lequel (or laquelle etc)

wherever [wɛər'ɛvər] adv où donc ▷ conj où que + sub; **sit ~ you like** asseyez-vous (là) où vous voulez

wherewithal ['wɛəwɪðɔːl] n: **the ~ (to do sth)** les moyens mpl (de faire qch)

whether ['wɛðər] conj si; **I don't know ~ to accept or not** je ne sais pas si je dois accepter ou non; **it's doubtful ~** il est peu probable que + sub; **~ you go or not** que vous y alliez ou non

○ **KEYWORD**

which [wɪtʃ] adj **1** (interrogative: direct, indirect) quel(le); **which picture do you want?** quel tableau voulez-vous?; **which one?** lequel/laquelle?
2: **in which case** auquel cas; **we got there at 8pm, by which time the cinema was full** quand nous sommes arrivés à 20h, le cinéma était complet
▷ pron **1** (interrogative) lequel/laquelle, lesquels/lesquelles pl; **I don't mind which** peu importe lequel; **which (of these) are yours?** lesquels sont à vous?; **tell me which**

you want dites-moi lesquels or ceux que vous voulez

2 (*relative: subject*) qui; (*: object*) que; sur/vers *etc* lequel/laquelle (NB: *à* + *lequel* = **auquel**; *de* + *lequel* = **duquel**); **the apple which you ate/which is on the table** la pomme que vous avez mangée/qui est sur la table; **the chair on which you are sitting** la chaise sur laquelle vous êtes assis; **the book of which you spoke** le livre dont vous avez parlé; **he said he knew, which is true/I was afraid of** il a dit qu'il le savait, ce qui est vrai/ce que je craignais; **after which** après quoi

whichever [wɪtʃ'ɛvər] *adj*: **take ~ book you prefer** prenez le livre que vous préférez, peu importe lequel; **~ book you take** quel que soit le livre que vous preniez; **~ way you** de quelque façon que vous + *sub*

while [waɪl] *n* moment *m* ▷ *conj* pendant que; (*as long as*) tant que; (*as, whereas*) alors que; (*though*) bien que + *sub*, quoique + *sub*; **for a ~** pendant quelque temps; **in a ~** dans un moment; **all the ~** pendant tout ce temps-là; **we'll make it worth your ~** nous vous récompenserons de votre peine; **while away** *vt* (*time*) (faire) passer

whilst [waɪlst] *conj* = **while**

whim [wɪm] *n* caprice *m*

whimper ['wɪmpər] *n* geignement *m* ▷ *vi* geindre

whimsical ['wɪmzɪkl] *adj* (*person*) capricieux(-euse); (*look*) étrange

whine [waɪn] *n* gémissement *m*; (*of engine, siren*) plainte stridente ▷ *vi* gémir, geindre, pleurnicher; (*dog, engine, siren*) gémir

whip [wɪp] *n* fouet *m*; (*for riding*) cravache *f*; (*Pol: person*) chef *m* de file (*assurant la discipline dans son groupe parlementaire*) ▷ *vt* fouetter; (*snatch*) enlever (*or* sortir) brusquement; **whip up** *vt* (*cream*) fouetter; (*inf: meal*) préparer en vitesse; (*stir up: support*) stimuler; (*: feeling*) attiser, aviver; *voir article*

whipped cream [wɪpt-] *n* crème fouettée

whip-round ['wɪpraund] *n* (Brit) collecte *f*

whirl [wə:l] *n* tourbillon *m* ▷ *vi* tourbillonner; (*dancers*) tournoyer ▷ *vt* faire tourbillonner; faire tournoyer

whirlpool ['wə:lpu:l] *n* tourbillon *m*

whirlwind ['wə:lwɪnd] *n* tornade *f*

whirr [wə:r] *vi* bruire; ronronner; vrombir

whisk [wɪsk] *n* (Culin) fouet *m* ▷ *vt* (*eggs*) fouetter, battre; **to ~ sb away** or **off** emmener qn rapidement

whiskers ['wɪskəz] *npl* (*of animal*) moustaches *fpl*; (*of man*) favoris *mpl*

whisky, (*Irish, US*) **whiskey** ['wɪskɪ] *n* whisky *m*

whisper ['wɪspər] *n* chuchotement *m*; (*fig: of leaves*) bruissement *m*; (*rumour*) rumeur *f* ▷ *vt, vi* chuchoter

whistle ['wɪsl] *n* (*sound*) sifflement *m*; (*object*) sifflet *m* ▷ *vi* siffler ▷ *vt* siffler, siffloter

white [waɪt] *adj* blanc/blanche; (*with fear*) blême ▷ *n* blanc *m*; (*person*) blanc/blanche; **to turn** or **go ~** (*person*) pâlir, blêmir; (*hair*) blanchir; **the ~s** (*washing*) le linge blanc; **tennis ~s** tenue *f* de tennis

whiteboard ['waɪtbɔ:d] *n* tableau *m* blanc; **interactive ~** tableau *m* (blanc) interactif

white coffee *n* (Brit) café *m* au lait, (café) crème *m*

white-collar worker ['waɪtkɔlə-] *n* employé(e) de bureau

white elephant *n* (*fig*) objet dispendieux et superflu

White House *n* (US): **the ~** la Maison-Blanche; *voir article*

white lie *n* pieux mensonge

white paper *n* (Pol) livre blanc

whitewash ['waɪtwɔʃ] *n* (*paint*) lait *m* de chaux ▷ *vt* blanchir à la chaux; (*fig*) blanchir

whiting ['waɪtɪŋ] *n* (*pl inv*: *fish*) merlan *m*

Whitsun ['wɪtsn] *n* la Pentecôte

whittle ['wɪtl] *vt*: **to ~ away**, **to ~ down** (*costs*) réduire, rogner

whizz [wɪz] *vi* aller (*or* passer) à toute vitesse

whizz kid *n* (*inf*) petit prodige

who [hu:] *pron* qui

whodunit [hu:'dʌnɪt] *n* (*inf*) roman policier

whoever [hu:'ɛvər] *pron*: **~ finds it** celui/celle qui le trouve (, qui que ce soit), quiconque le trouve; **ask ~ you like** demandez à qui vous voulez; **~ he marries** qui que ce soit or quelle que soit la personne qu'il épouse; **~ told you that?** qui a bien pu vous dire ça?, qui donc vous a dit ça?

whole [həul] *adj* (*complete*) entier(-ière), tout(e); (*not broken*) intact(e), complet(-ète) ▷ *n* (*entire unit*) tout *m*; (*all*): **the ~ of** la totalité de, tout(e) le/la; **the ~ lot** (*of it*) tout; **the ~**

lot (of them) tous (sans exception); **the ~ of the time** tout le temps; **the ~ of the town** la ville tout entière; **on the ~, as a ~** dans l'ensemble

wholefood ['həulfu:d] *n*, **wholefoods** ['həulfu:dz] *npl* aliments complets

wholehearted [həul'hɑ:tɪd] *adj* sans réserve(s), sincère

wholeheartedly [həul'hɑ:tɪdlɪ] *adv* sans réserve; **to agree ~** être entièrement d'accord

wholemeal ['həulmi:l] *adj* (Brit: *flour, bread*) complet(-ète)

wholesale ['həulseɪl] *n* (*vente f en*) gros *m* ▷ *adj* (*price*) de gros; (*destruction*) systématique

wholesaler ['həulseɪlər] *n* grossiste *m/f*

wholesome ['həulsəm] *adj* sain(e); (*advice*) salutaire

wholewheat ['həulwi:t] *adj* = **wholemeal**

wholly ['həulɪ] *adv* entièrement, tout à fait

 KEYWORD

whom [hu:m] *pron* **1** (*interrogative*) qui; **whom did you see?** qui avez-vous vu?; **to whom did you give it?** à qui l'avez-vous donné? **2** (*relative*) que; à/de *etc* qui; **the man whom I saw/to whom I spoke** l'homme que j'ai vu/à qui j'ai parlé

whooping cough ['hu:pɪŋ-] *n* coqueluche *f*

whore [hɔ:ʳ] *n* (*inf: pej*) putain *f*

 KEYWORD

whose [hu:z] *adj* **1** (*possessive: interrogative*): **whose book is this?, whose is this book?** à qui est ce livre?; **whose pencil have you taken?** à qui est le crayon que vous avez pris?, c'est le crayon de qui que vous avez pris?; **whose daughter are you?** de qui êtes-vous la fille?
2 (*possessive: relative*): **the man whose son you rescued** l'homme dont *or* de qui vous avez sauvé le fils; **the girl whose sister you were speaking to** la fille à la sœur de qui *or* de laquelle vous parliez; **the woman whose car was stolen** la femme dont la voiture a été volée
▷ *pron* à qui; **whose is this?** à qui est ceci?; **I know whose it is** je sais à qui c'est

 KEYWORD

why [waɪ] *adv* pourquoi; **why is he late?** pourquoi est-il en retard?; **why not?** pourquoi pas?
▷ *conj*: **I wonder why he said that** je me demande pourquoi il a dit ça; **that's not why I'm here** ce n'est pas pour ça que je suis là; **the reason why** la raison pour laquelle
▷ *excl* eh bien!, tiens!; **why, it's you!** tiens,

c'est vous!; **why, that's impossible!** voyons, c'est impossible!

wicked ['wɪkɪd] *adj* méchant(e); (*mischievous: grin, look*) espiègle, malicieux(-euse); (*crime*) pervers(e); (*terrible: prices, weather*) épouvantable; (*inf: very good*) génial(e) (*inf*)

wicket ['wɪkɪt] *n* (Cricket: *stumps*) guichet *m*; (: *grass area*) espace compris entre les deux guichets

wide [waɪd] *adj* large; (*area, knowledge*) vaste, très étendu(e); (*choice*) grand(e) ▷ *adv*: **to open ~** ouvrir tout grand; **to shoot ~** tirer à côté; **it is 3 metres ~** cela fait 3 mètres de large

wide-awake [waɪdə'weɪk] *adj* bien éveillé(e)

widely ['waɪdlɪ] *adv* (*different*) radicalement; (*spaced*) sur une grande étendue; (*believed*) généralement; (*travel*) beaucoup; **to be ~ read** (*author*) être beaucoup lu(e); (*reader*) avoir beaucoup lu, être cultivé(e)

widen ['waɪdn] *vt* élargir ▷ *vi* s'élargir

wide open *adj* grand(e) ouvert(e)

widespread ['waɪdspred] *adj* (*belief etc*) très répandu(e)

widget ['wɪdʒɪt] *n* (Comput) widget *m*

widow ['wɪdəu] *n* veuve *f*

widowed ['wɪdəud] *adj* (qui est devenu(e)) veuf/veuve

widower ['wɪdəuəʳ] *n* veuf *m*

width [wɪdθ] *n* largeur *f*; **it's 7 metres in ~** cela fait 7 mètres de large

wield [wi:ld] *vt* (*sword*) manier; (*power*) exercer

wife (*pl* **wives**) [waɪf, waɪvz] *n* femme *f*, épouse *f*

Wi-Fi *n* wifi *m*

wig [wɪg] *n* perruque *f*

wiggle ['wɪgl] *vt* agiter, remuer ▷ *vi* (*loose screw etc*) branler; (*worm*) se tortiller

wild [waɪld] *adj* sauvage; (*sea*) déchaîné(e); (*idea, life*) fou/folle; (*behaviour*) déchaîné(e), extravagant(e); (*inf: angry*) hors de soi, furieux(-euse); (: *enthusiastic*): **to be ~ about** être fou/folle *or* dingue de ▷ *n*: **the ~** la nature; **wilds** *npl* régions *fpl* sauvages

wild card *n* (Comput) caractère *m* de remplacement

wilderness ['wɪldənɪs] *n* désert *m*, région *f* sauvage

wildlife ['waɪldlaɪf] *n* faune *f* (et flore *f*)

wildly ['waɪldlɪ] *adv* (*behave*) de manière déchaînée; (*applaud*) frénétiquement; (*hit, guess*) au hasard; (*happy*) follement

wilful, (US) **willful** ['wɪlful] *adj* (*person*) obstiné(e); (*action*) délibéré(e); (*crime*) prémédité(e)

 KEYWORD

will [wɪl] *aux vb* **1** (*forming future tense*): **I will finish it tomorrow** je le finirai demain;

I will have finished it by tomorrow je l'aurai fini d'ici demain; **will you do it?** — **yes I will/no I won't** le ferez-vous? — oui/non; **you won't lose it, will you?** vous ne le perdrez pas, n'est-ce pas?

2 (in conjectures, predictions): **he will** or **he'll be there by now** il doit être arrivé à l'heure qu'il est; **that will be the postman** ça doit être le facteur

3 (in commands, requests, offers): **will you be quiet!** voulez-vous bien vous taire!; **will you help me?** est-ce que vous pouvez m'aider?; **will you have a cup of tea?** voulez-vous une tasse de thé?; **I won't put up with it!** je ne le tolérerai pas!

▷ vt (pt, pp **willed**); **to will sb to do** souhaiter ardemment que qn fasse; **he willed himself to go on** par un suprême effort de volonté, il continua

▷ n volonté f; (document) testament m; **to do sth of one's own free will** faire qch de son propre gré; **against one's will** à contre-cœur

willing ['wɪlɪŋ] adj de bonne volonté, serviable ▷ n: **to show ~** faire preuve de bonne volonté; **he's ~ to do it** il est disposé à le faire, il veut bien le faire
willingly ['wɪlɪŋlɪ] adv volontiers
willingness ['wɪlɪŋnɪs] n bonne volonté
willow ['wɪləu] n saule m
willpower ['wɪl'pauə'] n volonté f
willy-nilly ['wɪlɪ'nɪlɪ] adv bon gré mal gré
wilt [wɪlt] vi dépérir
win [wɪn] (pt, pp **won**) [wʌn] n (in sports etc) victoire f ▷ vt (battle, money) gagner; (prize, contract) remporter; (popularity) acquérir ▷ vi gagner; **win over** vt convaincre; **win round** vt gagner, se concilier
wince [wɪns] n tressaillement m ▷ vi tressaillir
winch [wɪntʃ] n treuil m
wind¹ [wɪnd] n (also Med) vent m; (breath) souffle m ▷ vt (take breath away) couper le souffle à; **the ~(s)** (Mus) les instruments mpl à vent; **into** or **against the ~** contre le vent; **to get ~ of sth** (fig) avoir vent de qch; **to break ~** avoir des gaz
wind² (pt, pp **wound**) [waɪnd, waund] vt enrouler; (wrap) envelopper; (clock, toy) remonter ▷ vi (road, river) serpenter; **wind down** vt (car window) baisser; (fig: production, business) réduire progressivement; **wind up** vt (clock) remonter; (debate) terminer, clôturer
windfall ['wɪndfɔːl] n coup m de chance
wind farm n ferme f éolienne
winding ['waɪndɪŋ] adj (road) sinueux(-euse); (staircase) tournant(e)
wind instrument n (Mus) instrument m à vent
windmill ['wɪndmɪl] n moulin m à vent

window ['wɪndəu] n fenêtre f; (in car, train: also: **~pane**) vitre f; (in shop etc) vitrine f
window box n jardinière f
window cleaner n (person) laveur(-euse) de vitres
window ledge n rebord m de la fenêtre
window pane n vitre f, carreau m
window seat n (on plane) place f côté hublot
window-shopping ['wɪndəuʃɔpɪŋ] n: **to go ~** faire du lèche-vitrines
windowsill ['wɪndəusɪl] n (inside) appui m de la fenêtre; (outside) rebord m de la fenêtre
windpipe ['wɪndpaɪp] n gosier m
wind power n énergie éolienne
windscreen ['wɪndskriːn] n pare-brise m inv
windscreen washer n lave-glace m inv
windscreen wiper, (US) **windshield wiper** [-waɪpə'] n essuie-glace m inv
windshield ['wɪndʃiːld] (US) n = **windscreen**
windsurfing ['wɪndsəːfɪŋ] n planche f à voile
windswept ['wɪndswept] adj balayé(e) par le vent
windy ['wɪndɪ] adj (day) de vent, venteux(-euse); (place, weather) venteux; **it's ~** il y a du vent
wine [waɪn] n vin m ▷ vt: **to ~ and dine sb** offrir un dîner bien arrosé à qn
wine bar n bar m à vin
wine cellar n cave f à vins
wine glass n verre m à vin
wine list n carte f des vins
wine tasting [-teɪstɪŋ] n dégustation f (de vins)
wine waiter n sommelier m
wing [wɪŋ] n aile f; (in air force) groupe m d'escadrilles; **wings** npl (Theat) coulisses fpl
winger ['wɪŋə'] n (Sport) ailier m
wing mirror n (Brit) rétroviseur latéral
wink [wɪŋk] n clin m d'œil ▷ vi faire un clin d'œil; (blink) cligner des yeux
winner ['wɪnə'] n gagnant(e)
winning ['wɪnɪŋ] adj (team) gagnant(e); (goal) décisif(-ive); (charming) charmeur(-euse)
winnings ['wɪnɪŋz] npl gains mpl
winter ['wɪntə'] n hiver m ▷ vi hiverner; **in ~** en hiver
winter sports npl sports mpl d'hiver
wintertime ['wɪntətaɪm] n hiver m
wintry ['wɪntrɪ] adj hivernal(e)
wipe [waɪp] n coup m de torchon (or de chiffon or d'éponge); **to give sth a ~** donner un coup de torchon/de chiffon/d'éponge à qch ▷ vt essuyer; (erase: tape) effacer; **to ~ one's nose** se moucher; **wipe off** vt essuyer; **wipe out** vt (debt) éteindre, amortir; (memory) effacer; (destroy) anéantir; **wipe up** vt essuyer
wire ['waɪə'] n fil m (de fer); (Elec) fil électrique; (Tel) télégramme m ▷ vt (fence) grillager; (house) faire l'installation électrique de; (also: **~ up**) brancher; (person: send telegram to) télégraphier à

W

wireless ['waɪəlɪs] (*Brit*) *adj* sans fil ▷ *n* télégraphie *f* sans fil; (*set*) T.S.F. *f*

wiring ['waɪərɪŋ] *n* (*Elec*) installation *f* électrique

wiry ['waɪərɪ] *adj* noueux(-euse), nerveux(-euse)

wisdom ['wɪzdəm] *n* sagesse *f*; (*of action*) prudence *f*

wisdom tooth *n* dent *f* de sagesse

wise [waɪz] *adj* sage, prudent(e); (*remark*) judicieux(-euse); **I'm none the ~r** je ne suis pas plus avancé(e) pour autant; **wise up** *vi* (*inf*): **to ~ up to** commencer à se rendre compte de

wish [wɪʃ] *n* (*desire*) désir *m*; (*specific desire*) souhait *m*, vœu *m* ▷ *vt* souhaiter, désirer, vouloir; **best ~es** (*on birthday etc*) meilleurs vœux; **with best ~es** (*in letter*) bien amicalement; **give her my best ~es** faites-lui mes amitiés; **to ~ sb goodbye** dire au revoir à qn; **he ~ed me well** il m'a souhaité bonne chance; **to ~ to do/sb to do** désirer or vouloir faire/que qn fasse; **to ~ for** souhaiter; **to ~ sth on sb** souhaiter qch à qn

wishful ['wɪʃful] *adj*: **it's ~ thinking** c'est prendre ses désirs pour des réalités

wistful ['wɪstful] *adj* mélancolique

wit [wɪt] *n* (*also*: **~s**: *intelligence*) intelligence *f*, esprit *m*; (*presence of mind*) présence *f* d'esprit; (*wittiness*) esprit; (*person*) homme/femme d'esprit; **to be at one's ~s' end** (*fig*) ne plus savoir que faire; **to have one's ~s about one** avoir toute sa présence d'esprit, ne pas perdre la tête; **to ~** *adv* à savoir

witch [wɪtʃ] *n* sorcière *f*

witchcraft ['wɪtʃkrɑːft] *n* sorcellerie *f*

 KEYWORD

with [wɪð, wɪθ] *prep* **1** (*in the company of*) avec; (*at the home of*) chez; **we stayed with friends** nous avons logé chez des amis; **I'll be with you in a minute** je suis à vous dans un instant

2 (*descriptive*): **a room with a view** une chambre avec vue; **the man with the grey hat/blue eyes** l'homme au chapeau gris/aux yeux bleus

3 (*indicating manner, means, cause*): **with tears in her eyes** les larmes aux yeux; **to walk with a stick** marcher avec une canne; **red with anger** rouge de colère; **to shake with fear** trembler de peur; **to fill sth with water** remplir qch d'eau

4 (*in phrases*): **I'm with you** (*I understand*) je vous suis; **to be with it** (*inf: up-to-date*) être dans le vent

withdraw [wɪθ'drɔː] *vt* (*irreg like*: **draw**) retirer ▷ *vi* se retirer; (*go back on promise*) se rétracter; **to ~ into o.s.** se replier sur soi-même

withdrawal [wɪθ'drɔːəl] *n* retrait *m*; (*Med*) état *m* de manque

withdrawal symptoms *npl*: **to have ~** être en état de manque, présenter les symptômes *mpl* de sevrage

withdrawn [wɪθ'drɔːn] *pp of* **withdraw** ▷ *adj* (*person*) renfermé(e)

withdrew [wɪθ'druː] *pt of* **withdraw**

wither ['wɪðəʳ] *vi* se faner

withhold [wɪθ'həuld] *vt* (*irreg like*: **hold**) (*money*) retenir; (*decision*) remettre; **to ~ (from)** (*permission*) refuser (à); (*information*) cacher (à)

within [wɪð'ɪn] *prep* à l'intérieur de ▷ *adv* à l'intérieur; **~ his reach** à sa portée; **~ sight of** en vue de; **~ a mile of** à moins d'un mille de; **~ the week** avant la fin de la semaine; **~ an hour from now** d'ici une heure; **to be ~ the law** être légal(e) or dans les limites de la légalité

without [wɪð'aut] *prep* sans; **~ a coat** sans manteau; **~ speaking** sans parler; **~ anybody knowing** sans que personne le sache; **to go** *or* **do ~ sth** se passer de qch

withstand [wɪθ'stænd] *vt* (*irreg like*: **stand**) résister à

witness ['wɪtnɪs] *n* (*person*) témoin *m*; (*evidence*) témoignage *m* ▷ *vt* (*event*) être témoin de; (*document*) attester l'authenticité de; **to bear ~ to sth** témoigner de qch; **~ for the prosecution/defence** témoin à charge/ à décharge; **to ~ to sth/having seen sth** témoigner de qch/d'avoir vu qch

witness box, (*US*) **witness stand** *n* barre *f* des témoins

witty ['wɪtɪ] *adj* spirituel(le), plein(e) d'esprit

wives [waɪvz] *npl of* **wife**

wizard ['wɪzəd] *n* magicien *m*

wk *abbr* = **week**

wobble ['wɔbl] *vi* trembler; (*chair*) branler

woe [wəu] *n* malheur *m*

woke [wəuk] *pt of* **wake**

woken ['wəukn] *pp of* **wake**

wolf (*pl* **wolves**) [wulf, wulvz] *n* loup *m*

woman (*pl* **women**) ['wumən, 'wɪmɪn] *n* femme *f* ▷ *cpd*: **~ doctor** femme *f* médecin; **~ friend** amie *f*; **~ teacher** professeur *m* femme; **young ~** jeune femme; **women's page** (*Press*) page *f* des lectrices

womanly ['wumənlɪ] *adj* féminin(e)

womb [wuːm] *n* (*Anat*) utérus *m*

women ['wɪmɪn] *npl of* **woman**

won [wʌn] *pt*, *pp of* **win**

wonder ['wʌndəʳ] *n* merveille *f*, miracle *m*; (*feeling*) émerveillement *m* ▷ *vi*: **to ~ whether/why** se demander si/pourquoi; **to ~ at** (*surprise*) s'étonner de; (*admiration*) s'émerveiller de; **to ~ about** songer à; **it's no ~ that** il n'est pas étonnant que + *sub*

wonderful ['wʌndəful] *adj* merveilleux(-euse)

won't [wəunt] = **will not**

wood [wud] *n* (*timber, forest*) bois *m* ▷ *cpd* de bois, en bois

wood carving *n* sculpture *f* en *or* sur bois

wooded ['wudɪd] *adj* boisé(e)

wooden ['wudn] *adj* en bois; (*fig: actor*) raide; (*: performance*) qui manque de naturel

woodpecker ['wudpekəʳ] *n* pic *m* (*oiseau*)

woodwind ['wudwɪnd] *n* (*Mus*) bois *m*; **the ~** les bois *mpl*

woodwork ['wudwəːk] *n* menuiserie *f*

woodworm ['wudwəːm] *n* ver *m* du bois; **the table has got ~** la table est piquée des vers

wool [wul] *n* laine *f*; **to pull the ~ over sb's eyes** (*fig*) en faire accroire à qn

woollen, (*US*) **woolen** ['wulən] *adj* de *or* en laine; (*industry*) lainier(-ière) ▷ *n*: **~s** lainages *mpl*

woolly, (*US*) **wooly** ['wulɪ] *adj* laineux(-euse); (*fig: ideas*) confus(e)

word [wəːd] *n* mot *m*; (*spoken*) mot, parole *f*; (*promise*) parole *f*; (*news*) nouvelles *fpl* ▷ *vt* rédiger, formuler; **~ for ~** (*repeat*) mot pour mot; (*translate*) mot à mot; **what's the ~ for "pen" in French?** comment dit-on "pen" en français?; **to put sth into ~s** exprimer qch; **in other ~s** en d'autres termes; **to have a ~ with sb** toucher un mot à qn; **to have ~s with sb** (*quarrel with*) avoir des mots avec qn; **to break/keep one's ~** manquer à sa parole/tenir (sa) parole; **I'll take your ~ for it** je vous crois sur parole; **to send ~ of** prévenir de; **to leave ~ (with sb/for sb) that ...** laisser un mot (à qn/pour qn) disant que ...

wording ['wəːdɪŋ] *n* termes *mpl*, langage *m*; (*of document*) libellé *m*

word processing *n* traitement *m* de texte

word processor [-prəusesəʳ] *n* machine *f* de traitement de texte

wore [wɔːʳ] *pt of* **wear**

work [wəːk] *n* travail *m*; (*Art, Literature*) œuvre *f* ▷ *vi* travailler; (*mechanism*) marcher, fonctionner; (*plan etc*) marcher; (*medicine*) agir ▷ *vt* (*clay, wood etc*) travailler; (*mine etc*) exploiter; (*machine*) faire marcher *or* fonctionner; (*miracles etc*) faire; **works** *n* (*Brit: factory*) usine *f* ▷ *npl* (*of clock, machine*) mécanisme *m*; **how does this ~?** comment est-ce que ça marche?; **the TV isn't ~ing** la télévision est en panne *or* ne marche pas; **to go to ~** aller travailler; **to set to ~, to start ~** se mettre à l'œuvre; **to be at ~ (on sth)** travailler (sur qch); **to be out of ~** être au chômage *or* sans emploi; **to ~ hard** travailler dur; **to ~ loose** se défaire, se desserrer; **road ~s** travaux *mpl* (d'entretien des routes); **work on** *vt fus* travailler à; (*principle*) se baser sur; **work out** *vi* (*plans etc*) marcher; (*Sport*) s'entraîner ▷ *vt* (*problem*) résoudre; (*plan*) élaborer; **it ~s out at £100** ça fait 100 livres; **work up** *vt*: **to get ~ed up** se mettre dans tous ses états

workable ['wəːkəbl] *adj* (*solution*) réalisable

workaholic [wəːkə'hɔlɪk] *n* bourreau *m* de travail

worker ['wəːkəʳ] *n* travailleur(-euse), ouvrier(-ière); **office ~** employé(e) de bureau

work experience *n* stage *m*

workforce ['wəːkfɔːs] *n* main-d'œuvre *f*

working ['wəːkɪŋ] *adj* (*day, tools etc, conditions*) de travail; (*wife*) qui travaille; (*partner, population*) actif(-ive); **in ~ order** en état de marche; **a ~ knowledge of English** une connaissance toute pratique de l'anglais

working class *n* classe ouvrière ▷ *adj*: **working-class** ouvrier(-ière), de la classe ouvrière

working week *n* semaine *f* de travail

workman ['wəːkmən] *irreg n* ouvrier *m*

workmanship ['wəːkmənʃɪp] *n* métier *m*, habileté *f*; facture *f*

work of art *n* œuvre *f* d'art

workout ['wəːkaut] *n* (*Sport*) séance *f* d'entraînement

work permit *n* permis *m* de travail

workplace ['wəːkpleɪs] *n* lieu *m* de travail

worksheet ['wəːkʃiːt] *n* (*Scol*) feuille *f* d'exercices; (*Comput*) feuille *f* de programmation

workshop ['wəːkʃɔp] *n* atelier *m*

work station *n* poste *m* de travail

work surface *n* plan *m* de travail

worktop ['wəːktɔp] *n* plan *m* de travail

work-to-rule ['wəːktə'ruːl] *n* (*Brit*) grève *f* du zèle

world [wəːld] *n* monde *m* ▷ *cpd* (*champion*) du monde; (*power, war*) mondial(e); **all over the ~** dans le monde entier, partout dans le monde; **to think the ~ of sb** (*fig*) ne jurer que par qn; **what in the ~ is he doing?** qu'est-ce qu'il peut bien être en train de faire?; **to do sb a ~ of good** faire le plus grand bien à qn; **W~ War One/Two, the First/Second W~ War** la Première/Deuxième Guerre mondiale; **out of this ~** *adj* extraordinaire

World Cup *n*: **the ~** (*Football*) la Coupe du monde

worldly ['wəːldlɪ] *adj* de ce monde

world-wide ['wəːld'waɪd] *adj* universel(le) ▷ *adv* dans le monde entier

World-Wide Web *n*: **the ~** le Web

worm [wəːm] *n* (*also: earth~*) ver *m*

worn [wɔːn] *pp of* **wear** ▷ *adj* usé(e)

worn-out ['wɔːnaut] *adj* (*object*) complètement usé(e); (*person*) épuisé(e)

worried ['wʌrɪd] *adj* inquiet(-ète); **to be ~ about sth** être inquiet au sujet de qch

worry ['wʌrɪ] *n* souci *m* ▷ *vt* inquiéter ▷ *vi* s'inquiéter, se faire du souci; **to ~ about** *or* **over sth/sb** se faire du souci pour *or* à propos de qch/qn

worrying ['wʌrɪɪŋ] *adj* inquiétant(e)

worse [wəːs] *adj* pire, plus mauvais(e) ▷ *adv* plus mal ▷ *n* pire *m*; **to get ~** (*condition,* *situation*) empirer, se dégrader; **a change for the ~** une détérioration; **he is none the ~ for it** il ne s'en porte pas plus mal; **so much the ~ for you!** tant pis pour vous!

worsen ['wə:sn] *vt, vi* empirer

worse off *adj* moins à l'aise financièrement; (*fig*): **you'll be ~ this way** ça ira moins bien de cette façon; **he is now ~ than before** il se retrouve dans une situation pire qu'auparavant

worship ['wə:ʃip] *n* culte *m* ▷ *vt* (*God*) rendre un culte à; (*person*) adorer; **Your W~** (*Brit: to mayor*) Monsieur le Maire; (: *to judge*) Monsieur le Juge

worst [wə:st] *adj* le/la pire, le/la plus mauvais(e); (*person*) adorer; **Your W~** (*Brit: to mayor*) au pis aller; **if the ~ comes to the ~** si le pire doit arriver

worth [wə:θ] *n* valeur *f* ▷ *adj*: **to be ~** valoir; **how much is it ~?** ça vaut combien?; **it's ~ it** cela en vaut la peine, ça vaut la peine; **it is ~ one's while (to do)** ça vaut le coup (*inf*) (de faire); **50 pence ~ of apples** (pour) 50 pence de pommes

worthless ['wə:θlis] *adj* qui ne vaut rien

worthwhile ['wə:θ'waɪl] *adj* (*activity*) qui en vaut la peine; (*cause*) louable; **a ~ book** un livre qui vaut la peine d'être lu

worthy ['wə:ði] *adj* (*person*) digne; (*motive*) louable; **~ of** digne de

 KEYWORD

would [wud] *aux vb* **1** (*conditional tense*): **if you asked him he would do it** si vous le lui demandiez, il le ferait; **if you had asked him he would have done it** si vous le lui aviez demandé, il l'aurait fait
2 (*in offers, invitations, requests*): **would you like a biscuit?** voulez-vous un biscuit?; **would you close the door please?** voulez-vous fermer la porte, s'il vous plaît?
3 (*in indirect speech*): **I said I would do it** j'ai dit que je le ferais
4 (*emphatic*): **it WOULD have to snow today!** naturellement il neige aujourd'hui! *or* il fallait qu'il neige aujourd'hui!
5 (*insistence*): **she wouldn't do it** elle n'a pas voulu *or* elle a refusé de le faire
6 (*conjecture*): **it would have been midnight** il devait être minuit; **it would seem so** on dirait bien
7 (*indicating habit*): **he would go there on Mondays** il y allait le lundi

would-be ['wudbi:] *adj* (*pej*) soi-disant

wouldn't ['wudnt] = **would not**

wound¹ [wu:nd] *n* blessure *f* ▷ *vt* blesser; **~ed in the leg** blessé à la jambe

wound² [waund] *pt, pp of* **wind²**

wove [wəuv] *pt of* **weave**

woven ['wəuvn] *pp of* **weave**

wrap [ræp] *n* (*stole*) écharpe *f*; (*cape*) pèlerine *f* ▷ *vt* (*also:* **~ up**) envelopper; (*parcel*) emballer; (*wind*) enrouler; **under ~s** (*fig: plan, scheme*) secret(-ète)

wrapper ['ræpə'] *n* (*on chocolate etc*) papier *m*; (*Brit: of book*) couverture *f*

wrapping ['ræpɪŋ] *n* (*of sweet, chocolate*) papier *m*; (*of parcel*) emballage *m*

wrapping paper *n* papier *m* d'emballage; (*for gift*) papier cadeau

wreak [ri:k] *vt* (*destruction*) entraîner; **to ~ havoc** faire des ravages; **to ~ vengeance on** se venger de, exercer sa vengeance sur

wreath [ri:θ, *pl* ri:ðz] *n* couronne *f*

wreck [rek] *n* (*sea disaster*) naufrage *m*; (*ship*) épave *f*; (*vehicle*) véhicule accidenté; (*pej: person*) loque (humaine) ▷ *vt* démolir; (*ship*) provoquer le naufrage de; (*fig*) briser, ruiner

wreckage ['rekidʒ] *n* débris *mpl*; (*of building*) décombres *mpl*; (*of ship*) naufrage *m*

wren [ren] *n* (*Zool*) troglodyte *m*

wrench [rentʃ] *n* (*Tech*) clé *f* (à écrous); (*tug*) violent mouvement de torsion; (*fig*) déchirement *m* ▷ *vt* tirer violemment sur, tordre; **to ~ sth from** arracher qch (violemment) à *or* de

wrestle ['resl] *vi*: **to ~ (with sb)** lutter (avec qn); **to ~ with** (*fig*) se débattre avec, lutter contre

wrestler ['reslə'] *n* lutteur(-euse)

wrestling ['resliŋ] *n* lutte *f*; (*also:* **all-in ~**: *Brit*) catch *m*

wretched ['retʃid] *adj* misérable; (*inf*) maudit(e)

wriggle ['rɪgl] *n* tortillement *m* ▷ *vi* (*also:* **~ about**) se tortiller

wring (*pt, pp* **wrung**) [rɪŋ, rʌŋ] *vt* tordre; (*wet clothes*) essorer; (*fig*): **to ~ sth out of** arracher qch à

wrinkle ['rɪŋkl] *n* (*on skin*) ride *f*; (*on paper etc*) pli *m* ▷ *vt* rider, plisser ▷ *vi* se plisser

wrinkled ['rɪŋkld], **wrinkly** ['rɪŋklɪ] *adj* (*fabric, paper*) froissé(e), plissé(e); (*surface*) plissé; (*skin*) ridé(e), plissé

wrist [rist] *n* poignet *m*

wrist watch ['ristwɔtʃ] *n* montre-bracelet *f*

writ [rit] *n* acte *m* judiciaire; **to issue a ~ against sb, to serve a ~ on sb** assigner qn en justice

write (*pt* **wrote**, *pp* **written**) [rait, rəut, 'ritn] *vt, vi* écrire; (*prescription*) rédiger; **to ~ sb a letter** écrire une lettre à qn; **write away** *vi*: **to ~ away for** (*information*) (écrire pour) demander; (*goods*) (écrire pour) commander; **write down** *vt* noter; (*put in writing*) mettre par écrit; **write off** *vt* (*debt*) passer aux profits et pertes; (*project*) mettre une croix sur; (*depreciate*) amortir; (*smash up: car etc*) démolir complètement; **write out** *vt* écrire; (*copy*) recopier; **write up** *vt* rédiger

write-off ['raitɔf] *n* perte totale; **the car is a ~** la voiture est bonne pour la casse

writer ['raɪtər] *n* auteur *m*, écrivain *m*

writhe [raɪð] *vi* se tordre

writing ['raɪtɪŋ] *n* écriture *f*; *(of author)* œuvres *fpl*; **in ~** par écrit; **in my own ~** écrit(e) de ma main

writing paper *n* papier *m* à lettres

written ['rɪtn] *pp of* **write**

wrong [rɔŋ] *adj (incorrect)* faux/fausse; *(incorrectly chosen: number, road etc)* mauvais(e); *(not suitable)* qui ne convient pas; *(wicked)* mal; *(unfair)* injuste ▷ *adv* mal ▷ *n* tort *m* ▷ *vt* faire du tort à, léser; *(answer)* être faux/fausse; *(in doing/saying)* avoir tort (de dire/faire); **you are ~ to do it** tu as tort de le faire; **it's ~ to steal, stealing is ~** c'est mal de voler; **you are ~ about that, you've got it ~** tu te trompes; **to be in the ~** avoir tort; **what's ~?** qu'est-ce qui ne va pas?; **there's nothing ~ with** tout va bien; **what's ~ with the car?** qu'est-ce qu'elle a, la voiture?; **to go ~** *(person)* se tromper; *(plan)* mal tourner; *(machine)* se détraquer; **I took a ~ turning** je me suis trompé de route

wrongful ['rɔŋful] *adj* injustifié(e); **~ dismissal** *(Industry)* licenciement abusif

wrongly ['rɔŋlɪ] *adv* à tort; *(answer, do, count)* mal, incorrectement; *(treat)* injustement

wrong number *n* (Tel): **you have the ~** vous vous êtes trompé de numéro

wrong side *n* *(of cloth)* envers *m*

wrote [rəʊt] *pt of* **write**

wrought [rɔːt] *adj*: **~ iron** fer forgé

wrung [rʌŋ] *pt, pp of* **wring**

wt. *abbr* (= *weight*) pds.

WWW *n abbr* = **World-Wide Web**

XL *abbr* (= *extra large*) XL

Xmas ['ɛksməs] *n abbr* = **Christmas**

X-ray ['ɛksreɪ] *n (ray)* rayon *m* X; *(photograph)* radio(graphie) *f* ▷ *vt* radiographier

xylophone ['zaɪləfəʊn] *n* xylophone *m*

Yellow Pages® *npl* (*Tel*) pages *fpl* jaunes

yelp [jɛlp] *n* jappement *m*; glapissement *m*
▷ *vi* japper; glapir

yes [jɛs] *adv* oui; (*answering negative question*) si
▷ *n* oui *m*; **to say ~ (to)** dire oui (à)

yesterday [ˈjɛstədɪ] *adv, n* hier (*m*);
~ morning/evening hier matin/soir; **the
day before ~** avant-hier; **all day ~** toute la
journée d'hier

yet [jɛt] *adv* encore; (*in questions*) déjà ▷ *conj*
pourtant, néanmoins; **it is not finished ~** ce
n'est pas encore fini *or* toujours pas fini;
must you go just ~? dois-tu déjà partir?;
have you eaten ~? vous avez déjà mangé?;
the best ~ le meilleur jusqu'ici *or* jusque-là;
as ~ jusqu'ici, encore; **a few days ~** encore
quelques jours; **~ again** une fois de plus

yew [juː] *n* if *m*

Yiddish [ˈjɪdɪʃ] *n* yiddish *m*

yield [jiːld] *n* production *f*, rendement *m*;
(*Finance*) rapport *m* ▷ *vt* produire, rendre,
rapporter; (*surrender*) céder ▷ *vi* céder; (*US
Aut*) céder la priorité; **a ~ of 5%** un rendement
de 5%

YMCA *n abbr* (= *Young Men's Christian Association*)
≈ union chrétienne de jeunes gens (UCJG)

yob [ˈjɔb], **yobbo** [ˈjɔbəu] *n* (*Brit inf*)
loubar(d) *m*

yoga [ˈjəugə] *n* yoga *m*

yoghurt, yogurt [ˈjɔgət] *n* yaourt *m*

yoke [jəuk] *n* joug *m* ▷ *vt* (*also*: **~ together**:
oxen) accoupler

yolk [jəuk] *n* jaune *m* (d'œuf)

---

yacht [jɔt] *n* voilier *m*; (*motor, luxury yacht*)
yacht *m*

yachting [ˈjɔtɪŋ] *n* yachting *m*, navigation *f*
de plaisance

yachtsman [ˈjɔtsmən] *irreg n* yacht(s)man *m*

Yank [jæŋk], **Yankee** [ˈjæŋkɪ] *n* (*pej*)
Amerloque *m/f*, Ricain(e)

yank [jæŋk] *vt* tirer d'un coup sec

yap [jæp] *vi* (*dog*) japper

yard [jɑːd] *n* (*of house etc*) cour *f*; (*US: garden*)
jardin *m*; (*measure*) yard *m* (= 914 mm; 3 feet);
builder's ~ chantier *m*

yard sale *n* (*US*) brocante *f* (dans son propre
jardin)

yardstick [ˈjɑːdstɪk] *n* (*fig*) mesure *f*, critère *m*

yarn [jɑːn] *n* fil *m*; (*tale*) longue histoire

yawn [jɔːn] *n* bâillement *m* ▷ *vi* bâiller

yawning [ˈjɔːnɪŋ] *adj* (*gap*) béant(e)

yd. *abbr* = **yard**; **yards**

yeah [jɛə] *adv* (*inf*) ouais

year [jɪəʳ] *n* an *m*, année *f*; (*Scol etc*) année;
every ~ tous les ans, chaque année; **this ~**
cette année; **a** *or* **per ~** par an; **~ in, ~ out**
année après année; **to be 8 ~s old** avoir 8 ans;
an eight-~-old child un enfant de huit ans

yearly [ˈjɪəlɪ] *adj* annuel(le) ▷ *adv*
annuellement; **twice ~** deux fois par an

yearn [jəːn] *vi*: **to ~ for sth/to do** aspirer à
qch/à faire

yeast [jiːst] *n* levure *f*

yell [jɛl] *n* hurlement *m*, cri *m* ▷ *vi* hurler

yellow [ˈjɛləu] *adj, n* jaune (*m*)

⊙ KEYWORD

you [juː] *pron* **1** (*subject*) tu; (*polite form*) vous;
(*plural*) vous; **you are very kind** vous êtes très
gentil; **you French enjoy your food** vous
autres Français, vous aimez bien manger;
you and I will go toi et moi *or* vous et moi,
nous irons; **there you are!** vous voilà!
2 (*object: direct, indirect*) te, t' + *vowel*; vous;
I know you je te *or* vous connais; **I gave it
to you** je te l'ai donné, je vous l'ai donné
3 (*stressed*) toi; vous; **I told you to do it** c'est
à toi *or* vous que j'ai dit de le faire
4 (*after prep, in comparisons*) toi; vous; **it's for
you** c'est pour toi *or* vous; **she's younger
than you** elle est plus jeune que toi *or* vous
5 (*impersonal: one*) on; **fresh air does you
good** l'air frais fait du bien; **you never know**
on ne sait jamais; **you can't do that!** ça ne se
fait pas!

you'd [juːd] = **you had**; **you would**

you'll [juːl] = **you will**; **you shall**

young [jʌŋ] *adj* jeune ▷ *npl* (*of animal*) petits
mpl; (*people*): **the ~** les jeunes, la jeunesse;
a ~ man un jeune homme; **a ~ lady**
(*unmarried*) une jeune fille, une demoiselle;
(*married*) une jeune femme *or* dame; **my ~er**

brother mon frère cadet; **the ~er generation** la jeune génération

younger [ˈjʌŋɡəʳ] adj (brother etc) cadet(te)

youngster [ˈjʌŋstəʳ] n jeune m/f; (child) enfant m/f

your [jɔːʳ] adj ton/ta, tes pl; (polite form, pl) votre, vos pl; see also **my**

you're [juəʳ] = **you are**

yours [jɔːz] pron le/la tien(ne), les tiens/tiennes; (polite form, pl) le/la vôtre, les vôtres; **is it ~?** c'est à toi (or à vous)?; **a friend of ~** un(e) de tes (or de vos) amis; see also **faithfully; sincerely**

yourself [jɔːˈsɛlf] pron (reflexive) te; (: polite form) vous; (after prep) toi; vous; (emphatic) toi-même; vous-même; **you ~ told me** c'est vous qui me l'avez dit, vous me l'avez dit vous-même; see also **oneself**

yourselves [jɔːˈsɛlvz] pl pron vous; (emphatic) vous-mêmes; see also **oneself**

youth [juːθ] n jeunesse f; (young man) (pl **youths**) [juːðz] jeune homme m; **in my ~** dans ma jeunesse, quand j'étais jeune

youth club n centre m de jeunes

youthful [ˈjuːθful] adj jeune; (enthusiasm etc) juvénile; (misdemeanour) de jeunesse

youth hostel n auberge f de jeunesse

you've [juːv] = **you have**

Yugoslav [ˈjuːɡəuslɑːv] adj (Hist) yougoslave ▷ n Yougoslave m/f

Yugoslavia [juːɡəuˈslɑːviə] n (Hist) Yougoslavie f

yuppie [ˈjʌpɪ] n yuppie m/f

YWCA n abbr (= Young Women's Christian Association) union chrétienne féminine

zany [ˈzeɪnɪ] adj farfelu(e), loufoque

zap [zæp] vt (Comput) effacer

zeal [ziːl] n (revolutionary etc) ferveur f; (keenness) ardeur f, zèle m

zebra [ˈziːbrə] n zèbre m

zebra crossing n (Brit) passage clouté or pour piétons

zero [ˈzɪərəu] n zéro m ▷ vi: **to ~ in on** (target) se diriger droit sur; **5° below ~** 5 degrés au-dessous de zéro

zest [zɛst] n entrain m, élan m; (of lemon etc) zeste m

zigzag [ˈzɪɡzæɡ] n zigzag m ▷ vi zigzaguer, faire des zigzags

Zimbabwe [zɪmˈbɑːbwɪ] n Zimbabwe m

Zimmer® [ˈzɪməʳ] n (also: ~ frame) déambulateur m

zinc [zɪŋk] n zinc m

zip [zɪp] n (also: ~ fastener) fermeture f éclair® or à glissière; (energy) entrain m ▷ vt (file) zipper; (also: ~ up) fermer (avec une fermeture éclair®)

zip code n (US) code postal

zip file n (Comput) fichier m zip inv

zipper [ˈzɪpəʳ] n (US) = **zip**

zit [zɪt] (inf) n bouton m

zodiac [ˈzəudɪæk] n zodiaque m

zone [zəun] n zone f

zoo [zuː] n zoo m

zoology [zuːˈɔlədʒɪ] n zoologie f

zoom [zuːm] vi: **to ~ past** passer en

trombe; **to ~ in (on sb/sth)** (*Phot, Cine*)
zoomer (sur qn/qch)
zoom lens *n* zoom *m*, objectif *m* à focale
variable
zucchini [zuːˈkiːnɪ] *n* (*US*) courgette *f*

Grammar

Grammaire

Using the grammar

The Grammar section deals systematically and comprehensively with all the information you will need in order to communicate accurately in French. The numbers → ❶ *etc* direct you to the relevant example in every case.

Abbreviations

fem.	*feminine*
infin.	*infinitive*
masc.	*masculine*
perf.	*perfect*
plur.	*plural*
qch	quelque chose
qn	quelqu'un
sb	somebody
sing.	*singular*
sth	something

Contents

Glossary

VERBS

VERB a 'doing' word which describes what someone or something does, is, or what happens to them, for example, *be, sing, live*.

ACTIVE a form of the verb that is used when the subject of the verb is the person or thing doing the action.

AGREE (to) in the case of adjectives and pronouns, to have the correct word ending or form according to whether what is referred to is masculine, feminine, singular or plural; in the case of verbs, to have the form which goes with the person or thing carrying out the action.

AUXILIARY VERB a verb such as *be, have* or *do* used with a main verb to form tenses and questions.

BASE FORM the form of the verb without any endings added to it.

CONDITIONAL a verb form used to talk about things that would happen or would be true under certain conditions, for example, *I would help you if I could*. It is also used to say what you would like or need, for example, *Could you give me the bill?*

CONJUGATE (to) to give a verb different endings according to whether you are referring to *I, you, they* and so on, and according to whether you are referring to the present, past or future.

CONJUGATION a group of verbs which have the same endings as each other or change according to the same pattern.

CONTINUOUS TENSE a verb tense formed using *to be* and the *-ing* form of the main verb.

DIRECT OBJECT a noun or pronoun used with verbs to show who or what is acted on by the verb. For example, in *He wrote a letter, letter* is the direct object.

ENDING a form added to a verb, for example, *go → goes*, and to adjectives, nouns and pronouns depending on whether they refer to masculine, feminine, singular or plural things or persons.

FUTURE a verb tense used to talk about something that will happen or will be true.

GERUND a verb form in English ending in *-ing*, for example, *eating, sleeping*.

IMPERATIVE the form of a verb used when giving orders and instructions, for example, *Shut the door!*

IMPERFECT one of the verb tenses used to talk about the past, especially in descriptions, and to say what was happening or used to happen, for example, *It was sunny at the weekend*.

IMPERSONAL VERB a verb whose subject is *it*, but where the *it* does not refer to any specific thing, for example, *It's raining; It's 10 o'clock*.

INDICATIVE ordinary verb forms that aren't subjunctive, such as the present.

INDIRECT OBJECT a noun or pronoun used with verbs to show who benefits or is harmed by an action. For example, in *I gave the carrot to the rabbit, the rabbit* is the indirect object and *the carrot* is the direct object.

INFINITIVE a form of the verb that hasn't any endings added to it and doesn't relate to any particular tense. In English the infinitive is usually shown with *to*, as in *to speak, to eat*.

INTRANSITIVE VERB a type of verb that does not take a direct object, for example, *to sleep, to rise, to swim*.

IRREGULAR VERB a verb whose forms do not follow a general pattern.

OBJECT a noun or pronoun which refers to a person or thing that is affected by the action described by the verb.

PASSIVE a form of the verb that is used when the subject of the verb is the person or thing that is affected by the action, for example, *we were told*.

PAST PARTICIPLE a verb form which is used to form perfect and pluperfect tenses and passives, for example, *watched, swum*.

PAST PERFECT see **pluperfect**.

PERFECT a verb form used to talk about what has or hasn't happened, for example, *I've broken my glasses*.

PERSON one of the three classes: the first person (*I, we*), the second person (*you* singular and *you* plural), and the third person (*he, she, it* and *they*).

PLUPERFECT one of the verb tenses used to describe something that had happened or had been true at a point in the past.

PRESENT a verb form used to talk about what is true at the moment, what happens regularly, and what is happening now, for example, *I'm a student; I'm studying languages*.

PRESENT PARTICIPLE a verb form in English ending in *-ing*, for example, *eating, sleeping*.

REFLEXIVE VERB a verb where the subject and object are the same, and where the action 'reflects back' on the subject. A reflexive verb is used with a reflexive pronoun such as *myself*, for example, *I washed myself*.

REGULAR VERB a verb whose forms follow a general pattern or the normal rules.

SIMPLE TENSE a verb tense in which the verb form is made up of one word, rather than being formed from *to have* and a past participle or *to be* and an *-ing* form; for example, *She wrote a book*.

STEM the main part of a verb to which endings are added.

SUBJECT a noun or pronoun that refers to the person or thing doing the action or being in the state described by the verb, for example, *My cat doesn't drink milk*.

SUBJUNCTIVE a verb form used in certain circumstances to indicate some sort of feeling, or to show doubt about whether something will happen or whether something is true. It is only used occasionally in modern English, for example, *If I were you*.

TENSE the form of a verb which shows whether you are referring to the past, present or future.

TRANSITIVE VERB a type of verb that takes a direct object, for example, *to spend*.

NOUNS

NOUN a 'naming' word for a living being, thing or idea, for example, *woman, desk, happiness, Andrew*.

FEMININE a form of noun, pronoun or adjective that is used to refer to a living being, thing or idea that is not classed as masculine.

GENDER whether a noun, pronoun or adjective is feminine or masculine.

MASCULINE a form of noun, pronoun or adjective that is used to refer to a living being, thing or idea that is not classed as feminine.

NOUN GROUP, NOUN PHRASE a word or group of words that acts as the subject or object of a verb, or as the object of a preposition, for example, *my older sister; the man next door*.

PLURAL the form of a word which is used to refer to more than one person or thing.

SINGULAR the form of a word which is used to refer to one person or thing.

ARTICLES

ARTICLE a word like *the, a* and *an*, which is used in front of a noun.

DEFINITE ARTICLE the word *the*.
INDEFINITE ARTICLE the words *a* and *an*.

ADJECTIVES

ADJECTIVE a 'describing' word that tells you more about a person or thing, such as their appearance, colour, size or other qualities.

COMPARATIVE an adjective or adverb with *-er* on the end of it or *more* or *less* in front of it that is used to compare people, things or actions.

INVARIABLE used to describe a form which does not change.

SUPERLATIVE an adjective or adverb with *-est* on the end of it or *most* or *least* in front of it that is used to compare people, things or actions.

PRONOUNS

PRONOUN a word which you use instead of a noun, when you do not need or want to name someone or something directly, for example, *it, you, none*.

REFLEXIVE PRONOUN a word ending in *-self* or *-selves*, such as *myself* or *themselves*, which refers back to the subject, for example, *He hurt himself*.

ADVERBS

ADVERB a word usually used with verbs, adjectives or other adverbs that gives more information about when, where, how or in what circumstances something happens or to what degree something is true.

COMPARATIVE an adjective or adverb with *-er* on the end of it or *more* or *less* in front of it that is used to compare people, things or actions.

SUPERLATIVE an adjective or adverb with *-est* on the end of it or *most* or *least* in front of it that is used to compare people, things or actions.

PREPOSITIONS

PREPOSITION a word such as *at, for, with, into* or *from*, which is usually followed by a noun, pronoun or, in English, a word ending in *-ing*. Prepositions show how people and things relate to the rest of the sentence, for example, *She's at home*.

CONJUNCTIONS

CONJUNCTION a word such as *and, because* or *but* that links two words or phrases of a similar type or two parts of a sentence.

NEGATIVES

NEGATIVE a question or statement which contains a word such as *not, never* or *nothing*, and is used to say that something is not happening, is not true or is absent, for example, *I never eat meat*.

QUESTIONS

QUESTION a sentence which is used to ask someone about something and which normally has a verb in front of the subject, for example, *Where are you going?*

Verbs

Simple Tenses: Formation of Regular Verbs

Simple tenses are one-word tenses which are formed by adding endings to a verb stem. The endings show the number and person of the subject of the verb. The stem and endings of regular verbs are totally predictable. For irregular verbs see p 50 ff.

There are three regular verb patterns (called conjugations), each identifiable by the ending of the infinitive.

First Conjugation

First conjugation verbs end in **-er**, e.g. **donner** to give. The stem is formed as follows:

TENSE	FORMATION	EXAMPLE
Present		
Imperfect	infinitive minus **-er**	**donn-**
Past Historic		
Present Subjunctive		
Future	infinitive	**donner-**
Conditional		

To the appropriate stem add the following endings:

		❶ PRESENT	❷ IMPERFECT	❸ PAST HISTORIC
	1st person	-e	-ais	-ai
sing.	2nd person	-es	-ais	-as
	3rd person	-e	-ait	-a
	1st person	-ons	-ions	-âmes
plur.	2nd person	-ez	-iez	-âtes
	3rd person	-ent	-aient	-èrent

		❹ PRESENT SUBJUNCTIVE	❺ FUTURE	❻ CONDITIONAL
	1st person	-e	-ai	-ais
sing.	2nd person	-es	-as	-ais
	3rd person	-e	-a	-ait
	1st person	-ions	-ons	-ions
plur.	2nd person	-iez	-ez	-iez
	3rd person	-ent	-ont	-aient

Examples

1 PRESENT
je donne
tu donnes
il donne
elle donne
nous donnons
vous donnez
ils donnent
elles donnent

I give, I am giving,
I do give *etc*

2 IMPERFECT
je donnais
tu donnais
il donnait
elle donnait
nous donnions
vous donniez
ils donnaient
elles donnaient

I gave, I was giving,
I used to give *etc*

3 PAST HISTORIC
je donnai
tu donnas
il donna
elle donna
nous donnâmes
vous donnâtes
ils donnèrent
elles donnèrent

I gave *etc*

4 PRESENT SUBJUNCTIVE
je donne
tu donnes
il donne
elle donne
nous donnions
vous donniez
ils donnent
elles donnent

(that) I give/gave *etc*

5 FUTURE
je donnerai
tu donneras
il donnera
elle donnera
nous donnerons
vous donnerez
ils donneront
elles donneront

I shall give,
I shall be giving *etc*

6 CONDITIONAL
je donnerais
tu donnerais
il donnerait
elle donnerait
nous donnerions
vous donneriez
ils donneraient
elles donneraient

I should/would give,
I should/would be giving *etc*

7

Verbs

Simple Tenses: Formation of Regular Verbs *continued*

Second Conjugation

Second conjugation verbs end in **-ir**, e.g. **finir** to finish. The stem is formed as follows:

TENSE	FORMATION	EXAMPLE
Present Imperfect Past Historic Present Subjunctive Imperfect Subjunctive	infinitive minus **-ir**	**fin-**
Future Conditional	infinitive	**finir-**

To the appropriate stem add the following endings:

		❶ PRESENT	**❷ IMPERFECT**	**❸ PAST HISTORIC**
	1st person	**-is**	**-issais**	**-is**
sing.	2nd person	**-is**	**-issais**	**-is**
	3rd person	**-it**	**-issait**	**-it**
	1st person	**-issons**	**-issions**	**-îmes**
plur.	2nd person	**-issez**	**-issiez**	**-îtes**
	3rd person	**-issent**	**-issaient**	**-irent**

		❹ PRESENT SUBJUNCTIVE	**❺ FUTURE**	**❻ CONDITIONAL**
	1st person	**-isse**	**-ai**	**-ais**
sing.	2nd person	**-isses**	**-as**	**-ais**
	3rd person	**-isse**	**-a**	**-ait**
	1st person	**-issions**	**-ons**	**-ions**
plur.	2nd person	**-issiez**	**-ez**	**-iez**
	3rd person	**-issent**	**-ont**	**-aient**

Examples

1 PRESENT
je fin**is**
tu fin**is**
il fin**it**
elle fin**it**
nous fin**issons**
vous fin**issez**
ils fin**issent**
elles fin**issent**

I finish, I am finishing,
I do finish *etc*

2 IMPERFECT
je fin**issais**
tu fin**issais**
il fin**issait**
elle fin**issait**
nous fin**issions**
vous fin**issiez**
ils fin**issaient**
elles fin**issaient**

I finished, I was finishing,
I used to finish *etc*

3 PAST HISTORIC
je fin**is**
tu fin**is**
il fin**it**
elle fin**it**
nous fin**îmes**
vous fin**îtes**
ils fin**irent**
elles fin**irent**

I finished *etc*

4 PRESENT SUBJUNCTIVE
je fin**isse**
tu fin**isses**
il fin**isse**
elle fin**isse**
nous fin**issions**
vous fin**issiez**
ils fin**issent**
elles fin**issent**

(that) I finish/finished *etc*

5 FUTURE
je fin**irai**
tu fin**iras**
il fin**ira**
elle fin**ira**
nous fin**irons**
vous fin**irez**
ils fin**iront**
elles fin**iront**

I shall finish,
I shall be finishing *etc.*

6 CONDITIONAL
je fin**irais**
tu fin**irais**
il fin**irait**
elle fin**irait**
nous fin**irions**
vous fin**iriez**
ils fin**iraient**
elles fin**iraient**

I should/would finish,
I should/would be finishing *etc*

9

Verbs

Simple Tenses: Formation of Regular Verbs *continued*

Third Conjugation

Third conjugation verbs end in **-re**, e.g. **vendre** to sell. The stem is formed as follows:

TENSE	FORMATION	EXAMPLE
Present Imperfect Past Historic Present Subjunctive	infinitive minus **-re**	**vend-**
Future Conditional	infinitive minus **-e**	**vendr-**

To the appropriate stem add the following endings:

		❶ PRESENT	**❷ IMPERFECT**	**❸ PAST HISTORIC**
	1st person	**-s**	**-ais**	**-is**
sing.	2nd person	**-s**	**-ais**	**-is**
	3rd person	**–**	**-ait**	**-it**
	1st person	**-ons**	**-ions**	**-îmes**
plur.	2nd person	**-ez**	**-iez**	**-îtes**
	3rd person	**-ent**	**-aient**	**-irent**

		❹ PRESENT SUBJUNCTIVE	**❺ FUTURE**	**❻ CONDITIONAL**
	1st person	**-e**	**-ai**	**-ais**
sing.	2nd person	**-es**	**-as**	**-ais**
	3rd person	**-e**	**-a**	**-ait**
	1st person	**-ions**	**-ons**	**-ions**
plur.	2nd person	**-iez**	**-ez**	**-iez**
	3rd person	**-ent**	**-ont**	**-aient**

Examples

❶ PRESENT

je vend**s**
tu vend**s**
il vend
elle vend
nous vend**ons**
vous vend**ez**
ils vend**ent**
elles vend**ent**

I sell, I am selling,
I do sell *etc*

❷ IMPERFECT

je vend**ais**
tu vend**ais**
il vend**ait**
elle vend**ait**
nous vend**ions**
vous vend**iez**
ils vend**aient**
elles vend**aient**

I sold, I was selling,
I used to sell *etc*

❸ PAST HISTORIC

je vend**is**
tu vend**is**
il vend**it**
elle vend**it**
nous vend**îmes**
vous vend**îtes**
ils vend**irent**
elles vend**irent**

I sold *etc*

❹ PRESENT SUBJUNCTIVE

je vend**e**
tu vend**es**
il vend**e**
elle vend**e**
nous vend**ions**
vous vend**iez**
ils vend**ent**
elles vend**ent**

(that) I sell/sold *etc*

❺ FUTURE

je vend**rai**
tu vend**ras**
il vend**ra**
elle vend**ra**
nous vend**rons**
vous vend**rez**
ils vend**ront**
elles vend**ront**

I shall sell, I shall be selling *etc*

❻ CONDITIONAL

je vend**rais**
tu vend**rais**
il vend**rait**
elle vend**rait**
nous vend**rions**
vous vend**riez**
ils vend**raient**
elles vend**raient**

I should/would sell,
I should/would be selling *etc*

Verbs

First Conjugation Spelling Irregularities

Before certain endings, the stems of some **'-er'** verbs may change slightly.

Below, and on subsequent pages, the verb types are identified, and the changes described are illustrated by means of a representative verb.

Verbs ending:	**-cer**
Change:	**c** becomes **ç** before **a** or **o** to retain its soft [s] pronunciation
Affects:	Present, Imperfect, Past Historic, Present Participle
Model:	**lancer** to throw → ❶

Verbs ending:	**-ger**
Change:	**g** becomes **ge** before **a** or **o** to retain its soft [ʒ] pronunciation
Affects:	Present, Imperfect, Past Historic, Present Participle
Model:	**manger** to eat → ❷

Verbs ending:	**-eler**
Change:	**-l** doubles before **-e**, **-es**, **-ent** and throughout the Future and Conditional tenses
Affects:	Present, Present Subjunctive, Future, Conditional
Model:	**appeler** to call → ❸

EXCEPTIONS:	**geler** to freeze; **peler** to peel → like **mener** (p 14)

Examples

❶ INFINITIVE
lancer

PRESENT PARTICIPLE
lançant

	PRESENT		IMPERFECT		PAST HISTORIC
je	lance	je	**lançais**	je	**lançai**
tu	lances	tu	**lançais**	tu	**lanças**
il/elle	lance	il/elle	**lançait**	il/elle	**lança**
nous	**lançons**	nous	lancions	nous	**lançâmes**
vous	lancez	vous	lanciez	vous	**lançâtes**
ils/elles	lancent	ils/elles	**lançaient**	ils/elles	lancèrent

❷ INFINITIVE
manger

PRESENT PARTICIPLE
mangeant

	PRESENT		IMPERFECT		PAST HISTORIC
je	mange	je	**mangeais**	je	**mangeai**
tu	manges	tu	**mangeais**	tu	**mangeas**
il/elle	mange	il/elle	**mangeait**	il/elle	**mangea**
nous	**mangeons**	nous	mangions	nous	**mangeâmes**
vous	mangez	vous	mangiez	vous	**mangeâtes**
ils/elles	mangent	ils/elles	**mangeaient**	ils/elles	mangèrent

❸ PRESENT (+ SUBJUNCTIVE)

j'	**appelle**
tu	**appelles**
il/elle	**appelle**
nous	appelons
	(appelions)
vous	appelez
	(appeliez)
ils/elles	**appellent**

FUTURE

j'	**appellerai**
tu	**appelleras**
il	**appellera** *etc*

CONDITIONAL

j'	**appellerais**
tu	**appellerais**
il	**appellerait** *etc*

Verbs

First Conjugation Spelling Irregularities *continued*

Verbs ending:	**-eter**
Change:	**-t** doubles before **-e**, **-es**, **-ent** and throughout the Future and Conditional tenses
Affects:	Present, Present Subjunctive, Future, Conditional
Model:	**jeter** to throw → ❶

EXCEPTIONS: **acheter** to buy; **haleter** to pant → like **mener** (*see below*)

Verbs ending:	**-yer**
Change:	**y** changes to **i** before **-e**, **-es**, **-ent** and throughout the Future and Conditional tenses
Affects:	Present, Present Subjunctive, Future, Conditional
Model:	**essuyer** to wipe → ❷

The change described is optional for verbs ending in **-ayer**
e.g. **payer** to pay; **essayer** to try.

Verbs ending:	**mener, peser, lever** *etc*
Change:	**e** changes to **è**, before **-e**, **-es**, **-ent** and throughout the Future and Conditional tenses
Affects:	Present, Present Subjunctive, Future, Conditional
Model:	**mener** to lead → ❸

Verbs like:	**céder, régler, espérer** *etc*
Change:	**é** changes to **è** before **-e**, **-es**, **-ent**
Affects:	Present, Present Subjunctive
Model:	**céder** to yield → ❹

Examples

❶ PRESENT (+ SUBJUNCTIVE)

je	**jette**
tu	**jettes**
il/elle	**jette**
nous	jetons
	(jetions)
vous	jetez
	(jetiez)
ils/elles	**jettent**

FUTURE

je	**jetterai**
tu	**jetteras**
il	**jettera** *etc*

CONDITIONAL

je	**jetterais**
tu	**jetterais**
il	**jetterait** *etc*

❷ PRESENT (+ SUBJUNCTIVE)

j'	**essuie**
tu	**essuies**
il/elle	**essuie**
nous	essuyons
	(essuyions)
vous	essuyez
	(essuyiez)
ils/elles	**essuient**

FUTURE

j'	**essuierai**
tu	**essuieras**
il	**essuiera** *etc*

CONDITIONAL

j'	**essuierais**
tu	**essuierais**
il	**essuierait** *etc*

❸ PRESENT (+ SUBJUNCTIVE)

je	**mène**
tu	**mènes**
il/elle	**mène**
nous	menons
	(menions)
vous	menez
	(meniez)
ils/elles	**mènent**

FUTURE

je	**mènerai**
tu	**mèneras**
il	**mènera** *etc*

CONDITIONAL

je	**mènerais**
tu	**mènerais**
il	**mènerait** *etc*

❹ PRESENT (+ SUBJUNCTIVE)

je	**cède**
tu	**cèdes**
il/elle	**cède**
nous	cédons
	(cédions)
vous	cédez
	(cédiez)
ils/elles	**cèdent**

Verbs

The Imperative

The imperative is the form of the verb used to give commands or orders. It can be used politely, as in English 'Shut the door, please'.

The imperative is the same as the present tense **tu**, **nous** and **vous** forms without the subject pronouns:

donne* give   **finis** finish   **vends** sell
* The final 's' of the present tense of first conjugation verbs is dropped, except before **y** and **en** → **❶**

donnons let's give   **finissons** let's finish   **vendons** let's sell

donnez give   **finissez** finish   **vendez** sell

The imperative of irregular verbs is given in the verb tables, pp 50 ff.

Position of object pronouns with the imperative:
- in *positive* commands: they follow the verb and are attached to it with hyphens → **❷**
- in *negative* commands: they precede the verb and are not attached to it → **❸**

For the order of object pronouns, see p 102.

For reflexive verbs – e.g. **se lever** to get up – the object pronoun is the reflexive pronoun → **❹**

Examples

① Compare:

Tu donnes de l'argent à Paul
You give (some) money to Paul

and:

Donne de l'argent à Paul
Give (some) money to Paul

②

Excusez-moi	Excuse me
Envoyons-les-leur	Let's send them to them
Crois-nous	Believe us
Expliquez-le-moi	Explain it to me
Attendons-la	Let's wait for her/it
Rends-la-lui	Give it back to him/her

③

Ne me dérange pas	Don't disturb me
Ne leur en parlons pas	Let's not speak to them about it
Ne les négligeons pas	Let's not neglect them
N'y pense plus	Don't think about it any more
Ne leur répondez pas	Don't answer them
Ne la lui rends pas	Don't give it back to him/her

④

Lève-toi	Get up
Ne te lève pas	Don't get up
Dépêchons-nous	Let's hurry
Ne nous affolons pas	Let's not panic
Levez-vous	Get up
Ne vous levez pas	Don't get up

Verbs

Compound Tenses: Formation

Compound tenses consist of the past participle of the verb together with an auxiliary verb. Most verbs take the auxiliary **avoir**, but some take **être** (see p 22).

Compound tenses are formed in exactly the same way for both regular and irregular verbs, the only difference being that irregular verbs may have an irregular past participle. The past participle of irregular verbs is given for each verb in the verb tables, pp. 50 ff.

The Past Participle

For all compound tenses you need to know how to form the past participle of the verb. For regular verbs this is as follows:

1st conjugation: replace the **-er** of the infinitive by **-é**

donner	→	**donné**
to give	→	given

2nd conjugation: replace the **-ir** of the infinitive by **-i**

finir	→	**fini**
to finish	→	finished

3rd conjugation: replace the **-re** of the infinitive by **-u**

vendre	→	**vendu**
to sell	→	sold

See p 40 for agreement of past participles.

Verbs

Compound Tenses: Formation *continued*

PERFECT TENSE
The present tense of **avoir** or **être** plus the past participle → ❶
(see pp 20-21)

PLUPERFECT TENSE
The imperfect tense of **avoir** or **être** plus the past participle → ❷
(see pp 20-21)

FUTURE PERFECT
The future tense of **avoir** or **être** plus the past participle → ❸
(see pp 20-21)

CONDITIONAL PERFECT
The conditional of **avoir** or **être** plus the past participle → ❹
(see pp 20-21)

PERFECT SUBJUNCTIVE
The present subjunctive of **avoir** or **être** plus the past participle → ❺
(see pp 20-21)

Examples of a verb that takes **avoir** and one that takes **être** are conjugated on pp 20 and 21.

For a list of verbs and verb types that take the auxiliary **être**, see p 22.

Examples

❶ PERFECT

j'ai donné	nous avons donné
tu as donné	vous avez donné
il/elle a donné	ils/elles ont donné

I gave, I have given *etc*

❷ PLUPERFECT

j'avais donné	nous avions donné
tu avais donné	vous aviez donné
il/elle avait donné	ils/elles avaient donné

I had given *etc*

❸ FUTURE PERFECT

j'aurai donné	nous aurons donné
tu auras donné	vous aurez donné
il/elle aura donné	ils/elles auront donné

I shall have given *etc*

❹ CONDITIONAL PERFECT

j'aurais donné	nous aurions donné
tu aurais donné	vous auriez donné
il/elle aurait donné	ils/elles auraient donné

I should/would have given *etc*

❺ PERFECT SUBJUNCTIVE

j'aie donné	nous ayons donné
tu aies donné	vous ayez donné
il/elle ait donné	ils/elles aient donné

I gave, I have given *etc*

Examples

❶ PERFECT

je suis tombé(e)
tu es tombé(e)
il est tombé
elle est tombée

nous sommes tombé(e)s
vous êtes tombé(e)(s)
ils sont tombés
elles sont tombées

I fell, I have fallen *etc*

❷ PLUPERFECT

j'étais tombé(e)
tu étais tombé(e)
il était tombé
elle était tombée

nous étions tombé(e)s
vous étiez tombé(e)(s)
ils étaient tombés
elles étaient tombées

I had fallen *etc*

❸ FUTURE PERFECT

je serai tombé(e)
tu seras tombé(e)
il sera tombé
elle sera tombée

nous serons tombé(e)s
vous serez tombé(e)(s)
ils seront tombés
elles seront tombées

I shall have fallen *etc*

❹ CONDITIONAL PERFECT

je serais tombé(e)
tu serais tombé(e)
il serait tombé
elle serait tombée

nous serions tombé(e)s
vous seriez tombé(e)(s)
ils seraient tombés
elles seraient tombées

I should/would have fallen *etc*

❺ PERFECT SUBJUNCTIVE

je sois tombé(e)
tu sois tombé(e)
il soit tombé
elle soit tombée

nous soyons tombé(e)s
vous soyez tombé(e)(s)
ils soient tombés
elles soient tombées

(that) I fell/have fallen *etc*

Verbs

Compound Tenses: Formation *continued*

Verbs Which Take the Auxiliary être

Reflexive verbs (see p 24) → **1**

The following intransitive verbs (i.e. verbs which cannot take a direct object), largely expressing motion or a change of state:

aller to go → **2**
arriver to arrive; to happen
descendre to go/come down
devenir to become
entrer to go/come in
monter to go/come up
mourir to die → **3**
naître to be born
partir to leave → **4**

passer to pass
rentrer to go back/in
rester to stay → **5**
retourner to go back
revenir to come back
sortir to go/come out
tomber to fall
venir to come → **6**

Of these, the following can be used transitively (i.e. with a direct object) and in such cases are conjugated with **avoir**:

descendre to bring/take down
entrer to bring/take in
monter to bring/take up → **7**
passer to pass; to spend → **8**
rentrer to bring/take in
retourner to turn over
sortir to bring/take out → **9**

ⓘ Note that the past participle must show an agreement in number and gender whenever the auxiliary is **être** except for reflexive verbs where the reflexive pronoun is the indirect object (see p 40).

Examples

1 je me suis arrêté(e)   I stopped
elle s'est trompée   she made a mistake
tu t'es levé(e)   you got up
ils s'étaient battus   they had fought (one another)

2 elle est allée   she went

3 ils sont morts   they died

4 vous êtes partie   you left (*addressing a female person*)

vous êtes parties   you left (*addressing more than one female person*)

5 nous sommes resté(e)s   we stayed

6 elles étaient venues   they (*female*) had come

7 Il a monté les valises   He's taken the cases up

8 Nous avons passé trois semaines chez elle   We spent three weeks at her place

9 Avez-vous sorti la voiture?   Have you taken the car out?

Verbs

Reflexive Verbs

A reflexive verb is one accompanied by a reflexive pronoun, e.g. **se lever** to get up; **se laver** to wash (oneself). The pronouns are:

	SINGULAR	PLURAL
1ˢᵗ person	**me (m')**	**nous**
2ⁿᵈ person	**te (t')**	**vous**
3ʳᵈ person	**se (s')**	**se (s')**

The forms shown in brackets are used before a vowel, an **h** 'mute' or the pronoun **y** → **1**

In positive commands, **te** changes to **toi** → **2**

The reflexive pronoun 'reflects back' to the subject, but it is not always translated in English → **3**

The plural pronouns are sometimes translated as 'one another', 'each other' (the *reciprocal* meaning). The reciprocal meaning may be emphasized by **l'un(e) l'autre (les un(e)s les autres)** → **4**

In constructions other than the imperative affirmative the pronoun comes before the verb → **5**

In the imperative affirmative, the pronoun follows the verb and is attached to it with a hyphen → **6**

Past Participle Agreement

In most reflexive verbs the reflexive pronoun is a *direct* object pronoun → **7**

When a direct object accompanies the reflexive verb the pronoun is then the *indirect* object → **8**

The past participle of a reflexive verb agrees in number and gender with a direct object which *precedes* the verb (usually, but not always, the reflexive pronoun) → **9**

The past participle does not change if the direct object follows the verb → **10**

Examples

1 Je m'ennuie — I'm bored
Ils s'y intéressent — They are interested in it

2 Assieds-toi — Sit down
Tais-toi — Be quiet

3 Je me prépare — I'm getting (myself) ready
Elle se lève — She gets up

4 Nous nous parlons — We speak to each other
Ils se ressemblent — They resemble one another
Ils se regardent l'un l'autre — They are looking at each other

5 Je me couche tôt — I go to bed early
Comment vous appelez-vous? — What is your name?
Il ne s'est pas rasé — He hasn't shaved
Ne te dérange pas pour nous — Don't put yourself out on our account

6 Renseignons-nous — Let's find out
Asseyez-vous — Sit down

7 Je m'appelle — I'm called (*literally*: I call myself)
Ils se lavent — They wash (themselves)

8 Elle se lave les mains — She's washing her hands (*literally*: She's washing to herself the hands)
Nous nous envoyons des cadeaux à Noël — We send presents to each other at Christmas

9 «Je me suis endormi» s'est-il excusé — 'I fell asleep', he apologized
Pauline s'est dirigée vers la sortie — Pauline made her way towards the exit
Ils se sont levés vers dix heures — They got up around ten o'clock
Elles se sont excusées de leur erreur — They apologized for their mistake

10 Elle s'est lavé les cheveux — She (has) washed her hair
Nous nous sommes serré la main — We shook hands

Verbs

Reflexive Verbs *continued*

Conjugation of: **se laver** to wash (oneself)

1 SIMPLE TENSES

Simple tenses of reflexive verbs are conjugated in exactly the same way as those of non-reflexive verbs except that the reflexive pronoun is always used.

PRESENT

je me lave	nous nous lavons
tu te laves	vous vous lavez
il/elle se lave	ils/elles se lavent

IMPERFECT

je me lavais	nous nous lavions
tu te lavais	vous vous laviez
il/elle se lavait	ils/elles se lavaient

FUTURE

je me laverai	nous nous laverons
tu te laveras	vous vous laverez
il/elle se lavera	ils/elles se laveront

CONDITIONAL

je me laverais	nous nous laverions
tu te laverais	vous vous laveriez
il/elle se laverait	ils/elles se laveraient

PAST HISTORIC

je me lavai	nous nous lavâmes
tu te lavas	vous vous lavâtes
il/elle se lava	ils/elles se lavèrent

PRESENT SUBJUNCTIVE

je me lave	nous nous lavions
tu te laves	vous vous laviez
il/elle se lave	ils/elles se lavent

Verbs

Reflexive Verbs *continued*

Conjugation of: **se laver** to wash (oneself)

2 COMPOUND TENSES

Compound tenses of reflexive verbs are formed with the auxiliary **être**.

PERFECT

je me suis lavé(e)
tu t'es lavé(e)
il/elle s'est lavé(e)

nous nous sommes lavé(e)s
vous vous êtes lavé(e)(s)
ils/elles se sont lavé(e)s

PLUPERFECT

je m'étais lavé(e)
tu t'étais lavé(e)
il/elle s'était lavé(e)

nous nous étions lavé(e)s
vous vous étiez lavé(e)(s)
ils/elles s'étaient lavé(e)s

FUTURE PERFECT

je me serai lavé(e)
tu te seras lavé(e)
il/elle se sera lavé(e)

nous nous serons lavé(e)s
vous vous serez lavé(e)(s)
ils/elles se seront lavé(e)s

CONDITIONAL PERFECT

je me serais lavé(e)
tu te serais lavé(e)
il/elle se serait lavé(e)

nous nous serions lavé(e)s
vous vous seriez lavé(e)(s)
ils/elles se seraient lavé(e)s

PERFECT SUBJUNCTIVE

je me sois lavé(e)
tu te sois lavé(e)
il/elle se soit lavé(e)

nous nous soyons lavé(e)s
vous vous soyez lavé(e)(s)
ils/elles se soient lavé(e)s

Verbs

The Passive

In the passive, the subject *receives* the action (e.g. I was hit) as opposed to *performing* it (e.g. I hit him). In English the verb 'to be' is used with the past participle. In French the passive is formed in exactly the same way, i.e.:

> a tense of **être** + past participle.

The past participle agrees in number and gender with the subject → **❶**

A sample verb is conjugated in the passive voice on pp 30 and 31.

The indirect object in French cannot become the subject in the passive: in quelqu'un m'a donné un livre the indirect object **m'** cannot become the subject of a passive verb (unlike English: someone gave me a book → I was given a book).

The passive meaning is often expressed in French by:
- **on** plus a verb in the active voice → **❷**
- a reflexive verb (see p 24) → **❸**

Examples

❶ Philippe a été récompensé

Philippe has been rewarded

Cette peinture est très admirée

This painting is greatly admired

Ils le feront pourvu qu'ils soient payés

They'll do it provided they're paid

Les enfants seront félicités

The children will be congratulated

Cette mesure aurait été critiquée si ...

This measure would have been criticized if ...

Les portes avaient été fermées

The doors had been closed

❷ On leur a envoyé une lettre

They were sent a letter

On nous a montré le jardin

We were shown the garden

On m'a dit que ...

I was told that ...

❸ Ils se vendent 3 euros (la) pièce

They are sold for 3 euros each

Ce mot ne s'emploie plus

This word is no longer used

Verbs

The Passive *continued*

Conjugation of: **être aimé** to be liked

PRESENT
je suis aimé(e)
tu es aimé(e)
il/elle est aimé(e)

nous sommes aimé(e)s
vous êtes aimé(e)(s)
ils/elles sont aimé(e)s

IMPERFECT
j'étais aimé(e)
tu étais aimé(e)
il/elle était aimé(e)

nous étions aimé(e)s
vous étiez aimé(e)(s)
ils/elles étaient aimé(e)s

FUTURE
je serai aimé(e)
tu seras aimé(e)
il/elle sera aimé(e)

nous serons aimé(e)s
vous serez aimé(e)(s)
ils/elles seront aimé(e)s

CONDITIONAL
je serais aimé(e)
tu serais aimé(e)
il/elle serait aimé(e)

nous serions aimé(e)s
vous seriez aimé(e)(s)
ils/elles seraient aimé(e)s

PAST HISTORIC
je fus aimé(e)
tu fus aimé(e)
il/elle fut aimé(e)

nous fûmes aimé(e)s
vous fûtes aimé(e)(s)
ils/elles furent aimé(e)s

PRESENT SUBJUNCTIVE
je sois aimé(e)
tu sois aimé(e)
il/elle soit aimé(e)

nous soyons aimé(e)s
vous soyez aimé(e)(s)
ils/elles soient aimé(e)s

Verbs

The Passive *continued*

Conjugation of: **être aimé** to be liked

PERFECT
j'ai été aimé(e)	nous avons été aimé(e)s
tu as été aimé(e)	vous avez été aimé(e)(s)
il/elle a été aimé(e)	ils/elles ont été aimé(e)s

PLUPERFECT
j'avais été aimé(e)	nous avions été aimé(e)s
tu avais été aimé(e)	vous aviez été aimé(e)(s)
il/elle avait été aimé(e)	ils/elles avaient été aimé(e)s

FUTURE PERFECT
j'aurai été aimé(e)	nous aurons été aimé(e)s
tu auras été aimé(e)	vous aurez été aimé(e)(s)
il/elle aura été aimé(e)	ils/elles auront été aimé(e)s

CONDITIONAL PERFECT
j'aurais été aimé(e)	nous aurions été aimé(e)s
tu aurais été aimé(e)	vous auriez été aimé(e)(s)
il/elle aurait été aimé(e)	ils/elles auraient été aimé(e)s

PERFECT SUBJUNCTIVE
j'aie été aimé(e)	nous ayons été aimé(e)s
tu aies été aimé(e)	vous ayez été aimé(e)(s)
il/elle ait été aimé(e)	ils/elles aient été aimé(e)s

Verbs

Impersonal Verbs

Impersonal verbs are used only in the infinitive and in the third person singular with the subject pronoun **il**, generally translated as 'it'.

e.g. il pleut it's raining
   il est facile de dire que … it's easy to say that …

The most common impersonal verbs are:

INFINITIVE	CONSTRUCTIONS
s'agir	**il s'agit de** + *noun* → ❶
	il s'agit de + *infinitive* → ❷
falloir	**il faut** + *noun object* (+ *indirect object*) → ❸
	il faut + *infinitive* (+ *indirect object*) → ❹
	il faut que + *subjunctive* → ❺
neiger/pleuvoir	**il neige/il pleut** → ❻
valoir mieux	**il vaut mieux** + *infinitive* → ❼
	il vaut mieux que + *subjunctive* → ❽

The following verbs are also commonly used in impersonal constructions:

INFINITIVE	CONSTRUCTIONS
avoir	**il y a** + *noun* → ❾
être	**il est** + *noun* → ❿
	il est + *adjective* + **de** + *infinitive* → ⓫
faire	**il fait** + *adjective or noun of weather* → ⓬
manquer	**il manque** + *noun* (+ *indirect object*) → ⓭
paraître	**il paraît que** + *subjunctive* → ⓮
	il paraît + *indirect object* + **que** + *indicative* → ⓯
rester	**il reste** + *noun* (+ *indirect object*) → ⓰
sembler	**il semble que** + *subjunctive* → ⓱
	il semble + *indirect object* + **que** + *indicative* → ⓲
suffire	**il suffit de** + *infinitive* → ⓳
	il suffit de + *noun* → ⓴

Examples

1 Il ne s'agit pas d'argent — It isn't a question/matter of money

2 Il s'agit de faire vite — We must act quickly

3 Il me faut une chaise de plus — I need an extra chair

4 Il me fallait prendre une décision — I had to make a decision

5 Il faut que vous partiez — You have to leave/You must leave

6 Il neige/Il pleuvait à verse — It's snowing/It was raining heavily/It was pouring

7 Il vaut mieux refuser — It's better to refuse; You/He/I had better refuse *(depending on context)*

8 Il vaudrait mieux que nous ne venions pas — It would be better if we didn't come; We'd better not come

9 Il y a du pain (qui reste) — There is some bread (left)
Il n'y avait pas de lettres ce matin — There were no letters this morning

10 Il est dix heures — It's ten o'clock

11 Il était inutile de protester — It was useless to protest
Il est facile de critiquer — Criticizing is easy

12 Il fait beau/mauvais — It's lovely/horrible weather
Il faisait nuit/du soleil — It was dark/sunny

13 Il manque deux tasses — There are two cups missing / Two cups are missing

14 Il paraît qu'ils partent demain — It appears they are leaving tomorrow

15 Il nous paraît certain qu'il aura du succès — It seems certain to us that he'll be successful

16 Il lui restait cinquante euros — He/She had fifty euros left

17 Il semble que vous ayez raison — It seems/appears that you are right

18 Il me semblait qu'il conduisait trop vite — It seemed to me (that) he was driving too fast

19 Il suffit de téléphoner pour réserver une place — You just need to phone to reserve a seat

20 Il suffit d'une seule erreur pour tout gâcher — One single error is enough to ruin everything

33

Verbs

The Infinitive

The infinitive is the form of the verb meaning 'to ... ' that is found in dictionary entries, e.g. **donner** to give; **vivre** to live.

There are three main types of verbal construction involving the infinitive:
- with the linking preposition **de** → **❶**
- with the linking preposition **à** → **❷**
- with no linking preposition → **❸**

Examples of Verbs Governing **de**

s'apercevoir de qch	to notice sth → **❶**
changer de qch	to change sth → **❷**
décider de + *infin.*	to decide to → **❸**
essayer de + *infin.*	to try to do → **❹**
finir de + *infin.*	to finish doing → **❺**
s'occuper de qch/qn	to look after sth/sb → **❻**
oublier de + *infin.*	to forget to do → **❼**
regretter de + *perf. infin.**	to regret doing/having done → **❽**
se souvenir de qn/qch/de + *perf. infin.**	to remember sb/sth/doing/ having done → **❾**
venir de* + *infin.*	to have just done → **❿**

Examples of Verbs Governing **à**

conseiller à qn de + *infin.*	to advise sb to do → **⓫**
défendre à qn de + *infin.*	to forbid sb to do → **⓬**
dire à qn de + *infin.*	to tell sb to do → **⓭**
s'intéresser à qn/qch/à + *infin.*	to be interested in sb/sth/ in doing → **⓮**
manquer à qn	to be missed by sb → **⓯**
penser à qn/qch	to think about sb/sth → **⓰**
réussir à + *infin.*	to manage to do → **⓱**

*The perfect infinitive is formed using the auxiliary verb **avoir** or **être** as appropriate with the past participle of the main verb. It is found after certain verbal constructions and after the preposition **après** after → **⓲**

Examples

1. Il ne s'est pas aperçu de son erreur — He didn't notice his mistake

2. J'ai changé d'avis — I changed my mind

3. Qu'est-ce que vous avez décidé de faire? — What have you decided to do?

4. Essayez d'arriver à l'heure — Try to arrive on time

5. Avez-vous fini de lire ce journal? — Have you finished reading this newspaper?

6. Je m'occupe de ma nièce — I'm looking after my niece

7. J'ai oublié d'appeler ma mère — I forgot to ring my mother

8. Je regrette de ne pas vous avoir écrit plus tôt — I'm sorry for not writing to you sooner

9. Vous vous souvenez de Lucienne? — Do you remember Lucienne?

10. Nous venions d'arriver — We had just arrived

11. Il leur a conseillé d'attendre — He advised them to wait

12. Je leur ai défendu de sortir — I've forbidden them to go out

13. Dites-leur de se taire — Tell them to be quiet

14. Elle s'intéresse beaucoup au sport — She's very interested in sport

15. Tu manques à tes parents — Your parents miss you

16. Je pense souvent à toi — I often think about you

17. Vous avez réussi à me convaincre — You've managed to convince me

18. avoir fini / être allé / s'être levé
    to have finished / to have gone / to have got up

    Après être sorties, elles se sont dirigées vers le parking
    After leaving/having left, they headed for the car park

35

Verbs

The Infinitive *continued*

Verbs followed by an infinitive with no linking preposition

the modal auxiliary verbs:

devoir to have to, must → **❶**
to be due to → **❷**
in the conditional/conditional perfect:
should/should have, ought/ought to have → **❸**

pouvoir to be able to, can → **❹**
to be allowed to, can, may → **❺**
indicating possibility: may/might/could → **❻**

savoir to know how to, can → **❼**

vouloir to want/wish to → **❽**
to be willing to, will → **❾**
in polite phrases → **❿**

falloir to be necessary: see p 32.

verbs of seeing or hearing e.g. **voir** to see; **entendre** to hear → **⓫**

intransitive verbs of motion e.g. **aller** to go; **descendre** to come/go down → **⓬**

The following common verbs:

adorer to love
aimer to like, love
aimer mieux to prefer → **⓭**
compter to expect
désirer to wish, want
détester to hate
espérer to hope
faillir → **⓮**

faire → **⓯**
laisser to let, allow → **⓰**
oser to dare
préférer to prefer
sembler to seem → **⓱**
souhaiter to wish
valoir mieux see p 32

Examples

1. Je dois leur rendre visite
   Elle a dû partir
   Il a dû regretter d'avoir parlé

   I must visit them
   She (has) had to leave
   He must have been sorry he spoke

2. Je devais attraper le train de neuf heures mais …

   I was (supposed) to catch the nine o'clock train but …

3. Je devrais le faire
   J'aurais dû m'excuser

   I ought to do it
   I ought to have apologized

4. Il ne peut pas lever le bras

   He can't raise his arm

5. Puis-je les accompagner?

   May I go with them?

6. Il peut encore changer d'avis
   Cela pourrait être vrai

   He may change his mind yet
   It could/might be true

7. Savez-vous conduire?

   Can you drive?

8. Elle veut rester encore un jour

   She wants to stay another day

9. Ils ne voulaient pas le faire

   They wouldn't do it/
   They weren't willing to do it

   Ma voiture ne veut pas démarrer

   My car won't start

10. Voulez-vous boire quelque chose?

    Would you like something to drink?

11. Il nous a vus arriver
    On les entend chanter

    He saw us arriving
    You can hear them singing

12. Allez voir Nicolas
    Descends leur demander

    Go and see Nicolas
    Go down and ask them

13. J'aimerais mieux le choisir moi-même

    I'd rather choose it myself

14. J'ai failli tomber

    I almost fell

15. Ne me faites pas rire!
    J'ai fait réparer ma voiture

    Don't make me laugh!
    I've had my car repaired

16. Laissez-moi passer

    Let me past

17. Vous semblez être inquiet

    You seem (to be) worried

Verbs

The Present Participle

Formation

1st conjugation:
Replace the **-er** of the infinitive by **-ant** → ❶
  - Verbs ending in **-cer**: **c** changes to **ç** → ❷
  - Verbs ending in **-ger**: **g** changes to **ge** → ❸

2nd conjugation:
Replace the **-ir** of the infinitive by **-issant** → ❹

3rd conjugation:
Replace the **-re** of the infinitive by **-ant** → ❺

For irregular present participles, see Irregular Verbs, pp 50 ff.

Uses

The present participle has a more restricted use in French than in English.

Used as a verbal form, the present participle is invariable. It is found:
  - on its own, where it corresponds to the English present participle → ❻
  - following the preposition **en** → ❼
  - ⓘ Note, in particular, the construction:
    verb + **en** + *present participle*
    which is often translated by an English phrasal verb, i.e. one followed by a preposition like 'to run down', 'to bring up' → ❽

Used as an adjective, the present participle agrees in number and gender with the noun or pronoun → ❾
  - ⓘ Note, in particular, the use of **ayant** and **étant** – the present participles of the auxiliary verbs **avoir** and **être** – with a past participle → ❿

Examples

1. donner to give → donnant giving

2. lancer to throw → lançant throwing

3. manger to eat → mangeant eating

4. finir to finish → finissant finishing

5. vendre to sell → vendant selling

6. David, habitant près de Paris, a la possibilité de ...

   David, living near Paris, has the opportunity of ...

   Pensant que je serais fâché, elle a dit ...

   Thinking that I would be angry, she said ...

   Ils m'ont suivi, criant à tue-tête

   They followed me, shouting at the top of their voices

7. En attendant sa sœur, Richard s'est endormi

   While waiting for his sister, Richard fell asleep

   Téléphone-nous en arrivant chez toi

   Phone us when you get home

   En appuyant sur ce bouton, on peut ...

   By pressing this button, you can ...

   Il s'est blessé en essayant de sauver un chat

   He hurt himself trying to rescue a cat

8. sortir en courant

   to run out (*literally*: to go out running)

   avancer en boîtant

   to limp along (*literally*: to go forward limping)

9. le soleil couchant

   the setting sun

   une lumière éblouissante

   a dazzling light

   ils sont déroûtants

   they are disconcerting

   elles étaient étonnantes

   they were surprising

10. Ayant mangé plus tôt, il a pu ...

    Having eaten earlier, he was able to ...

    Étant arrivée en retard, elle a dû ...

    Having arrived late, she had to ...

39

Verbs

Past Participle Agreement

Like adjectives, a past participle must sometimes agree in number and gender with a noun or pronoun. For the rules of agreement, see below. Example: **donné**

	MASCULINE	FEMININE
SING.	donné	donné**e**
PLUR.	donné**s**	donné**es**

When the masculine singular form already ends in **-s**, no further **s** is added in the masculine plural, e.g. **pris** taken.

Rules of Agreement in Compound Tenses

When the auxiliary verb is **avoir**:

> The past participle remains in the masculine singular form, unless a direct object precedes the verb. The past participle then agrees in number and gender with the preceding direct object → **❶**

When the auxiliary verb is **être**:

> The past participle of a non-reflexive verb agrees in number and gender with the subject → **❷**
> The past participle of a reflexive verb agrees in number and gender with the reflexive pronoun, if the pronoun is a direct object → **❸**
> No agreement is made if the reflexive pronoun is an indirect object → **❹**

The Past Participle as an Adjective

The past participle agrees in number and gender with the noun or pronoun → **❺**

Examples

1 Voici le livre que vous avez demandé
Here's the book you asked for

Laquelle avaient-elles choisie?
Which one had they chosen?

Ces amis? Je les ai rencontrés à Édimbourg
Those friends? I met them in Edinburgh

Il a gardé toutes les lettres qu'elle a écrites
He has kept all the letters she wrote

2 Est-ce que ton frère est allé à l'étranger?
Did your brother go abroad?

Elle était restée chez elle
She had stayed at home

Ils sont partis dans la matinée
They left in the morning

Mes cousines sont revenues hier
My cousins came back yesterday

3 Tu t'es rappelé d'acheter du pain, Georges?
Did you remember to buy bread, Georges?

Martine s'est demandée pourquoi il l'appelait
Martine wondered why he was calling her

«Lui et moi nous nous sommes cachés» a-t-elle dit
'He and I hid,' she said

Les vendeuses se sont mises en grève
The shop assistants have gone on strike

Vous vous êtes brouillés?
Have you fallen out with each other?

Les enfants s'étaient entraidés
The children had helped one another

4 Elle s'est lavé les mains
She washed her hands

Ils se sont parlé pendant des heures
They talked to each other for hours

5 à un moment donné
at a given time

la porte ouverte
the open door

ils sont bien connus
they are well known

elles semblent fatiguées
they seem tired

41

Verbs

Use of Tenses

The Present

Unlike English, French does not distinguish between the simple present and the continuous present (e.g. I smoke/I am smoking) → ❶

To emphasize continuity, the following constructions may be used:
être en train de faire, **être à faire** to be doing → ❷

French uses the present tense where English uses the perfect in the following cases:
- with certain prepositions of time – notably **depuis** for/since – when an action begun in the past is continued in the present → ❸
  Note, however, that the perfect is used as in English when the verb is negative or the action has been completed → ❹
- in the construction **venir de faire** to have just done → ❺

The Future

The future is generally used as in English, but note the following:

> Immediate future time is often expressed by means of the present tense of **aller** plus an infinitive → ❻

> In time clauses expressing future action, French uses the future where English uses the present → ❼

The Future Perfect

Used as in English to mean 'shall/will have done' → ❽

In time clauses expressing future action, where English uses the perfect tense → ❾

The Conditional

Used as in English to express what would happen, as well as (with **vouloir** or **aimer**) to express wishes or desires → ❿

Examples

❶   Je fume — I smoke *or* I am smoking
Il lit — He reads *or* He is reading
Nous habitons — We live *or* We are living

❷   Il est en train de travailler — He's (busy) working

❸   Paul apprend à nager depuis
     six mois — Paul's been learning to swim
     for six months (and still is)
Je suis debout depuis sept heures — I've been up since seven
Il y a longtemps que tu attends? — Have you been waiting long?
Voilà deux semaines que nous
     sommes ici — That's two weeks we've been
     here (now)

❹   Ils ne se sont pas vus depuis
     des mois — They haven't seen each other
     for months
Elle est revenue il y a un an — She came back a year ago

❺   Elisabeth vient de partir — Elisabeth has just left

❻   Tu vas tomber si tu ne fais pas
     attention — You'll fall if you're not careful
Ça va prendre une demi-heure — It'll take half an hour

❼   Quand il viendra vous serez en
     vacances — When he comes you'll be on
     holiday
Faites-nous savoir aussitôt
     qu'elle arrivera — Let us know as soon as she
     arrives

❽   J'aurai fini dans une heure — I shall have finished in an hour

❾   Quand tu auras lu ce roman,
     rends-le-moi — When you've read the novel,
     give it back to me
Je partirai dès que j'aurai fini — I'll leave as soon as I've finished

❿   Si j'avais le temps, je le ferais — If I had the time, I'd do it
J'aimerais t'accompagner — I'd like to go with you
Voudriez-vous autre chose? — Would you like anything else?

43

Verbs

Use of Tenses *continued*

The Imperfect

The imperfect describes:
- an action (or state) in the past without definite limits in time → ❶
- habitual action(s) in the past (often translated by means of 'would' or 'used to') → ❷

French uses the imperfect tense where English uses the pluperfect in the following cases:
- with certain prepositions of time – notably **depuis** for/since – when an action begun in the more remote past was continued in the more recent past → ❸
  Note, however, that the pluperfect is used as in English, when the verb is negative or the action has been completed → ❹
- in the construction **venir de faire** to have just done → ❺

The Perfect

The perfect is used to recount a completed action or event in the past. Note that this corresponds to a perfect tense or a simple past tense in English → ❻

The Past Historic

Only ever used in written, literary French, the past historic recounts a completed action in the past, corresponding to a simple past tense in English → ❼

The Subjunctive

In spoken French, the present subjunctive generally replaces the imperfect subjunctive. See also p 46 ff.

Examples

❶ Elle regardait par la fenêtre

She was looking out of the window

Il pleuvait quand je suis sorti de chez moi

It was raining when I left the house

Nos chambres donnaient sur la plage

Our rooms overlooked the beach

❷ Quand il était étudiant, il se levait à l'aube

When he was a student he got up at dawn

Nous causions des heures entières

We would talk for hours on end

Elle te taquinait, n'est-ce pas?

She used to tease you, didn't she?

❸ Nous habitions à Londres depuis deux ans

We had been living in London for two years (and still were)

Il était malade depuis 2004

He had been ill since 2004

Il y avait assez longtemps qu'il le faisait

He had been doing it for quite a long time

❹ Voilà un an que je ne l'avais pas vu

I hadn't seen him for a year

Il y avait une heure qu'elle était arrivée

She had arrived one hour before

❺ Je venais de les rencontrer

I had just met them

❻ Nous sommes allés au bord de la mer

We went/have been to the seaside

Il a refusé de nous aider

He (has) refused to help us

La voiture ne s'est pas arrêtée

The car didn't stop/hasn't stopped

❼ Le roi mourut en 1592

The king died in 1592

45

Verbs

The Subjunctive: When to Use it

(For how to form the subjunctive see p 6 ff.)

After certain conjunctions:

quoique **bien que**	}	although → ❶
pour que **afin que**	}	so that → ❷
pourvu que		provided that → ❸
jusqu'à ce que		until → ❹
avant que (... ne)		before → ❺
à moins que (... ne)		unless → ❻
de peur que (... ne) **de crainte que (... ne)**	}	for fear that, lest → ❼
de sorte que **de façon que** **de manière que**	}	so that (*indicating a purpose;* *when they introduce a result,* → ❽ *the indicative is used*).

ⓘ Note that **ne** in examples ❺ to ❼ has no translation value.
It is often omitted in spoken informal French.

After impersonal constructions which express necessity, possibility etc:

il faut que **il est nécessaire que**	}	it is necessary that → ❾
il est possible que		it is possible that → ❿
il semble que		it seems that, it appears that → ⓫
il vaut mieux que		it is better that → ⓬
il est dommage que		it's a pity that, it's a shame that → ⓭

After a superlative → ⓮

After certain adjectives expressing some sort of 'uniqueness' → ⓯

dernier ... qui/que		last ... who/that
premier ... qui/que		first ... who/that
meilleur ... qui/que		best ... who/that
seul ... qui/que **unique ... qui/que**	}	only ... who/that

In set expressions → ⓰

Examples

1 Bien qu'il fasse beaucoup d'efforts, il est peu récompensé — Although he makes a lot of effort, he isn't rewarded for it

2 Demandez un reçu afin que vous puissiez être remboursé — Ask for a receipt so that you can get a refund

3 Nous partirons ensemble pourvu que Sylvie soit d'accord — We'll leave together provided Sylvie agrees

4 Reste ici jusqu'à ce que nous revenions — Stay here until we come back

5 Je le ferai avant que tu ne partes — I'll do it before you leave

6 Ce doit être Paul, à moins que je ne me trompe — That must be Paul, unless I'm mistaken

7 Parlez bas de peur qu'on ne vous entende — Speak softly for fear that someone hears you

8 Retournez-vous de sorte que je vous voie — Turn round so that I can see you

9 Il faut que je vous parle immédiatement — I must speak to you right away / It is necessary that I speak to you right away

10 Il est possible qu'ils aient raison — They may be right / It's possible that they are right

11 Il semble qu'elle ne soit pas venue — It appears that she hasn't come

12 Il vaut mieux que vous restiez chez vous — It's better that you stay at home

13 Il est dommage qu'elle ait perdu cette adresse — It's a shame/a pity that she's lost the address

14 la personne la plus sympathique que je connaisse — the nicest person I know
l'article le moins cher que j'aie jamais acheté — the cheapest item I have ever bought

15 Voici la dernière lettre qu'elle m'ait écrite — This is the last letter she wrote to me
David est la seule personne qui puisse me conseiller — David is the only person who can advise me

16 Vive le roi! — Long live the king!
Que Dieu vous bénisse! — God bless you!

Verbs

The Subjunctive: When to Use it *continued*

After verbs of:

- wishing
  vouloir que
  désirer que ⎤ to wish that, want → **❶**
  souhaiter que ⎦

- fearing
  craindre que ⎤ to be afraid that → **❷**
  avoir peur que ⎦

ⓘ Note that **ne** in example **❷** has no translation value. It is often omitted in spoken informal French.

- ordering, forbidding, allowing
  ordonner que ⎤ to order that
  défendre que ⎦ to forbid that
  permettre que to allow that → **❸**

- opinion, expressing uncertainty
  croire que ⎤ to think that → **❹**
  penser que ⎦
  douter que to doubt that

- emotion (e.g. regret, shame, pleasure)
  regretter que to be sorry that → **❺**
  être content/surpris *etc* **que** to be pleased/surprised *etc* that → **❻**

After: **si (...) que** however → **❼**
  qui que whoever → **❽**
  quoi que whatever → **❾**

After **que** in the following:

- to form the 3ʳᵈ person imperative or to express a wish → **❿**
- when **que** has the meaning 'if', replacing **si** in a clause → **⓫**
- when **que** has the meaning 'whether' → **⓬**

In relative clauses following certain types of indefinite and negative construction → **⓭**

Examples

1 Nous voulons qu'elle soit contente — We want her to be happy (*literally:* We want that she is happy)

2 Il craint qu'il ne soit trop tard — He's afraid it may be too late

3 Permettez que nous vous aidions — Allow us to help you

4 Je ne pense pas qu'ils soient venus — I don't think they came

5 Je regrette que vous ne puissiez pas venir — I'm sorry that you cannot come

6 Je suis content que vous les aimiez — I'm pleased that you like them

7 si courageux qu'il soit — however brave he may be
si peu que ce soit — however little it is

8 Qui que vous soyez, allez-vous-en! — Whoever you are, go away!

9 Quoi que nous fassions, ... — Whatever we do, ...

10 Qu'il entre! — Let him come in!
Que cela vous serve de leçon! — Let that be a lesson to you!

11 S'il fait beau et que tu te sentes mieux, nous irons ... — If it's nice and you're feeling better, we'll go ...

12 Que tu viennes ou non, je ... — Whether you come or not, I ...

13 Il cherche une maison qui ait deux caves — He's looking for a house which has two cellars
(*subjunctive used since such a house may or may not exist*)

J'ai besoin d'un livre qui décrive l'art du mime — I need a book which describes the art of mime
(*subjunctive used since such a book may or may not exist*)

Je n'ai rencontré personne qui la connaisse — I haven't met anyone who knows her

49

Irregular Verbs

The verbs on the following pages provide the main patterns for irregular verbs. They are given in their most common simple tenses, together with the imperative and the present participle.

The auxiliary (**avoir** or **être**) is also shown for each verb, together with the past participle, to enable you to form all the compound tenses (see pp 18 ff). **Falloir** and **pleuvoir**, which are only used in the '**il**' form, are given below. The rest follow in alphabetical order.

falloir (to be necessary) / pleuvoir (to rain)

AUXILIARY: **avoir**

PAST PARTICIPLE	PRESENT PARTICIPLE	IMPERATIVE
fallu / plu	*not used* / **pleuvant**	*not used*
PRESENT	**FUTURE**	**IMPERFECT**
il **faut** / il **pleut**	il **faudra** / il **pleuvra**	il **fallait** / il **pleuvait**
PRESENT SUBJUNCTIVE	**CONDITIONAL**	**PAST HISTORIC**
il **faille** / il **pleuve**	il **faudrait** / il **pleuvrait**	il **fallut** / il **plut**

acquérir (to acquire)

AUXILIARY: **avoir**

PAST PARTICIPLE	PRESENT PARTICIPLE	IMPERATIVE
acquis	acquérant	acquiers
		acquérons
		acquérez

PRESENT		FUTURE		IMPERFECT	
	j'**acquiers**		j'**acquerrai**		j'**acquérais**
tu	**acquiers**	tu	**acquerras**	tu	**acquérais**
il	**acquiert**	il	**acquerra**	il	**acquérait**
nous	**acquérons**	nous	**acquerrons**	nous	**acquérions**
vous	**acquérez**	vous	**acquerrez**	vous	**acquériez**
ils	**acquièrent**	ils	**acquerront**	ils	**acquéraient**
PRESENT SUBJUNCTIVE		**CONDITIONAL**		**PAST HISTORIC**	
	j'**acquière**		j'**acquerrais**		j'**acquis**
tu	**acquières**	tu	**acquerrais**	tu	**acquis**
il	**acquière**	il	**acquerrait**	il	**acquit**
nous	**acquérions**	nous	**acquerrions**	nous	**acquîmes**
vous	**acquériez**	vous	**acquerriez**	vous	**acquîtes**
ils	**acquièrent**	ils	**acquerraient**	ils	**acquirent**

Irregular Verbs

aller (to go)

AUXILIARY: être

PAST PARTICIPLE
allé

PRESENT PARTICIPLE
allant

IMPERATIVE
va
allons
allez

PRESENT		FUTURE		IMPERFECT	
je	vais	j'	irai	j'	allais
tu	vas	tu	iras	tu	allais
il	va	il	ira	il	allait
nous	allons	nous	irons	nous	allions
vous	allez	vous	irez	vous	alliez
ils	vont	ils	iront	ils	allaient

PRESENT SUBJUNCTIVE		CONDITIONAL		PAST HISTORIC	
j'	aille	j'	irais	j'	allai
tu	ailles	tu	irais	tu	allas
il	aille	il	irait	il	alla
nous	allions	nous	irions	nous	allâmes
vous	alliez	vous	iriez	vous	allâtes
ils	aillent	ils	iraient	ils	allèrent

s'asseoir (to sit down)

AUXILIARY: être

PAST PARTICIPLE
assis

PRESENT PARTICIPLE
s'asseyant

IMPERATIVE
assieds-toi
asseyons-nous
asseyez-vous

PRESENT		FUTURE		IMPERFECT	
je	m'assieds or assois	je	m'assiérai	je	m'asseyais
tu	t'assieds or assois	tu	t'assiéras	tu	t'asseyais
il	s'assied or assoit	il	s'assiéra	il	s'asseyait
nous	nous asseyons or assoyons	nous	nous assiérons	nous	nous asseyions
vous	vous asseyez or assoyez	vous	vous assiérez	vous	vous asseyiez
ils	s'asseyent or assoient	ils	s'assiéront	ils	s'asseyaient

PRESENT SUBJUNCTIVE		CONDITIONAL		PAST HISTORIC	
je	m'asseye	je	m'assiérais	je	m'assis
tu	t'asseyes	tu	t'assiérais	tu	t'assis
il	s'asseye	il	s'assiérait	il	s'assit
nous	nous asseyions	nous	nous assiérions	nous	nous assîmes
vous	vous asseyiez	vous	vous assiériez	vous	vous assîtes
ils	s'asseyent	ils	s'assiéraient	ils	s'assirent

Irregular Verbs

avoir (to have)

PAST PARTICIPLE	PRESENT PARTICIPLE	IMPERATIVE
eu	ayant	aie
		ayons
		ayez

PRESENT		FUTURE		IMPERFECT	
	j'ai		j'aurai		j'avais
tu	as	tu	auras	tu	avais
il	a	il	aura	il	avait
nous	avons	nous	aurons	nous	avions
vous	avez	vous	aurez	vous	aviez
ils	ont	ils	auront	ils	avaient

PRESENT SUBJUNCTIVE		CONDITIONAL		PAST HISTORIC	
	j'aie		j'aurais		j'eus
tu	aies	tu	aurais	tu	eus
il	ait	il	aurait	il	eut
nous	ayons	nous	aurions	nous	eûmes
vous	ayez	vous	auriez	vous	eûtes
ils	aient	ils	auraient	ils	eurent

battre (to beat)

PAST PARTICIPLE	PRESENT PARTICIPLE	IMPERATIVE
battu	battant	bats
		battons
		battez

PRESENT		FUTURE		IMPERFECT	
je	bats	je	battrai	je	battais
tu	bats	tu	battras	tu	battais
il	bat	il	battra	il	battait
nous	battons	nous	battrons	nous	battions
vous	battez	vous	battrez	vous	battiez
ils	batten	ils	battront	ils	battaient

PRESENT SUBJUNCTIVE		CONDITIONAL		PAST HISTORIC	
je	batte	je	battrais	je	battis
tu	battes	tu	battrais	tu	battis
il	batte	il	battrait	il	battit
nous	battions	nous	battrions	nous	battîmes
vous	battiez	vous	battriez	vous	battîtes
ils	battent	ils	battraient	ils	battirent

Irregular Verbs

boire (to drink)

AUXILIARY: **avoir**

PAST PARTICIPLE	PRESENT PARTICIPLE	IMPERATIVE
bu	**buvant**	bois
		buvons
		buvez

PRESENT		FUTURE		IMPERFECT	
je	bois	je	boirai	je	**buvais**
tu	bois	tu	boiras	tu	**buvais**
il	boit	il	boira	il	**buvait**
nous	**buvons**	nous	boirons	nous	**buvions**
vous	**buvez**	vous	boirez	vous	**buviez**
ils	**boivent**	ils	boiront	ils	**buvaient**

PRESENT SUBJUNCTIVE		CONDITIONAL		PAST HISTORIC	
je	**boive**	je	boirais	je	**bus**
tu	**boives**	tu	boirais	tu	**bus**
il	**boive**	il	boirait	il	**but**
nous	**buvions**	nous	boirions	nous	**bûmes**
vous	**buviez**	vous	boiriez	vous	**bûtes**
ils	**boivent**	ils	boiraient	ils	**burent**

connaître (to know)

AUXILIARY: **avoir**

PAST PARTICIPLE	PRESENT PARTICIPLE	IMPERATIVE
connu	**connaissant**	**connais**
		connaissons
		connaissez

PRESENT		FUTURE		IMPERFECT	
je	**connais**	je	connaîtrai	je	**connaissais**
tu	**connais**	tu	connaîtras	tu	**connaissais**
il	connaît	il	connaîtra	il	**connaissait**
nous	**connaissons**	nous	connaîtrons	nous	**connaissions**
vous	**connaissez**	vous	connaîtrez	vous	**connaissiez**
ils	**connaissent**	ils	connaîtront	ils	**connaissaient**

PRESENT SUBJUNCTIVE		CONDITIONAL		PAST HISTORIC	
je	**connaisse**	je	connaîtrais	je	**connus**
tu	**connaisses**	tu	connaîtrais	tu	**connus**
il	**connaisse**	il	connaîtrait	il	**connut**
nous	**connaissions**	nous	connaîtrions	nous	**connûmes**
vous	**connaissiez**	vous	connaîtriez	vous	**connûtes**
ils	**connaissent**	ils	connaîtraient	ils	**connurent**

Irregular Verbs

coudre (to sew)

AUXILIARY: avoir

PAST PARTICIPLE
cousu

PRESENT PARTICIPLE
cousant

IMPERATIVE
couds
cousons
cousez

PRESENT

je	couds
tu	couds
il	coud
nous	cousons
vous	cousez
ils	cousent

FUTURE

je	coudrai
tu	coudras
il	coudra
nous	coudrons
vous	coudrez
ils	coudront

IMPERFECT

je	cousais
tu	cousais
il	cousait
nous	cousions
vous	cousiez
ils	cousaient

PRESENT SUBJUNCTIVE

je	couse
tu	couses
il	couse
nous	cousions
vous	cousiez
ils	cousent

CONDITIONAL

je	coudrais
tu	coudrais
il	coudrait
nous	coudrions
vous	coudriez
ils	coudraient

PAST HISTORIC

je	cousis
tu	cousis
il	cousit
nous	cousîmes
vous	cousîtes
ils	cousirent

courir (to run)

AUXILIARY: avoir

PAST PARTICIPLE
couru

PRESENT PARTICIPLE
courant

IMPERATIVE
cours
courons
courez

PRESENT

je	cours
tu	cours
il	court
nous	courons
vous	courez
ils	courent

FUTURE

je	courrai
tu	courras
il	courra
nous	courrons
vous	courrez
ils	courront

IMPERFECT

je	courais
tu	courais
il	courait
nous	courions
vous	couriez
ils	couraient

PRESENT SUBJUNCTIVE

je	coure
tu	coures
il	coure
nous	courions
vous	couriez
ils	courent

CONDITIONAL

je	courrais
tu	courrais
il	courrait
nous	courrions
vous	courriez
ils	courraient

PAST HISTORIC

je	courus
tu	courus
il	courut
nous	courûmes
vous	courûtes
ils	coururent

Irregular Verbs

craindre (to fear)

AUXILIARY: **avoir**

PAST PARTICIPLE	PRESENT PARTICIPLE	IMPERATIVE
craint	**craignant**	**crains**
		craignons
		craignez

PRESENT		FUTURE		IMPERFECT	
je	**crains**	je	craindrai	je	**craignais**
tu	**crains**	tu	craindras	tu	**craignais**
il	**craint**	il	craindra	il	**craignait**
nous	**craignons**	nous	craindrons	nous	**craignions**
vous	**craignez**	vous	craindrez	vous	**craigniez**
ils	**craignent**	ils	craindront	ils	**craignaient**

PRESENT SUBJUNCTIVE		CONDITIONAL		PAST HISTORIC	
je	**craigne**	je	craindrais	je	**craignis**
tu	**craignes**	tu	craindrais	tu	**craignis**
il	**craigne**	il	craindrait	il	**craignit**
nous	**craignions**	nous	craindrions	nous	**craignîmes**
vous	**craigniez**	vous	craindriez	vous	**craignîtes**
ils	**craignent**	ils	craindraient	ils	**craignirent**

Verbs ending in **-eindre** and **-oindre** are conjugated similarly

croire (to believe)

AUXILIARY: **avoir**

PAST PARTICIPLE	PRESENT PARTICIPLE	IMPERATIVE
cru	**croyant**	crois
		croyons
		croyez

PRESENT		FUTURE		IMPERFECT	
je	crois	je	croirai	je	**croyais**
tu	crois	tu	croiras	tu	**croyais**
il	**croit**	il	croira	il	**croyait**
nous	**croyons**	nous	croirons	nous	**croyions**
vous	**croyez**	vous	croirez	vous	**croyiez**
ils	croient	ils	croiront	ils	**croyaient**

PRESENT SUBJUNCTIVE		CONDITIONAL		PAST HISTORIC	
je	croie	je	croirais	je	**crus**
tu	croies	tu	croirais	tu	**crus**
il	croie	il	croirait	il	**crut**
nous	**croyions**	nous	croirions	nous	**crûmes**
vous	**croyiez**	vous	croiriez	vous	**crûtes**
ils	croient	ils	croiraient	ils	**crurent**

Irregular Verbs

croître (to grow)

AUXILIARY: **avoir**

PAST PARTICIPLE	PRESENT PARTICIPLE	IMPERATIVE
crû	**croissant**	croîs
		croissons
		croissez

PRESENT		FUTURE		IMPERFECT	
je	**croîs**	je	croîtrai	je	**croissais**
tu	**croîs**	tu	croîtras	tu	**croissais**
il	croît	il	croîtra	il	**croissait**
nous	**croissons**	nous	croîtrons	nous	**croissions**
vous	**croissez**	vous	croîtrez	vous	**croissiez**
ils	**croissent**	ils	croîtront	ils	**croissaient**

PRESENT SUBJUNCTIVE		CONDITIONAL		PAST HISTORIC	
je	**croisse**	je	croîtrais	je	**crûs**
tu	**croisses**	tu	croîtrais	tu	**crûs**
il	**croisse**	il	croîtrait	il	**crût**
nous	**croissions**	nous	croîtrions	nous	**crûmes**
vous	**croissiez**	vous	croîtriez	vous	**crûtes**
ils	**croissent**	ils	croîtraient	ils	**crûrent**

cueillir (to pick)

AUXILIARY: **avoir**

PAST PARTICIPLE	PRESENT PARTICIPLE	IMPERATIVE
cueilli	**cueillant**	**cueille**
		cueillons
		cueillez

PRESENT		FUTURE		IMPERFECT	
je	**cueille**	je	**cueillerai**	je	**cueillais**
tu	**cueilles**	tu	**cueilleras**	tu	**cueillais**
il	**cueille**	il	**cueillera**	il	**cueillait**
nous	**cueillons**	nous	**cueillerons**	nous	**cueillions**
vous	**cueillez**	vous	**cueillerez**	vous	**cueilliez**
ils	**cueillent**	ils	**cueilleront**	ils	**cueillaient**

PRESENT SUBJUNCTIVE		CONDITIONAL		PAST HISTORIC	
je	**cueille**	je	**cueillerais**	je	cueillis
tu	**cueilles**	tu	**cueillerais**	tu	cueillis
il	**cueille**	il	**cueillerait**	il	cueillit
nous	**cueillions**	nous	**cueillerions**	nous	cueillîmes
vous	**cueilliez**	vous	**cueilleriez**	vous	cueillîtes
ils	**cueillent**	ils	**cueilleraient**	ils	cueillirent

Irregular Verbs

cuire (to cook)

AUXILIARY: avoir

PAST PARTICIPLE	PRESENT PARTICIPLE	IMPERATIVE
cuit	cuisant	cuis
		cuisons
		cuisez

PRESENT		FUTURE		IMPERFECT	
je	cuis	je	cuirai	je	cuisais
tu	cuis	tu	cuiras	tu	cuisais
il	cuit	il	cuira	il	cuisait
nous	cuisons	nous	cuirons	nous	cuisions
vous	cuisez	vous	cuirez	vous	cuisiez
ils	cuisent	ils	cuiront	ils	cuisaient

PRESENT SUBJUNCTIVE		CONDITIONAL		PAST HISTORIC	
je	cuise	je	cuirais	je	cuisis
tu	cuises	tu	cuirais	tu	cuisis
il	cuise	il	cuirait	il	cuisit
nous	cuisions	nous	cuirions	nous	cuisîmes
vous	cuisiez	vous	cuiriez	vous	cuisîtes
ils	cuisent	ils	cuiraient	ils	cuisirent

nuire (to harm) conjugated similarly, but past participle **nui**

devoir (to have to, to owe)

AUXILIARY: avoir

PAST PARTICIPLE	PRESENT PARTICIPLE	IMPERATIVE
dû	devant	dois
		devons
		devez

PRESENT		FUTURE		IMPERFECT	
je	dois	je	devrai	je	devais
tu	dois	tu	devras	tu	devais
il	doit	il	devra	il	devait
nous	devons	nous	devrons	nous	devions
vous	devez	vous	devrez	vous	deviez
ils	doivent	ils	devront	ils	devaient

PRESENT SUBJUNCTIVE		CONDITIONAL		PAST HISTORIC	
je	doive	je	devrais	je	dus
tu	doives	tu	devrais	tu	dus
il	doive	il	devrait	il	dut
nous	devions	nous	devrions	nous	dûmes
vous	deviez	vous	devriez	vous	dûtes
ils	doivent	ils	devraient	ils	durent

Irregular Verbs

dire (to say, tell)

AUXILIARY: avoir

PAST PARTICIPLE	PRESENT PARTICIPLE	IMPERATIVE
dit	disant	dis
		disons
		dites

PRESENT		FUTURE		IMPERFECT	
je	dis	je	dirai	je	disais
tu	dis	tu	diras	tu	disais
il	dit	il	dira	il	disait
nous	disons	nous	dirons	nous	disions
vous	dites	vous	direz	vous	disiez
ils	disent	ils	diront	ils	disaient

PRESENT SUBJUNCTIVE		CONDITIONAL		PAST HISTORIC	
je	dise	je	dirais	je	dis
tu	dises	tu	dirais	tu	dis
il	dise	il	dirait	il	dit
nous	disions	nous	dirions	nous	dîmes
vous	disiez	vous	diriez	vous	dîtes
ils	disent	ils	diraient	ils	dirent

interdire (to forbid) conjugated similarly, but 2nd person plural of the present tense is **vous interdisez**

dormir (to sleep)

AUXILIARY: avoir

PAST PARTICIPLE	PRESENT PARTICIPLE	IMPERATIVE
dormi	dormant	dors
		dormons
		dormez

PRESENT		FUTURE		IMPERFECT	
je	dors	je	dormirai	je	dormais
tu	dors	tu	dormiras	tu	dormais
il	dort	il	dormira	il	dormait
nous	dormons	nous	dormirons	nous	dormions
vous	dormez	vous	dormirez	vous	dormiez
ils	dorment	ils	dormiront	ils	dormaient

PRESENT SUBJUNCTIVE		CONDITIONAL		PAST HISTORIC	
je	dorme	je	dormirais	je	dormis
tu	dormes	tu	dormirais	tu	dormis
il	dorme	il	dormirait	il	dormit
nous	dormions	nous	dormirions	nous	dormîmes
vous	dormiez	vous	dormiriez	vous	dormîtes
ils	dorment	ils	dormiraient	ils	dormirent

Irregular Verbs

écrire (to write)

AUXILIARY: **avoir**

PAST PARTICIPLE	PRESENT PARTICIPLE	IMPERATIVE
écrit	**écrivant**	écris
		écrivons
		écrivez

PRESENT		FUTURE		IMPERFECT	
	j'écris		j'écrirai		**j'écrivais**
tu	écris	tu	écriras	tu	**écrivais**
il	écrit	il	écrira	il	**écrivait**
nous	**écrivons**	nous	écrirons	nous	**écrivions**
vous	**écrivez**	vous	écrirez	vous	**écriviez**
ils	**écrivent**	ils	écriront	ils	**écrivaient**

PRESENT SUBJUNCTIVE		CONDITIONAL		PAST HISTORIC	
	j'**écrive**		j'écrirais		**j'écrivis**
tu	**écrives**	tu	écrirais	tu	**écrivis**
il	**écrive**	il	écrirait	il	**écrivit**
nous	**écrivions**	nous	écririons	nous	**écrivîmes**
vous	**écriviez**	vous	écririez	vous	**écrivîtes**
ils	**écrivent**	ils	écriraient	ils	**écrivirent**

envoyer (to send)

AUXILIARY: **avoir**

PAST PARTICIPLE	PRESENT PARTICIPLE	IMPERATIVE
envoyé	envoyant	envoie
		envoyons
		envoyez

PRESENT		FUTURE		IMPERFECT	
	j'envoie		**j'enverrai**		j'envoyais
tu	envoies	tu	**enverras**	tu	envoyais
il	envoie	il	**enverra**	il	envoyait
nous	envoyons	nous	**enverrons**	nous	envoyions
vous	envoyez	vous	**enverrez**	vous	envoyiez
ils	envoient	ils	**enverront**	ils	envoyaient

PRESENT SUBJUNCTIVE		CONDITIONAL		PAST HISTORIC	
	j'envoie		**j'enverrais**		j'envoyai
tu	envoies	tu	**enverrais**	tu	envoyas
il	envoie	il	**enverrait**	il	envoya
nous	envoyions	nous	**enverrions**	nous	envoyâmes
vous	envoyiez	vous	**enverriez**	vous	envoyâtes
ils	envoient	ils	**enverraient**	ils	envoyèrent

Irregular Verbs

être (to be)

AUXILIARY: avoir

PAST PARTICIPLE
été

PRESENT PARTICIPLE
étant

IMPERATIVE
sois
soyons
soyez

PRESENT		FUTURE		IMPERFECT	
je	suis	je	serai		j'étais
tu	es	tu	seras	tu	étais
il	est	il	sera	il	était
nous	sommes	nous	serons	nous	étions
vous	êtes	vous	serez	vous	étiez
ils	sont	ils	seront	ils	étaient

PRESENT SUBJUNCTIVE		CONDITIONAL		PAST HISTORIC	
je	sois	je	serais	je	fus
tu	sois	tu	serais	tu	fus
il	soit	il	serait	il	fut
nous	soyons	nous	serions	nous	fûmes
vous	soyez	vous	seriez	vous	fûtes
ils	soient	ils	seraient	ils	furent

faire (to do, to make)

AUXILIARY: avoir

PAST PARTICIPLE
fait

PRESENT PARTICIPLE
faisant

IMPERATIVE
fais
faisons
faites

PRESENT		FUTURE		IMPERFECT	
je	fais	je	ferai	je	faisais
tu	fais	tu	feras	tu	faisais
il	fait	il	fera	il	faisait
nous	faisons	nous	ferons	nous	faisions
vous	faites	vous	ferez	vous	faisiez
ils	font	ils	feront	ils	faisaient

PRESENT SUBJUNCTIVE		CONDITIONAL		PAST HISTORIC	
je	fasse	je	ferais	je	fis
tu	fasses	tu	ferais	tu	fis
il	fasse	il	ferait	il	fit
nous	fassions	nous	ferions	nous	fîmes
vous	fassiez	vous	feriez	vous	fîtes
ils	fassent	ils	feraient	ils	firent

Irregular Verbs

fuir (to flee)

AUXILIARY: **avoir**

PAST PARTICIPLE
fui

PRESENT PARTICIPLE
fuyant

IMPERATIVE
fuis
fuyons
fuyez

PRESENT	FUTURE	IMPERFECT
je fuis	je fuirai	je **fuyais**
tu fuis	tu fuiras	tu **fuyais**
il fuit	il fuira	il **fuyait**
nous **fuyons**	nous fuirons	nous **fuyions**
vous **fuyez**	vous fuirez	vous **fuyiez**
ils **fuient**	ils fuiront	ils **fuyaient**

PRESENT SUBJUNCTIVE	CONDITIONAL	PAST HISTORIC
je **fuie**	je fuirais	je fuis
tu **fuies**	tu fuirais	tu fuis
il **fuie**	il fuirait	il fuit
nous **fuyions**	nous fuirions	nous fuîmes
vous **fuyiez**	vous fuiriez	vous fuîtes
ils **fuient**	ils fuiraient	ils fuirent

haïr (to hate)

AUXILIARY: **avoir**

PAST PARTICIPLE
haï

PRESENT PARTICIPLE
haïssant

IMPERATIVE
hais
haïssons
haïssez

PRESENT	FUTURE	IMPERFECT
je hais	je haïrai	je **haïssais**
tu hais	tu haïras	tu **haïssais**
il hait	il haïra	il **haïssait**
nous haïssons	nous haïrons	nous **haïssions**
vous **haïssez**	vous haïrez	vous **haïssiez**
ils **haïssent**	ils haïront	ils **haïssaient**

PRESENT SUBJUNCTIVE	CONDITIONAL	PAST HISTORIC
je **haïsse**	je haïrais	je **haïs**
tu **haïsses**	tu haïrais	tu **haïs**
il **haïsse**	il haïrait	il **haït**
nous **haïssions**	nous haïrions	nous **haïmes**
vous **haïssiez**	vous haïriez	vous **haïtes**
ils **haïssent**	ils haïraient	ils **haïrent**

Irregular Verbs

lire (to read)

PAST PARTICIPLE	PRESENT PARTICIPLE	IMPERATIVE
lu	lisant	lis
		lisons
		lisez

PRESENT	FUTURE	IMPERFECT
je lis	je lirai	je lisais
tu lis	tu liras	tu lisais
il lit	il lira	il lisait
nous lisons	nous lirons	nous lisions
vous lisez	vous lirez	vous lisiez
ils lisent	ils liront	ils lisaient

PRESENT SUBJUNCTIVE	CONDITIONAL	PAST HISTORIC
je lise	je lirais	je lus
tu lises	tu lirais	tu lus
il lise	il lirait	il lut
nous lisions	nous lirions	nous lûmes
vous lisiez	vous liriez	vous lûtes
ils lisent	ils liraient	ils lurent

mettre (to put)

AUXILIARY: avoir

PAST PARTICIPLE	PRESENT PARTICIPLE	IMPERATIVE
mis	mettant	mets
		mettons
		mettez

PRESENT	FUTURE	IMPERFECT
je mets	je mettrai	je mettais
tu mets	tu mettras	tu mettais
il met	il mettra	il mettait
nous mettons	nous mettrons	nous mettions
vous mettez	vous mettrez	vous mettiez
ils mettent	ils mettront	ils mettaient

PRESENT SUBJUNCTIVE	CONDITIONAL	PAST HISTORIC
je mette	je mettrais	je mis
tu mettes	tu mettrais	tu mis
il mette	il mettrait	il mit
nous mettions	nous mettrions	nous mîmes
vous mettiez	vous mettriez	vous mîtes
ils mettent	ils mettraient	ils mirent

Irregular Verbs

mourir (to die)

AUXILIARY: être

PAST PARTICIPLE
mort

PRESENT PARTICIPLE
mourant

IMPERATIVE
meurs
mourons
mourez

PRESENT
je **meurs**
tu **meurs**
il **meurt**
nous **mourons**
vous **mourez**
ils **meurent**

FUTURE
je **mourrai**
tu **mourras**
il **mourra**
nous **mourrons**
vous **mourrez**
ils **mourront**

IMPERFECT
je **mourais**
tu **mourais**
il **mourait**
nous **mourions**
vous **mouriez**
ils **mouraient**

PRESENT SUBJUNCTIVE
je **meure**
tu **meures**
il **meure**
nous **mourions**
vous **mouriez**
ils **meurent**

CONDITIONAL
je **mourrais**
tu **mourrais**
il **mourrait**
nous **mourrions**
vous **mourriez**
ils **mourraient**

PAST HISTORIC
je **mourus**
tu **mourus**
il **mourut**
nous **mourûmes**
vous **mourûtes**
ils **moururent**

naître (to be born)

AUXILIARY: être

PAST PARTICIPLE
né

PRESENT PARTICIPLE
naissant

IMPERATIVE
nais
naissons
naissez

PRESENT
je **nais**
tu **nais**
il **naît**
nous **naissons**
vous **naissez**
ils **naissent**

FUTURE
je naîtrai
tu naîtras
il naîtra
nous naîtrons
vous naîtrez
ils naîtront

IMPERFECT
je **naissais**
tu **naissais**
il **naissait**
nous **naissions**
vous **naissiez**
ils **naissaient**

PRESENT SUBJUNCTIVE
je **naisse**
tu **naisses**
il **naisse**
nous **naissions**
vous **naissiez**
ils **naissent**

CONDITIONAL
je naîtrais
tu naîtrais
il naîtrait
nous naîtrions
vous naîtriez
ils naîtraient

PAST HISTORIC
je naquis
tu naquis
il naquit
nous naquîmes
vous naquîtes
ils naquirent

Irregular Verbs

ouvrir (to open)

AUXILIARY: avoir

PAST PARTICIPLE	PRESENT PARTICIPLE	IMPERATIVE
ouvert	ouvrant	ouvre
		ouvrons
		ouvrez

PRESENT		FUTURE		IMPERFECT	
	j'ouvre		j'ouvrirai		j'ouvrais
tu	ouvres	tu	ouvriras	tu	ouvrais
il	ouvre	il	ouvrira	il	ouvrait
nous	ouvrons	nous	ouvrirons	nous	ouvrions
vous	ouvrez	vous	ouvrirez	vous	ouvriez
ils	ouvrent	ils	ouvriront	ils	ouvraient

PRESENT SUBJUNCTIVE		CONDITIONAL		PAST HISTORIC	
	j'ouvre		j'ouvrirais		j'ouvris
tu	ouvres	tu	ouvrirais	tu	ouvris
il	ouvre	il	ouvrirait	il	ouvrit
nous	ouvrions	nous	ouvririons	nous	ouvrîmes
vous	ouvriez	vous	ouvririez	vous	ouvrîtes
ils	ouvrent	ils	ouvriraient	ils	ouvrirent

offrir (to offer), souffrir (to suffer) are conjugated similarly

paraître (to appear)

AUXILIARY: avoir

PAST PARTICIPLE	PRESENT PARTICIPLE	IMPERATIVE
paru	paraissant	parais
		paraissons
		paraissez

PRESENT		FUTURE		IMPERFECT	
je	parais	je	paraîtrai	je	paraissais
tu	parais	tu	paraîtras	tu	paraissais
il	paraît	il	paraîtra	il	paraissait
nous	paraissons	vous	paraîtrons	nous	paraissions
vous	paraissez	nous	paraîtrez	vous	paraissiez
ils	paraissent	ils	paraîtront	ils	paraissaient

PRESENT SUBJUNCTIVE		CONDITIONAL		PAST HISTORIC	
je	paraisse	je	paraîtrais	je	parus
tu	paraisses	tu	paraîtrais	tu	parus
il	paraisse	il	paraîtrait	il	parut
nous	paraissions	nous	paraîtrions	nous	parûmes
vous	paraissiez	vous	paraîtriez	vous	parûtes
ils	paraissent	ils	paraîtraient	ils	parurent

Irregular Verbs

partir (to leave)

AUXILIARY: **être**

PAST PARTICIPLE
parti

PRESENT PARTICIPLE
partant

IMPERATIVE
pars
partons
partez

PRESENT	FUTURE	IMPERFECT
je **pars**	je partirai	je **partais**
tu **pars**	tu partiras	tu **partais**
il **part**	il partira	il **partait**
nous **partons**	nous partirons	nous **partions**
vous **partez**	vous partirez	vous **partiez**
ils **partent**	ils partiront	ils **partaient**

PRESENT SUBJUNCTIVE	CONDITIONAL	PAST HISTORIC
je **parte**	je partirais	je partis
tu **partes**	tu partirais	tu partis
il **parte**	il partirait	il partit
nous **partions**	nous partirions	nous partîmes
vous **partiez**	vous partiriez	vous partîtes
ils **partent**	ils partiraient	ils partirent

plaire (to please)

AUXILIARY: **avoir**

PAST PARTICIPLE
plu

PRESENT PARTICIPLE
plaisant

IMPERATIVE
plais
plaisons
plaisez

PRESENT	FUTURE	IMPERFECT
je plais	je plairai	je **plaisais**
tu plais	tu plairas	tu **plaisais**
il **plaît**	il plaira	il **plaisait**
nous **plaisons**	nous plairons	nous **plaisions**
vous **plaisez**	vous plairez	vous **plaisiez**
ils **plaisent**	ils plairont	ils **plaisaient**

PRESENT SUBJUNCTIVE	CONDITIONAL	PAST HISTORIC
je **plaise**	je plairais	je **plus**
tu **plaises**	tu plairais	tu **plus**
il **plaise**	il plairait	il **plut**
nous **plaisions**	nous plairions	nous **plûmes**
vous **plaisiez**	vous plairiez	vous **plûtes**
ils **plaisent**	ils plairaient	ils **plurent**

Irregular Verbs

pouvoir (to be able to)

AUXILIARY: **avoir**

PAST PARTICIPLE	PRESENT PARTICIPLE	IMPERATIVE
pu	**pouvant**	*not used*

PRESENT		FUTURE		IMPERFECT	
je	**peux***	je	**pourrai**	je	**pouvais**
tu	**peux**	tu	**pourras**	tu	**pouvais**
il	**peut**	il	**pourra**	il	**pouvait**
nous	**pouvons**	nous	**pourrons**	nous	**pouvions**
vous	**pouvez**	vous	**pourrez**	vous	**pouviez**
ils	**peuvent**	ils	**pourront**	ils	**pouvaient**

PRESENT SUBJUNCTIVE		CONDITIONAL		PAST HISTORIC	
je	**puisse**	je	**pourrais**	je	**pus**
tu	**puisses**	tu	**pourrais**	tu	**pus**
il	**puisse**	il	**pourrait**	il	**put**
nous	**puissions**	nous	**pourrions**	nous	**pûmes**
vous	**puissiez**	vous	**pourriez**	vous	**pûtes**
ils	**puissent**	ils	**pourraient**	ils	**purent**

* In questions: **puis-je?**

prendre (to take)

AUXILIARY: **avoir**

PAST PARTICIPLE	PRESENT PARTICIPLE	IMPERATIVE
pris	**prenant**	prends
		prenons
		prenez

PRESENT		FUTURE		IMPERFECT	
je	prends	je	prendrai	je	**prenais**
tu	prends	tu	prendras	tu	**prenais**
il	prend	il	prendra	il	**prenait**
nous	**prenons**	nous	prendrons	nous	**prenions**
vous	**prenez**	vous	prendrez	vous	**preniez**
ils	**prennent**	ils	prendront	ils	**prenaient**

PRESENT SUBJUNCTIVE		CONDITIONAL		PAST HISTORIC	
je	**prenne**	je	prendrais	je	**pris**
tu	**prennes**	tu	prendrais	tu	**pris**
il	**prenne**	il	prendrait	il	**prit**
nous	**prenions**	nous	prendrions	nous	**prîmes**
vous	**preniez**	tous	prendriez	nous	**prîtes**
ils	**prennent**	ils	prendraient	ils	**prirent**

Irregular Verbs

recevoir (to receive)

AUXILIARY: avoir

PAST PARTICIPLE
reçu

PRESENT PARTICIPLE
recevant

IMPERATIVE
reçois
recevons
recevez

PRESENT	FUTURE	IMPERFECT
je **reçois**	je **recevrai**	je **recevais**
tu **reçois**	tu **recevras**	tu **recevais**
il **reçoit**	il **recevra**	il **recevait**
nous **recevons**	nous **recevrons**	nous **recevions**
vous **recevez**	vous **recevrez**	vous **receviez**
ils **reçoivent**	ils **recevront**	ils **recevaient**

PRESENT SUBJUNCTIVE	CONDITIONAL	PAST HISTORIC
je **reçoive**	je **recevrais**	je **reçus**
tu **reçoives**	tu **recevrais**	tu **reçus**
il **reçoive**	il **recevrait**	il **reçut**
nous **recevions**	nous **recevrions**	nous **reçûmes**
vous **receviez**	vous **recevriez**	vous **reçûtes**
ils **reçoivent**	ils **recevraient**	ils **reçurent**

résoudre (to solve)

AUXILIARY: avoir

PAST PARTICIPLE
résolu

PRESENT PARTICIPLE
résolvant

IMPERATIVE
résous
résolvons
résolvez

PRESENT	FUTURE	IMPERFECT
je **résous**	je résoudrai	je **résolvais**
tu **résous**	tu résoudras	tu **résolvais**
il **résout**	il résoudra	il **résolvait**
nous **résolvons**	nous résoudrons	nous **résolvions**
vous **résolvez**	vous résoudrez	vous **résolviez**
ils **résolvent**	ils résoudront	ils **résolvaient**

PRESENT SUBJUNCTIVE	CONDITIONAL	PAST HISTORIC
je **résolve**	je résoudrais	je **résolus**
tu **résolves**	tu résoudrais	tu **résolus**
il **résolve**	il résoudrait	il **résolut**
nous **résolvions**	nous résoudrions	nous **résolûmes**
vous **résolviez**	vous résoudriez	vous **résolûtes**
ils **résolvent**	ils résoudraient	ils **résolurent**

Irregular Verbs

rire (to laugh)

AUXILIARY: **avoir**

PAST PARTICIPLE	PRESENT PARTICIPLE	IMPERATIVE
ri	riant	ris
		rions
		riez

PRESENT		FUTURE		IMPERFECT	
je	ris	je	rirai	je	riais
tu	ris	tu	riras	tu	riais
il	**rit**	il	rira	il	riait
nous	rions	nous	rirons	nous	riions
vous	riez	vous	rirez	vous	riiez
ils	rient	ils	riront	ils	riaient

PRESENT SUBJUNCTIVE		CONDITIONAL		PAST HISTORIC	
je	rie	je	rirais	je	**ris**
tu	ries	tu	rirais	tu	**ris**
il	rie	il	rirait	il	**rit**
nous	riions	nous	ririons	nous	**rîmes**
vous	riiez	vous	ririez	vous	**rîtes**
ils	rient	ils	riraient	ils	**rirent**

rompre (to break)

AUXILIARY: **avoir**

PAST PARTICIPLE	PRESENT PARTICIPLE	IMPERATIVE
rompu	rompant	romps
		rompons
		rompez

PRESENT		FUTURE		IMPERFECT	
je	romps	je	romprai	je	rompais
tu	romps	tu	rompras	tu	rompais
il	**rompt**	il	rompra	il	rompait
nous	rompons	nous	romprons	nous	rompions
vous	rompez	vous	romprez	vous	rompiez
ils	rompent	ils	rompront	ils	rompaient

PRESENT SUBJUNCTIVE		CONDITIONAL		PAST HISTORIC	
je	rompe	je	romprais	je	rompis
tu	rompes	tu	romprais	tu	rompis
il	rompe	il	romprait	il	rompit
nous	rompions	nous	romprions	nous	rompîmes
vous	rompiez	vous	rompriez	vous	rompîtes
ils	rompent	ils	rompraient	ils	rompirent

Irregular Verbs

savoir (to know)

AUXILIARY: avoir

PAST PARTICIPLE	PRESENT PARTICIPLE	IMPERATIVE
su	sachant	sache
		sachons
		sachez

PRESENT

		FUTURE		IMPERFECT	
je	sais	je	saurai	je	savais
tu	sais	tu	sauras	tu	savais
il	sait	il	saura	il	savait
nous	savons	nous	saurons	nous	savions
vous	savez	vous	saurez	vous	saviez
ils	savent	ils	sauront	ils	savaient

PRESENT SUBJUNCTIVE		CONDITIONAL		PAST HISTORIC	
je	sache	je	saurais	je	sus
tu	saches	tu	saurais	tu	sus
il	sache	il	saurait	il	sut
nous	sachions	nous	saurions	nous	sûmes
vous	sachiez	vous	sauriez	vous	sûtes
ils	sachent	ils	sauraient	ils	surent

sentir (to feel, to smell)

AUXILIARY: avoir

PAST PARTICIPLE	PRESENT PARTICIPLE	IMPERATIVE
senti	sentant	sens
		sentons
		sentez

PRESENT		FUTURE		IMPERFECT	
je	sens	je	sentirai	je	sentais
tu	sens	tu	sentiras	tu	sentais
il	sent	il	sentira	il	sentait
nous	sentons	nous	sentirons	nous	sentions
vous	sentez	vous	sentirez	vous	sentiez
ils	sentent	ils	sentiront	ils	sentaient

PRESENT SUBJUNCTIVE		CONDITIONAL		PAST HISTORIC	
je	sente	je	sentirais	je	sentis
tu	sentes	tu	sentirais	tu	sentis
il	sente	il	sentirait	il	sentit
nous	sentions	nous	sentirions	nous	sentîmes
vous	sentiez	vous	sentiriez	vous	sentîtes
ils	sentent	ils	sentiraient	ils	sentirent

Irregular Verbs

servir (to serve)

AUXILIARY: avoir

PAST PARTICIPLE
servi

PRESENT PARTICIPLE
servant

IMPERATIVE
sers
servons
servez

PRESENT		FUTURE		IMPERFECT	
je	**sers**	je	servirai	je	**servais**
tu	**sers**	tu	serviras	tu	**servais**
il	**sert**	il	servira	il	**servait**
nous	**servons**	nous	servirons	nous	**servions**
vous	**servez**	vous	servirez	vous	**serviez**
ils	**servent**	ils	serviront	ils	**servaient**

PRESENT SUBJUNCTIVE		CONDITIONAL		PAST HISTORIC	
je	**serve**	je	servirais	je	servis
tu	**serves**	tu	servirais	tu	servis
il	**serve**	il	servirait	il	servit
nous	**servions**	nous	servirions	nous	servîmes
vous	**serviez**	vous	serviriez	vous	servîtes
ils	**servent**	ils	serviraient	ils	servirent

sortir (to go, to come out)

AUXILIARY: être

PAST PARTICIPLE
sorti

PRESENT PARTICIPLE
sortant

IMPERATIVE
sors
sortons
sortez

PRESENT		FUTURE		IMPERFECT	
je	**sors**	je	sortirai	je	**sortais**
tu	**sors**	tu	sortiras	tu	**sortais**
il	**sort**	il	sortira	il	**sortait**
nous	**sortons**	nous	sortirons	nous	**sortions**
vous	**sortez**	vous	sortirez	vous	**sortiez**
ils	**sortent**	ils	sortiront	ils	**sortaient**

PRESENT SUBJUNCTIVE		CONDITIONAL		PAST HISTORIC	
je	**sorte**	je	sortirais	je	sortis
tu	**sortes**	tu	sortirais	tu	sortis
il	**sorte**	il	sortirait	il	sortit
nous	**sortions**	nous	sortirions	nous	sortîmes
vous	**sortiez**	vous	sortiriez	vous	sortîtes
ils	**sortent**	ils	sortiraient	ils	sortirent

Irregular Verbs

suffire (to be enough)

AUXILIARY: **avoir**

PAST PARTICIPLE	PRESENT PARTICIPLE	IMPERATIVE
suffi	**suffisant**	suffis
		suffisons
		suffisez

PRESENT	FUTURE	IMPERFECT
je suffis	je suffirai	je **suffisais**
tu suffis	tu suffiras	tu **suffisais**
il suffit	il suffira	il **suffisait**
nous **suffisons**	nous suffirons	nous **suffisions**
vous **suffisez**	vous suffirez	vous **suffisiez**
ils **suffisent**	ils suffiront	ils **suffisaient**

PRESENT SUBJUNCTIVE	CONDITIONAL	PAST HISTORIC
je **suffise**	je suffirais	je **suffis**
tu **suffises**	tu suffirais	tu **suffis**
il **suffise**	il suffirait	il **suffit**
nous **suffisions**	nous suffirions	nous **suffîmes**
vous **suffisiez**	vous suffiriez	vous **suffîtes**
ils **suffisent**	ils suffiraient	ils **suffirent**

suivre (to follow)

AUXILIARY: **avoir**

PAST PARTICIPLE	PRESENT PARTICIPLE	IMPERATIVE
suivi	suivant	**suis**
		suivons
		suivez

PRESENT	FUTURE	IMPERFECT
je **suis**	je suivrai	je suivais
tu **suis**	tu suivras	tu suivais
il **suit**	il suivra	il suivait
nous suivons	nous suivrons	nous suivions
vous suivez	vous suivrez	vous suiviez
ils suivent	ils suivront	ils suivaient

PRESENT SUBJUNCTIVE	CONDITIONAL	PAST HISTORIC
je suive	je suivrais	je suivis
tu suives	tu suivrais	tu suivis
il suive	il suivrait	il suivit
nous suivions	nous suivrions	nous suivîmes
vous suiviez	vous suivriez	vous suivîtes
ils suivent	ils suivraient	ils suivirent

Irregular Verbs

se taire (to stop talking)

AUXILIARY: **être**

PAST PARTICIPLE
    tu

PRESENT PARTICIPLE
    se taisant

IMPERATIVE
    tais-toi
    taisons-nous
    taisez-vous

PRESENT		FUTURE		IMPERFECT	
je	me tais	je	me tairai	je	**me taisais**
tu	te tais	tu	te tairas	tu	**te taisais**
il	se tait	il	se taira	il	**se taisait**
nous	**nous taisons**	nous	nous tairons	nous	**nous taisions**
vous	**vous taisez**	vous	vous tairez	vous	**vous taisiez**
ils	**se taisent**	ils	se tairont	ils	**se taisaient**

PRESENT SUBJUNCTIVE		CONDITIONAL		PAST HISTORIC	
je	**me taise**	je	me tairais	je	**me tus**
tu	**te taises**	tu	te tairais	tu	**te tus**
il	**se taise**	il	se tairait	il	**se tut**
nous	**nous taisions**	nous	nous tairions	nous	**nous tûmes**
vous	**vous taisiez**	vous	vous tairiez	vous	**vous tûtes**
ils	**se taisent**	ils	se tairaient	ils	**se turent**

tenir (to hold)

AUXILIARY: **avoir**

PAST PARTICIPLE
    tenu

PRESENT PARTICIPLE
    tenant

IMPERATIVE
    tiens
    tenons
    tenez

PRESENT		FUTURE		IMPERFECT	
je	**tiens**	je	**tiendrai**	je	**tenais**
tu	**tiens**	tu	**tiendras**	tu	**tenais**
il	**tient**	il	**tiendra**	il	**tenait**
nous	**tenons**	nous	**tiendrons**	nous	**tenions**
vous	**tenez**	vous	**tiendrez**	vous	**teniez**
ils	**tiennent**	ils	**tiendront**	ils	**tenaient**

PRESENT SUBJUNCTIVE		CONDITIONAL		PAST HISTORIC	
je	**tienne**	je	**tiendrais**	je	**tins**
tu	**tiennes**	tu	**tiendrais**	tu	**tins**
il	**tienne**	il	**tiendrait**	il	**tint**
nous	**tenions**	nous	**tiendrions**	nous	**tînmes**
vous	**teniez**	vous	**tiendriez**	vous	**tîntes**
ils	**tiennent**	ils	**tiendraient**	ils	**tinrent**

Irregular Verbs

vaincre (to defeat)

AUXILIARY: avoir

PAST PARTICIPLE
vaincu

PRESENT PARTICIPLE
vainquant

IMPERATIVE
vaincs
vainquons
vainquez

PRESENT		FUTURE		IMPERFECT	
je	vaincs	je	vaincrai	je	vainquais
tu	vaincs	tu	vaincras	tu	vainquais
il	vainc	il	vaincra	il	vainquait
nous	vainquons	nous	vaincrons	nous	vainquions
vous	vainquez	vous	vaincrez	vous	vainquiez
ils	vainquent	ils	vaincront	ils	vainquaient

PRESENT SUBJUNCTIVE		CONDITIONAL		PAST HISTORIC	
je	vainque	je	vaincrais	je	vainquis
tu	vainques	tu	vaincrais	tu	vainquis
il	vainque	il	vaincrait	il	vainquit
nous	vainquions	nous	vaincrions	nous	vainquîmes
vous	vainquiez	vous	vaincriez	vous	vainquîtes
ils	vainquent	ils	vaincraient	ils	vainquirent

valoir (to be worth)

AUXILIARY: avoir

PAST PARTICIPLE
valu

PRESENT PARTICIPLE
valant

IMPERATIVE
vaux
valons
valez

PRESENT		FUTURE		IMPERFECT	
je	vaux	je	vaudrai	je	valais
tu	vaux	tu	vaudras	tu	valais
il	vaut	il	vaudra	il	valait
nous	valons	nous	vaudrons	nous	valions
vous	valez	vous	vaudrez	vous	valiez
ils	valent	ils	vaudront	ils	valaient

PRESENT SUBJUNCTIVE		CONDITIONAL		PAST HISTORIC	
je	vaille	je	vaudrais	je	valus
tu	vailles	tu	vaudrais	tu	valus
il	vaille	il	vaudrait	il	valut
nous	valions	nous	vaudrions	nous	valûmes
vous	valiez	vous	vaudriez	vous	valûtes
ils	vaillent	ils	vaudraient	ils	valurent

Irregular Verbs

venir (to come)

AUXILIARY: être

PAST PARTICIPLE
venu

PRESENT PARTICIPLE
venant

IMPERATIVE
viens
venons
venez

PRESENT		FUTURE		IMPERFECT	
je	**viens**	je	**viendrai**	je	**venais**
tu	**viens**	tu	**viendras**	tu	**venais**
il	**vient**	il	**viendra**	il	**venait**
nous	**venons**	nous	**viendrons**	nous	**venions**
vous	**venez**	vous	**viendrez**	vous	**veniez**
ils	**viennent**	ils	**viendront**	ils	**venaient**

PRESENT SUBJUNCTIVE		CONDITIONAL		PAST HISTORIC	
je	**vienne**	je	**viendrais**	je	**vins**
tu	**viennes**	tu	**viendrais**	tu	**vins**
il	**vienne**	il	**viendrait**	il	**vint**
nous	**venions**	nous	**viendrions**	nous	**vînmes**
vous	**veniez**	vous	**viendriez**	vous	**vîntes**
ils	**viennent**	ils	**viendraient**	ils	**vinrent**

vivre (to live)

AUXILIARY: avoir

PAST PARTICIPLE
vêcu

PRESENT PARTICIPLE
vivant

IMPERATIVE
vis
vivons
vivez

PRESENT		FUTURE		IMPERFECT	
je	**vis**	je	vivrai	je	vivais
tu	**vis**	tu	vivras	tu	vivais
il	**vit**	il	vivra	il	vivait
nous	vivons	nous	vivrons	nous	vivions
vous	vivez	vous	vivrez	vous	viviez
ils	vivent	ils	vivront	ils	vivaient

PRESENT SUBJUNCTIVE		CONDITIONAL		PAST HISTORIC	
je	vive	je	vivrais	je	**vécus**
tu	vives	tu	vivrais	tu	**vécus**
il	vive	il	vivrait	il	**vécut**
nous	vivions	nous	vivrions	nous	**vécûmes**
vous	viviez	vous	vivriez	vous	**vécûtes**
ils	vivent	ils	vivraient	ils	**vécurent**

Irregular Verbs

voir (to see)

AUXILIARY: avoir

PAST PARTICIPLE	PRESENT PARTICIPLE	IMPERATIVE
vu	voyant	vois
		voyons
		voyez

PRESENT		FUTURE		IMPERFECT	
je	vois	je	verrai	je	voyais
tu	vois	tu	verras	tu	voyais
il	voit	il	verra	il	voyait
nous	voyons	nous	verrons	nous	voyions
vous	voyez	vous	verrez	vous	voyiez
ils	voient	ils	verront	ils	voyaient

PRESENT SUBJUNCTIVE		CONDITIONAL		PAST HISTORIC	
je	voie	je	verrais	je	vis
tu	voies	tu	verrais	tu	vis
il	voie	il	verrait	il	vit
nous	voyions	nous	verrions	nous	vîmes
vous	voyiez	vous	verriez	vous	vîtes
ils	voient	ils	verraient	ils	virent

vouloir (to wish, to want)

AUXILIARY: avoir

PAST PARTICIPLE	PRESENT PARTICIPLE	IMPERATIVE
voulu	voulant	veuille
		veuillons
		veuillez

PRESENT		FUTURE		IMPERFECT	
je	veux	je	voudrai	je	voulais
tu	veux	tu	voudras	tu	voulais
il	veut	il	voudra	il	voulait
nous	voulons	nous	voudrons	nous	voulions
vous	voulez	vous	voudrez	vous	vouliez
ils	veulent	ils	voudront	ils	voulaient

PRESENT SUBJUNCTIVE		CONDITIONAL		PAST HISTORIC	
je	veuille	je	voudrais	je	voulus
tu	veuilles	tu	voudrais	tu	voulus
il	veuille	il	voudrait	il	voulut
nous	voulions	nous	voudrions	nous	voulûmes
vous	vouliez	vous	voudriez	vous	voulûtes
ils	veuillent	ils	voudraient	ils	voulurent

Nouns

The Gender of Nouns

In French, all nouns are either masculine or feminine, whether denoting people, animals or things. Unlike English, there is no neuter gender for inanimate objects and abstract nouns.

Gender is largely unpredictable and has to be learnt for each noun. However, the following guidelines will help you determine the gender for certain types of nouns:

Nouns denoting male people and animals are usually – but not always – masculine, e.g.

un homme a man
un taureau a bull
un infirmier a (*male*) nurse
un cheval a horse

Nouns denoting female people and animals are usually – but not always – feminine, e.g.

une fille a girl
une vache a cow
une infirmière a nurse
une brebis a ewe

Some nouns are masculine *or* feminine depending on the sex of the person to whom they refer, e.g.

un camarade a (*male*) friend
une camarade a (*female*) friend
un Belge a Belgian (*man*)
une Belge a Belgian (*woman*)

Other nouns referring to either men or women have only one gender which applies to both, e.g.

un professeur a teacher
une personne a person
une sentinelle a sentry
un témoin a witness
une victime a victim
une recrue a recruit

Nouns

Sometimes the ending of the noun indicates its gender. Shown below are some of the most important to guide you:

Masculine endings

-age	le **courage** courage; le **rinçage** rinsing
	EXCEPTIONS: une **cage** a cage; une **image** a picture; la **nage** swimming; une **page** a page; une **plage** a beach; une **rage** a rage
-ment	le **commencement** the beginning
	EXCEPTION: une **jument** a mare
-oir	un **couloir** a corridor; un **miroir** a mirror
-sme	le **pessimisme** pessimism; l'**enthousiasme** enthusiasm

Feminine endings

-ance, -anse	la **confiance** confidence; la **danse** dancing
-ence, -ense	la **prudence** caution; la **défense** defence
	EXCEPTION: le **silence** silence
-ion	une **région** a region; une **addition** a bill
	EXCEPTIONS: un **pion** a pawn; un **espion** a spy
-oire	une **baignoire** a bath(tub)
-té, -tié	la **beauté** beauty; la **moitié** half

Suffixes which differentiate between male and female are shown on p 78.

The following words have different meanings depending on gender:

le **crêpe** crêpe	la **crêpe** pancake
le **livre** book	la **livre** pound
le **manche** handle	la **manche** sleeve
le **mode** method	la **mode** fashion
le **moule** mould	la **moule** mussel
le **page** page(boy)	la **page** page (*in book*)
le **physique** physique	la **physique** physics
le **poêle** stove	la **poêle** frying pan
le **somme** nap	la **somme** sum
le **tour** turn	la **tour** tower
le **voile** veil	la **voile** sail

Nouns

Formation of Feminines

As in English, male and female are sometimes differentiated by the use of two quite separate words, e.g.

mon oncle my uncle   **ma tante** my aunt

There are, however, some words in French which show this distinction by the form of their ending:

Some nouns add an **e** to the masculine singular form to form the feminine → **1**

If the masculine singular form already ends in **-e**, no further **e** is added in the feminine → **2**

Some nouns undergo a further change when **e** is added.

MASC. SING.	FEM. SING.
-f	-ve → **3**
-x	-se → **4**
-eur	-euse → **5**
-teur	-teuse → **6**
	-trice → **7**

Some nouns double the final consonant before adding **e**:

MASC. SING.	FEM. SING.
-an	-anne → **8**
-en	-enne → **9**
-on	-onne → **10**
-et	-ette → **11**
-el	-elle → **12**

Some nouns add an accent to the final syllable before adding **e**:

MASC. SING.	FEM. SING.
-er	-ère → **13**

Some nouns have unusual feminine forms → **4**

Examples

1. un ami a (*male*) friend — une amie a (*female*) friend
2. un élève a (*male*) pupil — une élève a (*female*) pupil
3. un veuf a widower — une veuve a widow
4. un époux a husband — une épouse a wife
5. un danseur a dancer — une danseuse a dancer
6. un menteur a liar — une menteuse a liar
7. un conducteur a driver — une conductrice a driver
8. un paysan a countryman — une paysanne a countrywoman
9. un Parisien a Parisian (*man*) — une Parisienne a Parisian (*woman*)
10. un baron a baron — une baronne a baroness
11. le cadet the youngest (child) — la cadette the youngest (child)
12. un intellectuel an intellectual — une intellectuelle an intellectual
13. un étranger a foreigner — une étrangère a foreigner
14. le comte/la comtesse count/countess — le duc/la duchesse duke/duchess
    le maître/la maîtresse master/mistress — le prince/la princesse prince/princess
    le fou/la folle madman/madwoman — le Turc/la Turque Turk
    un hôte/une hôtesse host/hostess — le vieux/la vieille old man/old woman

Nouns

Formation of Plurals

Most nouns add **s** to the singular form → **❶**

When the singular form already ends in **-s**, **-x** or **-z**, no further **s** is added → **❷**

For nouns ending in **-au**, **-eau** or **-eu**, the plural ends in **-aux**, **-eaux** or **-eux** → **❸**
EXCEPTIONS: **pneu** tyre   (*plural*: **pneus**)
            bleu bruise   (*plural*: **bleus**)

For nouns ending in **-al** or **-ail**, the plural ends in **-aux** → **❹**
EXCEPTIONS: **bal** ball   (*plural*: **bals**)
            festival festival   (*plural*: **festivals**)
            chandail sweater   (*plural*: **chandails**)
            détail detail   (*plural*: **détails**)

Forming the plural of compound nouns is complicated and you are advised to check each one individually in a dictionary.

A word which is singular in the English may be plural in French, or vice versa → **❺**

Irregular Plural Forms

Some masculine nouns ending in **-ou** add **x** in the plural. These are:

bijou jewel	**genou** knee	**joujou** toy
caillou pebble	**hibou** owl	**pou** louse
chou cabbage		

Some other nouns are totally unpredictable. The most important of these are:

SINGULAR		PLURAL
œil	eye	**yeux**
ciel	sky	**cieux**
Monsieur	Mr	**Messieurs**
Madame	Mrs	**Mesdames**
Mademoiselle	Miss	**Mesdemoiselles**

Examples

❶
le jardin	the garden
les jardins	the gardens
une voiture	a car
des voitures	(some) cars
l'hôtel	the hotel
les hôtels	the hotels

❷
un tas	a heap
des tas	(some) heaps
une voix	a voice
des voix	(some) voices
le gaz	the gas
les gaz	the gases

❸
un tuyau	a pipe
des tuyaux	(some) pipes
le chapeau	the hat
les chapeaux	the hats
le feu	the fire
les feux	the fires

❹
le journal	the newspaper
les journaux	the newspapers
un travail	a job
des travaux	(some) jobs

❺
les bagages	the luggage
ses cheveux	his/her hair
le bétail	the cattle
mon pantalon	my trousers

Articles

The Definite Article

	WITH MASC. NOUN	WITH FEM. NOUN	
SING.	le (l')	la (l')	the
PLUR.	les	les	the

The gender and number of the noun determines the form of the article → **❶**

le and **la** change to **l'** before a vowel or an **h** 'mute' → **❷**

Uses of the Definite Article

While the French definite article is used in much the same way in French as it is in English, it is also found

with abstract nouns, except after certain prepositions → **❸**

in generalizations, especially with plural or uncountable nouns (those which cannot be used in the plural or with an indefinite article, e.g. **le lait** milk) → **❹**

with names of countries except after **en** to/in → **❺**

with parts of the body; 'ownership' is often indicated by an indirect object pronoun or a reflexive pronoun → **❻**

in expressions of quantity/rate/price → **❼**

with titles/ranks/professions followed by a proper name → **❽**

The definite article is *not* used with nouns in apposition → **❾**

à + le/la (l'), à + les; de + le/la (l'), de + les

	WITH MASC. NOUN	WITH FEM. NOUN
SING.	au (à l') → **❿**	à la (à l')
PLUR.	aux	aux
SING.	du (de l')	de la (de l') → **⓫**
PLUR.	des	des

The definite article combines with the preposition **à** and **de**, as shown above. You should pay particular attention to the masculine singular form **au** and **du**, and both plural forms **aux** and **des**, since these are not visually the sum of their parts

Examples

MASCULINE	FEMININE
1 le garçon the boy	la fille the girl
les hôtels the hotels	les écoles the schools
2 l'acteur the actor	l'actrice the actress
l'hôpital the hospital	l'heure the time
3 Les prix montent	Prices are rising
L'amour rayonne dans ses yeux	Love shines in his eyes
BUT:	
avec plaisir	with pleasure
sans espoir	without hope
4 Je n'aime pas le café	I don't like coffee
Les enfants ont besoin d'être aimés	Children need to be loved
5 le Japon	Japan
les Pays-Bas	the Netherlands
BUT:	
aller en Écosse	to go to Scotland
6 Tournez la tête à gauche	Turn your head to the left
J'ai mal à la gorge	My throat is sore, I have a sore throat
La tête me tourne	My head is spinning
Elle s'est brossé les dents	She brushed her teeth
7 4 euros le mètre/le kilo/	4 euros a metre/a kilo
rouler à 80 km à l'heure	to go at 80 km an hour
8 le roi Georges III	King George III
Monsieur le président	Mr Chairman/President
9 Victor Hugo, grand écrivain du dix-neuvième siècle	Victor Hugo, a great author of the nineteenth century
10 au cinéma at/to the cinema	à la bibliothèque at/to the library
à l'hôpital at/to the hospital	à l'hôtesse to the hostess
aux étudiants to the students	aux maisons to the houses
11 du bureau from/of the office	de la réunion from/of the meeting
de l'auteur from/of the author	de l'Italienne from/of the Italian woman
de l'hôte from/of the host	de l'horloge of the clock
des États-Unis from/of the United States	des vendeuses from/of the saleswomen

Articles

The Partitive Article

The partitive article has the sense of 'some' or 'any', although the French is not always translated in English.

	WITH MASC. NOUN	WITH FEM. NOUN	
SING.	**du (de l')**	**de la (de l')**	some, any
PLUR.	**des**	**des**	some, any

The gender and number of the noun determines the form of the partitive → **1**

The forms shown in brackets (**de l'**) are used before a vowel or an **h** 'mute' → **2**

des becomes **de** (**d'** + *vowel*) before an adjective → **3**
unless the adjective and noun are seen as forming one unit → **4**

In negative sentences **de** (**d'** + *vowel*) is used → **5**
EXCEPTION: after **ne ... que** 'only', the positive forms above are used → **6**

The Indefinite Article

	WITH MASC. NOUN	WITH FEM. NOUN	
SING.	**un**	**une**	a
PLUR.	**des**	**des**	some

In negative sentences, **de** (**d'** + *vowel*) is used for both singular and plural → **7**

The indefinite article is used in French largely as it is in English except:
  there is no article when a person's profession is being stated → **8**
  the article *is* present following **ce** (**c'** + *vowel*) → **9**

  the English article is not translated by **un/une** in constructions like 'what a surprise', 'what an idiot' → **10**

  in structures of the type given in example **11** the article **un/une** is used in French and not translated in English → **11**

Examples

❶ Avez-vous du sucre? — Have you any sugar?
J'ai acheté de la farine — I bought (some) flour
Il a mangé des gâteaux — He ate some cakes
Est-ce qu'il y a des lettres pour moi? — Are there (any) letters for me?

❷ Il me doit de l'argent — He owes me (some) money
C'est de l'histoire ancienne — That's ancient history

❸ Cette région a de belles églises — This region has some beautiful churches

❹ des grandes vacances — summer holidays
des jeunes gens — young people

❺ Vous n'avez pas de timbres/d'œufs? — Have you no stamps/eggs?
Je ne mange jamais de viande/d'omelettes — I never eat meat/omelettes

❻ Il ne boit que du thé/de la bière/de l'eau — He only drinks tea/beer/water
Je n'ai que des problèmes avec cette machine — I have nothing but trouble with this machine

❼ Je n'ai pas de livre/d'enfants — I don't have a book/(any) children

❽ Il est professeur — He's a teacher
Ma mère est infirmière — My mother's a nurse

❾ C'est un médecin — He's/She's a doctor
Ce sont des acteurs — They're actors

❿ Quelle surprise! — What a surprise!
Quel dommage! — What a shame!

⓫ avec une grande sagesse/un courage admirable — with great wisdom/admirable courage
un produit d'une qualité incomparable — a product of incomparable quality

85

Adjectives

Formation of Feminines and Plurals

Most adjectives agree in number and in gender with the noun or pronoun.

Feminines

Most adjectives add an **e** to the masculine singular form → ❶

If the masculine singular form already ends in **-e**, no further **e** is added → ❷

Some adjectives undergo a further change when **e** is added. These changes occur regularly and are shown on p 88.

Irregular feminine forms are shown on p 90.

Plurals

The plural of both regular and irregular adjectives is formed by adding an **s** to the masculine or feminine singular form, as appropriate → ❸

When the masculine singular form already ends in **-s** or **-x**, no further **s** is added → ❹

For masculine singulars ending in **-au** and **-eau**, the masculine plural is **-aux** and **-eaux** → ❺

For masculine singulars ending in **-al**, the masculine plural is **-aux** → ❻
EXCEPTIONS: **final**   (*masculine plural* **finals**)
                  fatal   (*masculine plural* **fatals**)
                  naval (*masculine plural* **navals**)

Examples

❶

mon frère aîné	my elder brother
ma sœur aînée	my elder sister
le petit garçon	the little boy
la petite fille	the little girl
un sac gris	a grey bag
une chemise grise	a grey shirt
un bruit fort	a loud noise
une voix forte	a loud voice

❷

un jeune homme	a young man
une jeune femme	a young woman
l'autre verre	the other glass
l'autre assiette	the other plate

❸

le dernier train	the last train
les derniers trains	the last trains
une vieille maison	an old house
de vieilles maisons	old houses
un long voyage	a long journey
de longs voyages	long journeys
la rue étroite	the narrow street
les rues étroites	the narrow streets

❹

un diplomate français	a French diplomat
des diplomates français	French diplomats
un homme dangereux	a dangerous man
des hommes dangereux	dangerous men

❺

le nouveau professeur	the new teacher
les nouveaux professeurs	the new teachers
un chien esquimau	a husky (*Fr*: an Eskimo dog)
des chiens esquimaux	huskies (*Fr*: Eskimo dogs)

❻

un ami loyal	a loyal friend
des amis loyaux	loyal friends
un geste amical	a friendly gesture
des gestes amicaux	friendly gestures

Adjectives

Regular Feminine Endings

MASC SING.	FEM. SING.	EXAMPLES
-f	-ve	neuf, vif → ❶
-x	-se	heureux, jaloux → ❷
-eur	-euse	travailleur, flâneur → ❸
-teur	-teuse	flatteur, menteur → ❹
	-trice	destructeur, séducteur → ❺

EXCEPTIONS: **bref**: see p 90

doux, faux, roux, vieux: see p 90

extérieur, inférieur, intérieur, meilleur, supérieur: all add **e** to the masculine

enchanteur: *fem.* = **enchanteresse**

MASC SING.	FEM. SING.	EXAMPLES
-an	-anne	paysan → ❻
-en	-enne	ancien, parisien → ❼
-on	-onne	bon, breton → ❽
-as	-asse	bas, las → ❾
-et*	-ette	muet, violet → ❿
-el	-elle	annuel, mortel → ⓫
-eil	-eille	pareil, vermeil → ⓬

EXCEPTION: **ras**: *fem.* = **rase**

MASC SING.	FEM. SING.	EXAMPLES
-et*	-ète	secret, complet → ⓭
-er	-ère	étranger, fier → ⓮

* Note that there are two feminine endings for masculine adjectives ending in **-et**.

Examples

1 un résultat positif — a positive result
une attitude positive — a positive attitude

2 d'un ton sérieux — in a serious tone (of voice)
une voix sérieuse — a serious voice

3 un enfant trompeur — a deceitful child
une déclaration trompeuse — a misleading statement

4 un tableau flatteur — a flattering picture
une comparaison flatteuse — a flattering comparison

5 un geste protecteur — a protective gesture
une couche protectrice — a protective layer

6 un problème paysan — a farming problem
la vie paysanne — country life

7 un avion égyptien — an Egyptian plane
une statue égyptienne — an Egyptian statue

8 un bon repas — a good meal
de bonne humeur — in a good mood

9 un plafond bas — a low ceiling
à voix basse — in a low voice

10 un travail net — a clean piece of work
une explication nette — a clear explanation

11 un homme cruel — a cruel man
une remarque cruelle — a cruel remark

12 un livre pareil — such a book
en pareille occasion — on such an occasion

13 un regard inquiet — an anxious look
une attente inquiète — an anxious wait

14 un goût amer — a bitter taste
une amère déception — a bitter disappointment

Adjectives

Irregular Feminine Forms

MASC SING.	FEM. SING.	
aigu	aiguë	sharp; high-pitched → ❶
ambigu	ambiguë	ambiguous
beau (bel*)	belle	beautiful
bénin	bénigne	benign
blanc	blanche	white
bref	brève	brief, short → ❷
doux	douce	soft; sweet
épais	épaisse	thick
faux	fausse	wrong
favori	favorite	favourite → ❸
fou (fol*)	folle	mad
frais	fraîche	fresh → ❹
franc	franche	frank
gentil	gentille	kind
grec	grecque	Greek
gros	grosse	big
jumeau	jumelle	twin → ❺
long	longue	long
malin	maligne	malignant
mou (mol*)	molle	soft
nouveau (nouvel*)	nouvelle	new
nul	nulle	no
public	publique	public → ❻
roux	rousse	red-haired
sec	sèche	dry
sot	sotte	foolish
turc	turque	Turkish
vieux (vieil*)	vieille	old

* This form is used when the following word begins with a vowel or an **h** 'mute' → ❼

Examples

❶ un son aigu
une douleur aiguë

a high-pitched sound
a sharp pain

❷ un bref discours
une brève rencontre

a short speech
a short meeting

❸ mon sport favori
ma chanson favorite

my favourite sport
my favourite song

❹ du pain frais
de la crème fraîche

fresh bread
fresh cream

❺ mon frère jumeau
ma sœur jumelle

my twin brother
my twin sister

❻ un jardin public
l'opinion publique

a (public) park
public opinion

❼ un bel appartement
le nouvel inspecteur
un vieil arbre
un bel habit
un nouvel harmonica
un vieil hôtel

a beautiful flat
the new inspector
an old tree
a beautiful outfit
a new harmonica
an old hotel

Adjectives

Comparatives and Superlatives

Comparatives

These are formed using the following constructions:

> **plus ... (que)** more ... (than) → **①**
> **moins ... (que)** less ... (than) → **②**
> **aussi ... que** as ... as → **③**
> **si ... que*** as ... as → **④**

* used mainly after a negative

Superlatives

These are formed using the following constructions:

> **le/la/les plus ... (que)** the most ... (that) → **⑤**
> **le/la/les moins ... (que)** the least ... (that) → **⑥**

> When the possessive adjective is present, two constructions are possible → **⑦**

> After a superlative the preposition **de** is often translated as 'in' → **⑧**

> If a clause follows a superlative, the verb is in the subjunctive → **⑨**

Adjectives with Irregular Comparatives/Superlatives

ADJECTIVE	COMPARATIVE	SUPERLATIVE
bon	**meilleur**	**le meilleur**
good	better	the best
mauvais	**pire** *or* **plus mauvais**	**le pire** *or* **le plus mauvais**
bad	worse	the worst
petit	**moindre*** *or* **plus petit**	**le moindre*** *or* **le plus petit**
small	smaller; lesser	the smallest; the least

* used only with abstract nouns

> Comparative and superlative adjectives agree in number and in gender with the noun, just like any other adjective → **⑩**

Examples

❶ une raison plus grave

Elle est plus petite que moi

a more serious reason

She is smaller than me

❷ un film moins connu

C'est moins cher qu'il ne pense

a less well-known film

It's cheaper than he thinks

❸ Robert était aussi inquiet que moi

Cette ville n'est pas aussi grande
   que Bordeaux

Robert was as worried as
   I was

This town isn't as big as
   Bordeaux

❹ Ils ne sont pas si contents que ça

They aren't as happy as
   all that

❺ le guide le plus utile

la voiture la plus petite

les plus grandes maisons

the most useful guidebook

the smallest car

the biggest houses

❻ le mois le moins agréable

la fille la moins forte

les moins belles peintures

the least pleasant month

the weakest girl

the least attractive paintings

❼ Mon désir le plus cher/Mon plus
   cher désir est de voyager

My dearest wish is to travel

❽ la plus grande gare de Londres

l'habitant le plus âgé du village/
   de la région

the biggest station in
   London

the oldest inhabitant in the
   village/in the area

❾ la personne la plus gentille que
   je connaisse

the nicest person I know

❿ les moindres difficultés

la meilleure qualité

the least difficulties

the best quality

Adjectives

Demonstrative Adjectives

ce (cet)/cette, ces

	MASCULINE	FEMININE	
SING.	**ce (cet)**	**cette**	this; that
PLUR.	**ces**	**ces**	these; those

Demonstrative adjectives agree in number and gender with the noun → ❶

cet is used when the following word begins with a vowel or an **h** 'mute' → ❷

For emphasis or in order to distinguish between people or objects, **-ci** or **-là** is added to the noun: **-ci** indicates proximity (usually translated 'this') and **là** distance 'that' → ❸

Interrogative Adjectives

quel/quelle, quels/quelles?

	MASCULINE	FEMININE	
SING.	**quel?**	**quelle?**	what?; which?
PLUR.	**quels?**	**quelles?**	what?; which?

Interrogative adjectives agree in number and gender with the noun → ❹

The forms shown above are also used in indirect questions → ❺

Exclamatory Adjectives

quel/quelle, quels/quelles!

	MASCULINE	FEMININE	
SING.	**quel!**	**quelle!**	what (a)!
PLUR.	**quels!**	**quelles!**	what!

Exclamatory adjectives agree in number and gender with the noun → ❻

For other exclamations, see p 128.

Examples

❶ Ce stylo ne marche pas — This/That pen isn't working

Comment s'appelle cette entreprise? — What's this/that company called?

Ces livres sont les miens — These/Those books are mine

Ces couleurs sont plus jolies — These/Those colours are nicer

❷ cet oiseau — this/that bird

cet homme — this/that man

❸ Combien coûte ce manteau-ci? — How much is this coat?

Je voudrais cinq de ces pommes-là — I'd like five of those apples

Est-ce que tu reconnais cette personne-là? — Do you recognize that person?

Mettez ces vêtements-ci dans cette valise-là — Put these clothes in that case

❹ Quel genre d'homme est-ce? — What type of man is he?

Quelle est leur décision? — What is their decision?

Vous jouez de quels instruments? — What instruments do you play?

Quelles offres avez-vous reçues? — What offers have you received?

❺ Je ne sais pas à quelle heure il est arrivé — I don't know what time he arrived

Dites-moi quels sont les livres les plus intéressants — Tell me which books are the most interesting

❻ Quel dommage! — What a pity!

Quelle idée! — What an idea!

Quels beaux livres vous avez! — What fine books you have!

Quelles jolies fleurs! — What nice flowers!

Adjectives

Position of Adjectives

French adjectives usually follow the noun → ❶

Adjectives of colour or nationality *always* follow the noun → ❷

As in English, demonstrative, possessive, numerical and interrogative adjectives precede the noun → ❸

The adjectives **autre** (other), **chaque** (each, every) and **quelque** (some) precede the noun → ❹

The following common adjectives can precede the noun:

beau beautiful	**jeune** young
bon good	**joli** pretty
court short	**long** long
dernier last	**mauvais** bad
grand great	**petit** small
gros big	**tel** such (a)
haut high	**vieux** old

The meaning of the following adjectives varies according to their position:

	BEFORE NOUN	AFTER NOUN
ancien	former	old, ancient → ❺
brave	good	brave → ❻
cher	dear (*beloved*)	expensive → ❼
grand	great	tall → ❽
même	same	very → ❾
pauvre	poor (*wretched*)	poor (*not rich*) → ❿
propre	own	clean → ⓫
seul	single, sole	on one's own → ⓬
simple	mere, simple	simple, easy → ⓭
vrai	real	true → ⓮

Adjectives following the noun are linked by **et** → ⓯

Examples

❶ le chapitre suivant — the following chapter
l'heure exacte — the right time

❷ une cravate rouge — a red tie
un mot français — a French word

❸ ce dictionnaire — this dictionary
mon père — my father
le premier étage — the first floor
deux exemples — two examples
quel homme? — which man?

❹ une autre fois — another time
chaque jour — every day
quelque espoir — some hope

❺ un ancien collègue — a former colleague
l'histoire ancienne — ancient history

❻ un brave homme — a good man
un homme brave — a brave man

❼ mes chers amis — my dear friends
une robe chère — an expensive dress

❽ un grand peintre — a great painter
un homme grand — a tall man

❾ la même réponse — the same answer
vos paroles mêmes — your very words

❿ cette pauvre femme — that poor woman
une nation pauvre — a poor nation

⓫ ma propre vie — my own life
une chemise propre — a clean shirt

⓬ une seule réponse — a single reply
une femme seule — a woman on her own

⓭ un simple regard — a mere look
un problème simple — a simple problem

⓮ la vraie raison — the real reason
les faits vrais — the true facts

⓯ un acte lâche et trompeur — a cowardly, deceitful act
un acte lâche, trompeur et ignoble — a cowardly, deceitful and ignoble act

Adjectives

Possessive Adjectives

WITH SING. NOUN		WITH PLUR. NOUN	
MASC.	FEM.	MASC./FEM.	
mon	ma (mon)	mes	my
ton	ta (ton)	tes	your
son	sa (son)	ses	his; her; its
notre	notre	nos	our
votre	votre	vos	your
leur	leur	leurs	their

Possessive adjectives agree in number and gender with the noun, not with the owner → **1**

The forms shown in brackets are used when the following word begins with a vowel or an **h** 'mute' → **2**

son, **sa**, **ses** have the additional meaning of 'one's' → **3**

1 Catherine a oublié son parapluie — Catherine has left her umbrella

Paul cherche sa montre — Paul's looking for his watch

Mon frère et ma sœur habitent à Glasgow — My brother and sister live in Glasgow

Est-ce que tes voisins ont vendu leur voiture? — Did your neighbours sell their car?

Rangez vos affaires — Put your things away

2 mon appareil-photo — my camera
ton histoire — your story
son erreur — his/her mistake
mon autre sœur — my other sister

3 perdre son équilibre — to lose one's balance
présenter ses excuses — to offer one's apologies

Pronouns

Personal Pronouns

	SUBJECT PRONOUNS	
	SINGULAR	PLURAL
1st person	**je (j')** I	**nous** we
2nd person	**tu** you	**vous** you
3rd person (*masc.*)	**il** he; it	**ils** they
(*fem.*)	**elle** she; it	**elles** they
	on one, someone; they	

je changes to **j'** before a vowel, an **h** 'mute' or the pronoun **y** → ❶

tu/vous
Vous, as well as being the second person plural, is also used when addressing one person. As a general rule, use **tu** only when addressing someone you know very well or when invited to do so. In all other cases use **vous**. For singular and plural uses of **vous**, see example ❷

The form of the 3rd person pronouns (**il/elle**; **ils/elles**) reflects the number and gender of the noun(s) they replace. **Ils** also replaces a combination of masculine and feminine nouns → ❸

On refers to someone whose identity is unknown, or to people in general → ❹

Sometimes stressed pronouns replace the subject pronouns; see p 103.

❶ J'arrive!	I'm just coming!
J'en ai trois	I've got three of them
J'hésite à le déranger	I hesitate to disturb him
J'y pense souvent	I often think about it
❷ Compare these questions:	
Vous êtes certain, Monsieur Leclerc?	Are you sure, Mr Leclerc?
Vous êtes certains, les enfants?	Are you sure, children?
❸ Donne-moi le journal et les lettres quand ils arriveront	Give me the newspaper and the letters when they arrive
❹ On m'a volé mon sac	Someone has stolen my bag
On dit que Berlin est très agréable	They say Berlin is very nice

Pronouns

Object Pronouns

	DIRECT OBJECT PRONOUNS	
	SINGULAR	PLURAL
1st person	**me (m')** me	**nous** us
2nd person	**te (t')** you	**vous** you
3rd person (*masc.*)	**le (l')** him; it	**ils** them
(*fem.*)	**la (l')** her; it	**elles** them

	INDIRECT OBJECT PRONOUNS	
	SINGULAR	PLURAL
1st person	**me (m')**	**nous**
2nd person	**te (t')**	**vous**
3rd person (*masc.*)	**lui**	**leur**
(*fem.*)	**lui**	**leur**

The forms shown in brackets are used before a vowel, an **h** 'mute' or the pronoun **y** → **1**

In positive commands **me** and **te** change to **moi** and **toi** except before **en** or **y** → **2**

le sometimes functions as a 'neuter' pronoun, referring to an idea or information contained in a previous statement or question. It is often not translated → **3**

The indirect object pronouns replace the preposition **à** + *noun*, where the noun is a person or an animal → **4**

The verbal construction affects the translation of the pronoun → **5**

Position of Direct Object Pronouns

In constructions other than the imperative affirmative, the pronoun comes before the verb → **6**

The same applies when the verb is in the infinitive → **7**

In the imperative affirmative, the pronoun follows the verb and is attached to it by a hyphen → **8**

For further information, see Order of Object Pronouns, p 102.

Reflexive Pronouns

These are dealt with under reflexive verbs, p 24.

Examples

1
Il m'a vu
He saw me
Ils t'ont caché les faits
They hid the facts from you

2
Avertis-moi de ta décision
Inform me of your decision
Avertis-m'en
Inform me of it
Donnez-moi du sucre
Give me some sugar
Donnez-m'en
Give me some

3
Il n'est pas là. – Je le sais bien.
He isn't there. – I know that.
Elle viendra demain. – Je l'espère bien.
She'll come tomorrow. – I hope so.

4
J'écris à Suzanne
I'm writing to Suzanne
Je lui écris
I'm writing to her

5
arracher qch à qn:
to snatch sth from sb:
  Un voleur m'a arraché mon porte-monnaie
  A thief snatched my purse from me
promettre qch à qn:
to promise sb sth:
  Il leur a promis un cadeau
  He promised them a present
demander à qn de faire:
to ask sb to do:
  Elle nous avait demandé de revenir
  She had asked us to come back

6
Je t'aime
I love you
Les voyez-vous?
Can you see them?
Elle ne nous connaît pas
She doesn't know us
Ne me faites pas rire
Don't make me laugh
Elle vous a écrit
She's written to you
Vous a-t-elle écrit?
Has she written to you?
Il ne nous parle pas
He doesn't speak to us
Ne leur répondez pas
Don't answer them

7
Puis-je vous aider?
May I help you?
Voulez-vous leur envoyer l'adresse?
Do you want to send them the address?

8
Aidez-moi
Help me
Donnez-nous la réponse
Tell us the answer

Pronouns

Object Pronouns *continued*

Order of Object Pronouns

When two object pronouns of different persons come before the verb, the order is: indirect before direct, i.e.

me			
te		**le**	
nous	before	**la**	→ **❶**
vous		**les**	

When two third person object pronouns come before the verb, the order is: direct before indirect, i.e.

le			
la	before	**lui**	→ **❷**
les		**leur**	

When two object pronouns come after the verb (i.e. in the imperative affirmative), the order is: direct before indirect, i.e.

		moi	
		toi	
le		**lui**	
la	before	**nous**	→ **❸**
les		**vous**	
		leur	

The pronouns **y** and **en** (see pp 104 and 105) always come last → **❹**

❶	Dominique vous l'envoie demain	Dominique's sending it to you tomorrow
	Est-ce qu'il te les a montrés?	Has he shown them to you?
❷	Elle le leur a emprunté	She borrowed it from them
	Ne la leur donne pas	Don't give it to them
❸	Rends-les-moi	Give them back to me
	Donnez-le-nous	Give it to us
❹	Donnez-leur-en	Give them some
	Je l'y ai déposé	I dropped him there

Pronouns

Stressed or Disjunctive Pronouns

	SINGULAR	PLURAL
1st person	**moi** me	**nous** us
2nd person	**toi** you	**vous** you
3rd person (*masc.*)	**lui** him; it	**eux** them
(*fem.*)	**elle** her; it	**elles** them
(*reflexive*)	**soi** oneself	

These pronouns are used:
- after prepositions → ❶
- on their own → ❷
- following **c'est**, **ce sont** it is → ❸
- for emphasis, especially to show contrast. For particular emphasis **-même** (*singular*) or **-mêmes** (*plural*) is added to the pronoun → ❹
- when the subject consists of two or more pronouns or a pronoun and a noun → ❺
- in comparisons → ❻
- before relative pronouns → ❼

❶ Je pense à toi
Partez sans eux

I think about you
Leave without them

❷ Qui a fait cela? – Lui.
Qui est-ce qui gagne? – Moi.

Who did that? – He did.
Who's winning? – Me.

❸ C'est toi, Simon? – Non, c'est moi, David.

Is that you, Simon? – No, it's me, David.

❹ Toi, tu ressembles à ton père, eux pas
Je l'ai fait moi même

You look like your father, they don't
I did it myself

❺ Lui et moi partons demain
Mon père et elle ne s'entendent pas

He and I are leaving tomorrow
My father and she don't get on

❻ plus jeune que moi
Il est moins grand que toi

younger than me
He's smaller than you (are)

❼ Ce sont eux qui font du bruit, pas nous

They're the ones making the noise, not us

Pronouns

The Pronoun en

en replaces the preposition **de** + *noun* → **❶**

The verbal construction can affect the translation → **❷**

en also replaces the partitive article (English = some, any) + *noun* → **❸**

In expressions of quantity **en** represents the noun → **❹**

Position: **en** comes before the verb, except in positive commands when it follows and is attached to the verb by a hyphen → **❺**

   en follows other object pronouns → **❻**

❶ Il est fier de son succès	He's proud of his success
Il en est fier	He's proud of it
Elle est sortie du cinéma	She came out of the cinema
Elle en est sortie	She came out (of it)
Je suis couvert de peinture	I'm covered in paint
J'en suis couvert	I'm covered in it
❷ avoir besoin de qch:	to need sth:
J'en ai besoin	I need it/them
avoir peur de qch:	to be afraid of sth:
J'en ai peur	I'm afraid of it/them
❸ Avez-vous de l'argent?	Do you have any money?
En avez-vous?	Do you have any?
Je veux acheter des timbres	I want to buy some stamps
Je veux en acheter	I want to buy some
❹ Combien de sœurs as-tu? – J'en ai trois.	How many sisters do you have? – I have three.
❺ Elle en a discuté avec moi	She discussed it with me
En êtes-vous content?	Are you pleased with it/them?
N'en parlez plus	Don't talk about it any more
Prenez-en	Take some
❻ Donnez-leur-en	Give them some
Il m'en a parlé	He spoke to me about it

Pronouns

The Pronoun y

y replaces the preposition **à** + *noun* → **❶**

The verbal construction can affect the translation → **❷**

y also replaces the prepositions **dans** and **sur** + *noun* → **❸**

y can also mean 'there' → **❹**

Position: **y** comes before the verb, except in positive commands when it follows and is attached to the verb by a hyphen → **❺**

y follows other object pronouns → **❻**

❶ Ne touchez pas à ce bouton — Don't touch this switch
N'y touchez pas — Don't touch it
Il participe aux concerts — He takes part in the concerts
Il y participe — He takes part (in them)

❷ penser à qch: — to think about sth:
  J'y pense souvent — I often think about it
consentir à qch: — to agree to sth:
  Tu y as consenti? — Have you agreed to it?

❸ Mettez-les dans la boîte — Put them in the box
Mettez-les-y — Put them in it
Il les a mis sur les étagères — He put them on the shelves
Il les y a mis — He put them on them

❹ Elle y passe tout l'été — She spends the whole summer there

❺ Il y a ajouté du sucre — He added sugar to it
Elle n'y a pas écrit son nom — She hasn't written her name on it

Comment fait-on pour y aller? — How do you get there?
N'y pense plus! — Don't give it another thought!

Réfléchissez-y — Think it over

❻ Elle m'y a conduit — She drove me there
Menez-nous-y — Take us there

Pronouns

Relative Pronouns

qui who; which
que who(m); which
These are subject and direct object pronouns that introduce a clause and refer to people or things.

	PEOPLE	THINGS
SUBJECT	**qui**	**qui**
	who, that → **①**	which, that → **③**
DIRECT OBJECT	**que (qu')**	**que (qu')**
	who(m), that → **②**	which, that → **④**

que changes to **qu'** before a vowel → **②/④**

You cannot omit the object relative pronoun in French as you can in English → **②/④**

After a preposition:

When referring to people, use **qui** → **⑤**
EXCEPTIONS: after **parmi** 'among' and **entre** 'between' use **lesquels/ lesquelles**; see below → **⑥**

When referring to things, use forms of **lequel**:

	MASCULINE	FEMININE	
SING.	**lequel**	**laquelle**	which
PLUR.	**lesquels**	**lesquelles**	which

The pronoun agrees in number and gender with the noun → **⑦**

After the prepositions **à** and **de**, **lequel** and **lesquel(le)s** contract as follows:
à + lequel → **auquel**
à + lesquels → **auxquels**   → **⑧**
à + lesquelles → **auxquelles**

de + lequel → **duquel**
de + lesquels → **desquels**   → **⑨**
de + lesquelles → **desquelles**

Examples

① Mon frère, qui a vingt ans, est à l'université

My brother, who's twenty, is at university

② Les amis que je vois le plus sont …

The friends (that) I see most are …

Lucienne, qu'il connaît depuis longtemps, est …

Lucienne, whom he has known for a long time, is …

③ Il y a un escalier qui mène au toit

There's a staircase which leads to the roof

④ La maison que nous avons achetée a …

The house (which) we've bought has …

Voici le cadeau qu'elle m'a envoyé

This is the present (that) she sent me

⑤ la personne à qui il parle

the person he's talking to

la personne avec qui je voyage

the person with whom I travel

les enfants pour qui je l'ai acheté

the children for whom I bought it

⑥ Il y avait des jeunes, parmi lesquels Robert

There were some young people, Robert among them

les filles entre lesquelles j'étais assis

the girls between whom I was sitting

⑦ le torchon avec lequel il l'essuie

the cloth with which he's wiping it

la table sur laquelle je l'ai mis

the table on which I put it

les moyens par lesquels il l'accomplit

the means by which he achieves it

les pièces pour lesquelles elle est connue

the plays for which she is famous

⑧ le magasin auquel il livre ces marchandises

the shop to which he delivers these goods

⑨ les injustices desquelles il se plaint

the injustices about which he's complaining

Pronouns

Relative Pronouns *continued*

quoi which, what

> When the relative pronoun does not refer to a specific noun, **quoi** is used after a preposition → **❶**

dont whose, of whom, of which

> **dont** often (but not always) replaces **de qui, duquel, de laquelle**, and **desquel(le)s** → **❷**

> It cannot replace **de qui, duquel** *etc* in the construction *preposition + noun +* **de qui/duquel** → **❸**

> If the person (or object) 'owned' is the *object* of the verb, word order is: **dont** + *verb* + *noun* → **❹**

> If the person (or object) 'owned' is the *subject* of the verb, word order is: **dont** + *noun* + *verb* → **❺**

ce qui, ce que that which, what

These are used when the relative pronoun does not refer to a specific noun, and they are often translated as 'what' (*literally*: that which):

> **ce qui** is used as the subject → **❻**

> **ce que*** is used as the direct object → **❼**

> * **que** changes to **qu'** before a vowel → **❼**

> Note the construction:
> **tout ce qui**
> **tout ce que**   everything/all that → **❽**

> **de** + **ce que** → **ce dont** → **❾**

> *preposition* + **ce que** → **ce** + *preposition* + **quoi** → **❿**

> When **ce qui, ce que** *etc* refers to a previous clause the translation is 'which' → **⓫**

Examples

1 C'est en quoi vous vous trompez
À quoi, j'ai répondu …

That's where you're wrong
To which I replied, …

2 la femme dont (= de qui) la
voiture est garée en face
un prix dont (= de qui) je suis fier

the woman whose car is
parked opposite
an award I am proud of

3 une personne sur l'aide de qui on
peut compter
les enfants aux parents de qui
j'écris
la maison dans le jardin
de laquelle il y a …

a person whose help one can
rely on
the children to whose
parents I'm writing
the house in whose garden
there is …

4 un homme dont je connais
la fille

a man whose daughter
I know

5 un homme dont la fille
me connaît

a man whose daughter
knows me

6 Je n'ai pas vu ce qui s'est passé

I didn't see what happened

7 Ce que j'aime c'est la musique
classique
Montrez-moi ce qu'il vous a donné

What I like is classical music

Show me what he gave you

8 Tout ce qui reste c'est …
Donnez-moi tout ce que vous avez

All that's left is …
Give me everything you have

9 Voilà ce dont il s'agit

That's what it's about

10 Ce n'est pas ce à quoi je
m'attendais
Ce à quoi je m'intéresse
particulièrement c'est …

It's not what I was expecting

What I'm particularly
interested in is …

11 Il est d'accord, ce qui m'étonne

Il a dit qu'elle ne venait pas, ce
que nous savions déjà

He agrees, which
surprises me
He said she wasn't coming,
which we already knew

Pronouns

Interrogative Pronouns

> **qui?** who; whom?
> **que?** what?
> **quoi?** what?

These pronouns are used in direct questions.

The form of the pronoun depends on:
- whether it refers to people or to things
- whether it is the subject or object of the verb, or if it comes after a preposition

Qui and **que** have longer forms, as shown in the tables below.

Referring to people:

SUBJECT	**qui?**	who? → ❶
	qui est-ce qui?	
OBJECT	**qui?**	who(m)? → ❷
	qui est-ce que*?	
AFTER PREPOSITIONS	**qui?**	who(m)? → ❸

Referring to things:

SUBJECT	**qu'est-ce qui?**	what? → ❹
OBJECT	**que*?**	what? → ❺
	qu'est-ce que*?	
AFTER PREPOSITIONS	**quoi?**	what? → ❻

* **que** changes to **qu'** before a vowel → ❷/❺

Examples

1 Qui vient?
Qui est-ce qui vient?

Who's coming?

2 Qui vois-tu?
Qui est-ce que tu vois?
Qui a-t-elle rencontré?
Qui est-ce qu'elle a rencontré?

Who(m) can you see?

Who(m) did she meet?

3 De qui parle-t-il?
Pour qui est ce livre?
À qui avez-vous écrit?

Who's he talking about?
Who's this book for?
To whom did you write?

4 Qu'est-ce qui se passe?
Qu'est-ce qui a vexé Paul?

What's happening?
What upset Paul?

5 Que faites-vous?
Qu'est-ce que vous faites?
Qu'a-t-il dit?
Qu'est-ce qu'il a dit?

What are you doing?

What did he say?

6 À quoi cela sert-il?
De quoi a-t-on parlé?

Sur quoi vous basez-vous?

What's that used for?
What was the discussion about?

What do you base it on?

Pronouns

Interrogative Pronouns *continued*

    qui who; whom
    ce qui what
    ce que what
    quoi what

These pronouns are used in indirect questions.

The form of the pronoun depends on:
- whether it refers to people or to things
- whether it is the subject or object of the verb, or if it comes after a preposition

Referring to people: use **qui** in all instances → **1**

Referring to things:

SUBJECT	**ce qui**	what → **2**
OBJECT	**ce que***	what → **3**
AFTER PREPOSITIONS	**quoi?**	what → **4**

* **que** changes to **qu'** before a vowel → **3**

lequel/laquelle, lesquels/lesquelles?

	MASCULINE	FEMININE	
SING.	**lequel?**	**laquelle?**	which (one)?
PLUR.	**lesquels?**	**lesquelles?**	which (ones)?

The pronoun agrees in number and gender with the noun it refers to → **5**

The same forms are used in indirect questions → **6**

After the prepositions **à** and **de**, **lequel** and **lesquel(le)s** contract as shown on p 106.

Examples

❶ Demande-lui qui est venu
Ask him who came

Je me demande qui ils ont vu
I wonder who they saw

Dites-moi qui vous préférez
Tell me who you prefer

Elle ne sait pas à qui s'adresser
She doesn't know who to apply to

Demandez-leur pour qui elles travaillent
Ask them who they work for

❷ Il se demande ce qui se passe
He's wondering what's happening

Je ne sais pas ce qui vous fait croire que ...
I don't know what makes you think that ...

❸ Raconte-nous ce que tu as fait
Tell us what you did

Je me demande ce qu'elle pense
I wonder what she's thinking

❹ On ne sait pas de quoi vivent ces animaux
We don't know what these animals live on

Je vais lui demander à quoi il fait allusion
I'm going to ask him what he's hinting at

❺ J'ai choisi un livre. – Lequel?
I've chosen a book. – Which one?

Laquelle de ces valises est la vôtre?
Which of these cases is yours?

Amenez quelques amis. – Lesquels?
Bring some friends. – Which ones?

Lesquelles de vos sœurs sont mariées?
Which of your sisters are married?

❻ Je me demande laquelle des maisons est la leur
I wonder which is their house

Dites-moi lesquels d'entre eux étaient là
Tell me which of them were there

Pronouns

Possessive Pronouns

Singular:

MASCULINE	FEMININE	
le mien	**la mienne**	mine
le tien	**la tienne**	yours
le sien	**la sienne**	his; hers; its
le nôtre	**la nôtre**	ours
le vôtre	**la vôtre**	yours
le leur	**la leur**	theirs

Plural:

MASCULINE	FEMININE	
le miens	**la miennes**	mine
le tiens	**la tiennes**	yours
le siens	**la siennes**	his; hers; its
le nôtres	**la nôtres**	ours
le vôtres	**la vôtres**	yours
le leurs	**la leurs**	theirs

The pronoun agrees in number and gender with the noun it replaces, not with the owner → ❶

Alternative translations are 'my own', 'your own' etc; **le sien**, **la sienne** *etc* may also mean 'one's own' → ❷

After the prepositions **à** and **de** the articles **le** and **les** are contracted in the normal way (see p 82):

> **à** + **le mien** → **au mien**
> **à** + **les miens** → **aux miens** → ❸
> **à** + **les miennes** → **aux miennes**

> **de** + **le mien** → **du mien**
> **de** + **les miens** → **des miens** → ❹
> **de** + **les miennes** → **des miennes**

Examples

❶ Demandez à Carole si ce stylo est le sien

Ask Carole if this pen is hers

Quelle équipe a gagné – la leur ou la nôtre?

Which team won – theirs or ours?

Mon stylo marche mieux que le tien

My pen writes better than yours

Richard a pris mes affaires pour les siennes

Richard mistook my belongings for his

Si tu n'as pas de disques, emprunte les miens

If you don't have any records, borrow mine

Nos maisons sont moins grandes que les vôtres

Our houses are smaller than yours

❷ Est-ce que leur entreprise est aussi grande que la vôtre?

Is their company as big as your own?

Leurs prix sont moins élevés que les nôtres

Their prices are lower than our own

Le bonheur des autres importe plus que le sien

Other people's happiness matters more than one's own

❸ Pourquoi préfères-tu ce manteau au mien?

Why do you prefer this coat to mine?

Quelles maisons ressemblent aux leurs?

Which houses resemble theirs?

❹ Leur car est garé à côté du nôtre

Their coach is parked beside ours

Vos livres sont au-dessus des miens

Your books are on top of mine

Pronouns

Demonstrative Pronouns

celui/celle, ceux/celles

	MASCULINE	FEMININE	
SING.	**celui**	**celle**	the one
PLUR.	**ceux**	**celles**	the ones

Celui agrees in number and gender with the noun it replaces → **❶**

Uses:

- preceding a relative pronoun, meaning 'the one(s) who/which' → **❶**
- preceding **de**, meaning 'the one(s) belonging to', 'the one(s) of' → **❷**
- with **-ci** and **-là**, for emphasis or to distinguish between two things:

	MASCULINE	FEMININE	
SING.	**celui-ci**	**celle-ci**	this (one) → **❸**
PLUR.	**ceux-ci**	**celles-ci**	these (ones)

	MASCULINE	FEMININE	
SING.	**celui-là**	**celle-là**	that (one) → **❸**
PLUR.	**ceux-là**	**celles-là**	those (ones)

- an additional meaning of **celui-ci/celui-là** *etc* is 'the former/ the latter'.

ce (c') it, that

> Usually used with **être**, in the expressions **c'est**, **c'était**, **ce sont** *etc*. Note the spelling **ç**, when followed by the letter **a** → **❹**

> Uses:
> - to identify a person or object → **❺**
> - for emphasis → **❻**
> - as a neuter pronoun, referring to a statement, idea *etc* → **❼**

ce qui, **ce que**, **ce dont** *etc*: see Relative Pronouns (p 108), and
Interrogative Pronouns (p 112).

cela, ça it, that

> **cela** and **ça** are used as 'neuter' pronouns, referring to a statement, an idea, an object → **❽**
> In everyday spoken language **ça** is used in preference to **cela**.

ceci this → **❾**

> **ceci** is not used as often as 'this' in English; **cela**, **ça** are often used where we use 'this'.

Examples

1 Quelle robe désirez-vous? – Celle qui est en vitrine.

Which dress do you want? – The one which is in the window.

Est-ce que ces livres sont ceux qu'il t'a donnés?

Are these the books that he gave you?

Quelles filles? – Celles que nous avons vues hier.

Which girls? – The ones we saw yesterday.

Cet article n'est pas celui dont vous m'avez parlé

This article isn't the one you spoke to me about

2 Comparez vos réponses à celles de votre voisin

Compare your answers with your neighbour's (answers)

les montagnes d'Écosse et celles du pays de Galles

the mountains of Scotland and those of Wales

3 Quel tailleur préférez-vous: celui-ci ou celui-là?

Which suit do you prefer: this one or that one?

De toutes mes jupes, celle-ci me va le mieux

Of all my skirts, this one fits me best

4 C'était moi

It was me

Ça a été la cause de …

That was the cause of …

5 Qui est-ce?

Who is it?; Who's this/that?; Who's he/she?

C'est mon frère

It's/That's my brother

C'est une infirmière*

She's a nurse

Ce sont des professeurs*

They're teachers

Qu'est-ce que c'est?

What's this/that?

Ce sont des trombones

They're paper clips

6 C'est moi qui ai téléphoné

It was me who phoned

7 C'est très intéressant

That's/It's very interesting

Ce serait dangereux

That/It would be dangerous

8 Ça ne fait rien

It doesn't matter

Cela ne compte pas

That doesn't count

9 À qui est ceci?

Whose is this?

Ouvrez-le comme ceci

Open it like this

* See p 85 for the use of the article when stating a person's profession

Adverbs

Formation of Adverbs

Most adverbs are formed by adding **-ment** to the feminine form of the adjective → **❶**

-ment is added to the *masculine* form when the masculine form ends in **-é**, **-i** or **-u** → **❷**
EXCEPTION: **gai** → **❸**

Occasionally the **u** changes to **û** before **-ment** is added → **❹**

If the adjective ends in **-ant** or **-ent**, the adverb ends in **-amment** or **-emment** respectively → **❺**
EXCEPTIONS: **lent**, **présent** → **❻**

Irregular Adverbs

ADJECTIVE	ADVERB
aveugle blind	**aveuglément** blindly
bon good	**bien** well → **❼**
bref brief	**brièvement** briefly
énorme enormous	**énormément** enormously
exprès express	**expressément** expressly → **❽**
gentil kind	**gentiment** kindly
mauvais bad	**mal** badly → **❾**
meilleur better	**mieux** better
pire worse	**pis** worse
précis precise	**précisément** precisely
profond deep	**profondément** deeply → **❿**
traître treacherous	**traîtreusement** treacherously

Adjectives Used as Adverbs

Certain adjectives are used adverbially. These include: **bas**, **bon**, **cher**, **clair**, **court**, **doux**, **droit**, **dur**, **faux**, **ferme**, **fort**, **haut**, **mauvais** and **net** → **⓫**

Examples

1 MASC./FEM. ADJECTIVE   ADVERB

heureux/heureuse fortunate   heureusement fortunately
franc/franche frank   franchement frankly
extrême/extrême extreme   extrêmement extremely

2 MASC. ADJECTIVE   ADVERB

désespéré desperate   désespérément desperately
vrai true   vraiment truly
résolu resolute   résolument resolutely

3 gai cheerful   gaiement or gaîment cheerfully

4 continu continuous   continûment continuously

5 constant constant   constamment constantly
courant fluent   couramment fluently
évident obvious   évidemment obviously
fréquent frequent   fréquemment frequently

6 lent slow   lentement slowly
présent present   présentement presently

7 Elle travaille bien   She works well

8 Il a expressément défendu qu'on parte   He has expressly forbidden us to leave

9 un emploi mal payé   a badly paid job

10 J'ai été profondément ému   I was deeply moved

11 parler bas/haut   to speak softly/loudly
coûter cher   to be expensive
voir clair   to see clearly
travailler dur   to work hard
chanter faux   to sing off key
sentir bon/mauvais   to smell nice/bad

Adverbs

Position of Adverbs

When the adverb accompanies a verb in a simple tense, it generally follows the verb → ❶

When the adverb accompanies a verb in a compound tense, it generally comes between the auxiliary verb and the past participle → ❷

Some adverbs, notably those of time and place, follow the past participle → ❸

When the adverb accompanies an adjective or another adverb it generally precedes the adjective/adverb → ❹

Some adverbs are used to form questions and precede the verb (see pp 126 and 127) → ❺

Comparatives of Adverbs

These are formed using the following constructions:

> **plus ... (que)** more ... (than) → ❻
> **moins ... (que)** less ... (than) → ❼
> **aussi ... que** as ... as → ❽
> **si ... que*** as ... as → ❾

* used mainly after a negative

Superlatives of Adverbs

These are formed using the following constructions:

> **le plus ... (que)** the most ... (that) → ❿
> **le moins ... (que)** the least ... (that) → ⓫

Adverbs with Irregular Comparatives/Superlatives

ADVERB	COMPARATIVE	SUPERLATIVE
beaucoup a lot	**plus** more	**le plus** (the) most
bien well	**mieux** better	**le mieux** (the) best
mal badly	**pis/plus mal** worse	**le pis/plus mal** (the) worst
peu little	**moins** less	**le moins** (the) least

Examples

1 Il dort encore
He's still asleep

Je pense souvent à toi
I often think about you

2 Ils sont déjà partis
They've already gone

J'ai toujours cru que ...
I've always thought that ...

J'ai presque fini
I'm almost finished

Il a trop mangé
He's eaten too much

3 On les a vus là-bas
We saw them over there

Elle revient demain
She's coming back tomorrow

4 un très beau chemisier
a very nice blouse

une femme bien habillée
a well-dressed woman

beaucoup plus vite
much faster

peu souvent
not very often

5 Comment va-t-il?
How is he?

6 plus vite
more quickly

plus régulièrement
more regularly

Elle chante plus fort que moi
She sings louder than I do

7 moins facilement
less easily

moins souvent
less often

Nous nous voyons moins fréquemment qu'auparavant
We see each other less frequently than before

8 Faites-le aussi vite que possible
Do it as quickly as possible

Il en sait aussi long que nous
He knows as much about it as we do

9 Ce n'est pas si loin que je pensais
It's not as far as I thought

10 Marianne court le plus vite
Marianne runs fastest

Le plus tôt que je puisse venir c'est samedi
The earliest that I can come is Saturday

11 C'est l'auteur que je connais le moins bien
He's the writer I'm least familiar with

Prepositions

Prepositions

It is often difficult to give an English equivalent for French prepositions, since usage varies so much between the two languages. The French preposition may not always be the one that the English sentence leads you to expect, and vice versa. A good dictionary will help you here → **❶**

English verbal constructions often contain a preposition where none exists in French, and vice versa → **❷**

English phrasal verbs (i.e. verbs followed by a preposition, e.g. 'to run away', 'to fall down') are often translated by one word in French → **❸**

❶ Il y a beaucoup de restaurants à Londres

There are lots of restaurants in London

Elle est allée à Londres — She went/has gone to London

donner qch à qn — to give sth to sb, to give sb sth

lancer qch à qn — to throw sth at sb

prendre qch à qn — to take sth from sb

à pied — on foot

une tasse à thé — a teacup

venir de Paris — to come from Paris

une boîte d'allumettes — a box of matches

une robe de soie — a silk dress

d'une façon irrégulière — in an irregular way

la plus belle ville du monde — the most beautiful city in the world

plus de cent personnes — more than a hundred people

je vais en ville — I'm going (in)to town

en janvier — in January

déguisé en cowboy — dressed up as a cowboy

je suis venue en voiture — I came by car

❷ payer to pay for   regarder to look at   écouter to listen to
obéir à to obey   nuire à to harm   manquer de to lack

❸ s'enfuir to run away   tomber to fall down   céder to give in

Conjunctions

Conjunctions

Coordinating conjunctions introduce a main clause, e.g. **et** (and), **mais** (but), **donc** (so), **ensuite** (then) and subordinating conjunctions introduce subordinate clauses e.g. **parce que** (because), **pendant que** (while), **lorsque** (when). They are used in much the same way as in English, but:

Some conjunctions in French require a following subjunctive; see p 46

Some conjunctions are 'split' in French:

et … et both … and → ❶
ni … ni … ne neither … nor → ❷
ou (bien) … ou (bien) either … or (else) → ❸
soit … soit either … or → ❹

si + il(s) → s'il(s) → ❺

que
- meaning *that* → ❻
- replacing another conjunction → ❼
- replacing **si**, see p 48
- in comparisons, see pp 92 and 120
- followed by the subjunctive, see p 48

aussi (so, therefore):   the subject and verb are inverted if the subject is a pronoun → ❽

❶	Ces fleurs poussent et en été et en hiver	These flowers grow in both summer and winter
❷	Ni lui ni elle ne sont venus	Neither he nor she came
❸	Ou bien il m'évite ou bien il ne me reconnaît pas	Either he's avoiding me or (else) he doesn't recognize me
❹	Il faut choisir soit l'un soit l'autre	You have to choose either one or the other
❺	Je ne sais pas s'il vient/s'ils viennent	I don't know if he's coming/ if they're coming
❻	Il dit qu'il t'a vu	He says (that) he saw you
❼	Comme il pleuvait et que je n'avais pas de parapluie, …	As it was raining and I didn't have an umbrella, …
❽	Ceux-ci sont plus rares, aussi coûtent-ils cher	These ones are rarer, so they're expensive

Sentence Structure

Negatives

ne ... pas not
ne ... point (*literary*) not
ne ... rien nothing
ne ... personne nobody
ne ... plus no longer, no more
ne ... jamais never
ne ... que only
ne ... aucun(e) no
ne ... nul(le) no
ne ... nulle part nowhere
ne ... ni neither ... nor
ne ... ni ... ni neither ... nor

Word Order

In simple tenses and the imperative:
- **ne** precedes the verb (and any object pronouns) and the second element follows the verb → **1**

In compound tenses:
- **ne ... pas, ne ... point, ne ... rien, ne ... plus, ne ... jamais, ne ... guère** follow the pattern:
  ne + *auxiliary verb* + **pas** + *past participle* → **2**
- **ne ... personne, ne ... que, ne ... aucun(e), ne ... nul(le), ne ... nulle part, ne ... ni (... ni)** follow the pattern:
  ne + *auxiliary verb* + *past participle* + **personne** → **3**

With a verb in the infinitive:
- **ne ... pas, ne ... point** *etc* (see above) come together → **4**
- **Rien, personne** and **aucun** can also be used as pronouns. When they are the subject or object of the verb, **ne** is placed immediately before the verb. **Aucun** also needs the pronoun en when used as an object → **5**
- **Jamais** and **plus** can be combined with some of the negative particles listed above → **6**

Examples

❶ Je ne fume pas

I don't smoke

Ne changez rien

Don't change anything

Je ne vois personne

I can't see anybody

Nous ne nous verrons plus

We won't see each other any more

Il n'arrive jamais à l'heure

He never arrives on time

Il n'avait qu'une valise

He only had one suitcase

Il ne boit ni ne fume

He neither drinks nor smokes

Ni mon fils ni ma fille ne les connaissaient

Neither my son nor my daughter knew them

❷ Elle n'a pas fait ses devoirs

She hasn't done her homework

Ne vous a-t-il rien dit?

Didn't he say anything to you?

Tu n'as guère changé

You've hardly changed

❸ Je n'ai vu personne

I haven't seen anybody

Il n'avait mangé que la moitié du repas

He had only eaten half the meal

Elle ne les a trouvés nulle part

She couldn't find them anywhere

❹ Il essayait de ne pas rire

He was trying not to laugh

❺ Je ne vois personne

I can't see anyone

Rien ne lui plaît

Nothing pleases him/her

Aucune des entreprises ne veut...

None of the companies want...

Il n'en a aucun

He hasn't any (of them)

❻ Je ne le ferai plus jamais

I'll never do it again

Ces marchandises ne valaient plus rien

Those goods were no longer worth anything

Ils ne font jamais rien d'intéressant

They never do anything interesting

Je n'ai jamais parlé qu'à sa femme

I've only ever spoken to his wife

Sentence Structure

Question Forms: Direct Questions

There are four ways of forming direct questions in French:

> by inverting the normal word order so that *pronoun subject + verb* becomes *verb + pronoun subject*. A hyphen links the verb and pronoun → **❶**
>
> - When the subject is a noun, a pronoun is inserted after the verb and linked to it by a hyphen → **❷**
> - When the verb ends in a vowel in the third person singular, **-t-** is inserted before the pronoun → **❸**
>
> by maintaining the word order *subject + verb*, but by using a rising intonation at the end of the sentence → **❹**
>
> by inserting **est-ce que** before the construction *subject + verb* → **❺**
>
> by using an interrogative word at the beginning of the sentence, together with inversion or the **est-ce que** form above → **❻**

Question forms: Indirect Questions

An indirect question is one that is 'reported', e.g. 'he asked me what the time was'; 'tell me which way to go'. Word order in indirect questions is as follows:

> *interrogative word + subject + verb* → **❼**
>
> when the subject is a noun, and not a pronoun, the subject and verb are often inverted → **❽**

n'est-ce pas

This is used wherever English would use 'isn't it?', 'don't they?', 'weren't we?', 'is it?' and so on tagged on to the end of a sentence → **❾**

Examples

❶ Aimez-vous la France? — Do you like France?
Avez-vous fini? — Have you finished?
Est-ce possible? — Is it possible?
Est-elle restée? — Did she stay?

❷ Tes parents sont-ils en vacances? — Are your parents on holiday?

❸ A-t-elle de l'argent? — Has she any money?
La pièce dure-t-elle longtemps? — Does the play last long?

❹ Robert va venir — Robert's coming
Robert va venir? — Is Robert coming?

❺ Est-ce que tu la connais? — Do you know her?
Est-ce que tes parents sont revenus d'Italie? — Have your parents come back from Italy?

❻ Quel train prends-tu? — What train are you getting?
Quel train est-ce que tu prends?
Pourquoi ne sont-ils pas venus? — Why haven't they come?
Pourquoi est-ce qu'ils ne sont pas venus?

❼ Je me demande s'il viendra — I wonder if he'll come
Dites-moi quel autobus va à la gare — Tell me which bus goes to the station

❽ Elle nous a demandé comment allait notre père — She asked us how our father was
Je ne sais pas ce que veulent dire ces mots — I don't know what these words mean

❾ Il fait chaud, n'est-ce pas? — It's warm, isn't it?
Vous n'oublierez pas, n'est-ce pas? — You won't forget, will you?

Sentence Structure

Word Order

Word order in French is largely the same as in English, except:

> Object pronouns nearly always come before the verb; see p 100

> Certain adjectives come after the noun; see p 96

> Adverbs accompanying a verb in a simple tense usually follow the verb; see p 120

> After **aussi** (so, therefore), **à peine** (hardly), **peut-être** (perhaps), the verb and subject are inverted → ❶

> After the relative pronoun **dont** (whose), certain rules apply; see p 108

> In exclamations, **que** and **comme** do not affect the normal word order → ❷

> Following direct speech:
> * the *verb + subject* order is inverted to become *subject + verb* → ❸
> * with a pronoun subject, the verb and pronoun are linked by a hyphen → ❹
> * when the verb ends in a vowel in the 3ʳᵈ person singular, **-t-** is inserted between the pronoun and the verb → ❺

For word order in negative sentences, see p 124.

For word order in interrogative sentences, see pp 126 and 127.

❶ Il vit tout seul, aussi fait-il ce qu'il veut

He lives alone, so he does what he likes

À peine la pendule avait-elle sonné trois heures que ...

Hardly had the clock struck three when ...

Peut-être avez-vous raison

Perhaps you're right

❷ Qu'il fait chaud!

How warm it is!

Comme c'est cher

How expensive it is!

❸ « Je pense que oui » a dit Luc

'I think so,' said Luke

« Ça ne fait rien » répondit Julie

'It doesn't matter,' Julie replied

❹ « Quelle horreur! » me suis-je exclamé

'How awful!' I exclaimed

❺ « Pourquoi pas? » a-t-elle demandé

'Why not?' she asked